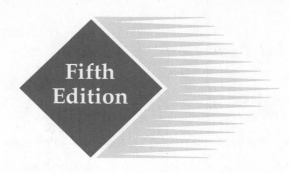

Fifth Edition

Research Methods in Psychology

John J. Shaughnessy
Hope College

Eugene B. Zechmeister
Loyola University of Chicago

Jeanne S. Zechmeister
Loyola University of Chicago

Boston   Burr Ridge, IL   Dubuque, IA   Madison, WI   New York   San Francisco   St. Louis
Bangkok   Bogotá   Caracas   Lisbon   London   Madrid
Mexico City   Milan   New Delhi   Seoul   Singapore   Sydney   Taipei   Toronto

McGraw-Hill Higher Education

A Division of The **McGraw-Hill** *Companies*

RESEARCH METHODS IN PSYCHOLOGY, FIFTH EDITION

This book is printed on acid-free paper.

2 3 4 5 6 7 8 9 0 QPF/QPF 0 9 8 7 6 5 4 3 2 1 0

ISBN 0–07–231260–2

Editorial director: *Jane E. Vaicunas*
Executive editor: *Joseph Terry*
Developmental editor: *Susan Kunchandy*
Editorial assistant: *Barbara Santoro*
Senior marketing manager: *James Rozsa*
Senior project manager: *Gloria G. Schiesl*
Senior production supervisor: *Sandra Hahn*
Coordinator of freelance design: *Rick Noel*
Photo research coordinator: *John C. Leland*
Supplement coordinator: *Sandra M. Schnee*
Compositor: *Interactive Composition Corporation*
Typeface: *10/12 Palatino*
Printer: *Quebecor Printing Book Group/Fairfield, PA*

Cover designer: *Jamie O'Neal*
Interior designer: *Kathy Theis*
Photo research: *Toni Michaels Picture Research*
Cover images: Pie Chart: © *Image Club Graphics;* Book Pages: © *Digital Vision Ltd.;* Glasses: © *Digital Vision Ltd.;* Keyboard: © *Image Club Graphics;* Background: © *Letraset*

The credits section for this book begins on page 548 and is considered an extension of the copyright page.

Library of Congress Cataloging-in-Publication Data

Shaughnessy, John J., 1947–
   Research methods in psychology / John J. Shaughnessy, Eugene B.
Zechmeister, Jeanne S. Zechmeister. — 5th ed.
      p.   cm.
   Includes bibliographical references and indexes.
   ISBN 0–07–231260–2
   1. Psychology—Research—Methodology.   2. Psychology,
Experimental.   I. Zechmeister, Eugene B., 1944–   .
II. Zechmeister, Jeanne S.   III. Title.
BF76.5.S46   2000
150'.7'2—dc21   99–15858
                                                          CIP

www.mhhe.com

About the Authors

JOHN J. SHAUGHNESSY is Professor of Psychology at Hope College, a relatively small, select, undergraduate liberal arts college in Holland, Michigan. After completing the B.S. degree at Loyola University of Chicago in 1969, he received the Ph.D. in 1972 from Northwestern University. He is a Fellow of the American Psychological Society whose recent research has focused on practical aspects of memory. He is coauthor, with Benton J. Underwood, of *Experimentation in Psychology* (Wiley, 1975). He was selected by students in 1992 as the Hope Outstanding Professor Educator; he serves as a mentor in the College's Faculty Development Program for younger faculty; and he has recently been chairperson of the Hope College Psychology Department.

EUGENE B. ZECHMEISTER is Professor of Psychology at Loyola University of Chicago, a large metropolitan university where he has taught both undergraduate and graduate courses since 1970. Professor Zechmeister completed his B.A. in 1966 at the University of New Mexico. He later received both the M.S. (1968) and Ph.D. (1970) from Northwestern University. A specialist in the field of human cognition, Professor Zechmeister authored, with S. E. Nyberg, *Human Memory: An Introduction to Research and Theory* (Brooks/Cole, 1982), and with J. E. Johnson, *Critical Thinking: A Functional Approach* (Brooks/Cole, 1992). He is a Fellow of both the American Psychological Association (Divisions 1, 2, and 3) and the American Psychological Society. In 1994, he was awarded the Loyola University Sujack Award for Teaching Excellence in the College of Arts and Sciences. Professor Zechmeister currently is the Undergraduate Program Director for the Loyola University of Chicago Psychology Department.

JEANNE S. ZECHMEISTER is Associate Professor of Psychology at Loyola University of Chicago where she has taught undergraduate and graduate courses in research methodology since 1990. Professor Zechmeister completed her B.A. at University of Wisconsin-Madison (1983) and her M.S. (1988) and Ph.D. (1990) in Clinical Psychology at Northwestern University. Her current research interests are in the area of psychology of religion, and she is conducting research on forgiveness. Her effectiveness as a teacher is evidenced by her many years of high teacher ratings and by her being identified consistently each year by graduating seniors as one of their best teachers at Loyola.

Brief Contents

Preface   *xi*

PART I

General Issues   **1**

   1   Introduction   2
   2   Ethical Issues in the Conduct
      of Psychological Research   41

PART II

Descriptive Methods   **83**

   3   Observation   84
   4   Correlational Research: Surveys   127
   5   Unobtrusive Measures of Behavior   176

PART III

Experimental Methods   **207**

   6   Independent Groups Designs   208
   7   Repeated Measures Designs   267
   8   Complex Designs   298

PART IV

Applied Research   **333**

   9   Single-Case Research Designs   334
  10   Quasi-Experimental Designs and Program Evaluation   368

Appendix A   Data Analysis and Interpretation   412
Appendix B   Questionnaire Construction   467
Appendix C   Communication in Psychology   479

Glossary   528
References   534
Credits   548
Name Index   551
Subject Index   556

Contents

Preface *xi*

PART I
General Issues 1

1 Introduction 2
PSYCHOLOGY AS A SCIENCE 3
THE SCIENTIFIC METHOD 5
  Scientific and Nonscientific Approaches
    to Knowledge 5
  Goals of the Scientific Method 20
SCIENTIFIC THEORY CONSTRUCTION
  AND TESTING 28
SCIENTIFIC INTEGRITY 32
GETTING STARTED DOING RESEARCH 33
THE ORGANIZATION OF THIS BOOK 36
  SUMMARY 37
  KEY CONCEPTS 38
  REVIEW QUESTIONS 38
  CHALLENGE QUESTIONS 39

**2 Ethical Issues in the Conduct of
  Psychological Research 41**
INTRODUCTION 42
THINGS YOU NEED TO KNOW BEFORE YOU
  BEGIN TO DO RESEARCH 43
  APA Ethical Standards 43
  Commentary 44
THE RISK/BENEFIT RATIO 47
  Determination of Risk 48
  Minimal Risk 50
  Dealing with Risk 50
  Obtaining Informed Consent 52
  APA Ethical Standards 53
  Commentary 54
DECEPTION IN PSYCHOLOGICAL RESEARCH 60

APA Ethical Standards 60
  Commentary 61
ADDITIONAL RESPONSIBILITIES TO
  RESEARCH PARTICIPANTS 65
  APA Ethical Standards 65
  Commentary 66
RESEARCH WITH ANIMALS 68
  APA Ethical Standards 68
  Commentary 69
REPORTING OF PSYCHOLOGICAL
  RESEARCH 72
  APA Ethical Standards 73
  Commentary 74
STEPS FOR ETHICAL DECISION MAKING 77
  SUMMARY 77
  KEY CONCEPTS 78
  REVIEW QUESTIONS 78
  CHALLENGE QUESTIONS 79

PART II
Descriptive Methods 83

3 Observation 84
OVERVIEW 85
CLASSIFICATION OF OBSERVATIONAL
  METHODS 86
OBSERVATION WITHOUT INTERVENTION 86
OBSERVATION WITH INTERVENTION 89
  Participant Observation 89
  Structured Observation 92
  Field Experiments 96
RECORDING BEHAVIOR 97
  Obtaining Qualitative Measures of
    Behavior 98
  Obtaining Quantitative Measures of
    Behavior 101

SAMPLING TECHNIQUES **108**
Time and Event Sampling 109
Situation Sampling 111
ANALYSIS OF OBSERVATIONAL DATA **111**
Data Reduction 111
Observer Reliability 113
PROBLEMS IN THE CONDUCT OF OBSERVATIONAL
RESEARCH **115**
Influence of the Observer 115
Observer Bias 121
SUMMARY 122
KEY CONCEPTS 123
REVIEW QUESTIONS 124
CHALLENGE QUESTIONS 124

**4 Correlational Research:
Surveys 127**

OVERVIEW **128**
CORRELATIONAL RESEARCH **129**
The Nature of Correlations 129
Correlation and Causality 131
Path Analysis 132
MEASURES IN CORRELATIONAL
RESEARCH **135**
Questionnaires as Instruments 135
Margin of Error 138
Reliability and Validity 141
Predictions and Decisions 144
USES OF SURVEYS **146**
CHARACTERISTICS OF SURVEYS **148**
SAMPLING TECHNIQUES **149**
Basic Terms of Sampling 149
Approaches to Sampling 152
SURVEY METHODS **157**
Mail Surveys 158
Personal Interviews 160
Telephone Interviews 161
SURVEY-RESEARCH DESIGNS **161**
Cross-Sectional Design 162
Successive Independent Samples
Design 163
Longitudinal Design 166
CORRESPONDENCE BETWEEN REPORTED AND
ACTUAL BEHAVIOR **169**

SUMMARY 171
KEY CONCEPTS 172
REVIEW QUESTIONS 172
CHALLENGE QUESTIONS 173

**5 Unobtrusive Measures of
Behavior 176**

OVERVIEW **177**
PHYSICAL TRACES **178**
Rationale 178
Types of Physical Traces 179
Problems and Limitations 183
ARCHIVAL DATA **185**
Rationale 185
Types of Archival Data 189
Content Analysis 192
Illustrative Uses of Archival Data 195
Problems and Limitations 197
ETHICAL ISSUES AND UNOBTRUSIVE
MEASURES **202**
SUMMARY 203
KEY CONCEPTS 203
REVIEW QUESTIONS 204
CHALLENGE QUESTIONS 204

PART III
Experimental Methods 207

6 Independent Groups Designs 208
OVERVIEW **209**
CHARACTERISTICS OF EXPERIMENTS **210**
WHY PSYCHOLOGISTS CONDUCT
EXPERIMENTS **211**
EXPERIMENTAL CONTROL **212**
RANDOM GROUPS DESIGN **217**
Random Assignment 217
Establishing External Validity 220
Challenges to Internal Validity 226
ALTERNATIVE INDEPENDENT
GROUPS DESIGNS **233**
Matched Groups Design 233
Natural Groups Design 235

ANALYSIS OF EXPERIMENTS   238
  Overview   238
  Confidence Intervals   239
  Null-Hypothesis Testing   243
  Limitations of Null-Hypothesis
     Testing   249
  Analysis of Variance (ANOVA)   250
  Effect Size   256
  Meta-Analysis   259
  SUMMARY   261
  KEY CONCEPTS   263
  REVIEW QUESTIONS   263
  CHALLENGE QUESTIONS   264

7   *Repeated Measures Designs   267*
OVERVIEW   268
REASONS FOR USING REPEATED MEASURES
  DESIGNS   268
PRACTICE EFFECTS   270
BALANCING PRACTICE EFFECTS   273
  Complete Design   274
  Incomplete Design   279
LIMITATIONS OF REPEATED MEASURES
  DESIGNS   284
  Irreversible Tasks   285
  Differential Transfer   287
ANALYSIS OF REPEATED MEASURES
  DESIGNS   289
  Sensitivity and Power   289
  Repeated Measures Analysis of
     Variance   290
  SUMMARY   294
  KEY CONCEPTS   295
  REVIEW QUESTIONS   295
  CHALLENGE QUESTIONS   296

8   *Complex Designs   298*
OVERVIEW   299
GUIDELINES FOR IDENTIFYING AN
  EXPERIMENTAL DESIGN   300
THE NATURE OF MAIN EFFECTS AND
  INTERACTIONS   302
ANALYSIS OF COMPLEX DESIGNS   312
  Logic of Analysis Plan   312

  Analysis with an Interaction   314
  Analysis with No Interaction   318
INTERPRETING INTERACTIONS   320
  Interactions and Theory Testing   320
  Interactions and Contradictory
     Findings   321
  Interactions and External Validity   323
  Interactions and Relevant Independent
     Variables   324
  Interactions and Ceiling and
     Floor Effects   326
  Interactions and the Natural Groups
     Design   327
  SUMMARY   329
  KEY CONCEPTS   330
  REVIEW QUESTIONS   331
  CHALLENGE QUESTIONS   331

PART IV
Applied Research   333

9   *Single-Case Research
     Designs   334*
OVERVIEW   335
THE CASE STUDY METHOD   336
  Characteristics   336
  Advantages of the Case Study
     Method   340
  Disadvantages of the Case Study
     Method   344
  The Case Study Method: Final
     Comments   347
  Applied Behavior Analysis   348
SINGLE-CASE ($N = 1$) EXPERIMENTAL
  DESIGNS   350
  Specific Experimental Designs   352
  Problems and Limitations Common to
     All Single-Case Designs   359
  Ethical Issues in Single-Case
     Designs   361
  SUMMARY   363
  KEY CONCEPTS   365
  REVIEW QUESTIONS   365
  CHALLENGE QUESTIONS   366

10 *Quasi-Experimental Designs and Program Evaluation* *368*

OVERVIEW 369
DIFFERENCES BETWEEN LABORATORY EXPERIMENTS AND EXPERIMENTS IN NATURAL SETTINGS 370
Control 370
External Validity 371
Goals 372
Consequences 372
TRUE EXPERIMENTS 374
Characteristics of True Experiments 374
Obstacles to Conducting True Experiments in Natural Settings 374
Threats to Internal Validity Controlled by True Experiments 376
Problems That Even True Experiments May Not Eliminate 380
QUASI-EXPERIMENTS 383
The Nonequivalent Control Group Design 385
Nonequivalent Control Group Design: The Langer and Rodin Study 387
Sources of Invalidity in the Nonequivalent Control Group Design 389
The Issue of External Validity 394
Interrupted Time-Series Designs 394
Time Series with Nonequivalent Control Group 398
AN EXTENSION OF SINGLE-CASE DESIGNS TO RESEARCH IN NATURAL SETTINGS 400
Rationale 400
The ABAB Design 401
PROGRAM EVALUATION 403
SUMMARY 407
KEY CONCEPTS 409
REVIEW QUESTIONS 409
CHALLENGE QUESTIONS 410

Appendix A *Data Analysis and Interpretation* *412*

INTRODUCTION 413
THE MULTIPLE STAGES OF DATA ANALYSIS 414
THE ANALYSIS STORY 415
COMPUTER-ASSISTED DATA ANALYSIS 415
A RESEARCH EXAMPLE 416
Stage 1. Getting to Know the Data 417
Stage 2. Summarizing the Data 421
Stage 3. Confirming What the Data Tell Us 426
CONFIRMATORY ANALYSIS USING NHST 427
Comparison Between Two Means 427
Summary of Confirmatory Analysis Based on NHST 432
CONFIRMATORY ANALYSIS USING CONFIDENCE INTERVALS 433
Construction of Confidence Interval for a Single Population Mean 434
Construction of Confidence Interval for Difference Between Population Means 434
Summary of Confirmatory Analysis Based on Confidence Intervals 437
COMPARISON OF TWO MEANS IN A REPEATED MEASURES DESIGN 437
RECOMMENDATIONS FOR COMPARING TWO MEANS 438
DATA ANALYSIS INVOLVING MORE THAN TWO INDEPENDENT GROUPS 439
Analysis of Variance (ANOVA) 439
Calculating Effect Size for Independent Groups Designs 442
Assessing Power for Independent Groups Designs 443
Analytical Comparisons 444
Confidence Intervals for Independent Group Designs 447
Error Bars and Confidence Intervals 448
SINGLE-FACTOR ANALYSIS OF VARIANCE FOR REPEATED MEASURES DESIGNS 449
Effect Size for Repeated Measures ANOVA 451
Using Confidence Intervals with Repeated Measures Designs 451
TWO-FACTOR ANALYSIS OF VARIANCE FOR INDEPENDENT GROUPS DESIGNS 452
Effect Sizes for Two-Factor Design with Independent Groups 456

Illustration of Simple Main Effect   456
TWO-FACTOR ANALYSIS OF VARIANCE
    FOR A MIXED DESIGN   458
STATISTICAL TABLES   460

*Appendix B   Questionnaire
    Construction   467*
INTRODUCTION   468
STEPS IN PREPARING A QUESTIONNAIRE   468
GUIDELINES FOR THE EFFECTIVE WORDING OF
    QUESTIONS   470
GUIDELINES FOR THE GENERAL FORMAT
    OF A QUESTIONNAIRE   473
    Questionnaire Design   473
    Ordering of Questions   475
ENHANCING RESPONSE RATE IN A
    MAIL SURVEY   477

*Appendix C   Communication in
    Psychology   479*
INTRODUCTION   480
THE INTERNET AND RESEARCH   482

GUIDELINES FOR EFFECTIVE WRITING   484
STRUCTURE OF A RESEARCH REPORT   487
    Title Page   488
    Abstract   489
    Introduction   490
    Method   493
    Results   495
    Discussion   500
    References   502
    Appendixes   503
    Author Note   503
    Footnotes   504
    Order of Manuscript Pages   504
ORAL PRESENTATIONS   504
RESEARCH PROPOSALS   506
A SAMPLE RESEARCH REPORT   508

Glossary   528
References   534
Credits   548
Name Index   551
Subject Index   556

Preface

As research psychologists, we relish the opportunity to discover something new about behavior and mental processes. Our curiosity stirs, for example, when we consider what kinds of effects watching *Sesame Street* may have on the intellectual growth of children. We wonder, too, to what degree do genes determine personality? Or, on the social-psychological level, what are some outcomes of racial stereotyping? These are the types of inquiries into human behavior that engage us, keep us wondering, and prompt our exploration. For us, gathering, delving into, and analyzing research is a much anticipated venture. Like an eager child anxious to open up a brightly wrapped birthday present, we ask ourselves, "What will we discover?"

When we decided—two decades ago—to write a research methods textbook, we wanted to capture this excitement of psychological inquiry as well as the importance of understanding the methods by which research is conducted. Twenty years later, our greatest satisfaction from writing this textbook and teaching research methods is seeing students who enter the course feeling mild trepidations, leave not only feeling competent and confident but also excited about their understanding of the research process.

ORGANIZATION AND APPROACH

As in previous editions, we begin with a general introduction to the scientific method and with suggestions for how to get started doing research in psychology. We then discuss descriptive, experimental, and applied methodologies. Although we have made some changes that we believe will benefit students in their study of research methods, the basic organization and content of the previous edition remains the same.

Our approach is based on our years of teaching experience. As instructors of research methods, we recognize that most students in our classes will be research consumers and not research producers. Yet we also understand that critical thinking skills are essential to both roles. As we have done in previous editions, we take a problem-solving approach to the study of research methods. Research begins with a question; an appropriate methodology must then be selected to answer that question. It is important to analyze the strengths and weaknesses of a methodology and to evaluate critically the nature of the evidence obtained.

We have drawn many examples from the rich psychology literature to help present research methods. Thus, students also learn much about psychology in general when studying research methodology. This approach is important because it helps students appreciate the critical link between research methods and psychological knowledge. We believe that it is this appreciation for research methods and their findings that makes the study of psychology even more fulfilling and meaningful.

ABOUT THIS EDITION

Many years have past since the first edition was published, but we continue to keep this text current and exciting:

- This time around, we added more than 100 new references to this edition in order to show students the most recent psychological findings.
- New photos and drawings have been added to stimulate students' interest.
- We echo a message that was heard in previous editions: A multimethod approach to hypothesis testing is necessary to meet the goals of scientific psychology. All methodologies are limited and it is only by gathering evidence using many different approaches that we will succeed in our task.
- We include Challenge Questions at the end of each chapter that permit students to test their critical thinking skills. Many of these questions were developed from reports of research findings in the media. We urge instructors to provide students with additional examples of research findings from popular news outlets that not only will increase students' reasoning skills but also help them appreciate the relevance of understanding research to understanding their world.

CHANGES IN THE FIFTH EDITION

The changes in this edition have made this text even more student-friendly and effective:

- **Bullet Points:** Users of previous editions will immediately recognize an important new pedagogical feature in this edition. Within each chapter we have added "bullet points" to the introduction of major sections. These bullet points represent summaries of the main ideas in each section and serve two major purposes. First, they provide an outline of the next section of text for the student. This alerts students to what will follow and guides their study. Over the years students have mentioned to us how much they like the many examples of "real" research methods and findings that we incorporate in the text, but they also have indicated that it is sometimes difficult to isolate what is the key idea of a text passage from what is meant to illustrate and amplify that idea. The bullet points should better enable students to identify the key ideas from their reading. A second purpose of the bullet points is to provide an easy method of review after the text has been studied. Students can make use of these outlines of key points to help summarize their knowledge of the chapter contents.

- **Tips and Strategies:** In Chapter 1 we expanded our coverage of "Getting Started Doing Research," making use of McGuire's (1997) interesting heuristics for generating testable hypotheses and Sternberg's (1997) guide to the selection of a research question. Most of us need help when learning to perform a complex task, and the tips given by these experts can help students begin to think about the complex task of doing psychological research. Instructors may wish to call attention to these strategies when discussing research studies used to illustrate various methodologies or to incorporate them when planning student research projects.

- **Approach to Statistical Analysis:** In the past few years there have been important challenges to the way psychologists traditionally analyze research results. A controversy has centered on the use of null-hypothesis significance testing. In fact, at one point, rumors of a "ban" by the APA on null-hypothesis testing were circulating in the field. At the same time, we have noticed an ever increasing sophistication in the statistical treatment of data. This is especially the case for correlational analyses. Path analysis and structural equation modeling techniques, for instance, are becoming more prevalent in the literature. As instructors we find it increasingly difficult to identify published articles that are approachable by undergraduates. And as authors of an introductory textbook on research methods, we find ourselves in a quandary. How do we introduce students to techniques of statistical analysis in a way that is sensitive to important issues in this area and also prepare them to digest current research reports? In part, this state of affairs represents the perennial problem of deciding how best to integrate research design and statistics, a problem every instructor of the research course (and every author of a methods textbook) has wrestled with. Recently, however, this challenge has become more salient and more difficult.

  Our response has been to make significant changes in the way in which we treat statistical analysis in this edition. The most obvious change will be seen in the appendix material, which has been completely rewritten. A new appendix is titled "Data Analysis and Interpretation" and replaces the previous appendix, which had mainly a how-to-do-it emphasis. The statistical appendix in this edition is a tutorial on analysis and interpretation of results based on our understanding of the issues as presented by experts in our field. We leaned heavily on Robert Abelson's ideas as elucidated in his published articles and book, *Statistics as Principled Argument* (1995/Erlbaum), the trenchant arguments made by Geoff Loftus advocating the use of error bars and confidence intervals, the report by the APA Task Force on Statistical Inference co-chaired by Abelson, Jacob Cohen, and Robert Rosenthal (see, for example, Azar, 1997), as well as the views of many others who tutored us so we could tutor students.

  Students will find in the new appendix an introduction to what is recognized as a necessary three-stage approach to analysis: an exploratory stage (getting to know the data); a summary (descriptive) stage; and a confirmation stage (confirming what the data tell us). We describe techniques for analysis appropriate to all three stages (including stem-and-leaf displays, traditional descriptive statistics, and various methods of confirmation ranging from error bars to confidence intervals to traditional inferential techniques such as analysis of variance). We walk students through a research study using actual data from a published article, illustrating the stages of analysis and informing students what may and may not be said on the basis of analysis techniques. For instance, we discuss at length through a series of questions posed to students what they may conclude (or not conclude) on the basis of traditional null-hypothesis testing techniques. The appendix also presents the rationale and guidelines for obtaining measures of effect size as well as conducting a power analysis. Power tables are now included in this edition. We expect undergraduate students to find some of these statistical issues challenging, but we are optimistic that careful study of the material in this appendix will give them the necessary background both to read critically published research articles and to analyze data from their own research projects.

- **Improvement by Chapter:** In the chapter material we continue in this edition to identify for students how statistical analysis and methods are intertwined. In Chapter 4 we open the door to more complex correlational analysis with a (new) brief illustration of path analysis. In the experimental chapters (6–8) we again emphasize analysis of variance techniques in conjunction with effect size analyses, but also (in Chapter 6) illustrate graphical interpretation and the use of confidence intervals when confirming what data tell us. For this latter example, we had the gracious cooperation of Judy DeLoache and her colleagues who provided statistical summaries of actual data from her cross-cultural research on children's cognition. In this way we were able to illustrate difficult statistical concepts in the context of interesting contemporary psychological research, which is our never-ceasing goal when revising.

- **A New Sample APA Manuscript:** The topic of the new sample paper is false memory and is written to illustrate the most current recommendations of APA regarding report writing (e.g., including power analyses and effect size measures when reporting results). Like its predecessor, however, the manuscript details an actual research study.

- **Web Site:** Both students and instructors using this edition will also benefit from a new web site that was designed for this book. Much of the material that was published before in a workbook written to accompany the major text is now found on this web site. There are interactive exercises and quizzes for students to test their knowledge of text material, as well as links to other important psychology web sites. Instructors will find an image bank to prepare transparencies for class use, and both students and instructors may easily contact the authors via this site. Please come see us at www.mhhe.com/shaughnessy.

WORDS OF THANKS

Many knowledgeable and discerning reviewers over the years contributed to this latest edition. Among the most recent to whom we are grateful are

Laura Bowman
Central Connecticut State University
Angela Farris Watkins
Spelman College
Joel Freud
University of Arkansas
Brenda Kirby
LeMoyne University

Laura Thompson
New Mexico State University
Terri Bonebright
DePauw University
David Basden
California State University–Fresno

If a change that was recommended didn't appear, it wasn't because we didn't consider carefully what these reviewers were telling us. We did. Thanks for pushing us to be better.

The cumulative contributions of many others to this and earlier editions are by now beyond easy acknowledgment. Yet, some people stand out as helping to prepare this latest edition. They include our colleagues at Loyola University Chicago, Emil Posavac and Scott Tindale, who read and critiqued the new appendix dealing with data analysis and interpretation, and Joe Sherwin, Director of Research Services at Loyola, who read carefully the ethics chapter and made important suggestions for changes. The secretarial staff at Loyola made many things easier. In particular we want to acknowledge Lillian Hardison, Anita Sissac, and Marilyn Domingo. And many thanks go to Paula Shaughnessy, who stood in below-zero wind chill to snap a picture of three silly people running around in shorts one cold December day. Andy Apodaca, with just a little supervision from Liz Zechmeister, did a marvelous job of proofreading, checking references, and preparing the indexes.

We also would like to acknowledge the editorial and production staff at McGraw-Hill. Jane Vaicunas, as editorial director, has been with us for several editions now. Joe Terry was the senior sponsoring editor who brought things together, with a lot of help from his editorial assistant, Barbara Santoro. Susan Kunchandy and Jim Rozsa helped develop and market the book, respectively. Our project manager, Gloria Schiesl, and production supervisor, Sandy Hahn, got us through copy editing and page proofing, and then out the door. The supplement coordinator, Lai Moy, worked with John Shaughnessy to develop the instructor's manual. Cover designer, Rick Noel, made us look smart outside and Toni Michaels helped with photos inside. Our copy editor, Bea Sussman, was very helpful and did a superb job. Finally, these last two editions have benefited from the beautiful drawings by our good friend Fran Hughes. She makes research methods something to look at!

John J. Shaughnessy
Eugene B. Zechmeister
Jeanne S. Zechmeister

PART

I

General Issues

Introduction

CHAPTER OUTLINE

PSYCHOLOGY AS A SCIENCE
THE SCIENTIFIC METHOD
Scientific and Nonscientific Approaches to Knowledge
Goals of the Scientific Method
SCIENTIFIC THEORY CONSTRUCTION AND TESTING
SCIENTIFIC INTEGRITY
GETTING STARTED DOING RESEARCH
THE ORGANIZATION OF THIS BOOK
SUMMARY

PSYCHOLOGY AS A SCIENCE

- The scope of scientific psychology has increased dramatically in the 100-plus years since its inception.
- The American Psychological Association (APA) and the American Psychological Society (APS) promote the science of psychology.

There is no record of who first observed behavior carefully and systematically, who conducted the first public opinion survey, or even of who performed the first psychology experiment. We don't really know exactly when psychology first became an independent discipline. It emerged gradually, with its roots in the thinking of Aristotle (the "father" of all psychology; Keller, 1937), in the writings of later philosophers such as Descartes and Locke, and, even later, in the work of early 19th-century physiologists and physicists.

The date usually taken to mark psychology's official beginning is 1879. In that year Wilhelm Wundt established a formal psychology laboratory in Leipzig, Germany. Wundt, like many scientists of his time, had a doctoral degree in medicine. He even published for a while in the fields of anatomy and physiology. These experiences gave Wundt a basis for his ideas about a "physiological psychology" that led to his scientific approach to psychology. Dozens of researchers from around the world came to his psychology laboratory to learn about the "new" discipline. As a consequence, from Wundt's laboratory a scientific psychology spread quickly to the intellectual centers of the world. According to one noted historian, Wilhelm Wundt was the first person "who without reservation is properly called a psychologist" (Boring, 1950, p. 316).

Whatever exact date one accepts for the beginning of a scientific psychology, we can see that the enterprise is little more than 100 years old. Near the end of the 19th century, in 1892, the American Psychological Association (APA) was formed, with G. Stanley Hall as its first president. Hall had been a student at

Wilhelm Wundt
(1832–1920)

William James
(1842–1910)

Harvard of the well-known American philosopher and psychologist William James. In 1878, James bestowed upon Hall the first Ph.D. in psychology given in the United States. After receiving his degree, Hall left the United States to study with Wundt in Germany (Boring, 1950). Still later, in 1887, Hall founded the first psychology journal in the United States, the *American Journal of Psychology*. The APA had only a few dozen members in its first year; 100 years later, in 1992, when the APA celebrated its 100th birthday, there were approximately 70,000 members (see American Psychological Association, 1991).

Psychology has changed significantly since its beginnings. Wundt and his colleagues were primarily interested in questions of sensation and perception—for instance, visual illusions and imagery. Experiments on reaction time also were conducted with the goal of measuring the time necessary for various cognitive processes, such as those involved in making choices (Boring, 1950). Psychologists continue to be interested in sensation and perception, and Wundt's procedures form the basis of some of the experimental methods in use today. However, research on sensation and perception represents but a fraction of the research undertaken in contemporary psychology. Today psychologists are interested in a myriad of topics, including those in such general areas as clinical, social, industrial, counseling, physiological, cognitive, educational, and developmental psychology.

Psychology has also not developed strictly as a laboratory science. Although laboratory investigation remains at the heart of psychological inquiry, psychologists and other behavioral scientists do research in schools, clinics, businesses, hospitals, and other nonlaboratory settings, including the Internet (see, for example, Smith & Leigh, 1997). Many research psychologists, for instance, are engaged in program evaluation, a type of research in which the impact of large-scale interventions on groups or institutions is evaluated. Program evaluators confront questions such as whether a new management–labor relations program will lead to increased employee morale and company productivity, or whether the nationwide Head Start program has significantly raised the IQ of hundreds of thousands of preschoolers (see Chapter 10).

Promotion of psychological research is a concern of the APA as well as the American Psychological Society (APS). Formed in 1988 to emphasize mainly scientific issues in psychology, APS has grown at a phenomenal rate. When APS celebrated its 10th anniversary in 1998, there were more than 15,000 members (see Ruksznis, 1998). Although many psychologists choose to join either APA or APS, many join both. APA and APS both sponsor annual conventions, which psychologists attend to learn about the most recent developments in their fields; each organization also publishes scientific journals in order to communicate the latest research findings to its members and to society in general; and both organizations encourage student affiliation, which provides educational and research opportunities for both undergraduate and graduate psychology students. By affiliating with APA and APS, students can subscribe to major psychology journals at a relatively low cost as well as become involved at an early stage in a career in psychology. Information about joining APA and APS as a regular member or as a student affiliate can be obtained by writing to the respective head offices, or by consulting their World Wide Web pages on the Internet at:

(APA) http://www.apa.org
(APS) http://www.psychologicalscience.org

Both the APA and APS web sites provide news about important recent psychological research findings, information about psychology publications, and links to many psychology organizations. Take a look!

THE SCIENTIFIC METHOD

- Psychologists use the scientific method to gain knowledge about human and animal behavior.
- The scientific method differs from nonscientific ("everyday") approaches to gaining knowledge.

There is one way in which psychology has not changed in the 100 years or so of its existence: The **scientific method** is still emphasized as the basis for investigation. The founding of Wundt's laboratory marked the beginning of the formal application of the scientific method to problems in psychology. This method is not identified with particular kinds of equipment, nor is it associated exclusively with specific research procedures. The scientific method is something abstract. It is an approach to knowledge that is best described by distinguishing it from what might be called *nonscientific* or "everyday" approaches to knowledge.

Scientific and Nonscientific Approaches to Knowledge

- The scientific method is empirical and requires systematic, controlled observation.
- To achieve control in a research situation, researchers manipulate independent variables or select levels of individual differences variables to determine their effect on behavior.
- Dependent variables are measures of behavior used to assess the effects of independent variables.
- Scientific reporting is unbiased and objective; clear communication of concepts occurs when operational definitions are used.
- Scientific instruments are accurate and precise; physical and psychological measurement should be valid and reliable.
- A hypothesis is a tentative explanation for a phenomenon; testable hypotheses have clearly defined concepts (operational definitions), are not circular, and refer to concepts that can be observed.
- Scientists adopt a skeptical attitude and are cautious about accepting explanations until sufficient empirical evidence is obtained.

TABLE 1.1   CHARACTERISTICS OF SCIENTIFIC AND NONSCIENTIFIC (EVERYDAY) APPROACHES TO KNOWLEDGE*

	Nonscientific (everyday)	Scientific
General Approach:	Intuitive	Empirical
Observation:	Casual, uncontrolled	Systematic, controlled
Reporting:	Biased, subjective	Unbiased, objective
Concepts:	Ambiguous, with surplus meanings	Clear definitions, operational specificity
Instruments:	Inaccurate, imprecise	Accurate, precise
Measurements:	Not valid or reliable	Valid and reliable
Hypotheses:	Untestable	Testable
Attitude:	Uncritical, accepting	Critical, skeptical

*Based in part on distinctions suggested by Marx (1963).

Several major differences between a scientific and a nonscientific approach to knowledge are outlined in Table 1.1. Collectively, the characteristics listed under "Scientific" define what is called the scientific method. The distinctions made in Table 1.1 between a scientific and a nonscientific approach are intended to highlight differences that frequently exist between an informal and casual approach that often characterizes our everyday thinking and thinking that is characteristic of the scientist's approach to knowledge. These distinctions are briefly summarized as follows.

General Approach   Many everyday judgments are made intuitively. This usually means that we act on the basis of what "feels right" or what "seems reasonable." Intuition is not based on a formal decision process, such as that of deductive logic, nor is it based on information that was taught to us or that we acquired through direct experience. The many everyday inferences and conclusions reached intuitively are the product of insight and of what we quickly perceive as true.

Intuition is a valuable cognitive process. We frequently have little to go on other than what intuition suggests is the right answer or the proper course to follow. Intuition can also help us make decisions in situations that we have not encountered before. Consider, for example, what intuition might suggest as the answer to a question based on the following situation:

> Assume that on two different occasions you are the victim of a street crime. Let us say that you are walking down the street and someone tries to grab your wallet or purse. The thief begins to wrestle with you in order to get it. You find yourself in need of assistance. On one occasion there is a crowd of bystanders who witness the attempted robbery. On the other occasion there is only one person who sees the event. The question is: In which situation would you be more likely to receive help, when many people are present or when only one person is present?

Intuition would suggest that the more people present, the greater the chances that at least one person would help. Surprisingly, social psychologists have determined that just the opposite is true. A bystander is more likely to act in an emergency when alone than when a group of people is present (Latané & Darley, 1970; see also Chapter 3).

Our intuition about what is true does not always agree with what is actually true because we fail to recognize that our perceptions may be distorted by what are called cognitive biases or because we neglect to weigh available evidence appropriately (Kahneman & Tversky, 1973; Tversky & Kahneman, 1974). One such cognitive bias, for instance, is called *illusory correlation*. This is our tendency to perceive a relationship between events when none exists. To illustrate this bias, Ward and Jenkins (1965) showed people the results of a hypothetical 50-day cloud-seeding experiment. For each of the 50 days, the research participants were told whether cloud seeding had been done and whether it had rained on that day. Ward and Jenkins constructed the results such that there was actually no relationship between cloud seeding and the likelihood of rain—rain was equally likely on days when seeding had and had not been done. Nonetheless, people were convinced that the evidence supported their intuitive supposition that cloud seeding and rain varied together. One possible basis for the illusory-correlation bias is that we are more likely to notice events that are consistent with our beliefs than events that violate our beliefs. Thus, in Ward and Jenkins' study, people may have been more likely to notice and remember the days on which cloud seeding was followed by rain than the days on which clouds were seeded in vain because they believe cloud seeding produces rain.

The scientific approach to knowledge is empirical rather than intuitive. An **empirical approach** emphasizes direct observation and experimentation as a way of answering questions. This does not mean that intuition plays no role in science. Any scientist can probably recount tales of obtaining empirical results that intuition had suggested would emerge. On the other hand, the same scientist is also likely to have come up with just as many findings that were counterintuitive. Research at first may be guided by what the scientist's intuition suggests is the proper direction to take. Eventually, however, the scientist strives to be guided by what direct observation and experimentation reveal to be true.

Observation   We can learn a great deal about behavior by simply observing the actions of others. However, everyday observations are not always made carefully or systematically. Most people do not attempt to control or eliminate factors that might influence the events that they are observing. As a consequence, erroneous conclusions are often drawn. Consider, for instance, the classic case of Clever Hans. Hans was a horse who was said by his owner, a German mathematics teacher, to have amazing talents. Hans could count, do simple addition and subtraction (even involving fractions), read German, answer simple questions ("What is the lady holding in her hands?"), and give the date, and tell time (Watson, 1914/1967). Hans answered questions by tapping with his forefoot or by pointing with his nose at different alternatives shown to him. His owner considered Hans to be truly intelligent and denied using any tricks to guide his horse's behavior. And, in fact, Clever Hans was clever even when the questioner was someone other than his owner.

Newspapers carried accounts of Hans's performances, and hundreds of people came to view this amazing horse (Figure 1.1). In 1904 a scientific commission was established with the goal of discovering the basis for Hans's abilities.

FIGURE 1.1   Top: Clever Hans performing before onlookers. Bottom: Hans being tested under more controlled conditions when Hans could not see the questioner.

The scientists found that Hans was no longer clever if either of two circumstances existed. First, Hans did not know the answers to questions if the questioner also did not know the answers. Second, Hans was not very clever if he could not see his questioner. It was discovered that Hans was responding to very slight movements of the questioner. A slight bending forward by the questioner would start Hans tapping, and any movement upward or backward would cause Hans to stop tapping. The commission demonstrated that questioners were unintentionally cuing Hans in this way.

This famous account of Clever Hans illustrates the fact that scientific observation (unlike casual observation) is systematic and controlled. Indeed, it has been suggested that **control** is the essential ingredient of science, distinguishing it from nonscientific procedures (Boring, 1954; Marx, 1963). In the case of Clever Hans, investigators exercised control by manipulating, *one at a time*, conditions such as whether the questioner knew the answer to the questions asked and whether Hans could see the questioner (see Figure 1.1). By exercising control, taking care to investigate the effect of various factors one by one, the scientist seeks to gain a clearer picture of the factors that actually produce a phenomenon.

The factors that the researcher controls or manipulates in order to determine their effect on behavior are called the **independent variables.** In the simplest of studies, the independent variable has two levels. These two levels often represent the presence and the absence of some treatment, respectively. The condition in which the treatment is present is commonly called the *experimental condition*; the condition in which the treatment is absent is called the *control condition*. If we wanted to study the effect of drinking alcohol on the ability to process complex information quickly and accurately, for example, the independent variable would be the presence or absence of alcohol in a drink that participants were given. Participants in the experimental condition would receive alcohol, while participants in the control condition would receive the same drink without alcohol.

The levels of the independent variable do not always represent the presence and the absence of some treatment; moreover, an independent variable may have more than two levels. What is critical is that the levels differ with respect to the variable of interest. For example, Heath and Davidson (1988) recruited female college students to participate in a study designed to aid in the development of a rape-prevention pamphlet. When volunteers appeared in the laboratory, they were asked to review one of three packages of materials that they were told was being considered for possible inclusion in the pamphlet. The three packages of materials varied in the manner in which rape was described. Specifically, the materials to be reviewed presented rape as being very controllable, somewhat controllable, or not at all controllable. After reviewing the materials, the women were asked a series of questions regarding their own perceptions of the risk of rape. The independent variable in this study was the degree of control emphasized in the pamphlet materials; it had three levels (high, medium, low).

Sometimes the levels of the independent variable are selected by a researcher rather than manipulated. This is typically the case when an **individual differences variable** serves as the independent variable. An individual differences variable is a characteristic or trait that varies consistently across individuals. For example, a researcher may be interested in how depression affects perceptions of other people (e.g., Albright & Henderson, 1995). Do depressed individuals, for instance, perceive others more or less accurately than individuals who are not depressed? Level of depression would be the independent variable in this study. Level of depression is an individual differences variable and typically is not manipulated by a researcher; rather, the researcher controls this independent variable by systematically selecting individuals who exhibit varying levels of naturally occurring depression. Intelligence, age, aggressiveness, gender, and fraternity or sorority membership are other examples of individual differences variables. Because individuals are selected from preexisting groups, such as those who are depressed, female, aggressive, and so forth, these variables are also sometimes referred to as *natural groups variables.*

The term *independent variable* is used both for individual differences variables when levels of the variable are selected (e.g., level of depression) and for manipulated variables when the levels are implemented by the researcher (e.g., type of booklet describing rape). Nevertheless, as you will see later in Chapter 6, there are important differences between these two kinds of independent variables.

The measures of behavior that are used to assess the effect (if any) of the independent variables are called **dependent variables.** In our example of a study that investigates the effects of alcohol on processing complex information, the researcher might measure the number of errors made by control and experimental participants when playing a difficult video game. Errors, then, would be the dependent variable. Most studies in psychology are done in order to discover the nature of the relationship between particular independent and dependent variables. In the Heath and Davidson (1988) rape study, there were several dependent variables, represented by the women's responses to questions on the rape-perception questionnaire. The results showed that women who read materials emphasizing rape as an uncontrollable event reported higher anxiety when outside on the street or inside their homes, and a greater intention to take precautionary steps, than did women who reviewed the materials describing rape as more controllable. Interestingly, results of additional experiments carried out by Heath and Davidson (1988) indicated that although uncontrollable rape is definitely viewed as anxiety producing, the "intent" to be more cautious reported by their research participants may not always be followed by actual changes in behaviors. Unfortunately, when rape is perceived as an uncontrollable event some women may view attempts to reduce their vulnerability to attacks as futile.

If changes in the dependent variable are to be interpreted unambiguously as a result of the effect of the independent variable, proper control techniques must be used. The story of Clever Hans was used to show how scientists use control to eliminate alternative explanations for a phenomenon (e.g., that Clever Hans was, in fact, clever). Throughout this text, we will be describing specific control procedures used by psychologists when carrying out research (see especially Chapters 6 and 7).

Reporting   If we ask someone to *report* to us about events that occurred in our absence, we probably want the report to be unbiased and objective. Otherwise we will be unable to determine exactly what happened. As you might imagine, personal biases and subjective impressions often enter into everyday reports that we receive. Ask anyone to describe an event to you and you are likely to receive not merely details of the event but also personal impressions. You may also find that the details reported to you are not the ones that you would have reported. We often report events in terms of our own interests and attitudes. Obviously, these interests and attitudes do not always coincide with those of others. The next time you take a class examination, poll several classmates on their impressions of the test. Their reports are likely to vary dramatically, depending on such factors as how well prepared they were, what they concentrated on when they studied, and their expectations about what the instructor was going to emphasize on the test.

When scientists report their findings, they seek to separate what they have observed from what they conclude or infer on the basis of these observations. For example, consider the photograph in Figure 1.2. How would you describe to someone what you see there? One way to describe this scene is to say that two people are running along a path with another person running in front of them. You might also describe this scene as three people *racing* each other. If you use this second description, you are reporting an inference drawn from what

FIGURE 1.2   How would you describe this scene?

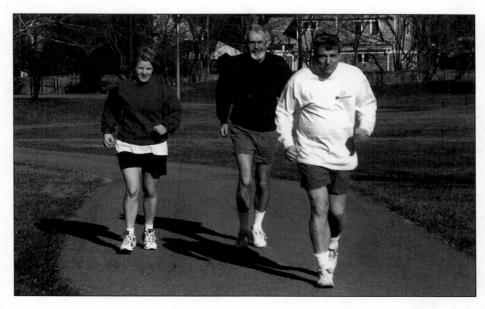

you have seen and not just reporting what you have observed. The description of three people running would be preferred in a scientific report.

This distinction between description and inference in reporting can be carried to extremes. For example, describing what is shown in Figure 1.2 as running could be considered an inference, the actual observation being that three people are moving their legs up and down and forward in rapid, long strides. Such a literal description also would not be appropriate. The point is that, in scientific reporting, observers must guard against a tendency to draw inferences too quickly. Further, events should be described in sufficient detail without including trivial and unnecessary minutiae. Proper methods for making observations and reporting them will be discussed in Chapter 3.

Scientific reporting seeks to be unbiased and objective. One accepted check on whether a report is unbiased is whether it can be verified by more than one independent observer. A measure of interobserver agreement, for example, is usually found in observational studies (see Chapter 3). Unfortunately, many biases are subtle and not always detected even in scientific reporting. Consider the fact that there is a species of fish in which the eggs are incubated in the mouth of the male parent until they hatch. The first scientist to observe the eggs disappear into their father's mouth could certainly be forgiven for assuming, momentarily, that he was eating them. That's simply what we expect organisms to do with their mouths! But the careful observer waits, watches for unexpected results, and takes nothing for granted.

Concepts   We use the term *concepts* to refer to things (both living and inanimate), to events (things in action), and to relationships among things or events, as well as to their characteristics (Marx, 1963). "Dog" is a concept, as is "barking," and so is "obedience." Concepts are the symbols by which we ordinarily communicate. Clear, unambiguous communication of ideas requires that we use concepts that are clearly defined. This means that the concepts we use should be free of unwarranted or surplus meaning. That is, a concept should not convey more meaning than was intended.

In everyday conversation we can often get by without having to worry too much about how we define a concept. Many words, for instance, are commonly used and apparently understood even though neither party to the communication knows *exactly* what the words mean. We are suggesting that people frequently communicate with one another without being fully aware of what they are talking about. This may sound ridiculous but, to illustrate our point, try the following.

Ask a few people whether they believe that intelligence is mostly inherited or mostly acquired. You might try arguing a point of view opposite to theirs just for the fun of it. After having engaged them in a discussion about the roots of intelligence, ask them what they mean by "intelligence." You will probably find that most people have a difficult time defining this concept. Yet people are frequently willing to debate an important point regarding intelligence, and even take a definite stand on the issue, without being able to say exactly what "intelligence" is. When someone does provide a definition, it is unlikely to be exactly the same as that given by another person. That is, "intelligence" means one thing to one person and something else to another. Clearly, in order to attempt to answer the question of whether intelligence is mainly inherited or mainly acquired, we must provide an exact definition that all parties involved can accept. On the other hand, we can talk about it, even argue about it, on an everyday basis without knowing exactly what it is we are talking about!

One way in which a scientist gives meaning to a concept is by defining it operationally. An **operational definition** explains a concept solely in terms of the operations used to produce and measure it. Intelligence, for instance, can be defined operationally by specifying a paper-and-pencil test emphasizing understanding of logical relationships, short-term memory, and familiarity with the meaning of words. Some may not like this operational definition of intelligence, but once a particular test has been identified, there can at least be no argument about what intelligence means *according to this definition*. Operational definitions facilitate communication, at least among those who know how and why they are used.

Although exact meaning is conveyed via operational definitions, this approach to communication has not escaped criticism. One problem has been alluded to already. That is, if we don't like one operational definition of intelligence, there is nothing to prevent us from giving intelligence another operational definition. Does this mean that there are as many kinds of intelligence as there are operational definitions? Each time a new set of questions is added to a paper-and-pencil test of intelligence do we have a new definition of intelligence? The answer, unfortunately, is that we don't really know. To determine whether a different procedure yields a new definition of intelligence, we would have to seek additional evidence. For example, do people who score high on one test also score high on the second test? If they do, the new test may be measuring the same thing as the old one.

Another criticism of using operational definitions is that the definitions are not always meaningful. For example, defining intelligence in terms of how long one can balance a ball on one's nose is an operational definition that most people would not find very meaningful. How do we decide whether a concept has been meaningfully defined? Once again, the solution is to appeal to other forms of evidence. How does performance on a balancing task compare to performance on other tasks that are commonly accepted as measures of intelligence? We must also be willing to apply common sense to the situation. Do people usually consider balancing a ball evidence of intelligence? Scientists are generally aware of the limitations of operational definitions; however, the clarity of communication that derives from this approach is assumed to outweigh the problems it raises.

Instruments   You depend on instruments to measure events more than you probably realize. The speedometer in the car, the clock in the bedroom, and the thermometer used to measure body temperature are all instruments that we would find it difficult to do without. And you can appreciate the problems that arise if one of these instruments is inaccurate. *Accuracy* refers to the difference between what an instrument says is true and what is known to be true. A clock that is consistently 5 minutes slow is not very accurate. Inaccurate clocks can make us late, inaccurate speedometers can earn us traffic tickets, and inaccurate thermometers can lead us to believe that we are ill when we are not. The accuracy of an instrument is determined by *calibrating* it, or checking it with another instrument known to be true. Thus, we periodically call the telephone company to check the accuracy of our clocks based on the recorded messages telling us the "time at the tone," which we assume represent the true time. The accuracy of speedometers can be checked using a combination of observations of roadside distance markers and the seconds ticking off on an accurate watch.

Measurements can be made at varying levels of *precision*. A measure of time in tenths of a second is not as precise as one that is in hundredths of a second. One instrument that yields imprecise measures is the gas gauge in most cars. Although reasonably accurate, gas gauges do not give very precise readings. Most of us have wished at one time or another that the gas gauge would permit us to determine whether we had that extra half gallon of gas that would get us to the next service station.

We also need instruments to measure behavior. Wundt used a reaction-time apparatus to measure the time required for cognitive processing. You can be assured that the precision, and even the accuracy, of instruments of this kind have improved significantly in the last 100 years. Today electronic counters provide precise measures of reaction time in milliseconds (thousandths of a second). Many other instruments are employed in contemporary psychology. To perform a psychophysiology experiment (e.g., when assessing a person's arousal level) requires instruments that give accurate measures of such internal states as heart rate and blood pressure. Tests of anxiety sometimes employ instruments to measure galvanic skin response (GSR). Other behavioral instruments are of the paper-and-pencil variety. Questionnaires and tests are popular instruments used by psychologists to measure behavior (see especially Chapter 4). So, too, are the rating scales used by human observers (see Chapter 3). For instance, rating aggression in children on a 7-point scale ranging from not at all aggressive (1) to very aggressive (7) can yield relatively accurate (although perhaps not too precise) measures of aggression. It is the responsibility of the behavioral scientist to use instruments that are as accurate and as precise as possible.

Measurement   Psychologists must deal with two types of measurement. The first type, *physical measurement*, involves dimensions for which there is an agreed-upon standard and an instrument for doing the measuring. Length is a dimension that can be scaled with physical measurement, and there are agreed-upon standards for units of length. For instance, 1 meter was at one time defined as 1/10,000,000 of the distance between the North Pole and the equator.

This proved impossible to measure precisely, so the definition of 1 meter was changed to the distance between two points on a platinum-iridium bar kept under controlled conditions near Paris, France. Although this provided accuracy to one part in a million, greater precision was sought. In 1960 the meter was defined as 1,650,763.73 wavelengths of the red-orange radiation of the inert gas krypton-86. But even this proved not precise enough for scientists. (When using the krypton measure to determine the distance from the earth to the moon, scientists found themselves in error by more than 1.5 meters.) The definition of the meter was changed to the length of the path traveled by light in a vacuum in 1/299,792,458 of a second.

In most research in psychology, however, the dimensions to be measured do not involve physical measurement. Rulers do not exist for measuring beauty, aggression, or intelligence. For these dimensions we must use a second type of measurement: *psychological measurement*. Agreement among a certain number of observers provides the basis for psychological measurement. If several independent observers agree that a certain action warrants a rating of 3 on a 7-point rating scale of aggression, we can say that we have a psychological measurement of the aggressiveness of the action. When Albright and Henderson (1995) asked individuals who were depressed and who were not depressed to evaluate other people, the researchers provided participants with an 8-point scale to judge the degree to which various statements about people were true. The rather counterintuitive finding was that depressed individuals provided more accurate ratings of other people than did those who were not depressed.

Of course, many dimensions that can be scaled physically can also be measured using psychological measurement. Observers can be asked to judge which of two lines is longer, and, if they consistently select the longer one, we know the observers can "measure" length. This type of measurement is called psychophysical measurement, and it represents one of the earliest areas of experimental investigation in psychology.

It is important that measurement be both valid and reliable. In general, **validity** refers to the "truthfulness" of a measure. A valid measure of a concept is one that measures what it claims to measure. We discussed this aspect of measurement when we mentioned possible operational definitions of intelligence. Intelligence, it was suggested, could be defined in terms of performance on a task requiring one to balance a ball on one's nose. According to the principle of "operationalism," this is a perfectly permissible operational definition. However, most of us would question whether such a balancing act is really a measure of intelligence. In other words, we would want to know if this is a valid measure of intelligence. Can intelligence actually be measured by how long we can keep a ball balanced on our nose? As we indicated earlier, evidence bearing on the validity of this definition would have to come from other sources. The validity of a measure is supported to the extent that people do as well on it as they do on independent measures that are presumed to measure the same concept. For example, if time spent balancing a ball is a valid measure of intelligence, then a person who does well on the balancing task should also do well

FIGURE 1.3   Balancing a ball on your nose may be an operational definition of intelligence, but is it a valid measure of intelligence?

on such measures as size of vocabulary, reasoning ability, and other accepted measures of intelligence.

The **reliability** of a measurement is indicated by its consistency. Several different kinds of reliability can be distinguished. When we speak of instrument reliability, we are discussing whether an instrument works consistently. The car that sometimes starts and sometimes doesn't when we engage the ignition is not very reliable. Observations made by two or more independent observers are said to be reliable if they show agreement—that is, if the observations are consistent from one observer to another. When several psychologists asked college students to rate the "happiness" of medal winners at the 1992 Summer Olympics in Barcelona Spain, they found that rater agreement was very high (Medvic, Madey, & Gilovich, 1995). They also found, somewhat counterintuitively, that bronze (third place) medal winners were perceived as happier than silver (second place) medal winners, a finding that was explained by a theory of counterfactual thinking. Apparently, people are happier just making it (to the medal stand) than they are just missing it (i.e., missing a gold medal).

In the context of psychological testing, researchers need to be concerned with test reliability. Are the results obtained on a test consistent from one administration of the test to another? When test scores are not reliable, we don't know what a particular score means. Suppose that in preparing to apply to graduate school in psychology you take the Graduate Record Examination (GRE), a test that is required of applicants to many graduate programs. Scores on this test are then sent to schools to which you are applying. Only if the GRE is a reliable test can a school trust that your score represents how you consistently perform on tests like this one. If a test is not reliable, then we have no way of knowing whether a particular score is high, low, or somewhere in the middle of scores you might possibly obtain on this test.

In subsequent chapters of this book, we will discuss various kinds of validity and reliability and introduce you to various methods for measuring them.

Hypotheses A **hypothesis** is a tentative explanation for something. It frequently attempts to answer the questions "How?" and "Why?" At one level, a hypothesis may simply suggest how particular variables are related. For example, consider the phenomenon of "depressive realism," which we have alluded to previously. This refers to the idea that in many situations depressed individuals make more accurate (or realistic) judgments than do individuals who are not depressed. Albright and Henderson (1995) wondered whether depressive realism would extend to depressives' judgments about people. They hypothesized that depressed individuals would judge other people more accurately than would those who were not depressed. That is, they hypothesized that level of depression and accuracy of judgments were *related*. You may remember that when these researchers asked participants to rate the degree to which various statements about people were true, the results supported their hypothesis: Depressed individuals gave more accurate ratings of other people than did those who were not depressed.

At a more theoretical level, a hypothesis may offer a reason (the "why") for the way that particular variables are related. For example, Albright and Henderson (1995) suggested that many of us avoid symptoms of depression by perceiving other people less favorably than is actually true. (This way we always look good!) Such a strategy may help us to feel good about ourselves. These researchers further hypothesized that depressed individuals, in contrast, may lose this ability to view people unfavorably. That is, depressed individuals make more accurate (realistic) judgments *because* they have lost the ability to view others unfavorably. Moreover, consistent with their reasoning, individuals who were not depressed (unlike depressed individuals) rated others less favorably than was objectively true.

Nearly everyone has proposed hypotheses to explain some human behavior at one time or another. Why do people commit apparently senseless acts of violence? What causes people to start smoking cigarettes? Why are some students academically more successful than others? One characteristic often distinguishes the hypotheses proposed by the nonscientist from those offered by the scientist: testability. As attractive as it might be, if a hypothesis cannot be tested, it is of no immediate use to science (Marx, 1963).

Hypotheses are not testable *if the concepts to which they refer are not adequately defined*. To say that a would-be assassin shot a U.S. president or other prominent figure because he was mentally disturbed is not a testable hypothesis unless a definition of mentally disturbed can be agreed upon. Unfortunately, psychologists and psychiatrists cannot always agree on what terms such as "mentally disturbed" mean. Often this occurs because an accepted operational definition is not available for these concepts. You may have learned in a psychology class that many of Freud's hypotheses are not testable. One reason has to do with the lack of operational definition for such concepts as *id*. As one prominent researcher has commented, "a criterion of whether or not a so-called empirical concept is a scientific concept is whether or not it has been operationally defined" (Underwood, 1957, p. 52). Therefore, in addition to facilitating clarity in communication, operational definitions offer a means of evaluating whether our hypotheses contain scientifically acceptable concepts.

Hypotheses are also untestable if they are *circular*, in which case the event itself becomes an explanation for the event. One scientist has pointed out that using a definition of an event as an explanation for the event—that is, a *circular hypothesis*—is something you can "catch the late-night talk show hosts doing" all the time (Kimble, 1989). Consider these examples:

— Your eight-year-old son is distractable in school and having trouble reading because he has an attention deficiency disorder.
— The stock market crash of October 19, 1987, was caused by widespread economic panic. (Kimble, 1989, p. 495)

Do you see that by saying a boy is "distractable . . . *because* he has an attention deficiency disorder" doesn't explain anything? An attention deficiency disorder is defined by the inability to pay attention. Thus, such a statement simply says that he doesn't pay attention because he doesn't pay attention! Or that by saying a "stock market crash . . . was *caused* by widespread economic panic" simply suggests that economic panic (as defined by the stock market crash) is due to economic panic?

This scientist goes on to say that "If [he] could make just one change in what the general public (and some psychologists) understand about psychology, it would be to give them an immunity to such misuses of definitions" (Kimble, 1989, p. 495).

A hypothesis also may be untestable if it *appeals to ideas or forces that are not recognized by science*. As we have shown, science deals with the observable, the demonstrable, the empirical. To suggest that people who commit horrendous acts of violence are under orders from the Devil is not testable because it invokes a principle (the Devil) that is not in the province of science. Such hypotheses might be of value to philosophers or theologians but not to the scientist.

Hypotheses in scientific research are often derived from a theory. We'll discuss the nature of scientific theories, their function, and how they are constructed and tested later in this chapter. But now, let us complete this description of a scientific approach by discussing the attitude you must have as a scientist.

Attitude   More than anything else, scientists are skeptical. Not only do they want to "see it before believing it," but they are likely to want to see it again, and again, perhaps under conditions of their own choosing. Behavioral scientists come to this skepticism by recognizing two important facts. First, behavior is complex, and often many factors interact to give rise to a psychological phenomenon. Discovering these factors is often a difficult task. The explanations proposed are sometimes premature, not enough factors having been considered or the existence of one or more factors having gone unnoticed. Second, the behavioral scientist recognizes that science is a human endeavor. People make mistakes. Human inference, as we have suggested, is not always to be trusted. Therefore scientists are often skeptical about "new discoveries" and extraordinary claims.

The skepticism of scientists produces a cautiousness that is often lacking in those without scientific training. Too many people are apparently all too ready to accept explanations that are based on insufficient or inadequate evidence. This is illustrated by the widespread belief in the occult. Rather than approach cautiously the claims of those who promote belief in the paranormal, many people are uncritical in their acceptance. According to public opinion surveys, a large majority of Americans believe in ESP (extrasensory perception), and many people apparently are convinced that beings from outer space have visited earth. About 2 in 5 Americans give some credibility to astrology reports, and as many as 12 million adults report changing their behavior after reading astrology reports (Miller, 1986). Such beliefs are held despite minimal and often contradictory evidence of the validity of horoscopes. This human tendency to ignore certain kinds of evidence is not new. When scientists successfully demonstrated the means by which Clever Hans was so clever, many people continued to believe in his superior reasoning ability (Watson, 1914/1967).

What is responsible for this tendency to propose explanations based on the occult and to resist obvious evidence to the contrary? Singer and Benassi (1981) suggest that an uncritical attitude toward such events has several sources. First, there are many distortions in the media. The public is constantly exposed to television shows, newspaper accounts, and other reports of events presumably caused by supernatural forces. These reports are often presented with little critical evaluation, and scientific evidence for alternative explanations is frequently ignored. The sheer pervasiveness of such reports may lend credibility to them.

Another reason for the widespread acceptance of the occult may be deficiencies in human reasoning. As we emphasized earlier in this chapter, everyday inferences are susceptible to many biases, including the tendency to seek only confirmatory evidence, to jump to conclusions, and to perceive causality in events when none is actually present (see, for example, Zechmeister & Johnson, 1992). Finally, Singer and Benassi find fault with science education. Too often, they suggest, science is taught as a set of facts rather than as a way of approaching knowledge critically and systematically. Thus, people are often impatient with the scientific process and even confused when scientists appear to change their minds or when they attempt to clarify earlier findings. Singer and Benassi also find that the general public exhibits woefully little general scientific knowledge. Many people believe that islands float on the ocean surface, for instance, and that the moon is fixed in the sky but only visible at night. Belief in astrology reports and "lucky numbers," for example, is stronger among people with little formal education than it is among college-educated individuals (Miller, 1986).

Scientists do not, of course, automatically assume that unconventional interpretations of unexplained phenomena could not possibly be true. They simply insist on being allowed to test all claims and to reject those that are inherently untestable. Scientific skepticism is a gullible public's defense against charlatans and others who would sell them ineffective medicines and cures, impossible schemes to get rich, and supernatural explanations for natural phenomena.

Goals of the Scientific Method

- The scientific method is intended to meet three goals: description, prediction, and understanding.
- Psychologists seek to describe events and relationships between variables; most often, researchers use the nomothetic approach and quantitative analysis.
- Correlational relationships allow psychologists to predict behavior or events, but do not allow psychologists to infer what causes these relationships.
- Psychologists understand the cause of a phenomenon when the three conditions for causal inference are met: covariation, time-order relationship, and elimination of plausible alternative causes.
- The experimental method, in which researchers manipulate independent variables to determine their effect on dependent variables, establishes time-order and allows a clearer determination of covariation.
- Plausible alternative causes for a relationship are eliminated if there are no confoundings in a study; a study free of confoundings has internal validity.
- External validity refers to the extent to which a study's findings may be used to describe different populations, settings, and conditions.

Description   Description refers to the procedures by which events and their relationships are defined, classified, cataloged, or categorized. Clinical research, for instance, has provided practitioners with many different sets of criteria for classifying mental disorders. Many of these are found in the American Psychiatric Association's *Diagnostic and Statistical Manual of Mental Disorders* (4th ed., 1994), also known as *DSM-IV*. Consider, as one example, the criteria used to define the disorder labeled *Dissociative Fugue* (formerly Psychogenic Fugue).

Diagnostic Criteria for Dissociative Fugue

A The predominant disturbance is sudden, unexpected travel away from home or one's customary place of daily activities, with inability to recall one's past.

B Confusion about personal identity or assumption of a new identity (partial or complete).

C The disturbance does not occur exclusively during the course of Dissociative Identity Disorder and is not due to the direct physiological effects of a substance (e.g., a drug of abuse, medication) or a general medical condition (e.g., temporal lobe epilepsy).

D The symptoms cause clinically significant stress or impairment in social, occupational, or other important areas of functioning. (*DSM-IV*, 1994, p. 481)

The diagnostic criteria used to define dissociative fugue provide an operational definition for this disorder. Like many other unusual mental disorders, dissociative fugues are relatively rare; thus, we typically learn about these kinds of disorders based on individual descriptions of people exhibiting them. These descriptions are called "case studies." Clinical research frequently makes use of case studies, a procedure that will be discussed in detail in Chapter 9. Research also seeks to provide clinicians with descriptions of the prevalence of a mental disorder and their relationship to variables including, but not restricted to, gender and age. According to the *DSM-IV* (1994), for instance, dissociative fugue is seen primarily in adults, and although it is relatively rare, it is more frequent "during times of extremely stressful events such as wartime or natural disaster" (p. 482).

Another example of description in psychological research is the work of Levine (1990) who described the "pace of life" in various cultures and countries of the world. Measures of a country's tempo were made by noting the accuracy of outdoor bank clocks in a country's cities, by timing the walking speed of pedestrians over a distance of 100 feet, and by measuring the speed with which postal clerks processed a standard request for stamps. The investigator frequently enlisted the help of students to make observations while they traveled during summer vacations or semester breaks. The results of this study are shown in Figure 1.4. The citizens of Japan exhibited, overall, the fastest pace of life; the citizens of Indonesia were the slowest. U.S. citizens were second overall.

Psychology (like science in general) develops descriptions of phenomena using the *nomothetic approach*. The objective of the nomothetic approach is to establish broad generalizations and "universal laws" that apply to a wide population of organisms. As a consequence, psychological research frequently consists of studies involving large numbers of participants with the purpose of determining the "average," or typical, performance of a group. This average may or may not represent the performance of any one individual in the group. Not all citizens of Japan or the United States, for example, are on the fast track. In fact, Levine (1990) and his colleagues found wide differences in the pace of life among various cities within a country. Inhabitants of large cities walked faster than did those of medium-sized cities in the various countries that were visited. In the United States, differences in a city's tempo were found depending on the region of the country. Cities in the Northeast (e.g., Boston, New York) had a faster tempo than did cities on the West Coast (e.g., Sacramento, Los Angeles). Of course, there will be individual variations within cities as well. Not all citizens of Los Angeles are going to be slow-paced, nor are all New Yorkers going to be fast-paced. Nevertheless, the Japanese move *in general* at a faster

FIGURE 1.4   Measures of accuracy of a country's bank clocks, pedestrian walking speed, and the speed of postal clerks performing a routine task served to describe the pace of life in a country. In the graph a longer bar represents greater accuracy of clocks or greater speed of walking and performing a task (from Levine, 1990).

pace than do Indonesians, and Americans on the West Coast exhibit, *on the average*, a slower pace of life than do residents of the Northeast.

The nomothetic approach does not deny that there are important differences *among* individuals; it simply seeks to identify the similarities that exist among these differences. For example, a person's individuality is not threatened by our knowledge that that person's heart, like the hearts of other human beings, is located in the upper left chest cavity. Similarly, we do not deny a person's individuality when we state that that person's behavior is influenced by patterns of reinforcement. Researchers merely seek to describe what organisms are like in general on the basis of the average performance of a group of different organisms.

Although the nomothetic approach predominates in psychological research, there is an alternative. Some psychologists, notably Allport (1961), argue that the nomothetic approach is inadequate—that the individual cannot be represented by an average value. Allport argues that the individual both is unique and exhibits behavior that conforms to general laws, or principles. He maintains that study of the individual, called *idiographic research*, is important. A major form of idiographic research is the case study method, which we will describe in detail in Chapter 9.

Researchers decide whether to make generalizations about groups of individuals or to look for the lawfulness found in one individual's behavior. This decision is largely dictated by the nature of the question being asked. And although many researchers do mainly one or the other kind of research, others may do both. A clinical psychologist, for instance, may decide to pursue mainly idiographic investigations of a few clients in therapy but consider nomothetic issues when doing research with groups of college students. Another decision that the researcher must make is whether to do quantitative or qualitative research. *Quantitative research* refers to studies whose findings are mainly the product of statistical summary and analysis. *Qualitative research* produces research findings that are not arrived at by statistical summary or analysis and lack quantification altogether (see, for example, Strauss & Corbin, 1990).

The data of qualitative research are most commonly obtained from interviews and observations and can be used to describe individuals, groups, and social movements (Strauss & Corbin, 1990). Qualitative research is often about "naturally occurring, ordinary events in natural settings" (Miles & Huberman, 1994, p. 10). Powell-Cope (1995), for instance, used qualitative methods to "describe the experiences of gay couples when at least one was diagnosed with symptomatic HIV infection or AIDS" (p. 36). Van Meter, Yokoi, and Pressley (1994) used a qualitative research approach to develop a theory of student note-taking. The researchers met with university undergraduates in small discussion groups, conducted both directed and undirected interviews, then developed and administered formal questionnaires. According to the authors, this qualitative approach to research on student note-taking yielded "many insights into note-taking dynamics that have not been identified in previous research" (p. 323). Other examples of qualitative research are found in Chapter 3 when we discuss narrative records of observed behavior; case studies described in Chapter 9 also are a form of qualitative research. Just as psychological research is more frequently nomothetic than idiographic, it is also more typically quantitative than qualitative. And although both kinds of research can be usefully employed to describe behavior, our emphasis in this book is mainly on quantitative research.

Prediction   Description of events and their relationships often provides a basis for *prediction,* the second goal of the scientific method. There are important questions in psychology that call for predictions. For example: Does the early loss of a parent make a child especially vulnerable to depression? Are children who are overly aggressive likely to have emotional problems as adults? Do stressful life events lead to increased physical illness? Research findings suggest an affirmative answer to all of these questions. This information not only adds valuable knowledge to the discipline of psychology but is also helpful in both the treatment and the prevention of emotional disorders.

An important occupation of many psychologists is the prediction of later performance (e.g., on the job, in school, or in specific vocations) on the basis of earlier performance on various standardized tests. For instance, we mentioned earlier the Graduate Record Examination or GRE. Scores on this test, as well as undergraduate grade-point average (GPA), can be used to predict how well a student will do in graduate school. Yet Sternberg and Williams (1997) suggest that there are limitations on this prediction. They found that while GRE scores predicted fairly well the first-year grades of graduate students at their institution, the GRE was not predictive of other, important performance criteria such as advisors' ratings of a student's creativity, ability to teach, and ability to do research. Not surprisingly, these researchers have sparked a debate by questioning the validity of the GRE, which is so widely regarded as a predictor of students' later professional development (see, for example, "Comment" section of *American Psychologist*, 1998, *53*, 566–577).

Interestingly, research has shown that faculty recommendations, which are usually required for graduate school admittance, are also a rather poor predictor of whether a student will successfully complete a doctorate degree (Willingham, 1974). On the other hand, there is research showing that the amount of undergraduate research activity and ratings by peers of a student's commitment to psychology are better predictors of later success in psychology (as measured, for example, by number of scientific publications) than are the more traditional measures, such as GRE scores and GPA (Hirschberg & Itkin, 1978).

When scores on one variable can be used to predict scores on a second variable, we say that the two variables are correlated. A **correlation** exists when two different measures of the same people, events, or things vary together—that is, when particular scores on one variable tend to be associated with particular scores on another variable. When this occurs, the scores are said to "covary." Consider a measure with which you likely have had some experience, namely teacher/course evaluations in classes that you have taken. College students are commonly asked to evaluate their instructors and the course material toward the end of a course. By the time a course is over, you probably have formed many impressions of a teacher (e.g., whether the instructor is supportive, enthusiastic, likeable). After all you have just spent as many as 12 or 14 weeks (perhaps more than 30 hours) in this instructor's classroom. Ambady and Rosenthal (1993) asked how well teacher evaluations by students *not* enrolled in the class would correlate with end-of-the-semester evaluations made by students in the class. They showed video clips (without sound) of teachers to a group of female undergraduates. But, and here is the interesting part, they showed the video clips for only 30 seconds, 10 seconds, or just 6 seconds (across several studies). The researchers found that teacher evaluations based on these "thin slices of nonverbal behavior" correlated well with end-of-the-semester teacher evaluations made by students who were enrolled in the class. These results indicate that people (in this case teachers) reveal much about themselves when their nonverbal behavior is seen only briefly, and also that we (as observers) can make relatively accurate judgments of affective behavior quite quickly. Ambady and Rosenthal's findings, of course, do not mean that all the information in teaching evaluations can be captured by this method as they focused only on judgments of affective behavior (e.g., likeableness).

We can cite one more example of correlational evidence from a study we introduced earlier. When studying the "pace of life," Levine (1990) found a positive correlation between a city's pace of life as measured by people's walking speed and its deaths from heart disease. This indicates that the faster the pace in a city, the more likely its inhabitants are to die from heart disease. Death rates from heart disease, in other words, can be predicted by simply measuring how fast a city's inhabitants typically walk 100 feet!

We are concerned with issues of correlation at various points in this text and discuss the more general topic of correlational research in Chapter 4. Correlational research, which seeks to describe predictive relationships among variables, is a major area of psychological research.

It is important to point out that successful prediction doesn't always depend on knowing why a relationship exists between two variables. Consider the report that the Chinese rely on observing animal behavior to help them predict earthquakes. Certain animals apparently behave in an unusual manner just before an earthquake. The dog that barks and runs in circles and the snake seen fleeing its hole, therefore, may be reliable predictors of earthquakes. If so, they could be used to warn people of forthcoming disasters. We might even imagine that in areas where earthquakes are likely, residents would be asked to keep certain animals under observation (as miners once kept canaries) to warn them of conditions of which they are as yet unaware. This would not require that we understand why certain animals behave strangely before an earthquake, or even why earthquakes occur.

You may remember that Levine (1990) showed that measures of the pace of a city can be used to predict death rates from heart disease. However, we can only speculate about why these measures are related. One possible explanation for this correlation suggested by the researchers is that people living in time-urgent environments engage in unhealthy behaviors, for example, cigarette smoking and poor eating habits, which increase their risk of heart disease (Levine, 1990). To account for the relationship between *non*student ratings and student teacher evaluations, Ambady and Rosenthal (1993) suggested that people are "attuned" to quickly picking up information about a person's affect because this information is important (adaptive) in real-life decision making. Without additional information, however, this idea must remain speculation.

Understanding Although they are important goals in themselves, description and prediction are only the first steps in understanding a phenomenon. Understanding is the third and most important goal of the scientific method. It is achieved when the cause or causes of a phenomenon are identified. The scientist sets three important conditions for making a **causal inference** and, hence, of understanding: *covariation of events; a time-order relationship; and, the elimination of plausible alternative causes.*

If one event is the cause of another, the two events must vary together—that is, when one changes, the other must also change. This is the principle of covariation that we noted was the basis of the goal of prediction. Further, the presumed cause must occur before the presumed effect. This is the second condition, a time-order relationship. Finally, causal explanations are accepted only when other possible causes of the effect have been ruled out—when plausible alternative causes have been eliminated.

Unfortunately, people have a tendency to conclude that all three conditions for a causal inference have been met when really only the first condition is satisfied. For example, research has suggested that parents who are stern disciplinarians and who use physical punishment are more likely to have aggressive children than are parents who are less stern and use other forms of discipline. Parental discipline and children's aggressiveness obviously covary. Moreover, the fact that parents are typically assumed to influence how their children behave might lead us to think that the time-order condition has been met—parents use physical discipline and children's aggressiveness results. More recent research has shown, however, that infants vary in how active and aggressive they are and that the infant's behavior has a strong influence on the *parents'* responses in trying to exercise control. In other words, some children may be naturally aggressive and require stern discipline rather than stern discipline producing aggressive children. Therefore, the direction of the causal relationship may be opposite to what we thought at first.

It is important to recognize, however, that the causes of events cannot be identified unless covariation has been demonstrated. The first objective of the scientific method, description, can be met by describing events under a single set of circumstances. The goal of understanding, however, requires more than this. For example, suppose that a teacher wished to demonstrate that so-called "active learning strategies" help students learn. She could teach students using this approach and then describe the performance of the students who received instruction in this particular way. But at this point what would she know? How do we know that another group of students taught using an approach that did not use active learning strategies might not learn the same amount? Before the teacher could claim that the performance she observed was caused by the use of active learning strategies, she would have to compare this method with some other reasonable approach that did not employ active learning strategies. She would look for a difference in learning between the group using active learning strategies and a group not using this method. Such a finding would show that teaching strategy and performance covary. As you will see in Chapter 6, this is one reason why manipulation is such an important method of control for scientists. By manipulating independent variables, such as type of learning strategy, the investigator can determine more clearly whether any subsequent covariation occurs in the dependent variable. If it does, a bonus results from using manipulation: The time-order condition has also been met, because the researcher changes the independent variable (e.g., teaching method) and *subsequently* measures the changes, if any, in the dependent variable (e.g., a measure of student learning).

By far the most challenging condition to be met in making a causal inference is eliminating other plausible alternative causes. For example, consider a study in which the effect of two different teaching approaches (active and passive) is to be assessed. You can see that one way not to assign students to teaching conditions in this study would be to have all men in one group and all women in the other. If this were done, the independent variable of teaching method would be "confounded" with the independent variable of gender. **Confounding** occurs when two potentially effective variables are allowed to covary simultaneously. When research is confounded, it is impossible to determine what variable is responsible for any obtained difference in performance. If males were assigned to one condition of our hypothetical teaching experiment and females to another, then we would not know whether any difference we observed was due to gender of the participant or to the independent variable of type of teaching. When no confoundings are present, a research study is said to have **internal validity.** Much of the discussion in this book will focus on developing skills in performing internally valid research by learning to identify and eliminate confoundings.

The internal validity of a study, which relates to our ability to make causal inferences based on it, must be distinguished from the study's **external validity.** External validity involves the extent to which the research results can be generalized to different populations, settings, and conditions. A research finding may be internally valid and have little external validity. Although free of confoundings, the study may not be able to be generalized. Questions of external validity in science often arise, for instance, when results obtained with animal subjects are claimed to apply to human participants as well. Researchers frequently depend on experiments with animals to obtain information about human psychopathology and other illnesses. Animal models have been used to study drug addiction, minimal brain dysfunction, and various forms of mild to severe psychopathology (Maser & Seligman, 1977), as well as psychosomatic factors in various human illnesses (see Hofer & Myers, 1996). A frequent focus of animal research has been the effect of stress on the development of mental and physical illness. And while these studies have yielded valuable information about the effects of stress in animals, it is not clear whether these findings can be easily generalized to situations involving human responses to stress (e.g., Weiner, 1996). Nevertheless, as Hofer and Myers (1996) emphasize, the goal of animal research is the "enrichment of clinical and human research," and while "in themselves animal studies can never settle questions about human nature, . . . they can allow clinicians and those who study normal humans to ask more highly focused research questions that can be tested in the limited studies that are possible with our own species" (p. 522).

Because laboratory research, in general, is often conducted under more controlled conditions than are found in natural settings, an important task of the scientist is to determine whether laboratory findings generalize to the "real world." This is often the goal of what is called *field research.* By performing in the "field" (outside the laboratory) an experiment that is similar to an experiment that has been carried out in the laboratory, a researcher can provide evidence bearing on the external validity of laboratory results. Research conducted outside the laboratory often requires methods and procedures that are specifically designed for this less well controlled environment. Later in this book we will introduce some of the methods used by psychologists to conduct field research (see especially Chapters 3 and 10).

SCIENTIFIC THEORY CONSTRUCTION AND TESTING

- Theories, proposed explanations for the causes of behavior, vary in their scope and their level of explanation.
- A scientific theory is a logically organized set of propositions that defines events, describes relationships among events, and explains the occurrence of events.
- Successful scientific theories organize empirical knowledge, guide research by offering testable hypotheses, and survive rigorous testing.
- Theories frequently posit intervening variables to explain observed behavior.
- Researchers evaluate theories by judging the theory's internal consistency, observing whether hypothesized outcomes occur when the theory is tested, and noting whether the theory makes precise predictions based on parsimonious explanations.

Theories are "ideas" about how nature works. Psychologists propose ideas about why behavior occurs the way it does (e.g., what causes schizophrenia), about the nature of cognition (e.g., how people solve problems), and so on. A psychological theory can be developed on different levels: For example, it can be developed on a physiological or on a symbolic level (see Anderson, 1990; Simon, 1992). A theory of schizophrenia may, in other words, propose biological causes (e.g., specific genetic carriers), psychological causes (e.g., patterns of emotional conflict, stress), or both. The propositions contained in theories may be expressed as verbal statements, as mathematical equations, or even as computer programs.

An important dimension on which theories differ is scope. The *scope* of a theory refers to the range of phenomena that it seeks to explain. A theory of "flashbulb memory," for instance, attempts to explain why the personal circumstances surrounding particularly surprising and emotional events, such as the explosion of the space shuttle *Challenger*, are remembered better than are details associated with everyday events (see, for example, Brown & Kulik, 1977; McCloskey, Wible, & Cohen, 1988). Many older adults, for instance, can apparently remember precisely what they were doing when they heard about the assassination of President Kennedy. The scope of a theory of flashbulb memory is relatively restricted, proposing as it does an explanation of the nature and cause of an interesting but very specific memory phenomenon. A theory of human love, such as that proposed by Sternberg (1986), is an example of a psychological theory of much greater scope. Sternberg shows how the amount and kind of love one experiences is a function of three critical behavioral components: intimacy, passion, and decision/commitment. Even broader in scope is Anderson's (1990; 1993; Anderson & Milson, 1989) theory of human cognition, which offers an account of how cognition works in general, including ideas about learning, memory, problem solving, and so on. Clearly, the scope of a theory can be quite large. In general, the greater the scope of a theory the more complex it is likely to be. Complexity may be a necessary characteristic of psychological theories

FIGURE 1.5   A theory of "flashbulb memory" seeks to explain why personal circumstances surrounding vivid, emotional events, such as the explosion of the space shuttle *Challenger*, are seemingly remembered so much better than are details of everyday events.

given the nature and range of phenomena psychologists try to understand. Complexity also can be a serious obstacle, however, to testing a theory. Most theories in contemporary psychology tend to be relatively modest in scope, attempting to account only for a limited range of phenomena.

The source of a scientific theory is a mixture of intuition, personal observation, and discovered knowledge (known facts and ideas). The famous philosopher of science, Karl Popper (1976, pp. 268–269), suggested that truly creative theories spring from a combination of "intense interest in a problem (and thus a readiness to try again and again)" and "critical imagination." *Critical imagination* is the ability to think critically, but there is more. It includes a readiness to challenge accepted ideas and an "imaginative freedom that allows us to see so far unsuspected sources of error" in previous thinking about a problem. Critical imagination, in other words, means traveling beyond what others have said are the boundaries (limits) of thinking about a problem. Assuming we have that important burning interest in a problem, one way we might approach constructing a scientific theory is by critically examining what is known, looking for flaws or unseen sources of error in that knowledge.

Whatever the nature and scope of a theory, whether it be expressed mathematically or verbally or developed at a physiological level or at some higher-order level, the theory includes certain assumptions and concepts that must be explained in order for it to be understood and tested. A theory of flashbulb memory, for instance, needs to state exactly what a flashbulb memory *is*, showing, for example, how flashbulb memory differs from other, more typical memory. A complete theory must also explain why in some cases a person's so-called flashbulb memory is clearly wrong, even though the individual expresses high confidence in the (inaccurate) memory (see Neisser & Harsch, 1992). To be complete, therefore, a theory must include definitions of various events or concepts (e.g., emotional events, test accuracy), information about relationships between these events (e.g., the relationship between degree of emotional involvement and amount remembered), and so forth. Thus, we can offer the following formal definition of a scientific **theory:** *a logically organized set of propositions (claims, statements, assertions) that serves to define events (concepts), describe relationships among these events, and explain the occurrence of these events.*

The major functions of a theory are to *guide* research and to *organize* empirical knowledge (Marx, 1963). In the early 1960s, Rotter (1966) developed a theory of internal versus external locus of control. In this theory, Rotter differentiates individuals who perceive a contingency between their behavior and what happens to them (internal locus of control) and those who perceive that their behavior has little consequence for what happens to them (external locus of control). Rotter developed a questionnaire to define this concept on the basis of the idea that individuals differ in locus of control because of the way they have been rewarded during their development. The theory suggests a relationship between perceived locus of control and anxiety, with greater anxiety associated with greater perceived external locus of control. The theory has guided researchers for many years and has served to organize a body of empirical literature regarding self-efficacy, or the feeling of being able to cope with the environment (see, for example, Myers, 1999). The success of a psychological theory such as the locus-of-control theory can be measured by the degree to which it achieves the two important goals of guiding research and organizing empirical findings.

A scientific theory guides research by suggesting testable hypotheses. You may remember that hypotheses, like theories, are explanations for behavior; however, a hypothesis typically is simpler and more tentative than is a scientific theory (Marx, 1963). We described earlier in this chapter several factors that affect the testability of hypotheses, including the important criterion of operational specificity of concepts. It is important that hypotheses derived from a theory attempt to meet these criteria.

Theories frequently require that we postulate intervening processes to account for observed behavior (Underwood, 1975). An intervening process is one that "mediates" between certain antecedent conditions and behavior. We have been discussing one such intervening process, memory. We can safely say that we have never "seen" memory. It is something that we infer based on observations of our own behavior and that of others when asked about a previous experience. We assume that there is some record of experiences somewhere inside us which we refer to when queried about a previous experience. The concept "memory" is proposed as an intervening process to explain the behavior we have observed. Mediating processes such as memory are called *intervening variables*. To be useful to the scientist, it is important that these concepts have a clear relationship to behavior (see Kimble, 1989). That is, although we might infer many kinds of unseen processes to help explain behavior, unless we tie down intervening processes to observed relationships between specific antecedents (independent variables) and behavior (dependent variables), our theories are scientifically weak. For example, a theory that proposes a "free-floating" process to explain behavior cannot be shown to be wrong. Because free-floating processes (e.g., "the little person inside me") are not tied to specific empirical relationships, they can be called into play in any and every situation to "explain" behavior.

How scientific theories should be evaluated and tested is one of the most complex and difficult issues in psychology and philosophy (e.g., Meehl, 1978, 1990a, 1990b; Popper, 1959). At least one scientist, however, suggests a rather straightforward procedure. Kimble (1989, p. 498) says quite simply, "The best theory is the one that survives the fires of logical and empirical testing." Although somewhat simplistic, this is a good starting point. A theory can be evaluated first on the basis of its organization, its logical consistency. Are its propositions arranged in a meaningful way? Is the theory free of contradictions? Can specific deductions about expected behavior be made from it easily? Theories are tested logically by exposing their internal structure to the critical eye of members of the scientific community. A particular theory's propositions, assumptions, and definitions are frequently the topic of debate in scientific journals. Ideas about the exact definition of flashbulb memories, for example, have been debated at length in the psychology literature (e.g., Cohen, McCloskey, & Wible, 1990; Pillemer, 1990; Winograd & Neisser, 1992).

Kimble (1989) suggests that a theory is strengthened or weakened according to the outcomes of empirical tests of hypotheses derived from it. Successful tests of a hypothesis serve to increase the acceptability of a theory; unsuccessful tests serve to decrease the theory's acceptability. The best theory, in this view, is the one that passes these tests successfully. But there are serious obstacles to testing hypotheses and, as a consequence, confirming or disconfirming scientific theories. For example, a theory, especially a complex one, may produce many specific testable hypotheses. Therefore, a theory is not likely to fall on the basis of a single test (e.g., Lakatos, 1978). Moreover, theories may include propositions and concepts that have not been adequately defined or suggest intervening processes that are related to behavior and to each other in complex and even mysterious ways. Such theories may have a long life, but their value to science is questionable (Meehl, 1978).

When constructing and evaluating a theory, scientists place a premium on parsimony (Marx, 1963). The *rule of parsimony* is followed when the simplest of alternative explanations is accepted. When choosing among theoretical propositions, scientists tend to favor the simplest of them. This rule is nicely illustrated by the comments made by Albert Einstein in response to a young psychology student's question about the cognitive "process that occurred when

[he] had [his] most productive thought" (Fromm, 1998, p. 1195). In 1932, Erika Fromm, who was then a student of Max Wertheimer, the founder of Gestalt psychology, wrote letters to 100 leading scientists and philosophers as part of a psychological study of productive thinking. Among the responses she received was one from Einstein. He described the nature of the thinking that led to his theory of relativity, a process which he then characterized in the following way:

> It was always the search for a logically simple meaning of empirically established relationships, propelled by the conviction that there existed a simple logical meaning. (Fromm, 1998)

Precision of prediction is another criterion by which a theory can be evaluated. Theories that make precise predictions about behavior are preferred to those that make only general predictions (Meehl, 1990a). For instance, a theory of flashbulb memory that predicts the precise nature and duration of a "forgetting function" for such a memory is clearly a better theory than one that simply states that these memories will be remembered "longer" than other memories. Stated another way, some tests are easier for theories to pass than are others. A good scientific theory is one that is able to pass the most rigorous tests. *Rigorous testing* includes more tests that seek to falsify a theory's propositions than ones that seek to confirm them (Cook & Campbell, 1979). While confirming a particular theory's propositions provides support for the specific theory that is being tested, confirmation logically does not rule out other, alternative theories of the same phenomenon.

Although theories can be difficult and challenging to work with, the process of constructing and evaluating scientific theories is at the core of the scientific enterprise and is absolutely essential for the continuation of the science of psychology.

SCIENTIFIC INTEGRITY

- Psychologists are obligated to conduct research of the highest integrity.
- The American Psychological Association (APA) has adopted a code of ethics to guide the professional behavior of psychologists.

Science is a search for truth. Fraud, lies, and misrepresentations should play no part in a scientific investigation. But science is also a human endeavor, and frequently much more is at stake than truth. Both scientists and the institutions that hire them compete for rewards in a game with jobs, money, and reputations on the line. The number of scientific publications authored by a university faculty member, for instance, is usually a major factor influencing decisions regarding professional advancement through promotion and tenure. Under these circumstances, there are unfortunate, but seemingly inevitable, cases of scientific misconduct.

A variety of activities constitute violations of scientific integrity. They include data fabrication, plagiarism, selective reporting of research findings, failure to acknowledge individuals who made significant contributions to the research, misuse of research funds, and unethical treatment of humans or animals (see Adler, 1991). Some transgressions are easier to detect than others. Out-and-out fabrication of data, for instance, can be revealed when, in the normal course of science, results are not able to be reproduced by independent researchers, or when logical inconsistencies appear in published reports. However, more subtle transgressions, such as reporting only data that meet expectations or misleading reports of results, are difficult to detect. The dividing line between intentional misconduct and simply bad science is also not always clear.

To educate researchers about the proper conduct of science, and to help guide them around the many ethical pitfalls that are present, most scientific organizations have adopted formal codes of ethics. In Chapter 2 we will introduce you to the APA ethical principles governing research with humans and animals. As you will see, ethical dilemmas often arise. Consider the research by Heath and Davidson (1988) mentioned earlier in this chapter. You may remember that they asked groups of university women to help prepare a new rape-prevention pamphlet. Their participants reviewed materials that presented rape as very controllable, somewhat controllable, or not at all controllable. Women who read the uncontrollable version reported greater levels of anxiety about rape than did women who read the other versions. However, the researchers did not actually intend to produce a new rape-prevention pamphlet. Participants in this research were deceived regarding the true purpose of the study: to investigate how perceived controllability of rape influences women's perceptions of vulnerability to rape. Under what conditions should researchers be allowed to deceive research participants?

Deception is just one of many ethical issues that researchers must confront. As yet another illustration of ethical problems, we mentioned that animal subjects sometimes are used to help understand human psychopathology. This may mean exposing animal subjects to stressful and even painful conditions. Again, we must ask about the ethical issues involved with this type of research. Under what conditions should research with animal subjects be permitted? The list of ethical questions raised by psychological research is a lengthy one. Thus, *it is of the utmost importance that you become familiar with the APA ethical principles and their application at an early stage in your research career, and that you participate (as research participant, assistant, or principal investigator) only in research that meets the highest standards of scientific integrity.*

GETTING STARTED DOING RESEARCH

— What to study?
— How do I find a hypothesis to test?
— Is my research question a good one?

There are many decisions that must be made before beginning to do research in psychology. The first one, of course, is, what to study. In what area of psychology do I wish to do research? Many students approach the field of psychology with interests in psychopathology and issues associated with mental illness. Others are intrigued with the puzzles surrounding human cognition, such as memory, problem solving, and decision making. Still others are interested in problems of developmental and social psychology. Psychology provides a smorgasbord of research possibilities to explore, as is illustrated by the literally hundreds of scientific journals that publish the results of psychological research. You can quickly find information about the many research areas within psychology by reviewing the contents of a standard introductory psychology textbook. More specific information can be found, of course, in the many classes offered by the psychology department of your college or university, such as abnormal psychology, cognitive psychology, and social psychology.

The next decision is a bit harder. How do I come up with a research hypothesis? McGuire (1997) believes that the ability to generate testable hypotheses can be described and taught to students. He identified 49 simple rules ("heuristics") for generating a hypothesis to be tested scientifically. We can not review all 49 suggestions here, but we can give you some insight into McGuire's thinking about scientific thinking by listing some of these heuristics. He suggests, for example, that we might generate a hypothesis for a research study by:

— thinking about deviations (oddities, exceptions) from a general trend or principle;
— imagining how *we* would behave in a task or faced with a specific problem;
— considering similar problems whose solution is known;
— making sustained, deliberate observations of a person or phenomenon (e.g., performing a case study);
— considering the opposite direction of plausible causality for a phenomenon;
— generating counterexamples for an obvious conclusion about behavior;
— exploring alternative labels for phenomena;
— "jolting one's conceptualizing out of its usual ruts" by shifting attention to the opposite pole of the problem or expressing a question in different modalities (e.g., pictures, words, symbols);
— coming up with multiple explanations for a given finding;
— thinking about how people need to function in a given environment;
— borrowing ideas or theories from other disciplines;
— looking for irregularities in previous results and attempting to reconcile conflicting outcomes;
— trying new modes of data collection such as performing qualitative analyses of a quantitative finding or carrying out new statistical analyses of old data.

No matter how or where you begin to develop a hypothesis for your research, at some point you will find yourself needing to peruse the published literature of psychological research. There are several reasons why you must search the psychology literature before beginning to do research. One obvious reason is that the answer to your research question may already be there. Someone else may have entertained the same question and provided an answer, or at least a partial one. It is highly unlikely that you will not find some research finding that is related to the research question you have chosen to answer. This should not discourage you; in fact, it should be a source of satisfaction. Finding that other people have done research on the same or similar idea will give you the "in" that is necessary to build the science of psychology. Doing research without a careful examination of what is already known may be interesting or fun (it certainly may be easy); perhaps you could call it a "hobby," but we can't call it science. Science is a cumulative affair: Current research builds on previous research. Once you have identified a body of literature related to your research idea, your reading may lead you to discover, as McGuire (1997) suggested, inconsistencies or contradictions in the published research. You may also find that the research findings are limited in terms of the nature of the participants studied or the circumstances under which the research was done, or that there is a psychological theory in need of testing. Having made such a discovery, you have found a solid research lead, a path to follow.

When reading the psychological literature and thinking about possible research questions, you might also consider how the results of psychological studies might be applied to societal problems. Later we discuss differences between basic and applied research (see especially Chapter 10). Suffice it to say that applied research typically focuses on improving the human condition. As you learn how to do research in psychology, you may want to consider ways this knowledge can be used to generate questions that when answered will make humankind just a little better off.

Searching the psychology literature is not the tedious task that it once was; computer-aided literature searches, including use of the Internet, have made identifying related research a relatively easy, even exciting task. In Appendix C of this book we outline how to search the psychology literature, including ways to use computer-based guides.

FIGURE 1.6 Computers have made reviewing psychological literature a relatively easy task.

Finally, as Sternberg (1997) points out, choosing a question to investigate should not be taken lightly. Some questions are simply not worth asking because their answers offer no hope of advancing the science of psychology. The questions are, in a word, meaningless, or at best, trivial. "How do I know if my research question is a good one?" Sternberg (1997) suggests that students new to the field of psychological research ask themselves several questions before deciding they have a good research question:

— Why might this question be scientifically important?
— What is the scope of this question?
— What are likely outcomes if I carry out this research project?
— To what extent will psychological science be advanced by knowing the answer to this question?
— Why would anyone be interested in the results obtained by asking this question?

As you begin the research process, finding answers to these questions may require guidance from research advisors and others who have successfully answered them in their own research. We also hope that your ability to answer these questions will be enhanced as you learn more about theory and research in psychology and as you read about the many examples of interesting and meaningful psychological research that we describe in this book.

Of course, identifying a research problem doesn't necessarily tell you *how* to do the research. What is it exactly that you want to know? Answering this question will mean that you must make other decisions as well. Should I do a qualitative or quantitative research study? What is the nature of the variables I wish to investigate? How do I find reliable and valid measures of behavior? What is the research method best suited to my research question? What kinds of statistical analyses will be needed? Do the methods I choose meet accepted moral and ethical standards?

A major goal of this book is to provide you with the information to help make these decisions and many others associated with the research process.

THE ORGANIZATION OF THIS BOOK

This book provides an introduction to the way in which the scientific method is applied in psychology. As you are probably aware, the scope of psychology is quite large, encompassing many areas of study. Moreover, no single research methodology can be said to answer all the questions raised in a particular area. Thus, the best approach to answering a question about behavior or mental processes is frequently a *multimethod approach*—that is, searching for an answer using different research methodologies.

The organization of the book follows loosely the goals for the scientific method. Following a discussion of ethical issues in research (Chapter 2), we introduce you to what are called *descriptive methods*. Naturalistic observation, for instance, is an important tool of psychologists who want to describe behavior in a natural context (see Chapter 3). Questionnaires are among the most commonly used instruments in psychology and frequently are the basis for making *predictions* about behavior. The nature of questionnaires and their use in survey research are discussed in Chapter 4. Several less commonly used measures of behavior—those based on the examination of archival records and those derived from the study of physical traces—are treated in Chapter 5. In the third part of the book we deal with *experimental approaches* to the study of behavior. The emphasis is on experiments done with groups of participants (see Chapters 6–8). Experimental approaches are aimed chiefly at discovering cause-and-effect relationships. However, experimental methods used in the laboratory are not necessarily the same as those used outside the laboratory.

Finally, in the fourth section of the book we introduce you to the methods employed in *applied research*. In Chapter 9 there is a discussion of experiments conducted with small numbers of research participants, in fact, with single individuals ($N = 1$). In that chapter we also discuss the important case study method. The last chapter deals with quasi-experimental designs and with the important topic of program evaluation, which is concerned with assessing the effects of "treatments" applied in natural settings (see Chapter 10).

SUMMARY

Psychology's official beginning is marked by the establishment, in 1879, of a formal psychology laboratory in Leipzig, Germany, under the direction of Wilhelm Wundt. With this beginning came the first applications of the scientific method to problems of psychology. As an approach to knowledge, the scientific method is characterized by a reliance on empirical procedures, rather than intuition, and by an attempt to control the investigation of those factors believed responsible for a phenomenon. Those factors that are systematically controlled in an attempt to determine their effect on behavior are called independent variables. The measures of behavior used to assess the effect (if any) of the independent variable are called dependent variables.

Scientists seek to report results in an unbiased and objective manner. This goal is enhanced by giving operational meaning to concepts. Scientists also seek to measure phenomena as accurately and precisely as possible. Measurement involves both physical and psychological measurement. Scientists seek both validity and reliability of these measures.

Hypotheses are tentative explanations of events. To be useful to the scientist, however, hypotheses must be testable. Hypotheses that lack adequate definition, that are circular, or that appeal to ideas or forces outside the province of science are not testable. Hypotheses are often derived from theories. More than anything else, scientists are skeptical. A skeptical attitude is not always found among nonscientists, who may rush to accept "new discoveries" and extraordinary claims.

The goals of the scientific method are description, prediction, and understanding. Both quantitative and qualitative research are used to describe behavior. Observation is the principal basis of scientific description. When two measures correlate, we can predict the value of one measure by knowing the value of the other. Understanding is achieved when the causes of a phenomenon are discovered. This requires that evidence be provided for covariation of events, that a time-order relationship exists, and that alternative causes be eliminated. When two potentially effective variables covary such that the independent effect of each variable on behavior cannot be determined, we say that our research is confounded. Confounding must be avoided if we wish to produce a study with internal validity. The external validity of a study involves the extent to which research results can be generalized to different populations, settings, and conditions.

Scientific theory construction and testing provide the bases for a scientific approach to psychology. Theories have the important function of guiding research and organizing empirical knowledge. Finally, many ethical questions are raised by psychological research; it is important that the science of psychology be carried out according to the highest standards of scientific integrity. Getting started doing psychological research requires us to make several important decisions, including those about what topic to investigate, what is the specific question I wish to answer, and is my question a good one? Finally, we must decide exactly how to *do* the research.

KEY CONCEPTS

scientific method
empirical approach
control
independent variable
individual differences variable
dependent variable
operational definition
validity

reliability
hypothesis
correlation
causal inference
confounding
internal validity
external validity
theory

REVIEW QUESTIONS

1 For each of the following characteristics, indicate how the scientific approach differs from nonscientific (everyday) approaches to knowledge: general approach, observation, reporting, concepts, instruments, measurement, hypotheses, and attitudes.
2 What is the major advantage of using operational definitions in psychology? What disadvantages are there in using operational definitions?
3 Distinguish between the accuracy of a measuring instrument and its precision.
4 What distinguishes physical measurement from psychological measurement?
5 What three shortcomings often keep hypotheses from being testable?
6 Why do behavioral scientists always seek to maintain a skeptical attitude?
7 What are the three goals of the scientific method?
8 What do we mean when we say that the nomothetic approach is used in science? How is the nomothetic approach different from the idiographic approach?

9 Provide an example both of quantitative research and of qualitative research.

10 What three conditions must be met if one event is to be considered the cause of another?

11 Distinguish between the internal validity and the external validity of a research study.

12 Describe how a scientific theory can be used to guide and organize empirical research.

13 Identify at least three characteristics used to evaluate a theory.

14 Explain the use of intervening variables in theory construction. What important quality should an intervening variable have?

CHALLENGE QUESTIONS

1 In each of the following descriptions of research studies, you are to identify the independent variable(s). You should also be able to identify at least one dependent variable in each study.

A A psychologist was interested in the effect of food deprivation on motor activity. She assigned each of 60 rats to one of four conditions differing in the length of time for which the animals were deprived of food: 0 hours, 8 hours, 16 hours, 24 hours. She then measured the amount of time the animals spent in the activity wheel in their cages.

B A physical education instructor was interested in specifying the changes in motor coordination with increasing age in young children. He selected six groups of children and gave each child a test of motor coordination. The groups of children differed in age—that is, one group was made up of all 5-year-olds, the next group was all 6-year-olds, and so on up to the sixth group, which was all 10-year-olds.

C A developmental psychologist was interested in the amount of verbal behavior very young children displayed depending on who else was present. The study he did involved selecting children who were either 2, 3, or 4 years old. These children were observed in a laboratory setting for a 30-minute period. Half of the children of each age were assigned to a condition in which an adult was present with the child during the session. The other half of the children were assigned to a condition in which another young child was present during the session with the child being observed. The psychologist measured the number, duration, and complexity of the verbal utterances of each observed child.

2 In the following description the independent variable of interest is confounded with a potentially relevant independent variable. Identify the confounding variable and explain clearly how the confounding occurred. Also state exactly what conclusion can be supported on the basis of the evidence presented. Finally, suggest ways in which the study could be done so that it would be internally valid.

A physiological psychologist developed a drug that she thought would revolutionize the world of horse racing. She named the drug Speedo, and it was her contention that this drug would lead horses to run much faster than they do now. (Forget, for the sake of this problem, that it is illegal to give drugs to racehorses.) She selected two groups of horses and gave one of the groups injections of Speedo once a week for 4 weeks. Because Speedo was known to have some negative effects on the horses' digestive systems, those horses given the Speedo had to be placed on a special high-protein diet. Those horses not given the Speedo were maintained on their regular diet. After the 4-week period, all the horses were timed in a 2-mile race and the mean times for the horses given Speedo were significantly faster than the mean times for those not given Speedo. The psychologist concluded that her drug was effective.

3 Two physicians did a study to try to determine why people who are allergic to cats still keep them as pets. They asked 67 patients (22 male and 45 female) with an average age of 40 years to complete a questionnaire concerning the nature of their attachment to their cat. Even though 11 people had a history of emergency room visits following exposure to cats, 38 said they would definitely replace their cat if it died, and an additional 16 reported they would have difficulty avoiding a new acquisition. Having someone to love and companionship were the most commonly selected reasons for having cats. The physicians concluded that cat ownership meets strong psychological needs in allergic patients. What comparison information is needed before reaching the conclusion that the psychological reasons for owning a cat are peculiar to allergic patients?

4 When presented with only correlational evidence, the investigator can only hypothesize about possible causal factors underlying a relationship between variables. A stage wherein the investigator thinks about possible causal factors and "tries them out" as explanations, perhaps during discussions with other researchers, is often a preliminary step to doing research that may provide evidence for the factors responsible for the reported relationship. For each of the following reports of covariation, identify a possible causal factor—that is, speculate on *why* these events are correlated.

   A   A study of nearly 5,000 Swedish women (20 to 44 years old) revealed that couples who live together before marriage have an 80% higher probability of getting divorced than do married couples who do not live together before marriage.

   B   Married women are found to suffer from depression more than men. However, the greater the marital compatibility, the less the risk of depression among women.

   C   In the late 1980s the National Institutes of Health sponsored a conference to assess available data regarding the healing power of pets. The idea is that having pets is good for you. One investigator reported that among 92 coronary patients, pet owners were more likely to be alive 1 year after discharge from a coronary heart unit than were people who do not own a pet.

Answer to Challenge Question 1

   A   IV: hours of food deprivation with four levels; DV: time (in minutes) animals spent in activity wheel

   B   IV: age of children with six levels (distinguish selection of levels from manipulation in part A); DV: scores on test of motor coordination

   C   IV: age at three levels and additional person present with two levels (again, distinguish selection and manipulation); DV: number, duration, and complexity of child's verbal utterances

Ethical Issues in the Conduct of Psychological Research

CHAPTER OUTLINE

INTRODUCTION
THINGS YOU NEED TO KNOW BEFORE YOU BEGIN
   TO DO RESEARCH
APA Ethical Standards
Commentary
THE RISK/BENEFIT RATIO
Determination of Risk
Minimal Risk
Dealing with Risk
Obtaining Informed Consent
APA Ethical Standards
Commentary
DECEPTION IN PSYCHOLOGICAL RESEARCH
APA Ethical Standards
Commentary
ADDITIONAL RESPONSIBILITIES TO RESEARCH PARTICIPANTS
APA Ethical Standards
Commentary
RESEARCH WITH ANIMALS
APA Ethical Standards
Commentary
REPORTING OF PSYCHOLOGICAL RESEARCH
APA Ethical Standards
Commentary
STEPS FOR ETHICAL DECISION MAKING
SUMMARY

INTRODUCTION

A scientist has an ethical responsibility to do the following:

— seek knowledge;

— carry out research in a competent manner;

— report results accurately;

— manage available resources honestly;

— fairly acknowledge, in scientific communications, the individuals who have contributed their ideas or their time and effort;

— consider the consequences to society of any research endeavor;

— speak out publicly on societal concerns related to a scientist's knowledge and expertise (Diener & Crandall, 1978).

In order to meet these obligations, the scientist must consider the numerous ethical issues and questions of proper scientific conduct. To help guide the ethical behavior of psychologists, the American Psychological Association (APA) has formulated an Ethics Code to aid ethical decision making in the context of doing research, as well as in other contexts, for example, when teaching, doing therapy, or serving as administrators (see American Psychological Association, 1992). The Ethics Code deals with such diverse issues as sexual harassment, fees for psychological services, test construction, classroom teaching, and expert witnesses.

As stated in the Preamble to the Ethics Code, psychologists are expected to make "a personal commitment to a lifelong effort to act ethically; to encourage ethical behavior by students, supervisees, employees, and colleagues, as appropriate; and to consult with others, as needed, concerning ethical problems" (p. 39). It is important for students of psychology also to make this commitment. They should familiarize themselves with the Ethics Code and make every effort to live up to its stated ideals and standards of behavior. (A copy of the complete APA Ethics Code can be obtained from the APA Order Department, American Psychological Association, 750 First Street, N.E., Washington, DC 20002-4242.)

Many of the ethical standards in the APA's Ethics Code deal directly with psychological research (see especially Sections 6.06–6.26 of the code), including the treatment of both humans and animals in psychological research. As with most ethical codes, the standards tend to be general in nature and require specific definition in particular contexts. Often more than one ethical standard applies to a research situation, and at times the standards may even appear to contradict one another. For instance, ethical research requires that human participants be protected from physical injury. Research, however, that involves drugs or other invasive treatments may place participants at risk of physical harm. The welfare of animal subjects should be protected; however, as we saw in Chapter 1, certain kinds of research may involve inflicting pain or other suffering on an animal. Solving these ethical dilemmas is not always easy and requires a deliberate, conscientious problem-solving approach to ethical decision making.

Ethical decisions are best made after consultation with others, including one's peers but especially those who are more experienced or knowledgeable in a particular area. In fact, review of a research plan by persons not involved in the research is legally required in some situations. In the remaining sections of this chapter, we identify those standards from the Ethics Code that deal specifically with psychological research. We also offer a brief commentary on some aspects of these standards and present several hypothetical research plans that raise ethical questions. By putting yourself in the position of having to make judgments about the ethical issues raised in these research proposals, you will begin to learn to grapple with applying particular ethical standards and with the difficulties of ethical decision making in general. We urge you to discuss these proposals with peers, teachers, and others who have had prior experience doing psychological research.

THINGS YOU NEED TO KNOW BEFORE YOU BEGIN TO DO RESEARCH

- Prior to conducting any study, the research must be reviewed to determine if it meets ethical standards.

Because research psychologists must consider a host of ethical issues, problems can be avoided only by planning carefully and consulting with appropriate individuals and groups *prior to doing the research.* The failure to conduct research in an ethical manner undermines the entire scientific process, retards the advancement of knowledge, and erodes the public's respect for the scientific and academic communities. It can also lead to significant legal and financial penalties for individuals and institutions. The following ethical standards spell out some things researchers must keep in mind as they begin to do psychological research.

APA Ethical Standards

6.06 Planning Research

1 (a) Psychologists design, conduct, and report research in accordance with recognized standards of scientific competence and ethical research.

(b) Psychologists plan their research so as to minimize the possibility that results will be misleading.

(c) In planning research, psychologists consider its ethical acceptability under the Ethics Code. If an ethical issue is unclear, psychologists seek to resolve the issue through consultation with institutional review boards, animal care and use committees, peer consultations, or other proper mechanisms.

(d) Psychologists take reasonable steps to implement appropriate protections for the rights and welfare of human participants, other persons affected by the research, and animal subjects.

6.07 Responsibility

1 (a) Psychologists conduct research competently and with due concern for the dignity and welfare of the participants.

(b) Psychologists are responsible for the ethical conduct of research conducted by them or by others under their supervision or control.

(c) Researchers and assistants are permitted to perform only those tasks for which they are appropriately trained and prepared.

(d) As part of the process of development and implementation of research projects, psychologists consult those with expertise concerning any special population under investigation or most likely to be affected.

6.08 Compliance With Law and Standards

Psychologists plan and conduct research in a manner consistent with federal and state law and regulations, as well as professional standards governing the conduct of research, and particularly those standards governing research with human participants and animal subjects.

6.09 Institutional Approval

Psychologists obtain from host institutions or organizations appropriate approval prior to conducting research, and they provide accurate information about their research proposals. They conduct the research in accordance with the approved research protocol.

Commentary

As you can see, the importance of consulting with others about ethical issues prior to doing research cannot be overemphasized. It is particularly critical that a researcher obtain prior approval from the proper institutional committee before doing research.

- Institutional Review Boards (IRBs) review psychological research to protect the rights and welfare of human participants.
- Institutional Animal Care and Use Committees (IACUCs) review research conducted with animals to ensure that animals are treated humanely.

The National Research Act, signed into law in 1974, resulted in the creation of the National Commission for the Protection of Human Subjects of Biomedical and Behavioral Research. This act requires that institutions, such as colleges and universities, seeking research funds from specific federal agencies, establish committees to review research sponsored by the institution. These committees, referred to as Institutional Review Boards (IRBs), review psychological research at these institutions in order to safeguard the rights and welfare of human participants. Federal regulations impose very specific requirements on the makeup and duties of these committees (see *Federal Register*, June 18, 1991). For example, an IRB must be composed of at least five members with varying backgrounds and fields of expertise. Both scientists and nonscientists must be represented, and there must be at least one IRB member who is not affiliated with the institution. Responsible members of the community, such as members of the clergy, lawyers, and nurses, are asked to serve on these committees.

FIGURE 2.1   Many ethical questions are raised when research is performed with humans and animals.

FIGURE 2.1   *(Continued)*

A psychology student seeking to do research with human participants is apt to be asked first to satisfy the regulations of a department committee charged with reviewing research conducted in the psychology department. Depending on the association of this departmental committee with an IRB, research falling into various well-defined categories is either reviewed at the departmental level or referred to the IRB, which has the authority to approve, disapprove, or require modifications prior to the approval of the research.

In 1985 the Department of Agriculture, as well as the Public Health Service, formulated new guidelines for the care of laboratory animals (Holden, 1987). As a result, institutions doing research with animal subjects are now required to have an Institutional Animal Care and Use Committee (IACUC), whose members minimally must include a scientist, a veterinarian, and at least one person not affiliated with the institution. Review of animal research by IACUCs extends to more than simply overseeing the research procedures. Federal regulations governing the conduct of animal research extend to specifications of animal living quarters and the proper training of personnel who work directly with the animals (Holden, 1987).

Nearly every college and university requires that all research conducted at the institution be reviewed at some stage by an independent committee. Violation of federal regulations regarding the review of research involving humans or animals can bring a halt to research at an institution, spell the loss of federal funds, and result in substantial fines (Holden, 1987; Smith, 1977). Given the complex nature of federal regulations and the policies of most institutions requiring review of research with humans and animals, *any individual who wants to do research should inquire of the proper authorities, prior to starting research, about the appropriate procedure for institutional review.*

THE RISK/BENEFIT RATIO

- A subjective evaluation of the risks and benefits of a research project is used to determine whether the research should be conducted.

In addition to checking if appropriate ethical principles are being followed, a major function of an IRB is to arrive at a consensus regarding what is sometimes called the *risk/benefit ratio*. Despite use of the term *ratio*, the risk/benefit ratio is nothing like a mathematical ratio with easily calculable components. The decision to do research must rest on a subjective evaluation of the costs and benefits both to the individual and to society. Failure to do research may cost society the benefits of the knowledge gained from the research and, ultimately, an opportunity to improve the human condition. To do research may at times exact a cost from individual participants—for example, research participants risk injury when exposed to potentially harmful circumstances. The principal investigator must, of course, be the first one to consider these potential risks and benefits. Nevertheless, determining the ratio, and hence the decision to do research, is most appropriately made by knowledgeable individuals who do not have a personal interest in the research. As we have indicated, this is often the role played by a department ethics committee or an IRB.

In its simplest form, the **risk/benefit ratio** asks the question, Is it worth it? When the inconvenience and risks to participants are considered, is there sufficient potential benefit to the individual and to society to carry out this research? Many factors affect a decision regarding the proper balance of risks and benefits of a research activity. The most basic are the nature of the risk and the magnitude of the probable benefit to the participant as well as the potential scientific and social value of the research (Fisher & Fryberg, 1994). When the benefits to an individual are clear and immediate, or when there is obvious scientific and social value associated with the research, a greater risk can be tolerated than when the benefits are less clear or their application is less immediate. For instance, in the context of research investigating the antecedents of psychotic behavior, the possible benefits to both the participants and society may be substantial if a proposed treatment has a good possibility of having a beneficial effect. Society will also benefit as psychologists come to understand more completely such behaviors as aggression, altruism, eating disorders, deviance, and suicide. The benefits to be gained by investigating these behaviors, however, must be continually weighed against the risks to the participants.

In determining the risk/benefit ratio, a researcher must also take into account the probability that valid and interpretable results will be produced. An established scientist with a history of successful research in her field, for instance, would reasonably be judged to have a greater chance of obtaining important results than would an undergraduate psychology major. Rosenthal (1994b) makes a clear point in this regard: "Everything else being equal, research that is of a higher scientific quality is more ethically defensible" (p. 127). More specifically, "If because of the poor quality of the science no good can come of a research study, how are we to justify the use of participants' time, attention, and effort and the money, space, supplies, and other resources that have been expended on the research project?" (Rosenthal, 1994b, p. 128). Thus, *an investigator is obliged to seek to do research that meets the highest standards of scientific excellence.*

When research involves risk, there are considerations beyond making sure the research is planned competently. When risk is present, a researcher must confirm there are no alternative, low-risk procedures that might be substituted or that previous research has not already successfully addressed the research question being asked. Without careful prior review of the psychological literature, for instance, a researcher might carry out research that has already been done, thus exposing individuals to needless risk.

Determination of Risk

- Potential risks in psychological research include risk of physical injury, social injury, and mental or emotional stress.
- Risks must be evaluated in terms of potential participants' everyday activities, their physical and mental health, and capabilities.

Determining whether research participants are "at risk" illustrates the difficulties involved in ethical decision making. Life itself is a risky affair. Commuting to work or school, crossing streets, and riding on elevators are all activities that have an element of risk. Simply showing up for an appointment to serve in a psychology experiment must be judged to entail some degree of risk. To say that human participants in psychological research can never risk injury would bring all research to a halt. Decisions about what constitutes risk must take into consideration those risks that are part of everyday life.

Any determination of risk must also consider the nature of the participants. Certain activities can reasonably be judged to pose a serious risk for some individuals but not for others. Running up a flight of stairs may substantially increase an elderly person's chance of suffering a heart attack; the same task would not be a serious risk for most young adults. Individuals who are exceptionally depressed or anxious might be expected to show more severe reactions to certain psychological tasks than would other people. Statements about what constitutes risk cannot be easily generalized to all individuals or populations.

Risk is often associated with the possibility of physical injury—that is, when bodily harm is threatened. More often, however, participants in social science research risk social or psychological injury. The potential for social risk exists when information gained about an individual through her or his participation in psychological research is revealed to others. Simply knowing that someone completed a questionnaire inquiring about deviant sexual practices could cause social injury if people react differently to that individual as a consequence of their knowledge. Information collected during the conduct of research may include important personal facts about intelligence, personality traits, and political, social, or religious beliefs. A research participant is not likely to want this information divulged to teachers, employers, or peers. Failure to protect the confidentiality of a participant's responses may significantly increase the possibility of social injury.

The potential for psychological injury exists whenever the procedures associated with a research activity are likely to induce serious mental or emotional stress in the participants. A participant in a social psychology experiment involving a simulated emergency, as when smoke enters a room where she is waiting, may experience a substantial amount of emotional stress until the true simulated character of the event is revealed. Merely participating in a psychology experiment is anxiety provoking for some individuals. After learning a list of nonsense syllables, a student participant once volunteered that he was sure the researcher now knew a great deal about him! The student assumed the psychologist was interested in his mental state as revealed by the associations he used when learning the list. In reality, this person was participating in a simple memory experiment designed to measure forgetting. *A researcher is under an obligation to protect participants from emotional or mental stress, including, when possible, that which might arise due to a participant's misconceptions about the nature of a psychological task.*

Minimal Risk

- When a research study involves procedures or activities that are similar to those experienced by participants in their everyday life, the study is described as having "minimal risk."

A distinction is sometimes made between a participant "at risk" and one who is "at minimal risk." One definition of minimal risk is that followed by IRBs in their review of biomedical and behavioral research (*Federal Register*, January 26, 1981; amended *Federal Register*, June 18, 1991).

Minimal risk means that the probability and magnitude of harm or discomfort anticipated in the research are not greater in and of themselves than are those ordinarily encountered in daily life or during the performance of routine physical or psychological examinations or tests.

As an example of minimal risk, consider the fact that many psychology laboratory studies involve lengthy paper-and-pencil tests intended to assess various mental abilities. Participants are frequently under time pressure to complete the tests and may receive specific feedback regarding their performance. No doubt some degree of mental or even emotional stress is associated with participation in these kinds of activities. Within limits, however, the risk of psychological injury in this situation would generally be assumed to be no greater than that of being a student. Therefore, college students would be judged to incur only minimal risk in such experiments. When the possibility of injury is judged to be more than minimal, individuals are considered to be "at risk." When this occurs, more serious obligations fall on the researcher to protect the welfare of such participants.

Dealing with Risk

- Whether "at risk" or "at minimal risk," research participants must be protected. More safeguards are needed as risks become greater.
- To protect participants from social risks, information they provide should be anonymous, or if that is not possible, the confidentiality of their information should be maintained.

Even when only a slight potential for injury exists, the researcher should try to minimize the risk and provide safeguards for the participants. For instance, stating at the beginning of a memory experiment that the tasks are not intended to measure intelligence or personality reduces the level of stress that some participants experience. When substances are to be taken internally, individuals should be screened prior to participation in order to identify and excuse any who might show unusual physical reactions. In situations where the possibility of harm is judged to be significantly greater than that occurring in daily life, the researcher's obligation to protect participants increases correspondingly. It is not unheard of for an IRB to require that a clinical psychologist be available to counsel individuals when, by participating in a psychology experiment, they are exposed to the possibility of serious emotional stress.

No research activity involving more than minimal risk to participants should be carried out unless alternative, low-risk methods of data collection have been explored. In some cases, descriptive approaches involving observation or questionnaires should be substituted for experimental treatments. It is also possible to take advantage of naturally occurring "treatments." For example, Anderson (1976) interviewed owner-managers of small businesses that had been damaged by hurricane floods. He found that the likelihood of problem-solving coping behaviors by the participants showed an inverted U-shaped function when related on a graph to perceived stress, indicating there is an optimal level of stress and that, when stress is higher or lower than this optimal level, performance decreases. A similar relationship has been demonstrated in a number of experimental laboratory tasks using experimenter-induced stress.

In order to protect research participants from social injury, the method of data collection should preserve the anonymity of participants or, when this is not possible, ensure the confidentiality of responses. Thus, if at all possible, a researcher should obtain information about participants in a manner that does not require individuals to be identified.

Simply not having participants sign their names to the test instruments is obviously one way to keep participation anonymous. When the researcher must test people on more than one occasion or otherwise track specific individuals, numbers can be randomly assigned to participants at the beginning of a study. Only these numbers need appear on participants' response sheets.

When anonymity cannot be preserved, confidentiality should be protected through some type of code system. If the information supplied by participants is particularly sensitive, such a scheme is necessary to minimize the risk of social injury. One procedure is to assign code numbers to participants. Names are then linked with the code numbers on a master list and access to this list restricted by keeping it under lock and key.

Assuring participants of their anonymity or the confidentiality of their responses can also benefit the researcher if such assurances lead the participant to be more honest and open when responding (Blanck, Bellack, Rosnow, Rotheram-Borus, & Schooler, 1992). It can be assumed that participants will be less likely to fabricate or withhold information if they do not have to worry about who will have access to their responses.

WHAT DO YOU THINK?

For each of the following research situations, do you think only "minimal risk" is present (i.e., risk not greater than that of everyday life) or is more than minimal risk present? If more than minimal risk is present, then participants are judged to be "at risk." In this case, you might think of what safeguards could be employed to reduce that risk. As you do so, you will undoubtedly begin to anticipate some of the ethical issues yet to be discussed in this chapter.

1 College students are asked to complete an adjective checklist describing their current mood. The researcher is seeking to identify students who

are depressed so that they can be included in a study examining cognitive deficits associated with depression.

2 Elderly adults in a nursing home are given a battery of achievement tests in the dayroom at their home. A psychologist seeks to determine if there is a decline in mental functioning with advancing age.

3 Students in a psychology research methods class see another student enter their classroom in the middle of the class period, speak loudly and angrily with the instructor, and then leave. As part of a study of eyewitness behavior, the students are then asked to describe the intruder.

4 A researcher recruits students from introductory psychology classes to participate in a study of the effects of alcohol on cognitive functioning. The experiment requires that some students drink 2 ounces of alcohol (mixed with orange juice) before performing a computer game.

Obtaining Informed Consent

- Researchers and participants enter into a social contract, often using an informed consent procedure.
- Researchers are ethically obligated to describe the research procedures clearly, identify any potential risks that might influence individuals' willingness to participate, and answer any questions participants have about the research.
- Research participants are ethically obligated to behave appropriately during the research by not lying, cheating, or engaging in other fraudulent behavior.

The success of most human psychological research depends on the willingness of students, patients, clients, and other members of the community to take part in a scientific investigation. At times, participants in psychological research are given money or other compensation for their time and effort. At other times, people simply respond to requests by researchers for volunteers to participate in a research endeavor and expect no compensation. Researchers obtain the **informed consent** of participants to ensure that the participants explicitly express a willingness to take part in the research after having been informed about the nature of the research, the consequences of not participating, and the factors that might be expected to influence their willingness to participate. Researcher and participant enter into a social contract. This contract is sometimes an informal one; however, in other circumstances, the contract includes statements signed by both researcher and participant, as well as by witnesses. As part of this contract, *a researcher has an ethical responsibility to make clear to the participant what the research entails, including any possible risk to the participant, and to respect the dignity and rights of the individual during the research experience.*

Although not often discussed, we wish to emphasize that the research participant also has an ethical responsibility to behave in an appropriate manner, for example, by paying attention to instructions and by performing tasks in the manner requested by the researcher. Taylor and Shepperd (1996) relate how in one study participants were briefly left alone by an experimenter who admonished them not to discuss the experiment among themselves. However, once alone, the participants talked about the experiment and obtained information from each other that in effect negated the value of the research. Moreover, when later asked by the experimenter about what they knew of the procedures and goals of the study, none admitted knowledge gained during their illicit conversation. We suggest that *lying, cheating, or other fraudulent behavior on the part of someone who has agreed to participate in a scientific investigation is as much of a violation of the scientific integrity of the research situation as is the failure of a researcher to fully explain to the participant the risks inherent in the research task.*

APA Ethical Standards

6.10 Research Responsibilities

Prior to conducting research (except research involving only anonymous surveys, naturalistic observations, or similar research), psychologists enter into an agreement with participants that clarifies the nature of the research and the responsibilities of each party.

6.11 Informed Consent to Research

(a) Psychologists use language that is reasonably understandable to research participants in obtaining their appropriate informed consent (except as provided in Standard 6.12, Dispensing With Informed Consent). Such informed consent is appropriately documented.

(b) Psychologists inform participants of the nature of the research; they inform participants that they are free to participate or to decline to participate or to withdraw from the research; they explain the foreseeable consequences of declining or withdrawing; they inform participants of significant factors that may be expected to influence their willingness to participate (such as risks, discomfort, adverse effects, or limitations on confidentiality, except as provided in Standard 6.15, Deception in Research); and they explain other aspects about which the prospective participants inquire.

(c) When psychologists conduct research with individuals such as students or subordinates, psychologists take special care to protect the prospective participants from adverse consequences of declining or withdrawing from participation.

(d) When research participation is a course requirement or opportunity for extra credit, the prospective participant is given the choice of equitable alternative activities.

(e) For persons who are legally incapable of giving informed consent, psychologists nevertheless (1) provide an appropriate explanation, (2) obtain the participant's assent, and (3) obtain appropriate permission from a legally authorized person, if such substitute consent is permitted by law.

6.12 Dispensing With Informed Consent

Before determining that planned research (such as research involving only anonymous questionnaires, naturalistic observations, or certain kinds of archival

FIGURE 2.2   When college students are asked to participate in psychological research as part of a course they are taking, equitable alternative activities should be provided for those who do not wish to participate.

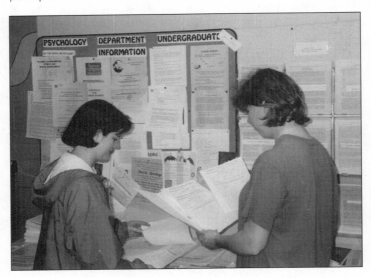

research) does not require the informed consent of research participants, psychologists consider applicable regulations and institutional review board requirements, and they consult with colleagues as appropriate.

6.13 Informed Consent in Research Filming or Recording

Psychologists obtain informed consent from research participants prior to filming or recording them in any form, unless the research involves simply naturalistic observations in public places and it is not anticipated that the recording will be used in a manner that could cause personal identification or harm.

6.14 Offering Inducements for Research Participants

(a) In offering professional services as an inducement to obtain research participants, psychologists make clear the nature of the services, as well as the risks, obligations, and limitations. (See also Standard 1.18, Barter [With Patients or Clients].)

(b) Psychologists do not offer excessive or inappropriate financial or other inducements to obtain research participants, particularly when it might tend to coerce participation.

Commentary

- Potential research participants must be made aware of all aspects of the study that may influence their willingness to participate.
- Research participants must be allowed to withdraw their consent at any time without penalties.

- Individuals must not be pressured to participate in research.
- Informed consent must be obtained from legal guardians for individuals unable to provide consent (e.g., children, mentally impaired individuals); assent to participate should be obtained from individuals unable to provide informed consent.
- Researchers should consult with knowledgeable others, including an IRB, when deciding whether to dispense with informed consent, such as when research is conducted in public settings. These settings require special attention to protecting individuals' privacy.
- Privacy refers to the rights of individuals to decide how information about them is to be communicated to others.

Ethical research practice requires that research participants be informed of all features of the research that reasonably might be expected to influence their willingness to participate and that researchers respond to any inquiries the participants might make about the research. In this way individuals can make an informed decision about their participation. Participants should also be informed that they are free to withdraw their consent at any time without penalty or prejudice. Consent must be given freely, without undue inducement or pressure. *Informed consent should always be obtained and is absolutely essential when participants are exposed to the possibility of more than minimal risk.*

True informed consent cannot be obtained from certain individuals, such as the mentally impaired or emotionally disturbed, young children, and others who are recognized as having limited ability to understand the nature of research and the possible risks. In these cases, formal consent must be obtained from the participants' parents or legal guardians; however, when feasible "assent" always should be obtained from the participants themselves. Developmental psychologists who want to test schoolchildren are often faced with the task of contacting dozens (if not hundreds) of parents in order to secure permission for the children to participate in psychological research. We should mention that ethical restrictions such as those involving informed consent also raise methodological issues (see Adair, Dushenko, & Lindsay, 1985). For example, results of one study revealed that children of parents who did not provide parental consent for a research project were academically less successful and less popular with their peers than were children of parents who did provide consent (Frame & Strauss, 1987). Thus, data gathered from the children whose parents gave consent may not always be generalized to children who did not have parental consent.

Consider the dilemma faced by one graduate student who was seeking to interview adolescents receiving services from a family planning clinic (Landers, 1988). Parental permission was not required for the teens to attend the clinic; thus, if the investigator asked the parents for permission for their children to participate in the study, she would be revealing to the parents the teens' use of the clinic's services. Yet obtaining permission of parents before conducting research with minors is standard ethical practice and also is mandated by federal laws. To help make a decision regarding proper ethical procedures in this difficult case, the graduate student correctly sought advice from experts, specifically, from members of APA's Committee for the Protection of Human Participants in Research. (In 1990, this committee was renamed Committee on Standards in Research, and the scope of its ethical concerns was enlarged [Grisso et al., 1991].) The student used the information obtained from the experts to formulate the procedures that she proposed to use as part of her dissertation research. Although advice should be sought from knowledgeable others whenever ethical dilemmas arise, *final responsibility for conducting research ethically always rests with the investigator.*

It is not always easy to decide what constitutes undue inducement or pressure to participate. Paying college students $5 an hour to take part in a psychology experiment would not generally be considered improper coercion. Recruiting very poor or disadvantaged persons from the streets with a $5 offer may be more coercive and less acceptable (Kelman, 1972). Prisoners may believe that any refusal on their part to participate in a psychology experiment will be viewed by the authorities as evidence of uncooperativeness and will therefore make it more difficult for them to be paroled. Parents of schoolchildren may fear that their children will be less well treated by teachers if they refuse to give permission for their children to participate in research. When college students are asked to fulfill a class requirement by serving as participants in psychology experiments (an experience that presumably has some educational value), an alternative method of earning class credit should be made available to those who do not wish to participate in psychological research. Such options should be equivalent, in terms of time and effort, with the requirements of research participation. Frequently employed options include reading and summarizing journal articles describing research, making informal field observations of behavior, attending presentations of research findings by graduate students or faculty, and doing volunteer community service (see Kimmel, 1996).

Serious ethical problems can arise when a researcher withholds certain information about a psychological treatment from a research participant. The reason for withholding information may be a legitimate concern on the part of the researcher that informing participants of all the details of the experiment will negate the effect of a particular treatment. For example, research on conformity behavior often requires participants to believe that responses of other persons in the situation represent those individuals' own opinions. Telling individuals before the experiment that responses made by other people will be purposely misleading would appear to make this type of research impossible. (We discuss the use of deception in psychological research later in this chapter.)

IRBs require investigators to document that the proper informed consent procedure has been followed for any research involving human participants. A sample informed consent form for use with a normal adult population is shown in Box 2.1. This form may be submitted to an IRB for approval when deception is not present and when no more than minimal risk is anticipated. *If the research involves more than minimal risk or if deception is used, the investigator has the responsibility to seek advice from those with experience in the particular problem area under investigation.*

BOX 2.1

SAMPLE INFORMED CONSENT FORM

[DATE]

I, [NAME OF PARTICIPANT], state that I am over 18 years of age and that I voluntarily agree to participate in a research project conducted by [NAME OF PRINCIPAL INVESTIGATOR, TITLE, INSTITUTIONAL AFFILIATION]. The research is being conducted in order to [BRIEF DESCRIPTION OF THE GOALS OF THE RESEARCH]. The specific task I will perform requires [DETAILS OF THE RESEARCH TASK, INCLUDING INFORMATION ABOUT THE DURATION OF PARTICIPANT'S INVOLVEMENT. ANY POSSIBLE DISCOMFORT TO PARTICIPANT MUST ALSO BE DESCRIBED.].

I acknowledge that [NAME OF PRINCIPAL INVESTIGATOR OR RESEARCH ASSISTANT] has explained the task to me fully; has informed me that I may withdraw from participation at any time without prejudice or penalty; has offered to answer any questions that I might have concerning the research procedure; has assured me that any information that I give will be used for research purposes only and will be kept confidential. [PROCEDURE FOR PROTECTING CONFIDENTIALITY OF RESPONSES SHOULD BE EXPLAINED.]

I also acknowledge that the benefits derived from, or rewards given for, my participation have been fully explained to me—as well as alternative methods, if available, for earning these rewards—and that I have been promised, upon completion of the research task, a brief description of the role my specific performance plays in this project. [THE EXACT NATURE OF ANY COMMITMENTS MADE BY THE RESEARCHER, SUCH AS THE AMOUNT OF MONEY TO BE PAID TO INDIVIDUALS FOR PARTICIPATION, SHOULD BE SPECIFIED HERE.]

_____
[Signature of Researcher]

_____
[Signature of Participant]

Members of an IRB also may be consulted to obtain advice on how to prepare a consent procedure that protects the rights of the participants. In some situations it may not be necessary to obtain informed consent. The most obvious example would be when researchers are observing individuals' behavior in public places without any intervention. An investigator, for instance, who wishes to gather evidence about race relations on a college campus by observing the frequency of mixed-race versus unmixed-race groups sitting at tables in the college cafeteria or walking across campus would not ordinarily need to obtain students' permission before making the observations. (We assume the identity of specific individuals will not be recorded.) Such student behavior can be considered public, and the method is naturalistic observation (see Chapter 3). However, deciding what is public or what is private behavior is not always easy.

Diener and Crandall (1978) identify three major dimensions to consider when deciding what information is private and what safeguards should be employed: sensitivity of the information, setting, and degree of dissemination of the information. Clearly, some kinds of information are more sensitive than others. Individuals interviewed about their sexual practices, religious beliefs, or criminal activities are likely to be more concerned about the dissemination of

FIGURE 2.3   Deciding what is public or what is private behavior is not always easy.

this information than those interviewed about who they believe will win the World Series. Similarly, organizations and businesses are likely to perceive some types of information about them as more sensitive than other types.

The setting in which behavior is observed is also a factor in defining what constitutes private activity. Individuals engaged in what reasonably might be considered public behaviors, such as attending a baseball game or other outdoor event, give up a certain degree of privacy. Yet, deciding what is public behavior is not always easy. Such behaviors as riding inside one's own car, using public bathrooms, or picnicking in a park are not easily classified. Decisions about ethical practice in these situations sometimes depend on the sensitivity of the data and the manner in which the information will be disseminated.

Dissemination of information in terms of group averages or proportions is unlikely to reflect on specific individuals. In other situations, code systems can be used to protect participants' confidentiality. *Dissemination of sensitive information about individuals or groups without their permission is a serious breach of ethics.* When information about individuals has been collected unobtrusively (e. g., by a concealed observer), one approach that has been suggested is to contact the individuals after the observations have been made and ask whether this information can be used by the researcher.

As Diener and Crandall indicate, the most difficult decisions regarding privacy involve situations in which there is an obvious ethical problem on one dimension but not on others and situations in which there is a slight problem on all three dimensions. For instance, the behavior of individuals in the darkened setting of a movie theater would appear to have the potential of yielding sensitive information about the individual, but the setting could be reasonably classified as public. **Privacy** refers to the rights of individuals to decide how information about them is to be communicated to others. Whenever possible, the manner in which information about participants will be kept confidential should be explained to participants in psychological research so they may judge for themselves whether the safeguards taken to ensure their confidentiality are reasonable. Implementing the principle of informed consent requires that the investigator seek to balance the need to investigate human behavior on the one hand with the rights of human participants on the other.

WHAT DO YOU THINK?

Although the APA Code of Ethics suggests that informed consent is not necessarily required in studies involving naturalistic observation of public behavior or "similar research" (see Standard 6.10), as we have just seen, deciding what is "public" is not always easy. Consider the following research scenarios and decide whether you think informed consent of participants should be required before the researcher proceeds to do the research. It may be that you want more information from the researcher. If so, what additional information might you want before deciding? You will see that requiring informed consent can change a research situation dramatically, making it difficult, for example, for a researcher to record behavior under "natural" conditions. Such are the dilemmas of ethical decision making.

1 In a study of drinking behavior of college students, an undergraduate working for a faculty member attends a fraternity party and records the amount drunk by other students at the party.
2 As part of a study of the gay community, a gay researcher joins a gay baseball team with the goal of recording behaviors of participants in the context of team competition during the season. (All games are played outdoors and may be watched by the public.)
3 Public bathroom behavior (e.g., flushing, hand washing, littering, writing graffiti, etc.) of men and women is observed by male and female researchers concealed in the stalls of the respective washrooms.
4 A graduate student seeks to investigate cheating behaviors of college students by concealing himself in a projection booth in an auditorium used for administering exams to very large classes. From his vantage point he can see with the aid of binoculars the movements of most students. He records head movements, switching papers, passing notes, and other suspicious exam-taking behaviors.

During the 1980s, the APA Committee for the Protection of Human Participants in Research became involved in a number of controversies over the ethical issues related to psychosocial research on acquired immune deficiency syndrome (AIDS) (Melton, Levine, Koocher, Rosenthal, & Thompson, 1988). Particularly salient among the ethical dilemmas posed by this research is that related to privacy. Control over knowledge about oneself and one's body is basic to respect for persons and is even constitutionally protected; on the other hand, the courts have supported the government's police power to curb threats to public health (Melton & Gray, 1988). The transmission of AIDS is known to take place via the sharing of body fluids, such as sexual contact or sharing of needles for intravenous injections. Thus, to understand fully the spread of AIDS requires gathering data regarding individuals' sexual practices, drug use, medical history, travel, and acquaintances. Unfortunately, confidentiality cannot always be guaranteed to participants in AIDS research because of laws requiring the reporting of AIDS cases and the fact that records can sometimes be legally subpoenaed (Gray & Melton, 1985). As in other areas when ethical dilemmas arise, the investigator is obligated to seek advice from knowledgeable others regarding the appropriateness of a research procedure. For example, consultation with members of IRBs, experienced researchers, members of ethics committees, and representatives of the population at risk (Melton et al., 1988) will help ensure that the rights of participants are protected when the psychosocial aspects of communicable diseases are investigated.

DECEPTION IN PSYCHOLOGICAL RESEARCH

- Deception in psychological research occurs when researchers withhold information or intentionally misinform participants about the research. By its nature, deception violates the ethical principle of informed consent, yet it is considered a necessary research strategy in certain areas of psychology.

No ethical issue related to research is more controversial than that of deception. There are those who would argue that participants should *never* be deceived in the context of psychological research. Deception runs counter to the principle of openness and honesty that ethical practice says should characterize the relationship between experimenter and participant. **Deception** can occur either through *omission*, the withholding of information, or *commission*, intentionally misinforming participants about an aspect of the research. Either kind of deception contradicts the principle of informed consent. To some, deception is morally repugnant; it is no different from lying. Nevertheless, despite the increased attention given to deceptive methodological practices over the last couple of decades, the use of deception in psychological research has not declined and remains a popular research strategy (Adair, Dushenka, & Lindsay, 1985; Sharpe, Adair, & Roese, 1992).

APA Ethical Standards

6.15 Deception in Research

(a) Psychologists do not conduct a study involving deception unless they have determined that the use of deceptive techniques is justified by the study's prospective scientific, educational, or applied value and that equally effective alternative procedures that do not use deception are not feasible.

(b) Psychologists never deceive research participants about significant aspects that would affect their willingness to participate, such as physical risks, discomfort, or unpleasant emotional experiences.

(c) Any other deception that is an integral feature of the design and conduct of an experiment must be explained to participants as early as is feasible, preferably at the conclusion of their participation, but no later than at the conclusion of the research. (See also Standard 6.18, Providing Participants With Information About the Study.)

Commentary

- Deception is a necessary research strategy in some psychological research.
- Deceiving individuals in order to get them to participate in the research is always unethical.
- Researchers must carefully weigh the costs of deception against the potential benefits of the research when considering the use of deception.
- Researchers are ethically obligated to explain to participants their use of deception at the conclusion of the study and remove any harmful effects of the deception.

It is simply impossible to carry out certain kinds of research without withholding information from participants about some aspects of the research. In other situations, it may be necessary to misinform participants in order to have them adopt certain attitudes or behaviors. As we explain in Chapter 3, participant observers may find it necessary to give false information in order to gain access to a particular group or setting. Rosenhan (1973) and his colleagues, for instance, posed as patients in mental hospitals in order to investigate the manner in which psychiatric diagnoses are made. Or consider that Rosenthal's (1966) well-known research investigating experimenter bias was based on the assumption that the participants believed they were experimenters working for a principal investigator. The "experimenters" were actually the participants. The data collected by these participant-experimenters sometimes differed because of the expectations they had about the research outcome. The results helped researchers better understand the role of "experimenter bias" in the conduct of psychological research.

Although deception is sometimes justified on methodological grounds, deceiving participants for the purpose of getting them to participate in research in which they would not normally take part, or research that involves more than minimal risk, is always unethical.

A basic assumption underlying the use of deception is that it is necessary to conceal the true nature of an experiment so that participants will behave as they normally would or so that they will act in accordance with the stated instructions and cues provided by the experimenter. If people come to realize (and perhaps many already have) that psychologists often present misinformation and serving in a psychology experiment means they are likely to be deceived, then the very assumption on which the use of deception is based will be lost. Participants will no longer act in accordance with the instructions of the experimenter because they will no longer believe the experimenter is telling the truth. Frequent and casual use of deception undermines the usefulness of deception as a methodological tool (Kelman, 1967). In fact, Epley and Huff (1998) demonstrated that participants given knowledge in an experimental debriefing that they were deceived later exhibited more suspicion about future psychological research than did participants who were unaware of the deception.

The fact that psychologists are often identified with deceptive practices, and the fact that deception may be the basis for experimental manipulations in natural settings, also may affect the way people react to emergencies or other events they witness. On one college campus a student was attacked and shot by another student. Witnesses did not try to help, and the assailant was not pursued. When bystanders were asked why they did not intervene, some said they thought it was just a psychology experiment (Diener & Crandall, 1978).

Kelman (1972) suggests that, *before using deception, a researcher must give very serious consideration to (1) the importance of the study to our scientific knowledge, (2) the availability of alternative, deception-free methods, and (3) the "noxiousness" of the deception.* This last consideration refers to the degree of deception involved and to the possibility of injury to the participants. In Kelman's (p. 997) view: "Only if a study is very important and no alternative methods are available can anything more than the mildest form of deception be justified." *When deception is*

FIGURE 2.4 Deception is sometimes the basis for experimental manipulations in natural settings; for example, to investigate helping behavior, psychologists may create a situation involving what appears to be a person in distress.

used, the researcher must inform participants after the experiment of the reasons for the deception, discuss any misconceptions they may have, and remove any harmful effects of the deception. One goal of this debriefing is educating the participant about the need for deception. For example, after female participants were deceived about the true purpose of a study investigating women's perceptions of vulnerability to rape (see Chapter 1; Heath & Davidson, 1988), the researchers explained the reasons for the deception and corrected any misperceptions that had been created.

One final note regarding what is or is not deception should be made. Those who are just beginning to do research sometimes believe that unless they tell participants exactly what they expect to find—that is, the hypothesis being tested—they are deceiving participants. This is not necessarily the case. Information about the specific hypothesis being tested is usually withheld from participants in order not to bias them to behave in a certain way. For example, simply telling a group of control participants that comparisons will be made between their responses and those of a group receiving a particular treatment may introduce an unwanted spirit of competition. In most situations, not telling participants exactly what the researcher is testing is simply considered good experimental procedure. Of course, the researcher can never ethically withhold information that might seriously influence a participant's willingness to participate (APA Ethical Standard 6.15). Debriefing provides an opportunity to inform participants about the specific goals of a study and to educate them about the need to do psychological research.

WHAT DO YOU THINK?

Deceptive practices in psychological research continue unabated (e.g., Sieber, Iannuzzo, & Rodriguez, 1995); however, debate in the scientific community concerning deception also has not abated (see, for example, Bröder, 1998; Fisher & Fryberg, 1994; Ortmann & Hertwig; 1997). It is a complex issue, with those taking part in the debate sometimes at odds over the definition of deception (see Ortmann & Hertwig, 1998). The debate was summarized by Fisher & Fryberg (1994) as follows: "Ethical arguments have focused on whether deceptive research practices are justified on the basis of their potential societal benefit or violate moral principles of beneficence and respect for individuals and the fiduciary obligations of psychologists to research participants" (p. 417). This is quite a mouthful; so let us see if we can break it down.

A moral principle of "beneficence" refers to the idea that research activities should be beneficent (bring benefits) for individuals and society. If deception is shown to harm individuals or society, then the beneficence of the research can be questioned. The moral principle of "respect for individuals" is just that: People should be treated as persons and not "objects" for study, for example. This principle would suggest that people have a right to make their own judgments about the procedures and purpose of the research in which they are participating (Fisher & Fryberg, 1994). "Fiduciary obligations of psychologists" refer to the responsibilities of individuals who are given trust over others, even if only temporarily. In the case of psychological research, the researcher is considered to have responsibility for the welfare of participants during the study and for the consequences of their participation.

These ideas and principles can perhaps be illustrated through the arguments of Baumrind (1985), who argues persuasively that "the use of intentional deception in the research setting is unethical, imprudent, and unwarranted scientifically" (p. 165). Specifically, she argues that the costs to the participants, to the profession, and to society of the use of deception are too great to warrant its continued use. Although these arguments are lengthy and complex, let us attempt a brief summary. First, according to Baumrind, deception exacts a cost to participants because it undermines the participants' trust in their own judgment and in a "fiduciary" (someone who is holding something in trust for another person). When research participants find they have been duped or tricked, Baumrind believes this may lead the participants to question what they have learned about themselves and to lead them to distrust individuals (e.g., social scientists) who they might have previously trusted to provide valid information and advice. A cost to the profession is exacted because participants (and society at large) soon come to realize that psychologists are "tricksters" and not to be believed when giving instructions about research participation. If participants tend to suspect psychologists of lying, then one may question whether deception will work as it is intended by the researcher, a point raised earlier by Kelman (1972). Baumrind also argues that the use of deception reveals psychologists are willing to lie, which seemingly contradicts their supposed dedication to seeking truth. Finally, there is harm done to society because deception undermines people's trust in experts and makes them suspicious in general about all contrived events. Of course, these are not the views of all psychologists (see Christensen, 1988; Kimmel, 1998). Milgram (1977), for instance, suggested that deceptive practices of psychologists are really a kind of "technical illusion" and should be permitted in the interests of scientific inquiry. After all, illusions are sometimes created in real-life situations in order to make people believe something. When listening to a radio program, people are not generally bothered by the fact that the thunder they hear or the sound of a horse galloping are merely technical illusions created by a sound effects specialist. Milgram argues that technical illusions should be permitted in the case of scientific inquiry. We deceive children into believing in Santa Claus. Why cannot scientists create illusions in order to help them understand human behavior?

Just as illusions are often created in real-life situations, in other situations, Milgram points out, there can be a suspension of a general moral principle. If we learn of a crime, we are ethically bound to report it to the authorities. On the other hand, a lawyer who is given information by a client must consider this information privileged even if it reveals that the client is guilty. Physicians perform very personal examinations of our bodies. Although it is morally permissible in a physician's office, the same type of behavior would not be condoned outside the office. Milgram argues that, in the interest of science, psychologists should occasionally be allowed to suspend the moral principle of truthfulness and honesty.

Those who defend deception point to studies showing that participants on the average do not appear to react negatively to being deceived (e.g., Christensen, 1988; Epley & Huff, 1998; Kimmel, 1996), and that although "suspiciousness" about psychological research may increase, the overall effects seem to be negligible (see Kimmel, 1998). Nevertheless, the bottom line according to those who argue for the continued use of deception is well summarized by Kimmel (1998): "An absolute rule prohibiting the use of deception in all psychological research would have the egregious consequence of preventing researchers from carrying out a wide range of important studies" (p. 805). No one in the scientific community suggests that deceptive practices be taken lightly; however, for many scientists the use of deception is less noxious (to use Kelman's term) than doing without the knowledge gained by such studies.

What do you think about the use of deception in psychological research?

ADDITIONAL RESPONSIBILITIES TO RESEARCH PARTICIPANTS

- Researchers are ethically obligated to seek ways to benefit participants even after the research is completed, for example, by using debriefing procedures.

Over the years, many researchers have fallen into the trap of viewing human participants in research chiefly as means to an end, as "objects" used to obtain data in order to meet the goals of a research study. While perhaps conscientiously giving participants the opportunity to give their informed consent and carefully safeguarding them from serious injury, researchers sometimes have considered their responsibility to participants to end when the last response was made or the final piece of data collected. A handshake or "thank you" was frequently all that marked the end of the research session. This meant the research participants likely left with unanswered questions about specific aspects of the situation and with only the vaguest idea of the role they played in the scientific endeavor. It is important both in the planning and in the conduct of research to consider how the experience may affect the research participant and the participant's environment after the research is completed and to seek ways in which the participant will benefit from participation. As we have just seen, these concerns follow directly from the moral principles of beneficence and respect of individuals.

APA Ethical Standards

6.16 Sharing and Utilizing Data

Psychologists inform research participants of their anticipated sharing or further use of personally identifiable research data and of the possibility of unanticipated future uses.

6.17 Minimizing Invasiveness

In conducting research, psychologists interfere with the participants or milieu from which data are collected only in a manner that is warranted by an appropriate research design and that is consistent with psychologists' roles as scientific investigators.

6.18 Providing Participants With Information About the Study

(a) Psychologists provide a prompt opportunity for participants to obtain appropriate information about the nature, results, and conclusions of the research, and psychologists attempt to correct any misconceptions that participants may have.

(b) If scientific or humane values justify delaying or withholding this information, psychologists take reasonable measures to reduce the risk of harm.

6.19 Honoring Commitments

Psychologists take reasonable measures to honor all commitments they have made to research participants.

Commentary

- Debriefing benefits both participants and researchers.
- Debriefing informs participants about the nature of the research, their role in the study, and educates individuals about research. The goal of debriefing is to have individuals feel good about their participation.
- Debriefing allows researchers to learn how participants viewed the procedures, allows potential insights into the nature of the research findings, and provides ideas for future research.

Earlier we mentioned that protecting the confidentiality of a participant's responses brought benefits both to the participant (safeguarding from social injury) and to the researcher (increasing the probability of honest responding). **Debriefing** participants at the end of a research session also carries benefits both to participant and researcher (Blanck et al., 1992). As we saw when discussing the use of deception, *debriefing is necessary to remove any harmful effects or misconceptions about participation (although see Baumrind, 1985), as well as to explain to participants the need for deception; however, debriefing also has the important goals of educating participants about the research (rationale, method, results) and of leaving them with positive feelings about their participation.* Whenever possible, a researcher should take the time to explain the nature of the participant's specific performance and to show how it relates to group or normative data. If this is not feasible, participants should be given the opportunity at some future time to learn about the general outcome of the research. Some researchers take it upon themselves to mail a written report of a study's results to the participants; others, especially when testing captive populations such as college students, invite participants to come back later (for instance, at the end of a semester) to obtain a report summarizing the study's findings. In this way, participants can learn more about their particular contribution to the research study and, in doing so, feel more personally involved in the scientific process.

Debriefing is an opportunity for participants to learn more about research in general—by having the study's methodology explained to them, for instance, or by being introduced to various tests or instruments used in psychological research. Because the "educational value" of participation in psychological research is one reason given to justify the use of large numbers of volunteers from college introductory psychology classes, researchers testing students have an important obligation to attempt to educate participants about psychological research. In addition to being debriefed, student participants have sometimes been asked by classroom instructors to write brief reports about their research experience, including details about the study's purpose, the techniques used, and the significance of the research to understanding behavior. One evaluation of such a procedure revealed that students who wrote reports were more satisfied with the research experience and experienced a significantly greater overall educational benefit from it than did students who did not write reports (Richardson, Pegalis, & Britton, 1992).

Debriefing can help a researcher by providing an opportunity to find out how the participant viewed the procedures and treatments that were administered. For example, a researcher may wish to know whether a particular experimental procedure was perceived by the participant in the way the investigator intended (Blanck et al., 1992). Studies of what is called incidental learning involve exposing participants to certain kinds of critical material (e.g., the contents of a room, another person, a list of words, and so on) and then later asking them what they can remember of this material. It is important that participants, when exposed to the critical material, be unaware that a memory test will later be given (otherwise, intentional, not incidental, learning will take place). Debriefing enables the investigator to find out how participants perceived the tasks given to them and whether they were aware that their memory would be tested.

Debriefing that seeks to discover how participants perceive a specific task or situation must be done in a manner that avoids pressing them to reveal information they believe they are not supposed to possess. Research participants generally want to help with the scientific process, and many realize that in any valid psychological study information may be purposely withheld from them (Orne, 1962). To tell the researcher that they really *did* know about these details may seem to participants to threaten the study's validity and hence "ruin" it. Thus, if questioned directly, participants may withhold information about their perceptions in a misguided, albeit well-intentioned, attempt to protect the scientific integrity of the study. Debriefing should thus be carried out in an informal manner, with the participant carefully led by the investigator to respond honestly and openly. This is often best accomplished by using general questions in an open-ended format (e.g., What do you think this study was about?) and following up with more specific questions that, as much as possible, do not cue the participant about what responses are expected (Orne, 1962). Debriefing provides yet another benefit to researchers. It can provide them with "leads for future research and help identify problems in their current protocols" (Blanck et al., 1992, p. 962). Debriefing, in other words, can provide clues as to the reasons for a participant's performance, which may help when discussing the overall results or may set the stage for another study. Errors in experimental materials—for instance, missing information or ambiguous instructions—are sometimes detected through postexperimental interviews with participants. As we said, *debriefing is good for both the participant and the scientist.*

RESEARCH WITH ANIMALS

Each year millions of animals are tested in laboratory investigations aimed at answering a wide range of important questions. New drugs are tested on animals before they are used with humans. Substances introduced into the environment must first be given to animals to test their effects. Animals are exposed to diseases in order that investigators may observe symptoms and test various cures. New surgical procedures—especially those involving the brain—are often first tried out on animals. Many animals are also used for behavioral research, for example, by ethologists and experimental psychologists. These investigations yield much information that contributes to human welfare (Miller, 1985). In the process, however, many animals are subjected to pain and discomfort, stress and sickness, and death. Although rodents, particularly rats and mice, are the largest group of laboratory animals, researchers use a wide variety of species in their investigations, including monkeys, fish, dogs, and cats. Specific animals are frequently chosen because they are good models of human responses. For example, psychologists interested in audition sometimes use chinchillas as subjects because their auditory processes are very similar to those of humans. In addition, animal models of the relationship between stress and diabetes have helped researchers to understand psychosomatic factors in this illness (Surwit & Williams, 1996).

Apparently, chimpanzees are the only nonhuman primates that can harbor the virus linked to AIDS (Landers, 1988). As a result, concern over the dwindling numbers of these animals has been expressed, not only by animal conservationists, who worry about the extinction of the species, but by biomedical researchers, who may have to depend on these animals for laboratory research aimed at finding a vaccine for AIDS (Booth, 1988; Goodall, 1987).

APA Ethical Standards

6.20 Care and Use of Animals in Research

(a) Psychologists who conduct research involving animals treat them humanely.
(b) Psychologists acquire, care for, use, and dispose of animals in compliance with current federal, state, and local laws and regulations, and with professional standards.

FIGURE 2.5 Research with animals increases our understanding of mental and physical health.

(c) Psychologists trained in research methods and experienced in the care of laboratory animals supervise all procedures involving animals and are responsible for ensuring appropriate consideration of their comfort, health, and humane treatment.

(d) Psychologists ensure that all individuals using animals under their supervision have received instruction in research methods and in the care, maintenance, and handling of the species being used, to the extent appropriate to their role.

(e) Responsibilities and activities of individuals assisting in a research project are consistent with their respective competencies.

(f) Psychologists make reasonable efforts to minimize the discomfort, infection, illness, and pain of animal subjects.

(g) A procedure subjecting animals to pain, stress, or privation is used only when an alternative procedure is unavailable and the goal is justified by its prospective scientific, educational, or applied value.

(h) Surgical procedures are performed under appropriate anesthesia; techniques to avoid infection and minimize pain are followed during and after surgery.

(i) When it is appropriate that the animal's life be terminated, it is done rapidly, with an effort to minimize pain, and in accordance with accepted procedures.

Commentary

- Animals are used in research to gain knowledge that will benefit humans, for example, by helping to cure diseases.
- Researchers are ethically obligated to protect the welfare of research animals and to treat them humanely.
- The use of animals in research is widely debated and involves complex issues.

The use of animals as laboratory subjects has often been taken for granted. In fact, the biblical reference to humankind's "dominion" over all lesser creatures is sometimes invoked to justify the use of animals as laboratory subjects (Johnson, 1990; Rollin, 1985). More often, however, research with animal subjects is justified by the need to gain knowledge *without putting humans in jeopardy* about aspects of nature that directly affect the human condition. Few cures, drugs, vaccines, or therapies have come about without experimentation on animals (Rosenfeld, 1981). It would be difficult to contemplate the consequences of doing research on such diseases as cancer or muscular dystrophy without the opportunity first to examine the course of the disease or try out a new cure on animal subjects. Feeney (1987), for example, has called attention to the contributions that basic research with animal subjects has made to the treatment of patients recovering from brain and spinal cord injury. He also points out that our understanding of the relationship between brain and behavior was advanced significantly by the now classic work in the 1960s of Roger Sperry, who won a Nobel Prize for his work on the "split brain" (the functioning of the brain after the corpus callosum has been cut). Early investigations by Sperry and others, using cats and monkeys as subjects, demonstrated that the two hemispheres of the brain can function independently in learning and memory. This knowledge permitted physicians to perform similar operations to treat humans suffering from intractable epilepsy. Maestripieri and Carroll (1998) suggest that investigation of naturally occurring infant maltreatment in monkeys can inform scientists about child abuse and neglect (see also Cicchetti, 1998).

Many questions, however, have been raised about the role of animal subjects in psychological studies (Novak, 1991; Shapiro, 1998; Ulrich, 1991). These questions include the most basic one, whether animals should be used at all in scientific investigations, as well as important questions about the care and protection of animal subjects. Clearly, according to the APA principles, *the researcher who uses animal subjects in an investigation has an ethical obligation to look out for their welfare and to treat them humanely.* Only individuals qualified to do research and to manage and care for the particular species being used should be allowed to participate. When the research exposes the animals to pain or discomfort, it must be justified by the potential scientific, educational, or applied goals. As we noted earlier when institutional review was discussed, animal review boards (IACUCs) are now in place at research facilities receiving funds from the Public Health Service. These committees are charged with determining the adequacy of the procedures for controlling pain, carrying out euthanasia, housing animals, and training personnel, as well as determining whether the experimental design is sufficient to gain important new information and whether the animal model is appropriate or whether nonanimal models could be used (Holden, 1987).

Partly in response to calls from members of animal rights groups during the 1980s, investigators must now meet a host of federal and state requirements, including inspection of animal facilities by veterinarians from the U.S. Department of Agriculture (Landers, 1987a, 1987b; see also National Research Council, 1996). These regulations are often welcomed by members of the scientific community, and many animal researchers belong to groups such as the APA Committee on Animal Research and Experimentation (CARE) that seek to protect laboratory animals. CARE has developed a list of specific guidelines to be followed when animal subjects are used in psychological research. (A copy of these guidelines may be obtained by writing CARE, c/o Science Directorate, American Psychological Association, 750 First Street, N.E., Washington, DC 20002-4242.) As with any ethically sensitive issue, however, it is clear that compromises must be made. For example, until alternatives to animal research can be found, the need to conduct research using animal subjects in order to battle human disease and suffering must be balanced against the need for adequate control over the way animals are treated in laboratory research (Goodall, 1987). As APA's chief executive officer, Raymond Fowler, pointed out, it is also important that the use of animal subjects not be restricted because the application of the research is not readily apparent (Fowler, 1992). "The charges that animal research is of no value because it cannot always be linked to potential applications is a charge that can be made against all basic research." Such an indictment "threatens the intellectual and scientific foundation" of all psychology, including both "scientists and practitioners" (p. 2).

Although few scientists would disagree that restrictions are necessary to prevent needless suffering in animals, most want to avoid a quagmire of bureaucratic restrictions and high costs that will undermine research. Feeney (1987) suggests that severe restrictions and high costs, as well as the negative publicity (and occasional terrorist acts) directed toward individuals and institutions by extremists within the animal activist groups, may deter young scientists from entering the field of animal research (see also Azar, 1994a). If such is the case, the result possibly could be to deprive the (presently) incurably ill or permanently paralyzed of the hope that comes through scientific research.

Clearly, the issues surrounding the debate over the relevance of animal research to the human situation are many and complex. As Ulrich (1992) has commented, discussion of these issues must be approached with "wisdom and balance" (p. 386).

WHAT DO YOU THINK?

Ethical decision making often pits opposing philosophical positions against one another. This is clearly seen in the debate over the use of animals in research. At the center of this debate is the question of the "moral status" of humans and nonhuman animals. As the Australian philosopher Peter Singer (1990, p. 9) points out, two generally accepted moral principles are:

1 All humans are equal in moral status.
2 All humans are of superior moral status to nonhuman animals.

Thus, Singer continues, "On the basis of these principles, it is commonly held that we should put human welfare ahead of the suffering of nonhuman animals; this assumption is reflected in our treatment of animals in many areas, including farming, hunting, experimentation, and entertainment" (p. 9).

Singer, however, does not agree with these commonly held views. He argues that "there is no rational ethical justification for always putting human suffering ahead of that of nonhuman animals" (p. 9). Unless we appeal to religious viewpoints (which Singer rejects as the basis of decisions in a pluralistic society), there is, according to Singer, no special moral status to "being human." This position has roots in the philosophical tradition known as utilitarianism, which began with the writings of David Hume (1711–1776) and Jeremy Bentham (1748–1832), as well as John Stuart Mill (1806–1873) (Rachels, 1986). Basically, this viewpoint holds that whenever we have choices between alternative actions we should choose the one that has the best overall consequences (produces the most "happiness") for everyone involved. What matters in this view is whether the individual in question is capable of experiencing happiness-unhappiness, pleasure-pain; whether the individual is human or nonhuman is not relevant (Rachels, 1986).

What do you think about the moral status of humans and animals and its relation to psychological research?

REPORTING OF PSYCHOLOGICAL RESEARCH

- Investigators attempt to communicate their research findings in peer-reviewed scientific journals, and the APA Code of Ethics provides guidelines for this process.

Generally, once a psychological investigation is completed, the principal investigator prepares a manuscript for submission to one of the dozens of psychology-related scientific periodicals. Publication in a psychology journal not only achieves the goal of communicating the results of a study to members of the scientific community and to society in general but, as we have seen, may also enhance the researcher's reputation and even the reputation of the institution that sponsored the research. But getting the results of a scientific investigation published is not always an easy process, especially if the researcher wishes to publish in one of the more prestigious scientific journals. Journals sponsored by APA, such as the *Journal of Abnormal Psychology*, *Journal of Educational Psychology*, *Journal of Experimental Psychology: Learning, Memory, and Cognition*, and *Psychological Review*, can have rejection rates approaching 90% (American Psychological Association, 1998). Manuscripts submitted for publication must be prepared according to strict stylistic guidelines (see Appendix C), meet rigorous methodological and substantive criteria, and be appropriate for the particular journal to which the manuscript is submitted.

Problems in any of these three areas may be sufficient to deny publication; however, manuscripts are more commonly rejected because of problems in the methodology of the study, problems in the statistical treatment of the results, or because the results do not make a significant enough contribution to scientific progress in the field. Decisions about the acceptability of a scientific manuscript are made by the journal's editors, usually on the basis of comments made by the experts in the field who have been asked by the editors for their opinions about the manuscript's scientific worth. This process is known as peer review, and many scientists have had their hopes of being published dashed along this difficult path. Despite the many pressures to publish in order to earn promotion or tenure at a university, it is imperative that all scientists adhere strictly to the code of ethics governing the reporting of results.

APA Ethical Standards

6.21 Reporting of Results

(a) Psychologists do not fabricate data or falsify results in their publications.
(b) If psychologists discover significant errors in their published data, they take reasonable steps to correct such errors in a correction, retraction, erratum, or other appropriate publication means.

6.22 Plagiarism

Psychologists do not present substantial portions or elements of another's work or data as their own, even if the other work or data source is cited occasionally.

6.23 Publication Credit

(a) Psychologists take responsibility and credit, including authorship credit, only for work they have actually performed or to which they have contributed.
(b) Principal authorship and other publication credits accurately reflect the relative scientific or professional contributions of the individuals involved, regardless of their relative status. Mere possession of an institutional position, such as Department Chair, does not justify authorship credit. Minor contributions to the research or to the writing for publications are appropriately acknowledged, such as in footnotes or in an introductory statement.
(c) A student is usually listed as principal author on any multiple-authored article that is substantially based on the student's dissertation or thesis.

6.24 Duplicate Publication of Data

Psychologists do not publish, as original data, data that have been previously published. This does not preclude republishing data when accompanied by proper acknowledgment.

6.25 Sharing Data

After research results are published, psychologists do not withhold the data on which their conclusions are based from other competent professionals who seek to verify the substantive claims through reanalysis and who intend to use such data only for that purpose, provided that the confidentiality of the participants can be protected and unless legal rights concerning proprietary data preclude their release.

6.26 Professional Reviewers

Psychologists who review material submitted for publication, grant, or other research proposal review respect the confidentiality of and the proprietary rights in such information of those who submitted it.

Commentary

- Decisions about who should receive publication credit are based on the scholarly importance of the contribution.
- Ethical reporting of research requires recognizing the work of others using proper citations and references; failure to do so may result in plagiarism.
- Proper citation includes using quotation marks when material is taken directly from a source and citing secondary sources when an original source is not consulted.

The ethical standards governing the reporting of the results of a scientific investigation seem more straightforward than in other areas of ethical concern. Even here, however, the lines cannot always be drawn clearly. Consider, for example, ethical issues related to assigning *publication credit* to those who make contributions to a research project. Research is often a collaborative effort, involving, for instance, colleagues who offer suggestions about a study's design, graduate or undergraduate students who assist a principal investigator by testing participants and organizing data, technicians who construct specialized equipment, and expert consultants who give advice about computer programs needed for statistical analyses. Because authorship of a published scientific study frequently is used to measure an individual's motivation and competence in a scientific field, *it is important to acknowledge fairly those who have contributed to a project.* However, deciding whether an individual should be credited by being an "author" of a scientific paper or whether that individual's contribution should be acknowledged in a less visible way, such as in a footnote, is not always easy (see, for example, Murray, 1998). If authorship is granted, then the order of authors' names must also be decided. "First author" of a multiple-authored article generally signifies a greater contribution than does "second author" (which is greater than third, etc.). There is a general consensus that contributions leading to authorship should be based mainly in terms of their scholarly importance (e.g., aiding the conceptual aspects of a study) and not by the time and energy invested in the study (Bridgewater, Bornstein, & Walkenbach, 1981; Fine & Kurdek, 1993).

A rather troublesome area of concern, not only for some professionals but frequently for students, is that of **plagiarism.** Again, the ethical standard seems clear enough: Don't present substantial portions or elements of another's work as your own. But what constitutes "substantial portions or elements," and how does one avoid giving the impression that another's work is one's own? This can be like walking a tightrope. On one side is the goal of achieving recognition for contributing to the solution of a problem; on the other side is the goal of recognizing others who have previously contributed to its solution. The fact that both professionals and students are too often caught in the act of plagiarizing suggests that many veer from the tightrope by seeking their own recognition at the expense of giving due credit to the work of others. Sometimes acts of plagiarism result from sloppiness (failing to double-check a source to verify that an idea that is presented did not originate with someone else, for example). Errors of this kind are still plagiarism; *ignorance is not a legitimate excuse.* On other occasions, especially among students, plagiarism can result from failure to identify literal passages through the use of quotation marks or to acknowledge the use of secondary sources. A *secondary source* is one that discusses other (original) work. Most textbooks can be considered secondary sources. Again, ignorance concerning the proper form of citation is not an acceptable excuse, and on unfortunate occasions researchers—professors as well as students—have seen their careers ruined by accusations of plagiarism.

Mistakes can be made all too easily. For example, what constitutes a "substantial" element of another's thinking is not always determined by quantity, as is sometimes assumed. That is, researchers occasionally ask "how much" of a passage can be used without putting it in quotation marks or otherwise identifying its source. A substantial element can be a single word or short phrase if that element serves to identify a key idea or concept that is the result of another's thinking. Students and other novices in an academic discipline, who may not yet be cognizant of important concepts and ideas in an area of knowledge, must be particularly careful when referring to the work of others. *Whenever material is taken directly from a source, it should be placed in quotation marks and the source properly identified.*

Because students and others new to a scientific field frequently rely on secondary sources, it is very important that they understand how to use and cite such sources, which include not only textbooks, but published reviews of research such as those that appear in scientific journals like the *Psychological Bulletin,* and other sources whose authors refer to another's findings and ideas. It is always unethical to present an idea or result from an article or publication found in a secondary source *in a manner that suggests you consulted the original work* when your only source of information about the critical material comes from the secondary source. For example, suppose you wish to discuss the interesting work done by Levine (1990) on pace of life that we discussed in Chapter 1 of this text. Unless you are able to locate and peruse the original article, it is unethical for you simply to acknowledge Levine when citing his work; you must also cite the authors of the textbook who discussed his work. It is also bad scholarship because if your readers rely on your report, they will be relying on your interpretation of the textbook authors' interpretation of the original (Levine's) work. It isn't difficult to see how building a base of scientific knowledge on interpretations of interpretations (and so on, when others interpret *your* work) would quickly produce inconsistencies and contradictions.

Citing work mentioned in a secondary source should be avoided whenever possible (e.g., by taking the time to locate and consult the original), but when it is necessary to do so, proper citation means informing your reader that you did *not* consult the original work (e.g., by using the phrase "as cited in . . ." when referring to the original work). This gives your reader fair warning that the identification and interpretation of the critical material did not originate with you. (Students of psychology are expected to be familiar with the stylistic rules and guidelines for manuscript preparation found in the *Publication Manual of the American Psychological Association*, 4th ed., 1994. See also Appendix C in this textbook.) As with other areas of ethical decision making, when in doubt get advice from others with experience in the area in which you have questions.

WHAT DO YOU THINK?

Ethical concerns associated with the assigning of authorship can take many forms. For example, not only is it unethical for a faculty member to take credit for a student's work, it is also unethical for students to be given undeserved author credit. This latter situation may arise, for instance, in a misguided attempt by a faculty mentor to give a student an edge when competing for a position in a competitive graduate program. According to Fine and Kurdek (1993), awarding students undeserved author credit may falsely represent the student's expertise, give the student an unfair advantage over peers, and, perhaps, lead others to create impossible expectations for the student. These authors recommend that faculty and students collaborate in the process of determining authorship credit and discuss early on in the project what level of participation warrants author credit.

As with many ethical issues, the process of making a good decision is not always easy. Consider the following scenario presented by Fine and Kurdek (1993) as part of their discussion of this important issue:

> An undergraduate student asked a psychology member to supervise an honors thesis. The student proposed a topic, the faculty member primarily developed the research methodology, the student collected and entered the data, the faculty member conducted the statistical analyses, and the student used part of the analyses for the thesis. The student wrote the thesis under very close supervision by the faculty member. After the honors thesis was completed, the faculty member decided that data from the entire project were sufficiently interesting to warrant publication as a unit. Because the student did not have the skills necessary to write the entire study for a scientific journal, the faculty member did so. The student's thesis contained approximately one third of the material presented in the article. (pp. 1141–1142)

What do you think? Should the student be an author on any publication resulting from this work? Or, perhaps, should the student's work only be acknowledged in a footnote to the article? If you think the student should be given author credit, do you think the student should be first author or second author?

STEPS FOR ETHICAL DECISION MAKING

Should research participants be placed at risk of serious injury to gain information about bystander apathy? Should psychologists use deception to learn about the causes of date rape? Is it acceptable to make animals suffer in order to learn about human drug addiction? These questions require answers; however, you no doubt realize by now that the answers do not come easily. Moreover, it is often unclear what the "right" answer is or even if there *is* a right answer. More often than not, at least in the context of doing psychological research, the answer is based on the reflective judgment of a group of individuals with varying backgrounds and experiences who are asked to review the study. The people who comprise a university IRB or IACUC, for instance, are one such group. Recommendations can be made regarding the steps to be taken in this review process (Keith-Spiegel & Koocher, 1985). We have prepared one set of recommendations based on our readings and on discussions with philosophers involved in ethical decision making.*

1 Find out all the facts of the situation. In other words, determine exactly what is involved in terms of procedure, nature of participants, and so on.

2 Identify the relevant ethical issues. An important part of this inquiry will be consulting ethical guidelines that are available, such as the APA Ethics Code we have excerpted in this chapter, as well as policy statements from various professional organizations. Also, make sure you are aware of local, state, and federal regulations or laws in this area.

3 Decide what is at stake for all parties involved (participants, researchers, institutions). This will mean taking different viewpoints, for example, by asking what is at stake from a scientific point of view, from society's viewpoint, from the view of participants, and from an overall moral viewpoint.

4 Identify alternative methods or procedures, discussing the consequences of each alternative, including their ethical implications. As part of this discussion, consider the consequences of *not* doing the proposed research. Examine the practical constraints of each alternative.

5 Decide on the action to be taken. Judge the "correctness" of your decision not in terms of whether it makes you feel happy (you may not), but, rather, in terms of the process that was followed. Is it the best that can be done given the circumstances?

SUMMARY

Psychological research raises many ethical questions. Thus, before beginning a research project, you must consider the specific ethical issues, as well as the various federal and state laws, relevant to your project. In most cases formal institutional approval—for example, from an IRB or IACUC—must be obtained

---

*We wish to acknowledge the contributions in this section of various members of the Loyola University of Chicago Center for Ethics, especially David Ozar, Mark Waymack, and Patricia Werhane.

before beginning to do research. One function of an IRB is to reach a consensus regarding the risk/benefit ratio of the proposed research. Risk can involve physical, psychological, or social injury. Informed consent must be obtained from human participants in most psychological research. Researchers must take special safeguards to protect human participants when more than minimal risk is present and to provide appropriate debriefing following their participation. Debriefing can also help human participants feel more fully involved in the research situation as well as help the researcher learn how the participants perceived the treatment or task. Serious ethical questions arise when researchers withhold information from participants. When deception is used, debriefing should include providing information concerning the reasons for having used deception.

Psychologists testing animal subjects must obey a variety of federal and state guidelines and, in general, must treat the animals humanely. Animals may be subjected to pain or discomfort only when alternative procedures are not available and when the goals of the research are judged to justify such procedures. Reporting of psychological findings should be done in a manner that gives appropriate credit to the individuals who helped with the project. Appropriate acknowledgment must also be made of those individuals whose ideas or findings have previously been reported in the published literature and who therefore contributed to the investigator's planning or thinking about the study.

KEY CONCEPTS

risk/benefit ratio	deception
minimal risk	debriefing
informed consent	plagiarism
privacy	

REVIEW QUESTIONS

1 Briefly summarize the role of Institutional Review Boards (IRBs) and Institutional Animal Care and Use Committees (IACUCs) in overseeing psychological research.
2 How is the risk/benefit ratio used in ethical decision making?
3 Differentiate among the following possible types of injury in psychological research: physical, psychological, social.
4 How is the possibility of social risk typically safeguarded against?
5 Under what conditions do the APA ethical standards indicate that informed consent may not be necessary?
6 What do Diener and Crandall (1978) say are three important dimensions to consider when making decisions about what information is private?
7 When is it unethical to deceive human participants?
8 What are the major benefits of debriefing, both to the participant and to the researcher?
9 What kinds of special knowledge are required by the APA standards for those working with animal subjects?

10 According to the APA standards, what circumstances must be present before animals may be subjected to stress or pain?

11 What allows an individual to claim "authorship" of a published scientific report?

12 What specific ethical procedure should be followed when it is necessary to cite information from a secondary source?

CHALLENGE QUESTIONS

NOTE: Each of the challenge questions for Chapter 2 includes a hypothetical research proposal involving a rationale and method similar to that of actual published research. To answer these questions, you will need to be familiar with the APA ethical principles and other material on ethical decision making presented in this chapter, including the recommended steps for ethical decision making that were outlined at the end of this chapter. As you will see, your task is to decide whether specific ethical standards have been violated and to make recommendations regarding the proposed research, including the most basic recommendation of whether the investigator should be allowed to proceed. Unlike other chapters, no answers to the questions are provided. To resolve the ethical dilemmas, you must be able not only to apply the appropriate ethical standards but also to reach an agreement regarding the proposed research after discussion with others whose backgrounds and knowledge differ from your own. You will therefore have to consider points of view different from your own. We urge you to approach these problems as part of a group discussion of these important issues.

Proposal 1

I. Assume you are a member of an Institutional Review Board (IRB). Besides yourself, the committee includes a clinical psychologist, a social psychologist, a social worker, a philosopher, a Protestant minister, a history professor, and a respected business executive in the community. The following is a summary of a research proposal that has been submitted to the IRB for review. You are asked to consider what questions you might want to ask the investigator and whether you would approve carrying out the study at your institution in its present form, whether modification should be made before approval, or whether the proposal should not be approved. (An actual research proposal submitted to an IRB would include more details than we present here.)

Rationale Psychological conformity occurs when people accept the opinions or judgments of others in the absence of significant reasons to do so or in the face of evidence to the contrary. Previous research has investigated the conditions under which conformity is likely to occur and has shown, for example, that conformity increases when people anticipate unpleasant events (e.g., shock) and when the pressure to conform comes from individuals with whom the individuals identify. The proposed research examines psychological conformity in the context of discussions about alcohol consumption among teenage students. The goal of the research is to identify factors that contribute to students' willingness to attend social events where alcohol is served to minors and to allow obviously intoxicated persons to drive an automobile. This research seeks to investigate conformity in a natural setting and in circumstances where unpleasant events (e.g., legal penalties, school suspension, injury, or even death) can be avoided by not conforming to peer pressure.

Method

The research will involve 36 high school students between the ages of 16 and 18 who have volunteered to participate in a research project investigating "beliefs and attitudes of today's high school students." Participants will be assigned to four-person discussion groups. Each person in the group will be given the same 20 questions to answer; however, they will be asked to discuss each question with members of the group before writing down their answers. Four of the 20 questions deal with alcohol consumption by teenagers and with possible actions that might be taken to reduce teenage drinking and driving. One member of the group will be appointed discussion leader by the principal investigator. Unknown to the participants, they will be assigned randomly to three different groups. In each group, there will be either 0, 1, or 2 students who are actually working for the principal investigator. Each of these "confederates" has received prior instructions from the investigator regarding what to say during the group discussion of the critical questions about teenage drinking. (The use of confederates in psychological research is discussed in Chapter 3.) Specifically, confederates have been asked to follow a script which presents the argument that the majority of people who reach the legal driving age (16), and all individuals who are old enough (18) to vote in national elections and serve in the armed forces, are old enough to make their own decisions about drinking alcohol; moreover, because it is up to each individual to make this decision, other individuals do not have the right to intervene if someone under the legal age chooses to drink alcohol. Each of the confederates "admits" to drinking alcohol on at least two previous occasions. Thus, the experimental manipulation involves either 0, 1, or 2 persons in the four-person groups suggesting they do not believe students have a responsibility to avoid situations where alcohol is served to minors or to intervene when someone chooses to drink and drive. The effect of this argument on the written answers given by the actual participants in this experiment will be evaluated. Moreover, audiotapes of the sessions will be made without participants' knowledge, and the contents of these audiotapes will be analyzed. Following the experiment, the nature of the deception and the reasons for making audiotapes of the discussions will be explained to the participants.

Proposal 2

II. Assume you are a member of an Institutional Animal Care and Use Committee (IACUC). Besides yourself, the committee includes a veterinarian, a biologist, a philosopher, and a respected business executive in the community. The following is a summary of a research proposal that has been submitted to the IACUC for review. You are asked to consider what questions you might want to ask the investigator and whether you would approve carrying out this study at your institution in its present form, whether modification should be made before approval, or whether the proposal should not be approved. (An actual research proposal submitted to an IACUC would include more details than we present here.)

Rationale   The investigators seek to investigate the role of subcortical structures in the limbic system in moderating emotion and aggression. This proposal is based on previous research from this laboratory which has shown a significant relationship between damage in various subcortical brain areas of monkey subjects and changes in eating, aggression, and other social behaviors (e.g., courtship). The areas under investigation are those that sometimes have been excised in psychosurgery with humans when attempting to control hyperaggressive and assaultive behaviors. Moreover, the particular subcortical area that is the focus of the present proposal has been hypothesized to be involved in controlling certain sexual activities that are sometimes the subject of psychological treatment (e.g., hypersexuality). Previous studies have been unable to pinpoint the exact areas thought to be involved in controlling certain behaviors; the proposed research seeks to improve on this knowledge.

Method

Two groups of rhesus monkeys will be the subjects. One group ($N = 4$) will be a control group. These animals will undergo a sham operation, which involves anesthetizing the animals and drilling a hole in the skull. These animals then will be tested and evaluated in the same manner as the experimental animals. The experimental group will undergo an operation to lesion a small part of a subcortical structure known as the amygdala. Two of the animals will have lesions in one site; the remaining two will receive lesions in another site of this structure. After recovery, all animals will be tested on a variety of tasks measuring their food preferences, social behaviors with same and opposite-sex monkeys (normals), and emotional responsiveness (e.g., reactions to a novel fear stimulus: an experimenter in a clown face). The animals will be housed in a modern animal laboratory; the operations will be performed and recovery monitored by a licensed veterinarian. After testing, the experimental animals will be sacrificed and the brains prepared for histological examination. (Histology is necessary to confirm the locus and extent of lesions.) The control animals will not be killed; they will be returned to the colony for use in future experiments.

PART

II

Descriptive Methods

Observation

CHAPTER OUTLINE

OVERVIEW
CLASSIFICATION OF OBSERVATIONAL METHODS
OBSERVATION WITHOUT INTERVENTION
OBSERVATION WITH INTERVENTION
Participant Observation
Structured Observation
Field Experiments
RECORDING BEHAVIOR
Obtaining Qualitative Records of Behavior
Obtaining Quantitative Measures of Behavior
SAMPLING TECHNIQUES
Time and Event Sampling
Situation Sampling
ANALYSIS OF OBSERVATIONAL DATA
Data Reduction
Observer Reliability
PROBLEMS IN THE CONDUCT OF OBSERVATIONAL RESEARCH
Influence of the Observer
Observer Bias
SUMMARY

OVERVIEW

As was mentioned in Chapter 1, scientists and nonscientists alike rely on observation to learn about behavior. What distinguishes scientific observation from nonscientific observation is the manner in which observations are made. Nonscientists are likely to observe casually and are often unaware of personal and situational biases that may influence their observations. Nonscientists rarely keep formal records of what they observe and consequently depend on memory for information about an event. Unfortunately, what one remembers about an event is not likely to be a literal record of what one experienced, and memory can be affected by information added after an event is observed (Bartlett, 1932; Loftus, 1997a, 1997b; Pezdek, Finger, & Hodge, 1997). Scientific observation, on the other hand, is made under precisely defined conditions, in a systematic and objective manner, and with careful record keeping. When observations are made in this manner, valuable information about behavior and its antecedents can be obtained. And, although observation is basic to all of psychology, we can distinguish among several types of observational studies.

An important task of the psychologist is to describe behavior in its natural context and to identify relationships among variables that are present. Changes in behavior are frequently observed to result from the context in which behavior occurs. For example, Schaller (1963) observed that mountain gorillas regularly eat meat when in captivity, but he found no evidence of meat eating by gorillas in the wild. Preschool children give longer and more evaluative narratives when reminiscing with their father than with their mother (Haden, Haine, & Fivush, 1997). By describing behavior in natural settings, the psychologist seeks to establish a basis for predicting future behavior.

Often, observation is also the first step in discovering the reasons why organisms behave the way they do. Observation, in other words, is an important step in hypothesis generation. For example, both animals and humans are known to display distinctive reactions to novel or unfamiliar situations. Observing a group of 2- and 3-year-old children in the presence of an unfamiliar person or object, Kagan, Reznick, and Snidman (1988) identified those children who were consistently shy, quiet, and timid and those who were consistently sociable, talkative, and affectively spontaneous. When the same children were observed at 7 years of age, a majority of the children in each group exhibited similar behaviors. The researchers hypothesized that shyness in childhood as well as extreme social anxiety in adulthood are the result of temperamental differences present at birth. In a similar vein, Caspi and associates (1997) used observational measures made at age 3 to successfully predict health-risk behaviors (e.g., abusing alcohol) of young adults. These results also support the idea that temperamental differences observed early in childhood are linked to distinct adult behavior patterns.

Systematic observation is an important tool not only of psychologists but of anthropologists, sociologists, and ethologists. In this chapter we examine observational methods used to investigate behavior—especially, but not exclusively, in natural settings. As you will see, the scientist-observer is not always passive, present merely to record behavior. Researchers sometimes intervene in the situation in which they are observing behavior. We'll take a look at scientists' reasons for intervening in natural settings. Methods for recording data and techniques for analyzing data are also illustrated, and some limitations and problems associated with the observation of behavior are explained.

CLASSIFICATION OF OBSERVATIONAL METHODS

- Observational methods can be classified as "observation with intervention" or "observation without intervention."
- Methods for recording behavior can be classified in terms of how much of behavior is recorded.

Observational methods can be classified according to the degree to which an observer intervenes in an observational setting as well as according to the way in which that behavior is recorded (see Willems, 1969). Hence we make an important distinction between observation with intervention and observation without intervention. Methods of recording behavior also generally differ in terms of whether all (or nearly all) of the behavior exhibited in a given setting is recorded or only particular units of behavior are recorded. In some situations an observer may seek a comprehensive description of behavior. This may be accomplished by the use of film, tapes, or lengthy verbal descriptions. More often, a researcher records specific units of behavior that are related to the goals of a particular study. An investigator, for instance, who is interested in prosocial behavior likely will concentrate on specific behaviors that define this type of behavior. For example, Chambers and Ascione (1987) observed children while they played either an aggressive video game or a video game with prosocial content. Children who played the aggressive game were later observed to put less money in a donation box and to volunteer to help sharpen pencils significantly less than did those who played the prosocial game.

We will discuss observational methods first in terms of the extent of observer intervention and then in terms of methods of recording behavior.

OBSERVATION WITHOUT INTERVENTION

- The goals of naturalistic observation are to describe behavior as it normally occurs and to examine relationships among variables.
- Naturalistic observation helps to establish the external validity of research findings.
- When ethical and moral considerations prevent experimental control, naturalistic observation is an important research strategy.
- Ethologists use naturalistic observation to describe innate patterns of behavior in animals and humans.

Observation of behavior in a more or less natural setting, without any attempt by the observer to intervene, is frequently called **naturalistic observation.** An observer using this method of observation acts as a passive recorder of what occurs. The events witnessed are those occurring naturally and have not been manipulated or in any way controlled by the observer. What exactly constitutes a natural setting is not easily identified (see Bickman, 1976; Willems & Raush, 1969). In general, we can consider a natural setting one in which behavior ordinarily occurs and that has not been arranged specifically for the purpose of recording behavior. Observing people in a psychology laboratory would not, for instance, be considered naturalistic observation. The laboratory situation has been created specifically to study behavior and, in a manner of speaking, is an artificial rather than a natural setting. In fact, an important reason for doing naturalistic observation is to verify relationships between variables that have been identified in the psychology laboratory. Observation in natural settings serves, among other functions, as a way of establishing the external validity of laboratory findings.

The major goals of observation in natural settings are to describe behavior as it ordinarily occurs and to investigate the relationship among variables that are present. Hartup (1974), for instance, chose naturalistic observation to investigate the frequency and types of aggression exhibited by preschoolers in a St. Paul, Minnesota, children's center. He distinguished hostile aggression (person-oriented) from instrumental aggression (aimed at the retrieval of an object, territory, or privilege). Although he observed boys to be more aggressive overall than girls, his observations provided no evidence that the types of aggression differed

FIGURE 3.1   Naturalistic observation is frequently the basis of psychologists' investigations of childhood behavior.

between the sexes. Thus Hartup was able to conclude that, with respect to hostile aggression, there was no evidence that boys and girls were "wired" differently.

Hartup's study of children's aggression illustrates why a researcher may choose to use naturalistic observation rather than to manipulate conditions related to behavior. There are certain aspects of human behavior that moral or ethical considerations prevent us from controlling. Researchers may be interested in the relationship between early childhood isolation and later emotional and psychological development. However, we would object strenuously if they tried to take children from their parents in order to raise them in isolation. Alternative methods of data collection must be considered if this problem is to be investigated. For example, the effect of early isolation on later development has been studied through experimentation on animal subjects (Harlow & Harlow, 1966), descriptions of so-called feral children raised outside of human culture, presumably by animals (Candland, 1993), case studies of children subjected to unusual conditions of isolation by their parents (Curtiss, 1977), and systematic observation of institutionalized children (Spitz, 1965). The nature of children's aggression is another aspect of behavior the investigation of which is subject to moral and ethical limitations. We would not want to see children intentionally harassed and picked on simply to record their reactions. However, as anyone knows who has observed children, there is plenty of naturally occurring aggression. Hartup's study shows how observation without intervention can be a useful alternative to methods of data collection that attempt to manipulate the behavior of interest.

Psychologists are not the only researchers who observe behavior in natural settings. Observation is a fundamental method of ethologists. Although related to psychology, **ethology** is generally considered a branch of biology (Eibl-Eibesfeldt, 1975). Ethologists study the behavior of organisms in relation to their natural environment. A major question they seek to answer is how natural selection has worked to produce particular behavior patterns in an animal species. The focus of an ethological investigation is often the development of an **ethogram.** This is nothing less than a complete catalog of all the behavior patterns of an organism, including information on frequency, duration, and context of occurrence for each behavior.

Ethologists adopt a comparative approach to understanding behavior and often seek to explain behavior in one animal species on the basis of innate patterns of behavior observed in species lower on the evolutionary scale. Speculations about the role of innate mechanisms in determining human behavior are not uncommon among ethologists. For instance, Barash (1977) observed whether male and female human pedestrians visually scanned both directions before crossing a dangerous intersection in Seattle, Washington. When a male adult and a female adult were together, adult males scanned more than females. This was true regardless of whether children were also present. The ethologist-observer suggested an evolutionary explanation: Adult male monkeys and baboons in the wild generally function as lookouts to warn the rest of the group of approaching danger. An ethological perspective has proved important for the understanding of both normal and abnormal human behavior. An interesting example is the ethological analysis of psychiatric problems based on comprehensive descriptions of facial behavior of schizophrenic patients (see Pitman et al., 1987).

OBSERVATION WITH INTERVENTION

- Most psychological research uses observation with intervention.
- The three methods of observation with intervention are participant observation, structured observation, and the field experiment.

It is characteristic of the scientist to "tamper" with nature, to intervene, in order to make a point or to test a theory. Intervention rather than nonintervention characterizes most psychological research. Kinds of intervention vary widely in psychological studies, depending on such things as the purpose for investigating behavior, the nature of the behavior under observation, and the ingenuity of the researcher.

Although the types of intervention employed by psychologists are too numerous and diverse to classify, their reasons for intervening are generally one or more of the following:

1 To precipitate or cause an event that occurs infrequently in nature or that normally occurs under conditions that make it difficult to observe.

2 To investigate the limits of an organism's response by varying systematically the qualities of a stimulus event.

3 To gain access to a situation or event that is generally not open to scientific observation.

4 To arrange conditions so that important antecedent events are controlled and consequent behaviors can be readily observed.

5 To establish a comparison by manipulating one or more independent variables to determine their effect on behavior.

These reasons for intervening are illustrated in three methods of observation: participant observation, structured observation, and the field experiment. As we review these major observational techniques, the investigator's reasons for intervening will become clear.

Participant Observation

- Undisguised participant observation is often used to understand the culture and behavior of groups of individuals.
- Disguised participant observation is often used when researchers believe individuals would change their behavior if they knew it was being recorded.
- Participant observation allows researchers to observe behaviors and situations that are not usually open to scientific observation.
- Participant observers may sometimes lose their objectivity or may unduly influence the individuals whose behavior they are recording.

Observation of behavior by someone who also plays an active and significant role in the situation or context in which behavior is recorded is called **participant observation.** In *undisguised* participant observation, individuals who are being observed know that the observer is present for the purpose of collecting information about their behavior. This method is used frequently by anthropologists who seek to understand the culture and behavior of groups by living and working with members of the group.

When the observer's role is not known to those who are being observed, we speak of *disguised* participant observation. As you might imagine, people do not always behave in the way they ordinarily would when they know their behavior is being recorded. Politicians, for instance, often make different statements when speaking to the press, depending on whether their comments are "for" or "off" the record. Our own behavior is likely to be affected by knowing that we are being watched. This problem associated with observational methods will be discussed more fully later in the chapter. For now, let us simply say that researchers may decide to disguise their role as observers if they believe that people being observed will not act as they ordinarily would if they know their activities are being recorded. Disguised participant observation typically raises ethical issues, for example, of privacy and of informed consent, which must be addressed prior to implementing the study. We will discuss these issues later in this chapter (see also discussion in Chapter 2).

Disguised participant observation was used by Rosenhan (1973) to investigate the basis of psychiatric diagnosis in the context of a mental institution. Eight individuals (including psychologists, a pediatrician, and a housewife) misrepresented their names and occupations and sought admission to twelve different mental hospitals. Each complained of the same general symptom: that he or she was hearing voices. Rosenhan (p. 251) described these symptoms and the rationale for their selection by the observers as follows:

> Asked what the voices said, he replied that they were often unclear, but as far as he could tell they said "empty," "hollow," and "thud." The voices were unfamiliar and were of the same sex as the pseudopatient. The choice of these symptoms was occasioned by their apparent similarity to existential symptoms. Such symptoms are alleged to arise from painful concerns about the perceived meaninglessness of one's life. It is as if the hallucinating person were saying, "My life is empty and hollow." The choice of these symptoms was also determined by the *absence* of a single report of existential psychoses in the literature. Beyond alleging the symptoms and falsifying name, vocation, and employment, no further alterations of person, history, or circumstances were made.

Immediately after being put in the mental ward, the researchers stopped complaining of any symptoms and refrained from acting abnormally. In addition to observing patient-staff interactions, the observers were interested in how long it took for a "sane" person to be released from the hospital. Length of hospitalization ranged from 7 to 52 days. The researchers were never detected as sane and, when they were discharged, their schizophrenia was said only to be "in remission." Apparently, once the pseudopatients were labeled schizophrenic, they were stuck with that label no matter what the nature of their subsequent behavior.

Participant observation allows an observer to gain access to a situation that is not usually open to scientific observation. In addition, the participant observer is often in a position to have the same experiences as the people under study. This may provide important insights and understanding of individuals or groups. The pseudopatients in the Rosenhan study, for instance, felt what it was like to be labeled schizophrenic and not to know how long it would be before they could return to society. In the fall of 1959, John Howard Griffin set out to research "what it was like to be a Negro in a land where we keep the Negro down." Griffin, a White man, darkened his skin using medication and stain in order to pass himself off as Black. For more than a month he traveled (walking, hitchhiking, riding buses) through Mississippi, Alabama, and Georgia. He described his experiences as a participant observer in his book *Black Like Me* (1960), which was an important precursor of the civil rights movement of the 1960s.

A participant observer's role in a situation can produce certain methodological problems. By identifying with the individuals under study, it is possible for an observer to lose the scientific objectivity that accurate and valid observation requires. Changes in a participant observer are sometimes dramatic and are not easily anticipated. Witness the experiences of a criminologist who used undisguised participant observation to study police officers at work. Kirkham (1975) went through police academy training like any recruit and became a uniformed patrol officer assigned to a high-crime area in a city of about half a million. His immersion in the daily activities of an officer on the beat led to marked changes in his attitudes and personality. As Kirkham (p. 19) himself noted:

> As the weeks and months of my new career as a slum policeman went by, I slowly but inexorably began to become indistinguishable in attitudes and behavior from the policemen with whom I worked. . . . According to the accounts of my family, colleagues and friends, I began to increasingly display attitudinal and behavioral elements that were entirely foreign to my previous personality—punitiveness, pervasive cynicism and mistrust of others, chronic irritability and free-floating hostility, racism, a diffuse personal anxiety over the menace of crime and criminals that seemed at times to border on the obsessive. A former opponent of capital punishment, I became its vociferous advocate in cases involving felony murder, kidnapping and the homicide of police officers—even though as a criminologist I continued to recognize its ineffectiveness as a deterrent to crime.

Participant observers must be aware of the threat to objective reporting that arises due to their involvement in the situation wherein they are recording behavior. This threat necessarily increases as degree of involvement increases.

Another problem with observer involvement is the effect the observer has on the behavior of those being studied. It is more than likely that the participant observer will have to interact with other people, make decisions, initiate activities, assume responsibilities, and otherwise act like everyone else in that situation. Whenever observers intervene in a natural setting, they must ask to what degree participants and events are affected by the intervention. Is what is being observed the same as it would have been if the observer had never appeared? It is difficult to generalize results to other situations if intervention produces behavior that is specific to the conditions and events created by the observer.

In the case of participant observation, the extent of an observer's influence on the behavior under observation is not easily assessed. Several factors must be considered, such as whether participation is disguised or undisguised, the size of the group entered, and the role of the observer in the group. Griffin, for example, was not known to be a White man even by most of the Blacks he associated with, and his entry into a subculture of literally thousands of disadvantaged Blacks could not reasonably be expected to influence the nature of Black-White interactions that he observed. Similarly, it does not appear that Rosenhan and his associates significantly affected the natural environment of the mental ward by assuming the role of mental patients. (However, some of the patients—though none of the staff—apparently detected the sanity of the pseudopatients, suggesting to the observers that they were there to check up on the hospital.)

When the group under observation is small or the activities of the participant observer are prominent, the observer is more likely to have a significant effect on participants' behavior. This problem confronted several social psychologists who infiltrated a group of people who claimed to be in contact with beings from outer space (Festinger, Riecken, & Schachter, 1956). A leader of the group said he had received a message from the aliens predicting a cataclysmic flood on a specific date. The flood was to stretch from the Arctic Circle to the Gulf of Mexico. The prophecy was reported in the newspapers, and certain psychologists who read the account saw an opportunity to test a theory of group cohesion and reaction in the face of unfulfilled prophecy. (The psychologists assumed that the flood was not going to occur.) Because of the attitudes of members of the group toward "nonbelievers," the researchers were forced to make up bizarre stories in order to gain access to the group. This tactic worked too well. Not only were the disguised participant observers welcomed into the group, which never consisted of more than a dozen hard-core believers, but their stories were taken as signs from the extraterrestrial beings. One of the observers was even thought to be a spaceman bringing a message. The researchers had inadvertently reinforced the group's beliefs and influenced in an undetermined way the course of events that followed. By the way, the flood never occurred, but at least some of the group members came to use this disconfirmation as a means of strengthening their initial belief. They began to seek new members by arguing that their faith had prevented the prophesied flood.

Thus, although participant observation may permit an observer to gain access to situations not usually open to scientific investigation, the observer using this technique must seek ways to deal with the possible loss of objectivity and the potential effects that a participant observer may have on the behavior under study.

Structured Observation

- Structured observations are set up to record behaviors that may be difficult to observe using naturalistic observation.

- Structured observations are often used by clinical and developmental psychologists.
- Problems in interpreting structured observations can occur when the same observation procedures are not followed across observations or observers, or when important variables are not controlled.

There are a variety of observational methods using intervention that are not easily categorized. Because researchers exert some control over the events, these procedures differ from naturalistic observation without intervention. However, the degree of control in these instances is often less than that seen in field experiments, which we will consider later. We have labeled these procedures **structured observation.** Often the observer intervenes in order to cause an event to occur or to "set up" a situation so that events can be more easily recorded than they would be without intervention. In other cases the observer may create quite elaborate procedures to investigate a particular behavior more fully.

Structured observations may occur in a natural setting or in a laboratory setting. Structured laboratory observations are often used by clinical psychologists when making behavioral assessments of parent-child interactions (see, for example, Hughes & Haynes, 1978). A parent and child who are seeking some sort of help come to a diagnostic clinic or laboratory and are asked to engage in specific tasks while being observed (often from behind a one-way window). Observations are made of various specific behaviors (for instance, tantrums or other emotional outbursts by the child) and of the general nature of the parent-child interactions. Partly on the basis of the results of this structured observation, the therapist plans a strategy to address the behavioral problems that exist. Leavens and Hopkins (1998) used structured observations of chimpanzees to investigate "gaze alternation," the behavior of alternating looking at a distant (and desired) object and the face of an experimenter who is in a position to retrieve the object. A banana was placed outside the cage of the chimpanzee by one experimenter, who then left the scene. A second experimenter approached, gave verbal greetings and established eye contact with the chimpanzee while ignoring the banana. Communication via gaze alternation was defined as alternating looking by the chimpanzee at the banana and the face of the experimenter. Vocal and pointing gestures were also recorded. The chimpanzees revealed high levels of what appears to be a form of intentional communication in goal-directed activities—a behavior, however, that clearly was present more often among older than younger animals.

Structured observations are also frequently used by developmental psychologists. Perhaps most notable are the methods of Jean Piaget (1896–1980). In many of Piaget's studies a child is first given a problem to solve and then given several variations on the problem to test the limits of the child's understanding. The observer acquaints the child with the nature of the problem and then usually asks questions to probe the child's reasoning processes. These structured observations have provided a wealth of information regarding children's cognition and are the basis for Piaget's "stage theory" of intellectual development. Piaget-type tasks are also frequently used by animal researchers to investigate

FIGURE 3.2   Jean Piaget (1896–1980) used structured observation to investigate children's cognitive development.

aspects of animal cognition. In one such study, orangutans outperformed squirrel monkeys on a classic test of the ability to represent the existence of an unperceived object or what has been called object permanence (de Blois, Novak, & Bond, 1998).

Structured observation is a compromise between the passive nonintervention of naturalistic observation and the systematic manipulation of independent variables and precise control that characterize laboratory methods. Such a compromise permits observations to be made under conditions that are more natural than those imposed in a laboratory. Nevertheless, there may be a price to pay. The failure to follow similar procedures each time an observation is made may make it difficult for other observers to obtain the same results when investigating a problem. Uncontrolled, and perhaps unknown, variables may play an important part in producing the behavior under observation. For example, the fact that structured observations like those used by Piaget do not always follow the same procedure from one observation to another can be viewed as a problem with these techniques (see Brainerd, 1978).

To reinforce this point regarding the possible influence of uncontrolled variables in structured observation, let us relate a historical anecdote about two well-known psychologists in the first half of the 20th century (see Cohen, 1979). In 1913, the same year he launched psychology on a new course with his remarks entitled, "Psychology as the Behaviorist Views It," John B. Watson set sail for the Tortugas islands off the coast of Florida. On a previous visit to the islands, he had begun observations of noddy and sooty terns in their natural habitat. Accompanying him was Karl Lashley, a student of Watson's who later did important physiological studies of brain function. Lashley went with Watson to help him make his observations and to help test the homing abilities of terns. At one point during the summer, Lashley removed 30 birds from their nests and took them with him on a boat trip to Mobile, Alabama, where he released 15 of them. Traveling more than 100 miles farther to Galveston, Texas, Lashley set free the remaining 15 birds. Watson waited on the island to record the arrival of the birds if, indeed, they were able to make it back as popular stories of the time suggested. Four days after Lashley released them, the birds began returning to the island. Watson and Lashley had demonstrated that terns could safely navigate across an open sea with no obvious landmarks from a distance of 1,000 miles. They were at a loss to explain how the birds managed their remarkable feat, and, as events transpired, Watson did not have the opportunity to carry out any more tests of the birds' homing abilities.

Suppose, however, that the procedure of taking the terns on board a ship caused some of the birds to become ill (something that had actually happened on a previous occasion, when the birds died in transit) and that their illness affected their homing behavior. When no birds returned to their nests after being released, the observers might have wrongly concluded that the animals had no homing instinct. This possibility does not seem that farfetched when you consider that more recent observations of bird navigation have revealed that homing pigeons make use of airborne odors to recognize the location of their lofts (see Wallraff & Sinsch, 1988). Birds who were allowed to smell only filtered air before being released did not show any tendency to return home.

Although structured observations are often important for gathering information about behavior, and even for testing specific hypotheses, researchers must be aware of the limitations they impose when they allow some variables to remain uncontrolled and when procedures differ with the circumstances or the behavior of the subject under observation.

Ethologists frequently use structured observation to study the limits of an organism's response by varying systematically the characteristics of a stimulus event. For example, observations by Nobel Prize-winning ethologist Konrad Lorenz led to the discovery of imprinting (see Eibl-Eibesfeldt, 1975). Imprinting is a process by which certain animal species form an attachment to an object encountered during a critical or sensitive period in their lives. Immediately after hatching, for example, the young graylag gosling will imprint on almost any moving object in its environment and follow that object for some time afterward. Under ordinary conditions, the object of the bird's imprinting is its parent, and the innately triggered response is important for the young bird's survival. To understand the imprinting response better, ethologists sometimes create models of both male and female parents and test the young animal's response when the models move, when they make a noise, or when the imprinting response is punished (see Eibl-Eibesfeldt, 1975). Lorenz himself served as a model; many students of psychology have been introduced to ethology by scenes of the famous ethologist being energetically pursued over land and water by the young birds who attached themselves (imprinted) to him.

Field Experiments

- In a field experiment, researchers manipulate one or more independent variables in a natural setting to determine the effect on behavior.
- A confederate is a research assistant who behaves in specified ways to create an experimental condition.

When an observer manipulates one or more independent variables in a natural setting in order to determine their effect on behavior, the procedure is called a **field experiment.** Although experimental methods will be discussed extensively in later chapters of this book, we mention the field experiment here because it represents one end of the nonintervention-intervention dimension that characterizes observational methods. In conducting a field experiment, the observer (now usually called the experimenter) seeks to control the antecedents of an event in order to measure systematically the effect of a variable on behavior. Control or comparison groups are used, and the experimenter usually dictates the assignment of participants to conditions. The field experiment is probably the most frequently used field-observation technique in social psychology (Bickman, 1976). In most cases individuals are unaware that they are participating in an experiment. In a field experiment researchers also typically make use of **confederates.** A confederate is someone in the research situation who is instructed to behave in a certain way in order to produce an experimental situation. Confederates, for example, have been employed by social psychologists to pose as robbers when bystander reaction to a crime has been investigated (Latané & Darley, 1970) and to mimic the behavior of individuals cutting into a waiting line in order to study the reactions of those in line (Milgram, Liberty, Toledo, & Wackenhut, 1986).

Field experiments sometimes yield valuable practical knowledge. For example, research by Latané and Darley and others helps us to understand the variables that affect a bystander's willingness to come to the aid of a victim. Interestingly, many studies show that a bystander is more likely to aid a victim when the bystander is alone than when other bystanders are present. Crusco and Wetzel (1984) also conducted a field experiment with the potential for practical application. They investigated the effect of touching on restaurant customers. Waitresses working as confederates touched restaurant customers on either the hand or the shoulder while returning change. The researchers speculated that a touch on the hand would produce positive affect toward the waitress whereas a touch on the shoulder, which may be seen as a sign of dominance, would not be viewed positively, especially by male diners. The participants were 114 diners from two restaurants who were randomly assigned to three levels of the independent variable: Fleeting Touch, when the waitress twice touched the diner's palm for 1/2 second when returning change; Shoulder Touch, when she placed her hand for 1 to 1 1/2 seconds on the diner's shoulder as she gave back change; and No Touch, when no physical contact was made with the customers. The major dependent variable was the size of the tip. Results showed that males tipped overall more than females but that both male and female diners gave a significantly larger tip after being touched than when not touched. The results did not show, as the researchers had expected, that the nature of the touch made a difference; male and female diners were affected equally by both kinds of touches.

RECORDING BEHAVIOR

- Researchers choose whether to obtain a comprehensive behavioral record or to record selected behaviors depending on the goals of the observational research.
- How the results of a study are ultimately summarized, analyzed, and reported depends on how behavioral observations are initially recorded.

We have mentioned two important characteristics of observational methods. One is the degree of observer intervention, the other the method of recording behavior. As we have tried to show, intervention is a dimension anchored at one end by the absence of any intervention, as is associated with passive observation in a naturalistic setting, and at the other end by the active and systematic manipulation of antecedent events that characterizes field experiments. Observational methods also differ in the manner in which behavior is recorded, particularly the degree to which behavior is abstracted from the situation in which it is observed (see Willems, 1969, for a thorough discussion of this aspect of observational methods).

In general, methods of recording behavior can be classified as those that seek a comprehensive description of behavior and the situation in which it occurs and those that focus on only certain kinds of behavior or events. Whether all behavior in a given setting or only selected aspects are to be observed depends on the purposes or goals of an observational study. Decisions regarding the manner in which behavior is recorded also depend on whether the investigator is doing qualitative or quantitative research. As we saw in Chapter 1, the results of a qualitative study are presented chiefly in the form of verbal description and logical argument, whereas quantitative research emphasizes statistical description and analysis of data to support a study's conclusions. The important point for you to remember is that how the results of a study are eventually summarized, analyzed, and reported hinges on the way in which the behavior is initially recorded.

Obtaining Qualitative Records of Behavior

- Narrative records in the form of written descriptions of behavior, audiotapes, and videotapes are comprehensive records of observed behavior.
- Researchers classify and organize data from narrative records to test their hypotheses about behavior.
- Narrative records sometimes include observers' inferences about individuals' motives or feelings, as in ethnography or ecological psychology.
- Field notes are records made by trained observers that describe particular events and behaviors of interest rather than comprehensive accounts of behavior.
- Narrative records should be made during or soon after behavior is observed, and observers must be carefully trained to record behavior according to established criteria.

Narrative records are intended to provide a more or less faithful reproduction of behavior as it originally occurred. Written descriptions of behavior made by an observer are one major type of narrative record. So are the spoken records produced by using a tape recorder and the visual records obtained with videotape or movie cameras. Ethologists are often interested in every detail of a behavioral event, so motion picture film turns out to be one of their most important means of recording behavior (Eibl-Eibesfeldt, 1975). For example, to study the function of the "eyebrow flash" in social interactions, ethologists made use of 67 hours of film showing individuals in naturally occurring social situations (Grammar, Schiefenhovel, Schleidt, Lorenz, & Eibl-Eibesfeldt, 1988). Across three different cultures, the eyebrow flash, usually accompanied by a smile, was found to be a universal social signal, for example, as a sign of factual "yes."

Once narrative records are obtained, the observer can study, classify, and organize the records at leisure. Particular hypotheses or expectations about the behaviors under observation can be tested by examining the data. This constitutes an important difference between narrative records and other forms of behavior measurement wherein the classification or coding of behaviors is done at the time of observation. Thus, researchers must choose methods for obtaining narrative records that will capture the particular information necessary for evaluating a study's hypotheses.

We have already mentioned how Piaget used structured observation to study the cognitive development of children. Having selected a problem to present to the child, Piaget then made a rather literal record of the child's attempts to solve the problem. The following narrative record was obtained by Piaget when investigating a 4-year-old child's understanding of volume.

In this structured observation, the child is given two containers, A and L, of equal height. A is wide and L is narrow. A is filled to a certain height (one-quarter or one-fifth) and the child is asked to pour the same quantity of liquid into L. The dimensions are such that the level will be four times as high in L as in A for the same amount of liquid. In spite of this striking difference in the proportions, the child at this stage proves incapable of grasping that the smaller diameter of L will require a higher level of liquid. Those children who are clearly still at this stage are satisfied that there is "the same amount to drink" in L when they have filled it to the same level as A. Here is a narrative record of one child's (Blas) response to this situation:

> Blas (4.0): "Look, your mummy has poured out a glass of lemonade for herself (A) and she gives you this glass (L). We want you to pour into your glass as much lemonade as your mummy has in hers.—(She poured rather quickly and exceeded the level equal to that in A that she was trying to achieve.)—Will you both have the same like that?—*No.*—Who will have more?—*Me.*—Show me where you must pour to so that you both have the same.—(She poured up to the same level.)—Will you and mummy have the same amount to drink like that?—*Yes.*—Are you sure?—*Yes.*" (Piaget, J. [1965]. *The child's conception of number*, pp. 11–12. New York: Norton. First published in French in 1941 under the title *Le Genèse du nombre chez l'enfant*.)

The narrative begins with the observer's comments to the child, Blas. The observer says, "Look, your mummy has poured out a glass of lemonade. . . ." After that follows an exact reproduction of what the observer said, what the child said, and what happened in this situation. The narrative contains little observer inference and the exact sequence of behaviors is recorded. His many observations of children's behavior led Piaget to a number of important conclusions about human cognitive development. As you can see, Piaget used the narrative record to illustrate that the 4-year-old has not yet mastered the principle of "conservation of volume." The two containers, which were of equal height but different width, were perceived by the child to hold the same amount of liquid when the level of the liquid was the same.

Hartup (1974) obtained narrative records as part of his naturalistic study of children's aggression. He investigated a number of different aspects of children's aggression, including the relationship between particular kinds of antecedent events and the nature of the aggressive episodes that followed. Consider this sample narrative record from Hartup's study (p. 339):

> Marian [a 7-year-old]. . . is complaining to all that David [who is also present] had squirted her on the pants she has to wear tonight. She says, "I'm gonna do it to him to see how he likes it." She fills a can with water and David runs to the teacher and tells of her threat. The teacher takes the can from Marian. Marian attacks David and pulls his hair very hard. He cries and swings at Marian as the teacher tries to restrain him; then she takes him upstairs. . . . Later, Marian and Elaine go upstairs and into the room where David is seated with a teacher. He throws a book at Marian. The teacher asks Marian to leave. Marian kicks David, then leaves. David cries and screams, "Get out of here, they're just gonna tease me."

Hartup (1974) instructed his observers to avoid making inferences about the intentions, motives, or feelings of the participants and to use precise language in describing behavior. Note that we are not told why David might want to throw a book at Marian or how Marian feels about being attacked. Hartup believed that certain antecedent behaviors were related to specific types of aggression. Because any inferences or impressions of the observers were strictly excluded, the content of the narrative records could be classified and coded in an objective manner. Thus, individuals coding the narrative would not be influenced by what the observer inferred was going on.

Not all narrative records are as focused as those obtained by Piaget or Hartup, nor do narrative records always avoid inferences and impressions of the observer. An important goal of **ecological psychology** involves the comprehensive description of individuals in everyday contexts. This approach has much in common with **ethnography,** which has long been a major descriptive tool of anthropologists and sociologists. Ethnographers frequently combine data obtained through various observational methods, such as naturalistic observation and participant observation, as well as that obtained through the examination of documents and interviews, in order to describe the context and meanings of everyday social situations (see Taylor & Bogdan, 1998). One example of ecological research is a study of "a day in the life" of a midwestern school girl (Barker, Wright, Schoggen, & Barker, 1978, pp. 56–58). Eight different observers took turns observing an 8-year-old girl from the time she awoke in the morning until she went to sleep at night. Because the researchers wanted to include information about the girl's motives, feelings, and perceptions, they required that the observers make a number of inferences. Generally, only the inferences that two or more observers agreed on were included. For example, people can often agree as to when someone is sad or happy or excited or calm. The narrative record of this little girl's day was about 100,000 words in length and was later determined to contain 969 different behavior episodes.

Narrative records are not always meant to be comprehensive descriptions of behavior as we have seen illustrated in the context of structured observations used by Piaget, or in the study of the day in the life of a young schoolgirl. Often the narrative records of an observer are merely running descriptions of the participants, events, settings, and behaviors. These records are generally called **field notes.** Field notes are nothing more than the verbal records of a trained observer. Used by journalists, social workers, anthropologists, ethnographers, ethologists, and others, they do not always contain an exact record of everything that occurred. Events and behaviors that especially interest the observer are recorded and are likely to be interpreted in terms of the observer's specialized knowledge or expertise. For example, in making notes about a particular patient, a psychiatrist might compare the client's symptoms with those of other patients or with a textbook definition. An ethologist might record how the behavior of one species appears to parallel that of another.

Field notes tend to be highly personalized (Brandt, 1972), but they are probably used more frequently than any other kind of narrative record. Field notes have generated numerous revelations about behavior; they are the basis of Darwin's theory of evolution as well as Rosenhan's description of being sane in insane places. Their usefulness as scientific records depends on the accuracy and precision of their content. These characteristics will be related to the training of the observer and the extent to which the observations that are recorded can be verified by independent observers and through other means of investigation.

Practical, as well as methodological, considerations dictate the manner in which narrative records are made. As a general rule, records should be made during or as soon as possible after behavior is observed. The passage of time blurs details and makes it harder to reproduce the original sequence of actions. Adjang (1986) used a portable cassette recorder to make narrative records of his spoken observations of the teasing behavior of young chimpanzees; however, he then transcribed these spoken reports onto paper "as soon as possible" (p. 139). This rule is sometimes not easy to follow when observations are made in natural settings. An ethologist who is trying to record the behavior of animals in the wild is sometimes hampered by bad weather, animal migration, dwindling daylight, and so forth. Notes may have to be made quickly—even while the observer is quite literally on the run. At other times observers may have to wait until they return to camp to make written records of behavior. When Festinger et al. (1956) infiltrated the group of people waiting for spacemen to rescue them from a cataclysmic flood, the participant observers sometimes found it difficult to take notes without being seen by members of the group. Excuses had to be made to leave the group (to go to the bathroom, for example) in order to make written records of the group's activities.

Decisions regarding the content of a narrative record must be made prior to observing behavior. We have seen, for example, that verbal narratives may differ according to the degree of observer inference or the completeness of the behavioral record. Thus, these aspects of a narrative record, as well as others, must be decided on prior to beginning a study (see, for example, Brandt, 1972). Once the content of narrative records is decided, observers must be trained to record behavior according to the criteria that have been set up. Practice observations may have to be conducted and records critiqued by more than one investigator before "real" data are collected.

Obtaining Quantitative Measures of Behavior

- When researchers seek to describe *specific* behaviors or events, they often obtain quantitative measures of behavior such as frequency of occurrence or duration of a behavior.
- Quantitative measures of behavior use one of the four levels of measurement scales: nominal, ordinal, interval, and ratio.
- Rating scales, often used to measure psychological dimensions, are frequently treated as if they are interval scales even though they usually represent ordinal measurement.
- Electronic recording devices may be used in natural settings to record behavior and pagers sometimes are used to signal participants to report their behavior (e.g., on a questionnaire).

When only certain behaviors or specific aspects of individuals and settings are of interest, the behaviors need to be defined prior to beginning an observational study. Decisions also should be made as to exactly how characteristics of their occurrence should be measured—that is, how the behavior can be *quantified*. For example, assume you wish to observe reactions to individuals with obvious physical disabilities by those who do not have such disabilities. In order to conduct your study, it would be necessary to define what constitutes a "reaction" to a physically disabled individual. Are you interested, for example, in helping behaviors, approach/avoidance behaviors, eye contact, length of conversation, or in some other behavioral reaction? As you consider what behaviors you will use to define people's "reactions," you will also have to decide how you will measure these behaviors. Assume, for instance, you are planning a study using naturalistic observation and that you have chosen to measure people's reactions by observing eye contact between individuals who do not have obvious physical disabilities and those who do. Exactly how should you measure eye contact? Should you simply measure whether a passerby does or does not make eye contact, or do you want to measure the *duration* of any eye contact? Of course, you may wish to make multiple measures, a research strategy that is recommended whenever it is feasible. The decisions you make will depend on the particular hypotheses or goals of your study, but they will also be influenced by information gained by examining previous studies that have used the same or similar behavioral measures. (Unfortunately, previous research indicates that reactions to physically disabled individuals frequently can be classified as unfavorable. See, for example, Thompson, 1982.)

Measurement Scales   Defining a behavioral measure involves deciding what scale of measurement to use. Thus, it is important for you to be familiar with the types of measurement scales used in behavioral research. There are four levels of measurement, or **measurement scales,** that apply to both physical and psychological measurement. The lowest level, or scale, is called a *nominal scale;* it involves categorizing an event into one of a number of discrete categories. For instance, we could measure the color of people's eyes by classifying them as "brown eyed" or "blue eyed." When studying people's reactions to individuals with obvious physical disabilities, a researcher might use a nominal scale by measuring whether persons make eye contact or do not make eye contact with someone who has an obvious physical disability. This type of category system is called a **checklist.** A checklist is used to record the presence or absence of specific behaviors, such as whether individuals make eye contact with a physically disabled person, whether children in a classroom are talking or are quiet, whether people use seat belts or do not use seat belts.

Characteristics of participants—such as age, race, and sex—are also frequently recorded using a checklist, as are features of the setting—such as time of day, location, and whether other people are present. It is often informative to observe behavior as a function of participant and context variables. Do males use seat belts more than females? Are people who drive inexpensive automobiles more likely to share a ride than people who drive expensive automobiles? These questions can be answered by observing the presence or absence of certain behaviors (seat-belt use or car pooling) for different categories of participants and settings (male and female, expensive and inexpensive automobiles).

Jenni (1976; also Jenni & Jenni, 1976) used a checklist to study the book-carrying behavior of male and female college students. Three types of book-carrying behaviors were defined: two major types and an "other" category. Figure 3.3 illustrates the two major types of carrying behavior. Students using Type I wrap one or both arms around the books, with the short edges of the books resting on the hip or in front of the body. Students using Type II support the books by one arm and hand at the side of the body, with the long edges of the books approximately horizontal to the ground. The "other" category included a variety of book-carrying methods that did not fit either Type I or Type II. For example, students occasionally hold books by the edges with both hands in front of the body (for instance, when reading while walking).

Observations of 2,626 individuals were made on six college campuses (three in the United States, one in Canada, and two in Central America). Individuals were observed as they passed a certain point on campus. Type of carrying behavior and sex of the student were noted. In terms of the arithmetic operations that we can perform on data recorded on a nominal scale, we can use only the relationships "equal" and "not equal." A common way of summarizing nominal data is to report frequency in the form of proportion or percent of instances in each of the several categories. Across the six college campuses, 82% of the females were observed to use the Type I method, whereas only 3% of the males used this method. On the other hand, the observers found that 96% of the males used the Type II carrying method compared with 16% of the females. The "other" methods were used 2% of the time or less by both male and female students. It appears that book-carrying behavior among college students is almost totally sex specific. Do you think there are sex-specific ways in which students carry backpacks?

FIGURE 3.3   Two methods that students were observed to use to carry books. In the Type I method, the short edges of the book rest on the hip or in front of the body. In the Type II method, the books are either pinched from above or supported from below by the hand or by both the hand and the arm (from Jenni & Jenni, 1976).

Type I   Type II

The second level, or scale, called an *ordinal scale*, involves ordering or ranking events to be measured. Ordinal scales add the arithmetic relationships "greater than" and "less than" to the measurement process. One common example of an ordinal scale is class rank. We can order students in a class from highest to lowest, but if we know only their ranks we have no information about how far apart the students are in academic performance. When we know that an Olympic distance runner won a silver medal, we do not know whether she finished second in a photo finish or trailed 200 meters behind the gold-medal winner. Tassinary and Hansen (1998) showed line drawings of female figures to male and female undergraduates. The figures varied on physical dimensions such as height, weight, and hip size. The undergraduates rank ordered sets of figures in terms of attractiveness and fecundity (i.e., capability of bearing children). According to evolutionary psychology theory, female attractiveness is defined on the basis of cues simultaneously signaling both physical attractiveness and reproductive potential. Interestingly, results of this study using ordinal measures did not particularly support this aspect of evolutionary psychology theory.

The third level, or scale, called an *interval scale*, involves specifying how far apart two events are on a given dimension. On an ordinal scale, the difference between an event ranked first and one ranked third does not necessarily equal the distance between those events ranked third and fifth. For example, the difference in grade-point averages (GPAs) between the first and third students in a class may not be the same as the difference in GPAs between the third- and fifth-ranked students. On an interval scale, however, differences of the same numerical size in scale values are equal. For example, the difference between 50 and 70 correct answers on an aptitude test is equal to the difference between 70 and 90 correct answers, and the ratio of these scale intervals is also meaningful. What is missing from an interval scale is a meaningful zero point. For instance, if your score were zero on a verbal aptitude test, you would not necessarily have absolutely zero verbal ability. On the other hand, the standard arithmetic operations of addition, multiplication, subtraction, and division can be performed on data that are measured on an interval scale. Whenever possible, therefore, psychologists try to measure psychological dimensions using interval scales.

In the context of an observational study, observers sometimes are called on to make ratings of behaviors and events. This usually involves making subjective judgments about the degree or quantity of some trait or condition (see Brandt, 1972). Generally a rating system requires an observer to evaluate some characteristic of an individual or situation on a psychological dimension. For example, Dickie (1987) asked observers to rate parent-infant interactions in the context of a study designed to assess the effects of a parent training program. The observers visited the home and rated both the mother and the father while the parents interacted with their infant child. During most of the observation period, the observers sat in the room with the infant and asked the parents to "act as normal as possible—just as if we [the observers] weren't here." Structured observations involving assigned play with each parent were also used.

Parent-infant interactions were rated on 13 different dimensions, including degree of verbal, physical, and emotional interaction. For each dimension a continuum was defined that represented different degrees of this variable. A 7-point scale was used, whereon 1 represented the absence or very little of the characteristic and larger numbers represented increasingly more of the trait. Table 3.1 outlines one of the dimensions used by the observers in this study: warmth and affection directed toward the child. Note that precise verbal descriptions are given with the four odd-numbered scale values to help observers define different degrees of this trait. The even-numbered values (2, 4, 6) are used by observers to rate events that they judge fall between the more clearly defined values. The investigators found that parents who had taken part in a program aimed at developing competency in dealing with an infant were rated higher than were untrained parents on many of the variables.

At first glance, a rating scale such as that used by Dickie would appear to represent an interval scale of measurement. There is no true zero, and the intervals seem to be equal. And, in fact, many researchers treat such rating systems *as if* they represented interval scales of measurement. Closer examination, however, reveals that most of the rating scales used by observers to evaluate people or events on a psychological dimension really yield only ordinal information. For a rating system to be truly an interval level of measurement, a rating of 2, for instance, would have to be the same distance from a rating of 3 as a rating of 4 is from 5 or a rating of 6 is from 7. It is highly unlikely that human observers can make subjective judgments of traits such as warmth, pleasure, aggressiveness, anxiety, and so forth in a manner that yields precise interval distances

TABLE 3.1 EXAMPLE OF RATING SCALE USED TO MEASURE A PARENT'S WARMTH AND AFFECTION TOWARD AN INFANT CHILD*

Scale Value	Description
1	There is an absence of warmth, affection, and pleasure. Excessive hostility, coldness, distance, and isolation from the child are predominant. Relationship is on an attacking level.
2	
3	There is occasional warmth and pleasure in interaction. Parent shows little evidence of pride in the child, or pride is shown in relation to deviant or bizarre behavior by the child. Parent's manner of relating is contrived, intellectual, not genuine.
4	
5	There is moderate pleasure and warmth in the interaction. Parent shows pleasure in some areas but not in others.
6	
7	Warmth and pleasure are characteristic of the interaction with the child. There is evidence of pleasure and pride in the child. Pleasure response is appropriate to the child's behavior.

*From materials provided by Jane Dickie.

between ratings. Classification of measures according to level of measurement is not always easy, and advice should be sought from knowledgeable experts when in doubt. In this way you will be prepared to make the correct choices regarding the statistical description and analysis of your data.

The fourth level of measurement is a *ratio scale*. A ratio scale has all the properties of an interval scale with the important additional quality of an absolute zero point. In terms of arithmetic operations, a zero point makes the ratio of scale values meaningful. For example, temperature as expressed on the Celsius scale represents an interval scale of measurement. A reading of 0 degrees Celsius does not really mean absolutely no temperature. Therefore it is not meaningful to say that 100 degrees Celsius is twice as hot as 50 degrees, or that 60 degrees is three times as warm as 20 degrees. On the other hand, the Kelvin scale of temperature does have an absolute zero, and the ratio of scale values can be meaningfully calculated. Physical scales measuring time, weight, and distance can usually be treated as ratio scales.

As an example of ratio measurement, consider an interesting study by LaFrance and Mayo (1976). They investigated racial differences in amount of eye contact between individuals of the same race engaged in conversation. Pairs of Black individuals and pairs of White individuals were observed in natural settings. The amount of time each member of the pair spent looking into the face of the other member was recorded. Duration of eye contact represents a ratio level of measurement. The researchers found that Blacks gazed less at another person while listening to conversation than did Whites. LaFrance and Mayo suggest that subtle differences in eye contact may be a source of social misunderstandings. White speakers may feel that lack of eye contact by a Black listener indicates untrustworthiness or lack of interest when it may merely be a manifestation of a cultural difference between the races.

Another important measure of behavior is *frequency* of occurrence. This measure sometimes produces confusion when attempting to identify the level of measurement. For example, in observing book-carrying behavior, Jenni (1976) made only one observation of each individual. As was noted, this represents a nominal level of measurement: Behaviors were recorded as falling in one of several mutually exclusive categories. Frequency of book-carrying behavior, therefore, was described in terms of the number (or percentage) of *different* individuals who used one method or another.

Checklists also can be used to obtain information about the frequency of particular behaviors in the same individual or group of individuals. In this case, repeated observations of the same individual or group are made over a period of time. The presence or absence of specific behaviors is noted at the time of each observation. In these situations, frequency of responding can be assumed to represent a ratio level of measurement. That is, if "units" of some behavior (e.g., occasions when a child leaves a classroom seat) are being counted, then zero represents an absence of that specific behavior. Ratios of scale values would be meaningful as long as, for instance, an individual with 20 units had twice as many units as someone with 10.

Consider, for instance, the Schedule for Classroom Activity Norms (SCAN), which is a checklist that divides classroom behavior into 27 discrete categories (McKinney, Mason, Perkerson, & Clifford, 1975). At repeated intervals of time, an observer records what each child in the classroom is doing. Many observations of the same child show which categories of behavior are most frequent for that child. In one study using the SCAN checklist, researchers looked for relationships between the frequency of certain classroom behaviors and performance on standard tests of academic achievement. Combining information obtained from observing the children's behavior with information obtained from IQ tests yielded a more accurate prediction of school achievement than could be obtained by using either observation or IQ information alone.

Table 3.2 summarizes the characteristics of levels of measurement that we discussed. You will need to keep these four types of scales in mind as you select statistical procedures for analyzing the results of the research you will be doing (see Appendix A).

Electronic Recording and Tracking   Behavior is sometimes measured by the use of various electronic recording and tracking devices. For example, in an observational study of family interactions of depressed women, the observers used portable microcomputers to record relevant behavior (see Hops et al., 1987). Family members were given codes, as were various behaviors and characteristics of the family interaction, and these were recorded using the hand-held electronic recording devices. As part of a study investigating the relationship between cognitive coping strategies and blood pressure among college students, participants were outfitted with an ambulatory blood pressure monitor (Dolan, Sherwood, & Light, 1992). College students wore the electronic recording device during two "typical" school days, one of which, however, included an exam. Participants also completed a questionnaire assessing coping strategies and kept detailed logs of their daily activities. The researchers compared blood pressure readings for different times of the day and as a function of coping style. Students classified as exhibiting "high self-focused coping" (that is, who showed tendencies "to

TABLE 3.2   CHARACTERISTICS OF MEASUREMENT SCALES

Type of Scale	Operations	Objective
Nominal	Equal/not equal	Sort stimuli into discrete categories
Ordinal	Greater than/less than	Rank-order stimuli on a single dimension
Interval	Addition/multiplication/ subtraction/division	Specify the distance between stimuli on a given dimension
Ratio	Addition/multiplication/ subtraction/division/ formation of ratios of values	Specify the distance between stimuli on a given dimension and express ratios of scale values

keep to themselves and/or blame themselves in stressful situations," p. 233), had higher blood pressure responses during and after an exam than did those who were classified as low in self-focused coping strategies.

Using an innovative procedure known as the Experience Sampling Method (ESM), researchers outfit participants with electronic beepers, usually for a week at a time, with the request they provide reports of their activities when signaled by the pagers (e.g., Csikszentimihalyi & Larson, 1987; Larson, 1989). In one study of adolescent interactions with their families, 220 middle-class youth provided reports at two periods in their lives, grades 5 to 8 and grades 9 to 12 (Larson, Richards, Moneta, Holmbeck, & Duckett, 1996). When "beeped," the adolescents used a checklist to indicate whom they were with, responded on 7-point scales regarding their emotional state and perceptions of the people they were with, and answered open-ended questions about their activities. As might be expected, the data revealed a sharp decline in the time adolescents spend with family members across grades 5 to 12. A surprising finding was that amount of adolescent-family conflict was not related to changes in family time, something *not* seen in other primates where conflict frequently leads to disengagement from the family group. The researchers argued that for human adolescents "the negative experience with family is as likely to be a stimulus for continued interaction—like one might see in an embattled, enmeshed family—as it is to be a stimulus for physical withdrawal" (p. 752). The ESM procedure also has been used to study the emotional states of chronic mental patients (e.g., Delespaul, 1995).

Because the ESM procedure relies on participants' self-reports of mood and activities, and not on direct observation of their behavior, it is important that techniques be devised to detect biases in data collection (e.g., possible omission or misrepresentation of personal activities by participants) (see Larson, 1989, for a discussion of possible biases using this method). Experience sampling has some of the problems associated with behavioral self-reports using survey methodology, which will be discussed in the next chapter. These problems can be weighed against the time and labor costs sometimes required to obtain a comprehensive description of behavior through direct observation (e.g., Barker et al., 1978).

SAMPLING TECHNIQUES

- When a complete record of behavior cannot be obtained, researchers seek to obtain a representative sample of behavior.
- The extent to which observations may be generalized, or external validity, depends on how behavior is sampled.

Before conducting an observational study, a researcher must make a number of important decisions about "when" and "where" observations will be made. In some cases, it might be possible to observe all the behavior of interest—for instance, the behavior patterns of certain short-lived organisms. In most cases, however, something considerably less than "all" of behavior will be observed. Imagine the task, if you will, that Barker et al. (1978) would have faced had they tried to record the behavior exhibited by an 8-year-old every day for a year. If she exhibited 969 behavioral episodes in a single day, we would expect more than 350, 000 episodes in 365 days!

Needless to say, in the vast majority of observational studies, the investigator must be satisfied with something considerably less than a complete record of behavior. Only certain behaviors occurring at particular times and in specific settings can generally be observed. In other words, behavior and settings must be sampled. The nature of these samples determines the extent to which generalizations are possible. Observations made of classroom behavior at the beginning of a school year, for instance, may not yield results that are typical of behavior seen at the end of the school year. Nor, for that matter, do observations made in the morning necessarily reveal the same pattern of classroom behavior as observations made in the afternoon. The frequency and type of aggression observed in children who are required to wear school uniforms may not be representative of the aggression found in children who do not wear school uniforms. As we saw in Chapter 1, our ability to generalize research findings depends upon the study's external validity. Results reasonably can be generalized only to participants, conditions, and situations similar to those in the study in which the results were actually observed. Time sampling, event sampling, and situation sampling are used to lend external validity to observational findings.

Time and Event Sampling

- Time sampling, systematic or random, refers to researchers' choice of time intervals for making observations.
- When researchers are interested in events that happen infrequently, they rely on event sampling to sample behavior.

Hartup (1974) used a combination of time and event sampling when studying children's aggression. In **time sampling,** the intervals at which observations are made are chosen either systematically or randomly with the goal of obtaining a representative sample of behavior. As examples, we might consider the application of these techniques in the context of observing a child's classroom behavior.

Suppose that observations are to be made for a total of 2 hours each day. As we indicated, restricting observations to certain times of the day (say, mornings only) would not necessarily permit us to generalize our findings to the rest of the school day. One approach to obtaining a representative sample is to schedule observation periods *systematically* throughout the school day. Observations might be made during four 30-minute periods beginning every 2 hours. The first observation period could begin at 9 A.M., the second at 11 A.M., and so forth. Another possibility would be to schedule 10-minute observation periods every half hour during the school day. A *random* time-sampling technique could be used in the same situation by distributing four 30-minute periods (or a dozen 10-minute periods) randomly over the course of the day. A different random schedule would be determined each day on which observations are made. Times would vary from day to day but, over the long run, behavior would be sampled equally from all times of the school day. A major advantage of the Experiential Sampling Method, discussed above, is that electronic beepers can be programmed to signal participants on a random time schedule (normal sleeping times are excluded). In their study of middle-class youth, Larson et al. (1996) obtained reports on the adolescents' experiences at "16,477 random moments" in their lives.

Systematic and random time-sampling procedures are often combined, as when observation intervals are scheduled systematically but observations within an interval are made at random times. For example, having scheduled four 30-minute observation periods at the same time each day (e.g., 9:00 A.M., 11:00 A.M., etc.), an observer might then decide to observe only during 20-second intervals that are randomly distributed within each 30-minute period. Or observation periods might be scheduled randomly during certain weeks of the school year but with weeks selected systematically from the early, middle, and late parts of the year. Whatever method is used, the observer must carefully scrutinize the schedule, noting both its limitations and its advantages in terms of yielding *a representative record of behavior*. Sampling plays a central role in conducting surveys. Many issues related to the topic of sampling are discussed in Chapter 4 when survey methods are introduced.

Event sampling may be a more efficient method of sampling behavior than time sampling when the event of interest occurs infrequently. In this case researchers want to maximize their opportunities to observe an event in order to get enough information about its occurrence to make investigating it worthwhile. Not only may time sampling cause precious instances of an event to be missed, but if the event is of significant duration, time sampling may not permit an observer to be present at the beginning of an event or to witness an event in its entirety. In event sampling the observer records each event that meets a predetermined definition. Researchers interested in children's reactions to special events in school, such as a Christmas play, would want to use event sampling. The special event defines when the observations are to be made. Researchers would certainly not want to use time sampling in this situation in the hope that a special event might occur during one of their randomly selected observation periods.

In many situations in which event sampling is used, a formally scheduled event like a school play is not the event of interest. Instead, researchers are often interested in events that occur unpredictably, such as natural or technical disasters. Researchers, for example, who are interested in victims' reactions to violent crimes are dependent on event sampling in selecting the occasions for making their observations. Whenever possible, observers try to be present in those situations and at those times when an event of interest has occurred or is likely to occur. Thus, in an ethological study of children's "rough-and-tumble" play, an observer positioned herself in the corner of a playground to observe members of a nursery school class (Smith & Lewis, 1985). Event sampling was the method of choice due to the relatively low frequency of this behavior, and the researcher made observations whenever rough play began. However, this manner of observing behavior can easily introduce biases into the behavioral record—as when, for instance, an observer samples at the times that are most "convenient" or only when an event is certain to occur. Characterization of events at these times may not be the same as at other times. In most situations, only through some form of time sampling is an observer likely to guarantee a representative sample of behavior.

Situation Sampling

- Situation sampling involves studying behavior in different circumstances, locations, and conditions and often with different participants.
- Situation sampling enhances the external validity of findings.

The external validity of observational findings can be significantly increased through **situation sampling.** Whenever possible—and when it is in keeping with the goals of a study—behavior should be observed under many different circumstances, locations, and conditions. By sampling different situations researchers reduce the chance that their results will be peculiar to a certain set of circumstances or conditions. It is clear that behavior often changes as a function of the context in which it is observed. Animals do not behave the same way in zoos as they do in the wild. Children do not always behave the same way with one parent as they do with the other parent. By sampling different situations, a researcher can also increase the diversity of the subject sample and hence achieve greater generality than could be claimed if only particular types of individuals were observed. As part of a naturalistic observation of beer drinking among college students, investigators purposely sampled behavior in various settings where beer was served, including five town bars, a student center, and a fraternity party (see Geller, Russ, & Altomari, 1986). When LaFrance and Mayo (1976) investigated racial differences in eye contact, they sampled many different situations. Pairs of individuals were observed in college cafeterias, business-district fast-food outlets, hospital and airport waiting rooms, and restaurants. By using situation sampling the investigators were able to include in their sample people who differed in age, socioeconomic class, sex, and race. Their observations of an apparent cultural difference in eye-contact behavior have considerably greater external validity than if only certain types of participants, or behavior in only a specific situation, had been studied.

ANALYSIS OF OBSERVATIONAL DATA

Data Reduction

- Observational data are summarized through the process of data reduction.
- Researchers quantify the data in narrative records by coding behaviors according to specified criteria, for example, by categorizing behaviors.
- Data are summarized using descriptive measures such as frequency counts, means, and standard deviations.

Analysis of Narrative Records Once they have been collected, narrative records can provide a wealth of information about behavior in natural settings. However, for meaningful information to emerge, data relevant to the goals of an observational study must be abstracted from the lengthy behavioral descriptions included in most narrative records. Results must be organized, and statements summarizing important findings must be prepared. This process of abstracting and summarizing behavioral data is called **data reduction.**

The first step in quantitative analysis of the content of narrative records often consists of identifying units of behavior, or particular events. This stage of data reduction involves **coding** behavioral records according to specific criteria. For instance, we previously noted that a narrative record describing a day in the life of a schoolgirl was found to contain 969 different behavior episodes (Barker et al., 1978, pp. 56–58). Hartup's (1974) 10-week observation of children's aggression yielded information about 758 units of aggression. As part of an ethological study of preschool children, McGrew (1972) identified 115 different behavior patterns. He classified patterns of behavior according to the body part involved, ranging from facial expressions such as bared teeth, grin face, and pucker face, to locomotion behaviors such as gallop, crawl, run, skip, and step. Coders classified these behavioral patterns while watching videotape records showing interactions of children attending nursery school.

Relevant units of behavior or events often are classified in terms of their apparent function or their particular antecedents. For instance, Hartup used nine categories to classify the nature of aggressive episodes. Antecedents of aggression were described using 18 different categories. Relationships between antecedent events and types of aggression were then summarized, and comparisons were made between different age groups. When derogation ("put-down") elicited aggression, more younger children than older children retaliated via some form of physical aggression (such as hitting). McGrew (1972) found that children exhibit a "pout face" after losing a fight over a toy. This ethologist-observer noted that young chimpanzees show a similar expression when seeking reunion with their mother. A "pucker face" was observed in children particularly after being frustrated (and often just prior to weeping). Interestingly, there seems to be no record of a pucker face in nonhuman primates.

Descriptive Measures   When events are classified into mutually exclusive categories (nominal scale), the most common descriptive measure is one of relative frequency. The proportion or percentage of times that various behaviors occur is expressed in terms of the total frequency of events observed. We have already seen several examples of this type of descriptive measure. Jenni (1976), for instance, reported the percentage of times that male and female students were observed to use three different book-carrying methods. Barash (1977) summarized his observations of pedestrian behavior in terms of the percentage of people in various social groupings who looked both ways.

When behavior is recorded on at least an interval scale of measurement, as frequently is the case when ratings are made, and when ratio measures of time (duration, latency) are used, one or more measures of central tendency are generally reported. The most common measure is the *arithmetic mean,* or *average.* The mean describes the "typical" score in a group of scores and is an important summary measure of group performance. Measures of variability or dispersion of scores around the mean are necessary to describe group performance completely. The *standard deviation* approximates the average distance of a score from the mean. (Measures of central tendency and variability, as well as confidence intervals for the mean, are discussed in Appendix A, as are additional guidelines for data summary and description.)

The mean and standard deviation as descriptive measures are illustrated in the results of the study by LaFrance and Mayo (1976). You may remember that these investigators observed other-directed looking behavior in pairs of Black and White conversants. The number of seconds that each listener in a pair spent looking into the speaker's face was recorded. Table 3.3 gives the means and standard deviations summarizing the results of this study. As we noted previously, White listeners spent more time looking into the faces of White speakers than Black listeners spent looking into the faces of Black speakers. This was found for same-sex pairs as well as mixed-sex pairs.

Observer Reliability

- Interobserver reliability refers to the extent to which independent observers agree in their observations.
- Interobserver reliability is increased by training observers and providing feedback about discrepancies, and by providing clear definitions about behaviors and events to be recorded.
- High interobserver reliability increases researchers' confidence that observations about behavior are accurate (valid).
- Interobserver reliability is assessed by calculating percentage agreement or correlations, depending on how the behaviors were measured and recorded.

In assessing the results of an observational study, we need to inquire about reliability of an observer. Would another observer viewing the same events obtain the same results?

TABLE 3.3 MEANS AND STANDARD DEVIATIONS DESCRIBING THE TIME (IN SECONDS) THAT LISTENERS SPENT LOOKING INTO THE FACE OF A SPEAKER PER 1-MINUTE OBSERVATION UNIT*

Group	Mean	Standard Deviation
Black conversants		
Male pairs	19.3	6.9
Female pairs	28.4	10.2
Male-female pairs	24.9	11.6
White conversants		
Male pairs	35.8	8.6
Female pairs	39.9	10.7
Male-female pairs	29.9	11.2

*From LaFrance and Mayo (1976).

Interobserver Reliability   The degree to which two independent observers are in agreement is referred to as **interobserver reliability.** Lack of agreement from one observer to another leaves us uncertain about what is being measured and prevents us from generalizing research results. Low interobserver reliability can be due to characteristics of the observers or to the procedures and methods of observing. When behavior is recorded, differences between observers in terms of experience, attitude, fatigue, boredom, and outcome expectancies are possible reasons for low interobserver reliability. Observer reliability is generally increased by training observers and giving them specific feedback regarding any discrepancies between their observations and those of other observers (Judd, Smith, & Kidder, 1991).

Low interobserver reliability may also result when the event to be recorded is not clearly defined. Imagine Hartup (1974) asking his observers to record aggressive episodes among children without giving them an exact definition of aggression. What exactly is aggression? Some observers might decide to define aggression as one child's physical attack on another; other observers might include verbal assaults in their definition of aggression. What is a playful push and what is an angry shove? Without a clear definition of behavior or of the events to be recorded, observers do not always agree—and hence show low interobserver reliability. In addition to providing precise verbal definitions, giving concrete examples of a phenomenon generally helps increase reliability among observers. Showing observers the pictures of book-carrying methods in Figure 3.3, for example, could be assumed to improve their ability to classify behavior according to this characteristic.

High observer reliability is not necessarily sufficient evidence that observations are accurate. We can imagine two observers of behavior who are both "in error" to the same degree. For instance, both might be influenced in a similar way by what they expect the outcome of the observational study to be. It is conceivable that the two observers would agree about what they saw but neither observer would provide an accurate record of behavior. Instances are occasionally reported in the media of several observers claiming to see the same thing (for instance, an unidentified flying object, or UFO), only to have the event or object turn out to be something other than what observers claimed it to be (for instance, a weather balloon). Nevertheless, when two independent observers agree, we are generally more inclined to believe that their observations are valid than when data are based on the observations of a single observer. In order for observers to be independent, each must be unaware of what the other has recorded. The chance of both observers being influenced to the same degree by outcome expectancies, fatigue, or boredom is generally so small that we can feel confident that what was reported actually occurred. Of course, the more independent observers who agree, the more confident we become.

Measures of Reliability   How observer reliability is measured depends on the way in which behavior is measured. When events are classified according to mutually exclusive categories, such as when individuals are classified in terms of whether they show a certain behavior, observer reliability is generally assessed via a percentage agreement measure.

A formula for calculating percentage agreement between observers is:

$$\frac{\text{Number of times two observers agree}}{\text{Number of opportunities to agree}} \times 100$$

Barash (1977) reported that observers were 100% reliable when classifying pedestrians as to the type of social group that was present (adult male and female, female with children, and so on) and in agreement 97% of the time when deciding whether pedestrians scanned both directions before crossing the street. Hartup (1974) reported measures of reliability that ranged from 83% to 94% for judges who coded narrative records according to type of aggression and nature of antecedent events. Although there is no hard-and-fast percentage of agreement that defines low interobserver reliability, a perusal of the literature reveals that researchers generally report estimates of reliability that exceed 85%, suggesting that agreement much lower than that is unacceptable.

Because in many observational studies most of the data are collected by one observer, or by several observers who collect data at different times, measures of reliability are often based only on a sample of observations for any one observer. For example, two observers might be asked to record behavior according to some time-sampling procedure and there might be only a subset of times during which both observers are present. Amount of agreement for the times when both observers were present can be used to indicate the degree of reliability for the study as a whole. For example, when studying beer drinking among college students, investigators reported the percent agreement for two independent observers who were present at slightly fewer than half of the 243 total observation periods; during the remaining periods only one observer was present (Geller et al., 1986). Observer reliability for home observations of family interactions involving depressed women was based on 86 (17%) of the 520 sessions (Hops et al., 1987).

When observational data are of at least an interval nature, as is often assumed when subjective ratings are made or when some variable such as time is measured, observer reliability can be measured using a Pearson Product-Moment Correlation Coefficient r. (Correlational measures, including the Pearson r, are discussed more fully in Chapter 4.) LaFrance and Mayo (1976) obtained measures of reliability when observers recorded how much of the time a listener gazed into the speaker's face during a conversation. The average correlation for observer reliability between pairs of observers was .92 in their study.

PROBLEMS IN THE CONDUCT OF OBSERVATIONAL RESEARCH

Influence of the Observer

- When individuals change their behavior when they know they are being observed ("reactivity"), their behavior may no longer be representative of their normal behavior.

- Research participants may use demand characteristics in the research situation to guide their behavior.
- Methods to control reactivity include unobtrusive (nonreactive) measurement, adaptation (habituation, desensitization), and indirect observations of behavior.
- Researchers must consider ethical issues when attempting to control reactivity.

Reactivity   The influence that an observer has on the behavior under observation is referred to as **reactivity.** Generally, we can think of reactive research situations as situations in which individuals "react" to the presence of an observer. Behavior in these situations may not be representative of behavior when an observer is not present. Underwood and Shaughnessy (1975) relate how a student, as part of a class assignment, set out to observe whether drivers came to a complete stop at an intersection with a stop sign. The student had hypothesized that drivers of high-priced cars would be less likely than drivers of low-priced cars to stop at the sign. The observer located himself on the street corner with clipboard in hand. However, he soon observed that all cars were stopping at the stop sign. He then realized that his presence was influencing the driver's

FIGURE 3.4   Reactivity refers to the influence that an observer has on the behavior under observation; for example, motorists are more likely to stop at a stop sign if an observer is visibly present.

behavior. When he concealed himself near the intersection, he found that drivers' behavior changed and he was able to gather data regarding his hypothesis.

Although human research participants may not exhibit innate reactions to an observer, as is the case with certain animals (e.g., see Moore & Stuttard, 1979), they can respond in very subtle ways when they are aware that their behavior is being observed. For instance, participants are sometimes apprehensive and more than a little anxious about participating in psychological research. Measures of arousal, such as heart rate and galvanic skin response (GSR), may show changes simply as a function of an observer's being present. Wearing an electronic beeper that signals when to record behavioral activities and mood also can be expected to affect participants' behavior (e.g., Larson, 1989).

Social psychologists have long been aware that behavior is affected by the presence of another person. Research has shown that performance on simple tasks can be facilitated by the presence of another person, a so-called facilitation effect, whereas performance on more complex tasks is often inhibited, a so-called social-impairment effect (see, for example, Bond & Titus, 1983). As you might suspect, whether social-facilitation and impairment effects are found depends not only on the complexity of the task but on who is present. For example, if the other person present is someone whose job it is to evaluate performance, as would be the case if an experimenter or observer were present, then effects due to another's presence are rather robust (see Guerin, 1986). In this case, social facilitation is usually attributed to increased arousal brought about by anticipation of being evaluated or to an increased desire on the part of the participant to gain approval and do what is socially acceptable. Social impairment would be produced if increased arousal interfered with performance, as sometimes happens when an individual facing tough competition "chokes," or if the presence of an observer distracts an individual and brings about poorer performance than that found when the person is alone. Although of interest as social psychological phenomena, these effects, of course, also help to define reactivity in a research situation and must be guarded against by the researcher.

Research participants may also attempt to behave in the way they think the researcher wants them to behave. Knowing that they are part of a scientific investigation, individuals usually want to cooperate and to be "good" participants. Being a good participant may be seen as doing what is expected by the observer. Orne (1962) has referred to the cues and other information used by research participants to guide their behavior in a psychological study as the **demand characteristics** of the research situation. Orne suggests that individuals generally ask themselves the question, "What am I supposed to be doing here?" By paying attention to cues present in the setting, including those that are part of the research procedure itself, or even by attending to implicit cues given by the researcher, the research participants can perhaps figure out what is "expected" of them and attempt to modify their behavior accordingly. An individual's reactions to the demand characteristics of a research situation pose threats to both the external and the internal validity of psychological research. When research participants behave in a manner that is not representative of their behavior outside the psychological research setting, our ability to generalize the results is restricted. Also, by behaving in a manner that they think is expected of them, participants may unintentionally make a research variable look more effective than it actually is or even nullify the effects of an otherwise significant variable. The problem of demand characteristics is often cited as a reason for limiting individuals' knowledge about their role in a study or about the study's hypothesis. By keeping participants unaware of important details regarding the study, the investigator hopes to obtain more representative behavior. However, limiting an individual's information about a study raises ethical concerns, which we discussed in Chapter 2, and about which we will have more to say later in this chapter.

Controlling Reactivity Problems of reactivity can be approached in several ways. Reactivity can be eliminated if observations are made in such a way that the presence of the observer is not detected by research participants. Measures of behavior in such circumstances are referred to as **unobtrusive (nonreactive) measures.** Obtaining unobtrusive measures may involve concealing the observer or hiding mechanical recording devices such as tape recorders and videotape cameras. LaFrance and Mayo (1976) observed people in conversation without their knowledge. Observations were made in a variety of natural settings, such as restaurants and waiting rooms, so we can imagine that observers had to keep their stopwatches and data sheets hidden behind menus and potted plants in order to obtain unobtrusive measures of behavior. Yet another approach is for researchers to use disguised participant observation and adopt a role in the situation other than that of observer. You may remember this procedure was used by social psychologists studying the behavior of individuals who claimed to be in contact with aliens from outer space (Festinger et al., 1956). Participants do not know that an observer is present, so we assume that they act as they ordinarily would. To investigate honesty, Hays (1980) worked as a clerk in a college student union. When patrons asked for change for a dollar bill, he gave them a nickel extra. Only 45% of those patrons who were judged by the observer to be aware of the extra nickel returned the extra money.

Another way of dealing with reactivity is to adapt participants to the presence of an observer. It can be assumed that, as participants get used to an observer being present, they will come to behave normally in that person's presence. Adaptation can be accomplished through either habituation or desensitization. In a *habituation* procedure observers simply introduce themselves into a situation on many different occasions until the participants cease to react to their presence. In order to film a documentary entitled *An American Family,* which was shown on public television in the early 1970s, observers (with their cameras) literally moved into a California home and recorded the activities of a family over a 7-month period. Although it is impossible to tell how much of their behavior was influenced by the observers' presence, the events that unfolded and remarks made by family members gave evidence of a habituation process having taken place. During filming the family broke up, the mother asking the father to move out of the house. When interviewed later about having the divorce announced to millions of television viewers, the father admitted that they could have asked the camera crew to get out but that, by this time, "we had gotten used to it" (*Newsweek*, 1973, p. 49).

Habituation may result when undisguised participant observers spend a great deal of time with the participants they are observing. Although they are still aware that an observer is present, participants may begin to behave as though the observer were not present. As part of a study of aggressive behavior in preschool children, Addison (1986) reported that before actual data were collected, a 5-day adaptation period was used to adapt the children to the presence of both the observer and the videotape equipment. Because the children often experienced classroom observers in the form of student teachers and other adults, there appeared to be no effect due to the presence of the researcher. Moreover, Addison (1986) stated that the children's interest in the videotape equipment diminished after a few days. Hart and Risley (1995) recorded children's vocabulary growth in their homes for more than 2 years. They began, however, "when the children were 7–9 months old so we would have time for the families to adapt to observation before the children actually began talking" (p. 28). Later, they were able to report that "Although no parent was unaware that the observer was there, over time the observer tended to fade into the furniture" (p. 35).

Desensitization as a means of dealing with reactivity is similar to the desensitization used in the behavioral treatment of phobias. In a therapy situation, an individual with a specific fear (say, an irrational fear of spiders) is first exposed to the feared stimulus at a very low intensity. The patient may be asked to think of things that are related to spiders, such as dusty rooms and cobwebs. At the same time the therapist helps the patient practice relaxation. Gradually the intensity of the stimulus is increased until the patient can tolerate the actual stimulus itself.

Desensitization is often used by ethologists to adapt animal subjects to the presence of an observer. Prior to a violent death in the land of her beloved subjects, Fossey (1981, 1983) conducted fascinating observational studies of the mountain gorilla in Africa. Over a period of time she moved closer and closer to the gorillas so that they would get used to her presence. She found that by imitating their movements—for instance, by munching the foliage they ate and by scratching herself—she could put the gorillas at ease. Eventually she was able to sit among the gorillas and observe them as they touched her and explored the research equipment she was using.

Finally, nonreactive measures of behavior can be obtained by observing behavior indirectly (see Webb, Campbell, Schwartz, Sechrest, & Grove, 1981). This may involve examining physical traces left behind or examining archival information, which are records kept by society about individuals and events. One researcher investigated the drinking behavior of people living in a town that was officially "dry" by counting empty liquor bottles in their trash cans. Another researcher used the records kept by a library to assess the effect on a community of the introduction of television. Withdrawals of fiction titles dropped, but the demand for nonfiction was not affected (see Webb et al., 1981). Physical traces and archival data are important unobtrusive measures that can be valuable sources of information about behavior. In Chapter 5 we discuss more fully these indirect methods of observation.

Ethical Issues   Whenever individuals are observed without their knowledge, as we saw may occur when an investigator seeks to control for reactivity, important ethical issues arise. For instance, in many circumstances, observing people without their consent can represent a serious invasion of privacy. As you saw in Chapter 2, deciding what constitutes an invasion of privacy is not always easy, and must include a consideration of the sensitivity of the information, the setting where observation takes place, and the degree of dissemination of the information obtained (e.g., Deiner & Crandall, 1978).

When individuals are involved in situations that are deliberately arranged by an investigator, as might happen in a field experiment, ethical problems associated with placing participants at risk may arise. Consider, for instance, a field experiment designed to investigate how college students' attitudes toward racial harassment are affected by hearing other students either condone or condemn racism (Blanchard, Crandall, Brigham, & Vaughn, 1994). More than 200 White undergraduate women attending various universities were "naive participants." The women were approached by a White interviewer as they walked across campus and were invited to answer a short series of questions about "how their college should respond to acts of racism" (p. 994). A female confederate, posing as a student, approached the interviewer so that she arrived at the same time as the naive participant. The interviewers asked both "students" the same five questions; however, the interviewer always questioned the confederate student first. At this point, the confederate responded by either condemning or condoning racists' acts. Of interest was the effect of these statements on the naive participants' responses to the same questions. The results were clear: Hearing another student condemn racism produced more condemning responses relative to a no-influence control group, and hearing another student condone racism produced more condoning reactions to racism than hearing no one else express an opinion. Thus, as the authors suggest, the findings "imply that a few outspoken people can influence the normative climate of interracial social settings in either direction" (p. 997).

Were the naive participants "at risk?" If you think the participants were at risk, what degree of risk was present? Did the goals of the study, and the knowledge potentially obtained, outweigh any risk? Although participants were "debriefed immediately" in this study, is that sufficient to address any concerns that the naive students might have about how they behaved when confronted with racist opinions, or even to restore confidence in a science that seeks knowledge through deception? Attempting to provide answers to these kinds of questions highlights the difficulty of ethical decision making. (Recommended steps in the process of ethical decision making are outlined in Chapter 2.)

Observer Bias

- Observer bias occurs when observers' expectations about behavior lead to systematic errors in identifying and recording behavior, and when researchers' biases determine which behaviors they choose to observe.
- Expectancy effects can occur when observers are aware of hypotheses for the outcome of the study or the outcome of previous studies.
- The first step in controlling observer bias is to recognize that it may be present.
- Observer bias may be reduced by keeping observers unaware ("blind") of the goals and hypotheses of the study.

You may remember that when Rosenhan (1973) and his colleagues observed the interaction between staff members and patients in mental hospitals, they found a serious bias on the part of the staff. Once patients were labeled schizophrenic, their behavior was interpreted solely in light of this label. Behaviors that might have been considered normal when performed by sane individuals were interpreted by the staff as evidence of the patients' insanity. For instance, note taking by the participant observers, which was done openly, was later discovered to have been cited by members of the staff as an example of the pseudopatients' pathological state. As a result of the staff's tendency to interpret patients' behavior in terms of the label that had been given them, the sanity of the pseudopatients was not detected. This example clearly illustrates the danger of **observer bias,** the systematic errors in observation that result from an observer's expectations.

Expectancy Effects   Although we might hope that scientific observations are free from the kind of observer bias documented by Rosenhan, we know that this is not always the case. In many scientific studies the observer has some expectancy about what behavior should be like in a particular situation or should result from a specific psychological treatment. This expectancy may be created by knowledge of the results of past investigations or perhaps by the observer's own hypothesis about behavior in this situation. Expectancies can be a source of observer bias—*expectancy effects*—if they lead to systematic errors in observation (Rosenthal, 1966, 1976).

An example of a study designed to document observer bias will illustrate this problem (see Cordaro & Ison, 1963). The study required college student observers to record the number of head turns and body contractions made by two groups of flatworms. The observers were led to expect different rates of turning and contracting in the two groups. The worms in the groups were, however, essentially identical. What differed was the observers' expectations about what they would see. Results showed that the observers reported twice as many head turns and three times as many body contractions when a high rate of movement was expected than when a low rate was expected. Apparently, the students interpreted the actions of the worms differently depending on what they expected to observe.

Other Biases   An observer's expectancies regarding the outcome of a study may not be the only source of observer bias. You might think that using automated equipment such as movie cameras would eliminate observer bias. Although automation reduces the opportunity for observer bias, it does not necessarily eliminate it. Consider the fact that, in order to record behavior on film, the observer must determine the angle, location, and time of filming. To the extent that these aspects of the study are influenced by personal biases of the observer, such decisions can introduce systematic errors into the results. Altmann (1974) describes an observational study of animal behavior in which the observers biased the results by taking a midday break whenever the animals were inactive. Observations of the animals during this period of inactivity were conspicuously absent from the observational records. Furthermore, using automated equipment generally only postpones the process of classification and interpretation, and it is perfectly possible for the effects of observer bias to be introduced when narrative records are coded and analyzed.

Controlling Observer Bias   Observer bias cannot be eliminated, but it can be reduced in several ways. As we mentioned, the use of automatic recording equipment can help, although the potential for bias is still present. *Probably the most important factor in dealing with observer bias is the awareness that it might be present.* That is, an observer who knows about this bias will hopefully take steps to reduce its effect.

Observer bias also can be reduced by limiting the information provided to observers. When Hartup (1974) analyzed the results of his observational study of children's aggression, the individuals who performed the analysis were not permitted to see all the narrative records. When the nature of the aggressive act was classified, the antecedent events were blacked out; and when antecedent events were coded, the nature of the aggressive act was blacked out. Therefore, in making their classifications, the coders could not be influenced by information related to the event that they were coding. In a manner of speaking, the coders were "blind" to certain aspects of the study. Observers are *blind* when they do not know why the observations are being made or the goals of a study. When Burns, Haywood, and Delclos (1987) observed the problem-solving strategies of children from two different socioeconomic groups, they first videotaped the children while they worked on five tasks selected from standardized intelligence tests. When task strategies were observed and coded from the videotape records, however, the observer-coder was blind to which group the child was from. When LaFrance and Mayo (1976) investigated eye contact between individuals conversing in natural settings, their observers did not know that possible differences along racial lines were being probed. Using "blind" observers greatly reduces the possibility of introducing systematic errors due to observer expectancies.

SUMMARY

Observational methods can be characterized in terms of both the degree of observer intervention and the manner in which behavior is recorded. Observation in a natural setting without observer intervention is called naturalistic observation. On the other hand, both structured observation (frequently used by developmental psychologists) and field experiments (often used by social psychologists) depend on some degree of observer intervention. The manner of record keeping in an observational study varies according to whether a comprehensive description of behavior is sought or the observer seeks only to describe certain predefined units of behavior. Whereas narrative records, including field notes, are used to provide comprehensive descriptions of behavior, checklists are typically used when it is simply of interest whether a specific behavior has occurred (and under what conditions). Frequency and duration of behaviors also may be recorded, and observers are sometimes called on to make subjective judgments, in the form of ratings, about the quality or degree of a characteristic of the subject or situation.

How quantitative data are described and analyzed depends on the scale of measurement used. The four levels of measurement used by psychologists are nominal, ordinal, interval, and ratio.

Observations can rarely be made of all behavior that occurs. Consequently, some form of behavior sampling (time or situation sampling) must be used. An important goal of sampling is to achieve a representative sample of behavior. When narrative records are made, some type of coding system is generally used as one step in the process of data reduction. Measures of frequency and duration, as well as ratings, are typically summarized, using descriptive statistics such as the mean and standard deviation.

It is essential to provide measures of observer reliability when reporting the results of an observational study. Depending on the level of measurement that has been used, either a percentage agreement measure or a correlation coefficient can be used to assess reliability. Possible influences of reactivity and observer bias must be controlled in any observational study. Finally, ethical issues must be addressed prior to beginning a research study, and they are especially salient when conducting observational studies using disguised participant observation, unidentified confederates, or other forms of participant deception.

KEY CONCEPTS

naturalistic observation
ethology
ethogram
participant observation
structured observation
field experiment
confederate
narrative records
ecological psychology
ethnography
field notes
measurement scale

checklist
time sampling
event sampling
situation sampling
data reduction
coding
interobserver reliability
reactivity
demand characteristics
unobtrusive (nonreactive)
   measures
observer bias

Review Questions

1 What three characteristics distinguish scientific observation from nonscientific observation?
2 What critical characteristics distinguish among naturalistic observation, participant observation, structured observation, and a field experiment?
3 What two dimensions can be used to classify observational methods?
4 There are five general reasons for intervening in conducting an observational study. Identify a study illustrating each reason—either from the studies cited in this chapter or from research you have read about in other psychology courses.
5 What factors in participant observation can be expected to influence the extent of the observer's influence on the behavior being observed?
6 What is the principal advantage of the structured observation method?
7 Name the four scales of measurement, and give an example of each.
8 What aspect of an observational study is the proper use of time sampling and situation sampling intended to ensure?
9 What are the most common descriptive measures (a) when events are classified into mutually exclusive categories and (b) when behavior is recorded on at least an interval scale?
10 What factors contribute to low interobserver reliability, and how can interobserver reliability be increased?
11 Does high interobserver reliability ensure the validity of observations? Why or why not?
12 Why are participants' reactions to demand characteristics a threat to both the internal and the external validity of psychological research?
13 What ethical issues must one address when using unobtrusive measures such as concealing the presence of an observer?
14 Give an example of each of the two ways in which investigators attempt to mitigate reactivity by adapting individuals to the presence of the observer.
15 What is the best procedure to reduce observer bias?

Challenge Questions

1 Students in a developmental psychology lab course conducted an observational study of parent-infant interactions in the home. When they first entered the home on each of the 4 days they observed a given family, they greeted both the parents and the infant (and any other children at home). They instructed the family to follow its daily routine and they asked a series of questions about the activities of that day to determine whether it was a "normal" day or something unusual had happened. The students tried to make the family feel comfortable, but they also tried to minimize their interactions with the family and with each other. For any given 2-hour observation period there were always two student observers present in the home, and the two observers recorded their notes independently of each other. There were six pairs of students who were randomly assigned to carry out the 8 hours of observation on each of the 12 families who volunteered to serve in the study. The same pair of observers always observed a given family, and two families were assigned to each pair of observers. The observers used checklists to record behaviors on a number of different dimensions, such as mutual warmth and affection of the parent-infant interaction.

A Cite two specific procedures used by the students to ensure the reliability of their findings.

B Cite one possible threat to the external validity of the findings of this study; once again, cite a specific example from the description provided.

C Cite one specific aspect of their procedure that indicated that the students were sensitive to the possibility that their measurements might be reactive. What other methods might they have used to deal with this problem of reactivity?

2 A naturalistic observation study was done to assess the effects of environmental influences on drinking by college students in a university-sponsored pub. Eighty-two students between the ages of 18 and 22 were observed. Observations were differentiated on the basis of whether the person being observed was with one other person or was in a group of two or more other people. The observations were made over a 3-month period; sessions were always from 3 P.M. to 1 A.M., and observations were made Monday through Saturday. Each participant was observed for up to 1 hour from the time he or she ordered the first beer. Two observers were always present during any observation session. The results showed that in terms of number of beers drunk per hour men drank more and faster than did women. Men drank faster when with other men, and women also drank faster with men present. Both men and women drank more in groups than when with one other person. These results do indicate that the environment within which drinking occurs plays an important role in the nature and extent of that drinking.

A Identify the independent and dependent variables in this study.

B What is the operational definition of a group in this study?

C Identify one specific aspect of this study that increases the external validity of the findings.

3 A friend of yours is absolutely convinced that he has a positive influence on the friendliness of conversations in which he is a participant. He has reached this conclusion on the basis of his everyday observations. You convince him that a systematic study is needed to confirm his hypothesis. Your friend (still smiling) carefully develops an operational definition of the friendliness of a conversation and records a rating for each of the next 50 conversations in which he is a participant. His results show that 75% of these conversations are rated "very friendly," 20% are rated "friendly" and 5% are rated neutral. Your friend returns to you—now convinced beyond a shadow of a doubt that he has a positive effect on the friendliness of a conversation. Although your friend won't be pleased with you, explain to him why the results of his study are essentially useless as a means of confirming his hypothesis. While you have this chance to teach your friend about research methods, explain to him why it would be better for you or someone else to rate the friendliness of the conversations in a proper study testing your friend's hypothesis.

4 The following description is based upon a study that was done as an assignment in a research methods class. You are to use this description to answer the questions that follow it.

The study was conducted to investigate one aspect of the pace of life at a small college. The measure of pace of life was the time it took a person to walk a distance of 70 feet. Researchers compared the walking speeds of people who did (called passers) or did not pass (called the nonpassers) someone while going through an area designated as the passing zone—the main path from the administration building continuing through the path that leads past the admissions office. Participants walked west in the passing zone up to a marker that indicated the start of the timing zone, which was 70 feet long. Observers worked in pairs with one observer timing the passer and the second observer timing the nonpasser. There were 24 pairs of observers who made a total of 83 paired observations (passer/nonpasser pairs). Observers positioned themselves so that they could see the passing zone and the timing zone but so they would not be noticed by the people walking along the path. The observers recorded the gender of the observed person, the context in which the observation took place (e.g., how crowded it was, weather conditions), and the date and time of the observation. Observations were distributed across the days of the week during which the study was done with more observations on Monday, Wednesday, and Friday than on Tuesday and Thursday. The results indicated that the passers' times through the 70-foot timing zone were faster than the times for the nonpassers.

A   Identify the type of observational method that was used in this study.

B   What is the operational definition of the dependent variable in this study?

C   Identify one aspect of the procedures in this study that would likely increase the reliability of the observations.

D   Identify one aspect of the procedures in this study that would likely limit the external validity of the findings of this study.

E   Identify one aspect of the procedures in this study that would likely decrease the reactivity of the observations.

F   What possible interpretations do you think are appropriate for the finding that passers walked faster than nonpassers? Try to come up with at least one interpretation based on a characteristic of the people in the categories of passer and nonpasser and at least one based on characteristics of the situation.

Answer to Challenge Question 1

A   The students' procedures that enhanced reliability were as follows: observing each family for 8 hours, using two independent observers, and using checklists to provide operational definitions.

B   One possible threat to the external validity of the findings was that the 12 families volunteered for the study and such families may differ from typical families.

C   The students' efforts to minimize interactions with the family and with each other suggested that they were sensitive to the problem of reactivity. Two other methods they might have used are habituation and desensitization.

Correlational Research: Surveys

CHAPTER OUTLINE

OVERVIEW
CORRELATIONAL RESEARCH
The Nature of Correlations
Correlation and Causality
Path Analysis
MEASURES IN CORRELATIONAL RESEARCH
Questionnaires as Instruments
Margin of Error
Reliability and Validity
Predictions and Decisions
USES OF SURVEYS
CHARACTERISTICS OF SURVEYS
SAMPLING TECHNIQUES
Basic Terms of Sampling
Approaches to Sampling
SURVEY METHODS
Mail Surveys
Personal Interviews
Telephone Interviews
SURVEY-RESEARCH DESIGNS
Cross-Sectional Design
Successive Independent Samples Design
Longitudinal Design
CORRESPONDENCE BETWEEN REPORTED AND ACTUAL BEHAVIOR
SUMMARY

OVERVIEW

Campaigns for political offices frequently are accompanied by media reports revealing the results of the "latest poll." A poll supposedly tells us which candidate is "ahead" at any particular time. Media analysts spend a lot of time interpreting poll results, giving us their opinions about what the latest "figures" mean for the candidates. You may even have seen debates about whether polls influence the political process; for example, analysts have argued that some people "switch sides" to support a front runner in the poll in order to be on the winning side. Although polls are intended to describe people's voting preferences at the time the poll is taken, they are also used to predict how people will vote at the time of the actual election. Candidates use poll results to help orchestrate their campaigns, for example, by identifying places they should visit and key public issues. Political polls involve the use of survey-research methods. As you will see in this chapter, however, surveys have a much broader application than their use in political polling; they are an important research tool of psychologists.

Survey research represents a more general approach to psychological research called correlational research. Correlational research, unlike experimental research (see Chapter 6), does not involve the manipulation of independent variables. Instead, **correlational research** assesses relationships among naturally occurring variables with the goal of identifying predictive relationships. The predictive relationships found in correlational research have implications for decisions such as diagnosing psychological disorders and selecting among job applicants. A decision to admit you to a university was likely made with the help of correlational research showing the relationship between various predictors (e.g., high school rank, academic test scores) and a measure of success in college (e.g., first-year college GPA).

Larose and Roy (1995) identified a predictive relationship in their study of students who were beginning college. Students completed a questionnaire that measured their personal approach to learning. For example, the questionnaire included items asking about students' attitudes toward teachers and the students' priorities regarding their use of time. Using students' responses to this questionnaire, Larose and Roy (1995) found they could predict students' academic success in the first year of college better than when only high school grade point average was used to predict college success. Their questionnaire was also useful in predicting which students were likely to be at risk academically in their first year of college. Correlational findings such as these can play an important role in decision making.

In this chapter we also introduce the basic logic and techniques of *sampling*—the process of selecting a subset of a population to represent the population as a whole—which is so often critical to successful prediction. You will then learn about the advantages and disadvantages of various survey-research methods and survey-research designs. We conclude the chapter with a brief discussion of the correspondence between people's reported behavior when completing surveys and their actual behavior. Do people really do what they say they do?

CORRELATIONAL RESEARCH

The Nature of Correlations

- A correlation assesses the extent to which two variables covary; the correlation coefficient is a quantitative index of the direction and magnitude of this relationship.
- The direction of a correlation coefficient can be negative or positive.
- The magnitude of a correlation coefficient ranges from −1.0 (a perfect negative relationship) to +1.0 (a perfect positive relationship); a correlation coefficient of 0.00 indicates no relationship.
- Scatterplots are graphical displays of the relationship between two variables.

Prediction, as you saw in Chapter 1, is an important goal of the scientific method. Correlational research frequently provides the basis for this prediction. A **correlation** exists when two different measures of the same people, events, or things vary together—that is, when scores on one variable covary with scores on another variable. For example, a widely known relationship exists between smoking and lung disease. The more individuals smoke (e.g., measured by duration of smoking), the greater their likelihood of contracting lung disease. Thus, smoking and lung disease covary, or go together. This correlation also can be expressed in these terms: The less people smoke, the lower their chances for contracting lung disease. Based on this correlation we can make predictions about lung disease. For example, if we know how long an individual has smoked, we can predict (to some degree) his or her likelihood of developing lung disease. The nature of our predictions and the confidence we have in making them depends on the direction and the strength of the correlation.

The direction and strength of a correlation are determined by computing a **correlation coefficient.** The correlation coefficient is a quantitative index of how well we are able to predict one set of scores (e.g., likelihood of lung disease) using another set of scores (e.g., duration of smoking). A correlation coefficient expresses the relationship between two variables in terms of both the *direction* and the *magnitude* of that relationship.

The direction of a correlation coefficient can be either positive or negative. A positive correlation indicates that, as the values for one measure increase, the values for the other measure also increase. As we've seen, measures of smoking and lung disease are positively correlated (more smoking, more lung disease). Another predictive relationship concerns Scholastic Aptitude Test (SAT) scores: SAT scores and college students' first-semester GPAs are positively correlated. Thus, we can predict that students with higher SAT scores should have higher first-semester GPAs, and students with lower SAT scores should have lower first-semester GPAs. With correlations, the "reverse" prediction can be made too. If we know only the first-semester GPAs of students, we can "predict" what their SAT scores were prior to entering college. Students with higher GPAs would be more likely to have higher SAT scores, and students with lower GPAs would be likely to have lower SAT scores.

In a negative correlation, as the value of one measure increases, the value of the other measure *decreases*. A national survey of high school seniors showed a negative correlation between the amount of time spent watching TV and the number of correct answers on an academic achievement test (Keith, Reimers, Fehrmann, Pottebaum, & Aubrey, 1986). Students who spent *more* time watching TV answered *fewer* questions correctly on an achievement test. What about the reverse prediction? Based on this finding, if you knew that a student scored very high on the achievement test, would you predict that the student had spent a "a lot" of time or "a little" time watching TV?

The magnitude (degree) of a correlation coefficient can range in absolute values from 0.0 to 1.00. A value of 0 indicates there is no correlation and there is no basis for making predictions. The relationship between intelligence and mental illness, for example, exhibits a zero correlation; we cannot predict the likelihood that a person will become mentally ill by knowing the person's IQ (nor can we predict a person's IQ based on his or her mental health). A value of +1.00 indicates a perfect positive correlation, and a value of −1.00 indicates a perfect negative correlation. When a correlation coefficient is either +1.00 or −1.00, we can make predictions with absolute confidence. Values between 0 and 1.00 indicate predictive relationships of intermediate strength and, therefore, we have less ability to predict confidently. Remember, the sign of the correlation signifies only its direction; a correlation coefficient of −.46 indicates a stronger (more predictive) relationship than one of +.20. (Note: In practice, only the sign of negative correlation coefficients is indicated; a coefficient without a plus or minus sign is treated as positive, that is, +.20 = .20.)

The nature of a correlation can be represented graphically using a scatterplot. Scores for the two variables are represented on the x-axis and y-axis. Each individual has a value (or score) for each variable (e.g., SAT score and first-semester GPA). A scatterplot shows the intersecting points for each pair of scores. Hypothetical examples of scatterplots showing strong positive, practically zero, and moderate negative correlations are shown in Figure 4.1. The magnitude or degree of correlation is seen in a scatterplot by determining how well the points correspond to a straight line; stronger correlations seem to form a straight line of points. Thus, the correlation is stronger in the first example (a) than in the other two examples; however, the correlation represented in the third example (c) is stronger than the second example (b). The direction of a correlation can be seen in the scatterplot by noting how the points are arranged. When the pattern of points seems to move from the lower left corner to the upper right (a), then the correlation is positive (low scores on the x-axis go with low scores on the y-axis and high scores on the x-axis go with high scores on the y-axis). When the pattern of points is from the upper left to the lower right (c), the correlation is negative (low scores on the x-axis go with high scores on the y-axis and high scores on the x-axis go with low scores on the y-axis). Whether represented in a scatterplot or in a correlation coefficient, the purpose of a correlation is to

FIGURE 4.1   Three scatterplots illustrating a strong positive (a), a zero (b), and a moderate negative (c), correlation between scores on two variables: X and Y.

(a) Positive relationship

(b) Zero relationship

(c) Negative relationship

determine how well we can predict one measure based on its covariation with another measure. A formula for calculating the most commonly used correlation coefficient, the Pearson *r*, may be found at the end of this chapter.

Correlation and Causality

- When two variables are related (correlated), we can make predictions for the variables; however, we cannot make inferences about the cause of the relationship.
- When a relationship between two variables can be explained by a third variable, the relationship is said to be "spurious."

A study by Lubin and his colleagues (1988) illustrates how useful correlational studies can be in psychological research. They investigated correlations among measures of physical and psychological health in their survey of 1,543 adults living in the United States. Respondents rated their physical health and provided information about health-related factors such as how often they visit a physician and the nature and frequency of any medications they were taking. The interviewers also collected data regarding respondents' occupation and religious affiliation, frequency of volunteer and social activities, and so forth. Each of the respondents also completed a paper-and-pencil test measuring both positive affect (e.g., happiness) and negative affect (e.g., depression). Measures of psychological health and physical health were found to be correlated. For instance, positive affect was positively correlated with self-ratings of physical health; happier people were more healthy. Additionally, frequency of volunteer activities correlated negatively with a measure of depression; people who were more active with volunteer activities experienced less depression. Correlations like these can be useful for predicting physical and psychological health-related problems.

Correlational studies are the method of choice when the goal of the research is prediction. There are serious limitations, however, on using results of correlational studies to infer causal relationships: *"Correlation does not imply causation."* For instance, there is a reliable correlation between being outgoing (socially active) and being satisfied with one's life (Myers & Diener, 1995). Based on this correlation alone, however, we could *not* argue convincingly that being more outgoing and socially active *causes* people to be more satisfied with their lives. Although it is possible that being outgoing causes people to be more satisfied with their lives, the "reverse" causal relationship also may be true: Being satisfied with life may cause people to be more outgoing and socially active. The causal relationship could go either way—being more outgoing causes greater life satisfaction *or* being more satisfied with life causes people to be more outgoing. It is impossible to determine the correct causal direction simply by knowing the correlation between the two variables.

Another causal interpretation may exist for this relationship. It's possible that a third variable, having more friends, leads people to be more outgoing *and* more satisfied with their lives. A correlation that can be explained by a third variable is called a *spurious relationship* (Kenny, 1979). In this particular example, "number of friends" is a possible third variable that could account for the relationship between being outgoing and being satisfied with one's life. Individuals with more friends may be more likely to be outgoing and satisfied with life than people with fewer friends. This isn't to say that the original positive correlation between being outgoing and life satisfaction doesn't exist (it certainly does), it just means that other variables (e.g., number of friends) may explain *why* the relationship exists. These problems with understanding causal relationships based on correlations should make it clear that *more than mere correlational evidence is necessary to make causal statements*.

Path Analysis

- Path analysis is a statistical technique used to help researchers understand potential causes of correlational relationships.
- Mediators are variables that help to explain the relationship between two variables.
- A moderator variable affects the strength and direction of the relationship between two variables.
- Although path analysis helps researchers to interpret correlational studies, they cannot make definite causal statements about the relationships between variables.

There are sophisticated statistical techniques that can be used to help with causal interpretations of correlational studies (Baron & Kenny, 1986; Holmbeck, 1997). One technique involves the identification of mediator variables and moderator variables. A *mediator variable* is a variable that is used to explain the correlation between two variables. A *moderator variable* is a variable that affects the direction or strength of the correlation between two variables. A study by

Valentiner, Holahan, and Moos (1994) nicely illustrates these concepts. The researchers carried out a correlational study to examine the relationship between parental support and students' adjustment to college. Parental support was measured by asking first-year students questions about their mother and father, such as "Does she (he) really understand how you feel about things?" and "Is she (he) critical or disapproving of you?" They measured changes in well-being and distress over a 2-year period, and observed a correlation between parental support and changes in psychological adjustment: Students' perceptions of positive support from their parents were associated with greater well-being and less distress over the 2-year period. In analysis terms, this relationship is called "direct" because one variable (parental support) is directly correlated with another variable (changes in adjustment); this is illustrated as Path a in Figure 4.2.

Valentiner and his colleagues sought to explain why this relationship exists, and predicted that how students cope with stress might mediate, or help to explain, the relationship between parental support and adjustment. Specifically, they measured the extent to which these students coped using "approach coping" more than "avoidance coping" for "the 'most important problem' they experienced in the past 12 months" (p. 1096). Approach coping strategies involve active efforts to solve problems or change one's thinking about a problem, whereas avoidance coping strategies involve trying to forget the problem exists or behaving in ways that don't address the root of the problem (e.g., yelling "to let off steam"). Generally, approach coping is viewed as more adaptive than avoidance coping. Consistent with their predictions, Valentiner et al. found that parental support was positively correlated with the percent of approach coping students used; this is illustrated as Path b in Figure 4.2. Thus, students' perception that their parents are supportive was associated with more adaptive, approach coping.

This is only part of the story, however. Valentiner et al.'s next step was to show that approach coping is associated with positive changes in psychological adjustment (Path c in Figure 4.2). This is exactly what their correlations demonstrated: Students who used more approach coping than avoidance coping had

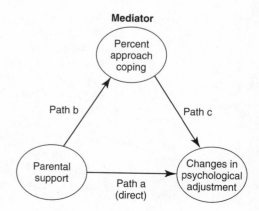

FIGURE 4.2 Illustration of direct (Path a) and indirect (Paths b and c) relationships between parental support and changes in psychological adjustment to college. Adapted from Figure 1 of Valentiner et al. (1994).

improved well-being and less distress over the 2-year period. With this pattern of relationships, Valentiner and his colleagues were able to say that parental support was directly associated with students' adjustment (Path a), and also that approach coping partially mediated, or explained, the relationship between parental support and psychological adjustment (Paths b and c). Thus, one possible reason why parental support was associated with positive adjustment is because parental support also was associated with the use of adaptive, approach coping strategies. In analysis terms, parental support is said to be associated with psychological adjustment *indirectly,* through the mediating variable of coping strategies.

Valentiner et al. (1994) also identified a moderator variable that affected the observed relationships between parental support, coping, and changes in students' adjustment. The moderator variable in their study was how controllable the participants thought their "most important problem" was, and the sample was divided into two groups: students who thought the occurrence of their problem was controllable and students who thought the event's occurrence was uncontrollable. The correlational analyses were then repeated separately for each group of students to determine if the same pattern of correlations would be obtained. Basically, researchers try to identify a moderator variable to discover the conditions under which a relationship exists and the conditions under which the relationship is weaker or does not exist.

What happened with students who reported their life event was *controllable?* The pattern of correlations changed: Perceptions of parental support were no longer directly related to changes in psychological adjustment (Path a). However, the indirect relationship between parental support and adjustment, through approach coping, was still observed (Paths b and c). Thus, for controllable problems, perceptions of parental support may help students to use more effective coping strategies, which are associated with positive changes in psychological adjustment.

Precisely the opposite picture emerged for students who reported their event was *uncontrollable.* In these analyses, parental support directly predicted changes in students' psychological adjustment over the 2-year period (Path a). Now, however, the indirect path involving correlations with approach coping was not associated with students' adjustment (Paths b and c). How can it be that adaptive, approach coping was not associated with students' adjustment in the face of uncontrollable events? Valentiner et al. explain this rather unintuitive finding by arguing that when events are uncontrollable, coping strategies that emphasize active problem solving may be counterproductive—much like hitting your head against a brick wall. When events are uncontrollable, the best strategy may be to *not* try to solve the problem because it can't be solved. In this situation, perceptions of supportive parents seem to be more important for students' positive adjustment.

The use of sophisticated statistical techniques like those we just described can greatly enhance our ability to interpret the results of correlational studies. However, it is important to remember that we still can't make definite causal statements based on an analysis of mediator and moderator variables.

MEASURES IN CORRELATIONAL RESEARCH

Questionnaires as Instruments

- Most survey research relies on questionnaires to measure variables.
- Demographic variables describe the characteristics of people who are surveyed.
- Self-report scales are used to assess people's judgments or to identify individual differences among respondents.
- Two methods to develop individual differences scales are the Likert method and factor analysis.
- The accuracy and precision of questionnaires requires expertise and care in their construction.

The value of correlational research (and any research) ultimately depends on the quality of the measurements that researchers make. The quality of these measurements, in turn, depends on the quality of the instruments used to make the measurements. The primary research instrument in survey research is the questionnaire. On the surface, a questionnaire may not look like the high-tech instruments used in much modern scientific research; but, when constructed and used properly, a questionnaire is a powerful scientific instrument for measuring different variables.

Demographic Variables Demographic variables are an important type of variable frequently measured in survey research. Demographic variables are used to describe the characteristics of the people who are surveyed. Religious affiliation and occupation, which Lubin and his colleagues (1988) measured in their study of psychological and physical health, are demographic variables. Measures such as race, ethnicity, age, and socioeconomic status are also examples of demographic variables. Whether we decide to measure these variables depends on the goals of our study, as well as on other considerations. Entwisle and Astone (1994), for example, provide a practical reason for including race and ethnicity as demographic variables in survey research. This practical reason is the ever-increasing diversity of the U.S. population. Entwisle and Astone (1994) point out that "The ethnic and racial diversity of the U.S. population is now projected to increase through the middle of the next century, so that by then the majority of the U.S. population will be persons whose ethnicity would now be classified as 'nonwhite'" (p. 1522). By asking respondents to identify their race we are able to document the racial mix of our sample and, if part of the research goals, compare racial groups.

Measuring a demographic variable such as race may at first seem very easy. One straightforward method is simply to ask respondents to identify their race in an open-ended question: What is your race? _____ Such an approach may be straightforward, but the resulting measurement of race may not be satisfactory. For example, some respondents may mistakenly confuse "race" and "ethnicity." Important distinctions in identifying ethnic groups may go unrecognized by respondents and researchers. For instance, Hispanic does not identify a race; Hispanic designates all those whose country of origin is Spanish speaking.

So, a person born in Spain would be classified as Hispanic. *Latino* is a term that is sometimes used interchangeably with Hispanic, but Latino designates people whose origin is from the countries of North and South America, excluding Canada and the United States. Distinctions like these can be confused. For example, a person known to the authors is of European Spanish heritage and correctly considers himself a Caucasian, and not Latino. His ethnicity is Hispanic.

In general, "quick and dirty" approaches to measurement in survey research tend to yield messy data that are hard to analyze and interpret. Entwisle and Astone (1994) recommend a more deliberate—and effective—approach when measuring race. They outline a series of nine questions to measure a person's race. One of these questions is, What race do you consider yourself to be? Other questions seek information such as what countries the person's ancestors came from, and whether Latino respondents are Mexican, Puerto Rican, Cuban, or something else. This more detailed series of questions allows researchers to measure race less ambiguously, more accurately, and more precisely. We use this example of measuring race to illustrate a more general principle: *The accuracy and precision of questionnaires as survey-research instruments depends upon the expertise and care that go into their construction.*

Preferences and Attitudes   Individuals' preferences and attitudes are frequently assessed in surveys. For example, a marketing researcher may be interested in consumers' preferences for different brands of coffee, or a political group may be interested in potential voters' attitudes regarding controversial public issues. Psychologists have long been interested in measuring people's thoughts and feelings on a vast array of topics, and often develop *self-report scales* for people to provide verbal or written responses to items on the scale.

Self-report scales are commonly used to measure people's judgments about items presented on the scale (e.g., coffee, divorce, political candidates, life events) and to determine differences among people on some dimension presented on the scale (e.g., personality traits, amount of stress). For example, respondents may be asked to rate different life events according to how stressful they perceive the events to be. The researcher then may develop a list of life events that vary on the dimension of stressfulness. This type of scale focuses on differences among the items on the scale. To measure individual differences, respondents may be asked to report how often during the past year they experienced different stressful life events listed on a scale. A total stress score can be obtained for each individual by summing responses to the items on the scale. Individuals can then be compared according to the amount of stress experienced during the past year.[1] Rozin, Markwith, and Stoess (1997) investigated individual differences among people who were "meat avoiders, vegetarians, and people reluctant to eat meat" (p. 68). They found that vegetarians who avoid meat for moral reasons find meat

---

[1]The area of psychological measurement concerned with scaling items or stimuli is known as psychophysics, and the area of measurement concerned with individual differences is referred to as psychometrics.

more disgusting and avoid a wider range of animal foods than do those who avoid meat for health reasons. Interestingly, though, both groups showed similar levels of dislike for the taste and smell of meat.

Individual differences scales are used to identify differences among respondents on the dimension measured in the scale (e.g., degree of meat avoidance) and are perhaps the most common scales in psychology. Two frequently used methods to develop individual differences scales are the Likert method and factor analysis. In the Likert method, a number of items are written to reflect the construct or domain of interest. For example, a researcher may be interested in individuals' willingness to forgive others. A 5-point rating scale is typically provided for individuals to respond by circling a number on the scale. One item that could be used to measure forgiveness is:

When people hurt me or make me angry, I can usually forgive them.

Many such items are administered to a large group of people (at a minimum, 100), and each individual's responses are summed to derive a total score. Items are then selected from the whole set of items to best represent the domain. Items are discarded if they don't discriminate individuals who are high on the dimension from individuals who are low (based on their total score). Each selected item should correlate well with the total scale score. Once the best items are chosen, an individual's scale score is obtained by summing her responses to these items. An important goal of scale development is reliability, and in the Likert method, each time the scale is used the researcher must demonstrate that the items in the scale consistently measure the domain of interest (reliability is discussed in greater detail later in this chapter). It is important to note that measures with 5-point rating scales are often called "Likert scales" (instead of, most correctly, "Likert-type scales," or more simply, "5-point rating scales"). A scale is only a Likert scale if it follows the method for scale development that we just outlined.

Factor analysis is similar in that it is designed to select the best items to represent the construct or domain of interest. An advantage of factor analysis is that a measure can be developed that assesses more than one construct. For example, the forgiveness researcher may be interested in "other-forgiveness" and "self-forgiveness," so her questionnaire may have items intended to represent each "factor." In factor analysis, responses for each item are correlated with responses for every other item (this represents many "intercorrelations," which is why factor analysis is best accomplished using a computer). The pattern of intercorrelations among items is used to determine which items are related to the factor(s) represented in the scale. Items that correlate poorly are dropped. As with Likert scales, the reliability of scales developed using factor analysis should be analyzed each time they are used.

Self-report measures, often in the form of a questionnaire, are among the most frequently used tools in psychology. Given their importance, it is critical that these measures be developed carefully. Important information on questionnaire construction, such as wording of questions, response options, questionnaire format, and order of questions, is found in Appendix B.

Margin of Error

- Although survey researchers select a sample to represent a population, they recognize that it is unlikely the sample will exactly describe the population due to sampling error.
- The margin of error represents a quantitative estimate regarding the difference between sample results on a measure and the likely population values.
- The margin of error is influenced by the sample size and the confidence level researchers choose for estimating the population value.
- Although the margin of error indicates how well survey results may describe a population, whether these results can be interpreted depends on the quality of the survey-research methods.

Survey results are often reported in terms of the percentage of respondents who prefer a certain candidate, agree or disagree with a certain position, or possess some particular demographic characteristic. We must be careful, however, when we translate this numerical information into a verbal description of the results. For example, a major metropolitan newspaper reported on the National Collegiate Athletic Association's (NCAA) 1995 Division I Graduation-Rates Report. The overall graduation rate within 6 years for all students entering in 1988 (both athletes and nonathletes) was 57%. For football players the graduation rate was 56%, and the newspaper reported the good news that this represented an increase from the 1987 graduation rate. In 1987, the graduation rate for football players was 55%. It turns out that the percentage increase in the graduation rate for football players, 1%, was not particularly impressive. The graduation rates for 1987 and 1988 were included in the newspaper article so there wasn't an effort to mislead the reader about the size of the increase. However, survey researchers need some way to translate these differences in percentages into appropriate verbal statements. Is a change from 55% to 56% a "meaningful" or "significant" increase? When it comes to describing survey results, an increase is not always an increase.

As we will describe more fully later in this chapter, survey research relies heavily on sampling. Survey research is conducted when we would like to know the characteristics of a population (e.g., preferences, attitudes, demographics), but often it is impractical to survey the entire population (we'd spend all of our time completing surveys!). Responses from a sample are used to describe the larger population. Well-selected samples will provide good descriptions of the population, but it is unlikely that the results for a sample will describe the population *exactly*. For example, if the average age in a classroom of 33 college students is 26.4, it's unlikely that the mean age for a sample of 10 students from the class will be exactly 26.4. Similarly, if it were true that 65% of a city's population favor the present mayor and 35% favor a new mayor, we wouldn't necessarily expect an exact 65:35 split in a sample of 100 voters randomly selected from the city population. We expect some "slippage" due to sampling, some "error" between the actual population values and the estimates from our sample. At issue, then, is how accurately the responses from the sample represent the larger population.

It is possible to estimate the **margin of error** between the sample results and the true population values. Rather than providing a precise estimate of a population value (e.g., "65% of the population prefer the present mayor"), the margin of error presents a *range* of values with the idea that the true population value is likely to be within the range (e.g., "between 60% and 70% of the population prefer the present mayor"). What specifically is this range?

The margin of error provides an estimate of the difference between the sample results and the population values due simply to chance or random factors. Let's consider a specific example using the hypothetical mayoral election referred to above. Assume that in a random sample of 100 voters, 63 people said they favor the present mayor and 37 said they want her replaced. (Let us assume we "know" that 65% of the people in the population favor the incumbent and 35% want a new mayor.) The question we must ask is, Is the difference between 63 and 65 (the sample estimate and population value, respectively) a *real* difference? That is, is the sample value of 63% an accurate description of the population, given that we expect some error? Another way of stating this is: Is the sample value of 63 *within the margin of error* that is expected when random samples of this size are taken? If it is, then the difference between 63 and 65 may not be a real difference but one due to sampling error.

The margin of error gives us the range of values we can expect due to sampling error—remember that we expect some error; we don't expect to describe the population exactly. To stay with the mayoral election example, let us assume that a poll of many voters is taken and a media spokesperson gives the following report: "Results indicate that 63% of those sampled favor the incumbent, and we can say with 95% confidence that the poll has a margin of error of 5%." The reported margin of error with the specified level of confidence (usually 95%) indicates that the percentage of the actual population who favor the incumbent is estimated to fall between 58% and 68% (5% is subtracted from and added to the sample value of 63%). Because the population value (65%) falls within the range of values indicated by the margin of error, it is reasonable to assume that the sample value of 63% accurately describes the population. It's important to remember, however, that we usually don't know the true population value. The information we get from the sample and the margin of error is the following: 63% of the sample favor the incumbent, and we are 95% confident that if the entire population were sampled, between 58% and 68% of the population would favor the incumbent. This can be represented on a graph by plotting the value obtained for the sample (63%), with error bars

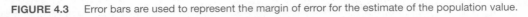

FIGURE 4.3   Error bars are used to represent the margin of error for the estimate of the population value.

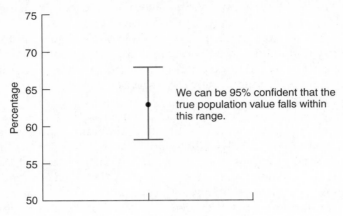

We can be 95% confident that the true population value falls within this range.

representing the margin of error. Figure 4.3 displays error bars around the sample estimate.

The margin of error is primarily determined by the size of the sample—the larger the sample size, the smaller the margin of error. This is because a larger sample is more likely to represent the diverse characteristics of the population. Thus, in order to reduce the margin of error (and more precisely describe the population), an obvious decision is to increase the size of the sample. This may make sense in some situations, but increasing sample sizes can make the cost of doing a survey too high. For example, if our margin of error is 5% with a sample size of 100, we would have to quadruple the sample size to 400 to decrease the margin of error by half!

The margin of error is influenced also by how confident we want to be when estimating the population value. Given a sample of specific size, we can be more confident about our estimate when we have a larger margin of error. As an illustration, think of what your weight is right now. Can you confidently estimate your weight within 5 pounds (a margin of error)? Would you be more confident of your estimate if you were allowed to be within 10 pounds? We could express the differences in the sizes of the intervals in terms of confidence. A person might say, "I am 99% confident that my weight is between 160 and 180, but I'm only 90% confident that my weight is within 165 and 175." When describing survey results, a 99% confidence level results in a larger margin of error (i.e., a larger range of values) than does a 90% confidence level (assuming the same sample size for the two different confidence levels).

The margin of error for a given sample can be computed using the sample size and a specified confidence level. In practice, however, a desired margin of error (e.g., 3%) and confidence level (e.g., 95%) are selected and the sample size necessary to achieve these two objectives is then calculated.

Margins of error are routinely included in media reports of national surveys. At this point, you should be able to estimate the population values from sample information presented in media reports. Remember that you can not know for sure the true population value based on sample information. The goal of surveys is to tell you "with a margin of error" what the true population value is.

Knowing the margin of error for a survey is not sufficient to assure that the survey results can be interpreted. Interpretable results also depend on factors such as how the survey sample was selected, how many selected for the sample actually responded to the survey, how the questions on the questionnaire are worded, and the training of the interviewers who administer the questionnaire (Converse & Traugott, 1986). Unfortunately, these important aspects of survey research usually are not reported in the media. Thus, we should be cautious in accepting interpretations of survey results unless we are well informed about critical characteristics of the survey. As you will soon see, problems can arise even in a carefully conducted survey.

Reliability and Validity

- Reliability refers to the consistency of measurement, and is frequently assessed using the test-retest reliability method.
- Reliability is increased by including many similar items on a measure, by testing a diverse sample of individuals, and by using uniform testing procedures.
- Validity refers to the truthfulness of a measure: Does it measure what it intends to measure?
- Construct validity represents the extent to which a measure assesses the theoretical construct it is designed to assess; construct validity is determined by assessing convergent validity and discriminant validity.

As we learned in Chapter 1, reliability and validity are vital characteristics of all psychological measurement. Thus, it makes sense that measurements in survey research must be reliable and valid. In this section we will describe some procedures researchers use to determine whether measures are reliable and valid.

We first discuss examples of assessing the reliability and validity of *tests*. Tests, like surveys, are commonly used instruments in correlational research. We chose to use tests for our examples because you already know a great deal about tests—they're probably a routine part of your life. You may even prefer a particular type of test because you believe you perform better on that type of test. Most of us experience emotional reactions when taking tests, ranging from exhilaration to terror! There are good reasons for these emotional reactions. Important decisions frequently are based in part on test results—admission to college, passing or failing courses, admission to graduate or professional schools. Although you have considerable experience with tests, what else do you know about the tests you take? For example, have you ever wondered whether the tests you take are reliable and valid? Consider that question for a moment. How would you be able to tell whether a test was reliable and valid? Asked a different way, what are the fundamental characteristics of a reliable and valid test?

Reliable tests, like reliable observers or any other reliable measurements, are characterized by consistency. A reliable test is one that yields similar (consistent) results each time it is taken. Tests must be reliable if they are to be used to make predictions about who will be selected for a scholarship, who will be hired for a competitive job, or who should be fired from a job. For example, Powell and Whitla (1994) developed a test they call MicroCog to measure normal changes in cognitive processes as people age. As part of the natural aging process, older adults experience some changes in memory and other cognitive functions. For instance, they may have trouble remembering people's names, which leads some older adults to wonder if they are "losing it." This question is important in the workplace. In 1994, it became illegal in the United States for an employer to compel a worker to retire because of age. Tests like MicroCog can be useful to older adults to allay their fears about memory loss and to employers when they make difficult decisions about the performance of older employees. When test results are used as part of the process of making such important personal decisions, it is essential that the tests be as reliable as possible—reliability is no longer just a measurement issue.

There are several ways to measure a test's reliability. One common method is to compute a *test-retest reliability*. Usually, test-retest reliability involves administering the same test to a large sample of people at two different times (hence, test and retest). For a test to be reliable, people need not obtain identical scores on the two administrations of the test, but a person's relative position in the distribution of scores should be similar at the two test times. The consistency of this relative positioning is determined by computing a correlation coefficient using the two test scores for each person in the sample. A desirable value for test-retest reliability coefficients is .80 or above, but the size of the coefficient depends on factors such as the number and types of items.

As we just mentioned, the reliability of a test is affected by the number of items on the test; in this case, more items is better. We are likely to have unreliable measures if we try to measure a student's understanding of material based on a single test item, or a baseball player's hitting ability based on a single time at bat, or a person's attitude toward the death penalty based on a single question on a survey. The reliability of our measures will increase greatly if we average the behavior in question across a large number of observations—many test items, many at-bats, and many survey questions (Epstein, 1979).

In general, measurements will also be more reliable when there is greater variability on the factor being measured among those individuals being tested. Often the goal of measurement is to determine the extent to which individuals differ. A sample of individuals who vary a great deal from one another are easier to differentiate reliably than are individuals who differ by only a small amount. Consider this example. Suppose we wish to assess soccer players' ability to pass the ball effectively to other players. We will be able to differentiate more reliably good players from poor players if we include in our sample a wider range of players—for example, professionals, high school players, and peewee players. It would be much harder to differentiate players reliably if we only tested professional players—they'd all be good! The range of skill level would not be that great. Thus, a test is often more reliable when administered to a diverse sample than when given to a restricted sample of individuals.

A third and final factor affecting reliability is related to actual test administration. Tests will be more reliable when the testing situation is free of distractions and when clear instructions are provided for completing the test. (You may wish to think about times when your own test performance was hindered by noise or when you weren't sure what a question was asking.) These three factors affecting the reliability of tests (number and type of items, variability in the sample, and testing procedures) apply equally to measurements made using questionnaires in survey research.

The reliability of a test is easier to determine and to achieve than the validity of a test. The definition of validity is deceptively straightforward—a valid test measures what it is intended to measure. For example, a valid test of research methods knowledge might ask you about the terms *reliability* and *validity*; we suspect you would question the validity of a research methods test that asked about the classical counterpoint in the fugue of Mozart's Symphony No. 4 in C Major (finale). Have you ever heard students complain that questions on a test didn't seem to address the material covered in class? This is an issue of validity.

At this point, we will focus on construct validity, which is just one of the many ways in which the validity of a test is assessed. The *construct validity* of a test represents the extent to which the test measures the theoretical construct it is designed to measure. Quantitative reasoning, intelligence, self-esteem, anxiety, and depression represent examples of theoretical constructs psychologists measure using tests. One approach to determining the construct validity of a test relies on two other kinds of validity: convergent validity and discriminant validity. These concepts can best be understood by considering an example.

Table 4.1 presents data showing how we might assess the construct validity of a measure of "life satisfaction." Lucas, Diener, and Suh (1996) note that psychologists are increasingly examining factors such as happiness, life satisfaction, self-esteem, optimism, and other indicators of well-being. However, it's not clear whether these different indicators all measure the same construct (e.g., well-being) or whether each is a distinguishable construct. Lucas and his colleagues conducted several studies in which they asked individuals to complete questionnaire measures of these different indicators of well-being. For our purposes we will focus on a portion of their data from their third study, in which they asked participants to complete three scales: two life satisfaction measures, the Satisfaction with Life Scale (SWLS) and a 5-item Life Satisfaction measure (SL-5), and a measure of Positive Affect (PA). At issue in this example is whether the construct of life satisfaction—the quality of being happy with one's life—can be distinguished from being happy more generally (positive affect).

The data in Table 4.1 are presented in the form of a correlation matrix. A correlation matrix is an easy way to present a number of correlations. Look first at

TABLE 4.1   EXAMPLE OF CONSTRUCT VALIDITY*

	SWLS	LS-5	PA
SWLS	(.88)		
LS-5	.77	(.90)	
PA	.42	.47	(.81)

*Data from Lucas et al. (1996), Table 3.
Note: SWLS = Satisfaction with Life Scale; LS-5 = 5-item Life Satisfaction scale; PA = Positive Affect scale.

the values in parentheses that appear on the diagonal. These parenthesized correlation coefficients represent the test reliabilities of the three measures appearing in the table (Satisfaction with Life Scale, 5-item Life Satisfaction, and Positive Affect, respectively). As you can see, the three measures show good reliability (each is above .80). Our focus, however, is on measuring the construct validity of "life satisfaction," so let's look at what else is in Table 4.1.

It is reasonable to expect that scores on the Satisfaction with Life Scale (SWLS) should correlate with scores on the 5-item Life Satisfaction measure; after all, both measures were designed to assess the life satisfaction construct. In fact, Lucas et al. observed a correlation between these two measures of .77, which indicates that they correlate as expected. This finding provides evidence for *convergent validity* of the tests; the two tests converge (or "go together") as measures of life satisfaction.

The case for the construct validity of life satisfaction can be made even more strongly when the measures are shown to have discriminant validity. As can be seen in Table 4.1, the correlations between the Satisfaction with Life Scale (SWLS) and Positive Affect (.42) and between the 5-item Life Satisfaction measure (LS-5) and Positive Affect (.47) are lower. These findings show that life satisfaction tests do not correlate as well with a test designed to measure another theoretical construct—namely, positive affect. The lower correlations between the life satisfaction tests and the positive affect test indicate that *different* constructs are being measured. Thus, there is evidence for *discriminant* validity of the life satisfaction measures because they seem to "discriminate" life satisfaction from positive affect—being satisfied with one's life is not the same as general happiness. The construct validity of life satisfaction gains support in our example because there is evidence for both convergent validity and discriminant validity.

Predictions and Decisions

- Actuarial prediction relies on correlational data to make predictions about people's average behavior.
- Predictions are improved when multiple sources of information are used.
- Statistical predictions, based on correlations, have been shown to be superior to predictions based on clinical judgment.

The results of correlational research have implications for decision making. Predictive relationships can be used in making diverse decisions such as who should pursue a career as a salesperson or who should be admitted to a psychiatric hospital. Making predictions based on correlational data is called **actuarial prediction.** As we described in the previous section, predictive relationships must be reliable in order to make good decisions. Based on highly reliable predictive relationships (i.e., strong correlations), we can accurately predict what people's average behavior will be. For example, students who score in the highest 20% on an academic aptitude test are *on average* more likely to succeed in college than are students who score in the lowest 20%. However, actuarial predictions do not necessarily tell us what an *individual* person will do in a particular situation. Thus, knowing a particular student's score on an academic aptitude test does not allow us to predict with certainty whether *that* student will graduate from college. We can only predict what students "like this student" will typically (on the average) do. Nonetheless, actuarial prediction can still be extremely useful.

Important decisions are rarely based on a single source of information. Instead, when more than one measure has been shown to have predictive value, we combine the information across measures to improve predictions. This is similar to the multimethod approach to research described in Chapter 1. When several different research methods are used to investigate a problem, we're more likely to achieve a valid conclusion. The same is true when making decisions: The use of several different predictors in the decision-making process increases the likelihood of making good decisions.

For example, applications to graduate and professional schools comprise several pieces of predictive information: GRE (MCAT, LSAT) test scores, undergraduate GPA, letters of recommendation, and personal essays. Similarly, employers selecting applicants in more applied settings rely on the use of multiple predictors. Broach (1992) reported that predictions of air traffic controllers' performance in radar-based training after 1 or 2 years in that occupation were better when biographical data (such as age and prior experience) were included than when the predictions were based solely on a civil service test.

Statistical prediction based on correlational research is sometimes contrasted with clinical prediction. Specifically, Meehl (1954) studied the task that clinical psychologists routinely face when they diagnose their clients' disorders. Statistical prediction and clinical prediction represent two different ways to combine information when making a decision. Clinical prediction occurs when a clinician reviews the available evidence pertinent to a case, including impressions gained from interviewing the client, and then makes a diagnosis (prediction) of the client's disorder. Clinical prediction relies heavily on the personal and professional *judgment* of the clinician.

Statistical prediction is essentially the same as actuarial prediction: Correlational research is used to identify predictive relationships. For example, a large amount of research has shown that the occurrence of "depression" is correlated with low energy, difficulty sleeping, and crying; the occurrence of "schizophrenia" is correlated with withdrawal and disordered thinking. Information about a given client is entered into this predictive (correlational) system, and a statistical prediction is made about which disorder is most likely experienced by the client. The distinguishing characteristic of statistical prediction is that it is based on empirical evidence (e.g., results of paper-and-pencil tests) rather than on the individual judgment of a clinician. Which of these two approaches yields more accurate predictions of psychological disorders?

Meehl (1954) compared the accuracy of statistical prediction versus clinical prediction when clinicians make these challenging diagnostic decisions. He found that, in an absolute sense, *neither* clinical prediction nor statistical prediction was very accurate—a not surprising finding given the complexity involved in diagnosing psychological disorders. Meehl did find, however, that statistical prediction was more accurate than clinical prediction. In fact, research has shown that statistical prediction is superior to clinical prediction (personal judgments) across a wide variety of areas, including predictions about who to admit to graduate school, who is a good risk for a bank loan, who is at risk for a heart attack, and who should be paroled from prison (Dawes, Faust, & Meehl, 1993). We should generally trust, therefore, what the data "say" more than what one person says when making important decisions.

Although this evidence suggests that we should rely on statistical prediction whenever possible, it is not always practical to do so. As Meehl (1993) emphasizes, "You could not choose a graduate school, buy a car, get married (or divorced), let alone invest money or vote for president, if you required all your choices to be derived rigorously from scientific proof" (p. 727). Empirical evidence simply is not available for many important decisions. When we have no basis for making a statistical prediction, then we must make the best decision we can based on our own judgment. However, when we do have the data for a statistical prediction, we face a different situation. Meehl (1993) argues that, *ethically*, we are making a questionable choice if we ignore the data and rely on personal judgment. Our hope is that the knowledge you have gained about correlational research and predictions will allow you to make a more informed decision about how you make decisions in your life.

USES OF SURVEYS

- Survey research is used to assess people's thoughts, opinions, and feelings.
- Surveys can be specific and limited in scope or more global in their goals.
- The best way to determine whether a survey is biased is to examine the survey procedures and analyses.

We discussed in Chapter 3 how psychologists use observational methods to infer what people must have been thinking or feeling to have behaved in a certain way. Survey research is designed to deal more directly with the nature of people's thoughts, opinions, and feelings. On the surface, survey research is deceptively simple. If you want to know what people are thinking, ask them! Similarly, if you want to know what people are doing, observe them! As we have seen, however, when we hope to infer general principles of behavior, our observations must be more sophisticated than our everyday, casual observations. So, too, survey research requires more than simply asking people questions.

The deceptive ease of conducting a survey is illustrated in a report by a young girl named Bridgette that was published in a suburban grammar school's newsletter. The report read, "I surveyed 50 people on which candy bar they liked best. Here are my results in order of preference: Hershey bar—35, Snickers—10, Whachamacallit—5." These results may please the makers of Hershey bars, but the supplier for the school's vending machine should be wary of stocking it based on Bridgette's findings. Who were the "50 people" surveyed? How were they selected? How was the survey conducted? Was each child interviewed separately? If other children were present during the interview, were they eating candy bars? If so, what brands? Do the children who claim to like Hershey bars best really eat them most often? These and many other questions must be answered before we can confidently interpret the results of this survey.

You may be thinking at this point that we are taking Bridgette's survey too seriously, and you are probably right. Nonetheless, these questions are typical of those that should be asked when we read or hear reports of surveys. A goal of this chapter is to help you to ask the right questions about surveys and to aid you in evaluating the answers provided to these questions.

Social scientists, such as political scientists, psychologists, and sociologists, use surveys for a variety of reasons. For example, Cherlin et al. (1991) conducted national surveys in Great Britain and the United States to investigate the effects of divorce on children. Myers and Diener (1995) reported the results of many studies that used surveys to study factors affecting people's personal sense of well-being.

Surveys are also used to meet the more pragmatic needs of political candidates, public health officials, professional organizations, and advertising and marketing directors. The scope and purpose of surveys can be limited and specific, or they can be global. For example, the Practice Directorate of APA conducted a survey with a limited and specific purpose (Peterson, 1995). The Practice Directorate is a branch of APA that focuses primarily on the concerns of clinical psychologists. Their national survey of 1,087 adults was designed to understand better what the public thinks psychologists do, what kind of education psychologists have, and in what settings psychologists practice. The survey produced many observations, including that 46% of respondents reported having seen a mental health professional or that someone in their family had, and 80% said that psychologists usually work in private practice. In fact, although more than half of psychologists do work in the mental health field, fewer than half of those work in private practice. Clearly, the public's estimate of 80% is high. Results from this survey will be useful to the Directorate in focusing their public education strategies.

Myers and Diener (1995), on the other hand, conducted a survey with a more global scope. They reported the results of a survey sampling people from 24 countries representing every continent but Antarctica. One of the research questions was whether people in wealthy countries have a greater sense of well-being than those in not-so-wealthy countries. Is being "well-off" associated with greater "well-being"? The survey results showed that national wealth, as measured by gross national product per capita, is positively correlated with well-being (.67). But this relationship is not simple because national wealth is also correlated with other variables that are themselves highly correlated with well-being, such as number of continuous years of democracy (.85). Thus, surveys can be used to address issues of global concern such as democracy, wealth, and well-being.

One of the ways that surveys can be used deserves mention because of ethical issues. An ethical dilemma arises when sponsors of survey research have vested interests in how the results turn out. Crossen (1994) highlighted this by stating, ". . . more and more of the information we use to buy, elect, advise, acquit, and heal has been created not to expand our knowledge but to sell a product or advance a cause" (p. 14). Crossen (1994) cites examples such as a national survey sponsored by the zinc industry showing that 62% of respondents wanted to keep the penny (which is zinc based), and a survey sponsored by a manufacturer of cellular phones showing that 70% of respondents (all of whom used cellular phones) agreed that people who use cellular telephones are more successful in business.

Is it reasonable to conclude that survey results are biased anytime the outcome of the survey is favorable for the sponsoring agency? Answers to ethical questions are rarely simple and the answer to this one certainly is not. High-quality and ethical research can be done when the sponsor has an interest in the outcome. Knowing the sponsor of the research is important when evaluating survey results, but is not sufficient for judging whether the study is biased. It is much more important to know whether a biased sample has been used, or whether the wording of questions has been slanted, or whether the data have been selectively analyzed or reported. Any of these aspects of survey research can bias the results, and unethical researchers can use these techniques to make the results "turn out right." The best protection against unethical researchers and poor-quality research is to examine carefully the procedures and analyses used in the survey research.

CHARACTERISTICS OF SURVEYS

- Survey research involves selecting a sample (or samples) and using a predetermined set of questions.

Though they differ in how they can be used, all surveys have some characteristics in common. These shared characteristics make properly conducted surveys an excellent method for describing people's attitudes and opinions. First, surveys generally involve sampling, a concept we introduced in our discussion of observational methods (Chapter 3) and will discuss more in the next section of this chapter. Surveys also are characterized by their use of a set of predetermined questions for all respondents. Oral or written responses to these questions constitute the principal data obtained in a survey. By using the same phrasing and ordering of questions, it is possible to summarize the views of all respondents succinctly.

When a representative sample of people is asked the same set of questions, we can describe the attitudes of the population from which the sample was drawn. Furthermore, when the same questions are used, we can compare the attitudes of different populations or look for changes in attitudes over time. An example of the latter comes from two surveys of animal rights activists, one taken at a national march in Washington, DC, in 1990, and another of activists attending a similar event in 1996 (Plous, 1998). Results revealed that a change had taken place in the priorities of people in the animal rights movement during this time. Specifically, in 1990 a majority of activists viewed animal research as the most important issue facing the movement; in 1996, animal agriculture was viewed as the most important issue. The researcher suggested that there now may be more room for dialogue between activists and researchers than there was previously. Thus, survey research can be used to study changes in people's attitudes by presenting the same questions to samples selected at different times.

SAMPLING TECHNIQUES

- Careful selection of a survey sample allows researchers to generalize findings from the sample to the population.

Assume you've decided your research question is best answered using a survey, and you've determined the population of interest for your survey. The next step is to decide who to interview. This involves selecting a sample of respondents to represent the population. The power and efficiency of sampling are aptly summarized by survey researcher Angus Campbell (1981, p. 17):

> The method of choice for portraying all the variety of a large heterogeneous population is clearly that of the sample survey. Ever since statisticians and social scientists learned how to draw a sample from a large universe in such a way that every member of the universe has an equal chance of being chosen, it has been possible to describe the national population accurately by obtaining information from a few thousand carefully selected individuals.

Whether we are describing a national population or a much smaller one (e.g., the students of one university), the procedures are the same. We explain in this section how to make that careful selection of individuals which Campbell describes.

Basic Terms of Sampling

- The identification and selection of elements that will make up the sample is at the heart of all sampling techniques; the sample is chosen from the sampling frame, or list of all members of the population of interest.

- Researchers are not interested simply in the responses of those surveyed; instead, they seek to describe the larger population from which the sample was drawn.
- The ability to generalize from a sample to the population depends critically on the representativeness of the sample.
- A biased sample is one in which the characteristics of the sample are systematically different from the characteristics of the population.
- Selection bias occurs when the procedures used to select a sample result in the overrepresentation or underrepresentation of some segment(s) of the population.

As we begin to talk about sampling techniques, we need to be clear about the definitions of four terms: *population, sampling frame, sample,* and *element.* The relationships among the four critical sampling terms are summarized in Figure 4.4. A **population** is the set of all cases of interest. If you were interested in the attitudes of students on your campus toward services provided by the library, your population would be all students on your campus. In a survey, we select a subset of the population to represent the population as a whole.

FIGURE 4.4   Illustration of relationships among four basic terms in sampling.

Next, we need to develop a specific list of the members of the population. This specific list is called a **sampling frame** and is, in a sense, an operational definition of the population of interest. In a survey of students' attitudes toward library services, the sampling frame might be a list obtained from the registrar's office of all currently enrolled students. The extent to which the sampling frame truly reflects the population of interest determines the adequacy of the sample we ultimately select. The list provided by the registrar should provide a good sampling frame, but some students might be excluded, such as students who registered late.

The subset of the population actually drawn from the sampling frame is called the **sample.** We might select 100 students from the registrar's list to serve as the sample for our library survey. How closely the attitudes of this sample of students will represent all students' attitudes depends critically on how the sample is selected. Each member of the population is called an **element.** The identification and selection of elements that will make up the sample is at the heart of all sampling techniques.

It is important to emphasize at this point that samples are of little or no interest in themselves. A new library is not going to be built for the sole use of the 100 students surveyed. Similarly, the social psychologist is not interested solely in the racial attitudes of the 50 people he surveyed, nor is the marketing director interested only in the preferences of the 200 consumers she surveyed. Populations, not samples, are of primary interest. The "power" of samples to describe the larger population is based on the assumption that survey responses in a sample are applicable to the population from which the sample was drawn.

The ability to generalize from a sample to the population depends critically on the **representativeness** of the sample. Clearly, individuals in a population differ in many ways, and populations differ from each other. For example, one population might be 40% male and 60% female, whereas in another population the distribution might be 75% female and 25% male. *A sample is representative of the population to the extent that it exhibits the same distribution of characteristics as the population.* If a representative sample of 200 individuals has 80 males and 120 females, which of the above-mentioned populations does it represent?

The major threat to representativeness is bias. A **biased sample** is one in which the distribution of characteristics in the sample is *systematically* different from the target population. A sample of 100 individuals that included 80 females and 20 males would be biased if the population was 60% female and 40% male. In this case, females would be overrepresented and males would be underrepresented in the sample. There are two sources of bias: selection bias and response bias. (We will discuss selection bias now and deal with response bias in the Survey Method section.) **Selection bias** occurs when the procedures used to select the sample result in the overrepresentation of some segment of the population or, conversely, in the exclusion or underrepresentation of a significant segment.

Charles Madigan, a senior writer for the *Chicago Tribune*, documented a selection bias in samples surveyed for the 1994 national election. He identified the selection bias by comparing the demographic characteristics of the voters interviewed in exit polls to characteristics of the population drawn from U.S. census data. Note that the U.S. census data, representing the entire population, includes voters and nonvoters, whereas the exit-poll sample comprises voters only. Madigan determined that the exit-poll sample differed in systematic ways from the U.S. population in terms of age, race, education, income, and the proportion of working women. These differences indicate that the sample was not representative of the population due to a selection bias. Although the voter poll accurately reflects the interests and attitudes of those people who voted, their votes and survey responses may not be used to characterize the attitudes of the population (which includes people who did not vote). Clearly, politicians cannot assume a "mandate" based on a biased sample of individuals who voted.

A general lesson from the above example is that what constitutes a representative sample depends on the population of interest. For example, if exit polls are concerned (as they usually are) only with people who vote, then an unbiased sample is one that is representative of *probable voters,* not all eligible voters. Similarly, when a university wishes to know college students' opinions about on-campus parking, then the target population is college students who bring cars to campus (not college students in general). An unbiased sample would, in this case, be one that is representative of the subset of students who have cars on campus.

Selection bias also threatens the results of surveys posted on the World Wide Web. As Schmidt (1997) notes, the web "presents survey researchers with an unprecedented opportunity to examine groups of people with questionnaires tailored to the investigation of both broad and narrow domains" (p. 274). Nevertheless, there are some problems and risks. For example, although the number of people using the web is increasing at a fast fate, the majority of users in the late 1990s could be characterized as young males (late teens to early thirties) with above-average socioeconomic status (Schmidt, 1997). Those who wish to use the web for survey research must therefore be aware of the characteristics inherent to the population of web users. But this is not something new. Survey researchers must be constantly alert to the threat of selection bias in sampling. Fortunately, as we will see, they have developed techniques that can minimize the risk.

Approaches to Sampling

- Two approaches to selecting a survey sample are nonprobability sampling and probability sampling.
- With nonprobability sampling techniques, accidental sampling and purposive sampling, there is no guarantee that every element in the population has an equal chance of being included in the sample.
- Accidental sampling relies on individuals' availability and willingness to respond to a survey; in purposive sampling, researchers select elements for the sample based on their special characteristics.

- With the probability sampling techniques, simple random sampling and stratified random sampling, researchers can estimate the likelihood their findings for the sample differ from the population.
- In simple random sampling each element of the population has an equal chance of being included in the sample; in stratified random sampling, the population is divided into subpopulations (strata), and random samples are drawn from the strata.
- Probability sampling is the method of choice for obtaining a representative sample.

There are two basic approaches to sampling—nonprobability sampling and probability sampling. In **nonprobability sampling** we have no guarantee that each element has some chance of being included and no way to estimate the probability of each element's being included in the sample. In our library survey, if a researcher interviewed the first 10 students who entered the library, she would be using nonprobability sampling. Clearly, not all students would be equally likely to be at the library at that particular time, and some students would have essentially no chance of being included in the sample.

By contrast, if the researcher were to select 10 students randomly from the registrar's list of enrolled students, she would be using probability sampling. In **probability sampling** all students (elements) have an equal chance of being included in the sample. We can describe this researcher's approach as probability sampling because her sampling procedure (i.e., random selection from a predetermined list) allows all students to have an equal chance of being selected for the survey. Probability sampling is preferred because it allows researchers to estimate the likelihood that their sample findings differ from the findings they would have obtained by studying the whole population. Probability sampling is far superior to nonprobability sampling in ensuring that selected samples represent the population. Thus, the researcher who selects 10 students randomly from the registrar's list of students is more likely to have a representative sample than the researcher who bases her survey results on the first 10 students who show up at the library.

Nonprobability Sampling

Two types of nonprobability sampling are accidental sampling and purposive sampling. **Accidental sampling** involves selecting respondents primarily on the basis of their availability and willingness to respond. Newspapers often interview "the person on the street" and publish their comments. Their comments may make interesting reading, but their opinions are not likely to represent those of the wider community because accidental sampling was used. Accidental sampling also is involved when people respond to surveys in *Cosmopolitan* or other magazines because the magazine has to be available (and purchased), and people must be willing to send in their responses.

Crossen (1994) describes the drawbacks of another variation of accidental sampling, call-in surveys. Call-in surveys are used by TV and radio shows to poll the views of their audience. Those who happen to be "tuned in" and who are willing to call (and sometimes to pay the charge for calling a 900 number) make up the sample for these call-in surveys. Thus, it should be kept in mind that people who make calls in response to a call-in request differ from the general population not only because they are part of the particular show's audience, but they are motivated enough to make a call.

Crossen (1994) discusses a prime-time TV-news show that conducted a call-in survey with a question concerning the preferred location for the United Nations. It turns out that another survey research study involving about 500 randomly selected respondents also asked the same question. The question was whether the United Nations (UN) headquarters should remain in the United States. Of the 186,000 callers who responded, a solid majority (67%) wanted the UN *out of the United States*. Of the respondents to the survey research study (a random sample of individuals), a clear majority (72%) wanted the UN *to stay in the United States*. How could these two surveys yield such different—even opposite—results? Should we put more confidence in the results of the call-in survey because of the massive sample size? Absolutely not! A large accidental sample is just as likely to be an unrepresentative sample as is any other accidental sample. As a general rule, you should consider that accidental sampling will result in a biased sample unless you have strong evidence confirming the representativeness of the sample.

A second type of nonprobability sampling is **purposive sampling,** in which the investigator selects the elements to be included in the sample on the basis of their special characteristics. The individuals selected are commonly those who have an expertise or experiences related to the purpose of the study. You can think of these people being selected, on purpose, so as to understand their special experiences.

Connors and his colleagues selected a purposive sample in their study of "restraint" in alcohol and substance use (Connors, Collins, Dermen, & Koutsky, 1998). Restraint was first studied with overeaters, and in that context, refers to individuals' preoccupation with food and methods used to control and regulate food intake. Importantly, when regulation methods fail, highly restrained individuals may be more likely to binge. Connors et al. thought the restraint construct could describe alcoholics and substance abusers. Their survey sample consisted of 193 individuals seeking inpatient treatment for alcohol and other drug abuse. The patients completed questionnaires and interviews as part of admission procedures. Correlations among their measures allowed the researchers to conclude that the restraint concept may also be applied to individuals who abuse alcohol or other substances, as their survey responses indicated they are preoccupied with their substance and likely to abuse when their regulation methods fail. As you can see, Connors et al. were not interested in restraint in the general population, but in a very specific population. So, purposive sampling was ideally suited to the purpose of their study.

Probability Sampling   The distinguishing characteristic of probability sampling is that the researcher can specify, for each element of the population, the probability that it will be included in the sample. Two common types of probability sampling are simple random sampling and stratified random sampling. **Simple random sampling** is the basic technique of probability sampling. The most common definition of random sampling is that every element has an equal chance of being included in the sample. The procedures for simple random sampling are outlined in Box 4.1.

One critical decision that must be made in selecting a random sample is how large it should be. Earlier in this chapter we described the relationship between margin of error and sample size; the smaller the desired margin of error, the larger the sample size needs to be. For now, we will simply note that the size of a random sample needed to represent a population depends on the homogeneity (variability) of the population. College students in Ivy League schools represent a more homogeneous population than college students in all U.S. colleges in terms of their academic abilities. At one extreme, the most homogeneous population would be one in which all members of the population are identical. A sample of one would be representative of this population regardless of the size of the population. At the other extreme, the most heterogeneous population would be one in which each member was completely different from all other members on all characteristics. No sample, regardless of its size, could be representative of this population. Every individual would have to be included to describe such a heterogeneous population. Fortunately, the populations with which survey researchers work typically fall somewhere between these two extremes. Thus the representativeness of samples, like the joy of eating a piece of chocolate cake, increases with increasing size—up to a point.

The representativeness of a sample can often be increased by using stratified random sampling. In **stratified random sampling,** the population is divided into subpopulations called *strata* (singular, *stratum*) and random samples are drawn from each of these strata. There are two general ways to determine how many elements should be drawn from each stratum. One way (illustrated in the last example of Box 4.1) is to draw equal-sized samples from each stratum. The second way is to draw elements for the sample on a proportional basis. Consider a population of undergraduate students made up of 30% freshmen, 30% sophomores, 20% juniors, and 20% seniors (class years are the strata). A stratified random sample of 200 students drawn from this population would include 60 freshmen, 60 sophomores, 40 juniors, and 40 seniors. In contrast, drawing equal-sized samples from each stratum would result in 50 students for each class year. Which sample of 200 better represents the population?

In addition to its potential for increasing the representativeness of samples, stratified random sampling is useful when you want to describe specific portions of the population. For example, a simple random sample of 100 students would be sufficient to survey students' attitudes on a campus of 2,000 students. Suppose, however, your sample included only 2 of the 40 chemistry majors on campus, and you wish to describe the views of students according to different majors. Although this accurately reflects the proportion of chemistry majors in the campus population, it would be risky to use the views of only 2

BOX 4.1

SAMPLES OF RANDOM SAMPLES

The following names represent a scaled-down version of a sampling frame obtained from the registrar's office of a small college campus. Procedures for drawing both a simple random sample and a stratified random sample from this list are described below.

Adamski	F	Jr
Alderink	F	Sr
Baxter	M	Sr
Bowen	F	Sr
Broder	M	So
Brown	M	Jr
Bufford	M	So
Campbell	F	Fr
Carnahan	F	So
Cowan	F	Fr
Cushman	M	Sr
Dawes	M	Jr
Dennis	M	Sr
Douglas	F	Fr
Dunne	M	So
Fahey	M	Fr
Fedder	M	Fr
Foley	F	So
Grossman	F	Jr
Harris	F	Jr
Hedlund	F	So
Johnson	F	Fr
Klaaren	F	Jr
Ludwig	M	Fr
Nadeau	F	Sr
Nowaczyk	M	Jr
O'Keane	F	Sr
Osgood	M	So
Owens	F	So
Penzien	M	Jr
Powers	M	Sr
Ryan	M	Fr
Sawyer	M	Jr
Shaw	M	Sr
Sonders	F	Sr
Suffolk	F	So
Taylor	F	Fr
Thompson	M	Fr
Watterson	F	Jr
Zimmerman	M	So

Drawing a simple random sample

Step 1. Number each element in the sampling frame: Adamski would be number 1, Harris number 20, and Zimmerman number 40.

Step 2. Decide on the sample size you want to use. This is just an illustration, so we will use a sample size of 5.

Step 3. Choose a starting point in the Table of Random Numbers in Appendix A (a finger stab with your eyes closed works just fine—our stab came down at column 8, row 22 at the entry 26384). Because our sampling frame ranges only from 1 to 40, we had decided *prior* to entering the table to use the left two numbers in each set of five and to go across the table from left to right. We could just as easily have decided to go up, down, or from right to left. We could also have used the middle two or the last two digits of each set of five, but one should make these decisions before entering the table.

Step 4. Identify the numbers to be included in your sampling by moving across the table. We got the numbers 26, 06, 21, 15, and 32. Notice that numbers over 40 are ignored. The same would be true if we had come across a repetition of a number we had already selected.

chemistry students to represent all 40 chemistry majors (2 is too few). In this case (and more generally when a stratum is small in number), you could sample more chemistry majors to describe their views better. We can't say precisely how many to sample because, as we learned earlier, the sample size needed to represent a population depends on the heterogeneity of the population.

Step 5. List the names corresponding to the selected numbers. In our case the sample will include Nowaczyk, Brown, Hedlund, Dunne, and Ryan.

An even easier system, called *systematic sampling*, can be used to obtain a random sample. In this procedure you divide the sample size you want into the size of the sampling frame to obtain the value k. Then you select every kth element after choosing the first one randomly. In our example we want a sample size of 5 from a sampling frame of 40, so k would be 8. Thus we would choose one of the first eight people randomly and then take every eighth person thereafter. If Alderink were chosen from among the first 8, the remaining members of the sample would be Cowan, Foley, Nowaczyk, and Shaw. Note: This system should *not* be used if the sampling frame has a periodic organization—if, for example, you had a list of dormitory residents arranged by room and every tenth pair listed occupied a corner room. You can readily see that, in such a list, if your sampling interval was 10 you could end up with all people from corner rooms or no people from corner rooms.

Drawing a stratified random sample

Step 1. Arrange the sampling frame in strata. For our example we will stratify by class standing, so our sampling frame now looks like this:

Freshmen	Sophomores
1 Campbell	1 Broder
2 Cowan	2 Bufford
3 Douglas	3 Carnahan
4 Fahey	4 Dunne
5 Fedder	5 Foley
6 Johnson	6 Hedlund
7 Ludwig	7 Osgood

Freshmen	Sophomores
8 Ryan	8 Owens
9 Taylor	9 Suffolk
10 Thompson	10 Zimmerman

Juniors	Seniors
1 Adamski	1 Alderink
2 Brown	2 Baxter
3 Dawes	3 Bowen
4 Grossman	4 Cushman
5 Harris	5 Dennis
6 Klaaren	6 Nadeau
7 Nowaczyk	7 O'Keane
8 Penzien	8 Powers
9 Sawyer	9 Shaw
10 Watterson	10 Sonders

In our example the strata are equal in size, but this need not be the case.

Step 2. Number each element within each stratum, as has been done in the foregoing list.

Step 3. Decide on the overall sample size you want to use. For our example we will draw a sample of 8.

Step 4. Draw an equal-sized sample from each stratum such that you obtain the desired overall sample size. For our example this would mean drawing 2 from each stratum.

Step 5. Follow the steps for drawing a random sample and repeat for each stratum. We used the previously determined starting point (column 8, line 22) in the Table of Random Numbers, but this time we used the last digit in each set of five. The numbers identified for each stratum were: Freshmen (4 and 1), Sophomores (6 and 4), Juniors (7 and 9), and Seniors (2 and 9).

Step 6. List the names corresponding to the selected numbers. Our stratified random sample would include Fahey, Campbell, Hedlund, Dunne, Nowaczyk, Sawyer, Baxter, and Shaw.

SURVEY METHODS

- Three methods for obtaining survey data are mail surveys, personal interviews, and telephone interviews.

Selecting the sample is only one of several important decisions to make when conducting survey research. You also need to decide how you will obtain information from the respondents. There are three general methods: mail surveys, personal interviews, and telephone interviews. As was true of sampling techniques, there is no one best method for all circumstances; each survey method has its own advantages and disadvantages. The challenge you face is to select the method that best fits the problem you are studying.

Mail Surveys

- Although mail surveys are quick and convenient, they may have the problem of response bias when individuals fail to complete and return the survey.
- Due to response bias, the final sample for the survey may not represent the population.

Mail surveys are used to distribute self-administered questionnaires that respondents fill out on their own. One advantage of mail surveys is that they usually can be completed relatively quickly. Because they are self-administered, mail surveys also avoid the problems due to interviewer bias (to be defined in the next section). Among the three survey methods, mail surveys are the best for dealing with highly personal or embarrassing topics, especially when anonymity of respondents is preserved.

Unfortunately, there are many disadvantages to mail surveys. Some of these disadvantages are less serious than others. For instance, because respondents will not be able to ask questions, the questionnaire must be completely self-explanatory. A second less serious disadvantage is that the researcher has little control over the order in which the respondent answers the questions. The order of questions may affect how respondents answer certain questions. A serious problem with mail surveys, however, is one of bias—namely, response bias.

Response bias is a threat to the representativeness of a sample because not all respondents complete the survey. There are many reasons why this occurs. For example, respondents with literacy problems, low educational background, or vision problems may not complete the questionnaire; therefore, people with these characteristics may not be represented well in the final sample of respondents. Often, people included in a sample are too busy or not interested enough in the study to return a completed questionnaire. Low response rate (i.e., failure to complete and return the survey) is the major factor leading to response bias in mail surveys.

Low response rates necessarily produce smaller samples than the researcher intended. Generally, however, the size of the sample is not the most serious concern. The problem is that low response rates typically suggest response bias. Because of response bias, a carefully selected probability sample may become a nonprobability sample—an accidental sample in which individuals' availability and willingness determine whether they complete the survey. For example, for a survey concerning introductory psychology courses, Zechmeister and

Zechmeister (2000) used *Peterson's Guide to Four-Year Colleges 1998* to randomly select 250 universities and colleges in the United States and then sent surveys to their psychology departments. The response rate was 56%—surveys were returned from 140 psychology departments.

Unless the return rate is 100%, the potential for response bias exists regardless of how carefully the initial sample was selected. The researcher must demonstrate the absence of response bias. That is, the researcher needs to show that the sample of respondents who returned the survey is representative of the population, and that no segment of the population is overrepresented or underrepresented. For example, in Zechmeister and Zechmeister's survey, information from *Peterson's Guide to Four-Year Colleges 1998* allowed them to demonstrate that colleges for which a survey was returned were not different from colleges for which a survey was not returned.

The typical return rate for mail surveys is only around 30%. There are things you can do, however, to increase the return rate. Return rates will be highest when the questionnaire has a "personal touch," when it requires a minimum of effort for the respondent, when the topic of the survey is of intrinsic interest to the respondent, and when the respondent identifies in some way with the organization or researcher sponsoring the survey. Warwick and Lininger (1975) describe a survey that met these requirements. About 100,000 members of women's religious congregations in the United States were surveyed. The study was sponsored and supported by the religious congregations, it was conducted by a visible and respected member of one of the religious orders, and the subject matter was of great interest to the respondents. The result was an almost saintly response rate.

FIGURE 4.5   The three general methods for conducting surveys (telephone interviews, personal interviews, and mail surveys) have both advantages and disadvantages.

Personal Interviews

- Although costly, personal interviews allow researchers to gain more control over how the survey is administered.
- Interviewer bias occurs when survey responses are recorded inaccurately or when interviewers guide individuals' responses.

When personal interviews are used to collect survey data, respondents are usually contacted in their homes or in a shopping mall, and trained interviewers administer the questionnaire. The personal interview allows greater flexibility in asking questions than does the mail survey. In a personal interview the respondent can obtain clarification when questions are unclear and the trained interviewer can follow-up incomplete or ambiguous answers to open-ended questions. The interviewer controls the order of questions and can ensure that all respondents complete the questions in the same order. Traditionally, the response rate to personal interviews has been higher than for mail surveys.

The advantages of using personal interviews are impressive, but there are also a few disadvantages. Increasing fear of urban crime and an increasing number of households with no one home during the day have reduced the attractiveness of using personal interviews in the home. A significant disadvantage of conducting personal interviews is the cost. The use of trained interviewers is expensive in terms of both money and time. Perhaps the most critical disadvantage of personal interviews involves the potential for interviewer bias. The interviewer should be a neutral medium through which questions and answers are transmitted. **Interviewer bias** occurs when the interviewer records only selected portions of the respondents' answers or tries to adjust the wording of a question to "fit" the respondent. For example, suppose a respondent in a survey about television states, "The biggest problem with TV shows is too much violence." Interview bias would occur if the interviewer writes down "problem with TV is violence" instead of the respondent's full response. In a follow-up question, interview bias also would occur if the interviewer asked, "By violence do you mean murders, muggings, and rapes?" A more neutral probe would allow the respondent to describe what he or she means by asking, "Could you elaborate on what you mean by violence?"

The best protection against interviewer bias is to employ highly motivated, well-paid interviewers who are trained to follow question wording exactly, to record responses accurately, and to use follow-up questions judiciously. Interviewers should also be given a detailed list of instructions about how difficult or confusing situations are to be handled. Finally, interviewers should be closely supervised by the director of the survey project. The decision to use personal interviews is not one survey researchers take lightly.

A frequently used variation of the personal interview is the *focused interview* (also called *focus group*). Rather than interviewing a single person, the focused interview is done in a group setting, and the researcher tries to learn from the respondents the reasons for the attitudes or opinions they hold. Focused interviews are used extensively in market research to determine consumers' reactions to current or new products and services. Focused interviews are increasingly being used as part of the strategic planning process by civic organizations, colleges and universities, and churches. There is less emphasis in this approach on obtaining a quantitative summary of the views across all respondents. Instead, the goal is to obtain a qualitative description of the ideas that emerge from a guided group discussion.

Telephone Interviews

* Despite some disadvantages, telephone interviews have become the method of choice for completing brief surveys.

The prohibitive cost of personal interviews and difficulties supervising interviewers have led survey researchers to turn to telephone interviews. Phone interviewing met with considerable criticism when it was first used because of serious limitations on the sampling frame of potential respondents. Many people had unlisted numbers, and the poor and those in rural areas were unlikely to have a phone. By 1979, however, more than 95% of all households had telephones, and households with unlisted numbers could be reached using random-digit dialing. Telephone interviewing also provides better access to dangerous neighborhoods, locked buildings, and respondents available only during evening hours (have you ever been asked to complete a telephone survey during dinner?). Interviews can be completed more quickly when contacts are made by phone, and interviewers can be better supervised when all interviews are conducted from one location.

The telephone survey, like the other two survey methods, is not without its drawbacks. A possible selection bias exists when respondents are limited to those who have telephones and the problem of interviewer bias remains. There is a limit to how long respondents are willing to stay on the phone, and individuals may respond differently when talking to a "faceless voice." Hippler and Schwarz (1987) suggest that people take less time to form judgments during phone interviews and they may have difficulty remembering the response options offered by the interviewer. Moreover, extensive use of phone solicitation for selling products and requesting contributions has led many people to be less willing to be interviewed. And many people who are working two jobs are rarely at home to answer the phone. In spite of these limitations and perhaps others you can think of, the telephone interview is the method of choice for nearly all brief surveys.

SURVEY-RESEARCH DESIGNS

* The three types of survey design are the cross-sectional design, successive independent samples design, and the longitudinal design.

You are no doubt developing a sense that doing survey research, like doing all types of research, requires making a series of choices and decisions. For example, survey researchers decide who to survey when they choose a sampling plan, and they decide how to administer the survey when they choose a survey method. In this section we describe one of the most important decisions survey researchers must make—the choice of a research design. A survey-research design is the overall plan or structure used to conduct the entire study. There are three general types of survey-research designs: the cross-sectional design, the successive independent samples design, and the longitudinal design. As you probably already suspected, there is no all-purpose research design that meets every survey need; the choice of design must be tailored to the objectives of the study.

Cross-Sectional Design

- In the cross-sectional design one or more samples are drawn from the population(s) at one point in time.
- Cross-sectional designs allow researchers to describe the characteristics of a population or the differences between two or more populations, and researchers can make predictions based on the correlational survey data.

One of the most commonly used survey-research designs is the cross-sectional design. In a **cross-sectional design,** one or more samples are drawn from the population *at one time*. Information collected from the sample(s) is used to describe the population at that point in time. A researcher who gave questionnaires to samples of 20-year-olds, 30-year-olds, and 40-year-olds, asking about solutions to the homeless problem in the United States, would be using a cross-sectional design. So, too, would a researcher who sampled male and female college students and asked their opinions about various career possibilities following graduation.

Goodman and her colleagues (1997) used a cross-sectional design in their nationwide study of mental disorders in 9- to 17-year-olds. The purpose of their study was to determine if youths who receive outpatient mental health services for their disorder differ in systematic ways from the larger population of children and adolescents with mental disorders. They questioned whether previous research findings observed for samples of youths who receive treatment ("clinical samples") may be generalized to describe youth who do not obtain treatment, particularly because only a small proportion of children and adolescents with mental disorders receive treatment.

To answer this question they examined data collected in a study sponsored by the National Institute of Mental Health (NIMH) on mental disorders in children and adolescents. A community-based sample of parent-youth pairs from Connecticut, Georgia, New York, and Puerto Rico completed surveys and were interviewed in their homes. A total of 1,285 parent-youth pairs participated. (Thus, you can see that even cross-sectional designs are not necessarily simple or quick.) The focus in a cross-sectional survey is description—describing the characteristics of a population or the differences among two or more populations. Goodman et al. made many observations to describe differences between youths with mental disorders who received outpatient mental health services and youths with mental disorders who did not receive treatment.

Of their sample, 747 (58%) of the youths had no mental disorder (within the past 6 months); however 25 (3%) of these had received mental health services. A total of 535 (42%) were diagnosed with some type of mental disorder based on the structured interview; of these, only 69 (13%) received outpatient mental health services. How did the 69 children and adolescents with mental disorders who received treatment differ from the 466 who did not? Goodman et al. looked at a number of variables, and found that the youths who received mental health services were more likely to be identified as non-Hispanic White relative to other ethnic groups, and were less likely to be prepubertal girls. They were also judged to be more impaired, less competent, and more likely to have two or more disorders. Their parents differed too. Parents of youths who received treatment were more educated but were less satisfied with their family life, did not monitor their children, and were more likely to use mental health services themselves. Based on these data, Goodman et al. concluded that research samples of youths who receive treatment are not representative of all youths who have a mental disorder. Thus, research based on clinical samples may have limited generalizability to the larger population of children and adolescents with mental disorders.

Cross-sectional designs are ideally suited for the descriptive and predictive goals of correlational research. Surveys are also used to assess changes in attitudes or behaviors over time and to determine the effect of some naturally occurring event, such as the passage of a law to raise the drinking age. For these purposes the cross-sectional design is not the method of choice. Rather, research designs are needed that systematically sample respondents over time. Two such designs are discussed in the next two sections.

Successive Independent Samples Design

- In the successive independent samples design, different samples of respondents from the population complete the survey over a time period.
- The successive independent samples design allows researchers to study changes in a population over time.
- The successive independent samples design does not allow researchers to infer how individual respondents have changed over time.
- A problem with the successive independent samples design occurs when the samples drawn from the population are not equally representative of the population—that is, the samples are not comparable.

In the **successive independent samples design,** a series of cross-sectional surveys are conducted over time (successively). The samples are independent because a different sample of respondents completes the survey at each point in time. There are two key ingredients: (1) the same set of questions should be asked of each sample of respondents, and (2) the different samples should be drawn from the same population. In this way, responses can be compared over time. This design is most appropriate when the major goal of the study is to describe changes in the attitudes or behaviors of members of a population over time. We already mentioned one such successive independent samples design, that by Plous (1998), who surveyed different groups of animal rights activists who attended a national march in 1990 and 1996.

As another example, consider how a researcher might examine the changes in values and goals of male and female college freshmen over time. One way to do this would be to survey students at one point in time (e.g., 1990), then 10 years later (i.e., in 2000) ask *different samples* of college freshmen the same questions. In fact, such a study has been conducted since 1966, and every year some 350,000 full-time freshmen from a nationally representative sample of over 700 colleges and universities are surveyed (Astin, Parrott, Korn, & Sax, 1997). This research represents the largest and longest empirical study of higher education in the United States, with over 1,500 universities and over 9 million students participating during the 30-plus years of the study. Students are asked approximately 40 questions covering a number of topics, and although some changes have occurred in the survey over the 30 years, many questions have been asked each year, making this an excellent example of a successive independent samples design.

What can be said about changes in students' values and goals during this time period? Astin et al. (1997) reported the results for the portion of the survey in which students are asked to rate the importance of different values. Two values were of particular interest: "the importance of developing a meaningful philosophy of life" and "the importance of being very well off financially" (p. 12). Figure 4.6 displays the results for the percentage of students who endorsed these values as "essential" or "very important." In the late 1960s over 80% of students indicated that developing a meaningful philosophy of life was essential—in fact, this was the top value endorsed by students. In contrast, being well-off financially was essential to less than 45% of the students, and ranked fifth or sixth among students' values during the late 1960s. In 1996, the position of these values was reversed. Being well-off financially was the top value, with 74.1% of students endorsing this as essential. At sixth place in 1996 was developing a meaningful philosophy of life, with 42.1% of students endorsing this as an essential value. As can be seen in Figure 4.6, these contrasting trends in values began to shift in the early 1970s, crossed in 1977, and traded places in the late 1980s. Since then they have remained relatively unchanged. Using mediational analyses (described earlier), Astin et al. attributed some of these changes to increases in television viewing during the same time period, and suggested that the materialistic values celebrated in televisions shows such as *Dallas* and *Lifestyles of the Rich and Famous* promote materialistic values among viewers. Astin et al. concluded that "for many young people today, the making of money has become a kind of 'philosophy of life' in itself" (p. 14).

The successive independent samples design does have limitations. As way of illustration, the data presented in Table 4.2 represent the results of a successive independent samples design measuring people's trust in government in 1972 and 1978 (You may recall that Watergate occurred during this time period). Clearly, more Americans were cynical in 1978 than in 1972. How can we interpret

FIGURE 4.6   Contrasting trends in values for college freshmen from 1966–1996.
Source: Figure 7 (p. 13), Astin et al. (1997).

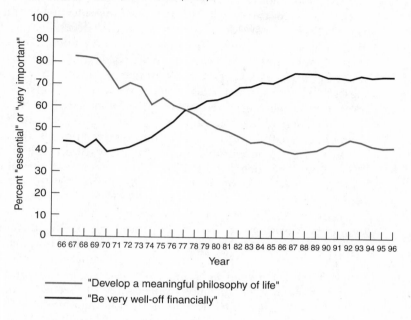

"Develop a meaningful philosophy of life"

"Be very well-off financially"

this finding? Consider the change from 36% to 52% in the "cynical" category from 1972 to 1978. We might be tempted to conclude 36% of the population still maintained their cynical views, and to that group we can add 16% of the population who changed their view to become more cynical by 1978. Who are these additional people? Well, we could also see that 38% of the population was trusting in 1972, but this dropped by 19% in 1978 (down to 19% "trusting" in 1978). Wouldn't it be easy to conclude that among the 19% of individuals who were no longer trusting, 16% changed their views to be cynical, 2% changed their views to "mixed" feelings, and 1% failed to answer? After all, that's how the numbers seem to add up!

TABLE 4.2   TRUST IN GOVERNMENT, 1972–1978*

	1972	1978
Cynical	36%	52%
Mixed	24%	26%
Trusting	38%	19%
Not answered	2%	3%
Number of cases	(2,285)	(2,304)

*Data taken from Campbell (1981), Appendix Table 8.

What we must remember, however, is that the people surveyed in 1978 were not the same people surveyed in 1972! The extent to which individuals change their views over time can be determined only by testing the *same* individuals on both occasions. We cannot determine in the successive independent samples design who has changed their views or by how much. The purpose of the successive independent samples design is to describe changes over time in the distribution of *population* characteristics (e.g., cynicism in the population), not to describe changes in *individual* respondents. Accordingly, the successive independent samples design is not very helpful in ferreting out the reasons for observed changes like those shown in Table 4.2. (As you will soon see, another survey design, the longitudinal design, is more appropriate in these situations.)

A second potential problem with the successive independent samples design arises when the successive samples are not representative of the same population. Imagine that the researchers who did the surveys reported in Table 4.2 had sampled affluent Americans in 1972 and poor Americans in 1978. Their comparisons of Americans' attitudes toward government over this time period would be meaningless. That is, they wouldn't be able to state that the population had become more cynical over time because it's possible that the degree of cynicism differs for affluent and poor Americans, which could also account for the difference between 1972 and 1978 results. The affluent and poor samples illustrate the problem of *noncomparable successive samples*. Changes in the population across time can be described accurately only when the successive independent samples represent the same population. Thus, it is important to assure that the successive independent samples are comparable. Although sophisticated statistical procedures exist to help unravel the problems associated with noncomparable successive samples, the best solution is to avoid the problem by carefully selecting successive samples that represent one population.

Longitudinal Design

- In the longitudinal design, the same respondents are surveyed over time in order to examine changes in individual respondents.
- Because of the correlational nature of survey data, it is difficult to identify the causes of individuals' changes over time.
- As people drop out of the study over time (respondent mortality), the final sample may no longer be comparable to the original sample or represent the population.
- Individuals' survey responses may be influenced by the fact that they have completed the survey on more than one occasion.

The distinguishing characteristic of the **longitudinal design** is that the *same* sample of respondents is surveyed more than once. For example, a researcher interested in changes in college students' attitudes about their college experience might give a questionnaire to a sample of students when they begin their college studies, and then give *the same questionnaire to the same individuals* after they complete each year of college.

The longitudinal design has two important advantages. First, the investigator can determine the direction and extent of change for individual respondents. Also, because changes in individuals' responses are assessed, it's easier to investigate reasons for attitude or behavior changes. Second, the longitudinal design is the best survey design when a researcher wishes to assess the effect of some naturally occurring event. For example, by measuring people's attitudes before and after a national election, the researcher can assess the effect of this event. (For further discussion of assessing the effects of naturally occurring events, see Chapter 10.)

Heatherton, Mahamedi, Striepe, Field, and Keel (1997) used the longitudinal design to investigate changes in attitudes and behaviors related to eating during the transition from college to early adulthood. Although much is known about eating disorders in adolescents and college students, Heatherton and his colleagues were interested in learning how disordered eating may progress over time as individuals settle down, marry, establish careers, begin families, and importantly, gain a stronger sense of identity. These researchers hypothesized that as individuals change their roles and life goals during their 20s, an emphasis on physical appearance may decrease, which would decrease the prevalence of eating problems. To test their hypothesis they randomly selected a sample of 800 women and 400 men from a private northeastern college in 1982 to complete a survey about eating and dieting. Their response rate was 78% ($N = 625$) for women and 69% ($N = 276$) for men. In 1992, they contacted these same individuals (with the help of the alumni office) and surveyed them again about their eating attitudes and behaviors. The distinguishing characteristic of the longitudinal design is the fact that the same individuals were surveyed in each phase of the study.

As you may imagine, longitudinal designs involve a massive effort. The potential power of such an effort, however, is that researchers can examine changes within individuals over time. In Heatherton et al.'s (1997) study, results indicated different changes in eating and weight gain for women and men. Survey responses suggested that during the decade since college, women's eating disorder symptoms, chronic dieting, and body dissatisfaction decreased. However, despite these decreases, women's dissatisfaction with their body and their desire to lose weight remained high. Men, in contrast, rarely had problems with eating and weight during college. Ten years later, however, they had experienced weight gain (an average of almost 12 pounds, compared to women's average gain of 4 pounds). Men also reported increased dieting and symptoms of disordered eating on the 1992 survey, although this was still low relative to women.

Heatherton et al. (1997) made some interesting observations that are relevant to our understanding of longitudinal surveys. Heatherton et al. proposed that decreases in women's eating problems reflect their maturation during their 20s, changes in their roles, and being away from the college campus (and the pressures to be thin that occur on college campuses). It's possible, however, that other processes may account for changes within the individuals in the sample. Using a successive independent samples design in which *separate* samples of college students were surveyed in 1982 and 1992, Heatherton, Nichols, Mahamedi, and Keel (1995) noted that eating-disordered symptoms and body dissatisfaction also were lower for the college students in the 1992 sample relative to the 1982 sample. These findings suggest that decreases in eating-disordered attitudes and behaviors may reflect changes that are occurring at a societal level. Heatherton et al. (1997) suggested that increasing information about eating disorders presented in the media (e.g., accounts of the late Princess Diana's struggle with bulimia) may explain these decreases. As you can see, one potential problem with longitudinal survey designs is that it is difficult to pinpoint the exact *causes* for individuals' changes over time, as it is not clear whether the longitudinal changes reflect maturational processes within the individuals, or societal changes about eating attitudes and behaviors.[2]

Another potential problem with longitudinal designs is that it can be difficult to obtain a sample of respondents who will agree to participate in a longitudinal study, which more often than not means a long-term study. In many studies the respondents may be asked to complete several lengthy surveys at regular intervals over a number of years. People are often hesitant to make the commitment of time necessary to complete such an extensive project.

Even when the respondents do agree to participate, there can be further problems. You might think this design solves the problem of noncomparable samples (i.e., when samples are drawn from different populations) that can occur when successive independent samples are used. After all, in the longitudinal design the same people participate over and over, so of course the sample represents the same population each time. Unfortunately, successive samples in a longitudinal design are identical *only if* all members of the original sample participate throughout the study. This is not likely to be the case. For example, in the Heatherton et al. (1997) study there were 901 participants in the original 1982 sample. In 1992, only 724 (80%) of the original participants returned a useable survey. Unless all the respondents in the original sample complete all phases of a longitudinal design, there is a possible problem due to *respondent mortality* (sometimes literal, but most often figurative). Respondent mortality is probably the most serious disadvantage of the longitudinal design because as samples decrease over time, they are less likely to represent the original population from which the sample was drawn. It is usually possible, however, to determine whether the final sample is comparable to the original sample in a longitudinal design. The characteristics of nonrespondents in the follow-up phase(s) are known because they participated in the original sample. Therefore, we can look at their original responses to see how these individuals may differ from those who continued their participation.

---

[2]Heatherton et al. (1997) noted that because the decreases in problem eating were larger among individuals in the longitudinal survey than in the successive independent sample survey, maturational processes likely were operating to decrease individuals' problem eating over time, in addition to societal changes.

Paradoxically, problems can also arise in longitudinal designs because the same respondents are interviewed more than once. One possible problem is that respondents may strive heroically to be consistent across interviews. This can be particularly troublesome if the study is designed to assess changes in respondents' attitudes! Although their attitudes have actually changed, people may report their original attitudes in an effort to appear consistent (perhaps they know researchers value reliability). Another potential problem is that the initial interview may sensitize respondents to the issue under investigation. For example, consider a longitudinal design used to assess students' concern about crime on campus. Once the study starts, participants may pay more attention to crime reports than they normally would. You might recognize this as an illustration of reactive measurement—people behaving differently because they know they are participating in a study (see Chapter 3).

Rather than trying to be heroically consistent in their eating attitudes and behaviors over time, Heatherton et al. (1997) noted that their participants may have been reluctant to report that they were having the same problems with eating as when they were in college. Thus, the decreases the researchers observed in problem eating during the 10-year period may be due to the fact that "women who are approaching their thirties may be embarrassed to admit they are experiencing problems typically associated with adolescence" (p. 124). When survey respondents are asked to report their attitudes and behaviors, researchers must be alert to reasons why their respondents' reports may not correspond to their actual behavior.

CORRESPONDENCE BETWEEN REPORTED AND ACTUAL BEHAVIOR

- Survey research involves reactive measurement because individuals are aware their responses are being recorded.
- Social desirability refers to pressure respondents sometimes feel to respond as they "should" believe rather than how they actually believe.
- Researchers can assess the accuracy of survey responses by comparing these results with archival data or behavioral observations.

Regardless of how carefully survey data are collected and analyzed, the value of these data depends on the truthfulness of the respondents' answers to the survey questions. Should we believe survey responses reflect people's true thoughts, opinions, feelings, and behavior? The question of the truthfulness of verbal reports has been debated extensively, and no clear-cut conclusion has emerged. Judd et al. (1991) note, however, that in everyday life we regularly accept the verbal reports of others as valid. If a friend tells you she enjoyed reading a certain novel, you may ask why, but you do not usually question whether the statement accurately reflects your friend's feelings. However, in everyday life there are some situations in which we *do* have reason to suspect the truthfulness of someone's statements. When shopping for a used car, for instance, we might not always want to trust the "sales pitch" we receive. Generally, however, we accept people's remarks at their face value unless we have reason to suspect otherwise. We apply the same standards to the information we obtain from survey responses.

By its very nature, survey research involves reactive measurement. Respondents not only know their responses are being recorded, but they may also suspect their responses may prompt some social, political, or commercial action. Hence, pressures are strong for people to respond as they "should" believe and not as they actually believe. The term often used to describe these pressures is **social desirability** (the term "politically correct" refers to similar pressures). For example, if respondents are asked whether they favor giving help to the needy, they may respond affirmatively because they believe this is the most socially acceptable attitude to have. As suggested in Chapter 3, the best protection against reactive measurement is to be aware of its existence.

Sometimes researchers can examine the accuracy of verbal reports directly by using archival data or unobtrusive measures (topics described more fully in Chapter 5). Judd et al. (1991) describe research by Parry and Crossley (1950) wherein responses obtained by experienced interviewers were subsequently compared with archival records for the same respondents kept by various agencies. Their comparisons revealed that 40% of respondents gave inaccurate reports to a question concerning contributions to United Fund (a charitable organization), 25% reported they had registered and voted in a recent election (but they did not), and 17% misrepresented their age. A pessimist might find these figures disturbingly high, but an optimist would note that a majority of respondents' reports were accurate even when social desirability pressures were high, as in the question pertaining to charitable contributions.

Researchers also assess the accuracy of verbal reports by directly observing respondents' behavior. The field experiment done by Latané and Darley (1970) illustrates the problem. They found that bystanders are more likely to help a victim when the bystander is alone than when other witnesses are present. Subsequently, a second group of participants was asked whether the presence of others would influence the likelihood they would help a victim. They uniformly said that it would not. Thus, individuals' verbal reports may not correspond well to behavior. A similar example comes from Milgram's (1974) series of experiments on people's obedience to authority. In one of his experiments, Milgram found that 63% of the men he tested (ages 20 to 50) complied fully with instructions to administer increasing levels of shock to a learner each time the learner made a mistake. The 63% who complied fully applied the highest level of shocks used in the experiment. Prior to doing this experiment Milgram asked a different group of people what they would do in this situation. Most said they would certainly stop before reaching the highest level of shock. Research findings such as these should make us extremely cautious of reaching conclusions about people's behavior solely on the basis of verbal reports. Of course, we should be equally cautious of reaching conclusions about what people think solely on the basis of direct observation of their behavior.

We want to make one final point about the usefulness of survey results. The process of doing a survey has much in common with the process of writing an essay. You often begin with a grand topic that must be focused so that it can be covered manageably. As you narrow your focus, you may sometimes have the feeling that your original topic has been lost or at least made trivial. No essay can capture all aspects of a given topic, nor can a 20-item or even 200-item questionnaire. Survey research, like the rest of the scientific enterprise, is built on faith that compiling reliable findings in a series of limited studies will eventually lead to increased understanding of the important broader issues we face.

SUMMARY

Correlational research represents a general approach to research that focuses on assessing the covariation among naturally occurring variables. The goal of correlational research is to identify predictive relationships by using correlations or more sophisticated statistical techniques. The results of correlational research also have implications for decision making, as reflected in the appropriate use of actuarial prediction. The greatest limitation of correlational research is the problem of interpreting causal relationships.

Survey research illustrates the principles of correlational research and it provides an accurate and efficient means for describing people's thoughts, opinions, and feelings. Surveys differ in purpose and scope, but they generally involve sampling. Results obtained for a carefully selected sample are used to describe the entire population of interest. Surveys also involve the use of a predetermined set of questions, generally in the form of a questionnaire.

Sampling is a procedure whereby a specified number of elements are drawn from a sampling frame that represents an actual list of the possible elements in the population. Our ability to generalize from the sample to the population depends critically on the representativeness of the sample, the extent to which the sample has the same characteristics as the population. Representativeness is best achieved by using probability sampling rather than nonprobability sampling. In simple random sampling, the most common type of probability sampling, every element is equally likely to be included in the sample. Stratified random sampling is used when analysis of subsamples is of interest.

There are three general survey methods: mail surveys, personal interviews, and telephone interviews. Mail surveys avoid problems of interviewer bias and are especially well suited for examining personal or embarrassing topics. The problem of response bias is a serious limitation of mail surveys. Personal interviews and phone surveys usually have higher response rates and provide greater flexibility. The phone survey is the method of choice for most brief surveys.

Survey research is carried out according to an overall plan called a research design. There are three survey research designs: the cross-sectional design, the successive independent samples design, and the longitudinal design. Cross-sectional designs focus on describing the characteristics of a population or the differences between two or more populations at one point in time. Describing changes in attitudes or opinions over time requires the use of successive independent samples or longitudinal designs. The longitudinal design is generally preferred because it allows the researcher to assess changes for specific individuals and avoids the problem of noncomparable successive samples.

Survey results, like those of other verbal reports, can be accepted at face value unless there is reason to do otherwise, such as pressures on respondents to give socially desirable responses. People's behavior does not always conform to what they say they would do, so survey research will never replace direct observation. However, survey research does provide an excellent way to examine people's attitudes and opinions.

KEY CONCEPTS

correlational research
correlation
correlation coefficient
margin of error
actuarial prediction
population
sampling frame
sample
element
representativeness
biased sample
selection bias
nonprobability sampling

probability sampling
accidental sampling
purposive sampling
simple random sampling
stratified random sampling
response bias
interviewer bias
cross-sectional design
successive independent
  samples design
longitudinal design
social desirability

REVIEW QUESTIONS

1 Describe the major goal of correlational research, and briefly explain how correlational research is different from experimental research.
2 What two types of information do you gain by knowing the sign and the numerical value of a correlation coefficient?
3 Describe the difference between a mediating variable and a moderating variable.
4 Describe the Likert method for developing a scale.
5 Identify at least two factors beyond the margin of error of the sample that you would need to know to be sure that a survey's results are interpretable.
6 Describe briefly one way you could measure a test's reliability and one way you could measure a test's validity.
7 Explain how clinical and actuarial prediction could be used in deciding which students to admit to your college or university. What is the relative predictive accuracy of these two approaches?
8 What information is needed to address the ethical issue that arises when the sponsoring agency of a survey has a vested interest in how the results turn out?
9 What two characteristics do surveys have in common regardless of the purpose for which the survey has been done?

10 What is the greatest threat to the interpretability of the results of a survey when an accidental sample is used?

11 Explain the relationship between the homogeneity of the population from which a sample is to be drawn and the size of a sample needed to ensure representativeness.

12 What factors would you consider in deciding whether to use a mail survey, personal interviews, or telephone interviews for your survey research project?

13 What aspect of a survey research project is threatened by response bias and what factor contributes most to the potential for response bias?

14 What would you need to be assured of before interpreting group changes in attitudes over time that were found in using a successive independent samples design?

15 Which survey research design would you choose if you want to assess the direction and extent of change over time in the opinions of individual respondents?

16 How would you respond if someone told you that survey results were useless because people did not respond truthfully to questions on surveys?

CHALLENGE QUESTIONS

1 Survey research is difficult to do well, and this can be especially the case when the topic is people's sexual attitudes and practices. For a book focusing in part on women's sexuality, an author mailed 100,000 questionnaires to women who belonged to a variety of women's groups in 43 states. These groups ranged from feminist organizations to church groups to garden clubs. The author's questionnaire included 127 essay questions. The author received responses from 4,500 women. Findings in this survey included that 70% of respondents married five years or more reported having extramarital affairs and that 95% of respondents felt emotionally harassed by the men they love.

  A The final sample in this study is large (4,500). Is this sufficient to assure the representativeness of the sample? If not, what survey research problem lessens the sample's representativeness?

  B Is it possible on the basis of your response to Part A of this question to argue that any conclusions drawn by the author from her data are incorrect? What could you do to determine whether the results were correct?

2 Dual-income couples now outnumber those with single incomes, and this has led researchers to examine how dual career demands affect relationships. A survey research study on this topic was described in *Psychology Today* (1988). The researchers found that among dual-career couples there was a positive correlation such that couples who spent greater amounts of time together found their relationship more satisfactory.

  A Presume that this finding is a reliable one. What two alternative explanations would you propose for why this correlation exists.

  B What moderator variables could you use to explore possible causal relationships underlying this correlation? Be sure to specify how you think the size or direction of the original correlation will change as you change the values of the moderator variable.

3 Two student researchers have been asked to do a survey to determine the attitudes of other students toward fraternities and sororities on campus. There are 2,000 students in the school. About 25% of the students belong to the Greek organizations and 75% do not. The two student researchers agree that they should use a cross-sectional

design for their study. But they disagree about what sampling plan is best for the study. One researcher thinks they should draw a stratified random sample of 200 students: 100 from among those students who belong to Greek organizations and 100 from among the independent students. The second researcher thinks they should draw one simple random sample of 100 students from the campus as a whole. Comment critically on these two sampling plans. Finally, develop your own sampling plan if you decide that neither of the ones proposed so far is optimal.

4   A task force has been established at a small liberal arts college under the direction of the Dean of Students to examine the quality of students' experiences on their campus. The task force decides to do a survey to determine students' knowledge of and their perceptions of the fairness of the judicial system used to enforce the rules in the living units on campus. The questionnaire for the survey included personal questions asking students to describe their own experiences when they had violated college policies or when they had known other students who had violated college policies. A stratified random sample was drawn from the Registrar's list of full-time students living on and off campus. The sample size was 400 on a campus with 2,000 full-time students. Questionnaires were returned by 160 students for a response rate of 40%. One important finding from the survey was that over a third of the respondents rated the judicial system as unfair. The task force met to decide whether to include the survey findings such as this one in its final report to the Dean of Students.

A   Was the initial sample of 400 students likely to be representative of the population of 2,000 full-time students? Why or why not?

B   Identify a potential survey research problem that could be present in this study that would lead the task force to be concerned that the final sample was not representative of the population of 2,000 students.

C   Using only the evidence that the response rate for the survey was 40% the task force concluded that the final sample was not representative of the population of students. They further decided that the ratings of the judicial system as unfair by more than a third of the students was an incorrect overestimate. Do you agree that the finding represents an incorrect estimate? Why or why not?

D   While the task force was meeting to discuss their final report, one member of the task force expressed the opinion that students' responses were unlikely to have been truthful and so the results of the survey were useless and should not be reported at all. The director of the task force calls on you to respond to this statement. What would you say?

Answer to Challenge Question 1

A   In general, larger sample sizes do make it more likely that the sample will be representative. The problem in this study is that the final sample (though large) represents a low response rate from the original sample of 100,000 (4.5%). The low response rate and the topic of the survey make it likely that a response bias is present in this survey such that the sample of 4,500 women cannot be considered representative.

B   The likely problem of response bias does not make it possible to argue that the conclusions drawn by the author are incorrect. Neither can the author argue on the basis of this sample that the conclusions are correct. We simply cannot know based on this evidence whether the conclusions are correct or incorrect. There is at least one good way to determine if the results of this survey were correct. You would need to obtain from the literature the results of one or more surveys on women's sexual attitudes and practices. It would be essential that these other surveys had used representative samples of women. Then, you would compare the results of this survey with those of the other surveys. Only if the results of the present survey corresponded to those of the surveys with the representative samples would we consider the results of the present survey correct. Of course, you could also carry out your own survey, one that avoids the problems that are present in this survey, and determine whether your results are similar to those of this author-researcher!

PEARSON PRODUCT-MOMENT CORRELATION COEFFICIENT *r*

The degree of relationship between two variables for the same sample of subjects is determined by calculating a correlation coefficient. If the two measures both represent at least an interval scale of measurement (see Chapter 3), then the Pearson Product-Moment Correlation Coefficient *r* is used. The computational formula for the Pearson *r* is as follows:

$$r = \frac{\sum XY - \dfrac{(\sum X)(\sum Y)}{n}}{\sqrt{\left(\sum X^2 - \dfrac{(\sum X)^2}{n}\right)\left(\sum Y^2 - \dfrac{(\sum Y)^2}{n}\right)}}$$

where
X = raw scores for the first variable,
Y = raw scores for the second variable,
Σ = sum of scores, and
n = number of pairs of scores.

Unobtrusive Measures of Behavior

CHAPTER OUTLINE

OVERVIEW
PHYSICAL TRACES
Rationale
Types of Physical Traces
Problems and Limitations
ARCHIVAL DATA
Rationale
Types of Archival Data
Content Analysis
Illustrative Uses of Archival Data
Problems and Limitations
ETHICAL ISSUES AND UNOBTRUSIVE MEASURES
SUMMARY

OVERVIEW

Thus far, we have emphasized how the behavioral scientist learns about behavior through some form of direct observation (Chapter 3) or from data obtained through survey research (Chapter 4). In this chapter we consider some alternatives to these major approaches to studying behavior. The alternatives, called **unobtrusive measures,** tell us about behavior indirectly. The researcher obtains data unobtrusively, frequently with the individuals being studied not present during the investigation. Although these alternative methods are often important in themselves, they also frequently provide a means of confirming the validity of conclusions reached on the basis of direct observation or surveys. Thus, unobtrusive measures can make important contributions to the multimethod approach to research.

One type of unobtrusive measure is the examination of **physical traces** produced by individuals' behavior. Consider, for example, the possibility that Latin Americans differ from North Americans in their concern for punctuality. Possible cultural differences in the importance of punctuality could be investigated by surveying people in both North American and Latin American countries as to how they feel about concerts or sporting events that begin later than the scheduled starting time. However, an alternative, unobtrusive, method would be to examine clocks in cities of North America and South America. It seems reasonable to assume that people's concern for time will be reflected in how accurately they set their clocks. In fact, researchers found that public clocks (those located in banks) in a Brazilian city were less accurate than those in a similar-sized city in the United States (Levine, West, & Reis, 1980). Although there may be alternative explanations for this finding, differences in this physical-trace measure support the notion that cultural differences in concern for being on time do exist. You may remember from the discussion in Chapter 1 that Levine (1990) also used accuracy of public clocks to help define the "pace of life" of cities and countries around the world. Direct observation revealed that the walking speed of a country's citizens correlated positively with the accuracy of the country's public clocks.

Archives constitute another important unobtrusive source of information about behavior. **Archival data** are obtained by inspecting the records and documents produced by society, as well as by analyzing reports in the media. For example, researchers have claimed that analyses of mortality data reveal a lower than expected frequency of deaths before important events, such as birthdays and religious holidays, and a higher than expected frequency of deaths after these important events. The general procedure for investigating the relationship between death and important occasions is to examine archival data revealing the death dates of individuals in relation to certain important events (see, for example, Schulz & Bazerman, 1980). Three major positive events have been examined by researchers: birthdays, national elections, and religious holidays. For instance, one of the early studies to offer data supporting a "death-dip hypothesis" used birth dates and death dates of persons listed in the book *Four*

Hundred Notable Americans (Schulz & Bazerman, 1980). Based on chance alone, one would expect that an individual's death is equally likely in any of the 12 months. However, the number of deaths during the month prior to the month of an individual's birth was found to be lower than the death rate for other months, thus, supporting the death-dip hypothesis. According to Schulz and Bazerman, a general explanation for this type of finding is that people somehow prolong their lives or delay death until a special event, such as a birthday, has been experienced. Exactly how one might do this is not particularly clear. One suggestion is that looking forward to a positive event creates a state of positive anticipation that precipitates beneficial neurochemical changes. Another possible explanation is that elderly persons are more likely to follow their health and medical regimens closely as an important date nears, so as to reduce the chances of dying before the event arrives.

In this chapter we present the rationale for using physical traces and archival data. Particular kinds of physical traces are identified and examples of their use in psychological studies are offered. Types of archives and the kinds of data that can be drawn from archival sources are also reviewed. Several important advantages of the use of physical traces or archival data are highlighted. There are some limitations and problems with these unobtrusive measures, and they, too, are discussed.

PHYSICAL TRACES

Rationale

- Unobtrusive measures of behavior such as physical traces do not have the problem of reactivity, in which people change their behavior because they know they are being observed.
- The investigation of physical traces represents a valuable component of the multimethod approach to hypothesis testing.

As everyone who has read a few detective stories knows, examining physical evidence of past behavior can provide important clues to the characteristics (or even identity) of individuals, as well as information about the conditions under which an event occurred. The size of footprints in the ground says something about the size and age of the person who stepped there. The distance between footprints can indicate whether the person was walking or running, and so on. As we have seen, physical evidence (in the form of clock settings) can be of value to behavioral scientists. Physical traces (as well as archival data discussed later in this chapter) are especially valuable because they provide nonreactive measures of behavior (Webb et al., 1981).

You will recall from Chapter 3 that a behavioral measure is reactive when participants' awareness of an observer affects the measurement process. This is often the case when direct observations are made, and it is nearly always the case when surveys are conducted. Aware that their responses are being recorded, participants may behave in a way that does not correspond to their normal behavior.

Survey data are particularly susceptible to reactive effects, because respondents may give answers that they feel the researcher wants to hear or may answer in a way that makes them (the respondents) look good. For instance, social scientists are well aware that responses to surveys asking about degree of political activity, such as past voting behavior, typically overestimate this activity (e.g., Endersby & Towle, 1996).

Physical-trace measures are unobtrusive because they are obtained indirectly, in the absence of the subject; thus, they are valuable alternatives to the reactive measures obtained via direct observation or surveys. Although a physical-trace measure might be the only measure of behavior in some studies, physical traces are more commonly used in combination with other measures. As we have emphasized previously, a research study can be strengthened considerably by including several different measures of behavior. A **multimethod approach** to hypothesis testing is recommended because it reduces the likelihood that research findings are due to some artifact of a single measurement process (Webb et al., 1981). There are few (if any) perfect measures in the social sciences. Therefore, the results of a study must be carefully scrutinized to determine whether some characteristic of the measurement instrument (such as its reactivity) has contributed to the results. Even then, it is possible that some artifact has been overlooked. *The most persuasive argument supporting the validity of a particular research hypothesis is one based on evidence obtained by applying a combination of measures.*

Researchers investigating cultural differences in time perception used such a multimethod approach. They surveyed individuals living in Latin America and in the United States to find out how frequently their subjects were late for appointments and to discover their attitudes toward being late (Levine et al., 1980). Citizens of Brazil reported themselves more often late for appointments and expressed less regret at being late than did citizens of the United States. However, a bias in these responses could be present if people described themselves in a way that fit their cultural "image," rather than as they actually behaved. As already noted, however, the researchers also found that public clocks were less accurate in Brazil than in the United States. Further, the researchers observed that watches worn by people in the United States deviated less from the correct time than watches worn by people in Brazil. The data obtained by examining public clocks and the watches worn by citizens of each country tended to confirm the validity of the survey responses and, in combination with the survey results, provided impressive evidence for the research hypothesis.

Types of Physical Traces

- Two categories of physical traces are "use traces" and "products."
- Use traces reflect the physical evidence of use (or nonuse) of items, and can be measured in terms of accretion or erosion and in terms of natural or controlled use.
- By examining the products people own or the products produced by a culture, researchers test hypotheses about attitudes and preferences.

Physical traces are the remnants, fragments, and products of past behavior. Two broad categories of physical traces are "use traces" and "products." *Use traces* are what the label implies—the physical evidence that results from use (or nonuse) of an item. Clock settings are an example of a physical-use trace. So are the remains of cigarettes in ashtrays and the marks made in textbooks. *Products* are the creations, constructions, or other artifacts of earlier behavior. Anthropologists are often interested in the surviving products of ancient cultures. By examining the types of vessels, paintings, and other artifacts that remain, the anthropologist can often describe precisely the pattern of behavior exhibited in a setting that is thousands of years old. Psychologists may also examine physical products in order to describe behavior or to test hypotheses. Psychologists who study animal behavior, for instance, may learn about the behavior of different species by examining the types of nests that are constructed. Newhagen and Ancell (1995) examined bumper stickers used by Black and White residents of a Washington, DC, suburb to investigate racial differences in degree of emotional expressiveness.

Use Traces   An examination of physical evidence provides measures of both accretion and erosion (Webb et al., 1981). *Accretion measures* are based on the accumulation of material. Measuring the amount of litter found on a college campus, for example, would be taking an accretion measure. *Erosion measures* are obtained when the physical evidence is the result of selective wear and tear. The degree to which a young child's dolls show signs of wear is an erosion measure that might indicate which dolls the child likes best. The distinction between accretion measures and erosion measures is not always so obvious. Settings of clocks, for instance, resist easy classification. Nevertheless, classifying physical-use traces in terms of accretion or erosion is often a meaningful description of physical traces, and the distinction calls our attention to two important dimensions of use traces.

Physical-use traces are also classified as either natural or controlled (planned). *Natural* use traces are produced without any intervention by the investigator. Their appearance is the result of naturally occurring events. *Controlled*, or planned, measures result to some degree from the intervention or manipulation of an investigator. A study by Friedman and Wilson (1975) illustrates the distinction between these two types of measures.

The investigators employed both controlled and natural accretion measures to investigate college students' use of textbooks. They affixed tiny glue seals between adjacent pages of textbooks before the students purchased the books for a course. At the end of the semester the investigators obtained the books from the students and recorded how many seals in the textbooks had been broken and where the broken seals were located. Because the researchers controlled the presence of glue seals in the books, this constituted a controlled (accretion) measure. It may be judged to be an accretion measure in that the researchers recorded the accumulation of broken seals (although one might reasonably argue that "erosion" was being measured). The investigators also analyzed the frequency and nature of underlining by students in the textbooks, something, of course, that is typically associated with textbook use. This constituted a natural accretion measure. Analysis of these physical-use measures indicated that students more often read (and presumably studied) the chapters that appeared early in the book than those appearing later in the book.

Table 5.1 contains examples of physical-use traces and the variables being measured. These measures either were used as part of an actual scientific study or represent suggestions by researchers of possible novel and nonreactive measures of behavior (see Webb et al., 1981). The examples given in Table 5.1 are organized according to whether they are accretion or erosion measures and whether their

TABLE 5.1 EXAMPLES OF PHYSICAL-USE TRACES AND VARIABLES BEING MEASURED*

Trace	Variable
Natural accretion	
Inscriptions (graffiti) on walls of public rest rooms	Sexual preoccupation
Radio dial settings	Popularity of radio stations
Fingerprints or smudges on pages of books	Book usage
Liquor bottles in trash cans	Alcohol consumption of households
Odometer readings in cars	Conservation of gasoline
Litter	Effectiveness of antilitter posters
Dust on books	Frequency or recency of use
Garbage	Food use and lifestyle
Locked/unlocked cars	Concern for property
Lengths of cigarette butts	Cultural differences in death rate due to cancer
Controlled accretion	
Glue seals broken (seals inserted prior to distribution)	Index of specific pages read
Nose prints on windows of museum exhibit (windows wiped clean each night)	Popularity (frequency) and age (height of points) of viewers
Natural erosion	
Wear on floor or steps	Amount of foot traffic
Wear on library books	Frequency of use
Food consumed	Eating behavior
Spots (produced by rubbing) on statues or religious objects	Level of religious belief
Controlled erosion	
Wear on children's shoes (measured at two points in time)	Activity level of children
Removal of "tear-away" tags on ads or notices	Interest in notice
Wear on mats or other floor coverings placed in specific areas	Amount of foot traffic
Change in statues or objects coated with substances sensitive to touching	Superstitious behavior

*From Webb et al. (1981).

use is natural or controlled. As you examine the contents of Table 5.1, can you think of other possible physical traces that could serve as measures of the variables listed?

Products   Physical products have been examined less frequently in psychological studies than have physical-use traces. Nevertheless, this category of physical traces has been used in interesting and meaningful ways to test hypotheses about behavior. A particularly good example of the use of physical products is found in a study by Coren and Porac (1977). They investigated the extent of human right-handedness in various cultures since ancient times. To determine manual preference, they examined more than 12,000 works of art, including paintings, sculpture, and other products that spanned more than 50 centuries of human endeavor. The researchers recorded instances of unambiguous tool or weapon use depicted in the artworks. They looked for any differential trend in the depiction of right- or left-handers in different cultures and at different times in human history. No differences were evident. Rather, across many cultures and in every epoch, 93% of the artworks examined showed persons using their right hand. The results provide evidence for a physiological rather than a sociocultural theory of handedness.

Brandt (1972) points out that the products that people own provide important clues to their lifestyle and behavior patterns. What personality differences, for instance, are reflected in the purchase of different models of cars or in the extras and options that are ordered with a car? Besides serving as a measure of social status or personality, the products a person owns can be used to assess the validity of certain kinds of verbal reports. Are individuals' statements about their attitude toward energy conservation, for instance, related to the kinds of products they own and use?

Consider the American driving public's interest in bumper stickers. You probably have seen stickers that state "Guns Don't Kill, People Do," or "Stop Abortion." As Newhagen and Ancell (1995) point out, bumper stickers are unique in that they "allow for the expression of highly personal opinions about strongly held views to a large audience without any real commitment to interact with them" (p. 313). And, unlike graffiti, which is often illegal and socially undesirable, bumper stickers permit an acceptable outlet for the expression of public emotion. When Newhagen and Ancell analyzed bumper sticker messages of suburban Blacks and Whites in the Washington, DC, area, they found overall frequency of bumper sticker usage was highest in low-income areas regardless of race. High-income White neighborhoods showed most evidence of positive and intense stickers, whereas bumper stickers were least frequently observed and, when they were, the messages were the most subdued, in high-income Black neighborhoods. The researchers suggested that the results illustrate examples of discretely different forms of public expression of emotion as a function of race and income. This conclusion seems to fit with Endersby and Towle's (1996) characterization of bumper stickers as reflecting "a form of identification and solidarity with a group sharing common beliefs" (p. 307).

Problems and Limitations

- Before concluding that a measure of physical traces is a valid indicator of behavior or attitudes, a researcher should make sure no sources of bias exist.
- Validity of physical-trace measures can be ascertained by examining converging evidence.

Physical measures offer a researcher valuable and sometimes novel means to study behavior, and the measures available are limited only by the ingenuity of the investigator. However, the validity of physical traces must be carefully examined and verified through independent sources of evidence. Bias can be introduced in the way physical-use traces are laid down and in the manner in which traces survive over time. Does a well-worn path to the right indicate people's interest in objects in that direction or simply a natural human tendency to turn right? Is the setting of clocks a good measure of people's regard for punctuality, or do inaccurate clock settings indicate poor artisanship, inadequate maintenance, or irregular electrical service? To what extent is frequency of bumper sticker usage affected by the recent success of local sports teams?

Problems associated with the analysis of physical traces are illustrated in a classic study of honesty carried out using the "lost-letter technique" (see Merritt & Fowler, 1948). We can consider the method as controlled accretion. The investigators "accidentally" dropped postcards and envelopes at various locations in cities of the East and Midwest. Two types of envelopes were "lost." One contained a written message, and the other contained a lead slug the size of a 50-cent

FIGURE 5.1 The classic "lost-letter technique" illustrates some of the problems with the analysis of physical traces (see text).

piece. All the letters were addressed and bore proper postage, but no return address was shown. Although 85% of the empty envelopes were returned, only 54% of the envelopes with a slug found their way to a mailbox. Further, more than 10% of the envelopes with a slug were returned after having been opened.

Before the researchers could conclude that the return rates represented a valid measure of the public's honesty (or dishonesty), several possible biases associated with this physical trace had to be considered. Postcards, for instance, were less likely than sealed envelopes to be returned, but the fact that postcards may be more easily disturbed by natural conditions than are larger envelopes may have contributed to this difference. On the other hand, envelopes with a slug are heavier and less likely to be blown away—and these were still less likely to be returned. Letters that were dropped in certain locations (e.g., where many children are present) or at certain times of the day (e.g., just before nightfall) are also likely not to be returned for reasons other than the public's dishonesty or apathy.

Some of these possible biases associated with the lost-letter technique were avoided by the methods of dispersal used by the researchers, whereas others were checked via direct observation of a letter's fate. Observation of a sample of dropped letters revealed that a letter was picked up 90% of the time by the first person who saw it, suggesting that dropped letters were soon in the hands of unknowing participants.

In an interesting twist on the lost-letter technique, Stern and Faber (1997) used the Internet to produce a "lost e-mail" technique. In one study the researchers investigated people's attitudes toward the 1996 presidential candidate, Ross Perot, by sending messages to randomly selected e-mail addresses across the country. They sent two different versions of what was supposed to look like a misdirected e-mail message. Both messages went to "Steve" and asked for help with fund raising; however, one version mentioned that the fund raising was for Ross Perot. Although return rates did not differ between the two versions, the researchers analyzed the contents of messages included with the returned e-mail. A number of people returning the Ross Perot message went out of their way to say they were voting for someone else, while none said they planned to vote for him. That informed consent is not part of this procedure, and that returned e-mail typically includes the sender's e-mail address, making an anonymous response impossible, introduces ethical concerns. What do you think? How would you address these ethical concerns?

Whenever possible, supplementary evidence for the validity of physical traces should be obtained (see Webb et al., 1981). Alternative hypotheses for changes in physical traces must be considered, and data must be collected that allow different interpretations to be dismissed. Care must also be taken when comparing results across studies to make sure that measures are defined similarly. When Newhagen and Ancell (1995) tallied bumper stickers, they included only those literally found on car bumpers; Endersby and Towle (1996) operationally defined bumper stickers as any message visible from the rear of the vehicle, which included rear window decals. Different operational definitions of a concept can easily lead to different results.

ARCHIVAL DATA

Rationale

- Archival data comprise the records or documents of the activities of individuals, groups, institutions, and governments.
- Archival data are used to test hypotheses as part of the multimethod approach, to establish the external validity of laboratory findings, and to assess the effects of natural treatments.
- Archival data represent a rich, plentiful source of observations for psychological studies.

When we were born, a record was made of our birth. Information on the birth record probably included the city and state in which we were born, the date and time of our birth, our parents' names, and our name. When we die, another record will be made. It will include such details as probable cause of death, date and time of death, and our age. In between these two events, innumerable records are made of our behavior. Physicians record visits. Hospitals keep a record of when we enter and when we leave. Schools record our grades and extracurricular activities. Businesses may record the number of times we are late or how often we fail to show up for work. Newspapers describe notable successes and failures. Local governments record when we get married and to whom, as well as when we buy a house and how much it costs. The federal government records, among other things, what we pay in income taxes.

Records are kept not only of individuals but also of countries, institutions, cities, and businesses. The gross national product of a country, its major exports and imports, the size of its defense budget, the distribution of its population, and the number of television sets owned by its populace are but a few of the facts that are frequently recorded. How much profit a company makes is part of its report to stockholders. Voting behaviors of state and federal legislators are recorded, as is the amount of money a city spends on social services. Analysis and interpretation of local and world events flood the media. The contents of the media and of documents and books (published and unpublished) are a source of information about current fads and prejudices, changing patterns of belief, and the ideas of important (and not so important) members of society.

Archives are records or documents recounting the activities of individuals or of institutions, governments, and other groups. As measures of behavior, archival data share some of the same advantages as physical traces. Archival measures are nonreactive and therefore provide an alternative to data collection via surveys. Like physical-trace measures, archival data can be used to check the validity of other measures as part of a multimethod approach to hypothesis testing. A nice illustration of the use of archival data in the context of a multimethod approach to hypothesis testing is Frank and Gilovich's (1988) investigation of the strong cultural association that exists between the color black and "badness," or evil.

As Frank and Gilovich point out, in vintage American Western movies you could always tell the good guys from the bad guys. The good guys, of course, wore white hats and the bad guys wore black hats. There is a strong cultural association between black and badness. We speak of people being "blackballed," "blacklisted," "blackmailed," and a person's reputation's being "blackened." When terrible things happen it is a "black day." Black is seen in many cultures as the color of death. The good and bad sides of human nature are also contrasted using black-and-white images, as was illustrated by the characters of the famous *Star Wars* movies. Viewers of these classic films likely will remember the confrontation between the villain, Darth Vader (dressed completely in black), and the young hero, Luke Skywalker (dressed in white or light colors). Vader, unfortunately, had "gone over" to the dark side.

Frank and Gilovich wanted to find out if this strong cultural association between black and evil would affect the way people behave. Specifically, they asked whether professional sports teams that wear black uniforms are more aggressive than those that wear nonblack uniforms. Using archival data obtained from the central offices of the National Football League (NFL) and the National Hockey League (NHL), Frank and Gilovich analyzed penalty records of each major professional team in these sports between 1970 and 1986. Yards penalized were analyzed in the NFL, and minutes that a player was assigned to the penalty box were calculated in the NHL. These particular measures were deemed more appropriate given the study's hypothesis than was number of infractions. Penalties for overaggressiveness are generally more severe (in yards or minutes) than are those for simple rule violations. The operational definition of a "black uniform" was that the colored version of the team's uniform (the one used typically for away games in the NHL and for home games in the NFL) was more than 50% black. (An exception was made for the Chicago Bears of the NFL, who wear dark-blue uniforms but whose uniforms many people mistakenly remember as black; thus, they were included among the black-uniform teams.) According to the authors' hypothesis, teams wearing black should be penalized more than would be expected simply by chance. And they were. Thus, teams with black uniforms, such as Oakland, Chicago, and Cincinnati in the NFL, and Philadelphia, Pittsburgh, and Vancouver in the NHL, were reliably more aggressive than were many other teams.

What psychological processes might account for these effects? Frank and Gilovich suggest that both social-perception and self-perception processes are at work. They argue that others (specifically, referees) "see" players in black as more aggressive than players not wearing black (and therefore award more penalties to players in black), and that players themselves behave more aggressively when they put on black uniforms. As part of their multimethod approach to this issue, they provided support for these explanations by collecting data from laboratory experiments. In one experiment, both college students and referees watched staged football games between teams wearing black or white uniforms and rated their aggressiveness. In a second study, students donned either black or white uniforms in anticipation of an athletic competition before choosing a game from a list of aggressive and nonaggressive games. In the first experiment, both referees and college students were more likely to rate a team wearing black as aggressive. The second experiment showed that students who donned black uniforms chose more aggressive games. By combining data obtained from archival analyses and laboratory experiments, the investigators provide an unusually strong case for their explanations of this interesting cultural phenomenon.

An examination of archival information may also provide a way to test the external validity of laboratory findings. Lau and Russell (1980) analyzed the contents of the sports pages in eight daily newspapers in order to test whether results obtained from laboratory-based experiments investigating *causal attributions* (the reasons people give for a certain outcome, or the cause they attribute the outcome to) were relevant to "real-world" settings. A major finding from laboratory studies of attributions is that people tend to make internal attributions (assuming that the outcome is due to some characteristic within themselves) for success and to make external attributions (assuming that the outcome is due to something beyond their control) for failure. Lau and Russell's analysis of explanations given by sportswriters or team members for the outcome of baseball and football games supported this conclusion. Specifically, they identified 594 explanations for success and failure involving 33 major sporting events. From the perspective of the winning team, 75% of the attributions were internal, whereas only 55% of the attributions of the losing team were internal. Support for this laboratory-based attribution theory also was obtained by analyzing letters and replies published in two widely syndicated newspaper advice columns: "Ann Landers" and "Dear Abby" (see Fischer, Schoeneman, & Rubanowitz, 1987; Schoeneman & Rubanowitz, 1985).

Other reasons for using archival data are to test hypotheses about past behavior and to assess the effect of a natural treatment. For example, given that sports teams typically play "at home" and "away" over the course of a season, researchers repeatedly ask how this difference affects a team's performance. Archival records play a central role in studies of the "home advantage" in sports competitions (see, for example, Courneya & Carron, 1992). The *home advantage* refers to the fact that in many sports competitions a team wins consistently more games played at home than it does games played away. An interesting and somewhat counterintuitive finding (because it goes against the well-documented home advantage), is that teams playing at home do not necessarily perform well in key games, such as those that decide a championship (Baumeister, 1995; Baumeister & Steinhilber, 1984). The "home choke" phenomenon, nevertheless, has not always found support through archival analyses (Schlenker, Phillips, Boniecki, & Schlenker, 1995a, 1995b).

Natural treatments are naturally occurring events that have significant impact on society at large or on particular members. Because it is not always possible to anticipate these events, the investigator who wishes to assess their impact must be prepared to use a variety of behavioral measures, including archival data. Assassinations of world leaders, drastic changes in the stock market, and the passage of new laws are examples of the kinds of events that may have important effects on behavior and that might be investigated using archival data.

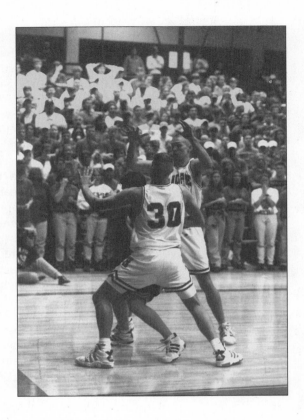

FIGURE 5.2   Archival records permit psychologists to study the "home advantage" in sports competitions.

So, too, are the naturally occurring events of a natural life history, such as death or divorce of parents, a chronic illness, or marital difficulties.

In 1921, Lewis Terman began a longitudinal study of intelligence by recruiting more than 1,500 above average children in the San Francisco and Los Angeles schools (see Friedman et al., 1995; also Terman & Oden, 1947). The children, 856 boys and 672 girls, were preadolescents at the time and have been followed at 5- to 10-year intervals since that time. The archival records associated with Terman's study of gifted children, and interviews with surviving members of this group, enabled investigators to study "psychosocial and behavioral predictors of longevity" (Friedman et al., 1995). One particular focus is the effect of parental divorce on individual behavior and longevity. Many studies in the psychology literature indicate that children experiencing parental divorce or conflict have more conduct and behavioral problems, greater academic difficulties, and poorer health than children whose parents did not divorce (see Tucker et al., 1997). Researchers used the archival records from Terman's study to examine the effect of parental divorce on mortality rates. The data are clear, at least in this homogeneous group of very bright (IQs greater than 135), nearly all White, mostly middle-class individuals: Parental divorce leads to premature death. Men from divorced homes were predicted to die at age 76, whereas those from intact homes were predicted to die at age 80; for women the corresponding predicted ages of death were 82 and 86 (Friedman et al., 1995). Reasons for this effect are complex and not completely understood. For example, children from divorced homes were also more likely to be divorced themselves, men were more likely to die from physical injuries, and women from divorced homes smoke more (Tucker et al., 1997). Results of these archival analyses indicate, nevertheless, that "parental divorce sets off a negative chain of events, which contribute to a higher mortality risk among individuals from divorced homes" (Tucker et al., 1997, p. 389).

Another reason for considering archival data as a behavioral measure is simply because archival data are so plentiful. We noted earlier the extensive records that society keeps on individuals, groups, and institutions. Through careful analysis of archival information, the industrious researcher can seek evidence to support numerous hypotheses. There are practical advantages as well. Archival data represent data that have already been collected; at times, initial summary descriptions may also be provided in archival records. Thus, an extensive data-collection stage may be circumvented. Because archival information is frequently part of the public record and is usually reported in a manner that does not identify individuals, ethical concerns are less worrisome. One goal of this chapter is to alert you to the possible rich rewards of analyzing archival data in the context of psychological studies of behavior. As more and more archival sources become available through the Internet, researchers will find it even easier to examine behavior in this way.

Types of Archival Data

- Types of archival data include running records, news media, and other types of records; archival data can consist of public or private documents.

The sheer diversity and extent of archival sources make their classification rather arbitrary. Records that are continuously kept and updated are frequently referred to as *running records*. Tax records and records of various government agencies are good examples, as are the myriad records of sports teams. Because of their continuous nature, running records are particularly useful in longitudinal studies or in the documentation of trends. Other records, such as personal documents, are more likely to be discontinuous or episodic (see Webb et al., 1981). Archival records can also be distinguished by the degree to which they are available for public inspection. Many records kept by government agencies are easily obtainable. Most records of private institutions and businesses, however, are not open to public scrutiny or can be obtained only after many requests and considerable patience on the part of the researcher.

The news media are yet another important source of archival information. Various records, ranging from stock market reports to crime statistics, are published in newspapers and reported on television. The content of media reports is also a form of archival record and is subject to analysis. Earlier we described how the contents of sports pages were used to test a theory of causal attribution.

The placement of "Found" advertisements in the Lost and Found section of a newspaper can be used to measure public altruism (see Goldstein, Minkin, Minkin, & Baer, 1978).

Phillips (1977) used running records of motor vehicle fatalities kept by the California Highway Patrol and a measure of suicide publicity derived from California newspapers to determine whether there is a significant suicidal component to motor vehicle fatalities. He hypothesized that a substantial number of deaths arising from motor vehicle accidents are actually the result of individuals using their cars to commit suicide. To test this hypothesis, Phillips investigated whether motor vehicle fatalities would, like suicides in general, increase after a well-publicized suicide story. Components of the publicity measure included the daily circulation of each newspaper and the number of days the newspaper carried the suicide story. This measure correlated significantly with changes in motor vehicle fatalities after each story. The number of motor vehicle fatalities increased significantly during the few days after a well-publicized suicide story, reaching a peak on Day 3. This result is shown in Figure 5.3. Changes in frequency were determined by comparing experimental periods (the week right after the story) with control periods that were free from suicide stories and were matched with the experimental periods in terms of day of the week, presence or absence of holidays, and time of the year. Phillips concluded that "suicide stories stimulate a wave of imitative suicides, some of which are disguised as motor vehicle accidents" (p. 1464).

Table 5.2 contains a list of selected sources of archival information and the nature of the data that might be obtained from them. The types of archival data shown in Table 5.2 are rather arbitrarily classified as running records, those pertaining to the media, and "other records," including records of businesses, schools, and other private institutions. An examination of the sources described in Table 5.2 will introduce you to the variety of possible measures that can be obtained from archival sources. Then, following a discussion of content analysis of archival sources, we will review several specific illustrations of the use of archival data in the context of hypothesis testing.

FIGURE 5.3   Daily fluctuations in motor vehicle accident fatalities for a 2-week period before, during (Day 0), and after publication of suicide stories. (From Phillips, 1977.)

TABLE 5.2 SELECTED SOURCES OF ARCHIVAL INFORMATION AND ILLUSTRATIVE DATA FOR THREE TYPES OF ARCHIVES*

Source	Illustrative data
Running records	
Congressional Record	Statements of position on particular issues
Telephone directories	Community ethnic group membership
Salaries of teachers or government employees	Community support
Government agency records (labor, commerce, agriculture departments)	Living trends
Judicial record	Uniformity in sentencing for antisocial behavior
Moody's Handbook	Corporate financial structure
Who's Who in America	Nature of cited accomplishments of successful people
Tax records	Regional differences in patterns of living
City budgets	Perceived value or extent of support of various activities
Media	
Society section of metropolitan newspaper	Upper-middle-class and lower-upper-class activities
Children's books on sale	Qualities of models (heroes and heroines)
Movie announcements in newspapers	Changing taboos and enticements
Want ads	Employer inducements
Obituary columns	Charity preferences
Published speeches	Political, social, economic attitudes
Newspaper headlines	Press bias
Other records†	
Absentee and tardiness records	Work habits or motivation
Military reenlistment and longevity figures	Morale indicator
Pay increase and promotion lists	Perceived value of individuals to an organization
Number of people one supervises	Measure of management responsibility
Production and other output figures	Performance of individuals, departments, and so on
Sales contest records	Selling effectiveness, effectiveness of incentive plans
Sales slips at Delegates' Lounge bar in UN	Tension indicator
Peanut sales at ball games	Excitement indicator (greater after than before seventh inning)
Sales level of consumer goods	Effectiveness of display location, advertisement, or style of packaging
Air trip insurance figures	Public concern before and after air crashes
Sales of layettes by color (blue or pink)	Sex preference in different social classes
Sale price of autographs	Popularity indicator
Club membership list	Indicator of segment of society involved
Committee reports	Institutional modification attempts
Actuarial records: birth, baptismal, death records; marriage licenses	Comparative demographic data (occupation, religion, time of day, cause of death, and so on)
Cemetery documents, burial-lot records	Family membership

*Adapted from Brandt (1972).
†Institutions, business, hospitals, schools, and so on; may or may not be opened to public inspection.

Content Analysis

- Content analysis refers to the process of making inferences based on objective coding of archival records.
- Steps for content analysis include identifying a relevant source of archival data, sampling data from the records, and then coding the contents of the records.
- Content coding includes classifying events and behaviors from archival records into clearly defined categories and recording the amount of time or words devoted to events and behaviors.
- Trained coders use rating scales to make qualitative judgments about the contents of archival records.

Although many sources of archival data can be identified, the usefulness of these sources depends ultimately on how their content is analyzed. In the simplest case, the analysis required may be minimal. Recording the votes of state legislators may be as simple as transcribing vote tallies found in legislative documents. Similarly, determining the win-loss record of sports teams playing at home or away is simply a matter of working with data found in one of the many sports digests that are on the market. In many cases, however, extracting relevant data from an archival source requires careful procedures and relatively complex analysis of the source's content. Furthermore, problems of sampling, reliability, and validity of measures must be addressed, just as these problems are addressed in situations where behavior is observed directly.

Content analysis is generally defined as any technique for making inferences by objectively identifying specific characteristics of messages (Holsti, 1969). Although it is associated primarily with written communications, content analysis may be used with any form of message, including television and radio programs, speeches, films, and interviews. Weigel, Loomis, and Soja (1980) used content analysis to study race relations as they are depicted on prime-time television. They analyzed the frequency of appearances of Blacks and Whites on evening television shows carried by all three major networks. In addition, they rated the quality of Black-White and White-White interactions. Carroll and Russell (1997) analyzed four major Hollywood films to test a biological theory of facial expression. An analysis of actors' portrayal of emotions such as disgust and fear did not provide evidence for "patterns" of facial components predicted by some theories. Finally, in a content analysis of a popular form of written communication, personal ads, researchers analyzed the descriptions of partner preferences among homosexual and heterosexual individuals (Bailey, Kim, Hills, & Linsenmeier, 1997). They related their findings to theories of sexual orientation and psychological adjustment of homosexual individuals who are not typically masculine or feminine.

There are several discernible steps in conducting research using content analysis. First is the identification of a relevant archival source. What is relevant, of course, depends on the goals of the study and the questions the researcher is asking. In some cases merely a statement of the purpose of the study is sufficient to pinpoint an appropriate archival source. A researcher who sets out to study humor in tombstone messages, the manifest content of suicide notes, or race relations on television has already identified the general source for content analysis. In other situations the identification of relevant sources depends on the ingenuity of the researcher. Lau and Russell's (1980) choice of the sports page represented an appropriate and clever use of archival sources as a test of the external validity of laboratory findings related to attribution. In the absence of films depicting emotional expression in everyday life, Carroll and Russell (1997) selected Hollywood films, such as *Ordinary People* (1980) and *Dead Poets Society* (1989), "noted for their realistic portrayal of modern life and for their highly emotional content" (p. 167).

Having identified an archival source, the researcher must sample selections from this source appropriately. Sampling procedures similar to those described in previous chapters can be used. As is the case when behavior or events are sampled, the goal of sampling is to obtain a sample that is representative of all the data of interest. To investigate race relations on television, Weigel et al. (1980) videotaped a full week's broadcasts by the three major networks in the spring of 1978. Only programs with a story line, but all product commercials, were included in the sample. The decision not to use documentaries, news broadcasts, and sports shows reduced the sample of viewing time by about 20%. As always, the extent to which the results of an archival study can be generalized depends on the nature of the sample that is used. Terman's study of genius was, as we saw, based on data collected from high IQ, mainly White, middle-class individuals. Thus, the external validity of subsequent, archival studies of longevity is necessarily less than it would be had a more heterogeneous sample been represented in the archives. Moreover, we might question whether the impact of parental divorce on children's lives at the beginning of the 20th century, when divorce was less frequent and less socially acceptable, is the same as it is today.

The next step in performing a content analysis is *coding*. This step is similar to the scoring of narrative records (see Chapter 3) and requires that relevant descriptive categories and appropriate units of measure be defined (see Holsti, 1969). As with the choice of the archival source itself, what determines a relevant descriptive category is related to the goals of the study. This aspect of a content-analysis task can be illustrated by examining the categories used by Weigel et al. (1980) in their study of race relations. Four major categories were defined: (1) human appearance time, (2) Black appearance time, (3) cross-racial appearance time, and (4) cross-racial interaction time. Each category was operationally defined. For instance, cross-racial interaction was defined as "the time during which black and white characters were engaged in active, on-screen interactions (talking, touching, or clear nonverbal communication)" (p. 886). The use of precise operational definitions permitted coders viewing the sample broadcasts to make reliable judgments of events.

In many content-analysis studies, the communication is written. The units of classification for quantitative analysis generally include single words, characters, sentences or paragraphs, themes, or particular items (Holsti, 1969). Lau and Russell (1980), for instance, determined the frequency of attribution statements that were categorized as either internal or external and were made by members of the winning or losing team. In a study of bereavement, researchers performed a content analysis of interview transcripts of men who had lost a partner to AIDS (Pennebaker, Mayne, & Francis, 1997). Use of insight and causal words predicted emotional well-being a year later.

Another unit of measure often used when newspaper content is analyzed is that of space—for instance, number of column inches devoted to a particular topic. This measure was used by Phillips (1977) when studying the relationship between publicized suicides and frequency of motor-vehicle fatalities. When television or radio broadcasts are studied, the unit of measure may be time. Such was the case for the study by Weigel et al. (1980). Both Black appearances and Black-White appearances were expressed in terms of the percentage of total human appearance time.

Qualitative measures are also used as part of content analysis. These qualitative assessments are frequently in the form of ratings. For example, in addition to measuring time of cross-racial interactions on prime time television, Weigel et al. sought to determine the "degree to which cross-racial interactions on television were characterized by the conditions that promote friendliness and mutual respect in face-to-face encounters" (pp. 886–887). To do this, they developed a series of rating scales that emphasized the interpersonal dimensions found to be important in previous race-related research. Broadcasts videotaped a year earlier were used to define levels of the scales, and coders were trained in the use of the scales before real data were collected. Newhagen and Ancell (1995) asked raters to judge on a 10-point scale the emotional valence (positive or negative) and intensity of bumper sticker messages.

Satterfield and Seligman (1994) used the CAVE technique to investigate the explanatory styles of George Bush and Saddam Hussein during several historical periods of conflict, including the Persian Gulf Crisis. The acronym, CAVE, stands for "content analysis of verbatim explanations" (see Schulman, Castellon, & Seligman, 1989). The CAVE guidelines help researchers identify causal statements in written or spoken verbatim messages. The statements can then be rated on dimensions of explanatory style, similar to those used by Lau and Russell in their study of causal attributions in sports. The content analysis of verbatim explanations by Bush and Hussein for periods preceding military actions or political conflicts produced an interesting result:

> When the leaders were pessimistic (relative to themselves), their subsequent actions were more cautious and passive. When the leaders were relatively optimistic, their subsequent actions were more aggressive and risky. (Satterfield & Seligman, 1994, p. 79)

The authors noted the many limitations of their study (e.g., a relatively small sample of verbatim messages and world events was analyzed). They also appropriately acknowledge that the correlational nature of their study means they must "leave open the large class of third-variable accounts before concluding that explanatory style itself causes cautious versus risky actions" (p. 79). For example, before a definitive conclusion regarding the relationship between explanatory style and political action can be reached, such issues as political demands on the leaders or cultural differences in rhetorical style need to be investigated further. Nevertheless, the data suggest that "shifts in explanatory style seem at least to signal corresponding shifts in aggressivity and risk taking" (p. 80). Archival research of this kind may help us better understand the psychological nature of political decision making and perhaps even help predict the course of world events.

Whenever possible, judges (coders or raters) should be blind to important aspects of the study, such as the main hypotheses, the source of the messages, and the immediate surrounding context. Judges in the Satterfield and Seligman (1994) study of explanatory style, for example, rated the world leaders' statements only after "all potentially biasing date information was removed" (p. 78) and after source material had been assigned random number codes. Measures of interjudge (interobserver) reliability also should be presented as part of a content analysis. (Measures of interobserver reliability are discussed in Chapter 3.)

Illustrative Uses of Archival Data

- Archival data are used to analyze communications and trends over time, and to assess the effects of natural treatments.

Analysis of Communications   Satterfield and Seligman's (1994) analysis of the explanations by George Bush and Saddam Hussein for world events is a good example of the use of archival data to analyze communications. So, too, is an interesting study by Osgood and Walker (1959), who compared the content of real suicide notes, simulated suicide notes (notes deliberately faked), and ordinary letters. Working under the assumption that language behavior changes as a function of heightened motivation, they suggested that suicide notes should differ from ordinary letters and faked notes in several ways. The investigators chose 16 different measures to test their hypotheses regarding the content of these messages (e.g., number of syllables per word and number of distress-expressing phrases). Many of these measures revealed significant differences between suicide notes and ordinary letters. Interestingly, suicide notes did not show greater disorganization. When quantitative measures that were successful in distinguishing between suicide notes and ordinary letters were used to differentiate between faked and real suicide notes, the analysis correctly predicted the real suicide note in 10 of 13 matched pairs.

Analysis of Trends   Over the years, women have frequently been underrepresented in businesses and professions. In the last few decades, however, significant attempts have been made to reduce any gender bias affecting hiring and promotion as well as entry into various professions. Scientific organizations, such as those in psychology, have taken steps to reduce discriminatory practices. The *APA Publication Manual* (American Psychological Association, 1994), for instance, includes specific guidelines for using inclusive language in APA journals (see also Appendix C). The APA Ethics Code, which was discussed in Chapter 2, clearly promotes respect for people's rights and for the dignity of all individuals without regard to gender (as well as to other cultural, social, or physical factors). According to General Principle D of the Ethics Code, "Psychologists try to eliminate the effect on their work of biases based on these factors, and they do not knowingly participate in nor condone unfair discriminatory practices" (American Psychological Association, 1992, p. 1600).

To what extent have psychologists been successful in reducing gender bias in their research activities? To attempt to answer this question, researchers reviewed nearly 5,000 scientific articles from eight psychology journals published between 1970 and 1990 (Gannon, Luchetta, Rhodes, Pardie, & Segrist, 1992). The journals were selected so as to represent various topic areas (developmental, abnormal, and so on) within psychology. With the exception of one journal that did not begin publication until 1978, the contents of all articles published in these journals in 1970, 1975, 1980, 1985, and 1990 were examined. Eight different variables were identified, and the contents of the articles were coded according to these variables. Among them were the gender of the first author, gender of the participants, the type of language (i.e., sexist or nonsexist) used, and the existence of generalizations based on gender (e.g., generalizations of results obtained from participants of one gender to both genders).

The results of this trend analysis of gender bias in published psychology articles revealed that while "sexism has clearly diminished in the past two decades," there is "continued evidence of discriminatory practices" (p. 389). For example, on the positive side, significant increases between 1970 and 1990 in the percentages of articles with female first authors were found in nearly every journal, while the percentages of studies that had male-only participants declined significantly in most journals. In addition, sexist language in these psychology journals was all but totally eliminated by 1990. On the negative side, a substantial percentage of articles showing gender bias were still being published in 1990. An article was considered gender-biased "if participants included only one gender for no obvious reason or with no reason explicitly stated, if sexist language was used, or if the discussion section contained inappropriate generalizations" (p. 393). Under this definition, gender-biased studies averaged about 85% in 1970 and about 30% in 1990. As the authors indicated, the archival analysis revealed an obvious reduction in gender bias in psychological studies during the period of this study, but it is evident from the data that, as of 1990, there was still room for improvement.

An analysis of APA journals by Graham (1992) revealed that there also is room for improvement in the manner in which psychologists approach the study of African Americans. Archival data obtained from six major APA journals indicated that the presence of empirical articles on African Americans decreased during the period between 1970 and 1989. The bottom line was highlighted in the title of her article: "Most of the Subjects Were White and Middle Class." This trend seems unfortunate when, as the author notes, "social concerns demand increased understanding of the psychological functioning of Black Americans, and pedagogical needs call for cultural diversity in our academic curricula"

(p. 629). In terms of publishing sex-biased studies and empirical studies of minority groups, one might well ask, where is psychology now?

Assessing the Effect of a Natural Treatment   A study investigating the effect of a natural treatment (one that we have mentioned previously) is that of Phillips (1977). In this study, the "treatment" was the publicity given by major newspapers to suicides, and the effect of this publicity on motor vehicle fatalities was assessed. In a subsequent study, Phillips (1978) used records of the U.S. National Transportation Safety Board (*Briefs of Accidents: U.S. Civil Aviation*) to show a relationship between well-publicized murder-suicides and changes in fatal aircraft accidents. This archival study revealed a sharp increase in multifatality crashes (implying both a murder and a suicide component) in the period following the widespread publicizing of a murder-suicide story. Interestingly, the peak increase in aircraft fatalities occurred on Day 3 following the story, just as was found when suicide stories were related to motor vehicle fatalities (see Figure 5.3). In yet another study, Phillips (1983) showed homicides increased significantly following heavyweight championship prize fights during the period between 1973 and 1978. Particularly intriguing is the fact that deaths due to homicides peaked 3 days following the prize fight, as had been found in previous analyses of motor vehicle and airplane fatalities following well-publicized suicide stories. As evidence that this effect is due to some type of modeling of aggression, Phillips carried out additional analyses showing that homicides increased as the level of publicity surrounding the event increased. He operationally defined level of publicity in terms of whether the fight was discussed on television network news. He found that the increase in homicides was significantly greater when the fight was given more publicity on the network news.

This series of studies by Phillips and his colleagues is an impressive demonstration of the use of archival data to provide external validity to the results of laboratory findings. Phillips noted that laboratory studies have shown that exposure to violent films and television produces brief increases in aggression by laboratory subjects. Often, however, neither the setting nor the nature of the violence studied (e.g., hitting inflatable toys) is similar to that found in the real world. In contrast, studies using archival data, although lacking the rigorous control possible in the laboratory, provide evidence of what happens to people who are exposed to real media instances of aggression.

Problems and Limitations

- Archival data may be biased due to selective deposit and selective survival.
- Selective deposit occurs when biases influence what information is recorded (deposited) in an archival record, or whether a record is made at all; selective survival occurs when archival records are missing or incomplete.
- Archival records are subject to errors and changes in record-keeping procedures.

- Although archival data are considered nonreactive, reactivity can influence the production of archival records; this is particularly true for public records.
- When interpreting the results of correlational analyses of archival data, researchers must be alert to the possibility of spurious relationships.

When discussing the validity of physical traces, we mentioned that biases may result from the way physical traces are established and from the manner in which they survive over time. These biases are referred to as selective deposit and selective survival, respectively, and they are no less a problem for archival records (see Webb et al., 1981). Either of these biases can impose severe limitations on the generality of research findings.

Problems of **selective deposit** arise when biases exist in the production of archival sources. An interesting example of selective deposit is that associated with suicide notes. We mentioned earlier the research of Osgood and Walker (1959), who performed a content analysis of suicide notes and compared real suicide notes to ordinary letters and to faked suicide notes. We might ask whether the thoughts and feelings expressed in suicide notes are representative of all suicides. It happens that fewer than a fourth of all individuals who commit suicide leave notes, so it is possible that those who do leave notes are not representative of no-note individuals (Webb et al., 1981).

Problems of selective deposit may also arise when individuals associated with archival sources have the opportunity to edit and alter records before they are permanently recorded. This is illustrated by legislators' use of the *Congressional Record*. Though the *Congressional Record* is ostensibly a spontaneous record of speeches and remarks made before the Congress, legislators actually have the opportunity to edit their remarks before they are published (Webb et al., 1981) and even to enter into the record documents and accounts that were never really read aloud. No doubt remarks that are, in hindsight, viewed as less than politically expedient are changed prior to publication in the *Congressional Record*. Researchers who use archival data must be aware of the biases that may occur when an archive is produced. Consider, for example, what types of biases might cause selective recording of crime statistics, income expense accounts, or sales figures.

Problems associated with **selective survival** arise when records are missing or incomplete (something an investigator may or may not even be aware of). It is important to consider whether there are reasons to suspect systematic biases in the survival of certain records. Are documents missing that are particularly damaging to certain individuals or groups? Following a change of presidential administrations, are some types of archives destroyed or misplaced? Are "letters to the editor" representative of all letters that were received? Schoeneman and Rubanowitz (1985) cautioned that when analyzing the contents of advice columns, they could not avoid the possibility of a preselection bias because advice columnists print only a fraction of the letters they receive. As one prominent group of researchers has commented, when one examines archival data, "the gnawing reality remains that archives have been produced for someone else and by someone else" (Webb et al., 1981, p. 140).

In addition to problems arising from selective deposit and survival, the researcher using archival sources must be aware of possible errors in the record keeping and changes over time in the manner in which the records were kept. It is important to demonstrate that the record keeping was relatively constant and stable over the period of the study. When running records are kept, there is always the possibility that the definitions of categories have been changed midstream. For example, had the U.S. National Transportation Safety Board made important changes in the definition of "noncommercial" aircraft during the period of Phillips' (1978) study, it would have seriously affected the statistics he used to implicate murder-suicides in aircraft fatalities. An interesting example of unintended bias appears in the debate over the "home choke" hypothesis. Critics argue that the archival data do not support the hypothesis that sports teams choke in key games when playing at home (Schlenker, et al., 1995a, 1995b). When defending the archival analyses supporting the hypothesis, Baumeister (1995) pointed out that during the archival period there had been a rule change for the World Series regarding the use of a designated hitter. The rule change favored the home team, and could have worked against the "home choke" hypothesis.

Although archives represent nonreactive measures of behavior, their classification as such applies only to archival analysis; it does not imply that reactivity was not a problem when the archive was produced. Statements made by public figures and printed in newspapers or reported by other media must be evaluated for their reactive components. Politicians and others who are constantly exposed to media publicity no doubt learn how to "use" the media, and their public stance may not match their private views. Lau and Russell (1980) had to consider whether the public statements made by players and coaches about a team's performance were really the same as those they made in private. They concluded that differences between public and private statements of attribution no doubt existed but that these differences do not invalidate their generalization of laboratory findings to real-world settings. The only way to control for reactive effects in archival data is to be aware that they may exist and, when possible, to seek other forms of corroborative evidence.

Yet another problem in the analysis of archival data is identifying spurious relationships. A **spurious relationship** exists when evidence falsely indicates that two or more variables are associated. Such evidence may be the result of inadequate or improper statistical treatment. This problem may exist in studies showing a relationship between frequency of deaths and important occasions. Although many people appear to endorse the view that individuals can somehow prolong their life in order to experience certain important events, such as birthdays, Schulz and Bazerman (1980) reanalyzed data from several studies to show that supportive evidence may be the result of statistical artifacts—for example, the way in which the period of time before and after a death was measured. This reanalysis of the data eliminated any evidence for the death-dip hypothesis. These researchers also reanalyzed data from other studies supporting the death-dip and death-rise hypotheses and showed how statistical artifacts could account for the results. Nevertheless, Schulz and Bazerman suggested that data supporting the death-dip hypothesis "may well be within reach if we use the proper methodologies and carefully select important events" (p. 261).

Spurious relationships can also exist when variables are accidentally or coincidentally related. This is sometimes the case when changes in two variables are the result of another, usually unknown, third variable. For instance, it has been noted that ice cream sales and the crime rate are positively correlated. However, before concluding that eating ice cream prompts people to commit crimes, it is important to consider the fact that both variables are affected by increases in temperature; neither eating ice cream nor committing crime directly affects the other.

Several studies (e.g., Baron & Reiss, 1985) have been done to determine whether Phillips' (1983) finding of a relationship between heavyweight prize fights and homicides in the United States is a spurious one. Critics suggested that statistical artifacts are present, while others questioned whether important variables were controlled. Baron and Reiss, for instance, suggested that the third-day peak, which Phillips (1983) admitted he could not readily interpret, was quite possibly due to the occurrence of holidays or weekends near prize-fight dates or even to fluctuations in the unemployment rate. Nevertheless, extensive reanalysis of Phillips' original data tended to reaffirm a link between violence portrayed in the media and violence acted out in society (see Miller, Heath, Molcan, & Dugoni, 1991; Phillips & Bollen, 1985).

There is no easy way to deal with spurious relationships except to gather, from independent sources, additional data that will help confirm a relationship and to subject the available archival data to more than one kind of analysis. This often is no easy task and explains why, as we have noted on more than one occasion, that researchers are appropriately cautious when giving their final conclusions about the outcome of an archival study (see, for example, Baumeister, 1995).

As one last example of the difficulties associated with interpretations based on archival data, consider the problems involving the outcome of archival studies examining the relationship between temperature and aggression (see, for example, Anderson, 1989). Psychologists frequently have used archival records of temperatures and of frequencies of aggressive or violent acts—such as assaults, rapes, and homicides—in order to test the hypothesis that aggression increases with increases in temperature. Data supporting the temperature-aggression hypothesis have been around for years. Nevertheless, researchers have also been aware of possible artifacts of tests of this hypothesis. For example, are aggressive incidents more likely when more people are outdoors, interacting in groups (shopping, playing sports, taking vacations)? If this is the case, and if we assume people are more likely to be outside in the warmer months, then a relation between temperature and aggression may be a spurious one. Temperature and violence would not be directly related but accounted for by some third variable such as opportunity for outdoor activities (see Anderson, 1989). You may recognize this argument as a variation on the ice cream sales–crime rate relationship mentioned earlier. Researchers responded to this criticism by looking at a wide variety of measures, collected during different historical periods, and across cultures. The relationship between temperature and aggression was similar in these studies, making an alternative explanation less plausible (Anderson, 1989).

The manner in which spurious relationships appear can be illustrated with another set of data collected to test the temperature-aggression hypothesis. One way to test this hypothesis is to examine frequency of violent acts as a function of month of the year, the expectation being that violent acts will be most frequent during the hottest months of the year, such as July and August. Anderson (1989) summarized the results of several studies that looked at this relationship. In the bottom panel of Figure 5.4, you can see data revealing the frequency of assaults across the 12 months of the year. The data in this figure appear to support the temperature-aggression hypothesis, frequency of assaults is least during the cold months and peaks during July and August. Now look at the data at the top of Figure 5.4. In this graph the monthly frequencies of homicides are graphed.

FIGURE 5.4   Summaries of data relevant to tests of the temperature-aggression hypothesis. Data on the bottom show monthly distribution of assaults; data on the top describe monthly distribution of homicides. (From Anderson, 1989.)

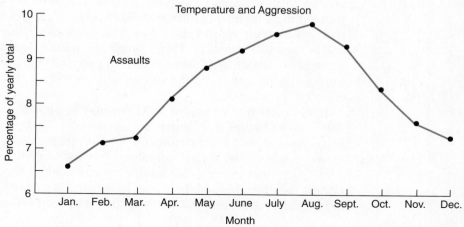

The frequencies of homicides and assaults are similar for the first few months of the year and, in fact, July and August reveal peak periods for both kinds of violent acts. However, the frequency of homicides is also very high in the cold month of December. Is the temperature-aggression hypothesis invalidated? Or, is there an artifact in these data? One possibility is that homicides increase in December due to an increase in family disputes during the holidays (see Anderson, 1989). Researchers must be constantly alert to possible artifacts in a data set and seek corroborative evidence for an hypothesis. For instance, showing that temperature is related to assaults and not to property crime argues for a specific relationship between temperature and aggression (Anderson, Bushman, & Groom, 1997). Finally, as we have emphasized previously, it is important to take a multimethod approach to hypothesis testing.

ETHICAL ISSUES AND UNOBTRUSIVE MEASURES

- Unobtrusive measures such as physical traces and archival data represent an important research method for psychologists to fulfill their ethical obligation to improve individual and societal conditions.

The APA Ethics Code makes clear that psychologists have an obligation to "promote integrity in the science," be "concerned about the ethical compliance of their colleagues' scientific and professional conduct," seek to "broaden knowledge of behavior and, where appropriate, to apply it pragmatically to improve the condition of both the individual and society." Moreover, "when undertaking research, they [should] strive to advance human welfare and the science of psychology" (see Preamble, Principles B, C, and F, of the *APA Ethics Code*; American Psychological Association, 1992, pp. 1599–1600). These goals apply, of course, to scientists in general and not simply when they use of one particular methodology, such as that associated with unobtrusive measures. Nevertheless, because several studies reviewed in this chapter highlight nicely the *proactive* nature of scientific research, these ethical principles are worth emphasizing. Research reviewed in this chapter illustrates, for instance, how psychologists have contributed meaningfully to our understanding of suicide, race relations, effects of parental divorce, conflict resolution, societal violence, sexual discrimination, and fair scientific practices. These contributions arise from one small part of psychological research, that having to do with physical traces or archival data. This impressive list testifies to the way in which psychologists strive to meet their ethical responsibilities.

It is important to remember that there may be a cost to society of *not* doing research (see Chapter 2). A better understanding of such social problems as violence, suicide, and race relations, for example, has the potential to improve many people's lives. Yet, ethical dilemmas arise when there are serious risks to participants that make certain kinds of research difficult to justify when considering a risk/benefit ratio. One way in which this dilemma may be resolved is to seek alternative, low-risk methods of data collection (see Chapter 2). In the present chapter, you saw how research can be carried out on important psychological problems under conditions where ethical issues are often minimal relative to more intrusive methods. Thus, in some situations, unobtrusive measures may represent an important low-risk methodology for research on important social issues.

SUMMARY

Unobtrusive measures such as physical traces and archival data are important alternatives to direct observation and surveys. Physical traces are the remnants, fragments, and products of past behavior. Physical-use traces are based on the accumulation of evidence (accretion measures) or are the result of selective wear (erosion measures). Furthermore, use traces can either result naturally, without any intervention by the investigator, or be planned by the investigator. Physical traces may provide important nonreactive (unobtrusive) measures of behavior and can be used as the sole dependent variable or in combination with other measures of behavior. Multimethod approaches to the study of behavior are particularly recommended because they reduce the chance that results are due to some artifact of the measurement process. In obtaining physical traces, an investigator must be aware of possible biases in the way in which traces accumulate or survive over time.

Archival data are found in records and documents that recount the activities of individuals, institutions, governments, and other groups. These sources of information are valuable because they provide a way of investigating the external validity of laboratory findings, assessing the effect of a "natural treatment" (such as a political assassination), analyzing the content of communications, and describing trends. Archival records are nonreactive measures of behavior and, like physical traces, can be used in multimethod approaches to hypothesis testing. The analysis of archival data typically requires some form of content analysis, a process that can involve problems of sampling and coding that are not unlike those that arise in the analysis of narrative records (see Chapter 3). Problems of selective deposit and selective survival must be investigated when archival data are used, and evidence should be presented showing that observed relationships are not spurious.

Unobtrusive measures can be an important alternative to more intrusive methodologies, permitting psychologists to do research on important issues with minimal risk to the participants.

KEY CONCEPTS

unobtrusive measures
physical traces
archival data
multimethod approach

content analysis
selective deposit
selective survival
spurious relationship

REVIEW QUESTIONS

1 What characteristic of physical traces and archival data makes them especially attractive alternatives to the direct-observation and survey method of measuring?
2 Why are multimethod approaches to hypothesis testing recommended?
3 What are the different kinds of physical-trace measures used by psychologists, and in what ways do they differ?
4 What possible sources of bias exist when physical-use traces are the dependent variable in a research study, and how can the validity of these measures be verified?
5 Identify and give an example of one of the four reasons for using archival data.
6 What dimensions distinguish the various types of archival sources used by psychologists?
7 What three basic steps must be taken in any research in which content analysis is done?
8 Explain the role of precise operational definitions in content analysis, and give one example of a quantitative unit and one example of a qualitative unit of measurement in content analysis.
9 Identify and give an example of the problems that researchers must be aware of when they make use of archival sources.
10 Explain the two ways in which evidence indicating spurious relationships most often arises.

CHALLENGE QUESTIONS

1 Suggest two sources of archival data for each of the following variables. Be sure to specify an operational definition of each variable.
  A   Public's interest in cultural events
  B   Students' political attitudes
  C   Community concern about crime
  D   Amount of mobility in a corporation
  E   Citizens' attitudes toward their schools
  F   Ethnic grouping of neighborhoods
  G   Current fads in dress
2 For each of the following archival sources, specify two kinds of data that might be useful in a psychological study. Once again, be sure to specify the operational definition that could be used for the variable you have identified.
  A   Weekly news magazine
  B   Television soap operas
  C   Classified section of newspaper
  D   Annual city budgets
  E   Student yearbooks
  F   List of donors to a university
  G   Television commercials
3 A bright female graduate student in psychology has been offered a job with both *Newsweek* and *Time*. The salary offers of the two companies are basically the same, and it appears that both the working conditions and the job responsibilities are similar. To help her decide which job to accept, she resolves to determine whether one magazine has a better attitude toward women than the other. She appeals to you to

help her with a content analysis of these two news magazines. What specific advice would you give her regarding each of the following steps of her content analysis?

A Sampling

B Coding

C Reliability

D Quantitative and qualitative measures

4 An educational specialist was convinced that schoolyard fights among young boys were more violent than those among young girls. To gather evidence relevant to her hypothesis, she checked the records at the nurse's office of her school. She found that, of the 100 injuries resulting from fights which were reported to the school nurse, 75% involved boys and only 25% involved girls. The investigator was convinced on the basis of these findings that her hypothesis was correct. Criticize this conclusion by showing how these very same findings could result if exactly the opposite of the investigator's hypothesis were true—namely, that fights among young girls are more violent. (Be sure to confine your answer to the adequacy of the data that the investigator has presented to support her conclusion.)

5 A researcher wishes to test the hypothesis that children attending private grade schools are not as "dirty-minded" as students attending public grade schools. He chooses two schools (one a parochial school and one public) that are located in the same neighborhood, approximately one mile apart. Both schools include grades 1 through 8. To test the hypothesis, the investigator decides to use measures both of natural accretion and of controlled accretion. Specifically, he operationally defines "dirty-mindedness" as the number of obscene words (from a predetermined list) that are found in the restrooms of each school. The natural accretion measure is simply the number of new target words appearing on the walls of the restrooms at the end of each week. As a measure of controlled accretion, the investigator obtains permission from the school authorities to place pads of paper and pencils in the toilet stalls of the restrooms at each school. On each pad of paper is written "Leave me a note." At the end of each week the investigator replaces the pad with a fresh one and examines the pages that have been written on for the appearance of obscene words.

A Comment on possible problems of selective deposit and survival for the physical-trace measures proposed in this study.

B Frame questions that might be asked concerning the external validity of this study.

C Suggest ways in which the investigator might use a multimethod approach to this problem.

Answer to Challenge Question 1

The sources of archival data listed below for each of the variables represent only illustrations and not definitive answers. Operational definitions are only sketched here; they should be developed more fully through discussion in class.

A Public's interest in cultural events—attendance figures for theater and concerts in the past calendar year; membership lists of organizations that support cultural events

B Students' political attitudes—records of participation by students at local, state, and national conventions; membership lists of organizations that advocate political positions

C Community concern about crime—police records of all calls reporting "suspicious" activities in the community; sales records for locks, burglar alarms, and firearms

D   Amount of mobility in a corporation—company records of average time spent by employees in various positions; company records with annual lists of promotions within the company

E   Citizens' attitudes toward their schools—records of the election results for millage requests for schools, including number of millage votes that passed and number of times each had to come up for a vote; membership lists for parent-teacher organizations with the implication that active participation suggests positive attitudes

F   Ethnic grouping of neighborhoods—analysis of the ethnic origins of the names in neighborhood phone directories; city licensing records for restaurants and food stores in the neighborhoods

G   Current fads in dress—sales records for selected articles of clothing that typify a particular fad; magazine, newspaper, and television advertisements for clothing

Experimental Methods

Independent Groups Designs

CHAPTER OUTLINE

OVERVIEW
CHARACTERISTICS OF EXPERIMENTS
WHY PSYCHOLOGISTS CONDUCT EXPERIMENTS
EXPERIMENTAL CONTROL
RANDOM GROUPS DESIGN
Random Assignment
Establishing External Validity
Challenges to Internal Validity
ALTERNATIVE INDEPENDENT GROUPS DESIGNS
Matched Groups Design
Natural Groups Design
ANALYSIS OF EXPERIMENTS
Overview
Confidence Intervals
Null-Hypothesis Testing
Limitations of Null-Hypothesis Testing
Analysis of Variance (ANOVA)
Effect Size
Meta-Analysis
SUMMARY

OVERVIEW

In previous chapters we discussed research methods that primarily fulfill the descriptive and predictive functions of the science of psychology. Psychologists use observational methods to develop detailed descriptions of behavior, often in natural settings. Survey-research methods allow psychologists to describe people's attitudes and opinions. Successful prediction is achieved when we discover measures of behavior that covary reliably; for instance, people who have many significant changes in their lives are also more stressed. Converging evidence for the validity of behavior descriptions based on observation and survey research can be obtained by analyzing archival data and physical traces, nonreactive means for describing behavior. However, as essential as they are to the scientific study of behavior, description and prediction are not sufficient. Psychologists also seek understanding—the "why" of behavior. Scientific understanding is achieved when the causes of a phenomenon have been identified. The next three chapters focus on the best available research method for identifying causal relationships—the experimental method. We will explore how the experimental method is used to test psychological theories as well as to answer questions of practical importance (e.g., whether an intervention worked to increase children's reading proficiency).

The distinction between experimental methods and descriptive methods should not be drawn too sharply. Observation, survey research, and archival data can certainly contribute to our understanding of the causes of behavior, and experiments certainly require observation. In fact, experiments are a kind of structured observation. Field experiments and longitudinal designs in survey research also embody the principles of the experimental methods, although we have discussed them in the context of descriptive research methods. Similarly, experimental methods can be used effectively to develop accurate descriptions of behavior, especially when the methods are applied to practical research problems such as the effectiveness of a behavior modification program (see Chapter 9).

As we have emphasized, the best overall approach to research is the multimethod approach. If we obtain comparable answers to a research question after using different methods, our confidence in our conclusions increases. Our conclusions are then said to have *convergent validity*. Each method has different shortcomings, but the methods have complementary strengths that overcome these shortcomings. The special strength of the experimental method is that it is especially effective for establishing cause-and-effect relationships.

In the present chapter we discuss the most commonly used experimental design—the random groups design. You will be introduced to the underlying logic of this design, the procedures for forming random groups, the ways in which the external validity of experiments can be established, and the challenges to internal validity that apply specifically to the random groups design. Two alternative experimental designs involving independent groups also will be considered: the matched groups design and the natural groups design. We conclude this chapter by describing how the results of experiments are analyzed.

Statistical analysis gives us the evidence we need to decide if our experiment worked to reveal the process we are investigating.

CHARACTERISTICS OF EXPERIMENTS

- Researchers manipulate an independent variable in an experiment to observe the effect on behavior, as assessed by the dependent variable.
- Good experiments can be identified by their internal validity, reliability, sensitivity, and external validity.

Imagine you are observing adults while they are reading. Would you be able to tell whether individuals are saying the words to themselves as they read silently? Most adult readers don't move their lips when reading, so it's unlikely you could tell whether they are saying words silently to themselves. Think now as you read these words. Can you mentally "hear" the words as you read them? This process of "hearing" words while reading is literally unobservable. However, Haber and Haber (1982) constructed a clever situation to study this unobservable process. The term they used for talking to oneself while reading was *subvocal articulation*. To examine this process, they gave college students two types of sentences to read, tongue-twisters (Francis Forbes' father fries five flounders) and control sentences that were not tongue-twisters (Mary Wright's uncle cooks red lobsters). Haber and Haber reasoned that, if the students did say the words to themselves as they read silently, the tongue-twister sentences would be harder to read and thus take longer to read than the control sentences. This is exactly what they found, so they concluded that we do "talk to ourselves" as we read.

Haber and Haber never did observe subvocal articulation directly. They constructed a situation in which a difference in behavior (reading time) was observed indirectly as a result of a process they presumed was occurring. The situation the researchers created allowed this process to "show itself." Much of the experimental research in psychology is like that of the Haber and Haber study. Theoretical processes are proposed [*we talk to ourselves when we read*], experiments are done in which outcomes are predicted on the basis of these explanatory processes [*tongue-twister sentences should take longer to read than control sentences*], and the outcomes of the experiments are used to make decisions about the existence of these unobservable theoretical processes [*because the tongue-twister sentences did take longer to read, we conclude that we do talk to ourselves when we read*].

A true experiment involves the *manipulation* of one or more factors and *measurement* (observation) of the effects of this manipulation on behavior. The factors the researcher controls or manipulates are called the **independent variables.** The measures used to observe the effect (if any) of the independent variables are called **dependent variables.** When Haber and Haber (1982) investigated subvocal articulation, they manipulated the independent variable of the type of sentence students read (tongue-twister or control). The dependent variable they observed was the amount of time it took students to read each sentence. (Although the term *experiment* is also used to describe studies with independent variables whose levels are selected [e.g., gender of participant or grade level in school] rather than manipulated, for reasons that will become clear, we treat these kind of "experiments" separately later in this chapter.)

There are many ways to distinguish experiments that are done properly from those done improperly, but we will emphasize four characteristics of experiments to consider: internal validity, reliability, sensitivity, and external validity. An experiment has *internal validity* when the cause and effect relationship is interpretable—that is, we can conclude that manipulating the independent variable caused a change in the dependent variable, and we can rule out other plausible causes for the outcome. In all cases, we want our experiments to have good internal validity because only then can we make claims about the causes of behavior. Second, the purpose of an experiment is to produce a difference in behavior; a *reliable experiment* is one in which this difference is likely to be observed again if the experiment is repeated. When our experiments are reliable, we can state with confidence that our conclusions are not arbitrary or due to chance factors. Third, independent variables differ in terms of how large an effect they have on behavior; a *sensitive experiment* is likely to detect the effect of an independent variable even when the effect is small. For example, Haber and Haber found that students take more time to read tongue-twisters compared to control sentences. However, a smaller mean difference in reading time might be observed when comparing students' reading times for sentences with familiar words and sentences with unfamiliar words. Our goal is to design sensitive experiments that allow us to observe the effects of our manipulation, even when those effects might be small. Finally, when an experiment has *external validity* the findings can be generalized to individuals, settings, and conditions beyond the scope of the specific experiment. That is, questions of external validity ask whether the findings observed in an experiment would be observed when other individuals participate, when other settings and conditions are used.

You will want to learn ways to enhance each of these characteristics in the experiments you do. However, this may not be easy because these four important characteristics of a good experiment cannot always be maximized simultaneously. For instance, procedures that increase the sensitivity of an experiment can reduce its external validity. Thus, planning an experiment is something of a juggling act. In what follows you'll find directions for managing this complex task.

WHY PSYCHOLOGISTS CONDUCT EXPERIMENTS

- Researchers conduct experiments to test hypotheses about the causes of behavior.
- Experiments allow researchers to decide whether a treatment or program effectively changes behavior.

A major purpose of conducting experiments is to test empirically the hypotheses derived from psychological theories. A hypothesis is a tentative explanation (e.g., an explanation for why some behavior occurs). If the results of the experiment are consistent with what is predicted by the hypothesis, then the explanation receives support. Such was the outcome of the experiment by Haber and Haber (1982). On the other hand, if the results differ from what was expected, then the proposed explanation may need to be modified and a new hypothesis developed and tested in the next experiment. Although testing and revising hypotheses can sometimes be a long and painstaking process, much like combining the pieces to a puzzle to form a picture, the self-correcting interplay between experiments and proposed explanations can become a challenging and satisfying approach to understanding the causes of the way we think, feel, and behave.

Besides providing empirical tests of proposed explanations derived from theories, experiments can be used to test the effectiveness of a treatment or program. For instance, experiments are often used to test the effects of medical treatments on particular illnesses. This role of experiments in this area has a long history (Thomas, 1992). Consider the fact that near the beginning of the 19th century, typhoid fever and delirium tremens were often fatal. The standard medical practice at that time was to treat these two conditions by bleeding, purging, and the administration of other, similar "therapies." An experiment was performed to test the effectiveness of these supposedly beneficial treatments. One group was randomly assigned to receive the standard treatment (bleeding, purging, etc.), and a second group was randomly assigned to receive nothing but bed rest, good nutrition, and close observation. Thomas (1992) describes the results of this experiment as "unequivocal and appalling" (p. 9): The group given the standard medical treatment of the time did *worse* than the group left untreated. Treating such conditions using early 19th-century practices was worse than not treating them at all! Experiments such as these contributed to the insight that many medical conditions are self-limited; the illness runs its course, and patients recover on their own. Many psychological disorders also will disappear when left untreated, a process known as spontaneous remission. Well-conducted experiments can provide vital information about the effectiveness of treatments and programs in a wide variety of areas. Seligman and his associates, for example, initiated an impressive series of experiments looking at the effect of teaching cognitive and social problem solving techniques on the prevention of childhood depression (e.g., Gillham, Reivich, Jaycox, & Seligman, 1995), a process they call "psychological immunization." Thus, experiments serve a useful purpose not only when we are testing theories but also when we are seeking solutions to society's problems.

EXPERIMENTAL CONTROL

- Control is the essential ingredient of experiments; experimental control is gained through manipulation, holding conditions constant, and balancing.
- Experimental control allows researchers to make the causal inference that the independent variable *caused* the observed changes in the dependent variable.

- An experiment has internal validity when it fulfills the three conditions required for causal inference: covariation, time-order relationship, and elimination of plausible alternative causes.
- Manipulation of an independent variable is used to establish a time-order relationship and allows for a clearer determination of covariation.
- When confounding occurs, a plausible alternative explanation for the observed covariation exists, and therefore, the experiment lacks internal validity.
- Plausible alternative explanations are ruled out by holding conditions constant and balancing.
- In an independent groups design, each group of participants in the experiment represents a different condition of the independent variable.

Experiments are effective for testing hypotheses because they allow us to exercise a relatively high degree of control in a situation. Control is used in experiments to meet the three conditions necessary for a causal inference—that is, to be able to state with confidence that the independent variable *caused* the observed changes in the dependent variable. The three conditions needed to make a causal inference are covariation, time-order relationship, and elimination of plausible alternative causes. When these three conditions are met, the experiment has internal validity.

The covariation condition is met when we observe a relationship between the independent and dependent variables. For example, when Haber and Haber (1982) manipulated the tongue-twister and control sentences, the time it took students to read the sentences differed. We can say that the time needed to read a sentence was related to (covaried with) the type of sentence (tongue-twister or control). The second condition, time-order relationship, is met when we manipulate an independent variable in an experiment and *then* observe changes in the dependent variable. We make a causal inference when the cause precedes the effect. Imagine bumping your head and experiencing a headache (a covariation). The time-order relationship is usually one in which you bump your head and then experience the headache, so you infer that bumping your head caused the subsequent headache. Similarly, in controlled experiments, the condition of time-order relationship will be met when manipulation is used and a subsequent change in behavior is observed.

The key to meeting the conditions of covariation and time-order relationship is the control technique of *manipulation*. When some factor (e.g., type of sentence) is presumed to cause an effect on behavior (e.g., time to read a sentence), the factor is manipulated as an independent variable with at least two levels. In Haber and Haber's experiment the investigators introduced two types of sentences: tongue-twister and control. Many experiments involve more than two levels of an independent variable; however, at least two conditions of the independent variable are necessary in order to compare the differences in observed behavior (the dependent variable).

The most challenging condition for making causal statements is the elimination of plausible alternatives. To infer that some factor caused an effect on behavior we must be sure that other explanations are not possible. To do this, we use two additional methods of control: *holding conditions constant* and *balancing*. These control techniques can be illustrated in an experiment investigating eyewitness behavior conducted by Loftus and Burns (1982).

Their experiment concerned the effect of viewing a violent scene on a person's memory for information in the film that was presented seconds before the individual witnessed the mentally shocking event. The experiment was done at the University of Washington, and 226 students volunteered to participate in order to fulfill a course requirement. The students participated in small groups, and each small group was randomly assigned to view one of two films. Approximately half of the students (115) were assigned to view a violent version of a film. Near the end of the film, these students saw a robber, while running to a getaway car, turn and fire a shot toward two men who were pursuing him. The shot hit a boy in the face, and the boy fell bleeding to the ground. The other half of the students viewed a nonviolent version of the film that was identical to the violent version until just before the shooting. At this point in the film, the camera switched back to inside the bank, where the students saw the bank manager telling the customers and employees what happened and asking them to remain calm. The two versions of the film (violent and nonviolent) represent the levels of the independent variable in the experiment.

After viewing the film, students in both groups answered 25 questions about events in the film. One question was critical: It asked for the number on the

FIGURE 6.1   Black-and-white representation of scene viewed by students, showing boy with the number 17 on his football jersey. (From Loftus and Burns, 1982.)

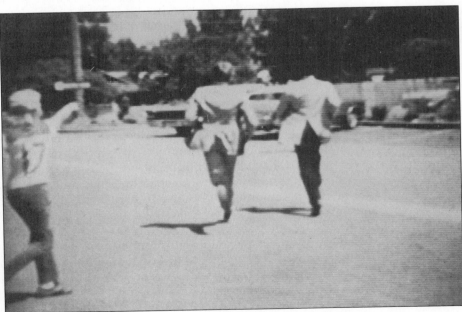

football jersey worn by a boy playing in the parking lot outside the bank. The boy wearing the jersey (see Figure 6.1) was visible for 2 seconds during the film—the 2 seconds before the shooting (violent version) or the 2 seconds before the scenes back in the bank (nonviolent version). The dependent variable was the percentage of students who correctly recalled the jersey number. The results were clear-cut: Just over 4% of the students correctly recalled the number in the violent condition, whereas nearly 28% did so in the nonviolent condition. Thus, Loftus and Burns concluded that a mentally shocking event can impair memory for details immediately preceding the event.

How did Loftus and Burns (1982) use the control techniques of holding conditions constant and balancing? *Holding conditions constant* is used to make sure that the independent variable is the only factor that differs systematically across the groups. In their experiment, the students viewed exactly the same film except for the critical incident; they were given the same experimental instructions at the beginning of the experiment and received the exact same questionnaire at the conclusion.

If the two groups had differed on a factor other than the film manipulation, then the results of the experiment would have been uninterpretable (i.e., lacking internal validity). For example, if the participants in the violent version had viewed a film depicting a boy in the background wearing a different jersey than that seen in the nonviolent version, then we wouldn't know whether the difference in recall was due to viewing the violent version of the film or to the fact that the jersey was different (e.g., a smaller number or less distinct). When the independent variable of interest and a different, potential independent variable are allowed to covary, a **confounding** is present. Holding conditions constant is used to avoid confoundings. By holding constant the boy playing in the background and the jersey (among other things) in the two versions of the film, Loftus and Burns avoided a confounding. A factor that is held constant so it does not change cannot possibly covary with the intended independent variable. More importantly, a factor that is held constant cannot possibly covary with the dependent variable either, making it possible to rule out the variable as a potential explanation for the observed results.

It is important to recognize, however, that we choose to control only those factors we think might influence the behavior we are studying—what we consider *plausible* alternative causes. For instance, Loftus and Burns held the setting constant by testing all their participants in the same room, but it is unlikely they specifically controlled the room temperature to be constant between groups because room temperature probably would not affect memory (at least when varying only a few degrees). They also tested students in "small groups," but there was no apparent attempt to hold constant the size of the group. Again, it doesn't seem plausible that small variations in the size of groups watching the film would have an effect on recall. The point is that we control only those factors we believe are potentially relevant—that is, those additional factors that might affect the behavior of interest. Nevertheless, we should constantly remain alert to the possibility that there may be confounding factors in our experiments whose influence we had not anticipated or considered.

Another example of holding conditions constant is apparent in the sentences used by Haber and Haber (1982) to examine subvocal articulation. The tongue-twisters (Francis Forbes's father fries five flounders) and control sentences (Mary Wright's uncle cooks red lobsters) have several features in common. Two important features held constant are the number of words in the sentences (six) and the number of syllables (nine). Imagine what would happen to our conclusions if the tongue-twister sentences always had more words and syllables than the control sentences; in this case, type of sentence (tongue-twister or control) would be confounded with number of words/syllables in the sentence. When the results indicate that tongue-twisters take longer to read than control sentences, would you be able to conclude subvocal articulation caused the difference? Could it be simply that longer sentences take longer to read? By holding constant the number of words and syllables in the sentence, we can rule out the plausible explanation that more time is needed to read tongue-twisters because they are longer. Can you see any other features of the sentences that were held constant?

The control technique of *balancing* is required because not all factors we want to control can be held constant. The most important factors in psychological research that cannot be held constant are the characteristics of the participants who are tested. Individual differences among participants cannot be eliminated—we simply can't make everyone exactly the same. As a result, differences across conditions on the dependent variable measure may be due to the fact that different people participated in the various conditions. An experimenter must find a way to make sure these individual differences do not confound the independent variable being investigated.

In an **independent groups design,** each group represents a different condition as defined by the independent variable. The experiment on eyewitness behavior is an example of an independent groups designs: The independent variable (i.e., the version of the film) varied across different groups of participants. To have internal validity it is important to balance individual differences among the different groups of the experiment. That is, we must make sure that one group is not smarter, more motivated, more conscientious, contains more females, has fewer psychology majors, and so forth, than another group. In the Loftus and Burns study of eyewitness behavior, if participants viewing the nonviolent film were also shown to be more attentive or have better recall ability than participants viewing the violent version, a plausible alternative explanation for the findings exists. It's possible that attentiveness (or memory ability) and not the version of the film could explain why participants in the nonviolent condition recalled more. By balancing subject characteristics across the groups, we rule out the alternative explanation that group differences on the dependent variable are due to characteristics of the participants. Exactly how this is done will be the major topic of the next section, where we will examine the most commonly used design involving independent groups of subjects, the random groups design.

Before turning to the next topic, however, consider one other characteristic of the methodology used in the Loftus and Burns experiment. The experimental manipulation involved a form of deception because the experimenters did not tell participants that they would see a boy being shot in the face. Moreover, we can imagine that this scene might be emotionally disturbing for some students. No doubt the researchers would argue that deception was necessary in order for memory following a traumatic event to be investigated in this manner. If participants knew they would see an emotionally disturbing event, then they might act differently than they would without that knowledge. For example, they might try to prepare themselves mentally for such an event. This may not only cause them to act differently from the way they would otherwise, but the event itself would perhaps no longer be as shocking as it would be without forewarning. As you learned in Chapter 2, debriefing participants about the experiment is always necessary when deception is used in order to help the participants understand the reasons why they were deceived and to clear up any misunderstandings that might arise from their role in the experiment. Does the experimenters' use of deception in this study of eyewitness behavior seem justified? Do you believe that participants viewing the film were placed "at risk"? If so, do you think the risk was justified?

RANDOM GROUPS DESIGN

Random Assignment

- One type of independent groups design, the random groups design, has comparable groups of individuals participate in different levels of the independent variable.
- The logic of the random groups design allows researchers to make causal inferences about the effect of the independent variable on the dependent variable.
- Random assignment to conditions is used to form comparable groups by balancing or averaging subject characteristics across the conditions of the independent variable manipulation.
- Block randomization balances subject characteristics and potential confoundings that occur during the time in which the experiment is conducted, and creates groups of equal size.

The simplest experiments involve one independent variable with two levels and one measure of the dependent variable. The effect of the independent variable is assessed by observing the difference in the dependent variable between these two levels. In the independent groups design, a different group of subjects participates in each level (i.e., the groups are independent of each other). In the experiment done by Loftus and Burns (1982), for example, one group of participants was assigned to view a violent version of a film while a second group of participants viewed a nonviolent version of the same film. Both groups' memory for details of the films was compared. The logic of the design is straightforward. *If* the two groups are similar on all important characteristics at the start of the experiment *and if*, in the experiment itself, the two groups are treated the same *except* for the level of the independent variable (e.g., violent or nonviolent film), *then* any difference in the performance (e.g., memory for details) between the two groups must be caused by the independent variable.

Clearly, one key to this logic behind the experimental method is forming comparable (similar) groups at the start of the experiment. In the **random groups design,** comparable groups are formed prior to implementing the independent variable. One way to do this is by sampling subjects in a way that ensures each subject in the population has an equal likelihood of being included in each group of the experiment. One possible procedure for accomplishing this goal is random selection, as, for example, when we sample randomly from a registrar's list of students to obtain a representative sample of students for a survey (see Chapter 4). Actually, random selection is rarely used to establish comparable groups in a psychology experiment. Random selection requires well-defined populations (e.g., a registrar's list of students), but psychology experiments usually involve accidental samples from ill-defined populations. For example, human adult participants are often students from introductory psychology courses who volunteer for experiments as part of the course. Individuals enrolled in a general psychology course just happen to be those students who are taking this course in a given school term. Similarly, animal subjects typically are those that happen to be shipped to the researcher by a supplier. The animal researcher may not be aware of the precise nature of the population from which the animals were obtained or how they were selected.

The most common solution to the problem of forming comparable groups when ill-defined populations are involved is to use **random assignment** to place subjects in the conditions of the experiment. A closer look at the details of the Loftus and Burns experiment illustrates both the procedures of random assignment and the power of the random groups design. The major benefit of randomly assigning subjects to groups is to balance or average out the characteristics of the students in the two groups. For example, as we noted previously, if the groups of participants viewing the two versions of the film differed in their memory ability, then we could reasonably argue that the observed difference in memory for details of the film was due simply to this characteristic of the participants and not due to the type of film viewed. In this example, participants' memory ability, and type of film would be confounded. However, because the two samples of over 100 students in the Loftus and Burns experiment were randomly assigned to conditions, they are unlikely to differ (on the average) in memory ability, in attentiveness, or in any other way that might influence individuals' performance on the memory test. That is, random assignment to conditions is used to ensure that the average memory ability, the average attentiveness, and so forth, were comparable for the two groups. Because other potential causal factors were controlled by holding them constant and because individual differences among the students in the two groups were controlled by balancing them using random assignment, we can conclude that the different versions of the film caused the difference in students' memory performance.

A common procedure for carrying out random assignment is block randomization. First, let us describe exactly how block randomization is carried out, and then we will look at what it accomplishes. Suppose we have an experiment with five conditions. A "block" is made up of a random order of all five conditions.

One block of conditions	➜	*Random order of conditions*
A B C D E		C A E B D

In block randomization, one subject is assigned to *each* condition in the block before a second subject is assigned to *any* one condition. That is, we assign subjects to conditions one block at a time. For example, if we want to have 10 subjects in each of five conditions, then there would be 10 blocks in the block-randomized schedule. Each block would consist of a random arrangement of the five conditions. You might think of this procedure as one where you take the first five people who show up for the experiment and assign each one randomly to one of the five conditions, then take the next five people and assign each to one of the five conditions, and so on, until you have done this 10 times. This procedure is illustrated below for the first 11 participants.

10 Blocks	Participants		Condition	
1) C A E B D	1) Cara	→	C	⎫
2) E C D A B	2) Andy	→	A	⎪
3) D B E A C	3) Jacob	→	E	⎬ First block
4) B A C E D	4) Molly	→	B	⎪
5) A C E D B	5) Emily	→	D	⎭
6) A D E B C	6) Eric	→	E	⎫
7) B C A D E	7) Anna	→	C	⎪
8) D C A E B	8) Laura	→	D	⎬ Second block
9) E D B C A	9) Sarah	→	A	⎪
10) C E B D A	10) Lisa	→	B	⎭
	11) Tom	→	D	

and so on for 50 participants

Block randomization is an important technique for randomly assigning subjects to groups because it produces groups that are of equal size while controlling for time-related variables. The number of observations in each group influences the reliability of the descriptive statistics for each group. Because you will be comparing descriptive statistics across groups in your experiment, you want these measures to be of comparable reliability. So, each group should ideally be of similar size. Block randomization accomplishes this. Also, because subjects are assigned to conditions one block at a time, events that occur during the time when the experiment is being done are likely to be experienced by equal numbers of subjects in all conditions of the experiment. This is important because experiments often take a substantial amount of time to complete and the behavior of participants can be affected by events that occur during the time the experiment is conducted.

For example, suppose that you are doing a Loftus-and-Burns-type experiment that requires 100 participants assigned randomly to four conditions (e.g., four types of film segments). Assume further that you are drawing participants from introductory psychology classes. Given the availability of participants and your own personal schedule, such an experiment may take several weeks to complete. What if, after beginning the experiment, an instructor in one of the introductory psychology classes happens to describe the Loftus and Burns experiment? An experiment just like yours! Some students participating in your experiment may now recognize the film of the bank robbery and be prepared for a memory test, which could affect their performance. If all participants with knowledge of the experiment are assigned to one particular experimental condition, this would produce a serious confounding. The beauty of block randomization is that it will balance (or average) any effect of participants' prior knowledge of the experiment across the four conditions. That is, participants from that particular introductory psychology class will be randomly assigned to the different conditions of your experiment in approximately equal numbers. Thus, although there may be more variability in the groups' performances (which, you will see, can be troublesome), you will avoid a confounding. Block randomization works to balance other time-related variables, such as changes in experimenters or even changes in the populations from which subjects are drawn. An experiment conducted across two semesters of a school year (e.g., both fall and spring semesters) is perfectly acceptable if a block randomization schedule is used.

The procedure of block randomization, like many procedures, is best learned by doing it. You can get an idea of what using block randomization is like by doing Challenge Question 1A at the end of the chapter.

Establishing External Validity

- When findings from an experiment can be applied to other individuals, settings, and conditions, the experiment has external validity.
- Although random assignment to conditions improves the internal validity of an experiment, it does not lead to representative samples that would increase the experiment's external validity.
- In some investigations (e.g., theory-testing), researchers may choose to emphasize internal validity over external validity; other researchers may choose to increase external validity using sampling or replication.
- Replication (usually partial replication) is an important method for establishing the reliability and external validity of research findings.
- Researchers often seek to generalize results about conceptual relationships among variables rather than specific conditions, manipulations, settings, and samples.

External validity refers to the extent to which findings from an experiment can be generalized to individuals, settings, and conditions beyond the scope of the specific experiment. Think for a moment about the Loftus and Burns experiment that we have been discussing. Can these findings be used to help us understand eyewitness behavior that might occur in a natural setting (and not on film)? When eyewitnesses are alone? When a different type of traumatic incident is involved? These are questions that ask about the external validity of the eyewitness study.

Although random assignment is the most commonly used procedure for carrying out a random groups design, it does not provide representative samples that allow researchers to generalize the results of an experiment beyond the particular subjects who happened to participate in the experiment. For example, we previously pointed out that participants in many psychology experiments form an accidental sample from an ill-defined population (introductory psychology students). Random assignment of subjects to conditions of an experiment will establish comparable groups *within* this accidental sample and, thus, help assure the internal validity of the experiment. But, how do we establish the external validity of experiments that involve random assignment? How do we generalize the findings for the different groups across individuals, settings, and conditions?

One answer to this question is a bit unsettling, at least initially. Quite simply, for some experiments we do not establish external validity. Mook (1983) argued that, when the purpose of an experiment is to test a specific hypothesis derived from a psychological theory, the question of external validity of the findings is irrelevant. An experiment is often done to determine whether subjects *can* be induced to behave in a certain way. The question whether subjects *do* behave that way in their natural environment is secondary to the question raised in the experiment. The issue of the external validity of experiments is not a new one, as reflected in the following statement by Riley (1962, p. 413): "In general, laboratory experiments are not set up to imitate the most typical case found in nature. Instead, they are intended to answer some specific question of interest to the experimenter."

There are circumstances, however, in which it is critical to obtain results that can be generalized beyond the boundaries of the experiment itself. There are several ways to proceed. First, and most obviously, you can attempt to include in your experiment characteristics of the situation to which you wish to generalize. For example, Ceci (1993) described a research program that he and his colleagues conducted on children's eyewitness testimony. He described how their research program was motivated in part because previous studies on this topic did not capture all the dimensions of an *actual* eyewitness situation. Ceci described how their research program included factors such as multiple suggestive interviews, very long retention intervals, and recollections of stressful experiences. Including these factors made the experiments more representative of situations that are actually involved when children testify.

Ceci (1993) also pointed out, however, that important differences remained between the experiments and real-life situations:

High levels of stress, assaults to a victim's body, and the loss of control are characteristics of events that motivate forensic investigations. Although these factors are at play in some of our other studies, we will never mimic experimentally the assaultive nature of acts perpetrated on child victims, because even those studies that come closest, such as the medical studies, are socially and parentally sanctioned, unlike sexual assaults against children. (pp. 41–42)

As Ceci's comments reveal, in some situations, such as those involving eyewitness testimony about despicable acts, there may be important ethical constraints on establishing the external validity of experiments.

A second way to increase external validity is by sampling people or events. When the external validity of an experiment can be established ethically and when external validity is a high priority for the research, a simple general rule should be followed: Include a representative sample on any dimension (individuals, settings, or conditions) in your experiment to which you want to generalize your results. For example, when you wish to generalize beyond the particular subjects who participated in the experiment, then random selection (when that is possible) is preferable to random assignment. However, even when a truly representative sample on a relevant dimension is not feasible, you can increase the external validity of your study beyond a particular version of a violent event in an eyewitness study, beyond a specific word list in a memory experiment, or beyond a single photograph in a facial recognition study, by including multiple instances of these events. Participants can be randomly assigned to the different versions of each condition and the results then averaged across the different versions. Our belief that the results will generalize to other situations is strengthened when we observe similar results across a variety of stimulus types.

A third way to demonstrate external validity is through replication. **Replication** means repeating all of the procedures used in a particular experiment in order to determine whether the same results will be obtained a second time with different participants. Most replications are done when an initial finding is unexpected or is judged to be especially important. Typically, replication is said to occur if the effect of the independent variable is present in both the original study and in the replication study. *Replication serves the important goal of providing evidence for the reliability of an experimental finding.* Establishing the reliability of experimental findings from experiments posted on the World Wide Web, for instance, has become a matter of serious concern since more research is now being done online by Web users who happen upon experiments at psychology-related sites (e.g., the site maintained by the American Psychological Society). A major question is: Are the results obtained from traditional laboratory experiments with college student participants the same or similar to those results obtained from experiments posted on the Web (see, for example, Krantz, Ballard, & Scher, 1997).

As you might imagine, an exact replication is almost impossible to carry out. The subjects tested in the replication will be different from those tested in the original study; the testing rooms, experimenters, and even apparatus also may be different. Thus, when attempting to replicate an experimental result, in nearly every instance the replication will be a partial replication. Nevertheless, there are distinct advantages to carrying out a partial replication. *Partial replications*, in fact, are commonly done as a routine part of the process of investigating the conditions under which a phenomenon reliably occurs. Let us examine why.

A partial replication can help to establish both experimental reliability (by demonstrating that a similar experimental result occurs when the *same* basic experimental procedures are repeated) and external validity (by showing that a similar experimental result occurs when slightly *different* experimental procedures are used). Consider the same basic experiment done in both a large metropolitan public university and in a small rural private college; the participants and the settings in the experiments are very different. If the same results are obtained even with these different participants and settings, we can say the findings can be generalized across these two populations and settings. Notice that neither experiment alone has external validity; it is the findings that occur in *both* experiments that have external validity.

In partial replications, some but not all of the conditions of the original experiment are repeated. This may also occur when an experimenter chooses to repeat some levels of an independent variable, and also add some new levels not previously tested. When the same results are observed for the levels of the independent variable that are repeated (replicated), evidence for the reliability of the findings is obtained (remember that reliability indicates *consistency*). For conditions that are different from the original experiment, observing similar findings demonstrates the external validity of those findings. For instance, suppose you decided to follow up the interesting results on subvocal speech obtained by Haber and Haber (1982). If you designed a new experiment that included their two types of sentences (control and tongue-twisters) but also included a new type of sentence that varied in some theoretically important way from the original ones, then you would be able to obtain information about the reliability of their results (did you find the same thing when using their sentences?) as well as the external validity of their results along the dimension you chose to vary.

A frequently asked question concerning external validity of psychological research findings is related to the nature of the "subjects." As you are aware, many studies in psychology involve college students who participate in experiments as part of their introductory psychology course. Dawes (1991), among others, argues that college students are a select group who may not always provide a good basis for building general conclusions about human behavior and mental processes. He suggests that the college environment tends to protect students from external problems, thereby enhancing their feeling of control over their lives. People living outside the college environment may not have the same sense of control that college students do. Thus, research on "locus of control" done with college students may not generalize to people living outside the college environment. On the other hand, research involving fundamental processes such as sensation or perception might reasonably be judged to generalize well to noncollege students despite the differences in environment. In general, the arguments raised by Dawes and others should lead us to exercise care in generalizing conclusions from all studies in which college students are participants.

FIGURE 6.2   Questions of external validity include those related to the nature of the participants in psychological research; for example, we might ask whether results of studies done with college students will generalize to people not in a college.

It would be virtually impossible to establish the external validity of each finding in psychology by performing partial replications across each of the dimensions over which we want to generalize (e.g., subjects, settings, tasks, and so on). But if we take arguments like those of Dawes seriously, as indeed we should, it would appear that we have an impossible task in front of us. How, for instance, do we show that an experimental finding obtained with a group of college students will generalize to groups of older adults, working professionals, less educated individuals, and so forth? Underwood and Shaughnessy (1975) provide an answer, or at least an approach worth considering. Their notion is that we should assume that behavior is relatively continuous across time, subjects, and settings unless we have reason to assume otherwise. For instance, most experiments are carried out in individual laboratory rooms, but we are not likely to argue that the results of the experiment apply only to those particular rooms. Similarly, the particular subjects tested in an experiment are considered, according to this reasoning, to be generally representative of other, similar individuals who might have been tested.

Underwood and Shaughnessy's (1975) assumption is not a call to blind faith in any experimental finding. The boundaries for generalizing experimental findings are set by consensus of the research community. The research community may agree, for example, that introductory psychology students who volunteer for experiments are representative of college students in general but not representative of young children or the elderly. Or, agreement may be reached for some phenomena and not others. For instance, generalizing results of a vision experiment based on a college student sample may be safer than generalizing results of a locus of control experiment. Underwood and Shaughnessy (1975) argued that the burden of proof regarding questions of external validity rests with the person claiming we should *not* generalize. Consider criticisms questioning the generalizability of results based on college students. One response to such criticisms is to place the burden of proof on the critics by requiring them to provide an empirical demonstration that results based on college students are, in fact, limited. Such direct tests using partial replications represent perhaps the best way to establish the external validity of experimental findings.

Yet another way to establish the external validity of experimental research conducted in laboratory settings is demonstrated by Anderson and Bushman's (1997) analysis of aggression research. They used meta-analysis, a procedure described at the end of this chapter, to compare findings from aggression experiments conducted in laboratory settings to correlational findings from "real-world" settings. Critics of laboratory experiments argue that "artificial" laboratory situations in which, for example, college students may be "aggressive" by rating a rude experimenter negatively, do not tell us much about real-life aggression in which people threaten, assault, and murder others. Critics of real-world studies argue that correlations, for example, between violence presented in media and crime statistics, do not tell us about the causes of aggression. Anderson and Bushman's approach to this controversy was to argue that both types of studies potentially tell us about aggression if we look at the psychological processes these studies are attempting to examine. That is, what we wish to generalize from any one study are *conceptual relationships* among variables, not the specific conditions, manipulations, settings, samples, etc. (see also Banaji & Crowder, 1989; Mook, 1983).

An example provided by Anderson and Bushman (1997) illustrates the idea of generalizing at the level of psychological processes. We could conduct a study with 5-year-old children to determine if a specific name-calling manipulation induces anger and aggression, and then conduct another study to determine if this name-calling manipulation generalizes to 35-year-old adults. As Anderson and Bushman state, this type of research is likely to have low external validity regardless of whether the studies are conducted in the laboratory or the real world because the specific name-calling manipulation, " 'Pooh-pooh head' just doesn't pack the same 'punch' for 5- and 35-year-old people" (p. 21). However, if we wish to generalize the general psychological process, "*insults increase aggressive behavior,*" we could use different words that would be meaningful insults for each population to determine if the psychological process regarding insults generalizes across populations.

To examine psychological processes related to aggression, Anderson and Bushman (1997) identified a list of individual differences variables and situational variables they believed are related to aggression. They then searched the psychological literature for laboratory studies and real-world studies to compare the effects of these variables in the two settings. Importantly, they focused on conceptual relationships in the studies rather than comparing studies that used the same specific operationalizations of variables. For each individual differences variable they examined, they found the setting of the research did not change the nature of the effect. In both laboratory settings and real-world settings, males were more physically aggressive than females, but males and females did not differ in verbal aggressiveness; trait aggressiveness was positively correlated with aggression; and people with Type A personalities were more aggressive than people with Type B personalities. Also, for each situational variable they examined, with the exception of temperature, they found the nature of the effects was the same in laboratory and real-world studies. In both settings, provocation, alcohol, violent media, and anonymity of the aggressor were found to increase aggression. Anderson and Bushman concluded that "artificial" laboratory experiments do provide meaningful information about aggression because they demonstrate the same conceptual relationships that are observed in real-world aggression. Furthermore, laboratory experiments allow researchers to isolate the potential causes of aggression and to investigate boundary conditions for when aggression will or will not occur.

What about when results in the lab and the real world disagree? In real-world studies (as was observed in the archival data presented in Chapter 5), hot temperatures are associated consistently with aggression, but temperature effects are inconsistent in laboratory studies. Anderson and Bushman (1997) argue that these discrepancies, rather than evidence for the weakness of either method, should be used to help us refine our theories about aggression. That is, the discrepancies should make us recognize that different psychological processes may be at work in each setting. When we increase our understanding of these discrepancies, we will increase our understanding of aggression.

Challenges to Internal Validity

- Randomly assigning intact groups to different conditions of the independent variable creates a potential confounding due to individual differences among participants in the intact groups.
- Block randomization increases internal validity by balancing extraneous variables across conditions of the independent variable.
- Whether extraneous variables are controlled by balancing or by holding conditions constant influences the external validity and sensitivity of an experiment.
- Selective subject loss, but not mechanical subject loss, threatens the internal validity of an experiment.
- Placebo control groups are used to control for the problem of demand characteristics, and double-blind experiments control both demand characteristics and experimenter effects.

Testing Intact Groups   Random assignment is used to assure comparable groups in the random groups design. There are times, however, when noncomparable groups are formed even when random assignment appears to have been used. This problem occurs when intact groups (and not individual subjects) are randomly assigned to the conditions of an experiment. *Intact groups* are those that were formed prior to the start of the experiment. For example, the different sections of an introductory psychology class are intact groups. Students are not randomly assigned to different sections of introductory psychology classes (although sometimes scheduling classes seems random!). Students often choose to be in a particular section because of the time the class meets, the instructor, friends who will be in the class, and any number of other factors. Problems arise, however, when individuals differ across the intact groups. For example, students who choose to take an 8:00 A.M. section may differ from students who prefer an 11:00 A.M. section. Random assignment of these intact groups to experimental conditions is simply not sufficient to balance the systematic differences among the intact groups. These individual differences, then, are almost guaranteed to confound the independent variable under investigation. The solution to this problem is simple—do not use intact groups in a random groups design. (As you will see in Chapter 10, there are situations when researchers use intact groups because random assignment of participants to conditions is not possible; however, this means that the problem of confounding must be dealt with, and is always a less desirable alternative to a random groups design.)

Balancing Extraneous Variables A number of factors in an experiment may vary as a result of practical considerations when carrying out the study. For example, to complete an experiment more quickly, a researcher might decide to have several different experimenters test small groups of participants. The sizes of the groups and the experimenters themselves become potentially relevant variables that could confound the experiment, making the results uninterpretable. For example, if all the individuals in the experimental group are tested by one experimenter and all those in the control group are tested by another experimenter, the levels of intended independent variable become confounded with the experimenters. One would not be able to determine whether an observed difference between the control group and experimental group on the dependent variable was due to the independent variable manipulation or to the fact that different experimenters implemented the study.

Potential variables that are not directly of interest to the researcher, such as different experimenters and sizes of groups, are such vexing sources of confounding that they have a special name: **extraneous variables.** But don't let the term fool you! An experiment confounded by an extraneous variable is no less confounded than if the confounding variable were of considerable inherent interest. For example, Evans and Donnerstein (1974) studied one such extraneous variable—the differences between participants who volunteer early in the term and those who volunteer late in the term. Their results indicated that those who volunteer early are more academically oriented and are more likely to have an internal locus of control (i.e., they emphasize their own responsibility for their actions rather than external factors). Their findings suggest it would not be wise to test participants in the experimental condition at the beginning of the term and participants in the control condition at the end of the term, as this would potentially confound the independent variable with participants' locus of control. As we have seen, block randomization should be used to balance characteristics of participants across the conditions of an experiment.

Block randomization provides an easy and effective way to control numerous extraneous variables by balancing them across groups. All that is required is that entire blocks be tested at each level of the extraneous variable. For example, if there were four different experimenters, entire blocks of the block-randomized schedule would be assigned to each experimenter. Because each block contains all the conditions of the experiment, this strategy guarantees that each condition will be tested by each experimenter. Usually, we would assign the same number of blocks to each experimenter, but this is not essential. What is essential is that entire blocks be tested at each level of the extraneous variable, which, in this case, is experimenter. The balancing act can become a bit tricky when there are several extraneous variables, but careful advance planning can avoid confounding by such factors.

Even when their potential effects have been controlled through balancing, extraneous variables affect the sensitivity and external validity of an experiment. For example, if five different experimenters test an equal number of participants in each of two conditions, the experiment will be free of confounding due any differences across experimenters. However, the performance of the participants within each condition is likely to vary more than if one experimenter had tested all the participants. Participants are likely, after all, to respond differently to the different experimenters, even when the experimenters try to treat all participants within a condition the same way. Similarly, using two different word lists in a memory experiment or five different perceptual displays in a perception experiment will increase variability relative to a situation in which only one instance was used. This increased variability within each group makes it harder to detect differences between the groups, thus reducing the sensitivity of the experiment. If a difference is obtained between the two conditions, however, this finding has greater external validity than, for example, if only one experimenter had done the testing (because the findings can be generalized across different experimenters).

This is the general principle that emerges: *Controlling extraneous variables by holding them constant leads to more sensitive experiments with less external validity, whereas controlling extraneous variables by balancing them leads to lower sensitivity but increased external validity*. Both balancing and holding constant extraneous variables are equally effective control techniques, however, in ensuring that an experiment is internally valid.

Subject Loss   Internally valid experiments involving the random groups design need to have comparable groups of subjects not only at the beginning of an experiment but, except for the addition of the independent variable, also at the end. When subjects begin an experiment but fail to complete it successfully, the internal validity of the experiment can be threatened. There are two types of subject loss: mechanical and selective. It is important to distinguish between these two ways by which subjects are lost because selective subject loss poses a threat to internal validity (Underwood & Shaughnessy, 1975).

Mechanical subject loss occurs when a subject fails to complete the experiment because of an equipment failure (in this case, the experimenter is considered part of the equipment). If a light bulb burns out, or if someone inadvertently interrupts an experimental session, or if the experimenter reads the wrong set of instructions, the subject who was being tested represents a mechanical subject loss. Mechanical loss is unrelated to any characteristic of the subject, so it should not lead to systematic differences between the characteristics of the subjects who successfully complete the experiment in the various conditions of the experiment. In a real sense, mechanical subject loss represents the effect of chance events (e.g., a projector bulb happens to burn out) and, thus, should be expected to occur equally across conditions of an experiment. Hence, internal validity is not typically threatened when data from such subjects are excluded from the experiment. When mechanical subject loss occurs, the name of the dropped subject and the reason for the loss need to be recorded. The lost subject is then replaced by the next subject tested.

Selective subject loss is a far more serious matter. **Selective subject loss** occurs (1) when subjects are lost differentially across the conditions of the experiment; (2) when some characteristic of the subject is responsible for the loss; and (3) when this subject characteristic is related to the dependent variable used to assess the outcome of the study. Selective subject loss destroys the comparable groups that are essential to the logic of the random groups design, and can thus render the experiment uninterpretable. This problem can arise in a variety of experimental situations, for example, physiological studies involving surgical or drug treatments, memory experiments testing retention over days or weeks, and longitudinal designs in survey research (see Chapter 4).

The problems associated with selective subject loss can be illustrated by considering a fictitious but realistic example. Assume that the directors of a local fitness center decide to do an experiment to test the effectiveness of a one-month fitness program they have developed. They identify 80 people who are willing to volunteer for the experiment, and they randomly assign 40 to each of two groups. Random assignment to conditions is used to create comparable groups by balancing characteristics such as weight, fitness level, motivation, and so on across the two groups. Members of the control group are simply asked to come to the center at the end of the month. When they arrive, they are given a fitness test. Those in the experimental group participate in a vigorous fitness program for one month prior to the test at the end of the month. Assume all 40 control participants show up for the fitness test, but only 25 of the experimental participants stay with the rigorous fitness program for the full month, and only these 25 people are given the test. The average fitness score is significantly higher for the experimental group, leading the directors of the fitness center to make the claim that: "A scientifically based research study has shown that our program leads to better fitness."

FIGURE 6.3   Selective subject loss occurs when participants fail to complete an experiment for reasons related to the dependent variable.

Do you think the fitness center's claim is justified? It's not. At least not on the basis of the study we have described. This hypothetical study represents a classic example of selective subject loss. The loss occurred differentially across conditions; participants were lost only from the experimental group. The problem is not that the groups ended up different in size. The results would have been interpretable if 25 people had been randomly assigned to the experimental group and 40 to the control group and all the individuals had completed the experiment. The problem is that the 25 experimental participants who completed the fitness program are not likely to be comparable to the 40 control participants. It is likely that only the more naturally fit experimental participants could complete the rigorous program; the less fit individuals likely dropped out. Thus, the loss is traceable to a characteristic of the participants—their original level of fitness—and this characteristic is relevant to the outcome of the study. The final fitness scores of the experimental participants might have been higher even if they had not participated in the fitness program because they were more fit when they began!

If selective subject loss is not identified until after the experiment is completed, little can be done except to chalk up the experience of having conducted an uninterpretable experiment. You can take some preventive steps, however, if you realize in advance that selective loss may be a problem. One alternative is to administer a pretest and screen out subjects who are likely to be lost. In our example, an initial test of fitness could have been given, and only those participants who scored above some minimal level allowed into the experimental and control groups. The cost associated with this alternative is decreased external validity because the results could be generalized only to people above the minimal fitness level. This cost may be well worth paying because an interpretable study of limited external validity is still preferable to an uninterpretable study.

The second way to minimize the risk of selective subject loss also involves a pretest. Here all subjects are given the pretest but are then simply randomly assigned to one of the conditions. Then, if a subject is lost from the experimental group, a subject with a comparable pretest score is dropped from the control group. In a sense, this approach tries to restore the comparability of the groups. This approach also entails a cost of decreased external validity because those subjects who finally end up in the study may differ from those in the original sample. The advantage of this approach is that external validity is lost *only if* selective subject loss *does* occur. When a pretest is used to check for selective subject loss, it is essential that the pretest measures the dimension responsible for the loss. In our example, a fitness pretest would be preferable to a pretest of visual acuity (which is likely to be unrelated to subject loss in this study). Thus, the researcher must be ready to anticipate possible reasons for selective subject loss and measure these factors prior to beginning the study.

Placebo Control and Double-Blind Experiments   The final challenge to internal validity we will describe arises because of expectations held by both participants and experimenters. In our discussion of the problem of reactivity in observational research (Chapter 3), we introduced the concept of demand characteristics (Orne, 1962). **Demand characteristics** refer to the cues and other information used by individuals to guide their behavior in a psychological study. For example, if research participants know they have been given alcohol, they may expect certain effects, such as relaxation or giddiness, and behave accordingly. In addition to potential problems due to demand characteristics, there are also potential biases traceable to the expectations of the experimenters. The general term used to describe these biases is **experimenter effects** (Rosenthal, 1963). Experimenter effects may lead the experimenters to treat subjects differently in the different groups of the experiment in ways other than those required to implement the independent variable. In the context of our example experiment involving alcohol, experimenter effects could occur if the experimenters treated people in the different groups differently by, for example, reading the instructions more slowly to individuals who had been given alcohol. Experimenter effects also include biased observations by experimenters when they know which treatment the subject has received. Biased observations due to experimenter effects would arise in the alcohol study, for example, if the experimenters were more likely to notice unusual motor movements or slurred speech among the "drinkers" (because they "expect" drinkers to behave this way).

The problems of demand characteristics and experimenter effects can never be eliminated, but there are special research designs that control these problems. Demand characteristics may be controlled using a research design that involves **placebo control** groups. A *placebo* (from the Latin word meaning "I shall please") is a substance that looks like a drug or other active substance but is actually an *inert*, or inactive, substance. Pishkin and Shurley (1983) used a placebo control group to demonstrate the effectiveness of two drugs (doxepin and hydroxy-zine). The drugs were tested to determine if they reduce arousal levels of psychiatric patients in response to stress. The placebo participants were given capsules identical to the two drugs, but the placebo capsules contained only lactose, a sugar found in milk. None of the participants in the placebo control group realized their pill contained no medicine so all groups had the same "awareness" of taking a drug, and therefore, the same expectations. That is, the demand characteristics were the same for the groups—all participants expected to experience effects of the drug. Any differences between the experimental groups and the placebo control group could legitimately be attributed to the *actual* effect of the drug taken by the experimental participants, and not the participants' expectations about receiving a drug. One group of researchers claims that a placebo effect is significantly related to the therapeutic effect of antidepressant drugs such as Prozac (Kirsch & Sapirstein, 1998).

Placebo control groups can be used in combination with a technique that controls for both demand characteristics *and* experimenter effects. The technique is called a **double-blind** procedure because both the participant *and* the observer are blind to (unaware of) what treatment is being administered. In an experiment such as the Pishkin and Shurley (1983) study, two researchers would be needed to accomplish the double-blind procedure. The first researcher would prepare the drug capsules and code each capsule in some way; the second researcher would distribute the drugs to the participants, recording the code for each drug as it was given to an individual. This procedure ensures there is a record of which drug each person received, but neither the participant nor the experimenter who actually administers the drugs (and observes their effects) knows which treatment the participant received. Thus, experimenter expectancies about the effects of the treatment are controlled because the researcher who makes observations is unaware of who received the treatment and who received the placebo. Similarly, demand characteristics are controlled because participants remain unaware of whether they received the drug or placebo. Note that using placebo control groups raises special ethical concerns, as research participants who expect to receive a drug may instead receive a placebo. Typically, the ethics of this procedure are addressed in the informed consent procedure prior to the start of the experiment. Participants are told they may receive a drug or a placebo. Only individuals who consent to receiving the placebo or the drug participate in the research.

ALTERNATIVE INDEPENDENT GROUPS DESIGNS

Matched Groups Design

- A matched group design may be used to create comparable groups when there are too few subjects available for random assignment to work effectively.
- Matching subjects on the dependent variable task is the best approach for creating matched groups, followed by matching subjects on a task that is from the same category as the dependent variable.
- After subjects are matched on the matching task they should then be randomly assigned to the conditions of the independent variable.

The random groups design is by far the most common type of independent groups design. To work effectively, however, the random groups design requires samples of sufficient size to guarantee that individual differences among subjects will be balanced through random assignment. Specifically, the assumption behind the random groups design is that individual differences "average out" across groups. But how many subjects are required to ensure that this averaging process works as it should? The answer is, "It depends." More subjects will be needed to average out individual differences when sampling from a heterogeneous population than from a more homogeneous one.

We can be relatively confident that random assignment will *not* be effective in balancing the differences among subjects when small numbers of subjects are tested from heterogeneous populations. However, this is exactly the situation researchers face in several areas of psychology. For example, some developmental psychologists study newborn infants; others study elderly people. These psychologists often have available only limited numbers of participants, and both newborns and the elderly certainly represent diverse populations.

FIGURE 6.4 Random assignment is not likely to be effective in balancing differences among subjects when small numbers of subjects from heterogeneous populations are tested (e.g., newborns). In this situation, researchers may want to consider the matched groups design.

One alternative that researchers have in this situation is to administer all the conditions of the experiment to all the subjects, using a repeated measures design (to be discussed in Chapter 7). Nevertheless, some independent variables require separate groups of subjects for each level. For instance, assume you are trying to assess the effects of participation in a special program for senior citizens. You will need to have a separate control group that does not participate in the program. Or suppose you wish to administer two types of postnatal care to different groups of premature infants. In these situations a repeated measures design is of no use.

The matched groups design is a good alternative when neither the random groups design nor repeated measures design can be used effectively. The logic of the **matched groups design** is simple and compelling. Instead of trusting random assignment to form comparable groups, the researcher makes the groups equivalent by matching subjects. In most uses of the matched groups design a pretest task is used to match subjects. The challenge is to select a pretest task (also called a matching task) that equates the groups on a dimension that is relevant to the outcome of the experiment. *The matched groups design is useful only when a good matching task is available.*

Researchers have several options when selecting a matching task. The most preferred option is to match subjects using the same task that will be used in the experiment itself. For example, if the dependent variable in the experiment is blood pressure, participants should be matched on blood pressure prior to the start of the experiment. The matching is accomplished by measuring the blood pressure of all participants and then forming pairs or triples or quadruples of subjects (depending on the number of conditions in the experiment) who have identical or similar blood pressures. After these matched sets are formed, the investigator must assign subjects within a set randomly to the different conditions of the experiment such that each subject in a matched set is assigned to a different condition. Random assignment (after matching the subjects) is used to balance individual differences other than those for which subjects were matched. The logic of the design is again straightforward. Participants in the different matched groups begin the study with average blood pressure equivalent across the groups. Assume, then, some treatment is applied to one group but not to others. Blood pressure is assessed again at the end of the treatment to determine the outcome of the study. Because average blood pressure across the groups was equivalent at the start of the study, any group differences in blood pressure at the end of the study may be attributed to the treatment (presuming other potential variables have been held constant or balanced).

In some experiments, the primary dependent variable cannot be used to match subjects. For example, consider an experiment that examines different approaches to solving a puzzle. If a pretest were given to see how long it took individuals to solve this puzzle, the participants would likely learn the solution to the puzzle during the pretest. If so, then it would be impossible to observe differences in the speed with which different groups of participants solved the puzzle in the experiment itself. After having experience with the puzzle in the pretest, all participants would likely solve the puzzle very quickly. In this situation the next best alternative to using the experimental task as the matching task is to use a task from the same class or category as the experimental task. In our problem-solving experiment, participants could be matched on their performance when solving a different puzzle from the experimental puzzle. However, it is important that performance on the experimental puzzle correlates positively with performance on the matching puzzle. The least preferred alternative for matching is to use a task from a class different from the experimental task. For our problem-solving experiment, participants could be matched on some test of general ability, such as an intelligence test. As is true for all effective matching tasks, this general matching task must correlate positively with performance on the experimental task. One must keep in mind that as the correlation between the matching task and the dependent variable decreases, the advantage of the matched group design, relative to the random groups design, also decreases.

There is an additional important issue that arises with the matched groups design even when a good matching task is available. Consider an experiment comparing two different methods of caring for premature infants. The matched groups design would work well for this type of experiment. Six pairs of premature infants could be matched on their body weight and on measures such as their scores on an infant motor coordination test. This experiment illustrates the conditions when a matched groups design is most helpful—the need to test separate groups with only small numbers of participants and good matching tasks available. We began our discussion of the matched groups design by saying it is useful when we have too few participants to allow randomization to form comparable groups. A matching task like the body weights of the premature infants ensures comparable groups *only* on the dimension measured by the matching task. Although the matched groups design serves a very important purpose by allowing us to form comparable groups on the significant dimensions reflected in good matching tasks (e.g., body weights of premature infants), there remain potentially relevant characteristics of the participants that are not matched. For example, the two groups of premature infants may not be comparable in their general health or in their degree of parental attachment. It is important, therefore, to use random assignment in the matched groups design to balance other potential factors beyond the matching task. For instance, after matching the infants on body weight and motor coordination, the pairs of infants would be randomly assigned to one of the two groups. In conclusion, *the matched groups design is a better alternative than the random groups design when a good matching task is available and when only a small number of (heterogeneous) subjects is available for an experiment that requires separate groups for each condition.*

Natural Groups Design

- Individual differences variables (or subject variables) are selected rather than manipulated to form natural groups designs.
- The natural groups design represents a type of correlational research in which researchers look for covariations between natural groups variables and dependent variables.

- Causal inferences cannot be made regarding the effects of natural groups variables because plausible alternative explanations for group differences exist.

Researchers in many areas of psychology are interested in independent variables that are called *individual differences variables* or *subject variables*. Individual differences variables such as gender, introversion-extraversion, or aggressiveness, are important independent variables in personality psychology, abnormal psychology, developmental psychology, and social psychology. These variables cannot be manipulated. We cannot randomly assign someone to be 20 years old or to be an introverted or aggressive person, or to be male or female. Instead, we *select* the levels of these independent variables.

It is important to differentiate experiments involving independent variables whose levels are selected from those involving independent variables whose levels are manipulated. Experiments involving independent variables whose levels are selected—like individual differences variables—are called **natural groups designs.** The natural groups design is frequently used in situations in which ethical and practical constraints prevent us from directly manipulating independent variables. No matter how interested we might be in the effects of traumatic events such as major surgery on subsequent depression, we could not ethically perform major surgery on a randomly assigned group of introductory psychology students and then compare their depression symptoms with those of another group who did not receive surgery! Similarly, if we were interested in the relationship between divorce and emotional disorders, we could not randomly assign some people to get divorced. By using the natural groups design, however, we can compare people who have had surgery with those who have not. Similarly, people who have chosen to divorce can be compared with those who have chosen to stay married.

The intent of studies using the natural groups design is to determine whether these natural "treatments" result in systematic differences in behavior. For example, studies have shown that people who are separated or divorced are much more likely to receive psychiatric care than are those who are married, widowed, or have remained single. In general, the natural groups design involves looking for *correlations* between subjects' characteristics and their performance. Because of this, the natural groups design represents a type of correlational research (see also Chapter 4).

Natural groups designs are highly effective in meeting the first two objectives of the scientific method—description and prediction. Serious problems can arise, though, when the results of natural groups designs are used to make causal statements. For instance, the finding that divorced persons are more likely than married persons to receive psychiatric care shows that these two factors covary. This result could be taken to mean that divorce causes emotional disorders that lead to the need for psychiatric care. Before reaching this conclusion, however, we must assure ourselves that the time-order condition for a causal inference has been met—namely, that divorce preceded

FIGURE 6.5 Do individuals who join fraternities differ in important ways from individuals who do not? This question can be answered using the natural groups design.

the emotional disorder. Demonstrating covariation does nothing to specify the direction of the causal relationship. Perhaps those who suffer from emotional disorders are more likely to get divorced because the disorder placed strain on the relationship or because the emotional disorder contributed to marrying unwisely in the first place.

The most critical problem in drawing causal inferences based on the natural groups design is meeting the third condition for demonstrating causality: eliminating plausible alternative causes. Do you see how this problem is especially troublesome with the natural groups design? Eliminating plausible alternative causes requires a high degree of control and the experimenter has far less control in the natural groups design. The individual differences studied in the natural groups design are usually confounded. This is because groups of individuals are likely to differ in many ways in addition to the variable used to classify them. For example, individuals who divorce and individuals who stay married may differ with respect to a number of characteristics other than their marital status. For example, they may differ in their religious practices or financial circumstances. Any differences observed between divorced and married individuals may be due to these other characteristics, and not divorce. The manipulation done by "nature" is rarely the controlled type we have come to expect in establishing the internal validity of an experiment.

In Chapter 8 we will discuss an effective approach for drawing causal inferences in the natural groups design. The approach requires that *individual differences be studied in combination with independent variables that can be manipulated.* This combination of more than one independent variable in one experiment requires the use of a complex design, which we cover in Chapter 8. For now, recognize that drawing causal inferences based on the natural groups design can be a treacherous enterprise. While we frequently refer to such designs as "experiments," there are important differences between an experiment involving an individual differences variable and an experiment involving a manipulated variable.

ANALYSIS OF EXPERIMENTS

Overview

- Descriptive statistics are not sufficient to summarize the results of a study because they provide no indication of whether the findings are reliable.
- Inferential statistics are used to determine whether an independent variable has a reliable effect on a dependent variable.
- Two methods to make inferences about sample data are null hypothesis testing and confidence intervals.

The purpose of an experiment is to determine whether an independent variable has had an effect on behavior as indicated by changes in the dependent variable. The foundation of the analysis of an experiment is the description of the results. Descriptive statistics begin to answer the question, "What happened in your experiment?" (See Appendix A for an overview of the major steps in data analysis.) Nevertheless, descriptive statistics are rarely sufficient to answer this question. The problem is that the data we typically are describing are based on samples we have selected and assigned to the conditions of our experiment. The situation would be entirely different if we were describing populations and not samples. A population represents all the data of interest; a sample is just part of those data. Rarely, however, do psychologists work with populations. Most of the time they sample behavior and seek to make a conclusion about the effect of an independent variable based on these samples. Sample characteristics can vary from one sample to another simply due to chance variation. Knowing this requires us to be very cautious about drawing conclusions based simply on calculating descriptive statistics for our samples. How do we know that the differences we "see" among our sample means are reliable?

The best way to determine whether the differences in means obtained in an experiment are reliable would be to replicate the experiment and see if the same outcome is obtained. We noted earlier that replications provide evidence both for the external validity of a finding and the reliability of the finding. Although replications, especially partial replications, do occur in the natural course of research on a topic, they would be a cumbersome and inefficient way to establish the reliability of experimental findings if they were to be required for every experiment done in psychology. Participants for experiments are a scarce resource, and each replication costs us a study that could be done to ask new and different questions about behavior. We need some alternative to replication for determining whether the differences obtained in a single experiment are larger than would be expected on the basis of error (chance) variation alone.

The typical approach to drawing conclusions based on sample data has been through the use of inferential statistics, and more specifically, the approach called null hypothesis testing. **Inferential statistics** provide a way to test whether the differences in a dependent variable associated with various conditions of an experiment can be attributed to an effect of the independent variable. Null hypothesis testing is the most common form of inferential statistics used to make these decisions. There are many critics of this approach, however, and psychologists have been urged to seek other ways to draw inferences about sample data (e.g., Cohen, 1995; Loftus, 1996; Schmidt, 1996). Thus, in what follows, we first introduce you to an important alternative to null hypothesis testing, one that makes use of confidence intervals around the means. Then, we will discuss the more common approach, one based on null hypothesis testing. At that time, we will identify some of the important limitations to null hypothesis testing that critics have highlighted. Our introduction will be brief; you will find more about these two approaches to the analysis of experiments in Appendix A.

Confidence Intervals

- Samples are used to estimate population values.
- Confidence intervals for a sample identify the range of values in which we can expect a population value to fall with a specified level of confidence.
- Researchers determine whether populations differ by noting whether the confidence intervals for different samples in a study overlap.

To illustrate the use of confidence intervals to analyze and interpret results, we consider a study on how infants "grasp the nature of pictures" (DeLoache, Pierroutsakos, Uttal, Rosengren, & Gottlieb, 1998). Have you ever wondered whether infants understand that a picture of an object is not the same thing as the object itself? DeLoache and her colleagues were intrigued by research demonstrating that infants as young as 5 months seem to recognize the similarity between objects and their pictures, but also seem to recognize they're not the same. However, these research findings do not correspond well to anecdotes of infants' behavior toward pictures in which infants and young children try to grasp or pick up the objects represented in pictures, and even try to step into a picture of a shoe! These anecdotal reports suggest that infants and children treat pictured objects as if they are real objects, despite the two-dimensional representation in the picture. In four studies, DeLoache et al. examined "to what extent infants would treat depicted objects as if they were real objects" (p. 205).

FIGURE 6.6   Infants' understanding of the nature of pictures was examined by observing how they investigate and point to pictured objects. (From DeLoache et al., 1998; used with permission.)

Although we will focus on the results presented for DeLoache et al.'s (1998) fourth study, it is helpful to highlight the findings from their first three studies. In Study 1, a structured observation, 10 9-month-old infants were observed as they explored a picture book with "eight highly realistic color photographs of individual objects (common plastic toys)" (p. 206). The results indicated that each infant manually explored at least one picture and 8 of the 10 infants tried to grasp a pictured object at least once (the average was 3.7 attempts). In their second study, the investigators sought to make sure that infants could distinguish between pictured objects and their real-life counterparts. In this study, eight 9-month-olds were presented with the pictured object and the real object simultaneously. Overwhelmingly, the infants reached first for the object instead of the picture (86% of the trials), indicating that infants' grasping at pictures in Study 1 was not because the infants could not discriminate between two- and three-dimensional objects. The purpose of Study 3 was to determine the external validity of these findings by observing the grasping of pictures by "Beng infants from severely impoverished and largely nonliterate families living in a rural village in the West African nation of Côte d'Ivoire (Ivory Coast)" (p. 207). (See Figure 6.6.) The results indicated that Beng infants manually explored and grasped at the pictures (including pictures of objects common in the Beng community) in the same way as American infants.

The purpose of the fourth study was to determine how children's behavior toward pictures changes with age. Three age groups were tested: 9-month-olds, 15-month-olds, and 19-month-olds. Each group had 16 children, 8 girls and 8 boys. In addition to observing children's behaviors of investigating the pictures with their hands (grasping and other investigative behaviors), the

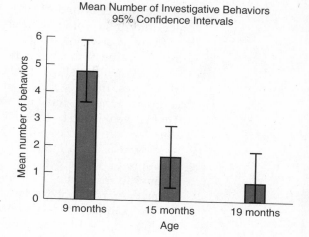

FIGURE 6.7   Mean number of investigative behaviors with 95% confidence intervals for 9-month-olds, 15-month-olds, and 19-month-olds. (From DeLoache et al., 1998; used with permission.)

researchers also coded instances of pointing at pictured objects. Their results for infants' investigative behaviors are shown in Figure 6.7.

The independent variable, age of the children, is a natural groups design with three levels: 9 months, 15 months, and 19 months. This variable appears on the horizontal axis (x-axis). The dependent variable was number of investigative behaviors and the mean number of these behaviors appears on the vertical axis (y-axis). As you can see in Figure 6.7, the mean number of investigative behaviors is highest for 9-month-olds, and much lower for 15-month-olds and 19-month-olds. The other important piece of information in the figure is the "bars" that surround each mean. We can use these bars to make decisions about whether the effect of the independent variable, age, is reliable.

The bars around each mean in Figure 6.7 represent confidence intervals. A **confidence interval** tells us the range of values in which we can expect a population value to fall with a specified level of confidence (see also "margin of error" in Chapter 4). We cannot estimate the population value precisely because of sampling error; the best we can do is estimate a range of probable values. The smaller the range of values expressed in our confidence interval, the better is our estimate of the population value. The bars in Figure 6.7 represent a 95% confidence interval. For 9-month-olds, the mean number of investigative behaviors for the sample was 4.75, and we can be 95% confident that the interval 3.61 and 5.89 (4.75 ± 1.14) contains the population mean for 9-month-olds. Thus, the sample of 16 9-month-old infants in this study is used to estimate the average number of investigative behaviors that would be demonstrated if the larger population of 9-month-olds were tested in this situation. For 15-month-olds, the mean number of investigative behaviors was 1.63, and we can be 95% confident that the interval between .49 and 2.77 (1.63 ± 1.14) contains the population mean. The sample mean for 19-month-olds was .69, and the 95% confidence interval has a lower bound of 0.0 (restricted by the range of permissible values) and an upper bound of 1.83 (.69 ± 1.14). Information about how to calculate and interpret confidence intervals is presented in Appendix A.

In many psychology studies, we are not really interested in estimating the specific value of the population mean. For example, we aren't really interested in knowing the average number of times 9-month-olds can be expected to grasp at pictures. Instead, we are interested in the *pattern* of population means and comparing the relationships among population means (Loftus & Masson, 1994). That is, we wish to be able to compare the behavior of the different age groups. This, too, can be accomplished using confidence intervals.

We can ask, do infants in the different age groups demonstrate different amounts of investigative behaviors, given our estimates of the population means? To answer this question, we examine the overlap of the bars in Figure 6.7. When the bars do not overlap, we can be confident that the population means differ. For example, the confidence interval for 9-month-olds does not overlap with the interval for 15-month-olds. From this, we can conclude that 9-month-olds differ from 15-month-olds in the number of investigative behaviors when looking at pictures (the means tell us that 9-month-olds investigate pictures more than 15-month-olds). The same conclusion can be made when comparing 9-month-olds and 19-month-olds. However, a different conclusion must be made when comparing 15-month-olds and 19-month-olds. Figure 6.7 demonstrates that the bars for these two groups overlap, indicating that the population means may not differ. For example, given our 95% confidence interval, it is possible that the true population mean for 15-month-olds is 1.63 (1.63 falls within the range of probable values, .49–2.77). It is also possible, given our 95% confidence interval, that the true population mean for 19-month-olds is also 1.63. Thus, even though the *sample* means differ (1.63 and .69, respectively), we cannot conclude that the *population* means differ (and in psychological research, we are more interested in describing the population than the sample). Based on the means and confidence intervals presented in Figure 6.7, we can conclude that 9-month-old infants investigate pictures with their hands more than 15-month-olds and 19-month-olds, and that these two older groups may not differ in the amount of investigative behavior they demonstrate.

DeLoache et al.'s (1998) data for infants' pointing at pictures are presented in Figure 6.8. What conclusions can you draw about the effect of age on infants' pointing based on the means and confidence intervals presented in this figure? Do 15-month-old infants differ from 9-month-old infants in their pointing behavior? Why or why not? Do 19-month-old infants differ from 15-month-old infants? Why or why not?

A final word of caution is necessary. Bars presented in graphs of data in journal articles sometimes represent *confidence intervals*, but may also represent the *standard error of the mean* or *standard deviations* (see Appendix A). Importantly, inferences about differences between means can only be made using confidence intervals. (A quick technique for *approximating* confidence intervals is to multiply the standard error of the mean by 2.) To complicate matters further, authors sometimes fail to inform readers what is presented. When bars are presented, it

FIGURE 6.8 Mean number of pointing behaviors with 95% confidence intervals for 9-month-olds, 15-month-olds, and 19-month-olds. (From DeLoache et al., 1998; used with permission.)

is important to inform readers what they represent and how they were calculated (Estes, 1997). (In Appendix A we discuss more fully the advantages of using confidence intervals when analyzing experiments.)

Null-Hypothesis Testing

- Null hypothesis testing is used to determine whether mean differences among groups in an experiment are greater than the differences that are expected simply because of error variation.
- The first step in null hypothesis testing is to assume that the groups do not differ—that is, that the independent variable did not have an effect (the null hypothesis).
- Probability theory is used to estimate the likelihood of the experiment's observed outcome, assuming the null hypothesis is true.
- A statistically significant outcome is one that has a small likelihood of occurring if the null hypothesis is true.
- Because decisions about the outcome of an experiment are based on probabilities, Type I or Type II errors may occur.

We introduce the idea of null hypothesis testing with the results from a classic series of studies by Asch (1951, 1955) on conformity to group pressure. The task in Asch's experiments was simple. Male participants were shown two cards. The first card contained one line, called the standard. The second card contained three lines of different lengths, only one of which matched the standard. The participants' task was to select the line that was the same length as the standard. Eighteen tests of this kind were given to each participant. During a test session, varying numbers of other men were present, all seated around a table. These men were introduced to the participant as fellow participants in the experiment, but they were actually working as confederates of the experimenter (see Chapter 3 for a discussion of the ethics of using confederates). For each card, the men were asked in turn which line they believed matched the standard. The confederates responded with incorrect responses on 12 of the 18 trials. When more than one confederate was present, each confederate gave the same incorrect response. Thus, the independent variable was the number of confederates present, and there were seven levels of this variable (0, 1, 2, 3, 4, 8, and 16). Participants were randomly assigned to a group representing one of these seven levels. The dependent variable was the degree to which the participant conformed to group pressure; this was measured by counting the number of trials in which the participant chose the incorrect response instead of the obviously correct choice. The maximum number of trials on which participants could conform by choosing the incorrect line was 12.

Two questions were addressed in Asch's experiment. First, would participants conform? That is, would they choose the incorrect line more in the conditions when others were present than when they were alone? Second, would conformity increase with increasing size of the dissenting (incorrect) majority? Asch conducted a properly controlled experiment, so it is possible to use the results of the study to answer these two questions.

As we have already seen in our discussion of confidence intervals, the first and most important step in analyzing an experiment is to summarize the results using appropriate descriptive statistics. The mean numbers of errors for the participants who had been randomly assigned to each of the seven groups in Asch's experiment are presented in Figure 6.9. The results seem clear. Fewer errors, on the average, were made when the participants were alone than when they were confronted with the incorrect responses of other "participants." And mean errors increased with increasing size of the dissenting majority, at least up to groups of four.

Descriptive statistics alone are not sufficient, however, to answer the two questions Asch's experiment addressed. In a random groups design, the problem rests with the nature of the control provided by balancing through random

FIGURE 6.9   Mean number of errors as a function of the size of the dissenting majority. (Adapted from Asch, 1951.)

assignment. Random assignment does not eliminate the differences among subjects. Random assignment simply distributes the differences among subjects (comparably, we hope) across the groups in the experiment. That is, the differences among subjects are not allowed to vary systematically across groups.

The nonsystematic variation due to differences among subjects within each group is called *error variation*. The individual differences within each group are reflected in the range of errors present in each condition. For example, Asch reported that when 16 confederates chose the incorrect line, at least one participant made no errors, while another participant made 10 errors. Thus, even though all the participants in this group received the same instructions and heard 16 confederates choose an incorrect line on 12 of the 18 trials, not all of the participants responded in the same way. This error variation is due in part to the different characteristics of the participants in the group (e.g., some may be more sensitive to social pressure). The presence of error variation in experiments poses a problem because the means of the different groups in the experiment may differ simply because of error variation, and not because the independent variable has an effect. Recall that we assess the effect of our independent variable by looking for differences among the means for the different conditions. However, if the means can differ because of error variation, and not necessarily because of the independent variable, we cannot be sure if the independent variable has had an effect. You will note that this is the same dilemma faced by researchers using a natural groups design (see our example above); however, in a natural groups design the chance variation between samples is due to the way samples were selected (not assigned). Thus, by themselves, the mean results of the best-controlled experiment do not permit a definite conclusion about the effectiveness of the independent variable. We have already examined one way out of this dilemma, the use of confidence intervals. Now let's look at another.

The primary approach in psychology to making a decision about the effect of an independent variable is called null hypothesis testing. This form of statistical inference is both inductive and indirect. It is inductive because we draw general conclusions about populations on the basis of the specific samples we test in our experiments, as we do when constructing confidence intervals. However, unlike the approach using confidence intervals, this form of statistical inference is also indirect because it begins by assuming the null hypothesis. The **null hypothesis** is the assumption that the independent variable has had *no* effect. Once we make this assumption, we can use probability theory to determine the likelihood of obtaining the difference observed in our experiment if the null hypothesis were true. If this likelihood is small, we reject the null hypothesis and conclude that the independent variable did have an effect on the dependent variable measure. Outcomes that lead us to reject the null hypothesis are said to be **statistically significant.** A statistically significant outcome means only that the difference we obtained in our experiment is larger than would be expected if error variation alone (i.e., chance) were responsible for the outcome.

Perhaps you can appreciate the process of statistical inference by considering the following dilemma. A friend, with a sly smile, offers to toss a coin with you to see who pays for the meal you just enjoyed at a restaurant. Your friend just happens to have a coin ready to toss. Now it would be convenient if you could directly test whether your friend's coin is biased (by asking to look at it). Not willing to appear untrusting, however, the best you can do is test your friend's coin indirectly by assuming it is not biased and seeing if you consistently get outcomes that differ from the expected 50-50 split of heads and tails. If the coin does not exhibit the ordinary 50-50 split (after several trials of flipping the coin), you might surmise that your friend is trying, by slightly underhanded means, to get you to pay for the meal. Similarly, we would like to make a direct test of statistical significance for an obtained difference in our experiments. The best we can do, however, is to compare our obtained outcome with the expected outcome of no difference. *The key to understanding null-hypothesis testing is to recognize that we can use the laws of probability to estimate the likelihood of an outcome only when we assume that chance factors are the sole cause of that outcome.* This is not different from flipping your friend's coin several times to make your conclusion. You know that, based on chance alone, 50% of the time the coin should come up heads, and 50% of the time it should be tails. Anything different from this probable outcome would lead you to conclude that something other than chance is working—that is, your friend's coin is biased.

A statistically significant outcome is one that has only a small likelihood of occurring if the null hypothesis is true. But just how small is small enough? Although there is no definitive answer to this important question, the consensus among members of the scientific community is that outcomes associated with probabilities of less than 5 times out of 100 (or .05) if the null hypothesis were true are judged to be statistically significant. The probability we elect to use to indicate an outcome is statistically significant is called the *level of significance.* The level of significance is indicated by the Greek letter alpha (α). Thus, we speak of the .05 level of significance, the .10 level, or the .01 level, which we report as $\alpha = .05$, $\alpha = .10$, $\alpha = .01$.

You must choose the level of significance *before* you begin your experiment, not after you have done the statistical analysis. Choosing the level of significance before doing the analysis allows you to avoid the temptation of using the probability of your obtained outcome as the level of significance you *would have chosen.* Strictly speaking, there are only two conclusions possible when you do an inferential statistics test: You either reject the null hypothesis or you fail to reject the null hypothesis.

When we take a strict approach to null-hypothesis (H_0) testing, we are essentially acknowledging the fact that it is impossible to prove something does not exist. For example, if we propose there is a monster in Lake Michigan, you would be unable to prove to us this is not so. Putting ecological considerations aside for the moment, you might drain Lake Michigan to show no monster is there, but we could simply assert that the monster dug into the bed of the lake. You might then begin to dredge the lake, and if you still came up with no monster, we could argue that our monster is digging faster than you are dredging. Becoming more desperate, you might fill the lake with explosives and if, after detonating them, you found no remains of the monster, we could calmly propose that our monster is impervious to explosives. So long as we are free to add characteristics to our monster, there is simply no test you could perform that would convincingly show us the monster does not exist. Practically speaking, however, if we continued to believe in our monster after reasonable efforts failed to yield evidence of its existence, we would be judged unreasonable and would lose credibility with other members of the community.

A similar practical problem faces the community of researchers in psychology. When we conduct an experiment and observe the effect of the independent variable is not statistically significant, we do not reject the null hypothesis. However, we do not accept the null hypothesis of no difference either. It's the same problem as occurs with the monster. There may have been some factor in our experiment that prevented us from observing an effect of the independent variable (e.g., few subjects, poor operationalization of the independent variable). Although we recognize the logical impossibility of *proving* that H_0 is true, we also must have some method of deciding which independent variables are not worth pursuing (to avoid losing credibility with our colleagues). Most often, experiments are done to show that an independent variable causes a change in behavior. We should not get too discouraged, however, if the particular independent variable we are studying does not produce a statistically significant difference in internally valid experiments with sufficient power. The discipline of psychology also progresses by identifying factors that do not influence behavior in particular situations.

Somewhat ironically, the standards for experiments that show an independent variable is irrelevant for behavior are even higher than the standards for those that show the independent variable is relevant. A *relevant variable* is one that influences behavior. Experiments that show effects are likely to be replicated, which allows researchers to determine the reliability of the effect. When an independent variable does not produce an effect, investigators may not pursue research with that variable any further. All too often, however, after failing to reject H_0, researchers do a small (and insensitive) "replication" to confirm their original conclusion of no effect. If anything, the second experiment should be *more* sensitive than the first if it is to strengthen the conclusion that the independent variable has had no effect (Tversky & Kahneman, 1971).

There are some instances in which researchers may choose to *accept* the null hypothesis (rather than simply fail to reject H_0). Yeaton and Sechrest (1986, pp. 836–837) argue persuasively that findings of no difference are especially critical in applied research. A few of the questions they cite to illustrate their point:

> "Are children who are placed in day-care centers as intellectually, socially, and emotionally advanced as children who remain in the home? Is a new, cheaper drug with fewer side effects as effective as the existing standard in preventing heart attacks?"

These important questions clearly illustrate situations in which accepting the null hypothesis (no effect) involves more than a theoretical issue—life and death consequences rest on making the correct decision. Frick (1995) argues that never accepting the null hypothesis is neither desirable nor practical for psychology. There are times when we want to be able to state with confidence that there is no difference. As a community, we need some way to assure ourselves that some monsters are just not worth searching for.

There is a troublesome aspect to the process of statistical inference and our reliance on probabilities for making decisions. No matter what decision you reach, and no matter how carefully you reach it, there is always some chance you are making an error. The two possible "states of the world" and the two possible decisions an experimenter can reach are listed in Table 6.1. The two "states of the world" are that the independent variable either does or does not have an effect on behavior. The two possible correct decisions the researcher can make are represented by the upper-left and lower-right cells of the table. If the independent variable does have an effect, the researcher should reject the null hypothesis; if it does not, the researcher should fail to reject the null hypothesis.

The two potential errors are represented by the other two cells of Table 6.1, and these two types of errors have the highly descriptive names of Type I error and Type II error. These errors arise because of the probabilistic nature of statistical inference. When we decide an outcome is statistically significant because the outcome's probability of occurring under the null hypothesis is less than .05, we acknowledge that in 5 out of every 100 tests, the outcome *could* occur even if the null hypothesis were true. The level of significance, therefore, represents the probability of making a *Type I error:* rejecting the null hypothesis when it is true. The probability of making a Type I error can be reduced simply by making the level of significance more stringent, perhaps .001. The problem with this approach is that it increases the likelihood of making a *Type II error:* failing to reject the null hypothesis when it is false.

The problem of Type I errors and Type II errors should not immobilize us. But it should help us understand why researchers rarely use the word *prove* when they describe the results of an experiment that involved inferential statistics. Instead, they describe the results as "consistent with the hypothesis," or "confirming the hypothesis," or "supporting the hypothesis." These more tentative statements are a way of indirectly acknowledging that the possibility of making a Type I error or a Type II error always exists. The .05 level of significance

TABLE 6.1   POSSIBLE OUTCOMES OF DECISION MAKING WITH INFERENTIAL STATISTICS

	States of the world	
	Null hypothesis is false	Null hypothesis is true
Reject null hypothesis	Correct decision	Type I error
Fail to reject null hypothesis	Type II error	Correct decision

represents a compromise position that allows us to strike a balance and avoid making too many of either type of error. The problem of Type I errors and Type II errors also reminds us that statistical inference can never replace replication as the ultimate test of the reliability of an experimental outcome.

Limitations of Null-Hypothesis Testing

- Null-hypothesis testing is frequently misinterpreted in terms of the meaningfulness of the results, the internal validity of the experiment, the truth of the null hypothesis, and the reliability of experiment outcomes.

Unfortunately, there are many misuses and misunderstandings of null-hypothesis testing. There are some common problems of null-hypothesis testing that you should avoid. For instance, you should be aware that:

— A statistically significant result is not the same as a practically meaningful result.
— A statistically significant result does not mean that the result is interpretable.
— A statistically significant result does not tell us whether the null hypothesis is true.
— A statistically significant result also does not tell us whether the experiment will replicate.

We will consider each of these problems in turn.

One common misuse of null hypothesis testing occurs when we confuse the statistical significance of a finding with the practical significance, or meaningfulness, of the conclusion based on that finding. The likelihood of obtaining a statistically significant finding is directly related to the sample size tested in the experiment. If we do an experiment with a very large number of subjects, almost any finding will be statistically significant. For example, suppose you ask participants to rate their life satisfaction on a 1 to 7 scale, with "1" indicating "not satisfied" and "7" indicating "very satisfied." Suppose further that a statistically significant difference was observed between mean ratings for a sample of 1,000 males and 1,000 females, with hypothetical mean ratings of 5.5 and 5.6. Although this difference in mean ratings may be "statistically significant," one may question the meaningfulness of such a difference in ratings. Later in this chapter we discuss ways to report the magnitude of an effect (measures of "effect size") which complement results from null-hypothesis testing. A measure of effect size tells us how big an effect our independent variable had on the dependent variable. We can use our knowledge of effect size to judge just how meaningful an effect is.

The statistical significance of a finding also says nothing about the internal validity of the experiment. Although we might be tempted to accept a conclusion if it is based on a "statistically significant" finding, we must remember that our ability to draw appropriate conclusions depends, most of all, on the internal validity of the study. In other words, confounded experiments can easily produce statistically significant outcomes! These "significant outcomes" should, of course, never be interpreted as valid when an experiment lacks internal validity.

J. Cohen (1995) points out two other common misunderstandings of what null-hypothesis testing tells us. The first misunderstanding is that a statistically significant finding tells us the probability that the null hypothesis is true. This misunderstanding is illustrated by the (incorrect) conclusion that "The probability of obtaining these results by chance alone is less than .05." With null-hypothesis testing, we never know the probability of the null hypothesis. What a statistically significant finding *does* tell us is the probability of our obtained difference *given that the null hypothesis is true*. Remember, our first step is to assume the null hypothesis is true; we do not determine the probability that the null hypothesis is true nor do we determine the probability that our obtained results are due to chance. An appropriate conclusion could be phrased, "The results occur with a probability less than .05 assuming the null hypothesis to be true."

A second misunderstanding involves the replicability of a finding that is associated with a certain probability under the null hypothesis. Suppose you conduct an experiment and the statistical analyses indicate the probability of your finding is $p = .01$. This probability *does not* indicate that the outcome would be replicated 99% of the time if the experiment were repeated. Or, stated slightly differently, we *can not say* with 99% confidence that the outcome is reliable—that is, it would be replicated. What we can say is that the finding we obtained in our experiment is an unlikely one if the independent variable had no effect. The only way to find out for sure if a finding will replicate is to replicate it!

You may be wondering at this point how null-hypothesis testing continues to be used when it has so many limitations. As Cohen (1995) says, "don't look for a magic alternative to NHST [null hypothesis significance testing], [or] some other objective mechanical ritual to replace it. It doesn't exist" (p. 1001). He advocates that researchers seeking to generalize from their data should use a variety of analysis techniques such as graphic data analysis and confidence intervals, as well as estimates of effect sizes (described at the end of this chapter). He also argues that improved statistical analysis in psychology requires improvements in psychological measurement and theory construction so that the hypotheses psychologists test will be more specific. Cohen (1995) concludes his critique of null-hypothesis testing with some sage advice: ". . . we have a body of statistical techniques, that, used intelligently, can facilitate our efforts. But given the problems of statistical induction, we must finally rely, as have the older sciences, on replication" (p. 1002).

Analysis of Variance (ANOVA)

- Analysis of variance (ANOVA) is an inferential statistics test used to determine whether an independent variable has had a statistically significant effect on a dependent variable.

- The logic of analysis of variance is based on identifying sources of error variation and systematic variation in the data.
- The *F*-test is a statistic that represents the ratio of between-group variation to within-group variation in the data.
- The results of the initial overall analysis of an omnibus *F*-test are presented in an analysis of variance summary table; analytical comparisons can then be used to identify specific sources of systematic variation in an experiment.
- Although analysis of variance can be used to decide whether an independent variable has had a statistically significant effect, researchers examine the descriptive statistics to interpret the meaning of the experiment outcome.

Statistical inference requires a test to determine whether or not the outcome of an experiment was statistically significant. The most commonly used inferential statistics test in the analysis of experiments is the *analysis of variance* (or ANOVA). As its name implies, the analysis of variance is based on analyzing different sources of variation in an experiment. In this section we will briefly introduce how the analysis of variance is used to analyze experiments that involve the random groups design.

There are two sources of variation in any random groups experiment. First, variation *within* each group can be expected because of individual differences among subjects who have been randomly assigned to a group. The variation due to individual differences can not be eliminated, but this variation is presumed to be balanced across groups when random assignment is used. In a properly conducted experiment, the differences among subjects within each group should be the only source of error variation. Subjects in each group should be given instructions in the same way, and the level of the independent variable to which they've been assigned should be implemented in the same way for each member of the group.

The second source of variation in the random groups design is variation *between* the groups. If the null hypothesis is true (no differences among groups), any observed differences among the means of the groups can be attributed to error variation (e.g., the different characteristics of the participants in the groups). As we've seen previously, however, we don't expect group means to be exactly identical. Fluctuations produced by sampling error make it likely that the means will vary somewhat—error variation. Thus, the variation among the different group means, when the null hypothesis is assumed to be true, provides a second estimate of error variation in an experiment. If the null hypothesis is true, this estimate of error variation between groups should be similar to the estimate of error variation within groups. Thus, the random groups design provides two independent estimates of error variation, one within the groups and one between the groups.

Now suppose that the null hypothesis is false. That is, suppose the independent variable has had an effect in your experiment. If the independent variable has had an effect, should the means for the different groups be the same or different? You should recognize that they should be different. An independent variable that has an effect on behavior should produce *systematic differences* in the means across the different groups of the experiment. That is, the independent variable should introduce a source of variation among the groups of the experiment—it should cause the groups to vary. This systematic variation will be added to the differences in the group means that are already present due to error variation.

The *F*-Test   We are now in a position to develop a statistic that will allow us to tell whether the variation due to our independent variable is larger than would be expected on the basis of error variation alone. This statistic is called *F*; it is named after Ronald Fisher, the statistician who developed the test. The conceptual definition of the ***F*-test** is the following ratio:

$$F = \frac{\text{Variation between groups}}{\text{Variation within groups}} = \frac{\text{Error variation} + \text{Systematic variation}}{\text{Error variation}}$$

If the null hypothesis is true, there is no systematic variation between groups (no effect of the independent variable) and the resulting *F* ratio has an expected value of 1.00 (since error variation divided by error variation would equal 1.00). As the amount of systematic variation increases, however, the expected value from the *F*-test becomes greater than 1.00.

The analysis of experiments would be easier if we could isolate the systematic variation produced by the independent variable. Unfortunately, the systematic variation between groups comes in a "package" along with error variation. Consequently, the value of the *F* ratio may sometimes be larger than 1.00 simply because our estimate of error variation between groups happens to be larger than our estimate of error variation within groups (the two estimates should be similar but can differ due to chance factors). How much greater than 1.00 does the *F* statistic have to be before we can be relatively sure that it reflects true systematic variation due to the independent variable? Our earlier discussion of statistical significance provides an answer to this question. To be statistically significant, the *F* value needs to be large enough so that its probability of occurring if the null hypothesis were true is less than our chosen level of significance, usually .05.

We are now ready to apply the principles of null-hypothesis testing and the procedures of the analysis of variance to analyze a specific experiment. We will use the Asch experiment we described earlier. The first step in doing an inferential statistics test like the *F*-test is to state the research question the analysis is intended to answer. Typically, this takes the form of "Did the independent variable have any overall effect on performance?" In the Asch experiment this question would be, "Did varying the size of the dissenting majority have any effect on the number of errors participants made?" Once the research question is clear, the next step is to develop a null hypothesis for the analysis.

The initial overall analysis of the experiment is called an *omnibus F-test*. The null hypothesis for such omnibus tests is that all the group means are equal (remember that the null hypothesis assumes no effect of the independent variable). The formal statement of a null hypothesis (H_0) is always made in terms of population characteristics. These population characteristics are indicated by Greek letters, and the population mean is symbolized as μ (mu). We can use a subscript for each mean in the Asch experiment to reflect the size of the dissenting majority (the levels of the independent variable). Our null hypothesis then becomes

$$H_0: \; \mu_0 = \mu_1 = \mu_2 = \mu_3 = \mu_4 = \mu_8 = \mu_{16}$$

The alternative to the null hypothesis is that one or more of the means of the groups are not equal. In other words, the alternative hypothesis states that H_0 is wrong, there is a difference somewhere. If the size of the dissenting majority does have an effect on conformity (i.e., if the independent variable produces systematic variation), we will reject the null hypothesis.

Analysis of Variance Summary Table The next step in an analysis of variance is to do the computations to obtain the estimates of variation that make up the numerator and denominator of the F-test. Computing F-tests is best done using a computer. Our focus now is on interpreting the results of the computations. The results of an analysis of variance are presented in an Analysis of Variance Summary Table. The summary table for the Asch experiment is presented in Table 6.2.

The means for each group that were presented earlier in Figure 6.9 are repeated at the bottom of the table. We examine the components of the summary table before looking at the outcome of the F-test for the experiment.

The left column of a summary table lists the two sources of variation described earlier. In this case the independent variable of the dissenting majority is a source of variation *between* the groups and the *within-groups* differences provide an estimate of error variation. The total variation in the experiment is the sum of the variation between and within the groups. The next column is the degrees of freedom (df). In general, the statistical concept of degrees of freedom is defined as the number of entries of interest minus one. Since there are 7 levels

TABLE 6.2 ANALYSIS OF VARIANCE SUMMARY TABLE

Source of Variation	df	SS	MS	F	p
Between Groups (Majority Size)	6	198.98	33.16	27.2	.0001
Within Groups (Error)	63	77.13	1.22		
Total	69	276.11			

			Size of dissenting majority				
	0	1	2	3	4	8	16
Mean Number of Errors	.08	.33	1.53	4.00	4.20	3.84	3.75

of the dissenting majority independent variable, there are 6 *df* between groups (7 − 1 = 6). There are 10 participants within each group, and so there are 9 *df* within each of the 7 groups. Because all 7 groups are the same size, we can determine the within-groups *df* by multiplying the *df* within each group by the number of groups (9 × 7) for 63 *df*. The total *df* is the number of subjects minus one (and also the sum of *df* between groups plus *df* within groups).

The sums of squares (SS) and the mean square (MS) are computational steps in obtaining the *F* statistic. The MS between groups (row 1) is an estimate of systematic variation plus error variation, and is calculated by dividing the SS between groups by the *df* between groups (198.98 ÷ 6 = 33.16). The MS within groups (row 2) is an estimate of error variation only, and is computed by dividing the SS within groups by the *df* within groups (77.13 ÷ 63 = 1.22). The *F* ratio is obtained by dividing the MS between groups by the MS within groups (33.16 ÷ 1.22 = 27.2). We are now ready to use the information in the summary table to test for the statistical significance of the outcome in the Asch experiment. You may anticipate the conclusion already, knowing that when the null hypothesis is assumed to be true (i.e., no effect of the independent variable), the estimate of systematic variation plus error variation (numerator of the *F*-test) should be approximately equal to the estimate of error variation only (denominator of the *F*-test). As we see here, the estimate of systematic variation plus error variation (33.16) is quite a bit larger than the estimate of error variation alone (1.22).

The obtained *F* value in this analysis appears in the second to last column of the summary table, and is reported as, $F(6,63) = 27.2$. An *F* statistic is identified by its degrees of freedom. In this case there are 6 *df* between groups and 63 *df* within groups. The probability of obtaining an *F* as large as 27.2 if the null hypothesis were true is shown in the last column of the summary table (.0001). The obtained probability of .0001 is less than the level of significance ($\alpha = .05$), so we reject the null hypothesis and conclude that the overall effect of the size of the dissenting majority is statistically significant.

Just what have we learned when we find a statistically significant outcome in an analysis of variance testing an omnibus null hypothesis? In one sense, we have learned something very important. We are now in a position to state that manipulating the independent variable produced a change in performance (i.e., participants' errors about the lines). In another sense, merely knowing our outcome is statistically significant tells us nothing about the *nature* of the effect of the independent variable. The descriptive statistics (in our example, the mean number of errors in Figure 6.9) allow us to describe the nature of the effect: As the size of the dissenting majority increased, up to 4 dissenters, the mean number of errors made by participants increased; with 8 and 16 dissenters, the number of errors decreased. Imagine if participants had made the most errors when they were alone. The results of the *F*-test could also have been statistically significant. The means, however, would lead us to draw a very different conclusion from the one we would reach based on the means in Figure 6.9. The point is, *never try to interpret a statistically significant outcome without referring to the corresponding descriptive statistics*.

Knowing that the omnibus test is statistically significant also does not tell us the *location* of the effect. We only know there is systematic variation *somewhere* in our experiment. On the basis of the omnibus test, we can only respond to a person who asked, "What happened in your experiment?" by saying, "Something." This response is not very satisfying and would almost surely prompt the exasperated reply, "Yes, but what?" Based on the omnibus *F*-test alone, however, we are unable to state which of the group means differed. Fortunately, there are analysis techniques that allow us to locate more specifically the sources of systematic variation in our experiments. These techniques are called analytical comparisons, and they are linked directly to the hypotheses that led Asch to do the experiment in the first place.

Analytical Comparisons   Asch did not do his experiment simply to find out whether something would happen when he manipulated the size of the dissenting majority. Instead, he had at least two specific questions to address in the experiment: Would participants choose the incorrect line more in the conditions when others were present than when they were alone? And would conformity increase with increasing size of the dissenting majority? **Analytical comparisons** are a way to translate these research questions into a form that allows us to locate a specific source of systematic variation in our experiment. We will illustrate this process with the first of Asch's two research questions.

The first step in doing an analytical comparison, like the first step in doing an omnibus analysis, is to state the null hypothesis for the analysis. The verbal statement of the null hypothesis for Asch's first research question is: The mean number of errors for the group when participants are alone is equal to the mean of all the groups in which other participants were present. This analytical comparison contrasts the performance of participants who are alone with the performance of participants when they are in a group. Note that we are not concerned with the particular number (1–16) of other people present, so we consider the mean for all individuals who participated with confederates present. More formally, the null hypothesis is:

$$H_0: \mu_0 = (\mu_1 + \mu_2 + \mu_3 + \mu_4 + \mu_8 + \mu_{16})/6$$

We can compute a mean square for this particular comparison. The mean square for the comparison reflects a combination of error variation and systematic variation due to this specific comparison. An *F* ratio can then be formed with the comparison mean square in the numerator and the mean square within groups in the denominator (estimate of error variation alone). Because this analytical comparison essentially involves the contrast between two means (participants alone and participants in groups), it has only 1 degree of freedom. We then determine the probability of the resulting *F* ratio by using the same procedures we described earlier for omnibus *F*-tests.

The computations for the first analytical comparison in the Asch experiment result in $F(1,63) = 57.53$ with a $p = .0001$. The obtained *p* is less than the conventional .05 level of significance, and so the analytical comparison is statistically significant. This outcome allows us to state that one source of systematic variation in the Asch experiment was that participants in groups performed differently from participants who were alone. Because the mean number of errors for participants in groups (2.94) was higher than that for participants alone (.08), we can conclude that Asch's first hypothesis was confirmed: Participants chose the incorrect line more in the conditions when others were present than when they were alone, suggesting these participants conformed to group pressure. Think again about your friend's question about "what happened" in your experiment. Can you see why you would be glad you know about analytical comparisons when you try to answer your friend's question?

Effect Size

- A problem with inferential statistics is that they are influenced by the sample size in an experiment.
- Measures of effect size indicate the strength of the relationship between the independent and dependent variables, but are not affected by sample size.
- One commonly used measure of effect size, d, examines the difference between two group means relative to the within-group variability.
- In addition to providing information about the amount of impact an independent variable has had, measures of effect size allow quantitative comparisons of results across experiments and estimates of the average effect of an independent variable.

When we do an inferential statistics test we are interested in determining whether the independent variable had an effect. One limitation of inferential statistics tests, however, is that the outcome of such tests is influenced by the sample size used in the experiment. That is, given an independent variable with an effect of a certain size, the value from the F-test used to test the effect of that independent variable will increase as the sample size increases. In other words, the F ratio can increase even when the effect size does not! Thus, the F-test (and other inferential statistics) does not directly tell us the effect size of the independent variable. This means that we need something other than an inferential statistics test to measure the size of the effect of an independent variable. What is needed to measure **effect size** is an indicator that reflects the strength of the relationship between the independent and the dependent variables and is independent of sample size. Several measures of effect size meet these criteria (e.g., Keppel, 1991). We describe how these different measures of effect size are computed in Appendix A. What we will do here is use one of these measures to describe the nature of an effect size and the way an effect size generally is interpreted.

One commonly used measure of effect size in experimental research is called d. It is a ratio that measures the difference between the means for the levels of the independent variable divided by the within-group standard deviation. The standard deviation tells us approximately how far, on the average, scores vary from a group mean. It is a measure of the "dispersal" of scores around a mean and, in the case of the within-group standard deviation, tells us about the degree of "error" due to individual differences (i.e., how individuals vary in their responses). The standard deviation serves as a useful metric to assess a difference between means. That is, the "size" of the effect of the independent variable (the difference between group means for the independent variable) is always in terms of the average dispersal of scores occurring in an experiment. If there is a lot of within-group variability (i.e., the within-group standard deviation is large), the denominator for d is large. To be able to observe the effect of the independent variable, given this large within-group variability, the difference between two group means must be large. When the within-group variability is small (the denominator for d is small), the same difference between means will reflect a larger effect size. Because effect sizes are presented in standard deviation units, they can be used to make meaningful comparisons of effect sizes across experiments using different dependent variables.

There are some guidelines to help us interpret d ratios. J. Cohen (1992) provided a useful classification of effect sizes with three values—small, medium, and large. Cohen (1992) describes the rationale for his classification of effect size (ES) as follows:

> My intent was that medium ES represent an effect likely to be visible to the naked eye of a careful observer. (It has since been noted in effect-size surveys that it approximates the average size of observed effects in various fields.) I set small ES to be noticeably smaller than medium but not so small as to be trivial, and I set large ES to be the same distance above medium as small was below it. Although the definitions were made subjectively, with some minor adjustments, these conventions . . . have come into general use. (p. 156)

Each of the classes of effect size can be expressed in quantitative terms; for example, a medium effect for a two-group experiment is a d of .50; a small and large effect are ds of .20 and .80, respectively. These expressions of effect magnitude are especially useful when comparing results from similar studies.

There are several advantages of using measures of effect size (see, for example, Chow, 1988):

1 Measures of effect size provide information about the *amount* of impact an independent variable has had. Thus, they complement tests of statistical significance which give only an indication of the presence or absence of an effect of an independent variable. In this way, we can use measures of effect size to rank several independent variables within the same experiment in terms of their relative importance.

2 Measures of effect size can be used to summarize a series of experiments that have included the same independent variable or dependent variable. This allows for a quantitative comparison of the outcomes across the series of experiments. For example, effect size can be used to find out whether a particular independent variable consistently had about the same amount of impact across the experiments.

3 Effect sizes can be averaged to provide an estimate of the overall effect size of an independent variable across a series of similar experiments. This comparison is especially important in applied research examining the effectiveness of treatments like an educational innovation or a new approach to psychotherapy.

None of the important questions addressed using effect size can be answered using the F ratios or p values obtained when inferential statistics tests are done. Nonetheless, measures of effect size and inferential statistics tests are complementary (Chow, 1988). For example, measures of effect size are more informative than are "p values" in helping researchers determine the substantive importance of experimental outcomes. At times, we want to know just how much of an "effect" our treatment had. Knowing the answer may help us decide whether to actually implement this treatment in an applied setting. When an experiment is being done to test predictions derived from a theory, however, the size of the effect of an independent variable is less critical. In this case, we are usually content with knowing that the independent variable "worked" in the way a theory said it should. In fact, as tests of a theory become more sophisticated, it is likely that small effects will be more critical. Inferential statistics tests are useful when experiments are done to test theories by confirming that an effect is present.

There is another reason not to discount small effect sizes. Consider the fact that studies have indicated there is a small positive effect of taking aspirin to try to prevent second heart attacks. Considering the large number of people who are at risk for recurrent heart attacks, the small positive effect of taking aspirin could still have an impact on thousands of people. In terms of the potential numbers of people who could benefit, the small beneficial effect of taking aspirin would not be a small effect at all.

Abelson (1985) identified another subtle aspect of interpreting small effect sizes. Abelson argues there are processes with tiny individual influences that can cumulate to produce meaningful outcomes. He uses a sports analogy to make his point. Abelson calculated how much of the variation in whether a batter got a hit in a single time at bat could be predicted on the basis of skill differences in major league batters. The skill differences were measured using the major league players' batting averages over 5 years. Basically, Abelson wanted to know if players' 5-year batting averages could be used to predict whether they got a hit on a particular occasion when facing a pitcher. Abelson found that less than 1% of the variation in a single at bat could be predicted by the batters' skill. If we interpreted the small value of this effect size at face value we would come to the very improbable conclusion that batting skill has almost nothing to do with batting success! However, when averages over 5 years are used to predict a subsequent *season's* batting average, rather than a single time at bat, batting skill is a much stronger predictor of batting success.

The problem here is a familiar one; Abelson is illustrating what happens if we try to predict the outcome of single observations—in this case, single at bats. Although researchers may be able to predict behavior *on average,* it is often quite difficult to predict behavior for a specific occasion. Abelson draws an apt analogy to the situation researchers face when interpreting an effect size based on a single experiment. A small effect size need not indicate that an independent variable is unimportant. Effect sizes can be used more effectively when they are based on a series of experiments. We conclude this chapter by describing a procedure for just this purpose: meta-analysis.

Meta-Analysis

- Meta-analysis uses measures of effect size to summarize the results of many experiments investigating the same independent variable or dependent variable.
- A critical aspect of meta-analysis is deciding which experiments to include in the analysis: The value of a meta-analysis depends on the methodological quality of the experiments that are included.

Each strand contributes to the strength of a rope. But the rope is stronger than any strand. Similarly, each properly done experiment strengthens our confidence in a particular psychological principle. But the principles of psychology are stronger than the results of any individual experiment. This is because principles of psychology (laws, if you will) emerge only after looking at the relationships among the results of many individual experiments. When a particular finding is found again and again under many different experimental situations, we are in a position to state with confidence a general law of behavior. This is the procedure used by Anderson and Bushman (1997) to identify the variables that consistently have been shown to impact aggression.

Meta-analysis is a valuable tool that makes it easier to summarize the results of experiments investigating the same independent variable or dependent variable. **Meta-analysis** is the analysis of the results of several independent experiments. In any experiment, the unit of analysis is the responses of individual subjects. In a meta-analysis, the unit of analysis is the results of individual experiments. These results are summarized using measures of effect size like those described in the previous section. Meta-analyses are used to answer questions like: Are there gender differences in conformity? What are the effects of class size on academic achievement? Is cognitive therapy effective in the treatment of depression? The results of individual experiments, no matter how well done, are not likely to be sufficient to provide answers to questions about such important general issues. We need to consider a body of literature (i.e., many experiments) pertaining to each issue. (See Hunt, 1997, for a good and readable introduction to meta-analysis.)

Prior to the use of meta-analysis, the results of previous research on a particular topic were summarized using some form of narrative review. These reviews were typically published in the *Psychological Bulletin*. The reviewers were often experts in the area of research under investigation. After reading and thinking about the relevant studies, the reviewers would draw conclusions that they thought were supported by the evidence. Meta-analysis is not intended to replace these narrative reviews; instead, it is meant to strengthen the evidence used to reach conclusions. For example, reviewers previously would tally the number of experiments that did or did not show a statistically significant effect of an independent variable. This "voting method" was a crude measure of the effect of the independent variable, particularly because of "publication bias." Publication bias occurs because research reports are more likely to be published (rather than filed in a cabinet) when statistically significant findings are reported; therefore, the "voting method" may overestimate the effect size of variables. Meta-analysis allows us to measure directly the average effect size for a given independent variable across experiments.

Rosenthal (1994a) used meta-analysis to summarize the results of 345 experiments on experimenter effects. Experimenter effects occur when the participants in an experiment respond in ways that correspond to the expectancies of the experimenter (see earlier section in this chapter on placebo control and double-blind experiments, as well as Chapter 3). Experimenter effects represent a specific instance of the more general category of interpersonal expectancy effects, which represent the effects of people's expectations on others' behavior. Table 6.3 presents the mean effect sizes for each of eight domains in which interpersonal expectancy effects have been studied. The table also includes a brief description of an example of a type of study done in each domain. The mean effect size across all 345 studies is .70, a medium effect using J. Cohen's (1992) scale. For four of the eight domains the mean effect size is greater than .80, indicating a large effect. Table 6.3 also shows that the interpersonal expectancy finding has considerable external validity because there is at least a medium size effect in six of the eight domains. Thus, we are in a position to state with confidence a general principle: Interpersonal expectancies can influence people's behavior.

Meta-analyses like the one summarized in Table 6.3 provide an efficient and effective way to summarize the results of large numbers of experiments. Nevertheless, the sophisticated statistical techniques that are used in meta-analyses are powerful only when the data from the studies being analyzed have been gathered in appropriate ways. The results of meta-analyses can be misleading

TABLE 6.3   ILLUSTRATION OF USE OF MEAN EFFECT SIZE IN META-ANALYSIS

Domain	d	Example of type of study
Laboratory interviews	.14	Effects of sensory restriction on reports of hallucinatory experiences
Reaction time	.17	Latency of word associations to certain stimulus words
Learning and ability	.54	IQ test scores, verbal conditioning (learning)
Person perception	.55	Perception of other people's success
Inkblot tests	.84	Ratio of animal to human Rorschach responses
Everyday situations	.88	Symbol learning, athletic performance
Psychophysical judgments	1.05	Ability to discriminate tones
Animal learning	1.73	Learning in mazes and Skinner boxes
Overall mean	.70	

Adapted from Rosenthal, R. (1994a). Interpersonal expectancy effects: A 30-year perspective. *Current Directions in Psychological-Science, 3*, 176–179.

when experiments with poor internal validity are included. Thus, important questions regarding meta-analyses ask: Which experiments should be included in the meta-analysis? Will only experiments reported in journals with high editorial standards be included, or will the meta-analysis include research reports that have not undergone editorial review? In general, the methodological quality of the experiments included in the meta-analysis will determine its ultimate value (see Judd et al., 1991).

Our hope is that this brief introduction to the analysis of experiments gives you an appreciation of the variety of ways statistical analysis can be done. Appendix A provides more details about statistical analysis, as well as a plan to follow when analyzing data. One theme emerges from our discussion of statistical analysis. There is no one best approach to analyzing an experiment, just as there is no one best research method. Analysis techniques, like any tools, are best used when we know their strengths and weaknesses. We need to recognize that statistical analysis does not determine the conclusions we draw from our experiment—we do that! Statistical analysis does help us constrain the conclusions we reach. Most of all, statistical analysis is not a necessary evil in experimental research; it is a critical step on the path from asking a research question to answering it.

SUMMARY

Experimental research allows us to observe the unobservable. Predictions based on proposed explanatory processes can be either confirmed or refuted by experimental outcomes. Properly done experiments are internally valid, reliable, sensitive, and externally valid. A major purpose of experiments is to test hypotheses derived from theories, but experiments can also be used to test the effectiveness of treatments or programs in applied settings. The experimental method is ideally suited to identifying cause-and-effect relationships when the control techniques of manipulation, holding conditions constant, and balancing are properly implemented.

In this chapter we have focused on applying these control techniques in experiments in which different groups of subjects are given different treatments representing the levels of the independent variable. In the most common design of this type, the random groups design, the groups are formed using randomization procedures such that the groups are comparable at the start of the experiment. If the groups perform differently, it is presumed that the independent variable is responsible. Random assignment is the most common method of forming comparable groups. By distributing subjects' characteristics equally across the conditions of the experiment, random assignment is an attempt to ensure that the differences among subjects are balanced across groups in the experiment. The most common technique for carrying out random assignment is block randomization.

Random assignment contributes to the internal validity of an experiment, but external validity must be established in some other way. One approach to enhancing external validity is to select representative samples of all dimensions on which you wish to generalize. Replication serves primarily as a check on the reliability of experimental findings, but replication also plays a key role in establishing external validity. When we obtain the same outcomes in two partial replications of the same experiment done in two widely different settings with different subjects, our confidence in the external validity of that finding increases. A partial replication, including the dimension on which you want to generalize as an independent variable, is perhaps the best way to establish external validity.

Testing intact groups even when the groups are randomly assigned to conditions should be avoided because the use of intact groups is highly likely to result in a confounding. Extraneous variables, such as different rooms or different experimenters, must not be allowed to confound the independent variable of interest. Even when such extraneous variables are controlled, however, they can contribute to the sensitivity and external validity of an experiment. Holding extraneous variables constant increases sensitivity and decreases external validity, whereas balancing extraneous variables decreases sensitivity and increases external validity.

A more serious threat to the internal validity of the random groups design is involved when subjects fail to complete the experiment successfully. Selective subject loss occurs when subjects are lost differentially across the conditions and some characteristic of the subject that is related to the outcome of the experiment is responsible for the loss. We can help prevent selective loss by restricting subjects to those likely to complete the experiment successfully, or we can compensate for it by selectively dropping comparable subjects from the group that did not experience the loss. Demand characteristics and experimenter effects can be minimized through the use of proper experimental procedures, but they can best be controlled by using placebo control and double-blind procedures.

The matched groups design is an alternative to the random groups design when only a small number of subjects is available along with a good matching task and when the experiment requires separate groups for each treatment. The biggest problem with the matched groups design is that the groups are equated only on the characteristic measured by the matching task. In the natural groups design, researchers select the levels of independent variables (usually individual differences or subject variables) and look for systematic relationships between these independent variables and other aspects of behavior. Essentially, the natural groups design involves looking for correlations between subjects' characteristics and their performance. Such correlational research designs pose problems in drawing causal inferences.

The purpose of analyzing an experiment is to determine whether an independent variable has had an effect on behavior as reflected by differences in the dependent variable across the levels of the independent variable. The identification of such differences begins with descriptive statistics. Because differences in the dependent variable can arise because of error variation alone, we need a way to help decide whether the obtained differences represent simply chance or also represent the effect of the independent variable. Confidence intervals may be constructed to help determine what happened in the experiment. Moreover, the inductive and indirect process of null-hypothesis testing provides a set of guidelines for deciding on the statistical significance of a finding. There are important limitations of null-hypothesis testing that prevent it from ever replacing replication; replication remains the ultimate test of the reliability of a research finding. The most commonly used inferential statistics test in the analysis of experiments is the analysis of variance.

Measures of effect size provide important information that cannot be obtained from inferential statistics tests. One strength of effect size is that it is a measure that is independent of the sample size in an experiment. Measures of effect size do have limitations, but effect size can be especially useful in meta-analysis. Meta-analysis provides a quantitative summary of the results of a large number of experiments on an important research problem.

KEY CONCEPTS

independent variables	placebo control
dependent variables	double-blind
confounding	matched groups design
independent groups designs	natural groups designs
random groups design	inferential statistics
random assignment	confidence intervals
block randomization	null hypothesis
replication	statistically significant
extraneous variables	*F*-test
mechanical subject loss	analytical comparison
selective subject loss	effect size
demand characteristics	meta-analysis
experimenter effects	

REVIEW QUESTIONS

1 Briefly outline the logic of the random groups design.
2 What issues would you consider if you wanted to establish the external validity of an experiment you were planning to do that involved random assignment?
3 Describe the role of partial replications and that of conceptual relationships among variables in establishing the external validity of a research finding.
4 What impact do extraneous variables have on the sensitivity and external validity of an experiment?
5 What preventive steps could you take if you anticipate that selective subject loss may pose a problem in your experiment?
6 Explain the logic of the two techniques that are used to control demand characteristics and experimenter effects.

7 Describe the conditions under which you would recommend that the matched groups design be used.

8 How do individual differences variables differ from manipulated independent variables, and why does this difference make it difficult to draw causal inferences on the basis of the natural groups design?

9 How would you use confidence intervals to reach conclusions about differences in performance across the conditions of an experiment?

10 How would you explain to a friend that statistical inference is inductive and indirect?

11 Explain what you have learned about the effect of an independent variable when you find out it has produced a statistically significant outcome. Is a statistically significant finding necessarily an important finding?

12 Distinguish between the information you gain from an omnibus *F*-test and from an analytical comparison.

13 Describe one advantage and one limitation of using measures of effect size.

14 What is the major difference between meta-analysis and narrative review in summarizing the results of previous research on a particular topic?

CHALLENGE QUESTIONS

1 An experimenter is planning to do a random groups design experiment to study the effect of the rate of presenting stimuli on people's ability to recognize the stimuli. The independent variable is the presentation rate, and it will be manipulated at four levels: Very Fast, Fast, Slow, and Very Slow. The experimenter is seeking your help and advice with the following aspects of the experiment:

A The experimenter asks you to prepare a block randomized schedule such that there will be four participants in each of the four conditions. To do this you can use the following random numbers that were taken from the random number table in Appendix A.

1-5-6-6-4-1-0-4-9-3-2-0-4-9-2-3-8-3-9-1-9-1-1-3-2-2-1-9-9-9

5-9-5-1-6-8-1-6-5-2-2-7-1-9-5-4-8-2-2-3-4-6-7-5-1-2-2-9-2-3

B The experimenter is considering restricting participants to those who pass a stringent reaction time test so as to be sure that they will be able to perform the task successfully with the Very Fast presentation rate. Explain what factors the experimenter should consider in making this decision, being sure to describe clearly what risks, if any, are taken if only this restricted set of participants is tested.

C The experimenter discovers that it will be necessary to test participants in two different rooms. How should the experimenter arrange the testing of the conditions in these two rooms so as to avoid possible confounding by this extraneous variable?

2 A researcher was conducting a series of experiments on the effects of external factors on people's persistence in exercise programs. In one of these experiments, the researcher manipulated three types of distraction while subjects walked on a treadmill. The three types of distraction were concentrating on one's own thoughts, listening to a tape of music, and watching a video of people engaging in outdoor recreation. The dependent variable was how strenuous the treadmill exercise was at the time the subject decided to end the session (the incline of the treadmill was regularly increased as the person went through the session, thereby making the exercise increasingly strenuous).

In an introductory psychology course, 120 students volunteered to participate in the experiment, and the researcher randomly assigned 40 students to each of the three levels of the distraction variable.

After only 2 minutes on the treadmill, each subject was given the option to stop the experiment (this option came before any of the subjects could reasonably be expected to be experiencing fatigue). Data for the subjects who decided to stop after only 2 minutes were not included in the analysis of the final data. Twenty-five subjects who were concentrating on their own thoughts completed the experiment; 30 subjects in the music condition completed the experiment; and 40 subjects in the video group completed the experiment. The mean strenuousness score was highest for the concentration group ($n = 25$), next highest for the music group ($n = 30$), and lowest for the video group ($n = 40$). These results did not support the researcher's prediction that the mean strenuousness score would be highest in the video group.

A What methodological problem may threaten the internal validity of this experiment? What factors indicate that this problem occurred?

B Assume that a pretest measure was available for each of the 120 subjects and that the pretest measured the degree to which each subject was likely to persist at exercise. Describe how you could use these pretest scores to confirm that the problem you identified in part A had occurred.

3 The newspaper headline summarizing research that had been reported in a medical journal read: "Study: Exercise Helps at Any Age." The research described in the article involved a 10-year study of nearly 10,000 men—and only men. The men were given a treadmill test between 1970 and 1989. Then they were given a second treadmill test 5 years after the first test and their health was monitored for another 5 years. Men who were judged unfit on both treadmill tests had a death rate over the next 5 years of 122 per 10,000. Men judged fit on both treadmill tests had a 5-year death rate of only 40 per 10,000. Most interestingly, men judged unfit on the first treadmill test but fit on the second had a death rate of 68 per 10,000. The benefits of exercise were even greater when only deaths from heart attacks were examined. The benefits from exercise were present across a wide range of ages—thus, the headline.

A Why is the newspaper headline for this article potentially misleading?

B Why do you think the researchers tested only men?

C Identify two different ways of obtaining evidence that you could use to decide whether the results of this study could be applied to women. One of the ways would make use of already published research and the other way would require doing a new study.

4 An experiment was done to test the effectiveness of a drug that is being considered for possible use in the treatment of people who experience chronic anxiety. Fifty people who are chronically anxious are identified through a local health clinic and all 50 people give their informed consent to participate in the experiment. Twenty-five people are randomly assigned to the experimental group, and they receive the drug. The other 25 people are randomly assigned to the control group, and they receive a placebo. The participants in both groups are monitored by a physician and a clinical psychologist during the 6-week treatment period. After the treatment period, the participants provide a self-rating on a reliable and valid 20-point scale indicating the level of anxiety they are experiencing (higher scores indicate greater anxiety). The mean self-rating in the experimental group was 10.2 and the mean rating in the control group was 13.5. The F-test for the mean difference between the two groups was $F(1,48) = 7.50, p = .01$.

A   Explain why a double-blind procedure would be useful in this experiment and describe how the double-blind procedure could be carried out in this experiment.

B   What information would you use to begin to describe "what happened" in this experiment?

C   Is the *F*-test for this experiment statistically significant? Be sure to provide the evidence on which you base your decision.

D   The effect size for this experiment is $d = .37$. What does this effect size tell you about the effectiveness of the drug beyond what you know from the test of statistical significance?

Answer to Challenge Question 1

A   The first step is to assign a number from 1 to 4 to the respective conditions: 1 = Very Fast; 2 = Fast; 3 = Slow; and 4 = Very Slow. Then, using the random numbers, select four sequences of the numbers from 1 to 4. In doing this you skip any numbers greater than 4 and any number that is a repetition of a number already selected in the sequence. For example, if the first number you select is a 1, you skip all repetitions of 1 until you have selected all the numbers for the sequence of 1 to 4. Following this procedure and working across the rows of random numbers from left to right, we obtained the following four sequences for the four blocks of the randomized block schedule. The order of the conditions for each block is also presented. The block randomized schedule specifies the order of testing the conditions for the first 16 participants in the experiment.

> Block 1: 1-4-3-2   Very Fast, Very Slow, Slow, Fast
>
> Block 2: 4-2-3-1   Very Slow, Fast, Slow, Very Fast
>
> Block 3: 1-3-2-4   Very Fast, Slow, Fast, Very Slow
>
> Block 4: 2-3-4-1   Fast, Slow, Very Slow, Very Fast

B   The investigator is taking a reasonable step to avoid selective subject loss, but restricting participants to those who pass a stringent reaction time test entails the risk of decreased external validity of the obtained findings.

C   The rooms can be balanced by assigning entire blocks from the block randomized schedule to be tested in each room. Usually, the number of blocks assigned to each room is equal, but this is not essential. For effective balancing, however, several blocks should be tested in each room.

Repeated Measures Designs

CHAPTER OUTLINE

OVERVIEW
REASONS FOR USING REPEATED MEASURES DESIGNS
PRACTICE EFFECTS
BALANCING PRACTICE EFFECTS
Complete Design
Incomplete Design
LIMITATIONS OF REPEATED MEASURES DESIGNS
Irreversible Tasks
Differential Transfer
ANALYSIS OF REPEATED MEASURES DESIGNS
Sensitivity and Power
Repeated Measures Analysis of Variance
SUMMARY

OVERVIEW

As we have emphasized, the experimental method involves at least two conditions (often a "treatment" condition and a "control" condition) in order to determine the differential influence of these conditions, if any, on behavior. Thus far we have considered experimental designs in which each condition is represented by a separate group of subjects. These independent groups designs (random groups, matched groups, and natural groups) are powerful tools for studying the effects of a wide range of independent variables. There are times, however, when it is inefficient to have conditions represented by different groups of participants. In such circumstances, it is still possible to do an interpretable experiment by having each participant experience all the conditions of an experiment. These designs are called **repeated measures designs** (or *within-subjects designs*). In an independent groups design, there is a separate group that serves as a control for the group given the experimental treatment. In a repeated measures design, subjects *serve as their own controls* because they participate in both the experimental and control conditions.

We begin this chapter by exploring the reasons why a researcher might choose a repeated measures design. We next examine practice effects in the repeated measures designs. Practice effects arise because participants undergo changes as they are repeatedly tested. Participants may improve with practice, for example, because they learn more about the task or because they become more relaxed in the experimental situation. They also may get worse with practice—for example, because of fatigue or reduced motivation.

We described in Chapter 6 that individual differences among participants cannot be eliminated in the random groups design, but they can be balanced by using random assignment. Similarly, temporary changes participants experience due to repeated testing in the repeated measures designs (i.e., practice effects) cannot be eliminated. Like individual differences in the random groups design, however, practice effects can be balanced across the conditions of a repeated measures design experiment. When practice effects are balanced the effect of an independent variable in a repeated measures design experiment is interpretable. Balancing *does not eliminate* practice effects from repeated measures designs. Balancing works by *averaging out* the practice effects across conditions. By doing this, we avoid confounding practice effects with the conditions of the experiment. This chapter discusses various techniques for accomplishing this balancing. We also describe potential limitations of repeated measures designs. We conclude the chapter with an introduction to procedures for analyzing the results of repeated measures designs.

REASONS FOR USING REPEATED MEASURES DESIGNS

- Researchers may decide to use a repeated measures design when few participants are available, to be more efficient when conducting the experiment, to increase the sensitivity of the research, or to study differences within subjects over time or across stimuli.

- Repeated testing of individuals to establish reliability of measurement differs from the repeated measures design because researchers manipulate an independent variable across the conditions of a repeated measures design.

There are at least four reasons why a researcher might choose a repeated measures design. First, repeated measures designs require fewer participants, so they are ideal for situations in which only a small number of participants is available.

The second reason for choosing a repeated measures design applies even when sufficient numbers of participants are available for an independent groups design. A researcher might choose to use a repeated measures design for the sake of convenience or efficiency. For example, Ludwig, Jeeves, Norman, and DeWitt (1993) conducted a series of experiments studying communication between the two hemispheres of the brain. The investigators measured how long it took participants to decide whether two briefly presented letters had the same name. The letters came from the set AaBb. Participants were to press the "match" key when the letters had the same name (AA, aa, Bb) and the "no match" key when the letters had different names (AB, ab, Ab). There were several different ways in which the pairs of letters were presented across four experiments, but there were two major conditions in these experiments. Either both letters were presented to one hemisphere (unilateral) or one letter of the pair was presented to each hemisphere (bilateral). Across the four experiments bilateral presentation led to faster response times than did unilateral presentation. In these experiments, two hemispheres were better than one!

Each trial in the Ludwig et al. (1993) experiment required only a few seconds to complete. They could have tested separate groups of participants for the unilateral and bilateral conditions, but this approach would have been horribly inefficient. It would have taken more time to instruct participants regarding the nature of the task than it would have to do the task itself! A repeated measures design in which each participant was tested on both unilateral and bilateral trials provided the experimenters with a far more efficient way to answer their question about how the brain processes information.

The third reason for choosing a repeated measures design for an experiment is that the experiment will generally be more sensitive than one that uses an independent groups design. As was noted in Chapter 6, sensitivity refers to the extent an experiment is able to detect differences in the dependent variable as a function of the independent variable. In repeated measures designs, the investigator tries to detect differences in the performance of the same participants under different conditions. In independent groups designs, researchers try to detect differences in the performance of different participants under different conditions. Repeated measures designs are generally more sensitive than are independent groups designs because the two types of designs differ in the amount of error variation that is present. Simply speaking, there is usually more variation *between* people than there is *within* people. That is, participants will vary within themselves over time (in a repeated measures design) less than participants will vary from other participants (in an independent groups design), and, thus, error variation is less in a repeated measures design. The less error variation, the easier it is to see the effect of an independent variable. The increased sensitivity of repeated measures designs is especially attractive to researchers who are studying independent variables that have small (hard-to-see) effects on behavior.

The fourth reason for choosing a repeated measures design is that some areas of psychological research require its use. When the research question involves studying changes in participants' behavior over time, such as in a learning experiment or in a longitudinal design (see Chapter 4), a repeated measures design is needed. Further, whenever the experimental procedure requires that participants compare two or more stimuli relative to one another, a repeated measures design must be used. For example, a repeated measures design would have to be used if a researcher wanted to measure the minimum amount of light that must be added before participants could detect that a spot of light had become brighter. It would also be called for if a researcher wanted participants to rate the relative attractiveness of a series of photographs. In general, the research areas of psychophysics (illustrated by the light-detection experiment) and scaling (illustrated by the ratings of attractiveness) rely heavily on repeated measures designs. Journals such as *Perception & Psychophysics* and *Journal of Experimental Psychology: Human Perception and Performance* frequently publish results of experiments using repeated measures designs.

Before continuing our discussion of repeated measures designs, we want to make a distinction between this type of design and other situations in which subjects are tested repeatedly. Psychologists frequently measure subjects on more than one occasion. There are important reasons for doing this, and these reasons usually have to do with reliability. First, as you saw in earlier chapters, a researcher may obtain two (or more) measures of the same individual in order to establish the reliability (consistency) of a measure. For example, a group of participants may be given the same aptitude test on two different occasions in order to assess the test-retest reliability of such an instrument. A correlation coefficient would likely be used to measure reliability in this situation. Another reason for testing subjects repeatedly is to obtain a more stable and, hence, reliable measure of behavior. For example, consider a study of individuals' current level of depression based on a self-report inventory. An investigator who measures depression would probably not want to use a questionnaire that has only one item asking about depression. Rather, such a measure will be more reliable if it is based on people's responses to many different items asking about their current mood. These situations, in which we test subjects repeatedly in order either to measure reliability, or to increase the reliability of our measurement, should be differentiated from repeated measures designs in which we contrast subjects' behavior in two or more conditions of an experiment.

PRACTICE EFFECTS

- In repeated measures designs, confoundings due to individual differences variables are eliminated because the same individuals participate in each condition (level) of the independent variable.

- In repeated measures designs, participants' performance may change across conditions simply because of repeated testing, not because of the independent variable manipulation; these changes are called practice effects.
- Practice effects may threaten the internal validity of a repeated measures experiment when the different conditions of the independent variable are presented in the same order to all participants.

At first glance, repeated measures designs might appear far superior to independent groups designs. The repeated measures designs require fewer participants than do the independent groups designs, and experiments can usually be completed more quickly when repeated measures designs are used. In addition to their greater efficiency, the repeated measures designs offer another advantage—the problem of confounding the conditions of the experiment with the characteristics of the participants within each condition is avoided. That is, in an independent groups design, one must take care to ensure that participants in different conditions of the experiment are essentially equivalent in terms of important characteristics (e.g., motivation, aptitude, etc.). An experiment is confounded if participants in various groups differ in ways other than the levels of the independent variable. In a repeated measures design, the same participants are tested in all conditions, so it is impossible to end up with brighter, more aggressive, or more anxious participants in one condition than in another condition. Stated formally, there can be no confounding by individual differences variables in the repeated measures designs.

The apparent superiority of repeated measures designs diminishes, however, when we realize that these designs require that the same participant must be tested more than once. Participants may change across repeated testings even if all tests are done under the same conditions. That is, participants may get better and better at doing a task if a skill is being developed, or they may get worse and worse at the task because of such factors as fatigue and boredom. The repeated testing of each participant in the repeated measures designs gives the participants practice with the experimental task. The changes participants undergo with repeated testing are called **practice effects.**

Kahneman, Frederickson, Schreiber, and Redelmeier (1993) used a repeated measures design in a series of experiments investigating people's perception of pain. They argued that the duration of an aversive experience plays a much smaller role in our perception of pain than do two other factors. They demonstrated that our evaluations of pain are influenced most by the worst moments and the final moments of the experience. In other words, we judge how painful an experience was by judging how painful it was at the point of most intense pain and by how painful it was at the end of the experience. These two factors were shown to be more important in the perception of pain than the amount of time the pain lasted. We will illustrate the balancing of practice effects using one of the experiments that Kahneman et al. (1993) did to determine the influence of the intensity of the pain in the final moments of the experience. Other experiments in the series addressed the second factor, the point of the most intense moments of pain in an experience.

There were two conditions in the experiment. In the first condition (short trial) students immersed one hand in cold water (14 degrees Celsius) for 60 seconds. In the second condition (long trial) the students also immersed their hand in 14-degree water for 60 seconds, but they then kept their hand immersed 30 seconds longer while the temperature of the water was gradually raised 1 degree (warmed) to 15 degrees. Each participant experienced both the short trial and the long trial only once. There was a 7-minute interval filled with another activity after each trial. One dependent variable was people's ratings of their degree of pain after each trial. The most important measure in the experiment, however, was the choice students made when they were asked to choose which trial they preferred to repeat.

The researchers found that the students' ratings of pain indicated that the 15-degree water was painful, but noticeably less painful than the 14-degree water. Overall, the long trial was rated by students as more painful than the short trial. Nonetheless, when students were asked which trial they preferred to repeat, 69% chose the more painful long trial. Kahneman et al. (1993) argued that the students chose the long trial because it was less painful in the final moments of the experience. The overall duration of the long trial was less critical in determining students' choice than was the fact that it was less painful at the end of their experience. To reach this intriguing insight the researchers had to make sure that practice effects were balanced in the experiment.

Suppose that Kahneman et al. (1993) had tested all the students by giving them the short trial first and then the long trial. In this case, practice effects would not have been balanced. The problem with using only one testing order is that differences between the two types of trials would be confounded with

FIGURE 7.1   In order to examine people's perceptions of pain, students in Kahneman et al.'s (1993) experiment immersed their hand in cold water.

the order in which they occurred: The short trial would always be the first trial and the long trial would always be the second trial. Students might become more familiar with the sensations resulting from having their hand immersed in cold water as they move from one trial to the other. Or maybe they would be less apprehensive about possible pain after they had experience with one trial. There are many important ways in which the students could change over the two trials. We call the summation of these changes *practice effects*. If only one order had been used, practice effects and the conditions of the experiment would be confounded. Thus, if people rated the two conditions differently, we wouldn't know if the difference in ratings was due to the type of trial (short or long) or the temporal order (first or second) in which the conditions appeared.

Kahneman et al. (1993) balanced practice effects by administering the conditions in two different orders. Half of the students received the short trial followed by the long trial and half received the long trial followed by the short trial. Since both orders were used equally often, the students' preference to repeat the long trial rather than the short trial cannot be attributed to the long trial always having been presented last. The changes due to practice effects that occurred for the students from the first trial to the second trial are likely to fall equally on each of the two conditions because half the students experienced practice effects during a long trial, and half on a short trial. Practice effects should average out across conditions. Any difference in performance, therefore, between the two conditions is the result of the nature of the short and long trials and not the result of practice effects.

BALANCING PRACTICE EFFECTS

- In the complete repeated measures design, individuals participate in each condition of the independent variable manipulation several times (in different orders) to balance practice effects *within* each individual.
- In the incomplete repeated measures design, individuals participate in each condition only once, and different individuals receive different orders of the conditions in order to balance practice effects *across* individuals.
- Because counterbalancing techniques differ for complete and incomplete designs, researchers must first choose which design they will use.

There are two types of repeated measures designs. In the *complete design*, practice effects are balanced for each participant. Balancing practice effects for each participant is accomplished by administering the conditions to each participant several times, using different orders each time. Each participant can thus be considered a "complete" experiment. In the *incomplete design*, each condition is administered to each participant *only once*. The order of administering the conditions is varied across participants rather than for each participant as is the case in the complete design. Practice effects in the incomplete design average out when the results are combined for all participants. This may seem a bit confusing at this point, but hopefully it will become clearer as we discuss these types of designs. The specific techniques for balancing practice effects, called **counterbalancing,** differ in the two repeated measures designs, so we will discuss the two designs separately. Just keep in mind that a major goal when using a repeated measures design is to control for practice effects; exactly how we do that depends on the specific repeated measures design that is used. Thus, the first step in controlling practice effects is to determine whether your experiment is based on a complete repeated measures design or an incomplete design.

Complete Design

- Practice effects are balanced in complete designs within each participant using block randomization or ABBA counterbalancing.
- In block randomization, the conditions of the experiment (a block) are randomly ordered each time they are presented.
- ABBA counterbalancing is preferred when it is not possible to administer conditions often enough for practice effects to be balanced using block randomization.
- In ABBA counterbalancing, a random sequence of all conditions is presented, followed by the opposite of the sequence.
- Block randomization is preferred over ABBA counterbalancing when practice effects are not linear, or when participants' performance can be affected by anticipation effects.

Does one side of your face express emotion more intensely than the other side? Sackheim, Gur, and Saucy (1978) used a repeated measures design to attempt to answer this question. Earlier research had shown that participants given photographs depicting posed facial expressions of six basic human emotions (happiness, surprise, fear, sadness, anger, and disgust) could readily and accurately identify the expressed emotion. Sackheim and coworkers took advantage of a technique developed in earlier work on facial recognition whereby a full photograph of a face can be constructed using only one side of a person's face. The technique involves developing both a photograph of a full face and a photograph of its mirror image. These two photographs are then split down the middle and two composite photographs are made—one from the two versions of the left side of the face and one from the two versions of the right side. Illustrative photographs are presented in Figure 7.2. In the center is a photograph of a person expressing disgust. The two composite photographs made from the center photograph are presented on either side of the original. Does one of the two composites in Figure 7.2 look more disgusted than the other?

Participants were shown slides of photographs like those in Figure 7.2 and were asked to rate each slide on a 7-point scale indicating the intensity of the expressed emotion. The slides were presented individually for 10 seconds, and participants were then given 35 seconds to make their rating. To increase the external validity of their experiment, the investigators had photographs of 14 different people depicting the 6 identifiable emotions and 1 neutral expression. The critical independent variable in the experiment, however, was the *version* of

FIGURE 7.2   (a) Left-side composite, (b) original, and (c) right-side composite of the same face. The face is expressing disgust. (From Sackheim et al., 1978.)

the photograph (left composite, original, or right composite). Each participant rated 54 slides: 18 left composites, 18 originals, and 18 right composites.

Participants' ratings of emotional intensity were consistently higher for the left composite than for the right composite. Sackheim et al. interpreted these findings in terms of hemispheric specialization of the brain. In general, the left hemisphere controls the right side of the body and the right hemisphere controls the left side of the body. Thus, the left composite reflects control by the right hemisphere, and the right composite reflects control by the left hemisphere. The higher ratings of emotional intensity for the left composite photographs suggest that the right hemisphere may be more heavily involved than the left hemisphere in the production of emotional expression.

The interpretation of the differences in the ratings depends critically on the order in which the slides were presented to participants. If all the original versions were presented first, followed by all the right composites, then by all the left composites, higher ratings for the slides shown at the end of this long sequence may reflect the intensity of the participants' boredom and fatigue rather than the intensity of the emotions actually depicted in the photographs. If you imagine yourself in this experiment making a rating for each of the slides in this long sequence (over 40 minutes), you will get a sense of what we mean by practice effects. Surely your attention, motivation, and experience in rating the emotionality of photographs will change as you work through the sequence of slides. Sackheim et al. used balancing techniques specifically developed for use with the complete design in repeated measures experiments to ensure that each of the three versions of the photographs was equally likely to appear at any point in the long series of slides.

In the complete design, participants are given each treatment enough times to balance practice effects for each participant. Of course, this is possible only when each treatment can be administered more than once. When the task is simple enough and not too time-consuming (such as judging the emotional intensity of photographs), it is possible to give one participant several experiences with each treatment. In fact, in some complete designs, only one or two participants are tested and each participant experiences literally hundreds of trials. More commonly, however, researchers use procedures like those used by Sackheim et al. That is, several participants are tested, and each participant is given each treatment only a relatively small number of times. In Sackheim et al.'s experiment, participants completed 18 trials with left composites, 18 trials with original composites, and 18 trials with right composites. Researchers have two choices in deciding how to arrange the order in which the treatments in a complete design are administered: block randomization and ABBA counterbalancing.

Block Randomization   We introduced block randomization in Chapter 6 as an effective technique for assigning participants to conditions in the random groups design. *Block randomization* can also be used to order the conditions for each participant in a complete design. For instance, Sackheim et al. administered each of the three versions of their photographs (left composite, original, and right composite) 18 times to each participant. The sequence of trials shown in Table 7.1 illustrates how block randomization could be used to arrange the order of the three conditions in their experiment. The sequence of 54 trials is broken up into 18 blocks of 3 trials. Each block of trials contains the three conditions of the experiment in random order. In general, *the number of blocks in a block-randomized schedule is equal to the number of times each condition is administered, and the size of each block is equal to the number of conditions in the experiment.*

If a participant rated the photographs following the sequence in the block-randomized schedule shown in Table 7.1, it is unlikely that changes in the participant's attention, motivation, or experience with rating photographs would affect any one of the conditions more than any other. The practice effects can reasonably be expected to average out over the three experimental conditions. Determining the average position of each of the three conditions in the block-randomized sequence gives a rough indication of the balancing of practice effects. This can be done by summing the trial numbers on which each condition appears and dividing by 18. For instance, the original version of the photographs appeared on trials 1, 5, 8, 11, 13, 18, 21, 24, 27, 28, 33, 34, 39, 40, 44, 48, 49, and 53. The average position of the original photographs, therefore, was 27.6. The corresponding values for the left and right composite photographs are 27.7 and 27.2, respectively. That these average values are so similar tells us that any one version of the photographs was not more likely to appear at the beginning, middle, or end of the sequence of 54 trials.

Block randomization is effective in balancing practice effects, but each condition must be repeated several times before we can expect practice effects to average out. We should not expect practice effects to be balanced after two or three blocks—any more than we would expect sample sizes of two or three in the random groups design to result in comparable groups. Fortunately, a technique is available to balance practice effects when it is not possible to administer each

TABLE 7.1 BLOCK-RANDOMIZED SEQUENCE OF TRIALS IN AN
EXPERIMENT WITH THREE CONDITIONS ADMINISTERED
18 TIMES EACH

Trial	Conditions	Trial	Conditions
1	O	28	O
2	L	29	L
3	R	30	R
4	R	31	R
5	O	32	L
6	L	33	O
7	R	34	O
8	O	35	R
9	L	36	L
10	L	37	L
11	O	38	R
12	R	39	O
13	O	40	O
14	L	41	R
15	R	42	L
16	R	43	R
17	L	44	O
18	O	45	L
19	R	46	R
20	L	47	L
21	O	48	O
22	L	49	O
23	R	50	R
24	O	51	L
25	R	52	R
26	L	53	O
27	O	54	L

Note: The conditions are the three versions of the photographs
used by Sackheim et al. (1978): L = left composite, O = original,
R = right composite.

condition often enough for the averaging process of block randomization to
work effectively.

ABBA Counterbalancing In its simplest form, ABBA counterbalancing can be
used to balance practice effects in the complete design with as few as two administrations of each condition. **ABBA counterbalancing** involves presenting
the conditions in one sequence (i.e., A then B) followed by the opposite of that
same sequence (i.e., B then A). Its name describes the sequences when there are

only two conditions (A and B) in the experiment, but ABBA counterbalancing is not limited to experiments with just two conditions. Sackheim et al. could have presented the versions of their photographs according to the ABBA sequence outlined in the top row of Table 7.2 labeled "Condition." Note that in this case it literally would be ABCCBA since there are three conditions. The order of the three conditions on the first three trials is simply reversed for trials 4 to 6.

The row of Table 7.2 labeled "Practice effect (linear)" illustrates how ABBA counterbalancing can balance practice effects. ABBA counterbalancing is appropriately used when practice effects are linear. If practice effects are linear the same amount of practice effects is added to or subtracted from performance on each successive trial. In our example, suppose that one "unit" of hypothetical practice effects is added to performance on each trial. Because there would be no practice effect associated with the first trial, the amount of practice added to Trial 1 in the table is zero. Trial 2 has one unit of hypothetical effects added because of participants' experience with the first trial; in Trial 3 there are two units added because of participants' experience with two trials, and so on. If you add up these hypothetical practice effects for each condition, you will see that all the totals are the same, namely, 5. The left composite condition gets the least (+0) and the greatest (+5) influence from practice effects; the right composite condition gets two intermediate amounts (+2 and +3). The ABBA cycle can be applied with any number of conditions, but there must be an even number of repetitions of each condition. (An unequal number of repetitions would end in the middle of an ABBA sequence—that is, AB would be the last two conditions of an ABBA series.) It balances practice effects even more effectively with larger numbers of repetitions of the cycle. Usually, however, ABBA counterbalancing is used when the number of conditions and the number of repetitions of each condition are relatively small.

Although ABBA counterbalancing provides a simple and elegant means to balance practice effects, it is not without limitations. For example, when practice effects for a task are not linear but involve abrupt initial changes followed by relatively little change thereafter, ABBA counterbalancing is ineffective. This is illustrated in the last row of Table 7.2, labeled "Practice effect (nonlinear)." In this example, the left composite receives a total of only 6 hypothetical units of practice effects, and the other two conditions receive a total of 12 units each. When practice effects of this type are anticipated, researchers often ignore performance on the early trials and wait until the practice effects reach a "steady

TABLE 7.2   ABBA COUNTERBALANCED SEQUENCE OF TRIALS IN AN EXPERIMENT WITH THREE CONDITIONS (LEFT COMPOSITE, ORIGINAL, AND RIGHT COMPOSITE)

	Condition:	Trial 1 Left	Trial 2 Original	Trial 3 Right	Trial 4 Right	Trial 5 Original	Trial 6 Left
Practice effect (linear)		+0	+1	+2	+3	+4	+5
Practice effect (nonlinear)		0	+6	+6	+6	+6	+6

state." Reaching a steady state is likely to take several repetitions of each condition, so researchers tend to use block randomization to balance practice effects in these situations. This problem should alert you to the fact that there are situations when you should not choose a repeated measures design, for example, if nonlinear changes cannot easily be eliminated from your analysis.

A second limitation of ABBA counterbalancing is the problem of anticipation effects. *Anticipation effects* occur when a participant develops expectations about which condition should occur next in the sequence. The participant's response to that condition may then be influenced more by this expectation than by the actual experience of the condition itself. For example, consider a time-perception experiment in which the participant's task is to estimate the length of time that has passed between when the experimenter said "Start" and when the experimenter said "Stop." (Of course, participants have to be prevented somehow from marking off time during the interval by counting or rhythmically tapping.) If the time intervals in such an experiment are 12, 24, and 36 seconds, then one possible ABBA sequence of conditions could be 12-24-36-36-24-12. If this cycle were repeated several times, participants probably would recognize the pattern and expect a series of increasing and then decreasing intervals. Their time estimates might soon begin to reflect this pattern rather than their perception of each independent interval. In general, block randomization should be used if anticipation effects are likely.

Incomplete Design

- Practice effects are balanced *across* subjects in the incomplete design rather than *within* subjects, as in the complete design.
- The rule for balancing practice effects in the incomplete design is that each condition of the experiment must be presented in each ordinal position (first, second, etc.) equally often.
- The best method for balancing practice effects in the incomplete design with four or fewer conditions is to use all possible orders of the conditions.
- Two methods for selecting specific orders to use in an incomplete design are the Latin Square and random starting order with rotation.
- Whether using all possible orders or selected orders, participants should be randomly assigned to the different sequences.

In the incomplete design, each participant is given each treatment *only once*. The results for any one participant, therefore, are uninterpretable because the levels of the independent variable for each participant are perfectly confounded with the order in which those levels were presented. For instance, the first participant in an incomplete design experiment might be tested first in the experimental condition (E) and second in the control condition (C). Any differences in the participant's performance between the experimental and control conditions could be due to the effect of the independent variable *or* to the practice effects resulting from the EC order. To break this confounding of the order of conditions and the independent variable, we can administer different orders of the conditions to different participants. For example, we could administer the conditions of our incomplete design experiment to a second participant in the CE order, testing the control condition first and the experimental condition second. In this way, we could balance the effects of order across the two conditions using two participants instead of one.

To illustrate the techniques for balancing practice effects in the incomplete design, we will use an experiment by Erber (1991) on the effects of people's moods on their perceptions of other people. There were two stages in this experiment. In the first stage, the independent variable of mood was manipulated using independent groups—that is, each participant was in only one mood group. In this first stage, participants read one of three stories about events in the life of a young female artist. These stories were previously shown to be effective in inducing positive, neutral, or negative moods in people. The story for the positive-mood condition included several events culminating in the artist's receiving a scholarship to college. The neutral-mood story described how the artist decided which college to attend. The negative-mood story described how the artist was overcome by a rare disabling illness at the end of her first year in college. Thus, after the first stage, participants are assumed to be in one of three moods: positive, neutral, negative.

At this point, the second stage of the experiment began. The participants believed that the second stage was a separate experiment, one in which they were asked to rate the likelihood of a person engaging in a particular behavior (welcoming a friend with a hug, getting depressed over the weather, and so on). Four individuals were described to the participants, and then the participants were asked to rate the likelihood that these individuals would demonstrate various behaviors. Four brief descriptions were provided to each participant, one for each "target" individual whom they would rate. For reasons that will become apparent, the descriptions were based on somewhat contradictory traits. Each of the four "target people" was described as (1) either moody and warm; (2) pessimistic and understanding; (3) unselfish and unsociable; or (4) trustworthy and possessive. A repeated measures design was used to implement the independent variable of the target person, which, of course, had four levels. Specifically, an incomplete design was used in which each participant rated all four target people *once*.

Before describing the techniques that can be used to balance practice effects for an independent variable in the incomplete design, we will take a brief look at the results of the Erber study. The dependent variable in this study was the participants' ratings of the likelihood that the target people would engage in certain behaviors. The researcher hypothesized that these ratings would be influenced by *participants'* mood (positive, neutral, or negative) as manipulated in the first stage of the experiment. Because the target people were described using both a positive (e.g., warm) and a negative (e.g., moody) trait, the researchers wanted to see if the participants' mood would determine which of the two traits most influenced their ratings. For example, the participants' task was to rate how likely it was for someone described as "warm and moody" to engage in positive behavior, such as "welcoming a friend with a hug," or in negative behavior, such as "getting depressed over the weather." Welcoming someone with a hug is something a "warm" person might do, while getting depressed is something a "moody" person is more likely to do. Perhaps you can anticipate what happened in this experiment.

The results revealed that if a participant was in a positive mood, then a "warm and moody" person was rated as more likely to engage in positive behavior (e.g., welcoming with a hug) than in negative behavior (e.g., getting depressed over the weather). If the participant was in a negative mood, the same "warm and moody" individual was rated more likely to engage in negative behavior than in positive behavior. The effect of mood on ratings of negative behaviors was larger than was the effect of mood on ratings of positive behaviors. These findings (along with other findings reported in the study) indicate that mood can influence the way we perceive other people in important ways. One such influence, Erber (1991) argues, is that negative mood may facilitate the accessibility of negative information about others. In other words, if you're in a bad mood, you're more likely to accentuate someone's negative traits!

The repeated measures independent variable in the Erber (1991) experiment was the four types of target people. In order to rule out practice effects as an alternative explanation for the findings it is essential that the order in which the targets are rated is balanced. We turn now to the balancing techniques that are used in the incomplete design. The general rule for balancing practice effects in the incomplete design is a simple one: *Each condition of the experiment must appear in each ordinal position equally often*. Several techniques are available for satisfying this general rule. These techniques differ in what additional balancing they accomplish, but so long as the techniques are properly used, the basic rule will be met and the experiment will be interpretable. That is, if appropriate balancing is carried out, then we will be in a position to determine whether the independent variable, and not practice effects, influenced the participants' behavior.

All Possible Orders   The preferred technique for balancing practice effects in the incomplete design is to use all possible orders of the conditions. Each participant is randomly assigned to one of the orders. With only two conditions there are only two possible orders (AB and BA); with three conditions there are six possible orders (ABC, ACB, BAC, BCA, CAB, CBA). In general, there are $N!$ (which is read "N factorial") possible orders with N conditions, where $N!$ equals $N(N - 1)(N - 2) \ldots (N - [N - 1])$. As we just saw, there are six possible orders with three conditions, which is 3! ($3 \times 2 \times 1 = 6$). The number of required orders increases dramatically with increasing numbers of conditions. For instance, for only five conditions there are 120 possible orders of the conditions, and for six conditions there are 720 possible orders. Because of this, the use of all possible orders is usually limited to experiments involving four or fewer conditions. With four conditions, how many possible orders are there?

Because there were four target people in the Erber (1991) experiment, 24 sequences would be required to obtain all possible orders of the conditions. These sequences are presented in the left half of Table 7.3. Using all possible orders

TABLE 7.3   ALTERNATIVE TECHNIQUES TO BALANCE PRACTICE EFFECTS IN AN INCOMPLETE REPEATED MEASURES DESIGN EXPERIMENT WITH FOUR CONDITIONS

All possible orders								Selected orders							
								Latin Square				Random starting order with rotation			
Ordinal position				Ordinal position				Ordinal position				Ordinal position			
1st	2nd	3rd	4th	1st	2nd	3rd	4th	1st	2nd	3rd	4th	1st	2nd	3rd	4th
M	P	U	T	U	M	P	T	M	P	U	T	P	U	T	M
M	P	T	U	U	M	T	P	P	T	M	U	U	T	M	P
M	U	P	T	U	P	M	T	T	U	P	M	T	M	P	U
M	U	T	P	U	P	T	M	U	M	T	P	M	P	U	T
M	T	P	U	U	T	M	P								
M	T	U	P	U	T	P	M								
P	M	U	T	T	M	P	U								
P	M	T	U	T	M	U	P								
P	U	M	T	T	P	M	U								
P	U	T	M	T	P	U	M								
P	T	M	U	T	U	M	P								
P	T	U	M	T	U	P	M								

Note: The four conditions are identified by the first letter of the first adjective describing each of the four target people in the Erber (1991) experiment: Moody-Warm (M), Pessimistic-Understanding (P), Unselfish-Unsociable (U), and Trustworthy-Possessive (T).

certainly meets the general rule of ensuring that all conditions appear in each ordinal position equally often. The first ordinal position shows this balancing most clearly: The first six sequences begin with the Moody-Warm (M) target, and each succeeding set of six sequences begins with one of the other three targets. The same pattern applies at each of the four ordinal positions. For example, the "M" target also appears six times in the second ordinal position, six times in the third ordinal position, and six times in the fourth ordinal position.

There is one other issue that must be addressed in deciding to use all possible orders. For this technique to be effective, it is essential that at least one participant be tested with each of the possible orders of the conditions. That is, at least one participant should receive the MPUT order, at least one should receive the MPTU order, and so on. Therefore, the use of all possible orders requires at least as many participants as there are possible orders. That is, if there are four conditions in the experiment, you must test 24 participants (or 48 or 72 or some other multiple of 24). This restriction makes it very important that you have a good idea of the number of potential participants available to you before testing the first participant.

Selected Orders   We have just described the preferred method for balancing practice effects in the incomplete design, all possible orders. There are times, however, when the use of all possible orders is not practical. For example, if we wanted to use the incomplete design to study an independent variable with seven levels, we would need to test 5,040 participants if we used all possible orders—one participant for each of the possible orders of the seven conditions (7! orders). We obviously need some alternative to using all possible orders if we are to use the incomplete design for experiments with five or more conditions.

Practice effects can be balanced by using just some of all the possible orders. The number of selected orders will always be equal to some multiple of the number of conditions in the experiment. For example, to do an experiment with one independent variable with seven levels, we need to select 7, 14, 21, 28, or some other multiple of seven orders to balance practice effects. The two basic variations of using selected orders are illustrated in Table 7.3. To allow you to compare the types of balancing more directly, we have illustrated the techniques for selected orders with the four-level independent variable from Erber's (1991) experiment that we described in the previous section.

BOX 7.1

HOW TO CONSTRUCT A LATIN SQUARE

More than one valid Latin Square can be constructed for an experiment. A simple procedure for constructing a square *with an even number (N) of conditions* is as follows:

1 Randomly order the conditions of the experiment.
2 Number the conditions in your random order 1 through *N*.

   Thus, if you had *N* = 4 conditions (A,B,C,D) and the random order (from Step 1) was B, A, D, C, then B = 1, A = 2, D = 3, C = 4.

3 To generate the first row (first order of conditions), use the rule:

   1, 2, *N*, 3, *N* − 1, 4, *N* − 2, 5, *N* − 3, 6, etc.
   In our example, this would yield 1, 2, 4, 3.

4 To generate the second row (second order of conditions) add 1 to each number in the first row but with the understanding that 1 added to *N* = 1.

   We would then have 2, 3, 1, 4.

5 The third row (third order of conditions) is generated by adding 1 to each number in the second row and again *N* + 1 = 1.

   The third row would be 3, 4, 2, 1.

6 A similar procedure is carried out for each successive row.

Can you construct the fourth row in this 4 × 4 square?

7 Assign the conditions to their corresponding numbers as determined in Step 2.

The Latin Square for this example would be:

B A C D
A D B C
D C A B
C B D A

If there is an odd number of conditions, then two squares must be constructed. The first can be made according to the rule given above for even-numbered squares. The second square is generated by reversing the rows in the first square. For example, assume *N* = 5 and the first row of the first square is B A E C D. The first row of the second square would then be D C E A B. The two squares are joined to make a *N* × 2*N* square. In either case, even or odd, subjects should be assigned randomly to the rows of the square. Thus, you must have available at least as many subjects as there are multiples of rows. (Procedures for selecting or constructing Latin Squares are also described in Winer, Brown, and Michels [1991, pp. 674–679].)

The first type of balancing using selected orders is called the Latin Square. In a *Latin Square*, the general rule for balancing practice effects is met. That is, each condition appears at each ordinal position once. For example, just to the right of the center of Table 7.3, we can see that in the Latin Square, condition "M" appears exactly once in the first, second, third, and fourth ordinal positions. This is true for each condition. Additionally, in a Latin Square each condition precedes and follows each other condition exactly once. Examination of the Latin Square in Table 7.3 shows that the order "MP" appears once, as does the order "PM." The order "PV" appears once, as does the order "VP," and so on, for every combination of conditions. (See also Box 7.1 on p. 283.)

The second balancing technique using selected orders requires you to begin with a random order of the conditions and to rotate this sequence systematically with each condition moving one position to the left each time (see the example on the right in Table 7.3). Using a random starting order with rotation effectively balances practice effects because, like the Latin Square, each condition appears in each ordinal position. However, the systematic rotation of the sequences means that each condition always follows and always precedes the *same* other conditions, which is not like the Latin Square technique. The simplicity of the random starting order with rotation technique and its applicability to experiments with more than four conditions are its primary advantages.

The use of all possible orders, Latin Squares, and random starting orders with rotation are equally effective in balancing practice effects because all three techniques ensure that each condition appears in each ordinal position equally often. Regardless of which technique one uses to balance practice effects, the sequences of conditions should be fully prepared prior to testing the first participant, and participants should be randomly assigned to these sequences.

LIMITATIONS OF REPEATED MEASURES DESIGNS

- There are some variables that cannot be studied using a repeated measures design.

The first obvious limitation of repeated measures designs is that they cannot be used to study individual differences variables such as age and gender. A 40-year-old person cannot be 20 years old, then 60 years old, and then 40 years old again (though we've all known people who act that way!). Second, repeated measures designs also are not appropriate when the levels of the independent variable represent an unfolding sequence of successive events. For example, a study of brain lesions would require controls such as Anesthesia Only and a Sham-Operated condition, and the sequential nature of these treatments seems to demand separate groups. That is, an animal could not be tested in the Anesthesia Only group once the animal was lesioned. Third, experiments in which each condition takes a great deal of time to implement are not likely to be suitable for repeated measures designs. For example, if the treatment involved participation in a year-long program, one ABBA sequence in a repeated measures design would take 4 years to implement! Finally, as you saw, a repeated measures design should not be used when practice effects are not apt to be linear. It is unlikely that the random groups design will be completely replaced by the repeated measures designs.

Irreversible Tasks

- Because individuals participate more than once in repeated measures designs, irreversible tasks cannot be used; instead, different versions of the task should be used.
- To balance practice effects when different versions of a task are used, the conditions of the independent variable of interest *and* the different versions of the task must be balanced.

We will consider a hypothetical but realistic experiment looking at the effects of marijuana use to illustrate a problem sometimes encountered in a repeated measures design, that of irreversible tasks. Participants in this hypothetical experiment are asked to come to the laboratory on four different days. Each day the participants smoke two cigarettes that contain one of four dose levels of marijuana—a placebo control (0) and doses of 50, 100, and 200 units. The experiment is an incomplete repeated measures design so each participant is given each dose once.

The experiment examines the effects of marijuana on people's ability to learn and remember new information. One way to carry out an experiment like this would be to give each participant a different list of words to learn under each dose of marijuana. A different list of words would be needed each time because a memory task of this type is an *irreversible task*—one that cannot be administered more than once without risking that the participant will master the task. Once participants master the task, their performance under subsequent conditions is not likely to vary. In a sense, irreversible tasks result in a "ceiling effect" for all conditions after the first one under which the task has been performed. When performance hits a "ceiling" there is no way to measure any further improvement in performance in the other conditions (see Chapter 8).

Suppose in this example that the researchers had given the *same* list of words to participants on each of the four days. Consider the performance of a participant who received the following sequence of doses: 0, 50, 200, and 100. Performance may not be all that good on the first day (0 dose) because the participant is learning the list of words for the first time. However, on the second, and following days, his or her performance is likely to be better because the list had been learned on Day 1. Note that this "improvement" would be seen just when the participant is receiving doses (50, 200, 100) of marijuana. This may make marijuana look like a drug that enhances memory! Of course, it would not be a valid finding because of the problem with irreversible tasks. Because the list was mastered early in the experiment, it would be impossible to know if marijuana had any effects on memory.

Thus, to control for problems associated with this irreversible task, memorizing a list of words, a *different* list of words should be used each time individuals participate in the experiment. This, however, creates a new problem if the same list is used for each condition of the independent variable manipulation. That is, if List A is always used for the 0-dose condition, and List B is always used for the 50-dose condition, and so on, the particular version of the list becomes confounded with dosage level. If the lists differ in important ways, for example, if one list is easier than the others, the effect of dosage level (the primary independent variable) cannot be interpreted.

The solution to the problem of irreversible tasks is outlined in Table 7.4. The solution requires two steps. The first step is to balance practice effects for the primary independent variable (in our case, the marijuana variable). A random starting order with rotation has been used to accomplish the balancing of the four dose levels (0, 50, 100, and 200 units); that is, each dosage condition appears in each ordinal position of the experiment. The sequences for the first four participants appear in the upper-left quadrant of the table. The first subject receives the conditions in the order 50, 200, 0, and 100 units with Lists A, B, C, and D, respectively. This order is then rotated for the second subject (200, 0, 100, 50), but note that this subject receives List A with the 200 dose, List B with the 0 dose, and so on. When the sequence of dosage levels is rotated for the third and fourth subjects, they too receive different lists for the dosage conditions. Because each dose appears with each of the four lists exactly once, the marijuana variable is also balanced for the possible effects of the list variable. Thus, if one

TABLE 7.4   BALANCING EXPERIMENTS WITH IRREVERSIBLE TASKS IN REPEATED MEASURES DESIGNS

	Ordinal position					Ordinal position			
	1st	2nd	3rd	4th		1st	2nd	3rd	4th
		List					List		
Subject	A	B	C	D	Subject	B	C	D	A
1	050	200	000	100	5	050	200	000	100
2	200	000	100	050	6	200	000	100	050
3	000	100	050	200	7	000	100	050	200
4	100	050	200	000	8	100	050	200	000
	Ordinal position					Ordinal position			
	1st	2nd	3rd	4th		1st	2nd	3rd	4th
		List					List		
Subject	C	D	A	B	Subject	D	A	B	C
9	050	200	000	100	13	050	200	000	100
10	200	000	100	050	14	200	000	100	050
11	000	100	050	200	15	000	100	050	200
12	100	050	200	000	16	100	050	200	000

Note: The numbers 000, 050, 100, and 200 refer to dose levels.

list happens to be easier for participants to learn, any one dosage level would not have an advantage due to being associated consistently with the easier list.

A problem would arise, however, if the researcher were to try to assess differences among the four lists. The lists for the first four participants are perfectly confounded by the ordinal position. That is, List A is always learned first, List B is learned on Day 2, List C on the third day, and List D is always last. The confounding of lists and ordinal position can be overcome by taking the second step in dealing with the problem of irreversible tasks. In general, this second step requires testing additional participants so that the list variable and ordinal position are also balanced. In our example, 12 additional participants need to be tested, with the order of the lists systematically rotated for each successive set of four participants. This also is illustrated in Table 7.4. Each quadrant of the table includes the same four orders of marijuana doses. However, by comparing the upper left quadrant with the three remaining quadrants, you can see that the order of the lists for each quadrant is different. The order of the lists has been determined using a random starting order with rotation, such that four different orders of the lists are used: ABCD, BCDA, CDAB, DABC. Thus, across the 16 subjects, each condition appears in each ordinal position with each version of the list. The two-step process of balancing in experiments involving irreversible tasks ensures that each of three variables (the independent variable of interest, stage of practice, and task) are balanced for the other two. Thus, the effects of all three variables are interpretable.

Differential Transfer

- Differential transfer occurs when the effects of one condition persist and influence performance in subsequent conditions.
- Because differential transfer threatens the internal validity of repeated measures designs, variables that may lead to differential transfer should be tested using a random groups design.
- Differential transfer can be identified by comparing the results for the same independent variable when tested in a repeated measures design and in a random groups design.
- An efficient method for determining whether differential transfer has occurred in an incomplete design is to compare the results for the independent variable at the first stage of practice to the results for the overall repeated measures design.

The most consistent and vocal critic of repeated measures designs has been E. C. Poulton (1973, 1975, 1982; Poulton & Freeman, 1966). While conceding that balancing techniques control practice effects, Poulton has argued that they do not eliminate a more serious problem. This problem arises when performance in one condition differs depending on the condition that precedes it. We call this **differential transfer.**

Consider a problem-solving experiment in which two types of instructions are being compared in a repeated measures design. One set of instructions (A) is expected to enhance problem solving, whereas the other set of instructions (B) serves as the neutral control condition. It is reasonable to expect that participants tested in the order AB will be unable or unwilling to abandon the approach outlined in the A instructions when they are supposed to be following the B instructions. Giving up the "good thing" participants had under instruction A would be the counterpart of successfully following the admonition "Don't think of pink elephants!" When participants fail to give up the instruction from the first condition (A) when they are supposed to be following instruction B, any difference between the two conditions is reduced. For those participants, after all, condition B was not really tried, and it becomes similar to a situation in which they participated in an "AA" condition, not an "AB" condition.

In general, the presence of differential transfer threatens internal validity because it becomes impossible to determine if there are true differences between the conditions. It also tends to underestimate differences between the conditions and thereby reduces the external validity of the findings. *Thus repeated measures designs should not be used when differential transfer may arise.* Differential transfer is sufficiently common with instructional variables to advise against the use of repeated measures designs for these variables (Underwood & Shaughnessy, 1975). Unfortunately, differential transfer can arise in any repeated measures design. For instance, the effect of 50 units of marijuana may be different if administered after the participant has received 200 units than if administered after the participant has received the placebo (e.g., if the participant has an increased tolerance for marijuana after receiving the 200 dose). There are ways, however, to determine whether differential transfer is likely to have occurred.

Poulton (1982) maintains that the best way to determine whether differential transfer is a problem is to do two separate experiments. The same independent variable would be studied in both experiments, but a repeated measures design would be used in one experiment and a random groups design in the other. The random groups design cannot possibly involve differential transfer because each participant is tested in only one condition. Poulton argues that differential transfer is not a problem if the repeated measures design shows the same effect of the independent variable as that shown in the random groups design. If the two designs show different effects for the same independent variable, however, differential transfer is likely to be responsible for producing the different outcome in the repeated measures design. When differential transfer does occur, the results of the random groups design should be used to provide the best description of the effect of the independent variable.

Perhaps the most efficient way to follow Poulton's advice is to do experiments involving a relatively large repeated measures experiment using the incomplete design. For example, if 48 participants were tested in a four-condition experiment with all possible orders of the conditions (i.e., 24 different orders), there would be 12 participants tested in each of the four conditions at the first stage of practice (i.e., the first ordinal position). That is, with 24 possible orders, each of four conditions (A, B, C, D) would appear six times in the first ordinal position, and since there are 2 participants tested in each sequence, there would be 12 receiving A first, 12 B first, and so on. So long as participants have been randomly assigned to sequences, the repeated measures design contains a random groups design for the first condition given to each participant. In other words, at this point in your repeated measures design (the first stage of practice), you have 12 participants assigned randomly to each of four conditions, making a random groups design within the first ordinal position. By comparing the results for the independent variable in the first ordinal position with the overall results for the independent variable in the repeated measures design, we can achieve the comparison Poulton recommends in one experiment.

ANALYSIS OF REPEATED MEASURES DESIGNS

Sensitivity and Power

- Sensitivity refers to the likelihood that an *experiment* will detect the effect of an independent variable when, in fact, the independent variable truly has an effect.
- Power refers to the likelihood that a *statistical test* will allow researchers to reject correctly the null hypothesis of no group differences.
- The power of statistical tests is influenced by the level of statistical significance, the size of the treatment effect, and the sample size.
- Repeated measures designs are likely to be more sensitive and to have more statistical power than independent groups designs because estimates of error variation are likely to be smaller in repeated measures designs.
- The primary means for researchers to increase statistical power are increasing sample size or using a repeated measures design, or both.

Before we describe the use of the *F*-test in the analysis of repeated measures designs, we will describe the concept of power in statistical analyses. The **sensitivity** of an experiment is the likelihood that it will detect an effect of the independent variable if the independent variable does, indeed, have an effect. As we have mentioned, repeated measures designs are generally more sensitive than independent groups designs. An experiment is said to have sensitivity; a statistical test is said to have power. The **power** of a statistical test is the probability that the null hypothesis will be rejected when it is false. The null hypothesis is the hypothesis of "no difference," and, thus, is false and should be rejected when the independent variable has made a difference. You may remember that in our discussion of Type I and Type II errors (see Chapter 6), we defined a Type II error as the probability of failing to reject the null hypothesis when it is false. Power can also be defined as 1 minus the probability of a Type II error. It is important to be aware of the factors in an experiment that affect the power of the statistical test that will be used to analyze the data *before* beginning to collect the data.

Keppel (1991) provides an excellent description of the factors affecting the power of a statistical test such as the analysis of variance. The power of a statistical test is determined by the interplay of three factors: the level of statistical significance, the size of the treatment effect, and the sample size. Keppel goes on to argue, however, that for all practical purposes sample size is the primary factor that researchers can use to control power. He describes how to use power charts to select an appropriate sample size for a given level of power with a certain level of significance and with an expected treatment effect that is either small, medium, or large. (We described the nature of small, medium, and large effects when we describe the measurement of effect sizes in Chapter 6.) The differences in sample size that are needed to detect effects of different sizes can be dramatic. For example, Cohen (1988) reports the sample sizes that are needed for an independent groups design experiment with one independent variable manipulated at three levels. It takes a sample size of 30 to detect a large treatment effect; it takes a sample size of 76 to detect a medium treatment effect; and it takes a sample size of 464 to detect a small treatment effect. It thus takes over 15 times more participants to detect a small effect than it does to detect a large effect!

Sample size is the major factor researchers can control to affect the power of the statistical analyses they use to analyze their experiments. Using repeated measures experiments can also affect the power of the statistical analyses researchers use. Repeated measures experiments are generally more sensitive than are independent groups experiments. This is because, as was mentioned earlier, the estimates of error variation are generally smaller in repeated measures experiments (see also next section). The smaller error variation leads to an increased ability to detect small treatment effects in an experiment. And that is just what the power of a statistical analysis is—the ability to detect small treatment effects when they are present.

To conduct a power analysis you must first estimate the effect size anticipated in your experiment. An examination of the effect sizes obtained in previous studies for the independent variable of interest should guide your estimate. Once an effect size is estimated, you must then turn to "power tables" to obtain information about the sample size you should use in order to "see" the effect. These steps for conducting a power analysis are described more fully in Appendix A. Power tables are also included at the end of Appendix A for you to consult. (Should you wish to investigate this issue further, Cohen [1992] provides a brief introduction to power, and, Cohen [1988] provides a more thorough introduction.)

Repeated Measures Analysis of Variance

- The general procedures and logic for null hypothesis testing using repeated measures analysis of variance are similar to those used for independent groups analysis of variance.
- Before beginning the analysis of variance for a complete design, a summary score (e.g., mean, median) for each participant must be computed for each condition.
- Descriptive data are calculated to summarize performance for each condition of the independent variable across all participants.

- The primary way that analysis of variance differs for repeated measures is in the estimation of error variation, or residual variation; residual variation is the variation that remains when systematic variation due to the independent variable and participants is removed from the estimate of total variation.

The analysis of experiments using repeated measures designs involves the same general procedures used in the analysis of independent groups design experiments. The principles of null-hypothesis testing are applied to determine whether the differences obtained in the experiment are larger than would be expected on the basis of error variation alone. The analysis begins with an omnibus analysis of variance to determine whether the independent variable has produced any systematic variation among the levels of the independent variable. Should this omnibus analysis prove statistically significant, analytical comparisons can be made to find the specific source of the systematic variation—that is, to determine which specific levels differed from each other. Because we have already described the logic and procedures for this general analysis plan in Chapter 6, we will focus in this section on the analysis procedures specific to repeated measures designs.

The first step in analyzing an experiment is preparing a matrix summarizing participants' performance in each condition of the experiment. In random groups designs, this means simply listing the scores of the participants tested in each of the conditions of the experiment and then summarizing these scores with some descriptive statistic such as the mean. Similarly, in complete repeated measures designs, we prepare a matrix in which the scores for each participant in each condition of the experiment are listed. An example of such a matrix appears in the upper portion of Table 7.5. The data represent performance of the five participants tested in a time-perception experiment done as a classroom demonstration of a complete repeated measures design. The purpose of the experiment was not to test the accuracy of participants' time estimates compared with the actual interval lengths. Instead, the purpose of the experiment was to determine whether participants' estimates of time increased systematically with increasing lengths. In other words, could participants discriminate between intervals of different lengths? Each participant was tested using all four interval lengths (12, 24, 36, and 48 seconds).

Each of the four interval lengths was tested six times in the experiment, and block randomization was used to determine the order in which the intervals were presented. Thus, each participant provided 24 time estimates, 6 estimates for each of the four interval lengths. Any one of the 6 estimates for a given time interval is contaminated by practice effects, so some measure that combines information across the 6 estimates is needed. Typically, the mean across the 6 estimates for each interval would be calculated for each participant to provide a single estimate of performance in each condition. As you may remember, however, the mean is influenced by extreme scores; it is quite possible that participants gave extreme estimates of the time intervals for at least one of the six tests of each interval. Thus, for this particular set of data, the median of the 6 estimates probably provides the best measure to reflect the participants' estimates

TABLE 7.5   DATA MATRIX AND ANALYSIS OF VARIANCE SUMMARY TABLE FOR A REPEATED MEASURES DESIGN EXPERIMENT

	Data matrix			
	Interval length			
Participant	12	24	36	48
1	13	21	30	38
2	10	15	38	35
3	12	23	31	32
4	12	15	22	32
5	16	36	69	60
Mean	12.6	22.0	38.0	39.4

Note: Each value in the table represents the median of the participants' six responses at each level of the interval length variable.

Source of Variation	df	SS	MS	F	p
Subjects	4	1553.5	—	—	—
Interval Length	3	2515.6	838.5	15.6	.0004
Residual (error variation)	12	646.9	53.9		
Total	19	4716.0			

of the time intervals. These median estimates (rounded to the nearest whole number) are listed in Table 7.5. The point of this illustration is that you must compute a score for each participant in each condition before you begin to do an analysis of variance.

Once an individual score for each participant in each condition has been obtained, the next step is to summarize the results across participants, using an appropriate descriptive statistic. The mean estimates across participants for each of the four intervals are listed in the row labeled "Mean" in Table 7.5. Even though the data for only five participants are included in the table, these mean estimates are reasonably accurate reflections of the actual interval lengths, at least for intervals up to 36 seconds. (Note that the mean is an average of medians. You may be used to seeing the mean and median as descriptive statistics summarizing a group's performance; however, as this example illustrates, these summary statistics also can be used to represent one person's performance when that performance is an "average" across trials or test occasions.)

The focus of the analysis was on whether the participants could discriminate intervals of different lengths. As you have probably already realized, we cannot confirm the participants' ability to discriminate intervals of varying lengths until we know that the mean differences in Table 7.5 are greater than would be expected on the basis of error variation alone. That is, even though it may *appear* that participants were able to discriminate between the different intervals, we do not know if their performance was different from that which would occur by chance. The null hypothesis for an omnibus analysis of variance for the data in

Table 7.5 is that the mean estimates for each interval are the same. To perform an *F*-test of this null hypothesis, we need an estimate of error variation plus systematic variation (the numerator of an *F*-ratio). The variation among the mean estimates across participants for the four intervals provides the information we need for the numerator. Even if these five participants had been tested on only one interval length several times, we would not expect their mean estimates to be identical. Thus, we know the mean estimates we have for each level of the interval variable reflect error variation as well. We also know, however, that if the different interval lengths did systematically affect the participants' judgments, then the mean estimates for the intervals would reflect this systematic variation. To complete the *F*-ratio, we also need an estimate of error variation alone (the denominator of the *F*-ratio).

One distinctive characteristic of the analysis of repeated measures designs is the way in which error variation is estimated. We described in Chapter 6 that for the random groups design individual differences among participants that are balanced across groups provide the estimate of error variation that becomes the denominator of the *F*-ratio. Because individuals participate in only one condition in these designs, differences among participants cannot be eliminated—they can only be balanced. In repeated measures designs, on the other hand, there is systematic variation among participants. Some participants consistently perform better across conditions, and some participants consistently perform worse. Because each individual participates in each condition of repeated measures designs, however, differences among participants contribute equally to the mean performance in each condition. Accordingly, any differences among the means for each condition in repeated measures designs cannot be the result of systematic differences among participants. In repeated measures designs, however, differences among participants are not just balanced—they are actually eliminated from the analysis. The ability to eliminate systematic variation due to participants in repeated measures designs makes these designs generally more sensitive than random groups designs.

If differences among participants cannot be the basis of estimating error variation in repeated measures designs, how do we get an estimate that involves only error variation in these designs? The source of error variation in the repeated measures designs is the differences in the ways the conditions affect different participants. Perhaps the best way to describe the way we get these estimates is to say that we do it "by default." We first determine how much total variation there is in our experiment. Then we subtract the two potential sources of systematic variation: the independent variable and participants. The remainder is called *residual variation,* and it represents our estimate of error variation alone. (For a more complete discussion of residual variation and why it is an estimate of error variation alone, see Keppel [1991].) As was the case in the random groups design when we used variation within groups as our estimate of error variation alone, residual variation serves as the denominator for the *F*-ratio in repeated measures designs (i.e., as an estimate of error variation alone).

The analysis of variance summary table for this analysis is presented in the lower portion of Table 7.5. As described in Appendix A, the computations of a repeated measures analysis of variance would be done using a statistical software package on a computer. Our focus now is on interpreting the values in the summary table and not on how these values are computed. Table 7.5 lists the four sources of variation in the analysis of a repeated measures design with one manipulated independent variable. Reading from the bottom of the summary table up, these sources are (1) total variation, (2) residual variation, (3) variation due to interval length (the independent variable), and (4) variation due to subjects.

As in any summary table, the most critical pieces of information are the F-test for the effect of the independent variable of interest and the probability associated with that F-test under the null hypothesis. The important F-test in Table 7.5 is the one for interval length. The numerator for this F-test is the mean square (MS) for interval length; the denominator is the residual MS. There are four interval lengths, so there are 3 degrees of freedom (df) for the numerator. There are 12 df for the residual variation. We can obtain the df for the residual variation by subtracting the df for subjects and for interval length from the total df (19 − 4 − 3 = 12). The obtained F of 15.6 has a probability under the null hypothesis of .0004, which is less than the .05 level of significance we have chosen as our criterion for statistical significance. So we reject the null hypothesis and conclude that the interval length was a source of systematic variation. This means that we can conclude that the participants' estimates did differ systematically as a function of interval length.

As we mentioned previously (in Chapter 6), it is good statistical practice to include measures of effect size for your analyses. A typical measure of effect size for a repeated measures design is the strength of association measure called eta squared (η^2) (see Appendix A). This measure is calculated by dividing the sum of squares for the independent variable by the sum of squares for the independent variable plus the sum of squares error. For our sample study, eta squared is 2515.6/(2515.6 + 646.9) = .80. This indicates the proportion of variance accounted for by the independent variable. Appendix A provides more information about the calculation of effect sizes and their interpretation.

This omnibus analysis of variance would almost certainly be followed by analytical comparisons (such as comparing the mean for each interval to the mean for the succeeding interval) to determine more exactly that mean estimates increased with increasing interval lengths. Once again, the logic of these analytical comparisons corresponds to the logic we discussed in Chapter 6 when we considered analytical comparisons in the random groups design. In most instances, the residual MS can be used as an estimate of error variation alone in computing the F-tests for the analytical comparisons. (See Keppel [1991], however, for a discussion of the complications that can arise in doing analytical comparisons in repeated measures designs.)

SUMMARY

Repeated measures designs provide an effective and efficient way to conduct an experiment by administering all the conditions in the experiment to each participant. Repeated measures designs are useful when only very few participants are available or when an independent variable can be studied most efficiently by testing fewer participants several times. Particular areas of psychological research (e.g., psychophysics) may also require the use of repeated measures designs. Finally, repeated measures designs may be used when a more sensitive experiment is required.

For any repeated measures design experiment to be interpretable, however, practice effects must be balanced. Practice effects are changes that participants undergo because of repeated testing. In a complete repeated measures design, practice effects are balanced for each participant. In an incomplete repeated measures design, each participant receives each treatment only once, and the balancing of practice effects is accomplished across participants.

Block randomization and ABBA counterbalancing can be used to balance practice effects in a complete repeated measures design. ABBA counterbalancing should not be used, however, if practice effects are expected to be nonlinear (and cannot be eliminated from the analysis) or if anticipation effects are likely. Techniques for balancing practice effects in an incomplete repeated measures design involve either the use of all possible orders or selected orders (the Latin Square and rotation of a random starting order). When irreversible tasks are used, three independent variables must be balanced (the independent variable of interest, stage of practice, and the task variable). The most serious problem in any repeated measures design is differential transfer—when performance in one condition differs depending on which condition it follows. Procedures for detecting the presence of differential transfer are available, but there is little that can be done to salvage a study in which it occurs.

The analysis of the results of repeated measures designs follows the same principles of null-hypothesis testing used to analyze independent groups designs. Estimates of error variation are determined differently, however, in the analyses of variance for repeated measures designs. The generally smaller estimates of error variation in repeated measures designs increases the sensitivity of these designs. The greater sensitivity of the experiments generally increases the power of the resulting statistical analyses in repeated measures experiments.

KEY CONCEPTS

repeated measures designs	differential transfer
practice effects	sensitivity
counterbalancing	power
ABBA counterbalancing	

REVIEW QUESTIONS

1 Researchers choose to use a repeated measures design for several different reasons. What are four of those reasons?
2 Distinguish between a complete design and an incomplete design for repeated measures designs.
3 What options do researchers have in balancing practice effects in a repeated measures experiment using a complete design?

4 Under what two circumstances would you recommend against the use of ABBA counterbalancing to balance practice effects in a repeated measures experiment using a complete design?

5 State the general rule for balancing practice effects in repeated measures experiments using an incomplete design.

6 What techniques can be used to balance practice effects in the repeated measures experiments using an incomplete design? Which technique is preferred?

7 Explain what is meant by an irreversible task in a repeated measures design?

8 For which types of independent variables are repeated measures designs unlikely to prove useful?

9 Describe how researchers can determine if differential transfer has occurred in a repeated measures experiment using an incomplete design.

10 Explain the different roles played by systematic differences across participants in the analysis of random groups designs and repeated measures designs.

11 What three factors determine the power of a statistical test? Which factor is the primary one that researchers can use to control power?

12 What is a common measure of effect size for a repeated measures analysis and what does this measure indicate about the independent variable?

CHALLENGE QUESTIONS

1 The following problems represent different situations in the repeated measures designs in which practice effects need to be balanced.

A Consider a repeated measures experiment using a complete design involving one independent variable. The independent variable has three levels (Low, Medium, and High). You are to prepare an order for administering the conditions of this experiment so that the independent variable is balanced for practice effects. You are first to use block randomization to balance the variable and then to use ABBA counterbalancing to balance the variable. Each condition should appear twice in the order you prepare. Use the first row of the random number table in Appendix A to determine your two random orders for block randomization.

B Consider a repeated measures experiment using an incomplete design. One independent variable is to be manipulated at six levels (A, B, C, D, E, and F). Present a table showing how you would determine the order of administering the conditions to the first six participants of the experiment. Be sure that practice effects are balanced for these participants.

2 Consider a repeated measures experiment using an incomplete design to manipulate an environmental variable, room temperature. There are three levels of the variable (60 degrees, 65 degrees, and 70 degrees). The dependent variable of interest is the amount of time taken to solve a list of word problems. Thus, three different word problem lists are required (designated as Lists A, B, and C). Present a table showing how you could administer the conditions of the experiment in order to determine the effect of the three independent variables: room temperature, stage of practice, and list. You have only nine people available for participants, but previous research indicates that you need not be concerned with problems of differential transfer.

3 The pursuit rotor is a test of perceptual-motor coordination. It involves a turntable with a disk about the size of a dime embedded in it. The participant is given a pointer and is asked to keep the pointer on the disk while the turntable is rotating. The dependent variable is the percentage of time on each trial that the participant keeps the pointer on the disk. Learning on this task in linearly related to trials over many

periods of practice, and the task generally takes a long time to master. A researcher wants to study the influence of time of day on the performance on this task with four different times (10 a.m., 2 p.m., 6 p.m., and 10 p.m.). The participants will receive a constant number of trials under each of the four conditions, and participants will be tested in one condition per day over four consecutive days. The researcher has 96 participants available.

A What design is being used for the time-of-day variable in this experiment?

B What research design is included in the first stage of practice of this experiment? How could the researcher use the results of the design in the first stage of practice as an indication of whether differential transfer had occurred?

4 The following table represents the order of administering the conditions to participants in a repeated measures experiment using an incomplete design in which the independent variable was the difficulty of the task given to the participant (High, Medium, or Low Difficulty). The values in parentheses represent the number correct for each participant in each condition. Use this table, when necessary, to answer questions that follow.

Participant	Order of conditions		
1	High (2)	Medium (9)	Low (9)
2	Medium (3)	Low (5)	High (7)
3	Low (4)	High (3)	Medium (5)
4	High (6)	Low (10)	Medium (8)
5	Medium (7)	High (8)	Low (6)
6	Low (8)	Medium (4)	High (4)

A What method was used to balance the stage-of-practice effects?

B Present the values you would use to describe the overall effect of the task difficulty variable. Include a verbal description of the effect along with the descriptive statistics that you use as a basis of your description.

C What would you conclude if the F-test for the effect of task difficulty was $F(2,10) = 4.25, p = .04$?

Answer to Challenge Question 1

A Assigning the values 1, 2, and 3 to the Low, Medium, and High conditions, respectively, and using the first row of the random number table in Appendix A beginning with the first number in the row, the block-randomized sequence is Low-High-Medium-Low-Medium-High. One possible ABBA counterbalanced sequence is Low-Medium-High-High-Medium-Low.

B Because there are six conditions, all possible orders is not feasible. Therefore, either a Latin Square or a random starting order with rotation is needed to balance practice effects. A possible set of sequences using rotation is:

Participant	Position					
	1st	2nd	3rd	4th	5th	6th
1	B	D	E	C	A	F
2	D	E	C	A	F	B
3	E	C	A	F	B	D
4	C	A	F	B	D	E
5	A	F	B	D	E	C
6	F	B	D	E	C	A

Complex Designs

CHAPTER OUTLINE

OVERVIEW
GUIDELINES FOR IDENTIFYING AN EXPERIMENTAL DESIGN
THE NATURE OF MAIN EFFECTS AND INTERACTIONS
ANALYSIS OF COMPLEX DESIGNS
Logic of Analysis Plan
Analysis with an Interaction
Analysis with No Interaction
INTERPRETING INTERACTIONS
Interactions and Theory Testing
Interactions and Contradictory Findings
Interactions and External Validity
Interactions and Relevant Independent Variables
Interactions and Ceiling and Floor Effects
Interactions and the Natural Groups Design
SUMMARY

OVERVIEW

In the last two chapters we described the basic experimental designs that psychologists use to study the effect of an independent variable. We discussed how an independent variable could be implemented with a separate group of participants in each condition (Chapter 6) or with each participant experiencing all the conditions (Chapter 7). We limited our discussion in these two chapters to experiments involving only one independent variable because we wanted you to concentrate on the characteristics of each research design. Experiments involving only one independent variable are not, however, the most common type of experiment in current psychological research. Instead, researchers most often use **complex designs** in which two or more independent variables are studied simultaneously in one experiment.

Consider, for example, a study by May, Hasher, and Stoltzfus (1993). These researchers used a complex design to study the effects of time of day on memory performance of younger and older people. In a preliminary study they determined that most younger adults (ages 18–22) were classified as "evening types" and most older adults (ages 66–78) were classified as "morning types." They reasoned on the basis of these results that the optimal time of day for doing a memory task would be in the afternoon for younger adults and in the morning for older adults. In their experiment they tested 11 older adults in the morning and 11 in the afternoon. Similarly, they tested 10 younger adults in the morning and 10 in the afternoon. All the participants first read 10 short stories. Immediately after reading the last story they were tested for their recognition of sentences that either were included in the story (old sentences) or were not included in the story (new sentences).

As indicated in the following diagram, this experiment involved four conditions: (1) older adults tested in the morning; (2) older adults tested in the afternoon; (3) younger adults tested in the morning; and (4) younger adults tested in the afternoon.

Age Group	Time of Testing	
	Morning	Afternoon
Older Adults	1	2
Younger Adults	3	4

In this complex design, one independent variable is an individual differences variable (age), with two levels: older adults and younger adults. The second independent variable is a manipulated independent groups variable, the time of testing, which also has two levels: morning or afternoon. In a complex design such as this one, the levels of each of the two independent variables are combined *factorially*. Factorial combination involves pairing each level of one independent variable with each level of a second independent variable. For example, older and younger adults are tested both in the morning and in the afternoon. The number of conditions in a complex design is always equal to the product of the number of levels for each independent variable included in the experiment. In the May et al. (1993) experiment there are two levels of age and two levels of time of testing so there are four conditions ($2 \times 2 = 4$). If these two age groups had been tested at three times of day, there would have been six conditions ($2 \times 3 = 6$).

Factorial combination in complex designs makes it possible to assess the effect of each independent variable alone (*main effect*) and the effect of the independent variables in combination (*interaction*). For example, May et al. found, as expected, that younger adults performed better overall on the recognition memory test than did older adults. This represents a main effect of the age variable. That is, "collapsed" across time of testing, younger adults performed better on the dependent variable than did older adults. More importantly, they found that recognition performance did not differ for younger and older adults in the morning (older adults' optimal time); but younger adults did much better than older adults in the afternoon (younger adults' optimal time). In other words, being tested at their nonoptimal time hurt older adults more than it did younger adults. This type of effect, called an *interaction effect*, can be discovered only when two or more independent variables are included in the same experiment. In general, an **interaction** occurs when the effect of one independent variable differs depending on the level of a second independent variable.

Complex designs may seem a bit complicated at this point, but the concepts will become clearer as you progress through this chapter. In what follows we describe the procedures for producing, analyzing, and interpreting main effects and interactions. We begin with a review of guidelines for identifying or selecting an experimental design. We then describe the basic concepts of main effects and interactions in complex designs. The analysis plans for complex designs are introduced along with the application of analysis of variance to complex designs. We give special attention to the interpretation of interactions in complex designs.

Guidelines for Identifying an Experimental Design

- Researchers use complex designs to study the effects of two or more independent variables in one experiment.
- In complex designs, each independent variable can be studied with an independent groups design or with a repeated measures design.

An experiment with a complex design has, by definition, more than one independent variable. Each independent variable in a complex design must be implemented using either an independent groups design or a repeated measures design according to the procedures described in Chapters 6 and 7. When a complex design has both an independent groups variable and a repeated measures variable it is called a *mixed design*. Before examining complex designs themselves, we need to review briefly the characteristics of the various experimental designs that can be used to study a single independent variable. You will be better able to understand descriptions of complex designs if you can quickly and accurately identify the independent variables, their levels, and the design used to implement each independent variable. Similarly, your ability to carry out your own experiments using complex designs will be enhanced if you can confidently select the most appropriate design for each independent variable in which you are interested.

The flowchart in Figure 8.1 summarizes the distinctions among experimental designs by taking you through a series of questions. The diagram will probably

FIGURE 8.1 Flowchart for identifying experimental designs.

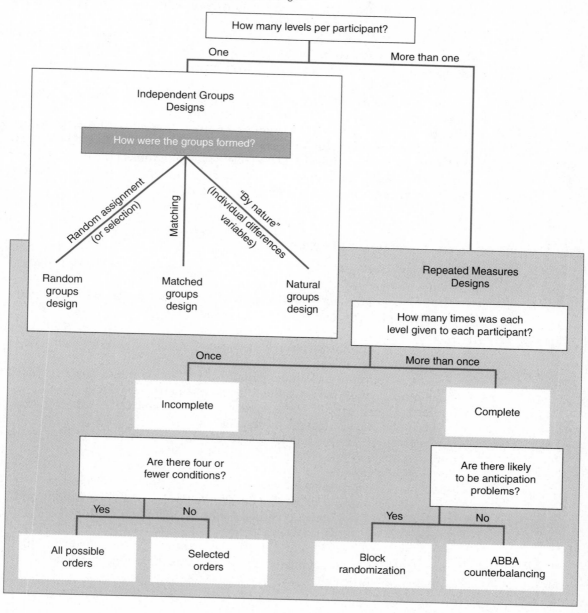

prove most useful to you when you are reading about a particular experiment in either your text or a journal article. As you identify each independent variable in an experiment, you can track the variable through Figure 8.1 to determine what design has been used to implement the independent variable. The first question at the top of the flowchart is the most critical one. The answer to the question, How many levels of the independent variable were administered to each participant?, determines whether an independent groups or repeated measures design has been used. Answering the subsequent questions for the independent groups designs will allow you to identify the particular type of design by examining the procedures used to form the groups. For the repeated measures designs, we have included questions to help you distinguish complete and incomplete repeated measures designs and to identify the appropriate balancing techniques for each type.

Complex designs require that you go through the flowchart in Figure 8.1 as many times as necessary to identify the design for each independent variable in the experiment. In a complex design, the two or more independent variables need not be implemented in the same way. For example, in the May et al. (1993) study, the age group independent variable (younger adults or older adults) represented a natural groups design. The time of day independent variable (morning or afternoon) was manipulated using the random groups design.

THE NATURE OF MAIN EFFECTS AND INTERACTIONS

- The simplest complex design is a 2 × 2 design—two independent variables, each with two levels.
- The number of different conditions in a complex design can be determined by multiplying the number of levels for each independent variable (e.g., 2 × 2 = 4).
- Complex designs allow researchers to examine interactions between independent variables.
- The overall effect of each independent variable in a complex design is called a main effect, and represents the differences among the average performance for each level of an independent variable collapsed across the levels of the other independent variable.
- An interaction between independent variables occurs when the effect of one independent variable differs depending on the levels of the second independent variable.
- Evidence for interactions can be identified using descriptive statistics presented in graphs (nonparallel lines) or tables (subtraction method), and the presence of an interaction is confirmed using inferential statistics (analysis of variance).
- More powerful and efficient complex designs can be created by including more levels of an independent variable or by including more independent variables in the design.

The simplest possible experiment involves one independent variable manipulated at two levels. Similarly, the simplest possible complex design involves two independent variables, each of which is manipulated at two levels. Complex designs are identified by specifying the number of levels of each of the independent variables in the experiment. A 2×2 (which is read "2 by 2") design, then, identifies the most basic complex design. Conceptually, there is an unlimited number of complex designs because any number of independent variables can be studied and each independent variable can have any number of levels. In practice, however, it is unusual to find experiments involving more than four or five independent variables. Regardless of the number of independent variables, the number of conditions in a complex design can be determined by multiplying the number of levels of the independent variables. For instance, as we saw in the May et al. study of age and time of day, there are two independent variables with each having two levels in a 2×2 design; thus, there are four conditions in a 2×2 design. In a 3×3 design there are two independent variables with 3 levels each so there are nine conditions. In a $3 \times 4 \times 2$ design there are three independent variables with 3, 4, and 2 levels, respectively, and a total of 24 conditions. The primary advantage of all complex designs is the opportunity they provide for identifying interactions between independent variables.

The nature of main effects and interactions is essentially the same in all complex designs, but they can be seen most easily in a 2×2 design. Consider an experiment by Hass, Katz, Rizzo, Bailey, and Eisenstadt (1991). They used a 2×2 design to investigate cross-racial evaluations. Cross-racial evaluations of performance is a research topic of both theoretical and practical importance. When given comparable information about a White and a Black applicant for a job, for instance, do evaluators rate the candidate of their own race (in-group) more favorably than the candidate of the other race (out-group)?

The students in the Hass et al. (1991) experiment (all of whom were White) were told by a White female experimenter that the researchers were developing a new quiz game for college students called Trivia Challenge. The participants were tested in small groups but one member of the group was always a confederate of the experimenter. The race of the group captain was the first independent variable. The two levels were Black and White captains. The experimenter made sure that an election among the group members always resulted in the confederate being selected as the captain of the group. The captain selected the questions that the group had to answer in the quiz game. The nature of these questions defined the second independent variable in the experiment, outcome, which also had two levels. In the success outcome conditions, the captain selected easy questions and the group easily reached the criterion for correct answers in the allotted time. In the failure outcome condition, the captain selected questions of such difficulty that the group failed to meet the criterion. Groups of participants were randomly assigned to the four groups formed by the factorial combination of the race of the captain (Black, White) and the outcome (success, failure). Can you identify the conditions of the experiment?

TABLE 8.1   EXAMPLE OF A 2 × 2 DESIGN WITH AN INTERACTION
(Mean Evaluation Scores for Captains in Each Group)

| Outcome | Race of Captain | |
	Black	White
Success	309.6	280.9
Failure	155.3	196.1

Adapted from Hass et al. (1991).

After the quiz game, participants completed a questionnaire that included several items requiring them to evaluate the captain of their group. The responses to these questions were combined into an overall evaluation score, with higher scores indicating more favorable evaluations of the captain. The mean evaluation scores for the four conditions of the experiment are presented in Table 8.1. We will use the data in this table to illustrate two critical concepts in complex designs: *main effects* and *interactions.*

In any complex factorial design it is possible to test predictions regarding the overall effect of each independent variable in the experiment while ignoring the effect of the other independent variable(s). The overall effect of an independent variable in a complex design is called a **main effect.** For example, the overall mean for success outcomes (295.2) can be obtained by averaging the two values for the Black and White captains in the two success conditions: [(309.6 + 280.9)/2] = 295.2. Similarly, the mean of the failure outcomes can be computed to be 175.7.[1] *The means for a main effect represent the overall performance at each level of a particular independent variable collapsed across (averaged over) the levels of the other independent variable.* In this case we collapsed over the race of the captain variable to obtain the means for the main effect of the outcome variable. The main effect of the outcome variable is the difference between the means for the two levels of the outcome variable—(295.2 − 175.7). In the Hass et al. (1991) experiment, the main effect of the outcome variable indicates that, overall, the evaluation scores for all captains were higher for success outcomes (295.2) than for failure outcomes (175.7).

Similarly, we can also determine whether there is a main effect of the second independent variable, race of captain. The procedure is exactly like that outlined for determining the effect of the outcome variable, but, of course, this time we must average across the success and failure conditions. The main effect for captain is the difference between the mean evaluation ratings for the two types of captains. You should be able to determine for yourself that these means were 232.4 and 238.5 for Black and White captains, respectively. Thus, it appears that

---

[1]The simple averaging of the values within each row and column to obtain the means for the main effects is possible *only* when there are equal numbers of participants contributing to each mean in the table. For procedures to use when the cells of the table involve different sample sizes, see Keppel (1991).

in the Hass et al. experiment, White captains were rated overall more favorably than Black captains. However, the difference was not great, and one would have to test whether the difference is statistically significant.

Analysis procedures for determining the statistical significance of main effects will be described in the next section. For now, we need only note that the interpretation of main effects is critically dependent on whether an interaction is or is not present. In general, main effects should be interpreted with caution whenever an interaction is present in the experiment. When no interaction occurs, the main effects of each independent variable can be interpreted as though they had been manipulated in two separate experiments, each of which involved only one independent variable.

The most important aspect of Table 8.1 is that it reflects an interaction between the two independent variables, race of the captain and outcome. If only successful outcomes had been tested in the experiment (first row of Table 8.1), we would have concluded that Black captains are evaluated more favorably than White captains. On the other hand, if only outcomes involving failure had been tested (second row of Table 8.1), we would have concluded that White captains are evaluated more favorably than Black captains. These results indicate that whether Black or White captains are evaluated more favorably *depends* on the type of outcome, success or failure. We discuss the statistical analysis of interactions in complex designs in the next section. For now, it is sufficient if you recognize that *an interaction is likely to have occurred when the effect of one independent variable changes depending on the levels of the second independent variable.*

When one independent variable interacts with a second independent variable, the second independent variable must interact with the first one (that is, the order of the independent variables doesn't matter). For example, we described the interaction in Table 8.1 by stating that the effect of the race of the captain varies with the type of outcome. The reverse is also true; the effect of the type of outcome varies with the race of the captain. Black captains were evaluated more favorably than White captains in the success condition, but White captains were evaluated more favorably than Black captains in the failure condition. Hass et al. (1991) chose to describe the interaction by emphasizing that the evaluation of the Black captains was more extreme than was the evaluation of the White captains (the Black captains' evaluation was more positive with success and more negative with failure). How you choose to describe the results of an interaction depends on which aspect of the interaction you want to emphasize. For example, Hass et al. emphasized the more extreme ratings given to the Black captains because they were testing the hypothesis that cross-race evaluation leads to more polarized (more extreme) responses for out-group members (White participants rating Black captains) than for in-group members (White participants rating White captains).

Mastering the concepts of main effects and interactions requires practice in identifying the various types of outcomes that can arise in a complex design. Box 8.1 provides an exercise that gives you an opportunity to begin to practice identifying main effects and interactions in 2 × 2 designs using only descriptive statistics. Inferential statistics would be required to confirm the statistical significance of any obtained effects, but the effects themselves can best be seen in a table or graph of the means for the conditions of the experiment.

There are three common ways to report a summary of the descriptive statistics in a complex design: tables, bar graphs, and line graphs. The procedures for preparing such tables and figures and the criteria for deciding which type of presentation to use are described in Appendix C. In general, tables can be used for any complex design and are most useful when the exact values for each condition in the experiment need to be known. Bar graphs and line graphs, on the other hand, are especially useful for showing patterns of results without dwelling on the exact values. Line graphs are particularly useful for depicting the results of complex designs because an interaction can be seen so readily in a line graph. *Nonparallel lines in the graph suggest an interaction; parallel lines suggest no interaction.*

BOX 8.1

HERE AN INTERACTION, THERE AN INTERACTION, EVERYWHERE AN INTERACTION

In the spirit of practice makes perfect, let us now turn our attention to the exercise we have prepared to help you learn to identify interactions. Your task is to identify main effects and interactions in each of six complex design experiments (A through F). In each table or graph in this box, you are to determine whether the effect of each independent variable differs depending on the level of the other independent variable. In other words, is there an interaction? After checking for the interaction, you can also check to see whether each independent variable produced an effect when collapsed across the other independent variable. That is, is there a main effect of one or both independent variables? The exercise will be most useful if you also practice translating the data presented in a table (Figure 8.2) into a graph and those presented in graphs (Figures 8.3 and 8.4) into tables. The idea of the exercise is to become as comfortable as you can with the various ways of depicting the results of a complex design.[2]

FIGURE 8.2   Mean number of correct responses as a function of task difficulty and anxiety level.

A.

	Task difficulty	
	Easy	Hard
Anxiety level — Low	3.34	3.34
Anxiety level — High	5.55	1.19

B.

	Task difficulty	
	Easy	Hard
Anxiety level — Low	6.25	3.10
Anxiety level — High	4.25	1.10

[2]Answer key for exercises in this box: An interaction occurs in A, D, and E.

When the results of a 2 × 2 design are summarized in a table, it is easiest to assess the presence or absence of an interaction by using the subtraction method. One determines the differences between the means in each row (or column) of the table and then compares these differences. If the differences are different, an interaction is likely. In applying the subtraction method, it is essential that the differences be calculated in the same direction. For example, to use the subtraction method for the data reported in Table 8.1, you could subtract the evaluation score for the White captain from that of the Black captain for the success outcome (+28.7) and then for the failure outcome (−40.8). The sign of the obtained difference should also be carefully noted. The subtraction method shows you that these differences are very different and, thus, an interaction between the two variables is likely. You can practice applying the subtraction method by determining the mean differences for the columns of Table 8.1. For more practice, see Box 8.1.

FIGURE 8.3   Mean number of errors as a function of type of task and brain hemisphere tested.

FIGURE 8.4   Mean reaction time as a function of set size and response type.

The opportunity to identify an interaction makes the 2 × 2 design more useful analytically than designs involving only one independent variable. Nonetheless, the 2 × 2 design barely scratches the surface when it comes to tapping the potential of complex designs. The 2 × 2 design can be extended in one of two ways. Additional levels of one or both of the independent variables can be included in the design, yielding designs such as the 3 × 2, the 3 × 3, the 4 × 2, the 4 × 3, and so on. Or additional independent variables can be studied in the same experiment with the number of levels of each variable ranging from 2 to some unspecified upper limit. The addition of a third or fourth independent variable yields designs such as the 2 × 2 × 2, the 3 × 3 × 3, the 2 × 2 × 4, the 2 × 3 × 3 × 2, and so on. We will describe one example of each of the two ways that a complex design can be extended beyond the 2 × 2.

Social psychologists are interested in the stereotypic beliefs people have about others. Eagly and Steffen (1984) describe one such stereotype pertaining to beliefs about men and women: "women are more communal (selfless and concerned with others) and less agentic (self-assertive and motivated to master) than men" (p. 735). In a series of experiments testing college students, Eagly and Steffen examined whether the social roles that women and men hold may contribute to the gender stereotypes. That is, if women are more likely to be working at home caring for children and men more likely to be employed outside the home, then men may be seen as more agentic and women are seen as more communal. Eagly and Steffen obtained results consistent with their social role interpretation.

In 1997, one of your textbook author's research methods classes tried to replicate one of Eagly and Steffen's (1984) experiments. They reasoned that Eagly and Steffen's results might not replicate because of the changes that had occurred over the past decade in men's and women's social roles. The experiment was a 2 × 3 design. College students were given a brief description of a target person and were asked to rate the target on 18 different traits. The first independent variable was the gender of the target: male or female. The second independent variable was the role assigned to the target person; there were three levels: unspecified, employed, or home care. The description for the employed male target, for example, was "An average man who is employed full-time." The measure participants used to rate the targets included 18 bipolar trait adjectives like "Not at all Aggressive" at one end of the scale and "Very Aggressive" at the other end of the scale. The participants marked one of five points along the scale to indicate which point best described the target person for that scale. The lowest possible score on the trait measure was 18 (a value of 1 for all 18 adjectives) and the highest possible score on the measure was 90 (a value of 5 for all 18 adjectives). Targets rated higher on the measure were judged to have more agentic characteristics; targets rated lower were judged to have more communal characteristics. Fifteen participants were randomly assigned to each of the six conditions of the experiment.

The results of the replication experiment are presented in Figure 8.5. An interaction is present in this experiment; the difference between the ratings for

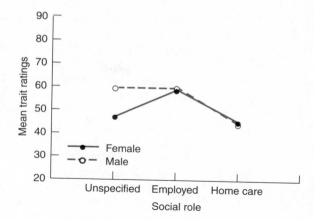

FIGURE 8.5 Illustration of an interaction in a complex design (2 × 3).

female and male targets varies with the different social roles. For the unspecified role, female targets are rated less agentic than are the male targets; this finding replicates a gender stereotype similar to that found by Eagly and Steffen (1984)—males are perceived as more agentic than females. For the employed role, however, female and male targets received comparable ratings, and both male and female employed targets were rated as agentic as the male target in the unspecified role. Similarly, for the home care role female and male targets were rated about the same and at about the same level as the female targets in the unspecified role. One way to summarize these findings is to say that if you are employed you are perceived to be more agentic (and more like a male) and if you are caring for children at home you are perceived as less agentic (and more like a female).

The experiment we just described illustrates how complex design experiments can be used to study intriguing issues like gender stereotypes. For our purposes now, however, the experiment illustrates that the concept of an interaction can be extended to complex designs beyond the 2 × 2, in this case to a 2 × 3 design. You should now be beginning to see how complex designs allow psychologists to test how two independent variables can work together to produce an interaction.

An even more powerful extension of complex designs arises when there are three independent variables in the experiment. Pingitore, Dugoni, Tindale, and Spring (1994) examined three independent variables in their study of possible discrimination against moderately obese people in a mock job interview. Participants in the experiment viewed videotapes of job interviews. The role of the applicant for the job in the videotapes was played by professional actors who were of normal weight. In the moderately obese conditions, the actors wore makeup and prostheses so that they appeared 20% heavier. Three of the independent variables in the experiment were: the weight of the applicant (normal or overweight); the gender of the applicant (male or female); and the participants' concern about their own body (high or low). The degree of concern with one's own body was called the body-schema variable. It was based on the participants' satisfaction-dissatisfaction with their own bodies and the importance of body awareness to their self-concept. For this part of the study, then, Pingitore et al. (1994) used a 2 × 2 × 2 design. The dependent variable was the participants' rating on a 7-point scale of whether they would hire the applicant (1 = definitely not hire and 7 = definitely hire).

As a first step in describing the results of the Pingitore et al. (1994) study we will examine an interaction of two independent variables that manipulated characteristics of the applicant: the applicant's weight and the applicant's gender. For normal weight applicants, male and female applicants were given very similar hiring ratings (means of 6.0 and 5.5 for males and females, respectively). For overweight applicants, however, mean hiring ratings were lower, especially the ratings of female applicants (means of 4.8 and 3.6 for males and females, respectively). The pattern of this interaction effect indicates that female applicants who are overweight may experience more job discrimination than male applicants who are overweight.

Pingitore et al. (1994) were able to refine their understanding of possible discrimination based on the applicant's weight even further when they included the independent variable of participants' body schema in their analysis. The interaction of the applicant's weight and gender described above occurred only with participants who were high in concern about their own bodies. That is, those high on the body-schema variable gave overweight female applicants especially low ratings. Participants who were low on the body-schema variable, on the other hand, gave lower ratings to overweight applicants, but their ratings for male and female applicants were about the same.

The results of the Pingitore et al. experiment for these three variables are shown in Figure 8.6. As you can see, displaying the means for a three-variable experiment requires a graph with more than one "panel." One panel of the figure shows the results for two variables at one level of the third variable and the other panel shows results for the same two variables at the second level of the third independent variable. Because there are only two levels of the third variable, we can show the means for all eight conditions in these two panels. If the third variable had three levels (i.e., 2 × 2 × 3 or 12 conditions), then we could use three panels in our graph for this comparison, one for each combination of the first two variables at each level of the third independent variable.

One way to summarize the Pingitore et al. (1994) findings we have just described is to say that the interaction of the independent variables of the applicants' weight and the applicants' gender *depended upon* the participants' body schema. We call this type of finding a three-way (or triple) interaction. As you can see, when we have a three-way interaction, all three independent variables must be taken into account when describing the results.

Let us summarize by saying that, in general, *when there are two independent variables, an interaction occurs when the effect of one of the independent variables*

FIGURE 8.6   Illustration of an interaction for a 2 × 2 × 2 complex design.

differs depending on the level of the second independent variable. When there are three independent variables in a complex design, a three-way interaction occurs when the interaction of two of the independent variables differs depending on the level of the third independent variable. Look again at Figure 8.6. You should easily see that the pattern of results for the first two independent variables (applicants' body weight and gender) differs depending on the level of the third variable (participants' body schema).

The power and complexity of complex designs increase substantially when the number of independent variables in the experiment increases from two to three. In the two-factor design there can be only one interaction, but in the three-factor design each independent variable can interact with each of the other two independent variables and all three independent variables can interact together. Thus, the change from a two-factor to a three-factor design introduces the possibility of obtaining four different interactions. If the three independent variables are symbolized as *A*, *B*, and *C*, the three-factor design allows a test of the main effects of *A*, *B*, and *C*; the two-way interactions of $A \times B$, $A \times C$, $B \times C$; and the three-way interaction of $A \times B \times C$. The efficiency of an experiment involving three independent variables is remarkable. Pingitore et al. (1994) would have had to perform three experiments involving two variables at a time (applicant's gender and applicant's weight; applicant's gender and participant's body schema; and applicant's weight and participant's body schema) in order to assess the three main effects and the three two-way interactions that they could examine in a single three-factor design. Furthermore, they could assess the simultaneous interaction of all three independent variables only by including all three variables in the same experiment. Complex designs are a very powerful tool in psychological research.

ANALYSIS OF COMPLEX DESIGNS

Logic of Analysis Plan

- In a complex design with two independent variables, the sources of systematic variation are the main effects for each independent variable and the interaction between the two independent variables.
- Descriptive statistics are needed to interpret the results of inferential statistics.
- How researchers interpret the results of a complex design differs depending on whether a statistically significant interaction is present or absent in the data.

The analysis of complex designs builds on the logic used in the analysis of experiments with only one independent variable (see Chapter 6). You may remember that the first step in analyzing such single-factor experiments is to perform an omnibus *F*-test to determine whether the independent variable has produced any systematic variation in the dependent variable. If the omnibus test is statistically significant, analytical comparisons can be used to pinpoint more precisely the source of the systematic variation.

The tracking of sources of systematic variation applies equally to the analysis of complex designs that involve more than one independent variable. The same basic tool—the analysis of variance—can be used for complex designs. In complex designs with two independent variables, however, there are three potential sources of systematic variation. Each independent variable can produce a main effect, and the two independent variables can combine to produce an interaction effect.

The experiment we will use to illustrate the analysis plan for a complex design involved a 3 × 3 design with nine groups of participants. Children of three

FIGURE 8.7   The experiment used to illustrate the analysis of a complex design involved a 3 × 3 design. One variable was an individual differences variable, age, and it had three levels: Children were 4, 5, and 6 years of age. The other variable was a manipulated variable, and it also had three levels: Children were tested with another child, alone, or with a parent. The dependent variable was time spent playing with unfamiliar toys.

different ages (4, 5, and 6) were tested under one of three situations (alone, with a parent, and with another child). Thus, the first independent variable, age, is an individual differences variable with three levels, and the second independent variable, situations, is manipulated using three levels. The dependent variable in the experiment was the amount of time the child spent playing with novel (unfamiliar) toys. There were 10 children of each age tested under each of the three conditions, so there were 90 participants in the experiment, 10 participants in each of the nine conditions.

Table 8.2 shows the mean times children in each group spent playing with novel toys. An analysis of variance summary table for this complex design is presented in Table 8.3. It was generated on a computer using a statistical software package that performs complex analyses of variance.

Let's look first at the analysis of variance summary table. There are three potential sources of systematic variation in this experiment: the main effect of age, the main effect of situation, and the interaction between the age and situation variables. The summary table indicates the degrees of freedom (*df*) for each of these effects. For the main effects, the degrees of freedom are equal to the number of levels of the independent variable minus one. Since there are three levels for both age and situation, the degrees of freedom for both main effects are 2. The degrees of freedom for the interaction are obtained by multiplying the degrees of freedom for each independent variable entering into the interaction. Thus, there are 4 degrees of freedom for the Age × Situation interaction (2 × 2 = 4). The degrees of freedom for the Mean Square Within Groups (the estimate of error variation for all three effects in the complex design) are obtained by multiplying the degrees of freedom within each group times the number of groups. In our example, there are 10 participants in each group and

TABLE 8.2 TABLE OF MEAN TIMES (IN MINUTES) SPENT PLAYING WITH NOVEL TOYS IN A 3 × 3 DESIGN

Situation	Age 4	5	6	Means for main effect of condition
Alone	5	5	10	6.7
With a parent	15	25	35	25.0
With another child	10	15	15	13.3
Means for main effect of age	10.0	15.0	20.0	

TABLE 8.3 ANALYSIS OF VARIANCE SUMMARY TABLE FOR A 3 × 3 DESIGN

Source of Variation	*df*	MS	*F*	*p*	η^2
Age (A)	2	35	3.5	.03	.07
Situation (B)	2	92	9.2	.0005	.19
Age × situation (A × B)	4	48	4.8	.002	.19
Error variation within groups	81	10			
Total	89	—			

therefore 9 degrees of freedom within each group. Because there are nine groups in the experiment, there are 81 *df* within groups.

The three *F*-tests entered in the summary table were computed by dividing the mean square (MS) within groups into the mean square for age, for situation, and for the interaction. The specific probabilities for each of the *F*-tests were part of the computer output for this analysis. If they had not been provided, we would have to use the value of *F* and the appropriate degrees of freedom for each effect (2 and 81 for each of the two main effects and 4 and 81 for the interaction) and consult a table of *F* values (see end of Appendix A) in order to determine their probabilities. Using the criterion of $\alpha = .05$ to determine statistical significance, we can see that the *F*-tests for each main effect and the interaction are statistically significant because the *p* value associated with each *F*-test is less than .05. A measure of effect size, eta squared (η^2) or proportion of variance accounted for, is also reported for each effect.

The information in the analysis of variance summary table is useful only in conjunction with the means reported in Table 8.2. The statistically significant *F*-test for the interaction indicates that the pattern of results across age differs for the three situations. As you can see in Table 8.2, the means reveal a larger increase across age in the time spent playing with a novel toy when the child is with a parent than when the child is either alone or with another child. The interaction can be seen clearly in the pattern of nonparallel lines shown in Figure 8.8. The means for the main effects of age and of situation on the outside of Table 8.2 also appear to differ, and these apparent differences are supported by the statistically significant *F*-test for each main effect.

The three *F*-tests in the summary table represent the counterpart of the omnibus *F*-tests we described when discussing the analysis of experiments with only one independent variable. In a complex design, just as in a single-factor design, follow-up analyses are needed to interpret the initial omnibus tests. The analysis plan for complex designs differs depending upon whether a statistically significant interaction is present.

Table 8.4 provides guidelines for interpreting a complex design experiment when an interaction does occur and when one does not. We will go through Table 8.4 twice, once describing an experiment in which there is an interaction and once describing a study in which there is no interaction.

Analysis with an Interaction

- If the omnibus analysis of variance reveals a statistically significant interaction, the source of the interaction is identified using simple main effects analyses and tests of simple comparisons.
- A simple main effect is the effect of one independent variable at one level of a second independent variable.
- If an independent variable has three or more levels, simple comparisons can be used to examine the source of a simple main effect by comparing means two at a time.

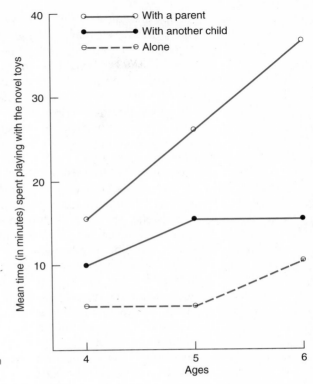

FIGURE 8.8 This graph shows results of complex design involving two independent variables, each with three levels.

TABLE 8.4 GUIDELINES FOR THE ANALYSIS OF A TWO-FACTOR EXPERIMENT

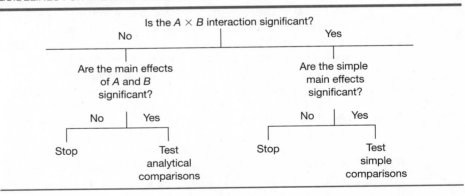

One of the many approaches psychologists have tried to use to understand depression is based on investigating the differences between the thought patterns of depressed and nondepressed people. You may remember that we touched briefly on this topic in Chapter 1. One aspect of this cognitive approach to depression deals with attributions, the causal explanations we use to try to account for our own behavior and the behavior of others. For example, depressed people exhibit a tendency to make attributions that are pessimistic, overgeneralized, and self-blaming (e.g., Myers, 1999). According to the cognitive approach, this tendency toward less optimistic thinking on the part of depressed people may be critically involved in causing the onset of depression, maintaining depression once it occurs, and alleviating depression by changing depressive thinking to be more optimistic. The study we will be using to illustrate the interpretation of the results of a complex design with an interaction represents one of the many experiments investigating the cognitive bases of depression.

Rodman and Burger (1985) investigated a particular phenomenon called the defensive attribution effect. In previous experiments, nondepressed participants read a description of an accident in which a person suffered mild or severe consequences. These nondepressed individuals attributed more responsibility to the perpetrator in the severe than in the mild accident condition. One interpretation of this phenomenon is that people do not want to attribute the cause of a severe accident to chance. If they did attribute the accident to chance, they would be increasing the perceived possibility that they themselves could be involved in a severe accident. Their attribution of greater responsibility to the perpetrator in the severe accident is a defensive attribution, allowing them to perceive themselves as protected against a likelihood of future severe accidents. Rodman and Burger reasoned that depressed people might be less likely to show this type of defensive attribution effect because their negative thinking would lead them to be less self-protective. Stated more formally, they tested the hypothesis that the defensive-attribution effect would decrease as a person's level of depression increased.

Rodman and Burger tested 56 college students in a 2 × 3 design. The first independent variable was the severity of the described accident (severe and nonsevere), and this was manipulated using the random groups design. The natural groups design was used for the second independent variable; students were selected on the basis of their scores on a paper-and-pencil test of depression to represent three groups: nondepressed, slightly depressed, and mildly depressed individuals. The dependent variable was a single item on a longer questionnaire that asked students to divide 100% among four potential sources of responsibility: each of the three drivers in the accident and uncontrollable "circumstances." The defensive-attribution effect would be reflected in a larger value assigned to uncontrollable circumstances for the nonsevere than for the severe accident. (Remember that it is protective to avoid making attributions to uncontrollable circumstances for severe accidents.) The mean percentage values for this uncontrollable factor for each of the six conditions are presented in Table 8.5.

As Rodman and Burger had predicted, there was an interaction between the two independent variables: as degree of depression increases, the differences between the percentage values for severe and nonsevere accidents change. (You may wish to use the subtraction method to see this.) Nondepressed students show the defensive-attribution effect and mildly depressed students do not. Analysis of these results using analysis of variance confirmed that the interaction was statistically significant.

TABLE 8.5 MEAN PERCENTAGE OF RESPONSIBILITY ATTRIBUTED TO UNCONTROLLABLE CIRCUMSTANCES

Type of Accident	Level of Depression		
	Nondepressed	Slightly depressed	Mildly depressed
Severe	7.00 (9.2)	14.00 (16.1)	16.90 (16.0)
Nonsevere	30.50 (22.2)	16.50 (12.7)	3.75 (3.5)

Note: Standard deviations appear in parentheses. Adapted from Rodman and Burger (1985).

Once we have confirmed that there is an interaction of two independent variables, we must locate more precisely the source of that interaction. As outlined in Table 8.4, there are statistical tests specifically designed for tracing the source of a significant interaction. These tests are called simple main effects and simple comparisons (see Keppel, 1991).

A **simple main effect** is the effect of one independent variable at one level of a second independent variable. In fact, one definition of an interaction is that the simple main effects across levels are different. We can illustrate the use of simple main effects by returning to the results of the Rodman and Burger experiment. There are five simple main effects in Table 8.5: the effect of the type of accident at each of the three levels of depression and the effect of the degree of depression at each of the two types of accidents. Rodman and Burger predicted that the defensive-attribution effect (the difference between the means for severe and nonsevere accidents) would decrease as severity of depression increased. Therefore, they chose to test the simple main effects of type of accident at each of the three levels of depression. They found, as predicted, that the simple main effect of type of accident was statistically significant for nondepressed students, but the simple main effects of type of accident for the slightly depressed and for the mildly depressed students were not statistically significant.

Two of the simple main effects in the Rodman and Burger (1985) study each involve three means. One can also examine how nondepressed, slightly depressed, and mildly depressed students differed in their attributions for severe accidents and how these three groups differed in their attributions for nonsevere accidents. That is, if statistical analysis reveals a significant simple main effect, then one concludes that there is a difference among the means (e.g., among the three groups for severe accidents). The next step, then, is to conduct *simple comparisons*, which are analytical comparisons that can be used to analyze simple main effects more fully (see Keppel, 1991). That is, once a simple main effect involving more than two levels of a variable has been shown to be statistically significant, simple comparisons can be done to determine the nature of the differences among the levels. In this procedure, means within the simple main effect are compared two at a time in order to identify the source of differences among levels. As you can see, simple comparisons only make sense when there is a simple main effect for an independent variable with three or more levels.

With two levels, a simple main effect compares the difference between the two means and no additional comparisons are necessary.

Once an interaction has been thoroughly analyzed, researchers can also examine the main effects of each independent variable. As we mentioned earlier in this chapter, however, the main effects are of much less interest when we know that an interaction is statistically significant. For instance, once we know that the effect of the type of accident varies depending on the level of depression, we have not added much when we learn that, overall, the nonsevere accident led to a higher mean percentage of responsibility attributed to uncontrollable circumstances than did the severe accident. Nonetheless, there are experiments in which the interaction and the main effects are all of interest. (Rosnow and Rosenthal [1995] describe additional procedures that can help you gain further understanding in analyzing and interpreting interactions and main effects.)

Analysis with No Interaction

- If an omnibus analysis of variance indicates the interaction between independent variables is not statistically significant, the next step is to determine whether the main effects of the variables are statistically significant.
- The source of a statistically significant main effect can be specified more precisely by performing analytical comparisons that compare means two at a time.

Dittmar, Berch, and Warm (1982) used a 3 × 3 design to test whether people who are deaf perform better on a visual-vigilance task than people who can hear. A visual-vigilance task requires a person to detect intermittent visual signals such as blips on a radar screen for a long period of time. Dittmar et al. expected that deaf people would have an advantage on such a task because their deafness would keep them from being distracted. The deaf people who participated were offered a prize if their vigilance performance was the best in their group. To assess the possible effect of the prize as an incentive, two additional groups of hearing people were tested, one offered a prize and one not. These three groups represent the levels of the first independent variable in the experiment. The participants were all tested in a 45-minute session divided into three continuous 15-minute periods, and these three periods were the levels of the second independent variable. Note that this is a mixed factorial design in that the first independent variable is an independent groups variable and the second is a repeated measures variable.

The mean percentage of correct detections across the three periods for the three different groups of participants is presented in Table 8.6. The same data are depicted graphically in Figure 8.9. The interaction, or more accurately the lack of an interaction, can best be seen in Figure 8.9. Although the three lines in the figure are not perfectly parallel, the mean percentage of correct detections appears to decrease in all three groups at approximately the same rate. That there was *not* a statistically significant interaction is confirmed by the results of

TABLE 8.6 MEAN PERCENTAGE OF CORRECT DETECTIONS ACROSS THREE PERIODS OF A VIGILANCE TASK FOR DEAF AND HEARING PARTICIPANTS

| | Period | | |
Group	1	2	3
Deaf	95	85	78
Hearing—Prize	93	82	70
Hearing—No Prize	93	74	68

Adapted from Dittmar et al. (1982).

FIGURE 8.9 Results of a 3 × 3 complex design in which there was no interaction effect but there were two main effects. (Adapted from Dittmar et al., 1982.)

the analysis of variance. As you have learned, nonparallel lines in a graph may *suggest* an interaction, but alone they are not sufficient evidence that an interaction effect is present. Like any observed difference among sample means, we must examine the results of our inferential statistical test before deciding that more than simply error variation is present.

The guidelines for the analysis of a complex design listed in Table 8.4 suggest that, when the interaction effect is not statistically significant, the next step is to examine the main effects of each independent variable. This can be done most easily by referring to the data in Table 8.6. By collapsing (averaging) across the three vigilance periods, we can obtain the mean detection rates for the main effect of the group variable. These means are 86.0, 81.7, and 78.3 for the Deaf, Hearing—Prize, and Hearing—No Prize groups, respectively. The overall analysis of the group main effect was statistically significant. As indicated in Table 8.4, the source of a statistically significant main effect can be specified more precisely by performing analytical comparisons (see Chapter 6 and Appendix A). For example, a comparison of performance in the Hearing—Prize and Hearing—No Prize groups (81.7 and 78.3) was not statistically significant, indicating that the presence of an incentive did not produce a difference between these two groups. However, the average performance of the two groups of hearing participants (80.0) was significantly lower than the performance of the deaf participants (86.0). These two analytical comparisons allow us to confirm that deaf participants were better at the vigilance task than hearing participants and that the offer of a prize did not affect the vigilance performance.

A similar approach would be followed in assessing the main effect of the period variable. By collapsing across the three groups of participants, we obtain the means 93.7 (first period), 80.3 (second period), and 72.0 (third period) for the main effect of the period variable. The main effect of this variable was statistically significant, and visual inspection of the means reveals that performance decreased, on the average, over time. Analytical comparisons could then be used to determine whether the decreases over each successive period (93.7 to 80.3 and 80.3 to 72.0) were significant. The analysis of Dittmar et al.'s vigilance experiment illustrates that much can be learned from a complex design even when there is no interaction.

INTERPRETING INTERACTIONS

Interactions and Theory Testing

- Theories frequently predict that two or more independent variables interact to influence behavior; therefore, complex designs are needed to test theories.

In Chapter 1 we described the critical role that theories play in the scientific method. In Chapter 6 we described how experiments are used to test hypotheses derived from psychological theories. Complex designs greatly enhance the researcher's ability to test theories because of the possibility in complex designs to test for both main effects and interactions.

For instance, the optimal arousal theory of motivation predicts that performance will be best when our arousal level is moderate—neither too low nor too high. If you have ever had to perform in either a highly competitive athletic or artistic event (or even a class exam), you have some sense of what is meant by optimal arousal. Your performance is not likely to be at its best if your arousal level is too low (you don't care how well you do) or too high (you are scared out of your wits). The optimal arousal theory further predicts that the level of arousal that is best depends on the complexity of the task to be performed. Specifically, the theory predicts that higher arousal levels will lead to better performance on simple or well-learned tasks, but lower arousal levels will lead to better performance on complex tasks. For example, you would probably be able to do simple arithmetic problems at a high arousal level, but the same arousal level would probably be disastrous if you were solving differential equations. Our focus for now is not on the details of optimal arousal theory but on the use of complex designs to test predictions derived from such a theory.

If we were to test the prediction that optimal arousal varied with task complexity, we would need to manipulate two independent variables, each with at least two levels. For example, if our experiment included arousal level (high or low) and task complexity (simple or complex) we would have four conditions.

Task Complexity	Arousal Level	
	High	Low
Simple	50	35
Complex	10	25

The values of the dependent variable entered in the body of our table are the mean number of problems completed correctly in each of the four conditions. As you can see, the effect of arousal level on performance depended on the level of task complexity—an interaction occurred. (You may want to use the subtraction method, or perhaps graph the results, in order to "see" the interaction.) For the simple task, high arousal led to better performance; however, for the complex task, low arousal led to better performance. This hypothetical but reasonable outcome supports the prediction derived from optimal arousal theory. The example also illustrates how interactions allow us to make more sophisticated tests of psychological theories.

Interactions and Contradictory Findings

- By testing for interactions between independent variables, often in the form of partial replications, researchers can identify reasons for contradictory findings in previous studies.
- Researchers manipulate an independent variable that is hypothesized to account for contradictory findings.

When only one independent variable is manipulated in an experiment, it is essential that all other potential independent variables be controlled by holding them constant or by balancing them across conditions (see Chapter 6). A problem can arise, however, if two researchers choose to hold the same potential independent variable constant at different levels in their respective experiments. For example, two memory researchers might be studying the relative effectiveness of two different learning strategies (A and B). These two strategies would represent the levels of the manipulated independent variable in both experiments. One potential independent variable that would clearly need to be controlled in these experiments is the difficulty of the material to be learned. The first researcher might decide to control the level of difficulty of the material by giving students in both conditions relatively easy textbook passages to learn. The second researcher, who is equally concerned with the problem of controlling the difficulty of the material, might decide to give students in both conditions relatively hard textbook passages to learn. It would not be surprising if these two researchers obtained different results. One such possible outcome is illustrated in the following diagram:

Passage Difficulty	Learning Strategy	
	A	B
Easy (Researcher 1)	50	50
Hard (Researcher 2)	25	10

The first researcher found that the two learning strategies are equally effective, while the second researcher found that strategy A is more effective than strategy B! Why couldn't these two researchers replicate each other's findings?

At first, we might try to account for the different outcomes in the two experiments by focusing on the difficulty of the textbook passages. We could argue that the two strategies are equally effective for learning easy textbook passages, but strategy A is better for learning hard passages. This argument would not be convincing, however, unless the two types of passages represented the only way that the two experiments differed. This seems highly unlikely. For example, the passages may very well have been studied for different lengths of time in the two experiments, the passages were probably on different topics, and the experimenters and participants in the two experiments were undoubtedly different. Clearly, the difficulty of the passages is not the only factor that could be responsible for the different effects of the strategy variable in the two experiments.

The best way to identify which factor is responsible for the different findings in the two experiments is to use a complex design in which you manipulate the factor you think is responsible along with the strategy variable in the *same* experiment. The use of a complex design to resolve discrepant findings follows a logic similar to the logic of doing a partial replication to establish the external validity of a finding (see Chapter 6). In both cases, you are examining whether the effect of the independent variable of interest depends upon a second independent variable; in this case, the variable of interest is the learning strategy (A or B), and the second independent variable is the difficulty of the passage. In an experiment in which the strategy variable and the passage-difficulty variable were both manipulated, there would be four conditions in a complex design: Strategy A—Easy Passage; Strategy A—Hard Passage; Strategy B—Easy Passage; and Strategy B—Hard Passage. By factorially combining the two independent variables, both easy and hard passages are tested using both learning strategies. Does the effect of learning strategy depend on the difficulty of the material?

Two possible outcomes of such an experiment are shown in the following diagram. The results outlined in Outcome 1 are the same as those observed for the two separate experiments when only the strategy variable was manipulated. That is, the strategies are equally effective for easy material, and strategy A is better than B for hard material. If you were to obtain this interaction, you could be confident that the difficulty of the text was responsible for the different effects of the strategy variable in the two original experiments.

Passage Difficulty	Outcome 1 Strategy		Outcome 2 Strategy	
	A	B	A	B
Easy	50	50	50	50
Hard	25	10	15	15

The situation would be very different, however, if you were to obtain results in your new experiment like those displayed in Outcome 2. In Outcome 2, the strategy variable had no effect when tested using either the easy or the hard text material. Because the strategy variable has the same effect with both types of material, it would logically follow that differences in degree of difficulty between the materials in the two original experiments cannot be responsible for the different effects of strategy in those experiments. You must select another variable that you "suspect" and manipulate it along with the strategy variable. Both trial and error and the guidance of theory are involved in the selection of the variable. The process can be a painstaking one, but complex designs are extremely useful in tracking down the reasons for the seemingly contradictory finding that the same independent variable has had different effects in two different experiments.

Interactions and External Validity

- When no interaction occurs in a complex design, the effects of each independent variable can be generalized across the levels of the other independent variable; thus, external validity of the independent variables increases.
- The presence of an interaction limits the external validity of a finding by specifying the conditions in which an effect of an independent variable occurs.

In Chapter 6 we discussed at some length the procedures for establishing the external validity of a research finding when an experiment involves only one independent variable. We noted at that time that partial replication was the primary means by which we establish external validity—that is, the extent to which our research findings may be generalized. We can now examine the role of complex designs in establishing the external validity of a finding. As you might have suspected, the presence or absence of an interaction is critical in determining the external validity of the findings in a complex design.

When no interaction occurs in a complex design, we know that the effects of each independent variable can be generalized across the levels of the other independent variable. For instance, the Dittmar et al. (1982) study that we just described showed that detection performance declined across three 15-minute vigilance periods, but the decline occurred at approximately the same rate for hearing and deaf participants. That is, there was no interaction of the hearing variable (hearing or deaf) and the period variable. Thus, declining performance in a vigilance task can be generalized to both hearing and deaf people.

Of course, we cannot generalize our findings beyond the boundaries or conditions that were included in the experiment. For example, the absence of an interaction between the hearing variable and periods in the vigilance task does not allow us to conclude that detection performance would decline at the same rate if young children or trained observers were tested. Similarly, we do not know whether the same decline across periods would occur if there were short breaks after each observation period. We must also remember that the absence of an interaction involves problems associated with the failure to reject the null hypothesis, such as the sensitivity of the experiment to detect any interaction that might be present (see Chapters 6 and 7). In other words, not finding a statistically significant interaction does not necessarily mean that an interaction is not really present; we may not have performed an experiment with sufficient sensitivity and power to detect it.

As we have seen, the absence of an interaction increases the external validity of the effects of each independent variable in the experiment. Perhaps more important, the presence of an interaction identifies limits for the external validity of a finding. For example, when they tested young adults, May et al. (1993) found that there was little effect of time of day on recognition memory performance. However, there was a substantial effect of the time of day when older adults were tested. This interaction clearly sets limits on the external validity of the effect that time of day has on memory performance. Given this finding, the best way to respond to someone's query regarding the general effect that time of testing has on memory is to say "it depends." In this case, it depends on the age of the person being tested. The presence of the interaction limits external validity but also specifies what those limits are.

Interactions and Relevant Independent Variables

- Relevant independent variables are variables that influence behavior.
- An independent variable can be a relevant variable either directly (a main effect) or by interacting with another independent variable to influence behavior.
- Researchers should be cautious about identifying an independent variable as irrelevant.

One of the primary tasks facing researchers who use the experimental method is identifying relevant and irrelevant independent variables. A **relevant independent variable** is one that has been shown to influence behavior; an irrelevant independent variable is one that has been shown not to influence behavior. Distinguishing between factors that affect behavior and those that do not is essential for developing adequate theories to explain behavior and for designing effective interventions to deal with problems in applied settings such as schools, hospitals, and factories (see Chapters 9 and 10).

If independent variables did not interact with one another, the task of identifying relevant independent variables would be a long one, but not a particularly challenging one. Each independent variable would simply be manipulated across a wide range of levels in separate single-factor experiments. The variables would be classified as either relevant or irrelevant depending on whether they produced a significant difference in the dependent variable. Independent variables do interact, however, and we must adjust our definition of relevant and irrelevant independent variables accordingly.

Consider the following example. Thousands of children in the United States receive drug treatment for hyperactivity every year. A reasonable question is whether dosage of the drugs is a relevant independent variable in determining the effectiveness of treatment. A hypothetical but typical experiment that could be done to address this question might include two dose levels (low and high) and three types of tasks (easy, moderate, and difficult). One possible outcome of such an experiment is summarized in the following table, with the dependent variable being the percent correct performance in each condition.

| | Dose Level | | |
Type of Task	Low	High	Overall Mean
Easy	75	90	82.5
Moderate	70	70	70.0
Difficult	65	50	57.5
Overall Mean	70	70	

The overall means for the main effect of dose level are identical (70), and this information could mistakenly be used to argue that dose level was an irrelevant independent variable because it had no main effect on children's performance. By now you recognize, however, that the dose level produced different effects depending on the difficulty of the task. For difficult tasks a low dose is better, for moderate tasks there is no effect of dose level, and for easy tasks a high dose is better. Dose level is a relevant independent variable because it interacts with the difficulty variable. In general, *a relevant independent variable is one that influences behavior directly (results in a main effect) or produces an interaction when studied in combination with a second independent variable.*

In general, be cautious about declaring an independent variable irrelevant. First, if an independent variable is shown to have no effect in an experiment, one cannot assume that this variable wouldn't have an effect if different levels of the independent variable had been tested. Second, if an independent variable has no effect in a single-factor experiment, this doesn't mean that it won't interact with another independent variable when used in a complex design. Third, as you are no doubt beginning to appreciate, null-hypothesis testing is limited in what it can tell us. The absence of a statistically significant effect may or may not mean that the effect is not present. Minimally, we would want to consider the power of our experiment before deciding that we have identified an irrelevant variable. (See Appendix A for more discussion about power analysis.) For now, it is best if you avoid being dogmatic about identifying any independent variable as irrelevant.

Interactions and Ceiling and Floor Effects

* When participants' performance reaches a maximum (ceiling) or a minimum (floor) in one or more conditions of an experiment, results for an interaction are uninterpretable.

Consider the results of a 3 × 2 experiment investigating the effects of increasing amounts of practice on performance during a physical-fitness test. There were six groups of participants in this plausible but hypothetical experiment. Participants were first given either 10, 30, or 60 minutes to practice, doing either easy or hard exercises. Then they took a fitness test using easy or hard exercises (the same they had practiced). The dependent variable was the percentage of exercises that each participant was able to complete in a 15-minute test period. Results of the experiment are presented in Figure 8.10.

The pattern of results in Figure 8.10 looks like a classic interaction; the effect of the practice time variable differed for the easy and hard exercises. Increasing practice time improved test performance for the hard exercises, but performance leveled off after 30 minutes of practice with the easy exercises. If a standard analysis of variance were applied to these data, the interaction effect would very likely be statistically significant. Unfortunately, this interaction would be essentially uninterpretable. For those groups given practice with the easy exercises, performance reached the maximum level after 30 minutes of practice, so

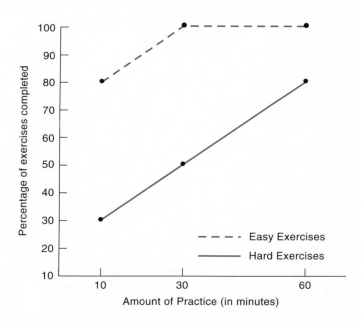

FIGURE 8.10   Illustration of a ceiling effect.

no improvement beyond this point could be shown in the 60-minute group. Even if the participants given 60 minutes of practice had further benefited from the extra practice, the experimenter could not measure this improvement on the chosen dependent variable.

The preceding experiment illustrates the general measurement problem referred to as a **ceiling effect.** Whenever performance reaches a maximum in any condition of an experiment, there is danger of a ceiling effect. The corresponding name given to this problem when performance reaches a minimum (e.g., zero errors on a test) is a **floor effect.** In general, one can avoid ceiling and floor effects by selecting dependent variables that allow ample "room" for performance differences to be measured across conditions. For example, in the fitness experiment it would have been better to test participants with a greater number of exercises than anyone could be expected to complete in the time allotted for the test. The mean number of exercises completed in each condition could then be used to assess the effects of the two independent variables without the danger of a ceiling effect.

Interactions and the Natural Groups Design

- Researchers use complex designs to make causal inferences about natural groups variables when they test a theory for *why* natural groups differ.
- Three steps for making a causal inference involving a natural groups variable are to state a theory for why group differences exist, manipulate an independent variable that should demonstrate the theorized process, and test whether the hypothesized interaction occurs between the manipulated independent variable and natural groups variable.

The natural groups design, which we described briefly in Chapter 6, is one of the most popular research designs in psychology. Groups of people are formed by selecting individuals who differ on some characteristic such as gender, age, introversion-extraversion, or aggressiveness. Researchers then look for systematic relationships between these individual differences variables and other aspects of behavior. The natural groups design is an effective one for establishing correlations between individuals' characteristics and their performance. As we also noted in Chapter 6, however, the natural groups design is perhaps the most challenging design when it comes to drawing conclusions about the causes of behavior.

The difficulty in interpreting the natural groups design arises when we try to conclude that differences in performance are caused by the characteristics of the people we used to define the groups. For instance, consider an experiment in which participants are selected because of their musical training. One group of participants includes people with 10 or more years of formal musical training, and one group includes people with no formal training. Both groups are tested on their ability to remember the musical notation for simple 10-note melodies. Not surprisingly, the results of these tests show that those with musical training perform far better than those without such training.

We can conclude on the basis of these results that memory for simple melodies varies with (is correlated with) amount of musical training. But we cannot conclude that musical training *causes* superior memory performance. Why not? There are probably many additional ways in which people with 10 years of musical training differ from those without such training. The groups may differ in amount and type of general education, family background, socioeconomic status, and amount and type of experience they have had listening to music. Also, those with musical training may have generally better memories than those without such training, and their superior memory for simple melodies may reflect this general memory ability. Finally, those who sought out musical training may have done so because they had a special aptitude for music. Accordingly, they might have done better on the memory task even if they had not had any musical training. In short, there are many possible causes other than individual differences in musical training for the difference in memory performance that was observed.

There is a potential solution to the problem of drawing causal inferences based on the natural groups design (Underwood & Shaughnessy, 1975). The key to this solution is to develop a theory regarding the critical individual difference variable. For example, Halpern and Bower (1982) were interested in how memory for musical notation differs between musicians and nonmusicians. Halpern and Bower developed a theory of how musical training would influence the cognitive processing of musical notation by those who had such training. Their theory was based on a memory concept called "chunking." You can get some sense of the memory advantage provided by chunking if you imagine trying to memorize the following strings of 15 letters: IBMTWASOSUSAFBI. Chunking helps memory by changing the same string of letters to a series of five more easily remembered chunks: IBM-TWA-SOS-USA-FBI.

Halpern and Bower theorized that musical training led musicians to "chunk" musical notation into meaningful musical units, thereby reducing the amount of information they needed to remember in order to reproduce the notation for a simple melody. Furthermore, if this process were responsible for the difference between the memory performance of musicians and nonmusicians, then the difference should be greater for melodies with good musical structure than for those with poor musical structure. Halpern and Bower manipulated the independent variable of musical structure to test their theory. To do this, they used three different types of melodies to test their groups of musicians and nonmusicians. They prepared sets of simple melodies whose notations had similar visual structures but that were either good, bad, or random in musical structure. The critical test was whether they would obtain an interaction of the two independent variables. Specifically, they expected that the difference in memory performance between musicians and nonmusicians would be largest for the melodies exhibiting good structure, next largest for the melodies exhibiting bad structure, and smallest for the random melodies. The results of Halpern and Bower's experiment conformed exactly to these expectations.

The obtained interaction allowed Halpern and Bower to rule out many alternative hypotheses for the difference in memory performance between musicians and nonmusicians. Such characteristics as amount and type of general education, socioeconomic status, and family background are not likely to explain why there is a systematic relationship between the structure of the melodies and the size of the difference in memory performance between musicians and nonmusicians. The interaction makes such simple correlational explanations much less plausible.

There are several steps that the investigator must take in carrying out the general procedure for drawing causal inferences based on the natural groups design.

Step 1: State Your Theory The first step is to develop a theory explaining why a difference should occur in the performance of groups that have been differentiated on the basis of an individual differences variable. Halpern and Bower theorized that musicians and nonmusicians differed in musical performance because of the way that these groups cognitively organize ("chunk") melodies.

Step 2: Identify a Relevant Manipulated Variable The second step is to select an independent variable that can be manipulated and that is presumed to influence the likelihood that this theoretical process will occur. Halpern and Bower suggested that type of musical structure was a variable associated with ease of chunking.

Step 3: Look for an Interaction The most critical aspect of the recommended approach is to strive to produce an interaction between the manipulated variable and the individual differences variable. Thus, the relevant manipulated independent variable is applied to both natural groups. Halpern and Bower sought an interaction between the individual differences variable (musician vs. nonmusician) and the manipulated variable (type of musical structure) in a 2×3 complex design. (The approach can be strengthened even further by testing predictions of interactions of three independent variables: two manipulated independent variables and the individual differences variable—see, for example, Anderson & Revelle [1982].)

SUMMARY

A complex design is one in which two or more independent variables are studied in the same experiment. A complex design involving two independent variables allows one to determine the overall effect of each independent variable (the main effect of each variable). More important, complex designs can be used to reveal the interaction of two independent variables. Interactions occur when the effect of each independent variable depends on the level of the other independent variable.

The simplest possible complex design is the 2×2 design, in which two independent variables are both studied at two levels. The analytical power of complex designs increases when additional levels of one or both of the independent variables are included in the design, yielding designs such as the 3×2, the 3×3, the 4×2, the 4×3, and so on. Additional independent variables can also be included to yield designs such as the $2 \times 2 \times 2$, the $3 \times 3 \times 3$, and so on. Experiments involving three independent variables are remarkably efficient. They allow us to determine the main effects of each of the three variables, the three two-way interactions, and the simultaneous interaction of all three variables.

When two independent variables are studied in a complex design, three potential sources of systematic variation can be interpreted. Each independent variable can produce a significant main effect, and the two independent variables can combine to produce a significant interaction. Interactions can be initially identified by using the subtraction method when the descriptive statistics are reported in a table, or by the presence of nonparallel lines when the results appear in a line graph. If the interaction does prove to be statistically significant (using an analysis of variance), we can interpret the results further by examining simple main effects and simple comparisons. When no interaction arises, we interpret the main effects of each independent variable, using analytical comparisons when necessary.

Complex designs play a critical role in the testing of predictions derived from psychological theories. Complex designs are also essential to resolve contradictions that arise when two experiments involving the same independent variable result in different findings. Investigators can trace the source of the contradictory findings by using a complex design in which both the original independent variable and the independent variable that is presumed to be responsible for the discrepant findings are manipulated in the same experiment.

When a complex design is used and no interaction occurs, we know that the effects of each independent variable can be generalized across the levels of the other independent variable(s). When an interaction does occur, however, limits on the external validity of a finding can be clearly specified. The possibility of interactions requires that we expand the definition of a relevant independent variable to include those that influence behavior directly (produce main effects) and those that produce an interaction when studied in combination with another independent variable.

Interactions that may arise because of measurement problems such as ceiling or floor effects must not be confused with interactions that reflect the true combined effect of two independent variables. Interactions can also be most helpful in solving the problem of drawing causal inferences based on the natural groups design.

KEY CONCEPTS

complex designs	simple main effect
interaction	relevant independent variable
main effect	ceiling and floor effects

REVIEW QUESTIONS

1 Use the Hass et al. cross-racial evaluation experiment to illustrate that there is one possible interaction in a 2 × 2 design but that there are two possible ways to describe the interaction.

2 Describe the method you would use to decide whether an interaction was present in a table showing the results of a 2 × 2 complex design.

3 Describe the pattern in a line graph that indicates the presence of an interaction in a complex design.

4 Outline the steps in the analysis plan for a complex design with two independent variables when there is an interaction and when there is not an interaction.

5 Explain how a complex design can be used to resolve contradictions that arise when two researchers obtain different results after manipulating the same independent variable in their respective single-factor experiments.

6 Use an example to illustrate how a complex design can be used to test predictions derived from a psychological theory.

7 How is the external validity of the findings in a complex design influenced by the presence or absence of an interaction?

8 What expansion in the definition of a relevant independent variable is required by the use of complex designs?

9 What potential solution is there for the problem of drawing causal inferences on the basis of the natural groups design?

CHALLENGE QUESTIONS

1 Consider an experiment in which two independent variables have been manipulated. Variable *A* has been manipulated at three levels, and Variable *B* has been manipulated at two levels.

 A Draw a graph showing an effect of Variable *B*, no effect of Variable *A*, and no interaction between the two variables.

 B Draw a graph showing no effect of Variable *A*, no effect of Variable *B*, but an interaction between the two variables.

 C Draw a graph showing an effect of Variable *A*, an effect of Variable *B*, and no interaction between the *A* and *B* variables.

2 A researcher has used a complex design to study the effects of training (untrained and trained) and problem difficulty (easy and hard) on participants' problem-solving ability. The researcher tested a total of 80 participants, with 20 randomly assigned to each of the four groups resulting from the factorial combination of the two independent variables. The data presented below represent the percentage of the problems that participants solved in each of the four conditions.

| | Training | |
Problem Difficulty	Untrained	Trained
Easy	90	95
Hard	30	60

A   Is there evidence of a possible interaction in this experiment?

B   What aspect of the results of this experiment would lead you to be hesitant to interpret an interaction if one were present in this experiment?

C   How could the researcher modify the experiment so as to be able to interpret an interaction if it should occur?

3 A psychologist is interested in whether older people suffer a deficit with respect to their reaction time in processing complex visual patterns. He selects a random sample of 65-year-old people and another random sample of young adults (such as college students). He tests both groups of 50 people in the same reaction time task. He presents a simple figure to each participant, then a complex pattern, and asks the participant to indicate as quickly as possible whether the simple figure is present in the complex pattern. Participants are timed only for their reaction to the complex patterns. This test is called an embedded figures test. As he had expected, the mean reaction time for the older adults was markedly longer than that for the young adults. By any standard the results were statistically significant.

A   Explain what minimal set of conditions the psychologist would have to include in his experiment before he could conclude that older adults suffered a deficit in their processing of complex visual patterns. That is, state what additional reaction time test must be given to both groups. Finally, describe an outcome of the test you propose that would support his position and one that would lead you to question his conclusion.

B   Recognizing that his original study is flawed, the psychologist tries to use post hoc matching to try to equate his two groups. He decides to match on general health (i.e., the better your general health, the faster your reaction time). Although he cannot get an exact matching across groups he does find that when he looks only at the 15 healthiest older adults, their reaction times are only slightly longer than the mean for the college students. Explain how this outcome would change the psychologist's conclusion concerning the effect of age on reaction time. Could the psychologist reach the general conclusion that older adults do not suffer a deficit in reaction time in this task? Why or why not?

Answer to Challenge Question 1

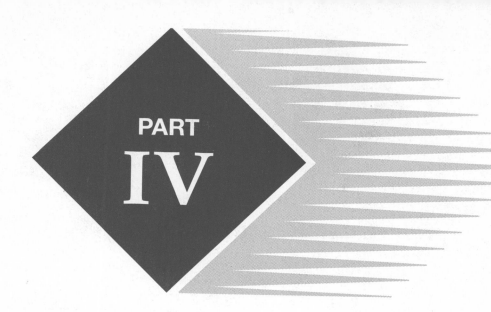

PART
IV

Applied Research

Single-Case Research Designs

CHAPTER OUTLINE

OVERVIEW
THE CASE STUDY METHOD
Characteristics
Advantages of the Case Study Method
Disadvantages of the Case Study Method
The Case Study Method: Final Comments
Applied Behavior Analysis
SINGLE-CASE ($N = 1$) EXPERIMENTAL DESIGNS
Specific Experimental Designs
Problems and Limitations Common to All Single-Case Designs
Ethical Issues in Single-Case Designs
SUMMARY

OVERVIEW

What do Sigmund Freud and B. F. Skinner have in common? They are, of course, among the best-known psychologists of the 20th century. However, having made this point, you may find it difficult to identify significant commonalities between these two psychologists. Freud introduced psychoanalysis. If we were to use the psychoanalyst's technique of free association, the mention of Freud would likely bring to mind concepts such as unconscious motives, defense mechanisms, and Freudian slips. Skinner developed the experimental analysis of behavior. Associations to Skinner's name are likely to include terms like behaviorism, reinforcement, and *Walden Two*. Interestingly, Freud and Skinner did have something in common: They based their research on the study of single subjects. And there the similarity ends!

Thus far in this book, we have emphasized *group methodology*—research designed to examine the average performance of one or more groups of subjects. This was particularly evident in the last few chapters, in which experimental methods were examined. The most common research design in psychological research is one involving many subjects, whose behavior is observed following one or more experimental treatments. A decision about the effectiveness of an independent variable is made when other potential independent variables have been controlled either within or between groups of subjects. Group methodology was emphasized when we discussed various kinds of independent groups designs in Chapter 6.

In this chapter we introduce an alternative methodology. The distinctive characteristic of this approach is its emphasis on a single subject or, at most, a few subjects (see, for example, Kratochwill & Levin, 1992). The approach is sometimes called "small *n* research." We use the name *single-case research designs* to identify this kind of psychological research. Single-case designs have been used since scientific psychology began in the 19th century. Psychophysical methods had their origin in the work of Gustav Fechner and were described in his 1860 book, *Elemente der Psychophysik*. Fechner, and countless other psychophysicists since, relied on data obtained through experiments with one or two individuals. You can find examples of single-case psychophysical experiments in journals such as *Perception & Psychophysics*.

Cognitive psychologists also have relied on single-case research designs. Most students of psychology know that Hermann Ebbinghaus initiated the scientific study of human memory with the publication, in 1885, of his monograph on memory. Ebbinghaus was both participant and experimenter; over a period of many months he learned and then attempted to relearn hundreds of series of nonsense syllables. His data provided psychologists with the first systematic evidence of forgetting over time (see, for example, Zechmeister & Nyberg, 1982). Closer to the present, Linton (1978) examined the retention of everyday events over a 6-year period by testing a single participant: herself. The study of expert performance, whether it be that of a ballet dancer, chess player, or musician, also relies heavily on small *n* research (e.g., Ericsson & Charness, 1994). Ericsson,

Chase, and Faloon (1980) studied the development of exceptional memory performance in a single undergraduate with average intelligence. The student practiced remembering sequences of random digits presented to him at the rate of one digit per second. Like most of us, he initially could remember only about seven digits, which is a typical adult "memory span" for digits. After more than 200 hours of practice, however, the student's memory span increased to nearly 80 digits! Single-case studies appear regularly in psychology journals, dealing with issues ranging from cognitive therapy for Vietnam veterans (Kubany, 1997) to the study of brain processes in amnesic patients (Gabrieli, Fleischman, Keane, Reminger, & Morrell, 1995).

In this chapter we discuss two specific single-case research methodologies. The first is the case study method. This approach, used by Freud and other psychoanalysts, is frequently associated with the field of clinical psychology, but as you will see, psychologists from other branches of psychology also make use of this important method. For example, Ruth Campbell's book *Mental Lives* (1992) is an interesting collection of case studies illustrating various aspects of human cognition. And the neurologist Oliver Sacks (1985, 1995) has captivated millions with his vivid descriptions of individuals with minds gone awry. Case studies are frequently the source of valuable hypotheses about behavior and can be an important complement to more rigorously controlled approaches to understanding behavior. Both the advantages and the disadvantages of the case study method will be reviewed.

The second single-case methodology we discuss is derived from Skinner's experimental analysis of behavior. Techniques derived from laboratory studies of animal and human behavior have been found to be effective in managing behavior in numerous applied situations, including schools, the home, hospitals, and businesses. Single-case experimental designs, also frequently called "$N = 1$ experimental designs," are characteristic of the approach called *applied behavior analysis*. We examine the rationale behind this approach and provide specific illustrations of the more common $N = 1$ experimental designs. These experimental designs represent a special case of the repeated measures design introduced in Chapter 7.

THE CASE STUDY METHOD

Characteristics

- Case studies, intensive descriptions and analyses of individuals, lack the degree of control found in $N = 1$ experimental designs.
- Case studies are a source of hypotheses and ideas about normal and abnormal behavior.

A **case study** is an intensive description and analysis of a single individual. Case studies frequently make use of qualitative data, but this is not always the case (e.g., Smith, Harré, & Van Langenhove, 1995). Data may be obtained from several different sources, including naturalistic observation (Chapter 3), interviews and psychological tests (Chapter 4), and even archival records (Chapter 5). A case study occasionally describes the application and results of a particular treatment, as, for example, when a new therapeutic technique is used to treat an emotionally disabled person. However, in the context of a case study, treatment variables are rarely varied systematically in an effort to control extraneous variables, and several different treatments are often applied simultaneously. Thus, case studies differ from $N = 1$ experimental designs in the degree to which variables are controlled (see, for example, Kazdin, 1998). The case study method has been used by child psychologists, memory researchers, and animal behaviorists, as well as by researchers in fields such as anthropology, criminology, neurology, and sociology.

In actual practice, the form and content of case studies are extremely varied. Published case studies may be only a few printed pages long or may fill a book. Kirsch (1978) described an attempt to implement "self-management training" with a woman experiencing low self-confidence and social inhibition. The case study, describing her treatment during nine therapy sessions and a 5-month follow-up, was presented in just four pages of one issue of the journal *Psychotherapy: Theory, Research and Practice*. In another case study, the personality psychologist Gordon W. Allport described the relationship between a mother and son as revealed in 301 letters that the mother wrote to friends. First reported in two consecutive issues of the *Journal of Abnormal and Social Psychology* (1946, Vol. 41, Nos. 3 and 4), this classic case study was published in 1965 as a 223-page book under the title *Letters from Jenny*.

Campbell's edited book, *Mental Lives* (1992), contains case studies of 15 individuals "with something 'abnormal' in the way they think, perceive, read, speak or remember" (p. 2). The focus of the book, however, is on what these cases reveal about *normal* cognitive functioning. For instance, Riddoch and Humphreys (1992) introduce us to Dennis, a 47-year-old man who experienced severe head trauma from a fall from a ladder. Dennis subsequently had difficulty recognizing familiar people (his own family) as well as common objects when he *saw* them (although his sight was good enough to watch TV); however, he could recognize people when he *heard* them speak and could identify common objects when he *touched* them. The authors of this case study use Dennis's experiences to teach us how visual recognition depends on stored knowledge. Emphasizing what we learn about normal behavior by examining unusual abnormal behaviors is, according to Campbell, what differentiates the case studies revealed in *Mental Lives* from those in other collections, such as those of Oliver Sacks. Sacks's collections of case studies focus mainly on detailed descriptions of individuals with peculiar, and rather fascinating, brain disorders. One of Sacks's best-known books is *The Man Who Mistook His Wife for a Hat* (1985). In it, as the title indicates, we are introduced to a man who quite literally, when searching for his hat, seized his wife's head, tried to lift it off and put it on. These "clinical tales," as Sacks calls them, not only provide insights into the relationship between mind and brain, but also reveal how individuals adapt, cope, and succeed when faced with profound neurological deficits. As you can see, case studies serve many important purposes.

Many aspects of the case study method make it a unique means of studying behavior. It differs somewhat from more experimental approaches in terms of its goals, the methods used, and the types of information obtained (Kazdin, 1998). For example, the case study method is often characterized as "exploratory" in nature and a source of hypotheses and ideas about behavior (Bolgar, 1965). Experimental approaches, on the other hand, are frequently viewed as opportunities to test specific hypotheses. The case study method has sometimes been viewed as antagonistic to more controlled methods of investigation. A more appropriate perspective is suggested by Kazdin (1998), who sees the case study method as interrelated with and complementary to other research methods in psychology. For instance, *Mental Lives* shows how case studies of abnormal lives can complement nomothetic studies of "normal" lives.

The case study method offers both advantages and disadvantages to the research psychologist (see, for example, Bolgar, 1965; Hersen & Barlow, 1976; Kazdin, 1998). Before reviewing its advantages and disadvantages, however, let us illustrate the method with a summary of an actual case study reported by Kirsch (1978), which was mentioned earlier. It is important that you read this slightly abbreviated version of a case study carefully because we will make reference to it when discussing the advantages and disadvantages of the methodology.

CAN CLIENTS BE THEIR OWN THERAPISTS? A CASE STUDY ILLUSTRATION

This article reports on the use of Self-Management Training (SMT), a therapeutic strategy which capitalizes on the advantages of brief therapies, while at the same time reducing the danger of leaving too many tasks not fully accomplished. . . . The essence of this approach involves teaching the client how to be his or her own behavior therapist. The client is taught how to assess problems along behavioral dimensions and to develop specific tactics, based on existing treatment techniques, for overcoming problems. As this process occurs, the traditional client-therapist relationship is altered considerably. The client takes on the dual role of client and therapist, while the therapist takes on the role of supervisor.

The Case of Susan

Susan, a 28-year-old married woman, entered therapy complaining that she suffered from a deficient memory, low intelligence, and lack of self-confidence. The presumed deficiencies "caused" her to be inhibited in a number of social situations. She was unable to engage in discussions about films, plays, books, or magazine articles "because" she could not remember them well enough. She often felt that she could not understand what was being said in a conversation and that this was due to her low intelligence. She attempted to hide her lack of comprehension by adopting a passive role in these interactions and was fearful lest she be discovered by being asked for more of a response. She did not trust her own opinions and, indeed, sometimes doubted whether she had any. She felt dependent on others to provide opinions for her to adopt.

Administering a Wechsler Adult Intelligence Scale (WAIS), I found her to have a verbal IQ of about 120, hardly a subnormal score. Her digit span (scale score = 12, raw score = 13) indicated that at least her short-term memory was not deficient. The test confirmed what I had already surmised from talking with her: that there was nothing wrong with her level of intelligence or her memory. After discussing this conclusion, I suggested that we investigate in greater detail what kinds of things she would be able to do if she felt that her memory, intelligence, and level of self-confidence were sufficiently high. In this way, we were able to agree upon a list of behavioral goals, which included such tasks as stating an opinion, asking for clarification, admitting ignorance of certain facts, etc. During therapy sessions, I guided Susan through overt and covert rehearsals of anxiety-arousing situations . . . structured homework assignments which constituted successive approximations of her behavioral goals, and had her keep records of her progress. In addition, we discussed negative statements which she was making to herself and which were not warranted by the available data (e.g., "I'm stupid"). I suggested that whenever she noticed herself making a statement of this sort, she counter it by intentionally saying more appropriate, positive statements to herself (e.g., "I'm not stupid—there is no logical reason to think that I am").

During the fifth session of therapy, Susan reported the successful completion of a presumably difficult homework assignment. Not only had she found it easy to accomplish, but, she reported, it had not aroused any anxiety, even on the first trial. . . . It was at this point that the nature of the therapeutic relationship was altered. During future sessions, Susan rated her progress during the week, determined what the next step should be, and devised her own homework assignments. My role became that of a supervisor of a student therapist, reinforcing her successes and drawing attention to factors which she might be overlooking.

After the ninth therapy session, direct treatment was discontinued. During the following month, I contacted Susan twice by phone. She reported feeling confident in her ability to achieve her goals. In particular, she reported feeling a new sense of control over her life. My own impressions are that she had successfully adopted a behavioral problem-solving method of assessment and had become fairly adept at devising strategies for accomplishing her goals.

Follow-up

Five months after termination of treatment, I contacted Susan and requested information on her progress. She reported that she talked more than she used to in social situations, was feeling more comfortable doing things on her own (i.e., without her husband), and that, in general, she no longer felt that she was stupid. She summarized by saying: "I feel that I'm a whole step or level above where I was."

I also asked her which, if any, of the techniques we had used in therapy she was continuing to use on her own. . . . Finally, she reported that on at least three separate occasions during the five-month period following termination of treatment, she had told another person: "I don't understand that—will you explain it to me?" This was a response which she had previously felt she was not capable of making, as it might expose her "stupidity" to the other person.

Three months after the follow-up interview, I received an unsolicited letter from Susan (I had moved out of state during that time), in which she reminded me that "one of [her] imaginary exercises was walking into a folk dancing class and feeling comfortable; well, it finally worked."*

* Source: Kirsch, I. (1978). Teaching clients to be their own therapists: A case-study illustration. *Psychotherapy: Theory, Research, and Practice, 15,* 302–305. (Reprinted by permission.)

Advantages of the Case Study Method

- Case studies provide new ideas and hypotheses, opportunities to develop new clinical techniques, and a chance to study rare phenomena.
- Scientific theories can be challenged when the behavior of a single case contradicts theoretical principles or claims, and theories can receive tentative support using evidence from case studies.
- Idiographic research (the study of individuals to identify what is unique) complements nomothetic research (the study of groups to identify what is typical).

Sources of Ideas About Behavior   The "power" of the case study method, according to Bolgar (1965), "lies in its ability to open the way for discoveries" (p. 30). It acts as a breeding ground for hypotheses that may subsequently be pursued with more rigorous methodologies. This aspect of the case study method was acknowledged by Kirsch (1978) in discussing the successful psychotherapy with the women named Susan. He stated that the "conclusions [of this study] share the limitations of any inferences drawn from case study material. At this point they should be viewed as tentative. It is hoped that the utility of [this technique] will be established by more controlled research" (p. 305). The case study method is a natural starting point for a researcher who is entering an area of study about which relatively little is known. In psychology, the development of psychoanalytic theory stands as a classic example of hypothesis formation based on the case study method.

Opportunity for Clinical Innovation   The case study method provides an opportunity to "try out" new therapeutic techniques or to attempt unique applications of existing techniques. In this way it offers an opportunity for clinical innovation. The use of self-management training (SMT) in psychotherapy changes the typical client-therapist relationship. The approach is based on teaching clients to be their own therapists—in other words, to identify problems and design behavioral techniques for dealing with them. The client is both client and therapist, while the therapist acts as supervisor. In a similar vein, Kubany (1997) reported the effect of a "marathon" 1-day cognitive therapy session with a Vietnam War veteran suffering from multiple sources of combat-related guilt. Therapy of this kind generally occurs over many hour-long sessions, but the fact that this intensive session appeared to be successful suggests a new way to conduct this type of clinical intervention.

Method to Study Rare Phenomena   Certain events appear so infrequently in nature that it is possible to describe them only through the intensive study of single cases. Many of the cases described in *Mental Lives* and in books by Oliver Sacks, for example, describe individuals with rare brain disorders. Other examples are found in the vivid case studies of so-called "feral children." These are children abandoned at an early stage who developed without significant human contact while living in the wild. Among the most celebrated case studies of a feral child is that of the "Wild Boy of Aveyron" (see, for example, *The Forbidden Experiment: The Story of the Wild Boy of Aveyron* [Shattuck, 1994]). Victor, as he came to be called, was captured in 1800 in the Aveyron district of France. Someone may have tried to kill him (as evidenced by the knife wound on his neck) and then abandoned him (perhaps had left him for dead) in the woods when he was about 5 years old. When he was captured, at about age 11 or 12, he was described as follows:

> He was human in bodily form and walked erect. Everything else about him suggested an animal. He was naked except for the tatters of a shirt and showed no modesty, no awareness of himself as a human person related in any way to the people who captured him. He could not speak and made only weird meaningless cries. (Shattuck, 1994, p. 5)

To many, Victor provided an opportunity to test what were then (and still are today) burning hypotheses about human nature. How are we different from animals? How do people learn language? What is "natural" and what is "cultural"? The story of Victor's reintroduction to society and his steps toward "humanity," under the tutelage of a devoted medical doctor and governess, in no way provides definitive answers to such abstract questions. Rather, in one author's view, this story "obliges us to reflect on how to live with those unsolved questions" (Shattuck, 1994, p. 182). Such can be the power of the case study.

FIGURE 9.1   Only surviving picture of the "Wild Boy of Aveyron."

Challenge to Theoretical Assumptions   A theory that all Martians have three heads would quickly collapse if a reliable observer spotted a Martian with only two heads. The case study method can often advance scientific thinking by providing a "counterinstance": a single case that violates a general proposition or universally accepted principle (Kazdin, 1998). Consider, for example, the theory that human language development depends on exposure to normal language during a *critical period*, from about 2 years of age to puberty (suggested by Lenneberg, 1967). A human child deprived of language exposure during this period would, then, not be expected to acquire language. Of course, depriving a child of language experience for purposes of testing this hypothesis would be immoral. Yet, there are "nature's experiments." You see why Shattuck's story of the Wild Boy of Aveyron was titled "The Forbidden Experiment." What was Victor capable of learning after such deprivation? Interest in Victor was stimulated by age-old theories about language development similar to the critical period theory. So, too, was interest in "Genie," a child discovered more recently (in 1970). Genie had been cruelly isolated from most human contact and normal language from about the age of 2 to age 13 (Curtiss, 1977). The circumstances surrounding Genie's imprisonment and abuse, as well as the attempts by psychologists and linguists to rehabilitate her, were chronicled by Rymer (1993). The scientists who surrounded her saw an opportunity to observe the results of a test (the forbidden one) of a critical period theory of language development:

> At best, Genie could have provided a flawed endorsement of Lenneberg's theory. But she was capable of a ringing refutation. If Genie could not learn language, her failure would be attributed ambiguously—either to the truth of the critical-period hypothesis or to her emotional problems. If Genie did learn language in spite of all that had happened to her, how much stronger the rebuttal! (Rymer, 1993, pp. 121–122)

According to the psychologist most closely associated with Genie's language training, Genie showed some language development but it was never completely normal. Thus, a "weak" version of Lenneberg's theory, namely, that *normal* language development would not appear after puberty without exposure during the critical period, "cannot be dismissed" by Genie's case study (Curtiss, 1977, p. 209).

Tentative Support for a Psychological Theory   Few researchers would accept the results of a case study as conclusive evidence for a particular hypothesis (see the discussion of disadvantages of the case study method that follows). The results of a case study generally must be viewed as tentative and must await investigation via more carefully controlled procedures before they are accepted by the scientific community. Nevertheless, the outcome of a case study can sometimes provide important evidence in support of a psychological theory, as we just saw occurred in the case of Genie and the weak version of Lenneberg's critical period theory. As another illustration, we can take an example from the memory literature.

In 1968, Atkinson and Shiffrin proposed a model of human memory that was to have considerable influence on research in this field. The model, which was based on principles of information processing, described both a short-term memory (STM) system and a long-term memory (LTM) system. Human memory, in other words, should be thought of as containing at least two structures, each with different characteristics and functions. STM was identified with "working memory" and represented the locus of conscious rehearsal and elaboration of information. It was the kind of memory we might use when looking up a telephone number and "holding" it until we had dialed it correctly. Information in LTM did not have to be actively processed in order to be remembered; rather, information in this memory system was stored on a relatively permanent basis, from whence it could be retrieved and brought into conscious memory (into STM).

Although results of numerous experiments provided evidence for this dual nature of our memory, Atkinson and Shiffrin considered the results of several case studies as "perhaps the most convincing demonstrations of a dichotomy in the memory system" (p. 97). These case studies involved patients who had been treated for epilepsy via surgical removal of parts of the brain within the temporal lobes, including a subcortical structure known as the hippocampus. Of particular importance to Atkinson and Shiffrin's theory was the case study of a patient known as H. M. (see Hilts, 1995; Scoville & Milner, 1957). Following the brain operation, H. M. was found to have a disturbing memory deficit. Although he could carry on a normal conversation and remember events for a short period of time, H. M. apparently could not put new information into long-term memory. He could not remember day-to-day events. He was able to read the same magazine over and over again without finding its contents familiar. It looked as though H. M. had an intact short-term memory system but could not get information into a long-term memory system. Subsequent testing of H. M. and patients with similar memory deficits revealed that the nature of this memory problem is more complex than originally suggested (see Zechmeister & Nyberg, 1982), but the case study of H. M. continues to be important whenever theories of human memory are discussed (for example, see Schacter, 1996).

Complement to the Nomothetic Study of Behavior   As we noted in Chapter 1, psychology is largely a **nomothetic** discipline. This means that psychology (like science in general) seeks to establish broad generalizations, "universal laws" that will apply to a wide population of organisms. As a consequence, psychological research is often characterized by studies that involve large numbers of subjects and that seek to determine the "average" or typical performance of a group. This average may or may not represent the value of any one individual in the group. Rather, a researcher hopes to be able to predict, on the basis of this mean performance, what organisms will be like "in general."

Some psychologists, notably Allport (1961), argue that a nomothetic approach is inadequate—that the individual is more than what can be represented by the collection of average values on various dimensions. Allport argues that the individual is both unique and lawful (operates in accordance with internally consistent principles) and that the study of the individual, called **idiographic** research, is an important goal (see also Smith et al., 1995). The need for an idiographic approach can be illustrated by the task confronting the clinical psychologist. As Allport points out, the clinician's goal "is not to predict the aggregate, but to foretell 'what any one man [sic] will do.' In reaching this ideal, actuarial predictions may sometimes help, universal and group norms are useful, but they do not go the whole distance" (p. 21). Allport suggests that our approach to understanding human nature should be neither exclusively nomothetic nor exclusively idiographic but should represent an "equilibrium" between the two. At the very least the idiographic approach, as represented by the case study method, permits the kind of detailed observation that has the power to reveal various nuances and subtleties of behavior that a "group" approach may miss. And, as you have seen, case studies have the ability to teach us about typical or average behavior by studying what is not average and is atypical.

Disadvantages of the Case Study Method

- Because extraneous variables are not controlled and several "treatments" may be applied simultaneously in case studies, researchers are unable to make valid causal inferences using this method.
- Observer bias and biases in data collection can lead to incorrect interpretations of case study outcomes.
- Whether results from a case study may be generalized depends on the variability within the population from which the case was selected; some characteristics (e.g., personality) vary more across individuals than others (e.g., visual system).

Difficulty of Drawing Cause-Effect Conclusions   You are well aware by now that one of the goals of science is to discover the causes of phenomena—to reveal in an unambiguous manner the specific factors that produce a particular event. However, cause-effect conclusions can rarely be drawn on the basis of results that are obtained from the case study method. The major limitation of the case study method in this regard is its failure to control extraneous variables. Numerous plausible hypotheses are generally present to "explain" behavior change.

Consider, for instance, the treatment of Susan through SMT reported by Kirsch (1978). Although Susan apparently benefited from the SMT therapy, can we be sure that this particular factor accounted for her improvement? Many illnesses and certainly numerous emotional disorders are known to subside spontaneously. That is, over the course of time a certain number of people generally report a decrease in symptoms and an overall improvement even without treatment. The case study method generally does not permit one to dismiss the hypothesis that improvement would have been observed even if the specific treatment had never been administered. In addition, numerous aspects of the situation may be responsible for Susan's improvement. Her care was in the hands of a "clinical psychologist" who assured her that she should not trust her own feelings and discussed with her the reasons for these feelings. The "insight" provided by a professional therapist may be sufficient to change Susan's attitudes toward herself. The therapist also asked Susan, as part of her therapy, to rehearse anxiety-arousing situations covertly and overtly. This technique is similar to rehearsal desensitization, which may be an effective therapeutic treatment in itself (see Rimm & Masters, 1979).

The fact that several "treatments" were used simultaneously makes it difficult to argue conclusively that the SMT therapy "caused" Susan's improvement. As we have seen, Kirsch himself was sensitive to the limitations of his results and suggested that the inferences drawn from his study should be considered tentative until they were investigated more rigorously.

The case studies associated with feral children such as Victor, and abused and deprived children such as Genie, illustrate well the difficulty with isolating causal factors. We can only try to imagine the kinds of terror experienced by a child left alone in the woods year after year or of that experienced by a child who is isolated and physically abused by an emotionally disturbed parent. How much of the failure to acquire normal language is the result of such emotional disturbance? What else don't we know about these children? One story which circulated about Victor, for example, was that he had been abandoned by parents at about the age of 5 because he had not shown normal language development by that age (Shattuck, 1994). Did Victor have difficulty learning language *before* he was deprived of human contact? Genie had been severely ill at age 14 months and an attending physician had commented that she showed signs of retardation (Curtiss, 1977). Was Genie destined to be developmentally delayed even without the horrible isolation she experienced? The data from case studies frequently leave us wondering about causal events.

Sources of Bias in Interpretation   The "outcome" of a case study often depends on inferences drawn by a researcher who is both participant and observer (see Bolgar, 1965). A therapist is an observer but is also certainly a participant in the therapeutic process. Problems of observer bias can arise in the context of the case study as they do in other types of observation (see Chapter 3). In the absence of independent measures, the outcome of a case study may be based mainly on the "impressions" of the observer (see Hersen & Barlow, 1976). Kirsch (1978) described the patient Susan's "feelings" about her ability to achieve her goals and told how she reported a "sense of control" over her life. He stated that his "impressions are that she successfully adopted a behavioral problem-solving method of assessment and had become fairly adept at devising strategies for accomplishing her goals" (p. 304). Interpretation of an outcome solely on the basis of the subjective impressions of the observer can be seen as a serious weakness in the case study method.

Possible Biases in Data Collection   The material of a case study often includes several kinds of information, some of it obtained from personal documents and psychological tests. Each of these sources of information must be carefully examined for possible biases. Archival records, as we described in Chapter 5, are open to several sources of bias. Further, when information is based on self-reports, there is always the possibility of distortion or falsification. Such was a possibility (although not necessarily a significant one) in the case of Susan's treatment. We have no way of knowing whether the patient's self-reports of improvement were exaggerated or even false.

Reports of even the most intelligent and well-intentioned individuals are susceptible to biases and reconstructions, especially when memory for remote events is concerned. Consider the following excerpt from a self-analysis by the well-known personality psychologist Alfred Adler (1973, pp. 179–180):

> Shortly after I went to a board[ing] school. I remember that the path to the school led over a cemetery. I was frightened every time and was exceedingly put out at beholding the other children pass the cemetery without paying the least attention to it, while every step I took was accompanied by a feeling of fear and horror. Apart from the extreme discomfort occasioned by this fear I was also annoyed at the idea of being less courageous than the others. One day I made up my mind to put an end to this fear of death. Again (as on my first resolve), *I decided upon a treatment of hardening* (Proximity of death!). I stayed at some distance behind the others, placed my school-bag on the ground near the wall of the cemetery and ran across it a dozen times, until I felt that I had mastered the fear. After that, I believe, I passed along this path without any fear.
>
> Thirty years after that I met an old schoolmate and we exchanged childhood reminiscences of our school days. It happened to occur to me that the cemetery was no longer in existence and I asked him what had happened to it remembering the great uneasiness it had at one time caused me. Astonished, my former schoolmate who had lived longer in that neighborhood than I had, insisted that there never had been a cemetery on the way to our school. Then I realized that the story of the cemetery had been but a poetic dress for my longing to overcome the fear of death.

Problem of Generalizing from a Single Individual   As Bolgar (1965) has stated, "Much of the criticism leveled against the case study method of research is based on the accepted canon that it is impossible to generalize from one case" (p. 30). The ability to generalize from a single case depends on the degree of variability in the population from which the case was selected. Psychologists who study visual perception are often able to make wide generalizations based on the study of one individual. The assumption is that visual systems in humans are very similar and are related to the biological makeup of all humans. Thus, as we mentioned earlier, many psychophysicists perform experiments with only a "small *n*." When significant variability exists among individuals, as would be the case when measures are made of learning and memory, emotionality, or personality, it becomes impossible to claim that what is observed in one individual will hold for all individuals. In this situation researchers often use the "average" performance of a large group for their interpretation.

Even if we accept the validity of Kirsch's (1978) conclusion regarding the effectiveness of the SMT technique of psychotherapy, we do not know whether this particular treatment would be as successful for other individuals who might differ from the patient Susan in any of numerous ways, including intelligence, age, family background, and gender. Also consider the "marathon" treatment of the Vietnam veteran which we mentioned earlier. Kubany (1997) noted that the client whom he treated for war-related guilt "was highly motivated to work on his guilt issues" (p. 241), and this, among other reasons, made him "a particularly good candidate for therapy" (p. 241). Thus, the therapist acknowledged that definitive evidence for the generalizability of the effectiveness of this treatment must await more controlled studies "with many veterans" (p. 241).

The Case Study Method: Final Comments

- When considering individuals' testimonials about the effectiveness of a particular treatment, we need to remember the limitations of the case study method.

Case studies sometimes offer "dramatic" demonstrations of "new" or "unusual" findings or provide evidence for "success" of a particular treatment. These reports are often highly persuasive (see Kazdin, 1998). Everyday examples are found in the media and in advertisements for various products. How many people who worry about their weight can resist the example of a formerly overweight individual who is shown to have lost considerable weight through "Treatment X." The persuasive value of case study examples are both an asset and a liability to the scientific community. Demonstrations of new or unusual findings based on a case study may lead scientists to rethink their original theoretical assumptions or may lead them into new and fruitful avenues of research. Learning techniques used by the French scientist, Itard, who worked with the feral child, Victor, are used today in special education classes and in Montessori schools (Shattuck, 1994). Genie's case study stimulated other studies of language in atypical children (Rymer, 1993).

Nevertheless, the results of case studies are often accepted by nonscientists with little regard for the limitations of such evidence. This is particularly likely when individuals are in a position to identify with the subject of the case study. A person who suffers from a life-threatening illness may see more than a ray of hope in the results of a dramatic "new cure" based on treatment of an individual with the same illness. If this treatment worked for this person, why wouldn't it work for me? For people who have (or think they have) few alternatives, this grasping at straws may not be totally unreasonable. However, too often people do not consider (perhaps they do not want to consider) the reasons why a particular treatment would *not* work for them. They fail, in other words, to recognize the limitations of the case study method. This may have unfortunate consequences. For example, during the early 1980s there was considerable controversy surrounding the supposed cancer-curing drug Laetrile (see Sun, 1981). Few respectable scientists or medical researchers considered this drug, which was made from apricot pits, to be beneficial in the treatment of cancer. Positive results, however, based on individual "case studies," were presented as evidence by advocates of the drug. Largely because of public (not scientific) pressure, the government carried out systematic tests of the drug under controlled conditions. No beneficial effect of the drug was found. As others have commented, by using Laetrile instead of traditional therapies, many patients may have postponed or interrupted valid courses of treatment and thus contributed to the spread of their cancer.

Applied Behavior Analysis

- Single-case ($N = 1$) research is used in the experimental analysis of behavior.
- In operant conditioning, reinforcement and punishment are used to change behavior.
- In the experimental analysis of behavior, control is demonstrated when an individual's behavior changes systematically with the manipulation of an independent variable.
- Operant techniques are used in applied behavioral analysis, as in behavior modification and behavior therapy.

A particularly important form of behaviorism that emerged in the 1930s is that associated with B. F. Skinner. Skinner's approach is synonymous with what is called an *experimental analysis of behavior*. It presents a unique behavioral view of human nature that not only contains prescriptions for the way psychologists should do research but also has implications for the way society should be organized. Several of Skinner's books, including *Walden Two* and *Beyond Freedom and Dignity*, describe how the principles of behavior control that have been and will be derived from an experimental analysis of behavior can be put to work improving society.

Operant conditioning is the process by which behavior is modified by its consequences. Changes in behavior are usually measured in terms of frequency of responding, although other measures (such as duration or latency) may be used. Thus, rate of responding is a major dependent variable in operant conditioning. The task of the operant researcher is to relate changes in rate of responding to changes in the environment. Generally, an increase in rate of responding is brought about by a procedure known as reinforcement. The giving of "rewards" (such as praise, candy, flowers, ribbons, or high grades) following a response is one way to increase the subject's rate of responding. Decreases in rate of responding are brought about by a procedure known as punishment. One way to punish an organism is to follow a response with an aversive (noxious) event. The laboratory rat that is shocked when it presses a bar will soon stop bar pressing. Another way to use punishment is, following a response, to remove something that an organism would normally want. The parent who takes away the keys to the family car after a teenager gets a traffic ticket and the teacher who denies recess privileges to students who misbehave are using this form of punishment.

In conducting the experimental analysis of behavior, experimenters frequently make observations of single subjects. As we said earlier, it is often the case in the experimental analysis of behavior (unlike the group methodologies discussed in previous chapters) that $N = 1$. Experimental control is demonstrated by arranging experimental conditions such that the individual's behavior changes systematically with the manipulation of an independent variable. As Skinner (1966, p. 21) commented,

> instead of studying a thousand rats for one hour each, or a hundred rats for ten hours each, the investigator is likely to study one rat for a thousand hours. The procedure is not only appropriate to an enterprise which recognizes individuality, it is at least equally efficient in its use of equipment and of the investigator's time and energy. The ultimate test of uniformity or reproducibility is not to be found in the methods used but in the degree of control achieved, a test which the experimental analysis of behavior usually passes easily.

There is a minimum of statistical analysis. Conclusions regarding the effect of an experimental variable are made by visually inspecting the behavioral record in order to observe whether behavior changes systematically with the introduction and withdrawal of the experimental treatment.

In *applied behavior analysis*, the methods that are developed within an experimental analysis of behavior are applied to socially relevant problems. These applications are frequently referred to as **behavior modification** but when applied to clinical populations the term **behavior therapy** is preferred (Wilson, 1978). Behavior therapy is seen by many as a more effective approach to clinical treatment than that based on a psychodynamic model of therapy. Therapists who use a psychodynamic model "seek to help people gain insight into the unconscious roots of problems and work through newly resurrected feelings" (Myers, 1998, p. 490). Therapies based on Freud's psychoanalytic theory are particularly representative of this approach. In contrast, behavior therapy focuses on observable behavior rather than hypothesized unconscious forces. For example, self-stimulatory behaviors (e.g., prolonged body rocking, gazing at lights, or spinning) that often characterize so-called autistic children may be conceptualized as operant behaviors. In this way, clinicians and teachers may be able to control their frequency of occurrence by using behavior modification techniques (see Lovaas, Newsom, & Hickman, 1987). Numerous studies have been published showing how operant techniques can be employed successfully to change the behavior of psychotic individuals, normal and mentally impaired children and adults, individuals diagnosed as schizophrenic, stutterers, psychiatric patients, and many others. Behavior-analytic approaches have also been successfully used by school psychologists in educational settings (see Kratochwill & Martens, 1994). A primary source for these published studies is the *Journal of Applied Behavior Analysis*.

SINGLE-CASE ($N = 1$) EXPERIMENTAL DESIGNS

- Researchers manipulate an independent variable in single-case experiments; therefore, these designs allow more rigorous control than case studies.
- There are several circumstances when single-case experiments may be preferred over multiple-group methods.
- In single-case experiments, baseline observations are first recorded to describe what an individual's behavior is like (and predicted to be like in the future) without treatment.
- Baseline behavior and behavior following the intervention are compared using visual inspection of recorded observations.

The use of a single subject, which we have seen is often characteristic of the experimental analysis of behavior, is also a hallmark of applied behavior analysis. The **single-case experiment,** as its name suggests, typically focuses on an examination of behavior change in one individual. This methodology can be extended, however, to treatments applied to single groups of individuals as well (Kazdin, 1998). Single-case experiments differ from the traditional case study method in that they contrast conditions within an individual whose behavior is being continuously monitored. That is, the independent variable of interest is manipulated systematically for each individual. Consequently, single-case experimental designs are an important alternative to the relatively uncontrolled case study method (Kazdin, 1982).

For certain kinds of applied research, $N = 1$ experimental designs may be more appropriate than designs based on multiple-group methodology (see Hersen & Barlow, 1976). This is likely to be true when research is directed toward changing the behavior of a specific individual. For example, the average response of a group of subjects will not necessarily be the same as the response of any one individual in the group. Therefore, the outcome of a group experiment may lead to recommendations about what treatments "in general" should be applied to modify behavior, but it is not possible to say what the effect of that treatment will be on any particular individual. As Kazdin (1982) commented, "Perhaps the most obvious advantage [of single-case experimental designs] is that the methodology allows investigation of the individual client and experimental evaluation of treatment for the client" (p. 482).

Another disadvantage of multiple-group methodology, particularly in the context of clinical research, is that ethical problems arise when a potentially beneficial treatment is withheld from individuals in order to provide a control group that satisfies the requirements of internal validity. Because single-case experimental designs contrast conditions of "No Treatment" and "Treatment" within the same individual, this problem can be avoided. Moreover, investigators doing clinical research often find it difficult to gain access to enough clients to do a group experiment. For instance, a clinician may be able to identify from a list of clients only a few individuals experiencing claustrophobia (excessive fear of enclosed spaces). The single-case experiment provides a practical solution to the problem of investigating cause-effect conclusions when only a few participants are available.

The first stage of a single-case experiment is usually an observation stage, or **baseline stage.** During this stage a record is made of the individual's behavior prior to any intervention. A typical measure is frequency of behavior per some unit of time, such as a day, an hour, or another recording interval. An applied researcher might record the number of times during a 10-minute interview that an excessively shy child makes eye contact, the number of headaches reported each week by a depressed migraine sufferer, or the number of verbal pauses per minute made by a chronic stutterer. The baseline record provides a description of behavior before treatment is provided and, most importantly, offers a prediction of what behavior will be like in the future without treatment (Kazdin, 1998). Of course, unless behavior is actually monitored we don't know for sure what future behavior will be like, but by taking baseline measures we can predict what the future holds. Figure 9.2 illustrates this function of the baseline record.

Once behavior is shown to be relatively stable—that is, it exhibits little fluctuation between recording intervals—an intervention (treatment) is introduced. Behavior immediately following an intervention is contrasted with that seen during baseline performance. The effect of a behavioral intervention is typically evaluated by visual inspection of the behavioral record. How did behavior change, in other words, following the experimental treatment? Keep in mind that we predicted what behavior would be like without treatment (see, for example, Figure 9.2). Traditionally, tests of statistical significance have not been used, although there is some controversy surrounding this aspect of single-case methodology (Kratochwill & Brody, 1978). Later in this chapter we will discuss some of the problems that arise when visual inspection is used to determine whether a treatment was effective (see also Kazdin, 1998).

Although there are numerous design possibilities for the researcher who uses a single-case experimental design (Hersen & Barlow, 1976; Kazdin, 1980), the most commonly employed are the ABAB and multiple-baseline designs (Kazdin, 1998).

FIGURE 9.2   Hypothetical example of baseline observations for the frequency of responses. Data in baseline stage (solid line) are used to predict the likely rate of responses in the future if treatment is not implemented (dashed line). (Adapted from Kazdin, 1998, p. 209.)

Specific Experimental Designs

- In the ABAB design, baseline (A) and treatment (B) stages are alternated to determine the effect of treatment on behavior.
- Researchers conclude that treatment causes behavior change when behavior changes systematically with the introduction and withdrawal of treatment.
- Interpreting the causal effect of the treatment is difficult in the ABAB design if behavior does not reverse to baseline levels when treatment is withdrawn.
- Ethical considerations may prevent psychologists from using the ABAB design.
- In multiple-baseline designs, a treatment effect is shown when behaviors in more than one baseline change only following the introduction of a treatment.
- Multiple baselines may be observed across individuals, behaviors, or situations.
- Interpreting the causal effect of treatment is difficult in multiple-baseline designs when changes are seen in a baseline *before* an experimental intervention; this can occur when treatment effects generalize.

The ABAB Design   The **ABAB design** seeks to confirm a treatment effect by demonstrating that behavior changes systematically with alternating conditions of No Treatment and Treatment. An initial baseline stage (A) is followed by a treatment stage (B), next by a return to baseline (A), and then by another treatment stage (B). Because treatment is removed during the second A stage, and any improvement in behavior is likely to be reversed at this point, this design is also called a *reversal design*. The researcher using the ABAB design observes whether behavior changes immediately upon introduction of a treatment variable (first B), whether behavior reverses when treatment is withdrawn (second A), and whether behavior improves again when treatment is reintroduced (second B). When variations in behavior follow the introduction and withdrawal of treatment in this way, there is considerable evidence supporting the conclusion that the treatment caused behavior change.

Horton (1987) used an ABAB design to assess the effects of facial screening on the maladaptive behavior of a severely mentally impaired 8-year-old girl. Facial screening is a mildly aversive technique involving the application of a face cover (e.g., a soft cloth) when an undesirable behavior occurs. Previous research had shown this technique to be effective in reducing the frequency of self-injurious behaviors such as face slapping. Horton sought to determine whether it would reduce the frequency of spoon banging by a young child at mealtime. The spoon banging prevented the girl from dining with her classmates at the school for exceptional children that she attended. The banging was disruptive not only because of the noise but because it often led her to fling food on the floor or resulted in her dropping the spoon on the floor.

A clear definition of spoon banging was made to distinguish it from normal scooping motions. Then, a paraprofessional was trained to make observations and to administer the treatment. A frequency count was used to assess the magnitude of spoon banging within each 15-minute eating session. During the initial, or baseline, period the paraprofessional recorded frequency and, with each occurrence of the response, said "no bang," gently grasped the girl's wrist, and returned her hand to her dish. The procedure was videotaped, and an independent observer viewed the films and recorded frequency as a reliability check. Interobserver reliability was approximately 96%. The baseline stage was conducted for 16 days.

The first treatment period began on Day 17 and lasted for 16 days. Each time spoon banging was observed, the paraprofessional continued to give the corrective feedback of "no bang" and returned the girl's hand to her dish. However, the paraprofessional now also pulled a terry-cloth bib over the girl's entire face for 5 seconds. Release from facial screening was contingent on the participant's not banging for 5 seconds. The first treatment phase was followed by a second baseline period and another treatment phase. Posttreatment observations were also made at 6, 10, 15, and 19 months.

Figure 9.3 shows changes in the frequency of the mentally impaired girl's spoon-banging behavior as a function of alternating baseline and treatment phases. Facial screening was not only effective in reducing this behavior during treatment phases, follow-up observations revealed that the target behavior was still absent months later. Following the final treatment phase, the girl no longer required direct supervision during mealtime at either school or home and was permitted to eat with her peers. The facial-screening technique was a successful procedure for controlling the maladaptive behavior of the young child when other, less intrusive procedures had failed. Because only one treatment was administered, and because visual inspection revealed that behavior changed systematically with the introduction and withdrawal of treatment, it can be

FIGURE 9.3 Frequency of spoon-banging responses across baseline, treatment, and follow-up phases of study. (Adapted from Horton, 1987.)

concluded that application of an aversive stimulus was responsible for eliminating spoon banging.

Methodological Issues Associated with ABAB Designs

A major methodological problem that sometimes arises in the context of an ABAB procedure can be illustrated by looking again at the results of the Horton (1987) study shown in Figure 9.3. In the second baseline stage, when application of the facial screening was withdrawn, spoon banging increased in frequency. That is, the improvement observed under the preceding treatment stage was reversed. What if spoon-banging behavior remained low even when the treatment was withdrawn? What can be concluded? If behavior in a second baseline stage does not revert to what it was during the initial baseline period, then serious problems of interpretation arise.

One reason why improvement in behavior may not reverse is that the behavior that is the focus of treatment would not logically be expected to become worse once improvement was observed. This might be the case if treatment involved training an individual in a new skill, such as tying one's shoes or commuting successfully to a job. Once the skill is acquired, it cannot reasonably be expected to be unlearned. The solution to this problem is one of foresight. That is, the ABAB design should not be used when the target behavior could not logically be expected to show reversal when treatment is withdrawn.

Given that the experienced researcher is likely to avoid using an ABAB design in situations wherein behavior would not be expected to reverse, the failure to observe a reversal of performance is probably due to one of two factors. One possibility is that a variable other than the treatment variable was responsible for the improvement in behavior in the first shift from baseline to treatment stages. For example, the individual may receive increased attention from staff or friends during treatment. This increased attention—rather than the treatment—may produce an improvement in behavior. If the attention persists even though the specific treatment is withdrawn, the behavior change is likely to persist as well. This explanation suggests a "confounding" between the treatment variable and some other, uncontrolled factor. On the other hand, it is also possible that, although the treatment caused behavior to improve, other variables "took over" to control the new behavior. Again, we might consider attention as a variable having an effect on behavior. When family and friends witness a change in behavior, they may pay increased attention to the individual. Positive reinforcement in the form of attention may maintain the behavior change that was initiated by the treatment.

In either case, when improvement in behavior does not reverse, it is not clear whether the experimental treatment or some other factor led to the initial behavior change; consequently, a causal claim for the effectiveness of the intervention can not be made (Kazdin, 1980, 1998). If behavior does not revert back to baseline when treatment is withdrawn, the researcher must examine the situation carefully with the hope of identifying variables that might be confounding the treatment variable or replicate the procedure with the same subject or with different subjects (Hersen & Barlow, 1976).

From an applied researcher's point of view, in some situations there is also an ethical problem in using the ABAB design. As you might imagine, the withdrawal of a beneficial treatment may not be justified in all cases. For example, although spoon-banging behavior would not be considered life-threatening or exceptionally debilitating, other kinds of behavior might be, and it would not be ethical in these cases to remove or even suspend treatment once a positive effect was observed. Some autistic children exhibit self-injurious behaviors such as head banging or face slapping. If a clinical researcher succeeded in reducing the frequency of such behavior, it would be unethical to withdraw treatment to meet the requirements of the ABAB design. Fortunately, there are other single-case experimental designs that do not involve withdrawal of treatment and that may be appropriate in such situations.

The Multiple-Baseline Design The multiple-baseline design demonstrates the effect of a treatment by showing that behaviors in more than one baseline change following the introduction of a treatment. There are several variations on the multiple-baseline design, depending on whether multiple baselines are established for different individuals, for different behaviors in the same individual, or for the same individual in different situations. In each case, the conclusion that an experimental variable produced a reliable effect rests on the demonstration that behavior changed only when the experimental variable was introduced. Although they sound complex, multiple-baseline designs are frequently used and easily understood. Let us refer to a specific example of each type from the applied research literature.

A **multiple-baseline design across individuals** is a procedure wherein more than one individual is observed simultaneously. Specifically, baselines are first established for different individuals. When the behavior of each individual has stabilized, an intervention is introduced for one individual, then for another individual, later for another, and so on. That is, the experimental treatment is introduced at a different time for each participant. If the treatment is responsible for changing behavior, then an effect in the behavioral record will be seen immediately following the application of the treatment in each individual.

An interesting example of the use of a multiple-baseline design across individuals comes from the field of sports psychology. This subdiscipline involves the application of psychological principles to the improvement of recreation and sports (see, for example, Browne & Mahoney, 1984). Specifically, the researchers investigated the effect that a coaching method based on several behavioral techniques had on the acquisition of specific football, tennis, and gymnastic skills (see Allison & Ayllon, 1980). To evaluate this new behavioral coaching method, they used a multiple-baseline design. Although their investigation was successful in each sport, we will examine the effects of behavioral coaching only as it was applied to the acquisition of a football skill.

The participants in this experiment were second-string members of a citywide football program chosen because they "completely lacked fundamental football skills" (Allison & Ayllon, 1980, p. 299). The skill to be acquired was blocking, which was defined operationally in terms of eight elements, ranging from the body's first being behind the line of scrimmage to maintaining body contact until the whistle was blown. Behavioral coaching involved specific procedures implemented by the team coach. The procedures included systematic verbal feedback, positive and negative reinforcement, and several other behavioral techniques. The experimenter first established baselines for several different members of the football team under "standard coaching" conditions. In this procedure, the coach used verbal instructions, provided occasional modeling or verbal approval, and, when execution was incorrect, "loudly informed the player and, at times, commented on the player's stupidity, lack of courage, awareness, or even worse" (p. 300). In short, an all-too-typical example of negative coaching behavior.

The experimenter and a second, reliability observer made observations of the frequency of correct blocks made in sets of 10 trials. Behavioral coaching was begun, in accordance with the multiple-baseline design, at different times for various football players. Results of this intervention are shown in Figure 9.4. Across four individuals, behavioral coaching was shown to be effective in increasing the frequency of correctly executed blocks. Observer agreement on blocking performance ranged from 84% to 94%, indicating that the observation of behavior was reliable. The skill execution changed for each player at the point where behavioral coaching was introduced. Thus it can be argued that this method *caused* the change in each player's performance.

When two or more baselines are established by observing different behaviors in the *same* individual, the design is called a **multiple-baseline design across behaviors.** A treatment is directed first at one behavior, then at another, and so on. A causal relationship between treatment and behavior is assumed if each behavior responds directly to treatment. For example, Gena, Krantz, McClannahan, and Poulson (1996) taught different appropriate affective behaviors to several youths with autism. As the researchers noted, children with autism often show inappropriate affective behaviors, which serve to limit their opportunities to communicate effectively with others and to develop interpersonal relationships. Treatment included verbal praise and tokens (exchangeable for rewards) delivered contingent on appropriate affective responses in three or four different behavior categories. Target behaviors were selected from the following: showing appreciation, talking about favorite things, laughing about absurdities, showing sympathy, indicating dislike. An inspection of the behavioral record showed for each child that the different affective behaviors changed immediately after introduction of the intervention.

The third major variation on the multiple-baseline design is that across situations. In a **multiple-baseline design across situations,** baselines are established for an individual's behavior in different situations. For example, a researcher might establish baselines showing frequency of a target behavior in the clinic and frequency of this same behavior in the home. As with other variations of this design, the treatment is applied at different times and the behavioral records are examined to determine whether behavior changes systematically with the introduction of treatment.

FIGURE 9.4 Multiple baselines showing percentage of football blocks executed correctly by four players as a function of standard coaching and behavioral coaching. (From Allison & Ayllon, 1980.)

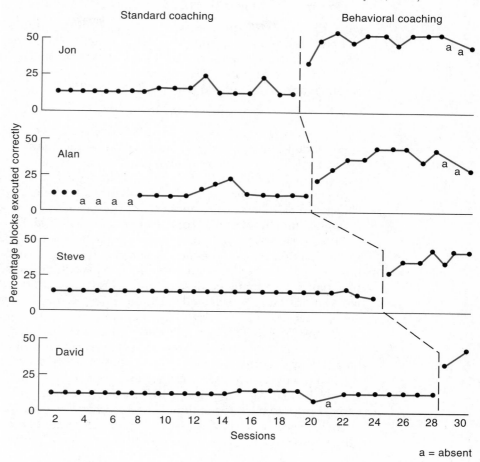

a = absent

In a study of verbal interaction among institutionalized mentally impaired persons, a multiple-baseline design across situations demonstrated that changes in the way meals were served influenced the frequency of mealtime language (VanBiervliet, Spangler, & Marshall, 1981). The investigators suggested that the typical institutional method of serving meals does not encourage peer interaction and that an alternative procedure, serving "family style," would increase verbal interactions. Baselines for frequency of verbalizations of five residents were made for three different situations (actually, three meals)—dinner, lunch, and breakfast. Behavior change was assessed in two ways: (a) by averaging the number of vocalizations made by the five residents, and (b) by examining individual behavioral records. Both measures showed that frequency of verbal behavior increased at each meal following the change in the way meals were served.

Methodological Issues Associated with Multiple-Baseline Designs

- How many baselines are needed?

Often the first question to arise when one is doing a multiple-baseline experiment is "How many baselines do I need?" As with many other aspects of single-case methodology, there are no hard-and-fast rules. The bare minimum is clearly two baselines, but this is generally considered inadequate. Three to four baselines are recommended (Hersen & Barlow, 1976).

- What if behavior changes *before* the intervention?

A convincing demonstration of a treatment's effectiveness rests on the observation that behavior changes immediately after the treatment or intervention is introduced. Thus, problems arise when changes are seen in a baseline *before* an experimental intervention. This may occur in any of the types of multiple-baseline designs we have considered, and the reasons are not always clear. When changes in baseline performance occur prior to an experimental intervention, it is often difficult to draw a conclusion about the efficacy of the experimental treatment. However, the multiple-baseline design can still be interpreted with some confidence when preintervention changes appear in only one of several baselines that are being recorded—so long as plausible explanations for the baseline change, explanations based on procedural or situational variables, are available. For instance, Kazdin and Erickson (1975) used a multiple-baseline design across subjects to help severely mentally impaired individuals respond to instructions. Participants who followed instructions were reinforced with candy-coated cereal and praise, and this intervention was introduced in each of four small groups at different points in time. Performance changed directly with the application of the positive reinforcement procedure in three groups, but not in the fourth. In this group, which had the longest baseline, behavior gradually improved prior to the intervention. The researchers reasonably suggested that this occurred because individuals in this group saw other patients comply with instructions and then imitated the treated participants' behavior.

- What if the treatment generalizes to other behaviors or situations?

Another problem sometimes seen in multiple-baseline designs occurs when changes in one behavior generalize to other behaviors or situations. For example, when researchers successfully increased the degree of verbal interaction of mentally impaired persons at a dinner meal, we might not have been totally surprised if the residents increased their amount of talking at other meals. Once behavior at dinner was changed, at other meals the sight of food being served or the act of sitting down beside an acquaintance might prompt an increased level of verbal interaction. Such generalization effects were not seen, however, so the effect of the mealtime intervention was clearly demonstrated (see VanBiervliet et al., 1981).

To circumvent possible problems of generalization, we must again bring foresight to bear. If altering the behavior of one individual is likely to affect the behaviors of others, if behavior in one situation is likely to influence behavior in another situation, or if changing one type of behavior is likely to affect other behaviors, then multiple-baseline designs may need to be modified or perhaps abandoned altogether (Kazdin, 1980, 1998). As we have noted, unless behavior improves directly following an experimental intervention, concluding that the treatment variable was effective is problematic. Unfortunately, anticipating when changes will occur simultaneously in more than one baseline is not always easy, but these problems appear to be relatively infrequent exceptions to the effects usually seen in a multiple-baseline design (Kazdin, 1998).

Problems and Limitations Common to All Single-Case Designs

- Interpreting the effect of a treatment can be difficult if the baseline stage shows excessive variability or increasing or decreasing trends in behavior.
- The problem of low external validity with single-case experiments can be reduced by testing small groups of individuals.
- Although psychologists can compare treatment and no-treatment conditions in single-case experiments, they cannot easily examine interactions among variables using this method.

Problems with Baseline Records   It is difficult to evaluate the effects of an intervention when there are increasing or decreasing baseline trends or excessive variability in behavioral records. An ideal baseline record and response to an intervention are shown in panel A of Figure 9.5. Behavior during baseline is very stable, and behavior changes immediately following the introduction of treatment. If this were the outcome of the first stages of either an ABAB or a multiple-baseline design, we would be headed in the direction of showing that our treatment is effective in modifying behavior. However, consider the baseline and

FIGURE 9.5   Examples of behavioral records showing possible relationships between baseline and intervention phases of a behavior modification program.

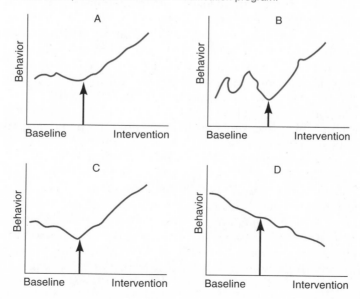

treatment stages shown in panel B of Figure 9.5. The baseline shows extreme variability, and, although the desired behavior appears to increase in frequency following an intervention, it is difficult to know whether the treatment produced the change or behavior just happened to be on the upswing. In this case it would be hard to decide whether our intervention successfully increased behavior.

There are several approaches to the problem of excessive baseline variability. One approach is to look for variables in the situation that might be producing the variability and could be removed. The presence of a particular staff member, for instance, might be causing changes in the behavior of a psychiatric patient. Another approach is to "wait it out"—to continue taking baseline measures until behavior stabilizes. It is, of course, not possible to predict when and if this might occur, but introducing an intervention before behavior has stabilized would jeopardize a clear interpretation of the experimental outcome. Another approach is to average data points. By charting a behavioral record using averages of several points, we can sometimes reduce the "appearance" of variability (Kazdin, 1978).

Another problem arises when the baseline record shows an increasing or a decreasing trend. In panel C of Figure 9.5, we see how behavior might change following an intervention when the initial baseline stage was characterized by a reduction in frequency of behavior. If the goal of the intervention was to increase frequency of behavior, the change described in panel C offers little problem of interpretation. An intervention that reversed the decreasing trend can be taken as evidence that the treatment was effective. However, should the goal of intervention be to reduce frequency of behavior, it would be difficult to know whether the decrease in frequency of behavior following the intervention is due to the intervention or to continuation of the baseline trend. This situation is illustrated in panel D. Here we see a decreasing trend in the baseline stage and continued reduction of frequency in the treatment stage. It is difficult in this case to know whether the experimental treatment had an effect. Generally speaking, when an intervention is expected to have an effect in the same direction as a baseline trend, the effect must be very marked in order to conclude that behavior was modified by the application of a treatment (Kazdin, 1978). Moreover, because a treatment effect in a single-case design is usually judged by visually inspecting the behavioral record, it is often difficult to say what constitutes a "marked" change in the behavioral record (see, for example, Parsonson & Baer, 1992). In such cases other means of evaluation should be employed, such as obtaining comparisons with "normal" individuals or asking for subjective evaluations from others familiar with the individual.

Questions of External Validity   When an effect is demonstrated using an $N = 1$ design, a frequent criticism is that external validity is limited. In other words, the $N = 1$ experiment appears to have the same limitation as the traditional case study method. Because each person is unique, it can be argued that there is no way of knowing whether the effect of a particular intervention will generalize to other individuals. There are several reasons why this problem may not be as serious as it seems. First, the types of intervention used in single-case studies are often potent ones and frequently produce dramatic and sizable changes in behavior (Kazdin, 1978). Consequently, these types of treatments are often found to generalize to other individuals. Other evidence for the generality of effects based on single-case studies comes from the use of multiple-baseline designs. A multiple-baseline design across subjects, for example, is often able to show that a particular intervention was successful in modifying the behavior of *several* individuals. Similarly, multiple baselines across situations and behaviors attest to the external validity of a treatment effect.

A treatment effect can also be shown to generalize to other individuals when a "single group" of subjects is used in a single-case experiment. As was mentioned before, the procedures associated with single-case designs are sometimes used with small groups of individuals as well. We have already seen two examples of this. VanBiervliet et al. (1981) showed that changes in a mealtime procedure were effective in increasing the average frequency of verbalizations of five mentally impaired individuals who were treated simultaneously. Similarly, Kazdin and Erickson (1975) found that positive reinforcement improved responsiveness to instructions in small groups of mentally impaired individuals. In both experiments, the researchers were able to demonstrate that an experimental treatment was, on average, effective for a small group of participants as well as for individuals in the group. In other words, an effect was replicated several times across members of a group each time an experimental manipulation was introduced. Such studies offer impressive evidence for both internal and external validity.

Interaction Effects   One limitation of the $N = 1$ methodology is not easily dismissed, and it illustrates again the lesson that no one research methodology is able to provide all the answers to questions that psychologists ask. The $N = 1$ experiment is not always appropriate for examining the effect of interactions among variables. For instance, although a single-case design can provide evidence of the effect of one variable (a main effect) by showing, for example, that behavior changes between conditions of No Treatment and Treatment, it is difficult to examine adequately the differential effect of combinations of various treatments and individual differences variables (Kazdin, 1998). In this situation, a large group design is often most appropriate (see especially Chapter 8). The experienced research psychologist realizes that there are problems and limitations associated with most methodologies. The methodology best suited to answering a particular question should be used. And, as we have stated previously, when possible, multimethod approaches to data collection are recommended.

Ethical Issues in Single-Case Designs

- Psychologists are sometimes faced with the ethical dilemma of removing an apparently effective treatment in order to demonstrate its efficacy.
- Psychologists must carefully consider the risk/benefit ratio when behavior modification treatments involve punishment.

Two particularly salient ethical issues associated with single-case research should be mentioned. One of these we have already discussed briefly, namely, the withholding of an effective treatment as is required in the ABAB design. Ethical issues arise when treatments aimed at reducing painful or harmful events are shown to improve behavior (e.g., in the first, or treatment stage of an ABAB design) and then are withdrawn (in the second baseline stage) to provide more conclusive evidence of the treatment's efficacy. As you saw, one solution is to change research designs and use a multiple-baseline design in which treatments need not be withheld. This would be an appropriate and obvious strategy in many situations, especially if previous research has demonstrated a treatment's worth and the behavior being modified is clearly harmful. In some situations, however, whether a treatment will be effective is clearly an unanswered question (after all, we do research to find out if a treatment *will* work!) and the benefits of the treatment may not be entirely clear.

Consider, for example, research aimed at increasing the use of designated drivers to reduce alcohol-related driving accidents (see Brigham, Meier, & Goodner, 1995). Researchers used an ABAB design in which the treatment involved placing posters and table signs offering free nonalcoholic drinks to designated drivers at a bar frequented by college students. The dependent measure was the number of persons on a given weekend evening who registered with the bartender as designated drivers. Visual inspection of the graphed results revealed a clear effect of the prompts and free nonalcoholic drinks during the first treatment stage, then a reversal to baseline frequency when the prompts and drink offer were withdrawn, and finally, an increase in frequency again when the prompts and soft beverages were reinstated. Thus, we can suggest that drivers leaving the bar were "safer" when the signs were in evidence. Should an alternative design have been used to avoid the reversal during the second baseline stage?

Another ethical problem sometimes associated with single-case research concerns the nature of the treatment. Behavior modification using a noxious or aversive treatment is one example. Lovaas, for example, has used "aversives" such as mild electric shock with autistic and schizophrenic children in order to develop appropriate social responses (e.g., Lovaas, 1993; Lovaas, Schaeffer, & Simmons, 1965). This research has generated considerable controversy despite the fact that the aversive treatments were used only when other methods had failed and the alternative appeared even more injurious. That is, the success of these treatments apparently saved some individuals from permanent institutionalization and little hope of successful therapeutic intervention. This type of research clearly illustrates the often difficult nature of ethical decision making. Is the risk to the participant outweighed by the benefit of the treatment? It is interesting to note that the French doctor, Itard, who tried to rehabilitate the "wild boy" of Aveyron faced a similar vexing ethical dilemma (see Shattuck, 1994). At one point during training the boy became so frustrated and upset that he threw tantrums, biting the mantelpiece, tossing burning coals around the room, even losing consciousness. When this behavior was continually repeated the doctor had to decide whether to halt training or try somehow to control the tantrums. Itard decided on a most unconventional, but, as it turns out, highly effective

FIGURE 9.6   Research using an ABAB design revealed that offering free nonalcoholic drinks to designated drivers increased the frequency with which people registered with the bartender as designated drivers (Brigham, Meier, & Goodner, 1995).

treatment: He forcibly held the boy (who was afraid of heights) out the fifth-floor window. The boy was clearly scared and apparently cried for the first time, but training was able to proceed. Determining whether a treatment is justified requires careful consideration of all relevant factors and, as we noted in Chapter 2, consultation with knowledgeable others when the risk/benefit ratio is not easily calculated. Of course, these questions must be raised whenever research involves a potentially harmful treatment, and is not just associated with the use of single-case designs.

SUMMARY

Two important single-case research designs are the case study and the single-case experiment, or $N = 1$ design. The case study method can be an important source of hypotheses about behavior, can provide an opportunity for clinical innovation (e.g., trying out new approaches to therapy), can permit the intensive study of rare phenomena, can challenge theoretical assumptions, and can provide tentative support for a psychological theory. The intensive study of individuals that is the hallmark of the case study method is called idiographic research, and it can be viewed as complementary to the nomothetic inquiry (seeking general laws or principles) that is also characteristic of psychology. Problems arise when the case study method is used to draw cause-effect conclusions, or when biases in the collection of, or interpretation of, data are not identified. The case study method also suffers from a lack of generalizability. How do we generalize on the basis of studying a single individual? Moreover, the "dramatic" results obtained from some case studies, though they may give scientific investigators important insights, are frequently accepted as valid by nonscientists who are not aware of the limitations of this method.

Behaviorism is an approach to the study of psychology that emphasizes the study of observable behavior under strictly controlled conditions. The behaviorism of B. F. Skinner is called the experimental analysis of behavior. Applied behavior analysis seeks to apply principles derived from an experimental analysis of behavior to socially relevant problems. The major methodology of this approach is the single-case experiment, or $N = 1$ design. Although there are many kinds of $N = 1$ designs, the most common are the ABAB design and the multiple-baseline design.

An ABAB design, or reversal design, allows a researcher to confirm a treatment effect by showing that behavior changes systematically with conditions of No Treatment (baseline) and Treatment. Methodological problems arise in this design when behavior that changed during the first treatment (B) stage does not reverse when treatment is withdrawn during the second baseline (A) stage. When this occurs, it is difficult to establish that the treatment, rather than some other factor, was responsible for the initial change. One may encounter ethical problems when using the ABAB design if a treatment that has been shown to be beneficial is withdrawn during the second baseline stage.

A multiple-baseline design demonstrates the effectiveness of a treatment by showing that behaviors across more than one baseline change as a consequence of the introduction of a treatment. Baselines are first established across different individuals, across behaviors in the same individual, or across situations. Methodological problems arise when behavior does not change immediately with the introduction of a treatment or when a treatment effect generalizes to other individuals, other behaviors, or other situations.

Problems of increasing or decreasing baselines, as well as excessive baseline variability, sometimes make it difficult to interpret the outcome of single-case designs. The problem of excessive baseline variability can be approached by seeking out and removing sources of variability, by extending the time during which baseline observations are made, or by averaging data points to remove the "appearance" of variability. Increasing or decreasing baselines may require the researcher to obtain other kinds of evidence for the effectiveness of a treatment—for example, measures of social comparison or subjective evaluation.

Finally, the $N = 1$ design is often criticized for its lack of external validity. However, because treatments typically produce substantial changes in behavior, these changes can often be easily replicated in different individuals. The use of single "groups" of subjects can also provide immediate evidence of generality across subjects. Treatments that are clearly aversive to the participants should only be used after careful consideration of the ethical implications, including the risk/benefit ratio.

The fact that the $N = 1$ design usually is not appropriate for testing the possible interactions of variables highlights the importance of selecting the research methodology that is most relevant for answering the particular question under investigation.

KEY CONCEPTS

case study
nomothetic approach
idiographic approach
behavior modification/
    behavior therapy
single-case experiment

baseline stage
ABAB design
multiple-baseline design (across
    individuals, across behaviors,
    across situations)

REVIEW QUESTIONS

1 Cite and give an example of the advantages of the case study method.
2 Distinguish between a nomothetic and an idiographic approach to research.
3 Cite and give an example of the disadvantages of the case study method.
4 What is the major limitation of the case study method in drawing cause-effect conclusions?
5 Under what conditions might a single-case ($N = 1$) design be more appropriate than a multiple-group design?
6 Distinguish between baseline and intervention stages of a single-case ($N = 1$) experimental design.
7 Why is an ABAB design also called a reversal design?
8 What major methodological problems are specifically associated with an ABAB design?
9 Outline the general rationale behind all the major forms of multiple-baseline designs.
10 What major methodological problems are specifically associated with multiple-baseline designs?
11 What major methodological problems are inherent in all single-case ($N = 1$) experimental designs?
12 How would you respond to the frequent criticism that single-case ($N = 1$) experimental designs lack external validity?
13 What types of research questions are not easily answered using single-case ($N = 1$) experimental designs?

CHALLENGE QUESTIONS

1 A case study showing how "mud therapy" was successful in treating an individual exhibiting excessive anxiety was reported in a popular magazine. The patient's symptoms included having trouble sleeping, loss of appetite, extreme nervousness when in groups of people, and general feelings of arousal that led the individual always to feel "on edge" and fearful. The California therapist who administered the mud therapy was known for this treatment, having appeared on several TV talk shows. He first taught the patient a deep relaxation technique and a "secret word" to repeat over and over in order to block out all disturbing thoughts. Then the patient was asked to lie submerged for two hours each day in a special wooden "calm tub" filled with mud. During this time the patient was to practice the relaxation exercises and to concentrate on repeating the secret word whenever the least bit of anxiety was experienced. The therapy was very costly, but after six weeks the patient reported to the therapist that he no longer had the same feelings of anxiety that he had had before. The therapist pronounced him cured and attributed the success of the treatment to immersion in the calming mud. The conclusion drawn by the author of the magazine article describing this therapy was that "it is a treatment that many people could benefit from." On the basis of your knowledge of the limitations of the case study method, answer the following questions:

   A What possible sources of bias were there in the study?
   B What alternative explanations can you suggest for the successful treatment?
   C What problem arises from studying only one individual?

2 A 5-year-old child frequently gets skin rashes, and the mother has been told by her family doctor that the problem is due to "something" that the child eats. The doctor suggests that she "watch carefully" what the child eats. The mother decides to approach this problem by recording each day whether the child has a rash and what the child has eaten the day before. She hopes to find some relationship between eating a particular food and the presence or absence of the rash. Although this approach might help discover a relationship between eating certain foods and the appearance of the rash, a better approach might be one based on the logic and procedures associated with $N = 1$ designs. Explain how the mother might use such an alternative approach. Be specific and point to possible problems that may arise in this application of behavioral methodology.

3 During the summer months you find employment in a camp for mildly mentally impaired children. As a counselor you are asked to supervise a small group of children, as well as to look for ways to improve their attention to various camp activities that take place indoors (e.g., craft making and sewing). You decide to explore the possibility of using a system of rewards (M&M candies) for "time on task." You realize that the camp director will want evidence of the effectiveness of your intervention strategy as well as some assurance that it will work with other children in the camp. Therefore you are to:

   A Plan an intervention strategy based on operant principles that has as its goal an increase in the time children spend on a camp activity.
   B Explain what behavioral records you will need to keep and how you will determine whether your intervention has produced a change in the children's behavior. You will need, for example, to specify exactly when and how you will

measure behavior, as well as to justify your use of a particular design to carry out your "experiment."

C Describe the argument you will use to convince the director that your intervention strategy (assuming that it works) will work with other, similar children.

4 A schoolteacher asks your help in planning a behavioral intervention that will help manage the behavior of a problem child in his classroom. The child does not stay at her desk when asked to do so, does not remain quiet during "quiet times," and exhibits other behaviors that disrupt the teaching environment. Explain specifically how a positive reinforcer, such as candy or small toys, might be used as part of a multiple-baseline across behaviors design to improve the child's behavior.

Answer to Challenge Question 1

A One source of bias in this case study was that the same individual served as therapist and as researcher with the commensurate problems of observer bias. A second source of bias is that the therapist based his conclusion solely on the self-reports of the patient.

B The successful treatment may have resulted from the relaxation technique alone; the use of the "secret word" in the face of anxiety; attention the patient received from the therapist; or even the high cost of the treatment.

C The major problem that arises from studying one individual is a potential lack of external validity.

Quasi-Experimental Designs and Program Evaluation

CHAPTER OUTLINE

OVERVIEW
DIFFERENCES BETWEEN LABORATORY EXPERIMENTS AND
    EXPERIMENTS IN NATURAL SETTINGS
Control
External Validity
Goals
Consequences
TRUE EXPERIMENTS
Characteristics of True Experiments
Obstacles to Conducting True Experiments in Natural Settings
Threats to Internal Validity Controlled by True Experiments
Problems That Even True Experiments May Not Eliminate
QUASI-EXPERIMENTS
The Nonequivalent Control Group Design
Nonequivalent Control Group Design: The Langer and Rodin
    Study
Sources of Invalidity in the Nonequivalent Control Group
    Design
The Issue of External Validity
Interrupted Time-Series Designs
Time Series with Nonequivalent Control Group
AN EXTENSION OF SINGLE-CASE DESIGNS TO RESEARCH
    IN NATURAL SETTINGS
Rationale
The ABAB Design
PROGRAM EVALUATION
SUMMARY

OVERVIEW

In the most general sense, an experiment is a test; it is a procedure used to find out something not presently known. In this sense we experiment when we add new ingredients to a chili recipe in order to see whether they improve its taste. We experiment with new ways to catch fish by changing the lures we use. We experiment when we take a different route to our job in order to find a faster way to commute. As you no doubt recognize, however, these kinds of informal "experiments" are much different from those experiments typically carried out in the conduct of psychological research. Experimental methods, unlike other research techniques such as observation and surveys, are viewed as the most efficient way to determine causation. But determining causation is not always easy, and in the last few chapters you were introduced to the complexity of the task facing the researcher who seeks to understand a phenomenon by discovering what caused it.

In this chapter we continue our discussion of experimental methods, but we focus on experiments as they are conducted in natural settings. You will see that the task of drawing cause-effect conclusions often becomes even more difficult, and that new problems arise, when an investigator leaves the confines of the laboratory to experiment in natural settings.

There are many reasons why experiments are carried out in natural settings. One important reason (mentioned in Chapter 6) for these "field experiments" is to test the external validity of a laboratory finding. We seek to find out if a treatment effect observed in the laboratory works in a similar way in another setting. Other reasons for experimenting in natural settings are more practical in that they are likely to be associated with attempts to improve conditions under which people live and work. The government may experiment with a new tax system or a new method of job training for the economically disadvantaged. Schools may experiment by changing lunch programs, after-school care, or curricula. A business may experiment with new product designs, methods of delivering employee benefits, or flexible work hours. In these cases, as is true in the laboratory, it is important to determine whether the "treatment" caused a change. Did a change in the way patients are admitted to a hospital emergency room cause patients to be treated more quickly and efficiently? Did a college energy conservation program cause a decrease in energy consumption? Knowing whether a treatment was effective permits us to make important decisions about continuing the treatment, about spending additional money, about investing more time and effort, or about changing the present situation on the basis of our knowledge of the results. Research that seeks to determine the effectiveness of changes made by institutions, government agencies, and other units of society is one goal of the discipline of *program evaluation*.

In this chapter we discuss the problems of conducting experiments in natural settings. We describe obstacles to doing true experiments in such settings, and we discuss ways of overcoming these obstacles so that true experiments are done whenever possible. Nevertheless, true experiments are sometimes not feasible outside the laboratory. In these cases, experimental procedures that only approximate the conditions of laboratory experiments must be considered. We discuss several of these quasi-experimental techniques. Problems with quasi-experimentation make us realize the value of true experiments, so we briefly consider alternatives to quasi-experiments in natural settings. One such alternative is the extension of single-case experimental designs (which we discussed in Chapter 9) to research in natural settings. We conclude the chapter by providing a brief introduction to the logic, procedures, and limitations of program evaluation.

DIFFERENCES BETWEEN LABORATORY EXPERIMENTS AND EXPERIMENTS IN NATURAL SETTINGS

- Experiments conducted in a laboratory setting differ from experiments conducted in a natural setting in terms of control, external validity, goals, and consequences.
- Researchers usually have less control over experimental conditions in natural settings than in laboratories.
- As control decreases, researchers' ability to make causal inferences also decreases.
- Research is conducted in natural settings to establish the external validity of findings from laboratory studies.
- Basic research is carried out with the goal of understanding a phenomenon, whereas applied research is usually done with the goal of improving the present situation.
- Research conducted in natural settings tends to have greater impact on the lives of more individuals than research conducted in laboratories.

There are some important considerations to keep in mind as we discuss experimentation in natural settings. Experimentation outside the confines of the psychology laboratory is likely to differ from laboratory research in a number of significant ways. Not every experiment in a natural setting differs from laboratory experiments in all of these ways, of course. But if you are thinking of doing research in a natural setting, we urge you to consider the following critical issues.

Control

More than anything else, the scientist is concerned with control. Only by controlling those factors that are assumed to influence a phenomenon can one make a decision about what caused it. As you have seen in previous chapters, control takes several forms. The random assignment of participants to conditions of an experiment is a method of control used to balance participant characteristics in treatment and no-treatment conditions. Other factors that are likely to influence a phenomenon may be controlled by holding them constant. In a natural setting, a researcher may not always have the same degree of control over conditions of an experiment or over assignment of participants as in a laboratory. A field experiment may have to be conducted according to the availability of participants or at the discretion of an administrator or government official. Natural settings place various restrictions on an experiment that limit the researcher's control. It is even possible that an investigator may not directly participate in the planning and conduct of the "experiment" but may be asked afterward whether a treatment "worked." This kind of situation is clearly the most difficult because important factors may not have been considered in planning or executing the intervention.

As an illustration, consider the following situation. As you saw in Chapter 1, many people frequently are too willing to believe in paranormal phenomena, including ESP and the claims of so-called "psychics." These beliefs may be due to deficiencies in human reasoning and in science education (e.g., Singer & Benassi, 1981). One response has been the creation of "critical thinking" and "science vs. pseudoscience" courses at the college level (e.g., Morier & Keeports, 1994). A reasonable question is, Do such courses "work"? That is, do students who take these courses acquire a more critical view of paranormal phenomena? The treatment in this case is exposure to the material and ideas presented in the course. The dependent variable might be responses to a questionnaire asking about belief in paranormal phenomena and the occult. We would like to know whether or not such courses "cause" a change in people's views of these ideas and events. However, you no doubt can see problems with this "experiment." Students are most likely not randomly assigned to take such a course. Are the students taking such a course already critical about paranormal claims, or did they take the course because of their interest and belief in paranormal phenomena? With whom do we compare the students in the course? Are there possible changes in students' views over time *that might occur independently of the course* and that need to be taken into account? What other events are not controlled in such a situation that might influence people's attitudes toward paranormal phenomena? In order to find out whether the treatment worked, a researcher faces a host of problems that arise due to the lack of control over the situation. Later, we will describe results of a published study that sought to answer this question: Can students be taught to be more critical of paranormal phenomena?

External Validity

Field experiments are sometimes conducted with the goal of establishing the external validity of a laboratory finding. The "artificial" environment of the psychology laboratory, which increases the internal validity of research because of the high degree of control, often decreases the external validity of the findings. Experiments in natural settings may therefore need to be conducted in order to generalize results beyond the laboratory situation.

On the other hand, as you saw in Chapter 6, the external validity of a laboratory experiment may not be all that important (e.g., Mook, 1983). This may be particularly true when an experiment is done simply to test a specific psychological theory. In contrast, the external validity of research done in natural settings is often very important because the focus of such research is frequently on a treatment's general effectiveness. This is especially true when social experimentation serves as the basis for large-scale social changes, such as trying out new ways to curb drunk driving or new procedures for registering voters.

If the results of a field experiment are to be used to plan further interventions or to implement similar programs in other locations or different regions of the country, then it is vital to know to what extent the treatment and results can be generalized. For example, legislators may wish to generalize to a different state certain procedures that have been shown to produce an increase in voter registration in one state. A method to increase employee morale that succeeded in one branch of a company may be considered by company officials for all branches of the company. Will the results of a reading program that is judged to be beneficial at one grade level in one school generalize to other grade levels, other schools, or situations where it is implemented by different personnel? Does a course found to improve students' critical thinking skills at one college also "work" at other colleges? These are, of course, all questions of external validity.

Goals

Experimentation in natural settings often has different goals from laboratory research. One major difference are the goals associated with basic and applied research. **Basic research** is often carried out with the single goal of understanding a phenomenon, of determining how "nature" works. It may be done to gain knowledge merely for knowledge's sake. **Applied research** is also directed toward discovering the reasons for a phenomenon, but it is likely to be done only when knowing the reasons for an event will lead to changes that will modify or improve the present situation. Experimentation in natural settings, therefore, is more likely to have practical goals. As you saw above, this is one reason why questions of external validity are more important for field experiments than they are for laboratory experiments.

Consequences

Sometimes experiments are conducted that have far-reaching impact on communities and society, affecting large numbers of people. For example, during the 1970s the U.S. government experimented with the "new town" concept. Thirteen new towns were created under government sponsorship. Beginning from scratch, designers tried to avoid all the problems of older unplanned urban communities. Towns such as Columbia, Maryland, and Reston, Virginia, are examples. Another example of an experiment by the U.S. government was a program designed to aid prisoners following release from incarceration (see Berk, Boruch, Chambers, Rossi, & Witte, 1987). Individuals released from prison often have little in the way of resources to help them begin a new life, and they frequently have difficulty finding jobs. This economic hardship can contribute to new crime. The program involved random assignment of ex-prisoners to groups that either received financial assistance on leaving prison or did not receive financial assistance. The program targeted as participants about 2,000 ex-prisoners in Texas and Georgia.

Clearly, these examples of society's "experiments," as well as those we might imagine being carried out on a smaller scale in natural settings (such as those conducted in schools or businesses), are likely to have consequences of greater immediate impact than those of laboratory research. Consider that the Head Start program for disadvantaged children and the *Sesame Street* television show were social experiments designed to improve the education of literally hundreds of thousands of children across the nation. Experiments in businesses may be carried out with the eventual goal of reducing the number of employees or in other ways affecting the quality of employees' lives. Moreover, as is true of all experiments, the consequences are not always those that were anticipated. Although a few planned communities worked, others did not, and planners and builders went bankrupt (see *Time,* October 16, 1978, p. 84). Although the prison release program produced some identifiable positive results, it was also found to be responsible for an *increase* in crime, apparently due to the ex-prisoners' freedom from having to work (see Berk et al., 1987).

In order to draw meaningful conclusions about the effects of these experiments, we must consider the design and implementation of these "treatments" and to do the best we can to assess as clearly as possible whether the treatments

FIGURE 10.1 As a social experiment, *Sesame Street* was designed to improve the education of hundreds of thousands of children.

worked. This is especially important because, as we have seen, the consequences of such experiments frequently are so great in terms of money spent and the number of people whose lives are affected. By contrast, the consequences of a laboratory experiment are likely to be minimal. They may directly affect only the lives of a few researchers and of those relatively few participants recruited to participate.

TRUE EXPERIMENTS

Characteristics of True Experiments

- In true experiments, researchers manipulate an independent variable with treatment and comparison condition(s) and exercise a high degree of control (especially through random assignment to conditions).

Although many everyday activities (such as altering the ingredients of a recipe) might be called experiments, we would not consider them "true" experiments in the sense in which experimentation has been discussed in this textbook. Analogously, many "social experiments" carried out by the government (such as the "new town" concept) and those that are conducted by company officials or educational administrators are also not true experiments. *A true experiment is one that leads to an unambiguous outcome regarding what caused an event.* True experiments exhibit three important characteristics:

1 In a true experiment some type of intervention or treatment is implemented.

2 True experiments are marked by the high degree of control that an experimenter has over the arrangement of experimental conditions, assignment of participants, systematic manipulation of independent variables, and choice of dependent variables. The ability to assign participants randomly to experimental conditions is often seen as the most critical defining characteristic of the true experiment (Judd et al., 1991).

3 Finally, true experiments are characterized by an appropriate comparison. Indeed, the experimenter exerts control over a situation principally in order to establish a proper comparison to evaluate the effectiveness of a treatment. In the simplest of experimental situations, this comparison is one between two groups that are treated exactly alike except for the variable of interest.

When the conditions of a true experiment are met, any differences in a dependent variable that arise can logically be assigned to the differences between levels of the independent variable.

Obstacles to Conducting True Experiments in Natural Settings

- Researchers may experience difficulty gaining access to participants and permission to conduct true experiments in natural settings.
- Although random assignment is viewed by some as unfair because it may deprive individuals from a new treatment, it is still the best way and fairest way to determine if a new treatment is effective.

Experimental research is an effective tool for solving problems and answering questions. Nevertheless, two major obstacles often arise when we try to carry out experiments in natural settings. The first problem is obtaining permission to do the research from individuals in positions of authority. Unless they believe that the research will be useful, school board presidents and government and business leaders are unlikely to support research financially or otherwise.

The second, and often more pressing, obstacle to doing experiments in natural settings is the problem of access to participants. This problem can prove especially troublesome if participants are to be randomly assigned to either a treatment group or a comparison group.

Random assignment to conditions appears unfair at first—after all, random assignment requires that a potentially beneficial treatment be withheld from at least some participants. Suppose that a new approach to the teaching of foreign languages was to be tested at your college or university. Suppose further that, when you went to register for your next semester's classes, you were told that you would be randomly assigned to one of two sections taught at the time you selected—one section involving the old method and one involving the new method. How would you react? Your knowledge of research methods tells you that the two methods must be administered to comparable groups of students and that random assignment is the best way to ensure such comparability. Nonetheless, you might be tempted to feel that random assignment is not fair, especially if you are assigned to the section using the old (old-fashioned?) method. Let's take a closer look at the fairness of random assignment.

If those responsible for selecting the method of foreign language instruction already knew that the new method was more effective than the old method at schools such as yours, there would be little justification for testing the method again. Under such circumstances we would agree that withholding the new method from students in the control group would be unjust. If we do not know whether the new method is better, however, any approach other than conducting a true experiment will leave us in doubt about the new method's effectiveness. Random assignment to treatments—call it a "lottery" if you prefer—may be the fairest procedure for assigning students to sections. The old method of instruction, after all, was considered effective before the development of the new method. If the new method proves less effective, random assignment will have actually "protected" the control participants from receiving an ineffective treatment.

There are ways to offer a potentially effective treatment to all participants while still maintaining comparable groups. One way is to alternate treatments. For example, Atkinson (1968) randomly assigned students to receive computer-assisted instruction in either English or math (the "treatment") and then tested both groups in English and math. Each group served as a control for the other on the test for which its members had not received computer-assisted instruction. After completing the experiment, both groups could then be given computer-assisted instruction in the subject matter to which they had not been previously exposed. Thus, all participants received all potentially beneficial treatments.

Establishing a proper control group is also possible if there is more demand for a service than an agency can meet. People who are waiting to receive the service can become a "waiting list" control group. It is essential, however, that people be assigned to the waiting list randomly. People who are "first in line" are no doubt different on important dimensions from those who arrive last (e.g., more eager for treatment). Random assignment is necessary to distribute these characteristics in an unbiased way between treatment and comparison groups.

There will always be circumstances in which random assignment simply cannot be used. For example, in clinical trials involving tests of new medical treatments, it may be extremely difficult to get patients to agree to be randomly assigned to either the treatment group or the control group. As you will see, quasi-experimental designs can be used in these situations. The logic and procedures for these quasi-experimental designs will be described later in this chapter.

Threats to Internal Validity Controlled by True Experiments

- Threats to internal validity are confoundings that serve as plausible alternative explanations for a research finding.
- The major classes of threats to internal validity include history, maturation, testing, instrumentation, regression, selection, subject mortality, and interactions with selection.

One way to evaluate an experiment is to determine what kinds of alternative explanations for a phenomenon have been controlled. Prior to doing an experiment, we might look to see what major classes of possible explanations are ruled out by our experimental procedure. Only by eliminating all possible alternative explanations can we arrive at a definite conclusion about cause and effect. In previous chapters, we referred to various uncontrolled factors that threaten the internal validity of an experiment as confounding factors (they are also called confounds). Several types of confounds were identified in earlier chapters (see especially Chapter 6). We will now list eight classes of confounds, using the terminology of Campbell and Stanley (1966; see also Cook & Campbell, 1979). You have already been introduced to some of these **threats to internal validity;** others will be new. After reviewing the major classes of confounds, we will be able to judge the extent to which various experimental procedures control for these kinds of alternative explanations of a treatment effect.

History   The occurrence of an event other than the treatment can threaten internal validity if it produces changes in the research participants' behavior. A true experiment requires that participants in the experimental group and in the control group be treated the same (have the same history of experiences while in the experiment) except for the treatment. In the laboratory, this is usually accomplished by balancing or holding conditions constant. For example, the same experimenter might be asked to test people in all conditions of an experiment. If different experimenters were to test experimental and control participants, we would confound the possible effect due to the experimenter and that of the treatment. That is, the "history" of the two groups in the experiment would differ if different experimenters were used for each group. When doing experiments in natural settings, the researcher may not always be able to exercise the degree of control associated with laboratory settings, so confounding due to history can be a threat to internal validity. For example, suppose that you set out to test whether a college-level critical thinking course did, in fact, change students' thinking. And suppose further that your test was simply to examine students' performance on a critical thinking test at the beginning of the critical thinking course and then again at the end of the course. History would be a threat to internal validity if events other than the treatment (i.e., the critical thinking course) occurred that might improve the critical thinking abilities of the students. For example, suppose that many students taking this course also took it upon themselves to view a video designed to teaching critical thinking that wasn't required for the course, and also purchased extra books and pamphlets to help them think more critically. This particular history of experiences would confound the treatment.

Maturation   Participants in an experiment necessarily change as a function of time. They grow older, become more experienced, and so forth. Change associated with the passage of time per se is called maturation. For example, suppose a researcher is interested in assessing children's learning over a school year using a new teaching technique. Without a proper comparison a researcher might attribute the changes in performance between a pretest and a posttest of a group of schoolchildren to the effect of the teaching intervention when, in reality, the changes were simply due to the normal processes of maturation.

Testing   Taking a test generally has an effect on subsequent testing. Consider, for example, the fact that many students often improve from the initial test in a course to the second test. The familiarity with the testing procedure and with the instructor's expectations that they gain during the first test affects their performance on the second test. Likewise, in the context of a psychology experiment in which more than one test is given (e.g., in a pretest-posttest design), testing is a threat to internal validity if the effect of a treatment cannot be separated from the effect of testing. Can you see how an attempt to assess the effect of a critical thinking course would be problematic if the assessment is simply the same students' scores on a pretest and a posttest?

Instrumentation   It is possible that changes over time take place not only in the participants of an experiment (e.g., maturation or increased familiarity with testing), but also in the instruments used to measure the participants' performance. This is most clearly a possibility when human observers are used to assess behavior. As you learned in previous chapters (see especially Chapter 3), observer bias can result from fatigue, expectations, and other characteristics of observers. For example, as a researcher becomes more experienced in making observations, there is likely to be a change in the quality of the observations that she or he makes. Unless controlled for, these changes in instrumentation can threaten internal validity by providing alternative explanations for differences in behavior between one observation period and another. Mechanical instruments also may change with repeated use. A researcher known to the authors once found that a machine used to present material in a learning experiment was not working the same at the end of the experiment as it was at the beginning. Measures made near the end of the experiment differed from those made at the beginning of the experiment. Thus, what looked like a learning effect was really just a change in the instruments used to measure learning.

Regression   Statistical **regression** is always a problem when individuals have been selected to participate in an experiment because of their "extreme" scores. As summarized by Cook and Campbell (1979, pp. 52–53), statistical regression

> (1) operates to increase obtained pretest-posttest gain scores among low pretest scores, since this group's pretest scores are more likely to have been depressed by error; (2) operates to decrease obtained change scores among persons with high pretest scores since their pretest scores are likely to have been inflated by error; and (3) does not affect obtained change scores among scorers at the center of the pretest distribution since the group is likely to contain as many units whose pretest scores are inflated by error as units whose pretest scores are deflated by it. Regression is always to the population mean of a group.

In other words, a very, very bad performance, or a very, very good performance (both of which we have all experienced), is likely to be followed by a performance that is not quite so bad, or not quite so good, respectively. Consider, for instance, your best ever performance on a classroom examination. What did it take to "nail" this test? It took no doubt a lot of hard work. But it is also likely that luck was involved. Everything has to work just right to produce an extremely good performance. If we are talking about an exam, then it is likely that the material tested was that which you just happened to study the hardest, or the test format was one you particularly like, or it came at a time when you were feeling particularly confident, and so forth (or all of these and more). Particularly good performances are, as Cook and Campbell (1979) stated, "extreme" because they are inflated (over our usual or typical performance) by chance (error). Similarly, an especially bad test performance is likely to have occurred because of some bad luck. When tested again (following either a very good or a very bad performance), it is just not likely that chance factors will "gang up" the same way to give us that super (inflated) score or that very poor (depressed) score. We will, as Cook and Campbell suggest, likely see a performance closer to the average of our overall scores.

Now, consider an attempt to raise the academic performance of a group of college students who have performed very poorly during their first semester of college (the "pretest"). Of course, participants are selected *because of their extreme performance* (in this case, extremely poor performance). Let us assume that a treatment (e.g., a 10-hour study skills workshop) is then applied. Statistical regression is a threat to internal validity since we would expect these students to perform slightly better after the second semester (the "posttest") *without any treatment* simply due to statistical regression. An unknowing researcher may mistakenly confuse this "regression effect" with a "treatment effect." Consider people who sign up to be treated first in a psychotherapy program. Are these individuals seeking treatment early because their symptoms are particularly bad at this time? If so, do you see how these people might show signs of improvement over their pretherapy screening when tested later, whether or not they received therapy?

Selection   When, from the outset of a study, differences exist between the kinds of individuals in one group and those in another group in the experiment, there is a confounding due to selection. That is, the people who are in the treatment group may differ from people in the comparison group in many ways *other* than their group assignment. In the laboratory, this threat to internal validity is generally handled by balancing participant characteristics through random assignment. When one is doing experiments in natural settings, there are often many obstacles to randomization of participants to treatment and comparison conditions. These obstacles prevent doing a true experiment and hence present a possible confound due to selection.

Subject Mortality   When participants are lost from an experiment, there is a threat to internal validity. (Possible reasons for participant loss were discussed in Chapter 6.) The threat to internal validity rests on the assumption that participant loss (attrition) changes the nature of a group from that established prior to the introduction of the treatment—for example, by destroying the equivalence of groups that had been established through randomization. This might occur, for instance, if an experimental task is very difficult and causes some experimental participants to become frustrated and to drop out of the experiment. Participants who are left in the experimental group will differ from those who dropped out (and possibly from those in a control group) if for no other reason than that they were able to do the task (or at least stuck it out).

Interactions with Selection   Several of the foregoing threats to internal validity can be a source of additional concern because they can interact with characteristics of groups of individuals selected for an experiment. Specifically, when comparable groups are not formed by random assignment, there are possible problems due to interactions between (1) selection and history, (2) selection and maturation, and (3) selection and instrumentation. Basically, this means that one or more groups of participants respond differently to effects associated with history, maturation, or instrumentation. For example, if groups of participants in an experiment mature at different rates, then differences between groups in the form of changes from pretest to posttest may be due to an interaction of selection and maturation rather than to any treatment. Such might be the case if first-year students in college who served as an experimental group were compared with sophomores who served as a control group. Changes in students that occur during their first year (as students gain familiarity with the college environment) might be presumed to be greater than such changes that occur during the second or sophomore year. These differences in maturation rates might explain any observed differences between the experimental and control groups, rather than any experimental intervention.

An interaction of selection and history results when events occurring in time have a different effect on one group of participants than on another. This is particularly a problem when intact groups are compared. Perhaps due to events that are peculiar to one group's situation, an event may have more of an impact on that group than on another. Consider, for example, research involving an investigation of the effectiveness of an AIDS awareness campaign involving two college campuses (one treatment and one control). Nationwide media attention to this problem might reasonably be assumed to affect students on both campuses equally. However, if a prominent student with AIDS died at one college during this period, and the story was featured in the college newspaper, we would assume that students at this student's college would be affected differently from those at the other. In terms of assessing the effect of an AIDS awareness campaign, this situation would represent an interaction of selection and history.

Finally, an interaction of selection and instrumentation might occur if a test instrument is relatively more sensitive to changes in one group's performance than to changes in another's. This occurs, for instance, when ceiling or floor effects are present. Such is the case when a group scores initially so low on an instrument (*floor effect*), that any further drop in scores cannot be reliably measured, or so high (*ceiling effect*) that any more gain cannot be assessed. As you can imagine, a confound would be present if an experimental group showed relatively no change (due to floor or ceiling effects), while a control group changed reliably because its mean performance was initially near the middle of the measurement scale.

A true experiment controls all these threats to internal validity. Quasi-experiments can be viewed as compromises between the general aim of gaining valid knowledge regarding the effectiveness of a treatment and the realization that true experiments (and hence control of the major factors threatening internal validity) are not always possible. As Campbell (1969) emphasizes, so-called true experiments should be conducted when possible, but if they are not feasible, quasi-experiments should be conducted. "We must do the best we can with what is available to us" (p. 411).

Problems That Even True Experiments May Not Eliminate

- Threats to internal validity that can occur in any study include contamination, experimenter expectancy effects, and the Hawthorne effect.
- Contamination occurs when information about the experiment is communicated between groups of participants, which may lead to resentment, rivalry, or diffusion of treatment.

- Threats to external validity occur when treatment effects may not be generalized beyond the particular people, setting, and time of the experiment.
- The Hawthorne effect occurs when people's behavior changes simply because they believe someone (e.g., researchers, persons in authority) is interested in them.

Before considering specific quasi-experimental procedures, we should point out that even true experiments may not control for all possible factors that might cloud the interpretation of an experimental result. Although major threats to internal validity are typically eliminated by the true experiment, there are some additional threats that the investigator must guard against, particularly when working in natural settings. We will use the term *contamination* to describe one general class of threats to internal validity. **Contamination** occurs when there is communication of information about the experiment between groups of participants. The result of this communication can be (1) *resentment* on the part of individuals receiving less desirable treatments, (2) *rivalry* among groups receiving different treatments, or (3) a general *diffusion of treatments* across the groups (see Cook & Campbell, 1979).

Consider a situation in which individuals have been randomly assigned to a control group. Further, assume that information is obtained by participants in this group indicating that "other" participants are receiving a treatment that appears to be beneficial. What do you think might be the reaction of the control participants? One possibility is resentment and demoralization. As Cook and Campbell explain, in an industrial setting the person receiving the less desirable treatment may retaliate by lowering productivity. In an educational setting teachers or students might "lose heart" or become angry. This effect of "leaked" information about a treatment may make a treatment look better than it ordinarily would because of the lowered performance of the control group that is demoralized.

Another possible effect that may occur when a control group learns about another group's good fortune is to generate a spirit of competition. That is, a control group might become motivated to reduce the expected difference between itself and the treatment group. As Cook and Campbell point out, this may be likely when intact groups (such as departments, work crews, branch offices, and the like) are assigned to various conditions. Realizing that another group will look better depending on how much it distinguishes itself from the control group, participants comprising the control group may be motivated to "try harder" so as not to look bad by comparison. Cook and Campbell call this problem compensatory rivalry. Like other contamination effects, it can potentially affect any experiment, but it can be of particular concern when experiments are done in natural settings.

Yet another possible effect of contamination is diffusion of treatments. According to Cook and Campbell, this occurs when participants in a control group use information given to others to help them change their own behavior. For example, control participants may use the information given to participants in the treatment group to imitate the behavior of individuals who were given the treatment. Of course, this reduces the differences between the treated and untreated groups and affects the internal validity of the experiment.

In addition to problems resulting from contamination, true experiments can be weakened by threats to external validity. As you have learned in previous chapters, the extent to which we can generalize across persons, settings, and times depends mainly on how representative our sample is of the persons, settings, and times to which we want to generalize. Representativeness is normally achieved through random sampling. However, because random sampling is used so infrequently, we can rarely say that our sample of participants, or the situation in which we are making observations, or the times during which we test individuals, are representative samples of all persons, settings, or times. Therefore, the investigator must be aware of possible interactions between the independent variable of an experiment and the type of individual, setting, or time of the experiment. Is a difference between an experimental group and a control group that is found when only volunteers are used, when the setting is an inner-city school, or when the experiment is conducted in the winter, also likely to be found when nonvolunteers are tested, when a suburban school is the setting, or when the experiment is performed in the spring of the year?

Cook and Campbell describe several approaches to evaluating threats to external validity, the foremost being determination of the representativeness of the sample. However, they point out that in the last analysis the best test of external validity is replication (see Chapter 6). External validity is an empirical question that is best answered through repetition of the experiment with different types of participants, in different settings, and at different times. Occasionally these replications can be "built into" an experiment—for example, by selecting more than one group to participate. Testing both schoolchildren from a lower socioeconomic group and a higher socioeconomic group in an experiment designed to determine the effectiveness of a new educational program would provide evidence of the generality of the treatment's effectiveness across these two socioeconomic groups.

Finally, true experiments do not always protect the experimenter from threats due to experimenter expectancy effects or to a "Hawthorne effect." Effects due to experimenter expectancies were discussed in earlier chapters. They occur when the experimenter unintentionally influences the results. Systematic errors in interpretation or mistakes in recording data can be the result of experimenter expectancy effects. Various ways to control experimenter or observer effects were outlined in Chapters 3 and 6 (e.g., using a double-blind procedure). The **Hawthorne effect** refers to changes in persons' behavior brought about by the interest that "significant others" show in them. The effect was named after events occurring at the Hawthorne plant of the Western Electric Company in Cicero, Illinois, near Chicago, between 1924 and 1932 (Roethlisberger, 1977). Studies were conducted to examine the relationship between productivity and conditions of the workplace. In one experiment, worker output was examined as a function of variation in the amount of lighting (illumination level) in the plant. Results revealed that *both* experimental and control groups increased their productivity during the study. Although there is some controversy surrounding the exact factors responsible for this effect (e.g., Parsons, 1974), a Hawthorne effect generally refers to behavior change resulting from participants' awareness that someone is interested in them.

As one example of the Hawthorne effect, consider a study in which prisoners are chosen to participate in research examining the relationship between changes in prison-cell conditions and attitudes toward prison life. If positive changes in prisoners' attitudes are obtained, the results could be due to the actual changes in cell conditions that were made, or they could be due to an increase in morale because prisoners saw the prison administration as expressing concern for them. The psychology investigator must be conscious of the fact that changes in participants' behavior may be at least partially due to their awareness of the fact that others are interested in them. Thus, you can see that a Hawthorne effect represents a specific kind of reactivity (i.e., an awareness that one is being observed), which we discussed in previous chapters (especially Chapter 3).

QUASI-EXPERIMENTS

- Quasi-experiments provide an important alternative when true experiments are not possible.
- Quasi-experiments lack the degree of control found in true experiments; most notably, quasi-experiments typically lack random assignment.
- Researchers must seek additional evidence to eliminate threats to internal validity when they do quasi-experiments rather than true experiments.
- The one-group pretest-posttest design is called a preexperimental design or a bad experiment because it has so little internal validity.

A dictionary will tell you that one definition of the prefix *quasi-* is "resembling." A quasi-government, for example, is one resembling, but not actually the same as, a true government. Similarly, **quasi-experiments** involve procedures that resemble those that are characteristic of true experiments. Generally speaking, quasi-experiments include some type of intervention or treatment and they provide a comparison, but they lack the degree of control found in true experiments. Just as randomization is the hallmark of true experiments, so *lack of randomization* is the hallmark of quasi-experiments. As Campbell and Stanley (1966, p. 34) explain,

> there are many natural social settings in which the research person can introduce something like experimental design into [the] scheduling of data collection procedures (e.g., the when and to whom of measurement), even though [the researcher] lacks the full control over the scheduling of experimental stimuli (the when and to whom of exposure and the ability to randomize exposures) which makes a true experiment possible. Collectively, such situations can be regarded as quasi-experimental designs.

Quasi-experiments are recommended when true experiments are not feasible. Some knowledge about the effectiveness of a treatment is more desirable than none. The list of possible confounds provided by Campbell and Stanley (1966; Cook & Campbell, 1979), which we reviewed earlier, can be used as a checklist in deciding just how good that knowledge is. Moreover, although a particular experimental procedure may not control for one or more possible types of confounds, the investigator must be prepared to look for additional kinds of evidence that might rule out a confound that is not specifically controlled by an experimental procedure. For example, suppose that a quasi-experiment explicitly controls for only six of the eight major classes of confounds that are eliminated by a true experiment. It may be possible, on the basis of supplementary data or through evidence offered by a logical analysis of the situation, to rule out the remaining two classes of explanations as implausible. In this case a strong argument can be made for the internal validity of the research design, even though a true experiment was not performed. What is important is that the researcher recognize the specific shortcomings of quasi-experimental procedures and be prepared to address these shortcomings through whatever evidence or logic is available.

With full knowledge of their limitations, then, we present the following information about specific quasi-experimental designs so that you will understand the routes remaining open to an investigator when the path to a true experiment is hopelessly blocked. At the same time, this presentation should help you appreciate the clarity of inference provided by the true experiment. Following a discussion of specific quasi-experimental designs, we look at an alternative to quasi-experimentation—the extension of single-case experimentation to research in natural settings. You may also want to refer to the previous discussion of obstacles to true experiments in natural settings. *The difference between the power of the true experiment and that of the quasi-experiment is such that, before facing the problems of interpretation that result from quasi-experimental procedures, the researcher should make every effort possible to approximate the conditions of a true experiment.*

Perhaps the most serious limitation on experimentation in natural settings is that the experimenter is frequently unable to assign participants randomly to conditions. This occurs, for instance, when an intact group is singled out for treatment and when administrative decisions or practical considerations prevent randomly assigning participants. Children in one classroom or school and workers at a particular plant are examples of groups that might be treated in the absence of any random assignment of individuals to conditions. If we assume that behavior of a group is measured both before and after treatment, such an "experiment" can be described as follows:

$$O_1 \times O_2$$

where O_1 refers to the first observation of a group, or pretest, $\times$ indicates a treatment, and O_2 refers to the second observation, or posttest.

Campbell and Stanley (1966) call this particular design the "one-group pretest-posttest design." Although it is sometimes used in psychological research, the design has very little internal validity. You should be able to see, for instance, that this design does not control for many factors that can threaten the internal validity of a study. For example, should a difference between pretest and posttest measures be found, how do we know that this difference was not due to some event other than the treatment (*history threat*), that it was not due to the fact that participants benefited from initial testing (*testing threat*), or that it didn't occur simply because the group of participants changed over time (*maturation threat*)? This particular design has so little going for it in terms of allowing cause-and-effect inferences that it is sometimes referred to as a "preexperimental design," or one that serves as a "bad experiment" to illustrate possible confounds (see Campbell & Stanley, 1966).

The Nonequivalent Control Group Design

- In the nonequivalent control group design, a treatment group and a comparison group are compared using pretest and posttest measures.
- If the two groups are similar in their pretest scores prior to treatment but differ in their posttest scores following treatment, researchers can more confidently make a claim about the effect of treatment.
- Threats to internal validity due to history, maturation, testing, instrumentation, and regression can be eliminated in a nonequivalent control group design.

The one-group pretest-posttest design can be modified to create a quasi-experimental design with greatly superior internal validity if two conditions are met: (1) there exists a group "like" the treatment group that can serve as a comparison group and (2) there is an opportunity to obtain pretest and posttest measures from individuals in *both* the treatment and the comparison groups. Because a comparison group is selected on bases other than random assignment, it cannot be assumed that individuals in the treatment and control groups are equivalent on all important characteristics (a selection threat arises). Therefore it is essential that a pretest be given to both groups to assess their similarity on the dependent measure. Campbell and Stanley (1966) call this quasi-experimental procedure a **nonequivalent control group design.** It can be outlined as follows:

$$O_1 \times O_2$$
$$\text{-----------}$$
$$O_1 \quad O_2$$

The dashed line indicates that the treatment and comparison groups were not formed by assigning participants randomly to conditions.

By adding a comparison group, threats to internal validity due to history, maturation, testing, instrumentation, and regression may be eliminated. A brief look at the logic of experimental design will help show why this occurs. We wish to begin a study with two similar groups; then one group receives the treatment and the other does not. If the two groups' posttest scores differ following treatment, we first must rule out alternative explanations before we can claim that treatment caused the difference. If the groups are truly comparable, and both groups have similar experiences, then we can assume that history, maturation, testing, instrumentation, and regression effects occur to *both* groups equally. Thus, we may assume that both groups change naturally at the same rate (maturation), experience the same effect of multiple testing, or are exposed to the same external events (history). If these effects are experienced in the *same* way by both groups, they cannot possibly be used to account for group *differences* on posttest measures. Therefore, they no longer are threats to internal validity. Thus, researchers can gain a tremendous advantage in their ability to make causal claims simply by adding a comparison group. However, these causal claims also depend on forming comparable groups at the start of the study, which then have comparable experiences, except for the treatment. Because this is difficult to realize in practice, as we'll see, threats to internal validity due to interactions with selection typically are not eliminated in this design.

A nonequivalent control group design was used by Morier and Keeports (1994) to assess the effectiveness of a college course designed to introduce students to the scientific method and to the "faulty, and often fraudulent, methods of pseudosciences" (p. 443). We referred to this situation and experiment earlier when we discussed the problems of control often found in natural settings. The situation met the requirements we just outlined for a nonequivalent control group design. There existed a group "like" the treatment group and it was possible to obtain both pretest and posttest measures from both groups. The investigators chose students enrolled in a "Psychology and Law" course at the same college to serve as a comparison group. Both courses were seminars and enrolled primarily nonscience majors. Students completed a questionnaire designed to measure belief in paranormal phenomena at the beginning of their respective courses and at the end. Although the two groups of students did not differ in their beliefs at the beginning of the courses, at the end of the semester the students in the "Science and Pseudoscience" course (the treatment group) scored significantly lower in their beliefs about paranormal phenomena than did the students in the "Psychology and Law" course (the comparison group). The researchers suggested that the course worked to reduce belief in paranormal phenomena because it explicitly confronted claims of the pseudosciences in the classroom.

As you approach the end of a course on research methods in psychology, you might appreciate learning about the results of another quasi-experimental study. This one examined the effect of taking a research methods course on reasoning about real-life events (VanderStoep & Shaughnessy, 1997), and it, too, used a nonequivalent control group design. Students enrolled in two sections of a research methods course (and who just happened to be using an edition of this textbook!) were compared with students in two sections of a developmental psychology course on their performance on a test emphasizing methodological reasoning about everyday events. Students in both kinds of classes were administered tests at the beginning and at the end of the semester. Results revealed that research methods students showed greater improvement than did students in the control group. Taking a research methods course improved students' ability to think critically about real-life events.

With that bit of encouraging news in mind, let us now examine in detail another study using a nonequivalent control group design. This will give us the opportunity to review both the specific strengths and weaknesses of this quasi-experimental procedure.

Nonequivalent Control Group Design: The Langer and Rodin Study

- Quasi-experiments often assess the overall effectiveness of a treatment that has many components; follow-up research may then determine which components are critical for achieving the treatment effect.

Langer and Rodin (1976) hypothesized that environmental changes associated with old age contribute, in part, to feelings of loss, inadequacy, and low self-esteem among the elderly. Of particular importance is the change that occurs when elderly persons move into a nursing home. Although they usually care for the elderly quite adequately in physical terms, nursing homes often provide what Langer and Rodin call a "virtually decision-free" environment. The elderly are no longer called on to make even the simplest decisions, such as what time to get up, whom to visit, what movie to watch, and the like. In a nursing home, many or most of these everyday decisions are made for the elderly, leaving them with little personal responsibility and choice.

To test the hypothesis that the lack of opportunity to make personal decisions contributes to the psychological and even the physical debilitation sometimes seen in the elderly, Langer and Rodin carried out a quasi-experiment in a Connecticut nursing home. The independent variable was the type of communication given to two groups of nursing-home residents. One group was given a communication stressing the many decisions that the patients needed to make regarding how their rooms were arranged, visiting, care of plants, movie selection, and so forth. These residents were also given a small plant as a gift (if they decided to accept it) and told to take care of it as they wished. This was the *responsibility-induced condition*. The second group of residents, the comparison group, was also called together for a meeting, but the communication given to this group stressed the staff's responsibility for them. These residents also received a plant as a gift (whether they chose to have one or not) and were told that the nurses would water and care for the plants for them.

Residents of the nursing home had been assigned to a particular floor and room on the basis of availability, and some residents had been there for a long time. As a consequence, randomly assigning residents to the two communication groups was impractical—and probably undesirable from the administration's point of view. Therefore the two communications were given to residents on two different floors of the nursing home. These floors were chosen, in the words of

FIGURE 10.2   Langer and Rodin (1976) used a nonequivalent control group design to study the effect of two different types of communication on the behavior of nursing-home residents. A major difference in the two types of communication involved the offer, and subsequent care, of a small plant (see text).

the authors, "because of similarity in the residents' physical and psychological health and prior socioeconomic status, as determined from evaluations made by the home's director, head nurses, and social worker" (Langer & Rodin, p. 193). The floors were randomly assigned to one of the two treatments. In addition, questionnaires were given to residents 1 week before and 3 weeks after the communications. The questionnaires contained items that related to "how much control they felt over general events in their lives and how happy and active they felt" (p. 194). Furthermore, staff members on each floor were asked to rate the residents, before and after the experimental communications, on such traits as alertness, sociability, and activity. The investigators also included a clever posttest measure of social interest by holding a competition that asked participants to guess the number of jelly beans in a large jar. Residents entered the contest if they wished by simply filling out a piece of paper giving their estimate and name. Thus, there were a number of dependent variables to assess the residents' perceptions of control, happiness, activity, interest level, and so forth.

The Langer and Rodin study nicely illustrates the procedures of a nonequivalent control group design. Moreover, differences between pretest and posttest measures showed that the residents in the responsibility-induced group were generally happier, more active, and more alert following the treatment than were residents in the comparison group. Behavioral measures such as frequency of movie attendance also favored the responsibility-induced group, and, although 10 residents from this group entered the jelly-bean contest, only 1 resident from the comparison group participated! The investigators point to possible practical implications of these findings. Specifically, they suggest that some of the negative consequences of aging can be reduced or reversed by giving the aged the opportunity to make personal decisions and to feel competent.

Before turning to the specific weaknesses associated with this design, let us call your attention to another feature of the Langer and Rodin study, one that characterizes many experiments in natural settings. The treatment in the Langer and Rodin study actually had several components. For example, residents were encouraged by the staff to make decisions about a number of different things (e.g., movies, rooms, etc.) and they were offered a plant to take care of. The experiment evaluated, however, the treatment "package." That is, the effectiveness of the overall treatment was assessed and not individual components of the treatment. We only know (or at least we assume based on the evidence) that the treatment with all its components worked; we don't necessarily know whether the treatment would work with fewer components or whether one component is more critical than the other. In the same vein, consider the results of the course confronting the claims of pseudosciences that we mentioned earlier (Morier & Keeports, 1994). There, too, investigators obtained evidence for the effectiveness of the treatment (the college course). Again, however, there were many components to the treatment: examples of legitimate scientific methods, introduction to logical fallacies and aspects of critical thinking, exposure to instructors skeptical of these claims, guest lecturers (including a magician posing as a psychic who then revealed himself as a fake). Again, the results of the experiment do not tell us about the effectiveness of these individual components.

Research in natural settings is often characterized by treatments with many components. Moreover, the initial goal of such research is often to assess the overall effect of the treatment "package." Finding evidence for an overall treatment effect, therefore, may be only the first stage in a research program if we want to identify the critical elements of a treatment. There may be practical as well as theoretical benefits to such identification. On practical grounds, should research reveal that only some of the treatment's features are critical to the effect, then perhaps the less critical features could be dropped. This may make the treatment more cost effective and more likely to be adopted and carried out. From a theoretical standpoint, it is important to determine whether components of the treatment specified by the theory as being critical are, indeed, the critical components. When you hear about research showing an overall treatment effect you might think about how additional research could reveal what specific components are critical to the treatment's effect.

Sources of Invalidity in the Nonequivalent Control Group Design

- To interpret the findings in quasi-experimental designs, researchers examine the study to determine if any threats to internal validity are present.
- The threats to internal validity that must be considered when using the nonequivalent control group design include interactions with selection, differential regression, observer bias, contamination, and Hawthorne effects.

- Although groups may be comparable on a pretest measure, this does not ensure that the groups are comparable in all possible ways that are relevant to the study outcome.

According to Cook and Campbell (1979), the nonequivalent control group design generally controls for all major classes of potential threats to internal validity except those due to interactions of (1) selection and maturation, (2) selection and history, (3) selection and instrumentation, and (4) those due to differential statistical regression. We will explore how each of these potential sources of invalidity might pose problems in an effort to interpret the results of the Langer and Rodin study. Then we will explain what evidence or argument the authors offered in defense of their interpretation, which was that the differential responsibility-induced communication *caused* the differences in posttest behavior between the two groups of residents. We will also examine how experimenter bias and problems of contamination were controlled, and we will comment briefly on problems of external validity inherent in the nonequivalent control group design.

First, it should be mentioned that Langer and Rodin found that the residents in the two experimental groups did not differ significantly on the pretest measures. Because the residents were not randomly assigned to conditions, it might not have been surprising to find a difference between the two groups before the treatment was introduced. Moreover, it is important to recognize that, even when pretest scores show no difference between groups, as Langer and Rodin reported, one cannot assume that the groups are "equivalent" (Campbell & Stanley, 1966). Why this is so will become apparent in the discussion that follows.

Interaction Between Selection and Maturation   An interaction between selection and maturation occurs when individuals in one group grow more experienced, more tired, or more bored at a faster rate than individuals in another group (Cook & Campbell, 1979). Campbell and Stanley (1966) illustrate this problem by describing a nonequivalent control group design using psychotherapy patients as a treatment group and individuals not in therapy as a comparison group. The psychotherapy patients would normally be expected to show some improvement without the treatment (called spontaneous remission), a change that could be falsely interpreted (given no change in the comparison group) as a treatment effect. Whenever the treatment group consists of individuals who are brighter or more competent than those in the comparison group, differences in rate of maturation may be a confounding factor.

An interaction of selection and maturation is more likely to be an actual source of invalidity (as are other sources) when the treatment group is self-selected (the members deliberately sought out exposure to the treatment) and when the comparison group is from a different population from the treatment group (Campbell & Stanley, 1966). This occurs when a particular group is singled out for treatment in order to determine whether behavior will improve as a function of the treatment. The example of psychotherapy patients who are compared with individuals not in therapy, which was mentioned earlier, is an example.

Before examining whether a selection and maturation interaction poses a problem for the Langer and Rodin study, we need to call your attention to another aspect of this issue. It is important to emphasize that, even when *pretest* scores are the same on the average for the treatment and control groups, we cannot conclude the groups are equivalent (comparable). This is true for two reasons. First, the pretest is likely to measure respondents on only one measure, or at best on a few measures. The mere fact that individuals do not differ on one measure does not mean they don't differ on other measures that are relevant to their behavior in this situation. Second, the natural growth rate of two groups from different populations might be different, but the pretest may have been taken at a time when both groups happened to be about the same. This problem is illustrated in Figure 10.3. The normal rate of change is greater in Group A than in Group B, but the pretest is likely to show that the groups do not differ. On the other hand, and again because of the differential growth rate, the groups would probably show a difference at the posttest that could be mistaken for a treatment effect. Langer and Rodin selected their groups (but not individuals) randomly from the same population of individuals. Consequently, their design more closely approaches a true experiment than it would if individuals in the two groups came from different populations (Campbell & Stanley, 1966), as would be the case if residents in a nursing home were compared with those attending a sheltered workshop program for the elderly.

Is there any reason to suspect an interaction of selection and maturation in the Langer and Rodin study? For instance, would residents on the treatment floor be expected to change naturally at a faster rate than patients on the no-treatment floor? Several kinds of evidence suggest that this would not be the case. First, the procedure of assigning residents to floors was basically random, and floors were selected randomly for treatment and no treatment. The authors also point out that various measures showed that the residents of the two floors were, on the average, equivalent in socioeconomic status and length of time at the nursing home. Finally, although it is not sufficient evidence in itself, residents on the two floors did not differ on the pretest measures. There is little in the Langer and Rodin study to suggest a confound due to an interaction of selection and maturation.

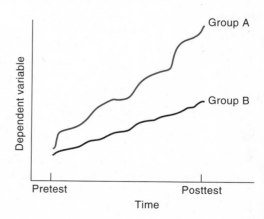

FIGURE 10.3 Possible differential growth rates for two groups (A and B) in the absence of treatment.

Interaction Between Selection and History   Another type of confound that is not controlled in the nonequivalent control group design is the interaction between selection and history. Cook and Campbell (1979) refer to this problem as *local history effects*. This problem arises when an event other than the treatment affects one group and not the other. Local history, for example, could be a problem in the Langer and Rodin study if an event affecting the residents' happiness and alertness occurred on one floor of the nursing home but not on the other. You can probably imagine a number of possibilities. A change in nursing staff on one floor, for instance, might bring about either an increase or a decrease in residents' morale, depending on the nature of the change and the relationship between the behavior of a new nurse and that of an old one. Problems of local history become more problematic the more the locations or settings of the individuals in the treatment and comparison groups differ. Langer and Rodin do not specifically address the problem of local history.

Interaction Between Selection and Instrumentation   An interaction of selection and instrumentation occurs when changes in a measuring instrument are more likely to be detected in one group than they are in another. Floor or ceiling effects, for instance, could make it difficult to detect behavior change from pretest to posttest. If this is more of a problem in one group than in another, an interaction of selection and instrumentation is present. Cook and Campbell point out that this confound is likely to be more of a problem the greater the nonequivalence of the groups. Because Langer and Rodin's groups did not differ on the pretest, and because performance of the groups did not suggest floor or ceiling effects on the measurement scales that were used, this confound seems implausible in their study.

Differential Statistical Regression   Finally, the nonequivalent control group design does not control for differential statistical regression (Cook & Campbell, 1979). As was noted earlier, this is especially a problem when one group has been singled out for treatment because of its poor performance on some measure. Whenever individuals are selected on the basis of extreme scores (the poorest readers, the workers with the lowest productivity, the patients with the most severe problems), regression toward the mean is to be expected. Changes in behavior from pretest to posttest that are due to regression may be mistakenly interpreted as a treatment effect if regression is more likely in the treatment group than in the control group. Because the groups in the Langer and Rodin study came from the same population and there is no evidence that one group's pretest scores were more extreme than another's, a problem of differential statistical regression is not plausible in their study.

Observer Bias and Contamination   It is worthwhile to consider how Langer and Rodin handled problems of observer bias and possible effects of contamination and to inquire whether a Hawthorne effect was present. If observers in their study had been aware of the experimental hypothesis, it is possible that they might inadvertently have rated residents as being better after the experimental communication than before. However, all the observers were kept unaware of the experimental hypothesis. Thus, observer bias appears to have been controlled. Langer and Rodin were aware of possible contamination effects. Residents in the control group might have become demoralized if they learned that residents on another floor were given more opportunity to make decisions. In this case, the use of different floors of the nursing home was advantageous; Langer and Rodin indicate that "there was not a great deal of communication between floors" (1976, p. 193). Thus, if one accepts Langer and Rodin's argument, contamination effects do not seem to be present, at least on a scale that would destroy the internal validity of the study.

Hawthorne Effect   A Hawthorne effect would be present in the Langer and Rodin study if residents on the treatment floor interpreted the responsibility-inducing communication as a form of special attention. Such an interpretation might lead residents on the treated floor to feel better about themselves. The changes in behavior Langer and Rodin observed could then be attributed to a change in morale due to a Hawthorne effect as easily as to the opportunity to make decisions and assume personal responsibility that was available to residents in the treatment group. It is difficult to rule out completely a Hawthorne effect in this study. According to the authors, however, "there was no difference in the amount of attention paid to the two groups" (p. 194). In fact, communications to both groups stressed that the staff cared for them and wanted them "to be happy." Thus, without additional evidence to the contrary, we can conclude that the changes in behavior Langer and Rodin observed were due to the effect of the independent variable and not to the effect of an extraneous variable that the investigators failed to control.

What should be apparent at this point is that for an investigator to decide, in the context of a particular experiment, whether an independent variable "worked," he or she must be something of a detective. Evidence for and against the interpretation that the treatment actually caused behavior to change must be systematically (and sometimes ingeniously) collected and carefully weighed. As Cook and Campbell (1979, pp. 55–56) explain:

> Estimating the internal validity of a relationship is a deductive process in which the investigator has to systematically think through how each of the internal validity threats may have influenced the data. Then, the investigator has to examine the data to test which relevant threats can be ruled out. In all of this process, the researcher has to be his or her own best critic, trenchantly examining all of the threats he or she can imagine. When all of the threats can plausibly be eliminated, it is possible to make confident conclusions about whether a relationship is probably causal. When all of them cannot, perhaps because the appropriate data are not available or because the data indicate that a particular threat may indeed have operated, then the investigator has to conclude that a demonstrated relationship between two variables may or may not be causal.

The Issue of External Validity

- Similar to internal validity, the external validity of research findings must be critically examined.
- The best evidence for the external validity of research findings is replication with different populations, settings, and times.

We must make the same systematic inquiry into the external validity of an experiment that we did into its internal validity. What evidence is there that the particular pattern of results is restricted to a particular group of participants, setting, or time? For example, although Langer and Rodin suggest that certain changes be made in the way the elderly are cared for, we might question whether the effectiveness of the responsibility-inducing communication would hold for all elderly residents, for all types of nursing homes, and at different times. That the particular nursing home selected by Langer and Rodin was described as "rated by the state of Connecticut as being among the finest care units" (1976, p. 193) suggests that the residents, facilities, and staff there would be different from those found in other facilities. For instance, if residents at this particular nursing home were relatively more independent before coming to the home than residents at other homes (perhaps because of differences in socioeconomic status), then the changes experienced upon moving into a home might have had greater impact on them. Consequently, the opportunity to be more independent of staff might be more important to these residents relative to residents in other homes. Similarly, if staff members at this home were more competent than those at other homes, they might be more effective in communicating the experimental communications than would the staff members at other homes.

As we indicated earlier, in the last analysis, the investigator must be ready to replicate an experimental finding under different conditions in order to establish external validity. The deductive process applied to questions of internal validity must also be used to examine a study's external validity. Moreover, *we must be ready to live with the fact that one experiment is not likely to answer all questions about an experimental hypothesis.*

Interrupted Time-Series Designs

- In a simple interrupted time-series design, researchers examine a series of observations both before and after a treatment.
- Evidence for treatment effects occurs when there are abrupt changes (discontinuities) in the time series data at the time treatment was implemented.
- The major threats to internal validity in the simple interrupted time series design are history effects and changes in measurement (instrumentation) that occur at the same time as the treatment.

In situations in which we can observe changes in a dependent variable for some time before and after a treatment is introduced, another quasi-experiment is possible. It is called a **simple interrupted time-series design** (Cook &

Campbell, 1979). The essence of this design is the availability of periodic measures before and after a treatment has been introduced. It can be outlined in the following way:

$$O_1 O_2 O_3 O_4 O_5 \times O_6 O_7 O_8 O_9 O_{10}$$

Situations such as this may arise when a new product has been introduced, a new social reform instituted, or a special advertising campaign begun. Campbell's (1969) analysis of the effect on traffic fatalities of a crackdown on speeding ordered by the Connecticut governor made use of an interrupted time-series design. Because statistics related to traffic accidents are regularly kept by state agencies, a wealth of archival data was available to yield pretreatment and posttreatment measures. Besides number of fatalities, Campbell looked at number of speeding violations, number of drivers having their licenses suspended, and other measures related to driving behavior. Figure 10.4 shows the percentage of suspensions of licenses for speeding (as a percentage of all license suspensions) before and after the crackdown. There is a clear discontinuity in the time graph that provides evidence for an effect of the treatment. Indeed, the discontinuity in the time series is the major evidence of an effect.

As Campbell points out, only abrupt changes in the time graph can be evaluated because gradual changes are indistinguishable from normal fluctuations over time. Unfortunately, changes often are not nearly so dramatic as those seen in Figure 10.4. In fact, Campbell's analysis of traffic fatalities over the same time period, while revealing evidence of an effect of the crackdown, did not show as abrupt a change as that associated with suspension of drivers' licenses (see Campbell, 1969, Figure 2).

A more typical outcome of an interrupted time-series design is illustrated by the findings of Ross and White (1987), who examined the effect of newspaper

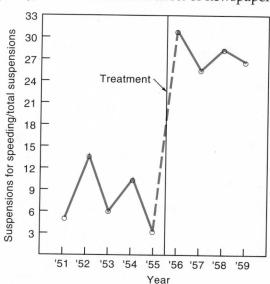

FIGURE 10.4   Suspensions of licenses for speeding, as a percentage of all suspensions. (From Campbell, 1969.)

publicity on subsequent crime rates. In June 1984, a metropolitan newspaper instituted a policy of publishing the court results of people convicted of shoplifting, impaired driving, or failure to take a Breathalyzer test. The published information identified the individual by name and also furnished details of the incident. For instance, in the case of shoplifting, the item that the individual attempted to shoplift and its value were also noted. Ross and White sought to assess the impact of this publication policy on the frequency of similar offenses. They obtained data from several police and government agencies detailing the incidence of these crimes over a time period beginning several years before the new policy was instituted and continuing for approximately 18 months after the new policy was implemented. The number of shoplifting offenses during this period is shown in Figure 10.5. Visual inspection, confirmed by the results of statistical analyses, revealed an effect of the publication policy on incidence of shoplifting. Interestingly, the policy showed no effect on the incidence of drinking and driving or refusing the Breathalyzer test. The investigators suggested that being associated with shoplifting carries a greater social stigma than does driving under the influence of alcohol.

FIGURE 10.5　Shoplifting offenses between January 1980 and December 1985. (From Ross & White, 1987.)

NOTE: Vertical line indicates start of publication policy.

Campbell and Stanley (1966) summarize the problem facing researchers using the simple interrupted time-series design: "The problem of internal validity boils down to the question of plausible competing hypotheses that offer likely alternate explanations of the shift in the time series other than the effect of $\times$" (p. 39). An effect of history is the main threat to internal validity in this type of design (Cook & Campbell, 1979). For instance, considering the results in Figure 10.5, is it possible that some factor other than newspaper publicity was responsible for the reduction in the frequency of shoplifting offenses?

Particularly threatening to the internal validity of the time-series design are influences of a cyclical nature, including seasonal variation (Cook & Campbell, 1979). For instance, when analyzing the effect of the Connecticut governor's crackdown on speeding, Campbell (1969) gathered data from neighboring states in order to rule out possible regional trends due to weather or the introduction of automotive safety features in order to strengthen his case for the effect of this particular social policy change.

Instrumentation must also be considered a threat to internal validity in the simple interrupted time-series design (Cook & Campbell, 1979). When new programs or new social policies are instituted, for example, there are often accompanying changes in the way records are kept or in the procedures used to collect information. A program intended to reduce crime may lead authorities to modify their definitions of particular crimes or to become more careful when observing and reporting criminal activities. Nevertheless, for an instrumentation threat to be plausible, it must be shown how changes in instrumentation could occur at exactly the time of the intervention (Campbell & Stanley, 1966). Ross and White (1987) showed that they were aware of possible influences due to instrumentation effects. They noted in their Method section that data collected more than 18 months after the newspaper's new policy went into effect were not comparable to prior data because the laws defining a shoplifting offense had been changed. Hence, data were collected only during the 18-month period immediately after the policy change.

Most other threats to internal validity are controlled in the simple interrupted time-series design. Problems of maturation, testing, and regression are pretty much eliminated by the presence of multiple observations both before and after treatment. None of these threats can be ruled out when only a single pretest and posttest measure is available, as in the single-group pretest-posttest design mentioned earlier. For example, an effect of maturation would not normally be expected to show a sharp discontinuity in the time series, although this might be possible in some situations (Campbell & Stanley, 1966). When only one pretest and one posttest observation are available, it is not possible to decide whether performance changes from pretest to posttest reflect a treatment effect or are simply due to maturational processes. The simple time-series design usually permits this decision to be made.

Threats to external validity in the simple interrupted time-series design must be examined carefully. It should be obvious that, if pretreatment observations of behavior are based on multiple tests, then an effect of the treatment may be restricted to those individuals who have had multiple test experiences. More-over, because only a single group is generally tested, one that was not randomly selected, it is always possible that the results are limited to people with charac-teristics similar to those who took part in the experiment.

Time Series with Nonequivalent Control Group

- In a time series with nonequivalent control group design, researchers make a series of observations before and after treatment for both a treatment group and a comparable comparison group.
- Archival data frequently provide the basis for time-series designs.

The interrupted time-series design can be enhanced greatly by including a control group. This procedure is identical to that followed in constructing a nonequivalent control group design, which we discussed previously. In this case the researcher must find a group that is comparable to the treatment group and that allows a similar opportunity for multiple observations before and after the time that the treatment is administered to the experimental group. This **time series with nonequivalent control group design** is outlined as follows:

$$\frac{O_1 O_2 O_3 O_4 O_5 \times O_6 O_7 O_8 O_9 O_{10}}{O_1 O_2 O_3 O_4 O_5 \quad O_6 O_7 O_8 O_9 O_{10}}$$

As before, a dashed line is used to indicate that the control group and the experimental group were not randomly assigned. This interrupted time series with nonequivalent control group permits one to control many threats due to history. As was mentioned earlier, Campbell (1969) used traffic fatality data obtained from neighboring states to provide a comparison with traffic fatality data following the crackdown on speeding in Connecticut. Although traffic fatalities in Connecticut showed a decline immediately following the crackdown, data from comparable states did not exhibit any such decline. This fact tends to rule out changes that might have been due to favorable weather conditions, improved automobile design, or other potentially positive factors.

Archival data, rather than direct observation, frequently provide the basis for time-series designs. For example, the extensive archival data in various fields of sport have furnished social psychologists with an opportunity to test the real-life implications of laboratory-based theories. In one study, researchers compiled statistics on baseball players who were traded in midseason to a new team (see Jackson, Buglione, & Glenwick, 1988). A quasi-experimental analysis revealed that the batting average of these players was higher when playing for the new club than for the old club, confirming a prediction made from a drive theory of social facilitation. The possibility that baseball players, regardless of whether they are traded, increase their batting average over the full-year season was ruled out as an alternative explanation for these findings by demonstrating that averages of a random sample of nontraded players did not show a similar rise.

A particularly good illustration of the interrupted time-series design is provided by McSweeney (1978), who analyzed the frequency of telephone calls asking for directory assistance following initiation of a charge for such calls. Directory assistance calls requesting information about phone numbers listed in standard directories cost the telephone company money, and they pay these expenses by charging more for other services. As McSweeney (1978) pointed out, an intervention that would effectively reduce the frequency of these unnecessary calls would benefit both the telephone company and the consumer.

In 1974, officials at Cincinnati Bell Telephone Company initiated charges for local directory assistance calls in excess of three per month. Subscribers were charged 20 cents for each additional call. Because the telephone company keeps extensive archival records, the effect of this intervention could be assessed using a time-series analysis. Furthermore, a simple time series could be expanded by seeking a comparison group. McSweeney chose to use as a control measure the long-distance directory assistance calls that were made from outside the Cincinnati area, for which no charge was made. Although the exact number of "participants" could not be known, it was estimated that the service charge for local directory assistance calls affected more than a million users. From data provided by Cincinnati Bell administrative records, McSweeney created the time-series graph shown in Figure 10.6. The frequency of local calls

FIGURE 10.6   Number of local and long-distance directory assistance calls placed per average business day before and after charges were introduced. (From McSweeney, 1978.)

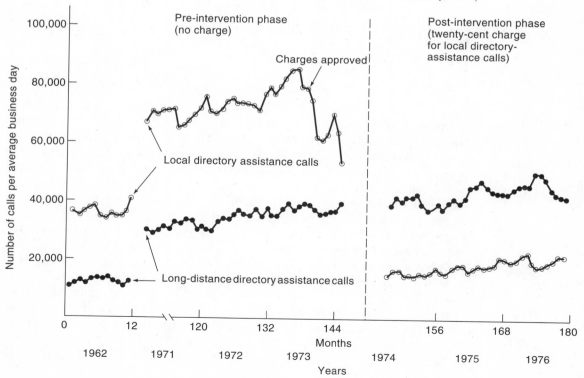

decreased dramatically after the charge was initiated; directory assistance calls from outside the area continued to increase gradually.

The time-series analysis revealed a small dip in frequency of local calls before the actual charges were levied. This was apparently in response to the announcement by telephone company officials of the upcoming cost to the user. McSweeney reasonably argued that this change was due to the fact that some individuals misunderstood the announcement in news reports and thought the charges were already being made. Others may simply have begun to change their calling habits in anticipation of the charges. The clear discontinuity in the time series associated with the treatment group, in conjunction with the absence of any decrease in calls by the comparison group, provides nearly incontrovertible evidence that the effect was due to the intervention made by the telephone company. A subsequent analysis showed that the decrease in local directory assistance calls resulted in an average savings of 65 cents on the telephone bill of each individual residential consumer.

AN EXTENSION OF SINGLE-CASE DESIGNS TO RESEARCH IN NATURAL SETTINGS

Rationale

- Both time-series designs and single-case experimental designs use observations before and after a treatment in order to make inferences about the effectiveness of the treatment.
- With both types of designs, researchers must consider history threats as a plausible alternative explanation for apparent treatment effects.
- Single-case experimental designs can be conducted as quasi-experiments when groups of individuals are tested using the ABAB design or multiple-baseline design.

You may have noticed a similarity between the simple time-series design and the single-case experimental designs discussed in Chapter 9. In both situations, observations made prior to a treatment represent a "baseline" that is compared with observations obtained after the treatment. If there is a clear discontinuity in the behavioral record following the application of a treatment, it is evidence for the effect of the treatment. Furthermore, for both types of design the major threat to internal validity is history. It is possible that some factor affecting the participants' behavior, other than the treatment, is responsible for the observed behavior change. However, the two types of design handle this threat differently.

When a simple time series is used, the investigator must search for historical factors (e.g., seasonal variation) that might explain a change in the behavioral record. The addition of a nonequivalent control group greatly enhances the internal validity of the time-series design but does not completely rule out a possible interaction with history or other threats, such as an interaction with instrumentation. Moreover, unless the discontinuity in the time-series record is abrupt and obvious, the investigator must consider the possibility that one of numerous subtle factors produced a change and must rely on sophisticated mathematical models to determine whether an effect is present (see, for example, McCain & McCleary, in Cook & Campbell, 1979). A single-case experimental design controls for effects due to history when changes in the behavioral record correspond systematically to the repeated introduction and withdrawal of an independent variable (as in an ABAB design) or to the staggered introduction of a treatment (as in a multiple-baseline design). Unless observed changes are very small, it may be possible to avoid using complex statistical procedures and to rely instead on visual inspection of the pattern of change associated with the sequential manipulation of a treatment.

Single-case experimental designs offer an alternative to quasi-experimental procedures when one is conducting research in natural settings (e.g., Horn & Heerboth, 1982). Although typically used to evaluate changes in a single participant, the single-case design strategy can be used for a group of individuals, such as a classroom singled out for treatment. Examples of single-case experimental designs using groups of participants are found in Chapter 9 (see, for instance, VanBiervliet et al., 1981). In some situations a *multiple-baseline design* can be employed (see Horn & Heerboth, 1982), as was done by Lyons and Ghezzi (1995) to evaluate the effect on the public's gambling behavior as a function of changes in state lottery games. Amount of dollars waged was measured in a multiple baseline "across states," Arizona and Oregon. To use an *ABAB design* the investigator must have control over the application and withdrawal of a treatment and an opportunity must be present for periodic observation both during no treatment (baseline) stages and during treatment stages. Clearly this is not always possible in natural settings.

Treatments are often initiated under the assumption that they will "work," and, unfortunately, their effects are often not evaluated. An energy conservation program, for example, is not likely to be applied, withdrawn, and then applied again in an attempt to measure its effectiveness. However, when control over the application and withdrawal of a treatment is feasible, a single-case ABAB design may be used to determine whether a treatment effect exists. The advantage to the researcher is a design whose internal validity is close to, if not the same as, that of a true experiment (see Horn & Heerboth, 1982). The following example illustrates the possibilities of using an ABAB design in natural settings.

The ABAB Design

- When the ABAB design is used as a quasi-experiment, treatment is alternately introduced and withdrawn (baseline) for a group of individuals.
- The effect of treatment can be observed by comparing records for observations made during treatment and baseline periods.

Schnelle and his associates used a single-case methodology to evaluate the effect of police procedures on reducing crime rate (see, for example, Schnelle et al., 1978). In one study they sought evidence for the effect of a combined police car and helicopter patrol in reducing the frequency of home burglaries in a neighborhood of Nashville, Tennessee. The area was selected because police records showed it had a chronically high number of burglaries. (Even though this "group" was selected because it was extreme, do you see how the *chronic* nature of the burglaries neutralizes the problem of statistical regression?) The plan was to increase surveillance of the area by adding a helicopter patrol to the usual police car patrol. When the helicopter was used, the pilots were told to fly low enough to observe suspicious activity. Pilots were in radio contact with the police in the patrol car. The helicopter was flown between 9 A.M. and 5 P.M. (weather permitting), a time that coincides with most home burglaries.

An ABAB procedure was used. Following a baseline observation of frequency of home burglaries in the experimental area, the helicopter was introduced for a period of time, then withdrawn, and then introduced again. The addition of the helicopter was an experimental program by the Nashville police, so the helicopter was again removed following the second treatment stage, providing an additional (and final) baseline period.

Figure 10.7 shows daily frequency of home burglaries during baseline and treatment periods. Visual inspection of the behavioral record clearly shows that the frequency of burglaries decreased when the helicopter was added to the police surveillance and increased when no helicopter was present. Interestingly, a check of police records showed no displacement of burglary activity to surrounding neighborhoods. That is, when the frequency of burglaries dropped in the experimental area, there was no corresponding rise in these types of crime in nearby neighborhoods, which served as a type of comparison group. Note that the dependent variable in this example is frequency based on a group of individuals—in this case, residents in an approximately 6-square-mile area. Except for this change in the way behavior is assessed, the design strategy is exactly the same as might be used with a single individual.

FIGURE 10.7　Daily frequency of home burglaries. Arrows indicate the days the helicopter was prevented from flying. (From Schnelle et al., 1978.)

PROGRAM EVALUATION

- Program evaluation is used to assess the effectiveness of human service organizations and provide feedback to administrators about their services.
- Program evaluators assess needs, process, outcome, and efficiency of social services.
- The relationship between basic research and applied research is reciprocal.
- Despite society's reluctance to use experiments, true experiments and quasi-experiments are the best approaches for evaluating social reforms.

Organizations that produce goods have a ready-made index of success. If a company is set up to make beach balls, its success is ultimately determined by its profits from the sale of beach balls. At least theoretically, the efficiency and effectiveness of the organization can be easily assessed by examining the company's financial ledgers. Increasingly, however, organizations of a different sort play a critical role in our society. Because these organizations typically provide services rather than goods, Posavac and Carey (1997) refer to them as *human service organizations*. For example, hospitals, schools, police departments, and government agencies provide a variety of services ranging from emergency room care to fire prevention inspections. Because profit making is not their goal, some other method must be found to distinguish between effective and ineffective agencies. One useful approach to assessing the effectiveness of human service organizations is the discipline of program evaluation.

Posavac and Carey (1997, p. 1) define **program evaluation** as a

"collection of methods, skills, and sensitivities necessary to determine whether a human service is needed and likely to be used, whether it is sufficiently intense to meet the unmet need identified, whether the service is offered as planned, and whether the human service actually does help people in need without undesirable side effects."

You should see that there are several components in their definition, and we will take up each of these components in turn. However, before doing so, we wish to note, as these authors emphasize, that the basic goal of program evaluation is *providing feedback regarding human service activities*. Program evaluations are designed to provide feedback to the administrators of human service organizations in order to help them decide what services to provide to whom and how to provide them most effectively and efficiently. Program evaluation represents a hybrid discipline that draws on political science, sociology, economics, education, and psychology. We discuss program evaluation at the end of this chapter on research in natural settings because it represents perhaps the most large-scale application of the principles and methods we have been describing throughout this book.

According to Posavac and Carey (1997), the questions asked by program evaluators are about needs, process, outcome, and efficiency.

An assessment of *needs* seeks to determine the unmet needs of the people for whom an agency might provide a service. If a city government were to consider instituting a program of recreational activities for senior citizens in the community, for example, it would first want to determine whether senior citizens actually need or want such a program and, if they do, what kind of program would be most attractive to them. The methods of survey research are used extensively in studies designed to assess needs. Information obtained in this type of program evaluation is also used to help program planning.

Once a program has been set up, program evaluators may ask about the process that has been established. Programs are not always implemented the way they were planned, and it is essential to know what actually *is* being done when a program is implemented. If the planned activities were not being used by the senior citizens in a recreational program designed specifically for them, it might suggest that the program was inadequately implemented. An evaluation that provides answers to questions about *process*, that is, about how a program is actually being carried out, permits administrators to make adjustments in the delivery of services in order to strengthen the existing program (Posavac & Carey, 1997). Observational methods may be employed in such evaluations.

An evaluation of *outcome* is just that; it asks whether the program has been effective in meeting its stated goals. For example, do senior citizens now have access to more recreational activities, and are they pleased with these activities? Are these particular activities preferred over other activities? The outcome of a community-watch program designed to curb neighborhood crime might be evaluated by assessing whether there were actual decreases in burglaries and assaults following the implementation of the program.

Evaluators might also ask about the *efficiency* of the program, that is, about its cost. Choices often have to be made among possible services that a government or other institution is capable of delivering. Information about how successful a program is (outcome evaluation) and information about the program's cost (efficiency evaluation) are necessary if we want to make informed decisions about continuing the program, how to improve it, whether to try an alternative program, or to cut back on the program's services. These evaluations may use both experimental and quasi-experimental methods for research in natural settings. An evaluator may, for example, use a nonequivalent control group design to assess the effectiveness of a school reform program by comparing students' performance in two different school districts, one with the reform program and one without. It is also possible to use archival data like those described in Chapter 5 to carry out evaluations examining outcome and efficiency. For example, examining police records in order to document the frequency of various crimes is one way to assess the effectiveness of a community-watch program.

Earlier in this chapter we described differences between basic and applied research. Program evaluation is perhaps the extreme case of applied research. The purpose of program evaluation is practical, not theoretical. Nevertheless, even in the context of blatantly practical goals, a case can be made for a reciprocal relationship between basic and applied research. Writing in the *International Journal of Psychology*, Salomon (1987) argues that each domain of research serves the other in an ongoing circular way. Specifically, basic research provides us with certain abstractions (e.g., scientifically based principles) that express certain regularities in nature. When these principles are examined in the complex and "dirty" world where they supposedly apply, new complexities are recognized and new hypotheses are called for. These new complexities are then tested and evaluated before being tried out again in the real world. Salomon's model is illustrated in Figure 10.8.

Salomon points to the work of Ellen Langer as a concrete example of this circular relationship. She identified a decline in elderly people's health once they entered nursing homes (see Langer, 1989; Langer & Rodin, 1976, described in this chapter). These naturalistic observations led her to develop a theory of mindfulness, which she has tested under controlled experimental conditions and which has implications for more general theories of cognitive development and of education (see, for example, Langer, 1989, 1997; Langer & Piper, 1987). The theory provides a guide for her applied work—designing new models of nursing homes. Tests of the practical effects of changes in the care given by nursing homes on the residents' health and well-being will undoubtedly lead to modifications of her theory of mindfulness.

Perhaps the greatest difference between basic research and program evaluation lies in the political and social realities surrounding program evaluation. Governments at both local and national levels regularly propose, plan, and execute various types of social reforms. Tax relief programs, work incentive programs, educational reforms, police reforms, and medical care for senior citizens are just a few of the types of social reform programs that a government might

FIGURE 10.8   Model illustrating reciprocal relationship between basic and applied research. (From Salomon, 1987, p. 444.)

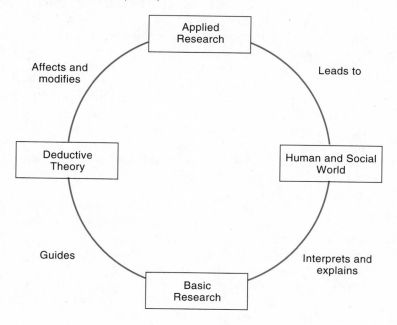

initiate. Unfortunately, as Donald Campbell (1969), a past president of the American Psychological Association, pointed out, the outcome of these social reforms often cannot be meaningfully evaluated. Did a change in police techniques lead to greater crime stoppage? Are more elderly people gaining access to public transportation after a reduction in fares? Does a work incentive program take more people off the unemployment rolls? The answers to such questions often cannot be found, said Campbell, because most social reforms are instituted in a political climate that is not ready for hardheaded evaluation. What public official, for instance, wants to be associated with a program that failed? As Campbell suggested, there is "safety under the cloak of ignorance" (pp. 409–410). Furthermore, many social reforms are begun under the assumption that they are certain to be successful. Otherwise why spend all that tax money? For many public administrators it is advantageous to leave that assumption in people's minds rather than face the truth about what happened.

Campbell (p. 409) put forth the argument that

> the United States and other modern nations should be ready for an experimental approach to social reform, an approach in which we try out new programs, in which we learn whether or not these programs are effective, and in which we retain, imitate, modify, or discard them on the basis of apparent effectiveness on the multiple imperfect criteria available.

Social scientists need to convince administrators to use true experiments, if at all possible, or quasi-experiments at the very least, when instituting new social programs. For example, a randomization procedure, perhaps based on public lottery, could be used to decide which group receives a pilot program or gains access to scarce resources. Groups not receiving the program or the available resources would become comparison groups. The effect of a social "treatment" could then be meaningfully evaluated. At present, decisions regarding who gets what are often influenced by particular interest groups—as the result of intense lobbying, for example—or made on the basis of political favoritism.

According to Campbell, the most significant change needed is for public officials to emphasize the importance of the problem rather than the importance of the solution. Instead of pushing for one certain cure-all (which, in most cases, has little opportunity for success), officials must be ready to execute reform in a manner that permits the clearest evaluation and must be prepared to try different solutions if the first one fails. Public officials must, in other words, be ready to use the experimental method to identify society's problems and to determine effective solutions.

Campbell's (1969) idea that social reforms and experimental methods be routinely brought together has had some impact on social policymakers, but it is still underutilized (see Berk et al., 1987). The reasons are some of the same ones initially identified by Campbell. Nevertheless, without social experimentation, especially that which makes use whenever possible of randomized field experiments, policymakers and the community at large may believe a treatment works when it doesn't or vice versa. Such incorrect decisions lead us to allocate money and resources to ineffective programs.

Not too many years ago, a show called "Scared Straight" was aired on national television. It described a juvenile education program implemented at Rahway State Prison in New Jersey. The program involved taking youthful offenders into a prison to meet with selected convicts from the inmate population. The goal was to inform juveniles about the reality of prison life and, thereby, the program leaders hoped, dissuade them from further illegal activity. Unsubstantiated claims were made for the effectiveness of the program, including some suggesting a success rate as high as 80% to 90% (see Locke, Johnson, Kirigin-Ramp, Atwater, & Gerrard, 1986). The Rahway program is just one of several similar programs around the country. But do these programs really work?

Several evaluation studies of the exposure-to-prison programs produced mixed results, including positive findings, findings of no difference between control and experimental participants, as well as results suggesting that the program may actually *increase* juvenile crime among some types of delinquents. There is a possibility that less hardened juvenile offenders may increase their criminal activity after meeting the prisoners. It has been suggested that because these less hardened offenders have recently begun a lifestyle wherein they are being recognized and reinforced by their peers for their toughness, this image is also reinforced by the tough image often projected by the prisoners. On the other hand, more frequent juvenile offenders, who have achieved a level of status among their peers for some period of time, may be more threatened by the prospects of prison life because it would mean loss of that status (see Locke et al., 1986).

Attempts to evaluate the effectiveness of this significant social program provide good examples of the difficulties inherent in evaluation research: the difficulty of randomly assigning participants, of getting administrators to cooperate with experimental procedures, and of dealing with loss of participants during the evaluation. Nevertheless, program evaluation based on sound experimental methodology offers policymakers at all levels (institution, community, city, state, federal) the information that can help them make more informed choices among possible treatments for social problems. Since resources inevitably are in short supply, it is critical that those that are available to help society be put to the best possible use.

Our hope is that your knowledge of research methods will allow you to participate knowledgeably and perhaps contribute constructively to the ongoing debate concerning the role of experimentation in society.

SUMMARY

Experimentation in natural settings differs in many ways from experimentation in psychology laboratories. There are likely to be more problems in exerting experimental control in a natural setting, and establishing external validity or generalizing results is more often a key objective. The stated goals of the research and its possible consequences also differ when research is conducted in natural settings. Reasons for doing experiments in natural settings include testing the external validity of laboratory findings and assessing the effects of "treatments" aimed at improving conditions under which people work and live.

Campbell and others have argued that society must be willing to take an experimental approach to social reform—one that will allow the clearest evaluation of the effectiveness of new programs. In many situations (for instance, when available resources are scarce), true experiments involving randomization of individuals to treatment and no-treatment conditions are recommended. However, if a true experiment is not feasible, quasi-experimental procedures are the next best approach. Quasi-experiments differ from true experiments in that fewer plausible rival hypotheses for an experimental outcome are controlled. When specific threats to the internal validity of an experiment are not controlled, then the experimenter, by logically examining the situation and by collecting additional evidence, must seek to rule out these threats to internal validity.

A particularly strong quasi-experimental procedure is the nonequivalent control group design. This procedure generally controls for all major threats to internal validity except those associated with interactions of (1) selection and history, (2) selection and maturation, (3) selection and instrumentation, and (4) threats due to differential statistical regression. In addition to the major threats to internal validity, an experimenter must be sensitive to possible contamination resulting from communication between groups of participants. Problems of observer or experimenter bias, questions of external validity, and Hawthorne effects are potential problems in all experiments, whether conducted in the laboratory or in the field.

When it is possible to observe changes in a dependent measure before and after a treatment is administered, one can carry out a simple interrupted time-series design. The researcher using this design looks for an abrupt change in the time series that coincides with the introduction of the treatment. The major threat to internal validity in this design is history—some event other than the treatment may have been responsible for the change in the time series. Instrumentation also can be a problem, especially when the treatment represents a type of social reform that may lead to changes in the way records are kept or data collected. By including a control group that is as similar as possible to the experimental group, one can strengthen the internal validity of a simple time-series design. A time series with nonequivalent control group, for example, controls for many possible history threats.

In this chapter we also discussed how the logic and methodology associated with single-case experimental designs (see Chapter 9) can be applied to experimentation in natural settings. For instance, an ABAB design may be used when a researcher can control the application and withdrawal of a treatment. In such cases the internal validity of the experiment can approach that of a true experiment.

A particularly important goal of research in natural settings is program evaluation. Persons other than psychologists (such as educators, political scientists, and sociologists) are often involved in this process. Types of program evaluation include assessment of needs, process, outcome, and efficiency. Perhaps the most serious constraints on program evaluation are the political and social realities that surround it. The reluctance of public officials to seek an evaluation of social reforms is often an obstacle to be overcome. Nevertheless, social scientists have called on individuals who are knowledgeable about the procedures of program evaluation to make themselves available to those who are responsible for the delivery of human services. By answering this call, we may help change society in a way that will bring the most effective services to those most in need.

KEY CONCEPTS

basic research
applied research
threats to internal validity
regression
contamination
Hawthorne effect
quasi-experiments

nonequivalent control group
   design
simple interrupted time-series
   design
time series with nonequivalent
   control group design
program evaluation

REVIEW QUESTIONS

1 What special reasons are there for carrying out experiments in natural settings?
2 Explain how laboratory experiments and those in natural settings differ in control, external validity, goals, and consequences.
3 What are the three distinguishing characteristics of true experiments?
4 What obstacles arise in trying to carry out experiments in natural settings?
5 How can participants be randomly assigned to conditions while still giving all participants access to the experimental treatment?
6 How might participants in a control group respond when contamination occurs?
7 What do Cook and Campbell (1979) consider the best test of external validity?
8 Why is the use of a pretest critical in the nonequivalent control group design?
9 Cite one example of a threat to internal validity that is controlled in the nonequivalent control group design and two examples of threats that are not controlled.
10 Explain why we cannot conclude that the treatment and control groups in a nonequivalent control group design are equivalent even when the pretest scores are the same for both groups.
11 What is meant by a "local history effect" in the nonequivalent control group design?
12 What is the major evidence for an effect of the treatment in a simple interrupted time-series design?
13 Explain how the addition of a nonequivalent control group to a simple interrupted time-series design reduces the threat to the internal validity of the design.
14 How can single-case experimental designs be used to determine whether an effect is due to a treatment or to the threat to internal validity called *history?*
15 What are the four types of assessment typically addressed in program evaluation?

CHALLENGE QUESTIONS

1 A quasi-experiment was used to determine whether multi-media instruction is effective. Two sections of introductory psychology were taught by the same instructor. In one section (the treatment group) the instructor used multi-media instruction. In the other section the instructor covered the same material but did not use multi-media instruction. Students did not know when they registered for the course whether multi-media instruction would be used. The students were not randomly assigned to sections. Students' knowledge of the course material was assessed using two forms of a comprehensive introductory psychology test. The students in both sections were tested on the second day of class (the pretest) and at the final (the posttest) on different forms of the test. The comprehensive test can be considered a reliable and valid test that can be used to compare the effectiveness of the instruction in the two sections.

 A   What quasi-experimental design is used in the study?

 B   Comment critically on the fairness of random assignment if you were arguing in favor of doing a true experiment to test the effectiveness of multi-media instruction.

 C   Identify and briefly describe one threat to the internal validity of this study if it had tested only the students who had received multi-media instruction.

2 A psychologist published a book describing the effects of divorce on men, women, and children. She was interested in the effects of divorce that occurred 10 years after the divorce. She found that even 10 years after a divorce half of the women and one-third of the men were still intensely angry. Although half the men and women described themselves as happy, 25% of the women and 20% of the men remained unable to "get their lives back on track." In only 10% of the divorced families did both the former husbands and wives have happy, satisfying lives a decade later. Finally, more than half of the children of divorce entered adulthood as underachieving and self-deprecating men and women. These findings were based on a 15-year study of 60 divorced couples and their 131 children living in Marin County, California (an affluent suburban area including mostly well-educated people). Explain how the use of a quasi-experimental design would have been helpful in order to specify which of the reported results are due to the effects of divorce.

3 The police force of a large city had to decide between two different approaches to keeping the officers on the force informed about the changes in laws. An enlightened administrator of this force decided to put the two approaches to test in a research study. She decided to use the random groups design and she assigned 30 officers randomly to each of the two programs for a period of 6 months. At the end of this time all the officers who successfully completed the training required under the two approaches were given a final test on their knowledge of the law. The 20 officers who completed Program A showed a reliably higher mean score on this test than did the 28 officers who completed Program B. The administrator wisely chose not to accept these results as decisive evidence of the effectiveness of the two programs. Using only the data reported in this problem, explain why she made this decision. Next, explain how her decision would have been different if 20 officers completed both programs (from the original 30 assigned to each) and there was still a sizable difference favoring Program A. Be sure to mention any limitations on the conclusions she could reach concerning the overall effectiveness of these programs.

4 A small undergraduate college with a new physical fitness center decided to introduce a health enhancement program for faculty and staff. The program is designed to take one semester to complete with three 1-hour sessions per week. Comment critically on each of the following questions regarding the evaluation of this program.

A How might an evaluation of needs have played a role in planning the program?

B What obstacles generally exist in real-world settings, and probably apply in this situation, that prevent the conduct of a true experiment to evaluate the outcome of the program? (Be sure to define the three characteristics of a true experiment.)

C As an alternative to a true experiment, a nonequivalent control group design is proposed in which a group of faculty who did not participate in the program agree to take the performance tests before the program begins and after the program has ended. Explain why this nonequivalent control group design is superior to a pretest-posttest design in which only the program participants would be tested. State one threat to internal validity that is controlled in the nonequivalent control group design.

Answer to Challenge Question 1

A The nonequivalent control group design was used in this study.

B Students may perceive random assignment to the two sections as unfair because they would not have a choice about which section they would take. If we do not know whether multi-media instruction is effective, however, then random assignment is the best and fairest method to determine whether multi-media instruction is effective.

C There are several threats to the internal validity of a pretest-posttest single group design. That is why it is referred to as a preexperimental design or a bad experiment. One possible threat in this study is maturation; that is, students are likely (we hope) to increase in knowledge of introductory psychology by the end of the course in which they are enrolled even if multi-media instruction had not been used. The nonequivalent control group design used in this study controls for this threat.

Data Analysis and Interpretation

CHAPTER OUTLINE

INTRODUCTION
THE MULTIPLE STAGES OF DATA ANALYSIS
THE ANALYSIS STORY
COMPUTER-ASSISTED DATA ANALYSIS
A RESEARCH EXAMPLE
Stage 1. Getting to Know the Data
Stage 2. Summarizing the Data
Stage 3. Confirming What the Data Tell Us
CONFIRMATORY ANALYSIS USING NHST
Comparison Between Two Means
Summary of Confirmatory Analysis Based
  on NHST
CONFIRMATORY ANALYSIS USING CONFIDENCE
  INTERVALS
Construction of Confidence Interval for a Single
  Population Mean
Construction of Confidence Interval for
  Difference Between Population Means
Summary of Confirmatory Analysis Based on
  Confidence Intervals
COMPARISON OF TWO MEANS IN A REPEATED
  MEASURES DESIGN
RECOMMENDATIONS FOR COMPARING
  TWO MEANS

DATA ANALYSIS INVOLVING MORE THAN TWO
  INDEPENDENT GROUPS
Analysis of Variance (ANOVA)
Calculating Effect Size for Independent Groups
  Designs
Assessing Power for Independent Groups
  Designs
Analytical Comparisons
Confidence Intervals for Independent Groups
  Design
Error Bars and Confidence Intervals
SINGLE-FACTOR ANALYSIS OF VARIANCE FOR
  REPEATED MEASURES DESIGNS
Effect Size for Repeated Measures ANOVA
Using Confidence Intervals with Repeated
  Measures Designs
TWO-FACTOR ANALYSIS OF VARIANCE FOR
  INDEPENDENT GROUPS DESIGNS
Effect Sizes for Two-Factor Design with
  Independent Groups
Illustration of Simple Main Effect
TWO-FACTOR ANALYSIS OF VARIANCE FOR A MIXED
  DESIGN
STATISTICAL TABLES

INTRODUCTION

The primary goal of data analysis is to determine whether our observations support a claim about behavior (Abelson, 1995). The claim may be that children of drug-addicted mothers exhibit more learning difficulties than those born to drug-free mothers, or that a program intended to prevent depression has worked. Whatever the claim, our case must be prepared with careful attention given to the quality of the evidence and to the way it is presented. When a quantitative research study is conducted, the evidence is primarily the numerical data we collected. To prepare a convincing argument, we need to know what to look for in these data, how to summarize that information, and how best to evaluate the information.

Data, of course, do not come out of thin air; we can assume results were obtained using a particular research methodology (e.g., observation, survey, experiment). If serious errors were made in the data collection stage, then there may be nothing we can do to "save" the data and it may be best to start again. Thus, we would like to assume that the data obtained for the analysis were generated after giving careful consideration to the statement of the research hypothesis (i.e., our tentative claim about behavior), the choice of a proper research design to test that hypothesis, selection of appropriate response measures, and assessment of statistical power. And, of course, we want to make sure that the data were collected in a manner that minimizes the contribution of demand characteristics, experimenter biases, confoundings, or other artifacts of the research situation. In short, we expect that a "good" research study was conducted, one that is internally and externally valid, sensitive, and reliable (see Chapter 6).

Consider what makes an experiment sensitive. A sensitive experiment is one that has a good chance of detecting the effect of an independent variable even if the effect is small. Several factors contribute to experimental sensitivity, including the number of extraneous variables held constant or balanced and the choice of research design. A concept related to experimental sensitivity is *statistical power* or the probability that we will reject a false null hypothesis. (Experimental sensitivity as well as the rationale and techniques associated with statistical power analysis were reviewed in Chapter 7.) Psychological research is frequently "underpowered." Too often research is done that has a high probability of missing a real effect; in other words, there is a high probability of making a Type II error (e.g., Cohen, 1990; Schmidt, 1996). *An assessment of the statistical power for your proposed study should always be part of a research plan.*

Power analysis begins by estimating the size of the effect you are seeking. This typically is done by calculating an effect size based on results of previous studies. We examine, in other words, the effect sizes other researchers obtained when studying the same or similar independent variables. Unfortunately, there is no one single measure of effect size used by researchers in all situations (see, for example, Kirk, 1996). One frequently reported measure of effect size, a standardized difference between means called *d*, was introduced in Chapter 6. Later in this appendix we discuss *d* as well as other popular measures of effect size.

Although power can be controlled in several different ways (see Chapter 7), the most common procedure is through adjustments of sample size. Consequently, once we estimate the size of the effect we are looking for (and choose an alpha level), we can consult "power tables," like the one at the end of this appendix, which identify the sample size needed to "see" (i.e., to obtain statistical significance for) that effect (see Tables A.5 and A.6). We will have more to say about power analyses later in this appendix.

THE MULTIPLE STAGES OF DATA ANALYSIS

Trusting we have obtained data based on a sound research study with sufficient power, what should we do next?

There are three distinct stages of data analysis:

I *Getting to Know the Data:* In the first stage we want to become familiar with the data. This is an exploratory or investigative stage (Tukey, 1977). We inspect the data carefully, get a feel for it, and even, as some have said, "make friends" with it (Hoaglin, Mosteller, & Tukey, 1991, p. 42). What is going on in this number set? Are there errors in the data? Do the data make sense or are there reasons for "suspecting fishiness" (Abelson, 1995, p. 78)? Visual displays of distributions of numbers are important at this stage. What do the data look like? Only when we have become familiar with the general features of the data, have checked for errors, and have assured ourselves that the data make sense, should we proceed to the second stage.

II *Summarizing the Data:* In the second stage we seek to summarize the data in a meaningful way. The use of descriptive statistics and creation of graphical displays are important at this stage. How should the data be organized? Which ways of describing and summarizing the data are most informative? What happened in this study as a function of the factors of interest? What trends and patterns do we see? Which graphical display best reveals these trends and patterns? When the data are appropriately summarized, we are ready to move to the confirmation stage.

III *Confirming What the Data Tell Us:* In the third stage we decide what the data tell us about behavior. Do the data provide confirmation of our tentative claim (research hypothesis) made at the beginning of the study? What *can* we claim based on the evidence? Sometimes we look for a categorical, yes-no, judgment, and act as judge and jury to render a verdict. Do we have evidence to convict? Yes or no: Is the effect real? At this stage we may use various statistical techniques to counter arguments that our results are simply "due to chance." Null-hypothesis testing, when appropriate, is performed at this stage of analysis. Our evaluation of the data, however, need not always lead us to a categorical judgment about the data (e.g., Schmidt, 1996). We don't, in other words, have to attempt a definitive statement about the "truth" of the results. Our claim about behavior may be based on an evaluation of the probable range of effect sizes for the variable of interest. What, in other words, is likely to happen when this variable is present? Confidence intervals are particularly recommended for this kind of evaluation (e.g., Cohen, 1995; Hunter, 1997; Loftus, 1996).

The confirmation process actually begins at the first or exploratory stage of data analysis, when we first get a feel for what our data are like. As we examine the general features of the data we start to appreciate what we found. In the summary stage we learn more about trends and patterns among the observations. This provides feedback that helps to confirm our hypotheses. The final step in data analysis is called the confirmation stage to emphasize that it is typically at this point when we come to a decision about what the data mean. Information obtained at each stage of data analysis, however, contributes to this confirmatory process (e.g., Tukey, 1977).

THE ANALYSIS STORY

Making a convincing argument for a claim about behavior requires more than simply analyzing the data. A good argument requires a good story. A trial attorney, in order to win a case, must not only call a jury's attention to the facts of a case, but also must be able to weave those facts into a coherent and logical story. If the evidence points to the butler, then we want to know "why" the butler (and not the cook) might have done it. Abelson (1995, p. 13) makes a similar point regarding a research argument:

> High-quality evidence, embodying sizeable, well-articulated and general effects, is necessary for a statistical argument to have maximal persuasive impact, but it is not sufficient. Also vital are the attributes of the research story embodying the argument.

Consequently, when data analysis is completed, we must construct a coherent narrative that explains our findings, counters opposing interpretations, and justifies our conclusions. (Guidelines to help you construct an appropriate narrative to accompany your data analysis are found in Appendix C.)

COMPUTER-ASSISTED DATA ANALYSIS

Today, most researchers have access to mainframe computers or microcomputers that include appropriate software to carry out the statistical analysis of data sets. This access to computers has led to a change in the approach taken to introduce students to statistical analysis. Stated simply, the availability of computer-assisted analyses has made knowing step-by-step computational procedures for complex analyses less important. Being able to set up and carry out an analysis using a statistical software package and being able to interpret the output have become essential skills that must be learned by researchers.

Carrying out statistical analyses using computer software requires two types of knowledge. First, the researcher must have a good knowledge of research design and statistics. Second, the researcher must be familiar with the requirements and capabilities of an appropriate statistical software package. Many software packages for statistical analysis are available for use both on mainframe computers and microcomputers. Some of the more popular ones are known by abbreviations like BMDP, SAS, SPSS, STATA, and SYSTAT. You may have access to one or more of these programs on the computers in your psychology department or at your campus computer center. Be sure to check with your instructor regarding the availability of these statistical packages on your campus. Should you decide to purchase a statistical software package for your personal computer, be sure to first obtain advice from an experienced researcher who is familiar with the characteristics of your computer and with the kinds of statistical analyses you want to perform.

In Chapters 6, 7, and 8 of this text we introduced various experimental designs and the logic of null-hypothesis testing and inferential statistics. This knowledge is essential if you wish to use computer-assisted analysis. A computer is not able to determine what research design you used or the rationale behind the use of that design (although some of the more user-friendly programs provide prompts to guide your thinking). To carry out computer-assisted data analysis, you must enter information such as the type of design that was used (e.g., random groups or repeated measures); the number of independent variables (e.g., single factor or multifactor); the number of levels of each independent variable; and the number of dependent variables and the level of measurement employed for each. You must also be able to articulate your research hypotheses and to plan appropriate statistical tests of your research hypotheses. For example, you should know what analytical comparisons you plan to do after performing an omnibus F-test. A computer will quickly and efficiently perform the computations necessary for obtaining descriptive and inferential statistics. To use the computer effectively as a research tool, however, you must give it specific directions regarding which inferential test you want it to do and which data are to be used in computing the test. Finally, when the computer has carried out the computations, you must be able to interpret correctly the output showing the results of the analysis.

A RESEARCH EXAMPLE

How many words do you know? That is, what is the size of your vocabulary? You may have asked yourself this question as you prepared for college entrance exams such as the SAT or ACT, or perhaps it crossed your mind as you thought about preparing for professional school exams such as the LSAT or GRE, as all of these exams emphasize vocabulary knowledge. Surprisingly, estimating a person's vocabulary size is a complex task (e.g., Anglin, 1993; Lorge & Chall, 1963; Miller & Wakefield, 1993). Problems immediately arise, for instance, when we begin to think about what we mean by a "word." Is *play*, *played*, *playing*, one word or three? Are we interested in highly technical or scientific words, including six-syllable names of chemical compounds? What about made-up words, such as the name of your dog, Tootles, or the word you use to call your significant other? One rather straightforward approach is to ask how many words a person knows in a dictionary of the English language. But even here we run into difficulties because dictionaries vary in size and scope, and thus results will vary depending on the specific dictionary that was used to select a word sample. And, of course, estimates of vocabulary knowledge will vary depending on how knowledge is tested. Multiple-choice tests will reveal more knowledge than will tests requiring written definitions of words.

One of the authors of your textbook was interested in the question of vocabulary size and conducted a study examining the vocabulary size of college students and older adults (see Zechmeister, Chronis, Cull, D'Anna, & Healy, 1995). A stratified (by letter of the alphabet) random sample of 191 words was selected from a modest-sized dictionary of the English language. Then a multiple-choice test with five alternatives was prepared. The correct meaning of the word appeared along with four lures or distractors chosen to make discrimination of the correct meaning difficult. For example, respondents were asked to identify the meaning of the word *chivalry* among the following alternatives: a. *warfare*, b. *herb*, c. *bravery*, d. *lewdness*, e. *courtesy*. The random sample of dictionary words was presented in booklets to 26 college age students (mean age = 18.46) and 26 older adults (mean age = 76). On the basis of previous studies, the older adult group was expected to outperform the younger group on the test of vocabulary knowledge.

Data from this study of vocabulary size will be used to illustrate the three stages of data analysis.

Stage 1. Getting to Know the Data

We want to begin by examining the general features of the data and edit or "clean" the data as necessary (Mosteller & Hoaglin, 1991). We check carefully for errors such as missing or impossible values (e.g., numbers outside the range of a given scale). Errors can arise because participants misuse a scale (e.g., by reversing the order of importance) or because someone entering data into a computer skips a number or transposes a digit. When typing a manuscript most of us rely on a "spellchecker" to catch our many typos and just plain misspellings. Unfortunately, there is no such device for detecting numerical errors that are entered into a computer. It is up to the researcher to make sure that data are clean prior to moving ahead.

Of particular importance is the detection of anomalies or what Abelson (1995) calls "klinkers." These are unusual or extreme values that don't appear to belong in the distribution of numbers. As we have seen, an anomaly sometimes signals an error in data recording, such as would be the case if the number 8 appears among data based on respondents' use of a 7-point scale, or if an IQ score of 10 was recorded in a sample of college student participants. Other anomalies are outliers. An *outlier* is an extreme number in an array; it just doesn't seem to "go with" the main body of data even though it may be within the realm of possible values. When doing a reaction-time study, for instance, where we expect most responses to be less than 1,500 ms, we might be surprised to see a reaction time of 4,000 ms. If nearly all of the other values in a large data set are less than 1,500, a value of 4,000 in the same data set certainly could be viewed as an outlier. Yet, such values are possible in reaction time studies when participants sneeze, absentmindedly look away from a display, or mistakenly think that data collection has halted and start to leave. A respondent completing a questionnaire may misread a question and submit a response that is far more extreme than any other response in our data set.

When anomalies appear in a data set we must decide whether they should be excluded from additional analyses. Those anomalies that clearly can be judged to be errors should be corrected or dropped from the data set, but, when doing so, a researcher must report their removal from the data analysis and explain, if possible, why the anomaly occurred. Consider a study by Haden (1998) which examined maternal styles of conversation with children. The researcher contacted 24 mothers who had one child about 70 months old and one child approximately 40 months old. The details of the study need not concern us except to note that homes of the participants were visited four times, with only a few days separating the experimental sessions. The researcher found that sessions three and four for one family were separated by 2 months instead of a few days. Scheduling difficulties with this family had caused the unintended longer interval between sessions. Further inspection during the initial data analysis stage revealed that this family's data consistently produced outliers. Haden (1998) decided not to include the data obtained from this family in further analyses and she explained in the "Participants" section of her published article the circumstances and rationale leading to her decision to exclude this family from her study.

In the first stage of data analysis we also want to look for ways to describe the distribution of scores meaningfully. What is the dispersion (variability) like? Are the data skewed or relatively normally distributed? One of the goals of this first stage of analysis is to determine whether the data require transformation prior to proceeding. Transforming data is a process of "re-expression" (Hoaglin, Mosteller, & Tukey, 1983). Examples of relatively simple transformations include those that express inches as feet, degrees Fahrenheit as Celsius, or number correct as percent correct. More sophisticated statistical transformations are also sometimes useful. (Information concerning the rationale and techniques for data transformation is found in many standard statistics textbooks. See also Emerson [1991].)

The best way to get a feel for a set of data is to construct a picture of it. An advantage of computer-aided data analysis is that we can quickly and easily plot data using various display options (e.g., frequency polygons, histograms) and just as easily incorporate changes of scale (e.g., inches to feet) to see how the data picture is altered. Minimally, by experimenting with different ways to visualize our data set we become more familiar with it. Which visual representation reveals the most about our data? What do we learn about our data when we compare plots with the axes defined differently? Is a polygon or histogram more informative? A picture is not only worth a proverbial 1,000 words, it also can quickly summarize 1,000 numbers. As we become more familiar with different pictures of our data, we learn that some pictures are better than others.

The data from the Zechmeister et al. (1995) vocabulary study represented the number of correct meanings identified out of a possible 191. Because participants without knowledge of the correct answer can be correct by chance on multiple-choice tests, a standard correction for guessing was applied to individual responses. However, two typographical errors appeared in the booklets given to the older adult group and so these items were deleted from further analysis. Also, examination of the test booklets revealed that several of the older participants omitted a page when working through the test booklet. Thus, the number of possible words was reduced for these individuals. Finally, the data were transformed to percentages to account for differences in the total number of possible responses among participants.

After cleaning the data set, the researchers obtained the following data in the first stage of the analysis. These data are expressed in terms of percentage correct multiple-choice performance for college students and older adults.

College (n = 26): 59, 31, 47, 43, 54, 42, 38, 44, 48, 57, 42, 48, 30, 41, 59, 23, 62, 27, 53, 51, 39, 38, 50, 58, 56, 45.

Elderly (n = 26): 70, 59, 68, 68, 57, 66, 78, 78, 64, 43, 53, 83, 74, 69, 59, 44, 73, 65, 32, 60, 54, 64, 82, 62, 62, 78.

A *stem-and-leaf display* is particularly useful for visualizing the general features of a data set and for detecting outliers (Tukey, 1977). A stem-and-leaf display obtains its name through the convention of using leading digits in a numerical array as "stems" and trailing digits as "leaves."

The following is a stem-and-leaf display for the college student data from our example vocabulary study:

2*	3
2	7
3*	01
3	889
4*	12234
4	5788
5*	0134
5	67899
6*	2

The leading digits are the first or tens' digits (e.g., 2-, 3-, 4-,) and the trailing digits are just that, those that trail the leading or most significant digits; in this example the trailing digits are the units' or ones' digits (e.g., -5, -6, -8). The display is made by arranging the leading digits in a vertical array beginning with the smallest at the top. A leading digit is followed, in ascending order, by as many trailing digits as appear in the distribution. Each line in the display is a stem followed by its leaves (Tukey, 1977). For example, the stem 3 in the above display has three leaves, 8,8,9, indicating that the numbers 38, 38, and 39 appear in the distribution. By convention, when many numbers are displayed, or when the entire data set contains only a few leading digits, a leading digit followed by an asterisk is frequently used to indicate the first half of an interval (see Tukey, 1977). For example, 5* would be the stem for leaves 0,1,2,3, and 4 (i.e., numbers 50–54); the leading digit 5 (without the *) would be the stem for leaves 5,6,7,8,9 (i.e., numbers 55–59). In the above display, for instance, the stem 2* has one leaf, 3, and the stem 2 has one leaf, 7, corresponding to the numbers 23 and 27, respectively. Leading digits may also be greater than one. For example, if scores varied between 50 and 150, single leading digits would be used for number less than 100 (8-, 9-, etc.), and two leading digits for numbers greater than 100 (10-, 11-, 12-, etc.).

As you might see, a stem-and-leaf display is something of a histogram on its side. It has an advantage over a histogram, however, in that each value is displayed; thus, specific item information is not lost, as occurs when a histogram is formed using class intervals (Howell, 1997). The most important advantage of a stem-and-leaf display is that it can clearly reveal the shape of the distribution and the presence, if any, of outliers.

Look carefully at the stem-and-leaf display for the vocabulary data of the 26 college students. What do you see? Is the general shape of the distribution "normal" (i.e., symmetrical and "bell-shaped") or skewed (i.e., asymmetrical with scores trailing off in one direction)? Does there seem to be a lot of dispersion or do the numbers tend to "center" around a particular value? Are anomalous values present? We suggest that the stem-and-leaf display for these data reveals that the data are concentrated around the 40 and 50 percentages with the distribution somewhat negatively skewed (note how the "tail" trails off toward the low or negative end of the distribution). Outliers do not seem to be present (e.g., there are no single digit percentages or percentages beyond the 60s).

It can be particularly revealing to display two stem-and-leaf displays side-by-side when comparing two groups of data. Consider the display pictured below. The same stems are used with trailing digits in one distribution increasing from right to left (e.g., 997 5) and leaves in the other distribution ascending (on the same line) from left to right (e.g., 5 67899). This indicates that the first distribution had scores of 57, 59, and 59, and the second distribution had scores of 56, 57, 58, 59, and 59. Side-by-side stem-and-leaf displays might be meaningfully used, for instance, to compare responses to a questionnaire item when a researcher is comparing two groups that differ in socioeconomic status, age, gender, or in some other meaningful way.

A side-by-side stem-and-leaf display for the two conditions of the vocabulary study looks like this:

Older Adults		College Students
	2*	3
	2	7
2	3*	01
	3	889
43	4*	12234
	4	5788
43	5*	0134
997	5	67899
44220	6*	2
98865	6	
430	7*	
888	7	
32	8*	

Look at the display on the left, the one for the older participants. How would you characterize it? The data seem to be somewhat normally distributed, although an extreme score, an outlier, appears to be present. The "32" doesn't seem to belong with the rest of the data. (There are ways to operationalize outliers in terms of their distance from the middle of the distribution and some computer programs will do this automatically.) Without additional information about the nature of the respondent (e.g., amount of medication taken that day, or possible reading problems) the experimenters could find no reason to exclude this score from the study. The presence of this possible outlier necessarily increases the amount of variability present in this group relative to what it would be without this score. Nevertheless, we must acknowledge that some data sets are naturally going to be more variable than others. For example, the older adults in this study simply may represent a more heterogeneous group of individuals than those in the college student sample. (There is a moral here: Obtain as much relevant information about your participants as is conveniently possible at the time you collect data. An extreme score has to be treated as a true score unless you know the reason it is extreme is due to error or to circumstances unrelated to the study.)

Now look at what the side-by-side stem-and-leaf display reveals about both distributions. You should immediately see that scores in the groups overlap to some degree, but there are many more scores above 60 in the older group than in the college group. This "picture" of the data begins to confirm the idea that the older adults performed better overall than the college students on this test of vocabulary size.

Conclusion   In the first stage of data analysis—the process of getting to know our data—we should identify:

a the nature and frequency of any errors in the data set, and, if errors were present, whether corrections could be made or data need to be dropped;

b anomalous values, including outliers, and if they are present, what reasons there might be for the presence of these values and what should be done about them (retained or dropped);

c the general features and shape of the distribution of numbers; and

d alternate ways to more meaningfully express the data.

Stage 2. Summarizing the Data

Data can be effectively summarized numerically, pictorially, or verbally. Good descriptions of data frequently use all three modes. In this appendix we will focus mainly on ways to summarize data numerically, that is, using descriptive statistics, although we do present some graphs. Information about drawing graphs to summarize data is also found in Appendix C. Verbal description of data also is a major topic of Appendix C (see especially guidelines for writing the results section of a research report).

The data from the vocabulary study will be summarized using measures of central tendency, dispersion, standard error of the mean, effect size, and power analysis.

Central Tendency   Measures of central tendency include the mean, median, and mode. These measures do just what their name implies: They indicate the score that the data tend to center around. The *mode* is the crudest measure of central tendency: It simply indicates the score in the frequency distribution that occurs most often. If two scores in the distribution occur with higher frequency than do other scores in the distribution, and if these two scores occur at different locations in the frequency distribution, this two-humped distribution is said to be *bimodal* (to have two modes).

The *median* is defined as the middle score in the frequency distribution. It is calculated by ranking all the scores from lowest to highest and identifying the value that splits the distribution into two halves, each half having the same number of values. The median is the best measure of central tendency when the distribution includes extreme scores because it is less influenced than is the mean by the extreme scores.

The *mean* is the most commonly reported measure of central tendency and is determined by dividing the sum of the scores by the number of scores contributing to that sum. The mean of a population is symbolized as μ (Greek letter mu); the mean of a sample is indicated by M when reported in text, for example, in a results section. (The symbol $\overline{X}$ [read "X bar"] is typically used in statistical formulas.) The mean should always be reported as a measure of central tendency unless there are extreme scores in the distribution.

Measures of central tendency for the two groups in the vocabulary study are:

	College	Older Adult
Mean (M or $\overline{X}$)	45.58	64.04
Median	46.00	64.50
Mode	38,42,48,59	78

As you can see, the mean performance of the college group is much lower than the mean or average performance of the older adults. This confirms what we saw in the side-by-side stem-and-leaf display: The older group performed better overall on the average than did the college group. Note that the mean and median in each group are similar; thus, even though we identified an extreme score in the older sample when looking at the stem-and-leaf display, the presence of this score does not seem to have "thrown off" the mean as a measure of central tendency. There is more than one mode in the college data, each appearing twice; the most frequent score in the older group is 78, and it appeared only three times. As you can see, the mode is not particularly helpful in summarizing these small data sets.

Dispersion   Whenever you report a measure of central tendency, it should always be accompanied by an appropriate measure of dispersion (variability). Measures of central tendency indicate the center of a frequency distribution; measures of dispersion indicate the breadth or variability of the distribution.

The crudest measure of dispersion (the counterpart of the mode) is the range. The *range* is determined by subtracting the lowest score in the distribution from the highest score. For example, in a small distribution made up of the scores 1,3,5,7, the range would be equal to $7 - 1$, or 6.

The most commonly used measure of dispersion (the counterpart of the mean) is the standard deviation. The *standard deviation* tells you approximately how far on the average a score is from the mean. It is equal to the square root of the average squared deviations of scores in the distribution about the mean. The standard deviation is defined as:

$$\sqrt{\frac{\sum(X - \overline{X})^2}{n - 1}}$$

where:

X = individual score
$\overline{X}$ = sample mean
n = sample size
$\sum$ = "sum of"

For reasons that need not concern us here the average of the squared deviations about the mean involves division by $n - 1$ rather than n so as to provide an unbiased estimate of the population standard deviation based on the sample. The standard deviation of a population is symbolized as σ (Greek letter sigma); the standard deviation of a sample of scores is indicated as *SD* when appearing in text, but it is often symbolized as s in statistical formulas. The variance, a measure of dispersion that is important in the calculation of various inferential statistics, is the square of the standard deviation, that is, s^2.

Measures of variability for the two vocabulary groups are:

	College	Older Adult
Range	23–62	32–83
Variance (s^2)	109.45	150.44
Standard Deviation (*SD* or *s*)	10.46	12.27

Note that the stem-and-leaf display showed greater dispersion among the older adults; with the *SD* we have a number to reflect that observation.

Standard Error of the Mean   In doing inferential statistics, we use the sample mean as a point estimate of the population mean. That is, we use a single value ($\overline{X}$) to estimate (infer) the population mean (μ). It is often helpful to be able to determine how much error there is in estimating μ on the basis of $\overline{X}$. The central limit theorem in mathematics tells us that if we draw an infinite number of samples of the same size and we compute $\overline{X}$ for each of these samples, the mean of these sample means ($\mu_{\overline{X}}$) will be equal to the population mean (μ), and the standard deviation of the sample means ($\sigma_{\overline{X}}$) will be equal to the population standard deviation (σ) divided by the square root of the sample size ($\sqrt{n}$). The standard deviation of this theoretical sampling distribution of the mean is called the *standard error of the mean*. Typically, we do not know the standard deviation of this population so we estimate it on the basis of a sample using the formula:

$$s_{\overline{X}} = \frac{s}{\sqrt{n}}$$

Small values of $s_{\overline{X}}$ suggest that we have a good estimate of the population mean, and large values of $s_{\overline{X}}$ suggest that we have only a rough estimate of the population mean. The formula for the standard error of the mean indicates that our ability to estimate the population mean on the basis of a sample depends on the size of the sample (large samples lead to better estimates) and on the variability in the population from which the sample was drawn, as estimated by the sample standard deviation (the less variable the scores in a population, the better our estimate of the population mean will be). As we will show later, the standard error of the mean plays an important role in the construction of confidence intervals and is frequently displayed along with sample means in a figure summarizing results of a research study. It is symbolized as *SE* when reporting results in a research manuscript.

Effect Size   The concept of effect size was introduced in Chapter 6. Measures of effect size or what are more generally called measures of "effect magnitude" (see Kirk, 1996) are important because they provide information about the strength of the relationship between the independent variable and the dependent variable that is independent of sample size. In Chapter 6 we described an effect size measure called *d* which is useful when we have performed an experiment involving two groups. The measure *d* yields information about the size of the mean difference in standard deviation units. Expressing the mean difference in terms of the standard deviation permits effect sizes to be compared across studies using different units of measure. For example, an effect size from a study of vocabulary knowledge that compared college students and older adults on tests emphasizing discrimination of word meanings (i.e., multiple-choice tests) and an effect size from a study contrasting performance of two similar groups using recall of word definitions could be directly compared. Such comparisons form the bases of meta-analyses, which seek to summarize the effect of a particular independent variable across many different studies.

The effect size measure, *d*, defined as the difference between sample means divided by the common population standard deviation, is called Cohen's *d* after the late statistician Jacob Cohen (see Cohen, 1988, for more information about *d*).

$$\text{Cohen's } d = \frac{\overline{X}_1 - \overline{X}_2}{\sigma}$$

The population standard deviation (σ) is obtained by pooling the within group variability and dividing by the total number (*N*) of scores in both groups. A formula for the common *population* standard deviation using sample variances is:

$$\sigma = \sqrt{\frac{(n_1 - 1)s_1^2 + (n_2 - 1)s_2^2}{N}}$$

where:
n_1 = sample size of Group 1
n_2 = sample size of Group 2
s_1^2 = variance of Group 1
s_2^2 = variance of Group 2
$N = n_1 + n_2$

Note: Researchers define the standardized difference between means in slightly different ways (see, for example, Cohen, 1988; Kirk, 1996; Rosenthal, 1991). Dividing the pooled within group variability by $N - 2$ rather than N in the above ratio produces a measure called Hedges's g (Hedges, 1981). The denominator in Hedges's g, in other words, is the pooled *estimate* of the population standard deviation, which is equivalent to the square root of the mean square error in a between-group analysis of variance. As sample sizes increase, the difference between d and g decreases.

Fortunately there are equivalency formulas that permit easy translation from one definition of effect size to another (see Rosenthal & Rosnow, 1991). For example, Cohen's d can be converted to Hedges's g by the formula:

$$g = \frac{d}{\sqrt{\dfrac{N}{df}}}$$

where:
$N = n_1 + n_2$
$df = N - 2$

Inconsistencies in defining effects size based on a difference between means have led some researchers to suggest that an effect size using the correlation coefficient, r, be used (e.g., Rosenthal, 1991). Knowing d, we can obtain r by the following:

$$r = \frac{d}{\sqrt{d^2 + 4}}$$

or directly from t, r is defined as:

$$r = \sqrt{\frac{t^2}{(t^2 + df)}}$$ (see Rosenthal & Rosnow, 1991).

An advantage of r is that it is interpreted in the same way that we interpret a linear correlation coefficient. When r is used, small, medium, and large effect sizes correspond to .10, .30, and .50, respectively (Cohen, 1988).

Which measure of effect size to use is a decision left up to the investigator. But, given the differences in measures appearing in the psychology literature, *it is very important to identify in a research report precisely how a measure of effect size was calculated.*

An effect size for the vocabulary study using Cohen's *d* is:

$$d = \frac{\overline{X}_1 - \overline{X}_2}{\sigma} = \frac{64.04 - 45.58}{\sqrt{\dfrac{(26 - 1)(150.04) + (26 - 1)(109.45)}{52}}} = 1.65$$

To interpret the value of 1.65, we can use J. Cohen's (1992) classification of effect sizes of $d = .20$ for a small effect size, $d = .50$ for a medium effect size, and $d = .80$ for a large effect size. Because our value is larger than .80, we can conclude that the strength of the relationship between the independent and dependent variable is large. "Age," in other words, had a large effect on vocabulary knowledge.

Power Analysis   Knowing the effect size we can determine the statistical power of an analysis. Power, as you will recall, is the probability that a statistically significant effect will be obtained. Suppose that a previous study of vocabulary size contrasting younger and older adults produced an effect size of .50, a medium effect according to Cohen's (1988) rule of thumb. We can use the power tables created by Cohen (1988) to determine the number of participants needed in a test of mean differences to "see" an effect of size .50 with alpha = .05. (See Table A.5 at the end of this appendix.) The table identifies the power associated with various effect sizes as a function of sample size. Looking at the power table we see that the sample size (in *each* group) of a two group study would have to be about 64 to achieve power of .80 (for a two-tailed test). Looking for a medium effect size we would need a total of 128 participants to obtain statistical significance in 8 of 10 tries. Had Zechmeister et al. been looking for a medium effect, their vocabulary study would have been underpowered. As it turns out, anticipating a large effect size, a sample size of 26 was appropriate to obtain power = .80.

Conclusion   In the second, summary stage of data analysis, we should identify:

   a the central tendency (e.g., mean) of each condition or group in the study;

   b measures of dispersion (variability), such as the range and standard deviation, for each condition of the study;

   c the effect size for each of the major independent variables; and

   d how to best present pictorial summaries of the data (e.g., figure showing mean performance across conditions);

Note: Although a graph showing mean performance in the two groups of the vocabulary study could be drawn, a figure usually is not needed when only two group means are involved. Pictorial summaries become more important when summarizing the results of experiments with more than two groups.

Stage 3. Confirming What the Data Tell Us

In the final stage of data analysis we evaluate the evidence for our claim about behavior. What, given these data, can we say about behavior? This stage is sometimes called confirmatory data analysis (e.g., Tukey, 1977). At this point we seek confirmation for what the data are telling us.

The traditional approach to confirmatory data analysis is null-hypothesis significance testing (NHST). It presently is the most common way of performing confirmatory data analysis. Nevertheless, criticisms of NHST have been persistent (e.g., Cohen, 1995; Loftus, 1991; 1996; Hunter, 1997; Schmidt, 1996), and for good reason. We psychologists have been misusing (and misinterpreting) it for decades, all the time ignoring warnings that we were doing so (e.g., Meehl, 1967). Some of the major misuses and misunderstandings associated with NHST were reviewed in Chapter 6. There are critics who suggest we discard NHST altogether (e.g., Hunter, 1997; Schmidt, 1996). Other experts, in what appears to be the majority view, suggest that we hang on to NHST but be cautious about its use (e.g., Abelson, 1995, 1997; Chow, 1988; Estes, 1997; Hagen, 1997; Muliak, Raju, & Harshman, 1997). Whatever the outcome of this debate within the psychology community, there is nearly universal agreement on the need (a) to understand exactly what it is that NHST can and cannot do, and (b) to increase our use of alternative methods of data analysis, especially the use of confidence intervals for effect sizes. Sometimes these alternative techniques will supplant NHST, at other times they will complement NHST.

The rationale both for NHST and for using confidence intervals was discussed in Chapter 6 and we strongly recommend that you review this information before proceeding. In what immediately follows we illustrate data analysis using traditional NHST, pointing out what we can and cannot say based on this form of data evaluation. Then, we will look at an evaluation of the same data based on an examination of confidence intervals for the effect size and contrast the information obtained from this evaluation with that provided by NHST. Finally, we will provide some recommendations for you to follow when evaluating evidence for a claim about behavior involving two means. The most common technique of confirmatory data analysis associated with studies involving more than two groups is the analysis of variance (ANOVA). The rationale for using an ANOVA and the interpretation of ANOVA results are discussed in the second half of this appendix.

CONFIRMATORY ANALYSIS USING NHST

Comparison Between Two Means

A t-test for independent groups was used to evaluate the difference between the mean percent multiple-choice performance of the college and older adult samples. We can define t for independent groups as the difference between sample means divided by the standard error of the mean difference ($s_{\bar{X}_1 - \bar{X}_2}$):

$$t = \frac{\bar{X}_1 - \bar{X}_2}{s_{\bar{X}_1 - \bar{X}_2}} \qquad \text{where} \quad s_{\bar{X}_1 - \bar{X}_2} = \sqrt{\left[\frac{(n_1 - 1)s_1^2 + (n_2 - 1)s_2^2}{n_1 + n_2 - 2}\right]\left[\frac{1}{n_1} + \frac{1}{n_2}\right]}$$

The obtained *t* was 5.84. An alpha of .05 had been chosen prior to doing the analysis. Table A.3 shows critical values of *t* associated with various *df*. The obtained *t* of 5.84 is larger than the critical *t* value with 50 *df* (the *df* = $N - 2$) and, thus, the obtained *t* can be said to be statistically significant. Statistical software programs typically provide the actual probability of an obtained *t* as part of the output, thus circumventing the need to consult a table of *t* values. In fact, the *Publication Manual of the American Psychological Association* (1994) advises that the exact probability be reported. Thus, the result of the inferential statistics test can be summarized as follows:

$$t(50) = 5.84, p = .000.$$

(*Note:* When the exact probability is less than .001 [e.g., $p = .0004$], only the first three zeroes are reported.)

At this point it is important to understand what we learned using NHST and what we didn't learn. Some of the information presented below is also found in Chapter 6; other information may well be new to you. Examine each of the following statements closely and decide if the statement is warranted given the results of NHST reported above. To get feedback about your knowledge regarding the subtleties of NHST we suggest that you mark each statement true or false before reading the discussion that follows.

Based on the above results ($p = .000$), are the following statements true or false?

1 The null hypothesis has a very low probability of being true. (That is, we can safely assume there is little chance, if any, that the difference between the population means equals zero.)

In many ways this is what we would like to say, but we can't (e.g., Cohen, 1995). The results of NHST tell us what the likelihood is of a difference of at least this size given that the null hypothesis of zero difference between means is assumed to be true. IF the null hypothesis is true and we obtain a result with $p < .05$ then we may conclude that the sample mean difference we obtained is an unlikely event given this assumption. This can be useful information (e.g., Abelson, 1997). Nevertheless, as we emphasized in Chapter 6, NHST tests our research hypothesis indirectly. We begin by assuming that the null hypothesis is true; the data do not tell us its probability of being true. Correct answer: False. *Bottom line:* Be careful when you claim what the outcome of NHST is really telling you.

2 The results provide evidence of a scientifically important finding.

Statistical significance does not indicate the scientific importance of a study. Whether the results of a study are important to the scientific community will depend on the nature of the variable under study (the effects of some variables are simply more important than those of others), how sound is the study (statistically significant findings are easily produced by poorly done studies), and other criteria such as effect size (see, for example, Abelson, 1995). Correct answer: False. *Bottom line:* Statistical significance is not the same as scientific significance.

3 The results are of practical importance. (For example, we might recommend that older adults rather than college students be hired in jobs requiring good vocabulary knowledge.)

The practical or clinical significance of a treatment effect depends on the external validity associated with the study, the size of the effect, and various practical considerations (including financial ones) associated with a treatment's implementation. A very large effect might be obtained as a part of a study that does not generalize well from the laboratory to the real world (i.e., has low external validity); thus, the results may be of little value to the applied psychologist. It is also possible that, given enough power, a small effect size will be statistically significant. Small effect sizes may not be practically important outside the laboratory. As you saw in Chapter 6, external validity is an empirical question. It is important to conduct a study under conditions similar to those in which the treatment will be used in order to see whether a finding is practically significant. We are not likely to carry out such an empirical test, however, if the effect size is small (although see Rosenthal [1990] and Prentice and Miller [1992] for some important exceptions). Finally, even a relatively large treatment effect might generalize well to real-world settings but never be applied because it is too costly, too difficult to implement, too controversial, or too similar in its effects to existing treatments. Correct answer: False. *Bottom line:* Remember that statistical significance (or effect size) is not the same as practical or clinical significance.

4 The smaller the p value, the larger the effect of the independent variable. (For example, because the actual probability of obtaining an effect in our example study was less than .001 we can assume that the magnitude of the effect is actually greater than if the probability had been .04.)

The p value does not tell you about effect size (see, for example, Muliak et al., 1997; Schmidt, 1996). Not being aware of this fact, researchers sometimes (incorrectly) believe that a result significant at $p = .01$ level is more important (i.e., the effect is "greater") than a result significant "only" at $p = .05$ level. Thus, when reporting results, researchers have been known to say such things as "the difference is highly significant, $p < .001$" (see Schmidt, 1996, p. 125). It is just as wrong to think that the null hypothesis is less likely to be true when an outcome occurs with $p = .01$ than, for example, one that occurs with $p = .05$ (Muliak et al., 1997). The p value tells you how likely is the outcome assuming the hypothesized value (usually zero) of your null hypothesis. It does not tell you the probability of the null hypothesis (see also discussion following statement 1). Correct answer: False. *Bottom line:* Do not confuse the p value with the effect size or with the probability that the null hypothesis is true.

5 The probability that the observed difference between the means reflects a real (true) mean difference in the populations is .95.

We cannot specify the exact probability for the difference between the means. The outcome of NHST reveals the probability of a difference this great by chance assuming the null hypothesis is true. It does not tell us about probabilities in the real world (e.g., Muliak et al., 1997). If results occur with a probability less than our chosen alpha level (e.g., .05), then, assuming the null hypothesis is true, all we can conclude is that the outcome is not likely to be a chance event in this situation (see also discussion following statement 1). Correct answer: False. *Bottom line:* Be sure you know what the outcome of NHST is really telling you.

6 The probability of mistakenly saying that an effect is present, when the effect is not really present, is .05.

When learning about NHST (e.g., see Chapter 6) we were taught that making a so-called Type I error is equivalent to alpha (.05 in this case). Logically, to make this kind of error, the null hypothesis must be capable of being false. Yet, critics argue that the null hypothesis defined as zero difference is "always false" (e.g., Cohen, 1995, p. 1000) or, somewhat more conservatively is "rarely true" (Hunter, 1997, p. 5). If an effect is always, or nearly always, present (i.e., there is more than a zero difference), then we can't possibly (or at least hardly ever) make a mistake by claiming that an effect is there when it is not. Following this line of reasoning, the only error we are capable of making is a Type II error (see Hunter, 1997; Schmidt & Hunter, 1997), that is, saying a real effect is not there. This type of error, largely due to low statistical power of most psychological studies, typically is much greater than .05 (e.g., Cohen, 1990; Hunter, 1997; Schmidt & Hunter, 1997). On the other hand, as you perhaps can easily imagine, there is always a possibility that researchers will claim an effect to be present when in fact one is not present. Thus, we must leave open the possibility for a Type I error, at least on the conceptual level. False alarms do happen, although it does not seem reasonable given the arguments of the critics of NHST always to assign .05 as the probability of a Type I error. Let us just suggest that Type I errors do occur. Correct answer: False, if the null hypothesis is taken literally; true, if there really is a zero difference between the population means or if we believe that in some situations it is worth testing an effect against a hypothesis of no difference (see Abelson, 1997; Muliak et al., 1997). *Bottom line:* The most common error in psychological research using NHST is a Type II error; nevertheless, as researchers we must be alert to the fact that in some situations it may be important not to conclude an effect is present when it is not (i.e., a Type I error).

7 If the results had *not* been statistically significant (i.e., $p > .05$), then we could correctly conclude that the null hypothesis is true.

By now you should recognize that this statement is false for two reasons. First, there is reason to believe that the null hypothesis is rarely, if ever, literally true. Second, we can always make a Type II error (and some experts, as we have seen, argue this is the only error we can make). Type II errors are likely when power is low, and low power has characterized many studies in the literature (see discussion following statement 6). Just because we did not obtain statistical significance does not mean that an effect is not present (e.g., Schmidt, 1996). In fact, one important reason for obtaining a measure of effect size is that we can compare the obtained effect with that found in other studies, whether or not the effect was statistically significant. This is the goal of meta-analysis (see Chapter 6). Correct answer: False. *Bottom line:* A nonsignificant finding does not tell us that an effect is absent. On the other hand, as we noted in Chapter 6, assuming that our study was conducted with sufficient power, a nonsignificant finding may indicate that an effect is so small that it isn't worth worrying about.

8 The results show that the effect is "reliable" and, thus, repeating this study with the same number of participants would produce a statistically significant result in at least 95/100 tries.

Researchers sometimes mistakenly say that when a result occurs with $p < .05$ that "this outcome will be obtained 95/100 times if the study is repeated." This is simply not true. Statistical significance does not tell us about the probability of replicating the results. The best way to determine the likelihood of replicating a finding is to replicate it. On the other hand, measures of power estimate the probability of obtaining statistical significance if the same study was repeated (Schmidt, 1996). Thinking that a significant result is easily replicated sometimes leads researchers to conduct a replication with fewer participants (i.e., less power) and, consequently, to reduce the chance of finding statistical significance. Correct answer: False. *Bottom line:* The level of statistical significance (i.e., the p value) does not tell us about the probability of replicating this result.

9 Statistically significant results prove that the research hypothesis is correct. (For example, the data from the vocabulary study prove that older adults have greater vocabulary knowledge than do younger adults.)

NHST cannot prove that a research hypothesis is correct. A statistically significant result is (reasonably) sometimes said to "provide support for" or to "give evidence for" a hypothesis, but it cannot prove that the research hypothesis is correct. There are a couple of important reasons why. First, NHST is a game of probabilities; it provides answers in the form of likelihoods that are never 1.00 (e.g., p greater or less than .05). There is always the possibility of error. If there is "proof" it is only "circumstantial" proof. As we have seen (see discussion following statement 1) the research hypothesis can only be tested indirectly by referring to the probability of these data given that the null hypothesis is true. If the probability that our results occurred by chance is very low (assuming a true null hypothesis), we may reason that the null hypothesis is really not true; this does not, however, mean our research hypothesis is true. As Schmidt and Hunter (1997, p. 59) remind us, researchers doing NHST "are focusing not on the actual scientific hypothesis of interest." Second, evidence for the effect of an independent variable is only as good as the methodology that produced the effect. The data used in NHST may or may not be from a study that is free of confounds or experimenter errors. It is possible that another factor was responsible for the observed effect. (For example, suppose that the older adults in the vocabulary study, but not the college students, had been recruited from a group of expert crossword puzzle players.) Evidence for a research hypothesis must be sought by examining the methodology of a study as well as considering the effect produced on the dependent variable. NHST tells us nothing about the soundness of a study's methodology. Correct answer: False. *Bottom line:* A statistically significant finding does not tell us the probability that our research hypothesis is correct.

10 The size of the treatment effect is directly related to the size of the test statistic (e.g., the value of t). (That is, in the example study above we may assume that the effect of the independent variable given $t = 5.84$ is not as large as it would be if $t > 5.84$.)

The size of a test statistic, such as t or F (or the p value; see discussion following statement 5) is not easily related to effect size. Test statistics are influenced by sample size; the same size effect of a variable will yield a larger test statistic if more participants are used. In fact, the development of effect size procedures was motivated by a desire to have a measure of the effect size that was independent of sample size (and, consequently, the size of our test statistic). Correct answer: False. *Bottom line:* Do not confuse the size of your test statistic (e.g., t or F values) with the size of the treatment effect.

Summary of Confirmatory Analysis Based on NHST

Perhaps you can appreciate why researchers urge caution when interpreting results based on NHST. The knowledge gained from NHST is limited, to say the least. Even when a result is "statistically significant," we don't know if the null hypothesis is true or false (although some argue that it is always false). Unless we have calculated an effect size, we don't know the size of the treatment effect. We don't know how likely it is we will be able to replicate the result. The only thing we can say when a result is statistically significant is that *"given these data, and assuming the null hypothesis is true, this outcome is unlikely due to chance."* We have obtained evidence for the fact that there is a nonzero difference between the population means and it is likely to be in the direction that we observed. This information is sometimes useful. There are times when we do want to know what NHST tells us (e.g., Abelson, 1995, 1997; Chow, 1988; Estes, 1997; Rindskopf, 1997). We may use a statistically significant outcome, for instance, as evidence that, as Abelson (1997, p. 14) says, "something surprising and interesting has occurred," and, thus, the effect may be worth pursuing.

If a result is *not* statistically significant we may *not* conclude that the null hypothesis is true (it rarely, if ever, is literally true, and Type II errors are the most common errors in psychological studies). A nonsignificant result leaves us in a state of uncertainty regarding the direction of an effect. *When results are not statistically significant, the information obtained from NHST is greatly improved if we report the power of our study.* Power tells us how likely we are to "see" an effect that is there and is an estimate of the study's replicability. Because power tells us the probability of rejecting a false null hypothesis, we know how likely we are to miss a real effect. For instance, if a result is not significant and power is only .30, we know that a study with these characteristics detects an effect only 3 out of 10 times. Therefore, 7 of 10 times we do this study we will miss seeing the effect. In this case we may want to suspend judgment until the study can be redone with increased power.

Measures of effect size tell us "how big" an effect the independent variable had on the dependent variable. When included with the outcome of NHST, we know what happened in the study independently of sample size and *p* values. This information can be summarized with effect size information from other studies looking at the effect of the same independent variable as part of a meta-analysis. Effect sizes will vary from study to study; a meta-analysis summarizes the results of many studies to reveal a typical effect size for this independent variable. *As recommended by the APA Publication Manual (1994), you should consider reporting a measure of effect magnitude whenever you describe the results of a study using NHST.*

Note: Cohen's *d* can be calculated from the outcome of the independent groups *t*-test, according to the following formula:

$$ d = \frac{2t}{\sqrt{df}} \qquad \text{(see Rosenthal \& Rosnow, 1991).} $$

Final Statement of Results Based on NHST for Vocabulary Study   We are now in a position to model a statement of results based on NHST that takes into account the information gained from all three stages of data analysis and the recommendations of the *Publication Manual of the American Psychological Association* (1994) regarding reporting results (see especially pp. 15–19 of the *Manual* and also Appendix C in this book).

> The mean performance on the multiple-choice vocabulary test for college students was 45.58 (*SD* = 10.46); the mean of the older group was 64.04 (*SD* = 12.27). This difference was statistically significant, $t(50) = 5.84, p = .000$. Older participants in this study had a greater vocabulary size than did the younger participants. The effect size based on Cohen's *d* was 1.65.

(If a figure was drawn showing the mean performance in the groups, then the statement of results should refer to the figure. See Appendix C.)

CONFIRMATORY ANALYSIS USING CONFIDENCE INTERVALS

We illustrated the use of confidence intervals in Chapter 6 in the context of a simple, one-factor experiment. Confidence intervals provide an important supplement to the information obtained through NHST, and, at other times, may replace NHST entirely. Confidence intervals are calculated for a single population mean or population mean difference. We first review the use of confidence intervals for one population mean. Then we introduce confidence intervals for the difference between two population means. After reviewing the procedures and rationale for constructing confidence intervals, we apply them to the data obtained in the two-group vocabulary study used previously to discuss NHST. The data and summary statistics are exactly the same; only the confirmatory stage of analysis has changed.

Construction of Confidence Interval for a Single Population Mean

Imagine you are having a physical examination at the campus health clinic. The technician reports that your pulse is 75 beats per minute. You are unlikely to be concerned that your heart is racing if you are also told the average pulse rate at rest for a person your age is 72 beats per minute. Your knowledge of the variability of pulse rates keeps you from being alarmed. In both physiological and psychological measurement we are often more interested in knowing a range of values that define a "normal" range than we are in specifying a single estimate of a population value. These normal ranges are based on the standard error of the mean and are called *confidence intervals*. In computing a confidence interval we specify a range of values within which we can have a certain degree of confidence that the population mean is included within the interval. As you may suspect, the larger the interval we specify, the greater our confidence that the mean will be included; but larger intervals give us less specific information about the exact value of the population mean. As a compromise, researchers have agreed that the 95% confidence interval and the 99% confidence interval will be used when an interval estimate of the population mean is desired. The confidence interval is centered about our point estimate of the mean ($\overline{X}$), and the boundaries of the 95% confidence interval can be calculated using the following formulas:

$$\text{Upper limit of 95\% confidence interval} = \overline{X} + [t(n-1)]_{\alpha=.05}\,[s_{\overline{X}}]$$
$$\text{Lower limit of 95\% confidence interval} = \overline{X} - [t(n-1)]_{\alpha=.05}\,[s_{\overline{X}}]$$

We have already described procedures for computing the sample mean ($\overline{X}$) and the standard error of the mean ($s_{\overline{X}}$). The unfamiliar symbols in the two equations for the limits of the 95% confidence interval are $[t(n-1)]$ and $\alpha = .05$. The level of significance, alpha (.05), may be familiar to you if you have studied the procedures for inferential statistics tests described in Chapter 6. In the case of confidence intervals, $\alpha = (1 - \text{level of confidence})$, expressed as a proportion. So, for the 95% confidence interval, $\alpha = 1 - .95 = .05$ and for the 99% confidence interval, $\alpha = 1 - .99 = .01$. The t statistic included in the equation is defined by the number of degrees of freedom $(n - 1)$, and the t is determined by looking it up in Table A.3.

Construction of Confidence Interval for Difference Between Population Means

The procedure and logic for constructing confidence intervals for a difference between means is similar to that for setting confidence intervals for a single mean. Because our interest is now in the difference between the population means (i.e., "the effect" of our independent variable) we substitute $\overline{X}_1 - \overline{X}_2$ for $\overline{X}$ and use the standard error of the mean difference rather than the standard error of the mean. To construct confidence intervals for the effect of our independent variable we use exactly the same information we used to carry out NHST for two means. The .95 confidence interval for the difference between two population means is defined as:

$$CI(.95) = (\overline{X}_1 - \overline{X}_2) \pm (t_{crit})(s_{\overline{X}_1 - \overline{X}_2})$$

where t_{crit} is found in Table A.3 with $df = (n_1 + n_2 - 2)$ at alpha $= .05$

We are now in a position to calculate the confidence limits for the difference between the two means in our example vocabulary research study. The .95 confidence interval for the population mean difference is:

$$CI(.95) = 18.46 \pm (2.009)(3.16)$$

thus,   upper limit $= 18.46 + 6.35 = 24.81$
lower limit $= 18.46 - 6.35 = 12.11$

We discuss the interpretation of confidence intervals in the context of the two group experiment or mean difference, but a similar interpretation also applies to the single sample case reviewed above. The following is what can be said based on these results.

1 The odds are 95/100 that the obtained confidence interval contains the true population mean difference or effect size.

As Muliak et al. (1997) point out, the confidence interval either does or does not contain the true effect. A .95 probability associated with the confidence interval for an effect size refers to the probability of capturing the true effect size if we were to construct many confidence intervals based on different random samples of the same size. That is, confidence intervals around the sample mean difference tell us what happens if we were to repeat this experiment under the same conditions (e.g., Estes, 1997). In 95 of 100 replications we would expect to capture the true mean difference with our confidence intervals. Confidence intervals do not require us to decide one way or the other about the truth of some hypothesis and thus do not force errors upon us. Decision errors arise in the context of NHST when we decide to accept or reject a null hypothesis. Note that data evaluation based on confidence intervals emphasizes what is of most interest: the effect of our independent variable. Confidence intervals give us information regarding the likelihood of the effect size.

2 The width of the confidence interval provides information about effect size.

Unlike NHST, by using confidence intervals we obtain information about the probable effect size of our independent variable. Obtained effect sizes vary from study to study as characteristics of samples and procedures differ. The confidence interval "specifies a probable range of magnitude for the effect size" (Abelson, 1997, p. 130). It says that the effect size likely could be as small as the value of the lower boundary and as large as the value of the upper boundary. Researchers are sometimes amazed to see just how large an interval is needed to specify an effect size with a high degree of confidence (e.g., Cohen, 1995). Thus, the smaller the width of the confidence interval the better job we have done at estimating the true effect size of our independent variable.

3 The size (width) of the confidence interval is directly related to sample size.

Interval size corresponds to power for NHST (e.g., Cohen, 1994; Loftus, 1996), and, like power, is affected by sample size. Increasing sample size will shrink the confidence interval. Note, however, that "*p* values" do not change as obtained *p* values do when increasing sample sizes using NHST. Confidence (e.g., .95) stays the same; what changes is the width of the interval to which our confidence refers. By increasing sample size we get a better idea of exactly what our effect looks like.

4 When establishing confidence intervals for a mean difference (as in this example), if the interval brackets zero, then we cannot say if an effect is present.

When a "zero" mean difference is a probable value for our effect, we must accept the possibility that an effect is not present. Confidence intervals give us a probable range for our effect. If zero is among the probable values, then we should admit our uncertainty regarding the direction of an effect (e.g., Abelson, 1997). Note the similarity of this situation to that when a nonsignificant result is found using NHST.

5 All the information obtained through NHST is found in confidence intervals.

Nothing is lost when constructing confidence intervals for an effect size; we get all the information found in NHST and more (e.g., Abelson, 1997; Cohen, 1994; Loftus, 1996; Schmidt & Hunter, 1997). As we saw above (see discussion following statement 2), when zero (mean difference) is in the interval, then we would fail to reject the null hypothesis were we using NHST. If we wish, we can use confidence intervals to make binary decisions as we do in NHST; all the information we need to make such a decision is present.

There are some things we should *not* say based on the use of confidence intervals. For example, we should not say:

1 The odds are 95/100 that the true mean difference lies in this interval.

At first blush this statement may seem to be identical to statement 1 on the previous page. It isn't. Keep in mind that the value in which we are interested is fixed, a constant; it is a population characteristic or parameter. As we noted previously, intervals are not fixed; they are characteristics of sample data. Intervals are constructed from sample means and measures of dispersion that are going to vary from experiment to experiment and consequently, so do confidence intervals. Howell (1997) provides a nice analogy to help understand how these facts relate to our interpretation of confidence intervals. He suggests we think of the parameter as a stake and confidence intervals as rings. From the sample data the researcher constructs rings of a specified width that are tossed at the stake. When using .95 confidence interval, the rings will encircle the stake 95% of the time and will miss it 5% of the time. "The confidence statement is a statement of the probability that the ring has been on target; it is *not* a statement of the probability that the target (parameter) landed in the ring" (Howell, 1997, p. 204).

2 The results provide evidence of a scientifically important study.

Data analysis follows the design and conduct of a research study. It is only one part of the research story. For all the same reasons we mentioned when discussing NHST, an evaluation of the numerical data alone does not speak to a study's scientific importance.

3 The results are of practical importance.

Again, data analysis by itself does not tell us whether a study has practical value. But, because confidence intervals yield estimates of the effect size, we have more information than we did following NHST (i.e., without effect size measures). There still may be issues of external validity or practical problems with applying a treatment in the real world, but confidence intervals for an effect size at least suggest the range of magnitude for probable effects we might expect under the conditions of our study.

Summary of Confirmatory Analysis Based on Confidence Intervals

We are now in a position to model a statement of results for the analysis of mean performance in two groups based on confidence intervals for the effect of the independent variable in the vocabulary study.

> The mean performance on the multiple-choice vocabulary test for college students was 45.58 ($SD = 10.46$); the mean of the older group was 64.04 ($SD = 12.27$). Older participants in this study had a greater vocabulary size than did the younger participants ($SEM = 3.16$). There is a .95 probability that the obtained confidence interval, $12.11 - 24.81$, contains the true population mean difference.

(Note that the confidence interval provides a range of effect sizes in terms of actual mean differences and not a standardized difference such as Cohen's *d*. The standard error of the mean (*SEM*) difference is given, although knowing the sample sizes, it may be calculated from the standard deviations of the groups. As a rule of thumb, the lower and upper .95 confidence limits are approximately 2 times the standard error of the mean. That is, 2 times 3.16 $\pm$ the mean difference approximates the .95 confidence limits.)

COMPARISON OF TWO MEANS IN A REPEATED MEASURES DESIGN

Thus far we have considered experiments involving two independent groups of subjects. As you are aware, experiments can also be carried out by having each subject participate in each condition of the experiment or by "matching" subjects on some measure related to the dependent variable (e.g., IQ scores, weight, etc.). Such experiments are called matched pairs, within-subjects designs or repeated measures designs (see Chapter 7). The logic of NHST is the same in a repeated measures design as it is in an independent groups design. However, the *t*-test comparing two means takes on a different form in a repeated measures design. The *t*-test in this situation is typically called a direct-difference *t* or repeated measures (within-subjects) *t*. When each subject is in both conditions of the experiment *t* is defined as:

$$t = \frac{\bar{D}}{s_{\bar{D}}}$$ where $\bar{D}$ = mean of difference scores or $\sum D/n$, and
$s_{\bar{D}}$ = standard error of difference scores, or

$$s_{\bar{D}} = \frac{s_D}{\sqrt{n}}$$ where s_D = standard deviation of difference scores, and
n = number of difference scores (i.e., number of pairs of scores)

The numerator of the repeated measures *t* is the mean of the difference scores (called "D bar") and is algebraically equivalent to the difference between the sample means (i.e., $\bar{X}_1 - \bar{X}_2$). Statistical significance is determined by consulting a table of critical values of *t* with $df = n - 1$ (see Table A.3). In this case *n* refers to the number of participants or pairs of scores in the experiment. You interpret the obtained *t* as you would the *t* obtained in an independent groups design.

Procedures for assessing effect size in a matched groups or repeated measures design are somewhat more complex than those we reviewed for an independent groups design (see Cohen, 1988; and Rosenthal & Rosnow, 1991, for information pertaining to the calculation of *d* in these cases).

Confidence intervals, too, can be constructed for the population mean difference in a repeated measures design involving two conditions. As with the *t*-test, however, the underlying calculations change for this situation. The confidence interval for the difference between two means in a repeated measures design can be defined as:

$$CI = (\bar{X}_1 - \bar{X}_2) \pm (t_{\text{crit}})(s_{\bar{D}})$$

RECOMMENDATIONS FOR COMPARING TWO MEANS

We offer the following recommendations when evaluating the data from a study looking at the difference between two means. First, keep in mind the final goal of data analysis: to make a case based on our observations for a claim about behavior. In order to make the best case possible you will want to explore various alternatives for data analysis. Don't fall into the trap of thinking that there is one and only one way to provide evidence for a claim about behavior. When there is a choice (and there almost always is), as recommended by the APA's Task Force on Statistical Inference (see Azar, 1997, p. 27), *use the simplest possible analysis.* Second, when using NHST be sure to understand its limitations and what the outcome of NHST allows you to say. Always consider reporting a measure of effect magnitude when using NHST, and, especially when a non-significant result is found, also a measure of power. Although there will be some situations when effect size information is not warranted—for example, when testing a theoretical prediction of direction only (e.g., Chow, 1988), these situations are relatively rare. In many research situations, and in nearly all applied situations, effect size information is an important, even necessary, complement to NHST. Finally, try to "break the habit" of relying solely on NHST and consider reporting confidence intervals for effect sizes in addition to, or even rather than, *p* values associated with *t* or *F*-tests. As we have seen, we get all the information found in NHST and *more.*

DATA ANALYSIS INVOLVING MORE THAN TWO INDEPENDENT GROUPS

Thus far we have discussed the stages of data analysis in the context of a two-group experiment. We can think of a two-group experiment as representing two levels of one independent variable. What happens when we have more than two levels (groups) or, as is often the case in psychology, more than two independent variables? The most frequently used statistical procedure for analyzing results of psychology experiments involving more than two groups is the analysis of variance (ANOVA).

Analysis of Variance (ANOVA)

An introduction to ANOVA was presented in Chapter 6. ANOVA is a special case of confirmatory data analysis examining statistical significance under the null hypothesis. Consequently, many of the problems associated with NHST reviewed earlier apply here as well. In the following sections we describe data analysis and interpretation of experiments using ANOVA. It is assumed that these analyses will be done using a computer (we did!), and thus emphasis will be on interpreting the output obtained from a typical statistical computer package. It should be noted that we consider only cases when all groups (or cells) in the experiment are the same size. We will also assume that the data in our illustrations have already passed through the first, exploratory stage of data analysis when data are inspected carefully, any anomalies are noted, and editing and cleaning have taken place as necessary. Prior to examining the ANOVA results, we summarize the results using major descriptive statistics. As we have emphasized, *appropriate summaries of the data should be performed before making any attempt to interpret the results of NHST.*

As we did when discussing data analysis of two-group experiments, we will point out ways to improve on the information obtained using NHST, especially through the use of effect size measures that complement results of NHST. The specific effect size measures used in multi-group experiments differ somewhat from those introduced in the context of analyzing results from two group experiments. We will also show how data from multi-group experiments might be evaluated using confidence intervals and what has been called the plot-plus-error-bar technique.

We consider four research designs: single-factor analysis of independent groups designs; single-factor analysis for repeated measures designs; two-factor analysis for independent groups designs; and two-factor analysis for mixed designs. *We recommend that, before proceeding, you read carefully the overview of the logic and rationale for ANOVA presented in Chapter 6, as well as the information found in Chapters 6, 7, or 8, that pertains to your specific research design.*

Single-Factor Analysis of Variance for Independent Groups Designs   The single-factor analysis of variance for independent groups designs is used to analyze the results of random groups and natural groups designs involving one independent variable with two or more levels. (The assumptions underlying the test strictly apply only to the random groups design.) The logic of this statistical test is described in Chapter 6.

The data in the following table represent the number of words correctly recalled (out of a possible 20) on a retention test in an experiment investigating memory training techniques. Five participants were randomly assigned to each of four groups (defined by the method of study that individuals were instructed to use to learn the words in preparation for the memory test). The control method involved no specific instructions, but in the three experimental groups participants were instructed to study by making up a story using the to-be-remembered words (story method), to use rhymes to remember the words (rhyme method), or to use visual imagery (imagery method). The independent variable being manipulated is instruction, and it can be symbolized by the letter "A." The levels of this independent variable can be differentiated by using the symbols, a_1, a_2, a_3, and a_4 for the four respective groups. The number of participants within each group is referred to as n; in this case, $n = 5$. The total number of individuals in the experiment is symbolized as N; in this case, $N = 20$. Finally, the number of groups is referred to as a; in this case, $a = 4$.

				Instruction (A)				
Subject	Control (a_1)	Subject	Story (a_2)	Subject	Imagery (a_3)	Subject	Rhymes (a_4)
1	12	6	15	11	16	16	14
2	10	7	14	12	16	17	14
3	9	8	13	13	13	18	15
4	11	9	12	14	12	19	12
5	8	10	12	15	15	20	12
Mean	10.0		13.2		14.4		13.4
Standard deviation	1.6		1.3		1.8		1.3
Range	8–12		12–15		12–16		12–15

An important step in the analysis of any experiment is to set up a data matrix like the one here. The number of correct responses is listed for each person in each of the four groups with each participant identified with a unique subject number. In order to understand the results of an experiment it is essential to summarize the data prior to examining the outcome of the ANOVA. Below the data matrix the mean, range (minimum and maximum scores), and standard deviation are provided for each group.

Before examining the "significance" of an F-ratio, try to get an impression of what the summary statistics are telling you. Look to see if there is a visible "effect" of the independent variable; that is, see if there is substantial variation among the means. (Later, we will show you how to calculate an effect size.) By examining the ranges and standard deviations, get a sense of the variability in each group. (Remember, the less scores vary around their sample means the better the chance of seeing an effect that is present.) The range, or difference between the minimum and maximum values, is useful in identifying floor and ceiling effects. Is the variability among the groups similar? (We want the variation to be relatively homogeneous as wide discrepancies in within-group variability can create interpretation problems when using ANOVA. Many computer programs provide a test of "homogeneity of variance" along with the ANOVA output.)

Our examination of the summary statistics reveals that there appears to be systematic variation among the means; the largest difference is seen between the Control (10.0) and the Imagery Group (14.4). All the experimental means are larger than the Control mean. You will want to refer to the means as you "read" the ANOVA summary table. Note that the range is similar for all the groups; the standard deviations, too, are fairly similar. This attests to the homogeneity of variance among the groups. Moreover, an inspection of the highest scores in each group shows that ceiling effects are not a problem in this data set (as total possible was 20). With these facts in mind we can proceed to an examination of the results of our F-test.

Interpreting the ANOVA Summary Table The ANOVA summary table for the omnibus F-test for the independent groups design described above is reported below. Remember that there were four groups of size $n = 5$ and, thus, overall $N = 20$.

ANALYSIS OF VARIANCE

Source	Sum of Squares	df	Mean Square	F-Ratio	p
Group	54.550	3	18.183	7.821	0.002
Error	37.22	16	2.325		

It is critically important you know what the ANOVA summary table contains. In Chapter 6 we described in detail the typical contents of an ANOVA table for a single-factor design with independent groups and we recommend that you review that information before proceeding.

The probability for the F-ratio in this experiment of .002 appears in the far right column of the summary table. Since this probability is less than the conventional level of significance (.05), we can conclude that this F-ratio is statistically significant. The results of NHST using ANOVA would be summarized in your research report as follows:

$$F(3, 16) = 7.82, p = .002.$$

At this point we know that the omnibus F-test was statistically significant. In other words, these results, assuming the null hypothesis is true, are unlikely in this situation. Thus, we conclude that there was an overall effect of the independent variable of type of memory training in the experiment. This tells us that something happened in the experiment, but it does not specify exactly what happened. It does not, for instance, tell us the degree of relationship between the independent and dependent variable, and thus we should consider calculating an effect size for our independent variable.

Calculating Effect Size for Independent Groups Designs

We mentioned earlier that the psychology literature contains many different measures of effect magnitude, which depend on the particular research design, test statistic, and other peculiarities of the research situation (e.g., Cohen, 1992; Kirk, 1996; Rosenthal & Rosnow, 1991). As we also noted, however, knowing one measure of effect magnitude we usually can translate it to another, comparable measure without too much difficulty. One measure, designed by J. Cohen, for independent groups is f (see Cohen, 1988). It a standardized measure of effect size not unlike d, which we saw was useful for assessing effect sizes in a two-group experiment. However, unlike d, which defines an effect in terms of the difference between two means, f defines an effect in terms of a measure of dispersal among group means. Both d and f express the effect relative to (i.e., "standardized" on) the within-population standard deviation. Consequently, f is defined as follows:

$$f = \frac{\sigma_m}{\sigma} \qquad \text{where} \quad \begin{aligned} &\sigma_m = \text{standard deviation of means} \\ &\sigma = \text{population standard deviation} \end{aligned}$$

Cohen has provided guidelines for interpreting f. Specifically, he suggests that small, medium, and large effects sizes correspond to f values of .10, .25, and .40. The calculation of f is not easily accomplished using the information found in the ANOVA summary table, but it can be obtained without too much difficulty from other measures of effect magnitude as we will show.

Another important class of effect magnitude measures that applies to experiments with more than two groups is based on measures of "strength of association" (Kirk, 1996). What these measures have in common is that they allow estimates of the proportion of total variance accounted for by the effect of the independent variable on the dependent variable. A popular strength of association measure is eta squared or η^2. It is easily calculated based on information found in the ANOVA summary table for the omnibus F-test (although many computer programs automatically provide eta squared as a measure of effect size). In this case, eta squared is defined as the Sum of Squares Between Groups divided by the Total Sum of Squares. In our example,

$$\text{eta squared} = \frac{SS_{\text{between}}}{SS_{\text{total}}} = \frac{54.55}{54.55 + 37.20} = .595$$

Eta squared can also be computed directly from the F-ratio for the Between Groups effect when the ANOVA table is not available (see Rosenthal & Rosnow, 1991, p. 441):

$$\text{eta squared} = \frac{F(df_{\text{effect}})}{F(df_{\text{effect}}) + (df_{\text{error}})}$$

or, in our example,

$$\text{eta squared} = \frac{(7.821)(3)}{(7.821)(3) + 16} = .595$$

Once eta squared is known, we can calculate f according to the following formula (see Cohen, 1988):

$$f = \sqrt{\frac{\text{eta squared}}{1 - \text{eta squared}}}$$

or, in our example,

$$f = \sqrt{\frac{.595}{1 - .595}} = 1.21$$

We can thus conclude that memory training accounted for .595 of the total variance in the dependent variable and produced a standardized effect size, f, of 1.21. Based on Cohen's guidelines for interpreting f (on previous page), it is apparent that memory training had a large effect on recall scores.

Assessing Power for Independent Groups Designs

Once the effect size is known we can obtain an estimate of power for a specific sample size and degrees of freedom associated with the numerator (between groups effect) of the F-ratio. In our example, we set alpha at .05; the experiment was done with $n = 5$ and $df = 3$ for the between groups effect (number of groups − 1). The effect size, f, associated with our data set is very large (1.21), and there really is no good reason to conduct a power analysis for this large effect which was statistically significant.

Let us assume that the ANOVA in the example on page 443 yielded a nonsignificant F and effect size was $f = .40$, a large effect. An important question to answer is: What was the power of our experiment? How likely were we to see an effect of this size given an alpha of .05, a sample size of $n = 5$, and $df = 3$ for our effect? Consulting the abbreviated power table, Table A.6, at the end of this appendix, we find that under these conditions power was .26. In other words, the probability of obtaining statistical significance in this situation was only .26. In only approximately one fourth of the tries under these conditions would we obtain a significant result. The experiment was clearly underpowered and it is unreasonable to make much of the fact that NHST did not reveal a significant result. To do so would ignore the very important fact that the effect of our independent variable was, in fact, large.

Although learning about power post hoc can be important, particularly when we obtain a nonsignificant outcome based on NHST, ideally *power analysis should be conducted prior to an experiment* in order to reveal the a priori (from the beginning) probability of finding a statistically significant effect. An experimenter who begins an experiment knowing that power is only .26 would appear to be wasting time and resources given that the odds of *not* finding a significant effect are .74. Let us assume, therefore, that the experiment has not been conducted and that the investigator examined the literature on memory training and found that a large effect was often obtained by previous researchers in this area. Let us further assume that the researcher wants power to be .80 in the experiment. Because power is typically increased by increasing sample size, we want to find out what the sample size should be in order to find a large effect with power $= .80$.

To find the sample size needed to see a large effect in 8 of 10 tries we use the power table to find n with $df = 3$ under the effect size heading of .40. Table A.6 shows that to achieve power of .80 we would need 18 participants *in each condition* of the experiment. The researcher should take this information into consideration *before* doing the experiment.

Analytical Comparisons

As we noted, knowing that "something happened" in a one-factor, multiple-group experiment is often not all that interesting. We generally do research, or at least we should, with more specific hypotheses in mind than "this variable will have an effect" on the dependent variable. Neither the results of the omnibus F, nor a measure of overall effect size, tell us which means are different from which other means. We can *not*, for instance, look at the four means in our experiment and judge that the "imagery" mean is significantly different from the "story" mean. The results of the omnibus F simply tell us there is variation present that is larger than would be expected by chance in this situation.

One way to learn more about what happened in a multiple-group, single-factor experiment is to perform analytical comparisons (see Chapter 6). Analytical comparisons help specify the source of the overall effect of the independent variable. Typically, a small set of comparisons is required to locate the sources of systematic variation in a single-factor experiment. *Analytical comparisons focus on the particular differences of interest.*

We will illustrate the procedure for doing analytical comparisons by describing the analysis of only one comparison. We will use as our example the analytical comparison of the control group with the average of the three experimental groups to see if this is one source of systematic variation contributing to the overall effect of the memory training variable.

Steps in Developing Coefficients for Analytical Comparison

1 State hypothesis in words: Compare control method with average of three experimental methods.

2 State null hypothesis for comparison:

$$\mu_{a_1} = \frac{\mu_{a_2} + \mu_{a_3} + \mu_{a_4}}{3}$$

3 Set null hypothesis statement equal to zero:

$$\mu_{a_1} - \frac{\mu_{a_2} + \mu_{a_3} + \mu_{a_4}}{3} = 0$$

4 Expand expression by taking minus sign inside brackets and isolating terms over common denominator:

$$\mu_{a_1} - \frac{\mu_{a_2}}{3} - \frac{\mu_{a_3}}{3} - \frac{\mu_{a_4}}{3} = 0$$

5 Eliminate fractions by multiplying expression by common denominator:

$$3\mu_{a_1} - \mu_{a_2} - \mu_{a_3} - \mu_{a_4} = 0$$

6 The coefficients for each group are the multipliers for each mean in this equation.

$$C_1 = +3$$
$$C_2 = -1$$
$$C_3 = -1$$
$$C_4 = -1$$

7 Computation check: The coefficients for an analytical comparison must sum to zero.

8 If a group is not included in a comparison, its coefficient is 0.

F-Test for Analytical Comparison   Once you have determined the coefficients for the analytical comparison you want to do, using the procedures described in the preceding section you are ready to run the program to compute the F-test for your comparison. Computer output for the analysis of the comparison of the control group to the average of the three experimental groups typically will resemble the following:

TEST OF HYPOTHESIS

Source	SS	df	MS	F	p
Hypothesis	50.417	1	50.417	21.685	0.000
Error	37.200	16	2.325		

The format of the summary table is very similar to that for the single-factor analysis we described earlier. In fact, the source of variation labeled "Error" is exactly the same as for the omnibus F-test for this experiment. In general, the error term for analytical comparisons in an independent groups design is the same as the error term for the omnibus test. The source of variation being tested in this analysis is labeled "Hypothesis." It reflects the potential systematic variation due to the analytical comparison being tested. Since analytical comparisons reflect the contrast between two means, they always have only one degree of freedom. In this case, the contrast is between the mean for the control group and the mean of the three means in the experimental groups. The F-ratio for testing the effect of the analytical comparison (called Hypothesis in the summary table) is the ratio of the Mean Square (MS) for Hypothesis over the MS Error. The resulting F shown in the summary table is 21.685. The probability of this F (with 1 and 16 degrees of freedom) under the null hypothesis is less than 1 in 1,000. This probability is less than the conventional level of significance (.05), and so we conclude that this analytical comparison is statistically significant. A report of the outcome of the analytical comparison would be written: $F(1, 16) = 21.68, p = .000$.

The mean for the control group was 10.0, and the mean across the three experimental groups was 13.7. These means along with the statistically significant F-ratio lead to the conclusion that the three experimental groups recalled more words than did the control group. This conclusion based on the test of an analytical comparison is much more specific than the conclusion based on the omnibus test that something happened in the experiment. Because the analytical comparison contrasts performance between two groups, we can obtain a measure of effect size for this comparison using Cohen's d or eta squared (η^2). When two groups are compared, eta (η), or the square root of eta squared, is equivalent to r, a measure of effect size sometimes recommended in this situation (see Rosenthal & Rosnow, 1991). We interpret r as representing a small, medium, or large effect size when r is .10, .25, or .40, respectively (Cohen, 1992). In this example, eta squared = .57, and eta (and r) = .75. How would you interpret the effect size?

Confidence Intervals for Independent Groups Design

As we saw in Chapter 6, the construction of confidence intervals can complement NHST and, at times, represent an alternative to NHST when performing confirmatory data analysis in an experiment involving more than two groups. The logic is similar to that which we outlined for the two-group designs described earlier in this appendix. Consider Figure A.1. We have plotted confidence intervals for each of the four means in our memory training experiment. When presenting confidence intervals for the four groups in our experiment we see immediately that we know more than the omnibus F-test revealed. Inspection of Figure A.1 reveals that the probable effect sizes for the three experimental groups do not overlap the confidence limits of the effect size for the control group. On the other hand, confidence intervals for the experimental groups do overlap; the probable (.95) effect sizes for the training groups are not all that different.

The calculation of confidence intervals for an independent groups design makes use of the error term for the omnibus F, that is, the MS within groups (see Loftus & Masson, 1994). Remember that the MS error is a pooled estimate of the sample variances. In our sample data set the MS error was 2.325 (see ANOVA summary table). The formula for computing confidence intervals around the sample means is:

$$CI = \bar{X} \pm \left(\sqrt{\frac{MS_{error}}{n}} \right)(t_{crit})$$

where n is sample size. The critical t value at .05 is obtained from Table A.3 using the df associated with the MS error. In our example, the values are:

$$CI = \bar{X} \pm \left(\sqrt{\frac{2.325}{5}} \right)(2.12) = \bar{X} \pm 1.45$$

FIGURE A.1 Means and .95 confidence intervals for the memory training experiment.

Note: Each of the four means are substituted for $\overline{X}$ in the above formula to obtain a confidence interval for each group.

Error Bars and Confidence Intervals

Researchers frequently plot the interval associated with the standard error of the mean rather than the confidence interval when describing mean results of an experiment. This technique is referred to as the *plot-plus-error-bar* technique (Loftus, 1993). The "bars" surrounding each mean indicate how much sampling error there is in estimating the population mean based on the sample mean. The smaller the error bar (i.e., the smaller the difference between the upper and lower bars), the better is our estimate of the population mean. Figure A.2 shows "error bars" based on 1 standard error of the mean for each of the four groups in our memory training experiment.

The bars surrounding the means in Figure A.2, based on plus or minus 1 standard error of the mean, differ from the bars revealing confidence limits (see Figure A.1) in a couple of important ways. First, comparing the bars in the two figures, A.1 and A.2, reveals that the bars are much smaller when drawn using 1 standard error of the mean. This is necessarily the case because .95 confidence limits are constructed by multiplying the standard error of the mean by the critical value of *t* for a two-tailed test at alpha = .05. Second, the interpretation of standard error bars and confidence limits differs (see, especially, Estes, 1997). As calculated from sample data, the standard error of the mean estimates the standard deviation of sample means around the population mean. If scores are normally distributed, approximately 68% of the scores will fall within plus or minus 1 standard deviation. The standard error of the mean thus provides a measure of dispersion (i.e., variability) around the population mean. It indicates approximately the average distance in the population a sample mean is from the population mean. The smaller the error bar the better is our estimate of the population mean. *We can consider error bars based on plus or minus 1 standard*

FIGURE A.2   Means plus error bars (±1 standard error of the mean) for the memory training experiment.

error of the mean (see Figure A.2) as telling us how well our sample mean estimates the population mean. Bars drawn using the standard error of the mean should *not* be interpreted to refer to the probability (e.g., .68) that replications will yield means within this interval (see Estes, 1997).

As we mentioned in an earlier section, confidence limits tell us the probability that this interval has captured the population parameter, in this case the population mean. We may assume that over replications of this experiment the population mean will fall 95 of 100 times within the particular interval we have constructed. We must always keep in mind the fact that the specific interval size changes with each replication due to variation in sampling. *We can consider bars drawn from confidence limits (see Figure A.1) as telling us how likely the population mean is to be within this range*, realizing that "this range" will vary from experiment to experiment. Like error bars, confidence limits give us information about the precision with which we have estimated the population mean (the smaller the interval the better is the estimate). Because, except for very small samples, .95 confidence intervals are approximately 2 times the standard error of the mean, it is not uncommon to see researchers construct plots based on 2 standard errors of the mean above and below the sample mean. This type of error bar permits you to say with (approximately) 95% confidence that the interval has captured the population mean.

You should note that the error bars in Figure A.2 are exactly the same size. This is because they (just like the confidence limits) were constructed using a "pooled" variance, specifically, the Mean Square within groups (error), from the independent groups ANOVA (see Estes, 1997). For our hypothetical data set, the Mean Square error is obtained from the ANOVA summary table. The formula for the standard error of the mean is thus calculated as:

$$\frac{\sqrt{MS_{error}}}{\sqrt{n}} \quad \text{where } n = \text{sample size}$$

As we advised you in Chapter 6, *be very careful when reviewing bar plots in the results sections of research reports*. Investigators (and the computer software programs they use) vary in their choice of bars to display and in the calculations on which the bars are based. We recommend that you display confidence limits rather than error bars whenever possible, but that in either case you *always explain to your research audience exactly how these intervals were constructed*.

SINGLE-FACTOR ANALYSIS OF VARIANCE FOR REPEATED MEASURES DESIGNS

The results of experiments that involve repeated measures (within-subjects) comparisons with one independent variable manipulated at two or more levels are analyzed using a single-factor analysis of variance. The within-subjects designs involve the repeated testing of subjects, and so the analyses of the within-subjects designs are also called repeated measures analyses. The underlying logic and the interpretation of the repeated measures ANOVA are the same as for the independent groups designs.

One distinctive characteristic is the procedure used to prepare the data matrix for repeated measures designs. These procedures were illustrated in Chapter 7 using an example of a time-perception experiment involving the complete repeated measures design. The independent variable was interval length, and there were four levels: 12, 24, 36, and 48 seconds. The means (and standard deviations) of the median time estimates for each of five participants for the four intervals were 12.6 (2.19), 22.0 (8.60), 38.0 (18.23), and 39.4 (11.78) seconds. Note that median time estimates represented individual scores because medians are affected less than means by extreme scores that sometimes appear when time is the dependent measure. This represents an example of "re-expression" (transformation) of raw data prior to further analysis that results from the important first stage of data analysis when we become familiar with the characteristics of our data set.

The data from the time-perception experiment outlined in Chapter 7 were analyzed with a single-factor ANOVA for repeated measures designs. The outline of a typical computer output is reported below:

Source	SS	df	MS	F	p
Interval	2515.600	3	838.533	15.555	0.000
Error	646.900	12	53.908		

The purpose of the analysis was to determine if the participants' estimates of the intervals changed with increasing interval length. Although the body of the ANOVA summary table looks pretty much like the one for the analysis of independent groups designs experiments, everything is not the same. The F-ratio is still made up of a numerator reflecting potential systematic variation and a denominator reflecting only error variation. As we described in Chapter 7, however, the error variation in the repeated measures designs is different from the error variation in the independent groups designs. In the repeated measures designs, error variation reflects the residual variation after the variation due to the independent variable and the variation due to subjects have been subtracted from the total variation in the analysis (see Chapter 7).

The Subjects Variation and the Total Variation do not always appear in the computer summary tables because neither is essential to computing the F-ratio for the independent variable. Thus we need to keep in mind that the sources of variation presented in the computer output may not represent all the sources of variation in the experiment.

When we examined the computer output for the data in our sample, we found that the probability associated with the obtained F-ratio of 15.55 was 0.000. Remember that when the probability of an obtained F is so low that it is beyond three decimal places a computer typically presents the probability as 0.000. Thus, do not be worried that something appears fishy; the probability that these results occurred by chance in this situation is simply so low that it would take at least three zeros to express it. Obviously it must be less than the conventional level of significance of .05, so we conclude that the effect of the interval length variable was statistically significant. Participants' time estimates did change with increasing interval length.

The statistically significant F-test for the overall effect of interval length is an omnibus F-test. As was the case in the analysis of independent groups designs experiments, analytical comparisons can be used to identify the source of the effect of an independent variable more specifically. Unfortunately, in the repeated measures designs, the Residual Mean Square is not necessarily the best error term for analytical comparisons and it is recommended that a new error term be calculated for each comparison (see Keppel, 1991, pp. 356–358, for more specific guidelines regarding appropriate error terms for analytical comparisons in repeated measures designs). When an analytical comparison involves only two conditions of a repeated measures design, for example, comparing the mean performance in Condition 1 with the mean in Condition 4 (i.e., performance is not averaged across conditions), the analytical comparison is safely done using a t-test for repeated measures.

Effect Size for Repeated Measures ANOVA

A common measure of effect size for the multiple-group repeated measures design, as it is for the independent groups design, is the strength of association measure, eta squared (η^2). It may be calculated from the Sums of Squares for the within-subjects effect and the Sums of Squares for the Residual or Error. In this situation,

$$\text{eta squared} = \frac{SS_{\text{effect}}}{SS_{\text{effect}} + SS_{\text{error}}} = \frac{2515.6}{2515.6 + 646.9} = .795$$

As mentioned previously, eta squared as a measure of effect size is the proportion of variance accounted for by the independent variable. However, it can be criticized when calculated with more than two conditions because its meaning is rather nonspecific (see Rosenthal & Rosnow, 1991). Like the omnibus F-test, it does not tell us exactly what we want to know. Whenever, possible, we will want to specify more clearly the source of an overall effect, and, as we saw, analytical comparisons with 1 df serve that purpose nicely. Eta squared is much more meaningful when there are only two conditions. As noted previously, in this case, eta(η), or the square root of eta squared, is equivalent to the correlation coefficient r, and effect sizes may be assessed using the guidelines for r. A small, medium, and large effect size based on r corresponds to .10, .30, and .50 (Cohen, 1988).

Using Confidence Intervals with Repeated Measures Designs

Figure A.3 shows confidence intervals around the means in the time-perception experiment. These intervals were constructed using the Mean Square error (Residual) in the omnibus ANOVA (see summary table on page 450) as

FIGURE A.3 Means and .95 confidence intervals for the time-perception experiment.

recommended by Loftus and Masson, 1994). Thus, calculation of the confidence interval was as follows:

$$CI = \overline{X} \pm \left(\sqrt{\frac{MS_{error}}{n}} \right)(t_{crit})$$

The interpretation of confidence intervals in the repeated measures design is analogous to that for the independent groups design, which we discussed above.

TWO-FACTOR ANALYSIS OF VARIANCE FOR INDEPENDENT GROUPS DESIGNS

The two-factor analysis of variance for independent groups designs is used for the analysis of experiments in which each of two independent variables was manipulated at two or more levels. The logic of complex designs with two independent variables and the conceptual basis for the analysis of these experiments are described in Chapter 8. We will focus in this appendix on the computer-assisted analysis of a complex design that involves F-ratios for the main effect of A, the main effect of B, and the interaction effect, A $\times$ B. Our example will involve a significant A $\times$ B interaction, and so we will also illustrate the computations for a simple main effect. The two-factor analysis for independent groups is applicable to experiments in which both independent variables are manipulated using a random groups design, in which both independent variables represent the natural groups design, or in which one independent variable represents the natural groups design and the other represents the random groups design.

The data in the following table summarize the number of correct responses on a simple motor learning task as a function of two independent variables. The first independent variable was the hand the participant used to perform the task, and the two levels of this variable were the dominant and the nondominant hand. The second independent variable was the delay (in seconds) between successive trials on the task, and it was manipulated at three levels (0, 30, and 60 seconds). The hand variable will be referred to as A, with the dominant hand being a_1, and the nondominant hand being a_2. The delay variable will be referred to as B with the 0-second delay as b_1, the 30-second delay as b_2, and the 60-second delay as b_3. Five college students ($n = 5$) were randomly assigned to each of the six groups ($N = 30$) resulting from the factorial combination of the two independent variables.

HAND DOMINANCE (VARIABLE A) $\times$ DELAY INTERVAL (VARIABLE B)

Dominant/0 sec		Dominant/30 sec		Dominant/60 sec	
Subject	a_1b_1	Subject	a_1b_2	Subject	a_1b_3
1	18	6	17	11	18
2	17	7	19	12	20
3	19	8	22	13	21
4	21	9	20	14	22
5	20	10	17	15	19
M	19.0		19.0		20.0
SD	1.58		2.12		1.58
Range	17–21		17–22		18.22

Nondominant/0 sec		Nondominant/30 sec		Nondominant/60 sec	
Subject	a_2b_1	Subject	a_2b_2	Subject	a_2b_3
16	9	21	15	26	16
17	11	22	17	27	19
18	10	23	16	28	18
19	11	24	27	29	20
20	12	25	14	30	18
M	10.6		15.8		18.2
SD	1.14		1.30		1.48
Range	9–12		14–17		16–20

Summary data represent mean (*M*) values for the dependent variable, in this case, number of correct responses (abbreviated as Response). A measure of dispersion, the standard deviation (*SD*), for each condition is also presented. Another measure of dispersion, the range (minimum and maximum scores) is shown for each group. The minimum and maximum values are useful in identifying basement and ceiling effects (see Chapter 8) when the absolute minimum and maximum possible values in the experiment are known. It is good practice to examine the means carefully to make sure they correspond to the correct cells of the design matrix. It is very easy to make a mistake when identifying variables and levels in a complex design. You might, for instance, want to use a calculator to verify that the means of specific cells in the data matrix are labeled correctly in the computer output.

The standard deviation provides helpful information about the variation in each group. Looking across the six groups, we can see that the largest standard deviation was in the dominant hand/30-second delay group (2.12) and the smallest standard deviation was in the nondominant hand/0-second delay group (1.14). The small difference between these two values indicates that there was little difference in the amount of variation across the six groups in the experiment. The fact that the largest standard deviation in any group was just over two correct responses indicates that there was not much variation within any of the six groups. We are almost ready to examine the ANOVA summary table for our two-factor experiment to see if there were any statistically significant sources of variation.

The means for the six groups are used to describe what happened in the experiment. When a complex design is carried out, it will nearly always be the case that interpretation of the results is greatly aided by drawing a graph. We have drawn one such graph in Figure A.4 (see Chapter 8 and Appendix C for more information on drawing graphs). The pattern of means should be reviewed carefully before examining the ANOVA summary table. A figure, or minimally, a table of means, and the ANOVA summary table are the essential tools needed to interpret the results of a factorial experiment.

As we inspect the ANOVA summary table we want to keep in mind the results of our summary analyses. This will help us to know what to look for in the output and how to interpret what we find there. For example, first look at Figure A.4. Note that the figure indicates that there was little change in the number of correct responses as a function of delay for the dominant-hand groups. For the nondominant-hand groups, however, there was an apparent change across the three levels of delay. The presence of a possible interaction is most easily detected by examining the graph of the means. Examination of Figure A.4 reveals that the two lines representing dominant and nondominant

FIGURE A.4   Mean number of correct responses as a function of the delay between trials (in seconds) and hand used to perform motor task (dominant, nondominant).

hands diverge (are not parallel) across the three delay intervals. Descriptively, an interaction between the two independent variables is suggested.

With this pattern of results in mind, we can turn to the analysis-of-variance summary table.

ANALYSIS-OF-VARIANCE SUMMARY TABLE

Source	Sum of Squares	df	Mean Square	F	p
Hand	149.633	1	149.633	61.075	0.000
Delay	93.800	2	46.900	19.143	0.000
Hand × Delay	60.467	2	30.233	12.340	0.000
Error	58.800	24	2.450		

The three F-ratios in a two-factor design take the same form as when the experiment involves a single independent-groups designs. The Mean Square Error is used as the denominator for all three F-tests. The Mean Square for each main effect and for the interaction are used as the numerators for three independent F-ratios. The three F-ratios appear in the summary table in the F column. It is best to evaluate the F-ratio for the interaction first (see Chapter 8). Interactions allow us to determine whether the effect of one independent variable differs depending on the level of a second independent variable (see Chapter 8).

The obtained probability of less than 1 in 1,000 for the F of 12.34 for the interaction is less than the conventional level of significance of .05. So, we can conclude that the interaction was statistically significant. A statistically significant interaction indicates that the effect of the delay variable was different as a function of which hand was used. This result confirms our impression of the pattern of mean performance seen in Figure A.4.

The pattern of means indicates the nature of the interaction. The delay variable had less of an effect on the groups using their dominant hand than on those using their nondominant hand. In the next section we will describe simple main effects, a type of analysis that can be used to specify the nature of an interaction even better. After examining the interaction effect, the two main effects should be examined. The F-ratio for the main effect of hand was 61.075, with a probability of less than one in a thousand. Because the probability is less than the conventional level of significance of .05, the main effect of hand was statistically significant. The means for this main effect can be obtained by averaging across the columns of the table, thereby computing a mean for the dominant hand of 19.3 and for the nondominant hand of 14.9. These means along with the statistically significant F-test indicate that those working with their dominant hand made more correct responses than those working with their nondominant hand. The F-ratio for the main effect of delay was 19.143, with a probability of less than 1 in 1,000. As was true for the main effect of hand, this probability is less than the conventional level of significance of .05, and thus the main effect of delay was statistically significant. The means for the main effect of delay are obtained by averaging across the rows of the table of means. These three means for the main effect of delay are 14.8, 17.4, and 19.1 for the 0-, 30-, and 60-second delays, respectively. These means and the accompanying statistically significant *F*-test for the main effect of delay indicate that the number of correct responses increased with increasing delay. Analytical comparisons could be used to specify the nature of the changes as a function of delay more precisely.

Effect Sizes for Two-Factor Design with Independent Groups

A common measure of effect size for a complex design using ANOVA is eta squared (η^2), or proportion of variance accounted for, which was discussed earlier in the context of single-factor designs. In calculating eta squared, it is recommended that we focus only on the effect of interest (see Rosenthal & Rosnow, 1991). Specifically, eta squared can be defined as:

$$\text{eta squared} = \frac{SS_{\text{effect of interest}}}{SS_{\text{effect of interest}} + SS_{\text{within}}}$$

(see Rosenthal & Rosnow, 1991, p. 352).

Thus, eta squared is obtained for each of the three effects in our sample experiment by the following:

Factor A (Hand):

$$\text{eta squared} = \frac{149.633}{149.633 + 58.80} = .718$$

Factor B (Delay):

$$\text{eta squared} = \frac{93.80}{93.80 + 58.80} = .615$$

Interaction (A × B):

$$\text{eta squared} = \frac{60.467}{60.467 + 58.80} = .507$$

As noted above (and see Rosenthal & Rosnow, 1991), when the sums of squares for the effects are not available, eta squared can be computed using the following formula:

$$\text{eta squared} = \frac{F(df_{\text{effect}})}{F(df_{\text{effect}}) + (df_{\text{error}})}$$

Illustration of Simple Main Effect

Simple main effects are used in the analysis of two-factor designs to identify more specifically the nature of statistically significant interactions (see Chapter 8). A simple main effect involves the overall effect of one independent variable at one level of a second independent variable. Statistical software packages vary as to whether they include the computation of simple main effects. We will illustrate the computation using calculations that can be done with a calculator. For these computations we will use the data for the three delay groups who used their non-dominant hand. These data are in the bottom half of the data matrix near the beginning of the section on the analysis of the two-factor design for independent groups. This simple main effect would be referred to as the effect of delay at the nondominant hand (or more generally, the effect of variable B at a_2). We will first present the computations and then briefly describe the interpretation of simple main effects.

Computing the simple main effect of B at a_2:

1 Compute SS_{B/a_2}

$$= \frac{\left(\sum X_{a_2b_1}\right)^2 + \left(\sum X_{a_2b_2}\right)^2 + \left(\sum X_{a_2b_3}\right)^2}{n} - \frac{\left(\sum X_{a_2b_1} + \sum X_{a_2b_2} + \sum X_{a_2b_3}\right)^2}{(b)(n)}$$

$$= \frac{(53)^2 + (79)^2 + (91)^2}{5} - \frac{(53 + 79 + 91)^2}{(3)(5)}$$

$$= \frac{2{,}809 + 6{,}241 + 8{,}281}{5} - \frac{(223)^2}{15}$$

$$= \frac{17{,}331}{5} - \frac{49{,}729}{15}$$

$$= 3{,}477.20 - 3{,}315.27 = 150.93$$

2 Compute $df_{B/a_2} = b - 1 = 3 - 1 = 2$

3 Compute $MS_{B/a_2} = \frac{SS_{B/a_2}}{df_{B/a_2}} = \frac{150.93}{2} = 75.47$

4 Compute $F(df_{B/a_2}, df_{WG}) = \frac{MS_{B/a_2}}{MS_{WG}} = \frac{75.47}{2.45} = 30.80$

The final computation of the F-ratio involved the use of the Mean Square Error (within groups) from the omnibus F-test. The computations for all the other values needed to compute a simple main effect are shown in the four steps we have outlined. As with any F-ratio, it is necessary to determine the probability of the F under the null hypothesis. The obtained $F(2, 24) = 30.8$ is associated with a probability of less than one in a thousand which is less than the conventional level of significance of .05. Thus, the simple main effect of delay at the level of nondominant hand was statistically significant. Although we will not illustrate the computations here, we did compute the simple main effect of delay for those persons using their dominant hand. The resulting $F(2, 24)$ was .68. An F-ratio less than 1 cannot be statistically significant so this nonsignificant simple main effect indicates that there was no statistically significant effect of delay when participants used their dominant hand. Together, the two simple main effects help us to specify the source of the statistically significant interaction of delay and hand dominance. As described in Chapter 8, the source of an interaction can be specified even more exactly by using simple comparisons to follow up statistically significant simple main effects.

TWO-FACTOR ANALYSIS OF VARIANCE FOR A MIXED DESIGN

The two-factor analysis of variance for a mixed design is appropriate when one independent variable represents either the random groups or natural groups design and the second independent variable represents the repeated measures design. The first independent variable is called the between-subjects factor (here symbolized as A). The second independent variable is called the within-subjects factor (symbolized as B). The two-factor analysis for a mixed design is somewhat of a hybrid of the single-factor analysis for independent groups and the single-factor analysis for the repeated measures designs. This particular complex design was not discussed in Chapter 8 and, therefore, we will present it in some detail here.

The data presented in the following table represent the mean frequency judgments participants gave to four brief segments of popular songs. The participants listened to a tape including several songs; half the individuals did not expect the frequency judgment test (incidental group), and half did expect the test (intentional group). In addition, all participants judged songs that had been presented either one, two, or three times. Thus, the experiment was a 2 × 3 design in which instructions were manipulated in a random groups design with five people assigned to each of two groups and in which the presented frequency variable was manipulated in a complete repeated measures design. The following data matrix shows the mean frequency judgments at three levels of presentation frequency for each participant in each group, as well as summary statistics in the form of means, standard deviations, and ranges, for each condition.

Group (A)	Subject	Presentation Frequency (B)		
		1 (b_1)	2 (b_2)	3 (b_3)
Incidental Group (a_1)	1	1.2	2.2	3.0
	2	.8	2.0	3.2
	3	1.2	1.8	2.8
	4	1.5	2.0	2.5
	5	1.2	2.5	3.2
	M	1.18	2.1	2.94
	SD	.249	.265	.297
	Range	.8–1.5	1.8–2.5	2.5–3.2
Intentional Group (a_2)	6	1.2	1.5	2.0
	7	1.0	2.0	2.5
	8	1.0	1.2	3.2
	9	1.2	2.2	2.8
	10	1.0	2.2	3.5
	M	1.08	1.82	2.80
	SD	.110	.449	.587
	Range	1.0–1.2	1.2–2.2	2.0–3.5

As you should now be aware, it is important to appreciate the trends in the data before looking at the ANOVA summary table. For instance, note that the mean frequency judgments increase in each group as a function of the presented frequency. Interestingly, there is not that great of a difference between group means (i.e., incidental vs. intentional) within each frequency presentation condition.

An outline of typical computer output for a two-factor analysis of variance for a mixed design is presented below; however, be aware that some computer programs separate the output of a mixed design, showing first the output for the between-groups analysis and then the output for the within-subjects analysis (which included the interaction effect). You may find that you have to scroll the computer screen to get all of the information.

Between Subjects					
Source	SS	df	MS	F	p
Group	0.225	1	0.225	1.718	0.226
Error	1.049	8	0.131		

Within Subjects					
Source	SS	df	MS	F	p
Present	15.149	2	7.574	58.640	0.000
Present × Group	0.045	2	0.022	0.173	0.843
Error	2.067	16	0.129		

The summary table is divided into two parts. The Between Subjects section includes the F-ratio for the main effect of groups. The form of this part of the table is like that of a single-factor analysis for the independent-groups design. The Error listed in this section is the within-groups variation. The F-ratio for the effect of group was not statistically significant because the obtained probability of .226 was greater than the conventional level of statistical significance of .05.

The second part of the summary table is headed Within Subjects. It includes the main effect of the within-subjects variable of presentation frequency and the interaction of presentation frequency and group. In general, any effect including a within-subjects variable (main effect or interaction) must be tested with the residual error term used in the within-subjects design. The F-ratio for the interaction is less than 1 and so was not statistically significant. The main effect of presentation frequency, however, did result in a statistically significant F. (As was true in the analysis of the single-factor within-subjects design, your computer output may include additional information than that presented here.)

Interpreting the results of a two-factor analysis for a mixed design follows the logic for any complex design (see Chapter 8). That is, the interaction is examined first, and if the interaction is statistically significant, then simple main effects and simple comparisons are used to identify the source of the interaction. The main effects are then examined, and analytical comparisons can be used to analyze further statistically significant main effects of independent variables with more than two levels.

Care must be taken when analyzing a mixed design to use the appropriate error term for analyses beyond those listed in the summary table (i.e., simple main effects, simple comparisons, and analytical comparisons). For example, if a significant interaction is obtained, it is recommended that simple main effects be analyzed by treating each simple effect as a single-factor ANOVA at that level of the second independent variable. If, for instance, we had obtained a significant interaction between group and presentation frequency in our sample

STATISTICAL TABLES

TABLE A.1   TABLE OF RANDOM NUMBERS*

Col. Line	(1)	(2)	(3)	(4)	(5)	(6)	(7)	(8)	(9)	(10)	(11)	(12)	(13)	(14)
1	10480	15011	01536	02011	81647	91646	69179	14194	62590	36207	20969	99570	91291	90700
2	22368	46573	25595	85393	30995	89198	27982	53402	93965	34095	52666	19174	39615	99505
3	24130	48360	22527	97265	76393	64809	15179	24830	49340	32081	30680	19655	63348	58629
4	42167	93093	06243	61680	07856	16376	39440	53537	71341	57004	00849	74917	97758	16379
5	37570	39975	81837	16656	06121	91782	60468	81305	49684	60672	14110	06927	01263	54613
6	77921	06907	11008	42751	27756	53498	18602	70659	90655	15053	21916	81825	44394	42880
7	99562	72905	56420	69994	98872	31016	71194	18738	44013	48840	63213	21069	10634	12952
8	96301	91977	65463	07972	18876	20922	94595	56869	69014	60045	18425	84903	42508	32307
9	89579	14342	63661	10281	17453	18103	57740	84378	25331	12566	58678	44947	05585	56941
10	85475	36857	53342	53988	53060	59533	38867	62300	08158	17983	16439	11458	18593	64952
11	28918	69578	88231	33276	70997	79936	56865	05859	90106	31595	01547	85590	91610	78188
12	63553	40961	48235	03427	49626	69445	18663	72695	52180	20847	12234	90511	33703	90322
13	09429	93969	52636	92737	88974	33488	36320	17617	30015	08272	84115	27156	30613	74952
14	10365	61129	87529	85689	48237	52267	67689	93394	01511	26358	85104	20285	29975	89868
15	07119	97336	71048	08178	77233	13916	47564	81506	97735	85977	29372	74461	28551	90707
16	51085	12765	51821	51259	77452	16308	60756	92144	49442	53900	70960	63990	75601	40719
17	02368	21382	52404	60268	89368	19885	55322	44819	01188	65255	64835	44919	05944	55157
18	01011	54092	33362	94904	31273	04146	18594	29852	71585	85030	51132	01915	92747	64951
19	52162	53916	46369	58586	23216	14513	83149	98736	23495	64350	94738	17752	35156	35749
20	07056	97628	33787	09998	42698	06691	76988	13602	51851	46104	88916	19509	25625	58104
21	48663	91245	85828	14346	09172	30168	90229	04734	59193	22178	30421	61666	99904	32812
22	54164	58492	22421	74103	47070	25306	76468	26384	58151	06646	21524	15227	96909	44592
23	32639	32363	05597	24200	13363	38005	94342	28728	35806	06912	17012	64161	18296	22851
24	29334	27001	87637	87308	58731	00256	45834	15298	46557	41135	10367	07684	36188	18510
25	02488	33062	28834	07351	19731	92420	60952	61280	50001	67658	32586	86679	50720	94953

*Source: Table of 105,000 Random Decimal Digits, Starement no. 4914, File no. 261-A-1, Interstate Commerce Commission, Washington, D.C. May 1949.

experiment, a simple main effect for the intentional group would involve carrying out a repeated measures ANOVA for only that group (see Keppel, 1991, for more information on these comparisons).

Effect size estimates in a mixed design also frequently make use of eta squared, that is, an estimate of proportion of variance accounted for by the independent variable. As in the independent groups design (see above), eta squared is defined as the *SS* effect divided by the *SS* Effect plus the *SS* Error for that effect.

Col. Line	(1)	(2)	(3)	(4)	(5)	(6)	(7)	(8)	(9)	(10)	(11)	(12)	(13)	(14)
26	81525	72295	04839	96423	24878	82651	66566	14778	76797	14780	13300	87074	79666	95725
27	29676	20591	68086	26432	46901	20849	89768	81536	86645	12659	92259	57102	80428	25280
28	00742	57392	39064	66432	84673	40027	32832	61362	98947	96067	64760	64584	96096	98253
29	05366	04213	25669	26422	44407	44048	37937	63904	45766	66134	75470	66520	34693	90449
30	91921	26418	64117	94305	26766	25940	39972	22209	71500	64568	91402	42416	07844	69618
31	00582	04711	87917	77341	42206	35126	74087	99547	81817	42607	43808	76655	62028	76630
32	00725	69884	62797	56170	86324	88072	76222	36086	84637	93161	76038	65855	77919	88006
33	69011	65795	95876	55293	18988	27354	26575	08625	40801	59920	29841	80150	12777	48501
34	25976	57948	29888	88604	67917	48708	18912	82271	65424	69774	33611	54262	85963	03547
35	09763	83473	93577	12908	30883	18317	28290	35797	05998	41688	34952	37888	38917	88050
36	91567	42595	27958	30134	04024	86385	29880	99730	55536	84855	29080	09250	79656	73211
37	17955	56349	90999	49127	20044	59931	06115	20542	18059	02008	73708	83517	36103	42791
38	46503	18584	18845	49618	02304	51038	20655	58727	28168	15475	56942	53389	20562	87338
39	92157	89634	94824	78171	84610	82834	09922	25417	44137	48413	25555	21246	35509	20468
40	14577	62765	35605	81263	39667	47358	56873	56307	61607	49518	89696	20103	77490	18062
41	98427	07523	33362	64270	01638	92477	66969	98420	04880	45585	46565	04102	46880	45709
42	34914	63976	88720	82765	34476	17032	87589	40836	32427	70002	70663	88863	77775	69348
43	70060	28277	39475	46473	23219	53416	94970	25832	69975	94884	19661	72828	00102	66794
44	53976	54914	06990	67245	68350	82948	11398	42878	80287	88267	47363	46634	06541	97809
45	76072	29515	40980	07391	58745	25774	22987	80059	39911	96189	41151	14222	60697	59583
46	90725	52210	83974	29992	65831	38857	50490	83765	55657	14361	31720	57375	56228	41546
47	64364	67412	33339	31926	14883	24413	59744	92351	97473	89286	35931	04110	23726	51900
48	08962	00358	31662	25388	61642	34072	81249	35648	56891	69352	48373	45578	78547	81788
49	95012	68379	93526	70765	10592	04542	76463	54328	02349	17247	28865	14777	62730	92277
50	15664	10493	20492	38391	91132	21999	59516	81652	27195	48223	46751	22923	32261	85653

TABLE A.2   VALUES OF *r* AT THE .05 AND .01 LEVELS OF SIGNIFICANCE*

df	.05	.01	df	.05	.01	df	.05	.01
1	.997	1.000	16	.468	.590	35	.325	.418
2	.950	.990	17	.456	.575	40	.304	.393
3	.878	.959	18	.444	.561	45	.288	.372
4	.811	.917	19	.433	.549	50	.273	.354
5	.754	.874	20	.423	.537	60	.250	.325
6	.707	.834	21	.413	.526	70	.232	.302
7	.666	.798	22	.404	.515	80	.217	.283
8	.632	.765	23	.396	.505	90	.205	.267
9	.602	.735	24	.388	.496	100	.195	.254
10	.576	.708	25	.381	.487			
11	.553	.684	26	.374	.478			
12	.532	.661	27	.367	.470			
13	.514	.641	28	.361	.463			
14	.497	.623	29	.355	.456			
15	.482	.606	30	.349	.449			

*Adapted from Table VII of Fisher and Yates, *Statistical Tables for Biological, Agricultural, and Medical Research,* 6th ed., 1974. Published by Oliver and Boyd, Limited, Publishers, Edinburgh, by permission of the authors and publishers. Published by Longman Group Ltd., London.

TABLE A.3   SELECTED VALUES FROM THE *t* DISTRIBUTION*

Instructions for use: To find a value of *t*, locate the row in the left-hand column of the table corresponding to the number of degrees of freedom (*df*) associated with the standard error of the mean, and select the value of *t* listed for your choice of α. The value given in the column labeled $\alpha = .05$ is used in the calculation of the 95% confidence interval, and the value given in the column labeled $\alpha = .01$ is used to calculate the 99% confidence interval.

df	$\alpha = .05$	$\alpha = .01$	df	$\alpha = .05$	$\alpha = .01$
1	12.71	63.66	18	2.10	2.88
2	4.30	9.92	19	2.09	2.86
3	3.18	5.84	20	2.09	2.84
4	2.78	4.60	21	2.08	2.83
5	2.57	4.03	22	2.07	2.82
6	2.45	3.71	23	2.07	2.81
7	2.36	3.50	24	2.06	2.80
8	2.31	3.36	25	2.06	2.79
9	2.26	3.25	26	2.06	2.78
10	2.23	3.17	27	2.05	2.77
11	2.20	3.11	28	2.05	2.76
12	2.18	3.06	29	2.04	2.76
13	2.16	3.01	30	2.04	2.75
14	2.14	2.98	40	2.02	2.70
15	2.13	2.95	60	2.00	2.66
16	2.12	2.92	120	1.98	2.62
17	2.11	2.90	Infinity	1.96	2.58

*This table is adapted from Table 12 in *Biometrika tables for statisticians,* vol. 1 (3d ed.), New York: Cambridge University Press, 1970, edited by E. S. Pearson and H. O. Hartley, by permission of the *Biometrika* Trustees.

TABLE A.4 CRITICAL VALUES OF THE *F*-DISTRIBUTION*

Instructions for use: To find the critical value of *F*, locate the cell in the table formed by the intersection of the row containing the degrees of freedom associated with the denominator of the *F*-ratio and the column containing the degrees of freedom associated with the numerator of the *F*-ratio. The numbers listed in boldface type are the critical values of *F* at $\alpha = .05$; the numbers listed in Roman type are the critical values of *F* at $\alpha = .01$. As an example, suppose we have adopted the 5% level of significance and wish to evaluate the significance of an *F* with $df_{num} = 2$ and $df_{denom} = 12$. From the table we find that the critical value of $F(2, 12) = 3.89$ at $\alpha = .05$. If the obtained value of *F* equals or exceeds this critical value, we will reject the null hypothesis; if the obtained value of *F* is smaller than this critical value, we will not reject the null hypothesis.

Degrees of freedom for denominator	Degrees of freedom for numerator																			
	1	2	3	4	5	6	7	8	9	10	12	15	20	24	30	40	60	Infinity
1	**161** 4052	**200** 4999	**216** 5403	**225** 5625	**230** 5764	**234** 5859	**237** 5928	**239** 5981	**241** 6022	**242** 6056	**244** 6106	**246** 6157	**248** 6209	**249** 6325	**250** 6261	**251** 6287	**252** 6313	**254** 6366
2	**18.5** 98.5	**19.0** 99.0	**19.2** 99.2	**19.2** 99.2	**19.3** 99.3	**19.3** 99.3	**19.4** 99.4	**19.4** 99.4	**19.4** 99.4	**19.4** 99.4	**19.4** 99.4	**19.4** 99.4	**19.4** 99.4	**19.4** 99.5	**19.5** 99.5	**19.5** 99.5	**19.5** 99.5	**19.5** 99.5
3	**10.1** 34.1	**9.55** 30.8	**9.28** 29.5	**9.12** 28.7	**9.01** 28.2	**8.94** 27.9	**8.89** 27.7	**8.85** 27.5	**8.81** 27.4	**8.79** 27.2	**8.74** 27.0	**8.70** 26.9	**8.66** 26.7	**8.64** 26.6	**8.62** 26.5	**8.59** 26.4	**8.57** 26.3	**8.53** 26.1
4	**7.71** 21.2	**6.94** 18.0	**6.59** 16.7	**6.39** 16.0	**6.26** 15.5	**6.16** 15.2	**6.09** 15.0	**6.04** 14.8	**6.00** 14.7	**5.96** 14.6	**5.91** 14.4	**5.86** 14.2	**5.80** 14.0	**5.77** 13.9	**5.75** 13.8	**5.72** 13.8	**5.69** 13.6	**5.63** 13.5
5	**6.61** 16.3	**5.79** 13.3	**5.41** 12.1	**5.19** 11.4	**5.05** 11.0	**4.95** 10.7	**4.88** 10.5	**4.82** 10.3	**4.77** 10.2	**4.74** 10.0	**4.68** 9.89	**4.62** 9.72	**4.56** 9.55	**4.53** 9.47	**4.50** 9.38	**4.46** 9.29	**4.43** 9.20	**4.26** 9.02
6	**5.99** 13.8	**5.14** 10.9	**4.76** 9.78	**4.53** 9.15	**4.39** 8.75	**4.28** 8.47	**4.21** 8.26	**4.15** 8.10	**4.10** 7.98	**4.06** 7.87	**4.00** 7.72	**3.94** 7.56	**3.87** 7.40	**3.84** 7.31	**3.81** 7.23	**3.77** 7.14	**3.74** 7.06	**3.67** 6.88
7	**5.59** 12.2	**4.74** 9.55	**4.35** 8.45	**4.12** 7.85	**3.97** 7.46	**3.87** 7.19	**3.79** 6.99	**3.73** 6.84	**3.68** 6.72	**3.64** 6.62	**3.57** 6.47	**3.51** 6.31	**3.44** 6.16	**3.41** 6.07	**3.38** 5.99	**3.34** 5.91	**3.30** 5.82	**3.23** 5.65
8	**5.32** 11.3	**4.46** 8.65	**4.07** 7.59	**3.84** 7.01	**3.69** 6.63	**3.58** 6.37	**3.50** 6.18	**3.44** 6.03	**3.39** 5.91	**3.35** 5.81	**3.28** 5.67	**3.22** 5.52	**3.15** 5.36	**3.12** 5.28	**3.08** 5.20	**3.04** 5.12	**3.01** 5.03	**2.93** 4.86
9	**5.12** 10.6	**4.26** 8.02	**3.86** 6.99	**3.63** 6.42	**3.48** 6.06	**3.37** 5.80	**3.29** 5.61	**3.23** 5.47	**3.18** 5.35	**3.14** 5.26	**3.07** 5.11	**3.01** 4.96	**2.94** 4.81	**2.90** 4.73	**2.86** 4.65	**2.83** 4.57	**2.79** 4.48	**2.71** 4.31
10	**4.96** 10.0	**4.10** 7.56	**3.71** 6.55	**3.48** 5.99	**3.33** 5.64	**3.22** 5.39	**3.14** 5.20	**3.07** 5.06	**3.02** 4.94	**2.98** 4.85	**2.91** 4.71	**2.85** 4.56	**2.77** 4.41	**2.74** 4.33	**2.70** 4.25	**2.66** 4.17	**2.62** 4.08	**2.54** 3.91
11	**4.84** 9.65	**3.98** 7.21	**3.59** 6.22	**3.36** 5.67	**3.20** 5.32	**3.09** 5.07	**3.01** 4.89	**2.95** 4.74	**2.90** 4.63	**2.85** 4.54	**2.79** 4.40	**2.72** 4.25	**2.65** 4.10	**2.61** 4.02	**2.57** 3.94	**2.53** 3.86	**2.49** 3.78	**2.40** 3.60
12	**4.75** 9.33	**3.89** 6.93	**3.49** 5.95	**3.26** 5.41	**3.11** 5.06	**3.00** 4.82	**2.91** 4.64	**2.85** 4.50	**2.80** 4.39	**2.75** 4.30	**2.69** 4.16	**2.62** 4.01	**2.54** 3.86	**2.51** 3.78	**2.47** 3.70	**2.43** 3.62	**2.38** 3.54	**2.30** 3.36
13	**4.67** 9.07	**3.81** 6.70	**3.41** 5.74	**3.18** 5.21	**3.03** 4.86	**2.92** 4.62	**2.83** 4.44	**2.77** 4.30	**2.71** 4.19	**2.67** 4.10	**2.60** 3.96	**2.53** 3.82	**2.46** 3.66	**2.42** 3.59	**2.38** 3.51	**2.34** 3.43	**2.30** 3.34	**2.21** 3.17
14	**4.60** 8.86	**3.74** 6.51	**3.34** 5.56	**3.11** 5.04	**2.96** 4.69	**2.85** 4.46	**2.76** 4.28	**2.70** 4.14	**2.65** 4.03	**2.60** 3.94	**2.53** 3.80	**2.46** 3.66	**2.39** 3.51	**2.35** 3.43	**2.31** 3.35	**2.27** 3.27	**2.22** 3.18	**2.13** 3.00
15	**4.54** 8.68	**3.68** 6.36	**3.29** 5.42	**3.06** 4.89	**2.90** 4.56	**2.79** 4.32	**2.71** 4.14	**2.64** 4.00	**2.59** 3.89	**2.54** 3.80	**2.48** 3.67	**2.40** 3.52	**2.33** 3.37	**2.29** 3.29	**2.25** 3.21	**2.20** 3.13	**2.16** 3.05	**2.07** 2.87
16	**4.49** 8.53	**3.63** 6.23	**3.24** 5.29	**3.01** 4.77	**2.85** 4.44	**2.74** 4.20	**2.66** 4.03	**2.59** 3.89	**2.54** 3.78	**2.49** 3.69	**2.42** 3.55	**2.35** 3.41	**2.28** 3.26	**2.24** 3.18	**2.19** 3.10	**2.15** 3.02	**2.11** 2.93	**2.01** 2.75
17	**4.45** 8.40	**3.59** 6.11	**3.20** 5.18	**2.96** 4.67	**2.81** 4.34	**2.70** 4.10	**2.61** 3.93	**2.55** 3.79	**2.49** 3.68	**2.45** 3.59	**2.38** 3.46	**2.31** 3.31	**2.23** 3.16	**2.19** 3.08	**2.15** 3.00	**2.10** 2.92	**2.06** 2.83	**1.96** 2.65
18	**4.41** 8.29	**3.55** 6.01	**3.16** 5.09	**2.93** 4.58	**2.77** 4.25	**2.66** 4.01	**2.58** 3.84	**2.51** 3.71	**2.46** 3.60	**2.41** 3.51	**2.34** 3.37	**2.27** 3.23	**2.19** 3.08	**2.15** 3.00	**2.11** 2.92	**2.06** 2.84	**2.02** 2.75	**1.92** 2.57
19	**4.38** 8.18	**3.52** 5.93	**3.13** 5.01	**2.90** 4.50	**2.74** 4.17	**2.63** 3.94	**2.54** 3.77	**2.48** 3.63	**2.42** 3.52	**2.38** 3.43	**2.31** 3.30	**2.23** 3.15	**2.16** 3.00	**2.11** 2.92	**2.07** 2.84	**2.03** 2.76	**1.98** 2.67	**1.88** 2.49
20	**4.35** 8.10	**3.49** 5.85	**3.10** 4.94	**2.87** 4.43	**2.71** 4.10	**2.60** 3.87	**2.51** 3.70	**2.45** 3.56	**2.39** 3.46	**2.35** 3.37	**2.28** 3.23	**2.20** 3.09	**2.12** 2.94	**2.08** 2.86	**2.04** 2.78	**1.99** 2.69	**1.95** 2.61	**1.84** 2.42
22	**4.30** 7.95	**3.44** 5.72	**3.05** 4.82	**2.82** 4.31	**2.66** 3.99	**2.55** 3.76	**2.46** 3.59	**2.40** 3.45	**2.34** 3.35	**2.30** 3.26	**2.23** 3.12	**2.15** 2.98	**2.07** 2.83	**2.03** 2.75	**1.98** 2.67	**1.94** 2.58	**1.89** 2.50	**1.78** 2.31
24	**4.26** 7.82	**3.40** 5.61	**3.01** 4.72	**2.78** 4.22	**2.62** 3.90	**2.51** 3.67	**2.42** 3.50	**2.36** 3.36	**2.30** 3.26	**2.25** 3.17	**2.18** 3.03	**2.11** 2.89	**2.03** 2.74	**1.98** 2.66	**1.94** 2.58	**1.89** 2.49	**1.84** 2.40	**1.73** 2.21

(*continued*)

TABLE A.4   CRITICAL VALUES OF THE *F*-DISTRIBUTION* (*Concluded*)

								Degrees of freedom for numerator											
		1	2	3	4	5	6	7	8	9	10	12	15	20	24	30	40	60	Infinity
	26	4.23	3.37	2.98	2.74	2.59	2.47	2.39	2.32	2.27	2.22	2.15	2.07	1.99	1.95	1.90	1.85	1.80	1.69
		7.72	5.53	4.64	4.14	3.82	3.59	3.42	3.29	3.18	3.09	2.96	2.81	2.66	2.58	2.50	2.42	2.33	2.13
	28	4.20	3.34	2.95	2.71	2.56	2.45	2.36	2.29	2.24	2.19	2.12	2.04	1.96	1.91	1.87	1.82	1.77	1.65
		7.64	5.45	4.57	4.07	3.75	3.53	3.36	3.23	3.12	3.03	2.90	2.75	2.60	2.52	2.44	2.35	2.26	2.06
Degrees of freedom for denominator	30	4.17	3.32	2.92	2.69	2.53	2.42	2.33	2.27	2.21	2.16	2.09	2.01	1.93	1.89	1.84	1.79	1.74	1.62
		7.56	5.39	4.51	4.02	3.70	3.47	3.30	3.17	3.07	2.98	2.84	2.70	2.55	2.47	2.39	2.30	2.21	2.01
	40	4.08	3.23	2.84	2.61	2.45	2.34	2.25	2.18	2.12	2.08	2.00	1.92	1.84	1.79	1.74	1.69	1.64	1.51
		7.31	5.18	4.31	3.83	3.51	3.29	3.12	2.99	2.89	2.80	2.66	2.52	2.37	2.29	2.20	2.11	2.02	1.80
	60	4.00	3.15	2.76	2.53	2.37	2.25	2.17	2.10	2.04	1.99	1.92	1.84	1.75	1.7	1.65	1.59	1.53	1.39
		7.06	4.98	4.13	3.65	3.34	3.12	2.95	2.82	2.72	2.63	2.50	2.35	2.20	2.12	2.03	1.94	1.84	1.60
	120	3.92	3.07	2.68	2.45	2.29	2.17	2.09	2.02	1.96	1.91	1.83	1.75	1.66	1.61	1.55	1.50	1.43	1.25
		6.85	4.79	3.95	3.48	3.17	2.96	2.79	2.66	2.56	2.47	2.34	2.19	2.03	1.95	1.86	1.76	1.66	1.38
	INFINITY	3.84	3.00	2.60	2.37	2.21	2.10	2.01	1.94	1.88	1.83	1.75	1.67	1.57	1.52	1.46	1.39	1.32	1.00
		6.63	4.61	3.78	3.32	3.02	2.80	2.64	2.51	2.41	2.32	2.18	2.04	1.88	1.79	1.70	1.59	1.47	1.00

*This table is abridged from Table 18 in *Biometrika tables for statisticians,* vol. 1 (3d ed.), New York: Cambridge University Press, 1970, edited by E. S. Pearson and H. O. Hartley, by permission of the *Biometrika* Trustees.

TABLE A.5   POWER TABLE FOR COMPARISON BETWEEN TWO MEANS (INDEPENDENT GROUPS) WITH ALPHA = .05 (TWO-TAILED TEST)

Note: The table shows the power associated with various effect sizes (.10–1.00) as a function of sample size for an independent groups *t*-test (α = .05, two-tailed test). Effect size is based on Cohen's *d*. The table may be used to assess power post hoc, that is, after a study has been completed. For example, when *n* = 20 in *each group* and the effect size is medium (.50), power is .33. (Decimal points have been omitted in table.) For the same sample size and a large effect size (.80), power is .69. The table may also be used in planning an experiment. Suppose that an examination of the literature suggests that the effect you are looking for is about .60, slightly greater than a medium effect size according to Cohen's (1988) rule of thumb. What sample size in needed to see this effect with power =.80? Looking at the column for this size effect (.60), you will see that power increases as sample size increases until .84 power is achieved when sample size is 50. To obtain power =.80 we can estimate that sample size should be about 45 (by interpolating between sample size 40 and 50). What sample size is needed to see this effect with power = .70? You should see that sample size must be 35 in each group to achieve power =.70. (Based on Cohen, 1988, pp. 36–37.)

		Effect Size (d)								
		(Small)				(Medium)			(Large)	
n	.10	.20	.30	.40	.50	.60	.70	.80	1.00
10	06	07	10	13	18	24	31	39	56
15	06	08	12	18	26	35	45	56	75
20	06	09	15	23	33	45	58	69	87
25	06	11	18	28	41	55	68	79	93
30	07	12	21	33	47	55	68	79	93
35	07	13	23	38	54	70	82	91	98
40	07	14	26	42	60	75	87	94	99
50	08	17	32	50	70	84	93	98	*
60	08	19	37	58	77	90	97	99	*
80	10	24	47	71	88	96	99	*	*
100	11	29	56	80	94	99	*	*	*

TABLE A.6   POWER TABLE FOR ANALYSIS OF VARIANCE FOR INDEPENDENT GROUPS WITH ALPHA = .05

Note: The table shows the power associated with various effect sizes (.05–.50) as a function of sample size in each group in an independent groups design. Effect size is assessed using Cohen's *f* (see Appendix A text). Power is summarized separately for an experiment with independent groups of 2, 3, 4, and 5. The table may be used to assess power post hoc, after a study is completed. For example, assume that an experiment was conducted with 3 groups (*n* = 30) and an analysis of variance performed on the data. Assume further that the effect size based on *f* was .40, a large effect according to Cohen's (1988) rule of thumb. What was the power associated with this test? Looking at that portion of the table that reveals power values for 3 groups (*df* = 2), and under the column .40, you can see that power = .93 when sample size is 30. (Decimal points have been omitted in the table.) The table also may be used to plan an experiment by determining the sample size needed to see an effect of a specific magnitude. Suppose that a review of previous studies revealed that on the average an effect size of .30 was obtained for the variable of interest. What sample size would be needed in a 4 group experiment to see an effect of this size with power = .80? Looking at the power values for an independent groups experiment with 4 groups, and under the effect size column .30, you will see that power increases as sample size increases and is .84 when sample size is 30. Power is .76 when *n* = 25; thus we can interpolate to estimate that sample size should be about 28 to achieve power = .80. If the effect size we are seeking is .10, a small effect size according to Cohen, you can see that power is only .22 even when sample size is 60. (Based on Cohen, 1988, pp. 311–318.)

2 Groups (*df* = 1)

				Effect Size (*f*)					
		(Small)			(Medium)			(Large)	
n	.05	.10	.15	.20	.25	.30	.35	.40	.50
5	05	06	07	08	11	13	16	20	29
10	05	07	09	13	18	25	32	40	57
15	06	08	12	18	26	36	47	57	76
20	06	09	15	23	34	46	59	70	88
25	06	10	18	29	42	56	69	80	94
30	06	11	21	34	49	64	77	87	97
35	07	12	24	39	55	71	83	92	99
40	07	14	27	43	61	77	88	95	99
50	07	16	32	52	71	85	94	98	*
60	08	19	38	60	79	91	97	99	*

3 Groups (*df* = 2)

				Effect Size (*f*)					
		(Small)			(Medium)			(Large)	
n	.05	.10	.15	.20	.25	.30	.35	.40	.50
5	05	06	07	09	11	14	17	22	32
10	05	07	10	14	20	27	35	45	64
15	06	08	13	20	29	40	52	64	84
20	06	09	16	26	38	52	66	78	93
25	06	10	19	32	47	63	77	87	98
30	06	12	22	37	55	71	85	93	99
35	07	13	26	43	62	79	90	96	*
40	07	15	29	48	68	84	94	98	*
50	08	18	36	58	79	92	98	99	*
60	08	21	42	67	86	96	99	*	*

(continued)

TABLE A.6   POWER TABLE FOR ANALYSIS OF VARIANCE FOR INDEPENDENT GROUPS WITH ALPHA = .05
(*Concluded*)

4 Groups ($df = 3$)

		(Small)			(Medium)			(Large)	
n	.05	.10	.15	.20	.25	.30	.35	.40	.50
5	05	06	07	09	12	16	21	26	40
10	06	07	10	16	23	33	44	56	78
15	06	09	14	23	36	50	65	78	94
20	06	10	18	31	47	65	79	90	99
25	06	12	23	39	58	76	89	96	*
30	07	13	27	46	67	84	94	98	*
35	07	15	31	54	75	90	97	99	*
40	07	17	36	60	81	94	99	*	*
50	08	19	40	65	85	96	99	*	*
60	09	22	47	74	91	98	*	*	*

5 Groups ($df = 4$)

Effect Size (f)

		(Small)			(Medium)			(Large)	
n	.05	.10	.15	.20	.25	.30	.35	.40	.50
5	05	06	07	10	13	17	22	29	44
10	06	07	11	17	25	36	48	61	83
15	06	09	15	25	39	55	70	82	96
20	06	11	20	34	52	70	84	93	99
25	07	12	24	43	63	81	92	98	*
30	07	14	29	51	73	88	96	99	*
35	07	16	34	65	80	93	98	*	*
40	08	18	39	68	86	96	99	*	*
50	08	21	44	71	90	98	*	*	*
60	09	24	52	80	95	99	*	*	*

*Indicates that power is greater than .995.

APPENDIX

B

Questionnaire Construction

CHAPTER OUTLINE

INTRODUCTION
STEPS IN PREPARING A QUESTIONNAIRE
GUIDELINES FOR THE EFFECTIVE WORDING OF QUESTIONS
GUIDELINES FOR THE GENERAL FORMAT OF A QUESTIONNAIRE
Questionnaire Design
Ordering of Questions
ENHANCING RESPONSE RATE IN A MAIL SURVEY

INTRODUCTION

In Chapter 4 we discussed procedures for administering a survey without describing in detail the nature of the most common survey research instrument: the questionnaire. Even if the sample used was perfectly representative, the response rate was 100%, and the research design was elegantly planned and perfectly executed, the results of a survey will be useless if the questionnaire was poorly constructed. Although there is no substitute for experience when it comes to preparing a good questionnaire, there are a few general principles of sound questionnaire construction with which you should be familiar before you do your first survey. In this appendix we describe six basic steps in preparing a questionnaire and then offer some more specific guidelines for writing and administering individual questions. This material will be most useful should you decide to make use of a questionnaire as part of a research project you are doing.

STEPS IN PREPARING A QUESTIONNAIRE

We can suggest six basic steps in preparing a questionnaire:

1 Decide what information should be sought.
2 Decide what type of questionnaire should be used.
3 Write a first draft of the questionnaire.
4 Reexamine and revise the questionnaire.
5 Pretest the questionnaire.
6 Edit the questionnaire and specify the procedures for its use.

Step 1   The warning "Watch out for that first step!" is appropriate here. *The first step in questionnaire construction—deciding what information is to be sought—should actually be the first step in planning the survey as a whole.* This decision, of course, determines the nature of the questions to be included in the questionnaire. It is important to project the likely results of the survey if the proposed questionnaire is used and then to decide whether these "findings" will answer the questions the study is intended to address. Surveys are frequently done under considerable time pressure, and inexperienced researchers are especially prone to impatience. Just remember that a poorly conceived questionnaire takes just as much time and effort to administer and analyze as does a well-conceived questionnaire. The difference is that a well-constructed questionnaire leads to interpretable results. The best that can be said for a poorly designed one is that it is a good way to learn how important careful deliberation is in the planning stages.

Step 2   *Once the information to be sought from respondents has been clearly specified, the next step is to decide on the type of questionnaire to be used.* For example, will it be self-administered, or will trained interviewers be using it? This decision is determined primarily by the survey method that has been selected. For instance, if a telephone survey is to be done, trained interviewers will be needed. In designing the questionnaire, one should also consider using items that have been prepared by other researchers. For example, there is no reason to develop your own instrument to assess racial prejudice if a reliable and valid one is already available. Besides, if you use items from a questionnaire that has already been used, you can compare your results directly with those of earlier studies.

Step 3 *If you decide that no available instrument suits your needs, you will have to take the third step and write a first draft of your own questionnaire.* Guidelines concerning the format and ordering of questions, as well as suggestions for wording questions effectively, will be presented in later sections of this appendix.

Step 4 *The fourth step in questionnaire construction—reexamining and rewriting— is an essential one.* Questions that appear objective and unambiguous to you may strike others as slanted and ambiguous. It is most helpful to have your questionnaire reviewed by experts, both those who have knowledge of survey research methods and those with expertise in the area on which your study is focused. For example, if you are doing a survey of students' attitudes toward the campus food service, it would be advisable to have your questionnaire reviewed by the campus food service director. When you are dealing with a controversial topic, it is especially important to have representatives of both sides of the issue screen your questions for possible bias. Sometimes no one particular wording can be agreed on by all. In such cases, the *split-ballot technique* is helpful. In this technique, different wordings of the same questions are used for equivalent samples of respondents. The effect of the wording can be directly examined by comparing responses made in these two (or more) samples. For example, Schuman and Bobo (1988) used the split-ballot technique to embed randomized experiments within their survey design. Their overall objective was to examine the opposition of Whites to the rights of Blacks to open housing. They used the split-ballot technique to assign subgroups within their samples randomly to different versions of questions. Comparing the responses of these subgroups led to the identification of factors that affect attitudes toward open housing, factors such as people's general resistance to government coercion.

Step 5 *By far the most critical step in the development of a sound questionnaire is Step 5, the pretest.* A pretest involves actually administering the questionnaire to a small sample of respondents under conditions as much as possible like those to be used in the final administration of the survey. Pretest respondents must also be typical of those to be included in the final sample; it makes little sense to pretest a survey of nursing home residents by administering the questionnaire to college students. There is one way, however, in which a pretest does differ from the final administration of the survey. Respondents should be interviewed at length regarding their reactions to individual questions and to the questionnaire as a whole. This provides information about potentially ambiguous or offensive items.

The pretest should also serve as a "dress rehearsal" for interviewers, who should be closely supervised during this stage to ensure that they understand and adhere to the proper procedures for administering the questionnaire. If major changes have to be made as a result of problems arising during the pretest, a second pretest may be needed to determine whether these changes solved the problems originally encountered.

Step 6   *After pretesting is completed, the final step is to edit the questionnaire and specify the procedures to be followed in its final administration.*

In the next two sections, we return to two issues pertinent to the third step in preparing a questionnaire: writing a first draft. We will consider two sets of guidelines: one for writing questions and one for the general format of a questionnaire.

GUIDELINES FOR THE EFFECTIVE WORDING OF QUESTIONS

Lawyers have long known that how a question is phrased has great impact on how that question is answered. Survey researchers need to be equally conscious of this principle. This point is illustrated in a survey Loftus (1979) conducted for the manufacturer of a leading headache remedy. She found that people reported having more headaches when they were asked "Do you get headaches frequently and, if so, how often?" than when they were asked "Do you get headaches occasionally and, if so, how often?" Unfortunately, the extent of the influence of the wording of questions in a given survey can almost never be determined precisely.

For instance, Clark and Schober (1992) suggest that survey respondents typically make what they call the "interpretability presumption," namely, that "each question means what it is obvious to me here and now that it means" (p. 27). This presumption on the part of the respondent, as they point out, has some important consequences. For instance, when a question includes a vague word, respondents often assume that the surveyor meant something very specific by this word. But because the word *is* vague, respondents produce various interpretations according to their individual biases and ideas of "what it is obvious to me." Thus, words like "few" or "usually," or terms such as "energy crisis," may be interpreted differently by different individuals. Respondents also tend to assume that a word is used in the way it is typically used in their subculture or culture. Clark and Schober (1992) cite as an example a surveyor who wanted to ask Mexican residents in the Yucatan the question, "How many children do you have?" When translated into Spanish, the surveyor used the word *niños* for children, but villagers in this area of Mexico treated *niños* as including living children and children who have died. The interpretability presumption may also lead respondents to assume that if the researcher asks a question, then it is one that the respondent can answer. Thus, respondents will often willingly give answers to questions that have no (valid) answers! For example, when asked to give opinions about nationalities that didn't exist, respondents nevertheless gave opinions.

Clark and Schober (1992) summarize well the problem of question wording facing survey researchers: "Surveyors cannot possibly write perfect questions, self-evident to each respondent, that never need clarification. And because they cannot, the answers will often be surprising" (p. 29).

The problem of question wording is clearer than the solution. Schuman and Scott (1987) argue that investigators should realize the limitations on assessing, in an absolute sense, people's opinions or attitudes based on any one set of questions. They encourage researchers to emphasize participants' responses to the same set of questions over time. At a minimum, *the exact wording of critical questions should always be reported along with the data describing respondents' answers*. The problem of the potential influence of the wording of questions is yet another illustration of why a multimethod approach is so essential in investigating behavior.

There are certain guidelines to follow to minimize problems arising from the phrasing of survey questions. These guidelines can be applied to *free-response* (open-ended) questions and to *closed* (multiple-choice) questions. Free-response questions, like the essay questions on a classroom test, merely specify the area to be addressed in a response. For example, the question "What are your views on the legalizing of abortion?" is a free-response question. By contrast, closed questions provide specific response alternatives. "Is police protection very good, fairly good, neither good nor bad, not very good, or not good at all?" is a closed question about the quality of police protection in a community.

The advantages of free-response questions are that they can be written more quickly and that they offer the respondent greater flexibility. However, these advantages are often more than offset by the difficulties that arise in recording and scoring responses to free-response questions. For example, extensive coding is frequently necessary before rambling responses to free-response questions can be summarized succinctly. Closed questions, on the other hand, are more difficult to write, but they can be answered more easily and quickly and fewer scoring problems arise. It is also much easier to summarize responses to closed questions because the answers are readily comparable across respondents. A major disadvantage of closed questions is that they reduce expressiveness and spontaneity. Further, the possibility exists that the respondent will have to choose a less than preferred response because no presented alternative really captures his or her views. Hence, the responses obtained may not accurately reflect the respondent's opinion.

Newcomb, Koenig, Flacks, and Warwick (1967) used both free-response and closed questions in a survey of students' attitudes. Their survey was done in two stages. In the first stage, student respondents were asked a series of free-response questions about how their lives had changed as a result of attending college. The trained interviewers used probes extensively and effectively in this stage. A self-administered questionnaire was then developed for the second stage of the survey. During this second stage, a different sample of students rated how much they had changed in each of a number of areas. The researchers wrote closed questions for the second stage of the survey using specific areas of change that had been indicated in the answers to the original set of free-response questions. This survey illustrates the complementary strengths of free-response and closed questions. The findings of the survey showed that one area in which change did occur was in the students' political views. What is more, these changes were shown to persist well after the students had left college.

Closed questions frequently include a scale which is used to measure the degree or amount of response to the question. A typical 5-point, Likert-type scale would include the categories "strongly agree," "agree," "neutral," "disagree," and "strongly disagree" (see Chapter 4 for more information on scaling methods). Alternatively, degree of response can be measured by asking respondents to rank several alternatives from "most preferred" to "least preferred." Rank-order scaling has the advantage that it forces the respondent to make discriminations among alternatives. Rank-order scaling is sensitive in measuring differences that respondents can detect.

The disadvantage of rank-order scaling is that it is not informative about the absolute judgment of any one alternative. For example, respondents could rank the beauty of 15 photographs even if they judged all the photographs to be ugly; they could reliably identify the least ugly (most beautiful) of the group even if they judged them all to be ugly. If they were asked to use Likert-type scales to rate the beauty of the photographs, it would be possible to measure the absolute level of rated beauty of each photograph. It would also be possible to interpret the relative distances between the ratings for different photographs, something that is not possible with rank-order scaling. (The winner and runner-up in a race can be decided in a photo finish or "by a mile," and the winner will still be first and the runner-up second.) The ability to obtain absolute judgments and to interpret distances between ratings are the primary advantages of Likert-type rating scales. The major disadvantage is that respondents may fail to make discriminations that they are capable of making. They may, for example, give the same rating of beauty to all the photographs. In general, rank-order scaling is preferred if the researcher is interested in relative preferences; rating scales are preferred if the researcher is interested in the absolute level of the respondents' reactions (e.g., the frequency with which items are rated as "poor," or the overall average rating for a stimulus event).

Regardless of the type of question used, the *vocabulary should be simple, direct, and familiar to all respondents. Questions should be as clear and specific as possible. Double-barreled questions should be avoided.* An example of a double-barreled question is: "Have you suffered from headaches and nausea recently?" A person may respond "no" if both symptoms have not occurred at exactly the same time or may respond "yes" if either symptom has occurred. The solution to the problem of double-barreled questions is a simple one—rewrite them as separate questions. *Survey questions should be as short as possible without sacrificing the clarity of the questions' meaning.* Twenty or fewer words should suffice for most survey questions. *Each question should be carefully edited for readability and should be phrased in such a way that all conditional information precedes the key idea.* For example, it would be better to ask, "If you were forced to leave your present job, what type of work would you seek?" than to ask, "What type of work would you seek if you were forced to leave your present job?"

Leading or loaded questions should also be avoided in a questionnaire. Leading questions take the form "Most people favor the use of nuclear energy. What do you think?" To avoid bias, it is better to mention all possible perspectives or to mention none. A survey question about attitudes toward nuclear energy could read either "Some people favor the use of nuclear energy, some people oppose the use of nuclear energy, and some people have no opinion one way or the other. What do you think?" or "What do you think about the use of nuclear energy?" *Loaded questions* are questions that contain emotion-laden words. For example, terms such as *radical* and *racist* should be avoided. To guard against loaded questions, it is best to have your questionnaire reviewed by individuals representing a range of social and political perspectives.

In summary, good questionnaire items should:

- include vocabulary that is simple, direct, and familiar to all respondents;
- be clear and specific;
- *not* involve leading, loaded, or double-barreled questions;
- be as short as possible (20 or fewer words);
- include all conditional information prior to the key idea; and
- be edited for readability.

GUIDELINES FOR THE GENERAL FORMAT OF A QUESTIONNAIRE

Two aspects of the general format should be considered in constructing the final copy of a questionnaire: the design or layout of the questionnaire, and the ordering of questions.

Questionnaire Design

An effort should be made to make the design of the questionnaire attractive, but the emphasis should be on making it as easy as possible to use.

A section of a questionnaire designed for personal or phone interviews is shown in Table B.1. This questionnaire was used by trained interviewers in a survey done by the Institute for Social Research at the University of Michigan. The aim of the survey was to examine the quality of American life (Campbell, Converse, & Rodgers, 1975). Several characteristics of this questionnaire are noteworthy. Each question is identified with a letter indicating the section of the questionnaire and a number specifying the individual question. This is done to facilitate later scoring and analysis of responses. The arrangement of the questions on each page is compact, but the structure is designed to make it easy to read the questions and to record responses. Whenever possible, questions with the same response format appear together. When closed questions are asked, a note is included to remind the interviewer to give the respondent a card listing the response alternatives so that the respondent can concentrate on the question and not on remembering the alternatives. At the beginning of the first question,

TABLE B.1   SAMPLE QUESTIONNAIRE FORMAT FOR PERSONAL OR PHONE INTERVIEW

Section A: City and Neighborhood

A1 In this study we are interested in measuring the quality of life of people in this country—that is, the things people like and dislike about their homes, cities, neighborhoods, jobs, and so on. The first question is: How long have you lived in (INSERT NAME OF COMMUNITY, OR OF COUNTY IF RURAL)? _____. (IF *LESS* THAN TWO YEARS, GET NUMBER OF MONTHS.)
_____ YEARS _____ MONTHS, OR SINCE_____

A2 And how long have you lived here in this (house/apartment)? (IF *LESS* THAN TWO YEARS, GET NUMBER OF MONTHS.)
_____ YEARS _____ MONTHS, OR SINCE_____

A3 I'd like to ask how satisfied you are with some of the main public services you are supposed to receive. (Hand R CARD 1, YELLOW) Please tell me how you feel about each thing I mention, using one of the answers on this card. First, how about the way streets and roads are kept up around here. Would you say this service is *very good, fairly good, neither good nor bad, not very good, or not good at all?*

1. VERY GOOD	2. FAIRLY GOOD	3. NEITHER GOOD NOR BAD	4. NOT VERY GOOD	5. NOT GOOD AT ALL

A4 How do you feel about the quality of the *public* schools that the children from around here go to—would you say it is *very good, fairly good, neither good nor bad, not very good, or not good at all?* [DK is don't know.]

1. VERY GOOD	2. FAIRLY GOOD	3. NEITHER GOOD NOR BAD	4. NOT VERY GOOD	5. NOT GOOD AT ALL	8. DK

IF R LIVES IN A CITY, TOWN, OR VILLAGE, ASK A5 AND A6: IF RURAL, TURN TO A7

A5 How good is garbage collection in this neighborhood? Is it *very good, fairly good, neither good nor bad, not very good, or not good at all?* [DK is don't know.]

1. VERY GOOD	2. FAIRLY GOOD	3. NEITHER GOOD NOR BAD	4. NOT VERY GOOD	5. NOT GOOD AT ALL	8. DK

A6 What about the parks and playgrounds for children in this neighborhood? Are they *very good, fairly good, neither good nor bad, not very good, or not good at all?* [DK is don't know.]

1. VERY GOOD	2. FAIRLY GOOD	3. NEITHER GOOD NOR BAD	4. NOT VERY GOOD	5. NOT GOOD AT ALL	8. DK

ASK EVERYBODY:

A7 How about police protection around here. Is it *very good, fairly good, neither good nor bad, not very good, or not good at all?* [DK is don't know.]

1. VERY GOOD	2. FAIRLY GOOD	3. NEITHER GOOD NOR BAD	4. NOT VERY GOOD	5. NOT GOOD AT ALL	8. DK

the respondent is given a brief rationale for the study as a whole, but this preamble is kept short so as to require as little of the respondent's time as possible.

The format of a questionnaire that is meant to be self-administered must be somewhat different. The first section of a self-administered questionnaire distributed to passengers on Amtrak trains is shown in Table B.2. The items are arranged in a clear and uncluttered manner, and the order of the questions is clearly indicated by the large boldface numbers. Each item is short and direct, and the instructions for each question are simple. The small numbers next to each blank are used to computer-code the responses. The numbers in parentheses indicate column numbers in a computer file, and the other numbers are the ones to be entered if the respondent checks that blank. Such prior coding saves time when the data are to be analyzed and helps reduce the number of errors in data entry. In designing a self-administered questionnaire, one should make every effort to make it visually appealing; visual appeal increases the response rate. It is most important that the questions be self-explanatory and that respondents be able to complete the questionnaire quickly and correctly.

Ordering of Questions

A crucial issue in deciding the order of the questions in a survey is which question or questions to ask first. The first few questions set the tone for the rest of the questionnaire and determine how willingly and conscientiously respondents will work on subsequent questions.

- Begin self-administered questionnaires with the most interesting set of questions in order to capture the respondent's attention. (Demographic data should be obtained at the end of a self-administered questionnaire.)
- In surveys involving personal or telephone interviews, on the other hand, demographic questions are frequently asked at the beginning because they are easy for the respondent to answer and thus bolster the respondent's confidence. They also allow time for the interviewer to establish rapport before asking questions about more sensitive matters.

The order in which particular questions are asked can have dramatic effects, as illustrated in a study by Schuman, Presser, and Ludwig (1981). They found differential responding depending on the order of two questions concerning abortion, one general and one specific. The general question was "Do you think it should be possible for a pregnant woman to obtain a legal abortion if she is married and does not want any more children?" The more specific question was "Do you think it should be possible for a pregnant woman to obtain a legal abortion if there is a strong chance of a serious defect in the baby?" When the general question was asked first, 60.7% of respondents said "yes," but when the general question followed the specific question, only 48.1% of respondents said "yes." The corresponding values for the specific question were 84% and 83% agreement in the first and second positions, respectively. The generally accepted method for dealing with this problem is to use *funnel questions*, which

TABLE B.2   SAMPLE FORMAT FOR SELF-ADMINISTERED QUESTIONNAIRE

Illinois Department of Transportation
Survey of Amtrak Passengers

Dear Amtrak Passenger:

The Illinois Department of Transportation is conducting a study of rail passenger service on the Chicago-St. Louis corridor to determine what improvements should be made to upgrade service on this route. This survey is designed to identify the preferences and travel needs of passengers on Amtrak trains. Your cooperation in filling out this questionnaire will be greatly appreciated.

A Department representative will collect the survey when you have finished. If you leave your seat before the representative returns, kindly leave the questionnaire on your seat. If you have filled out this survey previously, please take a few minutes to answer questions 1 through 7 and 21 through 26.

Have an enjoyable trip and thank you for your cooperation.

1 Please check the station where you boarded this train and the station where you will get off.

Station	Boarded	Will Get Off
Chicago	____ 01 (1–6)	____ 01(7–8)
Joliet	____ 02	____ 02
Pontiac	____ 03	____ 03
Bloomington	____ 04	____ 04
Lincoln	____ 05	____ 05
Springfield	____ 06	____ 06
Carlinville	____ 07	____ 07
Alton	____ 08	____ 08
St. Louis	____ 09	____ 09
Points in Missouri	____ 10	____ 10
Points in Arkansas	____ 11	____ 11
Points in Texas	____ 12	____ 12

2 Please indicate how you reached the station to board this train and how you will reach your next destination after you get off this train. (Check as many as apply.)

	To Station Where You Got On	From Station Where You Will Get off
Automobile	____ 01 (9–11)	____ 01(12–14)
Taxi	____ 02	____ 02
City Bus	____ 03	____ 03
Airline	____ 04	____ 04
Commuter Train	____ 05	____ 05
Amtrak Train	____ 06	____ 06
Amtrak Shuttle	____ 07	____ 07
Intercity Bus	____ 08	____ 08
Walker	____ 09	____ 09
Other	____ 10	____ 10

3 Is your car parked at or near an Amtrak Station during this trip?
Yes _____ 15.1   No _____ 15.2

4 What is the zip code of the place you left to get to this train? (If zip code is unknown, the city and a nearby major street intersection will be sufficient.)
Zip Code _____
  $\overline{16\ 17\ 18\ 19\ 20}$
OR: City _____
  Street
  Intersection _____

  _____

5 What is the zip code (or city and nearby street intersection) of the place where you will be going upon leaving this train?
Zip Code _____
  $\overline{21\ 22\ 23\ 24\ 25}$
OR: City _____
  Street
  Intersection _____

  _____

6 Which one of the following best describes the main purpose of this trip? (Mark only one)
26-1 _____ Business or work
  2 _____ Vacation or recreation
  3 _____ Travel to or from school
  4 _____ Personal business
  5 _____ Shopping
  6 _____ Visit family or friends
  7 _____ Entertainment/Spectator sport
  8 _____ Other (Please specify) _____

7 How long before the departure time of this train did you leave for the station?
27-1 _____ 10–15 minutes
  2 _____ 16–30 minutes
  3 _____ 31–45 minutes
  4 _____ 46–60 minutes
  5 _____ more than 1 hour

means proceeding from the most general to the most specific when ordering the questions pertaining to a given topic.

Problems resulting from the order of questions can also arise when several questions on the same topic are asked, all at the same level of specificity. For example, we might ask a series of questions regarding a person's views about several minority groups. Our interest might be in how the person's responses differ for the different minority groups. But responses could also be affected by the sequence in which the various questions were asked within each of the minority groups. A person's reaction to one question, for example, might influence how the next question is interpreted. Effects due to the order in which such questions are asked can be handled in one of two ways. The first technique is to use exactly the same order for all samples to be compared, thus holding the effect of order constant. This technique does not allow us to determine what the effects of order were. Alternatively, many different orders of the questions might be used within each of the samples to be compared, thus neutralizing the effect of order. This problem of dealing with order effects is discussed much more fully in Chapter 7.

The final aspect of the ordering of survey questions that we will consider is the use of *filter questions*—general questions asked of respondents to find out whether they need to be asked more specific questions. For example, the question "Do you own a car?" might precede a series of questions about the costs of maintaining a car. In this instance, the respondents would answer the specific questions only if their response to the general question was "yes." If that answer was "no," the interviewer would not ask the specific questions (in a self-administered questionnaire, the respondent would be instructed to skip that section). When the filter questions involve objective information (e.g., "Are you over 65?"), their use is relatively straightforward. Caution must be exercised, however, in using behavioral or attitudinal questions as filter questions. Smith (1981) first asked respondents whether they approved of hitting another person in "any situations you can imagine." Logically, a negative response to this most general question should imply a negative response to any more specific questions. Nonetheless, over 80% of the people who responded "no" to the general question then reported that they approved of hitting another person in specific situations, such as in self-defense. Although findings such as this suggest that filter questions should be used cautiously, the need to demand as little of the respondent's time as possible makes filter questions an essential tool in the design of effective questionnaires.

ENHANCING RESPONSE RATE IN A MAIL SURVEY

In addition to providing a well-designed questionnaire that is attractive (visually appealing), as well as easy to understand and complete, a survey researcher should consider the following procedures to enhance response rate in a mail survey:

- Include a letter summarizing the purpose of the survey, explaining the basis on which the respondents were selected, and assuring the respondents of confidentiality.

- Include a postage-paid return envelope along with the questionnaire.
- Mail a follow-up questionnaire. (And perhaps consider more than one follow-up mailing.)

As questionnaires are returned, the researcher should plot a cumulative response rate graph. Numbering the returned questionnaires in the order received allows researchers to make comparisons such as that between early and late respondents. Plateaus in the cumulative response rate graph indicate that a follow-up mailing should be sent. To obtain a high response rate, it is often necessary to send three mailings. These should be spaced about 2 to 3 weeks apart or when a plateau appears on the cumulative response rate graph. Because the original copy is likely to have been lost, a new copy of the questionnaire should be sent with each mailing.

APPENDIX
C

Communication in Psychology

CHAPTER OUTLINE

INTRODUCTION
THE INTERNET AND RESEARCH
GUIDELINES FOR EFFECTIVE WRITING
STRUCTURE OF A RESEARCH REPORT
Title Page
Abstract
Introduction
Method
Results
Discussion
References
Appendixes
Author Note
Footnotes
Order of Manuscript Pages
ORAL PRESENTATIONS
RESEARCH PROPOSALS
A SAMPLE RESEARCH REPORT

INTRODUCTION

Scientific research is a public activity. A clever hypothesis, an elegant research design, meticulous data collection procedures, reliable results, and an insightful theoretical interpretation of the findings are not useful to the scientific community unless they are made public. As one writer suggests most emphatically, "Until its results have gone through the painful process of publication, preferably in a refereed journal of high standards, scientific research is just play. Publication is an indispensable part of science" (Bartholomew, 1982, p. 233). Bartholomew (1982) expresses a preference for a "refereed" journal because refereed journals involve the process of peer review. Submitted manuscripts are reviewed by other researchers ("peers") who are experts in the specific field of research addressed in the paper under review. These peer reviewers decide whether the research is methodologically sound and whether it makes a substantive contribution to the discipline of psychology. These reviews are then submitted to a senior researcher who serves as editor of the journal. It is the editor's job to decide which papers warrant publication. Peer review is the primary method of quality control for published psychological research.

There are many journals in which psychologists can publish their research. *Memory & Cognition, Child Development, Journal of Personality and Social Psychology*, and *Journal of Clinical and Consulting Psychology* are but a few of the many psychology journals. As we mentioned, editors of these journals make the final decisions about which manuscripts will be published. Their decisions are based on (a) the quality of the research and (b) the effectiveness of its presentation in the written manuscript, as assessed by the editor and the peer reviewers. Thus both content and style are important. Editors seek the best research, clearly described. The editors of the 25 primary journals of the American Psychological Association reviewed about 6,000 manuscript submissions per year in the 1990s. Journal editors set rigorous standards; *only about one of every four submitted manuscripts is accepted for publication* (American Psychological Association, 1998).

Editorial review and the publication process can take a long time. A year or more may elapse between when a paper is submitted and when it finally appears in the journal. The review of the manuscript can take three to six months before a decision whether to accept the paper is made. Another seven to eight months is required for the publication process between the time the paper is accepted and when it is actually published in the journal. To provide a more timely means of reporting research findings, professional societies such as the American Psychological Association, the American Psychological Society, the Psychonomic Society, the Society for Research in Child Development, and regional societies such as the Eastern, Midwestern, Southeastern, and Western Psychological Associations sponsor conferences at which researchers give brief oral presentations or present posters describing their recent work. Such conferences provide an opportunity for timely discussion and debate among investigators interested in the same research questions. Research that is "in press" (i.e., waiting completion of the publication process) may be discussed, thus giving conference attendees a preview of important, but yet-to-be-published, research findings.

Researchers often must obtain financial support in the form of a grant from a government or private agency in order to carry out their research. Grants are awarded on the basis of a competitive review of research proposals. Research proposals also typically are required of graduate students when preparing a master's thesis or dissertation. A faculty committee then reviews the proposal before the thesis or dissertation research is begun. So, too, undergraduate students often are required to prepare a research proposal as part of a research methods or laboratory class in psychology. Finally, researchers at all levels will find that research proposals are required by IRBs in order to assess the ethical nature of proposed research at an institution (see Chapter 2). Research proposals require a slightly different style and format from a journal article that reports results of a completed study. We provide suggestions for preparing a research proposal later in this appendix.

What do journal articles, oral presentations, and research proposals have to do with you? If you attend graduate school in psychology, you will probably have to describe your research using all three of these types of scientific communication. Even if you do not pursue a professional career in psychology, the principles of good written and oral research reports are applicable to a wide variety of employment situations. For example, a memo to your department manager describing the outcome of a recent sale may have much the same content and format as a short journal article. Of more immediate concern, you may have to prepare a research proposal and write or deliver a research report in your research methods course. This appendix will help you do these things well.

The primary source for scientific writing in psychology is the fourth edition of the *Publication Manual* (1994) of the American Psychological Association. Editors and authors use this manual to ensure a consistent style across the many different journals in psychology. It includes chapters on the content and organization of a manuscript; the expression of ideas; APA editorial style; manuscript preparation; manuscript acceptance and production; and APA journals. The publication manual also includes information about ethical issues in scientific writing (see our discussion of this in Chapter 2) and instructions for submitting manuscripts in electronic form.

Throughout this appendix we have drawn heavily on the *Publication Manual* (1994).[1] This appendix is intended to help you complete successfully the writing you are likely to be doing in your research methods course. It is not intended as a substitute for the *Publication Manual* (1994). If advanced study in psychology is in your future, we recommend that you add the *Publication Manual* (1994) to your personal library. Another resource available from APA that you might find helpful is Gelfand, H., & Walker, C. J. (1994). *Mastering APA style: Student's workbook and training guide.* (You can order both from the American Psychological Association, 750 First Street, N.E., Washington, DC 20002-4242.) If you have reached that exciting point in the research process when you are preparing a manuscript for submission to a scientific journal, we urge you to read a brief article written by Robert J. Sternberg (1992), which was published in the monthly newsletter of the American Psychological Society, the *APS Observer*. Its title says it all: "How to Win Acceptances by Psychology Journals: 21 Tips for Better Writing."

Formal communication among researchers through journal articles and convention presentations is not sufficient to sustain the collaborative nature of science. Informal communication is vital to doing research. Research ideas are often formulated in research team meetings or in informal conversations with colleagues. Increasingly, researchers are collaborating at a distance using one of today's most exciting developments in scientific communication, the Internet and the World Wide Web (WWW). Researchers use electronic mail to discuss their research and access electronic databases through the Internet that make their research more efficient and more extensive. We describe some of the research-related features of the Internet in the next section.

THE INTERNET AND RESEARCH

— A researcher posts a questionnaire on the Internet . . .
— Clinical psychology graduate students participate in group discussions about managed health care with other graduate students on the Internet . . .
— Researchers working on the problem of alcohol abuse search databases on the Internet for statistics related to alcohol use and treatment . . .
— An undergraduate student obtains background information for a class project by e-mailing the author of a published study . . .
— Having completed the data collection phase of a psychology study, researchers prepare an article for publication in an electronic journal . . .

Access to the Internet has already become an indispensable tool for research psychologists. Although mainly used for communication via electronic mail (e-mail), the Internet also serves students and professional psychologists in many other important ways, including as a vehicle for conducting original research (see, for example, Azar, 1994b; 1994c; Kardas & Milford, 1996; Kelley-Milburn & Milburn, 1995). We describe here a few of the more important ways that the Internet is used by psychologists.

E-mail is, for many researchers, their primary means of communication with colleagues, journal editors, research collaborators, directors of granting agencies, and other professionals. Authors of published journal articles now typically list their e-mail addresses along with their regular mailing address. Have a question about an article you just read? Ask the author by sending an e-mail message. E-mailing is simple, efficient, and convenient. The authors of your textbook, for example, can be reached via e-mail by sending a message via Internet to:

John J. Shaughnessy (Hope College) at shaughnessy@hope.edu
Eugene B. Zechmeister (Loyola University of Chicago) at ezechme@luc.edu
Jeanne S. Zechmeister (Loyola University of Chicago) at jzechme@luc.edu

There is also a home page on the WWW dedicated to this textbook, which can be accessed for information about the authors, changes in editions, additional resources for doing psychological research, and errors or omissions in the current edition, publisher's address, ordering information, etc. Visit our page at www.mhhe.com/shaughnessy.

Discussion groups, called "Listservs," allow interested individuals to communicate with each other about various psychological issues. The group consists of a "list" of "subscribers" who wish to contribute to an ongoing discussion. List members are immediately "served" any message posted by a subscriber. (If the Listserv is large, the number of messages accumulating in your mailbox can be rather large. As a consequence, unless regularly attended to and edited, you may find your abilities to keep up with new information seriously challenged.) Listservs on the Internet focus on a wide variety of topics, including addiction, religion, and women's studies. The APA plans to create as many as 500 special-interest groups to link researchers around the world (Azar, 1995). Some Listservs are open to anyone who wishes to take part in the discussion, or who even just want to "lurk" (only passively participate), as many people do who follow the discussion "threads" (a group of messages focusing on a specific idea or issue). Other Listservs are open only to individuals with certain credentials (e.g., members of a particular APA division).

Of particular interest to graduate students in psychology are two discussion groups set up by and for graduate students. These forums allow graduate students to share information about graduate programs, research projects, as well as about postdoctoral and career opportunities. One discussion group, APSSCNET, is sponsored by the Student Caucus of APS (see Fiore, 1994). APA also sponsors discussion groups for students, which can be accessed through their web site (see next page).

Databases on the Internet are just that: collections of information (data) available via an electronic hookup. Databases related to medicine, alcoholism, and opinion polls are available, to mention but a few (see Kelley-Milburn & Milburn, 1995). Many databases are reached by using a TELNET command. TELNET allows you to connect your computer to a remote site. By following the rules laid out for you when you access a site, you can carry out searches and even download information to your own computer (see Kardas & Milford, 1996, for more information on using TELNET commands).

Electronic journals are here and more are on their way. Electronic journals such as *Psycholoquy, Psyche,* and *Prevention and Treatment* are examples. Subscribers receive articles in their electronic mailboxes to peruse and even to comment on should they have the expertise. Articles submitted to electronic journals for publication are professionally reviewed in the same manner as manuscripts submitted to print journals, but, of course it is all done via the Internet.

Original research can also be done electronically (see, for example, Kiesler, Walsh, & Sproull, 1992; and Smith & Leigh, 1997). Surveys, for example, can be conducted of individuals tied to a specific network or discussion group (Listserv) (see Schmidt, 1997, and also Chapter 4). Respondents usually have the option of replying electronically or printing a copy of the questionnaire and mailing the completed form to the survey administrator. As more and more people become connected to the Internet through commercial providers, there exists the potential for administering "treatments" electronically. Kiesler et al., for instance, describe a smoking cessation study carried out with CompuServe users. The University of Mississippi hosts a web site, PsychExps, where teachers and researchers can post experiments that can be accessed by students in psychology lab classes from around the world (see Bourke, 1998).

Where to begin? With all of the electronic resources now available, it's often hard to know where to begin. Internet service providers are commonly available at most universities and colleges. For those without this advantage, commercial services such as America Online, AT&T World Net, Earth Link, and MSN Premier provide access for a fee.

How useful you will find the Internet in planning and conducting research will depend both on your specific needs and on your level of expertise at accessing the Internet. If you are already experienced at using psychology-related information on the Internet, then there isn't much we can tell you. You are already on the cutting edge of what will be the main vehicle for information exchange at the beginning of the 21st century.

Both novices on the Web as well as experienced surfers can find a wealth of psychology-related information at the home pages of the American Psychological Association and American Psychological Society. These pages provide hyperlinks (Internet connections) to many other psychology-related sites and even permit you to be a participant "online" in a psychology experiment or survey.

To access APA via the Web: http://www.apa.org
To access APS via the Web: http://www.psychologicalscience.org

GUIDELINES FOR EFFECTIVE WRITING

Learning to write well is like learning to swim, drive a car, or play the piano. Improvement is unlikely to result solely from reading about how the activity is to be done. (Although listening to experts is an important place to begin. See, for example, the "21 Tips for Better Writing" by Sternberg [1992], which we mentioned earlier.) A person learns to write well by writing and then getting critical feedback from writing "coaches" (teachers, friends, editors). Lee Cronbach (1992), author of several of the most widely cited articles in the *Psychological*

Bulletin, writes:

> My advice must be like the legendary recipe for jugged hare, which begins, "First catch your hare." First, have a message worth delivering. Beyond that, it is care in writing that counts. . . . Rework any sentence that lacks flow or cadence, any sentence in which first-glance reading misplaces the emphasis, and any sentence in which comprehension comes less than instantly to that most knowledgeable of readers, the writer of the sentence. At best, technical writing can aspire to literary virtues—a change of pace from abstract thesis to memorable example, from brisk to easeful, from matter-of-fact to poetic. (p. 391)

Professional writer Jack Ridl provides the first maxim for effective writing: "Write, not assuming that you will be understood, but trying to avoid being misunderstood." Good writing, like good driving, is best done defensively. Assume that whatever can be misunderstood will be! To avoid these writing accidents, we offer the following tips to consider *before* you begin writing.

- KNOW YOUR AUDIENCE. If you assume your readers know more than they actually do, you will leave them confused. If you underestimate your readers, you risk boring them with unnecessary details. Either risk increases the likelihood that what you have written will not be read. But if you must err, it is better to underestimate your readers. For example, when you prepare a research report in a psychology class you might reasonably assume that your intended audience is your instructor. Writing for your instructor might lead you to leave a lot out of your paper because, after all, you assume your instructor knows all that anyway. It would probably be better to consider students in another section of your research methods course as your audience. This might result in your including more detail than necessary, but it will be easier for your instructor to help you learn to "edit out" the nonessential material than to "edit in" essential material that you have omitted. Whatever audience you choose, make the selection before you begin to write, and keep that audience in mind every step of the way.
- IDENTIFY YOUR PURPOSE. The principal purposes of a journal article are to describe and to convince. You want first to describe what you have done and what you have found, and second to convince the reader that your interpretation of these results is an appropriate one. Journal articles fall within the general category of expository writing. *Webster's Dictionary* defines exposition as "discourse designed to convey information or explain what is difficult to understand." The foundation of good expository writing is clarity of thought and expression.
- WRITE CLEARLY. The *Publication Manual* (1994) clearly outlines the road to clarity:

> You can achieve clear communication, which is the prime objective of scientific reporting, by presenting ideas in an orderly manner and by expressing yourself smoothly and precisely. By developing ideas clearly and logically and leading readers smoothly from thought to thought, you make the task of reading an agreeable one. (p. 23)

The *Publication Manual* cites three avenues to clarity:

1 economy of expression,
2 precision, and
3 adherence to grammatical rules.

- BE CONCISE. Economy of expression can best be achieved by saying only what needs to be said. Short words and short sentences are easier for readers to understand. Wordiness can best be eliminated by editing your own writing across successive drafts and asking others to edit drafts of your paper.
- BE PRECISE. Precision in using language means choosing the right word for what you want to say. The *Publication Manual* (1994) contains sage advice regarding precision of expression:

  > Make certain that every word means exactly what you intend it to mean. Sooner or later most authors discover a discrepancy between their accepted meaning of a term and its dictionary definition. In informal style, for example, *feel* broadly substitutes for *think* or *believe,* but such latitude is not acceptable in scientific style. (p. 28)

- FOLLOW GRAMMATICAL RULES. Adherence to grammatical rules is absolutely necessary for good writing because failure to do so distracts the reader and can introduce ambiguity. It also makes you, the writer, look bad, and, as a consequence, can serve to weaken your credibility (and your argument) with your reader. Economy of expression, precision, and adherence to grammatical rules do not guarantee effective writing. They do, however, greatly increase the likelihood that your writing will be effective.
- WRITE FAIRLY. As a writer you should also strive to choose words and use constructions that acknowledge people fairly and objectively. The American Psychological Association has developed guidelines (*Publication Manual,* 1994) regarding bias in the language authors use:

  > As a publisher, APA accepts authors' word choices unless those choices are inaccurate, unclear, or ungrammatical. As an organization, APA is committed both to science and to the fair treatment of individuals and groups, and policy requires authors of APA publications to avoid perpetuating demeaning attitudes and biased assumptions about people in their writing. Constructions that might imply bias against persons on the basis of gender, sexual orientation, racial or ethnic group, disability, or age should be avoided. Scientific writing should be free of implied or irrelevant evaluation of the group or groups being studied. (p. 46)

The *Publication Manual* (1994) describes several guidelines to achieve unbiased communication:

1 Describe the person or persons at the appropriate level of specificity. For example, the phrase *men and women* is more accurate than the generic term *man* when referring to all human beings. "Chinese Americans" or "Mexican Americans" would be a more specific reference for participants in a study than would be Asian Americans or Hispanic Americans.

2 Be sensitive to the labels we use to refer to people, for example, terms we use to refer to people's racial or ethnic identity. One of the best ways to follow this guideline is to avoid labeling people whenever possible. A label that is perceived by the labeled group as pejorative should never be used. In trying to follow this guideline it is important to remember that preferences for labeling groups of individuals change with time and that people within a group disagree about what label is preferred.

3 "Write about the people in your study in a way that acknowledges their participation" (p. 49). One way to accomplish this is to describe the people who participated in your study using more descriptive terms such as *college students* or *children* rather than the more impersonal term, *subjects*. Active voice is better than passive voice in acknowledging participation—"the students completed the survey" is preferred over "the survey was administered to the students." The *Publication Manual* (1994) includes several good applications and illustrations of these guidelines to the labeling of persons based on their gender, sexual orientation, racial and ethnic identity, disabilities, and age.

- WRITE AN INTERESTING REPORT. The *Publication Manual* provides useful advice about the overall tone of scientific writing:

  Although scientific writing differs in form from literary writing, it need not and should not lack style or be dull. In describing your research, present the ideas and findings directly, but aim for an interesting and compelling manner that reflects your involvement with the problem. (p. 6)

  One way to try to achieve an appropriate tone in writing your research reports is to strive to tell a good story about your research. Good research makes for good stories; and well-told stories are good for advancing research.

STRUCTURE OF A RESEARCH REPORT

The structure of a research report serves two major purposes. First, the structure provides an organization that the author can use to present a clear description of the research and a convincing interpretation of the findings. In this sense, the structure of a research report parallels the structure of a Shakespearean play. In a Shakespearean play, both the playwright and the audience share certain expectations about what should occur in each act as the play unfolds. For example "the stage is set" in the first act, and the climax can be expected in the third act. Similarly, in a research report both author and reader share expectations about the content of each section of the report. Similar to a play, the reader of a research report can expect to find specific information in each section. If you want to know how an experiment was done, you would look in the Method section; if you want information about the statistics used in the study, you would refer to the Results section. The structure is not intended to shackle the playwright or the author. It simply provides a vehicle to make it easier for the audience to focus on the particular point being made in the play or the research report.

A research report consists of the following sections:

Title Page
Abstract
Introduction
Method   } Body of
Results   } report
Discussion
References
Appendixes
Author Note
Footnotes

The body of the report is made up of four sections: Introduction, Method, Results, and Discussion (the four acts of the "play"). The title page and the abstract are like the playbill you see before the play itself begins, and the References, Footnotes, and Appendixes are analogous to the credits. In this appendix we will provide descriptions of the content and format of each of these sections; more complete descriptions are provided in the *Publication Manual* (1994). Neither this appendix nor the *Publication Manual* will suffice for teaching you how to write a research report. The best preparation for that is to read journal articles reporting research in an area of psychology that interests you. Ultimately, however, you will develop the skills for writing research reports only by actually writing them.

Title Page

The first page of a research report is the title page. It indicates what the research is about (i.e., the title), who did the research (i.e., the authors), where the research was done (i.e., authors' affiliation), and a brief heading to indicate to readers what the article is about (the "running head"). An illustration of a correctly typed title page and succeeding pages of a research report is presented in the sample paper at the end of this appendix. The sample paper includes notes to highlight several important aspects of the final typed draft of a research report.

The title is perhaps the most critical aspect of your paper because it is the part that is most likely to be read! The title should clearly indicate what the central topic of your paper is. In the words of the *Publication Manual:*

> A title should summarize the main idea of the paper simply and, if possible, with style. It should be a concise statement of the main topic and should identify the actual variables or theoretical issues under investigation and the relation between them.
>
> Titles are commonly indexed and compiled in numerous reference works. Therefore, avoid words that serve no useful purpose; they increase length and can mislead indexers. For example, the words *method* and *results* do not normally appear in a title, nor should such redundancies as "A Study of" or "An Experimental Investigation of" begin a title. (p. 7)

The byline for a research report includes the name(s) of the author(s) and the institution with which each author is affiliated. We discussed the criteria for authorship in Chapter 2; only those who meet these criteria should be listed as authors of a research report. Others who contributed to the research are acknowledged in an author note. The preferred form for an author's name is first name, middle initial, and last name.

The *Publication Manual* provides a succinct statement describing the last component of a title page, the running head: "The running head is an abbreviated title that is printed at the top of the pages of a published article to identify the article for readers" (p. 8). The running head should not exceed 50 characters, and it should appear on the title page typed in all uppercase letters one double-spaced line below the first line that includes the page 1 and the manuscript page heading (see sample paper). Note that the running head is *not* the same as the manuscript page heading that appears on every manuscript page. The running head appears once and only once in your manuscript, on the title page.

TIPS ON WRITING A TITLE

A common format for the title of a research report is "[The Dependent Variable(s)] as a Function of [the Independent Variable(s)]." For example, "Anagram Solution Time as a Function of Problem Difficulty" would be a good title. The title must not only be informative, but it should also be brief; the recommended length is 10 to 12 words. Most important of all, be sure your title describes as specifically as possible the content of your research.

Abstract

The second page of the report, the abstract, appears under that single word, which is typed as a centered heading (see sample paper). The abstract is a one-paragraph summary of the content and purpose of the research report. The abstract should be 100 to 120 words long (about 10 double-spaced typewritten lines). The abstract should identify four elements of your research:

a the problem under investigation;
b the experimental method, including tests and apparatus that were used, data gathering procedures, and pertinent characteristics of participants;
c the findings; and
d the conclusions and implications of the findings.

The abstract, in other words, should highlight the critical points made in the Introduction, Method, Results, and Discussion sections of the research report.

A well-written abstract can have a big influence on whether the rest of a journal article will be read. Abstracts are used by information services to index and retrieve articles. The fate of an article based on a reader's reaction to its abstract is well described in the *Publication Manual*,

Most people will have their first contact with an article by seeing just the abstract, usually on a computer screen with several other abstracts, as they are doing a literature search through an electronic abstract-retrieval system. Readers frequently decide on the basis of the abstract whether to read the entire article; this is true whether the reader is at a computer or is thumbing through a journal. The abstract needs to be dense with information but also readable, well organized, brief, and self-contained. Also, embedding many key words in your abstract will enhance the user's ability to find it. (p. 8)

TIPS ON WRITING AN ABSTRACT

Writing a good abstract is challenging. The best way to meet this challenge is to write it last. By writing the abstract after you have written the rest of the report you will be able to *abstract*, or paraphrase, your own words more easily.

Introduction

Objectives for the Introduction   The title of your report appears at the top of the third page as a centered heading, and then the first paragraph of the Introduction section begins immediately (see sample paper). The introduction serves three primary objectives:

1 to introduce the problem being studied;
2 to summarize briefly the relevant background literature that led you to the present research problem and approach; and
3 to state the purpose and rationale of the present study with a logical development of the predictions or hypotheses guiding the research.

The order in which these objectives are met in any given report may vary, but the order in which we described them here is the most common one. All three of these objectives share a common purpose: to give the reader a firm sense of what you are doing and why you are doing it.

The second objective, that of summarizing related research studies, is not to provide an exhaustive literature review. Instead, care should be taken to select the most pertinent studies to develop the rationale of your experiment. In summarizing these selected studies, you should emphasize whatever details of the earlier work will best help the reader understand what you have done and why. You must acknowledge the contributions of other researchers to your understanding of the problem. Of course, if you quote directly from another person's work, you must use quotation marks (see Chapter 2 for advice about citing others' work).

More commonly, however, reference is made to the work of other researchers in one of two ways. Either you refer to the authors of the article you are citing by their last names, with the year in which the paper was published appearing in parentheses immediately after the names, or you make a general reference to their work and follow it with both the names and the year of publication in parentheses. For example, if you were citing a study by David G. Myers and Jane R. Dickie that was published in 1996, you would write either "Myers and

Dickie (1996) found . . ." or "Recent research (Myers & Dickie, 1996) showed that . . ." Complete bibliographical information on Myers and Dickie's paper, including the journal title, volume number, and specific pages, would appear in the References section. Footnotes are not used to cite references in a research report in psychology.

You should include in your paper only those references that you have actually read. If you read a paper by Barney (1993) in which the research of Ludwig (1990) is described, you should not cite the Ludwig paper unless you have actually read that paper. Instead, you should use some form such as "Ludwig (1990), as reported by Barney (1993), found that . . ." You should use this approach for two reasons. The first and most obvious one is that you should accurately report what you have read. If this appeal to scholarly integrity does not suffice, you should recognize the risk you are taking. If Barney (1993) has misreported the work of Ludwig (1990) and you repeat this misrepresentation, you are equally subject to criticism. The general rule is simple: Cite only what you have read. (See also Chapter 2.)

TIPS ON WRITING THE INTRODUCTION

In order to write an effective introduction, be sure you can answer the following four questions *before* beginning to write:

- "What is the point of the study?
- How do the hypothesis and the experimental design relate to the problem?
- What are the theoretical implications of the study, and how does the study relate to previous work in the area?
- What are the theoretical propositions tested, and how were they derived?" (*Publication Manual*, p. 11).

Searching the Psychological Literature   In the long run, the best way to develop ideas for research and to become familiar with the relevant literature is to read the journals in your area of interest on a regular basis. If you are just beginning to do research in psychology, you may not have had a chance to read the research literature widely or to have settled on a principal area of interest in psychology. Or, even if experienced, you may wish to explore a new area of psychology, one found in a literature different than you are used to reading. For example, you may have an idea for an experiment and you may wonder whether the experiment has already been done. Or you may have read an article describing an experiment on which you would like to base an experiment, and you may be interested in finding other studies related to this topic. Whatever the case, there likely will come a time when you need to search the psychological literature. Resources for searching the psychological literature are available to help you answer these types of questions.

Modern methods of searching the psychological literature are built on *Psychological Abstracts*. The American Psychological Association has published

Psychological Abstracts since 1927. The abstracts, taken from over 1,000 national and international periodicals, are published monthly in the *Psychological Abstracts*. These abstracts are organized under 16 general categories, such as "Physical and Psychological Disorders." In the printed version of *Psychological Abstracts*, abstracts are arranged alphabetically under each category by the first author's last name, and the abstracts are numbered consecutively in one or two volumes each year. Searching *Psychological Abstracts* was often a time-consuming and cumbersome task before it became possible to use computers to search the psychological literature. Electronic databases have made the task of searching the psychological literature much less labor intensive.

PsycLIT is the CD-ROM version of *Psychological Abstracts*. PsycLIT includes *Psychological Abstracts* going back more than 25 years and is updated quarterly. One of the greatest advantages of PsycLIT is that it can be used so easily following only brief instruction. PsychINFO is the online version of PsycLIT. Other online databases that permit electronic searching are *FirstSearch* and *InfoTrac 2000*. Check with your local library staff to find out what online services are available to you. Joswick (1994) provides recommendations for electronic searches for those who want to move beyond the basics.

To illustrate the use of electronic databases to search the psychological literature, we describe a computer-assisted search done by one of our undergraduate students. The student was interested in conducting a survey to determine the incidence of rapes and other sexual assaults on dates (i.e., "date rape"). She came across a few references to this topic in her general reading in the area of women's studies, and then wanted to make a more systematic search of the psychological literature. A reference librarian helped her make a search of PsycLIT and the electronic database that included the *Social Science Citation Index*. The *Social Science Citation Index* records the reference history of an article. That is, once an article has been published, the citation index searches the references sections of all future articles in that area and notes whenever the original article is cited. The citation index can be used to determine how many times a given article has been cited or to identify the specific articles in which the original article is cited.

The student used a keyword search on PsycLIT and she had a chapter on rape by Klemmack and Klemmack (1976) to serve as the basis of her search of the *Social Science Citation Index*. An electronic database makes it possible to scan the titles and abstracts of articles in the database and to identify all those that contain particular keywords. The most effective approach to this type of search is to have intersecting keywords, both of which need to be present before the computer will "flag" an article. For example, the student used the keyword RAPE and the letter string DAT to guide her search. She chose the letter string DAT in order to catch such variants as DATE, DATES, and DATING. This intersection led to the identification of 75 references, 73 of which were written in English. The student also obtained 11 additional references that had cited the Klemmack and Klemmack (1976) paper when she did a computer search of the *Social Science Citation Index* database.

The major advantage of searching electronic databases is that they provide quick access to large amounts of information. The student completed both searches in less than half an hour. There are a few disadvantages. One disadvantage is that the quality of the search greatly influences the likelihood that you will obtain all the relevant references. When it comes to electronic databases, what you search is what you get. Estimates are that 30% to 50% of all users miss pertinent information in their search (Joswick, 1994). After searching such vast databases we may become unduly confident that we have identified "all that there is on the subject." These two potential problems are not problems with the *use* of electronic databases but with the *users* of electronic databases. Another possible disadvantage is that many of the references the computer locates do not prove useful. For example, the student obtained one reference on rape among mallard ducks on specific chronological dates. Keywords can also prove tricky. The string DAT identified all studies using the word DATA, so a number of the student's references provided data about rape—but not solely in the context of dating. When they are used properly, the advantages of searching the psychological literature with electronic databases like PsycLIT and Psych-INFO far outweigh their disadvantages.

Method

The second major section of the body of a research report is the Method section. The Method section is usually identified by a centered heading ("Method") with a double space separating it from the preceding and following text (see sample paper). The Method section follows right after the introduction. The introduction has provided a broad outline of the research you have done; the method fills in the nitty-gritty details. The *Publication Manual* presents a straightforward description of the goals of the Method section:

> The Method section describes in detail how the study was conducted. Such a description enables the reader to evaluate the appropriateness of your methods and the reliability and the validity of your results. It also permits experienced investigators to replicate the study if they so desire. (p. 12)

Writing a good Method section can be difficult. It sounds easy because all you have to do is describe exactly what you have done. But if you want to get a sense of how challenging this can be, just try to write a clear and interesting paragraph describing how to tie your shoelaces.

TIPS ON WRITING THE METHOD SECTION

The key to writing a good Method section is organization. Fortunately, the structure of this section is so consistent across research reports that a few basic subsections provide the pattern of organization you need for most research reports. Before describing the content of these subsections, however, we must address the question that students writing their first research report ask most frequently: "How much detail should I include?" The quality of your paper will be adversely affected if you include either too much or too little detail. The rule stated in the *Publication Manual* seems simple enough: "Include in these subsections only the information essential to comprehend and replicate the study" (p. 13). As we have said before, the best way to learn how to follow this rule is to read the Method sections of journal articles and to write your own research reports. Be sure to get feedback from your instructor concerning the appropriate level of detail for your research reports.

The three most common subsections of the Method section are participants, materials (apparatus), and procedure. Each of these subsections is introduced by an underlined subheading that usually begins at the left margin (see sample paper). The *Publication Manual* (p. 13) aptly summarizes the purpose and the content of the *participants* subsection.

Appropriate identification of research participants and clientele is critical to the science and practice of psychology, particularly for assessing the results (making comparisons across groups), generalizing the findings, and making comparisons in replications, literature reviews, or secondary data analyses.

When humans are the participants, report the procedures for selecting and assigning them and the agreements and payments made. Report major demographic characteristics such as sex and age. When a particular demographic characteristic is an experimental variable or is important for the interpretation of results, describe the group specifically—for example, in terms of racial and ethnic designation, national origin, level of education, health status, and language preference and use.

For nonhuman animal subjects, report the genus, species, and strain number or other specific identification, such as the name and location of the supplier and the stock designation.

Give the total number of subjects and the number assigned to each experimental condition. If any did not complete the experiment, state how many and explain why they did not continue. (pp. 13–14)

The *apparatus* or *materials* subsection is not always included in a research report. If the only equipment you used is paper, pencils, and a stopwatch, it is better to include this information in the procedure subsection than in a separate apparatus section. On the other hand, if the apparatus or materials played a central role in the study, a separate subsection is useful. If complex or custom-made equipment has been used, a diagram or drawing is helpful for both the reader and the writer of an apparatus subsection. In general, the label *Apparatus* is used when mechanical equipment is described. The label *Materials* is used when less mechanical instruments, such as a paper-and-pencil questionnaire, have been constructed or used. If you use equipment or materials developed by another investigator, you should cite the work of that investigator, but you should also include the general characteristics of the materials in your own report.

The *procedure* subsection is the most critical component of the Method section. In this subsection you describe what happened from the beginning to the end of the sessions in which you tested your participants. As the previous sentence implies, the organization of the procedure subsection is usually chronological. You should begin writing this subsection by outlining the important steps in testing participants in each group of your study. Next you can either describe the procedure for each group in turn or describe the procedures common to all groups and then point out the distinguishing features of each group. Whichever organization you choose (you may not learn which works best until you have tried to write both), it is best to begin writing only after you have prepared a checklist of the important features of your procedure. The instructions given to participants should be presented in paraphrase form unless they define an experimental manipulation, in which case they should be reported verbatim. The *Publication Manual* recommends that the Method section, and especially the procedure subsection, "should tell the reader what you did and how you did it in sufficient detail so that a reader could reasonably replicate your study" (pp. 14–15).

Results

The centered heading "Results" introduces this third major section of the body of a research report (see sample paper). Like the third act of a dramatic play, the Results section contains the climax of the research report—the actual findings of the study. For many students, though, the excitement of describing the climax is blunted by concern about the necessity of reporting statistical information in the Results section. The best way to alleviate this concern, of course, is to develop the same command of statistical concepts that you have of other concepts. While you are acquiring this mastery of statistics, however, you need a way to deal effectively with the problem of presenting statistical information. One solution to this problem is to adopt a simple organizational structure to guide your writing of the Results section.

You should use your Results section to answer the questions you raised in your introduction. However, the guiding principle in the Results section is to "stick to the facts, just the facts." You will have the opportunity to move beyond just the facts when you get to the Discussion.

Reporting Statistics The *Publication Manual* provides an excellent overview of the objectives of a Results section:

> The Results section summarizes the data collected and the statistical treatment of them. First, briefly state the main results or findings. Discussing the implications of the results is not appropriate here. Mention all relevant results, including those that run counter to the hypothesis. Do not include individual raw scores or raw data, with the exception, for example, of single-case designs or illustrative samples. (p. 15)

One way to meet these objectives is to use an organizational structure that is typical of paragraphs in the Results section. This structure is outlined in Table C.1, and an illustration of a paragraph from the Results section of a published article appears after the table.

TABLE C.1   STRUCTURE OF A TYPICAL PARAGRAPH IN THE RESULTS SECTION

1. State the purpose of the analysis.
2. Identify the descriptive statistic to be used to summarize results.
3. Present a summary of this descriptive statistic across conditions in the text itself, in a table, or in a figure.
4. If a table or figure is used, point out the major findings on which the reader should focus.
5. Present the reasons for, and the results of, inferential statistics tests.
6. State the conclusion that follows from each test, but do not discuss implications. These belong in the discussion section.

Sample paragraph

To examine retention as a function of instructions given at the time of study, the number of words recalled by each participant in each instruction condition was determined. Words were scored as correct only if they matched a word that had appeared on the target list. Thus, synonyms were not counted as correct; misspelled words were accepted if the spelling was sufficiently similar to a target item that it could be reasonably concluded that the intended word had actually appeared on the list. Mean numbers of words recalled were 15.6, 15.2, and 10.1 in the bizarre imagery condition, the standard imagery condition, and the control condition, respectively. Overall, mean recall differed significantly among the conditions, $F(2, 72) = 64.84$, $MSE = 0.44$, $p = .0001$, eta squared = .64. Two analytical comparisons were performed to determine the source of this effect. These tests revealed that the two groups given imagery instructions when averaged together differed significantly from the control condition, $F(1, 72) = 44.62$, $p = .0001$; the effect size (d) for this comparison was 1.57. However, the two imagery conditions did not differ significantly from each other, $F(1, 72) = 1.66$, $p = .20$. In conclusion, retention by participants instructed to use imagery was higher than that by participants given no specific study instructions, but retention did not differ for the two types of imagery instructions.

TIPS ON WRITING A GOOD RESULTS SECTION

We suggest you follow these steps when writing your results section.

- *Step 1.* A Results section paragraph begins by stating the purpose of the analysis. The reason(s) for doing an analysis should be stated succinctly; often, no more than a phrase is necessary. In the sample paragraph, for example, the purpose of the analysis is, "to examine retention as a function of the instructions given at the time of study." There are two reasons for making the purpose for each analysis explicit. It helps your reader follow the logic of your analysis plan. And, perhaps more importantly, it ensures that you will never try to report an analysis whose purpose you do not understand.
- *Step 2.* The second step in writing a Results section paragraph is to identify the descriptive statistic that will be used to summarize the results for a given dependent variable. For example, you might use the mean numbers of words recalled, as in the sample paragraph. Other possible descriptive statistics that could be used to summarize the results in each condition of your experiment are the median reaction time or the cumulative number of responses per minute.

- *Step 3.* The third step is to present a summary of this descriptive statistic across conditions. Whenever possible, measures of central tendency should be accompanied by corresponding measures of variability. If there are only two or three conditions in your experiment, this summary can be presented in the text itself. For instance, you could summarize the results of a two-group study by saying, "The mean number of correct responses for the experimental group was 10.5 ($SD = 2.1$), whereas that for the control group was 5.2 ($SD = 1.8$)." More commonly, however, you will have more data to summarize and you will need to present your findings in either a table or a figure (graph). We will describe the procedures for constructing tables and figures later in this section. The *Publication Manual* gives good advice regarding the use of tables and figures:

  > To report the data, choose the medium that presents them clearly and economically. Tables provide exact values and can efficiently illustrate main effects. Figures of professional quality attract the reader's eye and best illustrate interactions and general comparisons, but they are not quite as precise as tables.
  >
  > Summarizing the results and the analysis in tables or figures instead of text may be helpful; for example, a table may enhance the readability of complex sets of analysis of variance results. Avoid repeating the same data in several places and using tables for data that can be easily presented in a few sentences in the text. (p. 15)

- *Step 4.* We should not expect a table or figure to be self-sufficient. Your reader will need help to gain as much information as possible from a table or figure. You are in the best position to offer this assistance because you are the person most familiar with your results. You should direct your reader's attention to the highlights of the data in the table or figure, focusing especially on those aspects of the results that are consistent (or discrepant) with the hypotheses you proposed in the introduction. Usually the same data are not reported in both a table and a figure. Tables provide a more precise description of the results, but figures make it easier to see trends or patterns in the data. Whichever you choose, be sure to highlight in the text itself the critical results that the table or figure reveals.

- *Step 5.* The fifth step in writing a paragraph of the Results section is to present the results of inferential statistical tests. Three pieces of information should always be reported with any inferential statistics test: the name of the test (usually indicated by a symbol such as t, r, or F); the degrees of freedom for the test (presented in parentheses after the test is identified); and the value of the test statistic that you obtained. Three additional pieces of information are useful in reporting the results of an inferential test: the exact probability of the test under the assumption that the null hypothesis is true, the estimate of error variation for that test, and a measure of effect size (see Chapter 6 and Appendix A for information on effect sizes). For instance, you might see "The overall effect of the drug variable was statistically significant, $F(3, 64) = 7.15, p = .0005, MSE = 2.4$. The effect size ($d$) was .85." (When you write the Results section, you should assume that your reader has a basic knowledge of inferential statistics. Therefore, you do not need to refer to concepts such as the null hypothesis or mention whether your obtained probability is less than your chosen alpha level. All that is required is that you use the term "statistically significant" correctly.)

- *Concluding Step.* The final step in writing a paragraph in the Results section is to state a brief conclusion that follows from each test you report. This is accomplished by referring to the descriptive statistics on which the inferential test is based. For example, if the mean number correct in the experimental group is 10, that in the control group is 5, and this difference is statistically significant, an appropriate concluding statement would be "The control group did worse than the experimental group." In this simple example the conclusion may seem obvious, but appropriate concluding statements are essential in more complex analyses. It is not enough to string together a series of inferential statistical tests with appropriate commentary on the statistical significance of each test, and then never report the descriptive statistics or any conclusion. It is almost useless for your readers to know that an independent variable has had a statistically significant effect if you have failed to describe the nature of that effect. Descriptive statistics are essential in providing such a description.

Each paragraph of the Results section follows the structure outlined in Table C.1. The idea is not to overload your reader with statistics. The challenge is to select those findings that are most critical, being sure to report all the data pertinent to the questions raised in your introduction. Before concluding our discussion of the Results section, we will briefly describe the basic procedures for constructing tables and figures, two key tools in reporting results effectively.

Presenting Data in Tables   Tables are an effective and efficient means for presenting large amounts of data in concise form. The table should supplement and not duplicate information in the text of the paper, but it should be well integrated into the text. The tables in your paper should be numbered consecutively (Arabic numerals are used to number tables) so that they can be referred to easily in the text by their numbers. Each table should also have a brief explanatory title, and the columns and rows of the table should be labeled clearly. The data entries in the table should all be reported to the same degree of precision (i.e., all values should have the same number of decimal places), and the values should be consistently aligned with the corresponding row and column headings. An appropriately constructed table appears in the sample manuscript at the end of this appendix. When manuscripts are submitted for publication, each table is typed on a separate page and appears at the end of the paper after the references and footnotes sections.

Presenting Data in Figures   Figures, like tables, are a concise way to present large amounts of information. A figure has two principal axes: the horizontal axis, or x-axis, and the vertical axis, or y-axis. Typically, the levels of the independent variable are plotted on the x-axis and those of the dependent variable are plotted on the y-axis. When there are two or more independent variables, the levels of the second and succeeding independent variables serve as labels for the data within the figure or are indicated in a figure legend. In Figure C.1 the values of the dependent variable (mean number recalled) are plotted on the y-axis, the levels of one independent variable (serial position) are indicated on the x-axis. The levels of the second independent variable (Cued [C] or NonCued [NC]) label the data within the figures, and the levels of the third independent variable (instructions) serve as the headings for each of the two separate panels of the figure.

There are alternative ways to construct useful graphic presentations. All figures must include certain features, however. The x- and y-axes must be clearly labeled, with each label printed next to the corresponding axis. Selected points (called grid points) on each axis must be identified with labeled grid marks, and the grid labels are always printed horizontally. The grid scale for the x- and y-axes should be chosen such that the plotted data are legible and span the entire illustration. When a manuscript is submitted for publication, each figure

FIGURE C.1   Mean number of words recalled (of a possible ten) as a function of serial position within blocks, cuing (C = Cued; NC = Noncued), and instructional condition.

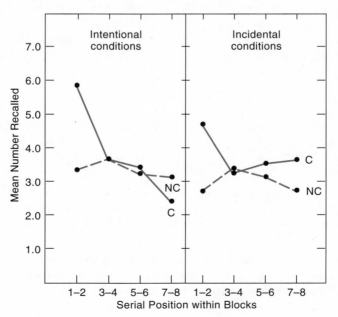

FIGURE C.2   Proportion recognition errors made by two groups of college students after rating verbal items for either familiarity or meaning. The items were nonwords (NW) and words appearing less than one time, one through ten times and more than forty times per million in the Thorndike-Lorge count.

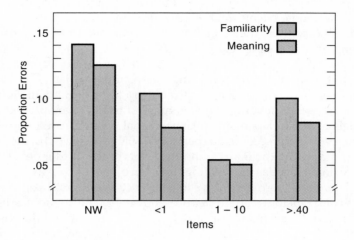

appears on a separate page but the figure captions do not appear on the figures themselves. They are presented on a separate page under the centered heading "Figure Captions." This page follows the tables at the end of the manuscript but precedes the figures, which are then presented in order (see sample paper).

Two general types of figures are commonly used in psychology: bar graphs and line graphs. A bar graph is often used when the independent variable plotted on the *x*-axis is a nominal-scale variable. For example, if you were plotting the mean GPA (dependent variable) of students enrolled in different academic majors (independent variable), you could use a bar graph. An illustration of a bar graph is presented in Figure C.2. The most common type of figure is the line graph shown in Figure C.1.

Discussion

The fourth section of the body of your report, the discussion, begins with a centered heading (see sample paper). The Discussion section, unlike the Results sections, contains "more than just the facts." In the words of the *Publication Manual:*

> After presenting the results, you are in a position to evaluate and interpret their implications, especially with respect to your original hypothesis. You are free to examine, interpret, and qualify the results, as well as to draw inferences from them. (p. 18)

(*Note:* For some research reports, when the results are relatively brief and discussion is straightforward and also not very lengthy, the two sections can be combined in a Results and Discussion section.)

The discussion begins with a succinct statement of the essential findings. You should give particular attention to how your findings support or refute your original hypotheses. You do not repeat the descriptive statistics in this summary, nor do you necessarily refer to the statistical significance of the findings. The *Publication Manual* provides good advice about what to do and not to do after the succinct summary of the findings:

> Similarities and differences between your results and the work of others should clarify and confirm your conclusions. Do not, however, simply reformulate and repeat points already made; each new statement should contribute to your position and to the reader's understanding of the problem. You may remark on certain shortcomings of the study, but do not dwell on every flaw. Negative results should be accepted as such without an undue attempt to explain them away. (pp. 18–19)

The discussion is written in a tone and style consistent with the introduction. Be careful, however, to keep the statements you make in the discussion consistent with the data reported in the results. For instance, you should not report that one group did better than another if the comparison between these groups was not statistically significant—at least not without some qualification of what you mean by "better."

As just noted from the *Publication Manual*, the discussion includes a description of how your findings relate to the relevant literature, most of which you will have cited in the introduction. If your results are not consistent with your original hypotheses, you should suggest an explanation for these discrepancies. Such post hoc (after-the-fact) explanations should be considered tentative at best. If the reasons for your results are unclear, you should not hesitate to say so. It sometimes is necessary and helpful to include a paragraph describing limitations or problems in the research. As noted in the *Publication Manual*, however, "do not dwell compulsively on every flaw." Do try to anticipate criticisms of your study that others might make.

If appropriate, conclude the discussion by proposing additional research that should be done on the problem you are investigating. Avoid cliches such as "Additional research on this problem is needed before definitive conclusions can be reached." Instead, be specific about what research should be done and why it needs to be done. That is, be sure to explain what the new research should reveal that we do not already know. The reader will not learn much if you say, "It would be interesting to do this experiment with younger participants." The reader can learn much more if you explain how you would expect the results to differ with younger participants and what you would conclude if the results of the proposed experiment were to turn out as expected. Remember, the watchword in proposing new research is to be specific. Your emphasis when writing your report should definitely be on quality, not quantity.

Tips on Writing the Discussion Section

Again, the *Publication Manual* gives good advice for authors beginning to write their Discussion section:

"In general, be guided by the following questions:

- What have I contributed here?
- How has my study helped to resolve the original problem?
- What conclusions and theoretical implications can I draw from my study?

The responses to these questions are the core of your contribution, and readers have a right to clear, unambiguous, and direct answers" (p. 19).

References

We have already described the procedure for citing references within the body of a research report by using the name(s) of the author(s) and the date of publication. The References section, which appears with a centered heading on a separate page after the discussion (see sample paper), includes the complete citation for each reference. "Just as data in the paper support interpretations and conclusions, so reference citations document statements made about the literature" (*Publication Manual*, p. 20).

There are three types of references that will cover almost all those needed for most research reports: journal articles, books, and chapters in edited books. In addition, with the availability of information on the Internet, there is a need to cite appropriately an Internet source. The format for each of these reference types is illustrated in Table C.2. As this table shows, the first line of each reference is indented. The journal article reference includes the authors, the year of

TABLE C.2   ILLUSTRATION OF FORMAT OF REFERENCE CITATIONS

Journal article

Loftus, E. F., & Burns, T. E. (1982). Mental shock can produce retrograde amnesia. <u>Memory & Cognition</u>, *10*, 318–323.

Book

Posavac, E. J., & Carey, R. G. (1992). <u>Program evaluation</u> (4th ed.). Englewood Cliffs, NJ: Prentice Hall.

Chapter in an edited book

Weiss, J. M. (1977). Psychological and behavioral influences on gastrointestinal lesions in animal models. In J. D. Maser & M. E. P. Seligman (Eds.), <u>Psychopathology: Experimental models</u> (pp. 232–269). San Francisco: W. H. Freeman.

Article in electronic journal

Kirsch, I., & Sapirstein, G. (1998). Listening to prozac but hearing placebo: A meta-analysis of antidepressant medication. <u>Prevention and Treatment</u> [On-line serial], *1*. Available: journals.apa.org/prevention/volume1/pre0010002a.html.

publication, the title of the article, the name of the journal, the volume number, and the page numbers. The book citation includes the authors, the copyright date, the title, the city in which the book was published, and the publisher. The reference for a chapter in an edited volume includes the author of the chapter, the date, the chapter title, the editors of the book, the title of the book, the page numbers of the chapter, the city of publication, and the publisher. The citation to an electronic journal identifies the specific Internet address.

When citing information from the Internet, especially Web sites, it is critical that you give the reader the specific information required to locate the electronic source. Be aware, however, that Internet addresses change regularly, as does the information that is found in them. It is recommended (e.g., Harnack & Kleppinger, 1997) that you indicate the date you accessed a Web site, for example in parentheses following the citation.

You can save your readers much aggravation if you follow the reference formats closely and proofread your reference list carefully. The references are listed in alphabetical order by the last name of the first author of each article. If there are two articles by the same author(s), they are arranged in ascending order by year of publication.

Appendixes

Appendixes are rare in published research articles, but they are a bit more common in students' research reports. When they are intended for a published article, each appendix begins on a separate manuscript page and they appear at the end of the paper following the references. (*Note:* Instructors may require you to submit an appendix including your raw data, the worksheets for a statistical analysis, or the computer printout of the analyses. The appendix can also be used to provide a verbatim copy of the instructions to participants or a list of the specific materials used in an experiment.) Each appendix is identified by letter (A, B, C, and so on), and any reference to the appendix in the body of the text is made using this letter. For instance, you might write, "The complete instructions can be found in Appendix A."

Author Note

The *Publication Manual* provides a concise description of the contents of an author note:

> The author note (a) identifies the departmental affiliation of each author, (b) identifies sources of financial support, (c) provides a forum for authors to acknowledge colleagues' professional contributions to the study and personal assistance, and (d) tells whom the interested reader may contact for further information concerning the article. (p. 21)

The author note appears on a separate page under the centered heading "Author Note" immediately after the References section (or after the appendixes, if there are any).

Footnotes

Because they are not used for citing references, footnotes are rare in journal articles and even more rare in students' research reports. When footnotes appear in the text they are of two types: content footnotes and copyright permission footnotes. Content footnotes supplement or expand upon the text material. Copyright permission footnotes acknowledge the source of quotations. Footnotes (of both kinds) are numbered consecutively in the text. In the typed manuscript, footnotes appear on a separate page following the references section under the centered heading "Footnotes."

Order of Manuscript Pages

The pages of your research report should be numbered consecutively in the following order:

> Title Page
> Abstract
> Text (introduction, method, results, discussion)
> References (start on a separate page)
> *Appendixes (start each on a separate page)
> Author note (start on a separate page)
> *Footnotes (list together, starting on a separate page)
> Tables (start each on a separate page)
> Figure Captions (list together, starting on a separate page)
> Figures (place each on a separate page).

*Appear only infrequently in journal articles.

ORAL PRESENTATIONS

Research psychologists regularly attend professional conventions at which they present brief oral descriptions of their research. Similarly, students may give oral presentations of their research either in class or at a department research symposium involving students from a number of different classes or at undergraduate research conferences. All of these settings share one characteristic—the time allowed for the presentation is usually no more than 10 to 15 minutes. In this length of time it is impossible to provide the detailed description that is included in a journal article. In general, as noted in the *Publication Manual*, "Material delivered verbally should differ from written material in its level of detail, organization, and presentation" (p. 339). To reach your audience the *Publication Manual* recommends that you:

> Omit most of the details of scientific procedures, because a listener cannot follow the same level of detail as a reader can. The audience wants to know (a) what you studied and why, (b) how you went about the research (give a general orientation), (c) what you discovered, and (d) the implications of your results. A verbal

presentation should create awareness about a topic and stimulate interest in it; colleagues can retrieve the details from a written paper, copies of which you may want to have available. (p. 339)

A colleague of ours in the biology department has developed five principles that he distributes to his cell physiology students to help them prepare the oral presentation required in his class. Like all good maxims these five sound simple enough, but they are all too frequently ignored even by experienced researchers.

FIVE PRINCIPLES FOR EFFECTIVE ORAL PRESENTATIONS

- AVOID THE TEMPTATION TO TELL EVERYTHING YOU KNOW IN 10 MINUTES. This temptation can best be avoided by limiting your presentation to one or two main points. What are the important "take home messages"? The brief time available for an oral presentation is barely sufficient to allow you to present the evidence supporting these main points. There simply will not be time to discuss any side issues.
- CULTIVATE A GOOD PLATFORM PRESENCE. This can best be achieved by developing public speaking skills. Most people need a written copy of their presentation in front of them while they are presenting, but your presentation will be more effective if you can appear not to be reading. Many people speak too quickly in front of an audience, particularly if they are reading; it is best to use simple, direct sentences presented at a moderate rate. Most important, speak loudly and clearly.
- USE EFFECTIVE VISUAL AIDS. The use of effective visual aids can help your listeners follow your presentation. Slides, overhead transparencies, and electronic presentations must be distinct enough to be seen clearly at a distance. The successful use of audiovisual aids is a skill and it can be improved with practice. Be sure that whatever visual aids you use are as close to self-explanatory as you can make them.
- LEAVE TIME FOR QUESTIONS. You need to keep in mind the fourth principle, leaving time for questions, because most professional conferences and classroom presentations will require that you reserve time for questions. Although questions from the audience can be somewhat intimidating, the opportunity for questions gives your listeners a chance to become actively involved in your presentation.
- PRACTICE YOUR TALK BEFORE A CRITICAL AUDIENCE BEFORE YOU GIVE IT. This final principle is perhaps the most important. Practicing your talk before an audience is more beneficial than simply rehearsing the talk over and over by yourself. Such private rehearsal is a good way to prepare for your "dress rehearsal," but it is no substitute for practicing before others.

These five principles provide a good coaching manual for oral presentations. The best way to develop this skill, however, is to deliver as many oral presentations as possible under "game conditions." Practice may not make perfect, but it is the best route we know to improvement.

RESEARCH PROPOSALS

In the last section of this appendix we discuss writing again—but this time the writing of research proposals. As we mentioned at the beginning of this appendix, researchers must often seek financial support for their research by submitting grant proposals to private or government agencies. Students in research methods classes are also sometimes required to submit proposals describing research they might do. Even if a written proposal is not required, only a foolhardy researcher would tackle a research project without careful prior consideration of related literature, possible practical problems, workable statistical analyses of the data, and eventual interpretation of the expected results. Without a carefully constructed plan for the research, the unprepared investigator is likely to produce an unworkable, unanalyzable, or uninterpretable piece of research.

The purpose of a research proposal is to ensure a workable experimental design that, when implemented, will result in an interpretable empirical finding of significant scientific merit. No research proposal, no matter how carefully prepared, can guarantee important results. Researchers learn early in their careers about Murphy's Law. In essence, Murphy's Law states that "anything that can go wrong will go wrong." Nonetheless, it is worthwhile to develop a research proposal, if only to avoid the research problems that are avoidable.

A written research proposal follows the general format of a journal article, but the headings of the various sections are slightly different. The proposal should include the following main sections:

Introduction
Method
Expected Results and Statistical Treatment
References
Appendix
Information for Institutional Review Board

An abstract is not included in a research proposal. The introduction of a research proposal is likely to include a more extensive review of the relevant literature than is required for a journal article. The statement of the research problem and the logical development of hypotheses in a research proposal are the same as required in a journal article. Similarly, the Method section in the proposal should be as close as possible to the one that will accompany the finished research. Thus our remarks about the format and content of the Method section of a research report apply equally to the writing of a proposal.

The section of the proposal entitled "Expected Results and Statistical Treatment" should include a brief discussion of the anticipated results of the research. In most cases the exact nature of the results will not be known. Nevertheless, you will always have some idea (in the form of a hypothesis or prediction) of the outcome of the research. The Expected Results section may include tables or figures of the results as you expect (hope) that they will come out. The results that are most important to the project should be highlighted. A statistical analysis plan for the proposed results should be in this section. For example, if you are proposing a complex design, you would need to indicate which effects you will be testing and what inferential test you will use for these tests. Reasonable alternatives to the expected results should also be mentioned, as well as possible problems of interpretation that will arise if the results deviate from the research hypothesis. Implications of the expected results (should they be obtained) often conclude a research proposal.

The References section should be in exactly the same form as the one you would submit with the final report. An appendix should complete the research proposal and should include a list of all materials that will be used in doing the experiment. In most cases this will mean that a copy of the instructions to participants will be included, as well as the type of apparatus used, a list of stimulus materials or a description of the stimuli, and so on. To repeat, all materials should be listed. For example, if you are doing a study involving students' memory for lists of words, the following must be included in the appendix: actual lists with randomizations made, type of apparatus used for presentation, instructions to participants for all conditions, and randomizations of conditions.

Finally, a research proposal should include material to be submitted to an Institutional Review Board (IRB) or similar committee designed to review the ethics of the proposed research (see Chapter 2).

A SAMPLE RESEARCH REPORT

First few words of title appear before page number.

5 spaces

↘ False Recall   1

Number pages consecutively, beginning with title page.

↱ Running head: FALSE MEMORIES

Type flush with left margin.

Type running head all in caps.

False Recall and Recognition of List Items Following Delay

Jeanne S. Zechmeister and Eugene B. Zechmeister

Loyola University of Chicago

Use upper and lower case for title, name, and affiliation (centered).

Note:
   Use one-inch margins at the top, bottom, right, and left of all pages.

Center, do not underline.

↓

No paragraph indentation for abstract.

Abstract

Abstract should be a single paragraph with no more than 960 characters, including punctuation and spaces (about 120 words).

Whether false memories persist over a delay was investigated using H. L. Roediger and K. B. McDermott's (1995) false memory procedure. College students ($\underline{N}$ = 19) studied 12 15-item lists and either recalled items immediately or following a 90-s delay. A first recognition test immediately followed recall of lists; a second test occurred 2 days later. The proportion of correctly recalled list items decreased with the 90-s delay, whereas the proportion of falsely recalled critical items increased. The overall proportion of items recognized as "old" was greater for false critical items than for correct list items, but both false recognition and correct recognition decreased over the 2-day period. These findings are compared to other studies that examined false memories following delays.

Note:
Double-space between all lines of the manuscript. There should be no more than 27 lines of text on each page.
When using a word processor, use left justification only (not full). Do not use italic and bold fonts, and use one font size throughout the manuscript.

Leave one space at end of all sentences, and after all commas, colons, and semi-colons.

Title appears centered on page 3, with first letter of major words in caps.

False Recall   3

False Recall and Recognition of List Items Following Delay

Roediger and McDermott (1995) captured the attention of memory researchers

by reminding us of the importance of examining participants' errors in recall and that

these errors can sometimes be quite predictable. Moreover, these "false memories" are

relevant to ongoing debates about false memories that may occur in more natural

settings (e.g., clinics, courtrooms). Roediger and McDermott, and many others, have

demonstrated that false memories are easily created and that participants'

phenomenological experience of these memories mimics their memories for actual

events (e.g., Mather, Henkel, & Johnson, 1997; Norman & Schacter, 1997; Payne, Elie,

Blackwell, & Neuschatz, 1996). The purpose of the present study was to replicate

Roediger and McDermott's (1995) findings and to extend their findings by examining

the persistence of false memories following delays. If false memories persist following

delays, important implications exist regarding courtroom testimony and recovered

memories in therapy. For example, memory retrieval in these cases follows varying

periods of delay and the accuracy of these memories may thus be questioned.

    In this false memory paradigm word lists are constructed such that each word is

highly associated with a critical, not-presented word. For example, participants may

hear the words bed, rest, awake, tired, dream, etc., but never the critical word, sleep.

False recall and recognition for the word sleep is quite high. Underwood (1965)

proposed that an implicit associative response (IAR) occurs when participants study an

associated word. For example, when participants hear "bed" they may think of "sleep"

(the IAR). With the next word, "rest," they again may experience "sleep" as an IAR, and

so on. When their memory is tested participants may have difficulty discriminating the

Identify all authors (surnames only) the first time you cite a source (five or fewer authors).

List multiple sources in alphabetical order, separated by a semi-colon.

Indent every paragraph five to seven spaces (consistently).

Abbreviated terms are first spelled out, followed by the abbreviation in parentheses.

Use Latin abbreviations (such as e.g. and i.e.) only in parentheses.

Use numbers to express amounts 10 and above, and when numbers are grouped with numbers 10 and above.

An "s" (with no period) is the abbreviation for second.

Use number for units of time or measure.

Note: Use past tense to describe the study.

Flush with left margin, underlined, only first letter in caps.

Always use words to express numbers that begin a sentence.

False Recall   4

IAR from the presented items, resulting in false recall or recognition. An alternative

account relies on the extent to which the lists of associated words activate a schema for

the words (e.g., a "sleep" schema). According to this account, recall after a delay may

be based on memory for the schema rather than the actual list presentation.

In the present study participants listened to 12 lists comprised of 15 words that

were associated to a critical, not-presented word. Participants were randomly assigned

to recall 4 of the 12 lists in either an immediate-recall condition or following a 90-s delay

in a single trial of free recall. When not recalling words (and during the 90-s delays)

participants completed distractor tasks consisting of math problems. Additionally, two

recognition tests were administered. The first recognition test followed the presentation

and recall of the 15 lists; the second was 2 days later.

We hypothesized that the proportions of correct recall and false recall would not

differ in the immediate-recall condition because of participants' inability to differentiate

their memory for the presented words from the IARs generated for the critical items. In

the delayed-recall condition, we expected the proportion of false items recalled to be

greater than the proportion of correct items recalled because of participants' activation

of a schema for the list to aid recall. This activation was assumed to lead to recall of the

highly associated, critical item. Furthermore, we anticipated that correct recall would

decrease over time but false recall would increase with the delay. Similar predictions

were made for participants' recognition of correct list items and false critical items.

Method   *Center, no underline, only the first letter in caps.*

Participants

Nineteen students (16 women, 3 men) from a research methods in psychology

Note: Method, Results, and Discussion sections do not begin on new page (unless coincidentally).

class at Loyola University of Chicago participated as part of a class project. Data for one student were omitted from all analyses because the student attempted recall for the wrong lists; recognition data for two students were omitted from analyses because they missed the second class session in which the experiment was conducted.

Materials

Word lists. We used 12 15-item word lists from Roediger and McDermott's (1995) study. They constructed 24 lists by selecting 15 words that were highly associated with a critical word that was not presented. Words were ordered such that the strongest associates were presented first, followed by more weakly associated words. For example, the list for the critical word, needle, was thread, pin, eye, sewing, sharp, point, prick, thimble, haystack, thorn, hurt, injection, syringe, cloth, and knitting. Six lists in the present study were identified by Roediger and McDermott as having a high likelihood of creating false memories (identified by the critical item): chair, mountain, needle, rough, sleep, sweet. The other six lists used in the present study for recall were randomly selected from their remaining lists (identified by the critical item): bread, cold, doctor, foot, music, slow .

Participants recalled words from 4 of the 12 lists in a single trial of free recall. In order to rule out the possibility that proportions of correct and false recall would be determined by the particular lists used for the recall task, the four recall lists were counterbalanced. The 12 lists were randomly divided into three sets of four lists, with the provision that two lists in each set have high likelihoods for creating false memories. Participants were randomly assigned to recall words for four lists. Seven participants recalled the chair, bread, slow, and sleep lists; seven participants recalled the needle,

---

Note: "Data" is plural.

Indented, underlined paragraph heading, followed by a period. Only first letter of first word in caps.

Use words to express numbers less than 10.

The word "participants" is preferred over "subjects."

False Recall 6

foot, doctor, and rough lists, and four participants recalled the sweet, music, cold, and mountain lists.

Distractor task. Participants completed a distractor task consisting of math problems when not recalling words and during the 90-s delay. We generated 20 pages of math problems. Each page had six complex math problems involving addition, subtraction, multiplication, and division.

Recall packets. We created six different packets to manipulate the recall condition (immediate, delayed) and counterbalance the lists used for recall. Four pages presented recall instructions based on those used by Roediger and McDermott (1995): "Please write down as many words from the list that you remember. A good strategy is to write down the last few items first, then the rest of the words in any order." Twenty pages had math problems. Between each page was a colored sheet of paper, which masked the participants' next task (recall or math problems). The order of the 24 pages depended on whether participants were in the immediate- or delayed-recall condition and which list set participants were assigned to recall. For example, the "music" list was presented first. Following the presentation of the list, participants assigned to recall the music list in the immediate condition opened their packet to a page with recall instructions; all other participants opened their packet to a page of math problems. After 90 s, a tone signaled participants to turn to the next white page (following the colored sheet). If assigned to recall the music list in the delayed-recall condition, participants' next sheet had recall instructions; all other participants received math problems. This sequence was followed for the remaining 11 word lists.

Recognition tests. Participants completed two different recognition tests, the first

Place periods or commas within quotation marks.

A comma separates authors' surnames and year of publication when citation is within parentheses.

Use ampersand to indicate "and" for references within parentheses.

Underline the anchors of a scale.

Numbers are used to indicate the levels of a design. Include one space to left and right of multiplication sign.

False Recall   7

followed the presentation and recall of lists (immediate), the second was 2 days later (delayed). Because three list sets were used for recall (to counterbalance recall lists across participants), we created three versions of the first recognition test (session 1) and three versions of the second recognition test (session 2). Following Roediger and McDermott's terminology, recognition-test items that were presented during the recall portion of the study are referred to as "studied," and new distractor items are referred to as "not studied." Each 72-item recognition test consisted of six different types of items: 10 Studied/Recalled items (5 each from two of the four lists participants were asked to recall); 2 corresponding critical items for these lists; 20 Studied/Not Recalled items (5 each from four of the eight lists participants did not recall); 4 corresponding critical items for these lists; 30 Not Studied Distractor items (5 each from six lists that were not presented); and 6 corresponding critical items for the distractor lists (these lists also were from Roediger & McDermott, 1995). The five items selected from the word lists for each recognition test were the first, third, fifth, seventh, and ninth words. The 72 words on each list were randomly ordered. Participants made recognition judgments using a 4-point scale (1 = sure new, 2 = probably new, 3 = probably old, and 4 = sure old).

Procedure

A 2 (condition) X 2 (memory type) mixed factorial design was used for the recall portion of the experiment. Students were randomly assigned to either the immediate-recall condition or the delayed-recall condition; thus, the condition variable was manipulated as a random groups design. Memory type was a repeated measures variable with two levels: correct and false memory. The recognition portion of the experiment was a repeated measures independent variable. Participants completed the first recognition test immediately following the presentation and recall of word lists and completed the delayed recognition test 2 days later. The dependent variables were proportion of correct and false recall and proportion of correct and false recognition.

The experiment was conducted during two scheduled class periods. In the first session, lasting 50 min, the experimenter gave students a consent form and a packet that corresponded to their condition when they entered the class (students were randomly assigned to conditions prior to their arrival). A participant number appeared on top of the packet. Instructions requested students not to open their packet. After students read and signed their consent form, they listened to tape-recorded instructions for the study. Following this, the experimenter stopped the tape recorder and asked if there were any questions. Tape-recorded word lists were then presented. The random order of the lists was as follows (identified by the critical item): music, needle, sleep, doctor, slow, mountain, rough, bread, sweet, cold, chair, and foot. Words were presented at the rate of approximately one word every 1½ s. Following the list presentation, participants heard a tone informing them to turn to the next white page. They then either recalled list items or completed math problems for 90 s. A tone then signaled participants to turn to the next white page. This page instructed them to recall the list items or complete math problems. This procedure was followed for all 12 lists.

After the study and recall phase of the experiment, the experimenter distributed the first recognition test and asked participants to record their participant number on the top of the recognition test. After completing the recognition test, participants were asked to write their participant number in their notebook; they were then dismissed. At the beginning of the next class session (2 days later), participants reported their number

"min" (without a period) is the abbreviation for minute.

Note: Words are not hyphenated at the end of a line.

Note: Always double-space. Do not insert extra spaces between sections.

Center, no underline.

and they were given the corresponding second recognition test. Each recognition test took approximately 5 min to complete. The instructor then fully debriefed participants regarding the purpose of the experiment.

Results

Results are presented first for participants' recall and then for their recognition of list items. The dependent variables were proportion of correct recall/recognition and proportion of false recall/recognition. Proportion of correct recall was determined by counting the number of words participants correctly recalled and dividing by 60 (the total number of list items they were asked to recall). Proportion of false recall was determined by counting the number of critical items falsely recalled and dividing by 4 (the total number of critical items for the four lists participants recalled).

Similar proportions were computed for recognition data. For ease of comparisons, participants' recognition responses were collapsed such that ratings of 1 or 2 indicated judgments that the word was "new" (i.e., not presented during the recall portion of the study), and ratings of 3 or 4 indicated the word was "old" (i.e., presented during the recall portion). The number of items judged "old" for each type of word (e.g., studied, recalled; not studied distractor) was counted and divided by the total number of words of that type presented on the recognition test.

Recall

Mean proportions for correct and false recall were entered into a 2 (condition) X 2 (memory type) mixed-design analysis of variance (ANOVA). Across the two recall conditions the proportion of falsely recalled critical items (M = .60, SD = .23) tended to be greater than the proportion of correctly recalled list items (M = .48, SD = .12), F(1,

M is the abbreviation for arithmetic mean

SD is the abbreviation for standard deviation.

MSE is the abbreviation for Mean Square Error.

Underline all statistical terms.

Do not capitalize names of conditions.

Footnotes appear on a separate page near end of manuscript (*not at bottom of the page*).

Do not abbreviate "Figure." Figure caption and figure appear on separate pages at end of manuscript.

Degrees of freedom for statistical tests are reported in parentheses (with no space after statistical term).

False Recall   10

16) = 4.38, p = .053 (MSE = .03, effect size r = .47).[1] The observed power to detect this large effect with the small sample size (n = 9 per condition), at alpha = .05, was estimated to be only .50. The main effect of condition was not significant, $F(1, 16) = .10$, p > .05 (MSE = .02, r = .10, power = .06). As predicted, however, recall condition and memory type interacted to influence participants' recall, $F(1, 16) = 9.50$, p < .01 (MSE = .03, r = .61). Simple main effects analyses revealed that recall differed in the immediate- and delayed-recall conditions in the predicted direction (see Figure 1). Participants in the immediate-recall condition did not differ in their proportions of correct recall and false recall, $F(1, 8) = .41$, p > .05 (MSE = .036, r = .22, power = .09); however, participants in the delayed-recall condition were more likely to recall a greater proportion of false critical items than correct list items, $F(1, 8) = 16.57$, p < .005 (MSE = .024, r = .82).[2]

A second set of simple main effects analyses examined the effect of delay for each type of recall. As expected, the proportion of correctly recalled list items decreased following delay and the proportion of false recall increased following delay (see Figure 1). For correct list items, participants in the delayed-recall condition recalled fewer items than participants who recalled list items immediately, $F(1, 16) = 15.42$, p < .005 (MSE = .008). The effect size (r) was .70, indicating a very large effect of immediate- vs. delayed-recall on participants' correct recall (see Cohen, 1988). In contrast, the proportion of falsely recalled critical items increased following the 90-s delay relative to the immediate-recall condition, $F(1, 16) = 3.77$, p = .07. The effect size (r) was .44; however, the estimated power to detect this large effect was only .45 (alpha = .05).

<u>Recognition</u>

Across two testing sessions separated by 2 days, we examined the proportion of items recognized as "old" as a function of whether items were correct list items or false critical items and whether the items were recalled (vs. not recalled) during the recall portion of the experiment (see Table 1).[3] Distractor items were excluded from the analyses because the proportion of these items judged "old" was generally low across item type and sessions, $\underline{M}$ = .18 ($\underline{SD}$ = .12). Main effects were observed for the time, memory type, and recalled/not recalled variables. As expected, memory for the items decreased over the 2-day period, as the proportion of all items recognized as "old" decreased at Time 2 ($\underline{M}$ = .71, $\underline{SD}$ = .14) relative to Time 1 ($\underline{M}$ = .87, $\underline{SD}$ = .11), $\underline{F}$(1, 14) = 16.40, $\underline{p}$ < .005 ($\underline{MSE}$ = .04, $\underline{r}$ = .73). Additionally, the main effect of memory type indicated that participants rated a higher proportion of false critical items "old" ($\underline{M}$ = .85, $\underline{SD}$ = .11) than correct list items ($\underline{M}$ = .73, $\underline{SD}$ = .13), $\underline{F}$(1, 14) = 14.72, $\underline{p}$ < .005 ($\underline{MSE}$ = .026, $\underline{r}$ = .71). Thus, in terms of proportions, false recognition was greater than correct recognition at Time 1 and Time 2. Finally, the proportion of items judged "old" was greater for lists participants were asked to recall ($\underline{M}$ = .87, $\underline{SD}$ = .09) relative to lists they did not recall ($\underline{M}$ = .71, $\underline{SD}$ = .14), $\underline{F}$(1, 14) = 23.57, $\underline{p}$ < .001 ($\underline{MSE}$ = .032, $\underline{r}$ =.79). This is the "testing effect" identified by Roediger and McDermott (1995), in which rehearsal during the recall portion of the experiment increases subsequent recognition.

There was also a Time X Recalled/Not Recalled interaction, $\underline{F}$(1, 14) = 7.49, $\underline{p}$ < .05 ($\underline{MSE}$ = .024, $\underline{r}$ = .59). This interaction indicated that recognition of words for recalled lists was slightly higher at Time 1 ($\underline{M}$ = .90, $\underline{SD}$ = .07) relative to Time 2 ($\underline{M}$ = .83, $\underline{SD}$ = .16), $\underline{F}$(1, 15) = 3.22, $\underline{p}$ < .10 ($\underline{MSE}$ = .013, $\underline{r}$ = .42, power = .39). In contrast,

False Recall   12

recognition of words from not-recalled lists dropped significantly at Time 2 ($\underline{M}$ = .60, $\underline{SD}$ = .18) relative to Time 1 ($\underline{M}$ = .83, $\underline{SD}$ = .18), $\underline{F}$(1, 15) = 18.63, $\underline{p}$ < .005 ($\underline{MSE}$ = .023, $\underline{r}$ = .74). Thus, rehearsal of the lists (through recall) increased the proportion of correct items and false critical items recognized as "old" even after a 2-day period, relative to lists that were not rehearsed.

As noted above, we observed differential effects of delay on the proportion recall of correct list items and false critical items. However, a similar effect was not observed for recognition data, as the Time X Memory Type interaction was not statistically significant, $\underline{F}$(1, 14) = .028, $\underline{p}$ > .05 ($\underline{MSE}$ = .014). The effect size, $\underline{r}$, for this interaction was quite small (.04, power = .05). Thus, the 2-day delay between the recognition tests resulted in similar decreases in the proportions of correct list items and false critical items that were recognized as "old."

Note: Make sure you use the "greater than" or "less than" sign correctly.

Center, no underline.

Discussion

Participants recalled list items in a single trial of free recall immediately after list presentation or following a 90-s filled delay. The proportion of correctly recalled list items decreased as a function of delay, but the proportion of false critical items recalled increased following the 90-s delay. Participants' recognition of correct list items and false critical items was tested following a 2-day delay. In terms of proportions, false recognition of critical items was greater than correct recognition of list items at Time 1 and Time 2, but recognition for both types of items decreased over the 2-day period. A testing effect occurred such that correct and false recognition were greater for lists participants had attempted recall relative to lists not recalled. The effects of rehearsal persisted over the 2-day period. In general, delay produced large effect sizes for both

Year of publication in parentheses after author's surname.

Do not use contractions such as "wasn't."

Year of publication is not repeated within a paragraph if it is clear that the same study is being described.

Year of publication appears in parentheses even when reference has appeared previously in manuscript.

Use "et al." following surname of first author for work with three or more authors.
Note: First citation to this work lists all authors (see p. 3).

---

recall and recognition.

McDermott (1996) used a 30-s filled delay to examine the effects of delay on participants' recall of correct list items and false critical items. Although she observed a decrease in correct recall following delay, her participants' false recall of critical items was not affected by delay. In contrast, we observed an increase in the proportion of false critical items recalled following a 90-s delay. One reason for this discrepancy may be derived from our differing findings for correct list recall. In McDermott's study the proportion of correct list items recalled following a 30-s delay was .50; in our study, the proportion of correct recall following a 90-s delay was .39. To the extent that a longer delay increased participants' forgetting of correct list items in our study, they may have had to rely more on schema-based recall, which we hypothesized to increase the occurrence of false memories. Alternatively, discrimination between IARs and memory for list items may become more difficult with longer delays. As a result, greater proportions of false recall would be expected (as was observed). This explanation is corroborated by McDermott's findings that after a 2-day delay, the proportion of falsely recalled critical items was greater than the proportion of correctly recalled items (similar to our findings for recognition). Thus, in both studies, participants demonstrated high levels of false recall that persisted over time.

Payne et al. (1996) examined participants' recognition memory for correct list items and false critical items in immediate (2 min) and delayed (24 hr) conditions. Similar to our recognition data, Payne et al. observed that false critical items were recognized with higher likelihood at both testing sessions than correct list items. However, they also observed an interaction between item type (correct, false) and "hr" (with no period) is the abbreviation for hour.

retention (immediate, delayed) for their recognition data that we did not. They observed more forgetting for correct list items than false critical items over the 24-hr period, whereas over our 2-day period we observed similar decreases for correct list items and false critical items. Differences in the retention interval (24 vs. 48 hr), the number of word lists (16 vs. 12), or other procedural differences may account for this discrepancy.

The findings of this study and those of other recent studies indicate that false memories are frequent and persist following delays. Moreover, there is accumulating evidence to suggest that false memories for highly associated information may exceed correct memory over time. These data are limited to individuals' recall for highly associated list items. Important areas for future research include false memories for natural categories such as people and events. Also, it is not clear to what extent individuals' emotions may affect correct and false recall. This question is particularly relevant to the issue of false memory in the emotionally charged situations of eyewitness testimony and therapy.

Note: References section begins on a new page immediately after the Discussion section.

Underline titles of books. Only first letter of first word and word following a colon in caps.

Publisher of book.

Use ampersand before last author's name.

First letter of questionnaire names in caps.

Use initials for first and middle names.

Period after year of publication (in parentheses).

Page numbers.

Use lower case for titles of articles and book chapters (except first word and word after a colon).

Underline journal name and volume number. Capitalize first letter of major words in journal name. Use comma after journal name and volume number.

Indent first line of each reference (same as paragraph).

Center, no underline.

False Recall   15

References

Cohen, J. (1988). <u>Statistical power analysis for behavioral sciences</u> (2nd ed.).
New York: Academic Press.

Keppel, G. (1991). <u>Design and analysis: A researcher's handbook</u> (3rd ed.).
Englewood Cliffs, NJ: Prentice-Hall.

Mather, M., Henkel, L. A., & Johnson, M. J. (1997). Evaluating characteristics of
false memories: Remember/know judgments and Memory Characteristics
Questionnaire compared. <u>Memory & Cognition, 25,</u> 826-837.

McDermott, K. B. (1996). The persistence of false memories in list recall. <u>Journal
of Memory and Language, 35,</u> 212-230.

Norman, K., & Schacter, D. L. (1997). False recognition in younger and older
adults: Exploring the characteristics of illusory memories. <u>Memory & Cognition, 25,</u> 838-
848.   Separate authors' names with a comma.

Payne, D. G., Elie, C. J., Blackwell, J. M., & Neuschatz, J. S. (1996). Memory
illusions: Recalling, recognizing, and recollecting events that never occurred. <u>Journal of
Memory and Language, 35,</u> 261-285.

Roediger, H. L., & McDermott, K. B. (1995). Creating false memories:
Remembering words not presented in lists. <u>Journal of Experimental Psychology:
Learning, Memory, and Cognition, 21,</u> 803-814.

Underwood, B.J. (1965). False recognition produced by implicit verbal
responses. <u>Journal of Experimental Psychology, 70,</u> 122-129.

Note: List references in alphabetical order using first author's surname. Double-space references, no extra space between references.

Center, no underline.

↓

Author Note

Authors' department affiliations in first paragraph.

Acknowledge people who assisted with the research and manuscript preparation.

Last paragraph in Author Note specifies author's address for correspondence. Use this form exactly with your name and address.

Jeanne S. Zechmeister, Department of Psychology; Eugene B. Zechmeister, Department of Psychology.

Portions of this research were presented at the Annual Meeting of the Psychonomic Society, November 1996. The authors thank the students in the first author's Research Methods in Psychology course at Loyola University of Chicago who participated in and discussed this study, and John J. Shaughnessy for his suggestions for this manuscript.

Send correspondence concerning this manuscript to Jeanne S. Zechmeister, Department of Psychology, Loyola University of Chicago, 6525 N. Sheridan Road, Chicago, IL 60626; e-mail: jzechme@luc.edu.

Footnotes

[1] The effect size, r, was derived from ANOVA output that presented eta^2 as a measure of effect size. Eta^2 represents the proportion of variance in the dependent variable that is accounted for by the independent variable. Eta^2 is analogous to r^2 in analyses involving one df for the effect. The square root of eta^2 represents r, the magnitude of linear relationship between two variables. Cohen (1988) offers the following guidelines for interpreting the size of an effect using r: small effect, $r = .10$; medium effect, $r = .25$; large effect, $r = .40$.

[2] Simple main effect analyses were calculated by treating the comparison as a one-way ANOVA, as recommended by Keppel (1991) for mixed designs.

[3] We also examined whether immediate- vs. delayed-recall conditions influenced recognition in the ANOVA. Because this variable did not produce any statistically significant effects in the recognition analyses, it will not be discussed further.

Note: Use footnotes sparingly in manuscript.

Type flush with left margin.

Line separates title from body of table.

Center column headings over appropriate columns.

Line separates headings from table data.

Line at end of table data.

Table "notes" are typed flush with left margin.

Table title, underlined, with first letters of major words in caps.

False Recall   18

Table 1

Mean Proportions for Recognizing Items as "Old" at Time 1 and Time 2 (48-hr Delay)

	Studied and Recalled	Studied and Not Recalled	Distractor
Correct List Items			
Time 1	.84	.79	.19
	(.12)	(.17)	(.12)
Time 2	.76	.56	.18
	(.22)	(.16)	(.16)
False Critical Items			
Time 1	.97	.88	.28
	(.12)	(.20)	(.13)
Time 2	.91	.64	.17
	(.20)	(.24)	(.10)

Note. Standard deviations are in parentheses. "Recalled" and "Not Recalled" refer to whether participants were asked to recall list items at Time 1, not whether these items were produced by participants during recall.

Note: Use double-space in table. Place only one table on a page.

Center, no underline.

↓

Figure Caption

False Recall   19

Flush with left margin. Do not abbreviate "Figure." ⟶

Figure 1. Mean proportions of correct and false recall in the immediate- and delayed-recall conditions.

Note: More than one figure caption may appear on a "Figure Captions" page.

The figure itself appears on a separate page at end of manuscript. If there is more than one figure, each appears on a separate page.

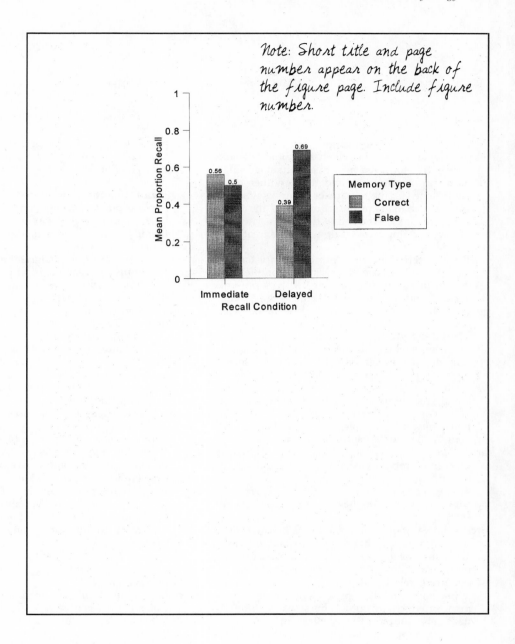

Glossary

ABAB design (reversal design) A single-case experimental design in which an initial baseline stage (A) is followed by a treatment stage (B), a return to baseline (A), and then another treatment stage (B); the researcher observes whether behavior changes on introduction of the treatment, reverses when the treatment is withdrawn, and improves again when the treatment is reintroduced.

ABBA counterbalancing A technique for balancing stage-of-practice effects in the complete repeated measures design that involves presenting the conditions in one sequence (e.g., AB) followed by the opposite of the same sequence (e.g., BA).

accidental sample A type of nonprobability sample that results when availability and willingness to respond are the overriding factors used in selecting respondents; generally low in representativeness.

actuarial prediction Prediction of people's typical or average behavior based on reliable correlations between variables (e.g., predicting students' college GPA based on SAT scores).

analytical comparisons A statistical technique that can be applied (usually after obtaining a significant omnibus F-test) to locate the specific source of systematic variation in an experiment.

applied research See **basic versus applied research.**

archival data Source of evidence based on records or documents relating the activities of individuals, institutions, governments, and other groups; used as an alternative to or in conjunction with other research methods.

baseline stage First stage of a single-case experiment in which a record is made of the individual's behavior prior to any intervention.

basic versus applied research Whereas basic research mainly seeks knowledge about nature simply for the sake of understanding it better, applied research seeks knowledge that will modify or improve the present situation; however, basic and applied research are considered to have a reciprocal relationship, for example, when basic research is used to identify abstract principles that can be applied in real-world settings, and when applied research is used to reveal possible limitations or extensions of these principles.

behavior modification (behavior therapy) The application of learning-conditioning principles in order to change behavior; the term behavior therapy is used when this application is with clinical populations.

behavior therapy See **behavior modification.**

biased sample A sample in which the distribution of characteristics is systematically different from that of the parent population.

block randomization The most common technique for carrying out random assignment in the random groups design; each block includes a random order of the conditions and there are as many blocks as there are subjects in each condition of the experiment.

case study An intensive description and analysis of a single individual.

causal inference Identification of the cause or causes of a phenomenon, by establishing covariation of cause and effect, a time-order relationship with cause preceding effect, and the elimination of plausible alternative causes.

ceiling (and floor) effect Measurement problem whereby the researcher cannot measure the effects of an independent variable or a possible interaction because performance has reached a maximum (minimum) in any condition of the experiment.

checklist Instrument used to record the presence or absence of something in the situation under observation.

coding The initial step in data reduction, especially with narrative records, in which units of behavior or particular events are identified and classified according to specific criteria.

complex design Experiment in which two or more independent variables are studied simultaneously.

confederate Someone in the service of a researcher who is instructed to behave in a certain way in order to help produce an experimental treatment.

confidence intervals   Indicate the range of values in which we can expect a population value to fall with a specified degree of confidence (e.g., .95).

confounding   Occurs when the independent variable of interest systematically covaries with a second, unintended independent variable.

contamination   Occurs when there is communication of information about the experiment between groups of participants.

content analysis   Any of a variety of techniques for making inferences by objectively identifying specific characteristics of messages, usually written communications but may be any form of message; used extensively in the analysis of archival data.

control   Key component of the scientific method whereby the effect of various factors possibly responsible for a phenomenon are isolated; three basic types of control are manipulation, holding conditions constant, and balancing.

correlation   Exists when two different measures of the same people, events, or things vary together; the presence of a correlation makes it possible to predict values on one variable by knowing the values on the second variable.

correlation coefficient   Statistic indicating how well two measures vary together; absolute size ranges from 0.0 (no correlation) to 1.00 (perfect correlation); direction of covariation is indicated by the sign of the coefficient, a plus ($+$) indicating that both measures covary in the same direction and a minus ($-$) indicating that the variables vary in opposite directions.

correlational research   Research whose goal is to identify predictive relationships among naturally occurring variables.

counterbalancing   A control technique for distributing (balancing) practice effects across the conditions of a repeated measures design. How counter-balancing is accomplished depends on whether a complete or an incomplete repeated measures design is used.

cross-sectional design   Survey research design in which one or more samples of the population are selected and information is collected from the samples at one time.

data reduction   Process in the analysis of behavioral data whereby results are meaningfully organized and statements summarizing important findings are prepared.

debriefing   Process following a research session through which participants are informed about the rationale for the research in which they participated, about the need for any deception, and about their specific contribution to the research. Important goals of debriefing are to clear up any misconceptions and to leave participants with a positive feeling toward psychological research.

deception   Intentionally withholding information about significant aspects of a research project from a participant or presenting misinformation about the research to participants.

demand characteristics   Cues and other information used by participants to guide their behavior in a psychological study, often leading participants to do what they believe the observer (experimenter) expects them to do.

dependent variable   Measure of behavior used by the researcher to assess the effect (if any) of the independent variables.

differential transfer   Potential problem in repeated measures designs when performance in one condition differs depending on which of two other conditions precedes it.

double-blind   Both the participant and the observer are kept unaware (blind) of what treatment is being administered.

ecological psychology   Has as its goal the comprehensive description of individuals in everyday contexts.

effect size   Index of the strength of the relationship between the independent variable and dependent variable that is independent of sample size.

element   Each member of the population of interest.

empirical approach   Approach to acquiring knowledge that emphasizes direct observation and experimentation as a way of answering questions.

ethnography   Branch of anthropology that focuses on the systematic description (e.g., using naturalistic observation and participant observation) of the context and meanings of social interactions in a particular culture. May share similar goals with ecological psychology.

ethogram   A complete catalog of all the behavior patterns of an organism, including information as to frequency, duration, and context of occurrence.

ethology   Study of the behavior of organisms in relation to their natural environment; generally considered a branch of biology.

event sampling   Procedure whereby the observer records each event that meets a predetermined definition; more efficient method than time sampling when event of interest occurs infrequently.

experimenter effects Experimenters' expectations that may lead them to treat subjects differently in different groups or to record data in a biased manner.

external validity The extent to which the results of a research study can be generalized to different populations, settings, and conditions.

extraneous variables Potential independent variables that are not of direct interest to a researcher, but, in order to avoid confounding, must be controlled (e.g., nature of experimenters, size of groups tested).

field experiment Procedure in which one or more independent variables is manipulated by an observer in a natural setting to determine the effect on behavior.

field notes Verbal records of a trained observer that provide a running description of participants, events, settings, and behaviors.

floor effect See **ceiling effect.**

F-test Statistical test based on the analysis of variance, specifically the ratio of systematic variation and error variation. Under the null hypothesis both sources of variation represent error variation only and the expected value of F is 1.00.

Hawthorne effect Changes in a person's behavior brought about by the interest shown in that person by significant others.

hypothesis A tentative explanation for a phenomenon.

idiographic approach Intensive study of an individual, with an emphasis on both individual uniqueness and lawfulness.

independent groups design Each separate group of subjects in the experiment represents a different condition as defined by the level of the independent variable.

independent variable Factor for which the researcher either selects or manipulates at least two levels in order to determine its effect on behavior.

individual differences variable A characteristic or trait that varies consistently across individuals, such as level of depression, age, intelligence, gender. Because this variable is formed from preexisting groups (i.e., it occurs "naturally") an individual differences variable is sometimes called a *natural groups variable.* Another term sometimes used synonymously with individual differences variable is *subject variable.*

inferential statistics Means to test whether the differences in a dependent variable that are associated with various conditions of an experiment are reliable, that is, larger than would be expected on the basis of error variation alone.

informed consent Explicitly expressed willingness to participate in a research project based on clear understanding of the nature of the research, of the consequences of not participating, and of all factors that might be expected to influence willingness to participate.

interaction What occurs when the effect of one independent variable differs depending on the level of a second independent variable.

internal validity Degree to which differences in performance can be attributed unambiguously to an effect of an independent variable, as opposed to an effect of some other (uncontrolled) variable; an internally valid study is free of confounds.

interobserver reliability Degree to which two independent observers are in agreement.

interrupted time-series design See **simple interrupted time-series design** and **time series with nonequivalent control group design.**

interviewer bias Occurs when the interviewer tries to adjust the wording of a question to fit the respondent or records only selected portions of the respondent's answers.

longitudinal design Research design in which the same sample of respondents is interviewed (tested) more than once.

main effect Overall effect of an independent variable in a complex design.

margin of error In survey research, an estimate of the difference between a result obtained from a sample (e.g., the sample mean) and the corresponding true population value (e.g., population mean).

matched groups design Type of independent groups design in which the researcher forms comparable groups by matching subjects on a pretest task and then randomly assigning the members of these matched sets of subjects to the conditions of the experiment.

measurement scale One of four levels of physical and psychological measurement: nominal (categorizing), ordinal (ranking), interval (specifying distance between stimuli), and ratio (having an absolute zero point).

mechanical subject loss Occurs when a subject fails to complete the experiment because of equipment failure or because of experimenter error.

meta-analysis Analysis of results of several (often, very many) independent experiments investigating the same research area; the measure used in a meta-analysis is typically effect size.

minimal risk A research participant is said to experience minimal risk when probability and magnitude of harm or discomfort anticipated in the research are not greater than that ordinarily encountered in daily life or during the performance of routine tests.

multimethod approach Approach to hypothesis testing that seeks evidence by collecting data using several different measures of behavior; a recognition of the fact that any single measure of behavior can result from some artifact of the measuring process.

multiple-baseline design (across subjects, across behaviors, across situations) A single-case experimental design in which the effect of a treatment is demonstrated by showing that behaviors in more than one baseline change as a consequence of the introduction of a treatment; multiple baselines are established for different individuals, for different behaviors in the same individual, or for the same individual in different situations.

$N = 1$ **designs** See **single-case experiment.**

narrative record Record intended to provide a more or less faithful reproduction of behavior as it originally occurred.

natural groups design Type of independent groups design in which the conditions represent the selected levels of a naturally occurring independent variable, for example, the individual differences variable age.

naturalistic observation Observation of behavior in a more or less natural setting without any attempt by the observer to intervene.

nomothetic approach Approach to research that seeks to establish broad generalizations or laws that apply to large groups (populations) of individuals; the average or typical performance of a group is emphasized.

nonequivalent control group design Quasi-experimental procedure in which a comparison is made between control and treatment groups that have been established on some basis other than through random assignment of participants to groups.

nonprobability sampling A sampling procedure in which there is no way to estimate the probability of each element's being included in the sample; two common types are accidental sampling and purposive sampling.

null hypothesis Assumption used as the first step in statistical inference whereby the independent variable is said to have had no effect.

observer bias Systematic errors in observation often resulting from the observer's expectancies

regarding the outcome of a study (i.e., expectancy effects).

operational definition Procedure whereby a concept is defined solely in terms of the operations used to produce and measure it.

participant observation Observation of behavior by someone who also has an active and significant role in the situation or context in which behavior is recorded.

physical traces Source of evidence that is based on the remnants, fragments, and products of past behavior; used as an alternative to or in conjunction with other research methods.

placebo control Procedure by which a substance that resembles a drug or other active substance but that is actually an inert, or inactive, substance is given to participants.

plagiarism Presentation of another's ideas or work without clearly identifying the source.

population Set of all the cases of interest.

power Probability in a statistical test that a false null hypothesis will be rejected; power is related to the level of significance selected, the size of the treatment effect, and the sample size.

practice effects Changes that participants undergo with repeated testing. Practice effects are the summation of both positive (e.g., familiarity with a task) and negative (e.g., boredom) factors associated with repeated measurement.

privacy Right of individuals to decide how information about them is to be communicated to others.

probability sampling Sampling procedure in which the probability that each element of the population will be included in the sample can be specified.

program evaluation Research that seeks to determine whether a change proposed by an institution, government agency, or other unit of society is needed and likely to have an effect as planned or, when implemented, to actually have an effect.

purposive sampling A type of nonprobability sampling in which the investigator selects the elements to be included in the sample on the basis of their special characteristics (e.g., recovering alcoholics).

quasi-experiments Procedures that resemble those characteristics of true experiments, for example, that some type of intervention or treatment is used and a comparison is provided, but are lacking in the degree of control that is found in true experiments.

random assignment Most common technique for forming groups as part of an independent groups design; the goal is to establish equivalent groups by balancing individual differences.

random groups design   Most common type of independent groups design in which subjects are randomly selected or randomly assigned to each group such that groups are considered comparable at the start of the experiment.

random sampling   See **simple random sampling.**

reactivity   Influence that an observer has on the behavior under observation; behavior influenced by an observer may not be representative of behavior when an observer is not present.

regression (to the mean)   Because some component of a test score is due to error (as opposed to true score), extreme scores on one test are likely to be closer to the mean on a second test, thus posing a threat to the validity of an experiment in which extreme groups are selected; the amount of this statistical regression is greater for less reliable tests.

relevant independent variable   Independent variable that has been shown to influence behavior, either directly, by producing a main effect, or indirectly, by resulting in an interaction in combination with a second independent variable.

reliability   A measurement is reliable when it is consistent.

repeated measures designs   Research designs in which each subject participates in all conditions of the experiment (i.e., measurement is repeated on the same subject).

replication   Repeating the exact procedures used in an experiment to determine whether the same results are obtained.

representativeness   A sample is representative to the extent that it has the same distribution of characteristics as the population from which it was selected; our ability to generalize from sample to population is critically dependent on representativeness.

response bias   Threat to the representativeness of a sample that occurs when some participants selected to respond to a survey systematically fail to complete the survey (e.g., due to failure to complete a lengthy questionnaire or to reply with a request to participate in a phone survey).

risk/benefit ratio   Subjective evaluation of the risk to a research participant relative to the benefit both to the individual and to society of the results of the proposed research.

sample   Something less than all the cases of interest; in survey research, a subset of the population actually drawn from the sampling frame.

sampling frame   Specific listing of all the members of the population of interest; an operational definition of the population.

scientific method   Approach to knowledge that emphasizes empirical rather than intuitive processes, testable hypotheses, systematic and controlled observation of operationally defined phenomena, data collection using accurate and precise instrumentation, valid and reliable measures, and objective reporting of results; scientists tend to be critical and, most importantly, skeptical.

selection bias   Threat to the representativeness of a sample that occurs when the procedures used to select a sample result in the over- or underrepresentation of a significant segment of the population.

selective deposit   Bias that results from the way physical traces are laid down and the way archival sources are produced, edited, or altered, as they are established; when present, the bias severely limits generality of research findings.

selective subject loss   Occurs when subjects are lost differentially across the conditions of the experiment as the result of some characteristic of each subject that is related to the outcome of the study.

selective survival   Bias that results from the way physical traces and archives survive over time; when present, the bias severely limits the external validity of research findings.

sensitivity   Refers to the likelihood in an experiment that the effect of an independent variable will be detected when that variable does, indeed, have an effect; sensitivity is increased to the extent that error variation is reduced (e.g., by holding variables constant rather than balancing them).

simple interrupted time-series design   Quasi-experimental procedure in which changes in a dependent variable are observed for some period of time both before and after a treatment is introduced.

simple main effect   Effect of one independent variable at one level of a second independent variable in a complex design.

simple random sampling (random selection)   Type of probability sampling in which each possible sample of a specified size in the population has an equal chance of being selected.

single-case experiment   A procedure that focuses on behavior change in one individual ($N = 1$) by systematically contrasting conditions within that individual while continuously monitoring behavior.

situation sampling Random or systematic selection of situations in which observations are to be made with the goal of representativeness across circumstances, locations, and conditions.

social desirability Pressures on survey respondents to answer as they think they should respond in accordance with what is most socially acceptable, and not in accordance with what they actually believe.

spurious relationship What exists when evidence falsely indicates that two or more variables are associated.

statistically significant When the probability of an obtained difference in an experiment is smaller than would be expected if error variation alone were assumed to be responsible for the difference, the difference is statistically significant.

stratified random sampling Type of probability sampling in which the population is divided into subpopulations called strata and random samples are drawn from each of these strata.

structured observation Variety of observational methods using intervention in which the degree of control is often less than in field experiments; frequently used by clinical and developmental psychologists when making behavioral assessments.

successive independent samples design Survey research design in which a series of cross-sectional surveys is done and the same questions are asked of each succeeding sample of respondents.

theory Logically organized set of propositions that serves to define events, describe relationships among events, and explain the occurrence of these events; scientific theories guide research and organize empirical knowledge.

threats to internal validity Possible causes of a phenomenon that must be controlled so a clear cause-effect inference can be made.

time sampling Selection of observation intervals either systematically or randomly with the goal of obtaining a representative sample of behavior.

time series with nonequivalent control group design (See also **simple interrupted time-series design.**) Quasi-experimental procedure that improves on the validity of a simple time-series design by including a nonequivalent control group; both treatment and comparison groups are observed for a period of time both before and after the treatment.

unobtrusive (nonreactive) measures Measures of behavior that eliminate the problem of reactivity, because observations are made in such a way that the presence of the observer is not detected by those being observed.

validity The "truthfulness" of a measure; a valid measure is one that measures what it claims to measure.

References

Abelson, R. P. (1985). A variance paradox: When a little is a lot. *Psychological Bulletin, 97,* 129–133.

Abelson, R. P. (1995). *Statistics as principled argument.* Hillsdale, NJ: Erlbaum.

Abelson, R. P. (1997). On the surprising longevity of flogged horses: Why there is a case for the significance test. *Psychological Science, 8,* 12–15.

Adair, J. G., Dushenko, T. W., & Lindsay, R. C. L. (1985). Ethical regulations and their impact on research practice. *American Psychologist, 40,* 59–72.

Addison, W. E. (1986). Agonistic behavior in preschool children: A comparison of same-sex versus opposite-sex interactions. *Bulletin of the Psychonomic Society, 24,* 44–46.

Adjang, O. M. J. (1986). Exploring the social environment: A developmental study of teasing in chimpanzees. *Ethology, 73,* 136–160.

Adler, A. (1973). *Practice and theory of individual psychology,* (P. Radin., Trans.) Totowa, NJ: Littlefield, Adams.

Adler, T. (1991, December). Outright fraud rare, but not poor science. *APA Monitor,* 11.

Albright, J. S., & Henderson, M. C. (1995). How real is depressive realism? A question of scales and standards. *Cognitive Therapy and Research, 19,* 589–609.

Allison, M. G., & Ayllon, T. (1980). Behavioral coaching in the development of skills in football, gymnastics, and tennis. *Journal of Applied Behavior Analysis, 13,* 297–314.

Allport, G. W. (1946). Letters from Jenny. *Journal of Abnormal and Social Psychology, 41,* (3, 4).

Allport, G. W. (1961). *Pattern in growth and personality.* New York: Holt, Rinehart and Winston.

Allport, G. W. (1965). *Letters from Jenny.* New York: Harcourt, Brace & World.

Altmann, J. (1974). Observational study of behavior: Sampling methods. *Behavior, 48,* 1–41.

Ambady, N., & Rosenthal, R. (1993). Half a minute: Predicting teacher evaluations from thin slices of nonverbal behavior and physical attractiveness. *Journal of Personality and Social Psychology, 64,* 431–441.

American Psychiatric Association. (1994). *Diagnostic and statistical manual of mental disorders* (4th ed.). Washington, DC: Author.

American Psychological Association. (1991). Five-year report of the policy and planning board, 1990; Five years of turbulence, change, and growth within APA. *American Psychologist, 46,* 678–688.

American Psychological Association. (1992). Ethical principles of psychologists and code of conduct. *American Psychologist, 47,* 1597–1611.

American Psychological Association. (1994). *Publication manual* (4th ed). Washington, DC: Author.

American Psychological Association. (1998). Summary report of journal operations, 1997. *American Psychologist, 53,* 983–984.

Anderson, C. A. (1989). Temperature and aggression: Ubiquitous effects of heat on occurrence of human violence. *Psychological Bulletin, 106,* 74–96.

Anderson, C. A., & Bushman, B. J. (1997). External validity of "trivial" experiments: The case of laboratory aggression. *Review of General Psychology, 1,* 19–41.

Anderson, C. A., Bushman, B. J., & Groom, R. W. (1997). Hot years and serious and deadly assault: Empirical tests of the heat hypothesis. *Journal of Personality and Social Psychology, 73,* 1213–1223.

Anderson, C. R. (1976). Coping behaviors as intervening mechanisms in the inverted-U stress-performance relationship. *Journal of Applied Psychology, 61,* 30–34.

Anderson, J. R. (1990). *The adaptive character of thought.* Hillsdale, NJ: Erlbaum.

Anderson, J. R. (1993). *Rules of the mind.* Hillsdale, NJ: Erlbaum.

Anderson, J. R., & Milson, J. R. (1989). Human memory: An adaptive perspective. *Psychological Review, 96,* 703–719.

Anderson, K. J., & Revelle, W. (1982). Impulsivity, caffeine, and proofreading: A test of the Easterbrook hypothesis. *Journal of Experimental Psychology: Human Perception and Performance, 8,* 614–624.

Anglin, J. M. (1993). Vocabulary development: A morphological analysis. *Monographs of the Society for Research in Child Development, 58* (10, Serial No. 238).

Asch, S. E. (1951). Effects of group pressure upon the modification and distortion of judgements.

In H. Guetzkow (Ed.), *Groups, leadership, and men* (pp. 177–190). Pittsburgh: Carnegie.

Asch, S. E. (1955). Opinions and social pressure. *Scientific American, 193*, 31–35.

Astin, A. W., Parrott, S. A., Korn, W. S., & Sax, L. J. (1997). *The American freshman: Thirty year trends.* Los Angeles: Higher Education Research Institute, UCLA.

Atkinson, R. C. (1968). Computerized instruction and the learning process. *American Psychologist, 23*, 225–239.

Atkinson, R. C., & Shiffrin, R. M. (1968). Human memory: A proposed system and its control processes. In K. W. Spence & J. T. Spence (Eds.), *The psychology of learning and motivation*, Vol. 2 (pp. 89–195). New York: Academic Press.

Azar, B. (1994a, December). Animal research threatened by activism. *APA Monitor*, 18.

Azar, B. (1994b, August). Computers create global research lab. *APA Monitor*, 1, 16.

Azar, B. (1994c, August). Research made easier by computer networks. *APA Monitor*, 16.

Azar, B. (1995, May). Board approves ways to spend science funds. *APA Monitor*, 25.

Azar, B. (1997, March). APA task force urges a harder look at data. *APA Monitor*, 26.

Bailey, J. M., Kim, P. Y., Hills, A., & Linsenmeier, J. A. W. (1997). Butch, femme, or straight acting? Partner preferences of gay men and lesbians. *Journal of Personality and Social Psychology, 73*, 960–973.

Banaji, M. R., & Crowder, R. G. (1989). The bankruptcy of everyday memory. *American Psychologist, 44*, 1185–1193.

Barash, D. P. (1977). Human ethology: Exchanging cheetahs for Chevrolets? *Environment and Behavior, 9*, 487–490.

Barker, R. G., Wright, H. F., Schoggen, M. F., & Barker, L. S. (1978). Day in the life of Mary Ennis. In R. G. Barker et al. (Eds.), *Habitats, environments, and human behavior* (pp. 51–98). San Francisco: Jossey-Bass.

Baron, J. N., & Reiss, P. C. (1985). Same time, next year: Aggregate analyses of the mass media and violent behavior. *American Sociological Review, 50*, 347–363.

Baron, R. M., & Kenny, D. A. (1986). The moderator-mediator variable distinction in social psychological research: Conceptual, strategic, and statistical considerations. *Journal of Personality and Social Psychology, 51*, 1173–1182.

Bartholomew, G. A. (1982). Scientific innovation and creativity: A zoologist's point of view. *American Zoologist, 22*, 227–335.

Bartlett, F. C. (1932). *Remembering: A study in experimental and social psychology.* Cambridge: Cambridge University Press.

Baumeister, R. F. (1995). Disputing the effects of championship pressures and home audiences. *Journal of Personality and Social Psychology, 68*, 644–648.

Baumeister, R. F., & Steinhilber, A. (1984). Paradoxical effects of supportive audiences on performance under pressure: The home field disadvantage in sports championships. *Journal of Personality and Social Psychology, 47*, 85–93.

Baumrind, D. (1985). Research using intentional deception: Ethical issues revisited. *American Psychologist, 40*, 165–174.

Berk, R. A., Boruch, R. F., Chambers, D. L., Rossi, P. H., & Witte, A. D. (1987). Social policy experimentation: A position paper. In D. S. Cordray & M. W. Lipsey (Eds.), *Evaluation Studies Review Annual*, Vol. 11 (pp. 630–672). Newbury Park, CA: Sage.

Bickman, L. (1976). Observational methods. In C. Selltiz, L. S. Wrightsman, & S. W. Cook (Eds.), *Research methods in social relations* (pp. 251–290). New York: Holt, Rinehart and Winston.

Blanchard, F. A., Crandall, C. S., Brigham, J. C., & Vaughn, L. A. (1994). Condemning and condoning racism: A social context approach to interracial settings. *Journal of Applied Psychology, 79*, 993–997.

Blanck, P. D., Bellack, A. S., Rosnow, R. L., Rotheram-Borus, M. J., & Schooler, N. R. (1992). Scientific rewards and conflicts of ethical choices in human subjects research. *American Psychologist, 47*, 959–965.

Bolgar, H. (1965). The case study method. In B. B. Wolman (Ed.), *Handbook of clinical psychology* (pp. 28–39). New York: McGraw-Hill.

Bond, C. F., Jr., & Titus, L. J. (1983). Social facilitation: A meta-analysis of 241 studies. *Psychological Bulletin, 94*, 265–292.

Booth, W. (1988). Chimps and research: Endangered? *Science, 241*, 777–778.

Boring, E. G. (1950). *A history of experimental psychology.* New York: Appleton-Century-Crofts.

Boring, E. G. (1954). The nature and history of experimental control. *American Journal of Psychology, 67*, 573–589.

Bourke, K. (1998, September). Now available on-line: Interactive experiments. *APS Observer*, 14–15.

Brainerd, C. J. (1978). *Piaget's theory of intelligence.* Englewood Cliffs, NJ: Prentice-Hall.

Brandt, R. M. (1972). *Studying behavior in natural settings.* New York: Holt, Rinehart and Winston: University Press of America, 1981.

Bridgewater, C. A., Bornstein, P. H., & Walkenbach, J. (1981). Ethical issues and the assignment of publication credit. *American Psychologist, 36,* 524–525.

Brigham, T. A., Meier, S. M., & Goodner, V. (1995). Increasing designated driving with a program of prompts and incentives. *Journal of Applied Behavior Analysis, 28,* 83–84.

Broach, D. (1992, June). Non-cognitive predictions of performance in radar-based air traffic control training. Paper presented at the Fourth Annual Convention of the American Psychological Society, San Diego, CA.

Bröder, A. (1998). Deception can be acceptable. *American Psychologist, 53,* 805–806.

Brown, R., & Kulik, J. (1977). Flashbulb memories. *Cognition, 5,* 73–99.

Browne, M. A., & Mahoney, M. J. (1984). Sport psychology. *Annual Review of Psychology, 35,* 605–625.

Burns, M. S., Haywood, H. C., & Delclos, V. R. (1987). Young children's problem-solving strategies: An observational study. *Journal of Applied Developmental Psychology, 8,* 113–121.

Campbell, A. (1981). *The sense of well-being in America.* New York: McGraw-Hill.

Campbell, A., Converse, P. E., & Rodgers, W. L. (1975). *The quality of American life; July–August, 1971.* Ann Arbor: ISR Social Science Archive.

Campbell, D. T. (1969). Reforms as experiments. *American Psychologist, 24,* 409–429.

Campbell, D. T., & Stanley, J. C. (1966). *Experimental and quasi-experimental designs for research.* Chicago: Rand McNally.

Campbell, R. (Ed.). (1992). *Mental lives: Case studies in cognition.* Oxford: Blackwell.

Candland, D. K. (1993). *Feral children and clever animals.* New York: Oxford University Press.

Carroll, J. M., & Russell, J. A. (1997). Facial expressions in Hollywood's portrayal of emotion. *Journal of Personality and Social Psychology, 72,* 164–176.

Caspi, A., Begg, D., Dickson, N., Harrington, H., Langley, J., Moffitt, T. E., & Silva, P. A. (1997). Personality differences predict health-risk behaviors in young adulthood: Evidence from a longitudinal study. *Journal of Personality and Social Psychology, 73,* 1052–1063.

Ceci, S. J. (1993). Cognitive and social factors in children's testimony. Master Lecture presented at the American Psychological Association Convention.

Chambers, J. H., & Ascione, F. R. (1987). The effects of prosocial and aggressive videogames on children's donating and helping. *Journal of Genetic Psychology, 148,* 499–505.

Cherlin, A. J., Furstenberg, F. F., Jr., Chase-Lansdale, P. L., Kiernan, K. E., Robins, P. K., Morrison, D. R., & Teitler, J. O. (1991). Longitudinal studies of effects of divorce on children in Great Britain and the United States. *Science, 252,* 1386–1389.

Chow, S. L. (1988). Significance test or effect size? *Psychological Bulletin, 103,* 105–110.

Christensen, L. (1988). Deception in psychological research: When is its use justified? *Personality and Social Psychology Bulletin, 14,* 664–675.

Cicchetti, D. (1998). Child abuse and neglect—usefulness of the animal data: Comment on Maestipieri and Carroll (1998). *Psychological Bulletin, 123,* 224–230.

Clark, H. H., & Schober, M. F. (1992). Asking questions and influencing answers. In J. M. Tanur (Ed.), *Questions about questions: Inquiries into the cognitive bases of surveys.* New York: Russell Sage Foundation.

Cohen, D. (1979). *J. B. Watson: The founder of behaviorism.* London: Routledge & Kegan Paul.

Cohen, J. (1988). *Statistical power analysis for the behavioral sciences* (2nd ed.). Hillsdale, NJ: Erlbaum.

Cohen, J. (1990). Things I have learned (so far). *American Psychologist, 45,* 1304–1312.

Cohen, J. (1992). A power primer. *Psychological Bulletin, 112,* 155–159.

Cohen, J. (1995). The earth is round ($p < .05$). *American Psychologist, 49,* 997–1003.

Cohen, N. J., McCloskey, M., & Wible, C. G. (1990). Flashbulb memories and underlying cognitive mechanisms: Reply to Pillemer. *Journal of Experimental Psychology: General, 119,* 97–100.

Connors, G. J., Collins, R. L., Dermen, K. H., & Koutsky, J. R. (1998). Substance use restraint: An extension of the construct to a clinical population. *Cognitive Therapy and Research, 22,* 75–87.

Converse, P. E., & Traugott, M. W. (1986, November 28). Assessing the accuracy of polls and surveys. *Science, 234,* 1094–1097.

Cook, T. D., & Campbell, D. T. (1979). *Quasi-experimentation: Design and analysis issues for field settings.* Chicago: Rand McNally.

Cordaro, L., & Ison, J. R. (1963). Psychology of the scientist: X. Observer bias in classical conditioning of the planarian. *Psychological Reports, 13,* 787–789.

Coren, S., & Porac, C. (1977). Fifty centuries of right-handedness: The historical record. *Science, 198,* 631–632.

Courneya, K. S., & Carron, A. V. (1992). The home advantage in sport competitions: A literature review. *Journal of Sport & Exercise Psychology, 14,* 13–27.

Cronbach, L. J. (1992). Four *Psychological Bulletin* articles in perspective. *Psychological Bulletin, 12*, 389–392.

Crossen, C. (1994). *Tainted truth: The manipulation of fact in America*. New York: Simon & Schuster.

Crusco, A. H., & Wetzel, C. G. (1984). The Midas touch: The effects of interpersonal touch on restaurant tipping. *Personality and Social Psychology Bulletin, 10*, 512–517.

Csikszentmihalyi, M., & Larson, R. W. (1987). Validity and reliability of the experience-sampling method. *Journal of Nervous and Mental Disorders, 175*, 526–533.

Curtiss, S. R. (1977). *Genie: A psycholinguistic study of a modern-day "wild child."* New York: Academic Press.

Dawes, R. M. (1991, June). *Problems with a psychology of college sophomores*. Paper presented at the Third Annual Convention of the American Psychological Society, Washington, DC.

Dawes, R. M., Faust, D., & Meehl, P. E. (1993). Statistical prediction versus clinical prediction: Improving what works. In G. Keren & C. Lewis (Eds.), *A handbook for data analysis in the behavioral sciences: Methodological issues* (pp. 351–367). Hillsdale, NJ: Erlbaum.

de Blois, S. T., Novak, M. A., & Bond, M. (1998). Object permanence in orangutans (*Pongo pygmaeus*) and squirrel monkeys (*Saimiri sciureus*). *Journal of Comparative Psychology, 112*, 137–152.

Delespaul, P. A. E. G. (1995). *Assessing schizophrenia in daily life: The experience sampling method*. Rijkjaniversiteit van Limburg (Maastricht, The Netherlands).

DeLoache, J. S., Pierroutsakos, S. L., Uttal, D. H., Rosengren, K. S., & Gottlieb, A. (1998). Grasping the nature of pictures. *Psychological Science, 9*, 205–210.

Dickie, J. R. (1987). Interrelationships within the mother-father-infant triad. In P. W. Berman & F. A. Pedersen (Eds.), *Men's transitions to parenthood: Longitudinal studies of early family experience* (pp. 113–143). Hillsdale, NJ: Erlbaum.

Diener, E., & Crandall, R. (1978). *Ethics in social and behavioral research*. Chicago: The University of Chicago Press.

Dittmar, M. L., Berch, D. B., & Warm, J. S. (1982). Sustained visual attention in deaf and hearing adults. *Bulletin of the Psychonomic Society, 19*, 339–342.

Divorce of the year. *Newsweek*, March 12, 1973, pp. 48–49.

Dolan, C. A., Sherwood, A., & Light, K. C. (1992). Cognitive coping strategies and blood pressure responses to real-life stress in healthy young men. *Health Psychology, 11*, 233–240.

Eagly, A. H., & Steffen, V. J. (1984). Gender stereotypes stem from the distribution of women and men into social roles. *Journal of Personality and Social Psychology, 46*, 735–754.

Eibl-Eibesfeldt, I. (1975). *Ethology: The biology of behavior*. New York: Holt, Rinehart and Winston.

Emerson, J. D. (1991). Introduction to transformation. In D. C. Hoaglin, F. Mosteller, & J. W. Tukey (Eds.), *Fundamentals of exploratory analysis of variance* (pp. 365–400). New York: Wiley.

Endersby, J. W., & Towle, M. J. (1996). Tailgate partisanship: Political and social expression through bumper stickers. *The Social Science Journal, 33*, 307–319.

Entwisle, D. R., & Astone, N. M. (1994). Some practical guidelines for measuring youth's race/ethnicity and socioeconomic status. *Child Development, 65*, 1521–1540.

Epley, N., & Huff, C. (1998). Suspicion, affective response, and educational benefit as a result of deception in psychology research. *Personality and Social Psychology Bulletin, 24*, 759–768.

Epstein, S. (1979). The stability of behavior: On predicting most of the people much of the time. *Journal of Personality and Social Psychology, 37*, 1097–1126.

Erber, R. (1991). Affective and semantic priming: Effects of mood on category accessibility and inference. *Journal of Experimental Social Psychology, 27*, 480–498.

Ericsson, K. A., & Charness, N. (1994). Expert performance: Its structure and acquisition. *American Psychologist, 49*, 725–747.

Ericsson, K. A., Chase, W. G., & Faloon, S. (1980). Acquisition of a memory skill. *Science, 208*, 1181–1182.

Estes, W. K. (1997). On the communication of information by displays of standard errors and confidence intervals. *Psychonomic Bulletin & Review, 4*, 330–341.

Evans, R., & Donnerstein, E. (1974). Some implications for psychological research of early versus late term participation by college students. *Journal of Research in Personality, 8*, 102–109.

Feeney, D. M. (1987). Human rights and animal welfare. *American Psychologist, 42*, 593–599.

Festinger, L., Riecken, H., & Schachter, S. (1956). *When prophecy fails*. Minneapolis: University of Minnesota Press.

Fine, M. A., & Kurdek, L. A. (1993). Reflections on determining authorship credit and authorship order on faculty-student collaborations. *American Psychologist, 48*, 1141–1147.

Fiore, S. (1994, May/June). The student notebook. *APS Observer*, p. 28.

Fischer, K., Schoeneman, T. J., & Rubanowitz, D. E. (1987). Attributions in the advice columns: II. The dimensionality of actors' and observers' explanations for interpersonal problems. *Personality and Social Psychology Bulletin, 13*, 458–466.

Fisher, C. B., & Fryberg, D. (1994). Participant partners: College students weigh the costs and benefits of deceptive research. *American Psychologist, 49*, 417–427.

Fossey, D. (1981). Imperiled giants of the forest. *National Geographic, 159*, 501–523.

Fossey, D. (1983). *Gorillas in the mist*. Boston: Houghton-Mifflin.

Fowler, R. D. (1992). Report of the chief executive officer: A year of building for the future. *American Psychologist, 47*, 876–883.

Frame, C. L., & Strauss, C. C. (1987). Parental informed consent and sample bias in grade-school children. *Journal of Social and Clinical Psychology, 5*, 227–236.

Frank, M. G., & Gilovich, T. (1988). The dark side of self- and social perception: Black uniforms and aggression in professional sports. *Journal of Personality and Social Psychology, 54*, 74–85.

Frick, R. W. (1995). Accepting the null hypothesis. *Memory & Cognition, 23*, 132–138.

Friedman, H. S., Tucker, J. S., Schwartz, J. E., Tomlinson-Keasy, C., Martin, L. R., Wingard, D. L., & Criqui, M. H. (1995). Psychosocial and behavioral predictors of longevity: The aging and death of the "Termites." *American Psychologist, 50*, 69–78.

Friedman, M. P., & Wilson, R. W. (1975). Application of unobtrusive measures to the study of textbook usage by college students. *Journal of Applied Psychology, 60*, 659–662.

Fromm, E. (1998). Lost and found half a century later: Letters by Freud and Einstein. *American Psychologist, 53*, 1195–1198.

Gabrieli, J. D. E., Fleischman, D. A., Keane, M. M., Reminger, S. L., & Morrell, F. (1995). Double dissociation between memory systems underlying explicit and implicit memory in the human brain. *Psychological Science, 6*, 76–82.

Gannon, L., Luchetta, T., Rhodes, K., Pardie, L., & Segrist, D. (1992). Sex bias in psychological research. *American Psychologist, 47*, 389–396.

Geller, E. S., Russ, N. W., & Altomari, M. G. (1986). Naturalistic observations of beer drinking among college students. *Journal of Applied Behavior Analysis, 19*, 391–396.

Gena, A, Krantz, P. J., McClannahan, L. E., & Poulson, C. L. (1996). Training and generalization of affective behavior displayed by youth with autism. *Journal of Applied Behavioral Analysis, 29*, 291–304.

Gillham, J. E., Reivich, K. J., Jaycox, L. H., & Seligman, M. E. P. (1995). Prevention of depressive symptoms in school children: Two-year follow-up. *Psychological Science, 6*, 343–351.

Goldstein, R. S., Minkin, B. L., Minkin, N., & Baer, D. M. (1978). Finders, keepers?: An analysis and validation of a free-found-ad policy. *Journal of Applied Behavior Analysis, 11*, 465–473.

Goodall, J. (1987). A plea for the chimpanzees. *American Scientist, 75*, 574–577.

Goodman, S. H., Lahey, B. B., Fielding, B., Dulcan, M., Narrow, W., & Regier, D. (1997). Representativeness of clinical samples of youths with mental disorders: A preliminary population-based study. *Journal of Abnormal Psychology, 106*, 3–14.

Graham, S. (1992). "Most of the subjects were White and middle class": Trends in published research on African Americans in selected APA journals, 1970–1989. *American Psychologist, 47*, 629–639.

Grammer, K., Schiefenhovel, W., Schleidt, M., Lorenz, B., & Eibl-Eibesfeldt, I. (1988). Patterns on the face: The eyebrow flash in crosscultural comparison. *Ethology, 77*, 279–299.

Gray, J. N., & Melton, G. B. (1985). The law and ethics of psychosocial research on AIDS. *Nebraska Law Review, 64*, 637–688.

Griffin, J. H. (1960). *Black like me*. New York: New American Library.

Grisso, T., Baldwin, E., Blanck, P. D., Rotheram-Borus, M. J., Schooler, N. R., & Thompson, T. (1991). Standards in research: APA's mechanisms for monitoring the challenges. *American Psychologist, 46*, 758–766.

Guerin, B. (1986). Mere presence effects in humans: A review. *Journal of Experimental Social Psychology, 22*, 38–77.

Haber, L. R., & Haber, R. N. (1982). Does silent reading involve articulation? Evidence from tongue twisters. *American Journal of Psychology, 95*, 409–419.

Haden, C. A. (1998). Reminiscing with different children: Relating maternal stylistic consistency and sibling similarity in talk about the past. *Developmental Psychology, 34*, 99–114.

Haden, C. A., Haine, R. A., & Fivush, R. (1997). Developing narrative structure in parent-child reminiscing across the preschool years. *Developmental Psychology, 33*, 295–307.

Hagen, R. L. (1997). In praise of the null hypothesis statistical test. *American Psychologist, 52,* 15–24.

Halpern, A. R., & Bower, G. H. (1982). Musical expertise and melodic structure in memory for musical notation. *American Journal of Psychology, 95,* 31–50.

Harlow, H. F., & Harlow, M. K. (1966). Learning to love. *American Scientist, 54,* 244–272.

Harnack, A., & Kleppinger, E. (1997). *Online! A reference guide to using Internet sources.* New York: St. Martin's Press.

Hart, B., & Risley, T. R. (1995). *Meaningful differences in the everyday experience of young American children.* Baltimore, MD: Paul H. Brookes.

Hartup, W. W. (1974). Aggression in childhood: Development perspectives. *American Psychologist, 29,* 336–341.

Hass, R. G., Katz, I., Rizzo, N., Bailey, J., & Eisenstadt, D. (1991). Cross-racial appraisal as related to attitude ambivalence and cognitive complexity. *Personality and Social Psychology Bulletin, 17,* 83–92.

Hays, R. (1980). Honesty requiring a self-initiated response. *Psychological Reports, 46,* 87–90.

Heath, L., & Davidson, L. (1988). Dealing with the threat of rape: Reactance or learned helplessness? *Journal of Applied Social Psychology, 18,* 1334–1351.

Heatherton, T. F., Mahamedi, F., Striepe, M., Field, A. E., & Keel, P. (1997). A 10–year longitudinal study of body weight, dieting, and eating disorder symptoms. *Journal of Abnormal Psychology, 106,* 117–125.

Heatherton, T. F., Nichols, P., Mahamedi, F., & Keel, P. K. (1995). Body weight, dieting, and eating disorder symptoms among college students 1982 to 1992. *American Journal of Psychiatry, 152,* 1623–1629.

Hedges, L. V. (1981). Distributional theory for Glass's estimator of effect size and related estimators. *Journal of Educational Statistics, 6,* 107–128.

Hersen, M., & Barlow, D. H. (1976). *Single-case experimental designs: Strategies for studying behavior change.* New York: Pergamon Press.

Hilts, P. J. (1995). *Memory's ghost: The nature of memory and the strange tale of Mr. M.* New York: Simon & Schuster.

Hippler, H. J., & Schwarz, N. (1987). Response effects in surveys. In H. J. Hippler, N. Schwarz, & S. Sudman (Eds.), *Social information processing and survey methodology* (pp. 102–122). New York: Springer-Verlag.

Hirschberg, N., & Itkin, S. (1978). Graduate student success in psychology. *American Psychologist, 33,* 1083–1093.

Hite, S. (1987). *Women and love: A cultural revolution in progress.* New York: Knopf.

Hoaglin, D. C., Mosteller, F., & Tukey, J. W. (Eds.). (1983). *Understanding robust and exploratory data analysis.* New York: Wiley.

Hoaglin, D. C., Mosteller, F., & Tukey, J. W. (Eds.). (1991). *Fundamentals of exploratory analysis of variance.* New York: Wiley.

Hofer, M. A., & Myers, M. M. (1996). Animal models in psychosomatic research. *Psychosomatic Medicine, 58,* 521–523.

Holden, C. (1987). Animal regulations: So far, so good. *Science, 238,* 880–882.

Holmbeck, G. N. (1997). Toward terminological, conceptual, and statistical clarity in the study of mediators and moderators: Examples from the child-clinical and pediatric psychology literatures. *Journal of Consulting and Clinical Psychology, 65,* 599–610.

Holsti, O. R. (1969). *Content analysis for the social sciences.* Reading, MA: Addison-Wesley.

Hops, J., Biglan, A., Sherman, L., Arthur, J., Friedman, L., & Osteen, V. (1987). Home observations of family interactions of depressed women. *Journal of Consulting and Clinical Psychology, 55,* 341–346.

Horn, W. F., & Heerboth, J. (1982). Single-case experimental designs and program evaluation. *Evaluational Review, 6,* 403–424.

Horton, S. V. (1987). Reduction of disruptive mealtime behavior by facial screening. *Behavior Modification, 11,* 53–64.

Howell, D. C. (1997). *Statistical methods for psychology* (4th ed.). Belmont, CA: Wadsworth.

Hughes, H. M., & Haynes, S. N. (1978). Structured laboratory observation in the behavioral assessment of parent-child interactions: A methodological critique. *Behavior Therapy, 9,* 428–447.

Hunt, M. (1997). *How science takes stock: The story of meta-analysis.* New York: Russell Sage Foundation.

Hunter, J. E. (1997). Needed: A ban on the significance test. *Psychological Science, 8,* 3–7.

Jackson, J. M., Buglione, S. A., & Glenwick, D. S. (1988). Major league baseball performance as a function of being traded: A drive theory analysis. *Personality and Social Psychology Bulletin, 14,* 46–56.

Jenni, D. A., & Jenni, M. A. (1976). Carrying behavior in humans: Analysis of sex differences. *Science, 194,* 859–860.

Jenni, M. A. (1976). Sex differences in carrying behavior. *Perceptual and Motor Skills, 43,* 323–330.

Johnson, D. (1990). Animal rights and human lives: Time for scientists to right the balance. *Psychological Science, 1,* 213–214.

Joswick, K. E. (1994). Getting the most from PsycLIT: Recommendations for searching. *Teaching of Psychology, 21,* 49–53.

Judd, C. M., Smith, E. R., & Kidder, L. H. (1991). *Research methods in social relations* (6th ed.). Fort Worth, TX: Holt, Rinehart and Winston.

Kagan, J., Reznick, J. S., & Snidman, N. (1988). Biological bases of childhood shyness. *Science, 240,* 167–171.

Kahneman, D., Fredrickson, B. L., Schreiber, C. A., & Redelmeier, D. A. (1993). When more pain is preferred to less: Adding a better end. *Psychological Science, 4,* 401–405.

Kahneman, D., & Tversky, A. (1973). On the psychology of prediction. *Psychological Review, 80,* 237–251.

Kardas, E. P., & Milford, T. M. (1996). *Using the Internet for social science research and practice.* Belmont, CA: Wadsworth.

Kazdin, A. E. (1978). Methodological and interpretive problems of single-case experimental designs. *Journal of Consulting and Clinical Psychology, 46,* 629–642.

Kazdin, A. E. (1980). *Behavior modification in applied settings* (rev. ed.). Homewood, IL: Dorsey Press.

Kazdin, A. E. (1982). Single-case experimental designs. In P. C. Kendall & J. N. Butcher (Eds.), *Handbook of research methods in clinical psychology* (pp. 416–490). New York: Wiley.

Kazdin, A. E. (1998). *Research designs in clinical psychology.* Boston: Allyn and Bacon.

Kazdin, A. E., & Erickson, L. M. (1975). Developing responsiveness to instructions in severely and profoundly retarded residents. *Journal of Behavior Therapy and Experimental Psychiatry, 6,* 17–21.

Keith, T. Z., Reimers, T. M., Fehrmann, P. G., Pottebaum, S. M., & Aubrey, L. W. (1986). Parental involvement, homework, and TV time: Direct and indirect effects on high school achievement. *Journal of Educational Psychology, 78,* 373–380.

Keith-Spiegel, P., & Koocher, G. P. (1985). *Ethics in psychology: Professional standards and cases.* New York: Random House.

Keller, F. S. (1937). *The definition of psychology.* New York: Appleton-Century-Crofts.

Kelley-Milburn, D., & Milburn, M. A. (1995). Cyberpsych: Resources for psychologists on the Internet. *Psychological Science, 6,* 203–211.

Kelman, H. C. (1967). Human use of human subjects: The problem of deception in social psychological experiments. *Psychological Bulletin, 67,* 1–11.

Kelman, H. C. (1972). The rights of the subject in social research: An analysis in terms of relative power and legitimacy. *American Psychologist, 27,* 989–1016.

Kenny, D. A. (1979). *Correlation and causality.* New York: Wiley.

Keppel, G. (1991). *Design and analysis: A researcher's handbook* (3rd ed.). Englewood Cliffs, NJ: Prentice-Hall.

Kiesler, S., Walsh, J., & Sproull, L. (1992). Computer networks in field research. In F. B. Bryant, J. Edwards, F. S. Tindale, E. J. Posavac, L. Heath, E. Henderson, & Y. Suarez-Balcazar (Eds.), *Methodological issues in applied social psychology: Vol. 2. Social psychological applications to social issues* (pp. 239–267). New York: Plenum.

Kimble, G. A. (1989). Psychology from the standpoint of a generalist. *American Psychologist, 44,* 491–499.

Kimmel, A. J. (1996). *Ethical issues in behavioral research: A survey.* Cambridge, MA: Blackwell.

Kimmel, A. J. (1998). In defense of deception. *American Psychologist, 53,* 803–805.

Kirk, R. E. (1996). Practical significance: A concept whose time has come. *Educational and Psychological Measurement, 56,* 746–759.

Kirkham, G. L. (1975). Doc cop. *Human Behavior, 4,* 16–23.

Kirsch, I. (1978). Teaching clients to be their own therapists: A case-study illustration. *Psychotherapy: Theory, Research and Practice, 15,* 302–305.

Kirsch, I., & Sapirstein, G. (1998). Listening to prozac but hearing placebo: A meta-analysis of antidepressant medication. *Prevention and Treatment* [On-line serial], *1.* Available: journals.apa.org/prevention/volume1/pre0010002a.html.

Klemmack, S. H., & Klemmack, D. L. (1976). The social definition of rape. In M. J. Walker & S. L. Brodsky (Eds.), *Sexual assault.* Lexington, MA: Lexington Books.

Krantz, J. H., Ballard, J., & Scher, J. (1997). Comparing the results of laboratory and World-Wide-Web samples on the determinants of female attractiveness. *Behavior Research Methods, Instruments, & Computers, 29,* 264–269.

Kratochwill, T. R., & Brody, G. H. (1978). Single subject designs: A perspective on the controversy over employing statistical inference and implications for research and training in behavior modification. *Behavior Modification, 2,* 291–307.

Kratochwill, T. R., & Levin, J. R. (Eds.). (1992). *Single-case research design and analysis*. Hillsdale, NJ: Erlbaum.

Kratochwill, T. R., & Martens, B. K. (1994). Applied behavior analysis and school psychology. *Journal of Applied Behavior Analysis, 27*, 3–5.

Kubany, E. S. (1997). Application of cognitive therapy for trauma-related guilt (CT-TRG) with a Vietnam veteran troubled by multiple sources of guilt. *Cognitive and Behavioral Practice, 4*, 213–244.

LaFrance, M., & Mayo, C. (1976). Racial differences in gaze behavior during conversations: Two systematic observational studies. *Journal of Personality and Social Psychology, 33*, 547–552.

Lakatos, I. (1978). *The methodology of scientific research*. London: Cambridge University Press.

Landers, S. (1987a, September). CARE urges protection for animals and labs. *APA Monitor*, 28–29.

Landers, S. (1987b, December). Lab checks: Rigid or reciprocal? *APA Monitor*, 6–7.

Landers, S. (1988, September). Adolescent study presents dilemma. *APA Monitor*, 6.

Langer, E. J. (1989). *Mindfulness*. Reading, MA: Addison-Wesley.

Langer, E. J. (1997). *The power of mindful learning*. Reading, MA: Addison-Wesley.

Langer, E. J., & Piper, A. I. (1987). The prevention of mindlessness. *Journal of Personality and Social Psychology, 53*, 280–287.

Langer, E. J., & Rodin, J. (1976). The effects of choice and enhanced personal responsibility for the aged: A field experiment in an institutional setting. *Journal of Personality and Social Psychology, 34*, 191–198.

Larose, S., & Roy, R. (1995). Test of reactions and adaptation in college (TRAC): A new measure of learning propensity for college students. *Journal of Educational Psychology, 87*, 293–306.

Larson, R. (1989). Beeping children and adolescents: A method for studying time use and daily experience. *Journal of Youth and Adolescence, 18*, 511–530.

Larson, R. W., Richards, M. H., Moneta, G., Holmbeck, G., & Duckett, E. (1996). Changes in adolescents' daily interactions with their families from ages 10 to 18: Disengagement and transformation. *Developmental Psychology, 32*, 744–754.

Latané, B., & Darley, J. M. (1970). *The unresponsive bystander: Why doesn't he help?* New York: Appleton-Century-Crofts.

Latané, B., Williams, K., & Harkin, S. (1979). Many hands make light the work: The causes and consequences of social loafing. *Journal of Personality and Social Psychology, 37*, 822–832.

Lau, R. R., & Russell, D. (1980). Attributions in the sports pages. *Journal of Personality and Social Psychology, 39*, 29–38.

Leavens, D. A., & Hopkins, W. D. (1998). Intentional communication by chimpanzees: A cross-sectional study of the use of referential gestures. *Developmental Psychology, 34*, 813–822.

Lenneberg, E. H. (1967). *Biological foundations of language*. New York: Wiley.

Levine, R. V. (1990). The pace of life. *American Scientist, 78*, 450–459.

Levine, R. V., West, L. J., & Reis, H. T. (1980). Perceptions of time and punctuality in the United States and Brazil. *Journal of Personality and Social Psychology, 38*, 541–550.

Linton, M. (1978). Real world memory after six years: An *in vivo* study of very long term memory. In M. M. Gruneberg, P. E. Morris, & R. N. Sykes (Eds.), *Practical aspects of memory* (pp. 69–76). New York: Academic Press.

Locke, T. P., Johnson, G. M., Kirigin-Ramp, K., Atwater, J. D., & Gerrard, M. (1986). An evaluation of a juvenile education program in a state penitentiary. *Evaluation Review, 10*, 281–298.

Loftus, E. F. (1979). *Eyewitness testimony*. Cambridge, MA: Harvard University Press.

Loftus, E. F. (1997a). Creating childhood memories. *Applied Cognitive Psychology, 11* (Special Issue), 575–586.

Loftus, E. F. (1997b). Memory for a past that never was. *Current Directions in Psychological Science, 6*, 60–65.

Loftus, E. F., & Burns, T. E. (1982). Mental shock can produce retrograde amnesia. *Memory & Cognition, 10*, 318–323.

Loftus, G. R. (1991). On the tyranny of hypothesis testing in the social sciences. *Contemporary Psychology, 36*, 102–105.

Loftus, G. R. (1993). A picture is worth a thousand *p* values: On the irrelevance of hypothesis testing in the microcomputer age. *Behavior Research Methods, Instruments, & Computers, 25*, 250–256.

Loftus, G. R. (1996). Psychology will be a much better science when we change the way we analyze data. *Current Directions in Psychological Science, 5*, 161–171.

Loftus, G. R., & Masson, M. E. J. (1994). Using confidence intervals in within-subject designs. *Psychonomic Bulletin & Review, 1*, 476–490.

Lorge, I., & Chall, J. (1963). Estimating the size of vocabularies of children and adults: An analysis of methodological issues. *Journal of Experimental Education, 32*, 147–157.

Lovaas, O. I. (1993). The development of a treatment-research project for developmentally disabled and autistic children. *Journal of Applied Behavior Analysis, 26*, 617–630.

Lovaas, O. I., Newsom, C., & Hickman, C. (1987). Self-stimulatory behavior and perceptual reinforcement. *Journal of Applied Behavior Analysis, 20*, 45–68.

Lovaas, O. I., Schaeffer, B., & Simmons, J. Q. (1965). Building social behaviors in autistic children by use of electric shock. *Journal of Research in Personality, 1*, 99–109.

Lubin, B., Zuckerman, M., Breytspraak, L. M., Bull, N. C., Gumbhir, A. K., & Rinck, C. M. (1988). Affects, demographic variables, and health. *Journal of Clinical Psychology, 44*, 131–141.

Lucas, R. E., Diener, E., & Suh, E. (1996). Discriminant validity of well-being measures. *Journal of Personality and Social Psychology, 71*, 616–628.

Ludwig, T. E., Jeeves, M. A., Norman, W. D., & DeWitt, R. (1993). The bilateral field advantage on a letter-matching task. *Cortex, 29*, 691–713.

Lyons, C. A., & Ghezzi, P. M. (1995). Wagering on a large scale: Relationships between public gambling and game manipulations in two state lotteries. *Journal of Applied Behavior Analysis, 28*, 127–137.

Madigan, C. M. (1995, March 19). Hearing it right: Small turnout spoke. *Chicago Tribune*, pp. 1–2.

Maestripieri, D., & Carroll, K. A. (1998). Child abuse and neglect: Usefulness of the animal data. *Psychological Bulletin, 123*, 211–223.

Marx, M. H. (1963). The general nature of theory construction. In M. H. Marx (Ed.), *Theories in contemporary psychology* (pp. 4–46). New York: Macmillan.

Maser, J. D., & Seligman, M. E. P. (Eds.). (1977). *Psychopathology: Experimental models*. San Francisco: Freeman.

May, C. P., Hasher, L., Stoltzfus, E. R. (1993). Optimal time of day and magnitude of age differences in memory. *Psychological Science, 4*, 326–330.

McCain, L. J., & McCleary, R. (1979). The statistical analysis of the simple interrupted time-series quasi-experiment. In T. D. Cook & D. T. Campbell (Eds.), *Quasi-Experimentation: Design & analysis issues for field settings* (pp. 233–293). Chicago: Rand McNally.

McCloskey, M., Wible, C. G., & Cohen, N. J. (1988). Is there a special flashbulb-memory mechanism? *Journal of Experimental Psychology: General, 117*, 171–181.

McGrew, W. C. (1972). *An ethological study of children's behavior*. New York: Academic Press.

McGuire, W. J. (1997). Creative hypothesis generating in psychology: Some useful heuristics. *Annual Review of Psychology, 48*, 1–30.

McKinney, J. D., Mason, J., Perkerson, K., & Clifford, M. (1975). Relationship between classroom behavior and academic achievement. *Journal of Educational Psychology, 67*, 198–203.

McSweeney, A. J. (1978). Effects of response cost on the behavior of a million persons: Charging for directory assistance in Cincinnati. *Journal of Applied Behavior Analysis, 11*, 47–51.

Medvec, V. H., Madey, S. F., & Gilovich, T. (1995). When less is more: Counterfactual thinking and satisfaction among Olympic medalists. *Journal of Personality and Social Psychology, 69*, 603–610.

Meehl, P. E. (1954). *Clinical versus statistical prediction: A theoretical analysis and review of the literature*. Minneapolis: University of Minnesota Press.

Meehl, P. E. (1967). Theory-testing in psychology and physics: A methodological paradox. *Philosophy of Science, 34*, 103–115.

Meehl, P. E. (1978). Theoretical risks and tabular asterisks: Sir Karl, Sir Ronald, and the slow progress of soft psychology. *Journal of Consulting and Clinical Psychology, 46*, 806–834.

Meehl, P. E. (1990a). Appraising and amending theories: The strategy of Lakatosian defense and two principles that warrant it. *Psychological Inquiry, 1*, 108–141.

Meehl, P. E. (1990b). Why summaries of research on psychological theories are often uninterpretable. *Psychological Reports, 66*, 195–244 (Monograph Supplement 1-V66).

Meehl, P. E. (1993). Philosophy of science: Help or hindrance? *Psychological Reports, 72*, 707–733.

Melton, G. B., & Gray, J. N. (1988). Ethical dilemmas in AIDS research: Individual privacy and public health. *American Psychologist, 43*, 60–64.

Melton, G. B., Levine, R. J., Koocher, G. P., Rosenthal, R., & Thompson, W. C. (1988). Community consultation in socially sensitive research. *American Psychologist, 43*, 573–581.

Merritt, C. B., & Fowler, R. G. (1948). The pecuniary honesty of the public at large. *Journal of Abnormal and Social Psychology, 43*, 90–93.

Miles, M. B., & Huberman, A. M. (1994). *Qualitative data analysis* (2nd ed.). Thousands Oaks, CA: Sage.

Milgram, S. (1974). *Obedience to authority*. New York: Harper & Row.

Milgram, S. (1977). Subject reaction: The neglected factor in the ethics of experimentation. Hastings Center Report, October.

Milgram, S., Liberty, H. J., Toledo, R., & Wackenhut, J. (1986). Response to intrusion into waiting lines. *Journal of Personality and Social Psychology, 51,* 683–689.

Miller, G. A., & Wakefield, P. C. (1993). On Anglin's analysis of vocabulary growth. *Monographs of the Society for Research in Child Development, 58,* (10, Serial No. 238).

Miller, J. D. (1986, May). Some new measures of scientific illiteracy. Paper presented at the meeting of the American Association for the Advancement of Science, Philadelphia.

Miller, N. E. (1985). The value of behavioral research on animals. *American Psychologist, 40,* 423–440.

Miller, T. Q., Heath, L., Molcan, J. R., & Dugoni, B. L. (1991). Imitative violence in the real world: A reanalysis of homicide rates following championship prize fights. *Aggressive Behavior, 17,* 121–134.

Mook, D. G. (1983). In defense of external invalidity. *American Psychologist, 38,* 379–387.

Moore, B. R., & Stuttard, S. (1979). Dr. Guthrie and *Felis domesticus* or: Tripping over the cat. *Science, 205,* 1031–1033.

Morier, D., & Keeports, D. (1994). Normal science and the paranormal: The effect of a scientific method course on students' beliefs. *Research in Higher Education, 35,* 443–453.

Mosteller, F., & Hoaglin, D. C. (1991). Preliminary examination of data. In D. C. Hoaglin, F. Mosteller, & J. W. Tukey (Eds.), *Fundamentals of exploratory analysis of variance* (pp. 40–49). New York: Wiley.

Mulaik, S. A., Raju, N. S., & Harshman, R. A. (1997). There is a time and place for significance testing. In L. L. Harlow, S. A. Mulaik, & J. H. Steiger (Eds.), *What if there were no significance tests?* (pp. 65–115). Mahwah, NJ: Erlbaum.

Murray, B. (1998, December). The authorship dilemma: Who gets credit for what? *APA Monitor, 1,* 31.

Myers, D. G. (1998). *Psychology* (5th ed.). New York: Worth.

Myers, D. G. (1999). *Social psychology* (6th ed.). New York: McGraw-Hill.

Myers, D. G., & Diener, E. (1995). Who is happy? *Psychological Science, 6,* 10–19.

National Research Council (1996) *Guide for the care and use of laboratory animals.* A report of the Institute of Laboratory Animal Resources committee. Washington, DC: National Academy Press.

Neisser, I., & Harsch, N. (1992). Phantom flashbulbs: False recollections of hearing the news about *Challenger.* In E. Winograd & I. Neisser (Eds.), *Affect and accuracy in recall: Studies of "flashbulb memories"* (pp. 9–31). New York: Cambridge University Press.

Newcomb, T. M., Koenig, K. E., Flacks, R., & Warwick, D. P. (1967). *Persistence and change: Bennington College and its students after twenty-five years.* New York: Wiley.

Newhagen, J. E., & Ancell, M. (1995). The expression of emotion and social status in the language of bumper stickers. *Journal of Language and Social Psychology, 14,* 312–323.

New town blues: HUD abandons a disaster. *Time,* October 16, 1978, p. 84.

Novak, M. A. (1991, July). "Psychologists care deeply" about animals. *APA Monitor,* 4.

Orne, M. T. (1962). On the social psychology of the psychological experiment: With particular reference to demand characteristics and their implications. *American Psychologist, 17,* 776–783.

Ortmann, A., & Hertwig, R. (1997). Is deception necessary? *American Psychologist, 52,* 746–747.

Ortmann, A., & Hertwig, R. (1998). The question remains: Is deception acceptable? *American Psychologist, 53,* 806–807.

Osgood, C. E., & Walker, E. G. (1959). Motivation and language behavior: A content analysis of suicide notes. *Journal of Abnormal and Social Psychology, 59,* 58–67.

Parry, H. J., & Crossley, H. M. (1950). Validity of responses to survey questions. *Public Opinion Quarterly, 14,* 61–80.

Parsons, H. M. (1974). What happened at Hawthorne? *Science, 183,* 922–932.

Parsonson, B. S., & Baer, D. M. (1992). The visual analysis of data, and current research into the stimuli controlling it. In T. R. Kratochwill & J. R. Levin (Eds.), *Single-case research design and analysis* (pp. 15–40). Hillside, NJ: Erlbaum.

Pennebaker, J. W., Mayne, T. J., & Francis, M. E. (1997). Linguistic predictors of adaptive bereavement. *Journal of Personality and Social Psychology, 72,* 863–871.

Peterson, J. (1995). How are psychologists perceived by the public? *APA Monitor,* 31.

Pezdek, K., Finger, K., & Hodge, D. (1997). Planting false childhood memories: The role of event plausibility. *Psychological Science, 8,* 437–441.

Phillips, D. P. (1977). Motor vehicle fatalities increase just after publicized suicide stories. *Science, 196*, 1464–1465.

Phillips, D. P. (1978). Airplane accident fatalities increase just after newspaper stories about murder and suicide. *Science, 201*, 748–750.

Phillips, D. P. (1983). The impact of mass media violence on U.S. homicides. *American Sociological Review, 48*, 560–568.

Phillips, D. P., & Bollen, K. A. (1985). Same time, last year: Selective data dredging for negative findings. *American Sociological Review, 50*, 364–371.

Piaget, J. (1965). *The child's conception of number.* New York: Norton.

Pillemer, D. B. (1990). Clarifying the flashbulb memory concept: Comment on McCloskey, Wible, & Cohen (1988). *Journal of Experimental Psychology: General, 119*, 92–96.

Pingitore, R., Dugoni, B. L., Tindale, R. S., & Spring, B. (1994). Bias against overweight job applicants in a simulated employment interview. *Journal of Applied Psychology, 79*, 909–917.

Pishkin, V., & Shurley, J. T. (1983). Electrophysiological parameters in anxiety and failure: Evaluation of doxepin and hydroxyzine. *Bulletin of the Psychonomic Society, 21*, 21–23.

Pitman, R. K., Kolb, B., Orr, S. P., deJong, J., Yadati, S., & Singh, M. M. (1987). On the utility of ethological data in psychiatric research: The example of facial behavior in schizophrenia. *Ethology and Sociobiology, 8*, 111S–116S.

Plous, S. (1998). Signs of change within the animal rights movement: Results from a follow-up survey of activists. *Journal of Comparative Psychology, 112*, 48–54.

Popper, K. R. (1959). *The logic of scientific discovery.* New York: Basic Books.

Popper, K. R. (1976). *Unended quest.* Glasgow: Fontana/Collins.

Posavac, E. J., & Carey, R. G. (1997). *Program evaluation.* (5th ed.). Englewood Cliffs, NJ: Prentice-Hall.

Poulton, E. C. (1973). Unwanted range effects from using within-subject experimental designs. *Psychological Bulletin, 80*, 113–121.

Poulton, E. C. (1975). Range effects in experiments on people. *American Journal of Psychology, 88*, 3–32.

Poulton, E. C. (1982). Influential companions. Effects of one strategy on another in the within-subjects designs of cognitive psychology. *Psychological Bulletin, 91*, 673–690.

Poulton, E. C., & Freeman, P. R. (1966). Unwanted asymmetrical transfer effects with balanced experimental designs. *Psychological Bulletin, 66*, 1–8.

Powell, D. H., & Whitla, D. K. (1994). Normal cognitive aging: Toward empirical perspectives. *Current Directions in Psychological Science, 3*, 27–31.

Powell-Cope, G. M. (1995). The experience of gay couples affected by HIV infection. *Qualitative Health Research, 5*, 36–62.

Prentice, D. A., & Miller, D. T. (1992). When small effects are impressive. *Psychological Bulletin, 112*, 160–164.

Rachels, J. (1986). *The elements of moral philosophy.* New York: McGraw-Hill.

Richardson, D. R., Pegalis, L., & Britton, B. (1992). A technique for enhancing the value of research participation. *Contemporary Social Psychology, 16*, 11–13.

Riddoch, M. J., & Humphreys, G. W. (1992). The smiling giraffe: An illustration of a visual memory disorder. In R. Campbell (Ed.), *Mental lives: Case studies in cognition* (pp. 161–177). Oxford: Blackwell.

Riley, D. A. (1962). Memory for form. In L. Postman (Ed.), *Psychology in the making* (pp. 402–465). New York: Knopf.

Rimm, D. C., & Masters, J. C. (1979). *Behavior therapy: Techniques and empirical findings* (2nd ed.). New York: Academic Press.

Rindskopf, D. M. (1997). Testing "small," not null, hypotheses: Classical and Bayesian approaches. In L. L. Harlow, S. A. Mulaik, & J. H. Steiger (Eds.), *What if there were no significance tests?* (pp. 319–32). Mahwah, NJ: Erlbaum.

Rodman, J. L., & Burger, J. M. (1985). The influence of depression on the attribution of responsibility for an accident. *Cognitive Therapy and Research, 9*, 651–657.

Roethlisberger, F. J. (1977). *The elusive phenomena: An autobiographical account of my work in the field of organized behavior at the Harvard Business School.* Cambridge, MA: Division of Research, Graduate School of Business Administration (distributed by Harvard University Press).

Rollin, B. E. (1985). The moral status of research animals in psychology. *American Psychologist, 40*, 920–926.

Rosenfeld, A. (1981). Animal rights vs. human health. *Science, 81*, 18, 22.

Rosenhan, D. L. (1973). On being sane in insane places. *Science, 179*, 250–258.

Rosenthal, R. (1963). On the social psychology of the psychological experiment: The experimenter's hypothesis as unintended determinant of experimental results. *American Scientist, 51*, 268–283.

Rosenthal, R. (1966). *Experimenter effects in behav-ioral research*. New York: Appleton-Century-Crofts.

Rosenthal, R. (1976). *Experimenter effects in behavioral research*. (Enlarged ed.). New York: Irvington.

Rosenthal, R. (1990). How are we doing in soft psychology? *American Psychologist, 45*, 775–777.

Rosenthal, R. (1991). *Meta-analytic procedures for social research* (rev. ed.). Newbury Park, CA: Sage.

Rosenthal, R. (1994a). Interpersonal expectancy effects: A 30-year perspective. *Current Directions in Psychological Science, 3*, 176–179.

Rosenthal, R. (1994b). Science and ethics in conducting, analyzing, and reporting psychological research. *Psychological Science, 5*, 127–134.

Rosenthal, R., & Rosnow, R. L. (1991). *Essentials of behavioral research: Methods and data analysis* (2nd ed.). New York: McGraw-Hill.

Rosnow, R. L., & Rosenthal, R. (1995). "Some things you learn aren't so": Cohen's paradox, Asch's paradigm, and the interpretation of interaction. *Psychological Science, 6*, 3–9.

Ross, A. S., & White, S. (1987). Shoplifting, impaired driving, and refusing the Breathalyzer: On seeing one's name in a public place. *Evaluation Review, 11*, 254–260.

Rotter, J. B. (1966). Generalized expectancies for internal versus external control of reinforcement. *Psychological Monographs, 80* (1, Whole No. 609), 1–28.

Rozin, P., Markwith, M., & Stoess, C. (1997). Moralization and becoming a vegetarian: The transformation of preferences into values and the recruitment of disgust. *Psychological Science, 8*, 67–73.

Ruksznis, E. (1998, July/August). 10th annual convention: A decade of success, a future of promise. *APS Observer, 1*, 8–10, 18–19.

Rymer, R. (1993). *Genie: A scientific tragedy*. New York: Harper Collins.

Sackheim, H. A., Gur, R. C., & Saucy, M. C. (1978). Emotions are expressed more intensely on the left side of the face. *Science, 202*, 434–436.

Sacks, O. (1985). *The man who mistook his wife for a hat and other clinical tales*. New York: Harper & Row.

Sacks, O. (1995). *An anthropologist on Mars*. New York: Knopf.

Salomon, G. (1987). Basic and applied research in psychology: Reciprocity between two worlds. *International Journal of Psychology, 22*, 441–446.

Satterfield, J. M., & Seligman, M. E. P. (1994). Military aggression and risk predicted by explanatory style. *Psychological Science, 5*, 77–82.

Schacter, D. L. (1996). *Searching for memory*. New York: Basic Books.

Schaller, G. B. (1963). *The mountain gorilla*. Chicago: University of Chicago Press.

Schlenker, B. R., Phillips, S. T., Boniecki, K. A., & Schlenker, D. R. (1995a). Championship pressures: Choking or triumphing in one's own territory? *Journal of Personality and Social Psychology, 68*, 632–643.

Schlenker, B. R., Phillips, S. T., Boniecki, K. A., & Schlenker, D. R. (1995b). Where is the home choke? *Journal of Personality and Social Psychology, 68*, 649–652.

Schmidt, F. L. (1996). Statistical significance testing and cumulative knowledge in psychology: Implications for training of researchers. *Psychological Methods, 1*, 115–129.

Schmidt, F. L., & Hunter, J. E. (1997). Eight common but false objections to the discontinuation of significance testing in the analysis of research data. In L. L. Harlow, S. A. Mulaik, & J. H. Steiger (Eds.), *What if there were no significance tests?* (pp. 37–64). Mahwah, NJ: Erlbaum.

Schmidt, W. C. (1997). World-Wide-Web survey research: Benefits, potential problems, and solutions. *Behavior Research Methods, Instruments, & Computers, 29*, 274–279.

Schnelle, J. F., Kirchner, R. E., Macrae, J. W., McNees, M. P., Eck, R. H., Snodgrass, S., Casey, J. D., & Uselton, P. H., Jr. (1978). Police evaluation research: An experimental and cost-benefit analysis of a helicopter patrol in a high-crime area. *Journal of Applied Behavior Analysis, 11*, 11–21.

Schoeneman, T. J., & Rubanowitz, D. E. (1985). Attributions in the advice columns: Actors and observers, causes and reasons. *Personality and Social Psychology Bulletin, 11*, 315–325.

Schulman, P., Castellon, C., & Seligman, M. E. P. (1989). Assessing explanatory style: The content analysis of verbatim explanations and the Attributional Style Questionnaire. *Behavioral Research and Therapy, 27*, 505–512.

Schulz, R., & Bazerman, M. (1980). Ceremonial occasions and mortality: A second look. *American Psychologist, 35*, 253–261.

Schuman, H., & Bobo, L. (1988). Survey-based experiments on white racial attitudes toward residential integration. *American Journal of Sociology, 94*, 273–299.

Schuman, H., Presser, S., & Ludwig, J. (1981). Context effects of survey responses to questions about abortion. *Public Opinion Quarterly, 45*, 216–223.

Schuman, H., & Scott, J. (1987). Problems in the use of survey questions to measure public opinion. *Science, 236*, 957–959.

Scoville, W. B., & Milner, B. (1957). Loss of recent memory after bilateral hippocampal lesions. *Journal of Neurology, Neurosurgery, and Psychiatry, 20*, 11–19.

Shapiro, K. J. (1998). *Animal models of human psychology: Critique of science, ethics, and policy.* Seattle, WA: Hogrefe & Huber.

Sharpe, D., Adair, J. G., & Roese, N. J. (1992). Twenty years of deception research: A decline in subjects' trust? *Personality and Social Psychology Bulletin, 18*, 585–590.

Shattuck, R. (1994). *The forbidden experiment: The story of the Wild Boy of Averyon.* New York: Kodansha.

Sieber, J. E., Iannuzzo, R., & Rodriguez, B. (1995). Deception methods in psychology: Have they changed in 23 years? *Ethics & Behavior, 5*, 67–85.

Simon, H. A. (1992). What is an "explanation" of behavior? *Psychological Science, 3*, 150–161.

Singer, B., & Benassi, V. A. (1981). Occult beliefs. *American Scientist, 69*, 49–55.

Singer, P. (1990). The significance of animal suffering. *Behavioral and Brain Sciences, 13*, 9–12.

Skinner, B. F. (1937). Two types of conditioned reflex: A reply to Konorski and Miller. *Journal of General Psychology, 16*, 272–279.

Skinner, B. F. (1966). Operant behavior. In W. K. Honig (Ed.), *Operant behavior: Areas of research and application* (pp. 12–32). New York: Appleton-Century-Crofts.

Smith, J. A., Harré, R., & Van Langenhove, L. (1995). Idiography and the case study. In J. A. Smith, R. Harré, & L. Van Langenhove (Eds.), *Rethinking psychology* (pp. 59–69). Thousand Oaks, CA: Sage.

Smith, M. A., & Leigh, B. (1997). Virtual subjects: Using the Internet as an alternative source of subjects and research environment. *Behavior Research Methods, Instruments, & Computers, 29*, 496–505.

Smith, P. K., & Lewis, K. (1985). Rough-and-tumble play, fighting, and chasing in nursery school children. *Ethology and Sociobiology, 6*, 175–181.

Smith, R. J. (1977). Electroshock experiment at Albany violates ethics guidelines. *Science, 198*, 383–386.

Smith, T. W. (1981). Qualifications to generalized absolutes: "Approval of hitting" questions on the GSS. *Public Opinion Quarterly, 45*, 224–230.

Sommer, R. (1968). Hawthorne dogma. *Psychological Bulletin, 70*, 592–595.

Spitz, R. A. (1965). *The first year of life.* New York: International Universities Press.

Stern, S. E., & Faber, J. E. (1997). The lost e-mail technique: Milgram's lost-letter technique in the age of the Internet. *Behavior Research Methods, Instruments, & Computers, 29*, 260–263.

Sternberg, R. J. (1986). A triangular theory of love. *Psychological Review, 93*, 119–135.

Sternberg, R. J. (1992, September). How to win acceptances by psychology journals: 21 tips for better writing. *APS Observer*, 12–13, 18.

Sternberg, R. J. (1997, September). What do students still most need to learn about research in psychology? *ABS Observer, 14*, 19.

Sternberg, R. J., & Williams, W. M. (1997). Does the Graduate Record Examination predict meaningful success in the graduate training of psychologists? A case study. *American Psychologist, 52*, 630–641.

Strauss, A., & Corbin, J. (1990). *Basics of qualitative research.* Newbury Park, CA: Sage.

Sun, M. (1981). Laetrile brush fire is out, scientists hope. *Science, 212*, 758–759.

Surwit, R. S., & Williams, P. G. (1996). Animal models provide insight into psychosomatic factors in diabetes. *Psychosomatic Medicine, 58*, 582–589.

Tassinary, L. G., & Hansen, K. A. (1998). A critical test of the waist-to-hip-ratio hypothesis of female physical attractiveness. *Psychological Science, 9*, 150–155.

Taylor, K. M., & Shepperd, J. A. (1996). Probing suspicion among participants in deception research. *American Psychologist, 51*, 886–887.

Taylor, S. J., & Bogdan, R. (1998). *Introduction to qualitative research methods: A guidebook and resource* (3rd ed.). New York: Wiley.

Terman, L. M. & Oden, M. A. (1947). *Genetic studies of genius: The gifted child grows up* (Vol. 4). Stanford, CA: Stanford University Press.

Thomas, L. (1992). *The fragile species.* New York: Charles Scribner's Sons.

Thompson, T. L. (1982). Gaze toward and avoidance of the handicapped: A field experiment. *Journal of Nonverbal Behavior, 6*, 188–196.

Tucker, J. S., Friedman, H. S., Schwartz, J. E., Criqui, M. H., Tomlinson-Keasey, C., Winograd, D. L., & Martin, L. R. (1997). Parental divorce: Effects on individual behavior and longevity. *Journal of Personality and Social Psychology, 73*, 381–391.

Tukey, J. W. (1977). *Exploratory data analysis.* Reading, MA: Addison-Wesley.

Tversky, A., & Kahneman, D. (1971). Belief in the law of small numbers. *Psychological Bulletin, 76*, 105–110.

Tversky, A., & Kahneman, D. (1974). Judgement under uncertainty: Heuristics and biases. *Science, 185*, 1124–1131.

Ulrich, R. E. (1991). Animal rights, animal wrongs and the question of balance. *Psychological Science, 2*, 197–201.

Ulrich, R. E. (1992). Animal research: A reflective analysis. *Psychological Science, 3*, 384–386.

Underwood, B. J. (1957). *Psychological research.* New York: Appleton-Century-Crofts.

Underwood, B. J. (1975). Individual differences as a crucible in theory construction. *American Psychologist, 30*, 128–134.

Underwood, B. J., & Shaughnessy, J. J. (1975). *Experimentation in psychology.* New York: Wiley: Robert E. Krieger, 1983.

Valentiner, D. P., Holahan, C. J., & Moos, R. H. (1994). Social support, appraisal of event controllability, and coping: An integrative model. *Journal of Personality and Social Psychology, 66*, 1094–1102.

VanBiervliet, A., Spangler, P. F., & Marshall, A. M. (1981). An ecobehavioral examination of a simple strategy for increasing mealtime language in residential facilities. *Journal of Applied Behavior Analysis, 14*, 295–305.

VanderStoep, S. W., & Shaughnessy, J. J. (1997). Taking a course in research methods improves reasoning about real-life events. *Teaching of Psychology, 24*, 122–124.

Van Meter, P., Yokoi, L., & Pressley, M. (1994). College students' theory of note-taking derived from their perceptions of note-taking. *Journal of Educational Psychology, 86*, 323–338.

Wallraff, H. G., & Sinsch, U. (1988). The role of "outward-journey information" in homing experiments with pigeons: New data on ontogeny of navigation and general survey. *Ethology, 77*, 10–27.

Ward, W. D., & Jenkins, H. M. (1965). The display of information and the judgement of contingency. *Canadian Journal of Psychology, 19*, 231–241.

Warwick, D. P., & Lininger, C. A. (1975). *The sample survey: Theory and practice.* New York: McGraw-Hill.

Watson, J. B. (1913). Psychology as the behaviorist views it. *Psychological Review, 20*, 158–177.

Watson, J. B. [1914] (1967). *Behavior: An introduction to comparative psychology.* New York: Holt, Rinehart and Winston.

Webb, E. J., Campbell, D. T., Schwartz, R. D., Sechrest, L., & Grove, J. B. (1981). *Non-reactive measures in the social sciences* (2nd ed.). Boston: Houghton-Mifflin.

Weigel, R. H., Loomis, J. W., & Soja, M. J. (1980). Race relations on prime time television. *Journal of Personality and Social Psychology, 39*, 884–893.

Weiner, H. (1996). Use of animal models in peptic ulcer disease. *Psychosomatic Medicine, 58*, 524–545.

Willems, E. P. (1969). Planning a rationale for naturalistic research. In E. P. Willems & H. L. Raush (Eds.), *Naturalistic viewpoints in psychological research* (pp. 44–71). New York: Holt, Rinehart and Winston.

Willems, E. P., & Raush, H. L. (Eds.). (1969). *Naturalistic viewpoints in psychological research.* New York: Holt, Rinehart and Winston.

Willingham, W. W. (1974). Predicting success in graduate education. *Science, 183*, 273–278.

Wilson, G. T. (1978). On the much discussed nature of the term "behavior therapy." *Behavior Therapy, 9*, 89–98.

Winer, B. J., Brown, D. R., & Michels, K. M. (1991). *Statistical principles in experimental design* (3rd ed.). New York: McGraw-Hill.

Winograd, E., & Neisser, U. (Eds.). (1992). *Affect and accuracy in recall: Studies of "flashbulb memories."* New York: Cambridge University Press.

Yeaton, W. H., & Sechrest, L. (1981). Critical dimensions in the choice and maintenance of successful treatments: Strength, integrity, and effectiveness. *Journal of Consulting and Clinical Psychology, 49*, 156–167.

Yeaton, W. H., & Sechrest, L. (1986). Use and misuse of no-difference findings in eliminating threats to validity. *Evaluation Review, 10*, 836–852.

Zechmeister, E. B., Chronis, A. M., Cull, W. L., D'Anna, C. A., & Healy, N. A. (1995). Growth of a functionally important lexicon. *Journal of Reading Behavior, 27*, 201–212.

Zechmeister, E. B., & Johnson, J. E. (1992). *Critical thinking: A functional approach.* Pacific Grove, CA: Brooks/Cole.

Zechmeister, E. B., & Nyberg, S. E. (1982). *Human memory: An introduction to research and theory.* Pacific Grove, CA: Brooks/Cole.

Zechmeister, J. S., & Zechmeister, E. B. (2000). *Introductory textbooks and psychology's core concepts. Teaching of Psychology*, in press.

Credits

Chapter 1 Page 3: Photo of Wilhelm Wundt © Corbis; photo of William James © Culver Pictures. Figure 1.1: Photos courtesy of Thomas A. Sebeok, Distinguished Professor Emeritus, Indiana University, Bloomington. Figure 1.2: Photo by Paula Shaughnessy. Figure 1.3: Original drawing by Fran Hughes. Figure 1.4: From Figure 3: page 453, of R. V. Levine (1990), "The pace of life," *American Scientist, 78*, 450–459. Copyright 1990 by Sigma Xi, The Scientific Research Society, Inc. Used with permission of the publisher and author. Figure 1.5: Photo © Corbis. Figure 1.6: Photo by Eugene B. Zechmeister.

Chapter 2 Figure 2.1: Photos by Eugene B. Zechmeister and John J. Shaughnessy. Special thanks go to Erica, Linda, and Hilary Bryant, Earron Henderson and members of his social psychology class, Candy Baguilat, Lynda Cafasso, and Peter Bergquist for being willing subjects for these photos; we thank Bill Shofner for helping us obtain animal pictures. And let us not forget to identify John's dog, Emma. We also wish to acknowledge the cooperation of the Parmly Institute of Loyola University of Chicago as well as Rich Bowen for providing experimental settings for some of these photos. Ethical principles 6.06–6.26 of the American Psychological Association (1992), "Ethical principles of psychologists and code of conduct," *American Psychologist, 47*, 1597–1611. Copyright 1992 by the American Psychological Association. Reprinted by permission of the publisher. Neither the original nor this reproduction can be republished, photocopied, reprinted, or distributed in any form, without the prior written permission of the APA. Figure 2.2: Photo by Eugene B. Zechmeister. We wish to thank Jen Brockway and Bess Anderson for posing as undergraduate students. Figure 2.3: Photo of Eugene B. and Jeanne S. Zechmeister by a friendly passer-by. Figure 2.4: Original drawing by Fran Hughes. Figure 2.5: Photo © Martin Rogers/Stock Boston.

Chapter 3 Figure 3.1: Photo by Eugene B. Zechmeister. Figure 3.2: Photo © Corbis/Farrell Grehan. Figure 3.3: Reprinted with permission from D. A. Jenni and M. A. Jenni (1976), "Carrying behavior in humans: Analysis of sex differences," *Science, 194,* 859–960. Figure 1, page 859. Copyright 1976 American Association for the Advancement of Science. Table 3.1: from J. R. Dickie, and S. C. Gerber (1980), "Training in social competence: The effect on mothers, fathers, and infants," *Child Development, 51,* 1248–1251. Materials from Jane Dickie, Psychology Department, Hope College, Holland, MI 49423. Table 3.3: From Table 2, page 550, of M. LaFrance and C. Mayo (1976), "Racial differences in gaze behavior during conversations: Two systematic observational studies," *Journal of Personality and Social Psychology, 33,* 547–552. Copyright 1976 by the American Psychological Association. Reprinted by permission of the publisher and author. Figure 3.4: Original drawing by Fran Hughes.

Chapter 4 Table 4.1: Adapted from Table 3, page 621, of R. E. Lucas, E. Diener, & E. Suh (1996), "Discriminant validity of well-being measures," *Journal of Personality and Social Psychology, 71,* 616–628. Copyright 1996 by the American Psychological Association. Reprinted by permission of the publisher and author. Table 4.2: From Appendix Table 8, of A. Campbell (1981), *The sense of well-being in America,* New York: McGraw-Hill. Copyright 1981 by McGraw-Hill, Inc. Reprinted by permission of publisher. Figure 4.2: Adapted from Figure 1, page 1095, of D. P. Valentiner, C. J. Holohan, & R. H. Moos (1994), "Social support, appraisals of event controlability, and coping: An integrative model," *Journal of Personality and Social Psychology, 66,* 1094–1102. Copyright 1994 by the American Psychological Association. Reprinted by permission of the publisher and author. Figure 4.5: Original drawing by Fran Hughes. Figure 4.6: From Figure 7, page 13, of A. W. Astin, S. A. Parrott, W. S. Korn, & L. J. Sax (1997), *The American freshman: Thirty year trends,* Los Angeles: Higher Education Research Institute. Used with permision of the author and publisher.

Chapter 5 Figure 5.1: Photo of Jeanne S. Zechmeister by Eugene B. Zechmeister. Table 5.1: Based on material from E. J. Webb, D. T. Campbell, R. D. Schwartz, L. Sechrest, and J. B. Grove, *Nonreactive measures in social sciences,* 2nd ed. (1981), Boston: Houghton Mifflin. Copyright 1981 by Harper &

Row, Publishers, Inc. (Copyright by Sage Publications, Inc. Adapted by permission of publisher and author.) Figure 5.2: Photo by Hope College Public Relations Department. Used with permission. Figure 5.3: Reprinted from Figure 1, page 1465, of D. P. Phillips (1977), "Motor vehicle fatalities increase just after publicized suicide stories." *Science, 196*, 1464–1465. Copyright 1977 American Association for the Advancement of Science. Reprinted by permission of publisher and author. Table 5.2: Adapted from material on pages 203–206 in R. M. Brandt (1972), *Studying behavior in natural settings,* New York: Holt, Rinehart & Winston. (Republished 1981 by University Press of America, Washington, D.C.). Used by permission of author. Figure 5.4: Adapted from Figure 2, page 83, and Figure 3, page 85, of C. A. Anderson (1989), "Temperature and aggression: Ubiquitous effects of heat on occurrence of human violence." *Psychological Bulletin, 106*, 74–96. Copyright 1989 by the American Psychological Association. Used with permission of publisher and author.

Chapter 6 Table 6.3: Adapted from Table 1, page 177, in R. Rosenthal (1994), "Interpersonal expectancy effects: A 30-year perspective," *Current Directions in Psychological Science, 3*, 176–179. Copyright 1994 by the American Psychological Society. Used with permission of author and publisher. Figure 6.1: From Figure 1, page 319, of E. F. Loftus & T. E. Burns (1982), "Mental shock can produce retrograde amnesia," *Memory & Cognition, 10*, 318–323. Copyright 1982 by the Psychonomic Society, Inc. Used with permission of publisher and author. Figure 6.2: Photo by Jeanne S. Zechmeister. We wish to thank members of Jeanne S. Zechmeister's Spring 1996 research methods in psychology class for permission. Figure 6.3: Original drawing by Fran Hughes. Figure 6.4: Photo © Herb Snitzer/Stock Boston. Figure 6.5: Photo by Eugene B. Zechmeister. Figure 6.6: Photo courtesy of Judy DeLoache and from Figure 2 of J. S. DeLoache, S. L. Pierroutsakos, D. H. Uttal, K. S. Rosengren, & A. Gottlieb (1998), "Grasping the nature of pictures," *Psychological Science, 9*, 205–210. Figures 6.7 and 6.8: Based on data provided by Judy DeLoache and her colleagues and adapted from Figure 3 of a study by J. S. DeLoache, S. L. Pierroutsakos, D. H. Uttal, K. S. Rosengren, & A. Gottlieb (1998), "Grasping the nature of pictures," *Psychological Science, 9*, 205–210. Used with permission of publisher.

Chapter 7 Figure 7.1: Original drawing by Fran Hughes. Figure 7.2: From Figure 1, page 434, of H. A. Sackheim, R. C. Gur, and M. C. Saucy (1978), *Science, 202*, 434–436. Copyright 1978 by American Association for the Advancement of Science. Used with permission of author and publisher.

Chapter 8 Table 8.1: Based on Table 1, page 86, of R. G. Hass, I. Katz, N. Rizzo, J. Bailey, and D. Eisenstadt (1991), "Cross-racial appraisal as related to attitude ambivalence and cognitive complexity." *Personality and Social Psychology Bulletin, 17*, 83–92. Copyright 1991 by Sage Publications, Inc. Adapted by permission of the publisher and author. Figure 8.5: Based on data provided by John J. Shaughnessy. Figure 8.6: Based on data in Table 2, page 913, of R. Pingitore, B. L. Dugoni, R. S. Tindale, & B. Spring (1994), "Bias against overweight job applicants in a simulated employment interview," *Journal of Applied Psychology, 79*, 909.917. Copyright 1994 by the American Psychological Association. Used with permission of publisher and author. Figure 8.7: Original drawing by Fran Hughes. Table 8.5: From J. L. Rodman and J. M. Burger (1985), "The influence of depression on the attribution of responsibility for an accident." *Cognitive Therapy and Research, 9*, 651–657. Copyright 1985 by Plenum Publishing Corporation. Used with permission of publisher and author. Table 8.6 and Figure 8.8: From Figure 1, page 341, of M. L. Dittmar, D. B. Berch, and J. S. Warm (1982), "Sustained visual attention in deaf and hearing adults," *Bulletin of the Psychonomic Society, 19*, 339–342. Copyright 1982 by the Psychonomic Society. Adapted by permission of publisher and author.

Chapter 9 Case study illustration: From I. Kirsch (1978), "Teaching clients to be their own therapists: A case study illustration," *Psychotherapy: Theory, Research and Practice, 15*, 302–305. Reprinted by permission of Donald K. Freedheim, Editor. Figure 9.1: Photo courtesy of Bibliotheque Nationale. Used with permission. Figure 9.2: Adapted from Figure 9.1, page 209, of A. E. Kazdin (1998), *Research design in clinical psychology* (3rd ed.), Boston: Allyn & Bacon. Used with permission of author and publisher. Figure 9.3: From Figure 1, page 60, of S. V. Horton (1987), "Reduction of disruptive mealtime behavior by facial screenings," *Behavior Modification, 11*, 53–64. Copyright 1987 by Sage Publications, Inc. Adapted by permission of publisher and author. Figure 9.4: From Figure 1, page 301, of M. G. Allison and T. Allyon (1980), "Behavioral coaching in the development of skills in football, gymnastics, and tennis," *Journal of Applied Behavioral Analysis, 13*, 297–304. Copyright 1980 by the Experimental

Analysis of Behavior, Inc. Reprinted by permission of publisher and author. Figure 9.6: Original drawing by Fran Hughes.

Chapter 10   Figure 10.1: Photo © Archive Photos. Figure 10. 2: Original drawing by Fran Hughes. Figure 10.4: From Figures 5 and 6, page 416, of D. T. Campbell (1969), "Reforms as experiments." *American Psychologist, 24,* 409–429. Copyright 1969 by the American Psychological Association. Reprinted by permission of publisher and author. Figure 10.5: From Figure 1, page 257, of A. S. Ross and S. White (1987), "Shoplifting, impaired driving, and refusing the breathalyzer," *Evaluation Review, 11,* 254–260. Copyright 1987 by Sage Publications. Reprinted by permission by publisher and author. Figure 10.6: From A. J. McSweeney (1978), "Effects of response cost on the behavior of a million persons: Charging for directory assistance in Cincinnati," *Journal of Applied Behavior Analysis, 11,* 47–51. Copyright 1978 by the Society for the Experimental Analysis of Behavior, Inc. Reprinted by permission of publisher and author. Figure 10.7: From J. F. Schnelle, R. E. Kirchner, J. W. Macrae, M. P. McNees, R. H. Eck, S. Snodgrass, J. D. Casey, and P. H. Uselton, Jr. (1978), "Police evaluation research: An experimental and cost benefit analysis of a helicopter patrol in a high-crime area," *Journal of Applied Behavior Analysis, 11,* 11–21. Copyright 1978 by the Society for the Experimental Analysis of Behavior, Inc. Reprinted by permission of publisher and author. Figure 10.8: Based on Figure 2, page 444, of G. Salomon (1987), "Basic and applied research in psychology: Reciprocity between two worlds," *International Journal of Psychol-*

ogy, 22, 441–446.   Reprinted by permission of Elsevier Science Publishers, Academic Publishing Division, and author.

Appendix A   Permission to use statistical Tables A.2, A.3, and A.4 in Appendix A is acknowledged with tables in Appendix A. Table A.5: Based on Table 2.3.5, pages 36–37, in J. Cohen (1988), *Statistical power analysis for the behavioral sciences* (2nd ed.), Mahwah NJ: Erlbaum. Used with permission of the publisher. Table A.6: Based on Tables 8.3.12, 8.3.13, 8.3.14, & 8.3.15, pages 311–318, in J. Cohen (1988), *Statistical power analysis for the behavioral sciences* (2nd ed.), Mahwah NJ: Erlbaum. Used with permission of the publisher.

Appendix B   Table B.1: Questionnaire used in a survey conducted by researchers at the Institute for Social Research (ISR), University of Michigan. Reprinted by permission of Willard Rodgers, ISR, Ann Arbor, MI 48106, and Sage Publications, Inc. Table B.2: Questionnaire given to authors, who were passengers on Amtrak's Chicago–St. Louis train, by representatives of the Illinois Department of Transportation.

Appendix C   Extensive quotations from *Publication Manual of the American Psychological Association,* 4th ed. (1994). Washington, DC. Copyright 1994 by the American Psychological Association. Reprinted by permission of the publisher. Neither the original nor this reproduction can be republished, photocopied, reprinted, or distributed in any form, without the prior written permission of the APA.

Name Index

Abelson, R. P., 258, 413–415, 417, 427–430, 432, 436
Adair, J. G., 55, 60
Addison, W. E., 119
Adjang, O. M. J., 101
Adler, A., 33
Adler, T., 346
Albright, J. S., 10, 15, 17
Allison, M. G., 355, 357
Allport, G. W., 22, 337, 343–344
Altmann, J., 122
Altomari, M. G., 111, 115
Ambady, N., 24–25
American Psychiatric Association, 20, 21
American Psychological Association, 4, 42, 63, 72, 195–196, 202, 428, 433, 480–481, 485–489, 491, 493–495, 497, 500–504
Ancell, M., 180, 182, 184, 194
Anderson, C. A., 200–202, 225–226, 259
Anderson, C. R., 51
Anderson, J. R., 28
Anderson, K. J., 329
Anglin, J. M., 416
Arthur, J., 107, 115
Asch, S. E., 243–245, 252–256
Ascione, F. R., 86
Astin, A. W., 164–165
Astone, N. M., 135–136
Atkinson, R. C., 343, 375
Atwater, J. D., 407
Aubrey, L. W., 130
Ayllon, T., 355, 357
Azar, B., 71, 438, 482–483

Baer, D. M., 190, 360
Bailey, J., 303–305
Bailey, J. M., 192
Baldwin, E., 56
Ballard, J., 222
Banaji, M. R., 225
Barash, D. P., 88, 112, 115
Barker, L. S., 100, 108, 112
Barker, R. G., 100, 108, 112
Barlow, D. H., 338, 345, 350–351, 354, 358
Baron, J. N., 200
Baron, R. M., 132
Bartholomew, G. A., 480
Bartlett, F. C., 85
Baumeister, R. F., 187, 199–200

Baumrind, D., 64, 66
Bazerman, M., 177–178, 199
Begg, D., 85
Bellack, A. S., 51, 66–68
Benassi, V. A., 19, 371
Berch, D. B., 318–320, 323
Berk, R. A., 372–373, 406
Bickman, L., 87, 96
Biglan, A., 107, 115
Blanchard, F. A., 120
Blanck, P. D., 51, 56, 66–68
Bobo, L., 469
Bogdan, R., 100
Bolgar, H., 338, 340, 345–346
Bollen, K. A., 200
Bond, C. F., Jr., 117
Bond, M., 94
Boniecki, K. A., 187, 199
Booth, W., 68
Boring, E. G., 3, 4, 9
Bornstein, P. H., 74
Boruch, R. F., 372–373, 406
Bourke, K., 484
Bower, G. H., 328–329
Brainerd, C. J., 94
Brandt, R. M., 100–101, 104, 182, 191
Breytspraak, L. M., 131, 135
Bridgewater, C. A., 74
Brigham, J. C., 120
Brigham, T. A., 362–363
Britton, B., 67
Broach, D., 145
Bröder, A., 63
Brody, G. H., 351
Brown, D. R., 283
Brown, R., 28
Browne, M. A., 355
Buglione, S. A., 398
Bull, N. C., 131, 135
Burger, J. M., 316–317
Burns, M. S., 122
Burns, T. E., 214–218, 220
Bushman, B. J., 202, 225–226, 259

Campbell, A., 149, 166, 473
Campbell, D. T., 32, 119–120, 178–181, 184, 189, 198, 376, 378, 380–385, 390–395, 397–398, 401, 406
Campbell, R., 336–337
Candland, D. K., 88
Carey, R. G., 403–404
Carroll, J. M., 192–193

Carroll, K. A., 70
Carron, A. V., 187
Casey, J. D., 401–402
Caspi, A., 85
Castellon, C., 194
Ceci, S. J., 221–222
Chall, J., 416
Chambers, D. L., 372–373, 406
Chambers, J. H., 86
Charness, N., 335
Chase, W. G., 335–336
Chase-Lansdale, P. L., 147
Cherlin, A. J., 147
Christensen, L., 64–65
Chow, S. L., 257–258, 427, 432, 439
Chronis, A. M., 417–418, 426
Cicchetti, D., 70
Clark, H. H., 470–471
Clifford, M., 107
Cohen, D., 95
Cohen, J., 239, 250, 257, 260, 290, 413–414, 424–428, 430, 433, 436–438, 442–443, 446, 451, 464–465
Cohen, N. J., 28, 31
Collins, R. L., 154
Connors, G. J., 154
Converse, P. E., 141, 473
Cook, T. D., 32, 376, 378, 381–382, 384, 390, 392–395, 397, 401
Corbin, J., 23
Cordaro, L., 121
Coren, S., 182
Courneya, K. S., 187
Crandall, C. S., 120
Crandall, R., 42, 57–58, 62, 120
Criqui, M. H., 188–189
Cronbach, L. J., 484
Crossen, C., 148, 153–154
Crossley, H. M., 170
Crowder, R. G., 225
Crusco, A. H., 96
Csikszentmihalyi, M., 108
Cull, W. L., 417–418, 426
Curtiss, S. R., 88, 342, 345

D'Anna, C. A., 417–418, 426
Darley, J. M., 7, 96, 170
Davidson, L., 9–10, 33, 63
Dawes, R. M., 146, 223–224
de Blois, S. T., 94
deJong, J., 89

Delclos, V. R., 122
Delespaul, P. A. E. G., 108
DeLoache, J. S., 239–243
Dermen, K. H., 154
DeWitt, R., 269
Dickie, J. R., 104–105
Dickson, N., 85
Diener, E., 42, 57–58, 62, 120, 132, 143–144, 147
Dittmar, M. L., 318–320, 323
Dolan, C. A., 107
Donnerstein, E., 227
Duckett, E., 108, 110
Dugoni, B. L., 200, 309–311
Dulcan, M., 162–163
Dushenko, T. W., 55, 60

Eagly, A. H., 308–309
Eck, R. H., 401–402
Eibl-Eibesfeldt, I., 88, 95–96, 98
Eisenstadt, D., 303–305
Emerson, J. D., 418
Endersby, J. W., 179, 182, 184
Entwisle, D. R., 135–136
Epley, N., 62, 65
Epstein, S., 142
Erber, R., 280–283
Ericcson, K. A., 335–336
Erickson, L. M., 358, 361
Estes, W. K., 243, 427, 432, 435, 448–449
Evans, R., 227

Faber, J. E., 184
Faloon, S., 335–336
Faust, D., 146
Feeney, D. M., 70, 71
Fehrmann, P. G., 130
Festinger, L., 92, 101, 118
Field, A. E., 167–169
Fielding, B., 162–163
Fine, M. A., 74, 76
Finger, K., 85
Fiore, S., 483
Fischer, K., 187
Fisher, C. B., 48, 63
Fivush, R., 85
Flacks, R., 471
Fleischman, D. A., 336
Fossey, D., 119
Fowler, R. D., 71
Fowler, R. G., 183
Frame, C. L., 55
Francis, M. E., 194
Frank, M. G., 185–186
Fredrickson, B. L., 271–273
Freeman, P. R., 287
Frick, R. W., 248
Friedman, H. S., 188–189

Friedman, L., 107, 115
Friedman, M. P., 180
Fromm, E., 32
Fryberg, D., 48, 63
Furstenberg, F. F., Jr., 147

Gabrieli, J. D. E., 336
Gannon, L., 196
Geller, E. S., 11, 115
Gena, A., 356
Gerrard, M., 407
Ghezzi, P. M., 401
Gillham, J. E., 212
Gilovich, T., 16, 185–186
Glenwick, D. S., 398
Goldstein, R. S., 190
Goodall, J., 68, 71
Goodman, S. H., 162–163
Goodner, V., 362–363
Gottlieb, A., 239–243
Graham, S., 196
Grammer, K., 98
Gray, J. N., 60
Griffin, J. H., 91–92
Grisso, T., 56
Groom, R. W., 202
Grove, J. B., 119–120, 178–181, 184, 189, 98
Guerin, B., 117
Gumbhir, A. K., 131, 135
Gur, R. C., 274–278

Haber, L. R., 210–213, 216, 223
Haber, R. N., 210–213, 216, 223
Haden, C. A., 85, 418
Hagen, R. L., 427
Haine, R. A., 85
Halpern, A. R., 328–329
Hansen, K. A., 104
Harlow, H. F., 88
Harlow, M. K., 88
Harnack, A., 503
Harré, R., 336, 344
Harrington, H., 85
Harsch, N., 30
Harshman, R. A., 427, 429–430, 435
Hart, B., 119
Hartup, W. W., 87–88, 99–100, 109, 112, 114–115, 122
Hasher, L., 299–300, 302, 324
Hass, R. G., 303–305
Haynes, S. N., 93
Hays, R., 118
Haywood, H. C., 122
Healy, N. A., 417–418, 426
Heath, L., 9–10, 33, 63, 200
Heatherton, T. F., 167–169
Hedges, L. V., 425

Heerboth, J., 401
Henderson, M. C., 10, 15, 17
Hersen, M., 338, 345, 350–351, 354, 358
Hertwig, R., 63
Hickman, C., 349
Hills, A., 192
Hilts, P. J., 343
Hippler, H. J., 161
Hirschberg, N., 24
Hoaglin, D. C., 414, 417–418
Hodge, D., 85
Hofer, M. A., 27
Holahan, C. J., 133–134
Holden, C., 47, 70
Holmbeck, G., 108, 110
Holmbeck, G. N., 132
Holsti, O. R., 192–193
Hopkins, W. D., 93
Hops, J., 107, 115
Horn, W. F., 401
Horton, S. V., 352–354
Howell, D. C., 420, 436–437
Huberman, A. M., 23
Huff, C., 62, 65
Hughes, H. M., 93
Humphreys, G. W., 337
Hunt, M., 259
Hunter, J. E., 414, 427, 430–431, 436

Iannuzzo, R., 63
Ison, J. R., 121
Itkin, S., 24

Jackson, J. M., 398
Jaycox, L. H., 212
Jeeves, M. A., 269
Jenkins, H. M., 7
Jenni, D. A., 103
Jenni, M. A., 103, 106, 112
Johnson, D., 70
Johnson, G. M., 407
Johnson, J. E., 19
Joswick, K. E., 492–493
Judd, C. M., 114, 169–170, 261, 374

Kagan, J., 85
Kahneman, D., 7, 247, 271–273
Kardas, E. P., 482–483
Katz, I., 303–305
Kazdin, A. E., 337–338, 342, 347, 350–351, 354, 358–361
Keane, M. M., 336
Keel, P. K., 167–169
Keeports, D., 371, 386, 389
Keith, T. Z., 130
Keith-Spiegel, P., 77
Keller, F. S., 3

Kelley-Milburn, D., 482–483
Kelman, H. C., 56, 62, 64–65
Kenny, D. A., 132
Keppel, G., 256, 289–290, 293–294, 304, 317, 451, 461
Kidder, L. H., 114, 169–170, 261, 374
Kiernan, K. E., 147
Kiesler, S., 484
Kim, P. Y., 192
Kimble, G. A., 18, 31
Kimmel, A. J., 56, 64–65
Kirchner, R. E., 401–402
Kirigin-Ramp, K., 407
Kirk, R. E., 413, 424–425, 442
Kirkham, G. L., 91
Kirsch, I., 232, 337–340, 344–345, 347
Klemmack, D. L., 492
Klemmack, S. H., 492
Kleppinger, E., 503
Koenig, K. E., 471
Kolb, B., 89
Koocher, G. P., 59–60, 77
Korn, W. S., 164–165
Koutsky, J. R., 154
Krantz, J. H., 222
Krantz, P. J., 356
Kratochwill, T. R., 335, 349, 351
Kubany, E. S., 336, 340, 347
Kulik, J., 28
Kurdek, L. A., 74, 76

LaFrance, M., 106, 111, 113, 115, 118, 122
Lahey, B. B., 162–163
Lakatos, I., 31
Landers, S., 55, 68, 70
Langer, E. J., 387–394, 405
Langley, J., 85
Larose, S., 128
Larson, R. W., 108, 110, 117
Latané, B., 7, 96, 170
Lau, R. R., 187, 193–194, 199
Leavens, D. A., 93
Leigh, B., 4, 484
Lenneberg, E. H., 342
Levin, J. R., 335
Levine, R. J., 59–60
Levine, R. V., 21–22, 24–25, 75, 177, 179
Lewis, K., 110
Liberty, H. J., 96
Light, K. C., 107
Lindsay, R. C. L., 55, 60
Lininger, C. A., 159
Linsenmeier, J. A. W., 192
Linton, M., 335
Locke, T. P., 407
Loftus, E. F., 85, 214–218, 220, 470

Loftus, G. R., 239, 242, 414, 427, 436, 447–448, 452
Loomis, J. W., 192–194
Lorenz, B., 98
Lorge, I., 416
Lovass, O. I., 349, 362
Lubin, B., 131, 135
Lucas, R. E., 143–144
Luchetta, T., 196
Ludwig, J., 475
Ludwig, T. E., 269
Lyons, C. A., 401

Macrae, J. W., 401–402
Madey, J., 16
Madigan, C. M., 151–152
Maestripieri, D., 70
Mahamedi, F., 167–169
Mahoney, M. J., 355
Markwith, M., 136
Marshall, A. M., 357–358, 361, 401
Martens, B. K., 349
Martin, L. R., 188–189
Marx, M. H., 6, 9, 12, 17, 30–31
Maser, J. D., 27
Mason, J., 107
Masson, M. E. J., 242, 447, 452
Masters, J. C., 345
May, C. P., 299–300, 302, 324
Mayne, T. J., 194
Mayo, C., 106, 111, 113, 115, 118, 122
McCain, L. J., 401
McClannahan, L. E., 356
McCleary, R., 401
McCloskey, M., 28, 31
McGrew, W. C., 112
McGuire, W. J., 34–35
McKinney, J. D., 107
McNees, M. P., 401–402
McSweeney, A. J., 398–400
Medvec, V. H., 16
Meehl, P. E., 31–32, 145–145, 427
Meier, S. M., 362–363
Melton, G. B., 59–60
Merritt, C. B., 183
Michels, K. M., 283
Milburn, M. A., 482–483
Miles, M. B., 23
Milford, T. M., 482–483
Milgram, S., 64–65, 96, 170
Miller, D. T., 429
Miller, G. A., 416
Miller, J. D., 19–20
Miller, N. E., 68
Miller, T. Q., 200
Milner, B., 343
Milson, J. R., 28
Minkin, B. L., 190
Minkin, N., 190

Moffitt, T. E., 85
Molcan, J. R., 200
Moneta, G., 108, 110
Mook, D. G., 221, 225, 371
Moore, B. R., 117
Moos, R. H., 133–134
Morier, D., 371, 386, 389
Morrell, F., 336
Morrison, D. R., 147
Mosteller, F., 414, 417–418
Muliak, S. A., 427, 429–430, 435
Murray, B., 74
Myers, D. G., 30, 132, 147, 316, 349
Myers, M. M., 27

Narrow, W., 162–163
National Research Council, 70–71
Neisser, I., 30
Neisser, U., 31
Newcomb, T. M., 471
Newhagen, J. E., 180, 182, 184, 194
Newsom, C., 349
Nichols, P., 168
Norman, W. D., 269
Novak, M. A., 70, 94
Nyberg, S. E., 335, 343

Oden, M. A., 188, 193
Orne, M. T., 67, 117, 231
Orr, S. P., 89
Ortmann, A., 63
Osgood, C. E., 195, 198
Osteen, V., 107, 115

Pardie, L., 196
Parrott, S. A., 164–165
Parry, H. J., 170
Parsons, H. M., 383
Parsonson, B. S., 360
Pegalis, L., 67
Pennebaker, J. W., 194
Peterson, J., 107, 147
Pezdek, K., 85
Phillips, D. P., 190, 194, 197, 199–200
Phillips, S. T., 187, 199
Piaget, J., 98–100
Pierroutsakos, S. L., 239–243
Pillemer, D. B., 31
Pingitore, R., 309–311
Piper, A. I., 405
Pishkin, V., 232
Pitman, R. K., 89
Plous, S., 149, 164
Popper, K. R., 29, 31
Porac, C., 182
Posavac, E. J., 403–404
Pottebaum, S. M., 130
Poulson, C. L., 356

Poulton, E. C., 287–289
Powell, D. H., 142
Powell-Cope, G. M., 23
Prentice, D. A., 429
Presser, S., 475
Pressley, M., 23

Rachels, J., 72
Raju, N. S., 427, 429–430, 435
Raush, H. L., 87
Redelmeier, D. A., 271–273
Regier, D., 162–163
Reimers, T. M., 130
Reis, H. T., 177, 179
Reiss, P. C., 200
Reivich, K. J., 212
Reminger, S. L., 336
Revelle, W., 329
Reznick, J. S., 85
Rhodes, K., 196
Richards, M. H., 108, 110
Richardson, D. R., 67
Riddoch, M. J., 337
Riecken, H., 92, 101, 118
Riley, D. A., 221
Rimm, D. C., 345
Rinck, C. M., 131, 135
Rindskopf, D. M., 432
Risley, T. R., 119
Rizzo, N., 303–305
Robins, P. K., 147
Rodgers, W. L., 473
Rodin, J., 387–394, 405
Rodman, J. L., 316–317
Rodriguez, B., 63
Roese, N. J., 60
Roethlisberger, F. J., 382
Rollin, B. E., 70
Rosenfeld, A., 70
Rosengren, K. S., 239–243
Rosenhan, D. L., 61, 90–92, 100, 121
Rosenthal, R., 24–25, 48, 59–61, 121,
    231, 260, 318, 425, 429, 433, 438,
    442–443, 446, 451, 456
Rosnow, R. L., 51, 66–68, 318, 425,
    433, 438, 442–443, 446, 451, 456
Ross, A. S., 395–397
Rossi, P. H., 372–373, 406
Rotheram-Borus, M. J., 51, 56,
    66–68
Rotter, J. B., 30
Roy, R., 128
Rozin, P., 136
Rubanowitz, D. E., 187, 198
Ruksznis, E., 4
Russ, N. W., 111, 115
Russell, D., 187, 193–194, 199
Russell, J. A., 192–193
Rymer, R., 342–347

Sackheim, H. A., 274–278
Sacks, O., 336–337, 340
Salomon, G., 404–405
Sapirstein, G., 232
Satterfield, J. M., 194–195
Saucy, M. C., 274–278
Sax, L. J., 164–165
Schachter, S., 92, 101, 118
Schacter, D. L., 343
Schaeffer, B., 362
Schaller, G. B., 85
Scher, J., 222
Schiefenhovel, W., 98
Schleidt, M., 98
Schlenker, B. R., 187, 199
Schlenker, D. R., 187, 199
Schmidt, F. L., 239, 413–414, 427, 429,
    430–431, 436
Schmidt, W. C., 152, 484
Schnelle, J. F., 401–402
Schober, M. F., 470–471
Schoeneman, T. J., 187, 198
Schoggen, M. F., 100, 108, 112
Schooler, N. R., 51, 56, 66–68
Schreiber, C. A., 271–273
Schulman, P., 194
Schulz, R., 177–178, 199
Schuman, H., 469, 471, 475
Schwartz, J. E., 188–189
Schwartz, R. D., 119–120,
    178–181, 184, 189, 198
Schwarz, N., 161
Scott, J., 471
Scoville, W. B., 343
Sechrest, L., 119–120, 178–181, 184,
    189, 198, 247
Segrist, D., 196
Seligman, M. E. P., 27, 194–195, 212
Shapiro, K. J., 70
Sharpe, D., 60
Shattuck, R., 341–342, 345, 347, 362
Shaughnessy, J. J., 116, 224–225, 229,
    288, 328, 386
Shepperd, J. A., 52
Sherman, L., 107, 115
Sherwood, A., 107
Shiffrin, R. M., 343
Shurley, J. T., 232
Sieber, J. E., 63
Silva, P. A., 85
Simmons, J. Q., 362
Simon, H. A., 28
Singer, B., 19, 371
Singer, P., 71–72
Singh, M. M., 89
Sinsch, U., 95
Skinner, B. F., 349
Smith, E. R., 114, 169–170, 261, 374
Smith, J. A., 336, 344

Smith, M. A., 4, 484
Smith, P. K., 110
Smith, R. J., 47
Smith, T. W., 477
Snidman, N., 85
Snodgrass, S., 401–402
Soja, M. J., 192–194
Spangler, P. F., 357–358, 361, 401
Spitz, R. A., 88
Spring, B., 309–311
Sproull, L., 484
Stanley, J. C., 376, 383–385,
    390–391, 397
Steffen, V. J., 308–309
Steinhilber, A., 187
Stern, S. E., 184
Sternberg, R. J., 23, 28, 36, 484
Stoess, C., 136
Stoltzfus, E. R., 299–300, 302, 324
Strauss, A., 23
Strauss, C. C., 55
Striepe, M., 167–169
Stuttard, S., 117
Suh, E., 143–144
Sun, M., 347
Surwitt, R. S., 68

Tassinary, L. G., 104
Taylor, K. M., 52
Taylor, S. J., 100
Teitler, J. O., 147
Terman, L. M., 188, 193
Thomas, L., 212
Thompson, T., 56
Thompson, T. L., 102
Thompson, W. C., 59–60
Tindale, R. S., 309–311
Titus, L. J., 117
Toledo, R., 96
Tomlinson-Keasy, C., 188–189
Towle, M. J., 179, 182, 184
Traugott, M. W., 141
Tucker, J. S., 188–189
Tukey, J. W., 414–415,
    418–419, 427
Tversky, A., 7, 247

Ulrich, R. E., 70, 71
Underwood, B. J., 18, 30, 116,
    224–225, 229, 288, 328
Uselton, P. H., 401–402
Uttal, D. H., 239–243

Valentiner, D. P., 133–134
VanBiervliet, A., 357–358, 361, 401
VanderStoep, S. W., 386
Van Langenhove, L., 336, 344
Van Meter, P., 23
Vaughn, L. A., 120

Wackenhut, J., 96
Wakefield, P. C., 416
Walkenbach, J., 74
Walker, E. G., 195, 198
Wallraff, H. G., 95
Walsh, J., 484
Ward, W. D., 7
Warm, J. S., 318–320, 323
Warwick, D. P., 159, 471
Watson, J. B., 7, 19
Webb, E. J., 119–120, 178–181, 184, 189, 198
Weigel, R. H., 192–194

Weiner, H., 27
West, L. J., 177, 179
Wetzel, C. G., 96
White, S., 395–397
Whitla, D. K., 142
Wible, C. G., 28, 31
Williams, P. G., 68
Williams, W. M., 23
Willems, E. P., 86–87, 97
Willingham, W. W., 24
Wilson, G. T., 349
Wilson, R. W., 180
Winer, B. J., 283

Winograd, D. L., 188–189
Winograd, E., 31
Witte, A. D., 372–373, 406
Wright, H. F., 100, 108, 112

Yadati, S., 89
Yeaton, W. H., 247
Yokoi, L., 23

Zechmeister, E. B., 19, 158–159, 335, 343, 417–418, 426
Zechmeister, J. S., 158–159
Zuckerman, M., 131, 135

Subject Index

ABAB (reversal) design, 352–355,
  401–402. *See also* Single-case
  experimental designs
  methodological issues, and,
    354–355
  natural settings and, 401–402
ABBA counterbalancing, 277–279
Accidental sampling, 153
Accretion measures, 180–183
Actuarial prediction, 144–146
Alpha. *See* Level of significance
American Psychological Association
  (APA), 3–5, 32, 42–43, 65–74,
  195–196, 202
American Psychological Society
  (APS), 4–5
Analysis of experiments, 238–261,
  289–294, 312–320, Appendix
  A. *See also* Analysis of
  variance; Coding; Data
  reduction; Descriptive
  statistics; Inferential statistics
  computer-assisted, 253,
    Appendix A
  confidence intervals, 138–141,
    239–243, Appendix A
  descriptive statistics, 238–239,
    Appendix A
  effect size, 256–259, Appendix A
  estimating error variation, 242,
    250–255, 292–293
  logic of, 245–249, Appendix A
  meta-analysis, 259–261
  null hypothesis testing, 243–250,
    Appendix A
  plot-plus-error-bar procedure,
    241–243, Appendix A
  power and, 289, Appendix A
  sensitivity, 211, 269–270, 289
Analysis of variance (*F*-test,
  ANOVA). *See also Appendix A
  for computational procedures*
  analytical comparisons, 255–256,
    317–318, 319–320, Appendix A
  complex designs, 299–329
  computer-assisted analyses, 253,
    Appendix A
  critical values, Appendix A
  degrees of freedom, 253–254,
    313–314
  effect size, 256–259
  error variation, 242, 250–255,
    293–294
  F-test, 252–253, 290–294, 312–314,
    Appendix A

independent groups design,
  252–253
interaction effects, 314–318
main effect, 312–314
null hypothesis, 243–256
omnibus *F*-test, 252–253, 290–294,
  312–314
random groups design, 252–253
repeated measures design,
  290–294
residual variation, 294
simple comparisons, 317–318
simple main effect, 317
summary table, 253–255, 292–294,
  313–314
systematic differences, 251–252
table of critical values,
  Appendix A
within-subjects design (*see*
  Repeated measures design)
Analytical comparisons, 255–256,
  317–318, Appendix A
ANOVA. *See* Analysis of variance
Anticipation effects, 279
Applied behavior analysis, 336,
  348–349
Applied research, 335–407
  versus basic research, 372,
    404–407
Archival data, 170, 177, 185–202
  content analysis and, 192–195
  illustrative uses of, 195–197
  problems and limitations of,
    197–202
  rationale for use of, 185–189
  types of, 189–191
Arithmetic mean (average), 112,
  Appendix A

Balancing, 214–216, 218–219,
  227–228, 273–284, 285–286
Baseline stage, 351–359
Basic *versus* applied research, 4, 372,
  404–407
Behavior modification, 349, 362
Behavior therapy, 349
Behaviorism, 335, 348–349
Bias
  archival data and, 197–198
  case study and, 345–346
  everyday inference in, 11–12
  experimenter (observer), 11–12,
    121–122, 392–393
  intentional, 32–33
  interviewer, 160

observer, 11–12, 121–122, 392–393
physical traces and, 183–184,
  198–199
questionnaires in, 135–138,
  158, 160
reporting and, 11–12
response, 158, 160
sampling, 161
selection, 150, 151–152
social desirability and, 170
survey, 151–152, 158,
  160–161, 170
Block randomization, 219–220, 228,
  276–277

Case study method, 335–348
  advantages of, 337–338, 340–344
  characteristics of, 336–338
  defined, 336–337
  disadvantages of, 338, 344–347
  illustration of, 338–339
  nomothetic study of behavior
    and, 343–344
Causal relationships (inferences)
  case study and, 344–345
  conditions necessary to establish,
    25–26
  correlational studies and, 24–25,
    131–132
  experimental methods and,
    212–213
  goal of scientific method and, 25
  natural groups design and,
    235–238, 327–329
  path analysis and, 132–134
  survey research and, 131–132
Ceiling effect, 326–327, 380
Central tendency, 112–113
Checklists, 102, 106–107
Classical (respondent) conditioning,
  347–348
Clever Hans, 7–9
Coding, 112, 193–195
Complex designs, 299–329
  advantages of, 320–326, 327–329
  analysis of, 312–320, Appendix A
  illustrations of, 299–300, 302–320,
    323–329
  interaction effects in, 300,
    302–311, 314–318, 320–329
  main effects in, 300–311,
    317–318, 320
Confederate, 96, 120, 243–244
Confidence intervals, 138–141,
  239–243, Appendix A

computational procedures, Appendix A
Confounding, 27, 215, 227–228, 270–271, 344–346, 376–380. *See also* Internal validity
defined, 27, 215
extraneous variables and, 227–228
individual differences (subject) variables and, 235–238
intact groups and, 226–227
internal validity and, 27, 215, 227–228
subject (individual differences) variables and, 235–238
Construct validity, 143–144
Contamination, 380–382, 392–393
Content analysis, 192–195
Control, 9, 370–371. *See also* Control condition; Control techniques
Control condition, 9, 210, 350, 370–371, 376
Control techniques
balancing, 212–215, 217–220, 227–228, 273–284, 286–287
block randomization, 219–220, 228, 276–277
double-blind procedure, 232
experimental, 212–217, 370–371, 375
holding conditions constant, 214–216, 219–220, 228
manipulation, 9, 210–211, 212–213, 375
placebo, 231–232
Convergent validity, 144, 209
Correlation
causal inference and, 132
defined, 24, 129
direction, 129–130
illusory, 7
magnitude, 129–130
path analysis and, 132–134
prediction and, 23–25, 129
reliability and, 115, 141–144
scatterplots and, 130–131
Correlation coefficient, 129–130, 175
computational procedures, 175
Correlational research, 128–146. *See also* Survey research; Tests
defined, 24–25, 128
path analysis, 132–134
Counterbalancing
ABBA, 277–279
block randomization, 276–277
complete within-subjects designs in, 273–279
defined, 273
incomplete within-subjects designs in, 279–284
Latin Square, 282–284
Critical value. *See* Statistical significance
Cross-sectional design, 161–163

d (as effect size), 256–257, Appendix A
Data analysis Appendix A. *See* Analysis of variance; Coding; Descriptive statistics
Data reduction, 111–112. *See also* Coding; Descriptive statistics
Debriefing, 66–68
Deception, 32–33, 60–65, 217
Degrees of freedom (df), 253–255, 313–314, Appendix A
Demand characteristics, 231
Dependent variable, defined, 10, 210–211
Description as a goal of scientific method, 20–23. *See also* Descriptive methods; Descriptive statistics
Descriptive methods, 84–206
archival data, 170, 177, 185–202
case study, 335–348
correlational, 128–171
experimental *versus*, 210–211
observational, 85–122
physical traces, 178–184
qualitative research, 23
survey research, 148–169
tests, 141–144
unobtrusive measures, 118–119, 177–203
Descriptive statistics, 112–113, 238–239, Appendix A
arithmetic mean (average), 112
central tendency, 112–113
computational procedures, Appendix A
plot-plus-error-bar procedure, Appendix A
standard deviation, 112–113
standard error of the mean, 242–243
variability (dispersion), 113, 241–242
Desensitization, 119
Differential transfer, 287–289
Discriminant validity, 144
Double-blind experiment, 232

Ecological psychology, 100
Effect size, 256–261, Appendix A
d, 256–257, Appendix A
eta squared, Appendix A
f, Appendix A
Element (in survey research), 151
Empirical approach, 7
Error bars, Appendix A
Error variation, 241–242, 252–253, 269–270, 293–294
eta squared, Appendix A
Ethical issues in psychological research, 32–33, 42–77, 121, 148, 195–196, 202–203, 355
animal research, 24, 68–72
APA code, 42–43, 195–196, 202

deception, 32–33, 60–65, 120
informed consent, 52–60, 111
plagiarism, 32, 73–76
privacy, 58–59, 120
reporting results, 32–33, 72–76
risk, 47–52, 120
risk/benefit ratio, 47–48
single-case research designs, 355, 361–363
surveys and, 148
unobtrusive measures, 202–203
Ethnology, 100
Ethogram, 88
Ethology, 88
Event sampling, 110
Expectancy (experimenter/observer) effects, 121
Experiment
defined, 210–211
quasi-, 383–385
sensitivity of, 211, 289–290
single-case, 350
true *versus* quasi-, 374
Experimental analysis of behavior, 336, 348–349
Experimental condition, 9
Experimental designs, 207–329. *See also* Quasi-experimental designs; Research methods; Single-case research designs
chart for identifying, 301
complex, 298–329
independent groups, 207–261
matched groups, 233–235
natural groups, 235–238, 327–329
quasi-, 383–400
random groups, 217–232
repeated measures, 268–294
single-case, 335–363
within-subjects (*see* Repeated measures)
Experimenter (expectancy) effects, 121, 231
External validity
case study of, 346
defined, 27, 211
establishing, 187, 220–226
experiments of, 211
interactions and, 323–324
interrupted time-series design of, 394–398
naturalistic observations and, 111, 371–372
nonequivalent control group design of, 398–400
single-case experimental design and, 360
Extraneous variables, 227–228

Factorial combination, 299–300
Field notes, 100–101
Field research (experiment), 27, 96–97
Floor effect, 326–327, 380

Focus group, 160–161
F-ratio. *See* Analysis of variance
F-test. *See* Analysis of variance

Generality of research findings. *See* External validity
Group methodology, 20, 21, 335

Habituation, 118–119
Hawthorne effect, 382–383, 393
History threat to internal validity, 376–377, 385
Holding conditions constant, 214, 219–220, 228
Hypothesis(es)
    defined, 17–18
    generations, 133–134
    multimethod approach and, 179
    null, 243–250
    scientific theories and, 30–31, 211–212
    testability, 17–18, 29–30, 211–212

Idiographic approach, 22, 343–344. *See also* Case study method
Illusory correlation, 7
Independent groups designs, 207–261
    analysis of, 238–261, 312–320, Appendix A
    complex design, 298–329
    defined, 216
    intact groups and, 226–227
    matched groups design, 233–235
    natural groups design, 235–238
    random groups design, 217–232
Independent variable
    confounding and, 26–27, 215, 227–228, 270–271
    defined, 9, 210–211
    potential, 215, 226–227
    relevant *versus* irrelevant, 227, 324–326
Individual differences (subject) variable. *See also* Analysis of variance
    complex designs and, 327–329
    defined, 10
    natural groups design, 235–238
    repeated measures designs and, 270–271
Inferential statistics, 235–259
Informed consent, 52–60
Institutional Animal Care and Use Committee (IACUC), 47
Institutional Review Board (IRB), 44, 47
Instrumentation threat to internal validity, 377–378
Instruments. *See also* Questionnaires
    accuracy, 13–14
    precision, 14
    reliability, 16, 141–144
Intact groups, testing, 226–227

Interaction effects
    analysis of, 314–318
    ceiling (floor) effects and, 326–327
    defined, 300, 311
    external validity and, 323–324
    interpreting, 302–311, 320–323
    natural groups design and, 327–329
    nature of, 302–311
    relevant variables and, 324–326
    with selection, 379–380, 390–392
    theory testing and, 320–321
Internal validity. *See also* Confounding; Control techniques
    defined, 27, 211
    double blind experiments and, 231–232
    experiments of, 211, 374
    extraneous variables and, 227–228
    history threats to, 376–377, 385
    intact groups and, 226–227
    placebo control, 231–232
    subject loss and, 228–231, 379
    threats to, 226–232, 376–380
Internet, 35, 184, 189, Appendix C. *See also* World-Wide-Web
Interobserver reliability, 114
Interrupted time-series designs, 394–398
Interval scale, 104–106
Intervening variables, 30–31
Interviewer bias, 160
Interviews, 160–161. *See also* Survey research
Intuition, role of, in science, 6–7

Latin Square, 283–284
Level of Significance, 246–247
Longitudinal design, 166–169

Mail survey, 158–159
Main effect, 300, 302–311, 318–320
    defined, 304
Manipulation, 10, 210–211, 212–213, 374–375
Margin of error, 138–141
Matched groups design, 233–235
Maturation threat to internal validity, 377, 385, 390–391
Mean. *See* Arithmetic mean
Measurement
    central tendency, 112–113
    nonreactive (unobtrusive), 118–120
    physical *versus* psychological, 14–15
    reactivity and, 116–120
    reliability of, 16–17, 114–115
    scales, 102–107
    scientific method and, 14–17

validity of, 15–16
    variability, 112–113
Measures of behavior. *See also* Archival data; Physical traces; Questionnaires; Tests
    nonreactive (unobtrusive), 177–203
    observation and, 101–108
    reactivity, 116–120, 178–179
Mediator Variable, 132–133
Meta-analysis, 259–261
Minimal risk. *See* Risk
Moderator variable, 132–133
Mortality. *See* Subject loss
Multimethod approach to hypothesis testing, 33–36, 170, 179, 209, 360
Multiple-baseline designs, 355–357. *See also* Single-case research designs
    across behaviors, 356
    across situations, 356–357
    across subjects, 355

N = 1 designs, 336–337, 348–349, 350–351. *See also* Single-case research designs
Narrative records
    analysis of, 111–112
    coding, 112
    considerations, 100–101
    defined, 98
    illustrations, 98–101
    improving quality of, 101
Natural groups design, 235–238, 327–329. *See also* Individual differences variable
Natural groups variable. *See* Individual differences variable
Natural treatment, 187–188
Naturalistic observation, 86–89
    defined, 87
    goals of, 87–88
Nominal scale, 102–103
Nomothetic approach, 21–22, 343–344
Noncomparable successive samples, 166
Nonequivalent control group design, 385–400
    characteristics, 385–386
    defined, 385
    external validity and, 398–400
    illustration, 387–389
    sources of invalidity, 389–393
    time series and, 394–400
Nonprobability sampling, 152–154
Nonreactive measures. *See* Unobtrusive measures
Null hypothesis
    analysis of variance and, 250–256
    defined, 245

limitations, 249–256, Appendix A
testing of, 243–250

Observation. *See also* Observational
methods
bias and, 11–12, 121–122
control and, 7–11, 121–122
ethical issues, 120
goals in natural settings, 85–86
scientific *versus* nonscientific,
7–11
Observational methods, 85–122
classification of, 85, 97
field experiments, 96–97
intervention and, 89–97
naturalistic, 86–89
participant, 89–92
problems in, 115–122
scientific *versus* nonscientific,
7–11
structured, 92–96
Observer (experimenter) bias, 112,
121–122, 231–232, 345, 392–393
controlling, 121–122
defined, 121
Omnibus *F*-test, 252–253, 290–294,
312–314
Operant (conditioning), 348–349
Operational definition, 13, 150
Ordinal scale, 104

Parsimony (rule of), 31–32
Participant observation, 89–92
disguised *versus* undisguised, 90
Path analysis, 132–134
Pearson Product-Moment
Correlation Coefficient,
115, 175
Physical traces, 178–184
problems and limitations of,
183–184
rationale for use of, 178–179
types of, 179–182
Placebo control, 231–232
Plagiarism, 32
Plot-plus-error-bar procedure,
Appendix A
Population, defined, 150
Power, 289–290, Appendix A
factors affecting, 289–290
tables, Appendix A
Practice effects, 270–284
anticipation effects and, 279
balancing, 273–284
controlling, 273–284
defined, 271
differential transfer and,
287–289
irreversible tasks and, 285–287
Prediction as goal of scientific
method, 23–25, 144–146
actuarial, 144–145
clinical, 144–146
statistical, 144–146

Privacy, 58–59
Probability sampling, 152–153,
154–156
Program evaluation, 4–5, 369,
403–407
Psychophysical methods
(psychophysics), 270, 335
Purposive sampling, 154

Qualitative research, 23, 97–101
definition, 23
versus quantitative research, 23
Quantitative research, 23, 101–108
definition, 23
versus qualitative research, 23
Quasi–experimental designs,
383–400
defined, 383
interrupted time–series designs,
394–398
nonequivalent control group
design, 385–400
simple interrupted time-series
design, 394–398
time series with nonequivalent
control group, 398–400
versus true experiments, 374–383
Questionnaires, 135–138, 157–161,
169–171
construction of, 136–138,
Appendix B

Random assignment, 217–220, 374
Random groups designs, 217–232
analysis of, 238–261, 312–320,
Appendix A
described, 218
external validity and, 220–226,
323–324
internal validity and, 226–232
Random numbers, table of,
Appendix A
Random selection (samples)
versus random assignment,
217–219
simple, 155
stratified, 155–156
techniques, 155–157
Ratio scale, 106
Reactivity, 115–120, 179
control for, 118–120
defined, 116
Recording behavior, 97–108. *See also*
Checklists; Measures of
behavior; Narrative records
classification of methods, 97
electronic, 107–108
Regression to (or toward) mean
defined, 378–379
threat to internal validity,
378–379, 392
Relevant independent variable, 227,
324–326
Reliability

defined, 16–17
experimental, 210–211, 220–225
instrument, 16
interobserver, 113–114
measures of, 113, 114–115,
141–144
observer, 113–115
test-retest, 142
Repeated measures designs,
268–294
analysis of, 289–290
complete, 274–279
defined, 268
incomplete, 273, 279–284
limitations, 284–289
practice effects and, 270–284
reasons for using, 268–270
sensitivity of, 269
Replication, 222–223
Report writing. *See* Research report
writing
Representativeness (of sample), 151,
154–156
Research designs, types of
correlational, 128–171
experimental, 209–329
observational, 86–122
quasi-experimental, 383–400
single-case (*N* = 1), 400–402
survey research, 148–169
Research methods
applied, 335–407
archival, 185–203
case study, 335, 336–348
correlational, 128–171
descriptive, 85–203
experimental, 209–329
experimental analysis of
behavior, 336, 348–349
field, 96–97
laboratory *versus* natural setting,
370–374
observational, 86–122
physical traces and, 178–184
psychophysical, 271
quasi-experimental, 383–400
single case (*N* = 1), 336, 350–363,
400–402
survey research, 148–169
Research report writing, 72–76,
Appendix C
Residual variation, 293–294,
Appendix A
Respondent (classical
conditioning), 348
Respondent mortality, 168. *See also*
Subject loss
Response bias, 158–159
Reversal design. *See* ABAB design
Risk (to participants), 47–52
definition, 48–49
minimal, 50
risk/benefit ratio, 47–48
Running records, 189–191

Sample
  defined, 151
  size of, 155, 256–261
Samples
  accidental, 153–154
  biased, 151
  noncomparable successive, 166
  purposive, 154
  random, 155–156, 217–220
  representative, 154–156
Sampling frame in survey research,
    150–151
Sampling techniques, 108–111,
    149–157
  accidental, 153–154
  behavior, 108–111
  event, 110–111
  nonprobability, 153–154
  probability, 152–153, 154–156
  purposive, 154
  random (simple), 155
  situation, 111
  stratified random, 155–156
  time, 109–110
Scatterplot, 130–131
Scientific integrity. See Ethical issues
    in psychological research
Scientific method, 5–27
  attitude of scientists and, 18–20
  characteristics of, 5–20
  communication and, 11–12,
    72–76. See also Appendix C
  concepts and, 12–13
  control and, 7–11
  empirical approach and, 7
  goals of, 20–27
  versus nonscientific approaches,
    6–7
Scientific psychology
  characteristics of, 5–27
  history of, 3–5
Selection bias, 151–152
Selection threat to internal validity,
    379–380
Selective deposit, 197–198
Selective survival, 198
Sensitivity, 211, 228, 289–290
Simple comparisons, 317
Simple interrupted time-series
    design, 394–398
Simple main effect, 317
Simple random sampling, 155
Single-case research designs, 335–363
  ABAB (reversal) design, 352–355,
    401–402
  case study, 335–348
  ethical issues, 361–363
  experiment, 350
  versus multiple group designs,
    350
  multiple-baseline designs,
    355–357
  natural settings and, 400–402
  problems and limitations of,
    359–361

Situation sampling, 111
Social desirability, 170
Spurious relationship, 132, 199–200
Stage-of-practice effects. See Practice
    effects
Standard deviation, 113, Appendix A
Standard error of the mean, 241–243,
    Appendix A
Statistical regression. See Regression
    to the mean
Statistical significance, 245–250, 305,
    Appendix A
  critical values, 246–247,
    Appendix A
  defined, 245
  effect size and, 260
  level of, 246
  limits of, 249–250
  power and, 289–290
  tables to determine, Appendix A
Statistical tests. See Analysis of
    variance; Correlation
    coefficient; t-test
Stem-and-leaf display, Appendix A
Stratified random sampling, 155–156
Structured observation, 92–96
Subject loss (subject mortality), 168,
    228–231, 379
  mechanical, 229
  selective, 229
  threat to internal validity,
    168–169, 228–231, 379
Subject selection threat to internal
    validity, 379–380
Subject variable. See Individual
    differences variable
Successive independent samples
    design, 163–166
Survey research, 148–169
  bias in, 151–152, 158, 160–161, 170
  correlational research and, 128
  designs, 161–169
  margin of error and, 138–141
  methods, 157–161
  questionnaire construction and,
    136–138, Appendix C
  sampling techniques, 149
  uses and characteristics of,
    146–149
  validity of, 169–171

Telephone survey, 161
Testing threat to internal validity,
    377, 385–386
Test-retest reliability, 142
Tests, 141–144
  correlational research and,
    141–144
  predictions from, 144–146
  reliability, 141–144
  validity, 141–144
Theory, 17–18, 28–32, 210, 212,
    320–321
  construction, 28–32
  defined, 30

  functions, 30
  intervening variables and, 30–31
  scope, 28
  testing, 31–32, 210, 320–321,
    342–343
Time sampling, 109–110
Time series with nonequivalent
    control group, 398–400
Treatment stage versus baseline, 351
t-test, Appendix A
Type I error, 248–249
Type II error, 248–249

Understanding as goal of scientific
    method, 25–27
Unobtrusive measures, 118, 177–203
  archival data, 185–202
  defined, 177
  ethics and, 202–203
  physical traces and, 179–182
  reactivity and, 118–119
Use traces, 180–182

Validity
  case study of, 344–347
  construct, 143
  convergent, 144, 209
  defined, 15
  discriminant, 144
  experiments of, 211, 212–232,
    270–284, 323–324, 371–372,
    374–380
  external, 27, 211, 220–226,
    371–372, 398–400
  internal, 27, 211, 226–232,
    374–380
  physical trace measures of, 179
  tests of, 141–144
Variability, 113. See also Error
    variation; Standard deviation
Variables, types of
  dependent, 10, 210
  extraneous, 227–228
  independent, 9, 210
  individual differences, 10,
    235–238, 270–271, 327–329
  intervening, 30–31
  irrelevant independent, 227–228,
    324–326
  matching, 233–235
  mediator, 132–133
  moderator, 132–133
  natural groups (see Individual
    differences)
  potential independent, 26, 215,
    226–227
  relevant independent, 227–228,
    324–326
  subject (see Individual
    differences)

Within-subject designs (see Repeated
    measures designs)
World-Wide-Web, 5, 222,
    Appendix C. See also Internet

CLIFFORD ODETS
American Playwright

MARGARET BRENMAN-GIBSON

CLIFFORD ODETS
American Playwright

The Years from 1906 to 1940

ATHENEUM
New York
1982

Library of Congress Cataloging in Publication Data

Brenman-Gibson, Margaret.
    Clifford Odets, American playwright.

    Bibliography: p.
    Includes index.
    1. Odets, Clifford, 1906–1963. 2. Dramatists,
American—20th century—Biography. I. Title.
PS3529.D46Z58 1981   812'.54 [B]   80-7927
ISBN 0-689-11160-6   AACR2

TO THE MEMORY OF MY FATHER
AND OF MY MOTHER AND WITH GRATITUDE
TO MY HUSBAND AND MY SONS

I will reveal America to itself by revealing myself to myself. CLIFFORD ODETS

Contents

PREFACE   xi

PROLOGUE   *The Problem*   3

PART ONE   *Soilbed and Seed 1890–1923*   15

PART TWO   *Quest for a Place 1923–1931*   65

PART THREE   *From Actor to Writer 1931–1935*   191

PART FOUR   *Survival in Public 1935–1940*   341

PERSONAL CHRONOLOGY OF CLIFFORD ODETS   615

WORKS BY CLIFFORD ODETS   619

NOTES AND COMMENT   621

ACKNOWLEDGMENTS   679

SOURCES AND REFERENCES   683

SELECTED BIBLIOGRAPHY   709

INDEX   719

Illustrations

Pearl Geisinger Odets, Clifford's mother
   (*Courtesy Freda Rossman*)
Clifford Odets at two
Clifford at four and father, Louis J. Odets
Esther Rossman, Pearl Odets, and Clifford
Clifford at five
Clifford and father in "bar mitzvah" portrait
Odets family at Boy Scout camp
Clifford's graduating-class picture (1921)
Clifford as "The Rover Reciter"
Scene from Harry Kemp production
   (*Courtesy Jerome Rosenberg*)
Dr. M. V. Leof, one of the best of Clifford's "surrogate fathers"
   (*Courtesy Madeleine Leof Ross*)
Clifford at twenty-three, an aspiring matinee idol
Actress-singer Tamara
   (*Culver Pictures*)
Actress Sylvia Field
   (*Culver Pictures*)
Actress Hortense Alden
   (*Culver Pictures*)
Actress Fay Wray in studio portrait
   (*Courtesy Fay Wray*)
Group Theatre directors Cheryl Crawford, Lee Strasberg, and
Harold Clurman
   (*Courtesy Robert Lewis*)
Group portrait of members of the Group Theatre
   (*Photograph by Ralph Steiner; courtesy Robert Lewis*)
Odets at height of his success
   (*Photograph by Alfredo Valente*)
Odets at twenty-eight
   (*Photograph by Carl Van Vechten*)
Odets as Dr. Benjamin in *Waiting for Lefty*
   (*Photograph by Alfredo Valente*)
Group actor Elia Kazan
   (*Photograph by Alfredo Valente*)
Group actress Paula Miller Strasberg
Group scene, *Waiting for Lefty*
   (*Theatre Collection, Museum of the City of New York*)
John Garfield and Morris Carnovsky in *Awake and Sing*
   (*Theatre Collection, Museum of the City of New York*)
Golden Boy
   (*Theatre Collection, Museum of the City of New York*)

Illustrations

Awake and Sing

The "firebug scene" from *Paradise Lost*
    (*Courtesy Robert Lewis*)

Rocket to the Moon

Robert Lewis in *Till the Day I Die*
    (*Photograph by Marian Post Wolcott; courtesy Robert Lewis*)

Luise Rainer*

Luise Rainer*
    (*Photograph by Carl Van Vechten*)

Luise Rainer and Clifford Odets at a concert*

Odets and Luise Rainer*
    (*Photograph by Carl Van Vechten*)

Luise Rainer, Clifford Odets, and Albert Einstein*

Odets on cover of *Time* magazine

        * Courtesy of Luise Rainer

Preface

As the study of life history emerges from that of case histories, it will throw new light on biography and thus on history itself.

ERIK H. ERIKSON

IN LATE July 1963, in a period of renewed hope that the nuclear-test-ban treaty had given all of us and our children an unexpected reprieve from the forces of evil, I was on vacation, reading in manuscript a colleague's book about Alger Hiss and Whittaker Chambers, two men whose relationship on the stage of history had engaged, moved, and mystified the entire world. For many years I had followed with fascination my colleague's painstaking gathering of information on their lives. On the basis of the internal consistency of his material, and before reading the manuscript, I had come to the conclusion that my colleague was about to deliver himself of the finest "psychoanalytic double-biography," as he called it, that had ever been written.

Still, I found myself troubled by what appeared to me to be his Freudian-fundamentalist approach to the unfolding drama of these two intertwined lives. I had found the raw data of both life histories—unearthed in detail by him with all the patience, wit, and resourcefulness of a detective—to be stunning, but it was now disconcertingly clear that even we two psychoanalysts did not agree on how the data should be organized, or on the motivations of these two men, let alone on the relation of their individual lives to the ongoing history.

In the midst of this task, a small package from playwright Clifford Odets arrived from California. My husband, William Gibson, and I had been good friends of Odets since 1950, when Odets chose Bill as one of a handful of budding American playwrights to participate in his writing seminar at the Actors Studio. Over the years we visited back and forth, and I in particular talked to him on the telephone once or twice a week into the small hours of the morning, especially when he was in despair about his work.

The package from Clifford proved to be another biography, this time not by a psychiatrist but by a professor of drama who, in his small volume, documented the thesis that in less than twelve months in 1935 Odets, not yet thirty years old, had "cut a swath in American theatre such as few are able to cut in a lifetime." He argued that Odets' historic stature as an American playwright did not rest only on the manifest social protest of his work, and that in any case the best of Odets' work was yet to come.

This was the second time in twenty-four hours that I had felt oppressed by the complexities of conceptualizing the story of any individual life, and of relating that story to the subject's work in such a way as to illuminate the problems of so-called psychoanalytic and psychohistorical biography. I had been struggling for years with this problem of oversimplification and schematization in day-to-day clinical work, and it had long been evident to me that there was a wide chasm between the vocabularies often used to describe a patient's case history and those used to tell the story of a neighbor's or a creative leader's life. To some of us this had always seemed not only conceptually but humanly pernicious.

Much later I retrieved from Odets' file a note I had written him after reading the little book he had sent. I spoke first of my unclarified dissatisfactions with the double-biography, saying I should have undertaken it myself; then I wrote of his biography, "You must admit it is quite a feat to deal with a guy like you and somehow turn it into a bland exercise," casually adding that his biography, too, was a book I would "maybe write some day." A few days later there had come a note from Odets: "I am on the way to the doctor just now for X-rays. There are some gastric troubles and we don't know what it is." I wondered why he made no reference to my letter with its careless offer "some day" to tell *his* life story. Two weeks later, at the Cedars of Lebanon Hospital in Los Angeles, he was dead, the autopsy revealing a massively metastasized cancer of the stomach.

Stunned by the death of a man whom my husband and I had admired and loved, I determined to find the meanings in his life and work. Long before we had become friends, this representative American playwright had been for me, as for many others of my generation, a culture hero. A clue to the significance his death held for me, and for many, appeared in my inability for days to rid my thoughts of a line from Gerard Manley Hopkins: "It is Margaret you mourn for."

This loss was more than a personal bereavement; it was more like one's own death. We had selected Odets as our spokesman, and his achievements and falls from grace, whether political or esthetic, were our own. I was perhaps proof, I thought, of Emerson's view that—despite all individuality—each new generation comes on as a "vast, solid phalanx," part of a "great destiny, colossal in its traits, terrible in its strength." It was clear that Alfred Kazin had had the same experience:

> Watching my mother and father and uncles and aunts occupying the stage in *Awake and Sing!* by as much right as if they were Hamlet and Lear, I understood at last. It was all one. . . . The unmistakable and surging march of history might yet pass through me. There seemed to be no division between my effort at personal liberation and the apparent effort of humanity to deliver itself.

Odets had helped those of us who were convinced we did not belong in our country to feel less estranged and assuredly more hopeful that we could transcend separateness and collectively take our place in a larger, more unified, and freer design than our individual lives promised. As we sat in the darkness, intent on the framed, lit space of the proscenium stage, we, in astonishment, *recognized ourselves and we knew we were at last being recognized.*

When, three decades later, I found myself involuntarily committed to the resurrection on paper of this life that in the thirties had so moved and enlivened us adolescents hungry for an ideology, I knew that only one approach to this undertaking was sufficiently comprehensive, and hoped I would not do violence in my account of an entire life span to Erikson's quantum jump in psychological theory, a formidable model of human development and of generational sequence whose growing body of integrated psychosocial principles is still regarded with suspicion in some quarters of the psychoanalytic establishment.

Upon receiving from the Odets Estate exclusive rights to his papers, I proceeded with some exhilaration to gather Odets' mountainous correspondence, notes, and files, and to interview dozens of people. It began to dawn on me that I had committed myself to the most exacting piece of research of my life, and I feared I was indeed venturing on ground where, as Leon Edel had put it in his stern warning to psychoanalyst poachers, not only do angels properly fear to tread but psychoanalysts had already left many large, muddy footprints:

> Possessing neither the discipline of criticism nor the methods of biography, they import the atmosphere of the clinic and the consulting room into the library.

To be sure, shaking an equally admonishing finger at his own literary colleagues, he had added:

> The other side of the picture has been inevitably the venture, on the part of critics and biographers, upon psychoanalytic ground, where they have been no less inexpert than the psychoanalysts on our ground. The use of the psychoanalytic tool involves high skills.

Edel had concluded, thus, with a territorial division whereby the species psychoanalyst, by definition, could treat only of "what's wrong with the artist's mental health" while the biographer, holding a monopoly on "reading the same pattern in the larger picture of the human condition," would seek to show "how the negatives were converted into positives: how, for example, Proust translated his allergies and his withdrawals from pain of experience into the whole world of Combray." Clearly this was a treaty I could not sign. It was precisely the "larger picture of the human condition," not a narrow pathology, which had become illumined by Erikson's consolidation of the Freudian revolution, an illumination as sorely needed by those of us to whom fractured people were turning for help as by those who were writing biographies.

As long ago as the mid-thirties Freud's celebrated statement that before the mysteries of the artist "psychoanalysis must lay down its arms" had become the defensive standard preface of the few biographies of gifted persons then being written by psychoanalysts. Nonetheless, each biography would proceed to claim, with utter banality, that the artist shared with the rest of us an out-of-time "oral fixation" or Oedipus complex, or suffered from "love-hate in human relations," or personified one or another antique diagnostic category.

The first ground-breaking model to appear was, of course, *Young Man Luther*. In that volume, which tackled only a circumscribed portion of a life cycle, Erikson described Luther's resolution of his own crisis of identity as roughly filling a "political and psychological vacuum which history had created in a significant portion of Western Christendom." He argued further that "such coincidence, if further coinciding with the deployment of personal gifts, makes for historical 'greatness.'" It seemed to me that this discovery, drawn not from the life of an artist but from that of a religious revolutionary and originator, provided a means for studying great, or even merely representative, originators *of any sort,* whether of action on the macrostages of history, of theories about the natural universe, or of plays on the microstage of the theatre. But a blazed path is not yet an easily traversed trail.

Odets had scribbled, "I will reveal America to itself by revealing myself to myself." He proposed to do this in his plays, and I now proposed to extend this revelation by a study of those plays in the context of his life story and of history itself. The task of distilling the huge pile of data I had collected about Odets' ancestry, infancy, childhood, adolescence, adulthood, and death and integrating it with the prevailing historical forces appeared monumental. When I confronted the additional task of considering *in microscopic detail* how all these data hung together with his plays, forming their context, I understood, first, why most clinicians restrict themselves to traditional case histories, and, second, why biographers who bravely entitle their life histories "The Life and Times of . . ." are usually reduced to parallel statements of a life, a time, and a body of work. The difficulty lies in discerning how all these hang together.

I now felt apologetic toward the drama professor and toward my colleague—who had by this time been severely drubbed by psychoanalysts, historians, and literary critics for his double-biography. It was by no means so clear to me as it had been on that summer day in 1963 that a *serious and detailed* joint charting of a life, a time, and a body of work could be accomplished by Erikson's method of "disciplined subjectivity" in a single lifetime.

I took comfort from the recollection that my old friend Henry Murray, a pioneer in psychoanalysis at Harvard, had repeatedly said that the "facts of personality" are to be found *only* in the life histories of whole human beings and that these are the "granite blocks on which to build a science of human nature." Nonetheless, had I foreseen the time and trouble it takes to attempt to set even one such small block in place, I should never have undertaken it, and I finally understand why so many biographies are never finished. It is possible that this biography also would have been abandoned but for the fact that, midway through, Erik H. Erikson, then my colleague on the Senior Staff of Austen Riggs Center, sat with me twice a week for six months, listening to me read aloud from the manuscript and offering invaluable comments. I cannot but express my profound gratitude to him now, and I hope that this life history reflects the spirit of those conversations.

A final point: this symbol [◖] in the text, with its accompanying footnote, refers the reader to "Notes and Comment," at the back of the book. This section is a compromise that removes from the narrative much of the thinking that comes as a reflex to a clinical researcher and indicates a way of working. Its contents are perhaps of more interest to the professional than to the general reader. They range back and forth over Odets' entire life, in an effort to see how the whole thing is of a piece, in Einstein's sense "invariant": an equation whose form is not changed under a group of transformations. And some of these comments explore the question of how the life of a culture hero reflects and expresses the "making and unmaking" of other twentieth-century Americans.

I hope even the general reader will risk reading them.

MARGARET BRENMAN-GIBSON

Cambridge Hospital, Department of Psychiatry
Harvard University School of Medicine
and Austen Riggs Center
July 1978

CLIFFORD ODETS
American Playwright

Prologue The Problem

1963 *Deathbed*

Dear American friend, that miserable patch of event, that melange of nothing, while you were looking ahead for something to happen, that was it! That was life! You lived it!

CLIFFORD ODETS, *1962*

I am like my mother who died, I think, of a broken heart.

CLIFFORD ODETS, *1950*

On a hot August day in 1963, Clifford Odets lay in a small private room in a Hollywood hospital fighting for what remained of his life. A sheet covered the lower half of his naked body, with its swollen abdomen; above it, his chest and arms, thin by now, still suggested the athletic vitality that had always characterized his walk and gesticulations. A tube was inserted in his nose; a second tube led from his side into a glass jar at the foot of the bed; both were removing the wastes his body could no longer eliminate. The gallons of iced apple juice he gulped down to moisten his cracked lips and dry throat reached only the stomach and flowed out into the jar. Nothing moved past the stomach level, below which there were intestinal obstructions, and because his body absorbed little, whether he drank, sucked lemons, or rubbed ice on his lips, his thirst was unslakable.

Compulsively he kept flexing his long, beautiful fingers, rippling them as though playing an instrument. Whenever the powerful sedatives pumped into his body threatened to overwhelm him, he would, in the words of a spectator, "wrench himself up and into consciousness," forcing himself to activity. At times he extended an arm at full length, shook his fist, and shouted, "Clifford Odets, you have so much to do!" More than once he said, "I want to yell, can I yell?" And then he shouted, "Yell!"— prolonging the word interminably like a fire siren. Those who heard it forgave its theatricality because it was evident there was something penultimate in this howl.

He put into words what he thought was the reason for waging his nightmare battle: "I may fool you all . . . you know, I may live. . . . Then perhaps Clifford Odets will do something to redeem the last sixteen wasted years."

It became a matter of utmost significance to him to know what time it was, and repeatedly he asked; once, after he was told, he said, "Why

don't they tell me the time, why do they keep it from me? Why do they do
that to a man's courage?" It was as though he were counting the minutes
that were still his. Next to the bed stood the metal hospital night table,
three metal chairs for visitors, and the standard spartan bureau. Over it,
on a shelf on the blank wall, a dark television screen looked straight down
at the bed.

     Six miles from the hospital, in the dinette-pantry of a white clap-
board New England house in Beverly Hills which Odets would never re-
enter, on a cheap maple table which was his customary work desk rested
his typewriter with a blank sheet of paper in it.
     Beside the typewriter he had himself placed two issues of *Time* dated
twenty-four years apart. One, from 1938, carries on its cover a photograph
of Odets at his desk, smiling, plump-faced, captioned with his cry, "Down
with the general fraud!" and inside is a long article in the theatre section.
This is one of the few instances of a *Time* cover story on an American
playwright. Comparing Odets' brilliant success with the arrival of Eugene
O'Neill "in the early twenties," the piece describes his "rich, compassionate,
angry feeling for people, his tremendous dramatic punch" and "his dialogue bracing as ozone," adding that in every Odets play "at least once or
twice during the evening, every spectator feels that a fire hose has been
trained on his body, that a fist has connected with his chin." His current
play, *Rocket to the Moon*, is summarized thus: "Heaving, racked, volcanic,
the play belches the hot subterranean lava of its characters' anger, helplessness, pain. It draws back their skin to leave every nerve exposed. . . .
Blisteringly real, its dialogue forks and spits like lightning from a scornful sky." The thunderous opening performance in 1935 of his one-act play
Waiting for Lefty, which by 1938 had circled the globe with over 300
productions, is again celebrated in the *Time* article, together with the
phenomenon of his having had three other plays produced that same year.
By the end of 1935, thus, "the Left theatre had become an exciting reality
for people in no wise Left-minded and when a 28-year-old Odets was not
being hailed as the Boy Wonder of the United States theatre, he was
acclaimed as its White Hope." The *Time* piece concludes that as of December 5, 1938, "his position remains unchallenged. . . . Odets is his country's most promising playwright."
     The other *Time* article, from 1962, headed "Credo of a Wrong-Living
Man," occupies less than a page under "Television" and carries a picture
of an older, sharper, more somber-faced Odets, again at his typewriter. It
reports an interview with the "dramatic laureate of the 30's" who says,
" . . . the American people don't know who they are or where they're
going," to which the interviewer rejoins, "Clifford Odets knows where he's
going—to NBC as a television writer."
     To more than one friend of Odets who had read with foreboding the
announcement of his contract to write twelve "teleplays" for a dramatic
series to star Richard Boone, it signaled a man nearing the end of his rope.
To him, however, the contract appeared to hold hope for a new beginning,
albeit a beginning about which he had considerable reservations. In his
diary he recorded a long talk with a friend "about how, with present materials available to beat one's way back to a creative life . . . I begin to
take the reins in my hands on all sides—it is that or perish!" adding rue-
fully, "Wolfgang Amadeus Mozart died on this day in the year of 1791.
And in the meantime in 1962 I was very busy projecting an NBC-TV
show," a show which, according to a television executive, would combine
"mass and class." The next day Odets wrote: "I feel innerly that the TV

will hone me sharp, be something that pulls me out of my sloth, that lays down gleaming tracks for my future more serious work. This fervidly is my hope—amen!" He talked continually of the six real plays he had "all laid out," and in a letter said, "I am bursting to be writing . . . my hand writhes and darts with words."

Secretly bolstering himself with Dexedrine, he plunged into a work schedule the pace and intensity of which no one who knew him had ever witnessed: devoting fourteen to sixteen hours a day, as "Story Editor" and "Playwright," to the preparation of scripts, interviewing of producers, writers, directors, and actors for the Boone television program, and working concurrently on a libretto, now long overdue, for a musical version of his 1937 success, *Golden Boy*. In spite of his longstanding terror of flying, he had flown to New York for conferences about *Golden Boy* and the Boone series, to be aired in September 1963. His television producer, who had had disquieting warnings about Odets' difficulty in finishing manuscripts, found him to be "the hardest-working guy I ever knew."

Odets had left New York early in 1955, immediately after the box-office failure of his last play, *The Flowering Peach*. For eight empty years he had assured himself that the reason he remained in Hollywood while his New York apartment gathered dust was to earn a living for his two motherless children, Nora, eighteen, and Walt, sixteen. In a letter to us, written before he signed the contract for the Boone television show, he said:

I am tired and miserable and my soul and all of its works follow behind two children and their needs; and, as much as I love them, resentments flare in me, resistances that prevent me fulfilling their needs properly. All of my plans to be working by now on the first and even second of a series of new plays have gone awry. And, willing to drudge for the mere living of it, I am unable at present to even find a movie job. . . . I am seething and swollen, lumpy, disordered and baffled, as if I were a woman 15 months' pregnant and unable to sleep or turn, crying aloud, "Oh, God, out, out!"

And in another:

When I think of the plays (so urgent inwardly) that I have written only in my head, instead of "sending" them, I shiverrr! . . . It is, of course, the *inner* climate that is bad; the rose bush below does not compensate for the bars on the window above. Secretly, however, with the aid of stealth and time, the bars are only an illusion now, for in many a perspiring night I have filed the bars thru and they hold together only by filaments of metal, waiting for one shove from me.

Friends, helplessly watching his misery and lack of productivity, knew there was something genuine and yet profoundly self-deceiving in his conviction that his long "tour of maternity," as he called it, was the sole reason he was not now writing plays.

By this time Odets had been forced to dispense with the luxury of a housekeeper and expected his now adolescent children to assume almost all the domestic responsibilities; he felt himself to be a "harsh old lunatic" of whom Nora and Walt were in mortal terror, and whose long lists of chores they both tried to evade.

The Beverly Drive house, accordingly, was a chaos, especially the living room. Before he had accepted the television job, Odets had puttered away anxious hours with his "hundreds of masterwork records drowning the piano top and spilling into chairs, a thousand books overflowing the shelves onto tabletops and floors, and everywhere scraps of notepaper overrun by his handscript, jottings to himself in red ink about fictional characters, the conduct of life, women, art and artists, childhood and fatherhood, his own nature and unsent letters, usually irate."

On the dining-room table stood teetering piles of magazines—the accumulation of thirty subscriptions ranging from *Life* to *Art News* and including *I. F. Stone's Weekly* and a technical journal, *Psychiatry*. There, too, were hundreds of stamp albums and loose stamps and catalogues from art galleries and from mail-order houses for cheap tobacco and detective stories, bags of freshly minted coins and crisp, new hundred-dollar bills hidden in books. Here also lay numerous drafts of the *Golden Boy* libretto, all so far unacceptable to the producer.

In the kitchen, on the sink stood a dozen half-emptied bottles of Médoc 1957; on the table, half-empty boxes of brown cigarillos and mail unopened for weeks. Here and there were scrubbed stains from the droppings of a wildly unhappy black standard poodle named Benjy and his competitor, a cat called Tiger Odets, the fourth and fifth members of the immediate family.

As his fifty-seventh birthday approached, Odets found he could no longer quiet a gastric distress of three and a half years' duration with his customary little white pills. His revered Beethoven had died in his fifty-seventh year, and so Odets finally decided on a secret visit to his family physician, who told him only that further studies would have to be carried out in a hospital.

Directly following his medical consultation, and without mentioning his illness, Odets astonished his beloved friends Jean and Dido Renoir by interrupting his ascetic work routine to give, with his children's help, what Renoir later called a "fairyland dinner" for them alone, in the unused garden beside the unused swimming pool. Delicate Japanese lanterns were strung in the garden, and wires hidden among the trees produced Mozart concerti to accompany the delicious food he himself had cooked and the 1953 Château Lascombes wine. This "Watteau evening," as the Renoirs described it—Odets' last dinner party—took place on July 14 (Bastille Day), a month to the day before he died, and four days before his fifty-seventh birthday. Only in retrospect were the Renoirs struck by the fact that he ate almost nothing and that he noted in wonder their own healthy appetites. Film-maker Jean Renoir recalled also how much Odets talked that evening about Renoir's father, Auguste, and how closely—almost relentlessly—he questioned him about old Renoir's capacity to paint to the end of his life despite a crippled hand. He appeared obsessed with the issue of how an artist maintains his work potency, and awed by the great painter's stubbornness. To Jean Renoir there seemed to be a self-disgust in Odets' reverence and wonder at Auguste Renoir's productivity in his life's final stage.

During the ensuing week Odets began to send communiqués to friends and relatives, telling them all that they might read in the papers that he was in a hospital, but it was just a matter of "dreary routines" and not alarming. To his daughter, Nora, vacationing in the East, he wrote that "the cat is eating very well. . . . My tummy still hurts so today I will be going for some x-rays and checkups. Don't worry about it, because it is nothing very serious. . . . You will hear from me again as soon as there is any news about all of these little items." It struck his son,

Walt, as odd that his father's note said he'd be gone only a few days, yet tucked into the envelope was a new hundred-dollar bill.

On the weekend before he went into the Cedars of Lebanon Hospital, he took to his bed. An old friend stopped in to see him and found that "Clifford had the whole ashen, grey thing in the face. I thought, 'the mark of death is upon him.'"

Odets called his producer at the Metro-Goldwyn-Mayer studio, where the television shows were being filmed, to say he had "some sort of belly-ache . . . colitis or something" and would not be in to work for a while.

On July 31 the exploratory surgery revealed that the primary site of what the Greeks called "the eating disease" was in the bowel, but that there were already extensive metastases to the stomach; neither the surgeon nor the family physician was surprised, as the five quarts of abdominal fluid withdrawn earlier had been teeming with alien cells. It was shortly after the surgery that the thirst commenced. He asked for his favorite Brouard la Rose 1955, interchanging it with apple juice and lemon tea. It should be stated as fact and symbol that he enjoyed with equal extravagance all of these drinks, which he called "ambrosia," but that he derived from them no sustenance.

The pace and concentration with which Odets now moved, physiologically and psychologically, until he became unconscious twelve days later were amazing. Although death is never a credible event, "this mountain blown to dust in two weeks," as his son put it, was overwhelming. His prolific activity seemed geared to maintaining as intensely as possible, with the aid of his special-duty nurses or of any woman he could draft, his hold on meaningful experience, on life itself. He dreaded, however, being left alone with this task.

Odets' absorption in his sensations and his frantic necessity to "make aesthetic order" of them impressed all the doctors and nurses. One recalled his extravagance about a patch of brilliant blue sky; another his grateful delight, indeed, his "ecstasy" in the "tiny, golden drops" of urine which now he was able only on rare occasions to produce without catheterization.

He was much preoccupied with the bouquets of flowers which arrived, insisting that the "sincere" ones be put where he could see, touch, and smell them, sending off immediately to another patient a yard-long carnation display from film actor Cary Grant which he labeled "phony." Often after inhaling long drafts of a bouquet he would take it apart, flower by flower, petal by petal, admiring in exquisite detail the scattered bright colors. He had performed this precise activity on a bed of white phlox in an impulsive attack thirty years earlier, and in a screenplay he wrote later had assigned this same symbolic performance to a young woman who was destroying herself. Sometimes he would shower his bare chest with the petals, like a child playing with leaves. And day after day he carried to his nostrils with his long fingers plump lemons grown for him by the Renoirs in their garden.

It was not enough for Odets simply to cling to the raw experience of these days. With the thrust of an artist, he tried to master it by expressing and recording it as well. His nurses were impressed into service to write out long memoranda he would dictate about himself, his family, his dreams, about a woman he felt he had wronged many years earlier, his observations on the psychosomatic aspects of his illness, and outlines for projected plays. Sometimes he tried to write these out himself on scraps of paper in barely decipherable hieroglyphs. Clinging to an artist's central lifeline for achieving wholeness, he steadily tried to provide esthetic form for his increasingly chaotic impressions, cataloguing as art works the people in his immediate world: one became "a Vermeer," and another "a Manet"; his doctor became "Joseph, son of Jacob," and the nurse a fairy-tale character.

Some of his impressions were more sinister, even terrifying. He whispered to his secretary, in words almost identical with those he had earlier used to describe his sense of being jailed in Hollywood, though humorless now, that he was "gripped by the feeling I have been kidnapped and am being held a prisoner here in the hospital," begging her to report this intelligence to his doctor, and to be on twenty-four-hour call for a rescue operation. This budding delusion disappeared quickly, only to return irreversibly later.

He could not rid himself of the conviction that there was great—perhaps mortal—hazard for him in his attention to his most minute feelings, most particularly in what he experienced as "the steady bliss" of the merging of himself and "the object." Finally he insisted that his former psychoanalyst fly out from New York at once because "she knows what's wrong with me, and unless we can work it out, this fascination with my own sensations may prove fatal."

Meanwhile, with the grace and style of a prince, Odets held court daily from his hospital bed, screening his visitors carefully. He gave his secretary, Virginia Rowe, a list of friends, scattered all over the world, whom he wanted to see or to phone—most of them talented, moneyed, and celebrated, a stellar array of theatrical royalty as well as family and old friends: the Jean Renoirs, Lee and Paula Strasberg, Harold Clurman, Elia Kazan, Marlon Brando, Shirley MacLaine, Cary Grant, Danny Kaye, Edie Adams, Kim Stanley, Lee J. Cobb, the author and her husband, Daniel Mann, Edith Mayer Goetz and her husband, William. It was Rowe's impression that Odets, with the awesome mood swings of the dying, held to the belief that these powerful, successful people provided a magical safeguard against death, but realized at the same time that he was saying his goodbyes. On occasion he made passionate accusations of neglect, sending to latecomers Edie Adams and Shirley MacLaine the petulant message, "How come you do me like you do do do?" Some—like Cary Grant, whom he now dubbed "Mr. Hollywood"—he punished; he often sent Grant away without seeing him, saying to the nurse, "I don't really know why I want *any* of them here."

He debated asking the Goetzes to bring along their close friend Frank Sinatra, whom Odets was then suing for breach of contract, wistfully fantasizing that if he and Sinatra were still friendly, "Frankie would see to it that I had anything I needed." Finally he decided not to send for Sinatra, and requested instead his dentist and confidant, William Goodley.

He asked for a hand mirror to ready himself for his guests. Each day, before any was permitted entrance, he would put in his dentures and carefully comb his graying halo of curly hair. Once, confronting his image appraisingly, he murmured to the nurse that he appeared to himself "after all, a distinguished man." She wondered if Odets had ever been on the stage, so impressed was she by his capacity to alter his face and voice for visitors, depending on how long he wanted them to stay and what emotional transaction he was planning. He would "go faint and weak if it were someone he didn't like. . . . Even in X-ray he kept performing and, somehow, name-dropping. . . ."

Jack Adler, Odets' "adopted brother," loyal jester and retainer, son of the great Jewish tragedian Jacob Adler, had stationed himself in the corridor to carry out the necessary legwork. He exchanged obscene jokes with Odets, kept him supplied with cracked ice, ran odd errands, and listened to him with maternal patience. Jay, as he was called, was one of the few persons of whose tolerance and devotion Odets was enduringly certain; on occasion Odets even permitted Adler to see him weep in desperation.

Odets asked Jay to talk about his great theatrical family and of the days when Jacob Adler owned a theatre on Second Avenue in "little old New York." It astonished and fascinated Odets that Jay, like Renoir, could talk so devotedly about his own father. Jay applied himself earnestly to the task of diverting him until he was no longer conscious: "A few days before he died, he asked me to bring in a young, fresh, gorgeous Irish girl named Betty. He just wanted to look at her. So I did." Jay added, "He tried to place me in a job even while he was dying; he called someone from the hospital. And I told Clifford, 'If you have a real job for me on the Boone show, okay, but I don't want just to be put on a payroll.'" Jay was aware that during these two weeks Odets had pressed money loans on some needy people who had come to say goodbye.

Among the steady visitors, some invited, some not, was the inevitable corps of personnel which mushrooms from the business side of the life of any contemporary artist: managers, lawyers, agents, each with his insistent task. One, protecting himself, wanted to be certain a "proper will" was drawn up, another was eager to collect a commission in advance, a third sought his signature to guarantee the priority of a debt claim, a fourth had a plan to reduce the estate taxes. Odets, to the nurses, referred to these callers as "the vultures." On one occasion, having struggled unsuccessfully with the problem of how to turn his dwindling collection of paintings and stamps into liquid assets for his children, Odets fell back exhausted on his pillow, saying, "Tell them I did the best I could."

Marlon Brando—an actor whose talent Odets felt was equaled only by that of his old friend Charles Chaplin, and for whom he had hoped to write a movie life of Beethoven—recalled his final visit:

I never knew what I meant to Clifford. To me, he *was* the thirties. I liked him because he was a wild man; even when he talked about the price of bottle tops, his eyes would flash. Clifford said life was a "one hand any way"—that's a term in weight-lifting where you get yourself off the ground in any way you can manage. I think he knew he was dying, and he knew I knew it. He didn't seem frightened, made many bitter, sardonic jokes, said once, "Life is about shitting in a towel." He was leaking from all parts of his body, his life running out in ugly fluids. The male nurse, who was imitating brightness, asked him lightly, "Do you want more apple juice?" Clifford couldn't stand his manner and flared at him. It was as if he were saying, "Look, don't interrupt me when I'm dying." . . . He *tried* to clarify [the meaning of life] right to the end, and *that's* the meaning of his life and death. He was a wild man and a noble man.

On August 10 Odets sent for his longtime friend Edith Mayer Goetz, daughter of the legendary Hollywood magnate Louis B. Mayer, a standard model for American writers creating a character to represent the triumph of the energetic drive in the illiterate American immigrant toward the realization of the American Dream. She came alone and was shown in by Danny Kaye, who warned her to "be strong." Odets went straight to the heart of his interview: "Danny, do you know her courage? Do you know how *she* stood up to *her* father and made a great life for herself and her husband?" Now, with astonishing vivacity, he enacted the complex and moving story of Edith Goetz's sticking to her guns with her husband against her father, a conservative Jewish Republican, during Adlai Stevenson's presidential campaign.

August 10 was to be his last consistently fierce, lucid, and desperately seeking day, a day in which his relentless activity never flagged. He left messages such as "Tell the Gibsons I love them and I know they love me." He put in a transatlantic call to Kim Stanley, then acting in a film in London. She recalled, "He was very articulate that night. He said, 'You know all those plays I told you I was going to write? I can't write them now because I'm dying.' " Miss Stanley, troubled by a guilty sense that she should have left her work and flown to California, later concluded that "I can't escape the feeling that he willed himself to die."

Odets then telephoned actress-singer Edie Adams at the *Today* television show in New York. The young widow of comedian-writer Ernie Kovacs felt she owed a great debt to Odets for his support after her husband's death. After talking to him, she knew he'd made up his mind to die: "He made all kinds of 'final' statements . . . like 'I really blew it, but you've got it all, don't waste it!' "

All of Odets' frenzied note-making, dictating, and final interviewing of celebrities and old friends and relatives became insignificant as he gathered his energies for his last two projects, one of which appeared to everyone natural, the other quite mad. The first was a desperate attempt at a "reconciliation" with his father, from whom he had been bitterly estranged for seven years. The second was a plan to save his life by marrying his former psychoanalyst; by telephone he implored her to fly to Los Angeles—which, without delay, she did.

Harold Clurman and Elia Kazan, veterans with Odets of the celebrated Group Theatre, had also flown to Los Angeles that morning. Before they came into his room at seven o'clock on this hot Saturday morning, Odets, according to his nurse, fluffed up his hair and straightened his gown, saying, "Don't let them stay long; I'm very tired." Clurman involuntarily began to weep when he saw him; Kazan was shocked by his appearance, even awestruck. Odets reached out, patted them, and said, "Don't talk—I'll do all the talking," and then he talked for many hours. Kazan recalled:

> When I went to his bedside I was shocked. His face had collapsed, the lower half of it, that is. His eyes still "stared," but they were a little glazed, too. His nose seemed sharper. "Gadg, I have the impression that all these visitors are being brought in here in an effort to divert me from the fact that I am dying." Cliff's head seemed to have shrunk. The quality of his face had changed. The softness and "poetry" had gone out of it. In the terrible swift final struggle, who can be or look anything but a wild animal fighting for his life? Whenever he dropped off into a barbiturate sleep, he'd pull himself out. Finally the moment came for him to tell Harold and myself what was on his mind: "I want to marry my psychoanalyst. I am *going* to marry her. Now you know what it is that's really in my thoughts. . . . I want some milk chilled, and some buttermilk chilled!!"—that very imperious to the nurse. Eight small cartons of milk and buttermilk were brought in. Cliff: "How do I feel? Dry and weak. No strength. No strength. Look at the shape of my lower leg!" He was always proud of it. "Don't let them see my birdie," to the nurse changing his sheets. "The taste of milk. The first thing you taste. There wasn't much bad about me. Maybe if there had been more bad about me, I would have written

those plays." Something was trying to carry him off and he was pulling himself back "in." He didn't want to pass out. "Death makes you
horny . . . I want to marry Dr. L."

The Renoirs arrived for their daily visit while Clurman and Kazan were
there. Kazan found Renoir to be

the most impressive figure of all his visitors. He was truly moved,
deeply and simply. He stood at Cliff's bedside, slightly stooped, a
bulky man like a big loaf of peasant bread. His concentration on Cliff
and his experience with Cliff was total. He bent over and kissed Cliff's
hand. He stayed another few seconds after his wife left, holding and
pressing Cliff's hand, and then bent over again, paying tribute to his
passing friend and, as Clurman said, also paying tribute to death.

Later Renoir recalled this day and Odets' extraordinary discourse on
the importance of "the detail" in art and in life. Struggling to find a way
to join his parched lips with some ice water in a glass, Odets showed
Renoir each detail of his maneuvers with a straw that at first would not
bend, until a few drops of the cold liquid finally ascended into his mouth.
Renoir recalled:

I watched this struggle as if he were involved in the most epic of undertakings . . . a detail. We talked of the unimportance of general
ideas and how they are contained inside the detail. Since then it has
become a kind of rule for me. His expression was of a man thinking
of profound things . . . of creation. He talked more of his *observations* of his Tante Esther and his Uncle Israel than of his work as
such. We spoke of how the making doesn't follow the conception
. . . no, they both happen together.

Clurman found him on this day

tying final knots . . . telling sharp, clear, dirty jokes. He kept repeating how good it is to have good friends like Lee, Gadg, and
Harold. "Harold knows more about my plays than anyone in the
world," or "Very foolish of you, Harold, for you to stick with Stella,
but something very good about it, too."

When Lee Strasberg, another old colleague from Group Theatre times,
flew in the next day, he knew that "it wouldn't last long." Odets repeated
several times that he was having a "life mask" made. The first time he
used the word "death," according to Strasberg, was in great bewilderment,
his hands out in a helpless palms-up gesture, saying, "How can Clifford
Odets die?" Continuing then, "Lee, my friend, give me a word for God,"
he motioned Paula Strasberg out of the room. Now euphoric, he said in a
half-whisper, "The juices are running through me. . . . I taste more."
Strasberg was moved and astonished. He said, "He kept wanting to
taste me. Then he'd sing and say, 'I'm wandering, I'm wandering.' This
is the first time I ever saw a person who seemed to know he was dying
. . . but it appeared as a terrific adventure. The emotion was excitement."
Sometimes Odets would yell, and then he would resume singing in
precisely the same manner as his Uncle Israel Rossman—the model for
Noah in *The Flowering Peach*—had done on *his* deathbed.

Odets' psychoanalyst arrived after Kazan and Clurman had gone to
lunch. Kazan described the scene on their return:

When we entered the room, there was a woman sitting at Cliff's
bedside. He was bent over, as much as he could, towards her, and

talking to her intently, his face charged with energy and fanatical desire. He looked like he was paying *frantic court* to someone. This went on for a moment before Cliff saw us. When he did, the woman also did. She rose and faced us. It was Dr. L., his psychoanalyst. Cliff was clearly supplicating her to marry him. He said, raising one hand in a dismissing gesture, "I'll say goodbye to you fellows now." We said goodbye and left. His face had been fierce, intent, not to be denied. His dismissal was curt and final and also not to be denied. We didn't demur. We left. That was the last time I saw Cliff. I suppose this was the last act of his life.

This unsuccessful suit, motivated by a wish to live and at the same time to leave a woman an imperishable legacy of guilt, was almost, but not quite, the last act of his life. The reconciliation with his father was steadily on his mind. One of Odets' sisters, knowing the gravity of his condition, had telephoned their father to suggest that, in view of the long alienation between him and his son, perhaps he should not visit the hospital. In the meantime, however, Odets had asked his doctor to phone his father, and the old man now came daily for passionate, ambivalent exchanges which occasionally overflowed into something desperately full of mutual promise.

Odets, in one of his many hieroglyph notes, wrote resentfully of his passive following of his father's "beat" in these sessions. Close upon this he has written as single words: "loathing," "anguished," and "angered." He told the young nurse, "I hate to say this, but I just can't stand him— my writing supports him and he didn't want me to be a writer." And to this same nurse Louis J. Odets spoke of his son's irresponsible youth, and how he had not followed his father's good advice: "He doesn't believe in God . . . used to get drunk as a boy and didn't make a penny until he was twenty-nine." He repeated his son's comment: "L.J., you're an old man! I didn't realize how old," then exclaiming, "But *he's* the old man, not me. *He's* older than *I* am!" She thought it was appalling that the two of them could still compete and fight under those conditions.

But there was quite another current flowing in this final transaction with his father: Odets told his secretary with high satisfaction that there was "good news" in the fact that he and his father were "making up," and that he had never really tried hard enough to understand L.J. He confided to his nurse that he could wish for a similar coming together between himself and his own son, but feared he had already made too many mistakes. He wondered whether he should have reared him more "as a Jew," and expressed envy of Shirley MacLaine's belief in God. Walt Whitman Odets knew of his father's concern about their mutual alienation and tried several times to reach him because, as he then told a family friend, "in recent months my father has come to think I *dislike* him . . . but every time I've gone to see him, he's been asleep."

On the one occasion when he was awake, Odets told his son, "I have had enough of beautiful, dopey women; when I get out of here, I am going to marry my psychoanalyst." The sixteen-year-old boy was mystified by this plan. He wanted to go more often to the hospital, as he, too, felt there was a mountain of "unfinished business" between himself and his father.

As his condition worsened, Odets became convinced the nurses were trying to poison him; when he grew unmanageable, the decision was made to give him massive doses of sedation instead of using mechanical restraints. Now he lay unconscious and unmoving, his face illegible, a damp cloth over his eyes obscuring his large, balding brow. He no longer called imperiously for his apple juice, his lemons, his buttermilk, his ice cream, or his reassuring court. Although the biological struggle continued another two days, the human struggle was over.

The public and the private responses to Odets' death were in curious contrast. The obituary notices adopted a variety of tones, some casually contemptuous, others faintly accusatory; *Time,* whose cover had immortalized him in 1938, dismissed his death with a few tasteless lines. Those publications which were above making a bad joke at a dead writer's expense offered a listless and stereotyped summary: A man of great early promise, having ridden a wave of social consciousness in the thirties, had sold out to the fleshpots of Hollywood. *The New York Times,* after listing most of Odets' ten full-length plays and five one-acters, concluded that "the artistic potential everyone expected to materialize was somehow never quite fulfilled." Almost all of them commented that in the thirties Odets had seemed the most promising playwright "since the flaming emergence of Eugene O'Neill." A man whose plays had been translated into nearly every known tongue, one of the few eminences in the Great Plains of American drama, was reduced to ash at Forest Lawn Cemetery in Los Angeles in a public atmosphere of casual journalistic quarter-truths, most of them shallow and devoid of historical perspective.

But the private responses were intense and peculiarly fresh, ranging from grief to bitterness. Alfred Kazin, one of America's leading critics, and his wife, novelist Ann Birstein, neither of whom had known Odets, confessed they had wept all day after hearing he had died. Zero Mostel, whose successful career had been seriously jeopardized by the blacklist resulting from the House Un-American Activities Committee witch hunts, expressed, with considerable passion and pain, the opinion that Odets had been one of America's great artists whose testimony before the House Un-American Activities Committee, in May 1952, had ended his creative capacity. Even grievers who were remote from the experience of political betrayal expressed a diffuse and elusive sense of having been betrayed. Elia Kazan said he could have forgiven Clifford anything except the grievous waste of his time and talent in writing films, for which activity he had scolded him almost to the day he died. Goldie Bromberg, widow of the actor J. Edward Bromberg, called it "a matter of self-preservation" not to talk about him at all. Kim Stanley said, "The death of Clifford Odets dictates a reexamination of my whole life—I don't know why."

In grievers and accusers alike there was a unanimity that America had lost not only a playwright of preeminent stature, but one whose personal force had polarized passions of mysteriously high intensity.

Odets himself had ventured a judgment in his diary two years before his death: "I may well be not only the foremost playwright manqué of our time but of all time. I do not believe a dozen playwrights in history had my natural endowment. . . . Perhaps it is not too late. . . . "

PART ONE

Soilbed and Seed

1890-1923

Chapter One

THEY hadn't known it, these Eastern European Jews, but each of them, pondering the momentous decision to leave the native country, was only a tiny drop in what became the Third Wave of Jews in Philadelphia. They were different in physique, culture, and class from the English Jews (the First Wave) and the German Jews (the Second Wave), both of whom, safely established in the City of Brotherly Love, were, in the main, hostile to these Jewish brethren. Not only did the newcomers threaten the status of those who had preceded them, but they were arriving in too great a number. Indeed, the Third Wave of immigrants to the United States made this the greatest mass immigration in all history.

Homeless and frightened, the Eastern European Jews had to manage their fear, their sense of isolation, estrangement, and rejection. Most were in dread of ridicule. Daily crucial decisions had to be made: what to call oneself, whether to speak Yiddish, German, Russian, or English, which neighborhood to live in, what songs to sing in public (even in private), what to read, whom to court, how to dress, how to cut one's hair, what foods to eat, and which, if any, of the 613 commandments to follow.

Should one imitate the Philadelphia establishment's Anglican-Church Jews, intermarry, take on the coloration of the new landscape and safely disappear into it, or, winding the ancient leather phylacteries around one's body in prayer, join battalions of disinherited brethren who were looking forward to "next year in Jerusalem"? If the latter, might this not lead to a new ghetto? But must a choice be made in this free land? Were there not German Jews in Philadelphia who were 32nd-degree Masons and who nonetheless prayed visibly at the most exclusive synagogue and were admitted to the Mercantile Club and to the golf links of the Philmont Country Club near Jenkintown? Perhaps one could remain a Jew, but of a certain kind.◖

Wholesale name-surgery—the simplest form of self-mutilation in the service of becoming American—was common in this Third Wave: Favoshenko became first Fabush and then Phillips; Rabinowitz, Robbins; Goldstein, Galdston; Horowitz, Harris; Cohen, Conn; Kaplan, Copland; and Russman, Ross.

Nose-surgery came later, with affluence. Some refused all such transformations as demeaning and hurried to build an extension of their immediate families in the form of the *landsmanshaft* (fellow-countryman's lodge) with other Ukrainian, Polish, Romanian, Galician, Austrian, or Lithuanian Jews, preferably all from the same town. The monthly dues, a considerable sacrifice, insured them against collective identity-dissolution and provided them with the more tangible benefits of legal advice, medical help, and, ultimately, burial plots. At the meetings they could talk about their past and of "America, America" or of *"Americhka, goniff"* (America, thief).

Among the Jews in this Third Wave to America were four who came to Philadelphia, "typical, typical, so typical," as Clifford Odets later said, and yet each quite different from the others: the two sisters named Esther and Pearl Geisinger and the two young men who would marry them. These four figures would re-echo through Odets' work from his first play to his last.

In Romania—often called "Austria" by the Geisingers—the two Geisinger girls had been part of a large, desperately poor family of peasants; twenty-eight children, most of them dead young from tuberculosis, were the issue of two marriages. Esther—to become Odets' beloved "Tante" (Aunt)—the eldest of the second marriage, was tall, carried herself like her Biblical namesake, was highhanded, and cursed "like a man." Pearl—to become his mother—the youngest, a vulnerable wisp of a girl with a chronic cough, was spoiled by her gaunt mother, who would secretly give her the giblets on the rare occasions when there was a chicken. There was something refined, dainty, and elegant about Pearl; even her small bones set her off from the rest of the children.

At seven, her mother had sent her to live with a well-to-do family where, in return for domestic work, she was to be fed and given the opportunity to learn to read and write. She had wept and refused to go; her mother, in the ancient Jewish esteem for literacy, had insisted because Pearl was so quick with words. But after a few weeks, her yearning for home unbearable, Pearl had slipped away from the grand house at night

◖ 1.1; this symbol refers the reader to the numbered "Notes and Comment" section, which appears at the back of the book.

and walked "for miles and miles, across a river and through a woods," running at last to her mother's arms. She could not be forced to return to the rich family.

Some think that her melancholy, stubbornness, shyness, and self-pity as an abandoned and grieving child began at this time. To her family she seemed dreamy, withdrawn, undemonstrative. Occasionally she was so sensitive to criticism that she would erupt in an outburst of temper. She turned increasingly to her straightforward, foul-mouthed, generous sister Esther, who made the decision to seek a new beginning in "Uncle Sam's golden land" and to take her baby sister with her. Esther thought she would send later for the rest, a pattern in this Third Wave.

Thus, at the turn of the century, these two, aged sixteen and eight, took the long trip in the evil-smelling steerage of a small vessel. Pearl's cough had become worse, the only symptom of the disease carried by so many of the "consumptive Geisingers." Esther was concerned that her little sister might fail the medical inspection on arrival and would, like many immigrants, be deported, but both sisters passed.

Resourceful, increasingly irritable and brash, Esther, who had never learned to read or write in any language, promptly got a job in a Philadelphia stocking factory; but the pay for this unskilled work was so meager that she soon commandeered Pearl to work there, too, interrupting her study of English. Pearl never forgave Esther, but money had to be accumulated for their mother, Freda, newly widowed, to come to America. Freda was "passed" by the receiving doctors, but was dead of tuberculosis, called "the white plague," four months after her arrival. She was thirty-five, a young death even then. Within a few years, with the need for labor in the United States now less urgent and the Great War beginning, the immigration gates would close to such "tempest-tossed" as the tubercular Freda Geisinger: illiterates, consumptives, and the indigent would be more strictly weeded out and sent back to Europe, steadily widening the gap between American idealism and everyday practicality.

Now orphaned, both girls were pleased when Esther received a proposal of marriage. It came from a strange, somewhat daffy, trigger-tempered young Russian Jew called Sroul (Israel) Rossman. Shorter than the queenly Esther, he had bright orange-red hair and green eyes "like a Cossack" (odd in a Jew), a tendency to bellow maniacally when excited or under the influence of schnapps, a strong streak of defiance and idealistic impracticality, and, most important, a beautiful singing voice. The rest of his family had already wandered away to become Richmans or Rosses in Boston. When Sroul agreed to house her little sister Pearl as part of the bargain, Esther married him.

They moved into a flat in a sunless red-brick "row house" at 207 George Street, one of the narrow, three-story, attached buildings in the Jewish neighborhood. It had a "storefront," which made it uglier than the others, but they hung a curtain over the large window, using the store itself as a bedroom. In their new home they were within walking distance of the State House (called by tourists Independence Hall), a reminder of the years when Philadelphia had been the proud capital of the newly independent colonies; there they could see the famous Liberty Bell, and near the river, where their street crossed American Street, they were in sight of Walt Whitman's Camden.

It was a step up for all three. Reviewing his life fifty years later on the new wire recorder bought by his nephew "the playwright," Odets' Uncle

◀ I.2.

Israel recalled prior days "in deh cheapest and doitiest neighborhood in Philadelphia by deh Mimma Molka [Aunt Molly] . . . slipping in deh same bed wid your uncle . . . nine people in two rooms, and widdout a toilet."

More bitter were the earlier memories of his father crying openly at the thought of having been the first Jew "chased out from his town ven dey put in de law in Russia dat Jews heff to live fifty versts [kilometers] avay from soitain places." His father had been a "big men, six feet tall, and a smaht men, who owned a flour mill . . . a men wid four hosses ov 'is own, four hosses nobody could bought dem! A big donation men . . . a men not to be ashamed . . . but dey gib him notice to move, so ver vill he move? He'll move to 'is fodder's in Shipskiva. But times started to go bed, and der was my liddle sisteh Faigele [Little Bird]. . . . " The decision had thus been precipitously made to flee to America. With "Uncle Sam, the king of the world," life would start afresh. Sroul confided to the wire recorder that he had dreamed of the day when he would learn to read and write; would go to a well-known cantor and study the ritual Hebrew prayers. With his extraordinary voice, he would then become a "chazzen" (cantor) in an "important" synagogue. In the meantime he was peddling fruit to support his bride and her sister.

Unlike some who had apprenticed themselves at home to watchmakers, tailors, shoemakers, ironmongers, he had no "balmaloochah" (craft) other than his gift for singing. His voice would be useful to him as a huckster, and you needed only a cart, a horse, and a two-dollar license. Lacking means for an education, Jews had been going into business this way for hundreds of years. Sroul's brother Kiva urged him to take a job making "bicycle suits" in the Philadelphia factory where he worked, but Sroul said: "Deh machinerry dere, deh noise, you can go outa yer mind dere. Awready I tried it in deh spool factory. Dey used to gib me t'ree dollahs a veek to start at seven and finish at six—I vas a greenhorn. No. Bettah I should be otside, so in a veek's time I gotta pushcaht. I bought it ten bonches benenas for two dollahs, and I'm ringing deh bells and hollerink, 'Benenas, ten cents a dozen, ten cents a dozen!' "

The humiliation in using his beautiful cantor's voice to peddle fruit was minor compared with that inflicted by both the Gentile establishment and the Second Wave, the German Jews. "Big shots—dey'd say, 'You're a Russian Jew, a hatable Jew.' I didn't know vat it means." One Jewish woman called him "a Russian pig" in German, telling him, "The trade never rings the *front* doorbell." When Sroul learned what she had said, he returned the next day and, turning his backside to her, invited her in English to "keess mine ess, pleass."

He spoke wistfully of his failure to become a cantor, saying it was now "too, too late" to take lessons.◖ "If I woulda stahted toity years ago, I'da loin meself good. I'll tell ya duh troot—ya t'ink I like my business? I don't like my business." It would have been good to have become "a second Yossele Rosenblatt," a famous cantor who "refused fifty t'ousand dollahs to shave off his black beard: not even for heff a million vould he do it."

Sroul took comfort in the fact that he had been asked over the years by his produce customers to sing: "Zingt, popele, zingt a bisele. Do us a favor, pliz, zingt. So I stand on deh veggon and sing." And he had acquired his horse, Joe, who, recognizing his voice "a block away," would whinny. The horse Joe, like the rest of the family, would appear in Odets'

◖ I.3.

plays. As Sroul seemed never able to collect from his customers, it was lucky that he had always had in America "a piece of bread . . . a tsibela [little onion], a knubela [little garlic], and a schnoppsela [little whiskey]." He was pleased with his sixty-nine-cent eyeglasses, and "Uncle Sam always gibs you a dollah if you need it in an emoygency . . . Uncle Sam doesn't let ya get losted."

Thus, Sroul Rossman established at 207 George Street one powerful current of values—of independent aspiration, personal integrity, and confidence in Uncle Sam. A significantly different current was introduced by the "wheeler-dealer" Lou—later changed to Louis—Odets, a stocky Russian Jew who would become Clifford's father. Lou, perceived at once by Esther as a real "macher," met Pearl at a neighborhood dance; he had already charmed the neighborhood with his "gift of gab," the latest dance steps, and his "snappy clothes." Esther found him to be suave, ingratiating, calculating, and insatiably vain. Aspiring to become "an important Jewish Elk" in the established B'nai B'rith, he was simultaneously determined to plow under forever his real name and his origins in Eastern Europe; he didn't dress like the rest of the "greenhorns," and his English—which he savored and from which he steadily sloughed off the Russian-Jewish accent —was excellent, if somewhat financial in its idiom ("You look like a half-million bucks in that dress") and marked by "rough, crude sex references." He was energetic, histrionic, enacting everything he said, and talked always "in exclamations." His son's written dialogue would be peppered with this same mark of punctuation.

Esther thought him a "phony show-off—a bullshitter" who was too particular about the crease in his pants "hitting right in the center of his shoe." He acted "like a king pounding on the table if the coffee or the fried matzoth wasn't just right," and he bragged constantly. On the credit side, he "always knew how to put his hands on a dollah, always made a good living." He had a sweet, scholarly father "from a balabatishe family . . . with a beautiful white beard, sort of a goatee," courtly manners, and a "real love for music." This Hebraic old gentleman, whom Odets never saw, would provide a model of ancient spiritual values for him in his life and his work. "But, oh, what a mother, so bossy, so selfish—just like Lou. He was ashamed that she talked with such a heavy Russian-Yiddish accent."

Lou had told Esther that his mother, Zipporah, had never recovered from the swift drop in her station when her husband went bankrupt, but she always "kept up a good front." He often said that "at six I had a governess, and at nine I was selling newspapers on the streets of Philadelphia while my father sold little bags of salt." Zipporah was a handsome woman, "like a queen," who wore her hair in thick braids coiled around her head and took great pride in her appearance. Indeed, the "keeping up of appearances" ("Will that look nice for the neighbors?" she often asked) was a central motive for Zipporah, who to Esther appeared to be the real boss of the family.

Into his ninetieth year of life Lou Odets would boast more of his having become a 32nd-degree Mason, "taken for an Irish-born American," than of his synagogue "donations" and his standing in the Jewish community. Both identities, however—as an American and as a Jew—were important to him. He was not trying to pass as a Gentile. He was intent on sweeping out of his way any obstacle to becoming a "big man." After his mother's death, however, he strictly forbade everyone to visit her grave, lest they see the name on the tombstone. Whenever he was asked what had been the original family name, he would firmly reply, "It has *always* been Odets." A disobedient in-law made a secret visit to the grave and was told threateningly by Lou Odets to "forget it or else." Naturally, the in-law did not keep this secret. The Odets children, however, would never tell their father when they learned of this discovery of their grandmother's grave ("like a skeleton in the closet"), where, carved for posterity on her tombstone, stands the name Zipporah Gorodetsky.* It is a measure of Lou Odets' desperate craving to "belong" in America—a craving internalized by his son—that he went to such extreme and atypical lengths to conceal his original identity even from his own family, and to pretend he was a "born American."◖

Esther remembered the one time Lou Odets' gentle father took a real stand: Lou came home from an amateur boxing match with a black eye, and his father became passionately angry, lecturing him about the impropriety of physical violence in Jews. Lou never mentioned boxing again, but continued to demonstrate his physical power to Esther, Pearl, and young men of the neighborhood; several recalled the brown leather strap he would place around his chest and tear asunder by inhaling. Esther looked on Lou's persistent exhibitionism with concealed admiration and unconcealed contempt.

Esther's disdain—she often called Lou "a hypocrite and a liar"—elicited from him a vindictive rage; many years after her death, still holding her responsible for all their difficulties, he said with obvious satisfaction, "The Good Lord punished her; he kept her sick and in pain for several years." He thought her a "bitch on wheels" who taunted him from the beginning as a fraud and then tricked him into marriage by maintaining he had made her sister, the sixteen-year-old Pearl, pregnant.

According to Pearl, it was with considerable misgivings that she married Lou Odets on March 6, 1905. To one close friend she confided that it was because she was already pregnant;† she told another that from the start she had felt imprisoned by him and had been courted simply as a sexual convenience who was never permitted "even to voice an opinion." Years later she would warn her two daughters to delay as long as possible having children lest they, too, be jailed in a bad marriage.

From the outset Lou made it clear to Pearl and to his colleagues at the Curtis Publishing Company, where he was a feeder in the print shop, that he felt himself to be above his job. He was determined "with the help of the Good Lord" to leave not only 207 George Street, where all four now lived, but the Philadelphia ghetto as well. A co-worker at the print shop later said, "While the rest of us were struggling for a foothold, Lou seemed always to have one already. He never feared failure. He thought he knew everything and was always interfering. Some tremendous ego that guy had—but he paid attention to *what* they were setting up in type, and vowed someday he'd have a printing business of his own." Lou enjoyed figures, was good at arithmetic, and was envied by his fellow work-

---

* The Russian-Jewish name Gorodetsky means "urban man." One branch of the family became Gordons, the other Odetses.

◖ 1.4.

† I have found no evidence that this was the case; perhaps there was a miscarriage.

ers for his "elephant-skinned self-confidence." He would often describe how he planned to insert a middle initial in his name someday and become what, all his life, he called "a big man—number one." He wanted to remain a Jew, but of a very specific kind: one who forbids the use of Yiddish in his home, reads only "American" newspapers, spends a fair sum on a social bar mitzvah for his son, and attends synagogue only on the high holidays in the expensive seats.

According to a niece, it vexed him beyond endurance that the girl he'd married was honest to a fault and did not understand the necessity for a certain amount of "hypocrisy in life" in order to make a good impression, to fit in, and to "get someplace in America." He always loved to tell a good story even if he had to trim the facts to fit it. He wanted his wife to "dress up nice and to run here and there like everybody else, but she couldn't, she was too shy." Always attractive to the ladies, Lou, in the niece's words, "found other ways out when Pearl wanted to stay home. But he really shouldn't have flaunted these other ones. That really hurt Pearl a lot, but she turned it all in, never said a word, never raised her voice . . . she just suffered."

There remains something shadowy and romanticized about Odets' mother, Pearl, regarded by some as "nunlike," by others as simply prudish, and by most as a model of sensitivity, good to a fault, always ready to forgive and forget, putting up with too much. But her husband described her as a person with all the faults everyone else attributed to him—"selfish, unfaithful, cold, demanding"—and her son Clifford in his diaries, letters, and plays offers persuasive testimony to her lifelong depression. Her buried anger can be read only in her chronic, demonstrative pain; it erupted only rarely, but, according to her niece, her refusal to fight with her husband exasperated him far more "than if she had hollered at him."

Relatives and former neighbors commented that Lou was always cruel in his philandering and that "it was a cold house, like a bunch of strangers—nobody communicated with anybody." One witness said it must have been a "spiritual crucifixion" for Pearl, adding that if she had not died early, she might have gone mad. Clifford could remember his mother saying often, "I think I will lose my mind."

Pearl's chronic physical illness, "a strict secret" later said by her husband to have been tuberculosis, was a steady source of debilitation; close friends described her as "asthmatic," but they knew her energy level was always low, her skin translucent, and her strength minimal. Excruciatingly lonely, she scrubbed, wept a great deal, stared out of windows, and talked often about death and the peacefulness of cemeteries.

Chapter Two

When I was a boy the whole promise
of American life was contained for
me in Xmas cards which showed a
warm little house snuggled in a snow
scene by night; often little boys and
girls were walking up the path of the
door and carrying bundles of good
things. This represented protection,
a home and hearth, goodness and
comfort, all things which become in-
creasingly more difficult to at-
tain. . . .

CLIFFORD ODETS, *1940*

AFTER not quite eight months of pregnancy, on July 18, 1906, Pearl gave birth to a three-and-a-half-pound boy. When Lou Odets came home for lunch, he found the baby "had slipped out too soon." No one could locate Pearl's doctor, so while a cousin ran for another, Esther worked hard to keep her sister's tiny son alive. Lou noticed that the premature infant had a split lower lip just like his, and that the feet looked flat like his: "the rotten Odets feet." Sixty years later he declared he was the first person to pin a diaper around his son's wrinkled posterior.◖ Lou decided to name the baby Clifford, a name he thought had an elegant ring. As Esther's daughter put it, "You know how it is—when Jews get classy, they *really* get classy."

Odets would later write that "no nightingales fell out of the Philadelphia trees" in honor of his birth; but when he was introduced to the writer Harry Kurnitz's father, he said, "I was born in the same year that Ibsen and Cézanne died." Mr. Kurnitz replied, "So what, so were twenty million Chinamen." Odets' heroes would always be men of the arts, and presumably he hoped that he might have been sent as a replacement for the playwright and the painter.◖

The struggle to keep their fragile firstborn alive promoted harmony between Lou and Pearl briefly. Together they watched with anxiety as he

◖ 2.1.
◖ 2.2.

turned into a "sickly little yellow monkey." When he was a month old, according to Odets, "a lady in a streetcar where my mother was carrying me told my mother that her sister's child had recently died of jaundice; my mother began to cry and my father, he tells me, wanted to hit the informative woman." However, Esther, neglecting a little her own two children, took a firm stand on feeding the little "yellow monkey," and presently he began to gain weight, the jaundice disappeared, and, with it, the détente between Pearl and Lou.

As always in a marriage, the overt arenas of struggle evolved gradually. According to former neighbors, although Lou continued, as a printer at the Curtis Publishing Company, to be "a nice provider," he increasingly expressed his multiple sexual and social dissatisfactions with Pearl by putting her on a small allowance and making her accountable to him for every penny. Often he would delay the allowance for a day or two, and sometimes it would slip his mind entirely. She became a shrewd manager and an indefatigable bargain-shopper who bought towels in the five-and-dime and, despite her chronic exhaustion, plodded for miles in the markets of Philadelphia to find, according to Esther's daughter, the cheapest cuts of meat. Thus she regularly freed a few pennies for her secret cash savings, which she called her "emergency fund." Half a century later her only son, feeling trapped in another prison, would waste hours in a more extravagant bargain-hunting: a simultaneous spending and hoarding of coins, fresh hundred-dollar bills, stamps, and paintings, out of which he established several separate "emergency funds." Pearl early supplied a model as an embattled prisoner who needed to make stealthy escape plans.

"While her husband the king was lying in bed sleeping," says Esther's daughter, Freda Rossman, Pearl would start the fires in the early morning to warm the house for her husband and baby, "shoveling the coal herself." Occasionally she'd grow angry, but there was mainly, as Lee Strasberg later saw it, "a softness, a quietness, and a sensitivity about her . . . an *acceptance* of suffering . . . a knowledge that suffering is the badge of human existence." But the consensus of relatives and friends was that in a quiet way Pearl could be antagonistic, to counter not only Lou's steadily expressed dissatisfactions but also his extramarital adventures. "He would make fun of her and try to shame her into being the kind of wife a 'big man' needed," claimed Freda Rossman. Pearl, in turn, would "go into her shell and not answer him at all for days at a time. He begged her to go places, but she'd never go."

Clifford, who watched or, more often, listened from his bed to these quarrels, would later record in his diary the memory of a despairing sense of impotence, of feeling he should rush to his mother's defense. Yet he was terrified of this juggernaut father whose physical strength, energy, and omniscience he envied and admired. From a file marked "L.J.," to which he kept adding all his life:

He has the insane belief that he must pass on (approve or modify) everything the other person is doing . . . full of petty and exasperating cautions . . . his life is perfect, it would seem, and he wants to

live everybody else's life to perfection for them! He will even caution
you on how to walk down the stairs.

His mother might herself have written the next paragraph:

> I had to fight him every inch of the way, not to be swamped and en-
> gulfed, to stay alive. Much of this struggle had to be done by silent
> resistance, for I was afraid of him and his wild energy, his volubility
> which could be so scathing and sarcastic. . . . Oh God, am I going
> to listen to this again? What I should do and I shouldn't do?

Pearl, Clifford concluded, had decided to become "staunchly silent and
proudly resentful."

To all who watched, it seemed evident, as one cousin declared, that
"Lou loved Lou at all times" and, as his son put it much later, "He always
saw himself as a charming and magnetic man. There was some truth in
it. Uninterrupted, not denied, he could sparkle on and on. But denied
these qualities by outsiders, he would grow depressed and shaky. Denied
them by his family, he would become engorged by indignation and rage.
. . . It was hell!"

Only as Clifford grew into puberty would he become conscious of how
his father's sexual peccadilloes contributed to his mother's pain.

Pearl confided to one close friend that she wanted to leave Lou, but
now that she had Clifford, she was doomed. "Besides," added the friend,
"she hadn't the will power to leave . . . nor anywhere to go. The only way
was to die of pain."

Once, in the house of his own gentle and scholarly father, Lou
shouted scathingly at Pearl that she was "no help," that her clothes
lacked "style," and that she would never know how to entertain a better
class of people than Esther did. Lou himself quotes his own father as
having cried out in horror, "*Ah zoi rett min tsu ah vibe?*" (Does one speak
thus to a wife?) The permanence and inviolability of at least the outer
form of the family, the Jewish family (to become a central theme in
Odets' plays), was a tenet never to be questioned. And so it was that,
despite the escalating war between them—with all its complexities accumulating as internal conflicts in their young son—Lou and Pearl remained husband and wife partly because, as in all human affairs, the
larger sweeps are obscured by the small oscillations of daily existence,
and also because, as Lou Odets said in the eighth decade of his life, "she
was, after all, the mother of my children and a warm body in bed . . .
even if she was no good there."

During these early days when, with eight people sleeping on the floor
in one room, private lives became public, many persons were witness to
Lou's roaring complaints in the small hours of the night that Pearl didn't
give him enough sex and to her whispered replies that her "sickness" had
left her with a weak bladder, making sexual life a constant embarrassment. Her best friend, Ida Mae Levine, recalled taking Pearl and her infant son to a train at three o'clock in the morning. Heartbroken at her
husband's appraisal of a night with her ("I coulda done better for a
quarter," he had said to her), she fled to a relative and remained for
several weeks, returning only when her money ran out.

Debilitated, fearful, and still confiding to Ida Mae her longing for her
dead mother (who had saved bits of chicken for her), Pearl, still in her
teens, wept often, unaware of her anger—with its attendant guilt—that
she had now become the trapped adult provider, the essential link to life
for her delicate, sickly son. Still, as the child grew strong and one day

took his first shaky step to grasp a broomstick held out by Ida Mae Levine, there came "a great joy on Pearl's face." From the start, there was something wrong with Clifford's feet, and he fell a good deal, but it was not anything of consequence.

Pearl watched her girlishly beautiful son's platinum-blond hair become curly, and his immense blue-gray eyes widen in a look of perpetual astonishment which would never leave him. With that curious conviction so often found in the mothers of gifted persons, Pearl told Ida Mae she was certain he would become a very special person, as he always had to find things out for himself. She early observed that her son was one of those rare beings whose gift carries with it the rejection of others' experience, and thus the capacity for fresh sight—a sense of playful wonder conveyed to the rest of us in their works.

Along with his insistence on seeing things his own way, it was evident he was paradoxically developing a strong need to please, even to placate, everyone. He was unusually obedient to Aunt Esther, Uncle Israel, and even to the neighbors, but most of all to his warring parents. The neighbors watched—some with amusement, others with concern—the development of engulfing intimacy between Pearl and Clifford. Deriving no emotional sustenance from her embattled relation to her husband, Pearl willy-nilly was nurturing a double-edged and mutually threatening relation to her son, a relationship that made promises without limit on both sides and carried a reproachful demand, equally without limit. Until Clifford was almost three, she kept his curls long and dressed him in extravagantly feminine lace-trimmed petticoats of a kind which, if they had been gifts from her husband, she would not herself have worn.

Tante Esther's daughter, Freda, thinks Pearl might have been happier with a man like her father, Israel. "He was honest, sang beautiful . . . never wanted to go anywhere . . . had no pretensions. On the other hand, my father wasn't educated and had a terrible accent. Also, by this time Pearl . . . was reading thousands of books in English and speaking without even a little accent." Pearl began early to teach her son how to spell. By the age of two or three he could spell "doll" and "baby."

Unlike either of his parents, Lou also was by now speaking a "real good American English." Exasperated by what he viewed as the vulgarity and ignorance of Esther and Israel ("*She* never lost *her* Jewish accent," he often said with contempt), Lou made the decision to escape the Rossmans and the Philadelphia ghetto in order to "get somewhere" in what he considered the only "real city" of the United States: New York. The move was, however, premature; he was unable to earn a living, and within the year he, his wife, and his small son were back in the same neighborhood, living briefly over a tailor shop near Clifford Street in West Philadelphia. There, according to scribbled notes for an autobiography he never wrote, Clifford Odets became, at age four, "first aware that I am alive, that I exist . . . like a movie shot fading into existence." It was in a small apartment over the tailor shop that water boiling on the two-burner gas stove scalded his arm; and here, too, that he watched boys catch fireflies and "impale them as tie-pins."

Lou's defeat in New York City was all the more intolerable because Esther and Israel had witnessed it. Back in Philadelphia in an ugly frame "porch house" at 510 Master Street, with the Rossmans downstairs and the Odetses upstairs, Lou was determined to tolerate this new exile with his wife's hated sister only until he would see a means to a firmer foothold in New York. There, he boasted, he would one day become a "big man," a man who could afford "silk-pongee shirts, a matched dining-room suite, an apartment with an elevator, and a Maxwell car." He might, he thought, even learn to play golf.

Unlike the Odets family, where Yiddish was rarely spoken and a Jewish newspaper was never seen, the Rossman household was a free-wheeling, lively place filled with Yiddish talk and Yiddish newspapers which, at first, neither Esther nor her husband could read. Freda recalled "lots of people always dropping in, some living with us for a few months if they had no work . . . always good food. Even Lou, much as he hated my mother and was ashamed she told dirty jokes in company and said things like 'sonofabitch'—even he came in for fried matzoth and to hear my prost [common] father sing songs in Hebrew and Yiddish."

Esther, like so many of her untutored sisters from Eastern Europe, learned many dodges to conceal her humiliating illiteracy. She memorized telephone numbers, which she would then pretend to look up in the directory. According to her daughter, it outraged Lou that the illiterate Esther, "who had no class, no style, an ignoramus," had such a strong hold on his son's heart: she was as demonstratively affectionate with Clifford as Pearl was not. Clifford seemed to prefer the Rossmans to his own family, and his Tante Esther referred to him with such frequency and so much pride as "my son" that her daughter chided her for hurting the feelings of her own son, Benny. Both boys were early assigned the task of asking the four traditional questions at the yearly Seder, the Passover feast, held in the Rossman house as a mark more of tradition and of generational continuity than of religious observance. Here Lou, freely mixing the platitudes of piety and business, made frequent reference to the "good Lord" and "his million-dollar promises." It is not certain when he began one of his favorite self-justifications: "The good Lord in Heaven and I are one."

Recalling later the acute anxiety of this time, Odets in his early twenties wrote of this period in West Philadelphia in a letter to an actress he was courting:

Do you remember that Stevenson poem, one of the children's things: "Late in the night——?" I've forgotten it, but the inflections are left in my mind . . . and the thought that it was always a little dreadful to go thru it, especially for a child who had been brought up on "a little brown goblin" under the bed. Oh for the nights when I awoke in the dark and the blood stopped in me for fright, when I was afraid to step off the bed because perhaps one of the goblins would seize me by the ankles. *Somehow I always arrived at my mother's bed safely* [italics mine]. . . . Oh that sharp, all filling dread: it comes back to me now with all the old potency . . . and nothing is lost but that I am bigger and older: the dread has remained. . . . We lived near a brickyard in West Philadelphia then. Trains ran thru it and all sorts of derricks and fallable (ability to fall, in case you'd like to know) things stood around in that brickyard. We children were told that the place was not only tenanted by goblins . . . but that it was overrun, thick, infested with goblins. If one of them caught a child he would immediately tie him to a stake and burn him. That must have been why we children traveled in pairs and trios. . . .

One afternoon we accosted one of the workmen in the yard and put the question to him forwardly and blankly: "Were there or were there not goblins in this particular yard?"

"Were there? Oh yes, dearie me, yes. Only yesterday my son . . . as big as you he was . . . was burned away to an ash."

"Oh," and a sickening feeling, "did you cry, Mister?"

"Did I cry?"—indignation—"Well I guess I did? I cried all night, that's what I did!"

"Well, why did you come to work today?" asks none other than Clifford Odets aged seven.*

And how that question did stump our man. . . . He walked away. But the matter did not end there, for your seven-year-old intellect (in the bud, my dear, in the bud) walked away sorely perplexed. At the dinner table he asked his mother, for the eleventh time, if she could tell why that man would come to work the day after his own son, his own dear sweet little son, had been burned, not to an overdone piece of toast, not to a fritter (corn or apple will do) over-carbonized enough to be rejected, but to an ash, an ordinary ash that would not even be salvaged from a garbage can by some hungry cat.

Even allowing for the retrospectively romanticized self-pity in this account—and the appeal in it—this is a surrealist model of unsupported and intense anxiety in the face of yearning for a united, protective, and reassuring pair of loving parents. It would remain with Odets, in endless nights of insomnia, until he himself was, like the workman's "dear little son," reduced to an unsalvageable ash.

Relatives and neighbors alike, according to Ida Mae Levine, accepted that "Pearl's baby," as Clifford was known, had divine rights very early in life, rights which continued until an event would shatter at the age of four his royal and exclusive status. Until this event Pearl, despite her lack of physical demonstrativeness, catered to her small, bright son as her mother had to her, and steadily taught him to say and to understand increasingly long words. Ida Mae thought there was something odd and extreme both in Pearl's pressure on him to learn and in her maintenance of his long yellow curls and lace petticoats. When Ida Mae finally persuaded her to give them up, they were replaced by velvet Lord Fauntleroy suits, Buster Brown rompers, and bangs.

Odets was able to recall dim images from the time before he was three: "toddling, unsteady on feet," "being on my father's chest" with feelings of "disgust." Then in his ears the mocking childhood jingle reverberating: "Cry-baby lipsy. Suck you mommy's titsy." He would beg to crawl up into Pearl's lap, saying, "Let me lay my head on your chesh [sic]." It was generally observed that he had a constant need for reassurance especially from his mother in physical contact, a contact from which she often drew back.

"Cricker Odex," as a neighbor on Master Street called Clifford, impressed everyone as not only a singularly beautiful child but also an unusually obedient one. Once he was put on a chair and asked to "wait until Mommy comes back" while Pearl lay down with a headache, for-

---

* Probably only five or six, as they had moved to New York by the time he was seven.

getting about the child. When she returned an hour later, there he still sat, not having uttered a sound of complaint. Although such dependent obedience was no doubt a convenience for a sickly and depressed mother, it presaged ill for Cricker's autonomy and self-reliance. His father now took to calling him "Putty."

Odets later wrote that the burden of this relationship lay so heavily on Pearl that "she tried to give me away to a farmer." There is no confirmation of this, and perhaps it was no more than a threat from a mother debilitated by chronic tuberculosis, or a child's fantasy, but there is evidence that in 1910 Pearl tried to enroll her bright boy in kindergarten at the age of four, demonstrating to the teacher how well he could recite poems and spell. He was rejected as too young.

It is clear that, aside from her ambitions for him (maternal pressures to master language are common in the life histories of writers), the critical event which led the exhausted Pearl to the need to "farm out" her son was the arrival of a second child in this same year, a girl whom Lou decided to name Genevieve. Lying now on Pearl's "chesh," instead of Clifford, was this small rival, who in her first year of life contracted a crippling infantile paralysis. Lou was certain she had caught it at the Rossmans', and added this to his list of grievances against Esther. Pearl, whose compulsive cleanliness had earned her the neighborhood title, "Sanitary Pearl," now became obsessed with scrubbing, disinfecting, and purifying. She was determined to keep further disease away from her family. One neighbor thought she was "becoming a little nutty on the subject."

Odets' autobiographical notes mistakenly state: "Gen born 1908, but this completely blank to me." For 1910–11, the period in which Genevieve was actually born, he has written: "Seder. Gordon. Park and Flowers. Girl's leg cut off." His cousin Freda had a dim memory of the children having witnessed a trolley-car accident where a girl's leg might have been amputated, but it is probable that Odets later substituted this screen memory for the actual birth of Genevieve. Half a century later he wrote in his personal notes: "Loneliness is the Anxiety Royal, king of them all. Couple that king with a queen called Jealousy and they spawn the princeling Murder!" And in another entry:

> The earliest image of a thread that makes trouble. At four or five I am forced to button and lace my own shoes and can't. My mother gives no help and is harsh and threatening. Sobbing bitterly, I tie up the shoes. (Shoes, feet, and the baby sister behind me is crippled.) I am helpless and no one helps.

Later he wrote in a letter to the author:

> I realized that when I was four or five, from then on I had a running battle with my mother. (She was 22 when I was five, you hear?) And from her side, too, the battle was joined. She wanted to be consoled; so did I. She was lonely, distressed and aggrieved; so was I. As a child, I expected to be petted, brought in (not cast out), consoled and comforted; and she begrudgingly would do none of these things for me; she was, after all, a child herself, in an unhappy marriage and, actually, was thinking about giving me away to a Pennsylvania farmer and his wife. This battle of who was the aggrieved, of WHO WAS THE POET, went on until she died, when I was 28 (I squirmed plenty over these years but never gave in and was glad (and sorry and sick-sad, too) when my father made pain for her!). And, you

know, it is not over yet. Any autumn will come, and dusk, and when I am one hundred and one, my heart will hurt that when the streets were cold and dark that, entering the house, my mother did not take me in her arms. (She had in her arms, of course, my sister crippled by polio.) No, till the day my mother died, she would say things like, "You'll forget me. You won't take care of me," etc., etc. And I, foolish child, wanted to be taken care of!

Almost half a century after the birth and crippling of his sister, as he struggled in his psychoanalysis to track the origins of his painful disconnectedness, he recalled the strategies he had evolved after her birth to cope with his emptiness, grief, and sense of worthlessness. Failing in making people sorry for what they had done to him, it seemed to him— and this, he thought, had become central to his impulse of art-making— that he had "the uncanny ability to put himself in a mood room and completely abstract himself away from where he was. "Didn't you dream yourself through windows even then? Weren't you always cut off from others, aside, shy, and reticent?" Neighbors confirmed his image of a withdrawn, lonely child. No one could recall seeing Pearl kiss him after Genevieve's illness.

Pearl, beside herself with observable guilt, grief, and probably covert resentment at her new burden, devoted herself now to her crippled daughter with a desperation which, according to neighbors and relatives, left "Cricker" abandoned. Esther's daughter said, "All his life Clifford claimed that Pearl devoted all her time to Genevieve. It was true." Genevieve said, however, that although her mother doubtless had to give her more time, and although she may have been her father's favorite, "Clifford was certainly always Mother's favorite." Ida Mae Levine was of the same opinion.◖ All agreed that Pearl's minimal demonstrativeness toward her son ended with the illness of her baby daughter.

In the year 1912—Clifford was six, Genevieve two—Lou Odets lost his job and, "fed up with that bitch Esther," decided to make another try at the rungs of the golden ladder of New York City; he wrote to the mother of a friend in the Bronx and asked if she could put up a family of four. He would at last become an American by burying his poverty and his Russian-Jewish roots in the dust of the Philadelphia ghetto, and by devoting the rest of his life to "the counterfeits of dignity and the false coinage embodied in his idea of success." Even after the move, however, Pearl made frequent secret visits to her sister in Philadelphia; there her small son absorbed the image of his Uncle Israel, whom as an adult he would identify as one "loved dearly, narrow and illiterate, but to this day, the single most eloquent human being I've ever met." Throughout his life, he, too, would return regularly to this branch of the Philadelphia family as his paradise lost.

Lou Odets—now preferring to be called "Louis" with the French spelling and pronunciation—began an active push toward affluence when he moved his family to 747 Southern Boulevard, then one of the few apartment houses in the quiet, open fields of the Bronx, still running with garter

◖ 2.4.

snakes. He was being swept along by a giant wave of economic expansion in the United States which had bred not only the giant landholders and industrialists celebrated by Theodore Dreiser, but also the body lice of the urban frontier: the gangsters and corrupt politicians of New York's Tammany Hall.

This was a time when the unchecked exploitation of land, forests, and people issued in what historians have seen as the most extraordinary carnival of waste yet recorded in history. In the struggle against such waste, the earliest conservationists came into being, along with a labor movement. Increasingly, legal restraints were applied to the most flagrant predators, a few of whose tenant-evictions were witnessed by young Odets. It astonished him even as a child that "nobody seemed to care that these people had no place to go."

In the presidential election of 1912 one of the million to cast his vote for the socialist Debs—who did seem to care about these evicted people—was Eugene Gladstone O'Neill, then twenty-four, a suicidal habitué (along with a collection of artists, anarchists, and thieves) of a rough bar in Greenwich Village called the Hell Hole. This place was known to Louis Odets through two young neighbors at 747 Southern Boulevard, Louis Rosenberg and Harry Horowitz. He liked to play poker and, after his evening classes in advertising at New York University, "enjoy a good time on Broadway" with these two amiable, small-boned "snappy dressers" and their tiny, good-natured girlfriends, who lived in the same block of flats. On Sundays the two young men and their girls, unsuitably garbed in high-heeled shoes and expensive dresses of gunmetal satin, played baseball in the open lot with some of the other tenants, Lou Odets among them.

Another tenant at "747," the mother of Sibyl Bowman (later, Broadway comedienne Sibyl Bowan), sensed that something was wrong with these tenants—"too many visitors, strange men at all hours"—and suggested to the police that they be dispossessed. But the police confidently told her she must be mistaken. They were carrying out their roles in what Lincoln Steffens called "the system," a loose coalition of New York crooks, policemen, and politicians.

Had it not been for the frequent visits to "747" of Lieutenant Charles Becker, the questionable tenants might have continued to live there. Tammany had granted the "Tenderloin" district to this young police lieutenant as his preserve. Becker had amassed a fortune in payoffs from madams, gamblers, and pimps in this glittering Sodom around Times Square. One independent spirit, a gambler named Herman Rosenthal, refused to "pay off a cop" and was promptly tracked down at Becker's behest. On a sweltering July evening in 1912 Rosenthal was shot through the heart in front of the Hotel Metropole by Lou Odets' well-dressed young card-partners, who, it turned out, were none other than "Gyp the Blood" and "Lefty Louie"—famous at this time, together with "Dago" Frank and "Whitey" Lewis, as "The Four Gunmen." Becker was determined to make of Rosenthal an object lesson in the folly of disobedience to a police officer.

Only now did Pearl become aware of Lou's excursions with the gunmen to the Hell Hole. The children were agog with interest, and although Clifford was only nine when Becker was electrocuted for the gambler's murder, he and his friends listened with fascination as the drama unfolded. The external image of a character for several of his plays, and especially for *Golden Boy*—the coolly detached gangster who, by following a murderous path of self-interest, "wears the best, eats the best, and sleeps the best"—began to take shape here. No one at "747" believed that Lou Odets was involved in anything but the good times of the Four Gunmen;

yet the image of these well-dressed, powerful gangsters and their ladies "in gunmetal satin" became a part of Clifford's fantasy of his own father "going downtown, making good, becoming a big man, and enjoying life."

Most of the tenants believed that Tammany Hall would protect the venal Lieutenant Becker, but they underestimated the dialectic counter-swing of the pendulum of history which had just nominated Woodrow Wilson for president of the United States. Through the efforts of District Attorney Charles Whitman, Odets' neighbor Mrs. Bowman identified Becker as a steady visitor to "747," and, as she put it, "the scandal which ensued became history." According to her daughter, "Mother was threatened that if she testified at Lieutenant Becker's trial, her children would be tarred and feathered, but she didn't scare easily." Thus did Lou Odets lose his silk-shirted poker partners, but he never lost the many lessons these tiny men had taught him of how one proclaims oneself a "big man," down to the solid-gold, three-initialed cufflinks for oneself or the black lace underwear for one's woman. His young son, with the porousness of the potential artist, took in all these details with avidity. District Attorney Whitman learned something, too: that a tide was turning. He was rewarded for this attack on the corrupt "system" by being made governor of New York.

Along with some of the more cynical tenants at "747," Lou did not believe there was anything more than personal rivalry in Whitman's crusade against "the system," and regarded the electrocution of the greedy Becker as cruel and unusual punishment for activities hitherto taken for granted as part of city life.

In a vacant store near the lot where the gangsters had played ball, the children now tried to master and give form to their recent experiences by "playing gangster." Sibyl Bowan believed that although Clifford was too young to have had a starring part in their frequent productions of "Jimmy Valentine"—wherein they would use the toilet as the safe to be cracked—he was doubtless involved in their plays, since he was already, in his sixth year, known at "747" for his talent in "elocution." Some of the time he was simply a member of the captive audience whose mothers had paid the older children a penny to keep the younger ones amused.

Unsure of their powers, these budding thespians would lock the store door until they could bring their lawless drama to a close and their charges back to "747," where they would encounter their neighbors, professionals from Broadway. There was an actress, Emma Dunn, who later went to Hollywood, and "Clinette, the Man in Black," a tall, thin, spellbinding magician-hypnotist whose sleight of hand was so expert that the local merchants were in terror that he would take back, without their knowing it, the money he had just paid for groceries. Clifford was awed and fascinated by these stage celebrities, even by Clinette's wife, a stunning young redhead with a resonant voice who taught diction and whose daughter Juanita later became the "Poetess of Greenwich Village."

The magician-hypnotist and his wife did not go to Hollywood, but were among the earliest to take the quite different path being beaten from the Bronx downtown to Greenwich Village, the low-rent enclave south of the Washington Square Arch, increasingly a refuge and meeting ground for escapees—criminal, political, or esthetic—from the confines of the rising American middle class. There bold men and women were groping in political and esthetic anti-establishment terms toward a realization of Emerson's seventy-five-year-old declaration of cultural independence: ". . . our long apprenticeship to the learning of other lands, draws to a close. The millions, that around us are rushing into life, cannot always be fed on the sere remains of foreign harvests. Events, actions, arise that must be sung, that will sing themselves. . . ."

In "the Village" young Eugene O'Neill was daydreaming of doing what Walt Whitman* had much earlier declared a necessity: "The entire stock in trade of rhyme-talking heroes and heroines must be discarded . . . and the songs of a free people sung." Another Village habitué was Theodore Dreiser, who would cajole one American playwright after another—Odets among them, three decades later—to undertake the heartbreaking task of making a film of his classic *Sister Carrie,* one of the most controversial pieces of indigenous American writing.

Waldo Frank, on whose talk of America Odets would feed in his mid-twenties, was also of this group, as was the strapping Harry Kemp, "hobo poet" and hero of adolescent Americans. Kemp would provide a bridge between O'Neill and Odets by acting in O'Neill's first play† and becoming Odets' first employer. Carl Van Vechten, liberal novelist, who two decades later would regard it a privilege to make photographic portraits of Odets and his bride, nested here along with such as Jack London, the precociously gifted revolutionist John Reed, Sherwood Anderson, Alfred Stieglitz, Max Eastman, and anarchist Emma Goldman. It was an American seedbed for the growth of those concerned with the progressive discard of "rhyme-talking heroes," and for the celebration of a new breed of artist whose carols, as Whitman put it, would be "stronger and haughtier than have ever yet been heard upon earth" and whose "materials of poems shall come from their lives."

Odets, still too young to concern himself with choosing a path to Hollywood, Greenwich Village, or anywhere else, lived in the world of his family and his intense relationships within it. In a nostalgic, wooing, self-conscious letter written later to Philip Moeller, director of Eugene O'Neill's plays—a man he would elect for a time as a mentor—he tries to sort out some of these complexities, in particular the quest for his father:

I was seven and it was early summer. When my family didn't "go away" in July and August, I knew delightful nights "around the block." The streets were crowded with boys and girls; women and men sat on the steps, on boxes, and talked of wonderful things to which children never listened (not that I ever so desired). Stores threw out light into the soft-edged night; people passed in and out to buy things like soda water. Everything was loose and "let go." It was summer and the night was a great mother with a tender face.

* Odets would name his only son after this great American poet.
† A street in Provincetown, Massachusetts, called Harry Kemp Way, commemorates the beginning of American drama in the Provincetown Players, whose chief function was to provide for Eugene O'Neill a professional home.

On Southern Boulevard the big red, open air trolley cars moved. The conductor swung himself along the narrow landing board and pulled on a bell. In the car women and men without coats leaned back indolently after the long hot day. Some people got off at our corner; and if it was some one's father he was greeted with a shout. The wife would look proudly at the neighbors, managing without the use of words to say that this was her man, faithful, loving, strong. Then she would go upstairs to make his supper.

I remember with a hurting joy the many nights that my father came home thusly, long after other men were finished with work. I remember my pride in his sudden appearance and how I quickly informed my mother—if she had not seen him—of his arrival. I was eager for my friends to see him, how intimately we were associated. Now, in this moment, I see how I loved him.

It comes as a revelation to almost everyone who has known Odets that he had ever had any feelings for his father besides terror, contempt, rage, or, at best, amused disdain. To Lou Odets, at the age of ninety, it was no surprise. The bewilderment he felt, rather, as he compulsively reviewed his relation to his famous son, was that sometime, without warning, a dreadful and mysterious chasm had opened and they were not "good buddies any more." It distressed him that no one would believe there was a time when his son not only respected and obeyed him, but also loved, admired, and desperately wanted to please him and be like him. He did not recall—if, indeed, he had ever known it—the erratic, unreliable, and frustrating nature of the bond. The son, on the other hand, wrote:

> The parent is indifferent or harsh with the child. Then, in conscious or unconscious expiation, he asks the child to kiss him and show affection. He really wants the child to tell him or her, the parent, that he is good, but now the child is afraid or indifferent and the parent gets angry and punishes again. An endless chain, with the child very desirous of pleasing, but it can't possibly know what is wanted or needed.

Odets' childhood regard for his father's "looks," his confident savoir-faire, his drive, his ability to make a good impression, and, above all, his formidable power is well documented; in another letter to Moeller he writes:

> My father was ambitious. In that squalid neighborhood he owned the only worldly polish. Everyone respected Lou Odets. He was then twenty-five or six, already a father of two children, handsome and probably, as foreman of a print shop, making a larger salary than all the others in our house, 747 Southern Boulevard, whose bricks I would kiss were they near.

I remember that when my father was late, I sensed a loneliness in my mother. She sat with the neighbors, the Wagners (who never could have children), the Bernsteins, the Beyers, but was only waiting for my father to come home. When he would not be home until very late there was always a feeling of sadness. I went to sleep with darkness in my eyes on those nights. My mother was laconic then, sitting by the window, or perhaps preparing laundry for next day's washing. Intimate friends of hers, Ida Levine, Lily Slatkow—her age, but not yet married—called her "Sanitary Pearl" . . . my mother who was always cleaning her house. Christ! What it stood for to her! The wonderful feeling that must have been in her heart! A husband and a boy and a girl and an apartment on the first floor. . . . "Ye shall lament for the fields of desire."

But most of those nights were glad ones. Around the corner, on 156th Street, my friend Herman and I played a kissing game with Annie and Sarah whose father drank and beat his wife, who once screamed for help so terribly that my father and some other men had to go to her assistance.

In fact it was "Cricker," not Pearl, who awaited Lou with yearning; Pearl now knew why Lou was so often late, and she knew also there was nothing to be done to fill her emptiness—except perhaps to indulge her one "passion" (as her friend Ida Mae called it): go to a movie and eat a treat afterward. These quasi-theatre outings, described by Odets later as brimming with "intake," for the eyes and ears as well as the stomach, were early models for the consolatory pleasures he would evolve:

> The best times of all were when the family would go to see an open air moving picture. As you passed into the theatre an attendant gave you a grass mat to make the wooden bench more comfortable. I remember seeing Clara Kimball Young very often, and Francis X. Bushman in that cinematic *Garden of Allah.* (Summer floods my room, Philip.) The stories of the pictures were nothing: it was the gallantries, the acting that was stirring. I can not remember duplicating the moving picture heroics in my dreams; none of them seemed to have left a deeper impression than that of the moment, or the next day when I might tell friends about what I had seen.
>
> Perhaps, on the way home from the theatre, my mother would stop into Drexler's bakery to buy some cheese cakes, or cream puffs. She did not think that ice cream was good for a boy at so late an hour (she has retained many such medical superstitions to this day), so we seldom stopped at Gottmacher's store which was my entire focus on the way home from Prospect Avenue. In those days ordinary candy stores did not keep ice cream; if they did, the ice cream was of an inferior sort. It remained for a specialized place known as an ice cream parlor to serve the neighborhood wants for such a luxury. . . .
>
> As soon as we arrived home from the theatre—unless, by a fluke, my father had bought a box of the ice cream—I was sent to bed. If we had ice cream I always made mine last as long as was humanly possible. My father took some strange delight in eating his right out of the box, and I often wished that he would change with me. Instead, as if he had noticed my wistful looks—which is what they must have been—he might heap another spoonful of the cream on my saucer.

Photographs of Clifford taken at this time by itinerant photographers show an ash-blond, girlishly delicate boy, large satin bow under his chin.◖

In a list of "what I remember as a child" made by Odets at forty-one for an autobiography, he notes "the magic of what a can was and the beans

◖ 2.6.

in it. Rice and milk. Cocoa. The first coconut pie. The first grapefruit. A plum dumpling." And a later memory of being "an earnest young man of eight at PS 39 playing in a little Greek play, *The Miraculous Pitcher* . . . a tale of a never-ending supply of milk." Neighbors in the Bronx and even Philadelphia who recognized themselves later in his plays said they had always watched how "with his beautiful, large blue eyes Clifford took it all in." One had always felt "he could even see through a wall."

As a steady backdrop to the reports of his special "vision" and his joy in intake stand eyewitness accounts by family, friends, and Odets himself of his sense of impotence in the face of his father's disparagement and his bottomless pride in his father's unusual strength. An example from his letter to Philip Moeller:

> On one particular night, after a picture show, I was told to go to bed. Instead I lingered in the dark dining room, looking pensively out the window. I did not answer when my mother called. "Where can he be?" I heard her ask. She struck a match and upon entering the dining room the match ignited the rope portieres which hung down in place of a door. Instantly they flared up. I stood there as if in a dream and in an instant my father sprang from the kitchen. With one movement he broke in half the pole upon which the ropes were hung and stamped them out under his feet.
>
> I suffered what I thought I did not deserve.* In five minutes the bed embraced me and I had sworn vengeance under my breath. It was distinctly one of the times I thought of dying and of how sorry they would be that I'd been licked for what was not my fault. . . . I knew the bitterness of injustice and vowed to myself that I would not forget the hurt. But slowly I began to think of my father's strength in breaking the pole in two. It didn't seem possible with a pole as thick as my leg. I got out of bed on the pretext of going to the bathroom for biological reasons. There I saw the pole broken in two. It was a marvellous sight, one that I never forgot and for many years it stood as a sign of my father's strength. I told all my friends about it. They in turn told the story to others, appending it with a view of half the pole. It is true that my father was very strong. He boxed and punched a bag inflated with air. He was very proficient with that bag, actually beating out a rhythm with it. But he never knew that his strength gave me a sense of inferiority. He was fond, too, of jestingly saying that I was afraid to fight. The iterated remark was not particularly helpful to my healthy mental growth.

It would take many years—more than for a simpler boy—before he would find, joining with brothers-in-art-and-politics, that under certain conditions he was not "afraid to fight." But his fight would be against the "bitterness of injustice," not in physical combat.◖

Pearl, chronically depressed by her relationship to her husband and exhausted by her tuberculosis, limited most of her maternal care to keeping

---

* Odets' sisters agreed that "Clifford was usually the one to be punished, whether he did it or not."
◖ 2.7.

her son and crippled daughter compulsively clean. She was determined she would have no more babies. Nonetheless, in the spring of 1916, when Clifford was almost ten, there arrived a little girl whom they named Florence. Pearl, in terror of the new polio epidemic, forced all three children to take mammoth doses of cod-liver oil and steadily syringed their ears "to keep the germs out." Lou decided everyone would be safer if they left the "filth of 747" and the rising "gangs of young hooligans." Accordingly, they moved around the corner to 783 Beck Street, twice as tall as "747" and one of the three apartment buildings in the Bronx that boasted an iron-grilled glass door, marble steps, an elevator, and a man to run it. Their apartment on the sixth and topmost floor cost more than the $18 a month they'd been paying, but, according to Lou Odets, they were among "a better class of people"—such as the Millsteins, who had "a colored live-in maid." The James Earles also moved from "747," but to New Jersey, shortly after one of the children had found an dead baby in a garbage can.

Almost half a century later, with an acute sense of the waste of his own life, Odets would file in a drawer marked "Full Length Plays" a note labeled "783 Beck Street":

> The American and dehumanizing myth of the steadily expanding economy. To move into this house was thought a terminal, a mission accomplished. But it became a mere wayside stop on the line and one moved to something higher and bigger. Where does America stop? When does it begin to make homes and sink nourishing roots? Will the best soon (always?) become slums and slag heap?
>
> Perhaps follow the rise and fall of the house by the Odets family moving in and then, several years later (now hating the place!) moving away. Oh, the waste of it all.
>
> The reflection of "social ideals" in the persons of the drama.
>
> And yet hope and growth and optimism should be shown from it all.

In the new neighborhood, with an equal mixture of Jewish and Irish, the two groups were ready, on the smallest provocation, to square off. Epithets new to the boy, like "kike," "sheeny," "Jewsonofabitch," "mick," and "shanty Irish," became part of Odets' everyday life. The reverberations of the impotent vulnerability he felt now, in his tenth year, whenever he walked as far as Springhurst ("the exact feeling of fight or run") would forever remain with him.

For a time he attended a parochial school with these feared and hated "strangers," and there absorbed, in spite of himself, a deep emotional resonance to the Old and the New Testaments.

Nearby, Sholem Aleichem, born Sholom Rabinowitz, was spending the last year of his life, a culture hero—"a Jew among Jews," as the Yiddish phrase has it. Living by the values of "Menschlichkeit" (humanness), he built a direct connection with the readers of a Yiddish newspaper for which he wrote, printing his address on its pages to make certain that "anyone who wished could contact him." Several tenants at 783 Beck Street did so, proudly reporting their correspondence to the others.

The new epidemic brought many European "specialists in polio" to the United States, and one of them, examining six-year-old Genevieve, concluded she would remain crippled for life. Relatives recalled that at this time Lou began, with anger and contempt, to call his handicapped daughter "Gimpty."

Years later, rehearsing on his typewriter what he should say to his psychoanalyst about the origins of what he felt to be his "cowardice," Odets wrote:

> . . . the dozens of times that I stood by while my father humiliated my mother and while he bawled out my sister Genevieve for being crippled and limping; he would put it that she could walk straight if she wanted to and he did not scruple to add that it made him personally ashamed when she limped. . . . I don't remember to my shame ever going to my mother's or my sister's aid against my father . . . I think I was too afraid—but I have a sneaking suspicion of having at times gained satisfaction from such scenes. Actually, in the bewildering conflicts between my mother and father I learned to *take neither side* and lived as if with blinders, pretending that I didn't know all the time that they were both fighting for my allegiance, for they were, among other things.◖

Pearl did not know that Lou was blaming her for their daughter's tragedy and telling the neighbors the fanciful tale that he had rescued his wife, who looked to them "ausgedahrt" (emaciated), from a Jewish orphan asylum on the assumption that out of gratitude to him she would be a hard worker. A neighbor recalled his saying that "the least one could ask of a wife is that she remove the bones from his fish; if he found one she had missed, the whole thing would go into the garbage." Having netted him, she had become, he said, "uppity, like a lady, and too good for housework." He would offer this fiction as a justification, as one put it, for "gadding about in his car, wearing custom-made suits, karakul-collared coats and gray spats. He was gone so much of the time we all thought he was a traveling salesman."

Lou's opinionated disparagement was not restricted to his family; anyone who crossed him at the print shop these days would become the target of his energetic sarcasm. "My father early taught me hatreds of the world," Odets later wrote. "If he said it was an apple, it was an apple—even if it was really an orange."◖

None of the three Odets children could recall that their mother ever encouraged anything but "respect"—a word frequently used by Lou—for their father. On the contrary, in a doomed effort to minimize the mortal split between herself and her husband, she would mechanically repeat, "You *must* respect your father," and would, despite the total absence of overt affection between herself and Lou, instruct them to greet him "with a kiss" when he came home from work.

There were three things Lou universally and relentlessly demanded: "admiration, respect, and appreciation." Frank Lubner, son of another Geisinger girl named Nettie, recalled that admiration of Lou's "outfits" was the easiest to muster. A standard dialogue between them would require that he say, "You're the due [duke], Lou," to which the routine response was, "Nothing's too good for Lou Odets." At such moments of relaxation Lubner found him pleasant, suave, and extremely entertaining when he told a story, jumping to his feet with a dramatic and athletic energy in order to enact it with humor and color. He would speak in a peculiar combination of original, off-beat images and pious platitudes.

Sometimes, as Lou watched his own advancement from feeder to pressman and could foresee buying a printing plant of his own, he would bring home a gift for his wife: a box of candy or, once, a piece of expensive black lingerie such as Harry Horowitz, alias "Gyp the Blood," had

◖ 2.8.
◖ 2.9.

bought his girl. Pearl hid it in a drawer, to be worn only once, when (under Lou's supervision) she was laid out in her coffin.

As often happens in an emotionally impoverished child, young Odets developed now a minor kleptomania which served both for the symbolic challenge of parental authority and the capture of the supplies of which he felt deprived.◄ In a letter written in his twenties to Philip Moeller, he offers four episodes describing his flirtations with delinquency:

> I was a thief of the first order up until the age of ten or twelve. It is possible that I got from an early reading of Robin Hood a romantic notion of robbery. The result was that at the age of ten I formed with two friends an organization called the "CCC." The first two C's represented Crook Club; the third's significance I can't remember. The three of us stole all manner of articles from coats hung in schoolroom wardrobes, pencils, erasers and occasionally a cent or two. It was very exciting work at which, fortunately, we were never caught.

He recalls with what guile he persuaded one of his friends to spend the purloined funds for both of them and the retribution when his mother caught him:

> In the same year I managed to completely rook a saving bank at home, one that my mother had filled by patient deposit of stray nickels and dimes. It was on a Saturday morning that she realized there had been some tampering with the bank. Attired in a white muslin nightgown, I was caught standing on my bed, backed against the wall, and lashed with a folded trouser belt. With a young cunning I screamed as loudly as possible. My mother would think of the neighbors and desist. But not until the buckle of the belt hit me across the waist did she stop. By that time I was badly bruised and bleeding slightly. There was a frightened look in my mother's face and I screamed out, on the strength of that look, that I would tell the whole world how I was beaten. My mother never stopped in her dramatic stride (it is from her that I inherit any acting ability) and answered, "go ahead, tell the world, tell everyone, tell everyone, you eater-out-of-hearts." A minute later two cousins and an uncle from Newark rang the door bell and I was saved from further lashing. To this very minute I remember Newark with much tenderness.

This is one of the few instances of Pearl's rage breaking through her soft, frightened melancholy; it shocked most of those who knew her. Perhaps there is some anti-feminine exaggeration in this communiqué from a young man catering to an older one presumed to have no interest in women. But the fact that this episode is again alluded to in Odets' private notes sixteen years later strengthens the credibility of this account.

Odets adds in his letter to Moeller his "passion of purpose" in obtaining supplies.

> From another incident of theft I realize a passion of purpose that is surprising to the more or less purposeless person that I am. I was an extremely sensitive boy: a harsh word made me cry. Yet when I think of the "book incident" I look with awe upon the resolution that must have filled me. My aunt took me for a visit to a family that had a son some three or four years my senior. Among his books I found an interesting one with that boyhood hero Tom Swift for protagonist. By the time my aunt had decided to conclude the visit, after the tea and

◄ 2.10.

quince jam, I was three quarters thru the book. The boy would not lend away the book, but instead put it in some closet. At the door, while my aunt was taking leave, I slipped back into the house on pretense of wanting a drink, and not only ripped the concluding chapters out of the book, but filled a capacious pocket with marbles. We arrived home in orderly fashion; my heart was in my face and ears and on my lips. Almost ready for bed, I heard the doorbell ring. Intuition told me that a messenger of doom was there. The family made passing comment on my sudden alacrity in answering the door. My mother said I was pale and sick looking. At the door was the owner of the book. Because his voice was loud and demanding my mother came to look over my shoulder. In that minute the world was stilled. But a lie from my lips saved the world's progress. "You gave me that yourself," I said. "You gave me the end of the book. But if you want it back you can have it." With that I shoved the pilfered pages in his hand and slammed the door. Mother said something about being polite. I had no answer; my voice had been lost somewhere between my toes and knees.

The boy had often seen such swift, lying maneuvers used by his father, a style of coping with life he came consciously to hate and would beg his own children to avoid; yet, as in the following childhood episode, it came to him quite "naturally":

There was a family upstairs that boasted three grown sons. When a fourth arrived they gave a great grand circumcision party. My party was in the bathroom, for to that family a litter of puppies was also born. The bitch's name was Dolly (later killed by a trolley car) and the bathroom smelled of something that lingers in my consciousness between the odours of library paste and wet leather.

The puppies were three or four days old and the one I took had a black face, of the entire litter the only one so distinguished. I brought him downstairs and put him in a shoebox under my bed. Back at the party it was not until much later that someone commented upon the fact that a puppy was missing. Did I know anything about it? No, I didn't, but I had heard of mother dogs carrying babies away in their mouths. Maybe, I suggested hopefully, that was what Dolly had done. No more comment was necessary: the circumcision was about to take place. I didn't see it for some reason or other. They kept me out in the kitchen where I proceeded to take nuts out of nut cake. Much later, when our family went home, when father was at a newspaper and mother was preparing salmon croquettes for a light supper, a clarion-like whimpering suddenly issued from my bedroom. I thought it would be a good idea to go to the store for my mother. Didn't she need some bread or some butter or something or something? No she didn't, but what was that in the bedroom. The dog was discovered. I was delighted, ah, I was delighted. See! Dolly wanted me to have that puppy so she had brought it down herself. Yes, said my father, and put it in the shoebox for me, too. So saying, he stopped reading his newspaper and began to do other things including a palm reading of the back of my anatomy. I knew a great remorse.

Confirmation of his childhood stealing is provided in Odets' record in 1950:

I stole steadily whatever I could lay my hands on: small change, picture cards, books, marbles, erasers, and pencils in school . . . later I stopped stealing, probably because of fear; I am still afraid of policemen and the law, and like all good radicals, have no use for the gendarmes!

He would, all his life, have a special empathy for the delinquent boy, most especially the orphan, writing in his notes, "The radical, the criminal, and the poet are all alike."

In addition to lying and stealing, he tried to resolve his sense of "belonging nowhere" by an inordinate investment—begun at this time and maintained throughout his life—in other families and other homes; the kitchen became his favorite room, not only for eating but for talking. A handful of sympathetic teachers◄ further supported him. The mothers and fathers of "the Beck Street Boys"—a gang of seventeen children with whom he would maintain some level of contact into adulthood—were often addressed by him as "Mom" or "Poppa"; he was often taken in and fed by a series of them—literally or spiritually. The luxurious spreads "Mom" Levy made available left an indelible impression not only on Clifford but on Herman Koblanov, whose mother had abandoned *him* by dying when he was five, a fact which drew these two boys close. From this time on, Odets was never without an adopted family and would enjoy his most richly productive period, two decades later, in the bosom of the Group Theatre.

Members of the Beck Street Boys remembered Clifford as a member of their brotherhood who appeared different from the rest of them only in his dreaminess and unique generosity: "If he had a dollar and you needed something, he'd give it to you without a moment's thought." Indeed, "Clifford started giving money away as soon as he had it to give, even if he stole it." He was still, however, enough one of them to play Prisoner's Base and Ring-a-lievio, distinguishing himself as a sprinter; there is a consensus, however, that "He wasn't much of a long-distance runner."◄ More impressive to the gang was the fact that he used to read "maybe a dozen library books a week," and many Beck Street Boys recalled with gratitude Clifford's ghostwriting their English compositions.

For Clifford himself, more memorable than his English compositions was his performance at Public School 52, at the age of ten or eleven, as the Prince in *Cinderella*. Years later he would tell John McCarten for a *New Yorker* profile that he had there and then determined to become an actor.◄ He was the only person who retained an indelible memory of this triumphant debut.

Much to her husband's shame, and over his protest, "Sanitary Pearl" called the Odets family to the attention of the neighbors by being the only housewife at 783 Beck Street who hung her mattresses out of the windows to air. Ignorant of her chronic tuberculosis, her depression, and her phobic need for "super-cleanliness," they assumed she was having difficulty in the toilet training of her children. This small, thin woman became an object of pity as she lugged around the heavy bedding, and all agreed her husband should spend more time at home helping her. When, however, a neighbor offered to take Pearl and the children for a ride in his brand-new open Ford, Pearl, in desperate terror of this high-powered machine, refused. Some neighbors thought she was so wedded to her suffering that she was fearful of trying *any* means of lifting it.

◄ 2.11.
◄ 2.12.
◄ 2.13.

The bonus of "my own room for the first time" at the Beck Street apartment and a gain in privacy for Clifford was accompanied by an increase in his father's oppression. His most intimate childhood friend, watching Lou's increasing affluence, recalled that "when he moved to Beck and Longwood, Lou decided he had really become a 'big man,' and that made worse not only his iron hold on his *own* family, but now he started telling *everyone else* how to live, too. He now became a two-bit czar, much worse than before . . . began to make fun of Clifford's rotten ball-playing, to snap his fingers in restaurants, and—if there were a moment's delay—to yell for 'Service!' "

As Clifford approached the Great Divide between childhood and adolescence, he could no longer restrict his defiance of authority to the covert activities of stealing and lying. His time of absolute obedience over, he daydreamed himself out of the windows of his classroom, and his grades began to fall in school achievement as well as in "Effort" and "Conduct." He later outlined a short story describing this time:

THE BOY WHO RAN AWAY: The whole morning, dressing after washing, shivering at the radiator (for in those days it was cold to get up in the March morning, and we hung our stockings on the radiator to warm them up), eating breakfast and unable to swallow the hot cocoa—that whole morning he was sick with thinking about what would happen when he got to school.

Miss Davis (cock-eyed, with freckles and eye glasses on a chain with a gold hairpin stuck in her hair) would ask him for his report card again, signed by his father, not his mother. It was a very bad card and complicated by the fact that he himself had signed it the month before. That time he had been sick with dread but had signed it, hiding it in a book under his bed until he had had the courage to bring it back to school. He was almost caught that time, Miss Davis asking, "Does your father always sign his name *Mr.* J. L. Ottman?"

And now this very bad card. Miss Davis forgot to ask him about it in the morning. But at noon it was the same thing, too sick to eat, standing on the sidewalk in front of the school before returning to the P.M. session. Standing on a manhole cover with the letters N.Y.C. on them. The whole city, policeman, officers, teachers—he stepped off the cover quickly. And in the class, as if making up for the morning lapse of memory, Miss Davis, "Where is your report card?" Very tart, no wasted words, sure he was lying. "Go home and get it signed and don't come back to school until you do!"

Terror! . . . What to do? Be licked, humiliated? A bad card—CCC! Go, run away, my child, run away from home. The day is warm, fly away from home. Where will you go? Go to the park, to the Bronx park. See the animals, the zoo—who cares about the animals? Terror, terror and starting to walk all the way to the zoo. Won't they ask you why you're not in school? What will you tell the policeman when he asks you who you are?

The park, a long walk. The animals viewed without pleasure. . . . My father would kill me if he got his hands on me. . . . Suddenly begin to run, running home. But people will think something's the matter if you run. Walk, walk rapidly, walking home, a whole six miles.

. . . And then the father seeing you. The chase. The horror of running in the middle of the street, the father shouting he won't hurt you and crying, crying—anything to blot that sound out of your mind.

Panting, hiding behind a fence. . . . Just go home. So climbing up the stairs and knocking at the door, faint-hearted, terrorized. Going in past the kitchen, the mother's eyes all red. Saying quietly to sit and eat; she is washing the dishes—they have all eaten. Still a little light out—it is *May*. And going to bed, thankful, oh so grateful, crying in the dark.

This edition of his terror of being unmasked before the judge and found to be a fraud—perhaps even a criminal—moved him closer to his adult terrors as an artist.

Although by this time there was much passionate talk in the neighborhood about the "world war" raging in faraway Europe, with people taking firm stands on whether "America should get involved," Clifford heard such discussions most often in the apartments of his friends. Lou preferred pinochle and Pearl was interested only in keeping her apartment free of bacteria, in coaxing her thin baby girl to eat, in helping her son with his schoolwork, and in evading her husband's rages.

In the debates at "783," President Woodrow Wilson was attacked by some as a simple warmonger ("He brought troops to Haiti, Santo Domingo, and Mexico") and by others—echoing men like Louis Brandeis, called "The Jewish Abraham Lincoln"—as part of a "yellow layer of Pacifist liberal cowardice." But there were those who hailed Wilson as the "man who kept us out of the war."◖ These bitterly opposed camps in the apartments of the Bronx mirrored the fact that imperialism everywhere was in crisis. The worldwide scramble for a division of the shrinking spoils spawned a successful revolution in Russia in 1917, and the governments of other nations were in terror of similar mutinies or, at least, low-level contagions. Odets' neighbors, like people everywhere, were divided between those backing and those opposing their rulers.

Odets recorded his fascination with these grownups' political discussions in a screenplay twenty-five years later: Wilson is called by one character "a man like a million." Another says, "He's got talent?" To which the reply is, "Gold." In a diary he wrote, "It was profoundly my opinion that a certain man living in our house was a criminal of a very dangerous order—he was a well-known socialist!" Thus a segment of history intersects with a life cycle and a groundwork is laid for an adolescent's ideology. Later he writes, "In a capitalist society, criminals, artists and revolutionists are brothers under the skin. For related reasons they are all men of opposition."* When the United States declared war on Germany and news came to 783 Beck Street that labor leader Eugene Debs had been jailed by the president for his opposition to the war and to the use of "a gun that shoots 70 miles," it confirmed for Clifford the equation of "socialist" and "criminal."

To Clifford's father, on the other hand, the war meant only that he could at last, in a booming economy, have his own printing plant, with a growing number of "direct mail" advertisers. By now he had become

◖ 2.14.

* This is similar to Walt Whitman's "I feel I am of them / I belong to those convicts and prostitutes myself / And henceforth I will not deny them / For how can I deny myself?"

"L.J.," the L to stand for Louis and the J, according to his daughter, for "nothing but class." "With his typical ego," he announced to a neighbor that soon his customers would want him to arrange their layouts and that ultimately he would even write the advertising copy. In the meantime, he boasted, he was earning enough to be able to send his family to the country for part of the summer. This coveted badge of rising middle-class status, which found expression in the ragtime song "My Wife's Gone to the Country," was for "Germ-proof Pearl" a terrible trial: she was afraid that flies would bring disease to her children. Her husband was more concerned that he could not afford such affluent accommodations as the Millsteins, who owned a Rolls-Royce, or their neighbor who dealt in wholesale scrap iron, much needed in the war.

In the summer of 1917—ignoring Pearl's protests—he sent her, Clifford, Genevieve, and Florence to Natkin's Farm at Hurleyville, New York, a small place which took guests. There Pearl's anxiety—ordinarily held somewhat in check by her compulsive ritual cleaning routines—ran rampant, and her sensitive eleven-year-old boy identified strongly with her. It was at Natkin's Farm that Clifford, filled with nameless terror and loneliness, commenced his compulsive masturbation, which he would later indicate for the rest of his life in his diaries and notes with a black-circled capital letter M. Then, as later, he regarded it as a burdensome "symptom," laden with shame and guilt, which he would repeatedly try, without success, to stop. Almost half a century later he writes: "When the child needs consolation (as all children do), and the mother will not give it, the child will later, thru youth and into adulthood move towards a series of consolations. These include such strange and disparate activities as sex, self-sex, distractions, arts, gourmandizing, beauty parlors, rich clothes, etc., etc." And, finally, he would see it as a corollary of the romantic artist's conscious necessity: "to seek his greatest excitement in himself."

Despite L.J.'s desperate wish to make a good impression on everyone he encountered, when he appeared at Natkin's Farm on weekends his temper was ignited by anything that threatened to mar his affluent image. Odets often recounted, in substance, the following "typical incident":

> Gen yelled out the window, "Here comes daddy, and he's had his car repainted." L.J. was ready to murder her because he wanted everybody to think he had a brand-new car. His anger about this went on for weeks; she had "disgraced" him in front of everybody. So then the whole vacation was spoiled. He relieved himself by his shouting and screaming, but had destroyed everyone else and then couldn't understand why they were so unhappy. . . . It was nice only when we were alone, without him.

L.J., still addressing Genevieve in public as "Gimpty," kept insisting not only to her but to others that she could walk straight if she wanted to, and that one day he would force her to walk straight. He would maintain his educational technique for many years, his open contempt and rage at his daughter astonishing all who witnessed it.◖

For the year 1917 Odets for the first time includes in his autobiographical outline a note of a death: the father of one of the Beck Street Boys. It was his first genuine awareness of his own mortality. In his list of "what I remember as a child" he concludes: "I wonder, wonder, ache and dream. That is my feeling memory of childhood: WONDERING, ACHING, AND DREAMING and every day ends with a long death of sleep!"

◖ 2.15.

Chapter Three

There was always, as a child, and right now as a man, something awesome to me about a tree . . . laden with fruit. . . . I think these things are related to the mechanism of what is a poet, because the thing keeps a firstness. . . . I still do what I did when I was twelve years old and saw an airplane fly over the Bronx. . . . There's no time I don't lift my eyes and look up in the sky.

CLIFFORD ODETS, *1961*

[California] . . . where an honest apple tree won't grow . . .

CLIFFORD ODETS, *1949*

ODETS was now moving into the identity crisis of adolescence, given in his case an edge both by the special innocence and porousness of the gifted and by the deadly struggle between his parents. Sexuality would remain essentially a solitary fantasy-activity for a year or two more, but as a vehicle for many of his deepest conflicts it began to assume the central importance for Odets it would hold for the rest of his life.◖

Ever, deep in his bones, "an outsider looking in"—the image is of an abandoned boy—Odets commenced at twelve the sharp and perverse pleasure of the spectator:

> One of the most exciting experiences of my boyhood was the time when we followed a young couple out to a field across the railroad tracks. We followed them cautiously, several of us, at a distance. Suddenly the pair disappeared in the field. Twenty years later I still remember the sound of the girl's voice when we finally discovered the pair had stretched out in a small pit. She was saying in a low, piteous voice, "Max, stop, Max please stop, stop it Max." She stopped with the voice, but he continued with what he was doing. We crept away,

awed, scornful and, I understand now, delighted. We were twelve or thirteen at the time. We knew the girl—the stepdaughter of Rabbi Weissbaum who was an amateur opera singer and lived on our block. As for the stepdaughter, Nellie by name, ever after she was referred to on our block as "Nellie the whore." What in the world did that girl of nineteen or twenty think when, walking down the street, her hair neat with braided coils, a little boy would dart out of an alley or cellar door and hiss, "Hey, Nellie the whore" and then run for all he was worth!

He began early to describe such episodes in his files marked "Psychology" or "Personal Notes," regaling friends over the years with accounts of what he had seen when a shade was not pulled, or what, on a lonely night, he had heard through a thin hotel-room wall.

Not long after this, at thirteen, he managed his first seduction, the first of hundreds, with a sister of one of the Beck Street Boys. From his scattered notes it appears that this initial excursion was brief and that it terminated unhappily: "Girls seem malicious and spiteful and are always telling parents about the bad things you do."

Six months before Clifford reached the Hebrew ritual age of passage from childhood to manhood, his father decided that disgrace lay not so much in being a Jew as in being a poor Russian-Jewish immigrant. Accordingly, Lou Odets seized upon a garbled solution which utilized some of the Americanizations of Reform Judaism. He began to attend High Holidays and Sabbath services (then held on Sundays, not Saturdays) no longer in a synagogue but in a "temple" reserved for wealthy Jews. At the same time he announced he had been born not in Russia but in Philadelphia,* and sent his son to a tiny red-bearded rabbi on Kelly Street for lessons in Hebrew, preparatory to a formal and expensive bar-mitzvah celebration.

Clifford and his friend Herman Koblanov (earlier Koblanovsky and later Kobland), who idolized him, appeared dutifully every day at the shabby railroad apartment where in the back bedroom the rabbi had installed a rickety wooden table and chairs as a makeshift Cheder (school) for his reluctant young "Yeshiva-niks." In this Bronx temple of Talmudic learning, puffing on one third of a Between the Acts cigar cut into three pieces for reasons of economy, the Malamud would "scream and smack down the stick on the table" to bolster his doomed pedagogical efforts.

Koblanov, nicknamed "Von" by Odets, recalled that neither he nor Clifford had even a remote notion of the meaning of the Hebrew words, and were impatient and disrespectful in the extreme. On one occasion Clifford was pursued under the rabbi's bed for "being so fresh." After three or four months of this sad slapstick, all participants gave up. Odets was thus never actually "bar-mitzvahed," but, once free of the cigar-smoking little rabbi, he experienced an intense wave of Jewish religiosity and decided to become a rabbi himself. He kept thinking of something his Uncle Israel often said: that up until thirteen a boy's sins are on his

* As late as 1938, Clifford Odets would repeat this myth to interviewers such as John McCarten of *The New Yorker*. It is unclear whether he then knew the facts. By 1961 he was telling the truth to interviewers.

parents, but that after that "the sins go off from the father and mother and goes in his own body."

Despite the fact that the bar mitzvah never took place, Lou Odets had formal photographic portraits made—the sort usually reserved in the Bronx middle class of this era for the commemoration of the ritual handing over of the Torah to a Jewish boy by his father. Looking much alike, Lou and Clifford appear in these portraits—in contrast to earlier snapshots—prosperous and overfed. Sitting together in twin rented tuxedos, they hold secular books, a smug smile playing on each mouth as, with lowered eyes, they pretend to be studying the book held by the boy. In this scene, with the father's arm around his boy's shoulders, we see no hint that the future will hold anything but an orderly unfolding of a "balabatish" (respectable, literally "like a boss") Jewish-American middle-class life cycle. The symbol here, however, is that of a father handing not the holy Torah to his young son, but passing on instead what Odets was to consider an odious set of imperatives on "how to live" in order to achieve the American dream of material security, status, and power. He began now to try to span the chasm between his father's values and those of his mother and his Uncle Israel.

In the summer of 1918, the war still raging, the self-deceiving and self-defeating Woodrow Wilson pleaded unsuccessfully with the American voter to agree at the polls that no "selfish ends" were being served in the war designed to end all war and make the world safe for democracy. Debate among the Bronx philosophers on Beck and Kelly streets was passionate. Many Jews—the Russian persecutions still fresh in their memories—had, from the beginning, opposed the United States joining forces with the Russians against the "civilized Germans." On November 11—with two million Americans sent to France and as many more in training; with 75,000 dead and 200,000 wounded or missing—Beck Street, along with the entire country, was overjoyed when Lloyd George expressed the hope, almost the belief, that "we may say that thus, this fateful morning, came to an end all wars."

To the lonely thirteen-year-old, more concerned this day by his father's tirade at one of his many withdrawn silences, these large events were an unfocused backdrop. His later notes state, "War ends. Parades." More important to him was the "move to 758 Kelly Street," a back-to-back twin to the apartment house at 783 Beck, and his being "adopted" by the parents of his friend Ernie Millstein, later president of the Mills Novelty Company.◖ Clifford and Herman were far more interested in being the first to let the young boy in on the facts of life than in the fact that the war had ended. Odets later wrote:

> Ernie . . . took to a retching sickness down in the cellar of the Longwood apartments, Beck Street side, when we first informed him of the amazing story of how babies were born. This sick feeling of his was transferred to me whenever I saw a big birthmark on my back. I used to shudder at the sight of it and finally decided that the way out

◖ 3.2.

of my dilemma was to never look at my back in the mirror while standing up in the bathtub. . . .

After he had become a leading playwright, Odets regularly told interviewers he should really have become a composer,◖ consciously linking the origin of this aspiration to his father's playing the pianola acquired during the war boom. "L.J.," a relative recalled, "worked those buttons like he was Paderewski." Odets later wrote:

> This was a mechanical piano which played mechanical paper rolls cut out into so-called "four-handed arrangements." The music galloped, wooden and mechanical, decorated all over with grace notes and embellishments. It was many years before I could listen to a mere pianist with two hands, alive and adding personal nuance and character to his playing; he seemed deficient in volume and energy, in music making. And yet it was from that crazy stupid pianola that I first acquired a love of music.

The pianola dumbly playing early Gershwin songs, the camera, the movie palaces—now swiftly replacing the nickelodeons—were all of a piece.

Pearl had a vague feeling there was something immoral here, and insisted that Clifford take "real, live" piano lessons. Along with Herman, he acceded dutifully for a short while in this undertaking, as doomed as their lessons in Hebrew; both boys found intolerable the practicing and memorizing of pieces chosen by the teacher. Pearl, never one to insist that her children carry disciplined responsibilities, confessed later that she, too, had found the practicing painful: "It hurt my ears." Yet an image which appeared regularly in the memories of people who knew Odets later is of Clifford seated at a piano. "Like a stage Beethoven," said Franchot Tone, "improvising lugubrious chords, sometimes singing along." Tone recalled also his real skill on the harmonica, on which he usually played sad, mournful little songs, occasionally lightened by a jig tune.

When the Gramophone and Typewriter Company was taken over by Victor, the Odets family acquired one of the first "talking-machines" on the block. Clifford often recalled how deeply moved he had been on hearing, on Red Seal records, the Sextet from *Lucia* and the *William Tell* and "1812" overtures, and how startled by the voice of Enrico Caruso. A dozen years later Odets would use Caruso's "O Paradiso" in a climactic moment of his first full-length play, *Awake and Sing!*, to accompany the exhortation and prophecy of Isaiah, put by him in the mouth of an idealized Bronx patriarch modeled after his grandfather: "Awake and sing, ye that dwell in the dust, and the earth shall cast out the dead." From this time of enchantment with the "talking-machine" and its records, Odets would, according to his friend Harvey Screbnick, "use music like a drug," experiencing a remarkable psychological intimacy with vanished composers —whom he called "the mighty dead"—whose message he was always eager to impart to others. In a letter to the author he wrote: "Would you believe that Haydn, Mozart, Beethoven, Schubert and Schumann are as alive to me

◖ 3.3.

as almost anyone I know? It has been true for many years, and there I am talking about men I do not know in life no less!"

In the context of a postwar disillusionment and recession, an emerging class of American intellectuals—Odets' ideological parents—was setting up battle lines against the American individualist who held that all forms of misery deriving from war or poverty were unchangeable by government action and were "natural outcomes of imprudence, idleness, improvidence or alcoholism." The outlets for the rising voices of humanist protest, opposed to injustice and to war, and enunciating a vague "anti-imperialism," were known as "magazines of dissent." One of them, bravely calling itself *The New Republic,* was publishing anti-war pieces by a young man named Maxwell Anderson, son of a Baptist minister. In this "radical" periodical, as later in another called *The Masses* (and still later *The New Masses*), the explicit intent was to wed socialist ideology and esthetic experiment.

Van Wyck Brooks, together with Waldo Frank, had founded a magazine entitled—in lower-case letters—*the seven arts,* advocating even bolder innovations in life and in art than the others did. The idealism in these small publications reflected a new brand of "popular radicalism" among working people who, by voting for general strikes and for the nationalization of mines, were nourishing apprehension in general and, in particular, a full-blown clinical phobia of Communism in William Howard Taft. In the midst of the postwar economic slump, educated and intelligent young men "of good families" were returning from Paris and Moscow full of the excitement of revolution: esthetic, psychological, and political.* One such young man, John Reed, a committed American Bolshevik, was the attractive and romantic enfant terrible of American journalism. Already a legendary figure, he would die of typhus in Moscow at thirty-three, and become a hero for Odets and many others of his generation.

President Wilson's attorney general, A. Mitchell Palmer, enlisted the aid of an eager, ambitious, and dedicated young bachelor named John Edgar Hoover to lay the groundwork for a roundup of these "revolutionary dissenters" who saw hope in the Russian experiment.† Almost ten thousand persons were arrested in order that their "caches of arms and explosives" could be seized. However, in what became known as the Palmer Raids, no dynamite could be located and only three guns were found, an anticlimactic outcome on the first day of January 1920.◖

Will Hays, an ordained Presbyterian elder, and national chairman of the Republican Party, later to superintend the morals of the film industry, earnestly recommended that, in the interest of "national security," the members of a labor fraternity be shot. The president and most mem-

---

* In the spring of 1919 Lincoln Steffens said to Bernard Baruch about the U.S.S.R.: "I have been over into the future, and it works." Theodore Dreiser, not yet a Communist, was being attacked for his "barbaric naturalism" and identified by the literary establishment as the "chronicler of vulgar American types." Discouraged by seventy-six rejections in one year, he was already looking to the film industry for a living.

† Many of them still met in the Hell Hole, the saloon where Eugene O'Neill was plunging into a suicidal depression and anesthetizing himself with alcohol.

◖ 3.4.

bers of Congress found this too extreme a measure and contented themselves with deporting to the Soviet Union the Greenwich Village anarchist
Emma Goldman. J. Edgar Hoover was commended for his effort and became the most continuously powerful individual in United States history,
whose reign over the Federal Bureau of Investigation ended only with his
death.

Young Odets, unaware of these roundups, was spending much of his
leisure raptly watching the movies of the hapless, homeless gentleman
tramp who twenty-five years later would become his close friend, Charles
Chaplin. First Chaplin and then Odets himself would become loosed foxes
in a precise repetition three decades later of a new postwar terror in high
places.

Odets, reading at twelve a dozen books a week—some of them popu-
larizations of the new and suspect "Freudian" psychology—knew almost
nothing of the nature of the history unfolding around him. Incarcerated
with mumps, he prevailed upon his friend Herman to ask his favorite
teachers (all of whose names he could remember two decades later) what
books he should read. It was in the climate of this time that a title often
mentioned by his teachers and recommended by the local librarian was
Les Misérables. Odets later described his reaction to this "find":

> Victor Hugo, the rich love of my boyhood days. ("Les Miserables"
> was the most, *is* the most profound art experience I have ever had: I
> was a boy who could give himself up without the slightest reserve
> when I was reading alone.) . . .
>
> Hugo . . . inspired me, made me aspire; I wanted to be a good
> and noble man, longed to do heroic deeds with my bare hands, thirsted
> to be kind to people, particularly the weak and humble and oppressed.
> From Hugo I had my first feeling of social consciousness. He did not
> make me a romantic, but he heightened in me that romanticism
> which I already had. I loved him and love him still, that mother of my
> literary heart. In the face of these famous gifts, it cannot matter that
> he taught me self-pity, too.

That champion of the wretched of the earth, Hugo, would become for
Odets what Nietzsche, the critic of Christianity, had been for O'Neill.
His was a familiar voice to a Jewish child. Odets later put in the mouth of
one of his characters: "Hugo's the one who helped me nibble my way
through billions of polly seeds—Hugo said to me, 'Be a good boy . . . love
people, do good, help the lost and fallen, make the world happy, if you
can!' "

At just this time Odets began to devote himself to the "humble and
oppressed" in his own family; first, to his younger sister. He superintended
the spiritual development of this two-and-a-half-year-old now and throughout her childhood, reading to her, teaching her to play the piano, comforting her and buying tiny dolls and books for her. He even conspired with
her against the parental "smell of authority" by promising not to tell that
she had poured her milk down the drain instead of drinking it. Often when
Pearl, in mute despair, took to her bed, he would secretly invent gourmet
dishes like fried raspberries, and once formed the letters C and O out of the
frankfurters he made for Florence. Neighbors said they had rarely seen a
boy so kind to a baby sister or so devoted to a sickly mother, the other
"miserable" in the family with whom he could identify.◖ Although he be-

◖ 3.5.

came impotently angry when his father taunted his crippled sister, Genevieve, he never took care of her in this way. She had, after all, displaced
him.

It was at this time he forbade his compulsively clean mother to tidy
his room because he had begun to rear tadpoles and fish, and to establish
an orphanage for a variety of animals ranging from turtles to homeless
cats. Florence remembered his whipping the turtle for devouring the tadpoles before they could become frogs. In the midst of the clutter of books,
papers, and animals in his room he always placed a single bright flower in
a vase—now and later a symbol for him of purity, beauty, and of a universal potential for "perfect form."*

This lavish caretaking, whose forms would change over the years,
stemmed now from an effort to master—by way of an active "helping
paternity"—his displacement by his crippled sister. In the larger world his
sense of "not belonging," of having no place, was that of a member of any
minority; in his family he was a deposed monarch, an abandoned child.
Decades later, trying to deduce universal truths from his own fifty years
of development, he wrote in his "Psychology" file:

> The early need to "father" comes, I think as follows. The oldest child,
> deposed (dethroned) by the arrival of the second, reaches past and
> over the latter to the third child and in solace, revenge, contempt, in
> the drive for self-esteem, for regaining status and position, etc., es-
> tablishes a rapport or entente with the third child (who is happy with
> the bargain, admiring), a sort of quasi-paternity—an acting out or
> restaging, etc., of the previous situation as it existed before the second
> child arrived. He will cut out the second in "his" "family" and even cut
> the third child away from the real mother and father. This is "devour-
> ment" of the third by the first. I think the first child must be (?) of the
> opposite sex to the later two. Also, to take care of the "baby" usually
> earns praise!

Characteristically, he emphasizes his revengeful, predatory, jockeying-
for-position motives in what appeared to the commonsense neighbors as
simply an uncommon generosity and sympathy for his baby sister. No
doubt, these angry devouring motives were indeed part of his fathering
of Florence. Equally important, however, was his growing capacity to put
himself in the place of the other, an empathy which informed his intense
love of music, his parlor "psychotherapy," especially of women, and, above
all, his plays.

In this same year L. J. Odets established his weekly card game (aped
secretly by his son, who used lima beans instead of money) and bought
the first wristwatch and the first Maxwell car with a self-starter in the
neighborhood. Also, he acquired a set of dining-room chairs which were, as
he put it to a nephew, "fit for the Prince of Wales himself to sit on." His
custom-made suits were by now many and expensive, and his initialed
shirts were finally of silk. According to his nephew, "In the summer it was
sailor straws . . . and in the winter he wore spats and was one of the
derby-hat clique." Like the three gangsters he had known, he was becoming
a real dandy. Moreover, he was now learning to play golf. His boasts were
an increasing embarrassment to his family, and a neighbor recalls that
"we wouldn't have had anything to do by now with that phony baloney
except for Pearl. She brought tears."

* He would call his last play *The Flowering Peach*.

In keeping with the unwritten American law of this time and place, that a change of apartment signaled an advancement of status (as Lou Odets put it, "With the good Lord's help, no grass growing under *my* feet"), the Odets family moved again, this time to 830 East 163rd Street, the only other apartment house in the Bronx with an elevator. Clifford and Genevieve were transferred to Public School 10. The next move would have to be a repeat if the status symbol of the elevator were to be maintained, and indeed it was—back to 758 Kelly Street. It was a time for the Odets family when, as Clifford put it, there was "all of America ahead . . . people moving on to 'bigger and better' things, places and other neighborhoods." Ultimately, here as everywhere, as each family moved on, the poor would move in, and the apartment house would lose its bright striped awnings and begin to deteriorate. Odets writes of this period, "Things growing up straight and crooked . . . the sorrow and the humor and the glory of life. And always America junking and looking and going ahead."

Although Pearl appears to have taken some pleasure in accumulating hand-embroidered linens and the "beautiful bedspreads that no one was allowed to sit on," her leading response to her husband's strenuous efforts to match their social life to their new dining-room suite was acute embarrassment over her lack of formal education and of social poise. She told her best friend that even her use of the German language was "low" (Plattdeutsch) and that she was in constant terror of ridicule by her husband. He disappeared for days at a time, and was often seen by one of the Beck Street Boys strolling on the Atlantic City or Coney Island boardwalk with some fashionable young woman of greater poise and literacy; these reports turned Pearl's embarrassment to despair.

Increasingly, Pearl told a friend, she could no longer endure her life and was planning to leave her husband. Indeed, on "one dreadful occasion" she mysteriously disappeared and was discovered alone in a cheap hotel room in Atlantic City armed with a small revolver. Sobbing, she confessed to her friend she had gone there to end her life.◖ She had reached this decision when, shopping for an inexpensive winter coat, she was told by the clerk that her husband had just bought a fur coat there for his blond secretary. With difficulty, her friend's husband took the gun from Pearl and brought her home in a profound depression. For a time she was mute, and when she resumed speech, her talk was of making "a new jailbreak" whether by suicide or by "just dying." Her steady sense of being imprisoned and her expression of it are eerily similar to her son's four decades later: "the rose bush below does not compensate for the bars on the window above."

Not long after this aborted suicide Pearl took two extended trips to California "for her asthma"; Genevieve and Florence went along, leaving Clifford behind. He summed it up telegraphically in his notes: "Mother to California twice. I live at 830. Adler family. *I go to Boy Scout Camp* [italics his]. Mother returns and goes again. I live with Cohens on Tinton Avenue and Tunick family on Union Avenue. Mother returns and visits at camp. I hear of secret operations."

Perhaps it is out of delicacy that no friend or relative can remember an "operation." Lou Odets vowed he had seen a "secret letter" which proved that in California Pearl had found a lover, "a no-good, a nothing,"* to whom she was returning on her second trip. Those who knew them both expressed the hope decades later that Pearl had indeed found a lover, as

◖ 3.6.
* Years later Clifford would use these same words to describe a rival for *his* wife's affections, and the term "secret operation" to describe an abortion.

she deserved a drop of happiness in her life. A snapshot taken in Los Angeles on one of these trips shows a faint smile on Pearl's usually somber face and suggests that, lover or no, she was more relaxed alone with her two little girls on the West Coast than with her husband in the Bronx.

For teen-age Clifford the departure of his mother and sisters, leaving him to a series of families and Boy Scout leaders, resulted in rushes of contradictory feelings: a reinforcement of his old terror and anger at being abandoned, together with renewed hope of finding substitute parents; and, most important, an exhilarating sense of freedom, particularly from his father's scorn and instructions.

Under these conditions he could enjoy times of cozy, pedestrian intimacy with his father, whom he still saw as powerful and knowledgeable, a man with whom he could dine at expensive restaurants and discuss the relative costs and merits of a Maxwell automobile and a Stutz Bearcat. From this time a memory later appears: "The man who told my father I was going to be 'a lady killer.' I was 14 and it was at a restaurant table. I was awed!" The use of the word "awed" here carries overtones of both wonder and terror at this clairvoyant vision of his own future power, not unlike his father's.

In the dreams and fantasies of this youngster there are hints of deeper intimacies of a masochistically voluptuous sort wherein he was, in a disguised form, the sexual "victim" of his father; often he is betrayed, like his mother, by this inconstant man. In his plays these unconscious fantasies would become a regular theme.

From the Scout camp the lonely boy sent an average of five letters a day to both boys and girls, starting to write them in the morning "after mess," soon to be interrupted "by the bugle asking me to come out swimming." When he returned, he would write only "a few more lines and then go to noonday mess." Describing this time a few years later, he wrote:

> Thus it was no wonder that sometimes it took three days to finish one lonely letter and the flower that I picked and labeled for that particular party had faded and then it would take another day or two to find a replica of the faded specimen. My record for writing letters in one day for myself was the high-water mark of nine letters. I was Ye Scribe for those that were demure and didn't know what to say to their best G's (meaning girls).

In these letters, as for the rest of his life, he would plead with all recipients to "answer sooner than is your usual wont" and then berate them when they failed to do this. The excessive need for a speedy reassuring response from his audience—to limit his creative risk-taking—had begun early.

A photograph of all five Odetses, taken at the Boy Scout camp when "Mother returned" with the girls, gives no hint of the cleavages within this family. All are smiling, Pearl with mouth closed, a bit stiff in her inappropriate dark dress. Her son, in high-button shoes and Boy Scout uniform, appears no more nor less strained than any adolescent. Genevieve's crippled leg is not obvious; only the fact that her prescribed high-lace shoes are black, not white like Florence's, offers a clue to her affliction. The Odetses look like any optimistic American family in the early 1920s which, having repudiated the intellectual President Wilson and his war, was now at ease with Warren Gamaliel Harding, a card-playing, small-town sport of a president, who was reputed to be a philanderer with a "bungalow mind," but who, as Odets said, "inspired confidence because he looked like a president."

It was the beginning of an energetic, pleasure-bent era when, as Odets later put it, "the whole town was hot and people were out for a good time." The war was over, there were many things to be bought. Although the sale of liquor was now forbidden by law—a short-lived interdiction pushed through by the recently enfranchised American woman, who thought thus to keep at least the domestic front under control—this prohibition served only to push the price up and the quality down. The twenties had nervously begun to roar, and Hendrik Van Loon was predicting a "renaissance of art" in the offing.

For Cassandras in the intellectual community, this frantic fiesta, with its miniskirts, bobbed hair, Charleston, bathtub gin—some of it made by Israel Rossman—and its by now stereotyped "Fitzgerald extravagances," carried a bitter postwar, pre-Deluge flavor. Far from feeling cheered by George Gershwin's music, with its message that "the war is over and jazz is here to stay," they were calling attention to Woodrow Wilson's predictions of a new world war to come in a generation if steps were not taken to prevent it. Moreover, these spoilsports, unamused by grand-scale sophomoric pranks and prodigious waste of natural and human resources, were asking people to share their shock at the international business machinations revealed in the recently opened archives as the background of the first worldwide war. They were asking also that "steps be taken."

What even these melancholy prophets could not foresee was that gestating within this "high plateau of permanent prosperity" was an international crisis of such terrifying proportions as to produce both the most monstrous attempt in the history of man to achieve a "final solution" and another, less final but more humane. While the gifted madman, architect in Germany of one solution, was counseling himself in 1923 to suicide should his "Beer-Hall Putsch" fail, Franklin Delano Roosevelt, crippled by poliomyelitis, was training himself to crawl along the floor. The world crisis to be called the Great Depression, an appellation which reflects its despair—would provide the piece of history which, intersecting with Odets' creative necessities, lifted him to a preeminent position among American playwrights.

But now, as business in the print shop kept improving, Louis J. Odets envisioned only the golden day when his bright son who wrote such good letters and compositions would become chief copywriter in a big advertising firm he himself would organize in the richest and most powerful city in the world.

During the business boom, hosts of American writers, painters, and composers exiled themselves to Europe, simultaneously in flight from what appeared to them a growing sense both of banality and of Evil; they were in quest of a cultural tradition and a continuity they had glimpsed there during the World War. Perhaps it was in response to this same sense of values unraveling that there occurred now a unique and brief chapter in the history of American film-making: the filming of classic European plays. Odets, talking to a graduate student half a century later, recalled what this had meant for him:

I came to Ibsen at about the age of 14 by being profoundly moved by seeing the actress Nazimova in a silent movie production of *A Doll's House*. I also saw her do—believe it or not—a silent movie of Oscar Wilde's *Salome*. And when this happened, when the picture excited me that way beyond myself, or beyond my knowledge of why or what, I would go to the library and get the plays out and read them. . . .

While young Odets was thus being introduced to the literature of European drama, Harold Clurman, soon to become for Odets the "witness of my life," was in Paris with his friend Aaron Copland.❮ Copland was learning in Paris to become an indigenous American composer, and Clurman was unwittingly preparing himself to organize the most influential production company in American theatrical history. Also in Paris was playwright John Howard Lawson, soon to write for the Group Theatre his *Success Story,* an American paradigm.

At this time Clurman knew only that he was rounding out, with his Sorbonne thesis on the French drama and his faithful attendance at the performances of the Moscow Art Theatre, a passion born on the Lower East Side for live theatre. There, at the Grand Street Theatre, he had often watched the princely Jewish actor Jacob P. Adler—called in Hebrew "nesher hagodel," the great eagle—performing Yiddish melodrama and spectacle and even a strange vehicle called *The Jewish King Lear.*

In the Yiddish theatre, begun in New York City in the 1880s, the essential, according to Jacob Adler's thespian children Stella and Luther, was the lively and passionate exchange between the actors and the audience. While the emotional content was often shallow, pretentious, or sentimental, the joyful mutuality between cast and spectators even in a vaudeville skit was probably more intense than in any other theatre in America. Only Italian opera would come close.

Stella and Luther Adler recalled that, despite their six-foot-tall father's noble flamboyance, he was an apostle of "realism." By this he meant that he regarded it a sacred duty of Jewish playwrights to bring to the stage in Yiddish the lives of what he called "ordinary Jews." His audiences did not share this essentially sophisticated view of theatre, and Adler never succeeded in persuading them that the realistic work of playwright Jacob Gordin was as good as the outsize spectacles of Jewish heroism to which they thronged. It remained for Odets, who would come to love the Yiddish theatre and the restaurants nearby, to bring not only these "ordinary Jews" but the prototype second-generation immigrant into the legitimate American theatre.

The nineteen-year-old Clurman becomes a general spokesman for the era when he recalls his sense of the American theatre of this time: " . . . what I actually see on the boards lacks the feel of either significant contemporaneity . . . or the sense of a permanent contribution to my inner experience. . . . Where is the best thought of our time in the theatre, the feeling of some true personal significance in any of its works?" There was in this widespread voluntary exile by creative Americans simultaneously a conscious reaching for positive esthetic values and a rejection of American materialism. Most of these young artists were more confident about what they wanted to avoid than what they needed to celebrate.

On the third day of February 1920 at 2:15 in the afternoon, on the stage of the Morosco Theatre, the curtain went up on the first play on Broadway by an American not in Parisian exile, whose intense and sorrowful honesty would be reflected in a body of work which finally would meet Clurman's plea for true personal significance: Eugene O'Neill's *Beyond the Horizon.* In a clumsy story—with an ending unusually sad for the American theatre—it told of a boy trying to become an artist in a materialist world which finds him full of "wild poetry notions." In the audience sat young Clurman, just back from Paris, and to a fellow student he

❮ 3.7.

expressed the conviction that this O'Neill matinee would prove to be a landmark in the history of American drama. More than a landmark, he said, it would inaugurate a new era in which American audiences could never again be content with plays imitative of European culture. Clurman's young companion dismissed this hot judgment as characteristic "Clurman extravagance." Not long after, however, Yale's Professor George Pierce Baker expressed the hope that the new public created by the war would stimulate a richer American drama within the next decade. With Theodore Dreiser now trying his hand at playwriting, it was evident that a footpath was being hacked out for the indigenous American dramatist. It would be another four years before Odets, now not quite fourteen, could even notice the path was there.

In the meantime Odets' dramatic fare consisted solely of a weekly movie; he was focused instead on his first "deep crush" on one Annie Baum, and preoccupied with an insuperable obstacle to its fruition: the underlined entry in his notes, punctuated with an exclamation mark, is *"Pimples!"* A few years later he would recall—in a letter to an older, homosexual man—the way this girl had mirrored his own growing dividedness:

> She was half Jew and part Gentile. She didn't know whether to associate with Clifford or not. Half of her said yes, the other portion frowned a no. . . . Perhaps [she] thought me a beggar. I was not ashamed and persisted. . . . I learned and am still learning by remaining a beggar. The man that will not eat hominy when there is not nectar, he is a fool. And the man who will not ask for nectar when it is to be had, he is yet a greater fool!

In a crumbling elementary-school graduation picture, where forty-three boys are seen grouped against the backdrop of a mammoth American flag hung on an outside wall of Public School 10—resembling, with its iron gratings on the windows, a prison—we see forty-three adolescent responses to a photographer's injunction to smile: some open, others masked. From this group of smiling boys emerged two murderers who were electrocuted, a labor racketeer, several thieves and muggers, a champion basketball player, and one playwright. Here, his wavy hair tightly groomed, his plump face offers a wary half-smile to the camera, and an expression that cannot be called other than "smart aleck." For the first time Clifford Odets' identification with his father—however partial, uncertain, and ambivalent—has become visible, and the biographer begins to hear occasional comments from neighbors that he was now "becoming a fresh kid." We are not surprised to hear as well that his speech melodies had begun to resemble his father's so closely that "sometimes over the telephone you couldn't tell if you were talking to L.J. or to Clifford."

The complexity of his task in integrating such overvalued aspects of his father as his narcissistic cocksureness with his mother's shy vulnerability is suggested by a different view of him, offered by a female fellow student:

> Gymnasium class. Clifford would be there (among all the other boys dressed in everyday clothes) dressed in a dark blue suit, a white shirt and ruffled collar and long sleeves with ruffles. Also always every day at class the blue suit, the white shirt and what is most outstanding in my memory was the white handkerchief. . . . After school Clifford would ask me to come to his home and go through his book collection. On one visit I came home with a book of poems—not by Clifford—

which he had autographed. Remember, he was only fourteen years old and most likely thought an autograph, even if it was someone else's work, meant something.

As is quite common in men whom history records, Odets' sense of his difference from others, his "specialness"*—hence the proffering of his autograph—commenced early: a sign of what Alfred Kazin calls "the gift of conviction."

At the same time that the father's smug smile was emerging on the son's face, the overt struggle between them was sharpening. Pursuing the muddiest of plans toward some sort of occupation during the summer after graduation from elementary school, Odets toyed with the idea of going to "dramatic school," but after a few tentative rounds on this topic with his father, he gave up that "impractical" idea and in September 1921 became, at fifteen, a freshman at Morris High School.

Morris High, named after a distinguished colonial family with large holdings in the Bronx,◖ was only twenty-five years old, but of New York public high schools was second in age only to Erasmus Hall in Brooklyn. Established at the same time as Boys High and Girls High, it was the "mixed" (coeducational) high school, boasting, according to one of its teachers, "a quality of forward-looking old-fashioned liberalism." It was top-heavy with "elderly people in whom conscience and propriety were strong." There was an unbreakable rule, for example, that the youngsters must be addressed by their surnames. The more flexible younger generation of teachers was still without influence.

On the surface, all was now in proper American order: the firstborn son was taking a general high-school course—preparatory, as L.J. planned it, to becoming a copywriter in his father's business—and the father was expanding this business to include not only a shop for job printing, called the Lincoln Press,† but, at long last, the dream of his own advertising agency, known as the Odets Company, specializing in "direct-mail advertising" as well as in something which he called "merchandising counseling."

In a small hard-cover book printed in 1922 (probably by L. J. Odets' own Lincoln Press) the credo of the Odets Company—with offices at 225 Fifth Avenue—was summed up under the title *Smoothing Out the Selling Path.*‡ In the space for the author's name appears, in modest print, "The Odets Company." This book was distributed, according to Louis J. Odets, "only to those institutions given a 3A-1 rating by Dun & Bradstreet. You know what that is? Well, *I'll tell you* what that is! 3A-1 means over-a-million-dollar rating . . . that means over a million business a year. To obtain that kinda business you gotta advertise it. Their credit is tops. They pay their bills on the first and the tenth of the month and they are checked every three, six, nine, twelve months for their standing."

His closest relatives were certain, however, that L.J.'s command of English grammar was at no time sufficient for him to produce even this

---

* Eugene O'Neill, no stranger to the subjective sense of apartness and uniqueness, in 1920 wrote a play devoted to this theme, called *Diff'rent.*

◖ 3.8.

† Odets would name his own later "firms" Jefferson: Jefferson Stamps, Jefferson Pictures, Jefferson Enterprises.

‡ Almost half a century later he would proudly and angrily produce this document as his proof—to his son's biographer, whom he counseled to "use your head for something besides a hat-rack"—that he had "always been a writer before you were born" and that his illustrious son "didn't grow on a tree" and "got his talent somewhere."

mass of advertising clichés, and that a hack copywriter in his employ must have ground out such incantations as: "Most advertising may be building good will but it isn't showing profits," or "Advertising, the modern miracle . . . is purely and simply salesmanship multiplied. There is no use in creating good will that does not sell, or in keeping one's name before the public if it does not sell. You must sell. . . ."

In a chapter entitled "The Method of a Poor Peddler," a garrulous buildup climaxes in the insight that a poor peddler makes much noise but few sales, concluding, "We wonder if a *few more sales and a little less good will* wouldn't do a lot more good" (italics mine). Odets was certain that if his father had actually written this booklet, instead of printing "The Odets Company" as the author, he would have printed "Louis J. Odets" in letters twice as tall as the title. Nonetheless, the old man's desperate claim to its authorship points to his longstanding grief, a grief incorporated by his illustrious son—namely, that he was a writer manqué.

Typically enough, the struggle between the father and the teen-age son was now crystallizing: the boy who had been conspicuously precocious and a source of pride with his public recitations was inexplicably becoming an embarrassing dunce. Clifford tried, without success, to persuade his father to let him change from the study of Spanish—recommended by L.J. because "someday we are going to do a lot of business with South America"—to French, which seemed to the son to be "the language of the poets." Accordingly, Clifford failed Spanish, and algebra as well. L.J. was nonplused that his bright and obedient son, always eager to please and to placate him, appeared now to be turning into an unrecognizably stupid, lazy, pimply, willful, and useless youth. He alternated between calling him an idiot and a bum. The pimply youth was puzzled, too, but helpless in the face of the upheavals within him, and in despair that he was no longer a source of pride to his father but rather a source of shame.

Although he could not resist the currents pulling him away from his father, he could not find the strength to oppose him openly in defense either of his own interest or of his mother's. L.J.'s publicly scandalous treatment of Pearl increasingly lacked restraint, and as Clifford was unable to defend her, his feelings of "cowardice and hypocrisy," as he later put it, were becoming unendurable. Family and neighbors agreed that "L. J. Odets was always a terrifying opponent . . . even if you were not his only son." Years later, pondering in guilt his high-handed treatment of his own son, Odets' memories would focus on this time when he himself was being disparaged or "cowed into convention" by his powerful and admired father. Clifford's friend Herman recalled most vividly the times when L.J. would discuss his son as though he were not present, saying contemptuously to neighbors, "He won't talk. Maybe he *can't* talk. Don't ask *me* what's the matter with him!" Odets often recalled that the best he could manage was "to protect myself from being hurt [by him] and extend this protection to others." It seemed to him he had to choose between a total disengagement and the panic which would result from "going to the aid of an humiliated other." As with all his earlier struggles, he resolved it both ways and neither way. The "humiliated other" to whom he obliquely refers is most often his long-suffering mother, though sometimes his crippled sister, both of whom he had always felt he was betraying each time he permitted an uncontested assault by his father. The configuration of a crucially experienced loss of integrity begins here to jell. Julian Drachman, drama teacher at Morris High, a keen and interested observer, noticed in Clifford at this time a characteristic manner paradoxically described as one of "sly innocence," his smile suggesting "he knew rather more than he was saying . . . a sort of chiel amang us takkin' notes."

Withdrawing progressively to his room—increasingly cluttered with books, tadpoles, tropical fish, and plants growing in Breakstone cheese boxes—Clifford struggled on for two years at Morris High, compiling five failures in major subjects, with four others, including English, on the razor edge. He failed in both art and music and for a short time managed still to do fairly well in two classes: in biology, taught by the "learned and clever" Dr. Israel Weinstein, and in a scholastically insignificant subject called by a name long since out of use, "elocution." He won the declamation medal with his recitation of Robert Service's "Spell of the Yukon," and struggled to maintain a patina of compliance, evident in his "citizenship rating" of A; his "initiative," called "helpful"; his "habits: good"; and "courtesy: very."

When even the patina disappeared, he was left with the one thing that truly engaged him: the Junior Dramatic Club, under Julian Drachman. Long after he had given up all of his classes, the bewildered sixteen-year-old who had begged his father to let him go to "dramatic school" continued with this activity.

Drachman, a sensitive and dedicated teacher who often quoted the Talmud, has clear memories of Odets:

> When the group met, one of those who turned up was a blonde-headed, sweet-faced little boy in knee pants and long black stockings. There was an unusually engaging expression of innocence about him; his look had a childlike, almost-baby-like freshness as though everything he saw in his newly discovered world filled him with wonder and excitement. His large blue eyes were constantly alight with interested observation and a quietly amused smile.
>
> In our over-crowded institution of almost 5,000 pupils, those in the upper grades who constituted a kind of juvenile aristocracy attended between 7:50 A.M. and 1:10 P.M. The younger children had to be present and scramble for their education after that, and their school day ended at 5:25 P.M. They could not possibly stay in after that dismal hour for meetings or rehearsals so we "PM-ers" had to come in before school if we were to have a club at all. Often because of the teaching schedules, they came as much as two hours before their own classes began—and greater love than this is unknown to the teenage school child. . . . It was not long before Odets showed himself as an outstanding member. There was nothing ostentatious, no self-propelled exhibitionism about his words or actions. On the contrary, he went modestly and efficiently about the business of preparing to play a part and he did it very well from the beginning without demanding any special consideration for himself.

Julian Drachman, one of those rare and invaluable mentors who confirm adolescents in their still inchoate aspirations, recalled the esthetic and the ethical values he tried to instill in the members of the Junior Dramatic Club:

> We studiously worked to avoid those terrible curses of the theatrical life associated with the star system: the exaggerated importance of the leading actor and the cruel elimination of the less gifted. We never forgot that our world was a school, not a marketplace, and that young actors were there to learn and to grow. . . . If Odets, who

clearly was the most gifted, had not cooperated fully in carrying out these principles, his dramatic career might have ended as soon as it began. For example, our basic method in casting a play was to select two complete casts. . . . One of our first productions was *Six Who Pass While the Lentils Boil* by Stuart Walker. Of course, Odets played the leading part, that is, Sir David Littleboy, in one of the casts.

It is curious that his first role should be that of "a boy who in the face of strong temptations does his duty and keeps his promise to his mother to watch the lentils until they should boil."◖

From a friend in the fermenting enclave of Greenwich Village a script came to Drachman which was a "highly sophisticated not to say salacious satire on the moral decadence of life during the corrupt period of Roman Imperial history." Although the children rejected the play as "boring because it was a lot of ancient history," it did not escape Clifford that young men were writing plays "downtown." For the time being, he was content only to act in them, confiding to his contemporaries that "one day I will write them, star in them and direct them." Drachman remembers him as particularly appealing in a "homemade costume with a white paper Buster Brown collar" as he struggled to work in his teacher's intuitively devised "Stanislavsky methods":

> Our method of conducting rehearsals stressed naturalness and vitality rather than strict accuracy. Our players never began to memorize their lines until they had been through dozens of rehearsals. . . . By this time they would so thoroughly have absorbed the action, character, and mood . . . that very little memorizing was needed. . . . Clifford could always be depended upon to learn his part not only with perfect detail, but also to understand the significance of what he was doing. . . .

The earliest hint of Odets' need to find a "container," a vessel of form, for his own dark struggles occurs in the account of a play tailor-made for his unconscious conflicts. Julian Drachman recalls his performance in this production:

> Probably our most spectacular success was *The Turtledove*, based on a Chinese legend about an emperor's son who disguised as a gardener loved the daughter of a haughty mandarin. When the lovers eloped, the infuriated mandarin pursued them, lashing the young man with a rawhide whip so that the latter fell down dead—and was raised to Heaven in the form of a turtledove. Cliff played the part of the lover with grace . . . but there was one thing he did that troubled me. During rehearsals, he soon realized that the thrilling climax of the play, his dropping dead, could easily be turned into a farcical anticlimax unless his fall seemed real. Over and over he practiced falling, hurling himself to the floor with such convincing violence that each time he did it I fully expected a serious accident. . . . He disregarded my . . . advice to take it easy and not risk broken bones. . . . He played in five performances of *The Turtledove*. I watched from the wings, and each time he fell like a thunderbolt a huge gasp broke from the audience and my heart, too, thumped in horror until a moment later it became clear that the good trouper . . . was still unhurt.

◖ 3.9.

Drachman could not have known that, in addition to wanting to give a persuasive performance, his young disciple was enacting one of the earliest of his demonstrative masochistic fantasies vis-à-vis his own father. Later versions of this underlying impulse (in automobile accidents) would have more serious results.

It took only one more event to persuade Drachman that this student was "destined to have a famous career in the theatre":

He was not a registered pupil in any class of mine, and I had seen no examples of his writing, but then something unprecedented took place. Cliff dropped into my late afternoon class one day and asked permission to stay and observe the lesson. Flattered by his interest, I readily agreed. He took an inconspicuous seat in the rear and remained there . . . glowing with rapt attention though being no member of the class he said nothing. He came often and sometimes took notes. Once he stayed after class and showed me his private notebook. It contained personal sketches of several of the teachers, and I was both thrilled and shocked to see with what insight and felicity he had analyzed my colleagues and me. . . . These faculty character descriptions were the only examples of his original writing that I saw during those years and they impressed me with his keen powers of observation and precocious skills. . . . That he would give up his own free time to sit in on a class for which he could not receive school credit seemed to me . . . evidence of an unusual devotion to literary scholarship. It was not until later that I began to suspect that he was perhaps not giving up his own free time but might be cutting other classes.

When this proved to be indeed the case, Drachman tried to persuade him "to more conventional attitudes." These efforts were in vain. "He would listen with respect and patience and then either make no response at all or a very sorrowful and brief one such as that most of the other teachers 'are such bores.'" There were, however, two exceptions: Ida Fischer of the Music Department, who took both a maternal and a teacher's interest in Clifford, and Charles Ballard, published poet and English teacher. Miss Fischer "was of Viennese descent and . . . possessed a full measure of *lebenslust*—joy of living. Lively, friendly, warm yet satirical, boisterous, throbbing with melody and fun, she was a sort of academic Elsa Maxwell in appearance as well as temperament."

Charles Ballard, tall, stooped, frail, kindly, and "ethereal," ate no meat because "he believed no man had the right to take the life of any creature." It was a concession for him to provide his dog with a prop bone, "licked over the years to the glow of alabaster." Mr. Ballard, overcome by Odets' ardent, if suicidal, performance in *The Turtledove,* had commemorated it by a tribute in Chinese rhetoric to match the play:

> For your shining eyes
> For your eloquent hands
> For your magic pictures
> I bow!

Ballard carried out in his English classes what he counseled himself in a concluding line of one of his poems: "I must be gentle with young things." Odets recalled:

I was ignorant enough not to know that there were monthly literary magazines or quarterly magazines. I saw something called *The Book-*

man on one teacher's desk, and I said, "What is that?" He says, "That's a book devoted to literature and the arts, a magazine." And I looked at it, and I said, "Gee, I'd like to buy something like that and look into it." I was a very ignorant boy and came from a very ignorant background.

Despite the best efforts of these three teachers, Clifford's grades continued to plummet. His father's enraged and frightened perplexity mounted, together with his shame that his son was making "such a bad showing." Pearl was by now also persuaded that something was irreparably amiss with her adored and golden son. Twenty years later Odets would reproduce characteristic dialogue of this time between himself and his mother:

Where are you going with the long pants? Can you hear me in there? Why aren't you in school today? (again no answer; after a wait) I'm warning you, no tricks! (only splashing answers her back) You know you're not so old I can't still give you with a strap! (merry boyish laughter is heard inside) What's so funny? (Sarcastically) Tell me so I'll laugh, too . . . (more ha ha comes back) In a minute I'll come in there. (putting her hand on the doorknob threateningly) You know I'm not afraid. (Then) He can't wash his own face and he's leaving the High School. Me you don't fool—I know you like a book.

In the spring of 1923 L. J. Odets could no longer ignore his sixteen-year-old son's steady downhill course. Julian Drachman witnessed the event:

One late afternoon I happened to be in the principal's office on another matter, and there I saw his father who had come on a mission of protest. . . . Mr. Odets was not there like so many parents to *defend* his son against the school's accusations, but *to complain against his son*, and what the school was doing to him. "I sent my boy to high school to get an education," he protested, "not to make a bum actor of him." . . . The stories that later drifted back to us seemed to corroborate the father's fears. I heard of his aimless dragging around, failing to find a job on Broadway, spending his time in pitching pennies on the sidewalk with younger boys, getting nowhere and apparently not even trying very hard.

Odets pleaded with his father for a short time "to let him go to college," but "L.J. would say, 'You can't go to college and just take nothing. If you want to be a lawyer or a doctor or a teacher, I'll send you.' Clifford would say, 'No, I don't want to be [any of those] I just want to go. . . . ' So this fight is going on and he's flunking algebra. They got him a tutor at a dollar a crack, but he'd come home and give the money back to his mother, saying, 'I didn't go. . . . ' If L.J. had said, 'I'll send you to college,' he would have worked at his algebra."

In the meantime the "ignorant boy," as Odets often later called himself, was devouring books with a greed that would never leave him: "anything at all from travel diaries of African explorers to occasionally an Ibsen play or Sherlock Holmes." By his seventeenth birthday he had read all of Victor Hugo and most of the Russians.

Now, too, despite the hooting of the kids on the block that he was being "show-offy," he devoted himself to the famed literary page of the *New York Morning World:*

. . . with Heywood Broun and F.P.A. and visiting columnists like William Bolitho, and then began to see that they were talking about a world that I would like to join. And, so to speak, my *first real* literary contact, for what it was, was with this page in the *Morning World* opposite the editorial page.

With Herman Koblanov, who of all the Beck Street Boys had the most generous spirit and the deepest appreciation of the originality of Clifford's being, he began to go to concerts in the Lewisohn Stadium on summer nights with "all the other kids thinking we were quite pretentious, that this was all bunk. . . . 'What's this about Choppen an' Brahms and all that? Well, come on! Cut the crap. . . . Who the hell do you think you are?' "◖

Once in a great while he "could rustle up a quarter" to see the local stock company, the Borani Players, in the Bronx, or for a Broadway play road-showing at the Bronx Opera House. Until much later, seeing a live play "downtown" was a rare happening. He was not aware, for example, that in the spring of 1922 O'Neill was expressing precisely the same sense of difference from his fellow man by having his "hairy ape," a stoker, die in the arms of a gorilla, with the curtain speech, "Even him didn't tink I belonged. . . . Where do I fit in?"

Odets continued to think of the silent movies as "inspiriting and inspiring" and full of "good acting." To express oneself publicly through the various masks of an actor appeared to him the acme of joyful creative attainment; he joined an amateur acting company, the Drawing Room Players, and was sometimes given parts in plays produced by the local library or at the Heckscher Foundation, a child-centered settlement house on the uptown extension of Fifth Avenue. He enjoyed acting because the response from the audience was immediate: if it was pleased, his hunger was instantly allayed; if not, he could quickly try another tack onstage or even a new part. In secret, he had begun to keep a diary and to write a few poems.

It was at this time, against Julian Drachman's counsel, that Clifford and his Bronx friend Jerry Rosenberg decided to do on their own an adult full-length play for an outside audience, selecting *The Return of Peter Grimm* by David Belasco, better known for his "realism" as a producer than as a playwright. The two boys worked for a couple of weeks as producer-director-actors until:

> Old Mr. Belasco let us know that he was still the owner of the copyright and that a whopping fee would be charged our group for each performance. The plea that ours was an educational group did not influence him and the plan simply folded not without a sense of relief. . . .

Imperceptibly, the time Odets spent at Morris High School dwindled as the time at the movies expanded. His Spanish teacher reported him as generally "indolent" and "irresponsible."

One day in November 1923, at seventeen and a half, to the profound dismay of the three teachers who "saw some kind of spark in me," he walked out of a classroom and never returned. He had seized a moratorium —a reprieve from irreversible commitment—and now commenced a battle for his creative life.

◖ 3.10.

PART TWO

Quest for a Place

1923-1931

Chapter Four

Each of us is an expression of the
will-to-power, but in America business is still the swiftest, surest
method of attaining great power. . . .
It never occurred to anybody that
greatness could be achieved as a
writer, a musician, an artist. Therefore all the potentially great men
poured into business.

THEODORE DREISER

. . . it reminded me of all those sad
boyhood days when autumn dusks
would come and a cold wind would
blow up the street and early the
streetlights came to life. I was a sad
boy and everything outside fed me.
That is what the perfect actor must
have, a constant feeding from outside of self. I think and I am, like
that, presto!

CLIFFORD ODETS, *undated fragment*

It was not immediately evident that a war of utmost gravity between
young Odets and both his parents had commenced. "True," his father later
said, "I couldn't see no way to get him back to Morris High, but, after all,
his friend Herman had quit, too, and Carl and Ernie, so I figured he could
join me in *my* business." Clifford at first protested that he wanted to go
into the theatre, but soon agreed to be trained by his father as a copywriter for the Odets Company. L.J. had no doubt it could be done: if
he could take his "stupid, ungrateful nephews from Philadelphia . . . out
of the goodness of my heart and make printers out of them," he could turn
his son into an advertising man. No matter that the nephews, as a direct
result of their humiliating apprenticeship, had left and never again addressed a word to him: "It was their own goddamn fault." They, in turn,
were left with an indelible image of "a man with a monumental ego, a

man who actually seemed to enjoy making you feel like two cents." Years later Clifford would recall, with the same "shame of cowardice" he had felt at being unable to defend his mother, how he had steadily echoed his father in transactions with the Philadelphia cousins, calling them "stupid loafers" and "ungrateful bums."

Louis J. Odets was expansive this year. It seemed that in this "permanent prosperity" come to America there was no limit to the future of the Odets Company. He brought home pads of colored paper and sheets of gold leaf and designed business stationery for himself which sported a white border around a field of soft green which, on closer inspection, turns out to be not a solid color but the words "The Odets Company" printed hundreds of times in tiny, tiny letters. On this stationery, with his father's typewriter, Clifford, going through the motions of an apprentice copywriter, began now his secret "literary" output. At first he restricted it to personal letters, of which, like many aspiring young writers, he kept carbons. Later he wrote poems, one-act plays, and reams of "Notes" on his father's elegant "business stationery." In a characteristically adolescent mélange of inhibited self-expression, affection for language, yearning, affectation, pomp, and condescension, he began, while "on the job," an active correspondence with a girl cousin in Philadelphia whom he had seen only twice in his life. It is evident that the mainspring of these letters is self-expression, with no specificity in the choice of correspondent. Yet it is equally evident that he hungers for a feminine response. The scars of his recent academic disasters jump off the page to us who know of them; also the hollow effort to assume his father's identity as a "busy business man" with the middle initial L. lifted from his father's first name. A typical letter—"typed," he explains in a postscript, "during business hours"—is a model of self-conscious seventeen-year-old preoccupations: to avoid convention, to show off, and, above all, to seduce.

October 30, 1923

Dear Irene:

Notice that I entirely dispense with the word cousin.

Cousin is a weak and futile word, anyhow and that is my reason for not using it.

My mother came home from Philadelphia the other day and told me that among others she had seen "The Fabians."

Well I said how are they—and Irene.

Oh fine my mother answered and Irene is a very nice girl.

Yes, so she is, I agreed; and I thought of long ago, when I had last seen you and how you had charmed me and how I had promised to write you, and—here we have that long lost letter.

The prodigal son has returned at last.

I find now that I hesitate and don't know what to say or write, or tell you about for I'm sure we have no mutual friends.

The span in miles between Philadelphia and New York is close on to a hundred miles and that is obviously a long way to travel.

And I'd like to come to PH. once in a while, but I'm a busy business man and business *is* business. So there you are.

Are you still one of the silent drama's enthusiasts?

You ought to know that whenever I hear that song, "In My Sweet Little Alice Blue Gown," my mind completes a circle and thinks of you. My memories always persist in delighting me.

Ah just a minute; to be sure, how is your friend, is it Pauline?

Here comes the conventional topic. How's school?

Do you take a language? I hope it's not Spanish for that's so practical. And there is a possibility of German. Let's hope that it is French that you take. For that's the tongue that has most all the romance of history, and romanticism, I'm sure appeals to you as it does to me.

Of course your mother and dad are in the best of health so I shan't ask that time-worn question.

My sincere regards to all.

It would be the acme of pleasure to receive an answer from you.

Yours as ever,
Clifford L. Odets

P.S.

Please excuse the typed letter as that is most convient [sic] during business hours.

The rest of this correspondence continues the controversy about the value of learning "practical" Spanish, with Clifford imploring his cousin to ask herself if there is "one character in Spanish, wait, en el historia de España (I didn't take five terms for nothing) who has been woven into a novel. No. Unless you would call Don Quixote historical."

To facilitate a prompt response, he sends her a catechism of questions in the form of a questionnaire usually sent by Louis J. Odets to his clients. A sample:

Your school life must be quite interesting. . . .
Let me know more about it. . . .
Do you belong to any sort of clubs? . . .
How are your parents? . . .
And yourself? . . .
Let me know what you term enjoyment. . . .
Have you many friends there? . . .
Who are they and of what sex? . . .
Do you dance and go to them? . . .
   ”   ”   ”   at parties? . . .

Throughout this correspondence, in an echo of his father's contempt, there occurs a barrage of scornful comment comparing, for example, Philadelphia and its "puny dirt plot they call (if it is called at all) Fairmount Park" to the "wondrous parks" like Van Cortlandt of New York City. The tone is as condescending and as self-enamored as L.J.'s in his most arrogant moments. Yet Clifford's scorn takes a turn quite different from his father's when he scolds Irene for not appreciating Zangwill's "fine play, 'The Melting Pot' " and adjures her to realize that "the foreigners are the backbone of this nation. . . . Were it not for the foreigners you would not have any streets to walk on. Who makes the city? Is it the Browns and the Joneses? No, it's the Palumbos and the Scaveretties."◖ Here, as when he would give the name "Joe Bonaparte" to the protagonist of his play *Golden Boy*, he displaces and masks his conflict about his Jewish identity. Yet the stand is the opposite of his father's: he promises his young cousin that if she will come to New York he will prove the value of the "melting pot" by taking her "to restaurants like The Samovar, The Armenian, and The Russian Inn to eat the fine things immigrants cook." Moreover, he asks, "Where can you find a 'Little Bohemia' that can equal our Greenwich Village, which we affectionately term 'The Village'?"

In response to her accusation that he is boasting, he writes:

◖ 4.1.

You say I brag. I pride myself upon being altruistic. I should hope that their [sic] is no egotism in me. When I laud our grimy old city that is not what should be called "bragging." That is undiluted patrism. (A new way to spell it) Amo mi ciudad. Tambien me pais.*

It is a revealing close-up of the disparate elements struggling for coherent shape in a shaky adolescent's quest for a supportable identity: the language ranges from a quasi-Elizabethan whimsy ("Thusly if this letter is off form, of course thou wilt not chide me") to misspelled Spanish, to a vernacular announcement that "Anne . . . is the bimbo for me." He describes this "Anne" as "an oliveskinned little Burma girl that Kipling wrote about in his 'On the Road to Mandalay,' which is a very beautiful poem I assure you." He promises his cousin to recite this for her, as "You see I'm quite a reciter myself, I won a couple of medals in school last term. And plays—oh plays—but what's the use. Only the conceited speak of their exploits."

One exploit of which he did not speak to Irene was his deception, directly upon leaving Morris High, of an English teacher at DeWitt Clinton High School. Pretending he was an enrolled student, he tried out for the lead part of François Villon in the school production of *If I Were King* and got it. "I was so crazy to act," he later said, that "I actually rehearsed it for three days before I confessed to the coach that I was not a member of the school." The teacher quickly enrolled him in two courses, "just enough to get by," and he proceeded to rehearse in the play every afternoon. But even the two courses were more than he could tolerate "at nine o'clock in the morning . . . coming all the way down from the Bronx"; thus, with regret the drama coach took him out of the play, and his brief matriculation at DeWitt Clinton ended.

In desperation to "be on a stage," he now presented himself to the Moss vaudeville-circuit office, which shortly hired him as a "ringer" elocutionist for Amateur Nights. On a given night he would be assigned to, say, the Alhambra or the Grand Theatre to participate as a bona-fide amateur contestant with his recitation of "The Face on the Barroom Floor," "The Shooting of Dan McGrew," or his favorite, "Fleurette."† The Moss office illicitly guaranteed him a minimum of three dollars in addition to any prize he could capture by eliciting audience applause. The first prize was ten dollars; second, seven; and third, five. Regularly he would round up the Beck Street Boys to swell his applause and thus give him a prize. At home, jingling the pocket money thus earned, he began to call himself an actor. Unimpressed, his father witheringly pointed out that more and more the Moss office wanted singers, not elocutionists, for Amateur Nights, and accurately predicted that his acting career in vaudeville would soon be at an end.

Later Odets recalled his sadness at the termination of these vaudeville recitations. As he lost himself in the passionate declamation of the crippled, ugly soldier who is redeemed by the love of a woman, he felt at

---

* Spanish: "I love my city. Also my country."

† This four-page Robert Service classic is told in the first person by a Canadian soldier more concerned about the fact that "folks shudder and turn away" from his face than that his leg is off at the knee. All of this has resulted from his smothering a bomb "that fell into the trench and so none of my men were hit / Though it busted me up a bit." It is climaxed by his transfiguration as a result of "Fleurette," a "graceful, slim" and "rare little queen" kissing the lips of his disfigured face: an extravagantly romantic Beauty-and-the-Beast tale with which Clifford deeply identified himself. In his more sophisticated years he would identify himself with the guillotined hero of Stendhal's *The Red and the Black*, whose severed head is reclaimed by the woman who loves him.

one with his audience and reassured. "More than the money . . . what was important is I never had that kind of self-confidence in any activity forever after."

Frequently in his correspondence the cocky surface—taken over from his father—cracks to reveal a painfully self-conscious youngster who sees himself through the eyes of the head of the Odets Company: "I look like a little fool and—oh what's the use of wasting space, you can tell what sort of simp I am by the stupid letter that I write. . . . If I show not that ability that you so rightly deserve, I beg you be lenient and remember that I am tired and don't show this letter to your friends. It is too FOOLISH."

Deep shyness, terror of ridicule, and urgent need to placate for an immediate reassuring response inform all his adolescent correspondence and would remain essentially unchanged for the rest of his life, whether with audiences, women, critics, employers, or members of a Communist-hunting congressional committee. His lifelong effort to master what he once called his "acidulated low self-esteem" now, and later, takes many forms: from a disarming penetration into the most secret places of a woman, to the creation of works of art. At seventeen, having already evolved this technique for binding a woman to his side, he offers his cousin Irene a brash, breezy, but emphatically shrewd summary of her "personality," guesses her secret vanities and fears, projects several of his own, and hints—often arrogantly—that by his insights he can open her to herself. On the day before Christmas 1923, with all the family except him visiting in Philadelphia, he threatens his cousin with "death by decapitation" if she delays in answering his letter, but concludes placatingly with a request for "some friends' pictures and I'll tell you all about them." On "the last day of 1923" he issues a final threat that he will "discontinue writing" if she is not more responsive, ending the year with an attack on womankind:

> You girls try to kid us poor fellows along and keep stringing them with hot air. You try to appear so artless, so naive. As for instance you read what I said about the mirror and you looking in it to see if you are growing more beautiful each day. You answered me that such a thing was impossible. However, down deep in your heart when you first read that sentence, your heart, or something akin to it, swelled with pride. You even may have read the thing over two or three times. Don't try and fool me. I can read a character like an open book. Now don't forget that.

Having begun to locate within himself the gift for seeing to the true hearts of people—later thought of by many as uncanny—he would, by turns, employ it in compulsive sexual campaigns and in creative work.◖

As the New Year opened, L.J. could no longer ignore the fact that his son, coming irregularly and late to the office at 225 Fifth Avenue, was passive, careless, moody, and of no use to the Odets Company. He could not ignore, either, the fact that Clifford had begun to reverse day and night, a schedule

◖ 4.2.

not calculated to fit into the world of business. Twenty years later, in retrospect, the son would see his own behavior as a "juvenile revenge."

As L.J. grew more hopeless about his son's future, his harangues grew more savage. Odets later recalled his father's voice fresh in his ear as though it had just been delivered:

> You don't listen to me. Oh, no, not you. Million dollar executives listen to your Dad—they *pay* him for his advice! You, you listen to the kids on your corner, your (snot nose) friends, but not to your father. Your father—he don't know a thing!

The boy met this torrent of abuse with a despairing and flushed silence, a "dogged passivity," as he called it, learned from his mother. It appeared to him later that "it became necessary to develop an even faster style of talking with which to strike back. Usually, however, one struck back at another person or thing, someone who would be apt to punish less in return." He began to strike at himself as well, now with self-accusations and later with suicide attempts. It became Odets' conviction that it was at this time he had come to detest the "go-getting father on my head" who kept roaring, "You'll get there if you'll only keep two feet on the ground." He liked to believe that his earlier bond with his father as the "strong protective adult" now vanished as L.J. moved in on him in the name of concern, shouting a dozen times a day, "I told you so!"

A copywriter in the employ of the Odets Company recalled from this time a characteristic exchange: "I said, 'You know, L.J., you remind me of a man in a book that a man named Sinclair Lewis has written.' L.J. replied, 'Yes? What's that? What's that? What book?' I answered, '*Babbitt*,' to which L.J. responded with elation, 'I'm like a man in a book!'" Although Odets frequently used this bitter anecdote to demonstrate how easy it was to resist as exemplar this caricature of a father, it's undeniable that by this time Louis J. Odets had become firmly entrenched within his son both as model and as antagonist. Simultaneously Odets needed to placate, submit to, defy, and outdo him. Two years before his death, at the age of fifty-five, he would say in all innocence: " . . . the man so twisted me, so sent me through a number of psychological wringers, that I'm sure some of the damage is still present," or, more urgently: "Most human beings spend the last two-thirds of their lives trying to eradicate and unlearn (resist, fight) the first painful third. So all is painful in the end!"

Clifford spent New Year's morning of 1924 watching a movie at the Rivoli with three of the Beck Street Boys. On the next day, back on the job at the Odets Company, he renews his urgent self-exploratory correspondence with his cousin. With that delicate balance of emphatic insight and projection characteristic of mistrustful but perceptive human beings, he analyzes her character. Calling himself "an even greater cosmic dreamer than you are" and a "sensitive, lofty thinker," albeit "sarcastic," he provides clues to the identity crisis building within him. When he describes himself as "weak in the fact that I am not practical," he is unaware that with part of himself he is surrendering to his father's bullying and contemptuous assessment. He concludes, with a bland and obtuse innocence, that "If a person of my type does not get business training while they are young, they will never make a success in business. Luckily I am getting the training." In passing, he mentions the three graphic artists *"we* employ" in his father's advertising agency. No one could predict from this statement of apparently placid conforming juvenile obedience that within the month this adolescent would leave the Odets Company and his father's employ forever, or, indeed, that within the decade he would emerge as *the* fiery American playwright-apostle of social revolt. Or, most important, that the conflict would continue throughout his life. Later he writes: " . . . the struggle in all of us between obedience and self-realization is central, perhaps the underlying structure, the basement of all human life."◖ And still later: "Anger integrates, mobilizes me . . . and insulates me against harm and virus in an irrational way."

He was now "bone-weary," enervated chiefly by the effort expended in trying to emulate and please his father. The first of his two tasks was to detach himself from his father—inside and out—while keeping them both alive. The second was to envision some occupation whereby he might earn a living and yet find the creative self-expression for which he hungered. His 1924 diary becomes a daily record of being physically spent and emotionally emptied. Hitting that "rock bottom" so often presaging a turning point in a gifted and endangered adolescent, he retreats, like his mother, into stony silence. Again and again in his diary occur the terms "ennui," "fatigue," "sloth," "weakness," "lassitude," "despair," and, most important, "a sense of fraudulence."

It would be many years before he would see in his battle with his father a distillation, a prototype of an American struggle. Thus would his private outrage be transcended and integrated into a system of values and an esthetic battle cry for the American artist, immortalized on the cover of *Time:* "Down with the general fraud!" In one form or another, over and over, his statement to newspaper reporters, interviewers, Ph.D. candidates, and to himself would be the same: "Man is an heroic being if he can only break through to fulfillment. . . . Nothing moves me so much as human aspirations blocked, nothing enrages me like waste. I am for use as opposed to abuse." How bitter, then, the fact that after his death the first word that occurred to an old friend, Elia Kazan, when asked to "think about Clifford," was the single word "Waste!"

The youth steadily consoled himself these days with masturbation and with fantasies of becoming a Great Actor, a Great Writer, and—almost as important—a Great Lover. At about this time he wrote a novel and burned it, "because it was so melodramatic," about a young pianist whose "promising career is cut short by an accident to his hand."◖

As his pimples receded and he emerged once more in photographs as a dreamy, softly appealing boy, he began to gather his forces toward achieving the basic strength of competence as an actor. At seventeen, it seemed to him later, his prime aim had been "to show how hep" he was and "what a pro": " . . . I don't know why almost. I think it really made you feel important, like smoking your first cigarettes. Why do you start smoking? You start smoking because you walk down the street with a cigarette: you're a big shot. You're grown up." Besides which, it was his conviction that he had had "a lot of flair, a lot of energy, and I could

◖ 4.3.
◖ 4.4.

really play the hide off a scene," but it would be another year before he would have consistent opportunity to do this, even as an amateur. He recalled to Robert Hethmon a premature, doomed effort:

> I had the bitter experience once of seeing the star of a stock company down at Proctor's Twenty-third Street. And I thought, "I'll just step in at the stage door." And they said they would be opening in two weeks with a play, a play called *A Prince There Was*. I think it was an old George M. Cohan play. And I walked in, and the whole company was assembled around the stage. They were working on a scene. And the stage manager came over and asked me what I wanted. And I said, "Well, I thought you might have some small part or something." He says, "You have experience?" I said, "Yes, of course." And then he spoke to the director, who was sitting down in the front rows, and they gave me the part of a messenger boy, and lo and behold, I was in the professional theatre. Well, I looked at this part and had never seen anything like it, because there were only the cues and then my three or four lines, and I couldn't make out what this was, a lot of dots ending in two or three words which was the cuing. And suddenly the director shouted at me, "That's you! Can't you see? Can't you hear your cue? That's you. You now knock at the door. You ring the bell." Of course, there were just chairs laid out on the rehearsal stage. And I couldn't make out this part. My hands were shaking. And the leading man came to the door and said something, and I did not answer him, because I could not see his speech on my page. I could just see the last two words. Well, anyway, I caught on very quickly because the stage manager was very nice, and he kind of, out of the side of his mouth, told me what to do. And then the director says, "Come in. Come downstage. Come down more." I didn't know what he was talking about: "Come downstage." Anyway, I didn't know what that meant. So he said, "This boy will never do. He has no acting experience at all." So I lost the job. And this was a bad blow to me.

Serious though his investment in becoming an actor now was, it is evident from the gravity with which he bought a diary for fifty-five cents and from his entries in it that he already entertained, however forlornly, a hope, mocked by his father, that someday he would be a writer. The presence of the strong wish to be an actor—taken directly from his histrionic parents—makes this an evolution significantly different from that of a playwright who, from the first, relies for self-expression and communication not on his own body but on the Word.◖

It is noteworthy that two editions of this diary are extant: the handwritten original and a much shorter one, typewritten later. Sample comparisons show on a minuscule scale how Odets worked "from life," even for a short public speech.* The original begins with a stereotyped entry dated January 7, 1924:

◖ 4.5.

* Odets, it turns out, prepared the doctored "diary" for reading on the occasion of the memorial meeting for Eugene O'Neill at the Actors Studio on December 21, 1953, where, according to a member of the audience, Odets "read from his boyhood diary to show how little one can predict about creativity." Juleen Compton recalled that "Clifford's idea was that there was potential in all young boys and no one knew 'which one of us is predestined to be geniuses.' He was showing how innocent a boy *he* was and no doubt O'Neill was the same and therefore we should all cultivate ourselves." In the one casual remark about O'Neill which he had manufactured for the occasion, he was demonstrating—he thought—the creative potential in all of us.

Bought this diary. Hope that I can use it to the best of advantage. Uneventful evening. (Two pipes full.) About time that I got a letter from Alma. I am anticipating a great deal of pleasure in my diary. Hope to make it really confidential. Eh what?

The doctored one, also marked January 1924, stops the biographer in her tracks with its bite and its prescience until she deduces it was rewritten long after the fact:

Bought this diary. Hope that I can use it to the best of advantage. Uneventful evening. Two pipesful. About time that I got a letter from Alma. Paul was around. He said he would change his name from Paul Greenbaum to Paul Green and be a playwright! I said there was a playwright by that name. He said it didn't matter. Then there would be two. I said I would be a playwright like Eugene O'Neill but wouldn't change my name. Must get to bed early next week.

On January 10, 1924, he records in his diary identity-fragments taken from each parent: his mother's prudery and his father's "gay-blade" investment and bodily grace:

Went to a dance with W. at the Martinique Mansion. What a cake affair—but such "belly whopping" (vulgaris). Well, well, I certainly do step better than I was wont to do. Horrors. I am gradually changing from a "collegiate" to a sharpy. Am going to *dances* more often. The A&S [Advertising and Selling] course was held at NYC—at Waverly & 8th Street. When I saw those college boys a gob came in my throat. To think that I am going to miss that. High School, too! Walked through Greenwich Village. Hope to rent a studio someday and make a sort of dreamer's den. The dance habit is getting in my system. Oh it's great to dance!

For the O'Neill evening Odets altered it thus:

Went to a dance with Walter at P.S. 54. What a cake affair! Well, well, I certainly step better than I was wont to. I am gradually changing from a collegiate to a sharpy. The Ad. & Selling Course was held at NYU, Waverly and 8th. When I saw those college boys a gob came in my throat. To think that I am going to miss all that! Walked thru Greenwich Village. It's where Eugene O'Neill hangs out. Hope to rent a studio some day and make a sort of Dreamer's and Writer's Den. Oh, it's great to dance!

The original diary of this endangered adolescent would not have been reassuring to a clinician: Odets is suffering from acute insomnia, sleeping later each day, and constantly determining to "get to bed earlier next week." During the days he is smoking too many cigarettes and pipes and making repeated vows to regulate this debilitating "bad habit."* He is dully trying, without success, to follow in his father's footsteps by taking a course at New York University in Advertising and Selling, attending to it only when the teacher fires his "guns of ambition by talking of O'Neill and the Barrymores." With more enthusiasm he plays pool and cards, determining to "record winnings or losses." He sets up numerous seductive and wary correspondences with girls and takes comfort from the prospect of "great doings ahead with Blanche," an anonymous girl whom he tele-

* During this same year Eugene O'Neill also is wrestling with his poisonous intakes—and on January 1, 1925, decides to "give up drinking and smoking forever."

phones, giving a pseudonym. He compulsively sees films—sometimes three in a day—admires the acting, and adjures himself repeatedly to "find out about playwrights . . . I still have that stage bug in my mind."

His diary records frequent battles with his father, and he describes a day when he escaped the chore of writing advertising copy and, instead, spent the afternoon in the 42nd Street library, deciding it would be "an ideal place to spend a vacation." On this same day he expresses wistful surprise that he "got a bid for some frat . . . all I remember is the last letter sounds like Zader." Now, as always, his yearning to belong to this, or to any, fraternity of brothers is high.◀

He feels himself to be "vegetating . . . and only pay-day gladens [sic] my weary heart." "My education," he writes, "is up to me. Books shall furnish it" and he has just bought "some little ones." He is becoming "tired of those phrases" his father uses, and "will see who asks ¼ first." Toward the end of January the "scraps" with his father come closer together, and, finally, a decisive entry on January 30: *"Today I have decided that I am going to leave my father's place."*

A psychotherapist-biographer, reading this, applauds—only to learn that the boy's attempt to resolve his crisis took the form of applying for a job—the first of several dreary positions this year—in another advertising agency precisely like his father's! His frightened acceptance of his father's aspirations and values had clearly become a piece of him. Years later he wrote:

> It is weird! The child raised by a dominating, authoritarian parent, develops both resistance and emulation. The thing, in other words, is bitterly fought but is simultaneously seen as some powerful thing, admirable, to be imitated. Hell results!

> For the grown person will now do exactly to others as he himself has been done to. Then a third quality enters: self-contempt and contempt for others. But in the "flaying" of others the self-contempt is dissipated.

> It is not the father over there of whom you must be careful—you can forget him. It is the father you have *incorporated*, his characteristics and hated elements—*that* is the father to be afraid of!

On the day he decides to leave his father's firm, the diary entries abruptly cease.

Seven months later the diary resumes with what must have been for this stagestruck boy a thunderous event. On August 30 he writes: "Saw 'The Miracle.' Stupendous. Superlative of every adjective that can describe it. Norman Bel Geddes is a wonder." Eyewitnesses of this Max Reinhardt spectacle report that no newspaper account of the time quite does justice to the luxurious opulence of the cathedral constructed by the tiny Austrian theatrical manager in the Century Theatre on Central Park West. Lit through stained-glass windows, it was, in the view of one observer, "a lavish combination of Europe and Paradise."

Herman Koblanov, who accompanied Odets on the first of his dozens of trips to *The Miracle*, recalls, "Clifford was so moved, it was somehow like a prayer." From August 30, 1924, until it closed, performances of the show were seldom without young Odets in the audience, at first as a paid customer (he used up his entire income from his work as a clerk at the

◀ 4.6.

H. C. Michaels Advertising Co. on tickets to this play) and later as a cloakroom employee whose sole compensation was to see *The Miracle* gratis. Odets recalled the play as a romantic tale of "a young, orphaned nun who dreams she is lured into the world where she learns much through suffering." She finds on her return to the cathedral from which she had fled that a compassionate Madonna has descended from her niche and has miraculously accomplished all of the nun's duties. Here was a resonating theme, and a protagonist with whom this boy could readily identify.

The nun was played by the tall, beautiful, and socially prominent Rosamond Pinchot, the same age as Odets, niece of a governor, only recently become an actress, and a great success in this, her first role. *The Miracle* was hypnotic for this aspiring young actor, the extent of whose investment in theatre was still a secret even from himself. In later years he often told the story of his intense yearning to communicate with the cast of this stupendous event: too shy to approach the remote, upper-class, Gentile Miss Pinchot—who eventually committed suicide—he one day accosted actor Schuyler Ladd, in full costume, curled blond wig and all. Blushing furiously and stammering, all Odets could think of to say to this god was, "What beautiful hair you have!" Ladd, he recalled, stared at him coldly "as if I were insane," then walked away.

On September 8, 1924, Odets records he has already lost two jobs since leaving the Odets Company and "If I could write a play, I would name it 'Sic Transit Gloria Mundi.'" He adds that his father's idea, still, " . . . of a liberal education is to work in *his* place."

He is reading many books, among them Thomas Beer's *Sandoval* and Hugo's *Toilers of the Sea*. In the latter he thinks he "may find material for a one-act play," but he is filled again with an "invisible ennui" and fears he "could fill this diary with ideas that were never reared to children."* He is compelled, instead, to play pinochle, "cursed game!" asking himself, "Are you condemned? Made a mistake? Blame it on temperament." There are repeated entries of remaining awake until the small morning hours, unable to sleep. He again and again blames tobacco for this symptom, "a very heavy cross. It makes me so listless." This insomnia, so frequent in youngsters who fear that any suspension in their consciousness may become permanent, was early begun and would remain with Odets for most of his life.

Right after his eighteenth birthday, as his money runs low, his desperate efforts to integrate a professional identity continue: "I am gradually realizing that money can consummate more dreams than all ambition and desire.† . . . These days one sees so many lifes [sic], and young ones too, scattered over the rocks of uncertainty and fear. . . . I often wonder if I really have the makings of an actor or an author in me. I compose bits every day but they are all disjointed, impromptu thoughts."

The big event each week, faithfully recorded in his diary—besides "Jean," whose "starved soul and body fairly vibrates as she speaks about her chronic ailment, Sex!"—is to read the "Lit. Review." He ponders that Jean's story "would furnish no little material for a story or a sketch." Without much confidence, he starts a novel and a few short stories, but these endeavors must be kept secret from his father and from his col-

---

* Odets' view of his generative difficulties commences early.

† Such avarice, often said to lie at the heart of the conflict in American writers, is not ordinarily a primary motive. Usually the writer is attempting to dissolve a sense of shame, guilt, inferiority, and identity-confusion by acquiring the trappings of success. The important thing is to be Somebody.

leagues in the bookkeeping department of the piece-goods factory where he is now employed.◀

As the fall of 1924 deepens, it appears clear to him, now working at the Commercial Investment Trust, that "I don't fool the bosses & they, not me. . . . As Steve says I don't seem cut out for work. At least not that kind." He, who routinely failed arithmetic even in the elementary grades, is dazed by figures he must daily confront. The word "unprofitable" occurs often in his diary and increasingly sums up a twenty-four-hour period: "The 'block' is dead. Walked up and down the avenue. My old friends are so unprofitable. Went to a 'chink joint.' Home 2 A.M."

In a sudden ascetic burst, as if to effect a magic resolution of his despair, he announces he has given up smoking cigarettes and cautions himself, "Never let love past the portcullis of your heart." And one day of "uselessness" follows another. His diary states: "If I was only making lots of money my mother would have a cook and a housemaid. Such a day. The sun lurked in moody clouds and so did the man."

Finally, we see an aborted impulse for theatre training: "Hope to call up the Neighborhood Playhouse for a tryout." In the next breath he negates it by pleading with normal "ambition" to "dispel these dreams that are as worthless as smoke rings. Beautiful—that's all. That is all." It is evident that in some unshakable part of his eighteen-year-old self he shares his powerful father's contempt for his aspirations as an artist.◀

For weeks on end, nonetheless, the music from *The Miracle* continues to haunt him: "it strums and palpitates in my mind." It seems to him "as if I were a child scores of years ago" and he longs "to tear away the cloud called 'the future.' " There is no hint that he has seen any play this year besides *The Miracle*—not even the daring anti-war play *What Price Glory?*, whose impact at its premiere has frequently been cited as the only precedent in the American theatre for the electric response in 1935 to Odets' *Waiting for Lefty*.

Finally, taking the day off for the Jewish New Year, he walks in brooding despair from Hunter's Island to the Boston Post Road and hitchhikes to Stamford, Connecticut, and back, in the rain, trying to decide whether he can quit his job. An outburst from his mother, who "rose from bed screaming" when he got home that she was tired of his late hours, determines him not only to "say farewell to the Commercial Investment Trust," but to leave home as well and ship out as O'Neill had. He determines he will go in the morning to the docks with Paul Greenbaum, who, "though humorless," also has aspirations in the theatre. A less manly thought intrudes itself as an alternative: perhaps he will meet a rich woman of eighty-two and marry her, as a twenty-eight-year-old colleague at the Commercial Investment Trust had just done. On the next day "Paul informs me that vis-a-vis [sic] and other passports are needed for abroad. *That is off,*" and the Odets family moves again, this time "to Apartment 6D" in the same building.

Clifford now hitchhikes to Philadelphia to visit Aunt Esther and Uncle Israel, who remain an organic part of him. There he is royally welcomed, admired, and fed, and returns to the Bronx, unemployed, bearing with him a bottle of his uncle's homemade "moonshine."

For three weeks life is "dull and oily" and he appears to have given up. Berating himself savagely in his diary with "Sluggard" and "Poseur," he plays handball mornings, deriving only minimal relief from his guilt

◀ 4.7.
◀ 4.8.

at such idleness by rehearsing, with Jerry Rosenberg, "thirteen one-act plays" for the amateur Drawing Room Players in the evenings. Smoking wildly, he fears for his health. He decides to "fix up" his new room with pipe racks, writes to pipe manufacturers for information, and plans to write a book on pipes! In the meantime he whistles in the dark: "No money. Oh well! An empty pocket gives me a light heart."

And now the husband of Pearl Odets' friend Rae comes forward with a new business opportunity for young Clifford, a job in the bookkeeping department of L. Bachmann and Co. Filled with guilt at his idleness, he writes in his diary, "Have the job! Figures. Enter in book. Figure interest. Perhaps I will acquire a greater love of figures, those jumbles I have always hated so! . . . Life still dazes me." And on his first day, "Oh such work!"

Now follows entry upon entry of the intolerable tedium of the job, and "Tired—tired—tired. Why always tired? . . . of life! . . . It is one damned rub and abrasion. . . . " He derives some pride from not having "been late yet on the job . . . which becomes clearer as no doubt will life in due times respectively" and hopes to gain some diversion from the girls he will meet at the dances of the Sigma Delta Phi social fraternity, to which he has just been elected, or maybe at the Victoria Athletic Club, an organization unrelated either to the English queen or to athletics. But he is in terror that as a result of this "fruitless" youth "I will have my play at 40— if I live that long." He has written vaguely to radio station WHN, "who have asked for young talent."

The longest entry of this year occurs in response to the death of an older man and issues in frightened resolutions that his next diary "will team [sic] with curses, moods, and detail. Each page shall afford me a record of youth . . . and I'll write you full, oh somewhat sacred diary." He is responding not only to the loneliness of the dead man's wife and children, but, more important to an aspiring young writer, to the threat of time running out. He records:

Learned this morning that Mr. Gus Cohen has died. Poor tired soul! . . . He seemed to typify an ideal American. Every now and then Mrs. Cohen would give vent to somewhat stifled combinations of a wail & sob. . . . Such horror in that word alone. Poor Mrs. Cohen. So she sits and wails, poor Mrs. Cohen. . . . Mr. Wiel lifted the cover from the deceased man's face. I was too timid to approach him. But from where I stood I saw over the edge of that dark coffin, the lifeless man's finely chiseled nostrils. They once had breathed fire. And in his moments of passion? And now but an inanimate doll; no better than common wax. How long oh Lord, how long will people come and go! For eternity, till a new race will be born—but not from sin or passion. Theirs will be a fleshless birth. So I sit here at twelve. The house too is shrouded in darkness. The shades crackle. My cigarette almost burns my finger tips. But I smoke and live. . . . Will I always be thus—cynical and tired of life. I wonder. I would believe in God if I had some proof. . . . Genevieve has just come from a dance at her school. Poor little chit. . . . Not many fellows dance with her. You see diary, she's slightly lame. I fight with her and call her vulgar names, but still I feel tender to her. She is, you know, my own sister. . . . Such ambitions as I cherish and have cherished, I am sure will never come to reality. . . . I have fixed up my cubicle tonight— Pennants 'n everything. . . . To Morpheus:—Treat me well and I advertise you.

The intention to communicate to an unseen future audience in this entry is evident. Although this glimpse of death may well have softened him even toward Genevieve, there is something self-conscious in his stated tenderness toward her—and certainly in his identifying her for his dear reader. The ascetic assumption that human misery is the outcome of "sin and passion," and that a "happy 'new race' will have a spiritual, fleshless birth," reflects one aspect of his adolescent struggle.

Toward the year's end he writes again, "Life dazes me" and he is "jaded, anxious and tense." His memory is failing, he thinks, "probably from smoking too much." Even at the parties, where he compulsively recites "The Spell of the Yukon," everything is "humdrum." There is a small smirk of excitement in a range of tobaccos for "my new tobacco table! Blue Boar, Imperial Cube Cut and Garrick." Quickly he tires of them all, as throughout his life he tires of such small consolations.

On Election Day he is depressed by "wasting the day off" and by over-hearing a friend's mother say, "If he comes in the house I'll kick him out," probably, he thinks, because he is smoking too much. He fears he is becoming a pariah. Maybe he will go blind from this addiction, his eyes are burning and aching already and "seem to smoulder in their sockets." And, finally, he has the fantasy that he will in fact become blind: "How meek I plan to be and how kind and gentle. Ha-ha. I smile sardonically."◖

And at work, more "Grind and grind and then some more grind. My head is weary as is my soul." And punctuating with a double exclamation mark, he has finally mailed a letter asking for a tryout at the Neighborhood Playhouse. There is a famine, a desperate hunger, and a terror in the soul of this eighteen-year-old who writes in his diary: "Smoke and smoke. What other joys in life. Possibly one other: not even that. It has lost its taste."*

Perhaps he should spend his week's pay to buy eyeglasses, as his eyes "dance a sluggish polka." For three weeks he makes no entries, apologizing on his return for a new and "peculiar sense of ennui" which totally immobilizes him. The depression he describes is the early model for the grave periods of breakdown in his later life.

A slight upturn commences at the end of 1924, when he takes "up my pen with a light heart" because he has started to coach plays at Morris High and has worked out a practical "social philosophy": "For the least, get the most you can from a girl." But on the debit side, he smoked forty cigarettes at a "blowout," and has been transferred to the shipping department of L. Bachmann and Co., where he now spends his days marking bales and cases.

On Christmas Day a long entry, expressing his fervent hope that he will write more in 1925, offers also a last will and testament:

Hello tiny diary. On this day I am bidding you a "hello." Your days are numbered as are mine. Only mine stretch far into the future—I hope. Do I hope? I wonder. Yesterday I bought, with part of my $25 bonus, your bigger brother. You see he was $.95 whereas you were only $.55. Let's hope that when he reaches your heaven each page will groan with the significance of words. Have twice indulged in that sport of beasts, since I last sullied your virgin whiteness.
CO—ha! ha!
(So—la! la!)
Should this vegetable that vegetates be torn from the soil of life by

◖ 4.9.
* It is clear that here he refers to masturbation.

a bony hand called death, distribute as follows all my world possessions and chattels.

To my *Mother*—all money and eternal love.

To my *Father*—My respect and love. Two calabash pipes that he
learn to smoke & love. My desire!

To *Sister G.*—That which she desires of my possessions & love.

To *little sister F.*—My love and a picture of me that I hope she
will always cherish. Little knick-knacks that she may desire. Friends.

Paul—Balance of my pipes and five books, except those mentioned in other gifts.

To any girls who come forward with the statements that they loved
me (and there are about a bakers dozen) to them present a small lock
of my hair. To all my male friends and others who will be notified via
all New York papers (dailys, morning only) that of my possessions
which they cherish mostly. Let them sometimes think of Clifford
whose *ashes* the four winds will toy with.

My files are for the consideration of my parents whom I will always
honor.

Signed

Clifford L. Odets.

The remaining few entries are concerned mainly with his determination
to best his friend Paul in their competition for a girl named Pearl, who
appears to be fickle. He writes, "You will learn to love me. I know that!
Years it may take, but you will." He insists that he has no "liking for her"
and means only "to develop Pearl into my own property." He has vowed
to do this as "it shall stand for all girls; hate them all. Loathe them but
crush their fragrances in your tender hands. Exclaim of their beauties and
virtues but under your breath, say, 'Pah.' " Addressing himself to "the
ladies": "I love your subtle perfumes, your wistful lips. The droop of your
shoulders and your smooth white breasts, tipped by flecks of wine, thrill,
fill me with vast yearnings—Pah!"

He protests that his interest in the girl Pearl is purely "predatory,
carnal," and a matter of regal conspicuous consumption: "I as well as
Paul am pursuing her for her body only. Her spirit means nothing to
Paul or I. If I write of ardent love to her, it is but to delude her into
passionate contact. Her body shall yet ride under mine. And so again I
solemnly give my deepest word of honor that I sponsor no love for her
. . . she of all would I have to grace my crown."◀

He appears to be fearful of permitting into awareness any but the
most cynically exploitive impulses, because "woman changes with every
tick of the clock." On New Year's Day, however, coming home drunk, not
having seen Pearl for several days, he writes at 5:30 A.M., with "father
after me": "I could, I think, learn to love her." He tries to maintain an
attitude of defensively detached, somewhat sadistic, and possessive conquest, much like his father's. "I am a house of women," he writes.

His experience with respectable work, on the other hand, as defined
by his father, leads him to conclude that "work and death" are the punish-
ments meted out to man for his "original sin," and that his own ancestors
could never have worked hard, for if they had, he, too, would love to work.
The absence of strong cultural institutions which dignify and support the
kind of work for which he has a gift leaves this youngster without an
anchor and inundated with rage, guilt, and one (uneasy) path to a sense
of competent manliness: girls.

◀ 4.10.

Desperately bored with writing lists of case numbers and styles at L. Bachmann and Co., he is on the point of abandoning his job. Had he known that he would never again seek a "real job," he would have been even more frightened of his father than he now was. Taking it for granted that there *must* be a solution to his son's indolence, Louis J. Odets, wrathful and mystified, began to interlard his oppressive pontification with a series of "how-to" books on business. For the rest of his life, in times of acute creative uncertainty Odets would desperately buy such booklets,* trying always, in the manner of his father, to turn a "real sparrow into a fake eagle."

His mother had become weakly irritable, focusing most of her attention on her thin younger daughter, forcing her to drink her milk, and to hang up her coat instead of leaving it draped over the red plush of the ornate dining-room chairs L.J. had bought. Clifford later described his mother in a diary:

Having a cold, towel around my shoulders, I think: This is the way your mother moved around the house, so slowly, gently melancholic, savouring small things, unconcentrated, weak because, partly of an extreme self-suggestibility which you yourself have inherited from her. So the mother, the dear dead mother, peers from behind the face of her living son.

Now and again what Odets called her "Italianate temper" would flare, but more often these days she would cry, feeling apparently in her loneliness that her sole source of leverage lay in an accusing and masochistic chant that "no one cares about me, no one helps," but that they would all remember her suffering after she was dead. Her son, who would later echo her cries for help, was disgracing her now with his wild hair, shabby clothes, late hours, and, above all, his lack of any activity that even hinted of an occupation. Dimly she believed it was her husband's fault and, in her moments of overt anger, referred to Clifford as "your son."

The son, years later, wrote a summary for his private file, called "Bullying." In it he concludes that "people have been bullying me all my life . . . negatively and positively they have been bullying me; and I have been submitting, responding and resenting it all my life. . . . I am very sensitive to being bullied and most likely fancy it is being done when it is not." Throughout this memorandum he traces reverberations of his father's "positive" and his mother's "negative" bullying. In another note he recalls: "My father urging and hurrying my child's dreamy, impressionistic mind along. The locked mind as a result, etc. Crowded, I began to crowd myself. His motto: do it *my* way!"

In this year he repeatedly complains to his diary that his collar is somehow too tight!

By his nineteenth year Clifford and his father were daily wrangling about "How should one live?" A strange son indeed, who could not earn his keep even during the golden glow of a steadily ascending American prosperity. L. J. Odets alternated between berating him and counseling him on "catching flies with honey in the world of business." Over and over he would recite variants of his litany: "You may not like the buyer . . . you may wanna see him in hell, but you smile . . . that's the way the world

---

* One of the most poignantly funny would be his purchase in 1940, long after he was successful, and directly after the failure of his play *Night Music*, of *How to Write a Hit Movie*.

goes . . . if you wanna learn, I'll tell ya . . . it's always nice to leave 'em smiling when you say goodbye." Or, in another mood, he would vilify and berate his son as "a worthless no-good."

The general tone of family life at the Odetses' these days was irritable, restless, and contentious. Odets' struggle, articulated much later in his work, was becoming increasingly overt and bitter. He was determined "not to have life nullified by . . . false values" and to maintain as a right of people that " . . . when their souls tell them where to go, they go."

His own soul's instructions were still unclear, but it commenced to guide his feet down a path dimly familiar to him from the days on Southern Boulevard when the magician Clinette and his wife had moved to "the Village." He spent increasing amounts of time wandering there, seeking kindred spirits. His father tried for a time to keep secret that he had spawned a disgrace, a bum, a "Greenwich Village dreamer," and the son years later would "shiver with shame" at the recollection of how "wild I was to get my name in front of the public" in order not only to appease his father but to reassure himself. A brief interlude as a Fuller Brush salesman met neither of these aspirations, and ended when his mother bought one of everything he had in his black case. He determined now to peddle instead his talents.

In collusion with one of his father's employees at the Lincoln Press, and purloining his father's name for an initial, he printed businesslike cards with "Clifford L. Odets" in the center, and in three corners what he considered his salable qualifications: "actor, elocutionist, drama critic." In addition, he wrote numerous witty squibs advertising himself as "The Rover Reciter," ready and willing to perform anywhere and anytime for a modest fee. New York *Evening World* columnist Karl K. Kitchen, a precursor of Earl Wilson, frequently published these, providing for him sometimes a dozen bookings a week, at first without pay, at small radio stations which were just beginning to find an audience.

The infant broadcasting industry, its stocks soaring, was beginning to evince the undiscriminating and insatiable appetite of all mass media for material, an appetite that even then could nibble at an indifferent elocutionist and swallow whole a young writer. Odets recalled:

In those days NBC was just a two-studio joint over Aeolian Hall on 42nd Street with just two microphones. I always remember NBC as a place having just two microphones. And I would appear at places like Gimbel Brothers radio station, all as the Rover Reciter. I'd get a fifteen-minute spot and do one or two of these things.

The Odets family had acquired the first radio in their apartment house, and occasionally L.J. was at home to hear his son's resonant voice reciting "The Face on the Barroom Floor." The son yearned for some affirmation from his father for this accomplishment, but none was forthcoming. Odets recalled their standard interchange: "Why didn't I get a haircut and stop looking like a Bolsheviki. They were about the same to him. And what was he going to tell his friends when they asked him what his only son was doing, a fine-looking American boy like myself, and he had to say 'Nothing'?" The son would answer, "Well, I'm on the radio," and the routine dead end would be reached with L.J.'s reply, "Yes, but what do you get paid for it?"

At this point the boy, feeling hopelessly trapped, would drink large quantities of gin and construct fantasies of dying, committing suicide, or, less extravagantly, leaving home for a foreign land, like Eugene O'Neill. He made do, however, with a less drastic move to Greenwich Village.

At the time I got to Greenwich Village, around 1925, most of the so-called great ones had gone. Floyd Dell had moved; George Cram Cook* was dead. I knew his daughter Nilla Cram Cook. Harry Kemp, they used to call him "The Tramp Poet," was still living down there. In fact, I was his leading man in something called The Poet's Theatre for two seasons. And O'Neill was part of this wonderful, glamorous world that a youth enters. . . . He was gone, but it was as if his fragrance, or the awesome sense of this man still lingered around the dirty alleys and streets. Macdougal Street meant the Provincetown Playhouse and Eugene O'Neill. In that sense I was influenced by Eugene O'Neill, but not directly by his work. I don't think that anywhere in my plays any influence of that kind shows.

In another place Odets describes a generational temper and the transmission of a Zeitgeist:

O'Neill gave me a "feeling" as a young man, not content or techniques. It is as if, permit me to say, sulfa drugs are invented and the whole stir and feeling for antibiotics are in the air—the man who finally discovers the mycin group has little to do with the inventor of the sulfa group—and yet the influence is there.
But, of course, if O'Neill had not come along when he did, when the U.S. was rolling over from, perhaps, a long provincial sleep —we should have had to invent him, I'm afraid.

Odets is describing the beginnings of a transition in American drama from themes and forms imitative of the European to something truly indigenous. A new play of O'Neill's, *Desire Under the Elms,* denounced as obscene by the time Odets went to see it, had begun a good run at the Greenwich Village Theatre.
There is no indication, however, that Odets was aware of John Howard Lawson's *Processional,* which opened on January 12, 1925, at the Garrick. He had not yet met Lawson, whose influence on him would be great.† *Processional,* with its early effort to dissolve the proscenium arch by an emotional fusion of actor and audience, was closer than any other American play to the impulse which would later catapult Odets' *Waiting for Lefty* into theatrical history.
Although O'Neill was gone from the Village, it was still a lively place, and people like Harry Kemp, who had acted for him, were providing links to the inspiring Provincetown Players. Superficially resembling Lou Odets, Kemp was intense, affectionate, rebellious, suspicious, physically powerful, a jealous bear of a man. He early married Mary Pynes, a beautiful, sad, tubercular woman like Clifford's mother. Like Clifford's father, Kemp loved prizefights and used to attend them with O'Neill. Unlike Lou Odets, he was regarded as an "eccentric idealist," a legendary Greenwich Village intellectual, erudite and with a great volume of mediocre poetry to his credit. One of the first of the American gurus for young writers and actors, Kemp achieved stature sufficient to elicit financial support from Theodore Dreiser and from Joseph Fels, a Philadelphia soap manufacturer with an interest in the arts, who provided most of the financing for his Poet's Theatre, later a cooperative venture.
Performing in the basement of the St. Mark's-in-the-Bouwerie Church

---

* Cook, a novelist, poet, and playwright, organized the Provincetown Players, O'Neill's first producing company. He died in 1924 at the age of fifty-one.
† In the cast of *Processional* was Lee Strasberg, soon to move into sketches in the *Garrick Gaieties,* stage-managed by Harold Clurman. These two men, together with Cheryl Crawford, would found the Group Theatre within five years.

at Fourth Street and Avenue A, this group had a repertoire consisting mainly of poetic English dramas, some by Shelley and some by Kemp. Clifford and his Bronx friend Jerry Rosenberg felt privileged to appear in these plays, even without pay. After much pleading with his father to come and see him perform, as "some day this will all lead to something," Clifford persuaded the entire Odets family to pile into Lou's new Packard, the longest car in the neighborhood, and drive down to St. Mark's. Only two memories of this evening survived: Florence recalled the bright-orange silk dress her brother had bought her for the event, and Lou Odets, in his ninth decade, declared, in his best possessive and narcissistic style, that "the play stank and so did Clifford," but that *he* (Lou) had made the evening a success by "telling the crowd I'd bust their heads in if they didn't clap." Clifford's efforts to win his father's support continued, however, until a debacle at another theatrical forum. For the Drawing Room Players, Clifford was playing the ghost in *Hamlet* (a part in which a neighbor found Clifford to be "very sincere"), and "when Lou saw the play would be given in a place sort of like a store, with boxes for benches, and some kind of dim lights hanging from the ceiling, he blew his top and made a terrible scene. He said it was degrading to be in a dump like that and Clifford was heartbroken."

Not long after this event, the *Bronx Home News* ran a story not only about Clifford's recitations of poetry on the radio but also about his participation in productions of the Drawing Room Players and Kemp's Poet's Theatre. He was for a brief moment a "neighborhood big shot," and he now determined to leave his father's house forever and become a stock-company actor. Lou began to form the judgment that his only son, his "kaddesh," was going mad.

In early March 1925 several of the Beck Street Boys repaired to employment agencies on Sixth Avenue looking for performing jobs at summer camps—the beginnings of the "Borscht Belt." Since these had already been snapped up, Clifford and Paul Greenbaum,* the other aspiring thespian in the gang, decided to accept menial jobs on Fishers Island, off the coast of New London, Connecticut. There at a "very fancy place called The Mansion House and Cottages" they received room and board, plus a $50 bonus for pulling satin bedsheets through the mangle. For years Odets relished telling how he had stuck it out for ten weeks, while Paul had "chickened out." Odets' fortitude was supported by his interest in a young waitress at the Mansion House, described by him later to *The New Yorker*'s John McCarten:

"There is no better way to measure your life," says Odets, "than to say 'I loved this girl then and she meant this or that to me.'" The girl by whom Odets measures this phase of his career was a school teacher from Springfield, Massachusetts, who was waiting on table at the hotel where Odets was employed. "It was," says Odets, "one of those horrible, exquisite, adolescent affairs, with something of the Sorrows of Young Werther about it." The Sorrows set in when the girl, to whom he had been sending poems daily, advised Odets that the man she was going to marry had just arrived at the hotel, driving his boss's limousine. Odets thereupon determined that someday, when he was a famous man, he would go to Springfield and make a speech from the observation platform of his train. Then if the girl jumped out of the crowd to speak to him, he intended to tell her coldly that she

---

* Paul Greenbaum became a manufacturer of "fur oddities," such as a "fur-handled can-opener."

had had her chance. He attributes a profound significance to the fact that although *Midnight,* in which he had the juvenile lead, in 1930, was short-lived, it lasted long enough for him to appear in Springfield in his only starring role. "She might have been in the audience," he points out.

Indeed, Reta Cooper might well have been in the audience, because the romantic nineteen-year-old boy had made—as always—a deep impression, so deep that she treasured his adolescent effusions,* showing them only to a few intimates until, at seventy-eight, she shyly and reluctantly gave permission for their use here.

Mrs. Cooper sorted Odets' poems to her into two piles. The second is headed, "This was after I told him I was going to marry Jimmy." This second batch, born of grief, is better and, on the whole, more honest,† with titles like "Dirge," "Retrospect," "Finale, Without Brasses." In one titled "Am I Dead or Dumb?" his anger and accusation erupts: "Your kiss is poison / I would be poisoned by a kiss / . . . Your eyes are as blue as waters deep / I would drown in water deep / Your head is the Medusa's head / I would strangle by your hair," etc.

His farewell letters to Reta are affectionate and wistful, addressing her as "Dear Raisin" or "Dearest Reta," and telling how he wept in the grass thinking of her and of Schubert's Serenade ("Through the leaves, the night winds moving murmur low and sweet"). He signs himself "Playboy" or "Clifford" and, chillingly, in the lower right-hand corner "L.O.," or "Clifford" and, again below, "L. Odets" (as in Louis Odets).

He tries to wish Reta well in her marriage, but "if Jimmy doesn't think he's lucky—just refer him to me." He calls himself a "sentimental Tommy" whose dreams "mean nothing." He implores her to "please write before you're married so that I can write you one more letter. Unconventional as I profess to be, it wouldn't do to write a Mrs. One try was sufficient." When apparently she does not reply, he tries to taunt her with his co-star in Harry Kemp's theatre, a "Salome" who was "stewed" at rehearsals: "I thought it lucrative to take her home. I did—It was!" Ever the abandoned one, now as always, he seesaws between grief and cruel, jealous rage.

Herman Koblanov was puzzled by his friend's intense involvement with this rather proper girl, adding that "he was, however, very serious with his romances when he was young." That it was a memorable event for him is suggested by the fact that twenty-five years later Odets started a new file called "Fishers Island Play," which opens with a boy who "pretends he took this job just for the experience, not because he needs a menial job." In his notes for this play, his boyfriend, whom he calls "Lew," ridicules him for romanticizing the relationship and tells him his chances for this girl are as good as that he will get "butterfly's wings for supper." A curious gourmet image of the devouring of one of God's more fragile creatures, an image that makes many of Odets' women laugh, sometimes bitterly.

---

* An example called "Tacit," which goes on for thirty-three lines, commences, "It was at a tryst / That he first kissed / Her flower stalk neck / And a moonlight flick / Lighted his heart / With quivering start." It closes, "It takes retrospect fears / From listless years / It brings tense joy / To a little boy. . . . " The poem breaks off abruptly with "Aw shut up!" He compares himself with self-disdain to Amy Lowell, whose poem he sends also to Reta, adding, "She smoked cigars and wrote poetry like that. Requiescat in Pace."

† ". . . But hurt is swift / And this very day / I have seen a smile / I know so well / An eye that shames / Shames the star / This very day."

On paper with the letterhead "Mansion House, Fishers Island," Odets, signing "C.L.O.," once again entreats his cousin Irene to respond: " . . . how considerate I am. I write, you don't answer, so I write again. But why don't you answer?"

As so often later, he is pleading for a woman's response. Had he known that his cousin had already turned her attention to the more practical offers of a "Mr. Steinberg," whom she would shortly marry, his Young Werther summer on Fishers Island would have been burdened with another sorrow. And yet mammoth shifts took place this summer, of such subtlety and complexity that there was inaugurated a series of profound reorganizations in Odets' inner and outer life.

Returning from the long summer exhausted and jobless, he determined never again to do menial or clerical work. Being again "on the outs" with his father, he would borrow a dollar here from Mom Levy, two dollars there from Herman Koblanov, and drink free Turkish coffee at Romany Marie's tearoom in Greenwich Village. Marie, though she dressed in the costume of a gypsy, was in fact, like his mother, a Romanian Jewess, with a heavy accent. Unlike Pearl, and in the caricatured tradition of a good Jewish mother, she prided herself on the fact that "there was never a question of anyone having enough to eat, as long as there was food on my stove." In her day Marie had fed an impressive list of painters, poets, and playwrights—among them, Rockwell Kent, Mark Tobey, John Sloan, Eugene O'Neill—who always came after the Hell Hole saloon closed for the night. Her small café, lit with candles and long a favorite meeting place for hungry young intellectuals, was warmed by Marie herself, one of the earliest in an extremely long line of appreciative female nourishers who respected Odets' talent. These women ranged from his Aunt Esther to Mom Levy in the Bronx to Communist leader "Mother Bloor,"* to the daughters of film magnate Louis B. Mayer, Paula Miller Strasberg, this writer, and many more.

He would complain to all these women in turn that not his mother nor either of his wives had ever "kept a full icebox." The first-act curtain line of his first full-length play (*Awake and Sing!*) is spoken by a man just rejected by a woman, a line which would become standard banter for decades: "What the hell kind of house is this it ain't got an orange!!"

* Ella Reeve Bloor was a top functionary in the American Communist Party during the thirties.

Chapter Five

---

*Without a home, homeless (or an
alien in the home of his parents—
alienated!) he went out to find or
make a home; and he attached himself to certain homeless others, men
or women who themselves did not
know what they lacked or sought.*

CLIFFORD ODETS, *1959*

As HE approached his twentieth birthday, Odets abandoned even the
motions of "getting a valuable business training," finally dropping the
middle initial L from his signature and restricting his "loans" from his
father to carfare and haircut money. The only material possession he
took from the house on his trial separations was his portable typewriter,
"Lovelorn Corona." His diary states he is still in the grip of "inertia and
ennui . . . just now the whole thing not very alarming, but maybe in
the future."◖

With what he later called "the vanity of a boy, energetic, strong and
spirited, passionately eager to be better and more original than others,"
he commenced to build a protective crust which in its "ambition and
bustle" had, he thought, a bullying quality much like his father's. Unlike
his father, however, he was unable to use as targets his crippled sister,
Genevieve, his baby sister, Florence, and his depressed, sickly mother. His
ambivalent identification with all these females induced a compassionate
defense in him which necessitated his looking elsewhere for targets.

As he began to move out of his father's orbit, something radical took
place: he began to show less of his mother's "dogged passivity" and now,
exactly like L.J., he consciously "wanted to be the whole cheese" and developed, in his own words, "a splendid conceit." Harry Kemp, finding him
"egotistical," fired him from the Poet's Theatre for that, as well as for his
ignorance of the works of Percy Bysshe Shelley. Strangely unruffled by
this, he writes, "So I shook his hand again and we parted—good friends. I
want to keep his companionship—a poet and too, a craven, at something—
I don't know what."

Just as someone in mourning for a dead mate tries to effect a resurrection by crystallizing within himself the lost mate's characteristics, so
did Clifford now try to integrate into the profession of "actor" his innocent

◖ 5.1.

(seen by him as feminine) sensitivity with his father's dramatizing cockiness, vanity, and go-getting energy, but he was unable to achieve his father's life-saving imperturbability. His uncertainty is reflected in a diary note about his friend Herman. "Von is a 'good fellow' that knows very little. I am a 'good fellow' who thinks he knows a lot. Which is better? He, I think." Whatever abysses of doubt and self-hatred yawned in L. J. Odets, he gave no sign of being aware of them, expressing only outrage that people (especially his children) showed insufficient "respect." Clifford's language synthesizes curiously his father's disdainful dismissal of everyone around him and the expanding, aspiring vocabulary of an uneducated youngster on a ravenous quest for culture. In proselytizing lectures he daily exhorts Herman to read poetry. In his diary he labels his fraternity meetings "rotten and puerile," adding, "I travel too big for them." (Into the ninth decade of Louis J. Odets' life the word "big" appeared more often than any other in his lexicon.) There appear, as well, startling and more sinister echoes of the father's self-hatred in Clifford's contemptuous references to "kike wenches" or "a low class of Jews." Years later, reviewing this time, Odets wrote:

> . . . college needed money, nonchalance, some classy clothes and a gift for being "wholesome" and democratic, a good mixer, none of which I had. What I did have was a pose—a firm Byronic pose, which attracted a few, particularly females from Brooklyn, but repelled most, chiefly males from everywhere. Don't ask me where I picked up that pose, but it was real, palpable and dreadfully obnoxious, in my earlier years even to actors, who are not themselves disinclined to postures and struts. . . .

It is sobering indeed that a quarter of a century later it would seem to Odets—totally unaware of the extent to which he had obediently taken over at the age of twenty so many of his father's character-armor values, attitudes, and defenses—that at this time he "detested the man, couldn't stand him." In retrospect he usually simplified his early relationships with all his family, but most especially that with his father: he liked to recall for friends and interviewers that he had hated, scorned, and rejected L.J. since adolescence. That it was more complex than this even on a conscious level is shown in a letter to Herman: "I fear he is a better man than his son by far . . . and I can do nothing better than try to emulate him in a number of matters."

Having established himself, still without fee, as a radio elocutionist who "could get thirty bookings in forty days" between Irish tenors singing "Mother Machree," Odets prepared his path to becoming "America's first real disc jockey" by "personally-styled" announcing at WBNY for a strange and colorful man named Sidney Norton Baruch. Regarded as a confidence man by some and a "mad genius" by others, "Doc," labeling himself "the black sheep of the family," claimed Bernard Baruch as his first cousin and insisted that, as one of his many accomplishments, by dint of his training as an electrical engineer he had invented the first depth bomb used in World War I.

A square, heavy set, powerful man, built like Louis J. Odets, Baruch impressed Clifford with his claim to be not only one of the first to experiment with the "crystal-set" radio, and a veteran of show business who had toured with Roxy's Gang (the famed S. L. Rothafel, American entrepreneur par excellence), but also to be the "discoverer" of the well-known "Silver-Voiced" and "Masked" radio tenors. He boasted that when the tour with Rothafel had ended, instead of returning the portable radio equipment, he—like many small-time brigands in this wide-open frontier industry—had simply kept it, wangling the call letters WBNY (later WBNX) from the government on the grounds that he was doing "experimental work."

In two small rooms on the top floor of the Tilmar Building at 145 West 45th Street, Odets made the original suggestion of playing entire programs of records, "popular and classical," with a "custom-made commentary" when there was nothing to announce over the airwaves. Local shops provided the discs in exchange for free advertising. Doc, "always looking for an angle," was so pleased with Odets' inventiveness that he said, "You can work for me any time," quickly adding, however, "There's no money in it. You'll get free meals from any restaurant you'll mention, and maybe, if you're good, a suit of clothes, but no money." This was in keeping with standard practice: amateur sopranos, yodelers, Swiss bell-ringers, were all glad for a chance to perform gratis.

"Old Faithful Herman," who would occasionally fill in for his friend Clifford at WBNY, recalled Baruch as a person "with the most fabulous gift of gab of anyone I've ever known. He could do anything. One day at Broadway and 46th Street he said, 'You see those two girls? I bet I can make both of them in five minutes!' In less than ten minutes they were up in his studio. He was incredible, could talk rings around anyone, even L.J." Herman recalls how deeply impressed Clifford was by Baruch's prowess, equally evident—like his father's—in business and in sexual exploits. Although Clifford refers to Baruch occasionally in his diary as a "liar" and a "swine," he notes also: " . . . today Doc gave me a copy of Roget's Thesaurus." Clearly, Sidney Norton Baruch, like Odets' father, was no simple villain.

In this year Clifford was sticking his neck out in all directions. He had had new cards printed advertising himself as a "dramatic critic," given confidence by Walter Winchell, who by now had said in his column that Odets was New York's "youngest critic." Each night after the broadcast at WBNY, according to Odets' diary, the two boys "would dash over on passes to see the voloptuous [sic] nude girls" in the second act of *Earl Carroll's Vanities*, the cast of which he tried, without success, to join.

He records, too, a young man's "strangeness and fumbling" in the initiatory sexual contacts with a woman: in short, "an exciting hell"; to friends he confided impressive sexual feats, "not the least of which was a method of contraception which avoided a blanketing of the sensory experience by the judicious use of adhesive tape on the tip of the penis." He states that he is "sex-mad" and "prurient," but can afford to "treat girls very coolly nowadays—aloft [sic]—let them come to me." But he records also in this year, as in almost every year thereafter, his romantic, self-lacerating quest for an unreachable madonna, a mysterious female whom he would peep at, adore from afar, call anonymously, write to, and chastely court, usually an actress. This year it was Nilla Cram Cook, married daughter of George ("Jig") Cook, discoverer of O'Neill. With Nilla he read poetry—sometimes his own, and lay beside her: " . . . no clamping. Just pure bliss . . . lovely wondrous Nilla!" He wrote her prayerful notes, sometimes in verse, stayed up late "mad almost, with thoughts of Nilla," called himself "an awful sentimental Tommy," and continued this courtship for months despite her repeated assurances that she loved her husband. A wrinkled scrap of paper, preserved for decades by Odets, records her plea: "So sweet child do try to recover from your avowed passion and be my friend—and my nice kitten-cat." His diary tells us he went to "ease my loaded heart" with Harry Kemp at his rectory home and was comforted by Kemp's sympathy as well as by his promise of the lead in his new play, *Don Juan in a Garden,* a work which the Poet's Theatre did not live to produce. He concludes, "God, love is terrible," but continues to write impassioned letters to Nilla.

There is more here than the usual adolescent split between "pure" and "sexual" women. What Odets adds to the standard conflict is the image of the young actress within *him* as a part of *his own* evolving identity structure. His attraction to, empathy for, and need to destroy actresses would remain to the end of his life.* In this complex reenactment he takes his father's role with him—acting by turns seductive, protective, and murderous. The feminine anima within him is strong; and he emulates and competes with his mother at least as often as with his father.

Although his central aspiration was still to become a great actor, he finished two crude one-act plays begun in 1925, entitled *Dawn* and *At the Water-Line,* later calling one "mawkish" and the other "melodramatic." Both have as protagonist, as do so many of Odets' plays, a desperately deprived character in crisis; in both he is saved by "a woman from his past." The more finished of the two was broadcast without fee over radio station WFBH in New York City on January 13, 1926, and later by other stations in New York and in Philadelphia. Odets' notation in his diary, however, sandwiched between "Nilla still crushing my thoughts" and "I *must* see Nilla," is the terse statement, "At F.B.H. Drawing Room Players put on my play, 'At the Water-Line.' Pretty decent affair." From this casual report of the premiere of his first play it is clear that writing plays is not yet at the heart of his aspiration. From its content, however, a biographer learns much. Odets later outlined the plot of *At the Water-Line:*

> The one part is the stoker on a ship, and alongside of me is a little Cockney stoker who is his particular pal. I guess I picked up the idea of this from the O'Neill plays. And they start talking, and the little Cockney wants to know why he's always so sad and silent, and he admits he once loved a woman who married another man. Anyway, there are a group of tourists investigating the bowels of the ship, and the ship crashes, and, lo and behold, one of the tourists who is trapped in there is the girl that left him behind. And now this man who never cared whether he lived or died, wants to live because he has this woman back. And her husband is conveniently killed up on top of the boilers, or something like that, and—believe it or not—they get out of the ship through something called an ash-expeller. They back into something that ejected hot ashes out of the ship under enormous pressure. I imagine a cat couldn't slip through it, but I kind of widened the dimensions so that the three of them got out, the Cockney and the leading man and his erstwhile lady friend got out to freedom and to happiness.

The manuscript of this primitive, now comical, barely disguised fantasy—in which Odets himself would later play the role of the hero, Garfield Grimes—includes an accusation of the materialistic, abandoning woman:

> GRIMES: There is one thing I've never forgotten . . . it has seared me like a hot iron . . . yes we were lovers . . . I was going to marry you. God but I was happy then. Just a smile from you and the whole day I walked in rapture. Rapture! (*He laughs*) Quite poetic,

---

* For years Odets kept adding notes to a bulging file for a play, never written, "Tides of Fundy," wherein an old playwright destroys a young woman playwright by undermining her self-confidence.

eh? Then . . . then Joe Bates bought you. That's the word . . .
BOUGHT. *He had the money and business and I had only the shadow
of a future.* (*In a low voice*) I left you one afternoon and the next
day I heard it . . . you had married Joe. Not a word to me when
you left me that day.*

The resemblance of this little melodrama to an early O'Neill play lies
mainly in its crudity. Odets always maintained that O'Neill's influence on
him had never been in formal terms but "in terms of aspiration . . . of
becoming a big American playwright . . . in terms of being some kind
of distinguished human being that people respect, in terms of shaking
audiences. . . ."
    Though bored on a second viewing this season by the "deep stuff"
in O'Neill's "great play, *The Great God Brown*," he was nonetheless affirmed in his direction as a playwright by the intense if awkward honesty
in what the Gelbs have called this "family epitaph," which indicted
material success and which stood in such contrast to most of what Odets
called "the fake plays" of the time.
    Closer to his creative heart this year, however, was a play not by an
American but by an Irishman whose folk connections, in his characters
and in their talk, resonated in Odets like the Yiddish language of the
neighbors at 747 Southern Boulevard. Of this drama, which he saw as
"a professional courtesy" at the Mayfair Theatre, he wrote in his diary:
"Wonderful play . . . beautiful humor and revengeful pathos. Best play
I've seen yet." He was describing Sean O'Casey's *Juno and the Paycock*, a
play essentially about the fortitude of a strong woman. It had finally
"dawned" on him, he writes, that as Doc Baruch's drama critic he might
(without buying a ticket) see live plays, not just movies, and that he
could "learn a lot" from them.
    We see from his diary that he did indeed learn a lot this year watch-
ing "live plays," one of which was by William Shakespeare. Lesser but
valuable expansions came by way of the *Garrick Gaieties of 1926* and
Walter Hampden in *The Servant in the House*. He scrutinizes intently
the work of an assortment of actors: men like Alfred Lunt, John Barrymore, Walter Huston, Rudolph Valentino, and Emil Jannings, and women
like Joan Crawford, Pola Negri, Bebe Daniels and Pauline Lord, Alice
Brady and Lya de Putti, and Mae West. In Hoboken, with the Rialto Stock
Company, the Bayonne Opera House or the Hudson Theatre in Union City,
New Jersey, he tried out their "techniques" for his own acting whenever
stock producer Jules Leventhal gave him a few insignificant "sides" to
play in Maxwell Anderson's *What Price Glory?* or Sidney Howard's *They
Knew What They Wanted*.† Meanwhile in the saloons of Bayonne he was
"mingling with real old actors."
    With his aide-de-camp, Herman, both now "film critics," he attended
movie premieres and was overwhelmed by seeing "lots of celebs." Herman
assured him at the opening of *Aloma* that "someday people shall throng
around us as they did there with Al Jolson and Alice Joyce." He concludes
in his diary, "Well? I hope and pray so." His aspiration remained to be not
a writer but a celebrated actor.
    With the same watchful intensity with which he studied the "stars,"
he observed the rehearsals of the Chrystie Players, a settlement-house

---

* Although this story is obviously rooted in a standard Oedipal fantasy, it is
likely that the immediate stimulus was his bitter defeat by the limousine driver in the
steaming laundry at Fishers Island.
    † With this warm, realistic melodrama about Italian-Americans, Howard had
nosed out O'Neill for the Pulitzer Prize.

group of amateurs led by a young Jewish actor named Lee Strasberg. Odets notes in his diary: " . . . the squalid East Side. Ugh—it teems with life, tho." Harold Clurman recalled a peculiarly ascetic, intellectual focus at these rehearsals presided over by the short, pale, lofty, and keenly intelligent Strasberg. His text was a direct antithesis to the clichés of thespian stagecraft Odets was learning from Jules Leventhal in the Union Stock Company: he appeared to believe that actors could consciously learn to use themselves creatively as instruments for the communication of authentic human experience rather than for an empty elocutionary facsimile. Odets felt drawn to, and threatened by, this rabbinical young man who had just replaced, as stage manager of the *Garrick Gaieties,* Harold Clurman, whom he was already proselytizing with his arguments for adaptations of the work of the innovative Russian actor-director Stanislavsky. In his diary Odets writes dubiously of the Chrystie Players, "Fair, but still I insist that I am a good actor." He never joined this group, and Strasberg remained unaware of his existence until five years later. Clurman, more interested in the literary content of a production than in its manner, had gone off to Europe again with composer Aaron Copland to gather more fuel for the warming fire he and Strasberg would start in the American theatre in the last days of 1930.

Odets records that he is trying to utilize, even in such unworthy parts as his radio role as Simon Legree in *Uncle Tom's Cabin,* the best of what he sees on the stage and on film; and that he is striving, in his recitations —which continue at the performer-hungry little radio stations—to project all the passion he so admires in the German UFA films, which "show the bareness of life and the immutability of fate."

Despite his new and elegant "renderings" of Dickens' "A Child's Dream of a Star" and his favorite, "Fleurette," he is beginning to tire of being The Rover Reciter. The essential reassurance in these recitations lay now in their guaranteeing him membership in what he calls "the big family of radio people" whom he encounters at WGBS, WRNY, WHN, or WFBH when he leaves what he grandiosely calls "my office" at WBNY.

Daily, saluting the marking system at Morris High, he gives himself a grade in his diary for his recitations, the highest being a "B-plus." It is as if he were trying to re-create the dilemma of his abandoned academic life and, this time, to master it. He writes, "If only it were a big station, with lots of talent." Then he not only would have a good family, but also would acquire a "real education," which he now flogs himself to achieve. Entries of "inertia and ennui" appear less often, however, than in the previous year, and in a singular entry he writes, "Work holds no terror for me—now. That is because the theatre looms big and solid on the horizon" and, moving on to more mundane ground, " . . . my face is a bit smoother today. Would to God that I were without these horrible blemishes. I always say wistfully, 'The girls used to call me baby-face.' "

"God never let me be blind as I once wanted to be," he records as he fills his vision with play after play and film upon film at the Rivoli, the Cameo, and the Criterion. This year he hears for the first time, presented by Warner Bros., music electrically recorded on discs to accompany a silent film—the first "Vitaphone production." The young critic says in advance of this event: "Warner's Theatre never has anything worthwhile. Their *Don Juan* with John Barrymore comes out soon and that will be good."

How astonished he would have been to know that his life and his work, and those of every other American writer, would be significantly shaped by this vast technological breakthrough to the mass market. Audible dialogue was on its way to becoming as widely salable as a cheap suit or, for that matter, his father's advertising copy, and the rate of pay would soon be astronomic.

Although throughout this year Odets wrote—usually in the small hours of the night—"filler columns" for newspapers, poems,¢ and two more one-act plays—one titled *Stolid Sam Stillson,* the other, *Three Potatoes and a Wormy Apple*—the focus of his daily activity at WBNY or pursuing his small "bits" in Leventhal's stock company was still geared to the prime goal of becoming "a good, good actor" who would "play my first lead" on the boards of the Lyceum Theatre, and who prayed "to God I will never be a ham." There is no indication that the professional identity "playwright" had yet begun to move to center stage.

His trip this year to Sixth Avenue for a summer-camp job netted three possibilities "in the acting field," and he chose the most profitable one: dramatics counselor for Camp Roosevelt, where for $200 (he would, at the height of his success, tell an interviewer it was $350) it would be his task, as "Uncle Clifford," to direct plays and to produce a vaudeville show for the campers. Along with a small army of budding actors, producers, writers, and directors who regularly swarmed upstate to the Borscht Belt, he collected a small nest egg for the winter, when he would make the rounds of the Broadway casting offices, looking for an acting job. For the next five years these summer-camp jobs would be his only real source of income.

In this year, until his father flew at him for being a "loafer," Clifford could afford some tenderness toward L.J., as at the Monday-night card game at the Koblanovs', recorded in his diary: "I stood in back of him and a [sic] urge came on to kiss his poor graying head. He lost some money. My store is low." A month later, idly stopping in at the office of the Odets Company at 9 East 38th Street, he found only his father's bookkeeper in this "sad and sombre" place and recorded in his diary:

> Brill and I to his office . . . and he tells me a tale that I will never forget. I have not put it here for fear it may be seen. He showed me things that I never knew about the Odets Company. Father's foibles were revealed and I cold and not knowing what to say . . . all night I thought of what Brill has told me and even now I think of it.

Six months after this episode L.J. had fled to Philadelphia, having given up for a salaried white-collar position in a boiler factory not only his cherished ownership of the Odets Company in his beloved New York City but also his career as a writer of advertising copy. The reason for this sudden move remains a mystery except for rumors of "dirty work at the crossroads." The only clue came from Louis J. Odets himself half a century later; in response to a biographer's casual question, "How did you happen to move back to Philadelphia in 1926?" he replied in anger, "I didn't do *nothin'* wrong in New York, nothin'!" Whatever the specifics of Brill's revelations this spring, Clifford was deeply disturbed by them.

A week later, no doubt deeply anxious himself, L.J. refused to advance "even a penny for a camp outfit" because Clifford was "corrupting" his friend Herman Koblanov by keeping him "from work and from sleep." When, moreover, Pearl joined her husband in this desperate and displaced anger at their son, Clifford again became acutely depressed.

On June 28, 1926, his diary records in Yiddish inversions, "Still cool are things. Almost I am not spoken to. A moral leper I am. With shamed face, I ask for carfare and then to dentist. Downtown, and Von [Herman]

¢ 5.2.

meets me at train station." At Browning King, "in return for future broadcasting, I get three lumberjack shirts," useful for camp, and a $15 commission for having sold a motion-picture projector. His humiliation at his continuing economic dependence and lack of profession merged with his disappointment in his father's moral rectitude and in his mother's withdrawal from him; the diary entries again regress below those of the previous year: "moody," "awful jaded," "tired," "lazy," "sombre," "dull," "meaningless," "empty," "indecision—mine always." Girls find him "brusque and somber," and one asks, "Don't you ever smile?" His list of guilts, never totally absent from the diary, mounts again. He fears that masturbation* and smoking are exhausting him, and finally determines to forswear the latter "for one whole year." After five abstinent days he resumed smoking and for the rest of the summer "used only one match for a pack and a half of Camels daily," reported Carl Heilpern, a close friend.

He is impatient with his young charges at Camp Roosevelt, near Monticello, New York, describing them as an "eager mass of pulsing lads and little girls" who "cry and sniffle on their first night away from home." Bending over backward from his own intense neediness, especially for succor from a woman, he decides to protect himself from "getting involved by being coldly exploitive" with girls. In spite of himself, he is drawn to a girl counselor, "nice and very much like myself," who tells him of her engagement and also of her dead mother, eliciting from him a romantically extravagant and somber poem, "To a Mother."◖ He cautions himself, "I must not let myself like her else I will be lost." All evidence suggests that he failed in his determination to remain detached from this Jean, and later he writes, "Splendid conceit badly damaged at Camp Roosevelt." His habitual preference to live at night is intensified by his depression and becomes so severe that his fellow counselors take it into their hands to get him working. Heilpern described their method:

> He was night people . . . they played various tricks on him to get him up . . . placing a foul-smelling herring on either side of his face on the pillow . . . and finally dousing him with a bucket of ice-water, after which he got the message . . . he worked very hard, smoked like a trojan and everything had to be perfect, and it couldn't be, because he was working with amateurs and although a gifted man, he was at the time an amateur himself.

One camper's memory of him was his performance as the Toff in Lord Dunsany's *A Night at an Inn,* and how he borrowed her brother's brilliantine which seemed the only effective agent for taming his "unruly, springy shock of hair."

On July 18 the diary entries abruptly cease with: "Clifford's birthday —20 years old today. 1906–1926." Not until October 19 is there a new entry; it is a joyous one: "Here—*this date* has *really* started my career as a professional actor. Leventhal has given me a week's job with the Rialto Stock Company—'Chuck' in 'Twelve Miles Out.' A 24-side part." His savior is an old acquaintance, producer Jules Leventhal of Hoboken, New Jersey, where he has done a few bits in a stock company. He describes Leventhal as a "strange, grimy and wonderful man . . . kindly but grasping who took a kind of shine to me and began to give me jobbing parts in stock." At last he has found acceptance from an older man who thinks he has talent and is willing to pay him for it. He is finally a "man of the theatre."

---

* Much later he would recall his impulse in self-stimulation both as "hostile" and as a wish to "get rid of something bad."
◖ 5.3.

It is some "counterweight," he later writes, to his being "completely on the outs with my family." Assuming that his work in life will be as an actor, he sees his quest for a place as almost completed.

Louis J. Odets had by this time bought a new house with a two-car garage for $15,000 in the middle-class residential section of Philadelphia called West Oak Lane. "Not knowing whether there would even be a room there for me," Clifford decided to remain in New York, uncertain, however, whether Jules Leventhal could give him enough acting jobs to keep him alive. He determined not to return to Philadelphia "unless I was really broke, unless I was really hungry, because it was my parents' house . . . I must refer to it that way because it was not my house . . . with a sense that I was not very welcome there, and that I was certainly the black sheep of the family."

On one of the many occasions when he was "really hungry," he journeyed to West Oak Lane, where he had an especially bloody battle with his father, who, according to his friend Herman, "was trying to set his own brain into Clifford's head" and who "threw him out and told him not to come back until he had a *real* job." Now he moved in with the Heilpern family on Tinton Avenue in the Bronx. His friend from Beck Street, Carl Heilpern, recalled, "My mother loved him like her own child, she used to touch everyone's head at night to see if we were all home, and he loved her like a second mother. He called her 'Mom.' " Pearl's grief at her son's radical break from the family was evident to everyone.

Odets tucked away for future use in his plays many sensory images of this warm, adoptive household—for example, Carl's father, a leather-worker, smelling a purse to see if the leather were genuine. It was during this time that Carl, always impressed by Clifford's "seeking for knowledge," became certain his friend was "destined for greatness."◖ The Heilperns well recalled his study of Yoga: "He was particularly interested in developing his powers of concentration, and in mind-over-matter experiments. He tried an experiment in the dead of winter, to concentrate on 'I am warm,' walking from 166th Street near Prospect Avenue to Katonah Park, about two and a half miles each way, without a coat!"

This effort at mastery through Yoga was the first of a long series of encompassing cosmic systems that Odets would assiduously study and test all his life, always with the aim of trying to control his Fate by discovering the secret Meaning of Life as well as its laws. He made an ingenuously catholic and impartial investment, over the years, in Eastern thought, astrology, graphology, face-reading, Marxism, psychoanalysis, and even Scarne's rules of gambling. He would seek illumination and guidance as well as the prediction and control of future events from any and all of these disciplines, sometimes from several at once, discounting whatever did not fit with his bent of the moment.

Sophisticated friends, touched to pity, wonder, and laughter by Odets' genuine reliance on these methods of control in a variety of life crises, were also impressed by the fact that institutionalized religion, given much lip service by his father, appeared to play no real part in Odets' life. What is omitted from this observation is his close study of the Bible, especially of the Old Testament, from which themes for later work would emerge.

Thus, in this year of his twentieth birthday, seeing himself at last as a professional actor, he was still without a sure sense of an "even place whereon to stand," and recorded for the first time his deep concern that he was "always blabbing too much—an open book." Dimly he understood

◖ 5.4.

this as a hungrily impatient, undisciplined, and dangerous leakage of his talent—not of his acting, but of his writing, talent. It was possible for him in the short run to use his father's "gift of gab" as an actor. This impulse for immediate response would forever war with his disciplined writing plans. As a writer, he knew there was always a longer wait for an inner integration and expression of his conflicts as well as for a response from an audience. His subsequent careers as actor, playwright, and screen-writer would represent a range of tormented attempts to stabilize these two sets of necessities. His dramatizations of even his day-to-day life, his steady need to "entertain" at parties, his enactments of plays he would never write were, at the age of twenty and forever after, attempts to achieve immediate mastery and to garner instant emotional returns. Even at this early age he understood what he was driven to do, but was rarely able to control his need for reassurance by an immediate response.

Chapter Six

---

*The loss of a sense of identity often
is expressed in a scornful . . . hostility toward the roles offered as
proper in one's family. . . . Life
and strength seem to exist only
where one is not, while decay and
danger threaten wherever one happens to be.*

ERIK H. ERIKSON

"THERE are two kinds of playwrights. Both can be excelling but it would be necessary to make a distinction between the playwright who was a theatre man and not a man of literature, not a man of the library. If I talk about past, very great playwrights, it's obvious from the very style and form and cut and shape and pattern of their work, that men like Molière and Shakespeare were men of the theatre. . . . And you see it on every page of any one of their plays. They write with their feet solidly planted on the platform." So Odets once said to a young man who was writing a Ph.D. thesis about him.

With the aim of consolidating his identity as an actor, not a play-wright, he now tried to plant his feet on "the platform," striving to feel at home in his own body so that he might know where he was going. Nonetheless, without quite knowing what other seed he was cultivating, he embarked at the same time on an erratic but energetic development of his writing. In what he called a "self-indulgence," in the small hours of the night he kept a diary, wrote poems, short stories, plays, and even a novel. Encouraged in this clandestine pursuit by Chamberlain Brown, an actors' agent, he collected this year many rejection slips from *Young's Magazine* and others, until he decided in frustration to burn them all along with his works, which he called "trash." At the same time he was expanding his "quest for culture" by listening insatiably to classical music and by reading and seeing plays.

His notes toward the end of this year focus on the desperation of his yearning to leave permanently his father's house in West Oak Lane, where (his brief engagement with the Rialto Stock Company having ended abruptly) he could daily hear the machine-gun rhythms and the clanking of the punching bags and weights with which his father was equipping the basement. Feeling that "something in Philadelphia doesn't like me," and that his "blood stands still here," he would have remained in New York with the Heilperns except that in Philadelphia was one of the "last stock queens in existence": Mae Desmond. Miss Desmond, with her husband, Frank Fielder, ran one company at the William Penn Opera House at 41st Street and Lancaster Avenue, another in the nearby town of Chester, Pennsylvania, and later a third in Camden, New Jersey. It is noteworthy that Clifford called his father from the Heilperns' in the Bronx and asked *him* to approach the Fielders, arguing that it was more convenient for L.J. in Philadelphia to make the first contact.

The Fielders recalled L.J.'s asking whether they would consider starting "a young boy recently graduated from high school in the business." Clifford's confidence in his father's "gift of gab" was not misplaced. They granted the boy an interview, and "he was forthright from the first. . . . All he wanted was a chance to work hard doing extra parts or 'walk-ons' and assisting the stage manager until we should decide that he was capable of handling speaking parts with a few lines. Perhaps then he could prove to us that he could handle dialogue and characterization. We explained to him that the work was hard, involving rehearsals every day with nine performances a week for each play and a different play every week for a forty-week season. This recital of a demanding schedule seemed to make Clifford even more anxious to join our group. Apparently the unremitting activity of a stock company was just what he was looking for in order to learn a profession he already seemed to love."

When Mae Desmond told him that the starting salary would be small, he replied that he would work even for nothing. One of their most affectionate memories was of "Clifford standing down front in the first entrance, watching the play unfold, with a book of plays . . . under one arm and a pad and pencil in the other. He would watch us with an intentness and fascination that became a gentle form of flattery." For years afterward the Fielders reared their son, Richard, on stories of how Clifford had stood in the wings "observing the plays night after night, as a fiery example of how an aspiring playwright should approach his art."

It appeared to Mae Desmond that Odets was more interested in the creative subtleties of putty noses, his "wig a day," and "all sorts of involved makeup" than in the dramatic structure of *Tess of the Storm Country*, the bill in which (with a four-side part) he made his audible debut with the Desmond Players. More memorable to him than the content of his first juvenile lead, however, was the depressing fact that on the program his name had been listed as "Mister Audette." The correction to "Odets" was subsequently made, and, according to his diary, he was himself mystified by the fact that he decided then to assume the name "Gordon"*—"hinting darkly that it was not my real name"—for his monologues and recitations at the Young Men's Hebrew Association in North Philadelphia, where, he records, "I am becoming a well-known personage" with "quite a following."† The tone is pleased, ironic, and self-mocking as

---

* He used the non-Jewish name "Gordon" for the family in *Paradise Lost*, his first box-office failure, written to meet the objection that the Greenberg family (later called Berger) in *Awake and Sing!* was "too Jewish." It is obvious that the name "Gordon," used by another branch of the Gorodetsky family, is an attempt at an acceptable "American" version of the original family name. Here, as always, names and name-changes act as barometers of the severity of an identity-struggle.

† His manner, as recalled by playwright Joseph Kramm, then in amateur theatricals at this same YMHA, was "austere and removed." Another member of this dramatic group remembered that he was "exceptionally good" in his monologues at parties, but was "aloof and never became part of the group."

at the same time he records with self-contempt the "lousiness" of the people running Philadelphia radio stations WIP and WFI, who are "ignorant enough" to want to give even *him* five whole dollars an evening to announce, and who are "hot about my rotten plays." Although there are several productions of *At the Water-Line* in Philadelphia, Odets makes little of them. Having come to the end of his stint as a radio performer, he writes disdainfully of his recitations and of his one-act plays.

As the Desmonds entrusted him with larger parts in plays like *Way Down East, Uncle Tom's Cabin,* and *What Price Glory?,* his watching in the "first entrance" became less frequent and he devoted himself, according to Mae Desmond, "to his characterizations," often having to take two or three parts in a single play. She recalled, as testimony to his sensitivity on stage, an episode from *Over the Hill to the Poorhouse* in which his attunement to her was so acute that a matinee audience consisting mainly of mothers burst into spontaneous applause when he softened the villainy of his character with an improvised gesture.

Odets took great pleasure in thus having won a sea of matinee mothers, since his own wan mother was still feeling baffled by, impatient with, and withdrawn from her impecunious son, most of whose income from the Desmond company disappeared for trolley fares or hotel bills in the small towns of Pennsylvania.

Martha Washington, the maid at the Odets house in West Oak Lane, whose central recollection was how much Clifford loved to eat ("He'd eat up all the carrots before I could peel 'em, and he loved my corn muffins and baked ham"), also remembered Pearl's deep fear that he would never be able to support himself and how often she would sadly shake her head when "Clifford would be lookin' at himself in the mirror, rehearsin' a play." Pearl would say, "There's Clifford up there, actin' crazy again."

"Mattie," as she was called by the Odets family, remembered Aunt Esther and Uncle Israel, whom Clifford visited often, as far more tolerant of his acting. Although he complains in his diary that the girl cousins he meets there "have big noses and those kinds of things," he was at ease eating Tante Esther's matzo balls and admiring the ingenuity with which she managed to be president of a Jewish social club, memorizing the minutes which she still had not learned to read. Esther's daughter, Freda, recalled that in this year "Clifford said, 'It was always in my mind to be a writer; someday I'll be that,'" and that "Whatever made 'Esther's boy' happy was fine with her." This is the sole hint that his professional identity was *consciously* shifting at this time. That he continued to make acting his central identity long after it became a "lousy, lousy grind" stemmed from his conviction, told to Freda, that he could "never earn a cent from writing."

It humiliated him that he could not send his friend Herman three requested dollars and he toyed with the "unbearable thought" of pawning his beloved typewriter, "Lovelorn Corona." "I have ceased to dream," he confides in Herman and, warming to the notion of what a practical planner he is becoming, continues his letter:

I have my future mapped out. After camp I come to New York and one of the agencies will get me another job in Stock. For two more years, I will play stock and spend summer at camp. After that I shall stock myself up with money (?) and clothes and hit the Broadway market. The highest bidder gets me.

Quite suddenly the bubble bursts, and he concludes, "I sadly fear they will not be very anxious to bid."

Odets' yearning to get back to New York issued from no grand creative plan to become a playwright there but, insofar as he knew, from his desperation to stop "my father driving nails into my head here" because he could not support himself.

Although he recorded this year his admiration for Dreiser's *American Tragedy*, there is no hint he had the slightest awareness of, or interest in, its social-political reverberations as an indictment of an immoral pecuniary culture. He had no difficulty, however, in identifying himself with Dreiser's hero ("poor bastard"), over whose tragic fate Dreiser himself had wept openly at the Longacre Theatre, where a dramatization was being enacted.

Further indication of his lack of awareness of political currents is the fact that Odets makes no comment on his father's fanatic devotion to the radio broadcasts by the priest of the Shrine of the Little Flower in the diocese of Detroit, Charles E. Coughlin. In the Depression years Coughlin, along with Senator Huey Long of Louisiana, would become an American demagogue, attacking "corporate interests" and faintly echoing the stance of the disappointed house-painter in Germany, who was still biding his time.

During this optimistic "boom" era, with young people throughout the land easily finding jobs and "belonging" to the society, Odets already felt beached and "disinherited." To be sure, there was some sustenance in acting parts with Mae Desmond's stock company as well as in his secret writing, but it would take the cataclysm of the Great Depression, with its vast wake of stranded people, to provide *his* spiritual salvation. He could become a "voice," however, for a disinherited generation *only* when it appeared. His own conflicts could become creative when history opened the door.

Historians are impressed by the fact that at this time "the business culture wanted nothing from the intellectual, had no use for him and gave him no sustenance." In Philadelphia this rejection was especially virulent with regard to Jews and artists, not because of religion or race per se, but in an amorphous terror of the apparently limitless upward mobility inherent in an ungovernable prosperity.*

Doggedly pursuing his ineluctable necessities in this upward push with that single-mindedness toward success that can occur only in a society of maximum social mobility, Louis J. Odets, deeply chagrined by the loss of his own business, was jockeying now for position in the Abram Cox Boiler Company. (Forty years later he said, "I would have become president there if I had been a Gentile.") He bought his wife black stockings with fleur-de-lis embroidered on them—which she tucked away along with the black lace underwear he had given her earlier—and joined the fashionable and well-endowed Knesseth Israel Synagogue, where most of the members were German Jews of status. His daughters, persuaded by him to attend, felt shabby and out of place. He was unable to induce either his wife or his son to follow suit, and as excuses cited his wife's health and his son's "out-of-town work."

* When newcomer Albert Greenfield was admitted to Philadelphia's elegant Mercantile Club, "a shudder went up" not only in old Philadelphia but in First Wave old Jewish families like the famous Wolfs.

Despite the brakes put on his ascension by Pearl and the children, Lou Odets managed to bask, along with the mayor, in the glory of a new Packard and of high office in the Philadelphia branch of the Ancient Arabic Order of Nobles of the Mystic Shrine. A photograph of these two royal Masonic gentlemen would cross the continent five times, finally coming to rest in the "place of honor" on the peeling beige walls of his small Los Angeles apartment, the last he would inhabit.

Pearl, while she expressed interest neither in her husband's organizational ambitions nor in his conquest of the Cox company, had begun to set the table nightly for her family with a linen tablecloth and matching napkins. The core of her daily existence was to try to make a nice home for her children, imposing no demands on them to share household responsibilities. She tried, instead, to induce them and her tropical fish alike to eat more than they wanted. Her "baby," Florence, probably on the edge of being clinically endangered, consistently refused food and brought home notes from school saying, "Your daughter is 30 pounds underweight; please do something about it." Hard as she tried, Pearl failed to fatten any of her children. Perhaps they sensed the desperate impulse (by now a stereotype) to engulf, so often found in depressed Jewish mothers of the Diaspora who hope to alter their feeling of emptiness and meaninglessness by cramming food into their children. Pearl had better luck with her tropical fish and in growing beautiful flowers.

Although on the surface Clifford resisted his mother, his internalization of her was profound: before long he was absorbed by his own fish tank, whose expectant mothers would often be aided by him, as surgeon-obstetrician, in delivering their young. And for all his life, flowers would be a magic source of hope. He would, whenever he could afford it, maintain one bright blossom in a vase in the center of his personal clutter, and often, in bursts of generous affection, would shower men and women alike with gifts of flowers.

Despite Pearl's flowers and matching napkins, her children dreaded bringing friends home because of the cold and unwelcoming atmosphere. Everybody bickered and ate breakfast at a different time. It would become a source of astonishment to all of them to learn as adults that there were families within which warm communication was the norm; families where the father would not insist that the children run to the door and kiss him on his arrival home, as did L.J.

Clifford, totally out of step with his family, spent as much time as he could away from West Oak Lane, acting in the Desmond company and avoiding his parents when he had no work by typing, drinking, smoking, and listening to Caruso records all night and sleeping most of the day. Two things now keep him from madness, he records: "music and girls." But even here something is amiss, as he writes to Herman that "I'm getting tired of women older than Clifford," like the "little brambler rose with the ancient ivy." Perhaps he attracts older women, he writes, because of his "new technique of conquest." In a recent instance he has put on "a kind of air that I find hard to explain. I think it was a bewildered one, and that would arouse her maternal instinct. . . . She is the second woman of the company and I think she would be awfully surprised if she were to see what I am writing here. . . . "

In his letters there is something chilling, both in his steady inconsolability and in the revengeful, cynically indiscreet descriptions to Herman of his calculated sexual campaigns to "scatter some meat around the landscape." This detached and predatory braggadocio about his sexual prowess would emerge throughout his life in times of stress, often to the surprise and consternation of even close male friends, who would remember it as "gross" and "adolescent."

There is some comfort for him in "Beauty and Godliness" ("a nobility in ourselves"), but these often vanish in self-disgusts. He has written in greasepaint on his grimy dressing-room wall the motto: "Grist to the mill" and a line from Pater, "The way to beauty is through a number of *disgusts*," adding, "For all those things that hurt me now, exalt me, drag and toss me, all those things are so much grist to the mill and when the finished product is ground out I know that I shall be glad for all my acrimonious hours and mute reflections."

Early in the year he writes a short and mysterious note to Herman from the Hotel Shober, "Chester's Best," in Chester, Pennsylvania, addressing him as "Dear Hound of Hell": "Spending a night here—and wife! What is life without a wife?" The tragic sequelae of this short note would appear two years later in a cryptic allusion to the suicide of this secret young wife, "Roberta," after she had shot their baby daughter, Joan.

By this time Herman, replacing Cousin Irene, is in the slot of the desperately needed "audience" who is flayed for delaying his response to Clifford's communiqués, typed—with carbon copies—in the dead of night, both as self-expression and to assuage his loneliness. The recipients of these hundreds of letters testified that at no time did he seem so genuine and so emotionally accessible as in his correspondence. To Goldie Bromberg, wife of Group Theatre actor J. Edward Bromberg, he later wrote of this letter-writing phase in his creative development:

> For many years I wrote them all the time. . . . I think it was all part of an effort to be considered a clever lad. I was clever, I am clever, but it was wrong to think that important. . . . I used to store my life inside me, give little of it out, make no contacts outside of me, participate in little but my own reverie. All that made necessary some sort of release and I used to sit far into the night hammering out letters. Only at night (and I remember sitting in my room and dancing with words) with a cerebrating worm crawling around in my head did I really live. And even that living, I think, was a kind of fiction that I seldom examined closely. . . . Had I done so I would have seen the falsity of the whole business. Maybe I was afraid to do that, knowing, as I did, that there was nothing with which to replace that fiction.

The needs to live and to communicate, if only symbolically, are stated, but inasmuch as the letter is often a steppingstone to the art form, he *must* perceive even this activity as "false" living, a substitute for actual relationships with people, an "as if" activity which stands in limbo between a human relationship and that more universalized and impersonal form of human communication we call art.

When the Desmond Players keep him busy and out of his father's house, his letters to Herman Koblanov become lighter and he jokingly signs the name of a current health crank and strong man, Bernarr Macfadden. The cannibalistic nature of his "humorous" attack on his friend is startling:

> Dear Von,
> There isn't the slightest reason for answering your letter . . . you don't deserve it. You should be boiled in oil. Then the oil should be boiled and your skin ripped off with forceps. After that they should rub salt over you and then bake you with a flour coating. Bake till brown and then serve with a paprika dressing. You hound!

Do you think that all I've got to do is to write you letters and wait several months for a reply? Stop thinking that, if you do!

Chester, Pa. How fondly I say those words and what dear memories I do not associate with it. One hundred mortal souls in this town and 98 thousand mill hands and that sort of thing. Clifford is getting along well these days. He is playing general business* with the Mae Desmond Players . . . plays every week too! Last bills . . . Uncle Tom's Cabin, three parts, Way Down East, one part and next week that old buzz saw, What Price Glory. I'll soon be able to revise the play. Playing the general, Gowdy and Lundstrum. Remember them?

If you for one moment think that WBNY is one of my worries, forget it! Too busy! Glad tho to here [sic] that the station is bigger and better. My love to S. N. Baruch and heartiest wishes too. I will be in town on Sunday, March 27th. Meet me at the station with roses and orchids. I don't know what train I will make but it will be the excursion one. I think that gets in New York about ten in the morning. Of course you'll be asleep!

Looking for camp job again. A letter from Camp Navajo on tap and it seems to Clifford that he has heard of it as one of the finest camps in the east. Going to see them on the above date.

Most of the above parts that I have played are old men. The management seems to have so queer hankerings to make a character man of me. I didn't do nothing, mister! This week, Way Down East, finds me playing an old, dried up hick of sixty with "my rheumaticky laig" and "my Long Life Bittersss" which is really whiskey in a tonic bottle. Hell, oh Hell why don't you yawn open and swallow your little boy friend, Clifford.

Philadelphia is only a half hour's ride from Chester but it is only on Sunday that I ride in and greet the folks. I didn't do that last Sunday because I took me a chorus girl off the Mutual Circuit and from Saturday night, after show and supper, until Sunday, before a noon day breakfast, I took her circuit and made it mutual property. It may be inferred that she did like wise with my circuit. That's when I wrote you that brief note. It may not be inferred that because she came from burlesk that she was old, fat, baggy and lousy. No sir! She was young, refreshing, supple, resilient, charming, healthy, hot, burning, scorching, a little drunk, all legs and such things, . . . well, she was!!! All the water is gone from my scuppers and the bilge is overflowing, Man overboard and save the life bouy [sic], I can tend to my own business. Incidentally, since I am coming to New York on the 27th it might be a good idea to put me on the Sunday afternoon program of that date. A good billing would not be amiss nor would some publicity make me sorrowfull [sic]. . . . Thank you (with an upward inflection). Ans: PDQ

Bernarr Macfadden alais [sic] ami Clifford.

In contrast, when he must return to his father's house between jobs, he is assailed by intense irritability, depression, and the feeling that he is buried alive in Philadelphia and belongs nowhere. In such times his hostile and defensive philandering rises:

* A technical term to describe one of the lesser acting jobs in stock companies. In descending order, there were five categories of actor: Leading Man, Second Man, Character Man, Juvenile, and General Business.

I think the trouble must be with me. I have a rather funny tempre-
ment [sic] . . . mispelled [sic] . . . trifles are what bother me.
Jeez, I'm no genius but I can't stand the constant bickering at home.
My mother is sure she is being aggravated to death by Clifford because he insists on sleeping. My damned nerves are so unstrung that
I can hardly type. Then the kids and their racous [sic] squawking
. . . arguments . . . noise . . . if I ever go crazy you alone will
know the cause . . . and this is no joke. If life would only allow
these trifles to stop bothering me. . . .

I think I dumped the apple cart this time. I have found, for
your edification, that life holds no joy for me unless it is to *philander*
along. To make believe that I am in love with life and women . . .
get me. So in Philly here, several months, I started my campaign
against women. Love 'em and leave 'em is the ticket. In other words
strive to be a miniature Don Juan. . . .

Odets' sense of asphyxiation was made more acute by the contrast
between the avant-garde intellectual ferment and freedom of New York's
Greenwich Village and the polite, well-padded small talk of even literate
Philadelphians, many of whom were still opposing Whitman's poetry as
"coarse."◄

It had become a commonplace for intellectual young Philadelphians
who could afford it to flee to Greenwich Village, and for their less fortunate
comrades to aspire toward New York City with the same fantasies of
"salvation in Moscow" as those held by the yearning characters of a
Chekhov play. The nature of the salvation maintained a straight line of
spiritual and intellectual continuity with O'Neill's early comrades in the
Hell Hole: a loose marriage of socialist-humanist politics with esthetic
experiment, all in the context of a skeptical rule-questioning and rule-
breaking, labeled "free" or "bohemian," according to one's lights.

Those who could not yet escape to New York huddled in line every
Saturday night at the famed Academy of Music for gallery seats to hear
Leopold Stokowski conduct the Philadelphia Orchestra; after the concert, if
there was no invitation to a private home, they would repair to a Horn and
Hardart restaurant across the street, nicknamed "The Heel." This was the
Philadelphia counterpart of Stewart's Cafeteria at Sheridan Square in the
Village. Here the talk was always so lofty, so passionate, and so declama-
tory that Eddie Wagner, a boxer who regularly went there to drink coffee,
was of the opinion that somehow "it lacked conversation."

Budding young physicians, archeologists, painters, architects, musicians, and writers formed a nucleus devoted not only to an exploration of
what Odets had called in his letters "Beauty and Godliness" but also to
ethics and social philosophy. Like their counterparts in New York, they
cannot be understood in terms of the stereotypes of the Roaring Twenties;
to be sure, many of them drank bathtub gin and danced the Charleston,
but they were fervently devoted also to creative personal growth, to social
justice, and to the avoidance of a new military conflagration. They debated the significance of the Russian Revolution for all of these. By this
time the brief moment of new hope, when "an iridescent apparition
seemed to be suspended over Moscow," had begun.

A young intellectual named Walter Lippmann was writing of the
social-psychological effects of the generally waning faith in religion, asking such rock-bottom questions as: how could mankind, "deprived of the

great fictions," meet the deep need which had made those fictions necessary? Soon it would become evident that the socialist dream of heaven-on-earth would be used to meet the need. In Philadelphia a few early apostles formed a club named after John Reed, the Byronic, crusading young American author of *Ten Days That Shook the World,* now several years dead, buried beside Soviet heroes in the Kremlin.

In August 1927 these apostles would shed bitter tears when two Italian immigrants were executed: they were convinced that Nicola Sacco and Bartolomeo Vanzetti had been found guilty of robbery and murder not because of the evidence presented at their trial but because they were philosophic anarchists. The apostles were equally convinced of the innocence of labor leader Thomas J. Mooney—later pardoned when the wheel of history turned—and outraged that he was doomed to spend over half of his short adult life in prison despite confessions that the testimony convicting him of bomb-throwing had been perjured.

Some of them would become obsessed in the same way, twenty years later, with the question of whether Alger Hiss had been unjustly convicted "in the court of public opinion." Their familiarity with the details of the Dreyfus case was intimate, and their identification with persons being politically extruded by American society ran deep.

It was inevitable that "the outsider" Odets, preoccupied with problems of values and ethics, and still nourished by Victor Hugo, would soon find these youngsters and feel less desolate and less lonely in their company.

Aunt Esther's neighbor in North Philadelphia, Mrs. Kahn, had a daughter named Rose, a plain girl who played the piano "like an angel." Everyone in the neighborhood knew that Rose was in love with Clifford, who visited often just to hear her play. Years later when he went to console her mother, "bitten deeply with the acid of grief" over Rose's death in childbirth, Odets wrote:

> I listened and tried to explain to her how useful and good her life could continue to be. (For the atmosphere she used to create in her home had been influential in the lives of a few musical and creative people, myself included); but it was difficult to talk against her real grief. . . .

The "atmosphere" consisted of her musicales after the Saturday-night concerts, with nourishment for the ear and for the stomach. Here Clifford luxuriated not only in good Jewish food and intimate live music, but in the fact that discussion, sometimes with girls, could reach beyond his father's Caruso records to include daring romantic "finds" of his own, such as Tchaikovsky and César Franck, Joseph Conrad and Dostoevsky. Here at last were "worthy" people who, he feared, "found me amusing and even perhaps to be pitied." He became "determined to wrest from them their admiration," and, looking back a quarter of a century later, "when finally I did, I was shy and embarrassed and knotted with tensions I could not resolve." He records, at twenty-one, that it continues to trouble him that so often he tries to resolve these tensions in withdrawn sexual self-stimulation. He does not seem to realize that the people he thought found him amusing and pitiable did in fact find him the electric talker, indeed the spellbinder he remained all of his life: a performer, like his father, but of another breed.

"It was love at first sight." This simple summary, offered in interview by several heterosexual men as a capsule account of their initial encounters with Odets, was also given by a regular attender of Mrs. Kahn's musicales: William Kozlenko, a deeply intelligent young man with a strong leonine head, recently graduated from Tchaikovsky and Conrad to Beethoven and Dostoevsky. He noticed the swift, intent, compassionate glance directed to his leg—crippled by infantile paralysis—by the shy, husky, blue-eyed Adonis introduced to him as a member of Mae Desmond's acting company. Only later, when he learned that Clifford had a crippled younger sister, did he lightly speculate that this fact might have contributed to Odets' taking the initiative in their relationship.

There were, however, more obvious attractions for Odets. First, Kozlenko was the precocious, soon-to-be-published author of a slender volume celebrating the defensively wisecracking, sad, and cynical magazine editor and drama critic George Jean Nathan, with whom Kozlenko identified at this time. In a fifty-page book called, with apologies to George Bernard Shaw, *The Quintessence of Nathanism,* young Kozlenko militantly supported the thesis that, in Nathan's words, "Art is a partnership between the artist and artist-critic. . . . Criticism is the windows and chandeliers of art; it illuminates the enveloping darkness in which art might otherwise rest only vaguely discernible and perhaps altogether unseen."

Despite his awe of Kozlenko's position as a published writer, Odets took strong issue not only with Nathan's thesis but with Kozlenko's conclusion that "Nathan has done more for the American theatre . . . than any of his American predecessors or contemporaries."

Odets conceded that Nathan's criticism was probably salutary in its opposition to a prevalent puritanism and provincialism (which saw Ibsen and Gorky as "sewers of vulgarity"), but felt that a critic, usually himself an artist manqué, can *never* be a *primary* force in the development of any art. Odets, initially grateful for the appreciator-critic in Kozlenko, so violently opposed Nathan's ideas that his relationship with Kozlenko gradually soured. His later savage bitterness toward Nathan as the prototype of the artist's prime enemy started here.

Kozlenko held the key to another world of prime importance to Odets, an anodyne already a source not simply of emotional and intellectual excitement but of sustenance. This was the great world of music. Kozlenko played the piano even better than Rose Kahn and owned many recordings; most were of Beethoven's works, about which he was planning another book. If this were not enough, he had written one of the earliest magazine pieces in America about Sibelius, and possessed a letter and a signed picture from this Scandinavian genius.

Odets was awed, and Kozlenko was flattered by such awe from this extraordinarily attractive and intelligent young actor who, according to Kozlenko, "without lessons could pick out simple lyrical pieces on the piano, improvising the harmonies intuitively. He actually did very well, sometimes enacting the role of a virtuoso. . . . His love of music was so genuine, I became what you might call his music-mentor." Night after night, when Clifford had no work with the Desmond company, they would listen to records, muting the sound with a towel to keep from waking L. J. Odets, who could understand an after-dinner interest in Caruso, but not this fanatical absorption.

Before long Odets began a novel about the power of music, using as a title the last five words of a sentence in Shaw's *Don Juan in Hell:* "Music is the brandy of the damned." Odets promoted Kozlenko from music-mentor to literary sounding board, and timidly told him after a concert that he had begun writing his first novel, a secret undertaking because his father bitterly disapproved as much of his "wasting time at the type-writer as he did of our listening to records." The hero of Odets' first opus was an old man named Carl Franck who "shuffled about the house in bedroom slippers, always stroking a cat in his arms."* Kozlenko assumed that the book would be a stereotyped juvenile salute to the composer César Franck, "but," he said, "I was stunned when I read it. Already he had that rich feeling for digging inside people. . . . It was set in a rooming house, a kind of Bohemian Grand Hotel of Philadelphia, occupied by re-bellious young men and girls—writers, actors, etc.—who broke away from their parental ties. Franck, a kind of benevolent father-figure, exuded advice and got in everybody's hair. There was passion and poetry, anger and nostalgia, a kind of dream-projection of a home which Cliff wanted very much to have, terribly romantic but full of talent. . . . He wouldn't believe he had talent. He worked secretly on this book all the time, but kept saying, 'After all, I'm an actor.' "

Although L. J. Odets was bitterly contemptuous, according to Kozlenko, of "those intellectual bums" his son would pick up at the Academy of Music, he tolerated occasional visits from his son's new friend, who was deeply moved by "the dreadful emotional discord in that family" and Clifford's fractured response to it. By this time Pearl was concentrating, as her personal expression, on the buying of beautiful bedspreads on which, her daughter recalled, no one was allowed to sit. She was pleased, as her son would be later in the purchase of a painting, "if she would get one at a good bargain." Kozlenko remembered her as a "tall, slender, sweet, taci-turn, shy woman with a lot of tenderness, withdrawn and attractive with the fair-haired sensitivity of Clifford's face. . . . He was deeply attached to her."

He recalled also the instant shift in emotional climate when L.J. would come home. Although he could be "charming and ingratiating, ob-serving all the amenities," he would instantly freeze into silence his fright-ened, smoldering, yearning son. Not being L.J.'s son, and by temperament a less obedient young man, Kozlenko occasionally engaged "this middle-class man who worshipped mercantile success" in a discussion of values. Usually in these scenes Clifford remained silent lest he "blow his top," deferring his tirades against his father "for not letting him become a musician" until he was alone with Kozlenko. L.J.'s social charm—much of it Kozlenko thought "transparently phony"—would unpredictably give way to a ranting explosion during which he would scream at Clifford, "You're living in *my* house, eating *my* food, and what are you?" On several occasions, according to Kozlenko, when the twenty-one-year-old Odets broke through his dogged silence to a bitter response, "his father slapped him so hard he staggered." Such physical assaults so unnerved Pearl that she would dissolve into sobs and run from the room, leaving Clifford de-termined never to speak to his father again.

Many times Odets fled to live with Kozlenko's parents, but more often he appeared at the home of his Tante Esther and Uncle Israel Rossman, where he was met with hugs, kisses, chicken soup, and knadlach. This home, to which he returned regularly until his aunt and uncle were

* There is something awesome in this prescient image of Odets' last years in Hollywood.

dead, provided the foundation for "the unique theatre vocabulary . . . that has infiltrated and salted our national dialogue" and ultimately for the characters of Noah and his wife in *The Flowering Peach*. There he put into Esther's mouth the judgment that he was "a boy one in between a million." In the presence of Tante and his uncle, Freda recalled, Clifford experienced an immediate expansion of spirit: "He would sit down at the piano, strike a few chords and break into song . . . frequently saying, '*This* is where I really feel at home.'"

Even during these periods of violent rejection by and of his father he longed to please him and, with a part of himself, shared his father's withering judgment that he was a lazy, worthless parasite. L.J.'s ideal for his son that he be a writer only of salable commodities was epitomized for him now in the demand that he become an advertising copywriter.*

His father's aspiration would forever remain entrenched in the impressionable boy as the sole route to paternal love and respect and, accordingly, to self-regard. This conviction, rarely conscious, would prove divisive for his creative development and would ultimately rend him asunder.◖

"Me, I'm all in a blur. Sometimes life seems so bitter that it isn't worth expending the effort necessary to breathe with. . . . One doesn't know what one is cut out for until one finds out. But they won't give you a chance to find out. Be like other people is what they ask of you. But damit I won't ever be a pattern on which millions more are designed." So wrote Clifford to Herman Koblanov to sum up his mood in the spring of 1927. He had just accepted a job as a dramatics counselor at Camp Arthur in Zieglersville, Pennsylvania, having been turned down at Camp Roosevelt, where his "splendid conceit" had been badly damaged the year before.

This summer at Camp Arthur, with its pit privies and its primitive stage (actually a platform without electricity at one end of an open field), would again fulfill the prime function of supplying a small nest egg for the fall, when his hope of "hitting the Broadway market" as an actor would revive. Yearning toward "the bigtime" in New York, he dreamed of coming in with "a vaudeville single"—maybe even in a one-act play called *The Very Naked Boy*. He managed, in this as in three camp summers to come, to remain spiritually alive by sneaking into the office nightly to type poems and letters to correspondents who became more desirable listeners in direct proportion to their distance from him. He confides that he is "making a collection of rejection slips."

Bored to distraction by directing all the plays he had acted in at Morris High School, he again consoled himself for "the strife we call life" with smoking, drinking, and girl-hunting. Even a visit from his father was welcome. He writes to Herman:

Last Saturday who should pop in but Father . . . and it was good to see him. . . . He travels around a lot and only today I got a card from the Palmer House in Chicago where he is now. The parents

* In 1940, feeling discouraged just before the opening of his last play with the Group Theatre (*Night Music*), Clifford would apply, under a pseudonym, for just such a position in an advertising agency!
◖ 6.3.

very nicely made up a gift of twelve beans for me and feeling as I did . . . first let me tell you how I felt. I felt just as if I were half in a grave. After two or three weeks camp always makes me feel that way. . . . I get little or no mail . . . there is nothing to remind me of the outside world and the sight of Nature begins to jar the old nerves. . . . Now you know the feeling that Clifford suffered. So I went out and got two pint bottles of rye and as I don't like it straight I got five bottles of ginger ale. That was enough and the boys plus C.O. were soon walking (?) down the road. They tell me that I insisted upon swimming in all the mud puddles and once or twice . . . I tried to stop a speeding automobile or so with my massive (?) body.* All I do know is that I woke up the next morning on a cot in the doc's office. My tongue was like flannel and I had a beautiful rainbow-like black and blue mark on my elbow and another on . . . well, an unmentionable spot. . . .

Shortly after his father's visit Clifford was urgently called from a rehearsal to hear his father sobbing helplessly over the phone the news of the death of *his* mother, Zipporah Gorodetsky, an event L.J. always insisted he "sensed" before it happened. This is the first hint that the terrifying "bulldozer father" had a yearning to reverse roles with his son.

While Clifford struggled with his charges at Camp Arthur, he was apparently unconcerned about the evolving history from which he would emerge as a spokesman for a generation. Theodore Dreiser was commissioned by William Randolph Hearst to visit the Soviet Union and to report on the Russian experiment. Despite his profound ambivalence, in this as in everything, Dreiser reported his hope that "this is truly the beginning of a brighter day for all." It pleased him that the Russians were enthusiastic about his "Americanskaya Tragedya." Sinclair Lewis and Dorothy Thompson, too, were taking soundings in Russia for many American intellectuals who very soon, during the Great Depression, would see in this model Communist country the sole hope for the future of man.

When Sacco and Vanzetti were sentenced to die in Boston, Massachusetts, on August 22, a demonstration on the Boston Common was organized to save these two lives. John Howard Lawson, though reluctant, joined his friends John Dos Passos and Edna St. Vincent Millay in this effort. The Defense Committee, headquartered at the Hotel Bellevue— where seven years later Odets would write *Waiting for Lefty*—was sending frantic wires: "Come and save Sacco and Vanzetti. This is the final call. They must be saved. The minute Sacco and Vanzetti die, there will die also the faith of millions in American justice."

The execution of these two men deeply stirred a significant portion of the intellectual community, which would never forget Vanzetti's prophecy at his trial: "Never in our full life can we hope to do such work for tolerance, for justice, for man's understanding of man as now we do by accident." Edna St. Vincent Millay, tried for "loitering" in this fruitless demonstration, said on the witness stand that she had never in her life walked with a more definite purpose.

---

* This is one of the earliest reports of his self-destructive recklessness.

By fall the young Philadelphians—Odets among them—gathering at the Heel would once again be full of the Sacco-Vanzetti case, and many would use it as a rallying point for left-wing teaching.* Although he took an active part in these discussions, Odets was more concerned with two personal problems: would Mae Desmond use him this season "on a weekly salary," so that he could escape living in West Oak Lane with his family, and how much compassion could he stir up for himself in how many women, in order to wage "my campaign against them"? To Herman he again writes, "Love 'em and leave 'em is the ticket."

During the fall of 1927 another kind of history was evolving: American schoolchildren were singing paeans to Charles A. Lindbergh, a young aviator who demonstrated not only his personal courage but his belief in a booming American technology by trusting himself, all alone, to pilot an airplane across the Atlantic Ocean, something never before achieved. Lindbergh, hailed as "Lucky Lindy," became a folk hero several rungs above singer Al Jolson, whose electrifying voice was heard in the first talking film, *The Jazz Singer*.◖ Each marked a significant human conquest and new dangers, one of space, the other of communication. But already a few Cassandras were noting signs of dreadful happenings to come: the economy was slowing down and perhaps, said some, a total decline of the West was on its way.

Odets' anxiety and depression were lifted somewhat by his being cast by a small touring company in the title role of *Abie's Little Rose*, a shameless imitation of Anne Nichols' famous *Abie's Irish Rose*, which celebrated the melting-pot integration of Jews and Irish in America. As Abie, he played all through the coalfields of Pennsylvania, but, to his dismay, without salary. Eventually, Odets reported to Herman Koblanov, the company discovered that the manager was a "dope fiend" and had spent the takings on cocaine, morphine, heroin, and "snow" instead of paying his cast.

Odets later told a *New Yorker* reporter that at the end of this tour, after exhausting all other possibilities, he had had to do the thing he least wanted to do: wire his father for money to get back to West Oak Lane, where he did not in the least want to go.

---

* Composer Marc Blitzstein, a member of this Philadelphia group, would struggle for the rest of his life to find a suitable musical form for this profoundly American story with immigrant protagonists.
  ◖ 6.4.

Chapter Seven

The question was really not one of knowing how to write, so much as knowing how to connect with yourself so that the writing is, so to speak, born affiliated *with yourself. . . .*

CLIFFORD ODETS, *1961*

THE year 1928 opened hopefully for the American theatre, for its leading playwright, Eugene O'Neill, and for twenty-one-year-old Clifford Odets. *Strange Interlude,* though dismissed by *The New Yorker* as a "stunt" and scolded by *The New York Times* as "twisted and macabre," was seen by others as a "giver of new scopes," a hewer of ways for truth and "a method to meet today's immense need for plays that can ably cope with Freud." Enough New Yorkers decided the play was worth seeing to keep it running for seventeen months, and it netted for O'Neill his third Pulitzer Prize, a movie sale, and the relatively untaxed fortune of $275,000.

Less visibly, and more impecuniously, Harold Clurman and Lee Strasberg were at the same time sowing seeds for what would prove to be a most influential force not only for Odets' writing but also for the development of an indigenous American theatre. Funded modestly by a real-estate man made rich during World War I and richer now on the "high plateau of permanent prosperity," Clurman and Strasberg first produced a morality play about contemporary life written by Waldo Frank, author of *The Rediscovery of America.* Next they worked on *Balloon,* a "delicate fantasy on the big world of success and the small world of the poet's heart" by Padraic Colum. It did not strike anyone as odd that their object of opprobrium, the American businessman, should also be the source of funds for all of their work.

By the end of this year Clurman—one of the few who saw O'Neill's *Strange Interlude* not as a stunt but as a breakthrough—was working as a play-reader for a respected organization most representative of this coming-of-age period: the Theatre Guild, whose historic function was, in Clurman's words, "to bring plays previously regarded as uncommercial to a big middle-class audience." Under the aegis of the Guild, the paths of Odets and Clurman would soon cross.

Whenever she could, Mae Desmond, still struggling to keep her stock company alive, gave Odets parts in plays like *The Cat and the Canary, Red Kisses, The Hunchback of Notre Dame,* and *Over the Hill to the Poorhouse.* By now, however, his aspiration to become a writer was taking discernible shape. With substantial encouragement from Chamberlain Brown, regarded by Clifford as a "big actor's agent" who frequently took handsome young men "under his wing," Odets determined to learn this year if he was finally to become an actor or a writer. He writes to friend Herman that he has a possible $80 acceptance from the even then prestigious *New Yorker* of "a profile considered by Brown a masterpiece, twice as long as they wanted"; such an acceptance, though only "possible," was no mean feat for a twenty-two-year-old high-school dropout. His spirits are high as he adds, " . . . don't be surprised if Odets gets some place on the stage and Kobland is called in to be his secretary . . . a delicious thought . . . eh?" The piece never appeared, and another seven years would pass before Odets' euphoric prediction would be fulfilled.

By the end of March, Mae Desmond had no future parts for him and he was desperately discontent in Philadelphia, but his mood continued briefly affirmative:

> . . . I have become so expert with make-up that with a wig, my own family don't recognize me. . . . I do my part well this week [a sizeable role, Judge Billings in *Over the Hill to the Poorhouse,* whom he played as an "oily heavy"] . . . I have been told that by the other members of the cast. There is not one of them that does not predict a fine career for me and more than one has voiced a desire to change places with me. They are stock hams and know it and will probably end their days in stock. . . . Clifford will not, for lately there has come to me the idea that I am going to be a truly good actor with a chance at greatness if such a thing is possible during one's life. . . . Don't call it vanity, Von, because I don't really have THAT. . . . If I have been able to make 13 characters in eleven weeks and make them convincing to old-time actors . . . then there must be something to me . . . those things don't swell me. They make me more sober and more careful to improve my technique. . . . I can't kick when I look back on the last year and see how much vital knowledge of the stage and its mechanics I have gained. Brown has as good as promised to see me to a job where I can make myself into a name.* . . . He said that a young man in order to succeed on the stage must have a mind, a personality, an education, feel life keenly, be buoyant and have a semblance of culture. Don't you think I have those things? So New York looms big. . . . To think I have at last, consciously, begun to mould my career. . . . Expect to hear from me within 10 days and in the meantime you MUST write and tell me what you honestly think about my chances. . . .

Despite Brown's "promises," by the spring of 1928, after a brief foray into Manhattan (where he lived at a West 57th Street rooming house remembered by Herman Kobland as a "horrible rundown fleabag called Raleigh Hall with miserable Broadway flotsam and jetsam characters"), he was stuck again in Philadelphia in his father's house. Listening to L.J.'s contemptuous attacks ("Boy, boy you sure do lead the life of Riley

---

* The American dream, "to make a name for oneself," was always strong in Odets, and it appears in all his work. Even in his first film, *The General Died at Dawn,* a Chinese warlord is bribed to give up his terrorism by the promise that he will "make a name" for himself.

. . . you should be ashamed of yourself!") and to his sister Gen's accusations that he is stealing money, he felt he was going to seed, and wrote, "There is too much flesh on me, so much that I think my sensitivity is gone."

His letters once again reflect a black depression relieved only occasionally now by self-mocking whimsy, or by a rhapsodic appreciation of music, rain, tomato omelets which he himself tosses, or by "the ever fresh miracle of an unfolding flower on my table. . . . "

In a rare burst of Whitmanesque well-being, to a newfound consoler named Betty he says: "Everywhere, in everything you see has Clifford lovers of a sort." To Betty he writes romantic, stiltedly literary letters just after having left her in the early morning for a long trolley ride home to 68th Avenue in West Oak Lane. Now, and forever, his freest communication is by way of the written word, as he reviews for her his having "stared and stared" at her that very evening at a party when he had longed "to kiss an inch of you, an inch below the angle of your cheek, where a shadow kept playing a game with the skin."

He is preoccupied with the fact of mortality, and envies "the poorest animal . . . for whom this is no issue and for whom there is as well no question of momentary compensations in his life." But, above all, he is boundlessly grateful to anyone who helps to dilute his sense of disconnection. To Betty he writes:

> In the orbit I have sloughed for months and months no one has been like you to make me glad, to make me think that life is not a cheat, is not a belly-stuffing jade. Futility is . . . a thing of . . . blackest thoughts. You killed it for me, in your room, while we talked and talked, and smoked and smoked. . . . There would be no lover's warmth in that kiss, but it would be to feel the nerves of you who so match the writer of these—and his nerves. That was why you made me glad: for I saw you as I was inside, and in that contemplation came to rest; futility dropped off from me as a garment that ceases to fit. Pick up your head! You have done some good in this world, making, as you did, a boy glad to feel the life that's his to do with as he will.
>
> A gracious thanks, a morning of the rarest sort for you. You'll never know how you have made me glad.

Struggling with the help of a psychoanalyst to overcome a disabling depression a quarter-century later, he would write in a diary of his life-long yearning "to get into people's love, into their hearts" and to be "accepted" by them. "I thought I saw that others, much less gifted, were being accepted where I was not. . . . This very feeling is almost the one that made me a playwright: 'Christ,' I used to think, 'if they think these are good plays I will show them that I can write better plays with my hands tied behind my back!'" But until he could be "let in" by reason of his writing, episodes such as this with Betty were his sustenance.

This sustenance, now and always, comforts him only briefly; his malaise overtakes him within the month, and he no longer writes of gladness and gratitude, but of pain, a renewed sense of futility, and his conviction that she will betray him: "I only wish Betty you had never said two lines. Once a girl said to me, in a summer night that sometime we'd go down to the sea and sit on a rock. I remembered that line for years; and so I am going to remember the two lines you said. I'm afraid they'll hurt me as the other one did. For we never went down to the sea, but I did

. . . alone." Like so many self-fulfilling prophecies he had made, and would make, this one shortly came to pass, and he retreated into Schubert's "lovelorn" music.

His experience of having been abandoned by his mother twice over —first as her grief in her marriage caused her to withdraw from him, and then as she turned to his crippled sister—would be courted and re-enacted by him with a dreadful regularity for the rest of his life. Time and again, as his defensive suspiciousness, along with his accusing and revengeful needs toward women, took precedence over the universal human need to master an original experience of defeat, he was indeed "betrayed," left alone, and deeply depressed. Always his best anodyne was either sexuality or the creation or devouring of Art.◀

Feeling "as impotent as a child just come from where it's born," he sustained himself this year by these letters to Betty in which he curses the poverty of living through language ("even the courage of ten millions will not help you kill this thing called Life") and uses words as his daily bread.

Even as he curses the emptiness and falseness of "stupid, lifeless" words, he is exploring them nightly, with high esthetic and intellectual excitement, and groping toward their mastery:

I am sick with being away from someone like you. I can't see to write any more . . . [crossed out] What's the use of talking . . . I can only see the hundred crying mouths that curve with pain in the dark. They are all of our mouths, we who shout and scream and yet are less than the murmurs of the insects under our feet. . . .

These words . . . and more words words words. We go from one to the other, with prayers to make us whole again. Christ!!!!!!*

This ambivalence toward the word, the *symbol*—that which is in place of the direct, unmanageable human exchange—is always found in writers, perhaps in all creators.◀

On the one hand, keeping himself warily detached, he grieves that he cannot trust the living, actual relationship and must fly to the universe of words. There he feels—at the price of a certain sense of fraudulence and isolation—more hope for a mastery of his daily experience. On the other hand, he celebrates the fact that the only true reality for him lies in the fictions he invents, the "lies like truth," dismissing life itself as "a dream."◀

Night after night, he pounds at his typewriter. A short story called "Twenty Minutes." "Three Dirty Poems," distilling in light verse his envy of the innocence of animals.† And, of course, letters, always letters, with the standard plea for an immediate, swift response. Not long after the completion of this short story, his typewriter was smashed.

Odets later told newspapermen many times that his father, enraged at the useless noise in the small hours of the night had arisen from bed and, with his boxer's powerful right hand, demolished the typewriter. His father offered several different versions of how "Lovelorn Corona" was destroyed. He told this writer:

◀ 7.1.
* Odets' lifelong and prodigal use of the exclamation mark is testimony both to his frantic search for genuine feeling and his sense of incompetence to articulate it.
◀ 7.2.
◀ 7.3.
† For example: "See the happy dog at play:— / He never has words to say; / Tepid or cold, shy or bold, / Never thinks of growing old; / Tearing off a little piece, / Never thinks, 'Might be my "niece" '; / See the happy dog at play."

You've heard his father broke his typewriter. . . . No . . . when I think of everything I done for Clifford . . . I'd never *tell* him what to do, I'd just suggest [said with obvious effort to remain calm]. Now, Gen was a cocky kid and one night at two o'clock she hollered she can't sleep. So I told him to close his door and windows, but the room was full of cigarette smoke; so I told him to cut out the cigarettes, but like a youngster he *didn't follow instructions* [now shouting in spite of himself]. So a fight started between him and Genevieve, and now his mother got up and bumped into the card table. The typewriter slid off and was damaged. I didn't break no typewriter, but I told him not to tell nobody what happened . . . to blame me, not to blame his mother [piously said] or that really *would* start a fight.

When Clifford's intense distress became evident to him, L.J. reported, "I went with him immediately to Schnellenberg's store and bought a new white Remington . . . and he threw his arms around me and kissed me two, three times." For Virginia Rowe, Odets' secretary, L.J. enacted another version in which the typewriter had caught on *his* sleeve and fallen to the floor, an accident pure and simple. Frank Lubner, Pearl's cousin, recalled her heartbroken account to him of Lou Odets in a towering rage smashing the typewriter "because he thought Clifford was wasting his time." Although the available evidence does not settle the question of who ruined the typewriter, there is no doubt that "Lovelorn Corona" was indeed a wreck, and that by this summer of 1928 L.J. had replaced it by a "new kind, finished in cream-color Duco." On a bloody battlefield, both father and son, it appears, were trying to reach an accommodation and, for a brief instant, were succeeding.

Clifford secretly named the new machine bought by his father "Ambition Corona," and wrote to his friend Herman:

. . . but Lovelorn is inconsolate so I take her out and play with her whenever I have the time.* Father bought me the new machine from the goodness of his heart. . . . Father and I are getting along splendidly. I like the old boy so much.

In a letter to Betty he expressed, with little apparent awareness, his yearning to emulate and to please his father on "Ambition Corona," and yet to write in such a way that the "writing is *born affiliated* with yourself." He writes:

Then I went to sit down at my typewriter. It is a good machine, but I have no love for it, it being nothing more than a tool with which I write. I had a machine once that I really loved. I called it "Lovelorn Corona" and treasured it beyond all reproach. How strange this machine is, was, as I looked at it in the early morning. It did not seem to be part of my life, part of my struggle, the struggle which will cease to be a struggle by the time camp is over this summer. For by that time I'll know whether I'm going to stay an actor or drop all the playing for a life of serious writing. *It has come to me that nothing will ever be settled if I remain satisfied to stay on the fence between the two, sighting both lands and yet being in neither of them.* [Italics mine]

---

* This is a striking image: of his own old typewriter as a woman whom he had abandoned (his Muse) in favor of a mate regarded by his father as more suitable ("Ambition Corona").

He was by this time on page 293 of his novel *The Brandy of the Damned*, about the anesthetizing uses of music. But his struggle to be done with "sighting both lands" would not cease during any season of his life. In later years he would repress not only his obedient compliance to his father but also his need for swift reassurance, and even close friends would believe he had always wholly detested his father and his father's values.

His heavy mood persists, and on one occasion he writes extravagantly to Betty that his "muse is recalcitrant" and that although the rain, "persistent marauder," has stopped, "yet am I sad to lacrimal plenitude, to heavy saliferous tears. Alack the fairest of peonies has gone to age [an actual white flower on his desk]: its petals belong to yesterday and its stalk lonely and naked, belongs to the ages of eternity."* Speculating that the "white as white" peony "must be some bewitched woman on a stalk . . . so fresh and live and real," he becomes defensive: "If it is effeminate to love flowers then mark me down as such. They and their fragrance are our closest links with Nature who runs the earth."◖

To be in command of himself "honestly and with honor" and to "sing the song," as he put it, of "one's nature" had become a seriously compromised undertaking from the moment Clifford had become the son of Louis J. and Pearl Geisinger Odets, immigrant Jews in twentieth-century America.

Awaiting his twenty-second birthday and his yearly stint as a dramatics counselor, this time at Camp Tioga in Lakewood, Pennsylvania, he slept late and filled his afternoons and evenings listening to Bill Kozlenko's records and his piano-playing. Or he and Kozlenko would take in a chamber-music concert and afterward go to Linton's restaurant for coffee and lively intellectual contests. He took special pleasure in silently watching newcomers make "intellectual mincemeat" of his friend Kozlenko by "drawing him out and pouncing on him . . . leaving him to suck the lollipop of consolation"; and his admiration and envy was unbounded for "a heavyweight who is a college student of the sort that win so many scholarships that he has to give most of them up." Painfully aware that he had never finished high school, Odets lacked confidence to be a contender in any of these contests. Yet he was totally absorbed by them, and used them for his self-expressive necessity by narrating them in letters of utmost detail during the small hours of the morning, on his "Lovelorn Corona" typewriter, who was "on her legs again, having decided to pick up her head and be a good girl." The image of this portable typewriter remained sharp for half a century in the memory of a camp director: "You rarely saw him without it. He was an imaginative youngster deeply wrapped up in all aspects of the theatre and determined to write. I must add he also had an unusual affinity for hard liquor and hard talk."

---

* He pleads with Betty for his immortality and in the same letter mocks at himself in doggerel that he cannot have animal freedom from human needs and guilts: "When I am dead don't write my name in water. Instead say, 'Poor, dear boy . . . there was a poet. One morning he left me and near his house a cat slunk by. This is what he sent to me: "The glorious tomcat walks along, / He has no sense of right or wrong. / He likes them thin, likes them fat, / Emulate the god-damned cat!" ' "

◖ 7.4.

Odets' wish to alleviate suffering was less obvious, but significant. He often said, "The first thing I think when I meet someone is what can I learn from him or how can I help him." During this summer of 1928 at Camp Tioga, the parents of Gerry Aronson, a ten-year-old camper afflicted with a formidable speech defect due to partial deafness, implored "Uncle Clifford" (between directing plays and minstrel shows) to cure their young son not only of his speech problem but of his inordinate willfulness and "blithe lying" to explain away his defect. In this first assignment to the kind of intuitive psychotherapy he would informally conduct all of his life, Odets demonstrated a remarkable delicacy of empathy and endless patience with the afflicted boy. This capacity would forever confound those who saw side by side with it his helplessness with his own children; or, for that matter, his inability to manage his obtuse, often desperately cruel impulses toward women, carbon-copied from his father.

"Uncle Clifford" gave young Gerry Aronson curative roles to play in his theatricals: for example, the part of a hopping frog, in which he was to croak at the top of his lungs, to the theme of Dvořák's "New World" symphony, the words of a popular song, "Crazy people, crazzzy people, crazy people like me like crazzzy people like you." As a respected psychoanalyst in Los Angeles, Dr. Gerald Aronson would recall "Uncle Clifford's" help with deep gratitude: "I never questioned the connection between Dvořák, crazy people, and a frog hopping. That was the magic of Odets."

For a few months during his twenty-second summer of life, it seemed that at long last he was integrating his warring elements into a cohesive identity. Beyond his actual work with the campers, he was assiduously exploring his gift as a writer and getting "lots of mail" in response to his letters. His diary records also great success with the girls across the lake at Camp Tabor, and a discarded girlfriend writes him desperately that she should have married him, not her husband of two weeks. As he grew in these achievements, critical for a young adult, his mood this summer was phenomenally good. He even had enough emotional leeway to welcome a visit from his father, and writes to Herman: "He's all right, that boy, and I can do nothing better than to try to emulate him in a number of matters. I fear he is a better man than his son . . . by far. I repeat, I am quite content."

It will not surprise us, however, to hear that his sinister demons were lurking not far off. In a savage letter to a girl nicknamed by him "Little Thing," written soon after his father's visit, he reviews the many "futile and wasted nights" he has spent with her until five in the morning, flaying her for the very attitude he had hated in his mother and was now beginning to sense as an ingrown part of himself: her passive withholding of herself, lack of assertion, and her cowardice:

> . . . futile because I never came to know you better altho I gave you my entire mentality on a plate. It was like a dish of chef-de-houevre (oi, oi) to be passed along for the dinner eater to take olives and delicacies from . . . but you were so afraid . . . Christ it makes me furious so that I am digging thru this paper with my typewriter keys and their metal letters . . . and I am smoking a Camel and the blood has left my head. I give you my word that if I had you here I'd throttle you, scar your face, or do something to you . . . never once did you tell me to go to hell or shut my face . . . instead there was always the sweet smile . . . good God, no assertion in you at all nothing that was stiffer than a lump of jelly. Why did you dare to let me walk all over your mind? . . . Jesu, a woman without courage.

. . . I'm tired of people like you . . . courage is what I'm talking about . . . the lyrical flights you might have started me on and did not . . . would not or could not I cannot say.

It is unlikely that the target of these harsh accusations actually deserved such a battering. This furious attack—to become characteristic—might be unleashed on *anyone* who exhibited signs of any conflict with which he himself was battling.◖ It is remarkable how much of the struggle among the members of his internal gallery of characters is distilled in this intemperate letter to "Little Thing."

Shortly after he had written this letter, his "vagrant thoughts that roam in the dark like beasts of prey" returned en masse, and he wrote to Herman of his vague homosexual anxieties regarding his agent, Chamberlain Brown: "I am afraid of that boy and must go so easily."

The summer over, Clifford must once again make plans to go to New York City from West Oak Lane to "search for the elusive job." With some of his Camp Tioga money he has bought "The Nutcracker" suite and is luxuriating in it and in radio station WJZ, "which will keep me filled with music until twelve." With all the family gone,* his father's house is depicted by him now as "a cozy home and a sweetly beautiful one," later once more as a "straightjacket." It is evident that, in spite of his acute loneliness, he takes pleasure in "drinking so deeply of music . . . music that flies and hurts . . . oh, hurt, music!" and in "books that cry for reading" and in writing thirty letters a week, headed by him "Odets Mansion. Oak Lane." He describes the flowered lampshades, cool woven-grass rugs on polished wooden floors, and ashtrays filled with his "matches charred with chagrin at having flared their lives away." Although the tone is needy and wistful, he is clearly enjoying his sense of belonging in a "family home" and his capacity to *nourish himself* in this home, even cooking his own "eggs battered up (with cheese) and spread in a hot-buttery pan . . . with much bread and salty butter and good coffee."

He has delayed his job-seeking in New York because

i have to stay here until sunday when they make my grandmother [Zipporah Gorodetsky] a present of a tombstone she died last year and she was nice and religious and a fine woman and my father cried to me over the phone because he had called me at camp after she was buried of course this business of graves and all that is not too nice to consider and besides i am being kept from being in new york when i should be there but father wants it and i am glad to please when i have the opportunity.

He explains the lower-case letters and lack of punctuation as the result of exhaustion.

Following a fresh attack in this letter on his "little thing old girl"

◖ 7.5.
* It is not known why there appears to have been a brief détente between his father and mother, who, he says, "are away on a second honeymoon," adding, "Father is a lover and his son Clifford is also a lover."

(Martha) for leaving him for so long "unanswered and mail-less," he jokes that he will never buy her an ice-cream cone, that he will write a poem against her, and finally that:

> i think i will smoke a camel the truest of friends thats what a camel
> is and like a baby going to sleep with a bottle your earnest friend goes
> to sleep with a camel maurice barrymore went to bed with a bottle
> and this humble boy goes to bed with a camel. . . .

While letters are not the same order of communication as free association, there is an obvious flow here from felt deprivation (he is mailless) to counter-starvation of the depriver (will never buy her ice cream), to indirect (esthetic) revenges (the poem "against" her), and on to a variety of consolatory solutions of "intake": music, smoking, eating, drinking. This pattern of intake remains constant throughout his life. Of his music addiction he said later, in a letter to this writer: "I write as one whose only unstinting, undepriving, fulsomely giving mother has been music,"* and again, "How happy an invention music. It is to be privileged to listen to the best conversation of great men of all temperaments and worlds." He might have added, "and to be under no demand for a response in the mutuality of a living relationship."

In his attempts to separate from his father, Odets had tuned seductive antennae toward older men with values different from L.J.'s who could appreciate him and on whom he could lean. Thus, he had turned to a succession of older men: the Village poet Harry Kemp; Doc Baruch; Mr. Brill, his father's employee; a series of columnists, including Walter Winchell; and now the worldly Floyd Neale, soon to be a staff announcer for the National Broadcasting Company. Neale, "grey at the temples, with dark theatrical eyebrows and an arresting face," became for Odets one of "the earliest signposts that life is not to the swiftest, but to the best educated." A man of means and of considerable taste in music and literature, Neale began to invite the appealing young elocutionist to drink with him on his balcony overlooking the East River. There, under an awning of "Venetian sailcloth, ice would tinkle in tall thin-blown glasses and we would drink to all that was beautiful and fine in life. . . . Floyd talked of many things, and I listened." There the young man experienced new "strange, stirring feelings" as he listened to Stravinsky's "Firebird" and "that living thing," the Bach D-minor Toccata and Fugue.

Neale, a confirmed bachelor known to take a particular interest in handsome and sensitive young men, would soon persuade a suspicious but impoverished young Odets to share his 59th Street studio apartment. Odets wrote of his debt to Neale, a man from whom "youth such as I am, knows its direction to be true. . . . In your face are written directions: You must climb the hill; there is only one road; after the muck, there is the beauty." On the other hand, in Neale's elegant apartment he would spend "some of the most miserable weeks of my young days and years." From there he writes to Sylvia Hoffman, a niece of the Millsteins, his former neighbors:

> I am sick and desolate . . . and I am writing to dear faces that
> seem, even now, to throng behind me and look over my shoulder as
> I write. . . . I could walk some fifty feet and from great windows

---

* It is possible that his addiction to music, like that of George Bernard Shaw, served as a protection against an addiction to alcohol or drugs. Although he drank heavily at times, this never became for him the problem it so often does become for writers (O'Neill, Dreiser, Faulkner, Inge, Hemingway, Fitzgerald, Dylan Thomas, Brendan Behan, Poe, Baudelaire, Rimbaud, and many writers still living).

look out on Central Park. But the Park is gleaming with rain and for once rain has no affinity with me. I could go into my room and finish half a bottle of gin that sits in its square bottle on my table. I could listen to great music; I am listening to poor radio music played by a string trio. . . . Or maybe I'll listen to that transformation music from Parsifal and feel holiness sweep thru me like some wave effacing writings on sand. . . .

I have been very busy with the Union City Stock company. This is our fourth week . . . Desire Under the Elms this week and because they are using most of the original company I'm playing something not much better than a walk on. But I don't care, these days, what I play. I live from one pay envelope to the next. No matter how, I live to eat and sleep and drink rotten gin that gives me the shakes for twenty hours after. . . .

What is good for loneliness, Sylvia? I mean the kind of loneliness that I have known on crowded dance floors, the kind I have had well within me when even dear faces were mine to have and hold, the poignant anguish I have known even among richness and in golden hours. The thing to do with a malignant cancer is to cut it out. But what of this eating loneliness? I don't think it can be cut out.

When Floyd Neale's intense interest in him, though vitally supportive, reached limits intolerable for this boy so ambivalently tied to his own father, he left. In a letter written to Neale later, Odets says:

I didn't and don't understand you. . . . If the music hadn't been there . . . I should have turned quite mad . . . and I had the music so little. I used to have to walk out at three and four in the mornings because I was afraid . . . I don't know what I was afraid of; only I was awakened several times by some disturbing thing and I had to go out into the Park to walk listlessly around until a policeman beckoned with his night stick . . . out. With the rain on the roof I used to imagine all sorts of things crawling in the dark and always I locked all the closet doors and the attic one, not neglecting to half turn the key in the lock so that it couldn't be forced out from the other side. . . .

He confided to his friend Herman that he had been wary of Neale's advances, but that Neale had valued their friendship sufficiently to retreat to conventional bounds after an initial skirmish, when he perceived the anxiety he was arousing.[*] There is little doubt that the unconscious homosexual conflict in Odets was severe all his life, a struggle unremarkable in sensitive, gifted men in our society. It manifested itself in a variety of ways in his life and in his work: in the excesses of his compulsive Don Juanism, by turns empathic and punitive toward his many female partners, no less than in the intensity of his dependence on a variety of strong men whose counsel he would at first seek and later reject with the charge they were bullying him.

Throughout Odets' life his work reflects his preoccupation with the corruption of the innocent, manifestly a boy, a girl, a child, or an artist. In every instance the possessive corrupter, be he projected as gangster, playwright, actor, director, factory owner, Chinese warlord, businessman, union official, fight manager, movie magnate, or Nazi, is modeled on some aspect of Odets' father. The aims of this ubiquitous character, who stands

---

[*] During his marriage to Luise Rainer, Odets told her that he had "near-murdered" an older man who made advances to him in his youth.

like a malignant monument over all, are multiple, but are geared to achieving visibly secure status and controlling power far more than to the simple accumulation of material goods.◖

At this time those elite circles of Philadelphia that had at long last come to accept Walt Whitman were also inclined to support the cultural manifesto of Van Wyck Brooks, a leading American critic and man of letters. Brooks pleaded with American writers to use American sources of life, not borrowed European ones, while sternly upholding the highest esthetic standards and values. This position was the steady topic of discussions in a household that became for Odets his intellectual oasis whenever he returned to his father's house in Philadelphia. A literate and sophisticated counterpart of his adopted home with Aunt Esther and Uncle Israel, the four-story Leof-Blitzstein "white brownstone" at 322 South 16th Street, called affectionately by the young intelligentsia of Philadelphia simply "322," became for him and for a small regiment of other youngsters—all, except Madi, Mickey, and Charlotte Leof, "on the outs with their families" —a spiritual haven, and he would always return to it for readings (before production) of his new plays.◖

Had Clifford been able to remake his own father, he thought he would have emerged with the figure of Dr. Morris Vladimir Leof, known throughout Philadelphia as Poppa but addressed by Jennie Chalfin—his common-law wife, a militant suffragette—simply as M.V. or Leof. Born Morris Vladimir Lipschitz in Russia in 1871, he had run away from his orthodox religious parents, first to Israel, then to Philadelphia, where an English teacher had persuaded him to change his name to Morris V. Leaf because it "would be terribly embarrassing in this country to be named Lipschitz." His careless handwriting, it is said, turned the *a* into an *o*, leaving the residue *Leof*. Perhaps it pleased him also that the name Leof had more visible links to his Russian-Jewish heritage, a heritage he had no intention of denying: indeed, despite his phenomenal intelligence, he never dropped his Russian-Jewish accent, and, in some contrast to L. J. Odets, who made frequent complaint that his Jewishness was a barrier to his success, Dr. M. V. Leof extolled the Jewish traditions of intellectual values, humanitarian service, and the "oneness of humanity."

He had early apprenticed himself to a small cigarmaker, and later to a banana-seller, literally saving pennies to go to high school and finally to the Philadelphia Medico-Chirurgical School, later proud to claim him as one of the first of its alumni to accumulate fifty years of medical practice. This was success and self-esteem of a different order from that to which Lou Odets aspired* and which involved discipline and energy of a sort foreign to Clifford's passive Uncle Israel, who had continued to sell bananas all of his life, instead of developing his talent as a cantor.

The stocky Poppa Leof, described as having a humorous and mobile

◖ 7.6.
◖ 7.7.
* When, two decades later, Odets wrote his famous indictment of the destruction of its artists by the American pecuniary culture (*The Big Knife*), he dedicated it, "For M. V. Leof, M.D., in his 78th year, with love." Dr. Leof good-humoredly protested that he was only seventy-seven.

face in a large head, with black hair and mustache, looked to his daughter Madi "like a Russian intellectual." A humanist, more interested in politics than esthetics, he had long been a member of the Socialist Party, but even within its ranks always disobedient, dissident. Several times he was threatened by the party with loss of his burial plot for his heresies. Confidence-inspiring and "willing to help anyone," Poppa Leof—despite the fact that he never married the mother of his three children, an act of socialist defiance—was in fact a Victorian moralist and rationalist who frequently contended that he simply did not "believe in alcoholics or homosexuals" even when they appeared in his parlor. He was considered to be one of the finest diagnosticians in Philadelphia.

"By no means a modest man," according to Madi, "he loved to be surrounded by intellects, especially younger ones." William Kozlenko, hurt that Clifford took him only twice to the intellectually prestigious Leof house, recalled him as a "gentleman of the old school, who would sit like Socrates and hold forth at regular Sunday night soirees." He tried to deflate Clifford by telling him that "Poppa Leof was a bit pompous." Testimony to Leof's intellectual honesty—a quality Clifford frequently and bitterly recorded as sorely lacking in his own father—was the fact that, having for years opposed, as an enlightened physician, the "irrationalities" of Sigmund Freud, he finally decided to look into this matter for himself. At seventy-five he commenced an intensive study of Freud's works and, on completing it at seventy-seven, announced, "I was wrong."

His helpmeet, an emancipated, tiny, slender schoolteacher with light-brown hair cut short, was also born in Russia; she was, her children report, "a pacifier, a mediator who felt anything her children would do was fine." Sometimes she quoted poetry written to Woodrow Wilson by her atheistic grandmother, pleading with him to stop the war. As M.V. held court from his blue velvet sofa, where he took a daily siesta, she "would wait on him hand and foot" while she chain-smoked cigarettes. She was markedly similar to Clifford's mother, and importantly different. Her husband's servitor, she nonetheless would never have thought of plunging into a passive depression as Pearl did in response to the hauteur of the German Jews of Philadelphia, "not one of whom," M.V. would later say, "marched in the first protest of American Jews against Hitler." Madi Leof's immense pride in her mother was still evident four decades later: "When someone painted '322' with red paint to prove we were Communists, my mother got up at seven A.M. and simply washed it off. She was a spitfire, but in relation to my father, he was without doubt the law."

The Leofs' son, Mickey (Dr. Milton Arno Leof), retained clear memories of young Odets. "It was obvious to all of us that Clifford looked to my father as a substitute father. It plagued and obsessed him that his own father thought of him as an idiot, a lazy bum. We couldn't understand what he was struggling about. Seems to me Clifford was a great sentimentalist. He really *wanted* to love his family and seemed to feel very guilty that he couldn't. He'd say, 'I can't stand their attacks' and would say over and over why couldn't his father understand that he *wasn't* an idle bum? When Poppa would come in the living room—always warm, intelligent—Clifford would mutter that he was not 'a stupid bastard' like his own father. It seemed like, later on, when *he* could give *them* money, he could be more affectionate with his family."

Whereas the other young people gathered at "322" felt equally alienated from their parents—some because they were ashamed of the parents' chicken stores or fruit wagons, some because of their illiteracy—most appeared to have managed a more comfortable integration than had Clifford.

It astonished Sabina, Mickey Leof's wife, known as "Tibi"—whose living and working quarters were on the fourth floor of "322"—that this young blond actor with a French-sounding name could be so opinionated in his public pronouncements. He would say things like, "One day I will tell H. L. Mencken and George Jean Nathan what theatre *really* is," breaking up everyone within earshot; whereas, "alone with me, he'd be terribly humble: he'd whisper shyly, 'Who am I to think of trying to write for the theatre?' He felt theatre should be about 'what one feels, presented so others will feel it.' His interest in politics was at this time nil."

Madi Leof, too, remembered his public protestations, given usually at the Heel and with a "meshugene look in his eye." On one occasion, when someone was praising O'Neill as a groundbreaker for American playwrights, the twenty-two-year-old Odets pounded the table with his fist and shouted, "I was born the year Ibsen died—you will hear from me!" With the artist's gift of conviction, Odets believed this extravagance as he uttered it, but, like so many artists, when he returned to his room at night he felt "subhuman." The swing between this sense of worthlessness and feeling "superhuman" when he was giving communicative form to his experience would characterize his entire life.

Clifford was fascinated by all members of the Leof clan as well as by their remarkable visitors: Sholem Asch with his daughter, Ruthie, and son, Nathan; the unique and independent journalist I. F. (called "Izzy") Stone; the Jewish tragedian Jacob Adler and his children; and even the Philadelphia millionaire and blueblood John Frederick Lewis, who so admired Poppa Leof that he would now and again lend him the Academy of Music for a liberal benefit. The first "integrated" party in Philadelphia was given by the Leofs, and Lewis thought Leof should be given the Bok Award as the outstanding citizen of that city. Sabina Leof and Lem Ward, both part of a small avant garde within this elite group, were busily reading Alfred North Whitehead as an answer to socialism; they were determined to prove to Poppa Leof that removing hunger would *not* solve all of the world's problems. One thing was certain, according to Madi Leof: "Whatever happened in the world was immediately reflected in that house." Clifford, ill-equipped to participate in these controversies, nevertheless fed on them: "You could breathe freely there."

Although he thought most of his daughter-in-law's painters, composers, and writers mad, Poppa Leof tolerated and counseled them all at one time or another: there was the collaborator of George Antheil, Abraham Lincoln Gillespie, described as "a hanger-on of Joyce, who talked as Joyce wrote, always with a greasy paper bag full of diabetic bread." There was the cadaverous court jester, young Harry Kurnitz, then editor and "complete staff" of *College Humor*, later to write a murder mystery that Hollywood wanted, and to be pushed onto the train taking him to Hollywood to become a screenwriter, the first from this group to "make it." Then there were musicians from the Philadelphia Orchestra. "We all idolized Stokowski," said Madi Leof Ross, and "our uncle Joseph Chudnowsky was one of his violinists." These, in particular, fascinated Clifford, although he was always astonished by their "poor taste in music."

Odets' favorite, however, among the young people at "322" was a gifted, sad, and mystifying young Jew with whom his bond was such that they continued an active correspondence even after the latter's incarceration in Lewisburg Penitentiary: Jack Schoenberg.* Brilliant and morose, said to have been graduated in his teens from the University of Pennsyl-

---

* This name has been changed to protect a family.

vania Law School and reputed to have had the highest intelligence quotient of any student in its history, Jack became a literate and expert forger of historic documents.

So erudite and skillful was Jack, known as "The Baron," that for some time he had the highest income in the group by selling such collector's items as "autographed" copies of *Leaves of Grass*, forging Walt Whitman's name. Even after his criminal record became known, his expert opinion was sought by respectable bookmen and merchandisers of autographs. Some swear that the manuscript of "The Star Spangled Banner" and possibly that of the Declaration of Independence now in the Library of Congress are his work.

An aspiring writer,* he appeared to the young people gathered at "322" frighteningly burned out, even as a young man. Often he would say in a flat tone: "I can't get excited about anything" or "I'm finished." Always on the edge of a cynical truculence and never ingratiating, he showed public animation only in card games; his real excitement—indeed, his "breathless suspense," as he wrote Odets—consisted in "carrying off slickly —with strategy and timing" a coup in the sale of a forgery "whose naturalness and exacting detail would have done credit to a general, or at least to an actor." The creative triumphs of his life consisted in manipulating the "sucker's delighted greed."

Mocking the heart of a merchandising society, he wrote: "The victims themselves would perpetuate the all-or-none character of the swindle." And if his victim's covetousness reached reckless extremes, he would "cram him, gorge him with swag, not just tickle his appetite," and then, expanding happily, he would cunningly promise his profit-bent customer "more bargains" and walk away "tingling with relief." All of this the Dostoevskian Jack would confide to Odets from prison.

A pioneer of the "put-on," Jack was strangely open with his friends at "322," even a little boastful of his secret chemical methods for aging paper—almost as though he were seeking to be apprehended. No one knew, however, when to believe him.

When one of his "bold ventures stung Kurnitz to invidious sneers," as he later put it, someone pointed out that "at least I was doing *some*thing about my life, I was earning *some* money, I was getting *some*where." Clifford, who was earning little money and getting nowhere, deeply admired and enjoyed the Baron's "chutzpah" in his criminal activity, which, after all, in its essence bore similarities to his father's machinations in the world of respectable business. Feeling totally incapable of such negotiations, he was in awe of their potency. The Baron, in turn, early recognized Odets' gift for prose and, over the years, expressed his esteem and affectionate envy for it, casting Odets in the role of a mentor and seeking Clifford's literary counsel on his work.

Jack, on the side, successfully administered a brothel on South 16th Street and once brought to the Leofs' a tall, battered blonde named Patsy, who, according to Sabina Leof, would serve as the external model for Lorna Moon in Odets' *Golden Boy*. He found it ironic and amusing in his glum way that, with this great range of illegal and highly remunerative enterprises, he managed to stay clear of the police until they caught him forging a five-dollar check.

For this he was imprisoned, becoming the co-inmate of William Annenberg, owner of the *Philadelphia Inquirer*, who was locked up for tax

* Like Odets, he was fond of quoting Whitman's paean to his kinship with criminals: "I feel I am of them / I belong to those convicts and / prostitutes myself / And henceforth I will not deny them / For how can I deny myself?"

evasion. In and out of jails over a span of almost twenty years, with Odets helping the nice Jewish girl he had married, Jack died in an Atlanta penitentiary in 1947.

From prison Jack had summed up in the proper, rounded, concealing script of a schoolteacher one of their discussions begun in the Leof living room in 1928:

> Friend Clifford, Sometimes I think Jews are consecrated in their very *existence* to imprisonment, for they look, they think, they talk, they move around, like prisoners; they brood, they hesitate, they cover despair, they shrink, as if it were tradition. Caution & sorrow are their chief reactions to the encroachments of outsiders: everyone is an outsider, caution is cunning & sorrow is stiffnecked. In a world like a consummate ghetto, everywhere, anywhere, there is only thwarting & revilement & surprise to be expected, & even Jewish laughter, anxious & unpent, is a cry of relief. Remember the insensate punishments the krauty beasts forced upon bearded & skullcapped old Jews, the newspictures of grinning louts prodding at exhausted old men to sweep faster & how natural, how recognizable both looked? Nothing seems to break Jewish loyalty to meekness; & it is consistent historical fact that the infrequent flares of violent defense against restriction & boycott & ostracism have occurred when human endurance was no longer possible, when the remaining alternative was extinction, & every other stubborn recourse of compliance or compromise had failed. . . . The Jewish prisoners I have known were not so glum as they were resigned, every one privately self-justified and entrenched in his attitudes toward his situation, his keepers, his loss of status, his chances. Only among his fellow Jewish prisoners did he relax, & that, as if obeying some immemorial instinct—sheepishly. We joked but shook our heads, in crises we irritably held that our Jewish dignity was more important than anything we could gain by deceit, our intimacy was the intimacy of hypodermic injections. At our services, sentimentality spilled mawkishly over; kaddish was always said for oneself. . . .
>
> Another weakling had been in the wholesale underwear business & had operated as a fence on the side. In a pique at his partners, who hadn't been tried & hadn't helped him very much, he renounced all Jews & Jewishness. He began to attend Christian Science meetings, refused to go to the Passover meal of chicken & delicacies because he thought it was a taunt, a flaunt, to the gentiles who couldn't have such a meal; he threatened on his release to go to one of the raucous antisemitic groups & give them real inside information about what Jews were really doing. Whenever one of us took him to task he upbraided us violently, said it was Jews like us who were responsible for bigotry. But, years later, I ran into him & he was back among his own kind, back at his business, squabbling, gesturing with his hands, happy. I reminded him of his apostasy. "Aah!" he waved a hand & blushed, "I was kiddin' you guys 'n' ya all bit!"

No one else in all of Odets' life would reflect for him with such forthright insights the nature of his own struggles, in his life and in his work, about being a Jew and an American.

Even the prisoner image was familiar to him in his unreachable mother, "jailed," as she said, in her marriage, staring out at the cemetery with the comment that there she would be free at last.◖

◖ 7.8.

In Jack, in a single bold identity, were concentrated most of young Odets' tabooed aspirations: the poet, the criminal, the revolutionary, and the reckless gambler "who tries to beat them at their own game." A "business success" until his arrest, Jack incorporated a maximum of disobedience, self-expression, and, for a time, even material power—all in a context of Jewish jokes and Jewish grief. Only in the penitentiary would he feel free to risk failure in his own creative work, instead of fraudulently signing his name to that of others. His letters to Odets from jail brim with sharp intellect and with a student eagerness for response to his writing. These two men deeply complemented and reflected each other. Each knew how like the other he was, and how similar were their struggles for liberation. And each knew what a chasm separated them: the one risking even his physical liberty in his efforts to "beat the system," the other forever playing it safe.

As post-war America sped on its innocent way to a major economic crisis, a lively dialectic had begun to polarize in its creative energies. In what Alfred Kazin has called "the opening phase of a revolution in world society," American artists were beginning to free themselves from the remains of "foreign harvests" and taking firm root in native ground. There was growing a self-acceptance of—indeed, pride in—the vitality of naturalistic American expression in all the arts. The Jewish-American Ernest Bloch had composed a musical history of America starting with the year 1620; in this year of 1928 it was presented by five leading symphony orchestras; and Aaron Copland was finding his voice in his American Festivals of Contemporary Music. Theodore Dreiser was no longer being dismissed as a "vulgar barbarian," and Hemingway and Dos Passos were finally being read.

On the other hand, an unprecedented relationship between art and commerce was evolving through the industries of the mass media, a marriage destined by its nature to sap the very vitality it needed to keep alive: a lethal paradox indeed. The situation would be summed up by the sophisticated foreign-born stage director Rouben Mamoulian, who, having turned to commercial films, was assailed for not bending his creative energies to a history of American labor. His reply was simple: "The picture industry is no different from the underwear business. It is completely governed by the law of supply and demand."

These same inexorable laws extended to American writers, who were now in short supply in relation to the film industry's gluttonous demand for dialogue, triggered the year before by the great success of the unprecedented sound film *The Jazz Singer*. The money steadily offered to American writers had begun to soar astronomically and even the Great Depression would not diminish these lavish salaries. The current joke was that Herman Mankiewicz was setting up in Hollywood an irresistible "Fresh-Air Fund for Authors." Over the next decades it would draw to Los Angeles *at some time* almost every American and refugee writer of any accomplishment: William Faulkner, F. Scott Fitzgerald, Theodore Dreiser, Robert E. Sherwood, S. N. Behrman, Philip Barry,

John Van Druten, Aldous Huxley, Dorothy Parker, Thomas Mann, Erich Maria Remarque, Lion Feuchtwanger, Antoine de Saint-Exupéry, Bertolt Brecht, Ernst Toller, Franz Werfel, Vicki Baum, Arthur Miller, William Gibson, Tennessee Williams, William Inge, Paddy Chayevsky.

In this fall of 1928 John Howard Lawson, still stinging over the failure of the ambitious New Playwrights group in New York, was already in Hollywood, soon to be followed by the gifted Francis Faragoh. John Dos Passos and Em Jo Basshe were still clinging to their experimental theatre in New York, but not for long. A bright young girl named Lillian Hellman would soon be in Los Angeles judging movie scripts for their commercial possibilities.

A vast and powerful empire, to become in its conspicuous consumption and waste the latter-day distillation of Mark Twain's "Gilded Age," was now being built in earnest in the clement air of California. By dint of its apparently limitless material resources, and the power flowing therefrom, it was fast becoming—sometimes consciously, sometimes not—a prime motivating goal in the psyche of the American writers, directors, and actors, a goal to be aspired to and reached; to be grappled with, be contemned, become resigned to, or, in the case of a handful of American writers, flee from.

Two young actors—both to become American playwrights—in whose psyches this determining and gripping fantasy was taking hold, whether they knew it or not, were in the last months of 1928 pursuing the more modest goals of trying to find acting jobs in the New York legitimate theatre. One of them, Joseph Kramm, would recall rooming in a cheap hotel at 44th Street and Sixth Avenue with the other, Clifford Odets:

> We had very little money. Cliff's family was better off financially than mine, and he never explained why he couldn't or didn't want to ask them for money. . . .
>
> We did a lot of talking, but not about writing. Each of us hoped to make it as actors. I had yet to get my first professional job, I wasn't Equity, but Cliff was, and he had had at least two years of work in different stock companies and possibly a show on Broadway. . . .
>
> We spent the days making rounds, but not together, because Cliff had given me the names of stock companies he had worked in, shows in which he played, and the names of parts it would have been credible for me to play. With that beginning in lying, I soon discovered that we lied to *each other*. A matter of pride. "I would have had the part, but . . . I read and he said I was great and I'll hear in a few days." That sort of thing. And that's why, to this day, I don't know if he had actually done a show on Broadway by then,* or only told me he had. But neither one of us had any luck, not even with Jules Leventhal, who, despite the low salaries he paid, proved the salvation of many an actor. In a few weeks we were broke. We moved to the Circle Hotel—on 60th Street, just west of Columbus Circle. We paid six dollars (three apiece) for a week's rent in advance for a room with a double bed. It was the kind of hotel whose rooms are rented three or four times a night, and I can only guess we were given a room because it was on the top floor, five flights up, and no elevator. We slept with the lights on, we never turned them out. We hoped that way to slow down the bugs.
>
> After paying the rent, we had less than a dollar in change between us. We bought a loaf of black bread (bread wasn't sliced in

* He had not.

those days) and a pound of American cheese, also unsliced, and we broke off a little each day. There was an old organ in the room, a church organ, one with a high bench. The bellows should normally have been operated by foot but for some reason they didn't work that way. I discovered that by sitting on the floor and moving the bellows with my hands we could produce a sound, so Cliff sat on the high bench and played the organ while I sat on the floor and moved the bellows. I can't tell you what he played, it sounded most like sonorous chords, but I know we found it pleasing.

At the end of that week, on Saturday, I received a money order . . . and Cliff and I went out and had our first meal in a week— we each ordered liver and onions. . . . We got into the next week without being asked for rent in advance. Then Cliff got a nibble, a real one, on a job in New York. His spirits soared, but when I say his spirits soared—well if you can think of someone austere and re- moved with a soaring spirit, that was Cliff. It was unmistakable, but it didn't change his air of austerity. How do I mean austere? Serious, distant, sometimes uncommunicative, not given easily to laughter.

As it became evident to Kramm that he was getting nowhere in New York, he decided, at Clifford's prompting, to go home and try his luck with the Mae Desmond company, one of the few stock groups not yet demolished by the film industry. Clifford advised him to say that "things are slow in New York, that Philadelphia is your home and you're just visiting, and that you thought you would drop around and see if they had anything for you."

Kramm concludes his account of this five-week intimacy:

I hitchhiked to Philadelphia, carrying in my bag a suit of clothes which Cliff had lent me because I didn't have a decent suit of clothes of my own. I changed clothes in Broad Street Station, went to the theatre, said exactly what Cliff had told me to say, and got a job. It lasted twenty weeks.

Now the strange thing is this—and it is only now, thirty-eight years later, that I wonder about it—for all our closeness in those weeks, about five weeks altogether—we didn't correspond. I wrote and told him I got the job, and that was it. I didn't hear from him. I know he worked that year, but I don't know where.

Perhaps Odets did work in New York as an actor in the fall of 1928. If so, it was not sufficiently memorable for him to note it. From his letters, however, we see that by January 1929 he was back in his father's house in West Oak Lane and almost at the end of his rope.

Chapter Eight

Ideologies serve to channel youth's forceful earnestness and sincere asceticism, as well as its search for excitement and its eager indignation, toward that social frontier where the struggle between conservatism and radicalism is most alive. On that frontier, fanatic ideologists do their busy work and psychopathic leaders do their dirty work; but there, also, true leaders create significant solidarities.

ERIK H. ERIKSON

No ONE knew at the beginning of 1929 that this year would constitute a continental divide in world history, the watershed between what seemed a limitless worldwide expansion by the natural forces of free enterprise—issuing, especially in the United States, in a "permanent affluence"—and the shattering economic contraction to which increasingly radical and savage solutions, one of them labeled "final," would be brought, all over the world.

With no inkling of what would befall them in the tenth month, imaginative men of affairs were building new buildings, hiring thousands of salesmen, and selling millions of paper shares in their enterprises. Holding company was piled upon holding company until "the pyramid threatened, like the Tower of Babel, to pierce the heavens." Dreiser's ruthless plungers and "grim crushers of the weak" had been replaced among the lords of creation by college men with good manners and well-advertised respect for religion.

A safeguard for all this busy business had been worked out the previous summer: the lion would lie down with the lamb and international disputes would be settled henceforth only by "pacific means."* Thus was it solemnly agreed by the nations which would be embroiled within the

---

* These are the words of the Kellogg-Briand peace pact signed by the U.S., Great Britain, France, Germany, Italy, and Japan and ratified by the U.S. Senate in January 1929.

next decade in what, with its genocide and nuclear devastation, must surely have been the penultimate struggle on this planet.

In such an enlightened, if perishable, vision of affluence a young man —now almost twenty-three and handsome—who could not "get in" anywhere and who could obtain only sporadic gainful employment as an actor appeared indeed a backward oddity—a source of murderous rage for his father, heartbreak for his mother, and scarlet shame for himself. They could not have known, as even Mae Desmond did not, that his jobs in her acting company were dwindling because the "all-talking" motion picture had fixed the death sentence not only on stock companies but also on small legitimate theatres such as O'Neill's Provincetown Players.* Miss Desmond remembered desperate efforts to remain alive:

We tried to stay in business by asking the stagehands to drop one man and the Stanley Company to lower our rent. Our requests were refused. But the Stanley Company had the Towers Theatre in Camden, New Jersey, an old vaudeville house that had failed. They offered this theatre to us on a 60–40 percentage basis. We accepted this offer. We gave our company at the William Penn Theatre the usual two weeks' closing notice, but told them we were going to reopen at the Towers Theatre in Camden without losing a day.

The members of the acting company, having no financial information or experience, decided that their individual reputations were sufficient to draw audiences to the William Penn Theatre, and they invited Odets to join them in their secession from the Mae Desmond company. He refused, explaining that Miss Desmond and her husband, Mr. Fielder, had given him his start and he would stay with them. The insurgent actors gave up in a few weeks. The Desmond company held out only a little longer.

The valedictory of the Desmond company provided Odets with his first creative step as professional playwright, in response to an economic emergency: the opening bill in Camden, *Madame X*, had a courtroom scene, and the expense of putting a full jury on the stage would be prohibitive. Mae Desmond recalled that after a heart-to-heart talk their "loyal Clifford" made a brilliant suggestion: make the audience the jury, thus saving the expense of hiring actors. He eagerly wrote the lead-in speeches for the new jury scene, and this was the start of his writing for the stage.

Although the stimulus in *Madame X* was economic necessity, this formal invention, to unite the actors with the audience and thus, as he said, to "make the proscenium arch disappear," would serve five years later as the model for just such a union in Odets' historic one-act play *Waiting for Lefty*.

"The more you look back, you are surprised about the little connecting things that brought you to some final and important terminal position." Odets described years later a "break which led me getting into the Group Theatre and perhaps even becoming a playwright." On one of his many— usually fruitless—trips to New York he ran into the agent Chamberlain

* In the half-century following Odets' birth, ninety percent of the 3,500 existing legitimate theatres in the U.S. would be swept away by the tidal wave of motion pictures and their least-common-denominator mass market.

Brown, who sent him to meet a well-known and gifted playwright named Vincent Lawrence because an actor from the Desmond company, now playing a small part and understudying the lead in Lawrence's play *Conflict*, was quitting. Odets described Lawrence as a man who "always had talent and always was what they call promising . . . later had a long career in movies and was quite embittered . . . always promised . . . he could write people and . . . scenes and his plays seemed to be about something live and real in a time when most plays were quite a fake." Lawrence, in his hotel room with a hangover, agreed, "Yeah, this boy will do, this boy will do."

From the hotel Odets went to the theatre to rehearse, as he would have to go on that night in two parts, an aviator and a Prohibition agent. As the Prohibition agent, he would raid a speakeasy where the leading man, Spencer Tracy (whom he described as "a small, wiry man, a wonderful actor, with a wonderful ability to talk and converse on the stage"), was being "very glum, morose, drunken." As Odets entered the speakeasy at the rehearsal, he heard the business manager mutter, "Who's that kid? He'll never do to play the Prohibition agent. That must be a man of forty-five or fifty." This comment led to what Odets, long after his success as a playwright, recalled as "one of the proudest moments of my life." Determined to be credible, he found in his stock actor's wardrobe a high, stiff collar such as an "older man would wear" and, rejecting his own supply of mustaches, spent his last money on a new iron-gray one, graying his temples to match.

As he waited nervously in the wings that night for his entrance, the business manager, not recognizing him, asked, "Who's that?" At the end of the scene he apologized to Odets, saying, "Son, you're a hell of an actor. I didn't even recognize you. You're good." It was a moment of highest vindication which he longed for his father to witness.

Conflict, the story of a war ace whose prestige declines as the war is forgotten, ran only for one more week, but, by an Actors Equity ruling, Odets received two weeks' salary, netting him the unprecedented total of $130, most of which would soon be spent on his hotel room, food, carfares to Philadelphia, and "non-orthophonic records of the two-dollar-grade to be had for only seventy-five cents each." Playing the Berceuse from Stravinsky's "Firebird" on a borrowed phonograph, he wrote to his resurrected mentor, Floyd Neale, that "my dressing room was instantly changed . . . from an unlovely place to your studio with its cool spaciousness where I listened so often to the Firebird spin its nest-like music."

Even more important than this financial windfall was the fact that he had met the "bluff, hearty, kind, friendly" actor Albert Van Dekker,* who in the fall of this year would be instrumental in his getting an acting job with a Theatre Guild road company. But before that tour, many empty and painful months were still to be endured.

By the spring of 1929 Odets had decided that his stock acting was "not for love of drama or art" but a "lousy, lousy grind" for the money. He declares that if he cannot "hit a production in the fall" he is "through with show

---

* Paramount Pictures would later delete the "Van" from his name.

business." To an acquaintance he reports in a defensively casual tone that he has written 65,000 words on his novel about music, *The Brandy of the Damned*, and that he is finding novel-writing far more difficult than he had dreamed it could be:

> You'll be interested to know that almost half of my book is finished. But the other half will take much longer to do, maybe months, and when I have it all assembled I'll probably have to cut great slices from it and rewrite for another month or two. But the book is shaping out and I begin to see my way more clearly. I always thought it was an easy matter to write a novel; that, it is fair to say, was before I sat down to write one. I imagine it is easy to write a mere story, but to turn out a smooth plot with motivation and characterization . . . that is not so simple. Then there is the dissection of the protagonists . . . oh dear!

His rebellious secret writing, no longer restricted to letters and diaries, emerges this year as an evolving world with increasing structure and gratification to which he nightly retreats in his father's house. It does not wholly assuage his continuing loneliness, which he thinks is sometimes "nothing more than a sex loneliness," adding that often he has "had sex and yet [has] been lonely." Labeling himself "juvenile," he concludes, "I want something to cleave to, some sort of anchor to keep me steady in any mental gale . . . that girl whose eyes will always read welcome for me . . . but I am lost in my search."

He ponders the reasons people find him "reserved" and, defending himself in a series of twists, suggests to a female correspondent that she "unconsciously resents my use of a typewriter for letters to someone as dear as you are." He explains that his handwriting is poor, not mentioning that, like so many writers, he is keeping carbons of his letters as part of his literary stockpile. He knows his friend Kozlenko thinks he is guarded, always keeping something back, and that he has "a peculiar formation of the eyelids, almost an insolent droop and stare to them," and in a disarming burst he adds:

> then there is this to consider: I am not at this age, almost entirely without attitude. Occasionally, I affect a smile or a pleasant disposition. I don't want people to think I'm some solemn-old fakir. Not that I care for their opinions, but opinions count in show business. . . . I'm not a paragon of naturalness, but I am myself as much as one can be that. I have no use for the little tricks of humanity: pretending you are 'what you ain't' . . . trying to make impressions, creating a pose. . . .

His aspiration to be an honest, whole human being, working and loving in a world where, he believes, "opinions count," is poignantly evident in all his letters of this time.

His yearning to merge with another person takes yet another tack as once again he warily seeks help from Floyd Neale:

> Your heart is big, yet why do you help chaps like me along? Is it not that you see in us a something that was you? Is it not that we all are subconscious, clinical cases to you who almost unknowingly peer at us and turn us around to be seen under the every whim of light and shadow—as Conrad does, with his men and women? What do I care about that—someday I'll do the same—but help a fellow along now, when he needs that help.

It is testimony to his desperation to be rescued from West Oak Lane that he asks help even from Neale, whose advances had once panicked him.

Thinking of Frost's line, "Home is a place where when you go they have got to take you in," he writes: "It is a hellish thing to have in you, embossed on your brain, a world pain, a morbid animal that writhes without provocation," adding then, "I would say, rather, a place where one goes to die." Wrestling with this passive surrender and with his own murderous impulses, he tries another formulation which also ricochets:

> But I come here to live, to scatter my mind on paper, to aim the machine gun bullets of my mind at some proper target. Thoughts are always like bullets spattering against the inside of my head.❬ They hurt. They lacerate nerves and flesh. I marvel at my wounds; one step further and we have arrived at self-pity. I must be careful to count my steps!

It would still be some time before he would creatively find a "proper target" besides himself at which to shoot. Two suicide attempts would come first.

In the spring of 1929 he writes, "I am a little mad, I think, as I sit here in the dark morning, in my underwear, with a silent sleeping household around me. . . . If I were to look now in my mirror I must necessarily ask myself: 'Clifford, do you dream all this? Are you alive and isn't it that these bitter mornings are only dreams?' " And yet along with his constant terror of his father and of his own feelings toward him, his glad descriptions of the spring grass and trees "daubed with blossoms like the little girls in confirmation dress" make clear the fact that he finds joy as well in being these days "fluid, receptive, aware," a state of mind which he senses is the matrix for creative thought. He writes in a letter to a girl:

> It is wonderful, here, for work. In the heavy, silent dark, when the entire household sleeps, when outside my window there is no sound but the muffled noise of night, then I can write almost without thought. I place sheet after sheet in the typewriter and when I "come to" I have written four or five thousand words. After that it is no effort to draw in a deep breath, button up my collar and go for a walk in the silent city. We are near the city line and I can step out of Philadelphia as fast as one is able to walk a half mile. And everywhere here, in city or out, is deep silence; I might be in a world by myself, with only the recondite musics that be half in me, half in the dark. The lovely, delphic night, my darkling mistress, she who embraces me with the loveliest language of all: Silence.

There is a self-romanticizing, even a masochistic quality in his image of himself as a lonely being who spatters bullets inside his own head and whose sole emotional bond is with the "delphic night"; at the same time it is reassuring to a clinician-biographer—who is cheering for his growth as an artist—that he now refers to his secret self-indulgence with his typewriter as "work." More engaged by it than ever before in his life, he is attempting an article for *The New Yorker*. Nonetheless, now without a hint of further work issuing from his brief appearance on the stage with Spencer Tracy, he continues to think of himself essentially as an unemployed, letter-writing actor, rejected as a "bum" by his father, yet impotently bound to him, economically and emotionally.

❬ 8.1.

Just before his twenty-third birthday, again a drama counselor at Camp Tioga, Odets had a black and mysterious experience. According to his diaries and letters, during the summer of 1928 in northern Pennsylvania he had met a sad, sweet, and possessive young person named Roberta, had made her pregnant, and then (he told Harold Clurman in 1931 and wrote to a friend two years later), after her father threatened to kill him, had secretly married her, with the intention of bringing her and their baby, Joan, to New York in the fall of 1929. Before he could accomplish this, he told Clurman (and subsequently several others) that on the fifth day of July 1929 Roberta shot their baby and herself, leaving him a legacy of agony that would take many years to soften.

A search for confirmatory evidence in his correspondence from these early July days of 1929 turns up a lode of fascinating but ambiguous material. First, a letter dated July 4 to an unknown "Mary Ann," identified by Odets only as "a rich Philadelphia girl met twice":

Dear Mary Ann,

Hello I say to you and yet am in no mood to say a word to none but myself. Already, for five days, I have said the most awful words to myself until the old, straining heart is heavy to overflow; for know that in all this time not once have we seen the mountains dim in the distance; that all this time there has been an ugly sky, no stars, no moon, no nothing but rain and a wind strong enough to almost blow the tents away from their moorings.

. . . Today, after dinner (the noon time meal here) I have begun to write to others out of necessity for release and relief from my taciturnity. What is graven on the sun dial's face must stay there, for words written in stone are not to be effaced as easily as the movement of a hand; and the brain, in case you didn't know, is not as perishable as stone; only Woman, innate morbidity or bad gin can erode the mind! And I, sad, oh sad to relate, have had all of those things; and shall die from them; and shall live by them; and do my little macabre dance again.

. . . Some one said that we can only be in love once, we can only see a picture once or hear music but one time. It is true—the futility of every first flush, every first cry of delight, is that never again can we experience that first feeling. You'll understand what I mean! And how soon we humans exhaust the world's possibilities, how soon we run the gamut of all that Life has to offer.

Do write me some words. I'll be very lonesome this year, for no minds are here to mingle with mine. They are not a very clever bunch here. There is a Harvard doctor, a few others, but an education is not necessarily a set of fine feelings.

I must go to direct my play now, it goes on Saturday night, the first one of the season and I must make it a good one. There is something to this "starting off with a rush" business. Hmmm, that might mean more than it sounds like, altho I won't say another word.

Be discreet, Mary Ann . . . what ever that means.

It is difficult to read unequivocally between the lines of this letter. Likewise, the crumbling carbon copies of his seven letters of this summer to a few half-intimates, carefully preserved and dated by Odets himself, make no direct reference to Roberta, to Joan, or to a suicide-murder. If they are read, however, with the premise of the tragedy in mind, they are full of double entendres.

In the first of them, dated July 5, 1929 (which he would later record as the day of the suicide-murder of his wife and child), he writes to his lost Betty:

> There is no humor in this place, there is no God and there are no Fates, only Furies who have been visiting us here for five days. For five days it has been costive weather . . . for almost a week we have not seen the mountains in the distance; and two hundred boys have been running thru wet grass which has lost all its spring and desire for life. . . .
>
> Today the air is quiet and my heart, quiet for all this time, is beginning to beat again; for it is warmer than usual. Once I took for myself a motto which said, "Sine sole silio," without sun I am silent— I have been silent and now am casting a weather eye towards the sky with the hope of breaking into speech of one kind or another. Speech makes us men and by that token I have been only a beast for all these five days, a shivering beast with dullness in his face and head. Oh well. . . .
>
> Now you know why I can't say that camp is nice, that I am not glad to be here and that I'm being healed by Nature, that Divine Unguent! There is no healing when there is protest; rather is recrudescence; and every old sore has turned unhealed and streaming. It is not that I complain, for I have learned that every drink brings with its warmth an accompanying tremor. But this is awful . . . and enough!

The rest of the letter is more normally chatty, if sluggish: he is working on mounting Lord Dunsany's *Night at an Inn;* he has visited the girls' camp across the way ("much as I tried to stay away from there") and

> In the meantime I should be mad but for my musical records which are playable here as we have several phonographs. Truly music is the brandy of the damned and I'm sure that my book is not misnamed. Incidentally, not a word is written in it since I've been here.

In the next, on July 7, to Martha ("Little Thing" from Camp Tabor the previous summer), the world has again been "costive and the skies cried without cease. . . . I . . . began to despair and the beast of morbidity began to parade through me—but enough." With the emergence of the sun, he says, comes contentment. If he knew that his young wife had killed herself and their child, it is not legible in this letter.

There occurs now a hiatus of almost two weeks in his correspondence, and on July 18 he writes in a mocking vein: ". . . with exulting pride, today is my birthday. I am a big, big man, reaching at this date a full maturity of twenty-three." He has kept it a secret lest his boys cheer him at the dinner table and "the management" bake him a cake.

"Your note made me glad," he writes, ". . . and but for the music I have here I should have wept." Describing his "peculiar existence" and his struggles with his passivity and his dependence on people:

> I don't receive more than two or three letters a week. . . . Now I am trying to make myself as complete as "the flower and stone" of the poet. Where is the self-development when one is dependent on others for happiness and contentment? What man can be an artist when his happiness hinges on the smiles, the words and whims of others, of those often far away or unavailable? . . . Perhaps someday I'll take for my credo, "go and get it.". . .

He is on a "sequestered mountaintop that pushes into the sky, where stars make the sky noisy and startlingly beautiful, where there is a silence

comparable to that of dusty tombs," adding, "I am alone, very much alone
. . . and that is good for the soul and brain." Moons are a symbol of
"mockery of every puny effort expended by crawling Man," and he envies
the thoughtless people about him. And finally:

> I'm not in any sort of mood for writing. I can only think of some music
> I've ordered . . . it'll be here in an hour or so and my thoughts jump
> so to the idea that I don't know what I'm about. There are almost fifty
> dollars worth of records coming, Beethoven and the two other Bs,
> Strauss, Wagner and others. Oh dear music.

Not from this nor from the remaining extant letter could we deduce
the tragedy he would later confide to Clurman and to a few others and
would record in his diary. Clurman had no doubt of the authenticity of the
dreadful events which he believes commenced in Chester, Pennsylvania,
when Odets was on tour with the Desmond stock company. "It was something I was to put away in some dark recess of my spirit and soul . . . he
said I wasn't to reveal it to anybody." Indeed, Clurman had, until now, kept
Odets' secret. Clurman doubted that Clifford and Roberta ever lived together
as man and wife;* rather, "it seemed to be a kind of boyish, hasty, youthful
mistake that occurred to a young fellow who doesn't know what life's about
and who gets overwhelmed by something that becomes much more serious
than he ever imagines anything in his sexual encounters to become. A
young boy doesn't necessarily think of consequences and the tragedies in
a relationship, and this may have possibly made a deep incision in his
psyche, so to speak: (a) to have a girl die because of him and (b) to
have a father, in a transport of anger and sorrow, to have threatened to
kill him." Clurman understood Odets' confidence as "a desire on his part
to reveal himself completely to me so I would know him to his depths, so
to speak."

A search of the Pennsylvania Bureau of Vital Statistics and of the
records of the State Police, as well as those of thirty town and county
clerks, reveals no marriage or death under the name Odets. However, even
were he not given to pseudonyms, it is likely he would have invented one
for this occasion. Unfortunately, early files of several northern Pennsylvania newspapers have been destroyed by fire or flood; thus, it is not surprising that no newspaper account of a murder-suicide from the summer
of 1929 has ever emerged. But Clurman's account and Odets' later references to this suicide-murder, widely spaced in time, have a coherence
which point to a genuine event, not a fantasy.

The letters of this time range from flat, depressed statements like
"It is a long time since . . . the desire to write animated my fingers and
mind . . . there is no Beauty in my heart," through full descriptions of
camp routine, to an account plausibly that of a man emerging from a depression.

> After breakfast the flicker began to stir in me and I found that song
> spurted from my lips, that I was greeting every one with glad cries
> and that my eyes were lifted from the ground. . . . The seedling has
> sprouted above the earth, the warm, fresh earth and for the first time
> saw that there was a sky, that there was something more to Nature
> than the press of earth, its darkness and damp.

---

* Inasmuch as this marriage was never publicly acknowledged by Odets and
never constituted a continuous domestic relationship, I do not count it as a real
"marriage."

Stapled to this letter is the following poem, again ambiguous as evidence for the truth of this horrendous tale:

Dawn in the Park
In all the confused music
of the birds who spill
Their lives from their throats,
like blood spilling from a wound—
so theirs the wound of life—
there is one far away bird
singing a clear three-noted song
that comes thru the confusion of post dawn,
clear, loud and unfailing,
sweet, fresh and unafraid
like something I in my life have never met.
I will sit on my bench and listen for that song.

At the end of July, "tired of myself, of the depths I contained, of all the words I kept repeating in my mind," he is set off by the perfume in a letter from Mary Ann and overcome with loneliness: "I am an easy lad to stir, when I am dead a word will bring me back to life I think, a word even whispered by some woman I have known better than I have known you, Marianna. . . ." Summing up his present feeling, he ends:

It is so easy with solitude to grow a shell. The face takes on lines that sweep downward and the small interests of life are lost in the admiration of self-development which later grows to discontent and bitterness. Man's tragedy starts when he learns to read; it increases when he faces his God without fear and writes in his book, "I do not know a God"; it goes on to bloom a malodorous flower, when man becomes sated with cloying pleasures; it grows, this tragedy of man, to a cruel sensitivity sharpened by added increase of knowledge and methods of living life. Thirst and answering drink only add to the overwhelming score and finally youth looks at the ground (long since has his gaze been removed from the sky) and wonders if the only rest from mental battle is to be there at his feet, worms around and in him, earth packing him away from the sky and breath hushed with the weight of death. Man stands on his little, lonesome mound then, knowing that there are no doctors to heal his mind, understanding that the greatest beauties and delights are but transitory, that even if there be no God there ought to be some thing to worship. . . .◀

And toward the end of the summer, after both Camps Tabor and Tioga have been emptied within twenty-four hours by "feral-faced" parents because of a typhoid epidemic, he writes again to Martha with less depression and some relaxation of style. In the context, however, of a melancholic young mother who has murdered his and her child, the account is chilling:

I saw parents come in at three in the morning, white-lipped, animal fear in their faces, come, wrap their boys in blankets and leave the camp as silently and hurriedly as they had entered it; I saw women wring their hands, call their husbands, cry, faint, scold. . . . They were little more than animals I have seen drawing back their lips and snarling. Theirs was the first instinct of Man and since the children were too young to understand self-preservation, the mothers, with all

◀ 8.2.

the maternal feelings they owned, drew their children to their bosoms and clutched them there as if the directors of the camp wanted to wrest them away.

Many confirmatory pieces of the Joan-Roberta tragedy are supplied by notes, diaries, and letters over the subsequent five years. This tragedy meshed with his conviction that both his parents had wished to abandon him or to see him dead.* All his life he held a vengeful grudge against them. Deep into the fall and winter of 1929 he was in a state of raging, despairing, and self-punitive guilt. The number and nature of his subsequent references to Roberta and Joan are impressive. In 1930 he writes in a letter to an actress he is wooing: "If I had a daughter, I'd call her Joan." In his diary on July 4, 1932, he writes:

Thinking at breakfast of Joan and Roberta a line came to my mind, also expressive of this day: "It was a damp fourth of July and sporadically fire crackers burst in the streets." . . . Tomorrow is July 5. Sleep, sleep sorrow sleep.

On the following day he adds in the diary:

Joan and Roberta are three years dead, gone gone gone. This summer I am beginning to live again in the present. The past is dead, bitterness, grieving are done. I am going to set this day aside and think calmly about everything. How I have lived these past three years since that time, half blind and half dead myself, inflicting fantastic tortures and gnawing to my head and heart. . . . The whole visible world is blowing in the wind. Grass will not stand up straight and leaves show their undersides. I stretched out and hugged the earth and buried my face down deep and cried, and then turned over and the hot sun dried the tears and I was strong again with the lovely day and all of life around me, myriad insects buzzing, working, vital grass pushing up and up, and I a Gulliver giant supine in a considerate world. Now I will go down and have lunch quietly. I will take a glass of water and consider its fluidity. Linger not here, thou static stone. Know better the ever moving, the flux of all life and living things. . . . It is so easy to write these words, but the inside corrosion does not go so easily. I don't ask when I look at Stella's little girl to be reminded of Joan, I would rather I saw only the little dark Ellen,† but Joan comes and her blue eyes under the black hair. And when I go for a swim at the pool I see clearly Robbie swimming up the way with me. I remember everything today, everything everything. I get so sad that I become as soft and gentle as a woman. I want to take people and kiss them and hold them close, all the people. It is so beautiful to have life in you, making you move, breathing clean warm air, having darting little thoughts. Come to me people, tell me your hearts and your hurts and I listen and hold your hands. Let me live with you people and know your thoughts and the dear stirring of warm feeling. From the ashes I say, up, alive, thrusting up all the time, up from a tree, profuse of foliage, eager for the sun, alive, lust lust for the sky, to touch other living things.

All right, I will pay back a trust. When I remember ever those

---

* Years later he would tell the author that his "first great betrayal" had been at the hands of his "child-mother," who, he thought, had wanted to get rid of him, to give him away. On another occasion he remarked that many "separate times" his father had driven him to suicide attempts.

† The daughter of actress Stella Adler.

two, child and child-mother, I will pay them for their existences by reaching out to other men and women, to loving people and giving to them what heart is mine, what human warmth. My days shall not be for nothing. Up and out you spread and give what there is of you to give. Their days, their days shall not be for nothing!!! Their days!

And in 1933 he writes to his current lover, the actress-singer Tamara:

. . . Darling, today, four years ago a girl to whom I was married was very unhappy. She had melancholia, jealousy, fears for the future. She lived in northern Pennsylvania and I spent most of my time in New York. I got a camp job and with the money saved from the job was going to bring her to New York in the fall, our baby too. I was at camp in upper Pennsylvania too. Her name was Roberta, the child's name was Joan. On July 5th she shot herself and the child. Every year since that time this day has been a horrible experience. Today I feel nothing, blankness. I think that old life is over now. I tell you all this so you'll know what it's all about. Harold [Clurman] knows and several of my friends, not even my parents. Secrets, but only because I was a young foolish boy. We won't have to talk about this any more. It goes like the river. . . .*

The configuration of the Roberta-Joan puzzle supports Odets' most negative attitudes, which provide a steady ground-bass for the repeated themes in his life and in his work: an innocent (often a young girl) is destroyed by a desperate, envious, depressed older person in a parental position; it becomes then incumbent upon him, the "author" of this tragedy, to "pay them for their existences by reaching out to other men and women, to loving people and giving to them what heart is mine. . . ." He will write often of the murder of children by parents, as metaphor and as actuality.

At the close of this embattled summer of 1929, coming back to life briefly, he praises silence and solitude:

. . . And this is the first time all season that I have really wanted to write letters. To really want to write a letter means that one must write not because he is lonesome, not because he has an obligation to full fill [sic], not because there is nothing better to do, but because the urge to write comes like a gripping thing, tosses all other things out to the exclusion of writing and then makes a complete regurgitation‹ in the victim. Let me send up a prayer to those on high—the gods that be—a prayer that says to always make me the victim of such discontent, the kind that fills one with thoughts and words and long paragraphs, that specie that makes one write write write and write!

But three years later in his diary he recalls the fall of 1929 as a nightmare:

I remember that autumn after when I went on the road with the Theatre Guild . . . horrible horrible days when I would have murdered the world in one swoop were it possible. I would have taken my flesh and rent it, tearing gaping wounds in it. It was anguish I knew, fear, hurt, bitterness and grieving.

So this is a new world on this day when they are dead three years, a new world. Up up out of the dust, and the face set another way. I feel so empty inside, a pull at my stomach. There I have had a cry. The day is so beautiful and blowing and I will go maybe to lie in

---

* This letter is dated August, not July, but Odets often confused dates on letters. ‹ 8.3.

the sun in the grass somewhere. Cry the tears if they are there, hold nothing in to turn and bite the vitals.

Fortified with his Camp Tioga money in September, still obviously depressed, he was again "cruising around looking for jobs" in New York. In a performance at Eva Le Gallienne's Civic Repertory Theatre on 14th Street he was surprised to see onstage his Philadelphia friend Joseph Kramm, with whom he had been bankrupt in New York. Visiting Kramm in his dressing room, he told him how envious he was that Kramm was clearly "on his way."

Shortly thereafter, in an unhappy frame of mind, feeling that he had lost his family and had no connection with it, he ran into the hearty Albert Van Dekker from the cast of *Conflict*. Van Dekker said that he was going on tour for the Theatre Guild, trouping three shows in repertory—*Marco Millions, Volpone,* and *R.U.R.*—and that Odets might as well call the casting director, Cheryl Crawford, and mention Van Dekker's name.

Odets recalled his first contact with the fresh-faced, sturdy girl from Akron, Ohio, a recent Smith graduate who would in the following year become one of the three visionary founders of the Group Theatre.

I went into a phone booth and called this lady, whom I'd never met before. . . . And she said to me on the phone, "Are you a big, strong fellow?" And I said, "Yes," and she said, "Well, come right over." So I went right over and asked for her and met her. By "big strong fellow" she meant was I homosexual or not, because they had plenty of homosexuals in the company, kind of chorus boy types, and she was looking for more *male* young actors, let me say. Well, I think I fitted that bill, because in two or three minutes I was down—we walked down some stairs, and there I was on the famous Theatre Guild stage, the stage of the Theatre Guild's theatre on West 52nd Street. And there were many famous people there who were very impressive. Mamoulian was directing one show, and Philip Moeller was polishing up *Volpone* and *Marco Millions*.

Cheryl Crawford, a serious young woman with an auburn "boyish bob," generally known for her executive tact, her practicality, and her moral intensity, was sufficiently impressed by this sincere, athletically built young man to hire him at $40 a week to play walk-on parts with the touring company. He was grateful to her, resolving to write back from the tour "just to keep her remembering that I was alive."

Another year would pass before Odets would meet Harold Clurman, to whom Cheryl Crawford was listening these days with respectful attention. Now a play-reader for the Theatre Guild, Clurman had quit the New Playwrights' Theatre of John Howard Lawson and Dos Passos to enroll, as Lee Strasberg had, in a course for directors given by a Russian named Richard Boleslavsky at the Laboratory Theatre.

The sensitively intelligent, midwestern Miss Crawford was finding steady nutriment and a new, more than exotic, more than political excitement in Clurman's reports of how the distant Moscow Art Theatre was linking the actor's work to the creative purpose of the playwright. Could it be, they wondered, that the promises in Russia's new national anthem to the international "prisoners of starvation, the wretched of the earth" were indeed to be fulfilled all over the world? Proclaiming a "better world's in birth," the anthem stated that if these prisoners would but arise, the entire planet would itself "rise on new foundations." A significant segment of young American intellectuals was indeed uniting in the wild hope that there was a world-view worthy to offer as response to O'Neill's desperate query, "God is Dead. Long Live What?" Had not the articulate Lincoln Steffens returned from this fabled land with the report that he had been to see the future and found that "it works"? At long last the promises of all previous revolutions, even those of Christianity, were to be kept here on earth. The post-war hunger for this vision was already acute long before one third of all Americans literally became, in the years to follow, "prisoners of starvation."

For both Odets and Crawford there was some ancient significance and appeal in the introspective social melancholy of this new promised land, evident, they agreed, even in the "bourgeois" playwright Anton Chekhov. The wild hopes implicit in Marxist ideology, inchoate in both of them when the twenty-two-year-old casting director from Akron hired the twenty-three-year-old son of a Russian-Jewish immigrant for this important Theatre Guild tour, made for an underlying chord of resonance. Odets asked Crawford if she would mind if he wrote her from the road; on the contrary, she said, she would be glad to hear from him.

There is no indication in his letters that Odets was yet deeply invested in the larger issues, nor that he even knew of the exuberant project in which Cheryl Crawford was becoming progressively involved with Clurman, Strasberg (as actor), and the Theatre Guild stage manager Herbert Biberman (as director): the production of the first Soviet play to reach the United States, called *Red Rust*. Welcomed more, according to Clurman, for its "tonic swing" than its ideology in the narrow sense, it was put on for respectable Guild subscribers, with an official blessing as an "exceptional play."

There was no organic connection between the later Group Theatre and this production by the "Theatre Guild Studio," as Clurman, Crawford, and Biberman decided to call their free-wheeling exploration. It is evident, however, that this project, like the abortive work the previous year on Waldo Frank's play, was moving these lively young people a critical step closer to the formation of the Group Theatre.

Odets, still significantly wrapped in his own private depression, gives no hint in his letters of this fall that he so much as noticed the catastrophic crash of that most reliable of economic barometers, the New York Stock Exchange. It began on Black Thursday and built to its first climax on the following Tuesday, October 29. Soon the word would be "panic," but, like so many emotional money-words, it was still a metaphor and only an early signal of the great recession now begun. The farmers had felt it coming, and President Hoover, in all sincerity, reassured them that this would be "just another panic," like the fifteen we had already triumphantly survived. The members of the Theatre Guild road company, delighted by the excellent business they were doing, chuckled over the headline in *Variety*, their trade newspaper: "Wall Street Lays an Egg."

Although historians date the official start of the Great Depression from this October day, its worldwide reverberations would not be apparent until the failure of the Bank of the United States in December of the following year. No one dreamed that within the next decade one out of three Americans would be suffering such acute want as to dictate the abandonment forever of that system of free enterprise from which this privation had issued. It was still inconceivable in 1929 that the United States would soon move into a "New Deal" giving the government vast and unprecedented responsibility for the welfare of its citizens.

Nor was it possible to foresee that by 1933 the aristocratic Franklin Roosevelt, an astute, valiant, and practical politician, would be, cigarette-holder poised, superintending from his wheelchair in the White House a bold plan to keep alive and employed the millions of citizens disinherited by social and economic arrangements insufficient to accommodate an advancing technology. Even his best efforts would be inadequate, however, to mobilize the economy; deliverance would come only with a declaration of war.

In Germany quite a different method would be applied to an already equally endangered economy. Millions of people would be withdrawn from the society and dispatched in sealed trains, thus stimulating the economy and simultaneously discharging a coolly organized savagery unknown within a species anywhere in the animal kingdom. The identities of individual human beings now evolving all over the world would, of necessity, express—subtly or obviously—either the totalistic or the pluralistic solution. The evolving cultural and esthetic forms, as always, were beginning to reflect these opposed world-views for changing the world.

A generation, some of whose members would become the messianic writers of the 1930s, had begun to gestate in the United States. By instinct, like most romantic artists, they were on the side of the underdog, the overturner; ugly ducklings all, they would find, ironically, that the Big Slump would be *their* salvation because it would provide a meshing of private despair with public event. Odets, like his ideological brothers, was beginning to feel he would merge "in some great aggregation of suffering men and women—the workers." The prevailing mood of these young people at the start was one of active "dismay and rebellion mingled with wild hopes for the future," their stance one of passion, their aim to change the world.◀ Ignorant of the moral catastrophes in the Soviet Union, they would find in it an egalitarian, quasi-religious model for the attainment of peace, social justice, and human dignity for the individual.

Odets, feeling himself to be a deprived, displaced person, a "homeless thing," by reason not of economics but of psychologics, had identified himself with Victor Hugo's "misérables" long before the Great Depression, but it was precisely this economic catastrophe that would provide him an initial bridge to his audience. This fall, however, still marooned on the island of his own private Big Slump, he restricted himself to a study of sonata form, sporadic efforts to write, and two abortive attempts to end his life.

The beginning of his spiritual rebirth, in 1930, would coincide almost precisely with the failure of the Bank of the United States; his creative apogee in the mid-thirties with the depth of the economic Depression; and the start of his malignant retreat to Hollywood with the resurgence of the economy when the United States declared war on December 8, 1941.

It was evident to members of the Theatre Guild troupe, as the Lincoln Limited clicked its way to Minneapolis, Chicago, St. Louis, that one of their extras, a withdrawn and romantic galley slave in *Marco Millions*, was desperately unhappy and shunning the company of women. Some thought it was because Odets loathed being an extra, others because he "had to dress with all the queers" and, being a sensitive boy trouping for the first time, found it intolerable. Odets described an incident that may have accounted in part for his lowly status as an extra:

◀ 8.4.

I once sat behind Mr. Alfred Lunt, an actor of remarkable gift, at a rehearsal of a Maxwell Anderson play, a bit in my hands, and when my moment came, retaining his vocal style, I pitched my voice two octaves lower than his. After the reading they took the part away.

A familiar figure in his pepper-and-salt suit, he is recalled as a sad and dreamy youngster leaving yearning love-notes and poems on the successive dressing-room cots of the leading lady, Sylvia Field (later Mrs. Ernest Truex), a tiny, exquisitely dainty young actress, obviously unattainable, on whom the entire company had something of a "crush."

For at least six weeks, to her great puzzlement, this lovely ingenue daily received a long epistle (copies of many are still extant) not only singing her praises in great detail, but presuming also to hold the key to the very heart of life in general, of her soul in particular, and of the professional work she was doing in her various roles. These were either unsigned or signed "a lad" or "one of the lads." Labeling himself a defeated and tired Cyrano, he compares his sadness to hers in *Marco Millions,* "where you are almost loved of Marco and yet go down to glorious defeat, the vanquished of gold pieces." He is drawn to watch her in this scene at every performance and "it hurts me more than I can say. Why, I don't know, but each time I watch it I feel that I'm being impaled on a spike and left quivering and wounded." To a psychoanalyst's ear there is here a reverberation of Odets' lifelong yearning to be loved by his own merchant father, just as there was in the play's author (O'Neill) when he used the thirteenth-century Venetian as his symbol for the lampooning of a twentieth-century American Babbitt, his own partial view of *his* father, and as there would be repetitively in Odets' plays. Her self-appointed physician, psychoanalyst, and director, Odets sends Miss Field a daily chart on how healthy, how happy, how tired, how rested she appears to be, and in addition how well she is acting. On one occasion: "It is good to note that you are one of the very few persons who seems to be steadily growing in 'R.U.R.,'" adding of one of her lines that "you strike in it the deepest note of your voice, the loveliest and most musical moment I have heard in any of your performances." It is evident (later even to him) that his identification with her runs deep and that he projects onto her not only many of his own qualities such as "your sad softness," but also his deepest aspirations, as well as his tragic sense of life. In the next paragraph of the same letter:

I have, here on my table, a large chrysanthemum. How great it stands before my eyes. It has opened as far as such flowers can go. First it was a seed, then a root, then a stalk, then a bud and now a flower long since culled from where it grew. Yet, in a vase, sunk stem first in water, it still lives with a fierce urge for Life. It spreads out its petals like a woman in love, until it must perish with ripeness. Always is fulfillment and then decay. The fruit ripens to glory and then sickens. . . .

It is easier to worship anonymously a "goddess" on the altar of a faraway stage than a real girl who is "nice to everyone." But this urgent twenty-three-year-old boy was unable to maintain his narcissistic dream of a goddess; and needing a direct human response ("Oh, how I hate silence!"),* he finally writes:

I must make apologies again, for it has come to me that by my lack of identity I have placed you in a very unfair position. You must wonder —if only occasionally—who is writing these thousands of words to

---

* On other occasions he pines for "silence," a universal yearning in the artist, who can explore himself only in the private space of protective silence.

you. You must be puzzled and at times conscious of that sharp eyes are watching you [sic]. For all of that I am very very sorry. But what do the metal scraps have to do with the magnet? Candidly, I do not think the metal filings can escape the lode stone. What to do . . . what to do.

I begin to see that I must either cease these letters and their meandering lines . . . or say to you that I am writing you letters . . . or ask that you come to have supper with me some night after the show, so that we can talk . . . or what . . . or what? Then I think that perhaps you have been far more clever than I and that all these days you knew full well who was writing to you. If only one might be certain of that! I think the best thing to do is to walk to your door some night and say: "Miss Field, this is the youngster who has been giving you failing sight from too much reading. Is he to continue writing? Is he to forget and forego what he cannot forget? Is he hurting your peace of mind? Do you care if he writes no more? Will you excuse him?". . . and more and more to which you can answer: "You damn fool!" or "You snake in the grass," or "Don't you need a new typewriter ribbon?". . . ad infinitum!

On the following day he takes the ultimate and irrevocable step of signing, with some flourish, "Believe me, Clifford Odets" to the following:

I am sick with my subterfuge, tired of trying to hiding [sic] my identity behind some phrase as stupid as "one of the lads" or by some silly mark on a typewriter key. I who have never lacked courage to do or say what is right, find now that all my strength is gone, has fled. There is more timidity in me than in a flock of lambs. . . . Forgive me that I have been so stupid and blundering, and excuse, if you will, that I have been some very young boy with more emotion than he is able to cope with. . . . I shall, shall, shall (that is a word of the future) speak with you tonight as if I were not a gauche boy, one who is "knotted like an oak with fierce sincerity." Enough! Enough . . . and I am bewildering you with more words when I should be almost blunt and say that here is my hand . . . and that I want so to be your friend . . . and you to be mine.

Quickly, wrapped in his own emotional universe, he follows this up by telling Miss Field she must not imagine "now that I have spoken my name . . . that I would not write to you again." He cannot help but write as "there is, for this boy, no surer way of releasing thought than by written words, no more certain escape from the pain and the gaol that are thoughts." He reviews having fled her dressing room the night before as she watched him drop his confession on her cot. He can liken her glance only to "the Leonardo Mona Lisa," which inundated his consciousness with "a kind of suspended animation." He ends with a review of the lives of Shelley, Keats, and Chopin, whose "George Sand nursed him and loved him and then left him to die of bitterness."* He begs her to "command me" to let him now become her "cavaliere servente." His heart shook as he awaited their face-to-face meeting.

From Miss Field's point of view, the events had no such importance: "I hadn't noticed Clifford until Albert Dekker and his wife told me that one of the boys watched me from the wings and wanted to meet me, but was

---

* At another time and place he would jot down in his heavy "X-file," a gallery of characters gathered for future use: " 'Pluck up courage, velvet fingers,' Sand said to Chopin."

too shy to speak," she recalled, adding, "They had us both to dinner and I liked him." From this point forward, during their trek, through Ohio to Detroit, Chicago, Minneapolis, and back to the East Coast, he continued the daily letters which embarrassed her: "I thought they were very funny . . . one poem to my throat, another to my 'twinkling heels' . . . but I was in love and engrossed in my beau. . . . Clifford was a very handsome boy but so intense, serious and tongue-tied."*

In this compulsive one-sided affair Odets was establishing this year's edition of what he called "the search for the lost part of me," an idealized "Nordic" image of the feminine side of himself.† In this year, as in others, his "ikon lady" would, of necessity, betray him by being a flesh-and-blood being with needs of her own: Sylvia Field was planning to marry someone else.

This Theatre Guild troupe was remarkable. Most of its members awed Odets, including the portly Sydney Greenstreet, Henry Travers, Ernest Cossart, and the kindly Earle Larimore, who, feeling sorry for this melancholy boy, would occasionally invite him to dinner with the object of his groveling adoration. After one such evening in Chicago he walked her home through the snow, Miss Field recalled. The next night she received a long letter saying he had walked back to his hotel "whistling Beethoven's Fifth." Later he desperately informed her that she must marry him because "I can make you glad." Miss Field, however, maintained her interest in her beau.

Soon, on a guilt-ridden, nervous, and ravenous evening, he wrote her his determination to bring it all to an end:

> I sat for almost an hour looking at an empty chair opposite me and imagined in it all the girls, young and old that I'd known. I make no idle boast here. I am little interested in boasts of any sort, affectation makes me sick to death and vulgar vanity that is without point has no place in my friendship. But I saw in that chair a ghostly troop, women who came one by one to sit there and leave after a brief perusal of each of them. With a stern code of life, with a realization of artistic creation, necessary creation with me, I have become hardened, have lost the urge to sing to every woman who attracted my eyes and other things, such as a need for feminine warmth and sympathy. I can see the change myself: From a boy of soft features and an easy manner in which every woman was a potential prey, I have grown to firmness and troubled face. I have kept away almost assiduously from the eternal, charming magnet that is Woman, have shunned it when ever possible.

He concludes that he sometimes feels "that I'd like to throw up the whole demanding business of life," adding:

> I am sorry . . . I have no right to send you all this. In my desolation I have become blind to decorous conduct, seem to have lost my native strength, my silence where silence is necessary. I think this is the place for it. . . . But be comforted. I shall never again write another word to you. . . . Here let me draw an end. Let me mark over all my words, let me say of them one word: "Obit."

It must have been shortly after this that Odets made his first suicide attempt, which, he later records, he himself stopped "midway." A second

---

* On one occasion he wrote a paean to her hands, "one of the most beautiful things about you" (he himself had extraordinary hands), expressing his fear "that they might do something not beautiful, that they would lapse into the silence of not being used."

† Odets comments often on his steady interest in "Nordic," non-Jewish women.

Wide-eyed innocent Clifford Odets, probably at two years of age.

Pearl Geisinger Odets, Clifford's mother; taken shortly before her death at the age of forty-seven in 1935.

Louis Odets and Clifford, age four, already captivated by the camera. See Notes and Comment 2.6.

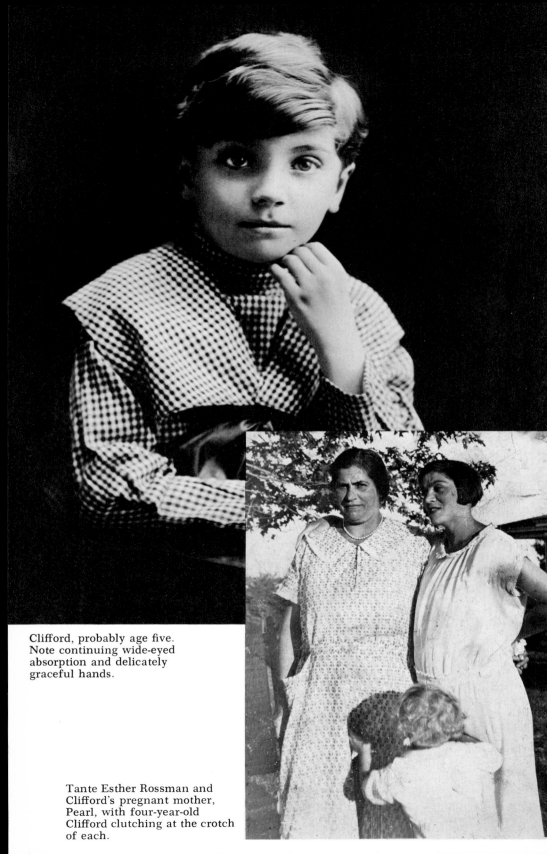

Clifford, probably age five. Note continuing wide-eyed absorption and delicately graceful hands.

Tante Esther Rossman and Clifford's pregnant mother, Pearl, with four-year-old Clifford clutching at the crotch of each.

Clifford, age 12½
(in knee socks), and his father,
Louis Odets, both in rented
tuxedos, pretending to prepare
for a bar mitzvah celebration
that never happened.

Odets family at Boy Scout camp. Left to right: mother,
Pearl, sister Florence, sister Genevieve, father, Louis J.,
and Clifford.

Clifford's graduating-class
picture from Public
School 10 in the Bronx,
1921. He is second row
from top, extreme left.

Clifford, age eighteen,
as vaudeville elocutionist
"The Rover Reciter"

"HOW DEATH CAME INTO THE WORLD" Scene from one of the dramatized American Indian spirit legends given before the veiled altar of the church of St. Mark's-in-the-Bouwerie under the direction of Harry Kemp, tramp poet. The playlets formed part of the church's Thanksgiving service. (Kadel & Herbert)

CLIFFORD ODETS

JEROME ROSENBERG

Scene from Harry Kemp production. Left to right: Clifford, Adrian Vanderhorst inside masked figure, Jerome Rosenberg, and two unknown players.

. M. V. Leof, one of the best of Clifford's "surrogate fathers," whose home provided intellectual and cultural sustenance in his twenties.

Clifford at twenty-three, an aspiring matinee idol in a studio portrait taken for the Theatre Guild.

Actress-singer Tamara, star of
Roberta, and Odets' lady in 1933–34.

Sylvia Field as Gwen in Jed Harris's
The Royal Family (George Kaufman
and Edna Ferber). The object of
twenty-three-year-old Clifford's
adoration on Theatre Guild tour.

Actress Hortense Alden, poetic
mirror-image of Odets in his
mid-twenties, and one of the earliest
of his hundreds of known lovers.

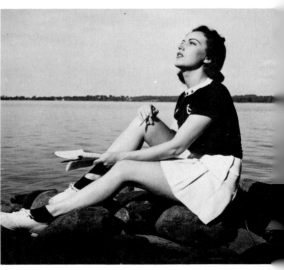

Fay Wray, studying a part for
summer theater in Skowhegan, Maine.

up Theatre directors at Brookfield Center in 1931. Left to
it: Cheryl Crawford, Lee Strasberg, and Harold Clurman.

e Group at summer camp, impersonating Rodin's *The Thinker* as instructed
photographer Ralph Steiner. Odets in third row on extreme right; Harold Clurman
d Lee Strasberg are in the last row on extreme right.

Odets in 1935 at the height of his success, photographed by Alfredo Valente.

Odets at age twenty-eight. This Van Vechten portrait was captioned by th Daily Forward "lyric poet of the Jewi middle-class."

Odets as Dr. Benjamin in Waiting for Lefty (1935).

p actress
a Miller Strasberg,
d wife of Lee.

Group actor Elia Kazan,
to become a famous stage
and film director, and later
a writer.

scene from *Waiting for Lefty;* at center, arms raised, Elia Kazan.

Awake and Sing, with John Garfield and Morris Carnovsky.

Golden Boy,
with Luther Adler,
Morris Carnovsky and
Frances Farmer.

A scene from Group
Theatre production of
Awake and Sing. Left to
right: John Garfield,
. Edward Bromberg,
Stella Adler, Morris
Carnovsky, Art Smith,
Sanford Meisner, and
Luther Adler.

The "firebug scene" from
Paradise Lost. Left to right:
Robert Lewis as the arsonist,
May; Morris Carnovsky
Leo Gordon; and Luther
Adler as Sam Katz.

Rocket to the Moon,
with Morris Carnovsky
and Eleanor Lynn.

Robert Lewis
as a Nazi orderly in
Till the Day I Die (1935).

Luise Rainer
expressing *joie de vivre*.

Luise Rainer in a waif-like mome

During intermission at a
concert, Clifford and Luise
—she signing autographs.

lets and Luise Rainer, c. 1937.

uise and Clifford being rowed by Albert Einstein to his cottage on Long Island Sound (1937).

FIFTEEN CENTS   DECEMBER 5, 1938

TIME

THE WEEKLY NEWSMAGAZINE

Peter A. Nyholm

CLIFFORD ODETS
Down with the general Fraud!
(Theatre)

VOLUME XXXII   (REG. U. S. PAT. OFF.)   NUMBER 23 attempt soon followed: desperately intoxicated not only with liquor but also with Tchaikovsky, he stood poised at a window of the Hotel Wolverine in Detroit, unsteadily climbing the sill to jump,◖ but was pulled back by actor Louis Veda, an effeminate member of the company who shared his passion for music. Years later he described this event as the outcome of "unrequited love" and tried to cast the unemployed Veda in his play *Night Music*, telling his sister that Veda had saved his life.*

Larimore, aware of his desperation, tried to cheer him by asking director Rouben Mamoulian to give him additional bit parts, usually to no avail. However, he must have been finding some relief in his writing, which, according to his letters, continued throughout this fall and winter. He devoted himself mainly to *The Brandy of the Damned*, but also found time to compose many poems for Sylvia Field. He is, he says, the passive instrument† through which *her voice* speaks:

> For, if the truth must be known, you are the author for all of them and use only my hand to set them down. Without you they were never written. There is something of the alchemist about you, you who take some elements in me, stir them to fancies, and make a new, strange compound that is poetry when it has left the tubes and retorts.

"Thoughts," he adds, that "had not been chained to form stabbed their way into my consciousness until now they have beaten their ways to paper, to black print on white." In this, as in his discussion of "thoughts like bullets," he expresses a belligerent quality which finds resolution only through his writing:

> . . . triolets and rondeaus and villanelles wait to be written, are massed now like armies of brave soldiers with flying banners. I do not know why they want to fight for an ideal (as all armies are sent to death and destruction) . . . but they do . . . these brave creatures . . . with their flying banners.

Further evidence that he is trying to perfect his "instrument" is the word lists he is making, a habit he would keep all his life. "Peripatetic," "pedestal," "desideratum"—all new and unmined.

As the year draws to an end, he is coming to terms with Miss Field's rejection. To his friend Herman he writes that he does not want to bore him with "some messy facts about unhappiness, ennui and world weariness" and that he is beginning to think Sylvia "is not a goddess, and that you must admit, is a departure point in any love affair." If *only* he had music for this long tour; it is like "being without a heart or pulse. . . . It is simply that I must have it; without music I am miserable all the time," concluding:

> You see there is some homeless Thing that wanders around in all of us. In some persons it's more pronounced. . . . To the thoughtful ones, those with sensitivity, there is no rest. We go on wondering about things, analyzing our very emotions and give‡ little from life but hurt. . . . The best thing of all would be for Man to remain unborn. . . .

◖ 8.5.

* In 1950 this actor, then known as Louis Veda Quince, was in the original cast of Odets' *Country Girl.*

† This fantasy of the Muse is frequently expressed by writers. (William Gibson commented of his play *Two for the Seesaw:* "God wrote the character of Gittel. I wrote Jerry.")

‡ Odets' slip, not mine.

From the Hotel Havlin in Cincinnati, Ohio, he writes to "Dear Miss Crawford" in that humorous and gossipy key often characteristic of homosexual men writing to women of whom they are fond. In a literate, newsy rundown on the work and lives of the members of the Guild company his scornful resentment toward the exclusive leading actors is evident. When he has run out of tidbits, such as the exciting rumor they will go to California to make a film of *Marco Millions*, he has the thought he would like to write to her as a friend but fears "an aspect of the sycophantic . . . considering as one must what is your position and what is mine."

The Christmas season with its "febrile gayness" is in full swing in damp, cold Detroit, and soon they will move on to Chicago, leaving "powder rings and empty cans" on dressing-room shelves, and towels covered with greasepaint. Those members of the company who can afford to spend $50 will go East for a welcome pre-holiday layoff at home, while those like Clifford will "pursue our ways to Chicago. . . . Personally," he assures Miss Crawford, "I am not one to be bothered with nostalgic aches and groanings. There is too much to live in oneself." Developing this brave and unpersuasive line of thought, he continues:

> Particularly this is true of the Jew who has always been a homeless thing anyway. It can not matter much to those people whether home is here or there. One or another it is of no matter.
> I had forgotten, incidentally, that I was a Jew until this week when a gentleman (one who is really a nice person) went below his skin and dragged up the furious invective, "You dirty Brooklyn Jew." There was nothing to do about that; I was so much stronger than he, could almost have broken him in my hands—so I turned the other cheek instead, but he had recovered completely enough to refuse the fleshly bait. However, it didn't matter. I've never lived in Brooklyn.

Considering that Odets would one day be hailed in the Jewish press as the "leading lyric poet of American Jewry," it is remarkable how few explicit references he makes to his origins. When he does, they are for the most part full of that self-contempt so frequently found in members of a minority group. In this comment the effort to separate himself from other Jews is evident in his reference to "those people" or earlier in his description of his "long-nosed cousins." The conflict within him about being a Jew was of sufficient proportions to permit him to "forget," on the one hand that he was a Jew and, on the other, to become a cultural spokesman for a generation of Jews.

From Cleveland he writes to an old Philadelphia friend at year's end that he is still "caught in the grip of one of those darker moods that you must have seen catch me by the throat and heart." It had seized him on the train from Pittsburgh as he looked out at the "fields stretched fallow, wherever one could look, their soil harder than an enemy's tongue." He has been reading Conrad and Zola, but finding it hard to concentrate, as he is thinking with anger of his futile efforts to win, proselytize, and educate Sylvia Field—a characteristic closing chapter in his relationships with women:

> Over a dinner table in Richmond I said suddenly: "How better if I had come to you as a man comes to a woman, instead of writing from afar as if you were something unobtainable." She answered a yes to that and I saw immediately my error. She was not understanding what I was writing, what my words were saying. I saw more: That she was afraid of my knowledge, so afraid that she continued to iterate, "I'm

just a goof." Stupid? Perhaps, but there is a gold in her the gleam of which I saw when I first came to know her. What will it matter if she can not discuss the weavings of Bach with me? I shall brush her eyes with my words of Beethoven and she'll see with my eyes, hear with my ears. But I have, if you please, given her an inferiority complex. In my company she won't be pinned down. I can get her to talk of nothing but what is fluffy and inconsequential. What of that? All I want is a woman, warm, sympathetic. . . . I begin to see that the psychologists are correct, that when one marries he is doing nothing more than taking a second mother to his bed.*

"The charm of our friendship is that in ten years we have met but three times." So comments a young man about his friendship with a young lady in the novel Odets was writing. As the now real Miss Field resisted seeing with his eyes and hearing with his ears, their relationship was at last drawing to a close. It would plague him, however, into the early months of 1930.

Tired of bridge, handball, the "Pagan Love Song" on the radio, smoking, the members of the Theatre Guild company, the piano rented by Sanford Meisner and Martin Wolfson, and, above all, of his "gin jags with their resultant shakes," he writes to Kozlenko:

I had some peace of mind in Cleveland this past Saturday night. I drank myself to a hysteria which was what I wanted to do. Then I deliberately sat down in an arm chair and cried and cried while one of the fellows tried to quiet me with his measurements of what life is, of how he was looking at the world and of his weariness. I filled two handkerchiefs with bitter, saliferous tears . . . and have been better all this week for it.

About Sylvia Field, he concludes with considerable insight:

I have been investing her with too much of what's in myself, have been seeing only (the usual case) those things I wanted to see. Now I've definitely set about to remedy that almost murderous mistake. In the past she has been puissant enough to almost divorce me from my work, from my writing and thinking; from now on you may be assured that she will slowly fade in my inner eye until her significance becomes nothing more than that of a laughing girl without too much profundity. I just couldn't afford to have her smashing into my scheme of life and living and doing and creating: I have cut out the tumor. . . . The wound has already begun healing for I am young and strong, still able to easily throw off malicious hurts. Good! you'll say. I echo your word!

In the remaining few days of 1929 he writes proudly to Sylvia Field that he has locked himself in his room at the Allerton House in Chicago and, "with the grace of the lash," his novel has grown ten thousand words heavier in one week. With high excitement and no evident awareness of the melodramatic flavor of this novel, he writes:

Karl [the central figure] meets love for the first time in his twenty two years. He is slightly puzzled, afraid, eager . . . and twenty things like that! A month later he says, in his nicest manner (he has blue,

---

* This pat assent to an Oedipus complex does much violence to the deeper meanings of his wishes, in their nature resembling an abandoned, frightened, self-absorbed, starving infant more than a boy in competition with his father for his mother's sexual favors.

astral eyes and a Latin's blue-black hair): "Consuelo, if love is a flame then I am the epitome of all conflagrations." But Consuelo Bianca, she of an Italian father and an English mother, had married by then a young meany. When her first baby came and died before its second yell, when the meany cursed her and the child and everything else and broke their love like a stick of kindling wood across his knee, then Consuelo saw that Karl was gone, that he would not and could not be called back. But these women are far more clever than the Chinese who are reputed to be "damn clever". . . so finally (it would take so long to tell) Karl came to know the glory that was, not ancient Greece, but that glory which was Consuelo Bianca.*

The reference to "the meany" breaking love "like a kindling stick" is an echo of his father's powerful breaking of the wooden pole in the Bronx; the demise of the baby, a reverberation of the Roberta-Joan episode.◖

He is tired and lonely in his cubicle, "quaking with nervous energy," writing at a fever pitch; he is sleepless and excessively hungry. He knows what T. S. Eliot meant with "I grow old . . . I grow old" and is, like Robert Louis Stevenson, locking himself in "triple armor" by writing letters and drowning people "in a cascade of words." He feels less impotent when he puts words to paper: ". . . she has to listen, she can't stop me from talking. . . . Therein is the peculiar charm of letter-writing . . . no one argues or breaks in on the flow . . . you talk and talk and talk. . . ."

* This is Odets' familiar dream of a pure, consolatory woman: Consuelo Bianca (white).

◖ 8.6.

Chapter Nine

*Art is history of an interior kind,
whose cardinal tenet is wholeness; it
woos wholeness by setting its limits,
and within them loosing truth against
contrary truth in a struggle to a quie-
tude which embraces and reconciles
both; to whatever degree it achieves
this, its matter lies beyond debate. It
seems to me no piece of writing is
worth its ink unless it thus marries
contrarieties and has issue.*

WILLIAM GIBSON

ODETS commences the New Year with a letter to "Darling Sylvia," describing his failure to "put you far behind me, so that not even a thought would
remain." Sharpening his pain and his self-pity with all the skills available
to his sado-masochistic character, he says he had stopped writing to her
with the "thought I might be able to keep from looking at you, that I would
kill the image of you that is written in me." He reminds her that he had,
in fact, once asked her "to kill me good and dead, but . . . you managed
instead to say several helloes that twisted in me like sharp blades." His
plea to her now to "kill this humble person" carries all the earmarks of
a masochistic resolution of resentment.◀

> Snub him when ever you can, walk by him with a tilted nose . . .
> snap your fingers at him and say "Pooh pooh, Mr. Odets. You're a fool,
> a jigger on a stick". . . oh something! Be angry with me for writing
> letters to you. Slap my face in public, call me an insolent hound, tell
> me that *I* am what's rotten in Denmark . . . oh something . . . and
> then I can grow to dislike you, can grow back to be the Clifford Odets
> who had never seen you. . . .
>   . . . Why don't you grab the helm and steer me for a big smash
> on the rocks? Then I can start salvaging the wreckage and begin again
> where I left off.* This aimless, hopeful, hopeless drifting is ter-
> rible. . . .

◀ 9.1.
* It would be a mistake to interpret this self-destructive fantasy entirely in the
terms of a conventional theory of masochism. It is also an expression of post-adolescent
confusion with its necessity for rebirth.

There are two more lengthy, stilted, and lacerated letters to Miss Field in January, both gory with bloody images of a helpless victim ("I am like the moth who is caught and mounted on the drying board with both wings and thorax pinned down: the greater the struggle the greater the damage and pain." Or "like some prowling animal caught in a trap . . . until the hunter arrives to end his life with a blow of a club or a winged, kindly bullet . . ."). He is now "Clifford, the vanquished, he who has lost his self, his pride . . . and had so little from you but silence," concluding: "when a woman is able to become more to me than Music, then I know something is wrong," because music has always been "as drink to a drunkard, dearer than life."

Desperately he makes a last attempt to make of himself a unique source of illumination by analyzing her character; finding this, too, of no avail, he bemoans the waste of his "nine billion words." Sylvia Field was, however, sufficiently immune to this approach—which he would refine with age—that in the early months of 1930, when the Guild troupe returned to New York, she left for Europe, thus ending Odets' frenzied courtship. Thirty years later Odets found himself compassionately interviewing a "little grey-haired grandmother" for a part in a film he was directing (*The Story on Page One*); her name was Sylvia Field Truex.

The Guild tour had provided him—despite his misery over his failure with Miss Field—the evocative prototype of what he called his "creative mood."* Sitting in the deserted theatre after one matinee, he wrote:

The theatre has long emptied itself of its quota of players; someone quietly threads down the steps, there is a jingle of a key and far away a door slams. There is a kind of spell over everything; it seems that this is the place in which the princess of the story is fast asleep, locked in slumber like to death, waiting for the prince to come and awaken her and all her handmaids and the household in which the cook has fallen asleep at her stove, the lackey at his sword-shining and the jester with a grimacing laugh on his drawn lips. So it is here, now, when I must certainly be alone. And it is in this time that I love most intensely the theatre with its quiet stage, the beacon of the pilot light and the dark house beyond the footlights, for all the world like some gaping mouth that might swallow stage, scenery banks and all.

There is a curious absence of alarm in his juxtaposition of these two role alternatives: either the sleeping princess (the playwright's feminine Muse) will be awakened by the prince (a masculine principle) to the creation of a rich and stratified life, or the entire stage will be devoured and thereafter be no more. Later he sharpens this image to include the subjective sense of incompletion, the experienced disconnection as a prime motivator of creative work. It becomes the "deed that cannot be left undone."◖ In a note for a full-length play he never wrote, called "I Heard the Music Start," he writes:

The creative syndrome: A strong impulse to visit bare, poor places, garish and lonely, like backstage with actors, subways, sitting in parked cars or in the waiting room of a railroad station—bleak corridor places on the way to somewhere else, places where you or no one else can be warmed or comforted and there is an unspoken sense of a shared

---

* Two decades later it would provide the setting for *The Country Girl*, a play about an alcoholic actor trying to make a comeback in the theatre. Again Odets (like Virginia Woolf) underscores, as a necessary condition for the creative mood, the need for being alone, a psychological room of one's own.

◖ 9.2.

minor misery. It is a disconnected mood that wants to meet with other disconnected and somewhat impoverished ones; an autumn in the soul, something bohemian and wayward, a thing of being homeless and footloose—an inner hankering and bareness which can't be named, a neither here nor there, a limbo, wayward and delinquent but not unpleasant. Finally there is nothing left to be or do but sit down and write. Thus the opening mood always of creativity for me.

His cousin Frank Lubner, son of Pearl's sister Nettie, was on leave from the Navy in New York a few days this winter and invited Clifford to dinner: "He said he preferred to take some food home from a delicatessen," Lubner recalled, "so we loaded up with delicacies and went home, which turned out to be a room he shared with five unemployed actors, which showed the unselfish, fine quality in him."

He picked up pocket money by filling out the cast of amateur productions in various Manhattan synagogues. Stanley Kauffman, later the drama critic for *The New York Times,* remembered the thrill of professional pride he experienced when as a youngster, in the basement of the Temple Rodeph Sholem on West 83rd Street, he was addressed by Odets, the only professional in the cast, as "Props" for his work as property man in an amateur production of Ludwig Lewisohn's *Adam.* From such income, occasional card winnings, and Pearl's occasional contributions— kept secret from his father—Odets survived for months on shredded wheat and cans of tomato-herring.

By spring, no longer having Sylvia Field to implore to "kill me good and dead," he undertakes the task himself. In letter after letter he elaborates on his "dismal failure to build myself to be a complete unit . . . to not need other people . . . to want nothing, to like isolation and desolation, to be constantly growing, to keep myself in a fluxionary state, to be sentient as a child's skin, to remain artless. . . ." He had thought that in the last five years, which he calls "all my conscious life," he had learned he "could sit still for hours in a room by myself* . . . 'as complete as a flower or a stone.' . . ." Now he sees that his independence was illusory and that, having "fallen in love," he no longer belongs to himself: "Most of me belongs to a woman who some months before was a complete stranger."❡ His only relief, "after I asked her a score of times 'to kill me, to kill my feeling,' " he confides, came "when I hit on the idea of cleverly insulting her."

Drifting from one cheap New York hotel to another, he first shares a filthy room with two racetrack touts and "hundreds of bedbugs," then moves back to the Circle Hotel, where his room was a tiny one "like a toilet." The Circle Hotel, known even by its more permanent residents as a place "to slip into for a quick cheap bang." In this "low cramped corner of an air shaft" there are, he says:

so many books . . . notes and yellow sheets of poems . . . an accumulation of newspapers fill one corner . . . ashes, dust, a counter-

* These are almost the same words used to describe his quiet obedience as a young child.
❡ 9.3.

pane that looks as if I'd wiped my feet on it, a glass with a rose in it, trousers hung up on nails, notebooks, pencils, letters, a faucet which is bubbling water just now . . . dirty socks, towels under the sink . . . and yet I can turn out my light [and have] . . . a profound black, a colour . . . [no other] more beautiful and satisfying.

The filth and chaos of this room became a nightmare image in the memory of Pearl's friend from Southern Boulevard in the Bronx, Ida Mae Levine, who had held out a broomstick to help Clifford take his first step. Almost four decades later she would recall Pearl's desperate and secret phone call to New York from Philadelphia. "For God's sake, I haven't heard from him for weeks. Please, please find him and bring him back to Philadelphia." Still in evident fear of Lou Odets' wrath, Ida Mae Levine responded guardedly to a biographer: "That wonderful self-sweet mother would have given her life to have her son home and near, but you may know that was impossible. . . . I can't say any more. . . . There was no one in this world . . . that had the kindness that boy had for anyone that was sick, or that loved a mother as he did. My tears for him and Pearl will be with us forever, . . . heartbreaking young years. . . ."

Ida Mae and her husband, Abe Levine, spent days "asking and walking night and day in the Village," and finally they found Clifford, half alive, starving, unhappy, sitting in the midst of "a thousand newspapers." They begged him to come home "for his sainted mother's sake, as it was her twenty-fifth wedding anniversary."

To the Levines he appeared to be in dread of seeing his father, but "finally he agreed for Pearl's sake, and we cleaned him up a little and took him in the back of our car to Philly. When we got there, he wouldn't walk in the house. It was heartbreaking." He went instead to the home of Tante Esther and Uncle Israel.

Soon after this humiliating trip to Philadelphia he writes to Bill Kozlenko that he has been "going through some sort of catharsis, some transition" which he does not understand, and that his creative work is at a standstill. His thinking is disorderly, he keeps pawning and redeeming his typewriter, he cannot pay his bill at the Circle Hotel, is drinking too much, and in another letter relates that he hasn't "slept a dreamless unhaunted sleep for months." At dawn he had found himself lying on the tiled bathroom floor, which "the mind had made . . . into a dream of a marble slab that fitted me with the precision of a tombstone." Continuing the dream, "I turned . . . to Cybele incarnated in a breasted woman. And in the dark I found that Cybele had shrunk to having the soul of a penny whistle."

Finally, the "verbal pile-up inside" having become unendurable, he impulsively writes to Cheryl Crawford that "my fingers begin to pain with desire to sit here for the better part of the night. I was never one to deny the potency of the creep of words . . . I must (oh must) justify this Jew: I really want to write to Cheryl Crawford; it doesn't matter why. Other times, in other ways, I will recommend myself to your attention . . . oh Diomedes,* why this constant justification? 'Afraid,' answers the counterpoint; I hear 'afraid' echoed in B-minor. . . ." He thinks that he may at last be becoming a man, "but I miss the self-pitying child . . . of course an actor never grows up."

The Millsteins' niece, Sylvia Hoffman, recalled visiting him in this vermin-ridden hotel room, concluding that "he had gone nuts. He was

___

* Greek legend: A Greek warrior at the siege of Troy who helped Odysseus steal the statue of Athena.

thin, wild-eyed, and desperately lonely . . . the whole thing was a horror. I was stunned that his father wouldn't give him a penny, and worried that he would kill himself with the Virginia Dare stuff he was drinking. When we went to the subway, he asked me quite seriously what I would say if he jumped in front of a train. I got hysterical." It was clear to her he was in the throes of a severe crisis, half realizing that he might be fatally over-committed to being an actor and that a new integration had to occur if he was to survive.

Recalling what he termed his "fit of depression," Odets thought that during the course of it he began to "understand really what writing was about in the sense of the personal affiliation to the material." He began a short story "about some young kid violinist" who was deprived of his violin by a hotel owner who kept it because he couldn't pay his bill. Odets thought he could average a thousand words a day on this story, but found to his despair that he was unable to manage this.

In the short story a "marooned kid" reminisces about his mother and his hard-working sister, and "although," Odets said, "I was not that kid, and I didn't have that kind of mother . . . or sister, I did fill the skin and outline with my own personal feeling, and made that kind of triple identification . . . and for the first time I realized what creative writing was, because, *there is no creative writing if it does not express the state of being of the writer himself*, *no matter what skins or masks he puts that state of being into*" (italics mine). His insight did not extend to an aware-ness of the role he assigns to his father in this fantasy: the hotel owner who takes the boy's means of creative expression (the violin) from him —as forfeit—unless he can "pay his bill." The same symbol recurs in his play *Golden Boy*.

Soon after this one, he commenced a short story of a pianist who goes to war and loses his right hand—again a loss of his creative "tool."

As he began to resolve his depression by finding "personal affilia-tions" with the life around him, he listened with sharp curiosity to his Circle Hotel neighbors talking just beyond the piece of burlap which served as the door to his room, becoming convinced he was living in a strange tragicomic world. Much moved by an unemployed young specialty dancer —probably the "mask" for Cleo in his play *Rocket to the Moon*—he lis-tened to her account of how *she* had lost confidence in *her* ability: it had happened in a Miami nightclub when a drunken Babbitt had dropped an olive into her navel as, in an exhibition of professional skill, she back-somersaulted near his table. Odets told her he could well understand how crushing such an indignity could be, but urged her to go on with her work and to trust her ability.

It was more difficult, however, to take such counsel unto himself and to trust his own materials and the self-healing process of his writing for the making of what William Gibson has called "interior history." Yet in this gloomy spring he began to be convinced that he must write "out of the kind of person you are," not as you should be, or "as another kind of person." Before this year's end it would come as a nourishing and freeing revelation that this was precisely the working premise of the "method acting" of Stanislavsky's Moscow Art Theatre, and of a gestating new theatre group to be revealed to him by Harold Clurman.

In the meantime, with the savings from his Theatre Guild tour de-pleted, he once again signed up (for the last time) as an "assistant social and dramatic director"—at the intellectual-Zionist Camp Scopus, "an adult camp of distinction on Trout Lake near Lake George in the Adiron-dacks"—and, filled with the passive fantasy of "becoming a sundial," he responds to the formidable masculine energies of the sun, frequently re-peating his motto, "Sine Sole Silio" (without sun I am silent).

He is convinced that in the "distance of Nature . . . I'll find the lost part of me* . . . the old songs will grow again in me, for without songs and singing I am lost. It comes to me that I don't want to be lost as Karl Franck [the hero of his unfinished novel] becomes lost." Writing to Kozlenko, still languishing in Philadelphia, Clifford quotes from his novel, to the writing of which he has returned:

> And in the end, when the singing years were done, he turned from being a Man and grew to the loneliness and silence of being a Great Hunger. He had finally found the philosopher's stone, a stone of such flinty substance that it could cut thru anything. On its polished, antique surface were imperishably graven the words: "We know only Silence. Why do you reach? There is only Silence."
>
> "This is truth," Karl said in his heart, "but perhaps Silence may have its music." Yet it could be seen in his eyes, sauternine [sic] eyes, that he knew he was bounded by the finite and that the infinite was a metaphysical term. On the face of the cosmic compass stood the word "finite" forever.
>
> So in the songless years, before the dark came, Karl was bitterly content to remain the questionable entity that all men must be. The search for the lost part of him mirrored futility, and he was sick with staring futility in the face. He knew: The lost part is Completion: Completion is Death.
>
> So in the last days Karl Franck was not a Man, but a Great Hunger.

This twenty-three-year-old boy, sitting in the clutter of his shabby hotel room and worrying about his receding hairline, would have been frightened indeed had he been aware of his clairvoyance about himself.

Before he left the Circle Hotel for Camp Scopus, he had met a shy, fragile actress about his own age named Hortense Alden, a most unusual young lady, then playing the part of Myrrhina in *Lysistrata* at the 44th Street Theatre. Becoming obsessed with her as he had been with Sylvia Field, he wrote dozens of letters to her, typed secretly in the small hours of the morning.

Forty years later her essential quality, recorded in 1930 by Odets, would still be apparent to a biographer: a literate, delicately lovely, clear-skinned, small-boned lady in a bohemian combination of black velvet cloche and white denim windbreaker with black skirt and stockings, she carried in a brown paper bag a volume of Shakespeare's plays. Explain-ing, "I am a very shy person," she refused to come up to my hotel room for an interview, preferring to sit in the public lobby. With the abrupt, precise movements of a wary woodland creature, *she* conducted the in-terview around the possible motives for my writing such a life story, ex-pressing the hope it would not be so "false a story" as Hemingway's post-humous *Moveable Feast*. Saying, "I don't know that I would ever talk to you about Clifford, for lots of reasons," she quickly and astutely summed up his life work, bringing the interview swiftly to a close with an imper-sonal discussion of the "dehumanization" attendant on the superhighway and big business.

By now the widow of another writer, she permitted herself the cau-

---

* Seven years later Odets would marry a girl who felt herself to be on an identi-cal search, and who described her incompleteness in almost identical language.

tious observation that "writers are hard to live with" and the innocent comment "I love a dead man, a man I never knew—Marcel Proust." Self-educated, beautiful, perceptive, sensitive, frightened, and successful early, Hortense Alden, then in her sixties—while suspiciously withholding all specific information—communicated clearly the fact that young Odets must have seen in her an idealized mirror-image of himself—like Sylvia Field a successful actress, but a more appropriate and accessible temporary partner. We do not know whether Odets knew he was in competition for her with author James T. Farrell.

From the first hours of his arrival at Camp Scopus, which he says is "filled with wild Hebrews,"◖ he longs to tell her that his handkerchief is still scented with the "wild bitter fruit flavor" of her amber-colored perfume, and his memory full of the beloved little "pits" behind her ears. Typing under a naked bulb in the camp office at one o'clock in the morning, in a cloud of gnats and "winging moths," he is obsessed with the mysteries of life and death, and decides that the only significance these insects can have is "to feed spiders."

He has created a small universe of snails in a sand-filled jar and sees "a whole tribe eaten by another." He has no difficulty, he writes, in understanding crickets,◖ "those musicians of the darker grass," their "singing dispositions" being for "lads with dreams." He knows this deluge of letters issues from an acute loneliness, and he pleads with Hortense to "sometimes think of me darling. . . . And for Christ's sake, write or I perish for a kindly word that not be given."

At this safe distance he can daily express his passionate attachment to her, now and again letting slip an ambiguity of his sexual identity: ". . . were I some sort of male Salome I should ask for the mouth of Hortense, nothing more. Where in this lousy dank night is the Herod who would want Clifford to dance for him?" He pleads with her to "make visions in me" as though she were indeed his impregnating personal Muse.

For all his complaints, this is assuredly a better summer than the last, and he sees "the promise of myself . . . with purpose, moving with a slow (less romantic, to be sure) deliberation," adding that "with each healing comes a new maturity," and he has an outline for a new short story:

"The Spirit of the Crane" I call it. No dear, it has nothing to do with Stephen, but with a bird, a grey crane that was killed with gun shot by a lad in a boat. He was one of those stupid individuals who kills any wild thing that he sees and he shot the crane from a boat while I was rowing. Then he proudly showed it around, holding it by the wing tips so that everyone could see what a great boy he was for having killed so large a bird. An hour later he threw it down the cellar and forgot it had ever existed.

But I liked to think, for weeks afterwards, that the spirit of the crane hovered over our lake. Sometimes, when the morning mists swirled over the spread of that lake, I liked to think that I saw the grey crane flap his wings and recede flyingly from the bow of my boat. I liked to think that any strange sound in the heavy nights was the crane's ululation, its despair made articulate to Nature who would surely punish the deed. Then, when summer was late, and pestilence came upon our camp, I knew that the grey crane was satisfied, that

◖ 9.4.
◖ 9.5.

I would never distinguish again the flapping figure of the mists, that nothing would cry in the night, and that one more winged creature had found rest.

I think, as an interesting factual, last remark, that the bird killer chopped off his trigger finger a month later while hewing down a young sapling because he wanted to make a rustic walking stick.

Again he is preoccupied with the theme of the brutal vulgarian who shoots down the "winged creature." This time the predator is punished by losing *his* power (to shoot).◖

Odets' roommate this summer at Zionist Camp Scopus, Mordecai Baumann, recalled him as a brooding "loner" with a friendly—sometimes knowing—smile, but never a laugh. He seemed always to be watching and listening: "A lot of his quality was in his eyes—unwavering, as though looking through you. It was as though he were searching for himself and hoping to find it in somebody else."

The management was not pleased with his aloofness from the female guests, but felt helpless to alter this as, by contract, only the waiters were required to dance with them. Many believed him to be homosexual, and were confirmed in this opinion when he attempted—by feminizing his part—to get some humor into his performance as the director in *The Potboilers*. When, however, the well-known actress Hortense Alden came up to visit him, it was decided he was probably straight.

As for his acting prowess, his colleagues thought it a shame he was so self-conscious, because with his beautiful voice, his curly light hair, and his handsome chiseled profile, he could have been a silent-screen matinee idol. They thought him only fair as an accused spy in O'Neill's *In the Zone*.

His duties in this extension of the Catskill Borscht Belt included producing variety shows which combined staff and guest talent. For these shows he relied heavily on three young people who seemed to have promise: a young dancer named Pauline Koner; his roommate, Mordecai, a baritone; and an ardent young Zionist named Meyer Levin. Also he had brought along, as an actress, Sylvia Hoffman, the niece of the Millsteins from the Bronx. As a sideline, "he was in charge of the horse-racing nights, with the social staff cutting in for about one-fourth of the total pay-off, on a rough pari-mutuel basis."

Once again his real life began late at night when the guests had gone to bed and the social hall was free. There, as in previous summers, he would commence by pounding out loud and mournful chords on the piano. The eighteen-year-old Baumann, seeing Romain Rolland's *Beethoven* under his arm, decided that Odets saw himself as the great and suffering romantic composer. "He was protective of me as if I were a younger brother or even like Beethoven's nephew—I think he liked the idea I was a singer and had won a scholarship to Juilliard." Odets' identification with Beethoven provided the theme for one of his earliest abortive plays.

Later he was seen sitting alone on the beach and still later in the

◖ 9.6.

camp office, either typing letters or jotting bits of dialogue heard that day on long strips of paper with which he covered the wall alongside his bed. He said these strips would one day appear in a novel or a "creative biography." He did not talk of writing plays and discussed the work of Tolstoy, not of Chekhov.

Gordon Lebowitz, athletic director for Camp Scopus, was astonished five years later to hear his own sentences, recorded on one of these long strips, in the mouth of an offstage voice in *Waiting for Lefty.*❨ This summer, and always, Odets' porous senses sucked in raw materials—photographing, recording, and storing them until he would transpose them into the meaningfully authentic images, sounds, symbols, and themes of his world. It was always a creative transposition, not a journalistic reportage.

He talked a great deal about his father this summer, but often "as if he were just an acquaintance, with amused pleasure," Baumann recalled. "When I met his father, it seemed he thought of himself as quite a guy—especially in regard to women. He was sort of like Willy Loman in *Death of a Salesman* in his blue jacket, white flannel pants, and sport shoes. They were somehow not like father and son. His father acted more like an older brother, and you could see this somehow tickled Clifford. L.J. was constantly taking all the credit for his son's accomplishments, even his good looks."*

On the one occasion when his sister Genevieve came to visit, Odets took "a kind of personal responsibility for her. He often expressed the hope that medical science would one day heal her disability." A crumbling program tells us that he permitted his younger sister, Florence, to come, too, at least long enough to be one of the "ladies" in *The Mikado, or the Town of Titipu,* directed by both Baumann and Odets.

In this Camp Scopus summer Odets steadily mourns the mortality of all life, but, more important, the fact that he has "lost wonderment." It troubles him that, except for "a few flashes," he has been unmoved by the "oestrus of a thousand whirring moths . . . or by the clear three-noted calls of field larks who rise to meet the sun." Not once has he "turned up a stone to see the crawling world underneath." It reassures him, however, on the occasion when he is deeply stirred by a luna moth, "who lives for a night . . . there is birth, and mating and death all of a moonlit night. The diaphanous spread of pale green wing lusts for life, gives life and dies with that giving." Moved by this moth, so "serene, young and already death shadowed," he concludes that he himself, after all, still has "the pulse of life," and writes a poem which wonders, "Oh, which way do we turn / When the dusk shall be gone / And the black stuff of night / Immures us without the light of a dream?"

He knows he has found in Hortense—in view of whose propped-up picture he writes these letters—a resonant audience, a girl who loves language and has written to him, in gratitude: "You gave me pity and kindness and wit and desperation." He expects her to understand him when he says that Nature's "divine unguent" is not healing him as he had hoped, and that he envies the brave, stiff, "green sappy stalks" of the phlox as it is dying. Full of gin, he has had a strange experience with these white flowers:

❨ 9.7.

* Whenever his son was earning money, L.J. apparently could afford to relax his terrifying and contemptuous assaults on him and even encourage a kind of competitive, "brotherly" camaraderie. After Clifford's death L.J. said to me that the title of this biography *must* be "Clifford Odets: How a Father Raised a Genius."

Up on the hill (I stood there in the fresh taunting air) there is a clump of phlox. I know there are red ones and other colours, for I've seen them by day, but now only the white ones stand out in the fresh darkness of the night. I pressed my hands to them, kissed them many times and lost my eyes in their fragrant wetness, and they were sweeter than flesh, more vinous than wine, as gracious and healing as your mouth. I stood there with those white flowers until suddenly I knew that I wanted to destroy them, to tear them off their branches: that urge came on me in a swoop, with a shivering fullness; and my hands would not be contained, I could not keep my fingers from clawing and pressing the blossoms to my palms with a crushing force.

And later in the same letter, "Darling, darling, I am so queer for flowers!"

In this episode, to be repeated literally by him on his deathbed, stood the distillation of one set of contrarieties within him: flower and destroyer of flowers, he would enact this scene in many forms in his life and in his work.

It pleases him that he can write Hortense he is immune to the "rapacious and predatory" females with which Camp Scopus is filled, shames him that he is drinking "to maudlinity" and crying in the grass. He sends her long poems, one marked "Opus 24," called "The Minuet of Futility: Some Variations on an Old, Old Theme." After an opening "Andante," there follow stanzas for violas, flutes, French horns, violins, bassoons, a tuba, an oboe, and even "a trombone choir," which proclaims: "Johann, Johann prolific and serene, / Wolfgang Mozart white-boned and clean / Ludwig, oh Fury, what did you mean? / 'Weep,' said the Music, 'Life's obscene!'"

In another, called "Frogs: A Truly Poetical Subject," he concludes, after describing these "inanimate green lumps": "This is Nature's secret: / That from the greatest ugliness / Springs the greatest Grace!"

In mid-August, just twenty-four and exhausted by his new duties as social director—and commiserating with Hortense over a mood of melancholy and a sore back—he writes her, "I've had such things the matter with me, and I know the resultant pain (But I always manage to get some devilish, sadistic pleasure out of pain—I tell you there are all sorts of queernesses about me!)." He sleeps, he adds, with his "hand touching your letter on the chair beside me."

Soon, for the amusement of the bridge-playing guests, "three of us men will dress up as women and parade around like three lala boys in drag"; but in less than three weeks, the silly potboilers over, he will be back in New York to make love to her and to take her for a ride on the Staten Island ferry. He is restless, irritable, and impatient.

A brief note to her with the Hemingway salutation "Dear Baby" reports, for the first time, a piece of physical violence, a fragment within him of his pugilist father, usually under strict control:

I am very depressed, Baby, because I hit a poor man in the eye this afternoon. He tried so bravely to smile after I hit him (he wouldn't cry, being twenty-six and a "man of the world") that I'm sure I'll see his face for years and years. And I was so wrong in hitting him, so vain, so stinkingly smug and satisfied with my strength, that now, hours later, I am ashamed and feel in myself a crawling of repugnance for what I did.

Ah, but I was furious . . . he threw a book at me and called me a God damned bastard . . . and then I go ahead and really act like one!

And once again he mourns his defensive toughening. Addressing her as "Dear Lovely," he sends his romantic valedictory for this summer:

Well, the summer is dying and all over there are portents of its death. . . . I can remember when I saw all the portents with inward tears, when a fluttering leaf could sting my eyes with almost weeping, when I was hurt to despair (yes) that flowers had gone to fruit and seed.

It is different now: what I see leaves me untouched. I see and am left unwounded. . . . An apathetic silence is left. Pity me, Lovely, for having lost tenderness. Be afraid for me that I can not be hurt. And give tonight, to your gods, one small prayer for this lad, a prayer that he may know, at least, pity.

Well, the summer is dying; the whole land wastes without wailing. Only the crickets* and the cicadas make their grief articulate. . . . Day and night, rainy times too, there are voiceful crickets, but only the nights know their full singing strength: they are less afraid of night. Night is a Great Heart; Night is a Great Mother.

Obsessed, pained, indeed infatuated—as poets have ever been—with the evolutionary chasm between the power of man's divine and boundless self-reflective awareness and the helpless terror of his animal mortality, he vainly tries to persuade himself (and us who read his careful carbon-copy record) that he is no longer wounded by the poignancy of the timeless life cycle, and is therefore only to be pitied for this loss of sensitivity. He is struggling to persuade himself that in death there are—after all—forgetfulness, silence, rest, peace, and comfort in Earth and in Night, the "Great Mother."

Finally, at summer's end, "wearied with standing alone on this stage that knows no ringing down of curtains," he feels small and alone and bursts forth, "Ah, why are you not here, Lovely Lady? . . . Next week, Lovely Lady. . . . And another kiss." And so, once again, back to New York and to the terror of being forced—by his waning funds—to return to his father's house in Philadelphia.

---

* Here again, the tiny night singer who breaks the silence with his "night music," title of Odets' last play for the Group Theatre. This is the first time he labels it an articulation of grief.

Chapter Ten

*I regard the Group Theatre as a kind
of outpost on a main line of American
experience which not only has not
come to an end but has barely begun.
If the impulse that gave birth to the
Group were to die out, the result not
merely would spell tragedy for a
handful of artists and workers in and
around the theatre, but would constitute something like a fatal wound in
the American spirit.*

HAROLD CLURMAN

*I'm sick of this dervish dance they've
got us doing on steel springs and a
General Electric motor. When it stops
—as it must—there will be dissolution and devastation; everything will
become as frightfully blank as today
everything is fiercely congested. . . .
Perhaps to rush out of line is to invite disaster. If so, let it come. . . .
We must help one another find our
common ground; we must build our
house on it, arrange it as a dwelling
place for the whole family of decent
humanity.*

HAROLD CLURMAN

FORTIFIED with his Camp Scopus pay, Odets joined the lines of Borscht
Belt performers at the casting offices in New York. With rare visits home,
he watched his money dwindle and his bill at the bedbug-ridden Circle
Hotel mount. Herman Kobland recalls his room, reeking of kerosene, as
enough to make even the healthiest person want to commit suicide. Odets,

in autobiographical notes, sums up this abode quite simply: "the disgrace!"

He found temporary relief from his melancholy paralysis on Second Avenue in the heart of the Yiddish theatre district. Lee Kozlenko, already committed though not yet married to Odets' Philadelphia friend Bill, recalls Odets taking her to the Café Royale, the hangout of the Jewish actors and intellectuals. Odets stood out among these Adlers, Schwartzes, and Tomashevskys with his golden hair and blue eyes, a handsome Nordic specimen. Smitten by both his physical beauty and his intellectual power, Lee was tongue-tied and withdrawn. Like Sylvia Field, she felt stupid in his presence, but so hypnotized by his discourse that she trailed along, silent, as, talking steadily, he led her on a long walk under the Third Avenue "El."

It seemed to her he was feeling guilty toward his friend Bill, and was thus simultaneously seductive and withholding. He told her how cruel and destructive he could be with women, and she was concerned that maybe his interest in her was psychological, perhaps clinical—or even that maybe Clifford liked to play with people. It seems that with the threat of geographic closeness, his relationship with Hortense Alden had instantly cooled and he was again lonely.

Soon after this, Odets invited Kozlenko to come and share his single cot in the Circle Hotel and to bring records. Each slept on the very edge of the cot because, according to Kozlenko, they couldn't bear to touch each other. Again his moods were black and he was preoccupied with thoughts of suicide. Their joint income consisted of Clifford's meager poker winnings and a few secret contributions from his mother, until he got a bit part in a new Theatre Guild play, *Roar China*.

In this year it did not appear remarkable that the successful and respectable Theatre Guild should ask Herbert Biberman*—later to become one of the ten famed Hollywood casualties of the periodic American hunt for Communists—to direct an anti-imperialist Soviet play he had seen in Moscow at the fabled Meyerhold Theatre. Both Cheryl Crawford, still the Guild's casting director, and Harold Clurman, in the play-reading department, found it an interesting project although difficult to cast and to produce. It needed mainly Chinese actors, and the action required that the uncurtained stage be flooded with sufficient water to float a facsimile of a British destroyer whose great cannon were to play out over the audience. Nevertheless, with the blessing of the gentlemanly Philip Moeller—fifteen years earlier an insurgent who had damned the commercialism of the American theatre—it opened on October 27 with "Clifford Odetts"† as one of the sailors from H.M.S. *Europa*. Biberman would recall him for his readiness to perform and for the totality of presence he lent to whatever he did. Although he had little or nothing to say in the play, he was a whirlwind of activity over the stage, the ship, and in the water. Despite gargantuan efforts, *Roar China* closed in two months.

Late in 1930 he was cast in a Theatre Guild play initially called *In the Meantime*. A work by Claire and Paul Sifton attacking the power of "the yellow press" to stimulate crime, it had a distinctly crusading tone. As a minor character, boastfully described by him years later as the "juvenile lead," Odets was paid $100 every Friday—a great deal of

---

* The Biberman cousins Herbert and Abner, from a wealthy Philadelphia dress-manufacturing family, would be held up to Clifford by his mother as models of deportment and success.

† Before 1935 Odets' name was invariably misspelled on programs: Odette, Audette, Oldett, Odetts. He would later jot on an envelope: "I may seem like Odets to you; to myself I am Gorodetsky."

money in 1931—for delivering his twenty-one sides of what he told Hortense Alden was balderdash. More important than his salary was his sense of being on the rise in the eyes of Philip Moeller, who was delighted by a critic's remark that Odets' playing was "completely understood and completely realized." He had developed a schoolboy crush on Moeller—a recluse generally thought to be homosexual—whom he now commenced to visit for long talks in the book-lined, record-filled, elegant apartment on Central Park South where Moeller often sat, a gray shawl about his shoulders, long cigarette holder in hand, listening to classical music. Moeller, a charming, cultured, intelligent man born of old New York upper-crust on fashionable lower Fifth Avenue, was by now secure in his eccentricities. Having failed in his aspiration to become a playwright, he had been a founder of the rebellious Washington Square Players, and had then established, mainly with Eugene O'Neill, the role of the director as kingpin in the American theatre, edging out the producer and set designer, hitherto the centers of power. Magnetized both by Moeller's personal qualities and by his unique position of power, Odets commenced to write long, intense, self-conscious letters to him several times a week, by turns tender and intellectually passionate. There are clear echoes in this relationship of his earlier troubled contact with radio announcer Floyd Neale, from whose physical approaches, he told Herman, he had fled. Moeller often discussed with him the difficulty of cutting a new "vexed" play by O'Neill in which the playwright, portraying himself as a young woman, struggles with withdrawal, guilt, and suicide. Moeller was doing for O'Neill what Clurman would later do for Odets. The final script would soon be delivered by O'Neill, with the title *Mourning Becomes Electra*. Odets felt honored that Moeller discussed such important issues with him.

On the eve of his departure for the pre-New York tryout of the Sifton play, Odets writes, in a drunken letter to Hortense Alden—now acting in *Grand Hotel*—that he is "doing the dirtiest trick that I've done in many years: I'm taking your phonograph with me for three weeks on the road . . . but I am desparation [sic] itself . . . and I know that you understand desparation." He will open in Baltimore and go from there to Washington and Pittsburgh. Assuring her that her phonograph will keep him from becoming an alcoholic or doing something even worse, he wonders whether this nepenthe in his ear will kill him as Hamlet's father was killed. A striking fantasy this is indeed, in view of the fact that snake venom was poured into the ear, and that Odets' next sentence says, "The music is Strauss' Don Juan with phallus erecti . . . and I will die with branding irons in my brain." The fantasy of being a painfully (but pleasurably) penetrated—and fulfilled—woman is on the surface.

A few days later, eating tabs of mocha chocolate, he writes her from Baltimore that he is lonesome to bitterness watching the pairs of dancers in a room off the lobby of his hotel. All he can do is "write you cold words that are so much dead ash immediately they are gone from me." How much more than ten thousand of his words is said by the lift of an eye, one pressure of the hand, or even a bar of Chopin. "Poor, poor is a man with words and nothing else. . . ."

Unaware of his necessity to starve himself literally and emotionally, a pattern frequently found in potentially creative young people "in order to let the grosser weeds die out" and "make way for the growth of their inner garden," he devoted himself to a period of asceticism in the effort to prove a total self-sufficiency. He was determined to believe he was an "island, entire of itselfe." To Moeller he writes that he will be father, he will be mother, and his works in this self-contained universe will be his children:

> Once I wrote something about a neuter-sexed artist who will develop from an androgynous human until finally all artists shall be born sexless. Only in that time . . . will lads cease to write such stuff as this. . . . Men who love men will go down into earth and from them will come men who love neither women or other men . . . all of their sexual stuffs will be sublimated in their work.

The price he would pay, in common with other creators, for this divine independence was a chronic difficulty, except through his art, in establishing intimate connections with other living beings.

At the Gaiety Delicatessen on 47th Street, after his opening performance at the Guild Theatre in the Sifton play, now called *Midnight,* Clifford asked an old Philadelphia friend, Ivan Black,—a Harvard-educated architect turned journalist—what he thought of his future as an actor. "I told him," Black recalled, " 'you'll never be an actor. On stage you have comedy eyes.' " Black saw that he had wounded his friend with this comment, and so added, "But don't be disheartened, you *can* become a playwright." Odets was much impressed by Black's genuine erudition, given extra weight by his powerful, athletic body, and by the fact that Black had had the strength to overcome a siege of Prohibition-period blindness; and so he fed Black's negative judgment of his acting into the hopper of his growing self-doubt.

Unaware that *Midnight* would close after forty-eight performances, Odets decided to move with Black (then an unemployed newspaperman) into a furnished room on West 82nd Street, east of Columbus Avenue. Although they had to share a bathroom in the hall, it was a relief to live in this old brownstone house with bay windows and mahogany sliding doors. Black recalls they existed on $40 a week, Clifford sending the remaining $60 to his mother to hide in her sewing basket for her "escape fund." It seemed to Black that Odets adored his mother and had no use for his father.

Odets tried hard not to dwell on Black's low opinion of his acting and, as a $100-a-week juvenile occupying one of the better dressing rooms, he relished for the first time, however briefly, some sense of importance. This was enhanced when one of the two play-readers of the Theatre Guild, an intense, darkly glowering young man with a roundish face and long sideburns, named Harold Clurman, came to his dressing room after a Saturday matinee and, as Odets was removing his make-up, began to talk to him. From behind his back he heard Clurman say in a shy voice —with a speech impediment—that he had come at Cheryl Crawford's suggestion and that he was inviting several Broadway actors to come to some meetings of "our group" because "we are going to make a kind of theatre."

Flattered by this visit from a man he regarded as learned and important, and mystified by his extravagant and passionate pronouncements that theatre must grow "in relation to a society, from significant and authentic life-experience," Odets responded to Clurman's tentative exploration by showing off a little. He dismissed the acting technique of the Lunts and, warming to Clurman's query, "So, what *is* your idea of acting?" responded, he recalled, this way: "Well, if you listen to much music, let's say, like Beethoven Quartets, that kind of polyphonic interweaving—" As Odets continued in this vein, Clurman regarded him gravely in the make-up

mirror until Odets burst into laughter, explaining, "I'm laughing because I don't know what the hell I'm talking about." It was then that
Clurman issued his invitation to attend the meetings now being held at
his room in the Hotel Meurice on 58th Street, but soon to remove to the
Steinway Hall studio of his composer friend Aaron Copland. There "our
group" would become the Group Theatre.

Although neither man knew anything of the history of the other,
there is no doubt that even in this first encounter, by a complex and
only partly conscious process—of the sort that makes instant lovers or
antagonists—they dimly sensed the significance each would have for the
other. Soon Odets would be saying of the intelligent, idealistic, fervent
man eyeing him in the make-up mirror, "Harold is my favorite character
outside of fiction." Much later, embittered, he would complain—as he
would with many older men—of being crippled by what he felt to be a
pontifical, engulfing, and exploitative paternalism: "Harold, with people,
is like a dog with bones. He licks 'em, bites 'em, chews 'em, eats 'em, and
when he is through with them, he moves away." Odets' bouquet as well
as his accusation would many times be relayed to Clurman, who would
forever regard the latter as unjust, but who—with a characteristic objectivity—would himself tell it to Odets' biographer.

In all significant human relationships there exists a dovetailing
which precludes a simple definition of villain and victim. The weight of
evidence here points to the probability that Odets' lifelong struggle with
the impulse to truckle in the face of power—a struggle which, learned
in terror at his father's knee, would leave him in turn cowering, murderous, or both—was at the heart of his accusation against Clurman. Clurman's need to control and to keep things going, though undoubtedly
strong, appears a less malignant character defect. Ultimately to become
one of America's leading directors—and, as a drama critic, a penetrating
cultural historian and philosopher—Clurman was already beginning
to exhibit some of the characteristics that caused actress-director Juleen
Compton later to say, "Harold is my substitute for a good society." This
included his conviction that it behooved him to pull the best out of others,
and to use it in the service of Art.

Harold Edgar Clurman,* born in 1901, was, like Odets, the child of Russian-Jewish immigrants. Quite unlike Odets, as the youngest of three
sons he was the apple of his physician father's eye and later "the staff of
his old age." A dedicated, sensitive man, Samuel Clurman had struggled
(like Odets' beloved Dr. M. V. Leof) to become a general practitioner in
the ghetto of New York's Lower East Side. He would steal time, however,
to take his six-year-old son to the Yiddish theatre on Grand Street, where the
child would watch rapt as Jacob Adler, father of Stella—later Harold's
bride—enacted tragic heroes from Shakespeare, Tolstoy, and Gorky. At
the Grand Street Theatre, a social center, the immigrant audiences would

---

* Sometimes he would use the nom de plume Harold Edgar or Harold Eager,
but, unlike the name Gorodetsky, the name Clurman was never fragmented or disguised. This says something about the integration and self-acceptance of the Clurman
family.

enthusiastically convene to gossip and to gain surcease from their problems by giving them voice.

Like Clifford's father a writer manqué, Dr. Clurman was given to frequent periods of deep melancholy. Impractical in the financial aspects of his medical practice as well as in his rearing of his sons, he would impulsively take young Harold to Grand Street to see such plays as *Uriel Acosta,* not because it was Art, but because it was fun. In a mixture of affectionate amusement, respect, and love, the son—in his sixties—would say of him, "My father had not educated me properly. He never showed me a dollar bill; he just sent them to me. It was quite a shock later to learn I was supposed to make a living." Odets would at first find Clurman's naïveté and helplessness in practicalities an appropriate attitude for the man he considered the only real intellectual in the American theatre. Clurman's attitude was not unlike that of the learned rabbi in a Hebraic community who takes it for granted, as do his wife and his disciples, that, being a fount of spiritual nourishment, he can dispense with physical adroitness and worldly accomplishment. The contrast between Clurman and Moeller cannot have escaped Odets.

Quite unlike L. J. Odets, who was convinced that life was indeed printed on dollar bills, Samuel Clurman was improvident and, according to his son, alien to the American scene. In his modest consulting room there were portraits of Shelley and Goethe and hundreds of books. Spiritual affluence was taken for granted by the Clurmans, but they would have laughed at L. J. Odets' imperious need to own the first car and the first radio on Beck Street. Young Harold did not, however, as he later recalled, draw conclusions from this about self-sacrificing, idealistic "Art with a capital A or Culture with a capital C." He learned rather that it is not necessary to be in the arts to be an artist, and that a person must learn what means most to him in life. Having established thus, like Emerson's hero, a self-respecting and immovable center, he can better trust his impulse, "whether that impulse lead him to shoveling manure on a farm, to painting pictures, or to making creative business 'deals.'" Ultimately Clurman would conclude from his experience that the esthetic need to join with the object derives from the same biological necessity as that which impels one human to join with another, with a painting, or, indeed, with a tree. He would spend a rich, sensuous—if often troubled—life making such connections, and would say in his sixth decade, "I do not say life is good; I say life is life," concluding that although "life is an adventure, it's no picnic."

The more evident it grew that Dr. Clurman's medical practice precluded his even trying to be a writer, he became increasingly irritable and critical of everything ugly, exploitative, shallow, competitive, fraudulent, and ruthless in the materialist American dream. Often his criticisms issued in a fierce wrangle with his wife, Bertha, and Harold—unlike Clifford, who was often dismissed by his Babbitt father as a kind of idiot—was routinely appealed to by both his parents as a young Solomon.

To his father Harold would by turns defend America and his mother by reciting what seemed noble chapters of history and repeating, "But she's a woman, Pop." He would beg of his mother, on the other hand, that she try to see the validity in some of his father's arguments and, above all, be patient with him. Harold steadily maintained this judicious parental role until, at the age of seventy-five, Dr. Clurman took his own life. Harold's role as preserver of a family and its peace was carried out not only in his home but as a mediating teenager in the organization of neighborhood theatricals and eventually as one of the three directors of the Group Theatre. Odets, grateful at first for Clurman's parental appreciation and illuminations, would ultimately shout bitterly at him, "Everyone's a child to you!" The essential identity of the director as "parent"—in contrast to the actor as "child"—has often been observed by clinicians.

In his early twenties, supported by his father's special respect for French culture—a respect characteristic of Russian intellectuals—Clurman became part of the general exodus to Paris. Many years later a tiny red ribbon in the lapel of his boulevardier's suit of dark silk would identify him as a Chevalier of France's Legion of Honor.

When he had completed a thesis on French drama at the Sorbonne, he attended closely to Copeau's talk of "serious theatre" and to his friend Aaron Copland's discussions of the critical necessity to find in America the "musical equivalent for our contemporary tempo and activity." For the first time in his life Clurman found himself deeply dissatisfied with theatre as an expressive form: "Either," he thought, "there is something inferior in the theatre *per se* or there is something wrong about the practical theatre of today that escapes me. I can't live without the theatre, but I can't live with it. The theatre gives itself lofty graces, claims a noble lineage, but has no more dimension than a bordello!"

With such disquiet he returned to the United States in 1924, feeling that the writing world had more dignity but that the theatre was somehow more available, and that he must accumulate some firsthand experience. The experience began as a $10-a-week extra in a play of Stark Young's produced by the new firm of Macgowan-Jones-O'Neill. He later recalled the inarticulate Robert Edmond Jones' impotent struggle, as a leader, to state his private grief that in this group he could perceive no dream, no revelation, and he recalled also "Gene O'Neill's silence."

Morbidly shy and stammering, Clurman found it difficult to land any kind of acting job. From his own account it would appear that only the persistence of his pleas finally so touched the heart of the Guild's kindly general stage manager, Philip Loeb,* that Loeb hired him as an extra in *Caesar and Cleopatra* to open the Guild's new theatre on 52nd Street. At a special performance there of a Pirandello play Clurman watched the effective, if "disagreeable," performance of a short, intense, pale-faced young man of intellectual demeanor who spoke with a faint foreign accent. Clurman found himself deeply interested in the face of this actor, which expressed not only a keen intelligence but also, as Clurman termed it, a suffering, ascetic control, with something old, withdrawn, and lofty about it.

As stage manager of the Guild's *Garrick Gaieties* in 1925, Clurman made friends with this young Russian Jew, Lee Strasberg, who was already concentrated on the technique of acting as is a "jeweler over the inner mechanism of a watch." Strasberg, too, was dissatisfied with the American theatre, but in a quite different way. Clurman learned from him the difference between literature and that group phenomenon which is theatre. By the time of his visit to Odets' dressing room Clurman had concluded, in continuous and passionate discussion with Strasberg, that what was needed was a total re-education of American theatre artists to include playwrights, directors, actors, musicians, lighting men, scene designers, costumers—a new vision truly indigenous to American life.

Still restless when the 1926 version of the *Garrick Gaieties* was in

---

* A gentle man with a tragic personal life, Loeb, three decades later, hounded by the House Un-American Activities Committee, jumped to his death from a hotel window.

preparation, Clurman once more went abroad with Copland, handing over the job of stage manager to Strasberg. At the Hofbräuhaus in Munich, Clurman and Copland, though apolitical at the time, were so frightened by the tone of a throng of beer-bloated, smoke-stewed, heavy-seated Germans that they beat a hasty retreat. No one was yet taking seriously the shrewd young politician and painter manqué named Schicklgruber.

In short order Clurman was back at the Theatre Guild advising director Philip Moeller about a new Werfel play, magnificently cast with many of the people with whom Odets would tour in 1929. Clurman, soon to become a Guild play-reader, was alive with dissatisfaction at the lack of organic happening in the Werfel production despite the considerable gifts of the director and actors. He confided both his distress and his proposed solutions to the third assistant stage manager, Cheryl Crawford, now on the verge of becoming the Guild's casting director.

Like young people in each new generation, Clurman began to find, along with his contemporaries, a characteristic voice, a voice increasingly critical of the successful Theatre Guild as "a Greenwich Village grown prosperous," with subscribers who could keep even a flop running for five weeks. He found its productions pretty, with a middle-class stuffiness lacking passion and point. The Guild could manage Sidney Howard, he felt, but on its stage Pirandello or Werfel became colorless or complacent, and O'Neill and Shaw decorative and fake-impressive. Later it would seem to him he had been especially severe with the Guild because it no longer satisfied the demands of the generation that was to burst forth in the thirties.

Long before the Friday-night meetings at the Hotel Meurice began, Clurman had gone to see Strasberg rehearse amateurs at the Chrystie Street Settlement House and, convinced of Strasberg's position that plays must be "artistic wholes," had enlisted his help in a series of abortive efforts to form a group that would take seriously what had now become for them both a clear necessity: "to link the actor as an individual with the creative purpose of the playwright."

In the summer of 1930, in love with Stella Adler and "intent on bringing my first years in the theatre to an issue," Clurman poured out his full heart to Aaron Copland:

Everybody is so clever in New York, I said. Ability, even talent, flashes at every turn and corner of the city. This was a fantastic world we were living in, electric with energy, feverish with impulse, gigantic with invention. It was a world full of sharp curiosity, quick assimilation, enormous activity, mountain-high with reward. . . . Nothing tied the fast-moving forces together, no governing principle, no aim, no deep and final simplicity. . . . Man no longer understood his own nature, his own dreams, even his own appetites. And despite the fact that he was constantly agitated, he was actually passive. He let everything be done to him. His consent was his habit, not his choice. . . . Perhaps to rush out of line is to invite disaster. If so, let it come. If enough of us try to form another line according to our true nature, ours may become the right line, one which others may follow and walk on more peacefully and gracefully. We must help one another find our common ground; we must build our house on it, arrange it as a dwelling place for the whole family of decent humanity. . . .

On and on I raved, clear and turbulent, mixing metaphors, categories, vocabularies, confident that out of this chaos I might achieve an order of meaning and ultimately of action. Copland listened silently. Finally I couldn't help noticing that his eyes had filled with tears and that he was suppressing a sob. "What's the matter?" I cried, bewildered. He positively couldn't say. He thought about it, and the next day he remarked that he had wept because he realized I was in for a load of trouble.

Subsequent events would bear out Copland's prediction. More important, however, was the fact that, according to Copland, "Harold is one of the few people I know who learns from experience." This gift, among others, would make of him a prime mover of a uniquely generative decade of theatrical history, called by Irwin Shaw "a glorious crusade." Clurman, like O'Neill, was in search of a new governing principle.

Despite Copland's misgivings, Clurman and Strasberg decided with Cheryl Crawford to start by organizing a permanent company of actors trained in a common technique, sharing a fresh esthetic vision, and unified by their craft in a "new" kind of theatre. Their choices of members hinged essentially on whether the actor seemed interested in hearing about "a theatre we hope to make." There was considerable question about Odets, as he was considered a mediocre actor by both men. Yet, said Clurman, "let's have him" because "something is cooking with that man. I don't know if it's potato pancakes or what, but what's cooking has a rich odor. Something will develop from that man." Clurman knew nothing at this time of Odets' aspirations as a writer.

Such, then, was the man who addressed Odets' reflection in the mirror of his Theatre Guild dressing room, who two years later would become his friend and, during the next decade, the primary witness of his life.

The psychological soil was now fully prepared for a radical conversion experience, an experience whereby, as William James put it, "a self hitherto divided and consciously wrong, inferior, and unhappy, becomes unified and consciously right, superior, and happy." Clurman had come bearing seeds for this soil, but not yet enough to prevent Odets' plunging once more into the nightmare abyss where what he called "the hydra-headed beast Morbidity" stalked.

His roommate, Ivan Black, acutely aware of Odets' preoccupation with suicide, would look at his grim face and listen to him at four in the morning play again and again at top volume the funeral music in Beethoven's "Eroica." It seemed to Black that Clifford was dying to be a genius but that, as he listened to Beethoven, he knew he could not create anything of that magnitude. Often Black would come in to find Odets in a morbid state staring down at the cement sidewalk from their rear window. He recalled his saying, "A guy could break his head if he jumped down there."

Odets' hopeless identification with Beethoven appeared to Black more than romantic, actually pathological. He confided to Black that as Beethoven had wanted to "conquer" as a tone poet, he aspired "to reign" in his creative life as a "literary song-cyclist." Believing that Beethoven was a "true genius," Odets labeled himself to his friend as "a lesser breed."

He began a file marked "Beethoven," noting the similarities between himself and the great composer and analyzing the sources and forms of his genius. Both, he felt, were shy, suspicious, essentially homeless, poor, and parentless—negative elements that Beethoven had changed into a positive but embattled idealism, a reaching out for "Bruderschaft." In his creative work he embraced the entire world, said Odets, making of it the home he had never had. For many years Odets used the figure of "my friend Louis" (as he called Beethoven) as his prime model of the artist: his interior and exterior struggles as well as his formal solutions. In one remarkably contemporary statement, written after his "conversion" to the Group Theatre, he sums up his own dilemma:

Bach was willing to serve the forms of his time. But Beethoven *began to make the forms serve him.* A fugue was no longer something to fill with content. Now, with him the fugue was shaped, pounded into serving his purpose in relation to a bigger thing—to the expression of his own individuality.

Beethoven was half master of the forms and half their servant. But about those who came after, what? Release from old social forms gave them a new kind of flight in which they were free to explore themselves completely. Artistic objectivity became to them a festival of extending their own individual personalities everywhere. But what happened after that, after Wagner and Debussy.

Weakness began to come because they were getting too far away from the roots and the nourishing earth of social form and life. They were no longer integrated with a social body. Lack of substantial form means the lack of a group. That is where we are today. Any time you find an expression purely an individual one you may be sure that quick death is not far behind. Sterility you will find in such an expression, lack of life and a sickness. An individual expression today is a danse macabre. Such an expression today will invariably be filled with disease, hunger, neurotic pleading and searching, perhaps a complete lack of caring covered with childish cynicism, bitterness, often hatred, lostness, tearing down.

But acceptance of a social form does something else, informs the artist's work with a feeling of life and love, gives him a sense of building up. The truth is that Beethoven in music may be called the first of the destroyers. Unconsciously he played his part, opening the first gates of an evolution towards the spiritual destruction that faces the world today, but is being met by a new type of person.

I think that is why Beethoven is so much our man today. Keenly, often with great bitterness and outbursts of futile rage, he felt the lack of a group, of his own kind of people who would be as intent as he on building up for themselves the same kind of world. He was the first great individualist in art. Today we are locked in a death grip with our individualities and coming back to a social thing again. Call it Communism, call it Group Theatre, call it the life of farms, but artists are coming back to the truth of root things, fundamentals again. Sophistication is dying a swift death on all sides. And our struggle is the same one that Beethoven knew in 1826 when he wrote his great fugue. Only with him there was no possible solution. He knew in the end that one could only suffer and realize suffering deeply in life, but go on and perhaps reach some rare spiritual level. Today we are confronted with solutions to our problem. Russia has helped many of us see with clearer eyes. Today we can do one of two things—go the way of the social trend—the communal way—or be dead in life while we feebly sing the ego and the pains of living with neurotic insistence on the fact that the world is doomed to death, a la Spengler.

Later he wrote a play in ten scenes about a composer named Louis (sic) Brant who might be a "monster or a genius," a man who aspired to replace Brahms in the lofty trio with Bach and Beethoven. He bought Beethoven's life mask and took it wherever he moved, ultimately climaxing his identification with this "first of the destroyers" by dying, like him, of an incurable gastrointestinal illness in his fifty-seventh year, and leaving behind instructions for a death mask of himself.

Ivan Black tried a variety of approaches with his "morbid" roommate, from affectionate teasing to stern lecturing on the thoughtlessness and self-indulgence of a suicidal preoccupation. He was feeling guilty for having contributed to the problem by voicing harsh judgment of Odets' acting ability, and by telling him that the novel he had recently begun "stank." Black recalled "this lousy thing where the protagonist commits suicide by walking into the sea at Brighton Beach with his violin in one hand and his bow in the other."❲ This scene, written first, closed the book. Black advised him again, "since he knew a lot about theatre," to try a play instead. But Odets' "malignant passivity" had gone too far. He could not even continue his novel.

"In the middle of the night," Black recalled, "some instinct woke me up, and there was Clifford at the window, this time with it wide open. I jumped up, pretended to joke about his being a fresh-air fiend, and told him about a suicide who had jumped to his death in Boston right next door to a museum. I said to Clifford then, 'Maybe he wouldn't have jumped if he had stepped into the museum first and had seen what was there.' " Clifford smiled sadly and, without a word, closed the window, soon saying, as he would in sincerity later say to Clurman, "You're the only big brother I ever had." In his notes for an autobiography he summarizes this event as "Ivan Black saves my life."

Black now embarked on a two-pronged therapeutic crash program: first, his own suicide-prevention formula—to expose Odets at the Metropolitan Museum to the thought and feeling of the world's greatest artists. Second, he invited him to collaborate on a play based on an unpublished novel he, Black, had just finished.

The first of these two endeavors bore immediate fruit. Every Saturday Black took Odets to the Metropolitan Museum. Systematically, starting with the hieroglyphics and sculpture in the Egyptian room, the burly Harvard athlete-architect-journalist shepherded him through, propounding his thesis that the artistic enterprise throughout history has gone hand in hand with a prospering economy. "When customers are available," he told the fascinated Odets, "the latent talent emerges." Demonstrating first the crudity of archaic Greek art, he went on to show its growing complexity as Athens developed a strong navy. When the Peloponnesian War with Sparta drained the treasury, the scene shifted, he said, to Asia Minor, and on he went to the Renaissance and the Elizabethans and down to the moderns. "Cliff was a very apt pupil, soaked things up like a sponge." He recalled pointing out links of architecture and history on a walk down West 44th Street one day, such as the "weird windows like the back of Spanish galleons on the second story of the New York

❲ 10.1.

Yacht Club—or the Georgian design of the Harvard Club. Clifford couldn't get over it."

Fascinated by ancient art forms, Odets, according to Black, found it difficult to accept anything much after Rembrandt, whom he loved. But then "he would remind himself what a bad reception Beethoven and Debussy had had because people were not yet accustomed to their sound. . . . So he kept looking at the moderns and later became America's foremost collector of Klees."

Frequently three others joined Black and his troubled ward on these Saturday fine-arts rounds: faithful Herman Kobland from the Bronx; Harvey Screbnick, a music devotee who played the violin (he would become Harvey Scribner, attorney and tax expert);* and Jacob Sandler, a wall-eyed gnome of a man whom Odets often fed and who called himself "the Jewish Peter Pan." Everyone in Greenwich Village called Sandler "Jake Shakespeare" because he had virtually committed to memory all of the bard's works. In addition, he had such a gift for language that he lived off of his conversation. Later he would complain of Odets' unacknowledged use of his lines, like the famous "I think I'll get myself a glass of municipal champagne" in *Rocket to the Moon* when a character goes to a drinking fountain, or "It's a cosmic frame-up!" when he stubbed an infected toe sticking out of a hole in his shoe. Sandler, quoting T. S. Eliot, would often repeat scornfully, "Mediocrities plagiarize. Geniuses steal boldly and bodily." On these educational Saturdays, as the Metropolitan Museum was beginning to fill with young people who could find no employment, such competitive resentments were still minimal among these five young men, all of whom democratically shared the growing—in some ways, relieving—belief of the thirties that success was not possible.

At this early phase of the deepening economic catastrophe, Odets, along with his contemporaries, carried the private conviction—however unconsciously—that his was strictly a personal failure. Depending on the particulars of a life history, a judgment was made that a man was useless to the world around him, a "superfluous person," as Caroline Bird has put it, for one of a variety of reasons. No one wanted this "superfluous person," perhaps because he was a Jew, an immigrant, a Negro, a cripple, a loafer, an angry person, an ugly person, a stupid person, an uneducated person, an artist, a misfit—or perhaps because he was a she. Few of these rejects knew that already the number of people who wanted to work and could find no job had tripled beyond the "normal" percent of idleness we are willing to tolerate. The relief when they would learn that one out of every four of them—sometimes one in three—was similarly afflicted would be incalculable. Perhaps, then, the fault was not to be located wholly within themselves, or by reason of anatomy or even national origin. Such is the seedbed of a revolutionary ideology.

Clifford found himself making vague links between Clurman's fanatic, often arrogant addresses at the Hotel Meurice meetings and these stirring Saturdays at the museum, recalling later:

I was an uneducated boy who was determined to educate himself. I did want to know everything there was to know about music, like a twenty-one-year-old boy wants to know all there is to know about women. He can't wait to put his hands in her hair, you know. In

* When asked how he interpreted the later vicissitudes of Odets' life, Scribner's reply was prompt: "If anything was defeating in his life, it was his tax relation to the U.S. government."

the same way I couldn't wait to put my hands on the body of music and on the body of art. What was this about Rembrandt? And what was this about French Impressionists? Who were they? What was all this mysterious thing? What was a movement of a symphony? What did that mean, a movement? What did that mean, *allegro con brio*? Everything was very mysterious to me and very wonderful. And part of this whole mysterious and wonderful thing was also contained in what he [Clurman] was talking about, because he was talking undoubtedly about art. And I had never associated art with the theatre myself. I didn't know what that meant. I knew that I wanted to make fifty bucks a week, that I wanted to make a living out of the theatre. As for writing, I could be as poetic as I liked in writing and could write this kind of short story, that kind of short story, all those things I was trying on the side.

The notion there could be any connection between making a living in the theatre and his writing, a secret self-indulgence where he could be as "poetic" as he liked, was a stunning insight, not yet usable.

Black recalled what a dismal failure was the other prong of his therapeutic program, his suggestion they collaborate on a play. Whereas Odets' depression permitted him to be a greedy consumer at the museum, he was at this point totally unable to be a producer. According to Black, Odets would simply sit at his typewriter in a bog of passivity, saying, "What do we say now?" Black's tolerance for this diminished as Odets began to pull out of the depths of his doldrums, and finally, in a burst of anger, Black tore their joint manuscript into shreds. He did not know that Odets' creative energies were being poured into his secret correspondence with Philip Moeller. He knew there was some peculiarly charged relationship between them because Clifford, when they walked through Central Park, would point to the high window of Moeller's apartment on Central Park South "as if God lived there." On one such occasion, at four in the morning, Odets was praising Alfred Lunt's stylized Mosca in the Theatre Guild's *Volpone* and, jumping lightly to the bandstand facing Moeller's dark apartment, he began playing the part, as if he were trying to show how much better a job he could do.

In his frequent visits to Moeller's apartment and in his seductive letters to him, sometimes two per day, the handsome, dependent boy of twenty-four continued to grapple with the monumental task of bringing some unity to his splintered, creative, and self-destructive self by being found worthy in the eyes of an older man. He saw in the urbanely witty high priest of the Theatre Guild a model to placate of quite another order from his father, or even from the boldly arrogant young fanatic Clurman, a "Jewish lad" not much older than himself.

Listening to Clurman talk at the meetings in what Odets called "his hungry way," he was fearful that here was not the beneficent Jehovah he was seeking, but one with "forked lightnings." Strasberg, too, when he returned from a road tour, appeared to Odets similarly lacking in both the kindness and the humility he had found in Cheryl Crawford and in Moeller. Nonetheless he found it impossible to stay away from the meetings. After almost three months he confessed to Clurman that he was just beginning to comprehend the difference between a production cooked up haphazardly for money-making purposes and a unified theatre founded on life values. It would take him longer to differentiate between Moeller's genteel taste and craftsmanship, on the one hand, and Clurman's loud, intemperate, and passionate pleas for a contemporary theatre expressing a unity of background, of feeling, of thought, of need. Designer Mordecai Gorelik, an early attender at Steinway Hall, often said with more than a trace of irony that the Group's favorite theme was "What shall it profit a man if he gain the whole world and lose his own soul?!" Nonetheless, and this would doubtless become a critical factor for Odets, "We were," according to Clurman, "lovers at heart." Aaron Copland wrote to him from a boat carrying him again to Europe, "If you succeed in your aims you can become the spokesman of our generation." Clurman had no real doubt that this was true.

In the meantime, increasingly uncertain of his acting ability as well as his commitment to it, and once again jobless, Odets ignored Cocteau's warning to beware of music, and began again to rely heavily on music, his nepenthe. Two and a quarter single-spaced pages written to Moeller distill some of his current struggle not only with his auditory addiction but also with his relationship to an older man known to be interested in young men:

Dear Philip Moeller,

I can not believe that you resent my writing to you, and since there are things clamouring for exodus—since there is no one to whom I would rather write than you—since I am full to bursting with much of Beethoven's last quartets—here is another letter. Remy de Gourmont says something about the sin being only in the consciousness of having sinned. . . .

But enough! It is strange to have to apologize for wanting to let go one's heart and mind about Beethoven. For tonight he has been the Bacchus of the Bourdelle head who "presses out for men his glorious wine." And I am drunk to sickness with more drinks than one of the 130 and 135 quartets. Four times I played the cavatina and remembered that this God (not only God but the entire Trinity) could say that everytime he remembered its melody it cost him tears. For me it negates the blitheness of the other movements; it tells me of the man who wrote a note to his nephew the same year he composed this opus 130, a note that says, "you will certainly kill me if you do not come." And yet here in the music there is not such bitterness. . . . Here is no tremendous psyche lost in a "raptus," no glittering heroics, no peasant humour with sleeping viola players and sotted bassoons, no virtuoso making idle runs with nimble fingers, no streaming haired fury, no parsimonious fellow whining about money, no egocentric maniac . . . no, here in this cavatina (titled "adagio molto expressivo" as if it were a Tschaikowsky hymn of pain) is the weary old man with blurred, salt-burned eyes that none might see. It is the man that some artist sketched on his death bed with his thin hair pasted to the already sunken temples seen in the death mask; it is the man who once said that he loved a tree more than a man; the man who left some letters that probably were never delivered because they spoke of a love that he might not have; the man who would improvise for an hour and then smash the keys with the flat of his hand because he had shown too much tenderness to his audience; here is Beethoven (Oh Ludwig, oh Louis and Lodovico I embrace you). . . .

You are fifty three now, Louis.* You complain, Louis that Vienna is forgetting you and your work. In the summer of this year

* It seems more than a psychoanalyst's self-indulgence here to notice that Odets frequently addresses Beethoven with his own father's name.

you do not sluice cold water over your head: there is chill enough in the blood that comes from your heart. You are sick unto death, Louis, and you write that the summer is cold and the winter is cold. You would like to have Karl by your side now, for you have learned the cost of the celibacy that came with being the high priest of your art whom you knew for the most jealous of all the wenches who ever quickened your pulse.

In another year you were sick and wrote a quartet in which you gave thanks to your idea of God: "Holy song of thanksgiving to the Godhead," you wrote. . . . Autumnal days have come Louis, and tomorrow you will allow a cheap publisher to change your writings: you will cut out the Great Fugue and substitute in its place some inorganic composition to please the public.

Now for the last time, with the cavatina's melody still in your ears, you are going to move to another house. Your tenth symphony, already in notes, lies in a drawer, and you have not gone on with it. But you write another quartet—do the close poignancy of the strings attract you—is there not enough strength for a painting, but yet enough for an etching—and in this quartet you admit that you have "cribbed from here and there." Louis, is it so that you are too weary to invent melody? True that you take pieces of Bach and Haydn and Mozart to develop with a cunning that not even fifty four years has dimmed? . . . Papa Haydn is dead now and you can not take chocolate with him ever again. Are you being revenged on Mozart by taking his melodies and doing things with them that he never could have done, revenged because he paid you scant attention when you were a lusty twenty? But Louis, Mozart is long dead and he would have loved you had he lived longer. Would you want Vienna to laugh at Mozart? Isn't it enough that they left him to die alone, that they lost his heart in some unfound hole, that his skull is perhaps side by side with those of street beggars and men who knew no music?

Look across to Baden from your window, Louis. The melody of your cavatina is caught in the wind, but your ears do not hear. Once, at the piano, you played a pianissimo so that whole groups of tones were left out. Your weary ears did not hear then; they are still unheeding. But the eyes see, and the heart remembers. It is autumn, Louis, and you have come to your last opus number. You write a jesting motto, "es muss sein," and for three notes you recall the cavatina of three years before. Your motto is a joke, but you have learned by now that it is best to teach the truth with a laugh.

Then you say something about your day's work being done. You are in bed, you are dying, Louis, but you have already said so in your cavatina. The physiology is all wrong, it is all tired. By your bed is a present of some bottles of wine that stand there like a symbol. Once you were able to drink wine. Now you are old, you are weary, you are dying Louis. "It is a pity," you say. The bottles of wine stand there, a mute symbol in the hushed room. You think of your cavatina and say, "When I think of that melody it costs me tears."

Oh Louis, my Love, my God, my Beautiful, one hundred and five years later it costs me tears. They tell me that you died in a room laden with lice, and I have seen a mask they made from your dead face, and I have read what many men say of you and your music. Loud is the praise of the musicologist. Your name is said in the public square and I have seen your face hung on the walls of schools.

You are "a Great Moral Force"; you "stormed the Citadel of the Gods"; you are the "Man who Freed Music": There is no clay in you and you are all good.

But Louis my dear, wink at me from your picture on the wall here. We—you and I—we know about your cavatina. Tell me, my friend, what kind of girl was this Giulietta Guiciardi? Do you think I would have liked her, Louis?

Sunday four thirty am

"I am desolate and lovelorn, where I was when I began this letter, except when I listen to music or write I must have someone at my side, someone feminine to love." So Odets concludes a later account to Moeller, equally long, written at three in the morning and expressing his own "speechless surprise" that he had chosen to be alone—and to write this long letter to Moeller despite the fact that he has at his disposal "four fond faces who would be here with the simple impulsion of a telephone call . . . such varied persons as a milliner, an actress, a lady belonging to a noted political figure, and a trim schoolteacher are all for Clifford . . . and all at one time. . . . He can be on occasion a fair bed-mate."

Detecting in himself a note of "fat and reeking complacency," he grows to hate the face he sees in the mirror. Yet he continues "to like himself secretly" when some lads get together and discuss their potencies. "Ah I can afford to smile at those lads, I remain wordless and think that once I was as young as they, and eager to prove my conquests, and as artless. But now by the grace of being twenty-four, I have acquired a Confucian silence." At least here, he reassures himself, is one area where, if he chooses, he can perhaps meet his father's contemptuous standards of masculine power.

He is concerned, however, by his "singular apathy from which it is impossible to be aroused by man or woman." The night before, arriving at a choice between a girl and the Beethoven quartets, "I had to send the girl home . . . she vows she'll never come again, but I still have the quartets!" He begins to realize "just how possible it is to feed music to a person until it finally becomes as an opiate, as demanding and despotic as a master with a lifted lash. No drug fiend knows better than I the fantastic torture of being without his nepenthe."

In his voluminous letters to Moeller he is reviewing his life, seeking to learn "why a youngster of twenty-four has need of a drug." (He does not mention the increasing frequency of his ingestion of gin as well as of Beethoven.) "A great sorrowful chord rolls back for my ears to hear . . . I feel myself as some homeless thing wandering until there is reason to stop." Why does he constantly "grieve vicariously for the world or . . . weep bitter tears because Mozart died as he did"? He is constantly on the "brink of lacrimal overflow" and always "sorry for everything, everyone who lives." Can it really be that he is happiest when he weeps, paining himself with "slavic-sad" thoughts?

Odets' tone is by turns seductive, apologetic, even sycophantic. He knows, however, that "I've written myself clear of many things" and is here trying to "think myself out of making a horrible failure of living a life that is still young and resilient."

Perhaps there can be no solution for him, he theorizes, until he is sexually "burned out." "I refuse to believe that the Life Force (Oh Jesus) can go wrong with so many people. Only when I explain twisted sexual impulses with the above theory can I agree that there is such a thing as a Force. . . ." It cannot have escaped Odets that he was addressing all of this to a man whose sexual adjustment was clearly not that of the average middle-class American.

He reads in the life of a Beethoven or a Brahms (quickly disclaiming his talent to be of their magnitudes) "the penalties of living" and closes with a plea that Moeller grant him "a simple hour of an afternoon" to pursue these large issues:

> You see, I have grown to be very fond of you. At rehearsals I came to see and realize that you were the kind of man I would grow to be in many respects. Liking you then was a selfish thing. You mentioned the Whistler butterfly and something jumped inside me. You saw Linda as a Boticelli [sic] woman . . . and again I was moved. The word "virtuoso" fell from your lips and the twitch came again. Often you would say something that no other person in the rehearsal room but myself got, things that took for me, foolishly, the shape of a personal message. There were scores of little phrases you dropped, all wrapped in the curious passionate quality you have (this is NOT silly), that I took to myself.
>
> When you used to excuse us from a night rehearsal I found myself wondering what concert you were going to hear. Would it be the Philharmonic or Iturbi or the Roth String Quartette? The next morning I would look at you to discover which you had heard. It was a silly game I'm afraid, one in which you never gave yourself away.
>
> Four times, however during the long period of rehearsing, you gave directions to some one else and called them by the name of . . . Clifford. I began to read some significance into the incidents, and finally told myself that you must be wondering what kind of person this Odets boy was—ordinary, queer, clever, stupid—a friend had recommended him and with a native curiosity you wanted to know what he was about.
>
> I said in my heart of hearts (I am being painfully truthful), I must convince this man that I have a worth. Once I left a book on Beethoven around where you might see it; once I whistled part of the Brahms' First; and once I lighted my face when you mentioned Boticelli.
>
> Ah well, I don't know what else, but I like you Philip Moeller.

The carbons of his letters to Moeller, similar in many ways to Freud's letters to Fliess, provide an excellent natural history of the rich chaos out of which he hopes, quoting Nietzsche, there will soon emerge a "dancing star."

Although we will soon hear of still another suicidal episode (the last for many years), there is no mistaking the exultant joy in his explorations of what he calls "the histology of myself," as well as in his finding "mighty friends" like Beethoven, Leonardo, Whistler, and Whitman. As he comes temporarily "up the hill, away from Apathy," he finds fearless lovers in the works of these men. Speaking of a poem:* "like an amoeba taking food, I broke around those lines so that now they're blood for me." He has "fifty ears" and is learning the sweet savor of simple foods, and can even write in one letter, "Life is lovely, Philip."

Still in regular, inflamed attendance at the Clurman-Strasberg-Crawford meetings, he is stimulated for the first time to work objectively on himself and commences to tabulate everything of his life he can re-

---

* "They told me, Heraclitus, they told me you were dead"—William Johnson Cory's paraphrase from Callimachus.

member. He begins to hope for a place in this group and to see "what its significance MIGHT [Odets' caps] be for me, for all of us!" and fiercely cleans house: "I threw out Tchaikowsky, Wagner, Chopin and Debussy, seeing that they were dangerous to me. . . ."

Thinking about the Group and himself in relation to it, he writes Moeller that there is a war within him between "The Aristocrat" and "The Peasant":

> On occasions both will accept certain strong predilections such as an insane love of music; but even in the passion there are different standards. The Peasant says of Tchaikowsky that he has much to give, that he is without banality in his finer work, that HE WAS A SUFFERING HUMAN BEING. The Aristocrat rails at listening to this Russian, says that he is full of rotten sentimentality, a quality which often fills the Peasant who often walks the street with tear filled eyes. . . .
>
> I have known the Aristocrat to weep but once, while seeing a performance of your "Hotel Universe." Otherwise he is contemptuous of dissolving into external emotion. . . . It is he who once wrote "Cry only hidden tears." He is pedantic, occasionally brilliant. He is never the sycophant that the Peasant is capable of being. Prayers he does not know. He likes to impress people with a sense of power and great knowledge. He is coldly, often shrewdly analytical. . . . Whereas the Peasant would be content with twenty-five dollars a week for the rest of his life, the Aristocrat wants hundreds a week and knows that he can get them.
>
> Both of these personalities are hungry always for Beauty and share alike all intellectual attainment. The Peasant is always in love with some*one*, building that person in its own image. The Aristocrat is always in love with some *thing*, building that thing in what he actually knows of it. The one takes what he can get; the other takes nothing that he has not examined with a cold probing mind.

In this sharp, proud, sycophantic, probing—and, withal, blind— document Odets states as best he can what he calls his dual personality. He is now caught in the value struggle between the rationalist, aristocratic Moeller of the successful and powerful Theatre Guild and the new vision presented on Friday nights at Steinway Hall by Clurman's earthy intellect and the growing "Bruderschaft" of actors, photographers, scene designers, dancers, and writers.

As Clurman saw it, the Theatre Guild directors, of whom Moeller was the most important, were—in the spirit of the decade before the crash—admirers rather than makers. They were imitators rather than initiators, buyers and distributors rather than first settlers. It seemed to him they had no "blood relationship" with the plays they dealt in: "They didn't want to say anything through plays, and plays said nothing to them, except that they were amusing in a graceful way, or, if they were tragic plays, that they were 'art.' And art was a good thing."

At Child's restaurant, after these meetings, Clurman would go on talking while Odets, having reached what he later called "an unhappy state of my life," would sit mute, though bursting to say things. Clurman privately thought him schizophrenic, not simply because he rarely spoke, but rather because when he did, it would be an incomprehensible, disconnected, unintelligible outburst. Clurman wondered whether he had made a mistake in having invited him in the first place.

"How long, how long must these uncertain days and nights go on

with life a dangerous and glittering questioning always in my mind?"
Odets asks Moeller on the first of March 1931, "the flowers" answering him
then: "Until your work be done," they say. "Until you bloom and go to
seed and your flesh grows withered on your bones."

Not until he finds "roots with which to fasten to the rich and fe-
cundating earth," nutriment in the soil, "for all the world like [a baby]
blindly reaching for a mother's swollen breast," will he do his work of
"writing out on paper the things I know and feel." Remarkable for a boy
in his twenties is the generative vow he adds: "And when I grow older
I'll be a gardener for the new lads on earth who'll be crying themselves
for attachment to earth." A long list of poets, painters, and young playwrights whom Odets would in fact later help—spiritually and materially—
testifies that this vow was not simply rhetoric. Thinking of "Cybele with
her plenitude," he suddenly realized, he records, "why I make a fetish of
Woman's breasts: They are all I ever see about a woman, all I know and
love." All his life he would imagine that he rejected and accepted significant women solely on this basis.

My window looks out on the back of a great apartment house the
wall of which is studded with windows. That wall brings a great sense
of the futile to me. The windows lighted, people moving behind them,
often seeing men and women loving and lusting in night clothes
. . . all of that and more bring to me a great yearning for people. I
want to be in an apartment as all of the people I see are. I too want
to have nights and days regular and orderly. I want to cut from my
life this sense of oneness, the quality of always being alone.

But what's the use; I've been alone in great crowds, and as sick
with sorrow. It's an awful thing to have to carry along with one,
this sense of being alone, of not being able to lose one's identity. I
stand out like a fleck of white on a modernist's painting. I think I'll
join the navy, that's what. I'll join the navy and become one of the
boys. I'll never say the name of Beethoven again; I'll drink rotgut
whiskey in the Philipines [sic] and know the sluts of Singapore. I'll
be one of the boys in every way and I'll even have my arms tatoed
(so what if I don't spell), but I'll have them tatoo a bleeding Jesus
on my chest!

In this outburst to Moeller, increasingly aware that he is struggling
to find what he calls "an elastic credo with which to live," he continues to
wrestle with the task he has set himself. He flies from his aspiration to
be "as all of the people I see are" to the position that "you must live
ascetically if you would produce violent art," and predicts that for the
coming weeks "I'll pace the floor and bite my knuckles. My head will
swim and my knees grow weak. Things will scream out within me."

As the antitheses within him sharpen, and as his (mainly unconscious) rage mounts, he permits himself small eruptions toward Moeller.
On his hapless roommate, Ivan Black—with whom he has to share his
bed—he silently begins to focus his impotent anger. About Moeller's
direction of a new Maxwell Anderson play he writes:

I saw your "Elizabeth the Queen" tonight and didn't somehow believe a word of it. Whether or no there were ever women as Miss F. [Lynn Fontanne] played Elizabeth, I can not say, but her performance had for me all the empty virtuosity of a Liszt Hungarian Rhapsody in performance. Constantly I felt the lady "eyeing her octaves," flexing her fingers in preparation for a difficult cadenza, counting the moments until she came to those awful tenths in the treble.

Ah well, what does my opinion amount to against those of the superior persons who've said such superlative things about Miss Fontanne?

Odets mentions neither Clurman nor the Friday-night meetings in these letters to Moeller. Here, as all his life, he was careful to keep people in separate compartments. It is evident from this, however, that the values of the rebellious Steinway Hall group have begun to color his vision of the Theatre Guild, and even of Moeller himself.

His interest in the vast shifts within himself is passionate, and for three solid months he continues to visit Moeller and to use him as a sounding board. He has made, he thinks, a momentous discovery: that "all my building up, polishing, and bettering of self was done to please the woman I would be if the feminine part of my nature dominated the rest of me." Alarmed by the implications of this partial insight into the feminine aspect of himself, he abandons it and moves on to his usual flirtation with Moeller. Has "dear Philip" noticed that Donatello's St. Lorenzo might have been modeled from the head of Jascha Heifetz? And in a dream he removed the "heavy tress of hair that modestly covered the virginal clitoris of Botticelli's Venus . . . what other man in the world can stand beside me now . . . we have been lovers!"

Time and again, in his struggle for a coherent world-view, he is convinced he is reaching "a sense of things" and pleads, "Of course I am young (and this is not boasting, as you seemed to think), but realization of a grievous lack that is in no sense my fault, but I have a precocity, one that I recognized even while in school." Because of that, "coupled with a fierce driving intellectual search," he has begun to sense a sequence of "chronology, with a feeling of humanity and kinship with all things that grow." Everything alive has "a cogwheel correlation. Winter is as necessary as summer. All urges are elemental . . . and not wanting in purpose—that's the word—PURPOSE! . . . Life is contained in a great unalterable form stricter than the symphonic form of Beethoven. . . ."

He sees just such form and purpose in the perfection of a tulip on his desk which, having been cut, has not been seeded: "its pistil has grown atrophied and the pollen on its anthers is of no more use . . . like all good artists and voluptuaries, it has cheated Nature of its due." The Greeks understood the perfect form in flowers, he thinks, "and that is why they made the legend of Narcissus who turned from boy to flower by a stream. . . ." Great artists, like Leonardo, Blake, Shelley, "crazy Van Gogh," and even "McDowell writing his little songs" could say about these blooms what he fears he cannot. He is sure Van Gogh, too, must have felt the "impulse to take these flowers and torture them with tearing because you can not define them or solve them or know them or get closer to them than touching."

This last sets off a characteristic grief over that sense of irremediable isolation which would be so frequent a visitor to his "sad heart." Still addressing Moeller:

> Tragical thoughts stalk my brain, thoughts about getting no closer than touching to all the world and what it contains. There's one thing I never wrote to you (a medallion of Schubert, like some strange affirmation, has just fallen from the wall), this intense desire for getting close to things, for being able to hold things inside you, for wanting to hold other people like the blood in your veins. Marvellous that Schubert should fall off the wall . . . the potency of my thought, the stirring strength of it. . . . Schubert, lovelorn, dying at thirty, wearied with trying to explain what he felt with melody . . .
>
> Mother of God . . . Schubert at thirty one and Mozart at thirty five, and both of them writing like mad and coming to greater, more beautiful things . . . and no one caring or knowing the shine of their genius . . . and zing with Mozart in a pauper's grave, a whore with her legs round his neck and his face on a dead drunkard's chest . . . and the fast growing grass sprouting from his skull and god knows the flower that sprang from his heart.
>
> And Schubert's brother paying for his funeral, saying "I hate to do this, and it's a hell of a bother, but he was my brother, albeit a fool and a wastrel" . . . and flip went the soil on the calm dead face of Franzerl who had rained manna on the earth's barren rock.

Doubtless his fantasy included the fear that if he were to die, his father would bury him in the same grudging spirit.

When such "tragical thoughts" took possession of him, his desperation, however extravagantly expressed, became an evident and moving reality to those about him. Indeed, this very extravagance and his sense of drama were recognized even by him to be a safety device:

> What to do, Philip, what to do! It is a very horrible thing, having energies and no wagon to hitch them to. With this past week I have been as near to suicide as I'll ever be without actually being a suicide. I find myself pulling up with a shudder (for life is often good) with a realization that I'd been unconsciously thinking about some lethal weapon and its use. Last night I lingered at my stove while cooking some chocolate. Asking myself why I stayed there, I understood that I'd been reflecting on the arrangement of the gas tubing. It is only when I contemplate a dramatic situation without a sense of drama that I am a dangerous person. . . .

These nights of passionate self-exploration, of "backward delving," desperate as they become, would nonetheless be marvelous, he adds, providing a sense of sequence, of "no longer missing ladder rungs in the dark," were it not for the "sordidly ugly" fact that "my blood keeps chanting lusty hours and the fever of my youth . . . making these young fresh fine girls a mere receptacle for a passion that, once sated, turns to brutal bantering intolerance. . . . I say to myself twenty times that such things won't happen again and two nights later my skin grows hot again." Then he calls an Ethel, a Harriet, a Sarah. Some girl is always available, and he carefully keeps Moeller posted:

> Afterwards we sit on the edge of the bed and drink hot chocolate. I write a couplet for her: "On each of her breasts was a star to see; so my lips studied astronomy." She is charmed to kissing me; she does not believe that a man can write poetry. And in a minute we are embroiled under the blankets, entangled in the sheets and what-

nots. She swears I must not bite her shoulders or other things. She has places to go and evening gowns to wear at them. But I know she has no evening gowns and I am suddenly sad for her and myself. My legs and arms grow passive and I turn away to the wall.

The girl now, characteristically, asks, "You are sad again? . . . You want me to go?" But he does not answer. "She knows me by now—and wearily she recaptures some silky thing from the floor . . . as if with pain. Then she'll come to my side saying softly, You are so funny, so funny. . . . The door closes with a gentle reverberation and she is gone. . . . A shame squirms gently in my tired hot brain. But presently there is the cool lucidity of a Beethoven quartet; and Louis smiles down from the wall with an understanding I've asked him for."

When the girl becomes pregnant and presses for marriage, he feels he is "the worst kind of bastard . . . unlovely and mouldy . . . but this marrying business is all wrong for me. I shudder (not figuratively) with knowing that some poor girl will marry me because I have 'nice eyes' and next stab me in our bed because I have taken her malleable life and irrevocably distorted it with my vagaries."

Odets gives no hint of awareness that part of his compulsive necessity to affirm and reaffirm his sexual prowess stems from the fact that he is dwelling on an ambiguous knife-edge in his relationship with Moeller. He does appear to feel a little uneasy, however, about the intensity of his feelings toward the older man. In his introduction to a new insight into "what is wrong with me," he writes:

Dear Philip, Just now I feel a special tenderness for you; I don't know why. . . . I smile when I think that this writing takes on the aspects of a love note. I don't care what it takes on! . . . I used to tell people that I was a lusty little pagan with no thought but that of impulse. It was not true, for I knew in myself a sense of reasoning and a sense of shame . . .

Proceeding to his discovery, he says, "Someone else has come to live in my body," and elaborates his meaning:

I started life as a boy with quick, intuitive perceptions, with an amazing artlessness. But a kind of pride came to me, one conditioned by squalid living and brutal contacts. I knew only that I must not show myself* to people, that I must encase my sensitivity with a shell. I must show rationality and sound intellect rather than naivete and intuition. I must appear complex and profound. Even my voice began to pitch itself to a depth not naturally mine.

The necessity, on the one hand, to conceal himself from the "brutal contact" of his contemptuous father lest he appear "an idiot" (or a girl) is obliquely alluded to here. Yet his unconscious yearning to be husbanded by him is clear.

At the end of March 1931 he had by no means given up the idea of being an actor, and was awaiting, with the others in the Group, "one of the main pillars of this theatre-to-be . . . some godlike creature who was somewhere out in the wilderness like John the Baptist who would come . . . and teach us things." (Lee Strasberg, who would be the

* All his life he was extremely sensitive about the size of his penis, which he judged to be too small, and often dangerously postponed medical examinations lest the doctor or nurse see his "birdie."

Group's acting teacher, was on tour playing the Jewish peddler in *Green Grow the Lilacs*.) Nonetheless there is an indication in the theme of a story Odets now wrote that somewhere he "knows" he had committed himself—in his acting—to being something he cannot be. It concerns a "dead and disappointed actress" whose grave is visited by maggots who hold "friendly conversation with the heart and brain." They, in turn, "repeat the heard story to the grass on the grave who tells it to a lone geranium." He was unable, he says, to sustain the "charm of the beginning of this tale"* and thinks he will, instead, dictate his boyhood to a friend, title it "The Days of My Boy Life," and sell it to the *American Mercury*.

If only, he thinks, one could recapture that wholeness, that oneness of purpose, that concentration of emotion that children have—like "a cat creeping up on a bird"†—then one could reach the "lyric peak . . . the unsaid words and the song that had to die when youth was reached." The tragedy of having irrevocably lost this singleness of thought lies in the fact that one can "never stand again and hear and see what adults have no awareness of." What adult, for instance, knows the terror of the boy "who waked in the dark of early morning, sensing that under his bed was a brown gnome lurking for fleshy game"? More to the point perhaps is the question which now follows: what boy, grown to manful stubbornness and to "a stiff pride," can find surcease from such inundating death-terror as he did when an artless, gullible child?

> The boy would not move in the darkness; frozen with terror he kept his eyes shut for as long as was possible—a time of infinity—and then with a sudden movement he leaped far out and clear of the bed —so that the gnome might not reach out to grasp his ankles—and fled without a backward glance to his mother's bed. The very quintessential of terror was in that flight, a terror that burned deeply into the young brain. And in his mother's bed the boy was so exhausted that the moment he felt her hand he fell asleep. He fell asleep because she was his mother and because her hand was good, a hand that had pulled him away from the brink of some abysmal chasm.
>
> Where today, when I live with the grown-up years and have garnered my life with futility, where today, my friend, is such a hand?◖

Having grown into the "splendour of 24," he can no longer take his mother's hand or even let someone tell him "what to do and how to do." Suddenly, set off from the body of the letter, he types a snatch of the 137th Psalm: "They required of us the words of a song, saying Sing us the songs of Zion. How can we sing in a strange land?" He closes this letter to Moeller with, "Jew and youth alike. I am sick with not being home and do not forget the Jerusalem of my boyhood years." Within a few short weeks, in the bosom of the Group Theatre, he would find a hand he could grasp, and, spared annihilation, he would once again find it possible in his New Jerusalem to let someone tell him what to do and how to do.

---

* He finds it a "bad story" and writes this letter as an inconsequential "dessert" after a "meal of soggy, mouldy potatoes and unsalted meat."

† "Like a murderer to his victim, silent"—Odets later said this about how a playwright must go to his work.

◖ 10.2.

It is enough to say that several times—without drama—I stuffed death behind me by several fortuitous happenings. And last night when I called you was the very, very end. I was very young and very defeated. I had finished a pint of most excellent wine; at eight thirty I found myself at Rachmoninoff's [sic] concert; at ten thirty I knew that I could not possibly go on; at eleven you were very kind, saying intuitive things, "Don't do something silly, get a good night's sleep."

In the telephone booth I began to think and smoke a cigarette. My brain was outraged, my sensibilities screaming with pain. And all of that from a jobless news reporter who had come to live at my house. For three weeks I hadn't been able to read or write or listen to music or anything else. Everytime he wrote some journalese piece he insisted upon reading it to me; he was full of vulgar tricks; he never took a bath; he left his dirty clothes all over the place and substituted my clean ones in their place . . . and more awful things. All this for three weeks while things began to mount up inside me; and I finding it impossible to say a word of protest to this amazing person, this ace of inconsideration.

In the telephone booth I knew that I must live long enough to say to this person, "Get the hell out of here, you god damned son of a bitch, you everything, you worse than scum, you you you!" I must live if only to say that to him. I hurried home. I rang the bell, but he was not in. I fumbled with my keys, got into the place, threw off my clothes (I would kill him) and finished the other quart of wine. I waited. I smoked a cigarette and waited some more. No sign of the gentleman. I wrote on a piece of paper the word "inexorable" and pasted it on the face of my clock. I listened to it tick for a long time. It began to bother me and I finally put it in the closet under a pile of clothes. Still no gentleman. I think I finally fell asleep.

I've forgotten to tell you that for the last three days I'd had a toothache of the worse sort. I hugged it close, keeping the pain as a religious flagellant to his lash. I had deliberately kept that toothache for three days. Now it waked me out of my sleep and for the rest of the night I could not sleep. Near dawn I fell asleep finally and was awakened at eleven. The gentleman was coming up: he had made a night of it somewhere. I said to him very calmly, "I'm sorry, you'll have to move. I can't stand it anymore." He said, "Yes, I guess so. It's no fun sleeping two in a bed. I've found it very uncomfortable." I said, "You are the worse (sic) kind of a son of a bitch. Get out." He said that I must be sick or something. I told him I was sick of him. An old friend came along at this time. The gentleman began to pack his stuff. When he was finished he asked me for a dollar. I gave him the change from my pocket. He went away. In the afternoon I went to a dentist far up town.

And now it's all over. I've had my tooth fixed and there are some fresh tulips in a vase, fresh red tulips one of which I'll take to bed with me tonight. I am coming back to sanity again. It is like a return from the dead.

So ran Odets' report to Moeller of the climax of this period wherein—emerging from his depression—he revolted against an older man by whom he felt exploited. Whatever the actual transgressions of his hapless roommate, Ivan Black, it is evident that Odets needed, in this anxious period of struggle, to clear the decks, assert his independence and his capacity to defend himself. He needed also to rid himself of this male bedmate.

By this time more than a hundred miscellaneous and enthusiastic theatre folk (most of them unemployed) were crowding into the Friday-night meetings at Steinway Hall. From this large group Strasberg, Clurman, and Crawford would select the few "chosen people" to spend the summer at Brookfield Center, Connecticut, where the new credo for living and work would be tried and, equally important, two plays would be re-hearsed for production in New York. There would be no pay for the summer beyond a bed, meals, and laundry; nonetheless all of these young people, feeling increasingly superfluous in, and alienated from, their contracting society, watched anxiously for a favorable sign. Finally, as he later told Robert Hethmon, it came:

> Now, there came the magical time when we knew. There had been a number of meetings down at Lee Strasberg's apartment in the London Towers, and a very impressive apartment to me. There was a full-size reproduction of a Gauguin painting, various women in various-colored dresses on a beach. And all this felt to me much more connected with art than the theatre. The fact that this man would have this reproduction of a Gauguin painting, a great big long panel it was. And some of us began to feel, "Well, if we'd been invited down to Strasberg's house" —there were only twenty-five of us: at the other place there might be a hundred and twenty-five—"that maybe we were people they were interested in." Now, I myself had great humility about this by now, because, well, Franchot Tone is there, and other leading people, and there was J. Edward Bromberg and Morris Carnovsky. I had seen them act, and they were wonderful actors. "Maybe we had some special kind of 'in.'"

By the end of March, it is plain from Odets' final letter to Moeller, he was dimly aware that this correspondence had had as a central function the locating of himself, creatively. With the hopeful portent of the invitation to Strasberg's apartment, his mood has perceptibly lifted. He scarcely dares to hope he is on the verge of becoming part of this splendid family, no longer a homeless failure, a despised disappointment. Is it possible, he wonders, to start a new life?

"I either warn you or promise you," he writes Moeller, "that as soon as I make up my mind which way to write prose, that soon I'll leave off writing these letters to you," adding his fear that, like the contemplative donkey stuck between two haystacks, he may write nothing and thus spiritually "starve to death."◖ Finding in his own work traces of Hugo, Conrad, Joyce, he supposes "I am without the courage necessary for the forming of any sort of artist precept."

Shortly thereafter Odets commenced the first draft of two acts of a play originally titled, in capital letters, "The Melancholic Gorillas" (later crossed out and replaced by "One of These Days" and several other titles, the last being "910 Eden Street"). This opus, whose original title clearly echoes O'Neill's *The Hairy Ape*, concerns itself, like the O'Neill play, with the romantic artist's despair that he does not belong in the world, that he has no place.◖

Set in a Philadelphia rooming house in 1930, *910 Eden Street* presents a set of aspiring, blocked young people all of whom seem slated for tragic ends. Mark Berke (shortened from Berkowitz), a Jewish poet—who appears to be Odets' central identification figure—has been a psychology

◖ 10.3.
◖ 10.4.

major in college and is "the nicest Jew" Linda, a well-born, virginal, non-Jewish, tea-drinking dance student, has ever met. Mark is counseled by a young and passionate Zionist, S. Theodore Manishevitz, known as "Tiny"* (whose wife has drowned herself and their child!), to "look homeward" and not at the blond, Gentile Linda.

Most who knew Odets believed that he thought little about his Jewish identity, knew no Yiddish, and was ignorant of Hebrew ritual. So it is remarkable how much excellent idiomatic Yiddish there is in this early play, and how many references to pogroms, "Gentile" women, anti-Semitism, and religious customs such as "kaddish," the Hebrew prayer for the dead.

In *910 Eden Street,* as is so often the case with early work, the unconscious fantasy is naked in its overdrawn statements, not only of the central identity-element, the Jewish poet, but also of the rest of the gallery of characters, all aspects of Odets' splintered unconscious image of himself: the young pianist who calls herself "one of the damned like all of us," damned because she fears she hasn't a first-rate talent; the prizefighter who wants to leave all this pretentious intellectual "slime" for life on a farm; the pedantic intellectual who advises him to do just that; the homosexual girl devoted to writing a novel; the young man who beats women down; another who, estranged from his wife and dying of stomach cancer, shoots his rival dead; a very young man who is through with women because they leave him "unfed"; a couple who commit suicide and of whom the Jewish poet says, "It is the most real thing they ever did."

Despite its romantic confusion, this play holds the seed for the poignant, richly variegated, funny characters—and their struggle—in Odets' later plays. A dialogue between Nick, the fighter, and Mark, the Jewish poet in his mid-twenties, crystallizes Odets' awareness of his own temptation to refuse his heritage and his yearning, inasmuch as he cannot believe in himself, for something to believe in:

ACT TWO

NICK: I'm telling you plain. You're not working for what you want. You're being romantic. You're wasting your life trying to be two other guys. It's gotta be one, not two. Stop wasting your time. Make up your mind—

MARK: You amaze me, Nick—talking Greek! I don't understand you. Don't look at me with those eyes. Let me alone. Let's have another drink. (*Goes to bottle*) How about it, St. George?

NICK: Three fingers. (MARK *starts as if to toast; looks up at ceiling*) Let's drink to the society dame with the veins in her eyelids. (*Smashes glass in fireplace*) (MARK *bursts into laughter,—?*)

MARK: (*Slowly*) I discovered something this afternoon. I looked at her face . . . It was like a mirror. I saw my own. I saw impotence, premature exhaustion. It's because she was born that way, exhausted and sterile. But I live that way. Sterile, both of us. And me all the time refusing my heritage, what is me, the Jew. Trying to refine myself. I mean the way sugar cane is refined to white crystals.

NICK: I'm a son of a gun, is this Mark Berke?

MARK: Yes, Mark Berke . . . nee Berkowitz—

NICK: I don't believe it.

MARK: Nick, you're as relentless as Nature. Have a drink. (*Starts for*

---

* William Kozlenko believed this character to have been modeled externally on playwright Joseph Kramm, also plump, bubbling, comical, and nicknamed as a youngster "Tiny."

a table, trips, falls to his knees.) I can't walk. Boy am I stinko!
(*Trying to get up, pulls down table scarf and several books. Looks
at one*) Doistoievsky . . . "The Idiot." Hha ha ha ha. (*Suddenly;
agitato*)

Doistoievsky speech [handwritten]

All this past year I have been thinking of these things—

MARK: Yes. Only think. I will liberate myself. That is what I want to
do all the time, liberate myself from what I think I ought to be
to what I am. Before I lose my hair I'll write a play. I'll call it
"Liberation." Yes. If I could write a play I'd call it "Liberation."
You see that 'is what I am, a Russian Jew, a plain blunt fellow,
yes, who loves his country men. Nick's right, only he doesn't
know how to say it. I can't read Doisoievsky [sic]. I used to sit
up at night and read him, but I can't do it, I can't. I am too much
like those people. I sit up all night and cry. Not for myself, but
for everything, for everything, for everything. I am Doisoievsky
[sic] people, only they have something to live for, a faith . . .
they believe in something. They sweat and stink and live low in
mud and water, but they believe in something. That's what we
don't have, something to believe in, a faith, a faith, a shining
faith. Then I brush my teeth when I go to bed and I sit on the
edge of my bed and can't sleep because all the time I am thinking
about those Doisoevsky [sic] people. My father was Russian and
my grandfather was Russian and they come down to me in the
blood. I am all of them and more. And then I come here and play
at being an American, a civilization I don't understand and believe in. Here I was born in Philadelphia and I feel all the time
a Russian Jew who can't speak English or anything. And I make
believe I am a poet and have beautiful thoughts and speak good
English. I change my name. Yes, I change my name . . . and
love white Gentile women with cold eyes and skin because the
others, my kind, make me see what I am. All the time I run
away from myself and hate people who are like myself. I live
low . . . low low low, deep in the stink and slime, like Doisoievsky [sic] people. Only with them it doesn't matter because first
they are living being themselves and second they have something to believe in. They believe, they believe, but me. . . . Oh
my God, my God, look down and forgive me for the wasted years
of my life. I have not justified my days and nights. I have walked
around in an empty world peopled only by my fever and
desire. . . .
(*He falls down on his knees, weeping against the couch*)
(*Here* NICK *falls down on his knees as if in prayer, saying these
are the first real words he's heard* MARK *say in two years.*) "Jesus!
Real at last."

The profound and universal human need to be part of something, to
believe in something—beyond one's fragile mortal self—is given an added
edge here by Odets' outcast position in relation to his father and, as an un-
employable Jew, in the larger society. He is now trembling on the edge of
his conversion.

He is finally convinced he has the stuff of literature in him and looks
forward to the day when he will know how to "canalize" it:

Every time I think of the day when I'll be able to write with concepts
behind me I experience a little shiver of joy. I think of nights without

restraint in which I'll just write and write. I'm not worried about what I'm going to say; that will take care of itself. The thing is, HOW to write! And I'm almost at the beginnings of a style of expression. Enough.

A double-spaced hiatus occurs now, and the last letter from Odets to Moeller concludes:

I'm glad now. A half hour ago I was not: I was obsessed with my childhood, having just then finished a Stevenson essay on the subject. But that always fresh Beethoven quartet, the 135th worked its usual miracle. . . . I'm going to look at the sky and count stars. I'll yell at the moon. I'll dance on my toes and kick in the air. I'll run out to Long Island, swim across the East River, and drag my newly married friend, Bill Kozlenko, from over or under his wife, and we'll dash into the night and talk about great things. . . . We'll look into each other's eyes and laugh and laugh and laugh. And we'll go to our beds.

That's how I feel, Philip! I "swing the world, a trinket at my wrist." Spring has come to me at last. The rain of yesterday has been soaked up by the hungry earth. I too am earth and I have drunk in the rain. Things are growing in me. I am pregnant with children, hosts of them with shining eyes and eagerness. Beautiful children with stars for eyes. Boy into flower, Philip. boy into flower!

He closes forever this mammoth sequence of letters with, "Oh that wonderful Beethoven quartet! Louis darling! [Signed] Clifford." He was at last to be let in, home free.

PART THREE

From Actor to Writer

1931-1935

ACT THREE FINALE.

PRESENT: PIKE, LEO, GUS, CLARA, JULIE, PEARL(?)—MR. PAUL.

Leo — I must make a confession!

THE DREAM IS OVER. ~~SLEEPING BEAUTY HAS BEEN AWAKENED.~~ FROM OUR PAST MISERY

AND BITTERNESS CAN COME A CLEAN FUTURE--IF THE PRESENT IS ACCEPTED FOR WHAT

IT IS. THE PAST WAS BASED ON IGNORANCE, ON MISCONCEPTIONS OF LIFE, ON FOOLISH

OPTIMISM AND BELIEF IN THE GOODNESS OF PEOPLE AND GOVERNMENT.

NOW THAT WE KNOW HOW BAD THINGS REALLY ARE WE CAN WORK FROM A TRUE

BASE OF EXPIERIENCE AND UNDERSTANDING TRUTHFULLY WHAT CAN HAPPEN TO

HONORABLE PEOPLE. *Gus, the good old days are gone.*

LIFE UNTIL NOW HAS BEEN A CLOUDY LIE IN WHICH EXPERIENCE WAS NOT

UNDERSTOOD FOR WHAT IT REALLY WAS. THE DREAM IS OVER. THE SLEEPING BRAIN

AWAKES! OUR SON BEN HAD AN AMERICAN DREAM. GUS HAS THE DREAM, MYSELF,

THE DREAM KILLS AND MAIMS. NOT SEEING REALITY CRIPPLES THE FINEST MAN.

YES, THE FALSE PARADISE IS LOST. FOR THERE NEVER WAS A PARADISE.

WHERE WILD ANIMALS MAY DEVOUR ONEON EVERY TURN, THERE IS *no* PARADISE, ONLY A

PLACE OF SHELTER. (A FAMILY TODAY IS ONLY A PLACE TO CLING TOGETHER AGAINST

A COMMON BLIZZARD, A MONEY BLIZZARD WHICH RAGES WINTER AND SUMMER--AND TO BE

TOGETHER IS TO LULL ONE TO SLEEP WITH A FALSE SENSE OF SAFETY AND COMFORT)

SO THAT OLD FALSE PARADISE IS LOST AND IN ITS PLACE--WE SHOULD BE VERY HAPPY,

JOYOUS AND REJOICING--THE REAL PARADISE IS REGAINED--THE ONE OF SURE KNOWLEDGE

AND TRUTH. NOW WE KNOW WHAT THE REAL WORLD IS, THE WORSE IT CAN BRING.

WE ACHIEVE NOW, IF YOU PLEASE, A NEW AND TRUE OPTIMISM. WE HAVE THE BOTTOM TO

(not a dream house).

OUR HOUSE AND WILL BEGIN NEXT THE BUILDING OF THE UPPER FLOORS AND ROOF.

IF THE PAST WAS A DREAM, THE PRESENT REALITY IS BRILLIANT AND HARD. WE SEE

WITH CLEAR EYES WHAT MUST BE DONE. WE MUST WORK!

We have been buried so long. Yes, grass was growing up on our door. Now we are in the sweet light and air of the new day!

Moles, soft little moles blind & underground.

A reduced reproduction of an original manuscript page from
the first draft of *Paradise Lost*, showing Odets' closing statement
for the play—changed in the final version (see page 296)

Chapter Eleven

When I brought up the racial questions I was not making a criticism; I was holding up an ideal. For I am a Jew myself. By blood I am a Gentile, but in a symbolical sense I am a Jew. That is, an outsider who longs to be part of the life around him. From childhood I have felt out of place in the world, particularly in America. . . . Like several of my friends, I had come to America by way of Russia. That is, by way of Russian liberation. . . . But such a love, based upon art rather than life, is apt to be a sentimental one. The country for Americans to love is America.

GERALD SYKES

I am done! done with chasing my febrile self down the nights and days. From the ashes the phoenix! The clamouring hatred of Life has been hushed to less than a whisper. On the pivotal point of a quarter of a century of living (sweet Jesus, twenty five years old this month!) I have begun to eat the flesh and blood of *The Group*. I partake of these consecrated wafers with a clean heart and brain; and I believe—as I have wanted to believe for almost ten years—in some person, idea, thing outside myself. The insistent love of self has died with strangulation in the night. The stubborn stupid lugubrious pride that one develops somewhere between the ages of ten and twenty has dissolved with some minor weeping. I who cried from my inverted wilderness for strong roots with which to fasten to the swarming sustaining earth have found them at last in The Group. I am passionate about this thing!!!

So Odets opened his entry in the Group Theatre's daybook, a public diary to which each member in turn contributed during this summer at

Brookfield Center, in the Berkshire foothills, five miles from Danbury, Connecticut. Lee Strasberg was taken aback by this "Wagnerian extravagance" coming from a peripheral young actor. He was offended not only by its romantic style but also by Odets' use of the Catholic mass as metaphor. He was unaware that Odets was undergoing a radical solution to a monumental personal crisis and that this formulation of his transport in the language of Catholic belief and ritual was more than metaphor. It is a self-consciously literary overflow, but it arises from the same archetypal necessity that issues in a genuine religious impulse, the loss of which O'Neill—the first alienated American playwright—was mourning in all his work.

Helen Deutsch, a spirited and discerning young writer soon to be deeply involved with Odets, and later to disappear into Hollywood, had attended the Group's final New York meeting at Strasberg's and given the members this notebook bound in black imitation leather with typed instructions to enter all events of the day: rehearsals, social events, guests, feelings, everything, in order to "create a permanent record of the summer." She had a reverence for history and for theatre and had just completed a first-rate account of O'Neill's Provincetown Theatre.

Visiting in midsummer with Virgil Geddes and Paul Green, she was astonished and delighted that her effort to provide in this diary "one source for a future history of the Group" had been so successful that she sat up all night reading it. While unsure whether the Group was already "too humble or too smug," she nevertheless wrote: "This book fairly sings. You've got something, you people, that most of us gave up looking for when we turned twenty-or-so and settled down to a life of quiet desperation. Those who have weakened into compromise can look at you, and blush, and take new heart." She pleads with them to record in detail their experiences with "the Method" (the Stanislavsky technique of acting). It is not enough, she tells them, to say simply, as one grateful actor did, "It is as clear and as sound as a theorem of Euclid," nor is it enough to record quasi-religious testimonials to salvation. They must all write with a sense of history because, said Group stage manager Alixe Walker, "we are in the biggest thing the American theatre has yet to see."

The official invitation to become one of the twenty-eight chosen people arrived when, in one of his characteristic ménage-à-trois arrangements, Odets was hiding out from his dunning landlord with Bill and Lee Kozlenko in Sunnyside, Long Island. Before departure from the Guild Theatre at 52nd Street, Odets, fearing he'd be late, stayed awake for forty-eight hours reading Waldo Frank's *Our America*. Crowded then with his records into the rumble seat of "some tennis-player-looking lady's car" on the rainy Monday of June 8, 1931, he records a few faint regrets at leaving behind Helen, Sylvia, Edith, and Mona, with one of whom he might have "burned out a love into that valuable friendship one may have with a woman," adding, "How I need such a thing for a final healing." At this moment his "love life" is a minor issue, however, because, although the scar tissue is still sore to the touch, "the catharsis is over."

Occasionally the depressed flavor of his life returns, but he smiles to himself: "the real adult life is before me for the first time in twenty-five years. A quarter of a century to reach this vista, clear, unafraid, steady and taking from life a simple nourishment." At last he has found the family "Bruderschaft" for which he had so steadily yearned as he had listened to Beethoven's Quartet.

After the first meeting of these fervent camaradas that night in the barn, Odets recorded:

A kind of hush falls on all of us and the habitual Strasberg suddenly goes leonine and paces around with his head in his hand. He opens the meeting as it were and admits that he's nervous. One suddenly feels something and a realization comes that here is life beginning. Harold Clurman talks after Cheryl who turns her face away and one knows that tears are behind her glasses. The air is surcharged with a strong feeling to which I find it difficult to apply a name. But something has happened, there is no doubt of that. Two of the fellows get up and say that they never realized the importance of this and that, they were not giving themselves wholly to group ideas, etc. It reminds me of nothing so much as saved souls giving testimonials at an evangelical meeting. It is true; there was an emotional upheaval there. I was awed a little and wanted to turn into sleep.

The significance of this summer to Odets is indicated by the fact that in his notes for an autobiography he omits any mention of the first half of 1931, and for that year enters only: "*The Group Theatre.* Brookfield Center."

When the Group's first play, *The House of Connelly* by Paul Green, was cast by Strasberg, Odets had only one line as a tenant farmer. He was disappointed and "something flares inwardly for a minute," but it quickly died down as he adjured himself to "let me learn completely to throw my energies into a harness with others and forget that I have only one line."

He continued to believe in his abilities as an actor: "I have a fierce energy and passion and a thinking brain and a powerful emotion. No one can take those things from me. The directors here will find that out. . . . " It is evident, in this shaky assurance, that he was still trying to maintain a strict separation between callings as actor and writer and has, as yet, no conscious thought of earning a niche in this extraordinary professional family as a playwright.

Indeed, no one here knew of his secret pursuit. Even Cheryl Crawford thought of him only as a faintly interesting actor who two years earlier had deluged her with sycophantic letters from the Theatre Guild tour. No one in the Group had an inkling that this blushing inarticulate would one day lay its golden eggs.

Considering that a career as an actor appeared to him, consciously, still his sole available vocation, it is the more remarkable that he could marshal his energies to weather the shattering impression (now conveyed to him by the acting company and, more important, by its high priest, Lee Strasberg) that, despite his paid jobs with the Theatre Guild, he is unable to ply his trade. In his own notes this critical revelation appears as, "I *can't act!* Tied up!"

Other Group members recall that he was adequate, but that in ad-libbing acting improvisations with one other person he appeared painfully shy, inhibited, rigid, and—as Franchot Tone said—"strictly stock—as though in a strait jacket" in his relation to an audience. When he tried to relax, his romantic quality would border on a hammy extravagance. Strasberg recalled that he and the others thought him somewhat crazy and that he had had the idle thought, "In a few years, at this rate, Odets will be sporting a cape." Another two years would pass before Odets would permit himself to face the fact that as an actor he was simply not up to the Group Theatre standard.

Testimony to the supportive powers of this Group and its Weltanschauung is that this uncertain young thespian, now under the analytically keen, merciless (some even said cruel) eye of a man thought by many to be the greatest acting teacher in the world—and rejected by him—could nonetheless continue to "chant renascence" and to record in his diary days of "broad calmness," with the past sad years "no longer in my eyes."

After they had been at Brookfield Center only eleven days, the perceptive Clurman recognized the curiously double-edged power of a committed and ideologically rooted group of people. He was experiencing the understandable alarm which occurs when the group organism threatens to supersede the integrity and sense of reality of its individual members.

> Everything is at a standstill and everything is going forward. Never have I so desired to cut myself off from time—past and future—and from the rest of the world. Never have I had so little desire to receive mail, to write letters or to acknowledge in any way the existence of a world outside the group! When I hear that one of our people has gone to N.Y. or requests permission to go I feel almost pained that they can remember other obligations and harbor desires unrelated to our immediate life here; and contact with other people in the hell of N.Y. inspires in me the dread of contamination. It is as if everything outside the group were somehow impure.
>
> But curiously enough something within me contradicts this feeling. The actors seem to have lost sight of the future more completely than I have. They appear to dwell more wholly in the present moment. Their confidence in the reality and perpetual continuance of the group—as sure as the reality of some planet—is exactly what I hoped for and what, for some strange reason, disquiets me. They act as if this were an eternal summer, as if they were going to be able to discuss their parts, do affective memory exercises, run the victrola, swim, play tennis and dress in pyjamas forever and ever. There is not enough—*pathos!*—in their enjoyment of their new life! I would have them realize for all their carefree pleasure how difficult the achievement of this summer's "paradise" has been, how terribly hard it is going to be to perpetuate it amidst the sterner realities of the winter and its N.Y. season.

On the same day Clurman pleads with the Group members for something less (and therefore more) than unquestioning faith:

> And more astonishing still is the naturalness—one might almost say the casualness—with which the actors take Lee's direction. They know he is good—in fact, practically perfect—so they work devotedly with him without, it would appear, an inner comment, a debate or a discussion leading even to praise. This astonishes me since I who have watched Lee before and worked with him am always struck anew with the originality and *daring* of his direction. For he is like a doctor who refuses to treat his patient except with the most natural, the most inevitable remedies and turns with disgust and even anger from the suggestion of some patent medicine (let us say, an obvious piece of business, a technical suggestion, a bit of external characterization or any preconceived means of expression). The patent medicine, says our doctor, may produce immediate relief but it may injure the patient's heart. . . . His method is daring because it places confidence in the actor's own capacity to develop in his gradual evolution into the character of the play, and finally because it refuses to admit a perfection of performance apart from this natural development of the actor. Lee is no "idealist": at bottom what he feels

amounts to this: "there is no perfection different from reality," in other words no actor can possibly play this part more "ideally" than the actor who is actually playing it or at any rate we have no right to assume anything else. The present actor in our hands is the best actor, and the inevitable reality of his personality is truer than the "ideal" conception of any director. I am convinced that no director —not even Stanislavsky—directs just this way.

Our actors do want to become better—they do want to work (they follow me with pathetic eyes, the small part actors who want additional training) and all of them because of this will become, within the limitations of their reality, what they ultimately desire to be. And that is all anyone can hope for. In short, everything is *really* beautifully ideal—ah, but a little more pathos, my brothers, a little more of the suffering and the struggle of a healthy and legitimate doubt!

One of the small-part actors who followed Clurman with pathetic eyes was, of course, Odets, who had by now given up his day-night reversal and was living, as he wrote to his friend Herman, a new life. Delighted that Clurman remembers a moment or two of his that was good in *Roar China* and in *Midnight,* Odets blushes with mixed terror and pleasure as he dreams of the time when he will become untangled as an actor by the fanatic Strasberg, who in his relentless hunt for true emotion, it is said, "can unlock doors within you you didn't even know were there."

Son of a garment-worker in Galicia, and now an artist, director, psychiatrist, ascetic, scholar, musicologist, rabbi, logician, Simon Legree, and Messiah, the intense Strasberg was revered and deeply feared by the actors. To suffer his wrath, whether it be a masked, stoical iciness or a shrill, maniacally enraged outburst, was each actor's nightmare; to be approved by him, the dream. The limitless power vested in him by these actors for their spiritual life or death was awesome.

Now only rarely visible in his face was the sad and tender vulnerability obvious in a photograph of only a few years earlier, before his young wife had died of cancer. Far more often "the people"—as he came to refer to this first American ensemble—would gauge his rising tension by the barely audible postnasal snort and brace themselves for the devastating eruption.*

In this first summer a few of the more rebellious members of the company tried to establish their independence of Strasberg by wisecracks to each other: "Be quiet, don't you know God just walked in?" or "How is the little tin Jesus today?" Or in a more worldly vein, "Here comes the Kremlin dictator." There was no doubt in Clurman's mind that "just as

---

* Strasberg thought years later that he had finally decided to eschew these tirades after someone told him the actors didn't understand from the outburst exactly what he wanted them to do. He supposed that many factors had contributed to his mellowing since this summer, concluding, with his characteristic half-smile, "To tell you the truth, we sometimes miss those outbursts. I think often they helped us in the work." His habitual use of the first person plural reflects simultaneously a bending over backward from personal vanity and a deep sense of the abdication of personal responsibility inherent in a regal position.

my talks of the winter meetings had brought the hope of a new kind of theatrical experience, the summer was sustained . . . by a worship of the new technique embodied in Strasberg's devoted ministrations."

For his part, Strasberg appeared to be more like a Puritan father hoping against hope to instill virtue in his somewhat lazy children:

> To watch life being born in any object is always a fascinating thing— but to watch it transform one person into another—under your very eyes—to know that you have helped to do it—that the thing is so near to you and yet so far—I wish the actor would sometimes realize how much the director's joy and happiness depend on him—maybe sometimes he might work even when he doesn't feel like it.

He aspires that his children become artists, not merely craftsmen like most actors, and adjures them that this can be achieved only by the cultivation of a work-discipline. Like Clurman, he fears that the actors are too much at ease in their paradisaical interlude. Perhaps, he thinks, it is part of the ethos of the time; his is the only daybook entry that takes the topic of work as a major theme.

> John Dewey remarks that despite all our industrial and scientific achievement our civilization persists in what he calls a "magical" attitude. We have a feeling that somehow things will happen—we gamble—we hope—we dream—but we don't *Work!* We have lost our self-respect, our faith in our own activity—we use Work only as a means—as a necessity—rarely as a *means to an End.* The actor wants everything to happen—he is so terribly hurt when it doesn't— his vanity—his self-confidence suffer—he unconsciously accepts the "magical" formula—he has a feeling that by being worried about it— by some kind of something that will happen he will create. He forgets he is a *doer*—an actor—creator and craftsman in one. I wish I could drive this into our actors in some way.

Taskmaster and often Cassandra, Strasberg—like Clurman—experienced with great excitement the affirmative sense of growth in this band of "primal Christians."

Sometimes the company took advantage of the inevitable competitiveness among the three directors, playing one against the other: Lee's "arrogant harshness and possessiveness of the actors"; Harold's impracticality and his "lapses into emotional coma," his "generalizations," and his usurpations of power; and Cheryl's "insufficient insight or her lack of authority."

For Odets, the child continued a miracle: "Lee Strasberg and Cheryl Crawford have some magical power," he wrote in his own diary, "the play has been in rehearsal for four days and the two scenes they did tonight already show an amazing power and strength and beauty and linear dimension." For other eyes he wrote, ". . . With more cogency than all the talks on theory during the past months . . . we see a young live thing off in first flight, but already with form, with a zest for living and wings for lifting. . . . " Manifestly referring to the Group and to the play, it seems evident he is also speaking of himself. The values inherent in self-exploratory work and creative growth were in the air he breathed daily, and even though his acting assignments were small, his spirits remained high and fermenting.

Odets, rejected now by Strasberg as an actor, would soon again be rejected by him as a playwright. It would be many years before what Odets referred to as "our strange friendship" would develop. During the much later course of that friendship Odets would be moved to say on one occasion that Strasberg is "the greatest director that America has produced," and on another that "his uneasy calm will crack his arteries prematurely."

Odets continued to struggle with his desperate pride—indeed, with what he was coming to regard as his sin of pride. Catching himself planning to be clever when it is his turn to write in the Group daybook, he solemnly vows to scuttle his need to impress people: "Oh this stinking urge to be well thought of! How it begins to control one's life, the inward as well as the outward." He seems totally unaware now of his father as a model in this necessity. Consciously, he thought he had forever repudiated his father—and his father's desperation to impress people—along with director Philip Moeller and his successful Theatre Guild.

In a revision of Odets' play *910 Eden Street* evidently done this summer, a young man named Nick looses a blast at the pretentiousness and cowardice of his cronies who "run away from Life" and hide in the "incensed rooms" of phony poetry and arty talk: "while you're making up your minds with pretty words, along comes death, T.B., a bum liver, crazy syphilis . . . and that's the end." Nick's long and impassioned sermon, clearly in the spirit of a new convert, orders these despairing "damned fools"—for whom in the earlier draft, written in the spring, there had been no solutions—to quit their fraudulence and "to get clean eyes that see plain what's in front of them." Odets' own conversion dictated a reorganization of this pained and hopeless early work.

It would be far easier now than ever after to maintain this Simon-pure dedication to honest observation and self-expression. Soon Odets' society would lay at his young feet the extravagant, misleading, and unreliable rewards of Success in America, rewards more complex, more confusing even than Louis Odets' new cars or his dining-room suite "fit for the Prince of Wales." At last he would be able to impress people and thus to be found worthy in his father's eyes as Somebody.

Only rarely now, he records, do his old ghosts return even for an hour, leaving him "maggoty with morbidity." When this does happen, a long look at his Beethoven mask or a replaying of the healing Quartet 135 suffices to set his feet once more on the new and pure path. Besides the central revelation—learning about a theatre of "true feeling"—he is playing ball, swimming in the pool, walking in the sunshine on beautiful country roads, having noisy philosophic discussions with J. Edward Bromberg, and listening to music ("but not too much," as he no longer "needs a drug"). The creative integration and sense of peaceful constructiveness is unmistakable in this summer, and it would be his view, according to his notes for an autobiography, that his first real writing had begun in this, his twenty-fifth year, with a short story. It appears to be true, as he said, that the entire first quarter-century of his life had built to this climax.

His generally monastic tone suggests he fears a dangerous leakage of creative powers, and he is even considering whether he could live a celibate life. "Unless I can find a girl who will match all that I can offer," he writes, "I will forego the whole business and stay to myself." Each time he comes to this conclusion, however, his loneliness becomes unendurable: "So much do I want to get out of myself and away from myself that every face takes on the value of a break in the wall," but he must be cautious now, lest he become "enmeshed in something that will do me no good. Passion for the sake of passion is of little value."

His dreams, which amuse him, reflect his ascetic view: in one, a charter member of the Group Theatre, Margaret ("Beany") Barker, daughter of the dean emeritus of the Johns Hopkins School of Medicine, is a "nun being kissed by a priest with evident relish." He finds her attractive, as well as socialite Eunice Stoddard, "who knows Emily Dickinson's poetry," but in the bosom of the Group, according to his diary, he no longer feels that desperation for a woman that earlier had brought him "inward twisting and entrail tearing." Soon he will try to forswear women entirely in order to keep "strong for the work to come, keep the brain cool and empty." Margaret Barker tells him he is impersonal, distant.

In the Group daybook he writes, "Only the girls bothered me for a while; they have white skin and I am young and it is summer. . . . " Privately he confesses to Herman Kobland that there are several girls who "stir my Hebraic blood." Even as the father had vowed Yiddish would not be spoken in his home and had thus expunged from his speech every trace of his Russian-Jewish accent, so now the son strives to conquer these "Nordics, blonde, cool, well-mannered, finishing school . . . having most everything that, I am sorry to say, we Jews wished we had." It is clearly as a confession that he continues, "It is so! Only in my choice of desirable women do I betray that I'm a Jew."

He had learned by this time that a deep scorn for his Jewish self contributed sizably to his self-contempt.◖ He is deeply attracted to Eunice Stoddard's fresh skin and the "selfish calm of her blue eyes." He fantasies what a "good wife and mother of healthy children who would be well brought up" she would make. Yet, as always, the situation is more complex than this. In another place he adds, "I like her, but I am afraid there is a peculiar whiteness there. Funny how my Jewish heritage betrays itself into being attracted to Nordic women. Otherwise, being a Jew does not bother me at all." This offhand and defensive disclaimer is patently unconvincing. Indeed, the bulk of his work would be peopled by overtly *non-Jewish* characters,* all having, however, what critics call a Jewish flavor. His most tenderly remembered play concerns itself with a Bronx family called first Greenberg, then Berger. Almost all the significant men, but not the women, in his life would be Jews. The two women he would later marry, however, would be Jewish, one partly, the other wholly.

The summer half gone, Odets finally writes a report to Kozlenko, who has sent him data on Brahms' Alto Rhapsody. His response symbolizes for him the radical reorganization he is experiencing: beautiful though the sounds are, Brahms does not "see life whole" as Bach did: "It is always an 'almost seeing.' . . . Many, many things are happening. Firstly, a sense of discipline has come to me . . . I am doing nothing to excess. I no longer make Life from Art. I make Art serve Life." He is acquiring, at long last, "one broad purpose in Life," and, like many young people who have found a unifying ideology, he pursues asceticism: cigarette-smoking "must go by the boards . . . romantic sloppiness must be replaced with a sort of monastic chastity. . . . " It is hard for him to articulate the precise nature of his newfound world-view, but he tries. Suffice it to say, "there is no such acting in America as is being done in our rehearsal barn."

◖ II.I.
* Cf. Arthur Miller, American-Jewish playwright, whose characters are mainly neutral, anonymous "Americans."

It is clear even in this fumbling letter to Kozlenko that he is over-whelmed by the genuineness of the "human emotion carefully regulated, chosen and put into the situation of the play," and fervently hopes that in *The Man with the Portfolio,* a Soviet play being adapted by Gerald Sykes, he will have "a nice part." If he does, perhaps his rapacious and jealous yearning to work with Strasberg will be satisfied. After a rehearsal, when Cheryl Crawford has paid him a small compliment, "such a trombone choir of feeling and love for life and lust and health surges up in me that I could scream with the exultation of the night. . . . " In all his entries now there is a legible shift from the strictly individual stance of the Romantic Artist to the Group-attuned consciousness characteristic of a spiritual community.

"I could not possibly write you the sort of words I wrote last sum-mer: sickly and cast over with the gloom of a dying fleshiness . . . this group is doing what I have never been able to do for myself when I was alone. . . . " So wrote Odets to Hortense Alden after two weeks at Brookfield Center. He records in his diary he has had "a lovely letter from Mother who is tremulous with love and emotion," and is deeply pleased that Margaret Barker has told Clurman and Strasberg "what they'll dis-cover in me once I'm untangled as she is being. . . . "

Even when he is given only a bit part instead of a major role in the new play, his heart is no more than "a little heavy," he writes Herman, and assures him that "every year our friendship grows closer and more joining." When he comes back, they must have a long talk, as "things that have been bothering us for years have been made clear here in one cumulative flash." He wants to pass them on, as "they will help us both to a new and finer life."

This wish to share his redemption, also characteristic of a spiritual community, was not peculiar to Odets. Almost everyone connected with what Clurman called "the beginners' honeymoon" was experiencing a reve-lation, a new turn in their personal and professional lives. Odets' paean of praise in the Group Theatre daybook was not singular in its extravagance.

Throughout its 114 pages the entries, with few exceptions, are grate-ful, awed, joyful, zealous, fervent, and curiously innocent. Temporal left-wing politics do not appear in these pages, and on the few occasions when Russia is mentioned, it is as a symbol of hope for a world of equality, jus-tice, moral wholeness, charity, and esthetic richness.

Again and again individuals writing in this Group diary use images and metaphors of birth, nourishment, creativity, growth, and salvation: "utopian," "paradisaical interlude," "a beggar suddenly handed a spiritual fortune," "a great unbelievable orchard," "a Garden of Eden," "fresh with the joy of living," "a raft in the open sea," "labor pains," "wholeness," "being part of a whole," and (over and over) *the part we will play in American life.*

All of them felt now, as Odets later put it, that "you belonged to some-thing very important and . . . that you were here to stay." Newspapers ran many feature stories about this band of young Americans of varying back-grounds, brought together from Baltimore, Galicia, Chattanooga, Seattle, the Bronx, Philadelphia, and the Lower East Side of New York City. All of the entries in the daybook speculate, with sympathy or with supercilious-ness, about its future.

Odets recalled, "It was almost like Walt Whitman's ideal of a school, where you sit under a tree and you talk about everything and famous peo-ple come and go." A frequent visitor under this tree was Maxwell Anderson, a big, shy man in his early forties who, for some unknown reason, took a shine to Odets, twice giving him money. More important than the money was his comment, made in ignorance of Odets' secret writing, ". . . you're not really an actor . . . you're going to be a playwright." As a member of the bottom group of actors, paid $35 a week, Odets was undoubtedly cheered by such reassurance from the highly successful Anderson, despite the fact that he had not believed a word of Anderson's *Elizabeth the Queen,* directed for the Guild by Philip Moeller.

Clurman held frequent and passionate colloquies with Anderson, who had begun, in *Elizabeth,* to create characters from far away and long ago who spoke in verse, the language of "the most exalted drama" of the past. Clurman exhorted him to find his heroes in contemporary America and to put in their mouths language—whether verse or prose—that bore an indigenous American stamp. In support of Clurman, a Group member remarked that "a good turn might be done Max if someone would steal his copy of Shakespeare." Anderson, apparently attracted by the buoyancy of this living theatre, and yet aspiring to write epic drama, would soon offer the Group a new play, thought by Clurman to be "bookish," called *Night Over Taos,* which combined a Racine plot line with an early New Mexico setting.

In this atmosphere Odets, drinking in all the arguments and counter-arguments, was steadily growing. He found himself less and less concerned with his father's opinion of him; he abandoned studying the want ads for a "real job" and began to fantasy that *he* might write a play in which not only the characters but the language rhythms and colors would bear the unmistakable "American stamp" Clurman was asking of Maxwell Anderson.

For the moment, however, he would content himself with learning along with the other actors—under Strasberg's whip and insight—how to substitute authentic human experience for the "clichés of stage deportment." Building on the Russian Stanislavsky's system of acting, they were daily exploring the excitement of improvisation, extemporizing scenes analogous to those in the play being rehearsed. More important for the quasi-therapeutic explorations of each person were what the austere Strasberg called "exercises in affective memory." In these the actor was asked to relive an event from his past that was relevant to the emotion required by the scene on which he was working. According to Clurman, the first effect on the actors of these new ways of mining genuine feeling for their work "was that of a miracle." The personal side-effects were more complex, and much later would become threatening for the viability of the Group organism.

The directors called in the actors one by one, making detailed analyses of their character defects and showing how these invaded their work. Odets thought later that his leading experience at the time had been "the sense that people cared for you, for your problems . . . about what you could bring to the totality of this theatre." Even those most critical of Strasberg's driving, autocratic zeal agree that he was unstinting of attention and real help when he had succeeded in stimulating an actor, through such exploitation, to authentic feeling. According to Clurman, however, Odets was concerned even this first summer that this curbstone psycho-analysis might be a mistake. At dinner one evening with Clurman he argued that it was precisely through his abnormality that the actor functioned, and it seemed to him the directors might be bent on creating "normal" human beings.

Nonetheless, to be part of *this* family meant—Odets later said to Robert Hethmon—"being connected with the best things in life . . . that

there was something special about you . . . that you were bringing something new." Three decades later he would believe not only that he had felt
himself to be in "the heartland of art and culture and creativity" that summer but also that there had been a "morality" there, unprecedented in his
experience.

At the end of this critical year the directors would make public announcement of their intention to create a theatre with a tradition of common values, "an active consciousness of a common way of looking at
and dealing with life." The aim of this theatre was to create an audience
that would feel itself to be "at one with" the company, each the answer
to the other, each leading the other. This would be theatre in its "truest
form" wherein the psychological separation between participant and observer would shrink or, ideally, disappear.

According to Clurman, there was very little political discussion during the summer of 1931. "Of radicalism there wasn't a spark." Clurman,
to be sure, spoke steadily of the "American problem." By this he meant
that "we were part of an unintegrated society of rich potentiality . . . we
wanted to explore the America in which we knew we were involved in the
sense that many of our 'personal' problems were part of the greater American problem." To make what he said more vivid, he sought living models of
"true men." He sought, for example, to bring these young people into contact with a "pioneer of the spirit," as he called his friend Alfred Stieglitz.
Stieglitz, a great photographer, devoted himself to helping people and
works "that gave authentic expression to what they felt and saw." But,
according to Clurman, most of the young Group people disapproved of his
attachment to Stieglitz as a "hangover from something soft and sentimental."

By the end of July the pain of close living and the approaching
anxiety of survival in New York are reflected in the daybook entries of
both Paul Green, whose *House of Connelly* would open the season, and
Clurman, whose paternal responsibilities were by now weighing heavily.
Addressing the company, Green writes: "Ye are the brethren, ye are the
sisters marching to Canaan Land! May you live to bless the thorns and
even like St. Francis be not angry with the fleas. . . . " He states that a
character in his play commits suicide because he has missed "the reality of
life," a reality for which they must work and pray.

Clurman expresses quite openly the complexity both of his struggle
and his hope:

> It is as if I were not permitted here to have a personal life outside
> the life of the group—which is the life of our actors. If I were in
> N.Y. I should be able to retire at moments into the dark of my apart-
> ment, go to a movie, commune with a non-theatrical friend, pos-
> sibly read a book that might take me away from the pressure of the
> group's demands. But here I have to draw strength constantly from
> within—and the supply doesn't always seem inexhaustible. . . . Per-
> sonally, I am hardly sustained in the struggle by anybody—conversa-
> tions with people are not sheltered, long or deep enough here to per-
> form their potentially tonic function. Yet there is something that gives
> me courage to go on—and that comes from the work itself. When I
> see the clear humanity of girls like Margaret and Dorothy in an im-
> provisation—and seeing it bless its purity and sweetness—when a re-
> hearsal becomes particularly alive, when Lee flashes an amazing
> intuitive perception of the "insides" of a part, a character or an actor,
> when one of the group warms with a new life to the urge of our talks,

when a visitor like Waldo Frank or Max Gorelik reflects the light of our enthusiasm and responds with a spontaneous yea to what they have seen here, I feel a fresh spurt of energy in my blood. That is why I am always encouraging Lee to complete "Connelly"—one *finished* piece of work (and when it is finished I know it will be good) would be as solid and objective a testimony of our activity as money in the bank. One play ready for the stage would be like a house into which I could enter, warm myself and cry "behold, we can live!" That one production—our first—is necessary to restore clarity in me and to heal something in me which for the moment is a little sore. . . . You are all my constant concern: I worry about you, make conjectures and respond to you all in pleasure and pain like a great father!

At the final run-through of *Connelly* at Brookfield Center, Clurman was deeply moved as "the actors poured forth a concentrated stream of fervor, that was like the pent-up rivers of all their young life's experience," and the following night he offered a "salute to the future" in which, praising both the company and Strasberg, he warned them of the resistance they would meet in New York, adding, "Our heat would melt the city's ice." He quoted "Beany" Barker, who had just turned down a manager's offer of a part: when asked "How long will you be busy with your present engagement?" she responded, "If our play is a success—twenty years. If not—twenty years." This was truly the sense of this collective, about which Odets would say three decades later, " . . . if only they could have lasted, we might have some kind of national theatre of extraordinary scope and of extraordinary gift . . . and not have to start anew."

Chapter Twelve

In my talks that winter I had cried out, as if in a paroxysm of discovery, that our theatre would be a theatre in search of essences. We were to find out what really mattered to us, seek out our own first principles. We were now primitives, dissatisfied with the elaborate surface wisdom of the day, eager to stand by what in our own honest simpleheartedness we found to be true. This called for a passionate scrutiny of our American environment; and theatrically speaking, it demanded a poetic rather than a factualist approach, for the attempt to capture essences is the mark of a poetic realism.

HAROLD CLURMAN

BACK in New York at the louse-ridden Circle Hotel, where he had once been suicidal, Odets, now far from suicidal, was deliciously alive to the hot life around him: the derelict tenants, the prostitutes, and, above all, to the concentrated beehive activity of his new family who "ate, slept, and drank nothing but the Group Theatre." Cast in a small part as a tenant farmer in *The House of Connelly*, he filled his afternoons and evenings with rehearsals and discussions. The Theatre Guild people—including Philip Moeller—were beginning to recoil from the Group as from a strange and rebellious child. Not ready, however, to disown it, the Guild offered to contribute half the production costs for *Connelly*. The other half, through the monumental efforts of Cheryl Crawford, was made up by Eugene O'Neill (who thought the new group sufficiently promising to be given a hearing), Franchot Tone, and an executive of Samuel French, play publishers. The child, in its turn, was becoming increasingly outspoken in its contempt for the parent's empty commercialism.

In the fruit of this growing and open rift Odets was finding an unprecedented security, opportunity for creative growth, and, finally, a legitimate vehicle for revolt against his father. Looking back two decades later, it would seem to him that he, like the others, had felt that through this rebellion against the "establishment" Theatre Guild the American theatre, in its highest possibilities, had at last its first champion. All his life he had been waiting for this opportunity to be simultaneously the rescued and the rescuer.

When the curtain came down to riotous applause on *Connelly*'s first night at the end of September, the Group associates repaired to an actor's apartment for an opening-night party free of the tension that would come when they began to appreciate the power of the press. Odets and Clurman taxied to Times Square to buy the morning papers and read such praise as they had hardly dared imagine. In later years Clurman would regret the congratulatory comparisons to the high skill of the Moscow Art Theatre, as, in his opinion, the central importance of *The House of Connelly* "lay in the fact that it was an American production—that is, a play and a performance that sprang from circumstances and conditions peculiarly indigenous at that time." The production was "revolutionary" in the sense that, as Clurman put it, "rarely if ever before on the American stage had a whole company so completely fused the technical elements of their craft with the stuff of their own spiritual and emotional selves."

It is striking that although the critical reception was, on the whole, excellent and the play ran for seventy-two performances (at that time not a hit, but also not a disaster), Odets' notes for his autobiography contain this entry alone: "House of Connelly fails in New York." Perhaps this reflected his competitiveness with its author, Paul Green, or simply his unquestioning acceptance of the hit-flop psychology of Broadway.

It was precisely this psychology the Group directors were militantly opposing. In an article written by Clurman for *The New York Times* of December 13, he announced the Group's determination to depart from the standard commercial custom of raising money "in dribs and drabs" for individual productions as gambler's investments. The Group was proposing, instead, to build a conscious audience "that would grow with the years and make a permanent contribution to our social-cultural life in the manner of certain state theatres abroad . . . or of the Reinhardt theatres in their heyday." To this end, it sought an endowment of $100,000, a naïvely modest sum even for those times. It hoped the endowment would take care of the hiatus which must occur when a show closed and a worthy script was not immediately available, or of the losses of a commercial failure.

To fill precisely such a hiatus, the directors had with considerable misgivings put into rehearsal, shortly after *Connelly* opened, a journalistic play they thought weak: *1931–* by Claire and Paul Sifton, which reflected the deepening Depression. It was, as Odets later remembered, about "the difficulty of getting married . . . of making a living . . . and of just keeping warm in a cold winter." In the bit part of a bum on a park bench, Odets recalled furnishing—by playing, with his back to the audience, a "little sad song" on his harmonica—the "mood obligato" for Franchot Tone, who was making love on another bench.

Perhaps it was in an effort to comfort himself for being trapped in so inconsequential a role, and at the same time to make an approach to Clurman, that Odets now asked him to read his play, *910 Eden Street*. Clurman agreed, and his subsequent response, given to Odets in the wings of the Martin Beck Theatre, was considerably short of what Odets had anticipated. Although sympathetic, Clurman said nothing about writing talent.

It gave evidence of an internal injury in the writer, I said. Something in his past life had hurt him. He was doubled up in pain now, and in his pain he appeared to be shutting out the world. His perception was disturbed because everything was seen in relation to his hurt. He had to learn to stand up straight and see the world more objectively.

Odets would never forgive either Clurman or Strasberg for their failure to perceive at once his singular gift for writing plays.

Odets later recalled Strasberg's production of *1931–* as "fantastically beautiful," if somewhat austere and filled with "black and white thinking." It closed after twelve performances, and was probably the last straw in the strained relations between the Theatre Guild and the Group.

Attacking the shortsightedness of critics like John Mason Brown, Clurman would say much later:

> From the standpoint of the "taster," with a museum or pastry-shop psychology, such crude documents from the life of the times are rather unappetizing. From the creative standpoint—that is, to those who are concerned in the making or doing of things that produce life—rough first efforts like *1931–* are most valuable.

Winding up what had been essentially the grounds for the Group's revolt against the safe and prosperous Theatre Guild, he concluded:

> In the theatre we are still a nation of beginners. If those seeds of life . . . often misnamed "experiments," are not fostered, nothing better is ever likely to follow. *1931–*, which Mr. Brown and others shunned, helped bring about plays over which they were quite enthusiastic four years later.

Indeed, *1931–* was the last such "experiment" to which the Theatre Guild contributed; its directors became increasingly cold to the notion of their delinquent offspring's stated aspiration to establish a theatre rather than merely a production organization. According to Clurman, once Philip Moeller had established the fact that the aim to form "a homogeneous body of craftsmen to give voice to a point of view which they shared with the dramatist" was as old as the Greeks, he stopped listening. Within a very few weeks Harold Clurman and Cheryl Crawford—called now "the fanatics" by Guild director Theresa Helburn—resigned their posts at the Guild, and the Group Theatre became an independent producing organization, still without its necessary endowment, and vulnerably headed straight for the eye of the economic storm. In a situation basically untenable, fiscal logic dictated that the crusade be abandoned. This was by now, however, out of the question.

The customers in the balcony of the Mansfield Theatre (the only customers there were for *1931–*) were emitting a strange and vociferous fervor, a "smoldering conviction," that Clurman found uncharacteristic of Broadway audiences. On the closing night, in an atmosphere of wild enthusiasm, a member of the audience shouted, "Long live the Soviet Union!" to which Franchot Tone, by now the "finest young actor" on Broadway, shouted back from the stage, "Hurrah for America!" Both outcries might be described as "irrelevant," Clurman said later, adding he felt there had been "something in the air beyond theatrical appreciation."

This "something in the air" became the social context within which the Group and its members formed "an active consciousness . . . a common way of looking at life." This consciousness, more moral and esthetic than narrowly political, would provide a sufficient bond between the fledgling Group and its emerging audience to provide a heady glimpse of a potential following for a national theatre.

On December 7 a helpless president refused to see an unarmed army of outcasts, the first of the "hunger marchers," who had come to Washington to demand jobs; later the marchers were routed by Generals MacArthur and Patton with the help of Major Dwight Eisenhower. Such headlined events were daily strengthening the affiliation of the Group Theatre with its new American audience. With the advent of the war ten years later, the possibility of a national theatre would again recede, but the quest for a form in which to embody the Group's Idea would continue long after the Group had dissolved.

In the meantime, far from abandoning its dedicated mission, the Group decided on the heels of *1931–* to revive *Connelly* for a short road tour of Philadelphia, Baltimore, Washington, and Boston, rehearsing Maxwell Anderson's heroic *Night over Taos* en route. This would serve the double function of providing a few weeks' pay for the company and keeping the "continuous activity" in motion. Odets could not have found difficult the transition from his bit as a sad bum in *1931–* back to that of a tenant farmer in *Connelly.*

Before they left New York for Baltimore (where critics found *Connelly* hostile to the old South), Clurman and Strasberg were treated to the controversial temper of the thirties. Speaking to a symposium held by the left-wing John Reed Club on "Revolution and the Theatre," Clurman presented the thesis that a play didn't have to deal with obvious social themes in order to have social significance. Derided for his blindness to their belief in theatre "as a weapon" and for the Group's "sentimentalization" of the South in *Connelly,* Clurman became infuriated and shouted at "these amateurs" that he had not come to be instructed by them. His rage stemmed mainly from the fact that their mechanical slogans were a caricature of all his earnest talks of the preceding year. The political splintering within the Group had not yet begun.

During this tour, on the strength of what he advertised to his father as a position in a permanent acting company, Odets felt he could emotionally afford to stay briefly at his father's West Oak Lane house in Philadelphia. There, with what he recorded as "missionary zeal," he was spreading the gospel among such heathens as Abner Biberman of the family that made L'Aiglon dresses, who had a genuine interest in theatre. Biberman, then just out of college, would recall Odets' immense pride in introducing him to the Group people, and also his encouragement to leave Philadelphia and find spiritual salvation by studying acting in New York City. Biberman, later to become an actor and director, scrupulously followed Odets' advice.

Before moving on with *Connelly,* Odets managed to obtain, as his chauffeur to Baltimore, a beautiful, high-cheekboned model named Pam, who found she could enhance her standing with these students of Stanislavsky by affecting a Russian accent. So taken was Franchot Tone by Pam that in Baltimore he "stole her away from [Odets] temporarily." He added thus to his respect for Odets' taste in music a new respect "for his taste in women." Even the aristocratic Tone had picked up some of the Group's Slavophilia. His competition with Odets for women would be revived off and on over the next twenty years. In Baltimore, Odets signed a hotel register with Pam as his wife and was overcome with anxiety about how the Group people would receive her. Clearly, the respect of his creative healing community was of prime importance to him.

In Boston, despite lavish praise in the *Transcript* for "the spirit and intention" of the new theatre, *Connelly* did very little business, and the better-paid members of the cast took severe salary cuts so that the poorer actors could be paid their pittance.

Notwithstanding these rigors, Odets' mood continued affirmative and, although he had no urgent need these days to write letters, he reported warmly to "Dear Lovely" Goldie Bromberg on her husband, Joseph, her "snake," now rehearsing the lead in the Maxwell Anderson play. He describes with good humor the "violent" arguments he, Bromberg, Bob Lewis, and the "sneering" Sanford Meisner have been having about Beethoven. But, more important, he explains to this strong and sympathetic young mother of two why he does not need the release of writing letters any longer: "I used to store my life inside me, give little of it out, make no contacts outside me, participate in little but my own reverie." Now the Group has replaced this fiction, and he, newborn like her babies (his hair falling out like theirs, too), has found "Faith in the Group, in Beethoven, and People."

As he had filially reported to Cheryl Crawford on the 1929 Theatre Guild tour, he now regales Goldie Bromberg with gossip of Max Anderson and his girlfriend, Mab; of the difficulties between Clurman and Stella Adler; and, most important, of "the joy" of being let in free to see Kreutzberg dance ". . . as artists to artists. All artists are brothers, and I would never make my brother pay to see me act."

Looking into his dressing-room mirror, he thinks that at last he may be beginning to lose his "boyish face," but "there's something . . . crazy about all this," as he does not really feel on the inside as he looks on the outside. But a "true harmony" of inside and outside is evolving, and "the way is paved with purpose and at the end there is some kind of rest."

The end of this cold February in 1932 found the Group and Odets back in New York, about to open and—after thirteen performances—to close Maxwell Anderson's *Night over Taos,* to the production of which Anderson had personally contributed $2,500. Odets once more took a room at the Circle Hotel, where the clerk, who had become fond of him, let him live on credit for a time. His mood now, though quieter than in the summer, remained optimistic. In a letter to the simulated-Russian model Pam (now replaced by a girl named Phyllis Rodin)* he reviews and apologizes for their "awful last night in Boston," where he had apparently been drunk, full of "bottled-up emotions," and had "worked most of it away on you."

In almost the same words Clurman had used in criticism of his subjective *910 Eden Street,* he writes to Pam: "Listen, Darling, know what the hell it's all about, that's all! See things as they really are. Sweet, objectify the outer world, objectify!!!!" His adjurations are addressed to Pam, and he makes no conscious link with the necessities of his own creative development. It is evident, however, that he was seeking a path from the confines of what he called "a harmful subjectivity." He was seeking a form for his romanticism, an externalization that would satisfy Clurman's—and his own—demand that he go beyond his own internal injury. With this, he hoped there would come a greater stringency of form, something more classic.

After offering Pam money he does not have, he concludes that we will all "yet live to kick Life one good kick square in the pants and take much joy out of everything."

---

* Disappeared abroad. Last seen in a newsreel showing a crowd on the banks of the Ganges River in India.

"Just now I told the hotel clerk, 'I can't sleep.' It came to me right then, as I said that, that I *can* sleep, but saying I can't immediately settles any attempt to sleep." From this opening of a memorandum to himself called "Some paragraphs . . . March 31, 1932. Anent CO," it is evident that although his depression was still in remission, his insomnia had returned. As he lies awake, "I find my salivary glands working and pulling at the stomach. I keep visualizing good things to eat: soft scrambled eggs, roast beef, a thick slice, pink in the middle and creamy buttery strawberry ice cream . . . other mornings just as I fall asleep I see a snake . . . I never see the whole snake, just a part of its body where it's thick. This should be a Freudian symbol. . . ." ❡ He is impatient with himself and decides he "must be careful not to think" since he is so suggestible: if he tells a white lie that he is sick, he becomes sick; if "I think for two minutes that my eyes hurt, they hurt," concluding then, "It is true: I tear a passion to tatters."

Only after he has typed over half a page does it become clear what has stimulated his sleeplessness, his hunger, and his preoccupation with suggestibility:

Today at a personal interview—Lee sat there wordless, seemingly uninterested, almost, I thought, a little annoyed. Harold said my work had been all right in "Taos," good. I did what I was to do in the play and had proved for the first time a value to the Group. But, he said, he didn't think I was yet ready for big parts because I held to my original emotion, the one with which I'd start a scene. I asked, "Incapable of sustained flight?" His answer was yes. I said I didn't believe that quite. Last year it might, would, have been true. Now I have come to a certain kind of liberation. That's what I'm doing all the time these days, liberating myself. The Group has helped as a mother might. It seems I'm not slated for large parts this coming season. All right, I must work on what I get and work. The truest thing to be said is what the directors have said of some people: "He or she is busy trying to be a great actor. No, be busy doing your work and what you have will come out, greatness or otherwise." I see that now as a blessed kind of thing. You don't worry or think except to do your job. Do your work. Other things will come if they're there. This goddam thinking all the time and thinking. Throw it overboard. It's easy enough to write here, but to do, TO DO! Yes, I see now that it's wise to hold yourself poised and ready for work, then work and let the rest of the burden fall on the directors. Let them say what you have, Lee and Harold, let them help you by being relaxed and open to them all the time. This is really belief.*

There is no question that Strasberg's silence and Clurman's assent that he was "incapable of sustained flight" had grievously wounded him. Again he would be consigned to bit parts. And yet there is considerable relief in accepting the relatively passive internal stance that one must relax and let "what you have . . . come out, greatness or otherwise."

In this same memorandum he wonders why he keeps thinking about being "at one with," about how much he longs to impress these fathers—

❡ 12.1.
* The first visible seedling of what eventually grew into *Awake and Sing!*, his first full-length play, appears here in a few lines of dialogue scribbled on the back of his diary note. See Notes and Comment 12.2.

"a Harold or a Lee"—with his worth. He is tired of logical analytical abstractions and is filled with a desire "to hear stories of people, to hear people talk about themselves and about other people." Throughout this spring, in his diary notes and in his few letters, he rejoices in the fact that since joining the Group he is no longer caught in "the American way of life wherein each one tries always to stay alone, to armour ourselves against the world . . . my face assuming the stiffness of a mask . . . unfriendly and brooding." In the Group "such nonsense drops off and the heart and brain and body turn naked to the good clean sun of friendship." He concludes with a desperate plea to himself to *be* himself:

> I am getting a great joy of eating these days. With the combination of an objective meal and a subjective hunger tied up to my ego I get a great joy. I find myself singing pieces of music.
> Will writing all these words help? Why are you writing them? To show to some one, or for your own good? Listen Clifford, if you are a fellow who likes just praise, be that fellow. If you're a jealous lad, don't lament it. If you find yourself ungracious, be that. Stop trying to make over what won't change. . . .
> But this summer will be a beautiful joyous summer. Open your face and chest and take a flap off your skull and let in good air and sun. How about the third act of "One of These Days"?*
> From whom, and where, will I get an explanation of this constant thinking of self. They say reverie is about nothing, mist, but my reverie seems actual and of thicker stuff. Why do I think this way about myself and about conduct. It is right to let conduct form itself by being yourself. Now stop, Jesus, stop, be yourself, let conduct come from that.

From his comment "my reverie seems actual and of thicker stuff" we can suppose Odets often felt precariously poised between creativity and out-of-hand madness.

Their first season having officially ended with the closing of Anderson's *Night over Taos*, the members of the Group—some with more, some with less, margin—were engaged in staying alive until June, when they would reconvene at Dover Furnace, New York, for their second summer. Even their "angel," millionaire Otto Kahn, complaining that he had been hard hit by the stock-market crash, was no longer helping, and Clurman remembered him dejectedly murmuring that "the capitalist system was not working very well."

The members of the Group, though shorter on food and furniture, were more cheerful than Kahn, and continued to maintain an intense activity. Clurman repeatedly delivered a sermon to the potential playwrights in the Group that they must catch up with "our thought" and begin to write "an essentially American view expressed through realistically conceived characters." He was having difficulty finding suitable plays and argued with outside playwrights, who charged that, on the one hand, the Group had none of the advantages of a commercial theatre and, on the other, was not "a real revolutionary theatre" either. Of two possibilities, he preferred John Howard Lawson's *Success Story* to a thin play by novelist Dawn Powell. They rehearsed both in the summer of 1932 at Dover Furnace.

---

* An alternate title for his early play *910 Eden Street*. Here, as so often later, he had written the first two acts of a play and stopped. His difficulties with sustained flight took the form always of third-act trouble, and he scribbled on an envelope, "Show me a man with third-act trouble and I'll show you a man who cannot commit himself."

Here in my room at the Circle Hotel in the morning of April 8th, 1932, I begin to come at last to the real essence of myself, of what I am, the good and bad, the stinking and the scented, the rotten and the astringent wholesomeness, all conjoined to make me what I am. Yes, I love my flesh and the bones inside that keep the flesh together. From this time on I know that organization is coming to Clifford Odets, that he needs only to let him be himself. How long to learn such a truth! Tomorrow, I think, I am not quite sure of where my next meal is coming. There is more than a half dollar in my pocket, left of a dollar that Joe Bromberg gave me at two this morning at his house in Sunnyside. I came back here to write and did one scene of John Brown. Since I have been puttering around, writing some on a short story about the starving Jew boy in a room like this. Then I began to read on Whitman in Ellis's book "The New Spirit" and suddenly it came to me—I was thinking all the time of a girl who's coming to bed with me tomorrow—that I am becoming myself. It was a thrill mixed with sexual ideas, for as I thought of that I saw the joy of feeling being wrapped in sex, of her heavy breasts and of her young eagerness. Of how she rode me as if I were a horse and of how she let her whole self fall and relax into her vagina and of how I was up and deep in her with my stiff blood-filled flesh. That is how to be in life, that is how to approach the earth, with no intellectual precepts made to follow. The body and the soul as one make everything for you to follow.

Now I'm glad and will brush my teeth and wash my face and go to sleep.   7:30 a.m.

This summer I will come to truth as a child. Yes, gladly, openly and with much love for grass and sun and growing things.

Scribbled in Odets' writing under this typewritten diary entry and in its margins are notes such as "Non-acceptance of self and its bad things is trouble" or ". . . the fundamental viewpoint of one's art based on self . . . not often possible of attainment by sensitive people today . . . tell why it was easily possible in people of other times and cultures —Emerson in our country . . . today, most personalities split some way or another. . . ."

This remarkable diary entry concentrates the qualities of the critical area between neurosis and creativity. Odets can work constructively now toward a solution of his identity crisis in the monastic order of the Group Theatre. He can afford to be philosophic that he is being steadily rejected as an actor precisely because he somewhere knows he is being thereby *rescued* from a commitment which is not his central gift.

He is accruing strength to become now a true explorer of himself, emboldened by his Group brethren and by Clurman, who had passionately encouraged Max Anderson to abandon his distant heroes and their quasi-Elizabethan language and to embrace, instead, a new voice in a native tongue. Soon Odets would listen raptly to the language of one of the earliest of such new voices in the American theatre when, at Dover Furnace in the summer, he would understudy the part of Sol Ginsberg in Lawson's *Success Story*. Lawson's play was, as Clurman put it, "a hectic poetry compounded from the slogans of advertisements, the slang of gangsterdom, and echoes of Old Testament music." This was the language Odets had grown up with and would soon be able to use in his work, with greater success than Lawson.

For another month—until he could no longer borrow money from the Kozlenkos, the Brombergs, or anyone—he remained at the Circle Hotel and soaked up all he could at Clurman's bare West 58th Street apartment. The spiritual nourishment there, much of it from distinguished guests, was always plentiful. In a file marked "Souvenirs" Odets preserved for three decades a four-page, single-spaced document marked "A Talk delivered by Waldo Frank, 4/10/32."

Frank—essayist, historian, novelist, and, earlier, co-editor with Van Wyck Brooks of the lively and dissenting literary magazine *seven arts*—had recognized early the talent in such writers as Frost, Dreiser, Sandburg, D. H. Lawrence, Dos Passos, Walter Lippmann, and Eugene O'Neill. *Seven arts*, because of its outspoken opposition, had been a casualty of World War I; by now Frank, a handsome man in his early forties, was known both for his enduring love affair with Hispanic culture ("These men and women had something to tell me, that they had roots very deep in the earth . . . that they knew a wholeness I did not know") and for his criticism of the American scene. Descended from cultivated German-Jewish Americans, he had been part of the European excursion, along with Lawson, Clurman, and Aaron Copland; and he had by now been feted in Latin America—though not in the United States—as a major writer.

The first to write seriously of Charles Chaplin, whom he had often entertained at his Greenwich Village flat, Frank, with Chaplin, had in 1920 in Paris been as impressed as Clurman by Copeau's new movement in the French theatre. All his life it would be Frank's conviction that Americans had so far settled for a second-rate culture in their worship of "The Machine." Independently of Clurman, and before they met, he had said, "With tragic need, America needs groups."

On this April evening, with an optimism rekindled by the Depression, his address was a plea to the audience—composed of Group members and their guests—to enable the Group "to live," as he could see in it a part of the hope "for creating a new world"—a world which would be new not only in its economics "but on the moral side of things . . . human beings who have different values . . . a different sense of the dignity of life . . . a different loyalty to the truth. . . ." He declared that pain, distrust, anger, and hatred must be replaced with "energy-making, miracle-making" creative impulses. Such impulses, he granted, had always existed "in scattered individuals," but for real creativity "they must find their expression in whole personalities and in groups of human beings." In the current theatre of both Hollywood and Broadway he saw only people "on the side of money" instead of "on the side of humanity."

The sophisticated Frank was quite aware that in the other art forms, the surge of an indigenous American art was already evident. There was the painter Thomas Hart Benton, teaching at the Art Students League in New York since 1926. In the first years of the Depression, Thomas Wolfe, John Steinbeck, and William Faulkner (from 1929 to 1939 a Hollywood screenplay writer) had each published his first major novel, soon to be followed by Dos Passos' despairing trilogy called *U.S.A.*, clearly influenced in its form by the film industry. With the country fractured and in an increasingly embattled state economically, American writers, painters, sculptors, dancers, were—paradoxically—at long last beginning to realize Emerson's prayer and prophecy that we should forswear the "sere remains" of foreign harvests. Within a year the crippled Franklin Delano Roosevelt, by means of a variety of "recovery measures," would commence—with the energy and precision of a surgeon—to try to heal this prostrate and divided society.

It can well be imagined how stirring to Odets, already familiar with Frank's writing, this address must have been. Very quickly he adopted him as one of his older male mentors, and Frank was one of the first to recognize his singular gifts.

> *. . . all my life I've been like the fellow who asked for a chocolate covered herring . . . the two don't go together.*
>
> CLIFFORD ODETS, 1932

It is half past six on Sunday afternoon, the first one in May, Mothers' Day. I think the day was first started by certain enterprising business men; a tremendous business is done by Florists and candy manufacturers. But this thing has a deeper start in me and I want to write now about what I am feeling.

My mother is extremely subjective and sentimental. So are all American mothers. I have not observed this day. Truthfully, if I had money I should have done so, altho not believing at all in its "sanctity." I got out of bed late, three o'clock in the afternoon. Immediately I was reminded from my mother's manner, of the import of today. She said briefly, "Your coffee is on the table." I made my breakfast. My father left for a club or something which makes me think he argued with my mother, a not uncommon thing in this house for as many years back as I can remember. There were always quarrels.

My sister G. upbraided my father for leaving my mother alone. She . . . says what ever she likes, full of . . . critical remarks about anyone and everything. My father said "You don't want her to be here when you entertain your friends." He left. I listened to some symphonic music all the time feeling, because it was in the air (my mother had gone to lie down on the bed in her room), my mother's thoughts: "What is my son going to do about today. What does my whole family care about me?" The thing goes on in her self-pitying mind, magnified beyond all importance. I saw her walk upstairs with a wrapped box of candy, probably a joint present from my sisters, or perhaps my father.

Not for hours has the thought of her own motherhood left my mother's mind. She turned on the radio, full blast so that I could hear it up in my room, turning to a program in which a man extolled the virtues of motherhood. Then they presented a play about George Washington coming home to his mother, a slushy treacle thing in which often is heard, "My boy, my boy." I did not say that there are Washington letters telling his mother to keep away from his house since the guests annoyed her and she annoyed them.

From this entry we see that Odets, almost twenty-six and once more penniless, had returned to his parents' home in Philadelphia to wait out the few weeks during which the Group directors were frantically searching for a place in which to reconvene for the summer.

As this sad Mother's Day drags on, the radio continues its sentimental playlets and Odets writes:

> The whole afternoon has made me sad beyond words. When I am away from home I send a telegram, but being here at home has been a harrowing mental experience today. In the first place, my mother is sentimental beyond compare. Secondly, it is I, an external object, who have made her bitter and unhappy. I can not do that consciously to anyone. Days before she was thinking about today. On her dresser—whether or not she placed it there for me to see I can not say—she put a telegram I had sent her for such a day a year or two ago. It says, "Dearest mother, much love for today and all other days." She had saved it, taken it out to read and it obviously shows that she was thinking about this Sunday before it came. Or about my relationship to her. Frankly, I can not cope with this thing. I think it's best to remain silent. Or is it better to say to her now, some of the things I'm writing here. . . .
>
> The viewpoints of this household are not mine. When I was here with "Connelly" my mother was grieved to tears that I did not have a new overcoat. She wanted me to visit my Uncle Willie, she said, but not with such an old ragged overcoat. I make her unhappy, she says, because she can not see me successful, having nice things, looking well, so she can be proud of me. Such viewpoints kill me. As bad as I am, in all her relationships with friends and relatives, she has never met a better young man, one who tries more sincerely and earnestly to be a good man, to lead a good life and reach a true spirituality thru living life. But no, a realization of such problems or distinctions do not exist for her, even tho she is able to recognize a mean selfish person almost on sight.
>
> I point out constantly to her that if her happiness depends on mine, as she says it does, that I have never been so happy in all my life as I am now. But no, it goes on as old; she looks at me and is torn between her kind of mother love and an unhappy mild bitterness that I am different from others and not materially rich. She says often that her cup would be filled to overflow if she could only see me happy. Well, I am happy and working industriously in life for further happiness and inner richness. What's the answer? I don't know.

That Pearl herself was divided, thus deepening her son's dilemmas, is evident from a diary note written later this spring; in this are reflected Pearl's honesty, her scorn for a life lived by middle-class values, her respect for learning and her sense of humor.

> My mother repeated an oft-told story of some wise student in Russia. For his wisdom he was greatly revered and respected, but he dressed shabbily, content with a tramp's habiliment. A family wanted to invite him to a party, but insisted that he dress properly for such an occasion. He agreed, dressing himself with unusual care and taste. Sitting at the festive board, he carefully began to spill his soup all over his coat and lapels. "What are you doing!" the host

exclaimed. "Well," said the student, "you invited my clothes so now I'm feeding them."

With great relief, even joy, Odets told his mother five days after the guilt-ridden Mother's Day that Cheryl Crawford had informed him that within the month the small band of zealots would set forth for a four-hundred-acre farm above Pawling, New York, called Dover Furnace. Meanwhile he must mark time; knowing, however, that he would soon rejoin his beloved Group, he maintained fair patience and good humor, writing some, visiting the Leofs and Marc Blitzstein, listening to Rose Kahn play the piano, attending concerts and recitals, and directing (and playing in) an amateur production in Philadelphia of *Precedent*, a play about labor leader Tom Mooney.

As the Group's Philadelphia evangelist, Odets was asked by his disciple Abner Biberman to do battle with his Theatre Guild cousin Herbert Biberman, now visiting from New York, who had directed Odets in *Roar China*. He describes the encounter in a wry and funny letter to Clurman announcing, "I had it out with the enemy today." It is evident from his account that there was some animosity and resentment between the two companies. Odets writes of their argument over the Guild production of *The Moon in the Yellow River*, and quotes Biberman's claim that in the production of the Broadway success *Another Language* a commercial manager "had done in four weeks . . . with no halloo, what the Group was trying to do in a year and a half and had not done." Odets states darkly: ". . . know that he is very bitter and angry about the Group. Mark him as Enemy # One."

To Clurman he sends an apologetic summary of his direction of *Precedent*, in which he will play a venal district attorney; his rejection of the Guild's Philip Moeller appears now complete:

> The production of "Precedent" is going well. I am making it like a news reel with held pictures before each black out.* I can do nothing with it as I would like to, not being able. But it's going to be as good as a Moeller production anyway. No, better is what I mean. The valuable thing from all this is that I'm learning about my own acting by seeing how rotten all this is.

In capital letters, as a postscript, he has typed, "I AM READING EMERSON OH I AM READING EMERSON." His father had left in his room as a message to him two volumes of a peculiar edition of Emerson "made for business men." In a gaily mocking account of this to Goldie Bromberg he says, "The devils quote and underline on every page glorious trumpet-sounding maxims about success. They make Emerson the first Bruce Barton of his country. But I am reading with a clear brain and no interest in success." Emerson is "certainly certainly the wisest American."

He was again writing energetically at night—short stories—to compensate for these "bloodless days" and sent to *Liberty* one about a "drunken boy walking around on a hot night." Another, called "Peggy of Dorchester," dealt with his unrequited love seven years earlier on Fishers Island.

Eating too much and feeling "bilious," he was listening to, and storing up in his diary, snatches of dialogue which would become his trademark:

---

* This is an adumbration of the *form* of *Waiting for Lefty* two years later.

My mother just came into my room here and put an apple on the table, saying, "Why don't you eat an apple once in a while, fruit." So I'll leave it lay. Yes, daytime here is a nuisance.

During these weeks he clearly was readying himself for the serious work of the summer by a steady self-searching inquiry—which he compares to that of Tolstoy—into basic life values and the means to achieve them. On a crumpled, yellowed scrap of paper is his scribbled exhortation: "Spirituality must come from physical suffering . . . you cannot be 'fat and comfortable' and gain spiritual sustenance. No. You must know deep fleshy hungers."

He is filled with contempt for the "Jewish fiddlers" he meets at the Leofs' who scrape away indiscriminately at Beethoven or Wagner; he has stopped speaking to one of them who, happily playing an early rococo piece of Beethoven, comments, "Beethoven was crazy when he wrote all the last quartets." It seems to him such musicians are "bad people" who have no judgment of this "greatest of all arts," and are either "vilely sentimental" or interested only in technical problems. They do not see the difference between the concise utterances of a Beethoven, who is saying something about himself and about life, and "the constant orgasmic music of Wagner."

He despairs of ever finding "an artist beneath a musician"; by an artist he means a kind of "priest"—not like the cellist he had met, "an urbane Jew of the sort who wear tailored clothes and are generous and insistent that you partake of their generosity." Although he appears to be unaware of the unconscious links, this is a set of self-admonitions.

Counseling himself against glibness, he says: "Be careful that you are not merely satisfied with a pithy phrase covering a pit of emptiness." He must not be too easily satisfied with learning an initial truth ("Once a thing is learned I cease to investigate it further").

Of prime concern is that he must not simply "trade one ideology for another" and must concentrate on "what is before us"—from kimmel seed on rye bread to the words of Emerson, who, he notes, had "also complained that our country was always interested in the biggest and the best."

In his diary on May 18—in love now with Emerson—he writes:

Looking at a photograph of Emerson reminded me early this morning of something I have often thought before: Beware of small nosed men. Seldom do they have generosity of spirit. You are apt to find them cramped and narrow, limited in their views. Just now I can not remember one great man who did not own a generous spread of nose. A large nose does not necessarily make a good man or a great one, but mostly good men or great ones have large noses.

I thought for a few hours that I would have liked to have known Emerson alive, to have sat in the grass at his feet and felt the pressure of his hand, seen the spread of what must have been a beautiful smile. But no, it is best this way. Sometimes it happens that the man refutes by his actions what he says. There was a little sorrow connected with personally knowing Waldo Frank. In his writing he holds back some of himself, a certain portion that is not admirable. Yet he is a large man and a good one. The slight colour of his vanity is not important beside his goodness.

Emerson loved me before I ever met him. (So with great men) When my father was yet a pubescent boy, this man was already the father of men like us. My father I say, and it is so! Particles of him we carry around with us, feed on them, are nourished. Emerson is of my flesh, I of his . . . if I do not fail him. This remains to be seen. Say this of Beethoven too, of all the others. How those men have never, will never die! Whitman roars in your ears all the time. When you swing your arm and the muscles flex, they are Whitman's muscles too.

This afternoon I dug up the front grass plot. Until I got into the work with a proper swing I disliked it. But after it went well and I worked with good will and lovely muscles, I was thinking of the birds who come down from all over, these sparrows, to grab at the worms and grubs you turn up. It could make a very nice parable. Here is this man turning up a plot of soil to plant grass. All the sparrows sit around, afraid of him, but eager for the worms and bugs turned up to daylight. They watch this man, wondering what he is doing. Then they realize he is doing his job for them, for their sakes, that they may have all this good food. He goes away and they swarm down and eat their full [sic] with much over to bring to the nests. No, first they fed the younglings in the nests. At night they meet. They are so overwhelmed by the goodness of this man—who must be a god —who worked an entire afternoon for them, that they send him a round robin of thanks and include him in their prayers . . . in fact make him the object and sole receiver of their prayers. . . .

Daily his father was at him for not getting "a real job," taunting him for his "religious" attachment to the Group. He fled from these attacks to his typewriter, where he recorded keen and compassionate accounts of his daily experience: a family friend is dying of the results of "sleeping sickness";* the next-door neighbors are a helpless young couple, unemployed and totally dependent on the young man's father, "out of Dostoievsky certainly."

A peculiarly long entry—almost 2,000 words—observes that "the American 'fag' has now entered the American home at last" through a radio program called *Myrt and Marge;* it astonishes him that his mother and sister laugh at the "fag" without realizing what they are laughing about. Parenthetically, "America is changing . . . breasts pop out of ads for toothpaste" and it all "may be for the best." Fundamentally, "people are not bad," but how few of them have Emerson's "uncorrupted behavior." There is something threatening to him in the overt homosexuality of the program, and he concludes with a self-comforting argument for phrenology:

Look at the Group's people and you will find them all broad across the cheekbones, with good foreheads and well-spaced eyes. There is something deep behind this. Anthropologists and psychology workers have found, I believe, that inward glandular structure and function is responsible for facial and cranial formation.

It appears he is reassuring himself that he, at least, is "uncorrupted."

To Clurman, less than three weeks before he will join him, he writes impassionedly and at length, almost as to a lover, that he fears the end of Christianity is near, that the materially rich American does not want to illustrate "The Passions of Man": "They do not care to be crucified for their opinions. Opinions! That is the key word."

Perhaps it was that Jew boy Heine who said originally that the reason we could no longer build Gothic structures was because they

* Odets' play *Paradise Lost* uses this material.

were built from convictions, and we had only opinions. Lacking today the communal life (culture?) that breeds convictions—no longer
desirous of abstaining and abnegating self for the greater glory of
sitting at the right hand of God, the Christian era is now dying, and
nothing is yet here to replace it. Men walk around with milky eyes;
artists torture their mediums and young men weep in the streets. . . .

Now I am coming to the question I want to ask, Harold. Here
comes the Group and all the time I kiss the ground where it walks.
Here stands The Group, with convictions; here is a communal life
from which already richness has resulted. There are other things
too I think: some few musicians, Waldo Frank and the others, Robert
Frost(!!!), some short story writers springing from their respective
places in the broad American country. What, I ask, what is the ideal
man for these people, for The Group, for us? . . . I suppose you
will say, "Don't ask, but work, work, work!" . . . Walking around
Philadelphia, meeting often horrible people (their intellect only a
foreskin to hide their sex), I have had actually these last weeks to
make a mark on my hand with mercurachrome, a red mark to be a
sign that I am not of these people, nor like them, nor falling into the
mire that holds them fast by night and day. I have bound a red sign
on my hand like our elder Jews with their boxes and binding of
straps. I match all the time their faith with mine in The Group and
when I think of thirty of us I want to weep with joy and remind
myself constantly that we are we and there is no earth or world
without us.

The record of the vicissitudes of his efforts to integrate a work-
identity continues almost to the day he leaves for Dover Furnace. In the
meantime he continues his sermons addressed mostly to himself. They
are geared to decreasing his vulnerability, his sense of uselessness, and
his alienation from a world which tends to defeat creativity by rigidly
closing down and contracting consciousness.

On all sides I am defeated and pressed back by my feelings and
senses. But it is only by going through them, and with them, that
one can reach salvation. To evade them is to stink with a living
death. No, through them. Not around them, but through them! Yet
hold a firm grip, an iron hand, and keep a stern discipline.

Get back to being a child, a child with an active intelligence and
curiosity. But all the time open. It is impossible that people can hurt
you now. You have more than the child; you have the sure knowledge of what people are and how valuable or valueless are their
qualities and words and behavior. In other words, you have now a
real sensitivity, not a sentimental one that boo hoos at every harsh
word pointed your way. Now you must get the simple, intuitive world
of the child to walk in again. And sleep peacefully, relaxed. Your life
is new and fresh. You are growing strong and enthusiasm is quickly
replacing the old romantic morbid shit. But be open. Let emotion
flow whenever it wants to. Be careful of forcing anything. In fact
force nothing!! Have the fluidity of water. Be a mirror of the passing
world and peoples. Be emotionally fluid. NOT STATIC. Your instincts
are right, the most valuable of all!

Filled with his love of Beethoven, Whitman, and now Emerson, he
writes: ". . . Have a hero! The self as hero is a dangerous matter. . . .
It may produce great art, but is apt to make life bitter and savourless. . . .

Make contact with the external object, with the tree, the mountain, the man and the woman. . . . Listening to one's own voice, watching one's own image—those are insidious matters. . . . When a man has a hero it is just as if he told you, 'I have clefted out for my self a road to travel.' . . . Most men who don't, most I say, are not of much use to life and the world. . . ."

The road he has clefted out is rocky indeed as he tries to avoid his father and absorb his mother's chronic pain. A note called "The Mother Mind" describes a typical scene, this one with Abner Biberman:

> He is shaved and fresh looking, appearing in white flannels and a smart jacket. He looks like a leisurely gentleman. I greet him, dressed in unpressed trousers, a leather jacket, hair uncombed and needing a shave. I see a pained look come into my mother's eyes at the disparity of us. She knows at that moment a great pain, contingent upon her standards. Then we go out to his car. All the time she is comparing the estates of the two young gentlemen, Abner, and her son. Thru her mind passes the pardonable idea that I am a much better man, more clever, etc., and yet, and yet.
>
> When we go into the house she makes the ace of justifications. "His fingernails were so black underneath," she says.

It does not please him that he observes in himself a certain "strong jealousy" whenever new members are taken into the Group: ". . . it is as if my girl has taken two strange men to her bed. But here it must be so: the world must flow between her thighs." The jealousy does not come, however, "from that those men may take my parts away.* No, it's a different thing."

A last scrap of typing, just before he leaves his parents' Philadelphia house to rejoin the Group at last in the woodlands of New York, states: "If there is a man you would know, set him up against a tree. He should compare favorably."

* Overtly, he refers here to acting parts in plays.

Chapter Thirteen

One thinks of The Group. In twenty-five, in fifty years where will it be? And we, the actors? Some dead, the others grey and toothless, ghostly, living in the past, worrying not about a summer and what feminine bed is for sleeping in: landmarks in a possible American theatre. I shudder at this. Yet I think of the new young boys and girls. We will talk to them, teach them the requisite cunning, make of them great actors too, and they will speak of us as we mention Stanislavsky now. . . . Not only are we living for truth, but that truth may be passed on: so be our work!

CLIFFORD ODETS, *1932*

Without the Group Theatre I doubt that I would have become a playwright. I might have become some other kind of writer, but the Group Theatre and the so-called "method" forced you to face yourself and really function out of the kind of person you are, not as you thought the person had to function, or as another kind of person, but simply using your own materials.

So Odets thirty years later recalled the central point for him of the scorching summer of 1932 at Dover Furnace, near Pawling, New York, where on June 19 he had arrived, along with Harold Clurman and Stella Adler, in Cheryl Crawford's car. Although he did not feel quite "the old turbulence, the old swift inner running" of the previous summer, he recorded how moved he was by "the gentleness of Cheryl toward me," and by the "joy that comes with such an arrival." He had once more won a respite from his father's house in West Oak Lane and from the only visible alternative to it: joining the millions of men in once respectable suits standing in dreary, self-demeaning lines, waiting for a handout. He meant now to face himself and to "do some writing with merit this summer," using his own materials.

On June 20 the Group—almost fifty members now—listened to Dawn Powell read her new play originally called "The Party," later to open and quickly close as *Big Night*. Although this "brutal picture" made a poor impression on Odets, he found Clurman's discussion brilliant, astonishing in its elucidation of layered meanings even in this slight work. He records in his diary: ". . . ideologies that come from genuine material, really participated in by the author, is the way to a good permanent literature."

This formula was easier to come by than was the "good permanent literature" itself. Knowing this, the Group directors had invited several writers, including a few playwrights, to be part of this summer in the conviction that a coherent theatre group that included the playwright was the matrix out of which plays would be born.* They had no inkling, however, that their own playwright would hatch not from these guests but from their bit-actor Odets, ignominiously relegated to understudying Luther Adler in John Howard Lawson's *Success Story*, now under pressured revision by its author. Previously rejected by the Theatre Guild under the title "Death in the Office," this play interested Clurman sufficiently that he wired an enthusiastic acceptance to Lawson in Hollywood.

Clurman regarded Lawson at this time as "the hope of our theatre," and saw as the essence of his play "what happens to an idealistic force when it finds no effective social form to contain it." The protagonist of *Success Story*, Sol Ginsberg, becomes, in Clurman's words, "a desperately destructive man because he sees no way his unusual energy, imagination, and sense of truth can operate in harmony with the society that confronts him. It is only by becoming society's enemy and the betrayer of his own deepest values that he can succeed in it."

An assistant statistician in the advertising firm of the easygoing "Nordic" Raymond Merritt, Ginsberg is a product of the East Side of New York who has established his efficiency by hard work. Sol, who "bristles with East Side mannerisms," is viciously resentful of the capitalistic class represented by Merritt; he gradually rises to a position of importance, casts aside Sarah Glassman, the Jewish girl who loves him and with whom he has shared his youthful ideals, and marries the mistress of his employer. He becomes the dominant head of the firm and still he is not satisfied. His soul's unrest is violently disturbing to him, as he finds no fulfillment in his success or in heaping clothes, jewels, and a beautiful house on his blond "Nordic" wife. Sarah mourns for the boy he once was—full of ideals, a radical. Reflecting on what has happened to him, he says that Christ, "who was a Jew dressed in a rainbow," gave him a choice of being a rebel (radical) or having "the earth" . . . he says he has "broken the chain with the past" (his Jewish heritage, "the blood of a race") . . . "then what am I . . . a missing link?" There is a tussle with a gun and Sol is shot dead by Sarah. Lawson appears to say in this play that when a Jew breaks his ties with his heritage, he ends up with nothing. He can find no peace or happiness either in a radical movement or in economic success. And pursuing "Christian values" has no meaning for him.

* Besides Maxwell Anderson and John Howard Lawson, who were in and out, there were Dawn Powell, George O'Neil, Philip Barber, Albert Bein, Gerald Sykes, and Ernest O'Malley.

In his autobiography Lawson recalled he had written this play in
pencil "at breakneck speed" and with a profound emotional involvement. He was wrestling, he believed, with "the problem of my identity,"
an important aspect of which was to come to terms "with the Jewish
aspect of my personality. . . . I could not be American without also being Jewish. . . . Sol Ginsberg has my idealism, my interest in social
struggle. He also has my driving desire for recognition and money and
success, which can be won only by spiritual bankruptcy and death."

Looking back in 1966 with the accumulated wisdom of thirty-four
additional years of living, Clurman would see Lawson's dilemma and its
subsequent resolution in Marxism differently: "I think Lawson *needed*
his corruption to be a playwright. He needed the struggle between his
power complex and his Jewish conscience. When he lost the conflict,
he lost his talent and, from then on, behaved like a converted Christian."❰

Odets' creative struggles of a similar nature—beginning to be visible
in his writing this summer—would for long periods be *enacted* on the
smaller stage of his daily life. Like all working artists, he would steadily
try to shift the battleground back to his art, a more controllable universe—sometimes.

Perhaps it was because Lawson's plays were, as Lawson himself
says, "deficient in psychological depth"—dealing with people as symbols
—or perhaps it was because he still lacked sufficient craft, that his *Success
Story* would be dismissed by many of the reviewers in the fall of 1932 as
the hackneyed story of a boy who makes good only to find "his victories
are vain." Odets, far from finding Lawson's play hackneyed, would sense
in it a cultural permission to unlock doors within himself he had hitherto
not dared even to acknowledge. He was disappointed indeed not to have
been cast in the leading role of Sol Ginsberg, a Jew torn between his
idealism and his drive for success.

It had been Lawson's determination in his teens, and steadily thereafter, to "write the crazy epic of this day," and *Success Story* was the
most "realistic" of many tries, his first having been produced when he
was twenty years old. His symbolic, expressionist *Processional* had created
a considerable stir in 1925. It was no wonder that the twenty-five-year-
old Odets, wrestling with variants of much the same identity issues (and
formal problems) as Lawson, and determined this summer to do "some
writing of merit," would find himself glued to Clurman's six-hour discussions and to Strasberg's rehearsals of this play. Although he knew
nothing of Lawson's personal history,❰ he was much interested by this
divided, dedicated, disputatious intellectual nearing forty, an unsuccessful
pioneer in expressionism in the American drama who had failed five years
earlier in his effort to keep the New Playwrights together. Some thought
his attempts to achieve a synthesis of Freud and Marx premature (he
had been trying all during the Jazz Age); others thought his specific talent
more didactic than creative.

When his pedagogic manner became annoying this summer, a Group
member described Lawson as a combination of "One-eyed Izzy and a
rabbi." To Clifford he appeared more "like some medieval figure, a
Borgia, with a good strong chest and great vitality" who was sufficiently
disciplined to "write with any sort of noise around him." Now he was
fresh from the fabled studios of Metro-Goldwyn-Mayer and RKO in the
film capital, and it was rumored he had acquired a beautiful home on

❰ 13.1.
❰ 13.2.

Long Island and a Russian wolfhound. The fact that Lawson had been injured in an auto accident and had a limp like Odets' competitor—his sister Genevieve—added charge to his interest.

On June 21, the day of the first reading of *Success Story*, Odets records in his diary that "there is a wonderful meaty part, a Jew who goes from Communism to riches and then realizes that his life has been lost on the way." J. Edward (Joe) Bromberg, who is Odets' choice for this part, said he thought Odets could play it, but Odets doubts it, as ". . . the directors have told me my worth and it doesn't seem to measure in any way to the requirements of such a role." That he is conscious of his investment in Lawson's theme is clear from the next sentence: "Every day would be a catharsis if I played that part, for it is much my own problem, the one of Mark Berke in my sad play 'One of These Days.' "*

On this same day he makes a nest in a drawer for "a lost little sandpiper who grieves of its lostness but does not stop its cheep-cheep noise for a minute." The next morning it is "stiff, legs drawn up to breast. . . . And that's how we bury him, nameless, markless."

Before Strasberg put the actors on their feet in *Success Story*, Clurman made a long analysis of it, "so brilliant," Odets later recalled, "that your mouth stood agape." Clurman, never a Communist, but ideological leader of the Group in a broad humanist and esthetic sense, fed the members' enthusiasm by detailing for hours on end what the theme meant for American life.

Lawson, later to be imprisoned as one of the "Hollywood Ten," but at this time opposed to party-line Communist doctrine, recalled, "I had no extended conversation with Odets, but remember his face as he watched and listened to rehearsals of the play. No one else responded in this way, and the intensity of his concentration touched me; he reacted to every line, every mood. . . . It was not the actor's problem that interested him but the social and aesthetic content of the play."

Pondering, in his seventy-third year, his influence this summer on Odets, Lawson concluded it was not simply his own "explosive rhetoric" that had stimulated the young man but something deeper: "a concept of the human personality thwarted ["alienated" is the modern word], fighting to get through to people, to assert himself in a hostile environment." While Lawson is "not suggesting that my work was successful in this," its central intention—like that of the body of Odets' subsequent work—was, in his opinion, the "agonized search for creativity." It is an "agonized" search in the twentieth century for writers because the society *invites* its creative youngsters into science and technology while frowning on those who take any art too seriously.

In the spring of this year Odets had scribbled to himself: "Spirituality must come from physical suffering." Now he must cope both with his disappointment and resentment that he had not been cast in either *Big Night* or *Success Story*, and with the fact that Clurman, on the basis of

---

* Mark Berke (nee Berkowitz), the doomed Jewish poet and "psychology major" in the Philadelphia rooming house, was Odets' chief identification figure in his play *910 Eden Street*. In *Success Story* Sol Ginsberg's corrupt job is in an advertising firm similar to the Odets Company.

910 Eden Street, did not think much of him as a writer. He was determined to accomplish two things this summer: to change Clurman's estimate of his writing and to deepen himself as an actor by no longer "skating across only the surface of myself." His diary records:

There is a compulsion that makes me do that, one that hinges on my attitude towards people. If one is to be an artist, particularly an actor who works by self exhibition, by self-exploration before an audience, he must indeed first learn to not let those people get in his way. That is what I do all the time: keep an attitude while I am working having a fear of being silly, of not being this or that. No, when I heard Chaliapin on records tonight, I realized that it was an absolutely necessary matter to wipe out this fear . . . it is a fear after all. Do away with the omnipresent thought of what *other people will think.* Comes this all back to: concentrate on what is before you. In justification, I must admit that I have made a slight improvement in this direction over last year. I am at least going the right way.

Like many gifted young men in crisis, he determined now to carry out this summer what he had only fantasied the year before at Brookfield Center: to make a "meditative descent into the inner shafts of mental existence,"⊄ in the hope he would be enabled to master and transform his appetites, angers, and conflicts, and thus to produce good work.

After a month of continence he writes:

Sometimes, as now, I contemplate with absolute amazement the fact that a man and woman together and naked can make such mad pleasure, So it is that nature makes of all of us indulgent monsters with Sir Instinct as chief pimp. And I have done monstrous things (if anything can be so adjectived) and will continue to do them as often as I have desire. I sense in myself as of old, every possible queerness: there is no sexual "depravity" in which I might not indulge at one time or another. I think the only sin is lack of selection, promiscuity, going from one to the other.

As he reviews the six girls with whom he has had sexual intercourse in the last year, he thinks the most important part of it is "that I have taken something away from each of them, some learned and deeply realized thing . . . and they from me . . . I am me and yet parts of all those girls." As he thinks of the particular splendors of each "of their secret places" and of the "lovely little ways they have stretched next to one" he thinks with love of Whitman, who said "something like oh the amplitude of the earth, and the coarseness and sexuality of it and the great goodness and charity of it."

It seems to him that "I never see a man or a woman—when I am happy—that I don't want to kiss them or at least touch them with my hand. I want to be doing things for people all the time when I am happy and overspilling. When I am unhappy or dumped, then it becomes a different affair." One Group member would recall Odets, full of applejack, confiding to him his discomfort over his sexual yearnings toward men.

His aim is not simply to master these struggles by repression or renunciation, but flexibly to shape the exploration of unconscious fantasies by way of Form into the confident and authentic communication we call Art. His diary records: "I have written down on a piece of paper in my

⊄ 13.3.

pocket: Be Fearless! It means more to me than the obvious significance."
Only a frightened man would thus address himself.

Odets envies the Group's leading actor, Franchot Tone, who appears to be unafraid, and who, "establishing an organic pitch with the other actors . . . is completely relaxed so that what comes is allowed through." He comforts himself that "there is a certain superficiality" in Tone, and that for him "to get the other dimension I feel lacking" he will have to change as a person.

Maxwell Anderson's girl, Mab, nightly brings him Anderson's type-writer (used by Anderson only on weekend visits), on which Odets hopes that "now I will find a stride." He tries not to be discouraged by writer Gerald Sykes' criticism of his short story, "One Hot Night," and is jealous of Sykes, whom Clurman thinks talented. The astonished religious ecstasy of the previous summer at Brookfield Center having cooled slightly, he records in the early part of this summer, "I am not using my-self enough." It helps his growing need for asceticism, however, that the actors are scheduled for strenuous and painful "body-work" with the dancer Helen Tamiris, whom Odets describes as "a goodly woman, a Jewess who has obviously struggled up from a Jewish meanness to what she is now, Amazonic and clipped of speech."

It helps his spiritual aspiration that he is assigned to work on difficult acting exercises and improvisations,* and that he has begun to make notes on what he calls a "Beethoven play"; but this is not enough. He must proclaim publicly and privately not only his determination to forswear aggressive as well as sexual expression, but also his capacity to rise above superficialities and vanities. His diary states:

> . . . what I must do is forget all thoughts of appearances. Cut off all my hair . . . forget how or why to dress, forget about the girls here and the desire for them . . . and get to real honest work and forgetfulness of being a social being in the bad sense.

Hoping thus to triumph over his fear of what people will think of his inadequacies, he will become worthy—as an actor—of Strasberg's and Clurman's attention. In his notes for an autobiography he later writes of this time:

> People laugh at *me*. . . . Sandy [Meisner] as example of people who jibe or scorn me; but they close me up or arouse murderous rage. (two kinds of people, those who accept me and those who reject me. But if they contribute to my growth, I hang on! This has never changed in me. . . .)

Although he was never to become a prime actor for the Group, he was now only a few steps away from taking precisely those risks as playwright he had been counseling himself to take: ". . . wipe out fear. Do away with the thought of what the people will think.† Concentrate on what is before you." But there were still several intermediate steps toward a monastic discipline and a relinquishment of pride: the shaving of his head on the second day of this hot July was the first visible one. It

---

* In one of these, designed to help people find their own materials, Odets por-trayed a sad organ-grinder and was encouraged by the high sense of mutuality he experienced with a new young apprentice of Greek origin, Elia Kazan, who played the adaptive monkey. In another he wakened to an alarm, rushed through breakfast and to an office, where, mocking a business executive, he lighted a cigar and put his feet on the desk—having rushed himself into exhaustion for nothing.

† Leo Garel, painter, has said, "One of the prime requisites of being an artist is the capacity to risk looking foolish." (Personal communication)

may well have served also as a kind of penance for the dreadful deaths of Roberta and Joan, his wife and daughter, three years earlier almost to the day.

His beautiful blond wavy hair shorn, he writes:

After lunch I make up my mind to get a haircut at Dover Plains. And it's all off now, completely bald, ascetic, but inwardly I feel (as I didn't want to feel) that it's not so bad to look at. If I were so ugly that no one ever looked at me, then I might be a much better person. Well, I'm glad the hair is off; it will do the scalp good and already has given me kind of psychical lift. I had to force myself (and that was a good thing to do) to walk past a group of people with that head. Now it's old and finished.

Desperate, no doubt, that his visions of Joan and Roberta be "old and finished" as well, he studies Frost's "Home Burial" and writes in his diary, "Sleep, sleep sorrow sleep."

He again takes up the "Beethoven play," calling it now *Victory*—this title probably borrowed from Conrad—or sometimes "The Brant Play" after its protagonist, Louis Brant, a uniquely gifted boy who, his mother dead, has been raised uncouthly by a brother and a father "in the country" on a farm.* He becomes a self-taught pianist, and is exploited by the entrepreneurs and agents of the world ("So many bugs on one flower"). He is, with Whitman, one of the "two great artists in this country"—and will, in Odets' fantasy, become "a ruthless man," replacing Brahms as the third in the trio with Bach and Beethoven. The boy has been discovered by the avaricious money-men as a performer, but throughout the play he struggles to persuade them he must give up this lucrative fame-making in order to be a serious composer.

There is in this early play a condensation (as in a dream) of Odets' current wish to please his own father and now the Group directors by being considered a valuable actor (a *performing* artist, like Brant). At the same time he holds the deeper aspiration to emerge as a Beethoven-like *primary* creative artist independent of people's immediate responses. Odets' experience of emotional abandonment by his mother (Brant's mother is dead) and the subsequent fear of, struggle with, and courtship of his father are all elaborated in *Victory*. The name "Louis Brant" includes not only his father's name but also his affectionate name for Beethoven, the Anglicized name of Brahms, and the well-known play-brokerage firm of Brandt and Brandt, to which he aspired as a client. To the Brandt agency he would soon grudgingly be giving ten percent of his income, as well as supplying income to his father. In this early play he, presciently enough, has Louis Brant supplying *his* father's income.

This opus, while a direct expression of Odets' own situation, is a naked paradigm of the struggles of the artist in America. Working feverishly on it all this summer—once it was clear he would be assigned no acting part—he began to use it as the creative, if cluttered, bridge to his first finished full-length play, *I Got the Blues*, later to become the classic *Awake and Sing!* In his diary he writes, "Now I see again in myself flight, always flight. Here I am writing on the Beethoven play, which—when it's finished—may not even be about Beethoven. What I should do is write that play about the Greenberg family, something I know better

---

* Two decades later he titles a play *The Country Girl*: the title referring to the rootedness, purity, innocence, and gullibility of Georgie, the wife of a washed-up alcoholic actor, with whom, according to his wife Luise Rainer, Odets consciously identified himself.

and is closer to me. . . ." In *Awake and Sing!* the name, originally Greenbaum after a Bronx family, would be changed to Berger.

In the pages of its crumbling manuscript, neatly filed away for three decades with *910 Eden Street* of the previous year, there stands a full and rich record not only of the fumbling explorations of a classically alienated young man into the mysteries of his vulnerable self, his family, his generation, and his world, but also into the formal problems of writing a play. This summer built to the climax of laying his manuscript before Clurman, whose literary judgment he valued beyond that of anyone else, and to whose criticisms he remained exquisitely sensitive: when Harold one evening was not favorable even to an acting improvisation, ". . . it threw me off center and how quickly I thought that I'd never get anywhere. One little such thing is tremendously discouraging."

The nine scenes of the play, taken together with the sixty-three pages of concurrent diary entries, reflect on every page the network of conscious and unconscious forces which moved Odets now to the writing of it. He has constructed the profile of his own life up to his conversion to the Group Theatre, its moral and esthetic values being a function not only of the worldwide economic debacle but also of a hunger for a home-grown American culture to compare favorably with that of Europe. Even his respectable mentor Philip Moeller was now in Russia, studying its theatre. The convergence of these forces of history with Odets' stage of development issued this summer in a high, if confused, productivity.*

With a water glass filled with black-eyed Susans on one side of him and fresh evergreen sprigs he had picked "crowning the Beethoven head," on the other, Odets pores over Turner's life of Beethoven to find materials for the Brant play. Intuitively sensing his own soft spots as a playwright, he tries to sort false heroics from nobility, introspection from sentimentality. Borrowing characters, names, and external events from the nineteenth-century life of his beloved "Louis," he moves back and forth from this embattled life to the universe of his own crude and often melodramatic work-in-progress called *Victory*, never certain what he actually wants to say with his play. He is in the grip of the major dilemma of any creative individual whose identity confusion is acute: does he seek to resolve his relationships essentially in human transactions with real people or in giving form to the fantasied relationships in characters he creates?

"In a flash," it seems to him he realizes the "whole blinding truth about Beethoven," writing in his diary:

> This is what Louis God sweet Beethoven did: He sacrificed completely the man to his art, so greatly, so completely as no man before or since has done.† All of his life and feeling and thought swept

---

* He turns also now to a distinction between the "practical reality" of any observation "such as the trickle of water I was just watching" and its "poetic value." He wants to participate simply in such immediate and innocent experience, uncluttered by rationality or defensive maneuvering, saying, "It's a big rain. The earth is hungry and takes in with its broad tireless mouth much nourishment. Would I might be so simple as a tree or a green field standing quietly in the rain."

† Odets knows that a gifted man must be propelled to the use of his gift by his own powerful motives, and that, moreover, it is frequently the case that productive artists of Beethoven's stature early abdicate the effort to live a "normal" life.

before him to come thru and be retained forever in his divine art. That is what Ludwig did. Every inch of him, every atom of sensitivity and brain tissue shot into his music like to some inspired orgasm and constantly he cohabited with music. It was that every minute, so that in the end the intercourse became to him as one who would walk cojoined forever with a woman. That was what it was. Music was a woman for Beethoven such as never existed really in flesh. Take the greatest possible of all loves of a man for a woman, one so severe and great that it has not yet been recorded, and then you have for the first time an understanding of what he gave to his music.⟨ Before I thought many of his statements were idle boasts, when for instance he said of Guiccardi [sic] that if he gave himself to her what would he have had left for his music. Now I see that he meant that and a score of other such remarks. Music was some deity alive to him and it was necessary that he serve her physically and spiritually at all times. He did! Now I realize, poor Clifford Odets, the full implication of the saying, "He sacrificed himself completely to his art."

During this summer his unconscious strategy, not unusual in creative men, is to try to achieve a relative autonomy from actual women, in the effort to consolidate his creativity and, accordingly, his participation in the world of men. The unconscious fantasy appears to be that fundamental nourishment will nonetheless be obtainable at the "breasts of the Muse." One must, however, beware, Odets says, of "incautious intake" of addiction, and he records this summer, as so often before and after, his profound struggles with smoking, drinking, eating, and, above all, with music.

He sees in the heroic model of asceticism the prime example of Emerson's comment that "heroes are bred only in times of danger," and is convinced that great artists are bred similarly. Now that, in 1932, the "world is drifting into dangerous times," he is waiting to see what heroes and artists will spring from the people, clearly doubting he is capable of sufficient renunciation of normal human involvement to become one of these heroes.

It is not simply the forswearing of appetites that stands at the heart of the matter. It is the loneliness consequent on a creative intransigence which the twenty-five-year-old boy, and later the fifty-six-year-old man, finds unendurable. He wants to say in his work that "Life is good" and yet he knows that this "goodness" probably cannot be found in the comforts and solaces of ordinary men.

Quoting Emerson, he writes in his diary, "One chooses in life either truth or repose; you can not have both," adding then, ". . . and I have chosen truth; without thinking I have chosen it. Strange that I have never considered for a moment the repose." Perhaps he sensed even then that repose was forever beyond his reach.

His current play, *Victory*, a composite caricature of the conflicts to occupy his life and his work, supplies a remarkable piece of psychological microscopy such as early literary work always provides, even for the specific nature of struggles toward form. He is made uneasy by its "glibness and melodrama," and by the fact that he cannot help working, as he sees it, from "detail to detail, never keeping the end in mind." It seems to him "the material becomes spotty this way and without focal direction." He is convinced that it is surely "wrong to work as I do" and that "be-

⟨ 13.4.

fore I do any more work, I must think and see the whole play and what it's about." He brands himself here, as frequently he would be branded later by drama critics, as a "scenewright."

Two decades later, standing on the more secure ground of his grasp of people, he defensively says, "I don't lay out plays—I lay out characters." But now, at twenty-five, he feels himself losing the battle for form, and at the mercy of his conflicts. He seeks a formal solution by using Beethoven's life as the spine of the play. The defensive function of this is that he once again sidesteps a direct confrontation with his own fantasies and conflicts. The price he pays, however, is that the work becomes stilted, schematic, lifeless, and lacking in personal idiom or symbol. Its reliance on the Beethoven story divorces it also from a contemporary context, thus rendering it romantically "self-expressive" and, accordingly, less communicative. Clurman is disappointed that *Victory* shows none of the talent earlier evident in Odets' *910 Eden Street,* where he had begun to deal with psychological materials closer at hand.

In an effort to impose on himself a work-discipline, he tacks on his wall outlines of ten scenes of *Victory,* only nine of which he writes. He writes out, as well, vignettes of all the characters, of Brant in particular, and a summary of the meaning of the whole play. These notes for *Victory* are supposed to serve as a means to a disciplined focus of the fundamental theme—as well as he can make it out—of this play: a person born into an individualistic society is doomed ("people hugging themselves to themselves"). The problem is "how to go down into the lowlands where other human beings are packed together" and, by understanding more than they, become their tongue and one of them? His view of this path to his audience shifts during these two summer months, and by the middle of August he writes that Hilda (the chief female character in *Victory*) lives a sinning "life of the flesh," going from one lover to another, while Brant "will go early to the life of the spirit." Both, he says, are after the same thing: to arrive ultimately "home." His play will try to show, he says, that one may reach this "high spiritual place," represented by "the old farmhouse," in *both* ways—an ingenuous simplification of the many passionate conscious and unconscious struggles visible in *Victory.*

Immediately following this discussion in his diary of his play he writes that he has been thinking of Hart Crane and of "how beautiful a death by drowning can be." Earlier in the day he had gone swimming and had reflected that the water was "like a mother, yielding and tender." From his swim he has "got a beautiful mood, and came out of it a better man. Truly." This day closes with Morris Carnovsky improvising "an old Jew praying and grieving for the world . . . that was nice." This is a mood not of despair but of a kind of Hebraic at-homeness with melancholy.

As the summer days follow one upon another, so do Odets' scenes for *Victory,* their several revisions, and his long, thoughtful, introspective diary entries. Eager for response, he frequently reads from his two plays to the other actors and to the visiting playwrights. To Goldie Bromberg he offers also his diary, and records then his shame after she has read of his secret marriage and its tragic finish. It is evident that he is steadily

231

asking a more general audience, "If I reveal myself to you, will you laugh at me and shun me, or will you accept me?"

A detailed splicing of the notes and revisions with this summer's diary again (as in his early novel about a composer) yields a chillingly prescient picture of the life yet to be lived by this frightened young actor now beginning to blossom as playwright. In the first scene "the money-men" discuss Brant's "mad calling card"—modeled after the one Clifford had earlier had printed for himself in his father's shop—which in self-mockery states: "Louis Brant—Concert Pianist, Conductor, Composer and Great Man. Dover, N.Y., U.S.A." Brant is described by Odets as "compactly but powerfully built," with "arrogance and pride and aspiration written all over him, particularly in the way he carries himself. The eyes are brilliant and show great vitality, the lips are determined. His movements are few, but quick and extremely energetic." The overt arrogance and athletic energy—to become more visible much later in Odets—were immediately observable in his father.

Composer Brant—in a clairvoyant scene which predicts Odets' life in Hollywood—says: ". . . every time I walked on the stage dressed up like a store dummy, I thought with shame in my heart that I was wasting my genius." Brant is certain that "no artist can go beyond his culture" and that Beethoven was able to express himself not because he had a "determined lip or fiery manners" but because "the times were ripe." All his life, plagued by the terror that he was a mediocre talent, too eager to please, Odets would make explicit the culpability of his society in his failure to achieve creatively what he might have in other circumstances.

Louis Brant's agents and managers understand the importance of his promise to his father that he will return to the farmhouse "in a silk shirt." Thus, they provide him with many silk shirts and assure him he'll soon get rid of his ideals. Brant goes on composing, however, asking his manager, "How can you call the one thing that gives me reason for life, a caprice? . . . there are a thousand millionaires, but only one Brant."

Brant, like Odets always seeking the "lost part of myself," peers into every woman's face for that life partner who will be a "winged victory" for him, a strong and nurturing woman who will shield an artist. Brant's effort is doomed, as Odets' will be. His wife dies in childbirth and the baby with her, leaving Brant deaf by now and feeling like a monster in his loneliness, his emotion burning itself out "like the heart of a cross-country runner."

There is confused indication here that because Brant the artist "feeds all into the mouth of his music," he cannot have the comfort of normal human relationships (home, wife, children). This, as with Beethoven, is his strength and his weakness. Brant is deprived by death of his son, whom he was going to call "Hosenknopf" (trouser button) "because he would stick so close to his father."

Odets' actual life progression is here prophesied: the loss of two wives by divorce and, a prime tragedy of his life, the father's alienation from his son. Unlike Beethoven, who achieved first rank as a creator as he fed all "into the mouth of his music," Odets (like Brant) would come to feel he had failed creatively *as well* as in his personal relationships, the proverbial donkey who starves between two haystacks.

In a mighty effort to synthesize his own and his father's emotional necessities, Odets includes in *Victory* a wealthy patron named Loeb in whose speech the melodies, idiom, and errors of grammar belong unmistakably to Louis J. Odets:

13.5.

Call it what you like—Brant needs me and I need him. Laugh, spit on me, I don't care, but Brant can't get along without me. I got money and he needs it. Great, not great, without capital you don't last long in this world. On the other hand, a man like me needs more from life than money and women. I used to think it was enough —women. But no! It don't take the place of what my father used to get when he went to synagogue. From Brant I get that. Believe me, when I listen to his music—if I know something about music or not—I get such a feeling. If I don't believe no more in the torah, in the holy scroll, I believe in Brant's music and I'm just as well off. It's a relative thing.

In the interchanges between Loeb and composer Brant we see Odets' recognition of the profound and mutually ambivalent investment with his father. The complexity of this relationship deepens with Clifford's later material success.

In this nightmare play (so much of which would actually unfold in Odets' life) the devastated, homeless Brant is clubbed by the police for his politics, is seen drunk in a "speakeasy." (Under two crossed American flags there is a sign, "No Trust.") The tough, world-weary, whorish, good-hearted woman appears, as later does Lorna Moon in *Golden Boy*, to ask, "Whatsa matter little boy, got the blues?" while a drunk shouts at him—as in the hallucinations of a paranoid schizophrenic—that he is "a pansy" and a "dirty Jew."

With friends committing suicide and his nephew (like Beethoven's) proving to be a tragic disappointment, Brant, the lonely composer, decides —in the absence of a religious heritage—that he must "chop from solid rock" his own life in this "foreign, alien world" which is full of betrayers, men and women alike. He has the fantasy that he will go to Europe, "where artists are loved and respected." Maybe he "just wants a paradise" where he is God (but, says Brant, all artists want that).

Just before the death scene, a violinist who esteems Brant's compositions suggests they get rid of all the women, and a quartet will play his music, "not for money."❡ Brant's nephew, now a wastrel, curses his uncle and his mother. If his mother hadn't abandoned him, he wouldn't be dependent "on this crazy old man." Odets would call himself a "harsh old lunatic" in relation to his own orphaned children.

As Brant is dying, he sings "in a harsh, wandering voice," just as Odets would sing "I am wandering" as *he* was dying. And Brant speaks precisely the words which would issue from Odets on his deathbed: "I can't die . . . I won't die. There is too much work left for me to do"— followed by "There is nothing on earth to satisfy my desires, but I have imagined for myself the loveliness I seek, and I will leave it in my music for others who also seek." The central resolution—like Beethoven's—is the abdication of the search for all satisfactions outside of creative work and its immortality. Throughout, the theme "Vergiss uns nicht" (Forget us not) returns. *Victory* ends, as would Odets' life, with Brant's final operation ("water gushing from my belly") and entrepreneurs on all sides beseeching him "from a pure business-angle" to write something commercial "like an opera."*

❡ 13.6.
* Odets' death interrupted his labors on a musical version of his play *Golden Boy*. This work was completed by his pupil William Gibson.

On July 18, his twenty-sixth birthday, Odets records in his diary that he has completed several scenes of the Brant play, is pleased with cigarettes sent from Philadelphia by Dr. Leof's daughter Charlotte, and was made furious "for the moment" by a telegram from his father "containing as usual a maxim for success, something like, 'We hope you are doing today what you expect to do tomorrow.'" One day he will "crack up in front of him and tell him what I think about that sort of gas. Every occasion he turns into a celebration of big business. I begin to feel insulted whenever I get near him." Immediately he feels guilty and adds:

> But this is nothing to feel permanently . . . the only thing about father is that his way of life, the means by which he lives have become completely re-fused with the end, and are one and the same. He realizes the end as a business one and does not see that it is controlling his life, not he it.

In the sanctuary of Dover Furnace, where he is not dependent on his father, he can afford such objective tolerance. His own "good impulses" are flowing, and although he hopes, like Balzac, to be famous and loved, he records his limitation on these ambitions:

> All right, I want those two, to which I add no plea for immortality, only enough light and sweetness here on earth—enough rest and friendly faces and hands where ever I look. How I grow tight and held-in when there are inimical people around me.

His only "bad impulse" is toward Franchot Tone, soon to deliver the Group a body blow by leaving: Odets has the frequent impulse to slap him on the mouth for his sulkiness, and speculates who would be the winner in a fist fight.

He is disappointed by Lawson's revision of the first act of *Success Story*, in which he understudies Luther Adler; he says it "has taken on glibness," and records that Clurman is advising Lawson to put back some of the old things because: "As it is now, it's been made more tight, more perfect in craftsmanship, but a certain succulent quality is gone, and a mood too." American art lacks, he says, this succulence, not to speak of "bigness, vitality, and health, and swing, and lust, and charity." Hearing Aaron Copland say he seldom writes more than a piece a year, Odets thinks of how contemporary artists "squeeze out a thousandth of an inch at a time," and that it will help—as Copland and Chávez have agreed —if recordings of American music are brought out "in daylight . . . instead of . . . a kind of ritual in the inner sanctum . . . like the necessity of a plum-tree for cross-fertilization to avoid stunted poor fruit . . . almost like a man living alone: something warps inwardly."

At the end of July, for two days running, Odets' diary records that "troops had routed out the Bonus Army in Washington" and that the president said "his calling out of the troops was constitutional, that mobs cannot rule the government." Sad at first, he is comforted by the thought that maybe "it was a valuable portent and helps hasten the day when the people will make a just government. One was killed and a score injured." The president thanked God that "we still have a government that knows how to deal with a mob."

As the economic catastrophe deepens, Odets, along with millions of disinherited Americans, begins to seek a world-view which will offer both an understanding of what is happening and a way out. Only later is this

13.7.

consciousness contained for him in a romantically adapted Marxist
ideology. As it seems to him the Enlightenment has eroded religious belief and traditional guides to conduct, he and his generation earnestly
search for alternatives.◖ Their only tangible undertaking, aside from
the exchange of ideas, would be in helping to establish—in this era of
unionization—the principle of collective bargaining for intellectuals.* A
very few, of whom Odets would become one, would work for Actors Equity,
and still fewer would briefly join the Communist Party, a pathetically
impotent political container for their idealism and their aspiration, which
boasted even during the depths of the Great Depression a membership of
only twenty-five thousand; it would acquire none of the political maturity
or practical potency of any of the European Communist parties.

During this Dover Furnace summer Odets records once more, with
a fresh insight, his debt to Beethoven in the maintenance of that innocence which lay at the heart of his world-view:

> I count myself a better man each time I feel B. with more truth. A
> thing I discovered: that all of the last quartets are written as if they
> were making an adjustment to a child. Take Brahms: he, in a sense,
> has an adjustment to a beautiful woman. But with B., he entered the
> crystal world of childhood in the end, felt all with the fluid emotional
> flow of a child—only with the depth of all his suffering and living—
> and as easily wrote it down. Truly truly one to enter the kingdom of
> heaven must go as a child.
> In the early B. things, say the third and fifth, it is as if he has an
> adjustment to challenge mountains and the sky. But in the end he
> comes back and speaks in a more hushed voice to children who
> themselves are able to communicate with things adults can not even
> see. *It's a kind of borderline of consciousness in which reality is
> part, but envisioning and the unconscious are also large parts*
> [italics mine].◖

By August, the Democratic Convention has nominated Franklin D. Roosevelt, whom H. L. Mencken now judges to be "the weakest candidate before
them," and a sharp black type appears in Odets' diary: Max Anderson (whose typewriter Odets uses) has bought a new ribbon for his machine in order to type his own new play, "all about Washington—graft and
politics."† And on the next night the cast reads the revised version of the
concluding two acts of *Success Story*. Lawson has by now "three different
versions of the second act," and Odets notes that, despite the dissatisfaction of a few Marxists, with whom he argues, Lawson is "a good
man indeed."

It is difficult for him to argue with the "important actors" who have

◖ 13.8.
* Lawson would be active in forming the Screen Writers Guild (1933), destined
to become a powerful and conservative body. Not long after this, Ronald Reagan, an
actor of indifferent talent, joined a similar organization for actors and would, in 1947,
become a "friendly witness" when Odets' name headed HUAC's list of "Hollywood
suspects."

◖ 13.9.
† *Both Your Houses* would open in New York on March 6, 1933, and win the
Pulitzer Prize.

power in the Group, but on this occasion, having done it successfully—
even winning Clurman's agreement to his points—he awakens the next
morning "with a great joyous feeling," marred by the news that one of
the guest playwrights, a cripple named Albert Bein, is missing, "probably
having jumped a freight to go wandering . . . miserable because of the
compromise he must make with life." Odets records:

> I got a pang during the rain tonight when I thought of him being
> somewhere in it, his little black worried eyes looking out of his
> Jewish face and the sad limp which he says nothing about very
> bravely. He tells me that sometimes he goes swimming at night so
> people won't see him legless.

The image on one level is of himself.

Startled by a surprise visit by actress Hortense Alden—object of his
adoration two years back—he greets her with "frenzied gladness . . . as
if I were a little dog greeting a long lost master," but he turns her over
to fellow actor Bobby Lewis and sees her no more. Feeling like a "holy
man in his little cell" and looking, with his beard and clipped head, according to Miss Alden, "like a Latin ecclesiastical student, something out
of Dürer," he feels suddenly quite alone, "isolated on a hill, but not unhappy . . . it's good to be thrown so completely on the Group. I want
it, want it to be part of my muscle and bone, beat of the blood, my
taciturnity and the look in my eyes. The Group means all that."

By the middle of August, with the "real writers" like Sykes and
George O'Neil gone, he uses Sykes' work-table to carry on with the Brant
play, but knows "a moment of little bitterness when I learned that Mab*
had given her typewriter over to Lawson for *his* use during the few days
he'll be here." It rubs in his lack of status as a writer. Worried about the
fall and winter, he "must ask the directors what they intend to do with
the people who are not playing parts in the two plays." If "not being
used here," maybe he can get some work with the Theatre Guild when
Philip Moeller returns from his tour of Russian theatres: "I have to live
and need money."

His restlessness, anger, and anxiety mount as he waits for a response
from Clurman: "I am beginning to resent everyone . . . all the time I
hear my heart in my ears and my blood either moves swiftly in my veins
or not at all." Angry with several girls for not giving him the nurturance
he now sorely needs, he has the fantasy of breaking the arm of one, recording, "Violence is no small part of me these nights." Anxiously seeing
"Harold pass with my script under his arm," he speculates that "tonight
or tomorrow I can expect some devastating comment. He has clear eyes
for seeing, that fellow. . . ."

As he waits for the blow to fall, his anger toward the girls mounts:
one ladylike "Nordic" in particular lacks "fibre, blood . . . I'll ask her
some day, 'How is your liver. Do you have kidneys?' " He would like to
provoke a slap in the face and then

> like a flash I would sink my fist in her belly. It would go right thru
> with a squash and hit her backbone which would collapse and make
> the head fall down off the top end to roll away in the grass like a
> pumpkin. Then I'd kick the pumpkin head and it would squash
> juicily, the mouth saying at the same time, "MY DEAR young man,
> what in the WORLD are you DOING?" It must be inherited, my dislike

---

* Now Maxwell Anderson's wife.

of her kind. I can just feel my fist in her soft belly, entrails streaming from my fingers. Ploosh! Slish!

This savage fantasy is directed at the same time at his own defensive
tendency to join the obedient, blond, belonging, "Nordic" establishment,
and thus to become himself safely cool, fiberless, bloodless, and liverless.

His insomnia has returned with his resentment, and while awaiting
Clurman's response to *Victory*, he writes a new scene wherein "Brant is
about to take a whore for a wife." His revengeful fantasies toward women
mount as he expects to be scorned by the father-person, Clurman, who
finally, after an interminable week, according to Odets' diary:

> told me of my play. He didn't like it, as I expected, but I saw this
> time that what he was criticising to a large extent was not the play
> I'd written, not that objective reality, but me, the man, as he knew
> him. He says for me not to deal so much with imaginative things,
> but to pin myself down to reporting actual and real things, such as
> people around here, what they look like, how they dress, etc. The
> last play [*910 Eden Street*], he said, was much better than this one.
> That's true, but has nothing to do with this one.
> When I got back I looked over the other play and was surprised
> at some of its qualities. It has real feeling and emotion, much of it
> actually lifting off the pages. Still, from the ordinary sense of play
> structure, it's a bad play, but I begin to believe that it's possible to
> make the weakness it represents (from a conventional point of view)
> into a strength. If action on the stage is not for me, but only inner
> feeling and conflicts expressed thru the words, then there must
> be some way of evolving my own form and style. I'll think about it.
> In the meantime I'm resting and thinking about several other
> ideas. It might be a good idea to change Brant to a fellow like
> George Gershwin* and make a modern play about Broadway pub-
> lishers and the yearning of such a fellow to be a classicist. Even
> better, I've begun to think about the Greenbaum family play.† I have
> much feeling for that sort of thing and could really do something
> with it. These past days I've been adding desultory notes and I see it
> already shaping in my mind. As I thought before I began the Brant
> play, the Greenbaum thing is much nearer to the truth of my own
> feeling and reality. I have bitterness and almost hate for them and
> what they stand for.

Twelve years later Clurman would recall *Victory* as "a very bad
play about a genius of the Beethoven kind." After what he felt to be "the
interesting if confused" start of *910 Eden Street*, it was surprising that
this one showed, he thought, "no trace of talent." Clurman had had no
way of knowing that this chaotic, romantic, and explosive work was one
of those product failures which are a necessary part of the growth
process of any artist.

It is instructive, however, to see how slanted Odets' account of
Clurman's response would become thirty years later. In 1961 he quotes
Clurman as having said,

> You know, I like you. I'm your friend . . . but you take my advice
> and don't waste your time writing plays, because you'll never be a

---

* Ten years later he wrote a 585-page screenplay for Warner Bros., not used
in *Rhapsody in Blue,* the film about Gershwin.

† Here is the first evidence that *Awake and Sing!* was beginning to take real
form.

playwright. You see, you don't know anything about people, he said. You don't see people. You're not objective. You don't hear what they're saying. Now, the best thing I would advise you to do is to keep a daily diary and write down your real and most objective impressions of people and what's going on around you. But don't waste your time writing plays, because you'll never write a play.

He makes it appear that Clurman had actively discouraged him from becoming a playwright, although his 1932 diary gives no hint of this. By 1961, estranged from him, Odets would need to show he had become a playwright in spite of Clurman. From the 1932 diary entry it is evident, however, that, while he had been wounded by Clurman's negative response, he had also been encouraged by him to leave off work on *Victory* and continue with the "Greenbaum family play," which became first *I Got the Blues* and later *Awake and Sing!*

He was at loose ends now, and his final diary entry for this same day has a certain spectator objectivity:

A lot of strangers were down at the pool, eight of them who looked as if they might be a Knights of Columbus chapter, Irish Catholics who carry their stamp on their shoulders. I sat on a rock at the water, watching them, trembling with feeling. There was I a primitive eyeing strangers not of my clan with a hate and fear. It was exactly like Clifford aged twelve walking over to Springhurst in the Bronx and meeting the shanty Irish there . . . the exact feeling of fight or run. Perhaps the one conditioned the other. These fellows turned out all right, making an effort to be friendly, beefy, like a lot of rookie cops and parochial school P.T. [Physical Training] teachers.

It is evident from his diary and from the vivid late-summer memories of other Group members that now, having failed to achieve status as actor or playwright, he was about to cut loose from the bind of his monasticism. His "wish to destroy," along with his sexual hunger, held in check during his sober waking hours, erupted climactically on August 30 in what his later notes call "the big drunk."

In his diary he writes, several days after the event:

Tuesday, August 30th.
      Virginia Farmer invited some of us to come up to her room to drink after the night class. She is leaving on the morrow to go on the road with "Real Folks," a radio sketch.
      I was eager to drink and got up there a little early. She was serious, that girl, for there was a gallon of applejack and gingerale and rye. One by one the people came in, and one by one I took the drinks quietly but steadily. Then began a drunk such as I've never had before. I ran from one room to the next kissing everyone and laughing. I took off my sweater and swelled out my chest and I was the lord of all creation . . . the last conscious thing I remember doing was bringing Franchot's bike upstairs. The rest I must piece together from what people told me I did, and from the few dim things I remember.
      Daisy tells me I fell terribly on my back and began to cry. She got a damp cloth and wiped my face with it. I told her I liked it and for her not to stop. The moment her back was turned I ran down the stairs and came back with a sugarbowl which I threw at her with bad aim. Butch tells me that I was running up and down

the stairs with superhuman energy, getting glasses and cups and throwing them out the window. . . . The next report is that I got over to the rehearsal hall and scattered everything there, throwing over the tables. Joe was somewhere out on the road, on his way to the pool and I called for him next. I found him out there, traded cigarettes and remember getting back to the main house where I decided to play the piano. It was two in the morning now. I played and then, passing thru the house, picked up two pool balls which I threw at Beanie's* door (!) with such violence that the dents are there now, deep and apparent. . . . Paula tells me that she thought I'd been hurt because I kept yelling, "Oh my god, oh my God." But Phil Barbour [sic] says that the conversation of we three in my room was brilliant and quick, the three of us talking very energetically and sharply (not at all like drunks) about three different things, I going on with what Beethoven tried to do in his music.

Finally they undressed me and I was dead in my bed, until I woke the next morning and found an orange squashed in my back pocket, my underwear ripped in half and Barton and Tony waking me with a letter from Phil Moeller, they thinking it was something about a job from the Guild. . . . I couldn't get over being drunk and my clothes hung from me. Humidity was in the air and everything was horrible and awful. On all sides people were telling me what I'd done the night before. It made me glad, I exulted in my deeds, really for the significance of this night is that it's the first time in my life I had an extroverted drunk and it is symptomatic of a new inner man, of a new line of life and conduct.

Although a "big drunk"—especially one where he would get hurt—had always had a calming effect on him, this one was especially relaxing and cleansing.

Stella Adler's comment on the episode, quoted for years, was, "If you don't turn out to be a genius, Clifford, no one will forgive you." And actor Joe Bromberg's scribbled insight, made earlier in the summer, remained on the wall: "Odets, born 1932."†

A few days before the end of this sticky hot summer Clurman brought Odets the heartening news he *would* be one of the eighteen actors out of thirty to have a job in New York: he would understudy Luther Adler in the Broadway production of *Success Story*, to be backed by the powerful theatre proprietor Lee Shubert, then almost sixty and a canny bargainer.

As Odets watched one of the last Dover Furnace rehearsals of the Lawson play, he was dismayed by the fact that "something had happened to the play since last I saw it, a false note has crept in somewhere. . . ." The Jewish Shubert had suggested several changes, "mainly those concerning the problem of a Jew being portrayed in so harsh and bitter a light," whereupon

---

* He had been attracted all summer to the "lovely, non-Jewish" actress Margaret ("Beany") Barker.
† Cf. Ralph Berger's statement in *Awake and Sing!* of being "born" from the suicide of his grandfather, Jacob.

Bing comes Jack Lawson and makes what seem unfeeling and un-
thinking dialogue changes, and on top of it apparently Lee [Stras-
berg] has changed the direction of Luther's performance. Where
before he was playing Sol with arrogance and bitterness, now that
is all softened and a romantic soft note has crept in, so that in the
third act Luther sounded like the Music Master patting a little girl
on the head.

Now, he concludes, the production is "neither here nor there."

He has learned a great deal this summer: from his own experiments in *Victory* with play architecture, he has developed a firmer
structural hand; from its failure to impress Clurman, he was encouraged
to return to the use of "the truth of my own feeling and reality." He is
strengthened in this resolve both by the vitality in *Success Story* and by
its evident diminishment when Lawson tried to tone down its "Jewishness." Moreover, it means a great deal to him that Clurman has actively
encouraged him to take up once more "the Greenbaum family play," for
which he had made many notes before starting on *Victory*. He is beginning to see that he can evolve a form for "the Greenbaum thing"
wherein the plots are interior.

His last diary entry at Dover Furnace concludes:

I stopped and thought of my own writing ability. I am sure of it
now, know the definite feeling of what to do and how. I am filled
with materials. Thoughts of "One of These Days" flashed thru my
mind and how I could make a book of it in the snap of a hand. Oh
young boy! And of how I could write a story of Pat and our road
trip. I have that talent and in a flash saw the entire thing spread before me. I must have time; time, oh give me more hours in the day
and a quiet space and a little food and white white paper and a flying
typewriter. I am coming to somewhere. Yes! Last night I was telling
Goldie of Walter and Edgar Jeidel,* of what kind of men they are
and of their family. They are the stuff of my art, people I know like
that. I am full of them and soon they'll be out, enriching me, and
I them.

Before the year was out, at twenty-six, he would have a draft of
the first act of *I Got the Blues*.

* The Jeidels, like the Greenbaums, were part of the Beck Street Boys in the
Bronx.

Chapter Fourteen

*Thus that historically cruel winter of
1932–3, which chilled so many of us
like a world's end, became for me a
time of renewed faith, because I appeared to be withstanding a sort of
test.*

HAROLD CLURMAN

*When I started to write "Awake and
Sing!" I didn't have a mission in life;
I wasn't going to change society.
When I came to rewriting it I was go-
ing to change the world—or help it.*

CLIFFORD ODETS, 1961

I am sitting here in the Groupstroy* at 440 West 57th Street in New
York City. This is three days after having left Dover Furnace and
a week since the last entry in this diary. The Groupstroy is an apartment for a dozen of us who have no money and no nothing. We have
beds here and food in the icebox and we are back in New York, I
with an empty feeling. Just now I am considering the advisability of
calling a girl on the phone and bedding with her tonight and I feel
my flesh jump up with the thought. So a flash when such a thought
has not been mine for days. But a flash now! And in my mind a
picture and a hunger, and such a hunger in my body and in my
fingers the sense of flesh and of parting lips with those fingers, lips
soft and warm and moist and not those of a face. Here I see in the
late afternoon, the sun almost receded from the window and I think
of a dark warm room and that girl next to me, she with full breasts
and young up to eighteen and eager for me and loving me and I
eager for her and the giving up of her body. But I won't phone her.
I will live my quiet way for a day or two more and then on a night,
at the Circle Hotel . . . the very name conjures up lewdness to my
mouth. . . .

I have a number of notes of the past week and will incorporate

---

* In Russian the suffix "stroy" means a construction or, loosely, a settlement.

them now and here. I won't call up that girl, perhaps a try when it grows dark. I want a girl to have by my side, to walk with; like Sol Ginsberg, "I want to love something," and I add, "I want to be loved."

While there is nothing remarkable in the sexual hunger of a young man—particularly in one concerned about both his manliness and his lovability, who has essayed an abstinent summer—the flow of associations here, and throughout, suggests something more. Frequently, for Odets the quickest solution to an anxious sense of his own emptiness was —instead of settling down to work—to "fill" a woman with whom he could identify himself. What is less clear is the relation of such instant solutions of anxiety to the motivational sources of creative work. That he himself often regarded the two energies as coming from the same source is clearly shown by his periodic retreats into asceticism when he was determined to work.

Now on the eve of the opening of *Success Story*, September 26, he is conserving his energy for the part of Sol Ginsberg, hoping against hope he will have a chance at least once to replace Luther Adler. It is all part of his imminent emergence:

One thing I'm sure of, that I can play Sol Ginsberg beautifully. There is no talk of Luther being better or worse. He is what he is and I am what I am. But of the two my performance can be better for the play and more the vision of what the playwright and production are both working for. I am very sure of this. All the time now I am getting nearer and nearer to the final word of Liberation! It is only around some corner now. I begin to feel my strength truly. I have learned to hold myself more, with sureness and purpose. I can tell a story of great growth during this past summer.

During an acting exercise with the "Nordic" young Group actress he felt his creative work in the scene inhibited until, by a violent argument about "doing the thing right," he reduced her to tears. At the moment she cried and he "felt the master," he was freed, and able "to go on and do the thing with my full personality. . . . The mastery impulse must be satisfied in me before I can fully do my work."

It appears that "to be the filler" or "fed" passively by identifying with his partner in sexual intercourse—in fact or fancy—is not enough; he must simultaneously assert his masculine (sometimes even sadistic) power: in short, to assume at one and the same time, however unconsciously, a feminine *and* masculine identification. He now *enacted* this as he renewed his compulsive pursuit of girls, gaining a reputation, on the one hand, as a ruthless, egocentric "lady-killer" and, on the other, as a lover empathically able to "put himself tenderly in the woman's place." Those who had known him only in his periods of withdrawn asceticism were astonished by what appeared to be his many faces. As playwright, he, of course, projected all of these complex identity-elements into the conflicting characters, the external resolutions in the play representing his internal integrations.

Mystery piles upon mystery for him as he pursues his fantasies toward creative freedom:

I want to make a fool of myself, I yearn for it, to debase myself and be laughed at, to lose my pride and the stiffness of the bones. It's something I've not been able to do ever and I find that now I long for it with an actual hunger. It's not an idea first from the head. My emotions suggested it to me long before I realized the thing in the brain. Take a girl, if you dare, you writer of words, and make a fool of yourself over her, in the open square where all may see. It would be a touching off of the last thing in me that prevents liberation. It would blow me up and then when I came down I would be clear and free of self and pride.

Although the masochistic fantasies here are complex indeed, it is likely that in this yearning to be debased, to lose pride, he is longing to be rid of the crippling terror of his lifelong need, learned from his father, to make a masterful "good impression,"* to be a Success. If he can dispense with this, he will no longer be pulled to pretentious writing about Beethoven-like characters. He will achieve that condition prerequisite for an artist: the free-swinging opening of interior gates that permit him, without fear or shame, to function out of the kind of person he is.

Although he never achieved his wish to play Sol Ginsberg in *Success Story*, he was significantly emboldened by Lawson's example, following upon Clurman's encouragement to use familiar materials. Within a few weeks, perching his typewriter on a breadbox in the kitchen of Groupstroy, he commenced to breathe life into the "Greenbaum family," now named Berger. A major creative turning point was under way.

It was, says Clurman, a "blow to the solar plexus of the Group" that, with a divided press, *Success Story* did not live up to its title. Despite organized efforts to counteract the reviews by publishing endorsements from prominent artists, campaigning for special audiences, and sending letters to editors, the purchase of tickets flagged and Lee Shubert withdrew his support. Thus, by New Year's Eve there was no pay for anyone, and Lawson prepared to flee once again to Hollywood with that particularly lonely sense of guilt felt by the author of a failing production. If only he had done a better job, he thought, all these fine actors would not now be homeless and unemployed. Whatever Lawson's deficiencies in *Success Story* may have been, the slender economic margin on which most Group members were living was directly related to the new financial panic which had forcibly struck in the fall, with banks crashing all over the country. The desperate President Hoover's efforts to avert this fresh and harrowing calamity had failed.

Nonetheless, the morale of the actors living on dwindling credit in the cold, damp, old ten-room railroad flat on West 57th Street was not low. Meals were prepared communally, with Clifford often frying potato pancakes. When he was not working on the Berger family in *I Got the Blues*† in the kitchen, he would retire to his tiny room, the coldest in the house (at one time occupied by a maid in this rundown brownstone) and emerge back into the kitchen with scenes to be read. Many of the actors

* In this fantasy of debasement there probably is a wish to submit to his father's assaults as well. There is a sexually tinged courting of pain here. Much later one of Odets' lovers, an extraordinary observer, said, "I always felt I was competing with pain for Clifford. . . . "

† To be copyrighted on November 21, 1933, under this title, and on May 15, 1935, as *Awake and Sing!*

remembered him assuring them "there will be parts for all," as though he were distributing food for his family. In his enthusiasm, he earned a few lifelong grudges by promising the same part to two actors.

Another place where he could enjoy the potent sense of the nurturer was downtown on 14th Street, where Eva Le Gallienne's valiant six-and-a-half-year-old Civic Repertory Theatre was fast unraveling under the impact of the cataclysmic economic crisis. Odets, as invited lecturer, was beginning to bring to many of Le Gallienne's young actor-apprentices—who were about to become homeless—some sense of the salvation he was experiencing in the Group Theatre, and getting from them a feeling of familial closeness to the rhythms of working-class people and an absorption in social ideals somewhat different from those of the Group.

During the month of December of 1932 the drafty old "Civic Rep" saw the last of the intrepid young Le Gallienne's efforts to offer at low prices serious theatre, most of it European. Appropriately enough in these surrealist times, her final offering was *Alice in Wonderland*. Within the year, in the same theatre, the newly formed left-wing Theatre Union would present the first of several plays by Americans, directly aimed at influencing the nightmare economic and political events: an anti-war play called *Peace on Earth*. One of its authors, Albert Maltz, after appearing fifteen years later before the House Committee on Un-American Activities, would be imprisoned as one of the "Hollywood Ten."

Molly Day Thacher, of early American stock, a Vassar graduate, and also the bride of Group apprentice Elia Kazan, had already begun to devote her energies to this rival organization, seeing in it the only hope for a counterweight to what she regarded as the Group's preoccupation with psychology and esthetics. She was one of those who, at this time, saw the theatre essentially as a social weapon, and the Theatre Union as the most promising company for this purpose. She did not interfere, however, with Odets' missionary work with the young actors. She was less tolerant, though, of a curious and repeated prank of his: he would incite actor Alan Baxter, Kazan's former rival for her hand, to call up the Theatre Guild's Philip Moeller, Odets' old mentor, in the dead of night. Pretending it was an emergency, Baxter, coached scene by scene by Odets, would berate him for his poor direction of O'Neill's plays. This was a strange and cruel game, directed by Odets, to torment a man to whom not long ago he had sycophantically surrendered.

Soon Odets would find himself deeply drawn to one of these Repertory actors: an affectionate, eager, eighteen-year-old Le Gallienne apprentice named Jules (Julie) Garfinkle. Characteristically, Odets was stirred to learn that this attractive roughneck, born on Rivington Street on the Lower East Side, had begun to play hookey and to run away from his stinking slum bedroom directly following his mother's death when he was seven. His father, a presser in a factory but, as Julie described him, "a cantor on weekends and holidays," had sent his precociously delinquent son—who was stuttering and stealing—to Public School 45 in the Bronx to be rehabilitated by the principal, Angelo Patri, noted for his success with wild, "mixed-up kids." Later, as film star John Garfield, Julie would become the American prototype of a grownup "Dead End Kid" and, more than any other member of the Group, make the melodies and rhythms of Odets' dialogue the common property of millions of Americans.

In the Bronx, as Odets would write the day after Garfield's death in 1952, Julie's "ardor for learning and growth" had become evident. His husky body, physical grace, shock of dark hair, candid face, and tough surface—always attractive to women—fitted him for the limelight he found as a Golden Gloves boxer, like Louis Odets, and as an actor, like Clifford himself. Ralph Berger, later described by Odets in "the characters of the play" for *Awake and Sing!* as "a boy with a clean spirit . . . ardent, romantic, sensitive, naïve," combines Julie Garfinkle and a large piece of Odets' own identity. "Ralphie," like the young actor, was "trying to find why so much dirt must be cleared away before it is possible to get to first base." Julie's family, despairing for his future, like Odets' father, had called him an "actor-bum" even after he had won scholarships to the Theatre Guild's American Laboratory Theatre and to Le Gallienne's Civic Repertory. Odets' bond with this delinquent orphan was sealed when he heard how Patri had finally succeeded in deterring him from escaping over the school wall, trampling flowers en route: he had said, according to Julie, "Son, don't you know those flowers have a right to live, too?" Julie never again jumped the wall.

In the black misery of the Depression, Julie Garfinkle was an optimistic, essentially non-political young learner, naïvely eager to develop his gift and to "spit from a penthouse." During this cold winter, as he yearned for permanent membership in the Group, Julie was supplying Odets' imagination with a piece of creative capital always treasured by a playwright: a gifted "mask" which acts as a vessel into which he can pour his own multiform materials. Odets would come to feed on the Group talents, and they on him. Seeing in each of them an aspect of himself, he was enabled to pull living, whole characters from his own depths ordinarily not available to his awareness or to his pen. "The real truth," he said, "is that with the Group Theatre ensemble acting company, I wrote not one or two leading parts with a lot of supporting players, but the early plays were written with equal-size parts for equal-size actors. So that a play like *Awake and Sing!*, let us say, has seven leading parts in it. And that form was dictated by the composition of the Group Theatre acting company."

The directors' morale this winter was less good than that of the actors: with the closing of *Big Night* after seven performances and Franchot Tone's departure for Hollywood, Strasberg had isolated himself in reading and rarely spoke. When he did, it was mainly to his new wife, Group actress Paula Miller, a delicate, generous girl with reddish-yellow hair, a lovely, sad, heart-shaped face, a vivid fantasy life, a fascination with intrigue and the supernatural, and a yearning to serve talent.

Paula, then and later, ran interference for Lee, at her best protecting him from—and connecting him with—the people of his world. One day as she was cooking cabbage and singing, she welcomed to Groupstroy an attractive young woman who, as Mrs. Robert Rockmore, had worked with O'Neill, James Light, and Stark Young at the Provincetown Players. The young woman had groped her way up the several flights of stairs, fighting down her allergic response to cabbage, in order to present to Strasberg for the Group a certified check for $50,000. This was a wedding gift from her husband-to-be, Motty Eitingon, a Russian-Jewish immigrant, now a successful furrier and passionate music-lover, who wanted to support with cash her conviction that the Group would be the next landmark in the American theatre. It seemed to some members that she herself, an extremely bright, if somewhat eccentric, woman "who didn't quite know where to put her energy," was hoping for some sort of future with this developing company.

"Paula brought in a man [Strasberg] who looked like a dried, salted herring," Bess Eitingon recalled. "I tried to explain to this person looking past me why I was bringing a check for fifty thousand dollars, but there was no response from him, nothing. I kept trying for a while and then ran down the several flights of stairs, crying. I felt terribly rejected and immediately called a friend to find out what was wrong with me. I could not for the life of me understand it. Did I have bad breath, or what?"

Strasberg, who has frequently told this story of his incredible blunder, explains his blank response with the innocent recollection, "I honestly couldn't think at the moment what we could use the fifty thousand dollars for." Persons close to him analyze this strange event differently: they see in it the extreme of Strasberg's necessity at this time to deny to himself that *he* had need of anything, operating competently only when he could define a situation in such a way that he was meeting the need of another. This dynamic of his would cost the Group Theatre a good deal.

In constant dread of an eviction notice from Groupstroy for nonpayment of the $50-a-month rent (it arrived early in February), Paula had begun to hunt for a small, cheap apartment for herself and her husband. In the back of her mind was the plea from the handsome blond actor typing on a breadbox placed on a kitchen chair: "Can I fly away with the two of you?"

Odets, setting up this nest with the Strasbergs, another of his many adopted families, was the first of a long parade of gifted people—to include Sidney Kingsley, John Garfield, James Baldwin, Shelley Winters, Kim Stanley, Geraldine Page, and Marilyn Monroe—for whom Paula would provide varieties of shelter over the next three decades. All of them would be profoundly grateful for the unstinting nourishment in her kitchens, which always included bagels, hot tea in a glass, fresh fruit, wit, encouragement, and companionship in the grief of mourning. No doubt many would also resent her blithe scheming to bring together, as Sidney Kingsley would put it in his eulogy of her, "the irreconcilables."

Working with people as her creative medium, Paula, who had a good sense of theatre, would often depart in her everyday life from the literal truth, in the service of a dramatic end-product. Those who loved her forgave her scheming, her distortions, and her tangential comments; those who did not, mocked her. To Sidney Kingsley, about to provide the Group's first hit play, she said later, "You know, Sidney, Clifford loved me. I'm not sure that he liked me, but he did *love* me." Thus, when Paula and "my Lee" —as she called him—moved above Sutter's Bakery at 285 West 11th Street, they took Clifford along. There, according to his own record, with prodigious intensity he wrote in two nights, again in the kitchen,* a draft of the second act of *I Got the Blues*.

By now he was steadily discussing the play's problems with the disconsolate Clurman, who was also without a home base and in terror that the work of the Group had come to an end. *The New York Times* had announced that the Group was out of business for the season and perhaps forever. Although Clurman wrote a defiant response, he later confessed he knew that the Group was in a state of rout, with a few of its actors already playing in other companies and most of them dependent on handouts.

Abruptly it was borne in on Clurman that since the Group's first meetings New York had become a mournful city, down at the heel. Even in his parents' middle-class home there was a pervasive sense of terror "as if soon the walls would disappear and they would remain naked and alone on the cold, empty street. . . . Yes, we could smell the Depression in the air."

---

* He wrote on a wooden table which he salvaged for use in later, more affluent years. On this same table William Gibson, after Odets' death had interrupted his work on it, wrote the book of the musical *Golden Boy*.

By now the desperate American people had decided by their votes that Herbert Hoover was not coping with the national catastrophe. Democrat Franklin Delano Roosevelt had polled 22.8 million votes to Hoover's 15.7 million. Odets and the Group—with all their reservations about this savior of capitalism—rejoiced in his victory. And during this bitter winter there began what Clurman has called "one of the most painful and one of the most pregnant periods of our Group life," a time in which he was "utterly wretched and, in some strange way, profoundly happy."

In his "disconsolate meanderings" he found Odets constantly by his side:

> We began to see each other nightly, and with hungry hearts wandered aimlessly through sad centers of impoverished night life. We would drop in at some cheap restaurant and over a meager meal make dreams of both our past and future. We would see a movie on a side street, pick up more friends, who, whether working or not, seemed equally at odds with the now consumptive city. We listened to queer conversations on street corners, visited byways we had never suspected before. There grew between us a feeling akin to that which is supposed to exist between hoboes in their jungles, and we were strangely attracted to people and places that might be described as hangdog, ratty, and low.
>
> At no other time before or since did either of us visit so many burlesque houses. The shows had no sex lure for us; they had the appeal of a lurid dejection. Somehow we felt close to the down-in-the-mouth comedians and oddly tender about the bruised beauties of the chorus. . . . Most of the jokes, aside from the usual rancid ones, concerned the low estate into which the world had fallen. An empty pocket, for instance, was called a Hoover dollar. . . .
>
> We heard that a special showing of a picture based on Hauptmann's *Weavers* was being given at the old Proctor's on Broadway and 28th Street. When we arrived at the theatre, we were overcome by an atmosphere of neglect, of damp, of cavernous emptiness. Only a few hollow-eyed people composed the audience.
>
> When we had seen the film and were ready to leave, a man, in a navy-blue flannel shirt with a suit and face that matched it, came out and addressed the audience with a simple conviction that must have been hard to maintain under the circumstances. He was a radical of some kind—the real article, not its phony counterpart—and he urged strong political action against the terror of the crisis, the unemployment, hunger, destitution of the day. Odets applauded with sudden spontaneity,—as if unprepared to do so and himself surprised that he had. I was no less surprised, but did not question him. I understood that his applause was not so much a matter of intellectual approval as almost a physical movement of union with the speaker who had uttered words that needed to be spoken one way or another.
>
> On this same platform, where I had once seen Stella Adler in a dramatization of Feuchtwanger's *Power*, in another two years *Waiting for Lefty* would be presented at a benefit for the taxi-drivers' union.

It was evident to everyone that Odets' political opinions stemmed directly from a humanist identification with these insulted and injured individuals rather than from a systematic logic of the sort John Howard Lawson used. Clurman, wisely and prophetically, assured him that he was not, and could never be, a real Communist and that he should never join the Communist Party because he would soon come to hate its members.

Usually after these excursions they would head for a place where they could meet with kindred spirits: Stewart's Cafeteria on Sheridan Square:

Here the poor and jolly have-beens, ne'er-do-wells, names-to-be . . . and sweet young people without a base, collected noisily to make a very stirring music of their discord and hope. Though this cafeteria must have represented a high degree of affluence to the really hungry, it struck me as a sort of singing Hooverville. For, strangely enough, this incubator of the depression, with many marks of waste and decay upon it, was in point of fact a place rank with promise. Some of the old Village (1915–25) was going to pot here, but also something new, not wholly aware of itself, and to this day still immature, was in an early state of gestation. . . .

Odets . . . was very sympathetic to such characters, as he was to many failures—those failures in whom he could discern former power, and those whose potentiality he felt threatened by unfavorable circumstances. Later he would say that he had written his first plays because he had seen his schoolmates, whom he had always thought cheerful good fellows, turn into either tasteless messes of nameless beef, or become thin, wan, sick ciphers. He wanted to explain what had happened to them, and, through them, to express his love, his fears, his hope for the world. In this way, instead of wallowing in his unhappiness, he would make it a positive force.

. . . He was younger than I, but he treated me as if he were an affectionate older brother. I liked him too perhaps because he listened to me so understandingly and responded warmly to my moods, but if I had been asked about him, I believe I should have confessed that I liked him for being so physical a person. He reacted to everything, not with words or articulate knowledge, but with his body. His senses were extraordinarily alive, though he was not professionally "sensitive." To be near him was like being near a stove on which a whole range of savory foods was standing ready to be served.

This metaphor of the promised feast in the famine of this cold winter matches precisely what Odets felt he was creating for the Group and its members.

The early months of 1933 saw throughout the Western world, at one and the same time, an acceleration of the collapse of a sense of life coherence and of moral values—to reach a climax after World War II—and an exhilarating determination to remake this disintegrating world. The models for this reconstruction differed. Odets' evolution as playwright cannot be understood without reference to this history.

On January 30—the birthday of the newly elected Roosevelt, who had recently said in a campaign speech that there were to be no more "forgotten men"—Hindenburg handed over the reins of the German government to Adolf Hitler, whom he called "that Austrian corporal," a man whom earlier he had publicly disavowed. Roosevelt and Hitler were each faced with the calamitous failure in his country of a policy of non-interference with the natural course of business enterprise; the choices that psychology and history would dictate for each would make inevitable their mortal confrontation. Stalin meanwhile, heir to the socialist mirage, publicly offered salvation to "forgotten men" all over the world while having already begun in secret his own program of mass murder.

Roosevelt's economic and social inventions, vigorous if improvisational, were all designed to tame the wild forces of individual enterprise and to knit together a fractured and economically depressed society. "Recovery" was his word. In the countries of Europe the crises would be variously met by ameliorative reform, policed states, the extrusion techniques of labor camps, genocide,◄ and, finally, by territorial conquest in a global war. At its close, within little more than a decade, American people would inflict on Japanese people, by then functionally a part of the Western scramble, massive mutilation and grotesque death of a kind undreamed of in 1933. The desperate and worldwide search for solutions, both provisional and "final," in the power universes of economics, politics, self-regard, identity, and morals had now arrived.

In each country there were dissenters to prevailing solutions:◄ In the United States there were, on the right, those who, in communion with Hitler, began to refer to "Rosenfeld, the Jew, the Red in the White House." The American dissenter on the left saw in the high-born Roosevelt's efforts only ultimate examples of cynically skilled "bourgeois" determination to preserve, in some form, free enterprise. Disbelieving that four million people were deliberately being starved to death in the Ukraine famine, these left-wingers had hotly recommended voting for William Z. Foster, the Communist candidate for President, as a way out of the nightmare. In the climate of this time many ordinarily cautious liberals were convinced the Russian solution might be adapted to the American situation. Even the respected playwright Sidney Howard—by no means regarded as a conspirator with the Soviet Union—was exasperated by the impotence of Republicans and Democrats in coping with the economic catastrophe, and announced that he would campaign next time on behalf of the Intellectuals Committee for Foster.

So deep was the rage and despair in some Americans that complex political alternatives were abandoned in favor of individual violence. A group of Iowa farmers warned that further attempts to foreclose on mortgages would be discouraged by lynching. A few weeks later a jobless anarchist, shouting, "Too many people are starving to death," shot at Roosevelt, not yet inaugurated; he missed him, but killed the mayor of Chicago. It was the era of the actual Bonnie and Clyde, poor, young bank-robbing killers celebrated as folk heroes in Texas.

On May 1, 1933, the Nazis staged one of their most impressive and effective propaganda coups. They took over, as if May Day were a Nazi invention, the celebration of the European Day of Labor by calling it "the Day of National Labor" and staging gigantic labor rallies in which the German working class and trade unions cooperated. The axe fell the next day, May 2, when the Nazis seized control of the trade unions, suppressed all labor newspapers, arrested trade-union leaders, and decreed their unions dissolved. From this moment on, collective bargaining was out of the question in the Third Reich. In place of the trade unions the German Arbeitsfront was formed. This party organization, which controlled labor in Nazi Germany, was under the direction of Dr. Robert Ley, who later announced: "We have done in a few hours and days what formerly would

◄ 14.1.
◄ 14.2.

have taken years or decades. Sometimes I fear lest the gods become jealous at all the tremendous things now being done by one poor human."

At this point of his *personal* history Odets' need for solutions to his economic and spiritual crises was being met by the Group Theatre. It is thus an irony that this playwright—to be celebrated as the "dramatist of social protest of the thirties"—had less necessity to locate a political formula for changing the world than to discover a creative concept of theatre that would elicit his profoundest talents. The tacked-on quality of his self-conscious Marxist metaphor is nowhere more apparent than in the work he was at this point engaged by: the successive drafts of *I Got the Blues* as it becomes the classic *Awake and Sing!* reflect his deliberate and cerebral effort to couch in Marxist lingo his rebellion as well as his hopes for the future.

Later he would puzzle over how he had damaged his early plays when he had "tried to take some kind of real life I knew and tried to press it into some kind of ideological mold." He felt he had "very easily, very fluently, and very naturally" given expression to a certain kind of life, but would "then try to tell the audience what it meant," and "what it meant in terms that I used was quite inferior to what the material really was saying." Here he refers to the final version of *Awake and Sing!* wherein his young protagonist gives up his personal rebellion against the constrictions of his life in order to become a political Marxist.

Equally apparent, however, in successive drafts—and in all of his subsequent work—is the deeper struggle born in his own family but inseparable from the larger sweep of developing history.◖

The form which Odets is now finally able to reach in order to convey his experience of life is, on the surface, realistic. However, the extraordinarily fresh, funny, and anguished characters in the Jewish-American Berger family of *I Got the Blues* take their places in a rich allegory which celebrates the grand passion of life, of death, and of resurrection. Broadly humanist and on the surface almost plotless, this bubbling play, sizzling with interior plot and conflict, would occupy him for the rest of the year.

To arrive at the stratified meanings of a play, it is necessary to pursue two complementary but separable lines of investigation: first, the life history of the playwright and the patterns of his life at the time he is writing the play; and, second, the history of his society and the stage of *its* life.◖ The second reflects, of course, the audience he is addressing.

Against this backdrop it becomes possible to see how a playwright scans his *internal* "gallery of characters," as Odets called them, loosing them against one another on the stage in a variety of ways, in an effort to master a set of lifelong conflicts. The remarkable and startling fact is that a body of work decoded this way reveals substantially the same personality themes and struggles repeated over and over. Each character occupies its own psychological territory within the playwright's identity and, despite external differences, can be discerned from play to play. Thus, a tyrannical mother in one play may represent the same identity-element expressed as

◖ 14.3.
◖ For a discussion of the author's method of play analysis see Notes and Comment 14.4.

a film magnate in another, or a dentist's sexy assistant may occupy the same psychological territory as a prizefighter with musical talent.

The other startling conclusion to which I have been led (initially by work on the evolution of *Awake and Sing!*) is that, whatever else a play is "about," it will also reflect the playwright's view of the very nature of his *own* creative processes: his celebrations and his conflicts.◖

All of my analyses of Odets' plays deal essentially with the underlying psychological conflicts and their resolutions; I do not undertake, for the most part, an analysis of the formal structure of the play.

I Got the Blues is manifestly about a Jewish "working-class family with middle-class aspirations," faced with the problems of a Depression society. Bessie and Myron Berger live with their children, Hennie and Ralph, and Bessie's father, Jacob, in an apartment in the East Bronx. When Bessie discovers that her daughter is pregnant and cannot locate the baby's father, she insists that Hennie marry Sam Feinschreiber, a gentle little man recently arrived from Europe. The son, Ralph, who works as a shipping clerk in the garment district, is in love and wants to marry, but his mother disapproves because the girl is too poor. Jacob, Ralph's grandfather, an artistic ex-barber with radical and idealistic ideas, encourages Ralph to seek a better and richer life for himself and society. At the play's climax he jumps from the roof of the house so that Ralph can collect his life insurance and escape from his materialist mother. At the end of the play the daughter, Hennie, is persuaded by an older man, the gangster Moe Axelrod, to run away with him, leaving husband and child behind; and Ralph, although he remains in the house, establishes his independence by vowing to make a new life in his grandfather's terms rather than his mother's.

Much would be altered in *I Got the Blues* before it would be presented as *Awake and Sing!* to a Broadway audience two years after it was first written. A major change is in the use of language: most of the phonetically spelled Yiddish—even Hebrew—dialogue in the manuscript of *I Got the Blues* is missing in the celebrated final version. "Meine schoene tuchter" becomes "my fine beauty," "mitzvah" becomes "blessing," etc.

Despite this surgery, the idiomatic, bluntly explosive Yiddish-American language would be experienced by the audience as authentic, fresh, and even lyrically uplifting. Unchanged in the two versions is the prodigal use of Yiddish-style humor and of the seeming irrelevancies and non sequiturs of "Yiddishkeit," which function as links between manifest and latent material, and as splendid ornament.

A strange example of this:

> BESSIE: Listen, Axelrod, in my house you don't talk this way. Either respect or get out.
> MOE: When I think about it . . . maybe I'd marry her myself.
> BESSIE: (*suddenly aware of* MOE): You could— What do you mean Moe?
> MOE: You ain't sunburnt—you heard me.

It is curious that far more has been made of Odets' influence on American and English "genre" playwrights than on Jewish-American writers generally.

Although time and space are formally contained within the traditional mold of a three-act naturalistic play, the sensory range and its intensity are not. In both versions the play population is acutely alive not only to the real sights, sounds, and smells of life, but to their symbolic, meta-

◖ 14.5.

phoric, and allegoric meanings. The pervading sense in the Berger family is simultaneously rich and claustrophobic.◄ Throughout, the pure and scholarly grandfather, Jacob, tells us that life is a "chulim" (a dream). For years Odets would say, "Verily, verily, I tell you, life is a dream."

Food deprivation and food intake are a steady obbligato. Many of the apparently casual exchanges center on eating and starving. A line quoted for decades afterward is Moe Axelrod's furious closing of the first act: "What the hell kind of house is this it ain't got an orange!!" Here, as throughout his work, Odets says that a house (read "home") must not only have an orange, but must itself be a Paradise, a Garden of Eden where an abundance of nourished seedlings become plants, producing flowers and fruit.

The ancient source of this image is, of course, the infant who trusts he will not be abandoned, but rather nourished to good and noble manhood by the food falling straight from mother to mouth. Moe calls Hennie "Paradise"; Jake plays over and over in his little room a record, "O Paradiso" sung by Enrico Caruso. This record—along with the rest—is smashed by the *mother* at the play's climax. Odets' next play, *Paradise Lost*, would be a neutralized, dreamlike, even more radically "de-Jewished" version of *Awake and Sing!* The "singer"—symbol for Odets of the artist, the poet— is a condensed representation of a pure being whose innocent mouth produces sustenance for himself as well as for others.

The sole meaning Odets offered for *Awake and Sing!* two years after he wrote it was that it represented a "fundamental activity: a struggle for life amidst petty conditions"◄—surely a sufficiently social theme to resonate with a Depression audience. Indeed, this manifest social meaning would become the sole meaning assigned to Odets in the history of the American drama. But Odets, unlike many socially committed playwrights of this time, wrote this play not as a conscious political tract but as an expression of his own personal "blues."

To be sure, the *form* of these blues—as well as his alternatives for their resolution—takes shape from the history in which he is struggling, changing over the period of his revisions until it ultimately reflects a radical political stance or, better, as Alfred Kazin put it, a "voluntary optimism."◄ This, however, is only on the most obvious level of meaning: the level of ideological commitment. It is this level which became dated most quickly.

In the continuing struggle, however, to a self-identity, Odets seeks in this work several other levels of meaning: in 1932, at twenty-six, the same age as the girl Hennie, he is still wrestling with the rock-bottom conflicts of his relation to all his family, but to his father in particular; not only his father's American business values, but a residue of far less obvious matters, such as his own sexual identity, are being explored. These other layers of meaning, in addition to the manifestly social meaning, would lead even the left-wing press to say: "It has been heralded as a play about a Jewish family in the Bronx. It is about them and about a great deal more. What that wider and deeper content is you have to feel out for yourself. . . ."

To illustrate: he represents in this play two concurrent—and, indeed, conflicting—fantasies addressed to his highly charged relationship with his father. These fantasies reflect, in a continuum of meaning, not only his most repressed struggles but also the observable idiosyncrasies of the

◄ 14.6.
◄ 14.7.
◄ 14.8.

Odets family. The manner in which each of them carries the character of his or her immigrant origins and generation is always thus simultaneously archetypal, representative (of a culture), and individual.

One element of Odets' identity◖ speaks through the character of Hennie, who, he says, "has had few friends . . . is proud of her body . . . won't ask favors . . . travels alone." She is "fatalistic about being trapped, but will escape if possible." In the play the original title, *I Got the Blues*, issues only from Hennie's and Ralph's mouths. Hennie must decide whether or not to remain one flesh with her contemptibly weak, innocent, and nervous husband, Sam Feinschreiber. This name means "fine (literally, in German, 'effete') writer." He represents another significant but humiliating identity-element of Odets himself, a composite of his verbal, anxious, depressed mother and a hidden aspect of his father, who, along with his Babbittry, aspired to be a "legitimate" writer. This self-image is of a "fine writer" who fathers an "illegitimate" child.

According to Odets' notes for this play, Sam "wants to find a home . . . a foreigner in a strange land, hypersensitive . . . conditioned by the humiliation of not making his way alone . . . *a sense of others laughing at him*" (italics mine). In the "old country" the Cossacks cut off Sam's father's beard as a practical joke. The old man went to bed, covered his face, and, on the third morning, died "from a broken heart . . . from *shame*." Feinschreiber "hears acutely all the small sounds of life" and he "*might have been a poet in another time and place*" (italics mine). For him, "Life is a high chill wind weaving itself around his head." In the original, he was described by Odets as a "poor mockie," only three years in the country, barely able to speak English. We do not hear that he speaks a fine Yiddish, German, or Russian.◖ Sam has no dignity, no pride, no guts; he is the kind of man for whom Odets had often heard his father express a withering contempt. Indeed, it is precisely Sam's lack of these strengths that makes him a candidate to be tricked by the mother into marrying Hennie without telling him she is *illegitimately pregnant* by a sailor (in the original version of *I Got the Blues;* in a later draft he becomes a salesman named Ben Grossman). Hennie says in the original that she would rather go to her grave without a husband than marry a "poor mockie like him." In the final *Awake and Sing!* she says "poor foreigner."

Jacob, in both versions, regards Bessie's plan to trick the youth as "the lowest from the low," spitting on the idea of "having respect" for Bessie's pocketbook or "for the neighbors' opinion." All three of these quoted items are standard in the vocabulary of Louis J. Odets. Bessie's overt enmity toward her idealist father, Jacob, has L. J. Odets' virulence in the first draft of *I Got the Blues:* she threatens to send him away to a "home" for old men where he will "rot in hell for all I care." She reminds him—as L.J. had often reminded his son—that he has never been able to hold a job, and she threatens (as L.J. had) to "break a chair on your head." Bessie deplores the fact that her father "don't believe in God" in much the same platitudes as L.J.'s attacks on Clifford's "atheism." She says she will "tear his tongue out and bury him . . . with Caruso and the books together." In the final draft of *Awake and Sing!* this is all considerably toned down. In both versions, however, Jacob quotes Marx as having recommended the abolition of "such families," "where there is so much hatred."

Odets' conflict about his own creative process is seen in the alternatives which he offers Hennie: she can remain true to Sam Feinschreiber,

◖ 14.9.
◖ 14.10.

the ridiculous, gullible, frightened poet manqué, a man who "does women's work," or she can run away to a sunny climate with "the boarder," a complex, powerful, mordant, cynical, yet intensely passionate *cripple*, Moe Axelrod.❶ Moe says, "In life there's two kinds—the men that's sure of themselves and the ones who ain't! . . . pick out a racket. Shake down the coconuts. . . . It's all a racket—from horse racing down. Marriage, politics, big business—everybody plays cops and robbers."

Hennie (the feminine identity-element in Odets) was made pregnant, she mockingly tells her father, by "the Prince of Wales," a name frequently used in the family for Lou Odets. The theme of her *illegitimate* baby and enforced marriage to the weak Feinschreiber—who is not the baby's real father—may have consciously taken as an external stimulus the story of Odets' mother marrying his father, according to him, because she was pregnant. Of more dynamic importance is the (probably unconscious) use of "baby" as equivalent to Odets' brain-children, his plays, which appear to be, in his view, equally illicit and born of "forbidden" passions, his unconscious wish to be "husbanded" by his own father* as Hennie wants Moe. That Hennie, in the final version, abandons her weak (fine writer) husband *and* her illegitimate baby to run off with Moe reflects Odets' life-long terror that his creative offspring were indeed illegitimate (counterfeit) and that he would do better to abandon serious writing for a life of passions and luxuries, the kind of life with which Moe is seducing Hennie. At the other end of the conflict stands his desperate need to devote himself ascetically to the gestation, delivery, and nurturance of his creative children, which, in some part of himself, he is convinced could be genuine, tall, and straight. In his later years he would often speak and write of his plays as babies "crying to be born."

In *both* versions of the play Hennie abandons her baby to the care of her mother and Sam. This highly condensed configuration expresses simultaneously many conflicts: Odets' chronic terror of abandonment and betrayal, plus his lifelong search for a woman who would not abandon him as he consciously felt his mother had when his sister became crippled. This incestuously romantic quest for a fantasied woman, often described by him in all of her unrealized perfection, who would protect not only him but also his baby (his work), would steadily alternate with a vengeful destructiveness toward women in both fantasy and fact. He would never trust himself or his women to cherish the childlike, creative innocence from which sprang his best work.

Hennie stands in admiration of Moe Axelrod's unique grand passions: not only does he have an imperative sexual need for Hennie, but she even may be his salvation. "Sometimes a girl stops your sickness," he says. He is, in addition, capable of murder, having "killed two men in extramartial [sic] activity." Before the play opens, he has all but raped Hennie, a teenage virgin, and then abandoned her crying on the bed, leaving a gift of expensive perfume to sweeten the scene. He says: "You won't forget me to your dyin' day—I was the first guy. Part of your insides. You won't forget. I wrote my name on you—indelible ink!"❶

In both versions Moe expresses in other ways a murderous vengefulness toward women. He says: "Don't make me laugh—when I get married! What I think a women? Take 'em all, cut 'em in little pieces like a herring in Greek salad. A guy in France had the right idea—dropped his wife in a

❶ 14.11.

* Several of Odets' ladies spontaneously expressed the view that "Clifford wanted to be husbanded more than wived."

❶ 14.12.

bathtub fulla acid. (Whistles) Sss, down the pipe! Pfft—not even a corset button left!" Moe cannot decide whether to devour his dismembered women in "Greek salad," to rape them, to serve them, or simply to make them vanish. Even old Jacob tells Ralph: ". . . a woman insults a man's soul like no other thing in the whole world!" All his life Odets would consciously pursue the quest for a supportive superhuman madonna with great breasts, often creating havoc when mortal women demonstrated their mortality or their small breasts.

Another major character in *I Got the Blues (Awake and Sing!)*, the mother, Bessie Berger,◖ appears to have been suggested by Odets' perception of Group actress Stella Adler. On old notes for *I Got the Blues* we see the name "Stella" changed to "Bella" to "Bessie," and from "Greenbaum" (literally "green tree") to "Greenberg" to "Berger," finally "Bessie Berger."◖ This ruler of the roost appears to be a condensation of identity-elements taken mainly from his father, but also from his mother and his Aunt Esther Rossman. Odets wrote that "Bessie Berger . . . is not only the mother in this home, but also the father."◖ Of Bessie, played by Stella Adler, Odets wrote also:

> She loves life, likes to laugh, has great resourcefulness and enjoys living from day to day. A high degree of energy accounts for her quick exasperation at ineptitude. She is a shrewd judge of realistic qualities in people in the sense of being able to gauge quickly their effectiveness. In her eyes all of the people in the house are equal. She is naïve and quick in emotional response. She is afraid of utter poverty. She is proper according to her own standards, which are fairly close to those of most middle-class families. She knows that when one lives in the jungle one must look out for the wild life.◖

The character of Bessie represents, thus, a synthesis of several of the identity-elements with which Odets was struggling. The relationship between Ralph and Bessie represents in the main, however, not that of Odets with his actual mother, but that aspect of Odets' relationship with his father which was related to, but distinct from, their mutual seduction: the struggle to decide who would be "the boss."

Thus, with a high-handed obtuseness quite like L. J. Odets', Bessie actively interferes with her son's relationship with his girl, a girl who has no parents, only "two aunts and an uncle." Bessie insists that her son's financial contribution is more important than his relation to his girl; he must learn that life *is* "printed on dollar bills." Above all, as L. J. Odets continued to say to the end of his life, he must be "shown respect."

The powerful Bessie threatens to abandon *her* weak husband and her children in order to "step in the street a free woman," self-sustaining ("In the nighttime I fry myself a little egg with a piece of bread"). She is tired of weak men like her husband, Myron; they are "mice from the kitchen," a "failure like rusty iron."◖ She says, "By me is no jumping off the roof" (her contempt for the quiet and scholarly Jacob—her father—and L. J. Odets' contempt for Clifford). She warns her family she will leave them all and do what? She will go to keep house for Morty! Morty is a two-dimensional venal version of Odets' father. Thus, just as Hennie leaves the weak Sam

◖ 14.13.
◖ 14.14.
◖ 14.15.
◖ 14.16.
◖ 14.17.

(fine writer) for the affluent, powerful Moe, so Bessie would like to leave her weak Myron to live with successful Uncle Morty.

The play reflects here Odets' covert but profound contempt for the passive, ineffectual, sensitive, ingenuous (equals "poetic failure") aspects of himself; the negative identity of his father, himself a writer manqué. To aspire thus to the professional identity Playwright is to run the risk of being a Sam Feinschreiber, a Myron, a weak, contemptible Nobody. Thus, Odets wants on the one hand to shed what he regards as the feminine (here, "schlemiel") part of himself—but, on the other, he must abandon his (creative and) illegitimate offspring if he does so.

The obverse of this is the idealist Ralph's wish to become autonomous, independent of his powerful parent. He can do this only by resurrecting within himself the redemptive power in the spiritual legacy left by his suiciding Hebraic grandfather, for whom the old traditions were no longer nourishing.◄ The powerful materialist Bessie's dominion over both her children and her husband (as well as the passionate Hennie's over *hers*) is far more credible than Ralph's last-minute voluntary, even forced claim on himself.

The minor characters seem to highlight *aspects* of the major ones: thus Bessie's husband, Myron, "thirty years a haberdashery clerk," knew he was "destined to be a failure in life the moment I began losing my hair"; he is the father of the naïve boy and pathetically hopes to win $80,000 by buying a fifty-cent ticket for the Irish Sweepstakes. If he wins—and he knows "someone's got to win. The Government isn't gonna allow everything to be a fake"—he will take his mother on a trip to Austria. (Odets had always fantasied taking his mother back to her homeland on a trip, away from L.J.) The immediate and current stimulus for Myron was probably Harold Clurman in his unhappy relationship with Stella Adler. But he reflects simultaneously an aspect of Odets' sad, gentle mother, who, like Myron, "is heartbroken without being aware of it." (Odets would say, "My mother died, I think, of a broken heart.")

Neither Bessie nor Myron has, in the play, a scintilla of the literacy, gift, intellectual depth, charm, or emotional complexity belonging to Stella Adler and Harold Clurman. The play characters borrow, as in the "day residue" of a dream, only fragments of these real people. The relationship between the powerful Bessie and the weak Myron is thus only a literal echo of Odets' conscious view in the summer of 1932 of Stella Adler's hold on Harold Clurman, for whom Odets was writing this play. But within Odets' own psychic economy, as well as in the *formal* structure of the play, the Bessie-Myron relationship is a variation on the same theme as the Hennie-Sam relationship. In both of these the multi-textured powerful character dominates the ineffectual, passive cipher, and always—however enriched and made lively by the persons in his actual world—these play characters are brought to life by his internal gallery of characters, not by the external people in his current life.

Another minor character, Uncle Morty (originally named Mordecai) —like Moe Axelrod and Louis Odets—drives a big car and smokes big cigars. Odets says of him:

> Uncle Morty is a successful American businessman with five good senses. Something sinister comes out of the fact that the lives of others seldom touch him deeply. He holds to his own line of life. When he is generous he wants others to be aware of it. He is pleased

◄ 14.18.

by attention—a rich relative to the Berger family. He is a shrewd judge of material values. He will die unmarried. Two and two make four, never five, with him. He can blink in the sun for hours, a fat tomcat. Tickle him, he laughs. He lives in a penthouse with a real Japanese butler to serve him. He sleeps with dress models, but not from his own showrooms. He plays cards for hours on end. He smokes expensive cigars. He sees every Mickey Mouse cartoon that appears. He is a 32-degree Mason. He is really deeply intolerant finally.

Uncle Morty, crippled emotionally as Moe is physically, is the skin-deep portrait of Odets' father, also "intolerant finally" and a "32-degree Mason." The passionate complexities of Odets' identifications with his father are reserved, however, for Moe Axelrod, in many ways the most richly alive character in the play. In his later work, Odets would struggle against his tendency to have the equivalent of the powerful Moe Axelrod character— his father within—"run away with the play."◖

Even the janitor, Schlosser (the one who locks up)—whose wife dies, leaving a daughter—becomes a vehicle for Odets' unconscious wish to be left alone with his father.◖ (The girl, his notes tell us, ran away to be a chorus girl in a "burlesque show"—as Odets did when he left his father's business to be an actor.)

Contrapuntal to the fantasy of a profane love affair with his father— as expressed in the relation between Hennie and Moe—he develops within the same work the fantasy of a sacred one through another of his internal gallery of characters. Odets is also Ralph Berger, the son, a boy without "guts" but with a "clean spirit . . . naïve," who wants to be "a headliner, his name in all the papers," rather than, as he puts it, "to sit around with the blues and mud in your mouth." Here the *idealized* father-symbol is in the person of the grandfather, Jacob, the name and exterior probably borrowed from Stella Adler's father, the famous Jewish actor, and, more remotely, from the Old Testament father of Joseph, the dreamer.◖ Odets says that "Jacob . . . is trying to find a right path . . . aware of justice, of dignity." He is an observer, reflective but impotent, "with no power to turn ideal to action." As a barber, the old man "demonstrates the flair of an artist" (like Ben Stark's "pioneering" in orthodontia in Odets' later *Rocket to the Moon*). He is "an old Jew with living eyes in his tired face."

The identity-elements in this character echo Odets' Uncle Israel Rossman, his mother, and his gentle, scholarly grandfather. Jacob is the Old Testament idealist who says, "In my day the propaganda was for God. Now it's for success. A boy don't turn around without having shoved in him he should make success." Chanting *in Hebrew*, he predicts that in Ralph's life "a Red Sea will happen again" and the evil Egyptians of the materialist world will be covered by it.

He is steadily trying to help his uncertain grandson not to become a failure like him, "an old man polishing stoves" (originally, "tools"): "For seventy years he talked with good ideas, but only in the head . . . a man who had golden opportunities but drank instead a glass tea."

Jacob counsels Ralph against such passivity (inactivation) and pleads with him to become himself through noble *action*: "I tell you—DO! Do what is in your heart and you carry in yourself a revolution!" ("Move yourself if you will move multitudes," Odets once said.) "Without a revolution, life is nothing. . . . Even Jesus Christ," says Jacob, "was a bolshe-

◖ 14.19.
◖ 14.20.
◖ 14.21.

vik," and advises his grandson: ". . . look on the world, not on yourself so much."

Ralph is, however, preoccupied with his personal lacks: he complains that "I never in my life even had a birthday party or a pair of skates," that he couldn't afford to "take up tap dancing," that he can't get his teeth fixed, sleeps on a daybed, has no room of his own, and that he generally can't stand this "cockeyed world." Ralph—like Odets—feels bullied by his parents, and his Gentile, impoverished, forbidden girl is an orphan.

Ralph is one of those slender, one-dimensional, work-horse characters in a play who never quite "comes alive" but who functions in an assigned slot: he carries on one level of meaning the generational role of transforming his grandfather's impotent revolutionary idealism into a contemporary salvation, inasmuch as the Hebraic grandfather himself, tired as "an old horse for hire," is fearfully incapable of such actions. In the first draft of *Awake and Sing!*, directly following a contemptuous order from his daughter to take their dog to the roof to urinate, Jake mocks himself bitterly: "Schmah Yisroeal. Behold! . . . For we are the chosen people . . ." and promptly jumps from the roof to his death, by the same means by which Odets two years earlier had come close to suicide.

Jacob leaves to the boy his insurance of $3,000 plus an ancient spiritual legacy to "do what is in your heart." Odets here states his contempt for his own cowardice as a man of thought instead of action, and his conviction that only the ultimate self-sacrifice (suicide) can issue in a "resurrection"—that is, the radical reorganization in himself for which he yearns. The implication is that a belief in God as well as the "Schmah Yisroeal" has become absurd, and that he must find a new way out. It is into this void that he moves his naïve version of a utopian socialist society in which, in the words of the Hebrew prophet Isaiah, "The earth shall cast out the dead" and all shall "awake and sing." In the original manuscript of *I Got the Blues* there is only a slight indication that the weak character Ralph intends to *use* the freedom gained by his grandfather's sacrifice in order to "change the world" politically. This was progressively elaborated in each new draft.

In both versions the major interior plots—corresponding to Odets' basic conflicts—lie in the contrapuntal relationships representing his two opposed fantasies about his father: primarily, in the "impure" and passionate one of Hennie and Moe, and secondarily, in the "pure" one of Ralph and Jacob. Hennie capitulates to the worldly Moe's seduction in *both* versions, but in *I Got the Blues* they are *separated* at the end by detectives leading Moe away to prison for some "crookedness" he has perpetrated, and Hennie must resign herself to a life with the effete Sam Feinschreiber. (L. J. Odets, it will be recalled, had left New York in a fog of mystery surrounding possible fraud in his business.) The father is, in short, revealed as a double-dealing fraud. This view of his father erupts *even* in the denouement of the *idealized* son-father story: Ralph discovers that his scholarly grandfather, presumably representative of the best in the older generation—and sensitive transmitter of a Hebraic love of learning—"has never read even one of his books." All the pages are uncut. In his final draft of *Awake and Sing!* Odets softened this indictment of Jacob by changing it to "Half the pages are uncut." Ralph says, "I certainly got the blues when I seen that." Odets can believe, thus, in neither "father" nor the worldly Moe nor the spiritual Jacob—and thus his young, aspiring foot cannot find an even place on which to stand.

By far the most energetic and dramatically compelling theme in both versions of *Awake and Sing!*—to be endlessly puzzling to critics and to

Ph.D. candidates—lies in the sensual Hennie-Moe relationship representing Odets' "profane" fantasy about his father. When in the original *I Got the Blues* Hennie gives Moe up, resigning herself to a life with the frightened, ineffectual, and scorned Sam Feinschreiber, this expresses Odets' fear that if he were wholly to give himself to his identity as Writer, he must renounce not only a wild sensuality but all passionate human relationships. Such a renunciation of the relationship to his fraudulent, passionate, seductive, high-stepping father, however, meant that he would exist only half-alive like his weak, depressed, withdrawn, tubercular mother. This is what Clurman in *The Fervent Years* calls the "masochistically pessimistic ending" of the early draft of *Awake and Sing!*

In the later revision of *Awake and Sing!* Odets manages to have it both ways: the intense sensuality of the profane love is consummated, and at the same time the sacred love—in all its idealism—is protected. Hennie and Moe (many of whose comments could have issued directly from the mouth of Lou Odets) are encouraged by the boyishly eager Ralph to seize their opportunity to run away together to Havana, a land of "moonlight and roses" where people bathe with "frenchie soap" and where champagne flows freely, a land not unlike the American dream of Hollywood.

This resolution of the Hennie-Moe relationship would for years confound and irritate critics and Odets scholars, especially leftist rationalists such as John Howard Lawson, who would find it structurally weak, "unmotivated," irrational, and totally lacking in economic or political logic. It is evident that Odets himself was in the dark regarding his unconscious reasons for *needing* to have Hennie and Moe run away together. He would later "confess" to *The New York Times*: "Pictures use romance as the solution for everything. That's routine. In *Awake and Sing!* I used the conclusion of the two running off to Bermuda* as the solution. But when I wrote it I knew it was a dirty lie."

This vehement insistence that he had written a "dirty lie" represents more than Odets' afterthoughts about the emptiness of movie romance as a solution. It is his disgust not only with his shameful "dirty" fantasy toward his father but also with his facile fulfillment of this latent wish: "taking the easy way out." The "dirty lie" of the Hennie-Moe resolution is countered by the purity in Ralph's rebirth as a potential earthly Messiah from his noble grandfather's suicide◖ (the "clean lie"). Ralph says:

> Right here in the house! My days won't be for nothing.◖ Let Mom have the dough. I'm twenty-two and kickin'! I'll get along. Did Jake die for us to fight about nickels? No! "Awake and sing," he said. Right here he stood and said it. The night he died, I saw it like a thunderbolt! I saw he was dead and I was born!◖ I swear to God, I'm one week old! I want the whole city to hear it—fresh blood, arms. We got 'em. We're glad we're living.

To this Moe replies, "I wouldn't trade you for two pitchers and an outfielder. Hold the fort!" Ralph is, as it were, starting from scratch; he has a second chance at life.

Thus, in this later and more optimistic revision, not only do Hennie and Moe consummate their lowbrow passionate yearning for each other, but now even the corrupt Moe, along with the pure Jacob, appreciates young Ralph as much as "two pitchers and an outfielder." This is Odets'

---

* He used Havana, actually.
◖ 14.22.
◖ 14.23.
◖ 14.24.

fulfillment of his yearning for the love of his baseball-fan father. The craft awkwardness in this glib denouement would leave many audiences unsatisfied, and the end of the play open to formal criticism.

Even the late John Gassner (always a sympathetic critic of Odets' work), having extracted for himself the clear and simple meaning of *Awake and Sing!* as a social-protest play, would all his life lodge his complaint that its fabric did not conform to its manifest meaning: "I could never believe that girl Henny who had slept with a traveling salesman under a boardwalk, gotten pregnant and fallen in love with Moe Axelrod, a petty racketeer. That little carrier of the proletarian revolt was certainly not convincing." Hennie's psychological function in the play has, of course, little to do with the proletarian revolt, and yet her relationship to Moe—full of a splendid superfluity of psychological energy and a texture of apparent irrationality—is, mysteriously, the most vital, most interesting, and most moving of all. The Hennie-Moe relationship stands closer to the heart of Odets' own psychological struggles than any other in the play, and could thus draw for its force from his relation to his father, the powerful taproot of his emotional life.*

The impact of *Awake and Sing!* derives not from its social protest against the horrors of poverty, but from the potency of spirit in its people. At last, although the language was English, not Yiddish, Odets was substituting for the consolatory spectacles and sentimentality in the Yiddish theatre the first deeply felt and formally achieved realism in America. He was daring to put on the stage the lives of recognizable people struggling for life amidst "petty conditions." And he was hoping their conflicts—by reason of their universality—would reach an audience not limited to Jewish-Americans.

Clurman's recollection that he and Odets were together nightly cannot have been quite literally true, as a number of beautiful women of good memory had vivid recollections of another kind of night life with Odets during this winter and spring. One of them, an orphan whom I shall call Alice, was then a lovely, volatile high-school virgin with a tough surface, resembling the feline actress Simone Simon. She recalls thinking, as Odets (still with his shaven head and Dürer beard) walked into the Village Vanguard café for a free Sunday-morning breakfast, "He's got to be a phony." As she listened to him talk, her precocious mind began to change, and shortly she agreed to let him come to her fifth-floor walk-up on 14th Street which she shared with several other penniless girls. There he asked her with what appeared to be genuine concern, "Where do girls like you come from?"—precisely the words he would put in the mouth of Joe Bonaparte in his play *Golden Boy*. Alice was touched by this inquiry and by his offer to help her as an actress by giving her improvisations to work on. Seating her on a chair in the center of the shabby room, he instructed her to concentrate on the fantasy: "You are desperate for this job, you need money so terribly you will probably commit suicide if you don't get this job." She wondered why he had chosen this theme. She responded so well to his

---

* English critics understand these universal psychological conflicts in Odets far better than do the Americans.

    ❆ 14.25.

efforts that he decided to educate her, commencing by taking her to her first foreign movie, in Russian. ("I was so impressed that he went to movies you can't even understand.") He talked to her about Dostoevsky, introduced her to Beethoven and to art museums, and finally invited her to his tiny room in the Strasberg apartment over Sutter's Bakery.

First there was dinner with the Strasbergs in their room, furnished Village style. No one said a word during dinner, listening instead to a record of classical Spanish music. When Lee and Paula went out for the evening, Clifford solemnly announced, "I am writing a play," and for almost three hours read to her from *I Got the Blues*. When he finished, he appeared to her exhausted and strangely, even nervously, eager to hear her opinion of it. It startled her that this learned and brilliant writer should so obviously need reassurance.

The reading and discussion over, he carried her "ever so gently to his bed" for her first sexual experience. From then on, she watched his bedrooms improve and was "madly in love with him" for several years, and distraught when she saw him with other girls. She felt—as would so many people, men and women alike, during the course of his life—that she was much more involved with him than he with her. There was in him, for all his tenderness and empathy, a separateness and the curiously impersonal quality of the spectator. He advised her not to break off with her concurrent boyfriend. She would be shocked two years later by the vengeful force with which she struck him in the face when she saw him sitting in a theatre audience with another girl as the cast was yelling, "Strike!" Something in her knew she had somehow been exploited.

It is Alice's impression that at about this time, "having something to do with Clurman's involvement with Stella Adler," Clifford became interested in Stella's younger sister Pearl, who did not return his interest. Odets noted: "Two kinds of reactions to me: I am special and wonderful; or I'm an idiot." Odets always had a special interest in Clurman's women.

As the Great Depression deepened and it became clear to the Group members that the directors were unable to assure them even the minimum subsistence their program of continuity called for, tension rose. The actors became increasingly critical and began to demand greater participation in the Group government.

All three directors were on edge. Clurman felt that Strasberg and Crawford feared real responsibility; Strasberg, in turn, was persuaded that Clurman's impracticality, his "middle-class" Theatre Guild experience, and his unrealistically exacting play standards were daily losing them their livelihoods. Strasberg, accordingly, wrote an impassioned address "To the directors of the Group," stating they had not planned things well, had not sufficiently considered the sensitivities of their audience, and had stuck too stubbornly to the production of new American plays. A good revival, he thought, might get them all through this dreadful winter. Recommending they face the fact that "we are fly-by-night producers," he suggested a more realistic theatre policy which would not wait for literary masterpieces but would aim at producing good "theatre." He called also for the formation of an actors' committee and the hiring of a business manager. Rereading this document thirty-five years later, Strasberg would be astonished

by his own perspicacity and would again conclude, "We might have survived had Harold been more realistic."

Clurman countered Strasberg's suggestion with the proposal that the
directorship be centralized in him. Instead, the Actors' Committee was
formed, became immediately inactive, and the triumvirate continued to
run the Group as before. However, there being no play in production, the
actors were increasingly asking permission to take any job that came
along.

Odets' total income—aside from an occasional secret contribution
from his concerned mother—came from a small nightclub called the Village Fair, where he was, now and again, paid two dollars an evening for
his old "Rover Reciter" recitations such as "Dangerous Dan McGrew" and
"The Face on the Barroom Floor." Ivan Black, master of ceremonies, recalls the poetry-loving customers' complaints at Odets' choice of material.
He recalls, too, Odets' joy this winter at landing the inconsequential part
of a Russian bureaucrat, Andrey Brikin, in a comedy, *They All Come to
Moscow*, on the strength of which he rented a small room in Greenwich
Village at Strunsky's well-known rooming house, which catered to improvident artists. The program, which lists Cornel Wilde in the cast, states that
"the appearance of Clifford Odets is by courtesy of the Group Theatre," and
that he was "a newspaper man well-known to radio audiences before the
stage claimed him."

This slight play about Americans in Moscow closed after twenty performances, but Odets' personal relationship with his stage wife, Natalya
Brikin, played by a lively young Russian-Jewish torch singer whose professional name was simply "Tamara," continued. Tamara, later this year
to make a sensation in the musical comedy *Roberta* with the song "Smoke
Gets in Your Eyes," had been born Tamara Drasin in Sorochintzy, Russia.
Darkly beautiful, with a sensitive, husky singing voice and a talent for the
guitar, she described herself for the program as having been named for a
Caucasian princess and having fled from the Russian Revolution. These
would have been sufficient qualifications for Odets. The fact, however,
that he saw her as a guileless, open-hearted innocent being mistreated by
his rival, Luther Adler, made her a necessity. He appeared not to notice
that Tamara was the first obviously Jewish girl he had courted in a long
time.

While Odets enviously thought of Adler not only as an arrived and
successful actor but as a reigning Don Juan, Adler thought of Odets as
"younger, taller, richer, blonder, and handsomer," someone with whom he
could not possibly compete for a woman. Indeed, Tamara broke off her relationship with Adler and commenced an intense affair with Odets, frequently meeting him in his small rented room at Strunsky's, where there
often occurred strange scenes which he stage-managed. Compulsively he
would arrange a situation wherein he made love to one girl while another,
sometimes weeping, watched. In his notes for an autobiography Odets jots
down for this period: "Want to sleep with two women."

This colossal and insatiable hunger is not different in its quality from
Jay Adler's description of Odets' ravenous devouring of Jewish bread made
by Adler's mother, or from his frequently expressed wishes to simultaneously smoke two cigarettes, listen to two symphonies, drink two wines. As
he would put it that fall, ". . . the trouble with me is that all my life I
looked for and wanted a full ecstatic day and night. It doesn't come that
way . . . but still I resent the loss."

Alice later became a waitress-dancer at the Village Vanguard, and
although Odets would appear there with Tamara or with the exquisite

actress Mary George, Alice never viewed his visits as deliberate cruelty. It is likely that there was in fact something unconsciously vengeful in such visits. He would arrange many such situations during the course of his life, sometimes as actor, often as audience. Beyond the misogyny expressed in such enactments, these caricatures of what Alice had complained of as his coldness and his "spectator personality" may be part of an "equidistance" from the principals of his life, probably necessary in varying degrees for dramatists.

"When I would visit Clifford on a Sunday in that characterless semi-suburban row house in Philadelphia, his father would make us listen—both of us sullen—to Father Coughlin, who, he thought, was going to save America." This is Abner Biberman's recollection of Odets, almost twenty-seven years old and once again penniless. Back, as he put it, "like a homing pigeon" at the West Oak Lane house, Odets talked a great deal about his work in progress, still called *I Got the Blues*. It was clear to Biberman he was desperate to finish this play and hoped against hope it might supply him enough income to rid him forever of his father's renewed, contemptuously withering assaults. Just out of college, Biberman asked Odets to arrange an audience with Strasberg. Clifford laughingly replied, "You say you want to talk to Strasberg. I've been living with that sonofabitch for five months and I haven't said five words to him!"

Whenever the two young men walked the many miles to the Odets home after an evening with the intelligentsia over the one cup of coffee they could afford at Horn and Hardart's restaurant, they would pray that Clifford's mother would awaken and, as she often did, quietly make them bacon and eggs. "If L.J. woke up, though," Biberman recalled, "it was really bad because he would storm down the stairs shouting"—at both young men—" 'Get out of my house!' " It was extremely puzzling to Biberman that most of the time, to his face, Clifford treated his father like "the greatest," often agreeing with his stands or, if he disagreed, saying, "You are absolutely right, but for absolutely wrong reasons." With part of himself, the son shared his father's contempt for him and continued, on one level, to be in abject terror of him.

In spite of what Biberman found to be "an alarming procession of girls" during this short stint (to be the last) of enforced living at home, Odets continued to work on *I Got the Blues* and steadily read it to Abner, who felt by now that Clifford was the most singular and important person in his life: "I'm sure he meant far more to me than I did to him."

Biberman, also scorned by *his* affluent-businessman father as a lazy misfit, was flattered that Clifford would take the trouble to introduce him to late Beethoven and to read him his play as he was writing it. He had never before experienced such a stirring "eloquence and inner certainty" in anyone, and would have been astonished by the lack of self-confidence Odets confided to his diary.

Finally, in the spring of 1933, Odets completed *I Got the Blues* and read it with "stunning effect" to a small group at the Kozlenko apartment in Sunnyside, Long Island, and again into the small hours of the morning at the Leof home in Philadelphia.

From his frantic love letters to Tamara, typed on his father's same old Odets Company stationery with the fine haze of tiny green print all over it saying "The Odets Company, The Odets Company, The Odets Company," it is evident he was afraid this first major work would be rejected and was fighting off a wave of the despair that had so often engulfed him before the days of the Group. Addressing her by turns as "Rainflower," "Lotus," "Darling, darling," "Russian Jewess," "Tartar Chink," and—when desperate for a response—"For Christ's Sake, Darling," he has left a record of these few weeks as he marked time.

"Even this goddam paper I'm writing on is of the past—sickening, of when I worked for a time in my father's old office . . . across the top is a border which reads 'All Genuine Odets selling copy is submitted on paper like this' . . . everything is awful as hell here." So Odets puts it to Tamara in a letter in which he quickly reassures himself with the recollection of the close of his diary from the last Group summer at Dover Furnace: "I'm reborn fresh and new as a child," to which he now adds, "I'm just about three years old—that is what you love a three year old child!" He refers, of course, to the fact that he had joined the Group family almost three years ago.

Perhaps it was a mistake, he thinks, to reread his boyhood diaries, "full of childish smoke, sickening, lost, unhappy . . . I feel just like them now, mediocre and sick and very adolescent . . . I have in me a death feeling now . . . all the futile wasted years." In an effort to muster counterforces, he visits Aunt Esther and listens to Uncle Israel sing in Hebrew; goes to a party at the Leofs'; picks two yellow irises; types long, affectionate letters to Harold Clurman and to Tamara. Somehow he thinks of Harold's "big face . . . good as bread" and Tamara as in "one whorl"; tries to take pleasure in the fact that his father has impulsively given him three "lovely white shirts . . . ones he'd bought for himself." It was done, he adds, "in a sudden swift gesture of glad giving, a thing I well understand since I'm so like him . . . you'll be surprised on meeting father how alike we are." Finally, he drinks wine and seltzer. This last simply makes him feel worse. It does not help that he is having teeth extracted. All his life the loss of hair and teeth would be a nightmare to him. A scribbled note, later to appear in *Awake and Sing!*, says, "As soon as he began to lose his hair, he knew he'd be a failure."

His almost daily letters to Tamara are a steady cry for help and for intimacy, accompanied, as always in his correspondence with a woman, by threats of violence if she is not more responsive: "Send me a note or I'll kill you dead quick certain!" or "I'll choke you with my useless hands and leave red marks on your throat. Go away, go away, go away from me." His effort to keep these threats humorous is forced and brittle.

When in the course of a single morning he asked his mother for the fourth time if there was mail and was "very quietly (no decoration or temperament to it) going insane" when she answered "no," he then "blew up and let my poor dear mother have all my rage and worry in some silly argument about whether or not to have a haircut." He tries to contact Tamara by listening to the radio in the hope of getting the broadcast from the Kretchma, in New York, where she sings, but tunes in "Gypsy Nina" instead. Frustrated, he ends up eating many platesful of ice cream with his sixteen-year-old sister, Florence, by now thin, irritable, and adoring of him.

From these letters to Tamara it would appear he has nonetheless written in three days a new draft of the third act of his play and will commence again on revisions of the first act. The second act, he writes, "can stand verbatim." It is evident his despair is no longer vanquishing him into paralysis as it used to do.

At long last, with definite word that the bankrupt Group will have a subsidized summer rehearsal period at an adult camp in the Adirondacks fifteen miles north of Lake George—in exchange for four nights a week of entertainment—Odets' spirits rise and the tone of his letters to Tamara becomes less romantic, less extravagant, but more convincingly committed than in any previous relationship: ". . . the truth is we're very cautious beings who are afraid of being bitten, stung. No doubt we both have been in past years, but I write now of a new year . . . we call out in each other the tread-slowly quality, the stop look and listen of two beings who want and are afraid of the wanting."

As his self-delineation grows firmer, he feels he can afford to risk more with a woman in the service of emerging from his painful and lonely isolation. And yet with Tamara, as with all other women, he cannot escape a certain romantic self-absorbed attitudinizing wherein his own fantasies and feelings, rather than the living relationship, are his essential focus.

He hopes she will seriously consider coming along with the Group to Green Mansions, described on its stationery as a summer camp "for moderns" at Warrensburg, New York, and would "like nothing better" than to share "the new lovely years before me" with her. "True," he writes, he is no more than a "twisted-headed Jew boy with blue eyes and a mouth and arms to love you" who only now in his twenty-seventh year is trembling "on the brink of maturity," but, he concludes, ". . . we must stop being afraid." He asks her if she will meet him in New York at the Strasbergs', where he will stay for two days before leaving with them for this third Group summer.

Chapter Fifteen

I surely felt that after that summer of 1933, that the Group Theatre would do my play. But they had not the slightest interest in it. And I now realized that I had real writing talent, when I saw that act up there on the stage, and right then I was not to be stopped or contained. *I still knuckled under, almost in the sense that the son in a family would knuckle under to his parents, despite the fact that he disagreed with them. You don't say, "Well, I'm leaving the family" quite, but my impulses ran that way.*
CLIFFORD ODETS, *1961*

We live in a strange, dry country. A strong heart is needed, iron nerves to continue to be a serious writer here.
CLIFFORD ODETS, *1961*

As THIS summer opened, Odets seemed more concerned about developing an intimacy with a real young woman than about living intensely with the fantasied characters of his new play. Early diary entries express a profound loneliness and make no mention of *I Got the Blues:*

Just now a letter to Tamara. I miss her more than sun on a naked body. She is as good, as nourishing. Sunday night in the city we were together and talked ourselves clean. Whatever I felt I told her, completely each inside thought. The doubts concerning myself and us . . . I say we are in love, I say we are for each other. She says so too, but has an edge of doubt in her mind concerning herself, me.

Well, I'm pretty damn full of her, not good for much else at this time. . . . I thought several times of J. and R.* Oh the pushing to

* These eight words are finally persuasive to a biographer that Odets' secret marriage to Roberta and their child, Joan, were fact, not fancy. This sentence addressed only to himself—with initials, not names, has the quality of an ordinary diary entry rather than a self-romanticizing communication. Erikson sees this event as a kind of "curse" carried by Odets for the rest of his life.

arriving at an at-oneness. Harold [Clurman] too. Last night to see him
standing around as the arrivals straggled in one by one, from all over
in different cars . . . no Stella for that boy and he surprised to learn
from me that she wasn't coming for another few days. The soft stillness of his face about it all . . . and she not worth the little hand
of him.

He felt now a brotherly closeness to his roommate, Clurman, who was
struggling with much the same human transactions, not only in the "blizzard" of his pained relationship with actress Stella Adler but also in a rift
with the other two directors. Clurman was in what he would later call "a
doleful withdrawal." Strasberg and Crawford were making decisions without him, one being that he was not ready to do any real directing, and
another that they would produce a play to which he was indifferent—
Crisis, by a new young playwright, Sidney Kingsley. Of this play Odets
records in his diary:

The new play? Our worst to date, but perhaps will make the most
money for us. A kind of "Counsellor-at-Law" in a hospital, only the
young author (who is here and seems quite a mediocre person) is not
so crafty as E. Rice.

As *Men in White*, this play would win a Pulitzer Prize, provide the
prototype for all future American medical drama on stage, screen, and
television, and—directed by Strasberg—be the Group Theatre's first hit.
Financed from Hollywood—by Franchot Tone, his new girl, Joan Crawford, and Doris Warner, daughter of Jack Warner (head of Warner Bros.)
—it would, paradoxically, keep the Group Theatre alive and provide a
target for attacks that it was now "going commercial." Tone, full of recollections of the creative satisfactions of the two summers he had spent with
the Group, was now reporting from Hollywood his humiliation and ennui
at having to say to Jean Harlow such lines as "Your hair is like a field of
silver daisies, I'd like to run barefoot through your hair." But he was in
love with Joan Crawford and could not leave a project that cost $9,000 for
three minutes of finished film and would cost over half a million to complete—an astronomic sum at that time.

The Group's main business of this summer was the reworking and
rehearsing of *Crisis* for a fall opening in New York. Odets was assigned
the small part of a businessman quite like his father, complete with cigar.
Kingsley would later recall Odets ad-libbing the line, "Say, what are we,
Boy Scouts?" "Knowing my own good worth," Odets defensively records in
his diary, "it doesn't bother me an inch" to have so small a role. However,
he persists in the fantasy, in much the same form as he yearned to astonish
his father with "success," that someday "by chance" he will be given a
good part and the directors will "then be surprised at my ability."

It is clear from his depressed account of his poor performance in
Maxwell Anderson's *Gods of the Lightning* that, although he had not yet
quite abdicated his identity as actor, he was moving steadily toward that
of playwright:

I went down to the social hall and on that stage worked so hard and
tried so honestly to give a good show . . . but all the time inside I
was battling to remember very difficult lines, exhausting work . . .
it was awful. I began to get depressed with being bad and slowly
dressed. The effort had been tremendous, the strain too, so I dressed
slowly and washed my face with dead hands. . . . Just this moment
Maxwell Anderson, the playwright of our show tonight, came in here

and has gone to sit in the corner booth. But not until I'd told him how I felt with the lines tonight. He's given me sympathy, telling me that in the original production the fellow who played the same part went almost mad with trying to remember what was what. Scant comfort when you hung by the fingertips for forty minutes on stage. . . . I'm going away now. . . . I can't sit here any more. I'm restless. I want, I want! But what. I haven't any idea. . . . Oh to be anchored to something, like a tree in the ground. . . . Did I tell you ever that I was destined in my flesh and spirit to be a musician but somewhere the spirit clutched wrongly. . . .

In his dissatisfaction, he asked Clurman to read *I Got the Blues;* perhaps it could be used as part of this summer's entertainment program for the Green Mansions camp, along with this old Anderson play, revue sketches, skits, cowboy songs, and outdoor performances of *The Emperor Jones*, in which he was cast as "Lem, a native chief." Harold's opinion, he records in his diary, is not so important to him as last summer, though "still important and valuable." He closes this entry, "Tamara, please come soon."

It is clear he misses her deeply and is genuinely trying to establish a viable human tie, ". . . almost as if one wondered where he'd left his left arm." Nevertheless he records that he is "otherwise calm and found." "Found!" he continues, "a large word for me to utter with any sort of truth. Here is truth." This large word reflects his new satisfaction with the writing he is doing. He feels he is moving closer to his ideal of attaining Emerson's "immovable center" as an artist.

Deeply stirred by a dreadful burst of sobbing from Clurman, who had participated in a demonstration of hypnosis by a visiting psychiatrist and had repeated over and over in the trance, "He worries for his wife, he takes his wife home," Odets records in his diary his concern for his friend's struggle to find his way with Stella Adler. And he renews his pleas to Tamara to come to Green Mansions; however, she is "all tied up with jobs now and promises (or hints) about coming up later." Luther Adler had warned him she was "career mad." In a longing letter he tells her how irritated he was with Stella's casual remark that "Most men fall for Tamara," and how he cannot rid himself of the image of her "lift of the shoulders, the part in the hair and how you comb and deftly turn a knot up in the back over the neck. . . ." In response, she advises him to start going out with other girls. Helplessly he writes, "You have me the way music was once in my life—everything . . . this is the first time I've ever been in love, truly in love, with someone outside myself, a girl clearly cut away from my so-called ideals, not some mental image." He is engaged, for all his posturing, in trying to establish a genuine intimacy with a woman who is not a fantasied madonna, a whore, or a neutrally blond "bloodless Nordic." But he senses something addictive and "not quite right" in his engulfed dependence on her.

Not until the second week at camp, on July 5—the anniversary of Roberta's death—does he mention in a letter to Tamara that Clurman likes *I Got the Blues*. This brief announcement follows the headline news that

Luther Adler has just arrived with his new wife and precedes the dreadful story, told apparently for the first time, of his young wife's suicide and her murder of their child. He concludes, "Harold knows and several of my friends, not even my parents. Secrets, but only because I was a young, foolish boy. We won't have to talk about this any more. It goes like the river."

Due to visit him in a month, Tamara has apparently asked for details of what Clurman thought of *I Got the Blues*. He replies:

> About my play? Harold liked it very much, but could only read the first act and a half since the rest is not typed so any other human eye but my own can read it with understanding. I'll show him the rest soon. In the meantime he wants me to put on the first act here sometime in August. I personally believe the play has stuff, but I know that it will be a long time before I find the proper form for my feeling. The feeling overspills the form . . . we'll talk of this sometime . . . of artists' problems there are not a few.

His diary records with what acute pain he watches the couples around him, especially those who appear to be solidly joined, like Group actors Morris Carnovsky and Phoebe Brand, or Joe and Goldie Bromberg. It is growing difficult for him to resist advances from several female guests at Green Mansions, one reminding him in "her coolness and violin string quality" of Tamara. He closes the entry with "I've got a swell talent and since life is becoming normal, there's no reason for me not to become a good artist. If Tamara Lotus were here I'd be indeed happy."

Within a few days, filled with "a sickness, hunger, a cloud in my head . . . it comes at night so strongly that I get black in the eyes," he records in his diary the crumbling of his resistance to "this woman standing against the railing outside the social hall . . . married, perhaps 34, tenderly, quietly, coolly, darkly, goodlooking, the face temperate, the smooth black hair touched with an oriental quality. . . ." Sometimes she shyly quotes poetry, "is uneasy with me often, laughs and shows small regular white teeth. . . . Her face is dark with sun and freckled, the hair not managed; she reminds me of Tamara. . . ." There is at last a harmony between his finally having left off "skating the surface of myself" in his play about a Jewish family in the Bronx and his attraction to these dark "oriental" girls. He had struck the roots which would nourish his best work.

He longs to remain in the country after the Group leaves for New York and writes in an adumbration of the consciousness of the next generation:

> This all reminds me deeply of an old wish, even a yearning, yes, yearning deep and strong, to some day spend all of the summer days into fall into winter, unto the first snow fall, in some country place. It comes to me, this feeling, again like homesickness, with an ache, as if in some distant past I lived that way, deep and good with nature and the flow of natural things. And the ache comes from that I have thwarted for long so many things natural and native to me. I am sure that the peasant Austrian stock which I partly come from moves supreme in my blood in such times as these; . . . you see I learned to live "away" from what I was and am, even did violence to myself. That's why I trust this mood of now, because I know what it stems from, the goodness of it and the rightness . . . containing of all the past and present and future in the moment which is now. Only men are fools enough to refuse the past, the born-in heritage . . . that is what I yearn for, the smooth flowing, the good complete acceptance of what is and always will be. . . . No rock dreams of being great,

shatters itself with desperation and discontent because it's not a flower. I mean perfection, being the bones and flesh you are and what racial matters flow fine with the corpuscles. *I want always the timeless evocations to be called out of me because I am!* [Italics mine]

In striking contrast to his contempt and rejection only a few years back of his long-nosed cousins and "dark women," he longs for Tamara's "Hebraic, biblical" face: ". . . this boy who jumped in and out of many beds is for one woman. The horror of polygamy is a burn in the face, a cough in the lungs." But, unable to tolerate her silence, "the idiocy of summer nights, the loneliness, the very urgency of being young," he records finally his capitulation to the older woman:

She talks with great sympathy of Max, her husband. She is content, gets much from her daughter. But a different life is slipping by her, she feels. Youth? She stands now on the top of the hill and it begins to go down for her. This she knows. . . .

We danced a dance. Would I walk? I would. We walked slowly up the hill. Two nights before I took her to her room. The beautiful child asleep on a cot and between two cots I kissed her and made an exploring game with my hands. She can't get over how quickly this thing happened, she says. She asks if I love her. I am truthful. "Like" I say. I would not want to make her unhappy. I become something for her to cling to—the other side of the hill stares her in the face. Nice, she is unspoiled, unaffected and simple, decent—what a word!

This night we walk up to her porch and sit there. She talks constantly about the beauty of the night. We are soothed with cool air and a cloudy moonlit night. She tells me she's lucky. All the girls look and flirt at me, with me, and why do I pick her out? I laugh softly, protestingly. Each time she makes such a remark I'm embarrassed. I suggest getting a blanket and lying close together somewhere. She goes in to her room, opens the back door. The child is asleep, but stirs. We get the blanket and climb the hill. What will happen? What CAN happen. We get mixed up. Her body belongs to a married woman, one who had a child and grew a little lax with the comfort of a steady husband. It expresses her simplicity, the face rougeless, altho in the late afternoon I saw she had rouged her cheeks, I think because I paid so little attention to her during the day. (It gave me a pang.) Her breasts are soft, spread, the nipples good. I have seen during the day her legs and thighs with the usual bursted purple capillaries in the flesh. She asks if I like her body. I do and say so. It comes to the point of a body being a body, only some are more firm than others.

After a time it becomes intolerable, but I can't ask her to take off her clothes and merely open my trouser front and press against her with buttons and tweed. It all bothers me, particularly when she says, "perhaps we ought to." I tell her of the danger to her and she agrees. She is relaxed nicely and talks softly, her voice changing with the whim of her heart's push. Such change in a voice I love. She talks and I answer yes and no. What is there to say, even when she demands I tell her something. "Let the night tell you something," I say, "or my hands." The hands are busy.

I took her to the back door and stepped over the threshold into her room. The child slept and turned twice, once sighed deeply in its sleep. We smiled together that the empty bright head could sigh with such concern. I've noticed that before in children. In the next room sleeps a young boy and his nurse. We must be careful of noise. The bed yelps when we sit on it. She says it would be nice if I just stayed there. I am in agreement. My blood agrees and all the senses, but not so much the head which is tired. We undress quickly. Her slight shame is like a willow curve in her body. There is a way a woman stands as the last garment slides off her body and the turn with which she slides into the bed. I had been sitting on the foot of the bed, already naked, my knees pressed together to hide the standing flesh and arched backward in the middle, I followed her into the bed. Here I forgot about the lovely child in the other cot, but in a flash got the feeling of what it would be like when that child grew up. One man's relationship with both daughter and mother, what would that be like—so I thought—and we were together naked under the heavy blankets. I missed mostly that I might move and swing myself with freedom. My bladder was distended and bothered me. The hardness of myself hurt too and it was not with utter content that I was there. Her face was very tender. A dull light came in from two windows. If you looked out you saw all the passive field and trees. When I said yes to her question, that I thought she DID have a lovely body, she told me that Max took the credit for it, saying he'd been kind to it during their married years.

There was danger of conception. Max always used something. They had found that best. Perhaps not being as close as one might wish, but best in the long run. I was in her now, quietly, strong, hard. But perhaps, she went on, a blue-eyed boy would be beautiful.

Don't move, darling, for Christ's sake don't move.

It requires such self-control, she said.

The slow inching, the smooth lubricated movements, cautious, not wanting to lose the being together. If I go I'm finished unless I can stay in you and keep firm and go ahead for a long time. That way is pleasure for you, darling, but to withdraw on the spurt is death for both of us. Don't move! No, she wouldn't and didn't. The shifting of the thighs. My distended bladder. The sweat from off my chest and the wet ran along our joined thighs. Her smell, the vaginal odour, my smell, the joining of them so old and familiar. How her face changed, deeply placid, unrecognized as if she had turned to some stranger in my arms. The mouth and the teeth which seldom opened to give me her tongue and the feel of the nipples as I kissed them. My fingers in her long pubic hair.

I said I'd go away and dressed stealthily. The boy in the next room muttered in his sleep and she was startled. Would I be careful. Night watchmen might stop me. I said don't worry and felt as if I was in a hot closed place. All down the hill to the other side I walked with the hot staining of her body on mine, the smell of her all over me. A little broken feeling in my body; my feet were heavy. When I came in the room Harold asked me the time. I said two thirty, but it was four thirty. I got in bed and for a few moments did not sleep, but that was over and it was morning before I knew.

After a week there is still no word from Tamara. He feels "dead inside" and in despair that "so little seems to touch me." He berates himself that he functions "like an animal. . . . Take this and move on." The dark married woman peers at him now from behind chairs and pillars, but he does not speak to her. To Tamara he writes in guilt, ". . . It's as if I don't love one particular person but instead a cloud of smoke, elusive and unable to be touched with a hand."

Shortly, his diary records with disgust and anger that the older woman has again approached him—"with her man ten feet away"—and now he feels as if all women are in a conspiracy against men. "I'm for the men against all women." Of Tamara he writes in his diary that there is "nothing, empty, as if she didn't exist" and he vows not to "make a game with life again if I can help it." He writes to her that she seems to have no feeling for him or she would respond, and on his twenty-seventh birthday he confesses the "shameful" episode of "bed-entering," describes his subsequent sense of emptiness, and concludes, "I don't want any more sadness in my life, not for the next ten years." He will turn now to "cleaning up my play," about which Cheryl Crawford has said to him, "You ought to be very proud to have written this play at the age of twenty-seven." This has cheered him a little.

Finally Tamara writes, questioning the entire basis of their relationship, and he feels "life is dead in the body." He replies, "I have nothing, have never had anything" except

What I felt for you I still feel. . . . Yes, I love you. Every word we said together—or I said (and I believe you too) is still as hot and active in me as ever. Only I close my eyes and go to bed. I don't question anything. If something ever happens between us—good, wonderful, beautiful as every star in the sky. But I don't want to hope and hope, yearn, to be sick in my heart and head and mouth . . . and then slide down to some hell. I'm a great boy for despair. I've despaired the last six or eight years of my life. When I despair I do it with all my strength and energy. I have much of both and could kill myself easily. I want to live. I want to be happy. I believe with you that together we could make some beautiful thing—a good life for both of us. I have been willing to try it with you for months. I'm still willing.

Tamara apparently was not willing, as within a week she arrived to tell him she was planning to marry someone else. Dimly recognizing how difficult it was for him to respond to the separate reality of another human being, he writes her defensively after their separation: ". . . really nothing has changed . . . we're as before . . . shadows for each other." In order to reduce his vulnerability, he is trying to retract the extent to which he had let her be a real and separate person and the hope he had had for a durable relationship. His letter ends in a self-conscious formulation of the artist's struggle:

. . . such beauty as you is not for me in life. I felt at that time that somehow all the lovely things, the warm comforts of love and a woman . . . all that's not for me, I thought. Can it be that I must forgo such things? What is it in me that turns me hard and lonely to my own small room and the hard bed? I can't say, but it happens so always. Is it the price I'll pay for my good art to come? In many things I'm soft and lax, but always an unconscious discipline goes on in me, just as if one half of my life were jealous of the other and controlled it with an iron grip. Of contentment and peace I've known so little, but when it came it was from little things, like last night when I sat before a fire and felt warm on the face and skin. But what other men get always eludes me. . . .

The attitudinized image dominating this letter is of the self-absorbed, lonely, self-pitying Beethoven who, from his ascetic isolation, sends noble communication to mankind. It is likely that in the nuances of their relationship Odets had unconsciously encouraged Tamara to mistrust and finally to abandon him at the same time that he was trying to weld a bond of intimacy. Paula Miller Strasberg recalled from this summer's end the mournful strains of "Bye Bye Blackbird," in Odets' not unpleasing voice, drifting to shore from the mists on a lake where he often rowed out, alone. It was both romantic and real. Paula was genuinely concerned he might drown himself.

In the midst of his mourning he heard from Tamara that her fiancé, whom he never met, had said that if something happened to him she should marry Clifford in his stead. Odets responded to this, "It touched me very deeply, almost brought tears . . . it was almost as if he shouted 'Brother!' across to me and I salute him with a warm feeling for it—a salute I suppose he'll never get."

At this point Harold Clurman decided to try his hand at direction for the first time with the second act of Odets' *I Got the Blues*. The other two Group directors, though not enthusiastic, did not object, since the risk was small in this informal setting. Despite his reservations about what he later called the "gross Jewish humor . . . the messy kitchen realism" of the first act, and the "almost masochistically pessimistic" quality of the third act, Clurman thought it worth a try. He was encouraged in this by the excitement it had generated in several Group actors who since spring had been urging the directors to option it; Odets himself assured Clurman it would play "like a house on fire."

Unable to lift himself from his depression over the loss of Tamara, Odets fought sleep, steadily exhausting himself, and suspected he had a deliberate desire to get sick, to break down. ("I remember the great joy of being a sick boy and being served with lovely oranges and toast.") In a last letter to her he describes the old and familiar passivity, which has once again paralyzed him:

> Really, so much is dead in me now. I can't begin to tell you. Only just now I'm beginning to understand what it is a man does with his life to kill dead all ambition and right to live. I have none of that now. Once I was so pushing and eager, but I see that the last few years have tired me. . . . To want to do something from a great physical inner push. Just as one would want to sleep with a loved woman, the same way one should be about life and art. But honestly I don't even want to sleep with a woman or go on with life. It's even worse. Resentment itself can move a man, but I don't have that, only the passive thing, something like a windless day in which clouds come close and nothing stirs. . . .◖
>
> Already the second act of my own play is in rehearsal, but I'm sick of it. I get from it nothing, no satisfaction, only a numb feeling. They all assure me it's a good piece of work. What about it, I say. I'd not be an ounce surprised to find that most of this unhealthy feeling comes from not being able to crowd a day into an hour. Women must be like this, wanting to bear a long line of good sons and daughters. Sometimes I feel like that about writing plays.

He wonders again, as he will for the rest of his life, whether an artist can—or should even try to—assuage his loneliness except through his work. It is certainly striking that in his later notes for an autobiography there is no mention of Tamara for this summer of 1933. The central event, at least in retrospect, was his coming together as a writer. In his paragraph headed "1933, second half," he notes only the activities of the Group and "putting on the second act of 'Awake.' "

◖ 15.1.

That he exaggerated, in his letters to Tamara, his indifference to the fate of his play is clear from the fact he invited Theatre Guild director Philip Moeller—about to start rehearsals of O'Neill's *Ah, Wilderness!*—to come to Warrensburg to see it. Moeller wrote that it was practically impossible, "as we expect to go into rehearsal on Monday on Gene's new play," but that he would do his best to have a look at the play, "hoping that it's a master-piece and that you have justified my faith in your ability to write." Odets invited his father, as well, for the public performance. His mother, in Atlantic City with Genevieve and Florence, was in the midst of a tortured relationship with a man met at a resort hotel, a relationship Louis Odets would later use to torment his children and exculpate himself.

During rehearsals of Act II of *I Got the Blues* Odets began to feel that something unprecedented in his life was about to happen. "As he listened to this family of fine actors rehearsing his lines, he began to laugh ecstatically," Clurman recalled. Luther Adler remarked, "Look at him, he's laughing at his own jokes." "But," said Clurman thirty-three years later, "that wasn't it at all. He was so excited to hear the dialogue that, until now, had only sounded like the tap-tap-tap of a typewriter, that he was laughing with joy!"

"I arrive!" So Odets, in notes written in 1934 after he had indeed arrived, summarized this premiere for the campers at Green Mansions of Act II of *I Got the Blues*. The audience identified completely with the actors, "roaring their enthusiasm and falling out of their chairs." Clurman was puzzled by the magnitude of the response, as he was still dissatisfied with the play, while Strasberg rather disliked this "small genre study" and was preoccupied with the larger problem of preparing *Men in White* for Broad-way.

But it quickly became apparent that the enthusiasm of the actors as well as of the guests warranted a second performance; and Louis Odets, who had visited his son here before, came to see what he described as his son's "one-acter." At seventy-eight, reviewing for his grandson his relation-ship to the Group Theatre, he reminisced: "Everyone in the Group Theatre knew L.J. There wasn't any other parents there—nobody. Every one of them knew me. Knew me? Hell, we were friendly. I should have so many good years left how many dinners as I bought those people there, both he's and she's."

Cannily watching the absorbed audience, the former head of the Odets Company began to sniff something negotiable in his son. As an actor, Clif-ford had never exuded such a promising aroma. Indeed, it had not been easy six years earlier to sell him to Mae Desmond's stock company. After a long life of unremitting braggadocio, Louis Odets would find it impossible after his son's death to persuade anyone except the present writer that he was the first to detect the sweet smell of success in this play. So convinced was he of the potential dollar value of the commodity shown this Saturday night to the Green Mansions campers that he determined, then and there, to prevent its theft. He immediately investigated copyright procedure and became the play's salesman. Sixteen years later, after the failure of Odets' comeback effort, *The Big Knife,* he would write to him nostalgically:

> Do you remember in the old days when L.J. would tell you and the Group Theatre boys when a play was good or bad? My record was 100%. Do you remember the Saturday in Green Mansion Camp, after I spent over two hours watching Lee Strassberg [sic] direct "Men in White"? I told him if he would build the play around Dr. Hockberg, make him the master, letting Dr. Ferguson play second fiddle, The Group Theatre would have the best show ever. Strassberg listened to me, I could tell the way he sat back and payed [sic] attention to my reason. That evening in the canteen *he* told *all* the boys and girls that L.J. said Men in White would be a success.
>
> Then came along at the same camp, a one actor [sic] "I Got the Blues" in the rough. I saw four or five hundred boys and girls who came to camp to play with each other and have fun for themselves— sit there spellbound, not remembering that they had a sweetheart along side of them—It was the first time I saw your script in action, not because you were my son I said it was good—because it was good, I said so.

Clifford himself, watching his inner being come to life before the applauding actors and campers, now realized that he had "real writing talent . . . and right then I was not to be stopped or contained."

Despite the fact that *I Got the Blues* had, in the opinion of the participating actors, all of the elements of a spontaneous hit, it soon became clear that the directors were consigning it to the same discard pile as the rest of the summer skits. Although Clurman and Crawford had learned from the performance that Odets was worth encouraging, neither of them thought enough of the play to push it through as a regular Group production in the face of "the Rabbi's" (Strasberg's) active dislike.

At first, as both Lou Odets and Clifford remembered it, the father counseled his son to play up to Clurman, hoping thus to sell him *I Got the Blues.* Not satisfied that Clifford was capable of carrying this off, he then recommended an indirect strategy: Clifford must "get on the good side" of Stella Adler and thus reach Clurman. It was Lou's impression, later denied by Stella Adler, that she was "really gone on Clifford," and that this would have been a successful maneuver. "Too bad," he told this writer in his seventy-ninth year, without a flicker of self-consciousness, "my idiot son wouldn't have anything to do with her." So there remained no alternative but for L.J. to peddle the property himself.

It was at this point that L.J. began to counsel Clifford that he must not trust these rival parents, the Group directors—Strasberg in particular. He declared that they were neglecting the play out of jealousy, and that Clifford must seek his fortune elsewhere.

Clifford, bitterly disappointed that Strasberg's dislike of his play was blocking its production in New York, was tempted to leave the familial Group. But he did have a small part in *Men in White,* to open within the month, and he needed more income than the dollar bills his mother occasionally tucked into her letters, so he felt he had to knuckle under to his adopted family.

A week before the company was to return to New York, he records that he is making notes for a new play—undoubtedly *Paradise Lost*—an allegory of the lost security of the American middle-class family. There is no hint he is aware that the immediate stimulus for this play is his personal grief over his own lost Garden of Eden in the Group. He conceives of it essentially as a neutralized, deracinated version of *I Got the Blues* which will be less offensive to Strasberg. "I doubt if it'll be a good play," he writes, "I have too 'intellectual' a feeling about it instead of an emotional one. But it goes ahead." He is bitingly tense and tired but determined to write what he calls a "richer 'Awake' which the Group *must* produce." He continues:

> I wake up most mornings with a tight sensation in the jaws, teeth clenched and often the eyes blind and hurting beyond endurance. Something takes place when I sleep, not relaxation, the very opposite. Sometimes I wonder if I ever get any rest at all—I don't know. But anyway I find myself tired in the mornings, as now, as many other grayish days when cigarettes are bitter to the mouth and I eat just because the food's there. By then it's usually time to go to rehearsal, but I have a free morning now; it's graced with rain and gloom and there's little singing anywhere.
>
> I'm full of ideas and sometimes it hurts to have your brain clicking without stop. Two new plays are in me, pressing for a first emergence. I think the one most emotionally close to me has already won and will soon be out with the help of sleepless nights, groans and the bedpost. I tried to dance twice last night but felt like a sleep walker on the floor. My legs didn't belong to my head and that latter thing was so busy clicking with the new play that I didn't know where I was. By the time I got to my bed—the brushing of teeth already behind, plus a vivid discussion with a gent who was sitting on a can while he extolled the great glory and nobility of Brahms (and I sneered youthfully)—practically the whole second and third acts were clear in my mind; also the presence in said play of a young rougue [sic], a minor Caliban by the name of "Turk" who is sweet and charming, a veritable unpolished gem, but nevertheless a crook and a liar. I smoked in bed, in the dark, and the two other gents snored, gently, with great satisfaction while I suffered the faint and wearying beauty of being very alive in the head while my body perished with fatigue. Then a third room mate came in, a new person, and there he stood with a lighted match over his head and he on tiptoes. I grunted. It all looked like that picture of the younger Handel caught at the clavier in the night. . . .

This concentrated tempo of work is characteristic for artists "hot" in a work. The "minor Caliban," conceived here two years before *Paradise Lost* was completed, would evolve from "Turk Kaplan" to "Kewpie Wolff," a wife-stealing gangster, to be played by Elia Kazan.

Lou Odets, having no such romantic image of his son's creative struggles, extracted from Clurman the name of a playbroker, an agent whose skepticism he would shrewdly counter, enlisting his aid in the selling campaign for *I Got the Blues*. For the first time in many years, father and son were, at least on the surface, united in common cause.

To everyone's astonishment, *Men in White*, the Group's sixth production, was an immediate hit in a rich theatre season. Of at least equal importance was the fact that the reviews were generally respectful not only of the play but also of Strasberg's distinguished direction, which, true to the Group's idealistic standards, had fused all the elements of theatre into what Joseph Wood Krutch called a "work of art." Even Odets, in his small part as a cigar-smoking businessman, was thought by many to be giving a vital, forceful, and incisive performance. There was some satisfaction for him in this, but not much. He had already begun to tell writer Waldo Frank how trivial an art he considered acting. Frank agreed with him not only on this, but also on his view of *Men in White* as commonplace and as possibly the beginning of a general "impurity" of standards creeping into the Group Theatre. Frank was unaware of Strasberg's conviction that the entire enterprise was in danger of dissolution *without* the "impurities" of plays sufficiently viable to keep the Group continuously active. Odets' standards were being steadily offended also by the fact that the directors remained firm in their decision not to produce *I Got the Blues* even though he showed them, for the part of Ralph, a perfect young actor from the apprentice group of the Civic Repertory named Jules Garfield.

Odets knew Garfield better by now, as he had been teaching him in his "course of acting based on the Stanislavski Method" at the studio formed from the ranks of the younger actors around the Theatre Union, now preparing the anti-war play *Peace on Earth* and soon to present *Stevedore*, an energetic exposition of what was then called "the Negro problem." Members of the Theatre Union—even those distrustful that he was smuggling in "the psychologizing" of the Group Theatre—would recall Odets' enormous impact on them. One, who entirely disapproved of the Group's approach to acting, remembered being deeply moved by Odets' "profound involvement, his candor, and his painstaking attention to *detail*."

"Where you have, for example, an emotion of deep anger and jealousy and try to re-create it," he had said, "you must try to re-create the *details* of the scene—not just thinking or remembering, but visualizing, for example, the notice on the hotel-room door when you have quarreled with your mistress."* He pleaded with the students not to substitute clichéd symbols for genuine experience. Although his subject was acting, undoubtedly he was thinking also of playwriting. None of these young actors thought him a particularly good actor, but they regarded him as "the best damn acting teacher that ever lived."

In an eight-page, single-spaced polemic entitled "Toward a New Theatre,"❰ Odets, emulating Clurman as an intellectual and spiritual leader and teacher, addressed himself to the young "proletarian" actors on 14th Street, taking essentially Clurman's line in his many inspired talks to the Group Theatre. He elaborated in considerable detail the Russian director Vakhtangov's definition of a *real* theatre as an "ideologically cemented collective." Tracing the history of the social function of theatre as ritual—expressing a "central and common purpose, a purpose deeply understood and realized by all present"—Odets brought his passionate address down to the practicalities of the fall of 1933. He devoted the last three pages to a discussion of "the finance and organization of the audience," "organization of playwrights and sources of revolutionary scripts," "the organization of directors," and, in the greatest detail, "the acting company" ("The actor is at all times the exact point of contact with the audience").

While his father continued, without success, to peddle the manuscript of *I Got the Blues*, Clifford—as he would later do repeatedly—thus seized on teaching as the antidote to the bitter humiliation of the Group's refusal of his play. While some of his intellectual formulations were becoming

---

* On his deathbed Odets would say to filmmaker Jean Renoir, son of the great painter, "It is *all* in the detail, Jean, all in the detail."
❰ 15.2.

more vocally Marxist and tied to the current Soviet model of salvation, his analyses remained fresh, provocative, and seldom doctrinaire.

So impressed were members of this Theatre Union acting class by his address on the theory and practice of a social theatre that they urged him to part company with the Group, form a permanent acting company, and become its director. He was determined, however, to finish his new play, *Paradise Lost,* and to persuade the Group to produce it. His determination to win an assent from the Group was fortified by a discouraging letter from Philip Moeller (fresh from directing O'Neill's new hit, *Ah, Wilderness!*) which said that *I Got the Blues* was not "quite up the Guild alley." Moeller invites him in this letter for "another of our confabs," but leaves no room for doubt that the Theatre Guild will have nothing to do with *I Got the Blues.* But Lou Odets proceeded with the copyrighting of the manuscript of the play. Off to Washington, D.C., went one of the six manuscripts of *I Got the Blues* which Clifford had spent a third of his $35 weekly salary to have typed.

Determined to use her $50,000 to produce plays, Bess Eitingon found two actors more willing to help her than Strasberg had been. With Louis Simon and an Irish sometime playwright, Frank Merlin, in an office at the Little Theatre on 44th Street (across from the Broadhurst, where Odets was playing in *Men in White*), she formed a producing firm in which, as she recalled, "despite my putting up all the capital, I had only one vote out of the three in our decisions." This was her wish after her humiliation with the Group Theatre: she had now decided to "take a back seat to the professionals." However, she read every playscript she could lay her hands on, since she did not quite trust her partners' taste.

"I shall never forget my enormous excitement," she recalled, "when I first read *Awake and Sing!* Motty and I had a place at Stamford, Connecticut, with a seventy-two-foot pool into the Sound, and there, in a little rowboat, I had retreated for uninterrupted privacy to read Clifford's play, brought me by Louis Simon, who knew Clifford from the Theatre Guild. The moment I finished it, I went ashore and cabled Motty, in Europe, 'I think I've found the white-haired boy of the American theatre. I want to buy an option.' Motty immediately called back, 'So—do what you want!' I told Simon and Merlin we ought immediately to give this young playwright five hundred dollars for a six-month option, and that I would like to talk with him."

As the young playwright entered the French doors of the Eitingons' penthouse apartment at 100 West 55th Street, Mrs. Eitingon, still smarting from her humiliation at the hands of Strasberg, was trying to appear a seasoned producer, at ease in a casual hostess gown. It was important to her, she recalled, to carry off with aplomb her first professional negotiation with a playwright. "Despite my intense excitement," she said, "at what this young man had managed—to bring to life with such authentic poetry my whole family—I was prepared to restrain my praise of his play in order not to seem amateurish as a producer." Mrs. Eitingon thinks her desperately cool and sophisticated manner may have contributed to the startling scene which followed.

Odets appeared to be stricken with wonder as his eyes swept over Motty Eitingon's dozens of record albums from ceiling to floor in the foyer, and he muttered, "This foyer would be enough for me to live in." As he slowly and silently made his way toward the vast living room surrounded by landscaped terraces, he cast a swift glance at a prized stained-glass window and then stared at his patroness in her hostess gown. "His face took on a look of puzzlement and pain," Mrs. Eitingon recalled, "as if he were saying, 'What do you want me to do?' And then, his face beet red, he blurted, 'What do you want me to do, fuck you?' I was shocked and disconcerted by the brutality of this, and astonished it had emerged from the author of so sensitive a play, but I managed to maintain my poise and replied, 'We'll come to that later, I guess.' " They did not, in fact, ever come to that. Despite this burst of machismo, this young playwright "gave off a terribly soft, vulnerable, even a girlish quality" which Mrs. Eitingon found not at all appealing. Her husband, she added, "had some of that same quality, to be sure, but he had steel as well."

Mrs. Eitingon had no way of knowing that Odets had come to her apartment fresh from having been almost thrown out by the Group Theatre directors in response to his ultimatum that he was on his way to accept the Eitingon option money if they were not going to produce *Awake and Sing!* From his frightened conviction that no one *could* want to produce his play came his self-consciously savage assault on her. In this twenty-minute episode is distilled a central theme in the story of this life: having taken into his self-image the contempt and rejection of the Group "fathers," he arrives at a potentially helpful mother, fearful that his art will not suffice and that she, too, will reject him. In a characteristically paranoid fashion he snarls at her, in effect asking, "Must I become a male prostitute to be rewarded for my work?"❨ This has, of course, contemporary sociological implications as well as ancient roots in his relation to his mother. "Even as he played this scene, I had the distinct impression he was observing it," Mrs. Eitingon concluded. "Maybe he was getting something to put in his notebook." She had an intuitive sense of the "witnessing" nature of all artists.

Mrs. Eitingon's partner Frank Merlin would much later rhapsodize to Odets and to other theatre people that *Awake and Sing!* had started an esthetic revolution in the American theatre, that his friend George Cohan "loved the lyric poetry in it," and that it reflected all of America: "The Irish and Italians as much as the Jews . . . people fighting and talking, talking and fighting." At this time, however, he fought to postpone its production until the firm had produced a "more practical" play, *False Dreams, Farewell*, which he was certain would triple Bess Eitingon's $50,000 and was besides, as he told her, "a helluva show." Accordingly, while he did not oppose the firm of Merlin, Eitingon and Simon giving Odets his first option money, $500, he insisted that *I Got the Blues* be their second, not their first, production. Thus, the "moneymaker" on which Bess Eitingon had been outvoted by her two partners was announced instead of *I Got the Blues* for January of 1934; a disastrous failure, it all but evaporated Mrs. Eitingon's $50,000 and her role as the deliverer to the American theatre of its "white-haired boy."

Dizzied by his option money, more than he had ever seen in his life, Odets first went to a liquor store and bought one bottle of every kind of liquor it had in stock. Next, despite his father's contempt for his choice of neighborhood, he paid a month's rent on a tiny, airless apartment—his first—next door to a stable, at 82 Horatio Street in Greenwich Village. The

❨ 15.3.

first piece of furniture he moved into the dark, divided living room and bedroom was a large phonograph. Pearl, who had been secretly sending money to her Bronx friend Rae Harber for an occasional spaghetti dinner for her son, arrived from Philadelphia bringing staples, cookies, and a pair of pongee curtains she had made to spruce up the airshaft window. L. J. Odets scathingly assured her they made no difference whatever in this "hole in the wall."

During this time of rising self-esteem, Odets brought to this make-shift apartment a chestnut-haired, seventeen-year-old Jewish girl named Dena, his first serious attachment since the catastrophe with Tamara (keeping in reserve Alice of the previous year, despite her taunts about his male equipment). Reared within the rich, if narrow, confines of what she would later call "Yiddishe Kultur," Dena was a chemistry major in college. Odets was the first representative of what she termed "the big outside world," which she was barely beginning to enter by way of the National Student League, a left-wing national organization open to high-school students. She met him at an NSL party where Bobby Lewis, Group actor and later director, was entertaining with his original rendition of Whitman's "I Sing the Body Electric"—as an old man convulsing in a cold shower—and his "Red Hamlet." Odets, attracted to her, wondered aloud why her boyfriend was not with her and then asked if he could call her. Presently, with some misgivings because Odets was ten years her senior, she decided to give up her current boyfriend for him. She saw him as an artist and a teacher as well as a lover. Dena, who later considered herself "one of the most self-absorbed persons I knew," would be remembered by her contemporaries at seventeen as "far more dynamic than Tamara," an honest, gifted, charming, and earnest girl with a great deal of anxiety covered by a patina of self-mocking, boyish, cavalier toughness: "the most genuine," Clurman said, "of all Clifford's many girls," and, according to Kazan, "not a girl to take a beating willingly as so many of Cliff's girls did . . . a strong and independent spirit." It is noteworthy that he could "handle" such a girl while he was feeling reasonably secure as a competent worker.

Over the next three years Dena maintained an erratic, stormy, and generally unhappy relationship with Odets, its pain punctuated by "lovely evenings when he would cook Wiener schnitzel, play music, and make love." Sometimes they were joined by actor Joe Bromberg and his wife, Goldie, or by Robbe and Julie Garfield. Odets frequently proposed marriage, but Dena steadily refused. "Lucky I didn't marry him" was her summary. It is likely this relationship suggested to him the core of a play he talked about for many years and never wrote, called "Tides of Fundy," about a playwright and a girl whom he offers to help. In the course of trying to help her, he destroys her.

From the last of his autobiographical notes for this year, it is clear Odets had not entirely forsworn his professional identity as an actor: "Directors' criticisms of my acting problems. Unfluid." Yet this note lacks the despair and the exclamation points of his 1931 note: "*I can't act! Tied up!*" He was more certain now of his talent as a writer, a security resting squarely on his $500 advance.

The New York Times of December 12, 1933, carries a small picture of him as a cynical, smug, cigar-smoking member of a hospital board in the successful *Men in White*. Under the picture, which might be Lou Odets, the caption identifies him as an actor who is "a playwright in his leisure moments." Like the character Ralph in his play, Odets had long wanted his name in the paper, and was pleased by his sale of *I Got the Blues*. Yet when

Group actress Ruth Nelson congratulated him on this good fortune, he winced and said, "But you know, Ruth, I wrote it for the Group, and they don't want to do it." He told her also that a Hollywood scout had suggested he might get $500 *a week* writing films, but that "Harold advised me to refuse—that I would be offered more later." He did refuse.

Frank Merlin announced at the end of 1933 that "casting problems of *I Got the Blues* force postponement until early next season," telling *The New York Times* in the same interview that he was planning to stage a play by E. P. Conkle called *Forty-nine Dogs in a Meathouse.*

This was only in part a subterfuge. According to Bess Eitingon, even a careful sieving of available actors, whether of Theatre Guild or Yiddish-theatre traditions, left her with a sense that all were somehow wrong for Odets' play. Although she did not realize it had been written by him specifically for the ensemble company of the Group Theatre, finely trained by Strasberg to work as a unit, she found herself imagining each of eight Group actors in his appropriate role. The acting company and the playwright had indeed sprung from the same soil and had grown together as Odets, in his Theatre Union lectures, had declared they should.

On the very first page of a five-cent school notebook still bearing a stamp from the Alliance Book and Stationery Store at 690 Eighth Avenue, Odets records on December 5, 1933, his first list of fourteen characters for his new "de-Jewished" play, *Paradise Lost*, with the name of a Group actor beside each. Under the title, alternatively penciled in as "The Fruit is Ripe," and opposite a printed list of "The Group Theatre Acting Company" pasted into the notebook, these initial pairings of the part with the actor give us some insight into the identity-elements of *Paradise Lost*. It is a process whereby a form evolves from the "actor masks" when a playwright works with an acting company. Listed first is the play's protagonist, "Mr. Judah Kantor—Morris Carnovsky." There can be no mistaking the Hebraic roots in this surname of Kantor or its translation as "singer." Its origins, as in a dream image are multiple: Clifford's Uncle Israel, who wanted to be a cantor, always stood as the self-expressive, impractical polar opposite of his father. Even better than prose is poetry, and still better is music. Yet there is always a danger here of biting hostility slipping through. Of Whitman, Odets, quoting from Emerson, said, "Half song thrush, half alligator."◖ Carnovsky would indeed play the part of this impotent, self-expressive liberal two years later in Odets' *Paradise Lost* after it had metamorphosed in successive drafts from "Judah Kantor" through "Leo Seltzer" to the neutral name "Leo Gordon" (a name adopted by one branch of the Gorodetsky clan).

Next Odets has written "Mrs. Clara Kantor—Stella Adler," who was cast as Leo Gordon's realistic and practical wife. After Judah Kantor's son "Ben," Odets has written his own name, then crossed it out and written that of Walter Coy, who in fact played Ben Gordon, named after Odets' cousin and childhood competitor, Ben, less gifted than Clifford. A second son, called "Julie"—taken from Julie Garfield—is slated for Sanford Meisner, who played the role. A daughter, here called "Judith"—later to become the frustrated pianist named "Pearl" after Odets' mother—symbol of the frustrated, doomed artist who will continue to create even as the world ends, whether by "ice, fire, or decay," is slated for Margaret Barker. Odets has both respect and contempt for this character.

The name "Turk Kaplan," the opportunistic, amoral gangster, has been crossed out to make way for the name "Kewpie Wolf." Odets lists Joe Bromberg first and himself second for this part. It would be played in

◖ 15.4.

Paradise Lost as "Kewpie" by Elia Kazan, whom Odets lists here only as one of four beggars.

Although Odets never portrayed any of the characters in *Paradise Lost,* it is noteworthy that he considered for himself only two parts. The first is the sweet and ingenuous all-American sprinter (Luther Adler once summarized Clifford's creative difficulties by saying, "He was a terrific sprinter, but not a long-distance runner"). This sprinter, like the ineffectual poet manqué Sam Feinschreiber in *Awake and Sing!,* is betrayed by his wife and then led to a suicidal death by the ambitious and seductive gangster who has done the betraying. The other part Odets considered for himself is that of the gangster, Kewpie, whose "spine"—"to get everything he wants"—Odets records now in his five-cent notebook. This character is the prototype of a long series of "wolves" whose sole aim is to get everything they want.

For each character Odets has written such a "spine," sometimes with its own "tag," a short snatch of dialogue which he considered a distillation of the character. Opposite these verbal descriptions are faces clipped from newspapers and pasted here to match his characterizations. Tucked between the pages are crumbling clippings from newspapers and magazines, many from the Communist *Daily Worker* supplying statistics on how many men were killed in World War I, detailing the rising suicide rate in the United States, and proclaiming in a full-page headline, "We must fight imperialist war before it breaks out; we must fight it daily hourly—Lenin." The article below the headline, dated February 10, 1934, describes how the "Roosevelt Administration Sails Full Speed Towards War." Letters from union members printed in the *Daily Worker* provide Odets with many direct quotations for the characters in *Paradise Lost.*◄

As he reached the middle of his twenty-seventh year, Odets worried constantly about his hairline, which was beginning to recede, and took as his central task the completion of this rich, large-canvas, less Jewish play. He was determined that the Group Theatre must produce it. However, the going was extremely slow and uninspired. Intellectually conceived to meet Strasberg's objections to "Jewish kitchen drama" and Clurman's criticisms of sentimentality, it became, in Yeats' words, "the will doing the work of the imagination."

He kept at it nonetheless, diverting himself, when he ground to a halt, with the writing of what he labeled "Some Notes on Music." In these he ponders with enormous acuity the psychological nature of the "real music between the notes" in the work of a variety of composers. Some are scribbled headlines only: "The hurt boy of Mozart. The final sensing of life . . . Gluck's dramatic overture and Beethoven's debt to Gluck. Hearing his operas as a boy. . . . The malice and definite spite of the Chopin mazurkas." His most extensive notes are, as always, on his ego-ideal, Beethoven, the "womanless man," the artist who, he writes, like all the greatest artists, dispensed with women "after the first period," a man who in his music "never asks . . . he always tells":

> Brahms tries to tell, but in reality he was an asker—a double reason for his being less a genius than Beethoven—the necessity of asking and the attempt to hide it. The greatest genius is the teller—the hero one. Why are there no tellers today. They will come from Communism!

This final exclamation suggests that by this time Odets had begun to embrace loosely, as a credo and panacea for all problems, whether economic, moral, or esthetic, Karl Marx's utopian vision of labor as "the

◄ 15.5.

source of the thought and energy which were to sweep all humanity into everlasting freedom and build a civilization shared by all." This utopianism was thought by Charles and Mary Beard to stem directly from the Christian ethic "which deemed of one blood all mankind, exalted labor, and emphasized the eternal brotherhood of the great and humble." The revolutionary Beethoven had created with sounds what Marx—nine years old when Beethoven died—would put into words: a fantasied vision of international Bruderschaft, a yearning toward a joined mankind quite different from the bloody facts of Stalin's regime. The people of the Soviet Union, still unaware of these facts, were once again receiving by the score equally unaware American pilgrims—Communists and non-Communists—all yearning for an international, inclusive human identity.

Odets, long on close terms with Whitman and Emerson, knew little of Marx beyond the stirring *Communist Manifesto*. He shared, however, with many of his generation an inchoate hunger to make sense of human society, a hunger progressively sharpening as the life meaning and hope supplied by religion ebbed. The resurgence internationally of a collective determination—grown flaccid since the Great War—to resist the tyrannies of a system which in this Great Depression was dramatically excluding so many took as its corollary the aspiration to erase one day all national, religious, and racial boundaries and thus all "pseudo-species" among humans. For a time it appeared to many that this next step in human awareness would first be taken in the Soviet Union, while its dialectic opposite —a barbarously divisive creation of a new pseudo-species—was, of course, gathering impetus in Nazi Germany.

Whereas in the United States, since Roosevelt's election, strikes were on the increase and in this year "the right to organize was itself becoming the crucial issue," in Germany collective bargaining—along with the right of a member of the "master race" to be employed in a Jewish household— had been outlawed.

Artists all over the world were stricken by the dark news of the closing down of the extraordinary Bauhaus, begun in Weimar after World War I with a passionate manifesto which had looked to "a new structure of the future, which will embrace architecture and sculpture and painting . . . and which will one day rise toward heaven from the hands of a million workers like the crystal symbol of a new faith." It had been a utopian vision not unlike that held by Americans wherein a brotherhood of man would contain a universal spiritual, as well as a material, unity. The "new faith" actually arising in Germany was, of course, of quite another order.

In this year a young journalist named Eric Sevareid, covering a truckers' strike for the *Minneapolis Star*, watched sixty-seven unarmed persons shot in ten minutes. "Suddenly I knew," he wrote, "I understood deep in my bones and blood what Fascism was." Arthur Schlesinger had the opposite reaction, saying of the strikers, "This—is revolution!" The filings were gathering at their opposite poles.

At one pole the work of many American writers had begun to reflect the longing for a path to redemption, and by the end of 1934 Odets would complete two redemptive plays: one, worked and reworked for nine months, would be a critical and box-office failure; the other, raced through to completion in a few nights, would establish his foothold as a luminary in the American theatre.*

* See Kenneth Burke on "redemption" in his brilliant essay "Ice, Fire and Decay."

Chapter Sixteen

*With dictatorship weighing heavily
on the public mind . . . Americans
again hurried to the theater to behold
"resistance to tyranny," to see the
resurgence and challenge of Caesar-
ism embodied in personalities and
events on the stage. . . .*

CHARLES AND MARY BEARD

*Unhappiness with Lee. I am stopped
as a writer and threaten to quit.
Harold stops me.*

CLIFFORD ODETS, *1934*

ON FEBRUARY 2, 1934, a tired New York taxi-driver checking into the
garage from the night shift early in the morning was thought to have
earned too little money for the company, and was immediately discharged.
A popular and attractive young man, he turned to several other drivers
bringing in their tickets and asked, "Well, boys, how long are we going to
take this?" According to Samuel Orner, elected within twenty-four hours
president of the Taxi Drivers Union of Greater New York, there now occurred a remarkable and totally spontaneous outburst: "First our garage
went on strike. They stopped the other boys from coming in. And not
only that . . . they told them to go to all the different garages and tell
them to strike, too. There was no union at this point . . . but the kind of
work cabbies do wisens them up, sharpens them up, so pretty soon they
managed to set up union halls in five boroughs."

Odets' historic one-act play *Waiting for Lefty* was derived, according
to him, from newspaper accounts of this forty-day strike involving forty
thousand men and nineteen thousand taxicabs. The strike, says Orner, "hit
everybody hard," and was "the bloodiest and most violent that had ever
taken place in New York." Cabs were burned; many men were wounded
and some killed. On the day Orner addressed a mass meeting in St.
Nicholas Hall, at 6oth Street and Central Park West, the police decided
"to mount machine guns on the roof across the street to meet expected
violence."

The violence came, as expected, and Orner himself did not escape it. After an initial settlement, in April the fleet operators, he recalled, began "reneging on their contracts." The taxi-drivers, again "very worked up" over what Orner felt were justified complaints, responded to a passionate address given by him in Germania Hall at Third Avenue and 17th Street by deciding to renew the strike. Orner says Odets, "brought perhaps by a Communist union organizer," attended this public meeting, "and he must have taken notes because so many lines in *Waiting for Lefty* were the same as in the meeting, almost word for word."

Waiting for Lefty, written by Odets months after this meeting, was drawn, Orner believes, from the climax of the taxi-drivers' strike in April 1934: "Mayor La Guardia, elected with the support of the liberals, had to maintain that image. So he took the clubs away from the police. Meanwhile he wanted to end that strike by hook or by crook. So he got a coupla guys—leaders in local chapters, hard-boiled guys lookin' for the almighty buck and ready to sell the men down the river—and convinced them to hold a big union meeting at Hunt's Point Palace in the Bronx. Then La Guardia got Judge Jacob Panken and Matthew Levy to come and sell the men a bill of goods trying to end the strike—a phony contract full of lawyer's language, phony as a two-dollar bill."

Informed at the last minute of this planned "sellout" of his men, Orner—who had been without sleep for seventy-two hours—made his way by subway to the Bronx. There he was waylaid by several cabbies from the Bronx local who told him he was early for the meeting and asked him to join them for a drink. "I was so tired I thought it was a good idea," Orner recalled, "but there must have been knockout drops in it, because that's the last I remember until some of my boys were dashing cold water on me and beggin' me to come up to Hunt's Point Palace to the meeting where Panken and Levy were selling the men out, trying to talk them into going back to work." Later he learned that while he slept the meeting had erupted "into a raging mob shouting 'No vote until we hear from Orner.' " A union member had announced, "Orner's down on the corner by the subway and it looks like he's been knocked out."

"I sure *was* knocked out," Orner concluded. "In *Lefty* I was found dead; actually, I was found unconscious. Somehow they brought me around and managed to get me up on the stage. Then I put an end to the whole trick." Eight months later, after he had again been drugged and this time beaten unconscious and left for dead by labor gangsters, he recovered and mounted another stage—at the Civic Repertory Theatre, where, introduced as "Lefty," he would join with columnist Heywood Broun in taking up a collection for the wounded cabbies in hospitals all over New York. Odets started a file during this period for a full-length play about "an agitator son brought home for dead."

There were many such strikes in 1934. After Roosevelt's election they were a significant element in the air Odets breathed, as were evictions, riots, hunger marches, and—in response—a sustained outcry against all poverty and injustice. It appeared that a national consciousness was being raised and a conscience reawakened. Since the abysmal rock-bottom of 1932 increasing numbers of Americans, in a wide spectrum of class backgrounds and political persuasions, were becoming convinced that nothing short of radical changes in society would suffice if man was to salvage a core of morality.

Aristocrat Franklin D. Roosevelt told a graduating class in Atlanta, "We need the courage of the young. Yours is not the task of making your way in the world, but the task of *remaking the world*. . . . " Communist Mike Gold, in the *Daily Worker,* headed his daily column: "Change the World."

As Odets struggled privately with the allegorically conceived inner and outer dilemmas of his disintegrating Leo Gordon in *Paradise Lost*—still trying to make it a "better and more mature *Awake and Sing!*"—fellow playwrights were seeking other paths to salvation. O'Neill—seeking internal, spiritual regeneration, in contrast to the materialist world-changing solutions of Marxism—had been persuaded by Jesuit priests not to have the hero of his *Days Without End,* John Loving (a remarkable name in those embattled days), shoot himself at the church altar; Loving resolves his "soul's sickness," instead, by a return to Catholicism via a romantically idealized marriage. Calling it a "modern miracle play," O'Neill said it revealed "a man's search for truth amid the conflicting doctrines of the modern world and his return to his old religious faith." At the very end the cynical, destructive self is vanquished by the now harmonious personality of John Loving, who, arms upstretched to a life-size crucifix, says, "Love lives forever! Death is dead! . . . Life laughs with God's love again! Life laughs with love!" After the disastrous reception of this clumsy and desperate affirmation—which he himself felt to be phony—O'Neill would not be heard from for twelve years.

Odets' mentor John Howard Lawson had become discouraged by the poor response to his play, *The Pure in Heart.** This work also was a desperate moral affirmation: even a promiscuous chorus girl can maintain her integrity, her purity, her innocence despite a surface of corruption. This was Lawson's last effort to dramatize the complexities and ambiguities of the general moral dilemma. In his play *Gentlewoman,* produced by the Group, which Clurman felt "possessed real qualities of emotional eloquence and social understanding," Lawson presented a resolution in which a sensitive, wealthy, educated, and neurotic woman is strengthened by an affair with a strong, daring, radical young poet who is both envious and contemptuous of her; the courageous young man shows the in-turned, egocentric woman that one must confront the real, the objective world. His awkward synthesis of Freud and Marx represented for Lawson, as for many other American middle-class intellectuals, a kind of halfway house on a nameless road leading to an unknown destination.

Clurman saw Lawson as the eloquent singer of a "divided conscience" and would later mourn—as would critic Joseph Wood Krutch—that Lawson's vitality and creativity as a playwright appeared to have ended when his troubled soul-searching was forsworn in favor of the comfortingly unambiguous stands of Communist doctrine. It would indeed appear that a sine qua non of creative writing is that neither pole of an unconscious conflict be repressively and totally plowed under.

Indicted by the left-wing press as a "bourgeois Hamlet" and by the uptown critics (prematurely) as a convert to Communism, Lawson sought clarity by accepting a newspaper assignment in the objective world of

---

* Clurman called this play Lawson's "swan song for the jazz-and-racket age."

Scottsboro, Alabama, where, in the context of a strike of field workers, eight illiterate, under-age Negro boys had been sentenced to death for the alleged rape of two white mill girls, both of uncertain virtue. The boys had clearly been railroaded, as part of the strategy to counter the strike, and rallies to raise money for their defense were held on almost every American campus as well as in Harlem, the Bronx, Dresden, Berlin, Cologne, Paris, Rome, and Buenos Aires. A play based on the case, *They Shall Not Die* by John Wexley, was produced by the Theatre Guild in February 1934.

Lawson's foray into this real world in Alabama resulted in his immediate arrest and an indelible impression of what he later described as

total terror . . . something like Fascism and Germany under Hitler. . . . I sat in the courtroom with two great bullies on either side of me, members of the White Legion, Alabama's version of the Ku Klux Klan. . . . After our release we started to walk along the street, a police car pulled up, a cop jumped out, tapped me on the shoulder and said "get in." . . . They kept me for another four or five hours grilling me, asked if I were Jewish, saying then, "That explains everything, you Jew agitators come down here and make trouble." . . . When the cops let me go, they told me to "get out of town, we can't protect you from the White Legion." . . . I was scared to death, because I had never imagined anything like that in the United States.

Lawson returned to Manhattan, where the New York *Post* had run front-page stories on his reports of the terror in Alabama; he tried without success to work on a new play optioned by the Group. Shortly he left for Hollywood to earn money, and to work for the Screen Writers Guild. Unionization being so much a part of the fabric of American life, no one had noticed his earlier efforts to organize Hollywood writers. Now, however, Harry Cohn, head of Columbia Pictures, reprimanded Lawson and instructed him to donate at least one dollar—or "never work again"—to the Merriam gubernatorial campaign opposing Socialist candidate Upton Sinclair's "End Poverty in California" platform. (Film tycoon Louis B. Mayer was meanwhile exacting a day's pay from each of his employees to stop the "Bolshevick sacking of California.") Lawson refused to obey Cohn's instruction and was discharged from Columbia Pictures. The story immediately made the rounds of the Group Theatre that Cohn's slogan was, "I am the king here. Whoever eats my bread sings my song." Odets, who became a Cohn employee two decades later, would learn the meaning of this dictum.

Group members were pleased when Lawson returned to the East; they hoped he would write them a new play. It was only during this deeply troubled period that Lawson began to resolve his conflicts by turning to Marxist theory.

Each of Lawson's moves was, of course, highly visible to Odets, and it did not escape him that Lawson—by now a kind of model for him—was not earning a penny from his writing for the theatre. It was equally clear that Lawson identified his sole source of income, the film industry, with a moral and esthetic tyranny not altogether distinct from the repression in Alabama.

With Budd Schulberg, a young idealist just out of college and son of a movie magnate, Lawson returned to Alabama with a delegation sent by the Committee for Constitutional Liberties and again was arrested. He was touched by an offer of help from a local Scottsboro lawyer. When it turned out that this man was working against him and for the Federal

Bureau of Investigation, he became convinced that the only persons who were consistently on the side of the angels in the Scottsboro nightmare were the young Communist leaders of the field strike. Historians have repeatedly observed that, in view of the energy and dedication of such radical leaders, the remarkable fact for the ten years between 1930 and 1940 is not that so many unemployed persons and anti-fascists became Communists, but that so few did. It is testimony both to the American character and to the awkward tactics of the amateur politicians in the American Communist Party.

Far smoother and more influential in *his* political maneuvers until World War II was L. J. Odets' idol, the "radio priest" at the Shrine of the Little Flower in Michigan, Father Charles Coughlin, named by a poll in this year as the most important public figure in the land except for the president. It would puzzle the elder Odets when his hero, initially a Roosevelt supporter, began to call the president a liar and betrayer and to suggest that he was in collusion with Jewish bankers in financing the Russian Revolution.

Lawson's *Gentlewoman* closed after twelve performances, and once more the Group was desperate for scripts. Odets' *Paradise Lost* was barely begun, and a rough draft of the only available play for the fall season, *Gold Eagle Guy* by a young man named Melvin Levy, was hotly attacked by the Group actors as being insufficiently progressive and contemporaneous,* perhaps even "reactionary." Defending himself, Levy prepared a statement for the theatre program discussing the lure of California gold for nineteenth-century voyagers.

In a forty-page response to the attack by his flock on *Gold Eagle Guy*, Clurman pointed out that the Group's aim had *never* been to become a political theatre like the Theatre Union, now running a play on the "Negro problem," *Stevedore*, and shortly to produce a celebration of Soviet courage, *Sailors of Cattaro*, the cast of which would be taught the Stanislavsky method of acting by Odets. The aim of the Group, said Clurman, was to make a "creative and truly representative American theatre."

He read this paper with characteristic fire to the entire company on the eve of the departure to the Soviet Union of Lee Strasberg, Sidney Kingsley, and Stella Adler, all eager to see for themselves whether it was true—as pilgrims had reported—that, in variety and scope as well as technical sophistication, the Russian theatre far surpassed that of the United States. They would be joined by Clurman in their Russian pursuit of the ideal "theatre collective" just before the Group embarked on its fourth rehearsal summer, in the Catskills of New York.

At the end of April excited reports from Moscow to Group members, still appearing in the successful *Men in White*, compared Russian acting techniques and theatrical productions to those in New York, Paris, Vienna,

---

* Melvin Levy would be called before the U.S. House of Representatives' Committee on Un-American Activities on January 28, 1952. There he testified to counsel Frank Tavenner, Jr., that his protagonist in this play was a "San Francisco man who . . . creates a shipping empire. . . . To me," Levy testified, "he was a very romantic and powerful, creative character. . . . He was both things. . . . On the other side, he was amoral, ruthless. . . . You must have both these things to make a character, to make a man. And if you leave out either thing, you're lying."

and Budapest. There is no mistaking in these letters, largely from Strasberg and Clurman, the vitality, range, and vigor of the Soviet theatre, a vigor reflecting both a longstanding, indigenous theatrical tradition and the work of such individual talents as Stanislavsky, Vakhtangov, and Meyerhold—all begun long before the Revolution.

Strasberg's spontaneously penciled seven-page record of his experiences at the Meyerhold Theatre in this spring of 1934 reflect an eager young spirit for whom theatrical innovations were fresh eye-openers—apolitical riches he would bring back to the Group.

One sits in the Meyerhold Theatre awaiting the start. There is no curtain. The scenery stares back at you. You do not know whether to smile or be impressed by the unusual feature. The audience babbles on quite unconcerned by now. A gong. The lights go out. On the stage the last props are brought on, candles are lit, positions are taken. A gong. The lights go on. The play is on.

As you don't know the language, you watch the scenery, the acting. You are annoyed and shocked by the latter. It looks old-fashioned. The actors move too much and posture and strut. You are sure you don't like it. It is all so unreal. You feel out of it. You don't know whether to be disappointed. It is certainly "different" and "unusual." But is this the man of whom Vakhtangov said, "He is a genius. Every production creates an epoch in the theatre." But the play goes on and before long you are thinking differently. You are caught by the scenic action, by its imaginativeness, by its flair. The entire life of the people begins to unfold. You feel you have misunderstood the scenery. It is not unreal. It actually makes possible more reality than would be possible in a realistic set. It stems from the desire not to be limited by the stage—the conventional set. Thus where a Meyerhold in *The Forest* can have the girl ironing, hanging clothes, chasing pigeons, people on a road, fishing, love scene on the road—marvelous in its effect of throb and pulse—the large swings used for the first love scene, the action on the see-saw, all these following one another or intertwining one with the other, creating the entire atmosphere of the life in the old Russian farmhouse, but bringing out and sharpening the drama—the taps of the rolling pins while drying the wash serve to accentuate the quarrel going on, the see-saw becomes a marvelous instrument to bring out the Freudian comment, the amazing leaps of the swing stress the latent conflict of the young people in love against their environment, making your own blood leap with them. None of this would be possible in a realistically confined set. . . .

Meyerhold's stage is not and actually never has been a mere striving towards theatricality—tho his effects are so brilliant and unusual that you forget the reason for it, and tend not to notice the new content uncovered or interpreted. Meyerhold's technical inventiveness derives from a desire to mirror and explore life more fully by means of the theatre. Meyerhold's form derives from his content.

The burden of these notes—later rewritten for an article in *New Theatre* magazine, unofficial organ for the insurgent movement in the American theatre—was Strasberg's ardent support of Meyerhold's effort to rediscover the "authentic traditions of real theatre" discarded in favor of the "theatrical rubbish of the second half of the 19th century." Strasberg's experiences in the Soviet Union were immediately translated into a note to Cheryl Crawford to explore authentic period songs, dances, and costumes for the Group's production of Levy's *Gold Eagle Guy*.

A postcard from Clurman dated June 10, 1934, and addressed to all the members of the company (Odets listed last) calls Moscow "very very stimulating." He finds that his ideas "about the Russian theatre and the Group (theatrical, technical problems) have crystallized." Most important, even in the shadow of Vakhtangov and the world-famous Moscow Art and Meyerhold theatres, he concludes that "The Group is an important theatre anywhere."

Of the personal influence of this trip, he later writes, "The effect of my Moscow trip was to release me. For four years I had lived, theatrically speaking, in Strasberg's shadow. . . . The variety of Soviet theatre styles helped me find myself by showing me concretely how many possibilities there were." Thus, as Odets continued with *Paradise Lost* to struggle toward a professional identity as a playwright, Clurman was commencing to pick his way as a director.

Odets, still clinging to the hope that Merlin, Eitingon and Simon would produce *I Got the Blues*, enlisted his father's powers of salesmanship in repeated visits to their office. L. J. Odets managed a renewal of the option and a promise to put the play into production by late August of 1934.

Apologizing for missing his best friend's wedding, Odets wrote on May 23 to Herman Kobland:

> Suddenly I'm here in Philadelphia, like a homing pigeon flying in a straight line. They gave me two weeks' vacation at the Group and since a vacation is necessary I came here and mean to spend the full of next week at Atlantic City. I expect one of Merlin's men out here and we must work together on some revision of my play—they really plan to start it in late August and this is my only chance to get the work done. Now that means I can't get to your wedding. I don't feel right about it, but what am I to do. However, I think you know what I feel for you without being there. You know our twenty years together had not been for nothing. . . . I won't keep on excusing myself.

Between the closing of *Men in White*—which by now had won a Pulitzer Prize for its unbelieving author—and the beginning of the Group's summer rehearsals of *Gold Eagle Guy*, in Ellenville, New York, Odets worked diligently on his revisions of *I Got the Blues* in Atlantic City, then the favored retreat for writers. In his loneliness he resumed his correspondence with Philip Moeller.

Moeller, addressing him as "Clifford Odette" at 82 Horatio Street, replied on stationery from the RKO film studio in Los Angeles. Calling him "My dear boy," Moeller's friendly letter encourages him to abandon acting for writing, and expresses the seductive hope that one day he, too, will experience Hollywood:

> I am glad you are still there writing and that you listened, though only halvedly to me about yourself as an actor. I have told you often and tell you again that you have too much mind for that sort of nonsense. Be a writer and a swell one. We need them. Why don't you let us have a look at your new play? I like the title tremendously. . . .
> Life out here is exciting and exhilarating but I have spent most of my off-moments wondering how anyone has ever compared this corner of the world to Italy—to Italy where it has taken thousands of

years to create the atmosphere and here where atmosphere is the one thing that is completely lacking. Somehow, I feel that the difference isn't solely the gimcrackery of it all . . . but there is a real frankness and sweetness about the people. Something young and gay and wide-eyed . . . and then flowers and flowers and trees and trees everywhere and everywhere. What it would all do to your sensuous sensuality someday I hope you will find out.

Eighteen months later Odets *would* be exploring what the film capital would do to his "sensuous sensuality."

By the time the Group convened in a ramshackle wooden hotel to prepare for a special season of three plays in Boston, guaranteed by the presidents of Radcliffe, Massachusetts Institute of Technology, and Tufts, plus assorted bankers and cultivated Bostonians, the summer was almost over. Odets' notes are terse: "I have my own room. Very discontent." His discontent stemmed directly from the fact that the Group was spending these few hot, damp weeks rehearsing not *I Got the Blues* but a play for which he felt contempt. Luther Adler summed up the company's feeling about *Gold Eagle Guy* when, at a rehearsal, he suddenly blurted, "Boys, I think we're working on a stiff." In this unworthy vehicle Odets had been assigned only two minor bits of play. When it now appeared that Merlin's production of *I Got the Blues* was again being postponed if not abandoned, his angry tension accumulated. Only a fraction of it was released by using as a dartboard a large photograph, tacked to his closet door, of Adolf Hitler, who by this time had begun to swallow Pearl Odets' homeland, Austria.

For the rest, he continued to work into the small hours of the mornings on *Paradise Lost*, still a Jewish-family play despite his ruthless excision of its Yiddish names and phrases. It was a work, as he later put it, "about a man, Leo, who was trying to be a good man in the world and meets raw, evil, and confused conditions where his goodness comes to nothing."

This play, uncertainly poised between psychological naturalism and allegory, deals manifestly with the same subject as *Awake and Sing!*: "the struggle not to have life nullified by circumstances, false values, anything."

In the grim inventory of dilemmas confronting the characters in *Paradise Lost*, a nullification of life resulting from the crippling economic impasse is the most immediately perceivable crisis. It is by no means offered, however, as the sole circumstance making for the "bitter black total" of men's lives. All plans go awry and "no one leads a normal life here, and every decent tendency finds its complement in sterility and futility." "No one," says Odets' revolutionary, Pike, an archetype of early American protest, "talks about the depression of the modern man's spirit." Perhaps it would be better to be at "the bottom of the ocean." It is "very quiet there, the light is soft and the food is free." Indeed, "the smell of decay may sometimes be a sweet smell."*

* Two decades later Odets wrote a bitter and excellent screenplay, based on a story by Ernest Lehman, about the corruption of show business, called *The Sweet Smell of Success* (1956).

Not far below this surface the allegory states that the growth of a human may be canceled equally by willful cruelty, covetousness, cowardice, or the adoption of false values. Neither *Paradise Lost* nor *Awake and Sing!* is a simple protest against material deprivation.

The historic frame in *Paradise Lost* is the First World War, and the central motive supplied by Odets for his radical voice, Pike, the furnace man who burns with a sense of injustice, is the death of two sons in that war and his prophetic vision of a new holocaust in the offing. In an early draft Pike argues, in loosely Marxist terms, that many more sons will be lost because man does not learn from his experience:

If we remain silent while they make the next war—who then are we with our silence?! Accomplices, Citizen! Let me talk out of my hungry heart! Don't stop me! Citizens, they have taken our sons and mangled them to death! They have left us lonely in our old age. The belly-robbers have taken cloth from our backs. . . . There's for idealism! For those blue-gutted bastards are making other wars while we sleep in silence. Snorin' in a bed while the Yankee Doodle buzzards plot another cycle of death and hunger! And if we remain silent while they make this war, we are the guilty ones. For we are the people and the people is the government, and tear them down from their high places if they dast do what they did in 1914 to 17. Cast them out as menstruous rags to be the food of dogs and vermin! Yes, kill or be killed! (*Slowly sits tremblingly*)

Paradise Lost is an intellectually ambitious, didactic, often eloquent, sprawling allegory of the decay of the American middle class. It is a work of which Odets remained always fond, but which he felt "spilled out of its frame."

Here again Odets conjures a "good part" of his father in Leo Gordon, a character who, in an early draft, describes his own rabbi father as having hair "black as coal," a silent man whose eloquence in the synagogue was as "beautiful as a storm in the mountains."◖ Leo opens the play, taking a stand against Hitler by abandoning his German canary* to a neighbor, who says, "I'll take care of her like a baby." The fact of its German origin has made the songbird ineradicably evil.†

Occupying the same psychological territory as the weak, frightened, idealistic Jacob in *Awake and Sing!*, Leo (who, like Jacob, would be played by Morris Carnovsky) reads books, does not vote (because both political parties are evil), is psychologically impotent and profoundly sad in the face of what he calls the "profound dislocation" of the world. He designs pocketbooks while his insensitive partner, physically strong and overtly hostile but sexually impotent and therefore childless (lacking creative power), sells them. Leo is a dreamer, he does not "see reality," and is unaware that there are gunmen at the union meetings. "Oh, you sleep, Boss," says one of his workmen to him. Embezzling joint funds (as Odets suspected his father had), the fraudulent partner plunges the honest and creative one into the play's climactic bankruptcy. Again and again and again, as Odets once wrote, "the Jewish father devours the Jewish prophet."

Like Bessie Berger (the mother in *Awake and Sing!*), who combines

◖ 16.1.
* To Odets a songbird means a poet.
† In *Awake and Sing!* a young woman abandons her illegitimate baby and her poet-manqué husband. The baby—that is, the creation, or even the innocent one within—is not legitimate and must be abandoned!

identity-elements of Lou Odets and Aunt Esther Rossman, Leo's wife in *Paradise Lost*, Clara, is shrewd, energetic, poker-playing, suspicious, materialist, and bossy. She counters Leo's gentle, trusting, conciliatory efforts "to understand" with suspiciousness plus a range of aggression from mild irony to "I'll knock out his teeth," urging her dreamy, imprac- tical husband to "for a change, stand up for your rights." From her chil- dren she *demands* respect (like L. J. Odets and like Bessie Berger), and to Leo's weak, idealist, generalized guilt she brings a tough matter-of-fact- ness and a character spine: "to have a good time." ("Why not?" says Clara. "Rich and poor—it's a natural condition!" "Don't act like the whole world's trouble's your fault.") She urges her son, Ben—much as Bessie Berger does in *Awake and Sing!*—not to marry until he can become a moneymaker. Ben defies her and marries a girl cut from the same sen- sual, demanding mold as Hennie in *Awake and Sing!* As Hennie abandons her gullible and ineffectual husband, that "mouse of a man" Sam Fein- schreiber, so does the psychologically equivalent Libby abandon Ben for life with the energetic, sensual, opportunistic gangster Kewpie.

Dialogues between Leo and Pike, written this summer and later, re- flect Odets' passionate absorption in *Paradise Lost* with his efforts to diag- nose and prescribe for life's fundamental ills, to find new meanings and a "new bible."◖ Repeatedly he asks, like the great Russian writers, why it is that "Never in my forty-seven years have I met a happy man. What is wrong?" And, like them, "What is to be done?" or "How should we live?" The innocently fervent religious ecstasy of Odets' first Group summer three years earlier has dimmed, and he obsessively mourns his lost Paradise on a variety of levels, starting with his own history and ending with that of the world. There are a few hints that in the "artistic" Leo Gordon, totally out of touch with the ugly realities of life, Odets is reflecting this quality not only in himself but also in the directors of the Group. After all, had not the "talmudic purveyor," as actor Lee J. Cobb called Lee Strasberg, blankly ignored Bess Eitingon's $50,000?

What Clurman called the "mist of twilight nostalgia" which envelops this play derives not simply from the disintegration of American middle- class life in the thirties, but also from the specific dilemmas of Odets' own family and from his current disillusionments with the Group. Thus, when Leo says that "never in my forty-seven years have I met a happy man," he is expressing Odets' experience of the human condition, not simply his reaction to the economic Depression.

While creating his two dozen characters as symbols of a dying order, Odets tried to infuse them, at the same time, with individual psychological life and interplay. It is an error, though, to see the interplay among the characters in a play as a simple reflection (or even a transposition) of the "real" people in a playwright's life. They *are* often that, but, far more important, *they are the internal warring elements of a playwright's char- acter.*

In *Paradise Lost* one son, Julie, a poignant caricature, is afflicted by terror and by an incurable "sleeping sickness":* as he slowly wastes away in his wheelchair, his face masklike, he amuses himself by scrutinizing everyone and by playing on paper the game of stock market, running up fortunes and losing them.† When his mother asks him what he is fright-

---

◖ 16.2.
* Odets often used "sleep" as a symbol of death in life—"Make a break or spend your life in a coffin." Kewpie in *Paradise Lost* will "wake up" Libby.
† Much later, in Odets' film *The Story on Page One*, the heroine's mother gambles on the stock market on paper.

ened of, his bizarre reply is, "No upward trend. I feel like a weak market." Occasionally he dresses up in evening clothes because it makes him feel good.

The third act opens with Clara paring her dying son's toenails and telling him the story of Moses on the mountain:

> Well, Moses stayed on the mountain forty days and forty nights. They got frightened at the bottom. Everybody was very nervous. "Where's Moses?" Nobody knew what happened. What did those fools do? They put all the gold pieces together, all the jewelry, and melted them, and made a baby cow of gold. Well, believe me, when God saw that he was very, very mad. Moses ran down the hill so fast . . . "What's the big idea!" he said. "Can't I leave you alone for two minutes?" He took the cow and broke it into a thousand pieces. Some people agreed, but the ones who didn't? Finished! God blotted them out of the book. Here today, gone tomorrow!

It is striking that Odets puts this highly moral, anti-materialist Bible story into the mouth of a character who, for the most part, takes a pragmatic, ambitious, distrustful, and money-wise role throughout the play. In *Awake and Sing!* the same function is served by old Jacob predicting that "the Red Sea will happen again," wiping out the materialist Egyptians.

In his original draft of *Paradise Lost* Odets concludes Clara's account of Moses with "This is the story of our people." That is, a people who—if they accede to the temptation to still their anxiety by the worship of gold —will be held in contempt by Moses and blotted out of the book by God, a high price. This view expresses the values of an Israel Rossman, not a Lou Odets. It was part of Odets' dilemma, insofar as gold represented to him power (an antidote to terror), the opportunity to "rescue" his mother from his father, and, above all, his father's respect.

The second son, Ben, appears at first to embody the distillation of the ingenuous American dream: a champion sprinter ("how like a god!"), a magnetic trophy-winner; indeed, in Odets' stage directions, a large statue of him—at which he later spits—commands the set. The all-American Ben is, however, also doomed because his "heart has turned to water" and he can no longer run. He is a "skyrocket" that "starts with a bang, ends with a fizz,"* but comforts himself that there is "a swell berth waiting for me in Wall Street." His extraordinary sweetness and innocence, apparently drawn by Odets both from the character of Julie Garfield and from himself, issue first in the loss of his wife to the petty gangster Kewpie,◖ a boyhood intimate, and finally in his "suicide" as he marches into a barrage of bullets while joining the gangster in his first holdup.† This robbery has been undertaken to cancel Ben's profound *shame* that— like Odets himself—he cannot make a living and must take money from his mother. "Without a dollar," Lou Odets always said, "you don't look the world in the eye." Stella Adler recalled the Group members discussing among themselves "how like a little embarrassed kid Clifford seemed this summer. He would say, 'I want to talk to you,' and when he tried to penetrate you, he was always a little phony, but also so babyish, sweet, and crazy."

---

* Van Wyck Brooks (whom Odets liked to quote) had said, "America is a land of first-acts."

◖ 16.3.

† A chillingly ominous note is sounded here by Odets for the future of his own personal American dream, as he sets his young people—who aspire to becoming champions—on the road to suicide or to being murdered by the powerful enemy. (See Notes and Comment 16.4.)

There exists a remarkable *formal* complexity in the multi-layered relationship between Ben, the innocent athlete—called by Clurman a "child of a baffled idealism"—and his boyhood friend Kewpie, described by Odets in his earliest *Paradise Lost* notebook as a secretive man whose "spine" is to get every single thing he wants"—"like Gadg."* The gangster tries to beat the world at its own game and knows, as does the mother in *Awake and Sing!*, that the world is a jungle where you must "look out for the wildlife." It differs from the jungle in that members of the same species devour one another. Lou Odets had often instructed his children that life consists of "dog eat dog."

On one level Kewpie is an obvious symbol of social corruption, the gangster often figuring in this role in the literature of this time. An illiterate cab-driver, he offers Ben an active alternative to passive resignation: proud survival is possible, he says, through bold, aggressively masculine criminal activity, like armed bank-robbery.

Defending himself after he has involved his friend in a holdup, thus engineering his death, he accuses the parents of having reared Ben as "a little kid in a man's world . . . he couldn't earn a living and he was ashamed." There is both a formal and a psychological overlap between the passive shame in the characters of Ben Gordon in *Paradise Lost* and the ineffectual, poetic Sam Feinschreiber in *Awake and Sing!*, also cuckolded by a gangster. *Both* characters reflect Odets' simultaneous affection and contempt for the poet resident within himself.

Although the identity-elements in Kewpie occupy in boldest outline the psychological territory held by petty racketeer Moe Axelrod in *Awake and Sing!* and, indeed, by all the powerful men in Odets' plays—and there would be many—Odets added during this summer several new shifts in his interior war. In *Awake and Sing!* the capitulation of the sensual girl (Hennie) to the petty racketeer (Moe) represents Odets' fantasy of a "profane" union with his high-stepping, seductive, corrupt father; in *Paradise Lost* the literal echo of that seduction is Kewpie's theft of his friend's wife, Libby. More important, however, is Ben's own capitulation to Kewpie's criminal get-rich-quick scheme, which issues not in a trip to Havana, as in *Awake and Sing!*, but in a suicidal death ("He stood there soakin' up cops' bullets like a sponge—a guy with fifty medals for running. Ben Gordon wanted to die!")◗ Although there is a great deal of overt tenderness between the two friends, Kewpie does not hesitate to steal Ben's wife. He is, however, enraged when someone calls his friend Ben a "nance." It is evident that the deeply significant relationship is not between a man and a woman but between the two men.

During this summer a lifelong friendship began to ripen between Odets and "a Greek from Turkey who seemed like a Jew": Elia Kazan, called "Gadget" because, as he himself put it, "I was so small and so odd." Odets admired Kazan's muscular intelligence, his fierce repudiation of his carpet-selling father, his degree from Williams College, and his ambitiousness. From the beginning, other members of the Group observed the special tenderness, almost a physical charge, between these two men. Odets began to collect notes for a short story to be called "My Friend, the Greek." He would never be satisfied with it, feeling it had not captured the complexities in his friend, whom he thought of as similar to the Old Testament Joseph, son of Jacob, whom he called "one of the first of the get-ahead boys."

In the work of this summer on the new play, *Paradise Lost*, it appears

* Elia Kazan.
◗ 16.5.

from Odets' regrouping of his own identity-elements evident in *Awake and Sing!* that he fears certain precious aspects of himself are in jeopardy (in particular, the innocence of the creative artist regarded by him as "moral" but also as feminine, weak, and passive). Other elements, taken from his father but consciously rejected by him, like the need for material power, sensual luxury, and visible status, are experienced as a deeply implanted and steadily seductive internal threat (Kewpie says to Ben: "I'm in you like a tapeworm").

Thus, when Ben agrees to Kewpie's plan of murderous armed violence as a method of getting what he wants, he cannot tolerate the consequent guilt, or his abdication of his innocent idealism and creativity, and therefore he successfully courts death. As is the case in most suicides, Ben is, in all likelihood, simultaneously murdering someone and acceding to that person's wish that he be dead.◄ Odets once said, "On three occasions in my life, all involving my father, I almost committed suicide."

Further evidence in *Paradise Lost* that Odets fears a capitulation of his innocence to his "gangsterism" is provided when Ben's wife, Libby, is sexually seduced by Kewpie, who—mocking Ben—supports her in the same style in which the petty racketeer proposes for Hennie in *Awake and Sing!*

It is unclear whether Odets knew by now of his mother's desperate and, as it would prove, final effort to find some small fulfillment with the man she had met the previous summer in Atlantic City and whom she now saw again. Not long after, Pearl became profoundly depressed. At this point she was withdrawn and unable to function. It was clear that Pearl Odets was by now severely embattled. The form of her marital crisis would be precisely repeated sixteen years later by her son.

Over many years Odets made notes for a play he never wrote, called "Private Treaty," about a man and a woman—each married—who try, in an Atlantic City hotel, to save each other by bringing "some kind of love" to their pinched lives. The play deals with betrayal, and with a yearning to help or to be helped, themes that reappear regularly in his plays.

> One night I had the idea for the scene in the play which I call the Fire Bug Scene. It just impelled itself to be written, and since I had no paper I wrote the whole scene as fast as I could on the white wall. The words just gushed out; my hand couldn't stop writing. Then later, I copied it down on the typewriter, but to this day the scene may still be on the wall of that old hotel.

So, many years later, Odets would describe the high point of this troubled, productive summer.

It is not clear why this scene—in which arson is proposed by Leo Gordon's crooked partner as a solution for their economic impasse—poured out of Odets with such insistence on this hot August night. Perhaps it combined, with an exciting formal economy, a wild and unchecked destructiveness (fire is a frequent image in his memories), a manifest dismissal of his father's attachment to the value of big business, and a way out through self-destruction (burn down the entire enterprise).

◄ 16.6.

In the proposer of the scheme, as well as in the strange little professional arsonist (to be played brilliantly by Group actor Bobby Lewis), there is an identity-element of Lou Odets: externally the arsonist is the very essence of propriety with his brown derby hat, his "oxford frame glasses on a ribbon," his umbrella, and his briefcase. The nightmare touch, supplied by Clurman, is a black fingerguard. A man with the "quantity of apricot cordial," the arsonist introduces his real business with Leo Gordon and Sam Katz (to burn down their Cameo Company so they can collect the insurance) by suggesting the advertising slogan: "Katz leather bags has nine lives." He quickly and "delicately" goes on to his "purely suggestive" proposal that he be paid the "triflin' fee" of $200 to incinerate their plant, having done such jobs fifty-three times before. The elliptical platitudes he offers, as well as his advertising slogan, could have come directly from the mouth of Lou Odets.

Leo Gordon is outraged by his crooked partner's scheme. But Katz defends himself by turning on his wife; like Pearl Odets, she is depriving him by always looking for bargains: "Did you ever see, a man like me should wear seconds in everything? Socks, shirts, everything is seconds!" Katz then moves on to his real agony: that he, "a man like an ox," can't have a son. "Better my eyes fell out from my head before I married you!" he screams.

Odets continues here his struggle with his father's business morality, the chasm between his parents, and, most important, his grief that he is not the kind of son his father wants. Leo Gordon decides—in the language of economics, so often interchangeable with that of feeling—to file "voluntary bankruptcy," a figure of speech reflecting Odets' despair at being a "good" man. Leo is sorely tempted to take the counsel of his corrupt partner and send their business up in flames; in a first draft of *Paradise Lost* it is Leo, "trying to be a good man in the world," who—like Jacob in *Awake and Sing!*—commits suicide. He cannot accept the fact that exploitation exists in his "Cameo Shop," protests that "I would not want my life built up on the misery of these people," and flirts with a bitter nihilism.

The dozens of brief encounters which inform this tragicomic, lyric, surrealist work add up to a futile, romantic, and rather mad account of the many ways life can go awry and the alternatives—almost all foredoomed—for salvation.

One can accept the system and try to operate within it (practically, like Clara Gordon, or corruptly, like Sam Katz) or one can go a step further and try to beat the system criminally, like the gangster Kewpie. Neither of these alternatives is acceptable to a humanist like Leo Gordon, in whom Odets has simultaneously collected his own idealism and his contempt for its ineffectuality in the "real" world.

In a world which Odets in this play called a "league of *notions*," Leo Gordon, in the briefest of affirmations, closes the first draft with a statement that "not seeing reality cripples a man." Pleading that we must work "from a true base of experience" and not permit life to be a "cloudy lie" or an "American dream," Leo introduces what Odets called this "Act 3 Finale" with "I must make a confession! The dream is over."*

In a later draft, doubtless written after he had become for a short time a member of the Communist Party, Odets' extravagantly expressed emphasis is not on fidelity to "reality" but to one's fellow man:

> Leo: No! There is more to life than this! Everything he said is true, but there is more. That was the past, but there is a future. Now we

* See facsimile of this manuscript page on page 192.

know. We dare to understand. Truly, truly, the past was a dream. But this is real! To know from this that something must be done. We searched; we were confused! But we searched, and now the search is ended. For the truth has found us. For the first time in our lives— for the first time our house has a real foundation. Clara, those people outside are afraid. Those people at the block party whisper and point. They're afraid. Let them look in our house. We're not ashamed. Let them look in. Clara, my darling, *listen to me.* Everywhere now men are rising from their sleep. Men, men are understanding the bitter black total of their lives. Their whispers are growing to shouts! They become an ocean of understanding! *No man fights alone.* Oh, if you could only see with me the greatness of men. I tremble like a bride to see the time when they'll use it. My darling, we must have only one regret—that life is so short! That we must die so soon. Yes, I want to see that new world. I want to kiss all those future men and women. What is this talk of bankrupts, failures, hatred . . . they won't know what that means. Oh, yes, I tell you the whole world is for men to possess. Heartbreak and terror are not the heritage of mankind! The world is beautiful. No fruit tree wears a lock and key. Men will sing at their work, men will love. Ohhh, darling, the world is in its morning . . . and *no man fights alone!* Let us have air . . . Open the windows.

Even Clurman, Odets' firmest supporter this summer, found in this romantic peroration the fundamental weakness of *Paradise Lost.* He could not believe so rapid a "forward movement" toward a new social order in the play's hero. Yet he remained steadily encouraging to Odets in the face of Strasberg's dismissal of him. At the end of this summer, deeply cut by Strasberg's rejection, Odets made the gesture of threatening to quit the Group: "I told Harold Clurman, who by then had become my particular friend among the three Group directors—he was a kind of older brother to me—I told him that since I had never got a part, I was leaving. He pleaded with me to stay, promising he would see that I got a good acting part in the coming season, and indeed I think I was leading him on a bit because I wouldn't have known where to go. Where else could you go? *All I really wanted was to have the Group Theatre do my plays*" (italics mine).

In his notes for an autobiography he writes, "Unhappiness with Lee. I am stopped as writer and threaten to quit. Harold stops me." Thus it was that he continued to wrestle with the ponderous *Paradise Lost,* his central project not only for this summer but for this entire year.

Odets did not realize yet that his own "unhappiness with Lee" was only a single reverberation of a growing resentment among a segment of the Group members toward all their directors, most sharply directed now at Strasberg. When Stella Adler returned from Paris, where, sitting under the trees in the Bois de Boulogne, she had helped Stanislavsky to recuperate from a severe illness, she was critical of Strasberg and talked about the "true Stanislavsky method." To this, Strasberg replied, "I don't teach the Stanislavsky method; I teach the Strasberg method."

It was in response to Strasberg, according to Robert Lewis, that Group actress Ruth Nelson became "a key figure in the history of the Group Theatre." He recalled the turning point in vivid detail:

Lee was directing *Gold Eagle Guy*—a play about the San Francisco earthquake. Joe Bromberg played a big tycoon; his wife was played by Margaret Barker (called "Beany"). One of the scenes contained a tea party in the fancy home which was wrecked when the earthquake came. (At the end of the play the whole set collapsed, and Dawn Powell, who was a very witty woman, said, "My God, why didn't they do that at eight-thirty, we could have all gone home!")

At one of the final rehearsals, during the scene in which Beany pours tea for the society ladies of the town (one of them played by Ruth Nelson), one of the ladies at the far end of the room suddenly gets a fainting spell and falls to the floor. When Beany saw that she made just a slight move, and then realized that that was not called for in her part; she was supposed to continue on with the tea—that was the point of the scene. So she quickly corrected herself and carried on with the rehearsal. Lee said, "What did you do that for?" She said, "I'm terribly sorry, Lee, I know I'm not supposed to react to that. I made a mistake. May we go on?" He said, "What did you do that for?" in a low, slow, menacing tone. She said, "I told you it was a mistake. I don't know why I did it. It was wrong, and I won't do it again—can we go on?" He repeated, "What did you do that for?" We all knew what he was trying to say and was unable to say. It's complicated to explain, but I will.

Beany was from a very fine family—her father was the head of Johns Hopkins, famous doctor, big heart-and-nerve man; Mrs. Barker, a distinguished leader of Baltimore society. Lee was brought up on the East Side—worked at the Henry Street Settlement House.

What Beany had done in that moment was what any "well-bred" hostess would do when she was pouring tea in her own house and one of her guests falls on the floor in a faint. What Lee was trying to get her to say was that a hostess might do that, even as a reflex, even though she was not supposed to—but she would not give him the satisfaction of saying that, because then he could really have made something out of it: he could say, shouting, something like: "This is not a play about Emily Post!" But, knowing that, Beany kept saying, "I don't know, it was a mistake." We all knew what she was trying to do—she was trying to get the run-through going, and to avoid all that screaming and yelling. Finally, Beany broke down and started to cry.

Ruth Nelson was always right on hand. If you broke your leg, she had splints—she always had everything—she was the Florence Nightingale of the Group—one of those people who is straight as a dye. Ruth had been watching this scene, and she couldn't stand it any longer when Beany started to cry. Ruth said, in a way that you knew she meant it, "I'm gonna kill him." No drama in it, just very simply and quietly. It was really scary. She started for him. Lee was sitting out in the theatre, across the orchestra pit, and she started to walk down the stage toward the pit. She was really blinded by rage and we saw she was going to walk right out across the pit—she could have broken a leg, really hurt herself. We all raced toward her. Lee saw her coming at him and saw genuine murder in her eye, and he turned around and ran out of the theatre, and never came back to the rehearsals of this play, which was finished by Harold. And that was the first directing Harold did—Lee refused to come back to the production. From then on, the air was cleared.

The news spread quickly throughout the Group that an unprecedented and frightening event had occurred. Strasberg had never before left a rehearsal. This outbreak by one actress, probably verbalizing the unspoken thoughts of her fellows, signaled a serious crack in the absolute power Strasberg had until then wielded.

Lewis quoted Katharine Hepburn as saying, when they were together in the film *Dragon Seed,* "You and Gadget [Elia Kazan] were the only two who were mean enough to go through the ten years of the Group and come out absolutely untouched." To which Lewis replied, "You are absolutely right, outside of three complete nervous breakdowns, *it didn't touch me at all.*"

On the day following his exuberant gush of words in the firebug scene, Odets said he "went into a liquor store and bought two cases of mixed liquor—two bottles of everything—Scotch, gin and rye, applejack, sherry, red port, and something called white port which I have not seen again to this day. And I and my particular chums in the Group Theatre, Elia Kazan, Art Smith, Bud [Roman] Bohnen, and one or two others, went to town on all that stuff."

Kazan, aspiring (like Odets and Art Smith) to be a writer, recalled this drunken spree in Ellenville: "We went shouting through the town, and when I threw a flower pot we were all put in jail. Clifford was drunk a lot this summer. The little money he had from Merlin went into the beginning of his study of wines. It was my first introduction to a guy having sherry in his room. It seemed so civilized. Clifford was depressed a lot, but he never let me see him made passive by it. He would become furious, never slumped or bowed down."

Kazan's memory of Odets is confirmed by Group actor Sanford Meisner, who was astonished to hear of Odets' conviction that Meisner had felt scornful of him. Meisner believes that it was rather an amazement at Odets' intensity: "He was desperately assertive in a purely fantasy way. . . . He came in the house one night and screamed, 'I am a genius!' I was caught off guard and must have giggled. Clifford picked up a bottle of gin and threw it at me with all that kind of ferocity. I ducked and it hit the wall. Then Clifford was horrified at what he had done." Two decades later in Hollywood, Odets told Meisner, as a kind of explanation for the early outbursts, that he finally had told his father off, but that "it took me fifty years to do it."

By the end of September the Group had moved up to Boston to offer a season of three plays: their successful *Men in White,* a revival of Lawson's unsuccessful *Success Story,* and the premiere of Levy's *Gold Eagle Guy.* Odets' mood continued to be in his word "ugly." Writing to Helen Deutsch, the Group's press representative in New York—addressing her as "Dear Comrade" or "well-breasted cat"—he says he is "bawling out the twirpy dames" and could "bite my own damn fingers off, but I need them for typing and hitting chords on the piano." He is determined to have a playing script of *Paradise Lost* finished by the end of the Boston run. Garfield's wife, Robbe, recalled Odets in a small dressing room, "looking angelic" with a halo of blond hair, complaining of his tiny part and saying, "This is the last year I'm going to sit around like this."

To Helen he sends five dollars, writing of his small part in the play:

The stupidity of sweating over six lines is breaking my heart. . . . How can a man, a full man of adult nerves and muscles stick around a place like this and work ceaselessly on lines, no matter how many. How can anyone stand it? . . . It's just as valuable as it might be to stand in a corner of a room and string beads. I can see by the token of my disrespect for all this that I am different from the others, worse or better I can't say, but different. The jaw of my brain is broken and hangs awry all these weeks!"

He thinks he is learning to drink in earnest and creating in himself "a hot blizzard," and surely his smoking will cause him to die of cancer. He is sleeping late, listening to recordings, and has yet to learn from Beethoven, he says, "the discipline of art." Without that "I'll remain a bum all my life, eager to play with the five senses, but no artist and worker." "Yes," he adds, "the winters'll get damn cold if I don't soon learn that discipline trick."

Indeed, the main reason he had remained in the Group this summer "was the damned fear that if I went to Hollywood I would drink like a bastard and brand the fleshpots too hot into my skin." It is clear that "no good work comes out of that unless you are really a genius, a Balzac at least, and I'm nothing like that. We breed them small in the first two decades of the 20th Century." He used to think the crazy ambition "to impress a virgin" (to be first in everything) was a disease only of the American Jew, "but now I see all the boys and girls have it." He is grateful that Helen has spoken to "that nice fellow [Guthrie] McClintic" about *I Got the Blues,* as it is now clear to him that neither the Group nor Merlin will produce it. He counts himself "miserable" and wants not to look at anything or see anything or live or wake, but to sleep, only to "crawl back in the dark cavern of the bed."

Despite these protestations, he continues to work late each night on *Paradise Lost,* and by mid-October has a new "scene-synopsis" for the entire play. He steadily torments Helen with banter about "a new girl every night," concluding, however, "I'm like a maniac about writing plays. I see a whole life stretched ahead. Don't write me about girls, Helen. I got HER in bed, the drama muse, and sucking like mad her breasts, the old bitch!" He can't tell whether his work is good or bad, but he is "thinking all the time," and is pleased with his growth as an artist over the last four years. The head is a "clicking machine, but not as regular or as foolproof." He is preoccupied with "matters political" and is convinced of "the new coming world." From R. Palme Dutte he is learning about the nature of Fascism. "If only," he says, "talk could change the world!!!"

His reflections are lively as he takes long walks in Boston and investigates his own awareness and its history with the adventurousness of a Columbus:

Getting out of the theatre, early, I took a long walk and worked off and into and out of moods. Look in a window sometimes and see there some article you wanted as a child, and could never get, and see what it does to you. Makes you understand something about ambition and success. This time I saw Halloween masks and marked out those that were always beyond my reach—the ones with trick moustaches and hair on them—and the other cheaper ones which sometimes fell into my hands. Very sad. I get that way too if I look into one of those ugly loaded Loft's candy windows. Oh dearie me, the coconut royals and the plantations and the parlays. Do you know what all those are? And the tin boxes in which some of the candy came, they too were prized very highly. No baby, the boy seldom yearned for things of the spirit! But once I wanted to be a rabbi! Yes, I was holy in my heart. Marxist holiness is better!

It dawns on him that he may have a special gift to wed in his thought the psychological and the historical:

We went to a party after the Saturday night show, given by one Strauss, society Jews, German Jews who are in a class all their own. Good for a sensitive young man like me to see all those different kind of people. If you told them that their activity is so strongly typical that it has deep social roots, they'd laugh. Constantly I am amazed at the depth of the social type, that if you know one society girl you understand them all; that one rich Americanized German Jew is exactly like another, that some where there must be other people like you and me. Appalling, but wonderful to see, to examine, to understand in relation to the social background. Intuitively I'm a smart boy. Someday I'll write a book. Which reminds me that in the act of making contact with a workers' theatre group here the other night . . . I met a lad . . . who is the only other one beside myself who has, to the best of my knowledge, applied a Marxian point of view to the history of music, especially to Beethoven. I sat there and listened to him talk to a girl and played dumb, but when he made a mistake I corrected. (Arrogant?) I would really have kept still, but he did make a mistake, several. I mention this because slowly I equip myself to write a good book on Beethoven, could even do it right this minute. Want you to know this so you won't get fresh with me.

The human relationships, on the other hand, around him are discouraging, whether among the homosexuals (male and female) or the heterosexuals. He fears that "Stella is tearing out Harold's heart: she takes a bite and spits the whole business away." He wishes Harold would "step on her more." ("The Bronx boys used to have it, 'Pick her up like a bowling ball.' Right!") His anger toward women simmers in his letters to Helen Deutsch, and it is evident he continues to debate the merits of living relationships with actual people against the more controllable world of art-making. He is concerned he may be "spoiling" Helen by his prompt replies to her letters, but continues nonetheless to write them and to amuse her with newspaper clippings from his growing collection. One is of an American Indian running for the Senate on the Communist Party slate in Texas. Under it he has written: "Am sending him a telegram telling him to 'go back where you came from.' The dirty sheeny! His uncle killed our Custer!"

It exhilarated him to wander in the late afternoons to the headquarters of the Marine Workers Industrial Union or to Boston's Faneuil Hall, a pre-Revolutionary meeting-place, one of the oldest in the country. There one afternoon he was transfixed by a young man exhorting coalboat workers from Spain to strike for a living wage against the American boat-owners. Speaking passionately in English and in Spanish, Joe Kelleher was so moving a figure that Odets approached him naïvely at the end of the meeting, saying, "You are marvelous. You should be an actor!"

He listened raptly to the Boston-born Kelleher tell of his shame and consternation when a Spanish anarchist, his co-worker at a sugar mill in Cuba, had accused him, as an American, of having murdered Sacco and Vanzetti. Recalling thirty-three years later his meeting with Odets at

Faneuil Hall, Kelleher said, "He was tremendously interested in the fact that this accusation had made me delve into the true story of the Sacco-Vanzetti case, and he was extremely interested also in Mendieta and Batista. I told him about Batista's vast real-estate holdings in Miami and in Daytona Beach, also about the 'ley de fuga.' That's the law of the fugitive, 'whoever has the gun rules.' Batista would shoot you in the back and then say you were trying to escape. That makes the murder legal."

So eager was Odets to embrace a hopeful world-image for the future of man that he, along with thousands of his generation, closed their senses to the indications of a developing nightmare in their humanist utopia, the Soviet Union. Stalin, no less competitive, paranoid, and ruthless than his opposite number in Nazi Germany, had already set in motion the machinery "to slake an implacable vengeance." This dislocation between theory and action has probably been exceeded nowhere in history and, according to Djilas, Stalin—an avid reader of Victor Hugo in his youth—was a monster "who, while adhering to fundamentally utopian ideas, in practice had no criterion but success—and this meant violence, and physical and spiritual extermination." Even had more facts been available in these desperate thirties, Odets' generation would have needed to shut them out, since to admit them in would have meant the death of hope.

Soon after the meeting in Faneuil Hall, Odets told his friend Clurman that he "wanted to belong to the largest possible group of humble, struggling men prepared to make a great common effort to build a better world. . . . He felt the need to share his destiny with the lowliest worker, with those who really stood in the midst of life. . . . He was driven by a powerful emotional impetus, like a lover on the threshold of an elopement."

Clurman's sense of the power of Odets' need to fuse with "struggling men" was accurate: by the end of October 1934 Odets proudly showed a few close friends his membership card in the Communist Party plus "a one-act workers' play" written in a four-day heat for a Boston union meeting. He hoped it would elicit a better response than his full-length plays, and believed it could become "a light machine-gun to be wheeled in as needed." The New Theatre League was steadily in need of such material for benefit performances. He wrote Helen that he had given up on *I Got the Blues* and that *Paradise Lost* had gone sour on him. "I thought about it too long . . . over ripe."

When Kelleher had told him he needed a "workers' play" to put on at meetings, Odets had got together a committee of five Group actors, all interested in writing, called "SKKOB," after their surnames: Smith, Kazan, (Alexander) Kirkland, Odets, Bohnen. It was to be a collaborative project entirely independent of the Group directorate, to be directed by Odets and Group actor Sanford Meisner. When the others tired of this small piece of "agit-prop" (agitation and propaganda), Odets continued to work on it alone and invited the other Group actors to play in it, sight unseen. "I didn't know at that point whether or not Clifford could even write a letter," actor Luther Adler recalled, "but I agreed to attend the reading in the basement of the Majestic [Theatre]."

It was a welcome diversion from the increasingly gloomy facts of their Boston season. *Men in White* was not doing nearly so well as it had in New York, and *Success Story*—in which Odets was again resentfully understudying Luther Adler—fared even worse. Some thought the dismal failure of Lawson's play was due to the nature of its demoniacally ambitious Jewish hero; it seemed to be echoing Hitler's anti-Semitism, and people wondered how a Jew could have created so unattractive a picture of a Jewish personality.

On the day before he read his "workers' play" to those few Group actors willing to listen, Odets described the opening night of *Success Story*:

You have by now read the notices of the Lawson play, but you should have seen the opening. The frozen silence, the terrorized silence, the stink of boiled cod in the air!!! Me, I was enraged by the bastards, so touched by the play that I went right home, quietly I went home and sat right down and wrote the first three pages, opening with a quote from the Bible.⟨ Yes, my lady, I needed that, sitting in the last row and when he said, "Once there was a guy named Christ dressed in a rainbow. He took me up on a mountain and showed me the world . . . he told the world plenty" . . . I cried a whole lot even tho Luther hammered, even tho even a dull person could feel the antagonism of the aristocratic audience. Which made my feeling even stronger, for what was being said on the stage was right there in the audience, which I didn't realize to this very minute. Yes, the whole thing on the stage was in the house. I was terrorized. Death in back and front, but I burn with a flame! Don't scare me one goddam bit. Until sundown will wiggle like a cut up worm and then make fruit trees where my ashes are.* This is the day of life, baby, the beginning and not the end. Let death be strong in Wagner, but we're burning daylight here. Right now! And damn far on in the future!

So that's how I felt when I got back to the room last night after the opening. I feel that way again and wish I were a musician to write it down. Of my own life that's the sorrow, not to write music. I was made for that as sure as rock is rock. The whole temperament is for that and as such a writer, I would have been a great one. The writer is not so hot. Maybe I'll learn to say what I feel, to find the exact way of doing it. *The word's the shadow, the note is it itself.* The stinker Pater was right (he knew something, that patie de foi [sic] gras): all the others aspire to the music art. What a wonderful feeling to believe beyond yourself. And not the Doistoievsky [sic] feeling wherein you could kill yourself for feeling this way, like the Karamazoff boy.

Despite heroic publicity efforts—including a humorous radio interview of Luther Adler by his competitive understudy (both parts of the dialogue were written by Odets)—business declined. The atmosphere became urgent.

The following night, even before the actors assembled unofficially in the cellar of the theatre to hear it, Odets began to understand what the writing of this collective workers' play meant to him. Writing to Helen from the Hotel Bellevue at five in the morning, "a towel on my head like one of the early Jews," he says,

This is what I learned from it: urgency creates its own art level, and not too bad at that. Particularly, if you gave a second draught [sic] to what you wrote at first. Yes, sit down and write, and some few good things will turn up. Certainly hot speeches, natural dialogue, and plus the simple basic dramatic situation—a good job.

Kazan later recalled how impressed he was, not so much by this trifling play as by the fact that Odets always "responded so fully to being

⟨ This refers to the opening of *Paradise Lost*, where the mother tells the story of Moses and the Golden Calf to her dying son. (See Notes and Comment 16.7.)
* Odets used this line at the end of *Waiting for Lefty*. He often borrowed phrases from himself, and from everyone around him.

needed." Even then Odets complained that if he had a theatre that wanted him to write for it, he would write much more. Still (and forever) poised between the identity of an actor (whose performance draws an immediate response) and that of a writer (for whom there is a delay of response), Odets flowered under the prod of the collaborative atmosphere of these five actors. Kazan thought even then that Odets was "too dependent on what was going on around him."

The "simple situation" in this play was drawn from the meetings of the taxi-drivers and coal-boat workers, called to decide upon the question of a strike.* The committeemen at a strike meeting wait for a leader who never appears (just as they had in fact waited for cabbie-organizer Sam Orner). As they wait for "Lefty," each of them shows in a blackout episode the crucial moment of his life which has brought him to this very platform. A corrupt union boss, a young hack and his girl, a husband and wife, a labor spy, a young doctor, and an actor demonstrate to the audience compelling reasons for taking a positive strike vote. The voice vote to strike after Lefty is found dead—taken by the actual audience in the theatre, which serves in the play as the union membership—is the climax of this forty-minute "agit-prop" play. Odets consciously drew its form from the standard blackface minstrel show he had so often seen in Bronx vaudeville houses with its interlocutor, end men, specialty men, and chorus. Of central formal importance was its improvisational quality and his utilization of the audience as part of the play, as he had done several years earlier for *Madame X* when Mae Desmond could not afford to hire actors for a jury. Then and now, actors, author, and audience become one.†

The central struggle in his heartbreakingly innocent and crude playlet (with its aside about anti-Semitism being a crime in the Soviet Union) is between Harry Fatt,‡ the "well-fed and confident" corrupt head of the union, and Lefty, the idealist young union leader whom the audience never sees. The audience is told at the end that Lefty has been murdered lest he lead the deprived cabbies to strike for a living wage. In his "notes for production" Odets singles out the character of Fatt for detailed discussion:

> Fatt, of course, represents the capitalist system throughout the play. The audience should constantly be kept aware of him, the ugly menace which hangs over the lives of all the people who act out their own dramas. Perhaps he puffs smoke into the spotted playing space. . . . He might insolently walk in and around the unseeing players. . . .

While Odets' recently embraced Marxist ideology dictated this symbol, he is at the same time dramatizing once again the outer struggle between himself and his father and the inner one between the warring identity-elements. Again the conflict is underscored by the character of a gunman, whose lethal weapon§ is answered by the Communist salute, "the good old uppercut to the chin."

---

* Odets would later tell the House Un-American Activities Committee he had never been involved in a strike and had written *Lefty* from his imagination. This was only literally true.

† The power of this fusion of author, audience, and performers is similar to a communal ritual and mobilizes the force of a religious experience. The Meyerhold Theatre used this technique also.

‡ Fatt occupies the same territory as Uncle Morty and Moe Axelrod (*Awake and Sing!*) and Sam Katz (*Paradise Lost*), while Lefty and Ralph (*Awake and Sing!*) are equivalent.

§ The gun and the powerful automobile are two of the most important symbols of virility in American culture.

Lefty's ultimate triumph in death (a positive strike vote in which the theatre audience joins) is mediated by his having been murdered by Fatt's henchmen. On one level this represents Odets' fantasy that his own death (or suicide) would represent the fulfillment of his father's wish and a final *revenge* on him. On another level it represents also, by way of a Christlike blood sacrifice, a transcendent communality with all the "deprived," and thus a "merger" into a loving oceanic consciousness. The union member who succeeds in eliciting the strike vote at the end of the play is Agate Keller, who has lost an eye in a factory (the name derives probably from agitator, glass-eyed—i.e., crippled—plus the real Joe Kelleher), that identity-element in Odets which, unlike Lefty, lives to proclaim its militancy. Agate, like Joe Bonaparte in the later *Golden Boy*, is "cockeyed"—has a glass eye.❿

> Agate (*crying*): Hear it, boys, hear it? Hell, listen to me! Coast to coast! HELLO AMERICA! HELLO. WE'RE STORMBIRDS OF THE WORKING-CLASS. WORKERS OF THE WORLD. . . . OUR BONES AND BLOOD! And when we die they'll know what we did to make a new world! Christ, cut us up to little pieces. We'll die for what is right! put fruit trees where our ashes are! (*To audience*): Well, what's the answer?
>
> All: STRIKE!
> Agate: LOUDER!
> All: STRIKE!
> Agate and Others on Stage: AGAIN!
> All: STRIKE, STRIKE, STRIKE!!!

Curtain

Underneath the fiery political message, Odets is counseling himself in *Lefty* not to wait passively for his personal success or salvation, but to join with his Group brothers and deliver an uppercut to "the enemy" responsible for *all* of their problems, ranging from betrayals by women to material deprivation, to his failure to get parts in plays. His indictment of a patently unjust social system is genuine; the personal steam, however, is supplied by his relationship to his parents and by his current yearning not only to overcome his loneliness, but also to deliver an "uppercut" to his surrogate fathers, the Group directors—most particularly to Strasberg, who, unlike Clurman, has not encouraged him in this project. He finds it a "blessed thing" to learn from the freedom of collaborative improvisation in working on this one-act play "how Bach must have felt sometimes":

> He was not so individual as we make him, wrote often what is called fingered bass.* A slight indication of the bass which allows improvisation by the player. That is how I felt when I had finished the Workers' Play—room for connectives between the scenes, collective discussion to decide what the boys wanted to do in the way of production ideas. No hugging to the breast here, the writer alone and happy in himself. No, do what you want, boys, change, cut, add. I said to myself—this is SOME thing.

It was a joy to have a few people to trust (Sandy Meisner, Art Smith, and Elia Kazan) and to whom thus he could make the gift of his love through his work. When he read to them and to a few more—who volun-

❿ 16.8.
* "Figured bass" is correct.

teered to rehearse this hasty one-acter by now entitled *Waiting for Lefty*—from his yellow sheets, he felt their intense responsiveness. Only much later did he learn that Luther Adler had privately commented to Clurman that "The Group has produced the finest revolutionary playwright in America."

In the meantime he sought reassurance and wisdom in an active and wooing correspondence with Waldo Frank, whom he encouraged to visit the Group more often, to become editor of the left-wing periodical *The New Masses*, to share his contempt for Marxist "intellectuals," and, most of all, to read his new play and be his friend. "In every large city of the country, I would have one Waldo Frank and a round dozen in New York," he writes, adding, "Younger men like myself would sleep a sweeter sleep in the night and not so often be sick at heart." Frank's response is prompt and grateful: " . . . one learns swiftly to know one's friends, and one carries them along, everywhere and forever . . . almost outside of time. Thus, I have a sure sense of you."

Odets confides to Frank, who has taken up the role once held by Philip Moeller, that "I'm going to stop acting shortly, and work only on writing . . . the acting thing is poor nonsense alongside good writing . . . I say it's not for an adult man." He clearly enjoys this intimacy by mail and describes to Frank how his central interest lies in self-realization for all far more than in material improvement:

> . . . workers invited a whole radio station to their party and soon had stopped the broadcast to send out a discussion on what kind of music they liked, the relative values of folk music and the classical composers. Then one man got up and recited a poem, "Lilacs in our Factory." I get tears with a story like that, but don't tell it to anyone. Some of the esteemed comrades would call it left deviation or some such bull nonsense! Really, I have not met one Communist who knows that a revolution is just not for bread, but beyond, beyond. I don't blame them here—the work they have heaped on their shoulders, the necessary activity—it all has a brutalizing effect on them and I have seen often that Communist organizers and workers are often as brutal and unfeeling as their opponents! And their understanding of just why man is mongrelized in America goes as deep as the thinness of a dime piece. But it has to be like that: they forge the Marxian abstracts into swords of action and need good brute hands for the work.
>
> There is some of that brutality in me too, Waldo, which is why I understand it. A long line of Russian and Austrian peasants is behind me, so shortly back that I am still hungry. On top of being a Jew! Allright, I know what I believe.

He concludes, "I know what men can be. Which is what I'll write about in my plays, forever and forever!"

None of the three Group directors took much interest in Odets' minor propaganda playlet, which, when they got back to New York, might or might not be included as one of several "acts" in a routine Sunday-night benefit for *New Theatre* magazine. Their concerns were quite properly focused on the gathering crisis of how the Group would survive if *Gold Eagle Guy* were to fail in New York, a looming possibility.

From the fact that Odets is suddenly at work on several other projects as well, we can judge that his impasse on a final draft of the third act of *Paradise Lost* is sizable. Still there is a zest in working, and he writes to Helen Deutsch, "A pox on the bastard day which flew like the wind . . .

must lengthen my working hours. . . . Can't do much work by day and the nights are too short." To himself he writes, "Helen is pursuing me"; yet he begs her to come up to Boston "to have dinner . . . talk about nice things." She must not think about "those nasty, sexy things," as in truth he is interested only "in a thick juicy steak, not sex." He feels eating is more in harmony with work than sexual activity is.

He is apparently, at the same time, pressing Dena for a marriage commitment. Dena writes him her own self-absorbed, mid-1930s feminist declaration of independence:

> Everything that happens between us must I think be contingent upon this fundamental premise, that you know what you want to do and that you're doing it and that I'm still dependent upon my family and upon school. The fact that I must go to school makes me a dependent person and I want very much to be independent. That those problems are, in the main, settled for you creates a barrier between us which under the present circumstances I can see no method of overcoming.
>
> I am only eighteen and it would only be childishness on my part to try and forget it.
>
> As to what we can do, I'll be damned if I know. I can't say how we can get together better, how we can achieve a greater intimacy, which is essential for two people to get along. Getting married wouldn't help at all.

She concludes by asking him to wait a year for her decision about marriage, adding that she is deferring also "equally important things" like whether or not to join the Young Communist League!

He is working on two articles for *New Theatre,* a little on the full-length play about "the agitator son brought home for dead," and on two short stories. He has completed in a single night one which he guiltily considers "cute and glib," written with *The New Yorker* in mind and dispatched there that day. "So fast it went I didn't make a carbon even. Hope it won't be lost." There is no trace anywhere of this small opus except for his own outline: "a gal I loved and how we had to camp in a tourist camp at night, she with a female friend, and how I drunk and weary in the next room heard thru the cardboard walls their lovemaking and knew I'd made a mistake. Fiction, not autobiography." He underscores the fictional nature of this story because it had in fact happened just this way, according to a diary entry.

Adding a third to his seductive enterprises, he now writes to a Lesbian with whom he had earlier been deeply smitten:

> You were awake for hours that night, and because the wall was thin I heard everything you said, and everything she said too. You were a little drunk too, the first night we got [there]. What I have felt about you . . . has not been exactly clear . . . a large portion of you I dislike intensely . . . [also] I lusted after your hide . . . but not only that . . . I wanted to help you, be helped . . . I always felt that I could be important in making a more "normal woman" of you . . . I see you pretty damn plainly . . . because you are . . . a sensitive recorder of your own personal history and I feel these records from you without conscious desire on my part. . . . Today, seeing your friend here . . . knowing what she is to you, understanding clearly the things involved, I resolved to write this letter to you. For your good? No, for my own, because I want to know clearly where I am or walk completely away from you . . . as a man bidding for

your affections. I know just how you're tied up . . . Wanting to be
something. . . . You can go right ahead and defeat me standing here
and I won't die. Only something between us will and that'll be too
bad. . . .

The second story continues the beginning he had made in the summer on "My Friend, the Greek," about Kazan. "Say, do you know I could
make a pile writing stuff like this?" he tells Helen. He is troubled, however, that the "glibness was highly pleasing to me"; maybe it is because
"the inside juice makes it come out crooked, up and down, but sometimes
powerful, and we want the refinement. Forced class distinctions made
that in us. Moussourgsky had it in a funny way. The only primitive I know
in music, and always yenning after slick Italian forms, to write like
Tschaikowsky." His preoccupation now with the hazards of glib, surface
writing and false values is reflected in a sample copy he sends Helen of
the first installment of someone else's novel, *Destiny*, in Street & Smith's
fifteen-cent weekly *Love Story Magazine*. Around the portrait on the
cover of an empty-faced, permanent-waved girl he has scribbled:

Dear Helen: Read this for its ideals of love and life, for its glibness—
and for its really amazing dexterity which not even Dostoievsky had.
The clarity is really astounding. If it can be gotten without the cliches
—a problem which is just now bothering me! And the snobbery! Is
that "Children's Hour"* really good? Clifford.

Within the next forty-eight hours he completed his short story about
Kazan, judged it to be "not good," and felt cheated:

If you don't connect with the main line of yourself no writing is
valuable. And with a thing like this you don't feel like rewriting. However, there is a good character here and some dramatic elements, like
discovering near the end of the story that the fellow who is telling
the story has only one arm.† Another time I'll read it and see if it's
worth a few more hours.

In his four-page letter, typed during the same twenty-four hours as
the six-page story about Kazan, he replies to what must have been a lonely
and despairing letter from Helen. In his admonitions and reassurances to
her we see—as so often through his life—the advice he offers one part of
himself from the other:

Don't I know how you are in that hotel room? Don't I know the
smooth nights with only maybe a cat screaming in the back yard and
that scream what we'd been saying for many hours, days, months?
But the way out is not to give up yourself, nor let the inside values fall
away. No, then keep them closer, use them, force them to function.
Look outside the self to clear work to do.
 Yes, I know the rooms. I'll write a character and show you soon.
I lived the American life too long to be forgetful. But I am juice,
I am life! Hold the world on my chest!‡ Draw life from people! Give
life. Eater of livers, flower out of good hot earth. You know me, kid!
 So long, Miss Runkel . . . Clifford.

But by now he cannot stop, and instead goes on to two long postscripts
which reflect his current dilemmas. In the first, a remarkable contem-

* A new play by Lillian Hellman.
 † Once more his protagonist is crippled.
 ‡ Odets often repeated as a child: "Lemme put my head on your chesh [chest],
Mommy."

porary comment, he leaps to attack the "phony ideals" of the "whole American thing."

> I forgot to say: that the lousiest American disease is dying for ideals. The cult of perfection. There we were youngsters. With all the phoney ideals we picked up, with a competitive system putting our most intimate lives upon a competitive basis; with the fine exigency of being young, the strength of early days. . . . We wanted all the time to be hitting the bull's eye. When we didn't we got disgusted, sick at heart. We wanted all the time to be right in the womb of the matter, to have the whole world right under hand . . . and when we failed in the face of all that desire, we called it inability to turn ideals into work. And because of those ideals (so called) we said death was better than this state of affairs. The great idealists gave up because everything could not be up high. Gave up rich life for that phoney desire engendered in us by the whole American thing.
>
> Well, I found that no bull's eye can be hit more than about once out of ten shots. The rest was resting and maturing new ideas and things. (But America taught us too that there was no time for waiting! Success, right now, in a big way. Which is just too bad for American art!) Why do we think slow growth is nothing? We know the answer. I learned it slowly. My trouble—have to experience everything slowly. Take each blame to self and bite the self with accusation.
>
> I found that this was no idealism, but phoney sterile stuff. Marx preached unity of theory and practise [sic]. We have busy theorizers here, but no one who seems to know the other side of the coin is there too . . . sentimental idealists. They'd rather have death than to work to make what they want. Fuck that lot! Bury them deep with horse turds for blossoms on the grave!

In the second postscript he tries to show Helen—and himself—how to avoid a "dislocation of theory and action" not in politics but in life itself:

> No Helen, don't be like that bunch of sick whelps! Be poor, but get what you want! Work for it the straightest way. I say those people never want the real thing; only the dusty ideals in the head . . . Frogs jumping from their mouths, no love, but hate, no building, only petty tearing down. No helping of anything, but reducing all to crumbled crap and in between cutting their bellies open with hot sharp liquor! What a stink the Broadway crowd makes. The idealists!
>
> This isn't Marxism, only something that all good artists knew instinctively. The few in this country know it too. No use, tho, to point out why economics make it difficult, impossible—you know that too. But Marx was right: where *there is dislocation of theory and action, there you find death in life and hopeless misunderstanding* [italics mine]. The Communists must succeed, because they know these tricks and use them. The others, the dusty boys, don't know how the inexorable logic of the dialectic moves up and grows strongly as a tree. To smash them down!
>
> We can take this to our lives. . . . Clifford.*

That he feels significantly threatened by what he calls the "unreal and preposterous" American dream is evident in his last letter to Helen from Boston:

* Twenty years later Odets said to a class of playwrights: "To talk about [maturity] is easy; to write about it is harder; but to *live* it . . . !"

Harold and I went to see "The Merry Widow" movie. You can't help feeling that life with those dopey problems would be wonderful for a while. When you kiss the girl she goes like this and you know everything is just right and ready for you to be a big success in your chosen undertaking. . . . Finding the true love settles every problem of your life. . . . Suddenly you're singing songs from a balcony, or maybe you find yourself in the back of a comfortable carriage (and you never need to pay the driver either), or it's walking thru gardens and tens of servants wait on a fellow and suddenly your girl comes smiling to you and HOW she is dressed! You never do a stroke of work and your pocket must be full, for you attend the most wonderful night clubs. No one cries about anything but the loved person who is really very faithful but seems dastardly at the moment. The man has nothing to do but dress in uniforms with the help of his valet. The king pins medals on your chest at the lift of an eye. In the Court of Justice everything is a great big joke. No one is really bad. Don't be silly, it's all in fun and at any moment a hot song will pop out of the lover's mouth to make you realize the deep pain in his heart. He parades thru rooms which would put any Gothic cathedral to shame. Buckingham Palace is a frizzle by comparison.

Millions of people see these pictures. And the same millions want everything the pictures show. . . . Not only is this ideal held up to us as the desideratum of life, but the cheapness and vulgarity of it is marked for most eyes and ears by the slickness and luxury around it. How unreal and preposterous the dream is, how lulling and insidiously poisoning. Poor poor Americans! . . . Poor poor Helen. Poor poor Clifford. Poor poor Gus.*

It is astonishing with what prescience Odets, on the threshold of immense success, perceives the range of jeopardy in store for him. "The American taint is all over," he writes, describing his "rising horror" at seeing it work everywhere—in the "best talents around you, in the erudite, in schools, in your own home . . . people don't know, but go where opinion is most concentrated for their own regard of an art work; they take someone else's word."

Whereas every housewife "feels a piece of cloth and her fingers tell her its worth," she turns to statements in print for her evaluation of an artist. Odets is contemptuous of himself that he is learning this "early lesson" so late, and explains to Helen that he is deeply preoccupied with these issues "because the temptation is so often on me nowadays to make a quick, cheap success."

The reason for this is obvious: his father had again been berating him and accusing his mother of giving money to their ne'er-do-well son. He had now forbidden her further visits or money doles. Pearl, in turn, despaired that she could no longer tolerate such severe pain on Clifford's account. She even determined for short periods, when Clifford had not written to her, to sever their relationship, but could not sustain this decision: she would say, "I'm fed up with him, I'm through, I'm finished." No one believed this for a moment, and the battle over Clifford between L.J. and Pearl Odets continued.

Odets writes to Helen:

In three ways I can do it, writing, directing or acting. For the first two I have good talent, for the last less. But in anyway [sic] a quick

---

* Gus is a character in *Paradise Lost*.

success is possible, and the bastardly joke is that it would impress even my Communist comrades as much as my own parents: Group people too. . . . We want really—all our kind—to smash down all opposition to every single part of us. We want to master people's regard for us, want to fix it high and indelibly, no matter if the medals be brass and the clamour tinny. The very insensitive mediocrity of most of the people among whom we move is a push to easy work, a jab in the neck to "Hurry, hurry, hurry." Mr. [Alfred] Stieglitz says that it's lucky God isn't an American or no babies would get born—an American God wouldn't wait nine months. Hurry, hurry, hurry! This is a very terrible country!!!

But there is something else on the horizon the young playwright has to "buck up against," something more terrifying, he thinks, than the hunger for success or the fear of poverty: the infinite life-and-death power of the critic:

The other stuff, the scorn for a lean pocket, the lack of curiously satisfying commodities like sweet soap and fat food, I don't mind all those lacks (even without a loving wife and soft bed I'll live, and her without fine clothes to wear), but to have to smack into that critical bunch in America!!!!

It is evident that on some level he knows how deeply vulnerable he is to immense power, and how strong would be his impulse to woo critics, kowtow, please, appease, truckle to, and, indeed, flee from them. He had tried all these stratagems in turns with his father.

After six miserable weeks in Boston a fearful Group company opened *Gold Eagle Guy* in New York. Although the press was cordial, the public was not, and once more the Group directors met in emergency session. Clurman has often described Strasberg's masked irritation with Clurman's "breathless professions of faith." Cheryl Crawford agreed with Strasberg that, in the absence of a new play, they should close down.

When Clurman told the actors in the basement of New York's Belasco Theatre that there would be no further work for them this season, he was met by Stella Adler's open contempt and her announcement, "We'll find our own play!" The entire company applauded her, and each in turn "threw the gauntlet down to the directors." The actors had won the day, and planned to start reading scripts. Odets spoke up shyly for his own play, *Awake and Sing!*,* arguing that he had cut the "messy" first act, that Harold had always liked the second act, and that the third act could be rewritten.

Luther Adler recalled that when Odets even offered to raise money for its production by the Group, Strasberg lost his temper and "laced it into Clifford in front of the whole company, saying, 'You don't seem to understand, Cliff. We don't *like* your play. We don't *want* to do your play. It has a small horizon.' " This assault instantly silenced Odets. None of the actors seemed to remember how enthusiastic had been their response to the production of his second act two summers earlier.

---

* This title seems to have become official at about this time.

According to Adler, the actors now read many scripts and agreed after a week that the situation was desperate. It was at this point that Odets called Adler into the property room and whispered to him that the Theatre Guild was interested in his play, adding, "You've got a big mouth. Get the Group company to read my play; they're reading all this crap, what can they lose?" Adler appealed to the actors on the grounds that "Cliff is one of our own; we owe it to him to hear his play," and although no one wanted to take the time to read it, the actors agreed to listen to a reading by Odets himself.

As Odets was performing the end of Act III of *Awake and Sing!*, Strasberg, Clurman, and Crawford walked in, and it was instantly evident to them that an event of importance was transpiring. "It was really impressive," Adler recalled. "I got up at the end and, without consulting the others, said, '*This* is the play we are going to do!'" The actors shouted for joy. Stella Adler, looking at Strasberg's sour expression, now shouted, according to Bobby Lewis, "Is it better to disband, and those who can get jobs will, and the rest go cold and hungry? What's the matter with this play, why shouldn't we do this play? Put it on!"

Suddenly there was no question about it. *Awake and Sing!* was to be the Group's next production, and Clurman, determined to restore the faith of the actors (Stella in particular) in him, decided to take a momentous plunge: he himself would for the first time officially direct a play for the Group. He arranged for a down payment of $225 to Odets. Frightened playwright and frightened director, by this time good friends ("Harold, I love you like a brother!" Clifford had often said), were now joined until the death of the Group Theatre would them part. Group secretary Ruth Young Eliot commented later, "I sometimes thought Clifford was really the creation of Harold."

It was not easy to raise the few thousands of dollars necessary to produce *Awake and Sing!* B. P. Schulberg, head of production at Paramount Pictures, and father of Budd (recently returned with John Howard Lawson from Scottsboro, Alabama), said to Luther Adler, "I'll give you seven reasons this play *must fail;* the most important is its Jewish messiness." "I invited him to put in five thousand dollars anyway and to sit in the front row and eat crow on opening night," Adler recalled, "so he did." Clurman, however, says, "He did *not* give us the money, but he did eat crow. He said, 'Somehow it seems so much better on the stage.'"

Clurman appealed also to Franchot Tone in Hollywood, and Cheryl Crawford to a responsive anonymous angel, and rehearsals began. Although Odets was modestly quiet during them, he kept Clurman awake night after night afterward in the shabby, bare apartment on Horatio Street, discussing the play's progress.

As 1934 drew to a close, Odets was shuttling between rehearsals of *Awake and Sing!* and his insignificant one-act "workers' play about a strike." The latter was loosely scheduled to be put on, following another one-acter and preceding a dance group, at a Sunday-night benefit for the *New Theatre* magazine, which, together with the left-wing *New Masses*, had recently run a contest for such propaganda pieces. Although Odets had not formally submitted it, *Waiting for Lefty* had been read by *New Theatre*'s discerning editor, Herbert Kline, who, lacking a better entry, had offered the $50 prize for the best forty-minute play to Odets.*

When Odets and Meisner had asked Strasberg's advice "about han-

---

* Philip Barber, later to replace Elmer Rice as the head of the New York Theatre Project for Roosevelt's Works Progress Administration, took the second prize of $25 for a fifteen-minute opus called *The Great Philanthropist.*

dling a group, an ensemble" for *Lefty*, which they were directing together, his replies had been curt. At a rehearsal which, according to Meisner, "absolutely crackled," the time came "when we had to pay our respects to the boss, the only one in the audience besides Clifford and me. We both looked eagerly at him, and Clifford said, 'Well?' Strasberg merely shrugged his shoulders. Clifford vowed that one of these days he would tell him off." To Clurman, Strasberg said privately, "Let 'em fall and break their necks."

Odets, speculating years later on Strasberg's attitude, would say,

. . . he always hated to go out on a limb. He must save face at all times. Almost Oriental. . . . Whenever the Group Theatre name was used or represented, it was as though his honor was at stake. He didn't like me, he didn't like what I had written, and he felt it would be in some way a reflection on him, on the entire Group Theatre. . . . It's almost like an older man of forty is married to a twenty-year-old girl who is gauche, he's always appalled; he, who had always lived so circumspectly, now had to stand for his wife in every area of mistake she makes . . . but Strasberg was this way about the entire Group Theatre. 'Don't use the Group . . . don't think you stand for Group Theatre . . . don't you talk about . . . ' Do I make my point? This tense, tender man, who could be so generous, sometimes could be niggardly and begrudging. It was with great trepidation I had proposed putting on this play at all.

Accordingly, the Group Theatre as such had nothing to do with the original production of *Waiting for Lefty*, although its entire cast was drawn from the company of *Gold Eagle Guy*. Odets gave up on the disdainful Strasberg, to whom he said, "You act just like my father," and decided, as the year was ending, "To hell with him. I'll just go ahead and do this myself." On New Year's Eve, Odets sent up a prayer that *New Theatre* would include *Waiting for Lefty* in its benefit evening on January 6.

Chapter Seventeen

My whole life changed in this period. Within three months I was not the same young man I used to be, but was trying to hold on to him.

CLIFFORD ODETS, *1961*

Nevertheless, we cannot but perceive that this winter did him great and lasting injury. . . . He had seen the gay and gorgeous arena, in which the powerful are born to play their parts; nay had himself stood in the midst of it; and he felt more bitterly than ever, that here he was but a looker-on, and had no part or lot in that splendid game. From this time a jealous indignant fear of social degradation takes possession of him; and perverts, so far as aught could pervert, his private contentment, and his feelings toward his richer fellows. It was clear to Burns that he had talent enough to make a fortune, or a hundred fortunes, could he but have rightly willed this; it was clear also that he willed something far different, and therefore could not make one. Unhappy it was that he had not power to choose the one, and reject the other; but must halt forever between two opinions, two objects; making hampered advancement towards either. But so is it with many men: we "long for the merchandise, yet would fain keep the price"; and so stand chaffering with Fate, in vexatious altercation, till the night come, and our fair is over!

THOMAS CARLYLE

*There seemed to be no division be-
tween my effort at personal liberation
and the apparent effort of humanity
to deliver itself.*

ALFRED KAZIN

ON THE night of the *New Theatre* benefit, Sunday, January 6, 1935, Odets
had a last-minute spat with the program committee. Its members had
finally agreed to include *Lefty*, but judged Anna Sokolow's dance group a
better climax for the evening's entertainment than this one-act play by
an unknown Group Theatre actor. The play was listed on the throwaway
leaflet without an author's name, simply as "Presented by the cast of
'Gold Eagle Guy.' " Tickets ranged from twenty-five cents to ninety cents.
Odets argued that his play would run almost an hour and that he did not
think anything should follow it, shouting in a burst of wild temper, "It
goes last, or it doesn't go on at all!" "It was very lucky they agreed," he
said later, "because there would have been no show after that."

Clurman recalled the evening:

The first scene of *Lefty* had not played two minutes when a shock of
delighted recognition struck the audience like a tidal wave. Deep
laughter, hot assent, a kind of joyous fervor seemed to sweep the
audience toward the stage. The actors no longer performed; they were
being carried along as if by an exultancy of communication such as
I had never witnessed in the theatre before. Audience and actors had
become one.

With this hastily improvised propaganda piece, which cost slightly
over eight dollars to produce, Odets, at the age of twenty-eight, had
achieved the artist's wildest dream: to present his experience to an audience in such a form that he and it would merge.◖

Odets recalled his bewilderment as *Lefty* was interrupted by wave
upon wave of tidal response from the audience:

What had happened was you were seeing theatre at its most primitive.
You were seeing it at its grandest and most meaningful. Because what
you were seeing that night in the theatre, when *Waiting for Lefty* went
on, and after each scene the audience stopped the show, they got up,
they began to cheer and weep. To my intense embarrassment. With
my friend Kazan sitting next to me—we were one of the voices in the
audience—I wouldn't have dared to take one of the parts myself, one
of the good parts. I should have liked to play the part of the young
doctor, the part Luther Adler was playing. What happened there was,
as I say . . . . the audience became the actors on the stage and the
actors on the stage became the audience, the identification was so at
one that you saw for the first time theatre as a cultural force, as perhaps in the history of the American theatre it has not been seen. . . .

◖ 17.1.

There have been many great opening nights in the American theatre, but not where the opening and the performing of the play were a cultural fact. You saw a unified cultural unit functioning. From stage to theatre and back and forth so that the identity was so complete, there was such an at-oneness with audience and actors, that the actors didn't know whether they were acting, and the audience got up and shouted "Bravo! Bravo!" and I was thinking, "Sh, let the play continue," but I found myself up on my feet shouting, "Bravo, Luther! Bravo, Luther!" In fact, I was part of the audience. I forgot I wrote the play, forgot I was in the play, and many of the actors forgot. The proscenium arch disappeared. That's the touchstone, the key phrase: *the proscenium arch disappeared.* Now later in the American theatre, and before, people have tried to do that by theatre in the round, theatre this way, theatre that way, but here, psychologically and emotionally, the proscenium arch dissolved away. When that happens . . . not by technical innovation, but when that happens emotionally and humanly, then you will have great theatre.

As he realized that the audience was expressing a passionate kinship with what he had written, Odets commenced to feel a bewildering mixture of joy, apprehension, acute embarrassment, and physical nausea so intense that he retired, trembling, to the men's room to weep and to vomit.

It is rare that a biographer finds that the memories of participants in any event are in accord. This performance of *Waiting for Lefty* is an exception: all testify that it was unique in the history of the American theatre. Professional theatre people as well as critics, searching their memories, find no premiere quite equal to it. It was not the twenty-eight curtain calls, which lasted almost as long as the play; it was not the "continuous cheering, screaming, yelling, and people going crazy," or the hats and coats people were hurling into the air at the end "like an Armistice Day," or even, as Kazan remembered it, that the "balcony, like a Niagara, seemed to roar down on the audience below." Rather, as Clurman saw it, the unanimity lay in an awareness of participating in a significant moment of history:

When the audience at the end of the play responded to the militant question from the stage: "Well, what's the answer?" with a spontaneous roar of "Strike! Strike!" it was something more than a tribute to the play's effectiveness, more even than a testimony to the audience's hunger for constructive social action. It was the birth cry of the thirties. Our youth had found its voice. It was a call to join the good fight for a greater measure of life in a world free of economic fear, falsehood, and craven servitude to stupidity and greed. "Strike!" was *Lefty*'s lyric message, not alone for a few extra pennies of wages or for shorter hours of work, strike for greater dignity, strike for a bolder humanity, strike for the full stature of man.

The audience, I say, was delirious. It stormed the stage, which I persuaded the stunned author to mount. People went from the theatre dazed and happy: a new awareness and confidence had entered their lives.

Waiting for Lefty would be more frequently produced and more frequently banned all over the world—from Union Square to Moscow, from Tokyo to Johannesburg—than any other play in all of theatre history.◖

*   *   *

◖ 17.2.

Sara Adler, wife of Jacob and mother of two leading Group members, could scarcely believe that this phenomenal evening had been provided by the mediocre young actor who used to devour her homemade bread as though he had been starved for a month. Jay Adler, who asked him for "your first autograph," recalled Odets' patient explanation to Mrs. Adler: "Well, I used to eat shredded wheat with mustard and catsup, and when I saw all that Jewish bread on your table, I'd just die." On this thrilling night this half-apology brought tears to Sara Adler's eyes.

Few members of this audience retired to their beds before dawn. They left the old Civic Repertory Theatre and drifted in joyous knots across town on 14th Street or up Sixth Avenue, walking in the street instead of on the sidewalks, kissing and hugging one another, talking and laughing, some even weeping—all too excited to go to sleep.

When someone thrust Odets' hat, its headband drenched with perspiration, into his wet hands, he and the Kazans joined one small group moving toward Stewart's Cafeteria. Sanford Meisner, his co-director of *Lefty*, retained an image "of Clifford at one of those long tables, very, very pale, tense, and absolutely quiet. He seemed almost like a person in shock . . . even depressed. It got to be quite early in the morning before we became exhausted enough to disperse. None of us had been prepared for what had happened."

Within twenty-four hours dozens of people, representing unions, anti-war and anti-Fascist student groups, and a variety of left-wing political parties, professional and amateur theatre companies, fraternal orders were besieging the offices of the New Theatre League and telephoning the Group Theatre with pleas for permission to produce *Waiting for Lefty*, and "for more plays from Odets." Herbert Kline requested photographs of the cast for the cover of *New Theatre* and announced he was writing a special article on *Lefty* to describe "the most thrilling hour I've ever spent in any theatre anywhere." In a letter to the directors of the Group Theatre he told of an unemployed man who had come to the New Theatre League office with a dollar, saying he had attended *Lefty* on a complimentary ticket and was ashamed not to have contributed anything in exchange for this phenomenal experience. Mark Marvin, head of the New Theatre League, reported that more than three hundred theatre groups had sent money for advance royalties.

A wire to Odets, signed The Workers Laboratory Theatre, states, "More guts than a slaughterhouse stop We almost wet ourselves." A follow-up letter concedes that "The Workers Laboratory Theatre, which has heretofore held the honors for vital proletarian theatre, must yield to the rank and file of the Group Theatre—and it does so gladly. But only temporarily!" It ends with a plea that Odets save it "from moral and financial bankruptcy" by providing new plays. No time was lost by the workers' theatre groups in casting Odets in the role of dramatist-Messiah for the Left.

As no one had expected anything more than an improvised *New Theatre* benefit composed of odds and ends, the "bourgeois press" had not been invited to the premiere of *Waiting for Lefty*. The dour Nathaniel Buchwald of the Communist *Daily Worker* was present, however, and, by accident, so were a critic from the Socialist *New Leader* and one from the *Morning Telegraph*.

Buchwald, with all the constricted and wary rationalism of a Communist Party member, confesses in his review that "it requires some effort to suppress the urge toward superlatives" but feels that "a sober appraisal will in the long run prove more useful to the young revolutionary dramatist

Cliff Odets."* He proceeds to congratulate him for his "uncommon ear for the American vernacular," and for turning it into "pithy, luminous and galvanizing dialogue." He approves also that the new young playwright is "propelled by his burning revolutionary fervor," which "swept the audience off its feet by the sheer power and sincerity of dramatic utterance." He must point out, however, that there is something naïve and "touchingly romantic" in this woefully loose play, whose "militant exhortations now and then deteriorate into mere sloganism." Its "strident overtones," he fears, may "vitiate his message." It is testimony to the profound negativism of the profession that this Communist critic focuses on the weaknesses in *Lefty*. Although he sees "something compelling and fascinating in the gushing fervor and driving sincerity," it rings, he says, "here and there with rasping 'leftist' overtones." He senses that here is a playwright who could be useful to the radical Left, but one who could also be a problem: a remarkable talent whose appreciation of Marxism and whose vision of a just society were more humanist and romantic than political. He is sanguine, however, that with guidance Odets will learn: "He is splendidly equipped for a young revolutionary dramatist. Technique and sober reasoning will come with practice. New as he is to the revolutionary theatre, he has already created a play that, for dramatic power and crackling dialogue, constitutes a high-water mark of the revolutionary drama and probably the most effective agit-prop play written in this country so far."

Buchwald apparently wrote to Odets, asking him to identify the cast members and, in passing, took the liberty of offering advice about the first episode in the play. Odets' immediate response, opening, "Dear Comrade Buchwald," is brief and businesslike, listing the actors in the premiere of *Lefty* (with Morris Carnovsky playing three parts, including that of Harry Fatt; Jules Garfield as Sid; Elia Kazan as Clancy; Luther Adler as Dr. Benjamin; and J. Edward Bromberg as Agate). But the letter is also deferential, closing with, "Many thanks for your valuable suggestions in reference to the first episode. With comradely greetings." Buchwald was the first, if only a minor one, of the army of critics he had long feared and from here on would try to appease.

It remained, ironically, for Henry Senber of the bourgeois *Morning Telegraph* (pinch-hitting for Whitney Bolton, who had a cold) to be the first critic to announce in no uncertain terms the arrival of an important new American playwright: "One left the theatre Sunday night with two convictions. The first was that one had witnessed an event of historical importance in what is academically referred to as the drama of the contemporary American scene. The other was that a dramatist to be reckoned with had been discovered." Unencumbered by the considerations of the *Daily Worker* critic, Senber was not troubled by "rasping leftist overtones" and could afford to say that, while *Waiting for Lefty* was "frankly revolutionary propaganda . . . it was the most exciting theatre this reporter has seen in many months," closing his review, "It has not been announced just where and when *Waiting for Lefty* will be presented again, but you can rest assured that it will be . . . soon. A play like this does not die."

Indeed, within a few days a benefit was announced for the United Workers Organizations at the Fifth Avenue Theatre, 28th Street and Broadway, featuring "two thrilling revolutionary plays." One, in protest of Hitler's false accusation of the Bulgarian revolutionary "Dimitroff," had been

---

* Odets routinely signed his letters "Clifford," not "Cliff," and never referred to himself by this nickname. Many years later his son, Walt Whitman Odets, would say, "People who refer to my father as 'Cliff' knew him as little as those who call me 'Walter.' "

written by two other members of SKKOB, Group actors Art Smith and Elia Kazan. Second billing was given to *Waiting for Lefty* and third place to the "fifty-piece symphonic orchestra of the Pierre Degeyter Club in a program of new Soviet music."

Between its first performance and the opening six weeks later of *Awake and Sing!* there were dozens of productions of *Lefty* all over the country; yellowing leaflets in Odets' scrapbook advertise performances in New York to benefit the Trade Union Unity Council, the *New Masses* and *New Theatre* magazines, and, on occasion, the Group Theatre Sinking Fund for Experimentation. Each successively dated announcement gives increasing prominence to the author's name, and finally the throwaway for the Broadway opening of *Awake and Sing!* announces it as a "new play by the author of *Waiting for Lefty*"—this despite the fact Broadway had not yet seen *Lefty*.*

One by one, the "bourgeois" drama critics were managing to attend one or another of these Sunday benefit performances even before their formal attendance at the press showing on February 10, and were reporting to their readers a turning point for the Group's role in the history of the American theatre. One said, "It can no longer be called the 'Grope Theatre.'" The critical turn issued quite simply from the fact that this articulate and gifted group of self-selected founding fathers and mothers, all pushed to the top of their considerable talent both by the economic necessity of the times and by their esthetic idealism, had now succeeded— almost in spite of its directors—in making visible its own uniquely gifted playwright.

Just before the opening of *Awake and Sing!* even the urbane and cautious John Mason Brown, critic for the New York *Post*, expressed his pleasure that at long last he had found grounds for actually "feeling the admiration" hitherto held by him in principle toward "this earnest band of players, one of the few theatrical organizations now functioning in New York which is animated by more than commercial aims." Reviewing the meritorious but somehow "forbidding" Group productions over the last four years, he contrasts them with the benefit performance of *Lefty* he saw at the Civic Repertory Theatre. Despite the fact, says Brown, that "the program was a simple one . . . which found the Groupers straying into the Red Pastures of the Theatre Union, and combining the political convictions of the Third International with the aesthetic principles of Stanislavsky . . . this benefit . . . did more than any other [production] to quicken my devotion to the Group ideal and to allow me to get some sense of what it is that as actors its players are driving at." However, he devotes as much space in his review to the initial improvisatory "five-finger exercises" as to *Lefty:* "the truly superb and completed gesturing which the Messrs. Odets, Bromberg, and Coy brought to their 'Improvised Operation to the music of Beethoven's Allegretto from the Seventh Symphony.'" From this it is evident that, with the innocence characteristic of critics, he had left the theatre without realizing that his "devotion to the Group ideal" had in fact been quickened by the arrival of a new playwright of stature.

Odets' morning mail included these days not only such elating reviews as Brown's but also a copy of *New Theatre* with photographs of *Lefty* on its cover and the full text inside. Many adulatory letters came also, one from a man Odets had earlier longed to please—a copywriter for the Odets Company. And, finally, there came an invitation from Erwin Piscator, then

---

* At the other end of the spectrum of response to Odets was a piece parodying Odets' speech rhythms, syntax, and choice of words, written by humorist S. J. Perelman for *The New Yorker* and entitled "Waiting for Santa."

president of an organization calling itself the International Union of the Revolutionary Theatre, to join in a "Fifth International Theatre Week" aimed at "uniting all revolutionary professional and non-professional theatres and attracting the widest circles of artistic intelligentsia. . . ." Clurman later said of Odets' work in this period:

> . . . the relation of his work to Marxism or Communism was of a special sort not to be understood in the terms of glib political commentary. . . . There was in it a fervor that derived from the hope and expectation of change and the desire for it. . . . "A tendril of revolt" runs through all of Odets's work, but that is not the same thing as a consistent revolutionary conviction. Odets's work is not even proletarian in the sense that Gorky's work is. Rather is it profoundly of the lower middle class with all its vacillation, dual allegiance, fears, groping, self-distrust, dejection, spurts of energy, hosannas, vows of conversion, and prayers for release. The "enlightenment" of the thirties, its effort to come to a clearer understanding of and control over the anarchy of our society, brought Odets a new mental perspective, but it is his emotional experience, not his thought, that gives his plays their special expressiveness and significance. . . . The feel of middle-class (and perhaps universal) disquiet in Odets's plays is sharp and specific; the ideas are general and hortatory. The Left movement provided Odets with a platform and a loud-speaker; the music that came through was that of a vast population of restive souls, unaware of its own mind, seeking help. . . . The quality of his plays is young, lyrical, yearning—as of someone on the threshold of life. . . .
>
> *Lefty* was not basically about the hackman's low wages, but about every impediment to that full life for which youth hungers. . . . On the one hand, Odets felt himself very close to the people—the great majority of Americans—even in his bent for the "good old theatre"; on the other hand, his heart was always with the rebels. But who precisely were the rebels, and what did they demand of him? Those he knew were a small minority, and they marked out a line for him that he could not altogether accept. . . .
>
> Perhaps the truth is that the vast majority, to which Odets felt he belonged as much as to any rebellious few, had not yet created for itself a cultural clarity or form, not to speak of other kinds of clarity or form—had not, for example, yet made for itself a theatre in which he could function freely. . . .

The battle lines, by now clearly articulated within Odets, had begun also to take shape without. The era of Roosevelt, Churchill, Hitler, and Stalin was building to a climax. And in this contracting period between two world wars his creative invention—its content and its form—reflected the international crises and tensions.

My first plays did not repair me from suicide, for by then it was no longer possible. Also, secretly not believing that the plays were good, I wanted to

*hang around and see what would
happen. Well, it turned out that I had
lighted off a couple of big firecrack-
ers; and no one was more surprised
and embarrassed than I was. Previously it was as an actor (hungering
for a good part) that I knew Lefty
and Awake and Sing were good. Acclaimed on all sides, I now knew as a
writer that the plays had real quality.
I made plans now to be a writer, not
an actor, but only with a wistful reluctance, for I was still itching for a
part.*

CLIFFORD ODETS, 1961

Despite the feverish pace of bookings for *Lefty* (even the shrewdly
commercial Shubert office wanted to read the play), Odets' focus of attention—along with the bone-weary Clurman's—was on reworking the
third act of *Awake and Sing!* for its opening on February 19 at the
Belasco Theatre. This would be his *"real* debut." Odets was building up
the boy Ralph "to a kind of affirmative voice in the end." He thought
there were "technical reasons for this change," but also, as he later said,
"the change had occurred in me too—a growing sense of power and direction. If I was going up, everything had to go up with me." Only much
later did he think he had at this time been trying "to take some kind of
real life I knew . . . and press it into some kind of ideological mold . . .
to make the materials of my plays say something they really were not
saying by tacking on certain ideological posture. . . . I think this did
damage. . . . I think very simply that the material was always richer
than the ideational direction that I tried to superimpose on it . . . it's
almost like not trusting the material." Or, more precisely, like not trusting oneself.

By this time many observers regarded Clurman and Odets as a
Damon-and-Pythias "union of egos"; they would talk in a shorthand of
half-sentences, intelligible only to each other. Clurman provided for
Odets some of the sense of morality and prophecy Tolstoy had for
Chekhov. In turn, Clurman often said, "I respect Clifford as if he were
dead." Group actors joked, "Harold is never so happy as when he is pregnant with a play of Clifford's." Waldo Frank recalled the precise moment
when it became quite clear to him, however, who was who: "One evening
Aaron Copland and I (we were both friends of Harold Clurman's)
dropped in on a rehearsal of *Awake and Sing!* I can remember Clifford
there silently glowering, but the thing that really stands out in my memory is the dialogue in the play. It had a big sign on it which said, 'This is
something important!' I whispered to Aaron that I had no doubt this production would be an historic *event.*" When Copland asked how he could
be so certain, Frank replied, "No one else alive is writing such dialogue."

Frank again and again expressed to Clurman his conviction that it
was a mistake "for so morally serious a theatre company to aspire to
Broadway." But everyone agreed that Waldo Frank was simply out of
step with the times. Had not even the staid Theatre Guild bought this

year from George Sklar and Paul Peters a piece called *Parade,* known as a "Bolshevik Revue"? As little as ten years later this purchase would seem incredible. To some it was even more incredible that Archibald MacLeish had written a poetic play called *Panic* about the banking crisis of 1933, expressing the conviction of this generation that human suffering was to be alleviated only by the extinction of the existing economic order and that such extinction was inevitable.

Even before the opening of *Awake and Sing!* Odets and Clurman abandoned their shabby place on Horatio Street for what was described as a large, modern apartment on the nineteenth floor at One University Place. With a tiny foyer, a kitchenette, a bedroom, and a large living room opening onto a terrace through two glass doors, it provided Odets with space for his burgeoning collection of books and records. "All I wanted was two clean rooms to live in, a phonograph, some records and to buy things for a girl. Nothing more I wanted," said Odets. He and Clurman were risking a joint commitment of $85 a month, more than four times the rent they had been paying. Odets paid the $16.50 for the moving truck, and caught them up on their back rent as well, out of the $225 option money he had received from the Group coffers. These expenses left them no money for furniture beyond a bed apiece, a desk and the late Beethoven quartets.

Although no production had resulted from *his* negotiations with Frank Merlin, Lou Odets was already beginning to watch ticket sales and make plans for consolidating his role in the success that was about to overwhelm Clifford. To his "genius son" he proclaimed his lifelong encouragement and his help in conceiving *Lefty* and *Awake and Sing!* He approved his son's "making a nice showing" by moving with Clurman to a "decent apartment." He would later reminisce to his grandson, "Where the hell do you think he got that play *Lefty*? There were taxi stands in the Bronx and they used to dispossess people up there . . . the rich bastards that owned those buildings would dispossess them. I remember two old Jews . . . they sold coffee cake. L.J. sent money so they could stay in their apartment another month. I used to pay those taxi chauffeurs, too. That's how it all got into *Lefty.*"

There came now many visitors to One University Place ("men like Sidney Bernstein* who attach themselves to men like Clifford"). All recall L.J.'s withering contempt for all other American playwrights: "What Clifford writes is bound to be better than those dopes Anderson, Kingsley, Sherwood, or Hellman." Some thought they detected a beginning of a childlike reflection in Odets of his father's patronizing views, and were surprised that he often let his father read his work before he put it on, and surprised, too, at how much it mattered to him still (at twenty-eight) to be finding favor in the eyes of his father.

The intensity of Odets' anger toward his father as well as his preoccupation with him seemed to the intuitive Stella Adler "girlish." To her and to many others L. J. Odets appeared to be a thick-skinned, histrionic, aggressive, and limited businessman, physically powerful and always on the move, capable of ingratiating, courtly charm and careful, correct manners. A few saw his obtuseness—indeed, his contempt. Stella Adler retained as her central image of him his paunch, his cigar, and a finger dramatically shooting out to clinch a triumphant conclusion about some business deal of his own or his son's. She was never persuaded by Clifford's

* Sidney Bernstein, lover of music, labor organizer, play producer, was the model for Lorraine Hansberry's play *The Sign in Sidney Brustein's Window.*

desperate attempts to dismiss him as "no longer important." To her it was astonishing "how long he took this father so very seriously."

Pearl Odets made it plain to her younger daughter that she, too, was anticipating a turning point. For the first time since the Depression had begun, she went shopping for herself and bought a dress to wear to the opening. More important, she hinted mysteriously to Florence that soon, soon, she would perhaps no longer be dependent on her husband, and that Clifford would not require any more secret handouts. In fact, there was a possibility (she could hardly bring herself to breathe it aloud lest God hear and cancel the whole thing) that her black-sheep son would soon have the power to rescue her from the interminable thralldom of her marriage and would set her up in an apartment in New York, free at last to have opinions of her own. She would no longer need to cover up for her incompetent son who had caused her such pain.

Lou Odets had no inkling of his wife's fantasies of escape. He was sorely missing being the "big executive of an advertising agency that did over twelve million dollars a year business." To the rabbi of the Temple Knesseth Israel in Philadelphia he explained that his son "has a vivid imagination" when the rabbi, after seeing Lefty, said, "You know, Mr. Odets, if I didn't know you, I would believe your son grew up in a poor family." Lou, despite his concern about his slipping credit rating, was still managing to impress the rabbi.

As the opening night of Awake and Sing! approached, the actors began to buzz and fret, but with that special vitality that infuses a company when it has some intimation it is about to bring forth vigorous issue. Abner of the Philadelphia Bibermans was "on the book," taking notes for Clurman during the rehearsals and recalled the high excitement running through the Group. Franchot Tone remembered Cheryl Crawford's joy in several long-distance phone calls to him in Hollywood, where he was busy playing a Bengal lancer in a film: "Harold's been working with Clifford," she told him, "and we have a fine full-length play." Bored with being a film star and lonely for the Group, Tone later said that he had sent $8,000 (Clurman says it was $5,000) without even reading Awake and Sing! "It seemed," Tone said, "it was a justification for my having stayed in Hollywood. I wish I had never left the East and the Group."

After the dissolution of his marriage to film star Joan Crawford, Tone would eagerly return to the Group; in the meantime it salved his creative conscience and fed his sense of potency to be the chief angel backing the Group's own playwright. Odets, ever competitive with Tone, was struck by the prodigious power his rival had acquired as a "movie star," a brand of power revered and coveted by Lou Odets.

For the opening night of Awake and Sing! on February 19 Clifford had invited his parents and sisters from Philadelphia. Florence recalled it as a uniquely festive occasion for the family. Through a business contact Lou Odets had got them two rooms at the Hotel Edison, and for several hours there was a truce between Pearl and Lou.

When Clifford met them at the Belasco, he appeared to his sister "bewildered, dizzy, excited" but glad to see Pearl, who for the first time in the memory of both daughters appeared happy and "so pretty in her new black long-sleeved chiffon, looking like Nazimova, and walking on air." Group actors, seeing her for the first time, were struck by her smallness, fragility, and vulnerability. "Like a shadow," Stella Adler recalled. "With Clifford's frame over her, she made him seem overpowering."

As the ensemble of nine superlative Group actors* began to create on the stage the life of the volcanic Berger family in the Bronx, the balcony, Odets said, "went wild." The orchestra audience was more restrained but sharply attentive. Alfred Kazin, who saw *Awake and Sing!* from the second balcony, speaks for those who shared it with him:

> . . . it seemed to me, sitting high up in the second balcony of the Belasco Theatre, watching Julie Garfield, J. Edward Bromberg, Stella and Luther Adler and Morris Carnovsky in Odets' *Awake and Sing,* that it would at last be possible for me to write about the life I had always known. In Odets' play there was a lyric uplifting of blunt Jewish speech, boiling over and explosive, that did more to arouse the audience than the political catchwords that brought the curtain down. Everybody on that stage was furious, kicking, alive —the words, always real but never flat, brilliantly authentic like no other theatre speech on Broadway, aroused the audience to such delight that one could feel it bounding back and uniting itself with the mind of the writer. I wanted to write with that cunning anger and flowing truth; the writer would forget his specialness, his long loneliness, and as he spoke to that mass of faces turning on in the dark, the crowd would embrace him, thank him over and over for bringing their lives out into the light. How interesting we all were, how vivid and strong on the beat of that style! Words could do it. Listening to Stella Adler as Mrs. Berger in *Awake and Sing,* I thought that never in their lives would my mother and the other Brooklyn-Bronx mamas know that they were on the stage, and that the force of so much truth could be gay. Odets pulled us out of self-pity. Everything so long choked up in twenty thousand damp hallways and on all those rumpled summer sheets, everything still smelling of the cold shadowed sand littered with banana peels under the boardwalk at Coney Island, everything that went back to the graveled roofs over the tenements, the fire escapes in the torrid nights, the food, the food, the pickle stands in the shadow of the subway and the screams of protest—"I never in my life even had a birthday party. Every time I went and cried in the toilet when my birthday came"—and now out in the open, at last, and we laughed.
> . . . Watching my mother and father and uncles and aunts occupying the stage in *Awake and Sing* by as much right as if they were Hamlet and Lear, I understood at last. It was all one, as I had always known. Art and truth and hope could yet come together— if a real writer was their meeting place. Odets convinced me. I had never seen actors on the stage and an audience in the theater come together with such a happy shock. The excitement in the theater was instant proof that if a *writer* occupied it, the audience felt joy as a rush of power.

* Art Smith (Myron Berger), Stella Adler (Bessie Berger), Morris Carnovsky (Jacob), Phoebe Brand (Hennie Berger), Sanford Meisner (Sam Feinschreiber), Jules Garfield (Ralph Berger), Roman Bohnen (Schlosser), Luther Adler (Moe Axelrod), and J. E. Bromberg (Uncle Morty), plus Tootsie Miller (Paula Strasberg's dog).

Kazin was convinced this night by Odets' play that he himself could become a writer "without giving up my people"; Odets was not quite convinced *he* could.

There were fifteen curtain calls—a remarkable response, but a comedown from the twenty-eight for *Lefty*. Afterward L.J., very much "the sport," invited his family and some of the actors to have "a bite to eat on me" and to sit out the interminable death-watch, waiting for the reviews. Three of Clifford's competing girls came along, vying with one another in their attentiveness to Pearl Odets, whose face was radiant. She whispered to her daughter Genevieve that she wanted to shout from the rooftops, "This is my baby." All recall Clifford, pale, restless, walking to the newsstand to see if the morning papers had yet arrived with their ultimate judgment on him.

The immediate critical response to *Awake and Sing!* in the "bourgeois press" was respectful, but the reviews were not generally what are called, in the world of theatre, "money notices," those which attract long lines of ticket-buyers on the day after an opening.

Brooks Atkinson wrote in *The New York Times* that "After experimenting with scripts from several different hands, the Group Theatre has found its most congenial playwright under its own roof," adding, however, that "Although he is very much awake, he does not sing with the ease and clarity of a man who has mastered his score." Four years later, after Odets' immense success, he would write in apology that *Awake and Sing!* cannot be "praised too highly." Walter Winchell, already ecstatic, predicted that Odets would one day be listed "among the theatre's Somebodies." Other critics thought he had already outstripped O'Neill and called him an American Chekhov. Pearl Odets was delighted when her son's name was coupled with the Russian playwright's; she had never heard of the other writer to whom he was compared, Sean O'Casey.

Even those who were unmoved by what one called his "synthetic Jewish realism" found his dialogue matchless and called him a playwright of "limitless promise." Several critics favorably compared his "hard and forceful" play to Shaw's "vague and gentle" *Simpleton of the Unexpected Isles*, produced by the Theatre Guild the same week. Critic Robert Garland wrote, "While its misguided mother, the Theatre Guild, runs around in circles with the retired old radical known as Bernard Shaw, its up-and-doing offspring takes up with the mettlesome young mischief-maker whose *Waiting for Lefty* is already the talk of the town below the Macy-Gimbel line."

The sensitive, often carping Stark Young wrote in the *New Republic* that *Awake and Sing!* showed great promise and exacted his "definite and constant" attention. Troubled, however, by the "stridency and ugliness" of the first act, he saw deeply into one aspect of Odets' personal struggle:

What the play lacks is a deep basis in the dramatist's own conception. What life, beneath the incidental, has he in mind? What, for instance, does he think of their constant patter about getting on, in money, in advantages when all the time there lie within his Jews' grasp their own marvelous inheritance? Are we to weep because this family that might have possessed one of the great racial traditions of the world, its poetry and prayer, are sour because they cannot have Packards?

Joseph Wood Krutch, on the other hand, told the *Nation*'s readers that this play, "despite its tragedies," was exhilarating because it had none of the "despairing sadism" of the Hemingway "hard-boiled school," adding, "As soon as one generation of writers has demonstrated to its own satisfaction that it is no longer possible to admire anything in human nature or to hope for anything in it, another comes along and does both." He saw Odets as standing at a personal crossroads and wondered whether he would go off into specifically "revolutionary drama" or would remain with the essentially humanist tradition he had followed in *Awake and Sing!*

John Gassner recalled a pained private visit from Odets, who had come to ask what the critic had meant when he expressed the hope that in Odets' future work there would be more "awaking and singing" than by a self-centered young woman running off to Havana with a crippled racketeer. Gassner had found inorganic, also, the "tacked-on political optimism" in the play. "Odets listened to me intently, to try to learn what I had in mind," said Gassner. "He knew I thought him a major talent. . . ."

The left-wing press was much harder on Odets. For example, the *Daily Worker* in English and the *Freiheit* in Yiddish, again represented by the doctrinaire Buchwald, apologized for this "politically muddled" play, explaining that it had been written before *Lefty*, and dismissed it as a "confused family play, a step backward for Odets" and "a comedown for the Group Theatre, an unimportant play whichever way you look at it." But Abe Cahan in the Jewish *Daily Forward* disagreed, calling it "one of the most important happenings in the life of the American Theatre."

Deeply wounded by Buchwald's attack, Odets ingenuously renewed his defensive correspondence with the Communist critic, in the first of a lifelong series of naïve and fruitless efforts to set up an exchange with the very group he felt to be his "natural enemy," the critics. His efforts to disarm the pompous Buchwald failed as completely as his later attempts with "bourgeois" critics who would take him to task for his revolutionary programs. Buchwald's response to Odets' defense of *Awake and Sing!* was to dismiss it patronizingly as "commercial drama" and "a step in the wrong direction."

Writing in the *New Masses*, the young left-wing critic Michael Blankfort told *his* readers that *Awake and Sing!* was peopled by "well-documented and well-observed puppets." However, despite its grievous *ideological* faults, which he proceeded to detail, he thought it worth seeing for its dialogue, which he found "pointed, fresh, and convincing . . . flowing with juicy images." He nonetheless experienced as a serious flaw in "a revolutionary play" its author's self-conscious studding of it with "wisecracks, gag lines and gag characters." Withal, Blankfort concluded that Odets' "sure theatrical sense" could one day be harnessed into "as sure a revolutionary understanding."

Decades later, reviewing Odets' development as a playwright, Blankfort would say:

Here, really without knowing it, I detected the first of the cleavages —the struggle between the outside and the inside, the reach to excite an audience and the need to be one's own man. How many tricks is an artist permitted before he becomes less the artist and more the pro? In my review I remarked about the forced dialogue for effect. . . . When I [later] reviewed *Paradise Lost*, a better play, I thought, I felt he had overcome this flashy fault. I was unpopular in some quarters with both reviews, since the communist group and fellow travelers, of whom I was one, liked the first play and hated the second one, and I was dropped as a reviewer.

It will be forever to the credit of playwright John Howard Lawson that, despite his own left-wing political convictions, he did not share the left-wing press's patronizing attitude toward Odets. Arthur Vogel recalled the Sunday following the opening of *Awake and Sing!*:

This writer happened to be a guest in Lawson's home in East Moriches, L.I., during that fateful week when Odets' *Awake and Sing* opened. When the Sunday *Times* Drama Section arrived, everyone was eager to learn what Brooks Atkinson had to say about the new author. Lawson, who had hitherto been the Group's foremost playwright, settled down to read about the Group's new star. One of our circle, who had already read Atkinson's piece, insisted on offering to show me the original draft of Lawson's *Success Story*, where I could find out who had created the type of dialogue credited to Odets. Suddenly Lawson looked up angrily and snapped, "Stop it! That isn't important. What is important is that a great new talent has arrived and has forced even the hostile critics to take notice of social drama."

Brooks Atkinson wrote in a Sunday piece in *The New York Times:*

If there is any trend in today's theatre it is the vigorous advancement of the drama of the Left. The revolutionary theatre is forging ahead. . . . In short the theatre of the Left is becoming increasingly dynamic and is no longer a skirmish on the fringe of the theatre, for it has a coherent program which the Broadway theatre has always lacked, and it is inflamed with a crusader's zeal. It knows where it intends to go; and it does not doubt its ability to get there. The Broadway theatre has no program and no convictions; and in the midst of a vast social upheaval it has no comment to make. . . .

During the 1930s, thousands of persons eager for such comment in the theatre attended "revolutionary" dance recitals, concerts, and plays, frequently in large theatres like the Center Theatre in Radio City, and often for the benefit of left-wing organizations like the Communist *Daily Worker*, the International Ladies' Garment Workers Union, or the Friends of Biro-Bidjan.*

Never before nor since has American drama so sharply reflected the great value cleavages history was creating. Symptomatic of a reaction against the crusading zeal of the drama of the Left was the formation of a company of talented newcomers to the theatre, calling themselves the Stage Associates. They could see the merit in working collectively and with continuity. They deplored, as the Group did, commercial type-casting and the hit-flop economics and psychology of Broadway, but they insisted that they wanted to convey "no message, no program of propaganda." This company, which included such gifted young actors as

---

* Biro-Bidjan, a desolate settlement in Siberia on the Trans-Siberian railroad, was the short-lived solution to the problem of Jewish self-determination in the Soviet Union.

Henry Fonda, James Stewart, Mildred Natwick, and Burgess Meredith, announced that it wanted only to present its members in new plays. Scolding the Stage Associates roundly for the assumption that plays "exist in a void," *New Theatre* predicted that "as the social crisis becomes more acute, they . . . will have to decide whether to support fascism and cultural reaction in the theatre . . . or whether to combat such destructive forces." The Stage Associates promptly went out of business.

Odets became in a few short weeks not only the hope of the vigorous movement on the Left in the theatre, but also the serious man of the hour on Broadway, where *Three Men on a Horse* was convulsing its audiences with laughter. In less than ninety days he would have three plays running simultaneously. Nonetheless, this first production of *Awake and Sing!*, despite a snowballing of excellent reviews and nominations for the Pulitzer Prize in weekly magazines and syndicated columns, closed after 184 performances—by no means a flop, but certainly not a smash hit.* Strasberg felt vindicated in his negative judgment of Odets.

The continuing wild response of audiences to *Lefty* determined the Group directors to bring it uptown, but since it was not even an hour long, Clurman asked his roommate to write a companion piece for it. Stella Adler recalled with what workmanlike alacrity Odets agreed to do this: "He was a real theatre man . . . where there was a need, he would always meet it. If you needed a part, a rewrite, a sketch, a monologue, you'd never be stranded. He'd start with a character and he'd burst with that. He'd always start with people, and people had other people." For this assignment he decided—in this second year of the Nuremberg racial laws—to dramatize what purported to be an actual letter from Nazi Germany which he had read in the *New Masses*.

With the dispatch of a journeyman Odets worked swiftly and steadily, as he had on *Lefty*, completing *Till the Day I Die* in five days. It was one of the earliest anti-Nazi plays† to reach the American stage and during World War II would document for the Office of War Information (rejecting his application for a writing job) that Odets had been a "premature anti-fascist." Some in the Group, though grateful for his speed, thought five days too short a time to result in anything but an "agit-prop" melodrama. Others, like Clurman, recognizing its faults, found in it qualities of "youthful sweetness and idealism."

The potent, presumably true story smuggled from Berlin to Prague was of a German Communist arrested for underground work. He was tortured, but told the police nothing, and after a few weeks was released before the rest of his comrades. Suspicious of his early release, the comrades in his district guarded against the possibility of his having turned informer by avoiding him. Arrested a second time and tortured to reveal names, he was mocked by the Nazis with the fact that his comrades no longer trusted him. The man continued silent, but less firm. Penniless, he accepted money and clothing from the Nazis and returned to his dis-

---

* An inconsequential miniature, *The Old Maid*, not considered by the critics to be even a contender for the Pulitzer Prize, won it.
† An earlier one was Elmer Rice's *Judgment Day* in 1934, inspired by the Reichstag fire trial in 1933.

trict. The Nazis followed him, and whomever he spoke to, they arrested. He realized he was becoming a traitor inadvertently. His life now intolerable, he asked his brother to kill him. His brother consented, and thus was the man destroyed by the bloody tyranny he sought to overthrow. A German writer, F. C. Weiskopf, had turned this agonized account into a quasi-documentary "letter" for the *Neuen Deutschen Blätter,* subsequently translated in the editorial office of the *New Masses.**

Odets' choice of this particular piece about the spreading nightmare was far from random. He had had no direct experience with German fascism or—despite his brief and romantic Communist membership —with any serious political underground. He was, however, on hotly familiar terms with the rising international anxiety infecting all, Jews and non-Jews alike, who opposed Adolf Hitler's proposals for meeting Germany's and the world's crisis. On a level less available to his direct awareness, he was no stranger to the struggles between an idealist (conceived in the play as weak, "shy as a girl") and a cruelly seductive tyrant. He knew also the sequelae involved in trust, betrayal, rage, guilt, fear of loss of integrity, and a wish to commit suicide. And, finally, this was the year during which the closed gates to the "gay and gorgeous arena" of Success appeared at last to be swinging open. He longed for this success and yet feared the consequent isolation from his comrades; in his heart he knew that they soon would feel betrayed by him, precisely as did the comrades toward his protagonist in *Till the Day I Die.*

Thus, even in these hastily written seven scenes protesting the outrages in Germany, Odets' old unconscious fantasies and his personal "character as fate" emerge. His hero, violinist Ernst Tausig, the innocent revolutionary, is interrogated by a musically literate, lonely, and homosexual Nazi, Captain Schlegel.† When it appears that the agonized Ernst—whose hands duplicate the delicacy of Odets' own—will not be a cooperative witness and will not identify his comrades, the Nazi interrogator begins by taunting him—as so often Odets' father had—and ends by destroying his capacity to create music with those hands. On the surface in this scene there is apparent the terror that Odets' father's values will overwhelm him, endangering his capacity to write. Less obvious is his half-wish to be thus sadistically overwhelmed and to be freed of active responsibility for his talent. He describes his hero, it will be recalled, as "shy as a girl." Even L.J.'s view of his wife is included in this scene ("your slut of a mother"):

SCHLEGEL: I hear you're a musician of sorts.
ERNST: Yes.
SCHLEGEL: Play an instrument?
ERNST: Formerly the violin.
SCHLEGEL: Such sensitive hands. Hold them up. (ERNST *does so.*)
    So filthy. Put them on the desk. (ERNST *does so.*) So, a scraper
    of catgut. Now, what I have against the communists is—
    (*holding and turning* ERNST's *jaw in his hand*)—the snout-
    like narrowness of their non-Nordic jaws. The nostrils display
    sensual and voluptuous self-indulgence, talking with the aid

---

* Four years later Weiskopf threatened suit, claiming Odets had lifted his material. Lawyer Arthur Krim settled this claim out of court for $250 and twenty-five percent of future income from *Till the Day I Die.*

† Almost the same words that Odets wrote for Captain Schlegel were used seventeen years later by the House of Representatives Committee on Un-American Activities in its interrogation of Odets in trying to determine which Group Theatre members had joined the Communist Party.

of hands and feet; non-Nordic characteristics. (*Walking away from* ERNST, *wipes his hands on a handkerchief.*) . . . A violin is an eloquent instrument. Perhaps you are familiar with Beethoven's Opus sixty-one, the violin concerto. Answer yes or no.

ERNST: Yes.

SCHLEGEL: In the key of D? (*Having taken rifle from* ORDERLY'S *hand, he suddenly brings down the butt of it on* ERNST'S *fingers, smashing them. Roars:*) With the JOACHIM CADENZA? (ERNST, *writhing with pain, puts his smashed right hand under his left armpit and almost faints.* CAPTAIN SCHLEGEL *now roars the rest:*) And if you think that's the end, let me tell you by tomorrow you'll find your neck half broken instead of three lousy fingers!!! Stand up straight! Do you hear me? (ERNST *straightens up.*) Put your hand down. Put it down!!! (ERNST *slowly does so.*) In ten minutes your old slut of a mother won't know you. (*Suddenly, softly:*) Unless you answer my questions. (*Waits.*) You refuse . . . ?

ERNST (*finally, controlling his pain*): I have nothing to say.

Once more in *Till the Day I Die*, and not for the last time,* Odets re-creates in a play a pure, moral being—be he an artist or a fighter against tyranny—who is rendered creatively impotent, driven to suicide, or simply murdered by a malignant power. Here, as later, he is fascinated by the character embodying this power and has to struggle formally to keep the Nazi captain from "running away with the play."

His rage at this power—be it his father, capitalism, a gangster, corrupt unionism, Naziism, or general Evil—and its interference with innocent growing things† is matched by a masochistically savage, even voluptuous, fantasy of submission to being crippled, castrated, or killed by this same power.◗ Odets identifies himself simultaneously with the predator and with his victim.

Odets' departures from, and elaboration of, the original *New Masses* letter offer glimpses into the transpositions inherent in the creative process. For example, he creates new characters: a stock, fat Nazi detective "in a trench coat and a brown derby" (played by a talented twenty-four-year-old unknown, born Leo Jacob, stage name Lee J. Cobb) and the sadistic but civilized Nazi, Captain Schlegel, "a man like Goering" who bemoans the fact his countrymen are afraid even to attend a concert of the lieder of Hugo Wolf. The freshness in this somewhat stereotyped character lies not so much in his sensitive musical taste, his homosexuality, or his eruptive violence, but in the combination of all of these with his acute and visible loneliness. To his limp-wristed partner, Adolph, he confides, "I'm lonely, I've got no one in the whole world." When Adolph responds, "You've got me, Eric," Schlegel says, most unexpectedly in this anti-Nazi play, "Hitler is lonely too. So is God." We can add this startling piece of empathy with Hitler to the growing evidence for a significant identity-element in Odets, drawn from his father and put into this central character. This second of the seven scenes closes with the cruel but seductive Schlegel's mistrust of all human relationships ("You're as fickle

---

* In *Golden Boy* Joe Bonaparte has the same internal struggle; here, as in *Lefty*, it is still formally externalized.

† A minor character (played by Elia Kazan) used to be, before Hitler, "a peaceful man who planted tulips" and played trios. His name is Baum, which in German means "tree."

◗ 17.3.

as a girl," he says to his homosexual partner. "You know that song by Hugo Wolf, I wish all your charm was painted"). As there is no hint in the original Weiskopf letter of a preoccupation with music or with homosexuality, it is clear this is Odets' contribution.

The third scene opens in the barracks room of the famous Nazi "Columbia Brown House" of torture, where two troopers are playing pinochle and hotly arguing whether it is better to be "practical" or more "on the student side . . . artistic." They punctuate their debate by savage assaults on an aged prisoner. The scene ends with the "practical" trooper reading a quotation in the newspaper from Herr Doctor Goebbels: "The head of a prominent Jew must be displayed on every telegraph pole from Munich to Berlin." He adds then, "No dreamy stuff, Weiner. That's practical," and the scene closes with "a scream heard from below." Odets represents here the fantasy that the cruel forces of practicality and anti-dreaminess will behead the dreamy Jew—the outcast, the artist: in short, himself. At the same time it is the powerful, practical father fighting the dreamy son's "idealistic self-determination. The communication is at once historical and familial, and the formal inventions which bind him to an audience accommodate to the creative necessities.

In the fourth scene we are introduced to a more conflicted and more cynical Nazi, Major Duhring, who is partly Jewish. This character, a more literal projection of the twenty-eight-year-old Odets' unconscious view of the struggling identity-elements in himself, is described as a "tired, civilized man" who has lost his "social ideals" and has married into a fine old (pure) German family. He becomes the mouthpiece for that part of Odets' inner dialogue which recommends a bitterly resigned joining with, and submission to, the powers that be, the "enemy." Protesting to the hero that "The work I do for the National Socialists harms no foe of the Nazi state," Duhring warns him that "They'll get what they want out of you," and that he will several times be beaten to "within an inch of death" and then nursed back to health in order to force him to "name names." Duhring is the apologist within Odets who is convinced that his cowardice forces him into compromises which, though in themselves harmless, are unendurably humiliating and point to tragic ends. When the revolutionary Ernst insists he will not turn informer ("I will remember my proletarian task"), the sad and tired Major responds, "It's possible you may forget your proletarian task. Don't smile. A man's made of flesh and bone."

Although Odets had no inkling of the grave moral tests, as man and as artist, which lay ahead of him, including even literal interrogations such as this one by a government official, he was here rehearsing a test he even then sensed as urgent: Would he, *in his work,* forget his self-defined "proletarian task"? He had already rejected several Hollywood offers and been congratulated in the press for his esthetic and moral integrity. The tired Major, accused by the idealist Ernst of being a man tortured by conscience, advises the young revolutionary that it would be easier to shoot himself at once than to struggle with betraying his comrades. At this point the all-German homosexual Nazi returns and taunts the melancholy part-Jewish Major with his "family tree," calling him a coward, as so often L. J. Odets had called his son. Captain Schlegel says, "The first instinct of the Jew is to run," whereupon the tired Major shoots the Captain dead (an action that says: *I am not a coward. Proof is that I kill you*).

Saying he is "slimed over with rottenness" and that "the contradictions of my own nature have backed up on me," the desperate Major

Duhring now begs the young revolutionary to have his smashed fingers fixed (this is Odets advising himself not to abdicate his creative life), and removing his Nazi armband, he commits suicide, putting the gun in his own mouth. (If you "murder" your father to prove your bravery, you will pay with your own life.)

Scene 5 opens with Ernst, temporarily released by the torturing Nazis, in the apartment of his girl. He has been mercilessly whipped. His shirt is stuck to his bloody back, and Tilly "holds him as a mother might do with a child," her slightest effort to cleanse his wounds being intolerably painful. At first, denying to her his terror of the cruel tyrants, he then bursts forth, "I'm afraid, Tilly. . . ."❡ He knows he will be seized again, and again the seductive bribing sessions will alternate with torture.

He wants "one hour of peace," and wistfully says he has remained alive only "because I knew my comrades were with me in the same pain and chaos." Yet he believes—and from this issues the play's title—that "till the day I die there is no peace for an honest worker in the whole world." To this, Tilly, who has counseled him not to be "afraid of softness, of sorrow," responds with, "Till the day we die there is steady work to do. Let us hope we will both live to see strange and wonderful things. Perhaps we will die before then. Our children will see it then." Odets here adjures himself to work and to resign himself to a steady struggle. His statement and her response are formally and psychologically equivalent to the title *I Got the Blues* becoming *Awake and Sing!*

Ernst is far more excited by Tilly's news that "In France they have joined to make a solid front against the fascists" than by her news she is carrying his child: "Our work is bearing fruit? In that beautiful classic country. The united front? Oh Tilly, oh Tilly!! (*And suddenly he is crying in the pillow for all his pains and for the joy of this news.*)" Tilly "soothes him with understanding." The fruit of their joint work—a brotherhood against tyranny—has far more significance for him than their biological child. These are the priorities of the artist.

The sixth scene opens with a meeting of the comrades, who, over his girl's protest, are blacklisting Ernst as an informer. A poignant note is sounded in the figure of a minor character (to be played by Lee Strasberg*), old "Stieglitz," named after the venerated photographer and guru whose American Place gallery had become a symbol of esthetic idealism in the United States. In Odets' play Stieglitz' "noble mind" has been broken by the Nazis. Arguing passionately that there is no reason to assume Ernst has turned informer, Tilly reads from his letter:

They are taking my life by the inch. Day and night they press me for an answer—identify prisoners or be killed. I cannot last much longer. The terrible truth is they do not kill me. I am enclosing money which they handed over to me yesterday after forcing me to sit beside their chauffeur when they made a street raid. You may be sure I have kept my mouth shut.

To the accompaniment of the andante of Mozart's Sonata in C-Major ("a very wholesome beautiful key") being played by an old uncle and his friend, whose "poor old hearts" have been turned . . . to water" in Hitler's Germany, Ernst's brother Carl recalls that this was "the first piece of Mozart my brother and I ever played together," apologizing for this "irrelevant excursion into sentiment." Carl, "suddenly turning hard,"

❡ 17.4.
* Under the stage name "Lee Martin."

asks bitterly if there is time for music today and concludes that in their struggle "for true democracy" many a comrade has learned that "he has no home, no brother—even no mothers or fathers!" Yes, "it is brother against brother." The betrayer must be exposed wherever he is met: "Whosoever looks in his face is to point the finger. Children will jeer him in the darkest streets of his life! Yes, the brother, the erstwhile comrade cast out!"

Here, as in *Lefty*, where a brother betrays a brother ("He's my own lousy brother," says Clancy), Odets identifies with the homeless men and women, the insulted and the injured of Nazi Germany, by way of his own sense of homelessness. Consciously he had replaced his own family with the Group Theatre, extending this—through his romantic membership in the Communist Party—to working people, generally. A comrade closes the scene with "There is no brother, no family, no deeper mother than the working class. Long live the struggle for true democracy!" Even Ernst's girl-comrade, Tilly, now slowly raises her hand in agreement that he be blacklisted. She, too, places this symbolic "brotherhood" above her personal tie to Ernst.

Odets was writing this not long after he had embraced Clurman, saying to him, "Harold, I love you like a brother." But in the meantime Clurman was increasingly troubled by phone calls he overheard from film companies to Odets, who, said Clurman, "like a conspirator" would conduct his end of the conversation in whispers. Although Odets was turning down all offers, his future as a playwright remained a central concern for Clurman, who was preparing for another brief trip to the Soviet Union.

Till the Day I Die closes with a confrontation between the two brothers. Ernst, his hand amputated, recognizes the practical necessity that he be blacklisted. But he is determined to persuade his brother privately that he is not a traitor* by telling him the true story of how the Nazis planned to force him to inform by turning his brothers against him:

> They dressed me up. That was the plan, to look like a paid stool pigeon. Then the first leaflet appears: "Ernst Tausig is a paid stool pigeon." Who printed them? Comrades? No, the Nazis. . . . They have a detective taking me home at nights. I live in his house. I can't understand. They did something to me. Sulphur is running in my veins. At night I wake up perspiring. My tongue is thick, my eyes won't open. . . . I must have someone believing me. I'm not a traitor. I'm not so far gone I don't understand the position I'm in. I see what you must do to me. Warn all party members against me. You can't know the truth. Yes, what is one person like me against the whole enslaved German working class? I know I must be cast away. But you two [Carl and Tilly] can believe me.

Directly following this speech, his brother notices the smell of perfume on him. Ernst, in a daze, explains:

> No, you see how it was. They gave me money. It falls out of my hands. My mind wanders like smoke. I passed the store the other day and it was in the window. Perfumed soap. I bought some. A man must have something. It smells like flowers.

---

* This sequence of events chillingly forecasts what Odets would do over the years and in 1952, when he distributed copies, reprinted from the *Congressional Record*, of the House Un-American Activities Committee proceedings to prove his innocence.

All his life Odets apologized this way for what he called his smaller "consolatory" pleasures: flowers, wine, French soap, talcum powder, Martinson's coffee.

Ernst now concludes that he has been tortured for so long that he is in fact about to betray his comrades; he pleads with his brother, "Kill me!" Carl refuses, saying Ernst must do this for himself. The change here, dictated by Odets' own psychological necessity, is that his brother does not kill him as in the original *New Masses* letter. Ernst commits suicide, having said: ". . . . soon all the desolate places of the world must flourish with human genius . . . a world of security and freedom is waiting for all mankind!" His last words are "Do your work, comrades." Although in the play this manifestly refers to political work, Odets doubtless means creative work.

The final exchange is between Ernst's brother and his girl:

TILLY (*for a moment stands still. Then starts for room.* CARL *stops her*): Carl, stop him, stop him. (CARL *holds her back.*)
CARL: Let him die. . . .
TILLY: Carl. . . . (*Shot heard within.*)
CARL: Let him live. . . .

SLOW CURTAIN

This is similar to the ending of two of Odets' later plays. In *Golden Boy* a boxing champion commits suicide and is, in death, "home, at last." And in *The Big Knife*, after the suicide of a movie star, his friend says, "He . . . killed himself . . . because that was the only way he could live. You don't recognize a final . . . a final act of faith . . . when you see one."

In the month between the opening of *Awake and Sing!* and that of the double bill of *Lefty* and *Till the Day I Die* at the Longacre on March 26, the Odets vogue gathered momentum. The telephone at the barely furnished University Place apartment was rarely silent. Newspapers carried reports of Odets lunching with publishers, with motion-picture executives, with columnists, with magazine writers, with his newly acquired agent, Harold Freedman of Brandt and Brandt. Small news items in his scrapbook report the astronomic weekly salaries for screen writing— ranging from $500 to $2,500—that he is daily refusing. One account describes an offer to take the entire Group Theatre to Hollywood for a filming of *Awake and Sing!*: the New York *World-Telegram* states in astonishment, "Not a word was said about deletions, nor was there any mention of tempering the old gent who preaches Marx and who sleeps under a pastel of Sacco and Vanzetti in the drama at the Belasco."

It was beginning to appear to the ingenuous Odets that he could dictate his own terms even in Hollywood, making no compromises. Nonetheless, "doping myself with music," he kept reiterating that he wanted to remain in New York and write plays "if I can make a living here." He had already begun to send money, in amounts entirely disproportionate to his actual income, not only to his parents but to Uncle Israel, Aunt Esther, and, at their request, to their son, Ben. For the first time in his life he was able to do what he had often seen his father do: "to be a sport and pick up the check" for half a dozen people in a restaurant. Candidates for this indiscriminate largess, as well as for large loans, were, in these impoverished times, plentiful. It was easy to accept money from Odets, since he seemed to take delight in giving it. He spent little on himself, and when he did, it was mostly on records and books. Occasionally he indulged himself in the secret luxury of a cake of Yardley soap or the public one of a pair of elegant suede gloves or a "really good suit."

It puzzled and disturbed Clurman that Odets appeared increasingly irritable, isolated, morose, and, in trifling matters, stingy. He began to snap at Clurman and to express resentment at being drawn into his endless difficulties with Stella Adler. With Strasberg he quarreled openly, calling him "a big shit" for insisting on casting his wife, Paula, in *Lefty*. Strasberg's earlier contempt for him as writer still gnawed at him. Moreover, as happens often in sudden fame and success, old friends backed off in defensive or competitive hostility while new ones intensified his isolation by treating him like a Messiah. Odets felt more alone than at any time since he had found the Group.

To Lucius Beebe, interviewing him in his bare apartment, he seemed bewildered. He confided that, walking down Broadway, a pile of press clippings in his hand, he had turned to his friend Jules Garfield, saying, "You know, it's like seeing my clothes walking in front of me with a hat stuck on top. Everybody is talking about Clifford Odets, but it doesn't seem to be me at all."

His bargaining power even as an actor had increased enough so that, at long last, he was able to persuade the directors to let him replace Luther Adler, now busy in *Awake and Sing!*, in *Waiting for Lefty*. As Dr. Benjamin, dropped from a hospital staff because he is Jewish, Odets filled the last acting assignment of his career.

Pearl Odets, delirious with joy and a bit bewildered, commuted from Philadelphia to see many performances of *Awake and Sing!* Her slender figure was often seen at the back of the theatre and in the ladies' room of the Belasco between acts, seated shyly, stiffly on a chair, her large eyes shining, simply listening to the praise for her son. Once she said, "After I heard them all say over and over, 'Isn't he wonderful?' I said to myself, 'Oh my God,' and went skipping down the street." This was remarkable behavior for a woman who, her daughter thought, "had not even *felt* like skipping since maybe she was ten years old."

In one of her two letters preserved by Odets she wrote:

Dearest Clifford,
    Just a few lines to let you know that we are well. Hope you are the same. don't say a word, but since I became a playwrites Mother I havent time to breath, not alone write, more people call me to congratulate on my Sons great success, than you have any Idia. Im just all talked out by now. . . . I really deserved of this happiness I only wish that somehow I could be near you. I hope you feel the same. I dont mean to be in your way in, but I feel in myself, something just tells me I can help you a great deal. At any I can truthfully say that tomorrow is thirty years that Im married, and this is the happiest time of all those years. Now understand me right, my Son, never once have I thought of the money end of it so help me God, to see you well and happy. Im coming to New York this weekend, please let me express some of my Idias to you, Im so nervous I cant write with ink pleas excuse, everybodys love
                                                                Mother

A week later she dares to put into words her earlier suicidal despair and her present joy at her approaching freedom:

. . . in my darkest moment in winter I thought not so long ago that I was through with life only God and I know how near I came to that. so you just a human being came in time and I am sure my God that I always believe in have in my heart and mind has given me beauty and happiness and taken me out of the dust and darkness and awake and sing, in true life . . . please dont ever for one moment think that its the money end Im thinking of, because after all, Im no boss over your money and thank God I havent bee [sic] in want for many years, it just simply has changed conditions for me already, I can see the change, I wont have to retrain [sic] my feeling anymore. I also will be able to voice my opinion and have a little freedom, Im no longer afraid, Im free thanks to you, and if I live Im going to see wer [sic] you are going to be considered the greatest writer of all, and you are going to think, that you have the greatest Mother of all if some day I can have day with you alone, and now I think I have about said enough for the present are you apt to think that your great success has afected [sic] my mind some, no fear Im sane, just very very happy, and luck be with you.

No doubt the son passed over his mother's conditional clause "if I live" as the standard, wary game Jewish mothers sometimes play with God and with their children.

On March 26, the opening night of the twin bill, Odets—greeted by an ovation when he appeared as Dr. Benjamin—appeared to many as if he were even more terrified of the critics than before. He feared that *Till the Day I Die* would be torn to pieces. Over and over he walked anxiously to the corner newsstand in the early morning hours to learn his fate. As he had anticipated, most of the critics found his anti-Nazi play melodramatic, secondhand, and discursive. The left-wing press again was much harsher in its critique than men like Brooks Atkinson, who respectfully concluded his *New York Times* review, "Even with these reservations, *Till the Day I Die* is unmistakably the work of a man indigenous to the theatre." The conservative Yiddish-language newspaper *Der Tag* found it "the best anti-Nazi play yet," adding, "You get paralyzed that what you see on the stage is possible in a civilized community. It is frightening."

To Odets' considerable surprise and relief, most of the critics focused their reviews on the fact that the "poet laureate of the Group Theatre" had now demonstrated he was "a comet," a "thunderbolt," a "white hope," a "future Goliath," a "prolific boy wonder." They thought he was writing "ironfisted and exciting stuff," and Richard Watts, Jr., of the *Herald-Tribune*, announced that not "since the flaming emergence of Eugene O'Neill" had the American theatre seen such talent for dramatic writing. John Mason Brown commenced a piece with, "You may disagree violently with Mr. Odets' ultimate solutions . . . you may even resent the constant angry jabs at the pit of your social stomach . . . but you cannot

fail to realize . . . he has a sweeping, vigorous power which is as welcome as it is thundersome when encountered in our theatre."

Brown, a self-confessed Polonius, soon counseled Odets in his New
York *Post* column to "put his playwriting first and his party allegiance
second," publishing then a rejoinder from Odets which was an obsequious,
almost servile wooing of the critic:

> Please let me explain my position as a writer. It all rests in the divi-
> sion you made—the short plays and the long ones. The short ones
> have, of course, immediate functional value and are quickly written.
> But I would like to explain that they are extremely helpful studies
> in play construction and have the value of helping me write the
> long plays more effectively. They help me sort my theatre knowledge
> which lies around unassorted in my head. There is a sort of general
> housecleaning going on in my mind, a search and a drive at present
> for a strong form to fit the content of what I hope will be at least
> one good play a year.

Odets' tone is that of a contrite schoolboy promising his father or head-
master he will try to do better. He continues his appeasement:

> Mr. Brown, I read Emerson for many years. I think he is the wisest
> American who wrote, he and Whitman. . . . I believe in the vast
> potentialities of mankind. But I see everywhere a wide disparity
> between what they can be and what they are. That is what I want
> to say in writing. I want to say the genius of the human race is
> mongrelized, I want to find out how mankind can be helped out of
> the animal kingdom into the clear sweet air. How it will be done
> God knows not this young man. But I know Huey Long won't do
> it nor Father Coughlin, and I know that war is brewing all over the
> world. How many fine young men will go in this next one—mil-
> lions more!

Clearly trying to ward off attack from these omnipotent authorities on
his next play, he adds:

> I tried to say some of this in *Awake and Sing!* In the new full-
> length play, *Paradise Lost*, I have said the same things in a richer
> and more mature manner, I think . . . but you are right up to the
> hilt: the playwright must come first. I'm studying full steam ahead.
> I have five long plays laid out and one is in the typewriter. . . .

Again apologizing, he concludes:

> Finally, the two short plays took three and four nights to write. The
> Belasco piece [*Awake and Sing!*] eight months, *Paradise Lost* nine
> months. No good baby can be born in four nights and I am out for
> good babies. Nine months seems a reasonable time to me.

This naïvely cajoling letter, made public by the critic, would not, as
Odets hoped, temper the critical assault on *Paradise Lost*. Brown himself would take him severely to task for not being Chekhov. In the meantime, however, despite the mixed response to *Till the Day I Die*, the fact
that he had three vital, "electric" plays running concurrently on Broadway was universally hailed as a "record," and, according to Clurman,
"Odets in the spring of 1935 was the man of the hour." A variety of
celebrities had begun to court him not only as the dramatic find of the
day, but also because his Communist beliefs added an exotically dangerous aura to his reputation. It was said that he was frequently seen with

writers, actors, newspapermen, and composers recently fled from Nazi Germany, and that he was influenced by their "agit-prop" methods whereby people on the street were drawn into a play without knowing it.* Even the left-wing critics agreed there were few propagandists to equal him in these short pieces.

By this time the public clamor, correspondence, and phone calls had become so steady that this overnight celebrity brought in his Bronx childhood friend Herman Kobland as a full-time paid secretary to help—as he had predicted when they were unemployed youths.

Odets accepted almost all the dizzying invitations in this "gay and gorgeous arena" which now deluged him. They came from such as Eleanor Roosevelt, Alfred Stieglitz, novelist and photographer Carl Van Vechten, Tallulah Bankhead, Beatrice Lillie, Clare Boothe (not yet Luce), Edna Ferber, Aline Bernstein, Helen Hayes and Charles MacArthur, Bernard Baruch, Communist Ella Reeve ("Mother") Bloor, Fannie Brice, Dorothy Parker, Sidney Howard, Billy Rose, Ruth Gordon, Jed Harris, Walter Winchell, Clifton Fadiman, Bennett Cerf, and a great range of other celebrities in theatre and publishing, on the left and on the right. At their parties in Manhattan and on Fire Island he appeared shy, silent, out of place, and intently watching. A young movie actress was puzzled that the wild-eyed, unkempt, and brilliant young playwright seemed so overimpressed by these famous people. Dena recalled his awe at the bold excesses, drunk or sober, of Tallulah Bankhead.

With actresses Ruth Gordon and Beatrice Lillie, Odets began to develop relationships of greater complexity, and he was at a loss now to know what to do about young Dena, who still maintained, along with Helen and Alice, an abiding, if troubled, interest in him.

By the end of April enthusiastic theatre societies were being formed all over the United States and in other parts of the world to present the three Odets plays. Announced in almost a hundred towns and banned in many of them, *Lefty* became a folk symbol of high intensity, and college presidents joined with labor lawyers to fight against its being censored. Odets was called "the poet of the Jewish middle class," "the proletarian Jesus," and "the voice of the thirties." When actor Will Geer was severely beaten by the "friends of the New Germany" for producing *Till the Day I Die* on the West Coast, Odets put a heavy lock on the door of the University Place apartment, where he was now alone, Clurman and Cheryl Crawford having gone off on another exploration of theatre in the Soviet Union.

Odets' work had by now aroused an unprecedented attention from all the metropolitan dailies. Harry Kurnitz, expressing how much "pleasure a play like *Awake and Sing!* would give a reformed and only recently reformed mockie like myself," teased him in a letter about "having a secretary named Herman," and about there being an opening on *The New York Times* as "Odets Editor." It had become a commonplace for theatre writers to commence a feature story on Odets with advice to all other American playwrights, especially O'Neill, to "look to their laurels."

Carrying the Group Theatre along with him, he had been graduated into the larger American scene. Meanwhile, as he found himself paralyzed in the face of the revisions of *Paradise Lost* suggested by Clurman, he became increasingly depressed and irritable.

When he was pressed into attending a "hard-times party" at the

---

* Although the content is different, this is exactly like the Living Theatre of the late 1960s.

Group Theatre's rehearsal hall in honor of scene designer Mordecai (Max) Gorelik, his irritability was magnified by what probably seemed to him the adhesive quality of a young blonde introduced to him by an editor of Emerson Publishing Company as a co-ed from Seattle who had just won a trip to Russia. He found the party unendurable and shortly went home. But to the vulnerable young blonde, Frances Farmer, the meeting was of great significance:

> I was immediately attracted to the playwright. He was brittle and snapping, and even though our conversation was brief, a little more than a curt nod in fact, just meeting him had a deep effect on me. I managed to stand within earshot of his voice most of the evening hoping to pick up the crumbs of his opinions on art, music, and, especially, the theater.
>
> He was a brilliant playwright, surrounded by a fascinating conglomerate of skilled professionals. . . . I'm sure I went unnoticed that evening, especially to Clifford, for during our later intimate relationship, he claimed no recollection of having met me.

Within the next two years this exquisitely beautiful, principled, and gifted young woman would become an overworked Hollywood star, the leading lady in Odets' play *Golden Boy*, and—aided by Odets' dark side —in her thirtieth year the tragic paradigm of a theatre artist in America.

PART FOUR

Survival in Public

1935-1940

Chapter Eighteen

*In a funny way, his real excellence as
an artist was obscured by the political
claque.*

IRWIN SHAW

*One is born with talent or with gen-
ius, but one makes himself an artist.
Nothing is more difficult than this
process of becoming an artist. For no
matter how profound the instincts of
the young artist, society and American folk ways are a strong befuddling
drink: the creative road is strewn
with wrecks, a veritable junk yard of
old rusted bodies. Some reason for
this.*

CLIFFORD ODETS, 1940

By MID-APRIL the pile of newspapers and magazine clippings had become an avalanche unmanageable even for his secretary, and Odets,
feeling strangely "depressed, nervous, sick at heart," fled to the Half-
Moon Hotel in Coney Island. Herman had not seen him so depressed
since the suicidal days at the Circle Hotel.

With "a real Yiddish feeling about the medicinal qualities of salt
water," he watched the waves and lay in a hot salt tub for hours on end,
praying for sleep and for creative repose. Articles in *Time* and the *Wall
Street Journal*, as well as in the *New Masses, New Theatre,* and the
Daily Worker, described him as the most exciting, promising, articulate,
original, illuminating, and hard-hitting spokesman of the American
theatre, who was "providing a new kind of theatre" and who, according
to the then thriving *Literary Digest*, was "irresistible to all for his humanity, regardless of political persuasion." On all sides he was hailed as
"a combination of O'Neill, Chekhov and O'Casey" who was "electrifying
apathetic theatre goers," and as the "only new dramatist of outstanding
potential."

From the Half-Moon Hotel he wrote a reassuring letter to Lee Strasberg ("You know I wouldn't make a step with Paradise Lost before first consulting you and the others"), but in it he expressed grave doubts about the wisdom of following *Awake and Sing!* with *Paradise Lost,* as the two plays are so similar. "It turned out this way because I thought we wouldn't do *Awake.* In which case I made up my mind to write the same play, but better." If there were "several plays locked up in the collective cupboard of the Group," he would not consider letting it produce *Paradise Lost* now. It will be bad for the Group and for him as a playwright. "For this reason I've been thinking about the new play and attempting to start some work on it." The letter closes with a plea to Strasberg that at the very least the casting of *Paradise Lost* should not accent the similarity of the two works by using the same actors in corresponding roles.

He privately agreed with Strasberg, who stood almost alone in his view that a suitable and practical alternative to *Paradise Lost* would be a new play offered the Group by Maxwell Anderson, then a Group Associate. Using the Sacco-Vanzetti case to talk about American injustice, it was called *Winterset.* But Harold Clurman and Stella Adler had mocked its sentimentality and the incredibility of its Elizabethan East Side. Moreover, Paula Miller Strasberg and the few others within the Group who regarded themselves as its Marxist conscience thought the play overly romantic. And most likely Odets was by now as competitive with Anderson as he was with O'Neill. Accordingly, the Group rejected *Winterset,* which would open in the fall under other auspices. This episode opened a growing rift between Strasberg, convinced that the Group should do *Winterset,* and Clurman, who rejected it.

Odets found it harder to settle down to work on his new play, *The Silent Partner,* than at any time since he had consolidated his identity as a writer.❡ The interference with his creative processes which he would bitterly describe five years later in his diary had already begun. He did not want "to be less than the other"; he was desperate "to appear complete and upright in the eyes of his fellow Americans" and, above all (had his father not contemptuously hammered this home a thousand times?), "never, NEVER ridiculous or at a loss."

Nonetheless, following the model for an artist—as he put it—"of the womanly woman, not the shrewd businessman," he earnestly tried to keep himself "open" and productive by working feverishly on *The Silent Partner.* In this ambitious play he was further exploring the use of symbolism, of "heightened realism," and of a richer, poetic kind of language. Although it used the manifest symbols of the class struggle (two brothers leading a strike against an increasingly vicious management, and vying for the same working girl), it expressed also the artist's tireless struggle to find a form in which to master a range of new and old conflicts, conscious and unconscious, lately reopened: most prominently that between his Hebrew prophetic and American expedient souls (vying for the same "working girl") *within him.* Flaring anew were transformations of ancient mistrusts, fears of insufficient masculinity and of ridicule, terror of human closeness, and a compensatory hunger for status and power.

Most accessible to awareness stood the terror that he would be unable to maintain his recently achieved status—so gratifying to his father —as the most promising of American dramatists. At the same time it appeared to him easy to displace Eugene O'Neill, who, in the opinion of many, was humorless, cold, pretentious, and, at this point, dying as an artist. It was columnist Heywood Broun's publicly stated opinion that Odets

❡ 18.1.

was "a far greater figure than O'Neill ever was or will be." Odets' secretary called his attention to all of these views.

There is something warily abstract, constipated, and even humorless in the early drafts of *The Silent Partner;* it is as if he knew, however, that he had to keep at it, with whatever constriction, if he were not to dry up completely. In this play he uses as a symbol a band of thugs who prevent a milk delivery to the hungry children of valiant strikers. Thus the bullying, ideal-less forces of brutish business (his father) threaten the very lives of the innocent children (his creative self).

At the apogee, thus, of the year of his greatest public acclaim he knew himself to be in severe creative peril and was sleepless and consumed with anxiety.

In the same mail in which he received a headline story from *Variety* stating that "Clifford Odets Snubs Films," there were urgent requests for money—which he instantly met—from his father, from his cousin Ben, from two actors, and from several left-wing organizations. Five motion-picture studios made him astronomic offers to write films, and Lewis Mumford wrote that "no one else writing for the stage in America today has achieved your combination of strength and direction, humanity, and tenderness." A newspaper piece from Eugene, Oregon, wonders whether the theatre's "latest darling will succumb like other American playwrights to Hollywood." Finally, there was a long letter from Clurman, still en route to Europe.

The burden of Clurman's letter is that, despite his fast-dwindling bank account, "You must not go to Hollywood, now or at any other time." It had hurt him to hear Clifford even discussing the possibility with his agent. The letter is long, passionate, and eloquent:

> There are many . . . [talented people] in NY. . . . They do nothing with it but put on a little weight, eat better meals, drink better cocktails, screw fancier women, and get invited around to better parties! This applies to practically everyone, with a single exception among playwrights. This means that tho there are talents, there are no *men*. And a talent without a man behind it (and by a man I mean a person who *believes* in something, loves something and is willing to make sacrifices for what he believes in and loves). Talent without a man, I say, is sterile and ugly. It's the kind of thing America has so much of and which makes our country so miserably meaningless and empty most of the time.
>
> Now you have talent, and you must cultivate it like a child. You must respect your talent. You must work on it. Your talent can become important, but Cliff my dear friend, if it were ten times what the critics say it is, *it would still be very easy to make little of it* . . . very little. . . . I want to see you grow—really—add stature to your work, depth, and to acquire beside your facility, an ability not only to judge your work by the *highest* standards but the ability to carry through your judgment on the work itself, to perfect it to the utmost, and to acquire standards of perfection for your own material. . . . This . . . takes a whole life-time . . . one's vigilance, intelligence, energy. And therefore you can't afford to waste *any* time. Hollywood is a waste . . . only one excuse for going to Hollywood—*dire* need of money. . . . People fool themselves in America. All the Greens, Behrmans, Andersons, Lawsons . . . and their little trips to Hollywood . . . are just pissing away what they have and turning their blood to ____!

The only American playwright of any real stature is still O'Neill (even though he has become academic and dead for other reasons). O'Neill at least stuck to his last. . . . Go . . . sit under a tree . . . do nothing . . . all this may serve you . . . but a day spent working in Hollywood is a betrayal of your talent. . . . It is the great American lie—this expediency business. This is the period when you've got to take hold of yourself and realize these things really—or you'll be realizing it retrospectively and sentimentally—but too late. . . .
        . . . because I respect your talent . . . I don't want you to whore around with it. . . . In a quiet moment away from Walter Winchell, the Pulitzer Prize and the rest of the great incubus . . . called New York theatre life, you could remind yourself of what I really think about your present problem.

Odets replied he was very happy to have read Clurman's welcome letter, as it made him feel needed and responsible. The immediate result, however, was that he abandoned the exploratory, risky *Silent Partner* and returned without heart to his revisions of *Paradise Lost* in order to provide a fall production for the Group Theatre. He feared it would be badly received by the critics, but, in view of his extraordinary fame, the Group had nothing else with so much commercial potential. Only later would he become aware of the depth of his resentment at feeling thus pressured and "milked" by his redeeming family, now become simultaneously demanding parents and clamoring children.

His anger stemmed from the double jeopardy of being diverted from work on the new play and of risking a production of the flawed *Paradise Lost*. Predicting that the critical wolves would tear him to pieces for this poetic, "less Jewish" echo of *Awake and Sing!*, he was filled with anxiety.

As he worked on *Paradise Lost*, he was flooded by fantasies for disarming the critics. He would phone them, he would write them, he would educate them about the need of the young artist to grow. Perhaps they would understand and pull in their claws. The possibility of losing face, the power of status, or a generalized "respect"—like L. J. Odets' steady nightmare of maintaining his credit rating—had now become a central preoccupation. It was Odets' desperate need to "hold on" to the self-esteem provided by his father's kind of American "Success"—rather than, as commentators would later declare, his yearning for cashmere shirts and rare Médoc wines—that had begun to gnaw at his vitals in this most critical time of his creative life.

As he tried to assuage his anxiety with salt water, music, and work at the Half-Moon Hotel, he took comfort from the fact that he had "called it quits" with nineteen-year-old Dena, who wrote that she "wants a human bond, not just going to bed," and told him how much she had missed him at the May Day parade in New York City. He replied that first he *must* find "stability, order, and schedule" in his work. It pleased him also that he had instructed his secretary, Herman, to proceed with plans to move his mother, by using the remainder of his modest earnings, from Philadelphia to New York.

He had Pearl in mind in this rescue operation, but at the same time she represented that aspect of himself which had to be freed from the tyranny of his father. He was, after all, engaged in a life-or-death struggle to preserve his creative capacity by preserving within himself the "womanly woman, not the shrewd businessman." His mother, according to Mattie Washington, was "delirious with joy" at the prospect of her imminent deliverance. This emotional setting could not have been more unfortunate for the tragic event which now took place.

Four months after the incredible fact of his mother's sudden death, Odets, with the instinct of the writer, tried to master the experience by recording it:

The Death of My Mother

How often does my little sister cry in the night for her mother? I can not tell, for I have not seen her since our mother died. When I walked away from the house where it happened I knew how Napoleon felt wandering around the lost battlefield of Waterloo. He was the champion of the world—Dempsey for instance—but when he lost a fight and went back to his dressing room and sat alone while the newspaper wires were flashing the news of his defeat around the world, he had a feeling and it was not good.

So when I walked out of the house where my mother had died I had a feeling and I knew to myself that I would never come back there again. Now I know I'll go back to the house, for I must find myself again. I mean in reference to my mother. For she has been dead for four months and I can't believe it. I didn't see her die and I can't believe it. I have been used for a long time not to seeing my family for months at a time. So in reference to my mother I keep thinking that when I go back to Philadelphia she will be there in the house and it will be one of our old reunions. She will look at me with brimming tender eyes and she will touch me with the hands of a woman who finds fulfillment only in her son's success in the world.

But I want to make this clear: when I go back to the house this time she won't be there, and I will know she is dead. Yes, she is forever dead. I have had certain incredulous moments in the night time when I said to myself, Impossible! Ridiculous! But then I remember how we buried her in a shiny coffin, and I remember the whole week and the many people who swarmed around her dead body, and how her dead face looked in the chapel.

Yes, my friends, this woman is dead. I have a hangover. It is Sunday afternoon. Before I was lying on the couch and suddenly I began to cry. I know why too. It was because it was a beautiful sunny day and I was thinking what a day it was to enjoy, that a living person could walk proudly and softly thru the streets and be happy. And then I had one of those moments of incredulity. Why, she can't be dead I was saying. So I began to cry because I knew at the same time that the sun had made her coffin so shiny and glittering.

What happened was that she got sick going to the funeral of a man who had died of sleeping sickness. There are so many goddam things people can die of. My mother caught a cold there and it got worse in a few days. When I came home she was in the front bedroom upstairs. There were nurses and several doctors. I didn't like my father's secrecy about it. He was figuring that I was a child. My mother's sister, my aunt, she was there too, and with my father she was sitting up all night in a big chair. If my mother moved, there she was for help. My mother didn't sleep. She would lie there all night with her big eyes moving in her pale face.

Several times in two days I talked gently with my mother, a few sentences at a time. She was not getting better, for complications were setting in. But I was helpful and made her happy. I had just made a great worldly success as a writer and she told me she was thankful she had lived long enough to see it. But she didn't want to die, she said. Maybe we could take a trip to Europe she added, or go to California where she had been twice in the past. I told her sure, and joked that I would give up my whole goddam artistic soul and sell out to the movies to take her there.

My father told me once, downstairs in the kitchen where we would gather after the long vigils upstairs, that his wife was scared to death that she would die. Then my aunt would come down and make sure that every one had remembered to eat, my two sisters and myself. The colored girl was forever laying out food it seemed and we were always eating. It seems that to be any where near death immediately heightens your respect and love for the living. We were all very kind to each other.

The next day was Sunday and in the paper I found a nice picture of myself and showed it to my mother. "Nice . . . ," she whispered, the one word, for it was difficult for her to speak. She was having great pain in her chest and they could not give her morphine because she was not strong enough. My father is an American business man of practicality and a variety of experience, but I noticed here that he was boyish in the face of what was happening. What ever the doctors said he would do, and all night we sat up in the chilly room and sometimes napped off and waked up with a start. My mother was only looking with her big eyes and her still painful face.

I asked her if she would mind if I went back to New York on some business and she insisted that I go. "You can't help me. Go,"* she said. Those were her exact words and I remember them because they were the last words I heard her say. I kissed her goodbye fiercely. It was fierce because behind the gentleness of my mouth I held back such strong emotion. I went away because I didn't know then how sick she was and my father wouldn't tell me. That's why I went to New York, and also because I couldn't stand being there in the house and having the phone ring every five minutes with people asking how is she.

I was very tired and nervously exhausted because I had made a success as a writer and people were jumping on my head from all points of the compass. What I am doing here is finding an excuse for having left my mother alone there. For she was pretty much alone without me. Her life really pivoted on me and I walked away. But I didn't know she was going to die. Here is how I found it out.

I was home in New York and called my father twice a day. He would always say that she was all right. Then I went to the Half Moon Hotel in Coney Island where I was resting by the ocean. My father knew I was there. I was walking along the dark boardwalk at night and suddenly started back to the hotel to call Philadelphia again. Just as I got to the hotel door a bellboy came running out and said there was a phone call for me, long distance.

---

* Odets often said that whenever he met someone new, two questions he asked himself were: "How can I help you? What can I learn from you?"

I spun thru the revolving door and the operator told me she would get the call back as it was being held for me. I knew what it was and she said with a sympathetic face that she was afraid it was too late. The phones stood in a row on a shelf and I picked up one. They were trying to rouse the long distance operator, but I told them what number to call in Philadelphia. Far off I heard one operator relaying the call to the other and a distant voice said to keep the wire clear, for it was a death call. I almost pressed the ear piece thru my head and then I heard my father's voice. He said your mother is dead and I said oh is it! Oh is it! And he said not to cry and I was filled with a great sucking down hole of anguish.

It was such a thing! There in the public lobby and getting this phone call and my bereft father on the other end and trying not to let anyone there hear what I was saying. He said to pack a bag and to come to Philadelphia to stay for a week. I said I would catch the first train and he said not to hurry now, for it wouldn't help. But get a night's sleep, he said, and come the first thing in the morning. That was the whole phone call. His voice was calm: he had gone thru all that already.

Well, when I asked the night clerk to cash a check I had to ask him to fill it out, for I couldn't write with that shaking hand. I spoiled a check and he wrote the second one and gave me the money and promised to call a cab. (A few weeks before my mother had visited me in New York. She was sitting right here on the end of this couch. After dinner I asked her where we would go. She said she didn't care. I insisted we go some place and suddenly she said, looking at me gently with her full eyes, I am going places by being here. That was how much that woman loved me.)

When I got upstairs to my room I cried and then stopped, and cried and stopped and while I was crying found that I was stacking newspapers on the radiator. Then I would go in the bathroom and look at my face in the mirror to look at the face of a man whose mother had just died. I kept saying to myself, it isn't possible! I don't believe it! It can't be! I kept talking to myself and found myself laughing because I was talking that way.

Just as you must surely have only an agonizing sense of your physical self if your arm or leg is being cut off, torn out, so it is with death. You are shut off with a great quality of self revolving in your head. Perhaps there are people who can go out to others and for others in such a moment, but I must be different. There is something exultant in such aloneness and I had it here. For in times like these life is lived most fully. Life is like a big fish in a dark ocean and sometimes this fish leaps high in the air and looks around for that flash at the whole world, and sees it fully, hot, aware. Then back down in the water.

When I got in the taxi cab I knew it was too late for the last night train to Philadelphia, so I told the driver to take me to my apartment in down town New York. Spring was here. Coney Island was coming to life. Many concessions were already open. I huddled in a corner of the dark cab; I was cold. We rode thru dark lush Prospect Park. Yes, it was spring all right. My poor mother had waited for this time—her life before had been a wintery life and now, when it was turning to something warmer, now she had died. I remembered how she had often courted death with a sort of wistful distant appreciation. She was always talking about death. But I knew that now she had not wanted to die. I kept thinking that if I found out she had died in pain that I would break down and cry for a week without stop. Somehow I could not stand that she had died in pain.

When I arrived at the apartment I began to walk up and down. I distinctly remarked to myself that the floor was hard. I played several Beethoven sonatas, but could not listen well. I would cry and stop, catch myself in the middle of a sob, firmly caught with incredulity. It could not be. The telephone rang. It was Bea Lillie who was at Tallulah Bankhead's apartment. Bankhead wanted to talk to me I was archly informed. She did. Would I come to a party at her place? No, I wouldn't. I told her I had to go to Philadelphia. She was insistent, in fact insulting. I merely insisted that I had to go to Philadelphia. She was drunk and it became like some sort of jittery telephone game between us. Finally it was over.

There was a train at four thirty in the morning. I couldn't find a bag to put some clothes in. I finally realized I had left them at the hotel. I used an old one left here by my friend Harold. I kept thinking I ought to apologize for taking it without asking. I stopped off at the corner cafeteria for something to eat. I ate well, eggs and coffee. Jack Adler came over to discuss some business project. I said I didn't feel like talking, but could I look at his paper. When he continued about an appointment I told him my mother had died and that I was going there and didn't know when I would come back. He immediately backed away in a curious manner, as if someone had told him then and there I was a leper.

I forgot that while still in the apartment I left a note for my secretary, Herman. I wonder what he did with that note. I would like to see it. I would like to see what I wrote. I cried a lot when I was writing it—it took me a half hour to write him a few sentences. Then I wanted to call someone up and tell them. I picked Joe Bromberg, but he wasn't home. His wife Goldie answered. I was being very calm. She wanted to know why I wanted Joe. I told her that my mother had just died and that I wanted to tell some one and suddenly she said oh Clifford and I was crying so I couldn't talk and I said I was sorry I had waked her. What womanly sympathy came from her. A phrase, my poor tired mother, kept in my mind all the time. I kept saying it, my poor tired mother.

When I looked over the press clippings about my plays I had a fresh shudder, and under the picture of which she had said nice* I wrote that word. At the beginning of the book I wrote "Call this 1935," for that would always be an historical year in my life. Everything has happened in this year, success, a new life to look forward to. And now the death of my mother.

The few sentences that had taken him so long to write, preserved by Herman, read:

Dear Von—

My poor dear tired mother died last night and I went there on the earliest train. Allright about it.

Dear Herman, call all the dates on the calendar off.

Clifford.

* The picture was a sketch in the *Herald Tribune* copied from a photograph in which Odets has the appearance of a thoughtful, gentle, middle-class, bespectacled college youth. He is dressed in a proper shirt and tie, and might be a young history teacher. The picture is captioned, "Champion of the under-dog."

Tell them this at the office. Also you must go to the Half Moon and get all my things. Please don't overlook any papers, etc. Will you look in all the drawers, etc. Please Thursday or Friday do it, and pay bills there.

The nightmare, according to Mattie Washington, the part-time cleaning woman in the Odets home, had begun one dreary morning with a loud and ugly argument between Pearl and her husband. L.J. was "yelling in a particularly horrible and mean voice" that he knew the reason his wife "did not want to sleep with him was that she was interested in someone else." Mrs. Washington noticed that at breakfast Pearl looked white. Still, since quarrels were commonplace in this family and Pearl often looked that way in the morning, her youngest, the only child still living at home, went off to her job as a secretary in a social-service agency. Her eyes brimming with tears, Mrs. Washington recalled the argument: "Mister Odets hollerin' at Mrs. Odets for visitin' Clifford in New York. They used to fight a lot about that, her givin' him money and all. This time he was accusin' her of makin' a secret trip to him of some kind and she, poor darlin', was denyin' it—I really think Clifford was fixin' to get her to New York. Lotsa times after their fights she'd stand at the window and say, 'I wished I was layin' over there in that cemetery.' Neighbors would say, 'Where's Lou?' and she'd say, 'Outa the city,' and then they'd see him in town with a woman. Then he'd come home and he'd say, 'Hi, darlin',' as if nothin' was wrong. Once he had a car accident and it came out some woman was with him. It was a terrible scandal for Mrs. Odets.

"On that terrible day," she went on, "it was one of their worst fights, and poor Mrs. Odets, she was always short of breath anyway, and this time he pushed her, I really don't think he meant her to fall down the stairs, but she did, and she took one of her attacks like asthma and heart, but by this time he had run out of the house and we couldn't find him. No one knew where he had gone. They said he had gone away on business. Dr. Myers was very mad because he thought she died a heartbroken woman. Later he said, 'Mattie, I really don't think she wanted to live any more, and that's why she died.' It was a few years before Aunt Esther told all this to Clifford, and that's when I think he *really* started hating his father."◖

Pearl Odets—although deathly ill throughout that night—waited until the next morning before awakening anyone, not wanting to frighten her daughter. In a wan and tired voice, she had said, "I don't feel good. I'm sick," adding that she had herself already called Dr. Howard Myers. Mattie recalled Tante Esther's alarm, and by the second evening a "lung specialist" was called. He decided she had had a lung hemorrhage, and later, as her abdomen was distended, a "stomach specialist" came; both thought Pearl should not go to the hospital, as "it was nothing serious." Pearl disagreed and said repeatedly to Mattie, "I'll never get better." She spent some time that evening with Esther and her daughter, appearing stronger, with bright pink cheeks. Within the week, to everyone's astonishment, Pearl was dead. It was May 8, 1935 and she was forty-seven years old.

On the death certificate the cause of death is given as "acute general peritonitis, a subphrenic abscess"—a strange diagnosis, forever after a mystery to physicians. Lou Odets later said that he had talked the doctor out of mentioning the lung hemorrhage on the certificate because it would have been a disgrace to suggest she might have died of T.B. It is not clear whether he invented his story because of the universal shame this era at-

◖ 18.2.

tached to tuberculosis, or whether it was to obliterate all possibility of his having played a role in Pearl's terminal illness.

Steadily weeping, Mrs. Washington described "Mrs. Odets' nest-egg wrapped in a piece of cloth in her little sewing basket. She was always puttin' away secret cash. I always kinda guessed it was somethin' for Clifford, or maybe to run away from her husband. I was real surprised to see how much she had saved—three thousand dollars. That was a whole lot in those Depression days."

Clifford thought the money should be divided between Florence and Genevieve, but L.J. deducted $1,000 to spend on lavish banks of calla lilies, their centers filled with violets, to put around her coffin. In the basket also, Esther's daughter remembered, "was the beautiful black shawl, embroidered with red roses" that Esther had given Pearl "because she loved it so."

Pearl's body was clothed in the black lace underwear brought her years back by her husband as a peace offering, which she had hidden and never worn; the outer garment was her "good black silk-chiffon" worn once, on the opening night of *Awake and Sing!*

On the Sunday of the funeral, which happened to be Mother's Day, the veteran Communist Ella Reeve Bloor was marooned in Philadelphia. "Reading in the newspaper," she later wrote to Odets, "the sad news of your beautiful mother's sudden death and that the funeral was about to take place in Rosenberg's synagogue uptown, I cried out I must go at once . . . Clifford is all alone at his mother's funeral. . . . You were there with your sisters and Stella Adler was there. I was quite right you were *alone* in that large gathering and I did help a little when I said very humbly, 'Clifford I just wanted you to know I was here with you' . . . and when we went back to New York City, I remember how we pledged together you would always be my son." The need and capacity to call forth such maternal response from a certain kind of woman had become a permanent part of him.

Strangely, Stella Adler was the only Group member who attended the funeral. "I have always been aware of tradition," she said. Recalling the oppressive airlessness of the Odets house in West Oak Lane, she added, "It was small and without distinction. I remember the suburban neighborhood and a sense of the lives of cigar-smoking salesmen and merchants . . . quite different from the Leofs' and Blitzsteins' where I had seen Clifford before—there was always an atmosphere of music and intellect there. You could breathe." "Poppa and Momma Leof" were also at Pearl Odets' funeral, although they had never met her. Odets said later, "No matter how I resented Stella's treatment of Harold, I could never hate her after that."

Miss Adler was impressed by the "aggressiveness and power in Clifford's father . . . a man who, whatever he had, he brought forward. Maybe a man who moved in limited circles, *but he moved!*" It was easy to believe that this man could burst a leather belt around his chest simply by exhaling.

Many members of L.J.'s Masonic Lodge and the Order of the Eastern Star, as well as the curious who had read the Sunday newspaper, came to the funeral and watched Odets enter the first car with his father and sisters for the procession to Montefiore Cemetery. In the second rode Tante Esther and Uncle Israel Rossman with their children and with Aunt Nettie's son, Frank Lubner, who thought Clifford appeared grief-stricken and close to collapse. Lubner was convinced that had it not been for Esther, Odets might have committed suicide after the death of his mother. Tante Esther, once again, as in his childhood, "became a mother to him, and . . . when he was about to give up hope, persuaded him to carry on." Until Esther's death in 1953 "Clifford visited the Rossmans regularly, sent them money, paid their hospital bills and their mortgage and never left them in want of anything." Esther, in turn, fed him chicken soup and knadlach, and put flowers on Pearl's grave every week, even if she had to steal them from another plot.

Clifford, at the funeral, warned Tante Esther and Uncle Israel not to start moaning in traditional style, as it might upset his sisters. For five years following, one of his sisters was unable to utter the words "mother" and "death," and the other felt that an "angel had left us."*

On the way back to New York, Clifford was enraged and obsessed by the idea that his father had not thought him adult enough to tell him his mother was dying, thus depriving him of a last exchange with her. For his part, Lou Odets was claiming bankruptcy, feeling sorry for himself, and vilifying his dead wife to his children, losing no time in expressing his conviction that their mother had had an affair in Atlantic City, and focusing on the fact that the man had no standing, was a nothing, a mere desk clerk in a hotel.†

The responses to a death close by are always intense, and each of us quickly finds a position from which to deal with this essentially unassimilable event. It appears that L. J. Odets was now under tremendous and desperate pressure to justify to his children his existence with his wife. It had become of critical importance to him that they know that not all the transgressions had been his. L.J. began to plan a trip around the world at his son's expense.

Back in his still-bare apartment, alone (Clurman was still in Moscow, where *Lefty* was being hailed as a masterpiece), Odets was grateful for the chore of writing a monologue, *I Can't Sleep*, to be performed on May 19 by Group actor Morris Carnovsky at Mecca Temple under the auspices of the Marine Workers' Committee and the American Union Against Reaction. Elia Kazan recalled Odets' despondence and his extreme sleeplessness on his return from Philadelphia, and his steady talk of his "poor, tired mother . . . of her beauty and idealism." Odets spoke of her as "a young Jewish girl with a petal-like freshness." In his father he saw only a driving materialism. Kazan, in a burst of empathy, said to Odets, "The worst thing we do to each other is what we are." Odets nodded in grief.

"Once he had decided to write it, he finished *I Can't Sleep* in one night," said Kazan. "At his best he wrote with such pleasure." Apparently he was able for this short sprint to mobilize himself: by four in the morning he had whipped off the three pages on his all-capital-letters typewriter, adding a short postscript to Carnovsky, who, he hoped, would enjoy the part. It would be his fourth presentation of this year, to be anthologized as one of the best pieces of writing of the thirties:

---

* Testimony to the general impact of Pearl's death on friends and relatives was a twenty-five-line poem written by the daughter of an old friend in which her "smile, her unselfish acts, her saintliness," and the joy she brought to others were extolled.

† The similarity of this outrage to Clifford's later outrage at the "unworthiness" of *his* last wife's lovers is eerie.

I Can't Sleep

Standing on a street corner, a beggar with the face of a dead man. Hungry, miserable, unkempt, an American spectre. He now holds out his hand in an asking gesture as a man walks by. The man stops, looks at the beggar, says:

MAN (*Angrily*): I don't believe in it, charity! Maybe you think I'm Rockefeller! (*He walks away briskly; the beggar lowers his hand and shivers. The man now returns and silently offers him some coins. The beggar refuses by putting his hands in his pockets.*)

Take it—don't be ashamed. I had a fight in the shop: I was feeling sore. Take the money . . . you're afraid? No, I'm giving it to you. (*Waits*) I mean it. Take it. (*Suddenly shouts*) Say, maybe you think I'll lay down on the ground and die before you'll take it! Look, he's looking at me! All right, I made a mistake. I yelled on you, too! Don't act like a fool—if a person gives you money, take it. I know, I made a mistake in the beginning. Now I'm sorry I yelled on you.

Listen, don't be so smart. When a man offers you money, take it! For two cents I'll call a cop in a minute. You'll get arrested for panhandling on the streets. You know this expression, "Panhandling"? You can't talk? Who says you have to insult me? I got a good mind to walk away. Listen, what do you want from me? Maybe I look to you like a rich man. Poverty is whistling from every corner in the country. So an honest man gets insulted cause he offers a plain bum money. Live and learn!

Look, he's looking at me. Maybe you think I'm not honest. Listen, in my shop the only worker the boss gives a little respect is Sam Blitzstein. Who's Blitzstein? Me!! Don't think I'm impressed cause he's a boss. I just said it to give proof. Everything, "he's tickled to death," a favorite expression by Mr. Kaplan. A very generous man, Mr. Kaplan—like all bosses: the end of the summer he gives away dead flies! Yes. Yes. . . .

Take the money—you'll buy yourself a hot meal. I'll take out a nickel for the BMT. I keep for myself five dollars a week and the rest goes in the house. In the old days I used to play a little cards, but in the last few years with such bad conditions I quit playing altogether. You can't talk? (*Laughs bitterly and shakes his head*) Even my wife don't talk to me. For seven years she didn't speak to me one word. "Come eat," she says. Did you ever hear such an insult?! After supper I go in my room and lock the door. Sometime ago I bought for myself a little radio for seven fifty. I'm playing it in my little room. She tells the girls not to speak to me —my three daughters. All my life I was a broken-hearted person, so this had to happen. I shouldn't get a little respect from my own children! Can you beat it?!

I'll tell you the truth:—I don't sleep. The doctor says to me it's imagination. Three dollars I paid him he should tell me it's imagination! Can you beat it? I don't sleep at night and he tells me imagination! Can't you die?! I eat healthful food. For a while I was eating vegetarian in the Golden Rule Cafeteria. It didn't agree with me. Vegetarian, shmegetarian, they'll have a good time anyway, the worms. Headaches, backaches—these things I don't mention—it ain't even important.

I like to talk to people, but I don't like political arguments. They think I'm crazy in the shop. I tell them right to their faces,

"Leave me alone! Talk politics, but leave me live!" I don't hide my opinions from nobody. They should know what I know. Believe me, I'm smarter than I look! What I forgot about Marx they don't know. (*Changes the subject*) Friday night regular as clockwork I go on the corner and take a shave for twenty cents. After supper I walk in Prospect Park for two hours. I like trees and then I go home. By this time the youngest girls is sleeping, but my oldest girl stays up late to do homework. A very smart girl in school. Every month A-A-A, she leaves the report card on the sideboard and I sign it. This will give you an idea she likes me. Correct! Last week I tried to talk to her, a sensible girl, fourteen years old. She ran in the kitchen to my wife. Believe me, my friend, in a worker's house the children live a broken-hearted life. My wife tells her lies about me.

Look, he's looking. What did I do to my wife? I suddenly got an idea the youngest girl wasn't my girl. Yes, yes, it happened before in history. A certain man lived in our neighborhood a few months. He boarded downstairs with the Bergers, next to the candy store, a man like a sawed-off shotgun. I saw in my young girl a resemblance. Suddenly he moved away. On the same day I caught her crying, my wife. Two and two is four! I remember like yesterday I took a pineapple soda in the store. For three weeks I walked up and down. Could I work? Could I eat? In the middle of the night I asked her. She insulted me! She insulted my whole family! Her brother came from Brighton Beach the next day—a cheap race horse specialist without a nickel. A fourteen carat bum! A person an animal wouldn't talk to him! He opened up his mouth to me. . . . I threw him down the stairs!

But one thing—I never laid a finger on the girls in my whole life. My wife—it shows you what a brain she's got—she gives my oldest girl a name: Sydelle! S-Y-D-E-L-L-E! Sarah she can't call her. Or maybe Shirley. Sydelle! So you can imagine what's happening in our house!

Oh, I don't sleep. At night my heart cries blood. A fish swims all night in the black ocean—and this is how I am—all night with one eye open. A mixed up man like me crawls away to die alone. No woman should hold his head. In the whole city no one speaks to me. A very peculiar proposition. Maybe I would like to say to a man, "Brother." But what happens? They bring in a verdict—crazy! It's a civilized world today in America? Columbus should live so long! Yes, I love people, but nobody speaks to me. When I walk in the street I can't stand I should see on every block some beggars. My heart cries blood for the poor man who didn't eat for a few days. At night I can't sleep. This is an unusual combination of worries. I say to myself, "It's your fault, Blitzstein? Let them die in the street like flies." But I look in the mirror and it don't feel good inside. I spit on myself!

I spoke last week to a red in the shop. Why should I mix in with politics. With all my other troubles I need yet a broken head? I can't make up my mind—what should I do? I spoke to a Socialist on the street. A Communist talked in my ear for two hours. Join up, join up. But for what? For trouble?

Don't look at me. I'll say it straight out—I forgot my mother. Also a dead brother for thirty years dead. Listen, you think I never read a book? "Critique of the Gotha Programme," Bukharin,

Lenin—"Iskra"—this was in our day a Bolshevik paper. I read
enough. I'm speaking three languages, Russian, German and English. Also Yiddish. Four. I had killed in the 1905 Revolution a
brother. You didn't know that. My mother worked like a horse.
No, even a horse takes off a day. My mother loved him like a bird,
my dead brother. She gave us to drink vinegar we should get sick
and not fight in the Czar's army. Maybe you think I didn't understand this.

Yes, my blood is crying out for revenge a whole lifetime!
You hear me talking to you these words? Is it plain to you my
significance? I don't sleep. Don't look at me. I forgot my working
class mother. Like a dog I live. You hear the truth. Don't look at
me! You hear me, do you?!

I watched last week the May Day. Don't look at me! I hid in
the crowd and watched how the comrades marched with red flags
and music. You see where I bit my hand? I went down in the subway I shouldn't hear the music. Listen, I looked in your face before and saw the truth. I'm talking to myself. The blood of the
mother and brother is breaking open my head. I hear them crying, "You forgot, you forgot!" They don't let me sleep. All night
I hear the music of the comrades. All night I hear hungry men.
All night the broken hearted children. No place to hide, no place
to run away. Look in my face, comrade. Look at me, look, look,
look!!!

Fadeout.

Dear Morris,
This last paragraph goes off a little I think. But it can be fixed
when I'm not so tired—four in the morning now. Will get it to you
this way and fix it up when my mind's fresher.

This short piece, listed as a "monodrama," was presented as the fifth
short attraction of *Spring Varieties*. The four items preceding it included
"West Coast Strike Songs," revolutionary dances, anti-war songs by Hanns
Eisler, and Odets himself performing "improvisations on the 2nd movement of Beethoven's 7th Symphony." The second half of the evening was
a one-act play, imitative of *Lefty*, based on the San Francisco marine strike
and written by Group actor Art Smith.

I Can't Sleep is an excellent example of a writer filling the vessel of
a generational ideology with his own unconscious family conflicts, ethical
struggles, and formal inventiveness. Clurman said that "the troubled conscience of the middle class in the depression period" was its source of inspiration. Again, true and incomplete.

In his personal depression Odets is struggling here—with all the
seeming contradictions of a dream—with at least three identity-elements
within himself. First, he is the "beggar with the face of a dead man . . .
an American spectre . . . a panhandler" who must ask in fear for handouts. Secondly, as a victim may identify himself with his persecutor, he is
also the man Blitzstein* whom the beggar approaches, a man in some
ways like his father and yet a tenderly fantasied figure like old Jacob in
Awake and Sing! ("What I forgot about Marx they don't know.") The
speaker uses his father's forms and rhythms of speech, he is a man who
plays cards, his wife, he says, "don't talk to me," and he longs for "respect"

* Clearly named after composer Marc Blitzstein's father, Sam, married to Madi
Leof, daughter of "Poppa" Leof, socialist physician in Philadelphia.

from his *three daughters;* he lives "a broken-hearted life" because his wife "tells lies" to the oldest "daughter," who would otherwise like him. There are, of course, three children in the Odets family, the oldest being Clifford, who would write of his father, "He had it all worked out that my mother and aunt poisoned my mind against him. He never realized (would not, could not, dared not) that *he* had poisoned my mind against him."

The speaker even suspects that—as Lou Odets told his daughter—his wife has betrayed him with another man. The speaker believes that the youngest daughter is not his. Odets here assigns to the wife the pretentious denial of Jewishness—actually so despised in his father and in himself— in naming a daughter Sydelle instead of the Old Testament name Sarah. Had not his father given *his* three children the names Clifford, Genevieve, and Florence?

Finally, in *I Can't Sleep* stand the troubled divisions *within* Sam Blitzstein. Like Odets, he is sleepless, lonely, and guilt-ridden and sees "on every block some beggars." He hates them and yet lives in them, longing to end his isolation, his sense of alienation, of being a stranger, by calling these wretched of the earth "brother." If he were not such a coward ("Why should I mix in with politics. With all my other troubles I need yet a broken head?"), he would "join up" with them, militantly demanding his rights and theirs, rather than permitting himself simply to be milked by them. On another level he sees his father and Harold Clurman—each in his own way —as "beggars" who, on the one hand, fill him with guilt and rage and, on the other, inspire in him an overwhelming wish to please each by meeting their diametrically opposed demands. Of his father he later wrote:

> When I became a successful money-earning playwright, my father, who had not been a father thought like many others that I was fair game. He began by announcing, "Don't forget that your Dad is used to living on his 15–20 thousand a year." I gave it to him. Thus this man, who had three times driven me to suicide attempts, retired at the age of 49.

Although the figures in Odets' "Debt Book" show that "15–20 thousand" a year is exaggerated, he records giving his father more than $100,000 over the next fifteen years, and to Clurman several thousands.◖

His current feeling toward Clurman was exceedingly complex: he had begun to resent Clurman's pressure for a rapid succession of plays for the Group, yet he was grateful to Clurman for making him feel needed and gifted.

The worst pain of all in *I Can't Sleep* is Blitzstein's guilt toward his mother. "I forgot my working class mother," he cries, and this is why he is sleepless and there is no place to hide. Odets now fears he will forget the "poor, tired" "womanly woman" who also represents his innocent, creative heart.◖

It is as if he feels himself guilty of conspiracy with his father in the destruction of his mother, thus magically jeopardizing his capacity as artist. When at the very end Sam Blitzstein pleads with the beggar, "Look at me, look, look, look!!!" it is Odets himself begging for that forgiveness which will restore both his uniqueness in his mother's eyes and his father's forbearance (when God is angry, he turns away his face). Odets is trying to strengthen within himself not only his capacity to work but also his endangered ability to sustain loyalties, what Erikson has called the cornerstone of identity—namely, "fidelity."

◖ 18.3.
◖ 18.4.

None of these considerations negates the genuineness of his long-standing conscious yearning to feed the starving, to help the fallen, to comfort the lonely and wretched of the earth, and, above all, to so change an unjust world that each child will be protected from abuse and have a chance to grow like a flower, quietly and "in conformity with its own nature."

Doubtless Odets took some comfort now from a reassuring event, uniquely integrating in the life of every writer: the publication (on the day before his mother's death) of his first book, with the dedication, written before Pearl's illness: "For my Father and Mother." The firm of Covici-Friede had advanced him $200 against royalties for the right to publish *Waiting for Lefty, Awake and Sing!* and *Till the Day I Die* under the title *Three Plays.* The hard-cover edition sold for $2.50, the paperback for $1.25.

It was enthusiastically received by leading literary critics, many of whom attacked the Pulitzer Prize committee for giving its award to *The Old Maid* instead of to *Awake and Sing!* One reviewer predicted, "The time will come when every library will have a shelf of his plays for he is the sole young American dramatist capable of filling O'Neill's now rather empty shoes." The *World-Telegram*'s Harry Hansen announced that this volume would "smash the vapid, lifeless Broadway stage into kindling, and start a new period of virile writing."

The left-wing press offered the volume as a "bonus" for subscriptions, and the respected Alfred A. Knopf wrote to Odets, expressing regret that he was not to be his publisher. Bennett Cerf asked him for an autographed picture and invited him to several elegant lunches, which culminated in Odets' transferring his contract, with better terms, to Random House. In his 1935 scrapbook he pasted Random House's booklist wherein he took his place beside O'Neill, Joyce, Proust, J. M. Synge, Robinson Jeffers, Gide, Gertrude Stein, and poets Auden, Spender, and C. Day Lewis.

During the week following Pearl Odets' funeral Clifford sent out numerous copies of this first book of plays, inscribing each with careful attention: to the Leofs, to the Kozlenkos, to Group Theatre members, and to his family. Two days after the funeral he wrote on the flyleaf of the copy he gave his father, "There should be two parents to give this to . . . but we are left alone, with love . . ." To his secretary, Herman Kobland, he wrote the inscription, "To my dearest and oldest friend, Herman, for whom fine words are not necessary. We understand together quietly and surely what friendship means. With love, Clifford." To his Philadelphia aunt and uncle he wrote, "Dear Aunt Esther and Uncle R., Whenever you need me you will call me. We will not forget where the blood is warmest. Love, from Clifford." Characteristically, in *his* time of grief and need he offers help and gifts, spending hours searching for precisely the "right" birthday clock to send to Corinne Steinberg, young daughter of the Irene to whom he had written romantic letters in his teens.

To the New York Public Library he sent drafts of original manuscripts of all three published plays, attempting thus to allay his self-doubt by establishing a public record of his place in the history of American drama.

In a remarkably judicious review in the left-wing *New Masses* the Marxist playwright John Howard Lawson wrote an earnest appraisal of this "talent of outstanding significance." Applauding Odets' "skill, vitality, and honesty rarely found in the current theatre," he developed a discerning argument: that it is a distortion of a Marxist approach to literature to see Odets' vitality simply (as *The New York Times*' Brooks Atkinson did) as a function of "crusader's zeal." On the contrary, says Lawson, Marxism "aims not to narrow, but to greatly broaden the cultural horizon." He concludes with the fundamental problem, "which no revolutionary writer has fully solved: the psychological activity of the individual in relation to the forces which are remolding society. . . . Odets succeeds in dramatizing the complex interaction of character and environment—but only in brief snatches. The next step is to master the sustained activity of the human will in conflict with the total environment. . . . *Waiting for Lefty* is a study in conversions. . . . This is the source of its power. . . . But Odets will undoubtedly go beyond this to mastery of more profound and more sustained conflict."

It was becoming increasingly difficult for Odets to refuse the invitations to speak which were inundating him. He felt it his duty to participate in "the struggle for justice," and these "performances" on the stage of "real life" doubtless diverted him as well from his increasing sense of disorganization and from the acute anxiety he felt when trying to work on *Paradise Lost* or *The Silent Partner*. Newspapers announce him as the principal speaker at numerous places: a "mass protest meeting against Germany's new military preparations"; at a meeting of the "unemployed members of the Writers' Union from the curb in front of 902 Broadway where there is picketing going on"; a protest against American shipments of scrap iron to Japan on "Pier Number 3, in Red Hook, Brooklyn."

Along with many other intellectuals of his time, he was convinced that dread events—already visible in Germany—were in the offing and could be impeded by such direct mass protest. He overestimated how much time remained for such action.

Yet, pairing dates, a biographer cannot escape the impression that in accepting these speaking engagements Odets was falling back on his old identity as a performer in a vain effort to cope with what he called his "extreme emotional exhaustion." He later recalled that after his mother's death he had feared he was going insane, and now he thought he had been having a complete "breakdown." He understood "the frenzy of Van Gogh's painting" and sometimes found in the dead of night that "I almost couldn't stop writing. The hand kept going"; yet "the hand" did not originate work which satisfied him, and his depression would not budge.

With strong urging from Helen Deutsch, who was staying in a large rented studio near the Henry Varnum Poors in the country village of New City, New York, he decided to retreat from Manhattan to the sanctuary of this writers' and artists' colony in order to work on *Paradise Lost*. With the handsome, articulate Helen he lived not far from Mab and Maxwell Anderson. Helen recalled how sad, remote, and irritable Odets appeared. A violent dialogue between Odets and Anderson about the chances for a humanist society in the Soviet Union remained clear in her memory. Anderson said quietly: "Russia will soon become a frank tyranny." In response, Odets began to pace, his enormous eyes glittering and characteristically bulging from their sockets. Patient at first, he finally lost control and shouted at Anderson, "What's bothering you is the income tax, the income tax! You are a damned reactionary, a fascist!"

Deeply disturbed by this assault on her best friends, Helen pulled Odets to her car and, spinning the wheels in the dust, tried to get away before the Andersons would hear Odets, like a madman, screaming over and over from the circular driveway, "Maxwell Anderson, you are a shit!" Anderson was receiving the brunt not only of Odets' repressed rage at his father (whose world cruise he was about to finance) but also of his own growing doubt that the Soviet Union was the utopian society he longed for it to be.

Helen left the next morning. Her depressed farewell note to the now withdrawn Odets, "who," she said, "wouldn't have cared if I turned green around the edges," tells as much of their relationship as of the earnest ideological perplexities of a young intellectual of this generation:

> Dear Clifford,
>   I am going away. I don't think I have to tell you why. They're the only people I know in the world who would care if anything happened to me; really the only ones I can depend on.
>   You're some wrong about Max. He's not an *active* fascist and it makes me angry to hear you toss that word about. . . . It's as bad as yelling sheeny at everybody with a different accent. I think he's horribly ignorant and too tired or too frightened to learn the truth. You were right to lose patience; they were disgusting in their willingness to believe rottenness. . . . But is that fascism? I really don't know. I've no doubt they'd tag along in a fascist state but I don't think they'd lift a finger to get one, and that's what makes an ACTIVE fascist, isn't it?
>   Just the same I've got to get out. I'm terribly ashamed of having been so lulled by them, so fat and sleepy with living in the country. . . . I feel I have a raison d'etre when I can make you physically comfortable, and do what I can to protect and further that goddammed-fuckingwhythehell talent. It's pretty hard to be strong in a vacuum, particularly when you're a woman. . . . You see I'm not a writer who can go off and write something and come back with his place in society. . . . It's romantic and stupid to tell me to go wrap copies of the New Masses for mailing . . . because that is not my work, any more than the work I'm now doing at the Group is. . . . Max and Mab were the only ones who ever tried to encourage me, to tell me I was a person. The only people I ever respected enough to believe them . . .

Thus did both young people abandon the moral and political "education" of the older Andersons. Helen arranged for Odets to move to the Poors' house nearby, where in their absence he looked after their pregnant dog, Sister, and worked on *Paradise Lost* and on an autobiography he would never finish. Helen continued with her work as a highly successful theatrical press agent in New York, numbering the Group Theatre as only one of many clients. Eventually she found herself in Hollywood writing screenplays.

On June 1, back in New York to see a performance of *Lefty* by the Negro People's Theatre at the Rockland Palace in Harlem, Odets wrote a dispirited apology to Helen:

> Dear Helen,
>   I wanted to drop you this note before to tell you many thanks for housing me those few days, for being solicitous about the Odets beast . . . everyone says I look very well, so it must be so, thanks to New City.
>   I still feel shredded inside, stepped on and will now really have to

rest myself or stop talking about it. Something is wrong with me, I don't know what. I keep thinking about my dead mother.

Well, I will see you soon.

Clifford.

It had been evident from the letters sent from Moscow by Harold Clurman and Cheryl Crawford that their visit had coincided with the apogee of the "short silver age" of Soviet literature. Under the friendly leadership of Maxim Gorky, comrade of Chekhov, the Convention of Soviet Writers had recently given earnest consideration to the creative problems of writers in a socialist state; Bukharin had even written in *Izvestia* on the problems of Soviet poetry, and Isaac Babel had been a respected voice.

To Clurman at this time the Soviet Union appeared to be extraordinarily sane and freely creative, a country where there was no conflict between "what their hearts dreamed and what their hands were doing." He records his delight and astonishment on a visit to the great film-maker Eisenstein, accompanied by photographer Paul Strand, a Group Associate, who was awed by this audience. Eisenstein told them he planned a piece for *Izvestia* which would state that Strand was "the greatest master of photographic art in the world today"—a distinctly non-competitive and internationalist comment. Although Clurman writes, "I felt . . . proud of ourselves as Americans," it is clear he was envious of a country where life derived meaning from the daily experience of everyone contributing to a shared end.

At the Meyerhold and Vakhtangov theatres, the theatrical fare was cosmopolitan and varied. Gordon Craig, also on this trip, argued the merits of the Soviet-Jewish *King Lear*. They saw productions of Chekhov, Shakespeare, Molière, plus a few Soviet plays, good "though not great." Clurman and Crawford report their pride in the work of their own company back in New York.

Soviet audiences wanted, however, "mostly comedy, color, romance, and *fun* in the theatre right now," writes Clurman to Strasberg. Indeed, "it is almost a *faux pas* to put on a political play at the moment." An exception was the work of Odets. The taste the Russians had had of *Lefty*, spoken in English, made them want Odets' new book of plays, then being translated into Russian. "They are panting for it here," Clurman adds.

With the characteristic lag of art behind the events of history, there was no visible hint that beneath the surface of this rich and free cultural parenthesis the "great terror" in Russia had already begun and that within a short time Gorky would be poisoned and Bukharin shot, and that Soviet culture would lose its creative openness and its attendant generosity of spirit. In the meantime, with the images fresh in his mind of a Broadway theatre critically impoverished and of one third of America literally starving, Clurman saw the Soviet Union as a society whose values and aspirations provided an inspiring contrast.

If the day-to-day fact was poor in comparison with the ultimate objective, it was because that objective was so great; but they had no trouble in seeing the relationship between the two. Every partial achievement, such as the opening of the Moscow subway, bore witness to that relationship and was illuminated and made meaningful through it.

On his return, Clurman assembled the Group members and, using his Soviet diary as a text, addressed them passionately on the importance of such central purpose and cautioned them that if the Group was "to become the recognized and honored first theatre of America" (the choice of words reflects his recent experience), they must not only achieve preeminent standards of excellence in their craft, but in their choice of plays "represent all of the creative aspects of our country . . . to make use of the widest and deepest traditions to which, as an American theatre, we are heir." He emphasized that America did not need to strengthen its "Left theatre," but needed to "sustain those forces that would contribute to the making of good theatre of whatever description." Further, he criticized the company for its growing sectarianism, its brashness, even its lack of manners.

At this point, to everyone's astonishment, Odets arose and loosed a thunderous diatribe at the assembled company and, by implication, at Clurman: they were all becoming complacent, stuffy, passive (all things he now feared in himself), and, above all, he shouted, they were not growing! His harangue, delivered with the volume and the manner of his father, expressed a dismissing contempt and disgust and went far beyond any chiding Clurman had had in mind. Its disproportion and inappropriateness embarrassed everyone in the same way his assault on Maxwell Anderson had done to Helen.

To a young Group actor, Lee J. Cobb, who felt himself not to be part of the "inner prime councils," Odets appeared to be "contained in a vessel which, if exposed to heat higher than room temperature, could burst. . . . It seemed almost necessary to relieve some of the pressure . . . a release of rage almost like an orgasm. . . . Clifford always had a stage presence, a sense of drama, and yet these outbursts were honest. It was part of his color." With Odets' sudden success as a writer, he added, "the dichotomy within himself regarding actors came out and the WRITER became the more important. . . . Actors are usually *hated* and used by writers, but Clifford had seemed up to this point to *love* us and to use us, which is better." Thus his outburst at the company was the more surprising. Clurman was now forced publicly to dissociate his own intent from this wild and mystifying eruption.

This was Odets' second such outburst in as many weeks. He, too, was dismayed and stunned by it, and after it he went back to his depression and, Helen recalled, "just sat." Neither Maxwell Anderson nor the Group company as target could provide release for his grief, rage, and terror. He could war with the father-oppressor, whether in action or in art, only if his ambivalence and guilt were stilled by a socially righteous idealism. On some inaccessible level he was doubtless resenting his mother's abandoning him by dying.

Shortly, a more suitable "enemy" was delivered to him by John Howard Lawson. Detailing the barbarous injustices of the reactionary Mendieta-Batista regime in Cuba, Lawson asked Odets to head a committee under the auspices of the League of American Writers to investigate labor and social conditions there, and in particular the status of Cuban students under this tyrant. Odets and fourteen others would sail on the Ward liner *Oriente*, and, according to Lawson, on this "trip of utmost importance . . . a prominent writer in the group would add tremendously to its significance. Not to mention that it would be exciting and valuable. . . ." Lawson was surprised when Odets immediately agreed to embark on this confrontation with President Carlos Mendieta.

This retreat to the salt sea doubtless had, as a central function for Odets, a self-healing effort. But, unlike his solitary, impulsive flight to the Half-Moon Hotel several weeks earlier, this excursion was motivated at least partly by his identification with "the wretched of the earth," an early gesture against what he perceived to be a growing, worldwide fascism. As he would truthfully tell the counsel for the House Committee on Un-American Activities two decades later: "The purpose that attracted me was that there were fears, oppressive measures taken against thousands of intellectuals and college students. They were thrown into jail. . . . I then was glad to go down in the sense of, if nothing else did happen, we would dramatize what the issues were down there."

Whenever he thought he might succor anyone who was oppressed, it met his own profound need for succor, reflected in a passionate wish for justice. As he had protected, fed, and taught his shy, cranky, thin little sister, so he now took pride in this first opportunity to "encourage and hearten certain sections of the Cuban people." It was not until the expedition was about to reach Havana that he learned he had been named its official chairman as "the idealist who had some kind of publicity value." A man obviously expert on Latin American affairs and on political tactics began to brief the small group of teachers, students, ministers, and union organizers on "what do you do when you get there, what happens, what kind of statements shall one give the press." The man spoke with such clear knowledge and authority that Odets concluded he must be a member of the Communist Party and the real head of this amateur delegation. "I was astonished to learn," he later testified, "that when we got to Cuba we were going to be arrested. This was news to me . . . on grounds that we were persona non grata in Cuba . . . accused of being a Communist delegation. Actually, there were a lot of people on this delegation who in my opinion had nothing to do with Communists or communism. . . ."

On July 5 the New York *Post,* under a half-inch banner headline, "Odets Tells Own Story of Cuban Arrest and Deportation," published his wireless dispatch describing what happened when he and the fourteen others,* including five women, were seized on arrival by Cuban officials. Two terrified young schoolteachers on a vacation trip to Mexico were sent to prison along with them. Despite cables from the *Post* to the Cuban government designating Odets a "special correspondent" and stating that "any courtesy that may be extended to him will be greatly appreciated," as well as protests from virtually every drama editor in the country, he was not permitted to send a dispatch until he and his companions were back aboard the *Oriente,* bound for New York. From shipboard he wrote:

Fifteen of us, representatives of more than twenty American organizations and periodicals, form the commission of investigation which headed for Havana to carry greetings to the Cuban people and to examine impartially Cuban social, political and economic conditions. Now we are on the way home without having had a chance to do any of those things except through a fence of machine guns.

As we dock at Havana, police and reporters swarm aboard the Oriente and lock us in the smoking room. We suspect our baggage has been examined on the way down. . . . All the time we are sur-

* Labor organizer Manning Johnson—later used by the House Committee on Un-American Activities as an informer, and unmasked as such by Odets in his 1952 testimony—was the secretary of this delegation.

rounded by Cuban secret police, by army and navy guards and by musical comedy detectives in straw hats.

The reporters tell us they are "waiting for Lefty" and inform us that a Cuban delegation of fifty organized to meet us has been arrested. But the city, we are told, is plastered with leaflets about our trip.

Secret service men are brutal in their handling of our two Negro delegates. The whole place bristles with guns. Paul Crosbie, one of the delegation, tries to insist on our rights as American citizens, but nobody listens.

A fight develops among the different groups of guards. The harbor police want us. So do the national police, a much tougher bunch.

Finally our landing cards are taken up and we are marched down to the customs. Our baggage is ripped open. All our papers, notes and books are confiscated.

Hundreds of police with rifles and sub-machine guns now are surrounding us.

I try to send twelve cables. Eleven of them, including two to the New York Post are stopped.

Agents provocateur dressed as laborers begin to circulate among us. One gives a Communist salute and laughs. I see he has a Young Cuba membership card.

We are herded to the dock and the police look at the five women as if undressing them with their eyes.

The police try to prove that the mechanism of Nathan Shaffer's false leg is a concealed weapon of some sort. Shaffer is a delegate from the International Workers' Order. They insist I must be Russian because of my long hair.

It is three hours before they are through with us at the customs. Then we are put in a launch, taken across the bay and marched a mile uphill to the Tiscornia prison camp.

Guards with sub-machine guns ready still surround us; we know that one false move cooks us. But we are careful to give no excuse.

The girls show a fine, courageous spirit as they are registered. We are herded into a large barracks. A captain suddenly curses, for no reason, and swings on Frank Griffin of the International Labor Defense, one of our Negro members.

Four marines stay constantly on guard in the barracks. We have bare springs to sleep on. American reporters hang around all day waiting for news.

Finally American Vice-Consul Edgar arrives in response to a request I had sent to the Consulate and Embassy.

"Apparently you are not wanted in Cuba," he says, and we have our first laugh in fifteen hours.

Then the Group Theatre calls from New York, and I am allowed to go to the telephone. I am assured that protests are going out from many sources and that action will be taken. But Vice-Consul Edgar tells me I cannot send a dispatch to the Post; I must wait until we get on the ship going home. This is the first time we know that we are to be summarily deported.

After supper we walk in the rain back down the hill from the prison camp and the launch takes us back to the Oriente.

Consul General Cameron is there. He seems thoroughly scared.

No official reason is given for our deportation, but we consider it to be in honor of our sincerity of purpose.

On the liner we are still surrounded by scores of detectives, but we are able to learn that hundreds of protest messages are pouring in on President Mendieta and United States Ambassador Caffery.

We are herded into the salon and our consular officials begin to act as glorified baggage collectors, gathering up our ripped open belongings. Then the detectives leave and only a black shirted machine gunner on the dock continues to watch to see that we do not get smuggled ashore.

Passengers seem dismayed as the ship pulls out and clumps of people on shore wave to us.

Some of the Havana papers are smuggled to us. They have distorted our releases. For instance, one says I have had three plays banned on Broadway; instead of that I have three running on Broadway.

The significance of the whole outrageous affair is clear.

The Mendieta-Batista dictatorship here is afraid of an honest investigation.

The American people must realize that now after what has happened.

So our mission on behalf of the Cuban people has been fruitful even though we were not allowed to investigate anything.

Thus, instead of remaining for their announced two-week survey, they had been hustled out of Cuba within twenty-four hours of their arrival.

J. David Stern, publisher of the New York *Post*, wired Secretary of State Cordell Hull a "formal protest at the . . . forcible detention of our correspondent. . . . I am astounded at the reported indifference of [U.S.] Ambassador Caffery," adding that "if our diplomatic representative cannot protect an accredited representative of a United States newspaper from such an outrage then such diplomatic representative must be replaced. . . ." Stern wrote on the same day a "Dear Marvin" note to Roosevelt's assistant secretary, Marvin H. McIntyre, enclosing his wire to Hull. McIntyre advised Stern he was "taking matter up immediately."

Of the hundreds of cables sent in protest by drama editors, politicians, relatives, writers, actors, to the naval prison in Havana, Odets preserved only a few: from Harry Saylor, editor of the New York *Post*, from Communist Congressman Vito Marcantonio, from the Group Theatre, from the incorrigible actress Tallulah Bankhead, and from his father. Miss Bankhead's message read:

Darling I regret having to quote the scriptures but Charlie MacArthur told you so stop goody goody I hope you stay in the dainty place until you have written my play or shall I be big and say our play stop no but really its too fantastic and ridiculous but you can't be a genius and have everything stop don't forget my postcard and be happy. Love, Tallulah

His father's two messages are in a different key. The first advises him, "Don't give interview don't let anyone photograph you will meet you love dad" and the second reminds him of his status: "You are a Post correspondent Dad." On this one, Odets has written, "Hot dog! Hotcha!"

When they arrived in New York, several hundred people with an eight-piece brass band were waiting at Pier 13 to welcome Odets and his American Commission to Investigate Labor and Social Conditions in Cuba. Some of them carried placards inscribed, "American Capital is Destroying Cuban Liberty"; others said simply, "Welcome Home!" Western Union messengers brought Odets dozens of welcoming telegrams. He preserved the one from Beatrice Lillie.

Addressing the impromptu street meeting, the Rev. Herman F. Reissig, a member of the deported delegation and pastor of the Kings Highway Congregational Church in Brooklyn, declared, "We who are not Communists have got to stop being afraid of being called Communists. What is going on in Cuba today is an omen of what will go on in this country to-morrow if we don't take means to stop it." He pointed out that four members of the commission were descended from heroes of the American Revolution and one was a past official of the American Legion.

Immediately mass meetings were organized in many American cities to protest not only the deportation of the commission but also the arrest and beating of the members of a native Cuban committee who had welcomed the Americans. Poet Archibald MacLeish and Roger Baldwin, of the American Civil Liberties Union, now joined Odets on the platform, along with Carleton Beals, with whom Odets collaborated on a long piece for the *New Masses* and on a nickel pamphlet called *Rifle Rule in Cuba*. This thirty-one-page document provides an excellent, politically sophisticated Marxist analysis of the background for Fidel Castro's successful Cuban revolution. Odets had begun also to make notes in his ever-present notebook for a play about a Cuban revolutionary hero, to be called "Law of Flight"—this title deriving from "a game the police and army play in Cuba (Ley de Fuga)," first described to him by the Boston union leader Joe Kelleher: "The police shoot you in the back and claim you were trying to escape. That was what we expected as we went up the hill."

While Odets was in Tiscornia prison camp near Havana, squads of police had raided Ukrainian Hall in Newark, New Jersey, to prevent a performance of *Waiting for Lefty*. It was the sixth such assault on the play in as many weeks. Back in New York, the deportees, along with others, protested the actions of the New Jersey police and also led a parade to the office of the Cuban Consul General, where they "demanded permission for another investigating group to enter Cuba." Some speakers linked the New Jersey event and the events in Cuba with the sinister happenings in Nazi Germany.

Odets' hot public indignation was directed more at the Cuban dictatorship than at the bans on *Lefty;* he wrote many pieces about the collusion of the United States with the Mendieta regime in the person of United States Ambassador Jefferson Caffery, who, he charged, "has a heart of sugar and works hand in glove with the Cuban government." Privately, after learning that his Cuban mission had been known to be potentially dangerous (the Communist Party had thought it too risky for Mother Bloor and had forbidden her to go), he became extremely resentful at having been kept in ignorance and thus used, and soon he resigned his membership of eight months' standing in the Communist Party. Three weeks later, however, he would once more lead a confrontation with a tyrant, solidifying his role as a left-wing hero. This time the enemy woud be fascist Italy; its representative, the playwright Luigi Pirandello.

By the end of July, until *Awake and Sing!* would reopen on a double bill with *Lefty* for a limited engagement in September with Odets again playing Dr. Benjamin, he was briefly "without a single play on the street." On the closing night Clurman wired him, "This end must be the beginning of a great beginning." And Odets made a strange note on a slip of paper: "Now that I am really a playwright, I will discontinue my scalp treatments to prevent baldness."

Maxwell Anderson, John Howard Lawson, and Paul Green had not, according to the *Herald Tribune*, supplied anticipated plays, and for the first time in four summers the Group was not rehearsing a play for the new season. Odets, though he thought it had some of his best writing, was still fearful of a production of *Paradise Lost* lest it seem repetitive of *Awake and Sing!*, but it was beginning to appear to the directors of the Group Theatre that they had no alternative. He postponed the decision by accepting speaking engagements to raise money for the Cuban people and for the *New Masses*.* Since his return from Cuba, his depression had significantly lifted. He was eating and drinking too much, however, and still suffering from severe insomnia.

When the New York *Post* announced in large headlines that "Pirandello Arrives Damning Ethiopians" and "Nobel Prize Winner Defends Duce's Acts in Africa," many Americans were shocked. When the aging and renowned playwright was further quoted as saying, "I am a fascist because I am an Italian" and that he never "mixes politics with literature," more than left-wing literary circles were profoundly distressed. Some knew, though most did not, that Pirandello had become exhausted, bewildered, and heartsick over tragedies in his family life and over his longstanding conflicts with Mussolini, who had always said that creative activity must serve the fascist state. For Odets, the final straw in Pirandello's public statement came when he said, "The American people have conquered a whole continent and made it a home for the prolific work of the white race," implying, Odets thought, that this was Mussolini's mission in Africa.

Odets, writing in *New Theatre*, replied,

Pirandello's shameless propaganda for war against the Ethiopian people reveals the complete bankruptcy of Italian fascist thought. There is a definite tie-up between Pirandello's art and the decadent culture of fascist Italy. Pirandello reflects the "civilization" he is ballyhooing in this country. As an artist he has nothing important left to say. All he can do is to repeat himself. As a man he can sink no lower than to be Mussolini's official fool.

John Howard Lawson added:

Every writer who respects the honor and dignity of his craft should protest this prostitution of a writer to the service of destructive reaction.

Rose McClendon, black actress and head of the Negro People's Theatre, added her voice:

I am glad to add my protest to those of men like John Howard Lawson and Clifford Odets against Pirandello and all he represents. Lawson did not hesitate to risk his life in Alabama out of sympathy for the Negro people and Odets recently faced physical danger in an effort to expose the terror directed against the Cuban people.

Sidney Kingsley, Elmer Rice, and other American writers joined in this condemnation by "all people who believe in liberty."

* Such people as Irving Berlin, Sidney Howard, S. N. Behrman, and Ira Gershwin sent him large checks, many of which he matched.

As so often in Odets' accusations, there is a discernible thread of fear that he himself is guilty of precisely that which he is condemning. When he states that as an artist Pirandello can only "repeat himself" he is expressing the fear he is facing if he lets the Group produce *Paradise Lost.* And when he states the conviction that "as a man he can sink no lower than to be Mussolini's official fool," he reflects his (justified) apprehension about the strength of that in himself which longs to submit to a powerful tyrant.

Ignorant of the hue and cry being raised against him, Pirandello received in his suite at the Waldorf-Astoria a letter signed by Lawson and Odets which simply requested an audience with him. He was pleased to grant it, anticipating, he said later, that "the appointment had been made in expectation that a few American playwrights desired to pay their respects and discuss dramatic and artistic questions." Herbert Kline, editor of *New Theatre,* and a member of the delegation,* recalled the event, described by one newspaper as "an ambush":

> Pirandello received us expecting the homage that he deserved as a playwright—but not expecting us to ask him to protest the Italian brutalities and mass murder in Ethiopia—which we did, saying he was safely outside of fascist Italy, that his work belonged to the world that loved his plays and revered him as a master. Odets commented that we expected from him the kind of humanity expressed by the great French writer Henri Barbusse, who had agreed to head the international "League Against War and Fascism."
>
> Of course, we were placing Pirandello in a terrible position— but he was a free man, and too old and famous to suffer personally if he did come out and join us in asking a stopping of Mussolini's attack on the Ethiopian people.
>
> He looked stunned by our request—then expressed himself sadly as unable to do so, and that he [had] thought he would be treated with more hospitality by people of the American theatre. Even though we were right in terms of humanity—and he was wrong —I remember having a coffee with Clifford later and both of us expressing how uncomfortable we felt, despite our righteousness, in badgering the old gentleman with our young, challenging views on life. Somehow it didn't seem right, even though we were right, as we had seen the hurt in the eyes of this beautiful old man. I tell this anecdote only to describe how Clifford expressed his deep humanity and respect for Pirandello even in conflict with his strongest beliefs at the period of their most affirmative public statement.

Pirandello had insisted the press be present at this meeting and, according to *The New York Times,* had argued that "Mr. Odets' plays were good plays not because they were social, but because they are artistic and that he believed a true artist wrote apart from the age he lives in." According to Lawson, ". . . when we started to argue about fascism, Pirandello almost collapsed. . . . This confrontation under such painful circumstances of the author of *Six Characters* and the author of *Lefty* had a sort of historical meaning."

Within the year Odets, despite his leading of American support for the Loyalist cause in Spain, would be attacked for having "sold out" his social conscience to Hollywood; Herbert Kline would be filming attacks by Mussolini's bombers on Barcelona, Valencia, and Madrid; and Pirandello would be dead.

* Odets, Lawson, Kline, Ivan Black, Henry Hart, and Mark Marvin.

There is a face to keep, a position to retain. Before you were free; you are a prisoner now. The story of the boy who hit the target's heart once, never trying again, is apropos.

CLIFFORD ODETS (*undated*)

. . . and then famous, MY POSITION BULLIES ME! *and I have a strong desire for anonymity, knowing that I could live better and more truly if not known.*

CLIFFORD ODETS (*undated*)

As the fall theatre season approached, with Maxwell Anderson's *Winterset* lost to the Group, with Strasberg in a state of what Clurman called "impassivity," and with Cheryl Crawford committed to an incomplete script called *Weep for the Virgins* as the Group's initial offering, it seemed to Clurman that Odets, despite the risk, must rework *Paradise Lost*, which Clurman would direct as the Group's second production. Odets saw the logic in this decision, but remained paralyzed. Instead of working on the play, he guiltily alternated between stuporous music-listening and a frenzied courtship of five women, two older and three younger than he, one of whom was his old standby Dena. Perhaps, he thought, he would locate in Dena the key to his old innocent and creative self before he was thirty years old. Since his success he was experiencing, to his dismay, a curtailment of powers, not an extension of them, and an intolerable anxiety that he could not even meet Clurman's request for a reworked third act of *Paradise Lost*.

Perhaps, he writes to Dena, sending her money, he should marry her. She thanks him for his check, telling him that until she received his recent letters she had been planning "to tell you to go plumb to hell and that I was sick of being kicked around, even by you," that she was "thrown on my ear" when his offer came and now she wonders "just how seriously you mean the whole thing?" If she had had any money, she would have wired him "Okay," because "I love you and you know that," but maybe he was under "all sorts of influences" when he wrote and is regretting his offer already. As for having babies, "they are only a minor consideration" and can wait. She adjures him to do "a lot of good work," to answer at once, "and don't think I'm not still sore at you, lots of love and kisses, you bum, Dena."

Two weeks later she writes sadly, "Some day, Cliff, after the revolution when we're both old and gray and we've both done really important things . . . we'll spend a weekend together," adding that she is leaving for Beacon, New York, "to rest" at Goldie Bromberg's place. From this it appears that Odets has withdrawn his offer of marriage.

The wryly witty Broadway star Ruth Gordon, ten years his senior, writes teasingly about his romantic fantasy of marrying Dena so that a "comfortable, healthy wife" and "formula children" might restore his soul; she counsels him that, on the contrary, Beethoven was right and that Odets should, like his hero, remain single. The intuitive Miss Gordon had moved him to tears when she said, "I think you are a lonely person," and now saw that he was toying with the possibility of trying to meet his creative anxiety by manufacturing a biological family to make up for his lost "brain-children." Shortly she would leave for London, stimulating a "cloudburst" of letters from him, mostly unsent.

In sudden desperate determination, he leaves all the women behind for New City, where the Henry Varnum Poors have lent him a place to work. From there he writes a lonely letter to the first correspondent of his adolescence, his cousin Irene (now married to a man named Steinberg). He tells her his father has visited him, dispensing managerial and literary advice, and that he is working on two plays, one called *Paradise Lost*, for immediate production. He closes with the hope that someday "I will have my own house" to which to invite the family, and "When I get that house, I'll plant a beautiful tree in front of it for my Mother."

From Cape Cod, Ruth Gordon writes to Odets in care of Henry Varnum Poor in New City:

Dearest Clifford,

This is a beautiful dreamy lazy afternoon full of Cape odors and soft colors and being here, I know for the first time what you meant when you said you were glad you are an American. This or the next town, Orleans is the home of my father's people and I have pride in belonging here. Cape people seem almost alone in the respect that they still have an integrity toward life. It isn't that they are just old-fashioned. They are different. I don't think they particularly want to be different and cultivate it. They just are that way and let it go at that. One bus goes through in the morning down to the tip end of the Cape, Provincetown, and returns decently at five o'clock at night on its way back to New Bedford and that is ALL the way of getting out of here unless you have your own car. No nervous little local jitneys or hacking busses, just nothing. The A and P could never get so much as a sample in here. They have a splendid General Store and Post Office, trimmed with fine old seamen's wood carvings and run by Mr. Goodspeed and his daughter and it is just not a place to shop; it is a minor and aromatic adventure. Cake and carrots and the mail and the New Bedford Times are all jostling around with Balsam chewing gum that I haven't thought of since I was a child. And fishing tackle and ladies' dusting caps all come out of the same cupboard.

From her reference to Odets' being glad he *is* an American it is evident that they have discussed their mixed feelings about identity. From her secure position as a non-Jewish daughter of pre-Revolutionary ancestry, she can afford a greater sense of outrage and shame at the inequities in her country. Celebrating a comforting era when it could still be said of the Cape, "There is nothing new as far as the eye can travel," she offers him in six subsequent pages an intimate Early American sampler both of this clear-light place and of herself.

On the day before Ruth sailed for Europe with Helen Hayes and Charles MacArthur, Odets commenced a daily account of his current life, in the form of letters to her. He retained both the original and the carbon, stating he would give them all to her at once.

The Group—filling in with a brief revival of *Awake and Sing!* plus *Lefty* in New York and five weeks in Philadelphia—now commenced its fall season, and the deadline for *Paradise Lost* was finally upon him. The thorniest problems with this work, as in the rest of his plays, lay in its third act.* Struggling nightly with it at the University Place apartment which he still shared with Clurman, he found himself writing, instead, those long letters to Ruth Gordon, actually addressed to the creative part of himself he called "feminine," of which he had lost track. In these letters—which would never have to run what he called "the gauntlet" of critics—he writes freely, spontaneously, playfully, catching the essence of a multitude of people and events.

The task of revising *Paradise Lost* feels to him monumental, but he ascribes the difficulty entirely to the fact that it is a finished play which has gone "cold." He cannot see now how large a contribution to his creative impasse is the terror of losing his magical Success. He writes:

What a bad bad summer it was, insecurity and maladjustments all over the landscape for me. Then Ruth Gordon and I meeting and being restless and unsettled from that. Dead dead summer, dead loss (but for Ruth), a season of adjustment making and few friends realize the difficulty of making adjustments to the new life which has come to me. I am amazed that a sensitive person like Harold is not aware of it. I assure you it is painful.

The artist will have to learn the technique and craft approach of going back to an already written and "cold" play. Or else write them so perfectly (at least with more care) that rewriting is not necessary. I think I can write such a play. My trouble, as some dame mentioned to Harold, is "quick writing." People think I work much harder than I do: I encourage the "white" deception. What more can I ask than the present awareness of my own artistic problems? In America, at 29, I am doing well, growing steadily. Ruth Gordon powdered it down fine and bitterly when she said to me yesterday—touching intuitively one of my sorest points, "Learn to be generous to yourself, Clifford." I flay myself incessantly, about everything. What a dumb brute!!!

After the first Group meeting, Clurman and Odets brought back to their apartment Stella Adler, Sanford Meisner, and photographer Paul Strand to listen to records of "extraordinary" Hugo Wolf songs. "They are," he writes, "romantic, decadent, like stretching out on a plushy oriental rug," but a "great discovery for me."

After dinner they all went to see the Russian film *Peasants,* with which he deeply resonates:

I'm a sucker for those pictures, but this one was good. Curiously simple and honest, but worth a carload of Hollywood's best. But what a hero they have to show! And that reminds me of a letter from Sidney Howard this morning, dinner with him tomorrow night.

---

* Odets often said later, "Show me a playwright with third-act trouble and I'll show you a man who cannot make a commitment."

I say that reminds me of him because he is a playwright looking for a hero to write about. All over America the artists looking for a hero to put in their workings, and all without allegiance or hero—like saying a man with his essential things cut off. Howard realizes it keenly. He tells me his new play, *Paths of Glory*, now in rehearsal, has 73 speaking parts in it. (I cry several times during every Russian picture—the human quality of the people is preserved with great love in all of them, the very opposite of American pictures wherein they work for the very opposite effect. In one an abundance of life, in the other sterility and lack of real life. What people will finally get to realize about my work—which is what I want—is the abundance of life the plays will reflect. It is not for nothing that I'm half Russian!!!)

Soon he would believe that he could bring such "an abundance of life" to American film-making. Right now he read and reread a *Vanity Fair* article which congratulated him for keeping away from Hollywood. Cut off for the time being from all the significant women in his life and obsessed with thoughts of his dead mother, he writes:

A thing that has reached terrifying proportions in my life is the fact that I seem to make little contact with living people. I know what has happened. From most of them there is so little to be learned, so little to be seen or discovered in them that is original and revelatory, that I have gotten into the habit of ignoring them. It was always that way with me: the inside teeming and quick rhythm was more important. It is even more so now, but how dangerous it is, how easily it will let one fall into the habit of peopling the world with one's own desires and images! I feel it happening all the time, but seem to do nothing to prevent this loss. I have paid a truly great price for the years of my young loneliness: I am forever locked in myself; deeply imbedded in the flesh and bones of myself is a hungry peering person, astigmatic, tired, alone.

Enviously he tries to unravel what establishes the contact between Ruth Gordon and Jed Harris (at thirty-five a successful director and/or producer of many plays like *The Royal Family* and *The Front Page*), with whom she has told Clifford she is "madly in love." It interests him that Harris was born in Vienna to Meyer and Esther Horowitz, and he wonders when the name was changed. He is envious also of Clurman, to whose intimacies with Stella he is listening as he types, and indeed of any pair that appears to be joined. He hopes writer Charlie MacArthur, husband of Helen Hayes, is jealous of *him* as a writer.

Pursuing his interest in Harris, he fantasies meeting him and questions people who know him, as he must know "what sort of fellow can impress Ruth and leave on her the mark that Harris apparently has," and concludes:

I see it this way: that she was a sort of intellectual virgin when he came along; she was a sensitive person, hungry, alone in a world of sort of semi-fools, and when he came along there was a conquest and a marking that she won't forget until the day she dies. That is the tribute we pay to people who have helped slap and shape us into the form of maturity.

Only four or five Group members, he writes, remain dear to him; the others might as well not exist. When, however, the entire company met on the Belasco stage on the first day, he notes with relief:

A great feeling flows between Gadget [Kazan] and me and when we met it was like a love making. He has been down south, to Cuba and Mexico. Cuba almost refused to let him in because he was a steerage passenger. Gadget will always go down to the bottom because he knows the values there are truer than up stairs—he has the instinct of the true artist for people and things. On the stage here he confessed to me (as I did too) that he had been looking forward to seeing me.

Suffering from what he calls "a kind of nervous exhaustion" and feeling "half-dazed," he makes restless stabs at the third act of *Paradise Lost,* at the "suffocating sea of notes"* he is accumulating on *The Silent Partner,* and at a possible series of radio sketches "with a Whitmanesque perspective on America." He cannot even "listen well" to music: "I keep hovering in that partition between two concentrated thoughts." It seems to him he is "like the old Jew who got both the lash and the rotten fish when he was asked which punishment he wanted—couldn't make a decision!"

The invitations continue to pour in, people wanting "to stroke the lion's mane" and he wants to accept them all:

So much to learn, so many different classes of people to see!!! If I could only practise patience . . .

From the outside my face looks still, but inside my heart races and the mind twists like a worm in a fire—I will really do the unusual thing of burning out my youth by sitting still in a chair. Right now I feel a sweep of energy flow down over my naked shoulders. What a stupid impasse this is: I make more trouble for myself than three or five girls could do!

Spoke to father on the long distance phone. He is all business again. I am so sorry to be tired of seeing him. He will sit there and talk nothing but business and my financial welfare. Which ever way this cat is dropped he will fall on golden paws. The problem arises from the fact that he is lonely, tired, bewildered and his wife and my mother for more than twenty-five years is recently dead. What can you do about that? Be a good son? . . .

Anything is possible with me now—the most fabulous kind of success. I really feel in myself an ability to do or be anything I desire to be. Except what is most difficult, being a serious and sober artist who progresses in his work from play to play. That is the most difficult.

Unable to shake his preoccupation with his older rival, Jed Harris, he finally arranges a meeting with him. He is convinced in advance that Harris shares with him the same "bad parts." A subtle atmosphere, initiated by Odets, hangs over their meetings, that of an interchangeable emotional triangle.

We proposed to meet each other after his rehearsal at night, eleven at the Vanderbilt. I told him I'd have to bring a girl along, a girl who was with me, but after an evening at home with her—and a luxuriant hour in bed in which we tore up the mattress—and after a dinner I left her and slowly sauntered in the warm air and got to the theatre where the rehearsal of Harris' show was still going on.

* Odets' son Walt's later comment: "My father always kept accumulating all these notes and books, thinking he'd find the key in one of them, thus synthesizing the whole thing. Instead, he became more and more confused and finally could synthesize nothing."

How very dully—the actors were very tired. Harris left them rehearsing, gave some whispered instructions to the stage manager, and we left the theatre together. He was wearing a sweat shirt under a well-cut blue flannel coat—said he couldn't see what was the use of collars and ties—he'd learned this in California. He was heated and put up his collar. I don't suppose any two people ever made such immediate acceptance of each other. Said he liked to walk a distance after rehearsals. Said he was tired—rehearsing from one till eleven at night. We walked down 6th Avenue.

He talks easily, fluently, not tapping himself very deeply. I can see he functions most deeply only in relation to some problem or specific task. There was none of that between us and he continued talking about political problems, as if that were the thing which would interest me most. A great deal of charm and easy relaxation came from him, his weariness acting as a sort of auto intoxication. He doesn't contact you fully—he is hearing himself more than he hears the outside. I mean that he doesn't actually listen to what he is saying, but to something else—he can think about two things at once, in fact does it most of the time. When he is really interested in a thing, then the two streams come together.

We walked all the way down to Luchow's on 14th Street. He has the facility of making physical contact with another person—it is the way he will touch you or guide you by the elbow across the street. It must be very pleasing to a woman to be touched like that. I understood immediately, when we sat in Luchow's under light, that to accept him this way was merely to accept myself. What I am saying is that I have never in my life met a person with whom I had so much in common. I mentioned Charlie MacArthur and he said, "Yes, Charlie wanted to be like us." We drank beer and he ate. We sat there until they closed the place and had to leave us out a side door already locked.

He is autoerotic, generates himself to activity more than outside objects do. I thought to myself with a great sense of relief, "When I look at him and listen to him I can see myself with sharp objectivity. How fortunate to have met him then!" The whole point of his life, it developed in conversation, is his sense of never having used himself or his talent. Directing plays and producing them he sees as some unimportant thing which has nothing to do with being creative. He feels he hasn't functioned in life. We got into a slight flurry about creative directors like Meyerhold. He refused or didn't see the dialectic process of the things he thinks not so good finally helping create the better things. There is something about him uncreative in the sense that he would rather have the whole damn theatre die than help build it up to what he wants it to be. For instance, he said that he had once had an idea for a permanent company, but that the leading actor figure in it—Holbrook Blinn—had died. So his idea had died too. Paul Green was a poor playwright, Jack Lawson, too. But he couldn't see that damning them was damning the only life and starting point we have in America and that you had either to work with them or die off into utter sterility and death. The death feeling about Harris is bad, mostly for himself, a good deal for the whole theatre.

Although Harris' easy charm, together with his damning of other American playwrights, was more sophisticated than Lou Odets', it is evident that Clifford, in the context of their shared relationship with Ruth Gordon, is responding to him much as to his father: a combination of feminine surrender ("It must be very pleasing to a woman to be touched like that") and at the same time a sharing of significant identity-elements ("I have never in my life met a person with whom I had so much in common").

The first meeting with Harris stimulated a long, self-exploratory letter wherein Odets continues to use the director-producer as the mask for his own conflicts:

> Working alone all these years he has had no identification with anything out of himself. He is the talented individual going on by himself, without relationship to a world, a group, an idea, an animating force. Attached to something he could still blossom out into a fine artist, but he doesn't see that as part of his problem. I don't think—as much as he understands himself—that he sees himself properly in relation to other American artists and the entire American life around us. He said, for example, that actors so often failed because their work had no continuity to it. Which hit the nail exactly on the head. But he failed also to see that the thing is true of himself. No, he did mention that, saying, "A guy like me should be working nine or ten months out of the year like any other worker. Instead I get one play and then there's five blank months in between." But he failed again to see that if his viewpoint were in relation to some thing else beside his personal views that there would be no blank months.
>
> He likes the New Theatre Magazine, spoke highly of it, said he wants to write a Hollywood article for them—I got his promise for it. He hates the bunk shooters, he hates the movie magnates. And there is the whole sad thing. For even tho his hate is proper, his critical attitude sharp, that is only half of the works, half of a man. The other half must be what he loves, what he admires, what he is willing to work for. Let him spurn the decay with sharp creativity, but where is the healthy part from which he must feed or die? So, no matter what one can say or do, Jed Harris with all his colours and complexity and talent, must always remain half a man until he finds the thing to which he can give his allegiance and affirmation.
>
> Right now, he said, he is thinking of getting on a freighter boat and taking a trip around the world. He'll land in the Orient, work his way over to Russia in a Ford and finally land up in Moscow. He wants to see for himself, he says—the reports and books are unsatisfactory. Yes, he'll walk out on the theatre, he says, what's it ever given him—the critics of course are only worth smiling at, etc. All that is right, but he doesn't quite see that he is playing their game perfectly—a series of small slams and a tearing down.
>
> He has in him all the good deep qualities of the Jew—even the moral fibre. But it doesn't function and instead one gets from his face a vulnerable look, even a sense of something crippled. A hunchback has that look in his face, if you know what I mean.

Odets' tone of masculine competition coupled with a feminine seductiveness toward Harris continues:

> We finally landed here in this room to hear some music. He sat down, Ruth (are you there yet?), in the same chair you sat when you were here last. You must know how I thought of the both of you

together. We talked and played music and suddenly I saw that he had picked up the poem book you sent me. "I have an edition home exactly like this," he said. I looked at him with curiosity, wondering what he would do or say if I told him that was probably his book. I didn't say a word about it. I think he knew tho, because it was with the other two books you sent and he saw the three together. Perhaps he didn't tie them up.

I told him we would do a play together. He wanted to know if I was a good actor, could I direct, etc. Told him I wanted to do a play for Ruth Gordon. He liked that, looked at me, told me what a fine woman she was, "a great person" he said, going on to explain why. We found ourselves in accord on her acting talent. He spoke with a burst about her, twice. We went to have coffee in a corner store. We talked about the movies. Would I be interested in doing a movie with him, about a strike? Sure I would if we had a free hand. "Of course we'd have to have a free hand," said he. Then he skipped off in a cab, with a side wave of an expressive hand, at five thirty in the morning. Said I'd look him up. Sure, he said.

Do you know, I forgot, there is a touch of Bohemianism still in him? A touch of the talented amateur. Perhaps that comes from never having taken very seriously the thing which was his art form. The talented artist stabilized in his work will seldom talk about it with such rapacity or brain-glinting.

His present show made him tired too. He knows what most actors are, he despises them, he laughs at them. But what will he put in their place?

When I got to bed I felt as if I'd spent a few hours with myself, something like having written a satisfactory letter.

He repeated the entire event the following night, this time "with Kazan thrown in for good measure." His identification with Ruth is palpable:

As the quality of Harris comes to life and wholeness under my hand and inside, so there is a stepping-up of my sense of you—and that is what I wanted. Almost I wanted to be with you by being with him. Altho wearied by the late hour both times I still managed to go to bed with a relaxed satisfied feeling both times.

He had given Harris his play *Paradise Lost* to read and has just heard, as he writes, that Harris—who says he has never said this before about a script of a living writer—"loved it":

Then, my sweet far-away Ruth, began a telephonic "wooing" that lasted an hour. He went all over the script and said some good things. He has talent. He knew what he would do with the script and he "wooed" in a soft voice the writer, trying to sever him from a background, trying to focalize him on Jed Harris. He wants to do the script. I don't blame him—all the junk he's worked with!

Finally he said he would come to see *Awake and Sing* two nights from now, instead of waiting until his own play opens, as he had said before. He also said (in a semi-serious-joking way) that he might bolster up soft spots in his present play with six or eight lines from my script. I told him I'd knock him down if he did.

Odets is enacting with Harris not only a standard sexual triangle, but also his submissive yearning to please his father in his work. Harris' response to *Paradise Lost* encourages him to proceed with this deeply feared production, but he cannot resume real work on it until he masters a constellation of anxieties and is deprived of the creative "income" he is still deriving from playing Dr. Benjamin in *Waiting for Lefty*.

Making a conscious link between his acting and his inability to write, he berates himself for the siphoning off of his creative powers by his "diversions"; he is convinced that his will-lessness, his compulsive "weakness" for women—what he calls his "monstrous indulgence in sexuality"—is at the cost of productivity, a view frequently found in men with work problems.

At the same time he manages some restraint and compassion in special situations:

I saw Tallulah Bankhead last night and for a couple of hours sat on the edge of her bed and told her all the dirty stories I know. She was much piqued that I wouldn't get into bed with her. Formerly, in the face of such masculine inactivity, she would spit like a bitch cat. Now she is a little amazed and respectful about it. I begin to think she is a very worthless person, but certainly blooming with all sorts of vices and manners which have deep social roots. She is always interesting to see, albeit a little boring at times. I can't quite make out what is wrong with her. To say she is in flight from something is to say an obvious thing. She suffers from an awful and big sense of "insufficiency." She feels all people are aware of that lack and she compensates for it by giving you her sex instruments for your use and possible pleasure. That is her way of binding you to her. She really knows nothing, hasn't the concentration of a fish on a dish. To see this dame sheathed in a silk nightgown is to be sorry for the human race and I was not afraid to tell her that I was ashamed of her, just as one fellow human to another. You cannot see anyone have such disregard for life without squirming. I know I can't. A human being is a great thing and is needful of respect! You will gradually understand and see in my work that always my direction and choice will be to find in people the progressive heroic elements. They are the parts of life which are going to help build a new great world. . . .

I can really act a streak if I'm relaxed on the stage and have marked out for myself at least the pattern of the part. In this role it is easy for me to improvise and I do it every performance, reshaping the words to the different rhythm and impulse which comes nightly. To be relaxed on the stage and know what you are saying and what it means—great satisfaction, for a real thing is built. In such a time an audience can see before its eyes exactly what I do when I sit down and write the page of a script.

At home—suddenly that strange weird red headed girl rang the bell and came in. She was feeling, she said, down. I am too tired now to write about her—an interesting person there, so unrelated to normal living things around her that she seems like an author's creation. She actually swore that she didn't remember two nights we bedded together in Boston, and they only last year! This night she'll remember. Or I'm wrong!

I kept thinking to myself, "Let me see you send this girl away. Give her up. Keep your hands off her." But then I thought I could if I wanted to. And so excused what is surely a weakness and monstrous indulgence. The sex urges of my body have long ago been satisfied, but the head is full of small boy burning ideas. I don't think I'll ever lose them. Well, I have SOME virtue: at least I don't run around LOOKING for girls!

Several interesting technical ideas came to me during the past hours—chiefly from listening to Beethoven. The false starts he makes are fine for tightening up dialogue. Goodnight. The notebooks are crammed—I am happy. Goodnight Ruth in England.

Such "consolations," as well as the substitute-writing of letters to Ruth Gordon, continue until rehearsals of *Paradise Lost* are well under way.

Loving her with "all the pores of my skin," he writes detailed salutations to Ruth Gordon's "heavy hair," her "ironical mouth," and sundry other items. The excesses in these letters, as in most from Odets to a woman, suggest a "willing," indeed, a forcing of feeling.

Contact with his father is now steady, and it is evident that Lou Odets, unsuccessfully struggling with his own middle-years crises of loneliness, stagnation, and despair, is regressively turning to his successful son for some repair of his economic and psychological bankruptcy. The son, deriving far more satisfaction than he is aware of from their reversal of roles, writes:

L.J. (which is what he likes to be called instead of Father, since it is a younger and more intimate thing) got here at after noon and stayed most of the afternoon trying to work up in me a sense of my position—I suppose that's what it would be called. I told him I wished I might feel as important about myself as he seems to think I am. He spoke with such energy that often (as it has always been) he danced as the words poured out. Herman had to ask him why he was dancing. Such zest for life! Such energy! And yet he looks older, a little rueful too. I would much rather he had the old arrogance of the successful American business man. He will make a wonderful character in a play. Often when I catch myself at the peak of some expression which works in my hands and face I know I look just as he does at a similar moment. He was tickled to death when I mentioned to him some time ago that we shared a bottom lip with a split in its center. He can't get over that.

He left with Herman about five and I stayed on. Ate out of the icebox. Had brought groceries to fill the shelves almost and got from it a comforting sense of being stored up for the long cold winter to come. Felt how I would (or could) stay here and write and write until the new play was out and wonderful to behold—I am thinking about it and the breaking point is near when it will begin to come. I haven't found out yet what makes the creative state in me, but I know readily enough when it's there.

The metaphor, now and always, is the delivery of a child "wonderful to behold."

This deluge of letters to Ruth Gordon, terminated by her return from England on the *Aquitania*, is counterpointed by an active effort to discover the secret of her tie to Jed Harris and to replace him. His identification with Harris has produced the same ambivalence as with his father: "There is something morbid in my curiosity, because it would be simple for me to match in a short time the bad parts of him. . . ."

When *Awake and Sing!* and *Lefty* moved at the end of September from
New York to the Broad Street Theatre in Philadelphia, Odets gave up his
part to Alexander Kirkland, leaving now no action-buffer between him
and his anxiety about the third act of *Paradise Lost*. He is pictured in the
Philadelphia Record at the opening night of the double bill standing outside the theatre with his bankrupt father, who now lived alone in a hotel
room. They look eerily alike, the son's face having filled out considerably
during this bewildering year.

After the curtain came down, L. J. Odets accompanied Clifford to
his old hangout on Locust Street for a reunion with the Leof crowd, many
of whom were now receiving money from him.

The complex experience for both father and son as they were now
changing places is distilled in this evening. Clifford, the reigning "sport,"
was paying for everyone—not only for his father but also for the friends
this same father had not long before contemptuously shouted out of the
house as parasitic "snot-nose bums." At the table L. J. Odets began to
discuss taking a trip around the world to assuage his grief about his wife's
death and his plans, at forty-eight, to retire when he returned, all at his
son's expense.

It was a swift and significant turnabout, wherein the frightened,
helpless, rejected failure was fast becoming the commanding monarch.
The triumphant, even vengeful sense of power flowing to Odets from his
meteoric success in the preceding months seemed to him a splendid and
yet insanely frightening dream. The death of his mother (at the apogee
of his "arrival" as an artist) and this changing of places with his father,
as he later understood, had triggered a severe identity-confusion and,
accordingly, a work stoppage which would forever compromise his creative growth. Two decades later, mired in Hollywood and working on what
was probably his best film, *The Sweet Smell of Success*, he writes of a
"fictional" character:

> This man has become a writer in terms of escape or rebellion from
> parental domination or an onerous situation which created in him
> unbearable tensions and anxieties. He perhaps feels swamped and
> nullified, etc. Now, a successful writer, he finds a work stoppage
> *because* he has, through his original neurotic patterns, worked him-
> self into (and is playing out) the original situation all over again.
> The situation is once again onerous—the parental domination has
> been replaced by a punishing (or suffocating) need to live up to a
> *now successful image*, to keep (before it was to *find*, to validate
> himself in the eyes of parents and others by becoming a success)
> intact what he has become; to simultaneously defy and placate critics
> and public opinion and esteem for his talent (all parental, authori-
> tarian and punitive!). Now he is more constricted and imprisoned
> than before. And, Art, his way of flight, has become the harshest
> reality of them all! Of course, it simply means that success did not
> remove the original neurotic problem; it merely realigned and re-
> stricted it, etc.

No small item in this realignment was the fact that, despite his staggering reception, his income for this year would total only $5,060.35, a sum
equal to two or three weeks' salary in the film-writing assignments he had
been refusing. With an army of relatives and friends—his father most
significantly—now dependent on him, the gap between his position of
power and his financial capacity to maintain it was widening. Whereas
his writing had originally supported his separation from and rebellion

against his father, it now was demanded by the father as well as by his father's replacement, Clurman.

At this point the Group directors decided to mount an immediate production of *Paradise Lost* because the motion-picture firm Metro-Goldwyn-Mayer, always on the scent of new talent, had agreed to provide $17,000 for it. Clurman urgently renewed his insistence that Odets finish revising the third act while the company in Philadelphia began rehearsals of the play.

For his part, Odets engaged instead in several worthy and diverting projects. Together with Jed Harris, Herman Shumlin, Sidney Howard, and John Howard Lawson, he was organizing a symposium and dinner at the Hotel Edison for the benefit of the left-wing *New Theatre* magazine, in honor of "its having widened the horizon of American theatre." He persuaded innumerable artists and writers to be sponsors: the Rev. John Haynes Holmes with thoughts on "The Theatre and War," poet laureate Archibald MacLeish to discuss "Poetry in the Theatre,"* while he himself would talk about "Dramatizing Our Times." In his own presentation he offered a passionate declaration that the distinction between "art" and "propaganda" is essentially false. Any "creative work artistically worth its salt" must "artistically tell the truth" about some aspect of life. "I consider a fine art work like the Bible excellent propaganda, or the Greek dramas with their poetic arguments against war. Propaganda comes into play wherever a writer expresses a definite—positive—point of view, whether it's his individually, or his as a member of a section of society. . . . No writer lives in a vacuum. His reactions must necessarily spring out of the life around him." It is evident that while Odets was genuinely pursuing his principled necessity to make some actual impact on the troubled "real world" of 1935, he was also strenuously avoiding work on *Paradise Lost*.

His next project was to amass 100,000 signatures to present to Secretary of State Cordell Hull for the release of labor leader Ernst Thaelmann from his dungeon in Nazi Germany. "America has its Lincolns, its John Browns, great men who fought against slavery. Germany today has its Ernst Thaelmann," he wrote, pleading for political asylum for the German.

Clurman, understandably impatient, continued to plague him for rewrites, and Odets determined to force himself to locate the weak spot in *Paradise Lost* by reading it to a group assembled at the Leof home in Philadelphia. Old Dr. Leof thought it magnificent, but it troubled Odets that some of the younger people had fallen asleep before he concluded at three in the morning. Accordingly, he returned to the safer arena of political action.

When there appeared a full-page advertisement labeled "A New Declaration of Independence" signed by a handful of industrialists excoriating him, among others, as a "dangerous radical" and "criminal," Odets responded with an open letter to the newspapers accusing them of "hiding behind the American flag." He adjures them to "read American

---

* It is difficult to convey the qualitative difference between the culture of the mid-thirties and *any* decade thereafter. The integration between a moral-political position and an esthetic one, between the "real" and the "created" worlds, was unprecedented. For example, for the Marxist *New Theatre* magazine Archibald MacLeish—to become Librarian of Congress—wrote a long piece, called "Theatre Against War and Fascism," in which he described Odets' as the best and most "actual and alive" work in the New York theatre. Because of these "worker's theatres," argued MacLeish, "the American theatre is as dead as we have been saying it was for many years and the American theatre is more alive than it has ever been in its history."

history. Read of Valley Forge and the valiant farmers who froze and starved while the profiteers stayed home . . . ," concluding, "The lover of REAL patriotism will not listen to these men and their hateful words. They are the killers of true democracy. WE ARE AMERICANS! We are lovers of the honest words of great Americans—Jefferson, Walt Whitman, and Abraham Lincoln! We are Revolutionists!" He began to buy books on American history, accumulating over the years hundreds of them, which he used to create outlines for plays on Benjamin Franklin, Lincoln, Jefferson, Woodrow Wilson, John Brown, Shays' Rebellion—none of them ever to be written.

On October 19 three thousand people crowded into the Manhattan Opera House for a program including a dashed-off one-act playlet, *Remember*, written and directed by him in the space of a week for the Negro People's Theatre. Describing it as dealing with the "horrors of home relief," a left-wing critic was disappointed that this short piece was "too psychological" and that "he convinced us more by emotion and individual characterization than by a thorough exposure of the problem." *Remember* pictures the miserable tenement flat of an unemployed family of Negroes. When the relief investigator comes to investigate whether they are entitled to home relief, the small daughter reveals that her father works one day a week, thus invalidating their claim. A "chatterbox" neighbor arrives to announce that the mother has just died in a charity hospital, "stunning the child." The father bursts out with a "grief-stricken protest" against a system which permits a poor woman to perish for lack of care. In what the Jewish *Daily Forward* called "a flaming monologue," the father adjures the child to "remember, remember, remember all her life" the evils of the world which had killed her mother and prevented her from "living like a human being," and to "fight against those responsible for our misery." Contrasting *Remember* with a one-act play by Paul Peters on the same program, the *Daily Forward* critic said Odets' "electric" characters "light up from within." Unlike the Communist reviewer, he was delighted with these characterizations.

The social-political form into which Odets has cast the refrain "Remember, remember, remember" reflects the documentary-advocate consciousness of his era. The personal source of it, as in *I Can't Sleep* (where he berates himself for having forgotten his dead "working-class mother") is also clear. Overtly, the antagonist who must be remembered and fought is the evil force in society that "blocks growth and crushes the innocent." The subtext, once again, accuses his father of murdering his innocent mother and his own innocent and creative self.

An old Bronx girlfriend, paying him an installment on a loan, comments in a letter that she has just seen *Remember* and was disappointed, since it did "not come to life except in the last few moments." It seemed to her, as to most of the critics, that even as propaganda it was a weak piece. As art Odets apparently dismissed it, never listing it among his works or even preserving a copy in his files.

With the rehearsals of *Paradise Lost* going full speed ahead under Clurman's direction, Odets, with sinking heart, finally gave the production his full attention; as the actors worked onstage, he looked for the weak spots in his play. He had withdrawn temporarily from the field of political action.◖

◖ 18.5.

> *If one says of creativity, of the creative (human in the best sense) life, of creative work, that it begins with the fullest empathic engulfment, that its very source is empathic relatedness with persons, things and situations* OUTSIDE *of one's self: If all this is true, as it is, what happens to the human or artist when he begins to consciously or unconsciously, as fixed pattern or attitude, say: "No, I withhold! I refuse to give myself over! I will no longer give myself to you, to them, to it!" Then, where is the human being or the creative man? He is rigid, costive, coagulated! He is sterile, dead: he is incapable of love, sympathy or human movement in his deepest centers.*
>
> *This is why it can be said truthfully that art (or the creative act) begins in love and giving, for there must always be present this empathy, this basic act of giving over. If we will say what in our present world is against this giving over we will have to write a large essay. What a problem! For there is scarcely a creative man in our time or place who has won his way through. Jesus did have wisdom: "Unless ye be born again . . ."*
>
> CLIFFORD ODETS *(undated)*

Despite Odets' misgivings, the Group actors at work on *Paradise Lost* found it deeply moving and thought it the richest of his plays. The young, elegant, and literate Stella Adler, though chafing at playing once again the mother of a family, preferred its symbolic underwater quality to the "fervent dramatic realism" of *Awake and Sing!* "We were unfortunately too young really to understand it," she recalled, "but even then I felt the destruction of the Gordon house [the setting for *Paradise Lost*] was the destruction of a way of life, like the Cherry Orchard going down*—the

---

* Interspersed in *Paradise Lost* are what have been called "Chekhovian irrelevancies" ("Take a few nuts," or "I shave and it comes right out again"). Had Odets never heard of Chekhov, the form and the peculiarly Russian melancholia which pervades *Paradise Lost*—despite his effort to make it affirmative and *déraciné*—would likely have emerged nonetheless. This style and this mood are particularly suited to a social allegory set in a disintegrating middle-class family which, for all its last-minute bravado, has, instead of individual dramatic confrontations, a generalized, desperate fin-de-siècle quality in the unraveling of a group. Although Clurman finds Odets' work closer to that of Sean O'Casey, Ph.D. candidates argue the point.

children had no destiny." It seemed to her that this summer Odets was trying to write "of a better class of people" than those in *Awake and Sing!* "This home was more like the Leof home in Philadelphia. There are artists, there is middle-class aspiration. It is a home of substance, and everyone is more articulate. They are still Jewish, but not in a ghetto sense."

Groping in what director Clurman told the actors was "a void full of terror," the characters in *Paradise Lost* are manifestly confronted by the documentary facts of actual bankruptcy and destitution. Clurman responded, however, to the latent symbol. Fresh from the Soviet Union, where he had been so impressed by the sanity of everyone, he was depressed by the "inner chaos" in New York, with people hankering for things they didn't really want and ambitious to "achieve ends they didn't respect." It seemed to him, as he watched people "struggling over mirages," that *Paradise Lost* reflected and explained this dreamlike lack of clarity in American life. Finally, said Clurman, with the house "empty of all its foolish and kindly furniture, forever shaken and damaged in its ancient comfort, nothing was left these people except their basic sweetness."

Odets, grateful for the dedication with which Clurman and the company were working on his play, anticipated that "for anyone who was sensitive" it would be their best all-around production. "It was rich, velvety, and gloomy and no one who acted in that production will ever forget it." Under the hot pressure of the opening night in the offing, he managed to bring into the third week of rehearsal revisions of the third act, changes geared mainly to reducing the gloom of the play by counseling courage and new hope for the future. His own hope that this play would locate enough "sensitive" people to constitute an audience even for a few weeks was exceedingly low.

In the meantime he writes to critic Richard Watts, Jr., of the *Herald Tribune*, what the latter calls an "ominous" letter. In it he asks Watts, "Why should playwrights, actors, and directors stay on Broadway instead of flying to Hollywood?" Answering his own question, he continues, "Except for a sentimental regard for 'theatre,' there is obviously no reason." It seems to him that any theatre person would have to have three good reasons to remain on Broadway and to "exclude Hollywood from his yearly schedule." He could do this, first, if he could make a living in New York; second, if the Broadway stage were actually possessed of an ideal; and, third, if by remaining in New York he could see a "steady and progressive improvement in his work, both as craftsman and artist." Pleading with Watts in advance, he adds that a playwright might even forgo Hollywood's "ducats" if he could be assured of only the last two of his three points. But, he concludes, until groups like the Group Theatre become secure, "there must be mourning and wailing in the theatrical streets and our children's children will have their teeth set on edge."

The kindly Watts publicly sympathized with "Mr. Odets in his period of melancholia" and reminded him that Broadway had, after all, lately seen a *Winterset*, a *Dead End*, and the emergence of Odets himself. He concludes, "Despite the admirable protests of the Screen Writers' Guild," the job of a screen writer is a "patchwork community task" which Odets would not like.

Two days later Odets submitted an application to the Guggenheim Foundation asking that it support his "writing of a play to be called *Silent Partner*, dealing with a state of industrial war in a small American industrial town." This is to be followed, his application tells us, by a play dealing with the love affair of an actress and a writer in which "class elements from the background of each is brought into play, not yet titled. Both, be it proposed, to be ready for stage production this time next year." He gives writer Waldo Frank as his only reference.

Jed Harris, back from a trip to Hollywood, took Odets to see the film of a young actress about whom he was enthusiastic. As they watched the wistful, elegant, and civilized Luise Rainer, a star fresh from Vienna, gazing with her large eyes at William Powell in *Escapade,* Odets whispered to Harris she would be ideal to star in his new play about the writer and the actress. Privately, he thought, "She is wondrous . . . if only *I* could meet such a woman." He was indeed soon to meet her and to embark on a relationship which, outside of his family, would be the most significant of his life.

Two weeks later a careful reader of the *New Masses* would have been puzzled by a tiny ad which stated, "Clifford Odets will be glad to advise during rehearsals of First Run Production of any 'valuable' play. No charge." In desperate need of reassurance and help himself as *Paradise Lost* neared the end of its rehearsal period, he was offering help to young playwrights.* Perhaps only working members of the theatre can appreciate how extreme a bending-over-backward was this defensive gesture. Ordinarily a playwright whose play is about to open is focused with a distilled singlemindedness on his own immediate work problems. The last thing he would do would be to run such an advertisement.

Fearful that Strasberg was probably right in his view that Odets' plays lacked a coherent plot line, he continued to try to tighten the third act of *Paradise Lost,* showing drafts to Helen Deutsch, the Group's press representative, even before he brought them to Clurman. In a wild panic on the eve of the opening, he decided to write to all the critics, trying to establish for them a frame of reference. In it he states that the hero of his play is "the entire middle-class of liberal tendency" and that

> the characters are bewildered. . . . The best laid plans go wrong. The sweetest human impulses are frustrated. No one leads a normal life here, and every decent tendency finds its complement in sterility and futility. Our confused middle-class today, which dares little, is dangerously similar to Chekhov's people. Which is why the people in *Awake and Sing* and *Paradise Lost* (particularly the latter) have what is called a 'Chekhovian quality.' Which is why it is so sinful to violate their lives and aspirations with plot lines. Plots are primer stuff, easily learned.

To find reassurance, he invited novelist Thomas Wolfe, with whom he had recently become friendly, to the dress rehearsal at the Longacre Theatre. According to an acquaintance, Wolfe was enthusiastic about Odets and his work, and Odets hoped Wolfe would understand what he was getting at.† Bracing himself for opening night, he compulsively read and reread a critique of the play from his father—still jobless and "unable to make any connections"—in which L.J. called his son "the World's Leading Dramatist."

---

* Fifteen years later, in a similar mood, he would organize his Playwrights' Workshop under the aegis of the Actors Studio.
    † Even as people "drop" famous names to bolster a shaky self-esteem or to win their public support, so did Odets deliberately rub elbows with famous and successful people.

Just before the curtain went up on December 9, Stella Adler peeked from behind it at the first rows of the orchestra seats. "I said to myself when I saw David Sarnoff," she recalled, "they'll die. These business people and bankers had paid loads of money to see a play which said to them, 'Your lives are junk. You will fail.' It seemed clear we were concerned with idealism and that this audience was at the wrong show."

There were, as always at an Odets play, two audiences. The one in the balcony, writer Irwin Shaw recalled, "was attentive, responsive, not only to the ideas, but to the heightened language." He was convinced by the "wild applause, screeching, and shouting at the end" that it was certainly "the biggest hit that ever was." That he was mistaken became abundantly clear the next day. Shaw remained convinced it was the "carriage-class part of the audience, very conscious of its position," that closed *Paradise Lost*. "For them the theatre was a place where you were entertained, where your preconceptions were nourished. They did not want to be told their lives were junk. O'Neill never really attacked anything as Odets did. Even in *The Hairy Ape*, all he said was, 'That's the way it is.'"

Odets' naïve entreaty to the critics, far from gentling them, had the same effect that the smell of a fresh wound in a fleeing animal has on a pack of bloodhounds. Almost to a man, they seized upon his reference to Chekhov as a starting point and, obviously enraged by his audacity, wrote generally sarcastic and negative reviews. "For all its moments of brilliance," they found *Paradise Lost* not only an echo but an eccentric parody of *Awake and Sing!*, overwrought, turgid, confused, and unbelievable. They were offended in a variety of ways: its stalemated and tragic sense of life was unpalatable, its "Marxist eschatology" hysterical, its people bizarre. Many made explicit their resentment of his indictment of the poor, asleep, dead lives of "the American middle-class of liberal tendency" in which several critics, in their reviews, defensively claimed membership. *The New York Times*' Brooks Atkinson closed his negative account with ". . . [it is] the work of a genuine dramatist," and a few others with variations of the *World-Telegram*'s statement that even in this formless fiasco Odets could not help but reveal he was still a "dramatist of definite talents" who would one day deliver "the great American play in a made-to-measure modern medium."

Odets' first response to their barrage was anguish. His second was to mount, with his colleagues, an energetic, two-pronged campaign, with a scope unique in the history of the American theatre, to keep his play from closing immediately: he initiated a prolific personal correspondence, placating and restrained in its tone, with all the major critics, and at the same time an advertising campaign in which he and a staggering array of the intellectual leaders of his time became copywriters!

Clurman, after a "council of war," announced the Group's decision to do battle:

> The Group Theatre calls Clifford Odets' *Paradise Lost* a great and important play. This assertion is not a mere challenge to persons less enthusiastic. As a matter of fact the reviewers have been extremely respectful and judicious in their comments. The difference between the Group's feeling about the play and those who make more qualified remarks is a difference in values, which means a different idea as to what really matters in the theatre.
>   Some critics complain that Odets is not as great as Chekhov; what we feel is that an American dramatist who can be compared

with Chekhov at all (correctly or not) bespeaks a history-making event on our stage. The Group does not think it necessary to maintain that *Paradise Lost* is a "perfect" play. It maintains that imperfect or not, its level of thought, emotion, imagination, understanding, is not only of a very high order but such as we find perhaps once in ten years in our theater. It is really astonishing to find plays that the reviewers obviously do not think about twice complimented as being a swell evening's entertainment, while they write reviews of a play by an author they unmistakably admire which give the impression that because the play is not quite immortal it is inferior to the run of here-today-gone-tomorrow amusements.

We believe it would show far more regard for the theater and for its best public to hold one's reservations of such a play as *Paradise Lost* for studied critical essays in the future and to say right away that it is one of the truly important contributions to our theatre—one of the plays that place the theater in the realm of deeply enjoyable art.

We believe that when an author of Clifford Odets' caliber writes so rich and varied a play as *Paradise Lost* the least that one might expect is a clear-cut statement to the effect that every sensitive theatergoer must by all means see it.

Sincerely,
Harold Clurman

To each of the critics Odets himself sent a night letter:

Dear Mr. _____. Theatre work for me is strictly on long term basis. An artist can't recognize failure, in the sense that failure is always forward moving if used creatively. The sincere critic can be very helpful to the sincere writer, specifically yourself and myself. Propose now to call *Paradise* rehearsals in effort to work several of your critical statements into concrete theatre practice. Week after next will you spare two hours from your busy schedule to look in again. Many thanks for obvious fairness and sincerity of your review.

Clifford Odets

Invitations to attend the play and form an opinion were now sent to a variegated list of over a hundred persons, all visibly significant in their own fields. Included in it, most of them accepting, were Albert Einstein, Rev. John Haynes Holmes, Eleanor Roosevelt, John Dewey, Rabbi Stephen Wise, Irving Berlin, Archibald MacLeish, Theodore Dreiser, Tallulah Bankhead, Sinclair Lewis, Walter Lippmann, Harry Emerson Fosdick, Mayor La Guardia, Leopold Stokowski, George Gershwin, Ernest Hemingway, Lewis Mumford, Clifton Fadiman, Dorothy Parker, Thornton Wilder, Franz Werfel, Robert E. Sherwood, Norman Thomas, Lou Holtz, and Harpo Marx!

From the positive responses Helen Deutsch compiled advertisements quoting, for example, S. N. Behrman: "It reveals his special genius beyond anything he has shown before"; Fadiman: *Paradise Lost* is "a pivotal American drama"; MacLeish: "The most sensitive ear in the city of New York"; and, standing by itself, Heywood Broun's statement:

There is in my opinion no play in New York at present which is as alive and vital and stirring as *Paradise Lost*. Clifford Odets has more to say and he says it better than any living dramatist in this country. I want to make no reservation in stating the opinion that this young man is a far greater figure than O'Neill ever was or will be.

It isn't enough to say that *Paradise Lost* is a promising play; it is the best our stage has to offer.

It is noteworthy that while most who responded were privately ambivalent about the play, they were all eager to help the Group and Odets to fight for their lives. Thus, few withheld permission to be quoted with reservations deleted.

Concurrent with what *Time* called this "extraordinary advertising campaign," Odets continued his steady didactic correspondence with the major critics, much of which they published in their own newspapers. In the meantime, taking advantage of the readiness to place blame (a routine phenomenon after a play fails), L. J. Odets counseled his son, "Take care of yourself. No one else will." L.J.'s campaign against his rivals, Clurman and Strasberg, had begun.

On December 22, Richard Watts, Jr., one of the critics most sympathetic to and understanding of Odets' work, printed Odets' latest letter in full in the *Herald Tribune*:

Dear Richard Watts:

I must confess I looked forward to your Sunday column and was not disappointed upon a reading of it. It was not that I expected to find in it a corroboration of my own opinion—that *Paradise Lost* is a good advance over the other plays—but rather looked for a clear-cut statement of the fact that defects or no *Paradise Lost* was definitely a play to see and discuss. I am grateful for such a statement from you.

I think many of the critics supposed that after earning some measure of success from their hands I had turned around and dashed off a "quickie." The truth about *Paradise Lost*: took nine months to write, was almost all written before *Awake and Sing!* was produced, was laid aside at the conclusion of its second act to give a weekend to the creation of *Lefty* in a Boston hotel room.

All this is mentioned, Watts, to situate the play's place in the general line of my work and development.

Where we are in agreement is in the fact that there is a similarity of character allotment between the people of *Awake and Sing!* and the current play. However, I find this a superficial resemblance instead of a profound one. The people of *Paradise Lost* are on a much higher plane of consciousness and their concern with physical details of life are considerably less than those of the other play. Also they are more summed up in symbols than in realistic characters who depend on a fairly conventional plot line for impulse and direction.

However, similarity of character allotment is a common practise in the work of playwrights with a content. The early plays of Ibsen, and even the later ones, are a signal example of this fact. Not to mention Tchekov who may be said to have constantly written the same play since he was constantly writing an expression of the same life, his own! O'Casey too!

Do not suppose that I mean by this to stay in one place and deal only with a single class. Since a well-grounded point of view translates all things and people into its own image, there is no reason why the American dramatist should not range from coast to coast, class to class. That is my intention for the future.

You speak next of "the Left Wing ideology clumsily expressed— as in the case of most of the speeches allotted to the furnace man." Well, he was meant to be clumsy, unable to formulate in any other way the things he had to say. He is no left winger. True, he is against war, bitterly, tragically, but his clear social theories are muddled in a very characteristic manner. No conscious left winger says he wishes he were dead at the bottom of the ocean. Nor does he say "I don't know the answers" when he is asked for social whys. Nor will a left winger do as little in a third act as Mr. Pike does in *Paradise Lost.*

Clurman, the director of the play, summed up this character as follows, rightly I thought: "He is not a Communist or a conscious revolutionary of any sort; he is a wraith-like figure as of some wounded but unyielding spirit of protest in the American soul." There have been many such characters in American history, John Brown for example, Garrison, dozens of others.

Anyway, your critical comments were very valuable and gratefully received. We've already received a great volume of mail on the play and mean to fight all along the line for it, in line with the Group statement you printed. I hope you will come to see it again. Truthfully, it seems to me to merit a second visit for a completer understanding of what it's about. I only hope some of the other critics will read your column of today and take some of its ideas to heart. Otherwise every time a valuable play has a defect it might as well be thrown into the ashcan before the opening night!

Incidentally, I may personally have to take a drastic step in order to support the planned advertising budget for the show, and will try to let you know about it in due time.

With best regards,

P.S. Of course you are free to use this letter for reprinting if you want, all or parts. Be better for us than you, I guess.

The drastic step he was considering was a reconnoitering trip to Hollywood without specific plans or commitments. All year he had steadily been offered unquestioning acceptance as a writer, as well as great sums of money by the film industry. Until now he had refused all offers. When his small bank account was reduced to $200, he asked publisher Bennett Cerf for $500 in order, he said, to make a down payment on his mother's tombstone. Although he was considering this temporary move solely in order to keep *Paradise Lost* alive, it is evident that a deeper motive was the necessity to hold on to the Success he had wrung out of this year, thus finally pleasing his father while turning the tables on him.

Clurman recalled an evening after the disastrous reviews of *Paradise Lost* when he, Stella Adler, and Odets were together, and Stella suddenly said, looking directly at Clurman, "I feel I need to sin and you make me feel I have no right to." Odets, pacing, wheeled and shouted, "She's right!" Clurman could not help thinking this meant Odets was considering a visit to "the Coast," where, he said, he would visit Franchot Tone, now married to Joan Crawford, and "maybe look up" J. Edward Bromberg, about whose forays to Hollywood he had been extremely righteous.

On December 28 Odets received a savage seven-page reply from his father to what must have been a brutal assault from him. In his letter L.J. forgets his long history of contempt for his son's early efforts to be a writer and launches an attack on "the Group," mainly directed at Strasberg and Clurman, who have turned down his offer to be the Group's "business manager":

Dear Cliff: . . . I hope I hurt you, like you hurt me, and if you have a wee bit of brains you will be hurt.

There may have been mispelled words in my letter to you. I typed it. Your sister is too "big" to write a letter for her father on an old typewriter. *Just like you.* Too "big."

Let us see who are you, what have you accomplished, and what are you making of your accomplishments. *Nothing but grief.* Up to the age of 28 you worked hard and did not earn a quarter enough to support yourself. You knew what you wanted and worked for it. I always admired you for it. The Group you were with did *not* give you a chance. *Would not* let you develop. That's what they were formed for, to develop artists. At 28 you had a show finished, they, because there was nothing better to do played an act of your show. It went across 100%, and what did they do for you, or with your play. They let you go hang. My impression was that the Group was formed to develop artists. I know that they make a bluff at developing directors, actors, etc. You were just Cliff, "able" yet playing bits. They had your play but turned it down for "Gold Eagle Guy" and when that was a flop and the Group was about to fall apart, accidently, only because they had *nothing else* to do, they put on "Awake and Sing" after two weeks rehearsing. Then the *Group developed a playwright.* So every body tells Clifford Odets and that donkey falls for it. The Group developed a playwright. It makes me laugh.

The Group are all wet they have had about 80% flops since they formed. They have *very* little brains these outside of acting and directing. They *don't* know a good play from a bad one. . . .

Tell me young man where have you gotten *all* the experience in the world, you think you have? I have seen men that was raised higher than you, and then seen them drop lower than that. . . .

Yes you are still the "White Hope" but you are dropping. *Please* wake up . . . I saw your ad of the 10 playwrights. It was a *very* good ad, and proved the play. I told you the same thing, but, you are *not* selling the show to playwrights, and therefore not getting your message to the people you wrote the play for.

Continuing accomplishments: Last season you turned out 3 shows all good. Cliff became the "White Hope of the Theatre" got more publicity than any other living man on Broadway. What happened— he supported the Group 35 people (the very same Group that would *not* give him a fighting chance, though he was one of them) and left him self with out a dime. He turned down $4,000 a week in the movies. For the new season the Group "Bulied" him around, turned down good plays, and picked out a flop, and at last three months after the season opened, they done "Paradise Lost" and "M.G.M. *paid* for it on account of Clifford Odets," at the cheapest theatre on Broadway. Then they spoiled the best show "Paradise Lost" on Broadway, because they know *nothing* of the people that go to shows. . . . Cliff—"Familiarity breeds contempt" by that I don't mean you would want to hurt me. I'm just to close to you. Cliff. I have proved my ability. Large business institutions have paid me (a fellow who don't even know how to spell) over $20,000 a year for nearly 25 years. Because, I do know right and wrong. Come to think of it I believe I told the Group and you every time they were going to have a flop. I also recall telling them that "Men in White" was going to be the best play they had up to that time, after Lee, and Joe B.* thought there was nothing in it.

I could have made "Paradise Lost" the *biggest success* on Broadway, by removing the weaknesses. I know the "I" public. I have studied

---

* J. Edward Bromberg.

them for 25 years.—I wonder why the movie industry hire executives at such large salaries when they don't know a thing about actors, directors, or how to make movies?—because, they know the "I" public who pay the bills. Of course your an artist, your not interested in money. I wonder what you would do if you had $25,000 now, that you could have had?

In writing this letter I'm not trying to be wise or rub it in. I'm trying to open your eyes. Clurman is *not* the best director for you . . . *Get WISE big boy. You need a manager besides an agent.* The Group will be no more in one year if they don't get a manager.

In my sales letter I asked for an interview. I thought you would ask all of the directors of the Group to come together and read the letter for them. You would not expect me to write in a letter what I would expect to do for them, that would come out in an interview. If I would save them one (1) flop I could earn mine, and believe me that's easy. With you fool artists. Yes sir—Yes sir—Yes sir—

No you darn fool.

Love,
L.J.

P.S. I spent 2 hours writing this and I expect you to spend 20 minutes to read it.

In the same mail Odets received a financial statement from his agent at Brandt and Brandt informing him that for this week he was owed a royalty of $32.89. He waived this for the advertising campaign, and the Group members took salary cuts. Also on this day came a letter from Ida Bernstein in the Bronx, wondering if he remembered how nice he was to her once when she was sick, and concluding, "What does your dad say now? . . . There is a Jewish saying that sons belong more to fathers."

On December 30 Odets gave Cerf's check plus $500 to the Paradise Lost Company; on December 31 he wired Thomas Wolfe a Happy New Year and asked, "Are you going to tell us what you thought of the play and let us quote you with Dreiser and Broun?" Also on the last day of this fateful year he wrote to George Bernard Shaw, his "spiritual father" in England:

Dear Mr. Shaw:

In writing to you without introduction I am carrying on a relationship which you yourself have established. The right to theatrically criticize society and social institutions is something which has been made possible in the 20th century English speaking world largely thru your efforts. And so you have bred a crop of wild sons in many places, and I am now writing to you as one of those sons.

You do not have to be told that there is not a first rate theatre critic in New York. There is not one who writes from a constant point of view, not one who looks at writers on a long term basis, not one who has in his work any continuity of ideas or approach to the theatre. Indeed, there is little first rate theatre. We have a few acting personalities, a few playwrights who are feebly identified with social impulses, chiefly in their negative aspects.

Five years ago there came into being The Group Theatre here. Its intention was a continuity of performance and growth based on a permanent acting company, three permanent directors and careful training in all phases of theatre. All of these people had generous theatre experience behind them. Their purpose was to express the progressive elements in American life.

For this purpose they soon received scripts from most of America's best writers—Paul Green, John Howard Lawson, Maxwell Anderson and several others. The acting company stayed together (only one of the boys went to the movies—Franchot Tone) and now has the distinction of being the foremost acting company in the land, one extremely well trained in the art of ensemble playing on a high level of creativity.

A year ago a playwright began to crawl out of the acting company and in short order had prepared two plays for presentation on Broadway by the Group. That was me. The first plays were "Awake and Sing!" and "Waiting for Lefty!" The critics gave us very good notices. Not intelligent or helpful, but good from a box office point of view. I was hailed as "the most promising theatre writer since Eugene O'Neill," "America's white hope of the theatre." . . . A great string of such balderdash. No where was there any evaluation of the plays. Demerits were pointed out, grave and glib warnings were given: we had American extremism at its worst. It was a silly case of "the biggest and the best" from beginning to end.

Four weeks ago The Group opened a new play of mine, "Paradise Lost." The critical reception was a fusilade! "Life is not like that," "a rotten confused liar with a confused warped point of view," "he has gone back and thinks Marxian ideas are true American life" . . . they have raised hell with a good deal of personal feelings and vehemence in their reviews. All agree that this last play is not as good as the first ones.

We have fought them back and are still doing so—with quotes from literary men like Dreiser, Thomas Wolfe, Heywood Broun, A. MacLeish, etc. And we are fighting, not on the basis of this one play, but on the basis of a fundamental difference between their negative points of view and our positive ones.

This is an old story and no one knows it better than you. And it is also an old story that our critical gentlemen talk of you and Ibsen now as if you have always been a smooth accepted product. What an insult!

This is not impertinence on my part, this writing to you, this demanding which follows. We are fighting here for our artistic and personal lives for the same points on which you fought. We are carrying on a full good work which has occupied most of your life and continues to do so. We are radicals with our work here, radicals in the sense that we insist on the right of critical opinion concerning people, life and government.

I am immediately sending to you under separate cover all the plays I've written to date. "Three Plays" came first; "Paradise Lost" is just off the press. Another one is in the typewriter and I would like to send it to you before production next season.

Can you say, will you say a critical word for these plays, something that we can reproduce and quote in America? A good blast from you would so unnerve our critical gentry here that for ever after they might tiptoe before shouting "Foul! Evil!" Yes, the very hills here shout out for a first rate critical mind to evaluate the "left" writers growing up here. It would be worth everything in the world to have one clear fine bugle at the head of the procession!

I am not losing sight of the fact that you may not like my plays. But I am certain of one thing—you will see much to help and encourage in them and the trend in American theatre which they represent.

Right now I have to go out to Hollywood to write movies for six weeks in order to get enough money for advertising bills for "Paradise Lost." Advertisements and stirring up a general discussion seem at present to be the only means we have found for fighting. The bugle is yet to come!

Your wild literary son,

Please answer soon.
P.S. The preface of "P.L." is written by one of The Group's directors. He seems as you can easily see, about the only theatre critic we have.

There is no record of a response from Shaw.

Planning to be in Hollywood only a few weeks, Odets left a note instructing Herman—still on full salary—to give Group mascot Jake "Shakespeare" Sandler whatever he wanted to eat from the icebox at One University Place, to let his sister Florence stay there, and to send all her bills to him. When he got back—which would be soon, he ended—he would let her be in a mob scene of a new play, *Silent Partner.* Just before he left New York, he dashed off an introduction to a new edition of Gogol's *Dead Souls* in which he celebrated the great twentieth-century Russian novelist's insistence that "a tree which produced such corrupt fruit needed chopping down."

When Herman—who knew he was now almost penniless—expressed concern, Odets assured him he would shortly return with a few thousand dollars, enough to keep alive not only Jake and Florence but *Paradise Lost,* his father, his Tante Esther and Uncle Israel, Herman, and himself. Had he not turned down dozens of movie jobs this year? Surely someone out there would still want him, if only briefly. A black sheep turned prodigal son always has a great deal of sorting to do. Odets was not now certain whether he more delighted in or resented this turnabout with his real and his Group families. To be thus cast in the central role of powerful protector and dispenser of largess, to his father as well as to the Group fathers, gave him a sense of potency and, simultaneously, of a demanded-upon imprisonment. ("I am bullied by my position," he later wrote while signing checks for small and large amounts to the order of relatives, poets, painters, directors, actors, cancer researchers, left-wing publications, and young playwrights.)

"Just before he left for Hollywood," recalled Herbert Kline, editor of *New Theatre,*

> he called me, took me to an expensive dinner, explained he was going out for the good of the Group, and help he could and did give to the New Theatre generally, to make money to return, to keep on writing for the Group Theatre the things that he and I believed in. Later, in his apartment at One University Place, he showed me his files for keeping notes—overheard dialogues—ideas for plays, characters, etc. And he talked about how much the magazine meant to him—and gave me a check for *New Theatre,* and asked if I needed any money personally. I did, but I never took any except for the magazine and told him so. Since Clifford knew that I drew only $15 a week "living money" for my work as editor, he seemed a little embarrassed that he would be earning a comparative fortune and said he hoped money he sent afterwards would help make things a little better. The magazine

was always broke, he knew, had no political or other financial support
—and Cliff was always one of the writers who supplemented our returns on subs and newsstand sales with generous checks. . . .

Thus he established early a pattern of meeting defensively with a representative of integrity whenever he feared he was about to breach his own.
    To his cousin Irene's small daughter, Corinne, Odets wrote that he
was going to Hollywood "for a very short while" and would be sure to send
her "a nice present." Throughout his life he would maintain such avuncular
gift-giving relationships with several children, identifying himself variously
as "Uncle Clifford" or "Uncle Stamps."
    With *Paradise Lost* failing and under steady critical attack in New
York, and his father vacationing at the Fleetwood Hotel in Miami Beach,
Odets continued to be obsessed with the necessity not only for gathering
public endorsements for the play from the great of America but also for
locating large sums of money to keep it alive. Its looming demise (which
occurred after seventy-two eked-out performances) significantly threatened
his role of Successful Playwright and Unstinting Provider. With old friends
in vicious competition for the yearly $1,440 paid by civil-service jobs, and
with his services as an actor no more in demand than before, it was clear
to him there was only one place in the world where he could conceivably
earn the money he felt he desperately needed: Hollywood.
    To the members of the Group he defensively explained that he was
broke and had to support not only his play but also his father and sisters,
his friend Herman, and his aunt and uncle. By accepting a temporary
movie job he could solve not only his own financial problems but those of
his family and of the Group Theatre.
    His father, planning his world tour, had just written complaining that
he had not received a letter in two weeks and got news of his son only
from the newspapers. In a conciliatory shift of tone, he continued, first
from Miami and then from Philadelphia, "The Good Lord is kind to me, to
have given me, you." He is very grateful, he says, for "the finest vacation
I ever enjoyed" and, advising his son on extending his salary as a screenwriter, he quotes Jed Harris: "Don't give them too much to read in a short
time. Even if you have everything finished, make them wait. They will try
to rush you." He expects his son will send him "according to our conversation in New York, $200 a week," adding, "Your parent needs that much
he has been spoiled in the last 20 years, spending more than that every
week. . . ."
    He sends regards from the Ritz Brothers, playing in his Miami hotel;
a plea for a long airmail letter he can read "twenty or thirty times"; and
an assurance that "God will repay you for not forgetting your family," a
melody in a key quite different from that of the preceding fifteen years.
    The central importance to Odets of maintaining the reversal of roles
in which his father was now dependent on *him* was probably the critical
factor in his decision to explore the film industry. At the same time, but
secondarily, he thirsted, he told Helen Deutsch, to learn something of the
technique of film-making, ingenuously believing (had they not earnestly
discussed this many times after seeing a movie on 42nd Street?) that he
could contribute to its becoming a "genuine art-form for the masses of
people" and not just a cheap commercial diversion. It was not yet evident
to him that this multimillion-dollar industry could not afford to risk its
high investments on a product which lacked a sufficiently low common denominator to entertain billions of people the world over. He would help to
create, he half believed, an international folk art. The pile of beached

talents come to Hollywood and unproductively stranded there had not yet mounted to the heights it would reach within the next decade.

The paradox lay in the fact that while he sought to bolster his new and shaky position as his father's father by this sortie to the film capital, he could simultaneously satisfy the other pole of his longing—namely, to be his father's accepted, even admired son. He knew that earning thousands of dollars a week would mean far more to L. J. Odets than any creative triumphs in the legitimate theatre.

Clifford had always been fascinated by the extravagant accounts brought back from Hollywood by John Howard Lawson, Franchot Tone, J. Edward Bromberg, and S. N. Behrman, of the awesome, capricious, and apparently limitless power of the heads of motion-picture studios—potentates with personal chefs, dining rooms, horses, cars, yachts, planes, custom-made clothes, masseurs, and harems. Tales of absolute rule and self-indulgence by such tyrannical emperors as Louis B. Mayer, Harry Cohn, the brothers Warner, and even the stripling Irving Thalberg filled him with admiration and revulsion. All of these Sun Kings were what his father called "big men." To be needed and admired by such men would satisfy a profound and archaic yearning far more important than to *have* their clothes, horses, yachts, dining rooms, or perhaps even their women.

Even as he prepared to leave for Hollywood, Odets' uncertainty that he would still be wanted by any of these dream-factory maharajahs had been such that he sent to the Guggenheim Foundation copies of *Awake and Sing!* and *Paradise Lost* to bolster his application for modest support ($3,000) for a year of writing plays "with no strings attached." Surely, he reasoned, his proposal was in consonance with Senator Simon Guggenheim's wish to "continue the influence of a young life of eager aspiration" (Guggenheim's son had died prematurely). Had there been no Hollywood, Odets would have had no option but to tell his father, Tante Esther, Uncle Israel, and the Group that he could no longer support any of them and to wait until the Guggenheim fellowships were awarded and see what strings were attached. The simple existence, however, of this golden bridge—unprecedented in human history—between the artist and the astronomic rewards of mass marketing opened quite a different alternative, one which would have an incalculable effect not only on Odets' creative development, but on that of every theatre worker of the century. The general phenomenon of the lure of the film industry and the accusation-guilt sequence (not special to Odets at all) is illustrated in a letter written by one Group actor to another, decrying the active hostility expressed toward him by Group members, as if he had defected to an enemy. He describes what he had gone through for the sake of the Group's ideals, and at the expense of his family's needs, in resisting lucrative offers from Broadway and Hollywood. He insists that he upheld the values of the Group and struggled as valiantly and as long as any of them to keep it going. He realizes that he is not the only one who held out against the promises of riches, and then asks why, since others, too, have finally traveled to Hollywood, he has been singled out for abusive attack. His sense of betrayal, outrage, righteous indignation, and crushing guilt is patent.

Only those protected by a lack of chameleon versatility would be entirely safe.*

---

* The paradigm is of an unknown writer on the lowest echelon at MGM in 1939 ($250 per week or less) who turned in an original screenplay about a Southern family only to be told he was a fool, as "We just made *Gone With the Wind*." The writer's contract was terminated, and the rejected screenplay became *The Glass Menagerie* by Tennessee Williams.

It would take some time before Odets would become aware of the invisible strings attached to the option he had now elected. To a newspaper reporter he naïvely explained that since he had found he could not make a living in New York by writing plays, he was going to see whether he could support himself by taking eight weeks out of the year to write a film. With a nine-dollar balance in his checking account, it seemed a reasonable idea. The few crisp bills he had hidden in books—like his mother's secret escape fund in her sewing basket—would not carry him far. Almost no writer dismissed out of hand an offer to work on talking pictures. Even Leo Tolstoy's imagination, it is said, had been stimulated:

> You will see that this little clicking contraption with the revolving handle will make a revolution in our life—in the life of writers. It is a direct attack on the old methods of literary art. We shall have to adapt ourselves to the shadowy screen and to the cold machine. A new form of writing will be necessary. I have thought of that and I can feel what is coming.
>
> But I rather like it. This swift change of scene, this blending of emotion and experience—it is much better than the heavy, long-drawn-out kind of writing to which we are accustomed. It is closer to life. In life, too, changes and transitions flash by before our eyes, and emotions of the soul are like a hurricane. The cinema has divined the mystery of motion. And that is greatness. . . .
>
> I am seriously thinking of writing a play for the screen. . . .

But he never did.

Chapter Nineteen

In order to gain time for a great work, I must first do plenty of scribbling for the sake of money, so that I may have enough to carry me over. . . .

LUDWIG VAN BEETHOVEN

A man like myself, of a lesser breed than Beethoven, had and has similar problems. I was not strong enough to stand the loneliness, the opprobrium—I could not look my Fate in the face, could not clasp it hand to hand. . . . In the creative sense I was never neurotic until I tried to live the "normal" life of other men. When I could not accept the harness, the prison cell—only then did I stop being free.

CLIFFORD ODETS, 1962

Herman Kobland, Harold Clurman, and Jed Harris (still wooing Odets) saw him off on his first trip to Los Angeles. Clurman recalled that after Odets had gone through the gate to his train, Harris turned and asked, "Have you ever really been in the money?" Clurman admitted he had not. "Then you don't know," said Harris, "how hard it is to remain a rebel."

Odets checked into the Chateau Elysee in Los Angeles, where his mentor Philip Moeller had stayed eighteen months earlier. Occupying most of his suitcases were his voluminous notes of his new play, *The Silent Partner*. He soon moved from the Chateau Elysee to the more prestigious Beverly-Wilshire Hotel and was shortly invited, through Franchot Tone, to a "real Hollywood party," where, shyly and with great interest, he watched such personages as George Gershwin, actresses Joan Crawford and Madeleine Carroll, and writer John O'Hara. Presently his gaze fell upon the distinguished face of a man of gentle mien, with the sharply defined and intelligent features of a "head on a Roman coin." The man moved toward him and in a faintly Russian-Jewish accent said, "Mr. Odets, are you here to work or are you here to take bows?" With that he moved away again. Odets, attracted by this obviously cultivated and worldly man addressed by others as "Millie," immediately set about discovering his identity.

He was awed to learn that the ironic gentleman was the director venerated by him and his post-war generation for the classic anti-war film *All Quiet on the Western Front*, Lewis Milestone. Franchot Tone informed him further that this modest and idealistic man was referred to as "the oracle of the film industry," and, incidentally, that he was first cousin to another of Odets' heroes, violinist Nathan Milstein. Before the evening was out Odets sought further contact with Milestone.

In this glancing first contact lies the paradigm of the means by which the serious American writer is eased into the film industry. Had a tough former junk-salvager, furrier, song-plugger, or glove salesman—a crude rogue elephant like Louis B. Mayer, Jack Warner, Harry Cohn, or Samuel Goldwyn—approached the conflicted Odets at this point, he would have recoiled in wary anger that someone so like his father might once more control him. Lewis Milestone, working at Paramount, was, however, another breed of man entirely: in no way a wily businessman, he was a gentle and earnest man of taste, breeding, liberal politics, a sensitive Jewish intellect who responded to the best in American writing. These were the attributes which best fitted him, unwittingly and ironically, to be the first to serve as Odets' Judas goat.

"I let him stew for a couple of hours," Milestone later recalled, "and then at about two in the morning I came back to him and asked him if he would be interested in adapting for the screen a story of an American who helps Chinese revolutionaries against a warlord. Actually, the original was somewhat pulp-paper material, with enough in it for six pictures. William Le Baron* of Paramount and I had earlier agreed that Odets was the only one who could do something with the one good thing in it, and I had been trying to locate him for days, not knowing he had come to California. . . . I was delighted to meet him at the party. . . . He agreed he would look at it."

The next day, with the delicacy of a career diplomat, Milestone relayed to Odets his honest conviction that his plays revealed genius and then sent a long black Cadillac from the Paramount studio to pick him up at the Beverly-Wilshire and bring him to Milestone's quietly elegant wood-paneled office, "just to talk things over." Odets immediately unburdened his heart to the kindly and sympathetic older man, told him that even his critically acclaimed plays were not earning money, described the financial obligations he had undertaken, and concluded—with a naïveté which touched Milestone—that, far from being in Hollywood "to take bows," he had come in the desperate hope of earning enough to send some money immediately to the Group and to his family. From the start Odets made it clear, Milestone recalled, that his central interest lay in writing stage plays, not films, and that his prime aim was to keep his play *Paradise Lost* running.

"I told him I understood his situation," Milestone continued, "and I shall never forget his face when I asked him whether ten thousand for four weeks work would be enough. He thought I was kidding. It was like putting steak before a starving man. When I told him it wouldn't surprise me that he could walk away with thirty thousand dollars for this first

* Producer Le Baron was himself a writer manqué.

movie, he looked stunned and shook his head. Actually, it turned out I was right." Or almost right—the figure would be $27,500.

Milestone found Odets, of all playwrights, the least cynical toward film-making. "[Films] were a great unknown to him, and he approached the prospect with interest, but in tremendous fear. Actually, in a way, he was lucky that his first venture into pictures was with me . . . because I understood his condition and I respected his work. I told him I would serve as his agent without a commission." By mid-February 1936 an agreement was drawn up between "Paramount Pictures," incorporated in Delaware for tax reasons, and Clifford Odets, wherein he agreed to work on a film to be called *The General Died at Dawn* for a period of four weeks at $2,500 per week "with no more than forty-five days additional without the writer's consent." At the same time he signed six copies of a statement for the California Unemployment Bureau, saying he did not intend to remain in California for six months or longer. He agreed, moreover, that "Paramount Pictures" would be the legal "author" of the screenplay, and it, in turn, agreed to provide him with a "first-class Pullman" back to New York!

After Milestone had repeatedly urged him not to be concerned about the film medium ("Write just as if you were working on a play. Leave the rest to me"), Odets' anxiety abated and he fell to on *The General Died at Dawn* with optimistic energy and discipline. The technology of movie-making interested him, and his self-regard—deeply eroded by the reception of *Paradise Lost*—was restored by Milestone's daily articulated respect.

Grateful for the three to four pages a day Odets was turning out, Milestone made certain that in the details of life he was provided not only with respect but also with a modicum of Hollywood pampering. Milestone knew it was important that he not feel, as John Howard Lawson had described the position of film writer, "like a glorified office boy," and arranged that he move into a comfortable house on Camden Drive, complete with Filipino houseboy; that he was introduced to the maître d's at the best restaurants; and that a studio car and driver were available to him at any time of the day or night. Not since the death of his mother had he felt looked after or catered to. But, far more important, he felt respected as he had not since the opening of *Awake and Sing!*

Before long, however, Milestone recalled, Odets' acute loneliness became evident, and Milestone and his aristocratic wife, Kendall, knew that something would have to be done. It occurred to Odets himself to invite his "favorite character outside of fiction," Harold Clurman, to visit California at his expense. He was longing for contact with his Group brothers. Although touched and grateful, Clurman was in an acute turmoil, both because of his steadily embattled relationship with Stella Adler and because the fractures within the Group appeared to be seriously widening. He replied that if he told Strasberg and Cheryl Crawford how he was feeling, they would advise him to avail himself of Odets' "beautiful generosity," but he did not want to bother them, in this difficult rehearsal period of the Group's production of *The Case of Clyde Griffiths,** with his private state

---

* This adaptation of Dreiser's *An American Tragedy* opened on March 13, 1936, and closed in three weeks, a failure.

of mind. It troubled him that he was feeling critical of Lee's direction, finding him "gentle and relaxed but quite prolix, lacking a certain taut concentration and creative sharpness that he has at his best."

"What concerns me most," he adds, "is the play problems for next season and having enough money for a summer session of rehearsal." Stella Adler, Elia Kazan, and Robert Lewis are on the production committee, and all are concerned about the urgent need for new plays. Reflecting the harsh economics of the situation (despite the wild acclaim for Odets' work, none of the Group's 1935 offerings had yielded a real profit), he writes that, besides *The Silent Partner*, the Group should produce a "modern commercial show of the kind Sherwood or Howard would write," and wonders whether Clifford would do a dramatization of Sinclair Lewis' anti-Fascist *It Can't Happen Here*. To finance it will be hard, he concludes, as "the movie rights have been disposed of," but perhaps they can "persuade the movie company itself to finance it." The influence of the film industry on the legitimate theatre—if only indirect—is evident in all of the Group's deliberations, and the steady demand on Odets to become the playwright-Messiah for the Group, financially and creatively, is unmistakable. This demand, while resented by him, nevertheless significantly supported his productivity for the next several years, as he referred to Clurman jokingly as "my conscience."

With remarkable sensitivity Clurman, as before, concludes with his concern about Odets' coming "fate as an artist":

I am glad you are making money—and hope you won't spend it all (even tho I am one of the beneficiaries of your "wealth!"). I am glad you are having a taste of movie work since, like our girl friend Stella, you have to have the taste of "sin" in order to be free of temptation! I felt during the weeks after *Paradise* that you would *have* to go to the Coast—no matter what disadvantages there might be in it, but now that you have gone and are there, I think you will have to get back to silence, quiet, simplicity and a certain "obscurity" to write the play you have in you. (Waldo Frank told me recently about a conversation he had with André Gide in Paris last summer. "All my life I have written in the quiet. And I assure you, my dear Waldo, that one writes very well in the quiet!") Your fate as an artist, as a creative being, depends on your ability to *order* your life. . . .

Your talent is turbulent and rich and the more of these precious qualities one has the greater the need for order, for retirement, for concentration, for modesty and for consecutive effort. . . . The whole problem of the artist in America (aside from economic security: which by and large you have) is the problem of avoiding distractions without living in an ivory tower. The distractions I speak of may not be merely such obvious things as Hollywood—wine, women and song!—they may be intellectual things—fads, movements, lectures, public appearances, causes and whatnot. The work of artistic creation even for the most sensuous, active and extroverted artist is in a sense an ascetic act, an act of withdrawal. . . . Talent itself is not unusual and like all forms of life is easily destroyed and wasted—in the war which is our daily life.

. . . And your talent, what you may give the theatre and through it the American world—are vital matters to me—nearly always on my mind. I see them in conflict with a world that can destroy even while it embraces and I see the possible loss not simply as a personal tragedy but as a truly historical calamity! . . . I have great confidence in your fundamental livingness—but do not blame me for looking on with anxiety at the moving line of your life and for contemplating your destiny with awe. I know people are not accustomed any more to thinking about anything present and immediate in these terms but isn't that why life has lost some of its savor and has acquired the character of a workaday, mechanical routine rather than a passionate, exalted, magnificent drama. . . .

Harold was pleading for the creative soul of his lonely brother as well as for his own. The survival of their family, the Group Theatre, appeared to him to be a necessary condition for both.

Impulsively, during one intolerably lonely evening Odets called Dena in New York and asked her to come out to Los Angeles to live with him, telling her his secretary would supply her with a train ticket. Despite her mother's anxious questions about marriage, Dena—just out of Hunter College—decided to make the trip, and when she arrived at 727 North Camden Drive, she was disappointed to find it a "stiflingly dreary middle-class house." She was not certain whether to be more amused or embarrassed by the Filipino houseboy, who, in a formally elegant accent, addressed her at once as "Mrs. Odets."

An enraged letter soon came from Dena's father saying she and Odets should marry immediately. Odets replied, "We'll see." He was depressed, she thought, not enjoying his work on the film, and extremely ill at ease in the Hollywood setting. Yet it seemed to her he desperately wanted to be liked by the people there—especially by "accepted" writers like John O'Hara and S. N. Behrman. At the same time he proselytized them with red-faced passion about the values of the Group Theatre. He was determined to be, in their eyes, an accepted American playwright of quality, "like Sidney Howard or Robert Sherwood," not merely a propagandist.

Dena was struck by Odets' effort, while writing the screenplay for *The General Died at Dawn*, to continue at night with *The Silent Partner* and the Cuban play, *Law of Flight*, which he considered his "real work." He always carried his notebook and was steadily clipping items and pictures of people from newspapers for these plays and for future works. It seemed odd to her that he would never sit down to work on these plays without first carefully washing his hands.

Columnist Sidney Skolsky was a frequent visitor to the beige house on Camden Drive, and his wife, Estelle, tried to help Dena with her hair and her clothes, which by Hollywood standards seemed severe. It struck the straightforward young leftist Dena that although Odets initially was thoughtful, warm, and sexually attentive, there was something peculiarly middle-class, dried-up, dull, unnourishing, and, indeed, oppressive in the situation. She remained as "Mrs. Odets" until quite abruptly Odets' sexual advances to her ceased and they commenced having bitter battles, apparently about trifles, during which Odets would savagely pound his fist against the wall, screaming, "I am an evil, black, bad person!" She would soon learn what lay at the root of his withdrawal and of these bitter self-accusations. In the meantime the atmosphere between them had become so obviously hostile that the Filipino houseboy stopped calling her "Mrs. Odets" and addressed her now as "Miss K."

At this point, "my stock dropping fast," Dena tearfully asked Clifford for a train ticket back to New York, where, unable to face her frightened and irate parents, she moved into the Hotel Brevoort at Odets' expense and

—having just returned from Hollywood—was now thought qualified to work under a pseudonym as a film critic for the *Sunday Worker*. En route East, she had stopped in Chicago, where the Group touring company was playing *Awake and Sing!*, and been comforted by Clurman, who found Odets' behavior toward her outrageous and mystifying. Elia Kazan, stage-managing the road company, was usually more lenient in such matters than Clurman, but this time he found it puzzling that Odets would send home such a "real woman," so "genuine an article" as Dena. Both men were more concerned, however, with whether or not the Group tour of Odets' play would conclude with a deficit than they were with their friend's capacity for enduring intimacy. They were both exceedingly interested in what Dena could report on the progress of Odets' new play, *The Silent Partner,* and were pleased to hear he was continuing to work on it.

Soon the newspapers cleared up the mystery of Odets' behavior toward Dena with a steady stream of items such as, "Radical young playwright Odets and beguiling young Viennese actress Luise Rainer are seen everywhere together, in cafés, on the streets, on the beaches, always arm-in-arm." Odets had finally met the woman with whom he had been smitten on the screen.

*Like Odets, Luise Rainer had been a premature baby. "I guess I often look for those two months of warmth they deprived me of," she said, laughing, but meaning it. Born between two boys to a well-to-do family, she soon learned the meaning of "a woman in a man's world." She was a shy girl with great, dark, expressive eyes in a mobile, wistful face topped by a mass of shiny black hair. Feeling lost and out of place in an "average bourgeois surrounding," she, like Odets, came early to seeking solace for an intense need for affection in an interior world.

Heinz Rainer, her possessive, tempestuous father, settled in Europe as a successful businessman after having spent most of his childhood and youth in America, where as a six-year-old orphan he was sent to the home of a prosperous uncle. He often wondered if his "Mausele" (Little Mouse), as he called Luise, was eternally absent-minded and "in the clouds," or ignorant, or simply very different. In contrast to his lack of interest in his two boys, his affection and concern centered on his slight daughter, at home demure, in school an immensely athletic imp, a champion runner, and, later on, an intrepid mountain-climber. Luise was her father's secret pride and his "Augapfel," the apple of his eye. However, Luise experienced "his controlling love, his disciplinary actions—which he felt necessary at the slightest provocation—and his tyrannical possessiveness" ultimately as a burden. Already as a child Luise was saddened to see her mother, "a beautiful pianist, and a woman of warmth and intelligence and deeply in love with her husband, suffering similarly." Luise recalled one of her many ill-fated efforts to make her family understand her:

As a kid of so-called good family I was chased into museums. To antiquity then I took an instant dislike. To me it seemed to consist of old bones and old spoons. Good God, why did I have to look at it!

* The text of the account of the Rainer-Odets relationship is somewhat uneven because of Miss Rainer's insistence on retaining her own wording.

Not so with modern art. It was vivid in the twenties; and then there had been the famous Fauve movement, fantastic shapes, fantastic colors. I would come home and sit in my chaste all-cream room and to me it looked lifeless, like butter. I saved the pennies of my pocket money, bought tubes and tubes of oil paint. Color, color, I yearned for color! The first thing I did was paint a big sign and hung it outside the door of my room: "No entrance." Then I locked myself into my butter-cream haven. I painted and painted. Walls, bed, chairs, table, everything. Reds, emeralds, fiery blues, shining yellows. The fumes of turpentine made my head ache. Never mind, this was my Sistine Chapel. All finished, the family was invited in. A reverberating storm developed. Father Rainer thundered, my beloved Mummy aired her fury with some temperamental slaps into my face and I don't remember any more where else. I must admit, even then I knew: the colors hadn't quite come out as I had intended. Well, I guess it *was* a catastrophe!—Shortly after that, at fourteen, I secretly started dancing lessons with a beautiful pupil of the famous dancer Mary Wigman. She had watched me during the intermission of a concert and thought me good material. She invited me to her studio and she worked with me. That was wonderful.

Yet these were for her difficult years. Like Odets in his early suicidal period, Luise was enduring a desperate time. She was, as she put it, "possessed to give back to people the images and feelings which people and things gave to me," without having yet, however, discovered the security of a form, a medium. "I became an actress," she said later, "only because I had quickly to find some vent for the emotion that inside of me went around and around, never stopping. I would have been happy, instead of turning to the stage, to write, to paint, to dance, or, like my mother, to play the piano beautifully. If only it had been easier to acquire the necessary techniques for such professions quicker." She knew she could never expect emotional or financial support for a career in the arts. An army of critics agreed from the time she was sixteen that she had unusual acting talent, and she must herself have known it. The one indisputable fact for her as an adolescent was that she *had* to become an artist of some kind.

Emmy Rainer—who came from an upper-class German-Jewish family, a number of wealthy industrialists, including the head of I. G. Farben, one of Germany's chemical giants—helplessly watched her withdrawn daughter, who, though she had friends, seemed to be becoming a loner. She wondered now, as she later told Luise, if she had been overly insistent on fastidiousness and controlled upper-class proprieties with her rebellious daughter. It began to appear doubtful that Luise would fulfill her father's wish that, above all, she should attend a good finishing school and "marry the right man." She appeared to be, on the contrary, becoming a tomboy while developing her mother's "inferiority complex."

Emmy and Heinz Rainer, planning to do some traveling and with their two boys in boarding school, entrusted the eleven-year-old Luise to the care of her grandparents. The atmosphere in her grandparents' elegant house was stiffly upper-class; meals were served silently by white-gloved servants, and the table was always set with the most delicate china and heaviest silver. The precisely arranged heirloom bedspreads were a daily challenge to Luise until on one occasion she pranced up and down on a few of them "simply to destroy the suffocating upper-class order of things." What Luise actually revolted against was not the delicate china on the table or the heavy silver or the silent movement of white-gloved servants but, something she had in common with Odets, a dislike for the "lack of an innate awareness of those who have not, and a caring." Her grandmother, aghast, scolded her, implying that her "near-delinquencies" must surely have come from her father's side.

To illustrate her father's temperament, Luise told the story of Emmy and Heinz's wedding day. The bridegroom, appalled by the propriety and mountains of lace finery in his bride's trousseau, had, as a practical joke, loosed a lion cub to race through the halls, terrifying the guests. He had then taken his bride high into the mountains with no more than her going-away outfit. "Now," he said to his bride, "I can teach you how to live." "Like Cliff, my father was impossible and marvelous," Luise later commented. Emmy was enchanted; her family was not. And now Emmy's mother was confronted with the issue of that marriage: a defiant, obstinate, histrionic girl, intelligent but hard to handle, and so delicate that for a whole year she had "stayed in a children's rest home (Kinderheim) on an island in the North Sea called Wyck-auf-Föhr in order to stabilize my health." She spent endless hours, happy to be alone, listening to music, dancing, painting, and writing. Now and again Luise went about her grandmother's house deliberately stopping the steady tick-tock of the countless antique clocks. She recalled, "The silent order in my well-behaved grandparents' house bored me to distraction. The clean dresses I had to wear daily embarrassed me in school in front of other children who were not all that clean, and to get rid of pent-up feelings I would sneak out in the early evening to follow a little man who dutifully turned on the gas lamps on the street, and approximately three or four steps behind him I would turn off each one again."

Five years later, at sixteen, after Luise had made up her mind to try to become an actress and had heard of a famous theatre and theatre school in Düsseldorf, a town near her grandparents' home, she asked to be permitted to stay with them. Then, behind closed doors and "by no means aware of the facts of life, I studied the part of Lulu by Wedekind, one of the most sensual, sexy female characters ever written, as well as the demure character of Francisca in Lessing's *Minna von Barnhelm*." After Luise auditioned, no one could believe she had had no previous training, and the next day Louise Dumont, a famous actress who had known Eleanora Duse, signed her to a two-year contract. This was not long after Odets' stint with the Mae Desmond company had ended.

During this time Luise's family refused to see her act; they believed that performing was a career fit only for vulgar people. Although Luise had assured them that she would become a great actress but would retain her integrity, they were deeply concerned about life in the theatre world. In fact her dedication to her work had at this time a cloistered quality, and the intensity of purpose she demonstrated was remarkable, as was her immediate success.

She knew by now that when she stood on the stage and expressed what she felt, she was able to connect to other human beings. She could feel, as she put it, "the warmth and the love coming to me from the audience and yet I could remain at a protective distance. It was what I needed."

In 1930 there occurred an event potentially comparable to Odets' finding the Group Theatre: the famous Russian-Jewish Habimah players, acting in Hebrew, came to Düsseldorf. Luise was stunned by their abilities. They saw her in *Peer Gynt*, in the role of Anitra, and a mutual admiration developed. After their guest appearance, whenever possible, Luise followed them in their travels. Just before the company finally left Germany, the chief actors asked Heinz Rainer if Luise could come along as one of them. His reply was "I have nothing against the Jewish theatre, but this is going too far." Luise was unable to defy her father, and the Habimah left without her.

Luise now virtually disappeared into Vienna and Berlin, whence news soon came that the fabled Max Reinhardt was starring her in the plays of Shakespeare, Ibsen, Shaw, Schiller, and Pirandello. Theatrical columns called her the "wonder-child of the drama" and boasted, as a continent away they did of Odets, that she was repeatedly rejecting offers of a career in Hollywood.

Luise Rainer's determination to resist these flattering offers held firm until a talent scout, sent by Louis B. Mayer to approach another actress, was told that he was a fool not, first and above all, to see Luise Rainer playing Roberta in Dreiser's *An American Tragedy*. He did. Next morning he telephoned Mayer and reported what he had seen. That very evening the scout, a tall man with an American accent that Luise could barely understand, appeared in her dressing room and reported that Mr. Louis B. Mayer was determined to bring her to America. It happened at a propitious moment. Luise had just experienced her first real tragedy: the man she loved and was about to marry was killed flying his own airplane. Film magnate Louis B. Mayer's entreaties promised an escape from the immediate context of her grief. Accordingly, she accepted his offer to come to the land she had heard of since early childhood, a land whose citizenship her father had adopted, a land filled with fascination.

Thus in 1935, just nineteen years old,* speaking fluent French and German but only the barest school English, this dark-haired, wide-eyed young girl found herself in an elegant train compartment speeding westward in an enormous new country. Accompanied by a dear companion, her Scottie dog Johnny, she was captivated by the landscape of America that bore all the forms and shapes she had seen in Europe, only, as she said later, "more vast, more wild." She was anticipating a new, rich, seriously creative life.

For his part, Mayer was embarked on a campaign to wipe out the damaging portrait of America that Sinclair Lewis had presented in *Main Street* and *Babbitt*. Movies featuring wholesome characters—Andy Hardy, Dr. Kildare, and the dog Lassie would become the most successful— would balance, Mayer thought, the disagreeable representations not only by Lewis but also by writers he thought crude, like Dreiser, Upton Sinclair, Sherwood Anderson, and John Dos Passos. For this mission Mayer needed all the talent he could find, and thus gave a six-month contract to this young European who could barely speak English.

Luise later recalled her arrival in Hollywood:

> I was collected and photographed. It seemed a bit like a fingerprint. I was seated on a heap of luggage, not mine but supposed to be mine! I was asked to coquettishly cross my legs. Someone came over and shifted my skirt a bit higher. He stepped on Johnny, my dog, who howled and was ready to snap. They too snapped their cameras, one picture, and another, and another (not that they had the faintest idea who I was). Finally satisfied, they disappeared as fast as they had appeared. For two days after this I was put on ice in the Beverly-Wilshire Hotel. Then one of their big funeral cars was sent to whisk me to the studio. There I met a variety of executives or

* Luise Rainer's records of her birth date vary.

their executives or their assistants or "yes-men." They all seemed equally important and most of them looked surprised, wondering, it seemed, who I was, surprised no doubt at my simple, unglamorous appearance, surprised therefore that I was there altogether. Everyone said politely: "So glad to meet you" and I believed they were. Leaving, they said: "See you later," at which I could only imagine that a party was planned. However, shortly after, I found myself again quite alone in the big funeral car that now drove me through the Metro lot. Within minutes I passed Napoleon, Tarzan, Clark Gable, a camel, a lake with an ocean liner on it, and we drove through a piece of African desert, as well as a part of New Orleans. Long after we had left the lot, when we finally reached Beverly Hills, I thought this, too, was still a lot and more sets of Metro-Goldwyn-Mayer!

A small beach house was rented for Luise, and then came a silence of two months.

At first Luise was convinced that there had occurred some dreadful misunderstanding; perhaps, she thought, it was her language difficulty. The fact was that no one on the Metro lot appeared to know she was there, much less to realize who she was, or of what renowned European repertory company she was a member. Although paid a weekly salary, she was not even asked to read for parts. Unable to comprehend the obscene wastefulness of the American film industry, it took her some time to realize that it really did not matter to Mayer or to anyone else that she, touted to reporters as "a new Garbo," schooled in the classics, had been persuaded to leave Vienna in order to play in "fine American films." She was simply an inventory item in cold storage, and her salary, though ever so small for Hollywood, troubled her, since she felt she was not earning it. It was, however, provided, by contract, to keep her steadily available.

In her tiny house she read, played Beethoven sonatas, took long walks along the beach, talking with her dog, reciting old parts and poems, often in contest with the wind and the pounding waves. By now she had only one wish: "to get back home and to the European theatre as quickly as possible."

As she was wondering how she could simply leave and return to the real creative work and life of Vienna, a young star named Myrna Loy, testing her power, left her leading man, William Powell, standing on a movie set, thus creating a crisis amounting to thousands of dollars a day. Anita Loos, highly regarded as a screenwriter, now remembered the Viennese import in the Metro-Goldwyn-Mayer warehouse, and Luise Rainer was given Miss Loy's role in *Escapade*.

When the grosses piled up because of Luise's capacity in this film to make millions weep, she was given the part of Anna Held in *The Great Ziegfeld*. While this picture was being filmed, according to a reporter, "she even made the case-hardened electricians on the sound-stage catwalks shed a volume of tears," a feat something like "making Il Duce give Ethiopia back to Haile Selassie, only much more difficult." To be sure, neither of these roles could compare creatively with parts in the Pirandello, Ibsen, and Shakespeare plays she was used to; still there was some compensation for her in the fact that at long last she was working. Everyone agreed she would receive an Academy Award for her performance as Anna Held. She finally had emerged from the shadows of the Metro lot to the limelight of the Brown Derby restaurant, where, seated one evening with songwriters E. Y. Harburg and Harold Arlen, she noticed heads turning. Someone whispered, "Clifford Odets just came in." Luise had never heard of him.

Director Lewis Milestone had often said that these two shy, lonely, gifted intellectuals, described in the film magazines as music-loving, publicity-shy "enigmas," would have a great deal in common. But on this night, although Odets—after scanning the room—sat down beside her, he did not address a single word to her all evening. "As he was sitting there not speaking to me, I felt a strange and extraordinary attraction and at the same time, instantaneously, I felt a strange sense of doom." She could not know how enchanted he had been by her image on the screen and by accounts of her from Jed Harris. Luise later reminded him of this occasion: " . . . when you looked at me as if I was a fascist and Joan Crawford tied in one person."

Their second meeting was at a party at the house of Dorothy Parker some weeks later. Surrounded by others, Odets' eyes remained on Luise, who sat in a corner in conversation with a guest. "I felt his eyes on me like a laser beam," she said. "The next day he telephoned me, saying, 'Can one never see you alone?' " They met, and from then on were inseparable.

Shortly, Odets moved into Luise's house, now on Cliffwood Avenue in Brentwood. Luise was hard at work on *The Good Earth*, her third film within the first eighteen months of being in Hollywood. She had not as yet met any member of the famous Group Theatre.

When Harold Clurman arrived and came to stay with Clifford and Luise, he eyed Luise suspiciously, as he claimed Odets as the lifeblood of the Group, the provider of its, and especially his, needed materials. It seemed to Luise that he felt an instantaneous resentment toward her, and a kind of competition between them commenced at once. Moreover, Luise felt that Clurman was a bit of a sponger, "feeding on a tree named Odets." Yet, as she put it later, "with obvious intelligence and shrewdness, he created an appearance that was less sponger than donor." Luise mentioned this to Clifford, and she recalled, "To his own distress, he found himself aware of this fact." However, Clurman's stay ended before any overt antagonism developed. The Group coffers had been depleted by the brief road tour of *Awake and Sing!* and Clurman had decided to make a trip to "the Coast" in order to replenish them from the incomes of Group members, many of whom now had well-paid "temporary" jobs in motion pictures. At the same time, he thought, he could explore the film industry, a citadel of glamour and mystery, a "mirror of magic" even to so purehearted a man as he.

Odets, with his characteristic need for a sounding board, talked to Luise about his secret and creatively revolutionary ideas for making a "real" film of *The General Died at Dawn*. Actually, his day-night reversal and her strenuous long days at the studio left them little time together. As they went separately to their work, each would leave fervent love notes for the other. Luise felt that Clurman was trying to "put a wedge between us, for what he pronounced to be the good of the Group Theatre and therefore the good of Odets."

Her first film had made her a star, but she felt that the work, compared with her work in the theatre, was mechanical and fragmented. "They don't need an actress here," she said to Odets. "What they need and want is a face and the camera to go around it. Louis B. Mayer's statement

'Give me a good-looker and I make her an actress' sure seems to be right." Odets felt and told her she was "the Duse of our time," and promised that he would write the longed-for plays for her to do in America. And Luise assured him with equal sincerity that he was America's most gifted young playwright. The vehemence of their feeling, "the happiness at having found each other culminated in a hunger for one another, a fiery passion hard to surmount."

Luise listened and encouraged Clifford in a broken English that he found irresistible. There was something dependent, even helpless, in her inability to speak which increasingly touched and attracted him. He was always drawn to a woman, as he put it, "with tremors." And here was one who, at the same time, was intelligent, beautiful, and becoming a luminary.

"To try and talk through these ideas with a good, but old-line director like Lewis Milestone was almost impossible because when it all boiled down he saw things rather conventionally," Odets said later. Inspired by Clurman's reports of film-making in the Soviet Union, Odets had visions of harnessing the technology of the sound stage and the camera to cinematic experiments never tried before.*

He earnestly believed, as did Luise, that, whatever commercial limitations might be set by the studio, the producer, the director, the technicians, or the mass market, he could emerge with a creative, personal statement of which he could be proud. Accordingly, he threw himself wholeheartedly into this first film project, working often around the clock.

He found himself deeply and genuinely interested in the central character of the Chinese warlord General Yang, whom he described as "a talented man, but very, very corrupt." Yang's core was vanity, and Odets gave him a line directly from his own father's mouth: "You will see —I *big* man." Indeed, as Milestone recalled, "It began to appear that this character was running away with him." Akim Tamiroff, who played Yang, was impressed by Odets' intimate and rich understanding of the warlord and emerged grateful for his help in creating a persuasive performance.

As Odets worked furiously on the screenplay, Milestone became concerned at its length; moreover, he told Odets, he had an odd sense that he had heard some of General Yang's speeches before. Odets confessed that he had adapted them from newspaper reports of recent addresses by Adolf Hitler. It seemed to him, he explained, that their spirit was just right for this tyrant who was "a heartbreaker, a headbreaker, a strikebreaker—a four-star rat!" and who was destroying the land while he exacted impossible taxes from the peasants.

It is startling how even in this adaptation of a pulp-paper story Odets managed to use documentary anti-establishment materials from the history around him and, at the same time, to project with such animation his ceaseless struggle with his father. Even as in *Awake and Sing!* the role of the businessman had captured him, issuing in a rich character, so in this film General Yang, the powerful "big man" (sometimes idealized), outdistances the vitality of the other characters. Of the rich gallery within him, the identity-element of Lou Odets was always the one most readily available to Clifford in his writing.

General Yang's antagonist, O'Hara, played by the young and handsome Gary Cooper, was modeled by Odets on his protégé, actor Jules (not

* Later another "Wunderkind," whom he considered to be a better organizer than he, independently hatched the same "revolutionary film ideas," made *Citizen Kane*, and was subsequently devoured by the industry. Orson Welles would eventually earn his living as an actor by peddling Perrier and wine on television commercials.

yet John) Garfield: he had run away from an orphan asylum, sold news-papers, boxed ("I didn't like smackin' other kids around, so I quit"), and is now trying to help the poor Chinese to revolt against their oppressor. Odets loved the name "O'Hara"; it meant to him "a real American writer." In gratitude for his name, he cast his friend, novelist John O'Hara, in the minor role of a newspaper reporter in *The General Died at Dawn*. Both were affectionately tolerant of Cooper, whose sole comment on the script was "It's a lot of words, but I'll learn 'em."

Opposing the peasants' revolt is not only the almost credible Yang but also the father of the beautiful heroine (played by Madeleine Carroll), a character who, as often in Odets' work, uses the girl as bait for trapping and subduing the rebellious, justice-seeking young hero. In a parody of Odets' stage dialogue, the heroine finally offers her own "worthless life" to save O'Hara, saying, "I got a solid chunk of anguish in me." Characteris-tically, even in this derivative film Odets' hero trusts a woman and loses everything. When she betrays him and he thinks they are both to be exe-cuted by General Yang, he says, "You kicked out one of my lungs on the train," adding the famous lines (quoted by young couples for decades afterward, seriously or ironically, depending on their generation, as a symbol of harmonious merging): "Judy, darling, we could have made won-derful music together—a circle of light and warmth," and "Someday, maybe there'll be a law to abolish the blues, maybe a constitutional amend-ment, for all of us."

Before this pulp-fiction story finally ends, the hero kills the girl's father and Yang threatens him with death ("You will eat fresh fish tonight. When you arrive in Shanghai tomorrow, fresh fish will eat you"). O'Hara outwits a dying Yang by appealing to his outrageous vanity: "If you kill us all, who will be left to tell the story of your greatness?" The young man seductively describes how he will place Yang's picture in "the London *Times, The New York Times*"; this image persuades the warlord, who finally releases both hero and betraying heroine instead of executing them. Safe now, O'Hara says: "You are a small noise at the end of a parade . . . interested only in yourself. . . . " It is clear throughout that Odets is strongly identified *both* with the warlord and with his revolution-ary antagonist.

Thus the young people are liberated by the deaths of two oppressive fathers, and, according to Odets, instead of revolutionizing film-making as he had fantasied, "on a set of clichés we made some good birthday decorations." When the melodramatic *The General Died at Dawn* opened, Odets' left-wing devotees loyally clapped for the few stereotyped militant speeches he put in the mouth of O'Hara. The reviewers jeered at these same lines, and Frank Nugent of *The New York Times*—who enjoyed the film and recommended it—said irritably in his headline (actually imitating the title of an earlier magazine piece by Robert Garland), "Odets, Where is Thy Sting?" and closed with "Odets Takes a Holiday."

Representative Martin Dies, a pioneer in American witch-hunting, duly recorded in a growing dossier on Odets the "left-wing character" of this innocuous film at the same time that he noted the rumors (which were baseless) that Odets—whose *Waiting for Lefty* had just been per-formed at San Pedro, the working-class harbor of Los Angeles—was per-sonally responsible for the efforts of the screen writers to unionize in a strong guild. Noted also was columnist O. O. McIntyre's statement that Odets was still a member of the Communist Party, to which Odets sent a blistering and truthful denial. Informal blacklisting had now begun.

Odets' political activity at this point was in fact restricted to giving occasional addresses at meetings dedicated to forming a united front to oppose "war and fascism." With the clouds of World War II already on the horizon in Morocco—as followers of Francisco Franco pursued conspiracies to topple the duly elected government of Spain—Odets had an ominous feeling, which he frequently confided to friends, that there was a grave danger in the growing alliance between Hitler, Mussolini, and the Spanish general. His fears were dismissed, however, even by the very writers (except Robert E. Sherwood, soon to be in government) and actors organizing the anti-war meetings in Los Angeles.◖ After a long and humiliating trek from the ornate door to the platformed desk which everyone knew had been literally copied from Mussolini by Columbia Pictures head, Harry Cohn, in 1933, they could observe on Cohn's wall a picture personally autographed by Mussolini, from one man of power to another. It was said Walter Wanger had an identical photograph on his wall. Only a few would notice, when Odets' fears became nightmares, that the pictures of Mussolini unobtrusively disappeared.

By early April, his "ten weeks in films" almost over, Odets received pleas from Group members, besides Clurman, for the new play; and he told Luise he must settle down to a revision of the fifteen choppy scenes he had written for *The Silent Partner,* a play which had an increasing hold on him, but whose complex ills he could not diagnose. It was imperative that he finish by the first of June, as Clurman wanted it for the Group's second production of the fall season or, "if nothing else materializes, the first." There were possible plays forthcoming from Irwin Shaw, Arthur Kober, Vincent Lawrence, Samson Raphaelson, and an American version of *The Good Soldier Schweik** to be written by Paul Green, with music by Brecht's gifted collaborator, the refugee Kurt Weill, of *Threepenny Opera* fame. Clurman hoped also that Maxwell Anderson could be prevailed upon to give the Group his new "contemporary comedy in verse." The Group had not had a financial success since *Men in White.*

That Odets had grave doubts about his new play is clear from the fact that he now writes Clurman once more asking whether *The Silent Partner* will "*definitely*" be given summer rehearsal. The reply comes at once: "What a question! Of course, of course, of course," but Clurman quickly adds, "But to rehearse the play . . . it must be written. And you must also remember your own resolve to do a clear job—revision, editing, shaping everything carefully so that there may be no criticisms of any technical loose ends. The burden of the effort is now on you, not on us: we are prepared and *waiting.*"

Clurman has spoken to Aaron Copland about writing music for the play, and he writes, "Aaron is excited about the promise of a finished *Silent Partner* and would like to get to work on . . . it." Copland has been sleeping in Odets' bed at One University Place since "he was kicked out of his apartment" for "too much modern music." Clurman closes with a personal plea: "Is it possible to write Stella a good part?" One that fits her (not a mother as in *Awake and Sing!* or *Paradise Lost*). He thinks it

◖ 19.1.
* This became *Johnny Johnson,* directed by Lee Strasberg, to the production of which Odets contributed $1,500. It was a financial disaster.

"would be a great help," as the Group may otherwise lose Stella. If Odets is having trouble with *The Silent Partner,* might he not write "the piano-store play"* as a vehicle for Stella? It is evident, apart from his personal investment in the discontented Miss Adler, that Clurman was reluctant to open a new Group season with a serious labor play and longed for a good comedy. He was accurately sensing the fact that the American theatre was slowly becoming a place in which to be likable, not serious, and that without a popular offering the Group Theatre would soon perish.

In another letter Clurman urges Odets to forge ahead, but assures him that if he does not think *The Silent Partner* is ready, it will not be done: "I will never use one of your plays as an organizational stopgap." This sentence did not reassure Odets, who would complain for years to come that the Group—and Harold in particular—always pressured him for a play, whether or not he thought it was ready for production.

The Group, for the relief of whose difficulties a "New Group Plan" would be unveiled by Clurman on the second day of July, had now decided once more to "sing for its supper," this time at an adult camp called the Pinebrook Club in Nichols, Connecticut. Clurman wonders whether Odets and Elia Kazan might like to share with him and Stella the expenses for a house, as the common "Group house" would not be a good place for Odets to work on his new play. It is evident that Odets had not yet told Clurman that Luise Rainer, not Kazan, would be Odets' partner in their summer household.

Finding it difficult to come to grips with the vexed problems of *The Silent Partner,* Odets found his usual escape in making notes for future plays and in letter-writing, especially to his Philadelphia family. To Cousin Irene's small daughter, Corinne, he sends an account from the *Hollywood Citizen-News* of his "impossible interview" with child star Shirley Temple in her "doll-house portable dressing room." When the columnist introduced Odets to her as "also an actor. He acts on the stage," the child, who had never seen a stage play, replied, "People don't act on the stage, they act in the movies." The story underscored Luise Rainer's sad and bitter feeling about the film industry. Odets assured her that they would soon leave Brentwood and be back East in the bosom of the Group, where serious artists worked, as she had, differently from these people in "show biz," and were making serious plans for the fall, the most important being his new labor play, which he regarded as his most ambitious and humanly significant so far. As it began to appear that her film *The Good Earth* would drag on interminably, Luise hoped Odets could wait for her so they could go East together.

As Odets reread Kazan's report of the Chicago company's first-night audience for *Awake and Sing!,* his confidence in his ability to move an audience with a serious statement was further diminished. "If you walked out on stage," wrote Kazan, "facing an orchestra half-full of stodgy Guild subscribers, ice-packed into tux and evening clothes, you caught cold. They were mildly interested in the play, but there was no 'audience response.' They didn't get the local jokes, the Jewish jokes, the horseracing jokes, the street jokes, any of the jokes. The speech to them was just a blur of unusual color."

Thus as Odets set to the task of revising *The Silent Partner,* he was flooded with the same fear he had felt after *Awake and Sing!* when he

---

* In the folder in Odets' files labeled "Piano Store Play" is a dreary scenario about a pathetic effort on the part of a colorless character to find intimacy. Described by Odets in his notes as a "liar like Paula Miller," he is a person who lives in fantasy.

had told Clurman, quoting Strasberg, "I have a serious artistic problem. I don't feel I write completely American characters, they always come out a little Jewish." Clurman had replied, "There is no American character separate. The American character is mixed in with the Anglo-Saxon character, Dutch character, Russian character, Irish character, and the Jewish people have made a contribution which has given us people like George Gershwin, and a lot of things which are very Jewish, but are also one hundred percent American, just as Sinclair Lewis is." This had appeased Odets, but he had nonetheless determined that *Paradise Lost* would not have this drawback. Clurman's distaste for the "vulgar Jewish jokes"— which he had excised—in the first twenty pages of *Awake and Sing!* had been painful to him. Thus, a part of Odets shared Louis B. Mayer's aspiration to erase the images of an immigrant America and to substitute for these the more accepted, more palatable images of white Anglo-Saxon Protestants who had been in America a long time and had forgotten why they had come. But another part of him longed to celebrate his Tante Esther and his proud uncle Israel, the "songer," who wouldn't "kiss no one's ess for not'ing" and who knew full well why they had come. But the Chicago reception of *Awake and Sing!* produced in him a corroding sense that not even in the legitimate theatre of America did he have a reliable forum in which to express this core of himself.

Odets had taken the title for his new play about a strike from a statement attributed to tycoon Andrew Carnegie: "Where the wealth of a nation is honorably accrued, the people are always the silent partner."* This statement, put in the mouth of a character in the play who applauds Hitler's example of "putting troublemakers in detention camps," is followed by "Democracy is not a privilege to scatter before swine."

Group actor Morris Carnovsky, impressed by the symbolic density and poetic quality in this "anti-Fascist play," called it "an ode to the working class." Odets thought, however, that the play was also critical of the working class.◖ The point was, he said, addressing people generally: ". . . stop the foolishness. For God's sake get serious or die. You're going to die for lack of seriousness." Clurman described it as a play about "an old order of benevolent capitalism that had grown lame, a new order of monopolistic capitalism that was growing vicious (fascist), and a still unorganized and spiritually unformed working-class . . . the old world of money and power becoming decrepit . . . while the new world was in America still raw, unclear, undisciplined. . . . " In the universe of critical discourse reserved for a rationalist conception of history, this was indeed what the play was "about." Odets, however, was reaching for more.

In *The Silent Partner,* as in *Paradise Lost* and, more crudely if more successfully, in the quasi-documentary *Waiting for Lefty,* he was consciously trying to create on the stage a psychohistorical—even a mythic— reality which would include not only the psychological richness, complexity, and detail of the life of "real people," but would also set them

---

* There is no indication Odets knew of Elizabeth Ward's novel *Silent Partner,* which decried conditions in factories.

◖ 19.2.

allegorically, even ritually, in a particular moment of the history of man's world-image.*

As in his *Paradise Lost,* he mourns the loss of a secure oneness of mother and child and, consequently, of innocence. In *The Silent Partner* he continues also an exploration of form, begun in *Paradise Lost,* of what he called a "heightened realism, a very tense fullness and richness . . . naturalistic and yet existing on a symbolic level."

Odets' initial impetus away from what Clurman had called the "messy Jewish-kitchen realism" of *Awake and Sing!* had resulted in making his next work, *Paradise Lost,* less naturalistic, less ethnic, and, for some serious critics, less significant. An unexpected bonus, however, in this work purged of its Jewish flavor had been his foray into symbolism and into the use of language with an underwater—some thought, poetic—quality which Odets himself found rich in color and very rich in mood. He regarded *The Silent Partner,* which again explored the uses of such symbolism, as presenting the problems of a symphony, in contrast to his less ambitious "chamber works" like the later *Rocket to the Moon.*

He knew it was more difficult to create a psychologically detailed picture of a universal human struggle (whether Jewish or non-Jewish), filled with its vitality, its ambiguities, and its paradoxes, than to abstract it either in the simple terms of the class struggle, as in *Waiting for Lefty,* or in the more complex terms of individual motivation, as he would later in *Rocket to the Moon.* But in *The Silent Partner,* as in *Paradise Lost,* he was determined to wrestle with a larger canvas, with the use of heightened language, and with the mammoth problem of uniting individual motivation with its wider social and historical context.†

He would never abandon the impulse to express an allegory in his plays, but the fate of *The Silent Partner* would substantially discourage him from a forthright pursuit of this impulse.‡ Except for the last work of his life, his plays hereafter maintained a surface of literal realism without, however, the authentically Jewish ring which in *Awake and Sing!* had become his unique American voice.⁣

In the fifteen somewhat disjointed scenes which comprise *The Silent Partner* (each titled, as in a novel)§ the protagonist, Mr. Gracie, is a member of an old American, Anglo-Saxon, Protestant family being ousted from the management of an industrial plant by a "fascist" absentee ownership. Although this impotent and alcoholic man is the son of the corporation's founder, he is being displaced from above by unseen, merciless, and omnipotent powers while his employees—who call him "Lord Plushbottom"—are conducting a dangerous strike against him from below. His will being insufficient to control the forces above *or* below him, he is caught in the middle, is in charge of nothing, and, deeply ashamed, bitterly calls himself "the Admiral of the Swiss Navy."

---

* Much later a student in his playwriting class would ask about this play, "Was it like the work of Thornton Wilder?" and Odets would reply, "That's just not having any blood."

† Precisely the same difficulty is reflected in the history of the attempts to synthesize psychoanalytic views of individual motivation and the life cycle with observations of social and historical processes.

‡ He would say to writer Ted Allan in 1939 that even the eager young Cleo Singer in *Rocket to the Moon*—symbol of the aspiring soul of the artist—was looking for "a socialist world." Neither Allan nor anyone else could see this in the play.

⁣ 19.3.

§ These shrank to nine, of which Odets thought only eight were really "finished." Like his last play, *The Flowering Peach,* the final draft of *The Silent Partner* has never been published, except for one scene (Act II, scene 2) in *New Theatre and Film,* March 1937.

Like the fractured Major Duhring in Odets' anti-Nazi play, *Till the Day I Die*, Mr. Gracie is ridden by doubt, committed to nothing, and thus impotent. Divided, helpless, and passive, he knows he "cannot stop the strikers from being killed" any more than he can stop the scab "thugs from replacing them and destroying their brotherhood. He wants to "have his cake and eat it, too."

In Mr. Gracie the playwright has established the battleground for the opposing forces in the play, not only, as Clurman suggests, in terms of the class struggle but also in terms of Odets' current creative crisis precipitated by the death of his mother, by his recent success, and by his profound fear of failure as judged by his father.

Dictating a remarkably authentic and tender letter to his son, in which he renews his subscription to *Time*, the torn Gracie expresses this fear of failure, telling his son "how life begins to terrorize me." He cannot, in his heart, be "against those workers." He is "dispossessed," he feels, and "in the same boat" as the strikers, but is as controlled by "invisible wire-pulling financiers as they are." He ends: "The Plant has been taken away from me. It's an age of speed-up and monopoly and only the biggest fish, sharks can roam the once-free ocean. The minnows are swallowed, without dressing. . . . Eat or be eaten." Odets' father had always said, "It's dog eat dog."

Odets' pervasive sense of smallness, impotence, and will-lessness—with none of the free choices of a "big man"—steadily wars here, as in the rest of his life and work, with his adherence to an image of a world in which a man may courageously and responsibly transcend his individuality and find strength in a rebellious—nay, a creatively—revolutionary brotherhood whose members succor each other. Indeed, he may even sacrifice his life in its service. Although Odets no longer thought of himself as a Communist, he still called himself "a man of the left," "a radical playwright." At the same time his feeling of helplessness was reflected in his renewed interest these days in astrology: how the heavenly stars and planets invisibly pull the strings of one another's destinies, as well as that of every human. Simultaneously he expressed a fear and awe of *all* authority, of celebrity, and of psychology, and defensively scorned all these "forces," proclaiming a fearless and creative sense of being "in control" of his life. He assigned to a variety of characters in *The Silent Partner* both ends of this conflict.

Summarizing its plot for a Ph.D. candidate twenty-five years later, Odets chose, of the many characters (sometimes twenty-four, sometimes forty-five) who roam the pages of its several inchoate drafts, the dispossessed plant-manager, who has a hopeless foot in each camp, as the chief protagonist. His inner division is echoed by a minor character, a sheriff who is supposed to swear in thugs as deputies but, being in his heart on the side of the strikers, will not do so.

In the variegated and mythic panorama of this rough, fluid, social, expressionist play, one could equally choose as central characters the two strike-leaders, Cliff and Christie Love, who are brothers.* Their surname—

¶ 19.4.
* This was the only time Odets used his own name for a character in a play. Throughout, "Cliff" is usually referred to by the nickname "Lovey." His brother's name, "Christie," seems to derive from the name of Christ, who proclaimed equality for all brothers, who pleaded with them to love one another, and who died for their redemption. It is not clear why Odets needed to split this identity-element into two parts: perhaps the introspective intellectual represents thought and the impulsive fighter, action. Setting the play in "twin cities" (Apollo and Rising Sun) is again a "pairing." (See Notes and Comment 19.11.)

which underwent a series of revisions, from "Love" to "Lovell" to "Love-land" to "Lovelace" to "Ellis"—is reminiscent of O'Neill's "John Loving" in *Days Without End,* which O'Neill had called a "modern miracle play" revealing "a man's search for truth amid the conflicting doctrines of the modern world and his return to his old religious faith." Perhaps Odets had copied the name from O'Neill; more likely each of these alienated and personally torn men was dealing with the necessity to find, during a cultural era of identity-vacuum, a path of a sustaining brotherhood, a loving communality.

O'Neill had tried to resuscitate his Catholicism; Odets was clinging to something between a primal Judaeo-Christianity and Marxism. In the simple, almost ritual *Waiting for Lefty* he had achieved a primitive merger with his audience where Lefty, the union organizer, was also, like Jesus, a Messiah who became a blood sacrifice. In *The Silent Partner,* Cliff Love, another messianic strike-leader, is the blood sacrifice. The subtexts of all three plays are strikingly similar. O'Neill's John Loving at the end stands in front of a cross: his hating, "death-seeking" self is conquered and, arms outstretched, *in the form of a cross,* he dies. At this point his "life-seeking" self rises from his knees and stands before the cross, arms outstretched, affirming his newfound faith in God. The struggle with an underlying impulsive hostility is part and parcel of the search for an ideological or a religious integration; the purpose of such an integration is to keep hatred in check and to permit love to flow without becoming the sentimentality which is the mark of a repressed cruelty.

With significant exceptions, the related themes of what might loosely be called "the search for love," the betrayal, and the blood sacrifice are steadily present in Odets' work. In this context "love" refers not to adult sensuality but to an image of a communal, innocent, egalitarian brotherhood—like Beethoven's—where, Odets says, all "the children" are on the same safe footing: ". . . no difference, Jew Gentiles, Gentiles, Jews (flips his open hand around) like flapjacks . . . no difference."* In order to restore this paradisiacal state it may, however, be necessary, he adds, that the "anvil become hammer," as in a strike, a revolution, a murder of a warlord, or even a suicide. In the course of such overturn the climactic event is frequently the uncorrupted self-sacrifice of a "son."◖

Lovey makes it explicit what "organizing a union" and the strike mean to him (and here Odets quotes Luise Rainer):

> I was a seven months' baby, and all my life I was looking for that extra two months. I felt unborn, incomplete. The church didn't help, work didn't help, reading didn't—maybe having children and a wife might have—but organizing a union *did.* I tell you this: *the strike is a mother.* I'm born now. Does that sound funny?

Perhaps he should have said reborn.

---

* Erik H. Erikson, to whom I introduced Odets, saw in him "something of the primal Christian" who longed to sit with his brothers and sisters "knowing transcendence" without murderous envy. Odets' statement in the summer of 1931 (see p. 193) reflects a longing for such communion.

In a screenplay called "The Actor," begun shortly before his death but before he consciously knew he was ill, Odets' intense yearning to believe in what he called "the inherent nobility and love in people" was evident. In this play all his friends gather "as brothers" to help the dying man. Shortly afterward, as Odets himself lay dying, he called his friends, Lee Strasberg, Gadg Kazan, Harold Clurman, Cary Grant, Marlon Brando, Danny Kaye, Jean Renoir, William Goodley, and others ("all brothers"!).

◖ 19.5.

One of the most psychologically impressive scenes in the play occurs when the nearby farmers bring milk to the starving strikers for their children and sick families. The stage directions describe it:

ALL the women are standing motionless, focused on the milk cans. Their eyes and mouths making love to the milk. Slowly ROXIE comes forward to one of the milk cans and looks down at it as she will in later life at her first baby.* Suddenly she falls to her knees, throws her arms around the can and begins to sob. This is something which all the other women understand.

When the company thugs enter *with guns* and pour the milk "into the gutter," this mobilizes even the most reluctant of the women to affirm the strike. She spits in the face of the thug, and whereas previously she had pleaded for an end to the strike, she now says, closing the scene, "May any man who votes to end our strike burn in hell forever! Forever . . . !" It has become clear that only through the communal solidarity of the strike (brothers cease killing one another) can the children be fed and a life with creativity and dignity for successive generations be restored. In addition to the overt political meanings here, the unconscious symbol is of a joining with brothers and sisters to restore for all that sustenance originally provided by the mother. It is a symbol of the path of "brotherly love" and of the feminine "milk" of human kindness, not of the fear of a wrathful Old Testament God.

Odets brings in a minor character, a "writer of prize novels and movies," who is vacationing nearby and who wants to report sympathetically on the strike for a magazine. His contempt for this man, most obviously like his current manifest self, but like Dreiser and Lawson also, is unmistakable. A "famous writer and a big influence in America," Philip Bliss (sic) arrives dead drunk and has to be carried in by his secretary and his uniformed Negro chauffeur. As the famous writer snores, the black chauffeur does a "dance of Death" accompanied by music which has in it "the music of war, of murder, all of these things taking place six blocks away at this moment."

The "war and murder" taking place on this Fourth of July—the day of celebrating American liberation from another absentee landlord—are the scabs shooting their way into the plant, and throughout Mr. Gracie, the plant-manager, descended from the earliest American patriots, hears his ancestors turn in their graves as they wonder why they fought in 1776. The United States of America, into whose constitution was written the right to pursue happiness,† is a paradise lost in which Odets—first American-born member of a Jewish family—yearns for a "true" egalitarian American identity.

The yearning for a restoration of his innocent paradise lost is also echoed as the second act closes when Cliff, the older, more intellectual and introspective of the two brothers—who does not "feel like a man" and is "too much with the head"—is shot by the scabs and dies, "sitting in his own blood," and pleading for immortality: "tell them, tell them, boys and girls, remember us." His brother, Christie, "a figure of great wrath and fearless," shouts to the others who are praying, "Stay on your knees! Cry

* It is startling that Odets sees so clearly that in man's lost paradise an infant nourishes a mother even as she nourishes him.
† Elaine Dundy points out that in no other country is the "pursuit of happiness" taken so seriously as in the U.S.A. From this point of view, she argues that Odets was perhaps the first serious *American* playwright, as his plays are full of concern for this concept. (Personal communication)

out to your mother! Ask her to get me bullet-proof skin for an hour! *I wanna break bones! I wanna kill them! Tear out their hearts!* Christ God, as Samson did it—lemme smash their brains on these walls! God, listen to me. *Gimme bullet-proof skin for one hour."* (Later Christie will go off with Pearl* . . . like a new Adam and Eve.◀) Typed in red capital letters (the only time such type is used in this manuscript) is the stage direction: "The great writer Philip Bliss is slowly carried out of the Labor Temple by his fearful Servants." It is as if Odets is here issuing a stern warning to himself. Later this direction was crossed out by Odets.

In a desperate plea for murderous power and invulnerability,◀ for a tough hide like his father's—and its accompanying capacity to "tear out hearts"—Odets expresses the obverse side of his "search for love," for the innocence of the lost communal paradise, and for what he would later call the "merging of subject and object." It is the vengeful side of the artist's impulse: he wants to "knock his audience dead," or, as he put it in another place: "Art works should shoot bullets." To Luise Rainer he said, "An artist should go to his work silently like a murderer to his victim."

Act III opens with what Odets labels "The Death Watch." Actually, the strike-leader, Cliff, is already dead, his body on display alongside his "Five Foot Shelf" of red-bound books. His mother wanders about the room, exactly as Pearl Odets often had, "in a torment of habitual unconcentration," looking for the shoebox (a coffin?) for her son's now empty shoes. "They won't fit Christie," she says, and since Cliff "only wore them twice," they "oughta be returned." She fears that Cliff, though "a reader of magnificent books," is "burning, burning he won't rest!" because, like his father's, his death was a violent one, and besides, "he never did even his Easter duty."

A minor character now announces the title of Sunday's sermon as: "Did the Lord really command Abraham to slay his own son Isaac?" Odets continues to wrestle here both with his ancient and his current relation to a father and his values, and concomitantly with the larger issues of the human condition in this time. His urgent fear is that in his anxiety to maintain his success he will lose what he calls his "unique self," meaning, of course, his creativity.

This struggle is carried out in the play by steady bickering among the death-watchers," who offer a variety of answers to the question, "God, who is He . . . the word which signifies this Unknown Quantity?" One naïvely says, " . . . people with all study don't find out what is, life. People is searching their brain day and night to come to the answer, to the point!" For himself, this same character asks only that "I will die before my two boys pass on, and will work till I die. Tonight I stop work, in the morning I die. That is all what I ask." Another cynically mocks all effort to make any meaning of life, contemptuously labeling the one who is trying to do so "Lord Chesterfield of Hershey Bar."

Closing the play, Odets tries to create a last-minute affirmation, and, as in his earlier work, it is by way of the triumph of action over intellect: there is news that a militantly active woman striker, feared to be in a terminal coma from injuries inflicted by the scabs, will *live*, whereas the introspective* intellectual Cliff is dead. An old Italian baker sadly picks up one of his books and, looking at the title, says, "Anthropology," and "suddenly he is crying in his fine hands."

Odets has appended an "alternate ending" which is less sentimentally

---

* Odets' mother's name.
◀ 19.6.
◀ 19.7.

affirmative. The dead boy's mother makes a bitter speech: "The children, the children, *they* know and the parents don't. So *they* think. What is it the young ones want, the world in one bite?❮ They won't listen till the end of the earth . . . the young fools . . . children turn a body's heart to stone. . . . "

At this point the mother, who keeps insisting that the strike-breaking company meant her dead boy "no harm," at last finds the resting place for his shoes, the shoebox she has been hunting. It is clear they will not be filled, and "she slowly breaks into tears." In the background, throughout the act, the flicker of candles by the coffin is as steady "as the distant music of a carnival calliope which alternates between a brassy jazz tune and a sentimental ballad." It is notable that, preoccupied as Odets is with the death of his mother, it is not the mother but the son who dies. This reversal suggests not only a profound identification with his mother but also a pervasive belief that he shared with his father the wish to murder her.* The son is again the blood sacrifice, the one who dies for the sins of many, the Messiah.

The style of *The Silent Partner* is on the whole humorless, static, at times bombastic. Occasionally, however, Odets' capacity to stand back wryly from his own epic, even mythic, romanticism emerges even here ("How sad I am to think how sad I used to be!" says one character), and there appear hints, even in early drafts, of potential size, richness, freedom, and compassion.

Odets was beginning to think it could become his best work, and he would compulsively return to it during the next three years. Indeed, this play had become the battleground for his current struggles with form, with campaigns visible on a variety of fronts in its many drafts. How ambitious dared he be (the symphony or the chamber work)? Wherein lay the greater risk, in using the familiar Jewish-American idiom of his Tante Esther and Uncle Israel, or in abandoning it for a universal kind of heightened speech? How privately "psychological" or how publicly documentary should his work be? Should it be carefully plotted as a "well-made play," or could it present the simple confrontation of characters loosed at each other? Should he concentrate on making it commercially practicable, or allow creative elbow room for exploration of new aspects of himself and of new forms? Most important of all the private issues visible on this giant canvas is the fundamental paradox probably common to all artists: the will to create (in short, to be as God) must include the will to destroy and then to rebuild.❮ The play mourns his lost paradise when he was his mother's only and adored child, a paradise forever lost with the appearance of a crippled sister; he expresses at the same time his repressed rage toward both women.

Eager to show *The Silent Partner* to his "brother Harold," Odets began to make plans to work with his Group family for the summer even though

❮ 19.8.
* It will be recalled that their maid reported grave apprehension that L. J. Odets had pushed his wife down the stairs just before she died. On the flyleaf of *Paradise Lost* Odets published the dedication "For My Dead Mother."
❮ 19.9.

Luise was still hard at work filming. She would join him later at the house he rented for them in Shelton, near the Pinebrook Club in Nichols, Connecticut.

She was anxious because *The Good Earth* was beginning to appear to be a jinxed and interminable project. Its original director, George Hill, had committed suicide, its next had fallen ill, and now director Sidney Franklin, with the help of Irving Thalberg, had been asked by the studio to do the work of an international diplomat in order to allay the fears of the Chiang Kai-shek Nationalist government, which thought the film would emphasize the miserable conditions of the Chinese peasants. Some were convinced that Mme. Chiang's anti-Communism was at the root of the problem.

At Thalberg's suggestion, the Chinese government had sent as observer a young Nationalist Army general with his wife and two children, all of whom rapidly became part of the company. When he and his family suddenly disappeared, he was replaced by the Chinese consul, who explained that the first man had been suspected of permitting a politically dangerous picture to be made. The alert Albert Lewin, professorial assistant to the energetic young Thalberg—who was then feuding with Louis B. Mayer—immediately invited writer Lin Yutang and scholar Hu-Shi to look at what was finished of the film. Mme. Chiang Kai-shek could not believe Luise Rainer was not herself Chinese, and Pearl Buck later wrote: "I was much moved by the incredibly perfect performance of Luise Rainer . . . marvelling . . . at the miracle of her understanding." *The Good Earth* was thus given a seal of approval, the Chinese government's objections were withdrawn, and the film proceeded. It would be Thalberg's last. The original young general was never again heard from, and Luise was long delayed in joining Clifford in Connecticut.

As for Clifford, he found himself again entertaining the resentful thought that Clurman was indeed "fattening on him," as Luise had said. Clifford had impressed on her the unique importance of the Group Theatre and the salvation it held, in his opinion, for *both of them* as artists. To Clurman, on his visit to Hollywood, Odets had seemed confused and oddly cut off from the Group. He had not been certain Odets would finish either *The Silent Partner* or *Law of Flight* in time for the fall season.

Just before boarding the eastbound Santa Fe with the same suitcase again filled with drafts of *The Silent Partner,* Odets stopped at a florist's and at a record shop to send to Luise a bouquet of roses and Beethoven's Seventh Symphony. The weekend they had spent together, he wrote her, was "very good, nourishing and I . . . better and happier than I've been for a long time. . . . It would be terrible if something happened, if in the end we went different ways. . . . I give you Beethoven's 7th because it is mostly like what I feel for you, not forgetting the slow movement. How terrible and how wonderful this feeling . . . How wonderful our last night together . . . " He read and reread a scribbled note she had passed to him at the Brown Derby restaurant: ". . . let's show them that this *is* a world for poets!"*

Clurman wrote at length to Strasberg, asking him to "personally guarantee a production to Maxwell Anderson of the next play he sees fit to write for us," adding then apologetically, "Even if it's another *Winterset,* I'll vote for it. I should live so." He was apprehensive about the new labor plays by Odets and by John Howard Lawson (*Marching Song*) as

---

* She referred to American poet Hart Crane's frequently quoted suicide note, "This is *not* a world for poets."

possibly dated. The Congress of Industrial Organization had by now made great strides, and Clurman was afraid unionization was becoming a dead issue. Later, however, he would write, "Some of the more brutal scenes of *The Silent Partner* were to be enacted during the coming spring in the Chicago Memorial Day massacre."

Clurman's letter to Strasberg is deeply troubled on many counts: Stella Adler is carrying too much of a burden (being financially responsible for her aging mother and her young child), and there is a growing cleavage within the Group between the actors and directors. The central issue, however, which opens and closes it—as in all his letters to Odets— is the urgent need for new playwrights and new plays.

Before Odets left Hollywood for Connecticut, he had worked with great satisfaction on further revisions of *The Silent Partner* (the original draft, he often said, having been finished in three or four days) and, with no satisfaction whatever, on the Cuban play, a work he would always regard as the only really poor play he ever wrote.

He thought to title it "The Morgue at Miramar" after the place to which the dead body of his revolutionary hero—based on the real Antonio Guiteras, an anti-Batista guerrilla—had been taken. Guiteras, a native Cuban who tried to do what Castro later did successfully, was betrayed and shot, with his Irish-Cuban girlfriend, on the beach at Miramar. "When their bodies were taken there, democracy and liberty in Cuba were taken there to that morgue," said Odets.

Although "The Morgue at Miramar" again expresses Odets' enduring themes of betrayal and murder (blood sacrifice) of the potential deliverer, work on it did not nourish him. He felt far away from its place and from people whom he had known, after all, for only a few hours; the images which came to him were stale and the people lifeless. Soon it became clear that he was unable to open his internal "gallery of characters" creatively for this material, and he abandoned it.❡ Not so with *The Silent Partner*.

A biographer who pores over the more than three hundred files of what Odets called "projects in work" (plays in various stages of incompletion) with their rich "social types," short scenes, summaries, and sometimes full acts, comes away with the dizzying impression that Odets was occupied each night with the creation of a gigantic psychological and historical mural which, if he could finally synthesize it all, would reflect his "true experience" of man's fate and his own. At times he felt he could control no more than a square inch of this giant canvas, and he would then spend the night writing "notes" for one of these "projects in work," or, less ambitiously, snatches of dialogue or a description of a "typical character" for his general storehouse of material. At other times he would essay a sketch of the whole, as in *Paradise Lost, The Silent Partner*, and *The Flowering Peach*. But the fundamental materials, from play to play, are, in a crucial sense, interchangeable.

For example, in a file marked "Agitator-Son Play" (begun in 1934 and continued in this spring of 1936 concurrently with *The Silent Partner*)

❡ 19.10.

he works on a more transparent edition of Cliff Love from *The Silent Partner*. In the "Agitator-Son Play" he is the older of two brothers(and "has never earned a nickel except at odd jobs." His father is a "very average businessman" of the lower middle class "who once might have been a poet or an artist." The father "tried to work him into his business, but it all failed." The boy has writing talent and has had several short stories published, but "the father sneers at this. . . . A little afraid too he is. He dominates the house and wants to keep it that way." Odets' summary continues:

The mother in the family is or was a cultured woman, the mediator between son and father, and it was she, so long as she lived, who kept capitalist life tolerable and kind and human and charitable. She represents the best of the liberal bourgeoisie, but is sick or dying, or will have died as the first act curtain goes up. Perhaps the end of the first act.

The father will not support his son, or does it grudgingly. With the mother's death the son has come home to stay. The father asks if he is not ashamed to be supported at his age, and son says no . . . he is a rational, realistic, humanistic person. Radical.

The play becomes a struggle of two men for domination of a household. Then in comes a younger son, back from Cornell or something like that. Or from a military academy and the father wanting him to end up at West Point. The two men struggle for the ultimate development of the boy, right or left, and the second act goes down with the older son having his first novel accepted as a big prize novel and published to wide critical acclaim. The father has lost so far. At the same time the father's business goes bankrupt. It is the second time; the first was seventeen years before and he was honest and made good with all the creditors.

This time there is no hope.

The father takes correspondence course in English, etc. (Biographical data).

The mother's spirit hovers over the household. Perhaps she is brought downstairs and dies downstairs at end of act one. And some sign or token that she is happy that the older son is victorious in the end.

Father accuses son—"What were you doing in the Negro maid's room last night for two hours?" Son was talking to her as a Negro about Negro problems. "We spoke of the Scottsboro boys, and Angelo Herndon," etc. Don't believe it? Ask her. Father sputters, "Ask her?!! Me?!"

Third act opens with father saying that he supposes the son will leave now that he is a success. Also borrows some money. The son wins in other ways, etc.

Older son plays piano—his mother taught him, etc. So we bring out what the mother was throughout the play. Father had little to do with sons' good things.

In this "Agitator-Son" file Odets has underlined sentences in an article by Lewis Corey, "The Minds of the Middle-Class": " . . . the final destruction by the depression of the 1930's of the employment security . . . of professionals" reveals that they are "a new proletariat" and that " . . . the old ideological lumber in their minds must be thrown out, for it was used to build a house in which they no longer live" or "the mind of the old middle-class, as it clings to property, thinks in terms of compromise and survival, moves toward state capitalism and fascism. That mind sheds all its old progressive ideals and becomes wholly reactionary." Odets had penciled at the top of the article: "Here is an important play."

His conscious thought about the "Agitator-Son Play" is largely in terms of the class struggle, as, indeed, it is in *The Silent Partner*. Yet in both he is working at the same moment with the intensely personal materials of his own family and, as in the early plays of O'Neill, with the creative dilemmas of the American playwright.

Just before leaving Hollywood to join the Group Theatre in Connecticut, he writes to Helen Deutsch:

> The thing that comes with easy living—I mean when the first shot of ambition goes . . . is a great tolerance. Or as you write it, thinking all people are wonderful and good. What goes—and this is very bad—is a loss of the sense of the unique self; forgetting to keep one's point of view, forgetting an essential difference between one's self and most other people. One says to other movie writers . . . "what the hell we are all writers." But that is a bad lie. They are writers, and the self is an artist. And to forget that difference . . . is the first step in the downfall. What makes it doubly difficult is trying to be nice. When one is in a spot of just the slightest recognition, he is anxious to prove that he is nice, unspoiled, democratic. . . . The thing that stiffens one against all stars and big shots out here is that tremendous effort of theirs to be nice: it is an essential activity with them. Nothing breaks down the moral tissue with greater ease. . . .
>
> You know about California. . . . Have no original ideas about it except that for plain normal living it is fine. But the artist can't be a normal liver, and surely the sources of his material are not in the good feeling in his lungs, the ease and softness in the air, and the profusion of fresh vegetables and fruit; and not in the great salary checks!
>
> Milestone and I got on very well. He is a nice fellow, albeit a little dulled by California, as all talented people are. . . .

Working in the lower berth of his Pullman (he had bought an upper for sleeping, a lower for working), he received in Albuquerque, New Mexico, a birthday wire from Luise four days early: "I give you the stars, the heavens, the sun and the moon and me." Chiding her humorously for her mistake, he concludes she will have to send another wire on July 18, when he will be thirty years old. Better still, she must join him and the Group in Connecticut. Writing her in an archaically romantic style, he says they will be a "wonderful pair," he will write plays for her and she will have in him "a true deep friend, a lover, a helper in all things." She must not say, as she often has, "Don't think you have to help me," as a large part of love is to "serve and to help the loved one. And it must be added—to be helped!" Although he is convinced that "the nature of love is poignance, sadness, a sort of despair in which the more one loves the more one despairs," he is ready, he thinks, to overcome his "bad small pride," his mistrust, his competitiveness, his revengefulness, and concludes, "I give you love, temperament, talent, youth, brightness, hunger, love . . . and I take the same from you." When the train stopped at Dodge City, Kansas, he mailed a note telling Luise she is not "alone in America, not today and not tomorrow," nor is he—and a postscript: " . . . but you *so alone* in a foreign strange country!!! No more Luise, no more alone!!!" Feeling thus joined to a woman, and with his bag bursting with new work for the Group, he arrived at his New York apartment, on the day before his thirtieth birthday, with greater happiness than for a long time.

Eager though he was for a reunion with his Group brothers and sisters, he had first to touch home base by listening to his records. The next morning he read with grief of the deep response in the Soviet Union to the death of Maxim Gorky, and with anxious foreboding of the bitter fighting in Madrid between General Francisco Franco's Fascist Insurgents and the Loyalist government of Spain. He felt he must talk with Luise at once. Wild with anxiety when he could not immediately reach her by phone in California, he sent wire after wire and kept calling steadily until, many hours later, she answered. His ordinarily extreme suspiciousness and jealousy now exacerbated, he insisted that she come East immediately. She could not; she was still at work.

The press, always hot on the scent of clay feet, especially on a self-proclaimed Marxist, heard that Odets was back and within forty-eight hours was doing its best to expose him as a fallen angel. A black headline in the *Herald Tribune* announced, "Odets Returns, Denies 'Sellout' to Hollywood," with three subheads saying, "Took $28,500* in Eleven Weeks, True but Only to Support His More Serious Work"—"Also His $85 Apartment"—"And He's Found Time to Do a Play on Industrial War." The tone of the long piece—a model for dozens to follow—is mocking, shallow, cynical,† in contrast to Odets' guileless replies. "I've just seen some of those wisecracks," he says. "Odets sells out to Hollywood and the like. Well, it's a lot of claptrap. People like to say bad things about anyone I suppose. Look, I produced three or four plays here in New York, and the money I get for them you could put in a thimble," adding of his eleven weeks' work in Hollywood, "Why, that will underwrite my work here for a full two years. I can't see any reason why a writer shouldn't accept such an assignment, give them the very best quality of work that he can, and let that salary pay the freight for his other work." He was quick to add, however, that the "marvelous" technical resources were so expensive that "they are dependent on the export market. They won't risk offending anyone. You work within limits and everyone knows it; you don't hear any phony talk about art. . . . I'm lucky to have something to look forward to, lucky to have people like the Group to come back to—people who understand what I'm working at and trying to do. I feel sorry for any playwright who doesn't have that advantage." He had no doubt that his "real work" lay in the East and in the Group's anticipated productions of *The Silent Partner, Law of Flight,* and a short satirical farce he had begun—about the pathetic private lives of street-corner Santa Clauses—called *The Blizzard Men.*

Pursued by newsmen to the rambling frame house he had rented not

---

* His income-tax record says $27,500.

† In their play *Stage Door,* Edna Ferber and George S. Kaufman parroted this view, presenting an undisguised portrait of Odets as an opportunistic, arrogant boor who sold out to Hollywood, leaving his friends with their principles and artistic integrity to shift for themselves.

far from Bridgeport, he continued good-humoredly to answer the same questions. When asked for the tenth time, "How do you reconcile writing for decadent Hollywood when your pen is dedicated to the proletarian cause?" he smiled and said, "Suppose a man were accustomed to writing novels for adults. He is asked to write a children's story. There you have it." He could afford to be contained and undefensive, as right after the welcoming party given him by the Group he had confidently given Clurman the plump manuscript of *The Silent Partner*. In the Group's fall schedule it would follow Paul Green's and Kurt Weill's poetic play *Johnny Johnson*, which lamented the world's trend toward war. Moreover, Luise had now agreed to join him and the Group within the week. His life was in hand.

As he eagerly awaited Clurman's response to *The Silent Partner*, he entered into the Group's lively discussions of its financial and organizational crisis and proposed reorganization which designated Clurman, despite his impracticality, as the central authority with executive decision; in addition, there would be a democratically elected Actors' Committee, consisting of Elia Kazan, Stella Adler, Morris Carnovsky, and Roman Bohnen. Many Group members believed these administrative maneuvers would prove of no avail in meeting the profound lacks in American culture; others thought of the Group's struggle to survive on a platform of humanist ideals as a small edition of the increasingly savage confrontations in Spain. When he heard that the French novelist André Malraux had decided to participate in that struggle by laying his body on the line as a flier for the Loyalists, Odets wondered whether that didn't make more sense than writing plays. Gorky, too, had participated directly in the history around him. Still fresh, however, was the memory of his terrifying Cuban fiasco, when he had felt duped and used by the Communist Party with an amorality which had shocked him. Like many young American intellectuals, he fantasied joining the suicidal brigade (which would name itself after Abraham Lincoln) leaving for Spain to fight Franco, Hitler, and Mussolini. But he did not act on this fantasy. Perhaps he feared becoming one of the many young American volunteers being memorialized after their deaths in Ukrainian, Polish, and Finnish halls as well as in union headquarters all over the country. Or, more likely, with his identity as a writer firmly established, he had withdrawn much of his investment in direct political participation. He had no way of knowing what evil and grievous times were already launched in the utopian Soviet Union, and he joined in the affectionate nicknaming of the tempestuous Stella Adler as "La Pasionaria" after the Communist heroine of the Spanish Civil War, unaware that the woman, Dolores Ibarruri, was engaged at this time in a ferocious assault on the heretical Marxist party of Catalonia, socialists opposed to Stalin's bloody methods.

Clurman lost no time in reading *The Silent Partner* and was dismayed to find it "at once his most ambitious and his most incomplete script." He told Odets that although the play was "intuitively sound in its basic perception, it was very weak in all its central characters and situations" and that it revealed "more rough substance than created form," advising him finally that "if he could imbue these central characters with the life he meant them to have, this would be his most important play and he would indeed be the writer everybody hoped he would become."

It seemed to Clurman that Odets listened "as if bemused." In fact Odets was having a hard time concealing his bitter disappointment that the Group would not immediately put his play into production, and, like all artists under criticism, his defensive anger that the work had not been hailed as a masterpiece. Moreover, he was preparing to meet Luise in New York, where she had arrived with a severe sore throat and happy anticipations at meeting the Group. It was plain to him that it would now be extremely difficult to withdraw into a concentrated reworking of the play.

Their need for each other was intense, and their union had a luminous power evident to everyone. However, living for a fortnight in the house Clifford had rented, Luise said, "Wherever we looked there seemed to be Group Theatre members. . . . They seemed pretentious to me, conceited, compared with the European acting companies to which I belonged. Cliff was shocked when I said to him: 'Just because they leave one button open on their shirts doesn't make them artists!' " It was strange to Luise to watch this multitude of competitors for Odets' badly strained emotional resources. "Cliff was ardent, wild, loving, raging, and ranting. . . . As I flew back to California, my sore throat became an acute tonsillitis."

Some of the gifted Group actresses, in an effort to expose what they regarded as a core of narcissistic indomitability, relentlessly parodied what seemed to them a wistfully wide-eyed, little-girl helplessness in Luise. They refused to believe that she was truly shy and that she was not interested in going to parties without Odets when he was busy working. Even her illness, they decided, was histrionic. "Luise," one said, "is one of those actresses who is acting all the time." She, in the meantime, was at the Cedars of Lebanon Hospital in Los Angeles with a raging fever and a great sadness that things had not gone well between her and Clifford or with the Group members. Her quarrels with Clifford were vividly with her.

The hot bickering between Clifford and Luise over the Group, the rights of women, the ugliness of the rented frame house, and the provinciality of Bridgeport remained vivid in the memories not only of Group members but also of visitors like Mrs. Henry Varnum Poor (novelist Bessie Breuer) and Lewis Milestone. Milestone had come east on a double mission: to persuade Odets to make a film of a psychological melodrama derived from a work of the Russian Ilya Ehrenburg (*The Loves of Jeanne Ney*) and to help the Group raise the production costs for Paul Green's anti-war play, still incomplete.

Luise, who always had impeccable taste, maintained that she "preferred living in a whitewashed empty room to living in a place cluttered with ugly provincial furniture and a great heap of bric-a-brac," and that the house Clifford had rented for them had been "a sore to my eyes." When she tried to rearrange things, she felt this "was utterly resented by Odets." John Howard Lawson was left with a memory of Luise and Clifford which penetrated below the surface bickering: "I have a strong picture in my mind of Odets and the woman standing by a lake and a sort of sadness about them that moved me."

By the time playwright Paul Green returned to Connecticut from North Carolina with a manuscript for the Group, the summer was almost over. Odets had enjoyed refugee Kurt Weill's lectures to the Group about music in the theatre, had half enjoyed the Group's presentations of Chekhov to the adult campers of the Pinebrook Club, and had enjoyed not at all his own efforts to rework *The Silent Partner* along the lines Clurman had recommended. He was deeply offended that even in the safe, unpressured atmosphere of this summer camp, so different from the life-and-death stakes of a Broadway opening, the Group had not put his play "on its feet" so that he could see for himself what it needed. He blamed Clurman, burdened by recurrent collapses in his stormy relation to Stella Adler, for a planless summer, for his impracticality ("Harold can't button his fly by himself," he said), and for his reliance on "inspiration." It appeared to him unjust, after a year in which he had been the Group's mainstay, that Paul Green's equally imperfect play should be given precedence over his. Yet with all this, as autumn neared, his mood, reflected in the voluminous and ardent correspondence with Luise (how radiant a relationship whenever they were separated by three thousand miles!), was once more "fresh and alive"; he was happy to stay on alone in the country, to ride his bicycle for an hour each day, and to ready *The Silent Partner* for a New York production in mid-October. In a typical letter to Luise, addressing her as "Darling," he writes of intimacy, of marriage, and of sharing with her her mother:

Summer is over here now. The Labor Day week end crowd has gone home from the camp and the country side is quiet. Slowly slowly the fields, the woods and lake will relax back to their native stillness and with it autumn will come and colder air and a disappearance of birds and flowers. And it is sad, every end of summer is sad, sad with fulfillment, for it is a time when many things complete their bloom and have lived long enough to drop their seed and make more life. . . . And more life and works for writers and artists. . . .

Oh to work, Darling, to work on and take each small idea out of the jewel case of the head and polish and develop it into a whole art work. Oh the delight of all the parts, of each character, of each spoken line . . . and on to the great tired satisfaction of looking at a completed work and knowing it is good and full and ready to be put in the world with an independent life of its own. When a woman has her baby by slow growth and much pain and delight, then she's done what the artist has done.

All this, most beautiful Luise, is about the fact that I'm working on "The Silent Partner" and have made approximate plans for the rest of the next six months. The play will be finished in four weeks, perhaps three. Then I am going to do a picture with Milly [Milestone] for W. Wanger, but do it in New York so that I can be near the rehearsals of the play. When the play goes on I'll come out to the coast and start on another picture, but will try to map out and start working on the two short plays. . . .

You see I've planned a full schedule for myself; and it makes me very happy. To work, even the mere prospect of work, makes me very happy. Then I will try next to make a really good picture, and the prospect of such an attempt is pleasant. What I want to do now is stop wasting time. Work, work, work, and to see each thing will come well from the heart and head with a proper mixture of cunning (meaning technique) and emotion.

What do you think of all that, Darling? Will you wait for me in California? Not go out with too many men? Do your own work quietly, surely, with a sense of increased technique and value, and patiently wait for me? . . . will you rest, rest, sleep soundly and deeply, eat well, and store up in yourself great wells of strength . . .

Luise Darling, my sorely missed wonderful girl, will you think of us together in life, in the world, on your back mountain path, on the ocean, scanning Europe with our clear fresh eyes, walking beaches with our young strong legs? Will you see us together in all positions, all loves, all hates, will you see us in grass with the crickets singing in our hair? . . . Darling, be with me for fifty years, and if we live to be a hundred, even then together, knowing always the onward flowing of the river which is our lives, not minding the small times of turning bends and coursing over obstructions.

Now Darling, I do not leave you go. I know it. I will fight for you. When I am alone this way I know the truth of us together, that we can not be apart once we know we want to be together. You are right about the marriage and that it should have been in the beginning. For then one knows one has said, "YES! SO IT MUST BE! SO IT IS! SO WE DESIRED IT!" . . . How is your dear Mother? Let us take care of her and give her good things and mostly the best of our kindness and feeling for human beings. We will listen to music with her, the Schnabel records. . . .

Yes, I have so much feeling for your Mother, Luise, and I never even saw her. But don't tell her this, really, for she will be frightened by so much affection from a stranger. Let it be that suddenly one day, a year later perhaps, she will suddenly say to you, "Do you know, Luise, that boy really likes me very very much." Just like that. And you answer, "Why, it is more than like; he loves you because you are his Mother."

I must go to Philadelphia this Saturday because on Sunday they are unveiling my Mother's tomb stone. So you know how I feel. When I wrote "Paradise Lost" and it was printed I was going to say on the front page, "Look inside, Mother dear, and see how you are mixed forever among the warm sweet words." But I didn't for several reasons.

Luise Darling, how happy I am that I know you. . . . Right now I would call you on the phone, but it is so bad and I can't hear you. No, I change my mind—I call you.

Five minutes later—AND I CALL AND YOU ARE NOT IN. THE OPERATOR SAYS IT HAS BEEN STATED ON THE OTHER END OF THE PHONE THAT YOU HAVE GONE TO A PICTURE AND SHE DOESN'T KNOW WHEN YOU'LL BE BACK. LET IT BE SOON DARLING, come back soon and speak to me on the phone.

Clifford.

6 A.M.—No one home yet. And so to bed. Darling, you must be all all better to be staying out so late.

Although Odets does not mention it in his letter to Luise, contributing to his well-being is an event vividly recalled by Lewis Milestone: "I had two tickets to the Canzoneri-Ambers championship fight, and knowing Clifford had never seen a prizefight, I invited him to come along. During the prelims he paled and pulled out his notebook. When it seemed to me he was too busy writing to see the main event, I complained that I had bought two very expensive seats and that he could write at home. His reply was, 'You have just given me a very fine play, and what's more it will make money for the Group.' He appeared to be very happy."

Odets confided to Elia Kazan, whom he was seeing often, that within the year he would have a "hit show" for the Group to be called "The Manly Art" or perhaps "Golden Gloves." The following fall his play, finally to be called *Golden Boy,* would indeed save (once more) the life of the Group Theatre.

Halfway into September, just before the disappointing opening of *The General Died at Dawn,* Odets and Milestone were walking down Broadway and looked up to see the moving ribbon of light bulbs around the top of the *New York Times* building announcing the death of Luise's producer, Irving Thalberg. Milestone was astonished to see Odets weeping. "I asked him did he know Thalberg so well," Milestone recalled. "His reply was, 'I never met the man. He was successful, influential, willful, and corrupt— but he died so young.'" What he called a "young death"—that is to say, the cessation of a life which, in his view, had not reached its full flowering—was always a dread reminder to Odets. To Luise he wrote,

Darling . . . Thalberg, of course, meant little or nothing to me, but to see an extremely successful young man suddenly cut down and dead—to have a harrowing sense of what can happen to any one— accidents, sickness and the rest—to see the sudden wailing and distress which comes with such things—well, it sickens one at the heart a little.

But there is the good thing which comes with this. It is to honor and fight for the living, to have tenderness for those who carry precious life in them. For a man like myself it is to be together with a loved woman like you to help one another in life and work.

So I say, for reasons of love as well as those of loneliness, for us to have firm strong allegiance to each other. I say that from each to the other must flow strength, help, stability, firmness of purposes, growth, joy, giving, taking. Darling, it must develop to that point where you look on me as a well-stocked shelf, and you come to it and take whatever you need or desire. And I expect the same from you. Such a future is not easy to attain, but it is worth fighting for, worth having petty struggles about.

For what is work and effort without a friend, a lover, a mother and father and brother and sister all rolled into one. Darling, let me be all those things for you (and you for me). And together let us cut thru the essential and necessary facts which constitute life and come to the best possible conditions of going on, but always together, fearless and working constantly to express for large audiences of people a new optimism and courage in an otherwise dark bitter world which is trying to cut its own throat. . . .

And to help us in this worthy work of living a realistic useful life we will have the aid of a few good friends, of someone like your mother, and of Beethoven and Mozart and looking at the work of others who went before us and left the best of their living days in paintings and writing.

For the present, Luise, I send you my softest most tender self and the strength of my arms and mouth all of which are very much in love with you.

The practical significance for Luise of Thalberg's sudden death from pneumonia was immediately apparent: Louis B. Mayer seized the opportunity to rid his citadel of all executives suspected of disloyalty and of "highbrow interests." This included, of course, all those involved with *The Good Earth.* It was too late to change this film into one of his "happy pictures about happy people and their happy problems happily resolved."

Luise, now in dread of what assignments she would have to fulfill in order to meet her contractual obligation, wished Odets were in California to help her get out of her onerous seven-year contract in which she felt like "nothing but a bolt in their machinery." She will perish as an artist, she writes, if she is forced to make films under conditions in which she has no choice of script, of director, " . . . no rights altogether."

Odets, in turn, spurred by Clurman, was determined to have an acceptable draft of *The Silent Partner* ready for rehearsal directly following the Green-Weill play, *Johnny Johnson,* the production of which had already commenced what would soon promote an irreconcilable cleavage within the Group. Discouraged and overwhelmed by personal difficulties and by the Group's administrative and financial problems, Clurman had relinquished the direction of this play to Strasberg, who, he thought, was becoming increasingly touchy and defensive. Strasberg, in turn, was critical of Clurman's inadequate provision for "a serious consideration of all scripts which were possible for production." It seemed to Strasberg, and Cheryl Crawford agreed with him, that Clurman's patronizing attitude toward manuscripts by men like Maxwell Anderson, S. N. Behrman, and Sidney Kingsley was unrealistic—indeed, "somnambulistic." For his part, Clurman found Strasberg's unwillingness "to admit his artistic shortcomings or difficulties" intolerable. The rupture between them was the most bitter since the Group had begun, and *Johnny Johnson* gave no hint it could be the artistic or financial triumph that could heal it.

Characteristically, Strasberg tried to master the problem by writing a defensive and intelligently didactic analysis of the problem:

> As long as the Group was not in existence, the people are concerned only with their hopes and their dreams, but once the Group becomes organized, then certain contradictions appear between the people and the needs of the Group. . . . There is always a disproportion between what each individual demands for his own development and what the Group activity demands from each individual. . . . This conflict is not necessarily dangerous except that being totally an unconscious activity it is able to work without awareness, leading to the formation of rifts, splits, cliques, bureaucratic alignments, based on personal interests, masquerading as Group needs . . . etc.

The period of what Clurman would call the "breakdown" of the Group had begun.

It is striking how little Odets wrote to Luise of this major Group crisis. He was probably embarrassed to let her see his family's dirty linen, and, moreover, he was about to bring deliverance, he thought, with the revised version of *The Silent Partner*, which he has stayed on in Nichols, Connecticut, to finish.

In the dark about Odets' revisions, Clurman writes him his reaction to having seen, with Kazan, *The General Died at Dawn.*

> Our greatest lesson was to hear lines so characteristic of you become almost imperceptible and without the quality of experience when said by actors (?) with no relation to them. . . . The applause was not for the author of a Paramount Picture but for a boy who wrote "Awake and Sing," "Paradise Lost," etc., in obscurity. Gadg pointed out that the cost of the picture could back six productions like "Johnny Johnson" or "The Silent Partner" and that Lewis Milestone's weekly salary was more than either he or I earn in a year. *That's* America!

Clurman is disappointed

not to have a rough copy of the play [*The Silent Partner*] so I can be of help in making the play RIGHT—removing all the brilliant excrescences, the gay dross, the colorful excesses and expanding the significant omissions. . . . However, I am sure you know most of the things that have to be done yourself, and I hope you are working hard doing them.

It is clear he is hurt that Odets has withdrawn from him somewhat since his liaison with Luise. He closes with, "Can you send the rest of the salary money ($1250) [for a half-week's rehearsal pay for *Johnny Johnson*] . . . you have been swell about the money." According to Odets' income-tax return for 1936, he contributed almost $5,000 to this production. By this time the indomitable Mrs. Motty Eitingon had once more appeared, and this time her offer of $40,000 toward the production costs of *Johnny Johnson* had been accepted, but the actors still needed to be paid. Odets would have been dismayed to know how vital it was to him to be at long last a man of sufficient means to pay even a part of their salaries. From the moment he had become a "big man," father to the Group and even to his own father, he had poured into the maintenance of that controlling position a magic belief that through derivatives like loans, gifts, pedagogy, and the like, he could redress his own alienations. Even now, as he struggled to achieve an intimacy with Luise, occasionally succeeding, he wished he "might be all new—all the parts, all the thoughts." As it is, he writes to her, " . . . you make me feel so new that mostly I feel like a stranger to myself—I look in the mirror with a strange fine feeling."

That his strange feeling was not entirely "fine" is suggested by a peculiar figure of speech embedded in one of his daily (sometimes two or three a day) effusions to Luise in which he talks of his "imagined fears" of her. "The good thing about being in love is that all one's thoughts turn in that direction—their energies, impulses and desires are not scattered all over the city, *but fly straight out as a bullet* to the loved girl*" (italics mine). Throughout this extravagant correspondence there is a desperate, even primitive urge toward complete union: "altogether both of us being one rich person." However, Odets was often fearful of such a merger as a betrayal of his creative energies.

Luise, out of the hospital now and mending, supported his decision to remain in the East until he had a finished version of *The Silent Partner*. In her romantic, talented way and with her newly acquired language (she is learning ten new words a day) often phonetically spelled, she tries to express her view of his situation and her wish that he should not be distracted by their relationship or by the steady stream of offers that he become a film writer on a long-term contract.

Darling, Cliff, afar lover— . . . My impatient, restless boy—Why it is important that your next play must especially be a good and *finished* one, you ask me? Because till now darling you could show it in your own fine way that you live and experience and that you are able to express your mind—what is wonderful all ready—but now you shall show and they beg you to show because they need you—that your work was not only the product of momentary event but the beginning of a helping explanation and the wonderful ability of seeing and *understanding!* Then, you really are good for all those people

* In another place he writes, "Art should shoot bullets." Beethoven had said of Napoleon, "If I knew as much about strategy as I do about counterpoint, I'd make short shrift of that fellow."

who love you already, and so *you are good to yourself!* Darling, do you understand what I mean? Oh, I don't care what you mean to them if I wouldn't know how important it is for *you*, for your happiness to know and to *see* that you are able to give—and Darling what I want is your happiness because it is OURS!! THAT'S WHY! So, be quiet, my sweet, be patient, I'll wait for you, wait gladly till you come with a free head and conscience, till you have finished what must be finished. Be patient darling and if I have to do with it be very very patient.

The loneliness in this airmail "Spezial Deliverie" letter from Luise, addressed to "Clifford Odets, Nichols, Conn., USA," is unusually intense. She had tried, before sending it, to speak to him that morning on the phone, but "Cliff was half asleep and didn't quite understand what I wanted." She had been sleepless thinking of Thalberg's death, of his wife's pain ("this poor Shearer girl"), of the bloody killing in Spain, of a visit from a German refugee and from two "important members of the Anti-Nazi Party who told heart-breaking things about what is allready happening in America." Rumor had it that some actors had been denied jobs by having been placed by various studios on an informal blacklist for presumed dissenting political opinions. This, she writes, is extremely difficult to believe in the United States of America.*

Luise recalled of this time: "There was no doubt in my mind that I didn't fit into film-Hollywood. Although having climbed to the top with enormous speed, I had never dreamed the American girl's dream of success as a film star. My intuition told me that this very speed of success and adulation was somehow in contrast with the solid development necessary to a lasting career. With the man I loved three thousand miles removed, and not feeling like seeing many people just by myself and outside of my work, I was nothing less than uprooted. My one dream, in contrast to what I had written to him, was to have Clifford, my man, beside me.

"I felt lonely and alone in spite of my work. Even at the time of my greatest success I was in need of personal reassurance. Clifford O. was no Rock of Gibraltar, he needed one!"

Steadily lamenting her poor English and his lack of German, she is convinced she must stop her "Salvation-Army complex" and must lock her door, for a short time at least, not only to all of the tragic world-happenings, but to the private crises of all the many, many people who come into her house, every one with his own little or big trouble, needing support. She does not want to be inundated as she has steadily been with why, for instance, Oscar Levant fritters away his talent and strength; why George Gershwin's neurasthenic and analyzed (oh, so analyzed) soul, or what remains of it, is screaming for redemption—"I wish I had someone to explain me my own why's"—and so has decided to rest by scaling the mountains behind her house.

On the tenth day of November 1936, Luise writes:

I'm not going away darling—I stay right here and go ahead, go through. It would not make me really happy just now to go away because my thoughts and my deep thirst would go with me. Thirst for everything! I have to stay here and make this town, this surrounding,

* Odets by this time had begun to turn down public appearances on the same platform with known Communists, as they would, in his opinion, "harm my chances of drawing a broad popular audience to my plays—which is my best way of working for 'a good life.'" At no time "ever" had he mentioned to Luise Rainer—who, of course, realized that he was decidedly left in his political views—that he was a Communist and had held membership in the party.

that seems hell to me, into a paradise for me. But that one sometimes loses courage does not even surprise me who has all all will to make good and there are really *facts* and not only imagination that can let one despair. You know, darling, yes you must know it that there are times when you are working so much that you think that you cannot go on, and still you find time and happiness to absorb and to do other things. . . . As if one is in love: then our eyes are so much more wide-open for other human beings, for everybody's feelings; one is so much more impressionable for all happenings. And then come times when your work does not satisfy you and then your "doings" and all you are makes you unhappy . . . and you feel paralyzed. Sure one has to awaken oneself at such moments, but it is bad to awake and the first you see and feel is the (very) thing that paralyzed you. Darling, my love for art (even if Mr. Dietz* says it is absurd to speak about art), yes, this love burns in me, it burns and burns and sometimes I think I can't stand it not to be able to bring out. If I ever will, I don't know. I'm afraid nothing will ever really satisfy me because I know how high the Heaven is. . . . My longing is so big—Yes it goes around the world and it goes through the world and it tries to reach into the sky and to bring it closer, but it does not work. Everything I do is so "human" so tied to the earth—how can I ever hope to do something only a God can do? You will laugh about me my beloved. I speak aloud out what I think and feel, but even your laughing makes me happy because I love you. . . . I will fill myself with songs (please send me the songs of Kurt Weill), I will go to an exhibition and I will listen to music (dear music which makes me so sad because I feel how imperfect I am).

                                                              Your Luise

Luise was deeply grateful for every reassurance and for every sign of warmth and understanding that came from Clifford, but they seemed to her ever so rare. In fact, she sadly remembered that when, "like most other women would and do," she would ask, "Do you really think you love me?" his answer could come out "in vehemence": "It's sugar, sugar, sugar . . . that's all you want!"

Odets, in turn, was grieved when he wrote her daily and, as he says, "only silence answers as if one might drop a stone in the ocean and get no reply but the same steady sound of waves and the lonely seabirds wheeling and crying overhead in the darkening sky," or, in a more active vein, "When I quickly eat three juicy peaches in one bite, whom do I think of . . . ?"

Longing for Clifford, Luise struggled on in the Hollywood she had begun to detest. She found comfort in the golden slave bracelet he had given her engraved with both their names and "I love you." More often than not, her letters and telegrams are contained, with such closings as " . . . it seems a lifetime we separated. Work good and come soon. Please! Darling, dear, dear Cliff. Oh, take all the kisses I have." Or later: " . . . why if you really love me don't you come to me why why why?"

If he could have, he would have replied from the depths of his ambivalent terror that, despite his profound loneliness, it appeared to him safer to maintain this ardent, yearning, long-distance romance than to exchange it for the more demanding, difficult, and pedestrian challenge of a daily face-to-face relationship. We can only guess at his unconsciously punitive motives: as with all his women, "the abandoned becomes the

* Howard Dietz, head of publicity for Metro-Goldwyn-Mayer in New York.

abandoner"—and is then, once more, abandoned. Moreover, he could not leave New York until *The Silent Partner* was safely in rehearsal under Clurman's direction. In this, his thirty-first year, he was nonetheless consciously determined to wrest a creative life, a living, and a family from his existence.

True, his beloved Beethoven (he later wrote) had been able to achieve only one of these, and "crying out against his Fate, that he is imprisoned in his task (i.e., himself); that he cannot be like other men in the normality of their relationships, in their marriage and homes, in growing children beside them," had said of a woman, "Yes, she meant very much to me. But if we had stayed together, what would have remained for my work?"

He, however, was not reconciled to such a choice as Beethoven's, and in response to Luise's yearning "whys," wrote and wired her steady reassurances and pleas to be patient. His letters continue to be characteristically rich, pedagogical, and highly ambivalent:

> Here is the idea I spoke to you about on the phone, the idea that excited me so much about building up a character, an idea which it seems to me might have as much use for an actress as for a playwright.
>
> This principle: Often in complex people one will find that unconsciously, without their own knowledge, they are living their life in reference to some one person, an event or incident, or some one thing in their past life. This thing or person makes in their life what I call "a root experience" for lack of a better name. This "root experience" makes itself into the shape of a "spearhead" in the personality. Later experiences array or line themselves up behind this "spearhead" taking their direction and significance from it. And so the entire personality (or person) forges ahead, blindly (altho sometimes dimly or brilliantly aware) following the "spearhead" cutting thru life in a predestined pattern. . . .
>
> This can be a good thing, as it is the mainspring of the artist of our day. And it may be very bad, often making for evasion and misunderstanding of simple things, spoiling and preventing a talent (if only for simple normal clean living) from reaching its full bloom, and making a person do many bad things he doesn't intend to do. . . .
>
> I hope the above is not too abstract, but I've limited myself to omitting particular details. But if you try this with anyone you know well—yourself, myself—you will see how well it works. At the same time I suddenly call to mind an idea which Stanislavsky, the Russian director, gave out. He said, "Find out—what does the character want?" This is related to my idea. I would like sometimes to sit down and discuss acting of parts with you. It is really very much related to the art of writing.

Just before Luise arrived for a visit in November for the opening of *Johnny Johnson*, Odets ("in my loneliness") asked the Metro-Goldwyn-Mayer publicity man to bring him a "large leather case of about 500 pictures" of Luise as O-Lan, the Chinese peasant in *The Good Earth*, and as herself. "The pictures," he writes, "of your small, delicate bones and plump underlip, made me very happy and very sad." His loneliness is such, he continues, that he doesn't leave the house for days on end except to go to the dentist. "Writing is a very lonely job as it is—to sit alone night after night at a typewriter is one of the cruelest jobs a man may choose for himself! Make no mistake about it." He is becoming like "a wild animal in a cage," impatient enough "to tear my desk apart, to suddenly hurl a typewriter against the wall, to suddenly walk into this sleeping building and pound on all the apartment doors, to go out into the street and run and run until I feel exhausted." The flowers with which he fills his apartment don't help, as their self-contained perfection, he feels, shuts him out.

He had by now secretly supplied graphologist Lucia Eastman—whom he revered—with a specimen of Luise's handwriting, asking whether a Mr. "Von Delf" (himself) should marry the woman who had written it. Miss Eastman found Luise "most charming" but "very complex" with some "deep hurt in her youthful days" and a consequent mistrust and "inverted vanity," concluding—from her extra-graphological knowledge of Odets—that she could give the marriage her blessing only if it were "properly managed" and hedged by very special conditions:

> Neither of these two people would be satisfied with purely emotional marriage, as each has too strong an individuality to be absorbed completely in each other, even though they might think so at first. The only way in which they can be bound together in a perfect whole is for each one to be absolutely free—this sounds like a paradox but is the truth. They should each have separate rooms with a common gathering place and be as punctilious about entering without permission as though they were strangers or casual friends. The minute love becomes commonplace and routine it will begin to die with people of these complex types who will never be satisfied with the commonplace. They should both keep on doing creative work as that will give them a safety valve. . . . I do not mean that they would live always in "perfect peace" as that would be equally boresome. But even in their squabbles there should be perfect truth. . . .
>
> This will be more difficult for her than for Mr. Von Delf because of early unhappiness and repression of her real self. She will also have to be both wife and mother to this man, as he is still very much of the small boy—sensitive and imaginative and still inclined to believe in Santa Claus in spite of the fine logical mature mind which he possesses. If she will try to remember that a hurt child is often apt to try to hurt the mother he loves—an unconscious reaction—she will find it easier to keep from magnifying small pin pricks into deep wounds. If he will remember the differences in her temperament and his and make allowances for that, they could find a joy and thrill which is unfortunately rare. . . .

Miss Eastman, who was associated with the Louise Rice Institute of Graphology, was a wise and experienced woman, and Odets valued her judgment more than that of his several female astrologers, as later he would depend on the counsel of his female psychoanalyst. Thus, when she added a separate postscript recommending a postponement of the marriage until Luise can "face the facts," it troubled him. When Luise checked into the Waldorf-Astoria Hotel on her arrival in New York instead of coming to Odets' apartment, it likely confirmed, for Odets, Miss Eastman's assessment of her profound wariness.

Luise's recollection of this experience is different: "I was tired from making three major films within those first eighteen months in Hollywood, and more than tired from the emotional turmoil of my private life. I was hating the phony film-world of Hollywood and its cigar-eating executives that now, after I had been a completely different character in each of three films, said, 'She's difficult to cast,' instead of saying, 'This girl can do anything!' When therefore, for my peace' sake, I went to stay at the

Waldorf-Astoria Hotel instead of in Clifford's apartment, it seemed to him a slight. At no time was Clifford able or willing to see the necessity for my own need of peace—during or after my work just as he, at all times, demanded this for himself. His immediate reaction was therefore to want me more than ever! Also, only three miles separated us now from each other instead of the usual three thousand; thus we seemed more apart than ever. The magnetic drawing power each of us had for the other brought us together again in less than two days. The result was that we decided to marry."

Odets now wrote a letter to the European parents he had never met, asking for permission to marry Luise. The letter's ponderous formality has a touching quality. As Luise later said, "It read as though he, who never cared to dress up, was exposing himself on a podium, dressed in tails, carefully conducting a minuet."

November 21st, 1936.

Dear Mr. and Mrs. Rainer,
     It is with some little difficulty that I begin this letter to you, the reason being that we are not personally acquainted as yet. But I have met you both so often and so happily thru Luise that I feel even now a warm friendship for you both. More than "warm friendship" I quickly add, for to be in love with Luise is necessarily a state of affairs which makes friendship a poor word and substitutes in its place something more definite and closer! In any case, please accept my heartiest and warmest greetings!
     Luise is here in New York now for a few days, having arrived yesterday. We are going to see many of the new plays here and then she will fly back to the west coast to start work on a new picture. In the meantime I must stay on here for another two weeks to see that a new play of mine gets safely into rehearsal; and then I'll join Luise again out in California. Once we are out there together, both working on a picture, being in love, deeply interested in each other's welfare and happiness, it would be a good idea for us to get married and settle down to make the best possible kind of life together for ourselves. I wish I might tell you personally how enthusiastic I am about this possibility instead of writing it on a typewriter in cold words. Luise tells me that she has already written to you both of her feelings in the matter, and since I am sure you value her judgment as highly as I do, you can be sure that we are not dealing here in Hollywood fantasy but wonderful reality and happiness combined. God knows that nowadays reality and happiness are a rare combination indeed!
     I keep asking Luise when you are coming here for a visit. And tonight at the dinner table I asked her (a little timidly) if she thought you would like me. She answered yes very quickly and when I asked her why she said because she has written to you about me many times and said only the best things. Which made me eat my dinner with a better appetite! Seriously, I look forward to meeting you both as eagerly as I looked to seeing Luise again after a two months' separation—and may it be soon.
     In the meantime my compliments for having had and raised so beautiful and wonderful a daughter as Luise. Surely she has inherited her fine character and qualities from both of you. In all of Hollywood she seems to me to be the only woman of high character and talent and it is very possible, very probable, that in the com-

ing years she will develop into a great artist. I hear you say that I am prejudiced in the matter, but it is a prejudice we all share together, isn't it? How proud I am to be able to write these things to you and to know that Luise loves me.

Yours,

Three weeks later, after they have lived again in close proximity, he feels the necessity to write the following to Luise:

Darling, we both agree that a marriage between us can be wonderful. And we both agree that there will be difficulties, but that we will work on the difficulties and try to get rid of them.

Now there is one thing I would like the privilege of asking: do you think that I alone will be responsible for those difficulties, or do you see as I do, that we are both difficult persons and that both of us together make the difficulties, instead of just me. Do you understand this to be the truth?

It can not be a successful mating where you think:
I am generous and he is not.
I am thoughtful and he is not.
He has to change himself and I do not.
He is overproud and I am not.
He is immature; I am mature.
I am honest and he is not.
He lies and I do not.
He thinks about sleeping with strangers and I do not.
He is not interested in a permanent marriage and I am.
He is impatient and I am not.
He has a quick temper and I do not.
I can criticize him but he can't criticize me.
I can tell him what to do, but he can't tell me what to do.
He wants to hurt my feelings, but I don't want to hurt his.

I also think—and you probably agree—that we should not spend the entire year together, but every year should spend some weeks apart.

I think—and you agree with this—that we should not try to possess or own each other completely. You yourself have said this often.

And we must not insist that each be like the other or change habits to suit the other. We must realize that we are highly individualized persons each with long lives and personal experiences behind us.

And above all we must must have complete trust and faith in each other and remember always that we are in love and have the strongest possible desire for a continually growing developing marriage.

12/10/36.

Better never never to begin a life together if you suppose that between us you have all the virtues and I all the vices.

He did not send this letter to Luise, and instead jotted down some notes for himself:

She strikes out like a child when hurt.
jealousy—resentment against conditions, etc.—
learn to take things normally and naturally—
I won't bind you—you are free—

break down defense mechanism—
possessiveness—(fear of losing what she has)
torn between bourgeois or artistic—
she fights what she needs—stability, etc.—
develop a sense of relative values—relative—
Anna Held—lessons for L and myself from Ziegfeld—

Treat her as a problem child. (a puppet)

Find out what's in back of her opinions.

A hobby for her.

Nonetheless he concludes in a letter he does send: "even our quarrels have magically become love in my mind . . . one does not quarrel about what is unimportant and casual . . . How polite we can be with a stranger."

Three weeks later he received a sweet letter of assent from Emmy Rainer which expresses not only her wish that they will bring each other happiness and peace, but also her acceptance of him as a fourth child in the Rainer family. She closes with a hope to hear "about your own mother that you loved so much!" No reply could have been more welcome to (as he often called himself) this old-fashioned "family man without a family." Emmy Rainer's letter was followed by a similar letter from her husband. Clifford and Luise had come together in a welcoming family.

As the year pulls to an end, Odets' spirits are lifting. He writes Luise he has only "one and a half scenes more" for the *final* revision of *The Silent Partner* and is encouraged that his usually impassive agent, Harold Freedman, was "shaken" by what he already has. Whatever his discouragement as a result of Clurman's doubts about its timeliness, it has been much allayed by word from a Czech theatre director, Hans Burger, who tells of his German group of actors playing *Lefty* in the Nazi sectors of Czechoslovakia. Nazi youths in the audience had come up to join left-wing trade unions, saying, "If *that's* what strikes and communism mean, we're in the wrong army." Burger closes by urgently requesting a copy of *The Silent Partner* for immediate translation into several European languages. As in Spain, where theatre people promise they will get busy with plays for the Teatro Popular as soon as "the streets are cleared," Burger is eager to enlist the theatre to "crush the forces of reaction." Odets—making notes for a "real anti-Nazi play" about Carl von Ossietzky, a pacifist imprisoned and tortured for three years by the Nazis and this year a Nobel Prize winner—is of the opinion that no one has yet exposed in dramatic form "the real nature of this evil."

He has in the meantime agreed to do, with Lewis Milestone directing, a swift and remunerative rewrite of the Ehrenburg-Pabst film *The Loves of Jeanne Ney*, changing its characters from Russian émigrés in Paris to Spaniards in Paris who feel they must go back to fight for the Loyalists in Spain "as a matter of honor." He tells Milestone it will be a "romantic drama against a revolutionary background."

Despite the seething unrest and survival-anxiety in the Group office, with the tension between Strasberg and Clurman mounting and the

Actors' Committee beginning to hold secret meetings—presumably to analyze the principal artistic and administrative blunders of the disastrous *Johnny Johnson*—in late November, Odets confidently brought *The Silent Partner* to a point where he felt it was ready to be copyrighted and rehearsed. He knew that the Group had no other satisfactory new play and that, despite his reservations, Clurman was ready to go forward with this one. Odets worked on a cast list of the approximately forty-one characters, giving major parts to Jules Garfield, Elia Kazan, Morris Carnovsky, Albert Van Dekker, Roman Bohnen, and Luther Adler, with lesser parts for almost every other Group member, including Lee J. Cobb, Margaret Barker, Ruth Nelson, and Sanford Meisner. The most striking omission is Stella Adler. Heading his personal "Opening Night List"—relatives and friends invited to the first public showing of a play—was his father, listed as "L. J. Odets."

By the time he left New York in mid-December for California, where he planned to marry Luise, he had bought a Hammond organ and rehearsals of *The Silent Partner* were in progress under Clurman's direction. Seldom in his life had Odets been so filled with happy expectation in all departments.

Chapter Twenty

Margaret, I want to tell you now, after a night of crying: millions and millions of years ago when all being was in a sea of tears: tears, because all yearned to be "born" and help— and hope—was slow, and waiting long, he and I were ONE, *we were that algae that split and separated in painful process of being born, of being male and female, man and wife. No other knew the other better than he and I knew each other, and where we were split asunder we were bleeding; always bleeding, and when we saw each other we knew we were* THAT *other and we were still bleeding, and we knew that his blood was my blood and my blood was his blood and we thought that if* one *in this world could help either of us it was* WE *who could do it to each other. But we could* NOT. *Because a God had decided for us to be the* HE *and the* SHE *and we could* no *more come together and could* no *more heal our wounds; and seeing our bleeding made us know of our faintness and made us the* ONLY OTHER *hate the other in desperation of the knowledge that* NEVER NEVER *could we heal. And therefore we screamed.* IN PAIN. AL-WAYS IN PAIN.

> LUISE RAINER, March 22, 1964, ("after a sleepless night, in an effort to explain my tragically wild and explosive union with Odets")

CHRISTMAS dinner at Luise's house on Cliffwood Avenue was a strained affair. She had invited, besides Clifford, only four others, all Europeans: her brother, her part-time secretary, Hannah Braun, with her husband, and Joachim Maas, a well-known novelist and friend of Thomas Mann. Odets felt awkward as he opened wonderful presents from Luise, whereas all he had given her was ". . . seven dressing gowns, all fit for a seven-foot-tall model, and breasty at that," all of which Luise was not. Hannah Braun remembered, "Odets went on and on carping about how he simply couldn't understand why everyone thinks Europeans are so wonderful, that in fact the old country stank and was dilapidated and that Luise simply must learn English for the sake of her career."

Luise recalled that only days before this her brother had beseeched her not to marry Odets, and that Maas, meeting her on Sunset Boulevard, had mockingly gone down on his knees, begging her not to bind herself to "that man." Her studio bosses had told her they were against it as well, and her parents—by now well aware from her letters of the problems in this stormy courtship—were also advising her not to marry him.

A few days later Luise went—accompanied by Bess and Motty Eitingon —to Palm Springs to "think things over," and Odets moved to the Beverly-Wilshire Hotel. The Christmas dinner had climaxed two weeks of building unhappiness which Odets summarized in a businesslike three-page letter to Luise, dated December 29, 1936.*

My Darling,
      Sometimes a little hardness is necessary. . . .
      Now I don't know by now where you stand or what you think. . . .
      Blaming myself equally with you—and it is very important that you see that you are as much to blame as I am—I think the events and discussions since I left your house have been sheer foolishness and rot. . . . Personally I am of the opinion that the reasons which make us respectively a good actress and a good playwright are the reasons that we make difficulties out of simple normal things. We have a tendency to dramatize small situations and happenings, giving them too much significance and importance. That is a fact.
      Now here is the simple truth; I came to California prepared to marry you. But immediately, in fact before I left New York on the train, I found myself with a half-hysterical girl who cried and laughed in one breath, kissed me and pushed me away in the next. I had planned completely in my mind that we would shortly be married, but it seemed you wanted it carefully said in well chosen words. Such an idea did not occur to me, but if you had told me you wanted me to say it in certain words I certainly would have done so. But you were in such a mood that you kept always saying the opposite of what you meant and it always happened that if something was on your mind on Monday I wasn't told about it until Wednesday.
      . . . I began to feel that nothing I was doing or would do could please you . . . and furthermore that you refused to tell me what would please you. In fact, again, you often said the opposite, even to writing me a note in German (which I can't read) and then being saddened because I didn't go to the store and buy a German dictionary to translate it. (Things like that, Darling, I may never do, for I don't

* It is Luise's view that the tone and the exaggerations in this letter were dictated by Odets' finding it "unbearable" that *she* had left *him*. There is supporting evidence for this in his relationships with other women. Again the theme here is abandonment.

think that I have to go buy a German dictionary to prove I love you.)

By this time two things had happened. A week had passed by almost and I was beginning to get very worried about the great amount of work I had to do and still have to do at the present time. Secondly I said to myself—*and I was not examining you!*—if this keeps up like this it might be a fatal mistake for both of us to get married. . . .

You ask me why and if I did not think out all these things in New York. Marriages, I must tell you, are not made in heaven, and they are not made in New York away from the loved one. . . .

Now I tell you this. If we are going to be married—and I am by no means certain that you want to marry me at all now—you will have to take yourself with firm hands and be very clear now and later about all that is involved. You must not tell me "I am happy if you work" and then be so unhappy behind my back that you are sick and I am sick and all normal intercourse between us gets more and more impossible. . . . Excuse me for seeming hard, Luise, and seeming to leave out all my own foolish faults, for I don't mean to be. . . .

Now, I sent you a telegram in which I said, "How about three weeks from today." You didn't answer, so I sent another one asking you to send me "a happy word." Finally, at two in the morning, I get a wire which said, "Cliff Cliff Cliff." It doesn't interest me. The point is simply this—do you want to marry me three weeks from today? But you must think and make sure that I can take care of you and make you happy, in which case I will be happy. Personally, truthfully, I am not sure I can make you happy. But I can hope and try my best. *But it is for you to determine if my best will be good enough.* . . .

Now everything is said. I have purposely made this letter unemotional as possible, leaving out the natural sentiments and love messages that come up so easily in me about you. Perhaps you have already decided that I am no good for you. In that case I want to know that. But don't misunderstand me—I am not telling you to throw me away. I am asking you to make up your mind, and what I want is simple clear thought, not suffering or emotion or pain.

Your,
Clifford

Until now you have been of the opinion that I did not make up my mind—and if so, it was a fault. But I think this letter clears up everything, step by step, as it developed inside me. You say I was indecisive the few days here in the hotel? You are right—I will always be like that and never make up my mind in a minute or an hour. That is part of my character or lack of character, Darling.

P.S. Wanger is trying hard to get you for this picture. Mayer thinks maybe yes!

Obsessed with their relationship, Odets wrote letter after letter to Luise, mostly unsent. In one he begins to despair:

Yes, I came to California simple and clear and determined that we would be married at the first possible chance. Then, it is true, I no longer felt exactly that way. Our relationships, our being together began to get so mixed up—you were so full of so many fears that I found myself sharing them. You took me in your arms and the next minute said something to me which came like a knock on the head with a club. You said in one breath, "We'll be married, we won't be married." I began to feel like a clock you were winding and unwinding and the truth is that finally I didn't know where I was standing. Then you disappeared from the house for a day—you had gone to a hospital to rest.* You left me a sweet note, and the night before you had told me a dozen contradictory things. . . . I asked you about what was the matter, if you were always like this—and you said no, that I ought to understand the position you were in, being worried about contracts, movies, etc. . . .

In the end—this is what I believe—I don't think I am strong enough to take care of you. It seems to me that I can't manage my own work and you. If what you want is an older man (or any man) to devote most of his hours awake to you, then I'm the wrong fellow. Marriage with us will have to be a love, a romance, a business, a companionship, all together. We must not be together all the time; we must both take side trips here and there, very often together, sometimes alone. We must both be free to do our work and whims must not break the chain of the work. . . .

Yes, I am impatient and have a temper, but I am not bad or mean on purpose and it is never my intention to consciously do some thing to hurt you. I saw my mother hurt and wounded and crying silently at the window for fifteen years. I wouldn't want to make such a life with my own wife . . . I would rather kill myself first. . . .

. . . I can not promise that once we are married I will be an angel or that I will do every small thing to please you. Also you will get out of your mind soon, I hope, that in ten or fifteen years I am going to run away from you and find a young girl to live with. And I don't agree with what you said on the phone last night—that when you said that it proved you loved me! Nonsense! Or if I didn't suspect you that it meant I didn't love you. Even worse nonsense!

Most important between us, I believe, is this—that we must positively know that one person does not react as another. To make an example—you may think that love means for a man to kiss you on the mouth; but the man may not think that—he may think that a kiss on the hand proves he loves you.

Frankly, you have begun to convince me that I'm not a very good person. (My father and family did that for a number of years while I still lived at home!) I know you don't mean to do it, but you make me feel I'm uncouth, vulgar, a savage, impolite, ten years old, knowing nothing about people or their habits. . . .

The truth is that, as in the old days, I begin to wish a little bit that I were dead dead dead!

I seem to have committed so many unpardonable sins towards you in the last two weeks that by now I have a constant fear of making more sins. So I find myself treading on eggs—on my word of honor I am always afraid that at any moment a simple natural thing I do or say is going to plunge you deep in sadness—like smoking a cigarette while talking to you, like not attaching as much importance to some small thing as you do.

I am sorry, Darling

Although he formulates it as her decision to make, it is evident that these two weeks had seriously shaken his courage. Echoing his doubts, graphologist Lucia Eastman's secret warnings had more than once returned to him. Nonetheless, his telephone calls to the Eitingons pleading for their

---

* She had in fact gone to visit the well-known architect Richard Neutra and his wife, Dione, not to a hospital.

help in persuading Luise to return were unremitting. It was intolerable that *she* should abandon *him*. After she received an extremely ardent letter assuring her of his love and the beauty of the life they would create together, Luise wired, "Tomorrow I come and hold your arms open to take your girl—Luise" and a few days later the Los Angeles press carried the news she had won the Film Critics Circle award as best actress, and that they had filed their intention to be married on the eighth day of January, 1937.

On the seventh, his anxiety raging, he received from Clurman a stunning blow: the Group was abandoning (Clurman says "postponing") *The Silent Partner*. In a long and stilted letter, prefaced by a keenly ambivalent acknowledgment of the announced marriage plans, Clurman tried his best to demonstrate that the bitter crisis within the Group was not solely responsible for this decision.

Dear Cliff,

I think it is swell for you to have taken the decisive step to marry. You have been a "free man" for too long, and a "free man" is only half a man! Marriage means a certain responsibility—no matter how you slice it!—even a certain "compromise," a certain giving up of oneself, a certain loss of oneself which really engages one with life. . . . I think marrying will even be good for your playwriting and artistic understanding (you've never written women's parts as good as Gus, Myron, Sam F., Uncle Morty). It will make you suffer and sweat—and it will bring you great happiness, too, I hope, and Luise is a swell girl, a match for you, a woman to combat, to frighten you, to struggle with and for, to admire, respect, love. The fact that she fished you out of your romantic torpor (as far as women go I mean) is a great tribute to her power and a sign of her rightness for you.

Things have been happening fast and furious—and all somehow linked together. The directors and actors of the Group have unanimously decided to postpone "Silent Partner" till next season—unless you insist on giving it to someone else to be produced this season. . . . I told you many times that for your work to be good it would have to be the *best* you can do, and the same is true of the Group company itself. It is obvious that the "Silent Partner" is not the best (in its present state), not even one-half as good as it can be, and that is due to the fact that you were harrassed, uncertain, confused all the time you were writing it on account of conditions in your life. You did not work on it from the first because you could not work on it, you were not in the psychological state—in that state which is patiently humble even when you are passionately pressing forward and fundamentally clear and controlled even in the midst of the fever of creation—you were not in the proper state, I say, to turn out the best. Nor are you now. You cannot under present conditions do the rewriting—a really creative job of the first magnitude—without settling down to a *long* daily routine needing deliberation and cool judgment. And it would be unfair to yourself as well as to the actors *who love your work* to let your play come out half-baked. For despite its great power and beauty even now it would be savagely repudiated and it would hurt your development after "Paradise Lost" to be thus represented.

But just as you have had your problems involving money, love, career, etc., etc., the Group company has had its upheavals recently of an even more complex nature because so many people are concerned. . . .

Just as you *want* passionately to finish "Silent Partner" right now, so there are actors in the Group who insist that we ought to continue thru hell and all right now. But such insistence (on your part as well as theirs) would lead to a breakdown from which there would be no recovery—for it would mean an effort made under continuously false conditions. . . .

As for you and your plays etc: I shall be happy to work on "Silent Partner" with you on the coast—and Gadget would too. Or, if you prefer, not. I still say it would be best for you to do *completely* and *entirely* your coast work—pictures—and then come back to writing your plays which you must then do also *completely* and *entirely* without interruption by coast offers of any sort. Because as you say, you can't do two things at one time. Nobody of your peculiar makeup could. . . .

Deeply discouraged, Clurman is ready, like Odets (and now Kazan, too), to seek his fortune in Hollywood, to which promised land Stella Adler, disgusted with the Group, had already fled and become the less Jewish-sounding Stella Ardler for a subsidiary company of Paramount Pictures. His letter ends with a plea to Odets for help in finding work in the film industry:

As for myself: I must find a job on the coast. I need the money. If I were subsidized I should not look for a job on the coast. But I am not and I intend to do as good work as I possibly can on anything I do—as you say much can be learned from the medium of the movies. I have not yet done anything about getting a job. . . .

A few days later Odets had managed to arrange for Clurman to work with him and Milestone on the Ilya Ehrenburg material, now titled *The River Is Blue*.

Several years later it would appear to Clurman that the central reason for dropping *The Silent Partner* had lain in script difficulties. In truth, the Group Theatre had reached a crisis which a commercial hit might have resolved. It is unlikely, however, that even had it been a more finished play, *The Silent Partner* would have offered the needed healing of the profound wounds described in a landmark document formulated by the Actors' Committee, consisting now of Elia Kazan, Morris Carnovsky, Roman Bohnen, and Stella Adler.

Opening with "We are writing this paper so that the Group will go on," this formal and passionate analysis of the current breakdown first credits the three directors with "wrenching" the company out of the American theatre six years earlier by the "sheer force" of their collective will. However, "It is inescapable," they continue "that the directors have not solved the Group problem," most particularly how to provide a living for its members. It has been, they say, only the "dogged faith" and determination of the actors—not the directors—that has kept the Group alive. There follows a merciless dissection of the three directors. Of Strasberg they write that "he has been the greatest artistic force in the American theatre during the last five years" and that the famous "Method"—supposedly Stanislavsky's—has in reality been "Lee's own method of work." But while they admire his courage, his doggedness, even "the brute domineering of his will," the time has passed when the Group needs his "clannishness, removal from life, arbitrariness, his need to be right, and his hysterical force." In the new Group which they envision, Strasberg would be relieved of "all but purely artistic tasks."

Of Clurman they say that "despite the fact that his regime as managing director is a failure, he is the logical man for the position at the head of the theatre" as he is the "clearest and the most whole of the three." They conclude, therefore, that if an "iron-clad and completely worked-out plan" can be prepared in advance, this would be insurance against his organizational impracticality and his tendency to collapse under the weight of his own and the Group's difficulties. They express sympathy for the "martyred" Cheryl Crawford, who should be replaced by a "business manager," leaving Miss Crawford—whom they call a "disappointed artist"—to the "creation of scripts."

In a conclusion headed "What's to be done," they speak of having only "one tattered bond" remaining to all—"a passionate concern for the Group idea"—and offer the alternatives of trying to patch up the existing organization or "dissolution, to allow a new and more fit Group to rise from the ashes. . . ."

Clurman, Strasberg, and Crawford agreed to resign, and the actors called for a new committee to draft future plans before Clurman and Kazan left for Hollywood. With Clurman exhausted and able to commit himself to nothing, not even to a promise that he would return from Hollywood to the Group, the few joint meetings of directors and actors came to nothing, and the New York press announced the end of the Group Theatre —an announcement which Clurman denied. It cannot have escaped Strasberg's notice that Odets, Clurman, and Kazan were grouping together, leaving him and Cheryl Crawford in New York to await developments.

By this time Odets had received not only the report of the Actors' Committee but also a variety of private, less-tempered accounts; Group actor Art Smith, for example, addressing him as "Dear Cliffritz" with "thanks for the check," concludes about *The Silent Partner:* "I don't believe the directors will ever consent to proceed with the true artistic faith and conviction which characterized the actors when we decided to do 'Awake and Sing' or when we did 'Lefty' without assistance from Olympus."

Luise later recalled her wedding and honeymoon:

> Doubtless I was very romantic. Like most young girls, I longed to find the right man and to get married to him. Like many young girls, I had pictured myself in flowing white for the occasion. That, I knew, was out. So I was to wear a little traveling suit.
>
> But the night before the great day I lay awake. I thought that my living room, the stage of the ceremony, though always filled with flowers, did not look festive enough. I jumped out of bed and grabbed a large bedsheet, I went down stairs and carefully pinned it against a similarly large window. Onto the sheet I drew the outline of an enormous heart, cut little holes into this outline and filled each with a red carnation. This was to be the background.
>
> At the hour of the ceremony Lewis Milestone and his wife, best man and best woman, and I waited for Cliff. He arrived looking as though he had run all the way from Beverly Hills to Brentwood. Not a flower in his hand. True, he had sent, the day before, a fabulous long ermine coat a friend's wife had ordered and didn't want. That was wonderful. But I dreamed of a tiny bouquet! Anyway I did not say a word.

Hearts beating hard, we stood in front of the enormous bedsheet listening to the ceremonial words. Suddenly a great big BANG. The newspaper people, kept far and away, had pressed and run down the tall wooden door that locked the walled-in garden, and through the open entrance stormed into the house and ceremony, flinging cameras, ready to shoot. The ring did not fit, good God the ring didn't fit! It was too small. Clifford pressed hard and got it over. My finger started swelling. We could not wait for all to be done to race to the jeweler and have it cut off. Then, I guess, we lunched with the Milestones. And then we went off: the honeymoon!

Clifford didn't drive. I did, and rather fast. Not that it was not hot enough where we had come from, but down south we went. Johnny, my dog, was sitting in the rear. Clifford had often wished, and wished now, that Johnny was dead and he told us so, Johnny and me. Johnny under his onslaught seemed to get uglier and uglier. In fact, Johnny didn't like Clifford and Clifford didn't like me loving Johnny. Before reaching the border to Mexico I got a speeding ticket and the policeman, unmoved by the delicate air of a young bride, felt I deserved it. Late that evening we arrived at the Rosa Rita Hotel, an enormous box of a thing, at Ensenada, a tiny town on the ocean at the northern tip of Mexico. Off-season, the big hotel was completely empty except for a troupe of midgets recouping after a vaudeville tour. Once in our room Clifford, permitting no exception from his usual habit to work through the night, had gotten his typewriter out and started to work. I was, as one may say, a bit at loose ends. Dream and reality seemed to have little in common.

Next morning—with no one else to talk to, as Clifford had started his daily sleep—I thought I had better make friends with the midgets. They had recognized me and surrounded me. They were impressed, which helped my dented mood. Amongst them I looked like Goliath. They introduced themselves and each other to me: "This gentleman" —he was well combed and came up to my navel—"does our tightrope act"—"This lady"—she stood in a well décolleté lace dress and was the size of my legs—"has done a film, in fact, to tell you the truth, we have often thought she looks a bit like you!" I agreed, but decided to go for a long walk along the beach. Hours later I saw from afar Clifford coming towards me. He looked rather grim. Maybe he was annoyed I had not sat in the room waiting for him to waken. After all, it was his wedding night—I mean day—I had no business not to be at his side. But I, I had needed fresh air. Throughout my life, whenever I was miserable, if I could, I would go out where there were flowers, trees, mountains, or sea. It would heal me. All this meant little to Clifford. We walked towards the hotel and the midgets seemed to be all over the place and were most anxious to meet Clifford as well. But Clifford said he resented the midgets and left me sitting in their midst while he went upstairs to his room. Those are the facts I remember of my honeymoon.

Luise's unhappiness deepened when, on their return to the house on Cliffwood Avenue, her husband immediately announced (secretly following his graphologist's advice) that they would have separate rooms. Once he locked himself in his room and shouted through the door, "If we have to live together all our lives, there simply isn't enough in me to last!" There was the steady implication that he feared that sexual activity in marriage would drain off his creative energy. Luise would listen to the tapping of his typewriter into the small hours of the morning. In her diary she wrote: "His fear of non-renewal! So he says: 'spending our lives together we must beware of giving out continuously.' What does he mean? I have never been afraid of giving out. I hope I never will be."

Using his notes on the Ambers-Canzoneri fight, he had begun a new play, one he fervently hoped would save from extinction the Group Theatre and his role in it; he called it at first "The Manly Art." For the first time in his life he had consciously determined to write a "hit play."

Luise, feeling he was unaware of her comings and goings, left early in the morning for the studio while he was, as usual, still asleep after a night of work. Their only contacts until evening were his extravagant love notes, signed alternately "Your master" and "Your obedient servant." Her loneliness mounted, and she, quite naturally, became more responsive to overtures from other people. Even when these exchanges were entirely innocent, however, Odets became pathologically jealous. On one occasion before they were married, George Gershwin, drawn to her quicksilver vitality, had engaged her in a chat, and "Clifford," according to Luise, had "made a terrible scene, shouting and throwing things." Now she became uncertain how long she could tolerate this relationship, and instead of coming home in the evening after work, she would go, as long as there was light, up into the hills behind her house, feeling, as she told him, that she had been "chased out of her own house." Odets, in turn, became depressed, wondering if he could sustain *any* human relationship. Later he jotted on an envelope,

> Any relatedness or relationship with another is taxing, a form of taxation; and to resent it is to delimit or make the relatedness impossible. Paid over fully, it is the most rewarding of all taxes; refused, it makes "relating" and human contact and unification impossible.

From his father, back from his world tour, Odets received a long letter in the mixed style of a "pal" and a Jewish Polonius:

> Well "ole scout" how does it feel to be a married man? Once more I want the pleasure to congratulate you, not because you were married, but, because you married a woman who loves you, and whom you love. There is nothing greater in life, then love. With love in your heart, you can have a mind that is clear, you can soar, transcend. Happiness that you have been seeking is yours, at last—but, this love is only a loan to you. If you want to keep it, you must earn it. You can believe your old father when he tells you, it takes two to love. I know you well, better than you think I do. Your life, and the life of your beautiful wife is in your hands. She is a wonderful little person. I have carefully analyzed her. Her thoughts are beautiful. Of course as an artist, she may be temperamental, or moody at times—but, so are you. Thru her many interviews, her wire to me, her action at City Hall when you were obtaining your marriage license, her air of reverence with which she answered all questions—she has proved that she possesses that tender or passionate affection of love—Now "big boy" you are a God chosen person. You own love. Very few people in all the World possess it. No one can be real happy without it— What I would do to "earn" keep it. I would honor and obey, never belittle, *always respect*, never forget that my wife comes first at all times, I would never look for, or find faults, I would always try to make her happy, and keep her in a loveable condition, I'd make her want me more than any one else, I'd love her, and let her know about it. I would tell her nice things before someone else would, I would not forget that its the

little things in life that counts, I would learn what she likes and would see that she has them, I'd make her feel that I mean to please. Again *always respect*— Of course, I'd teach her to do the same things, but women are so frail, delicate—just like the springs in a fine watch—sometimes harsh words, actions, etc. "warp" their little minds, and like the springs in a fine watch—are never the same.

I wrote this letter "big boy" because as your father and a man of experience I have a right too [sic]. You may feel you know all I wrote you, maybe you do—but I want you to live it. Lots of Love for two. L.J.

Perhaps, if his wife had been an Academy Award winner, Lou Odets would have expressed such rhapsodic rhetoric about his own marriage. His son, who had witnessed the ugliness between his parents and the open sadistic contempt directed at his mother, found it shocking.

The Los Angeles and New York press as well as the national magazines had been in some awe of the puzzling relationship between Clifford and Luise, highly atypical for the movie colony ("These two lonely, shy, music-loving intellectuals spurn the usual glitter of Hollywood nightlife, preferring to walk hand-in-hand on the beach at sunset . . . ," etc.). Now they began to nip at this "bourgeois romance," lying in wait for an opportunity to bring the elusive pair down to a level where, as one put it, "they would type easier." Most often they taunted Odets for accepting "capitalist gold" for his "communist ideas," or for having ceased being "a Moses—even a Messiah." He had become, one said, a "Lost Leader taking profits from movie slaves, and actually married to a star of the silver screen." The Saturday *Home Magazine* section of the Hearst news chain was particularly concerned that Odets maintain an untainted Marxist allegiance, concluding one of its many feature articles about them (headed "Gold—and Lovely Luise for the Leftist Dream Man") with the following:

> Frankly, I am worried. I am mortally afraid that some night I shall be standing on a curbstone in the Forties when Clifford Odets comes driving up in a big, shiny car with his pretty bride, and when I give him the old upraised right fist and a cheery hail of "Hi, Comrade Odets" he will just give me a vague look and a shiny dime!

Odets' publicly militant stand—in his plays and in his activities—with the insulted and injured of these suffering times had been sufficient to stimulate many members of the bourgeois press into a punitive campaign of ridicule. His new capacity to earn great sums of money during this Great Depression, plus his marriage to an Academy Award winner, provoked a spate of sarcastic, mindlessly righteous newsprint. Now and again a columnist such as his old friend Walter Winchell would come to his defense, saying he had been "shoved around plenty by Broadway managers and critics alike" and was entitled to earn whatever he could.

The Group Theatre members, many of them now working in California under contract to the suave, polo-playing film producer Walter Wanger (cousin of writer Lion Feuchtwanger), had their own reasons to keep in sharp focus Odets' falls from grace. They saw in him at one and the same time the realization of their own aspirations (many of them were steadily borrowing money from him) and their conscience pangs about working in the film industry. Many viewed his marriage to a film star as a danger to his creativity. "You begin to live your life for the columnist," said one, "and as for a playwright marrying a movie star, unless he is out to destroy her—which experience might be useful to him as a writer—it *has* to be damaging to him."

"After all," as writer Irwin Shaw put it, "if Luise Rainer is going to be in a junky little picture which they're putting a million dollars into, even though you might be writing *A Doll's House*, everything is geared to making her little piece of junk seem overpoweringly important and what the writer is doing seem piddling." Indeed, it seemed to Ira Gershwin that there was something shaky and defensive in Odets' impassioned shout in response to teasing on this score: "I am now working on six plays at one time, and one of them is the best play about labor ever written in this country!" But *The Silent Partner* had just been shelved by the Group, and even Odets did not believe the brave announcement that it would be produced in the fall. Clurman, now working for Wanger, gave no sign of returning East, or even of concern for the Group.

The astute Irwin Shaw has described an aspect of what happens to a less than confident writer in the situation in which Odets now found himself:

Any writer married to a movie star has a tendency to meddle in the star's life—that's what the star wants—all these women out there are looking for men to tell them what to do and take care of them. Taking care of a movie star is like taking care of a delicate, large, sick dog. First of all, they're frightened—somebody is going to say something nasty about them—they're losing their looks—somebody is going to swindle them into doing the wrong part—they lean on the husband and say take care of this, read this, do this—it's hard enough to read the things you want to read yourself—you have to read her movie scripts. Your brain rots—you're committed to being places you don't want to be at that time—the location of the movie star's work is fixed —it has to be.

By this time Odets had set forth to slay Luise's particular dragon, Louis B. Mayer, head of the Metro-Goldwyn-Mayer studio. This was a role for which Lewis Milestone found him singularly unfit. "Clifford," said Milestone, "was no match for those men." But it was far more than simple meddling in his wife's business that led him to do repeated battle with this powerful man and his representatives. It was, by identification, his own business, and far more important to him than he knew to establish his own worth and masculine strength with such moguls as Mayer. To the extent that he could insist that Luise's serious creative aspirations be met in her films, he felt that even his own conflict would be easier to resolve, and his own creative future rendered less vulnerable. Indeed, his reiterated appeal to the "money-men" at Metro-Goldwyn-Mayer was that they respect Luise as "the Thomas Mann of actresses."

It is the paradox and the power of art that even while Odets was enacting with Mayer his own deepest conflicts, he was simultaneously trying to bring them to creative resolution by writing a play about a young violinist seduced away from music-making and into the highly paid violence of the prizefight ring, where he forever cripples his artist's hands. On the success of this play hinged the life of his brotherhood, the Group Theatre, and his identity as a playwright.

To many of his friends it appeared that Odets now desperately needed a wife who could nurture *his* talent and not an artist who had her own creative obligations. Although Clifford adored and respected Luise's cultivation and her decidedly European civilized manner, he felt certain that what he was writing about at this time was fundamentally alien to her. Steadily protesting that he wanted "an equal and not a wife," he nonetheless left Luise with the feeling he very much wanted a *full-time* wife.

Moreover, according to Mrs. Henry Varnum Poor, it appeared to mat-

ter terribly to Odets that Luise never had time to stock the refrigerator.
When once she asked him if he could wear his brown shoes instead of his
black ones with his light slacks, he felt this was an "absolutely uncalled-
for criticism." On the other hand, Clifford, though arguing for equality,
really believed, said Mrs. Poor, that "a woman should be subservient to the
male." Thus, in these first weeks of their marriage the battle was joined.
Their scribbled notes, preserved by each, reflect the struggle. In the possession of Luise Rainer, written, she thinks, after her husband had been raging about the empty larder, is the following:

> Dear Clifford—first please let me tell you that more than 50 times you
> told me you don't eat anything for breakfast. 2. Since a few days roles
> [sic] are ordered and I have not seen you eat any bread. 3. There was
> this one package of bread and it is very probable that it became bad
> overnight. Even if I would have looked into your breadbox I probably
> would have thought that this one package would be enough in case
> you would like to eat bread. But these points all are very unimportant,
> what is much more important to me is this: *what* gives you the *right*
> to ask any duties from me?? All I do and will do I will do freely, if I
> forget to do something and you tell me, believe me I *love* to make it
> right the next time but you will get nothing but opposition from me if
> you DEMAND. Clifford what are you doing for me that you have the
> right to say: "it is your duty" to see that there is bread. Is it because
> you are a man and I a woman? Or what is it? Is it that you are sooo
> bourgeois to demand this as "duties" from your wife? And what is this
> phantastic line: "what do you think you are here a concubine?" Clif-
> ford are you completely nuts!? I have to be here and on your side
> much much more than "concubine" or housewife, I have to be on your
> side a very mature and understanding person. . . . I am a person
> who has to stay for herself, who works, makes money, takes care of
> herself, and I want you to know that I will do everything *for love for
> you, nothing* for duty. I thought "these times are past??" And *you*
> don't want me to be old fashioned!!! I don't understand such behav-
> ing from a person which always speaks so differently theoretically.
> My darling, I will do everything for love, nothing for "duty" as long as
> I have to be a "modern" girl. And I want you to know and appreciate
> that I am more than a concubine and that I love to be a housewife too
> if you appreciate it and don't demand things like that! Kiss.

and at other times Luise would write notes like:

> Dear Clifford please tell me if I do things wrong because I want to
> learn how to do them right! And I will try to do them right. Luise.

A note jotted down by Clifford for himself:

> Conversations with Luise. Me . . . How do you want me to be, dar-
> ling? She . . . Be as you want, darling. I don't want you to be any
> way except as you want to be. You do not have to be any certain kind
> of way for me. As you want. Really, sweet.

Odets was persuaded he was doing all the giving and Luise all the
taking, as she was certain of the converse; each found the other's "ego"
uniquely self-involved and unwilling to make concessions. Luise maintained that Odets swung from incredible sweetness and desire for her to
"being a monster of fury about nothing." When once he said to her in greatest tenderness: "If ever you want to commit suicide, do it while lying in
my arms," she could not believe she had heard right. He, in turn, com-

plained to intimates like Kazan that she steadily taunted his weaknesses ("I couldn't climb mountains, do a hundred-yard dash, or even drive a car") and that he never knew when he awoke whether he would find himself living "with a superiorly boyish Joan of Arc or a helplessly despairing Chekhov sister."

That she was not interested in the refrigerator or in cooking for him became an enraging symbol of abandonment and deprivation in this marriage. Sometimes he thought the only being she cared for was her Scottie dog. And yet in their passionate struggles and reconciliations their physical merging remained for each a unique life-experience, a powerful bond which perpetuated their troubled relationship.

They had been married less than a month when, after an especially violent quarrel—begun with the question of women's rights and concluding with whether or not Luise "really" wanted him to be interested in his work or, indeed, in anything but her—she impulsively boarded a train for New York, shouting, "If I were a man I would visit every whorehouse in New York!" Odets later discussed Luise's strength as a covert male toughness which had frightened and excited him, even as his covert femininity may have provided for her a maternal tenderness which vexed her in its passivity and delighted her in its empathy.

The movements of a contender for an Academy Award were grist for newspaper mills, and Luise stepped off the Twentieth Century Limited in New York into a swarm of reporters. Clifford had asked his father to meet her at the station, but after a few brief comments Luise slipped away from them all—her father-in-law, the forty-odd reporters, uniformed police, and hordes of onlookers. Newspapers reported she was surrounded by a squad of MGM press agents who had "coached" her in the stateroom before she left the train (presumably protecting Louis B. Mayer's dictum that the breath of "scandal" must never touch a star's domestic life).

On the West Coast, according to the papers, Odets "banished rumors of disharmony" by explaining he had not accompanied her because he was busy on a new script. On the East Coast, Luise remained in seclusion. Odets sent wire after wire pleading for a reconciliation. He sent friends to her and, persuaded by them, she finally responded to Odets' pleading. As she prepared to return to California, she was seized by a violent sore throat and a fever just as she had been the previous summer during their troubled vacation in Nichols, Connecticut. Nonetheless she wired him to meet her in Pasadena. She was longing to see him: "It is so difficult without my man among so many people." On the journey home, although filled by his affectionate protestations with new hope for their future together, Luise, recalling the murderous hatred in his great eyes just before she left, could not shake off the feeling that she had married a man of immense imbalance.

This man meets a young girl, fresh unspoiled; he despoils her. It is as if he met his own talent at the age of seventeen (the girl of this age now) and began to corrupt her.

Out of his sense of frustration he takes this virginal girl and teaches her every trick of sex and life he knows. He purposely, for reasons of revenge, out of rage at seeing his own face in the mirror, ruins this girl and cripples* forever the possibility of her acquiring a valuable sense of values. He delights in her sadistically. After breaking her maidenhood, after the first few sex excitements his real excitement comes from corrupting her wilfully and completely, in every way. Often the man is disgusted with himself.

In the end he shows her what she is. This is a parable, a whole history of America. It is the story of those men with split personalities, the Sol Ginsbergs and Joe Bonapartes† who do one thing and mean something else inside.

So wrote Odets a few days after Luise's return to California, in a page-and-a-half outline labeled "A novel, short, brutal, of the modern man in America." "The so-called hero," he writes, with no apparent insight into the desperately autobiographical sources of this short summary, "is a sort of George Jean Nathan" (a critic loathed and condemned by Odets) and the girl is a singer, "a Deanna Durbin type of girl" whose mother arranges for her daughter to be seduced by Nathan while all attend a play called *Golden Boy*. The girl understands that "she must suffer sex experiences" (with this and future powerful men) "for the sake of the art of singing." Instead of her effecting this bargain, however, the "willful corruption" of the girl by the man proceeds. The man "becomes her Svengali," and the mother and he "fight for the control of the girl."‡ Interrupting himself now, in caps he writes, "Or is the father still alive and the parable is this: The father-artist fighting the corrupt system for the soul of a young artist who wants both things—Joe Bonaparte again?"

He wonders whether "the girl goes to Hollywood and there the last stages of corruption are put on her?" and concludes with a caution to himself:

BE CAREFUL. There are two stories here and they must be carefully joined to make one. One story is the corruption of an artist. The other story is the one of the rage of an artist already impotent. This means that the critic must have at one time been a brilliant novelist or playwright.

The essential elements in these two stories, written concurrently with *Golden Boy*, are transparent. Although, as always, he projects an external seducer (here the arrogant critic George Jean Nathan, who expresses many of Odets' identity-elements, drawn from his father), he perceives that the struggle is internal. "It is the story," he says, "of the Sol Ginsbergs and Joe Bonapartes . . . of the young artist who wants both things." As so often in his plays, he reverses the roles of the mother and father, making her the manipulator and him the "father-artist." In this he recognizes L. J. Odets' bitter disappointment that his own literary talent has so far issued only in a false claim to the authorship of the hack booklet *How to Smooth the Selling Path*.

While a father usually participates vicariously in the success of a talented son (the "Deanna Durbin" character here), the unremitting necessity in L. J. Odets to become controlling manager, mentor, marital advisor, and even collaborator—born of his blocked aspiration and creative impotence—had now become in all ways excessive. When L. J. Odets read, for example, in *Variety* of Luise's "tilt with MGM," he immediately dispatched

---

* Odets jots, "The crippled becomes the crippler!"

† Sol Ginsberg is John Howard Lawson's divided protagonist in *Success Story;* Bonaparte, Odets' in *Golden Boy.*

‡ This is one of the central themes of Odets' *Rocket to the Moon, Clash by Night, The Country Girl,* and *The Big Knife.*

a two-page letter to his son, instructing him: "now read carefully," and offering Odets and Luise instant surcease from all their problems if they would hire *him* in the place of their many business representatives, all of whom he steadily indicted as dishonest, self-seeking, and incompetent:

> Being a parent I'm on the wrong side of the fence! Forget you ever heard of me before. . . . I am writing this letter as a business counsellor. I want both Luise and you to treat it so. I am not looking for favors. Generally speaking, successful children rightfully feel that a parent has little to offer them in the ways of ideas or service . . . I flatter myself to the extent of believing I offer a rare exception to this general rule.
>
> I am a business executive for over twenty-five years. I have been responsible for many, many millions of dollars worth of business. *Not* as a manufacturer, but as a sales and advertising executive, *agent*. Selling a service—other peoples merchandise, ware, art, etc.
>
> I know that if I could get Luise and you to speak your secret thoughts you would tell me that you are awed by the growing size of your business problems, and further I know how you both hate business, and still further we all know that it is impossible to burn a candle at both ends, to success. It is logical that if business will worry you, your art will suffer.
>
> I am offering my services. . . .

Of course, Clifford and Luise did not avail themselves of this offer. It would have astonished and gratified the father, however, could he have read his son's bitingly critical letters to his agents and manager written soon after and almost in the same words, indicting them for his "bad contracts" with Walter Wanger and with Paramount Pictures. No matter that Harold Freedman of the Brandt and Brandt agency points out that Odets was paid more "for a first picture by a young playwright" than anyone had ever been paid. Odets held all his hangers-on responsible for their share in the crippling blows to his musician's hands—which is to say, his esthetic integrity. In the play he was writing (*Golden Boy*) these hangers-on appear as a ring of exploiting middle-men, all greedily wanting—like his own father—"a piece" of the boy.

Within a few days there arrived a new eight-page diatribe from his father, written in the heat of his outraged vanity, his loss of face, over Luise's recent trip to New York. Apparently one of a series of unanswered letters, it commences with the account of his car accident,* caused, he says, by his son, "the dummist [sic] chunk of humanity I have ever come in contact with."

> You start your letter with; "I'm in no mood or position for writing letters."—Well, I demand that you place yourself in a position, and get into the mood to read this letter three (3) times. I am still your father and I demand it. There is a God in Heaven that takes care of the blind and the dumb. With your eyes wide open you are blind, and with all your intelligence, you are dumb. God does not take care of people like you. He helps people like you, when they help themselves. I was in N.Y. last weekend. I always listen in on Walter Winchell Sunday night, expecting to hear Luise's or your name mentioned—and of course knowing how you two are in love with each other I expected to hear something that would make me happy too—To my surprise he mentions your names, and tells the world at large, that after only a

---

* Odets would have many car accidents for which he would blame his father.

few weeks of married life Clifford Odets moved back to his hotel, away from his wife's home—I tell the truth if I was sitting in a chair I would have fainted, but I was driving in my car, I got *sick,* stalled the car and a fellow in the back ran into me, and ripped my fenders. I never fainted before in my life. The only way for me to forget it, was to cut my heart out.

Continuing with a muddled emotional logic more revealing than any confession, he takes his thirty-year-old son to task, once more shaming him mercilessly:

I felt sure that you were a *big* enough *man* to be with your wife of four weeks, that you would not let her travel alone . . . The husband is supposed to be a *big man* in the world. Hitler, he too thinks he is a big man. A dictator who thinks he is smart, the selfish brute, *to reach his own goal,* he would walk over everybody and anything in the world. If he reached "that" goal he would not know what to do with it, because he would not be happy. *You answer me,* could Hitler feel that he has attained good fortune and success? Could he have that feeling arising from the consciousness of wellbeing or of enjoyment, or contentment? Your answer is NO. Your answer is no, because you know that Hitler is a scoundrel, to obtain his *selfish* goal he has no love in his heart, and therefore he steps over every body, every thing, even those things that he loves—and *you* further know that if he reaches his goal, he can not be happy.

Now young man, and *young* you are. What is your aim in life? What goal are you trying to reach? *At what* expence?—You impress the people that your aim in life is love for all, happiness to all. You have told me 101 times, that the reason you don't like the movies are because they are not true "honest." They wont show what makes people unhappy. I don't understand. (and I'm as smart as you are). Hitler preaches love and happiness to 65 million people, even to the youngest children as long as they can understand. . . .

With a mind that is bemuddled as yours is, you will *never* get any where, that a mind like yours can take you. You are at a peak in life *now,* that you will never again attain. You are a man, and you have a *real* woman that *loves* YOU. . . . Men with millions, and better brains than yours (who have been married) have died of loneliness. Again I say: Love that costs nothing, is a gift of God. Fools throw love away, only to be heartbroken untill their dieing day—

Cliff, at this minute you are the dearest I have in the world and I must speak, yell at the top of my voice at you—your actions are such that *I'm ashamed of you.* You are the dummist chunk of humanity I have ever come in contact with. What in hell do you want? Do you know? NO you don't. Your just a great big fool. You don't know what you want, don't know how to get it, and will never get anything, compared to what you are entitled to get. Your all ass backwards, and sitting on your brains.

The naked parody here of American "bigness" as power is startling; the struggle between this as an aspiration and the fear of turning evil, like Hitler (and dying of loneliness), is even more startling. It does not occur to him that these very aspirations and terrors might be his own.

Gathering a second wind for this assault, he continues:

You married in your class, an artist. An artist that is as big as you are. At 25 she is outstanding. A kid in age. In her third performance she is as good as Garbo—and there is none better, she is going places in this world. Everybody loves her, and she is loveable. I saw her in Good Earth and tears rolled down my cheeks. She is wounderful not good, but perfect—This little sweet bunch of joy loves you, wants to make you happy, and you love her, and during her honeymoon which should be not less sixty days—*you you* the man finds work to do in two weeks, so that it is too hard to enjoy his *bride,* and you think your a man with brains—What do you think, you married a washwoman. I think your so smart, that you don't know what its all about.

The rift between Clifford and Luise provides him also with an opportunity to express his competitive hatred toward the members of the Group Theatre as evil influences, a hatred that would continue unabated long after his son's death:

What kind of friends have you down there, don't they say anything to you? or are they selfish feinds instead of friends. . . . Your a big boy, from a small town. Any one you meet that appeals to you, can sell you a bill of goods. Your father knows nothing, I know, he means well, but don't know. . . . I know Cliff she might be tempermental and if she is, as your father I'd say your much worse—I'll tell you that its all your fault, and tell you why. I figured when you'd marry the girl you love, you would change. What kind of happiness can you have in life, living as you do. You get up at 2 P.M. attend to a few things business untill about midnight 10 hours—then you sit down to write, after your all tired out up to about 6 A.M. . . . The proof is you got very little done in the last year in a half your way. Try my way. Cliff you will be the happiest man in the world with Luise. She is different, she is a find, she will help you. But, remember she is a "Big" person, she is *not* a washwoman. She is as big as you are. RESPECT makes happiness. Love her she wants you. Give all friends up for her.

This avalanche of accusation and advice would have had little contemporary significance for Odets were it not for the fact that his father's voice, by now firmly established within him, echoed all of it. And, as when he was a small boy and, later, a vulnerable adolescent, the voice repeated, "You should be *ashamed* of yourself . . . You are a bad little boy . . . Give up those nasty habits and those false friends . . . Your father knows best . . . How do you ever expect to be a BIG MAN?" In spite of himself, he began to wonder whether the Group people—and Clurman in particular —were indeed parasitic and "taking advantage." Even Luise thought so.

Odets must have relented somewhere in his stubborn silence: shortly after Luise's conciliatory return to Hollywood, his father thanks them both for "your telegram and letter," adding now happily, "respect to a parent is a prayer to God" and "I read about both of you in the papers *every* day." All was now right in L.J.'s world.

By the end of March, however, this happy state of affairs had ended; father and son are again exchanging furious letters, with L.J. occasionally trying to appease Clifford:

I know that both of you are made up of the same temperment, and both your tempers are awful, horrible, yet you are both fine people of good heart and fine character.

Nowhere are the father's literary aspirations and his effort to control by psychologizing—a pattern emulated by the son—more evident than in these letters counseling him on how to maintain his marriage:

I say, getting "under the skin" of some people is quite a job. They go around armored as old gruff-and-tough, brick-baked inside of a crust of alleged hard-boiledism. . . . "Self conceit.". . . The harder the crust seems to be, the greater the chances that the man inside of it is a pretty soft proposition. Of course there are some people "egotists," whose innards are so dried up and whose think-tanks so filled with set-concrete, that even trying to break through is a waste of time, but I'm not concerned with petrified people. I am thinking of a beautiful star, and a brilliant playwright. Two loveable people, in love with each other. . . . Even the bitterest misanthrope who ever drew breath cannot make the grade alone.*. . . Of course as a parent I don't know anything, and I'm too old, and old-fashioned, and can't see things your way. . . . Your in a hurry. Where are you going? You'll be dead a long time. Teach each other the meaning of Sacrifice, you'll love it, and you will both enjoy life as it was meant to be enjoyed.

It was intolerable to Lou Odets that his son might lose this star, this prized possession, this "big woman."

In a long and depressed postscript starting, "Now, big boy," he pleads for a letter, brings him up to date on family news (Florence is studying drama, Genevieve is expecting a baby), chides him for not writing letters ("Are you a brother, are you afraid to make them happy?"), and concludes on a melancholic note that he cannot seem "to make connections, anywhere" and is, at forty-nine, an old man:

I'm getting very tired and very very lonesome. Every day feels that it has 36 hours in it, and every hour feels like a day—but, what's the use, I'll live untill I die, and then who cares. My health is good, but I have bad tonsils, and I'll have to have them removed.

When all else failed, this hardy man, who would long outlive his son, characteristically fell back on his physical ailments as a conscience-prod.

"Up to my ears here in nothing." So wrote Odets from California to Helen Deutsch, now press-relations officer for the Theatre Guild in New York. His overlong, not quite commercial film adapted from the Ehrenburg material is being postponed "perhaps forever . . . unless they can get big stars to make it box office."† He will spend eight more weeks in Hollywood on a picture for Paramount to be called *Gettysburg* and then will have the capital and "go in a corner and write a new play . . . revise Silent Partner and am all set for the coming Broadway season." He asks Helen to get him a job at the Theatre Guild or at least an acting part in Ben Hecht's new play, *To Quito and Back*. "Perhaps," he writes, "Gadget [Kazan] and I can play the two leading parts and have some fun out of the theatre for a change. I used to get fun out of the theatre and now I get bubkas!"

It is clear from all his correspondence that he regards New York and the theatre as his home base and his work for the film industry as a brief piratical raid. Indeed, Luise was aware that he always came out with one

---

* It is not usual for L. J. Odets to use words like "petrified" or "misanthrope." It is possible he cribbed portions of this letter.

† This material would be reworked by playwrights John Howard Lawson and Lillian Hellman to become the internationally controversial film *Blockade*, dealing no longer with Russians in Paris but with the struggle against fascism in Spain.

tiny little suitcase, showing that he didn't intend to stay very long, "knowing ever so well that a marriage, difficult at best, would hardly be manageable if the partners are always separated by three thousand miles." And, according to a business manager, "His bags were always packed, in case New York called him." To the end of his life he would maintain a New York apartment and, on all public records, call it his "permanent residence."

At this moment, however, *his* New York, the key figures of the Group Theatre, except for Strasberg, were in Hollywood, too. Most of them were there to work in Odets' now-shelved film. Those not already signed by Walter Wanger were trying to find a niche in any movie studio that would accept them. Clurman, finding his work on the film "not in the least dull," had taken a house with two servants, where he lived with Stella Adler, whose "new nose," according to Kazan, "is a huge success, and she should photograph marvellously." Indeed, he adds, "if she makes a big hit in movies, Harold will have to make the Inescapable Choice" between Hollywood and New York.

In this same letter to Strasberg (who also inquires eagerly about *his* chances for work in the film industry—he doesn't care whether it is with Wanger or with Warner Bros.) Kazan sets forth for him and for the remaining East Coast Group Theatre members what he regards as "the true state of affairs." This document, a crucial one for the Group, starts with the "small matter" of why the Group members now found themselves "holding the bag" in relation to Odets' abandoned film. Kazan shrewdly details his reasons for thinking their own lawyer was secretly on the other side of the bargaining table ("To put it tersely, we were represented by the Boss' agent"); he presents precisely the same picture of self-seeking, ambitious men, eager to manipulate, to exploit and control artists as commodities, that Odets was creating in the play he was writing, at this moment called "Golden Gloves."

For himself, Kazan tries to state simply and clearly his own position in regard to working in the Group:

> I believe myself entirely now when I say that I have no interest here at all. This goes, even though I know that I could and others have and can, produce distinguished films here. But such work is so hedged in by opposing circumstances, that when it does appear, it has been the combination of lucky turns—like throwing ten coins in the air and having them all come down heads. And beyond this, even under *ideal* Hollywood conditions—which by the way do not exist for anyone, even for Capra—I'm not interested. I will stay here about two or three weeks more just to see if I can make up a little bundle of cash, without killing a lot of time waiting. If I can go to work fairly soon, I'll stay. I need the money. If not, I'll be right back.
>
> When I get back, I'm going to Russia for a couple of months—it looks like it might be a last chance before they slam the gate over there. Then I should be back in N.Y. in the late summer. And then with whatever forces can be gotten together—I will work in a Group theatre. I'm not interested in anything else and would not do anything else. I know I can work in a Group this fall—but—
>
> The one thing I will not embark on again is an organization where the organization and relation of people was as unhealthy as it was in our Group in its last year and a half. I believe that now, in this intermediary period, many people are being motivated by a certain kind of fear. This impulse says "Let us cling to what we have, it is better than nothing . . . we can slowly iron out its faults as we work

along . . . we had the best people and we had the best relation and adjustment between these people . . . for chrissake lets not lose what we have." I believe this attitude to be a panicy one and also extremely dangerous. I believe that if we got together this summer, the same people in the same relations etc.—the same clashes and diseases would grow up and then there would come a really terrible explosion! . . .

Furthermore, I believe the time has come to deeply and with all the fruit of our experience, reorganize the Group. We need fresh blood; we need to take chances again with new people. If for no reason than the fact that we are losing our old people, in one form or another, to whatever varying degree. . . . We must have new material to work with and material in whom we feel *potentiality*. . . . Loyalty is no longer enough. The struggle is too fierce. . . .

About Stella and Harold. I talked with Harold two nights ago. I told him frankly that I thought that he was in a comatose state, that he seemed to have lost his own appetite, desire and personal dynamics . . . that he seemed to be further embedded in his concern for Stella than he had ever been before. To this he simply answered that I was right. . . . Also, to be frank and clear, he seems to be no more determined about his relation to Cheryl and yourself. Luther [Adler] says to this that we, the Board members will see that the grating working parts, clear and work separately. This I believe to be mechanical and bad theatre theory. The theatre is a collective art and the working parts have to work or else. . . . For the possibility that a new basis will be evolved by time, circumstances, talks, new relations, etc. . . . for this too, I'm willing to wait . . . everyone longs for the Group; all await leadership . . . I'm calm and full of confidence about what I want . . . I'm eager to go to Russia now that I have a real chance and I know I'll not miss. Then to come back and work. However I know there must be leadership . . . nothing will arise that's good from the will of the majority.

At this point it appeared to be a toss-up as to whether the future, if any, of the Group Theatre would be superintended by Strasberg or by Clurman. Kazan was not aware that by now Strasberg and Cheryl Crawford had together made an irrevocable decision to leave the Group, a decision based—according to Strasberg—explicitly on the planlessness of the Group with regard to playwrights and their plays. The struggles between Clurman and Strasberg had been bitter, Strasberg believing "that the existence of the Group could be respectably based on plays that were not necessarily of the first-grade and yet that could be on the stage first-rate theatre . . . like 'Men in White.' " All of this he wrote in a long position paper.

Even Paula Miller Strasberg, recently arrived in the film capital and thrilled with her own possibilities for a "term contract" with a major studio, did not know how close to the end of his connection with the Group her husband was. "Although," she adds, "all the Group people are anxious to work here, the Group is the important thing. . . . The Group gives us prestige here." Morris Carnovsky, whose screen test consisted of scenes from Odets' *Paradise Lost*, has joyously landed the part of Anatole France in a new film about Emile Zola. His wife, Phoebe Brand, although eager to do a picture, hopes for a part in Clifford's new play. They have a car and "a sweet house," all quite different, says Paula, from the marginal existence provided at best by the Group in New York. Yet, she writes, it all feels temporary.

Earlier and maligned Group defectors to films, like J. Edward Bromberg and Franchot Tone, had by now begun shyly and apologetically to invite Group people to dinner at poolside. Even Clurman confessed he found the sunny routines of California pleasant. And Paula writes that refugee composer Kurt Weill, excited at his new friendship with Charlie Chaplin, "loves Hollywood because he feels that here people know their jobs thoroughly and are experts." Further, she does not believe Kazan's stated indifference to film-making; it seems to her he is eager to direct pictures. However, everyone is pointed toward a new Group Theatre season in New York as Odets works on his new play. Jules Garfield has written confidentially that he is to play Odets' violinist-prizefighter who must decide between his music and success in the ring.

The flood of passionate letters, personal and ideological, between East and West Coast Group members leaves no doubt that the powerful pull of the film industry was inescapable (for everyone except Molly Day Thacher, Kazan's wife, a Puritan conscience for all) and that the longing to reconstitute the Group on some basis was warring with that pull. Odets was by no means alone in his hope that income from film activities could support serious Group work in the New York legitimate theatre.

Within a twenty-four-hour period Paula Strasberg received two shattering letters: a short one from Cheryl Crawford stating simply, "I have decided to leave the Group. The internal situation seems to me incapable of solution," and a longer one from her husband, saying he has also decided to leave the Group and that he may join Cheryl in her new producing unit in the theatre ("If she can't make money at that," he adds, "she can then go into the movies").

To Elia Kazan, Strasberg writes scathingly and at great length about "the vicious circle of responsibility and irresponsibility":

> It is, unfortunately . . . , a little too late to start talking things over. . . . So I will try to be . . . frank in my expression. . . . I absolutely agree with practically everything you say. If you were somebody else I would feel greatly encouraged. But *you* are now the Group theatre.** What are you doing to carry all that out? . . . Perhaps I am slighting your activity but who is going to do all this work? You plan to go to Russia and when you come back you'll be ready to start work. And what about the other people who are not going and must make their plans in the meantime. . . . It isn't the inside of the Group theatre—*that* may need reorganization if only because of the very bad lack of authority on anyone's part. But will that make the Group situation much different? That as far as I am concerned is the real problem and towards that you all manifest a not utterly charming naivete (forgive the irony—Cliff doesn't like that in me—an expression of my feeling of superiority). . . .
>
> As far as I'm concerned I shall not write you personally about the Group anymore. . . . My regards to Cliff and Luise. (You shouldn't have criticized the Good Earth—I hear she cried.)

Although Strasberg wanted to believe that his decision to leave the Group was "objective," it's evident from this letter to Kazan that he is wounded; that he feels excluded and unappreciated. Out of patience with Clurman's passivity, Strasberg had come to the decision that he could wait no longer.

It cannot have been easy for a man who felt himself to have been the founding father of the Group Theatre to thus relinquish it. To his wife he

---

* Here he means the Actors' Committee.

wrote in his usual defensive first-person plural: "since we in the East anticipated the possibility of the picture being put off, it perhaps doesn't hit
us with the same personal shock." This vulnerable and deep-feeling man
could never afford to be caught off guard. Odets would see past this shield
only much later. Until then their relationship would remain, as it was now,
distant.

Clurman, close geographically and spiritually to the unwitting pivot
of power in this situation—namely, Odets, who was writing a new play—
concluded that Strasberg's accusation that the actors had destroyed the
Group's leadership "was itself an admission of incapacity for leadership."
Thus he accepted the resignations from Lee Strasberg and Cheryl Crawford
"with a kind of friendly fatalism." It would take several more weeks of
fruitless struggle with Stella Adler, of "profound unhappiness" at the
thought of facing once more his father's despair about his economic problems, and of encouraging letters to return (now from both Kazans) before
Clurman would risk coming back East as sole director of the Group and of
Odets' new play, its title changed again to "Golden Fleece."

Odets discussed this Group crisis with Luther Adler, with Kazan, with
Clurman, and (for endless hours, to Luise's immense irritation) with
J. Edward Bromberg and his wife, Goldie. But in a curious way Odets stood
outside the underlying struggle between Strasberg and Clurman. Although
he confided to Luise his resentment that "Harold is always trying to be my
intellectual father," and that "he is a schnorrer, never pays me the money
he owes me," his deep and dependent respect for Clurman was never
stronger than it was as he continued to work on the prizefighter play. To
Group actor Bobby Lewis, Odets writes an impulsively affectionate letter
projecting into Lewis his own lonely need:

> Bobby darling, what are you doing and where are you? Can you use a
> hundred dollars? Are you in any want? Are you unhappy? Write and
> confess all to your friend of old, Clifford, and your friend of new—
> Luise. . . .
>
> Saw Harold the other night and we were both dissatisfied with
> The Silent Partner as the first of our new Group productions because
> it hasn't in it the elements of popular success and you know what I
> mean.
>
> So I ran upstairs and brought down a sheet of paper I had sketched
> in a cab coming home from Paramount the day before—my Para-
> mount!—and lo and behold we both agreed that it was the play to do
> first and that very night I wrote the first half of the first ten scenes,
> altho Harold doesn't know it yet. Here is the thing—if we have a good
> popular play (and this one has more audience appeal than even Awake
> and Sing!) we don't need to work out new Group problems and plans
> —the success of the first production will take care of so much! . . .
>
> Wherever you are now—do not despair of anything. Perhaps in
> this quiet night you are despairing somewhere and that is the thing
> which was winged to me and made me suddenly, for no practical rea-
> son, sit down and start this letter to you. We will all be together soon
> and with the good ones of The Group should make something even
> better than before.
>
> Write soon and I send you love and friendship,
>   Clifford

In this early version of *Golden Boy* the protagonist is an uncertain,
passive, diffident boy of seventeen or nineteen, terrified of coming to grips
with his idealist father, who wants him to pursue a career in music rather

than in the punishing, moneymaking prizefight ring (a reversal, of course, of Odets' overt history with his father). This respectful young man is significantly different from the final version of the twenty-one-year-old character of Joe Bonaparte who is urgently—if defensively—belligerent, clearly rent by the contradictions within him, and warily resentful of being steadily used by a variety of men who are manipulating him for their own ends. Odets is simultaneously trying to master in this play the social and historical dimension (he calls it a "modern allegory") as well as the personal conflicts in his complex relation to his father, to his new wife, to the Group, and also to the hard world of "big business" he had lately entered in Hollywood.

As he diligently worked also on the screenplay of the Civil War film *Gettysburg* for Paramount, Odets exhibited a naïve sincerity of application and a singular depth of purpose. The film's producer, Albert Lewin, a man of dry intelligence, had been recently booted out of MGM by Louis B. Mayer, who disapproved of his having been a member of the late Irving Thalberg's snobbishly intellectual court. Accustomed to cynicism in a serious playwright turned screenwriter, Lewin was startled by Odets' hopes that *Gettysburg* would be much better than his two previous film efforts and would "have some sadness of life in it." The humor, Odets thought, was "only movie humor," but, he told Group actor Bobby Lewis, "the sadness is real, oddly enough, or naturally enough."

To Jay Adler he writes of his salary of $2,500 a week: "Abe Lincoln and I ain't worth that much together." As would become his obsessional practice, Odets let this film script become longer and longer as he tried to improve it. He seemed unable to accomplish this, and the mammoth screenplay, with its torrent of colorful, lively dialogue, would soon be shelved, along with *The Loves of Jeanne Ney*.

Despite his writing talent and his keen interest in the craft of filmmaking, Odets found it difficult to adapt his gift efficiently to this production line. Had he been more versatile (or less), his life's struggle would not have become so pained. He seemed unable to learn, as his fight-promoter in *Golden Boy* put it, that an Einstein belongs "in a college" and that "in the prizefight ring the cash customer don't look for stoodents." Like the torn young hero in *Golden Boy*, which he was bootlegging on studio time, he could not throw himself wholeheartedly into the work of writing a motion picture. To write a "hit play" for the Group Theatre was another matter. He was determined it would be entertaining, earn money, and yet be a serious and honest statement of his own state of being.

Before starting his night shift of work, he would frequently abandon Luise for a card game with Ira Gershwin, or for a conference with Kazan, Clurman, or Luther Adler about *Golden Boy*. It was a male camaraderie such as he had enjoyed in the Bronx with the Beck Street Boys. These meetings even had a conspiratorial quality as the manuscript of *Golden Boy* grew on studio time—in Kazan's words, "under the very nose of Paramount." Kazan recalled the atmosphere as similar to that in 1934 when the writer-actors who called themselves SKKOB had, in defiant revolt against the three Group directors, worked on Odets' swiftly accomplished propaganda piece *Waiting for Lefty*.

In the collaborative atmosphere of a rebellious brotherhood, which always diluted his loneliness and nourished his productivity, Odets could half-perform the scenes he was writing rather than face alone the anxious limbo of a writer whose current work has not yet taken fire. There was a safety for him in such collaboration, standing thus between the professional identities of actor and writer, and the reassurance he derived from an immediate and positive response from a rebellious Group "family" was incalculable. Besides, as he often said, "Anger, defiance mobilize me."

When Kazan left for New York, it appeared likely to him that Odets would soon follow to deliver his new play, or most of it. Kazan enlisted the aid of Jules Garfield, playing then on Broadway in Arthur Kober's *Having Wonderful Time*. From Garfield, Odets promptly received the kind of encouragement on which he thrived:

> If only we could open our reopening with a play by you it would be ideal—the new "one" seems like a swell story. Oh, if only you could bring it to life by September, we'd do anything. I mean myself, Gadget, Molly.* I feel frankly, that no important American play has been written since "Lefty" and "Awake" and that's no shit! You should see the crap that's being handed out here.
>
> I do want to say that in order to point a play socially in these days it's important to remember that the punch and drive of real honest facts can no longer be fed to the theatre—they want to laugh and I feel the point can be made and they can still laugh. I think that's the new trick . . . I shall keep writing semimonthly to check up on the new play—Perhaps it will serve as a small reminder that there is one guy who's hoping, praying and laying awake nites, that, that new child of yours will come to life!

Garfield, like the others in the Group, was concerned that Odets' new play be a commercial success. He took it for granted that he would play the lead role, not, as it would turn out, the minor comedy character Siggie, symbol of the uncomplicated, lusty, normal American young man about whom Odets had written in his bulging separate file for *Golden Boy* characters: "The halvah king of Brooklyn gives a bar mitzvah party for his son and prominently displayed is a bust of his son in halvah."

L. J. Odets writes again about Clurman, "Harold is your worst enemy," and from Luise, Clifford hears, "You surround yourself with people who lie to you or look up to you and say you are a genius. . . . Awake and sing! and get as clear a sense of critique for yourself as you have for others. . . . I cannot live on your side because I would only be happy with you if I would lie to you. I won't do it . . . you have the greatest talent of any one person I know. Grow, develop and open your eyes."

Meanwhile, in growing despair at her own lonely struggles with Louis B. Mayer ("Why," he had asked her, "do you not sit on my lap when we talk contracts, like my other stars do?") she tried a variety of strategies with her husband. When she demanded his advice about her dealings with Mayer, he would frequently walk out of their ensuing discussions, especially when she accused him of siding with "Mayer and his henchmen"; sometimes he would counsel her that "big industries like the movies are not something to have tremendous hopes and ideals about," and "when one is dealing with manufacturers and merchants, what is completely necessary is REALISM . . . to hold in front of you like a shield!" Luise would reply, "You don't argue reasonable." Somewhere she knew that even when he talked to her he was not actually focused on *her* problems with Louis B. Mayer but on his *own* life and work.

Their greatest relaxation had long been listening to records, but Luise found bizarre her husband's compulsive necessity constantly to play music at top volume. She felt that his need for loud music stemmed from the fact that there was little harmony in him. "This steady intake of music became such an irritant to me that it created more a wall than a bond," said Luise.

---

* Elia Kazan and his wife, Molly Day Thacher.

Sometimes all protective buffers would collapse, and at times, she recalled,

> Cliff's rages and his screaming seemed unbearable, I was not permitted to open my mouth. After work when I was dead tired from ten hours at the studio I did not dare go to my own house. He would be there sulking. He was jealous of everything. I did not know what to do. I would drive past my own house and slowly go up alone for walks in the hills. Much later I would return frightened. He was able not to talk for days.

Finally, after an especially bitter exchange, he shouted at Luise, "You will have to earn my love to deserve it!" He later recorded, ". . . when I wanted to hit Luise in the heat of an argument, I hit myself instead, pulled my own hair, banged my fists against the walls." This time, after Luise insisted that he "leave my house," he did, taking with him only a toothbrush, establishing himself on Van Ness Avenue as "C. Oak." Three years later he reconstructed the event in his diary:

> In my loneliness here last week I remembered a secretary I had met who worked at one of the studios. Split from Luise, I moved to two ugly hot rooms near the studio and lived there in even a deeper stupor than the one in which I find myself now. This young lady was helpful; in the afternoon she took my dictation at the studio; in the evening she came to my rooms in California slacks, a silk shirt and a red ribbon twisted in her chestnut hair. We slept together painfully and passionately—I think she was sorry for me in part. We drank scotch and water out of green glasses and she called me Mr. Odets even while we were in bed, until I suggested otherwise. She admired me, her eyes big and frightened, said she thought me charming. She had shaved off her pubic hair. I asked her why—"Summer, cool," she said. I suspected that it made her feel devilish, artistic and creative, since she mentioned several times that artists' models always did that. Sultry excitement, outstanding breasts (the adjective exact!), more scotch and water, pantingly hot nights—we lasted that way for several weeks. Early one morning Luise came there. . . . I was living there under an assumed name (oh, the disgrace of everything then!).

Luise recalled this one-room kind of "garlow"* as a dingy, dirty place which was appalling. Nonetheless, "as I loved him, I got him out of it."

In this distressed period a letter arrived for Luise from photographer–art dealer Alfred Stieglitz that clearly resonated with her own view of her relationship with Odets:

> My dear Luise Rainer:
>   The day before I left New York your beautiful letter came . . . I understood only too well. I knew when you were in New York what was inevitable. And your first letter to me, what a cry it was for a love worthy of your own love. In the papers I read you had signed up with Hollywood for 7 years and I hoped that this time (it was) on your own adequate terms. Then somebody said to me that you were with child—and in a way I was horrified for I didn't believe that C. was worthy to be the father of *your* child—that is, that he had not earned that right. And then I thought, but Luise Rainer is a woman throughout and all of her cries out for a child from the man she loves. And even if she sees the man truly and knows his love is not equal to hers, in her

---

* A Midwestern word which combines "garage" and "bungalow."

madness she feels she might gain the kind of love she needs by giving him the privilege of becoming father of her child. So you see, I saw you as pregnant and happy, too, with a seven-year contract—even though I knew that in reality you were not happy. How one struggles to get a glimpse of real light anywhere. . . .

I see by the newspapers that your film is announced in New York for tomorrow night . . . I like to think of you. It gives me a nicer feeling about the world when my spirits are low and life seems as unnecessarily sad. O'Keeffe is here. She leaves for New Mexico in a week—I'll be here all summer.*

By the middle of July, Odets had submitted several movie ideas,◖ and had refused a $500-a-week raise offered by Paramount to keep him in Hollywood. On one brightly sunlit California morning, he boarded the Super Chief with Luther Adler, en route to his apartment in New York, leaving his marriage behind again, to pursue his work. To Adler he said of his marital problems, "It's always us, us, us. Fuck us!"

Luise wanted to call it "permanent quits," and Clifford—in a peculiarly detached letter written as he was leaving Hollywood—begged her to reconsider.

He could not tolerate it when she called it quits, nor could he bear the shame, outraged vanity, and human failure in a divorce. Part of him was still, in his words, "a family man without a family." He writes:

You don't want me to see you. You are wrathful, indignant. At what, Darling? That one tried to make something good? I can't believe that.

Luise, I have never stopped feeling married to you in these past weeks. I shall go on feeling that way until you say *no*. And you have practically said *no* in a hundred different ways by now. You do not want to wait until the Summer is over. You want immediate stability. . . . Write to me please, to N.Y., at the apartment. We have been painful to each other. But mostly you have suffered. No further pain is needed or wanted. If you are afraid of continuance, write and tell me so. If you can't or don't want to be apart for two more months, write and tell me. If you want to say, "Rather than more pain I say no—finished—this minute," tell me so.

Please write me your plans. Will you go to Europe? to N.Y.? I want to know for myself—and secondly I want to be able to tell people what you are doing when they ask—no one knows we are apart. Unless you want people to know it—I don't think that is wise for you at the moment. . . .

You burn in me with a steady flame, Darling, but don't let my feeling influence you. . . .

Anyway, Darling, openly, hands down and sadly, Your Clifford . . . . Tell me anything you want me to do for you, Luise.

From Hutchinson, Kansas, he sent her an unsigned wire: "How painful, how painful, how very painful."

In the same mail she received a copy of *Modern Screen* containing a long piece about her headed "Rainer the Rebel," with the subheading "Luise wouldn't give a dime for glamor but she'd spend a fortune fighting for happiness." It is remarkable how in this shabby monthly, proud of its "largest circulation of any screen magazine," the writer manages to cap-

---

* As this book was going to press, Miss Rainer sent this 43-year-old letter requesting its inclusion: "I think it is rather *very* relevant!! and Stieglitz, in those days, as also today, was and is as vital a personality as Clifford."
◖ 20.1.

ture much about this "arresting personality, this small, unpretentious dynamo in slacks and short-sleeved blouse, with dark eyes and windblown bob."

It is evident from the interview that Luise is obsessed with her development as an artist and her embattled position at the Metro-Goldwyn-Mayer, where she is refusing "to play trash." "They call me a Frankenstein that will destroy the studio," she said. "What can I spoil if I'm true to myself? I cannot do what for me is wrong," concluding that the day she compromises herself she will have to commit suicide, and that "it is more important to me to be a human than to be an actress." She is sorry that the press regards her as "high-hat." It is just that she prefers to be known through her work. "I don't want success that goes—swish—up and then down. Does that sound proud? It is only the proudness of an honest shoe-maker in his shoes." In spite of her strength, she concludes, "It is so easy for me to have an inferiority complex. Mr. Odets always laughs about that. . . . Success does not have much to do with happiness."

Arrived in New York, Odets called a girl he had known as a child in the Bronx. She, a bright, sad-faced orphan, had been in their dining-room "shows" and become a worker for the Theatre Union and now for Orson Welles' energetic and thriving Mercury Theatre. During Odets' abortive and hostile effort to seduce her, he told her his ideas for a play about a dentist. It had occurred to him as he sat that day in a dentist's chair, "How many dentists did I pass on my way from the West Coast? All the time I am going here, there, everywhere—seeing new things—these little dentists all over remain in the same office with the same chair, same equipment, same spittoon—all half dead or submerged like an iceberg." When she showed interest in the idea, he generously offered it to her "free of charge," only to become furious when she later made it into a play which was considered for production; Odets then denied he had given her permission to use it.

This plot is the first hint of his own quite different "dentist play" that evolved this year as *Rocket to the Moon*. It would center, he thought, on the hapless, drab, meek, frustrated little dentist who is unhappy because his work has no meaning. He derives from it only the "pleasure of a crafts-man." The dentist's painful, unsuccessful efforts to leave his nagging wife and to find love with his silly little technician would make up the bulk of the play. Its center of gravity would shift radically, however, with the cur-rents of Odets' relationship to Luise.

It appears that neither Odets nor Luise was ready to dissolve their union, even though both suffered equally and felt equal responsibilities toward their work. Two weeks after he went East she flew to New York to make plans for a summer with Clifford where the newspapers were hailing him as "the unextinguished White Hope of the American Theatre." In a rented cottage on Fire Island and one in Southampton he had finished al-most two acts of *Golden Boy*, and appeared to her to be in much better spirits than in Hollywood and, creatively, she thought, "in full strength."

Chapter Twenty-One

When did you look in the mirror last?
Getting to be a killer! You're getting
to be like Fuseli! You're not the boy I
cared about, not you. You murdered
that boy with the generous face—God
knows where you hid the body! I don't
know you.

CLIFFORD ODETS, 1937

WITH the writing of *Golden Boy*, subtitled in the earlier draft "a modern allegory," Odets was returning to New York on what he called his "schedule of a couple of plays and one picture a year," and to what he knew to be his central calling, that of Writer for the Legitimate Theatre. Awed by the creative potential in films, he thought, however, he would express and celebrate the American spirit in *both* media. But even now, still innocent of the corrupting nature of the film industry, he knew he felt freer writing for the stage.

The bitter autobiographical paradox inherent in every line of this terse, tightly constructed, funny American morality play lay in its growing creative mastery and its prophecy of the step-by-step unfolding of the doom of a talented young violinist determined to become "Somebody" in America.◖ Not quite twenty-one, the hero (seventeen years old in Odets' first draft) finds himself unable to tolerate the risks and the humiliation of being an impotent if gifted "freak" in a savagely competitive society. Another early title was "A Cockeyed Wonder." The protagonist, Joe Bonaparte, son of an Italian immigrant, expresses his enraged and vengeful determination to become a normal American, to belong, to gain power, and, above all, "not to be ashamed of my life." He can be unashamed only if he "makes it" with a great "success." Joe abandons his artistic conscience and irrevocably cripples his musical talent by breaking his musician's hands in the prizefight ring. Finally, having murdered an opponent in the ring, he seeks peace, perhaps redemption, in suicide. By destroying himself he accomplishes at the same time his revenge on those who have made of him a negotiable commodity, whether as a "silver mine" for his fight manager or as a "gun" for his owner, a gangster. As Joe drives to his death with his boss's mistress in a powerful automobile which "mows down the night," he not only destroys himself but also, in grief, stills forever the

◖ 21.1.

inner voice of his creative conscience represented by his father, who wants his son to do only "whatsa in his true nature." His suicide is an effort to restore in death the sure sense of belonging, of the "paradise lost" of infancy. Odets once more is trying to offer proof for the proposition he enacts in his life: that twentieth-century America destroys its artists and prophets.

Clurman, of whom Odets said, "He understands *Golden Boy* better than I do," put its theme in a somewhat different way:

> The story of this play is not so much the story of a prize-fighter as the picture of a great fight—a fight in which we are all involved. . . . What the golden boy of this allegory is fighting for is a place in the world as an individual; *what he wants is to free his ego from the scorn that attaches to "nobodies" in a society in which every activity is viewed in the light of a competition* [italics mine]. He wants success not simply for the soft life . . . which he talks about, but because the acclaim that goes with it promises him acceptance by the world, peace with it, safety from becoming the victim that it makes of the poor, the alien, the unnoticed minorities. To achieve this success, he must exploit an accidental attribute of his make-up, a mere skill, and abandon the development of his real self.

Odets himself downgraded the dense and contrapuntal projection of the struggles among his "gallery of characters" in *Golden Boy*, seeing it essentially as a craftily engineered melodrama with a sharply compelling story line."* In truth, its expression of American consciousness is of a subtler order than the dashed-off *Waiting for Lefty*, routinely reprinted in college anthologies as representative not only of his work but also of the best of the "social drama of the thirties."

The metaphors in *Golden Boy*—representing the conflict between authentic human experience and simply "making it" as an art-technician—so vividly expressed, according to Elia Kazan, "what all of us felt at the time" that they would be copied and recopied until they would finally become the stale movie clichés of Artistic Integrity versus Material Success. Nonetheless, these Odets characters, their wisdom, their pain, and their jokes, remain richly alive, as their derivatives, in the countless formula plays and films which came after, do not. Thirty years after it was written, *Golden Boy* would be recognized as one of the first American existentialist plays.

It is indeed a prophetic paradigm of the unraveling of the American Dream, a world-image of redemption through Success on a rapidly changing path of upward mobility, a road unthinkable without the Gun and the Machine. It is not fortuitous that Joe Bonaparte's wasteful and meaningless death is a self-destruction in his powerful and expensive automobile, his beloved Duesenberg. The "winner" ends as a "loser."

America was still in the grip of the economic Depression and Roosevelt's ameliorative New Deal, and the flirtations with full-scale war had not yet reached proportions significant enough to revive economic support for the Dream. In the 1920s, after one worldwide military victory, the Dream *had* revived, as it shortly would again with the necessity to bring about a second such victory, and falteringly thereafter into the days of the New Frontier. Perhaps *only* in this period of as yet warless Depression was it possible for a playwright to set forth so sharply as did Odets the beginning of the end of the American Dream.◖

---

* In his personal copy of the published play he wrote, "My copy—poor as it may be. Xmas, 1937."

◖ 21.2.

From the first line of the twelve scenes of *Golden Boy*—often called by critics "cinematic"—the people Odets looses at one another are highly condensed in their psychological reality and in their representation of his own warring identity-elements. Odets always said to his students, "Go for the jugular!"

The play opens with a man saying to a woman, "Pack up your clothes and go! Go! Who the hell's stopping you?" He is the fight manager Tom Moody, and he combines in his person conscious aspects of Odets' identity-elements ("I was always a *moody* child," he often said) and his current struggle, like that of his parents, to preserve and to abandon his marriage. Most important, Moody's personality is derived from that aspect of Odets' father which was eager to seduce anyone, even a son, into being his "silver mine." Yet, writes Odets in the stage directions, reflecting another side of his resonance with this character, his "explosiveness covers a soft, boyish quality, and . . . he has a certain vulnerable quality which women find very attractive."

Moody's mistress, an orphan named Lorna Moon (her first name deriving from the words "forlorn" and "lovelorn,"* her surname from the eternal symbol of cool, inhospitable, unattainable Woman◖), has a "quiet glitter" about her, and if she is sometimes hard, "it is more from necessity than choice." Her eyes, however, often "hold a soft, sad glance" (again like Odets' depressed mother's and his own). Lorna Moon is like most of the significant women in Odets' life: feminine, vulnerable, and psychologically or actually "orphaned." At the same time she is tough (even "masculine") in her capacity to fend for herself in a competitive world and to become involved in casual sex.

Moody and Lorna Moon are battling; the woman—a "tramp from Newark" whom he has rescued ("Misery reached out to misery")—is pleading to cement their bond in marriage, the man giving reasons why it is not possible.† Moody says he needs (like Odets' father) a "resurrection" in order to restore his 1928 pre-Depression "gold standard." "Find me a good black boy,"‡ he says, "and I'll show you a mint."

Instead of a mint in the form of a "good black boy," Fate delivers to fight manager Moody a *disrespectful* outcast ("*Respect* is all I ask from children," L. J. Odets always said), a lonely "cock-eyed wonder" named Joe Bonaparte, "like in Napoleon." The fragmented chief protagonist of the play, he is on the one hand small, shy ("like a wild animal"), inferior-feeling, and on the other a would-be conqueror. The name "Bonaparte" suggests both "the good part" and "apart," a son of the revolution and its enemy. Moody must sing a "siren song"§ to this boy in order to seduce him into real fighting. For this he uses Lorna, as well as promises of fame and fortune. At the play's climax this oddball, cross-eyed child of an Italian immigrant (read a Russian-Jewish-American artist) kills in the fight ring an innocent "good black boy," a "poor guy with . . . sleepy little eyes," symbol once again for the playwright's murder of his own natural, inno-

---

* He called his first typewriter "Lovelorn Corona" and talked of it as of a mistress.

◖ 21.3.

† Thirteen years later Odets recalled during his psychoanalysis the "stickiness" when as a child he could not give his mother the adult loving response she was demanding. By this time L. J. Odets had told him—as immediately after Pearl's death he told his daughter—that their mother was "a tramp" who had given him a venereal disease.

‡ Symbol of the victimized outcast.

§ Psychoanalyst Henry A. Murray has noted the bisexual symbol of the siren, as a minor god associated with Death, depicted with the head, bust, and arms of a woman but the body of a bird!

cent, and creative self, "that boy with the generous face." It is precisely this murder of an outcast, a "nobody," which makes Joe "a contender." The formal line of this play—from beginning to end—is tight and consistent. Joe Bonaparte's demonstrated capacity (and wish) to destroy the "good black boy" (the innocent outcast within himself) ends his capacity to create music. As he cannot tolerate the murderer within him, or return to his violin, he must join in vengeful death the older, maternal Lorna, a "tramp" who belongs to his father-surrogate, fight manager Moody. Joe's father (actually a maternal figure) closes the play with, "Come, we bring-a him home . . . where he belong." Like Eugene O'Neill,* Odets maintained the fantasy that only in death could there be a restoration of that union, that secure belonging, that lost paradise of mutuality inhabited by a mother and an infant son.

One of Joe Bonaparte's first wisecracks is about another fighter who has just broken his hands: "If Kaplan's mother fed him milk, he wouldn't have those brittle bones." (A man breaks—becomes fragmented—if he has not been well nourished by the first woman in his life.) The second-act curtain and turning point of the play is Joe's breaking *his* musician's hands in the ring. "Hallelujah!" he wildly shouts. "It's the beginning of the world!" This breaking of his bones is the beginning for him of one world, the murderously competitive one, and the end of another, the creatively fulfilling one. His violin case becomes now, indeed, "a coffin for a baby," a baby whose bones would not have been brittle had his mother not abandoned or betrayed him. Odets often expressed the conviction that a steady and strengthening legacy of unambivalent mutuality with his mother would have enabled him to withstand the terrifying, seductive, and engulfing Power of the world of his father. He would thus have been content to be "a real sparrow," and not have been driven to become a "fake eagle." Whether or not it is literally true, as he always maintained, that his mother had wanted to abandon him to a farmer, the determining fact is that Odets *believed* she had. In *Golden Boy*, Mama Bonaparte is dead and "was a big nuisance right up till the day she died."

Odets distributes his father's complex identity-elements, and accordingly his own, among several characters besides Moody, the fight manager. By far the most interesting and significant of these is Eddie Fuseli, "a renowned gambler and gunman" who "shoots you for a nickel—then for fifty bucks he sends you flowers." (In Clurman's words, "Clifford's father, like all cruel men, is extremely sentimental.") Modeled physically after radio announcer Floyd Neale,† who years back had taken a paternal interest in Odets and who, he said, had tentatively tried to seduce him, Fuseli is lean and graying at the temples. His interest in owning "a piece of that boy"— seventy percent, in fact—is not, like manager Moody's, primarily for the money, but for the narcissistic triumph of owning someone who is, like himself, a downtrodden "Eyetalian" who could be "a contender for Number One" and who could even "win the crown." The gunman, who had acquired his weapon in "the war," is described as a "queer" and, in Odets' production notes, as "the loneliest man in the play." Fuseli's misogyny is explicit and bitter ("Don't ask me which is worst, women or spiders"), as are his seductive overtures to Joe, from his possessive forms of address ("Sweet," "Sweetest," "Sweetheart") to his lavish praise and gifts. Says Eddie to Joe: "He wears the best, eats the best, sleeps the best. He walks down the street respected—the golden boy . . . and I done it for him!"‡

---

* Compare O'Neill's *Diff'rent* and *The Hairy Ape*.
† We know this from Odets' scattered notes for the characters of *Golden Boy*.
‡ This sentence is eerily like L. J. Odets' wild claims after his son's death.

Odets gave Elia Kazan, whom he chose to play Fuseli, a profile of the lonely reptilian gunman who "really understands" Joe. He regarded as central to this seductive gangster in his narcissistic and possessive love of the boy an identity-element drawn from his own father. Indeed, the life-long, overt, physical tenderness between Odets and Kazan led many who did not know either man to believe mistakenly that they were lovers. To himself he writes of Fuseli:

> His main activity is to hunt for possession. In order to understand the activity you must understand the background. It is the background of the downtrodden Wop. It develops a furtiveness. Every actor can find the equivalent because every one has something about which he is sensitive. Eddie was brought up in a rough neighborhood where the boys used to fight. His homosexuality may be only partly conscious. In the war he found the way out in the hunt for possession. His dominant mood is loneliness. The war taught him that no one does anything except from fear and a desire for power or gain. He distrusts everyone, even the people he loves. Also distrusts Joe. This gives him adjustments of furtiveness, carefulness, and watchfulness. He doesn't pal around with other gangsters or with anybody except if he needs them. He is a bird of prey. He should be as tall as possible, taller than Luther. Eddie should be the most stylised performance in the play. There is no vulgarity of the bum in him. Life has created something evil out of him. He has developed a personality which doesn't even mingle with his own racket. People don't trust him, and he doesn't mind it. He has developed a certain pride and almost elegance. He has a refined way of talking, not vulgar. Almost delicate in an aloof way, but back of it is a lot of dynamite. He is completely shut off from other people. Doesn't even want to handle the details of the fight. The reason he is anxious to have a champ is that he would be *Eddie's boy to be proud of* [italics mine]. He would have dominance over him and possession. His love has a certain element of pride. "He depends on me and he needs me." The part should be carefully dressed. Elegant without too much vulgarity. A real nattiness—George Raft. When Joe gets dressed up it is more vulgar than when Eddie gets dressed up. Eddie's clothes are just a little bit off. His good dress comes from pride and disdain. He is sharp and careful. His room is probably neat and bare, almost classic in bareness and sharpness. His gun and knife are right at hand, and very handsome.

The symbolic charge on Fuseli's possession of the gun and the knife in his ascetic room is high. Toward the end of the play, when Joe's desperation erupts, he sees "a crowd of Eddies all around me, suffocating me, burying me in good times and silk shirts," and he cries, "I want some personal life." Eddie's response to this is, "I give Bonaparte a good personal life. I got loyalty to his cause . . ." and Joe finally shouts, "*You use me like a gun!* [italics mine] Your loyalty's to keep me oiled and polished!"

A gun, like a knife, is an archetypal symbol of intrusive, destructive masculine power, used to kill or to defend against a sense of impotence.* It has become a commonplace even outside the psychoanalyst's office that in fantasy or dream the gun, the knife, the rod, the sword, the locomotive, the powerful automobile may represent an intrusive phallus. Thus, when Joe screams his frantic accusation at Eddie ("You use me like a gun!"), it

---

* Ten years later, in his play *The Big Knife*, as well as in an unfinished piece, "Manslaughter," the same symbolism emerges: the wish for and terror of being "screwed" by a powerful father.

is no longer simply Odets' grief and rage at being generally used by his father, but specifically his sense of having been narcissistically groomed as a well-oiled and destructive bodily appendage to compensate for his father's felt deficiencies—sexual and otherwise—and certainly to express his rage at, and his need to dominate, women. ("I don't like no one to laugh at that boy," says Eddie.) Joe says, "If music shot bullets I'd like it better." Odets is having difficulty integrating his yearning to create esthetic harmony with his need for raw, male, aggressive power.◖

Odets yearns to be not his father's conforming gun but an appreciated expressive instrument like his Uncle Israel's voice or Joe's violin; it is the same psychological ground that was occupied by Ralph and his idealist grandfather in *Awake and Sing!** As Jacob wanted his grandson honestly to explore his own nature, so Poppa Bonaparte wants his son to find "truthful success."

Joe has taught this immigrant father that "Music is the great cheer-up in the language of all countries," and having practiced for ten years, he has won a scholarship and a gold medal for playing "the best in the city." During this time his father has painfully managed to scrape together $1,200 (a fortune in the Depression) to buy his son a good violin for his twenty-first birthday. The father's sweetness and innocent hopefulness are nowhere more poignant than when he learns his son is planning a career in prizefighting instead, and thus he is unable to surprise him with the wherewithal for a career as a musician. The pessimistic, misogynous philosopher Carp† sadly says:

> Fortunes! I used to hear it in my youth—the streets of America is paved with gold. Say, you forgot to give him the present.

MR. BONAPARTE
(*Slowly, puzzled*)

I don'ta know . . . he say he gonna fight. . . .

This slow, gentle, sad, and loving man who introduces himself, "My name is Joe Bonaparte's father," has a strong maternal quality, reminiscent often of Pearl Geisinger Odets, and provides one of the most wrenching father-son confrontations in the literature of American drama as Joe makes clear to him his choice:

MR. BONAPARTE
(*Brings the violin case from its
hiding place in the buffet.*)

Joe, I buy you this some time ago. Don't give cause I don't know whatta you gonna do. Take him with you now. Play for yourself. It gonna remember you your old days of musical life. (JOE *puts down the suitcase and picks up the violin. He plucks the strings, he tightens one of them. In spite of the tension his face turns soft and tender.*)

LORNA
(*Watching intently*)

We better not miss the train—Tokio's waiting.

MR. BONAPARTE
(*Of violin*)

Take him with you, Joe.

◖ 21.4.
* In notes for the play Odets says "Poppa Bonaparte is sort of a Jacob character."
† Carp is the character who has said no word to his wife in seven years and wonders can it be natural to play baseball ("Hit a ball, catch a ball . . . believe me, my friend—nonsense!").

JOE

It's beautiful. . . .

MR. BONAPARTE

Practise on the road. (JOE *abruptly turns and with the violin exits.*
The others listen, each standing in his place, as rich violin music
comes from the other room. JOE *returns. There is silence as he places*
the violin on the table in front of his father.)

JOE
(*In a low voice*)

Return it, poppa.

ANNA
(*Hugging* JOE)

Have a good trip, Joey.

CARP

Eat in good restaurants. . . . (*There is silence: the* FATHER *and* SON
look at each other. The others in the room sense the drama between
the two. Finally:)

JOE

I have to do this, poppa.

MR. BONAPARTE
(*To* JOE)

Be careful fora your hands.

JOE

Poppa, give me the word—

MR. BONAPARTE

What word?

JOE

Give me the word to go ahead. You're looking at yesterday—I see tomorrow. Maybe you think I ought to spend my whole life here—you
and Carp blowing off steam.

MR. BONAPARTE
(*Holding himself back*)

Oh, Joe, shut your mouth!

JOE

Give me the word to go ahead!

MR. BONAPARTE

Be careful fora your hands!

JOE

I want you to give me the word!

MR. BONAPARTE
(*Crying out*)

No! No word! You gonna fight? All right! Okay! But I don't gonna give
no word! No!

JOE

That's how you feel?

MR. BONAPARTE

That'sa how I feel! (MR. BONAPARTE's *voice breaks and there is noth-*
ing for father and son to do but to clutch each other in a hasty em-
brace. Finally MR. BONAPARTE *disentangles himself and turns away.*
JOE *abruptly grabs up his suitcase and exits.* LORNA *follows, stopping*
at the door to look back at MR. BONAPARTE.)

The maternal identity-element in Joe's father is underscored by his
alliance with Lorna (the fight manager's mistress), who, like him, does not
really want to "use" Joe as a commodity. Mr. Bonaparte, unlike the other

men, does not hate women or, indeed, life itself. When Carp, the angry philosopher who sells penny candies, asks him, "What's the use to try . . . for every wish we get, ten remains unsatisfied. Death is playing with us as a cat and her mouse," he replies, "You make-a me laugh, Mr. Carp. You say life'sa bad. No, life'sa good." Odets himself believed firmly in both positions, a stand similar to O'Neill's "hopeless hope" in *The Iceman Cometh.*

Carp asks about Joe's brother, Frank (the ghost of Odets' idealist union organizer Lefty), "What's it his business if the workers in textiles don't make good wages?" In sharp contrast to Joe's individual, ambitiously self-centered fighting, Poppa Bonaparte replies, "Frank, he fighta for eat, for good life. Why not!" Carp snaps, "Foolish!" It is here that the old man delivers the famous Odets trademark line, "What ever you got ina your nature to do isa not foolish!" In this vestige of Odets' earlier hope for salvation, redemption, through membership in a revolutionary Christian brotherhood, there is a deep and wistful sense of loss. *The Silent Partner*, with its united striking workers, was still in his "active" file. Before leaving Hollywood, however, Clurman and he had agreed that "it hasn't in it the elements of popular success."

As when he was writing the film script of *The General Died at Dawn* and found the character of the Hitlerian Chinese warlord "running away with him," as Milestone put it, so now he found it difficult to detach from Eddie Fuseli and his seduction of Joe. "There is in this part," he wrote, "a dialectic contradiction. In Eddie, who "shoots like a Roman candle," it is

that when a man is completely self-possessed but not completely satisfied, there is some little place where he gets hysterical: the fright of being caught and discovered as a racketeer. The loneliness frightens him. Therefore he has a desire to own, to possess, to completely have something. He knows Lorna is the most dangerous person to him, and he hates her. He knows Joe depends on her. He wants to offer the girl to the boy. That is part of his pride. If that could be arranged he would offer Lorna as a shining beauty. Then he could dominate both . . . He doesn't want her to stay with Joe too long because that would divide his possession. And far back in his mind is the fact that Joe might some day get fed up with girls altogether. . . .
There are two ways of playing this part. If the actor conceives this part as a man, he can play it tenderly and beautifully. But that is wrong thematically. It must be pure lust for possession which makes it a terrible kind of love and maniacally insistent. Kewpie* had a certain naïvete, but this boy has only bitter knowledge and a ruthlessness. If he were ever caught by the police he would commit suicide . . . Only wise people would know he is homosexual. . . . In the last act when he gets hysterical it is because this man has become a business interest. There is a peak of love which leaves the loved one completely free. But this love becomes evil when it is too possessive. Eddie is only tender when Joe is serving him. (Must take out the word nance.)†

Even minor characters, despite their individual color, derive much from the character of Lou Odets. Roxy Gottlieb (God-love), for example, is an entrepreneur (like the original "Roxy," S. L. Rothafel). Odets describes him as follows:

All struggle for food. Roxy horns in. This activity comes in in a special way due to his character. This horning in on business affairs and

* The gangster in *Paradise Lost*, a similar character.
† At this time used for a homosexual man.

discussions is that he is always unemployed, although he is very busy.
Another quality which is linked up is that he is instructing and telling
the world . . . He is given to fits of depression because the results
that he wants don't always come and also because of an injured ego.
Every once in a while it becomes clear to him that people don't really
take him seriously. Like theatrical agents. Most of the things he says
are repeatings of what he heard, which he believes is his own knowledge. This gives him a certain cowardice, physically and otherwise.
. . . He is very lonely. No one cares about him very much . . . Another thing that relates to the instructive attitude is that he is a great
moralist and believes in God. Like the Jew who will gyp people in business and always go to synagogue on Yom Kippur. He likes sermons in
the synagogue because the rabbi always tells the world how to behave.
It is a dependence on the rabbi and God because after all what is there
to believe in. There must be some basis, and that is it. He thinks in
terms of moral slogans. Everything is that way. "The password is
honey," etc. He is very unconscious of his vulgarity. When he says,
"A woman's place is in the hay," this is really a moral idea. His most
sincere line in the play is "Can I ask you a civil question?" and "Without a dollar can you get along?"

Joe's maternal trainer, Tokio, on the other hand, embodies the qualities Odets most admired in workers in the motion-picture industry: those
of the honest craftsman-technician. He wrote of Tokio (who—like Poppa
Bonaparte—is a piece of his conscience):

He is a worker and he works. To work is his spine. He has every characteristic of a worker. He has a certain modesty. It goes to actual deference. The really good worker who is a craftsman is interested chiefly
in working. It becomes so much his life that he has no time for certain
types of quarrels or to think of his pride. The worker who is working
is very contented. There is a certain deference, not ass licking, which
comes from serving thru his work. No bitterness and little sentimentality. If he died he would say to God "I did what I had to do." He likes
Joe and is nice to him because of his workmanlike attitude towards
materials. He never gets involved in the machinations around him,
but goes on doing his business of training. He doesn't even question
the people very much. He just works honestly . . . When he is tender
(often) it is rather quiet and inexpressive. When Joe cries, he doesn't
ask why. He doesn't even think it is peculiar. He is not embarrassed by
it. He tries to encourage him, but just by working on. If Joe gets killed
in the last act he would not slop over it. He has no philosophy of life.
He is the real American that Cheryl talks about. He doesn't know
where he is but he is never lost. He has a lot of instinctive knowledge,
but in a quiet, unaffected way. He knows his boss and that he is his
boss. He has a quiet pride in his handiwork . . . He knows the bosses
want results and don't know how to get them. He can get results and
they will see when he finishes the work.

Moreover, Tokio understands the deep sensitivity in this young prizefighter:
"If you want the goods delivered," he says, "you have to treat him delicate,
gentle—like a girl." Lewis Milestone had understood this about Odets.

Defending himself to reporters, Odets would often insist that there
was no harm in perfecting his craft, and in earning a living as just such
an honest technician when he could do so no other way. (Carp: "Nowadays
is it possible for a young man to give himself to the Muses? Could the
Muses put bread and butter on the table?") Odets' simile between the

prizefight ring and the film industry would be evident to the critics, many protesting it.

Towards the end of Act II, Joe—having been betrayed by his girl—says to his trainer, "Now I'm alone. They're all against me . . . you're my family now, Tokio—you and Eddie!" When, in the ensuing fight, he closes the door on his music, even with some relief, by breaking his hand, he is released from his familial bonds *and* from his need to create music not only to ride on the powerful "Millionaire Express" but, more important, to become "the monarch of the masses" by crushing his opponent with the murderous "fury of a lifetime." His ambitious hatred, the "wild wolf inside," now has the upper hand, he wants singlehandedly to "beat up the whole damn world" and, indeed, he kills his adversary, "The Chocolate Drop." "What," he now asks in anguish, "will my father say when he hears I murdered a man?" And he knows he has symbolically smashed himself. He can fight no more (his guilt at destruction), nor can he return to creating beautiful music. He says, "What's left, Lorna? Half a man, nothing, useless. . . ."

Lorna tries (unpersuasively) to reassure him with the kind of forced optimism that had closed *Lefty*, *Awake and Sing!*, and *Paradise Lost*:

No, *we're* left! Two together! We have each other! Somewhere there must be happy boys and girls who can teach us the way of life! We'll find some city where poverty's no shame—where music is no crime!—where there's no war in the streets—where a man is glad to be himself, to live and make his woman herself!

As they take off across the Triborough Bridge, following this affirmative speech, it is clear that Joe's tragic need remains to embody within himself the gravity-defying, phallic power of a destructive and self-destructive flying thing:

When you *mow down the night* [italics mine] with headlights, nobody gets you! You're on top of the world then—nobody laughs! That's it—speed! We're off the earth—unconnected!

Poppa Bonaparte's position on prizefighting is that "If they wasa fight for cause or for woman, woulda not be so bad." His other son, bandaged (in the actual staging, like the familiar "Spirit of '76" picture) because of a strike fight, personifies a historically ethical American position for the release of hate, to be a real son of the revolution, a fighter for justice, not an ambitious Napoleon. Says fight manager Moody: "Every man here enjoys life, liberty and the pursuit of happiness."

The father is filled with compassion for the "poor color' boy" whom his son has killed, and as he awaits the return of Joe and Lorna, he mourns that his son "usta coulda be great for all men."* The suicidal death of the hero in Odets' earlier plays had had the significance of a blood sacrifice—like that of Christ—by reason of which a brotherhood of men would gain redemption and immortality. Whereas in *The Silent Partner* the strike is called "a mother"—a force which unites sons—there is no such nurturant mother in *Golden Boy*. Symbolically, Odets disappoints both maternal figures (Bonaparte and Lorna) and can join with them only in death.† The death of Joe Bonaparte, a man fighting *against* his brother, is despairing and personally vengeful, a meaningless "waste."

* When Poppa Bonaparte says this of his son, he means as an artist, a mysterious being who, like Jesus, combined humanity and divinity.

† A quarter of a century later he would write of the death of his friend Marilyn Monroe, thought to have committed suicide: "Now this girl has peace, for she is with Magna Mater at last."

It is the two-dimensional union organizer Frank (candid, sincere—named after Odets' cousin) who gets the news that Joe and Lorna are both dead in a crash in the town of Babylon ("I oughta burn," Lorna had said) and announces it thus: "You're all killers!" adding, "What waste!"

Poppa Bonaparte standing, "his head high," closes the play with "Joe. . . . Come, we bring-a him home . . . where he belong. . . ."

The rich, compassionate, emotional flow in *Golden Boy*, with its layers of meaning, its cornucopia of American image, of symbol, of character, and its ornamenting grace notes of oblique dialogue and humor, would perhaps never be surpassed by Odets. Although in his work he would again and again confront the same moral dilemma in a variety of manifest forms, all of them deeply humane, he would not again illuminate it as intensely and profoundly as here.◖

It is worth asking what were the special inner and outer circumstances of *Golden Boy* that provided this optimal level of conflict, of anxiety,* of ambiguity, of free access to his unconscious fantasies, and of hope for the resolution of a crisis of identity. The overflow of character and image was so copious that he had begun a new file entitled "Siggie and Anna," stating in his notes that this new play "would open with the last scene of *Golden Boy*."

A critical factor in all such prodigality always is the extent to which the playwright is, as it were, invited out by his potential audience. With *Lefty*, the invitation to become the spokesman for a righteous hatred of injustice had successfully allied his private rage to a socially shared and constructive end. In a subtler way this had happened with *Awake and Sing!*, celebrated by audiences for helping them to feel more "real." However, in the larger and more abstract canvases of *Paradise Lost* and in *The Silent Partner* he was unsuccessful in persuading an audience that his anger spoke *for them*. Perhaps it was because in both those plays he sacrificed his unique gift for detailed immigrant-American characterizations and dialogue to his conscious need to depart from this idiom and to make abstract formulations which would transcend his Jewish-American identity. He often said he wanted the respectability of a Sidney Howard, a Maxwell Anderson, a Robert E. Sherwood.

William Gibson has put it well: "If you can love yourself for hating, which you can do only if people love you for doing it, then you're able to open up creatively."

Another stimulus to a playwright in discovering the rich variety of characters within him is the existence of a company of gifted actors, each of whom exerts a magnetic pull on a different aspect of his Self. "I always know what a person is by what he brings out in me," said Odets. Thus it was not simply that the new Group urgently needed him now as *its* playwright; each of the members provided for *him* what he called a "mask," a formal container for the release of his inner gallery of characters.◖

Having discovered in the actors the "masks" for aspects of his own dividedness, he could set about, not only with love but with a willingness to sacrifice some personal ego, to seek a resolution of their (outer) struggles and, accordingly, of his inner ones.◖

His brothers in the Group—Clurman and Kazan in particular—were

◖ 21.5.
* O'Neill said that when the tension rose "beyond a certain point" he could not work.
◖ 21.6.
◖ 21.7.

eagerly awaiting *Golden Boy* for their salvation and his redemption. "He needed to feel we were all in this together and that the rest of us were waiting, and relying on him. It was youthful, beautiful, and clear we were all in the same danger"—so Kazan described this time. Odets, like Kazan, knew he was perfecting himself as a craftsman and could earn a living by means of that craft. He had, however, just escaped from the bondage of selling this skill in Hollywood, and was euphoric that a play born not of formula but of his genuine human experience, his state of being, was coming to life under his hand. Thus he sought in the creative mastery of this play to rescue himself from the tragic end of his hero, whose "death at impasse"◖ followed inevitably the closing of both doors: to his creative life and to his vengefully competitive livelihood.

Although he was having his usual third-act difficulty at the time Luise arrived in the East, Odets and the other Group members had high hopes they would have a potentially successful play for the fall. The reconstituted Group Theatre, headed by Clurman, had added Odets to its executive council (Kazan, Luther Adler, and Roman Bohnen), making of him at last an integral family member. And although Clurman saw Luise's arrival as a threat, it renewed Odets' hope that their relationship might yet be salvaged for good. It was Odets' fervent hope, also, that Luise would consider becoming part of the Group.

> MR. BONAPARTE: *In the modern man you will find two things which grow up side by side; a love to build, and a love to tear down—a love to love, and a love to have revenge. This depends on where comes the man from. These twins in a certain time of a man's life separate—one stays and one goes out of his life forever. Joe is not at such a point. He has in him to make revenge on everybody for his past life of humiliated and ashamed and inferior feeling.*
> CLIFFORD ODETS, 1937

One of the first things Odets had done on arrival in New York was to go with Luther Adler to see Jules Garfield in Arthur Kober's hit comedy, *Having Wonderful Time*. He had some gnawing doubts that the handsome young actor had the emotional depth and complexity he wanted in Joe Bonaparte. After a few minutes he whispered to Adler, "Julie can't play this part; it'll have to be Gadg." It would in fact be not Kazan but Luther Adler himself who would play the Golden Boy, a choice which would bitterly disappoint Garfield. Until Clurman arrived from Hollywood on Au-

◖ 21.8.

gust 23, feeling like a hero returning from exile, Odets, Adler, and Kazan busied themselves with revising and casting *Golden Boy*—and, far more difficult, trying to raise its production money. Odets began to blame Adler for his third-act problems. "You hung me up for weeks," he later told him, "with that remark, 'Again fruit?' " Adler, noting that Poppa Bonaparte was a fruit-vendor, had asked Odets, to no avail, why he was so preoccupied with fruit trees and fruit. Odets did not know, but he was obsessed with it—and temporarily hung all his doubts about the play on this question.

Even though the play was still not finished at the end of August and there was no money for Mordecai Gorelik to start building sets, the mood of the Group members continued high as Odets remained optimistic. From the moment he had conceived *Golden Boy* as a "popular success," he had had no doubt it would be one. It helped also to hear that Clurman was recruiting from Paramount the intelligent, shapely, honey-haired beauty Frances Farmer to play Lorna Moon. Someone said of her that she's "like a golden ear of corn"; another, "She has a virginal honesty." Already well known for her performance in the smash-hit film *Come and Get It*, she would take her place with Luther Adler, Elia Kazan, Lee J. Cobb, Morris Carnovsky, Phoebe Brand, Jules Garfield, Robert Lewis, and Roman Bohnen in this historic production. Even the minor parts looked like plums to such young newcomers as Howard Da Silva, Martin Ritt, Michael Gordon, and Karl Malden, all of whom would remember *Golden Boy* as a crucial event in their lives. They all assumed that production money would soon materialize.

Luise was exhausted from completing two films since *The Good Earth*, one of them with Spencer Tracy, when she finally arrived in the East, but her reunion with Odets was a joyful one. They spent a weekend with friends in a house on Long Island Sound filled with laughter. Most of their time, however, to the annoyance of their hosts, was spent in the seclusion of their room.

The other guests were jealous of both of them and particularly "of how we couldn't let go of each other, of how Cliff always carried me—literally on both arms, as his woman—into the bedroom." Each was acutely aware of the other's magnetism. Even Marlene Dietrich had, according to Luise, found Clifford interesting, while Clifford complained steadily of the attention paid *her* by a variety of gifted and famous men, like writers Erich Maria Remarque and Carl Van Vechten, and the fabled Alfred Stieglitz, founder of the American Place gallery, who had just written to Luise in a vein which greatly reassured her and disturbed her husband:

. . . What a magnificent human being you are. Why am I not a wizard to give Clifford the power to see—to feel—*what* he actually has in you . . . I can hardly believe that you sat here twice but a few days ago. It all seems so dreamlike. . . . I still hear your voice—see your face—see all of you as you told me about your meeting with those men. . . . Oh I know what yearning—longing—mean. I too have lived. And you young as you are have lived—lived hard from the moment of birth. And you will continue to live hard till the end—artist and woman. The most difficult combination in the world as I told you. I think of your work what you have already given to so many tens and hundreds of thousands of people. And of what you will give to millions more—A great Woman . . . O'Keeffe* is eager to see you. I told her about our two sessions. What a giant and beautiful soul you were. When you come again you two must meet.

I hope you are a bit quieter than you were. It is such a terrific struggle to keep oneself even half-way in order. Old as I am there is the constant struggle. Sometimes maddening. "Creative work! Highest comprehension and momentary redemption." I have stared at that statement of yours for a long long time. Yes that's it. How we all seek redemption. I must laugh at Clifford's idea of you as romantic—I fear he is quite as romantic, but not from the same angle. If you are romantic I say hurrah for romanticism of that order. You are a great Lover—the personification of Love—that too he might call romantic —Great heavens. Ever labels. How I hate all of them.

"I have so much to learn, so much," of course you have. And you will learn much, very much. But there is one thing that can't be learned and you have—have forever—love—Love. Your very being exudes it. Some people fear its power. Not merely yours but all love. I wish you could see The Place now. The pictures are hung. The walls with the pictures are pictures—very beautiful ones—in themselves. O'Keeffe is a marvel in hanging. She and I work beautifully together. And Mrs. Einstein is helpful too. Remember you have become an integral part of The Place which translated means you have given me unbounded strength. . . .

So I am ever in your debt. And I enjoy that feeling. And I hate being in debt as a rule!

Stieglitz' identity was indissolubly bound into the American Place, not simply as an art gallery but as an international hearth for young artists.

During this period, on a sunny Sunday afternoon, a friend of Luise's, Billy Rosenwald, "of Sears and Roebuck," came in his yacht to transport Luise, Odets, and other guests to a small cottage Albert Einstein was renting at Peconic on Long Island Sound. The purpose of the trip was to enlist the aging scientist's aid for a group of Jewish refugees fleeing Hitler. On arrival, it appeared the yacht was too large to dock at the tiny pier. Promptly, his white hair flying in the wind and a radiantly innocent smile lighting his face, Einstein arrived in order to debark the passengers in what one of them recalled as "something that only with great euphemism could be called a rowboat. It was more like a few pieces of wood hammered together." When it came Luise's and Odets' turn, it was evident to Odets, from the fact that he playfully pulled her hair, that Einstein found Luise attractive. She, flustered, capsized the boat and "almost drowned the great scientist." On one of the snapshots taken directly after this slapstick episode and retained by Luise, Odets, in a burst of jealous anger, has, with a scissors, carefully decapitated the picture of Einstein.

Such outings were rare, as Odets was hard at work on the final act of *Golden Boy*. Luise and he were usually in seclusion at One University Place, going for walks only in the evening, having meals in little restaurants in the neighborhood. It was difficult for them to maintain such seclusion, inasmuch as they were both celebrities and people would steadily try to hobnob with them.

* Georgia O'Keeffe, celebrated American artist, wife of Stieglitz.

Luise recalled a trip at this time to Saratoga with Motty and Bess Eitingon. Both "loving old Motty, but not appreciating in similar fashion his wife to the same degree, we soon felt out of our element, which became the start of new quarrels." Fleeing to their own quarters, Luise could be melted instantly by her husband kneeling and addressing her as "Baby" while comparing her sad eyes and her fragility to his mother's. They immersed themselves in each other, but only a few days later they were at odds once more. "Lo and behold! She wants to hog the act! She forgets that not only she but I too have to be saved!" So wrote Odets in a scribbled note to himself.

Luise, convinced that she would have become "an idol, a goddess to him—like his mother—if I had died," wrote her husband a note: "You want me dead. You think you love me but you love only what does not disturb you or does not have any life itself." He, in turn, desperate at his snail's-pace progress in finishing *Golden Boy*, lashed out at what he felt was the relentless insatiability of this sad-eyed, vulnerable, and powerful waif. Always, according to him, she insisted on a total "togetherness." Later he described in his journal what he regarded as her efforts "to capture love."

Now I can see what I fought in Luise so desperately albeit instinctively. I fought her attempt, not deliberate on her part, to close me up and so destroy me as an artist. Or shall I say I fought her attempt to keep me *only for herself*, which amounts to the same thing! If she had wisely permitted me to stay open for all and everything I would have been all open for her . . .

It appears each of them was making the same accusation. Odets, however, insisted there were times (and this was one, as Clurman, Kazan, and Adler anxiously waited on the sidelines for the third act of *Golden Boy*) when

What I want and have wanted for the last week is a simple clear thing —twelve to sixteen hours a day of good concentrated work. You will have to allow me that, and perhaps you will have to allow me not to spend an hour with you a day. I am sure there is nothing wrong with that. And there is nothing wrong with it if YOU have to do it (and there are times when you will!) in your work.

As it began to appear they might have to commence rehearsals of *Golden Boy* without either a third act or the $19,000 needed for production, Luise seemed to the Group the arch-enemy, a distracting witch who must not be crossed. When, for example, Elia Kazan arranged for Odets to have lunch "with old man Beck" to sell him on giving the Group the Martin Beck Theatre—a "class house," said Kazan—he apologized for "bothering" him when Luise was in town.

Odets, in turn, his anxiety mounting, also blamed Luise for the delayed third act. What he came to call her "horrible vacation" at One University Place became in his view the source of his third-act problem. In his frustration with his work difficulties, Luise became the scapegoat. He wrote her daily diatribes instead of working on the play. In one he opened, "Dear Luise, What is wrong is simple," and proceeded in two vigorous single-spaced typed pages to describe the problem:

You are an energetic girl with much temperament and emotion and life inside you. And you have no job at present. . . . Normally that is quite all right. But at present I am doing a hard job which requires much patience and concentration. The simple fact, without wasting words, is that I must either take care of you and all your emotions or energies; or I must do the job. Both I can not do together . . . In the meantime, I tell you to go out and live a normal healthy life and to have a good time . . . You immediately interpret that in a bad way and tell me that it means I want you to go out with men in public places. Well, I don't mean anything of the sort and you are a fool for thinking it. . . .

There are two things you do which are very bad for both of us. One is that you insist that we are one and the same and that we must react in the same way to everything . . . or there is no love from me, according to your way of thinking: Another thing—which you write in your note—is that if you do something to me, then that is what you want me to do to you. But I don't act the same as you. I have my own behavior patterns—I express myself differently and am a different personality. But you seem to insist that I do everything as you do it. I can't and I won't. . . .

A good example is the telegram from Kolisch. The fact is that I was not in the least jealous of you or him about that. I am afraid to tell you this because you have shown me that to you my jealousy is an expression of love. I don't happen to think that jealousy means love at all. And the reason here that I wasn't jealous of Mr. Kolisch was because I have enough faith and trust in your character to know that you won't be off in a corner kissing him or making eyes at him. I trust you . . .

. . . A big essential difference is that you are a woman and I am a man. A woman generally thinks that she can go presto with a wave of her hand and make a seed grow into a flowering tree in a minute. Her emotions and quick responses and sympathies make her think that. Unfortunately, it is not true.

Please! Let there be less suffering between us, less talk about what one is giving, less talk about great sacrifices made. That is all the bunk. You are greatly mistaken if you think I am any more happy than you, that I give less, that I give more. You are mistaken if you think you have less anger than me, or more patience. We are two people—make no mistake about this—with plenty of temperament, plenty of anger and impatience. Both of us! Not just you, not just me!

Whatever difficulties Odets could not hold Luise responsible for were Clurman's fault. "When did Harold ever raise any money for the Group?" he cried. Indeed, in this fall of 1937, with an intensification of the Depression, investors were afraid to risk anything on a play which lacked Broadway stars and which ended with the suicidal destruction of its hero and heroine in an automobile accident. As the scheduled opening date approached, Clurman became desperate, and Odets' awareness that it was essentially *his* responsibility to "bring in a hit" for the economic survival of the Group all but stopped him in his creative tracks.

Luise's experience of this "horrible nine-week vacation" was that it was indeed "horrible." Having fled the Metro-Goldwyn-Mayer lot and Mayer's demands that she use her talent in "complete nonsense," she had come East hoping she would be warmed by the love of her husband in a city where the Group was involved in making good theatre, not "movies." Arrived at the black-leathered bachelor apartment, she found her husband asleep in the mid-afternoon. Herman Kobland told her Odets had been working all night and had instructed him to buy many jars of pickled chestnuts, a favorite of hers, but not to waken him until five in the afternoon.

She did her best "to become invisible" by disappearing into innumerable art galleries, shopping, listening to music, or visiting with Alfred Stieglitz and other friends. Her real need, she recalled, was for "renewal from Hollywood" and being with the man she loved. Each day, however, it became more apparent that this was not happening. Loving people as she did, she would go out to see people in cafes, restaurants, at exhibitions. Sometimes she would even go down to the Bowery and "mingle with the poorest of the poor," delighted that there she was not recognized.

One of her happier experiences of this summer came when, at the time of the Japanese invasion of China, Luise spoke at Madison Square Garden and twenty-two thousand people rose to their feet and cheered her words. It was, according to the press, a thrilling occasion. However, Odets refused to be there and behaved as though the event had never occurred.

When Odets refused to acknowledge what seemed to her his obvious jealousy, and called her suggestions for his third act "shit," her sense of uselessness must have become intolerable to her. She confided her grief to Alfred Stieglitz, who offered her steady and extravagant reassurance. Apparently she felt far from being able to return like a "baby kangaroo to its mother's pouch," as, according to Odets, she had told him she would like to feel. Thus she reached the end of her vacation and flew back to Hollywood, where she daydreamed of a long tour of Europe and of playing once more in serious plays in a serious theatre company.

The rehearsal period of *Golden Boy* has become a peak experience in the memories of most members of the Group company. Lee J. Cobb, cast as Carp, recalled, "It became, *for all of us*, back from Hollywood, a time to take a unifying second breath." He recalled Odets as simultaneously "an awe-inspiring Titan and everyone's older brother," whose fierceness of language and singularity of gift "in an era when mediocrity was not disproportionately rewarded, as it is now," lifted the actors even beyond their considerable talents. They were all soaring, he felt, with the sense of regained freedom and creative concentration. "If this play were to fail," said Cobb, "we would conclude only that the public was not ready for it. If it were to succeed, so what?" This self-respecting, artistic independence, in contrast to the paper-doll servility of film acting, was a source of exhilaration to all of them. To twenty-one-year-old Martin Ritt,* given a small part because he could punch a bag, it was evident he had become a part "of the greatest acting company in the world." Unaware that the production money had yet to be raised, the actors were blissful in their regained creative liberation.

When the opening date was upon them and still only small sums had been raised, Odets' anxiety began to erupt wildly. Luise, back in California to meet her contractual obligations to Louis B. Mayer, felt she had left her vexed marriage up in the air and was now working on sterile commercial projects. Presently her husband wired her for $5,000 for *Golden Boy*, which she sent immediately. He himself had already put in $4,625 for

---

* Ritt later became a leading Hollywood producer-director.

thirty shares of the production. He told her he was frantically rounding up a variety of motion-picture people to invest; among them was producer Walter Wanger, who contributed $2,000 to settle his contract with the Group actors, most of whom had returned to New York as Hollywood "failures." Ignoring telegrams offering him "expensive" movie jobs and trying to revive his interest in the film *Gettysburg*, Odets continued his money-raising efforts as well as obsessional work on his third act.

A few days before dress rehearsal Odets made a proposal to Clurman for last-minute revisions of the central meaning of the play. In a scene where the gangster Fuseli is berating Lorna for leading Joe on "like Gertie's whoore" ("You turned down the sweetest boy who ever walked in shoes . . . the golden boy, that king among the juven-niles! He gave you his hand—you spit in his face!") Odets, in a misogynous burst, decided, as Clurman recalled, that "Fuseli brings out his gun with the intention of shooting Lorna." When Clurman heard this idea, he became enraged. Purple and choking, he began to scream, "That's all wrong! You can't change it now! That's not what you meant at all!" Finally, as in an epileptic convulsion, he fell upon the floor, rocking, rolling, screaming, and, in his misery, pounding the floor with fists and feet. The cast, thinking their director was truly in a fit of epilepsy, or psychotic, looked on aghast. No one moved until Odets said quietly, "All right, we'll do it the way it is." Clurman arose with dignity and continued the rehearsal. Group actor Sanford Meisner, impassively smoking a cigarette in his long holder, smiled and remarked coolly, "I wouldn't be in any other business."

By late August Odets had collected enough of the production money and apparently had his third act well enough in hand to consent to be interviewed by a reporter from the Communist *Daily Worker* in its small office between 12th and 13th streets, off University Place. He had been refusing interviews for weeks because he had been working nights and sleeping days. The startling theme of the interview was that, according to the reporter, Odets had stated, "Social drama isn't dying. It never really lived," adding in his characteristically passionate style, "The critics created a straw man and knocked it out themselves." The reporter described their "supper of 14th Street hot dogs," continuing then his account:

> "I don't think the left theatre belongs on Broadway," he said with a frown. "It should be all over the country in the Federal Theatre, in union halls, in the hinterland. What's the sense in writing plays for a few bourgeois intellectuals on Broadway at $3.30 a head?
>
> "Right now the Federal Theatre is the best medium offered for the social theatre—even if it is crude at times. No matter how bad it is, it's still better than paying $3.30 on Broadway.
>
> "All these twerps get together and talk about saving the theatre. All they want to save is their own jobs. All that's left of the theatre is entertainment and the movies took all that away."

Throughout, Odets expresses his conviction that a creative marriage between social drama and commerce is essentially not viable and says he will not return to Hollywood "unless I am broke." It is a place where

> "You never can get started working. It's a good place for a vacation. You feel like you're in Atlantic City. All the quacks in the world are out there."
>
> Most of the actors, directors and others in flicker center have a "cynical, negative attitude towards the joint; make the money and get the hell out, is the way a lot of them feel."

Almost as an apology, he adds a redeeming feature:

"You can get any number of well-known names behind an anti-Nazi affair," he declared. "We ran four parties for the Scottsboro boys last fall and got 200 people at five and ten dollars a head."

Odets, who talks and acts like "one of the boys," emphatically denied the many stories floating around saying that Hollywood shekels had gone to his head and that he was on the "outs" with the left theatre.

"All that stuff comes from people who don't know me. Sometimes it gets me sore. The people who know me don't say those things.

"I got away with some stuff in *The General Died at Dawn* and in the other two scripts I did—*The River Is Blue*, and *Gettysburg*. But they've been careful with me. They go over my stuff with a fine tooth comb. It's difficult to do anything with social significance."

Odets optimistically outlines his creative hopes and plans for the immediate future:

The Group will not have a permanent company under the new set-up and will not have to shoulder the burden of livelihood for a company of 30 all year round. "They can produce shows as cheaply as any theatre now," Odets said.

The interview concludes:

Odets is planning a third script for the Group for next season. It's called *Night on Steel Mountain* and will be a melodrama about the CIO in a company town. Odets is going to see John L. Lewis before he starts working on the play.

The greatest hope of the American Theatre who has been compared to Eugene O'Neill in his early days has one bone to pick with his fellow travelers in the left theatre.

"The trouble with most left wing playwrights is that they got the Broadway bug. They want bourgeois glory and in some ways you can't blame them. But the real theatre isn't on Broadway—it's to be played on the back of a wagon and in a union hall.

"We need more agit-prop plays like *Lefty*. All left wing plays should be written like that. No expensive scenery or costumes. Take a play like *Private Hicks*. You got to spend, say, about $80 for costumes and another $100 for scenery when what you want is a $10 play.

"Our left wing playwrights can learn a lot from the movies. It's a training school in technique. I know I'm a better writer now than when I wrote *Lefty*. The movies teach you how to please people, how to entertain them, and—most important—how to change their minds. That won't do any left wing writer any harm."

It is evident that his vision of a lively creative situation with a ready bridge to a communal audience, as in those times of history when religion provides the unifying forms and symbols between creator and audience, involves a divorce from commerce, not only in the film industry but in the legitimate theatre as well.

Luise now became the catch-basin for his terror that *Golden Boy*, written to be a "hit play," might fail as *Paradise Lost* had. Meanwhile he grieved over *The Silent Partner*. His disproportionate fear and anger, much of it transferred from times long gone, was now focused on his distraught wife, who was asking *his* help to prevent her from being cast in a commercial film for which she had only contempt. Instead of helping her, he wrote her draft after draft of irately accusing letters, sending only those which in his judgment had some base in rationality, and which he felt to be sufficiently restrained. To be sure, his obsessed review of their relationship and of their correspondence, all preserved in his files, reflects his insightful concern over the increasingly sharp battle lines they were actually drawing. Yet there is no mistaking the fact that its irrational crescendo rose sharply as the opening night of *Golden Boy* approached. The unsent drafts are bald, angry, and threatening.

To one of his many disquisitions Luise replied with an "extra rush" telegram saying, "It will take me a little time to answer as I want to answer and answer exactly."

In a representative eight-page handwritten letter ending, "What shall I do?" (one of many such letters), she tries to convey to her husband her experience of trying to be of help to him and her misery at his calling her efforts "nothing but shit":

> Cliff darling—everything is down again, you tore me right down and smashed me to pieces . . . I deeply hoped . . . felt: that my help to you in those 6 weeks was more than 13 typewritten pages. I envy you for having another person* besides me so deeply and actively interested in your work . . . I believe that the interest I tried to give *was* more than that. Was more than shit . . . "The duty of a wife"? Darling, do we live "the duties of a wife and a husband"? If I ask you for something you don't like to do, you just don't do it, or if you do I sure have shortly later to hear that I should have married a gigolo, because I only need a warm sweater. . . . You say I spoke only with you about Lorna! Darling, if I really spoke mostly of Lorna it was because I had the feeling that here I was the surest in any kind of criticism, and because I wanted this womensfigur to be as alive and good as possible because I know that it always was more difficult for you to write women's parts, and here I felt sure that if you need it I could give. Yes darling, I am in the defense because I see that you feel about whatever I did or said was as unimportant as shit. We spoke about every character in the play, spoke about the scenes . . . darling when we for instance went downstairs through the park, do you think I thought anything else than about your play? . . . And all I did was shit?!
>
> But what more you must know Cliff [is] that till now you holded every work of yours far away from me—you didn't want me to know of it or hear what I thought. Don't you know that it is very difficult for me to find so quick and suddenly the right way? . . . I don't know so well most of the American characters you write about, not because I don't know the language so well, but because I don't know *you* in your *work* so well, surely Harold knows your work *much* better than I do and besides he knows he is asked . . . And still I helped you, Cliff . . . I think I helped you more than any person ever helped you . . . But as you feel about it as nothing as shit, I am no good for you. I would not know where to start again as I have the assurance from you once again that what I try for us is shit.
>
> And a word about Mr. Katz.† Yes Cliff, I said it and am happy to know a person who has real interest in me and tries to help me. . . . Don't you understand that I needed it because *you don't listen to me,* to everybody else, *yes,* but with me you feel it like a strain. You told me

---

* She means Harold Clurman.
† A painter friend devoted to Luise.

once in Hollywood when I asked to speak with you about something "don't you remember you spoke yesterday at least an hour about it" . . . You have not one Mr. Katz, you have a whole Group of Mr. Katz's and you let me feel it often enough and deep. But . . . I didn't care to have a Mr. Katz, I wanted us to have him. Yesterday Katz said he wants to make a portrait of me for you because he wants you to be his friend as I am . . . still I wished you would give me what Katz does—it is little, little—but I know you don't want it—as probably I never will be able to give you what Harold and the Group can give you. Darling everything you said is so ugly. Cliff I am young yet and can build up again and again but what shall I do when I have not the strength to rebuild and rebuild again. . . .

She wishes him and the Group "a great honest success* as it is important for all of you," continues with the advice that he "take a good rest darling even if it is only short," and closes with "take a good handshake and a deeply good look."

Odets somehow managed in this period to read and rank, as a judge in a contest, a hundred passionate essays on the Soviet Union written by high-school children. And on the night before the play opened, he went to hear Jascha Heifetz play his violin.

The opening-night audience at the Belasco Theatre on November 4 was at first restless, noisy, coughing, and rudely self-absorbed, but when the final curtain came down and the audience cheered, the company knew that it had done a superb job. Most of the Group members, including Odets, wept. Clurman, in director's terror, had absented himself from the performance, but joined the Group to read the critics' judgments, which, though mixed, agreed that Golden Boy had been worth waiting for. There were enough "money reviews," hailing Odets' work as the "most exciting stuff being written for the American theatre," to make it the greatest financial success in the history of the Group. With its sale to pictures for $70,000, it would be their mainstay for two seasons. Once more the members would look to the Group for, as Clurman put it, "what society itself failed to provide . . . full lives disciplined by a unified moral and intellectual code that would direct them toward smiling goals of spiritual and material well-being . . . merely everything."

Although it had been Odets' hope that the press would be unanimous in proclaiming, as some did, that with Golden Boy he had stepped into the empty shoes of the now silent O'Neill, he was gratified by his rousing welcome back to the legitimate stage. Both the left-wing and the bourgeois press rediscovered that, despite his tendency toward romanticism, "no playwright alive can touch him when it comes to the relentless vigor and humor of his dialogue"; that "the force and telegraphic brevity with which he delivers a scene or an individual" was unique; and that "among his high talents, he can count a gift for revealing everything by the uncanny use he makes of humanizing details." Despite a few comments that the plot of Golden Boy resembled at times a "melodramatic motion picture,"

* Poppa Bonaparte in Golden Boy wants his son to have a "truthful success" on his violin, not a violent, competitive victory in the ring.

they celebrated the "reclamation of Clifford Odets from the dreamland into which he had lately wandered." It is evident from the eager controversy in the press that there was widespread, if grudging, relief at seeing once more an Odets play "quick with life, pungent in dialogue and character- ization, stirring and comic and ruthlessly authentic" ("the best of the Odets genius," said Burns Mantle). In its "amazing variety" from the "hard, funny, jaunty talk of taxi drivers and gunmen" to its "sensitive, subtle talk between the boy and his unhappy girl," thoughtful critics saw a unique American theatrical event, and Richard Lockridge of the *Sun* concluded: ". . . it is Mr. Odets' evening. It is good to have him back where he belongs."*

For weeks following the opening, critics on the right and on the left— and there were many in those days†—continued to discuss *Golden Boy.* Some of them triumphantly announced that the Group had finally come to see that entertainment was more important than propaganda; others mourned that Odets was no longer a revolutionary playwright, but most agreed with Burns Mantle that there had been "enough said about Odets' selling out to Hollywood to make his return to Broadway important." Even the conservative *Herald Tribune* expressed relief that "after whisperings of doom, the Group Theatre has come together again and Odets is perma- nently a playwright."

The honest and insightful reviewer for the *Telegraph,* Whitney Bolton, impatient with the defensive and competitive sarcasm so often expressed about Odets by his fellow critics, asked why they did not celebrate "with Thanksgiving and advance cheers" the return to the stage of a major dramatist who would help the ills afflicting the theatre. "Instead," he went on, "they say, 'All right, come on, but it had better be good, better than any- thing you've ever done or we'll murder you!'" Then "they shiver with de- light in the opportunity to point jeering fingers and say 'Look, look! another good boy ruined by Hollywood. Isn't it wonderful?'" Bolton, unable to hold with them, concluded they should all be thankful for a playwright who "in an uncannily exact idiom" had brought them "one of the most exciting and moving first acts this town has seen in a long time."

Cheered by the good business at the box office of the Belasco, and troubled by being so often the target of sharp criticism, Odets wrote a serious essay for *The New York Times,* trying to place his new work in its historical context vis-à-vis the film industry:

"DEMOCRATIC VISTAS" IN DRAMA
BY CLIFFORD ODETS

In his essay "Democratic Vistas" written in 1871, Walt Whitman wrote: "Of what is called the drama, or dramatic presentation in the United States, as now put forth at the theatres, I should say it deserves to be treated with the same gravity, and on a par with the questions of ornamental confectionery at public dinners, or the arrangement of curtains and hangings in a ballroom. . . .

"I feel with dejection and amazement that among writers and talented speakers, few or none have yet really spoken to this people, created a single image-making work for them, or absorbed the central

---

* The closing line of *Golden Boy* is: "Come, we bring-a him home . . . where he belong. . . ."
† New York's daily newspapers alone at this time accounted for eleven active critics: *The New York Times, World-Telegram, Herald Tribune, Daily News, Daily Mirror, Journal-American, Post, Sun, Telegraph, Daily Worker,* and *Freiheit.* Added to this were many periodicals of varying political complexions.

spirit and the idiosyncrasies which are theirs—and which, thus, in the highest ranges, so far remain entirely uncelebrated and unexpressed."

Let us, for once, give the movies some credit. They have spoken to this people. The movies have explored the common man in all of his manifestations—out of the Kentucky mountains, out of the Montana ranch house, out of the machine shop, from the docks and alleys of the great cities, from the farm, out of the hospitals, airplanes, and taxicabs.

The movies are now the folk theatre of America. But they are still not what Whitman asked for in 1871. . . . Hollywood producers will tell you gladly that they are not interested in presenting their themes "significantly." They are not interested in interpretation or criticism of their material. Their chief problem, they contend, is the one of keeping the level of human experience in their pictures as low as possible. They keep to primary colors with the expected result: The good will be rewarded, the wicked punished; success lurks around every corner; love is only a matter of the right man looking the right girl in the eyes; and so on and so on and so on. . . .

But the experience of . . . cinema heroes and heroines is still something virginal and wondrously young. The treatment of the themes is puerile in every respect. The American gallery remains, as Whitman said, "uncelebrated and unexpressed."

It is sad to consider what movies are doing to America's consciousness of itself. Men are simple, credulous, imitative animals for the most part. Hollywood has set our citizens examples of conduct and behavior patterns fit only for the lower animals. Movies have imposed upon the land a glossary of experience definitions which would make the humble monkey howl. Every week 80,000 watchers are instructed in these standards of living and conduct by Hollywood.

What does all this have to do with playwrights and the stage? Merely that it is about time that the talented American playwright began to take the gallery of American types, the assortment of fine vital themes away from the movies. This was attempted in *Golden Boy*. Some critics were surprised at the choice of theme. Where is there a more interesting theme in this country than a little Italian boy who wants to be rich? Provided, of course, you place him in his true social background and show his fellow-conspirators in their true light, bring out the essential loneliness and bewilderment of the average citizen, do not blow trumpets for all that is corrupt and wicked around the little Italian boy, do not substitute a string of gags for reality of experience, present the genuine pain, meaning and dignity of life within your characters. . . .

Here is the essential point: a playwright might follow the movie trend of themes with great profit. But in each he would have to tell the truth where the film told a lie, starting each time where the picture left off. A writer of talent could begin a great career that way—as "celebrator and expresser." Great audiences are waiting now to have their own experiences explained and interpreted for them. Walt Whitman's plea is still unrealized.

It was clearly Odets' fervent hope that he would be the man to meet Whitman's plea.

The play seems to have caught on. But I want to write a play for *you*. That will give me real happiness, not this one! We will open OUR play out of town for two or three weeks. It is still a promise of love that we will startle New York together! I am a bad fellow—with a fearful temper and an impatience which comes from ardour—but I don't forget my love for Luise, and the ache of love for her never leaves me. Our play will be one of love, of growing devotion, of deepening accord, of maturing and coming together. Luise, I love you with a love which gives me a shake in the head and throws the glasses off my nose!

So wrote Odets from a dingy, dark room in Philadelphia, where he had gone to visit Tante Esther and Uncle Israel. He debated whether to see his father, whom he was now subsidizing in a mammoth mattress-manufacturing fiasco called Doctors of Sleep. (Later the father would say, "I gave *him* his first mattress to sleep on!" and the son would rejoin, "That mattress cost me $25,000!") L. J. Odets was about to marry a childless, maternal woman called Lillian who found him to be "a gentleman" whom she could baby.

With the ordeal of the opening successfully past, and three thousand miles separating Odets from Luise, the correspondence shows that Clifford no longer needs to destroy his wife, that he is concerned for her health, which, as always in her periods of emotional distress, was now actually poor, and that for the first time in a long while he is restlessly fantasying in detail their "wonderful life ahead":

What are you doing about eating good solid food and not being too thin? Did you throw Rosenbluth's diet out the plane window when you left New York? (Altho I couldn't blame you for throwing anything out of the plane window then!) Keep healthy, darling. For if you keep healthy we can both work with a free mind and earn a big bunch of money and with it buy a house in the country here and then hide ourselves there like two thieves and do some magic things and suddenly out of it comes an enormous and healthy baby which we keep secret and hidden there! Finally we calmly ride back to New York and everybody exclaims, "What a wonderful beautiful baby! What human beings produced that baby?" But we smile and shuffle our feet and talk about the weather, but we don't tell them anything! Get me? We get immediately busy on another play, but rush home every once in awhile to play the Beethoven 7th for the baby. Also, the baby starts taking piano lessons at the age of five. God knows what our first child will turn out to be, but piano lessons are good to have!

Luise sadly recalled that at this point she was so mired in her own impotence to develop as an artist, and in her fierce determination to break out of her Hollywood serfdom, that she was not ready even to think about "an enormous and healthy baby." "Perhaps," she pondered, "the story would have been different if I could have."

Odets sends his wife a book on Eleanora Duse ("But you are your own Duse," he adds), dozens of ardent and vivid love notes, and a copy of his dedication for the published *Golden Boy*: "For Luise, Artist, Wife, Best Friend!" She replies with equal ardor, and in witty, whimsical letters —perfectly attuned to Odets' long-distance love and sensuality—tells him of her new apartment in Westwood ("no Hollywood atmosphere and many students in the neighborhood") and includes a photograph of herself.

Luise was about to become an American citizen, apparently ready to settle down with her American husband, and awaiting eagerly his coming to her defense against the executives of Metro-Goldwyn-Mayer. What she now was asking of the studio was the right to limit her number of pictures to one a year, to have a veto on them, to spend at least half her time in New York with her husband, and to be in his plays. While none of these demands appears humanly unreasonable, they were at this time contractually outlandish, and Louis B. Mayer assured her that if she remained thus arrogant and stubborn about her parts or the number of pictures she would make a year, his reprisals could be devastating. Odets decided that legal counsel from Morris Ernst would be useful. Perhaps they could cite Luise's actual anemia and her general depression about the quality of the pictures she was contracted to make as grounds for breaking her contract. (The studio physician recorded that she might have been pushed by now to "suicidal tendencies.")

Relaxed by the steady build-up in business of *Golden Boy* ("It is like an hour-old baby and needs a lot of watching," Odets writes), he addresses her as "Dearest, finest, gentlest, sweetest, most beautiful girl," compares her to a Schubert song, and is clearly ready to ride to her rescue so that they may commence on their "cooperative of two, two to begin with! Our own collective society." He is envious that actress Sylvia Sidney has already bought a house in the country, where, it appears, she and Luther Adler will live after their marriage. The fantasy of a motherly but independent wife drawing a circle of warmth and safety for the artist-husband pervades his thinking.

There is clearly building now in Odets a hot anticipation of crossing swords with the powerful Mayer, delivering Luise from his predatory clutches, and settling down with her to an idyll. He writes with male assurance, "I can settle the entire contract in several simple moves . . ." and begs her to "forget all worry about studio affairs. Leave all those worries to me . . . all this movie trouble will soon be past history for both of us." He suggests that Luise meet him somewhere "in the middle of America. Just you and I in a strange place alone, together joyful." It is a genuine wish.

Finding it impossible to leave the studio, she asks that he come to her and wires him:

> Dearest, and may you travel speedy and when you see clouds, they are my warmth which streams out to you, and when you see birds they are loving parts of my soul flying through the winds to bring you my kisses. Your girl.

They did not meet in the middle of America, but in West Los Angeles, where Odets arrived on the Santa Fe Chief three days before Christmas, once more with early drafts of *The Silent Partner* and the Cuban play, *Law of Flight,* in his suitcase. In addition, he had brought his large file of notes marked "The Dentist Play."

Chapter Twenty-Two

DENTIST: *Full of quiet despair. For years he has been trying to deaden and kill himself with hard work, late at night falling into bed exhausted. His marriage with Belle is loveless but neither will admit it although both know it.*

CLIFFORD ODETS, 1938

ON THE wave of the Group Theatre's greatest hit, *Golden Boy,* Odets was, as his agent put it, "hot as a pistol" when he arrived in the film capital to visit his wife. Studios were besieging him to "write his own ticket"; but although he was concerned about the thousands of dollars he was pouring into his father's failing Doctors of Sleep mattress shop, he did not consider any of their offers. The left-wing as well as the "bourgeois" press—each grinding a different axe—agreed that he and Luise Rainer were once more providing excellent copy. *Life* celebrated his return to the legitimate theatre with a two-page spread and the announcement that "Hollywood, contrary to prediction, has not broken Clifford Odets." Rather, it had "matured his art, disciplined his style, taught him to tell a story and helped him to become indisputably as good as the best the U.S. theatre has to offer."

Even *The New Yorker* decided the time had arrived for their special canonizing of a celebrity: in a "profile," entitled "Revolution's Number One Boy," John McCarten presents a supercilious, obtuse, and jibing portrait of Odets that could have been written by critic George Jean Nathan, who was steadily taunting him in the press for his "affected," "phoney" love of music, his "ignorance" of it, and his general lack of writing talent. In the *New Yorker* piece Odets is portrayed as a pretentious, hypocritical, arrogant Communist party-liner, now out for "Hollywood gold" while creating characters "always badgered by the Capitalist System who can get out of their unhappy predicament only by means of 'The Revolution.'" His records, books, Hammond organ, and busts of Beethoven and Lenin are condescendingly noted.

Odets, deeply wounded, wrote McCarten a note saying, "Next time you need a couple of hundred bucks, you don't have to cut anybody's heart for it. Come to me and I'll be glad to give it to you." McCarten defensively told a friend he had only been trying to write a lively piece "in the *New Yorker* style." So doubtful, however, was Odets of his own value that he had his secretary clip out the profile and make of it for his bookshelf a slim, leather-bound volume reassuringly lettered in gold.

Although Odets' champion, the *World-Telegram*'s columnist Heywood Broun, had, he said, "wept copiously all over the floor of the Belasco" at the "grave and gay" *Golden Boy* and now stated his gratitude fully, he added nevertheless that Odets would do well to study Orson Welles' Mercury Theatre production of *Julius Caesar* to see how Shakespeare had managed to "weave the story of the individual into the larger pattern," thus achieving "top tragedy." Broun's profound response to this Mercury Theatre *Julius Caesar*, as he himself recognized, was reinforced by Welles' staging it in such a way that there could be no mistaking the universality of the fascist threat now gathering momentum in Europe. Along with many other serious-minded critics, Broun was, however, underscoring his relief that Odets had brought to the stage something other than the "fluff of the last several seasons." It had been Broun's steadily expressed conviction that Odets was "within sight of becoming a great playwright."

Meanwhile, in the London *Observer*, Ivor Brown was of the opinion that Odets' picture of the "home of the shabby, dissatisfied Jews" in *Awake and Sing!* had been lively, all right, but only because "Jewish backchat is naturally quick and queer, racy and inventive." He thought it significant of the "poor state of the drama in New York that Mr. Odets should be accepted as the Young Hope." Within a few months, however, when the Group Theatre's production of *Golden Boy* opened in London, theatre workers and many of Brown's colleagues would respond to its vigor as to a blood transfusion which brought them a surge of new life and introduced a new genre of writing to the English theatre.

Odets' stay in California was brief. He was preoccupied with a plan to have Hallie Flanagan's Federal Theatre mount simultaneous productions of his unproduced labor play, *The Silent Partner,* all over the United States. Film star Sylvia Sidney had expressed interest in appearing in it, and with a beautiful star and a subsidized national theatre, he dreamed of his work reaching great masses of ordinary people. Miss Flanagan describes in her book, *Arena,* her bold, serious-minded, and phenomenal experiment, conceived to provide eight thousand jobs for unemployed theatre people. Odets was convinced that under these auspices he would convey the kind of authentic human experience for which Broun was pleading. It was a dream of a serious national American "folk-theatre." To be sure, even numerous Federal Theatre productions of *The Silent Partner* across the nation would reach considerably less than the eighty million regular moviegoers. Still, he thought, the genuineness of content in this "people's theatre," part of Roosevelt's New Deal for artists, would make up for the smaller audience. It was his fantasy that it would begin to approximate Walt Whitman's theatre vision. To actress Helen Hayes, wife of writer Charles MacArthur, he excitedly described what he called a "Charlie Theatre." When Miss Hayes asked what he meant by a "Charlie Theatre," Odets replied, "Well, you're an actress married to a man named Charlie. I'm a playwright and I have a brother-in-law named Charlie. So-

and-so is a director and he has a son named Charlie. Suddenly the government passes a law everybody named Charlie is going to be electrocuted at midnight, New Year's. So you and I, so-and-so, the director, all of us who have Charlies threatened, get together and we write, direct, stage, and act a play and the audience comes and everybody in the audience has some Charlie in his life whom he's trying to save and then you get something going on between the people on stage and the people in the audience that I call a Charlie Theatre, and that's what we need."❡

The "Charlie Theatre" which he envisioned would combine the best of everything: the immediacy of *Waiting for Lefty*, the universal symbols of human salvation, and the individual psychological dimensions for which he had striven in *Golden Boy*. He had been recently impressed by the "Miracle Plays" performed by the Federal Theatre on a truck at Tenth Avenue under the roar of the elevated trains, an early form of American street theatre. A procession of Wise Men—actors keeping alive under the Works Progress Administration—had made their way against the lighted façade of International House, the open windows letting out the sound of hundreds of carolers inside the building, with a frieze of black as well as white angels in halos and golden robes. But the Federal Theatre, as Odets well knew, was responsible for far more than creative Christmas improvisations. Miss Flanagan had, for instance, gained permission from the crusty George Bernard Shaw to perform his plays for a royalty of $50 a week, and Eugene O'Neill was "thrilled," he said, to accept the same. And with the Living Newspaper productions as well—a form of unprecedented social documentary—the Federal Theatre was thus at one and the same time a "Charlie Theatre" and a medium for introducing live, serious drama to millions of people in more than forty states. *The Silent Partner*, once more coming to life on his desk, seemed to Odets an ideal vehicle for production under the energetic Miss Flanagan's bright, bold eye.

In a radio interview after his return to New York, Odets said, "The *business* of the American theatre is in a bad way." Making it clear that "by business I mean entertainment," he left no room for doubt that "the American movies are the best purveyors of entertainment in the world." "But," he continued,

> . . . from the point of view of significant theme, the theatre has come to a sort of rebirth in the last five years. A whole generation of former actors, directors and writers are now comfortably entrenched in Hollywood with the theatre completely left behind. For several reasons these once mighty theatre names are not to be blamed for their exodus. There were several reasons they might have stayed on Broadway. One reason would be a deep and compelling interest in the themes of the plays in which they were interested. A second would have been a feeling of growth in their chosen crafts and the final would have been a satisfactory earning power. In most cases none of these elements were present in the Broadway theatre.

Asked by the interviewer whether he would advise "the younger generation of dramatists" to try their luck in Hollywood, he replied:

> . . . Flatly, the answer is they must stay where they are, myself included. The movies by reason of their business set-up—consider the fact that Hollywood pictures derive over fifty percent of their income from foreign sources—cannot and will not give any expression to controversial themes. Controversial themes include what one thinks of

❡ 22.0.

Fascism, what one thinks of President Roosevelt's drive for a higher living standard for most Americans, includes an opinion of John L. Lewis, and the hundreds of thousands behind him. On the other hand, a strict censorship exists in Hollywood and it is difficult for a writer to express even the simpler pains and tragedies of life—what for instance really happens between a man and woman in love. Any adult treatment of thousands of simple life situations are forbidden by this censorship. No, let the theatre craftsmen with any real sense of life stay in the theatre.

Adding that he had been "an object of suspicion" when writing *The General Died at Dawn,* he described, in addition to the studio censorship, that of the Hays Office and even, as with Luise Rainer's *The Good Earth,* the necessity to obtain the approval of the Chinese government! He concluded, "At the present moment Germany would also have to give its seal of approval." Indeed, he said, *The Forty Days of Musa Dagh* had been canceled because Turkey had protested to Great Britain.

Asked whether he was now more concerned with "instruction or entertainment" as against "lasting qualities of literature," he responded forthrightly:

Yearnings for immortality are an old headache with the race. I always suppose that's why a man raises a family. However, I have a strong feeling that the dramatist who is worth his salt is far more interested in good sharp pencils and quiet to begin with. Next, given a theme in which he is really interested, in which he participates (and that is really the first requirement of an art work), he knows his work must be exciting and entertaining since in time a play must make an immediate impression on an audience. A dramatist who thought in terms of posterity's attitude toward his work would be in the singular position of a man who attempted to predetermine what part of his body was going to be nourished by the steak he was eating. . . . *

My formula is simple, I write what I believe! Many writers write what they think the audience believes. The function of an artist in any medium should be to tell the truth completely, from top to bottom. *Truth is a revolutionary force.*

Mr. Weinstein of station WOR closed by wishing him "all success in your devotion to the stage and to the presentation of the Truth." Odets went home and added to his bulging file of "General Notes":

A first rate exuberance will always make up its own words, vocabulary! That is a way of going around the thing, the object, and expressing its essence, the feeling it engenders! Poetry!

The truth is that there are few men who can afford *not* to get married.

What a poor life where the meal becomes the chief verification of security and actual existence!

A poet is a man who trusts no experience but his own.

Art is to make life less superficial. (H. Clurman)

Odets was now trying to restore to his work the wholehearted "conviction of innocence," the uncritical idealism that had provided such joy, hope, even faith—in himself and in his audience—when it had

---

* The writer nourishes his *Self* with his own words! Compare Odets' statement to that of Thomas Wolfe, who wrote that he would one day die of gluttony by devouring his own (overly abundant) words.

merged with him three years earlier in shouting, "Strike!" To be sure, his hero, union leader Lefty, had been found dead with a bullet in his head, murdered by an external enemy, a corrupt leader, but he had died *meaningfully*, in order that "all men should be free." The fragmented Joe Bonaparte's death had had no such meaning ("What waste!" says Frank at the close of *Golden Boy*).

The prescient Roosevelt, seeing war ahead, had, however, begun to rearrange his priorities. The Works Progress Administration must be whittled away; thus, the Federal Theatre would disappear within the year, and with it Odets' hope that it would produce *The Silent Partner* in forty states. In some desperation, he returned to his abandoned play about Cuban revolutionaries, begun in 1936, *Law of Flight*. He changed his hero's name from Guiteras to Lorca, but this play remained dead on his desk. He could not breathe life into any of these brave Cubans who, in this trial universe, were trying to subdue on their tiny island the fascist and military tidal wave now threatening to leave its rehearsals in Spain and engulf the world. Even the confused *Silent Partner* appeared to him a far more possible creative venture.

It was not simply, as Clurman thought, that Odets' stay in Cuba had been too brief to give him sufficient background for a credible play. Rather, the intertwining of Odets' own crisis of intimacy with that of world history was shifting his creative center of gravity. As the war came closer, even the face of the external enemy was changing, and he could no longer be ignited by the simplified problems and solutions of *Lefty* or even of *Awake and Sing!*, wherein the vanquishment of the corrupt union leader, the boss, the Nazi, the merchandising world, or even of what he called in *Awake and Sing!* the "petty conditions of life" leads automatically to the self-verification, the joyous self-realization of Everyman, a "Paradise" regained.

Like many artists at this time, Odets felt an impulse simultaneously to express the acute social crisis and to withdraw totally into his own hectic inner life. Still struggling to resolve his protracted twin crises of identity and of intimacy in his marriage, he found himself thinking about the pathetic efforts of an obedient little dentist to break out of the stifling bonds of his childless marriage and constricted life to a genuine intimacy and generativity. Moreover, in fear, Odets was beginning to suspect that the Broadway audience which supports a "hit" was, as he put it, "like a whore that pretends to be an aristocrat"—tasteless, naïve, sentimental, and unable to comprehend the larger patterns of the human condition. To Luise he expressed the opinion that audiences were probably far superior in her civilized Vienna, a city on the brink of one of the most savage periods in its history.

Thus, he found himself scribbling notes for the play which ultimately he titled *Rocket to the Moon*—about Ben Stark, a meek and repressed dentist. The stale, frightened Stark finds himself half asleep, half dead in life, no longer a creative "pioneer" in orthodontia, and caught between his duty to a controlling, depressed, and carping wife and his attraction to a young, aspiring, and sexually exciting girl who is simultaneously being courted by a worldly old man. The external enemy, clear in *Waiting for Lefty* as the oppressive ruling class, has here become amorphous: the obediently constricting identity of the American middle class. These few notes represented, however, Odets' growing need to investigate from the inside, more sharply than in *Golden Boy*, the relationship of his own psychology to life-fulfillments. He puts into the dentist's mouth a sentence which precisely sums up his own creative struggle as playwright:

"When I have to talk price with a patient [read, "an audience"] it cuts me off immediately from his needs. . . . This is a *business* when it should be a fine human service. . . . Just let them pay me a living wage. And in that service . . . I will regain . . . my stature as a man. . . ."

Along with these notes for *Rocket to the Moon*, Odets again took up work on the Cuban play, journeying to Philadelphia to work alone on it in the house of his Aunt Esther. Then, with great misgivings, he read it to the Group. Clurman's pronouncement that it was "a blank cartridge" elicited the unanimous conclusion that it "needed more work," always a euphemism in the theatre for a fundamentally negative judgment. Still his need to connect overtly in his work with the history and, accordingly, with the group-identity about him remained; he was not ready to give up work on *Law of Flight*. In his notes he wrote:

I am not interested in portraying human nature—that is easy—but in portraying human nature as modified and conditioned by society and social conditions. It is the only way I set out to work. A character is a social type when I set out. On this foundation an individual appears.

The daily headlines by this time were becoming almost intolerable. "My God," writes Luise from California, "where shall all the Jews go?" The sinister signs of what still lay ahead were gradually becoming sharper. Yet the methods evolving for a "solution of the Jewish problem" defy comprehension to such an extent that, beyond what Erikson has called "abortive fits of revulsion," nobody—be he American, Jew, or German— could maintain any consistent emotional reaction to them.

Odets now interviewed "one long parade of Cubans, a peculiar race, hard and soft at the same time." He located also an expert on the Cuban revolution, and continued to wrestle with his Spanish-speaking characters, "who are shot while trying to escape" after being offered amnesty by a cynical dictator who thus betrays them. Clurman, Irwin Shaw, and Kazan's wife, Molly, took a trip to Cuba without Odets, to "soak up the atmosphere" in preparation for a Group production of Odets' play.

As he finds this play resisting him, Odets reads and rereads a long and passionate letter from Harold Clurman, deeply concerned that Clifford is so often leaving New York to be with his wife in Hollywood; in the letter Clurman adjures him to work harder that he may better seize and project the "American and international reality." Although its content deals with Odets' productivity and discipline, the tone of this communication is highly personal, almost the tone of a lover:

Hotel Stafford
Baltimore, Md.

Clifford Darling,
   I am obeying a sudden impulse in writing you. I feel the need to say once more what I have said so often. . . .
   . . . I have just finished reading a play by Hemingway—don't know yet exactly what I think of it—it's "problematic" . . . but it gives me to think not only of the subject matter—which is really Hemingway's subjective feeling about himself and his kind in Spain —but of the problem of contemporary American writers. Last night I saw Behrman's "Wine of Choice" and tho it is only a slight thing and it doesn't quite come off (not yet at any rate) it has a spark of talent, a note of seriousness, a muffled tingle of reality . . . and that reality is so rare on our stage and so important that we must learn to show it, discuss it, understand it, sing it. . . .

But when I think how far these plays are even from their own standards—from being clear, visible, significant . . . when I think how vital the realities they suggest or point to (?), when I think of the American and international reality they are connected with I cry out that we *must* all learn to seize this reality, understand it better, penetrate it more deeply and project it more boldly and beautifully. We *must* do it not for art's sake, but for the sake of our own hearts and guts, our own lives which are so immortally connected with and significant of all the life that is around us. . . .

And of all people *you* Clifford Odets are the nearest to understand or *feel* this American reality . . . the reality only half experienced but nevertheless present for most Americans like us—of whom there are many millions. . . . *You* are nearer to that reality than anybody I know, nearer to it I believe than all the American novelists and playwrights—Yes I say this advisedly. You are the *Man.* You have more chaos in you than Eugene O'Neill and chaos is good and creative to begin with. You have more goodness than Jack Lawson and without goodness nothing good can come. You have more scope than such as O'Casey, more warmth and immediacy than most of the novelists. But don't be flattered for the more you have the greater the responsibility, the greater the shit you are if you do not make the best of it—give the most of it in the finest way. You have a hard task because you were given so much. . . . You must work all the time. No, you don't work enough, you don't write enough. . . . Write small plays moderate in scope—as well as big ones. All your plays are relevant, are real . . . especially those laid in America! . . .

Don't be afraid of "Silent Partner"—it is full of wonderful things but it is half born still—no matter what it is in comparison with the others (get over the habit of thinking about "others." That is *critic* stuff—not creative). . . . Write—write—write—because we need it so much. "We" is not the Group alone, not the American theatre (pfui! on the American theatre) but our folks, we Americans, we guys who live on University Place, Hester St., Fifth Ave., Central Park West, Santa Monica Blvd., Oshkosh, and Kalamazoo.

You always say you can't write unless you feel there is a need for your work. Darling the need is so *great* that it is terrifying—the need is for 100 Clifford Odets and 100 plays by all of them would not be enough for what work has to be done—unless we all go to our doom. You are a Voice—we need millions of articulate Voices to rouse our sad bewildered, bloody, horror-stricken world. You are the *Best* Voice we have in America today . . . for the love of your brothers—*give out!!*

If your plays can't be "perfect" or perfectionist, let them be plentiful—like Balzac's novels (the man was crude but he was a torrent). Sometimes I think the best American art—Whitman, Marin, etc.—is characterized by a certain roughness, speed, helter-skelter quality and maybe your plays have to be a little imperfect. . . .

. . . You know that I can't tell you always what I feel and think even when we are alone together, kidding or being serious, drinking or exchanging looks and thoughts. But you must know that above all things I have this great desire to shape the world in my own way to the realization of what is the truth about the life of our times and all times—so that the world can *live.* We must all work in trades, in politics, in the arts toward this end . . . some call it the revolution! . . . You have the stuff to really *serve* . . .

and that is what I am asking you to do. You must work like a coal-heaver. You must sweat from the exertion of it all. . . . Don't be a renegade to your talent . . . And, if for some reason, you are stopped at an impasse—then move to where you are not known, move to where you will get no publicity no matter what you do or whom you see—get lost somewhere in a sea of American life. . . .

Harold.

I'll be home by Saturday night.

In the Group, once again was circulated a comment that provoked both laughter and serious thought: "Harold is never so happy as when he is pregnant with a new play of Clifford's." Odets considered making Harold happy by accepting an offer from a left-wing group to fly to Spain, "all expenses paid," and write a play about the civil war there; it would be of material help, this group said, to the struggling Loyalist forces. But his lifelong terror of flying was a serious deterrent; the other was his strong wish to be with his wife, to whom he wrote from New York that he has been thinking, "How you walked into this room one night. You were wearing a pink sweater and your unbound breasts shook as you crossed the room and I said 'oh dear' to myself."

Odets turned his thoughts once more to the "dentist play" and to something else, the drab piece he called "the piano-store play," thinking to star Luise in at least one of them. Their love would issue, he hoped, in a historic collaboration for the theatre. Still, despite his best efforts, the characters in neither of these were coming to life any faster than in the Cuban play.◖ He called it a "work-stoppage," complained bitterly to his secretary, paced the New York streets at night, going sometimes to eat chicken soup at Moskowitz and Lupowitz restaurant, or to the East Side Jewish theatre, where he delighted in the acting of the Adler family and the great Tomashevsky. Sometimes, when he needed to be reassured that he was Somebody, he went to the Stork Club. If a columnist noticed him there with a "real" celebrity and wrote a squib about him in the newspaper, it would cheer him.

Not a day passed now without some form of communication between Clifford and Luise, most of it, on both sides, ardent, tender, and complaining. He says she doesn't write enough; she is apologetic and fervently prays for the end of their separation as she is not a letter-writer. Why is her line always busy, he asks, or "out of order"? Has she taken the phone off the hook? He scolds that she "waits" for a sign, and over and over he apologizes for his quick temper. Of course, he says, his many aversions are ridiculous. She must do as she likes. But her mistrust of him is most painful and her lack of response shames him in front of his secretary:

Permit me to record the melancholy fact that when you ask the secretary if he writes my telegrams to you, you make me very unhappy. Such news makes me turn pale, and believe me this is no exaggeration. One other thing which makes me ashamed in front of the secretary is that he sees so many telegrams leave here for California and so very few ever come back in answer. . . .

◖ 22.1.

Luise's response is immediate and filled with yearning for their ("Soon!") reunion. She cannot, she says, maintain a relationship by mail; she wants a personal, private, and secret relationship. He reassures her that as soon as the Group's new play, *Casey Jones*, by Robert Ardrey, has opened, he will bring to California Luise's mother, who is about to arrive from Brussels for a visit. Addressing her variously and always affectionately as "Dearest Mozart Sonata," "Dearest Babe—Fiery-Girl," "Darling Luisechen," "Loved Girl," "Best girl and wife," he confides his anticipation that Emmy Rainer will be *his* mother too:

> I just know what your mother is going to be like and she is going to get a big American Walt Whitman hug from me. I'm getting to be such a damn little polished gentleman that I won't even miss flowers for her. To be in love with you as I'm in love with you is to feel that we both were born from the same mother—love always seems to have some of that, and perhaps that's why the mother-in-law so often is jealous of the new child. Well, here the field is clear—you have the only mother of the two of us, sadly enough. It amazes me, as I happen to think of it now, how often I think of my mother. Often, during one day, I'll have two or three short shocks of remembering her—it runs thru me like a snatch of some twisted tune.

Speaking of mothers and of music, he hopes in the next sentence that with *Don Giovanni* he will convert her to Mozart's operas, "the tenderest passages of music ever written in opera, and I don't mean the fake sloppy Italian kind." Two things he needs in order to sleep well these days: "You and good work." Repeatedly, and in many forms, he says, "Love is wanting to do something for the loved girl. Tell me, baby, write me, send me a message and tell me what I can do for you."

She writes that she is taking vitamins and "swallowing good ocean air" so that when the time comes for them to start a family, "our baby will be a giant." She wishes he would in the meantime write her a good screenplay for a film of Joan of Arc. He, in turn, sends enthusiastic snapshots of Elia and Molly Kazan's new infant, describes with pleasure Paula Strasberg "carrying her baby around inside," and gives envious news that his secretary and longtime friend, Herman Kobland, is soon to become a father.

Luise, however, was now working on her seventh film in three years and, clearly, earlier had not been the time to start a family. Paula Strasberg recalled many conversations with Odets in which he expressed the hope that the time was not far off. Now that her hammered-out agreement with MGM permits her to be in New York with her husband from October until April of each year "until 1942," Luise appears to be rethinking her priorities. First, she lays out a clear schedule of plays and films for both, and an itinerary for a trip together in Europe. The Chinese government has appointed her arbiter of a documentary Archibald MacLeish and Joris Ivens will make. "Why," she writes to Odets, "can't these ghastly agents understand that the freedom to function in life, and to work for important issues that history is presenting at this time are more important than the million dollars" that the agent keeps telling her she could have gotten were she less stubborn? And, finally, she now seems to consider it possible to start a family. Elated, Odets replies, "Did I hear you say something about a baby?"

In the meantime he is nurturing "babies" of his own: he has begun to support—from his "Pearl Fund," named after his mother—a variety of promising young playwrights, painters, and poets, enabling them to do their own work. This provides him solace for his current writing problems. He writes graphologist Lucia Eastman of these difficulties and she advises him to try to do "*some* creative work each day as it is the only real outlet people of your type can find entirely satisfactory and unselfconscious." Beyond the terror of failure, he is again persuaded that an important factor in his "work-stoppage" is his resentment of the turnabout in his relationship with his father. He decides several times not to send Lou Odets any more money for the doomed Doctors of Sleep, and he is conscious on occasion of a wish to disappoint, even to shame him. Nonetheless, for the leaflet of his father's luckless mattress enterprise he writes its advertising slogan: "Civilization harasses people."

Luise appears to understand her husband's desperation and has rented a small and private work-cottage for him at Lake Arrowhead, California. Their correspondence continues ardent and tender. Just before leaving New York, Odets receives from her a long letter:

In a few weeks I have to start work and I am looking forward to it. I don't know why they push all their pictures constantly into distance—and they release so many people, much uncontentment is among the employed. I had a long talk with the car drivers on the lot and you don't know how much hatred there is, and hatred against the *Jews* too. The drivers thought I can help them a little but I spoke to them and said that they have to be unionized and only so can come to anything, but they said that the union is not doing a God damned thing that their union absolutely is sticking together with the bosses; and I must say darling—I feel so too, it's terrible, even out of that develops a racket here in America. The Screen Actors Guild too is completely *ridiculous* and seems employed by the producers, they haven't pressed through a *single* point for the actors. . . . Oh, there is so much work to be done. Sometimes I wish I would be stronger physically, *not* a man but a *woman* with very wide shoulders and fight for the things which I feel have to be fought for. As I don't believe in the voices of St. Catherine and other saints I believe in wide shoulders, but as mine don't feel wide enough I will be quiet for a while. But sometimes I feel like a burning flame and sometimes that comes out, and those are the times when they suddenly want me to help them, this group and that group and another group, it was always like that in my life, but then I say no, no, not yet, I am my man's girl because he wants me to be and I want to be! and he will do; and the strength I have I will give to him, but that doesn't mean that I don't have it—and I'll tell you right now something else: I think only women like me with the inside strength I have are more worth then any man ever can be! Because they combine besides strength the knowledge of a snake with the tenderness of a flower and with all that they can fly like a bird. Now tell me a man who can do that!!

My dearest dearest darling kiss me. I am yours, I am your girl, hold me in your arms warm and tender and strong and let me see your eyes, your eyes looking at me. My darling, my dearest, my everything. Do you know that you make the world go round for me? Luise.

Like her husband, perhaps like all artists, Luise longed to be simultaneously a man and a woman, to "fly like a bird" with the "knowledge of a snake," and yet to be tender as a flower. For her work, she said, "May I have my feet in the ground and the fist of God in my back."

*   *   *

When Odets arrived "on the Coast," Luise took him up to San Francisco. Luise recalled: "He had never been there, while I knew it well and loved it, and wanted him to see it as well." It did not work out quite as she hoped. He had explained to her that he "could go around the world just by reading books about it all," so he was not really interested "to walk about, see the Bay, enjoy the up-and-down of trolley cars and all else. 'Everyone has their own rhythm,' he declared. 'You have yours, I have mine!' They returned to Los Angeles, stopping in Santa Barbara, from where Luise phoned her home in Brentwood to find out if there was any important news. "News there was indeed," Luise recalled. "It was the evening of the Academy Award presentations. The newspapers had been on the phone all afternoon as news had spread that Luise might win the award for the second time in successive years, this time for her work as O-Lan in *The Good Earth*. Was she snubbing the Academy Award dinner? Did she even think of not coming? the papers asked. It was six P.M.; the drive back would take a good two hours. Odets, hiding his competitiveness behind a mask of indifference to such vulgar honors, suggested they skip the affair. Luise knew she could not do that. A fierce fight started. Luise drove, Odets shouted."

Arrived home, they were greeted by a giant mattress that all but filled the bedroom. It was a gift from "Papa" Odets' Doctors of Sleep Shoppe. A shipping charge of $248 was attached. For Luise the mattress became part of the "weird nightmare of the evening."

> Clifford was furious, eyes rolling. I was in jeans and sneakers. I had to change, I had no time to appease Clifford. In fact, I did not want him to come down to Los Angeles and the Biltmore Hotel with me. I felt upset and miserable and he was the cause. Why, if he thought it was so "nothing," should he share this triumph with me! He insisted on coming, and he came. Arriving at the Biltmore Hotel, all lit up for the great evening, I could not face going in. It was raining and I was crying. We walked around the hotel four or five times. We went in just as it was announced I had won the award for the second time, the second year running. It made history. Clifford's face remained grim throughout. I made my thank-you speech. I smiled for the countless cameras and reporters. Here I was at dizzying heights, admired and envied: I was as low as I had ever been in my life. I did what I had to do mechanically, I hardly realized I had got the award. Clifford, who would say to me: "You are Duse" and "You are the only true actress" and what not—when I was at the top of my fame, it just seemed to provoke him. He broke what he could break. Had I not grown up with a decent sense of values within a stable environment, I might well have done away with myself. Years later I felt deeply sorry for Marilyn Monroe, I understood her suicide.

Dimly, Odets understood Luise's despair, but could not afford to act upon his empathy. Instead, in one of his hundreds of files of works in progress, he entered the note "The Actress Play": "a star lives in public isolation." The newspapers recorded in a combination of surprise and annoyance that he had come to this formal and important occasion in an ordinary business suit.

The day after the Academy Awards, Hitler marched into Austria and Luise exhausted herself making plans to receive fleeing refugees, many of them writers, actors, artists. The new Exodus had now begun in earnest.

> *It was his duty to keep the Kingdom*
> *of the Movies free from the ancient*
> *enemy of the people—Art.*
>
> BEN HECHT *on Louis B. Mayer*

Odets did not know that Luise had sent for her mother from Europe to seek her counsel about their immensely difficult marriage. With a little-girl longing not unlike her husband's—to get, as she later put it, "only what a mother can give"—Luise sat down alone with Emmy Rainer. She recalled that before she could mention anything about her own affairs, her mother sadly and quietly said to her: "Darling, you cannot imagine how difficult it is to live with Father; I don't think I am able to bear it much longer." (Luise's father had many qualities reminiscent of Odets.) "My poor mother sought the counsel from me that I had so hoped to get from her." It was apparent to Luise that her mother was at least as needy as she, and her own sense of isolation deepened. It did not help significantly that she was attracting many interesting men.

Her oblivious agent meanwhile wrote Odets that to him she seemed "very happy since her new contract" with MGM. Her husband, on the other hand, with three thousand miles once more separating them (he had returned to New York to the Group), was now able to send her flowers and all kinds of warm and exquisitely written commitment. ("The roses are staying in my bedroom," she wires, "giving me a lot of warm looks.")

Relieved, after bitter struggle, that she is not being farmed out to another producer to do a film she "loathes" ("How dreadful to be a property," she writes Odets, a chattel who can be disposed of at the whim of Louis B. Mayer), she is still in dread of her assignment as Mrs. Johann Strauss in *The Great Waltz,* to be done directly after completion of her current film, *The Toy Wife.* Despite her agent's efforts to have the script rewritten, she still thinks it a very poor script and, according to the agent, feels as though the six months in Hollywood to which she has agreed by contract are "like a jail term." The agent assures Odets the studio will have to be more flexible with Luise because, "after all, this, her next film *The Great Waltz,* is a super-colossal epic [Luise did *not* think so] and . . . it's going to cost about a million and a half, which is one of the most expensive pictures . . . and they are not likely to throw that money away." Eventually he hopes to solve it by "keeping her away from them [the heads of the studio] entirely and only use her [in negotiations] when it is necessary as a trump, if she avoids getting into arguments. It's silly to think of her intentionally ruining herself. She's too valuable an asset for them to intentionally destroy."

By the end of April Luise has fled briefly, "without permission," from her Hollywood prison to New York, seeking asylum and her husband's protection both from the studio and from her agents, who, she says, sound "more and more like they are working for Metro-Goldwyn-Mayer than for us." Her assigned role in *The Great Waltz* is, she believes, "shallow, ridiculous and intolerable." She will *not* be a mindless marionette, no matter what her contract states.

Her husband agrees and, after several drafts, sends a note to the senior partner of her agent's firm, Berg-Allenberg:

Dear Phil,
  The functions of an agent are exactly those of field interferers in a football game. And now you just ain't doing no interference on our behalf. When the moguls of Metro give you an order you deliver it verbatim instead of taking them out! Pooh to that, Phil, absolutely and positively Pooh! Please always be interference for our side! This goes for Luise's vacations and it goes for parts and pictures and everything else. Yours in absolute sorrow and chagrin.

  When her agent wired Luise that she would be suspended from the studio payroll if she did not *"immediately"* fly back to California, she did so, but only for a few days of retakes on *The Toy Wife*, after which she returned to New York for what was to be a happy spring vacation with her husband. That it did not unfold as planned is attested to by a playful wire from Luise, sent a week later on May 16 from California, saying in part, ". . . it is not allowed to hit the girl over the head. But of course it's not allowed either that the girl packs and runs away. However, I would have come back the very next day wouldn't I have been frightened of your rolling eyes. . . ."
  Odets, it appears, was not to be so easily mollified by this peace offering, instead typing out on yellow paper on the same day a furious note to his wife, no salutation and unsigned. He now reproaches her with accusations he steadily made against himself:

You have no kind of concentration and you lack completely all working habits both in and out of your work . . .

He has patiently waited now for two years, he says, for her to become aware of her own failings, to no avail. He continues:

I am slowly going crazy from that queenliness. . . . Only Christs and Lenins are permitted such acute awareness of the faults of others in this world!
  Until that day when you are free from those faults you are forever finding in me and all the others near you, until then I don't permit you to make one word of criticism of me, not one word!
  You are wilful and capricious, unreasonable and absolutely primitive in your dependence on blind feeling. You seem to lack all reasoning powers. . . . You live for the minute instead of the year. . . .
  You are the one who has to do the growing up. . . . A movie director doesn't give you direction because he is afraid of you, not because he is completely dumb.
  Me, I don't want to be married to a perfectionist who is herself full of faults!

  For his file called "General Notes" he jotted, "A man and a woman must be constantly inventive in relation to each other. When they refuse, there is trouble."
  As he sat depressed, waiting in vain in his New York apartment for some mending words from his wife, Odets' rage and despair mounted. Perhaps the marriage, he thought, was truly at an end. Instead of writing this to Luise, he lashed out at his publisher, Bennett Cerf, for insufficient advertising and improper distribution of his plays, and was not appeased by Cerf's prompt reply that he considered "you and O'Neill the two most important playwrights in America."
  On May 25 a letter from his father assures him that "Floating Com-

fort Is Here to Stay," and that if he will give him an additional $1,000 for Doctors of Sleep, "this business will go over big as it is the talk of Philadelphia."

On the back of this letter Odets has written, "You talk like a con man . . . I did not and do not like to be stuffed with vague optimistic halftruths." To his father he wrote:

Dear L.J., I have your letter of yesterday and my answer to it is that I don't think I want to give you the money. There are several reasons for this, the chief one being that in the past two years I have handed over to you 20,500 dollars. That is a lot of money in any language you choose.

I did not want to go in any business, but for your sake I agreed that I would put 5 thousand dollars in the present shop. You insisted that was not enough, and added that a few thousand more would see you thru. Reluctantly I agreed to that. Next you took 2 thousand dollars more, bringing my cash outlay to 10,000. Now that you want 4 thousand more and write as if it is an easy and understandable fact that I'll turn it over . . . And above that this giving can go on forever, with no stop.

You are coming to me now as a business man, not a father, and when you come that way you must bring with you the facts and figures and safety devices to cover *my* investments. Thruout the dealings in this business you have been talking to me like a gold mine salesman and completely excluding from your plans and my investments all chances of possible failure. . . .

Frankly, I don't like this business of being pushed around with super-salesmanship. It mortifies me and makes me uneasy. . . . Since I do not feel that you are completely frank with me (and have not been so before) it is impossible for me to go along further with you. You will have to know that you are not being backed up by a bank.

Maybe, as you write, "We are going places with Doctors of Sleep," but my share is done by now. "Going places" has to be explained to me on a much more practical basis instead of on a general air of goodfellowship and salesmanship. . . .

That is all I can say at present. If you have some answer please let me hear it—write it instead of telling me. When you knock me down with your terrific energy I usually don't hear a word you say.

In the meantime he eagerly awaited in sleepless anxiety, anger, and suspicion an overture from his wife. Instead, he received by return mail a six-page reply from his father on stationery with an inch-high block heading stating, "Sleep's the Only Medicine That Gives Ease—Sophocles," the paper covered by a fuzzy green shadow-picture of doctors and nurses contentedly looking down on a presumably happy customer lying on one of his father's mattresses. L. J. Odets denies with many underlinings that he is untrustworthy, trying to justify the further large sums he is asking of his son, concluding, "I did not and don't intend to tell any untruths to you."

Only in this context of profound unhappiness and a chronic conviction that he was being deceived, unfairly treated, indeed guilefully exploited (he was still loaning large sums not only to Group members but also to his sister Genevieve's husband, to his old Bronx buddies, and to colleagues in the theatre) can one understand Odets' response to the first communication from Luise in almost two weeks. On May 28, 1938, he received a wire without a salutation: "I am going to have a baby. Luise."

His immediate response to this was hostile disbelief. The return cable Luise received came as a sledgehammer blow: "Dear Luise will wire you Monday because now I don't know what to say love Clifford." (In the rough draft, "tomorrow" was crossed out and "Monday" substituted, and the word "love" was penciled in as an afterthought.) Upon reading this, she decided with a leaden heart to have an abortion immediately and to file for divorce.

Tragically, Odets had typed out a different wire, never sent:

Dear Luise, if you are sure you are going to have a baby, finish the present picture and then come east and we will live in a country house while the baby grows and I try to be a productive playwright once again. But you must come not as a critic and you must not complain because I am Clifford Odets and you must not load me with fatigue and worry so that I can't write. And if I hear you ever again talk about the great sacrifices you make for me, I will be the one to fly away that time.

Luise, shown this unsent wire three decades later, was certain that her response, had he sent it, would have been instantly to break her contract with Metro-Goldwyn-Mayer, to fly east, and to await their baby.

On Monday, May 30, she received from Clifford a long wire marked, "Send and deliver immediately! Retain all punctuation!" It further solidified her dread and bitter decision:

Dear Luise, please be very clear. You have been most critical against what you call my selfishness and lack of appreciation of you. You have often stated how I am responsible for your great unhappiness. Numerous times you have packed your bags and flown away. Before those things I have been fearful or nervous or angry and completely unproductive and I keep asking myself what good is a man's life to himself or another if he can not work. Now I am finally convinced, against my emotions and pride, that you married the wrong man in the hope that you could mould and change him to your pleasure. Above all this I think your delicate health and secret feminine trouble, about which you did not tell me, forbids a child at present. Finally, I must ask you again to be very clear for your own sake. If in your opinion I am so poor a husband how can you expect me to be ready for parenthood? Will your message make a new person of me? Will being a parent change anything? Will it change our essential clashing natures, yours or mine? I am very sad to say I don't think so and under the circumstances it is possible to send nothing but a sick sad heart which you doubtlessly share. Clifford.

His mention of her "secret feminine trouble" referred to his having vaguely heard from a friend that Luise had a tipped uterus, which was untrue. It is his way of telling her she is lying, that she *could not* have become pregnant until this presumed anomaly was corrected, or that if she were truly pregnant, it could not be safe for her. Thus she *must* be conniving, he thought, to trap him into a renewal of their marriage with this false news. He will not, he states, be trapped. She, in turn, wires back that she has not told him earlier of the pregnancy as "I didn't want this to interfere with your decisions," and she tells him now "So you'll be proud that the woman in me received completely the man in you."

In his "General Notes" that evening, he jots: "The big bribe of

Christianity is that Christ will be responsible for anything you do—you need be responsible for nothing!"

On the following day it is clear that a deeply troubled and perceptive Luise has received his implied central message about "responsibility":

Dear Clifford with great sadness I must say you are right, that it is good we are apart, as it is true that I was so often very unhappy on your side. And it is true that I hoped and hoped often against my own belief that you will stop finding fault with me and making demands on me and start to change yourself. Your wire is brilliant and you really relieve yourself of every kind of responsibility. But Clifford, what great unbelievable unkindness to speak now about some kind of secret feminine trouble I should have. Would your remark not be so sad because it belittles so tremendously the memory of a man I had loved I should laugh a little about this, but so I must tell you that never in my life I had any kind of trouble like that and I hope I never will dear Clifford I wish a world of good for you and that you will become very happy and do great work. Luise

On June 1 Odets received from obstetrician Dr. Rudolph Marx in Los Angeles the surprising report, sent "at the request of Miss Luise Rainer," that her uterus is "normal" and that on May 26 he had indeed found her to be pregnant. Clearly taken aback by this evidence that Luise was not deceiving him, he writes her a pained, perplexed letter, every line of which suggests that, while he is by no means ready for fatherhood, neither is he indifferent to his wife:

Dear Luise,

For the love of goodness, do you think I am trying to find out something bad about you? Or to look for secret bad things? Or that I want to make accusations? I was only angry, even bitter, to find that you had a doctor's report about your insides and had passed the information along to strangers without thinking it necessary or wifely to mention them to your husband. The real truth is that I love your insides, up-placed, down-placed, inside out or any way. I would be very happy to be proven wrong, but I get a sense from you that you think I am some mean low fellow who is trying to do you harm and slander.

Beautiful girl, what do you think it is? That I dislike you, even hate you? You are in me like an ache and anguish and I easily remember every good and wonderful quality you have. Don't send me these cold doctor reports, since you did not choose to tell them to me before, you yourself. I know you better than this report, better than the doctor. Also, I am not looking to blame you for anything, am not looking to dodge this responsibility or that—those are all unessential and ugly activities—not that you or I are without blemish.

My feeling, Luise, is to help you, to give you what I can, to work out this love for you in some way or other. And that last only because I don't seem to be able to give you a husband, myself. All the love for you doesn't help—we don't get along.*

For the past two years we haven't helped each other as artists, have perhaps even damaged each other a little—altho it is all marked up in the end to growth and new perceptions, not loss.

But just believe me, Luise—when I am tired out and as ex-

---

* In a later interview Luise commented, "I wholly agreed with this last sentence. I took the consequences!"

hausted out as I find myself now, it is out of love for you, not hate, certainly not indifference or injured feelings!!! How can I say you are the woman I loved? The word is love, the tense is the present, now, here, today and tonight. Which is why everything is so painful and I feel so lumped-up in the chest and head and all over, and surely you must feel the same way!!!

Angry, calm, sober, drunk, here or west, I know those good dear things which move inside you, and don't love them less now. But we can't live together with justice and equity to both—or it has never seemed to work out that way. We seem to repress each other, distress and throw each other off balance. There would be great hope if it happened to only one of us, but always it happens to both—we can't be quiet against each other and both of us need quiet above many other things.

No, Luise, take back the doctor's report. Tell the doctor and yourself that I love your insides and don't probe them with suspicious unfriendly fingers. Don't think anything like that, Luise, unless you want to make me more miserable than I am right now. But you don't want to do that. Perhaps I pained you before, during the past few weeks. But it wasn't my intention to do that. My silence came from being hurt (permit us each our hurt), from the bag-packing and the moving out.

Well Luise, if we can't grow up together, we must grow up independently. But it just is no joke all around and you must know how painful it is. In the meantime, if you permit it, I am not impressed by the doctor's. "The general condition of Miss Rainer was excellent." Take care of your delicate health. . . .

Perhaps I will go to London next week. It seems the Golden Boy Company is going there to play for from two weeks up to two months. Perhaps the trip will have a refreshing effect. Anyway I certainly have to come up from under the water and shake my head clear. Right now you probably feel as useless as I do. If only I were not so wilful, or you were not—if only one of us was different—but no man or woman can throw a whole past life out of the window.

Goodnight, Luise [written in].

Clifford.

Several days before setting sail on the *Queen Mary* with Clurman and Stella and Luther Adler for the London opening of *Golden Boy*, Odets wrote Luise an unhappy, stalling farewell in answer to a short note from her:

Dear Luise, The only thing left for me is to agree with your short calm note which arrived late tonight, and that last agreement is only a masculine conceit. Since you have already spoken with a lawyer there is nothing left to be said. Wednesday I'm leaving for London and will be gone four or five weeks. Please don't do anything until I return; then I'll do anything you want done. In the meantime I haven't and won't say a word of this to anyone—that will leave you free to present the break in any way you choose. I am assuming that you will want to present the break first since you have gone to a lawyer so quickly, so very quickly quickly quickly. As soon as I return I'll send you a wire asking you what you want done and how.

Goodbye for now, Luise. Please accept all hopes for every good normal beautiful thing you ask from life, and so really richly deserve. Yes. Clifford.

He followed the letter by a wire:

Suggest you do everything possible to get your citizenship papers in the meantime.

His ledger records that on this same day he sent $1,000 to his father and $500 to Harold Clurman.

Luise now wrote:

Clifford,

My darling—I still believe you don't know why I want to get this divorce. Things which are going around in my mind are not conscious to you at all and I think to a certain degree I owe you some explanations for this, as you call it quick, quick, quick decision.

I will admit freely that I probably would never have thought so quick quick quick to do this step, had not something happened which shocked me so terrificly that I think nothing could make me overcome it. It was the way you reacted when I told you that I am having a baby. Your baby. Since years let me say, I dreamed of having it, it was my greatest wish and since many months I told you so. And we both planned on having it. And again and again I had asked you: "Darling where will you put my baby," because already the pure childish thought of it gave me much great happiness. And then one day I knew I was carrying your baby. And Clifford, you could have hit me harder, or kicked me more or could have said still more terrible things to me, all that was forgotten over this wonderful event, which I always thought is one of the greatest and deepest moments between a woman and her man, and a man and his woman. I knew, when I was going to have this baby, I was going to be quiet and calm inside and I would have become stronger, too, and could have faced more, smiling at all the things which had troubled me so much before. Yes, my darling, I strongly felt that. And then I sent you this news and your answer was: "Don't know what to say will let you know in two days." Everything that followed was no more important to me, though, believe me, it broke my heart to pieces, when I got the answer concerning my "feminine trouble."

All right darling, you decided you didn't want the baby, but the way you let me know was so unbelievable that it no more fitted into the picture I had made of my Clifford. And this answer after two days of thought—from then on I knew that this I could never forget in my whole life. It still would have been different if we both would not have spoken so often of it and had wished our baby.

How little, how idiotic became all our quarrels when I knew that here the first great thing between us had happened. I tell you Clifford, after I received your wire I knew what I had to do. What I had to do for myself. But I still didn't know what I should do with my baby. I had received it in so great happiness and great belief and great trust and I had no reason to forget that so quick. But then I knew I had to disconnect every tie to you. I know you never knew it, but I was always so tremendously there for you. And now, to protect myself from greater hurt, I had to pull myself completely away. When a few days ago I was lying on the operating table, conscious and trembling in my whole body, not from fear, but from terrible unhappiness, I decided that this was the most I could ever stand from a man, who I thought loves me. And that made me decide so "quick, quick, quick."

Thinking he had a month's grace, Odets said nothing of his trouble to his Group brothers aboard the liner on this, his first and last trip abroad. Clurman, noticing his friend's utter silence and extreme melancholy, said to him, "I don't say life is good, I say life is life." He urged Odets to accompany him to Paris after the opening in London, telling him that composers Aaron Copland and David Diamond would be there, a special lure to Odets.

On the same afternoon that Sylvia Sidney had seen Luther Adler and the Group off to London, she was horrified upon returning home to read large black headlines which proclaimed that "Luise Rainer Sues Odets for Divorce as a Sulker,"* the newspaper story adding that he had "an ungovernable temper, stayed away from home all night, and wanted her to give up her career." Miss Sidney immediately radio-telephoned the *Queen Mary,* by now far at sea, and was connected to the stateroom Clurman shared with Stella Adler. Clurman (once described as a *"tragic* W. C. Fields"), on hearing "It is Miss Sylvia Sidney," replied in confusion, "Send her right up." She reminded him she was still in New York and said she was calling to warn Clifford of the terrible news that would greet him in the London press. Clurman now understood his friend's silent melancholy; Stella decided she must tell Odets.

Soon after, Clurman found him at the rail as he was taking his wedding ring from his finger and casting it into the Atlantic Ocean. Thinking to stiffen his friend's spine, Clurman said quietly, "How romantic." Odets made no reply.

Within a few hours there came a radiogram from Luise:

Dearest Clifford I hope you will understand that I could not have selfrespect anymore if I would go through any longer what I have gone through as always the best to you in all friendship. Luise

This was quickly followed by one from her lawyers explaining that "our client requires filing of action quickly in order to relieve tension and permit resumption of normal life." Luise's parents in Brussels assured her in a cable, "Cliff not worthy your devotion. Divorce will be extreme relief. Do not be miserable or fearful. Life will bring you a thousand times better." Luise in turn wired her father-in-law:

L.J. Dear—I wished I wouldn't have to write this letter. All I can say is that I wished so deeply that Cliff and I could have become happy. But it didn't go and so to save both our health and future happiness this step had to be done. I will be allways a friend of your "big boy" if he let me be it. . . .

Though disapproving of Odets, Metro-Goldwyn-Mayer had regularly dispensed idyllic press releases about the marriage. The recent batch had fitted especially well into their advertising campaign for her forthcoming film, *The Toy Wife.* Moreover, Odets' gangplank interview just before sailing for London—which, the newspapers reported, "made it clear he was leaving only because of business assignments and that he and Miss Rainer were very much in love"—now made Odets' friends aware how difficult would be his arrival in London. Writer John O'Hara, in London, radiogrammed Odets that he would sneak him off the *Queen Mary* on his arrival to avoid embarrassment. To Luise, Odets cabled, "How painful everything must be for you and how sorry I am."

*   *   *

* Luise Rainer said these were not her words.

As they neared the end of their sea journey, the Group members became anxious. It was well known that plays which succeeded on Broadway usually failed in London. No one, they feared, would understand the characters of *Golden Boy*, the American argot, or the play's social theme. Odets was apprehensive not only of the genteel British audience but also of humiliating questions from the London reporters about the failure of his marriage.

Opening night of *Golden Boy* at the St. James's Theatre, contrary to all expectations, was a stormy success. Never before had an audience applauded through the singing of "God Save the King." The London theatre world, and most particularly its insurgent forces—such as the amateur working-class Unity Theatre (on whose council were Sean O'Casey, Harold Laski, Paul Robeson, Sir Stafford Cripps, and Tyrone Guthrie)—perceived at once the dynamic vitality of the play and of this non-academic American company which presented a consistently vigorous ensemble and, in Harold Clurman's words, also "professed ideals of life as well as art." Even editorial columns in London papers hailed Odets as the "white hope of English dramatic letters," and the Group was entertained at a Parliament tea after the social meaning of *Golden Boy* had been discussed on the floor of the House of Commons.

Interviewed in the Mayfair apartment he had rented with Luther Adler, Odets expressed incredulity that he was being compared with Shakespeare and Bernard Shaw. "I could have been a first-class composer," he said, "but will always be a second-class playwright." Then turning quickly to the explosive issues of the history around him, he detailed his astonishment that so many English people had stated to him the opinion that the civil war in Spain was a small and local affair and that Hitler was "not really serious" and *surely* would never dare to bomb London. This in the face of reports in the British press of large-scale movements of Austrian Jews to a place near Munich, called Dachau, and of arrogantly heiling Nazis and followers of the fascist Franco staying, along with most of the Group, at London's elegant Dorchester Hotel.

"It seems to me," said Odets, "that the English stage needs a new kind of hero, one who will say, 'I will *not* carry on!'" According to one critic, Odets' work "started all the John Osbornes and the rest of England's angry young men."

Odets now began to outline a new "anti-Nazi play" and another about refugees. His personal resolve took, at first, the form of a virulent face-to-face attack, supported by Elia Kazan and Luther Adler, on Clurman's passivity as Group director. "Why," shouted Odets, "does Harold talk, talk, talk? Why does he raise no money?" And directly to Clurman, echoing his own self-accusations, "You're lazy. You don't respect your talent. The Group does not develop, they do not make artists of themselves!" Chairs, fists, and English bone china began to fly in the expensively furnished apartment in this, the opening skirmish of a battle that would continue for the rest of the life of the Group.

Odets meanwhile mailed off another $1,000 to his father, an equal amount to his sister Genevieve, just become a mother. And to one of the Bronx boys he lent $5,000 for an auto-sales business. It is hard to say whether these grand and powerful handouts filled him with as much triumph as anxiety.

To Kermit Bloomgarden, the Group's business manager, it appeared Odets was now convinced that Harold, in his weakness, was jeopardizing the Group's future because of the vanity and caprice of a powerful woman, Stella Adler. "All night," according to Odets, "Harold would harangue, click and grind his teeth, screaming all the critical and jealous things he could not, in the daytime, say to Stella." For her part, Miss Adler's conviction that Clurman's investment in the Group had reached absurd and fanatic proportions was underscored when Clurman insisted that Odets, Kazan, and Bloomgarden accompany them from London to Paris for a week. Just as Luise Rainer had felt she could not shake these omnipresent Group competitors, so apparently did the immensely attractive Stella Adler, who had adopted her own feminine means of fighting back at Clurman by taking on numerous gifted and famous lovers.

In Hollywood, under the half-inch headline "My Opinion is She Still Loves Him," columnist Louella Parsons quoted Luise as saying the Group was "Clifford's whole life, he was like a man with two wives, only I feel his first love was his greatest . . . some way, I didn't fit into that part of his life."

Returning to the United States on the *Champlain,* Clurman thought Odets slightly less depressed than on the way over, noted from a shipboard affair that he regarded his marriage as having truly come to an end, and, most important and alarming, observed that his work-stoppage continued. Clurman kept encouraging him to write "the dentist play," which, he told Odets, from its sketchy outline promised to be "infinitely tender and humbly truthful." Privately, Clurman was concerned that this story of a dentist ravaged by love for a silly girl might be a bit drab, but nonetheless he told Odets he would direct it if Odets could but mobilize himself. Although Clurman was hoping to put into effect a new Group plan for a four-play season, to include a work by Irwin Shaw and one by William Saroyan, there was as yet no finished play with which to open in the fall.

The London company and an American road tour of *Golden Boy* were, however, bright spots on the horizon, with Elia Kazan as the young fighter Joe Bonaparte and Lee J. Cobb as Joe's idealist father. Cobb, perceiving the deep bond between Odets and Kazan, recalled how well Kazan played Joe Bonaparte: "He was never a man at peace, and for the understanding of Joe's conflict, had much to draw on in himself. Kazan, like Bonaparte, was always trying to get somewhere, and it seemed to many of us in the Group he would do *anything, really, anything* to get there."

Back in New York, and once more against a stone wall in raising money for the new season, Clurman decided to journey to Hollywood to persuade Franchot Tone to come back and play in a new anti-Fascist play by Irwin Shaw, and to find a female star for Odets' "dentist play." Advance sales would doubtless be easier to build if the Group could advertise film stars. Although he was successful in persuading Tone to return for a year, and in locating a lovely young actress, Eleanor Lynn, just released by Metro-Goldwyn-Mayer, Clurman remained disquieted by Odets' continuing "restless, rootless, uncertain mood." He was pleased, however, to hear his friend had just refused to write an "extremely well-paid and important film."

With Kazan and his family, Odets rented for the summer the home of the Henry Varnum Poors in New City, New York, but could not settle down to work. For days on end he would disappear in a new and expensive car which he was barely able to drive. Clurman, back from California, awaited Odets' new play at this house. He recalled an evening when, having been absent for days, Odets careened up the road late at night and, bursting into the living room, shook a furious finger at him and shouted,

"Harold, you're dead wrong!" The problem in *Golden Boy,* he yelled, was not at all his lack of familiarity with the world of the prize ring, as Clurman had suggested in his preface to the published version. Rather, it was the immense problem of trying to combine "psychology and character" with a strong narrative line. If you get the first, he argued, it *must* slow down the second, and only a very few playwrights had ever succeeded in doing it, perhaps only Shakespeare. Chekhov had succeeded somewhat, he thought, but his narrative was pretty slow. And "as for Ibsen," he went on, shouting at top volume, "instead of architecting soaring buildings, he wasted his life on bourgeois cottages like *Hedda Gabler.*"

It was evident that Odets was wrestling not only with his painful personal problems, but with profound creative issues of dramatic content and form, not to speak of commercial viability. He knew that the great success of *Golden Boy* rested solidly on its driving—indeed, in his opinion, "melodramatic"—story. And if it were not a sufficiently complex task to wed narrative and significant individual motivation, there remained steadily in the back of his head the additional aim of honestly setting these rounded characters in the context of history and the consequent broader meaning of their values. Clurman, finding himself in essential agreement with this diatribe, said nothing. Instead, he dreamed soon after that he was in an insane asylum in which "Boleslavsky and Stanislavsky were also inmates of long standing."

As this melancholy September drew to a close, Odets heard with horror that novelist Thomas Wolfe was gravely ill. When, from Chattanooga, Sidney Bernstein wired him that Wolfe had died, Odets immediately got into his car to drive to the funeral, where he would serve as one of the pallbearers. As he neared Asheville, North Carolina, he was seized with anxiety at the thought of Wolfe's ungainliness, his loneliness, his speech defect, his immense talent, and, above all, of his having died "on the threshold of genius." As he ruminated thus, he lost control of the car and drove it off the road, demolishing it and severely lacerating himself. A week later he wrote in his file labeled "Social Types":

> When a person fails to gain attention and satisfaction from life (a prime need!) the person is often apt to bid for those things by sensational methods or eccentricities. An elaborate suicide is one such, curious behavior patterns demanding general attention (illness, etc.) are another. Montreal. . . . 9/30/38

Sidney Bernstein recalled his astonishment that Odets had survived the accident and anticipated, fearfully, the next one.

Kazan vividly recalled the tense September 30 of 1938. President Roosevelt was urging all Americans to pray for peace, and there was still no script of the new "dentist play" from Clifford. Finally, a night letter from Odets was delivered to the Harris Theatre in Chicago, where the road company of *Golden Boy* was playing. Addressed to "Harold Clurman or Kazan," it stated:

I am too dispirited to work well. The play won't be ready for a Chicago reading but will join you and company in Detroit with the revised script. Am moving around in Canada now and will come over at Windsor then, Clifford.

In the evening, alone in his small Montreal hotel room, Odets—now buying six newspapers a day for some hint of Luise's whereabouts—read with foreboding that on this day the Nazis had decreed that the licenses of all Jewish physicians be revoked. In Munich the earnest British prime minister, seeking "peace in our time," had—after a frantic two weeks— had a conciliatory meeting with Adolf Hitler, Benito Mussolini, and a representative from France. There, drinking champagne, all had agreed that a useful solution of Germany's economic depression would be its appropriation of a piece of her small, independent, democratic neighbor, Czechoslovakia. Hitler had given his word that this small concession would make war unnecessary. The British prime minister, a man who, Odets noted, enjoyed listening to Beethoven sonatas, found Hitler a ruthless man, but one who could be trusted, he thought, to keep this promise. The astute Roosevelt had no such illusions and told the idealistic young men around him, among them Alger Hiss, that Hitler would try to conquer Europe. Thus it would be that, without breaking stride, Roosevelt would soon become a war leader, no longer urging Americans to "pray for peace." Odets was steadily clipping from the newspapers samples of these developments and experimenting with ideas for his new "American" anti-Nazi play.

The Nazi Propaganda Ministry had distributed in the United States, through the German-American Bund, material designed to make clear that this expansion of Germany—along with the extermination of Jews, Catholics, dissenters, and the labor movement—was the most effective roadblock to the worldwide advance of Communism. The American Bund, making local application of this thesis, applauded the creation of a committee designed to do a job many historians believed could not be done legally. Under the chairmanship of Congressman Martin Dies, Jr., of Texas, however, there now came into being in the House of Representatives the Special Committee on Un-American Activities, with the catch-all purpose of investigating "the extent, character, and objects of subversive and un-American propaganda activities . . . from foreign countries or of a domestic origin . . . and all other questions in relation thereto that would aid Congress in any necessary remedial legislation." Odets began assiduously to collect, in addition to newspaper accounts, the official records of this committee's proceedings.

Republicans as well as Democrats in Congress who hated Roosevelt's New Deal reforms—and there were many—had begun to unite under the banner of "anti-Communism" for a repressive, even totalitarian political solution to the critical American economic problem and to the growing power of organized labor. It was clear to Odets that although these foes of Roosevelt were unwittingly aping Hitler, such political repression in the United States would have to assume an indigenous form; he made a note of populist Huey Long's prediction that fascism in America—like Hitler's "Aryanism"—would be built on a program of Americanism.

Thus it was that, using the respected investigative power of Congress, this as-yet-inconsequential committee could publicly oppose the "socialist" reforms of Roosevelt's Brain Trust. Lumping together collective bargaining, social security, the minimum wage, and the Federal Theatre, the committee set a tone which for over a quarter of a century would consistently push for constrictive, repressive, death-affirming solutions for all the evolving crises of the United States.

Representative Dies had a favorable response in the United States, not only from the German-American Bund, the Silver Shirts, and the Ku Klux Klan, but also from many of the major newspapers. In Nazi Germany, as well as in fascist Spain and Italy, he was hailed as a messiah who would bring deliverance to the United States from "Pres. Rosenfeld, the Communist Jew." Odets' files of clippings on the accelerating exodus of intellectuals from Germany and on the work of the Dies Committee were simultaneously growing. He was hoping his new "anti-Nazi" play would transcend the critical events in Germany as his swiftly written *Till the Day I Die* had not. For the moment the small "dentist play," about a stifled little man who sought to renew his own creativity, could not mobilize his energies.

The "House Un-American Committee," as its victims came to call it, was immediately labeled by Roosevelt as "sordid, flagrantly unfair and un-American." The energetic young men around him, such as Rexford Tugwell, Thomas Boyle, and Alger Hiss—feeling labor behind them—did not take it so seriously as did the President, at least not until Boyle was gerrymandered out of Congress for his opposition to the committee. To them, according to Alger Hiss, Dies appeared at first a "pipsqueak enemy," indeed silly, in pinpointing targets such as Odets' little Hollywood friend Shirley Temple or the long-dead Elizabethan playwright Christopher Marlowe, ably defended by Hallie Flanagan of the Federal Theatre. The reason given by the committee for "exposing" these allegedly subversive artists was that they had enormous public influence. Perhaps of equal importance to the committee was its dim realization that most often the artist is on the side of freedom, of life-affirming forces, and therefore an enemy of repression, be it internal or external. Odets longed to write a play on this theme.

The daily demonstrated illiteracy and ruthlessness of Dies and his colleagues filled Odets with rage and dread far in excess of the committee's actual power at this time, and despite the fact he no longer had organizational ties to Communism, he would remain to the end of his life emotionally vulnerable to this threat. His fear was in direct proportion to his long-established awe and hatred of highhanded tyranny.

Traveling alone in Canada, Odets was carrying, along with his file of notes for the "dentist play," the manuscripts of his labor play and the Cuban play. It is evident that his necessity was to work, preferably on material tied to the ongoing historic upheavals. In his "General Notes" for 1938 he wrote:

The invasion of Prague, from news dispatches. Crowds of thousands stood, weeping silently, and then spontaneously broke into their national anthem! A policeman outside the city hall tried desperately to direct traffic but was too blinded by his tears. Many of the Czechs covered their faces with their hands and turned away at the first sight of the German troops. Well, can a writer write in the face of these things? Yes, he *must* write in the face of these things!

It troubled him, however, that a form for uniting these somber events to his own urgencies continued to elude him. Finally, he stopped work on his "social-historical" plays—all of which took as their theme the beginning of the end of the American Dream—and concentrated instead on his "dentist play"; this appeared to be about the "merely personal" struggles of ordinary and lonely people, with Ben Stark, the passive, submerged dentist, trying to find sufficient courage to "take life by the throat" by having an affair with his childlike and aspiring secretary, Cleo Singer. Odets implies that Ben's stifled growth will thereby be given new impetus and he will escape the feeling that he has "blown it."

In Odets' original outline, written only a few weeks after his wedding and during the first of many separations, the dentist's secretary succeeds in detaching him from his wife, Belle. More than a year later, with Odets' divorce all but arranged, he found as he was rewriting this play that the secretary, Cleo, had begun to take center stage away from the dentist, Ben, and to evolve as the "identity-element" by now familiar from his earliest writing: the aspiring, unformed, even damaged artist.◖

The dentist, a "second-class professional" who reads Shakespeare, but who would be frightened "even to get a passport," and who "plays it safe" in his own work, is in competition for Cleo (Odets' Muse) with his father-in-law, Mr. Prince, who decisively proclaims, with no trace of his son-in-law's shame and doubt, "*I want what I want!*" This is the conflict between that aspect of Odets which is, like his proper mother, deadened by a frightened paralysis, and that part of himself which insists on a joyful and maximal experience of life which excludes nothing, but which he fears is "evil."

Advising the meek Ben Stark that he is an iceberg, half dead, the older man, Judah Prince, makes a bold proposal: "Explode, take a rocket to the moon!" supplying here the title for the play eagerly awaited by Clurman and Kazan.

The other pole of Odets' conflict is jotted in a "production note" in the margin: "Motto: 'You don't easily give up a home if you have been an orphan.'" This caution issued from a person terrified to make a great leap lest he fall into an abyss.

When Odets arrived in Detroit, the actors were so delighted that he had finally brought his new play that they swallowed their disappointment at his having completed only two acts. All agreed the three major characters were among his best and most mature. Clurman found himself, however, unsettled by what appeared to be a shift away from the original plan of the play, which Odets had told him was to be about "love and marriage in America," and in which the constricted dentist, "awakened" by his love for Cleo, would undergo a ravaging depth of experience, increasing his stature as a man and propelling the growth hitherto blocked. Now, with a new prominence for the worldly Prince (a man who recommends himself as someone who "don't look foolish before authority"), a quite different triangle had been created, with the aspiring girl at its apex. The theme appeared to have moved from the frightened dentist to the girl, even as Odets had moved from his failed struggle for intimacy with his wife to the broader issues of his own creativity: carrying the responsibility for the recent destruction of his unborn biological child, he feared that his stagnation would extend to his "brain-children" as well. The character Cleo, his Muse, now bore the burden of re-establishing his generativity. Clurman devoutly hoped the third act would dispel his fear that the character Cleo had run away with the play, confusing its formal structure sufficiently to sabotage both its esthetic unity and its commercial success.◖

◖ 22.2.
◖ 22.3.

515   *Group Theatre/1938*

Although by the first of October Odets had copyrighted three acts of *Rocket to the Moon*, he continued to be plagued by its resolution. Luise had earlier thought it a mistake that the searching Cleo should reject all the men in the play and had advised him to have her accept the rich old sybarite, as the girl Hennie had taken the businessman Moe Axelrod in *Awake and Sing!* Clurman was still troubled that it was unclear whether the dentist or the girl was "the hero" of the play. And Odets was once again obsessively undecided and privately resentful on several other counts: that Clurman was so "full of ideas as to what my play was about" and still had not raised the production money; that once more he was under emergency pressure to provide the Group with a commercially viable brain-child which it would immediately gobble up; that he could not protect his newborn progeny by directing the play himself; and, most important, that he was by now convinced that plays of any psychological complexity were not made for the Broadway commercial theatre. The memory of this time and his anger toward Clurman was still fresh much later:

. . . He finally got to think that I was kind of like a cow who dropped a calf, didn't know anything about it. Because this is what happened in the Group Theatre and I was very resentful of it. I dropped this calf and some people would rush up and grab it, wipe it off and take it away, and I would be left there bellowing. And while they were hustling this calf around you'd think that I had no relationship to it. I let them, too. I would let them do it, but with a great deal of resentment. I never would have let any private producer do anything of this sort. . . .

All the time I wanted to direct the play myself. But in order to direct the play I would have to have at least some decent distance between myself and the play. Well, that never happened. They had to have those veal chops on the table. For the next week, or everybody would go hungry. So in a certain way this gifted calf that I'm talking about, that I dropped, was also veal chops for everybody to eat. They would discuss casting with me. When they deferred to me it was really just to be polite. Nobody meant to be more than polite to me. They really didn't care what I thought. Every once in awhile, I would put my foot down. I would say, "No, I don't want that actor there." But most of the time I agreed with Clurman. . . .

It was Odets' conviction that Clurman and his "sturdy crutch," Kazan, together with Group business manager Kermit Bloomgarden, "ran everything, had all the fun, all the excitement, and I would just stand there on my legs like a bellowing mother cow who couldn't locate that calf I just dropped." Yet Odets was grateful for Clurman's steadfast principles, and carefully typed out for his own files a copy of a four-page letter from Clurman—trying to plan the rest of the Group season—to John (no longer Jules) Garfield, now becoming a film star in California. Garfield had just turned down a part in Irwin Shaw's play *The Gentle People,* written for the Group. Once again, as in his sermons to Odets, Clurman was simultaneously trying to preserve a spiritual foundation for the work of the Group Theatre and to hold on to his artistic capital:

Dear Julie:

I told you I wasn't sore when I said alright you needn't play "Gentle People." And I wasn't. I wasn't and I ain't. I told you too that the people in the Group like Gadget,* myself and others understood you

* Elia Kazan.

—but didn't agree with the course you've taken. No one feels vindictive about it either—no one at least who can alter the shape of your career.

But I think in friendship to you and as a Group person I ought to tell you more, together with our understanding of your problem, why we believe you are wrong and how you are doing yourself an injury.

You wanted to go out and taste the fruits of a strange world—Hollywood. You wanted to feel how it is to be a star and be flattered and talked about and make a lot of money and feel safe with plenty of dough in the bank. . . .

. . . Because you're a sound kid and you were well-trained in the Group you aren't fooled by it all. That is true, that is what your publicity says, and that is what I sense.

And yet how are you thinking of your future? You're thinking of it in terms of a series of fat parts for yourself—a lot of luscious plums that you will pick at your ease and your leisure from the garden of the theatre.

To Odets, it was arresting that Clurman was raising precisely the same issues with Garfield as with him—indeed, the same issues Odets himself was raising with the Group and with his wife: who was taking, who giving more?

Clurman, somewhat righteously, preaches a guilt-provoking sermon to Garfield:

That is different from the spirit of the actors in the Group—or from the spirit of any bunch of really creative people who try to give at least as much as they take. It is a different spirit from that which is expressed in Stanislavsky's motto "Love the art in yourself; not yourself in art."

Please believe me, Julie, I am not preaching to you. Other actors have left us—you say you have not left us and I believe you—and the Group has gone on and made progress, and those who stayed on at the job despite frequent bitter disappointments and dissatisfactions grew stronger and finer both in their jobs and as people because of their ability to stick to the job and through their understanding of what that job is which is not only playing attractive parts . . . but of working toward strengthening the Group which was created for the by no means small task of shedding some light and suggesting some spiritual order in the lurid anarchy of Broadway, New York and generally all around us. . . .

But to show how much of a free individual you were you signed a contract which allows you one show a year in New York. And now that you have signed you are free—to do what? To play one choice show a year and to have yourself photographed for the rest of the time in masterpieces by the Warner Brothers. You are now free to spend eight to ten hours a day shooting a one-minute scene in a pool or in an automobile or on a freight train and the rest of your time musing over the part you will choose to play in New York . . . and now and again organizing some semi-political thing for Spain, etc. (This is a worthy cause, but it's lots easier than fighting in Spain or just sticking to the job anywhere else.)

Driving his points home, Clurman pressed on with his review and his appeal to Garfield:

You were impatient with the Group because it wasn't enough of a collective, you were unhappy in the Group because it screwed you out of playing a part *you* decided you could play better than an actor who has been on the stage for years,* an actor who played "lousy little parts" in the Group whenever he was cast in them, . . . you were skeptical of the Group because after all it didn't do so many progressive plays like "Waiting for Lefty" to warrant so many sacrifices . . . in other words, . . . you were a great collectivist, a finer actor, more industrious and more idealistically radical than any of us. I don't believe it for a moment, Julie, and neither do you. Because if this were true or only half true your course wouldn't be a five-year contract with Warner's giving the theatre the benefit of all these virtues only once a year from two weeks to maybe six months! You did what you did because inside and outside pressures—such as all of us have—urged you to seek the beautiful land of opportunity—for money, for reputation, for novelty and for general turkish bath comfort—or to do what you wanted to do without any responsibility.

And finally, trying to be objective and minimally righteous, he concludes:

I am not an enemy of Hollywood. When I was there it acted on me like a long sleep. It helped me get out of my most pressing debts and it gave me a respite to draw strength for the tough road back to the Group. A lot of people—actors, writers, directors—can't for one reason or another do anything else but work in Hollywood and what they do in Hollywood is the best they can do—more power to them, and let them work to make themselves happy there and to make Hollywood a more human place or pictures more digestible entertainment. For a man not to disintegrate he must constantly do the best he can do, give of his strongest and most complete self. And I have enough respect for your talents and your background and your fundamental nature . . . to believe that your place is still with the Group. . . . But, dear Julie, the Group to do you any good or for you to be genuinely valuable to it must not be a stopping off place . . . but a place where you work—and struggle if need be . . . —taking your chances with the other people. . . .

I can tell that even in your confusion you are one of us. Even your bad reasons and your hesitant rationalizations about Hollywood —the great medium of pictures and the social films like Zola, etc., etc.—convince me that you are still close to us. That is why I would welcome you amongst us if and when you come back. But then you must come with a real understanding of your action, not as a guest favoring us with a visit for the benefit of auld lang syne and a part that Sandy, Gadget, Luther, Leif† or one of the other boys might covet, but as a true part of our free and disciplined group of actors. If you come you would have to resolve yourself to fight to get free of Warner's (at the proper time according to the tactics necessary for the occasion); you would have to free yourself of your desire to be free the way you are now . . . because the man who wants to be free to do only what is agreeable to his sense of comfort and his lazy ego is a piece of mush—and consequently a willing or cynical slave to those machines called moving picture companies on the coast.

* This refers to Garfield's bitter disappointment at not having been given the lead role in *Golden Boy*, played by Luther Adler.
† Sanford Meisner, Elia Kazan, Luther Adler, Leif Erickson.

Clurman ignores here that it is far easier for a plain girl than for a comely one to maintain her virtue, and that few of the Group's actors, directors, or writers had, in their Hollywood excursions, found themselves so vigorously and so seductively courted as had Franchot Tone, John Garfield, and Odets. Elia Kazan's turn—he was still learning his trade as a director—was yet to come.

Fearful of the preview audiences, unfocused on his third act, and steadily flooded with yearning fantasies of Luise, Odets puttered with the last scenes of *Rocket,* wrote a fan letter to Laurette Taylor, an appeasing invitation to critic John Mason Brown to have a drink with him and listen to music, and offered loans to a variety of people in trouble who had not asked his help. In addition, together with Sylvia Sidney and Luther Adler, he signed contracts to supply most of the capital for the production of *Rocket to the Moon.* He resented Clurman's disagreements with him about the motivations in the play and tried to intervene directly by reminding the actors what Stanislavsky would have said: "Every time you don't believe what he's saying or that you don't think he's talking to you in the first place, you stop him and say you don't believe him."

Another tenant at One University Place, composer Aaron Copland, was sharply aware of Odets' distress and recalled a late-evening encounter when Odets, who had been anxiously walking the streets, bumped into him: "Without the customary 'hello,' he said merely, 'Aaron, I'll bet Beethoven had third-act troubles too!' " For his file marked "Full-Length Plays" Odets wrote:

> The struggle to give myself up. The pain of not doing so, not being able to. There is a whole life story in this—it ties up with many modern things. A play in this—the obvious symbol being jail and giving up to the "authorities." Not to be able to give up to a woman, a man, a friend or group or party. To hold on to one's self, different, aloof, alone, but developing in one's work. And to always be wanting to give up, not to be different, not to be alone! The constant struggle of this, the aching balance!
>
> And its real value to an artist. If it comes from a bad thing, he makes it into good. Perhaps this is the whole story of "Crime and Punishment," but he gives up to Christ.
>
> Ibsen in other ways deals with this theme. He says to give up the self to get the self. Is that correct? Isn't that what Peer is about?
>
> This personality must start with an *essential difference* from other men. Joe's cock-eyes. Byron's crippled foot.

and on the same page:

> In our time: D. H. Lawrence, dying wanting a group, isolated bitter, sensitive, dying.

and then:

> Cleo in California

By this time he was certain *Rocket to the Moon* would be a failure.

It appeared to him that life consisted in a steady oscillation of ambivalent choices between one prison (one haven) and another: on the one hand, the isolated and ascetic fulfillment of a creator or, on the other, the security of being an old-fashioned family man. His romantic identification with Beethoven thus contained not only the ideal of a form-bursting revolutionary genius, but also that of an embattled and lonely man who had valiantly chosen the prison cell of the artist. He frequently quoted Beethoven: "But if I had married her, what would have been left of my work?" He further wrote down for himself:

I am a writing creature. My purpose in living is to write increasingly better plays which mirror the fast life around us today. I need a wife to help me live; not to help me write, except insofar as she is a woman living life today and I will come to know her and what she thinks and is.

I need a healthy self-reliant woman for a wife, one who . . . must know . . . that I am not a water faucet ready to be turned on and off at her instant desire. She must love me, be faithful in all ways. She must make a home for me, creating an island of quiet and calm for both of us and a child or two which both of us want and create between us. She must help me, compel me.

These may be difficult things for a woman to give, but in return for them I promise gladly to give the following: my love and fidelity always. An ardent impulsive nature, intelligent and sensitive; but by the same token some impatience and temper brothed over by inarticulate brooding. She will have all or most of my earnings, good earnings. She will be the mistress of the house. We can afford servants. I will respect her privacy exactly as my own. We will discuss as husband and wife all of her problems, mine, our family's, but in their time and place; the time is never during my working hours. I will give sympathy when ever I can; my heart is good-intentioned.

And I have in me a deep desire to improve myself both as man (husband) and artist.

These things I will give and do as long as I live.

10/14/38

By mid-October his loneliness seemed unendurable. Feeling acutely jealous of his old competitor Luther Adler, who had just married Sylvia Sidney, he decided to ask attorney Louis Nizer to find out whether Luise would entertain the possibility of a reconciliation.

It seemed to Luise that Louis Nizer, a wise man, did not relish the task of urging her to continue this union. However, he had promised Odets to do so. Luise recalled that her inner reply, "at all times unable to keep up a grudge, certainly not with a loved one," was by no means unambiguous. During their six-month separation her longing for him had been acute; so, however, had been her relief. Crucial in her decision was the fact that at this time she had decided to leave Hollywood and had, in any case, planned to go to New York on the way to Europe. Tired of the esthetic shallowness and the ennui of film acting ("I wanted to become whole once more with stage work," she said), Luise had confided one afternoon to her studio hairdresser even before Nizer's arrival that she could no longer abide the film capital in general and Metro-Goldwyn-Mayer in particular. She had decided, she said, "soon to leave." Before that day had ended, she was summoned to "the front office," where Mayer sat, coldly furious. "I hear you're gonna want to leave us," he commenced.

Luise recalled the scene: " 'Mr. Mayer, I cannot work any more. It simply is that my source has dried out. I have to go away. I have to rest.'

Whereupon the answer came: 'Whadda ya mean? Whadda ya need a source for? Don't you have a director?'"

Luise fell silent. This answer from Mayer seemed as extraordinary to her as it seemed natural. One was not a human being, one was far from being an artist. All one was was a tiny cog in a huge machine. "If not a complete release, at least give me a leave of absence," Luise continued.

Mayer stared at her and then he said slowly: "Luise, we've made you, and we're gonna kill you."

Luise's answer was: "Mr. Mayer, you did not buy a cat in a sack. Though young, I was already a star on the stage before I came here. And you know it. Besides, God made me, not you. I shall tell you something: all your great actresses in this country are between the early forties and fifties, Katharine Cornell, Helen Hayes, Gertrude Lawrence, Laurette Taylor, etc. I am in my mid-twenties. You, Mr. Mayer, must be in your sixties! In twenty years from now you will be dead. That is when I am starting to live!"

That was their last conversation. She walked out and went off without permission to New York.

In Boston a distraught Odets acted out for the cast a new third act of *Rocket to the Moon* for which Clurman and Kazan had been pressing him. So fearful was he of their response that he tried in this performance to compensate with an athletic Thespian energy for what he felt were the play's remaining structural deficiencies. Two years later he recalled this time:

> I was in Boston when we put Rocket into rehearsal. I was unhappy because of Luise, unhappy because of the play and the hurry-up work attendant upon putting it into production. I was lonely, confused, wrathful, repressed, nervous, tense and unhappy. To none of these things did I give much surface expression. One morning I was combing my hair in front of the mirror. Suddenly I almost fell to the floor with a pain in my back so intense that I would have sworn on the witness stand that a stranger had crept up behind me and buried an axe* in my back. The pain was treated by massage and x-rays and examinations by an eminent specialist. He told me to keep my arm in a sling so that there would be no weight on the muscles of the back. And it was in this fashion that I attended the first rehearsals of the play. Now, while all this was happening I had the unflagging sense that the pain lacked sincerity and truth, for there can be a truth to pain, too.
>
> I mean that I was unable to convince my mind that the pain had genuine physical or organic sources. All this while, of course, the pain was truly agonizing, so much so that I groaned every time I turned in the bed. But, I noticed, it was very comforting for me to surrender to the pain—I lay back in it like the softest and most pleasurable of beds—which was what aroused my suspicions. Back in New York I was plied with friendly concern and electric heating pads, not to neglect mention of a high stiff collar which was supposed to make my backbone straighten itself out. I made use of all these devices and

---

* Compare this with the title of his later play *The Big Knife*, which indicts the commerce in filmmaking as a "knife."

ministrations, but inwardly smiled a grim smile to myself and that was the end of it; the pain dwindled away and in a week was gone.

While his lonely and wrathful playwright surrendered to pain, Clurman, in one of his esthetic sermons, told the cast, "This is the first love play the Group has ever done, but more extraordinary is the fact that it is the first love play by a modern playwright." Moreover, "love means connection . . . with all things" and that "both religion and art are intended to help man's separation, his isolation." Thus "the opposite of love is not hate, it is loneliness," and "Death is the greatest connection . . . you go back to the soil." Odets wrote in the margin of the long typescript of Clurman's production notes, "indifference, disconnection" and "It is the indifference which makes a man who once had a woman's love want to kill her . . . murder comes from rejection."

The wife of one of the actors who had invested some money in *Rocket* felt less than sanguine about its chances, saying in Yiddish to her husband: "In der erd das gelt." ("There into the ground goes the money.") The Group members began to smell a failure, comforting themselves that there were still three weeks before the play would open and that Odets was still at work on it. Had they known how distracted their playwright was by the news that his wife had checked into the Waldorf-Astoria, and how much time and energy he was expending on getting his secretary and other friends to spy upon her, they would have begun to panic.

On November 3, a few days after Luise's flight from Louis B. Mayer, newspapers in Los Angeles and in New York proclaimed, "Luise Rainer and Clifford Odets Reconciled and She Wants World Told in Big Headlines." Credit for the reconciliation was given to attorney Louis Nizer, and the papers showed Clifford and Luise gazing tenderly at each other. Interviews with the "tousle-haired movie star and the bushy-haired playwright"—in the usual mélange of journalistic half-truth and shrewd observation— informed "untold thousands of admirers of the brilliant young American playwright and the brilliant young (and she will be American by naturalization on November 18) actress to stop worrying a little while about two of their favorite people." The *World-Telegram* reporter found that "the delirious, entirely human conflict between two of the most star-cros't lovers American show business has recently encountered, made fascinating hearing as Miss Rainer analyzed it."

Despite the banal sentimentality of all these newspaper accounts, there was no mistaking the mutual joy in the reunion. Louis Nizer had asked Luise to see *Abe Lincoln in Illinois* with him and to meet at Sardi's a "very dear and charming friend." It turned out to be Odets. Luise's and Odets' jubilation was felt and described by all the reporters. She was quoted by one as saying that obviously she must be "the one to change," and that "Mr. Odets is strong . . . He has strong ideas, some of them wonderful . . . I, of course, have strong ideas, too. This is obviously very bad . . . What it was was that Mr. Odets was sure I didn't love him. And I was sure he didn't love me." They were discussing the possibility of moving to a larger apartment so that, as Luise put it, "I won't be in his way." There was banter about renting separate quarters for the dog.

Within a few days Luise had to return to Hollywood for retakes on her picture; however, not a day passed now without a tender and ardent exchange between them. Clifford to Luise: "I looked happily at your fur coat in the closet. Still working on third act of my play." Dozens of flowers greeted Luise when she came home.

She has read the two acts of *Rocket* he gave her and writes:

Darling your play is beautiful. It is poetic and nearly epic in its description of this class sterilized by convention, yearning for the form which brings solution. I wonder how your 3rd act will be. After reading this two I nearly want to beg: help them, let them be open to themselves and to each other and even if it hurts let them face completely and decide so they will become clean and clear in themselves and with that, find and prepare the way to what must become our future. As there is a solution even for this class, and there is strength and health in many of them if one only helps to clear confusion and gives to them—the most confused—love and patience . . .

The personal plea in her critique seems evident to me. She is much reassured by his declaration, "I am your particular rocket," and by the fact he is not only searching for a "good, solid play" for her to act, but is writing one himself especially for her—"perhaps about George Sand or Joan of Arc." His summaries of what their reunion has brought him bring her to tears:

. . . This is what our love is to me, how it helps me. All the time I have a simple-deepdown-warm-quiet feeling of confidence. Had a bite to eat with Irwin Shaw and a few others after the rehearsal and there I sat in Sardi's with this simple crown of confidence on my hair. All I have to do is sit there with the little crown and a glass of beer and I am very happy. You are a most beautiful girl, inner and outer, and I love you dearly.

With less than two weeks left before the opening of *Rocket*, Odets confided to Group members that, in his opinion, Clurman's physical staging was all wrong. Perhaps, he thought, it was wrong to address the company as a group. Lee Strasberg never used to do this. Still working on the last three pages, it troubled him that at a hectic, alcoholic reading of the play at the Leofs' in Philadelphia the only one who remained awake until four in the morning, when he came to the end of what he had, was Poppa Leof.

It troubled him still more that the preview audiences were cool; it seemed to him they were not responding to the psychological complexities of his characters. Moreover, he could not decide how to end *Rocket* and kept working on a peculiar little coda in which, as he later put it, "a third kind of man, a little unimaginative travelling salesman," happily married, a man "who has found love and can't wait to get home to his wife," comes in shouting, "War is declared!" It turns out the salesman means only that war is declared on "unsafe tires" and he—this loving, settled, and secure husband—is selling safe ones. It is a little joke.

In this coda, which he would later delete, Odets was unsuccessfully condensing his current conflict. This salesman whose function, Odets said, was to "demonstrate that love is possible," is an insensitive clod of small reach who is declaring war on the fast, bold, and dangerous living recommended by the worldly Mr. Prince. ("Explode! Take a rocket to the moon!") His "safe tires," unlike the lethal ones in *Golden Boy*, will lead no one to destruction. Neither will they provide much of a ride. This, then, is the fly in the ointment of reconciliation with his wife. In the background hovers the encompassing Angst of this time. ("War is declared!" shouts the little salesman just as the civil war in Spain appears to be drawing to a close with the victory of Fascist Franco and the defeat of the Republic.)

Luise reads her husband's subtext well, and writes him:

The conduct of your hero becomes unsatisfying. I don't understand the solution, I don't know *why* does he return to his wife? For poor weakness? Or convenience? Or for fear or for why? If he loves the girl why is he thrown overboard like that by a senile fellow like Prince, Prince can talk a lot but who says that *that* is right for the girl? *She* didn't say so!! And Stark believes all of this? Why?—Or does he love his wife? Why for God's sake doesn't he speak then, open his mouth like a human being should do to someone he loves (and so does not want to hurt)? Why does he not say that the girl shall have patience because this might only be a fire and will pass? What made him change so quick? There is one thing definitely missing to me, one speech in the end which says why he goes back, otherwise this going back is another suicide (see Golden Boy). And that is no solution. I wished you would have shown where his wife really is unfit for him, but shown this not only in small outside things which mostly are only the result of repeated irritations and misunderstandings, but what really is the source and reason for this. And why, besides the pure animal instincts, he feels pulled to the young girl. If you don't show that, then the play is nothing but another story of one man between two women. And for that a young highly talented writer like you should not spend his time. I would have liked to see that this young girl shows Stark thru her whole being that living in personal satisfaction like his wife wants to live and like his wife makes him live too, living like that does no more belong in our time. I wished she would show him that we have to live for more than ourselves, that we have to work for all. That the standard of value of living is no more the possibility to buy a new hat or not, but the real understanding for Man around you, the knowledge for their needs and the complete willingness to give. And seeing and feeling all this it is for Stark as tho he awakes for the first time in his life—he has to leave his wife and begin to this new and right life. But of course that needs courage!! We want to see more than suicide solutions from Clifford Odets, we want to see courage as our times needs it!

Luise's plea that the play reflect an "understanding for Man around you" was written a few days after details of the awesome carnage of the Kristallnacht ("Night of Broken Glass") had reached her, and she wired her husband: "Am sick over happenings in Germany. Many friends . . . newly imprisoned." She followed this with a letter beseeching him to "concentrate on a new anti-Nazi play." He told her this was not so easy to do as she thought, and that many people had been urging him also to write a play supporting a third term for President Roosevelt.

On the day before being granted her citizenship ("Tomorrow I am going to be an American girl," she writes) and only a few days before she would leave Mayer's fiefdom, Luise had dinner with her agent and that night had a liberating dream—which she describes in a letter—in which she vanquished "seven at one blow":

I dreamt of agents last night and the agents and Louis B. Mayer and Hitler had all together only one swell head but were moving with uncounted feet and finally I decided that they were the Marsians and I pinched the head-Marsian in one leg which was 2 times as big as I and all the Marsians got very afraid and blew up and became little red baloons which I tied together on a string. By that time it was morning and I drunk it all down with a cup of coffee and a piece of wry-crisp.

The only figure missing in Luise's condensed image, thought Odets, was his own father, who had just heard in anger of Clifford's refusal of a remunerative offer to write a screenplay at Columbia Pictures for his own *Golden Boy,* an offer he turned down two days before *Rocket* opened.

Harry ("King") Cohn, head of Columbia Pictures, playing the favorite Hollywood game of "making a deal" with the Broadway director Rouben Mamoulian, learned that the only Columbia "property" in which Mamoulian had any interest was Odets' *Golden Boy;* Cohn said it had already been assigned. The deadlock between them ended when Cohn learned Mamoulian owned something *he* wanted, a short story much admired by director Frank Capra.* Cohn offered to buy it for $75,000; Mamoulian refused to sell. After much wrangling, Cohn agreed to assign *Golden Boy* to him in return for the short story. Cohn was amazed when Mamoulian would accept only what he had paid for it: $1,500. This move confused Cohn—it violated the rules of the Hollywood game. And so did Mamoulian's next step: in view of Odets' refusal to write the screenplay, he hired Daniel Taradash and Lewis Meltzer, two New York playwrights in their mid-twenties, who required, said Mamoulian, "at least one hundred dollars" each per week. "Are you crazy?" Cohn asked him, adding that *Golden Boy* required a "four-thousand-dollar-a-week writer." When Mamoulian then suggested he pay the two young playwrights $2,000 apiece, Cohn with great misgivings settled instead on $200 apiece and, with no idea how important these two men would become in the film industry and to him personally, began referring to them as "those fucking Theatre Guild writers" and urging them, to Mamoulian's great irritation, to make *Golden Boy* sound "like Capra."

When Odets heard this story through the grapevine, it strengthened his determination to stay away from "that factory" and to rescue his wife from hers.

The position of *Rocket to the Moon* in Odets' personal history, as well as in the history of American drama, is pivotal. While it is true that even in his openly agitational *Waiting for Lefty* Odets' characters and dialogue were already electric and original, the shift from the emotional currency of politics to that of psychology first becomes evident in *Rocket to the Moon.* Unlike Odets' early plays adjuring the oppressed proletariat to "awake and sing" in economic liberation, *Rocket* makes an appeal for creative and psychic liberation.

History was changing his audience:◖ those who three years earlier had looked for ultimate salvation to the theory of Marx and the model of the Soviet Union were becoming cynical and wary. The peace-loving Russian comrades—hitherto embraced by many idealistic Americans as apostles of self-realization—had lately made a pact of mutual defense with "imperialist" France and, worse, had begun the systematic extermination of their own domestic enemies. The barbarous Moscow trials were straining the loyalty of even the most devoted American fellow travelers. In short, there no longer existed so credulous an audience as the one that had risen in joyous unison in 1935 at the close of *Waiting for Lefty* to shout "Strike!"

* This became the motion picture *Mr. Smith Goes to Washington.*
◖ 22.4.

Odets' first jottings for *Rocket to the Moon*, made the year before, when he was thirty, outline a play whose sensory quality is immediately reflected in its wasteland setting: in sharp contrast to the play's title, the space is tightly, even suffocatingly, bounded. People and flowers alike thirst for nourishment, and there is little room for growth. With fewer characters than ever before, Odets again gives them neutral "American" names of indeterminate national origin.

Writing this play in the context of his then-crumbling marriage, it must have appeared to Odets that, despite his loneliness and shame at this failure, he had a second chance, a fresh start in his primary—his most "real"—self-identity as an honest artist, if not as a husband or father. His anima—Cleo—says, "It's getting late to play at life; I want to *live* it. Something has to feel real." It is as if Odets falls back to an earlier stage and hopes this time for a firmer resolution at least of his work-identity and for a renewal of his generativity as playwright. He will find the "real reality" in his brain-children—a safer fatherhood, he feels, than of a flesh-and-blood baby.

In *Rocket to the Moon*, for the first time in his life, Odets was writing a play which does not culminate in some kind of crippling or catastrophe: on this occasion there is no injury to his creative "hands," no suicide, no death.

In *Rocket*'s turn to a psychological instead of an economic deliverance can be seen an adumbration of the reach thirty years later in American cultural history toward self-actualizing (inner) values. In *Golden Boy*, Joe Bonaparte, who has irrevocably lost himself as a violinist by crippling his hands in a prizefight, cries out in a climactic defiance of gravity while driving his car, "We're off the earth!" and while the "money-men" are dividing shares of him, the speeding automobile destroys Joe and his girl in Babylon, Long Island. It is the paradigm of the price paid for the machine and the worldly values inherent in the American Dream.

Here, while there recurs the image of an escape from the constricting pull of a "Mother Earth," it is in a rocket, a machine even more powerful than an automobile and possessing the intrepid thrust of a virile, technological world-power. The emotional tone of the rocket image is *not* suicidal but freely adventurous and open. The image is of a twentieth-century American conquistador, liberated from the constrictions of immigrant terror, planting his flag in unmapped territory, the feminine moon. Wholly different from the apocalyptic locomotor image which closes *Golden Boy*, or even from that of a businesslike astronaut, a "rocket to the moon" is filled with hope, initiative, and even a promise of a peak experience of freedom.

With a pace and a focus of intent rare in dramatic literature, Odets manages in the first distilled "beat" of the very first scene to get into the heart of the play's conflict and its apparent theme: there is an immediate confrontation between the frightened, isolated dentist, Ben Stark, and his scolding wife, Belle. Their conflict commences in a sensory web of heat and claustrophobic imprisonment. Ben wants to "specialize," to grow, and Belle, like Odets' father, gives practical reasons which stifle his growth. By a most economic exchange, Odets ends the first round with the controlling wife, Belle, the victor. Indeed, she has won even before the play opens, and when she concludes the opening beat with, "Any day now I'm expecting to have to powder and diaper you," she has established herself as the parent, the boss, the obstacle in the path of the aspiring Ben Stark's

22.5.
22.6.

creative growth. As the play opens, the conflict between these two—husband and wife—appears to be its theme.

The connective tissue of the play, as in a musical fugue, derives from fragments of this announced theme: Belle says her husband must not simply agree to do as she says; he must also "see that I'm right," *play it safe,* and not try to expand his practice and creative work. He, who was once a "pioneer with Gladstone in orthodontia" (in making straight and whole that which is crooked), has already lowered his creative sights to tooth-pulling and to cultivating petunias in a flower box, and his income to one tenth of what "men with half my brains and talents are making." "If he had to go get a passport, it would become a terrific event in his life."

The fact that he is "only" a dentist, not a doctor, is already a comedown in the "good prototype" of Jewish middle-class life. But Belle does not approve of Ben's creative collaboration with Gladstone in dentistry, any more than did Odets' father approve of Harry Kemp, or his wife, Luise Rainer, approve of his association with Clurman in the Group Theatre. Even Ben's last-ditch attempts to nurture (to generate) his sadly drooping little flowers, which his secretary calls his "orphan babies," are immediately revealed in the first few minutes as fumbling and inept.

> STARK: I wanted to do something . . . what was it? Not a drink.
> . . . Oh, the flowers! (*He fills a paper cup, puts his pipe between his teeth and tries without success, one hand full, to fill a second cup.*)
> BELLE: Try one at a time, dear.
> STARK: (*Coolly*) One at a time is a good idea. (*At the window, right, he pours the water on a window box of drooping petunias. As he turns for more water, he faces* BELLE *who has brought him the second cupful.*) Thanks.
> BELLE: (*Smiling*) Any day now I'm expecting to have to powder and diaper you.

Even in these few lines Odets juggles and adjusts the basic conflicts and the "moves" of his internal "gallery of characters."◖

In this short exchange is reflected Odets' conviction, when he commenced this play, that Luise—like his father—wished to criticize, denigrate, and control him and his work (Ben's petunias), as well as to convert, reform, and direct him. And Odets has condensed in the dentist's relation to his controlling, depressed wife his own response not only to his father's tyranny, but also to the mood of his melancholy mother and the steady (internalized) combat between his parents.◖ In his production notes Odets writes of Stark, "He is a man who suffers because he can't make important decisions easily . . . fears scenes and fights . . . if he feels it is a matter of principle, he can stand up, otherwise, he may cave in. . . . Principle is a shield where the self can be forgotten."

Ben Stark's physical ineptitude, his indecisiveness (an expression of Odets' own sense of incompetence, like his mother's) take their contemporary external shape from Clurman's clumsiness in practical undertakings. It was a steady source of banter in the Group Theatre that Clurman could scarcely open a package of cigarettes, was unable to use a can-opener, and would say "Hello" without picking up the telephone receiver. Odets often said, "Gadg Kazan is Harold's muscle and his legs."

Odets consciously thought of Ben Stark's meek obedience to his wife's disdainful will ("You win, you win!" he says to her wearily) as simply a

◖ 22.7.
◖ 22.8.

literal copy of Clurman's compliance with the powerful Stella Adler. But these characters are all configurations within Odets' own self, organized long before he met Clurman or Stella Adler. Such are the complexities of joining an inner gallery of characters with the playwright's actual contemporaries from whom he is said to have "taken" his cast of characters.◖

As the play moves on through this first act, with the playwright keeping the polyphonic conflicts alive while offering expository material, minor characters, crackling dialogue, and lovely jokes, there are reverberations not only of Odets' struggles with Luise and of his grief about their aborted child, but also of his own earlier trail of dead or aborted children, creative as well as biological. This is a play in which the people steadily reveal themselves. Belle Prince Stark, ironically calling herself "your terrible wife"—as Odets' wife often had—says to Ben, in Luise's actual words, "A woman wants to live *with* a man—not next to him," adding that she has been "blue all morning," thinking of their dead baby.

Throughout this first act it is evident that Odets initially intended the central question to be: Will this frightened individual, Ben Stark, summon the courage to break his bondage and fulfill his life by a love affair or will he play it safe, abdicate his growth, and be like the enslaved immigrant who continues till the end (in the words of Bob Dylan, born Robert Zimmerman) to "passionately hate his life and likewise fear his death"?

After the initial victory of the wife over the husband, the girl Cleo enters and the play appears ready to move forward again. We are forewarned, however, of the increasing imbalance in the play's structure by the fact that Ben, the protagonist, is from the beginning the least interesting character. He is the quiet observer, the static center.

Obviously unsuited to her job and as inefficient in it as Odets in his youth had been in all of his, Cleo is, like him, an insecure name-dropper and fabricator; she lies that her mother was an opera *singer* (her surname) in Europe and that "I come from a well-to-do family . . . I really don't need this job." Later Ben says to her, "Everyone tells little fables, Cleo. Sometimes to themselves, sometimes to others. Life is so full of brutal facts . . . we all try to soften them by making believe." Cleo, the storyteller, the artist, becomes now (*psychologically*) the central identity-element in the play, though not yet the central character in its *formal* structure. The fables she tells are the effort to make life bearable by "making believe." Precisely this is the work of a playwright: to make himself and other people believe in a reality he creates. However, at this early stage of the game Cleo appears to be no more than a shallow rival to the oppressive wife, who is simultaneously patrolling many beats, strengthening her hand not only against the girl in this first triangle, but on all those who are making her husband's office "inefficient." She is calling everyone to heel and trying to hold her barren fort in a status-quo position. As she leaves the office, we are introduced to the play's third major character, Judah Prince. Odets describes him in terms clearly recognizable as belonging to L. J. Odets, yet with more affection and empathy than usual. Consciously, he thought he had modeled this character after the tragedian Jacob Adler, the attorney Max Steuer, and the Yiddish actor Tomashevsky:

He is near sixty, wears an old panama hat, a fine Palm Beach suit of twenty years ago and a malacca cane. There is about him the dignity and elegant portliness of a Jewish actor, a sort of aristocratic air. He is an extremely self-confident man with a strong sense of humor

◖ 22.9.

which, however, is often veiled. He is very alive in the eyes and mouth, the rest of him relaxed and heavy.

His daughter no longer speaks to him because of the dreadful life he had given her dead mother, a punitive silence to be meted out much later by Odets to his own father. "I am the American King Lear," says Prince, whose dreams of self-realization—like the secret aspiration of the senior Odets to be a writer—have come to nothing: "In our youth we collect materials to build a bridge to the moon," Stark comments, "but in our old age we use the materials to build a shack."

There are early hints that a new triangle is building, with the two men competing for the girl. While it is difficult to care what will happen between Ben and the sexy, stockingless Cleo Singer, dressed in "angel-skin satin," the interchange between the passionate old man (Prince) and Cleo is from the outset arresting, enlivening, and involving. Clearly, it is in their relationship that Odets sees the formidable threat to the American artist: in the struggle between worldly and creative values. To the extent that it would be difficult for the audience to see Cleo as a symbol of creativity would the play fail.

The charged excitement between the sensual, worldly old man and the aspiring young Cleo—as so often in an Odets work—is immediate and unmistakable, as it was between the equivalent characters of Moe and Hennie in *Awake and Sing!* or gangster Eddie Fuseli and fighter-musician Joe Bonaparte in *Golden Boy*. The old man tells the girl he likes her honesty and that "everything that's healthy is personal." He adds (as Odets' father often said of himself and his son) that he and she are identical. She aspires to being a dancer; and he regards himself as having been an idealist and believes that, without marriage, he could have been a great actor. In all of this the old man is clearly making a move toward the girl. Structurally, by dint of this move, the play has shifted ground: alongside the original triangle of husband, wife, and aspirant girl stands now a new one: husband, aspirant girl, and father-in-law. Prince, like Odets' father, announces he has been made to "play safe" by *his* wife even as Belle (his daughter) now urges her husband to do. "A housewife rules your destiny," says Prince to son-in-law Stark, adding that he lives a dull life "where every day is Monday." Prince feels that he himself has "disappeared in the corner, with the dust, under the rug."

Although Judah Prince boasts that he still earns money, he bitterly asks to whom shall he leave it all, "to Jascha Heifetz"? Addressing himself and simultaneously his son-in-law, he asks, "Is this the life you dreamed?" The answer is no, he thinks, for both of them, and the path to salvation is clear:

PRINCE: (*Suddenly turning, hand on door knob, pointing his cane at* STARK *and lowering his voice to a near whisper*) Iceberg, listen . . . why don't you come up and see the world, the sea gulls and the ships to Europe? (*Coming back into the room*) When did you look at another woman last? The year they put the buffalo nickel on the market? Why don't you suddenly ride away, an airplane, a boat! Take a rocket to the moon! Explode! What holds you back? You don't want to hurt Belle's feelings? You'll die soon enough—

STARK: I'll just have to laugh at that!

PRINCE: Laugh. . . . But make a motto for yourself: "Out of the cof-

22.10.

fin by Labor Day!" Have an affair with—with—with this girl
. . . this Miss Cleo. She'll make you a living man again.

By making himself one flesh with an innocent, growing girl, Prince
assures Ben, he will be creatively activated by sex, a formula which Odets
in his own frenzied life often alternated with sexual abstinence. It is as
if (some of the time) he regards the feminine aspect of himself as the
source of his generativity which would be brought to life by sexual union.
This element is in conflict with that of the worldly American businessman
who, though magnetic, is ruthless, exploitive, senses-bound, self-centered,
lonely, and fundamentally out of touch with his own creativity, with the
"play" in himself. By reason of his richness, this character, Judah Prince,
threatens to "run away" with *Rocket to the Moon*, as does his equivalent
character in so many of Odets' plays.

Act I closes with the inhibited Ben Stark looking out at the Hotel
Algiers, modeled on the seamy Circle Hotel of Odets' youth, a symbol to
him of sexual vitality and forbidden freedom. At the windows of this teeming place he used literally to peep at "real life," in order, he reasoned, to
gather material for his plays.

As Cleo leaves, she reminds Ben of his dreary coffin of an existence:
"Mrs. Stark says she expects you home at seven o'clock." It is not these
routines Odets fears; rather it is that in the "real" intimacy of marriage he
will disappear as an artist. ("A man falls asleep in marriage," says Ben.)
Thus Odets, on some level, is convinced that a continuing intimacy with
a woman threatens his creativity.

The second act of *Rocket to the Moon* opens in sharp contrast to the
first: Cleo is offering Ben cool water to comfort him in the hellish heat of
this summer.◖ Unlike his wife, who wants him to play life safe, she does
not deprive him, fight him, seek to reform and ultimately to possess and
control him as though he were her lost baby. Indeed, Cleo expresses her
own reassuring determination never to marry: "It's too sordid," she says.

By now it is becoming apparent to Prince that his obsessive son-in-law
—whose mentor for a fuller life he has tried to be—will not leave his wife,
or even seek to renew himself by having an affair with Cleo. Accordingly,
Prince makes his own dramatic "move" and, in a richly ornamented (indeed, brilliant) scene of power and restraint, he is on the seductive attack.
Like Odets himself, he is a "student of the human insect," flirting, teasing,
and promising. He tells Cleo she is "talking to a man with a body like silk"
who "possesses the original teeth, every one" (*he* has no need for a dentist!), and "in all the multitudes of your acquaintanceship you won't find a
man with younger ideas than your present speaker." True, he wears high-
heeled shoes because "I don't like to be so small," but if she will put herself
in his hands, he will help her to learn and to grow.

Just as in *Awake and Sing!*, where the powerful racketeer Moe Axelrod offers Havana on a silver platter to the girl Hennie, or in *Golden Boy*,
where gangster Eddie Fuseli promises fame and fortune to the violinist-
fighter Joe; or the gangster Kewpie, a soft life to Libby in *Paradise Lost*, so
now does Prince offer Cleo not only his money but his deep understanding
of her needs ("My girl, I studied you like a scientist").◖

Cleo, like one identity-element of Odets himself, is naïve, quick to take
offense, frightened, fragile, and unsupported. She fears ridicule for her
yearning to become a dancer (a clear echo of L. J. Odets' taunts when his

◖ 22.11.
◖ 22.12.

son aspired to being an actor) and is convinced no one loves her: "Millions of people moving around the city and nobody cares if you live or die." She will, in revenge (as Odets had often contemplated), "fall down on them all" from a high building.

It takes courage, says the girl, a courage she is not sure the dentist has, "to go out to things, to new experiences," to seek an expansion, an intensification of life: of one's consciousness and expression. ("Don't you think," she says, "life is to live all you can and experience everything? . . . Shouldn't a wife help a man do that? . . . your wife broke up your courage.")◖

A minor character cries, "Diphtheria gets more respect than me! . . . Why can't they fit me in, a man of my talents?" And to Stark's gathering gloom the nineteen-year-old Cleo replies, "Just because you're sad you can't make me sad. No one can. I have too much in me! . . . I have a throat to sing with, a heart to love with! Why don't you love me, Dr. Stark?" Ben, like Odets, smiles when he can't meet a situation. As this first scene in Act II ends, Cleo announces that not Stark "or any other man" deserves her. This statement turns the central theme of the play from an inhibited dentist's struggle over whether to have an affair to the aspiration of a young, unfulfilled artist. Taking this initiative, Cleo's answer to the question "How should one live? Boldly or timidly?" is unmistakable:

> CLEO: (*Shyly*) I'll call you Benny in a minute! (*After a throb of hesitation*) Ben! Benny! . . . (*They are standing off from each other, poised on needles*) Don't be afraid. . . .
> STARK: . . . No? . . .
> CLEO: Love me. . . . Love me, Ben.
> STARK: . . . Can't do that. . . .
> CLEO: (*Moving forward a step*) Put your arms up and around me.
> STARK: Cleo. . . . (*Now they move in on each other. Everything else gone, they are together in a full, fierce embrace, together in a swelter of heat, misunderstanding, loneliness and simple sex.*)

The initiative *must* come from the girl; had Odets left it to the paralyzed identity-element represented by the character of Stark, nothing would happen. Cleo, like Odets always afraid of repudiation, is for the moment confirmed, and Ben Stark is breaking his long sleep to give rein to his impulse with this girl. Perhaps, he dreams, as Frenchy has expressed it, it will restore his "power for accomplishment" lost through "unhappy marriage." A man who "don't get much personal satisfaction out of his work . . . is a lost man."

Another minor character who functions psychologically as a negative identity-fragment in the play "glistens with arrogance." He, too, is trying to seduce Cleo, whose "jingling body" is a magnet. She is impressed by this man, whose very name suggests a smooth, shiny surface: Willy Wax. "A man who gets his name in the paper so often," she says, "must be important to some people." Willy Wax is a caricature of the sexual predator who is at the same time a Spurious Artist. This is Odets' unconscious fear of what he could become were he to accede to the worst of his father within himself. Group Theatre actor Sanford Meisner, cast in this part, recalled the character with utter distaste, a man "with no redeeming feature." "Movies," says Wax, "started me off on my path of painless perversion." Clurman told the cast that this character "plays with his talents.◖ His adjustment is a constant perversion of himself," and Odets has added in

◖ 22.13.
◖ 22.14.

the margin of the production notes, "He likes to astound and impress . . . actually he is worn out, alienated." Not yet thirty-three, Odets tucked a terrified vision of his future into this minor character.

It is not accidental that the play's motion has been taken from the middle-aged, imprisoned dentist, Ben, and given to the nineteen-year-old anima, Cleo. Odets found himself at this time in a new edition of his central—essentially unresolved—adolescent identity-crisis: whether to play life safe and to become the kind of stereotyped householder his father wanted him to be, obediently writing advertising copy for the Odets Company and rearing a family; or, in the style of a priest (or a romantic artist), to give first priority to the creation and communication of *his* vision of life. This had not, of course, been a conscious, voluntary decision when he was nineteen, nor was it now at thirty-two. Art deals not in a deliberate choice among a number of possibilities, only in necessities. The necessity in this play is reflected first in the creation of the submerged dentist as the central character. He is a man who has abandoned his creativity. But, it emerges, Odets could not emotionally "afford" to open up this static man and risk a violent confrontation with the powerful Mr. Prince.◖

Faced with this emotional dilemma, Odets tried thus in midstream to find a safe structural solution by placing the heart of the play in the hands of the Artist, trapped in a family that laughs at her wish to be a dancer. Here he ran no risk of an unmanageable confrontation. However, it is precisely in this shift of focus that the play's structure became confused. Odets did not succeed in persuading even the Group members that Cleo represented their longing for creative fulfillment. They were not prepared to see so large a responsibility put on the shoulders of a stockingless girl who wears "angel-skin satin."

With the Aspiring Artist, Cleo, at the center of the action, she is wooed by all the men in the play: Odets' Muse is torn between the sybarite Prince (Artist Manqué); the safe Ben, who has sacrificed creativity for security; and the Corrupt Artist, Willy Wax, who warns her she is "living in the city of the dreadful night" wherein "a man is coarse or he doesn't survive." As for Cleo, "even her breasts stand at attention. Alas, she is not yet wise in the ways of the world."

When the dentist's controlling wife, who counsels security, suddenly appears in his office, Ben is touched—as Odets had often been by his own wife—by her loneliness and by her efforts to stir his jealousy. But her offer to replace Cleo as his assistant is an intolerable invasion—exactly like Odets' experience, as he later said, of Luise's efforts "to help" him in his work and to make a mutual career of their marriage. ("A man's office is his castle," says the dentist.)

His compassion and his tolerance come to an end as she states her suspicions. Finally he blazes out:

> Will you stop that stuff for a change! It's about time you began to realize there are two ends to a rope. *I* have needs, too! This one-way street has to end! I'm not going to stay under water like an iceberg the rest of my life. You've got me licked—I must admit it. All right, I'm sleeping, I don't love you enough. But what do *you* give? What do you know about *my* needs?

Again, in the beginning of Act III, in duplication of many such dialogues Odets had had with Luise, Ben continues his argument: "It's like we're enemies. We're like two exposed nerves! . . . These scenes go on.

◖ 22.15.

We're always worried . . . we're two machines counting up the petty cash. Something about me cheats you—I'm not the man to help you be the best woman it's in you to be." The theme here is the struggle between the passive, deadened, and demobilized identity-element of Ben Stark— which oppressed Odets' mother and now does him—and his Muse, Cleo Singer, the "radium girl" who gives off heat, light, and creative energy.

The second act closes with the dentist making a declaration of love to Cleo; he is now desperately jealous of both his rivals, the urbane Prince as well as the Spurious Artist, Willy Wax. He says, "You're more important to me than anything I know. Cleo, dear . . ." and her closing plea is, "Don't let me be alone in the world, Ben. . . . Don't let me be alone." The girl is using all power at her disposal to force the relationship with the dentist into an overt sexual affair. Again these externalized relationships mirror the internal struggle.

If this exchange is understood solely on its manifest level, it is hard to understand what has moved the dentist to the conviction that this storytelling, naïve child who is steadily "making believe" has become more important than anything in his life. If, however, we assume the identity-element of the innocent Cleo to be Odets' anima, the Aspiring Artist, rather than simply the "jingling body" of a lovely girl, his capitulation to her makes sense. The confusion of these two levels of meaning has issued in many baffled discussions of *Rocket to the Moon* in drama textbooks.

The third act opens with the dentist and his wife silent, "each one revolving in his own tight little world." She is ready, in her desperation, to forget his affair with the girl if he will agree "it was only a thing of the moment." Impulsively ("anything to blot out this pale ghost before him") he cries, "Yes, yes!" but immediately finds himself twisting and saying, "It can't be settled in a minute, Belle. . . . I have a responsibility." He cannot agree to his wife's scream, "Your first responsibility's to me! You hear that?" Again, unless we seek a meaning beyond the manifest level, Ben's statement about responsibility is baffling.

The key to this mysterious exchange lies in the word "responsibility." On the surface it makes no sense that a man uses this word to his wife to describe his "duty" to a nineteen-year-old paramour. The latent meaning of the word "responsibility" refers to Odets' allegiance to his own talent ("Talent must be respected," he often said). Their heated exchange sums up the position of an artist battling for his creative life. The struggle is only manifestly against his wife's demand that he give up the girl.◖

Unaware that his underlying dilemmas in the play issue in part from his own current struggles, Odets has his protagonist, the dentist (who is almost forty and yet feels "like a boy"), ponder what people get out of life "anyway" when he asks Frenchy, a bachelor chiropodist,◖ if he does not want marriage and children. In their ensuing dialogue on the nature of love and the difficulty of discovering it "in this day of stresses," this "nervous time," Frenchy declares that happy marriages are "rare, like the dodo bird," and sternly advises his friend to be practical: "Leave the morals out. . . . Never mind the shame and guilt."

> FRENCHY: (*With extreme seriousness*) Love? Depends on what you mean by love. Love, for most people, is a curious sensation below the equator. . . . The girl I want . . . she'd have to be made in heaven. . . .

◖ 22.16.
◖ 22.17.

STARK: You're that good, you think?

FRENCHY: (*Correcting him*) That *bad* Doc! *She'll* have to be the good one. This is why: Love is a beginning, a jumping-off place. It's like what heat is at the forge—makes the metal easy to handle and shape. *But love and the grace to use it!*—To develop, expand it, variate it!—Oh, dearie me, that's the problem, as the poet said!

What Odets had called his "slow exhaustion, this shame" over his then-failed marriage and his fear of intimacy, is promptly retracted by Frenchy:

In this day of stresses I don't see much normal life, myself included. The woman's not a wife. She's the dependent of a salesman who can't make sales and is ashamed to tell her so. . . .*

Odets thus tried to understand his marital failure, his isolation, and the nature of his creative struggles in terms of the stresses of the time. He was, of course, both right and wrong.

As the cynical chiropodist leaves this scene with the injunction that the dentist must choose between the girl and his wife—reviving the manifest conflict which opened the play—the latent meaning is once again underscored: the playwright must choose between his own development as an artist and the demands of a "normal married life." His dilemma lies in whether he is wedded to the "real" world of relationships with other living humans or to a constructed world peopled by the characters into whom *he* breathes life, who are, of course, the distribution of *himself*. It is a world he hopes to control. When the dentist's wife, Belle, pushes her husband to make this choice, it is more on the basis of a moral obligation than a mutually nurturant relationship. Moreover, real children, unlike brain-children, "break too easy," he says, and become (in Bacon's words) "hostages to fortune."

At this point the other major threat to Odets' creativity reappears: carrying an umbrella with a "fancily carved dog's head of ivory" for a handle ("A quiet dog always bites," he says, smiling smoothly), Judah Prince, calling himself "King Midas," confidently announces *his* intention to marry "Miss Cleo." Having dreamed "the secret of the world"— namely, that "it is not good for Man to live alone"—he is determined to capture his prize by offering her "maturity and experience in everything —love, what to eat, where, what to wear and where to buy it . . . an eye turned *out* to the world!" (italics mine). That aspect of Odets which is flooded with desire for sensual and material fulfillment and power competes now with creative aspiration: the eye turned in.

When the dentist says, "And you dare to think you'll buy that girl? You're a damned smiling villain!," Prince replies with a remarkable and passionate speech which would signal the bewildered critics that the play's theme must be "man's search for love":

Listen, a man in the fullness of his life speaks to you. I didn't come here to make you unhappy. I came here to make *myself happy!* You don't like it—I can understand that. Circumstances insulted me enough in my life. But *your* insults I don't need! And I don't apologize to no man because I try to take happiness by the throat! Remember, Dr. Benny, I want what I want! There are seven fundamental words in life, and one of these is love, and I didn't have it! And another

---

* This line antedates *Death of a Salesman* by almost a decade.

¢ 22.18.

one is love, and I don't have it! *And the third of these is love, and I shall have it!* (*Beating the furniture with his umbrella*) De corpso you think! I'm dead and buried you think! I'll sit in the long winter night with a shawl on my shoulders? Now you see my face, Dr. Benny. Now you know your father-in-law, that damned smiling villain! I'll fight you to the last ditch—you'll get mowed down like a train.◖ I want that girl. I'll wait downstairs. When she returns I'll come right up, in five minutes. I'll test *your* sanity!—*You,* you Nobel prize winner! (*He stops, exhausted, wipes his face with a large silk handkerchief, does the same to the umbrella head and then slowly exits.*)

Prince is not simply the negative aspect of Odets' identification with his salesman father. Indeed, when this many-faceted character protests he *will* have love, it is Odets' own passionate statement that he cannot live a life *without* human intimacy. ("I *love* your needs," Prince says to Cleo.) But this longing for genuine intimacy wars with his wish to be a self-sufficient artist responsible *only* for what he generates on the stage, and not for a flesh-and-blood wife or their children. Just as Prince is more interesting than Ben Stark precisely because he harbors many strong polarities, so is *Rocket to the Moon* a more interesting play than the political *Waiting for Lefty,* in which one end of a conflict is plowed under, leaving a cast of simple characters in a simple play, all on one note.

There occurs now a short interlude between the dentist and the Spurious Artist, Willy Wax. The latter, just come from his own unsuccessful attempt to seduce the girl, says, "Your little Neon light spluttered right in my face," adding that she is old-fashioned and belongs "somewhere in the last century."◖ This is Odets speaking not so much of a sexpot as of the virtues of integrity and of creative conscience. Ben Stark pleads with Wax, here representing artistic prostitution, not to corrupt the aspiring girl, to "keep away from her," as she is "young, extremely naïve. . . . You might warp her for life. . . . She's a mere mechanism to you." This sentence expresses Odets' steady fear that the Spurious Artist within him could be seduced into an abdication of his gift. Cleo, however, turns in a fury on this would-be seducer, the Spurious Artist, saying:

Mr. Wax, we don't want you around this office. You make love very small and dirty. I understand your type very well now. No man can take a bite out of me, like an apple and throw it away. Now go away, and we won't miss you.

When she turns back to the helpless dentist, a man "as mixed up as the twentieth century," she finds him evasive, collapsed, on the point of tears, and unable to leave either his wife or the "prison office" of his life. He can say to her only, "Help me. . . ."◖ Only the small voice of that fragment of himself represented by the chiropodist Frenchy asks the opposite question, "What can I do for the girl, for Cleo? What will she be in ten years, with my help?"

Cleo, attempting to obtain a clear answer, both for herself and for Stark, asks the dentist if he will leave his barren wife, and he—consumed with fear and guilt—can say nothing at all. He is chained and sterile. The dentist's "decision" occurs by default; it is helplessly passive, not

◖ 22.19.
◖ 22.20.
◖ 22.21.

active. With the character of Stark having clearly gone beyond his emotional depth and unable to handle the "mistake" of his intimacy with the girl, he is inarticulate. When Cleo asks, "What do you say, Ben?" Odets writes, "STARK (*lost*): Nothing. . . . I can't say . . . Nothing."

Here the play is overburdened and reflects Odets' inner fractures. Given the premises of the opening of the play (a man who will be forced to a choice between a wife and a mistress), the closing climax *should* be Ben choosing between Belle and Cleo. But, as we have seen, there was slowly superimposed on this initial triangle a second one—Ben, Prince, and Cleo—and the play took on the fuzziness of a "double exposure," with the playwright emotionally unable fully to resolve the struggle in *either* triangle. Thus, with Ben—the character originally at the play's center—immobilized, it falls to Cleo and Prince to propel the play to its end. Prince says of Stark, "He won't leave her. That needs courage, strength, and he's not strong."

Cleo makes a last stab at passing the initiative back to the evasive, lost Ben. His response is soft and defeated:

> Listen, Cleo . . . think. What can I give you? All I can offer you is a second-hand life, dedicated to trifles and troubles . . . and they go on forever. This isn't self-justification . . . but facts are stubborn things, Cleo; I've wrestled with myself for weeks. This is how it must end.

When Judah Prince asks Cleo what she'd have to lose by a union with *him*, she replies, "Everything that's me." The underlying meaning here is Odets' conviction that the core of his identity lay in resisting his father's bids to surrender to him and to his values, and to become instead an honest artmaker.

As in the closing of Odets' earlier play *Awake and Sing!*, the powerful older man moves in, making a real "pitch" for the girl: "And I offer you a vitalizing relationship: a father, counselor, lover, a friend!"

In *Awake and Sing!* the "equivalent" girl, Hennie—mother of an illegitimate child and subsequently married by a weak man called Sam Feinschreiber (fine writer)◀—succumbs and runs off with another old sybarite called Moe (roughly the equivalent of Judah Prince). In *Rocket to the Moon*, however, the Aspiring Artist (Cleo) makes the final *active* statement of the play. Manifestly, she is "looking for love," but Prince sees beyond this: he tells her she will never get what she is looking for— namely, a life with the purity of an esthetic creation: "You want a life like Heifetz's music—up from the roots, perfect, clean, every note in place. But that, my girl, is music!"

In other words, says Odets, only in that transcendent distillation of experience we call Art can there be found the precision, the intensity, the confident joy and serenity, and, above all, the integrated and liberating wholeness she seeks.

When Prince says to her, "You'll go down the road alone—like Charlie Chaplin?" Cleo's response and Prince's rejoinder finally clinch the idea that this girl represents for Odets the Aspiring Artist:

> CLEO: Yes, if there's roads, I'll take them. I'll go up all those roads till I find what I want. I want a love that uses me, that needs me. Don't you think there's a world of joyful men and women? Must all men live afraid to laugh and sing? Can't we sing at work and love our work? It's getting late to play at life; I want

◀ 22.22.

to *live* it. Something has to feel real for me, more than both of
you. You see? I don't ask for much. . . .
PRINCE: *She's an artist* [italics mine].

Whereas Odets' initial intention had been for the character of Ben
to emerge with greater stature and confidence from the overwhelming
experience of his love for this girl, it is Cleo who announces such growth:
"Experience gives more confidence, you know. I have more confidence
than when I came here. Button my coat, Ben."

It is *she* who escapes the airless constriction of the dental office, not
he. It is clear he will *not* return to "creative orthodontia," whereas her
future is open-ended.

Prince says, "Yes, you love her. But now, my iceberg boy, we both have
disappeared."

In these two short sentences there is a paradox filled with grief. The
Aspiring Artist determinedly walks away, free alike from the vacillating,
timid dentist lacking self-esteem, *and* from the sensual, worldly predator,
both of whom have abandoned their creativity. Manifestly, Prince is saying
both men have lost their chance for "love" ("we both have disappeared").
Beneath the surface, however, Odets is saying that he stands now in
mortal dread that if this Muse escapes him—as Cleo does in the play—
he will be left with only the internal war between the elements of a
weak, constricted, and guilt-ridden indecisiveness and a strong, aggressive, and commanding sensuality. In their actual lives both Odets and his
father consciously felt themselves till the end of their days to be artists
manqués from whom their creativity had somehow slipped away.

Stark, in a desperate postscript, eyes flooded with tears, says:

I insist this is a beginning. Do you hear?—I insist. . . . For years
I sat here, taking things for granted, my wife, everything. Then just
for an hour my life was in a spotlight. . . . I saw myself clearly,
realized who and what I was. Isn't that a beginning? Isn't it? . . .
And this is strange! . . . For the first time in years I don't feel
guilty. . . . But I'll never take things for granted again. You see?
Do you see, Poppa?

The play closes with Stark "almost laughing," confessing his ignorance of life: "Sonofagun! . . . What I don't know would fill a book!"
The final image is of an empty room, lit only by the lights of a hotel
(where real—forbidden—life is lived), the locale of so much of Odets'
actual peeping and listening:

PRINCE exits heavily. STARK turns out the last light, then exits, closing the door behind him. The room is dark, except for red neon
lights of the Hotel Algiers and a spill of light from the hall. Slow
curtain.

This last stage direction distills Odets' sense of the playwright as
"witness," the man who, like all artists, cannot help distancing himself
and watching his life's experience—and transposing it by way of Form
—even while he lives it.◖

Although there is evident strain and self-doubt in Ben Stark's triumphant announcement that his identity has been significantly illumined
and integrated by the play's events ("for an hour my life was in a spotlight"), it does affirm that aspect of Odets which takes nothing for
granted (a creator). Ben declares, moreover, that "For the first time in

◖ 22.23.

years I don't feel guilty." While neither of these affirmations of enlightenment and freedom is persuasively buttressed in the play, we can decode Odets' wish: he is saying (defensively) for the first time in any of his plays that he is determined not to surrender his creativity to the other pulls within him. The identity-element of his Muse (Cleo) rejects not only the weak identity-element which has fearfully abdicated creative powers (Ben), but also those which have "sold out" to the vulgarizations of Art (Willy Wax) and to worldly fulfillment (Judah Prince). Moreover, in *Rocket to the Moon* he is liberated from that guilt evident in all his work wherein the moral idealist—after compromising himself in his creativity —commits suicide, is murdered, or meets violent death.

Just before the opening night of *Rocket to the Moon*, in what was meant to be a humorous fantasy of how her loyalty and devotion could be tested, Luise closed her letter with:

As for me personal I wish from you for Christmas: *one terrific flop* just to show you that I am there for you and fight for you. Goodbye my darling, in a few days I'll be there—and God help you—for good. The dame.

Although Luise's conscious intent was to demonstrate her fealty, a trembling playwright—about to open a play not yet finished—may not have received his wife's message simply as the conventional "Break a leg" wish usually offered on an opening night.

On November 24, as the curtain went up on the first scene of *Rocket to the Moon*, its author stood in terror over a toilet in the basement of the Belasco, vomiting convulsively. He expected a total failure with this, his sixth play for the Group Theatre. He took the cast and the Leofs, who had come from Philadelphia, to his small apartment at One University Place to provide them with champagne as they awaited the verdict of the daily reviewers. He sat on his black desk, designed to slope for his work, and said little.

Although almost all the critics complained of the play's length and its indecisive third act, they by no means dismissed it as he had feared. Brooks Atkinson, for *The New York Times*, found it "A play torn out of the quivering fabric of life," "electric with the anguish of rebellion of human beings . . . written with the hard brilliance of his past work." He affirmed once more that "among our serious dramatists, there is no one to equal Mr. Odets' gift for dialogue . . . phrases that burn and others that burst with sardonic humor." Nonetheless, he concludes, "Although Mr. Odets' rocket leaves the stage in the first act with a shower of sparks and a roar of glory, it busts before it touches the moon."

Reflecting the same audience-sense of having been somehow betrayed, Richard Watts, Jr., for the *Herald Tribune*, wrote, "Mr. Odets continues to be the most exciting and the most exasperating of the younger American dramatists . . . a writer of really brilliant first acts, fine and moving dialogue, true and breathing characters, of brooding power and of plays that end by being curiously disappointing." Watts found the first act "the finest thing Mr. Odets has ever written," and the play, despite the confusion of its ending, as "eloquent and stirring as anything in the recent theatre." For the most part, the critics granted Odets' "brilliance," while battering him for the play's third act. Words like "tantalizing," "cruelly disappointing," "exasperating," "provocative," were steadily used, and George Jean Nathan triumphantly announced that Odets' "someday" genius "alas, still remains in the future."

Several critics announced with relief that he had outgrown his old conviction that an economic revolution would settle everything, applauded the new depth and maturity in his psychological perception, and called *Rocket* his wisest and best play. "This man is no everyday dramatist," said John Mason Brown, and Richard Lockridge of the *Sun* was pleased that "at last, he is adrift with the rest of us in human puzzlement." Tagging him "a fugitive from Hollywood," Walter Winchell was impressed, even a little awed, at "his advent" into the "broad fields of Psychology, Philosophy and Logic," and concluded that this play would be "of greater interest to the student of theatre than to the general public." Only Arthur Pollock, critic for the *Brooklyn Daily Eagle*, judged that "Odets has another hit on his hands," and ended: "a play those who care about the best in the theatre will not think of missing, certainly. A landmark in the growth of Clifford Odets. Something for him to be proud of as he grows up."

This notion that the work of an artist has continuity and a curve of growth was most explicitly stated by the thoughtful Joseph Wood Krutch in the *Nation:*

> The tendency still persists to make of Clifford Odets and his plays a political issue. That, I think, is a pity from any point of view now that the facts are becoming increasingly clear. Whatever his opinions may have been or, for that matter, may still be, those opinions are shared by many, while Mr. Odets reveals a gift for characterization and a gift for incisive dialogue unapproached by any of his Marxian fellows and hardly equaled by any other American playwright.
>
> *Rocket to the Moon* . . . carries him at least one step farther along the road he is traveling, and to my mind at least makes the best of the other new plays now current on Broadway seem pallid indeed. . . .
>
> Not one of the personages is a story-book cliché; not one of the situations seems other than freshly imagined; and Mr. Odets exhibits, among other things, two gifts not often combined—the gift for a kind of literal realism which makes his characters recognizable fragments of reality, and the gift of endowing these same characters with an intensity of life which lifts them into another realm. . . .
>
> Like the best scenes in previous works, *Rocket to the Moon* is in one sense not a "pleasant" play. . . . The broken spirit of the middle-aged failure, the desperate gallantry of the old man trying to pretend that he can accept the emptiness of his own life, and the unconscious cruelty of the girl who cannot even imagine what it is like not to have a whole lifetime before one, are realities which nothing can explain away. . . . Yet the intensity which makes the play at moments almost unbearable is responsible also for the fact that it is more than a tale of frustration and rises above mere realism toward the tragic level. . . .
>
> The political implications of the play, if they exist at all, are even less intrusive and less explicit than they were in *Golden Boy*. . . . Mr. Odets is welcome to any opinions he may care to hold so long as he can write as impressive a play as the present one.

The left-wing press, while still recognizing Odets' unique talent, did not hold with Krutch that Odets' political opinions did not matter or with Watts that they had become more subtle and implicit. In the stereotyped jargon of a political partisan, Ruth McKenney, writing in the *New Masses*, announced that although "*Rocket* is a good play, a moving one, full of blithely poignant moments," its author has taken to writing plays about "problems people solved the day before yesterday." Unconvinced that ordinary people like Ben Stark, the dentist, could still be wrestling with such pedestrian emotional problems as, in Odets' words, "the long sleep of life," she continues her juvenile attack:

> For the people of our country have learned how to be bold and brave in the last three years, and Clifford Odets has not. The dentist and his wife and his friends have been jolted out of their narrow vision of life by history, but Mr. Odets sees them today as they were long ago before the workers of Spain went out to fight Fascism, before the workers of America organized to fight reaction in our nation.

While Odets recognized the youthfully narrow zeal and doctrinaire optimism in this attack, it troubled him to see the growing alienation between himself and his adherents on the Left. In the meantime, from the "bourgeois weeklies" the assault on him continued also, until—out of patience with his colleagues—*New York Times* critic Brooks Atkinson wrote a new piece about Odets:

> When an established writer falls short of his best work the Broadway misanthropes cry: "Beat him! Let him have it right on the button!" They have a spuriously quixotic impulse to coddle the mediocrities and abuse the geniuses. When Clifford Odets followed *Awake and Sing!* with a piece of muddled mysticism labeled *Paradise Lost*, the reviewers were urged to denounce him furiously. Now that he has followed *Golden Boy* with *Rocket to the Moon*, which expires in a state of loquacious confusion, the reviewers are again urged to dance jubilantly on his grave. For every man who pokes his head above the dead-level of uninspired competence arouses malicious resentment in the minds of his inferiors. They would be pleased to see him kicked back into obscurity. Genius is a disquieting element in a phlegmatic neighborhood.

It was by now apparent that *Rocket* would not last long, and the specter of keeping the play alive "so at least my friends can see it" was plaguing Odets. He knew his intolerable vulnerability to criticism was like his mother's; yet he continued to bleed. Bearing $19,000 in bonds to the Group's business office, he threw them down on a desk, shouting, as Luther Adler recalled it, "I'm *not* a genius. I can't write like a genius. With these reviews, they're driving me out of the theatre. Whatever I do is not good enough for them. They want me to write a masterpiece!" He had brought his bonds hoping to prolong the play's life, as he had done with *Paradise Lost*. *Rocket*, later alternating with *Awake and Sing!*, would end nonetheless after 131 performances.

It was cold comfort that on December 5 he received his second canonization of this year: first had come the *New Yorker* profile, and now appeared a cover story in *Time*. His picture on the cover of *Time* showed him seated at his typewriter, looking plump, balding, and wearing a forced smile: the caption read "Down with the General Fraud!" The long story on him, titled "White Hope," reviews his wild success three years before with *Waiting for Lefty*, saying he had arrived then "for good and all" just as O'Neill had in the twenties, and that "his position remains unchallenged." The *Time* writer holds that

> The reason that Odets has gained and held a public that, by and large, does not share his Leftish ideas is obviously not the ideas themselves but his rich, compassionate, angry feeling for people, his tremendous dramatic punch, his dialogue, bracing as ozone. In every Odets play, regardless of its theme or its worth, at least once or twice during the evening every spectator feels that a firehose has been turned on his body, that a fist has connected with his chin.

Turning specifically to *Rocket,* the piece continues:

> Odets does not encase this eternal situation in the snug, tight frame of the well-made Broadway "domestic drama." Heaving, racked, volcanic, the play belches the hot subterranean lava of its characters' anger, helplessness, pain. It draws back their skin to leave every nerve exposed. In its best scenes *Rocket to the Moon* is blisteringly real, its dialogue forks and spits like lightning from a scornful sky. . . .

The account closes with a word on Odets' reconciliation with Luise:

> Just before they separated, Luise Rainer obtained a new film contract allowing her six months off each year to be with Odets in Manhattan. The idea was that, among other things, she might act in his plays. Said he: "But for our separation, she would be playing in one now." He expects to write one for her soon, calls her "a terrific actress." He talks of the long happy life they are going to lead together. He talks of the house they are going to build in the country. He talks of "the desideratum of marriage"—children. He talks. And he also writes.

This idyllic account of a securely arrived playwright about to build a long and productively happy life in the country with his beautiful and gifted wife and children bears little resemblance to the experience of the principals. Odets was bitter about the reception of his play and steadily finding fault now with Clurman's casting, direction, and revisions. Unable to tolerate the consensus that it was a "brilliant failure," Odets made new cuts and redirected a scene in the second act. As with *Paradise Lost,* he wrote a personal letter to all the critics, inviting them to see it again, as "to the Company and myself it seems a better show now than then." Once again he is almost obsequious:

> My frank opinion is that a second visit to the play may have valuable ramifications. Certainly any further critical evaluation of the play cannot help but be useful to the young developing playwright who sends these lines.

To critic John Gassner alone he wrote in gratitude:

> Dear John Gassner—Your review of "Rocket to the Moon" gave me a great feeling—admiration for the piece first—second, happiness that somewhere there is a theatre critic who understands a play above the cut of musical comedies. You are a great help to young theatre artists like myself, and may you continue to look and listen with the same penetration—*and may you get on a daily paper soon!* (or move out into the world) Let me know any time I can help.

And finally he sent an invitation to Theodore Dreiser, who replied that he was bogged down in Hollywood, trying for film assignments, but would see *Rocket* "if it is still running when I return to New York."

It was characteristic of Odets when he was intensely anxious to set up a quasi-intimacy with a "big man," a person he might think of as a father. Now, after reading in *The New York Times* an especially stirring speech by President Roosevelt, he wires him:

> Dear Mr. President. Two American citizens who admire you very much send their sincere appreciation of your speech of yesterday. Luise Rainer, Clifford Odets.

Roosevelt's secretary, Missy LeHand, responds to Luise:

> My dear Miss Rainer:
>   It was indeed thoughtful of you and Mr. Odets to send the President that nice message of December sixth. He asks me to assure you that he is much pleased to know that you liked his address at Chapel Hill, North Carolina.

Despite everyone's calling to his attention the superlatives being lavished on him wherever *Golden Boy* played on tour, he was, like most artists, obsessed only with the negative opinions of the critics. Although, similar to all playwrights, he reminded himself that many reviewers were limited newspapermen who had come "roaring up from the sports page," he could not rid himself of the feeling that in public print their words were God's judgment, penetrating to the core of his evil and his incompetence. Luise was back in New York, and later she recalled this troubled time:

> Out of the blue Cliff was fighting with me. After that there would be silence for days. He was not speaking. As for myself, I had to write down whatever I thought the fight was about because I simply could not remember it later on. Sometimes it seemed as though Cliff actually enjoyed these fights, that for him they nearly seemed to be something sensual and essential.

Their bitter battles were, she recalled, often resolved by their "love-making that was really in a strange way as spiritual as they were physical. He seemed like a holy disciple, and the idea of bearing him and bearing *for* him seemed to me at this point the greatest possible fulfillment."

Aside from his intense and ambivalent exchanges with Luise, Odets saw almost no one. Producer Sidney Kaufman remembered a paid audience of almost six hundred people awaiting Odets at the New School for Social Research, where he had agreed to talk to a film class at eight o'clock. Just before he was due, he telephoned to say he'd be late. The class waited almost an hour, and then Kaufman, not knowing how close to the edge Odets was, announced, "We have been kidded by an irresponsible maniac and I will refund your money." Later Odets, with apology, sent him his collected works with gratitude "for your complete absence of bile."

Suddenly it appeared to Odets that if he and Luise could flee the eviscerating critics, the resentful Group, and the "betrayed" left-wingers, their marriage and his sanity would have a chance. Accordingly, overcoming his deep reluctance to uproot himself, he wrote to the acting consul-general of the Union of Soviet Socialist Republics, requesting two visas for "a month from now." They would go and see for themselves whether people there were actually leading the whole, mature, joyful, creative, and peaceful lives about which Ruth McKenney was dreaming in the *New Masses*. Besides, in Russia his work was being welcomed, not rejected. He knew the Russians would feel honored by a visit from him.

It is possible that if the Soviet consul had been prompt in granting visas, the melancholy course of events would have been different.

Chapter Twenty-Three

*Fear of failure is a corrosive that eats
at the fiber of many good Americans.*

HAROLD CLURMAN

*I lay in high grass and thought of
Clifford. He hated to walk; he would
have thought such joys utter foolishness—coming from me, anyway. He
was beset with physical fear, of hurting himself, or getting hurt. New
vistas opened by the woman he
wanted to master were unacceptable
because they made him feel weak instead of offering new strength. And
yet it was strength he was in search
of always. I would say that human
strength and human creation was to
him what to me is the far sky and the
silhouette of the rugged mountain
against it. . . . His lack of ever relying on anything but himself was
the source of his restlessness and self-
destruction. Only the deep realization to belong, to be whole as an image, but to be part of a whole greater
than oneself, can be momentary solace and respite. . . . There in the
high grass all was calm. In my phan-
tasy Clifford sat beside me and only
then could I lean my head against
him without fearing that he would
move. Tomorrow it will be a year that
he is dead.*

LUISE RAINER

IT IS a commonplace of clinical observation that in the Christmas season, with its extremes of demand and expectation, the emotional hungers and angry disappointments that have successfully been dammed all year may overflow—sometimes with disastrous consequences for those whose balance of the moment is tenuous. Thus it was with a heightened resentment that within a seventy-two-hour period Odets paid his old friend Herman and his sister Florence their salaries as, respectively, secretary and "typist"; irritably told his wife to mark in a catalogue with an X what she wanted for Christmas *and* for her approaching birthday; agreed to lend a Group actor $100, and two Theatre Guild players $50 apiece; sent to an old Bronx comrade $2,000 for his failing business; and paid to Aaron Copland the first installment on a commission for a piano sonata (Copland had said, half-joking, "Is a dedication and a presentation of the manuscript worth five hundred dollars?" Odets, recognizing the composer's straits, had offered his friend $3,000, which, with *Rocket*'s failing box office, he was now unsure he could pay). Most important of all, he received a doleful letter from his father proclaiming the disastrous end of the mattress firm Doctors of Sleep and announcing that his bank balance had shrunk from the $20,000 Clifford had given him to $25.65. He needed more cash, he said, to seek his fortune with his new wife in Los Angeles. Odets sent him $1,500 and stayed out all night drinking, while Luise waited.

The "bellowing cow" whose calf had been taken from him felt he was being milked dry. Yet he ambivalently encouraged these demands because to be a nurturant rescuer countered his sense of empty neediness and isolation. On some level the rescuer always identifies with the rescued, the feeder with the fed. But when, as now, he was not working, the emotional yield of being the feeder was insufficient, and his anger, not to speak of his own hunger and thirst, steadily rose within him. Luise recalled him staggering into the apartment now, exhausted and drunk. She thought, moreover, that he might again be seeing writer Helen Deutsch, from whom there were many messages.

Ever since the unhappy opening of *Rocket to the Moon*, Luise had been discussing with Alfred Stieglitz that her worry about her marriage was once more deepening. She felt it was impossible even to breathe in the small apartment with Odets asleep most of the day and the secretary trying to catalogue Odets' piles of records when he wasn't playing them full blast. Now and again, in desperation, she would slip off and rent a room at the Waldorf-Astoria Hotel, tour the art galleries, or take long walks. She was happiest when strangers—not recognizing her—talked to her and she felt free.

Odets, alternating between a blazing rage and his characteristic look of wide-eyed astonishment, kept repeating in his mother's soft voice that he wanted her to be self-reliant and respectful of his privacy; yet it appeared that the moment she wanted to go anywhere a typical enraged note would appear mysteriously, e.g.: "Europe is out of the question because I . . . can't go with you and you must be here to help me work and live and to be a man. . . ." It infuriated him once again that she paid no attention to stocking the refrigerator, whereas he had put in a supply of pickled chestnuts, her favorite delicacy. Luise, who fasted occasionally, recommended it to her husband, as she felt it cleansed the system. The emotional fasts now imposed on her by him were, however, intolerable to her.

When, after a silence of several days, she sought out old friends, Odets' jealousy assumed paranoid proportions.

In his "Short Story" file he recorded one such contest:

"Fight in the Snow":

The fight in the snow with Luise, plunging in and out of cabs on the way to a meeting with friends. It is snowing, early December, Sunday night and lower 5th Avenue is deserted. The passing policeman, the wind, forcing her into a doorway, the snow growing deeper—a dead, snow-filled world, and riding back home. The astonished cab driver. Coming home and taking drinks. Phonograph music. "Oh God, how I love that hateful woman!"

Luise recalled the cabdriver's comment, "Good riddance, Madam, of the bastard!" It seemed to her that any reassurance she could find, even the attentions of her fans, competitively angered him. As her isolation became public knowledge, while her husband, in his furious moods, accused her of hungering for constant adulation and company, she grew increasingly depressed. It appeared to her, as Odets tried in vain to rework *The Silent Partner,* that only from his records and his books was he deriving any pleasure or even bare emotional sustenance. He wrote: "The virtue of a ghost is its silence. Stay silent, dear, remain a ghost."

Odets felt especially disconnected and guilty when—directly after writing several irate notes accusing his agent of being only a "collection agency" for himself—he was on hand to celebrate the arrival in New York of the S.S. *Paris* returning a hundred American veterans of the Spanish Civil War. Members of the welcoming crowd—little knowing how imminent was Fascist Franco's victory—carried placards: "Madrid will be the Tomb of Fascism!" and "Lift the Spanish Embargo!" Perhaps, thought Odets, he should not content himself with money contributions to the Abraham Lincoln Brigade, composed of American volunteers fighting with the Loyalists against the insurgent Franco. Rather, like his friend, the poet Edwin Rolfe, he should go to Spain and engage in direct combat with the oppressive general.

His fear of another box-office failure, his growing sense of disconnection from the Group, now called by *The New York Times* "our leading art theatre," and his resentment toward Clurman (who was beginning to represent all of the "parasitic demands" on him) were augmented by the conclusion in the long *Time* article: "Actually, Odets has most of the time carried the Group on his back." Clurman's later rejoinder was that "if this was true, one might have added that he carried the Group as a son carries his father." Precisely so, but this son who had indeed been carrying his own father for more than three years, and simultaneously struggling with a wife whom he quoted in his own terms as wanting to be sheltered in his pocket "like a baby kangaroo," was reaching his limit. Their life increasingly had a desperate and violent quality, simultaneously a frantic effort to merge with and to destroy one another.

She could not recall the content of their bitterly climactic quarrel on Christmas Day of 1938, but in her memory "it was the worst yet." She decided it would be impossible to join Frances and Rockwell Kent in the country for New Year's Eve as they had planned, and once more she moved from One University Place to the Waldorf-Astoria Hotel. A note from Clifford to Luise on January 12 says:

Dearest Darling Luise—Today is your birthday. Well I thought for several days about something nice to get you—but nothing is nice except flowers and so I put those beside your sleeping place. One great wish for your birthday, Darling—that you develop in every way the great talent in your hands—then you will be the great artist, great woman, great wife and great mother! All love today and always from your C.   P.S. The phonograph I must pick carefully—early next week.

By the end of January 1939 Luise was in the hospital running a high fever, ill—as so often in the wake of these battles—with a severe upper respiratory infection. She hid then in the apartment of her old friends Ida and Volodya Pozner, not telling her husband where she was. There were reports that Clifford had precipitously taken off in his Cadillac with his manuscript of *The Silent Partner* and was speeding south in the direction of the University of North Carolina, Key West, or Mexico. Herman had instructions to say nothing of his whereabouts. Luise had decided not to wait for the Russian visas for herself and her husband and to go abroad instead with the Pozners. She asked Odets' secretary to leave her farewell on her husband's night table:

Dearest Clifford—there is little to say. I feel very sad about you. I feel you behaved horrible during these past two months. You know, one can not just do anything one wants oneself, and inspite of *many words* against it—demand that the other too does what one wants, take everything for granted what the other does but the same time is unwilling to do the smallest thing oneself, throw everything over board every 3 day and then be "depressed" and "unhappy" if there is a strange relationship. I can not understand, Cliff, that you, who criticises it so in others are that romantic! I could not open your letter. So many beautiful words had come all ready from you, so little had been done to realise them, and horrible words and accusations came and you didn't even realise what you had said or done and were surprised or disturbed when I was broken to pieces. No, Clifford, it's really a shame and it makes me very sad. One would wait for such behavior from a bad little bourgeois haustyrant—never from the Clifford whom I gave my selve to happily again and again.

I am going to England now—as you always say: to get my head cleart! I think I will do a play there, I am going allready on a contract but I am not bound. If I don't like the play or plays I go to France and skying in Switzerland. Breathing fresh air! Luise

Luise recalled, "I went to the south of France to the castle of Renaud de Jouvenel. Together, with other friends, we were able to bring children out of war-torn Spain."

Her energetic efforts to find temporary havens for the Spanish children were being supported in Washington by Eleanor Roosevelt, who was desperately trying to persuade her husband to help. ("Franklin frequently refrained from supporting causes in which he believed because of the political realities," she said.) Roosevelt, seeking a billion dollars from an isolationist Congress to expand the U.S. Air Corps, was inhibited from bringing in these thousands of refugee children (Spanish and Jewish) by the sixty anti-alien bills before the Seventy-sixth Congress.

Ignoring the immense pressure on him, especially to save the lives of children, was not easy for Roosevelt, especially when it came from people to whom he was politically indebted. Correspondence preserved in the Roosevelt Library at Hyde Park poignantly states the historical context. A "Dear Marvin" letter from comedian Eddie Cantor in Beverly Hills to President Roosevelt's secretary, Marvin H. McIntyre, implores him to barter his (Cantor's) cooperation in the president's "infantile paralysis drive" for permission for 10,000 child refugees, "Christians and Jews," to come into the United States. He assures McIntyre that there are 10,000 families willing to receive and to adopt them immediately ("These children would have to come in within the next year . . . otherwise they would not be worth-while saving"), adding, "My dear Marvin, for generations to come, if these boys and girls were permitted entry into this country, they would look upon our leader as a saint,—they would bless the name of Franklin D. Roosevelt."

McIntyre, on Roosevelt's advice, sends the letter to Under Secretary of State Sumner Welles, commenting on how hard Cantor had worked for the infantile-paralysis fund and don't they owe him a "discreet little note of appreciation"? Two weeks later Welles drafts a letter which McIntyre sends on to Cantor as his own. A long and cordial letter, it conveys the president's interest and sympathy "towards the situation in which so many thousands of persons find themselves abroad," but concludes that there are difficult "legislative and administrative problems" of such dimension that the president must "continue to give it his careful thought." Of which nothing came.

It was hard for many American citizens to understand why in the great expanse of the United States no room could be found for any of these small outcasts, already being welcomed in Belgium and the Netherlands, where Hitler's new prophecy, made on January 30, of the "annihilation of the Jewish race in Europe" was a close and credible threat. Luise became caught up in the survival of refugee children from Spain, and later (with Eleanor Roosevelt) she assisted European victims of the Holocaust.

Film director Julien Duvivier wanted Luise to star with Louis Jouvet in a film written by Selma Lagerlöf. She recalled, "I could not now imagine being put again in front of a camera. Already in Hollywood I could not bear to look at my eyes on the screen. They looked so blasted sad. Many weeks later I was in England, where then various plays were offered to me, and I starred in a play by Jacques Deval. There, after months of monstrous misery, pressed by my mother and a dear friend, I went to a party. I met the man with whom I fell in love. He was a most handsome English diplomat. It felt like a new spring." For the first time she felt that she "had once more eyes and ears."

When in the midst of her work Luise received a clipping describing an auto accident suffered by Odets in Key West, she knew it was "suicidal" and had to do with his "immense confusion" and their separation. She nevertheless had no wish to return to him. Once more she had found the type of man familiar to her from her early youth, "completely different from Odets, strong but without the need for tantrums. It was pure balm." It was an important relationship that lasted throughout the war.

Her husband, on his flight south, had stopped at the University of North Carolina and, discussing with students the parochial and illiterate nature of American criticism, had earned the irritation of a reporter on the *Greensboro News* not only by his attacks on critics but by the casual statement that "If a youngster has any talent, a college course will certainly kill it." He had concluded the interview by saying he was working on a play which "he has to finish in two weeks or else." The outraged reporter had responded with, "This lion of the limelight seems to be a little confused by the glare."

Actually this lion was more than a little confused; he was once more battling the familiar symptoms of his old depression, which ranged from a sense of stale boredom, dullness, and apathy to an actively suicidal despair. The freedom his Cleo had won in *Rocket* was beginning to sour within him. Seeing himself mirrored emotionally in the disadvantaged blacks of the South, he wrote a remarkably astute note in a Chapel Hill hotel room:

> In the case of the dull southern Negro—I say that the mechanism of the type, at a very early age, deliberately throws itself (altho gradually) into a comatose state from which it never recovers—and this to escape the future pain and constant denial and reprisals of future life which it dimly (or intuitively) felt and knew from childhood on. One of the chief things the early personality seems to do (and throughout life indeed) is to put armour on the vulnerable spots. It is exactly as a constant bruised joint will grow a callous—and a callous has no sensitivity; it is merely a mechanism of pain-avoidance. That is the phrase—the mechanism of pain-avoidance.

He found himself thinking a great deal about pride, vulnerability, and about Waldo Frank, reading his books and recalling Frank's moving accounts of beatings in Cuba, Mexico, and South America, where he had fought tyranny. No real pain-avoidance, thought Odets, in that enterprise. This despite the fact that Frank was both vulnerable and proud. To Sidney Bernstein, his old music-listening companion (now a committed labor organizer in Chattanooga, called variously Sidney Benson or Ted Wellman), Odets wrote he would meet him in Miami and together they would visit Key West, where Ernest Hemingway would tell them about *his* experiences fighting fascism in Spain. In his notebook he jotted:

> Shakespeare's characters have a sense *only* of their importance; never of their unimportance; this despite all their weary talk of fate and destiny and mortal coils.

> Pride as a chief characteristic. Richard III as pure pride. Even villain's chief characteristic is pride.

Lacking his usual source of both sustenance and anesthesia, his music recordings, he found himself reading avidly and consuming unwonted amounts of gin. "The small consolations," he called them.

From Miami, Odets and Bernstein drove to Key West, where Ernest Hemingway, in open shirt and khaki shorts, greeted them warmly. Hemingway, just returned from Spain's civil war, was more knowledgeable than the hopeful placard-bearers in New York; his first words after his greeting were "Spain is in its last stages: fascism is *really* on the march now." Bernstein recalled how seriously and sadly he said this and with what profound respect Hemingway described the work of the Spanish Communist Party in trying to prevent Franco's fascism from engulfing not only Spain but the rest of the world. He recalled, too, Odets' gravely scrutinizing interest not only in Hemingway's moving narrative of Spain but in his bowlegs, his marriage, and his two children. Odets correctly judged Hemingway's marriage also to be "in its last stages," and wondered aloud whether artists have more trouble in their human ties than do other people. Later Odets wrote what he called a "souvenir":

Hemingway. Full of pride and honor, bristling, he was at bottom always partly a liar and knew it. Poor man, what was wrong was that he could not forgive nor live easily with this relatively small incompatibility in himself. And, unable to accept it himself, he nevertheless wanted you to accept it. I knew he was a self-nag the moment I looked at him; I saw instantly that he held high a self-image of himself, but a boyish one rather than an adult one. The boy had been stuck forever in his crop.

With muckraker journalist Robert Allen, collaborator with Drew Pearson and brother of playwright Paul Peters, they all bowled and drank. Hemingway daily insisted they all go fishing, but Odets steadily refused. He preferred, he said, "just to watch people." Hemingway advised him in that case, "not to hang around here. Go to Cuba, to the hotel Ambos Mundos, it's a great place—not a tourist joint."

Bernstein recalled how talkative Hemingway was when he came to see them off, and how quiet, in contrast, Odets. When Hemingway made a joke about a real prince who would be sailing with them ("I call him the fairy prince," he said), Odets did not smile, and on the four-hour boat ride to Cuba he appeared to his friend Bernstein very low in spirit. He spoke only twice—once to wonder whether his marriage was indeed finished, and again to inform Bernstein that this was literally the same boat from which Hart Crane, saying, "This is no time for poets," had jumped. Bernstein, whose neglect of his work as union-organizer was troubling him, decided nevertheless to remain with his melancholy friend for two weeks in Cuba. He was deeply concerned that Odets had recently had two car accidents. In one he had been severely lacerated, and Bernstein feared that the next car accident might be the last.

Arrived in Havana, they went first to the famed Zaragozana restaurant, where they ate dinner and bought several cartons of cigarettes. (Hemingway had said, "You buy a package of cigarettes and you're a businessman in Havana.") Next Odets wanted to see "what the Cuban Communist Party headquarters looked like." Having established that, like all such headquarters, it was a small, drab office with a few desks, one typewriter, and piles of literature "in doctrinaire Spanish instead of English," they moved on to what Bernstein recalled as "the most marvelous cathouse in Havana, run by a stout American Negro woman who elegantly served drinks and then asked us, 'What would be your pleasure?'" To Bernstein's astonishment, Odets announced he would "just watch." The proprietress now ran down the possibilities: "Two men, two women, a man and a woman, a pony and a woman." In hasty conference, said Bernstein, "we decided on two girls." When the girls' performance had reached its climax by means of a strapped-on dildo, "the madam asked us whether *we* now wanted these two girls." He was disappointed that Odets sadly shook his head, muttered something about venereal disease, and suggested they leave. The madam was clearly puzzled and angry as both men departed.

The strangest episode of the evening, in Bernstein's opinion, occurred after he returned with a pretty young girl to a nightclub where he had left Odets drinking alone. Odets commandeered the girl and disappeared for several hours. Early in the morning Bernstein's phone rang.

It was Odets, describing how "he had made the girl go down on him, how shocked he had been she was willing to do this as she seemed such a nice, well-bred girl, and, above all, his concern that I might resent his contact with this girl I barely knew just because I had seen her first." Bernstein added that he was always taken aback by the eccentricity of Odets' naïvely middle-class morality: "He always tried to elicit this particular piece of sexual activity from a woman and was regularly shocked when the girl was willing to humiliate (Odets' word) herself this way." Over the years, according to Bernstein, "he would boast about this or that middle-class girl from a good family or a good college and express his amazement she would 'do a thing like that.' I think he often preferred that because it was always connected in his mind with a fear of clap." Not to speak of a far deeper fear of that dark feminine cavern which he so often celebrated in his secret poems as putrid, rank, revolting, and dangerous—a treacherous hole which could swallow a helpless man.

In his "Havana Notebook" he wrote:

> We do not grow into this adult world; we are *shocked* into it. Last night I had a dream. I was walking beside the President. Suddenly I put my head on his shoulder. "I want you to be my father," I said. Suddenly men, adult, find themselves alone, afraid, motherless, fatherless, hesitant of accepting responsibility: all of the men are afraid and alone. They quickly raise families. Havana 2/22/39

He defensively told a newspaper reporter that his wife had gone to Paris "to be in a play," confiding that he had always found her bourgeois expectations silly: "How can any wife expect her husband to open the car door for her? Once in a while, all right, but always? For a wife?"*

> *On March 28, 1939, Madrid fell to the fascists. Concurrently with this event came an almost unrecognizable change in the spiritual scene of American life. A certain flatness, a falling off of aspirational force, a kind of treadmill progression subtly characterized the environment from this time till after the outbreak of the war in September.*
>
> HAROLD CLURMAN

Odets continued to work doggedly on *The Silent Partner*, and when Bernstein went back to Chattanooga, he journeyed on to Mexico City. There he made contact with a small American colony of literati, dancers, newspaper correspondents; above all, he busied himself with the Mexican-American theatre. As he continued to struggle with what he called the "symphonic form" of *The Silent Partner,* with its now forty-five char-

---

* Luise laughed when she later heard this. "The opposite was the truth. I always thought it idiotic that strong American girls needed such attention."

acters (he called *Rocket* a "chamber piece"), he distracted himself with
his "General Notes" and with outlines for a variety of full-length plays.

One play was a social satire about an impostor president; another
was about a quartet of musicians, each driven away from the harmonious
creative whole of the group by his own needs; and a third, begun in 1937
and resumed periodically over two decades, was conceived as taking
place in "Harlan, Kentucky . . . a southern state, Spain, Germany or
Italy." Called *Night on Steel Mountain*, the third play is a panoramic
drama about "a conflict of classes and of social types and their typicali-
ties which come from various backgrounds." Like *The Silent Partner*, it
is peopled with Gogol characters and deals once more with the twin
themes of trust and betrayal in personal and in social history. Characteristically, the protagonist meets a violent death brought on essentially by
his own inner fragmentation. Psychological and historical "fascism" over-
hangs the whole. Odets' notes, often including striking adumbrations of
social philosophers like Marcuse, grapple with his own sense of rootless-
ness—in his work, his love, and his life—and, above all, with the search
for a way of life that will help each man rise to his potential. He writes:

Notice a curious fact—the American men have no past, no present,
only a future. They have no memory; the present irks them because
all of the possibilities and expansions of their lives are not in it; only
the future do they live for. This is very important; in fact I believe
that in this fact is contained all the vices and virtues of the typical
American. In it is contained the typical rejection of himself and what
he is; in it is contained his complete lack of sense of his own experience (see most plays or movies or art). In it is contained the
whole utilitarian philosophy of the American: "Can it be used?" . . .

Now what does this come from? Perhaps the following is an
explanation. It is a raw, unexplored, unrealized country—it is a
century or two ago. What was your past? In colonial days it was a
running away from a painful past—you were a shoemaker, a criminal from Europe, religiously persecuted. No matter what, at any
rate you resolutely turned your back on the past. Then you considered your immediate present: hardship, hacking out of the wilderness, settlement-making, hostility from Indians, from nature—a
complete conspiracy. But you hold on, you fight and chop for the
sake of what? For the sake of a future; and the more you realize the
possibilities of a future the more you look forward to it, aiming to it.
There are also social inferiorities which plague you, colonial inferiority, if you please, and these too catapult you into a visionary future.
AND SO YOU HAVE determined for yourself and your ancestors a kind
of avid contemplation of the future, forgetting present and past. . . .

The future was very often called the American dream; and only
when one begins to realize (when we, the people begin) that there
is no future, only then will the past and present be accepted, only
then will our men and women begin to accept themselves, taking for
granted what they are, living deeply and pleasurably, without nerves,
without aspirational mainsprings . . . in a word, with deep and
fundamental acceptance of the being and the life in which it moves.
May the day come soon when we reach that civilization level!

His appreciation, in this pre-Erikson time, of the interweaving of individual conflict in the context of history is startling.

He described the satire on the impostor president in his file marked
"Full-length Play":

> The dictator of a fascist country has been dead for a year. Three substitutes who look like him are parading as him, doing his work. The people don't know it; the state exists.

This play is a parable wherein Odets expresses his own suspicious sense of being fraudulently used, whether by his father, the Group Theatre, or the United States government. One of the "doubles" (himself, of course) comes to life and wants to outwit "The Board," to be a "true democrat," and really to run the government. But they watch him with "spies and guards" and supply him with "plenty of booze and women." It is their intention, he discovers, to kill him when his usefulness is over. He determines publicly to reveal the plot, knowing "it means death." He lives long enough to tell the world that all "The Board" wants is a "rubber-stamp, a servant of finance." As he is announcing "Gentlemen of the press, the president of the United States died fourteen months ago," he is himself shot dead.◀

Once again in this play the torn protagonist is a blood sacrifice and the story is, yet again, an account of how an honest, if divided, creator—who feels himself to be on one level an impostor—is destroyed by those identity-elements within himself which *want* him to be a servant of evil ("of finance"). The stereotypy of image in these never-to-be-written plays reflects his sense of impasse.

As *Rocket* was ailing at the box office, Luther Adler had suggested that the Group revive *Awake and Sing!* and play the two alternately. It would mark a step in the direction of a repertory theatre. With Odets still incommunicado in Mexico City, this plan was put into effect without him. To everyone's astonishment, *Awake and Sing!*—in a production inferior to the original four years earlier—was received as an honored classic. *The New York Times'* Brooks Atkinson now found that it could "not be praised too highly" and concluded that it was "one of the most stirring plays of this generation." The *Herald Tribune's* Richard Watts, Jr., agreed, calling it "deservedly a classic of the modern theatre." Richard Lockridge of the *Sun* thought "it goes without saying that anyone who missed it four years ago is under obligation to see it now," and John Mason Brown found it to be "literally quivering with vitality" and "even better than it was four years ago . . . really genius when Mr. Odets is functioning at his best." It seemed to Brown that "those who fail to see it may be said in truth to dwell in the dust."

It was not primarily because he was so far away (Odets never saw this production and read only a few reviews) that these encomiums meant little to him. The problem went much deeper: he was in a steady terror that he was indeed, as he now wrote in his notebook, "the boy who hit the target's heart once, never trying again," adding, "America keeps you keenly conscious of success . . . there is a face to keep, a position to retain. Before you were free; you are a prisoner now." All of which has less to do with a need for Cadillacs, cashmere sweaters, or French soap, and more with being an American son of an immigrant salesman who feels himself to be a failure and a writer manqué.

◀ 23.1.

Hearing rumors that the Group was planning to spend the summer making a film, he wrote Clurman the first letter since his breakup with Luise. In it he expresses his outrage that even this last sanctuary for "satisfying, fulfilling work in the theatre" is now in jeopardy. In his conclusion—"Pictures equal fame and money. Yes, but leading to what?"— lies his plea that the Group remain a protector of his talent, a buffer against the relentless pressures to merchandise it. He expresses the universal aspiration of the serious artist: to hold a secure place by way of created form in an esthetically moral and unified family wherein his own role is freely but firmly and integrally rooted. It is a need to transcend one's individual identity and to offer integration to others by way of one's self-integration:

Huichapan, 21
Mexico, D.F.

Dear Harold,

Is there some one in the Group Theatre, or its office, perhaps yourself, who might be kind enough to sit down and dictate a letter to a stenographer? It would be a point of kindness, in this letter, to tell me what the Group is doing, what its plans for the summer are, and all such information which a friend might think I'd like to know. Newspapers are notoriously unreliable and I get them very late here, in the bargain.

Every once-in-awhile I like to know what I'm working for. I like to know about the productions being contemplated, about the movie plans, about play contests, about important decisions. It also pleases me greatly when my opinions of matters are inquired after. Apparently it is thought around the Group that only a decision to close a play of mine is important to me; or some one will make an inquiry by mail or telegram, can he borrow some cash, can he have this or that; or am I working hard on that play which is so badly needed. That, to all extents and purposes, about concludes my relationship with the Group Theatre.

That, you must know, is a very unsatisfactory relationship. It puts me in the singular position of the pretty girl who stays in her room and gives out when a man decides he wants a night-full. I abhor this position, I deplore it, I despise it and conditions which make it; and I'll have to do something about it. Don't answer back with the old saw—none of you want to bother me—for, I'm bothered very promptly when someone there wants something.

Here, in short, is what I'm talking about. The pleasure I get out of life is of a very limited sort, special and very little. For years now I have had the very difficult lonely task of sitting in an empty room and writing plays for months of nights. When the plays were finished they were promptly seized and put in other hands, myself cast away and out like you throw old furniture out. I told you about that in Boston. Next, when vital decisions were to be made, concerning my plays or others, or any Group affairs, I was consulted concerning them to even a lesser extent than was the office secretary, the girl, Ruthie.

Again, in short, I am in the anomalous position of being the Group's main dynamo and at the same time as far out of the texture of the Group as I was eight years ago in Brookfield Center. Don't like it, doesn't suit me, doesn't use me, doesn't please or give me pleasure — abhor it!

What are you going to do about this problem, Harold? I want, psychologically and materially, to be in the Group Theatre. You will have to assume more responsibility towards my personal welfare than you've been doing. You will have to see to it that I get some personal pleasure out of the Group. You will have to include me more in all organizational plans. Believe me, Harold darling, this letter contains one of the most serious problems of the Group Theatre, altho you or no one else may be aware of it. My growing discontent is going to shortly become an unpleasant explosion, as displeasing to myself as to you and the others. One of the main reasons I go away from New York (as now) is that there is no work for me in New York. I am beginning to be genuinely isolated from the theatre. What I am looking for instead, is a satisfying fulfilling relationship in the theatre. You are too clever, I know, to suppose that the success, fame and publicity of the last few years has been in anyway nourishing to my deepest necessities.

The standard of work has decreased several hundred percent; (last production with any depth was Paradise Lost) and it is sad to record that the more proficient our actors become, the deeper they become as men and women, the less are they called upon to bring to their actual stage work. This is also true of the director.

The spiritual life, to use an old fashioned word, of all of us has become as sounding brass. And do not think that radical insight into life is precluded from the word spiritual.

The asp of success, in my opinion, has bitten deeply into the Group Theatre members; and it is most curious that lapses, plans which each member would not permit for himself, he permits the Group Theatre as a unit. Which of you would go to the movies when an active theatre program was before you? Not one. Then why permit the theatre to do it? You say this is a different kind of movie program. Pray, what difference? That we are acting together? Is that the end of the Group's work, that we will be acting together? Is it not time to ask again, "Acting together for what"? What is the "What for" of our work at present? What has it been during the last few years? Not important. Once it was important to keep us together: Golden Boy did it. But now we are even sick with togetherness! Is our end to remain "togetherness"?

You have often heard it spoken around the Group that we are interested in continuity of work, a continuity of this life. But now ask what life?

Revenue is the only excuse, but there is a place where even revenue must cease and make way for program. Will this money be used for repertory. Of course not; we won't use our own money in any case. Then why not spend some time raising rep money, plays, plans. But apparently it's more pleasant to do a film. Why for God's sake? What's a film? Who is interested in doing a weak sister like Gentle People in the films? What's it good for? A redefinition of this theatre is necessary, even a rededication, in my humble opinion. I mean humble—humility before what we could be and the use to which our theatre could be put in the American scene. We are beginning to "fit things in." Certain extra-artistic elements (hunger for success and worldly approbation) are beginning to dominate. The tone of the Group smells somewhat.

Summer is for plays like Silent Partner, not for movies. Pictures equal fame and money. Yes, but leading to what? I will tell you like

Jacob, "If this theatre leads to a people's theatre, to repertory, to a radical critical attitude to the society around it, it's for something. Otherwise it's nothing!"

I am putting this problem up to you, not to add headaches (of which you have enough, and I know!), but because it is the most honest way of approaching it. Dishonestly, I could burrow underground and come up with some perfectly amazing prizes; there are some matters in which you would absolutely have to permit me a free hand, particularly in relation to my own plays. Let us, to be short, be brightly honest: you and I are the indispensable members of the Group Theatre, no others.

What, by the way, prompted this letter? Do you ask that? Simply sitting at the typewriter and being unable to work on the play; getting no pleasure from it; asking myself "What for?"; and longing to be home. But home for me is a theatre in which I take an active working part, work which oils the head and heart. (I can't keep going on newspaper approbation.) And you must help me get deep into the texture and mechanism of the Group's functioning. You must think that perhaps I'd like to play good parts, direct interesting experimental productions, help make decisions, etc., etc., and be permitted to at least assist in casting my own plays! In short, for a final time, I want to enjoy myself within the Group Theatre and the framework of its possibilities. For most of you there has been liberal enjoyment and deep pleasure in the formation and growth of our theatre; seldom for me, and you will have to believe me when I say it.

Here: Success, for me, has been a curtailment of Group Theatre life and pleasure. Now I must make it into an extension, and you must help me.

Right now I must know the Group summer plans. It was all set to put S. Partner into summer rehearsal. Now I hear something about a movie in the summer. What about that?

Have you ever been here? Why don't you come now—be my guest for a week or two, even three, and we can ride back together. Do you need a rest? This place is just like California, but with a thousand times more character and clarity and moral tone and possibility. Send me a wire and say you are coming—a new plane service has just been started from N.Y. to here. Really, there is no place like this one to rest your head and see the true values of things. Whole Group Theatre ought to work here in the summer—five Mexican dollars for one of ours. But I mustn't get too friendly—I forgot I'm very displeased with you!!!

Love,
Clifford

4/8/39

Three days later, after finishing a bottle of brandy with the Mexican painter Carlos Mérida, he all but demolished his Pontiac in the worst accident of his life. He had later only a dim memory of swerving into a telephone pole to avoid an oncoming car, and of the length of time it took his rescuers to extricate him from the wreckage. In the hospital it seemed to him miraculous he had escaped with only severe lacerations of the face and a torn shoulder. It was alarming to composer Hanns Eisler and his wife, now refugees from Germany, as well as to others in the intellectual community of Mexico City, that Odets was steadily being reckless with his life.

To all of them, and to visiting artists from New York such as singer

Mordecai Baumann or the Anna Sokolow dance troupe, he appeared, as Baumann put it, "lost, unconnected, with no commitment to anyone or anything." One of the dancers recalled his "taking all the girls in the company to dinner." However, it surprised her that "he didn't really seem interested in any of us. He seemed to prefer picking up a waitress in a café." On one occasion he told her how he had "gone through the Mexican girl's family apartment to her bedroom, but only to see how they live."

On April 12 Clurman, ignorant of the accident the day before, replied warmly to Odets' plea that the Group Theatre abandon the plan to make a film in the summer; he was clearly trying to reconnect, to recommit him:

Dear Cliff:

I hasten to answer to tell you how much I love you, how much in all things I would like you to be happy, how much I am willing to work to make you so. Yes, when we get together we must definitely have an understanding of how, and by what means, you can feel more tied in with the Group. My desire to assure you of our anxiety to have you work with us as closely as you desire, at this moment far outweighs any quibble or argument I may have as to details, justifications, and recriminations about past events. All I could say if I wanted to make a blanket statement is that I might have written you a letter in an emotional mood, bitterly complaining from my, and the Group's standpoint, about your not being as close to the Group as you should and show you how in certain respects some of the burden of that problem was yours. . . .

Yes, the Group intends to have a summer. We propose to rehearse for about eight to ten weeks in the country before opening in New York. Right now we have no plays at all for next season. I will consider that we have "Silent Partner" when a script is in my hands. . . .

There has been a movie proposition put to us. This has not been absolutely set and in no case would it interfere with our summer plans as I consider the Group summer, which means rehearsals in the real, old-fashioned Group way, the paramount need for the Group Theatre as a whole. I am sure you agree with this. . . .

We need more good plays, and we must encourage more talented playwrights. I think we ought to do one or two productions in a new vein—Possibly a revue or a classic. Incidentally, apropos of some of the things I have written about morale and fascistic tendencies of our day, I was thinking about your idea for a quartet play; the image there of the quartet and of the factors that drive the people to decay into their own individual cells, is exactly what I am thinking of when I try to define the Group problems. . . .

There has been an offer from some people in Denver to take 25 of us out there, pay all our expenses for the summer, transportation, etc., in return for one performance a week for about six weeks. We have done nothing about this yet. We are gathering more information concerning it, but so far it is the only concrete thing that has come up as to our summer activities. . . .

In the meantime, I want again to convey the spine of this letter which is

    a) I want to help you toward your aim as stated in your letter
    b) It is really not our fault that things are as they are
    c) It doesn't matter a damn whose fault it is, I still want to help you because
        a) I love you

    b) I admire you
    c) I think you are important to the human race, to the
        American people, to the Jews, . . . which means that
            a) I respect you
            b) I admire you
            c) I love you
I hope this is clear.

          Love,
            Harold

    Clurman's letter was sufficiently clear that Odets determined to return to the United States, to provide, if necessary, the basic financing for another Group summer and, above all, to furnish it with a script, be it *The Silent Partner, Night on Steel Mountain,* or a wistful play about two trained monkeys "escaped from Hollywood" and a boy who is sent to recover them.

    To Clurman, a week after his accident, Odets wrote a long letter reflecting that relief often experienced by a guilt-ridden, depressed person who has managed to obtain for himself an optimum expiation in an "accident," and who can now afford to enjoy not only the fact of his survival but life itself:

                                                4/18/39

Dear Harold, Friend, Brother,
    What made me most happy in your letter of last week was the fact that the Group is going to have a summer. The news that we might do a picture over the summer was so depressing to me that I was unable to write for three days; I limped along for a time after that and then got into my stride again. Then I wrote you that letter and said in it only a fraction of the things I wanted to say. By now I have a peculiar pattern of behavior—I write a hot letter (and I can write hot, baby!), I leave it on my desk, the next morning I tear it up, the next night I write there more temperately and much more to the point.

    Well, then there was the accident: the car ruined (but fixable) and myself so badly shocked that I was dazed for two days, mooning around in a dressing gown. Very interesting psychologically, that accident! The worse that happened to the body was some small cuts, a torn ligament in the right shoulder and A CURIOUS LITTLE PIECE OF TONGUE bitten right off one edge. It's better now—tongues heal quickly. But the actual shock I found very interesting, a new experience, the intense jitters, the acute awareness which is followed by complete exhaustion and blackest depression and uncontrollable tears . . . but all the time a very enjoyable sense of all parts of the personality being alive and moving together.

    Well, the accident has taken a week out of my writing schedule, that's what I want to say. Now, with luck, with hard work is what I mean, this draft can be finished in ten days. The Silent Partner is what I'm talking about. It has been a lesson in discipline for me. For weeks I kept repeating a paragraph from one of Lord Byron's letters to myself. (The key to the whole romantic temperament is in those letters.) He says that when he writes it's like a tiger leaping out of the jungle. If he hits, he says, it is a wonderful hit, but if he misses there is nothing for him to do but slink back into the jungle and leave that particular piece of work alone forever. That's me, says I—impossible to rewrite. Better start something new, better throw S. Partner away to the dogs. . . . Anything for an excuse not to work! Even sent back to New York for two new files of notes and delighted myself with looking over the notes of the Two Monkeys play.* Yes, yes, I say, what a smash hit this play is going to be, movie sale and all—can't miss, sure fire, and yet interesting, moving, a good play. Even graphed out the scenes, shook the single sheet of paper in my hands, bellowed out to the landlord here, "Do you know this one damn sheet of paper is conservatively worth a quarter of a million dollars?!" So the next night I started on The Silent Partner. It will be ready for summer rehearsal; and don't go cagey with me, that stuff about you will know you have it when you have it in your hands. Did you have G. Boy in your hands when you knew you had it? Rocket? Paradise Lost? Look, the momser! Or are you beginning to believe all those press stories about it being necessary to have three Group members sitting on my head in order to get a play? Ha, here I sit, worrying about the casting, and he tells me his hand is empty! Go scratch yourself with it!

I'm not in a serious mood tonight, so I can answer your letter with nothing but affection and fun, even tho I'm tired. . . .

For here is a good thing: This Mexican trip and certain definite personal decisions (and you know what I mean) have given me my first rest and quiet in four years. Yes, during these past few weeks I've had exactly *the inner calm* I had when I sat down in a warm quiet hotel room and wrote Lefty. I tried to tell this to a certain Mexican girl in outlandish Spanish but she said pass the cognac and pushed me out of the other side of the bed. Yes, Yes, real shivers of delight—the horizon lifts slowly and surely, the way you swing back a very heavy safe door after years of fumbling with the goddam combination; and a quiet calm fellow inside there, sitting with clear eyes and a quiet heart. You will see good things coming soon, Harold dear. How eager I find myself for fresh new problems! How few of them are personal and subjective. I really think the auto accident was a kind of final polishing off process—don't you know the medicos are now using insulin shock for relief of dementia praecox? Enough. . . .

Your comment on how . . . Group problems tie up with the projected quartet play was very interesting. I found that out for myself when I went over my Group file, for I have a Group theatre play, too; the thesis was the same, I saw, exactly the same, so much the same that it seemed foolish at the time. But, I guess, a few people will have to die before I can ever write that Group play with any feeling of comfort: in England they'd get us on the libel laws!

You speak of a classical play. I spent my first month away from New York in constant reading. In one week I carefully read eleven Shakespeare plays, twenty Tchekoff stories, two John Webster plays and the second volume of Parkington. No, it was two weeks to tell the truth. . . .

The two John Webster plays are interesting and extraordinary works. I mean "The White Devil" and "Dutchess of Malfi." Orson Welles announced the latter, but that's no reason why we shouldn't be interested in it. I'm always ready to service an Elizabethan like Webster, cutting, adding a line here and there and so forth. Webster, compared to Shakespeare, is more a man of my kidney and ball, if I may say so. . . . A lot of Shakespeare is sheer drivel and bunk and his mind is not first class even tho much of his poetry and EMO-TION is. . . .

At least one and possibly both of the Webster plays have parts

* This will become *Night Music.*

in them for Stella, the name parts in fact. I haven't thought too much
about what the Dutchess means, but it was certainly written in a
world on its way to doom, breaking down with corruption and greed
and all that. . . .

Within a week Clurman shot back his answer; its content can leave
no doubt as to the nature of the practical problems inherent in the development of a serious American theatre. His fervent and understandable wish
is to be "backed by Warner's or someone like that"—this although Clurman
had a profound and detailed understanding of the merchandising core of
all motion-picture companies. With the brief dream of a national American
theatre now dissolving under the pressure of a rising defense budget, a
theatre producer could choose either to be the entrepreneur for an independent "floating crap game" or to accept the relative security—in whatever form—of backing from the film industry, which would attach its own
visible or invisible strings.

Despite Clurman's demurrer to Odets that he does not mean "to whack
you into doing a commercial play for us," the desperate wish is apparent:

I was happy to find you in what seems to be a mood of growing
confidence and comparative inner peace. . . .

I cannot give you the exact figures of our losses for this season
but they have been considerable. "Awake and Sing" lost some money
almost every week and I assure you that it was not due to poor exploitation. The notices and separate articles written all the time were
alone a terrific source of publicity, but they had the effect of praise
for a classic author and a fine institution, but not the effect of making
people buy tickets. We spent money in a large ad in all the newspapers on various occasions, all to no avail, due to the fact that the play
was never, as you remember, a commercial hit. When we toured the
play on the road, the notices were much more enthusiastic than the
first New York notices but we rarely grossed over $6,000. The Jewish-
ness served as a limitation, etc., etc. . . .

I don't mean to depress you with all this, or to whack you into
doing a commercial play for us—actually, despite the fact that we
probably have only 7 or $8,000 in the bank, our position is not as ter-
rible as this figure would indicate. Critically, we have arrived—really
and truly! Last week, Watts, apropos of "My Heart's in the Highlands"
called us "The outstanding theatrical organization of this country";
and at the critics dinner, which I attended, praise for our organization
was heaped upon me by even such recalcitrants as George Jean
Nathan, who incidentally, praised me personally as a director. A little
embarrassing. . . .

Our serious problem, as always, is getting scripts. Naturally, I
am very encouraged by what you write but please permit me to be
hard boiled until the scripts are before me. Unless I am, I get into
that mood of passionate eagerness from which you suffered during
"Rocket to the Moon.". . .

I am going to read the plays you suggest. I have always heard
about "Duchess of Malfi" as a good play and as a play for Stella, only
I would like her reappearance here to be in a new play by somebody
like yourself or Shaw.

Enough for today, let's keep on exchanging these notes until you
come back. I don't know yet if I will be able to get down to Mexico. . . .

Love,
Harold

Clurman's letter stimulated Odets to hard work and to a kind of manic excitement about the coming reunion with his Group family. An intersplicing of his letters and personal notes in the subsequent weeks reveals a fascinating underground stream. First, he writes an adulatory letter to President Roosevelt (about whom he has lately dreamed as his father) offering filial help for a re-election.

4/25/39
Mexico, D.F.

Dear President Roosevelt,

Pardon this letter, if you see it, and it won't hurt to see it. But in going over the resumes of the week's news, I was struck again by the character and quality of your actions and your writings. And this makes me send verbal admiration to you and to tell you how you have just plain damn sewed up the affections of so many of your citizens. Despite the roars of our own local money men, you will live a very long time in the hearts of all fair-minded-and-hearted men and women of our country.

If you are going to run for a third time, please permit me to help with my good writing hand. Excuse the tone, but my hand writes well and can add a little assistance when ever you need it. For months I have been thinking of a "Pro-Roosevelt" play to tour around the country, but it isn't easy to plan or write, unless one means to be superficial.

Again, pardon this note, and please accept the gratitude of so many of us that you are the president of our country.

Sincerely,
Clifford Odets
Playwright.

Huichapan, 21.

Two weeks later Roosevelt replies without accepting his offer:

May 6, 1939

PERSONAL
Dear Clifford Odets:

Please accept my thanks for that cordial note of yours. It is pleasant, but withal startling, to read such encomiums.

Very sincerely yours,
Franklin D. Roosevelt

Mr. Clifford Odets
Huichapan, 21,
Mexico, D.F.

Two days later Odets is filled with sad thoughts of his dead mother and has a dream:

File Personal.

All day of the eighth of May I was thinking of my mother, because on that day she was dead four years. But I did not dream about her that night. I went to a cheap night club that night and sat at a table with a friend and his girl and I drank too much and went home and slept badly that night.

On the evening of the ninth I lay down for an hour's nap and had a beautiful dream. A large group of people had been invited to the house of some great professor, a sort of Einstein I imagine altho he was more unspecified in the dream. I took my mother along, probably because recently I had separated from my wife.

When we arrived at the address we were surprised to find that it was a kind of old fashioned eating place; we learned we were expected to go in and eat our dinner alone, at any table we chose. We went in and one table was much too large. Also we encountered Mrs. Watson, an American woman who has just left Mexico where she came for a rest. During this time she nursed me thru the shock of an automobile accident, taking, as she said, the exact relationship to me that she would take to her son, a young man almost my age.

Then, because we could not find the right table apparently, we found ourselves at the left side of the room where there was a large bunk against the wall. My mother stretched herself on the bunk. Myself I found in the middle of the bunk, my feet between the heads of my mother and Mrs. Watson. I sat up and put a blanket or coat up to my mother's chin. She was very tired and said very little. Now I noticed the peculiar style of the room. "This looks like the Avon period," I said to Mrs. Watson, "It's Shakesperian style, isn't it?" Mrs. Watson said that it was. I turned to my mother with a glad cry, telling her the room was in Shakesperian style, saying *this* is it, as if we had recently discussed it. My mother smiled quietly and said nothing.

So we lay that way for a few minutes and suddenly I felt Mrs. Watson taking off first one of my shoes and next the second. She was trying to make me more comfortable, but I apologized profusely, thinking how rude it had been to keep my shoes on. At the same time I thought, Mrs. Watson helps me and my own mother doesn't.

It had grown dark in the room and now I heard my mother's voice. "Cliff, dear," she said. I quickly bent over to her.

"Yes, mother."

In a tired voice she said, "Kiss me . . ."

A whole wave of pity and concern and tenderness ran over me: "Why, of course," I said, "certainly I will, certainly."

Then I woke up and saw it was all a dream, understood very quickly, immediately, it was a dream.

But I kissed her anyway.

Mexico City, May 9th, 1939

On one level it was the dream of a boy who longs, usually without success, to please his father and, failing that, to be taken care of by his mother. He told Hanns Eisler and his wife in Mexico City that he was not abandoning them and would help soon to bring them to New York to be part of the Group Theatre.

A few days later he wired his cousin Minnie Fabian a warm Mother's Day greeting. He also began his file for the "anti-Nazi play" on the nightmare account of the last emigrant ship to leave Germany, the *St. Louis;* the ship had been bound for Cuba with its cargo of almost a thousand doomed Jewish souls, but all were soon to be returned by a series of countries, including the United States, to the Holocaust. Odets was seized with an intense need to return to his Motherland and to write with "radical insights into life."

May 16 found him in San Antonio, Texas, with a handsome new mustache and beard to hide his unhealed scars from the accident. Two days later he arrived in Tyler, Texas, visiting Louis Veda Quince, the Theatre Guild actor whom he credited with keeping him from suicide ten years earlier when they were touring in the Theatre Guild's *Marco Millions*. In Tyler, Odets submitted to a newspaper interview in which he was critical of Hollywood, evasive about the state of his marriage, and confident that the "Silent Partner would be somewhere on June 15." Of his long hair, mustache, and beard he quipped, "I like to reveal new aspects of myself. I'd rather look like a phony writer than a phony businessman," a joke he would repeat to columnist Leonard Lyons for his column.

In his "General Notes," he wrote:

> After four months in Latin America: evidently the keynote of the American town is: things to sell and the means and instruments with which to sell them; store fronts, window displays, advertisements, monstrous neon lights—each bigger than the next—amazing cheap trashy world! When things are not to sell but *to keep,* we will begin to have a civilized life in our country! San Antonio, Tex. 5/16/39.

Before leaving Texas, he offered a loan to the improvident Louis Veda Quince, who could not resist.

In Chattanooga, Tennessee, he picketed briefly with striking reporters of the American Newspaper Guild and stopped off for a few days to see Sidney Bernstein. Together they listened to the late Beethoven quartets and discussed *The Silent Partner*. Bernstein recalled Odets' mood as unusually optimistic and his readiness to work as high. "From the way he described *Silent Partner*, it could have been a really good play," he judged. The House Committee on Un-American Activities would, thirteen years later, suspect that on this trip to Chattanooga Odets had conspired with Bernstein in a Communist plot to overthrow the government.

Actually, the only turmoil being created by Odets was in the theatre. From Mexico City, correspondent Ted Allan wrote a communiqué for Joseph North on the staff of the *New Masses*, saying, "That man Odets always drops a bombshell. . . . There had been little theatre in Mexico City of any kind before he arrived. And things haven't been the same since." He quoted Odets as having said before leaving Mexico City that "Hollywood in performance but not in promise is an odorless gas like carbon monoxide," and said Odets had explained to the Mexican press that he still believed the film medium held a great and fluid potential if it could ever be liberated from the stranglehold of big business.

In the same communiqué Allan said Odets had not produced his Cuban play because it had been, in his opinion, "a piece of brutal theatrical pamphleteering," and that he regarded *Golden Boy* as his weakest work, but thought its dialogue made it "better than mediocre." After *The Silent Partner*, Odets' next would be "either a proletarian love story or, if Roosevelt runs, a pro-Roosevelt play." Allan closed with a spirited account of Odets' visionary plan for a "lightning theatre group to tour every town of the United States," putting on plays relevant to the problems of each region. It was his "Charlie Theatre" all over again, and would emerge three decades later as the innovative street-and-guerrilla theatre.

"I first openly disputed with Clifford at a meeting on theatre at the Third Congress of Writers, held in New York from June 2nd to 4th in 1939. . . . There was quite a clash between us about art and social responsibility, and I warned him that the present (psychological) trend of his work—*Golden Boy* and *Rocket to the Moon*—was weakening his art. . . . A friend only recently mentioned the shock of my words to him." Thus, thirty years later,

John Howard Lawson described Odets' first public appearance after his return from Mexico. This assault from his old mentor wounded Odets and contributed to his immediate decision to flee once more, this time to Skowhegan, Maine, where he would prepare a final draft of his "socially responsible" play, *The Silent Partner,* for the Group Theatre to work on during the summer. His struggle to unite in his work a world-view that would integrate the radical insights of Marx and Freud continued. Encounters like this one with Lawson alienated him from his left-wing comrades. And yet their externalized, simplistic view of world order did violence to his subjective experience of a steady conflict and ambiguity in life. It seemed evident to him and to Clurman that Lawson was going creatively dead as he became politically more and more doctrinaire. Odets' passion to synthesize the contradictions of the psychological and the historical would continue to plague him. Indeed, his last play, on the Biblical theme of Noah, would be his ultimate effort at a solution of this problem.

Before leaving New York, he managed to sign, among many others, checks for his old Bronx boyhood friend Ernie Millstein ($1,000 to Mills Strap Novelty Co.), to actors Louis Veda Quince and Grover Burgess, as well as to the Rocket to the Moon Corporation ($4,000) and to the Northern Trust Co. of Philadelphia for payment on the mortgage on Tante Esther's and Uncle Israel's house on Sixth Street in Philadelphia. To Alfred Stein in Mexico he sent two pairs of requested earplugs, usually used to guard his own fitful sleep. To his handwriting expert he regularly sent samples for her analyses of friends as well as of public figures.

He instructed Herman to send his father a check for $200 with a note that "there will be only two more checks of equal amounts." "He asked me to be quite sure," wrote Herman to Louis Odets, "that I make it clear to you that the September first check will be the last one." Odets' savings account, consisting mainly of $22,000 worth of government bonds bought three years earlier with his Paramount salary, was fast dwindling and at this point there was no income from his plays. Bennett Cerf hoped his plan to publish six Odets plays in one "cheap edition" would result in some.

Within the first few hours of his arrival at Skowhegan's summer theatre, where Sinclair Lewis was trying out a new play, Odets learned with an odd twinge that Sylvia Field, the actress he had ardently worshipped ten years back on the Theatre Guild tour, and now a mother, was part of the company. Another member of this lively group, which included comedian Ed Wynn, was Fay Wray, a bright, gentle, beautiful, and self-effacing young film actress. Miss Wray was already a kind of myth for her performance six years earlier in the Beauty-and-the-Beast classic *King Kong,* wherein she had struggled and screamed interminably in the grasp of a fifty-foot gorilla atop the Empire State Building. Odets was immediately attracted by her modest, sad dignity, and by a curiously virginal quality she conveyed despite the fact that—still in her twenties—she was estranged from her writer husband and the mother of a small girl.

To others in the company Miss Wray ("the most womanly woman I have ever known," he would repeat for years after) seemed smitten at once by the handsome "white hope of the American theatre." She appeared to feel for artists, and especially for writers, a kind of wonder; and, like many young and eager "appreciators," she was passionately ready to learn from him about everything: music, politics, literature, playwriting. She began to read his plays one after another, and was deeply moved, she told him, by the lyric tenderness in them, which matched, she thought, the way he would gravely kneel in front of her tiny daughter, Susan, saying, "Hello,

dearest," giving her a book or a doll. From the start it seemed he was fundamentally unknowable, but perhaps, she once wrote, this was characteristic
"where a great and burning talent exists." Her many notes and airmail
special-delivery letters to him, after he left, sound half young-girl-in-love,
half fan. She speaks steadily of her longing to share with him the Group
Theatre atmosphere of "real work," so different, she feels, from the shallow
Angela Is 22 by Sinclair Lewis, or the other "inconsequential" play she was
playing in here before it reached New York, called *Life with Father.**

William Kozlenko, summoned by Odets, vividly recalled that he
seemed to be in torture with his work. One scene in *The Silent Partner*
obsessed and dominated him. "He knew that, however theatrically sensational the scene might be, you cannot build an entire play around one
scene. And yet he could not shake loose from it. The scene was a coffin
with a dead man and a woman talking to the dead man. It kept bothering
him."

It was as though Odets had concentrated here the core of his concern
that he was himself dead as a creator, needing the transfusion of a maternal love to bring about a hopeful and productive resurrection—an old
theme in his repertoire. Kozlenko tried to help, but until the day Odets left
for Lake Grove near Smithtown, Long Island, to join the Group Theatre
for its eighth (and last) summer, Odets talked of little else. He did not
tell his friend his other obsession—namely, the magical fantasy that if
Fay Wray were an ample-bosomed woman, he would marry her, thus
solving all his difficulties. There was something archaic, indeed unbal-
anced, in the critical importance he always gave to this single part of the
anatomy. For him, more than for most men, it promised a source of emotional and creative replenishment, a literal feeding mother. Sometimes he
counseled himself, however, not to await the ample bosom of the Magic
Mother, but to be one-pointedly faithful to a writer's central business in
life: to feed himself and others with his own words.

Stopping at One University Place before going on to Lake Grove, a Christian Science children's school near Smithtown, where the Group was gathering, Odets found a letter from Fay Wray describing her heavy-heartedness
and Ed Wynn's tears at his departure from Skowhegan, where he had en-
deared himself to everyone. She has been worrying "again" about his prone-
ness to automobile accidents and pleads with him to "slow down."

Another was from his father, responding to his son's ultimatum that
he become self-supporting:

> Please don't "Bust" family relations up. It's God's will that all family
> relations should always be kept in tact. You have but two sisters and a
> father, all of the same blood, regardless of their positions in life com-
> pared to yours, you should be one of them. Suppose you were the father
> of three children and they did not turn out all alike and as smart or
> clever as you think they should, would you dissown them? No. You
> would love them just the same. The good Lord has been very kind to
> you. He has given you, what only one man in millions possess. A brain

* The amiable *Life with Father* would play 3,000 performances on Broadway.

and how to use it— Please Clifford don't ween away from your immediate family. In their hearts they love you. You can make them happy,
and they can make you happy. Money doesn't buy happiness, and your
heart is bigger than all the money in the world. . . . I'v allready
started to look for a job. Anything thats worthwhile, I'll be glad to
take, and I'm looking for it. . . .

The sanctimonious tone of his father's letter angered and depressed him.
Neither he nor Herman believed that Odets senior would ever try to find
work. Odets junior promptly received a summons for speeding and reckless driving.

> *This theatre is a theatre of meaning.*
> HAROLD CLURMAN

What Clurman called "the falling off of aspirational force" preceding the
outbreak of World War II subtly underlay the Group's surface of bus-
tling activity and self-exploration this summer. On every page of the
mammoth and passionate logbook kept by the wife of actor Michael Gordon
until the fateful first day of September there stands clear evidence of a
tense, unraveling, humorless, and desperate mood. Assembled here in the
dreamy Gothic buildings of a Christian Science school, not far from a Nazi
Bundist camp, were more actors, playwrights, and apprentices than ever
before in the history of the Group Theatre; and it was their fervent hope
that during this six-week period the Group would, as actor Leif Erickson
(husband of Frances Farmer) put it, "get back to its roots."
     Some expressed in whispers that the Group Theatre was dying, and
Clurman, in one of his candid and exuberant monologues, expressed his
fear of, and wish for, the Group's dissolution. He had, in the view of a
Group actor, become a "shouting, whirling dervish" who had appointed
himself the prolix Asker of Basic Questions for everyone, like "What is
Life? Where are you going? What is Art?" It was as if he had decided,
despite his admitted ambivalence about the Group, that, "so help me, this
is *going* to work." Some, like the rudderless Frances Farmer, were grateful
for Clurman's fanatic, almost apoplectic direction and dedication; others
irritably decided that "Harold is mystical, long-winded, and just wants
everyone to be his slave." He had, after all, put it to them at eleven o'clock
in the morning of their second day, "Are you willing to let me be the
absolute dictator for a season?" Was it a tongue-in-cheek question? Many
were enraged at "Harold's megalomania," and a few dismissed it with
"Harold talks too much and too loud."
     There were daily Group meetings to discuss both professional and
deeply personal problems; many of these confrontations foreshadowed
what would later be called, in the world of psychiatry and psychology,
"encounter" or "sensitivity-training" groups. They talked of individualism
within a collective; of the nature of genuine commitment, whether to a
person or to a group; and steadily, through Stanislavskian exercises, of
themselves. For some this was life-saving, for others devastating. As always, the Group was full of gifted people living on a knife edge in all their
relationships.

The Farmer-Erickson marriage, it was clear to some, was in extreme jeopardy. Equally clear to all was that Odets was dazzled by the golden beauty and intelligence, as well as the strange purity, of Miss Farmer. Private wagers were being made that his presence would be the final stress on her strained relations with her husband. It was known that four years earlier she had been deeply attracted to Odets.

"The truth sessions that last summer were really cruel," in the opinion of Kermit Bloomgarden, business manager for the Group. He recalled one in which "actor Bud Bohnen was violently attacked, relentlessly stripped, for even *considering* a Hollywood job. John Garfield and J. Edward Bromberg were already out there and Lee J. Cobb was back and forth. They shouldn't have driven these people out like black sheep, but sent them to Hollywood with blessings, and invited them back to be in plays." Questions had been raised also of Bloomgarden's divided loyalty between the Group and commercial producer Herman Shumlin, for whom he was working on the side in order to eke out a living; the Executive Council (then consisting of Clurman, Odets, Kazan, Bohnen, Carnovsky, and Luther Adler) told him he must choose, and Bloomgarden advised Clurman, in a large public meeting, that "he better kiss my ass and beg me to stay." Although Clurman declined this recommendation, Bloomgarden retained both his Group and his commercial commitments.

A well-known actress whose husband was a Group member saw in such episodes a lack of professional dignity, "a real beginning of the end." She was revolted by the atmosphere and decided "they were all eating and killing each other that summer."

Clurman pleaded with them to desist, to make *him* their target instead. They obliged until he, too, felt that these "truth sessions" were becoming overly cruel. On one occasion he screamed to the assemblage, as though insane, that "it is simply not the Group's business if I've had a fight with Stella. And it's not your business, either, if I want to make up with her." The boundary between what was properly Group business and what was not was becoming fuzzy indeed as its identity lost what Clurman called "a religious coherence." An inevitable result was a steep rise in the general level of anxiety. In one breath the members looked forward to a decade of esthetic renewal and consolidation; in the next, to the Group's immediate demise. That the coming year would mark an upheaval was apparent.

As in any communal enterprise, Bloomgarden recalled, "the relation of the individual to the Group, its responsibility to him and his to it, was constantly hashed over" and, according to him, "issues of personal selfishness were steadily discussed." When the well-known actress went home to New Jersey leaving her husband in Smithtown with the Group, she was swiftly branded as "selfish." Odets was more difficult to pigeonhole. Said Bloomgarden, "He always wanted his ten-percent royalty, even when he recommended cuts for everyone else, but he practically underwrote that whole summer himself with thousands of dollars." Lee J. Cobb, who longed for an intimate friendship with Odets, saw something niggardly not so much in Odets' royalty demands as in his emotionally withdrawn reserve.

Even the purists found it increasingly difficult to make clear-cut decisions about how much sacrifice the individual owed the Group, who was being venal and selfish, and, more specifically, whether it was admissible to have "stars" or even inequities in a collective such as this. To Morris Carnovsky it appeared that if the Group were to survive, it would need to "reach beyond itself," go into something like poetic drama, "which is bigger, which expands our personality somehow." He sensed that the Group was laboring not only for its survival as a professional theatre but, in a curious way, for the preservation of the collective humanist meaning and ethic that had initially inspired all of them.

Three days before his thirty-third birthday Odets heard Clurman announce to the Group in booming tones that he was happy to be reading the revised version of *The Silent Partner*, and that additional new plays would soon be coming from Irwin Shaw, John Howard Lawson, Robert Ardrey, and Victor Wolfson. Before starting rehearsals of *The Silent Partner*, Clurman was eager, he said, to proceed with the generalized discussion of "What is a Group member?" Kazan, on the other hand (identified in the Logbook only as "Gadget"), with his genius for the emotionally specific, the personal, and the concrete, came in bearing a large placard on which he had lettered "Remember your resolution!" It was addressed to Clurman, who had promised not to shout so loudly any more. Kazan, as always, transformed the discussion into a lively and direct statement of each one's experience, thus allowing Clurman to explore the prime immediate issue that was obsessing him: how to reconcile the contractual agreements of the film actors among them (like Franchot Tone, John Garfield, J. Edward Bromberg, Lee J. Cobb, and Roman Bohnen) with their duty to the Group and to their own development as artists. It was clear to Clurman that if anything were to be salvaged, the Group's new arrangements would need to be looser and that it could not return to "that peculiar kind of religious coherence that we wanted to have in 1931."

It had hurt him, he said, that Odets had flared in London and again in Boston, saying that he was becoming "bored with Group actors and would prefer to write a play for Jimmy Cagney." Luther Adler, tired and feeling "stale," thought perhaps he should stop acting for a time, and Bobby Lewis agreed that the company might be becoming a bit "stodgy." Still, they wrestled with the problem of how to evolve a genuine collective (not a merchandising) discipline and yet maintain personal freedom. Throughout the logbook of this summer the central issue (stated and restated) is how, without losing independence, to maintain democratically an esthetically and socially moral and meaningful theatre in a commercially competitive society. The aim was a creatively working collective, not a proving ground for individual success. Clurman ended one of his many long and passionate addresses, "If I intended to make stars of you for Broadway and Hollywood, I wouldn't go about it by creating a Group Theatre."

On his birthday, July 18, Odets wrote a preface for the Modern Library edition of his six "first-period" plays: *Waiting for Lefty, Awake and Sing!, Till the Day I Die, Paradise Lost, Golden Boy,* and *Rocket to the Moon,* with three appended introductions by Clurman. Whereas his first published volume of three plays had carried on its flyleaf "For my Father and Mother," this dedication, "For Pearl Geisinger, My Mother," omitted even the name bestowed on her by his father. The preface was brief:

> At the ripe age of thirty-three (to the day!) I have the pleasure of writing a few prefatory words to a collection of my first six plays. However, the talent represented in these plays is essentially synthetic, not analytic; and for this reason it is not my intention to do as Oscar Wilde said of a friend, "He has nothing to say and he says it." My belief, in other words, is that the plays will say whatever is to be said; most of them have bones in them and will stand up unsupported.
>
> Notwithstanding, a writer must be permitted to express preferences in terms of his own work. *Paradise Lost,* poorly received as a

practical theatre work, remains my favorite play in this group. While not unmindful of its harsh and ungracious form, I must be permitted to say that our modern audiences, critics included, still must have their plays, like salt-water taffy, cut to fit the mouth. *Paradise Lost* shares with *Rocket to the Moon* a depth of perception, a web of sensory impressions and a level of both personal and social experience not allotted to the other plays here. True, at least two of the other remaining four plays are more *immediately useful*, but my choice still stands.

Now, since we are on the subject, much of my concern during the past years has been with fashioning a play immediately and dynamically useful and yet as psychologically profound as my present years and experience will permit. To some extent this pressing problem (pressing since we are living in a time when new art works should shoot bullets) has been most closely approached in a new play not included in this volume, *The Silent Partner*. Rightfully that play belongs in this collection in the place of *Rocket to the Moon*, for of the two it was conceived and written first. Revisions have changed it, but in terms of inner and outer progression it belongs among the first six, part and parcel of a "first-period" group. Theatre exigencies being what they are . . .

When these plays were written it was almost impossible for me to do more or differently with them. Much of them was felt, conceived and written out of a personal need. Now after the fact, after the melancholy facts, the writer is a better craftsman, his horizon lifting wider. That temptation to improve upon these plays is often present. Nevertheless, none has been rewritten in part or whole: let them stand, crudities and all, as a small parade of a young talent discovering and shaping itself. If you have acquired by now the distressing sense that I am situating myself historically, correct! Talent should be respected.

Two more items remain to be mentioned. I have insisted on retaining, in the form of an appendix, the original introductions of these plays. This insistence stems from a conviction that two of these introductions by Harold Clurman, Group Theatre Director and constant good friend, are among the first-class theatre writing of our time.

Lastly, a pair of acknowledgments. Fortunate is the writer in this strange and inimical world who finds a devoted helpful obstetrician for births and beginnings. Harold Clurman and I have stood in this relationship, groaning mortal and devoted Persian surgeon. This is not to forget the Group Theatre actors and actresses, all dear and good friends, who have given such inspired performances of all these plays.

It is clear he regarded *The Silent Partner* as a neglected infant still in process of painful birth, but a significant one that, with Clurman's help, would meet his creative need to fashion a play not just "immediately useful" like *Lefty*, but, in his words, "psychologically profound" as well. Clurman was, as he put it, "stunned" when Odets presented him simultaneously with this volume and a new car.

Also on Odets' birthday, the fourth day of the Group's reconvening, Clurman initiated a discussion of the first two acts of the "final" draft of *The Silent Partner*. He opened defensively by saying he respected Odets "as if he were dead," and invited the Group "to wander, to grope with me . . ." as it is more difficult, he said, to know what one thinks of something "brilliant than when it is lousy or flat." It was evident that Clurman was profoundly disappointed with Odets' revisions.

Carnovsky—clearly hoping against hope—asked that Odets first summarize for them the content of the third act, on which Odets was still at work. It was evident, he said, that although it dealt with a strike, this was no run-of-the-mill propaganda piece. Indeed, he had decided that his earlier view of *The Silent Partner* as an "antifascist ode to the working-class" was narrow and simple. He had now decided that "it is broader and deeper, a far bigger thing . . . like the celebration of the good life, a very poetic play." Some thought—despite its "labor-play" surface—that its spine was the choice between Life and Death, or Good and Evil. Odets contributed the intelligence that there had been "two strikes like this down in Sid Benson's territory. . . . The working class is cut off from a large part of the entire country . . . but these are not just workers, each one is a different kind and it's my intention that each of them be educated *as an individual* within that class struggle" (italics mine).

The discussion continued all morning, as animated, informed, and thoughtful as one could wish of any acting company. Finally, Clurman wondered aloud whether New Yorkers would pay the astronomic sum of $1.50 to see a play that appeared at least on the surface to be simply "the strategy of a strike." It was clear he thought not. Moreover, he was calculating to himself the salaries of forty-three actors and the cost of building five sets. He concluded that the play would not be a success, would surely lose money, and would bolster the false impression that "we are a Red theatre." On this note they adjourned until the afternoon. A small group accompanied Odets to his room to inveigh with him against Clurman's negative view of *The Silent Partner*. Odets was hurt and furious, and found himself thinking instead about his outlined play "Quartet," in which a harmoniously working group is rent apart by the antithetical needs of individual members. When asked by Clurman to summarize the last few days, he replied:

You said a great deal and all the time you were talking I was thinking and when we left a meeting walking back to the house it would be very difficult to abstract the content of tonight's meeting when I write a play that I have in my files. This is a play about a string quartet. Let me tell you briefly something about the play. I must first talk about myself a little bit. I find myself in Mexico and I think what am I doing here. You are far away from home. Where is home. When I think of home I think of the Group Theatre and I have for a number of years. But being alone in Mexico and cut off from the Group Theatre I had an old feeling. That old feeling is related to being unneeded, unwanted, unloved, unconnected. That's a very modern feeling. A great many pieces of literature have been written about that in the last few years. It's my contention, by the fact of the Group Theatre's being together and being what it is that men must not be alone, they must not be unconnected. I think that one of the great glamors about war—and you can't deny that there is a glamor about war—is that for the first time men are *working and fighting together side by side focussed by common work upon a common enemy or toward a common aim* [italics mine]. However, again typical, since we are modern men of the 20th century, there is so obviously something in modern life, a conditioning which tears men apart from each other and makes them work separately. I want to write a play about that, about what is still a kind of feeling. I thought, what is the exact, most precise image of some work in which men *must* work together and I thought the string quartet was one such because we certainly must agree that there, above everything, 4 men must play together. Then I want to take that image and translate it into a dramatic story and show how despite the deep human and even professional need for working together there were nevertheless extraordinary forces around them which prevent their working together and break the quartet apart. All of the things in this play, all of the deeply personal, the creative idiosyncrasies of these four men, all of the problems of these four men exist and have existed in the Group Theatre for the nine years they have been together and we have seen how various members of the original Group left it, how the Group once went completely out of existence and how of its original three directors only one is left.

It is obvious Odets was thinking of Clurman, Strasberg, Kazan, and himself. As the life history of each character in the play unfolded, it would become increasingly evident from their struggles that Clurman, Strasberg, Kazan, and he himself were indeed, for him, the core "quartet" that was progressively dissolving. He went on:

When that happens with people it's only symptomatic of deep social causes. A man like Lee Strasberg, gifted and talented—and I shall in my play try to prove that living in a social climate is what made him wrong. Harold Clurman as I see it has for years been watching the individual growth or retrogression of all the members of the Group and he has seen that even in the cases of the most deeply socially minded members of the Group there still are elements, I am saying this advisedly, of what goes to make a fascist and by that I mean what goes to make an *irresponsible uncreative person because essentially that is what fascism is* [italics mine].

I can't write plays in a void. I must write because you need my plays. If you don't need my plays I would never have written them.

Despite his own resentments, he concluded with a defense of Clurman against the rampant charges of dictatorial attitudes:

Harold Clurman has seen and has seen with very good eyes—certain 20th century idiosyncrasies in all of our people or most of them which slowly and surely engulf and devour the Group Theatre. He sees even better that perhaps a great deal of that has been his feeling that perhaps he has been assuming too much responsibility for the personal and professional lives of the people in the Group Theatre. What he really said the other night to my mind was that now you become responsible men and women for the Group Theatre. You now have charge of yourselves. I was therefore amazed when someone said Harold had become Lee Strasberg overnight. When for the first time he was saying that we are now equals. Now you must understand as adults, the short and long term effect of every single act you commit, of every situation which you create. He was saying I give you the Group now. He has been saying that out of what I feel to be his sense that unless the 30 odd members take the Group in their hands and make it always aware of their part in the creation of it, in a short time there will be no Group Theatre. That was my understanding of what he said.

Clurman now made his own summary, emphasizing that all in the Group were simultaneously beginners and teachers, adding:

I consider Clifford Odets one of the important writers or artists in any country right today. At the same time I hope that when Clifford Odets is 40 that he will look at the 6 or 7 plays he has written as minor works of his young years. That I hope he will be able to do that through my work with him, through your work with him, through the lessons he learns from all of us and what that means ultimately is the opportunity that we all give him to work with himself.

He ended the session by saying, "Now let me tell you something that will shock you." He had been thinking, he said, of "how to get Lee Strasberg back to work with us," continuing:

The idea is fraught with many dangers. All I want to tell you about now is that this bad boy, Clurman, was so vindictive that behind everybody's back he talks about everybody, with the full knowledge that the same compliment is paid to him by all concerned. This same person is always trying to figure how all the people he believes in creatively, who have something to give can really come to give it in this organization.

Clurman was by now aware of a depletion and deepening discouragement within himself. It was his fantasy that Strasberg might supply for the Group the energy and fresh enthusiasm that Clurman could not muster. Neither he nor any one of them realized that their growing sense of the end of an era accurately reflected a turn of history already menacing the entire world. The Federal Theatre was all but gone, and the Group would be the next casualty in a world now shifting its energies from creation to destruction.

Still smarting from John Howard Lawson's accusation that his interest in matters psychological was endangering his "social responsibility," Odets was doing his best to ignore Clurman's view that *The Silent Partner* still suffered serious defects and, more important, "had lost most of its topical value." However, when Clurman said, "Let's say it's a great play, but a bad work of art," Odets knew his "devoted Persian surgeon" considered this child stillborn and would not produce it. He persuaded himself, despite his strong wish to use this play to show people like Lawson that he had *not* abdicated his social responsibility, that Clurman was right. On August 8—Odets having left to lick his wounds and to visit Fay Wray in Maine—Clurman called a solemn meeting to announce that "after a series of discussions and conferences with Clifford Odets, *he* has decided not to have us produce *The Silent Partner* at the present time," giving as Odets' reason that "the play does not represent the intention that he really set himself . . . and the various versions were compromises from his original intention." At the same time he announced Odets' plan to start on "a new play which takes place in New York, unlike anything he has done before which he hopes to have finished in December. He doesn't wish to be rushed. He doesn't wish to bring to me incomplete scripts which I then spoil but . . . plays as complete as he can make them. I for one shall be happy to spoil plays only by directing them." Quickly he added that Odets, in order to meet the financial emergency, had already set to work on a new acting version of Chekhov's *Three Sisters*, and that he expected Irwin Shaw to finish a new play within the week. Clurman's cool and collected delivery belied his underlying awareness of Odets' resentment and of the Group's acute peril.

When, at long last, Irwin Shaw's new play, *The Golden Years*, was ready, Clurman quickly read it and, with sinking heart, decided he had to reject it. A parable, it intended to show through the falling fortunes of a middle-class family in the Depression how fascism could come to America. These nondescript "ordinary citizens," hitherto decent and honest, turn in desperation to criminal means to recapture their lost position. It had been Clurman's secret hope that, with a good new play from Shaw, it would not be necessary to put into production Odets' adaptation of Chekhov; now there was no choice. With a sense of foreboding, he cast *Three Sisters* and commenced rehearsals with Frances Farmer, Leif Erickson, and Morris Carnovsky. Almost at once, as he recalled it, "my work became halting, indecisive." There was no money for a New York production, especially since this was the third projected revival of the same play. Moreover, a "poisonous feud" had begun between Stella Adler, who was co-directing, and Morris Carnovsky. ("You are not a truthful actress. I just don't believe you!" he shouted at her.) It did not help morale when two visitors arrived at Lake Grove with faces which had been battered by members of the police department of New York City, where this pair had protested a large meeting of the American-Nazi Bund in Madison Square Garden. Clurman was filled, he later said, with a "foreboding about the future . . . a loosened feeling in the air."

On August 22, 1939, to the utter disbelief of thousands of Americans, it was announced on the radio that Hitler's emissary, Ribbentrop, was flying to Russia to sign a nonaggression pact with Stalin and that the swastika was already flying over the Moscow airport.

Two days later there were convivial pictures in the newspapers of Stalin toasting Hitler's health in champagne ("I know how much the German nation owes to its Führer," he said); this was in celebration of a formal decision "to relieve the tension of political relations, to eliminate the war menace and to conclude the non-aggression pact." The Second World War had now in fact begun, and with it the decline of an indigenous, energetic, life-affirming American culture.

Gloom descended at Lake Grove. People stood around in dismal, stunned clusters, discussing whether this Russian-German amity meant that the hopeful era of a popular humanist front against war and Fascism was at an end.⊄ Some, unable to tolerate disillusionment with the Soviet Union, scrambled desperately to rationalize what had happened. Bereft, Frances Farmer repeated dully, "Stalin must know what he's doing," in the fashion of a mourner uttering disbelief in the face of death, and faith in God's wisdom. She and the others took little comfort from the confident newspaper announcements that the Group would, after all, have a winter season, opening with Odets' adaptation of Chekhov's *Three Sisters*, to be followed in December by a new Odets play, *Night Music*.

Clurman had seen Odets in troubled conversation with the rigidly uncompromising Frances Farmer in the morning and had been uncertain whether they were talking of the Nazi-Soviet pact or of their own intense and visibly embattled relationship. He wondered idly whether Leif Erickson—absorbed in a game of tennis—knew his marriage to Miss Farmer was at an end. "In the afternoon," said Robert Clurman, Harold's young nephew, "Odets came bounding in, his manner desperately bright, and proclaimed the Russians had effected a brilliant stroke and that now the

⊄ 23.2.

English imperialists could fight it out with the Nazis. I couldn't tell whether he had come to this position on his own or worked it out in committee." Miss Farmer, recalling her teen-age prize-winning essay on the virtues of the Soviet Union, appeared to be relieved by Odets' position on the Hitler-Stalin alliance. Deeply respectful of him—indeed, by now reverently in love with him—she was happy to share his elaborate political rationale for the entente. She felt it brought them closer in a Group now rent by differences.

Half a world away, Odets' wife, involved with her Englishman, was listening with him to the Verdi Requiem at the music festival in Lucerne. "We came out of the concert hall after the beauty and harmony to hear on loudspeakers the screaming dissonance of Hitler's voice shouting his agreement with Russia. Shortly after, when he marched into Poland (on the first day of September), people knew that the Second World War was upon us and began grabbing in panic for passports." By the third day Luise's English friend received orders from his government to return at once to London; England and France had declared war on Germany. They returned to London together. "Get your divorce," he said. She left for America. History had stepped between them. Luise heard from a friend in Hollywood that already the American movie magnates were terrified that their foreign actresses—even Greta Garbo—were becoming an unprofitable commodity to stock, especially if they spoke with anything like a German accent. Clark Gable and Vivien Leigh were a far safer investment.

For many years Louis B. Mayer's involvement in history and politics had been an open secret on the MGM lot, and it was widely known that Mayer had arranged a private screening for the German consul in Los Angeles of an MGM film written by F. Scott Fitzgerald, for the purpose of learning what to delete as possibly offensive to the Nazi regime. By this time all the other studios had ceased distributing films in Germany, and the market was therefore wide open for MGM. It was well known also that, far from dismissing Congressman Dies and his committee as buffoons, Mayer was using their help to destroy unions and to establish secret blacklists in the film industry which, in the opinion of many, have not been entirely eliminated forty years later. To those anti-Nazi artists whom he still needed, Mayer was making it clear that "when you are in business, you can't afford to express yourself freely; you go along with whatever is there. If it's Hitler, you salute, say Heil Hitler, smile, and go on about your business." The others he dismissed without explanation. Many in the industry were convinced that if Mayer were not Jewish, he would actively join hands with Hitler and with the Ku Klux Klan. It was rumored also that he was flirting with a conversion to Catholicism.

One actor recalled being summoned to "God's apartment" for one of what Mayer called his "cozy chats." Mayer told him the German distributors had agreed to distribute the actor's latest film only if he retracted anti-Nazi comments he had recently made in a public meeting. Starting with fulsome compliments for the actor's talent, he moved on to bribes ("Your wife is an actress. Maybe she wants to play in the movies"), then to advice ("If you want to give them [anti-Fascists] money, give it under the table"), and finally to threats ("If you keep doing this, you'll get no more jobs. We'll see what happens at the box office!"). The actor refused to make a retraction and concluded with, "Oh, tear up the contract!"

There appeared to be sinister similarities between studio heads, especially Mayer, and many European entrepreneurs who had now become Nazis.

The pact between Nazi Germany and the Soviet Union, far more than most political transactions, triggered for many American intellectuals a spiritual life-crisis. Friendships of long standing ended now in violent and bitter rupture, with some (like Odets) staunchly supporting the self-protective canniness in Stalin's move, while others, convinced they had been cynically betrayed, mourned the passing of what they had believed to be man's last humanistic bastion. The significance of the accord between the two leaders, one publicly committed to genocide, the other to a "flowering destiny," reached deep into the Weltanschauung of anyone who thought about such things.

In one of his characteristic roles, this time as mentor to an innocent, Odets continued to instruct Frances Farmer and simultaneously, by correspondence, Fay Wray in the intricate moral reasoning which led to the conclusion that the United States should have no part in what in its first phase was called a "phony" war. He, along with others, found it impossible to believe that a holocaust was in the making. Convinced that Russia's truce with Germany would help to end the squaring off of England and France against Germany, Odets signed a public letter, later to haunt him, calling for cooperation with Soviet Russia in its effort "to maintain world peace." At the same time he continued to write fulsome letters to Roosevelt, sincerely praising his policies. By the end of August he had fled to Canada to work on his new play as Roosevelt prepared his speech proclaiming "a limited national emergency." From Fay Wray he heard that a newspaperman, on a tip from the Dies Committee, had come to Skowhegan to question her and ask about Odets' "interest in Communism"; he had heard they might each be subpoenaed. For the next thirteen years this threat would remain a steady menace in Odets' life. Even in 1939, absurd as he knew it was to think of the committee as having any real political muscle, he was seized by terror.

The growing irresolution and fragmentation within the American theatre, a mirroring of the evolving world history, was reflected in the Group's last moves for survival. Indeed, Odets had decided, with the exquisite prescience of the artist, to call his new work *Night Music;* it would be a lyrically wistful eulogy for a dying aspect of himself in a dying time. He would express, in what he called "a song cycle on a given theme," not only his personal sense of homelessness and impermanence but that of a generation in search, as Clurman later described this play, of "something real, secure, dependable in a slippery, shadowy, noisy, and nervous world." He had lost hold of who the enemy was, and was unsure about the meaning of the spreading war, which now began with Hitler marching into Poland. On September 23 Odets noted that Sigmund Freud, Jewish conquistador of the human mind, having finally been persuaded to leave Vienna and to flee the Holocaust, had died in London. On the same day a letter from Fay Wray assured him that "the clear hard plays you write will survive through all this changing world." He was not so sure.

Despite his uncertainty about his place in history, Odets still believed he could earn a living as a playwright and keep the Group alive through even these increasingly treacherous times; it appeared to him that, in order to do this, he must stay away from the film industry and its "deals."

In mid-September, however, he received a letter from an old friend, the professorial Albert Lewin, long one of Irving Thalberg's lieutenants. Lewin suggested that Odets should become, as screenplay writer, the fourth member of a new motion-picture company, with all to share the net profits. The others in the company would be Lewin himself, a director "of the calibre of King Vidor," and David Loew, one of the sons of Marcus (Max) Loew, who had risen from the Lower East Side of New York to become at first a gambler in furs and later a tycoon in films.

Lewin and Loew had met when both were studying English literature at New York University. They were representative of a new generation, sons of the shrewd Loews, Zukors, Schencks who had struggled out of fur, garment, junk-peddling, or scrap-iron businesses into the vast empires of mass entertainment. There they could combine a boundless commercial ambition with something more revered in their tradition: a Hebraic respect for a wise man, an artist, a writer, a cantor (a "songer," as Odets' Uncle Israel called himself). Whereas the pioneering magnates like Marcus Loew had become essentially and overtly buyers and sellers and often ruthless potentates, the sons carried forth the less conscious aspect of the father's aspiration: to keep a long tradition of learning, of creativity, alive. Thus it happened that in the generation of Marcus Loew's son David there were many young men who sought to maintain the fiefdoms of their fathers, but at the same time to struggle against them by restoring a creative and esthetically self-respecting identity in film-making. Indeed, since the advent of the spoken word in motion pictures, an entire generation of producers was emerging with precisely such a mixed aspiration. For many of them, the psychological "sons" of the original barons of the industry, the writer was becoming a Messiah to be lured with the promise of success and money power. Through him would come a spiritual redemption for all. The sons sought, while making fortunes, to re-establish the values and virtues not of their fathers, but of their grandfathers, even as Odets had done in the character of the intellectual grandfather in *Awake and Sing!* The irony thus is that precisely in this new generation of "civilized" film-makers lay the greatest danger to Odets' creativity. The confluence they established with his own struggle against and identification with Louis J. Odets would ultimately make it possible for him to deceive himself in carrying out their "idealistic" projects. Such self-deception would have been more difficult in transactions with Max, the tough father of David Loew, who made no bones about the fact that film "grosses" were his central concern.

Lewin's correspondence with Odets provides a prototypic example of this characteristic effort to synthesize art and commerce against which Odets was steadily struggling:

Dear Clifford:

I recently settled my contract with Paramount, although it had nearly a year still to go, because it became clear to me that my ideas and theirs about what constitutes a good picture were irreconcilable. If I stayed, it could only be at the risk of making pictures that would make me hang my head in shame, and fortunately the many years I spent with Irving Thalberg made it financially unnecessary for me to make this sacrifice of my self-respect. I seem to recall that you, with admirable acumen, prophesied, and even recommended, some such denouement for me and Paramount. Such an ending, in fact, became inevitable when they refused to go ahead with "Gettysburg."*

* A screenplay Odets had written in 1937.

Now I have an extremely important proposal to make to you: David Loew is an old friend of mine. Not only is he a swell guy personally, but in his business dealings utterly honest and scrupulous. . . . Now he and I have been discussing a cooperative plan which has, I think wonderful possibilities. . . . Let me give you an idea of the possibilities of this arrangement. Eddie Small made a picture, released by United Artists, the most important name in the cast being Adolphe Menjou; the picture was a bust, but it grossed $700,000. The picture cost Small $400,000—without the producer, writer, director savings which I outlined above. It is my conviction that with these savings we can make a "class" picture for between $200,000 and $350,000. Let us take the extreme cost and the minimum return. Say the picture costs $350,000 and grosses $700,000. The distributor takes 25%, leaving $525,000. We are charged $75,000 for prints and advertising, leaving $450,000. Dave takes his negative cost, leaving $100,000. If the picture is an absolute bust, we each stand to take $25,000 for our pains. If we have a fair success and gross $1,000,000, we each earn $80,000. If we have a substantial success and gross a million and a half, which is not unreasonable to expect, we each earn $175,000. At the very worst we can count on some return for the investment of our time and effort (and Dave for his money), at the best we can count on a much greater return than we could get for a handsome studio contract. Beyond that we have the fun of working in freedom, collaborating on something that is entirely our own, under conditions not unlike those of the theatre, but with, I believe, much surer expectations of profit. . . .

Lewin went on to suggest stories that might interest Odets, to inquire about his "Monkey" play (*Night Music*), and to discuss, in the same blend of art and cash, possible actors.

Nine days later Odets replied: "Unfortunately I am not in the mood or the position to do pictures at the present time—otherwise I should find your proposal very exciting. I have so much work to do here, including Group Theatre organizational work, that it would be impossible for me to come to the coast." He concluded with "a sincere hope that you find some happiness in your work—it is very necessary to a man of your intelligence and nerves." For the moment, he felt himself to be safe from these sons.

In October Clurman publicly announced that Odets' adaptation of *The Three Sisters* had been shelved. As *Night Music* was far from ready to put into rehearsal, he decided to produce a new play by the exceedingly talented Robert Ardrey, despite a hostile response to it from most of the Group actors. Odets agreed to help with the out-of-town tryouts. Called *Tower of Light* and then *Thunder Rock*, Ardrey's play was to be designed by Mordecai Gorelik and directed by Kazan.

Like Irwin Shaw's *The Golden Years*, *Thunder Rock* was a parable of the times. Reflecting the profound doubts gripping all thoughtful persons, it asked whether it might not be more honest to retreat into the "ivory tower" of self-examination than to rush into some ill-understood, violent confrontation. The negative response of the New York critics to this play, his fourth commercial failure, was exceedingly discouraging to Ardrey, and although Robert E. Sherwood, Maxwell Anderson, S. N. Behrman, and Elmer Rice of the Playwright's Company awarded him a special prize, in memory of their recently dead colleague Sidney Howard, for "the most promising play of the season by a young American playwright,"

Thunder Rock closed after twenty-three performances. Within a few weeks Ardrey would disappear, like so many others before and after him, into the maw of Hollywood. Ardrey avoided the legitimate theatre for many years, and then made one last unsuccessful try before retiring forever into anthropological research. As Odets later put it, "We live in a strange dry country. A strong heart is needed, iron nerves, to continue to be a serious writer here."

It appeared to Odets a bitter irony that only playwrights sufficiently slick and "commercial" to earn a living in the theatre were safe from the seductions of the film industry. In this theatre season of 1939–40, for example, with the Depression not yet ended by a war economy, *Tobacco Road* was in its seventh year, *Hellzapoppin* had played 1,000 times, *You Can't Take It With You* more than 800, and Robert E. Sherwood's *Abe Lincoln in Illinois* had passed the 400 mark.

The fate of the thoughtful if imperfect *Thunder Rock* in this season of long-run hits depressed and frightened Odets. He had grave doubts that the gently serious, essentially plotless play on which he was at work would fare any better. He expressed "shivers," as he called them, in his letters to Fay Wray. She tried to comfort him by telling him he towered above all these writers and by pointing out the judgments of such discerning critics as Brooks Atkinson and Joseph Wood Krutch, who found his talent to be "unique," and Otis Ferguson, who had just announced in the *New Republic* that Odets "already holds a corner on the genius of serious writing for the theatre today." But he took as little comfort from this as he did from his name in great lights on the marquee of the Radio City Music Hall as the author of *Golden Boy*, starring Barbara Stanwyck and a newcomer, William Holden. He tried to bolster his shaky self-regard by sending an inscribed copy of his collected plays to Franklin D. Roosevelt. The President autographed it for posterity* and sent, by way of Missy LeHand, a thank-you to Odets.

When Herman Kobland brought the afternoon papers to Odets, just arising at five P.M. on October 26, they remained untouched until early the next morning when he returned from the Laurelton Hotel, where he had been with Frances Farmer. To Odets' astonishment, staring up from all the papers was his wife's wistful face, suffused with that smiling radiance which becomes a public reflex in a professional actress. She had just arrived from Europe on the *Rotterdam*. Although she had already filed for divorce, she declined to discuss this with the reporters. Despite her assurances to them that "I will see my husband later," black headlines—some extremely sarcastic—announced that "Luise Returns, Odets 'Busy' Staying Away." The newspapers did not print what the worldly newsmen had privately asked her, nor her replies to them. Luise Rainer was barraged with reporters' questions about Odets' new relationship: "Do you know your husband is living with Frances Farmer?" Hearing of this relationship, she replied, "I have been away a long time. A man has a right to do what he wants if a wife is gone so long."

Odets' eye fell upon a new lapel watch in the newspaper photographs and, knowing his wife had an aversion to all timepieces, correctly concluded that this one must be a gift from a new lover. Seized with a desperate and characteristic determination *not* to lose Luise and be the one abandoned, he called the Waldorf-Astoria, leaving word for her to contact him "immediately." He followed the message with a telegram. He called

---

* It reposes in the Roosevelt Library at Hyde Park, New York.

relentlessly every ten minutes for hours, telling the switchboard girl he would continue this throughout the night. The harassed operator begged Luise to accept one of the calls; she finally did, but refused her husband's plea that he come to her. Nonetheless, he was shortly pounding furiously on the door of her room and she let him in. She was exhausted and had retired. She noticed his great staring eyes travel to the photograph of her handsome Englishman on the night table, and his first "terribly unhappy" words to her were, she recalled, "I knew there was someone else." "He started now a terrific bombardment," she added, "telling me he loved me, he respected me as an artist and he wanted me back. But as I was deeply in love with someone else by now, I did not waver for a moment. I was determined not to go back to him. I hoped that the 'phony war,' as it was called, would be over in a month or two and I could get a divorce and return to England to my friend.

"I wanted to sleep and told him so," Luise continued, "but Odets stayed and announced he was spending the night. Well, he did, but he sat on a chair all night while I slept in my bed. No word passed between us all night."

When Luise awoke, her husband had not moved from his chair and was staring at her "with great sadness." "I asked him now," she said, " 'What of Frances Farmer?' To this he replied, 'So, what of it?' It made me furious. 'What of the girl,' I said, 'does she think, "So what?" ' "

Once more an abyss had opened, and Luise remembered having said to him, "You have to respect other human beings. You cannot call a person Duse as you did me and then make it impossible for them to function." "Everyone," she added later, "has his own capacity for pain. Clifford had hurt me as much as one could hurt. If one gets hurt more, one simply cannot feel more. I told Clifford that we cannot remain married, we would never be happy. I knew I would go through with the divorce." Indeed, within a few months Metro-Goldwyn-Mayer had acceded to Luise's long-standing entreaties to release her from her contract. Her contract with MGM was dissolved, as were those of all other "foreign" stars; and she was granted in Los Angeles—by Judge Thurmond Clarke, who had married them—an interlocutory decree.

While Odets sat on a chair staring at his sleeping wife, Frances Farmer anxiously awaited him in her room at the Laurelton Hotel. They had planned to have dinner together. When she received a note saying only, "This affair is now ended as my wife has returned from Europe," she was stunned. There had been no previous hint, she later said, that theirs was anything but a genuinely committed relationship. Soon after, she barricaded herself in this hotel room, reading, weeping, and drinking.

Much later she summarized her tragic deterioration as an artist in the film colony: "My artistic id was clobbered to shreds and the emotional trauma with Odets finished the job." From the time he had asked her to play Lorna Moon in *Golden Boy,* she was, she said, "mesmerized."

He would insult me in front of everyone, belittling my performance, and he was satisfied only when he had reduced me to tears and sent me sobbing to my dressing room.

There were times after such incidents when he would not speak to me for two or three days. At other times, he would force his way into my dressing room and make a great point of not only locking the door behind him, but further securing the room by propping a chair under the doorknob, and then he would tear off his clothes and scream his love and need for me with all the fire and passion of a Rococo

Thespian. He would threaten to take his life and mine, unless I loved him. The fact that I was genuinely attached to this man compelled me to try to gratify his physical appetite. His sexual behavior was a complicated maze of weird manipulations. He would deftly maneuver me to a point of fulfillment, then withdraw and mock what he termed my base and disgusting desires. After searing my feminine spirit in this bed of humiliation and degrading me in every possible manner, he would begin again with the shyness of an innocent lad and explore me with tender fascination.

This was no ordinary man. He was a creature who pried open the psyche with the intention of sticking it with pins. I cannot say that I loved him; a more apt description would be a passionate hatred coupled with a physical fascination. Whatever it was, it did much to destroy me. . . .

When *Golden Boy* closed, I went into rehearsal of a play called *Thunder Rock*, but I was no longer able to cope with the building pressures and I found myself trying to keep my stability by drinking even more.

Looking back, Group members, all of whom had watched the affair with unusual concern, agreed that this seemed to be the trigger for her life's descent, during which she became addicted to alcohol and to drugs, was jailed, reviled, beaten, and, for seven years, institutionalized by her mother as a lunatic. Before her grief climaxed, however, she fled to California, where, determined at least to regain her status as a powerful film star, she rented actress Dolores del Rio's luxurious home, bought dozens of Balmain gowns and a Cadillac (in place of her usual tweeds and ratty Chevrolet), and invited Harold Clurman to come and live with her. There was something savagely revengeful in her paranoid and bitter parody of the life of a star in del Rio's mansion; the rage she leveled at "Hollywood phoniness" was steady and indiscriminate.

According to Miss Farmer's biographer, Lois Kibbee, "Odets had played *all* the significant roles in her life. It was almost a Svengali thing. He had been, for this essentially simple and fatherless girl, a great and extraordinary man, and to be wanted by him had been for her, despite her quick intellect, like climbing a mountain. After being married to a handsome, talented, spoiled, endearing young actor whom she called 'Mrs. Erickson's little boy, Leif—the boy next door who laughed a lot'—it had been for her an immense experience to have as her lover this attractive and celebrated playwright, seven years older than she, and in her view, a genius." Several Group members dated their antipathy to Odets from this time; one recalled her astonishment that "so kind and tender a man who obviously revered his dead mother and whose empathy with women could be so delicate, could nevertheless be so exploitively cruel with some women."

Miss Farmer herself did not, as did most of the Group, ascribe her later breakdown sheerly to the rupture of her relationship with Odets. It seemed to her that the bottomless sense of work-futility, even what she called a "prostitution" of her talent, which had begun with the Group's unraveling and the war's beginning, intensified as she continued to work in the film industry. What she experienced as a steady erosion of integrity reached its climax two years later in Mexico, while she was being "rented out" for ten times her salary to be in a film which she actively loathed and had tried to avoid. Daughter of a powerful, spiritually intense and rebellious woman, "a pioneer in the Northwestern Freethinkers movement, a high-strung woman who had read Nietzsche," she had written, at fourteen, a defiant composition entitled "God Dies," in praise of rationalism. Like Luise Rainer, she had always aspired to be an artist—a writer, she thought, or perhaps a "creative actress." Her throwing off the "yoke of a producer's chattel-slave" now took the form of a donnybrook with Mexican police in a hotel lobby, thus ending her work on the film. Deported from Mexico to California, it was not long before she was once again in violent struggle with her enraged studio. Finally, after a suicidal, drunken drive, she was subdued by six police and hospitalized by court order. Odets kept a steady cumulative file, clipped from newspapers, labeled "Frances Farmer," whom he described as "this unhappy, stiff, rude and uncontrollable girl, but with a real purity." He planned, one day, to write her story—the "Actress Play," about "the way America treats its artists."

For seven years Miss Farmer remained, stubborn and despairing, in what she recalled as a "snake pit," where, of all her humiliations, she found "by far the worst was the insulin shock treatment." Released in her late thirties, she was still talented, still beautiful, still thoughtful, but profoundly damaged. She made her way back to her hometown, Seattle, and, under an assumed name, worked in the valet service of a hotel. After three failed marriages, the last of which brought her to the Midwest, she earned a living by hosting a television movie program; as a hobby she took in stray cats. In her fiftieth year the former young idealist-revolutionary was named Indiana's "Business Woman of the Year." On August 3, 1970, she died alone in Indianapolis at fifty-six, of cancer of the esophagus.

By December Odets had sent a copy of *Paradise Lost* to actress Fay Wray, now living at the Chateau Elysee in Hollywood with her small daughter, awaiting the final court hearing of her divorce action against writer John Monk Saunders. In a despairing mood Odets tells her of his failure with Luise and of his tired, tortured misgivings about the "monkey play" he is calling *Night Music*. Not only does the new play not yet seem to him quite what he had intended it to be, but he is unspeakably humiliated that even at this point of his career, as he writes a play tailored to the urgent production needs of the Group, it appears that Clurman will have difficulty in obtaining financial backers for it. In the last four weeks he has turned down, not without anxiety, highly lucrative offers to work in Hollywood on a Hitchcock film, to write a screenplay of Vincent Sheean's life, to write an "original" screenplay, and to adapt a novel for film.

Fueling both his anxiety and his rage are his father's continuing financial demands for himself and his wife, Lillian, both about to leave for Los Angeles, where L. J. Odets hopes to be in the "bond business" and try *his* hand at "writing screenplays"! As so often in his correspondence with his father, Odets has kept in his file the original irate draft of a letter marked "not sent" and a copy of the toned-down version actually mailed. In the original he writes:

Dear L.J.,
   Enclosed is a check for two hundred and fifty dollars. I am sending you this against my will and can tell you why, without argument. I told you, when you insisted on that foolish business (and it was foolish to me from the first minute you had the idea), that if I gave you money for the business I could not later give you money for

weekly living expenses too. I made that very clear to you at the time— we were standing in my bedroom. Then the business went over ten thousand dollars more than I had originally planned to give you for it. My good will (perhaps you don't realize it even yet) was extremely taxed and strained, to say the least. But I was very surprised to find that after that business fiasco you still expected me to give you a weekly allowance and did not hesitate to ask for it. The business swallowed up fifteen thousand dollars, which on a weekly allowance basis of fifty dollars a week would have covered you for almost seven years. In other words, you wanted to eat your cake and still have it. On top of that I have STILL NOT HAD AN ACCOUNTING OF WHAT HAPPENED TO THAT FIFTEEN THOUSAND DOLLARS which you say the business swallowed up. On top of that you tell me, after I have handed over to you 28 thousand dollars in four years, that you have spent another seven thousand which your wife had. Well, you must have been living like a prince. That is all I can say to that. One of two things is quite apparent: either you have been living with riotous extravagance (I mean for one who has not been earning a salary for five or six years), or you have saved some money on the side and even now have a bank account. Which is true I don't know—you know for yourself.

In this relentless assault, his effort to shame and defeat his father as well as his own "American Dream" is evident:

It is another one of those big shot things—another one of those big golden dreams—and does not smack to me of honest sober work. Honest sober work to me is when some one gets a job for forty or fifty dollars a week and forgets about the dreams of big salaries and being the big boss or the big sales manager. Don't forget, I am not talking to a man who has been looking for a job for a month—you have been looking for years. What is that bug you have in your mind about being a boss of men? . . . I'm afraid that in your job hunting you have been very strongly influenced in what you looked for by what neighbors and friends would think if L. J. Odets took some simple unassuming job.

Odets' Group friends would later be astonished to learn that Odets had been at this time not only supporting his father but also handing over to him vast sums "for investment." Odets senior had always conveyed to them the impression that he was himself a "Big Success and a Sport." Indeed, even after his son's death he would have no compunction in telling his biographer, "Clifford owes me thousands of dollars and that ain't buttons and shoestrings."

Odets' close-mouthedness was in part a reflection of his own deep shame that he had incorporated as part of his own identity L. J. Odets' fantasies of the Big Deal, the overnight success, the Quick Killing. On the small scale of his movie negotiations and his stamp and, later, painting collections, Odets would try to enact his father's fantasied role of the canny tycoon—always without confidence and never with real success.

Within a few weeks, while financing for *Night Music* was still shaky, he would write an engagingly innocent letter, applying under the name of "C. Oakes" (a name he had used in Hollywood when he had separated from Luise) for a position as an "ad-man" on a newspaper. "He wanted to see," said Herman Kobland later, "whether his writing ability could land him a job writing advertising copy." The files do not hold, nor can Kobland recall, any reply.

In the meantime he was up each night writing and furiously rewriting *Night Music*, promising Clurman he'd have it ready for the current season and assuring Elia Kazan and Morris Carnovsky of the two leading male parts. Indeed, he thought consciously of each of them as he wrote. The actress who thought she was to be the leading lady recalled her disappointment when "rather cruelly he confided, 'I think I need a shiksa* for the girl.'" He was considering for this leading lady his Cleo from *Rocket to the Moon*, the winsome Eleanor Lynn; or, he thought, he might offer it to screen actress Margaret Sullavan, also a "Nordic girl, clean, wholesome, stabilized and competent. . . ."

"All these months my pain has been double: one, because I did not have you and two, because it was completely my fault. You must forgive me dearest Luise. I will not let you go." This was one of the batch of unanswered wires Odets was still firing off to his wife, often sending them in the small hours of the morning while reworking *Night Music*. There were stacks of telephone messages from him to her at the Waldorf-Astoria, many marked by the switchboard "Call not accepted." He had clearly not yet given up, and was steadily seeking to impress into service mutual friends who might once more help bring about a reconciliation. He recognized her uniqueness and he could not permit *her* to be the abandoner. She recalled, "I, however, finally felt now free from Clifford." As he received no encouragement from her, and as the time drew near for *Night Music* to go into rehearsal, his anxiety mounted; he feared that, for lack of funds, *Night Music*, like *The Silent Partner* and his Chekhov adaptation, would be shelved. He set about to raise money for the play himself.

He was becoming increasingly angry with Clurman for not having raised the capital for this twenty-second Group production, *his* seventh for the Group. "Everybody was papa to Clifford once they had power," Clurman later observed. "He thought somehow I *could* have raised that money if I but would." When, in this discouraging context, a canny inquiry arrived from film producer Al Lewin asking for a script of *Night Music*, Odets immediately sent one off to California. Within four days he received a long telegram from Lewin saying that "the play is beautiful. Excited about its screen possibilities." Moreover, Lewin adds, "I hate the idea of another writer tying synthetic dialogue to your breathing characters." A young playreader named Stanley Kramer, who years later spoke of Lewin as "one of the most intelligent men I've ever met in the film business," had also made a strong recommendation that Odets should write the screenplay. Before the week was out, Odets had agreed, in exchange for a substantial and immediate chunk of his play's backing on Broadway ($20,000), to write the screenplay of *Night Music* for the new film-producing firm of Loew-Lewin, in which Odets had earlier refused partnership. It is clear that had he not agreed to do this, there would have been no production of *Night Music*. Even with this advance from Lewin, Odets had to provide most of the remainder—$21,000—from his dwindling bank account.

Lewin followed his initial ecstatic and reverent response to *Night Music* with the cool appraisal of a motion-picture producer. In a four-page

* A Gentile woman.

letter to Odets he discusses act by act and scene by scene how to "improve the narrative pace," arrogating to himself a license he would have labeled sacrilegious the week before when he was courting Odets for "the property." Odets was dismayed by these clichéd ideas, as he was by Lewin's suggestion to change the title from *Night Music* to *Mating Call.*

In this twentieth century, artists of the theatre have evolved a means of avenging themselves for humiliations such as these script suggestions from a movie producer. It is called "the deal." Odets has scribbled in his copy of Lewin's proposed contract (sent not to him but to his agent, Harold Freedman) many penciled marginal suggestions to "make a better deal."

Employing his own doctor-father's world-view and the special language of the film industry, Harold Clurman assured Odets, as director Lewis Milestone had earlier, that he was no match for "the money-men." But to his last breath Odets—always without success—would try to outsmart them: he demands "$2,000 each week after the fifth or tenth week up to 80 thousand, all this against 7½ percent of the movie gross, etc., etc."

Despite the demands of his disciplined and rapid work on the last rewrites of *Night Music,* he managed to send almost daily wires of warm encouragement plus a Mexican blanket to Fay Wray, involved in the last throes of her divorce; to write thanks to Tante Esther for her "fine knishes," enclosing a check to his "red-head Uncle" for a winter coat; to send $400 to Clurman for a trip to "the Coast" to interview actresses for the feminine lead in *Night Music;* to send another large check to his father, who was finally en route to Hollywood; and to sign his name on a petition "to defend the Constitutional rights of communists."

Found in his files for this period just before the opening of *Night Music* was a document historic for the American theatre, called "An Analysis of the Problems," which outlined a prospectus whereby dedicated theatre workers who share "a common world view and a common acting technique" might conceivably survive.◖

In a letter to Fay Wray he continued to express his anxiety that, despite his best efforts, *Night Music* was not all he had wanted it to be. She replied warmly that she understood all too well the "deep tortured tired yearning," even despair, he was feeling, but nonetheless had unshakable confidence in him and in his work.

Odets knew he had not solved in *Night Music,* as he had not in *The Silent Partner,* the fundamental problem he had set himself: to create, within a panoramically historical sweep, richly alive people who would tell both a generational and a personal story. It did not comfort him that other American playwrights failed even to grasp the problem. "Forgive me, but I get a real sense of power," he later writes, "when I go to the Broadway theatre. Alone, by myself, I am apt to think what a small talent I have. But when I look around at these boys I can only think that I am a giant."

As so often happens to playwrights, Odets began now to shift his anxiety about his play to issues of casting and, disproportionately, to a struggle with Clurman about the theatre in which to house it. "Clifford was so childish in some ways," Clurman recalled. "I said to him, 'Your play is intimate, it's like a conversation. I don't want it in a big theatre. Let's put it in the Lyceum.' Clifford's response was 'Look, that's an old theatre. I want it in the Broadhurst!' It seems he didn't want to be relegated to a small, old theatre; he didn't want to be Jewish, he didn't want to be the child of immigrants, he didn't want to be ghetto-ized. Somehow he thought if his lovely little play were put in the Broadhurst on that street of successes he would be in 'the class of the Robert Sherwoods, the Sidney

◖ 23.3.

Howards'! In the same way, he had to buy a big car and hang around those lousy places like the Stork Club and the 21, places where he shouldn't have been. He really had a better time eating knishes at Moscowitz' and Lupowitz' restaurant."

Clurman remembered this and many other times when he had said to Odets, "Listen, a ghetto man is not always a Jew . . . everybody has a ghetto, his own ghetto. Artists have ghettos if they feel 'Yes, I've always been the second, not the first.' They make their own ghetto. . . . I'd tell him he would never be a Robert Sherwood . . . 'not because you are inferior but because you're in a different kind of world'! But he didn't understand it. I would give him examples from history. I said Balzac was never in the French Academy but he was the biggest novelist of his time. Ravel was never given the Prix de Rome. I told him over and over, 'Look, write one play a year for ten years. Seven will be flops. Now, some of those seven will be better than the three that will be successful, and all seven which will flop will have wonderful things in them. The point is,' I told him, 'that you have written them, and *that* is the immortal thing.' " Directly following such an address, it seemed to Clurman that "Clifford's heart would have an orgasm, so to speak, and he would agree." But presently he would "start to shiver all over again, almost as if he had been ripped untimely from his mother's womb.* He was always cold and moving up to a stove for warmth."

Clurman concludes his passionate statement: "I knew the whole process because, you see, I felt all the same things, all the fears. . . . I am not above them, but I found the capacity to confess them to myself, to struggle with them, strangle them, and generally win a victory over them. Clifford didn't have the stamina. . . ." In fairness, it must be noted that not only were the values of their respective fathers antithetical, but also Clurman had never been offered the enticements of fame and fortune steadily dangled before Odets. It is easier to maintain one's purity in the absence of temptation. By this time even composer Aaron Copland was living in Los Angeles, writing scores for films.

Odets' view prevailed, and it was decided that *Night Music* would be shown at the larger, newer, more fashionable Broadhurst, and that Jane Wyatt, described in the press as "the only Class A debutante ever to make it on the legitimate stage," would play the feminine lead. It cheered Odets considerably that the entire Group company appeared to have a genuine affection for his play, and all the actors were exhausting themselves to make it an artistic success.

Odets' need, which arose after *Awake and Sing!* had been criticized as "overly Jewish," to write what he thought of as "American plays," and thus to be accepted as a "regular American playwright," not as a "Jewish lyric poet," is clearly reflected once again in *Night Music*. Although his remarkable ear could not help but reflect the explosive language melodies of New York City, he was conscious of trying to purge it of its "Yiddishkeit." In this effort to neutralize his Jewishness (he thought it was in order to broaden and to universalize his work) he sacrificed one of the wellsprings

---

* Clurman was surprised to learn that Odets and his wife, Luise, had both indeed been premature babies, weighing in at three and a half pounds!

of his uniqueness as a playwright. Only toward the end of his life, after planning innumerable plays on Biblical themes, would he turn once more to this source for a play about Noah, *The Flowering Peach*, finding it still available, if somewhat impoverished.

The wistful, expressionistic *Night Music*, signaling, as he put it, "the nighttime of civilization," reflects also the beginning of the end of his home in the Group Theatre, of his marriage, and of his romantically held political ideology. It still strains, however, toward the optimism for aspiration, growth, and survival which he had expressed in *Rocket to the Moon*. Its title is derived from an exchange between members of two generations: the "fine old relic" detective Abraham Lincoln Rosenberger, representative, like Clurman, of the best "old-fashioned" values in American culture, and Fay Tucker, the aspiring girl who seeks self-realization. "Do you hear what I hear?" she asks. And to his "What?" she replies: "The last cricket, the very last. . . . Crickets are my favorite animals in all the world. They're never down in the mouth. All night they make their music. . . ." Rosenberger, who has an unreal and charismatic quality, shrugs and asks, "Say, what kind of problems can a cricket have . . . ?" Seemingly unresponsive, Fay replies, "Night music. . . . If they can sing, I can sing. I'm more than them. *We're* more than them. . . . We can sing through any night!" ◖ The artist is better than an animal and can try to restore hope by whistling through the dark.

Thus, just as his passively plaintive title *I Got the Blues* gave way to the active adjuration to *Awake and Sing!*, so in this "jazz lullaby," subtitled *A Comedy in Twelve Scenes* and dedicated to the memory of the lively liberal columnist Heywood Broun, Odets makes the existential plea that we humans find the strength to "sing" (to create) through our night of pain, be it a war, a Depression, a broken love, a stifled act of creation, or a dying. Let us demonstrate, he asks, that in this jungle of life, this "sordid wilderness," this meaningless sideshow, we are as strong and resourceful as a cricket; more, because we are human, we can "make beauty come from sordidness." Ten years earlier he had written to actress Hortense Alden of his lifelong terror of the dark and of the crickets who sang through it, adding, "and yet strangely I love the dark as passionately as I love Music and Woman." And later: "Three (4) things should not be done by day: loving, music, thinking and writing." Crickets, cheerful little creatures who can "sing" through the darkest of nights, are celebrated over and over in Odets' correspondence.

He chose to present this serious statement (Clurman, later persuaded that it was an early American example of the "theatre of the absurd," called it "a melody, not a thesis") in a tender, charming, even a farcically improvisatory key.

Odets' thirty-odd characters explore in twelve scenes, on one weekend, and in eight sets, that part of the "sordid wilderness" he knows best: New York City ("the greatest city in the world" or, as he called it, "the city of the dreadful night," which gives you a "heartbroken feeling"), where plays "fall like sparrows" and actors, prototypes of homelessness, are a "flock of birds in passage."

On a scrap of paper he had jotted early in the year, under the heading "Night Music," two short items: "the last individualist" and "against conformity." In the "micro-reality" of a stage play he tries to re-create and to master his recent as well as ancient sense of deprivation, guilt, estrangement, and hopelessness.

◖ 23.4.

*   *   *

The play is set on "a chilly October evening" in a place to maintain law and order, "the Police Station of a New York City precinct." Here the authorities are "wrestling with two real live squirming monkeys"—"the two most famous trained monkeys in the United States," who must be taken to sunny California—where they are needed by "Federal Pictures' "—by "Suitcase Steve" Takis. Takis, the play's defensively brash, homeless protagonist, owes his nickname to the fact that, unable to take hold in the world, he lives "out of a suitcase." If the monkeys are not delivered to the West Coast by this impertinent and isolated young man (who boasts falsely that he is a junior executive "with Al Lewin's eye on me"* "tryin' to make good after years in the tunnel"), he will lose his livelihood and his chance to become a senior executive, landing once more "on the street." It is evident that, despite his bravado, he is "shivering in his boots."

Thus in the first few pages Odets establishes the fearful, ironically taunting, and self-chiding metaphor of his own (and simultaneously his wife's) current life-situation. "They're makin' a picture," Steve says, "an' the last minute they discover they need two wonderful trained monkeys. Well, those monks are up in New Haven, in the East." As he is about to take them to Hollywood on a plane, the animals hurl a monkey wrench into the plan: in the heart of the Manhattan theatre district (44th Street and Broadway) one throws away Steve's wallet containing his ticket, his money, and his "credentials";† the other reaches out to steal a locket around the neck of Fay Tucker (who is perhaps a "society girl"). When she screams, Detective Abraham Lincoln Rosenberger, who is dying of cancer, comes to her rescue and brings everyone to the police station. The detective's name fuses a Hebrew patriarch with a great American who freed slaves; this is crowned by a surname, Rosenberger, meaning "flowering hills." Mainly concerned with establishing good values in the next generation, Rosenberger represents an identity-element akin to the Biblical grandfather in *Awake and Sing!* Fay is an earnest, womanly twenty-one-year-old, determined "to better herself in every honest way possible," whose aspiration is similar to that of the young dancer Cleo in *Rocket to the Moon*. One of the "outer masks" for this character was the quiet Fay Wray. Odets' description of Fay Tucker as a courageous girl ("Taking chances doesn't frighten me!") who is "earnest . . . flexible, realistic and practical, every inch a womanly queen," matches his expressed conscious view of the actress. Both Rosenberger and the girl are, of course, aspects of Odets' identity as artist: at one point, Fay is referred to as "a thing of beauty . . . delicate . . . flowers on the hill." Thus, the creative identity-element ("flowering hills") resides in *both* these characters, Rosenberger and Fay.

In *Night Music* an overtly cocky but deeply frightened boy is helped by an older man to restore valuables (creative gifts) to their rightful owner. Harold Clurman (the "witness of my life") had long served this function. Odets' steady contempt not only for the film industry but for all American Business and those who participate in it (its "trained monkeys") is expressed metaphorically in wry humor on every page of this play.

It is clear that Rosenberger wants to establish the boy and girl together in a crusade to save themselves and their land from the nullifications of commerce and technology: "You had the wisdom and foresight to be born

---

* It is artless of Odets to use here the real name of the film executive who is trying at this very moment to seduce him back from the New York stage to Hollywood.
† Since the year of his great success (1935) Odets had had the ongoing fantasy of changing his name, giving away his money, and anonymously "starting all over again."

in the twentieth century," he says. "Go, go with love and health—your wonderful country never needed you more. . . ." He is the vessel both for generational continuity and for what Erikson has called "generativity."

From the police station the girl, now apologetic, offers the boy a haven in her shabby Hotel Algiers. (Odets used this same grimy, "exotic" name for a hotel in *Rocket to the Moon.*) This scene, drawn from Odets' experience a decade earlier at the Circle Hotel in Manhattan, is a rich repository of melancholy, disconnected souls who make "up and down the airshaft amazing conversation, obscene and amatory, often pitiful." Fay's middle-class Philadelphia parents, she says, "would have kittens if they ever saw this place." ("A kangaroo wouldn't live here.") She is in fear her father will find her here, and soon he does.

The affair between a "rude, rash, uncontrollable" Greek-American boy from Brockton, Massachusetts (a "wild animal"), and a gentle, well-bred, middle-class WASP girl from Philadelphia represents for Odets at least three faces of a central conflict: his own longstanding if ambivalent wish to achieve a real intimacy with just such a secure female member of America's non-Jewish "elite" (as Kazan in his marriage already had); his intense current relationship with the Greek-American Kazan; most important, his effort to integrate *within himself* all of these diffused identity-elements. On the one hand, he is the repudiated minority-group member who must pretend importance to save face and thus behaves cockily; but he has those "nobody-nothing blues" and feels like "the King of the Jews." On the other, she is the honest girl who has more acting talent than she thinks. In its long series of Manhattan vignettes, mainly concerning the old detective and the young couple, lies the story of a lonely young man in terror for his life's work: that will deliver his freedom and his talent to those "in authority" (Federal Pictures or the army) by turning *himself* into a "trained monkey." Beyond this, Odets explores a rich variety of complex psychological and historical issues in this prescient play of youthful alienation and decline; its central theme, however, is that of the boy who is helped by the *dying* detective, a lonesome, high-principled, wise man of a disappearing generation who unravels mysteries, who stops evildoers, and who quotes George Washington on the "preservation of the sacred fire of liberty."

The merchandising identity-element within Odets, in conflict with the values of Abraham Lincoln Rosenberger, is the girl's father, who describes the man his daughter "was engaged to marry" in the vocabulary of L. J. Odets:

> Draw your own conclusions when you meet him. The boy's making his six thousand every year. . . . Why? I'm the one *who loses face* in the community [italics mine], not you. . . . All those pitying looks your mother and I get when we go down to the Building Loan.

Fay replies:

> But I draw the line when they insist that I must live the same lives they live. I can't admire their way of living and I don't care for their ideals. That seems to be a crime. Every relative I have tells me I'm a criminal. But I think *they're* criminals. Because they don't live—because their alphabet's from A to B—because their lives are narrow, petty and small!

Throughout the play Suitcase Steve is closely followed by the detective and is furious. ("I'm sore on that Dick. He's followin' me an' I don't like it.") Rosenberger, "one of the most famous detectives in the city," is the embodiment of Odets' creative conscience. He is, in addition, "a partisan of the pursuit of life, liberty and happiness." "The whole world thinks I'm a criminal—he's on my trail," cries the boy, adding, "Am I a crook? Con man? Suppose it gets in the papers?" Here, as in *Awake and Sing!*, Odets questions the "legitimacy" of his creative activities. Rosenberger is not simply a source of guilt, but is a feeder and protector as well. However, when he sends up sandwiches and coffee for both young people, he elicits at first a proud and angry outburst from the boy: "What's he think we are, that Dick? Orphans of the storm?" In this scene, as so often in Odets' work, deprivation or hunger is the emotional motor of the dialogue. Indeed, just before Steve *refuses* sustenance from the detective and, in fact, declares "a moratorium on the eating," he has sung for Fay an improvised "home-made" composition about eating, accompanying himself (as Odets often had at the Circle Hotel) on a broken-down harmonium. "It is," writes Odets in the stage direction, "the music of a lost boy, gloomy, apprehensive, lonely." The strange blues lyric matches the music:

It was hunger, hunger alone, that caused Steve Takis to leave his home. . . . Move over, Mr. Horse. Gimme room in your stall. How are the oats, Brother Horse? Gimme room in your stall. Didn't you ever wish you was dead? Brother Horse, giddiap, Brother Horse! I got those nobody-nothing blues! I'm feelin' like the King of the Jews! Oh, you Brother Horse, eating oats by the peck. Brother Horse, Brother Horse, send a dish over to me. How's your father? How's your mother, Brother Horse? Got no mother, got no father, anywhere! Some fun, Brother Horse!

Odets' intense envy of the animal—who cannot suffer like "the King of the Jews," and who dumbly (without conflict) eats "oats by the peck" provided by his master—is stated here as clearly as in any of his writings.

Now and again Odets' rage overflows in Steve's sudden outbursts at the ethical old detective, symbol of a dying generation. ("You broke a boy's career in two. An' you can die for all I care," cries Steve.) He is, however, immediately filled with contrition when he is told the old man is in fact dying and, after "thirty-two honorable years,"* has been retired "like an old horse." Steve listens to the detective's rather remarkable prescription for handling his rage:

There are two ways to look, Mr. Takis—to the past or the future. We know a famous case in history where a woman kept looking back and turned to a salt rock. If you keep looking back on a mean narrow past, the same thing can happen to you. You are feeling mad. Why shouldn't you feel mad? In your whole life you never had a pretzel. You think you have to tell me it's a classified world? There is an old saying, "A hungry man is an angry man." We understand that. But your anger must bear children or it's hopeless. The man next to you has nothing, and you fight with him. Why should two bald men fight about a comb? You have the materials to make a good man. But stop breaking things with your fists. Look ahead, Mr. Takis. What did the doctor prescribe for society? Boys like you! God gave you a fine head—use it, dear boy. (*An afterthought*) Sincerely yours, A. L. Rosenberger, your old Dutch Uncle. . . . (*Then*) Good night, Mr. Takis.

The recommendation for Steve to *use* his capacity to love as well as his creative gift ("Your anger must bear children") and not to become a

* This was written around the end of Odets' thirty-second year.

trained monkey for the army or for Federal Pictures is stated and restated by Rosenberger. On the surface Odets adjures himself to make another try at intimacy, at love. (FAY: "Steve, where are your eyes? Don't you see you're at war, right now, yesterday, last year—*and right here?!*") Rosenberger supports her:

> *You* are ignorant. Because your fight is *here*, not across the water. You love this girl? And you mean it? Then fight for love! You want a home? Do you?—then fight for homes! Otherwise, excuse me, you are a rascal and a liar!

Rosenberger guides Steve into seeing that in this "wilderness of uncertainty" there are solid alternatives in love and in work to delivering himself to the Moloch of Bureaucracy (be it the film industry or the military): he can gamble on himself.

It is some time before Steve can drop his face-saving maneuvers and confess to the girl that he does not own "seven suits, two English," and that he has been pretentiously playing the "big shot" who can get her a screen test when he is in fact nobody, nothing: "Petty cash tryin' to be a mint." He continues that although he is the monkeys' keeper, they control *him* ("Here's these monks. They're not with me. *I* travel with *them!* They got the big future . . ."). He goes on: "I threw it around like a toreador to you—who I was an' how I was. But I'm nobody, nothing—I want you to know it. . . . Can't get you no shoe, no hat, no room, no nothin'!" He wails, "Fay, money's my worse enemy—he don't come near me!" Her response is valiant and reassuring: "I want you to realize what a wonderful man you are! . . . Nothing ventured, nothing gained."

His confession opens the possibility of a genuine relationship with the girl, of doing free and honest work and of making music on his clarinet (a gift from his mother, dead of cancer!). At the last minute it is revealed that Federal Pictures can dispense with the trained monkeys, since the company has discovered "they had two trained monkeys out there all the time. . . . Right on our own lot!" Thus the play has come full circle.

It had opened with the central character forced to deliver the escaped animals (i.e., conform to the demands of a merchandising bureaucracy) and it closes with his escape as he remains "in the East" with his good "witness" (the detective) and his confident and loving girl, with whom he hopes for a durable relationship. He links arms with the detective and the girl, and the "trio starts out as one."* Truly a new beginning, but with roots in the past. It should be noticed, however, that the boy's escape from the obedient and frightened conformity of returning to Hollywood is not by his own will and choice. He is fired from his job because Federal Pictures already has enough trained monkeys! Thus the triumph of this "last individualist" is a *passive* event.

Throughout the play the war provides a massively conflicted and surrealist backdrop: at times as an illusory way out, a means for the boy "to ditch" the girl; or as a metaphoric home that provides food and shelter, where one can be passive. More often it is a simple nightmare. One of the many minor characters, for example, is a "Little Man," Mr. Watson, of the Watson Construction Company, who constructs "bridges an' cathedrals on paper, but no one's interested"; he is sixty years old and, like the detective, is ailing. He, too, thinks much of "youth" and at first offers them his wisdom: "If you got money, you got nerve. . . . If you ain't got money, you ain't got nerve." He continues, in a dreamlike exit speech:

---

* In this condensed image the generations are linked and Odets' unconscious wish for a loving reunion with (a good) father and "wife-mother" is realized.

But no doctor'll tell you that. When you think about it the old days were best. . . . Eggs two for a cent. . . . Free liver for the dog. Uptown was just a wilderness in the old days. Now the *whole* town's a wilderness. . . . I'd like to tell my wife what I think of her. You don't know me, do you? That's no way to talk about your wife. . . . I'm the man nobody knows. I'm very bold, but some nights I'm gripped by unbearable shame and shyness. . . . Well . . . Good night, boys an' girls. Come on, you naughty girl. Good night, good night, my dear. . . . (*Suddenly stopping and turning aghast, horror in his voice*) What about the war?!!

STEVE: What about it?

LITTLE MAN: Terrible! . . . Terrible!! (*He walks out, leaving silence behind him.*)

Soon after, Steve says, "The more I think about it, the better I like Roy's idea to join the war. Are you cold?" It is the voice of Odets' profound and desperate conflict. What a relief it would be to join a mindless, passive fraternity engaged in a communal effort to destroy a clean-cut embodiment of Evil (Hitler), and thus to externalize all of one's inner struggles. Even as in *Lefty*, where there had been no doubt who the Enemy was, thus releasing a guilt-free flow of anger (indeed, of hatred) in Odets, so now how mobilizing, how integrating it would be to join wholeheartedly the family of Americans "fighting for their liberty." But there are all kinds of paradoxes, inner and outer, which brake this anger and confuse him. Dimly in this play of impermanence he perceives the war as an oncoming major crisis for America and in world history. The adjustment of his characters to it is already conflicted, but his own *conscious* political ruminations come only later.

It had been much simpler in the early thirties for an entire generation, first, to identify the Enemy as the domestic capitalist establishment (or one's mercantile father) and, second, to join in a group-identity which opposed it and its tool of expansion: war. Now the situation was cloudier. The war appeared to be, from one point of view, a penultimate scramble for power, a struggle in which Odets felt no investment (he had said in August, "Let the imperialists fight it out among themselves"!).

The dilemma was by no means Odets' own. Theodore Dreiser, at sixty-eight living in a shabby apartment in Hollywood and trying in vain to break *into* successful film writing, saw the war at first as "the same old thing," a "financial hook-up between big American finance and big British finance—Threadneedle Street and Wall Street." Until the Soviet Union entered the conflict, this isolationist sentiment was strongly felt by many American intellectuals, especially if they were not Jews. The lead editorial in the October 1939 issue of the left-wing *Theatre Arts Committee* magazine carried the headline "Keep America Out of War." The later German invasion of Russia, according to his biographer, would "all but unhinge Dreiser," who then abandoned his isolationism. Odets, however, unlike Dreiser, could not help being threatened from the start by Hitler's "final solution." The emotional complexities inherent for him in this evolving history were becoming obsessive and paralyzing.

On the surface, the "conclusion" of *Night Music* is a desperate effort to return to a simple Marxist frame, to an uncomplicated and romantic "domestic" revolution. Rosenberger says, "You are the people. Whatever you want to say, say it! Whatever has to be changed, change it! Who told you not to make a new political party? Make it and call it 'Party-to-Marry-

My-Girl!' " Below the surface Odets is adjuring himself not to lose sight of the fact that the Enemy he must conquer, if he is to be free to love and to work, is not only external but also internal, and that he must overcome the Hitler within himself if he is not to be forever enslaved and alone.

It is curious that this play, full of foreboding and dark presentiment, written in a watershed year in Odets' life and in the history of the world, climaxes with a youthful vigor and optimism rare in his work. Absent are the usual deaths and suicides, and with a firm vote of fatherly confidence* from the fine old detective, Steve's line which closes the play is "Make way! This girl's got a crush on me! Make way!"

The final stage direction reads, "Overhead the airplanes are zooming and singing." Among them is the plane that will *not* take Steve or the monkeys to the West Coast. He is united with his courageous girl, and they review their qualifications for an autonomous, self-respecting life: "Taking chances doesn't frighten me!" she says. "Otherwise I'd stay in Philly, wrapped up with the mothballs." She continues: "For several years I ran my father's stationery store," adding, "I'm a manicurist . . . an expert stenographer . . . I can even act, although I'm not an actress. I know you're talented on the clarinet. Can't you wrap a package? Address envelopes? Squeeze oranges for juice?" He replies, "I drove a cab for five months." He has here outwitted the dehumanized technology, its film-industry bureaucracy, and even the army. The "night music" of the lowly but invincible cricket has drowned out "the twentieth-century music" of the planes.

* Compare the end of *Awake and Sing!,* where Ralph is given a similar vote by Moe Axelrod (he's as good "as a baseball player").

Chapter Twenty-Four

The biggest shock I have experienced since the auto crash in Mexico a year ago was the reviews of the play today. . . . My feelings were and are very simple. I felt as if a lovely delicate child, tender and humorous, had been knocked down by a truck and lay dying.

CLIFFORD ODETS, 1940

ON THE first day of 1940, when the downstairs buzzer sounded in his apartment at One University Place late in the afternoon, Odets was still sound asleep. Since it was New Year's Day, Herman was not there to answer it. When Odets, half asleep and cranky, finally asked who it was, a girl's voice, soft and extremely frightened, replied over the speaker, "Mr. . . . uh . . . Clurman sent me." Odets later recalled thinking, "Another of Harold's impositions," but decided to let the girl come up.

When he opened the door, there stood a lovely young teen-age girl with a large, gentle, and generous mouth, her dark, wistful eyes wide with awe. Odets' glance was, however, immediately riveted to the sight revealed by her open coat and low-necked dress. Here were the two largest, most beautiful breasts he had ever seen, "like great juicy melons," he thought. When he could bring himself to say "Come in," he noticed the long, speckled feather sticking straight up from her hat, and began to laugh. As he watched her walk into the living room, her long arms hanging awkwardly, he muttered to himself, "Renoir." The girl—to become his wife and mother of his two children—painfully self-conscious and timid, said, "No, Grayson, Bette Grayson. Mr. Clurman thought maybe you could use me for something in your new play." Within the hour he had promised her she could understudy the feminine lead in *Night Music* and they were making love furiously in Odets' bed.

Two weeks later he wrote in his diary that the innocence of the girl, whose "hands are cold and energy low," reminded him of his character Cleo Singer and "of the Sparks girl in John Howard Lawson's *Pure in Heart*." He calls Bette "a nice sweet little girl fresh from California," "a rosebud," adding:

She is living here with a crushed sour girl, her sister, who is that way because she's been freshly divorced. She has a two and a half year old girl who's been sick for a week. I was very touched to hear of this unhappy young mother with a sick child. They didn't need any help when I offered it. Now the child is at Mount Sinai Hospital, dying of uremia. I am engaged in the whole thing as if the child were mine. That's my nature and one can't go against his own nature I suppose, but I am depressed that I am depressed. Am dressing and washing to go up now and meet Betty [sic] outside the hospital.

I notice that the unhappier and lonelier I am, the more I want to mix into other people's lives and be as generous to them as possible. I am not sure that the impulse is an unselfish one, but I won't worry about that.

His instant identification with a dying child and its relationship to his inner perception of his own creativity are readily apparent. There can be little doubt that within his statement "I am engaged in the whole thing as if the child were mine" lies a deep concern for his own endangered child—his talent.

He has also swiftly repressed the threatening recognition that his instant identification with the deprived one issues in part from a need to feed, comfort, instruct, even rescue the Cleo Singer—the needy aspirant—within himself. His steady necessity as artist—to play Pygmalion to his own *inner* Galatea◖—could sometimes be externalized and enacted with a living girl if she were sufficiently childlike and malleable. The complex Luise Rainer had had, to be sure, the necessary vulnerability and neediness for this transaction, but her strength, conviction of talent, and intellectuality had often pushed her from the position of sorrowing waif into being herself a taming Pygmalion, thus upsetting the balance between them. Still haunted by Luise's accusations that she was the sole "giver" in their marriage, Odets was relieved by this eager, admiring, and grateful child spectacularly adorned with the anatomy of a nursing mother.

He confirms this view in a diary entry three days later when he ponders his intense attraction to this "darling, sweet and gentle girl, Bette," who listens with him "so givingly" to the records he steadily plays on his powerful, newly reorganized player. He speculates that whereas his marriage to Luise had been from the first "a great mistake" ("We both were looking to a staunch rock out of a turbulent sea"), he believes that:

My interest now, I think (how can I ever be sure of something while it is happening—I'm an after-the-fact boy!), is a young girl to whom *I* can give form and shape. This, I think, is why I am so attracted to Betty. Much of love for me is in giving. Unfortunately, I am not one of the receivers in life. I receive badly, restlessly, shamefully. How much easier it is to give than to receive. It is strange to me that people are not aware of that fact.

It pleases him that Clurman and Kazan agree on Bette's essential sweetness and on her "givingness," and his entry concludes:

She was very self conscious in Sardi's tonight. I held her hand to give her a little reassurance. The thought of her lifts me out of this room a little.◖

◖ 24.1.
◖ 24.2.

In a matter of days Odets had established Bette as an understudy to Jane Wyatt, which the company seemed willing to tolerate, inasmuch as she appeared to be Odets' new girl. Everyone agreed she had much beauty, and they listened indulgently while she talked about how well things were going, how much she enjoyed Hanns Eisler's incidental music for the show, and how she was "developing" in these rehearsals, "just listening to Harold talk." Her childlike self-absorption seemed extreme even for an actress, and her talent was minuscule; they were hopeful she would never have to go on as their leading lady.

Had a recording angel been observing from afar the intensity and dedication with which Clurman and Odets set to work on *Night Music*, he might have concluded they knew not only that this might be their last chance to work together but also that the life of the Group Theatre hung by a thread. Yet the morale of the company was unusually high. Later, several agreed, "We were counting on *Night Music* to pull us out."

Clurman was still trying to persuade Odets that his protagonist, Steve Takis, was an "unsympathetic" character—too boastful, loud, impertinent, complaining, and generally unappealing. Odets argued that his play consisted precisely in Steve's change from a defensively cocky, frightened, self-pitying phony to a more courageous and more honest person, and that it was up to Clurman to convey this to Kazan, who was playing him. At this point he announced his determination "not to change a single line." Still, such disputes were to be expected in this collaborative art.

It is curious that on every day of this critical, mid-century year Odets would keep a remarkably lively and detailed private journal, something he had never done before and would not do again. That he undertook this journal reveals not only his need to be a responsible chronicler of this crucial time, but also his longing to be able to earn a living not as a playwright but from an autonomous, non-collaborative form of writing. The style of the journal, though expressively intimate and self-therapeutic, is careful, thoughtful, and clearly aimed at publication and posterity. There is no doubt he was exploring, as part of his mid-life crisis of generativity, the possibilities of the journal both as a psychological life-preserver and as an alternative to writing for the changing film industry, should *Night Music* fail. He confined his growing anxiety about the production to his journal entries. Now and again he mailed to Fay Wray in Hollywood a carbon copy of an entry, asking her to "take it as a letter" in response to her many loving airmail specials reassuring him about *Night Music*.

Three weeks before the Boston tryout he is investing—somewhat frantically—in yet another form of life insurance by simultaneously outlining three new plays. One is a "sextette, about six or seven homeless men"; another, called "The Actress Play," is the story of the reconciliation of a film star with her writer husband. In the journal he writes of the third, to be called at first *Trio* and finally *Clash by Night:*

> I was thinking, for the modern murder love play—the couple must go to out of the way movies and restaurants like the ones I took Betty [sic] to tonight. Illicit love lives in the submerged half-lit world of de-

pressing joint-like places, everything on the sneak and faintly ribbed with terror.

As an afterthought, the day's entry concludes, "Confidence is repose."

Luise, he notes, is finally returning his long-ignored telephone messages, "but I didn't call back, for I don't want to speak to her or see her. I go deader and deader on her each day, but it is a protective thing, out of an ego scorned. How amazing to me was my reaction when she told me about her Englishman when she returned to New York from London a couple of months ago." With Arthur Krim, who is his lawyer and Luise's, he notices that he tries to appear to be impartial, casual, reasonable, cool. "I was trying," he writes, "to disavow a real thread of feeling which still connects me with her."

As the opening of *Night Music* approaches, Odets—exhausted from his chronic insomnia—writes, "I dream and dream, empty vacant bits and shards of dreams." In one of them "the brain was taken out of my head and I didn't feel badly at all, only a faint whirring but silent headache and general emptiness . . . the doctor on this extraordinary case was my father. What can that mean?" And the next day:

> Much deeper and fuller than I ever admit to myself consciously, is the fear of running the gauntlet—for opening a play in New York City is really the equivalent of running the gauntlet. That is what I don't want to face, that is one of the things that disturbs me deeply. I even find it militates against sitting down to the typewriter and starting a new play.

Perhaps, he thinks, it is Clurman who is decerebrating him. Surely his play is not so heavy, so drab, nor his hero so oafish, as it now seems. As the rehearsals proceed, with Odets silent and unable to tell Clurman his violent criticisms of his directing, he trembles with anger and writes in his journal:

> He is still indecisive and shaking about actual physical staging, but as splendid as ever about explaining the character's psychology to the actor. He has the patience of a devil (not a saint) for his patience is somehow involved with what he wants, something which comes from the ego. He is the supreme type of a man who has made a virtue and strength from every weakness.

And again later:

> Harold has the whole first act up on its feet by now. I sat thru the whole rehearsal, watching, listening, minding my business and thinking that I could do an excellent job of direction myself. My ensembles would be much more dynamic than Harold's, more brusque, more impatient, more dash and verve, but not as excellent psychologically.

He is deterred from expressing his views by a dim awareness of the depth —and, in part, the irrationality—of his hostile mistrust, for which he feels guilty. Clurman had no inkling of Odets' profound misgivings about the production, and would, in his memoirs five years later, express his belief that Odets' doubts had begun with the reviews.

Obsessed not only by his failed marriage but by his steady longing "to give himself over" to his director, to the Group, to a wife, even to the president of the United States, Odets reasons that perhaps his apprehension is ill-founded and it is his ancient fear that holds him apart and resistive even toward a director:

> The terror of my childhood was that either or both of my parents or my sisters might die. Many nights I stayed awake as child and boy, fearful that my parents had been killed in an auto wreck, etc. These thoughts really terrorized my youth. And that terror is one of the reasons that now I am so chary of forming permanent relationships of an intimate or personal nature. I can't face the possibilities of serious illnesses or death to others close to me; for myself I am not much mindful. This is really one of the things which makes it so difficult for me to give myself over to others.

Sometimes in time of stress, he writes, "I feel I am bleeding from the eyes . . . I have not the slightest capacity for happiness. Woe to my wife!" His persistent psychologizing and attempts at self-analysis reflect his steady effort to cope somehow with his massive and increasing anxiety as the time nears for his public exposure with *Night Music*. He appears to be aware on some level of its esthetic and psychological confusions.

On almost every page of this journal emerges his lifelong preoccupation with the question of whether or not he is courageous enough (like Beethoven) to go it independently as an artist, or whether he needs, as he thinks, "a good wife." "Marriage," he says, quoting a French philosopher, "is the only adventure open to the coward." He continues:

> Usually the man of talent and imagination finds the most difficult thing in life is the one of necessary adjustment to other people and their ideas. Adjustment, however, is the very essence of a successful or creative marriage. The talented man then finds it necessary—if he wants to be happily married—to tamper with his own personality which is his chief working source (and that includes his wife's tampering!); or he must make a compromise by marrying below himself, in a good sense, where the shallow level of contact makes only a shallow level of adjustment necessary. There are exceptions to this, but they are few and far between, very few and very far. . . .

Perhaps, he writes, a slim, handsome young person like his leading lady, Jane Wyatt, "competent, very Catholic and . . . womanly in a small, neat way," would be good for "a maniac like myself." She is a "woman with form, a woman with clarity," unlike a "nice girl like Betty who resolves nothing in my intensely personal life." And yet Jane Wyatt elicits from him something of which he is bitterly ashamed:

> I am a dastard! Several times I found myself talking to Jane Wyatt about Jews, trying to show her how objective and impersonal I was about the problems of Jews; really trying to disavow being a Jew if the truth must be told. *I yearn for acceptance like a youth of eighteen* [italics mine], and in a curiously twisted way (altho she doesn't know it) I reach out to her for her form and clarity, even tho I know it is young and quite incomplete.

It is an old story.

Steadily plagued by feelings of guilt for his behavior toward women, he pleads with himself that perhaps "creative uneasiness excuses everything." If this is not so, then

> my inability to follow up assumed personal responsibilities would be another strong item to make my life unhappier than it is. Everything-for-the-work is practically the only way I can feel and think. . . .

He closes the day's entry in what he calls this "lazy journal" with a "fine quote from the Talmud"—actually another self-accusation:

> In the distance, as I was walking, I saw what looked like a beast. When I got closer I saw it was a man. But when I got still closer I saw it was my brother.

The company arrived for the Boston tryout of *Night Music* on an exceedingly cold, snowy day and immediately arranged an appeasing cocktail party at the Ritz-Carlton for the drama critics. "Not one living face did I see among them. They have so much vanity, these provincial newspaper people!" writes Odets. It gives him a bleak feeling to find himself more anxious than five years earlier when he had dashed off his acclaimed propaganda piece *Waiting for Lefty* in the same hotel where he is now staying.

By the time he arrived at the evening rehearsal, Hanns Eisler was already at work with his musicians in the basement.

> That is what made my heart go banging, the music! Not the new scenery. What an excellent little workman Hanns is! How he whipped those fellows into shape, turned them, taught them, flattered and pushed them—got exactly the results he wanted, altho he can't make a musician of a man who has played a clarinet for twenty years without knowing what music is.

Harry Robin, an assistant of Hanns Eisler, then in his twenties, recalled the "remarkable electronic music"—revolutionary in its form for this time—and the relationship between the composer and Odets:

> I helped Eisler as a technician with the electronic music instruments which Eisler had scored for his incidental music to Odets' beautiful play *Night Music*. . . . I can remember . . . in the interchanges between Eisler and Odets a sense of their very warm admiration for each other; the concentrated, attentive way in which Odets would listen to Eisler's music and comments; occasional, beautifully modulated rantings by Odets on the progress of the rehearsals. . . . I remember what Odets looked like at the time . . . he was a beautiful human being, in his expression—very alert to words, intonation, very much inside the métier he had chosen and quite evidently loved.

But it was not the music that worried Odets, or even the ponderous scenery, which he thought might be overloaded with details "exactly as some of the small-part actors are overloading the delicate line of the play with over-expressiveness." What concerned and enervated him was his impotent, tongue-tied hostility toward Clurman's heavy-handed direction of his play:

> Harold C. and I never face each other when I have to criticize some of his work, as tonight. I am unhappy about some of the scenes, but it is next to impossible to talk to him about them. I did say a few words of what I meant. Tomorrow I'm taking a line rehearsal while he attends the technical run thru. He suggests I make the changes I suggest while the actors are reading. Which I'll do. But what is needed is certain restagings. This time I'll see it thru and it will be the first time since I've been a playwright. To see something which is obviously wrong and to permit it to pass for fear of hurting a friend's feelings . . . what soft stupidity! And yet all my life I have been unable to say, in troubled times, what is on my mind without first

getting angry and then letting the anger act like gunpowder behind bullets. Yet that is the very thing which helped and started me as a playwright.

Odets' greatest concern was his friend Kazan's performance as Steve Takis: "Every time he was being the most brilliant actor on the American stage, my play went out the window." It seemed to him Kazan was being so misdirected by Clurman that he was throwing the delicacy of the play out of focus. Of Kazan he writes:

What gets him by with any audience is his winning personality. In N.M. his characterization is very incomplete and more or less mechanical. In most places it is as if he walked out of his dressing room in his street clothes and shoes, Elia Kazan, not Steve Takis. He lacks variety of approach, variety of voice, altho his perceptions are good; he has flashes of genuine charm, too. The audiences, I think, will like him, but he is far from satisfactory to me personally. A certain uncouthness hits me, too, a sort of boisterous quality; real shyness he does not give, altho he simulates it mechanically. In the middle of the rehearsal period he did have some of the Pierrot quality which Harold was working for, but now it's all gone—the play suffers for it.

"But he was a friend, we couldn't replace him," he said twenty-five years later to director Peter Bogdanovich, "so he stayed in and the play stayed out the window."

In his journal he writes:

I am half Cleo Singer even up to this day of 33 years and 6 months. I am Steve Takis and the file of boys and men behind him. And I am in love with any abstract statement which abstracts my painful experience for me, whether stated by myself or another, often Harold Clurman who is always doing that when he discusses, interprets or directs a play of mine. Also, that is the only way I explain and interpret myself to myself—by writing a play. Perhaps this constant uncovering of the self is one of the prime impulses in the creative mechanism—it and the constant effort to relate the self to persons, things—a woman—outside the self. All of the characters in my plays have the common activity of "a search for reality."

Night Music opened in Boston on a bitterly cold night to poor business and mixed notices. Odets discounts these reviews, however, as "provincial . . . which means afraid of New York opinion, timid, captious in a petty way, written out of heartfelt inferiority, never honest reactions but rather what one is SUPPOSED to write! A woman critic who told me three dirty stories at the party objected to the hero of the play for his . . . generally immoral behavior." In any case, he reasons, it is not these provincials who hold his future in their hands. Dispirited, he writes:

Seemingly the most intelligent of the Boston reviewers, an Elliot Norton, wrote a two column interview with me, but it turned out to be all about my "changing political beliefs" and scarcely a word about my plays and their various qualities. This gentleman admired me as "an intense serious person whom it was a pleasure to meet"; and kept breathing thru his piece one long sigh of relief that I was not really a communist at all—meaning, apparently, that I was not considering blowing up any dams or bridges at the moment. And that is called dramatic criticism in America! That is why, by the way, when a play of mine gets fine notices, it nevertheless does about one quarter the business of the average potboiler. By now the theatre audiences have an idea that I write political tracts—and who can blame them? —would you pay good money to hear the average political tract?

Odets had become, especially since his marriage to an Academy Award–winning film star, a uniquely newsworthy offstage character and a handy target, made more tempting not only by the "tract" nature of his early plays but also by his public and controversial pronouncements on political morality in world events. Precisely because he had made of himself so visible and audible a symbol of moral aspiration, the reporters— especially of the Hearst chain—who had discovered afresh the Great Menace of Communism were again eager to shoot him down as either a dangerous revolutionary or a hypocrite. On the other side—but to him equally irrelevant and damaging to his position as an "American play-wright"—stood the kind and liberal men, like Elliot Norton, who "defended" him. Thus it was that while the changing political stances of a variety of serious American writers—many of them, like F. Scott Fitz-gerald and Theodore Dreiser, trying to earn a living writing films—were of no special interest to a reading public, Odets, by reason of the provoca-tive public symbol he had become, was still elected to be, by turns, a redeeming Jesus, a betraying Judas, or simply a fraud. The demand on him in all these roles was extravagant. It is no wonder he yearned to start all over again, anonymously, as "C. Oakes."

This steady moralizing assault from the press touched and wounded him because, like any caricature, it derived from something recognizable. Even the discerning Clurman, however, did not comprehend the com-plexities of the profound characterological and creative struggle within him, a struggle which led him day after day to lacerate himself as "a very ordinary fellow . . . vain, dishonest, morally lax, proud, self-indulgent" but most of all as one who is exceedingly passive: "You seldom 'intend' your thinking and activity," he scolds.

On the day after the Boston opening he writes:

You are constantly excusing yourself for all these patent deficiencies by saying this sort of jelly-fish existence is a prime requisite of the creative personality. Is that true? Is no self discipline necessary? Aren't you really sinking deeper every week into the feather bed of a successful career? Right now, friend, you are excusing yourself by saying, "Here again is this old foolish American cry for competence and result every minute!" These are the whispered thoughts which will ruin you. The amused expression on your face right this minute denotes a certain lack of seriousness which is beginning, like an odour of dead flowers, to suffuse thru your entire personality. Read this again in a week, in another week, again. Don't be afraid of harassing yourself, of nagging yourself. The wife is dying out in you and only the self-indulgent husband will soon be left.

It is yet another way of stating his fear that he is passively permitting the powerful identity-element within him of his father—without whose esteem he can have no *self-esteem*—to slowly kill that of his sensitive, vulnerable, language-loving mother. His ancient yearning for acceptance by his father, whose very being was a distillation of the values of a mer-cantile society, and his fear that he could never "measure up" to him as a man are forces of a quite different order from what Clurman would later call Odets' wish for "the congratulations of the boys at '21' . . . and the votes of *Variety*'s box-score." Clurman saw Odets' "deep-seated disorder" as issuing from the dilemma of wanting "to occupy two different places at the same time." He called it the desire "for this-and-that. . . . Odets wanted to run with the hares and hunt with the hounds . . . to be the great revolutionary playwright of our day and the white-haired boy of Broadway." This is a partial truth, but it is an overly simple formulation which does violence to the complexities of human organization.

Years later, whenever Odets was asked whether Clurman's account of his role in the Group Theatre was accurate, he would usually respond, with a wistful smile, "It's as honest as it can be from one man's point of view." Occasionally he would add that it seemed a somewhat righteous, simplistic, and holier-than-thou account with little self-searching. Harold, he writes, usually says of himself, *"That's* how I am."

With the crucial opening in New York only two weeks off, Odets became recklessly eager to cut and change his play; Clurman opposed him in this. Odets writes:

> The whole effort now is to make the play a success, a pitiful effort. Even we forget about the charm of the play, its delicacy and poignancy. . . . Everything drives towards success. The American Theatre, excuse me, is vile and a stench hangs over it. Here is one young man who would* weep at its death! What a life, what a life! A dog's life, believe me, veritably a dog's life! And what of the play form? Very easy—in the end it will never be a satisfactory form, never very subtle, never possible of fulfillment for an artist as in painting or music. And here it is complicated by a thousand business details, necessarily, hopelessly, disgustingly!!

Doubtless not the least disgusting of the "business details" was the fact that, according to his financial ledger, he was drawing thousands of dollars for running expenses from his savings account (in total, even more than the film company of Loew-Lewin was contributing).

His concern has many aspects: he fears not only a critic like George Jean Nathan, who, it seemed to him, had made it his mission to hold him up to public ridicule, but his own friends on the Left, like John Howard Lawson, who had already seen in *Rocket to the Moon* a dangerous decline into "individual psychology" and away from contemporary history. Stimulated now by the arrest of a Communist leader, Odets writes:

> Yesterday they gave Browder four years in jail for a minor offense which usually would go by unmentioned. Obviously the Roosevelt Government has decided to put up Browder's head on a pike, to satisfy the clamour of reactionaries who think Fascists and communists paddle the same canoe. Browder is out on bail and spoke last night at a Lenin memorial meeting in the Garden. I think it was mistake of taste, a real error, to say, as he did, that Roosevelt is interested in war and munitions because a son of his married a Dupont girl. They will probably find some other silly misdemeanor with which to convict another communist leader or two and then call it quits.
>
> Communism needs to be Americanized before it will have any effect in America. My personal feeling about social change is this. I have one opinion as a private citizen. But in the world of the theatre, in relation to my plays and audiences for them, Leftism as understood by the communists is impossible. Any excessive partisanship in a play defeats the very purpose of the play itself. To be socially useful

---

* The implied "not" is missing from the original. This could have been a typo—or an interesting slip.

in the theatre, one cannot be more left than, for instance, La Guardia. Unless one is writing pamphlets or agitational cartoons, only clear but broad generalizations are possible. But one must make sure to write from a firm core even tho, in my opinion, an attempt to reach as broad an audience as possible should always be taken into consideration. I thought once that it would be enough to play in a small cellar, but I soon saw that those who would come to the cellar were not the ones in need of what I could say. Personally I am of the opinion that Steinbeck and myself are the two young American writers who see clearly what must be done and are doing it, each in our own way.

It was difficult now for any writer to remain aloof from the alienating tide of world history. Even the withdrawn O'Neill, "horrified at Hitler," had lately outlined a play "dramatizing his hatred of statism" and had half jokingly sent it to Louis B. Mayer and Sam Goldwyn with a price tag of a million dollars! At the same time the splintered Zelda Fitzgerald was toying with the notion that fascism might be a way of holding the world together.

Quite apart from political considerations, Odets suspects that—because audiences "have been corrupted by the movies and cheap magazines"—even in the American legitimate theatre, let alone in the film industry, the aspirations of a serious writer are increasingly in jeopardy, as, two decades later, one of his successful students, William Gibson, would affirm:

. . . one might say many enthusiastic and truthful things about the rewards of the professional theater, such as the money, and the comradeship, and the money, and the self-espials, and the money, but to me they all lay in the arms of the truth that the theater, in this country, in this decade, was primarily a place not in which to be serious, but in which to be likeable; and it behooved each of us in it to do careful bookkeeping on his soul, lest it grow, like the dyer's hand, subdued to what it works in.

Halfway through the Boston tryout, restless, impatient, and drinking a great deal of scotch, Odets writes a long journal entry that is lively and revelatory:

It is getting to be "another day" here. Harold sort of pecked at the lack of rehearsal discipline at the rehearsal he called for today. The show was very slow and unconcentrated last night. By now, of course, the whole thing bores me almost beyond endurance; so I left the rehearsal and walked up the avenue and bought some shirts and some toilet water and French soap for some of the people. Then there was a late dinner and the evening performance which I watched with a hypnotic glare born out of absolute boredom. Some of the Theatre Guild people were over to see our show which they seemed to like. Tomorrow and Thursday there will be exchange matinees— their company sees our show and we see theirs.

After the show, while Harold, Gadget [Kazan] and I sat over drinks at the Ritz bar, I kept thinking about my real need for a certain kind of woman, one who would be able to control me and help give this blasted life of mine some kind of form. I feel sure she is hiding in an Eskimo igloo! This way, alone, half of my life is wasted, without definition and clarity. How a good woman could help me; for I seem unable to help myself.

The other day I was realizing what had happened to me as a child in school and that the same thing must happen today to children. The school system and the teachers bred in me such a respect for authority that it amounted in the end to a sort of systematic terrorization. Most of the time in school I was so numbed by fear that my ability to think and see what they put in front of me was close to nil. I distinctly remember my fear of competition, too—if I had to work rapidly and competitively it was all over with me before I started. Actually those early school years taught me to immediately reject what was not immediately simple or soluble for me. The fear of failure and concomitant disgrace, censure and punishment actually made a sort of half wit of me. For years afterwards the ordinary smell of library paste made my heart beat faster, for that smell meant school. Those early school years have left a permanent mark on my mind: I think with difficulty altho my logical sense is fine and my feelings and intuitions are first rate. It is only in the last few years that I am able to follow a difficult thought out to its resolution.

"Open for me, open, darling—open the door!" That, if you please, is the cry of youth, the cry of the poet, my personal cry. When you stop crying that, you are getting old.

ABOUT SELF INDULGENCE: When you look for accommodation from every one and everything, when you demand comfort and affirmation from all contacts, then you are what is called self indulgent. That has its value and its place, but it is ruinous as a steady diet, for it develops nothing of genuine importance in the personality. Au contraire, it pinches off, chokes off thousands of new experiences, and finally imprisons one in the strongest jail of all—the human senses: it is as if one lived in a cushioned cell with never a new book to read: it is never meeting people in their amazing variety. Development comes from directly dealing with what irks and troubles one; self indulgence forbids such direct dealing.

Jane Wyatt sits around at rehearsals, her skirt slightly lifted. I yearn to see her legs. Finally after weeks, her skirt lifts high enough for me to see them. I quickly turn my head away, I can't look.

There is a favorite expression in our country: "Be Yourself." Which means exactly the opposite of what it says. It means be like me and my friend, not like yourself. Conform, it means!

The mysterious K—the magic C!

Wyatt comes from the American aristocracy. In herself she shows some of its best qualities, but her relatives who visited her after the opening, they show some of its worse. Their faces are handsome, blank and brutal. They remind one of the Italian aristocracy as painted by the great Italian painters. The face of Doris Duke, often seen in the newsprint, is a good example. There is little or no nuance in the face; it shows a lack of inner life and experience, a lack of values of the spirit. The men and women behind these faces will brook little or no opposition, accept no "incomplete" values, entertain no complexity of emotion or situation. Finally, they are not really open to life, but only to the known, to that which is simply understood and grasped immediately, to all that is already digested, already conquered, already certain. The wages of their sins are in what they are: they are deeply punished for their easeful wealth and position!

Father Coughlin said on the radio, last Sunday, that only two choices are open to the world today—Christ or Marx. Selah!

I used to worry about this question: "Is this my best play to date?" Now I say, "This is another play."

More and more I grow to have deep respect for good workmanship. It is almost impossible to accept sincerity and sensitivity in its place, particularly when they are generalized under the heading of "art" or "artiness."

Self indulgence may come, too, from an ardent (but secret) desire to bring a divided personality together. In other words, you have nagged and despised yourself, refused to accept yourself for so many years—now accept, do not refuse any impulse.

Luise Rainer was one of the several persons in my life who prepared me for life. She is alive in me in many ways, some excellent. Our brief time together was necessary for both of us.

I am crying out for form (and a person to give it) in a confused wilderness of many feelings and contradictions. This problem in myself, a minor artist, makes me understand the same problem in a major artist, Beethoven. This is true of his personal life and his work: Every time he found a form for his content he simultaneously found that his content had progressed in depth and a new form was necessary—a very tantalus of life! He, however, had the hard-headedness to see it thru to the very bitter end—He obviously died looking for a new form—and he died having pushed music to a level which before had never been attained nor has yet been equalled. Great unhappy man!

With two performances to go in Boston, he concludes, "This hasn't been a pleasant experience, for several reasons."

One is that we haven't profited from the tryout period, and the other reasons all stem from Harold's character. He has a deep lack of capacity for work. He falls into certain doldrums, certain saragossas of the senses. Twice he sat at afternoon rehearsals and permitted the company to rattle thru their lines. Later, when I asked him why he hadn't used each rehearsal for some particular purpose (work on characterizations, etc.) he stammered out some feeble apology, flushed into silence, and that was the end of that. There are periodic times in Harold's life when he falls into a sort of profound bafflement; they are bad for the people he is working with, myself included, for they drag all of the work down to the level of these sub-normal phases of his life. In the end, now at least, I will have to say this about him: He is no organizer, one half director, great critic when and if one of his clear phases meets material before it. His inability to establish discipline, for rehearsals and other purposes, is shocking. With some exaggeration of fact, the merest member of the company is able to gain more personal respect from his fellow actors than is the director of the play! This has one good effect—it relaxes the players so that their most creative feelings and ideas are permitted free play. But as you watch, week after week, you discover that the actor needs a firm hand to guide and tie up his ideas into proper forms and finished performances.

I think he is extremely fortunate to have Group actors with whom to work; other actors would show up his fatal flaw in him almost as soon as he started with them. This flaw or split in Harold's personality seems to me explainable by the quality of his genius or talent, altho genius is close to the proper word. That quality is best explained by the phrase "The Russian temperament" as it was used in the old sense when talking of Doistoevsky characters. They are men of moods, not of action; they are deeply intuitive, "irrational," and their experience comes slow and whole; nothing in life, not life itself is utilitarian in any sense of the word; they bathe in their impressions, they stammer, are incoherent nine tenths of the time, and yet their inner climate is one of intense spirituality and truthfulness; they are mostly completely the opposite of the average American male—inefficient, inept, clumsy, never impatient of results, never "complete," trusting an inner "instinct," lacking clarity, general instead of concrete . . . in short, the Russian soul!!!

He is much preoccupied with Clurman's limitations, as though a psychological mastery of his friend's dynamics would offer him a modicum of relief from his own anxieties:

He, as usual, was non-committal, as he always is when he is not able to handle actual material from which to start reacting. He is the best reactor I know, but with no actual material as a base he is hopeless and lost. His talent is deeply analytic, never synthetic, as I more and more find out, from day to day. He cannot build or put together; he can only take apart, analyze, interpret what is in front of him to be interpreted. In a curious way he is only half a man, a kind of centaur, a sort of Rodin man half out of the block of marble; but the man half is amazingly alive and real, sensitive, struggling in some mysterious dark fashion which I only half understand. . . .

Then, with considerable guilt and some sense of proportion, he adds that in himself there is an "unyielding quality" which is his misfortune "as a person" but which "will be in the end my salvation as an artist." He writes:

All this about Harold is troubling me, altho I don't take it as seriously as it sounds on the page. Firstly, I share myself some of these "faults" I find in him; and secondly, he is nevertheless enormously gifted as a stage director. But what troubles me is his kind of philosophical detachment about his faults, i.e., "that is how one is and that is how one goes."

Despite his serious reservations about Clurman's staging, there is no hint in his journal that he (or anyone in the Group) is in that special kind of theatre panic which overcomes a company when, rightly or wrongly, it feels itself to be "in trouble" before a New York opening. Indeed, he is gratified that the cast of Hemingway's Spanish Civil War play, *The Fifth Column,* also trying out in Boston, seemed to like his play. Franchot Tone, Katherine Locke, and Lee J. Cobb came backstage with Lee Strasberg, their director, "a bearer of a terrible uneasy calm which will crack his arteries prematurely." Strasberg, Odets writes, "gave snatches of criticism to Gadget, but he has so little courage to directly front something that everything he says comes out in mysterious bits and fragments which add up to making no sense whatsoever." Indeed, it seems to him that Lee is increasingly

A peculiar character, more and more withdrawn into himself each year. He knows more about actors and their working problems than any man in this country; but he is something like a great pianist who dries up before a concert audience. At present, from the Theatre Guild, he is taking orders meekly enough, keeping his mouth shut and minding his own business. In the Broadway theatre he is a fish out of water; for one who knows his talent he is a moving figure. But he has made all his problems for himself, including his break with the Group.

At the "very last hour" in Boston, an idea for a new play comes to him: a "little play but amusing and sad . . . a 'bad girl' named Mae or Julia wants to marry and settle down." In two hours he has laid out the first two acts. "That is the nature of my talent—bing—and there is a play." But for the New York opening, he would remain in Boston, certain that within two or three weeks he would have a "very presentable first draft." He could call it *She Wants to Marry*. He has tucked the notes for safe-keeping into the inside pocket of his jacket, and will continue it in New York unless a different play he is mulling, "one of bigger feeling and intention," will come to life.

In seven hours, with Bette beside him in his Cadillac, he drives back to New York, where once more the day will "cluster around the work and thought about *Night Music*"—restaging certain bits, changing a line here and there, and watching the preview audiences. One is "poorish," the next—with "an intelligent audience for a wonder!"—goes well. He could not tell what the young playwright Bill Saroyan thought, as he was "very cordial and very restless under his youthful face. His mind as he talks to you is always tinkling like a tinkle-toy, but not with what he happens to be saying to you at the moment." Tired, he writes, "If the show goes as well tomorrow night as it did tonight, we are in for a run."

On February 22, 1940, Odets' journal entry is restless but cheerful:

This is the time for opening the play. Harold gave the cast a brief line run-thru, but I stayed at home, sleeping, resting, lounging it out against my slowly constricting nerves. Restless, finally, I jumped into the roadster and rode out to Sunnyside to take Bill [Kozlenko] and Lee to dinner. I chattered away, quite calm, really to that peculiar point of indifference which comes from having done all that one can do in a situation. We rode into New York and had dinner across the street from the theatre, at Sardi's. A lot of the people who were going across to the show were eating dinner there—it was like running the gauntlet. Stella Adler was there with a party, smoke-eyed and neurotic—usually when *you* are dying *she* is more dramatic about the event than you are! Finally I pushed my way thru a lot of well wishing people and went over to the theatre. The cast was in fine shape, quietly making up in their own rooms; no noise, no excitement backstage, things routined and orderly.

The audience was no better or worse than the usual opening night crowd. If anything they were an edge more respectful. Harold I had met outside the theatre for a moment—he was white and tired and was going to see a musical comedy, true to his habit of never attending an opening. I, on the other hand, get a kind of perverse spiteful pleasure from attending an opening. I saw none of the critics but shook hands with several friends.

The performance of the play was tiptop—the cast had never been better. The play suffered from what had always been wrong with it because of a certain lack in the direction—a lack of clear outlining of situations, a lack of building up scenes, a certain missing in places of dramatic intensity. But none of these things were enough to do vital harm to a beautiful show, smooth, powerful and yet tender, fresh, moving and touching, with real quality in all the parts. But I could see during the first act that the audience was taking it more seriously than it deserved; and I knew that the old thing was here again—the critics had come expecting a King Lear, not a small delicate play. I knew again that their preconceptions had armed them against this play. It all made me very tired, but at the end I thought to myself that it didn't matter, for the show was more or less what I intended; it was lovely and fresh, no matter what the critics said. And I knew, too, that if another and unknown writer's name had been on the script, there would have been critical raves the next day.

People surged back stage after the curtain—they all seemed to have had a good time. There were the usual foolish remarks from many of them, "Enjoyable, but I don't know why," etc., etc. Also a good deal of insincere gushing from a lot of people who would like nothing better than to stick a knife in your ribs, God knows why!

I invited some people down to the house for a drink. Along came the Eislers, Kozlenkos, Betty, Julie Garfield, Boris Aronson, old Harry Carey and his wife, Morris and Phoebe [Carnovsky] later, Harold, Aaron Copland and Victor, Bobby Lewis and his Mexican bitch, etc. etc. We drank champagne, scotch when the wine ran out, talked, smoked, filthied up the house, listened to some music. Then they went and I dropped into bed, dog-tired, unhappy, drunk, knowing what the reviews would be like in the morning. In and out I slept, in and out of a fever—all of modern 20th century life in one day and a night.

The next morning came as a dreadful lightning bolt, and this journal entry is the last for ten days:

The biggest shock I have experienced since the auto crash in Mexico a year ago was the reviews of the play today. Perhaps it was the serious lack of sleep which kept me so calm and quiet. I wanted to send the Times man a wire telling him I thought his notice stupid and insulting, but I gave up that idea after a while. Equally distressing to me was the attitude at the office, an ugly passivity—they are quite inured there to the humdrum commercial aspect of doing a play this way—close if the notices are bad.

My feelings were and are very simple. I felt as if a lovely delicate child, tender and humourous, had been knocked down by a truck and lay dying. For this show has all the freshness of a child. It was Boris A.* who called the turn. He said, "this show is very moving to me, a real art work, but I don't think they will get its quality—it is not commercial."

In the morning I cashed fifteen thousand dollars worth of the baby bonds I hold. I thought to spend it on advertising, to keep the show open, etc., but by the time I finished at the office in the afternoon it was easy to see the foolishness of that; the show costs almost ten thousand a week to run.

So, friend, this is the American theatre, before, now and in the future. This is where you live and this is what it is—this is the nature of the beast. Here is how the work and delight and pain of many months end up in one single night. This is murder, to be exact, the murder of loveliness, of talent, of aspiration, of sincerity, the brutal imperception and indifference to one of the few projects which promise to keep the theatre alive. And it is murder in the first degree—with forethought (perhaps not malice, perhaps!) not second or third degree. Something will have to be done about these "critics," these lean dry men who know little or nothing about the theatre, despite their praise of the actors and production. How can it happen that

* Set designer Boris Aronson.

this small handful of men can do such murderous mischief in a few hours? How can it be that we must all depend on them for our progress and growth, they who maybe drank a cocktail too much, quarreled with a wife, had indigestion or a painful toe before they came to see the play—they who are not critics, who are insensitive, who understand only the most literal realism, they who should be dealing in children's abc blocks? How can the audience be reached directly, without the middleman intervention of these fools?

I think now to write very inexpensive plays in the future, few actors, one set; perhaps hire a cheap theatre and play there. Good or bad, these "critics" must never be quoted, they must not opportunistically be used. A way must be found to beat them if people like myself are to stay in the theatre with any health and love. Only bitterness results this way, with no will or impulse for fresh work. The values must be sorted out and I must see my way clearly ahead, for I mean to work in the American theatre for many years to come.

I have such a strong feeling—a lovely child was murdered yesterday. Its life will drag on for another week or ten days, but the child is already stilled. A few friends will remember, that's all.

Two decades later Odets would freshly recall his sorrow when, having brought his $15,000 to the Group office, he realized "the fight had gone out of them all, and I saw they were beaten." At this point, he told Peter Bogdanovich, "I went to the men's room and I cried. I cried for five minutes. And that was the end of the Group Theatre."

After twenty-two performances and two weeks of merciless beatings from critics on the Left and on the Right (the reviews had a hostile edge even worse than those of *Paradise Lost*), *Night Music* would close. The attacks overwhelmed Odets, with phrases ringing in his head like "a foolish play from a man of great talent," "The White Hope Grows Paler," "When Odets Imitates Saroyan Doomsday Is Near," or (throwing back at him his quoting of Oscar Wilde) ". . . having nothing to say and saying it." The content of the onslaught ranged from criticism of its "confused" political as well as its dramatic content to its stylistic immaturity, uncertainty, and sentimentality. Especially bitter to Odets were the attacks from those middle-class critics who had earlier decried his political dogmatism as a youthful limitation. Now they missed it:

Obviously the play belonged to a new development in Mr. Odets' career. It still had about it that vitality in phrasing and attack which is the unique stamp of Mr. Odets' talent. Its writing was frequently pungent. Its images were often driven home as with a pneumatic drill. Its characters were from time to time established with incisive vigor which is Mr. Odets' pre-eminent aesthetic possession. But the old dogmatism, which in large part was responsible for the force of the earlier Odets dramas, was missing.

Without it Mr. Odets seemed lost. So was his play. The absence of the erstwhile cocksure conviction may be taken as a proof of intellectual growth. It is a good thing always for an artist to realize that black and white are not the only colors. Still, without his former blinders, Mr. Odets appeared to be looking out on a world which (for him) was strangely gray. . . . Somehow, as one listened to these pallid words crudely stated, one missed the old, brave dream of a new world; the angry cries of "Strike, Strike, Strike!!"; and the sudden spiritual rebirths which, in the pattern of Mr. Odets' earlier plays, have put in their appearance almost with the regularity of the marines.

It comforted him not at all that John Mason Brown in this savage review granted that, even "indifferent or poor, Odets is far more exciting to listen to than what the majority of playwrights can turn out." Brown called him an "under-achieving" but gifted youngster who still promised much ("one wonders when the lightning will strike next").

A few days after the opening, a letter came from his father in Los Angeles, no longer on the old Doctors of Sleep stationery: instead, a newly printed banner headline in large red capital letters advised the world to "LITE THE WAY TO BUSINESS—AT THE POINT OF SALE" and under it, in even larger black capitals, "ODETS SALES COMPANY COLD LITE SIGNS." The letter commenced—like a character in an Odets play—with the hollowest of reassurances, its content and its reiteration of the word "big" not unlike Odets' whispers to himself:

> Dear Cliff:
> Just received a letter and clippings of the show. There not so good, but they are not bad. The show rates much better.—I can recall when I read the first write-up on "Golden Boy" in the Herald T. It was pretty bad, you know the results.
> I believe that "Night Music" will go over *Big*. I am not just writing this to try and make you feel good—I honestly believe it will. It is a good show, tender, full of fire-crackers, effective scenes and according to the critic's, the acting is good. I don't mean that critic ??(shit ass)?? Col'd'eman.* You wait and see.
> You know "big boy," every prominent person must pay. If some "cluck" wrote the play, the critic's would probably say, in fact I feel sure they would say "a very intertaining show, scenes packed full of dynamite"—but Mr. Clifford Odets America's leading dramatist wrote it. Therefore no good. We expect the World's best drama from him, not just good entertainment.
> Cheer up. The Sun shines, then shines again. Remember the "old man" is telling you that "Night Music" will be successful. Please, Cliff, don't let that worry you. It's just another step in your life. There never lived a human, who was big enough to make steps, that some people did not knock and kick. The Sun keeps shining.
> Let me know what you expect to do. Let me live with you in thought since I can't be with you all the time in person. Be happy "big Boy" the world moves fast.

It was important to L. J. Odets on practical grounds that *Night Music* be a commercial success, since

> My business has got me stymied. I can get plenty of sales, but the manufacturing is off. On account of the war the raw material used in the signs is not pure enough. They are trying to clean it up. In the mean time I have to wait.

With the writer's weapon of choice, Odets tried now to hit back at the critics in a mocking, revengeful piece for the *World-Telegram*. Basing it on his perceptions of the actual personalities of the critics who had, after mowing it down, left his "child" to die by the roadside, he wrote a composite "interview":

* Critic Robert Coleman of *The Daily Mirror*.

THE MOROSE MR. MORGAN
OR
INTERVIEW WITH A CRITIC
BY
CLIFFORD ODETS

Last week, after the opening of my new play, *Night Music,* I decided to track down a great mystery to its source. I wanted to find out what a drama critic is, how he works, what makes him go and "where he lives" in general. . . .

Altho we had not met face to face, the morose Mr. Morgan was very gracious when I rang his doorbell hard by the East River. . . .

"What do you want?" he asked. . . .

"I came," I answered, "to examine and understand the psychological progression of a drama critic." . . .

"Of course," he said with a certain trick of abrupt perception, "you were dissatisfied with the notices we gave your *Night Music.*"

"True, true . . . ," I said, growing accustomed to the gloom of this eagle's nest. "Not only that," I added, "but I want one intelligent man to explain to another altho younger man from what standards the critics review the work of a playwright whose talents they profess to admire." . . .

"Here's your first question, Mr. Odets." He ran a small tongue precisely across his lips. "You want to know why we don't distinguish in our reviews between the ordinary commercial showpiece and plays of genuine merit and importance, incomplete tho they may be. Your complaint is that we lump both together and fail to distinguish the difference of creative level for the reader. Correct?"

"Correct, Mr. Morgan. Why?"

"Because we have a duty to our readers, too, not only to the theatre. We have to tell them where they get their money's worth."

"What constitutes 'their money's worth'?"

"Some show, some trifle that amuses them for an hour."

"Then how about leading public theatre appetite instead of following behind it? Will there ever be a serious American theatre of real substance and depth so long as the serious theatre workers are not given the same helping hand which is extended to the Broadway shrewdlings?"

"Whoa," Mr. Morgan said, lifting a gentle hand, "you're going too fast for me. But I do agree with you to some extent; we seem to approve whole-heartedly only when a play has nothing to say and says it well."

"Why is that?" I asked. . . .

"Perhaps," he said, "because a complete thing is always more satisfying to one's human enough nature. Perhaps because we assume that our ability as critics is measured by our abilities to gauge a success from a failure. Maybe because the bird who flies high is most open to a shot. Fellows like yourself, Anderson and a handful of others are trying to express serious and important ideas in the world today. Perhaps you yourselves force us to approach you over-critically." . . .

"One of your brother jurists," I went on, "famous for his seasonal collection of 'The Best Ten Plays,' has frequently given my opening plays a two star plus rating; then had to include them in his collection at the end of the year. How do you explain that, Mr. Morgan?"

"Am I my brother's keeper?" was the gentle reply. Then, "But be content, Mr. Odets . . . he seldom gives more than two stars to Shakespeare. . . .

"Critics here run from the curtain to the typewriter—there are such things as deadlines. . . . Add to that the fact that few of us have space for second reviews or comments. Often, come to think of it, we are lucky that our reviews make downright sense. . . .

"And we have other faults," he continued sadly. "Sometimes we come to a play with a preconception of what we are about to see. If several of us had not been forewarned that O'Neill's *Ah, Wilderness* was a little comedy," the results might have been extremely disastrous for all concerned. Likewise, as ordinary human beings, can we not be excused for writhing before the third military academy play in one short season? Or let us say that the season has been very dull; isn't it understandable that we are apt to rave about the first fairish play which comes along?" . . .

"And remember this," I said, quickly for I could see a certain morose look coming to Morgan's face, "you are always making easy frames of reference for yourselves by saying my plays are like Tchekov or O'Casey. . . ."

"Yes, yes," Morgan murmured sadly, "just as you say . . . an easy frame of reference. But we're tired men, Mr. Odets, over worked. . . ."

In the deepening gloom I lighted a cigarette and turned to the door. It was plain to see that Mr. Morgan was well out of this world. He was talking, half to himself it seemed.

"I'd rather be a playwright," he was saying. Again and again he repeated that simple haunting phrase, "I'd rather be a playwright . . ."

It seemed shameful to listen. As softly as possible, I closed the door behind me. . . .

Suddenly I understood the world of Mr. Morgan and was feeling very guilty.

It is clear from his next journal entry, the first since the reviews, that his self-purging article on the critics had not brought much relief:

I have no heart to sum up the week—it has been one of blind fury for me, with a hard tautness of nerves. I am still smarting from this strange so-called critical drubbing which I took at the hands of the reviewers. Everything they wrote was beside the point.

The pain of the past week has been a double one for me. On one side are the reviews and the really irresponsible men who wrote them; and on the other side is my profound dissatisfaction with Harold's direction of the play and the general condition of the Group at present. Harold must lessen the gap between his first rate critical perceptions and production intentions with a play of mine, and what he finally produces on the stage. There is something positively weird and ununderstandable about his inability to work into a production the brilliant ideas with which he starts rehearsals. For instance, he starts with an idea that Steve Takis is a Pierrot and must be played that way. It finally ends up with Gadget Kazan getting brilliant notices for a clumsy, brutal clodhopperish performance of the part.

And now comes the first step in discharging his debt to the motion-picture firm of Loew-Lewin, without which, after all, the production would not have taken place:

Al Lewin flew in with his entourage to see the play. He was dissatis-fied, as above, with the production, but he expressed delight that the script was exactly what he thought it. Al and I had a few talks about the movie and I begin to see headaches ahead. Al, despite a certain gentleness and sensitivity, is just as much a Hollywood man as a Mayer or Zanuck.

This is immediately followed by "No, I have no patience to write anything here. I am restless and squirming all over." Having said this, he moves into a long discussion of how easy it is for Sylvia Sidney to turn Luther Adler "against his best self" because, in his opinion, Luther, "a young growing artist," is always "looking for support and a steel wrist to guide him." As always, his insight is keenest into problems which mirror his own.
     After a long psychological analysis of Sylvia Sidney's relationship to her mother, he comes back to his own struggle and to his efforts to deal with it:

Don't ask me to write here clearly about myself and the failure of "Night Music." I am much too confused. In the meantime I took over last week's losses, between three and four thousand. For this coming week we have taken ads which announce the closing. Losses will be another three or four, I imagine.
     In the midst of all this I began rereading Stendahl [sic], C of Parma. I learn much from him and am entertained greatly. He offers, by the way, an absolutely indispensable picture of his Times for an understanding of Beethoven. B has a great deal in common with Stendahl heroes, so have I, so has many a modern middle class youth a hundred years later. Class lines are very well drawn in Stendahl, too. The issues which agitated the surface of that life are all written out and explained by S. Haydn, for instance, wore a powdered wig and Beethoven did not. That seems a small trifle, but read S. and you find that wearing one's own hair unpowdered was the sure sign of the radical of the day, etc., etc.
     At the moment, because of this production catastrophe, I have no direction, only confusion. My one desire is to get out and away from this painful treading on water. Also, I am torn between my friendship for Harold and my loyalty to my own development as a writer. Harold no longer helps me, rather hinders me. And no friend-ship can help me excuse the lamentable bungling of my last two scripts under his hands. You must learn to speak the most important things in your mind, not the unimportant but easy and comfortable ones. You have a despised weakness this way—change it, fix it, make it better!!!
     But this horrible experience has not been all dead loss and waste. No, I learned a few indelible (!) items from this production. One is never never [to] trust an American audience to understand a char-acter whose psychology is in any way involved. Absolutely indis-pensable to Night Music was what is nicely enough called in Holly-wood "A rooting interest." This had to be aroused in Steve's behalf in the audience by very clearly stating to them at the opening, "This boy is the hero, I want you to know that he is a nice boy, like him, laugh at him, don't take him too seriously." Without this greased slide

into the play an average audience in this country (not Europe) is unable to relax and sit back and enjoy the play. An American audience wants everything clearly explained and labelled before a scene starts. Otherwise they will not hear a line of the scene and they will complain that the play is confused and unclear. Nor, once you have shown them the type, must a character indulge in "unpredictable" behavior. That was the trouble for them with Rocket To The Moon. I showed them familiar types but their end behavior was not familiar at all. For this reason they said the first half of the play was brilliant, but the second half was confused. The second half was not confused at all, but it contained MY conception of the behavior and meaning of the familiar types. It was the conception which they could not follow, would not or could not take. Ibsen had this same trouble. In fact, I seem to remember that this is what Shaw's Essay on Ibsen is about. I must reread it. But right now I know that Ibsen overcame this problem in a rich craft way. His "A Doll's House" and others will bear rereading and study. I can remember that the way he leads up to Nora's final act makes you accept that final act, unconventional as it was at the time. That is what I must learn to do. Even at that, my audience will not accept the unconventional point of view, for they understand, with that intuitive sense that all audiences have, that what I am saying is really opposed to them and their interests as respectable citizens of society. The freezing of a wealthy benefit audience at a first performance of Paradise Lost I can never forget! Yes, great craft cunning is necessary and you are not working enough on it.

Now one beautiful thing this past week was a boyhood sense of the seasons of the year which suddenly came upon me. I found I was keenly aware of the succession of seasons. It gave me a deep feeling to sense the winter going and spring rains coming. It is March now and wind and rain is here and the rightness of it makes me feel very good, just as it did when I was a boy. I would be missing a good deal to give up the imminent spring by going south or to California now. It has been raining for two days. Warm March rain, warm in feeling but cold in fact as wires and poles are coated with ice. Warm to me, for it is the beginning of spring and I hope a useful healthy spring: There is so much work to be done, so much work oh work work and use of the self in earnest sincere useful work!

Nine months earlier, on his thirty-third birthday, Odets had written a preface to a collection of his six plays, calling them a "first-period" group. Now, in this "healthy spring" of 1940, it was not given him to know how many endings he had come to. He had been, in the 1930s, "the playwright of the decade"; the decade had ended. In a matter of weeks the great powers would be convulsed in a war (no longer "phony") which would alter the face of the globe; the world which had shaped Odets, and for which he had written, was ended. The Depression was lifting, and the moral simplicities of that time were ended, and the individual soul's unshackling in the liberation of the working class was no longer a tenable faith. The wild hopes in the title *Awake and Sing!* had given way to the grim mood of the final stanza of Matthew Arnold's "Dover Beach," the last three words of which he would take as the title of his new play:

> . . . the world, which seems
> To lie before us like a land of dreams,
> So various, so beautiful, so new,
> Hath really neither joy, nor love, nor light,
> Nor certitude, nor peace, nor help for pain;
> And we are here as on a darkling plain
> Swept with confused alarms of struggle and flight,
> Where ignorant armies clash by night.

Closest to hand, the Group Theatre had ended, and with it Odets' explosively productive years as an artist; the "first period" group of six plays produced in four years would be succeeded by several films and only four plays produced during the twenty-three years that were left to him. And in these twenty-three years, hounded in turn by political witch-hunters and by his own demons, he would restlessly move from East Coast to West Coast and back until his final ending in the only cemetery in the world with gold funerary boxes.

Personal Chronology of Clifford Odets

Born July 18, 1906; Died August 14, 1963

July 18, 1906	Clifford Odets born (prematurely) to Pearl Geisinger Odets and Louis Odets at 207 George Street, Philadelphia.
1908–1916 (Age 2–8)	Family makes three moves: to the Bronx, New York; to Philadelphia; and back to New York. Sister Genevieve born 1910; sister Florence, 1916.
1921–1923 (Age 15–17)	Enters Morris High School; wins first place in declamation contest; acts in school plays. Leaves school in 1923.
1924–1929 (Age 18–23)	Member of Drawing Room Players; becomes "The Rover Reciter"; acts in Harry Kemp's Poet's Theatre; "youngest drama critic in New York" (Walter Winchell); first disc jockey on radio (WBNY); also recites on various other New York and Philadelphia stations; writes radio play, *At the Water-Line,* produced by two radio stations in New York and one in Philadelphia. Joins Mae Desmond Players, also acts with Union City Stock Company; drama counsellor at summer camps. Presumably marries Roberta (surname unknown), who allegedly shoots their child, Joan, and commits suicide.
1929–1930 (Age 23–24)	Understudies Spencer Tracy in Broadway production of *Conflict;* an extra with Theatre Guild touring company. Works on a novel, *The Brandy of the Damned* (unpublished). Juvenile lead in Theatre Guild production of *Midnight.* Early meetings of Group Theatre.
1931 (Age 25)	Group Theatre officially formed; Odets invited to be a charter member; given a few small parts. Writes plays, *910 Eden Street* and *Victory* (both unpublished).
1932 (Age 26)	Understudies Luther Adler in John Howard Lawson's *Success Story.* Starts writing plays: *I Got the Blues,* to become *Awake and Sing!* Directs and acts in *Precedent* (about Tom Mooney) in Philadelphia.
1933 (Age 27)	Has lead in *They All Come to Moscow.* Second act of *Awake and Sing!* presented by Group Theatre at Green Mansions, New York (summer camp). Has part in Sidney Kingsley's *Men in White.*
1934 (Age 28)	Commences writing *Paradise Lost.* Writes one-act play, *Waiting for Lefty,* in three nights during Group Theatre rehearsals of another play in Boston. *Waiting for Lefty* wins *New Theatre* magazine play contest. *Awake and Sing!* accepted for production by Group Theatre.
1935	
January	*Waiting for Lefty* presented at benefit performance for *New Theatre* magazine (Odets becomes an overnight sensation).
February	*Awake and Sing!* opens at Belasco Theatre. Odets writes *Till the Day I Die* (one act).
March	*Waiting for Lefty* and *Till the Day I Die* open as double bill at Longacre Theatre. *Waiting for Lefty* awarded George Pierce Baker Drama Cup, Yale University.
April	Publication of *Three Plays by Clifford Odets* by Covici-Friede.

May	Death of mother, Pearl Geisinger Odets. Odets writes monologue, *I Can't Sleep* (published in *New Theatre*, February 1936).
July	To Cuba with protest group—arrested and deported.
December	*Paradise Lost* opens at Longacre Theatre.
1936	Odets to Hollywood; writes screenplay *The General Died at Dawn;* meets Luise Rainer; commences play *The Silent Partner;* returns to New York.
1937	Odets and Luise Rainer married in Los Angeles, January 8. Odets writes several screenplays (unproduced). Returns to New York. Writes *Golden Boy,* which opens at Belasco Theatre in November.
1938	*New Yorker* profile, January 28; Odets commences new play, *Rocket to the Moon;* to London for opening of *Golden Boy;* separation from Luise Rainer; *Rocket to the Moon* opens in November at Belasco Theatre; reconciliation with Luise Rainer; *Time* cover story, December 5.
1939	Odets and Luise Rainer separate. Traveling in Cuba and Mexico; working on *The Silent Partner* (unpublished, except for one scene in *New Theatre and Film,* March 1937). Publication of *Six Plays of Clifford Odets* by Random House. Commences new play, *Night Music.*
1940	Meets Bette Grayson, whom he will later marry. Opening of *Night Music* at Broadhurst Theatre in February. Keeps a daily journal during entire year; commences a new play, *Trio,* to become *Clash by Night;* spends a few months in Hollywood writing screenplay of *Night Music* (unproduced).
1941	Finishes first draft of *Clash by Night* in January; however, most of the year spent rewriting and seeking backing for the play. Odets' withdrawal of this play from Group Theatre participation marks final dissolution of the Group. Billy Rose produces the play, starring Tallulah Bankhead, Joseph Schildkraut, and Lee J. Cobb. After a two-month road tour, *Clash by Night* opens at the Belasco Theater on December 27.
1942	To Hollywood to write screenplay for Warner Bros. on life of George Gershwin; the Odets screenplay was tabled, but was later revised and used in a film entitled *Humoresque* starring John Garfield and Joan Crawford. Returns to New York City, and adapts *The Russian People* by Simonoff, for the stage. The play was produced by the Theatre Guild.
1943	Works on adaptation of Franz Werfel's *Jacobowsky and the Colonel,* to be produced as a play and later as a movie. Marries Bette Grayson on May 14. To Hollywood to write screenplay *None But the Lonely Heart* for RKO Pictures, based on the novel by Richard Llewellyn, and subsequently to direct the film, starring Cary Grant, Ethel Barrymore, and Barry Fitzgerald. Both Grant and Barrymore won Academy Awards for their performances.
1944–1948	Writes screenplay of *Deadline at Dawn,* based on novel *Welcome to the City* by William Irish, to be directed by Harold Clurman. Continues living in Hollywood, writing screenplays. For RKO Pictures: *Sister Carrie* (shelved); *The Greatest Gift* (after many revisions by various writers, finally produced as *It's a Wonderful Life* with Jimmy Stewart and Donna Reed); *All Brides Are Beautiful,* to have starred Joan Fontaine (shelved); *Sister Kenny* and *Notorious* (revised further by other writers). For Metro-Goldwyn-Mayer: *The Whispering Cup,* based on Mabel Seeley's novel, to have starred Katharine Hepburn (shelved); and an original screenplay, *April Shower* (never produced).
	Begins an extensive art collection, including paintings and drawings by such artists as Utrillo, Soutine, Braque, Picasso, Matisse, Marin, Cézanne, Rouault, and many others. Develops one of largest collections of Paul Klee works in the United States.

Produces a large volume of his own small watercolors, which are shown in art galleries in New York City and Los Angeles.

A daughter, Nora, born April 18, 1945, and a son, Walt Whitman, born February 4, 1947.

In October 1947 is named by House Un-American Activities Committee as one of seventy-nine "active in Communist work in film colony." In December, Odets attacks the Thomas committee in a letter published in *Time* magazine.

Begins writing *The Big Knife*. Returns to New York City. Writes article for *New York Times*, "On Returning Home" (April 25, 1948).

1948–1954   Living in New York City. *The Big Knife,* starring John Garfield, opens at National Theatre on February 24, 1949; *The Country Girl,* starring Uta Hagen and Paul Kelly, opens at the Lyceum Theatre on November 10, 1950; *The Flowering Peach* opens at the Belasco on December 28, 1954.

Bette Grayson Odets obtains a divorce in November 1951; dies February 1954.

Odets is questioned by the House Un-American Activities Committee in May 1952.

1955–1963   To Hollywood with two children to write screenplay for Columbia Studios *Joseph and His Brethren,* to have starred Rita Hayworth (shelved). For Hecht-Hill-Lancaster: revises screenplay *Sweet Smell of Success,* starring Burt Lancaster and Tony Curtis; writes screenplay based on A. B. Guthrie's novel *The Way West* (shelved). For Jerry Wald at 20th Century-Fox: writes original screenplay and directs *Story on Page One* starring Rita Hayworth and Gig Young (1958–59), *Wild in the Country* (1960) starring Elvis Presley. For Columbia Studios (1961) works on revision of *Walk on the Wild Side,* from the Nelson Algren novel. Receives gold medal award (1961) from American Academy of Arts and Letters. Commences revisions of *Golden Boy* for a musical to star Sammy Davis, Jr. (1962–63). As story editor for NBC-TV dramatic series, "The Richard Boone Show" (1962–63), writes three teleplays and supervises development of story material until death, on August 14, 1963, of cancer.

Works by Clifford Odets

Published and/or Produced Plays, Screenplays, Teleplays
(*Life Works: 1925-1963*)

COLLECTIONS:

Three Plays by Clifford Odets. New York: Covici-Friede, 1935.
Six Plays of Clifford Odets. New York: Grove Press, 1979; Random House, 1939;
    Modern Library, 1939.
Golden Boy, Awake and Sing!, The Big Knife. London: Penguin Books, 1963.

INDIVIDUAL PLAYS:

AWAKE AND SING! New York: Covici-Friede, 1935. In: *Three Plays by Clifford
    Odets; Six Plays of Clifford Odets;* Penguin Books edition. Also in many
    anthologies.
WAITING FOR LEFTY. In: *New Theatre,* Vol. II, No. 2, February 1935. *Three
    Plays by Clifford Odets; Six Plays of Clifford Odets; Representative Ameri-
    can Plays,* ed. Robert Warnock (Oakland, N.J.: Scott, Foresman, 1952);
    and in many other anthologies.
I CAN'T SLEEP. In: *New Theatre,* Vol. III, No. 2, February 1936; *The Anxious
    Years,* ed. Louis Filler (New York: Capricorn, 1964).
PARADISE LOST. New York: Random House, 1936. In: *Six Plays of Clifford Odets.*
TILL THE DAY I DIE. In: *Three Plays by Clifford Odets; Six Plays of Clifford
    Odets;* also in various anthologies.
GOLDEN BOY. New York: Random House, 1937. In: *Six Plays of Clifford Odets;*
    Penguin Books edition; many anthologies.
ROCKET TO THE MOON. New York: Random House, 1939. In: *Six Plays of Clifford
    Odets;* anthologies.
NIGHT MUSIC. New York: Random House, 1940.
CLASH BY NIGHT. New York: Random House, 1942.
THE BIG KNIFE. New York: Random House, 1949; Penguin Books edition.
THE COUNTRY GIRL. New York: Viking Press, 1951; *Theatre Arts,* May 1952.
THE FLOWERING PEACH. In: *The Best Plays of 1954-55* (condensed), ed. Louis
    Kronenberger (New York: Dodd, Mead, 1955). Playing script: Dramatists
    Play Service, New York.
Adaptation: *THE RUSSIAN PEOPLE,* from a play by Konstantin Simonov
    (1943). In: *Seven Soviet Plays,* ed. Henry Wadsworth Longfellow Dana
    (New York: Macmillan, 1946).

SCREENPLAYS (all adapted from previously written material, except for *The
    Story on Page One*):

The General Died at Dawn (Paramount), 1936 (directed by Lewis Milestone).
None But the Lonely Heart (RKO), 1944 (directed by Odets). In: *Best Film
    Plays, 1945,* ed. John Gassner and Dudley Nichols (New York: Crown,
    1946).
Deadline at Dawn (RKO), 1945 (directed by Harold Clurman).

The Sweet Smell of Success (Hecht-Hill-Lancaster), 1957 (directed by Alexander Mackendrick).

The Story on Page One (20th Century-Fox), 1959 (directed by Odets).

Wild in the Country (20th Century-Fox), 1960 (directed by Philip Dunne).

TELEVISION SCRIPTS (NBC, 1963–64): *The Richard Boone Show,* Clifford Odets, Editor)

"The Affair"
"Big Mitch"
"The Mafia Man"

RADIO PLAY:

"At the Water-Line" (1925–26)

MUSICALS BASED ON ODETS' PLAYS:

The Golden Boy Musical (1965), reworked from Odets' libretto by William Gibson after Odets' death (New York: Bantam Books, 1966). (Directed by Arthur Penn.)

Two by Two (1970), (from *The Flowering Peach*), book by Peter Stone. (Directed by Joe Layton.)

(See Bibliography for partial listing of Odets' published articles.)

Completed But Unpublished and/or Unproduced Works*

PLAYS:

"Victory" (1931)
"910 Eden Street" (1931)
"Remember" (one-act) (1935) (no ms. extant)
"Mother's Day" (with Elia Kazan) (1936)
"The Silent Partner" (1936–39). Act II, scene 2 in *New Theatre and Film,* March 1937
"The Cuban Play" or "Law of Flight" (1937–38)
"Three Sisters" (adaptation from Chekhov) (1939)

SCREENPLAYS (adapted from previously written material):

"The River Is Blue" (1936) (later rewritten by John Howard Lawson and Lillian Hellman and produced as *Blockade,* 1938). (Directed by William Dieterle.)
"Gettysburg" (1937)

RADIO PLAYS:

"Dawn" (1925–26)
"The Show Must Go On" (1939)

Various Odets materials may be found in the special collections of the following libraries: Boston University Library, Columbia University Library, New York Public Library (Berg Collection and Research Library for the Performing Arts), University of Pennsylvania Library, Yale University Library, University of California at Los Angeles, University of California at Irvine, University of Texas.

* These include writings up to and including 1939 only; subsequent works will be listed in Volume II of this biography. All manuscripts are part of the Literary Estate of Clifford Odets.

Notes and Comment

MATERIAL RELEVANT TO THIS SECTION IS MARKED
WITH THE SYMBOL ⟨ IN THE TEXT.

p. 18 1.1 Israel Zangwill gave voice to the confused and solitary struggles
of immigrants in his play *The Melting Pot*, first produced in
1908, contributing its title to America. Stung by a critic who
dismissed this play as "romantic claptrap" which rhapsodized
over "crucibles and Statues of Liberty," Zangwill replied that
the critic, "never having lacked Liberty, nor cowered for days
in a cellar in terror of a howling mob, can see only theatrical
exaggeration in the enthusiasm for a land of freedom." Soon
after, Abraham Cahan, editor of the *Jewish Daily Forward* for
fifty years, would write *The Rise of David Levinsky* and Mary
Antin, *The Promised Land*.

p. 19 1.2 Cf. Ella Quinlan O'Neill and Eugene O'Neill—or Odets' love of
Klee's "Dance of the Grieving Child."

p. 20 1.3 It is an irony of history that a majority of this Third Wave of
Jews who had fled Eastern Europe for the Land of Opportunity
would become so occupied with the necessity of earning a living that they would never have the chance to cultivate their
individual talents. It is precisely *their* sense of "missed opportunities" that increased the pressure on their children for high
accomplishment. For some, this pressure was onerous; for
others supportive and liberating.

p. 22 1.4 The following excerpts from original interview notes are taken
from a 200-page record of verbatim dialogue. It is an instructive
privilege for a clinical biographer to experience the direct impact of a personality so formidable and archetypal as L. J. Odets.
This experience illuminates the staggering sentence Odets wrote
less than a year before his death, a sentence which sums up
his internal struggle and his lifelong relationship to his father:
"Hapless and helpless. The Jewish prophet is being eaten alive
by the Jewish father in me, and if somewhere it doesn't stop
soon, I shall be indeed dead."*

For almost two years Louis J. Odets ignored my letters requesting an interview. To Odets' former secretary and then to
Odets' son, both of whom tried to help, he would make such
comments as: "Those shit-ass" Gibsons and Strasbergs had
some nerve "trying to tell *me* what to do. . . . First thing you
know they'll be letting me sweep the floor."† "Who the hell died
and left him [William Gibson] boss? . . . A couple of tricky
snotnoses, ignorant. . . . Clifford was *somebody*. I could see

---

* Letter to Margaret Brenman-Gibson, October 23, 1962.
† L. J. Odets to Virginia Rowe, telephone conversation, July 15, 1964.

him bigger than he could see himself. . . . Are they trying to bully me or outsmart me? After all, we're talking about a character the Good Lord endowed with gifts he gives to only one in a hundred million. . . . That man made millions, millions, and now he leaves buttons and shoestrings. . . . There is a beautifull story there. . . ."*

After numerous transcontinental phone calls this lonely old man finally relented, saying, ". . . but use your head for something besides a hatrack—it won't do you any good whatsoever." I flew out to Los Angeles on the chance. Then seventy-nine years old, this widower, living on Social Security in a seedy, small apartment, picked me up in a long black Chrysler (probably rented), opening the door for me in a tyrannical, even bullying caricature of courtly ingratiation. Once in the car, there immediately ensued hostile, crude sexual advances of such magnitude that the sentence (often recorded by Odets in his diary as his own response to his father) "How dare you!" kept running through my head. The total disregard of one's essence was the most outrageous part of the experience.

The most revealing incident—partly because it was so unnerving—occurred after I had listened to four hours of his monologue about everyone's indebtedness to him for all he had done for them, and what evil, ungrateful, and envious children he had, and the details of his sexual relationship with both his wives, and how his son had "pauperized" him by his economic dependence all his life (the reverse was, of course, the fact). I now asked rather casually, "When did the name change from Gorodetsky to Odets?" At first, incredulous, he flatly denied that his father's name had ever been Gorodetsky. When he saw that I knew there had been a name-change, the ingratiation and flirtation ceased. Replacing it was a mounting white fury in which he screamed and pounded the furniture: "If you put *that* in your book, I'll make life for you totally miserable. . . . If you *dare* to put that in the book, I'll make such trouble for you as you've never had in your life . . . trouble like you never saw before. You'll destroy Clifford's reputation. Don't you dare! I'll . . . I'll . . . [sputtering, almost apoplectic] . . . I'll [screaming] *disown* you!" When I told this episode to one of his daughters, she said, "I'm not surprised. He won't admit he was not born in this country, but there is a photograph of him as a young child in Russia in a funny hat, with Russian printing on the back." Clearly, for Lou Odets a claim to being "Somebody" in America rested on having been born on United States soil and showing no trace of having been a Jew in Eastern Europe. It was my challenge to this claim that aroused in him such intense anxiety. Such is a "melting pot."

p. 24 2.1   Maintaining in his seventy-ninth year that "In my heart I have always been a writer," Louis J. Odets recalled the scene of his diapering his son as a good opening for a biography of his son, to be entitled "Clifford Odets: A Father Rears a Genius." In *his* book he would say "very little about Pearl" and would not "even mention" his sister-in-law Esther, her husband, or, indeed, any-

_____
* L. J. Odets to Walt Odets, April 1964.

one else, because "writing a biography is the same as manufacturing a piece of merchandise and you got to stick to one subject, and one subject only, if you want to make any sales. . . . It's how good it is for everybody, not just a few. . . . Charlie Chaplin is a big man. He wrote *his* autobiography to make a lot of money, but he was known to fifty-one percent more people than Clifford. . . . Clifford wasn't a big enough man for anybody to care about him. He never joined any organizations, not even B'nai B'rith . . . so you got to get an entertaining story to have a best-seller that will make a big movie about how a father raised a genius, from birth to death."

p. 24 2.2 Of central significance for Odets' creative fate was the fact that in this year of his birth a scientist named Lee De Forest saw a practical means to amplify sound. De Forest's tube would inaugurate an unprecedented era in human communication. Millions of people—educated, uneducated, old, young—across vast distances would simultaneously hear the same words, laugh and cry at the same instant, thus establishing a least common denominator—and, accordingly, rewards, conflicts, and complexities for artists—that neither Ibsen nor Cézanne would have dreamed possible. In this year, too, occurred the actual American tragedy on which Theodore Dreiser based his classic novel, the story of a boy who, in pursuit of material success, destroys an innocent young girl and ultimately himself: a capsule of the beginning of America's fall.

On yet another level of the trajectory of history, to become part of the daily discussions in immigrant households—and, accordingly, to be woven gradually into Odets' emerging consciousness—were the momentous upheavals in the lands they had all left. This year 1906 followed the first try to turn their world upside down, made in 1905 by the "insulted and the injured," many fresh from the Kishinev pogroms, in Lou Odets' native Russia. They had intended to create the model of a utopian society, based on Marx's theory of work, wherein physical and spiritual enslavement would be forever ended. In such a world all would equally "belong" and become one free and peaceable species, and the generations would strengthen and replenish each other. Marxist thought, which first gave political form to this unsuccessful attempt at revolution in Russia—and to the sucessful one a decade later—would in the 1930s provide for Odets' generation what Malcolm Cowley has called "a wild hope for the future" in the form of the Union of Soviet Socialist Republics.

On another frontier, a different revolution had been set into motion, a radical view of Man's body and mind which held out another kind of hope for freedom: Sigmund Freud, just past his fiftieth year, had within the same decade unveiled "the Mystery of the Dream" and, accordingly, opened a path to the discovery and conquest of Man's *internal* impoverishments and enslavements. A "better world was in birth" on all fronts.

p. 27 2.3 Odets often said, "A poet is a man who trusts no one's experience but his own."

p. 31 2.4 The monumental task, spared to no one, of interweaving inborn drives, needs, and gifts with internalizations of a series of external models and events has sometimes been oversimplified as the "resolution of the Oedipus complex." Actually, each successive stage of life from infancy through adolescence to old age provides its own psychological crisis with its resultant strengths and antipathies or deficits.*

Each child (male or female) has far more to do than to compete with the parent of the same sex, resolving it by an "identification," as Freud taught, with that parent. In living reality, each little girl or boy competes with, emulates, internalizes, and establishes boundaries vis-à-vis *both* mother and father. This complementary intermeshing of systems—wherein the river forms its banks as the banks form the river—is, of course, made even more complex by the advent of the tributaries of sisters, brothers, and any other important members of a household. If this were not enough to integrate, conceptually, there exists *simultaneously from the beginning* in all of these family members the world-view of the society into which the infant is born. Sometimes these cultural institutions support the potential creativity of a given child, sometimes not. Or, worse, there is a conflict and the resultant identity-elements steadily war with one another. For young Clifford, at one end stood the image of a powerful, active, energetic male who could break a pole in half and reign over a household of cowed women and, at the other, a passive, vulnerable, and innocent woman trampled by her husband. To add further complexity: having been the "chosen child," he is cast out by a new arrival and will spend the rest of his life oscillating between the need to "get back," to "belong," and a willingness to make peace with an "inner identity" which Freud thought to be at the core of Jewishness—namely, the capacity to live and to think in isolation from the compact majority.† The aggrieved boy who could not managed to button his shoes or even to pull on his long black stockings felt, by turns, fused with, deserted by, identified with, and in competition with his mother, his father, and his crippled sister. He came to seek union—later given form in his work—with the aggrieved of his world and to believe on one level that a passport to being loved was to be, like his little sister, a cripple. The reverberations of these early realities and fantasies would appear regularly from this time on. Although *material* deprivation, as such, played no significant role in his own grievance at this point, it would later provide an emotional and a creative bridge to the impoverished.

Wiseacre commentators, totally misunderstanding the basic nature of his grief, would, in the years of his great success, profess astonishment that anyone reared in the middle class could sincerely make common cause with the "prisoners of starvation." This is a misunderstanding of the creative process which can transpose any human experience into a symbolic equivalent.

p. 35 2.5 Pearl's only intimate, Ida Mae Levine, apologizing for her spelling in the eighth decade of her life ("I never made the third grade, even"), writes that she helped Pearl "every night and

* E. H. Erikson, "The 'Works.'"
† Freud, "Address to the B'nai B'rith" (1926).

day" and that "no novel could be written" that would have "more heartbreaking young years than the real life story about Clifford as we saw it." Having made only elliptical references to Lou Odets' character and to his philandering, she retreats in fear ("I can't say any more . . . I'm afraid I've said too much . . .") and concludes, ". . . no son ever loved a mother as he did and suffered most of his young life wanting to see her well, be near her, give her everything. . . . My tears for him and Pearl Odets will be with us forever."

p. 36 2.6   The contrast between these early-twentieth-century photographs and those of young Eugene O'Neill, pad and pencil in hand, taken at the same age a few years earlier, sums up the new paths for writers being prepared by American technology. The need of immigrants in a melting-pot culture was for a medium of mass entertainment which required no language. Silent, least-common-denominator pictures projected on a screen were universally understandable, even by those of Pearl's neighbors who could not speak English or read or write in any language.

As the technology which substituted the picture for the word was expanding, another set of historic forces was coming into play. Already, George Cram Cook was in revolt against what he called the "commercialism of the Broadway theatre." He helped to build the Washington Square Players, nucleus for the Theatre Guild, later to spawn the Group Theatre; and he already dreamed of the play-space in which a "young culture could find its voice." In this space, which he in fact would provide, America's first playwright of stature, Eugene O'Neill, would emerge, declaring his private war against business enterprise and technology. Odets, America's second playwright of stature, would follow close on his heels.

p. 37 2.7   True to the best in Jewish tradition, the conscious acceptable "enemy" for Odets would become an impersonal set of unjust and corrupt societal conditions, and the means of battle would be waged largely in words within the controllable arena of social conscience within a work of art. This is a resolution significantly different from the masochistic one of his childhood wherein his fantasied form of vengeance is to suffer the hurt (like his mother) unto death, when "they will be sorry." Recognizable features of this childhood fantasy remain, however, in the plays. He is, of course, innocent of the cultural institutions at this moment evolving which will impede these infantile conflicts from becoming creative. The marriage between art and commerce, on a scale unprecedented, was now emerging in the infant motion-picture industry, an industry initiated by fur-gamblers and garment-traders; it would soon manufacture "product" subject to the same laws of supply and demand as ready-to-wear coats and dresses.

p. 39 2.8   Despite the fact that he was deeply identified with his mother's vulnerability, his "satisfaction" in these scenes probably issued from a revengeful triumph in seeing both his abandoner and his crippled competitor punished. A long series of women in his life would become the targets of this blind vengeance.

p. 39 2.9 It was vital to him to find favor in the eyes of his "all-powerful dynamo" father, whom he would by turns emulate, seek counsel from, voluptuously submit to, as his mother did, and then coldly turn from, in a burst of murderous rage or of self-destruction.

p. 40
2.10 It is my impression that this symptom occurs frequently in children of minority groups, regardless of economic class. These feel themselves to be "homeless" in the world. But it is not uncommon, either, in those who feel deprived, rebellious, or "outside" on whatever grounds—like Theodore Dreiser, whose account of his stealing has become a classic.*

p. 42
2.11 Note letter from Ida Fischer to Odets (1926) that he was "an artist student who let fine teachers live. . . ."

p. 42
2.12 Years later Group Theatre actor Luther Adler, knowing nothing of this history, commented on him as a creative artist: "Clifford was a sprinter . . . not much good for a long haul." The quality of psychological wholeness or integrity that gives *anyone*—artist or no—*durability* or stamina for the long haul issues from a series of good fortunes in the successive crises of a developing human being, leaving a residue of basic strengths like hope, will, purpose, competence, fidelity, love, care, and wisdom.

p. 42
2.13 It appears that Odets' determination to become an actor had begun quite early as he watched his self-dramatizing mother. He had been both attracted and repelled by her, thinking her to be, on occasion, "crazy." Yet, and of crucial significance for a boy, he had precisely the same conflict regarding his father, also a dramatizer. This fluid diffusion of the precursors of identity is often found in actors. Some professional actors report that when the boundaries become too fluid and the distinctions between reality and fantasy blur, they have a fear of going insane. In some cases, they give up acting as a profession.

At his mother's behest, Odets for years recited poems for the Bronx neighbors and was enthusiastically applauded by his mother and her friends: an early edition of the "other" to whom the artist addresses himself: his audience.

p. 44
2.14 Lou Odets, in his characteristic blend of shrewdness and naïveté, would later recall in a letter (May 20, 1940) *his* views while trying to dissuade his son from bothering with such a "nonentity as Wilson as the subject for a play": "About Pres. Wilson . . . some thought he was alright, others thought he was a sucker for the ladies. It's the old story. In this world, when you're out of sight, you're out of mind." In a long discussion of Wilson's campaign and his unsuccessful efforts to become a Mason (an aspiration in which Lou had succeeded) his competitiveness with Wilson is evident.

p. 45
2.15 The complexity and subtlety of human development were never better demonstrated than in the fact that Genevieve, supposedly the most handicapped of the Odets children, would emerge nearly impervious to insult, having incorporated many of

* Swanberg, *Theodore Dreiser.*

her father's values. She would marry, raise a family, teach school, and become conventionally the best "adjusted"—certainly the happiest—of the three Odets children. She would "disgrace" L.J. for the last time in August 1963 when she arrived in Los Angeles as her famous brother lay dying. Enjoying her work for the state of New Jersey, she was indiscreet enough to mention it to L.J.'s neighbors. L.J. was appalled that she would "admit you have to work" and berated her until she went home to New Jersey. Genevieve, understandably, rejoices today in her own son and daughter, who "live normal lives." She is glad her son is not "a miserable genius like Clifford" and is convinced that he'll even "get ahead of Clifford some day." At this writing, her son is on the editorial staff of the *National Enquirer,* and her daughter, although married and a mother, is an honor student at Montclair State College in New Jersey. In 1978, upon reading my description of her and the above comment, Genevieve wrote to me, "[Your] statements make it appear that I was severely handicapped. I am not—I walk with a limp, but this has not stopped me from doing anything I wanted to do. I have had a good life with a wonderful husband." (Her husband died two days after she had written this.) In recent years Genevieve learned to drive a car, especially adapted for her use.

p. 46 3.1   In a seductive pursuit of literally hundreds of women over the course of his life, Odets in a concentration of underlying purpose would try actively to master a variety of undigested experiences. On the one hand, there stood his early-begun humane and compassionate identification with his mother in her innocent vulnerability, self-centeredness, and blocked aspiration to "study languages." Simultaneously he had to bend over backward in order to deny these "feminine" (weak) aspects of himself—often equated with his creativity—by means of this self-same Don Juanism and of a defensive arrogance,* both observed in his father. If this were not enough complexity, he had already commenced his compulsive quest for "the ideal woman" who would rescue him. Having long since, however, come to the angry and depressed conclusion that no woman could be trusted to meet his wild hunger, and that every woman would, like his mother, betray and abandon him, he commenced early—with the precision of a computer—to choose women who could not in the long run nourish him, and whom, one after another, he would feel justified in betraying or, indeed, destroying.† Often while enacting his father's predatory contempt, he experienced his victim's pain, as he had his mother's. In scattered notes, on napkins, envelopes, match folders, he repeatedly scribbled, "The abandoned becomes the abandoner" or "The crippled, the crippler."

There would be many permutations of this pattern, however, and thus instances wherein a sequence would shift and a

* Writer Abe Burrows, a man of wit and insight, later observed, "Clifford had the arrogance of an unarmed man."
† According to Edmund Bergler (*Psychology of the Writer*), this unconscious conflict is characteristic of many writers, some reaching better, some worse resolutions. Although he reduces life's complexities to an oversimple psychoanalytic scheme, Bergler has discussed with great cogency this multi-layered defense structure and its relation to masochism. The life of O'Neill supports this hypothesis.

configuration alter, permitting the woman to escape the grim climax—and to be left only with an image of "a lovely, gentle boy" or of that rarest of men who, as one woman put it, "can truly put himself in a woman's place and know just what to say and do, in or out of bed." Although he would later achieve some mastery over these conflicts by shifting the arena to his plays, the pain throughout his actual life in his driven, compulsively repeated and mostly losing struggle for a livable resolution of his early crises would be inordinate.

p. 48 3.2 The name Millstein likely became Mills for reasons similar to those behind the transformation of Koblanovsky to Kobland, and Gorodetsky to Odets. The complexities of turning oneself inside out in the quest for an acceptable identity are further indicated by the fact that these three boys in "our detective and spying games" adopted as code names their own names spelled backward (Namreh Von Albok, Niet Slim and Droffilc Stedo). This is not so remarkable as the fact that the last mentioned would be used by Clifford Odets as one of his adult nom de plumes and later by his father, when, masquerading as a screenwriter, L. J. Odets would submit manuscripts to motion-picture studios; unproduced, they would be stored for eternity in the same vaults as his eminent son's unproduced screenplays.

p. 49 3.3 Many writers have expressed the wish to compose. Both Thornton Wilder and William Gibson have suggested that it is related to the poetic and the architectural impulses (personal communication). It is curious, in this context, that there is no mention of his Uncle Israel's singing, a topic which frequently appears in his plays and in his conversation in later years.

p. 50 3.4 The Palmer raids of January 1920 occurred just a year before a postwar murder which, according to Hannah Arendt, "became the watershed between two eras in Germany" and, accordingly, in the morality of the world: under the eyes of the socialist regime then in power, a paramilitary organization shot and tossed into a canal the leftist-humanist, *anti-terrorist* Polish Jewess, Rosa Luxemburg. From this organization Hitler would soon recruit his most promising killers.*

p. 51 3.5 As long as he lived, Odets would maintain in his orbit someone —often a promising young female artist—who had been victimized by life, one way or another, and whom he was helping— with or without sex—to grow. All the more bitter for each such orphan, as it was later on for his baby sister, when he was driven to abandon her and to move on to the next. Had his initial promise to the one in need been less, so accordingly would have been the subsequent disappointment.

p. 53 3.6 In Odets' file of unfinished plays, there is one (1949–1963) called "Private Treaty" or "By the Sea" (also called "Sonatina," "Horner in a Corner," or "Harry"). It is about a man, Merle Horner, who has discovered his wife's infidelity (in some versions, with his business partner). He drives to Atlantic City,

* Arendt, review of *Rosa Luxemburg* by J. P. Nettle.

after taking his little daughter to his favorite aunt in Philadelphia, and checks into a hotel there. He has a gun and plots the murder of his wife and her lover. In one version he has taken a fur coat, a recent gift to his wife, and as it hangs on the door of his room, he fires bullets into it. Among the few guests of the hotel there is a schoolteacher, Doris Beck,* who is also in the throes of marital discord. The two are drawn together and they share not only their personal torments but, for a few moments, the comfort and loving warmth of their bodies. Through this "brief encounter" they find the strength to go back to their separate lives. Odets describes Merle as an "average American guy" who never cared for his father, and whose "mother died young."

p. 56 3.7 Copland's family name, Kaplan, has been changed by an immigration official on Ellis Island to whom it had seemed "a disadvantage."

p. 58 3.8 Odets read in the newspapers that a descendant of this family, Gouverneur Morris, had been recruited by the enterprising movie magnate Samuel Goldwyn shortly after the end of World War I as one of his stable of "Eminent Authors" along with Rupert Hughes and Mary Roberts Rinehart, and, "not to be outdone," Paramount had captured Sir James Barrie, Joseph Conrad, Arnold Bennett, and Somerset Maugham.† The Hollywood drain on international literary talent began early. *This* "path to success" was thus clearly marked for this impressionable, bright youngster who knew he had taken over both his mother's and his father's gift for the Word. Thus, a bridge is established between observed social role and the intrapsychic business of identity-formation.

p. 61 3.9 The author of this juvenile play was here expressing the conflict so often found in writers: whether to distill life's meanings in spiritual or in worldly terms. The universal wish to keep a promise—usually to one's mother, to become in fact the "special redeeming person" she early knew one to be—is felt as a kind of spiritual, even religious (in the broadest sense) "duty," different from heeding the sterner, more authoritative voice of one's father. Here the symbol (cooking lentils) of creating sustenance for oneself and for others is particularly transparent.

p. 64 3.10 It is a frequent occurrence in youth that an individual destined to become outstanding, whether as an artist or as a spiritual leader (Gandhi), finds a kind of psychical ballast in a comrade who acts as sounding board or "straight man." Odets' childhood friend Herman Kobland, later his devoted secretary, served this function as well as, on occasion, that of being a whipping boy.

p. 69 4.1 While Odets in a victorious nation is offering this melting-pot thesis—essentially an argument to end the murderous national divisions within humanity—Hitler, a disappointed young painter in a defeated Germany, is devoting his time to its opposite: the proposition of the salvation of the German people through the

---

* Named after Beck Street, in all likelihood.
† MacGowan, *Behind the Screen.*

creation of a new pseudo-species, the Aryan. He had failed in his Beer-Hall Putsch, but instead of killing himself as he had promised, he ran away to hide and to bide his time.

p. 71 4.2 The gift of empathizing, central to such diverse arts as psychotherapy and playwriting, is little understood. The special kind of imagination that permits one person to put himself "in the place of the other" involves at the very least some experience of incompletion on the part of the "I," with some hope of closure by way of identification with the "thou," thus often thought of in Western culture as a feminine quality. But there is more than this. There is a diffusion of identity to accommodate—as Odets put it—an inner "gallery of characters," and there is a detached "witnessing" of the entire process. Put to creative use, such a "gallery" may issue in the career choice of writer, actor, playwright, or any other artist. Given different dimensions, the outcome may be the practice of psychotherapy. With less good fortune, a self-effacing, indecisive chameleon emerges, with a chronic sense of weakness, suggestibility, fraudulence, or hypocrisy. Odets would ultimately know all of these uses of his extraordinary capacity to empathize.

p. 73 4.3 It seems to me, rereading Genesis, that Odets is correct, and that the original sin is, after all, disobedience.

p. 73 4.4 It is remarkable how early, even in his one descriptive sentence —which is all we have of this adolescent novel—there are visible the fundamental conflicts and attempts at creative mastery in an entire body of work. The themes here, often to be repeated in more sophisticated form in his adult plays, operate on many levels from that of childhood anxiety to "Zeitgeist": most legible is the *fear* that his creative life will be destroyed by some external "accident" (the pianist's hands are damaged). There would be, however, in this dreaded event also a relief: namely, an absolution from the responsibility for developing his talent. If his creative hand is broken, he *cannot* ply his art, and will be thus "forced" to turn to some more practical means—approved by his father—of acquiring a remunerative work-identity and material power. Thus, he hopes by this very loss to gain his father's love and his own self-regard. At the same time, the "accident" rids him of two separate guilts of self-absorption: the self-feeding and self-stimulation in his private "impractical" writing as well as in his consolatory masturbation, both accomplished by hand. ("If thine hand offend thee . . .") Thus, the fantasy of being deprived of his gift is both feared and hoped for as a deliverance.* The accident obliterates both gift and guilt. Moreover, if he can become a cripple like his baby sister, he can restore, perhaps, his central position in the family. The metaphor of an artist whose creative career is ended by an "accident" to his hands is repeated by Odets in many forms throughout his work, most explicitly in the successful *Golden Boy*, where

* Compulsive handwashing is a symptom familiar to clinicians as a less productive means of trying to resolve such a conflict. Additional evidence for this general thesis is offered by the image of the artist (pianist) Pearl in *Paradise Lost,* who, in her loneliness, "sucks her breast." (Modern Library, 1939, Act II, p. 199.)

a violinist breaks his hand in the prizefight ring and then commits suicide. The central meaning of this play was usually seen simply as "a struggle between Art and Material Success." Actually, the metaphor (of being crippled or of crippling—or killing—oneself) is not idiosyncratic for Odets and is broader. World literature is studded with heroes (not so often heroines) who lose their power by having limbs lopped off, by becoming blind, crippled, or by being in one way or another sacrificed or crucified. Perhaps the struggle with the impulse to surrender the responsibility of manhood (by these symbolic castrations or deaths) is an expression of the steady battle from infancy on between the strengths of will, purpose, and competence and the antipathies of dependency, inhibition, and inertia. This is further complicated by the conflict between the wish to defeat and to emulate the father. There is also in this struggle something, still elusive, that stems from the bisexuality in the act of creating a work of art. Odets often discussed the "androgynous" nature of the artist. This last remains conceptually unclear to me, especially with regard to the differences between men and women in the evolution of the creative impulse, whether for biological or other kinds of procreation.

p. 74 4.5   The playwright who, from the beginning, puts his primary investment in the Word and not in his own body—as a performer —is probably closer to the existential concerns of a homo religiosus.* He is more preoccupied with high-minded matters of ideology, utopian outlook, and "cosmic mood" than is the actor turned playwright. Odets, in this as in everything, always had one foot, uncertainly, in each camp.

p. 76 4.6   After Odets' death Erik Erikson commented to the author that the playwright—whom he knew personally—had always seemed to him in some significant way like a "primal Christian" in his innocent and generous ardor to "do good," to "know transcendence," and to be joined to a community of brethren wherein "all may learn and all may be comforted."

p. 78 4.7   According to Erikson, ". . . it is of great relevance to the young individual's identity formation that he be responded to, and be given function and status as a person whose gradual growth and transformation make sense to those who begin to make sense to him. . . . Such recognition provides an entirely indispensable support to the ego in the specific tasks of adolescing."†

p. 78 4.8   A number of other American playwrights were growing into manhood during this "bourgeois Nirvana" before the economic dam would burst in 1929. Accordingly, there would appear in the 1930s many plays, besides Odets' *Golden Boy*, with the theme "For what is a man profited if he shall gain the whole world and lose his own soul?" By the time these plays were actually produced (*Success Story, Men in White, Gold Eagle Guy*, etc.) very few young intellectuals were being offered even routine jobs for their souls, let alone "the whole world." Yet the theme found a

---

* Cf. E. H. Erikson, *Young Man Luther*.
† E. H. Erikson, "Identity and the Life Cycle."

resonating audience composed of those whose identities had been in formation during the prosperous 1920s. John Howard Lawson, already writing plays by 1923, saw "America prostrate before the false gods of wealth and success . . . and more terrible, the great god, conformity."* This sentence is in a direct line of descent from Dreiser's "I would not give the bells that ring/ For all the world of bartering."†

p. 80 4.9 Odets' fantasy of going blind from smoking contains some of the same elements as the fear (the wish) to become a cripple. The fear of becoming a helpless dependent is no less real than the longing to be legitimately in a position to abdicate all responsibility for his livelihood, for his talent, and for his human relationships.

p. 81 4.10 A quarter of a century later he would try to trace the tightly braided complexities of his lifelong campaigns of seduction: "To be SEDUCTIVE means to be trying to bring into being or focus a person who is not there for you; it is to replace the cold, depriving one with a person more in line with your permanent or temporary needs. (A person who rejects you, even a stranger, is a depriving and threatening person.) To SEDUCE is an effort to transform the unwilling to the willing, the ugly to the beautiful —ugly, of course, because it is resistant or denying—the resistant to the compliant, EVEN THE ENEMY TO THE ACCOMPLICE! Often it is to MITIGATE the harsh, the unfriendly, the cold, the critical and unsafe. (At present I am leaving out the denigrating contained in seduction, the cutting one down to one's previous image of the worthlessness of women, etc., etc.) Seducing and seductive—there is much in the above that goes on in and is related to the Don Juan type. Seduction (with its implication of resistance and unwillingness in the other) is an act of *transformation* when it happens, of MAGIC, in which all the past unhappy matters of one's life are routed and disappear. Lack becomes gain, emptiness seems filled, deprivation seems satisfied: the illusion is of an ABSOLUTE OBTAINED! (I have known women who, giving themselves freely to many men, thought that they had conquered 'wolves'!)"‡

p. 88 5.1 There is here a good object lesson in the evolution of a self as we trace the identity confusions in a creative boy barely out of his teens, destined within ten years to become, as playwright, "the American poet of the Jewish middle-class"§ and the "white hope of the American drama." Externally he is struggling to separate from a first-generation middle-class Jewish-American immigrant family during the prosperous third decade of the twentieth century. He is a boy whose characteristically adolescent task of establishing a workable identity is in some ways more difficult than for many. In the effort to pull together into a coherent whole the conflicting diversities within him, he must not only sort out constitutional givens, maturing sexual needs, creative gifts, and effective defenses, he must also integrate

* Lawson, "Rebellion in the 1920s," p. 20.
† Swanberg, *Theodore Dreiser.*
‡ Odets, Notes, "Psychology" (undated).
§ Warshow, "Poet of the Jewish Middle Class."

positive and negative identity-elements from both (conflicted) parents and establish consistent roles within the family and in the wider world.* The late adolescent's critical quest for a place in the social order is usually aggravated in a twentieth-century artist. Odets' exploration of the available forms and cultural institutions in work and love is eloquently and painfully documented in the material of this period.

p. 94 5.2 Inspired by his excitement over a girl cellist at the radio station whose group plays "The Kashmiri Love Song," he writes several thin romantic paeans to love. A fragment: "And when I am covered with dust / Shall my tribute be any less to you / Who dwell among the stars? / I know my heart will live / When even the wind shall scatter it / To the four corners of the earth / And perchance some will blow to you / Up there and you will say, 'Alas I am blinded.'"

p. 95 5.3 Odets' intense, ambivalent, and guilt-laden relationship with his mother is clear in this poem. More important, perhaps, is the evidence of this early expression by a nineteen-year-old boy of a genuine gift for language. His being "in love with her" was obvious to his friend Herman, and an oft-repeated comment was: "My first betrayal was at the hands of my mother," who had abandoned him for her crippled daughter. "To a Mother— You are an October sun, mellowed and gold. / Your flowing smile is an amber wine / To warm the night cooled by the moon / Who has forgotten the world as she lies with her love. / Yours are thoughts of yesterday / And wraiths of the day before. / Like a youth that goes without goodbye / Is that day of long ago. / The colours of falling leaves / Is the blend of your soul, / Scarlet and gold and a crisp of brown. / Still you do as the sun dial says, 'I count only sunny hours,' / And without the sun of a memory / You are silent. / You are as one who waits / For a salt laden breeze from nameless seas, / While your pale, solemn eyes / Still flicking with light / Look into the mirror of self content. / Your sweet, tired voice / Ripened by love and child / Echoes like a vibrant whisper of yesterday / As a harp that still reverberates / After the hand of the musician has flown. / YESTERDAY LOVE WAS LUSH / AND PULSE BEAT FAST AT THE FLASH OF A STAR. / TODAY LOVE HAS GONE TO MORE FERTILE GROUND / TO BEGET AND TO KNOW YOUR SORROW. / As a velvet-soft rain spattering softly / On an upturned, parchèd face / Are the words you drop from mellowed thought. / Nothing stirs when your voice, / Like a leaf tossed in winds / Croons on of yesteryear / What you have lost you have gained / In the seed that is yours and is not yours. / For that is your sorrow, this your regret; / That ever you shall be known / As the Mother of Living who know you not. / And then too, is there not joy / In the pain of that thought? / Your work is finished. You may go. / You were a flower, your seed is gone / To beget, to beget and to know your sorrow. / You are pod, well-tossed and fumbled with / On the sere stubble of yesterday's / Seething, singing grass, / Dried by yesterday's passionate sun, / Cooled by tonight's moon /

---

* E. H. Erikson, *Identity: Youth and Crisis.*

Who has drawn a veil across her sphere / While she burns in bliss with her lover. / NOW ONLY THE MOONLIGHT IS HERE ON THE STUBBLE / WHILE AN EMPTY POD RATTLES BY. / WAS THAT POD MAKING MUSIC? / OR WAS THAT THE WIND . . . SIGHING / AS THE WIND MAY SOMETIMES DO? / And who knows but that when Death clutches / A memory shall soften, / Gloved in pity, / Immured in understanding / Even that hand." (From a letter to Herman Kobland, May 6, 1928.)

p. 96 5.4 Although such prescience is frequently maintained by participants in a biography, it has often been observed that in some subtle way individuals destined to become personages do indeed convey a high sense of "speciality" to others, sufficient to stimulate the taking of notes and the conserving of documents.

p. 98 6.1 The day-night reversal, with its relieving sense of freedom from demand, is characteristic for people who feel detached from, or oppressed by, the world around them. It provides a kind of nonconforming rebellious and private limbo, a private world.

p. 105 6.2 By the mid-1920s the history of American dramatic literature was being stretched prematurely by the American-Jewish playwright John Howard Lawson, who, together with John Dos Passos, Michael Gold, Em Jo Basshe, and Hungarian-born Francis Edwards Faragoh, had organized "The New Playwrights' Theatre," financed by the Maecenas Otto Kahn (called "Old Fountain Pen" because he signed so many generous checks). They were trying to create a "revolutionary" theatre such as Bertolt Brecht and Erwin Piscator were already successfully managing in Germany—"revolutionary" with regard both to its humanist content and to new forms, a theatre largely non-imitative, *to be run by playwrights.* (Odets knew nothing of this.) They were bent on going beyond what they felt were the confines of the "psychological symbolism" of Eugene O'Neill, who, tied to the Theatre Guild, refused to have anything to do with them. For three seasons they struggled against the prevailing winds, earning for themselves such contemptuous titles as "the Revolting Playwrights." Theodore Dreiser, friendly to the New Playwrights, saw on his trip to the Soviet Union in 1928 theatrical experiments similar, he thought, to theirs.*

p. 109 6.3 We know, as yet, little of the *decisive* circumstance which enables some of us and not others to make a livable integration of the disparate and fractionated models, or what Erikson calls "identity-elements and fragments," which confront all of us from the moment of birth. The late George Klein offered the interesting hypothesis that where a significant one of them excites chronic terror in the child, the difficulty of such an integration is magnified and the "introject" remains as a kind of festering foreign body.†

p. 111 6.4 Interestingly enough, the technological shift that made "talking pictures" possible was not, by itself, enough to capture the Amer-

* Lawson, "Rebellion in the 1920s."
† Personal communication.

ican audience. Thomas Edison, expert though he was on problems of synchronizing sound and film, could not appreciate the law that complements psychodynamics with history. Still lacking was a popular unconscious fantasy carried by a gifted individual. Accordingly, Edison had announced, after several box-office failures, that there was simply "no field for talking pictures." Film historians have been puzzled by the sensational success in the following year by a sound film which dramatized the actual life history of its star, Al Jolson, born in the Russian village of Srednicke: the story of a cantor's son who "leaves the sanctity of the synagogue" for a career on the stage despite his father's despair that "the stage is no life for a man."* Though the producers were fearful of a movie about the struggles of a minority group, they were emboldened by the unique talent of their singing star, born as Asa Yoelson, son of Naomi and Moses, a "greenhorn" who thought he ought to say a prayer for the dead when his son went into vaudeville. With great apprehension, thus, Warner Brothers opened in New York City on October 6, 1927, a film, *The Jazz Singer*, with spoken dialogue and songs that would electrify its heavily first- and second-generation audiences. We can suppose that Clifford, nephew of "the songer" Sroul Russman, cantor manqué, was deeply impressed by the content of this sound film, by the dizzying success of Al Jolson, and by the American promise that had become his theatrical trademark: "You ain't heard nothin' yet!" The interwoven universes of psycho-dynamics, history, technology, and individual talent had now joined in such a way that a new cultural era— the era of the collaborative mass media—had begun in earnest: the end of 1927 would see only fifty-five theatres wired for sound on film, and two years later, 8,741!† By the time of the Great Depression the success of the "talkies" was sufficiently clear to persuade the Rockefellers to build the great Radio City Music Hall, to buy through their Radio Corporation of America—which manufactured sound-on-film equipment—a film-producing company as well as the Keith-Albee-Orpheum vaudeville-theatre corporation. By 1930, it is estimated, ninety million Americans were regular moviegoers and their hunger for dialogue was insatiable. This situation would go beyond all imagination within the next several decades. Millions of souls scattered all over the planet would demand that their home screen show them something, anything, around the clock, preferably imported from the United States.‡

p. 115
7.1

We know too little of what in the external world, uniting with what special sensitivities in a child, issues in so many periods of deep life-despair as Odets had. Possibly a genetically less sensitive, less porous, and less gifted youngster would have responded with greater resilience to his family and would have achieved a more comfortable day-to-day "adjustment." The laws not only of artists, but of all humans, which govern the precise ways in which the nested complementary systems of biological givens

* Sieben, *The Immortal Jolson.*
† MacGowan, *Behind the Screen.*
‡ Letter to M. Brenman-Gibson from Television Information Office, March 28, 1967.

interweave with stimulations and deprivations remains largely terra incognita. Careful developmental work with newborns and children is beginning to blaze trails.

Beyond the "pleasure principle" in day-to-day functioning there stands the "repetition-compulsion." This complex and little-understood principle of human functioning advanced by Freud has been variously discussed as a death instinct, as an atavistic return to the stereotyped behavior of insects, or as a perverse "fate neurosis." The thriftiest hypothesis states: ". . . the individual unconsciously arranges for variations of an original theme which he has not learned to overcome or to live with: he tries to master a situation which in its original form had been too much for him by meeting it repeatedly and *of his own accord*" (italics mine.)* It must be added that in the complexity of human development it sometimes happens that the experience of the "original situation" is lost sight of, no longer comprehended, and thus only the unsuccessful maneuvers devised to cope with the underlying problem are externally repeated to no avail. Odets, attempting to master the experience of abandonment, becomes wary, accusatory, and abandoning.

p. 115
7.2

Shakespeare often reveals his understanding of this process: For example, when Hamlet flays himself for being "pigeon-liver'd" and lacking sufficient gall to revenge his father's murder in *action*, he says: "Why, what an ass am I! This is most brave, / That I, the son of a dear father murder'd, / Prompted to my revenge by heaven and hell, / Must, like a whore, *unpack my heart with words*. . . ." (II, i). Or again, in *Troilus and Cressida:* "Words, words, mere words, no matter from the heart: / The effect doth operate another way. . . . My love with words and errors still she feeds; / But edifies another with her deeds" (V, iii).

I think also of a painter who, looking at his father's corpse in an open coffin, is assailed by profound guilt as the detached thought comes to him, "How paintable he is now." In some marvelous way, the esthetic *form* contains or insulates the potentially explosive feeling in the unconscious fantasy. Indeed, *until the form is found, the artist often reports, the feeling is not available.*

p. 115
7.3

On one occasion Odets said, ". . . yes, this year I wrote: 'Verily, verily, life is a dream,'" adding, "I wrote verily, verily, because I didn't make up this saying. . . ."† One of his characters echoes this: "I don't enjoy my life . . . I enjoy only the dream of it."‡ The preoccupation with the nature of reality is a regular theme in Shakespeare's plays, most explicitly in *A Midsummer Night's Dream.* ("Life's but a stage," or, says Shakespeare, "call it Bottom's dream, for it has no bottom.")

The decision to place the process of creating at the center of one's life, whether as artist, scientist, or religious prophet, takes as its premise the idea that whereas the material world is impermanent, transient, and essentially "unreal," the transcen-

* E. H. Erikson, *Childhood and Society.*
† Odets to William Gibson, Tape #4, p. 23.
‡ Odets, *Clash by Night,* scene 3 (eighth draft, October 1941, unpublished).

dent world of the spirit is the realest reality, the Absolute. Thus, an artist, like a mystic, quite naturally takes up the basic position of a witness, a "second man," an observer, not an "overshadowed" participant. This is essentially the same as the "witnessing" described in Eastern thought as a regular indication of higher or transcendent states of consciousness.*

p. 117
7.4

Odets' core-image of himself as a growing plant remained until the last moments of his life. On his deathbed he picked the last petal from the last yellow rose on his night table. The struggle to maintain the incorruptible innocence of the unfolding flower, always threatened by what he saw as his father's "false" values of ingratiation and salesmanship, is steadily projected in his work: in the aspiring young girl, the murdered child, the suiciding youngsters,† a man crippled by a Nazi, a singing mouse who commits suicide, and in a variety of other plays never to be written, except as outlines: David, the poet, versus Saul, the predator; the jaded playwright who destroys the young girl playwright, and many, many more. *In none of his plays is the tyrant destroyed—it is always the "innocent."* As he grows older and his dependence on his father is transferred to a series of significant men, his *conscious* distaste for his father comes to the fore. It is a source of astonishment to his sister that, while expressing disdain and contempt for their father, Clifford, until he was fifty years old, nonetheless secretly confided in and steadily sought counsel from him!

The image of his aspiring self as an "innocently" evolving organism is reflected in the last interview of his life, televised in Los Angeles. When he was asked what he had come to see as the "sum and substance," his response at fifty-six, though more sophisticated, is essentially the same as in his letters at twenty-one: "I would want to talk, in our country particularly, about the fulfillment of each individual human being. I would like to make a statement about what, in our American world, develops all of the inherent possibilities of each man and woman and what holds them back, what stymies them. . . . I find our American world today lacks innocence; I find it lacks the conviction of innocence. We pick up those techniques in which we are the richest. Those are the techniques of conciliation and ingratiation, the techniques of selling yourself—all of which necessarily means that innocence goes and experience, perhaps, shrivels our souls. . . . By innocence I mean that quality, that uncorrupted quality, with which all children are born—what Emerson called uncorrupted behavior and ended by saying that only animals and children seemed to have it. It's that quality of uncorrupted behavior when nothing outside of yourself influences you, when you are in command of yourself with honor, without dishonesty, without lie; when you grasp and deal and are permitted to deal with exactly what is in front of you in terms of your best human instincts. . . . This is what I mean

* See Gibson, *A Season in Heaven.*
† In a rough outline called "The Suicide Play" Odets tells the horrendous story of a series of mysterious suicides in a school wherein the grownups are actually responsible for these deaths of their children.

by innocence."* The image of the innocent (often a girl in conflict with a tough, mercantile world) is one frequently used also
by two other American literary ground-breakers: Dreiser and
O'Neill, who, in their work—as well as in their actual complex
relations with women—identify an important identity-element
of themselves in this image. O'Neill writes to Carlotta Monterey:
"Daughter, you are my secret, shy, shrinking one, my pure and
unsoiled one, whom the world has wounded."†

p. 119
7.5

The passivity in his mother vis-à-vis his father—internalized by
Odets as both a negative and a positive feminine anima—erupts
in his final accusation that she has not activated him ("the
lyrical flights that you might have started me on and did not").
The fantasy, not uncommon in creators, of being thus passively
activated is carried further in the notion that he then produces
edible brain-children which provide him and others with sustenance ("I give you my mentality like a dish of chef-de-hoeuvres";
later he likens his plays to a calf cut into veal chops while the
mother cow stands bellowing).‡ There is both terror and triumph in this "feminine" passivity.

p. 122
7.6

In Odets' *Golden Boy*, the seductive voice of the Devil in Eddie
Fuseli, the gangster whose promises to young Joe Bonaparte
(torn between art-making and prizefighting) that he will "eat,
sleep and wear the best" are secondary to the promise that he
will reign as "the champ," "the Monarch of the Masses," or like
his small historic predecessor Napoleon, as the "conqueror." This
theme is central also in the work of other American writers, like
Mark Twain, Theodore Dreiser, Eugene O'Neill. In every case,
*while the writer is indicting the "Titan," he is also envying and
admiring him.*§

p. 122
7.7

There is some ambiguity about the date of the earliest contact
of Odets with the Leof-Blitzstein families. It is certain, however,
that he did not meet composer Marc Blitzstein, stepson of Madi
Leof Blitzstein, until 1932. Marc, aged 23 at this time, was, like
all proper American artists, seeking spiritual nourishment in
Europe. He studied with Arnold Schoenberg and Nadia Bou-
langer. Within a few years he would join the generation of composers that gave America its first musical identity, abandoning
his Schoenberg and Stravinsky styles and stating that "music
should teach as well as entertain." Like Odets—who envied him
his calling of composer—his emergence as an American artist
of the thirties would be facilitated by the emotional bridge to an
audience of the Great Depression and by the rehearsal in the
Spanish Civil War for a stand against Hitler and Mussolini.
After he was robbed and murdered in 1964, the manuscript of
a new work, begun in his twenties—based on the lives of Sacco

---

* Odets in "Sum and Substance," an interview with Herman Harvey, televised by
KNXT, Los Angeles, February 3, 1963. Reprinted in *University of Southern California
Alumni Review.*
† Gelb, *O'Neill*, p. 765.
‡ Interview by Arthur Wagner, October 1961.
§ Swanberg, *Theodore Dreiser*, p. 176.

and Vanzetti and entitled "The Condemned"—was found in his parked car.*

p. 126
7.8

At the end of his life he would describe his own intention to leave Hollywood and return East as a jailbreak plot.†

p. 127
7.9

F. Scott Fitzgerald went to Hollywood to write a screenplay for Constance Talmadge at United Artists (even before Al Jolson and sound) for which he would get $12,000 if they liked it and $3,500 if they didn't. When, after eight grueling weeks, he finished it and United Artists decided it was not good enough to use, he told his wife that he would "never write another picture because it is too hard." The newspapers announced he had come back East, where his editor, Maxwell Perkins, thought he "could work better on a novel."‡

p. 134
8.1

Critics have used the phrase "machine-gun bullets" to describe Odets' dialogue. His own image of "bullets spattering inside my head" is strikingly similar to O'Neill's "radical" poem published in *The Masses* in 1917, where he likens his soul to a submarine whose "aspirations are torpedoes" with targets outside himself: namely, the obese and grimy "galleons of commerce." O'Neill lurks "menacingly in green depths" of the sea to obliterate these "dull, heavy-laden merchant ships." Again a violent and anti-mercantile world-view, an artist's personal integration of his old rage with a generational ideology.

p. 138
8.2

Odets' view that "even if there be no God, there ought to be something to worship" again reflects a "Zeitgeist," a world-view strikingly similar to that of O'Neill (significantly different from Odets in personality and as a playwright), who during this same period was struggling with the rest of his trilogy, begun with *Dynamo*, to be entitled "God is Dead! Long Live—What?"§ In this, O'Neill had intended to dramatize the failure of rationality and materialism to supply whatever sense of significance or meaning religion had provided. The symbols of twentieth-century materialism and technology and O'Neill's unconscious view of his own destructive and self-destructive mother became intertwined in a complex manner. This process deserves close study if we are to illuminate the systematic unfolding of the individual conflict as it interweaves with the ongoing history and is creatively expressed by the *specific gift* of the writer.

p. 140
8.3

This use of the word "regurgitation" to describe his own writing is strange unless we pursue the hypothesis that the production of form in words as a means of mastering experience is deeply and universally rooted in our feelings about what goes into and comes out of our mouths, what we "swallow," what we cannot "stomach," what calls for "biting wit," what "nourishes" us, and what makes us "spill our guts." Odets says that "the urge to write comes like a gripping thing . . . and then makes a com-

---

* J. Peyser, Columbia University *Forum*, Winter 1966.
† Odets, letter to M. Brenman-Gibson, July 1, 1961.
‡ Milford, *Zelda*, p. 130.
§ Gelb, *O'Neill*, p. 679.

plete regurgitation in the victim." On the positive side of this statement of a creative burst stands the awesome and welcome sense of "involuntariness," often described by writers when they are "hot." "It is as if," Odets once said, "my hand were being guided by some unseen Force." On the negative side stands the sense of formlessness in the word "regurgitation." It is like a "diarrhea" of the mouth. In the creator there is a vital difference between an *active inner* openness—even a sense of being the passive instrument of an automatic process—and the *passive* surrender of the total self, with a sense of helplessness, whether to outer or to inner forces. The writer often thinks of himself as a closed system who, with his words, provides his own *nutrition* which he does *not* "regurgitate." If he is fortunate enough in the course of this self-sustaining mastery to feed others (his audience), they will, in turn, feed him not only with their money but with their love. He is after his self-feeding, *primarily*, but welcomes an Other who finds his words sufficiently nourishing that—like that First Nourisher, his mother—"she" will nourish him.

p. 143
8.4

Within three decades of the Great Depression the aim in a significant portion of young people (outside of totalitarian countries) would shift from changing the world to changing oneself: the Marxist theoretician, as high priest, would be supplanted first by the psychoanalyst until he, too, as a member of the Establishment, would become suspect. By the 1960s there would emerge around the world a new, young voice, disillusioned with the political possibilities for changing the world, but intent—often with the aid of drugs—on resisting the "disappearance of the individual in the downward suicidal spiral of Western civilization"* by reorganizing the Self. The new methods, aimed inward more than outward, would range from protests like the "put-on" with its rejection of the Word, to electronically amplified celebrations of "flower power." Sandals, beards, costumes, unisex dungarees and hair styles, handcrafted beads, woven cloth, folk music, poetry, home-baked bread—and some tool for silently transcending analytical thought—would become the logos of an international protest against the mass manufacture of death, whether in robot living, food additives, schoolrooms, or instant nuclear annihilation. The vitality in this counter-culture would be unmistakable, and police forces all over the world would be astonished at the pacific nature of their festivals. A wide variety of paths for "raising" or "expanding" consciousness would emerge, and the quest for self-realization and for international social institutions to renew hope would be called by some "America's new spiritual awakening," and by others the "new narcissism." This vitality would then be threatened in the 1970s (the Vietnam war over) by a more pragmatic conservative wave.

p. 147
8.5

He was approximately the same age as O'Neill was when, in his early twenties, being a hopeless alcoholic bum, he took what he believed to be a lethal dose of Veronal. For both, this was a life-cycle turning point.

* Watts, *Psychotherapy East and West.*

p. 150
8.6

The death of a child is often used as a symbol for the loss of a sense of wholeness and innocence; Odets uses it throughout his work. Tennessee Williams, in his classic *Streetcar Named Desire,* dates the emptiness of the life of Blanche (again white) DuBois (Williams' central identification-figure) from the time that the boy she adored, "too fine to be human," blew the back of his head off by inserting a gun barrel into his mouth and pulling the trigger. The death of this vulnerable, sensitive boy, secretly having become a homosexual—also an identity-element for Williams—appears also to represent for him a loss of integration and innocence.

p. 151
9.1

Although every psychoanalyst has observed the clinical evidence that some persons seek triumph through defeat and are stimulated even by suffering physical pain, our theory is still insufficiently systematized to provide a clear picture of how this happens.* One of Odets' lovers said, "I always felt I was competing with Pain for Clifford." Although Odets here rationalizes his wish for torture as a means of obtaining release from his captor, there is a paradoxical gratification—as in many passive adolescent boys—in the fantasy of controlling a powerful woman by being in her clutches. Often, as with alcoholics and compulsive gamblers, there is involved a significant "J'accuse."

p. 152
9.2

The "disconnected mood" which strains for closure more in the artist than in the rest of us is the same bridge that had earlier joined Odets to Victor Hugo's "misérables." His emotional starvation would thus welcome as a brother the literal starvation of the Depression Years, as it would aid him in that central necessity for any artist: to find a communicative Form whereby he can simultaneously heal his inner disconnections and end his disconnection from others. His gift permits him, while integrating the contrarieties within, to provide such integration for his audience as to unite him with it. This is the self-healing and other-healing function of all art. It is ultimately what Odets, on his deathbed, kept calling "the merging of subject and object."

p. 153
9.3

Erikson's classic discussion illuminates Odets' shaky sense of himself: "True 'engagement' with others is the result and the test of firm self-delineation. Where this is still missing, the young individual when seeking tentative forms of playful intimacy in friendship and competition, in sex play and love, in argument and gossip, is apt to experience a peculiar strain, as if such tentative engagement might turn into an interpersonal fusion amounting to a loss of identity, and requiring, therefore, a tense inner reservation, a caution in commitment. Where a youth does not resolve such strain he may isolate himself and enter, at best, only stereotyped and formalized interpersonal relations; or he may, in repeated hectic attempts and repeated dismal failures, seek intimacy with the most improbable partners. *For where an assured sense of identity is missing even friendships and affairs become desperate attempts at delineating the fuzzy outlines of identity by mutual narcissistic mirroring: to*

---

* I have explored this in a paper on masochism: Brenman, "On Teasing and Being Teased: And the Problem of 'Moral Masochism.' "

fall in love then often means to fall into one's mirror image, hurting oneself and damaging the mirror. During lovemaking or in sexual fantasies, a loosening of sexual identity threatens: it even becomes unclear whether sexual excitement is experienced by the individual or by his partner, and this in either heterosexual or homosexual encounters. The ego thus loses its flexible capacity for abandoning itself to sexual and affectual sensations, in a fusion with another individual who is both partner to the sensation and guarantor of one's continuing identity: *fusion with another becomes identity loss.* A sudden collapse of all capacity for mutuality threatens, and a *desperate wish ensues to start all over again,* with a (quasi-deliberate) regression to a stage of basic bewilderment and rage such as only the very small child knows" (italics mine).* It is likely that in that minority who become originators, whether in art, in science, or in history, such a self-delineation is a longer and more complex process than in the simpler, more obedient members of a society (who experience fewer choices). Erikson's observation that in these circumstances "to be a suicide" can become *in itself* an identity choice is echoed by Odets' comment: "He killed himself because that was the only way he could live."† It would be interesting to see how the progression is different in artists like Mozart, where the development of an artist commences as an obedience, not as a rebellion.

p. 157
9.4

Testimony to the sharpness of his ambivalence is the fact of his tears that same evening—so bitter he had to leave the room—when one of these same "wild Hebrews" read aloud the poem of Exile, the 137th Psalm, which he recorded, reading and rereading it.

p. 157
9.5

Repeatedly, Odets uses the cricket, the humble bug that makes "night music," as a symbol for innocent self-expression. He would call his last work for the Group Theatre *Night Music.*

p. 158
9.6

It would take a militant anti-Freudian and anti-Jungian to ignore the archetypal phallic symbols here. The great "winged creatures" in all of literature defy gravity and plant the seeds of life. Odets feared that his father's immense power could destroy his capacity to "fly"—as a man, and as a creator.

p. 159
9.7

In the play, a character identifies his own brother as a labor spy. Lebowitz recalled then a day when he had been in a violent argument with his brother, up for the weekend. Odets, nearby, "wondered why I was fighting with one of the guests. . . . I replied, 'I know that bastard very well . . . I slept in the same bed with him for ten years. He's my brother.'"

In the closing moments of the labor-spy episode, Clancy (who has changed his name to the more elegant "Clayton") says: "I got nothing to hide. Your own secretary knows I'm straight." An unidentified voice then says, "Sure, boys, you know who this sonofabitch is?" Clayton replies: "I never seen you before in my life!!" To which the voice responds: "Boys, I

* E. H. Erikson, "Identity and the Life Cycle."
† In Odets' play *The Big Knife.*

slept with him in the same bed sixteen years. HE'S MY OWN LOUSY BROTHER!!"

p. 172
10.1

The theme of the doomed (or crippled) young artist/musician/actor would frequently appear in his plays (Pearl in *Paradise Lost, Golden Boy, Rocket to the Moon, Till the Day I Die, The Big Knife, The Country Girl*).

p. 184
10.2

Cf. Eugene O'Neill to Carlotta Monterey: ". . . Mistress, I desire you, you are my passion, and my life-drunkenness, and my ecstasy, and the wine of joy to me! Wife, you are my love, and my happiness, and the word behind my word, and the half of my heart! *Mother, you are my lost way refound*, my end and my beginning, the hand I reach out for in my lonely night, from my ghost-haunted inner dark, and *on your soft breasts there is a peace for me that is beyond death!* . . ."*

p. 186
10.3

The unconscious fantasy once again is that the writer must "eat his words," subsisting on them or, as Thomas Wolfe often said, perishing by gluttony or self-poisoning.

p. 186
10.4

In O'Neill's play, a decade earlier, the protagonist named "Yank" dies in the arms of a gorilla in the zoo, which he greets as "brother," saying, "Even him didn't t'ink I belonged . . . where do I fit in?" O'Neill concludes that in death ". . . perhaps the Hairy Ape at last belongs."†

p. 200
11.1

A five-year-old black girl, asked in a psychological study some years ago to paint a "perfect picture," covered the entire page with white paint!

p. 210
12.1

Such quasi-hallucinations of delicious food are commonly found in patients whose emotional hunger is such that they alternate between an extravagant intake of food and self-starvation, the latter often being a desperate ascetic effort to control the former. The archaic hunger in this pattern is dynamically more important than its overtones of adult sexuality.

p. 210
12.2

On the back of this journal entry for March 31, 1932, there is a scrap of dialogue by a character called "Ralph." It is remarkable that even in this brief snatch of dialogue from *I Got the Blues*, to become the very beginning of *Awake and Sing!*, the formal and emotional stamp of Odets is legible, as are the central themes of his life and work. He pleads for a solution to overt conflict (people who don't want war), for unblocked perception ("open eyes"), for group-consciousness ("people on the side of people"), for honest people who say "the money-men are wrong." In short, he seeks "brothers who want a new world!"

p. 223
13.1

Clurman's observation that Lawson lost his talent when he plowed under one end of his conflict supports my conviction that creative tension is sustained when an artist has sufficient tolerance for ambiguities to permit him to maintain a diversity,

* Gelb, *O'Neill*, p. 760.
† Gelb, *O'Neill*, p. 489.

even a struggle, within the unity he creates in form.* If the conflict is intolerable and one or the other pole of it disappears (as with Lawson's conversion to a doctrinaire Marxism which served to keep him from the spiritual bankruptcy he feared), there is no live dynamic conflict available, and thus the work goes dead and becomes logical argument (Yeats' "rhetoric") instead of emotional communication.† The plays are consequently stillborn. Perhaps creativity in a given culture rests similarly on the existence of such a dialectic: where one end of the conflict is abolished (as in a totalitarian state), there is little genuine creativity in the arts. The ubiquitous unconscious conflict between the feminine and masculine sides of an identity found in the romantic artist (perhaps in all artists) is relevant here.‡ Another way of conceiving this issue is to say a working artist maintains a high tension between the syntonic and dystonic aspects of himself. Thus, he may have a delicate balance between trust and mistrust, autonomy and shame, industry and inferiority, initiative and guilt, identity and identity confusion, intimacy and isolation, etc.§

p. 223   Lawson's grandfather, a Mr. Levy with a first name unknown
13.2   even to his grandson, was part of the Second Wave in 1848, a Russian-Polish Jew. He settled in Springfield, Massachusetts. His son, whom he called Simeon, became a cowboy, a rare calling for a Jew, and rode herd from Houston, Texas, to Mexico City as part of his general preparation for becoming the head of the successful Reuters Press Cables in New York City in 1846.

Simeon married a cultivated and idealistic German-Jewish woman whose choice of names for her children reflected her self-conscious investment in America: one was Wendell Holmes, another Adelaide Jeffrey, and a third was named after an American prison reformer, John Howard.

Simeon Levy found it easier to obtain school admissions for these children (or even hotel reservations) when he signed his letters "S. Levy-Lawson"; thus he determined to change his name. This name-change embodied a characteristic attempt at a Jewish-American synthesis Odets would also evince, even in such details as the naming of the central character in his play *Night Music*, Abraham Lincoln Rosenberger (how like the names of American blacks: "Martha Washington Jones"), or in the naming of his only son, Walt Whitman Odets. Lawson (presumed to be the model for the central character in *Most Likely to Succeed*, written by his old friend John Dos Passos) had been the first American playwright to struggle vainly in 1928, at Dreiser's request, to make an honest screenplay of *Sister Carrie*, the story of the corruption of an innocent. Sixteen years later Odets, again at Dreiser's request, would also try in vain to accomplish this task, and subsequently another attempt would be planned by American playwright Lillian Hellman, only to be

* Brenman-Gibson, "Notes on the Study of the Creative Process." Also: Brenman-Gibson, "Creation of Plays: With Specimen Analysis."
† Wyatt, "The Reconstruction of the Individual and of the Collective Past."
‡ Brenman-Gibson, ibid.
§ E. H. Erikson, "The 'Works.' "

thwarted by the terror of the blacklist.* And twenty years after that, Odets' pupil William Gibson would be invited to make a stab at it, but he would have the good sense to refuse.

p. 225
13.3

In his monumental account of Martin Luther, Erikson says: "The aim of monasticism is to decrease the wish . . . to destroy . . . to an absolute minimum. 'I was holy,' Luther said. 'I killed nobody but myself.' "†

p. 229
13.4

Odets' wives would learn in painful experience that on some level he was quite literal in the conviction that whatever he spent on a woman sexually was taken from his creative energy. Immediately after their marriage he set severe limits on his sexual relationship with Luise Rainer, and he abandoned Bette Grayson sexually for the first several months of their married life. Apparently, premarital sex, except for this monastic period at Dover Furnace, carried less threat of creative damage.‡

Thirty years after writing this "Beethoven play," having undergone many years of psychotherapy, he would turn once again to a consideration of Beethoven's art in relation to his embattled life, trying to use it as a whip on his own back.§

p. 231
13.5

Cf. Odets' *Golden Boy* (1937).

p. 232
13.6

Precisely this theme, ten years later, inspired Odets' play *Trio*, which became *Clash by Night*.

p. 233
13.7

During my interviews of L. J. Odets, which totaled eighteen hours, I have noted that my leading and steady thought was, "How dare you!" My experience of outrage was not simply the repeated response of an "underling" to the repeated affronts of an "executive" of big business. It was his intrusive, narcissistic *disregard of what I am* that was so offensive. In vivo, I had experienced what the Odets children had grown up with.

p. 234
13.8

For Odets and for most Group members—and, indeed, for Eugene O'Neill—as happens in many a fragmenting society, the attempt is to consolidate a utopian enterprise, diffusely aimed at upholding the Judaeo-Christian ethic by opposing commercialism, "spiritual materialism," and war. Such attempts usually have psychological roots in a Beethoven-like aspiration toward "Bruderschaft," as well as in a social activism. They are of an entirely different order from the powerful, tough, savvy political artillery which had brought about the Russian Revolution. They are also quite different from the destructive parochial politics that was played within the next two decades by congressional investigators, who humiliated, imprisoned, or destroyed many of those in and out of the Group who were earnestly en-

---

* Gould, *Modern American Playwrights*, p. 179.
† E. H. Erikson, *Young Man Luther*, p. 109.
‡ Luise Rainer, interviewed by M. Brenman-Gibson, March 20, 1964; also Robbe Garfield Cohn, interviewed by M. Brenman-Gibson, May 28, 1964.
§ Cf. Odets' long memorandum on Beethoven, written in 1962 (Odets Literary Estate).

gaged, like Odets, in trying to locate—with a curious innocence —the significance and the moral core of their existence.*

p. 234
13.9

In this statement of the experience of an altered state of consciousness we see what psychoanalyst and art historian Ernst Kris would later try to abstract for the creative process under the rubric "a regression in the service of the ego." In countless ways, throughout his life, Odets would trace the interferences (in himself) of this "fluid emotional flow."

p. 248
14.1

Herbert Bayard Swope (originally Schwab), editor of the New York *World,* who would become known as a "foul-weather Jew," early saw the growing threat as far worse even than the Crusades.

p. 248
14.2

The complex Theodore Dreiser, for example, in impotent negotiation about a "picture idea" for Mae West with Hollywood film magnates—many of them Jewish—had begun to express his private conviction that Jews should be deported. "The world's quarrel with the Jew," he said, "is not that he is inferior, but that he is superior." In public—together with his fellow *American Spectator* editors Sherwood Anderson, Ernest Boyd, James Branch Cabell, George Jean Nathan and Eugene O'Neill—he published in September of 1933 a mythical "Editorial Conference (With Wine)," supposedly a whimsy, on the subject of the Jews and the "rising question of a Jewish homeland."† Dreiser argued that Jews were internationalist rather than nationalist and thus formed an "unassimilated racial group that threatened to overrun America." Nathan belittled Jewish poetry and music. O'Neill proposed a homeland in Africa, while Boyd suggested giving the Jews the state of Kansas. Dreiser recommended a handicap for Jews: a limitation on numbers in given lines of work. Thus, "100,000 Jewish lawyers might be reduced to ten and the remainder made to do farming." Many of Dreiser's friends, Jews and Gentiles alike, saw no humor in this "editorial conference"; they had already begun to respond to pained pleas for help from fellow artists—Jews and non-Jews—fleeing from Germany. Hutchins Hapgood, Hy Kraft, and Jerome Blum were outraged.

One of the earliest to seek help was the poet-playwright Bertolt Brecht, a Gentile who left Germany for Denmark the day after Hermann Goering's Reichstag fire, contrived by Hitler to seem the work of left-wing intellectuals and Jews, the prime dissenters in Germany. Brecht told Lee Strasberg‡ he had been among the first seven of Hitler's "wanted men." Millions of them, less far-sighted or perhaps less mobile than Brecht, would shortly vanish in smoke. Brecht, forced to run just ahead of the German army, would live briefly in Sweden and in Finland, finally landing in 1941 in the United States, where he applied at once for citizenship and soon became a staunch admirer of Odets' *Waiting for Lefty.* In September 1947 he would be inter-

* Cf. Halsey, *The Pseudo-Ethic.*
† Swanberg, *Theodore Dreiser,* p. 408.
‡ Interviewed by M. Brenman-Gibson, March 3, 1968.

rogated by the House Committee on Un-American Activities. In
1948 he left for East Berlin, where he died in 1956.

p. 249
14.3

It is against this history that Eugene O'Neill in the 1920s—long
before the Great Depression—had already begun the American
dramatist's protest: the many-sided sense of being blocked (inside and out) from meaningful life and from direct perception,
the feeling of not belonging in a shapeless world rapidly dehu-
manizing itself through technology and the piratical values of
business and war. To O'Neill it mattered greatly that the meaning, strength, and solace earlier supplied by the coherence of
religious belief was fast slipping away. Other American dramatists after World War I tried to construct a non-religious Weltanschauung by combining the insights of Freud and Marx—or,
to put it more accurately, to show how the dilemmas of human
experience derive simultaneously from both "inner" and "outer"
serfdom.

Even before World War I, O'Neill in published poems was
passionately calling on "comrades" not to "bleed and groan for
Guggenheim" or "to give your lives for Standard Oil" but rather
to "awaken to new birth," to "rise up in your might and cry 'All
workers on the earth are brothers and we will not fight.' "* It is
striking, however, that during this rock-bottom period of the
Depression the usually melancholy O'Neill, removed to his Sea
Island mansion, responded with a defensively pleasant and sentimental comedy (*Ah, Wilderness!*) and a desperate, divided,
and awkward effort to affirm the ready-made solutions of the
Catholic Church (*Days Without End*). O'Neill would not be
heard from again until after World War II.†

p. 249
14.4

Erikson, in constructing his view of the human life cycle, describes the extremes of play. At one end, he said, there stands
the microsphere of the child's "small world of manageable toys
. . . (a harbor to return to when he needs privately to overhaul
his ego)" and at the other end the productions of the artist. He
describes our visionary propensity: "I would postulate that the
infant's *scanning* search with his eyes, and his recognition of
what is continuously lost and found again, is the first *significant
interplay* (just consider its later dramatization in peek-a-boo)."
For my purpose here, this first dramatization in the game of
peek-a-boo can be considered a paradigm for the transaction between playwright and audience.

It begins to appear possible to construct, at least theoretically, a playwright's line of development starting with "the first
significant interplay"—that is to say, the infant's scanning and
filtering of the "buzzing, blooming confusions" both within and
without, and moving on hopefully from the gestalt of the mother's face to efforts in dramatic, enacted childhood play to construct the future while reconstructing the past.‡ Finally, blessed
with a gift for symbolic play construction (playing with thoughts
and states of consciousness) and provided that his guilt at such

* Gelb, *O'Neill*, p. 245.
† Lawson, *Hidden Heritage*.
‡ E. H. Erikson, *Toys and Reasons*.

play with the fires of creation is not disabling, the playwright will, by way of form, create a vision that will evoke a communal response from an audience. In this regard, a play is assuredly first cousin to a ritual. Lacking the support of a communal tradition, however, a contemporary playwright must succeed in creating an immediate interplay with his audience, as he has little leeway for recovery.

After many false starts, I decided to restudy Erikson's innovative outline of dream analysis with a view to adapting it for the microscopic analysis of plays.

Just as the child reveals through play the infantile form of the human ability to deal with experience by creating model situations and to master reality by experiment, thus redeeming failures and strengthening hopes, and the adult dreamer is likewise driven to accomplish the "deed that cannot be left undone,"* it now began to appear that the playwright is doing all of this and something more. As he activates or "moves" himself, revealing himself to himself, bringing about not simply revelation but also renewal—called, in other areas, "enlivening," "healing," "holy inspiration," or "recreation"—so is his audience revealed to itself, restoratively reached, touched, moved, and at best unified and liberated, at least for a time. We think of motion as the essence of life. Thus we are grateful to the playwright who manages to leap the abyss separating him from us and in so doing to bring us to new life by "moving" us.

Like a child's play construction or a dream, the play is ingeniously transposed, and it is far more cunning than either. It uses all the primary thought processes of the dream: displacing, condensing, reversing, and substituting within the basic container we call form all the identity-elements, themes, images, and crises of life.†

p. 250   Throughout Odets' work the conflict between the wish for mate-
14.5   rial success and creative expression is evident. There are less explicit examples in contemporary drama. For example, in Pinter's *The Homecoming* the playwright's struggle and his fear of what happens to his own creativity is symbolized by his wife, who is a fashion model and the mother of his three sons. In the second act the play *appears* to have gotten out of hand when the family—the father and brothers—who have been trying to seduce the wife now invite her to stay with *them* and to earn money by becoming a whore (prostituting the playwright's talents). The terms of the "deal" are discussed. The father's "kiss me" to his daughter-in-law at the end is not unlike Hennie's going off with Moe Axelrod in Odets' *Awake and Sing!* or Cleo's *refusal* to go with Mr. Prince in his *Rocket to the Moon*. Pinter's play is all in reverse (emotionally), like a "negative" of a picture. Pinter expresses his credo as *observer* through the Ph.D. son.

p. 251   Dr. Leslie Farber suggests‡ that this feeling of having minimal
14.6   freedom of movement reflects Odets' feeling not only about his

* E. H. Erikson, *Toys and Reason.*
† Brenman-Gibson, "Creation of Plays: With Specimen Analysis."
‡ Private communication.

own family but about the Group Theatre and the constricting tone of the Depression era.

p. 251
14.7

Two decades later Odets would *still* say, "All my plays deal with one subject: the struggle not to have life nullified by circumstances, false values, anything."*

p. 251
14.8

In 1967, according to the director of a revival of *Awake and Sing!* at the Charles Playhouse in Cambridge, Massachusetts, the "adjustment" the actors would take for rehearsals was an underlying conviction that *nothing* would really work out "for the best." Only thus could the performers make the play credible to themselves.

p. 252
14.9

Erikson calls them "identity elements." Perhaps the term "identity fragment" should be used only for an *unassimilated* element.†

p. 252
14.10

Compare Odets' sense of Yiddish as a mother tongue with the speech about Dostoevsky and "I pretend to be an American" in his early play *910 Eden Street* (p. 20).

p. 253
14.11

There is something automotive and virile in the name Axelrod. It not only carries the flavor of L.J.'s actual powerful, expensive automobiles, but also the series of such autos in which a long list of Odets' characters would murder innocents or would commit suicide. That Odets creates this powerful "big-car" man *as a cripple* suggests his unconscious appreciation of his father's secret and frustrated longings to be a "real big man" as a rich and successful writer (L.J.'s advertising agency, his "book," *How to Smooth the Selling Path*—actually written by a hack in his advertising agency—and his plays written under the name "Stedo"). Although as a child Odets consciously thought of his father as a paragon of virility to be emulated, there are many indications that he understood his father's unconscious vulnerabilities, and his consequent need to keep "proving" himself by whatever fraudulent means. L.J. (so often away on jaunts) must have seemed "a boarder," like Moe Axelrod.

p. 253
14.12

"Indelible ink" indeed. Odets' unconscious fantasy of submitting himself in every way to his powerful, venal, and attractive father returns over and over: for example, in his later *Golden Boy*, where the pugilist-violinist succumbs to the blandishments of the gangster who brings him silk shirts (he must then commit suicide); in *Rocket to the Moon*, where the aspiring young dancer Cleo Singer (translate: a girl who "sings"—that is, who creates art—"Cleopatra," beloved of the conqueror) must decide whether to run away with a man very like the crippled sybarite Moe Axelrod in *Awake and Sing!*, a "Mr. Prince" (L. J. Odets' reiterated comparison of himself and the "Prince of Wales"), who intrigues her with elegant handkerchiefs and gardenia toilet water at "forty dollars an ounce," etc., etc. There were adumbrations of this *struggle against seduction and cor-*

* Hyams, "Twenty Years on a Tightrope."
† E. H. Erikson, *Identity: Youth and Crisis.*

ruption by the father in Odets' earliest writing, and it continues throughout his works.

p. 254
14.13

Bessie Berger occupies the same emotional "territory" as Belle Stark in Odets' later play *Rocket to the Moon*. Both derive externally from actress Stella Adler.

p. 254
14.14

The Greenbaum family were Bronx neighbors; Paul also had been an aspiring writer. Originally Odets, in his diary, called this play "The Greenbaum Play." Noteworthy that all of the names here except Axelrod are German-Yiddish (mother's side), not Russian (Berger, Feinschreiber, Grossman, Schlosser). Note: Grossman means "big man"—this is the name of the man who raped and impregnated Hennie. Odets was always profoundly ashamed he was not a "big man" genitally. He called his penis, however, "the President" or "presidential timber." L.J. was always talking of successful and important men as "big men."

p. 254
14.15

L. J. Odets said this of *himself* to me about diapering, feeding the children cod-liver oil, etc.*

p. 254
14.16

L.J. often commented, "It's a world of dog eat dog." Odets' character Joe Bonaparte in *Golden Boy* says, "When I go down the street, it's a war."

p. 254
14.17

This is Odets' image of his father's *most unconscious* view of *himself*, but quite consciously L. J. Odets' image of his actor-son, Clifford.

p. 255
14.18

In an early draft of *Awake and Sing!* Odets has crossed out ". . . every day is like the kid who stood in the synagogue while the rabbi sang sad songs."†

p. 256
14.19

Odets' internalized father is in the Chinese warlord in the film *The General Died at Dawn;* the "fascist" in *The Silent Partner;* Fuseli in *Golden Boy;* Mr. Prince in *Rocket to the Moon;* Earl in *Clash by Night;* Marcus Hoff in *The Big Knife;* Bernie Dodd in *The Country Girl.*

p. 256
14.20

In Odets' play *Victory* (1932) the *mother is dead also,* leaving a boy alone with his father.

p. 256
14.21

Joseph, son of Jacob, is, like Joe Bonaparte in *Golden Boy,* the corruptible dreamer or artist. Jacob occupies the same psychological ground as the fine old Italian father of Joe Bonaparte (translate: the "good part," but also the conqueror), who wants his son to conquer with his music, not by his murderous physical strength. Later Odets wrote "Joseph and His Brethren," a screenplay about the great "dreamer" who, abandoned by his brothers to die, became a powerful ruler in Egypt. Joseph was one of Odets' Biblical favorites, along with Noah, Saul, and

---

* Interview, June 19, 1965.
† Manuscript, *Awake and Sing!,* Research Library, The New York Public Library at Lincoln Center.

David. He thought of Elia Kazan as a "Joseph"—"a dreamer and an opportunist."

p. 258
14.22

I have noted that years later, stuck in a creative impasse, Odets would say, "Hapless and helpless . . . the Jewish prophet is being eaten alive by the Jewish father in me; and if somewhere it doesn't stop soon, I shall be indeed dead."* This is the central struggle of his creative life. In *Awake and Sing!* the "Jewish prophet" commits suicide (as do so many of Odets' idealist-innocents in his gallery of play characters) and is resurrected in the boy Ralph. The title changes then from *I Got the Blues* to *Awake and Sing!* (". . . ye that dwell in the dust, for thy dew is as the dew of herbs and the earth shall cast out the dead"— Isaiah, 26:19).

p. 258
14.23

Cf. Odets' 1932 diary, where Odets writes of his secret dead wife and daughter: "Their days won't be for nothing!"

p. 258
14.24

Group actor J. Edward Bromberg wrote on the wall at Dover Furnace: "Clifford Odets born, 1932."

p. 259
14.25

The direct historical line between the early Yiddish theatre described by Irving Howe† and the work of Odets emerges as a surprise which Howe does not indicate. Odets' moving of the drab lives of ordinary Jewish-Americans onto the Broadway stage so that they occupied it "with as much right as Lear" provided an evolutionary step from a kind of folk sentiment or grandiose spectacle to serious indigenous drama of a sort different from O'Neill's, whose spiritual ancestry in Strindberg was very different from any folk tradition. The collective identity of Americans who were second-generation immigrants (Jews and non-Jews), as well as of those other "homeless cosmopolitans," was first given articulate voice by Odets.

p. 272
15.1

This letter to Tamara is a good example of Odets' struggle. On the one hand, he re-enacts what was for him an experience of having been abandoned; this is followed by accusation and punishment: his blackmailing threats of suicide. On the other hand, it is leavened by optimism ("I have faith in life and people").

p. 276
15.2

Herewith an abbreviated representative example of Odets' didactic talks at the Theatre Union in the fall of 1933; it distills a significant turning point in the history of the American theatre:

TOWARD A NEW THEATRE

To most of us the theory of real theatre has been lost. I would not like to wrangle about this statement, but quote instead a paraphrase of a section of the Communist Manifesto: "Don't wrangle with us so long as you apply to an intended revolutionary theatre the standards of your bourgeois notions of theatre. Your very ideas of theatre are but the outgrowth of your contact with only bourgeois theatre." And this is why the theory

---

* Letter to M. Brenman-Gibson, October 23, 1962.
† Howe, *World of Our Fathers*.

of real theatre has been lost to us. Because the bourgeois theatre is truthfully the only theatre we know and IT IS NOT REAL THEATRE, but instead a highly disjointed bastardized form of entertainment worthy of no name but Death and Corruption. . . .

But in isolated cases real theatre still does exist. The old traditional Japanese and Chinese theatres are some such, altho they are really defunctive elaborate forms concerned with a dead content. . . .

The earliest form of such theatre existed in primitive societies, exists even today. From the ordinary everyday life of such a society sprang a need to express itself and its problems. There was no rain: it became necessary to organize a ceremonial dance, an elaborate ritual in which certain members of the tribe became the chief actors. A ceremonial to call on the gods for rain. But a curious condition is here observed—that in such rituals the audience played as large a part as did the actors. *There were no passive watchers in those theatres* and their mobility and participation came from the fact that they were as deeply interested in the theatricalized theme as those who carried it out as actors. At the same time the setting, the actual size and structure of the theatre, the properties to be used, the words and incantations . . . *all of these expressed a central and common purpose, a purpose deeply understood and realized by all present.* It was the same in hunting rituals before and after the hunt, in the spring planting festivals, at harvest time In other words, let us say that the entire performance was always motivated and animated thruout by a social need. The ceremony became thus a social expression. So understood, a real theatre is always a social theatre used to express a communal idea or necessity.

Now when we move away from this so-called lower level of human society and come to feudal existence we shall find the same conception of theatre holds true here. . . . In fact this collective conception is the base of all the great arts of that time. The social need produced Homer as surely as it did the Bible. And the Catholic church produced not only Gregorian chant, but a long string of very great painters. Not to neglect the church dramas, the so-called "mysteries," and the great Gothic cathedrals, an art completely anonymous and communal to which few individual names can be attached. Indeed, all that art is a monument to the memory of the masses, of collectives, not to some particular artist. And it is all illuminated, even up into the music of Bach (who is practically the last of those days) by an impersonality expressing only the collective or social intention.

But here comes the French revolution. The rise of the bourgeoisie. Free trade. The stressing of the individual above that of the common or collective good. Shakespeare's theatre is already left behind. So is Molière's. The great star actors now come on the scene. Heine is able to answer a friend who asks, as they look at a Gothic cathedral, "Why is it that today we cannot build such structures?" he answers, "Because they were built out of convictions and we today have only opinions."

This is a very prophetic remark. . . .

But what has happened to the theatre in all this time? The single artist, the one who works with himself, as painter, writer, musician, he has been able to keep himself and his point of view integrated. One painter on a single canvas still knows that his color, line, design, subject matter—all must be organized towards one common result. He himself makes that organization. But the theatre is a collective art, consists of many different artists working towards a finished production. Before, as in the primitive ceremonies or church mysteries, *the ideology was common to all.* The playwright, the actor, the director, the scenery man—all unconsciously shared a common approach to their work. But today? No sir, there is no common approach because there is no longer a common viewpoint. So we have the Theatre Guild presenting first a Catholic play, next a Marxist play, next a play upholding the most terrible reactionary standards of life, and all with no sense of any point of view in agreement or opposed to them. . . .

Now here I have gotten a little off the track, but let us take a look at the present day Soviet Russia theatre and see by what accident it managed to get on the right track. . . . None at all, but by the fact of a revolution which was no accident. By the fact of a new society coming into existence. By a need to give expression and meaning in theatrical terms to that society. By a new common ideology. By a new NEED, a social need. . . .

Today in America there is no theatre anywhere with a collective statement. America has never had a cultural ideology in the first place. In each place where this may seem misstatement you will find those people brought over European culture and grafted it to their present environment. In the second place, since they are completely under the domination of big money men, the American theatre and movie is frantically apologizing for instead of criticizing the economic system. Thirdly, they are only interested in making money.

Because of the fact that we are liable to still limit ourselves to the bourgeois notion of theatre, let us (and since we are agreed that the American theatre is not a cultural unit organized to express a basic sense of life around it except negatively) —make a working definition of theatre, based on this present discourse. Vachtangov, a very talented Russian director who has since died, put it very neatly when he said, "*A theatre is an ideologically cemented collective.*" He adds, "Only where such a collective is present is the creation of a real theatre possible. The subject of creative work in a theatre is not the director, not single actors, but the collective as a whole; and if this collective does not unite by ideological and artistic aims common to all its members, if all the members are not brought up on the basis of the same principles and methods, if it is made up—as theatrical companies are generally made up—of actors picked up in a casual manner, such a collective will not be the subject for genuine theatre, a theatre valuable artistically and socially, but a corpse instead.". . .

The Communist Manifesto accuses the bourgeoisie of reducing the family relationship—in fact all cultural relationships too—to the same money relationship. So in the capitalist theatre, it is natural to find the actor in this role as completely as any other worker. Why is it important that the actor have more than a mere money relationship to our theatre? The answer is obvious. Firstly, because he is the most important part of the theatre. The actor is at all times *the exact point of contact with the audience.* We hear you say "The director's conception?" Yes, but it is only the actor who will carry out that conception. . . .

Our theatre's work is undoubtedly the communication of a materialistic sense of life, and surely *this work must develop progressively* in clarity, intensity, and scope with each play produced. Only a permanent acting company will make possible such progress. For this reason and others soon to be mentioned, the slick Broadway actor is valueless. He brings dust, no belief, no truth. He brings stale old technique, stagnant tricks, and sonorous stale platitudes of acting, which surely had their roots in our present decaying society. He brings type casting, artistic sterility, and all the old stage hokum and bunk. . . . Exactly as the social unit grew in the capitalist society to one—that is, to the individual instead of the group and common good—exactly has the theatre or any other art followed the same road, and it would be easy to show you how in this respect and others, the theatre mirrors completely economic change down through history. Ensemble playing is in itself a revolutionary thing derived from the common approach to work, as opposed to the individual one. When you hire individual actors for a single production, each actor is playing with a stranger, instead of being integrated in an ensemble in which each is to the other a comrade and a deep friend. . . .

We do not believe that the usual period of four weeks is sufficient for the preparation of a production. On Broadway where chiefly the only work done with actors is the giving of positions and memorizing of lines, this period is sufficient—in fact, over sufficient; but for our ideal—a true laying open of a script—a true formation of a production from the starting point of a script and its meaning should take longer than the four weeks allotted by custom. For this reason also, a permanent company is valuable. While working in one production, they are rehearsing in another. In fact, often two may be rehearsed simultaneously. *Our theatre must be organized to assure itself an unbroken line of activity. All plans should point toward continuity of performance, if a true social value is to be expressed.* Again for this reason, a permanent company should be formed in which there are no leading actors, and no class distinction of small parts and big parts. Here we must be workers with a common goal in mind.

In closing, it might be wise to mention the financial elements involved in the forming of a permanent company, since as we mentioned some time ago, an already established audience predicates the same possibilities as a financial subsidy, it is almost possible even now—granting a summer in which to prepare at least one production, to promise a group of actors employment for at least twenty or thirty weeks. In worrying about the actors' financial status, we must not forget that many of them would still remain unemployed when not employed by the Theatre Union.

p. 278
15.3

The closing of what may be Mel Brooks' best film, *The Twelve Chairs*, asks the same question when the performer must undergo an epileptic convulsion for a crowd in order to collect a few pennies.

p. 280
15.4

It is thus that the title *I Got the Blues* becomes *Awake and Sing!*, and in a later play the character symbolizing the poet is a young girl called Cleo Singer (*Rocket to the Moon*). Still later, *Night Music*, and when all seems lost, music turns to war (*Clash by Night*).

p. 281
15.5

Cf. *Paradise Lost* in *Six Plays of Clifford Odets*, Grove Press, 1979:

I:1, p. 185   SCHNABEL: In the shop the girls work for one dollar a day—nine hours. Forty-five-hour week. Five dollars for girls a week, seven dollars for men. But on payday Mr. Katz makes us sign statements we get more—thirteen and seventeen. . . .

I:1, p. 186   LUCY: We keep the lunches under the table where the cockroaches run all over it.

II:1, p. 206   PIKE: This *system!* Breeds wars like a bitch breeds pups!

p. 291
16.1

The unifying force in the fantasy of belonging to Old Testament Jewry is similar to that of novelist Henry Roth, precisely the same age as Odets, who in this year would complete his first work, *Call It Sleep*—a novel to be ignored for thirty years—about the terror of a young son in an immigrant family in a New York Jewish ghetto. Roth would stop writing, marry a "shiksa," and retire to an impoverished life in the Maine hinterlands.*

p. 292
16.2

From an early draft of *Paradise Lost* (Act II, p. 18), a sample dialogue:

LEO: Tell me, my friend. You went around the country many times. You saw many kinds of people. Down in their cellars—

PIKE: Your cellar's got spiders. I told your wife: hot water! For birth and death, plenty of hot water.

LEO: Take a few nuts.

PIKE: Don't mind if I do. (*Starts eating and cracking them from bowl at elbow*)

LEO: What is to be done? I keep asking myself this question. Never in my forty-nine years did I meet a happy man. What is wrong?

PIKE: A great man said, "The weight of dead centuries presses down on the brain of the living."

LEO: This means . . . ?

PIKE: Examine a drop of ocean water under microscope. Know about the whole ocean.

LEO: It sounds reasonable.

PIKE: Then examine the ones in your family. Scrutinize hard, citizen. Examine the family basis today. What's the germs

* Irving Howe, "Life Never Let Up," *The New York Times Book Review*, October 25, 1964. Also, "The Belated Success of Henry Roth," *Life*, January 8, 1965; Roth, *Call It Sleep.*

you see in that ingenious microscope? Why, those strepto-cocci is wiggling out one message with their fiery tails—"Everything on a money basis—S.O.S. !"

LEO: True enough!

PIKE: Our society makin' the ideals and they so rotten that a hungry cat'd shy from them! And not even those maggoty parcels of ideal allowed to mature in the cold breath of com-petition and private production for profit. . . . How you got your food and shelter was that factor which determined what you'd think and write and play for music!

LEO: Yes, this is Hegel's materialistic conception of life.

PIKE: But not enough for Major Hegel to find that out, not by a damn sight! Got mixed up some his self. But then comes along a great prophet. Jew man with a fiery heart. Takes Hegel's words and ideas and forges his self a mighty fight-ing sword!

LEO: Marx, no?

PIKE: Brigadier-General Karl Marx. There's your new Bible, Citizen!

LEO: Yes, we had great men—Spinoza, Marx—

PIKE: Wait! That cycle ain't finished yet. All you Jews'll have to be great men or get your brains scattered around by these so-called Fas-sists.

GUS (*Entering*): I shave and it comes right out again.

Little of this remained in *Paradise Lost* on Broadway.

p. 293
16.3

Even as in the Bible shame plagues Man after he has eaten the forbidden fruit, so in Odets' twentieth-century *Paradise Lost* shame becomes the central hurdle for the innocent boy Ben, pursuing the American dream. He tries to resolve this nullifica-tion of his life by a reluctant alliance with the gangster Kewpie, originally called Kewpie *Wolf* (the devourer), who will help him to find "the dollar" which will wipe out his shame. Kewpie calls him "yellow in his heart" (as Clifford's father often had), and he adds, "I am in you like a tapeworm."* In an early draft of *Paradise Lost* there is the cat who eats her own kittens!

p. 293
16.4

The theme of suicide occurs also in: *Awake and Sing!*, *Waiting for Lefty*, *The Silent Partner*, *Golden Boy*, *Clash by Night*, *The Big Knife*, *The Country Girl*, and even in the character of "the gitka," the singing mouse who has no mate, in Odets' last play, *The Flowering Peach*.

p. 294
16.5

There are remarkable continuities as well as changes in the body of Odets' work offering a range of resolutions to a basic moral dilemma: the principled one of old Jacob in *Awake and Sing!* (who commits suicide) as put forth by Ralph and later by Leo Gordon, or that of the unprincipled gangster who seizes what he wants (as in *Victory*, *910 Eden Street*, *Awake and Sing!*, Kewpie Wolf in *Paradise Lost*, and most clearly in Joe Bonaparte/Eddie Fuseli versus Poppa Bonaparte in *Golden Boy*, and Charlie Castle /Marcus Hoff versus Hank Teagle in *The Big Knife*). By this scheme, *Rocket to the Moon* is Odets' most truly optimistic play:

* Act II, scene 1. Cf. Moe to Hennie in *Awake and Sing!*, "I'm written in you like indelible ink . . . part of your insides," and Odets to the author, "The Jewish prophet is being eaten alive by the Jewish father in me."

Cleo leaves the pallid, cowardly Ben Stark (Ben again!), but she leaves also the seductive, corrupt "old man" Mr. Prince and *goes her own way!*

p. 295
16.6

In the long list of suicides in Odets' plays, there is implied a steady masochistic accusation of his father as the prime cause: "*You* are *killing* me." It was his mother's lifelong message to her husband. For example, Joe Bonaparte, having acceded to the gangster Fuseli, does the same in *Golden Boy*. See also *The Big Knife* and *Clash by Night*.

p. 303
16.7

It is not surprising that the story of Moses and the Promised Land always intrigued Odets. The tale of the great tough Liberator and Ethical Integrator, much occupied with spiritual over material values, is archetypal. He is a street man of vision who, by his insights, points the way to the Promised Land (is it Paradise Regained?), but cannot himself enter it, according to Scripture, because he and his congregation have not trusted in or been sufficiently respectful to God ("Ye have been rebellious since the day that I knew you," says God). Unacquainted with Odets' interest in Moses, Hillard Elkins, producer of the musical version of *Golden Boy*, which Odets did not live to finish, commented, "I was always deeply moved by Clifford. He always seemed to me somehow like Moses who was permitted to catch a glimpse of the Promised Land, but would never enter it."*

p. 305
16.8

The symbol of "cock-eyed" for Odets is always something wrong, askew, to be ashamed of, mocked: something wrong with his masculinity.

p. 315
17.1

Testimony to the angry despair of the contemporary young artist of the 1960s, as old forms were breaking down, was the defensive and transparent necessity to proclaim the opposite of a union with the audience. The playwright might try to assault or to outrage the audience, turn his back on it (often literally), or make a cinematic shadow play of defecating on its members. Still, the playwright invited them to join in the "happening," never quite certain who was "putting on" whom. The ineradicable impulse to effect a union of artist and audience remained. It is the archetypal impulse in both artist and audience to expand (even to erase) boundaries and to rediscover that ancient unity, lost by us all when we had to learn separateness.† It cannot surprise us that the extremes of *this* form of defense are short-lived.

p. 316
17.2

Waiting for Lefty continued as a political tool‡ in the United States and all over the world for years: in the U.S.S.R. in 1935 and 1936; in November 1936 in Czechoslovakia it influenced young workers to join trade unions instead of Nazi political organizations. There was an official German threat to arrest the

* Conversation with the author, September 7, 1965.
†Cf. Eric Bentley, "I Reject the Living Theatre," *The New York Times*, October 21, 1968. Also, Megan Terry, "Who Says Only Words Make Great Drama?" *The New York Times*, November 10, 1968.
‡ The Communist Manifesto is now omitted from productions of *Lefty*.

actors, and efforts were made, as in many American cities, to interrupt the performances. None of these succeeded. The University of Chile asked the U.S. State Department in 1943, in order to celebrate the Fourth of July, for permission to present *Lefty;* in Japan in 1946, under the supervision of the American occupation forces, *Lefty* launched a democratic theatre in Japan; in Ceylon, translated into Sinhalese, it was adapted to a busmen's strike in May 1948; in Paris, in June 1948. How seductive to a man like Odets to feel he could be a "power for good" and progress *all over the world,* and still be on good terms with the United States State Department!

p. 330
17.3

A satisfying understanding of the creative processing of such fantasies of murder or suicide—despite the vast literature on the topic—remains, in the particular instance, elusive. It seems likely, however, that as long as his society provided a socially shared and thus impersonal "enemy" (like capitalism, or Nazism, or American injustice) that could be opposed without guilt, he was rerouted, despite his disclaimer ("My first plays did not repair me from suicide"), from paralyzing fantasies of eliminating himself. Moreover, the relief in the message "See what you have done to me" is universal in masochism, as is the "victory in defeat."*

p. 332
17.4

The correspondence of this with William Gibson's scene in which Will Shakespeare has been whipped (*A Cry of Players*)— also, au fond, a representation of the struggle of a young man *with the authority* of his father—is the more remarkable in light of the fact that Gibson had not seen or read *Till the Day I Die* when he wrote his play. It suggests a universal theme of the relation between the father, the son, and the mother. The same scene, used also by O'Neill, is recognizable in both Odets' and Gibson's stagings as similar to the climax of a Passion Play where another son, scourged and bleeding, is comforted by "the women" after being crucified by "the men."

p. 336
17.5

According to Erikson, the data are accumulating that suggest that the mother of a creative man who achieves prominence has conveyed to her son a feeling of great "specialness" in herself, which she has passed on to him. It is as if she says, "You have something unique, better than your father, and you get it all from me." This identification with the mother (at least of a boy) can thus become a source of great creative strength, but also of a confusion of gender identity.†

p. 344
18.1

In play therapy, a child *cannot play* when he or she is flooded by an emotion that cannot be "handled" by the child; just so— I am coming to believe—is it in the self-curative process we call "creative." The easy, relaxed "playfulness" prerequisite for originating *anything* appears too risky to a person gripped by fear of outcome. It begins to feel dangerous to open up, to "hang loose," to experiment. In child therapy we call such a freezing of free

* Reik, *Masochism in Modern Man.*
† Personal communication.

movement a "play-disruption." Odets called his creative freezing a "work stoppage."*

p. 351
18.2
Florence Odets Kabaker later recalled that another cleaning woman, Ruth Jackson, not Mattie Washington, had come in on this day.† In biography, as in all life history, it devolves upon the interviewer to judge the credibility of the witness and the way an event (always a Rashomon phenomenon) hangs together. In this instance, Mattie Washington's account (perhaps borrowed in part from Ruth Jackson) appeared to be basically coherent and accurate.

p. 357
18.3
It would remain forever a dilemma for Odets—staged and re-staged in his life and in his plays—on which of his parents revengefully to affix his crippling sense of betrayal. Many of the important men of his life, fiercely rejected by him as "a bully" or "a tyrant," said to me, "He must surely have hated his father." On the other hand, the women who feel sexually used, conquered, patronized, and exploited by him say with equal conviction, "A man who hated women so much must have had a bad time with his mother." Even the simplest life is, however, more complicated than the most complex case-analysis. Otherwise, how to account for the other side of the ledger: the men who report having received a unique, maternal nurturance from him and the grateful women who are convinced that, but for Odets, they would have taken their own lives.

Odets always took the public position that he had adored his saintly, heartbroken mother who had died young of grief, and had rejected his bully-Babbitt father who philandered, exploited, bossed, and extorted money from him. Again, true and incomplete. He identified with, resented, admired, rejected, and competed with elements in *both* his parents—as do we all. The integration, however, of this particular mix—with his specific gifts—into a solid and confident identity was severely freighted with difficulty, and all of Odets' plays reflect this struggle. Is the villain Lorna or Fuseli in *Golden Boy*? Belle or Mr. Prince in *Rocket to the Moon*? Mae Wilenski or the boarder in *Clash by Night*? Frank or Georgie in *The Country Girl*?

p. 357
18.4
If indeed the mother of a creative man has established a special kind of tie with her (usually eldest) son and has led him to believe that his creativity stems from something *she* has given him (bypassing his father), then to "forget" her is dangerous for his creativity.‡

p. 381
18.5
There are cyclic times in history when young people—who are the carriers of new ideologies in *any* given generation and in any culture—look to internal states of consciousness for salvation, and others when they look to political solutions. Whereas in the

* See E. H. Erikson, *Toys and Reasons*. Also, Brenman-Gibson, "War on Human Suffering."
† Florence Odets Kabaker, interviewed by M. Brenman-Gibson by telephone, October 1, 1978.
‡ E. H. Erikson, personal communication.

1930s the prevailing world-view issued in a range of proposed *political* solutions, in the 1960s there was a division between political activism and an "expansion of consciousness"—whether by drugs or by spiritual practices—as a "way out." It would be overly facile to suppose that an enthusiasm for political solutions stems solely from a perceived hope they can actually work (as with the new model of Soviet Russia in the 1930s—and far less with China in the 1960s and 1970s). A close study of periods of political revolution and of great "spiritual awakenings" should teach something about this.

p. 409
19.1

Robert E. Sherwood wrote in a preface to his anti-war play *Idiot's Delight* the following: "During the past two weeks (this is March 16, 1936) the Italians have made a great offensive in Ethiopia; there has been an outburst of assassination and hara kiri by Fascists in Japan; the British Foreign Secretary, Mr. Eden, has said in the House of Commons that the current situation is 'dreadfully similar to 1914.'. . . What will happen before this play reaches print or a New York audience, I do not know. But let me express here the conviction that those who shrug and say, 'War is inevitable,' are false prophets. I believe that the world is populated largely by decent people, and decent people don't want war.

"If decent people will continue to be intoxicated by the synthetic spirit of patriotism, pumped into them by megalomaniac leaders, and will continue to have faith in the 'security' provided by those lethal weapons sold to them by the armaments industry, then war *is* inevitable; and the world will soon resolve itself into the semblance of an ant hill, governed by commissars who owe their power to the profundity of their contempt for the individual members of their species."

p. 411
19.2

Odets intended in *The Silent Partner* to make a bolder experiment than usual in carrying out Walt Whitman's credo: ". . . the true use for the imaginative faculty of modern times is to give ultimate vivification to facts . . . and to common lives, endowing them with the glows and glories . . . which belong to every real thing, and to real things only.* William Stott's brilliant discussion *Documentary Expression and Thirties America* is a piece of cultural history that captures the "feel" of this time, and the impulse to endow common lives with glory.

p. 412
19.3

In *The Flowering Peach*, written as Odets neared fifty, the Jewish idiom and speech melodies returned in the mouths of Noah and his wife, characters fashioned after his Philadelphia Aunt Esther and Uncle Israel. In this Old Testament story of hope he tried once again—almost twenty years after *The Silent Partner* —to synthesize the broad, abstracted aims of the allegory and the poetic myth with the vitality of psychologically authentic human beings.

p. 413
19.4

In his own copy of Erikson's *Childhood and Society* Odets has underlined many paragraphs which discuss the experience of smallness and impotence.

* Whitman, *Complete Poetry and Selected Prose*, p. 455.

p. 414
19.5

It is to be expected that the most powerful psychosocial records of human experience (in all cultures, Scripture) universally deal with rock-bottom issues between parents and children, husband and wife, brothers and sisters, and all with some ultimate Other. As dreams are an individual "royal road to the unconscious," so Scripture is a royal road to the collective unconscious.

Odets' regular use of the theme of a Messiah who becomes a blood sacrifice takes its small place in an ancient and evolving account of the moral evolution of humankind away from a self-centered aggression—even cannibalism—and toward a "putting oneself in the place of the other," called love. In the West, from the opening of the Old Testament, God is usually testing and punishing more than He is rewarding. His successive covenants are variations of a bargain, a long account of promises and broken promises. ("If you will do *this* for me, I will do that for you," or, "I will *refrain* from harming you.") As the nature of the bargain changes, the name of God and the image change. There is thus much to be divined from these evolving bargains about the people who are making them. In general, it appears that the Judaeo-Christian image of God moves from a powerful, *tyrannical,* wrathful, and vengeful Male Being who issues commandments and demands total attention, respect, and *obedience* to an image which is softer, more compassionate, empathic, generous, peaceful, inclusive, and self-sacrificing.* The Christian promise in exchange for fidelity finally includes life everlasting.

After the first primitive (broken) contract in Paradise, the next one of significance—after God has destroyed the world—is with Noah, to whom He promises great fertility and safety from destruction if Noah, in turn, will promise *to obey* (again) and *not to kill human beings.*† Maybe the sacrifice of (only) a small piece of vulnerable flesh is a mini-castration, but, more important, it is a substitute for sacrificing an entire person. Circumcision, after all, is not murder. Abraham, however, is again tested to the limit: God asks him to prove *his* obedience by agreeing to give *as a blood sacrifice* his son Isaac. As soon as Abraham agrees, he is, of course, permitted to sacrifice, instead, an animal. But how complex and dreamlike a tale! If we look at the story from God's point of view, he is testing Abraham's surrender to *Him;* from Abraham's point of view it is a test not only of obedience to the Father, but of *self*-reassurance that he *will* be able to kill his son (before his son kills him). If from Isaac's, it is the threat that his father is quite ready to kill him, like Laius with Oedipus, if the situation becomes sufficiently threatening. The Scripture writer's central identification here is with Abraham, who is reassuring *himself* that he need not fear *his father or his son,* and can thus afford *to obey the one and spare the life of the other.*

We come now to Moses. Although God still exacts from him strict obedience to 603 variations on ten themes (a prime one being "no more killing of children"), he now promises, as

* Shatan and Brenman-Gibson, "The Biblical Story of Sarah, Isaac, and Abraham Reconsidered, etc."
† Noah will be the central figure in Odets' last play, *The Flowering Peach.*

YHWH, to be slow to anger, quick to mercy, and compassion-ate.* And the account describes a God who, at the time of the Babylonian Exile, weeps that the Egyptians are drowning in the Red Sea after the children of Israel are safely across. He says, "Are the Egyptians not my children, too?"† Whether one believes that Moses failed to enter the Promised Land because he had impatiently *disobeyed* God (by smiting the rock to get water) or whether, as Freud and Goethe believed, he was slain by the children of Israel who were tired of his righteous com-mandments, Moses, too, is in the line of deliverers who meet with a cruel end.

And, finally, there is Jesus. Perhaps not "finally," but most recently in the West. He is a curiously condensed and subli-mated version of the pre-patriarchal days when Baal, Moloch, and Chemesh actually devoured sons, a story which has been integrated with the later construction of Abraham's willingness to sacrifice Isaac. (Some apocryphal accounts say Isaac, like Jesus, was in fact sacrificed and resurrected.)‡ In any event, there is a large evolutionary step in the image of God when he appears in *human form* in this *first son* (always the sacrificed one in Biblical history).§ This son offers *himself* as a sacrifice, is killed by men, and ministered unto by women. The heart of the matter is that he is "chosen" by God to be crucified so that all may live into eternity. Like the ancient animal sacrifice, *he* is the scapegoat on whom all sins can be piled. It has lately been argued that, on a collective level, the Jewish people serve pre-cisely the same function.‖

Freud once said that if we could totally understand a single dream of an individual, we would understand his entire life history. So, if we understood the whole of even one piece of Scripture, like the evolution of child-sacrifice, we should know human history.

p. 416 19.6	Cf. Steve and Fay in Odets' *Night Music* or the young couple in *Clash by Night*.
p. 416 19.7	The plea in *The Silent Partner* is specifically for invulnerability against the gun, a history-changing invention whereby one man can kill another from a long distance, with energy supplied by an extra-bodily source.
p. 417 19.8	Odets offers here the image of man's "biting" propensity (that is to say, his aggression more than his sexuality) as the source of his expulsion from Paradise. He savagely adjures himself not to become mired in this infantile sadism, but to move on to the next developmental task: to become autonomous and to develop a will. Indeed, the old Italian baker replies that people too often live life as "an accident . . . instead of a will . . . a will to see, to understand, a will to *do*."#

* This is from the Hebrew Masoretic text.
† From the Midrash.
‡ Spiegel, *The Last Trial*.
§ Schlossman, "God, the Father and His Sons."
‖ Littell, *The Crucifixion of the Jews*.
Act III, scene 1, p. 6.

p. 417
19.9

It is likely that the formlessness and sentimentality of *The Silent Partner* reflects Odets' repressed and undigested will to destroy, the blood sacrifice of his hero an unconscious effort to "earn the right to create," a right given to women biologically both by their monthly blood sacrifice and by the labor of childbirth.

p. 419
19.10

It is interesting to see how lacking in creative fulfillment for the playwright is the creation of a work whose basic, high-charged unconscious conflict is a permanent part of his psychic life, but which, for whatever reason—formal or psychological—he is unable to "bring to life." There must be a convergence of the universal, the personally experienced, and the solution of what we call "formal problems" in order to set into motion a creative process whose product is live people, not dogma. Odets described the blocked creative process in himself as "looking at these matchsticks on my desk and wondering what could bring them to life." If something goes awry in *any* of these variables, the play is doomed. *Merely working on the unchanging unconscious fantasy is clearly insufficient for a creative process.*

We are still a long way from being able to describe positively in any detail what are the "necessary and sufficient" conditions which transform a stale effort at mastering an unconscious conflict—or expressing an unconscious fantasy—into a creative one which formally and emotionally satisfies the playwright and "speaks to" an audience. In the course of this study it has become clear, however, that some conditions—beyond the indispensables of native talent and a profound, if unconscious, bisexuality—are significantly facilitating for the bringing forth of live young: the presence of an *unresolved unconscious conflict* with an optimum *"openness"* of its materials to a pre-conscious level (not under rigidly embattled repression or defensive operation); the choice of a *form* for the expression of the conflict—and consequent fantasy—which is not too distant from the playwright's self-identity and which provides a psycho-historical bridge to a social matrix which *invites and supports the expression of this* form of mastery.*

p. 420
19.11

The "pairing" of characters and plots throughout literature, especially dramatic literature, is common and expresses the dialectical polarities, the opposed forces, the ambivalences in all of human existence. Often the "mirrorings" are two sides of the same coin.†

The prime source of such pairing is the Old Testament.‡ Again and again there is the story of a pair of brothers locked in competition: Cain and Abel, followed by Ishmael and Isaac (which inaugurates the special relationship between Jehovah and the Jews). There follow then Esau and Jacob, Reuben and Joseph, and finally Joseph's sons, Menasseh and Ephraim. From the New Testament, there stand Jesus and Judas. That this pairing occurs so regularly throughout history reflects the arche-

---

* Cf. Gibson, "Confessions of a Turtle." Also, Rose, "The Power of Form."
† William Gibson has discussed this phenomenon in detail in his probing structural analysis of Shakespeare's plays, *Shakespeare's Game.*
‡ Cf. Schlossman, "God, the Father and His Sons."

typal nature not only of the love and murder from brother to brother, but also of the relationship between these competitive brothers and God, the father.*

p. 463
20.1

We get occasional glimpses like this "movie idea" of Odets' difficulties in the film industry:

"There is a town full of dogs and for a long time these stray dogs—hundreds of them—were useful to the town. They scavenged, ate garbage, were an important part of the sanitation department of the town. Even ate big rats.

"Now there is no longer a need for these workers and the town tries to dispose of them. No one has the heart to kill them, etc., and they decide to ferry them all out to a small deserted coastal island and let them starve to death there. (They are dispossessed workers—machinery has replaced them.)

"This is done. All night their howlings can be heard. Several times some kind hearted people bring them food, but it is a hopeless job to feed so many. Now we start a love story like that of the ordinary movie. One big strong male dog takes the part of a girl dog against a male bully. He is hurt in helping and the girl licks his wounds.

"The love story begins and develops. The male dog—hero—becomes leader of the island. Some other dogs plot his overthrow and plan to take his position. Food is getting low and things look bad. Perhaps then there is sudden news that some edible plant has grown up with the heavy spring rains—perhaps mushrooms.

"Then a boat ventures near and the dogs swim out and in their quest for food overturn the boat and drown two men, both of them nasty villainous brutes.

"Then the dogs die and are eaten by the others. (Perhaps occasionally cut back to the mainland and show humans in regards to these animals.) Only the girl and boy are left and they at last are rescued. (But they had children and they disappeared—eaten by other dogs.)

"How can we suggest here workers and what happens to them?"

p. 465
21.1

If one does not become a "Somebody" in America, one remains "Nobody." Writing by Jews, blacks, and even by the children of Irish or Italian immigrants routinely reflects this sense of being "Nobody," not only in not belonging, but in forever being "out of the running" in an intensely competitive world. The work of black writers, in particular, in the late 1940s eloquently described a nameless, faceless, invisible, inaudible branch of the human race. Discussing this phenomenon, Erikson offers the provocative idea that the painful and extreme identity-consciousness, often at the heart of the creative expression of ethnic minorities, may be seen not simply as alienation, but as a corrective trend in historical evolution. Such tolerance of identity-consciousness, he argues, may provide us with the insights necessary to heal ourselves of the very things which divide us group

* See also footnote, p. 413.

from group into a number of pseudo-species, a division which threatens our very survival.*

p. 466
21.2

The curve of history would see the children of Odets' generation born in the West of their migrating parents returning East on their motorcycles seeking another kind of redemption, convinced their fathers were on the wrong path. The burden of their message would be to abandon this struggle for Success. Far from striving to become a "Somebody" who is "Going Places" in a big car, like L. J. Odets' Maxwell or Joe Bonaparte's Duesenberg, they would seek the reclamation of their individual humanity by choosing to be a "Nobody" in anonymous dark glasses and long unisex hair, mockingly clad in the castoffs of army and navy uniforms, looking like Jesus' disciples, or American soldiers from Valley Forge. They would recommend—like the immigrant Poppa Bonaparte's "whatsa in his nature"—"doing our own thing" and "making love not war."

Erik Erikson has suggested† that a film of the late 1960s, *Easy Rider*, was the American sequel to *Golden Boy*. The last line of *Easy Rider* was poignantly like that of Odets on his deathbed: "We blew it!"

p. 467
21.3

In his next play, *Rocket to the Moon*, there is again the same symbol. In 1937 the quintessence of impossible attainment was to send a rocket to the moon. In 1969 the high excitement in watching the thrusting vehicle which escapes the orbit of Mother Earth and plants itself a quarter of a million miles away on the pale "feminine" planet—which reflects the light of the sun—transcended even the technological triumph.

p. 470
21.4

There is rich and varied confirmation not only from his plays, but also from his drawings and his watercolors that, on a primitive and (largely) unconscious level, Odets did indeed think of himself—his whole body—as a phallus. On rare occasions his self-image was of a proud, polished weapon but more often the image was of an ineffectual, dismembered, and bleeding creature. In his many drawings and watercolors there are snakes cut into fragments and dripping blood, watched by wistful birds; birds with broken wings, "doves in flight" (Joe says, "I was a real sparrow, and I wanted to be a fake eagle!");‡ "cock-eyed" bisexual men and women (if he does not draw one eye up and one down, he does so with their breasts).§

To his dying day Odets would be pathologically ashamed of his own "birdie," always fearful that nurses and doctors

* E. H. Erikson, *Identity: Youth and Crisis.*
† Personal communication.
‡ Cf. Freud on Leonardo da Vinci's preoccupation with birds flying (and the vulture); also the myth of Perseus, who—equipped with Mercury's winged shoes—cut off the head of Medusa, silencing the hissing serpents. Her blood, sinking into the Earth, produced Pegasus, the winged horse tamed by Minerva for the Muses. Also, Shakespeare's similar bird imagery (Spurgeon, *Shakespeare's Imagery*).
§ Compare *Waiting for Lefty* and *Paradise Lost* ("cut me in little pieces"—"Plant fruit trees where my ashes are," etc.)—that is to say: from my fragments, from my torn masculinity and femininity, shall come finally whole, organic children (works of art).

would see how "tiny" it was. It was physically (by all medical reports) average, but not what in his view "a big man" should have. Taken together with his plays and the details of his life, this body of material provides a staggering array of data.

When an audience responds to any complex play, a resonance is established—*by way of its form*—not only with its manifest content (as in *Golden Boy*, the wish to free oneself from the scorn that attaches to "nobodies" in a competitive society) but simultaneously with primitive, archetypal (deeply unconscious) levels. Odets was doubtless not the first son in history to be persuaded that Doom would result from his inadequate anatomy or from having become his father's destructive—indeed, murderous—tool; nor was he the first son to long for, and fight against, the kind of enveloping union with his father that Eddie, the gambler-gunman, was trying to foist on Joe Bonaparte. Nor, indeed, was he unique in his vengefulness toward Woman as the prime betrayer.

All of this may be of interest to the psychologically curious reader. Let there be no mistake however: Such decoding does not "explain" the miraculous gifts for imagery, character, humor, and, above all, for Form which transpose the unconscious conflicts into creative communication.

p. 475
21.5

The maternal Mr. Bonaparte is "Europe" (representing old and good values), while the son Joe is "America" (the new and competitive values of "success"). There are many layers of meaning in their relationship: European history; the family as a parable of forces in American society; Odets' personal family story; and his own internal drama.

p. 475
21.6

Thus, the bodies, faces, and the very beings of so wide an assortment of actors as Morris Carnovsky, Elia Kazan, Stella Adler, Sanford Meisner, Luther Adler, Robert Lewis, Lee J. Cobb, John Garfield, Roman Bohnen, Franchot Tone, Ruth Nelson, Phoebe Brand, Frances Farmer, Margaret Barker, Art Smith—indeed, every last one of his Group brothers and sisters—informed the range in these Odets characters, giving them an uncannily whole quality rarely seen in actors on a stage. The special unity of his inner with these outer faces stimulated in him what William Gibson calls "a creative love."* On *Golden Boy* he worked fast and joyfully, with high excitement, creating a small world of abundant, unforgettable inhabitants.

p. 475
21.7

It is, as in Erikson's parallel of a Gandhian nonviolent political struggle with a nonviolent resolution of inner conflict: if one can heal the breaches by empathizing with, and thus elevating, *both* poles of any conflict, the result is expansionary and liberating.†

p. 476
21.8

See Leon Saul's excellent paper, "Sudden Death at Impasse," which suggests that when a person is in a context whose meaning for him spells "no exit," he may die as a way out.

* The artist asks in his created "micro-realities": "How shall we live?" (Tolstoy); the political leader, in his: "What is to be done?" (Lenin).

† William Gibson, interviewed by M. Brenman-Gibson, August 19, 1964. Also, E. H. Erikson, *Gandhi's Truth.*

p. 492
22.0
Odets' description (in 1938 to Helen Hayes) of the "Charlie Theatre" wherein the playwright, actors, director, and all *merge* with the audience when there is a pre-existing emotional bond —indeed, a conviction and an aim—which unites them all is fundamentally the same as the "ideologically cemented collective" which was the Group Theatre.

It is the eternal quest of mankind to which the artist or the spiritual leader gives voice: the merging of subject and object, the yearning for a collective spirit, a spirit largely lost with the rise of individualism. This wish in our time—to become part of a bigger whole—wars with the wish to maintain diversity within this unity. We are therefore suspicious of totalistic solutions like those in the Communist countries.

p. 497
22.1
We understand little of that confluence of inner and outer circumstances that transforms the images and fantasies of the artist from an inchoate wool-gathering—in initial quality, not different from the daydreams of the rest of us—into the structured, communicative ordering of the polarities of existence which we call esthetic form. Any working playwright recognizes the successive shifts from the initial image, the amorphous daydream, or even the isolated fragment of dialogue, to the deliberate and active collecting of characters, situations, scenes, and, finally, acts.

When he manages to set up a confrontation sufficient that the characters take on a life of their own, he happily becomes their passive scribe. We are barely beginning to explore the nature of the saturation process that transforms the fantasy into a play. It is, at the very least, an optimal balance among several things: first, an urgent need to master some part of experience; second, to find the psychological "safety" of a formal vessel for it; and, finally, a potential audience which invites it out of him. *After* writing the above, I came upon the following note written by Odets in his fifty-third year (August 28, 1959):

THE ARTIST, THE PROPHET, ETC.

His simultaneous task:
1. To express as it is being born in outward form the inward truth or statement of experience.
2. To shape and form it (or use a form) for purposes of communication, including that the form is integral and organically with and at one with the experience.
3. To parabalize (in the Jesus sense), so that the message is safe or socially acceptable by the lords and masters. (Message is then given and messenger is not killed!)
4. To sustain the self-image in terms of good and ideal, leaving behind the disliked and unfavorable image of the self.
5. ?To stay in balance and not, like Jesus, go out of balance (which is really why Jesus was crucified!).
6. ?To live conformably to one's "nature." A form, I believe, of squaring the self.

The very prodigality of Odets' rich files covering all stages of this process (there are hundreds of "projects" and thousands of characters) leaves a biographer with the impression that, given a shift in his inner or his outer circumstances, this man could indeed have been, as Clurman often said, a "Balzac of the theatre." However, because his steady need for immediate reassurance was inordinately high, he was always holding back, stopping short, in terror both of his rage and of losing face, of being ashamed, and of becoming Nobody.* Moreover, as Odets put it, "Engaged, but hold back the rage, say nothing but finally hold back even the work and turn the rage against the self or a few intimates."

p. 514
22.2

In the character of the pathetically aspiring Cleo Singer there is distilled the symbol of the exhausted American artist, still yearning to realize her creative potential and steadily—like L. J. Odets—verging on fraudulence: she lies pretentiously and is tempted by the fame and fortune held under her nose by the minor character Willy Wax. The beginning of the dissolution of the Group Theatre was already now evident as only one of the many casualties of the end of the American Dream. Given the fact that all civilizations have a "dream" which rises and falls, it is important for us as observer to note that this playwright conceives this play at a time when his own creative "descent" is more or less in synchrony with that of his culture.

p. 514
22.3

An interesting question for study here is: How had an experienced playwright of great skill begun with one play and ended with another?

For over a year Odets had been seriously blocked in his work, had had a dismaying sense of loss of emotional connection to his wife and of creative connection to the growing crisis in the immediate events of world history. He sensed only dimly that the deeper connection of his current work to the unfolding of history lay in its reflection of an increasingly urgent conflict between the values of salesmanship and an innocent creativity. His notes suggest he was seeing both his wife and his father as "the enemy," while finding it increasingly difficult to identify "the enemy" as a simple, political-economic order with which he could do battle as he had in the past. The references in *Rocket* to the villainy of the economic system are perfunctory and hollow.

In the discussion which followed my initial presentation of the analysis of *Rocket*,† both playwrights present (Arthur Miller and William Gibson) agreed that such a specific "distribution of the author" in the form of identity-elements—not merely a general projection of himself—does indeed exist in every play, and that during the writing of the play these elements are seen only dimly, if at all, by the playwright. Miller commented, "When I'm writing the thing, it's as if somebody else is writing those notes. And I think that balance is crucial

* Directly on concluding this sentence, I am handed by Virginia Rowe, my intelligent and alert research assistant, Granville Hicks' review of a biography of poet Vachel Lindsay, written in 1935 and saved by Odets, wherein Hicks concludes (and Odets has underlined it): ". . . *it was the lack of external support that made his inner weaknesses fatal.*" She says, "How's *that* for validation!" It occurs to me that in this series of events, there is a clue to refining a method for "psychohistorical" studies.

† Brenman-Gibson, "Anatomy of a Play."

. . . because if you *know* something, something you *really* solve, then writing the whole play becomes unnecessary." The restorative function of the creative act is evident in this observation.

p. 524
22.4

The creative process is not finally consummated until the artist's experience—given form on paper, canvas, or stone—has reached an audience. Most particularly the dramatist, that most topical and perishable of artists, must feel that he has succeeded in obliterating boundaries and established a union with the group physically assembled to watch his play. In the contemporary theatre, where alienation was for some long time the guiding theme, the improvisers (or writers) express on the surface their indifference, even their contempt, for the audience. But even here the acting group is bitterly disappointed when no audience—from whom they can estrange themselves—appears in their theatre, thus "closing down" their "play."

p. 525
22.5

A key tragedy of his childhood, it will be recalled, was the "abandonment" of him by his mother in favor of his crippled sister. It had been this personal sense of disinheritance which had cogwheeled with the collective sense of disinheritance in the Depression era.

p. 525
22.6

These names reflect a variety of identity-fragments and elements: Odets took the name "Ben" from his lively Tante Esther's "ordinary" son, a man whose life was indeed, in Odets' view, "a long forgetting." The word "stark," according to Webster, means "desolate, bleak, unadorned or rigid, as in death." The wife's maiden name, "Belle Prince"—as with "Bessie Berger" in Odets' *Awake and Sing!*—condenses the word "belle" ("beauty") with the name of actress Stella Adler (Odets had scribbled "Stella, Bella, Belle, Bessie" when making notes); she was seen as a Jewish princess in a long succession of actors in the royal Adler family, and, like Ben's wife, a powerful, even a tyrannical figure. The conflict, as in a dream, is densely overdetermined: it is simultaneously between a controlling parent (or wife) and a child (or husband).

p. 526
22.7

This is an excellent example of the principles of playwriting described by William Gibson in his *Shakespeare's Game*.

p. 526
22.8

Were it not for the fact of Odets' own struggle between his longing to surrender, abdicating all autonomy, initiative, and responsibility (as he had long ago sat obediently for hours on his little chair, waiting), and his impulse to "explode," there would be no conflict and no play.

p. 527
22.9

This is a good example of how misleading it is to make a one-to-one biographic correlation between the playwright as protagonist and the people in his life as "supporting cast." To be sure, those in the playwright's life-space, most especially members of a family, or even of a gifted acting company like the Group Theatre, call out his own internal "gallery," providing the masks for the characters who people his play. It is no accident, for example, that actor Morris Carnovsky always played the "spiritual" parts in Odets' plays, while Kazan was usually cast, as Odets put it, as the "original get-ahead boy." Odets regularly used the Group Theatre members as masks for his own warring identity-elements and -fragments, and was actually helped to create whole persons (lovingly and fully) by reason of the independent existence of these excellent actors.

p. 528
22.10

Her name, "Cleo Singer," combines that of a sexually irresistible young "Queen of Sheba" (Cleopatra) for whom men would well lose worlds and Odets' image, steadily drawn from music, of the artist (a *singer* like his Uncle Israel). "Clio" is also the name of the Muse of poetry and history. Odets says, "Whitman is half songbird, half alligator," and the gitka, a mouse, in Odets' last play, *The Flowering Peach*, has a high, sweet singing voice, but, having no mate, commits suicide. Also, *Cleo* = Cl. Odets: Odets had, in adolescence, often put an "L." in his signature as a middle initial, doubtless after his father's name, "Louis." Again, the products of creative transcendence, akin to dreams.

p. 529
22.11

Cf. Kenneth Burke on Odets in his classic essay "Ice, Fire, and Decay."

p. 529
22.12

This same identity-element would assume the form of the Hollywood film executive in Odets' play *The Big Knife*. The price in each play for material power (that is, attachment to the *senses*, not to money) is surrender of one's integrity and freedom.

p. 530
22.13

Cleo expresses here Odets' struggle to establish himself as "the center of awareness in a universe of experience," unfettered by arbitrary inner and outer restriction. It is an innocent expression of the very nature of "I-ness."*

p. 530
22.14

Freud commented on Dostoevsky's gambling as a kind of "playing with himself." Odets was also a gambler.

p. 531
22.15

In the discussion which followed my original presentation of this material to a small group, playwright Arthur Miller said, ". . . *There is a terror underneath* (this play), *which stopped it from being written.* . . . There is a phantom-like quality about it, which was one of the things that always drew me to Odets. I could never understand how he was equated with realism, naturalism or even social drama, after *Waiting for Lefty*. I think he is dealing with phantoms. . . . In this play, he is raising conflicts which he never engages in. . . . This play is a measurement—not in a moral sense, but in another sense— of values, life-values . . . and it seems to me that the showdown, the climax, the unveiling which he is always promising, will have to engage a real knock-down fight, between the dentist and that old man. . . . Now there is a conceivable end to his play where the *Life Force* escapes all of them, and they are left in effect with no Force. Cleo, ridiculed, with her make-believe and lying, a fairly pathetic creature, walks out and with her walks out (ironically enough) all their lives, because she some-

* E. H. Erikson, "Psychosocial Identity."

how embodied their aspirations. There is a fear which is probably very complicated, of just the conflict he proposed . . . which is a very common thing in playwrights.

"It would involve some disaster which is *too great a price to pay*,* and consequently the conflict is aborted before it got started. He can let Cleo be free because her struggle is not a menace to him, that's a free-flowing thing. He can create enough distance towards it to allow it to happen. But these other two (the old man and his son-in-law)—he has too much of an investment in, and *they would really knock him to pieces if he would allow them to come to blows, and there would be nothing left of him* [italics mine]. That's the kind of terror that casts a pall over the vividness."†

The biographical data of Odets' life support Miller's impression of an overload of anxiety attached to the *unconscious aspects* of Odets' conflicts among the identity-elements, experienced as the "corrupt" materialist (Prince), the innocent "idealist" (Cleo), and the obsessively blocked intellectual (Stark).

p. 532
22.16

Dynamically, this is identical with Elena's position in Gorky's *Country People*. She, a wife-mother, is tolerant of her husband's sexual affairs in order, she says, "not to put obstacles in the path of his beautiful inner life." Thus, in Gorky's play the "affairs" are more obviously the artist's journeys into himself. In Pinter's *The Homecoming* the wife's otherwise mystifying role is similarly illuminated if again we see her as the playwright's creative anima in danger of becoming a whore.

p. 532
22.17

All his life Odets had trouble with his feet, his hair, and his teeth. Continually seeking help for these difficulties, he came to see them as representing his steady sense of disintegration.

p. 533
22.18

The name "King Midas" serves again to highlight the struggle between material and spiritual values.

p. 534
22.19

This is a playwright's gift for eccentric metaphor: the content of Prince's threat reflects Odets' unconscious fear and guilt in competing with this powerful father.

p. 534
22.20

In a play he would never finish, "An Old-Fashioned Man," Odets expressed his yearning for the traditional values in art and in life that his world was steadily losing. Erikson has observed that the steady identity-confusion in American life gives it chronically a somewhat adolescent quality (private communication).

p. 534
22.21

Profound issues of the polarities of activity and passivity as well as initiative and guilt are here condensed. Compare this with Odets' later play *The Big Knife*, which closes with a despairing repetition of the word "Help!"

* This idea may be related to the central theme of Miller's *The Price*.
† Brenman-Gibson, "Anatomy of a Play: With Specimen Play-Analysis," November 6, 1971. Discussion participants were Joan Mowat Erikson, Erik H. Erikson, Leo Garel, Margaret Brenman-Gibson, William Gibson, Ann Birstein Kazin, Alfred Kazin, Bessie Boris Klein, Rachel Klein, Betty Jean Lifton, Robert Jay Lifton, Inge Morath Miller, Arthur Miller, Peggy Mowrer Penn, Arthur Penn, Virginia Rowe, and Hellmut Wohl.

p. 535
22.22

This image expresses Odets' fear that *all* his creative children are "illegitimate."

p. 536
22.23

Odets said, "In making art one is free from inhibition and masking of emotions and fear of encounter. One ranges freely, taking *painlessly* all sides. Inactive, incapacitated, passive, arid, and sterile, aware but unable and helpless—in art one becomes freely a man of action and all is possible!

"In this world, one may always be the hero—loved, pitied, magnanimous, stern, strong, successful against men, women, and dragons; one may forgive and even pity others—it is something god-like and absolute that the artist becomes with the exercise of what is usually his only talent. . . ."* This statement should be compared to Gandhi's description of the "Truth Force" or what he called "Truth in Action."†

p. 552
23.1

Odets has externalized here his own conflict, even as does a political figure who mirrors his inner "play" not by *writing* a play, but by *enacting* it on the "stage of history."

p. 572
23.2

Poet Robinson Jeffers responded to the signs that a world conflagration had begun by writing "The Soul's Desert (August 30, 1939)":

They are warming up the old horrors; and all that they say is echoes of echoes.
Beware of taking sides; only watch.
These are not criminals, nor hucksters and little journalists, but the governments
Of the great nations; men favorably
Representative of massed humanity. Observe them. Wrath and laughter
Are quite irrelevant. Clearly it is time
To become disillusioned, each person to enter his own soul's desert
And look for God—having seen man.‡

p. 583
23.3

Although this document may have been written by someone else, it is clearly representative of Odets' thinking and was probably drafted in collaboration with him:

I believe that the Group Theatre is now passing through the deepest and most crucial period of its existence. Years of "muddling through," of constantly yielding to spontaneity and taking the path of least resistance have finally culminated in creating a crisis the outcome of which will determine the form of the Group in the future, and perhaps whether or not it will exist at all. . . . This is not simply a crisis of . . . hard times. Such a crisis could be solved now, as were previous ones . . . by tightening belts and making the necessary sacrifices. . . .

In short, things simply cannot continue in the same old way any longer. There seem to be three possibilities or alternatives.

* Odets, Personal Notes, "Romantics," 1957.
† E. H. Erikson, *Gandhi's Truth.*
‡ Jeffers, *Selected Poems.*

First, that the crisis will cumulate to the point of dissolution; second, that the present trend will end in a more or less rapid change into a sort of semi-artistic, semi-commercial producing company of the Abbot type (tho dealing with a higher type of production); or third, that there will be a rapid and planned transformation of the Group into the kind of theater which is the ideal of everybody involved, and which alone can fulfill the role set itself by the Group throughout its existence.

The first alternative needs no elaboration. The second in effect equals the first, since no actor or writer wants to make continuous financial sacrifice to a theater in which he does not feel the sense of participation and belonging, which does not make for a continuous and varied growth and development of the membership, which only consists of being hired for specific productions and nothing more.

What is the third alternative, the one which I and everyone else is deeply and anxiously concerned with. What is the nature of the Group Theater which everyone is hoping to salvage and build up into THE American Theater, what are its activities, and what should be its obligations to its personnel.

I think it should be a theater with a full and rounded life, . . . with an inner life and vitality growing out of the application of this program. . . . I think that this program should encompass at least the following main categories:

1. A main line of major productions for Broadway production. These plays should reflect contemporary American life, and more truly than any other theater present the traditions, problems and aspirations of the American people.

This main line of productions will of course provide the theater with its basic financial income, and must of course be considered as the major expression before the general public of the Group Theater as a producing organization.

These productions must therefore be most carefully selected with the utmost consideration of their adaptability to the audience expected, both with regard to their content and box-office appeal. Costly experiments in this line of plays should be avoided as much as possible, as witness the examples of "Casey Jones" and "Quiet City," and as few risks taken as possible. At the same time, too many concessions to the "right," in the form of "money names," etc. should also be avoided. It has been proved that these of themselves offer no guarantee for financial success, and they detract from the ensemble playing to the point where they might actually hamper the production as a whole. Furthermore, this is not the type of production expected from the Group Theater, which is noted for its ensemble playing rather than star system playing, and which is judged by a separate standard by both critics and audience. This policy also has a bad effect on the regular company unless special reasons make it imperative.

2. While the foregoing is the main line of Group productions, it cannot be considered as the sole activity of the Group. There must be continuous and planned activity for the improvement of the technique and craft of every individual actor, as well as the improvement of the collective technique of the entire acting company. This can only be accomplished through the

agency of classes and studio work of a continuous nature, which critically examines the individual and collective acting problems of the actors. . . . Without regular and permanent activity along this line, it is not possible for the Group to develop its acting to constantly higher standards. . . .

3. In connection with this class and studio work comes the problem of training young actors having common ideals with the Group Theater. There are numbers of young actors of varying degrees of talent who look to the Group as an ideal, and for whom there is no room in the Group at present. . . .

4. Special attention must be paid to the problem of developing young playwrights capable of producing the best type of plays. Talented young playwrights should be drawn to the Group and be given careful individual attention in the form of personal discussion with the Director, etc. Regular discussions should be organized with a small group of the most promising of the younger playwrights taking in all phases, direct and indirect, of the problem of writing the best type of American plays of the present era. These young playwrights should be further encouraged by the playing of scenes from their plays in the class and studio work, and by studio and experimental production of their plays. In this way the Group can serve as the center for the best of the younger playwrights, training them, giving them some type of production, thus developing playwrights for the American theater in general, and the Group in particular.

5. In connection with all these activities, I think that the work of the Group should be marked by the production of a second line of plays. This should be a line of Sunday night productions of plays which deserve production for any one of a number of reasons, and upon which it is not thought suitable to make a big advance financial outlay, or take any large scale risks.

These productions should include revivals of all sorts, from Shakespeare to Chekhov to Odets, which would enrich the theater. These productions should also include productions of young playwrights whose work is not yet thought mature enough to warrant a commercial showing involving a large financial risk. These productions should also include the bolder and more daring experiments, whether in form or content. . . .

Without such a line of plays I do not think the Group will attain the many-sided and rich life it needs, nor realize its function as really the first theater in America.

* * * * *

It is further my firm opinion that the whole problem of the future form of the Group Theater will have to be settled this season. If there is no solution of the general type outlined above, there will either be dissolution, or deterioration into a semi-commercial production office. The latter will certainly cause a drift of the most valuable actors away from the Group. The actors are willing to sacrifice financial prosperity and well-being and the full exploitation of their money-making ability. In return they must have that type of theater which furnishes a rich, varied, integrated vital and functional life, with constant growth and development, a life that will fill the need of the actor to realize himself both as an artist and collective human being. . . .

Nor is the solution of the problem dependent solely, or even mainly, on the success of the major productions. A big financial success can sometimes lull the company into a false sense of security, cause a loosening of activity based on a temporary sense of well-being, prosperity and smugness. Under such circumstances a big financial hit can have an adverse effect on the rounded development of the Group.

Only when a money hit is accompanied by an intensive program of work and activity, when it is treated as a breathing spell which supplies especially favorable conditions to the development of the whole program of the Group, can we say that the Theater is really forging ahead. . . .

To relegate the Group Theater to just sort of a producing company would be to relegate the actor from a participant in a vital and living organism for which he would make any sacrifice into an employee, playing in plays as they are produced and nothing more. Since there is no advance guarantee for permanent and unbroken financial success, more must be furnished than the latter, which breeds the same approach as does the ordinary commercial theater.

*   *   *   *   *

To sum up somewhat. The present burning problem is the production of NIGHT MUSIC in the most efficient and most effective way. . . . All other matters must for the time be subordinated to this major immediate task.

The successful production of NIGHT MUSIC opens the opportunity of re-organizing the life of the Group to insure its future existence as a Group. No resting on laurels, no false sense of security, can be permitted to interfere with this basic task of radically overhauling the whole method of work and inner life of the theater.

Classes and studio work should be started at once, initiated by the leadership, and participated in by the entire acting company, those in and those not in NIGHT MUSIC, plus those young actors in whom the Group has some interest.

Work towards a Sunday night production out of the class and studio work should be started as soon as is feasible. I would recommend this as more suited to the solution of the inner problems of the Group than the immediate launching of another major commercial undertaking. For such Sunday night production I recommend offhand the following: THREE SISTERS, which the Group owes public presentation; PARADISE LOST, in a simpler production; and perhaps one of the plays of Rella, Greendale, etc. Should a studio production create such an effort that a public demand for a run is aroused, it would of course be in the nature of a major victory, and can be complied with minus the risk connected with a commercial undertaking.

*   *   *   *   *

Needless to say, the type of theater here outlined is based on a common world view, a common view of the relation of the theater to society, and a common acting technique. This can only be possible in a theater able to absorb and assimilate its experiences, and enrich itself from them. This in turn demands a continuity of artistic experience and development which can only be fulfilled by a continuity of personnel, by a permanent acting company. . . . This does not preclude an actor occasionally, with agreement in advance, seeking temporary employment elsewhere. The latter should be the exception rather than the rule.

* * * * *

A few concluding remarks on leadership and administration. The theater here outlined of necessity demands a high degree of planning and organization. These in turn demand a high degree of authority in the leadership, and of discipline among the membership.

However, this leadership must rest firmly on its ability to give the best leadership and guidance, to maintain the direction and perspective of the Group, to successfully steer the theater thru all the difficulties and problems, always driving on to the common goal.

The leadership must also recognize the voluntary nature of the association of the Group, and that leadership cannot be won or maintained by force. Nor can the Group be treated as the private property of the leadership. If it is, the membership will also treat it thus, and the whole feeling of common participation will yield to an employee-employer relationship between leadership and membership which will obliterate the real purpose of the Group. . . .

On the other hand the leadership must recognize its accountability to the theater as a whole, and the right of the membership to be consulted and participate in the adoption of major policies. This can be accomplished through the agency of occasional (annual or semi-annual) meetings in which perspectives and major policies are discussed, in which the leadership gives an account of its past stewardship, makes its plans for the new. The membership has the right to pass judgment on the work accomplished, to assist in formulating plans, and thus bound to carry out to the ability of every member the tasks assigned to him. Other than that, the collective nature of the Group is expressed by each member doing his job to improve his work and the general level.

These are some of my thoughts, crudely expressed and perhaps too dogmatically, concerning the Group Theater.

A decade later Odets was teaching young playwrights— among them William Gibson—in the Actors Studio.

p. 585
23.4

It cannot be a coincidence that in the years 1939–41, during which worldwide death-forces appeared to be in the ascendance, Eugene O'Neill—horrified by Hitler and by his sense of the increasing evils of "statism" and worldwide war—wrote two major plays using the symbol of night as death: *Long Day's Journey into Night* and *The Iceman Cometh*. The latter, begun in June and finished in November of 1939, is set in the year of O'Neill's attempted suicide (whose non-consummation he often regretted) and expresses O'Neill's philosophy of "hopeless hope."

O'Neill told a friend that the "iceman" is death, that "final orgasm," and we know that "The night cometh when no man can work." Clinicians, too, are familiar with the equation of night, sleep, and the "death" (les "petits morts") in orgasm. While working on *Long Day's Journey into Night*, O'Neill said, ". . . like anyone else with imagination, I have been sunk by this damned world debacle. The cycle is on the shelf [his historical plays] and God knows if I can ever take it up again, because I cannot foresee any future . . . to which it could spiritually belong."*

p. 593
24.1

It is probable that the original Pygmalion story and its derivatives are all statements of the artist and his "creation." In a painting, "Pygmalion," at the Metropolitan Museum of Art, the male is embracing the "female," whose body is in fact that of a young boy—broad-shouldered and muscular, clearly another edition of the Narcissus story, with more sublimation.

p. 593
24.2

Psychoanalysts have pondered—unsatisfactorily—the fundamental difference between "narcissistic" and "genuine" generosity; indeed, it has proved difficult to draw a sharp division between the two. In a life-struggle, however, when the recipient of such giving as Odets describes begins unaccountably to feel enslaved, trapped, and somehow deprived of autonomous life and growth, we can be quite certain that the recipient's separate existence has been at least threatened, if not violated, and that we have stepped from "generosity" (the model is the mutuality of a nursing mother and child) to something controlling, limiting, growth-arresting, and, therefore, exploitive or "selfish." It would take many years, however, before Bette Lipper (at sixteen, she had named herself "Grayson" for a career on the stage) would begin consciously to feel her relationship with Odets as no longer a support, but a tightening noose, and Odets to feel he had been swindled by the visible promise of her body and by her pliancy. At that point, even before they were married, the battle between them would be joined.

* Gelb, *O'Neill*, p. 831.

Acknowledgments

AMONG the many people to whom I am indebted for immeasurable help in the preparation of this life history, I must first mention Clifford Odets' children, Nora and Walt Whitman Odets, who gave me the exclusive rights to his literary estate—which included masses of papers: complete unpublished plays, as well as plays in all stages of incompletion, "idea" files, his own notes on his psychoanalytic sessions, correspondence, diaries and journals, scrapbooks, ledgers, check stubs and registers (to convey some sense of the extent and richness of the primary documents immediately at my disposal).

I have written at length in my Preface of my debt to Erik H. Erikson, and I will add here my deep gratitude for the early encouragement and steadfast support of the then Medical Director of the Austen Riggs Center in Stockbridge, Massachusetts, Dr. Robert P. Knight, who has since died, leaving a great hole in the world.

Concomitantly, this book would literally not have been possible without the initial vote of confidence and the later (mostly unambivalent) support and sympathy of my husband, William Gibson, whose acute observation of the creative process and his own personal knowledge of Clifford Odets have illuminated and informed every page of this book. Indeed, I often wonder if most of the good ideas in it are his and not mine.

My parents, both now dead, applauded this undertaking from the start, and my father, in particular, translated into English articles and magazine pieces from Russian or Yiddish newspapers and magazines.

George S. Klein, before his death, provided steady encouragement and lent his brilliant intellect to the critique of the material in the early chapters. His wife, Bessie Boris Klein, my oldest friend, was the first after my husband to read a first draft. Her sharply critical mind and her enthusiasm helped me stick with it.

Many thanks to Leo Garel, whose understanding of the creative process in its social contexts is unparalleled.

Virginia Rowe, Odets' secretary and confidante in the last six years of his life, moved from California to Massachusetts to assist in the preparation of this biography and has lent invaluable assistance at all stages of the work and at all levels: from yeoman secretarial and research jobs to highly sophisticated editorial work. Besides me, she has worked harder on this book than anyone.

The late Harold Clurman played an important role in the forming of this story with hours of discussion not only about Odets, but also about the American theatre. These hours were among the most real education I have had—and a delight besides. I cannot adequately express my thanks for his permission to quote freely from all his relevant letters, as well as from his many writings, most particularly his brilliant book *The Fervent Years* (both the published and unpublished versions).

To Luise Rainer, now living in Switzerland with her publisher husband, Robert Knittel, I am indebted for the days—which were painful to her—she spent with me in Stockbridge (shortly after Odets' death), telling me of her stormy relationship with him. Her subsequent revisions of my manuscript corrected whatever factual inaccuracies had crept in, and, in some instances, substituted for her initial account her experience as seen by her fifteen years later. I deeply regret the reopening of old wounds consequent upon her cooperating in this study, and I am grateful she was willing to help. I thank her for her permission to quote from her letters to Odets, and also from correspondence and interviews with me.

Lee and the late Paula Strasberg were generous in the extreme, contributing many hours of memories, lending me letters, papers, and documents, and recommending other informants. I am beholden to Lee for his permission to quote from these letters and papers.

Herman Kobland, a childhood friend and steadfast companion of Odets who later became his secretary, was of invaluable assistance, generously turning over the files and papers he had meticulously kept through the years, giving me, as well, the benefit of his recollections from childhood on.

Reconstruction of the family life of Clifford Odets would have been impossible, of course, without the help of his sisters, Florence Odets Kabaker and Genevieve Odets Levy. I am indebted to them, and to Clifford's father, the late Louis J. Odets, for permission to quote from their letters and interviews. There is no way, as she must know, that I can adequately express my thanks to the most admirable Mrs. Effie Fincher, Louis Odets' nurse in his last days. She, after many nurses in succession had quit, made life bearable for an unhappy old man without compromising her principles one iota.

Other members of the family who were helpful were Freda Rossman, who told me about her mother and father, Esther and Israel Rossman, Odets' "substitute parents," his beloved aunt and uncle. Frank Lubner, a cousin, wrote to me of his memories of Odets and his family.

Julian Drachman's keen memories of his pupil in high school, as well as his published piece about Odets, "Genius in Embryo," provided me with a priceless glimpse into Odets' adolescence. I thank him for his permission to quote from his material.

Particularly helpful in fleshing out Odets' relationship with the Group Theatre were his friends Elia Kazan and Luther Adler, and I am grateful to them. I especially thank Elia Kazan for permission to quote from his letters.

Special mention must be made of the contribution of the late John Howard Lawson to this project, not only his personal experiences but also his insights into the political climate of the time. We had many discussions, both in person and through correspondence, and he generously sent me the rough draft of his autobiography (which, sadly, has never been published). I am beholden to his daughter, Susan Amanda Lawson, for permission to quote from his papers.

Alger Hiss, on several occasions, helped enormously in clarifying and delineating the political climate in the Roosevelt era.

I particularly treasure my talks with Jean and Dido Renoir, who made the last years of Odets' life more tolerable.

I am indebted to professors Robert Hethmon, Michael J. Mendelsohn, and Arthur Wagner for making available to me typescripts of their interviews with Odets, and Professor Baird Shuman has steadily cheered me on.

For their invaluable help in the herculean task of interviewing informants for this study, I thank Mark Harris, Peggy Maurer Penn, Virginia Rowe, and the late Dr. Meyer Zeligs.

I am grateful to Charles Stiles for his excellent survey of the psychoanalytic literature on creativity, and to Elaine Dundy for her summaries of much of the Odets correspondence.

For the provocative ideas offered in a group discussion of my analysis of *Rocket to the Moon*, I thank Leo Garel, Alfred Kazin, Robert Jay Lifton, Arthur Miller, and Arthur Penn.

I am indebted to Herman Gollob for his ideas and editing suggestions throughout.

In addition to those I have already mentioned, whose lives touched Odets' life over a long span of years, and who have been so generous in contributing their recollections, I would like to mention the people who have given me information relating to specific periods of his life:

For information surrounding Odets' last days, I am indebted to the recollections of Edie Adams, Jack Adler, Mac Benoff, Marlon Brando, Catherine Corcoran, Dr. Hyman Engelberg, Edith Mayer Goetz, Dr. William Goodley, Buck Houghton, Daniel Mann, Alfred Ryder, Kim Stanley, and Gladys Stell.

For Odets' early history, childhood events, family background, and continuing family relationships, the following people have contributed invaluable information: Ida Mae Bernstein (Levine), Sibyl Bowan (Stapleton), Maurice

James Earle, Minnie Fabian, Rae and Leo Harber, "Pinky" Goodman (Kruger), Blanche McCabe (Reasor), Dr. David Meranze, Rose Satinsky, and Martha "Mattie" Washington.

For recollections pertaining to Odets' adolescence and young manhood, I am indebted to Hortense Alden, Dr. Gerald Aronson, Mordecai Baumann, Harold Beker, Herbert Biberman, Ivan Black, Mrs. Reta Cooper, Albert Dekker, Mae Desmond (Fielder), Frank Fielder, and their son Richard, Sylvia Field (Truex), Anna Mae Franklin, Paul Greenbaum, Carl Heilpern, Frieda Heilpern (Beck), Stanley Kauffmann, William and Leonore Kozlenko, Joseph Kramm, Gordon Lebowitz, Sabina and Dr. Milton Leof, Madeleine Leof (Ross), Sylvia Hoffman Regan, Jerome Rosenberg, Harvey Scribner, Sarah Singer, Irene Steinberg, Martha "Mattie" Washington, and Martin Wolfson.

The remembrances of many people contributed to the reconstruction of Odets' life during the Group Theatre years. I am acknowledging here with heartfelt thanks all those who helped in re-creating for me the turbulent years from 1931 to 1940: Jay Adler, Stella Adler, Julia Algaze, Boris Aronson, Philip Barber, Mordecai Baumann, Phil Berg, Walter and Judith Bernstein, Sidney Bernstein, Abner Biberman, Michael Blankfort, Kermit Bloomgarden, Peter Bogdanovich, Hannah Braun, Bessie Breuer (Mrs. Henry Varnum Poor), Abe Burrows, Ben Burns, William Challee, Robert Clurman, Lee J. Cobb, Roberta Garfield Cohn, Juleen Compton, Aaron Copland, Cheryl Crawford, Dena, Helen Deutsch, Melvyn Douglas, Bess Eitingon, Florence Eldridge, Ruth Young Eliot, Leif Erickson, Waldo Frank, Gene Frankel, B. B. Gamzue, John Gassner, Ira Gershwin, Mordecai Gorelik, Stymean Karlen, Sidney Kaufman, Joseph Kelleher, Lois Kibbee, Sidney Kingsley, Herbert Kline, Stanley Kramer, Albert Lewin, Robert Lewis, Stefan Lorant, Leonard Lyons, Fredric March, Sanford Meisner, Lewis Milestone, Ruth Nelson, Samuel Orner, Arthur Penn, Dr. Sandor Rado, Martin Ritt, Harry Robin, Richard Roffman, Alfred Ryder, Janet Sachs, Irwin Shaw, Eleanor Scherr Shibley, Sylvia Sidney, Sidney Skolsky, Carolyn Slaski, Delos Smith, Frances Stark, Ralph Steiner, Franchot Tone, Andreas Voutsinas.

For permission to quote from their letters, I am indebted to Ted Allan, Phil Berg, Cheryl Crawford, Dena, Helen Deutsch, Ruth Gordon, Herbert Kline, Robert G. L. Waite, and Fay Wray. For permission to quote from letters of those who have died, I am grateful to the executors of the Tallulah Bankhead Estate, and to Jean Frank for letters of Waldo Frank. My thanks to Roberta Garfield Cohn for John Garfield's letter, to the executors of the Estate of Albert Lewin; and to Georgia O'Keeffe for Alfred Stieglitz's letter to Luise Rainer.

Among the libraries and librarians who rendered great assistance, I must first express my thanks to those gems, Jane Haase and Eileen Linton, librarians at Austen Riggs Center in Stockbridge, Massachusetts. I am also indebted to Phyllis Zack and Ruth White of the Reference Department of the Berkshire Atheneum, Pittsfield, Massachusetts. I received valuable help from Paul Myers and the late George Freedley of the New York Public Library's Research Library of the Performing Arts, as well as permission to quote from letters in that library's Berg Collection. Important material was obtained from the Franklin Delano Roosevelt Library at Hyde Park, the American Jewish Archives, from Helen D. Willard, Curator of the Harvard University Library, and from Neda Westlake of the University of Pennsylvania, to whom I am grateful for permission to quote from the letters of Theodore Dreiser and Waldo Frank. The Academy of Motion Picture Arts and Sciences was most generous with its help.

For secretarial help, I thank Miriam Jacoby, Catherine Rauscher, Frances Northrup; and for their generous volunteer assistance, Beala Schiffman and Hilda Flamm.

There are many others whose contributions fall within the scope of the second volume of this biography, and whose help will be acknowledged in that volume.

Without the support of the following foundations, this book would not have been possible; it is part of a long-range inquiry into the nature of the creative process, and has been funded in part by the Austen Riggs Center, The Robert P. Knight Variable Floating Research Fund (Charles Murphy), the Foundations' Fund for Research in Psychiatry, the National Endowment for the

Humanities, the Guggenheim Foundation, the Grant Foundation, the Foundation for Research in Psychoanalysis, the Whitney Foundation, the American Association of University Women, the Rockefeller Foundation, and the Anne Pollock Lederer Foundation. I offer my heartfelt thanks to all.

To Professor John Mack, psychoanalyst-biographer and my first "boss" in the Cambridge Department of Psychiatry of Harvard University School of Medicine, my deep gratitude for his steady affirmation. And to the late (so very prematurely to be called "the late") Professor Lee Macht, who replaced John Mack, for his humanist values. And finally, to my colleagues, both at Austen Riggs Center and at Cambridge Hospital, an incalculable debt for providing an atmosphere that encourages both basic and applied research into those mysteries of the human heart on an understanding of which our survival may hinge.

Sources and References

FOR the sake of smoother reading, I have dispensed with the system of numbers within the text, and have adopted the following method of citing references. Shown before each specific reference in this listing are the number of the page and a few of the words to which the citation refers. For a full listing of sources given in abbreviated form, see the Bibliography.

To have cited the name of every informant and the date of a specific interview (and, also, in a few cases, the names of the interviewers, other than myself) or the name of a correspondent and the date of a letter from which I have quoted would have resulted in an unmanageably long reference section. I have, therefore, tried to identify my informant in the text, and/or in the Acknowledgments.

Page numbers cited for *Night Music* refer to the Random House edition; those given for all other Odets plays refer to the Grove Press edition of *Six Plays of Clifford Odets* (1979).

Following are abbreviations used in the reference list for frequently cited sources:

CO	Clifford Odets
LJO	Louis J. Odets
HC	Harold Clurman
MB-G	Margaret Brenman-Gibson
LR	Luise Rainer
HK	Herman Kobland

PREFACE

Page	Quote	Source
ix	"history itself"	To MB-G, personal communication
ix	"another biography"	Shuman, R. Baird, *Clifford Odets*
x	"deliver itself"	*Starting Out in the Thirties*, p. 82
xi	"involves high skills"	*Literary Biography*
xii	"myself to myself"	CO, Personal Notes, undated

PROLOGUE

3	"You lived it!"	CO, Notes, "General"
3	"a broken heart"	CO, Notes, "Moi"
4	"Wrong-Living Man"	*Time*, 11/14/62
4	"an NBC-TV show"	CO, Diary, 12/5/62
5	"my hope—amen!"	Ibid., 12/6/62
5	"darts with words"	CO, letter to MB-G, 1962–63?
5	"shove from me"	CO, letter to MB-G and William Gibson, 7/1/61
6	"letters, usually irate"	Gibson, Preface, *Golden Boy Musical*, p. 5
7	destroying herself	Life of George Gershwin (never produced)
13	"not too late"	Personal Notes, 1961

CHAPTER ONE

Page	Quote	Source
17	"full fruitfulness"	*Philadelphia—Holy Experiment*
17	"I know so well"	CO, Journal, 3/20/40
19	Esther married him	Israel Rossman, wire recordings made by CO
20	"widdout a toilet"	Ibid.
20	"ten cents a dozen"	Ibid.
21	"doesn't let ya get losted"	Ibid.
22	According to Pearl	Pearl Odets, letter to CO, 3/5/35

CHAPTER TWO

Page	Quote	Source
24	"difficult to attain"	CO, Journal, 3/24/40
27	"capacity for fresh sight"	Cf. E. H. Erikson, *Toys and Reasons*
27	"doll" and "baby"	CO, Notes, "Moi," 9/47
27	"impale them as tie-pins"	CO, Notes, "What I Remember," 9/47
29	"by some hungry cat"	CO, letter to Hortense Alden, 7/13/30
29	"you mommy's titsy"	CO, Notes for an Autobiography, 1935
30	"Girl's leg cut off"	Ibid.
30	"the princeling Murder!"	CO, Notes, 1962
30	"no one helps"	CO, Notes, "Moi," 9/58
31	"taken care of"	4/20/55
31	"shy, and reticent?"	CO, Analytic Notes, 12/28/51, p. 4
31	"his idea of success"	Miller, A., Introduction, *Collected Plays*, p. 34
31	"I've ever met"	Mendelsohn, p. 10
32	recorded in history	Beard, *Basic History*, p. 415
32	"and sleeps the best"	*Golden Boy*, Act II, Scene 1
34	"will sing themselves"	Ibid., p. 228
34	"a free people sung"	Ibid.
34	"heard upon earth"	Whitman, "Starting from Paumanok," *Leaves of Grass*, p. 12
35	"how I loved him"	CO, letter to Philip Moeller, 3/6/31
35	"wanted or needed"	CO, Notes, "L.J.," 11/55
36	"go to her assistance"	CO, letter to Philip Moeller, 2/22/31
36	"cream on my saucer"	Ibid.
37	"a plum dumpling"	CO, Notes, "What I Remember," 9/47
37	"healthy mental growth"	CO, letter to Philip Moeller, 2/22/31
38	"shown from it all"	CO, Notes, "783 Beck Street," 1/59
38	"fight or run"	CO, Diary, 8/23/32
38	"contact him"	Waife-Goldberg
39	"among other things"	CO, note to his analyst, 11/14/51 (unsent)
40	"with much tenderness"	CO, letter to Philip Moeller, 2/22/31
41	"toes and knees"	Ibid.
42	"no use for the gendarmes!"	CO, Notes, "Moi," 4/18/50
44	reply is, "Gold"	CO, screenplay, Life of George Gershwin, 1942 (unpublished), p. 94
44	"well-known socialist!"	CO, Journal, 2/6/40
44	"men of opposition"	Ibid., 7/11/40
44	"can I deny myself?"	Whitman, "You Felons on Trial in Courts," *Leaves of Grass*, p. 304
45	"rich clothes, etc., etc."	CO, Notes, "Psychology" (undated)
45	"long death of sleep!"	CO, 9/47

CHAPTER THREE

Page	Quote	Source
46	"up in the sky"	Mendelsohn
46	"tree won't grow"	*The Big Knife*
47	"all he was worth!"	CO, Journal, 3/24/40
47	"bad things you do"	CO, Notes, "What I Remember," 9/47
47	of *The New Yorker*	"Revolution's Number One Boy"
48	"goes in his own body"	Israel Rossman, wire recording, 7/1/49
48	"to an end all wars"	Beard, *Basic History*. Cf. Schlesinger, Vol. I
49	"in the bathtub"	CO, Journal, 3/24/40
49	"a love of music"	Ibid., 11/11/40
50	"in life no less!"	7/1/61
50	"or alcoholism"	Beard, *Basic History*, p. 395
50	"and it works"	Schlesinger, I, 13
50	guns were found	Ibid., I, 43
50	himself with alcohol	Gelb, pp. 188, 368
51	"me self-pity, too"	CO, Journal, 3/24/40
51	had been for O'Neill	Gelb
51	" 'if you can!' "	*The Big Knife*
52	"usually earns praise!"	2/57
53	"and going ahead"	CO, notes for Gershwin screenplay, 1942
53	"on the window above"	CO, letter to MB-G and William Gibson, 7/1/61
54	"I was awed!"	CO, Notes, "Moi," 1962
54	"(meaning girls)"	CO, letter to Irene Steinberg, 12/10/23
54	"looked like a president"	CO, screenplay, Life of George Gershwin, 1942 (unpublished), pp. 146–47
55	"out for a good time"	Ibid., p. 147
55	"and read them"	Mendelsohn, p. 10
56	an American paradigm	Lawson, "Rebellion"
56	"any of its works?"	HC, *Fervent Years*, p. 5
57	within the next decade	Gelb, pp. 408 ff.
57	"yet a greater fool!"	CO, letter to Floyd Neale, 3/6/29
59	"language of the poets"	Hethmon, p. 2
59	"the matter with him!"	CO, Personal Notes
59	"an humiliated other"	CO, Chronology for autobiography, 1934
60	"consideration for himself"	Drachman, pp. 32–33
61	"was still unhurt"	Ibid.
62	"cutting other classes"	Julian Drachman, "Genius in Embryo" (unpublished)
63	"very ignorant background"	Hethmon, p. 5
63	"like a book"	CO, screenplay, Life of George Gershwin, 1942 (unpublished), p. 21
63	"or Sherlock Holmes"	Hethmon, p. 5
64	"the editorial page"	Ibid.
64	" 'think you are?' "	Ibid.
64	"sense of relief"	Julian Drachman, "Genius in Embryo" (unpublished)

CHAPTER FOUR

Page	Quote	Source
67	"into business"	Interview in *The World*, 1914 (cf. Swanberg, p. 176)
67	"like that, presto!"	Undated fragment
69	"at parties?"	11/21/23
70	"Tambien me pais"	12/31/23
70	"member of the school"	Mendelsohn
70	DeWitt Clinton ended	Ibid.
71	"don't forget that"	12/31/23
72	"don't know a thing!"	CO, Notes, "L.J.," 1961
72	"is still present"	Hethmon, p. 6
72	"painful in the end!"	CO, Notes, "Psychology," D, 30, 4
73	"all human life"	Ibid., 1954?
73	"an irrational way"	CO, letter to MB-G, 11/21/60
73	"the general fraud!"	12/5/38
73	"opposed to abuse"	CO, letter to G. Gross, 12/18/47 (unpublished thesis)
74	"hide off a scene"	Hethmon, p. 9
75	"and smoking forever"	Gelb, p. 573
76	"Hell results!"	CO, Notes, "Psychology," 9–1
76	"self-contempt is dissipated"	Ibid.
76	"to be afraid of!"	Ibid., 8/57
77	"on temperament"	CO, Diary, 9/9/24
80	"lost its taste"	Ibid., 11/6/24
81	"Clifford L. Odets"	Ibid., 12/25/24
82	"a fake eagle"	*Golden Boy*
82	"her living son"	CO, Journal, 6/29/40
82	"do it *my* way!"	CO, Notes, "Moi," 1950s?
82	By his nineteenth year	The 95-cent diary for 1925 having disappeared, we are less certain of details here than in 1924
83	"to go, they go"	Hyams
83	"Greenwich Village dreamer"	Hethmon, p. 8
83	"front of the public"	Ibid., p. 12
83	"two of these things"	Ibid.
83	"get paid for it?"	Ibid., p. 8
84	"that kind shows"	Mendelsohn, p. 12
84	"I'm afraid"	CO, letter to Edw. T. Herbert, 6/12/63
87	"food on my stove"	Gelb, p. 299

CHAPTER FIVE

Page	Quote	Source
88	"they lacked or sought"	CO, Personal Notes, 9/59
88	"maybe in the future"	CO, Diary, 3/26
89	"He, I think"	Ibid., 5/11/26
89	"postures and struts"	CO, Notes, "Places We Knew," 5/61
89	"couldn't stand him"	Hethmon, p. 6
89	"a number of matters"	7/30/28
90	to perform gratis	Landry
91	"and to happiness"	Hethmon, p. 12
92	"shaking audiences"	Mendelsohn, p. 12
92	this "family epitaph"	Gelb, p. 579
92	"real old actors"	CO, Diary, 4/29/26
93	"I am a good actor"	Ibid., 5/23/26
93	"immutability of fate"	Ibid., 6/22/26
93	"with lots of talent"	Ibid., 5/3/26
93	"on the horizon"	Ibid., 1/21/26

Page	*Quote*	*Source*
93	"that will be good"	Ibid., 6/25/26
94	"My store is low"	Ibid., 5/3/26
94	"and from sleep"	Ibid., 6/26/26
95	motion-picture projector	Ibid., 6/28/26
95	"something bad"	CO, Notes, "Sex" (undated)
95	"parts in stock"	Hethmon, p. 10
96	"black sheep of the family"	Ibid.

<h2 style="text-align:center">CHAPTER SIX</h2>

98	"happens to be"	*Identity and the Life Cycle*, p. 129
98	Ph.D. thesis about him	Mendelsohn, p. 1
98	identity as an actor	CO, letter to HK, 3/21/28
100	"anxious to bid"	Ibid., 6/16/27
101	"no sustenance"	Schlesinger, Vol. I, p. 150
101	like the famous Wolfs	Burt, p. 567
103	"mute reflections"	CO, letter to Sylvia Hoffman, 3/9/27
103	"without a wife?"	CO, letter to HK, 3/13/27
103	baby daughter, Joan	CO, letter to Tamara, 8/4/33
103	"replace that fiction"	CO, letter to Goldie Bromberg, 1/27/32
104	"ami Clifford"	3/18/27?
105	"miniature Don Juan"	CO, letter to HK, 5/10/27
105	poetry as "coarse"	Burt, p. 397
105	"suspended over Moscow"	Beard, *Rise of American Civilization*, III, 657
106	those fictions necessary	Schlesinger, Vol. I, p. 151
106	"court of public opinion"	Halsey. See also Hiss; Zeligs
106	"her real grief"	CO, Journal, 3/20/40
106	"I could not resolve"	CO, Notes, "Moi," 9/53
106	sexual self-stimulation	CO, Chronology, 1927
109	"our national dialogue"	Vogel
109	"between a million"	CO, Boston notes for "The Flowering Peach" (unpublished), 1954
109	distance from him	CO, letter to Sylvia Hoffman (undated)
110	"an unmentionable spot"	7/27
110	"brighter day for all"	Swanberg, p. 330
110	"in American justice"	Lawson, "Rebellion," p. 347
111	least want to go	McCarten

<h2 style="text-align:center">CHAPTER SEVEN</h2>

112	"*affiliated* with yourself"	Wagner
112	"cope with Freud"	Gelb, p. 661
113	"of the poet's heart"	HC, *Fervent Years*, p. 22
113	"delicious thought . . . eh?"	Undated—1928
114	"about my chances"	CO, letter to HK, 3/21/28
114	"sensitivity is gone"	CO, letter to "Betty," 6/19/28
114	"made me glad"	Ibid., 5/20/28
115	"but I did . . . alone"	Ibid., 6/4/28
116	"old boy so much"	8/28
116	"neither of them"	6/19/28
118	"I am quite content"	7/30/28
119	"I cannot say"	"Martha," 8/18/29

Page	Quote	Source
119	"must go so easily"	7/30/28
119	"music until twelve"	CO, letter to "Martha," 9/4/28
119	"also a lover"	Ibid., 9/1/28
120	"with a camel"	Ibid., 9/8/28
120	"has been music"	11/16/51
120	"an arresting face"	CO, letter to Ed Thompson, 1/18/29
120	"the best educated"	CO, letter to Sylvia Hoffman, 11/15/29
120	"and I listened"	Ibid.
120	Toccata and Fugue	Ibid., 3/6/29
120	"young days and years"	CO, letter to Floyd Neale, 8/7/28
121	"can be cut out"	6/24/26? (probably misdated later by CO)
121	"from the other side"	CO, letter to Floyd Neale, 8/7/28
125	"I deny myself?"	Whitman, "You Felons on Trial in Courts," *Leaves of Grass*, p. 304
125	Odets from prison	Correspondence of CO and "Jack Schoenberg"
126	"you guys 'n' ya all bit!"	Letter to CO, 2/8/46
127	"in world society"	Kazin, *On Native Grounds*, p. 283
127	"supply and demand"	Beard, *Rise of American Civilization*, III, 594
128	but not for long	Lawson, "Rebellion"

CHAPTER EIGHT

Page	Quote	Source
130	"significant solidarities"	*Young Man Luther,* p. 42
130	"pierce the heavens"	Beard, *Rise of American Civilization,* III, 12
131	wave of motion pictures	Elliot Norton, lecture at Boston University seminar, Windsor Mountain School, Lenox, Mass., 6/25/67 (unpublished)
131	"becoming a playwright"	Hethmon, p. 13
132	"quite a fake"	Ibid., p. 14
132	"moments of my life"	Ibid.
132	"You're good"	Ibid.
132	"nest-like music"	Ibid.
132	"lousy grind"	CO, letter to Ed Thompson (undated)
133	"oh dear!"	Ibid.
133	"[has] been lonely"	Ibid.
133	"creating a pose"	CO, letter to Sylvia Hoffman, 4/2/29
133	"needs that help"	3/6/29
134	"count my steps"	CO, letter to "Martha," 5/8/29
134	" 'only dreams?' "	CO, letter to Ed Thompson, 3/22/29
134	for creative thought	CO, letter to Floyd Neale, 3/6/29
134	"of all: Silence"	CO, letter to "Martha," 5/8/29
135	two years later	CO, letter to Tamara, 8/4/33
135	"what ever that means"	7/5/29
136	"awful . . . and enough!"	7/5/29
136	" 'go and get it' "	CO, letter to Alex, 7/18/29
137	"Oh dear music"	Ibid.
137	"Beauty in my heart"	CO, letter to "Betty," 7/22/29
137	"darkness and damp"	Ibid., 7/24/29
138	"thing to worship"	7/30/29
139	"wrest them away"	8/18/29
140	"Their days!"	7/5/32
140	"like the river"	8/4/33

Page	*Quote*	*Source*
140	"heart is mine"	CO, Diary, 7/5/32
140	"write and write!"	CO, letter to "Martha," 8/18/29
141	"bite the vitals"	Diary, 7/5/32
141	recent Smith graduate	HC, *Fervent Years,* p. 13
141	"and *Marco Millions*"	Hethmon, p. 16
142	according to Clurman	HC, *Fervent Years,* p. 25
142	"exceptional play"	Ibid., p. 24
143	"women—the workers"	Cowley, "1930s"
143	"hopes for the future"	Ibid.
144	"took the part away"	CO, Notes, "Places We Knew," undated
144	"quivering and wounded"	Letter #3, 1929
145	"ad infinitum!"	1929
145	"you to be mine"	Wed. eve., 1929
145	"cavaliere servente"	Letter #9, 1929
145	"Sand said to Chopin"	Typed 10/65, p. 16
146	"Nordic," non-Jewish women	CO, letter to HK, 6/25/31
146	"when ever possible"	11/28–29/29
146	"one word: 'Obit' "	Ibid.
147	passion for music	Notes for an Autobiography, 1934. Also personal communication to MB-G; Personal Notes; letter to "Martha," 3/13/31
147	"unrequited love"	Letter to "Martha," 3/13/31
147	"tubes and retorts"	CO, letter to Sylvia Field, #9, 1929
147	"their flying banners"	Ibid., #4, 1929
147	"Man to remain unborn"	11/21/29
148	"what is mine"	11/29
148	"lived in Brooklyn"	12/14/29
148	"an enemy's tongue"	CO, letter to Philip Lottman 12/2/29
149	"mother to his bed"	Ibid.
149	"week for it"	12/11/29
149	"echo your word!"	Ibid.
150	"Consuelo Bianca"	Letter #13, 12/29
150	"talk and talk"	Ibid.

CHAPTER NINE

151	"and has issue"	*The Seesaw Log,* p. 273
151	"written in me"	1/1/30
151	"drifting is terrible"	Ibid.
151	theory of masochism	Brenman, "On Teasing"
151	necessity for rebirth	E. H. Erikson, "Identity and the Life Cycle"
152	"banks and all"	CO, letter to Sylvia Field, 1929
153	"a complete stranger"	CO, letter to Philip Lottman, 1/26/30
154	"beautiful and satisfying"	CO, letter to Louis Veda, 3/12/30
154	"a penny whistle"	CO, letter to Cheryl Crawford, 5/30
154	"never grows up"	Ibid.
155	being an actor	E. H. Erikson, *Young Man Luther,* p. 43
155	"to the material"	Wagner, p. 1
155	"of being into"	Ibid., p. 2
155	tragicomic world	McCarten
155	trust her ability	CO to MB-G (private communication)

Page	Quote	Source
155	"interior history"	Gibson, *Seesaw Log*
155	"kind of person"	Wagner, p. 1
156	"Sine Sole Silio"	CO, letter to William Kozlenko, 5/11/30
156	"a Great Hunger"	Ibid.
156	receding hairline	Ibid.
157	"with wild Hebrews"	CO, letter to Hortense Alden, 7/3/30
157	"that not be given"	Ibid., 6/24/30
157	"dance for him?"	Ibid., 6/27/30
158	"rustic walking stick"	Ibid., 7/1/30
159	"wit and desperation"	Quoted by CO in letter to Hortense Alden, 6/30/30
160	"a crushing force"	7/31/30
160	" 'Life's obscene!' "	8/30
160	"the greatest Grace!"	Ibid.
160	"chair beside me"	8/13?/30
160	Staten Island ferry	Ibid.
161	"act like one!"	8/20/30
161	"a Great Mother"	8/28/30
161	"And another kiss"	Ibid.

CHAPTER TEN

Page	Quote	Source
162	"American spirit"	HC, *Fervent Years*, p. 28
162	"decent humanity"	Ibid., xii
163	"the disgrace!"	1934
163	the American theatre	Gelb, p. 306
163	"I am Gorodetsky"	CO, Notes, "Moi" (undated)
164	was balderdash	12/4/30
164	*Mourning Becomes Electra*	Gelb, pp. 721 ff.
164	father was killed	12/4/30
164	"their inner garden"	E. H. Erikson, *Young Man Luther*, p. 44
165	"in their work"	1/27/31
165	sense of importance	Hethmon, p. 18
165	"kind of theatre"	Ibid.
166	"outside of fiction"	CO to MB-G, personal communication
166	"he moves away"	HC to MB-G, personal communication
167	"creative business 'deals' "	HC, Boston University lecture, 7/64
168	observed by clinicians	Weissman
168	"tempo and activity"	HC, *Fervent Years*, p. 5
168	"O'Neill's silence"	Ibid., p. 8
168	"mechanism of a watch"	Ibid., p. 10
169	for five weeks	Chinoy
169	"of the playwright"	HC, *Fervent Years*, p. 21
169	"to an issue"	Ibid., p. 27
170	"load of trouble"	Ibid.
170	"a glorious crusade"	Ibid., p. ix
170	"superior, and happy"	James, p. 186
172	"saves my life"	CO, Notes for an Autobiography, 1934
173	Caroline Bird	*Invisible Scar*
174	"trying on the side"	Hethmon, p. 19
174	manuscript into shreds	Ibid.
174	"forked lightnings"	CO, Diary, 6/12/31
175	"lose his own soul?!"	HC, *Fervent Years*, p. 32
175	"of our generation"	Ibid., p. 92

Page	Quote	Source
177	"four thirty am"	CO, letter to Philip Moeller, 1/24/31
177	"feminine to love"	Ibid., 4/27/31
177	"without his nepenthe"	Ibid., 1/27/31
178	"like you Philip Moeller"	Ibid.
178	letters to Fliess	*Origins of Psychoanalysis*
178	"a dancing star"	2/11/31
178	" 'you were dead' "	Ibid.
178	objectively on himself	CO entry in Group Theatre Daybook, p. 3
179	"cold probing mind"	2/17/31
179	"a good thing"	HC, *Fervent Years*, p. 24
179	"state of my life"	Hethmon, p. 21
180	"swollen breast"	3/1/31
180	"Jesus on my chest!"	2/26/31
180	"out within me"	2/11/31
181	"about Miss Fontanne?"	Ibid.
181	"have been lovers!"	2/15/31
181	"things that grow"	2/17/31
181	"form of Beethoven"	Ibid.
181	"Nature of its due"	3/5/31
182	"earth's barren rock"	Ibid.
182	"a dangerous person"	2/26/31
183	"turn away to the wall"	3/6/31
183	"with my vagaries"	3/13/31
183	"sense of shame"	3/11/31
183	"not naturally mine"	Ibid.
183	"teach us things"	Hethmon, p. 22
184	"a lone geranium"	3/23/31
184	"youth was reached"	Ibid.
184	"such a hand?"	Ibid.
184	"my boyhood years"	Ibid.
185	"return from the dead"	3/25/31
186	"special kind of 'in' "	Hethmon, p. 22
186	"sort of artist precept"	3/29/31
189	"style of expression. Enough"	CO, letter to Philip Moeller, 3/29/31
189	"boy into flower!"	Ibid.

CHAPTER ELEVEN

Page	Quote	Source
193	"to love is America"	Group Theatre Daybook, 8/9/31, p. 114
193	"about this thing!!!"	CO in Group Theatre Daybook, 7/12/31
194	Provincetown Theatre	Deutsch and Hanau
194	"take new heart"	Helen Deutsch in Group Theatre Daybook, p. 88
194	"has yet to see"	Alixe Walker in Group Theatre Daybook, p. 62
194	"catharsis is over"	CO, Diary, 6/8/31
194	"a simple nourishment"	Ibid.
195	"turn into sleep"	Ibid.
195	"I have only one line"	Ibid.
196	"N.Y. season"	HC in Group Theatre Daybook, 6/19/31, pp. 17–20
197	"and legitimate doubt!"	Ibid.
197	a new life	6/25/31
197	and in *Midnight*	CO, Diary, 6/16/31
198	"devoted ministrations"	HC, "Fervent Years," uncut ms., p. 106
198	"feel like it"	Group Theatre Daybook, 6/27/31

Page	Quote	Source
198	"actors in some way"	Ibid.
198	"and linear dimension"	CO, Diary, 6/12/31
198	"wings for lifting"	Group Theatre Daybook, 6/12/31
199	"America has produced"	Hethmon, p. 29
199	"his arteries prematurely"	CO, Journal, 1940
199	"as the outward"	CO, Diary, 6/8/31
199	"in front of them"	CO, fragment, undated, filed under 910 *Eden Street*
199	"maggoty with morbidity"	CO, Diary, 6/14/31
200	"and entrail tearing"	6/11/31
200	"brain cool and empty"	CO, letter to HK, 6/25/31
200	"it is summer"	Group Theatre Daybook, 7/12/31
200	"my Hebraic blood"	6/25/31
200	"well brought up"	CO, Diary, 6/19/31
200	"bother me at all"	Ibid., 6/16/31
201	report to Kozlenko	7/2/31
201	"exultation of the night"	CO, Diary, 6/19/31
201	"when I was alone"	6/23/31
201	"as she is being"	6/16/31
201	"and more joining"	7/24/31
201	"here to stay"	Hethmon, p. 26
201	"come and go"	Ibid., p. 27
202	a shine to Odets	Ibid.
202	by Philip Moeller	CO, letter to Philip Moeller, 2/11/31
202	"most exalted drama"	HC, *Fervent Years*, p. 71
202	American stamp	Ibid.
202	"copy of Shakespeare"	HC, "Fervent Years," uncut ms., p. 114
202	"stage deportment"	HC, *Fervent Years*, p. 40
202	"that of a miracle"	Ibid., p. 41
202	"of this theatre"	Hethmon, p. 25
203	"something new"	Ibid.
203	in his experience	Ibid.
203	"dealing with life"	HC, *Fervent Years*, p. 41
203	"greater American problem"	HC, "Fervent Years," uncut ms., p. 187
203	"soft and sentimental"	Ibid., p. 189
203	"with the fleas"	Pp. 95–97
204	"like a great father"	Group Theatre Daybrook, pp. 100–101
204	"young life's experience"	HC, *Fervent Years*, p. 49
204	"have to start anew"	Hethmon, p. 39

CHAPTER TWELVE

Page	Quote	Source
205	"poetic realism"	"Fervent Years," uncut ms., pp. 91–92?
205	"the Group Theatre"	CO to MB-G, personal communication
206	its first champion	Ibid.
206	"at that time"	HC, *Fervent Years*, p. 56
206	"emotional selves"	HC, "Fervent Years," uncut ms., p. 141
206	"warm in a cold winter"	Hethmon, p. 32
207	"world more objectively"	HC, *Fervent Years*, p. 63
207	"are most valuable"	Ibid., p. 66
207	"four years later"	Ibid.
207	"with the dramatist"	Ibid., p. 63
207	Theresa Helburn	HC, "Fervent Years," uncut ms., p. 160

Page	*Quote*	*Source*
207	"looking at life"	HC, *Fervent Years,* p. 67
208	Idea would continue	HC, "Fervent Years," uncut ms., p. 161
208	"missionary zeal"	CO, Notes for an Autobiography, 1934
209	"Beethoven, and People"	1/27/32
209	"kind of rest"	Ibid.
209	"away on you"	2/24/32
209	"a harmful subjectivity"	CO, Diary (fragment), 5/25/32
209	"out of everything"	Ibid.
210	"is really belief"	"Some paragraphs . . . March 31, 1932. Anent CO"
211	"sun of friendship"	CO, letter to Margaret Barker, 4/23/32
211	"come from that"	CO, "Some paragraphs . . . ," 3/31/32
212	"and growing things"	CO, Diary, 4/8/32
212	neurosis and creativity	E. H. Erikson, *Young Man Luther,* p. 47
213	"I did not know"	Waldo Frank obituary, *New York Times,* 1/10/67
213	in the French theatre	Chaplin, pp. 248–49
213	"America needs groups"	HC, "Fervent Years," uncut ms., p. 115
214	"don't go together"	CO, letter to Mary Morris, 5/20/32
214	"she annoyed them"	5/8/32
216	"I'm feeding them"	5/25/32
216	"Enemy # One"	5/32
216	"rotten all this is"	Ibid.
216	"no interest in success"	5/13/32
217	"here is a nuisance"	Diary, 5/13/32
217	"the last quartets"	Ibid., 5/25/32
217	"investigate it further"	5/18/32
217	"biggest and the best"	5/17/32
218	"of their prayers"	5/18/32
218	"Dostoievsky certainly"	5/25/32
218	"ads for toothpaste"	5/18/32
218	"and cranial formation"	Ibid.
219	"world without us"	5/27/32
219	"most valuable of all!"	5/27/32
220	" 'underneath,' she says"	Ibid.
220	"it's a different thing"	Ibid.
220	"should compare favorably"	5/29/32

CHAPTER THIRTEEN

221	"so be our work!"	CO, Diary, 7/29/32
221	"your own materials"	Wagner
222	his own materials	CO, Diary, 6/19/32
222	"good permanent literature"	6/20/32
222	and Ernest O'Malley	HC, *Fervent Years,* p. 86
222	"can succeed in it"	Ibid., p. 93
223	"bankruptcy and death"	Lawson, "Rebellion," p. 393. See also Levant (cf. "I am not an American," p. 262)
223	"psychological depth"	Lawson, "Rebellion"
223	"victories are vain"	HC, *Fervent Years,* p. 93
223	"noise around him"	Diary, 8/31/32
224	"mouth stood agape"	CO to MB-G, personal communication

Page	Quote	Source
	Page	*Quote* — *Source*

Page	Quote	Source
224	"search for creativity"	Lawson to MB-G, personal communication
225	"the right way"	6/27/32
225	"of mental existence"	E. H. Erikson, *Young Man Luther,* p. 109
225	"one to the other"	7/20/32
225	"a different affair"	Ibid.
226	"obvious significance"	6/24/32
226	"change as a person"	7/2/32
226	clipped of speech	6/22/32
226	"in the bad sense"	6/28/32
226	"what is before you"	6/27/32
227	"old and finished"	7/2/32
227	on a farm	CO to MB-G, personal communication
228	"closer to me"	7/8/32
228	"tremendously discouraging"	8/7/32
228	"in the rain"	7/4/32. See also E. H. Erikson, *Insight and Responsibility,* pp. 164 ff.
228	"the Beethoven head"	7/1/32
228	with his play?	8/6/32
229	" 'to his art' "	7/16/32
229	world of men	E. H. Erikson, *Insight and Responsibility,* p. 183
229	"breasts of the Muse"	CO, letter to Helen Deutsch, fall 1934
229	"incautious intake"	E. H. Erikson, *Insight and Responsibility,* p. 184
229	spring from the people	CO, Diary, 7/26/32
229	"Life is good"	Ibid.
229	"moment the repose"	7/29/32
230	"what it's about"	7/4/32
230	"lay out characters"	*Theatre Arts,* December 1950
230	"that was nice"	8/11/32
231	"wasting my genius"	"Victory" (unpublished), p. 24
231	"times were ripe"	Ibid., Scene 4, p. 5
231	"only one Brant"	Ibid., Scene 1, p. 22
231	"cross-country runner"	Ibid., Scene 4, p. 21
231	"close to his father"	Ibid., Scene 4, p. 25
232	"a relative thing"	Ibid., Scene 5, p. 7
232	later material success	E. H. Erikson, *Young Man Luther,* p. 65, of Hans and Martin Luther
232	a "dirty Jew"	"Victory," Scene 6, p. 30
232	"who also seek"	Ibid., Scene 9, p. 2
233	"people around me"	7/19/32
233	"and a mood too"	Ibid.
233	"lust, and charity"	7/28/32
233	"inch at a time"	Ibid.
233	"rule the government"	7/29/32 and 7/30/32
233	"deal with a mob"	Bendiner
234	"also large parts"	7/31/32
235	"see him legless"	8/10/32
235	"means all that"	8/13/32
236	"Ploosh! Slish!"	8/22/32
236	"whore for a wife"	Ibid.
236	"what they stand for"	8/23/32
237	"never write a play"	Hethmon, p. 35
237	"P.T. teachers"	8/23/32

Page	*Quote*	*Source*
237	"the big drunk"	CO, Notes for an Autobiography, 1934
238	"life and conduct"	8/30/32
238	grandfather, Jacob	Act III
239	"feeling and reality"	Diary, 8/23/32
239	"and I them"	9/5/32

CHAPTER FOURTEEN

240	"sort of test"	HC, *Fervent Years,* p. 112
240	"or help it"	Wagner
241	" 'I want to be loved' "	CO, Diary, 9/12/32
241	"this past summer"	Ibid.
241	his internal integrations	Brenman-Gibson, "Creation of Plays"
242	"of self and pride"	CO, Diary, 9/12/32
242	"pain for Clifford"	Brenman, "On Teasing"
242	calamity had failed	Beard, *Basic History,* p. 453
243	"weekends and holidays"	*New York Times,* 5/25/52
243	"learning and growth"	Ibid.
244	"get to first base"	*Awake and Sing!,* p. 38
244	"acting company"	Mendelsohn
245	"the irreconcilables"	5/1/66
246	"profoundly happy"	HC, *Fervent Years,* p. 105
246	"cavernous emptiness"	Ibid., pp. 107–108
246	"taxi-drivers' union"	Ibid.
247	"state of gestation"	Ibid.
247	"ready to be served"	Ibid., p. 111
247	no more "forgotten men"	Oglethorpe University, Atlanta, Georgia, 5/32
248	mass murder	Tucker. See also Alliluyeva
248	undreamed of in 1933	Lifton
248	the Ukraine famine	Halsey, p. 67
248	Committee for Foster	HC, *Fervent Years,* p. 112
248	mayor of Chicago	Bendiner
249	"one poor human"	Robert G. L. Waite, letter to MG-B, 12/3/68
249	"really was saying"	Wagner, p. 18
250	"you heard me"	*Awake,* Act I, Scene 1, pp. 56–57
251	"ain't got an orange!!"	Ibid., p. 58
251	"amidst petty conditions"	Ibid., Author's Notes, p. 37
251	"feel out for yourself"	*New Theatre,* March 1935
252	"escape if possible"	*Awake,* Author's Notes, p. 37
252	"laughing at him"	Ibid., p. 39
252	"poor mockie like him"	"I Got the Blues" (Copyright 1933, unpublished), Act I, p. 25
252	"poor foreigner"	*Awake,* Act I, Scene 1, p. 55
252	"lowest from the low"	"Blues," Act I, p. 25
252	"chair on your head"	Ibid., p. 26
252	"don't believe in God"	Ibid., p. 25
252	"the books together"	Ibid., p. 26
252	considerably toned down	*Awake,* Act I, Scene 1, p. 55
252	"such families"	"Blues," Act I, p. 26
253	"cops and robbers"	*Awake,* Act II, Scene 1, p. 71
253	"your sickness"	"Blues," Act III, p. 67
253	"indelible ink!"	*Awake,* Act III, p. 97
254	"a corset button left!"	Ibid., Act I, Scene 1, p. 56
254	"in the whole world"	Ibid., p. 48

Page	Quote	Source
254	"for the wild life"	Ibid., Author's Notes, p. 37
255	"losing my hair"	Ibid., Act II, Scene 1, p. 87
256	"deeply intolerant finally"	Ibid., Author's Notes, p. 38
256	a "burlesque show"	Ibid., p. 39
256	"in all the papers"	Ibid., Act I, Scene 1, p. 41
256	will be covered by it	Ibid., Act II, Scene 1, p. 72
256	"instead a glass tea"	Ibid., Act II, Scene 2, p. 78
256	"yourself a revolution!"	Ibid.
257	"the chosen people"	"Blues," Act II, p. 39
257	"change the world"	Ibid., Act III, p. 63
258	economic or political logic	Lawson, *Theory and Technique*
258	"it was a dirty lie"	*New York Times*, May 3, 1936
258	"glad we're living"	*Awake*, Act III, pp. 100–101
259	than do the Americans	Cf. Eric Mottram, Introduction to Penguin edition of CO's *Three Plays*
260	"I'm an idiot"	CO, Notes for an Autobiography, 1934
261	"I resent the loss"	CO, letter to Cipe, 9/1/33
262	necessary . . . for dramatists	E. H. Erikson, private communication, 2/24/68
263	"awful as hell here"	6/3/33
263	"new as a child"	Ibid.
263	"how alike we are"	Ibid., 6/5/33
263	"go away from me"	6/8/33
263	"to have a haircut"	6/13/33
264	"can stand verbatim"	6/7/33
264	"stop being afraid"	6/14/33

CHAPTER FIFTEEN

Page	Quote	Source
265	"ran that way"	Wagner
265	"serious writer here"	Ibid.
265	rest of his life	Private communication, 5/20/68
266	"little hand of him"	6/20/33
266	"crafty as E. Rice"	6/25/33
266	"Boy Scouts?"	Leonard Lyons, "Lyons's Den," *New York Post*, 8/16/63
266	"surprised at my ability"	6/26/33
267	"spirit clutched wrongly"	CO, letter to Cipe, 8/33
267	"Here is truth"	CO, Diary, 6/26/33
267	"over the neck"	6/27/33
267	with other girls	7/19/33
267	"not some mental image"	6/26/33
268	"goes like the river"	7/5/33
268	"not a few"	Ibid.
268	"I'd be indeed happy"	7/5/33
268	"reminds me of Tamara"	7/8/33
269	"because I am!"	CO, letter to Cipe, 8/33
269	"cough in the lungs"	CO, Diary, 6/25/33
270	"morning before I knew"	Ibid., 7/8/33
270	"seems to touch me"	CO, letter to Tamara, 7/10/33
270	"touched with a hand"	Ibid.
271	"against all women"	7/15/33
271	"if I can help it"	Ibid.
271	"next ten years"	7/19/33
271	"I'm still willing"	7/26/33
271	"always eludes me"	8/4/33

Page	Quote	Source
272	"he'll never get"	8/9/33
272	"oranges and toast"	Ibid.
272	"about writing plays"	Ibid.
273	"ability to write"	8/23/33
273	"laughing with joy!"	Playwrights' Seminar, Windsor Mountain, Lenox, Mass., 7/14/66
274	"I said so"	10/19/49
274	"stopped or contained"	Wagner
275	"it goes ahead"	CO, letter to Cipe, 8/29/33
275	"Group *must* produce"	CO, Notes for an Autobiography, 1934
275	"clavier in the night"	CO, letter to Cipe, 9/1/33
280	"half alligator"	CO, Journal, 11/28/40
281	"between the notes"	1/1/34
281	"come from Communism!"	Ibid.
282	"pseudo-species"	Cf. E. H. Erikson. See *Notes and Comment* 21.1
282	"the crucial issue"	Schlesinger, II, 385
282	had been outlawed	Nuremberg Decrees, 5/2/33
282	"symbol of a new faith"	Wingler
282	"what Fascism was"	Schlesinger, II, p. 388
282	"This—is revolution!"	Ibid.
282	path to redemption	Beard, *Rise of American Civilization*, p. 688

CHAPTER SIXTEEN

Page	Quote	Source
283	"events on the stage"	*America in Mid-Passage*, p. 638
283	"Harold stops me"	Notes for an Autobiography, 1934
284	"home for dead"	CO, letter to Helen Deutsch, 10/24/34
285	*"remaking the world"*	Rosenman, p. 65
285	"mature *Awake and Sing!*"	Letter to Robert Garland, 12/11/35
285	"laughs with love!"	Gelb, p. 762
285	"jazz-and-racket age"	Krutch, *American Drama*
285	"social understanding"	HC, *Fervent Years*, p. 124
285	stands of Communist doctrine	Krutch, *American Drama*
287	"you're lying"	House Un-American Activities Committee in Hollywood, 1/28/52, p. 2316
288	"representative American theatre"	HC, *Fervent Years*, p. 127
287	"derives from his content"	CO Estate files, "Special Materials—1934"
289	*Gold Eagle Guy*	Letter to Paula Strasberg, 5/7/34
289	"important theatre anywhere"	Letter to Group at Broadhurst Theatre, 6/10/34
289	"possibilities there were"	HC, *Fervent Years*, p. 131
290	"you will find out"	7/19/34
290	"false values, anything"	Hyams
290	"sterility and futility"	*Time*, 12/23/35
290	"modern man's spirit"	*Paradise Lost*, Act II, p. 199
290	"the food is free"	Ibid., Act I, p. 192
290	"a sweet smell"	*Paradise Lost*, Act II, p. 199
291	"(*Slowly sits tremblingly*)"	Ibid., Act I, pp. 46, 46A
291	"you sleep, Boss"	Ibid., p. 186
292	"life in a coffin"	*Awake*, Act III, p. 99
293	"gone tomorrow!"	*Paradise*, Act III, p. 219
293	"ends with a fizz"	"Paradise," original draft, Act I, p. 22

Page	Quote	Source
294	"he was ashamed"	Ibid., p. 223
294	"wanted to die!"	Ibid.
295	"committed suicide"	CO to MB-G, personal communication, 8/53
295	severely embattled	Ibid., private communication
295	"that old hotel"	Wagner
296	fifty-three times before	*Paradise*, Act II, p. 209
296	he screams	Ibid., p. 213
296	his "Cameo Shop"	Ibid., Act I, p. 187
297	"Open the windows"	Ibid., Act III, pp. 229–30
297	"do my plays"	Wagner
297	"Harold stops me"	1934
299	"all that stuff"	Wagner
300	"all these weeks!"	9/7/34
300	"or as foolproof"	10/18/34
300	"change the world!!!"	Ibid.
301	"holiness is better!"	CO, letter to Helen Deutsch, 10/24/34
301	"fresh with me"	Ibid., 11/30/34
301	"whole business away"	Ibid., 10/18/34
301	"killed our Custer!"	Ibid.
302	"implacable vengeance"	Conquest
302	"spiritual extermination"	Ibid., p. 67
302	"an elopement"	HC, Seminar at Windsor Mountain, Lenox, Mass., 1966
303	"the Karamazoff boy"	CO, letter to Helen Deutsch, 10/30/34
303	"a good job"	Ibid., 10/24/34
304	"notes for production"	*New Theatre*, 2/35
305	"SOME thing"	CO, letter to Helen Deutsch, 10/27/34
306	"sick at heart"	10/30/34
306	"what I believe"	Ibid.
307	"steak, not sex"	11/5/34
307	"help at all"	11/12/34
307	"not autobiography"	CO, letter to Helen Deutsch, 11/5/34
308	"a few more hours"	Ibid., 11/7/34
308	protagonist is crippled	Niederland
308	"Miss Runkel . . . Clifford"	CO, letter to Helen Deutsch, 11/5/34
309	"our lives . . . Clifford"	Ibid.
310	"Poor poor Gus"	11/7/34
310	"quick, cheap success"	11/21/34
311	"very terrible country!!!"	Ibid.
311	"bunch in America!!!!"	Ibid.
313	"this play at all"	Wagner
313	"do this myself"	Ibid.

CHAPTER SEVENTEEN

314	"hold on to him"	Wagner
314	"fair is over!"	*The Life of Robert Burns* (passage marked by CO in his copy)
315	"to deliver itself"	*Starting Out in the Thirties*
315	"no show after that"	Wagner
315	"had become one"	HC, *Fervent Years*, pp. 138–39
316	"great theatre"	Wagner

Page	Quote	Source
316	and to vomit	CO to MB-G, personal communication
316	"entered their lives"	HC, "Fervent Years," uncut ms., p. 248
317	"only temporarily!"	1/7/35
318	"country so far"	1/8/35
318	"had been discovered"	1/7/35
320	"could function freely"	HC, "Fervent Years," uncut ms., pp. 321 ff.
321	"itching for a part"	CO, Notes, "Moi," 7/61
321	"go up with me"	Wagner
321	"trusting the material"	Ibid.
322	extinction was inevitable	*New Theatre*, 3/35
324	"a rush of power"	Kazin, *Starting Out in the Thirties*, pp. 80–82
325	"giving up my people"	Ibid., p. 83
325	"mastered his score"	2/20/35
325	"praised too highly"	3/8/39
325	"theatre's Somebodies"	*Daily Mirror*, 2/20/35
326	"cannot have Packards?"	3/13/35
326	"you look at it"	2/20/35
326	"of the American Theatre"	3/30/35
327	" 'of social drama' "	Letter to LeRoy Robinson, *Jewish Currents*, 3/64
327	"no comment to make"	3/17/35
328	in new plays	*New Theatre*, 2/35
328	"destructive forces"	Ibid.
329	of the *New Masses*	*New Theatre*, 5/35
330	"have nothing to say"	*Till the Day*, Scene 2, pp. 118–19
330	"So is God"	Ibid., p. 119
331	"the Nazi state"	Ibid., Scene 4, p. 130
331	"flesh and bone"	Ibid., p. 133
332	"with a child"	Ibid., Scene 5, p. 137
332	"of sorrow"	Ibid., p. 138
332	"kept my mouth shut"	Ibid., Scene 6, p. 144
333	"smells like flowers"	Ibid., Scene 7, p. 152
334	"drama at the Belasco"	3/11/35
335	"me at all"	*Herald Tribune*, 3/31/35
335	"everybodys love Mother"	3/5/35
336	"luck be with you"	3/12/35
336	"It is frightening"	4/2/35
336	"exciting stuff"	John Anderson, *New York Journal*, 3/27/35
337	"in our theatre"	*New York Post*, 3/27/35
338	its being censored	Miscellaneous newspaper items, Scrapbook for 1935, Odets Estate
339	"of having met me"	Farmer, p. 65

CHAPTER EIGHTEEN

Page	Quote	Source
343	"political claque"	To MB-G, personal communication, 10/17/64
343	"reason for this"	CO, Journal, 9/7/40
343	"sick at heart"	CO, letter to "Dena," 4/20/35
343	"political persuasion"	4/6/35
343	"outstanding potential"	Miscellaneous newspaper and magazine stories, 1935 Scrapbook, Odets Estate

Page	Quote	Source
344	"you and the others"	4/25/35
344	"at a loss"	CO, Diary, 9/7/40
345	"playwrights to Hollywood"	Scrapbook items, Odets Estate
346	"your present problem"	4/18/35
351	"pay bills there"	5/9/35
352	"always be my son"	4/6/49
357	"mind against him"	CO, Notes, "L.J.," 8/60
357	"the age of 49"	CO, Notes, "Moi," 8/61
358	"rather empty shoes"	*Jewish Daily Bulletin* (1935 Scrapbook, Odets Estate)
358	"of virile writing"	5/15/35
358	of American drama	Lingel, letter to CO, 5/20/35
359	"sustained conflict"	7/2/35
359	"picketing going on"	Miscellaneous newspaper items, 1935 Scrapbook, Odets Estate
359	"emotional exhaustion"	Wagner, p. 16
361	"see you soon. Clifford"	6/2/35
361	"hands were doing"	Letter to Lee Strasberg, 5/11/35
361	a shared end	Ibid.
361	"panting for it here"	Ibid.
362	"meaningful through it"	HC, "Fervent Years," uncut ms., p. 256
362	"we are heir"	HC, *Fervent Years,* p. 153
362	"exciting and valuable"	Letter to CO, 6/6/35
363	"were down there"	P. 3467
363	"of publicity value"	Ibid., p. 3465
363	"or communism"	Ibid.
365	"to investigate anything"	*New York Post,* 7/5/35
365	"matter up immediately"	Correspondence, 7/3/35, National Archives, Hyde Park, N.Y.
365	"meet you love dad"	7/5/35
366	"went up the hill"	P. 28
366	"group to enter Cuba"	Newspaper reports, 7/7/35
366	"a great beginning"	7/27/35
367	conflicts with Mussolini	Freedley and Reeves
368	"artistic questions"	*New York Times,* 7/24/35
368	"age he lives in"	Ibid.
369	"is apropos"	CO, Notes, "success," undated
369	"if not known"	CO, Notes, undated
369	"you bum, Dena"	8/5/35
369	"a weekend together"	8/19/35
370	remain single	8/14/35
370	"for my Mother"	8/31/35
370	"the same cupboard"	8/14/35
371	"What a dumb brute!!!"	9/3/35
372	"I'm half Russian!!!"	Ibid.
372	"astigmatic, tired, alone"	9/4/35
372	"the form of maturity"	Ibid.
373	"forward to seeing me"	9/3/35
373	"concentrated thoughts"	9/6/35
373	"make a decision!"	Ibid.
373	"the most difficult"	Ibid.
374	"for the whole theatre"	9/7/35
375	"know what I mean"	Ibid.
376	"a satisfactory letter"	Ibid.
376	"for good measure"	9/9/35
376	"feeling both times"	Ibid.
376	"down if he did"	Ibid.
377	"new great world"	9/15/35
378	"Ruth in England"	9/10/35

Page	Quote	Source
378	"when it's there"	Ibid.
378	"bad parts of him"	9/6/35
379	"restricted it, etc."	CO, Notes, 4/57
380	"Dramatizing Our Times"	*World-Telegram*, 10/7/35 (Scrapbook, p. 143, Odets Estate)
380	"the life around him"	Scrapbook, p. 140, Odets Estate
381	"We are Revolutionists!"	*Daily Worker*, 7/12/35 (Scrapbook, p. 134, Odets Estate)
382	" 'be born again' "	CO, Notes, undated
383	"they didn't respect"	HC, *Fervent Years*, p. 156
383	"their basic sweetness"	HC, "Fervent Years," uncut ms., p. 353a
383	"ever forget it"	CO to MB-G, personal communication, 9/53
385	"modern medium"	Robert Garland, *World-Telegram*, 12/10/35
386	"Sincerely, Harold Clurman"	*World-Telegram*, 12/11/35
386	"your review. Clifford Odets"	12/10/35
387	"stage has to offer"	*World-Telegram*, 12/18/35
387	"No one else will"	12/15/35
390	"more to fathers"	12/28/35
393	"that every week"	3/21/36
394	"eager aspiration"	Foreword, *Directory of Fellows 1925–1967*
395	"play for the screen"	Macgowan, p. 375

CHAPTER NINETEEN

Page	Quote	Source
396	"carry me over"	From a letter (1811?)
396	"stop being free"	CO, Notes, "Moi," 1/16/62, Beverly Hills, Calif.
398	six months or longer	2/20/36
399	"at his best"	2/26/36
399	Group's deliberations	Ibid.
400	"exalted, magnificent drama"	Ibid.
405	"much more difficult"	*Motion Picture*, 9/36
406	"tied in one person"	Letter to CO, 10/17/36. See E. H. Erikson, *Identity: Youth and Crisis*, p. 219
408	earlier magazine piece	*Current Controversy*, 2/36
409	"materializes, the first"	HC, letter to CO, 1/18/36
409	"comedy in verse"	HC, letter to Lee Strasberg, 5/11/36
409	"prepared and *waiting*"	4/2/36
410	to be likable	Gibson, *Seesaw Log*
410	"blur of unusual color"	5/36
411	"scatter before swine"	"Silent," Act II, Scene 1, p. 9
411	"lack of seriousness"	Wagner, p. 19
411	"unclear, undisciplined"	HC, *Fervent Years*, p. 170
412	"not having any blood"	William Gibson, 1951
412	"a symbolic level"	Mendelsohn, p. 19
412	less significant	Warshow
412	in the play	Ted Allan, letter to Joe North, *New Masses*, 5/29/39
413	twenty-five years later	Wagner, p. 19
414	"flapjacks . . . no difference"	"Silent," Act III, Scene 1, p. 14
414	murderous envy	Private communication
414	"that sound funny?"	"Silent," Act II, Scene 3, p. 65

Page	Quote	Source
415	"women understand"	Ibid., Act II, Scene 2, p. 34
415	"at this moment"	Ibid., Scene 3, p. 65
415	concern for this concept	Private communication
416	*"for one hour"*	Ibid., Scene 4, p. 76
416	Adam and Eve	HC, *Fervent Years*, p. 170
416	"by his fearful Servants"	"Silent," Act II, Scene 4, p. 76
416	"should shoot bullets"	*Golden Boy*
416	"his Easter duty"	"Silent," Act III, Scene 1, p. 3
416	his creativity	CO, letter to Helen Deutsch, 6/20/36
416	"to the point!"	"Silent," Act III, Scene 1, p. 6
417	"heart to stone"	Ibid., p. 17
417	"sentimental ballad"	Ibid., p. 18
418	Thalberg's last	Crowther, p. 238
418	"should live so"	5/2/36
419	"Memorial Day massacre"	HC, *Fervent Years*, p. 179
419	"to that morgue"	Mendelsohn, p. 18
421	"talented people are"	6/20/36
421	"the moon and me"	7/14/36
422	"no more alone!!!"	7/17/36
423	Stalin's bloody methods	Conquest
427	"love with you"	9/16/36
427	"happily resolved"	Shulman, *Harlow* (New York: Dell Publishing Co., 1964), pp. 294–99
428	"Group needs . . . etc."	CO files, "Special Materials, 1936," Odets Estate
429	"about the money"	9/21/36
429	"strange fine feeling"	9/36
429	"to the loved girl"	9/11/36
429	"one rich person"	9/16/36
429	"of that fellow"	Ludwig
430	" 'a good life' "	CO, letter to Joe Greeman, 11/4/36
430	behind her house	9/16/36
432	"children beside them"	CO, Notes, "Beethoven," 1/16/62
432	"for my work?"	Ludwig, p. 85
433	"shuts him out"	11/6/36
436	"with a stranger"	Ibid.
436	"loved so much!"	12/10/36
436	"forces of reaction"	*New Theatre*, 11/36
436	"nature of this evil"	CO Files, "Anti-Nazi Play," Odets Estate

CHAPTER TWENTY

Page	Quote	Source
438	"IN PAIN"	Stockbridge, Mass., 3/22/64
442	"your girl—Luise"	12/30/36
443	"makeup could"	1/5/37
443	"getting a job"	Ibid.
443	and Stella Adler	12/36, Odets Estate
443	"purely artistic tasks"	Ibid. Also, HC, *Fervent Years*, p. 182
444	"creation of scripts"	Ibid.
444	"from Olympus"	2/31/37
446	"unification impossible"	CO, Notes, "Psychology," 1963
447	"Love for two. L.J."	1/21/37
447	"a shiny dime!"	*New York Evening Journal*, 1/23/37
450	"in New York!"	CO, Journal, 8/25/40
451	"something else inside"	2/22/37

Page	Quote	Source
451	"novelist or playwright"	Ibid.
452	"offering my services"	2/27/37
452	"bad contracts"	Correspondence with Bert Allenberg and Harold Freedman, 1937
453	"cut my heart out"	2/5/37
453	"sitting on your brains"	Ibid.
454	"what its all about"	Ibid.
454	"up for her"	Ibid.
454	"papers *every* day"	3/11/37
454	"fine character"	3/26/37
455	"meant to be enjoyed"	3/25/37
455	"have them removed"	Ibid.
455	"now I get bubkas!"	3/8/37
456	"the Inescapable Choice"	Letter to Lee Strasberg, 3/15/37
457	"will of the majority"	Ibid.
457	long position paper	Group Theatre file, Odets Estate
458	"and are experts"	3/12/37
458	"go into the movies"	3/16/37
458	"I hear she cried"	3/18/37
459	"same personal shock"	3/10/37
459	"friendly fatalism"	HC, *Fervent Years*, p. 191
459	"love and friendship, Clifford"	5/22/37
460	"naturally enough"	Ibid.
461	"come to life!"	5/27/37
461	"open your eyes"	Fragments, spring 1937, Odets Estate
461	"ideals about"	Spring(?) 1937
462	"against the walls"	CO, Journal, 3/14/40
462	"of everything then!"	Ibid., 7/27/40
463	"here all summer"	7/7/37
463	"for you, Luise"	7/13/37
464	"with happiness"	7/37
464	"pleasure of a craftsman"	CO, Notes, "Dentist's Love Play"

CHAPTER TWENTY-ONE

Page	Quote	Source
465	"don't know you"	*Golden Boy*, Act III, Scene 1
466	"his real self"	Introduction to *Golden Boy*, p. 430
466	existentialist plays	John Gassner, interviewed by MB-G 11/66
467	a venereal disease	CO to MB-G, personal communication, 1954
467	body of a bird	H. A. Murray, *Myth and Mythmaking*, p. 62
468	"done it for him!"	*Golden Boy*, Act III, Scene 1, p. 309
469	"oiled and polished!"	Ibid., Scene 2, p. 309
470	"truthful success"	Ibid., Act I, Scene 2, p. 250
470	"a Jacob character"	1937
470	"he gonna fight"	*Golden Boy*, Act I, Scene 2, p. 253
470	"my friend—nonsense!"	Ibid., p. 250
471	"*at* MR. BONAPARTE"	Ibid., Scene 5, pp. 271–72
472	"life'sa good"	Ibid., Scene 2, p. 249
472	"hopeless hope"	Gelb, p. 831
472	"isa not foolish"	*Golden Boy*, Act I, Scene 2, p. 250
472	"popular success"	CO, letter to Robert Lewis, 5/22/37
472	"the word nance"	CO, Production Notes, *Golden Boy*, pp. 2–3
473	" 'can you get along?' "	Ibid., p. 1

Page	Quote	Source
473	"finishes the work"	Ibid., pp. 2–3
473	"like a girl"	*Golden Boy*, Act I, Scene 3, p. 255
473	"butter on the table?"	Ibid., Scene 2, p. 249
474	"fury of a lifetime"	Ibid., Act III, Scene 2, p. 312
474	"his woman herself!"	Ibid., p. 316
474	"earth—unconnected!"	Ibid.
474	"not be so bad"	Ibid., Act II, Scene 4, p. 300
474	"pursuit of happiness"	Ibid., Act III, Scene 3, p. 320
474	"Magna Mater at last"	Diary, 8/5/62
475	"What waste!"	*Golden Boy*, Act III, Scene 3, p. 320
475	he could not work	Gelb, p. 838
476	"inferior feeling"	*Golden Boy*, Author's Notes, No. 7
477	"a virginal honesty"	Farmer
478	"debt as a rule!"	10/21/37
479	"all open for her"	CO, Journal, 9/7/40
479	"in your work"	10/20/37
479	Luise was in town	Letter to CO (undated)
481	"its mother's pouch"	CO, Journal, 9/11/40
482	the film *Gettysburg*	Letter to CO, 10/18/37
483	" 'left wing writer any harm' "	8/23/37
485	"merely everything"	HC, *Fervent Years*, p. 197
486	"where he belongs"	11/5/37
486	"to Broadway important"	11/14/37
486	"permanently a playwright"	12/26/37
486	"seen in a long time"	11/7/37
487	"still unrealized"	11/21/37
488	"glasses off my nose!"	11/14/37
488	"good to have!"	Ibid.
488	"students in the neighborhood"	11/26/37
489	"a lot of watching"	12/5/37
489	"collective society"	11/29/37
489	pervades his thinking	12/5/37
489	"for both of us"	12/14/37
489	"together joyful"	Ibid.
489	"Your girl"	12/20/37

CHAPTER TWENTY-TWO

Page	Quote	Source
490	"both know it"	CO, Notes, "Dentist Play," 7/37
490	"theatre has to offer"	1/17/38
490	"give it to you"	Quoted by Ted Allan in letter to Joe North, *New Masses*, 5/29/39
491	"the Young Hope"	2/27/38
492	to accept the same	Flanagan
493	"stay in the theatre"	1/18/38
493	"*revolutionary force*"	Ibid.
495	"my stature as a man"	*Rocket*, Author's Notes
495	"an individual appears"	CO, Notes, "Playwriting," p. 38
495	reaction to them	E. H. Erikson, "The Legend of Hitler's Childhood," *Childhood and Society*
497	"by Saturday night"	1/28/38
497	" 'oh dear,' to myself"	2/12/38
497	"come back in answer"	2/20/38
498	"some twisted tune"	2/19/38
498	"can do for you"	Ibid.
499	"unselfconscious"	3/3/38

Page	*Quote*	*Source*
499	"for me? Luise"	2/28/38
501	"of the people—Art"	CO, Notes
501	"most expensive pictures"	Philip Berg, 5/7/38
501	"intentionally destroy"	Ibid.
502	"sorrow and chagrin"	4/24/38
502	"there is trouble"	5/10/38
502	"playwrights in America"	5/19/38
504	as an afterthought	5/29/38
504	"fly away that time"	5/28/38
504	"the man in you"	Undated
505	"responsible for nothing!"	5/30/38
505	"do great work. Luise"	5/31/38
506	"Goodnight, Luise. Clifford"	6/1/38
506	"deserve. Yes. Clifford"	6/6/38
507	"papers in the meantime"	6/6/38
508	"in all friendship. Luise"	6/9/38
508	"normal life"	6/9/38
508	"if he let me be it"	6/9/38
508	"very much in love"	Leonard Lyons, *New York Post*, 6/14/38
508	"how sorry I am"	6/14/38
510	"humbly truthful"	Letter to CO, 5/7/38
510	"important film"	Bert Allenberg, letter to CO, 7/29/38
512	"at Windsor then, Clifford"	9/30/38
512	keep this promise	Shirer
513	"unfair and un-American"	Pomerantz
515	"agreed with Clurman"	Wagner, pp. 22–23
515	"I just dropped"	Ibid.
516	"garden of the theatre"	10/11/38
517	"on the coast"	Ibid.
518	"don't believe him"	CO, Notes, 10/19/38
518	"Byron's crippled foot"	10/7/38
521	"a week was gone"	CO, Journal, 3/26/40
521	"comes from rejection"	Discussion, 10/19/38
521	"their favorite people"	*World-Telegram*, 11/3/38
521	"he didn't love me"	11/4/38
521	"in his way"	Newspaper report, 11/4/38
521	"of my play"	11/9/38
522	"love and patience"	11/10/38
523	"times needs it!"	11/15/38
523	"newly imprisoned"	11/16/38
523	"piece of wry-crisp"	11/17/38
524	"sound 'like Capra' "	Thomas
526	"event in his life"	CO, Notes, "Dentist Play," "X" (character), 10/26/38
526	"diaper you"	*Rocket*, Act I, p. 330
527	"by making believe"	Ibid., Act II, Scene 1, p. 372
528	"relaxed and heavy"	Ibid., Act I, p. 339
529	"living man again"	Ibid., Act II, Scene 1, p. 350
530	*"simple sex"*	Ibid., pp. 379–80
530	"a lost man"	Ibid., Act II, Scene 2, p. 383
530	"to some people"	Ibid., p. 382
530	"painless perversion"	Ibid., p. 386
531	"ways of the world"	Ibid., p. 384
531	"about *my* needs?"	Ibid., p. 393
532	"in you to be"	Ibid., Act III, p. 400
532	"let me be alone"	Ibid., p. 397
533	"as the poet said!"	Ibid., p. 404
533	"to tell her so"	Ibid.

Page	Quote	Source
534	*"then slowly exits"*	Ibid., p. 408
534	"won't miss you"	Ibid., p. 411
535	"how it must end"	Ibid., p. 415
535	"my girl, is music!"	Ibid., p. 416
536	"She's an artist"	Ibid.
536	"Button my coat, Ben"	Ibid., p. 417
536	"Do you see, Poppa?"	Ibid., p. 418
536	"Slow curtain"	Ibid.
537	"The dame"	11/17/38
537	"fabric of life"	12/4/38
537	"his past work"	11/25/38
538	"remains in the future"	*Newsweek*, 12/5/38
538	"to the general public"	*Daily Mirror*, 11/25/38
538	"as he grows up"	11/25/38
538	"as the present one"	12/3/38
539	"in our nation"	12/6/38
539	"phlegmatic neighborhood"	12/4/38
540	"he also writes"	12/5/38
540	"sends these lines"	CO, letter to Richard Watts, Jr., 1/17/39
540	"any time I can help"	1/9/39
541	"return to New York"	1/17/39
541	"Luise Rainer, Clifford Odets"	12/6/38
541	"North Carolina"	12/7/38

CHAPTER TWENTY-THREE

543	"many good Americans"	HC, *Fervent Years*
543	"that he is dead"	Letter to MB-G, 8/13/64
546	"early next week"	1/12/39
546	"fresh air! Luise"	2/4/39
546	Seventy-sixth Congress	Morse, p. 208
547	"worth-while saving"	1/12/39, National Archives, Hyde Park, N.Y.
547	"certainly kill it"	2/5/39
548	"pain-avoidance"	1/39
548	"characteristic is pride"	2/39
549	"forever in his crop"	11/61
550	"war in September"	HC, *Fervent Years*
551	"various backgrounds"	CO, Notes, 6/11/37
551	"civilization level!"	CO, Notes, "General—Mexico City, 4/39"
552	"the state exists"	3/39
552	a blood sacrifice	Play analyses by MB-G, 1934–38
552	"a prisoner now"	4/39
557	"Love, Harold"	4/26/39
561	to the Holocaust	Morse
561	"insights into life"	CO, letter to HC, 4/8/39
562	"the same since"	5/29/39
563	"the last one"	6/29/39
564	book or a doll	Letter to CO, 7/24/39
564	"burning talent exists"	8/15/39
565	"looking for it"	7/39
565	"theatre of meaning"	HC, Group Theatre Logbook, 1939
565	"dictator for a season?"	Group Theatre Logbook, 7/16/39
567	"to have in 1931"	Ibid., 7/15/39
567	"creating a Group Theatre"	Ibid., 7/18/39
568	"lousy or flat"	Ibid.
569	"a very poetic play"	Ibid.

Page	*Quote*	*Source*
569	"that class struggle"	Ibid.
570	"written them"	Ibid., pp. 3–6
570	"what he said"	Ibid.
571	"work with himself"	Ibid., p. 7
571	"in this organization"	Ibid., p. 13
571	"bad work of art"	CO, Diary, 1939
571	"at the present time"	Logbook, 8/8/39
574	Frances Farmer	Farmer, pp. 192–93
574	the spreading war	Introduction to *Night Music*, p. viii
576	"expectations of profit"	9/19/39
576	"come to the coast"	9/28/39
577	"the theatre today"	10/4/39
578	"finished the job"	Farmer, pp. 192–93
579	"drinking even more"	Ibid., pp. 194–95
580	"with a real purity"	CO, Journal, 1/13/40
581	"simple unassuming job"	10/19/39
581	as an "ad-man"	12/16/39
582	"stabilized and competent"	CO, Journal, 1/17/40
582	"your breathing characters"	12/6/39
583	"I am a giant"	CO, Journal, 1/23/40
585	"through any night!"	*Night Music*, Act II, Scene 4, p. 160
585	"from sordidness"	Ibid., Production Notes, 1/12/40
585	"Music and Woman"	7/1/30
585	Odets' correspondence	Letters to Hortense Alden, 7/21/30 and 8/18/30
585	"heartbroken feeling"	*Night Music*, Act I, Scene 1, p. 21
585	"micro-reality"	E. H. Erikson, "Ontogeny of Ritualization in Man"
586	"doesn't frighten me"	*Night Music*, Act III, Scene 2, p. 228
586	"a womanly queen"	Ibid., Author's Notes
586	"flowers on the hill"	*Night Music*, Act III, Scene 2, p. 227
587	"needed you more"	Ibid., p. 236
587	"wouldn't live here"	Ibid., Act II, Scene 2, p. 131
587	"King of the Jews"	Ibid., Act I, Scene 4, p. 75
587	"petty and small!"	Ibid., Act II, Scene 3, p. 146
588	"liberty and happiness"	Ibid., p. 154
588	"gets in the papers?"	Ibid., Act I, Scene 4, p. 70
588	"Orphans of the storm?"	Ibid., p. 77
588	"apprehensive, lonely"	Ibid., p. 75
588	"Brother Horse!"	Ibid., pp. 74–75
588	"for all I care"	Ibid., Act II, Scene 5, p. 187
588	"Good night, Mr. Takis"	Ibid., p. 189
589	*"and right here?!"*	Ibid., Act III, Scene 2, p. 234
589	"rascal and a liar!"	Ibid., pp. 234–35
589	"wilderness of uncertainty"	HC, Introduction to *Night Music*, p. x
589	"to be a mint"	*Night Music*, Act III, Scene 2, p. 225
589	"don't come near me!"	Ibid., p. 228
589	"nothing gained"	Ibid., p. 229
589	"on our own lot"	Ibid., Scene 1, p. 217
589	"starts out as one"	Ibid., Scene 2, p. 237
589	"no one's interested"	Ibid., Act I, Scene 5, p. 96
590	*"silence behind him"*	Ibid., p. 97
590	"and Wall Street"	Swanberg, pp. 469–70
590	"unhinge Dreiser"	Ibid., p. 476
591	" 'Marry-My-Girl!' "	*Night Music*, Act III, Scene 2, p. 235
591	"Make way!"	Ibid., p. 237

Page	Quote	Source
591	"with the mothballs"	Ibid., p. 228
591	"for five months"	Ibid., p. 229

CHAPTER TWENTY-FOUR

592	"and lay dying"	CO, Journal, 2/23/40
592	"Harold's impositions"	CO to MB-G, personal communication, 7/53
593	"worry about that"	CO, Journal, 1/13/40
593	"out of this room a little"	Ibid., 1/17/40
594	should *Night Music* fail	Jacques, "Death and Mid-Life Crisis"
595	"Confidence is repose"	CO, Journal, 1/14/40
595	"couple of months ago"	1/20/40
595	"connects me with her"	1/27/40
595	"What can that mean?"	1/20/40
595	"starting a new play"	1/21/40
595	"strength from every weakness"	1/20/40
595	"not as excellent psychologically"	1/21/40
595	begun with the reviews	HC, *Fervent Years*, p. 246
596	"over to others"	CO, Journal, 1/21/40
596	"Woe to my wife!"	1/15/40
596	"very few and very far"	2/6/40
596	"maniac like myself"	1/21/40
596	"my intensely personal life"	2/12/40
596	"quite incomplete"	Ibid.
596	"I can feel and think"	1/21/40
597	"it was my brother"	Ibid.
597	"provincial newspaper people!"	2/5/40
597	"what music is"	Ibid.
598	"as a playwright"	Ibid.
598	"play suffers for it"	2/18/40
598	" 'a search for reality' "	1/27/40
598	future in their hands	2/9/40
599	"average political tract?"	2/17/40
600	*That's* how I am"	2/15/40
600	"hopelessly, disgustingly!!"	2/9/40
601	"in our own way"	1/23/40
601	a million dollars!	Gelb, p. 830
601	holding the world together	Milford
601	"movies and cheap magazines"	2/17/40
601	"what it works in"	Gibson, *Seesaw Log*, p. 140
603	"Great unhappy man!"	2/13/40
604	"the Russian soul!!!"	2/17/40
604	"only half understand"	2/15/40
604	" 'how one goes' "	2/17/40
604	"his arteries prematurely"	2/14/40
605	"break with the Group"	Ibid.
605	"at the moment"	2/21/40
607	"remember, that's all"	2/23/40
608	"regularity of the marines"	Brown, pp. 182–83
608	"playwrights can turn out"	Ibid.
608	"lightning will strike next"	Ibid.
608	"world moves fast"	2/26/40
608	"I have to wait"	Ibid.
610	"feeling very guilty"	CO, *World-Telegram*, 3/2/40
610	"performance of the part"	CO, Journal, 3/3/40
611	"a Mayer or Zanuck"	Ibid.
612	"sincere useful work!"	Ibid.

Selected Bibliography

Aaron, Daniel, *Writers on the Left: Episodes in American Literary Communism.* New York: Harcourt, Brace & World, 1961.

Abell, Walter, *The Collective Dream in Art.* New York: Schocken Books, 1957.

Adams, Joey (with Henry Tobias), *Borscht Belt.* Indianapolis: Bobbs-Merrill, 1966.

"Agit-Prop," *Time,* June 17, 1935.

Alliluyeva, Svetlana, *Twenty Letters from a Friend,* tr. Priscilla Johnson McMillan. New York: Harper & Row, 1967.

Arendt, Hannah, review of *Rosa Luxemburg* by J. P. Nettle, *New York Review of Books,* October 6, 1966.

Arnheim, Rudolf, *Picasso's Guernica: The Genesis of a Painting.* Berkeley: University of California Press, 1962.

———, *Toward a Psychology of Art.* Berkeley: University of California Press, 1966.

Barron, Frank, *Creativity and Psychological Health.* Princeton: D. Van Nostrand, 1963.

———, "Diffusion, Integration, and Enduring Attention in the Creative Process," in *The Study of Lives,* ed. R. W. White. New York: Atherton Press, 1964.

Beard, Charles A. and Mary R., *A Basic History of the United States.* New York: The New Home Library, 1944.

———, *The Rise of American Civilization,* Vol. III, *America in Midpassage.* New York: Macmillan, 1966.

Becker, Margaret, "Clifford Odets: The Development of a Playwright." Ph.D. thesis, University of Colorado, 1956 (unpublished).

Beebe, Lucius, "The Prolific Mr. O." New York *Herald Tribune,* March 31, 1935.

Bendiner, Robert, *Just Around the Corner.* New York: Harper & Row, 1967.

Bentley, Eric, *The Playwright as Thinker.* New York: Harcourt, Brace, 1955.

Bergler, Edmund, *The Writer and Psychoanalysis.* New York: Robert Brunner, 1954.

Bernstein, Barton J., ed., *Towards a New Past: Dissenting Essays in American History.* New York: Pantheon Books, 1968.

Bird, Caroline, *The Invisible Scar: The Great Depression, and What It Did to American Life, From Then Until Now.* New York: David McKay, 1966.

Blau, Herbert, *The Impossible Theater: A Manifesto.* New York: Macmillan, 1964.

Block, Anita, *The Changing World in Plays and Theatre.* Boston: Little, Brown, 1939.

Bowen, Catherine Drinker, *Biography: The Craft and the Calling.* Boston: Little, Brown, 1969.

Brecht, Bertolt, *The Messingkauf Dialogues.* London: Methuen, 1965.

Breit, Harvey, ed., *The Writer Observed.* Cleveland: World Publishing Co., 1956.

Brenman, Margaret, "On Teasing and Being Teased: And the Problem of 'Moral Masochism,'" in *The Psychoanalytic Study of the Child,* Vol. VII. New York: International Universities Press, 1952.

Brenman-Gibson, Margaret, "Anatomy of a Play: With Specimen Play-Analysis." Presented in seminar, November 6, 1971. Discussion (unpublished).

———, "Creation of Plays: With Specimen Analysis," in *Psychoanalysis, Creativity, and Literature,* ed. A. Roland. New York: Columbia University Press, 1978.

———, "Notes on the Study of the Creative Process," in *Psychology Versus*

Metapsychology, Vol. IX, No. 4, Monograph 36. New York: International Universities Press, 1976.
_____, "Odets: Failure or Not?" *The New York Times*, June 13, 1965, Section II, p. 1.
_____, "War on Human Suffering: A Psychoanalyst's Research Odyssey," in *The Human Mind Revisited*, ed. Sydney Smith. New York: International Universities Press, 1978.
Brody, Sylvia, *Passivity: A Study of Its Development and Expression in Boys.* New York: International Universities Press, 1964.
Brook, Peter, *The Empty Space.* New York: Atheneum, 1968.
Brooks, Van Wyck, *The Ordeal of Mark Twain.* New York: E. P. Dutton, 1920.
Brown, John Mason, *Broadway in Review.* New York: W. W. Norton, 1940.
Brustein, Robert, *The Theatre of Revolt.* Boston: Little, Brown, 1964.
Buchwald, Nathan, in *Daily Worker*, January 8, 1935.
Burke, Kenneth, "Ice, Fire and Decay," in *Philosophy of Literary Form.* New York: Vintage Books, 1941, 1957.
_____, "Revolutionary Symbolism in America," in *The Proletarian Novel (American Writers Congress)*, ed. Henry Hart. New York: International Publishers, 1935.
Burt, Maxwell Struthers, *Philadelphia, Holy Experiment.* New York: Doubleday, Doran, 1945.
Campbell, Joseph, *Hero with a Thousand Faces.* Princeton: Princeton University Press, 1968.
_____, *Masks of Gods* (4 vols.). New York: Viking Press, 1964–68.
_____, *Myths, Dreams, and Religion.* New York: E. P. Dutton, 1970.
Cantor, Harold, *Clifford Odets: Playwright-Poet.* New York: Scarecrow Press, 1978.
Chaplin, Charles, *My Autobiography.* New York: Simon & Schuster, 1964.
Chinoy, Helen Krich, ed., "Reunion: A Self-Portrait of the Group Theatre," *Educational Theatre Journal*, December 1976.
Clemens, Samuel, *The Autobiography of Mark Twain*, ed. Charles Neider. New York: Harper and Bros., 1959.
Clurman, Harold, *All People Are Famous (Instead of an Autobiography).* New York: Harcourt Brace Jovanovich, 1974.
_____, "Around Night Music," *New Republic*, April 30, 1951.
_____, "Clifford Odets," in *The Universal Jewish Encyclopedia*, Vol. VIII
_____, ed., *Famous American Plays of the 1930s* (1959). New York: Dell, 1968.
_____, *The Fervent Years* (1945). New York: Hill & Wang, 1961.
_____, "Interpretation and Characterization," *New Theatre*, January 1936.
_____, *Lies Like Truth.* New York: Macmillan, 1958.
_____, *The Naked Image.* New York: Macmillan, 1966.
_____, *On Directing.* New York: Macmillan, 1972.
_____, "Sins of Clifford Odets," *New Republic*, March 14, 1949.
_____, "Three Introductions," in *Six Plays of Clifford Odets.* New York: Random House, 1939.
Cohn, Ruby, and Bernard F. Dukore, *Twentieth Century Drama: England, Ireland and the United States.* New York: Random House, 1966.
"Communist Infiltration of the Hollywood Motion Picture Industry," Part 8, in House Committee on Un-American Activities *Hearings* (Clifford Odets' Testimony), May 19–21, 1952.
Conquest, R., *The Great Terror.* New York: Macmillan, 1968.
Cowley, Malcolm, *Exile's Return.* New York: Viking Press, 1951.
_____, "The 1930s Were an Age of Faith," *The New York Times Book Review*, December 13, 1964.
_____, *Think Back on Us.* Carbondale: Southern Illinois University Press, 1967.
"Credo of a Wrong-Living Man," *Time*, December 14, 1962.
Crosse, Gordon, *Shakespearean Playgoing 1890–1952.* London: A. R. Mowbray, 1953.
Crowther, Bosley, *The Lion's Share.* New York: E. P. Dutton, 1957.
Deutsch, Helen, and Stella Hanau, *The Provincetown: Story of a Theatre* (1931). New York: Russell & Russell, 1972.

Deutsch, Helene, *A Psychoanalytic Study of the Myth of Dionysus and Apollo: Two Variants of the Son-Mother Relationship.* New York: International Universities Press, 1969.

DeVoto, Bernard, review of *Proletarian Literature in the United States* (Granville Hicks and others, eds.), *Saturday Review of Literature,* October 5, 1935.

Dostoevsky, Fyodor, *The Notebooks for the Idiot,* ed. Edward Wasiolek, tr. Katherine Strelsky. Chicago: University of Chicago Press, 1967.

Drachman, Julian, "My Most Famous Student," *National Retired Teachers Association Journal,* January/February 1975.

Dudek, Stephanie Z., "The Artist as Person, Generalizations Based on Rorschach Records of Writers and Painters." Ph.D. thesis, New York University, 1960 (unpublished).

Edel, Leon, "The Biographer and Psycho-Analysis," *The International Journal of Psycho-Analysis,* Vol. XLII, Parts IV–V, 1961.

_____, *Literary Biography.* Garden City: Anchor Books, 1959.

Eissler, K. R., *Leonardo da Vinci: Psychoanalytic Notes on the Enigma.* New York: International Universities Press, 1961.

_____, "Psychopathology and Creativity," *American Imago,* Vol. XXIV, Nos. 1 & 2, Spring-Summer 1967.

Erikson, Erik H., *The Challenge of Youth.* New York: Anchor Books, 1963.

_____, *Childhood and Society.* New York: W. W. Norton, 1950.

_____, *Dimensions of New Identity: The 1973 Jefferson Lectures in the Humanities.* New York: W. W. Norton, 1974.

_____, *Gandhi's Truth.* New York: W. W. Norton, 1968.

_____, *Identity: Youth and Crisis.* New York: W. W. Norton, 1968.

_____, "Identity and the Life Cycle," *Psychological Issues,* Vol. I, No. 1, Monograph I, 1959.

_____, *In Search of Common Ground: Conversations with Erik H. Erikson and Huey P. Newton.* New York: W. W. Norton, 1973.

_____, *Insight and Responsibility: Lectures on the Ethical Implications of Psychoanalytic Insight.* New York: W. W. Norton, 1965.

_____, *Life History and the Historical Moment.* New York: W. W. Norton, 1975.

_____, "Ontogeny of Ritualization in Man," *Philosophical Transactions,* Royal Society of London, Series B, No. 772, Vol. CCLI, 1966.

_____, "Psychosocial Identity," in *International Encyclopedia of Social Science.* New York: Crowell-Collier, 1968.

_____, *Toys and Reasons: Stages in the Ritualization of Experience.* New York: W. W. Norton, 1977.

_____, "The 'Works.'" Unpublished chart prepared for the National Institute for Mental Health and presented in rough draft at the Erikson Conference on "Psychosocial Development Reconsidered," Bennington College, Bennington, Vt., July 9–16, 1978.

_____, *Young Man Luther: A Study on Psychoanalysis and History.* New York: W. W. Norton, 1958.

Erikson, Joan, *The Universal Bead.* New York: W. W. Norton, 1969.

"Exciting Dramatist Rises in the Theater, An," *Literary Digest,* April 6, 1935, p. 18.

Faber, Seymour M., and Roger H. W. Wilson, *Conflict and Creativity.* New York: McGraw-Hill, 1963.

Fadiman, Clifton, "The Problem Play from Ibsen to Odets." *Stage,* February 1936.

Fagin, N. B., "In Search of an American Cherry Orchard." *Texas Quarterly,* Summer-Autumn 1958.

Farmer, Frances, *Will There Really Be a Morning?* New York: G. P. Putnam's Sons, 1972.

Farrell, James T., "More About Clifford Odets," *New Theatre,* June 1935.

Ferber, Edna, and George S. Kaufman, *Stage Door.* New York: Doubleday, Doran, 1936.

Ferguson, Otis, "Pay-off on Odets," *New Republic,* September 27 and October 4, 1939.

Flanagan, Hallie, *Arena* (1940). New York: Benjamin Blom, 1965.

Flatter, Richard, *Hamlet's Father.* New Haven: Yale University Press, 1949.

Flexner, Eleanor, *American Playwrights: 1918–1938.* New York: Simon and Schuster, 1938.

Freedley, George, and John A. Reeves, *The History of the Theatre.* New York: Crown, 1963.

Freud, Sigmund, "Address to the B'nai B'rith" (1926), *Standard Edition of Complete Works,* Vol. XX. London: Hogarth Press, 1959.

———, *The Interpretation of Dreams.* New York: Basic Books, 1955.

———, *The Origins of Psychoanalysis: Letters to Wilhelm Fliess, Drafts and Notes, 1887–1902,* ed. Marie Bonaparte et al. New York: Basic Books, 1954.

Frisch, Max, *Biography: A Game.* New York: Hill & Wang, 1969.

Fromm, Erich, *Heart of Man.* New York: Harper & Row, 1964.

Gallaway, Marian, "A Comparative Study of the Development of Skills in Plot Construction by a Group of Living American Dramatists." Ph.D. thesis, University of Iowa, 1941 (unpublished).

Gard, Robert, Marston Balch, and Pauline Temkin, *Theatre in America: Appraisal and Challenge.* New York: Theatre Arts Books, 1968.

Gassner, John, *Masters of the Drama.* New York: Dover Publications, 1954.

———, "Paradise Lost and Theatre of Frustration," *New Theatre,* January 1936.

———, "Playwrights of the Period," *Theatre Arts,* September 1960.

———, *Producing the Play with the New Scene Technician's Handbook.* New York: Holt, Rinehart & Winston, 1953.

———, *The Theatre in Our Times.* New York: Crown, 1954.

———, Philo M. Buck, and H. S. Alberson, eds., *A Treasury of the Theatre,* Vol. II, *From Ibsen to Odets.* New York: Dryden Press, 1940.

Gay, Ruth, *Jews in America.* New York: Basic Books, 1965.

Gelb, Barbara and Arthur, *O'Neill.* New York: Harper and Bros., 1960, 1962.

Gibson, William, "Confessions of a Turtle," *Psychological Issues,* Vol. IX, No. 4, 1976.

———, *A Cry of Players.* New York: Atheneum, 1969.

———, Preface, *Golden Boy Musical.* New York: Bantam Books, 1966.

———, *A Season in Heaven.* New York: Atheneum, 1974.

———, *The Seesaw Log.* New York: Alfred A. Knopf, 1959.

———, *Shakespeare's Game.* New York: Atheneum, 1978.

Gilder, Rosamond, Hermine Rich Isaacs, Robert M. MacGregor, and Edward Reed, eds., *Theatre Arts Anthology.* New York: Theatre Arts Books/Robert M. MacGregor, 1948.

Glatzer, Nahum N., *Hammer on the Rock.* New York: Schocken Books, 1948.

Goertzel, Mildred George, Victor Goertzel, and Ted George Goertzel, *300 Eminent Personalities: A Psychosocial Analysis of the Famous.* San Francisco: Jossey-Bass, 1978.

Goldstone, Richard H., "The Makings of Americans: Clifford Odets's Implicit Theme," *Proceedings,* IVth Congress of the International Comparative Literature Association, 1966.

Goodman, Ezra, *The Fifty Year Decline and Fall of Hollywood.* New York: Simon and Schuster, 1961.

Gorelik, Mordecai, *New Theatres for Old* (1940). New York: E. P. Dutton, 1962.

Gould, Jean, *Modern American Playwrights.* New York: Dodd, Mead, 1966.

Greenacre, Phyllis, "The Childhood of the Artist," in *The Psychoanalytic Study of the Child,* Vol. XII. New York: International Universities Press, 1957.

———, "The Family Romance of the Artist," in *The Psychoanalytic Study of the Child,* Vol. XIII. New York: International Universities Press, 1958.

———, *The Quest for the Father.* New York: International Universities Press, 1963.

Gross, Gene, "A Study Based on the Plays of Clifford Odets." Ph.D. thesis, Department of Theatre, Smith College, Northampton, Mass., 1948 (unpublished).

Grotjahn, Martin, "The Defenses Against Creative Anxiety in the Life and Work of James Barrie," *American Imago,* Vol. XIV, No. 2, 1957.

Guttmann, Allen, *The Jewish Writer in America: Assimilation and the Crisis of Identity.* New York: Oxford University Press, 1971.

Halsey, Margaret, *The Pseudo-Ethic.* New York: Simon and Schuster, 1967.

Harvey, Herman, "The Sum and Substance," interview of Clifford Odets, televised February 3, 1963, on KNXT in Los Angeles. Published in University of Southern California *Alumni Review,* Spring 1963.

Haslam, Gerald W., "Odets' Use of Yiddish English in *Awake and Sing*," *Research Studies of Washington State University*, Vol. XXXIV, 1966.

Hatterer, Lawrence J., *The Artist in Society*. New York: Grove Press, 1965.

———, "A Psychotherapeutic Dimension: Creative Identity," in *Current Psychiatric Therapies*, Vol. V. New York: Grune & Stratton, 1965.

Hegel, G. W. F., *Reason in History*. New York: Bobbs-Merrill, 1953.

Hellman, Lillian, *An Unfinished Woman*. Boston: Little, Brown, 1969.

Hethmon, Robert, interview of Clifford Odets, September 30, 1961. Unpublished. Transcript in the Odets Estate.

Hicks, Granville, ed., *Proletarian Literature in the United States*. New York: International Publishers, 1935.

Hiss, Alger, *In the Court of Public Opinion*. New York: Harper & Row, 1960.

Holland, Norman N., *The Dynamics of Literary Response*. New York: Oxford University Press, 1968.

Holton, Gerald, "On Trying to Understand Scientific Genius," *The American Scholar*, Winter 1971–72.

———, "The Roots of Complementarity," *Daedalus*, Fall 1970.

———, ed., *The Twentieth Century Sciences*. New York: W. W. Norton, 1970.

Hopkins, Gerard Manley, *Poems*. London: Oxford University Press, 1961.

House Committee on Un-American Activities. *Hearings* in Hollywood, January 28, 1952, p. 2316.

Housman, A. E., *The Name and Nature of Poetry*. Cambridge: Cambridge University Press, 1950.

Howe, Irving, *World of Our Fathers*. New York: Harcourt Brace Jovanovich, 1976.

Hoy, Cyrus, *The Hyacinth Room: An Investigation into the Nature of Comedy, Tragedy, and Tragicomedy*. New York: Alfred A. Knopf, 1964.

Hughes, Catharine, "Odets: The Price of Success," *Commonweal*, September 20, 1963.

Hughes, H. Stuart, *History as Art and as Science: Twin Vistas on the Past*. New York: Harper & Row, 1964.

Hyams, Barry, "Twenty Years on a Tightrope," *Theatre Arts*, April 1955.

Isaacs, Edith J. R., "Clifford Odets, First Chapters," *Theatre Arts*, April 1939.

Jacobson, Edith, *The Self and the Object World*. New York: International Universities Press, 1964.

Jaques, Elliott, "Death and Mid-Life Crisis," *International Journal of Psychoanalysis*, 1965.

———, *Work, Creativity, and Social Justice*. New York: International Universities Press, 1970.

James, William, *Varieties of Religious Experience* (1901–1902). New York: Modern Library, 1929.

Jeffers, Robinson, *Selected Poems*. New York: Vintage Books, 1969.

Jones, Ernest, *The God Complex: Essays in Applied Psychoanalysis*. London: Hogarth Press, 1951.

Kakar, Sudhir, *The Inner World*. New York: Oxford University Press, 1978.

Kanzer, Mark, "Literature, Arts, and Aesthetics," *The Annual Survey of Psychoanalysis*, Vol. VIII, 1957.

Kaplan, Donald M., "Reflections on Eissler's Concept of the Doxaletheic Function," *American Imago*, Vol. XXIX, No. 4, 1972.

Kauffmann, Stanley, "Is Artistic Integrity Enough?" *New Republic*, February 8, 1960.

Kazan, Elia, *America, America*. New York: Stein & Day, 1962.

———, *The Assassins*. Greenwich, Conn.: Fawcett Publications, 1973.

Kazin, Alfred, *Contemporaries*. Boston: Little, Brown, 1962.

———, *On Native Grounds* (1942). New York: Anchor Books, 1956.

———, *Starting Out in the Thirties*. Boston: Atlantic–Little, Brown, 1965.

Kempton, Murray, *Part of Our Time: Some Monuments and Ruins of the Thirties* (1955). New York: Dell, 1967.

Kiell, Norman, *Universal Experience of Adolescence*. New York: International Universities Press, 1964.

Klein, George S., *Psychoanalytic Theory: An Exploration of Essentials*. New York: International Universities Press, 1976.

Kline, Herbert, "The New Plays; New Masses–New Theatre Winners," *New Theatre*, March 1935.

Koestler, Arthur, *The Act of Creation*. New York: Macmillan, 1964.

Kohlberg, Lawrence, "Psychological Analysis and Literary Form: A Study of the Doubles in Dostoevsky," *Daedalus*, Spring 1963.

Krutch, Joseph Wood, *American Drama Since 1918*. New York: George Braziller, 1957.

_____, "Mr. Odets Speaks His Mind," *The Nation*, April 10, 1935.

_____, review of *Rocket to the Moon, The Nation*, December 3, 1938.

Lampell, Millard, *True Story Magazine*, September 1961.

Landry, Robert J., *This Fascinating Radio Business*. New York: Bobbs-Merrill, 1946.

Langness, L. L., *The Life History in Anthropological Science*. New York: Holt, Rinehart & Winston, 1965.

Lawson, John Howard, "Blockade," second draft, 1938. Unpublished. In the archives of Southern Illinois University.

_____, *Film: The Creative Process*. New York: Hill & Wang, 1967.

_____, *Hidden Heritage*. Secaucus, N.J.: Citadel Press, 1968.

_____, "Rebellion in the 1920s: A Theatre Chronicle." Unpublished autobiography.

_____, *Success Story*. New York: Farrar & Rinehart, 1932.

_____, *Theory and Technique of Playwriting and Screenwriting*. New York: Hill & Wang, 1960.

Lesser, Simon O., *Fiction and the Unconscious*. Chicago: University of Chicago Press, 1975.

_____, "The Role of Unconscious Understanding in Flaubert and Dostoevsky," *Daedalus*, Spring 1963.

Levant, Oscar, *Memoirs of an Amnesiac*. New York: G. P. Putnam's Sons, 1965.

Levin, Sidney, and Ralph Kahana, eds., *Psychodynamic Studies on Aging: Creativity, Reminiscing, and Dying*. New York: International Universities Press, 1967.

Lifton, Robert Jay, *Death in Life*. New York: Random House, 1968.

Littell, Franklin, *The Crucifixion of the Jews*. New York: Harper & Row, 1974.

Ludecke, Kurt G. W., *I Knew Hitler*. New York: Charles Scribner's Sons, 1938.

Ludwig, Emil, *Beethoven: Life of a Conqueror*. New York: G. P. Putnam's Sons, 1943.

MacGowan, Kenneth, *Behind the Screen: The History and Technique of Movies*. New York: Delacorte Press, 1966.

Mann, Thomas, *Freud, Goethe, Wagner: Lectures Delivered at the New School for Social Research in New York, April 1937*. New York: Alfred A. Knopf, 1937.

_____, *The Story of a Novel: The Genesis of Doctor Faustus*. New York: Alfred A. Knopf, 1961.

Marcuse, Herbert, *Eros and Civilization*. New York: Vintage Books, 1955.

_____, *One-Dimensional Man*. Boston: Beacon Press, 1968.

Marx, Karl, and Frederick Engels, *Literature and Art*. New York: International Publishers, 1947.

Maurois, André, *Aspects of Biography*. New York: Frederick Ungar, 1957.

Mazlish, Bruce, ed., *Psychoanalysis and History*. Englewood Cliffs, N.J.: Prentice-Hall, 1963.

McCarten, John, "Revolution's Number One Boy," *The New Yorker*, January 22, 1938.

McCormack, Thomas, ed., *Afterwords: Novelists on Their Novels*. New York: Harper & Row, 1969.

McGraw-Hill Encyclopedia of World Drama, Vol. III. New York: 1972.

McPeek, James A. S., "Richard and His Shadow World," *American Imago*, Vol. XV, No. 2, 1958.

Mendelsohn, Michael J., interview of Clifford Odets, November 10, 1961, for thesis. Excerpts published in *Theatre Arts*, May and June 1963. Additional excerpts published in Mendelsohn, *Clifford Odets: Humane Dramatist* (De Land, Fla.: Everett/Edwards, 1969). Transcript of interview in the Odets Estate.

Mersand, Joseph, "Clifford Odets: Dramatist of the Inferiority Complex." *Players'* *Magazine*, May 1940.

Milford, Nancy, *Zelda*. New York: Harper & Row, 1970.

Miller, Arthur, Introduction, *Collected Plays* (1957). New York: Viking Press, 1973.

Miller, J. W., *The Modern Playwright at Work*. London: Samuel French, 1968.

Morse, Arthur D., *While Six Million Died*. New York: Random House, 1967.

"Mr. Odets is Acclimated," *The New York Times*, May 3, 1936, Sec. X, p. 4.

Muensterberger, Warner, "The Creative Process: Its Relation to Object Loss and Fetishism," in *Psychoanalytic Study of Society*, Vol. II, W. Muensterberger and Sidney Axelrad, eds. New York: International Universities Press, 1962.

Munro, Thomas, *Scientific Method in Aesthetics*. New York: W. W. Norton, 1928.

Murray, Edward, *Clifford Odets: The Thirties and After*. New York: Frederick Ungar, 1968.

Murray, Henry A., *Explorations in Personality*. New York: Oxford University Press, 1938.

———, *Myth and Mythmaking*. Boston: Beacon Press, 1968.

Nannes, Casper, *Politics in the American Drama*. Washington, D.C.: The Catholic University of America Press, 1960.

New Masses, June 1939 (for story of dispute between John Howard Lawson and Clifford Odets at Third Writers Congress, June 2, 1939, in New York).

"New Play in Manhattan—*Paradise Lost*," *Time*, December 23, 1935.

Niederland, William G., "Clinical Aspects of Creativity," *American Imago*, Vol. XXIV, Nos. 1 & 2, 1967.

Odets, Clifford, "All Drama Is Propaganda," *Current Controversy*, February 1936.

———, "Awakening of the American Theatre," *New Theatre*, January 1936.

———, "Clifford Odets Capitalizes His Own Life," *New York World-Telegram*, March 19, 1935.

———, "Critics a Mystery to Clifford Odets, So He Finds Mr. Morgan and Gives Him the Works," *New York World-Telegram*, March 2, 1940.

———, " 'Democratic Vistas' in Drama," *The New York Times*, November 21, 1937, Sec. XI.

———, "Genesis of a Play," *The New York Times*, February 7, 1942, Sec. IX, p. 3.

———, interview, *Theatre Arts*, December 1950.

———, Introduction to *Dead Souls* by N. Gogol. New York: Modern Library, 1936.

———, "Odets Tells Own Story of Cuban Arrest," *New York Post*, July 5, 1935, p. 1.

———, "Some Problems of the Modern Dramatist," *The New York Times*, December 15, 1935, Sec. XI, p. 3.

———, "Tribute by Clifford Odets to the Late John Garfield," *The New York Times*, May 25, 1952, Drama Section, p. 3.

———, and Carleton Beals, *Rifle Rule in Cuba*. New York: Provisional Committee for Cuba, 1935.

O'Hara, Frank, *Today in American Drama*. Chicago: University of Chicago Press, 1939.

Pack, Richard, "Censors See Red," *New Theatre*, May 1935.

Peckham, Morse, *Man's Rage for Chaos*. Philadelphia: Chilton, 1965.

Penrod, John A., "American Literature and the Great Depression." Ph.D. thesis, University of Pennsylvania, 1954 (unpublished).

Perkoff, Leslie, "I Would Like to Tell the Truth" (interview of Clifford Odets), *World Film News*, August 1938.

Polanyi, Michael, *The Tacit Dimension*. New York: Doubleday, 1966.

Pomerantz, Charlotte, ed., *A Quarter-Century of Un-Americana, 1938–1963*. New York: Marzani and Munsell, 1963.

Powdermaker, Hortense, *Hollywood: The Dream Factory*. Boston: Little, Brown, 1950.

Rabkin, Gerald, *Drama and Commitment: Politics in the American Theatre of the Thirties*. Bloomington: Indiana University Press, 1964.

Raymond, Aron, *The Century of Total War*. New York: Doubleday, 1954.

Reik, Theodore, *Masochism in Modern Man*. New York: Pyramid Publications, 1976.

Robbins, Michael D., "On the Psychology of Artistic Creativity," *The Psychoanalytic Study of the Child,* Vol. XXIV, 1969.

Rogow, Arnold A., *James Forrestal: A Study of Personality, Politics and Policy.* New York: Macmillan, 1964.

Roper, H. Trevor, *Hitler's Secret Conversations.* New York: Signet Books, 1953.

Rose, Gilbert, "The Power of Form: A Psychoanalytic Approach to Aesthetic Form." *Psychological Issues,* Monograph 49, 1980.

Rosenberg, Bernard, and Norris Fliegel, *The Vanguard Artist.* Chicago: Quadrangle Books, 1965.

Rosenman, Samuel, *Working with Roosevelt.* New York: D. A. Cato, 1952.

Roth, Henry, *Call It Sleep.* New York: Avon Books, 1964.

Rothenberg, Albert, "Creativity: A Survey and Critique of Major Investigation," *Psychoanalysis and Contemporary Science,* Vol. III, 1974.

———, *The Emerging Goddess: The Creative Process in Art, Science, and Other Fields.* Chicago: University of Chicago Press, 1979.

———, "The Iceman Changeth: Toward an Empirical Approach to Creativity," *Journal of the American Psychoanalytic Association,* Vol. XVII, No. 2, 1969.

———, *The Index of Scientific Writings on Creativity: Creative Men and Women.* Hamden, Conn.: The Shoe String Press, 1974.

Ruitenbeek, Hendrik M., *The Creative Imagination: Psychoanalysis and the Genius of Inspiration.* Chicago: Quadrangle Books, 1965.

———, *Psychoanalysts and Contemporary American Culture.* New York: Delta, 1964.

Salzman, Jack, ed., *Years of Protest: A Collection of American Writings of the 1930s.* New York: Pegasus, 1967.

Sand, George, and Gustave Flaubert, *Letters,* tr. Aimee L. McKenzie. New York: Boni and Liveright, 1921.

Sander, Marian, "Several Worlds of American Jews," *Harper's,* April 1966.

Saul, Leon, "Sudden Death at Impasse," *Psychoanalytic Forum,* Vol. I, 1966.

Schafer, Roy, *Aspects of Internalization.* New York: International Universities Press, 1968.

Schlesinger, Arthur M., Jr., *The Age of Roosevelt.* Boston: Houghton-Mifflin Co. Vol. I, *The Crisis of the Old Order* (1956). Vol. II, *The Coming of the New Deal* (1958). Vol. III, *The Politics of Upheaval* (1960).

Schlossman, Howard, "God, the Father and His Sons." Unpublished manuscript.

Schneider, Daniel E., *The Psychoanalyst and the Artist.* New York: Farrar, Straus and Giroux, 1950.

Seidel, George J., *Crisis of Creativity.* University of Notre Dame Press, 1966.

Seligmann, Kurt, *The Mirror of Magic.* New York: Pantheon Books, 1948.

Shatan, Chaim, and M. Brenman-Gibson, "The Biblical Story of Sarah, Isaac, and Abraham Reconsidered, etc." Presented at the Erikson Conference on "Psychosocial Development Reconsidered," Bennington College, Bennington, Vt., July 15, 1978 (unpublished notes).

Shirer, William, *The Rise and Fall of the Third Reich.* New York: Simon and Schuster, 1960.

Shuman, R. Baird, *Clifford Odets.* New York: Twayne Publishers, 1962.

Sieben, Pearl, *The Immortal Jolson: His Life and Times.* New York: Fell Publishers, 1962.

Slochower, Harry, *No Voice Is Wholly Lost.* New York: Creative Age Press, 1945.

———, "Symbolism and the Creative Process of Art," *American Imago,* Vol. XXII, 1965.

Spiegel, Shalom, *The Last Trial.* New York: Pantheon Books, 1967.

Spurgeon, Caroline F. E., *Shakespeare's Imagery.* New York: Macmillan, 1936.

Stein, Morris I., and Shirley J. Heinze, *Creativity and the Individual.* Glencoe, Ill.: The Free Press, 1960.

Steiner, Gary A., *The Creative Organization.* Chicago: University of Chicago Press, 1965.

Stern, Daniel, *Final Cut.* New York: Viking Press, 1975.

Storr, Anthony, *The Dynamics of Creation.* New York: Atheneum, 1972.

Stott, William, *Documentary Expression and Thirties America.* New York: Oxford University Press, 1973.

Sugrue, Thomas, "Mr. Odets Regrets," *American Magazine,* October 1936.

Swados, Harvey, *The American Writer and the Great Depression*. Indianapolis:
    Bobbs-Merrill, 1966.
Swanberg, W. A., *Theodore Dreiser*. New York: Charles Scribner's Sons, 1965.
Sypher, Wylie, *Loss of the Self in Modern Literature and Art*. New York: Vin-
    tage Books, 1964.
Taylor, William E., *Modern American Drama: Essays in Criticism*. DeLand, Fla.:
    Everett/Edwards, 1968.
Thomas, Robert J., *King Cohn: The Life and Times of Harry Cohn*. New York:
    G. P. Putnam's Sons, 1967.
Trotsky, Leon, *Trotsky's Diary in Exile—1935*. New York: Atheneum, 1963.
Tucker, Richard, "Svetlana Alliluyeva as Witness of Stalin." Seminar at Prince-
    ton University, May 31, 1968 (unpublished).
Tynan, Kenneth, "To Divorce Art from Money-making," *The New York Times
    Magazine*, December 1, 1963.
Van Hettinga, William L., "The Theme of Nonfulfillment in Three Plays of
    Clifford Odets." Ph.D. thesis, Duke University, 1960 (unpublished).
Vernon, Grenville, "The Case of Clifford Odets," *Commonweal*, June 10, 1938.
_____, "Mr. Odets' Plays Are Jewish," *Commonweal*, December 16, 1938.
Vogel, Arthur, "Clifford Odets: The Tragic Dilemma," *Jewish Currents*, January
    1964.
Waelder, Robert, *Psychoanalytic Avenues to Art*. New York: International Uni-
    versities Press, 1965.
Wagner, Arthur, interview of Clifford Odets for doctoral dissertation, October 9,
    1961. Excerpts published in *Harper's*, September 1966. Original typescript
    with Odets' corrections in the Odets Estate.
Waife-Goldberg, Marie, *My Father, Sholom Aleichem*. New York: Simon and
    Schuster, 1968.
Ward, Aileen, *John Keats: The Making of a Poet*. New York: Viking Press, 1963.
Warshow, Robert S., "Poet of the Jewish Middle Class," *Commentary*, May 1946.
Watts, Alan, *Psychotherapy East and West*. New York: Random House, 1975.
Weissman, Philip, *Creativity in the Theatre*. New York: Basic Books, 1965.
Wellworth, George E., *The Theater of Protest and Paradox*. New York: New York
    University Press, 1964.
White, Robert W., *Lives in Progress: A Study of the Natural Growth of Per-
    sonality*. New York: Holt, Rinehart & Winston, 1975.
_____, "Sense of Interpersonal Competence: Two Case Studies and Some Re-
    flections on Origins," in *The Study of Lives*, ed. R. W. White. New York:
    Atherton Press, 1964.
"White Hope," *Time*, December 5, 1938.
Whitman, Walt, *Complete Poetry and Selected Prose*, ed. James E. Miller, Jr.
    Boston: Houghton Mifflin, 1959.
_____, "Starting from Paumanok" (1860) and "You Felons on Trial in Courts"
    (1860), in *Leaves of Grass*. New York: Modern Library, 1950 (pp. 12 and
    304).
Willett, Ralph, "Clifford Odets and Popular Culture," *South Atlantic Quarterly*,
    1970.
Wilson, Edmund, *The Wound and the Bow: Seven Studies in Literature*. New
    York: Oxford University Press, 1965.
Wilson, Robert N., "Albert Camus: Personality as Creative Struggle," in *The
    Study of Lives*, ed. R. W. White. New York: Atherton Press, 1964.
_____, "Poetic Creativity Process and Personality," *Psychiatry*, May 1954.
Wingler, H., *Bauhaus*. Cambridge, Mass.: Massachusetts Institute of Technology
    Press, 1968.
Wolfle, Dale, ed., *The Discovery of Talent*. Cambridge, Mass.: Harvard Univer-
    sity Press, 1969.
Woodbridge, Elisabeth, *The Drama: Its Law and Its Technique*. Boston: Allyn
    and Bacon, 1898.
Worringer, Wilhelm, *Abstraction and Empathy: A Contribution to the Psychology
    of Style* (1908). New York: International Universities Press, 1963.
"Writer as Independent Spirit, The," *Proceedings of the XXXIV International
    P.E.N. Congress*, New York, June 12–18, 1966.
Wyatt, Frederick, "The Reconstruction of the Individual and of the Collective

Past," in *The Study of Lives,* ed. R. W. White. New York: Atherton Press, 1964.

Yarbrough, Camille, "Today I Feel Like I Am Somebody," *The New York Times,* March 18, 1971, Section D, p. 3.

Young, Stark, "Awake and Whistle at Least," *New Republic,* March 13, 1935.

———, "Lefty and Nazi," *New Republic,* April 10, 1935.

———, "New Talent," *New Republic,* May 29, 1935.

Zangwill, Israel, *The Melting Pot.* New York: Arno Press, 1932.

Zborowski, Mark, and Elizabeth Herzog, *Life Is with People.* New York: International Universities Press, 1953.

Zeligs, Meyer, *Friendship and Fratricide: An Analysis of Whittaker Chambers and Alger Hiss.* New York: Viking Press, 1967.

Index / Digest

The use of this symbol ⦗ refers the reader to the Notes and Comment section beginning on page 621

Abie's Irish Rose (Nichols), 111
Abraham Lincoln Brigade: return to New York, 545
activity/passivity, ⦗22.21, ⦗22.23
Actors' Equity, 234
Adams, Edie, 8, 10
Adams, Franklin P. (F.P.A.), 64
Adler, Jack (Jay), 8, 317, 350, 460
Adler, Jacob P., 56, 124
Adler, Luther, 56, 222, 261, 267, 268, 273, 281, 290, 302, 303, 305, 311–12, 315, 318, 335, 459, 463, 476–77, 489, 506, 508, 509, 518, 519, 539, 552, 567, 611
Adler, Pearl, 260
Adler, Sara, 317
Adler, Stella, 56, 238, 246, 254, 255, 266, 267, 274, 280, 287, 297, 311–12, 328, 344, 352, 371, 382, 385, 388, 399, 423, 443, 456, 506, 508, 510, 559, 572, 605
Aeolian Hall, 83
aggression: and paradise, ⦗19.8
Alden, Hortense, 156–57, 159–61, 163, 164, 201, 235
Aleichem, Sholem (Sholem Rabinowitz), 38
Alhambra Theatre, 70
Alice (CO's friend), 259–60, 261–62, 338
Alice in Wonderland, 243
Allan, Ted, and interview of CO, 562
Allen, Robert, 549
All Quiet on the Western Front (Remarque), 397
Aloma (film), 92
Ambers-Canzoneri prize fight, 426, 446
ambivalence: in literature, Old Testament, and pairing of characters, ⦗19.11
American Civil Liberties Union, 366
American dream, the, 77n, 113n, 199; beginning of end of, 466; end of, ⦗22.2; CO's view of, 38, 309–10, 311; and price paid for, 525

American-Nazi Bund, 572
American Newspaper Guild, 562
American Place, the, 477–78
American Tragedy, An (Dreiser), 101, 110, 398
Ancient Arabic Order of Nobles of the Mystic Shrine, 102
Anderson, Gertrude Maynard (Mab) (Mrs. Maxwell), 226, 235, 359–60
Anderson, Mab. See Anderson, Gertrude Maynard
Anderson, Maxwell, 50, 201–2, 209, 212, 226, 234, 267, 344, 359–60, 367, 409, 418, 428
Anderson, Sherwood, 34, 404
anorexia-bulima, ⦗12.1
anti-Semitism, ⦗14.2
Ardrey, Robert, 498, 567, 576–77
Arena (Flanagan), 491
Arlen, Harold, 405
Aronson, Boris, 606
Aronson, Gerald, 118
art in America, 309–10, 311, 428; craft vs. art, 233; and the Depression, ⦗7.7; as expression of common lives, ⦗19.2; legitimate stage vs. film, 486–87; and mass media, 127; mercantilism and, ⦗15.3; and musicians, ⦗7.7; rise of indigenous forms in, 213
artist in America, 375, 430–31, 466, 515; Clurman on, 345–46; Clurman's view of problems of, 399–400; and commerce, 606; and communal ethos, ⦗13.8; and "deals" with film industry, 583; and the film industry, 519–20, 524; and indigenous naturalistic expression, 127; and lack of cohesive worldview, 372; and lure of mass market, 394; and Hollywood, 516–17; and instant success, 430; lack of social affirmation for, 101; and mercantilism, 394, 516–18; mer-

artist in America (*Cont.*)
chandising of, 553; paradigms of, 227, 339; Luise Rainer, 464; and technology, ❪2.2
Asch, Sholem, 124
Atkinson, Brooks, 327, 359; on *Awake and Sing!*, 325; on *Awake and Sing!* revival, 552; on CO's work, 539; on *Paradise Lost*, 385; on *Rocket to the Moon*, 537; on *Till the Day I Die*, 336
AT THE WATER-LINE (radio play) (Odets), 91–92, 100
AWAKE AND SING! (Odets), 49, 87, 227–28, 237, 242, 249, 250–59, 277–78, 281, 338, 366, 379; analysis of, 250–59; cast of, 324n; and Chicago audiences, 410; and deleted dialogue, ❪14.18; and ending of forced optimism, 258–59, 326, 474; excerpts from, 250, 258; family as paradise, 251; to be filmed, 334; and Group's decision to perform, 311–12; and Group tour, 401; and later revivals, ❪14.8; manifest and latent meanings, 251–52; and CO's profane vs. sacred fantasies of father, 256, 257–58, ❪14.12; opening of, 321, 323–25; plot of, 250; reviews of, 325, 326; compared to Chekhov, 325; revival by Group, 552; and "simplified" solutions, 494; Yiddish-American language in, 250; and Yiddish names, ❪14.14
    identity-elements: artist manqué (Sam Feinschreiber), 252; dead mother (Schlosser's wife), ❪14.20; depressed mother (Sam Feinschreiber), 252; father-symbol (Moe Axelrod), ❪14.11; "feminine" anima (Hennie), 253; idealized father-symbol (Jacob), 256–57; innocent weakling (Ralph), 256; Jewish prophet (Jacob), ❪14.22; as loner, afraid of being trapped (Hennie), 252; misogynist (Moe Axelrod), 253–54; paternal/ maternal image (Bessie Berger), 254, ❪14.15; powerful cripple (Moe Axelrod), 253; ruthless mother (Bessie), 252; *identity-fragment:* CO's mother (Myron), 255; *themes:* rebirth, family, 250–59, ❪14.24. *See also* I GOT THE BLUES

Babbitt (Lewis), 404
Bachmann and Co., L., 79, 80, 82
Baker, George Pierce, 57
Ballard, Charles, 62
Bankhead, Tallulah, 338, 350, 365, 377, 386
Barber, Philip, 238, 312n
Barker, Margaret (Beany), 200–1, 204, 238, 280, 297–98
Barry, Philip, 127
Barrymore, John, 92, 93
Baruch, Bernard, 50n, 89, 338
Baruch, Sidney Norton, 89–90
Basshe, Em Jo, 128, ❪6.2
Batista, Fulgencio, 302
Bauhaus, the, 282
Baum, Vicki, 128
Bauman, Mordecai, 158, 556
Baxter, Alan, 243
Bayonne Opera House, 92
Beals, Carleton, 366
Beard, Charles and Mary, 282, 283
Beck Street Boys, 42, 47, 64, 85
Becker, Charles, 32, 33
Beethoven, Ludwig van, 49, 228–29, 234, 260, 396, 432, 512
Behrman, S. N., 127, 367, 386, 394, 400, 428, 495
Bein, Albert, 222, 235
Belasco, David, 64
Belasco Theatre, 321
Bel Geddes, Norman, 76
Benton, Thomas Hart, 213
Bergler, Edmund, 627n
Berlin, Irving, 367n, 386
Bernstein, Aline, 338
Bernstein, Ida Mae Levine. *See* Levine, Ida Mae
Bernstein, Sidney, 322, 511, 548–49, 562
Betty (CO's friend), 114, 115, 116, 117, 136
Beyond the Horizon (O'Neill), 56
Biberman, Abner, 163n, 208, 216, 220, 262, 323
Biberman, Herbert, 142, 163, 216
BIG KNIFE, THE (Odets), 122, 274, ❪14.19
Big Night (Powell), 222, 244
Birstein, Ann, 13
Black, Ivan, 165, 170, 172–73
Blankfort, Michael, on *Awake and Sing!*, 326–27
Blitzstein, Marc, 111, 216, ❪7.7
Blockade. See RIVER IS BLUE, THE
blood sacrifice, ❪19.5; and *Silent Partner* (Odets), ❪19.9
Bloomgarden, Kermit, 509, 515, 566
Bloor, Ella Reeve ("Mother Bloor"), 87, 338, 352, 366
Bogdanovich, Peter, 598, 607

Bohnen, Roman (Bud), 299, 302, 443, 476–77, 566, 567
Bolitho, William, 64
Bolton, Whitney, on *Golden Boy*, 486
Bonus Army, 233
Boone, Richard, 4
Booth, Clare. *See* Luce, Clare Booth
Borani Players, 64
Borscht Belt, 85, 94
Bowan, Sibyl. *See* Bowman, Sibyl
Bowman, Sibyl (Bowan), 32, 33
Boyd, Ernest, and anti-Semitism, ◖14.2
Boyle, Thomas, 513
Brady, Alice, 92
Brand, Phoebe (Mrs. Morris Carnovsky), 457, 477, 606
Brandeis, Louis, 44
Brando, Marlon, 8, 9
Brandt & Brandt, 334
Braun, Hannah, 439
Brecht, Bertolt, 128, ◖14.2
Brenman-Gibson, Margaret, 8, 10, 87
Breuer, Bessie (Mrs. Henry Varnum Poor), 424, 448–49
Brice, Fannie, 338
Brill (bookkeeper at Odets Company), 94
broadcasting industry, 83; early programming, 90
Bromberg, Goldie (Mrs. J. Edward), 13, 103, 230, 239, 279, 350
Bromberg, J. Edward, 13, 103, 186, 199, 209, 238, 279, 280, 297, 318, 388, 394, 458, 459, 566, 567, ◖14.24
Bronx Home News, 85
Bronx Opera House, 64
Brookfield Center, 186; and Daybook, 193, 194, 201
Brooklyn Daily Eagle, 538
Brooks, Mel, ◖15.3
Brooks, Van Wyck, 50, 293n
Broun, Heywood, 64, 284, 344, 585; on *Golden Boy*, 491; on *Paradise Lost*, 386
Browder, Earl, 600
Brown, Chamberlain, 98, 113, 119, 131–32
Brown, Ivor, on *Awake and Sing!*, 491
Brown, John Mason, 518; *Awake and Sing!* revival, 552; on *Night Music*, 607–8; on *Rocket to the Moon*, 538; on *Till the Day I Die*, 336–37; on *Waiting for Lefty* and the Group, 319
Bruderschaft, aspirations toward, ◖13.8
Buchwald, Nathaniel on *Awake and Sing!* 326; on *Waiting for Lefty*, 317–18
Buck, Pearl, 418

Bukharin, 361
Burger, Hans, 436
Burgess, Grover, 563
Burke, Kenneth, ◖22.11
Burrows, Abe, 627n
Burt, Maxwell Struthers, 17
Bushman, Francis X., 36

Caffery, Jefferson (ambassador to Cuba), 364, 365, 366
Cagney, James, 567
Cahan, Abraham, ◖1.1; on *Awake and Sing!*, 326
Call It Sleep (Roth), ◖16.1
Cameo, The, 93
Camp Arthur, 109–110
Camp Roosevelt, 94, 95
Camp Scopus, 155
Camp Tioga, 135–38
Cantor, Eddie, 546
Capra, Frank, 524
Carey, Harry, 606
Carlyle, Thomas, 314
Carnegie, Andrew, 411
Carnovsky, Morris, 186, 230, 280, 318, 353, 356, 411, 443, 457, 477, 566, 569, 572, 582, 606
Carroll, Madeleine, 396, 408
Caruso, Enrico, 49
Case of Clyde Griffiths, The, 398
Casey Jones (Ardrey), 498
Castro, Fidel, 366
Century Theatre, 76
Cerf, Bennett, 338, 358, 388, 506, 563
Cézanne, Paul, 24
Chalfin, Jennie, 122, 123, 352
Chambers, Whittaker, ix
Chaplin, Charles, 9, 51, 213, 458
"Charlie theatre," 491–92, 562; as ideologically cemented collective, ◖22.0. *See also* drama
Chayevsky, Paddy, 128
Chekhov, Anton, 142, 159, 343, 558
Chiang Kai-shek, 418
Chiang Kai-shek, Madame, 418
Childhood and Society (Erikson) ◖19.4
Children's Hour, The (Hellman), 308
"Child's Dream of a Star, A" (Dickens), 93
Christianity, 505
Chrystie Players, 92
Chrystie Street Settlement House, 169
Circle Hotel, 128, 153, 154, 155, 156, 162, 163, 205, 209, 212, 213, 240
Citizen Kane (film), 407n
Civic Repertory Theatre, 141, 243, 284, 317
CLASH BY NIGHT (Odets), 594, ◖13.6; *identity-element:* internalized father (Earl), ◖14.19;

CLASH BY NIGHT (Odets) (*Cont.*)
symbol: young couple as Adam and Eve, ◄19.6
"Clinette, the Man in Black," 33
Clurman, Harold, 8, 10, 11, 155, 186, 205, 245, 255, 260–61, 267, 388, 396, 495, 506, 508, 509, 510, 511, 570–72, 593; and Stella Adler, 266, 301, 410, 425, 457, 509–10, 566; on aim of Group, 287; on American theatre, 56, 168, 169; on artist in America, 345–46; on audience response to *Waiting for Lefty*, 315–16; on *Awake and Sing!*, 258; on *Beyond the Horizon*, 57; on Chrystie Players, 93; concern with CO as artist, 399–400; concern for Strasberg's direction, 399; and concerns re Group, 398–400; and concerns about *Rocket to the Moon*, 514; and criticism of, by Actors' Committee, 443–44; on dangers of Group's over-optimism and obedience, 196–97; and decision to direct *Awake and Sing!*, 312; discouragement of, 571, 572; as director, 289; and distrust of Luise Rainer, 406; and dream of "new age," 169–70, 203; as Harold Eager or Edgar, 166; early theatre work, 112; on fall of Madrid, 550; on fear of failure, 543; and first meeting with CO, 165; friendship with Aaron Copland, 170; on getting work in Hollywood, 443; on *The General Died at Dawn*, 428–29; on *Golden Boy*, 466; and Group concerns, 418–19; on Group, *New York Times* article, 206; and Group problem, 459; on Group Theatre in America, 162; as head of Group Theatre, 476; in Hollywood, 456; and hopes for CO and Luise Rainer, 442; and *I Got the Blues*, 268–270; ineptitude of, 425; letter to John Garfield, 515–18; letters to CO, 345–46, 399–400, 442–43, 495–97, 556, 559, and meaning of Group, 565–67; and media statement supporting *Paradise Lost*, 385–86; in Moscow, 361–62; on New York City, 245–47; on *Night Music*, 574, 585; on *910 Eden Street*, 206–7; as "obstetrician" to CO's plays, 568; and CO's admiration for, 568; on CO's belief re analysis and creativity, 202; as CO's "favorite character outside of fiction," 398; CO's image of, 166; on CO's

problems with *Silent Partner*, 442; on CO's *Victory*, 236; CO's view of, 222, 224, 515, 595, 603–4; on CO's work, 320; in Paris, 56; personal history of, 166–70; on plans for last Group summer, 556; play-reader for Theatre Guild, 141, 142, 163; rejects *Winterset*, 344; and relation to CO, 321, 496; relinquishes direction of *Johnny Johnson*, 428; resigns from Theatre Guild, 207; and respect for CO, 568; returns from Hollywood, 476; on Roberta-Joan mystery, 137; on *Rocket to the Moon*, 521; on role of actor in the Group, 515–17; Russian theatre vis-à-vis Group Theatre, 289; and search for investors, 480; on sense of responsibility towards Group, 203–4; on *Silent Partner*, 411, 423; as stage-manager, *Garrick Gaities*, 84n; on Lee Strasberg, 196–97; on *Success Story*, 212, 222; and temperamental outburst, 482; on the Theatre Guild, 179; and Theatre Guild Studio, 142; on a time of renewed faith, 240; and trip to Russia, 287–88; 289; on upholding Group standards, 362
Clurman, Robert, 572
Clurman, Samuel, 166–67
Cobb, Lee J., 8, 362, 477, 510, 566, 567, 604
Cohen, Gus, 79
Cohn, Harry, 394, 397, 409, 524
collective bargaining, 242, 282
Colum, Padraic, 112
Commercial Investment Trust, 78
Communism in America, 286–87; and anti-Communism, 512, 513; and growing disenchantment with, 524
Communist Manifesto, 282
Communist Party (American), 234, 287, 363, 366; and CO's membership in, 296, 302; and organizers, CO's view of, 306
Compton, Juleen, 74n
Conflict (Lawrence), 132
Conrad, Joseph, 186
Cook, George Cram, 84, ◄2.6
Cook, Nilla Cram, 84, 90–91
Cooper, Gary, 407
Cooper, Reta, 86
Copeau and French theatre, 213
Copland, Aaron, 56, 93, 127, 166, 169, 170, 175, 321, 409, 508, 518, 544, 584, 606
Corey, Lewis, 420
Cossart, Ernest, 146

Coughlin, Charles E., 101, 262, 287, 602
COUNTRY GIRL (Odets), 147, 152n, ⊄14.19
Country People (Gorky), ⊄22.16
Covici-Friede, 358
Cox, Abram, Boiler Company, 101
Coy, Walter, 280
Craig, Gordon, 361
Crane, Hart, 230, 549
Crawford, Cheryl, 84n, 141–42, 148, 154, 163, 169, 186, 195, 207, 221, 266, 271, 312, 323, 361, 444
Crawford, Joan, 92, 266, 323, 388, 396
creative process, activity/passivity in, ⊄8.3; and aggression, ⊄8.1; in arena of history, ⊄23.1; and audience, ⊄22.4; and avoidance of direct conflicts, 230; and bisexuality, 499, ⊄4.4; and child's play, ⊄14.4; collective unconscious in, ⊄19.5; conflict resolution through form, 223, 225, 285, 475, ⊄4.4, ⊄7.2, ⊄13.1, ⊄14.5, ⊄21.4, ⊄21.7, ⊄22.3, ⊄22.7, ⊄22.8, ⊄22.15; and "connection with self," 112; and death of child as symbol, ⊄8.6; and dream analysis, ⊄14.4; and equidistance, 165; fluid consciousness in, 234; gift of conviction, 124; and healing, ⊄14.4; and "holy inspiration" ⊄14.4; and hubris, 431; and identity-elements, ⊄22.9; and identity confusion, ⊄9.3; and isolation, 518–19; lack of affirmation in society, 224; and the life cycle, ⊄2.4; life vs. art, 228–29; male and female components in, ⊄19.5; and masturbation, ⊄4.4; as means to bridge "disconnection," ⊄9.2; and merging of subject and object, 304, 491–92, ⊄22.0, ⊄22.4; and need for silence, 144n; CO's view of, ⊄22.1; and prerequisites for, 382, 442; and ongoing history, ⊄13.1; and orality, ⊄8.3; oral metaphor in, ⊄10.3; overdetermination of symbols, ⊄22.10; and phallic symbols, 469, ⊄21.4; and plays, ⊄14.4; and playwright and audience, ⊄14.4; and playwright as observer, ⊄14.5; in playwrights, ⊄22.1, ⊄22.15; and playwriting, ⊄19.10, ⊄22.9; psychohistorical factors in, ⊄9.2; and Pygmalion story, ⊄24.1; quest for self-integration, ⊄9.2; and recreation, ⊄14.4; regression in the service of the ego, ⊄13.9; and relation to mother, ⊄18.4; and responsibility, ⊄4.4; restorative use of ⊄22.3; role of mother in, ⊄17.5; role of playfulness in, ⊄18.1; and sadomasochism, ⊄17.3; in scripture, ⊄19.5; self-witnessing in, 278; sense of involuntariness in, 147n, ⊄8.3; and sense of reality, ⊄7.3; and symbolic castration, ⊄4.4; symbolic representation of, in dramatic themes, 249–50, 253, ⊄14.5; transparency in early works, 187; and transposition of experience, ⊄2.4; as uncovering of self, 598; and unity of "inner" with "outer" characters, ⊄21.6; words as substitute for feelings, ⊄7.2. *See also* Odets, Clifford, *Work-related issues*, CREATIVE PROCESS; play analyses
Crisis. See Men in White
Criterion, The (theatre), 93
critics in America, 311, 385, 386, 391, 447, 606–7, 609–10; CO's view of, 107
Cry of Players (Gibson), ⊄17.4
Cuba, 301–2, 362–66
"Cuban play, the." *See* LAW OF FLIGHT
Curtis Publishing Company, 22
Czechoslovakia, 512, 513

Daily Forward, The, 326, 381, ⊄1.1
Daily Worker, 281, 285, 317, 326, 343
Daniels, Bebe, 92
DaSilva, Howard, 477
Days Without End (O'Neill), 414
Dead Souls (Gogol), 392; introduction to (Odets), 392
Debs, Eugene V., 32, 44
Declaration of Independence, 125
DeForest, Lee, ⊄2.2
Deity, the, and blood sacrifice; image of; in Old and New Testament, 661–62n, ⊄19.5
Dekker, Albert, 132, 141, 145
Dell, Floyd, 84
del Rio, Dolores, 579
"'Democratic Vistas' in Drama," 486–87
de Jouvenel, Renaud, 546
Dena (CO's friend), 279, 307, 338, 346, 369, 400–1
"Dentist Play, The" (Odets), 464, 489, 510, 511, 513–14. *See also* ROCKET TO THE MOON
Depression, the Great, 55, 101, 142–43, 245–48, 466
de Putti, Lya, 92
Der Tag, 336
Desire Under the Elms (O'Neill), 84, 121

Desmond, Mae (Mrs. Frank Fielder), 99, 113, 304
Deutsch, Helen, 194, 299, 359–60, 384, 386, 421, 455, 544
Dewey, John, 386
DeWitt Clinton High School, 70
Diamond, David, 508
Diaspora, the, 102
Dies Committee, and Odets, 574
Dies, Martin, Jr., 408, 512, 513
Dietrich, Marlene, 477
Documentary Expression and Thirties America (Stott), ¶19.2
Doll's House, A (Ibsen), 55, 612
Don Juan (film), 93
Don Juan in a Garden, 91
Dos Passos, John, 110, 127, 128, 141, 213, 404, 634
"Dover Beach" (Arnold), 613
Drachman, Julian, 59–63, 64
drama. *See* theatre; theatre in America
Drasin, Tamara. *See* Tamara
Drawing Room Players, 64, 79, 85, 91
Dreiser, Theodore, 32, 34, 50n, 57, 67, 84, 110, 127, 386, 404, 541, 590, 599, ¶2.10, ¶6.2, ¶7.4, ¶7.6, ¶14.2
"Dr. L." (CO's psychoanalyst), 10, 11, 12
Dunn, Emma, 33
Dutchess of Malfi, The (Webster), 558
Duvivier, Julien, 547

Earl Carroll's Vanities, 90
Earle, James, 38
Eastman, Lucia, 433, 441, 499
Eastman, Max, 34
Easy Rider (film), ¶21.2
Edel, Leon, xi
Edison, Thomas, ¶6.4
Ehrenburg, Ilya, 455
830 East 163rd Street, 53
Einstein, Albert, xii, 386, 478
Eisenhower, Dwight D., 208
Eisenstein, Sergei, 361
Eisler, Hanns, 356, 561, 555, 597
Eislers, the, 606
Eitingon, Bess (Mrs. Motty Eitingon), 244–45, 277–78, 280, 429, 439, 479
Eitingon, Motty, 244, 277, 439, 479
Eliot, Ruth Young, 312, 553
Eliot, T. S., 150
Elizabeth the Queen (Anderson), 202
Elkins, Hillard, ¶16.7
Emerson, Ralph Waldo, 34, 216, 217–18, 280
empathy: psychotherapists and writers, ¶4.2
Erickson, Leif, 565, 566, 572, 579

Erikson, Erik H., ix–xii, 98, 130, 266n, 357, 414n, 551, 587, ¶4.6, ¶6.3, ¶9.3, ¶13.3, ¶14.4, ¶14.9, ¶17.5, ¶21.1, ¶21.7, ¶22.20
Ernst, Morris, 489
Escapade (film), 405
Ethiopia, invasion of by Italians, 367–68

Fabian, Irene. *See* Steinberg, Irene
Fabian, Minnie, 561
Fadiman, Clifton, 338, 386
Faragoh, Francis Edwards, 128, ¶6.2
Farber, Leslie, ¶14.6
Farmer, Frances, 339, 477, 565, 572, 574, 577, 578–79, 580; and involvement with CO, 566, 572, 578–79
Farmer, Virginia, 237
Fascism, 282, 367–68
Faulkner, William, 127, 213
Federal Bureau of Investigation (FBI), 51, 286–87
Federal Theatre, 491, 492, 494, 512
Fels, Joseph, 84
Ferber, Edna, 338, 422n
Fervent Years, The (Clurman), 258
Feuchtwanger, Lion, 128
Field, Sylvia (Mrs. Ernest Truex), 144–153, 563
Fielder, Frank, 99
Fielder, Mrs. Frank. *See* Desmond, Mae
Fielder, Richard, 99
Fifth Column, The (Hemingway), 604
film industry, the ¶20.1; advent of, ¶6.4; advent of sound, 93; and antecedents, 575; and appeasement of Fascist governments, 418, 492–93; art and commerce in, 575; and avoidance of controversy, 492–93; and blacklisting, 430, 573; collusion of unions with, 499; and costs, 428; and creativity, 575; and Diaspora identity, 411; and driving out of small theatre companies, 129, 131; and effect upon artists, 428, 456, 464, 516–17, 519–20, 579–80; and fear of scandal, 450; and filming of classic European plays, 55; vs. legitimate stage, 486–87; and life of film star, 448; and mercantilism, 334, 335, 393, 397–98, 405, ¶2.7; movies as folk theatre, 487; CO's view of, 310, 421, 371–72; precursors of, ¶2.6; as purveyor of the American Dream, 310, 404; and right-wing politics, 286; and the "sun kings," 394; and writers, 127–28, 395, 397, 524, 575, ¶3.8

Fischer, Ida, 62
Fishers Island, 85, 86, 92n
Fitzgerald, F. Scott, 55, 127, 599, ❡7.9
Fitzgerald, Zelda (Mrs. F. Scott), 601
510 Master Street, 27, 29
Flanagan, Hallie, 491, 492, 513
FLOWERING PEACH, THE (Odets), 5, 11, 52n, 102, 109, 585, ❡19.3
Fonda, Henry, 328
Forest Lawn Cemetery, 13
Fosdick, Harry Emerson, 386
"Four Gunmen, The," 32
Frank, "Dago," 32
Frank, Waldo, 34, 50, 112, 142, 204, 213–14, 219, 276, 306, 321, 384, 399, 548; "A Talk," 213
Freedman, Harold, 334, 436, 452, 583
Freiheit, the, 326
Freud, Sigmund, xi, 574, ❡2.2, ❡2.4, ❡22.14
Frost, Robert, 134, 219

Garden of Allah (film), 36
Garfield, John (Julie), 276, 279, 280, 318, 335, 458, 476–77, 514–18, 566, 567, 606; and letter to CO, 461; CO's view of, 243–44
Garfield, Roberta (Robbe) (Mrs. John) (later Mrs. Sidney Cohn), 279
Garfinkle, Jules (Julie). *See* John Garfield
Garland, Robert, 408; on *Awake and Sing!* 325
Garrick Gaieties of 1926, 84n, 92, 93, 168
Garrick Theatre, 84
Gassner, John, 259; on *Awake and Sing!* 326
Geddes, Virgil, 194
Geer, Will, 338
Geisinger, Freda (CO's grandmother), 19
Gelb, Arthur and Barbara, 92
GENERAL DIED AT DAWN, THE (Odets), 113n, 398, 400, 406–8, 483; John Garfield as "outer mask" for O'Hara, 407–8; release of, 428; reviews of, 408
    identity-element: corrupt "big man" (Gen. Yang), 407; powerful father (Gen. Yang), ❡14.19; *theme:* betrayal by trusted woman, 408; revolt against the oppressor, 408
generosity vs. narcissistic giving, ❡24.2
Gentle People, The (Shaw), 514
Gentlewoman (Lawson), 285–87
George, Mary, 261
German-American Bund, 512, 513
Gershwin, George, 55, 386, 396, 411, 430, 446

Gershwin, Ira, 367n, 448, 460
Gettysburg (film), 460, 483
Gibson, William, ix, x, 8, 10, 128, 151, 601, ❡3.3, ❡13.2, ❡17.4, ❡21.6, ❡22.3
Gide, André, 399
Gillespie, Abraham Lincoln, 124
Gimbel Brothers, 83
Gods of the Lightning (Anderson), 266–67
Goetz, Edith Mayer (Mrs. William), 8, 87
Goetz, William, 8
Gold Eagle Guy (Levy), 287, 289, 290, 297–98, 299, 306, 311
Gold, Michael, 285, ❡6.2
GOLDEN BOY (Odets), 69, 155, 426–27, 456, 459, 460, 492, ❡13.5; as American existentialist play, 466; analysis of, 465–75; and casting, 476–77; and Harry Cohn, 524; early version of, 459; excerpt from, 470–71; film of, 485, 577; financing of, 481–82; "gallery of characters" and Group Theatre actors, ❡21.6; and Group rehearsals, 481–82; last-minute change, 482; latent and manifest meanings, 465–66, 469–70; and London production, 509; and London tour, 506; Lorna, external model for, 125; as model for movie clichés, 466; CO's descriptions of Fuseli, Roxy, and Tokio, 469, 472–73; and CO's fear of loss of creativity, ❡4.4; CO, on integrating narrative and psychology, 511; CO's profane vs. sacred fantasies of father, ❡14.12; opening of, 485; origin of, 426; origin of gangster image, 32; plot of, 465, 470; reviews of, 485–86, 491; road tour of, 510, 541
    identity elements: compassionate mother-symbol, (Poppa Bonaparte), 470–72; corruptible dreamer (Joe Bonaparte), ❡14.21; disrespectful outcast (Joe Bonaparte), 467; father-surrogate, 468; honest craftsman (Tokio), 473; internalized father (Fuseli), ❡14.19; Jew (Roxy), 473; homosexual (Eddie Fuseli), 468; maternal anima/orphan (Lorna Moon), 467; misogynist (Fuseli), 468; possessive corrupter (Eddie Fuseli), 468–69; seductive father-surrogate (Tom Moody), 467–68; *symbol:* moon as

GOLDEN BOY (Odets) (*Cont.*)
     unattainable Woman (Lorna
     Moon), 467, ◖21.3; murder
     of innocent as destruction of
     creative self, 467; self/gun
     as phallus, 469, ◖21.4;
     theme: need to be Somebody,
     465, ◖21.1; death as belong-
     ing, 475; death at impasse,
     476, ◖21.8; death as restora-
     tion of lost paradise, 468;
     destruction of self/creative
     "tool," 468, 474; material
     vs. spiritual values, 470, 474
Golden Boy musical, 5
"Golden Fleece." *See* GOLDEN BOY
"Golden Gloves." *See* GOLDEN BOY
Golden Years, The (Shaw), 571
Goldman, Emma, 34, 51
Goldwyn, Samuel, 397
Good Earth, The (film), 406, 410, 418,
     427, 500
Goodley, William, 8
*Good Soldier Schweik, The. See Johnny
     Johnson*
Gordin, Jacob, 56
Gordon, Michael, 477, 565
Gordon, Mrs. Michael, 565
Gordon, Ruth, 338, 370–71
Gorelik, Mordecai (Max), 175, 204,
     339, 576
Gorky, Maxim, 361, 423
Gorodetsky, Zipporah (CO's grand-
     mother), 21, 110, 119
Gorodetsky (CO's grandfather), 21,
     26
Grand Theatre, 70
Grant, Cary, 7, 8
Grayson, Bette (née Lipper) (later
     Mrs. Clifford Odets), 592–94, 605,
     606, 645, 677
Great God Brown, The (O'Neill), 92
Great Waltz, The (film), 501
Great Ziegfeld, The (film), 405
Green, Paul, 194, 203, 367, 409, 424
Greenbaum family, the, ◖14.14n
"Greenbaum family play," 236, 237,
     239, 242. *See also* AWAKE AND
     SING!
Greenbaum, Paul, 78, 85
Green Mansions, 264–74
Greenstreet, Sydney, 146
Greenwich Village, 33, 69, 83, 84, 87,
     105, 247
Group Theatre, the, 56, 84n, 142; and
     actors' committee, 261, 423, 436–
     37, 443; and actors' search for
     play, 311; analysis of current
     breakdown, 443–44; and com-
     munal ethos, ◖13.8; and attacks
     on Clurman, 509; and attitude

toward "defectors" to Hollywood,
515–18; and attitudes toward CO's
marriage, 447; and *Awake and
Sing!* and *Waiting for Lefty*
in Philadelphia, 379, beginnings,
170, 173, 174, 175, 179, 186;
beginning of breakdown of, 428;
chrysalis of, 169; Clurman on, in
New York Times article, 206; in
crisis, 423, 443–44, 672–76;
critical acclaim for, 559; and
"defections" to Hollywood, 394;
and demands on CO, 346, 399;
dissension within, 260–61; end of,
607; "end of," announced by
press, 444; and failure of *Gold
Eagle Guy,* 311; first season in
New York, 205–6; first summer,
Brookfield Center, 193–204; and
Golden Boy in London, 509;
Golden Boy as peak experience,
481; and guest playwrights, 222;
and Hollywood, 456–59, 516–18;
ideological conflicts within, 423;
as ideologically cemented collective, 203; and improvisations,
226, 230; as independent producing organization, 207; Kazan's
report on Hollywood, 456–57; last
plan for reorganization of, ◖23.3;
and loss of "religious" coherence,
566, 567; meaning to CO of, 193–
95, 197, 201–3, 221, 235, 274,
297, 346, 392, 553–54, 570; *Men
in White,* first hit, 266, 275; and
need for plays, 418–19; *Night
Music* as last chance for, 594; CO
as new playwright of, 319; and
CO's financial support of, 429,
545; and CO's sense of pressure,
515; CO's view of, 553–55; and
Paradise Lost campaign, 385–86;
politics in, 287; and problems of
survival, 398–99, 566–67; and
production of *Paradise Lost,*
382–83, 384–85; and Luise
Rainer, 424, 479; and recognition
by "bourgeois" press, 319; reconstituted, 476; need for reorganization of, 456–57; revival of *Awake
and Sing!* and *Waiting for
Lefty,* 371; *Rocket to the Moon*
as first love play of, 521; season
in Boston, 299–311; and second
summer, Dover Furnace, 221–
239; as spiritual experience, 201;
Lee Strasberg and Cheryl Crawford resign, 457, 458–59; summer
at Lake Grove, Long Island, 564–
73; and summer rehearsals at
Ellenville, NY, 289, 290, 297–99;

and suspicion from establishment theatre, 205; as theatre of meaning, 565–67; and "truth sessions," 565–67; a turning point in, 297; waits for CO's *The Silent Partner*, 409; and working as unit, 280
Guggenheim Foundation, the, 383, 394

Habimah Players, 404
Hairy Ape, The (O'Neill), 186, ¢10.4
Half-Moon Hotel, 343, 348
Hampden, Walter, 92
Hansen, Harry, 358
Harburg, E. Y., 405
Harding, Warren G., 54
Harlow, Jean, 266
Harris, Jed, 338, 372–76, 380, 384, 396, 406
Harvey, Herman, 638n
Having Wonderful Time (Kober), 461, 476
Haydn, Franz Joseph, 49
Hayes, Helen, 338, 491, ¢22.0
Hays, Will, 50
Hecht, Ben, 501
Heckscher Foundation, 64
Hedda Gabler (Ibsen), 511
Heifetz, Jascha, 485
Heilpern, Carl, 95, 96
Heilperns, the, 96, 99
Helen (CO's friend), 338
Hell Hole, the, 32, 50n, 87
Hellman, Lillian, 128, 455n, ¢13.2
Hemingway, Ernest, 127, 386, 495, 548–49
Hepburn, Katharine, 299
Hethmon, Robert, 74, 186, 202
Hiss, Alger, ix, 106, 512, 513
Hitler, Adolf, 55, 247–48, 512, 574, ¢4.1
Holden, William, 577
"Hollywood Ten," the, 243
Holmes, John Haynes, 380, 386
Holocaust, the, 547
Holtz, Lou, 386
"Home Burial" (Frost), 227
Homecoming, The (Pinter): and creative conflicts in, ¢14.5, ¢22.16
Hoover, J. Edgar, 50, 51
Hopkins, Gerard Manley, x
Hotel Meurice, 166, 173, 174
House of Connelly, The (Green), 195, 203, 204, 206, 208, 209
Horowitz, Harry ("Gyp the Blood"), 32, 39
Howard, Sidney, 248, 338, 367, 371, 380, 576
Howe, Irving, ¢14.25
House Un-American Activities Committee (HUAC), 13, 243, 287n, 304n, 363, 512–13, 562
HUAC. *See* House Un-American Activities Committee
Hudson Theatre, 92
Hugo, Victor, 51, 106, 186
Hull, Cordell, 365
"hunger marchers," 208
Huston, Walter, 92
Huxley, Aldous, 128

Ibsen, Henrik, 24, 55, 124, 612
"Ice, Fire, and Decay" (Burke), ¢22.11
I CAN'T SLEEP (Odets), 353–57; *analysis of*, 356–57; *identity-element:* beggar, 356, 357; idealized father-symbol (Sam Blitzstein), 356; coward, 357; Jew, denial of, 357; *symbol:* of fidelity, 357
Iceman Cometh, The (O'Neill), ¢23.24
identity: American, 73, 370, 411, 415, ¢22.20; and salesmanship and innocence, ¢7.4; collective, as outcast (in 1930's), 173; confusion, ¢5.1; elements, ¢14.9; -elements and fragments, ¢6.3, ¢22.6; -elements and "splitting," ¢22.3; evolution of, 624; gender confusion and creativity, ¢17.5; German-American, 512; and "I-ness," ¢22.13; Jew, "outsider's" identification with, 193; Jewish, 126, 222, 238, 300, 302, 390, 404, ¢14.1; Jewish-American, ¢1.1, ¢16.1; Jewish: Freud on, ¢2.4; minority groups and self-contempt, 148; and name changes, 18, 99n, 122, 372, ¢3.2, ¢3.7, ¢13.2, ¢14.1; nationalities, 237; in nations, 247–48; and nose surgery, 18; precursors of, in actors, ¢2.13; and psychological wholeness, ¢2.12; and self, ¢5.1; and self-identity in American minorities, ¢21.1–21.2; and social roles, ¢4.7; and survival, ¢21.1–21.2. *See also* Odets, Clifford, *Self-Identity Issues*, IDENTITY-ELEMENTS
ideology: Christianity, 505; Communist, 282; international "Bruderschaft," 282; Marxist, 142, 359, ¢2.2; and millenarianism, ¢18.5; and postwar "popular radicalism," 50; and revolutionary idealism, 474; and theatre, ¢22.0; and utopianism, 281–82
Idiot's Delight (Sherwood), ¢19.1

I GOT THE BLUES (Odets), 227, 239, 242, 245, 249, 250, 252, 253, 254, 257–58, 260, 262, 263, 267, 268, 271, 272, 273–74, 276, 277, 278, 289, 290, 300, ◖12.2. *See also* AWAKE AND SING!

Inge, William, 28

internalization, 249–50, ◖2.4. *See also* Odets, Clifford, *Self-Identity Issues* and *Work-Related Issues*, IDENTITY-ELEMENTS

Izvestia, 361

Jackson, Ruth, ◖18.2

Jannings, Emil, 92

Jazz Singer, The (film), 111, 127, ◖6.4

James, William, 170

Jean (CO's friend), 95

Jeidel, Edgar, 239

Jeidel, Walter, 239

Jews, identity and tradition, 122

Jewish-Americans, and pressure to succeed, ◖1.3

Jewish immigrants: differences between German and Russian, 18; First Wave, 101n; Third Wave, 17–18, ◖1.3

Jewish King Lear, The, 56

Jewish problem, the, 495, 512, 547, 561, ◖14.2

Johnny Johnson (Green and Weill), 409, 423, 428–29, 432, 437

Johnson, Manning, 363n

Jolson, Al, 92, 111, ◖6.4

Jouvet, Louis, 547

Joyce, Alice, 92

Joyce, James, 186

Juanita, "Poetess of Greenwich Village," 33

Judgment Day (Rice), 328n

Junior Dramatic Club, 60

Juno and the Paycock (O'Casey), 92

Kahn, Otto, 211, ◖6.2

Kahn, Rose, 106, 216

Kauffman, Stanley, 153

Kaufman, George S., 422n

Kaufman, Sidney, 541

Kaye, Danny, 8

Kazan, Elia ("Gadg" or "Gadget"), 275, 281, 302, 303, 305, 353, 426, 443, 456, 459, 476–77, 498, 511, 515, 518, 567, 570, 576, 582, 593, 610; Lee Cobb's impression of, 510; and friendship with CO, 294, 373; as Fuseli in *Golden Boy,* 469; and impression of CO, 299; and impression of Jean Renoir, 11; in London, 509; and CO's

death, 10–11, 13; on CO and "waste," 73; CO's view of, ◖14.21 (in *Night Music*), 598; and response to *Waiting for Lefty,* 315–16

Kazan, Molly. *See* Thacher, Molly Day

Kazin, Alfred, x, 13, 58, 127, 315, 324–25

Kelleher, Joseph (Joe), 301–2, 305, 366

Kellogg-Briand Peace Pact, 130n

Kemp, Harry, 34, 84, 88, 90

Kent, Rockwell, 87, 545

Kent, Frances (Mrs. Rockwell), 545

Kibbee, Lois, 579

King Kong (film), 563

Kingsley, Sidney, 245, 266, 287, 368, 428

Kirkland, Alexander, 302, 379

Kishinev pogroms, ◖2.2

Klein, George S., ◖6.3

Kline, Herbert, 312, 317, 368, 392

Knopf, Alfred A., 358

Kober, Arthur, 409

Kobland, Herman (Koblanov) ("Von"), 36, 47, 49, 59, 64, 76, 86, 87, 89, 94, 96, 100, 103, 109, 162, 173, 200, 201, 289, 338, 350, 358, 392, 498, 546, 563, 577, 581, ◖3.10, ◖5.3

Koblanov, Herman. *See* Kobland, Herman

Koner, Pauline, 158

Kozlenko family, the, 358

Kozlenko, Leonore ("Lee") (Mrs. William), 163, 194, 605, 606

Kozlenko, William, 107, 117, 123, 154, 163, 189, 194, 200, 564, 605, 606

Kramer, Stanley, 582

Kramm, Joseph, 99n, 128, 141

Kris, Ernst, ◖13.9

Kristallnacht (night of broken glass), 523

Krutch, Joseph Wood, 276, 285; on *Awake and Sing!,* 326; on *Rocket to the Moon,* 538

Ku Klux Klan, 513

Kurnitz, Harry, 24, 124, 125, 338

Laboratory Theatre, 141

Ladd, Schuyler, 77

LaGuardia, Fiorello, 284, 386

"La Pasionaria" (Dolores Ibarruri), 423

Larimore, Earle, 146, 147

LAW OF FLIGHT (Odets), 366, 400, 419, 489, 494, 495

law of flight (*ley de fuga*), 302

Lawrence, D. H., 518

Lawrence, Vincent, 132–33, 409

Lawson, John Howard, 110, 141, 212,

222, 223–24, 234, 239, 242, 258, 285–87, 358, 367, 380, 394, 418, 424, 455n, 567, ◖4.8, ◖6.2, ◖13.1; on *Awake and Sing!*, 327; background of, ◖13.2; Clurman's view of, 285; and dispute with CO, 563; to Hollywood, 128; identity as Jew, 223; and material vs. spiritual values, 222–23; CO compared to, 496; and CO's trip to Cuba, 362–63; CO's view of, 223; in Paris, 56

LeBaron, William, 397

Leaves of Grass (Whitman), 125

Lebowitz, Gordon, 159, ◖9.7

LeGallienne, Eva, 141, 243

Leof, Charlotte, 122, 233

Leof, Madi. *See* Ross, Madeleine Leof

Leof, Milton Arno (Mickey), 122, 123

Leof, Morris Vladimir ("Poppa"), 122–24, 352, 380, 522

Leof, Sabina (Tibi), 124

Leof family, the, 358

Les Misérables (Hugo), 51

Levant, Oscar, 430

Leventhal, Jules, 92, 93, 94, 95, 96, 128

Levin, Meyer, 158

Levine, Abe, 154

Levine, Ida Mae (Mrs. Abe), 26, 27, 29, 31, 35, 154, 390, ◖2.5

Levy, Matthew, 284

Levy, Melvin, 287

Levy, "Mom," 87

Lewin, Albert, 418, 460, 575–76, 582–83, 611

Lewis, John Frederick, 124

Lewis, Robert (Bobby), 209, 279, 296, 298–99, 312, 399, 460, 477, 567, 606

Lewis, Sinclair, 110, 386, 404, 563

Lewis, "Whitey," 32

Lewisburg Penitentiary, 124

Lewisohn Stadium, 64

life-cycle: adaptations in, ix–xii, ◖2.4, ◖2.15

Life magazine, 490

Life With Father (Day), 564

Lillie, Beatrice, 338, 350, 366

Lincoln Press, 58

Lindbergh, Charles A., 111

Lin Yutang, 418

Lipper, Bette. *See* Grayson, Bette

Lippmann, Walter, 105, 386

Literary Digest, 343

Living Newspaper, the, 492

Locke, Katherine, 604

Loeb, Philip, 168

Loew, David, 575–76

Loew, Marcus (Max), 575

London, Jack, 34

London Observer, The, 491

Long Day's Journey into Night (O'Neill), ◖23.4

Long, Huey, 101, 512

Longacre Theatre, 101

Loos, Anita, 405

Lord, Pauline, 92

"Lovelorn Corona" (typewriter), 100, 115–16, 117, 467n

Loves of Jeanne Ney, The (Ehrenburg), 424, 436, 460. *See also* RIVER IS BLUE, THE

Loy, Myrna, 405

Lubner, Frank (CO's cousin), 39, 116, 153, 352

Lubner, Nettie Geisinger (CO's aunt), 39

Luce, Clare Booth, 338

Lunt, Alfred, 92, 144, 174

Luxemburg, Rosa, ◖3.4

Lyceum Theatre, 94

Lynn, Eleanor, 510, 582

Lyons, Leonard, 562

Lockridge, Richard, on revival of *Awake and Sing!*, 552; on *Golden Boy*, 486; on *Rocket to the Moon*, 538

Maas, Joachim, 439

Mab. *See* Anderson, Gertrude Maynard

MacArthur, Charles, 338, 372, 491

MacArthur, Douglas, 208

MacLaine, Shirley, 8, 12

MacLeish, Archibald, 322, 366, 380, 386

Mae Desmond Players, 99–100, 101, 102, 103, 129, 131

Main Street (Lewis), 404

Malden, Karl, 477

Malraux, André, 423

Maltz, Albert, 243

Mamoulian, Rouben, 127, 141, 147, 524

"Manly Art, The." *See* GOLDEN BOY

Mann, Daniel, 8

Mann, Thomas, 128

Mantle, Burns, on *Golden Boy*, 486

Marcantonio, Vito, 365

Marco Millions (O'Neill), 141, 142, 144

Martha ("Little Thing") (CO's friend), 136, 138

Marvin, Mark, 317

Marx, Harpo, 386

Marx, Karl, 281

Marx, Rudolph, 505

Mary Ann (CO's friend), 135, 138

mass media, and cultural history, 93, 129, 131, 487, 515, 586, 600, 606, ◖6.4, ◖8.2

Masses, The. See New Masses, The

Mayer, Louis B., 9, 394, 397, 404, 427, 448, 461, 489, 519–20, 573–74
McCarten, John, 42, 47, 85, 490
McClendon, Rose, 367
McClintic, Guthrie, 300
McIntyre, Marvin H., 365, 546
McIntyre, O. O., 408
McKenney, Ruth, on *Rocket to the Moon*, 539
Meisner, Sanford, 149, 209, 226, 280, 302, 305, 312, 317, 371, 482, 530
Melting Pot, The (Zangwill), ◀1.1
Meltzer, Lewis, 524
Mencken, H. L., 124
Mendieta-Batista regime, 362–66
Mendieta, Carlos, 362
Men in White (Kingsley), 266, 275, 279, 289, 299, 302
Meredith, Burgess, 328
Merida, Carlos, 555
Merlin, Frank, 277, 278, 280, 322
Metro-Goldwyn-Mayer Studios, 7, 405, 489, 508
Meyerhold Theatre, 361, 288–89
Michaels, H. C., Advertising Company, 77
Midnight (Initially, "In the Meantime") (Sifton), 86, 163
Milestone, Kendall, 398
Milestone, Lewis, 397–98, 406, 407, 424, 426, 436, 444, 448, 583
Millay, Edna St. Vincent, 110
Miller, Arthur, 128, ◀22.3, ◀22.15
Mills Novelty Company, 48
Millstein, Ernie, 48, 563
Milstein, Nathan, 397
"Miracle Plays." *See also* theatre, 492
Miracle, The, 76–77, 78
Modern Screen, 463
Moeller, Philip, 34, 37, 40, 141, 163, 164, 174, 207, 228, 235, 243, 273, 289
Monroe, Marilyn, 474n
Mooney, Thomas J., 106
"Morgue at Miramar, The," 419. *See also* LAW OF FLIGHT
Morosco Theatre, 56
"Morose Mr. Morgan, The," 609–10
Morris High School, 58, 59, 64, 93
Moscow, 105, 361
Moscow Art Theatre, 56, 141, 155, 289
Moscow Trials, 524
Moses, and the Promised Land, ◀16.7
Moss vaudeville circuit, 70
Mostel, Zero, 13
Most Likely to Succeed (Dos Passos), ◀13.2
Mourning Becomes Electra (O'Neill), 164
Mozart, Wolfgang Amadeus, 49, 182
Mumford, Lewis, 345, 386

Murray, Henry, xii
Mussolini, Benito, 367–68, 409
"Myrt and Marge," 218

Nathan, George Jean, 107, 124, 451, 490, 538, 559, 600, ◀14.2
Nation, The, 326, 538
National Broadcasting Company (NBC), 4, 83
National Day of Labor (Germany), 248
Natwick, Mildred, 328
Nazi Germany, 248, 282, 512–13
Nazi-Soviet pact, 572, 574
Nazimova, 55
Neale, Floyd, 120, 121, 132, 133, 164
Negri, Pola, 92
Negro People's Theatre, 367
Neighborhood Playhouse, 78
Nelson, Ruth, 280, 297–98
New City, 359, 370
New Leader, 317
New Masses, The, 50, 312, 326, 328, 343, 358, 367, 384, 539, 562
New Playwrights' Theatre, 128, 141, ◀6.2
New Republic, The, 50, 325, 577
New Theatre League, 317
New Theatre, 288, 306, 307, 312, 313, 319, 328, 343, 367–68, 380, 392
New Theatre and Film, 412n
New York City, 27, 31, 32, 33, 105
New York Herald Tribune, 350n, 383, 387, 422, 486, 537, 552
New York Morning Telegraph, 317–18
New York Morning World, 63
New York Post, 319, 337, 363, 365
New York Public Library, 358
New York Sun, 538, 552
New York Telegraph, 486
New York Times, 13, 112, 245, 258, 279, 327, 336, 368, 385, 408, 537, 539, 552
New York University, 75
New York World-Telegram, 334, 358, 385, 521, 608–9
New Yorker, The, 42, 47n, 85, 111, 112, 113, 134, 307, 490–91
Nietzsche, Friedrich Wilhelm, 51
NIGHT MUSIC (Odets), 82n, 147, 572, 574, 580, 582, 583–91, 594; as an "American" play, 585; analysis of, 585–91; and Boston tryout, 597–605; closes after 22 performances, 607; Eisler's music for, 597; and ending of youthful optimism, 591; excerpt from, 587, 588, 589, 590; and financing, 582; latent and manifest meanings, 585–91; and New York opening, 605–6; CO's doubts about, 583; CO on open-

ing and reviews, 605–6; opening
in Boston, 598; review of, 607–8;
as "Two Monkeys Play," 557–58
  identity-element: aspiring
  feminine anima (Fay
  Tucker), 585, 587; dying
  representative of traditional
  values (Rosenberger), 585,
  587; feeder and protector
  (Rosenberger), 588; Jew/
  Greek, 587; merchant father,
  afraid of losing face (Mr.
  Tucker), 587; proud, lonely
  outsider (Steve Takis), 587;
  symbol: cricket as singer/
  artist of the night, 585; young
  couple as Adam and Eve,
  662, ◀19.6; *theme:* to conquer the Enemy within, 591;
  the drive for an autonomous,
  self-respecting life, 591;
  generational continuity, 586–
  87; to transpose "sordidness
  into beauty," 585; struggle
  against sterile conformity,
  587, 588, 589
Night at an Inn (Dunsany), 95, 136
Night Over Taos (Anderson), 202, 208,
  209, 211
1931 (Sifton), 206, 207
910 EDEN STREET (Odets), 186–88,
  199, 206, ◀14.10
Nizer, Louis, 519, 521
Norton, Elliot, 598–99
Nugent, Frank, on *The General Died
  at Dawn,* 408
Nuremberg racial laws, 328

obedience, ◀19.5
O'Casey, Sean, 92, 325, 343

ODETS, CLIFFORD. This entry is divided
into the following sections:
Chronology
Family
CO Quoted
Self-Identity Issues
  LETTERS TO OTHERS
  OTHERS' IMAGE OF
Work-Related Issues
  CRITICAL EVALUATION OF AND
    RESPONSE TO
  WRITINGS

Chronology
  BIRTH, 24; EARLY FAMILY LIFE,
  25; INFANCY AND EARLY CHILD-
  HOOD: first step, 27; spells "doll"
  and "baby," 27; first move to
  N.Y.C., 27; earliest memory, 27;
  return to Philadelphia, 27; birth of
sister Genevieve, 30; second move
to N.Y.C., 31; childhood, 35–46;
birth of sister Florence, 38; move
to 783 Beck Street, 38; plays the
Prince in *Cinderella,* 42;
ADOLESCENCE, 44; period of
Jewish religiosity, 47; Hebrew
instruction, 47; first seduction
(at 13), 47; piano lessons, 49;
discovers Victor Hugo, 51; to
Boy Scout Camp, 53; discovery of
classic plays, 55; enters high
school, 58; wins declamation
medal, 60; acts in school plays,
60–61; leaves school, 64; joins
Drawing Room Players, 64; employed by father, 67; secret
"literary" output, 68; elocutionist,
70; diary (1924), 73; (says)
begins first novel, 73; loses first
acting job, 74; takes course at
New York University in Advertising and Selling, 75; leaves
father's employ, 76; begins day-
night reversal, 77; recites on
radio, 83; becomes "The Rover
Reciter," 83; in Greenwich Village
milieu, 84; joins Harry Kemp's
Poet's Theatre, 84; performs in
amateur theatre, 85; menial job
and romance on Fishers Island,
85–87; abandons "business" jobs,
88; first real disc jockey, 89; "New
York's youngest critic," 90; first
production of radio play, *At the
Water-Line,* 91; moves to Philadelphia, 94; leaves new home in
Philadelphia, 96; writes more,
98; obtains job with Mae Desmond Players, 99; unverified
marriage to Roberta, 103; (says)
begins first novel (second time),
108; dramatics counselor, Camp
Arthur, 109–10; in *Abie's Little
Rose,* 111; ADULTHOOD, 112;
struggles for existence in New
York City, 113; writing novel,
Brandy of the Damned, 117;
dramatics counselor at Camp
Tioga, 117; spends time with the
Leofs, 122; shares room with
Joseph Kramm, 128–29; in *Conflict* with Spencer Tracy, 132;
Roberta presumably shoots
daughter and self, 135; hired for
Theatre Guild tour, 141; infatua-
tion with Sylvia Field, 144–50;
plays galley slave in *Marco
Millions,* 143; "rebirth" in De-
pression, 143; first and second
suicide attempt, 146–47; lives

ODETS, CLIFFORD, *Chronology (Cont.)*
in Circle Hotel, 153–54, 155;
start of self-identity crisis, 154,
155; affair with Hortense Alden,
156–59; Camp Scopus, 156–61;
in *Roar China,* 163; in *Midnight,*
163, 165; shares room with Ivan
Black, 165; beginnings, conversion experience, 170, 179, 189;
suicide attempt, 172; "educated"
by Ivan Black, 172–73; attends
pre-Group Theatre meetings, 173,
174, 178, 179, 186; friendship
with Philip Moeller, 174–85, 186,
188–89; begins writing play, *910
Eden Street,* 186–88; resolution
of identity crisis in "conversion"
to Group Theatre, 193; departure
for first Group Theatre summer,
194; return to New York, 205;
tours with *House of Connelly,*
208; back to Philadelphia, 214–20;
directs *Precedent,* 216; writing
short stories, 216; to Dover
Furnace, 221; shaves head,
226–27; writes play, *Victory,*
228–32; begins *I Got the Blues,*
(*Awake and Sing!*), 237; understudies lead in *Success Story,*
238; lives with Strasbergs, 245;
develops close friendship with
Clurman, 246; in *They All Come
to Moscow,* 261; returns to family
in Philadelphia, 262; completes
I Got the Blues, 262; first attempt
at intimacy (Tamara), 264–65;
goes to Green Mansions, 264–74;
Roberta-Joan mystery, 265; plays
businessman (*Men in White*),
266; teaches at Theatre Union,
276–77; meeting with Bess
Eitingon, 277–78; receives first
option money (*I Got the Blues*),
278; moves to 82 Horatio Street,
278; affair with Dena, 279, 307,
369; offer from Hollywood, 280;
plans for production of *I Got the
Blues,* 289; to Ellenville, N.Y.,
with Group, 290, 294, 295, 297,
299; writes *Paradise Lost,* 290;
threatens to quit Group, 297;
with Group to Boston, 299–311;
joins Communist Party, 302;
writes *Waiting for Lefty,* 302;
reads *Waiting for Lefty* to Group
actors, 303; returns to New York
with Group, 311; rejection by
Strasberg, 311, 312, 313; *I Got the
Blues* becomes *Awake and Sing!,*
311–12; Group decides to produce
Awake and Sing!, 312; *Waiting
for Lefty* wins prize, 312; *Waiting
for Lefty* as instant success, 315;
opening of *Awake and Sing!,* 321,
323–25; moves to One University
Place, 322; has three plays on
Broadway, 328, 334; plays Dr.
Benjamin (*Waiting for Lefty*),
335, 377; is lionized; offers from
Hollywood, 334, 337–38; hires
Herman Kobland as secretary,
338; death of mother, 347–53;
publication of *Three Plays,* 358;
appears as speaker at protest
meetings, 359; political activity
in Cuba, 362–66; resigns from
Communist Party, 366; confrontation with Pirandello, 367–68;
leaves cast of *Waiting for Lefty,*
379; involvement in causes,
380–81; *Paradise Lost* goes into
production, 382–83; applies to
Guggenheim Foundation, 383;
launches campaign to save
Paradise Lost, 385–92; goes to
Hollywood, 396; contracts to write
The General Died at Dawn, 398;
works on *The Silent Partner* and
The General Died at Dawn, 400;
meets Luise Rainer, 406; leaves
California for Nichols, Connecticut, 418, 421; accused by press of
"selling-out" to Hollywood, 421–
22; in Nichols, Connecticut,
revising *The Silent Partner,* 425;
discusses marriage with Luise
Rainer, 426; release of *The
General Died at Dawn,* 428;
works on *The Silent Partner* in
New York, 431; contemplates
marriage with Luise Rainer,
433–36; Luise Rainer arrives in
New York, 433–34; rehearsals
begun for *The Silent Partner,*
437; second trip to Hollywood,
439; files intention to marry
Luise Rainer, 442; *Silent Partner*
production postponed, 442; marries Luise Rainer, 444–45; begins
writing "The Manly Art" (*Golden
Boy*), 446; writing *Golden Boy,*
452, 459; leaves for New York,
463; finishes two acts of *Golden
Boy,* 464; becomes member of
executive council of Group, 476;
reunion with Luise Rainer in
New York, 477; *Golden Boy* opens
and is a hit, 485; brief trips to
Hollywood, 489–92, 500; returns
to New York, 492, 501; sails to
London, 506–8; Luise Rainer sues
for divorce, 508; returns to United

States, 510; rents Henry Varnum Poor house, 510; buys expensive car, 510; has car accident, 511; is pallbearer at Thomas Wolfe's funeral, 511; travels in Canada, 512; in Detroit with Group, 514; finishes *Rocket to the Moon*, 499, 515; in Boston with *Rocket to the Moon*, 520; reconciliation with Luise Rainer, 521; attempts to keep *Rocket to the Moon* open, 539; cover story in *Time* magazine, 539–40; requests visa to Russia for Luise Rainer and himself, 541–42; leaves New York for the South, 546; separation from Luise Rainer, 547; has car accident in Key West, Florida, 547; visits Ernest Hemingway, 548–49; trip to Cuba, 549–50; stays in Mexico City, 550–61; has car accident in Mexico, 555–57; travels to Texas, 561; travels to Chattanooga, Tennessee, 562; meets Fay Wray, 563; works on *Silent Partner* at Skowhegan, Maine, 563; spends summer with Group at Lake Grove, Long Island, 564–73; writes preface for *Six Plays*, 567–68; visits Fay Wray in Maine, 571; adapts Chekhov's *Three Sisters*, 571; works on *Night Music* in Canada, 574; his interest in Communism questioned, 574; adaptation of *Three Sisters* shelved, 576; divorced by Luise Rainer, 578; Frances Farmer affair, 577–79; refuses various film offers, 580; writes *Night Music*, 580–82; writes letter applying for copywriting job, 581; renews courtship of Luise Rainer, 582; arranges financing for *Night Music* through film deal, 582; agrees to write screenplay of *Night Music*, 582; meets Bette Grayson, 592; starts writing a daily journal for 1940, 594; to Boston with *Night Music*, 598; returns to New York for opening of *Night Music*, 605; *Night Music* closes, 607; HOLLYWOOD PERIODS, 5–13, 396–421, 439–63, 489–92, 500; LAST DAYS (1963), 3–13; physical health, 6, 7; "Watteau evening" with Renoirs, 6; hospitalization, 6; visits from friends and celebrities, 7–11; paranoid delusions, 8, 12; attempts to master experience, 7–9; Elia Kazan's description of, 10, 11;

Harold Clurman's description of, 11; reconciliation with father, 10, 12; marriage fantasy, 10, 11–12; Jean Renoir's description of, 11; Lee Strasberg's description of, 11; and Louis J. Odets, 12; relation with son, 12; death, 13;

Family

BIRTH OF FLORENCE, 38; BIRTH OF GENEVIEVE, 30; CONFLICTS WITHIN, 39, 102, 105, 108, 214, 262, ⏴13.7; DEVOTION TO MOTHER AND SISTER, 51; DISPLACEMENT BY SISTER, 30, 31; EVENTS, 35–38, 39–45, 47–49, 51–54, 85; theatre and movie outings, 36; AND HISTORICAL BACKGROUND, 17–20; HISTORY OF, 18–23; JEWISH TRADITION AND IDENTITY IN, 26; "LAST WILL AND TESTAMENT" (1924 DIARY), 80–81; RELATIONS BETWEEN FATHER AND MOTHER, 23, 25, 26, 36, 39, 40, 119, 351; RELATIONS WITH FATHER, 71, 72, 218, 227, 233, 322, 353, 373, 388, ⏴2.9; accommodation between, 67, 116, 159; assaults by, 96, 108, 115–16; both as "artists manqué," 59, ⏴14.11; as "chums," 109; conflicts between, 63, 82; and his corruptibility, 94; father as model and antagonist, 72; dependence on him as go-between, 99, 393; father's image of son as "coward," 37; fear of/pride in his strength, 25, 37, 59, ⏴22.19; hatred of, in retrospect, 89; identification with him, 57, 378; image of, as "big man," 33, 35–36; inscription to him, 358; money to him, 357, 393, 488, 499, 503, 507, 509, 544, 563, 580–81, 583; mutual ambivalence, 232; positive feelings for him, 12, 35, 54, 94, 118; "profane vs. sacred" fantasies of him, 54, 61, 256, 258, 294, ⏴14.12; called "Putty" by father, 30; reconciliation (last days), 10, 12; role reversal, 12, 110, 357, 379–80, 393–94, 503, 564–65; as source of shame to, 43, 59, 63, 83, 85; yearning towards, 83, 144, 394; RELATIONS WITH MOTHER, 63, 78, 214–16, 220, 310, 323, 335–36, 498, ⏴1.2, ⏴2.5, ⏴10.2, ⏴18.5; and her ambitions for him, 27, 29, 30; beaten by, 40; dedication of *Six Plays* to, 567; and a dream, 560–61; as disappointment to, 100; and

ODETS, CLIFFORD, *Family* (*Cont.*)
his "divine rights," 29; engulfing
intimacy of, 27, ◖5.3; and his
guilt, 357; and image of her,
82; internalization of, 102; other's
image of, as tender, 154; and
plan to move her to N.Y.C., 351;
and his poem to, 95; response
to her death, 347–50; sense of
abandonment by, 30, 31, 46, 115,
362, ◖5.3; and his "specialness,"
27; AND RELIGIOSITY, OUTER
TRAPPINGS OF, 48; ROSSMAN
HOUSEHOLD: Jewish tradition and
identity, 28; Yiddish spoken in,
28; SURROGATE BROTHERS: Jay
Adler, 8; "Beck Street Boys," 42;
Ivan Black, 172; Harold Clurman,
297, 312, 475, 557; Elia Kazan,
294, 373, 475; SURROGATE FAMI-
LIES: Adlers, 53; "Beck Street
Boys," 42; Blitzsteins, 352;
Cohens, 53; Group Theatre, 333;
Heilperns, 96; Kahns, 106; Leofs,
122–24, 216, 217, 352; Levys,
42; Millsteins, 48; Rossmans, 28,
100, 108–9, 154, 352–53, 358,
488, 495, 563, 583; Strasbergs,
245; Tunicks, 53; SURROGATE
MOTHERS, Ella Reeve Bloor, 87,
352; Margaret Brenman-Gibson,
87; Edith Mayer Goetz, 87; "Mom"
Levy, 87; "Romany Marie," 87;
"Tante Esther" Rossman, 87,
352–53; Irene Mayer Selznick,
87; Paula Miller Strasberg, 87,
245; Mrs. Watson, 561; SURRO-
GATE FATHERS: Sidney Norton
Baruch, 89–90, 120; Mr. Brill,
94, 120; Harold Clurman, 210,
236, 582; Waldo Frank, 214, 306;
Jed Harris, 372–76; Harry Kemp,
84, 120; M. V. Leof, 122–23, 124;
Philip Moeller, 164–65, 174; Floyd
Neale, 120; Lee Strasberg, 210,
313; Walter Winchell, 120;
VALUES, MATERIAL VS. SPIRITUAL,
21, 27, 28, 31, 48, 53, 83, 122

CO Quoted
ON ACTING: and auditioning, 144;
dissatisfaction with, 266–67,
299; ON ACTOR AND "SUPPLIES,"
67; ON AMERICAN "ARISTOCRACY,"
602; ON THE AMERICAN TOWN,
562; ON ANALYZING CHARACTER,
432; ON ANGER, 73; ON "THE ARIS-
TOCRAT AND THE PEASANT," 179;
ON ART: vs. life, 396; making as
freeing, ◖22.23; as propaganda,
380; ON ARTIST: in America, 265,

343; asceticism in, 271; as hero,
◖22.23; ON AT THE WATER-LINE,
91; ON AWAKE AND SING!, 251;
and "Bessie," 254; ending of, 258,
321; intentions in writing, 240;
and "Uncle Morty," 255–56; ON
TALLULAH BANKHEAD, 377; ON
SIDNEY BARUCH, 90; ON BEETHO-
VEN, 171–72, 175–77, 228–29,
234; ON BEING BULLIED, 82; ON
BLOCKED HUMAN ASPIRATIONS,
73; ON BUYING LIQUOR, 299; ON
CALIFORNIA, 46; ON CHRISTIANITY,
505; ON HAROLD CLURMAN, 165–
66, 283, 595, 610; and *I Got the
Blues*, 268; and the "Russian
soul," 603–4; and *Victory*, 236–37;
AS COMFORTER, 106; ON COMMU-
NISM IN AMERICA, 600; ON CHERYL
CRAWFORD, 141; ON CREATIVE
PROCESS, 155, ◖22.1; and prob-
lems, 371, 379; wellspring of,
382; ON CRITICS IN AMERICA,
606–7; IN DAILY WORKER INTER-
VIEW, 482–83; ON DEATH OF
MOTHER, 347–50; ON DESIRE FOR
ANONYMITY, 369; ON DIFFICULTY
OF WRITING NOVEL, 133; ON
DREAM ABOUT PRESIDENT ROOSE-
VELT, 550; ON EARLY RADIO, 83;
ON EFFECTS OF SCHOOL, 602; ON
HANNS EISLER, 597; ON EVILS OF
SELF-INDULGENCE, 602–3; ON
EVOLUTION OF THE AMERICAN,
551; ON FAMILY LIFE, 24; ON
FATHER, 25, 26, 39, 72, 94;
demands of, 357; internalization
of, 76; relation to, 35; ON FEAR: of
appearing foolish, 225; of failure,
595–96; of intimacy, 596; ON
FEDERAL THEATRE, 482; ON FEEL-
ING UNWELCOME IN FAMILY, 96;
ON FILM INDUSTRY, 421, 482–83,
562; and strictures on writer,
492–93; ON HIS FISHERS ISLAND
ROMANCE, 85–86; ON LYNN FON-
TANNE, 181; FROM "GENERAL"
NOTES, 493; ON GIVING UP THE
SELF, 518; ON GOLDEN BOY:
excerpt from, 465, 476; and
"Fuseli," 469, 472; and "Roxy,"
457, 472–73; and "Tokio," 473;
ON GREENWICH VILLAGE, 84; ON
GROUP THEATRE: being chosen
for, 186; "conversion" to, 193;
first summer, 194–95; meaning
of, 202–3, 221; threatening to
leave, 283; wanting his plays done
by, 297; ON HEMINGWAY, 549;
ON JED HARRIS, 373–76; ON
VICTOR HUGO, 51; ON HUMAN

RELATIONSHIPS, 446; "I ARRIVE," 273; ON IDENTITY AS ACTOR, 73–74; ON IMAGE OF COW WHO HAS DROPPED A CALF, 515; ON HIS IMAGE AS POLITICAL WRITER, 598–99; ON INNOCENCE, ❡7.4; ON "INNOCENCE" OF POET, 46; "INTERVIEW WITH A CRITIC," 609–10; ON INVASION OF PRAGUE, 513; ON JEWISH IDENTITY, 57; ON JOYS OF COLLABORATIVE WORK, 305; ON ELIA KAZAN, 598; ON D. H. LAWRENCE, 518; ON JULES LEVEN-THAL, 95; ON LIFE-CRISIS, 314; ON LONELINESS ("THE ANXIETY ROYAL"), 30; ON LONELINESS OF WRITING, 432; ON MEMORIES: at age three, 29; at age four, 27; at age five, 30; at age eight, 36–37; at age thirteen, 53; of childhood, 45; ON MEN IN WHITE, 266; ON MERGING OF ACTOR/AUDIENCE, 315–16; ON MIDDLE-CLASS LIVES, 17; ON MOTHER: identification with, 3; internaliza-tion of, 82; ON NEED FOR AGIT-PROP PLAYS, 483; ON NEED FOR PERFECT WIFE, 519; ON NEED TO WRITE LETTERS, 103; ON NIGHT MUSIC: opening night per-formance, 605–6; shock over reviews of, 592, 606; ON NON-ACCEPTANCE OF SELF, 212; ON NOT BELONGING, 88; IN "NOTES FOR DENTIST" (ROCKET TO THE MOON), 490; ON EUGENE O'NEILL, 84; ON PARADISE LOST, 275, 387–88; doubts *re* timing of, 344; "fire bug" scene of, 295; ON PIANOLA AND MUSIC, 49; ON PIRANDELLO AND FASCISM, 367; ON PLANS FOR FUTURE, 100; ABOUT HIS PLAYS, 562; ON PLAY-WRITING: and American audi-ences, 611–12; origins of his characters, 244; tacked-on ideol-ogy, 249; ON A POET, ❡2.3; ON HIS "POSE," 89, 133; ON PSYCHO-HISTORY AND WRITING, 495; ON RAGE TOWARD ROOMMATE, 185; ON LUISE RAINER, 479, 545, 595, 603; ON REALIZATION OF WRITING TALENT, 265; ON ROBERTA AND JOAN, 139–40; ON RUSSIAN FILMS, 371–72; ON SEDUCTION, ❡4.10; ON SELF-DESTRUCTIVENESS, 511; ON SELF-IMAGE, 241, 583; ON SELF-LIBERATION, 210–11, 212; ON SENSE OF: aloneness, 180; being exploited, 515; isolation, 181–82; mortality and work con-

continuity, 221; ON "783 BECK STREET," 38; ON SEXUAL EPISODE, 462; ON SEXUALITY, 225; ON SHAKESPEARE, 548, 558; ON SIBLING RELATIONS, 52; ON SOUTH-ERN BLACKS, 548; ON SPIRITUAL-ITY AND SENSUALITY, 138; ON SPYING ON COUPLE IN FIELD, 46; ON STENDHAL, 611; ON LEE STRASBERG, 262, 283, 604–5; and his "face-saving," 313; ON "SUCCESS," 320–21, 369, 552; ON "THE SUM AND SUB-STANCE," ❡7.4; ON SURROGATE FAMILY (KAHN), 106; ON SWINGS OF SELF-ESTEEM, 260; FROM THE TALMUD, 597; ON TAMARA, 265; ON THEATRE IN AMERICA, 492, 600–1; ON THOUGHTS AS BULLETS, 134; ON TRIP TO CUBA, 363–65; ON TURNING POINTS—ACTOR TO PLAYWRIGHT, 131–32; ON TWO KINDS OF PLAYWRIGHTS, 98; ON UNCLE ISRAEL, 31; ON UNLIVED LIFE, 3; ON "VON" (HERMAN KOBLAND), 89; ON "WHO WAS THE AGGRIEVED . . . ," 30; ON WON-DER OF THEATRE AS ART, 173–74; ON BEING A WRITER, 112; ON YEARNING FOR ACCEPTANCE, 596

Self-Identity Issues
ACTIVITY/PASSIVITY, 72, 155, 172, 174, 183, ❡4.9, ❡7.5; AMERICAN DREAM, THE, 92, 113n, 309–10, 311; ANGER AS MOBILIZING, 461; ANONYMITY, WISH FOR, 462, 581, 599; ATTEMPTS AT SELF-MASTERY, 96; AWARENESS OF NATIONAL PREJUDICE, 38; BROTHER TO ALL, 179, 194; CAPACITY FOR FRESH SIGHT, 27, 184; CLAIRVOYANCE, 156; AND COMMUNAL ETHOS, ❡13.8; AND COMPETITIVENESS, 344; CONFLICT: actor vs. writer, 77–78, 175, 184, 195, 196; ado-lescent, 70, 73; innocent vs. cor-rupter, 121; intimacy vs. creativ-ity, ❡13.4; as Jew, 411; Jewish father vs. Jewish prophet, ❡14.22; "masculine" vs. "feminine," 181; material vs. spiritual values, 470; obedience vs. self-realization, 73; re responsibility, 596; theatre vs. films, 383 (*See also* AND IDENTITY-ELEMENTS); CONSOLATORY PLEAS-URES: 229, 334; drinking, 84, 108, 110, 149, 177, 237–38, 299, 367, 548, 601; eating, 30, 120, 367; love of flowers, 7, 28; masturba-tion, 45, 73, 95; music, 49, 98, 107, 108, 120, 136, 137, 152, 175,

ODETS, CLIFFORD, *Self-Identity Issues* (*Cont.*)

177, 378, 461; reading, 42, 51, 63, 548; sex, 240–41, 377, 462, 549–50; smoking, 73, 80, 95, 120; use of stimulants and drugs, 5; DEATH, PREOCCUPATION WITH, 79, 80, 161, 427; DEPENDENCE ON OTHERS, 136; DIVIDEDNESS, 116; EFFORTS TO INTEGRATE WORK-IDENTITY, 219; AND EVOLUTION OF SELF, ¶2.4, ¶5.1; GENERATIVITY, IMAGERY OF, 180, 488; GENERATIVITY, THROUGH SUPPORT OF ARTISTS, 498; GENEROSITY, 9, 42, 129, 334–35, 345, 358, 392–93, 429, 459, 507, 509, 544, 562, 563, 568; and retraction of, 464; vs. narcissistic giving, ¶24.2; AND GIFT FOR LANGUAGE, ¶5.3; AND GROUP THEATRE, 184, 193–95, 197, 201–3, 208, 210, 221, 235, 274, 297, 312, 346, 392, 553–54, 570; AND GUILT, 357, 474, 588, ¶4.4; AND HATRED AND FEAR OF TYRANNY, 513; IDENTIFICATION WITH: artists, criminals and revolutionists, 42, 44n, 124–27, 246, 381; Beethoven, 49, 158, 171–72, 175–77, 178, 189, 218, 519, 603, 645n; composers (in general), 49; Emerson, 217–18; ethnic minorities, 69; helpless, dependent women, 407; mother, 417, 426; Mozart, 4, 49, 177; the oppressed, 51, 247, 302, 333, 362–66, ¶2.4; Whitman, 125n, 225, 486–87; AND IDENTITY: confusion and creative growth, 151n, 379; crisis of, 194, 494; AND IDENTITY-ELEMENTS, ¶14.22: the abandoned/abandoner, 30, 86, 115, 149n, 431, 439–40, 442, 463, 582, ¶3.1; actor, 37, 42, 61, 64, 67, 73–74, 85, 92, 94, 95, 99–100, 103–4, 113, 142, 163, 212, 222, 279, 377; actor at one with audience, 70–71; actor/elocutionist/drama critic, 83; actor-identity, precursors of, ¶2.13; actor/writer, 94, 100, 224, 225, 304, 460, ¶4.5; aggrieved one, 30, ¶2.4; American, 370, 381, 415; artist, 24, 227, 295, 525; artist (androgynous), 165; artist (manqué), 13, 552; artist (minor), 603; ascetic, 240–41; aspiring innocent, ¶7.4; "bad boy," 454; "big man," 233, 429, 581; child, 184; collector, 6, 7, 9, 25; composer, 49; consoler, 459; coward, 39; craftsman, 473, 476;

cripple/crippler, 70n, 235, 451n, ¶2.4, ¶3.1; "family man," 119, 436; flower/"destroyer of flowers," 160; healer, 307, 358; the innocent vs. corrupter, 121; the isolate, 372; Jew, 12, 57, 69, 100, 146, 184, 187, 188, 200, 217, 237, 281, 303, 306, 325–26, 373, 411, 414, 583–84, 596, ¶9.4, ¶14.10, ¶14.18; Jew, and command of Yiddish, 187; Jew, and conflict, 148, 411; Jew, and name-change, 99; Jewish-American, 475; Jewish prophet/father, ¶14.22; "masculine"/"feminine" persona, 88–89, 91, 241; nurturer, 243, 247, 392, 574, ¶3.5; outsider, 46, 173, 186, 514; performer, 359; playwright, 77, 92, 186, 236, 279, 379, 448, 486–87; playwright (adolescent), 61; playwright (American), 583–84; playwright (second-class), 509; playwright (as self-witness), 536; poet, 30; prisoner, 5, 126, 396, ¶7.8; "psychoanalyst," 144, 435–36; Pygmalion to inner Galatea, 593; reborn child, 263; rescued/rescuer, 206, 544, 593; spectator, 262; voyeur, 46–47; writer, 54, 62, 74, 94, 108, 115, 150, 188–89, 274, 344, 408, 423, 465; IDEOLOGY: adolescent, 44; Christian brotherhood, 472, 569; communal solidarity, 415; Communism, 246–47, 281, 296, 600–1; Communism and CO's view of Nazi-Soviet pact, 572–73, 574; Marxism, 233; and roots of socialism, 44; INTIMACY, 225, 264–65, 267; and creativity, 429, 445, 534; crisis of, 494; fear of, 429, 439–41; and isolation, 534; and need for distance, 431–32; problems with, 165, 271–72 435–36, 461–62, 500, ¶13.4; and Luise Rainer, 421–22, 425–26, 427; as threat to creativity, 529; words as substitute for, 164; ISOLATION, 181–82; "MASCULINE/FEMININE" ISSUES, 91, 157, 450; attempts to integrate, 89; internalization of, 88–89; MISTRUST, 595; and holding back, ¶22.1; and hostility, 160, 359, 362; and sense of being exploited, 503, 544, 552; MOBILIZATION THROUGH ANGER, 598; OBEDIENCE, 27, 29, 43, 76, 153; PHYSICAL HEALTH, 6, 7, 24; AND POLITICAL ACTIVITIES, 359, 363–66, 380–81; RELATIONS WITH MEN: Ivan Black, 170, 172–73,

185; Harold Clurman, 246, 321, 406, 459, 495–97, 509, 553–55, 556–59, 568, 583, 597, 610; Hanns Eisler, 597; Waldo Frank, 306; Jed Harris, 372–76; Elia Kazan, 294, 373, 469; William Kozlenko, 107–8; Philip Moeller, 164–65, 174, 175–79, 180–85, 186, 188–89; Floyd Neale, 120–21; RELATIONS WITH LUISE RAINER, AND MARRIAGE, 406, 418, 425–26, 449, 463, 483; ambivalence, 431–33; competitiveness, 500; courtship, 421–22; divorce, 508; giving and getting, 449; growing rift in, 502, 503–6; intimacy problems, 435–36, 446, 488–89, 497–98, 499, 522, 544–45, 500; her pregnancy, 504–7; renewed courtship, 582; sense of being abandoned, 439–40, 450, 577–78; sexual relations in, 450; violent interactions in, 424, 446, 461–62, 477, 478, 479–81, 500, 541, 545; vis-à-vis Group Theatre, 424; RELATIONS WITH WOMEN (GENERAL): attraction to childlike women, 592; breast "fetish," 180, 564, 592, 593; choice of partners, ◀3.1; cynicism, 102; Don Juanism, 121, 182–83, 225, 269–70, 271, 578, ◀3.1, ◀4.10; exploitiveness, 80, 81, 95, 177, 260, ◀24.2; fantasies of marriage, 10, 369; intimacy, 225, 264–65, 267, 270, 271–72; misogyny, 71, 91, 105, 118, 235–36, 262, 263, 550, ◀2.8; quest for ideal woman, 8, 86, 90, 133, 489, 519, 601, ◀3.1; seduction, 71, ◀4.10; sense of betrayal by women, 114, 422, 521; RELATIONS WITH WOMEN (INDIVIDUALS): Hortense Alden, 156–57, 159–61; Alice, 259–60, 261–62; Betty, 114–15; Nilla Cram Cook, 90–91; Reta Cooper, 86; Dena, 279, 307, 369, 400–1; Helen Deutsch, 300, 301, 307, 360; Frances Farmer, 572, 574; Sylvia Field, 144–52; Ruth Gordon, 370–78; Bette Grayson, 592, ◀24.2; Leonore Kozlenko, 163; Pam, 208; Luise Rainer (*see above*); Phyllis Rodin, 209; Tamara, 262–63, 264–65, 267, 268, 270, 271, 272; "RELIGIOUS" ROOTS, 96; SADOMASOCHISM, 134, 151–52, 160, 241–42, 243, 462, 520–21, 557, 578–79, ◀17.3; fantasies of, 103, 164, 181, 235–36, 253–54, 329, 330, ◀9.1; and father as destructive, ◀16.6; and longing

to submit to tyrant, 368; and profane vs. sacred fantasies of father, 54, 256, 258, 294, 469–70, ◀14.12; and scapegoating others, 452, 479, 480; and self-accusation, 597, 599; and self-destructiveness, 110, 511, 555, ◀22.1; and sense of being abandoned, 468; and sense of betrayal, 503; and suicide attempt, 172; and suicide, preoccupation with, 84, 170, 182; AND SELF-ADJURATIONS, 435–36; AND SELF-ANALYSIS, 153, 596; AND SELF-ASSESSMENT, 113; SELF-ESTEEM ISSUES: and capacity for love, 225; and fear of becoming Nobody, ◀22.1; fear of critics, 311, 326, 336; fear of death of creativity, 564; fear of failure, 336, 344, 346, 384, 483, 539, 541, 545, 552, 577, 582, 594, 595; fear of fraudulence, 43, 78; fear of loss of integrity, 59, 393; fear of internalized father, 599; fear of losing face, 226; fear of own rage, ◀22.1; fear of "repeating self" as artist, 368; need to be accepted as "American" playwright, 400, 584; need to belong, 76, 476, 551, 553–55, 569, 596, ◀2.4; need to be "big man," 497; need for brotherhood, 201, 247, 302; need for "fidelity," 357; need to impress, 199, 210, 241–42; need to "parent," 52, 118, 393; need for reassurance, 54, 71, 157, 228, 384, 433, 460, ◀22.1; need for self-concealment, 183; need to be "special," 58, 109, ◀5.4; need for supplies (food), 449; sense of disintegration, ◀22.17; swings in self-esteem, 6, 10, 42, 59, 71, 73, 99–100, 103, 124, 177, 258, 398, 415, 448, 577, 583–84, ◀14.14, ◀19.4; and vulnerability to criticism, 336–37, 346, 539, 541; SEXUALITY, 46, 90, 212, 377, 450; and asceticism, 240, ◀13.4; breast "fetish," 180, 564; childhood aversion to, 48; conflicts, 79; Don Juanism, 121, 269–70, 271, 578; fear of vagina, 550; homosexual anxieties, 119, 121, 183, 218, 225; identification with woman, 164; and masculine power, 177; misogyny, 550; and older woman, 269–70; tenderness, 225; SYMBOLS: earth/night/death as "the great mother," 161; flowers as perfect form, 52, 102, 117, 136,

ODETS, CLIFFORD, *Self-Identity Issues* (*Cont.*)

144, 181; injury to creative "tool," 73, ◖4.4; life as a dream, ◖7.3; night as mistress, 134; phallus/ body/self/snake (interchangeable), ◖21.4; plays as children, 253, 489, 593, 606, ◖22.22; words as bullets, 598; words as nourishment, 493n, 564; words as substitute for feelings, 115; SYMPTOMS, ◖22.17; childhood lying, 41, 70; childhood phobias, 28–29; childhood stealing, 40–41, ◖2.10; day-night reversal, 77, 134, 445–46; depression, 5, 78–80, 88, 95, 114–15, 135, 136, 137, 140, 272, 275, 343, 353, 508, 510, 512, 547, 549; fear of insanity, 359; insomnia, 75, 210, 367; moodiness and quarrelsomeness, 335; pain, 520–21; phobias, 5, 497, 585; VALUES, MATERIAL VS. SPIRITUAL, 109, 218–19, 310–11, 470, ◖15.3; WHOLENESS, STRUGGLE FOR, ◖15.1; WILL: gift of conviction, 58, 124; "passion of purpose," 40; WORLD-VIEW, STRUGGLE FOR, 181, 187–89. *See also Work-Related Issues,* "GALLERY OF CHARACTERS"/IDENTITY-ELEMENTS; play analyses

LETTERS TO OTHERS: Hortense Alden, 28–29, 157–58, 159–61, 164; Phil Berg, 502; Betty, 114, 115, 116, 117, 136; Margaret Brenman-Gibson, 30, 49, 120; Goldie Bromberg, 103, 209; John Mason Brown, 337; Harold Clurman, 217, 511–12, 553–55, 557–58; Reta Cooper, 86; Cheryl Crawford, 148, 154; Dena, 307; Helen Deutsch, 299–301, 302, 303, 306–7, 308–10, 311, 360, 421; Sylvia Field, 144–47, 149–52; Waldo Frank, 306; John Gassner, 540; Mr. and Mrs. William Gibson, 5; Ruth Gordon, 371–78; Elia Kazan, 511–12; Herman Kobland, 89, 103–5, 109, 110, 113, 147, 289, 350–51; William Kozlenko, 133, 149, 154, 156; Robert Lewis, 459; Martha ("Little Thing"), 118–19, 136, 138; Mary Ann, 135, 138; Philip Moeller, 34–35, 36, 37, 40, 165, 174, 175–79, 180–85, 186, 188–89; Floyd Neale, 121, 133; Louis J. Odets, 503, 580–81; Pam, 209; Mr. and Mrs. Heinz Rainer, 434–35; Luise Rainer, 425–26, 427, 432, 439–41, 463, 479–80, 488, 497–98, 502, 504, 505–7, 522, 545–46; Sylvia Hoffman Regan, 121; Franklin D. Roosevelt, 541, 560; Irene Fabian Steinberg, 68–70, 71, 72, 87; Lee Strasberg, 344; Tamara, 140, 263, 264, 267–68, 270, 271, 272; Richard Watts, Jr., 383, 387

OTHERS' IMAGE OF: as actor, 8, 60–62, 165, 170, 195, 210, 276; as "angelic"/"babyish," 293; as having "the arrogance of an unarmed man" (Abe Burrows), 627n; as artist, 108, 170, 224, 278, 570; as artist manqué, 73; as an artist/student, 172–73, ◖2.11; as artist/teacher, 276, 279; as ascetic, 235; as austere, 99n, 128; as awe-inspiring, 481; as bewildered, 335; as "brittle" (Frances Farmer), 339; as budding dramatist, 117, 165; as "champion of the underdog," 350n; as "civilized" (Kazan), 299; as Communist, 447; as "concentrated," 224; as creation of Harold Clurman, 312; as eloquent, 262; as emotionally niggardly, 566; as empathic, 246, 247; as enjoying conflict (Luise Rainer), 541; as everyone's older brother, 481; as fallen idol, 447; as "family man," 123; as feeling "special," 57; as "finest revolutionary playwright," 306; as guarded, 133; as hard-working, 5; as healer, 118; as holy disciple (Luise Rainer), 541; as humane, 368; as irritable, 359; as leftwing hero, 302, 317, 366; as a "loner," 158; as "middle class," 550; as a misogynist, 579; as more important to other than vice versa, 260; as "Moses," ◖16.7; as most important person in other's life, 262; as mother's favorite, 31; as musical, 49, 108; as no match for "money men," 448, 583; as overly dependent, 304; as romantic, 170; as "phony," 64, 259; as "primal Christian" (Erikson), ◖4.6; as propagandist, 338; as responding to being needed, 303, 328; as "schizophrenic," 179; as having "sly innocence," 59; as having "special" vision, 37; as a "sprinter," 281, ◖2.12; as suicidal, 170, 172;

as a Svengali, 579; as having swings in self-esteem, 124; as a "vessel ready to burst," 362; as vulnerable, 278; as "wild and noble" (Marlon Brando), 9

Work-Related Issues

PLAYS. *See* individual titles (complete listing on page 619)

AS ARTIST IN AMERICA, 515, 606–7; and lack of affirmation, 231, 411; the merchandising of, 553; AUDIENCE AS PARTICIPANTS, 131; CORE CONFLICTS IN, ◖14.5; CRAFT TECHNIQUE, 611–12; CREATIVE PROCESS: activity/passivity in, ◖8.3; adolescent self-expression, 68, 73; and aggression (unconscious), 134, 416; and asceticism, 199–200; and blood sacrifice, ◖19.9; commerce, 495; commitment and 3rd-act problems in, 371; and conflict, ◖22.8; and conflict resolution, 448, 475, ◖3.1; and conflict, unconscious aspects of, ◖22.15; and continuity in themes, ◖12.2; and creative vs. political concepts, 249; and defect, 202; and dialogue with the self, 416; and drama, problems in, 511; "equidistance from others" in, 262; and equilibrium, 558; evolution of, 228; and "feminine" perspective, 415, 529, ◖7.5; and formal problems, ◖22.3; and generativity, 5, 77, 189, 272, 425, 514, 515, 525, 527, 568; and generativity gestation, imagery of, 239, 337, 378; and hubris, 417; and importance of "the detail," 11; and injury to creative "tool," ◖4.4; and "inspirational burst," 275, 605; interferences with, 344; and isolation, 518–19; as in jeopardy, 345–46; and lack of self-confidence, 82; lack of social support for, in adolescence, 81; and leakage of talent, 97, 594; life vs. art, 431–32, 445, 519, 522, 531, 533, 596; loneliness of, 229, 432; and "madness," 211; marriage as drain on, 445–46; marriage as restorative of, 370; and merging of subjejct and object (actor/audience), 131, 304, 315–16, 491–92; and need to communicate, 103; and need for excitement in self, 45; and need for form, 7; and need for loneliness and disconnection, 152–53;

and need to be needed, 569–70; and need to "objectify," 209; and need for rebirth, 382; and neurosis, 212; and orality, 140, 300; oral metaphor in, ◖8.3, ◖10.3; origins of need to write, 114; and outer stimulus, 475; as own "witness" in, 278; productivity and rebellious brotherhood, 460–61; products of, ◖22.10; and psychohistory, 251, 320, 407, 411, 494, 513, 551, 563, ◖9.2, ◖22.2; reflection of inner struggle, 522; and regression in service of ego, ◖13.9; relation to inner needs, 494; and relation to mother, ◖18.4; and responsibility, ◖4.4; and risk of confrontation, 531; and sadomasochism, ◖17.3; and search for form, 603; and self-exploration, 494; and sense of involuntariness in, 140, 147, ◖8.3; and sensory porousness, 96; and shift from politics to psychology, 524; and shifts in creative center, 494; sublimation of rage in, 588; symbolic representation of, 249–50, 252–53; transpositions of experience in, 330, 624; as uncovering of self, 598; and unity of inner with outer characters, ◖21.6; and values, material vs. spiritual, 528; words as self-nourishment, 493; and working on demand, 353; and work-stoppage, 5, 379, 419, 497, 510; ENDINGS OF FORCED OPTIMISIM, 258–59, 297, 326, 416, 474; EXPRESSING ALLEGORY IN, 412; "GALLERY OF CHARACTERS," 255, ◖4.2; as archetypal, representative and individual, 252; early signs of, 119; and "outer masks," 125, 231, 232, 244, 280–81, 407, 468, 475, 526–27, 586, 587, ◖14.13, ◖14.21, ◖21.6; and "splitting," ◖22.3; "GALLERY OF CHARACTERS"/IDENTITY-ELEMENTS, 249, 292, 407, ◖14.9, ◖22.6, ◖22.9; "feminine" anima, 253, 467, 527, 585, 587; artist, 514, ◖10.1, ◖14.21; artist manqué, 252, 525, 528, 536; "Artist, Spurious," 530; beggar, 356, 357; composite mother/father, ◖14.15; coward, 331, 357; craftsman, 473; cripple, 253, 305, 308; father, 252, 256, 330, 407, 467–68, 525, 526, 527, 528, 536, 587, ◖14.11, ◖14.19; father, idealized, 256–57, 291, 356;

ODETS, CLIFFORD, *Work-Related Issues* (*Cont.*)

feeder, 588; gangster, 294, 468–69; homosexual, 330, 468; idealist, 291, 304, 329, 330, 413, 525–26, 585, 587; the innocent, 256, 293; Jew, 324, 412, 473; Jew, denial of, 357; Jew/Greek, 587; Jewish prophet, ◀14.22; loner, 252; masochist, 294, 295; misogynist, 253–54, 468; mother, 252, 255, 470–72, ◀14.20; outsider, 467, 587; tyrant, 254, 292, 293, 304, 329, 330, 407; "HEIGHTENED REALISM," 412; IDEOLOGY: Marxist, 296–97, 304; religious, 416; revolutionary idealism, 474; IMAGE OF FATHER'S UNCONSCIOUS SELF-IDENTITY, ◀14.17; INTEGRATING MARX AND FREUD, 563; NEED FOR COLLECTIVE THEATRE, ◀15.2; AND PSYCHOHISTORICAL PERSPECTIVE, 301, 570; AND PSYCHOSOCIAL CONFLICTS, ◀2.7; RELATION TO FILM INDUSTRY, 422, ◀20.1; decision to work in, 393–95; difficulty in adapting to, 460; perceived pitfalls, 421; and possibility for art-making, 393, 407, 460; RESPONSE TO CRITICS, 318, 326, 337, 346, 384, 385, 386, 490–91, 540; SYMBOLS, 344–45, ◀16.8; blood sacrifice/Christ, 414, 552, ◀19.5; children as plays, 253; creative anima, ◀22.16; cricket as singer/artist, 585, ◀9.5; critic as artist manqué, 451; fidelity, 357; moon as unattainable Woman, 467, 525, ◀21.3; music, ◀15.4; self/gun/winged animal as phallus, 469, ◀9.6, ◀19.7, ◀21.4; singer (Cleo) as creative impulse, 251, 514, 532, ◀22.2; sleep as death in life, 292; strike as "brotherly love," 415; suicide as "resurrection," 257, 258; words as bullets, ◀8.1; young couples as Adam and Eve, ◀19.6; THEMES, ◀16.4; activation through sex, 527, 528–29; antiwar, 291; aspiration of unfulfilled artist, 530; betrayal, 232, 295, 333, 408, 414; biblical, ◀19.3; blood sacrifice, 305, 414, 417, ◀19.9; "brotherhood of man," 296–97, 333, 413, 414, 474; death, 468, 474, 475, 476, ◀21.8; filicide/patricide/suicide, 332, 416; generational continuity, 586–87; injury to creative "tool," 155, 158, 329, 330, 468, 474; the innocent vs. the possessive corrupter, 121; life vs. art, 232, 233, 533; loss of innocence, 412; material vs. spiritual values, 230, 292, 293, 451, 470, 474, 528, 529, 591, ◀16.5, ◀22.12; murder of innocent as destruction of creative self, 467; need to be Somebody, 465, ◀21.1; profane vs. sacred fantasies of father, 54, 256, 258, 294, 469–70, ◀14.12; rebirth, ◀14.24; redemption, 282; revolt against the oppressor, 408; search for love, 414, 533; search for wholeness, 535; sense of impotence, 413, 527, 530; shame, ◀16.3; struggle against nullification of life, 290, 305, 332, 451, 525, 587, 588, 589, ◀14.7; suicide as "blood sacrifice," 305; suicide as "resurrection," 334; to transpose sordidness into beauty, 585; violence, 416; yearning to help/be helped, 295; yearning for "lost paradise," 415; UNDERLYING ACCUSATION AGAINST FATHER IN SUICIDE THEME, ◀16.6. *See also* artist in America; creative process; play analyses; individual playwrights

CRITICAL EVALUATION OF AND RESPONSE TO: 316–20, 324–27, 336–37, 338, 343, 358–59, 491, 547, 577; attacks by press, 447; *Awake and Sing!*, 324–25; *Awake and Sing!*, as deserving of Pulitzer Prize, 358; *Awake and Sing!*, revival of, 552; comparison with O'Neill, 4, 506, 540; as controversial figure, 598–99; as early indigenous voice, 56, ◀14.25; English critics, 259n; Otis Ferguson, 577; John Gassner, 259; *Golden Boy*, 485–86; *Golden Boy* in London, 509; as "great new talent," 327; *Life* magazine, 490; Lewis Mumford, 345; *The New Yorker*, 490; *Night Music*, 607–8; CO's position, 495–97; CO's death, 13; CO's dialogue, 321, 324–25; *Paradise Lost*, 385–86; "poet of the Jewish middle class," 338; *Rocket to the Moon*, 537–40; school teacher, 62; sense of betrayal by, 13; Strasberg/Clurman, 281; *Time* magazine, 4, 539–40; unawareness of CO's influence on Jewish-American writing, 250; as "voice of the thirties," 338;

Waiting for Lefty as political tool, ◀17.2; as "white hope of American theatre," 4, 464. *See also* listings of individual plays

WRITINGS: (unpublished or incomplete plays, stories, and notes mentioned or discussed in the text): "Actor, The," 414n; "Actress Play, The," (notes), 594; "Agitator-Son Play," 284, 419–20, 421; "anti-Nazi play," 512, 513, 523, 561; "Artist, the Prophet, etc., The," ◀22.1; "Beethoven play," 226; "Boy Who Ran Away, The," 43; *Brandy of the Damned, The,* 108, 116, 133, 147, 149–50, 156; *Dawn,* 91; "Fishers Island Play," 86; "a gal I loved . . .," 307; "I Heard the Music Start," 152–53; "imposter president," 551–52; incident with older married woman, 268, 269–70; *Joseph and His Brethren,* ◀14.21; "movie idea," ◀20.1; "My Friend, the Greek," 294, 308; "Night on Steel Mountain," 483, 551; 1924 diary (doctored), 74; "Old-Fashioned Man, An," ◀22.20; "One Hot Night," 226; Outline for a novel, 450–51; "Peggy of Dorchester," 216; "Piano Store Play, The," 410n; poetry, 85–86, 115n, 138, 160, ◀5.2, ◀5.3; "Private Treaty" or "By the Sea," 295, ◀3.6; "Quartet," 569–70; "She Wants to Marry," 605; about six or seven homeless men, 594; "Some Notes on Music," 281; "Spirit of the Crane, The," 157–58; *Stolid Sam Stillson,* 94; "Suicide Play, The," 637n; *Three Potatoes and a Wormy Apple,* 94; "Tides of Fundy," 91n, 279; "To a Mother," 95; "Toward a New Theatre," 276, ◀15.2; "Twenty Minutes," 115

Odets Company, The, 58, 94
Odets, Florence (Mrs. Alvin Kabaker) (CO's sister), 38, 51–52, 85, 88, 159, 323, 352, 392, ◀18.2
Odets, Genevieve (Mrs. Howard Levy) (CO's sister), 30, 31, 38, 39, 45, 52, 79, 88, 159, 325, 352, ◀2.15
Odets, Lillian (Mrs. Louis J.), 488
Odets, Louis J. (CO's father) as "American-born," 47; and American dream, 39, 446–47; as American Jew, 21, 23, 47; as artist manqué, 459, ◀14.11; and attitude towards son, 35; as "big man," 23, 43, 581; as boxer, 22, 37; breaks CO's typewriter, 115–16; and closing of Odets Company, 94; conflicts with son, 82; and concealment of origins, 622, ◀1.4; and contempt for son's actor identity, 83; as "dandy," 52; and demands for "respect," 89; and devotion to Father Coughlin, 101; and Doctors of Sleep, 488, 490, 499, 500, 503, 544; expands business, 58; feeder in print shop, 22; and financial demands on CO, 357, 393, 488, 499, 503, 507, 509, 544, 563, 580–81, 583; and imperturbability, 89; and interview with author, ◀1.4; and jealousy towards Group members, 387, 388–90, 454, 461; and lack of Jewish accent, 21, 27; and letters to CO, 274, 389, 446–47, 452–54, 455, 564–65, 608; and letter from Luise Rainer, 508; and male chauvinism, 446–47; and marriage to Pearl Geisinger, 22; megalomania of, 622–23; and mid-life crisis, 378; and need to impress, 45, 581; and offers to manage Group/CO/LR, 389, 452; and opinion of son, 59; other's image of, 39, 43, 67–68, 72, 108, 159, 322, 352; other's response to, ◀13.7; and Pearl's death certificate, 351–52; paradoxical personality of, 21, 22, 23, 26, 39; as philanderer, 23, 53, 351; and physical ailments, 455; physical prowess, 22, 37; and the pianola, 49; and piety, 28, 393; plans for advertising firm, 55; plans to retire, 379–80; psychologizing of, 452–54, 455; publishes *Smoothing Out the Selling Path,* 58; and response to *I Got the Blues,* 273–74; and response to wife's death, 353; Esther Rossman's opinion of, 21; and Russian-Jewish identity, denial of, ◀1.4; and second wife, 488; and self-hatred, 89; as self-proclaimed catalyst of son's success, 322; "selling" *I Got the Blues,* 274, 275; and suspicion of Pearl's infidelity, 53; as Mason, 21; and treatment of Genevieve, 38, 39; and self-identity as failure, ◀14.17, 650; upward mobility of, 27, 28, 31, 38, 45, 52, 68, 101–102; on Woodrow Wilson, ◀2.14; as writer, 58n

Odets, Nora (CO's daughter), ⊄5.6
Odets, Pearl (Geisinger) (Mrs. Louis J.)
   (CO's mother), 18, 154, 214–15,
   310, 323, 324, 325, 335–36, 346,
   470, 567; as aggrieved child, 30;
   childhood of, 18; and compulsive
   cleaning, 30, 35, 38; death of,
   347–53; and depression, 19, 37,
   53, 295; dramatic flair of, 40; and
   "emergency fund," 25; and flight
   from L. J., 26; and impulse to
   engulf, 102; and letters to CO,
   335–36; marriage to Louis J.
   Odets, 22; and masochistic personality, 23, 25, 82; and her
   "nest-egg," 352; other's image of,
   42, 108, 324, 353; and passion
   for reading, 27; physical health,
   19, 26, 30, 37; and piano lessons
   for CO, 49; as prisoner, 53; as
   "Sanitary Pearl," 30, 35, 42; and
   sense of inferiority, 53; Lee
   Strasberg's impression of, 25; and
   suicidal trend, 53; suicide plan,
   53; sympathy of neighbors for,
   52; and trips to California, 53
Odets (?), Roberta (presumed wife
   of CO and mother of Joan), 135–
   40, 227, 265, 267–68. *See also*
   Roberta-Joan mystery
Odets, Walt Whitman (CO's son), 5, 7,
   12
Office of War Information, 328
O'Hara, John, 396, 400, 408, 508
O'Keeffe, Georgia, 463, 477, 478
Old Maid, The, 358
O'Malley, Ernest, 222
One University Place, 322, 478, 518
O'Neill, Eugene, 13, 32, 34, 50n, 58n,
   64, 112, 205, 343, 492, 601, ⊄2.6,
   ⊄7.4, ⊄7.6, ⊄10.2; anti-mercan-
   tilism in, ⊄14.3; and anti-
   Semitism, ⊄14.2; and aspirations
   toward Judeo-Christian ethic,
   ⊄13.8; and *Days Without End,*
   285; as first alienated American
   playwright, 194; and ideology of
   international brotherhood, ⊄14.3;
   and life turning point, ⊄8.5; and
   mercantilism, ⊄8.1; CO compared
   to, 386, 496, 506; and psycho-
   history, ⊄8.2; relation to father
   compared with CO's, 144; and
   symbol of night, ⊄23.24
O'Neil, George, 222, 235
"O Paradiso," 49
Orner, Samuel, 283–84, 304
Ossietzky, Carl von, 436
Our America (Frank), 194

Palmer, A. Mitchell, 50
Palmer Raids, 50, ⊄3.4
Pam (CO's friend), 208
Panken, Jacob, 284
PARADISE LOST (Odets), 277, 300, 306,
   326, 338, 346, 359–60, 367, 369,
   377, 379, 380, 380–81, 393; analysis of, 290–97; as "Chekhovian,"
   384; ending of forced optimism,
   297, 474; excerpts, 291, 293,
   296–97, ⊄15.5, ⊄16.2; the "fire
   bug" scene, 295; first reference
   to, 274–75; and Group Theatre
   actors, 280–81; Group Theatre
   production of, 382–83, 384–85;
   manifest meanings, 290–91; and
   CO's doubts re timing, 344; as
   CO's favorite among first six
   plays, 567–68; others' image of,
   382–83, and psychohistorical
   reality, 411; reviews of, 385; and
   "Russian" quality, 382n; and third
   act problems, 371
      identity-elements, 280–
      81; controlling materialist
      (Clara Gordon), 292; "the
      corrupter" (Kewpie), 294;
      destructive father (the
      arsonist), 296; idealized
      father-symbol (Leo Gordon),
      291; "the innocent" (Ben),
      293; the passive masochist
      (Ben), 294, 295; weak
      idealist (Leo Gordon), 291;
      themes, 290, 291, 292; loss
      of innocence, 412
Paramount Pictures, 397, 398, 452,
   460
Parker, Dorothy, 128, 338, 386
Parsons, Louella, 510
Patri, Angelo, 243–44
Patton, George, 208
Peace on Earth (Maltz), 243
Perkins, Maxwell, ⊄7.9
Peters, Paul, 322
Philadelphia, 17, 18, 19, 20, 27, 31,
   47
Philadelphia Orchestra, 105, 124
Philadelphia Record, 379
Pinchot, Rosamond, 77
Pirandello, Luigi, 366, 367–68
Piscator, Erwin, 319
play analyses: AWAKE AND SING!,
   250–59; GOLDEN BOY, 465–75;
   identity-elements as "gallery of
   characters," 249–50; method of,
   249–50; I CAN'T SLEEP, 356–57;
   NIGHT MUSIC, 285–91; 910 EDEN
   STREET, 186–88; PARADISE
   LOST, 290–97; repetitions of
   themes, 249–50, ⊄4.4; and repre-

sentation of creative process it-
self, 249–50, 253, ◀4.4; ROCKET
TO THE MOON, 525–37; THE
SILENT PARTNER, 411–17; TILL
THE DAY I DIE, 329–34; VICTORY,
227–28, 229, 230, 231–32;
WAITING FOR LEFTY, 304–5
playwright. *See* creative process;
writer in America
Playwright's Company, 576
Poet's Theatre, The, 84, 85, 88, 91
Poland, invaded by Hitler, 574
Pollock, Arthur, on *Rocket to the
Moon,* 538
Poors, the Henry Varnum, 359, 360,
370. *See also* Breuer, Bessie
Powell, Dawn, 222, 298
Powell, William, 405
Pozner, Ida and Volodya, 546
Precedent (Mooney), 216
Processional (Lawson), 84, 223
Promised Land, The (Antin), ◀1.1
Provincetown Players, 84n
psychoanalysis, and Freud's "Mystery
of the Dream," ◀2.2
psychohistory, need for, ◀8.2; Odets
view of, 301, 569–570; and diffi-
culties therein, 412n. *See also*
creative process; Odets, Clifford,
Work-Related Issues, CREATIVE
PROCESS
psychosocial crisis, ◀2.12
Public School #10, 53, 57
Public School #39, 37
Public School #52, 42
Pulitzer Prize, 92n, 112, 266, 285, 328,
358
Pygmalion story, as a version of
Narcissus story, ◀24.1
Pynes, Mary, 84

Quince Louis Veda, 147n, 561, 563
Quintessence of Nathanism, The
(Kozlenko), 107

Rabinowitz, Sholem. *See* Aleichem,
Sholem
Rainer, Emmy, 402, 403, 436, 498, 501
Rainer, Heinz (Luise Rainer's father),
401, 402, 403
Rainer, Luise, 121n, 384, 418, 438, 476,
543, 582, 593, 595, 603, ◀13.4; as
Academy Award winner, 405, 447;
and account of wedding and
honeymoon, 444–45; as Anna
Held (*The Great Ziegfeld*), 405;
and background history, 401–5;
becomes American citizen, 523;
and Harold Clurman, 484, 485;

CO's image of, as "Thomas Mann
of actresses," 448; comes to
Hollywood, 404–5; and disillusionment with film industry, 410; and
divorce from CO, 508, 578; in
England, 547; and first separation
from CO, 450; graphological
profile of, 433; and Group as
competitor, 510; and Group
members, 424, 479; leaves for
France, 546; and letters to CO,
429–31, 449, 484–85, 499, 505,
507–8, 537, 546; and magazine
profile, 463–64; and Louis B.
Mayer, 461, 519–20, 523; meets
CO, 406; and the midgets, 445;
negotiations with studio, 489;
and pregnancy, 504–7; and
reconciliation with CO, 521–22;
and relations with M-G-M, 428,
498, 501; relations with CO, 407,
424, 429–31, 433, 446, 461–62,
463, 477–79, 484–85, 497–98,
499–500, 541, 544, 545–46; 577–
78; released from contract with
M-G-M, 578; on *Rocket to the
Moon,* 522, 523; and second
Academy Award, 500; start of
acting career, 404; and Alfred
Stieglitz, 462–63, 477–78; in
Switzerland, 573; and vacation
in New York, 480–81; warns CO
about Group members, 461; wins
Film Critics Circle award, 442;
work with refugee children, 546,
547
Random House, 358
Raphaelson, Samson, 409
Reagan, Ronald, 234n
Red and the Black, The (Stendhal),
70n
Red Rust, 142
Rediscovery of America, The (Frank),
112
Reed, John, 34, 50, 106, 208
refugee children, 546–47
Regan, Sylvia Hoffman, 121, 154, 158
Reinhardt, Max, 76, 404
Remarque, Erich Maria, 128, 477
REMEMBER (Odets), 381
Renoir, Jean and Dido, 7, 8; Elia
Kazan's description of Jean, 11;
the "Watteau evening," 6
repetition-compulsion, ◀7.1
"Revolution's Number One Boy"
(McCarten), 490–91
Rialto Stock Company, 92, 95, 98
Rice, Elmer, 368
"Richard Boone Show," 4
Rise of David Levinsky, The (Cahan),
◀1.1

Ritt, Martin, 477, 481
ritual, and theatre, ¶15.2
RIVER IS BLUE, THE (formerly *The Loves of Jeanne Ney;* later, *Blockade*) (Odets), 443, 455n, 483
Rivoli, The, 93
Roar China, 163
Roberta-Joan mystery, 150, ¶14.23; Clurman on, 137
Robin, Harry, 597
ROCKET TO THE MOON (Odets), 4, 155, 173, 256, 489; and activity/passivity, ¶22.21; analysis of, 525–27; early development of, 494; early outline of, 514; and echoes of CO's personal life, 526; as ending with creativity uncompromised, 537; excerpts from, 526, 527, 528, 530, 531, 532, 533–34, 535–36; and formal problems, ¶22.3; latent meanings, 529, 530, 531, 532, 533, 534, 535, 536, 537; manifest meaning, 532; Arthur Miller's view of, ¶22.15; and the name "Cleo Singer," ¶22.10; and CO's doubts about, 522; CO's profane vs. sacred fantasies of father, ¶14.12; CO's views of, 568; opening of, 537; origin of "Cleo," 155; origins of, 464; and production money, 518; and rehearsals in Boston, 520; reviews of, 537–40; and rocket image, 525; structural defect of, 514, 527, 528, 531, 535; as turning point for CO, 524; relationship of conflict to structural defect, 531, ¶22.15

> *identity-elements:* artists manqué (Ben Stark and Mr. Prince), 525, 528, 536; aspiring feminine anima (Cleo) (CO's Muse), 527; internalized father (Mr. Prince), ¶14.19; powerful, controlling figure (father-symbol) (Belle Stark), 525, 526; sensual, worldly predator (father-symbol) (Mr. Prince), 527, 528, 536; Spurious Artist (Willy Wax), 530; weak, constricted one (aspect of mother) (Ben Stark), 525–26; *symbol:* Cleo Singer as American artist, 514, 532, ¶22.2; moon as unattainable Woman, 525, ¶21.3; *theme:* aspiration of unfulfilled artist, 530; life vs. art, 533; man's search for love, 533;

material vs. spiritual values, 528, 529, ¶22.12; struggle of aspiring artist against bondage, 525, 527; sex as creative activation, 527, 528–29; search for wholeness, 535; sense of impotence, 527, 530
Rockmore, Mrs. Robert. *See* Eitingon, Bess
Rodin, Phyllis, 209
Roosevelt, Eleanor (Mrs. Franklin D.), 338, 386, 546
Roosevelt, Franklin Delano, 55, 214, 234, 246–48, 511, 512, 513, 541, 546–47, 560, 577
Rose, Billy, 338
Rosenberg, Jerry, 64, 79, 85
Rosenberg, Louis ("Lefty Louie"), 32
Rosenthal, Herman, 32
Rosenwald, Billy, 478
Ross, Madeleine Leof (Madi) (Mrs. George), 122, 123–24
Rossman, Benjamin ("Benny"), 28
Rossman, Esther Geisinger ("Tante Esther") (Mrs. Israel) (CO's aunt), 18, 78, 87, 100, 108–9, 331, 352, 353, 358, 488, 495, ¶19.3; as a girl, 18; Jewish accent of, 27; personality of, 19, 28
Rossman, Freda (CO's cousin), 25, 30, 100; and description of Israel Rossman, 27
Rossman, Israel (CO's uncle), 11, 78, 100, 108–9, 280, 352–53, 358, 488, ¶3.3, ¶19.3; and anti-Semitism in Russia, 20; aspiration to cantor identity, 20; as fruit peddler, 20; CO's image of, 31; oral history of, 19–21; personality of, 19, 27; values of, 21
Roth, Henry, ¶16.1
Rothafel, S. L. ("Roxy"), 89
Rowe, Virginia, 8, 116
Russia. *See* USSR
Russian Revolution, 105; early attempts of, ¶2.2
Russian theatre, 287–89. *See also* Clurman, Harold; Strasberg, Lee
R. U. R. (Capek), 141

Sacco, Nicola, 106
Sacco-Vanzetti case, 110–11, 301–2, 344
sadomasochism, ¶17.3
Saint-Exupéry, Antoine de, 128
St. Mark's-in-the-Bouwerie Church, 84
Salomé (Wilde), 55
Sand, George, 145
Sandler, Jacob ("Jake Shakespeare"), 173, 392

Sandoval (Beer), 77
Saroyan, William, 510, 605
Saul, Leon, ¢21.8
Saunders, John Monk, 580
Saylor, Harry, 365
Schlesinger, Arthur, 282
Schoenberg, Jack, 124–27
Schubert, Franz, 49, 182
Schulberg, B. P., 312
Schumann, Robert, 49
Scottsboro Boys case, 286
Screbnick, Harvey. *See* Harvey
    Scribner
Scribner, Harvey, 49, 173
scripture, "feminine" and "masculine"
    principles in, ¢19.5
Selznick, Irene Mayer, 87
Senber, Henry, on *Waiting for Lefty*,
    318
Servant in the House, The, 92
Sevareid, Eric, 282
seven arts, the, 50, 213
783 Beck Street, 42
758 Kelly Street, 48, 53
747 Southern Blvd., 31, 35
Shakespeare, William, 92, 558–59,
    ¢7.2
Shakespeare's Game (Gibson), ¢22.7
Shaw, George Bernard, 120n, 492
Shaw, Irwin, 170, 343, 385, 409, 447–
    48, 495, 510, 522, 567, 571
Shelley, Percy Bysshe, 88
Sherwood, Robert E., 127, 386, 409,
    ¢19.1
Shrine of the Little Flower, 101
Shubert, Lee, 238
Shumlin, Herman, 380, 566
Sibelius, Jean Julius Christian, 107
Sidney, Sylvia, 489, 491, 508, 518, 519,
    611
SILENT PARTNER, THE (Odets), 344,
    345, 346, 383, 396, 400, 401, 409,
    410, 424, 431, 472, 489, 491, 492,
    494, 550, 556, 557–58, 562, 567,
    568, 569, ¢19.2; analysis of, 411–
    17; as belonging in *Six Plays*, 568;
    Carnovsky's view of, 569; cast list,
    437; and Chicago Memorial Day
    Massacre, 418; doubts about
    production of, 568; final revision
    of, 436; latent and manifest mean-
    ings of, 344–45, 411; not to be pro-
    duced, 571; plot of, 412; ready for
    production, 423; rehearsals begun
    for, 437; and revisions for produc-
    tion, 425; shelved by Group
    Theatre, 448; source of title, 411
        identity-element: internalized
        father (fascist), ¢14.19;
        passive, impotent man (Mr.
        Gracie), 413; *symbols of,*

344–45; strike as "brotherly
    love," 415; the strike as
    mother, 414; *themes;* be-
    trayal, 414; blood sacrifice,
    414, 417, ¢19.9; Christian
    brotherhood, 413, 414, 474;
    loss of innocence, 412; the
    search for love, 414; strug-
    gle for power, 413; violence,
    416; yearning for lost
    paradise, 415
Silver Shirts, the, 513
Sinatra, Frank, 8
Sinclair, Upton, 404
Sister Carrie (Dreiser), 34, ¢13.3
Six Characters in Search of an Author
    (Pirandello), 368
SIX PLAYS OF CLIFFORD ODETS: publica-
    tion of, 567; CO sends to President
    Roosevelt, 577
"SKKOB," 302, 319, 460
Sklar, George, 322
Skolsky, Sidney, 400
Slatkow, Lily, 35
Sloan, John, 87
Smith, Art, 299, 302, 305, 319, 356,
    444
Sokolow, Anna, 315, 556
"Soul's Desert, The" (Jeffers), ¢23.2
Southern Boulevard, 35
Spanish Civil War, 423; return of
    Lincoln Brigade, 545
"Spell of the Yukon" (Service), 60
"splitting": and characters in a play,
    ¢22.3; and identity-elements,
    ¢22.3
Stage Associates, 327
Stage Door (Ferber and Kaufman),
    422n
Stalin, Josef V., 248, 302, 572
Stanislavsky, Constantin, 93, 155, 202,
    297
Stanislavsky method, the, 194, 202,
    221, 297
Stanley, Kim, 8, 10, 13
Stanwyck, Barbara, 577
"Star Spangled Banner, The," 125
Steffens, Lincoln, 50n
Steinbeck, John, 213, 601
Steinberg, Corinne, 358, 393, 410
Steinberg, Irene Fabian (CO's cousin),
    68–70, 87, 358, 370, 393
Steinway Hall, 166, 175, 179, 186
Stendhal (Marie Henri Beyle), 70n
Stern, J. David, 365
Stevenson, Robert Louis, 28, 150
Stewart, James, 328
Stieglitz, Alfred, 34, 203, 338, 462–63,
    477–78, 481, 544
Stoddard, Eunice, 200
Stokowski, Leopold, 105, 124, 386

Stone, I. F. ("Izzie"), 124
STORY ON PAGE ONE, THE (Odets) (film), 152
Strand, Paul, 361, 371
Strange Interlude (O'Neill), 112
Strasberg, Lee, 8, 11, 25, 84n, 93, 186, 195, 239, 260–61, 266, 275, 343–44, 570, 571, 604–5, ¶14.2; and analysis of Group problem, 428; in Richard Boleslavsky's class, 141; critical of Clurman's judgment, 428; and criticism of, by Actors' Committee, 443; description of, 197–99; early theatre work, 112; in *Green Grow the Lilacs*, 184; leaves rehearsal of *Gold Eagle Guy*, 298; letter of Kazan, 458; on Meyerhold Theatre, 288; CO's unhappiness with, 297; CO's view of, 174; refuses $50,000 check, 244–45; and rejection of *Awake and Sing!*, 311; relation with Clurman, 168–69; response to CO, 194; and Theatre Guild Studio, 142; and trip to Russia, 287–88
Symbols, of creative anima, ¶22.16; night as death, ¶23.4; phallic, ¶14.11, ¶21.4; social, ¶21.5. *See also* Odets, Clifford, *Self-Identity Issues* and *Work-Related Issues*, SYMBOLS
Strasberg method, the, 297
Strasberg, Paula Miller (Mrs. Lee), 8, 11, 87, 238, 244–45, 272, 344, 457, 458, 498
Streetcar Named Desire (Williams), ¶8.6
Success Story (Lawson), 56, 212, 222, 233, 234, 238, 241, 242, 299, 302–3
"Sudden Death at Impasse" (Saul), ¶21.8
Sullavan, Margaret, 582
SWEET SMELL OF SUCCESS (Odets), 290n
Swope, Herbert Bayard, ¶14.1
Sykes, Gerald, 193, 222, 235

Taft, William Howard, 50
Tamara (Drasin), 261, 262–63, 264–65, 267, 268, 270, 271, 272
Tamiris, Helen, 226
Tamiroff, Akim, 407
Tammany Hall, 32, 33
Taradash, Daniel, 524
Taylor, Laurette, 518
temper of the times: Abraham Lincoln Brigade, 423; acceptance of radical themes in theatre, 163;

and changing history, 524; early 1930s, 282; early 1930s and world crises, 245–48; generational shift from "change the world" to self-realization, ¶8.4; the Great Depression, 142–43; isolationism, 590; late 1920s, 101; and the Jewish problem, ¶14.2; Nazi propaganda ministry and rise of HUAC, 512–13; Nazi-Soviet pact and beginning of World War II, 572–74; need to deny Stalinist vengeance, 302; 1920s, 110–111; 1929, 129–30; Philadelphia "intellectuals," 105–6; and political corruption, 32–33; post–World War I, 50–51, 55; pre–World War I, 44; and refugee children, 546–47; resistance to news of spreading Fascism, 509; return of Abraham Lincoln Brigade, 545; rising social consciousness, 207–8; in the South, 286; strikes and "conscience-reawakenings," 284; the "united front against war and Fascism," 362–66, 380, 409
Temple, Shirley, 410, 513
Ten Days That Shook the World (Reed), 106
Tess of the Storm Country, 99
Thacher, Molly Day (Mrs. Elia Kazan) 243, 317, 458, 495, 498
Thalberg, Irving, 394, 418, 427, 460, 575
theatre: "Charlie Theatre," 491–92; as collective art, ¶15.2; as ideologically cemented collective, ¶22.0; merging of subject and object (actor/audience), 491–92, ¶22.0, ¶22.4; "Miracle Plays," 491–92; as political force, 436; as ritual, 304n, 483, 491–2, ¶15.2
theatre in America, 33, 84, 93, 410, 583, 601; acceptance of radical themes in, 163; and "Charlie theatre," 491–92; Christ symbol in, ¶17.4; collective vs. individual expression in, ¶15.2; commerce and technology in, 515, 586, 600, 606; during the 1960s, ¶17.1; ensemble playing in, ¶15.2; and hit-flop psychology, 389; merchandising of, 559; and merging of subject and object (actor/audience), 84, ¶17.1; CO's view of, 492; and politics, 600–1, ¶19.1; reaction against political activism in, 327; and revolt against commercialism in, ¶2.6; and rise of theatre of the Left,

327; as ritual, 315–17; and themes re spiritual vs. material values, ◄4.8; turning point in, ◄15.2
Theatre Guild, 112, 132, 141, 146, 163, 169, 205, 207, 222, 321, 325, 455
Theatre Union, 243, 276–77, 287, ◄15.2
They Knew What They Wanted (Howard), 92
Third Congress of Writers, 562
Third Reich, the, 248
Thomas, Norman, 386
Thompson, Dorothy, 110
Threepenny Opera, The (Weill), 409
THREE PLAYS BY CLIFFORD ODETS, 358
Thunder Rock (Ardrey), 576–77, 579
TILL THE DAY I DIE (Odets), 338; analysis of, 329–34; excerpt from, 329–30, 334; and idea of patricide/suicide, 332; manifest and latent meanings, 329; as early anti-Nazi play, 328; opening of, 334, 336; plot of, 328–29; reviews of, 336–37
        identity-element: half-Jewish coward (Major Duhring), 331; sadistic homosexual (Capt. Schlegel), 330; seductive tyrant (Capt. Schlegel), 329, 330; shy, moral idealist (Ernst), 329, 330; *themes:* betrayal, 333; brotherhood, 333; destruction of creative "tool," 329, 330; suicide as "resurrection," 334; struggle to prevail, 332
Time Magazine, 4, 13, 73, 343, 387; cover story on CO, 539–40; on CO's reconciliation with Luise Rainer, 540; on *Rocket to the Moon,* 540
Tiscornia prison camp, 364
Tobey, Mark, 87
Toilers of the Sea (Hugo), 77
Toller, Ernst, 128
Tolstoy, Leo, 159; and plans to write screenplay, 395
Tone, Franchot, 186, 195, 205, 207, 208, 226, 233, 244, 266, 312, 323, 388, 394, 396, 397, 458, 510, 518, 567, 604
To Quito and Back (Hecht), 455
Tracy, Spencer, 132, 134, 477
Travers, Henry, 146
"Trio." *See* CLASH BY NIGHT
Truex, Sylvia Field (*See* Field, Sylvia)
"Truth Force" (Gandhi), ◄22.23
Tugwell, Rexford, 513
Twain, Mark, ◄7.6

Twelve Chairs, The (film), ◄15.3
207 George Street, 19, 22

UFA Films, 93
Uncle Tom's Cabin, 93, 100
Union City Stock Company, 93, 121
United Workers Organization, 318
University of North Carolina, 547
USSR (Union of Soviet Socialist Republics), 50, 110, 228, 287, 302, 361, ◄2.2

Vakhtangov, 276, 288, 289
Vakhtangov Theatre, 361
Valentino, Rudolph, 92
Van Dekker, Albert. *See* Dekker, Albert
Van Druten, John, 128
Vanity Fair, 372
Van Loon, Hendrik, 55
Van Vechten, Carl, 34, 338, 477
Vanzetti, Bartolomeo, 106
Variety, 345
Veda, Louis. *See* Quince, Louis Veda
VICTORY (Odets), 227, 228, 229, 230–32, 236, 237; analysis of, 227–28, 229, 230, 231–32; *identity-element:* dead mother (Brant's mother), ◄14.20; and prophetic nature of, 231, 232
Vogel, Arthur, 327
Volpone (Johnson), 141, 174

WAITING FOR LEFTY (Odets), 4, 78, 84, 110, 246, 302, 303–6, 315–21, 335, 366, 379; and actual taxi-driver strike, 283–84; analysis of, 304–5; as best of social dramas of '30s, 466; and blocking of performances, 366; cast of, 318; as "Charlie Theatre," 492; early model for, 131; excerpt from, 305, ◄9.7; and the "external enemy," 494; as folk symbol, 338; manifest and latent meanings, 304–5; merging of subject and object, 304; origin of a dialogue, 159; origins of, 283; plot of, 304; as political tool, worldwide, ◄17.2; and popularity in Russia, 361; produced in Nazi sectors of Czechoslovakia, 436; productions of, around world, 316, 317, 319, 338; and psychohistorical reality, 411; reviews of, 317–19; and simplifications, 494; as source of hope, 493; as "study in conversions," 359; wins prize, 312–13

WAITING FOR LEFTY (Odets) (*Cont.*)
identity-element: corrupt
head of union (Harry Fatt),
304; cripple (Agate Keller),
305; idealist (Lefty), 304;
themes: fight against depri-
vation, 305; power in group
identity, 305
Walker, Alixe, 194
Wall Street Journal, 343
Wanger, Walter, 409, 447, 452, 456,
482
Ward, Lem, 124
Warner Brothers, the, 394
Warner, Doris, 266
Warner, Jack, 397
Warner's Theatre, 93
Washington, Martha (Mattie), 100,
351–52, ◄18.2
Washington Square Players, ◄2.6
Watts, Richard, Jr., 383, 387; on
Awake and Sing!, revival, 552;
on Group Theatre, 559; on *Rocket
to the Moon,* 537, 539; on *Till
the Day I Die,* 336
Way Down East, 100
WBNY (later WBNX), 89, 90, 93
Weep for the Virgins, 369
Weill, Kurt, 409, 424, 458
Weinstein, Israel, 60
Weiskopf, F. C., 329
Welles, Orson, 407n, 558
Welles, Sumner, 547
Werfel, Franz, 128, 386
West, Mae, 92
WFBH, 91, 93
WFI, 100
WGBS, 93
What Price Glory? (Anderson), 78, 92,
100
White Devil, The (Webster), 558
Whitehead, Alfred North, 124
Whitman, Charles, 33
Whitman, Walt, 34, 44, 125, ◄19.2
WHN, 79, 93
Wilder, Thornton, 386, ◄3.3
William Penn Opera House, 99
Williams, Tennessee, 128, 394n, ◄8.6
Wilson, Earl, 83

Wilson, Woodrow, 33, 44, 48, 50, 54,
55, ◄2.14
Winchell, Walter, 90, 325, 338, 447;
on *Rocket to the Moon,* 538
Winterset (Anderson), 344, 369
WIP, 100
Wise, Stephen, 386
Wolfe, Thomas, 213, 384, 390, 493,
511, ◄10.3
Wolfson, Martin, 149
Wolfson, Victor, 567
WOR (radio station), 493
Workers Laboratory Theatre, 317
world-views, pluralistic vs. totalistic,
142–43
World War II, 328; end of, 48
WPA (Works Progress Administration), 494
Wray, Fay, 563–64, 571, 574, 577, 580,
583, 594
writer in America, 265; and ambivalence toward mercantilism, ◄7.6;
Clurman's image of, 495–97;
The Depression as salvation, 142;
and expression of ethnic self-
identity, ◄21.1; and film industry,
127–28, ◄7.9; and materialism
and technology, ◄8.2; and rise of
technology, ◄2.6; zeitgeist of, ◄8.2
writers: and empathy, ◄4.2; psychology
of, 627n, ◄3.3; spiritual vs. material values, ◄3.9
WRNY, 93
Wyatt, Jane, 584, 594, 596, 602
Wynn, Ed, 563–64

Yale University, 57
Yeats, William Butler, 281
Yiddish theatre, CO's roots in, 56,
◄14.25
Young, Clara Kimball, 36
Young Man Luther (Erikson), xi,
◄13.3
Young Men's Hebrew Association, 99
Young, Stark on *Awake and Sing!,* 325

Zangwill, Israel, ◄1.1

Margaret Brenman-Gibson, Ph.D., psychoanalyst and diplomate in Clinical Psychology, is a research associate and a visiting professor in the Department of Psychiatry, Harvard Medical School at Cambridge Hospital. She has been a senior staff member at Austen Riggs Center, Stockbridge, Massachusetts, and a training analyst at Western New England Psychoanalytic Institute for many years. The first American non-medical person to receive full training as a psychoanalyst, and to be appointed as a training analyst, she is an active member of the American and of the International Psychoanalytic Associations, and a fellow of the American Psychological Association. Formerly the director of the Psychology Division at the Menninger Foundation, she is currently engaged in a long-term investigation of the creative process and of non-ordinary states of consciousness, and continues her teaching and clinical practice both in Stockbridge and Cambridge. Dr. Brenman-Gibson has written more than fifty articles and books, including a classic essay on masochism and, with Merton Gill, M.D., two volumes on hypnosis and related states. In addition to being a Guggenheim Fellow in 1970, she has been awarded the C. F. Menninger Memorial Award for "outstanding research in psychoanalysis," and the Morton Prince Award for research on states of consciousness, and has received numerous research grants from such donors as the Carnegie Corporation, the National Endowment for the Humanities, the Rockefeller Foundation, the American Association of University Women, the Foundations' Fund for Research in Psychiatry, the Foundation for Research in Psychoanalysis, and the Grant Foundation.

Dr. Brenman-Gibson is married to writer William Gibson and is the mother of two grown sons.